BRITANNICA

Book of the Year

1969

Encyclopædia Britannica, Inc.

WILLIAM BENTON

Publisher

Chicago, Toronto, London, Geneva, Sydney, Tokyo, Manila

THE UNIVERSITY OF CHICAGO

The Britannica Book of the Year is published with the editorial advice
of the faculties of The University of Chicago

BRITANNICA VIEWS A PERPLEXING YEAR

As publisher of the Britannica, I am pleased with the comprehensive array of provocative feature articles in this *Book of the Year* 1969. They are designed to help achieve perspective for the curious reader—or to help restore it for the perplexed.

We have just lived through a turbulent year; crises and violence have besieged us. Can we now seek the perspective we need by drawing lessons from the immediate past as a guide to the evolving future? To this question, Britannica's Yearbook editors have devoted themselves. I feel they have given us a new landmark, the most instructive and revealing Yearbook in its 30-year history.

Foremost among this year's features is the extended essay by Lyndon B. Johnson, completed just as he prepared to relinquish his responsibilities. Last summer I presumed on my role as his ambassador to UNESCO (a post I have just vacated after six years) and asked him to prepare for the Britannica Yearbook his reflections as he left office. Where could he find a more receptive audience, I asked him, than the million subscribers to the Yearbook? I knew this request to be a great imposition on his most precious commodity—time. On the other hand, I hoped he would welcome an opportunity to "tell it as he sees it"—from his unique perspective.

I am delighted that the President agreed. This is the first article by him to be published since he entered the White House —his first published words to posterity as he leaves the White House—his first major venture in his new role as teacher and preceptor to the U.S. and the world.

Thus I proudly refer you to his "Agenda for the Future: A Presidential Perspective." I take greater pride in offering you this remarkable article than in any that has appeared in any Yearbook before—including three essays of my own! [1]

This historic and thought-provoking book-length article will be summarized in several installments in the *Reader's Digest* as well as published in full as a paperback by Bantam Books.

Former Chancellor Ludwig Erhard of West Germany, a celebrated economist as well as one of the leading politicians of Europe, draws on his visit to Latin America of last year for an absorbing and optimistic look at Latin America's economic, land, and population problems (p. 427).

Dr. Erhard foresees the possibility that land distribution and other necessary government policies—given proper leadership and government actions and reactions—can unlock the immense untapped resources of South America and can beat back starvation, defuse the "population bomb," and create a truly viable economy for the 200 million citizens who are our neighbors to the south and for whom we have created the Alliance for Progress.

A Soviet scholar, Yevsei Grigorievich Liberman, head of Kharkov A. M. Gorky State University and professor of eco-

nomic sciences, presents a defense of economic planning Soviet style, arguing that for the Soviet Union its managed economy is necessary and explaining how and why it works. His feature is "Economic Reform in the Soviet Union" (p. 295). A second article on Soviet affairs interprets the changes in Soviet foreign policy before and since the Czechoslovakian crisis of August 1968. It is "Crisis in the Communist World" (p. 764), by François Fejto of *Agence France-Presse,* a noted commentator on the U.S.S.R.

Further, I commend to those of you interested in money a brilliant and lucid special report by the New York economist Miroslav Kriz explaining the cause, nature, and dimensions of the gold crisis that has intermittently plagued the Western world. Dr. Kriz, a world authority on monetary matters, is a frequent *Book of the Year* contributor. His title this year is "The Gold Crisis and Its Aftermath" (p. 302).

The developing likelihood of a new kind of transatlantic commercial relationship between the United States, Canada, and Great Britain on one hand, and Western Europe on the other, is discussed in "Atlantic Free Trade Association," a feature article explaining the current rise of international trading unions (p. 212). Its author, H. Edward English, is director of the School of International Affairs at Carleton University in Ottawa.

The tumultuous highlights of the 1968 election year are covered in a most provocative special article. As its title states, it was indeed "An Incredible Year in U.S. History" (p. 781), reported for us by the former executive director of the Fair Campaign Practices Committee, and author of the book *Dirty Politics,* Bruce Felknor. Another article helps provide the background of the major role in the disjointed politics of 1968 played by "Youth in Revolt" (p. 313). Its author, John R. Seeley, dean of the Center for the Study of Democratic Institutions, explores what America's impatient young people are seeking and how they are seeking it.

Along with the revolt of youth, racial conflict plagued the United States; but we often tend to forget the degree to which the problem is equally or even more delicate and divisive elsewhere. The London *Observer's* Commonwealth correspondent, Colin Legum, examines the perils of black-white relations in Africa in a special feature titled "Africa: A Divided Continent" (p. 71).

Even the Olympic Games at Mexico City (themselves the subject of still another feature article, by the sports authorities Ross and Norris McWhirter) were boycotted by some young black American athletes, and Mexico City was the scene of armed conflicts between Mexican students and the police. The less violent Winter Olympics are reviewed by the editor-writer Howard Bass (p. 691).

1969 has been set apart by the United Nations as Human Rights Year, and a special report by Sir Dingle Foot gives the background on this UN proclamation (p. 775). The author is queen's counsel and chairman of the UN Human Rights Seminar on Freedom of Association.

There is also a report on the fourth assembly of the World

---

[1] Publisher William Benton contributed "The Voice of the Kremlin" as the featured article in the 1956 Yearbook, "The Voice of Latin America" in the Yearbook of 1961, and "The Teachers and the Taught in the U.S.S.R." in the 1965 Yearbook. All three were later expanded into books, *This Is the Challenge* (1958), *The Voice of Latin America* (1961), and *The Teachers and the Taught* (1965).

Council of Churches by J. Robert Nelson, professor of systematic theology at Boston University (p. 651).

Unfortunately, the world continues to place at least as much emphasis on destruction as on rights and ecumenism, as a frightening article on biological weapons makes clear (p. 253). Its authors are the editor of London's *Science Journal*, Robin H. Clarke, and Robert E. Hunter of the London School of Economics. They note that while it is theoretically possible to prevent nuclear weapons from falling into the hands of the tiniest or least responsible of nations, the devastatingly dangerous potential of biological warfare is within the reach of any nation large or small, responsible or not.

Our editors report some intriguing new information on earlier civilizations that failed to survive. I'm sure many of our readers will be interested in the special feature on early peoples of North America. This is by Charles E. Borden of the department of anthropology at the University of British Columbia. Borden presents new evidence of early American primitive peoples and their cultural links with Siberia (p. 101).

Two of the most troublesome problems of modern civilization are shelter and transportation. The preeminent Japanese architect Kenzo Tange discusses his philosophy of building design and how it should relate to the realities of urban living. His title is "New Space and New Structures for Modern Man" (p. 106). Another special feature reveals the urgency of the essential need to untangle our urban transportation snarl before it brings our increasingly metropolitan society to a dead stop (p. 749). This feature is by the editor of the British magazine *Traffic Engineering and Control*, Ernest Davies.

Movement of quite another sort is considered in a feature on modern ballet. Dance critic Walter Terry of the *Saturday Review* tells us that what now are startlingly avant-garde features will, surprisingly, soon be old and traditional (p. 248). Art, this time in the sense of painting and sculpture, is considered in yet another special report from a growing yet provocative perspective: as an investment. The article addresses itself to the increasingly frequent practice of buying paintings as one would buy shares on the stock market. It is aptly titled "Art as a Growth Stock" (p. 115). Its author is Geraldine Keen of the editorial staff of *The Times* of London.

Divergent as the titles and topics of these special reports may seem, I think as you read them you will discover the thread that ties many of them together. For example, the report on youthful turmoil probes the quest of youth for identity and purpose in modern society. Yet is not that search often frustrated by the urban problems outlined in the transportation feature? By the racial troubles of the African article? By the political problems in the review of the U.S. election year, and the human rights problems of the United Nations feature? The architectural report stresses the importance to man's quest for identity and purpose of the structures he makes—that they please and serve him, rather than overwhelm him.

Youth, like its elders, is concerned and apprehensive over the threat to mankind in the world's growing stockpile of atomic weapons. How, then, are young people to react to the special report of the gruesome threat posed by biological and chemical weapons available to any nation?

If we can agree that almost every major issue in today's world is interrelated with others, we must ask ourselves several questions. How can broad-scale solutions best be sought to the ills of contemporary world society? Are some solutions within sight? How can society proceed so that we may understand the solutions and achieve them before the problems become unmanageable?

President Johnson's essay deals with many of the problems addressed by the shorter special reports. Calling on his vast experience, he has given us what he believes and hopes are political and economic answers or clues to many of the urgent questions confronting us. We can be grateful for his insight and judgment, and we can—as of course he does—wish his successor, Pres. Richard M. Nixon, well in the task we face together. It is a task to which I hope this volume will contribute. I am sure it can contribute greatly to the reader's understanding of the task if he will peruse this yearbook thoughtfully.

William Benton, Publisher

How to Use the Book of the Year

THE *Britannica Book of the Year* is carefully planned for ready availability of reference material.

Three devices aid the reader to find information he seeks in the main section, which begins on page 65: first and most important, the Index; second, hundreds of cross-reference entries grouped alphabetically in the margins of the pages for quick and convenient information; and third, inserted frequently in or after the articles, the suggestion to *"see also"* other specific articles for further related information.

The reader will be repaid richly if he learns more of the contents than just the answers to an occasional reference question about an event of the year. In the pages of this volume, including the special articles which begin on page 16, there are many features to be noted.

The first thing to catch the attention of the reader as he thumbs through the volume will be the many pictures and other illustrations. These include many of the outstanding news photographs of the year, gathered from all over the world, and they constitute a remarkable pictorial record of the year's events.

OTHER FEATURES OF SPECIAL INTEREST:

* A list of the authors of the articles
  in the *Book of the Year*
  . . . starts on page 7.

* Calendar of major religious and national
  holidays scheduled or expected to
  occur in 1969
  . . . is on page 50.

* Chronology of 1968 — the major events of
  the past year listed day by day as they
  happened
  . . . starts on page 51.

* Obituaries — sketches of scores of prominent
  individuals who died in 1968
  . . . starts on page 566.

* Biographies of many prominent living figures
  whose activities dominated the news in 1968
  . . . starts on page 140.
  Government officials are named in articles
  on their countries. Hundreds of
  other persons are mentioned in articles.

* Statistical data of all types, the latest
  available, appear in many articles.

Above all, remember to use the Index (starting on page 806) whenever you wish information in the *Book of the Year*. The alphabetical arrangement of the book enables a reader to find subjects easily; the Index tells not only where articles appear but often guides the reader to other related subjects.

Before using the Index be sure to read the instructions that precede it.

Contents

Editorial Staff

CONTRIBUTORS

Initials and names of contributors to the Britannica Book of the Year *with the articles written by them.*
The arrangement is alphabetical by initials.

A.C.Ge./Geography
ARCH C. GERLACH. Chief Geographer, U.S. Geological Survey, Washington, D.C. Editor, *The Professional Geographer,* 1951–54.

A.D.Bu./Honduras
ALLEN D. BUSHONG. Associate Professor of Geography, University of South Carolina.

A.D.C.H./Industrial Review *(in part)*
ALAN DAVID CHRISTIE HAMILTON. Director, Technical Division, International Paints (Holdings) Ltd., London.

A.D.Fi./Religion *(in part)*
A. DALE FIERS. General Minister and President, Christian Church (Disciples of Christ). Author of *This Is Missions, The Christian World Mission.*

A.Dr./Industrial Review *(in part)*
ALFRED DAWBER. Chairman and Editorial Director, Emmott and Company, Ltd.; Kennedy Press Ltd., technical publishers, Manchester. Editor, *Textile Manufacturer.* Compiler of *Mechanical World Year Book; Electrical Year Book.*

Ae.B./Literature *(in part)*
ANNIE J. M. BRIERRE. Literary Critic, *Les Nouvelles Littéraires; La Revue des Deux Mondes; France—U.S.A.* Author of *Ninon de Lenclos.*

A.G./Malta
ALBERT GANADO. Lawyer, Malta.

A.G.A./Investment, International; Trade, International *(in part)*
ALAN GORDON ARMSTRONG. Research Officer, Department of Applied Economics, Cambridge University; Fellow of Selwyn College, Cambridge.

A.G.Bl./Music *(in part)*
ALAN GEOFFREY BLYTH. Music Critic, London.

A.G.R./Religion *(in part)*
ARTHUR GUY REYNOLDS. Registrar and Associate Professor of Church History, Emmanuel College, Toronto.

A.J.A.M./Turkey
ANDREW JAMES ALEXANDER MAN-GO. Orientalist and broadcaster.

A.J.Z./European Unity
ARNOLD J. ZURCHER. Professor of Comparative Politics, Graduate School of Arts and Sciences, New York University.

Al.Gr./Fuel and Power *(in part)*
ALLAN GRIERSON. Senior Lecturer in Mining, Imperial College of Science and Technology, London University. Author of *Design and Use of Belt Conveyors in Mines.*

Al.Ha./Medicine *(in part)*
SIR ALEXANDER HADDOW. Professor of Experimental Pathology, University of London. Director, Chester Beatty Research Institute, Institute of Cancer Research, Royal Cancer Hospital, London.

Al.Pa./Medicine *(in part)*
ALEXANDER PATON. Consultant Physician, Birmingham Hospital Group, Eng. Postgraduate Clinical Tutor, University of Birmingham, Eng.

A.N.F./Publishing *(in part)*
ANTHONY NICHOLAS FAITH. Industrial Editor, *Sunday Times,* London.

A.P.Kl./Religion *(in part)*
ALFRED PAUL KLAUSLER. Executive Secretary, Associated Church Press. Author of *Censorship, Obscenity and Sex; Growth in Worship.*

A.R.A./Cricket
ARTHUR REX ALSTON. Broadcaster and Journalist. Author of *Taking the Air; Over to Rex Alston; Test Commentary; Watching Cricket.*

Ar.C.B./Indonesia
ARNOLD C. BRACKMAN. Writer and Consultant on Asian Affairs. Author of *Indonesian Communism: A History; Southeast Asia's Second Front.*

A.R.G.G./Australia; Biography *(in part)*
ANTHONY ROYSTON GRANT GRIFFITHS. Lecturer in History, Flinders University of South Australia.

A.R.R./Money and Banking
ALAN RAYMOND ROE. Research Officer, Department of Applied Economics, University of Cambridge.

A.R.W./Panama
ALMON ROBERT WRIGHT. Former Senior Historian, U.S. Department of State.

A.R.Y./Algeria
ANTOINE R. YARED. Correspondent, *New York Times,* Algiers.

A.S.M./Medicine *(in part)*
ABRAHAM SAMUEL MARKOWITZ. Director, Department of Experimental Immunology, Hektoen Institute for Medical Research; Associate Professor of Microbiology, University of Illinois Medical School.

A.Th./Libraries
ANTHONY THOMPSON. General Secretary, International Federation of Library Associations. Author of *Vocabularium Bibliothecarii; Library Buildings of Britain and Europe.*

A.Tl./Industrial Review *(in part)*
ARTHUR TATTERSALL. Cotton Trade Expert and Statistician, Manchester, Eng.

A.T.M./Historical Studies
ALEXANDER TAYLOR MILNE. Secretary and Librarian, Institute of Historical Research, University of London. Compiler of *Writings on British History* (annual).

A.W.Bs./Japan
ARDATH WALTER BURKS. Professor; Director, International Programs, Rutgers University, New Brunswick, N.J. Author of *Far Eastern Governments and Politics; The Government of Japan.*

A.W.O./Nicaragua
ARDEN W. OHL. Instructor of Geography, Modesto (Calif.) Junior College.

A.W.Wo./Medicine *(in part)*
ALAN WALLER WOODRUFF. Wellcome Professor of Clinical Tropical Medicine, University of London, Physician, Hospital for Tropical Diseases, London. Co-author of *Recent Advances in Tropical Medicine.*

Ay.K./Literature *(in part)*
(THOMAS) ANTHONY KERRIGAN. Editor and translator of Miguel de Unamuno's *Collected Works* (for the Bollingen Foundation).

B.Ar./Ireland
BRUCE ARNOLD. Free-lance Journalist and Writer, Dublin.

B.B.M./Fuel and Power *(in part);* **Mining** *(in part);* **U.S. Supplement:** *Mining Table; Power: Mineral Fuels Table*
BERENICE BARRICK MITCHELL. Supervisory Statistical Officer, Division of International Activities, Bureau of Mines, U.S. Department of the Interior, Washington, D.C.

B.C.N./Fuel and Power *(in part)*
BRUCE CARLTON NETSCHERT. Director, National Economic Research Associates, Inc., Washington, D.C. Author of *The Future Supply of Oil and Gas;* Co-author of *Energy in the American Economy: 1850-1975.*

B.D./Biography *(in part)*
BRENDA DAVIES. Head of Information Department, British Film Institute.

B.El./Biography *(in part)*
BÉLA ELEK. Journalist, Paris.

B.Gr./Music *(in part)*
BENNY GREEN. Jazz Critic, *Observer,* London; Record Reviewer, British Broadcasting Corporation. Author of *The Reluctant Art; Blame It on My Youth.* Contributor to *Encyclopedia of Jazz.*

B.Hi./Biography *(in part)*
BARBARA HILBORNE. Journalist.

B.M.G./Czechoslovakia; Hungary; Romania
BERNARD M. GWERTZMAN. Staff Correspondent, the *New York Times.*

B.M.H./Religion *(in part)*
BEN MOHR HERBSTER. President, United Church of Christ.

B.N.D./Trade, International *(in part)*
BARRIE NICHOLAS DAVIES. Director, Statistical Division, Economic Commission for Europe, Geneva.

B.S.Ka./Biography *(in part)*
BERNARD S. KATZ. Writer, Office of Information, Department of the Navy, Washington, D.C.

C.Ce./Psychology *(in part)*
CONRAD CHYATTE. Associate Professor of Psychology, DePaul University, Chicago. Author of *Brain Blood-Shift Theory.*

C.C.O./Engineering Projects *(in part);* **Industrial Review** *(in part)*
CARTER CLARKE OSTERBIND. Director, Bureau of Economic and Business Research, University of Florida. Co-author of *Florida's Older People.*

Cd.H./Religion (*in part*)
CLIFFORD HAIGH. Editor, *The Friend*, London.

C.E.R./Timber
CHARLES EDGAR RANDALL. Assistant Editor, *Journal of Forestry*. Author of *Famous Trees; Our Forests*.

C.F.Sa./Biography (*in part*); **Finland**
CARL FREDRIK SANDELIN. Foreign News Editor, Finnish News Agency. President, Society of Swedish-speaking Writers in Finland.

C.H.J./U.S. Supplement: *Church Membership Table.*
CONSTANT HERBERT JACQUET, JR. Director of Research Library and Research Associate, National Council of Churches. Editor, *Yearbook of American Churches, 1967*.

C.I./Industrial Review (*in part*)
COLIN ISAACSON. Industrial Editor, *Plastics*.

C.J.Ay./Motor Sports (*in part*)
CYRIL J. AYTON. Editor, *Motorcycle Sport*, London

C.L.Be./Conservation (*in part*)
CHARLES LEOFRIC BOYLE. Lieutenant-Colonel, R.A. (ret'd). Chairman, Survival Service Commission, International Union for Conservation of Nature and Natural Resources, 1958–1963; Secretary, Fauna Preservation Society, London, 1949–1963.

C.L.F.W./Biological Sciences (*in part*)
CHRISTOPHER LEONARD FRANK WOODCOCK. Post Doctoral Fellow, Department of Biology, Harvard University.

Cl.M./Engineering Projects (*in part*)
CLAUDIO MARCELLO. Consulting Engineer; Honorary President, International Commission on Large Dams; Expert in dams for the International Bank for Reconstruction and Development.

C.M.Jo./Bowling and Lawn Bowls (*in part*)
CLARENCE MEDLYCOTT JONES. Editor, *World Bowls; British Lawn Tennis*. Author of *Winning Bowls; The Watney Book of Bowls*. Co-author of *Tackle Bowls My Way; Bryant on Bowls*.

Co.L./Biography (*in part*)
COLIN LEGUM. Commonwealth Correspondent, *Observer*, London. Author of *Must We Lose Africa?; Bandung, Cairo and Accra; Congo Disaster; Pan-Africanism— A Short Political Guide*. Co-author of *Attitude to Africa; South Africa: Crisis for the West; The Bitter Choice*. Editor of *Africa —A Handbook to the Continent*.

C.U.L./Religion (*in part*)
CHAIM URI LIPSCHITZ. Managing Editor, Jewish Press; Vice-President, Yeshiva Torah Vodaath and Mesivta; President, National Information Bureau for Jewish Life. Author of *The Shield of Israel; The International Date Line in Relation to Jewish Law*.

C.W.Mi./Dominican Republic; Uruguay
CLARENCE W. MINKEL. Associate Dean, School for Advanced Graduate Studies; Professor of Geography, Michigan State University.

Cy.W./Industrial Review (*in part*)
CYRIL WEEDEN. Assistant Director, Glass Manufacturers' Federation, London.

D.A.K.B./Medicine (*in part*)
DOUGLAS A. K. BLACK. Professor of Medicine, University of Manchester. Physician, Manchester Royal Infirmary. Author of *Essentials of Fluid Balance*. Editor of *Renal Disease*.

D.A.S.J./Employment, Wages, and Hours
DUDLEY ANTHONY STEPHENSON JACKSON. Junior Research Officer, Department of Applied Economics, University of Cambridge.

D.Az./Literature (*in part*)
DINA ABRAMOWICZ. Librarian, Yivo Institute for Jewish Research Library, New York, N.Y.

D.B.J.F./Football (*in part*)
DAVID BROUGH JAMES FROST. Rugby Union correspondent, *Guardian*, London.

D.D./Economics
DUDLEY DILLARD. Professor and Head, Department of Economics, University of Maryland. Author of *The Economics of John Maynard Keynes; Economic Development of the North Atlantic Community*.

D.Da./Morocco
DAVID DAURE. Chief Correspondent, Agence France-Presse, Rabat, Morocco.

Dd.H./Inter-American Affairs
DAVID HUELIN. Manager, Economic Intelligence Department, Bank of London and South America Ltd., London.

De.C./Industrial Design
DENNIS CHEETHAM. Lecturer in Liberal Studies, Faculty of Graphic Design, Leicester College of Art and Design, Eng.

D.F.C./Metallurgy
DONALD FREDERIC CLIFTON. Professor of Metallurgy, University of Idaho.

D.Fo./Biography (*in part*); **Immigration and Emigration** (*in part*)
DAVID FOUQUET. Staff Writer, *Congressional Quarterly*.

D.H.C.P.-B./Sailing
DOUGLAS HEXTALL CHEDZEY PHILLIPS-BIRT. Associate Member of the Royal Institution of Naval Architects. Consulting naval architect. Author of *Sailing Yacht Design; Motor Yacht and Boat Design; The Waters of Wight*.

D.J.I./Medicine (*in part*)
DWIGHT J. INGLE. Professor of Physiology and Professor, the Ben May Laboratory for Cancer Research, the University of Chicago. Author of *Physiological and Therapeutic Effects of Corticotropin (ACTH) and Cortisone; Principles of Research in Biology and Medicine*. Editor of *Perspectives in Biology and Medicine*.

D.J.Ro./Paraguay; Peru
DAVID JONATHAN ROBINSON. Economic Research Officer, Bank of London and South America Ltd., London.

D.K.R.P./Sporting Record
DAVID KEMSLEY ROBIN PHILLIPS. Assistant Editor, *World Sports*. Co-compiler of *The Guinness Book of Olympic Records*.

D.K.Wi./Chronology (*in part*)
DAVID K. WILLIS. State Department Correspondent, the *Christian Science Monitor*, Washington, D.C.

D.L.-Be./Astronomy
DONALD LYNDEN-BELL. Senior Principal Scientific Officer, Royal Greenwich Observatory, Herstmonceux, Eng. Visiting Reader in Astronomy, University of Sussex.

D.L.Bi./Insurance (*in part*)
DAVID LYNN BICKELHAUPT. Professor of Insurance, College of Administrative Science, Ohio State University. Author of *Transition to Multiple-Line Insurance Companies*. Co-author of *General Insurance*.

D.M.L.F./Canada
DAVID M. L. FARR. Professor of History and Dean of Arts, Carleton University, Ottawa. Author of *The Colonial Office and Canada, 1867–1887; Two Democracies; The Canadian Experience*.

D.M.Pa./Biography (*in part*)
DOROTHY MARGARET PARTINGTON. Editorial Assistant, *Encyclopaedia Britannica*.

D.O.M./Photography
DOUGLAS O. MORGAN. Publisher of photographic books: President Morgan & Morgan, Inc. and Morgan Press Inc., Hastings-on-Hudson, N.Y.

D.P.B./Industrial Review (*in part*)
DONALD P. BURKE. Senior Editor, *Chemical Week*.

D.T.K./Merchandising
DAVID T. KOLLAT. Associate Professor of Marketing, Ohio State University. Contributor to the *Journal of Marketing Research*. Author of *Consumer Behavior; Cases in Consumer Behavior; Research in Consumer Behavior*.

D.Wn./Burma; Dependent States (*in part*); **Nepal**
DOROTHY WOODMAN. Staff Contributor on Asian Affairs, *New Statesman*, London. Author of *Himalayan Frontiers; The Republic of Indonesia; The Making of Burma*.

E.A.J.D./Transportation (*in part*)
ERNEST ALBERT JOHN DAVIES. Editor of *Traffic Engineering and Control; Roads and Their Traffic; Traffic Engineering Practice*. Author of *National Enterprise*.

E.B.Br./Religion (*in part*)
EDWIN BLAINE BRONNER. Professor of History and Curator of the Quaker Collection, Haverford College, Haverford, Pa. Author of *William Penn's Holy Experiment*. Editor, *American Quakers Today*.

E.B.Nn./Rubber
EDWIN BOHANNON NEWTON. Former Manager, Advanced Rubber Technology, B.F. Goodrich Company, Brecksville, O.

E.Di./Austria
ELFRIEDE DIRNBACHER. Austrian Civil Servant.

E.G.Es./Fuel and Power (*in part*)
ERIC GEORGE ELLIS. Petroleum Technologist and Consultant. Author of *Lubricant Testing; Fundamentals of Lubrication*.

E.H.Ha./Vital Statistics (*in part*)
EVELYN HUNTINGTON HALPIN. Writer and consultant on vital statistics programs.

Ei.K./Cities and Urban Affairs (*in part*)
EISSE KALK. Research Officer, International Union of Local Authorities, The Hague, Neth.

El.G.B./Philately and Numismatics (*in part*)
ELSTON GORDON BRADFIELD. Editor Emeritus, *The Numismatist*. Co-editor, *Selections from The Numismatist*. Editor, *Introduction to Numismatics; Franklin and Numismatics*.

E.L.Ll./Molecular Biology (*in part*)
ELIZABETH LUKE LLOYD. Associate Biophysicist, Radiological Physics Division, Argonne National Laboratory, Argonne, Ill.

E.St./Medicine (*in part*)
ERWIN STENGEL. Emeritus Professor of Psychiatry in the University of Sheffield, Eng.

E.T.Ch./Medicine (*in part*)
EMIL THEODORE CHANLETT. Professor of Sanitary Engineering, Department of Environmental Sciences and Engineering, School of Public Health, University of North Carolina. Contributor to *Air Pollution*.

E.To./Antarctica (*in part*)
EVELYN TODD. Publications Officer/
Editor, British Antarctic Survey.

Ev.R./Domestic Arts and Sciences
EVELYN GITA ROSE. Home economics
consultant; Broadcaster; Food Historian;
Cookery Editor, *Jewish Chronicle*.
Contributor to *Home Economics; Guardian*,
London. Author of *More Fun with Your
Food; Evelyn Rose on the Jewish Home*.

E.W.M./Religion (*in part*)
ERIK W. MODEAN. Director, News
Bureau, Lutheran Council in the U.S.A.

F.A.Ri./Archaeology (*in part*)
FRANCIS ALLEN RIDDELL. State
Archaeologist for California.

F.Br./Boxing
FRANK BUTLER. Sports Editor,
News of the World, London.

F.G./Italy
FABIO GALVANO. London
Correspondent, *Epoca*, Milan.

F.H.Ka./Religion (*in part*)
FREDERIK HERMAN KAAN.
Information Secretary, World Alliance of
Reformed Churches, Geneva, Switz.

F.H.Li./Religion (*in part*)
FRANKLIN HAMLIN LITTELL.
President, Iowa Wesleyan College; Adjunct
Professor, Chicago Theological Seminary.
Author of *The Origins of Sectarian
Protestantism; From State Church to
Pluralism*.

F.J.Se./Medicine (*in part*)
FREDRICK J. STARE, M.D. Professor
of Nutrition and Chairman, Department of
Nutrition, Harvard School of Public Health.
Author of syndicated newspaper column
"Food and Your Health."

F.L./Swimming
FRANK LITSKY. Assistant to the
Sports Editor, the *New York Times*; Co-
editor, the *New York Times Official Sports
Record Book 1965, 1967, 1968, 1969*.

F.L.Lr./Medicine (*in part*)
FRANCIS LOEFFLER LEDERER,
M.D. Emeritus Professor of Otolaryngology,
Former Head of the Department of
Otolaryngology, University of Illinois
College of Medicine, Chicago. Author of
Diseases of the Ear, Nose and Throat.

F.N.He./Zoos and Botanical Gardens (*in part*)
FRANK NIGEL HEPPER. Principal
Scientific Officer, Herbarium, Royal Botanic
Gardens, Kew, Eng. Editor of *Flora of West
Tropical Africa* (vols. ii and iii).

F.P.P./Fairs and Shows
FREDERICK P. PITTERA. Chairman,
International Exposition Consultants Co.
Member, Board of Trustees, New York
Institute of Technology. Member, Board of
Governors, National Business and
Professional Council. Director, New Nations
Exposition and Development Corporation.
Author of *The Art and Science of
International Fairs and Exhibitions; The
Fairs of the United States and Canada*.

F.S.Rl./Biological Sciences (*in part*)
SIR FREDERICK STRATTEN
RUSSELL. Director, Plymouth Laboratory,
Marine Biological Association of the United
Kingdom, 1945–65. Author of *The Medusae of
the British Isles*. Co-Author of *The Seas*.

F.W.N./Medicine (*in part*)
FRANK W. NEWELL. Professor of
Ophthalmology, The University of Chicago.
Author of *Ophthalmology, Principles and
Concepts*. Editor, *Transactions of Glaucoma
Conferences*, vol. i-v.

F.W.Rr./Meteorology
FRANCIS W. REICHELDERFER.
Aeronautical and Marine Meteorology
Consultant. Former Chief, Weather Bureau,
U.S. Department of Commerce,
Washington, D.C.

G.C./Literature (*in part*)
GIOVANNI CARSANIGA. Lecturer in
Italian, University of Sussex, Eng.

G.C.Cu./Jamaica
GLORIA CLARE CUMPER. Chairman,
Council of Voluntary Social Services; Mem-
ber, Judicial Services Commission, Kingston,
Jamaica.

G.C.L./Ethiopia
GEOFFREY CHARLES LAST. Adviser,
Imperial Ethiopian Ministry of Education
and Fine Arts, Addis Ababa. Author of
*A Regional Survey of Africa; A Geography of
Ethiopia; Beginning Secondary School
Geography*.

Gd.Sn./Information Science and
Technology
GERARD SALTON. Professor of
Computer Science, Cornell University.
Author of *Information Organization and
Retrieval*.

G.F.R./Industrial Review (*in part*)
GEORGE FRANK RAY. Senior Research
Officer, National Institute of Economic and
Social Research, London.

G.F.Sh./Biography (*in part*)
GEORGE FRANCIS SHERMAN, JR.
Diplomatic Correspondent, *Washington
(D.C.) Star*.

G.H.St./Yugoslavia
GEOFFREY HOWARD STERN. Lecturer
in International Relations, London School of
Economics and Political Science. Author of
50 Years of Communism.

G.H.v.E./Netherlands
GERRIT HENDRIK van ES. Associate,
Institute for Political Science, University
of Amsterdam.

G.O.K.B./Immigration and Emigration
(*in part*)
GUNTHER O. K. BEIJER. Secretary,
Social Sciences Council, Royal Netherlands
Academy of Sciences and Letters,
Amsterdam. Author of *National Rural
Manpower; Adjustment to Industry; Rural
Migrants in Urban Setting; Some Aspects of
Migration Problems in the Netherlands*.

Go.M./Industrial Review (*in part*)
GORDON MINNES. Secretary, Canadian
Pulp and Paper Association.

G.P./Literature (*in part*)
GABRIEL PREIL. Writer. Hebrew and
Yiddish poet. Author of *Israeli Poetry in
Peace and War; Nof Shemesh Ukhfor*
("Landscape of Sun and Frost"); *Ner Mul
Kokhavim* ("Candle Against the Stars");
Mapat Erev ("Map of Evening"); *Lieder*
("Poems"); *Haesh Vehadmama* ("The Fire
and the Silence").

G.P.M.H./Medicine (*in part*)
GERARDUS PETRUS MARIA HOR-
STEN. Professor of Neurophysiology,
University of Nijmegen, Neth. Executive
Chief Editor, Excerpta Medica Foundation.

G.S.Mo./Zoos and Botanical Gardens
(*in part*)
GEORGE SAUL MOTTERSHEAD.
Director-Secretary, Chester Zoo, Chester,
Eng.

G.Sr./Literature (*in part*)
GUY SYLVESTRE. National Librarian,
Ottawa. Author of *Sondages; Anthologie de
la Poésie Canadienne*.

G.U./Thailand
GOVINDAN UNNY. Thailand Correspondent, Agence France-Presse, Bangkok.

H.A.Ru./Medicine (*in part*)
HOWARD A. RUSK, M.D. Chairman,
Department of Rehabilitation
Medicine, New York University
Medical Center, New York City. Con-
tributing Editor, the *New York Times*.
Author of *Rehabilitation Medicine*.

H.A.Ta./Transportation (*in part*)
HAROLD ANTHONY TAYLOR. Air
Transport Editor, *Flight International*,
London.

H.B./Biography (*in part*); Hockey (*in part*);
Ice Skating; Skiing
HOWARD BASS. Editor, *Winter Sports
Annual*. Winter Sports Correspondent, *The
Daily Telegraph*, London; *The Christian
Science Monitor*, Boston. Author of *The
Sense in Sport; This Skating Age; The Magic
of Skiing; Winter Sports*.

H.C.Cl./Literature (*in part*)
HENRY CUMMINGS CAMPBELL.
Chief Librarian, Toronto Public Library,
Toronto.

H.D.M./Engineering Projects (*in part*)
HORACE DENTON MORGAN. Senior
Partner, Sir William Halcrow and Partners,
London.

H.Du./Historic Buildings; Museums and
Galleries (*in part*)
HIROSHI DAIFUKU. Chief, Section for
the Development of the Cultural Heritage,
UNESCO, Paris.

He.B.H./Food (*in part*)
HENRY BERNARD HAWLEY.
Consultant, Human Nutrition and Food
Science, Sherborne, Eng.

He.Se./Medicine (*in part*)
SIR HERBERT (JOHN) SEDDON.
Professor of Orthopedics, University of Lon-
don, 1965–67. Author of *Nerve Injuries*.

H.Go./Chess
HARRY GOLOMBEK. British Chess
Champion, 1947, 1949, and 1955. Chess
Correspondent, *Times* and *Observer*, London.
Author of *Penguin Handbook on the Game
of Chess; Modern Opening Chess Strategy*.

H.H.Sa./Propaganda
HOWLAND H. SARGEANT. President,
Radio Liberty Committee. Author of *The
Representation of the United States Abroad*.

Hi.P./Union of Soviet Socialist Republics
HENRI PIERRE. Moscow
Correspondent, *Le Monde*.

Hi.S./Housing
HIDEHIKO SAZANAMI. Chief, Urban
Facilities Research Group, Building Research
Institute, Ministry of Construction, Tokyo.
Author of *Housing in Metropolitan Areas*.

H.Ko./Communist Movement
HANS KOHN. Emeritus Professor of
History, City College of New York. Author of
*Prologue to Nation-States: the French and
German Experiences 1789-1815*.

H.L.En./Conservation (*in part*)
HERBERT LEESON EDLIN. Publica-
tions Officer, Forestry Commission of Great
Britain. Author of *Trees, Woods and Man;
Wayside and Woodland Trees; Man and
Plants*.

H.M.F.M./Industrial Review (*in part*)
HUGH MICHAEL FINER MALLETT.
Editor, *Weekly Wool Chart*, Bradford, Eng.

Ho.S./Literature (*in part*)
HOWARD SERGEANT. Lecturer and
writer. Editor of *Outposts*, London. Author of
*The Cumberland Wordsworth; Tradition in the
Making of Modern Poetry*.

H.R.Mo./Music (*in part*)
HAZEL ROMOLA MORGAN. Assistant
to Administrative Manager, International
Sales Division, E.M.I. Records, London.

H.R.Sh./Agriculture (*in part*); **Food** (*in part*);
U.S. Supplement: *Principal Crops Table*
HARVEY R. SHERMAN. Research
Associate, Legislative Reference, Library of
Congress.

H.Sa./Biological Sciences (*in part*)
HAROLD SANDON. Formerly Professor
of Zoology, University of Khartoum, Sudan.
Author of *The Protozoan Fauna of the Soil;
The Food of Protozoa; An Illustrated Guide
to the Fresh-water Fishes of the Sudan;
Essays on Protozoology.*

H.S.N./Fisheries
HAROLD STANLEY NOEL. Editor,
World Fishing, London.

H.T.Ch./China; Taiwan
HUNG-TI CHU. Expert in Far Eastern
Affairs. UN Area Specialist and Chief of
Asia-Africa Section and Trusteeship Council
Section, 1946–67; Professor of Government,
Texas Tech University, Lubbock.

H.Y.S.P./India
HOLENARASIPUR Y. SHARADA PRA-
SAD. Deputy Information Adviser, Prime
Minister's Secretariat, New Delhi.

I.A.B./Portugal
ILONA ANTONIE BEER. Economic
Research Officer, Bank of London and South
America Ltd., London.

I.C.C./Argentina
IVOR CECIL COFFIN. Economic
Research Officer, Bank of London and
South America Ltd., London.

I.H.M./Alcoholic Beverages (*in part*)
IRVING H. MARCUS. Editor-Publisher,
Wines and Vines. Author of *Dictionary of
Wine Terms.*

I.Ka./Mathematics
IRVING KAPLANSKY. Professor,
Department of Mathematics, The University
of Chicago.

I.M.L./Somali Republic
IOAN MYRDDIN LEWIS. Reader and
Tutor in Social Anthropology, University
College, London. Author of *Peoples of the
Horn of Africa; The Modern History of
Somaliland.*

I.Pr./Stock Exchanges (*in part*)
IRVING PFEFFER. Professor of
Insurance and Finance, Graduate School of
Business Administration, University of
California at Los Angeles. Author of
*Insurance and Economic Theory; The
Financing of Small Business.*

I.S.F./Development, Economic
IRVING S. FRIEDMAN. The Economic
Adviser to the President of the International
Bank for Reconstruction and Development.
Author of *Exchange Controls and The Interna-
tional Monetary System; U.S. Foreign
Economic Policy.*

ITU/Telecommunications (*in part*)
INTERNATIONAL TELECOMMUNI-
CATION UNION, Geneva.

Ja.C.C./Molecular Biology (*in part*)
JAMES CLINTON COPELAND.
Assistant Geneticist, Division of Biological
and Medical Research, Argonne National
Laboratory, Argonne, Ill.

Ja.Co./Horse Racing (*in part*)
JAMES COLEMAN. Columnist,
Southam Newspapers, Canada.

Ja.E.M./Motor Sports (*in part*)
JAMES EDWARD MARTENHOFF.
Boating Editor, *Miami* (Fla.) *Herald.*
Author of *How to Buy a Better Boat;
Handbook of Skin and Scuba Diving.*

Ja.G.S./Medicine (*in part*)
JAMES G. SHAFFER. Associate Dean
and Professor of Microbiology, The Chicago
Medical School. Author of *Amebiasis: A
Biomedical Problem.*

J.A.Kr./Chemistry (*in part*)
JAMES ALISTAIR KERR. Lecturer,
University of Birmingham, Eng.

Ja.Ma./Television and Radio (*in part*)
JAMES MAGEE. Assistant Editor,
European Broadcasting Union, Geneva.

J.A.O'L./Biography (*in part*)
JEREMIAH ALOYSIUS O'LEARY.
Latin America Correspondent, *Washington
Evening Star*, Washington, D.C. Author of
Dominican Action—1965.

Ja.R.E./Belgium; Biography (*in part*)
JAN ROBERT ENGELS. Editor, *P.V.V.
Flitsen* (Journal of the Belgian Party for
Freedom and Progress).

J.B.A./Religion (*in part*)
JACOB BERNARD AGUS. Rabbi, Beth
El Congregation, Baltimore, Md. Visiting
Professor of Religion, Temple University,
Philadelphia, Pa. Author of *The Evolution of
Jewish Thought; The Meaning of Jewish
History.*

J.B.Be./Industrial Review (*in part*);
Transportation (*in part*)
JOHN BERESFORD BENTLEY. Staff
Writer, *Flight International.*

J.Be./Baseball (*in part*)
JACK BRICKHOUSE. Manager of
Sports, WGN, Inc., Chicago. Publisher of
*Jack Brickhouse's Major League Baseball
Record Book.*

J.B.Kr./Medicine (*in part*)
JOSEPH BARNETT KIRSNER, M.D.
Professor of Medicine, The University of
Chicago School of Medicine.

J.B.St./Religion (*in part*)
J. BUROUGHS STOKES. Manager,
Committees on Publication, the First Church
of Christ, Scientist, Boston.

J.C.B.B./Sweden
JOAN CARROLL BOONE BULMAN.
Writer and translator. Author of *Strindberg
and Shakespeare; Jenny Lind.*

J.C.Bd./Costa Rica; Venezuela
JOANNA CATHERINE BERESFORD.
Research Officer, Bank of London and South
America Ltd., London.

J.C.Y./Chemistry (*in part*)
JOHN COLIN YOUNG. Lecturer in
Chemistry, University College of Wales.

J.E.E.Le D./Contract Bridge
JOSE EMMANUEL EDOUARD Le
DENTU. Bridge Correspondent, *Le Figaro*,
Paris. Lawyer. Author of *Memento du jeu de
la carte; Bridge a la une; Le Championnat
du monde.*

Je.Ho./Baseball (*in part*); **Basketball** (*in part*);
Football (*in part*)
JEROME HOLTZMAN. Sportswriter,
the *Chicago Sun-Times.*

J.E.Ka./Industrial Review (*in part*)
JULIAN EDWARD KASTROP.
Publication Manager and Editor, *Petroleum
Engineer*, Petroleum Engineer Publishing
Co., Dallas, Tex.

J.E.McK./Sociology
JAMES EDWARD McKEOWN. Professor
and Chairman, Department of Sociology,
DePaul University, Chicago. Co-editor of
The Changing Metropolis. Author of *Study
Guide For Economics; Study Guide for
Sociology.*

J.E.Ro./Commercial Policies
JEAN EMILE ROYER. Former Deputy
Executive Secretary, General Agreement on
Tariffs and Trade; Consultant to various
international organizations.

Je.S.B./Tourism
JEREMY SPENCER BONNETT.
Research Officer, International Union of
Official Travel Organizations, Geneva.

J.Fa./Engineering Projects (*in part*)
J. FAUCHART. Ingénieur des Ponts et
Chaussées; Service Central d'Etudes Tech-
niques du Ministère des Travaux Publics,
Paris.

J.F.Ba./Biography (*in part*)
JOHN FREDERICK BARTON. Asian
Affairs Correspondent, United Press Interna-
tional, Washington, D.C.

J.F.Ss./Veterinary Medicine
J. FREDERICK SMITHCORS. Associate
Editor, American Veterinary Publications,
Inc., Santa Barbara, Calif. Author of *Evolution
of the Veterinary Art; The American Veterinary
Profession.*

J.F.Th./Refugees (*in part*)
JOHN FREDERICK THOMAS. Director,
Cuban Refugee Program, Department of
Health, Education, and Welfare,
Washington, D.C.

J.F.V.A./Literature (*in part*)
JOSE FRANCISCO VAZQUEZ
AMARAL. Professor of Romance Languages,
Rutgers University, New Brunswick, N.J.
Author of *Mexico, Datos Para Su Biografia.*

J.G.M./Consumer Expenditures
JAMES GEORGE MORRELL. Chairman,
James Morrell and Associates Ltd.; Economic
Adviser to a number of leading companies;
Economic Editor, *Management Today.*

J.Gr./Religion (*in part*)
JOHN GRACE. National Chief Secretary
and Lieut. Commissioner, Salvation Army.

J.G.S.M./Gardening (*in part*)
JOHN GRAHAM SCOTT MARSHALL.
Horticultural Consultant.

J.H.Bo./Biological Sciences (*in part*)
JEFFERY HUGH BOSWALL. Producer
of Sound and Television Programs, British
Broadcasting Corporation Natural History
Unit, Bristol, Eng.

J.J.A./Bowling and Lawn Bowls (*in part*)
JOHN J. ARCHIBALD. Sportswriter, the
St. Louis Post-Dispatch. Author of *Bowling
for Boys and Girls.*

J.J.Ac./Fuel and Power (*in part*)
JOSEPH JOHN ACCARDO. Washington
Editor, Chilton Publications; Columnist,
Gas.

J.J.Gm./Advertising (*in part*)
JARLATH JOHN GRAHAM. Editor,
Advertising Age.

J.J.Ho./Anthropology
JOHN JOSEPH HONIGMANN. Professor
of Anthropology, University of North
Carolina. Author of *Understanding Culture;
The World of Man; Personality in Culture.*

J.K./Biography (*in part*); **Israel**
JON KIMCHE. Editor, *The New Middle
East.* Expert on Middle East Affairs, *Evening
Standard*, London. Author of *Seven Fallen
Pillars: The Middle East 1945–1953; Spying
for Peace: General Guisan and Swiss
Neutrality.* Co-author of *Both Sides of the
Hill: Britain and the Palestine War.*

J.Ki./Museums and Galleries (*in part*)
JOSHUA B. KIND. Assistant Professor
of Art History and Humanities and Lecturer,
School of the Art Institute of Chicago.
Author of *Rouault.*

J.Kn./France
JEAN MARCEL KNECHT. Assistant
Foreign Editor, *Le Monde*, Paris. Formerly
Permanent Correspondent in Washington
and Vice-President of the Association de la
Presse Diplomatique Française.

J.K.R./Agriculture (*in part*)
JOHN KERR ROSE. Senior Specialist in
Natural Resources and Conservation,
Legislative Reference Service, Library of
Congress, Washington, D.C.

J.Me./Religion (*in part*)
JOHN MEYENDORFF. Professor of
Church History and Patristics, St. Vladimir's
Seminary; Professor of History, Fordham
University, New York City; Adjunct-
Professor of Religion, Columbia University.
Author of *The Orthodox Church; A Study of
Gregory Palamas; Orthodoxy and Catholicity.*

J.M.Ka./Religion (*in part*)
JOSEPH M. KITAGAWA. Professor of
History of Religions, The University of
Chicago. Author of *Religions of the East;
Religion in Japanese History.*

J.M.Th./Toys and Games
JOHN MICHAEL THEWLIS. Industrial
Journalist.

J.N.B./Religion (*in part*)
JOHN NICHOLLS BOOTH. Minister,
The Unitarian Church of Long Beach,
Calif., co-founder Japan Free Religious
Association. Author of *The Quest for Preaching
Power; Fabulous Destinations; Introducing
Unitarian Universalism.*

Jn.Ky./Religion (*in part*)
JOHN KIELTY. Secretary, General
Assembly, Unitarian and Free Christian
Churches, London.

Jn.M./Social Services
JOHN MOSS. Barrister-at-Law. Author
of *Hadden's Health and Welfare Services
Handbook.* Editor of *Local Government Law
and Administration.*

J.No./Theatre (*in part*)
JULIUS NOVICK. Assistant Professor
of English, New York University, New
York City; Guest Lecturer, Drama Division
of the Juilliard School. Dramatic Critic for
the *Village Voice* and "The Humanist" (TV);
Contributor to *The Nation;* the *New York
Times.* Author of *Beyond Broadway: The
Quest for Permanent Theatres.*

Jo.A./Religion (*in part*)
JOSEPH ANDERSON. Secretary to the
First Presidency, Church of Jesus Christ of
Latter-day Saints (Mormons), Salt Lake
City, Utah.

Jo.A.K./New Zealand
JOHN ARNOLD KELLEHER. Editor,
the *Dominion,* Wellington, N.Z.

Jo.B.W./Cycling
JOHN BORLAND WADLEY. Editor,
International Cycle Sport.

Jo.Hn./Ceylon
JOHN HOCKIN. Formerly London
Editor, *Times of Ceylon,* Colombo.

Jo.H.S./Nuclear Energy (*in part*)
JOHN H. STUMPF. Special Projects
Editor, Atomic Industrial Forum, Inc.

Jo.N./Mountaineering
JOHN NEILL. Chemical Engineer.
Author of Climbers' Club Guides: *Cwm
Silyn and Tremadoc, Snowdon South;* Alpine
Club Guide: *Selected Climbs in the Pennine
Alps.*

Jo.W.McL./Medicine (*in part*)
JOHN WATT McLAREN. Radiologist in
charge of the X-ray department, St.
Thomas's Hospital, London. Editor of
Modern Trends in Diagnostic Radiology,
Series 1, 2, and 3.

J.R.El./Medicine (*in part*)
JOHN ROGERS ELLIS, M.B.E.
Physician, the London Hospital; Principal
Medical Officer, Ministry of Health, London;
Secretary, Association for the Study of
Medical Education.

J.S.M./Defense
JOHN STEPHEN MAXWELL. Research
Associate, Institute for Strategic Studies,
London, 1967–68. Author of *Adelphi Paper
No. 50: Rationality in Deterrence.*

J.S.Sw./Molecular Biology (*in part*)
JAMES STOUDER SWEET. Science
Editor, Office of Planning and Development,
Northwestern University, Evanston, Ill.
Executive Editor, *Rand McNally Illustrated
Atlas of Today's World* (1967). Author of
Poverty in the USA (pamphlet). Co-author of
Poverty amid Affluence.

J.T.B./Cinema (*in part*)
JOHN TEAL BOBBITT. Writer and
Producer of Encyclopædia Britannica Films:
*The Bill of Rights of the United States;
The Congress; The Constitution of the United
States; The Declaration of Independence by
the Colonies; The Supreme Court.*

J.T.G./Psychology (*in part*)
JOHN T. GOODMAN. Assistant Professor
of Psychiatry (Psychology), Department of
Psychiatry, McMaster University, Hamilton,
Ont.

J.T.K./Medicine (*in part*)
JAMES THEODORE KALIVAS. Clinical
Fellow in Dermatology, Massachusetts
General Hospital, Boston; Research Fellow
in Dermatology, Harvard University.

Ju.W./Alcoholic Beverages (*in part*)
JULIUS WILE. Senior Vice-President,
Julius Wile Sons & Co., Inc., New York City.
Vice-President, New England Distillers, Inc.,
Teterboro, N.J. Vice-Chairman, Wine Con-
ference of America. Lecturer on wines,
School of Hotel Administration, Cornell
University.

J.Whi./Industrial Review (*in part*)
JEAN WHITSON. Technical Information
Officer, British Federation of Master
Printers, London.

J.W.Ma./Alcoholic Beverages (*in part*)
JOHN WILLIAM MAHONEY. Secretary,
Wine and Spirit Association of Great Britain;
Wine Development Board; Director, Society
of Friends of Wine, London. Author of *A
Guide to Good Wine* (Introduction); *Wines;
Spirits and Liqueurs; Wine Guide* (as
Luke Bayard).

J.W.Mw./Chronology (*in part*)
JOSEPH W. MARLOW. Lawyer.

Jy.L./Postal Services (*in part*)
JERRY LIPSON. Reporter with the
Chicago Daily News.

K.de la B./Arctic Regions
KENNETH de la BARRE. Executive
Officer, Arctic Institute of North America.

K.E.P./Government Finance
KENYON EDWARDS POOLE. Professor
of Economics, Northwestern University,
Evanston, Ill. Author of *Public Finance and
Economic Welfare.* Editor of *Fiscal Policies and
the American Economy.*

K.F.C./Philately and Numismatics (*in part*)
KENNETH FRANCIS CHAPMAN.
Editor, *Stamp Collecting;* Philatelic
Correspondent, the *Times,* London. Author
of *Good Stamp Collecting; The Handybook of
Stamp Collecting.*

K.H.W./Religion (*in part*)
KENNETH H. WOOD. Editor, *The
Review and Herald.* Author of *Meditations for
Moderns.* Co-author of *His Initials Were
F.D.N.*

**K.I./Congo, Democratic Republic of the;
Dependent States** (*in part*)**; Kenya; Malawi;
Rhodesia; Rwanda; Tanzania; Uganda;
Zambia**
KENNETH INGHAM. Professor of
Modern History, University of Bristol, Eng.
Author of *Reformers in India; The Making of
Modern Uganda; A History of East Africa.*

K.J.Z./Medicine (*in part*)
KEVIN JEROME ZILKHA. Consultant
Neurologist, King's College Hospital; Consul-
tant Physician, The National Hospital,
London.

K.K.Mi./Basketball (*in part*)
KEITH KIRKMAN MITCHELL.
Lecturer, Department of Physical Education,
Leeds University; Hon. General Secretary,
Amateur Basket Ball Association.

K.L.O./Rowing
KEITH LANGFORD OSBORNE.
Editor, *Rowing,* 1961–63. Hon. Editor,
British Rowing Almanack, 1961–.

K.Ra./Medicine (*in part*)
KAREL RASKA, M.D. Director, Division
of Communicable Diseases, World Health
Organization, Geneva.

K.Sm./Albania; Biography (*in part*)**;
Bulgaria; Economic Planning** (*in part*)**;
Intelligence Operations; Mongolia; Poland;
Political Parties**
KAZIMIERZ MACIEJ
SMOGORZEWSKI. Writer on contemporary
history. Founder and Editor, *Free Europe,*
London. Author of *The United States and
Great Britain; Poland's Access to the Sea.*

L.C.Br./Cities and Urban Affairs (*in part*)
LEWIS CHARLES BRAITHWAITE.
Frederick Soddy Research Fellow,
Department of Regional Studies, University
of Sussex, Falmer, Brighton.

L.Ch./Fuel and Power (*in part*)
LUCIEN CHALMEY. Adviser, Union
Internationale des Producteurs et Distribu-
teurs d'Énergie Électrique, Paris.

L.F.R.W./Afghanistan; Iran; Pakistan
LAURENCE FREDERIC RUSHBROOK
WILLIAMS, C.B.E. Fellow of All Souls
College, Oxford University, 1914–21; Professor
of Modern Indian History, Allahabad, India,
1914–19. Author of *India Under the Company
and the Crown; The State of Pakistan; What
About India?; Kutch in History and Legend.*
Editor of *Handbook to India, Pakistan,
Burma, and Ceylon.*

L.H./South Africa
LOUIS HOTZ. Formerly editorial writer,
the *Johannesburg* (S.Af.) *Star.* Co-author
and contributor to *The Jews in South Africa:
a History.*

L.J.Re./Race Relations (*in part*)
LAWRENCE J. REDLINGER. Research
Assistant, Center for Urban Affairs,
Northwestern University, Evanston, Ill.

L.Ke./Cooperatives
LOTTE KENT. Editor, *Cooperative News
Service,* International Cooperative Alliance,
London.

L.M.Gd./Antarctica (*in part*)
LAURENCE M. GOULD. Professor of
Geology, University of Arizona. Chairman,
Committee on Polar Research, National
Academy of Sciences. Author of *Cold: The
Record of an Antarctic Sledge Journey.*

L.M.M./Seismology
LEONARD M. MURPHY. Chief,
Seismology Division, Coast and Geodetic
Survey, Environmental Science Services
Administration, U.S. Department of
Commerce, Washington, D.C.

L.On./Geology
LAWRENCE OGDEN. Professor,
Geography and Geology Department,
Eastern Michigan University.

L.O.T./Tennis
LANCELOT OLIVER TINGAY. Lawn
Tennis Correspondent, *Daily Telegraph,*
London.

L.R.Bu./Education
LEONARD RALPH BUCKLEY.
Assistant Editor, the *Times Educational
Supplement,* London.

L.Sh./U.S. Supplement: *Major Legislation Table*
LYN SHEPARD. Congressional Correspondent, the *Christian Science Monitor.*

L.Ze./Literature (*in part*)
LEIF ZERN. Editor, *Bonniers Litterära Magasin.* Author of *Poems 1963.*

M.A.K./Economy, World; Payments and Reserves, International
MIROSLAV A. KRIZ. Vice-President, The First National City Bank of New York, N.Y. Author of *The Price of Gold; Gold in World Monetary Affairs Today; Gold: Barbarous Relic or Useful Instrument?*

Ma.Ka./Music (*in part*)
MAUD KARPELES. Hon. President, International Folk Music Council, Copenhagen. Author of *Cecil Sharp: His Life and Works; Folk Songs from Newfoundland.* Editor of *Journal of the International Folk Music Council,* vols. i–xiii and xvi; *English Folk Songs from the Southern Appalachians.*

Ma.S./Track and Field Sports
MAXWELL STILES. Sports Editor, the *Hollywood Citizen-News.* Author of *Football's Finest Hour; The Rose Bowl; Back Track.*

M.B.A./Libya; Sudan
MICHAEL BOGHOS AGOPIAN. Deputy Chief of Bureau, Agence France-Presse, Cairo.

M.By./Industrial Review (*in part*); **Transportation** (*in part*)
MICHAEL BAILY. Shipping and Transport Correspondent, *The Times,* London.

M.C.G.I./Medicine (*in part*)
MARTIN C. G. ISRAËLS. Director, Department of Clinical Haematology, University and Royal Infirmary, Manchester. Author of *Atlas of Bone Marrow Pathology; Diagnosis and Treatment of Blood Diseases.*

M.C.MacD./Agriculture (*in part*); **Transportation** (*in part*)
MALCOLM CHARLES MacDONALD. Director, Econtel Research Ltd., London. Editor, *Factual Series.*

M.Ct./Laos
MAX COIFFAIT. Correspondent, Agence France-Presse, Vientiane, Laos.

M.D.Bu./Publishing (*in part*)
M. DALLAS BURNETT. Associate Professor of Communications, Brigham Young University, Provo, Utah.

M.E./Electronics
MARCELINO ELECCION. Editor and Staff Writer, Institute of Electrical and Electronics Engineers.

M.F.B.B./Parks
MERVYN FRANCIS BERNARD BELL. Secretary, Countryside Commission.

M.Fd./Medicine (*in part*)
MAXWELL FINLAND, M.D. George Richards Minot Professor of Medicine, Harvard University. Emeritus Epidimeologist, Boston City Hospital.

M.F.F./Income, National
MICHAEL FREDERICK FULLER. Assistant in Research, Faculty of Economics and Politics, University of Cambridge.

M.Fi./Medicine (*in part*)
MORRIS FISHBEIN. Editor of Medical World News. Emeritus Professor, The University of Chicago; University of Illinois, College of Medicine. Author of *Modern Home Remedies and How to Use Them; Handy Home Medical Adviser; Concise Medical Encyclopedia.*

M.F.S./Switzerland
MELANIE F. STAERK. Executive Editor, *Swiss Review of World Affairs* (*Neue Zürcher Zeitung*), Zürich.

M.J.A./United Kingdom (*in part*)
MICHAEL JOHN ARTIS. Editor, *National Institute Economic Review.* Author of *The Foundation of British Monetary Policy.*

M.Mr./Barbados; Botswana; Burundi; Commonwealth of Nations; Dependent States (*in part*)**; Ghana; Lesotho; Maldive Islands; Mauritius; Nigeria; Swaziland**
MOLLY MORTIMER. Journalist on Commonwealth and International Affairs. Contributor to *The Quarterly Review.* Author of *Trusteeship in Practice; Kenya.*

M.N.Y./Religion (*in part*)
M. NORVEL YOUNG. President, Pepperdine College, Los Angeles. Editor, *Twentieth Century Christian* and *Power for Today.* Author of *Churches of Today.*

Mo.M./Greece
MARIO (S.) MODIANO. Athens Correspondent, *The Times,* London.

M.Pan./Prices
MILIVOJE PANIC. Economic Adviser, National Economic Development Office, London.

M.Pl./Industrial Review (*in part*)
MAURICE PLATT. Consulting Engineer. Formerly Director of Engineering, Vauxhall Motors, Ltd. Author of *Elements of Automobile Engineering.*

M.Pu./Mexico; Spain
MANUEL PULGAR. Senior Economic Research Officer, Bank of London and South America Ltd., London.

M.R.-R./Literature (*in part*)
MARCEL REICH-RANICKI. Literary critic, *Die Zeit.* Author of *Deutsche Literatur in West und Ost; Literarisches Leben in Deutschland; Wer schreibt, provoziert; Literatur der kleinen Schritte; Die Ungeliebten.*

M.R.S./Astronautics
MITCHELL R. SHARPE. Science writer. Author of *Living in Space: The Environment of the Astronaut; Yuri Gagarin, First Man in Space.* Co-author of *Applied Astronautics; Basic Astronautics.*

M.S.R./Malaysia; Singapore
MAHINDER SINGH RANDHAVA. Sub-editor, *The Straits Times,* Kuala Lumpur, Malaysia.

Mu.L./Advertising (*in part*)
MURRAY LEASK. Advertising Consultant.

M.W.Wi./El Salvador
MURAT WILLIS WILLIAMS. U.S. Ambassador-Retired. Formerly ambassador to El Salvador.

M.W.Wo./Religion (*in part*)
REVEREND MAX W. WOODWARD. British Secretary, World Methodist Council.

Mx.B./Vatican City State (*in part*)
MAX BERGERRE. Deputy Director, Vatican Affairs Department, Agence France-Presse, Rome.

Mx.H./Biography (*in part*)
MAX HARRELSON. Chief of United Nations Bureau, The Associated Press.

My.B.B./Nauru; Western Samoa
MARY BEATRICE BOYD. Senior Lecturer in History, Victoria University of Wellington, N.Z.

N.B.Wi./Dentistry
NED B. WILLIAMS. Professor of Microbiology and Director, Center for Oral Health Research, School of Dental Medicine, University of Pennsylvania.

N.Cr./Biography (*in part*)**; Germany** (*in part*)
NORMAN CROSSLAND. Bonn Correspondent, *Guardian.*

N.F.C./Medicine (*in part*)
NEIL FRANCIS CAIRNCROSS. Assistant Under-Secretary of State, Home Office, London.

N.H.K./Religion (*in part*)
NATHAN HOMER KNORR. President, Watch Tower Bible and Tract Society of Pennsylvania.

Ni.B./Literature (*in part*)
NIELS BARFOED. Editor of *Vindrosen.* Literary Critic, *Politiken,* Copenhagen. Author of *Den tøvende dag* (poems); *Ajourføringer* (essays on literature).

N.M.H./Law (*in part*)
NEVILLE MARCH HUNNINGS. Senior Research Officer, British Institute of International and Comparative Law, London. Author of *Film Censors and the Law.*

N.R.U./Commodities, Primary
NORMAN RICHARD URQUHART. Assistant Vice-President, in charge of Commodity Section, First National City Bank, New York City.

N.Si./Horse Racing (*in part*)
NOEL SIMPSON. Managing Director, Night Trotting Co., Ltd., Prestatyn, Wales.

N.Sy./Music (*in part*)
NICOLAS SLONIMSKY. Member of the Advisory Panel of Experts to the State Department in the Cultural Presentation Program. Author of *Music Since 1900; Music of Latin America.*

O.F.K./Norway
OLE FERDINAND KNUDSEN. Editor, *Norway Exports,* Oslo.

O.H.H./Guatemala
OSCAR H. HORST. Professor of Geography, Western Michigan University.

O.K./Industrial Review (*in part*)
ORLAND BENJAMIN KILLIN. Associate Professor of Industrial Education and Technology, Eastern Washington State College.

O.Pl./Medicine (*in part*)
OGLESBY PAUL, M.D. Chief, Division of Medicine, Passavant Memorial Hospital, Chicago, Ill. Professor of Medicine, Northwestern University Medical School, Chicago.

O.Tr./Biography (*in part*)**; Theatre** (*in part*)
OSSIA TRILLING. Vice-President, International Association of Theatre Critics. Co-editor and contributor, *International Theatre.* Contributor, *The Times,* London.

P.A.H./Religion (*in part*)
REV. PETER ANTHONY HEBBLETHWAITE, S.J. Editor, *The Month.* Author of *Bernanos; The Council Fathers and Atheism; Understanding the Synod.*

P.A.W.-T./Golf
PERCY AINSWORTH WARD-THOMAS. Golf Correspondent, *Guardian,* Manchester.

P.Bs./Art Sales (*in part*)
PIERRE BERÈS. Managing Director, Hermann Publishing Company, Paris. Founder and Editor in Chief, *Sciences.* Expert in rare books.

P.B.St./Publishing (*in part*)
PHYLLIS B. STECKLER. Director of Bibliography, R. R. Bowker Company. Editor of *Textbooks in Print; Children's Books for Schools and Libraries; Book Publishing Record Annual Cumulatives.*

Pe.M./Tobacco
PETER MACNAB. Editor, *Tobacco.*

P.F.Y./Mining (*in part*)
PAUL FREDERICK YOPES. Mining
Engineer, Bureau of Mines, U.S. Department
of the Interior, Washington, D.C.

P.Gl./Religion (*in part*)
PAUL GLIKSON. Secretary, Division of
Jewish Demography and Statistics, Institute
of Contemporary Jewry, The Hebrew University, Israel.

Ph.D./Africa (*in part*); Biography (*in part*);
Cameroon (*in part*); Central African
Republic (*in part*); Chad (*in part*); Congo,
Republic of (*in part*); Dahomey; Dependent
States (*in part*); Equatorial Guinea
(*in part*); Gabon; Guinea; Ivory Coast;
Malagasy Republic (*in part*); Mali (*in part*);
Mauritania (*in part*); Niger (*in part*);
Senegal; Togo (*in part*); Tunisia; Upper
Volta (*in part*)
PHILIPPE DECRAENE. Member of
editorial staff, *Le Monde*, Paris. Editor in
Chief, *Revue française d'Études politiques
africaines*. Research assistant at the Centre
d'Études des Relations Internationales de
l'Institut d'Études Politiques de Paris.
Author of *Le Panafricanisme; Tableau des
Partis Politiques Africains*.

Ph.K./Biography (*in part*); Prisons and
Penology
PHILIP KOPPER. Free-lance writer,
Washington, D.C.

P.H.M.J./Cambodia; Korea; Southeast Asia;
Vietnam (*in part*)
PHILIP HUMPHREY McNAIR JONES.
Publications Editor, *Far Eastern Economic
Review*, Hong Kong.

P.Md./Iraq; Jordan; Kuwait; Lebanon;
Middle East; Saudi Arabia; Southern
Yemen; Syria; United Arab Republic;
Yemen
PETER (JOHN) MANSFIELD. Former
Middle East Correspondent, *Sunday Times*,
London. Free-lance writer on Middle East
affairs.

P.M.Ha./Cities and Urban Affairs (*in part*)
PHILIP MORRIS HAUSER. Professor of
Sociology and Director, Population Research
Center, University of Chicago. Editor of
Urbanization in Latin America. Co-editor of
The Study of Urbanization.

P.M.Re./Industrial Review (*in part*)
PHILIP MORTON ROWE. Press Officer,
British Man-Made Fibres Federation,
Manchester.

P.Os./Biography (*in part*)
PAT OSBORNE. Producer and Script-
writer, Gramophone Department, British
Broadcasting Corporation, London.

P.R./Medicine (*in part*)
PATRICIA S. REMMELL. Instructor in
Nutrition, Department of Nutrition, Harvard
University School of Public Health.

P.Ss./Insurance (*in part*)
PERCY STEBBINGS. Insurance
Correspondent of *Investors' Chronicle*;
Post Magazine; The Review, London.

P.V.-P./Biography (*in part*)
PIERRE VIANSSON-PONTÉ. Political
News Editor, *Le Monde*, Paris. Author of *Les
Gaullistes; The King and His Court; Les
Politiques*.

P.W.Ga./Industrial Review (*in part*)
PETER WILLIAM GADDUM. Chairman,
H. T. Gaddum and Company Ltd., Silk
Merchants, Macclesfield, Cheshire, Eng.
Author of *Silk—How and Where It Is
Produced*.

P.W.He./Cosmetics; Fashion and Dress
PHYLLIS WEST HEATHCOTE. Paris
Correspondent on women's topics, *Guardian*,
Manchester.

P.W.Mi./Biological Sciences (*in part*)
PETER WALLACE MILES. Reader in
Entomology, University of Adelaide, Austr.

R.A.Cr./Literature (*in part*)
ROBERT A. CROMIE. Book Editor,
the *Chicago Tribune*, Chicago.

Ra.Pa./Philippines
RAFAEL PARGAS. Computer Operator,
National Geographic Society, Washington,
D.C.

Ra.R./Dependent States (*in part*); Guyana;
Trinidad and Tobago
RANDOLPH RICHARD RAWLINS.
Post-graduate Student, Institute of Latin-
American Studies, University of London.

R.B.Gt./Medicine (*in part*)
ROBERT BENJAMIN GREENBLATT,
M.D. Professor and Chairman, Department
of Endocrinology, Medical College of
Georgia, Augusta. Author of *Office
Endocrinology; The Hirsute Female; Ovulation*.

R.B.Le./Colombia; Ecuador
RAYMOND BASIL LEWRY. Senior
Research Officer, Bank of London and South
America Ltd., London.

R.Ca./Biography (*in part*)
ROBERT CAHN. Staff Correspondent,
the *Christian Science Monitor*. Co-author
of *Perle: My Story*.

R.C.LeB./United Nations (*in part*)
RICHARD CHARLES LeBLANC.
Public Information Officer, Press Division,
UNESCO, Paris.

R.d'E./Brazil
RAUL d'ECA. Formerly Fulbright Visiting
Lecturer on American History, University of
Minas Gerais, Belo Horizonte, Brazil. Co-
author of *Latin American History*.

R.D.Ho./Andorra; Liechtenstein; Luxem-
bourg; Monaco; San Marino
ROBERT DAVID HODGSON. Assistant
Geographer, U.S. Department of State,
Washington, D.C. Author of *The Changing
Map of Africa*.

Rd.R./Cinema (*in part*)
RICHARD ROUD. Program Director,
London and New York Film Festivals. Film
Critic, the *Guardian*, Manchester. Author of
Max Ophuls: an Index; Godard.

R.E.E.H./Religion (*in part*)
REUBEN ELMORE ERNEST HARK-
NESS. Emeritus Professor of History
of Christianity, Crozer Seminary, Chester,
Pa. Professor of History of World Religions,
History of Christianity, Baptist History,
Ellen Cushing Junior College,
Bryn Mawr, Pa.

R.F.Br./Medicine (*in part*)
R. F. BRIDGMAN, M.D. Chief Medical
Officer, Organization of Medical Care, World
Health Organization, Geneva.

R.F.G.C./Religion (*in part*)
RALPH FORMAN GODLEY CALDER.
Secretary, Overseas Appointments Bureau,
Christian Education Movement, London.

R.F.Mi./Philately and Numismatics (*in part*)
RICHARD F. MILLER. Director, Divi-
sion of Language and Literature, Eastern
Washington State College.

R.H.Be./Hockey (*in part*)
RICHARD HERBERT BEDDOES.
Sports Columnist, the *Toronto Globe and
Mail*.

R.H.Tr./Stock Exchanges (*in part*)
ROBERT H. TRIGG. Manager,
Institutional Research, New York Stock
Exchange.

R.Hy./Peace Movements
RICHARD HATHAWAY. Teaching
Faculty, History and International Studies,
Goddard College, Plainfield, Vermont;
Consultant, The Center for War/Peace
Studies, New York City.

Ri.B./Economic Planning (*in part*)
RICHARD BAILEY. Partner, Gibb-
Ewbank Industrial Consultants, London.
Author of *Problems of the World Economy;
Managing the British Economy*.

Ri.T.S./Biography (*in part*)
RICHARD TALBOT STOUT. Washington
Correspondent, *Newsweek*.

Ri.W./Liberia; United States
RICHARD WORSNOP. Writer, Editorial
Research Reports, Washington, D.C.

R.J.B./Archaeology (*in part*)
ROBERT J. BRAIDWOOD. Professor of
Old World Prehistory, the Oriental
Institute and the Department of
Anthropology, The University of Chicago.

R.J.Fe./Motor Sports (*in part*)
ROBERT JOSEPH FENDELL. New
York Correspondent, *Automotive News*.
Automobile Columnist for *Scholastic Roto;
Action*.

R.K.R./Medicine (*in part*)
RICHARD K. RICHARDS, M.D. Professor of Pharmacology, Northwestern University Medical School, Chicago. Editor of
Clinical Evaluation of Drugs.

R.L.Hs./Hockey (*in part*)
RICHARD LYNTON HOLLANDS.
Hockey Correspondent. Editor, *Hockey
News*, London. Co-author of *Hockey*.

R.L.R./Religion (*in part*)
ROGER LEWIS ROBERTS. Editorial
Consultant, *Church Times*, London.

R.L.Ro./Chile
ROBERT L. ROSS. Manager, Adela
Investment Company, Lima, Peru.

R.M.Gn./Horse Racing (*in part*)
ROBERT MARSHALL GOODWIN.
Assistant Editor, London. *Encyclopædia
Britannica*.

Rn.C./Bolivia; Cuba; Haiti
ROBIN CHAPMAN. Economic Research
Officer, Bank of London and South America
Ltd., London.

R.N.S./United Nations (*in part*)
RICHARD N. SWIFT. Head, Depart-
ment of Politics, New York University, New
York City. Author of *International Law:
Current and Classic; World Affairs and the
College Curriculum*. Editor of *Annual
Review of United Nations Affairs*.

Ro.Go./Vietnam (*in part*)
ROBERT GORALSKI. NBC News
Pentagon Correspondent.

R.Pn./Alcoholic Beverages (*in part*)
RENE PROTIN. Director, International
Vine and Wine Office, Paris.

R.R.No./Biological Sciences (*in part*)
RONALD RICHARDS NOVALES.
Associate Professor of Biological Sciences,
Northwestern University, Evanston, Ill.
Contributor to *Neuroendocrinology*, vol. ii.

R.S.Mi./Engineering Projects (*in part*)
RAYMOND SPENCER MILLARD.
Deputy Director, Road Research Labora-
tory, Ministry of Transport, Crowthorne,
Berkshire, Eng.

R.W.Cr./Television and Radio (*in part*)
RUFUS WILLIAM CRATER. Editorial
Director, *Broadcasting*, New York City.

R.W.Ma./Race Relations (*in part*)
RAYMOND W. MACK. Director, Center
for Urban Affairs, Professor of Sociology,
Northwestern University, Evanston, Ill.
Visiting Scholar 1967–68, Russell Sage
Foundation. Author of *Transforming
America: Patterns of Social Change; Our
Children's Burden: School Desegregation in
Ten American Communities*.

R.W.Sm./Religion *(in part)*
REUBEN WILLIAM SMITH. Assistant Professor of Islamic History, The University of Chicago.

R.W.T./Religion *(in part)*
RONALD WILLIAM THOMSON. Assistant General Secretary, Baptist Union of Great Britain and Ireland. Author of *Heroes of the Baptist Church; William Carey; The Service of Our Lives; A Pocket History of the Baptists.*

R.Y.C./Medicine *(in part)*
ROY YORKE CALNE. Professor of Surgery, Cambridge University. Author of *Renal Transplantation.* Co-author of *Lecture Notes in Surgery.*

Sa.B./Architecture; Art Exhibitions; Biography *(in part)*
SANDRA BLUTMAN. Assistant Curator of Drawings, Royal Institute of British Architects.

S.A.F./Medicine *(in part)*
STANLEY ANTHONY FELDMAN. Consultant Anesthetist, Westminster Hospital; Adviser, Postgraduate Studies, Royal College of Surgeons, London. Author of *Tracheostomy and Artificial Ventilation.* Co-author of *Principles of Resuscitation.*

S.B.P./Physics
STUART BEAUMONT PALMER. Assistant Lecturer, Department of Applied Physics, University of Hull.

Se.H./Political Science
SERGE HURTIG. Former Secretary General, International Political Science Association, Paris. Professor, Institute of Political Studies, University of Paris.

S.E.S./Germany *(in part)*
STEPHAN E. SCHATTMANN. Economist, London.

S.G.J./Crime *(in part)*
SVEND GRAM JENSEN. Research Associate, Institute of Criminal Science, University of Copenhagen.

S.H.Bo./Medicine *(in part)*
SAMUEL HUNTINGTON BOYER. Associate Professor of Medicine, the Johns Hopkins University School of Medicine. Author of *Papers on Human Genetics.*

Sh.P./Race Relations *(in part)*
SHEILA CAFFYN PATTERSON. Senior Staff Member, Institute of Race Relations, London. Author of *Colour and Culture in South Africa; The Last Trek; Dark Strangers; Immigrants in Industry.*

S.Ls./Biography *(in part)*
SOPHIE LANNES. Editorial Staff Member, *L'Express.*

S.M.Aa./Biography *(in part)*; **Denmark**
STENER MØRCH AARSDAL. Economic Editor, *Børsen.* Press Officer, Chamber of Commerce, Copenhagen.

S.M.Mc./Philosophy
STERLING M. McMURRIN. E. E. Ericksen Distinguished Professor of Philosophy, Dean of the Graduate School, University of Utah. Co-author of *A History of Philosophy.*

S.Pa./Furs
SANDY PARKER. Fur Editor, *Women's Wear Daily.*

S.S.G./Medicine *(in part)*
SYDNEY S. GELLIS, M.D. Professor and Chairman, Department of Pediatrics, Tufts University School of Medicine, and Pediatrician-in-chief, Tufts-New England Medical Center, Boston. Author of *Current Pediatric Therapy.* Editor, *Year Book of Pediatrics.*

S.Tf./Television and Radio *(in part)*
SOL TAISHOFF. President, Editor and Publisher, *Broadcasting,* Washington, D.C.

St.F.B./Horse Racing *(in part)*
STANLEY F. BERGSTEIN. Executive Secretary, Harness Tracks of America Inc.; Vice President, United States Trotting Association.

Sy.Ho./Nuclear Energy *(in part)*
SIDNEY LEE HOLLANDS. News Writer, *Nuclear Engineering,* London.

T.B.F./Medicine *(in part)*
THOMAS BERNARD FITZPATRICK. Professor of Dermatology, Harvard Medical School. Author of *Dermatologic Differential Diagnosis.*

T.C.J.C./Industrial Review *(in part)*; **Telecommunications** *(in part)*
THOMAS CHARLES JOHN COGLE. Technical Editor, *Electrical Review.*

T.L.T.L./Medicine *(in part)*
THOMAS LOFTUS TOWNSHEND LEWIS. Obstetric Surgeon, Guy's Hospital; Surgeon, Queen Charlotte's Maternity Hospital; Surgeon, Chelsea Hospital for Women. Author of *Progress in Clinical Obstetrics and Gynaecology;* (jointly), *The Queen Charlotte's Textbook of Obstetrics.*

T.M.R./Savings and Investment
TADEUSZ MIECZYSLAW RYBCZYNSKI. Economist, Lazard Brothers, London.

Tm.S./Gardening *(in part)*
TOM STEVENSON. Garden Columnist, *Baltimore News American; Washington Post; Washington Post-Los Angeles Times News Service.* Author of *Pruning Guide for Trees, Shrubs and Vines; Lawn Guide; Gardening for the Beginner.*

T.M.Sc./Conservation *(in part)*
THEODORE M. SCHAD. Senior Specialist, Engineering and Public Works, and Deputy Director, Legislative Reference Service, Library of Congress.

To.S./Literature *(in part)*
TORBJØRN STØVERUD. W.P. Ker Senior Lecturer in Norwegian, University College, London.

T.R.Sh./Speleology
TREVOR ROYLE SHAW. Commander, Royal Navy. Vice-President, British Speleological Association.

T.R.T./Biography *(in part)*
TRUMAN R. TEMPLE, JR. Public Information Officer, U.S. Atomic Energy Commission.

T.Sc./Alcoholic Beverages *(in part)*
TILMAN SCHMITT. Brewery Engineer. Editor of *Brauwelt; Brauwissenschaft.*

T.W./Biography *(in part)*; **Football** *(in part)*
TREVOR WILLIAMSON. Sports sub-editor, *Daily Telegraph,* London.

T.W.Me./Engineering Projects *(in part)*
T. W. MERMEL. Assistant to Commissioner for Research and Chief, General Engineering Division, Bureau of Reclamation, U.S. Department of the Interior, Washington, D.C. Chairman, Committee on World Register of Dams, International Commission on Large Dams. Author of *Register of Dams in the United States.*

Va.K./Iceland
VALDIMAR KRISTINSSON. Editor of *Fjármálatidindi; Iceland 1966.*

V.Gr./Crime *(in part)*
VAGN GREVE. Research Associate, Institute of Criminal Science, University of Copenhagen.

V.J.P./Cyprus
VERNON JOHN PARRY. Senior Lecturer in the History of the Near and Middle East, School of Oriental and African Studies, University of London. Contributor to *New Cambridge Modern History; Cambridge History of Islam; Encyclopaedia of Islam.*

V.L.A./Labour Unions
VICTOR LEONARD ALLEN. Senior Lecturer in Industrial Economics, University of Leeds. Author of *Power in Trade Unions; Trade Union Leadership; Trade Unions and the Government; Militant Trade Unionism.*

V.W.P./Crime *(in part)*; **Police** *(in part)*
VIRGIL W. PETERSON. Executive Director, Chicago Crime Commission. Author of *Gambling—Should It Be Legalized?; Barbarians in Our Midst.*

W.A.Ha./Publishing *(in part)*
WILLIAM A. HACHTEN. Professor, School of Journalism, University of Wisconsin.

W.A.Ka./Publishing *(in part)*
WILLIAM A. KATZ. Professor, School of Library Science, State University of New York. Author of *Introduction to Reference Magazines for Libraries.*

Wa.Ls./Art Sales *(in part)*
WILMA LAWS. Journalist, London. Member, International Association of Art Critics.

W.A.Ni./Oceanography
WILLIAM AARON NIERENBERG. Director, Scripps Institution of Oceanography, La Jolla, Calif. Co-author of *Modern Physics for the Engineer.*

W.A.P.M./Industrial Review *(in part)*
WILLIAM ARTHUR PEETE MANSER. Consultant, International Iron and Steel Institute, Brussels.

W.B./Horse Racing *(in part)*
WILLIAM BONIFACE. Sports writer, the *Baltimore Sun,* Baltimore, Md.

W.B.Mi./Religion *(in part)*
WILLIAM B. MILLER. Manager, Department of History, United Presbyterian Church, U.S.

W.C.Bo./Motor Sports *(in part)*
WILLIAM CHARLES BODDY. Editor, *Motor Sport.* Full Member, Guild of Motoring Writers. Author of *The Story of Brooklands; The 200 Mile Race; The World's Land Speed Record; Continental Sports Cars; The Sports Car Pocketbook; The Bugatti Story.*

W.D.Hd./Law *(in part)*
WILLIAM D. HAWKLAND. Dean, Provost, and Professor of Law, School of Law, State University of New York, Buffalo. Author of *Sales Under Uniform Commercial Code; Cases on Bills and Notes; Commercial Paper; Transactional Guide of the Uniform Commercial Code; Cases on Sales and Security.*

W.D.Hi./Telecommunications *(in part)*
WILLIAM DALE HICKMAN, JR. Washington (D.C.) News Correspondent, McGraw-Hill Publications.

W.Ei./Populations and Areas *(in part)*
WARREN WOLFF EISENBERG. Administrative Assistant to Rep. William J. Green.

W.H.Is./Gambia, The; Sierra Leone
(WILLIAM) HAROLD INGRAMS. Former Adviser on Overseas Information, Colonial Office, London. Author of *Arabia and the Isles; Hong Kong; Seven Across the Sahara; Uganda; The Yemen Imams: Rulers and Revolution.*

WHO/Medicine *(in part)*
WORLD HEALTH ORGANIZATION, Geneva.

W.H.Ta./Religion *(in part)*
WINSTON HOWARTH TAYLOR. Associate Secretary, Commission on Public Relations and Methodist Information. Director, Washington Office. Author of *Angels Don't Need Public Relations; Ending Racial Segregation in the Methodist Church; Toward an Inclusive Church.*

W.H.Ts./Biography *(in part)*; **United Kingdom** *(in part)*
WILLIAM HARFORD THOMAS. Deputy Editor, the *Guardian*, London and Manchester.

Wi.D./Television and Radio *(in part)*
WILLIAM I. DUNKERLEY, JR. Assistant Secretary, American Radio Relay League, Inc., Newington, Conn.

W.L.We./Literature *(in part)*
WILLIAM LESLIE WEBB. Literary Editor, *Guardian*, London and Manchester.

W.P./Religion *(in part)*
WILLIAM ASHWORTH PRATT. Director, Salvation Army International Information Services, London.

W.So./Africa *(in part)*
WALLACE SOKOLSKY. Assistant Professor, History Department, Bronx Community College, the New School for Social Research, New York University, Division of Adult Education. Co-author of *Contemporary Civilization; African Nationalism in the Twentieth Century.*

W.Te./Dance
WALTER TERRY. Dance Critic, *Saturday Review.* Author of *The Dance in America; The Ballet Companion.*

W.Vö./Religion *(in part)*
WALTER ALFRED VÖLKNER. Minister, Evangelical Lutheran Church of Tanzania, Northern Diocese, Kibaya, Tanzania.

W.W.E./Vital Statistics *(in part)*
WINSTON WALLACE EHRMANN. Professor of Sociology, Cornell College, Iowa. Author of *Premarital Dating Behavior.*

Y.S./Bowling and Lawn Bowls *(in part)*
YRJÖ SARAHETE. Secretary, Fédération Internationale des Quilleurs, Helsinki, Finland.

AUTHORS OF THE SPECIAL REPORTS
IN THE 1969 BOOK OF THE YEAR

AFRICA

(Africa: A Divided Continent)
Colin Legum
Commonwealth Correspondent
Observer
London

ARCHAEOLOGY

(New Evidence on the Early Peopling of the New
  World)
Charles E. Borden
Lecturer in Archaeology
University of British Columbia
Vancouver

ARCHITECTURE

(New Space and New Structures for Modern Man)
Kenzo Tange
Architect
Tokyo

ART SALES

(Art as a Growth Stock)
Geraldine Keen
Journalist
The Times
London

COMMERCIAL POLICIES

(Atlantic Free Trade Association)
H. Edward English
Director
School of International Affairs
Carleton University
Ottawa

DANCE

(The Avant-Garde Tradition)
Walter Terry
Dance Critic
Saturday Review
New York City

DEFENSE

(Chemical and Biological Warfare)
Robin H. Clarke
Editor
Science Journal
London
  and
Robert E. Hunter
Lecturer in International Relations
London School of Economics

ECONOMIC PLANNING

(Economic Reform in the Soviet Union)
Yevsei Grigorievich Liberman
Professor of Economic Sciences
Head
Kharkov A. M. Gorky State University

ECONOMY, WORLD

(The Gold Crisis and Its Aftermath)
Miroslav Kriz
Vice-President
First National City Bank
New York City

EDUCATION

(Youth in Revolt)
John R. Seeley
Dean
Center for the Study of Democratic Institutions
Santa Barbara, Calif.

INTER-AMERICAN AFFAIRS

(Toward a Sound Economy in Latin America)
Ludwig Erhard
Former Economic Minister
and Chancellor of the Federal Republic of
  Germany
Bonn

RELIGION

(Uppsala: 1968)
J. Robert Nelson
Professor of Systematic Theology
Boston University

SPORTING RECORD

(The 1968 Olympics: Grenoble and Mexico City)
Norris and Ross McWhirter
Commentators
British Broadcasting Corporation
London
  and
Howard Bass
Editor
Winter Sports
London

TRANSPORTATION

(Urban Transportation Systems)
Ernest Davies
Editor
Traffic Engineering and Control
London

UNION OF SOVIET SOCIALIST REPUBLICS

(Crisis in the Communist World)
François Fejto
Commentator on Communist Affairs
Agence France-Presse
Paris

UNITED NATIONS

(Human Rights)
Sir Dingle Foot
Queen's Counsel
Chairman
UN Human Rights Seminar
on Freedom of Association
London

UNITED STATES

(An Incredible Year in U.S. History)
Bruce L. Felknor
Former Executive Director of the U.S.
Fair Campaign Practices Committee
New York City

AGENDA FOR THE FUTURE:
A Presidential Perspective
by President Lyndon B. Johnson

"Every President comes to live with history—to probe why and how events occurred as they did. His purpose is not to understand it for its own sake, but to turn it forward, as if it were a powerful lamp, searching the darkness where the future lies."

When I returned to Washington on the tragic night of November 22, 1963, the agenda I found waiting for me as a new President was not greatly changed from the agenda which had faced the American people and their government a quarter century earlier when I arrived at the Capitol as a newly elected member of Congress.

It seemed that each Cabinet officer who came to brief me on the challenges before us spoke as a voice from the past. Most of the national problems which they laid before me were problems which American Presidents and Congresses—and generations of the American people—had been facing throughout my own years of public life. Those first moments in the Presidency did more than any other to influence the course of my service in that office until I relinquished it on January 20 of this year.

As I saw it, there was a clear reason for moving—and moving with dispatch and energy—to act while the sobering influence of national tragedy caused men of all walks of life to think of the country's interests, rather than their own lesser interests.

I recognized—as did many others, including some of my advisers and some of my old and trusted counselors from Capitol Hill—that an activist program involved great political risks. I was a new President, with no electoral mandate, and barely a full month of preparation was available before it would be necessary to face a reconvening Congress that had consistently denied to Pres. John F. Kennedy many of the programs for which he had spoken so eloquently and fervently. I knew that the effort to break the logjam might be foredoomed. Furthermore, I was acutely aware that if the effort were undertaken and failed to produce results, the consequence might be fatal to all future hopes of surmounting the pattern of opposition and obstinacy that had developed.

But without real hesitation, I came to this conclusion: that if any sense were to come of the senseless events which had brought me to the office of the Presidency, it would come only from my using the experience I had gained as a legislator to see if the legislative process could be made to function as the modern era required. While I knew all too well from long experience that it would not last, I believed that there was a consensus—a very broad, deep, and honest consensus—among most groups within our diverse society that would hold together long enough for the imperatives to be accomplished. That faith was fully justified.

I seriously doubt that any other President in our history ever enjoyed the breadth of earnest, willing, and selfless support that was accorded to our efforts in those early years to deal with the unfinished business on the American agenda.

But the agony and the cruelty of the American Presidency in the last half of the 20th century is that, whatever the purposes of its incumbent at home, the world will not permit the occupant of the office—nor the American people themselves—to attend the needs of this society without diversion.

As a legislator, I had seen first Franklin D. Roosevelt and then, one by one, each of his successors—Harry S. Truman, Dwight D. Eisenhower, and John F. Kennedy—undertake to meet the needs of this volatile society only to have the tug of far distant events turn them and the people to the tasks of defending freedom and pursuing an always elusive peace. In his inaugural address in 1933, Franklin Roosevelt could devote only a few lines to the world and set the first priority of his administration as affairs at home. Yet neither he nor any who have followed him could, in the end, maintain such a priority. Neither the force of world events nor the conscience and intelligence of the American people would permit that choice. In the first weeks and months of my term, I was constantly thinking of this pattern—and praying in my heart that we might escape it.

When, late in 1964 and early in 1965, it became apparent that North Vietnam—like other foes of freedom in other years—was bent upon escalating aggression against its neighbors, I recognized the choice with which I might ultimately be faced—and made a basic decision regarding the course of my administration.

Given the options available, I thought there was only one course appropriate to the trust of the office I held: to respond as the aggression of freedom's adversaries required us to respond in Vietnam, while, at the same time, continuing to carry forward the effort at home to put in place the foundations for America's future.

In the sections to follow in this article, I have attempted to set forth my personal observations on the problems that have dominated my attentions and energies for five years—and what I believe they foretell for the future. In writing of these, I hope to make some limited contribution to the fuller understanding of the perspective offered by the position of national leadership that it has been my privilege to share with 35 other Americans.

THE TUG OF WORLD EVENTS

Woodrow Wilson once observed that every new President would like to write his own record from the start, on a blank sheet of paper. But he cannot. He must begin by writing between the lines of what past Presidents have written. Their achievements, their commitments, their initiatives, and their mistakes are the material with which he must start.

This is nowhere so true as in foreign affairs. A President does not enter the Oval Office of the White House free to create, out of his own ideas and notions, a new framework of relations with other countries.

There are treaties on the statute books—which, because a healthy world community is built on reliance and trust, he must honor.

There are commitments to other nations—political, economic, and military—which he must satisfy.

There are developments in the world—diplomatic, ideological, and scientific—to which he must respond.

There are realities here at home—political and economic—that limit or extend his range of choices.

Finally, there are some universal realities that shape the world he sees from the Oval Office. One is the possession of nuclear weapons by at least five nations. Another is the race against want—the race to escape the Malthusian trap. A third is the existence of totalitarian Communist power in much of the Eurasian land mass—power that continuously threatens to disrupt such order as the world has managed to achieve.

All these things are part of the conditions that any modern President confronts when he begins his term of office.

Perhaps the greatest single lesson a President learns is that America's power to control events in the world is limited. Because we have, in our nuclear arsenal, the power to destroy the world, some have been misled to believe that we also have the power to shape the world to our wishes—to compel cooperation and respect.

The truth is that neither our nuclear power and aerial might nor our great wealth and productive economy can force events into a mold of our making. Our nuclear power can deter massive aggression and nuclear assault. Our resources can help other nations develop their own self-defenses. Our diplomats, backed by America's strength and guided by our commitment to order in the relations among states, can help to forge agreements that reduce the threat of war. But our power cannot change men who are determined to satisfy old hatreds or new ambitions. It can help to limit the scope of a conflict that has already begun, as it did in the Middle East in June 1967, but it cannot prevent conflict from breaking out.

Having learned these lessons in the limitations of power, a new President also learns to live with the knowledge that American

power, whatever its limitations, is still the most critically important element in the preservation of world peace.

And in time he learns to live with his own responsibilities as the chief executive of that power. Knowing that his information is always incomplete, that his human fallibility may lead him to misjudgment, and that generally he must seek to persuade, rather than demand, he begins a day-and-night watch over the international involvements of the United States.

If he is to a great degree bound by the commitments of past Presidents, he is also strengthened by the policies they formed. The alliances they helped to create, the trade relations they fostered, the military strength they developed help him to meet the challenges of *his* day.

But the most important instrument at his command is history itself—and particularly, America's experience in this century. Because change has become so rapid in our time, the past is no longer an infallible guide to the future. But it is still the most reliable guide we have—and it has been well said that those who do not understand it may be condemned to repeat it.

Every President comes to live with history—to probe why and how events occurred as they did. His purpose is not to understand it for its own sake, but to turn it forward, as if it were a powerful lamp, searching the darkness where the future lies.

In what follows, I shall briefly examine some of the principal events of this century that have, I believe, lessons in them for our future.

I shall then describe the most critical areas of international concern during my Presidency.

Then I shall try to project into the decade ahead, offering no simple solutions, for there are none, but describing what I believe to be the choices we and the world will face and suggesting the goals we should be striving to attain. My purpose is not to define the course of action that a particular administration should take but to describe, as best I can, what I believe the universe of choice is now and what it will be in the coming years.

For several hundred years what stability existed in the jungle of world affairs was maintained by the power of a few nations of Western Europe.

Throughout the 19th century, we were safe in isolation. We lived by the precepts of George Washington's Farewell Address, without realizing that our safety was protected by the efforts of others. The European nations conducted a system of politics which provided a condition of general peace. We lived within that system, without taking an active part in its decisions.

There was no need for us to be concerned about external threats, for there were none. We were free to devote our energies to developing our continent.

But the European system of world peace began to crumble in 1914. We went to war in 1917 without fully realizing what was at stake. Our slogans rallied the nation to fight tyranny and make the world safe for democracy. But we were really fighting to protect a national interest most Americans at the time did not understand—our interest in the balance of power.

In 1920, we rejected President Wilson's advice and tried to crawl back into the 19th century. For nearly 20 years, we did little to safeguard our stake in what was happening abroad and pretended that the world had returned to "normalcy."

We now know that the "normalcy" of Pres. Warren Harding was an illusion. Russia had come under the control of a Communist Party, dedicated to an ominous creed. Asia and Africa, inspired by the ideas and example of Europe and the United States, had begun to stir against imperial control. And Britain and France, weakened by the war, could not alone restore the order that had prevailed in the 19th century.

The world was breaking out of its old form. And we stood to one side, prisoners of our past, unable to play our part in the effort to achieve a new and more stable international system.

When World War II ended in 1945, we confronted a world without a frame. The old European system of peace had been destroyed by the tragedies of Fascism and war. Exhausted by a

Chief Justice Earl Warren administering oath of office during inauguration ceremonies, Jan. 20, 1965.

second great war in two generations, the nations of Europe were no longer large enough, or strong enough, to establish a system of peace in the world.

The Soviet Union had become a huge modern nation, controlled by Joseph Stalin through an iron dictatorship committed to a Communist world revolution.

China was stirring. In the aftermath of war, it too was seized by a Communist Party, linked to the Soviet Union in an uneasy alliance.

Through Asia and Africa, a retreat from empire began—a painful process that led to the emergence of many newly independent states, many of them weak and vulnerable to attack or subversion. In the two decades after the war, Britain, France, Belgium, and the Netherlands withdrew from their colonies and protectorates. The end of empire was a moral necessity. It was a historical process that recognized the fundamental equality of men. But it created problems of instability that have dominated the last 20 years and that promise to remain difficult and dangerous in the years ahead.

Another event of tremendous proportions occurred at midcentury. America's development of the nuclear bomb and Russia's subsequent acquisition of this weapon multiplied the consequences of any mistake in the management of world affairs.

Europe and Japan were nearly prostrate, facing colossal problems of physical reconstruction; Asia and Africa, weak and un-

certain, were emerging from the shadow of empire and eager to master the secrets of modern wealth; the Soviet Union, strong and ambitious, was seeking to take advantage of every opportunity for expansion. What was America's interest in this panorama of difficulties?

The United States has a fundamental interest in the way the world is organized. That interest is nothing less than our capacity to survive as a free and open democratic society. Our democracy, and our freedom, can be assured only if we and our allies and associates achieve a system of peace in the world—a system of wide horizons, within which we can move, and trade, and live in freedom.

At the end of the war, we sought to build such a system in collaboration with the Soviet Union, our associate in the war against Adolf Hitler, through the new United Nations Organization. We offered the Soviet Union aid for reconstruction, including that of the Marshall Plan. And we proposed putting the nuclear weapon, and nuclear technology, under international control. The Baruch Plan for eliminating the threat of nuclear destruction was surely one of the boldest and most farsighted proposals for consolidating the peace which has ever been made. The Soviet rejection of that plan was one of the grimmest turning points in postwar history. It started a nuclear arms race that has not yet been brought under control.

This, then, was the world President Truman faced. The Soviets rejected his offers of cooperation in peace and embarked on a policy of expansion. Through the veto, they paralyzed the United Nations as a peace-keeping agency, and they confronted us with a series of crises, in Iran, Turkey, Greece, and Berlin, that threatened the very possibility of peaceful coexistence.

In response to this awesome challenge, President Truman established between 1947 and 1949 the foundations of a foreign policy that his three successors, a bipartisan majority of the American Congress, and the American people have followed ever since. He promulgated the Truman Doctrine—which in effect told the Soviet Union, "Thus far, and no further." He assured Western Europe of our military and economic support, through NATO and the Marshall Plan. He supported the movement toward Western European unity and encouraged the reentry of Germany and Japan into the community of peaceful nations. In his Point Four program, and later through the Mutual Security Program, he began the task of assisting the developing nations—cut loose from the old European empires—to achieve real independence and growth. He supported the effort to build a viable world economic system through the World Bank, the International Monetary Fund, the General Agreement on Tariffs and Trade, and other means. These powerful acts were indispensable to our quest for a new system of peace.

The first stage in building such a system was to arrest Soviet expansion and to provide a climate in which reconstruction and development could go forward. But the goal of American policy is not containment and deterrence alone. Our aim is something more fundamental—the building of a reliable peace, which of course requires the achievement of understanding with our adversaries on the basic rules we must all respect if we hope to live on this tortured planet.

The history of the last 20 years is more than a story of threats and border wars, from Greece and Berlin to Korea and Vietnam. It is the story, too, of our persistent efforts to find a path to agreement with the Soviet Union and China and with other nations controlled by Communist parties.

Those efforts have not wholly succeeded, but they have not wholly failed either. The Baruch Plan was rejected, but the Nuclear Test Ban Treaty and the Outer Space Treaty have been ratified, and the Nuclear Nonproliferation Treaty is, as I write this, hopefully on the way to ratification—not only by the United States, but by most, if not all, of the potential nuclear powers.

The key to the future of our relations with the Communist nations, however, is their acceptance of the peaceful principle of live and let live. Thus far, they have not done so. They expect us not to intervene in Communist states allied to them, but they show no such restraint with regard to countries in the free world.

The Truman Doctrine represents the idea of minimal order in the world, which could and should evolve toward a condition of true peace. Carried out with firmness and restraint, it has given us a quarter of a century without a surrender and without a great war. Western Europe, for centuries the cockpit of war, has enjoyed a period of unprecedented growth.

But the tension between the orderly system that the Truman Doctrine made possible and the threat of Communist intervention in the affairs of other states has continued to this day. The resolution of this tension through agreement will be the most critical problem my successors will face during the next few years. The state of incipient crisis in Europe and the Middle East makes that clear.

With this background in mind, let me turn to a number of specific areas where the path to the future is defined by the possibility of achieving change in the attitudes of our allies, the nonaligned nations, and rulers of the nations governed by Communist parties.

Europe, Japan, and the United States: The Indispensable Coalition. The maintenance of peace requires the continued knitting together of the three great power centers of the free world—Western Europe, Japan, and the United States. Here are the reservoirs of strength and skill on which our hopes for order and prosperity depend. If these three work together to deter aggression, and to promote peaceful advance, I believe that sooner or later China and the Soviet Union will decide to accept our patient offers of peaceful cooperation. But if we fail to weld our present cooperation into a true coalition, the future will become dangerously uncertain—despite the great power of the United States.

The West's confrontations with Soviet power in Europe and the Middle East—beginning with Iran and Berlin in the late 1940s—have been tense and dangerous. Soviet control of this vast complex of men and resources would place any possibility of world peace in mortal peril. We have treated each confrontation with the determination—and with the care—that the stakes required.

During my tenure as President, we lived through two episodes of confrontation—the Middle East crisis of 1967 and the invasion of Czechoslovakia in 1968.

The Middle East. The six-day war in June 1967 had its roots in a local dispute, but it could not have occurred without the provocation of massive Soviet arms shipments to the United Arab Republic, Syria, Algeria, and Iraq. The crisis was the product of false rumors which swept the Middle East—rumors of an impending Israeli attack on Syria. At a critical moment, United Nations forces were withdrawn from the borders between Israel and the United Arab Republic, and the government of the U.A.R. announced that it was closing the Strait of Tiran to Israeli shipping. This step repudiated the international understandings on the basis of which the Suez crisis of 1956–57 was settled. It was an act of open hostility to Israel.

We worked desperately in every forum to head off the war. We sought a Security Council resolution calling on the U.A.R. not to use force to close the Strait of Tiran. That failed. The nations of the world were not willing to take responsibility for preventing war in the Middle East.

We sought to initiate direct discussions to avert the crisis. As the situation grew more threatening, we prepared naval and air forces to escort vessels through the Strait of Tiran. We were prepared to insist on the international character of that waterway, assured by the understandings of 1957.

But our efforts were overtaken by the steady mobilization of Arab forces in the hostile ring around Israel The armed forces of Jordan were put under Egyptian command. The U.A.R. moved its tanks into the Sinai Desert. The cry went up that Israel would be destroyed.

In this tense and menacing atmosphere, the explosion occurred, with results we all know.

Our effort, from the first day of the war, was not only to bring

hostilities to an end, but to move to a condition of peace in the Middle East. Our view was, and is, that the continued tension between Israel and its neighbors has become a burden to world peace. The world community must insist, at long last, on the right of each nation in this area to live in peace—free from terrorism, threats, and boycotts. And peace must be achieved by the will of the parties, and on their responsibility. Though other nations can help, an imposed solution that did not represent the real views of the nations involved would not last.

For a long year and a half, we pressed, in the United Nations and elsewhere, for a just and even-handed peace in the area—a peace that protected the dignity and rights of Arab and Israeli alike. We sought justice for the Palestinian refugees, secure and recognized boundaries, the guarantee of maritime rights, the limitation of arms, and a new regime for Jerusalem that protected the national and international interests in that holy city.

As I write these lines, I cannot report success. The hostility and suspicion between the parties is still too great. So the stalemate continues, as does the threat that it will burst into renewed violence. Though there are cool-headed men on both sides of the conflict, there is also the ever-present heat of inflamed public opinion—playing on an area saturated with misunderstanding, old grievances, and fears for survival.

The United States has mutual security agreements with none of the nations involved. Yet our old friendship with the Arab states, and our profound emotional attachment to Israel—together with our knowledge that this conflict could easily come to involve the major powers—has involved us deeply in the search for an enduring settlement.

My successors will have to continue the struggle for true peace in the Middle East. Too much is at stake for us, and for our friends, to rest until it is won. We must try to limit the danger that its absence poses—by seeking tacit or explicit agreement with the Soviet Union about shipments of arms to the area, new involvement in its disputes, and the exclusion of nuclear weapons from the area.

Czechoslovakia. The Czechoslovakian crisis of 1968 also threatened the stability of world peace.

In August 1968 the Soviet Union and four of its allies invaded Czechoslovakia to put down a tentative movement of liberalization in that country, designed to give its people some ordinary human freedoms. Czechoslovakia was not seeking to withdraw from the Warsaw Pact or to achieve neutrality.

This was not the first such suppression in Eastern Europe. In 1948, in 1953, and in 1956 the Soviet Union had brutally put down movements of national freedom in Eastern Europe.

Each time aggression or repression occurs, an American President must weigh the danger to world peace involved in that act and the consequences of responding to it with force or other acts of reprisal. Presidents Truman and Eisenhower and I were each confronted with Soviet acts of brutality in Eastern Europe, and each of us chose not to intervene and threaten the precarious balance of peace. On the other hand, we made it clear to the Soviets that our will to peace and detente by no means included a willingness to abandon our own interests or to qualify our commitments. There must be no miscalculation on their part.

They must realize the depth of our commitment to the people of West Germany and to West Berlin and to the other members of NATO. They must realize, too, that while the members of the NATO alliance will continue to exercise every restraint in order to avoid fictitious claims of provocation, they are likewise determined to increase their ability to meet the enlarged threat that has been posed.

In the face of the Czechoslovak and Eastern European situation, the Western allies must improve their methods of cooperation and strengthen the combat readiness of their collective defenses. The achievement of closer concert in our alliances, both in Europe and in Asia, should remain the first principle of our political strategy.

Such a development is important for many reasons. It should

result in a more equitable sharing of the burdens of responsibility than now prevails. That would establish a base for American action less vulnerable to isolationist attack than is the case at the present time. (Less than a year before the Czechoslovak crisis, many members of the Senate were ready to withdraw the bulk of American forces from Europe.)

With their alliance thus placed on a stronger and more enduring basis, the North Atlantic allies could renew their quest for conciliation with the Soviet Union through reciprocal policies intended to reduce tensions. They could also give an unmistakable signal, through actions rather than words alone, of their determination to defend Western Europe against aggression.

Our relationships with Europe, and with Japan, are not limited to the problem of security. Behind the shield of our collective security arrangements, we are cooperating in building a unified world economy and monetary system and in establishing patterns of joint action to help the developing countries of the third world.

When President Truman launched the Marshall Plan, he faced a basic policy decision. He could have dealt with Europe country-by-country. Or he could have encouraged the Western Europeans to cooperate and unify their efforts. He chose the latter course, because it was far more effective, and because it was the American people's desire to seek partners in the world, not satellites. The United States became the great friend of those Western Europeans who wanted to see Western Europe strong, united, and once again a major power in the world. President Eisenhower, President Kennedy, and I followed that lead, steadily, despite disappointments and difficulties.

There is no other hopeful way for Western Europe. The problems of defense, of East-West negotiations, of dealing with the crises and possibilities in the developing world are too big for countries of fifty million, acting by themselves, to make a significant impact.

I deeply regret that Western European unity did not move forward during my term in office. The reason, quite simply, was the policy of the government in France.

I had and I have great faith in the underlying strength of the friendship between France and the United States. Moreover, I believe that France will one day again be a leader in the movement toward Western European unity. But in the 1960s its policy took another course. I saw my task as acting so that, whatever the differences were between France and the United States, I did nothing to make them greater.

I was troubled by the withdrawal of France from the integrated arrangements of NATO, but the alliance could manage—and did.

What most troubled me was that French policy prevented the effective unity of Western Europe—when that was the only realistic road to the dignity and stature that the French government proclaimed as its European objective, and that as a great nation it deserved.

And so, when critical issues arose, such as the Middle East crisis, Western Europe's voice was divided. It could not organize itself to do what it needed to do in Latin America and in Africa, where major abiding European interests are involved. And it virtually withdrew from Asia, where more than half of the world's people live, and where issues are at stake which will shape Europe's future as well as Asia's.

I remember feeling this European impotence acutely in the Congo (Kinshasa) crisis in 1967. With white mercenaries pushing back Congolese forces, there was a real danger that the people of that country would turn in reprisal on some 10,000 white Europeans in the Congo. Pres. Joseph Mobutu needed a few military transport aircraft so he could bring his best forces to bear against the mercenaries. It was obviously a task for Europeans to undertake. But no government in Europe would take it on. Nevertheless, the danger to human lives and the danger of chaos were real and would not wait. So I sent three C-130s to the Congo.

There was a considerable outcry in the Senate and in the press about American overcommitment. But the job that urgently needed doing was done. The situation quieted down. The planes came out.

But it troubled me—and it still troubles me—that even in such a relatively minor matter Western Europe could not move.

During the Kennedy Round negotiations, we saw how much could be done between the United States and a unified Western Europe when a common basis of action existed. Much of the negotiation was conducted between the United States and the officials of the European Common Market. It resulted in the largest single round of mutual tariff reductions in history.

Cooperation among the United States, Japan, and the free countries of Europe was essential to carry the international monetary system through a series of dangerous crises in 1967–68. Despite some difficulties, we found that cooperation did the job—though the crisis of the franc in late 1968 showed how much is still to be done in achieving a dependable world monetary system.

As we look ahead, I am convinced that strengthening the Atlantic Alliance and Western European unity remains, after 20 years, still the right policy for Europe and for the United States.

I believe that the events of August 1968, when the Soviets invaded Czechoslovakia, may help to reinvigorate the alliance, as external danger often does. It is a tragic irony that men often shoulder their responsibilities only when threatened, and when further complacency seems dangerous.

It is also possible that rising concern over the "brain drain" to America, and the American challenge in managerial and technological fields, may propel the people of Western Europe toward unity—toward creating an entity capable of a stronger role in world affairs. That is highly desirable from America's point of view, as well as from Europe's.

As for the other great center of free world strength, Japan, its revival after World War II is the miraculous achievement of a vital, determined, and greatly talented people. We Americans can also take a certain pride in Japan's success. Our occupation was as wise as any occupation is likely to be. Our assistance was well used. Our protection of Japan through the Mutual Security Treaty has permitted that country to concentrate on its own development.

Now it is time for Japan to think of its relations to the rest of Asia—and the developing world—in terms of even greater responsibility.

Japan is the world's third ranking industrial power. There is no reason why it should abandon—and every reason for it to maintain—a policy of peace and friendship with all. But there is every reason why the Japanese people and its political leaders should move even further away from the habits of mind that grew when it was occupied, protected, and isolated. The key question for today's booming Japan is: What duties and obligations to others is it prepared to assume, particularly in aiding the economic growth of South and Southeast Asia?

The new Asia that is emerging is going to need the resources and wisdom and strength of Japan, operating within the new multilateral institutions that are being built. In the Asian Development Bank, Japan and the United States took up equal proportions of the capital: 20%. That is as it should be.

I am confident that, if Western Europe and Japan can accept the doctrine of fair shares and partnership, there is little danger that the American people will relapse into isolationism.

Vietnam. Vietnam has been the most frustrating of all the crises we have faced since coming out of isolation in 1941. Expressions of anguish about it—which I share with compound interest—have been accepted, wrongly, as statements of alternative policies. Hopes for an end to it have been converted into beliefs that there are easier ways out.

I do not believe that President Eisenhower had any real choice but to originate our commitment. I do not believe that President Kennedy could have done otherwise than deepen our commitment when the Communist aggressors escalated their campaign to seize the country. And—though I demanded and received a painstaking analysis of every alternative course—I believe now, as I did in 1964 and 1965, that we had no acceptable option but to intensify our effort when the enemy mounted an all-out drive to take South Vietnam and unhinge much of Asia.

Critics of our involvement have said that South Vietnam is "obscure" and in no way relevant to American interests, but every President who has surveyed the situation has believed otherwise.

Two months before his death, John F. Kennedy stressed in a television interview the immense importance of preventing a Communist victory in the region. In March 1963 he said that abandonment of our commitment would give the "Communists control of all of Southeast Asia with the inevitable effect this would have on the security of India, and, therefore, really begin to run perhaps all the way toward the Middle East."

The two Presidents who preceded him pronounced the security of Southeast Asia vital and directly related to America's interests.

Franklin Roosevelt also recognized the importance of the area. His secretary of state, Cordell Hull, described the area of South Vietnam as "pointing like a pudgy thumb toward the Philippines, Malaya and the Dutch East Indies." In a speech he drafted for the President, Secretary Hull wrote, "It is manifest that control of the South Sea area by Japan is the key to control of the entire Pacific area, and therefore to the life and commerce and other invaluable interests and rights in the Pacific area."

I would like to recall the situation that existed in 1965.

The monsoons were about to begin in South Vietnam. So effective was the Communist terror campaign, and so threatening was the enemy's buildup of troops, including large units of North Vietnam's regular Army, that every experienced observer believed that the country might well be under Communist control when the clouds lifted in the fall.

There was even more to it than that. Laos was two-thirds conquered by a Communist army led by the North Vietnamese. That

army was still advancing. The Communist Chinese foreign minister, Chen Yi, had publicly affirmed the intention to make Thailand the next target. By the spring of 1965, a guerrilla force was at work in northeast Thailand—separated by a mere 60 miles from the source of men and supplies in North Vietnam.

Moreover, Red China was preparing the Communists of Indonesia, the fifth largest nation in the world and one of the most strategically placed, to seize the government of that vast archipelago. In the fall of 1965 the Communists made their bid. The fact that it was eventually beaten back does not change the Communists' intent or the consequences that would have flowed throughout Asia and the Pacific from their victory.

It was evident to me that if we did not undertake the job of preventing the seizure of South Vietnam, there might have been no stopping short of India, then threatened by famine and other troubles.

It was then that I said to the American people, "We did not choose to be the guardians at the gate, but there is no one else."

The form of aggression in Vietnam—infiltration down jungle trails—was more difficult to understand than the crossing of the 38th parallel by North Korean armies in 1950 or the placing of Soviet missiles in Cuba in 1962. Although the National Liberation Front is a wholly owned subsidiary of Hanoi, there was—after decades of French colonial rule and a long, wasting war against that rule—a genuine element of civil war in the South.

Progress and setbacks were difficult for our people to comprehend, because there was no fixed front. The nature of guerrilla war requires a positive economic, social, and political response from the government under attack, and so the building of a postcolonial nation in the South—with all its difficulties—was interwoven with the military conflict. And, finally, guerrilla war is by its nature a slow combat of attrition, often appearing endless and without hope—the way Hanoi wished it to appear.

In the winter and spring of 1965, the North Vietnamese began to escalate the war—pouring thousands of combat troops down from the North, through Laos, Cambodia, and across the Demilitarized Zone. They were clearly moving in for the kill.

Confronted with this situation, I received this assessment from my advisers in mid-July 1965:

> We must choose among three courses of action with respect to South Vietnam:
> 1. Cut our losses and withdraw under the best conditions that can be arranged—almost certainly conditions humiliating the United States and very damaging to our future effectiveness on the world scene;
> 2. Continue at about the present level, with U.S. forces limited to, say, 75,000, holding on and playing for the breaks while recognizing that our position will probably grow weaker; or
> 3. Expand substantially the U.S. military pressure against the Viet Cong in the South and the North Vietnamese in the North and at the same time launch a vigorous effort on the political side to get negotiations started.

We made the decision to throw the weight of our air power against North Vietnam and to bring our own forces into the battle on the ground.

It was not a decision arrived at on a single day. For weeks we searched for alternatives—conscious that we were for the second time since 1945 committing American troops to battle against a Communist aggressor. During this time, I went twice to my retreat at Camp David, and there turned the painful choices around in my mind—trying to make sure the decision was right, having taken counsel with all who I believed might contribute wisdom.

The last thing I wanted, when the responsibilities and opportunities of the Presidency were thrust upon me, was to become a "wartime" President. There was too much to be done in our own country, and in helping to strengthen our ties to Europe and the developing world. But history determined that I should face the awful choice of intervention or retreat in Southeast Asia. I could not escape or delay it.

During the next three years, the situation markedly improved. Our military strength on the ground in Vietnam grew rapidly. The measures we had taken in the early 1960s, to expand and diversify our forces, began to pay off. Our soldiers and Marines were, by common consent, the equal of any who had ever taken the field

under our flag. They were also the best-equipped. Their firepower and mobility exceeded those of any previous forces in our history.

By the end of 1967, the enemy's main forces had been defeated in battle after battle. And South Vietnam had a government freely elected under a new Constitution—a situation far different from those days, after the assassination of Pres. Ngo Dinh Diem, when coup followed coup and Saigon's authority was constantly under challenge.

Still the enemy retained the power to launch heavy attacks against the main cities of South Vietnam—to inflict heavy casualties and to create hundreds of thousands of refugees. His assault during the Tet holidays at the end of January 1968 failed to achieve its objective of inspiring a revolt and bringing down the government. But it did inspire pessimism among many people—particularly here at home—about the prospects for ending the war on acceptable terms.

At the meeting in Manila in October 1966, the seven nations fighting the war agreed on four principles:
1. Aggression must not succeed.
2. We must break the bonds of poverty, illiteracy, and disease.
3. We must strengthen economic, social, and cultural cooperation within the Asian and Pacific region.
4. We must seek reconciliation and peace throughout Asia.

These were not merely guideposts for a time of war. They expressed our common vision of Asia's future.

The first requirement is a secure and well-monitored settlement in Southeast Asia. Only such a settlement can justify the terrible costs incurred by the people of Vietnam and Laos—as well as those borne by the people of the United States and by our allies. This time the peoples of free Asia and the Pacific must determine that it shall not happen again.

As I set down these thoughts, I cannot know what the situation in Vietnam will be at the time they are printed. But I do know that if the United States remains steady, a satisfactory peace will come. And the task for the future is to make it stick. That should be a task not merely for the United States—not merely for the nations which have assumed responsibility under the Geneva Agreements of 1954 and 1962—but for all the governments and peoples of Asia and the Pacific.

Second, in Vietnam itself we must do all we can to make representative government succeed. It is one of the miracles of our time that the people of South Vietnam, in the midst of war, created a constitutional government. We have learned in these years how hard it is for a developing nation to maintain stable constitutional government. In this century we have seen democratic governments collapse even in advanced Western Europe. We know in Latin America what a struggle it is to make democracy work and to gain the habit of passing power peacefully on constitutional terms. We know the troubles of democratic government in Africa, the Middle East, and in other parts of Asia.

In Vietnam the job was particularly difficult. The country was split in 1954. Even in South Vietnam, there are strong historic divisions among the people based on region and religion and race. French colonialism had tended to fragment the society rather than pull it together. With this background, what was done in the period 1966–68 was all the more remarkable—even heroic.

The vital, strongly individualistic people of South Vietnam want the dignity of constitutional democratic government. And to the extent that we can help them stay on this course, we should do so.

Third, Southeast Asia has made considerable economic and social progress in recent years. South Korea, Taiwan, Thailand, Malaysia, and Singapore are progressing with high momentum and confidence. Indonesia is slowly climbing out of the bankruptcy in which Sukarno left it and is beginning to glimpse the future that its remarkable resources make possible, if political stability is sustained. In Vietnam, despite the war, postwar plan-

ning has gone forward. I have not the slightest doubt that South Vietnam can become an economic success story, just as South Korea has. We in the United States, the Japanese, the Australians, the New Zealanders, and all others who might help must assume responsibility to keep this momentum in Southeast Asia moving.

Finally, we must not for a moment give up the dream and the fact of the new Asia. In the days when I bore the day-to-day burden of Vietnam, my greatest comfort, aside from the performance of our men in the field, was the fact that we were helping to bring about a new spirit of cooperation and confidence in free Asia and the Pacific. The peoples and governments of Asia had never cooperated before throughout their long history, except when under a single master. After our troops were committed in 1965, they began to come together.

Moreover, the peoples of Australia and New Zealand made a critical decision about the time that they put their forces into South Vietnam: that their fate was now tied to Asia's. I went to Manila and toured Asia in the autumn of 1966 to spur this new spirit. No one believed in it more deeply than my friend Harold Holt, whose death in late 1967 was a tragic blow to me. The task for tomorrow—for Australians, New Zealanders, and Americans —is to carry forward the policies of interdependence that Harold Holt and those of us who worked with him began.

We cannot withdraw from our security commitments to Asia. In supporting the Nuclear Nonproliferation Treaty, we are asking these nations, among others, to forgo the manufacture or receipt of nuclear weapons. That treaty—which is greatly to the interest of the American people—carries with it also American responsibilities, in Asia as elsewhere.

But we can hope that the new spirit of cooperation in Asia will in time permit its people to do more for themselves, so that we can do less. If they work together, they have the manpower and capacity largely to assure their own security and prosperity, with the United States a supporting partner in the enterprise.

Finally, reconciliation. Reconciliation must first, somehow, be carried out inside South Vietnam and within Laos, if we are to have peace. I believe the peoples of South Vietnam and Laos are ready for reconciliation, if Hanoi leaves them alone.

But the spirit of reconciliation must cross frontiers that are now battle lines, too. In a talk at Johns Hopkins University in April 1965 I offered the North Vietnamese a share in peaceful economic collaboration with their neighbors and with us. I hope that they will come to accept this. They do not wish to become a province of China. North Vietnam is, essentially, a small, underdeveloped nation with its future still to build. I was encouraged when Pres. Nguyen Van Thieu talked of a postwar period in which decent relations could be established between North and South Vietnam. For the sake of its own people, North Vietnam should join with its neighbors in Southeast Asia in making the most of the Mekong and all the other resources in that potentially rich region. We look forward to the day when our investment in Southeast Asia will be not in war but in aiding its peaceful development.

The tasks for tomorrow include the improvement of our relations with Communist China. China is a great nation with a long sense of identity and importance. It came late into the modern world and under bitter circumstances. Now it is working its painful way through a period in which it will ultimately find that the world has a place for a China that will modernize its life, in its own way, and respect its neighbors as it seeks respect for itself. No American postwar President—and, for that matter, no recent Soviet leader—has had to be told that mainland China is a reality. Each President has known that our international institutions will be incomplete until the day when mainland China takes its place among us in the world community. But there must be, on the part of China's leaders, respect for the right of China's neighbors to live in peace, and acceptance of the facts of life on Taiwan.

In summary, we went to fight in Vietnam because Southeast Asia was threatened by aggression—and, therefore, Asia's future was at stake. In the years to come, our policy must be addressed to progress throughout the region, on the basis of the cooperation that this tragic war has inspired. If we do this, the sacrifices of our men will not have been in vain.

The debate over Vietnam has long since degenerated into a shouting of slogans, and one popular slogan is "No More Vietnams." Those words express my profoundest hope. I hope that America's resistance in Vietnam will discourage future aggressors. Yet if aggression is undertaken and endangers the peace in a vital region of the world, it must be resisted. Otherwise disastrous consequences may follow—not only for that region, but for all those like ourselves who have a stake in peace. We had better face up to Adlai Stevenson's statement of the situation, "The contest with tyranny is not a hundred-yard dash—it is a test of endurance." And "retreat leads to retreat, just as aggression leads to aggression in this still primitive international community."

If word were to go out that the U.S. is abdicating its stabilizing role—and playing such a role does not mean that misleading slogan, "policing the world"—it would simply invite aggression by those who need little invitation now. It would be a deadly blow to the young nations seeking an independent footing in the world. Its consequences in Europe would be just as catastrophic.

A hard-pressed President finds that he must often fall back on the instinct of the American people for his support, and that instinct is sound. It will not long permit a President to retreat into irresponsibility. The penalty I paid for facing duty in Vietnam was a high one, but it was nothing compared to the penalties that would have been exacted had I not done so.

The United Nations. Ideally, the United States should never have to take unilateral action in a foreign crisis at all. Ideally, the organization set up to deal with international crises—the United Nations—should take over the responsibility of dealing with each critical threat to peace and, if necessary, send a force to the region involved to supervise a settlement.

But the effectiveness of the UN has not grown as rapidly as any of us wished. In the Security Council the Soviet veto has remained an obstacle to action in many cases. In the General Assembly the great influx of new nations—which often seem determined to make the UN into a forum only for protest against the dead vice of colonialism—has diluted the organization's effectiveness.

America's effort to make the UN effective has, I believe, been without parallel. We have tried so hard to strengthen its peacemaking efforts that on occasion we have voted against our own allies, as in the Suez crisis of 1956. We have even voted against our own narrow interests, as happened in the payments crisis of 1965, when we yielded to the refusal of France and the Soviet Union and some others to pay their shares for peace-keeping operations in the Middle East and in the Congo.

Some critics of our involvement in Vietnam have repeatedly suggested that we take the crisis to the UN—ignoring the fact that we have done so. At the 20th anniversary of the founding of the UN in 1965, I pleaded with its members to deal with the issue. Two of our distinguished ambassadors to the UN have made the same plea, but the UN refused. And for its part, North Vietnam has steadily rejected the intercession of the UN in what it professes to consider an "internal" struggle.

As a result of the UN's failure to cope with problems such as Vietnam, many Americans have become disenchanted with it, and a few have proposed that it be allowed to die. I cannot agree. Though it does not meet our hopes of maintaining world order, its value remains considerable. Its subsidiary organizations do a great amount of good work. As a forum where offended nations may talk out their grievances, it has been serviceable on many occasions. Perhaps the sensible way to look at the UN—until it does become more effective on its own—is as one more channel of contact among nations who are separated by competing interests in the various regions of the world. For example, during the Arab-Israeli war of 1967, Premier Aleksei N. Kosygin and I talked on the "hot line," and discussed the possibility of bringing a compromise resolution to the UN.

The time may soon be at hand for considering reforms of the UN. I would hope that reforms would contemplate at least one possibility. At present a few extremely strong and many extremely weak nations dominate the organization—the strong nations by veto in the Security Council, the weak by their sheer numbers in the General Assembly. May it not be time to consider ways of urging more responsibility on nations of middle size and power? Why not ask those nations to assume a larger share of the costs? The amount would not be a great additional burden for them, and among other benefits it might diminish some of the resentment felt by Americans at paying the lion's share. It would also permit nations like Australia, Yugoslavia, Sweden, and Italy to increase their voice in world affairs.

I recommend patience to my successors. Any future American leader who let the UN die would probably soon have to open negotiations to re-create it, or something very like it. I also recommend a search for reforms that will take some power away from the two extremes where it now resides.

It is often forgotten that from time to time we and the Soviets have found it possible to agree on actions, as in the Suez crisis, in the Congo, in Cyprus, and with respect to Kashmir. When the Soviet Union sees that we have a common interest in preventing any local crisis from bringing about a confrontation between the two strongest nations, the habit of agreement may grow. And with it would grow the effectiveness of a world body in which so many hopes were invested almost a quarter of a century ago.

Creating Local Strength. The basis for political, spiritual, and military strength in the new nations is economic strength. Aid from the rich nations to the poor nations is an essential means to this end. Those who decry America's aid program point to its failures. These exist, and have been inevitable in the beginnings of a program new to world history, but the fact is that the program's successes have been far more significant than its failures. And its urgency was never greater than it is today.

American economic aid literally saved Western Europe. In other parts of the world, where institutions and traditions are less suited to quick results, the results have nonetheless been impressive. A considerable number of relatively poor, unstable nations have been hoisted to the foot of the escalator—where their economies can begin to grow faster than their increases in population. Once this position has been achieved, there is no end to progress in sight.

Turkey is an example. It has achieved an annual economic growth rate of 6%. South Korea, wallowing in stagnation just a few years ago, now has an annual growth rate of 10%. Malaysia and Iran are at this point. Taiwan has worked itself out of the position of receiving American economic aid.

It is true that the nations that have not yet reached a point of inevitable momentum include India and Pakistan, Indonesia, and much of Latin America. However, there is hope in those nations, provided the spirit of aid does not die—as it sadly threatens to—in some of the nations best equipped to provide aid.

During my Presidency, I sent realistic foreign aid requests to Congress. Yet even these requests were reduced below the peril point. Eminent economists and planners have spoken of certain disaster in the next decade or two, unless the "have" world contributes more of its wealth, resources, and skills to the "have-not" world. Yet congressional support for a modest foreign aid program was virtually nonexistent, even among those who rejected military action as an appropriate response to aggression. One would have thought they would prefer economic assistance as a means of strengthening free nations. But no—they were among its most vociferous critics.

I believe my successors will find no more urgent task in the Presidency than that of creating a new basis for public support of foreign aid. Perhaps a greater emphasis on encouraging private investment would help. In any event, some way must be found to convince the American people that assistance to the developing world now is the best and least-expensive means of preventing chaos in the years to come.

Food. The bone structure of a strong economy is adequate production of food. But for years the lagging production of food has been the nightmare of the new nations, and, until very recently, it seemed destined to grow worse. The threat took two forms: chronic undernourishment and malnutrition.

The size of the problem can be put in large figures. By 1980, world population will, on present trends, grow from 3,400,000,000 to 4,500,000,000. Nearly three-fourths of this increase in mouths to feed will occur in those nations least equipped to take care of it. To feed them will require an annual increase in food production of 4% in those nations. In fact, their recent annual increase has been but half that, 2%.

The task of becoming self-sufficient in food has to be attacked from two sides. In the long run, population control measures must be made widely available. For a long time this matter was considered too delicate to be discussed forthrightly. I began, early in my Presidency, to speak about it—first only a few words, then a paragraph or two, then an extended call for a major commitment.

Making information and facilities available for family planning is the duty of the individual nations themselves, but they need help. In my term, the amount of American aid to help them meet their duty was increased from $2 million a year to $35 million a year. Future Presidents may have to increase the emphasis.

However, population control takes time. There are barriers which are harder to overcome than mere lack of funds. The underdeveloped world cannot wait, however, so the problem has to be attacked from the other side, too—increasing the production of food.

Nothing more hopeful happened in the world in the 1960s than a genuine breakthrough in food production. New varieties of grain have been produced under American auspices—wheat in Mexico, rice in the Philippines, other grains in India. A few years ago some of these new varieties were introduced experimentally in several nations. In the 1964–65 growing season, a few hundred acres were planted. A year later, 23,000 acres were planted. So successful was the result that the number of acres planted in 1967–68 was around 20 million, and as I left office we expected to see that figure doubled.

The new rice is being planted universally in the Philippines. In South Vietnam, rice production is now five times what it was before the new strain was introduced. Also, the growing season for the new rice is appreciably shorter—so that the same land may be used to grow other crops as well.

India's food problem has been of particular concern to me, as it was to President Kennedy. When I was in Asia in 1967, I radioed to Prime Minister Indira Gandhi that "I suspect that I follow the course of the rains and the Indian harvest almost as closely as you." That same season, our concern was amply rewarded. The Indian grain crops were 30% above what they had been the previous year—and some 12% higher than they had ever been in history.

In Pakistan, crops were 30% above the best year in the past. In South America, which is the continent with the largest yearly increase in population, the continent as a whole by last year was producing food at double the rate of increase in its population.

The new varieties of grain are the trigger mechanism. They are to the new agricultural revolution in Asia what the steam engine was to the industrial revolution in Europe.

Our so-called "short tether" policy of giving food aid has helped. We have granted food to needy nations at short intervals and on condition they give food production—mainly the manufacture of fertilizers—a priority that many nations have wished to give instead to heavy industry.

As is usual, the solution of one problem will create new ones. There is the possibility of class frictions, as better-off peasants make better use of the new varieties of grain, while poorer peas-

Premier Aleksei N. Kosygin, U.S.S.R.

Pres. Charles de Gaulle, France, and Pres. Heinrich Lübke, West Germany.

Prime Minister Levi Eshkol, Israel.

Chancellor Kurt Georg Kiesinger, West Germany.

Premier Nguyen Cao Ky, South Vietnam.

Prime Minister Eisaku Sato, Japan.

ants cannot. Price instability may become a problem. But none of these problems nearly equals the benefits. The need of the developing nations to double the rate of food production can now be met. A major source of turbulence that could lead to more wars of insurgency can be eliminated.

On the agenda for the future must be a campaign to see the food-growing revolution extended to all the developing nations. That task will often prove as much psychological as technical. And meanwhile, help in family planning must be increased—unless the problem of food, solved at the producing end, is to be revived by a too rapid increase in mouths to be fed, minds to be educated, and people to be usefully employed.

Growing Together Is Faster and Surer. The leaders of the subversive movements of the developing world are rarely hungry peasants. They are usually members of something like a middle class, who feel that society is stagnant and that they have no place in it. So even when the problem of food is met, there remains the problem of general economic growth.

One of the clear lessons of the past two decades is that the old nation-state is not an adequate unit for development.

One of the major efforts of my administration was to apply the principle of regional cooperation to those parts of the world where Vietnams might occur.

At Mexico City in April 1966 I said: "The drawing together of the economies of Latin America is critical to this hemisphere's future. Only in this way can the hemisphere develop truly efficient industries, expanded foreign exchange earnings, and a sound foundation for full Latin-American partnership in building a peaceful world community."

In the Pan-American conference at Punta del Este in 1967, the leaders of Latin-American governments formally committed themselves to move toward economic integration beginning in 1970 and to complete the process by 1985. At that meeting I deliberately withdrew from the United States' traditional role of a senior partner, to that of a junior partner in a process in which Latin America must take the lead. At this point, all that is certain is that a commitment has been made.

The habit of noncooperation left over from the past is deeply imbedded. Today a man in Lima, Peru, who wishes to telephone a man in Rio de Janeiro, Braz.—just across the Andes—must go through the exchange in Miami, Fla., or New York City. The trip from southern Brazil to Rio—roughly the same distance as from Boston to Washington—may take as much as two or three days. And the nations throughout the continent have great natural resources which their neighbors cannot or do not use. Locked behind the mountains, rain forests, and deserts of South America are fertile lands and unknown resources. Only a tremendous cooperative effort in road and rail building will make them available to Latin America's millions. And if Latin America's effort is to succeed, American policy will have to remain active in support of the integration movement.

The Central American nations have already begun a common market, a common bank to provide funds for regional projects, and a monetary council. They have multiplied trade among their members by seven times in the past seven years. With an annual economic growth rate of 6%, they have been able to increase funds for education by 50%. None of this would have been possible without integration.

Progress is still not rapid enough in the whole of Latin America, but a mood is growing within to force the pace. In the fall of 1968, a working paper for the Council of Latin American Bishops said with unusual bluntness: "A lack of technical development, blind oligarchic classes and foreign big business block necessary reforms and offer active resistance to everything that could work against their interests, and, in consequence, create a situation of violence. . . . A tiny minority receives the great part of income . . . while the great masses have a minimum income and are subject to the constant peril of unemployment." Strong words like these, from a source once considered extremely conservative, show the force for change in Latin America.

Some U.S. businesses in Latin America have begun to move with this force—actively seeking Latin-American participation in ownership and management, trying to be progressive citizens who give as much to their host countries as they gain. Others have not done so, and their shortsightedness has helped to make all U.S. businesses in Latin America subject to attack. The "colossus of the north" is a convenient enough scapegoat for the ills of Latin-American economies, without providing extra cause for criticism.

Success in the years ahead—for both U.S. business and Latin America—obviously depends upon greater cooperation, understanding, and joint participation. Motives of simple aggrandizement on the one hand, and confiscation on the other, will serve the interest of neither.

Success will depend, just as well, on the willingness of wealthy Latin Americans to keep their capital at home—investing it in their countries' future—instead of banking it elsewhere.

In the spring of 1966 I addressed the ambassadors to Washington from the African nations—the first speech ever given by an American President on Africa. We offered help in the development of regional projects on that continent. We then conducted a major study, led by former Ambassador to Ethiopia Edward Korry. He consulted a broad range of experts, public and private,

YOICHI OKAMOTO

here and abroad. As a result we began restructuring our aid program to Africa, moving away from individual and general assistance and toward specific regional aid. We are by no means the principal givers of aid to that vast continent. Yet we have a great interest in its stability and progress—an interest that is sure to grow in the coming decade.

As I said earlier, history forced me to develop a special interest in Asian regionalism. I am convinced that future Presidents and Congresses will find the trend toward regional concentrations of strength the most useful means of filling the dangerous voids on the map left by the old European empires.

The Soviet Union. Aside from the race against want and the need for joint action to preserve the peace and stimulate development, two other facts dominate the decisions of a President of the United States from his first moment in office.

One is that America has within call a nuclear firepower that works out to the equivalent of about 30,000 tons of TNT for every human being alive.

The other fact is that the Soviet Union is the only nation on earth that possesses a similar destructive force. Theirs is somewhat less in size, but the average human being would not be able to detect the difference in being hit by 30,000 tons of explosive

or 15,000 tons of it. No matter how much our patience is strained, no matter how many suspicions are aroused and revulsions created, we must find a way to live in peace with the Soviet Union—without either nation being forced to sacrifice its legitimate interests.

In my term in office I gave special priority to what came to be called "bridge building" between the two nations. I had not been in office a month when I drafted a letter to Premier Nikita S. Khrushchev proposing negotiations to limit armaments. And in a speech in New York City on October 7, 1966, I said that the wound running through Europe—the iron curtain—"must be healed peacefully. It must be healed with the consent of the Eastern European countries . . . and of the Soviet Union. This will happen only as East and West succeed in building a surer foundation of mutual trust." In the period that followed, West Germany began recognizing diplomatically, and seeking agreements with, the Soviet Union and the nations of Eastern Europe.

I soon lost count of the number of prophets who foretold failure for this effort, because of our commitment in Vietnam. In the pauses between their forecasts, we concluded the most remarkable series of U.S.-Soviet agreements since the cold war began: a treaty outlawing nuclear weapons in outer space; a treaty establishing consular relations, which was the first bilateral treaty negotiated between the two nations since 1933; a civil air agreement; and most important of all, a treaty to ban the spread of nuclear weapons. In addition, it has been agreed to try to negotiate a limitation of the two nations' missile armaments. I had intended to announce a meeting with Soviet leaders to begin these negotiations, when their tanks rolled into Czechoslovakia. And in spite of that brutal setback to accommodation between the two superpowers, turning down the arms race between us remains an urgent necessity.

The main obstacle between our two great nations—who have no claim whatever of a territorial or material nature against one another—has been the Communist ideology. During the 1960s, there were promising signs that this ideology was growing tired and outdated and might wither from its own irrelevance. Both in the Soviet Union and in the satellite nations of Eastern Europe, a progressive liberalization became one of the most hopeful developments since the end of World War II. The Soviet invasion of Czechoslovakia badly damaged the world's hopes and ours. I am inclined to believe that the act was ultimately self-destructive. Nothing in a half century of Communism has so badly fragmented and soured its parties in the non-Communist world.

To my successors, I leave a promising foundation of agreements that meet several elemental requirements of both nations. I recommend that they be guardedly built upon. If the world can survive another decade without permitting regional crises to develop into a global catastrophe, I believe that changes within the Soviet Union will help to lessen the tension between it and the rest of mankind. But a key element in moving that evolution forward is an unmistakable signal from the major non-Communist powers that adventurism that threatens the peace will not be tolerated.

Carrying the People. To my successors, I offer the following judgments for such use as they care to make of them.

They should experiment with new ways to explain foreign policy to the American people and win their understanding support. Through most of world history, foreign policy was the exclusive province of the aristocratic few in government. In our time everyone has become involved. The American press has multiplied its reporters covering our State Department and foreign capitals. Every evening, television brings into every home the most vivid pictures of foreign policy in action—in Europe, in Vietnam, in Panama, in the Middle East. Once largely a stay-at-home people, Americans since 1941 have traveled the world as soldiers, then as tourists and students, in soaring numbers. There are many instant authorities now, with clear opinions on every crisis. A democratic leader has to make new exertions to win their understanding. The gap between the intelligence information that a President deals with daily and the public's grasp of foreign events as reported by the media must somehow be narrowed.

The stress I place on informing the public may sound odd to those persuaded by the myths about secretiveness that have grown up in recent years—"managed news" in President Kennedy's years, "credibility gaps" in mine.

In fact, during my years in office we tried in a wide variety of ways to explain our foreign policy decisions to the American people. Secretary of State Dean Rusk held regular briefings for editors and journalists invited to Washington from all over the nation, and the frankest exchanges took place.

The point has been made that had I been more eloquent on the subject of foreign affairs, and shared more of Winston Churchill's qualities as a speaker, I might have been more successful. Churchill was unquestionably the most eloquent statesman in modern history. Yet he was just as eloquent as a member of Parliament in 1937, 1938, and 1939 as he was as prime minister in 1940. Nevertheless, his eloquence was unable to get a hearing until his nation was in mortal danger. (Indeed, had he been heeded earlier, and had Britain made a stand when Nazi troops moved on the Sudetenland, he would probably have been politically roasted for involvement in an obscure, faraway place—and for putting credence in the ridiculous dominolike theory that if the Sudetenland went, then Czechoslovakia, Poland, and France and all of Europe would not be far behind.)

There is a stock, popular criticism of foreign policy which recurs with the regularity of the seasons: "We never have the initiative. We always react to our opponents' initiatives. We run from one brush fire to another and lack a long-range policy to prevent brush fires."

Yet the only way to have the initiative in a crisis is to be the cause of the crisis. Aggressors "have the initiative" as well as the odium for their deeds. A democratic nation, dependent on public opinion, is in the nature of things essentially on the defensive in such situations. However, as crises have developed, we have developed initiatives that have ended most of them successfully.

We do have a long-range policy to prevent brush fires, but the trouble with long-range policies is that they *are* long range. They take time and patience and persistence, in the face of inevitable setbacks, to carry through. And I believe we can say that our policies work—both our long-range policies and the immediate tactics we have applied to successive individual crises.

Our initial action in the Dominican Republic, taken on the recommendation of our ambassador, was intended to assure the evacuation of some 5,000 endangered foreigners, most of them Americans, from a situation of chaos and breakdown of public authority. When that was accomplished, we ordered additional troops to the Dominican Republic to prevent Communists from capitalizing on the bloody civil strife and achieving a take-over—such as occurred only a short time ago in Cuba.

We reported our action to the OAS and obtained its support in the reestablishment of peace and normal conditions in the Dominican Republic. The 10th Meeting of Foreign Ministers of the OAS, called at our initiative, authorized an Inter-American Peace Force, including contingents from five nations and officers from a sixth, who joined with units of the United States to make up the first temporary peace-keeping force ever established by members of the inter-American system.

An Ad Hoc Committee of Foreign Ministers, during three months of patient negotiations, laid the groundwork for a provisional government and free elections, thus preserving for the Dominican people the right to make their own choice of leaders. The result has been a government with broad-based popular support and greater stability than any of its post-Trujillo era predecessors. Contrast that with Soviet intervention in Czechoslovakia to put a halt to freedom and the result it produced of very nearly wrecking the Communist bloc of nations.

Our role in South Vietnam has persuaded the nations of Asia that they have a future in freedom and independence. Contrast the soaring growth of nations we have aided—South Korea and Taiwan—with the mediocre progress of Communist-aided nations like North Korea and, even before their aggression, North Vietnam.

We have had aggravating problems, but contrast them with the Soviet Union's problems in Eastern Europe. Our Western alliance has loosened because of success. But there has been nothing in it like the raging conflict between the Soviet Union and China with actual territorial claims, as well as violent abuse, being heaped on one another.

Our problems in the developing countries have been frustrating. But note the collapse of what once seemed a growing Chinese prestige among the nations of Asia and Africa. Leaders who were prepared to be Communist clients have, one by one, been overthrown by their angry peoples: Sukarno, Nkrumah, Ben Bella.

When we consider the state of the world eight years ago, when John Kennedy and I came into office, we gain a better perspective on America's problems in foreign policy today.

Then, the Congo was in flames, ready for a Communist adventure. Cuba had fallen to a Communist regime—the first, and I pray last, breach in the wall of the Americas. Communist China—unified and aggressive—was challenging India's northern provinces. Laos was threatened with a Communist take-over. Indonesia was slipping toward Communist rule. President Eisenhower's proposed visit to Japan was canceled, for fear of violent demonstrations. Vice-Pres. Richard M. Nixon's trip to Latin America had been met with violent discourtesy. A confrontation in Berlin was imminent. There seemed no early hope for meeting the immense food shortages in the developing nations. Fallout from atmospheric tests of nuclear weapons was threatening to become a severe health hazard.

I cite these facts only to suggest that every American President has faced, and will face, a continuing series of challenges to world peace and American security. John Kennedy experienced the Bay of Pigs, Khrushchev's blunt attempts at intimidation in Vienna, a threat in Berlin that caused him to call up the reserves, the Cuban missile crisis, and the first terrible decisions over Vietnam. He knew what world leadership entailed for an American President and people: some opportunity, tremendous and inescapable responsibilities, and a succession of emergencies. President Roosevelt, President Truman, President Eisenhower, and I have known these things as well. One certainty in this uncertain world is that our successors will know them too—and they will struggle, as we did, to be wise enough and brave enough to bear them.

"It is," John Kennedy said at a time when criticism was rising against him, "a very dangerous, untidy world. But we have to live with it."

We shall live with it much better if our leaders succeed in communicating the political and moral necessities of their decisions to our people; and if the people, and the press, grant our leaders a measure of compassion and a degree of patience. That— and the determination to maintain the quest for progress and a stable peace in "a very dangerous world."

THE QUALITY OF LIFE

When America celebrated its first hundred years, the fireworks that lighted the skies revealed a nation confident that it had been specially blessed by Providence. A way of government that the world had considered an experiment had survived even the test of Civil War. Its industrial production was charging ahead at a rate no nation in history had ever known. On the Fourth of July in 1876, Americans knew that we were going to make it. They no longer thought of their nation as experimental. Neither did the nations of old Europe who were in the process of dismantling aristocratic structures and beginning to emulate our way of government of, by, and for the people.

YOICHI OKAMOTO
With J. Edgar Hoover, Nicholas Katzenbach, and aides.

Our second centennial is close upon us now. What are we going to be thinking on that milestone Independence Day eight years from now? Will we be looking forward to a third century with the same confidence, but on a higher and more advanced level? Or will we sense in our hearts that, in the face of accumulating new problems, our dream is failing?

It will be one or the other, I believe. Time, which was our friend so long, is impatient now.

Rarely in our history have the crossroads for America been so clearly marked. Rarely has so much depended on the turn we now take.

The point should be made that there is no God-given assurance that we are going to succeed. What happens to us will depend on what individual American men and women resolve to do—or what they neglect and lose heart in doing. It will depend on leadership being right and courageous, and on citizenship being constructive both in deed and criticism.

Let me state the problem we face in general terms before going on to details.

After the Civil War our growth in wealth and power was simply fantastic. The world had seen nothing like it before. Between Appomattox and the turn of the century, we hewed out of the wilderness enough new farms to fill twice the combined areas

of Britain and France. We transformed ourselves from a minor industrial power into one that could produce in 1900 twenty times as much steel as the entire world had produced thirty years before.

If our development in those days could be likened to a prairie fire of growth, it has in the present century taken on aspects of an explosion of growth. Barbara Ward, the British commentator and economist, noted that in the four years of World War II "the Americans built on top of their old economy another one of almost equivalent size." And in the quarter century that followed, we built on top of *that* old economy another twice as big again.

We have created a prosperity that no people before us have known, but two facts mar it.

One is that our phenomenal progress brought its own problems, and we did not pay enough attention to them while they were developing.

Perhaps the clearest case of neglect and delay was in our response to the tremendous migration of rural Americans—many of them Negroes—to the cities, beginning in the 1940s. In the 1950s alone, nearly ten million people made that move. Many lacked the skills that city life requires. They thought they were moving from hopelessness and discrimination to prosperity and freedom. They sought a fair share in the growing affluence of American life.

But they were not ready for the pressures of the cities, and the cities were not ready for them. City budgets and services were simply unprepared for their new residents, and as more prosperous families moved to the suburbs, the cities' tax base was steadily diminished. The problem was of national dimensions, but the national government, like most city and state governments, did not respond in time.

Another problem of prosperity, long neglected, is the threat it has posed to our environment. We have physical comforts and industrial might beyond the dreams of any previous generation. Yet the more we produce, the more wastes we pour into the rivers and poisons into the air, the more we deface great stretches of a beautiful country. Pollution has such a grip on the nation now that it menaces virtually all our rivers and lakes, and at least one of our Great Lakes might be beyond reclamation.

There is congestion on our magnificent road system, too. The automobile was invented to liberate man and speed his movement. But in the cities, it has hobbled him with an almost endless traffic jam.

The second blot on our record of prosperity is inequity. Even as our expanding affluence has enriched the lives of most of us, some are left behind in poverty—with little chance of working their way out on their own.

Prosperity alone does not help the man who cannot fill out a job application because he is illiterate or who is not trained to do anything more complicated than push a broom. It does not help the boy whose skin bars him from the opportunities open to others of his generation.

An estimated 22 million poor Americans still live in the squalid shadows of our wealth. In some of them—in those who see no stake for themselves in our society—a desperate anger burns. It has already broken out in mass violence and destruction. If it continues to burn, we can see on the horizon the gathering threat of a divided America: two nations, confronting each other across the ruins of our democratic dream. That must not be. No President—no people—can allow it to be.

The problem we face is to make the quality of American life—and I mean life for all Americans—match the quantity of our wealth.

The basic philosophy for achieving this aim was formed and elaborated by many great Democrats—especially by Franklin Roosevelt, Harry Truman, and Adlai Stevenson. When John Kennedy and I won the election of 1960, we were given the opportunity of transforming that philosophy into reality. Tragic fate struck down President Kennedy, and it was left to me—and to Hubert Humphrey, one of the foremost fighters for human rights of our time—to begin the transformation.

I do not believe there is a precedent in our past for the flow of legislative acts since 1964 designed to meet the problem: the first federal aid and incentive toward improved education; civil rights acts that broke the back of powerful legal obstacles to equality; the first concentrated efforts to begin rebuilding our cities and to crack open the hard core of poverty; conservation acts to rescue air, water, and open spaces from ruin; all this and much more, including the most concerted campaign ever to bring local government into intimate collaboration in carrying out all these programs.

We in the administration were more aware than our critics of the pitfalls on the way. The mere announcement of programs that had been needed too long aroused expectations that could not be quickly met. The first opening of doors to opportunity that had been too long shut produced impatience and even rebelliousness in those who wanted to charge through those doors. Not everything we tried resulted in instant success—and sometimes there was no success at all. For we were experimenting on the outer edge of understanding where necessary trial is bound to produce a good deal of error.

However, we could not wait until our understanding was complete and our procedures were perfected. We had to act. We had to begin. And we did—aware of the immensity of our undertaking, but certain that inaction and timidity were worse than occasional failure.

I remember each commitment—from that almost paralyzing day in November 1963 when the Presidency was thrust upon me, until the 90th Congress adjourned in 1968.

I remember how we struggled to shape each commitment into the language of a bill that began, "Be it enacted." I remember the long weeks of inactivity as our program rested in committees on Capitol Hill, and then the sudden bursts of bargaining, amending, reshaping, and rallying support—in the Congress, and in the nation at large.

I remember the young men who had swept into office in the election of 1964, voting bravely and conscientiously for change, breaking the logjams of years, sending bill after bill back down Pennsylvania Avenue for the President's signature.

I remember those happy summer mornings in the Rose Garden, or in the East Room of the White House, when a commitment was signed into a law.

These were the people's triumphs. Wise men helped to devise them; courageous and farsighted men voted for them; but they came into being because the people needed them and demanded them and finally won them.

But none of what we have achieved is self-executing. Laws that require equal justice must be enforced. Programs that express our commitment to progress must be funded. An education act cannot teach a single child. A housing act cannot give shelter to a single family, nor can a manpower act provide a single job, nor can a civil rights act give one human being the dignity and respect he deserves.

The real test of our commitment is whether we are willing to achieve, over a period of years, what those acts only promise.

I know very well that many Americans resist the idea of further federal efforts in these fields.

Some believe that "enough has already been done." But our problems persist—and are not going to disappear by themselves.

Others are troubled by the fact that, while practical and obvious improvements do not always come quickly, emotions that have been charged by change rise to the surface at once.

The answer to this concern may not be comforting, but it is true. It is that from the beginning of time, men have begun to demand more from life—democracy, or education, or a chance to live decently—only when a better life has seemed possible. Only when the door to hope is set ajar, do men thrust to enter. In our time, a progressive nation, a modern economy, and mass communications have joined to set that door ajar—to create hope and instill determination in many millions who had never dared to hope before.

The certain fact is that there is no turning back—no closing of that door. We can weather our troubles now—because the kind of America we seek is right, and because the alternative, denying just hopes and risking a divided and hostile nation, is intolerable.

By the time we enter our third century, or very soon thereafter, we can, if we will, make the commitments of the 1960s a reality for all our people.

We can virtually eradicate poverty as it is known today.

We can place a college degree within the reach of every young man and woman who has the ability and the desire to obtain one.

We can guarantee every expectant mother and infant child good medical care.

We can eliminate officially condoned discrimination of every kind.

We can provide a decent job for every worker and a decent home for every family.

Today, most Americans are not poor; most young people have an opportunity for college education; most mothers and babies have access to good medical care; most able-bodied workers are employed; and most families are well housed.

For this more fortunate majority, the issues that determine the "quality of life" are not so elemental as food, jobs, and shelter—the fundamental concerns of the poor and the disadvantaged. The majority is concerned—and will be increasingly concerned

—with whether there are enough *meaningful* jobs;

—with the quality of the education their children receive;

—with the cost of public services and medical care;

—with safety on their streets and in their homes;

—with finding and securing privacy when they need it;

—with the standard of conduct in their communities, and with a sense of understanding between the generations;

—with making the voice of the individual heard in the tumult of mass society.

Some of these concerns cannot be met by the adoption of a program by Congress, or even by the states and cities. They will be answered only by the choices that individuals and groups of private citizens make to shape their lives and institutions.

But national choices, public choices, will also affect the quality of their lives.

No matter how far a family moves from the heart of urban trouble, it cannot escape the consequences of our failure to help those who need help most. The riots of the past few years have made that clear.

No matter how prosperous or poor urban Americans may be, they must breathe the same air—air that is either clean and clear or loaded with chemical danger to their lives.

We will all walk streets that are either safe or dangerous, attractive or eyesores, welcoming or forbidding. We will all have a chance to know the joys of forests and shores set aside for our careful use, or none of us will. Our schools, colleges, and hospitals will either be good for all or for almost none.

We are, for all our mobility, one people—fated to enjoy a prosperous, secure, and enlightened life together or to hurt each other in mutual mistrust and anger.

Therefore, the choices we make on the great public issues of our time will affect not only those living in poverty and blight but also those who have escaped it or have never known it.

In what follows, I shall give my ideas about some of the continuing public concerns of our people—that affect our private lives. I shall talk of the choices that we shall have to make in the years ahead—if we are to achieve, by the beginning of our third century, the goals we have set for ourselves.

ECONOMIC GROWTH

The first condition for achieving these goals is the steady expansion of our national production. Prosperity alone may never be a cure-all for our problems, but it is the indispensable vehicle for overcoming them. It enriches the lives of about 85% of our people directly—through higher pay and higher profits—

and gives government the needed funds to carry out programs to help the other 15% living in poverty.

This may seem obvious to most Americans in 1969, but it was only recently that the policies that express this understanding began to play a role in our national policy.

For a century prior to 1961, the United States suffered recurrent recessions. When John Kennedy and I entered office, a large part of the nation's productive capacity was going unused. Our national production was growing at a rate of only 2% a year—the lowest rate of all the major industrial nations of the world.

As a result, by 1961 unemployment had risen to 7% of our work force. There were more than 38 million people living in poverty. And government revenues were woefully inadequate to meet our mounting problems at home.

When Premier Khrushchev threatened in the late '50s to "bury" us economically, few Americans laughed. Our economy—beset by recession, spotty growth, and unemployment—was too sluggish for easy confidence.

The "new economics" which we began to practice in the 1960s has been described as prosperity with a social conscience.

Whatever it was called, it worked.

For the first time, the Council of Economic Advisers, the secretary of the treasury, and the budget director operated as an integrated team. Their job was to help our free market economy protect itself from either sharp decline or dangerous overheating—to give us an early warning system for trouble and to steer us away from problems before they occurred.

Some thought the "boom and bust" cycle was unbreakable. I disagreed. I believed that with the cooperation of business and labor, and with a finely tuned fiscal and monetary policy, we could break it. The Council shared my view.

Compiling mountains of statistical data from every sector of our national life, they left as little as possible to chance. In 1964 and 1965, when it became apparent that the economy needed an extra stimulus, we obtained tax reductions totalling about $24 billion a year, in today's economy. In 1968, with the economy moving too fast and prices rising at a rate of 4% a year, we raised taxes and took back less than half of that—about $11 billion.

One of the most troublesome aspects of our economy grew out of the costs of the Vietnam war.

This was the most difficult part of our budget to predict, because we had no experience in estimating the cost of this kind of war. The extra military expenditures that we found we needed placed tremendous pressures on our economy—and on wage-price stability.

But even here our early warning system worked. We experienced an inflationary spiral, but we were able to keep it within reasonable bounds.

In fact, prices rose an average of only 2.1% per year during the 1961–68 period—an identical increase to that of the eight years of the Eisenhower administration.

During the Korean War, when the government actually controlled wages and prices, the consumer index rose significantly higher than during the Vietnam buildup, when there were no government controls of any sort.

When I left office, the nation was in the 95th month of the longest period of uninterrupted economic growth in its history.

For America, those years of prosperity meant that median family income rose to a record high—from $6,000 to above $8,000 a year. These gains were shared by every major group—workers, farmers, businessmen, stockholders, and professionals.

But just as important, our prosperity gave us the funds to launch an attack on the root causes of poverty and the other serious problems that confronted us.

If we ever return to the outdated economic notions of the past—and I pray we shall not—we will find ourselves without the jobs or the private and public investments we need for social

progress. We will almost certainly see a rise of social tensions beyond anything we have ever known.

But even as our economy expands, we must be on constant guard against inflation. When the economy is growing, labor tends to demand wage increases that are too high, and business tends to raise the prices of its goods too much. Dollars are poured into the economy faster than the economy turns out goods. Prices are pulled and pushed upward, and people get less for their money. Inflation amounts to an unseen tax which in fact takes part of the benefits of prosperity away from the people.

I know of no effective way to force business and labor to show restraint in their demands. Our experience during World War II and Korea proved that government controls were unsatisfactory. They placed an artificial burden on the economy and resulted in shortages of goods and deterioration in their quality.

I have always believed in the free operation of the market. The government can exhort. It can provide detailed information to persuade all sides that restraint is in their best interest. But I do not believe it is healthy for the government to enforce its judgments through rigid instruments of restraint.

Theodore Roosevelt once called the White House a "bully pulpit," and I had plenty of opportunities to find out what he meant. It seemed to me sometimes that I spent half of my time pleading and cajoling and reasoning with labor leaders and corporate presidents, trying to get them to hold the wage and price line. And every time, it occurred to me how much better it would be if they worked out their own guidelines for responsible wage and price actions.

The question of inflation aside, the real problem is, how do we maintain and increase production and growth? Later I will describe some positive things that can be done. They add up to getting money into the people's pockets in reward for work, so that in spending it they stimulate industry to produce more and better goods.

But there are several direct methods of regulating the economy that ought to be available to an executive.

Our experience in the 1960s proved that lowering taxes when the economy is sluggish and raising them when the economy starts to "overheat" is a successful method of influencing economic growth. However, in the case of both the tax reduction of 1964 and the tax increase of 1968, debate and controversy over my proposals lasted far too long in Congress. On both occasions, we carried the economy into dangerous waters before action was finally taken.

This was especially true of the tax increase, which I wanted to recommend to Congress as early as 1966. The Council of Economic Advisers recommended then that Congress be asked to pass a modest tax increase in order to combat inflationary trends in the economy. Their reasoning was compelling. The facts were there—hard and uncompromising.

Two meetings followed—both of them disheartening.

First I called our leaders of Congress together in the White House. I told them of the Council's recommendation and my own judgment that a tax increase was needed. Would Congress support it? The answer was that it would be "folly" to recommend it. It would get, at most, 4 votes out of 25 on the House Ways and Means Committee. This was an election year. You couldn't expect support for increasing taxes—even if it was only a fraction of the tax reductions of the past two years—in that political climate.

Hoping to appeal to the country over the heads of Congress, I asked more than 125 business leaders to come to the White House on March 30, 1966. The entire Cabinet, the CEA, and the chairman of the Federal Reserve were there. After briefings on foreign developments and our economic situation, I put this question to the business leaders: "How many of you, if you were President, would recommend a tax bill to Congress tomorrow? Raise your hand if you would." Not a hand went up. Not one hand. So the outlook for a tax increase was not just bleak. It was impossible.

When the surtax was finally passed, two years later—after a delay that further jeopardized the economy—we had to accept a cut of $6 billion in an already tight budget before Congress would approve our bill. Fortunately, in carrying out our responsibilities under the act, we were able to allocate the cut in such a way that it did not imperil most of our urgently needed social programs.

The surtax experience convinced me that we must assure prompt action on tax measures. This can be done in a number of ways. Presidents could be allowed a limited discretion to adjust taxes by executive action—something on the order of 5% up or down. This authority might be conditioned by giving Congress a period of time to acquiesce in the adjustment or to veto it. Alternatively, the Congress might amend its rules to provide that a Presidential bill calling for a tax increase or decrease be given priority over other pending legislation and acted on within a specified time.

I also believe we should strengthen our fiscal-monetary team to give us greater control over fluctuating interest rates. I would make the term of the chairman of the Federal Reserve Board coincide with the President's term of office. The board would still have its independence, but a chairman appointed by an incoming President is likely to be more sensitive to the overall policies of his administration.

In the next few years, we shall have to deal with a number of other troublesome economic issues that will affect the lives of most Americans. Among them are: the rising cost of medical care; the increasing cost of public services; spiraling land values, which make it difficult to build the housing units we need at acceptable costs; and building costs, particularly when they are inflated by obsolete or unnecessary building codes.

Neither federal fiscal nor monetary action can be as effective in dealing with most of these issues as can local governments and institutions. If our people want relief from increased costs in these areas, they will have to begin making their voices heard, not only in Congress, but in their state capitols, their city halls, county and city councils, and planning commissions.

POVERTY

I came out of the hardscrabble country of central Texas, where everybody was poor. If there was a rich man in town when I was growing up, I didn't know who he was. Johnson City's leading banker made $300 a month. A schoolteacher was lucky to get $100. I never went hungry, and I grew up in a clean and decent home, but I knew what poverty was.

I was a young man, heading up the National Youth Administration in Texas, when Franklin Delano Roosevelt saved the nation from disaster by using its power and resources to help poor and hungry citizens. I saw what a unique opportunity—and responsibility—the government had to help poor people help themselves.

But there were still 35 million Americans living beneath the poverty line when I became President—in an era of growing prosperity. The poor were, and are, a continual ache in the nation's heart.

There are hard economic, as well as humane, reasons why widespread poverty is intolerable. How much faster our businesses would expand, how much profits and jobs would grow, if we were able to develop the enormous potential market right here at home: among those millions of Americans who can buy very little because they are poor. If they were converted into prosperous consumers, the national economy would get a lift that no gain in foreign markets could supply.

I was determined that in my administration we would begin to take concerted action against poverty in America.

The final decision to wage what came to be known as the War on Poverty was made over the Christmas season of 1963—just a month after I took office—at my ranch in Texas. I called down from Washington my budget director, the chairman of the Council of Economic Advisers, and two of my special assistants.

I laid out three broad objectives: to prevent people on the margin from slipping into poverty; to help those trapped in poverty lift themselves out; and to make life easier for the poor who could not hope to escape poverty because of the handicap of age or disability.

I told my advisers I wanted the major effort to be directed toward children and youth—and that I did not want a program of make-work. I wanted to take poor young people, with most of their lives ahead of them, and train them and teach them so they might move into the mainstream of American life.

I knew that we would have to break new ground. No society had ever really launched a large-scale attack on poverty before. Even the New Deal did not touch the basic roots of poverty. It was confronted with vast unemployment and a direct national emergency. The New Deal had to concentrate on supplying temporary jobs and funds to laborers and white collar workers who were facing hard times.

The hard-core poor are a special kind of people. Many of them have never had real jobs, and they are not trained or equipped to handle them. Many have never had adequate incomes and do not know how to spend money wisely. Born into poverty to parents who had never known hope or who had given up hoping long ago, many simply have no motivation to reach up for something better. Broken families, delinquency, boredom, waste—a conviction of helplessness—this is their bitter heritage.

The programs which we initiated under the Office of Economic Opportunity—Head Start, Community Action, VISTA, Job Corps—were only part of the overall effort to reach the disadvantaged and hard-core poor. They were supplemented by a host of other programs designed to break up the kind of poverty that perpetuates itself generation after generation. For we conceived of the War on Poverty as an integrated attack, along many fronts, on the wretched living conditions of the entire poor community.

The OEO programs are the most experimental part of that attack—and deliberately so. They go beyond the tangible and familiar symbols of jobs and medical treatment. They work with more fragile things—awakening in a slum child the desire to learn, stirring in a discouraged man a sense of his own importance, giving a poor community a voice in directing its own affairs and consequently an interest in its future.

We had plenty of disappointments—and God knows we made mistakes, because we were in new territory. We trusted some people who did not deserve that trust. Trying to reach delinquents among the poor, a few Community Action Programs found themselves merely subsidizing delinquency. A few others discovered that they were supporting nihilists in the name of self-expression. But though these were the programs that generally made the news, they were a small minority among the hundreds of programs in communities across the land.

Not all of our poverty programs were running smoothly when I left office. They are still too new. Not all the experimenting is behind us.

But our people should not become disillusioned with temporary setbacks and occasional mistakes. The *easy* problems of unemployment yield to a prospering economy and to conventional programs of education and training. The problems that remain are the ones that baffle the experts. And the closer we get to eliminating all poverty, the more difficult the job will become. But that does not offer the slightest justification for failing to help people become the best they are capable of becoming.

In the long sweep, the results are what really count. And I think those results, by any standard, are spectacular. Since 1963, 13 million Americans—almost 40% of those whose family income was under $3,000 in 1964—have been lifted out of poverty. Almost three times faster than before, families have been escaping from the want in which they were trapped for so long.

But the figures of progress also help to define the problem. We estimated at the end of 1968 that 22 million Americans—two-thirds of them white—were *still* very poor. They must be rescued.

In four short years we mobilized the collective determination of our people to overcome this national blight. We enlisted half a million volunteers to take an active part in the battle.

But there were signs, by the time I left office, that our resolve was weakening. There was a growing reluctance in the Congress to appropriate the funds we needed to operate these programs. There was a grumbling around the country that we were wasting our time and resources.

Well, we can turn our backs if we wish. We can congratulate ourselves for having even made the effort in the first place, and then conclude that the task is just too big for us. But those 22 million people will still be there, sinking deeper and deeper into the morass of despair. And before long, some of those 13 million whom we helped over the poverty line will be slipping back.

And future generations will say of us: At the very moment when they had more wealth than any civilization in history, they allowed poverty to become a permanent part of the American way of life.

I reject that course. I hope all of us will reject it.

As I left office, my advisers told me the goal of eliminating poverty by 1976 was well within our grasp, if we want to reach it badly enough. Continued economic growth can reach part of the poor—perhaps reducing their number to 15 or 16 million people by that time.

But a growing economy alone will not be enough. Here is what I think should be done in the years ahead:

More jobs must be developed, particularly in needed public and community services.

Family-planning services should be made available to all the poor who desire them. Only one out of five low-income women have this service available to them now—and the result last year is estimated at nearly half a million unwanted pregnancies.

We must continue to improve schools in the ghettos and to expand Head Start and its follow-through programs. The classroom can be the surest route out of the slum.

In 1967, I recommended that the Congress enact a 15% Social Security increase, with a $70 monthly minimum. This would have moved two million Americans out of poverty in a single stroke. As it turned out, the Congress enacted a smaller increase, with a $55 floor. This moved a million people out of poverty.

I believe that the Congress, over the next few years, should increase Social Security benefits by approximately 50%, with a minimum monthly benefit of $100. Doing this would lift four million more people above the poverty line.

Health services for the poor must be improved. All discrimination in jobs and housing must be ended.

And finally, something must be done about the system of public welfare in America.

The welfare system, as I stated to the Congress last year, pleases no one. The cost of administering welfare is far too high, because workers must spend 90% of their time investigating recipients to make sure they are not cheating. The investigations themselves are an affront to the dignity of the applicants. And the benefits are tragically irregular: a dependent child in Mississippi receives $8 a month, compared to a rate of $52.50 a month in Minnesota.

I have recommended a number of important changes in our welfare system. Congress did not adopt them, and the states were no more receptive to reform than before.

Dissatisfaction with welfare has directed attention to other methods of making sure the poor have enough money for subsistence—methods such as a guaranteed annual income, or a reverse income tax.

I set up a commission last year to study these and every other concept for maintaining an income floor for poor families. I asked them to review our existing income maintenance pro-

Negro poverty was a major target of the Johnson administration's domestic policy.

grams—Social Security, veterans' pensions, unemployment and workmen's compensation, food stamps, and so on. When that commission's work is completed, we should proceed to hammer out a new system of income security for Americans.

It is not, I hope, prejudicial to the commission's study to point out that any scheme—if it is to succeed—will have to convince the Congress, and the nation, that simple grants of money will not remove the incentive to search for work. The plan we adopt must be one that commends itself to the nonpoor as more rational, more effective, more humane, and less wasteful than our present patchwork of income security programs.

Eliminating poverty once and for all in the years ahead will not be cheap. But it is well within our means. And I believe we should pay the price rather than pass along an even costlier burden to our children and grandchildren.

In considering our next steps, we should remember this fact: economists figure that every poor, unemployed male costs the American taxpayers $140,000 over his lifetime. When we spend just a fraction of that to train and motivate and employ that man, he stops consuming that money out of our pockets and becomes a taxpayer with the rest of us.

BREAKING THE COLOR BARRIER

Nigger."
That one terrible word contains so much that is wrong in our society: the hatred, the divisiveness, the prejudice, the cold indifference.

And now another ugly word has come along, made of the same stuff: "honky."

It is true, as I wrote earlier, that there is a very real danger of our becoming two separate societies: one white and one black.

And there are extremists of both colors who would like nothing better. But the progress we have made in the past 15 years—since the *Brown* decision—suggests that we can and will choose another course.

In 1964, 1965, and 1968, we struck hammer blows at legally sanctioned segregation in America.

We made sure that men and women of all races could register and vote—free from harassment, tricks, or fear.

We wrote into law a requirement that public accommodations—hotels, motels, restaurants, amusement parks, and the like—which offer services to the public, must offer them to *all* the public. Many people thought there would be widespread resistance to this law, and we created a committee of private citizens to seek compliance with it if that occurred. The committee, thank God, has had little to do.

We said that public funds would no longer go to subsidize discrimination of any kind—that federal grants-in-aid would not be used to finance racial bias.

We declared that jobs and promotions must be open to all, regardless of race or sex. We created an Equal Employment Opportunity Commission, to persuade employers to comply with this law, and we authorized action in the courts if conciliation failed.

We prohibited discrimination in the sale or rental of housing, determined that we would help minority Americans break the ring of bias that surrounds the central city.

We convened a White House Conference—"To Fulfill These Rights"—bringing together more than a thousand white and black Americans to chart a course of racial justice.

In the courts, in the Congress, in high federal office, and throughout the civil service, there was movement to include Negro Americans in the democratic system.

The first Negro Cabinet member was named; the first Negro Supreme Court justice was designated; the first Negro mayor of a great city was appointed, and others were soon elected; the United States Senate received its first Negro member since Reconstruction.

Negro families began to move into middle-income levels at an unprecedented rate. The education gap between white and Negro young people almost closed. Negro voter registration in the South grew by the hundreds of thousands. And, in 1968, it seemed that the percentage of Negroes living in urban poverty areas was actually declining.

These are tremendous achievements in so short a time. What brought them about?

—The awakened social conscience of millions of white Americans.

—The incredible bravery and perseverance of young white and black civil rights workers.

—The public's outrage over the brutality with which some communities responded to the civil rights movement.

—The dignity and good sense of many Negro leaders—in civil rights organizations, business and labor, and the churches.

—Most important, the efforts of millions of Negroes to improve their conditions of life.

My own concern for human rights had its beginning in my home—where I was taught that every man had a dignity and a worth of his own.

A few years later, as a schoolteacher in Cotulla, Tex., I saw

what happens to people when that dignity is denied. I saw bright, eager Mexican-American boys and girls whose spirits had already been crippled by discrimination. And I came to understand that what was bad for Mexican-Americans was just as bad for Negroes.

For generations minorities had been beaten down—humiliated—barred—and ignored. Their pay was lower, their education inferior, their opportunities almost nonexistent.

For many years, I had to wait for the opportunity to express my convictions fully about civil rights. I did what I could, quietly. I tried to reduce the heat of racial bias where I found it. But in the '30s and '40s, men in public life from my section of the country did not invite defeat at the hands of bigots by taking "advanced" public positions on this issue.

Then, as a senator, in 1956, I refused to sign the "Southern Manifesto" that condemned the *Brown* decision. In 1957, and again in 1960, I worked as Senate majority leader to pass the first civil rights acts since the early 1870s. They were not as effective as they became, by amendment, in the '60s but they started us on our way.

Equality for all became my first domestic priority when I assumed the office of President. I believed the time was ripe for a full-scale attack on racial discrimination in America. Many courageous and decent people—some of them in Congress, some who never achieved public fame—joined with me to start America on its way toward freedom for all its people. And one of the earliest champions was Hubert Humphrey, the man I chose to help me lead the fight for social justice.

Despite the progress we have made, two things should be remembered.

One is that our work for racial justice is far from done. The average Negro's income is still only about 60% of average white income. A Negro baby is twice as likely to die in his first year as a white baby. Negro ghetto areas remain bleak, ugly, and crowded, the air heavy with failure. Great numbers of all-Negro schools remain, too, 15 years after the *Brown* decision. And the children who attend those schools are far less likely to perform at "grade level" than white children—or than Negro children who attend successfully integrated schools. For the sake of the whole society, America must vigorously enforce the mandate of the 14th Amendment that segregation in the public schools—both North and South—be ended. Finally, the humiliations of racism persist. Thousands of acts of racial discrimination—some petty, some great—occur every day in America. They are beyond the reach of law. But they wound. They deprive. They build bitterness and resentment among millions of people who are fellow human beings and citizens of the same United States.

The second thing to remember is that large numbers of white Americans believe that their government, and leaders in private life, have given far too much attention to lifting the Negro out of poverty and discrimination. They believe they have been forgotten by their leaders.

And they fear. The legacy of slavery and second-class Negro citizenship is hard for both races to overcome. When riots in the cities break out, and when vehement, radical voices call for violence against the "honkies," the fears of white Americans are increased and compounded.

The essential contradiction between these two facts—the continuing deprivation of many Negro Americans and the resistance of many white Americans to efforts to end Negro deprivation—has caused some people, in both races, to believe that separation is the only practical answer to our dilemma, despite the fact that it was separation which brought us to this crisis point in the first place.

"Black Power" has become the rallying cry of many Negroes. "Law and order," a desirable condition in any society, has become the all-important catchword for many whites.

If "Black Power" can be taken to mean increased economic strength, job opportunities, political participation, self-reliance, and pride in race, I am for it. But some have used it to justify

the violent eruptions that have scarred many cities. Others use it to express the idea that black people can develop sufficient economic and political strength entirely separately and apart from the nation as a whole. This is a delusion—and a diversion from the real tasks of the Negro people.

"Law and order" has always been necessary for long-term human progress, whether in city streets or on the old frontier. I shall have something to say later on about the real problem of crime in our cities. Here, I shall say only that the term "law and order" has become, for many whites, a code word for enforcing separation between the races—or worse, a means of justifying brutal suppression and disregard of civil liberties. That, to my mind, is a perversion of the term.

I believe that race relations in America will improve in the future, despite the anxiety and division we feel in the air today.

But we must not succumb to the counsels of separatism. We must press forward, through times that strain our unity and disturb our confidence, to a better America for all the races that history has brought together on this continent.

The stakes are enormous; they involve the very survival of our free society, for as Lincoln said, "A house divided against itself cannot stand."

HOUSING

One day in a meeting on America's urban problems, I asked my advisers to examine the state of housing in America. I instructed them:

First, find out how many substandard houses there were in the United States.

Second, find out how many houses we would have to build to take care of our immediate and future needs—not just for the poor, but for all Americans.

Third, find out how this could be done.

Fourth, find out how *fast* it could be done.

Incredible as it seems, no one—inside the government or out—really knew how many dilapidated housing units there were in city slums and depressed rural areas. Estimates varied between three and ten million. So the first task was to pin that number down. I told my staff to get the best authorities in the country working on our total housing problem—practical men as well as

Conferring with the Rev. Martin Luther King, Jr.

YOICHI OKAMOTO

theorists; men who knew how to put a house in place, as well as those who understood city planning and development.

I also asked our housing people to begin work on an idea I brought to the Presidency with me. I thought it should be possible to build an attractive, comfortable house for a small family for about $5,000—not just a dull, spirit-depressing concrete cell, but a house that would permit its owners to live in dignity.

For five years, I prodded government agencies, architects, and builders to produce designs for such a house. Finally, late in 1968, the first prototypes were opened in Austin, Tex. I hope future administrations will seize on this development, improve on it, and help many thousands of families to acquire decent homes at prices they can afford.

The statistics which shape our housing problems—for the poor and well-off alike—are overwhelming. By 1980, when we are four years into our third century, there will be 40 million more Americans than there are now—enough people to fill 80 cities the size of Denver, Colo., or 3,300 suburbs as big as Levittown, N.J.

Our present rate of more than one million housing starts a year could never meet this burgeoning demand. And underlying the need to prepare a place for future citizens was the immediate necessity of giving *today's* poor families a better place to live.

The goal of giving every American a decent home has eluded this nation's efforts for many years. We have had public housing programs since the days when I was a young congressman, back in the 1930s.

But by the 1960s it was clear that those programs were having little impact on the poor, and often bypassing them. Our legislative tools were far too few—basically, public housing and urban renewal. Public housing units were few in number and often unattractive. And because of our chronic shortage of low-income housing, the leveling of slums frequently meant that their inhabitants were packed into worse slums, while the "renewed" areas were turned into office buildings and high-rise apartments.

During my administration, we first set about to organize our urban efforts. We created a new Cabinet Department of Housing and Urban Development—to give city affairs a voice at the Cabinet table.

We began a program of rent supplements to help low-income families rent better homes—privately constructed and operated units, with public funds making up the difference between what families could afford to pay and what the rent had to be.

The Model Cities Program was launched to enable cities to plan whole new neighborhoods, repair old homes or build new ones, improve schools, provide health centers, create play areas, stimulate employment, and aid businesses. Our purpose was to attack the problem of slum neighborhoods on a broad front—not just through more steel and concrete, but through the creation of healthy communities.

A modern President finds himself virtually sealed off from the day-to-day events that shape the life of the central cities, so far as personal visits are concerned. He must ask others to act as his eyes and ears.

In the winter of 1966–67, I began to send members of the White House staff into the ghetto areas of several large cities. I asked them to spend several days and nights in cities such as New York City, Philadelphia, Chicago, Oakland, St. Louis, Detroit, Baltimore, and Washington, talking to ordinary citizens, poverty workers, police forces, businessmen, welfare clients, and local officials. I wanted reports that "told it like it is"—and I got them. They did not make comfortable reading. In stark terms, they made it clear that we have far to go in removing not only the physical blight of the slums but also the blight of lost years in men's lives. By 1968 some of our programs were beginning to do this, but the gap between the promise and the reality of change remained wide and deep.

We needed more than improved public housing, rent supplements, and model cities programs. We needed a program that would enable America to meet—at long last—the housing needs of all our people.

In the fall of 1967, I asked some of the most thoughtful and influential men in America to consider such a program. They represented many concerns and professions—with men like Edgar Kaiser from industry and George Meany from labor working with Secretary Bob Weaver of the new Housing Department, members of the CEA, and my staff.

The result of their efforts, and those of housing specialists in HUD, was a massive and realistic plan. It became the Housing Act of 1968—an act that is so sweeping in scope, and so directly responsive to the urgent needs of our time, that I believe it qualifies as one of the ten most important legislative achievements of the last fifty years.

It lays the foundation for the construction of 26 million single homes and apartment units over the next ten years—$2\frac{1}{2}$ times as many as we would build at the present rate. Six million of these units would be for poor families and would wipe out every slum dwelling that now exists. (That is the number our search disclosed: six million substandard homes in America.)

To do all this will require almost a trillion dollars in investment—most of it private, some of it public. I believe our expanding economy will produce these funds. The 1968 Housing Act establishes the basic financial machinery for generating them. A main instrument for putting those funds to work in the low-income-housing field is the new National Housing Corporation. It will give builders of low-income housing the financial help and technical assistance they need to produce our goal of six million units.

Other parts of the plan will encourage builders to construct new towns—not suburbs, but independent communities with a life of their own. I believe surplus government lands can be used for some of these communities. Also included in our plan is the machinery to guarantee that businessmen and homeowners in the center city are protected by adequate insurance.

So the blueprint is there. The legal foundation is in place. The goal is no longer elusive or visionary. It is in sight, and practical men—in Congress, in the home-building industry, in banking institutions, in the labor unions, and in city halls—have said it can be reached.

Now Congress must authorize the funds, year by year, that will keep the Housing Act alive. Those funds are necessary not only to help pay the rent of the poor tenant, or to enable him to buy a home of his own, but also to ease the burden of the developer.

But money alone can accomplish very little, if we do not know how to spend it.

Bob Weaver, my secretary of housing and urban development, used to say that the urban problem broke down into three B's—bucks, bodies, and brains. We are going to have to answer some tough questions, and make some hard decisions, if the Housing Act is to achieve its goals. Here are some of them:

1. Who is going to build the homes?

A program of the dimensions of the 1968 Housing Act calls for a tremendous increase in the construction labor force. Yet many workers in the construction industry are approaching retirement age. Securing adequate manpower will require a massive recruitment and training program, as well as much easier access to the building trades by minority groups.

2. How are housing units going to be built in communities with restrictive building policies?

Most communities have building codes and zoning regulations designed for an earlier day. These are completely unrealistic now. They inhibit the development of a new housing technology. Last fall, we asked several firms to develop some ideas for good low-cost housing. Though they came up with some models that broke through the cost barrier, none of them could be built in most American cities today because of current building codes.

A drastic overhaul of those antiquated regulations is long overdue.

3. Where will these 26 million new homes be built—particularly the six million to replace the slums?

Frankly, we don't know. Some of them undoubtedly will go up on the sites of the razed tenements and hovels. But unless we want simply to gild the ghettos in America, and freeze forever the separation of our races, we cannot just put them all back, new brick for old.

Moreover, half of the dilapidated units are in rural America. It is not just a matter of replacing these, either, for many of the families in those shacks are going to want to move into urban areas.

Nor can we continue just extending the suburbs indefinitely. In heavily populated areas, that expansion devours the land, strangles our transportation system, and starves the cities of taxes.

New communities will drain off some of the problem—but where will they be located?

America needs an urban land policy, if we are to have rational and orderly growth. I believe the states, with the aid of federal incentives, will have to develop land banks. Acreage can be held in those banks for future development both in expanding urban areas and in new communities. Tied in with this will be the need for very careful and comprehensive planning, not only at the metropolitan level but by regions. As a people, we have never quite got over our distaste for the word "planning," but the time is clearly upon us when we must.

4. How can we produce enough low- and moderate-income units?

If we achieve the goal of the 1968 Housing Act—600,000 low-income units a year—we shall have to build at about ten times our present rate. Clearly there will have to be technological breakthroughs if we are to accomplish this—as well as breakthroughs in the use of labor. In addition, we must stress quality and innovation in design. There is no reason why public housing must be drab and dreary. People are entitled to live with dignity and in pleasant surroundings.

Research is also a key. A few years ago, I was told that we were spending about $350,000 annually on housing and urban research—hardly enough to pay the architect's fee on a great office building. Today the figure is $10 million. It will have to go even higher.

Finally, we shall need to have, as I suggested earlier, a more flexible fiscal policy. For if we are not allowed to control inflation by prompt and modest tax increases, we must resort to higher interest rates. That means a greater burden on both builder and buyer, and consequently fewer housing starts. The housing needs of our people should not have to wait while Congress delays action on a tax increase that spreads the burden fairly.

RURAL-URBAN BALANCE

Rural America has provided a steady stream of migrants to the cities ever since the Civil War. This stream has ebbed and flowed over the years. It became a flood in the decades following World War II, and, as I said at the beginning, the public response to it was slow and insufficient.

While many deprived people moved out of poverty by moving to the city, many others failed to realize their hopes. They are the ones who have attracted the most notice, for in moving they shifted the burden of poverty to the cities.

If we ignore the needs of our rural areas, while rebuilding the nation's cities and eliminating urban poverty, we will risk starting a new major flow to the city by the 45% of our poor who do not live in big city areas. We must avoid this kind of forced rural-urban migration.

When we talk about problems of rural America, we are talking about more than our farm people. Less than one-fifth of the rural poor live on farms. The others live in small communities and in mountain hollows—along the bypassed crossroads of America.

Rural America's problems are not going to be solved by farm programs alone. Farm programs help insure the nation's capacity to produce food and fiber, and we have strengthened and improved them in recent years, particularly through the Agricultural

Act of 1965. But we cannot ask our commodity support programs to do the impossible.

We are going to have to upgrade public services in rural areas and create new job opportunities so that rural youth will not be compelled to go to town to find work.

Community and area resource development programs provide the keys to improving the economic environment in rural America.

We began developing such programs during my administration. We started loan programs for community water and sewer projects, rural housing, rural electricity, rural telephone facilities, and manpower training. Only those who have lived in rural areas *without* electricity or telephones or job opportunities—as I have—can know what the coming of these things can mean to people. We encouraged the establishment and growth of nonfarm jobs in the more rural parts of our country.

But we have only begun to improve living conditions in the countryside. It is a difficult area in which to make rapid progress, and we have not been able to make as much headway as I had hoped.

Undoubtedly helping to improve the quality of life in rural America will occupy more of our energies in the years ahead.

Building on the assets of rural America, we must attract new industries, research centers, and training schools.

We must encourage the increased use of regional planning—and fuller participation by local people in the planning process—to determine the sensible location of schools, hospitals, shopping centers, and outdoor recreation.

We should experiment with low-interest-rate farm and home loan programs to help returning GI's settle in rural and small town areas if they desire to do so.

The fates of rural and urban America are linked together. What we plan and do for one will strongly affect the other.

Our aim to banish poverty from America requires that we attack poverty wherever it exists. Americans ought to have the opportunity to get and hold a decent job at a decent wage in the kind of community they prefer to live in—whether a large city or a small town. We should help each community acquire the facilities it needs to provide decent living conditions for all its citizens. And we should make certain that no community is prevented from sharing in America's prosperity because it is too poor to educate its young.

JOBS

Thirty-seven years ago, when I came to Washington, I carried with me a conviction that every man and woman who wanted to work ought to be able to get a job. My beliefs have not changed since then, but the dimensions of the job problem have.

By the early 1960s the economy began to gather strength. The results were more jobs—at higher wages and more security than ever before.

With a healthy economy, there were some remarkable gains. Over the past several years, for example, ten million jobs were created. Eight million covered those coming into the work force for the first time. The remaining two million thinned the ranks of the unemployed. The unemployment rate dropped steadily—to less than 4%. For adult males—the family breadwinner—it was under 2%.

This prosperity helped most Americans find work. But it also made the contrast more vivid in those sectors where unemployment had become a way of life.

Who were these chronically unemployed? There was the teen-age dropout, with no place to go. There was the migrant worker. There was the victim of a lifetime of racial discrimination. There was the man or woman without any marketable skill, and with little or no education. Many of these people are likely to be slow learners, to be accident-prone, to require more supervision. A

surprising number have never even been counted in the census. It is almost as if they did not exist, but they do.

Considering this situation, I always came back to my conviction that every citizen who wants a job should have one. A man who has a useful job for which he is reasonably paid is a man with a purpose in life—a purpose essential to human nature.

I believe that full employment is good, not only for the hard-core unemployed, but for the whole nation. I have never held with the theory that increasing unemployment is an appropriate cure for inflation. A progressive government and a responsible business and labor community can take care of inflation in more intelligent ways.

The period of economic growth and prosperity gave us, I felt, not only the opportunity but the obligation to tackle the problem of the hard-core unemployed.

In the '60s, we developed a new network of job programs—the Neighborhood Youth Corps, the Job Corps, the Manpower Training and Development Act, for example. But I was not satisfied. I believed that our manpower training programs were still not reaching the hard-core unemployed in sufficient numbers and with sufficient impact. All too often men and women were trained—only to find that when they completed training, there were no jobs for them.

In discussing this with some of the leaders of American business and labor, I learned that a most effective key to the manpower problem was on-the-job training, where men were first put on the company payroll and then trained on an assembly line or factory bench or in an office for a specific job. I also knew that six out of seven jobs in America were in private industry. This was a clear signal to me that American business would have to take a leading role in any new job program.

But the hard-core unemployed posed a severe problem, because they would require special and often costly services—in basic education, in grooming, in learning how to manage their money, and in correcting the health defects that were bars to their productive employment.

Late in 1967 I discussed the idea of a new manpower program with Henry Ford II and other industrialists, built around these essentials:

A nationwide network of businessmen, operating in the 50 largest cities, would act as the spearhead of a job program that would reach the hard-core unemployed.
The government would take a special census and locate the hard-core unemployed.
Business would hire them first, train them, and retain them.
Cutting red tape, the government would pay the extra costs of training: costs that business would not otherwise normally incur.

This approach had many advantages from the standpoint of our national economy. It could mean a new source of workers for American industry and new consumers for its products. It could give people, previously out of work, a meaningful stake in society, and so reduce tensions and frustrations. It could move men and women from the dependency of a welfare check to the rewards of a payroll check.

On a cold January Saturday in the Cabinet Room, the new National Alliance of Businessmen was born.

With the leaders of the industrial community, I reviewed the great changes that had taken place in business and government during our time. The days of the robber barons were long past. I believed that the business leadership of our nation had passed into the hands of enlightened men who were concerned with the general welfare of our people—not just with private gain.

Gone, too, was the notion that government could tackle a job as big as this one without business cooperation. After 35 years of intensive, if intermittent, effort, we have learned something about the limits of government power.

I told Mr. Ford and the others that they faced an awesome challenge. Their alliance was launching the most massive and difficult peacetime job program in all our history.

They accepted that challenge. Together, we set this target: jobs for half a million hard-core unemployed by June 1971, with 100,000 the first year. I also sought the alliance's help in finding

summer jobs for tens of thousands of boys and girls who lived in the slums. For our part, I asked Congress for $350 million in special funds to support this venture in its first year.

Armed with computers, flow charts, and the methods of modern business, the alliance moved into full swing, led by executives from corporations such as Ford, Coca-Cola, General Electric, Ling-Temco, IT & T, Bell Telephone, and Safeway, and with active support and participation of the labor movement—from George Meany and Walter Reuther on down.

Under the banner of "Hire—Train—Retain," the alliance persuaded businesses all over the nation to comb their production lines and offices for jobs for the hard-core unemployed.

By the end of 1968, progress was encouraging. Leo Beebe, a Ford vice-president who is the operating manager of the new program, reported to me that business had responded magnificently. Over 100,000 hard-core unemployed were at work in specific jobs on company rolls. They were being hired at the rate of 20,000 a month. At this pace, the alliance will more than double its first-year quota of 100,000, and possibly reach a quarter of a million jobs.

And it is significant that the retention rate for these "un-employees" equals or exceeds that for the ordinary worker.

I know that the eyes of Congress, and the people, will be on the National Alliance of Businessmen in the months ahead. I will be watching it closely, myself. Every failure will be reported, while successes may be ignored.

And there *will* be failures. We are dealing, after all, with human beings who have had almost everything going against them. There will be dropouts and setbacks. But if we stick with it, there will be many successes.

I hope that this adventure and others like it find a spot behind the workbench for every citizen who wants a job. It is, in my opinion, the most promising way ever devised of eliminating the tragic waste of our human resources.

As we look to the future, I would like to see the National Alliance of Businessmen expanded from the largest cities to every city in America with a population of 50,000 or more.

I would hope that a counterpart to the National Alliance of Businessmen could be set up in the public sector—at the federal, state, and local government levels—to hire and train the hard-core unemployed for jobs in the community: in hospitals, in schools, in offices.

Finally, we must recognize that some men and women will be left behind, despite all we do. All the special training programs will not help them, and they will simply not be able to compete in the job market. If industry cannot find a place for them, then their government must. There are plenty of areas in the public service that are crying for manpower—in hospitals, in parks, in recreation areas, to name only three.

One way or another, those who want to work must have jobs.

Two decades ago America made a pledge in the Employment Act of 1946: a decent job opportunity for every person willing to work. Now, when our economy is producing thousands of new jobs, and when we have the machinery for employing those who have never held a steady job before, we can finally redeem that pledge.

EDUCATION

Though our government operates programs that cost billions of dollars and enforces laws that affect millions of people, sometimes a simple story about one individual can put more of our efforts into perspective than all of the statistics we can gather in a year.

Pancho, a little Mexican-American, at the age of five had the physical development of a two-year-old. He was listless and withdrawn. Everyone assumed he was mentally retarded. It took a local Head Start program to discover that Pancho was suffering from a severe thyroid deficiency. Head Start doctors began treating him, and within a year and a half he had grown to normal size. He absorbed all his teachers could give him, and, in time, he became a happy leader in his class. I saw Pancho myself. He came to the White House in 1967—and I was never more proud of anything our programs had done.

There is also the story of a 17-year-old illiterate in Los Angeles. He couldn't get a truck driver's license, because he couldn't pass the written test. He was ashamed to take his girl friend to the movies, because he couldn't read what was playing on the marquee. A local poverty program taught him how to read and write. Suddenly a new world burst open to him—a world he never knew existed. He discovered that just by being able to read, he could begin to live and work and enjoy life in its fullness.

And finally, there is the story of a 62-year-old man who enrolled in one of our adult education programs. The first thing they taught him was how to write his name. That was a wondrous moment in his life—so wondrous that he didn't do another thing for the next hour but write it over and over again.

During the 62 months of my administration I signed more than 60 education bills. They covered every conceivable aspect of the education field: from Head Start to adult education, from fine arts to vocational education, from the biggest ghetto schools to the smallest rural schools.

The most powerful act of all is the one I signed on the front steps of my old Junction school, a few hundred yards from the house where I was born: the Elementary and Secondary Education Act. I felt then and I feel now that "I will never do anything in my entire life that excites me more." For one who had taught poor children in school 35 years before, that was a red-letter day.

I think this bill offers a perfect example of how our country always seems to catch up with enlightened leadership. The first general aid to education bill was introduced in the 1870s. Nothing happened. When Pres. Harry Truman recommended federal aid to education in 1948, his proposal was greeted with cries of outrage. He was accused of a rank invasion of states' rights and of attempting to put the federal government in control of the nation's schools. A congressman who had the temerity to find some good in the Truman plan might as well have endorsed sin.

That was almost the situation in Congress when I became President.

But this was the situation in the country:

In inner-city schools, 60% of the pupils who made the 10th grade dropped out before completing the 12th. A poor child was, on the average, a year behind in schoolwork by the time he reached the third grade. And if he made the eighth grade, he was three years behind the national average.

More than two of every three public elementary schools had no libraries. Nearly 18 million adults in America had finished only eight years of schooling. Almost five million were totally illiterate. The number of young men who failed the Selective Service mental examination was shocking. Clearly America's school system needed help.

Finally, after two years of the hardest kind of work, we were able to get legislation through the Congress in 1965—nearly 20 years after Harry Truman had proposed it. Federal moneys were made available to rescue the school systems, mainly in poor districts. A formula was worked out that minimized the church-state problem.

Passing that bill had somewhat the effect of the first four-minute mile. It wasn't long before there were others. After one of the real achievements of modern legislative history, we were on our way.

The value of an educated citizenry to a nation cannot be measured, but the value of education to an individual can be. A man with a high-school diploma earns appreciably more in his lifetime than one who fails to finish high school, and his average annual income rises sharply if he has a college education.

I wish I could say that the nation's education problems were solved by my administration. But in fact only a wide range of starts were made. Meanwhile, the needs of education were growing swiftly.

Head Start has proved of spectacular value to many slum children. I'll never forget Lady Bird's reaction after she had visited her first Head Start class. She said, "This is the finest thing we have done. They are taking some of the most deprived children in the land and are giving them hope. If you do nothing else, I hope you will nurture and expand this program."

We began Head Start in the hope that it would launch a revolution in elementary education. We started it outside the school system because of my concern that the vast majority of elementary schools around the country were not equipped to begin a special program for preschoolers of four and five years of age. Moreover, Head Start was not limited to traditional classroom instruction—through Head Start, the slum child might get his first nutritious breakfast and see his first doctor.

From the outset, it was my hope—as it is today—that Head Start would become a part of every elementary school district in this country, and thus ultimately every American boy and girl would begin school at the age of four, when the learning process is so critical.

I should like to see Head Start expanded to reach all children of low-income families—and eventually made a universal program for all preschool children.

The beginnings we have made in upgrading all elementary and secondary schools have not gone far enough. Most youngsters in slum schools are still denied a quality education. More money, better-trained teachers, more teachers' aides, and improved methods are still badly needed.

And I think we may find that a better classroom environment is not enough. Counseling families and helping them create a better home environment may also be essential. One thing seems clear about the desire and ability to learn. It is affected by the student's classmates, by his family situation, and by the image he has of himself. The quality of his whole life, and of the life about him, may be more important than modern teaching equipment and new buildings.

The military services, I believe, can play an important role in widening the educational horizons of underprivileged young men. Secretary of Defense Robert McNamara and I discussed this great potential at the ranch in early 1965. There was some opposition to the idea both in the Pentagon and on Capitol Hill, but I nevertheless directed the secretary to start two experimental ventures that I believe will pay great dividends in the future. One is "Project 100,000," through which men previously rejected for physical or educational handicaps are taken into the service and given intensive training. The other is "Project Transition," which prepares separating servicemen for meaningful careers in the civilian economy.

Finding good teachers for schools in both city and country slums is a special problem. We started the Teacher Corps to recruit able young student teachers to work in such areas. Congress has been slow to provide funds for this program. But if we are going to give poor youngsters the instruction they need, Congress's opposition has to be overcome and the corps greatly expanded.

We have come to recognize the increased importance of good elementary and secondary education. I believe grade-school and high-school teachers should be given the opportunity to take a refresher year away from their duties, for advanced scholarship and training, at suitable intervals.

College education faces a special crisis. Space demands and costs are soaring faster than resources are coming in. In June 1968 the heads of 42 leading colleges and universities mapped out their needs and concluded that they cannot meet the future with present sources of income. They felt that they must have permanent and continuing support from federal sources.

Some educators fear that federal dollars mean limited freedom for their institutions. Indeed, that is a threat we must always guard against. But I am encouraged by the words of Dr. Alexander Heard of Vanderbilt University: "Federal money is the freest money we get." Since the number of students in colleges is destined to rise by 50% in the next few years, and the cost of educating each individual student will grow, this problem cannot wait long for attention.

Federal funds for education have been tripled in the past five years—and our programs have only just begun. I believe we are going to have to triple them again by 1976 if we expect to achieve our education goals. This means that the federal government should be spending more than $30 billion on education by 1976.

Let us not begrudge the cost of these programs. The funds we provide do not simply disappear, never to be recovered. A highly educated population creates far more wealth than it consumes. Our experience with the GI Bill proved that, once and for all.

When we first broke the dam against federal aid to education in 1965, I said: "I am going to use every rostrum to tell the people that we can no longer afford the great waste that comes from the neglect of a single child." I mean to do that—not only for children, but for their parents, because I believe that the chance to learn and grow ought to be available to every person, from the time he is able to reason through old age. National resource and social benefit though it is, education is first and last an inexhaustible treasure for the human spirit.

So let us find ways to use our schools more than nine months of every year, and eight hours of every day. Let us make them a constantly available resource of pleasure, understanding, and gain for all our people.

HEALTH

One afternoon in the closing months of my administration, I sat in the Cabinet Room with the secretary of health, education, and welfare, Wilbur Cohen, talking about the country's health needs. Wilbur, who had been in on the takeoff for Social Security in 1935, was also one of the chief architects of Medicare in 1965. He carries the scars of a great many fights for social progress. And every one of them shines like a medal.

Remembering meeting after meeting with doctors before Medicare was started, I asked him how many doctors were cooperating in the program in late 1968.

"About 300,000," he replied.

"Out of how many?"

"About 350,000."

Six out of seven. And out of the 50,000 not cooperating, he said, most are administrators and not directly engaged in the practice of medicine. "I would say that 98% of the doctors actually practicing are cooperating."

I sat there and reflected. Few ideas in our time had had so bumpy a road as Medicare. As far back as 1935, President Roosevelt considered a federal health insurance plan. But he threw up his hands when he realized it would be impossible to get it through Congress.

President Truman revived the idea a decade later. And for 15 years, the labor movement spearheaded the drive for passage. But medical associations and insurance companies ran up the two biggest lobbying bills in our history to defeat it—$1.5 million in one year and $1.3 million the next. They produced a great advertising slogan—"Socialized medicine"—and scared people into believing that health insurance would bring regimentation of doctors, poor medical care, and so on. A sensible and compassionate way to help people defend themselves against crushing medical bills became "socialistic" and "un-American."

When we began our drive to get Medicare through Congress in 1965, we heard the same loud voices of opposition. Some doctors predicted there would be lines a mile long outside their offices. Others maintained it would be abandoned as a hopeless mess in six months' time.

I suppose no voices of opposition ever changed their tune so fast. "I wouldn't have believed it," a doctor told me last year, "but somehow this thing works."

I don't know how many of those 300,000 physicians he spoke for, but I do know he spoke the truth. Medicare does work.

In the first two years of Medicare's life, 20 million older people gained their freedom from financial fear, at a time of life when their medical bills are likely to be highest and their income

lowest. About 10 million hospital bills and 45 million doctor bills were paid out during that period.

Those bills—totaling about $8 billion—would once have had to be borne by the sons and daughters of the aged if the patients themselves could not afford them. Some of those without sons and daughters simply went without treatment. So Medicare has worked to everyone's advantage. It is one program—like Social Security and the minimum wage—that will never be taken away from the American people. In its brief life, it has already become too important to all of us.

Medicare was not the only breakthrough in the field of health care during the 1960s.

We launched Medicaid to provide medical help to seven million people of low incomes, whatever their age.

We tripled the federal investment in health research, in training medical personnel, and in bringing health services to the people. That investment has already paid off: fewer babies die at birth every year; more mothers are saved in pregnancy and childbirth; youngsters are spared the crippling effects of rheumatic fever and other heart diseases. Hardly anyone dies now from measles. The TB death rate has dropped by one-third. And every year fewer and fewer patients enter mental hospitals.

All of this is gratifying. But no American with a conscience can escape being haunted by an awareness of the distance yet to go. The nation that trained the surgeon who made the first heart transplant, whose scientists have practically created life in a test tube, and that has wiped out polio has still not assured the right of good health to all its people.

Although we are the richest nation on earth, we still are the 15th in infant mortality. I proposed a "Kiddy-Care" plan to give medical help to poor families from the time of pregnancy until the child is a year old. I believe that is still urgent business. And I believe that eventually it should be extended to all American families—as Medicare is.

YOICHI OKAMOTO

The President's office on the first night of the 1967 Detroit riots.

We have opened more medical schools, and with financial grants have assured the education of more doctors and the training of more health workers. But population is still increasing faster than the supply of doctors and dentists. If present trends continue, we will be short 41,000 physicians and 28,000 dentists by 1976. And as usual, it will be the poor who suffer most from those shortages.

This is a problem that does not demand sophisticated and difficult solutions. We need to expand the capacity of our medical schools and we need to put medical training within the reach of more people.

I believe it should be our national policy to offer the opportunity for an education in medicine and dentistry to every young man and woman who wants it and who has the qualifications to pursue it.

Another worrisome problem is soaring medical costs. If present trends continue, they will increase by 140% by 1975.

When I sat with Wilbur Cohen that late October day last fall, we discussed what we thought this nation could reasonably hope to accomplish in the next decade, building on the progress that has been made so far.

Here are the basic tasks, as we saw them:

First, making sure that all children, and their mothers, have adequate medical care from the time of the mother's pregnancy until the child is six years old. A great many adult social problems would be easier to deal with today if those adults had received the proper medical care when they were infants and young children.

Second, developing a program of health insurance to take care of medical bills in the event of the catastrophic, long-term illness of children.

Third, providing good medical care for all. This is sure to require more trained medical personnel—not just doctors and nurses, but others who can do many of the tasks that profes-

sionals must now perform. Delivering medical care and health services to every neighborhood is also critically important. Our experience with the anti-poverty programs' Neighborhood Health Centers suggested one way of doing this; and with federal help, more university hospitals could develop emergency and child-care stations in poor neighborhoods.

Fourth, slowing down the accelerating costs of medical care. Through the Medicare program, we ought to experiment with incentives to hospitals that lower their costs, as I proposed to Congress last year. And we should encourage prepaid, comprehensive plans for large groups of workers.

Fifth, working toward the elimination of large state mental hospitals, we should increase our support for community mental health centers. In the past few years, advances in treatment have sharply reduced the number of people who must be confined in mental institutions. Every effort ought to be made to make their care more effective and more humane—and that means in smaller institutions, close to home.

RESCUING THE ENVIRONMENT

For 37 years, I lived and worked in one of the most beautiful cities in America, and one of the most handsome capitals in the world. Thanks to limitations on the height of office buildings, and to a number of wide, tree-lined avenues and an extensive park, Washington retained a spacious dignity even as its population multiplied.

Yet its river is so polluted that only the most foolhardy person would swim in it.

Though it has little industry, its air is poisoned by hundreds of thousands of commuting automobiles.

The number of public parks and seashores within easy driving distance is small, and most are overcrowded.

For years an old dump burned in a poor section of town, endangering the health of many innocent people.

So—despite its beauty, and though it is the seat of government—Washington has most of the environmental problems of every other American city.

In the past few years, we have begun to do something about the American environment. We were not the first Americans to try, but we were probably the first generation to understand that if we did not move at once, and massively, the *next* generation might be confronted with a hopeless situation: its air too fouled to breathe in safety, its water too polluted to sustain life, much of its natural beauty lost to the public forever.

Theodore Roosevelt understood the danger of unlimited private exploitation of America's forests and lands. With the stroke of his pen, he put millions of Western acres into the public trust. His Congress may have resented it—old Speaker Joe Cannon vowed that he would appropriate "not one cent for scenery"—but Theodore Roosevelt got away with it, to his everlasting credit.

His kinsman, Franklin Roosevelt, continued the work of saving and restoring the American earth. His great interest was in soil conservation, and through the Civilian Conservation Corps and agricultural programs, the waste of good land was sharply slowed.

Still, conservation in the early 20th century usually meant setting aside areas like the Grand Canyon and Yellowstone Park—beautiful places, but remote. Only families on vacation could enjoy them. For many families, they were simply out of reach.

In the 1960s we set about to rescue areas near the cities, so that city people could spend their weekends away from congestion and in touch with nature. Assateague Island, Fire Island, and Cape Hatteras, three seashore areas within easy reach of the East Coast cities; Padre Island in Texas; Indiana Dunes on the Great Lakes; and what may be the most important of all, the Redwoods National Park in California—these were the people's triumphs in that time.

And in 1968, we committed, for the first time, some of the proceeds from offshore oil deposits for the preservation of land for the people's enjoyment. We earmarked a billion dollars for the purchase of new lands over the next five years. With land values skyrocketing today, it offers a vital assurance that we can pay for what we want to save.

It is ironic that the same Congress that passed this act reduced funds for Lady Bird's Highway Beautification Program from $85 million to $25 million. I hope future Congresses will show more interest in making roadside areas attractive—instead of permitting junk, signs, and careless construction to scar our country with ugliness.

Meanwhile, we have begun—but only begun—to rid the air, lakes, and streams of the pollution that threatens our health and safety.

The Connecticut River is a case study. It was once a clear stream of potable water. Industry and people turned it into a kind of sewer where few fish live—and those that are caught taste like gasoline when they are cooked. The master plan to reclaim that river is a model—available to all future administrations to follow in restoring health to great bodies of American water.

Other antipollution plans have been worked out across the nation, but there has been no turnaround yet. A bill that might have started us on our way to halting water pollution was vetoed in 1960. People talked about "local responsibility," when water conditions in many communities depended on what was happening hundreds of miles upstream, or down the lake. Help for the construction of treatment plants and for comprehensive planning was required, but it was not forthcoming, despite the farsighted efforts of men like Sen. Ed Muskie.

There is plenty of room for local responsibility in fighting water pollution. Businesses must come to regard the price of depolluting the water they use as part of their normal operating costs. Local agencies must develop stricter water-quality standards in their own areas, so that they do not impose poisoned water on their neighbors. Working together, federal, state, and local governments must spearhead the development of a better antipollution technology than now exists. And they must attack water pollution from stream source to river mouth—without regard to political boundaries.

Air pollution presents an even greater problem—one that has already threatened the health of several cities.

The automobile is probably the greatest single poisoner of the air. The number of internal combustion motors pouring waste into our atmosphere increases radically by the decade. An expert at the University of California has predicted that at the present rate of increase of pollutants, this continent will not be able to sustain life within a hundred years. Obviously, we must tighten up our automobile emission standards, but we may also have to consider seriously replacing part of our combustion vehicles with electric or steam automobiles.

Other revolutions in transportation will be necessary for America's mobile people. We have begun plans for rapid rail trains, similar to those in Japan but more advanced. These can help reduce the pollution that would come from millions of new automobile exhaust pipes.

Just slowing down pollution from the automobile, however, will not clean the atmosphere. Industrial waste is also a major contributor to smog and bad air. And here again our technology is behind. We must find more effective ways to take the sulfur out of the fuels that industry burns, or to filter it out of stacks.

The work of making our nation more beautiful, and of cleaning its air and water, must proceed. It is vital to our health and happiness. Driving to and from work each day through a brown haze of smog, seeing ugliness on all sides, can be as damaging to the spirit over a period of time as poverty, illness, or ignorance.

Rescuing the American environment is bound to be mostly a local and community effort. But the example can come, as my wife has shown, right from the White House.

Looking ahead, I believe one of our prime objectives should be to save the remaining unspoiled outdoor playgrounds for our children and grandchildren. We are still losing thousands of acres daily to new suburbs and industries—and once they are lost, they are almost never reclaimed. In the next few years, we should double the size of the wilderness system, create new national trails, and add substantially to the systems of national parks and scenic rivers.

A program to save our remaining unspoiled islands should also be on the agenda.

I believe that we should begin a national system of scenic parkways, financed from the Highway Trust Fund.

We should invest in more "vest pocket" parks—small areas in cities where people can rest a while from the pressures of urban life.

We must plan now, not for a decade or two ahead but for the next century. We should consider reorganizing the federal government so as to bring together all our environmental and natural resource efforts into a new Department of Natural Resources.

We can still save the American environment. The next generation may not have that opportunity.

THE THIRD FORCE

In the first third of this century, the strongest nongovernmental force in the nation was big business. Sometimes it was, stronger than government. In the second third of the century, Pres. Franklin D. Roosevelt helped organized labor come into its own as a "countervailing force." In the past few years, we began to strengthen another balancing force—the American consumer.

President Truman once said that hundreds of lobbyists represented special interests in Washington, but only the President of the United States represented the general interest of the consumer. Over the years a great deal of lip service was paid to protecting the interests of the consumer. But too little protection was actually provided.

Less than two months after assuming office, I reaffirmed these basic rights of the American consumer: the right to safety, the right to be fully informed, the right to choose, and the right to be heard.

I told Betty Furness and Esther Peterson, my consumer assistants, that the most important thing they had to do was to help focus the attention of the media and the nation on consumer problems. For without strong public support, we could never hope to get out of Congress the consumer-protection legislation that was needed.

A hundred years ago, consumer protection was largely unnecessary. We were a rural nation, and most products were locally produced. Products were uncomplicated, and it did not take an advanced degree to tell when one was bad or inferior. If you had a complaint, you could go directly to the source: to the miller, the blacksmith, the tailor down the street, or the grocer on the corner.

Today that has changed. A manufacturer may be thousands of miles away from his customer—separated by long chains of distributors, wholesalers, and retailers. Products are likely to be so complicated that only an expert can pass judgment on their quality. In addition, poor and ill-educated people in slums are easy prey for unscrupulous or negligent sellers.

Now, ours has always been a "producers' economy." The producers decide what shall be produced, how much of it, and what quality it shall have. Their size and wealth enable them to mount overwhelming sales campaigns. Their organizations make their voices heard in Washington. Unorganized consumers are often helpless before this force.

Investigations produced alarming facts. "Large economy-sized" containers turned out to contain proportionately less than small sizes. Uninspected fish, processed in dirty, uninspected plants, caused 400 cases of food poisoning on a single weekend in 1966. Shops have advertised installment rates at 1.5%—without making it clear that the rate was monthly and amounted in fact to a usurious 18% a year.

Slowly, our citizens—and the Congress—came to recognize that the government has an important role to play in consumer protection. This is not to say that our people wanted a super-arbiter of their tastes or a superregulator in the marketplace. But there are areas where the government—and only the government—can protect the interests of the American buyer, and we began to do that in the past five years.

We created the first auto and highway safety program in American history, to help reduce the outrageous death toll on our roads. Heated controversy surrounded that measure as it worked its way through Congress. But safety had to come first. The blood of 50,000 Americans who died each year on the highways was proof that we could afford inaction no longer.

During that time—with the unceasing support of American labor and consumer organizations—we saw a host of specific laws passed, from a Wholesome Meat Act and another dealing with poultry to acts assuring the safety of children's toys and the very clothing we wear. After almost a decade of deadlock, we finally passed the Truth-in-Lending Act, requiring lenders of money and sellers on the installment plan to make it clear to borrowers and buyers exactly how much, in dollars and cents, they would have to pay in interest and carrying charges every year. We began extensive research on the health effects of cigarette smoking, and Congress required cigarette packages to bear labels warning the public of the hazards of smoking.

So we began to give the buyer—which means all 200 million of us—new power in the marketplace.

For the immediate future:

1. We need a law to reduce the high charges many investors pay when they buy mutual funds.
2. We need a law to keep diseased and unwholesome fish off the dinner table.
3. We need to crack down on fraudulent and deceptive sales practices, especially in home repairs.
4. We need to guard against massive power failures, of the kind that have already struck New York City and the Eastern states.

Looking further ahead, it is time to recognize that services are playing a bigger and bigger role in our economy and in our daily lives. We must examine our whole system of warranties and guarantees to make sure the long-suffering citizen can get repairs and servicing when he needs them on the appliances that have become such an important part of his daily life.

But it takes more than government protection to serve the consumer interest. It takes an educated and fully informed public. We have too often neglected consumer education—particularly among our poor. We are going to have to place greater emphasis on this practical and needed education at all levels of government, and in our schools, in the years ahead.

THE FIGHT AGAINST CRIME

The one issue of recent years that has attracted more political demagoguery than any other—as well as more genuine and justified concern—is crime in the streets.

A visitor coming to America for the first time during the election season of 1968 might have been forgiven for assuming that the President of the United States commanded all the city police departments and that control of the courts was his personal responsibility.

The first point that must be made—and apparently made again and again, to the point of exhaustion—is that crime is a *local* problem. Its control is a *local* responsibility. Except for a few functions clearly spelled out by law, the federal government has little or no power to deal with the problem.

Nor should it have. Giving Washington such authority would require the creation of a national police force. Wise men have guarded against that for two centuries. Surely the centralized police states we have witnessed around the globe in our time have given ample proof of their wisdom.

Still, I am fully aware of the public's anxiety over the increasing crime rate. I share it.

Early in my administration, I asked a number of concerned citizens—lawyers, judges, district attorneys, educators, criminologists, journalists, and public officials—to examine the challenge of crime to our society. It seemed clear to me that, whatever arguments there might be over crime statistics and reporting, the incidence of crime *was* increasing. I asked these people to find out why.

Their report, for all who were interested in the facts instead of the mythology about crime, was a shocker. It said, in effect, that our whole law enforcement and criminal justice system is unable to meet the challenge of crime today, and unless some profound changes are made in that system, it will be even more ineffective tomorrow.

The report revealed that while our nation expects and demands effective protection from its police, it is reluctant to commit either the resources or the imagination that would help law enforcement do that job. The result is that the patrolman on the beat in most cities is woefully underpaid, undertrained, and underequipped. Too often, as a consequence, police careers attract men without the qualifications we should expect from them. In some of our biggest cities, one out of every five members of the police force did not finish the eighth grade.

Too often, the Crime Commission found, our lower courts are bogged down in procedures that have not changed for a hundred years or more. Assembly-line "justice" was the rule in others. A tawdry, careless atmosphere pervaded many courtrooms.

Small wonder that only about a quarter of the serious crimes in our communities led to arrests, only a tenth of those arrested were convicted, only a small fraction of those convicted were imprisoned, and thousands left imprisonment to return to a life of crime.

Looking over the crime statistics, two facts really leap out.

The first is that most victims of violent crimes are acquaintances of the offenders or members of their families. The second is that the principal contributors to the increase in America's crime rate are juveniles and repeaters.

The high rate of juvenile crime suggests a breakdown in family life, in schools, and in the power of the community to discipline its young. It also suggests a failure to produce enough jobs for the wave of teen-agers that has come upon the scene in the 1960s.

There is the clearest kind of correlation between the incidence of poverty and the incidence of juvenile crime. Take a map of any major city in the United States. Mark where unemployment is highest and income is lowest. Mark where the schools are poorest, housing most crowded and unsanitary, and where mental and physical health problems are greatest. Then mark where the juvenile crime rate is highest. The two areas will coincide—every time.

As for the repeaters, the failure of our correctional institutions is clear. About 40% of all the serious crimes in America are committed by people who have served time at least once. The attorney general told me once: "Mr. President, we turn more people to crime in our correctional institutions today than we rehabilitate." What an indictment—of our whole society.

Any long-range solution to our crime problem is probably going to depend on massive changes in slum living conditions and on improving the techniques of rehabilitation.

But we can't wait for those events before doing something about the rising crime rate in America. That "something" doesn't mean the unfettered use of the nightstick or the unchained abuse of the Supreme Court. It means much more work than that—more money, imagination, and willingness to experiment.

The Crime Commission emphasized the need for improving not just the salaries, education, and training available to local police forces but their equipment and organization. It suggested federal assistance in developing that equipment and planning better use of law forces.

Help is needed for local courts, as well. If law is to be respected, people must believe in the fairness of the lower courts. There are many places in America where this is not so—where cases are handled only after long delays or in a perfunctory way that breeds contempt for the law.

Today, few courts or law enforcement agencies have enough specialists to help them—probation officers, community relations officers, and youth counselors, to say nothing of psychologists and other highly trained social scientists. We go on expecting high-school-graduate police officers to decide some of the most difficult and demanding human issues on the spot, often in emergency situations, without any expert guidance or support.

And we continue to maintain vast, costly prison systems, frequently without giving them anything like the professional help they need to do the job of rehabilitation. There have been some experiments—but nowhere near enough—with rehabilitation in smaller institutions located in the community, using a broad range of professional services, and helping prisoners prepare to reenter normal life.

It was this knowledge—that local and state criminal justice systems needed immediate help—that inspired the Safe Streets Act of 1968.

Its forerunner, the Law Enforcement Assistance Act of 1965, has already had an effect on police training, equipment, and techniques. With the stronger and broader assistance of the new act, I think we can help bring about innovations in law enforcement and corrections that will substantially improve the safety of many cities. I regard the Safe Streets Act as the most significant tool the federal government has ever developed to help fight crime in America. To do its job, however, it must be fully funded in the next few years.

In the mid-1960s we also mounted an increasingly successful attack on organized crime and drug abuse.

Through a concentrated effort of federal and local officers, we were able to multiply indictments of those engaged in organized crime—from 19 in 1960 to over 1,150 in 1968.

In the fight against drug abuse—which is in itself a major cause of violent crime—we organized a new and powerful bureau of drug control in the Justice Department, and established heavier penalties for the misuse of hallucinogenic drugs.

Congress added several unwise provisions to the Safe Streets Act. I objected particularly to a provision that authorized wiretapping and eavesdropping in a considerable range of cases, by officials at every level of government. I signed the bill only because I was convinced that the federal government could retain administrative control of such invasions of privacy, so far as its own investigations were concerned.

Indiscriminate wiretapping and "bugging" have no place in a decent society. I tried to make this clear early in my administration, and reaffirmed it in a memorandum to my Cabinet officers on June 30, 1965. I said any wiretapping and eavesdropping should be restricted to national security cases.

With the regional directors of the Internal Revenue Service in 1966, I made the same point. People were disturbed by reports of wiretapping in income tax evasion cases. If that was being done, it ought to be stopped at once.

I have never believed we could open the door to widespread invasions of privacy without ultimately destroying the right of privacy. And if we do that, we shall lose one of the hallmarks of a free society.

There is another area where federal authority can clearly help reduce crime: effective gun controls. After a long-drawn-out struggle in Congress, we finally were able to get legislation outlawing the mail order sale of weapons and ammunition.

For a while, when public sentiment for effective gun control was high following the assassinations of the Rev. Martin Luther King, Jr., and Sen. Robert Kennedy, it appeared that we might even get the only really effective control—licensing and registration. But in the end, the gun lobby was too powerful. A flood of letters from hunters, convinced by the gun lobby that we intended to confiscate all weapons, hit Congress. The outrage of other citizens—sick of seeing national leaders cut down by gunmen—subsided after a while. And the issue faded away.

I cannot believe it has been permanently defeated, however. The Congress will not continue forever to ignore the will of the majority. It will become clear, even to those who have resisted the fact for so long, that we will never be able to control crime until we can keep guns out of the hands of those who should not have them. If we are really serious about maintaining law and order in America, we will register all weapons and license their users. Most civilized countries do, and their crime rates—which are considerably lower than ours—reflect it.

There is no single solution to crime any more than there is to poverty. Human behavior is too varied for that, and the causes of crime are too many.

But there are some things that can, over time, reduce the crime rate and make our streets, shops, and homes safer. Among them are:

Supporting local police, not just with bumper stickers and political speeches but with higher salaries, better training, better equipment, efforts to improve police-community relations, and more assistance from professionals in both the social and physical sciences.
Making our courts more efficient; reducing their criminal dockets; seeing to it that they also have the professional help they need.
Experimenting widely with new methods of rehabilitation, and increasing the number of probation officers.
Adopting strong gun control laws—including licensing and registration.
Evaluating all the juvenile delinquency control programs we have conducted over the past few years, under various authorities—including the comprehensive Juvenile Delinquency Act we enacted last year—and providing massive funds for those that have proved most successful.
Continuing our anti-poverty, employment, health, housing, and education programs at a high level.

Former Supreme Court Justice Tom Clark used to say: "I am convinced that every boy in his heart would rather steal second base than an automobile."

I agree. And if we provide support and appropriations for the

laws now on the books, we can save a good many youngsters from jeopardizing their lives and ours.

COST

There is one certainty about solutions to our problems. They won't come cheap. They will involve the expenditure of many billions of dollars in the years ahead. But every competent economic analyst I have ever talked with believes that if we have the wisdom to keep our economy strong and growing, we can afford them.

At the present rate of growth, we will have, at the very minimum, an additional $60 billion a year by 1976 to spend on new programs, on the expansion of existing ones, or on helping the states to develop their programs. Sixty billion dollars more a year, invested in the future of America.

There are many people who would look upon such spending as a waste and as a threat to individual incomes. That is a static way of looking at a dynamic economy, and it is wrong. Investments—in job training programs, in better health, in better education, in more housing, in more efficient transportation—don't diminish our economy. They add to it. They make it stronger and more productive. Creative reforms increase our national wealth.

I cannot leave the subject of costs without a mention of our commitment in Vietnam. It has been argued that paying for that commitment inevitably cuts down the money we should devote to meeting our urgent problems at home.

But there is no material reason why that should be so. I have said repeatedly—with the facts at hand to back me up—that we have enough national wealth to meet both categories of problems, foreign and domestic. However unhappy any cost of war is, the fact remains that Vietnam has taken up but 4% of our national income—compared to the 14% that was taken by the Korean War.

Over this period, investments in job training programs grew by more than six times. Outlays for health doubled. Expenditures for education grew two and one-half times. Federal aid to urban areas more than doubled. But all in all, total budget expenditures increased by only about 55%.

There are more than enough resources to deal with poverty and housing and jobs, if the people are ready to commit them with their taxes and if Congress will fund the people's programs.

We have, compared to nations in Western Europe, a relatively low tax schedule—federal, state, and local taxes added together. And it is a fact that, despite Vietnam, most Americans have enjoyed steadily higher personal incomes. The truth, I fear, is that many members of Congress who opposed domestic improvements before Vietnam, and will oppose them after Vietnam, have simply used Vietnam as an excuse to go on voting the way they always have.

It is not—I cannot say too often—our strength or our wealth that is being tested by the problems of this age. It is our will.

THE FOURTH ESTATE

To achieve the national goals I have described, the American people must understand them.

The President and his Cabinet officers have a number of instruments for conveying their policies to the people. Television addresses, press releases, public speeches, and private meetings with concerned groups of leaders are the main tools of communication available to government.

Yet what happens to their explanations of policy in print, or on the television screen, may be something far different from what they intended. Policy may be distorted. Rumors of dark motives, or of unspecified dissent, may be given equal prominence with the expressed purposes of the administration. Failure and conflict will certainly be emphasized wherever they can be found or presumed.

The theory on which much of the press seems to operate is that expressed by an old friend of mine one day in the Oval Office. When I asked him why the press seldom reported success and

seemed to concentrate on mistakes and controversy, this man—a distinguished and experienced publisher—said, "Mr. President, good news is no news. Bad news is news."

I recognize that every public figure wants everything reported about him to be favorable. Presidents are no exception—and indeed, the stakes with which they deal, and the cost of misunderstanding their intentions, make them all the more concerned to receive even-handed treatment by the Fourth Estate.

But even given the special interest of political leaders, there is now, it seems to me, a serious imbalance in the reporting of news.

During the 1968 campaign, a newspaperwoman wrote a brilliant satire on the kind of reporting some of her colleagues were then producing. It began:

A group of idealistic young people chanting "shut up and drop dead" was interrupted four times by Vice President Humphrey. The interruptions were part of a speech which the youths charged had been "planned." . . . The episode was further evidence of the Vice President's continuing failure to identify himself with the aspirations of the young.

To those who had carried great public responsibilities over the past five years, this satire seemed perilously close to being a typical "straight-news" story.

There is no simple answer to the problem I am describing. Good journalists try to give "color" to their stories, and to relate today's events to yesterday's. This can make for more informative reporting, and it certainly adds interest to the cold objective facts. But there is a dividing line between elaboration that enlightens and sensationalism that succeeds merely in confusing the issue and creating the impression of conflict where none exists.

Criticism of the errors committed by public leaders is a necessary function of a free press in a democratic society. Criticism of their character, in terms so stark that it makes them appear monsters who have imposed themselves on a helpless people, is likely to destroy any hope that they might unite and lead the nation toward the goals it must achieve for greatness.

The Presidency has always been the favorite target of the press, from the time of Washington and Jefferson to Kennedy and Johnson. The very fact that a man has had the temerity to aspire to that office, and to grapple with the immense problems that find their way to his desk, seems to inspire a degree of criticism unequaled in the Western world. Everything from the generation gap to the price of bread becomes his responsibility.

Each President must handle his press relations in his own way. Frankly, I believe one of the shortcomings of my five years in the Presidency was my inability to establish better rapport with the communications media. If I had it to do over again, I would try harder. My only stipulation would be an appeal to the news media to try harder also.

Although I held 140 news conferences—more than 50 of them filmed or televised live—during my five years in office, some elements in the press expressed discontent because there were not enough "formal" conferences. They did not like my practice of calling the regular White House reporters into my office or the Cabinet Room for an on-the-record news conference, without providing an opportunity for "live" broadcast or attendance by outside reporters because of short notice. These published criticisms nearly always included gratuitous insults to the White House correspondents: they were somehow "afraid" to ask penetrating questions.

I often wished that these critics had to subject themselves to the questions of these bashful reporters. I assure them they would be singing a different tune.

But in retrospect, I believe I should have held more regular televised news conferences. I was always more comfortable meeting with reporters around my desk, as President Roosevelt did, because it often gave us the opportunity to explore questions in greater depth than in a televised spectacular. Yet broadcast news conferences are an effective means of communicating with the public and should be widely used by national leaders.

Anti-Vietnamese war protesters.

UPI COMPIX

While I averaged more news conferences per week in office than either President Eisenhower or Kennedy, the image persists that I curtailed Presidential exposure to the press. Nevertheless I think most Washington reporters will agree that the White House during my administration did establish a hallmark for availability to the press. I met privately with individual newsmen or groups of newsmen several times each week—virtually always at their request, and frequently with some of my harshest critics.

My press secretaries—each of them with intimate knowledge of my activities—conducted more than 1,500 regular briefings and countless thousands of individual interviews. Cabinet officers had frequent news conferences and background sessions. In other efforts to communicate with the American people, I conducted nearly 100 briefing sessions for members of Congress on such issues as taxes and Vietnam. So I did attempt—with only occasional success—to communicate through the media.

I am well aware that no President escapes abuse from the press—especially after that honeymoon he usually has at the beginning of his term. But I do believe most Presidents would prefer a little moderation and restraint from the press throughout their administrations. Most Presidents would have preferred to ride on an even grade—instead of on a roller coaster that carried them from unreasonable heights at the beginning of their tenure to unreasonable depths once the honeymoon was over.

The qualifications of a good newspaperman or television commentator have increased substantially in the past three decades.

In the first place, government and politics have become vastly more sophisticated and complex than they used to be. Economy, science, sociology and psychology, and the intricacies of foreign affairs—all are increasingly interwoven through this nation's business.

As a result, a man who has to keep his readers well informed on government in our time should possess an abundant fund of background information. While many of the reporters who covered government affairs in my time did possess the information needed to judge the acts and purposes of today's government, I am afraid that many others did not, and showed little interest in obtaining it.

I have two thoughts for the press to consider or dismiss. They are the musings of a man who has seen the press in recent years only from the open end of the gun barrel—an angle from which the press rarely has occasion to see itself.

First, journalism is one of the professions. Yet, it is the only profession that has no entrance examinations or requirements.

Since these would probably be impractical, the task of maintaining high personnel standards remains a continuing and urgent one for the press itself.

I think that a good journalist should know American and world history as intimately as does a competent historian. He should have a substantial and specific understanding of economics and politics and foreign affairs, especially under the most recent five or six Presidents. He should be able to find the meaningful material in the welter of data that is thrown at him—and not simply rely on someone's cynical evaluation for a sensational lead sentence.

Second, I suggest that it may be time to change the basic attitude of journalism. Too little attention is devoted to the common everyday problems that plague society and to the efforts that succeed and therefore contain lessons we need to know.

Contrary to a notion that spread during my tenure, my relations with the press were at all times interesting and stimulating. I confess to a fascination with the news. Wire service news machines ticked away behind my desk within arm's reach. A bank of three television screens was also available for news and commentary.

I believe I was the only President in this century who presided over a war in which there was no censorship whatever of news dispatches. The effect of bringing Vietnam and all its travail onto the evening news screen will not be known, I believe, for a long time. It made the reality of that war more vivid, certainly. It may also have intensified the public's frustration over not being able to finish it off quickly, or at least to see battle lines on a chart changing as our troops moved forward from town to town. Showing the suffering and the savage combat with an elusive enemy was the price we paid for a free press. It was a price worth paying, all things considered, but it was still a heavy price for the nation.

I believe that journalism has been steadily improving in quality. Yet, I do not believe it has improved as rapidly as our responsibilities have grown heavier and more complex. Americans need to know, and they need to understand, and journalists are the main instruments who can meet these needs.

I do not think our government should or can do a thing about this situation. It is a matter purely for the free press itself. I have offered a suggestion for improving the competence and the professionalism of the press; the further task of imposing a degree of moderation on itself—lest in the search for the scandalous it neglect the real and the enduring—is a matter for the conscience of editors and writers everywhere.

These last few years have been turbulent. But contrary to an impression given by some of our recent street demonstrators, dissent was not invented in our country in 1967 and 1968. Americans have been practicing it with vigor since the day George Washington watched veterans of the Revolutionary War demonstrating outside his presidential mansion in Philadelphia. It was then that he decided to build the federal government a city of its own on the isolated Potomac. Had he but known it, he was merely creating a better lighted stage for dissent. From the White House, Lincoln watched dissenters proclaiming their causes. So did FDR. So did I.

Contrary to another impression given by recent demonstrators, the federal government has not the slightest inclination to defy or to stifle dissent. Indeed, no government has been so concerned throughout its history to assure dissent a hearing. Our close, free-world friends, Britain and France, have on occasion confiscated editions of periodicals for reasons of state. Our government has never done that. Both those two great friends of ours have in times of emergency such as war suspended the ultimate formal act of dissent—elections—until the emergency was over. America has never allowed civil or foreign war, or anything else, to prevent the holding of regular elections.

If we should ever deny ourselves essential liberties for security's sake, we will have neither. History is marred by the ruins of nations that have fought change with suppressive force. To do so is perhaps as instinctive as self-preservation. But it is, in the long run, self-defeating. If a nation cannot change peacefully when its people call for change, it risks violent change later on—and the loss of the civil liberties and property of all its citizens.

Dissent is legally protected in our nation. The Constitution clearly states the right to disagree and to assemble and demonstrate disagreement. Moreover, dissent is desirable for our political health. A democratic society needs the challenge and friction of differing arguments in order to find the right courses of action.

I am bound to say, however, that a small portion of recent dissenters have carried their dissent beyond the limits a lawful and civilized society can countenance if it wishes to remain lawful and civilized. A small fraction of those who should be our most enlightened people—members of the academic community—has carried dissent to the point of intolerance of any views that differ

from theirs. They have seemed determined not to debate or support reforms, but rather to break up and destroy, with no clear notion of what they wish to put in place of policies or institutions they oppose.

When small minorities have drowned out speakers, it has been called heckling. In fact heckling is a British term, and it is something of an art in which speaker and audience debate one another. But the sustained hooting and chanting of slogans—not to mention trying to smear paint on automobiles carrying officials, or in some cases, to overturn the cars—has a different origin: Germany in the '20s and '30s when Nazis appeared at meetings of opposing parties not to test speakers but to prevent them from speaking.

Inevitably this kind of behavior provokes its own reaction. It causes a polarization of views around extremes. That is the great danger of this kind of intolerant dissent.

There are three things which must be said about the extreme behavior of a few.

First, because ours is an organized democracy, because we know that chaos is the condition in which all rights are threatened, we cannot tolerate paralysis and violence, no matter what its causes. Social stability is absolutely essential to social progress. The common reaction to violence is not a public conversion to social progress, but more violence. Politicians who emerge in a time of violence are not likely to be those who can lead the nation in improving social conditions, or who urge the adoption of the dissenter's goals. They are likely to spring forth instead from the fears of the majority, and to promise to smash dissent and quell dissenters.

Second, violence must be professionally controlled by officers who carefully distinguish the lawbreaker from the dissenter—no matter how unpleasant the latter may be. Wherever possible, violent confrontations must be prevented or avoided, for out of them usually comes still more bitterness and outraged pride. Sometimes those confrontations cannot be avoided, since they are exactly what the dissenters seek and will not be denied. But when they do occur, the response of democratic authority must be just as controlled as the rioters are uncontrolled.

Third, the extreme behavior of a few should not cause us to

YOICHI OKAMOTO

dismiss dissent and demonstrations as baseless. We must have the will to communicate with those who show their rage with the way they live and with their powerlessness to change it through peaceful means. We must become able to listen—truly listen, not as a condescending gesture to the alienated young and the poor, but so that we may learn as well as guide. From even the most frustrated may come the "germ of inarticulate truth" that any society needs for refreshment and new understanding.

I do not believe that the causes most often cited for the divisiveness of these times are in fact the main causes. For example, some have said that Vietnam has been responsible. I have no doubt that the anguish of Vietnam contributed to it. But the fact is that the same divisiveness has appeared, violently, in countries not involved in Vietnam, such as France and Germany and Mexico.

Some have said that we have done nothing, or done too little, about our pressing social problems. Those who say that to me are straining their backs pushing against an open door. I, too, want to proceed faster. We have moved faster than ever before—but I must add that sometimes the demonstrators have provoked Congress and state governments into impeding the programs of the administration. I cannot forget that a member of Congress proposed cuts in our Demonstration Cities program on grounds that "we have had too many demonstrations in cities already." We changed the name of the program from Demonstration Cities to Model Cities, and tried again.

The "generation gap" is blamed for the mood of the times. I am sure it played a part, for it always does: it is a permanent feature of life. But I doubt that the gap between generations that have grown up since the New Deal is nearly as great as the gap that separated the first New Deal generation from those that preceded it in the 1920s.

I am inclined to believe that progress has something to do with the mood of dissent. In a stagnant society, people do not rebel. It is in a dynamic society where progress is being made that those at the bottom, impatient to participate, do rebel.

I think that a loss of national memory has something to do with it. After four decades, the Depression has become something to read about in textbooks, not a painful personal experience that causes young people to realize that great progress is being made. World War II, and the great need to prevent an aggressive tyranny from expanding beyond control, is a topic for old movies and not an aching personal fear replete with lessons for the present time.

Finally, there is a cause that deserves more attention than it has had: with our rapidly growing population and the growing size of government and of industry, our institutions are tending to become distant from the individual. The citizen feels the gap and a sense of frustration about influencing events.

High on any agenda for the future must be action to bring our institutions back to the people. The restiveness that demands this is a potentially healthy and creative force. Individuals are laying a claim to a greater role in deciding their destinies, and the claim must be met.

TOMORROW'S AGENDA

Only a relatively few years hence, when my grandchildren are beginning to form their families and advance in their careers, the United States will be a nation of 300 million people—half again as many citizens as now, almost four times more than when this century began. If life for Americans living then is to be meaningful, if freedom is to have any substance, if opportunity is to have any promise, if life in a complex urban society is to have any quality, it is apparent that we now, at this point in our national life, must overcome the impasses in our public processes —and make it possible for the talent, energy, and creativity of our society to begin fashioning rational responses.

Scientists often find it necessary to execute "midcourse corrections" in the flight of rockets exploring space. No matter how carefully programmed the rocket might be when it was propelled from the earth, it becomes essential midway along the route to recheck its bearings, reassess its directions and performance, and make adjustments to assure that it will continue on a true course to the target. I believe this is what we have been doing—or are beginning to do—in the present decade: making the midcourse corrections in the course of our government—and, hopefully, of our society—which are necessary if we are to remain on the true American course.

The American agenda for the future is not easily or adequately expressed in the familiar terms of today's political dialogue. Tomorrow's agenda, far more than that of the present decade, will be less of an agenda for politics than for society as a whole.

What I mean is this: over the postwar years, we in the United States have brought into being a society unlike any other in mankind's experience. There is no adequate way to measure it or describe it. The often-repeated statistics of affluence tell only a small part of the change which has been wrought.

Americans now are living very different lives from any other Americans in the past. They are seeing very different visions; they are coming to very different images of themselves and of the world in which they live. As never before, Americans of today are asking very different questions, experiencing very different doubts, stirring to very different impulses within the many institutions on which this society stands.

It is becoming ever more apparent, I believe, that as it has been necessary for *government and politics* to strive to overcome the burdens of the past, so it is necessary now for all our *institutions* to follow much the same course. The viability, authority, and relevance of our private institutions are at stake. Either we move into a new awareness of the new needs of our people—and their new capacities—or else many of the institutions and values imperative to our progress will become massive irrelevancies.

Unlike some, I do not myself believe that this is a society giving evidence of inner decay or moral rot at the core. Those who perceive a sick society are themselves, in my opinion, suffering from a sickness of vision if not of soul.

What I do see, at this point in time, is a vibrant, vital, vigorous society stirring with the realization that there must be—and that there can be—far better ways in which to serve our goals and purposes than we now have.

For two decades, we have grown at a breathtaking pace. Now, quite clearly, the institutions, arrangements, and concepts adequate in earlier times may be inadequate and obsolete for the times ahead. In many respects, we are more nearly at a time of beginning anew than we have been since the birth of the republic. With the foundation in place for the future, I suggest that we must—in private life as much as in public life—begin to give new thought, new attention, new interest to what we are to construct upon a new base.

We need to guard against the ever-present impulse to return to the quieter times of an irrecoverable past. Certainly, we must guard against the inadvertent return of an isolationist America, preoccupied with home to the exclusion of the world. We must no less be careful lest, in our focus upon problems of the moment, we neglect those investments in research, knowledge, and application of our ingenuity which sustain the engine of our progress. Quite apart from what the institution of government does or can do, on any level, the momentum of America will continue only *if all* our institutions are vigorous.

A far greater involvement of all sectors of our society is essential if we are to realize the fullness of the American promise. In our private organizations and institutions, Americans must not shy from questioning what has been done or what is being done because we may, very often, find that the predicate of the past— while vital to understanding—is no longer valid in today's conditions. An innovative, creative, open spirit is vital to the fashioning of our response to the vastly larger dimensions of the future.

BRITANNICA

Book of the Year

1969

1969 **Calendar**

1968 **Chronology of major**

international events

1968

JANUARY

S	M	T	W	T	F	S
	1	2	3	4	5	6
7	8	9	10	11	12	13
14	15	16	17	18	19	20
21	22	23	24	25	26	27
28	29	30	31			

FEBRUARY

S	M	T	W	T	F	S
				1	2	3
4	5	6	7	8	9	10
11	12	13	14	15	16	17
18	19	20	21	22	23	24
25	26	27	28	29		

MARCH

S	M	T	W	T	F	S
					1	2
3	4	5	6	7	8	9
10	11	12	13	14	15	16
17	18	19	20	21	22	23
24	25	26	27	28	29	30
31						

APRIL

S	M	T	W	T	F	S
	1	2	3	4	5	6
7	8	9	10	11	12	13
14	15	16	17	18	19	20
21	22	23	24	25	26	27
28	29	30				

MAY

S	M	T	W	T	F	S
			1	2	3	4
5	6	7	8	9	10	11
12	13	14	15	16	17	18
19	20	21	22	23	24	25
26	27	28	29	30	31	

JUNE

S	M	T	W	T	F	S
						1
2	3	4	5	6	7	8
9	10	11	12	13	14	15
16	17	18	19	20	21	22
23	24	25	26	27	28	29
30						

JULY

S	M	T	W	T	F	S
	1	2	3	4	5	6
7	8	9	10	11	12	13
14	15	16	17	18	19	20
21	22	23	24	25	26	27
28	29	30	31			

AUGUST

S	M	T	W	T	F	S
				1	2	3
4	5	6	7	8	9	10
11	12	13	14	15	16	17
18	19	20	21	22	23	24
25	26	27	28	29	30	31

SEPTEMBER

S	M	T	W	T	F	S
1	2	3	4	5	6	7
8	9	10	11	12	13	14
15	16	17	18	19	20	21
22	23	24	25	26	27	28
29	30					

OCTOBER

S	M	T	W	T	F	S
		1	2	3	4	5
6	7	8	9	10	11	12
13	14	15	16	17	18	19
20	21	22	23	24	25	26
27	28	29	30	31		

NOVEMBER

S	M	T	W	T	F	S
					1	2
3	4	5	6	7	8	9
10	11	12	13	14	15	16
17	18	19	20	21	22	23
24	25	26	27	28	29	30

DECEMBER

S	M	T	W	T	F	S
1	2	3	4	5	6	7
8	9	10	11	12	13	14
15	16	17	18	19	20	21
22	23	24	25	26	27	28
29	30	31				

1969

THE YEAR 1969 of the Christian Era corresponds to the year of Creation 5729–5730 of the Jewish calendar; to the year 1388–1389 of the Muslim hegira; to the 193rd year of the United States; and to the 201st year of the *Encyclopædia Britannica.*

JANUARY

S	M	T	W	T	F	S
			1	2	3	4
5	6	7	8	9	10	11
12	13	14	15	16	17	18
19	20	21	22	23	24	25
26	27	28	29	30	31	

FEBRUARY

S	M	T	W	T	F	S
						1
2	3	4	5	6	7	8
9	10	11	12	13	14	15
16	17	18	19	20	21	22
23	24	25	26	27	28	

MARCH

S	M	T	W	T	F	S
						1
2	3	4	5	6	7	8
9	10	11	12	13	14	15
16	17	18	19	20	21	22
23	24	25	26	27	28	29
30	31					

APRIL

S	M	T	W	T	F	S
		1	2	3	4	5
6	7	8	9	10	11	12
13	14	15	16	17	18	19
20	21	22	23	24	25	26
27	28	29	30			

MAY

S	M	T	W	T	F	S
				1	2	3
4	5	6	7	8	9	10
11	12	13	14	15	16	17
18	19	20	21	22	23	24
25	26	27	28	29	30	31

JUNE

S	M	T	W	T	F	S
1	2	3	4	5	6	7
8	9	10	11	12	13	14
15	16	17	18	19	20	21
22	23	24	25	26	27	28
29	30					

JULY

S	M	T	W	T	F	S
		1	2	3	4	5
6	7	8	9	10	11	12
13	14	15	16	17	18	19
20	21	22	23	24	25	26
27	28	29	30	31		

AUGUST

S	M	T	W	T	F	S
					1	2
3	4	5	6	7	8	9
10	11	12	13	14	15	16
17	18	19	20	21	22	23
24	25	26	27	28	29	30
31						

SEPTEMBER

S	M	T	W	T	F	S
	1	2	3	4	5	6
7	8	9	10	11	12	13
14	15	16	17	18	19	20
21	22	23	24	25	26	27
28	29	30				

OCTOBER

S	M	T	W	T	F	S
			1	2	3	4
5	6	7	8	9	10	11
12	13	14	15	16	17	18
19	20	21	22	23	24	25
26	27	28	29	30	31	

NOVEMBER

S	M	T	W	T	F	S
						1
2	3	4	5	6	7	8
9	10	11	12	13	14	15
16	17	18	19	20	21	22
23	24	25	26	27	28	29
30						

DECEMBER

S	M	T	W	T	F	S
	1	2	3	4	5	6
7	8	9	10	11	12	13
14	15	16	17	18	19	20
21	22	23	24	25	26	27
28	29	30	31			

1970

JANUARY

S	M	T	W	T	F	S
				1	2	3
4	5	6	7	8	9	10
11	12	13	14	15	16	17
18	19	20	21	22	23	24
25	26	27	28	29	30	31

FEBRUARY

S	M	T	W	T	F	S
1	2	3	4	5	6	7
8	9	10	11	12	13	14
15	16	17	18	19	20	21
22	23	24	25	26	27	28

MARCH

S	M	T	W	T	F	S
1	2	3	4	5	6	7
8	9	10	11	12	13	14
15	16	17	18	19	20	21
22	23	24	25	26	27	28
29	30	31				

APRIL

S	M	T	W	T	F	S
			1	2	3	4
5	6	7	8	9	10	11
12	13	14	15	16	17	18
19	20	21	22	23	24	25
26	27	28	29	30		

MAY

S	M	T	W	T	F	S
					1	2
3	4	5	6	7	8	9
10	11	12	13	14	15	16
17	18	19	20	21	22	23
24	25	26	27	28	29	30
31						

JUNE

S	M	T	W	T	F	S
	1	2	3	4	5	6
7	8	9	10	11	12	13
14	15	16	17	18	19	20
21	22	23	24	25	26	27
28	29	30				

JULY

S	M	T	W	T	F	S
			1	2	3	4
5	6	7	8	9	10	11
12	13	14	15	16	17	18
19	20	21	22	23	24	25
26	27	28	29	30	31	

AUGUST

S	M	T	W	T	F	S
						1
2	3	4	5	6	7	8
9	10	11	12	13	14	15
16	17	18	19	20	21	22
23	24	25	26	27	28	29
30	31					

SEPTEMBER

S	M	T	W	T	F	S
		1	2	3	4	5
6	7	8	9	10	11	12
13	14	15	16	17	18	19
20	21	22	23	24	25	26
27	28	29	30			

OCTOBER

S	M	T	W	T	F	S
				1	2	3
4	5	6	7	8	9	10
11	12	13	14	15	16	17
18	19	20	21	22	23	24
25	26	27	28	29	30	31

NOVEMBER

S	M	T	W	T	F	S
1	2	3	4	5	6	7
8	9	10	11	12	13	14
15	16	17	18	19	20	21
22	23	24	25	26	27	28
29	30					

DECEMBER

S	M	T	W	T	F	S
		1	2	3	4	5
6	7	8	9	10	11	12
13	14	15	16	17	18	19
20	21	22	23	24	25	26
27	28	29	30	31		

RELIGIOUS, NATIONAL, AND OTHER MAJOR HOLIDAYS

January 1969

1 New Year's Day
1 Cameroon, Haiti, Sudan
4 Burma
6 Epiphany (Twelfth Night)
11 Chad
26 Australia, India

February

2 Candlemas Day
2 Septuagesima Sunday
4 Ceylon
6 New Zealand
14 St. Valentine's Day
16 Lithuania
18 Shrove Tuesday, Mardi Gras
18 Nepal
19 Ash Wednesday
23 First Sunday in Lent
24 Estonia
25 Kuwait
27 Dominican Republic

March

3 Morocco
4 Purim (Jewish Feast of Lots)
7 Ghana
11 Denmark
15 Ides of March
17 St. Patrick's Day
17 Ireland
20 Muslim New Year (1389)
23 Passion Sunday
23 Pakistan
25 Annunciation Day
25 Greece
30 Palm Sunday

April

1 April Fools' Day
3 Pesach (Jewish Passover), 1st day
4 Good Friday
4 Hungary, Senegal
6 Easter Sunday
13 Eastern Orthodox Easter
14 Pan American Day
17 Syria
23 Israel
26 Tanzania
27 Sierra Leone, Togo
29 Japan
30 Netherlands

May

1 May Day, International Labour Day
9 Czechoslovakia
11 Rogation Sunday
11 Laos
14 Paraguay
15 Ascension Day
17 Norway
23 Shabuoth (Jewish Feast of Weeks), 1st day
24 Commonwealth Day, U.K.
25 Pentecost (Whitsunday)
26 Whitmonday
27 Afghanistan
30 Memorial Day, U.S.
31 South Africa

June

1 Trinity Sunday
1 Tunisia
2 Italy
5 Corpus Christi
10 Portugal
11 Kamehameha Day, Polynesian peoples
12 Philippines
14 Trooping the colour in honour of the sovereign's birthday, U.K.
17 Iceland
23 Luxembourg
24 Midsummer Day
30 Congo (Kinshasa)

July

1 Burundi, Canada, Rwanda, Somali Republic
4 United States
5 Venezuela
6 Malawi
9 Argentina
12 Orangeman's Day, N.Ire.
14 France, Iraq
15 St. Swithin's Day
18 Spain
20 Colombia
21 Belgium
22 Poland
23 Ethiopia, U.A.R.
26 Liberia
28 Peru

August

1 Lammas Day
1 Dahomey, Switzerland
4 Jamaica
6 Transfiguration Day
6 Bolivia
7 Ivory Coast
10 Ecuador
15 Assumption Day
15 Korea
17 Gabon, Indonesia
23 Romania
25 Uruguay
31 Malaysia, Trinidad and Tobago

September

1 Labor Day, U.S. and Canada
7 Brazil
9 Bulgaria
13 Rosh Hashana (Jewish New Year, 5730)
15 Costa Rica, El Salvador, Guatemala, Honduras, Nicaragua
16 Mexico
18 Chile
22 Yom Kippur (Jewish Day of Atonement)
22 Mali
23 Saudi Arabia
26 Yemen
27 Sukkoth (Jewish Feast of Tabernacles), 1st day
29 Michaelmas Day

October

1 Cyprus, Nigeria
2 Guinea
9 Uganda
10 China
13 Thanksgiving Day, Canada
14 Malagasy
24 United Nations Day
24 Zambia
26 Austria, Iran
29 Turkey
31 Halloween

November

1 All Saints' Day
1 Algeria, Vietnam
2 All Souls' Day
3 Panama
5 Guy Fawkes Day, U.K.
7–8 U.S.S.R.
11 Martinmas
11 Sweden
14 Jordan
18 Latvia
22 Lebanon
27 Thanksgiving Day, U.S.
28 Mauritania
29 Yugoslavia
30 First Sunday in Advent

December

1 Central African Republic
5 Hanukkah (Jewish Feast of Lights), 1st day
5 Thailand
6 Finland
8 Conception Day
11 Upper Volta
12 Kenya
18 Niger
24 Libya
25 Christmas Day
26 Boxing Day, U.K.
28 Childermas (Feast of the Innocents)
31 New Year's Eve

JANUARY

1

U.S. Pres. Lyndon B. Johnson imposed mandatory restrictions on most direct investments overseas by U.S. corporations.

Sékou Touré was reelected without opposition to another seven-year term as president of Guinea.

British Prime Minister Harold Wilson announced the selection of C. Day-Lewis as poet laureate.

2

New Year's truce, described as the "worst truce ever" by U.S. authorities, ended in Vietnam.

Pres. Johnson signed an omnibus social security bill that would raise the benefits of 24 million persons by at least 13%.

Sheikh Muhammad Abdullah of Kashmir was freed from house arrest by the government of India.

Mississippi seated Robert Clark as its first Negro legislator in 74 years.

Philip Blaiberg, a 58-year-old retired dentist, became the third recipient of a transplanted heart in an operation performed in Cape Town, S.Af., by Christiaan N. Barnard.

3

Cuba began the rationing of petroleum for public and private use.

Data released by the U.S. Atomic Energy Commission on the Chinese nuclear test of Dec. 24, 1967, indicated that the test might have been a failure.

4

Cambodia received a shipment of planes and antiaircraft guns from Communist China.

North Vietnamese mission in Paris repeated Foreign Minister Nguyen Duy Trinh's Dec. 30, 1967, statement that, if the U.S. would stop the bombing of North Vietnam, Hanoi would "start conversations with the United States . . . on relevant problems."

5

Five men, including author and pediatrician Benjamin Spock, were indicted on charges of conspiring to counsel young men to violate the U.S. draft laws.

Alexander Dubcek succeeded Antonin Novotny as first secretary of the Czechoslovak Communist Party.

U.S. command in Saigon reported that the U.S. military buildup in South Vietnam had reached 486,000 men; plane losses passed 1,000 with the loss of 4 planes over North Vietnam.

8

Arab summit parley scheduled to be held in Rabat, Mor., was postponed indefinitely.

Israeli Prime Minister Levi Eshkol and Pres. Johnson completed two days of talks at the latter's ranch in Texas.

Israeli and Jordanian forces fought for several hours on a 13-mi. front south of the Sea of Galilee, their most serious clash since the June 1967 war.

9

Sweden granted asylum to four U.S. Navy men who had deserted in Japan.

U.S. spacecraft Surveyor 7 made a successful landing on the moon and began transmitting pictures to earth.

10

John Grey Gorton was sworn in as Australia's 20th prime minister.

Prince Norodom Sihanouk of Cambodia, following talks with Chester Bowles, Pres. Johnson's special envoy, stated that the U.S. would not adopt a policy of hot pursuit across Cambodia's borders.

11

U.S. Vice-Pres. Hubert H. Humphrey returned to the U.S. after a tour of nine African nations.

International Committee of the Red Cross announced that Israel and the U.A.R. had agreed to a general exchange of prisoners of war.

Pres. Johnson asked the U.S. Agency for International Development to reduce its dollar expenditures by one-third, or about $100 million.

12

U.S. Atty. Gen. Ramsey Clark reported that 952 men had been convicted in 1967 for violating the Selective Service laws.

Four young Soviet intellectuals were convicted of anti-Soviet activity following a five-day trial in Moscow.

Cuban Prime Minister Fidel Castro called for world unification against "Yankee imperialism" in a speech closing a nine-day International Cultural Congress in Havana.

15

Second session of the U.S. 90th Congress convened in Washington, D.C.

U.S. Supreme Court gave final approval to the merger of the Pennsylvania and New York Central railroads.

Laotian garrison at Nambac, 60 mi. N of the royal capital of Luang Prabang, was taken by the Pathet Lao in the worst defeat suffered by Laotian government forces.

16

Urho K. Kekkonen was elected to his third six-year term as president of Finland.

Two U.S. military attachés were shot to death in Guatemala in a series of terrorist attacks.

Prime Minister Wilson announced that Britain would withdraw its military forces from east of Suez by the end of 1971; he also announced a series of cutbacks in home and defense spending.

17

Pres. Johnson in his annual state of the union message to Congress outlined an expanded program of legislation for the cities and the hard-core unemployed, gave a harder definition of his position on peace talks with North Vietnam.

18

U.S. and the U.S.S.R. submitted to the UN Disarmament Committee in Geneva the complete draft of a treaty to ban the spread of nuclear weapons.

British House of Commons, by a vote of 304–9, formally approved Prime Minister Wilson's program to reduce Britain's role as a world power and cut domestic welfare spending.

19

Colombia and the U.S.S.R. resumed diplomatic relations after a lapse of 20 years.

Pres. Johnson nominated Clark M. Clifford to succeed Robert S. McNamara as U.S. secretary of defense.

U.S. Defense Department officials estimated that 302,000 men would be inducted into the Army in 1968, compared with 230,000 in 1967 and 383,000 in 1966.

U.K. and the U.S.S.R. signed in London an agreement to cooperate in the fields of applied science and technology.

21

Communist forces began a siege of the U.S. stronghold of Khe Sanh, 6 mi. from the Laotian border and 14 mi. S of the Demilitarized Zone.

Mapai, the government party in Israel, merged with the Rafi and Ahdut Haavoda parties to form the Israel Labour Party.

Attempt by 31 North Korean infiltrators to kill South Korean Pres. Pak Chung Hi was broken up in Seoul; 5 of the raiders were killed and several others captured.

Bank of Canada increased the bank rate from 6 to 7% in a move to tighten the national money supply.

22

U.S. B-52 bomber carrying four unarmed hydrogen bombs crashed near Thule, Greenland, scattering bomb fragments over the ice.

Engine misfiring in orbit marred the first unmanned flight of the spacecraft lunar module, designed to ferry astronauts to the moon.

23

USS "Pueblo," a U.S. Navy intelligence ship, was seized off the Korean coast by North Korean patrol boats and taken into the port of Wonsan.

U.S. resumed normal relations with Greece; relations between the two countries had been suspended following the flight of King Constantine six weeks earlier.

24

Pres. Johnson in a special message to Congress made another plea for passage of his civil rights measures.

Jens Otto Krag resigned as prime minister of Denmark following heavy Socialist losses in elections held the preceding day.

Prime Minister Wilson and Soviet Premier Aleksei N. Kosygin, after talks in Moscow, issued a joint communiqué urging a political settlement of the war in Vietnam.

25

Pres. Johnson ordered 14,787 Air Force and Navy reservists to active duty as concern mounted over seizure of the "Pueblo."

Two Israeli soldiers were killed when gunfire raked the Allenby Bridge between Israeli occupied territory and Jordan.

26

U.S. appealed to the UN Security Council to obtain the safe return of the "Pueblo" and her crew and to restore the Korean armistice agreements to full effectiveness.

29

Pres. Johnson submitted to Congress a record budget for the fiscal year ending June 30, 1969; expenditure was estimated at $186.1 billion.

Pres. Nguyen Van Thieu of South Vietnam canceled the scheduled lunar New Year (Tet) cease-fire because of widespread Viet Cong attacks.

Twenty-four persons were reported killed in several days of communal rioting between Indian Muslims and Creoles on Mauritius.

30

Israeli and U.A.R. forces exchanged artillery fire across the Suez Canal.

USS "Pueblo" crew in custody . . . January 23

Viet Cong launched heavy attacks in Saigon and elsewhere in South Vietnam.

Japanese Prime Minister Eisaku Sato defended Japan's defense alignment with the U.S. during a heated debate in the Diet.

31

State of martial law was declared throughout South Vietnam as Viet Cong guerrilla attacks continued; Viet Cong commando units entered the presidential palace and the U.S. embassy in Saigon, holding the embassy for six hours.

Demonstrators in Seoul urged the U.S. to take stronger action against North Korean infiltration raids.

Kenya and Somalia resumed diplomatic relations, broken since 1963 as a result of border clashes.

West Germany and Yugoslavia resumed diplomatic relations after a break of ten years.

South Pacific island of Nauru, a former UN trust territory, became an independent republic.

FEBRUARY

1

Canadian government's draft bill of rights was tabled in the House of Commons.

Pres. Johnson in his annual economic report to Congress stressed the need for a tax increase and for restraint in wage and price decisions.

New coalition Cabinet was formed in Denmark by Radical Liberal Hilmar Baunsgaard.

Canada's three military branches —the Army, the Royal Canadian Navy, and the Royal Canadian Air Force—were unified into the Canadian Armed Forces.

Second UN Conference on Trade and Development (UNCTAD) opened at New Delhi, India.

2

Pres. Johnson stated that the Viet Cong's Tet offensive in South Vietnam was a complete failure both militarily and psychologically.

Pres. Johnson announced that North Korea had rejected a second U.S. demand for the return of the "Pueblo" and her crew.

3

Viet Cong forces held fast to positions on the edge of Saigon's Tan Son Nhut air base and in suburban Gia Dinh Province in the face of U.S. air strikes and helicopter strafing.

4

U.S. Defense Department stated that the Joint Chiefs of Staff had reported to Pres. Johnson that the U.S. Marine base at Khe Sanh could and should be defended.

5

Federal-provincial constitutional conference to begin the process of constitutional reform in Canada was opened in Ottawa by Prime Minister Lester B. Pearson.

6

U.S. nuclear aircraft carrier "Enterprise," sent to Korean waters following capture of the "Pueblo," was reported to have been withdrawn.

South Korean government protested to the U.S. government against unilateral U.S. discussions with North Korean officials concerning the "Pueblo."

7

North Vietnamese troops captured the U.S. Special Forces camp at Lang Vei, southwest of Khe Sanh.

All ten provincial premiers approved Prime Minister Pearson's proposal for a long-term program to give the French language equal status with English throughout Canada.

Pres. Johnson proposed to Congress a series of measures to deal with rioting, crime, drug traffic, law enforcement, and justice.

Government of Belgian Prime Minister Paul Vanden Boeynants resigned as the result of a language dispute in which Flemish students demanded that French-speaking students and faculty of the Catholic University of Louvain leave the Flemish-language area.

Six Latin-American nations signed a convention at Bogotá, Colombia, establishing the Andean Development Corporation.

8

Yemeni republican forces lifted the royalist siege of San'a', the capital.

Abdullah Yafi became prime minister of Lebanon, succeeding Rashid Karame, who resigned February 5.

South Korea announced a military expansion program to cope with stepped-up infiltration from North Korea.

Pres. Johnson in a special message to Congress requested authorization for $3,040,000,000 in foreign aid during the fiscal year ending June 30, 1969.

Three Negro students were killed in a racial disturbance at Orangeburg, S.C., springing from the attempts of students at two predominantly Negro colleges to desegregate a local bowling alley.

9

U.S. infantry troops were brought into Saigon to help clear the city of guerrillas.

U.K. Prime Minister Wilson and Pres. Johnson completed two days of talks in Washington, D.C.

U.S. and West Germany canceled plans for joint development of a vertical take-off fighter plane; work on the project had been under way since 1964.

10

Special commission studying the summer 1967 riots in New Jersey charged that Newark police, state police, and national guardsmen used excessive and unjustified force against Negroes.

Nine-day strike of New York City garbage collectors, which had led city officials to declare a health emergency, ended.

11

South Vietnam began the mobilization of an additional 65,000 troops.

Gen. Alfredo Stroessner was elected to another five-year term as president of Paraguay.

13

U.S. was revealed to be rushing an additional 10,500 combat troops to South Vietnam.

Council of the Organization of American States voted to elect Galo Plaza Lasso of Ecuador as secretary-general.

14

U.S. government announced that it would resume arms shipments to Jordan, suspended since June 1967.

Mayor of Hue said the Viet Cong had executed 300 civilians, including government officials, on February 9.

15

U.S. presidential emissary Cyrus R. Vance completed three days of talks with Pres. Pak and other South Korean officials.

16

U.S. National Security Council abolished draft deferments for most graduate students and also suspended occupational deferments.

Cease-fire ended a serious clash between Israeli and Jordanian forces on both sides of the Jordan River.

Pres. Johnson designated C. R. Smith, chairman of the board of American Airlines, to succeed Alexander B. Trowbridge as secretary of commerce.

18

Britain shifted from Greenwich Mean Time to the time of western Europe, one hour ahead.

Viet Cong began coordinated rocket and mortar attacks on U.S. and South Vietnamese military installations and cities from the Central Highlands to the Mekong Delta.

19

Canada's Liberal government was defeated in the House of Commons by a vote of 84–82 on a major tax bill.

Jacobus J. Fouché was elected without opposition as president of South Africa by a joint session of Parliament.

Agreement by U.S. airlines to reduce fares by 50% for foreign

WIDE WORLD

Soviet embassy in Washington, D.C., bombed . . . February 21

visitors was announced by a presidential task force on travel.

Viet Cong struck Saigon's Tan Son Nhut air base with mortar and rocket fire.

Three-man arbitration commission awarded about 300 sq.mi. of the Rann of Cutch, 350 mi. NW of Bombay, to Pakistan; the remaining 3,200 sq.mi. went to India.

20

Motion to cut off debate in the U.S. Senate on the administration's civil rights bill fell seven votes short of the necessary two-thirds majority.

Communist forces attempting to slip antiaircraft guns into the outskirts of Saigon were foiled by air observers.

South Korea announced plans to organize veterans, reservists, and ordinary villagers into a national militia and counterintelligence network.

South Vietnamese Vice-Pres. Nguyen Cao Ky resigned as head of that country's Emergency Recovery Committee, established to aid recovery from the Tet offensive.

21

Bomb of undetermined origin exploded at the Soviet embassy in Washington, D.C.

Switzerland announced that its ambassador to Peking would also act as representative to Hanoi.

22

Laotian Premier Souvanna Phouma charged that North Vietnam had 40,000 men in Laos.

Pres. Johnson in a special message to Congress proposed a program to provide six million new low- and middle-income housing units in urban centres during the next ten years.

23

North Vietnamese and Viet Cong made their first attack on Khe Sanh.

Pres. Johnson asked Congress to abolish visa requirements for tourists and businessmen from certain nations who wished to visit the U.S.

24

South Vietnamese troops captured the imperial palace in the walled Citadel of the city of Hue.

25

Archbishop Makarios was elected to a second five-year term as president of Cyprus.

South Vietnamese government arrested more than 20 political opponents between February 20 and February 25.

Léopold Sédar Senghor was re-elected president of Senegal for another four-year term.

26

Second attempt to cut off debate on the civil rights bill in the U.S. Senate failed by six votes.

27

House of Commons passed, by vote of 372–62, legislation drastically curtailing the right of Asians with British nationality to emigrate to Britain.

Nine British-protected Persian Gulf amirates agreed to form a union when British troops were withdrawn, probably in 1971.

28

Canadian House of Commons voted 138–119 in favour of the Liberal government's confidence motion, ending the government crisis.

Gov. George Romney (Rep., Mich.) announced his withdrawal as a candidate for president.

U.S. State Department ended restrictions on travel by U.S. citizens to Syria.

29

Pres. Johnson's National Advisory Commission on Civil Disorders, headed by Gov. Otto Kerner of Illinois, warned that the U.S. was moving toward two societies—one white and one black, separate and unequal.

MARCH

1

Clark M. Clifford took office as U.S. secretary of defense.

South Vietnamese House of Representatives rejected, by a vote of 85–10, a request by Pres. Thieu that he be given emergency powers to rule by decree for one year.

Third attempt to cut off debate on the civil rights bill in the U.S. Senate fell four votes short of the necessary two-thirds majority.

3

U.A.R. Pres. Gamal Abd-al-Nasser vowed that the Arabs would liberate all areas occupied by Israel.

4

U.S. Senate voted, 65–32, to cut off debate on the civil rights bill.

U.S. State Department was revealed to have denied a visa to Rhodesian Prime Minister Ian D. Smith.

5

Viet Cong guerrillas stormed into the capital of South Vietnam's southernmost province and occupied a hospital for several hours.

6

Rhodesian government hanged three Africans in defiance of the British government.

U.S. protested what it called the suppression of free speech in the Soviet Union by the imprisonment of dissenting writers.

7

South Vietnamese Senate rejected, by a vote of 40–3, the government's request for emergency economic powers.

U.A.R. turned down a proposal by UN envoy Gunnar Jarring that it send representatives to Cyprus to meet representatives of Israel.

U.S., the U.S.S.R., and the U.K. formally committed themselves to take immediate action through the UN Security Council against an actual or threatened nuclear attack on any nation that renounced nuclear weapons.

Lesotho's College of Chiefs revoked King Moshoeshoe II's declaration pledging to stay out of politics.

9

Viet Cong made seven coordinated attacks on the southern edge of Saigon.

10

North Vietnamese artillery attacks struck U.S. outposts just south of the Demilitarized Zone.

Seven nations belonging to the London Gold Pool reaffirmed their intention to maintain the price of gold at $35 an ounce in an attempt to end the wave of gold speculation that had begun March 1.

Tentative agreement was reached between two major copper producers and a coalition of 26 unions, the first break in the nationwide U.S. copper strike that began July 15, 1967.

11

U.S. and South Vietnamese troops launched the largest offensive of the war thus far against enemy forces in the Saigon area.

U.S. Senate, after seven weeks of debate, passed by 71–20 a major civil rights bill containing open-housing and antiriot provisions.

Tens of thousands of Poles, protesting government interference in cultural affairs, fought with police and armed militiamen in several parts of Warsaw.

12

British colony of Mauritius in the Indian Ocean became an independent state within the Commonwealth.

Sen. Eugene McCarthy (Minn.) made an unexpectedly good showing against Pres. Johnson in the New Hampshire Democratic presidential primary, winning about 42% of the vote.

13

University students and the police clashed in Cracow and Poznan as student demonstrations spread across Poland.

Worst epidemic of foot-and-mouth disease in British history was declared over by the Agriculture Ministry; more than 400,000 head of livestock had been slaughtered since the outbreak began in October 1967.

14

U.S. Federal Reserve Board raised its discount rate from 4½ to 5%; Bank of Canada raised its discount rate from 7% to a record 7½%.

UN Disarmament Committee ended its discussions in Geneva on a proposed treaty to end the spread of nuclear weapons.

U.S. command in Saigon reported that the number of U.S. casualties in Vietnam had exceeded those in the Korean War.

U.S. Agency for International Development ordered new, tighter controls over foreign aid spending.

15

London gold market was closed at the request of the U.S. to halt heavy selling of gold.

Panamanian Pres. Marco A. Robles declared that he would defy the National Assembly's attempt to impeach him for violating the constitution by interfering in the presidential election campaign.

British Foreign Secretary George Brown resigned and was replaced by Michael Stewart.

Canadian House of Commons approved, by a vote of 122–106, a bill that imposed a 3% surcharge on personal and corporate income taxes.

16

Sen. Robert F. Kennedy (N.Y.) announced his candidacy for the Democratic presidential nomination.

Eugene McCarthy . . . March 12

WIDE WORLD

More than 200 persons were injured in a clash between right- and left-wing students at Rome University in the latest of a series of student disturbances in Italy.

17

Seven nations belonging to the London Gold Pool agreed to stop buying and selling gold in the international market in an effort to prevent further loss of their monetary gold to private speculators; monetary gold would continue to be valued at $35 an ounce, but the price of gold sold privately would be permitted to fluctuate.

18

Heavy fighting broke out in South Vietnam's northernmost province of Quang Tri.

UN Security Council voted unanimously to extend the UN peace-keeping force in Cyprus until June 26.

U.S. Department of Health, Education, and Welfare announced that Northern school districts must end segregation caused by factors other than housing and take steps to assure Negro children the same educational advantages as white children.

19

British Chancellor of the Exchequer Roy Jenkins presented to the House of Commons the budget for the fiscal year ending March 31, 1969, which estimated revenue at £11,952 million and expenditure at £11,312 million.

Pres. Johnson signed into law a bill eliminating the requirement that 25% of U.S. currency be backed by gold.

20

French Pres. Charles de Gaulle renewed his call for a return to the gold standard.

Attempted army coup was suppressed by the government of Pres. Qahtan al-Shaabi of Southern Yemen.

U.A.R. Pres. Nasser named 14 civilians to an expanded Cabinet of 32 members.

21

Large force of Israeli troops crossed into Jordan and conducted a day-long retaliatory raid against alleged Arab terrorist bases.

South Vietnamese Pres. Thieu announced plans to increase the South Vietnamese armed forces by 135,000.

Gov. Nelson Rockefeller of New York announced that he would not seek the presidency.

Bank of England lowered the bank rate from the "crisis level" of 8% to 7½%.

22

Pres. Johnson announced the appointment of Gen. William C. Westmoreland, U.S. commander in Vietnam, as army chief of staff.

U.S. Senate approved, by a vote of 67–1, a code of ethics to govern senators and Senate employees in their financial dealings.

Antonin Novotny, already ousted as Communist Party first secretary, was forced to resign from the largely ceremonial position of president of Czechoslovakia.

Pres. Johnson nominated Wilbur J. Cohen to succeed John W. Gardner as secretary of health, education, and welfare.

Cuba and the U.S.S.R. signed an agreement providing for a 10% increase in trade in 1968.

23

King Husain of Jordan stated that neither he nor his government would accept responsibility for the safety of Israel or of Israeli troops occupying the West Bank.

Summit meeting in Dresden, E.Ger., of leaders from most Eastern European countries called on First Secretary Dubcek of the Czechoslovak Communist Party to explain the liberalizing changes taking place in Czechoslovakia.

24

UN Security Council unanimously adopted a resolution condemning Israel's attack on Jordan and all other attacks in violation of UN cease-fire agreements.

Panamanian Pres. Robles was voted out of office by the National Assembly but, with the support of the National Guard, he ignored the move.

25

U.S. and South Vietnamese troops clashed with enemy forces in a day-long battle 28 mi. NW of Saigon.

26

Zalman Shazar was elected to a second five-year term as president of Israel.

27

U.S. planes bombed a railroad yard 18 mi. from the Chinese border.

Indonesian Consultative Assembly elected acting Pres. Suharto to a five-year term as president.

28

Agreement for the resumption of U.S. arms shipments to Jordan was signed in Amman.

Protest march led by the Rev. Martin Luther King, Jr., in support of striking Memphis, Tenn., garbage collectors ended in violence in which one Negro youth was killed.

Opposition Conservative Party won all of four by-elections held in the U.K.

29

Israeli and Jordanian forces engaged in a six-hour artillery duel along the Jordan River.

30

Canada and the U.S. signed an agreement extending the North American Air Defense Command arrangement for an additional five years.

Gen. Ludvik Svoboda was elected president of Czechoslovakia by a 288–282 vote of the National Assembly.

Nine major industrial nations, including the U.S. and the U.K. but excluding France, voted to reform the world monetary system by eventually creating new reserve assets, popularly called "paper gold."

31

Pres. Johnson announced in a nationwide TV address that he would not seek or accept another term as president and announced simultaneously that he had ordered limitations on the bombing of North Vietnam.

APRIL

1

U.S. Supreme Court, by a vote of 5–3, extended its one-man, one-vote doctrine to cover local governments.

London gold market reopened; during the day the price of gold fell from $38 to $37.70 per ounce.

Jordan opposed a proposal in the UN Security Council to increase the number of observers in Israeli-occupied territory.

2

U.S. identified the 20th parallel in North Vietnam as the line north of which all air and naval bombardment had been halted.

Sen. McCarthy won 57.6% of the vote in the Wisconsin Democratic presidential primary, as against 35.4% for Pres. Johnson.

Soviet Premier Kosygin arrived in Teheran on an official visit to Iran.

3

U.S. and North Vietnam agreed to establish direct contact between their representatives as a first step toward ending the fighting in Vietnam.

U.S. House of Representatives passed, by a vote of 406–1, a resolution establishing an ethics code for House members and employees.

British government detailed the tougher policies by which it hoped to hold increases in wages, salaries, and dividends to 3.5% a year.

4

U.S. civil rights leader the Rev. Martin Luther King, Jr., was shot to death by a sniper in Memphis, Tenn.

Second test launching of the Saturn V rocket, designed as the launch vehicle for U.S. manned flights to the moon, was regarded as unsuccessful because of engine failures.

5

Siege of Khe Sanh was officially declared lifted.

Racial violence broke out in several cities following King's assassination; Pres. Johnson ordered federal troops into Washington, D.C., to halt disorders there.

"Action program" allowing freedom of the press and the expression of minority views within the Czechoslovak Communist Party was issued by party First Secretary Dubcek.

Soviet government endorsed the agreement of North Vietnam to start discussions with the U.S.

Prime Minister Wilson made a number of shifts in his Cabinet.

6

Canadian Justice Minister Pierre Elliott Trudeau was elected to succeed Prime Minister Pearson as leader of the Liberal Party.

Federal troops were ordered into Chicago to halt racial violence.

French government agreed to sell 54 supersonic fighter-bombers to Iraq.

7

Federal troops moved into Baltimore, Md., to quell racial rioting.

8

Five-nation force of 100,000 troops began the biggest allied drive of the war to eliminate Communist forces in the 11 provinces around Saigon.

Oldrich Cernik, who succeeded Josef Lenart as Czechoslovak premier after Lenart was ousted April 4, presented his Cabinet to the National Assembly.

9

British government proposed far-reaching legislation to outlaw racial discrimination in housing, employment, and many services.

South Africa announced that it would not sell gold, either in the official or in the free market.

10

Pres. Johnson announced the designation of Gen. Creighton W. Abrams as U.S. commander in Vietnam; he also named White House aide W. Marvin Watson to succeed Lawrence F. O'Brien as postmaster general.

Third new record established since April 1 for volume of shares traded was set on the New York Stock Exchange; the previous record had been set when the market crashed in 1929.

Algeria, Mali, Mauritania, and the Congo (Brazzaville) resumed diplomatic ties with Great Britain, broken during the dispute over Rhodesia in December 1965.

Central Committee of the Soviet Communist Party endorsed an intensive ideological campaign to combat what it called subversive efforts by the West.

11

U.S. Secretary of Defense Clifford announced the call-up of 24,500 military reservists.

Pres. Johnson signed the civil rights bill prohibiting racial discrimination in the sale or rental of about 80% of U.S. housing; passage of the bill had been speeded in the House of Representatives following the King assassination.

White House rejected North Vietnam's proposal of Warsaw as the site for holding preliminary peace talks.

Polish Parliament unanimously elected Marshal Marian Spychalski as chief of state.

12

U.S. troops hurled back a heavy assault on an artillery base about 40 mi. NW of Saigon.

13

North Vietnam objected to sites for preliminary peace talks suggested by the U.S.

Tanzania became the first country to grant recognition to the Nigerian secessionist state of Biafra.

West German Chancellor Kurt Kiesinger went on nationwide TV to warn of tougher police measures as demonstrations by left-wing youths continued in many major cities; the disorders had been set off by an assassination attempt against student leader Rudi Dutschke on April 11.

14

Police in West Berlin broke up a peace march by nearly 4,000 students.

North Korean soldiers crossed the truce line and ambushed a U.S. truck.

15

U.S. planes made the second heaviest attack of 1968 on North Vietnam.

Two unmanned Soviet satellites found each other by radar in earth orbit, maneuvered together, and docked automatically.

16

Pres. Johnson conferred in Honolulu with U.S. military commanders in South Vietnam.

17

Pres. Johnson and South Korean Pres. Pak conferred in Honolulu.

18

U.S. Federal Reserve Board increased the discount rate from 5 to 5½%.

Noncommissioned army officers in Sierra Leone staged a successful coup d'etat against the military government.

U.S. B-52 bombers hammered a North Vietnamese supply stronghold south of the Demilitarized Zone.

Israel requisitioned an area of about 29 ac. near the Wailing Wall in the Arab section of Jerusalem.

U.S. released figures showing that the South Vietnamese government had lost effective control over 1.1 million persons as a result of the North Vietnamese Tet offensive.

19

North Vietnam rejected all sites proposed by the U.S. for preliminary peace talks, including ten proposed the preceding day.

U.S. troops launched a major offensive against what was believed to be a large North Vietnamese force in the A Shau Valley in northern Thua Thien Province.

20

Pierre Elliott Trudeau was sworn in as Canadian prime minister to succeed Lester Pearson.

Citizens' Board of Inquiry issued a report charging that hunger and malnutrition were widespread in the U.S.

23

Soviet Communist Party asserted that the very existence of the Chinese Communist Party had been put in jeopardy by its present leadership.

Methodist and Evangelical United Brethren churches merged to form the United Methodist Church, the second largest Protestant body in the U.S. with more than 11 million members.

24

Czechoslovak Premier Cernik outlined his government's new program to the National Assembly.

Motion of censure against the government of French Premier Georges Pompidou failed by eight votes in the National Assembly.

Nine West African nations, including both French- and English-speaking countries, formed a West African Regional Group to promote economic unification in the area.

U.S., the U.S.S.R., and the U.K. presented to the UN General Assembly the draft of the treaty to prohibit the spread of nuclear weapons.

Campus of Columbia University in New York City was closed after two days of tumultuous student demonstrations.

25

King Olav V of Norway arrived in Washington, D.C., on a state visit.

Pres. Johnson designated George W. Ball to succeed Arthur J. Goldberg, resigned, as U.S. representative to the UN.

26

U.S. Secretary of Defense Clifford announced the establishment of a riot-control centre in the Pentagon.

White House announced the creation of an Urban Institute as an independent but government-supported centre devoted to the problems of the nation's cities.

U.S. Atomic Energy Commission exploded an experimental hydrogen bomb, the largest yet tested in the U.S., 3,800 ft. below the desert 100 mi. NW of Las Vegas, Nev.

27

Vice-Pres. Humphrey announced his candidacy for the Democratic presidential nomination.

UN Security Council voted unanimously to ask Israel to cancel a projected military parade through Arab sections of Jerusalem.

U.S. B-52 bombers carried out heavy raids near Saigon as an aftermath to renewed fighting around the capital.

28

Israeli patrol killed 13 Arab infiltrators on the occupied West Bank of the Jordan River.

Columbia University . . . April 24

CHARLES GIUGNO—PIX FROM PUBLIX

Right-wing National Democratic Party made its best showing to date in West German state elections, obtaining almost 10% of the vote and 12 seats in the legislature in the Land of Baden-Württemberg.

30

Gov. Rockefeller of New York announced his candidacy for the Republican presidential nomination.

New York City police forcibly removed Columbia University students and nonstudent supporters from five university buildings that they had held for several days.

MAY

1

Sixteen major trading partners of the U.S. agreed to a one-year acceleration of their tariff cuts on U.S. exports and to a one-year deferment of reciprocal tariff reductions by the U.S.

2

Israeli armed forces staged a military parade in Jerusalem as part of the nation's 20th anniversary celebration in defiance of a UN Security Council resolution.

Pres. Nasser's proposed reform program for the U.A.R. received overwhelming support in a national referendum.

Militant leftist students of the University of Paris occupied a lecture hall on the university's suburban Nanterre campus.

3

U.S. and North Vietnam agreed on Paris as the site for their preliminary peace talks.

South Vietnamese troops and U.S. helicopter crews killed 194 Viet Cong in a day-long battle 28 mi. SW of Saigon.

South African House of Assembly voted to abolish parliamentary representation for the country's Cape Coloureds.

Fighting broke out between students and police in the Latin Quarter of Paris; the Sorbonne was closed because of the disturbances.

4

Soviet government announced ratification of the consular treaty with the U.S.

5

Communist forces launched a major ground attack inside Saigon, which was coordinated with the shelling of other large cities in South Vietnam.

Bell Telephone and Western Electric Co. and the Communications Workers of America ratified a new contract, ending a nationwide telephone strike that had begun April 18.

6

Representatives of Nigeria and Biafra met in London to start negotiations aimed at ending the ten-month civil war.

7

Latin Quarter in Paris was cordoned off by riot policemen in an attempt to avert further student rioting.

Sen. Robert Kennedy won the Indiana Democratic presidential primary, the first primary contest he had entered since declaring his candidacy.

South African Liberal Party disbanded in anticipation of passage of a bill that would, in effect, bar multiracial parties.

Tunisia broke diplomatic ties with Syria, citing alleged Syrian attempts to foment subversion inside Tunisia.

9

Soviet Army troops were reported to be staging major movements near the Czechoslovak border.

Pres. Johnson and Thai Prime Minister Thanom Kittikachorn completed two days of talks in Washington, D.C.

10

U.S. and North Vietnamese negotiating teams, led by W. Averell Harriman and Xuan Thuy, respectively, began talks in Paris.

Prime Minister Trudeau stated that Canada should increase its contacts with Communist China for its own economic advantage and for the good of world order.

British Defense Minister Denis Healey announced that Britain was increasing by 40% its troop commitments to NATO.

U.S. Department of the Interior issued a permit to leaders of the Poor People's Campaign authorizing erection of a plywood "city" near the Lincoln Memorial in Washington, D.C.

11

U.S. and North Vietnamese negotiators completed procedural arrangements for their talks.

12

Presidential election was held in Panama following a bitterly fought campaign. Results were not immediately known.

Mrs. Martin Luther King, Jr., officially opened the Poor People's Campaign in Washington, D.C.

13

Hundreds of thousands of French workers and students joined in a nationwide 24-hour strike.

U.S. and South Vietnamese commands claimed that allied troops had overcome the main thrust of the Communist offensive in and about Saigon.

U.S. and North Vietnamese negotiators began substantive talks toward ending the war in Vietnam.

Poor People's Campaign . . . May 12

14

Pres. de Gaulle arrived in Bucharest on a state visit to Romania.

Thousands of French students occupied the Sorbonne in Paris.

International Committee of the Red Cross appealed to national Red Cross societies to assist victims of the civil war in Nigeria where famine was said to be widespread.

15

Soviet Union and the U.A.R. signed in Cairo an agreement providing for Soviet aid in building an $800 million industrial project at Helwan, 15 mi. S of Cairo.

16

AFL-CIO suspended the United Auto Workers for failure to pay dues.

Poland and Hungary signed in Budapest a new 20-year treaty of friendship and mutual aid.

17

Estimated 100,000 strikers took over dozens of factories in France.

Soviet Premier Kosygin and a high-level military mission arrived in Prague for what was officially described as a continuation of the exchange of views with Czechoslovak leaders.

18

South Vietnamese Pres. Thieu appointed Tran Van Huong to replace Nguyen Van Loc as premier.

Pres. de Gaulle returned to Paris from Bucharest a day ahead of schedule as strikes and demonstrations continued throughout France.

19

Nigerian federal government announced the capture of Port Harcourt in Biafra.

Viet Cong fired several rocket and mortar shells into the centre of Saigon.

20

France headed toward virtual paralysis as millions more of its workers occupied factories, mines, and offices.

U.S. Supreme Court in five decisions that overturned its own precedents broadened the rights of criminal defendants and convicted persons.

21

Pres. Johnson asked Congress for a supplemental $3.9 billion in new obligational authority for the war in Vietnam.

UN Security Council adopted a resolution opposing Israel's administrative unification of the Jordanian and Israeli sections of Jerusalem.

Attempt by exiles to invade Haiti and overthrow the government of Pres. François Duvalier was crushed by the Haitian government.

22

Motion to censure the French government failed by 11 votes in the National Assembly.

23

Rioting broke out again in Paris' Latin Quarter as rebellious students and other youths clashed with riot police.

Peace talks opened in Kampala, Uganda, between Nigeria and Biafra.

24

Pres. de Gaulle asked the French people to give him a personal vote of confidence and said he would resign if he did not receive it.

26

Sir Henry Tucker of the United Bermuda Party was named Bermuda's first prime minister.

U.S. command in Saigon confirmed that it had called for an all-out effort against the enemy in a secret directive.

Small but violent battles broke out on the edges of Saigon.

27

U.S. Supreme Court upheld, by a vote of 7–1, a 1965 amendment to the Selective Service Act that made it a criminal offense to burn or otherwise mutilate a draft card.

U.S., the U.K., and France agreed to surrender vestigial occupation rights in West Germany as soon as new laws giving the German government emergency powers in time of national danger went into effect.

28

Pres. Johnson sent Congress a message urging freer world trade and requesting international trade legislation.

Allied troops repelled an attack on the resort city of Dalat in South Vietnam.

Sen. McCarthy defeated Sen. Robert Kennedy in the Democratic presidential primary in Oregon.

29

Pres. Johnson signed the truth-in-lending bill requiring that consumers be informed of the cost of credit.

UN Security Council unanimously adopted a resolution urging all UN members to impose a total embargo on all trade and financial relations with and travel to Rhodesia.

Unified Socialist Party led by Pietro Nenni, having lost seats in the Italian parliamentary elections of May 19–20, voted to withdraw from the coalition government.

New and bitter fighting erupted in South Vietnam's northernmost province.

30

Pres. de Gaulle announced the dissolution of the National Assembly, preparatory to the holding of new elections in June, and pledged to prevent a Communist dictatorship by all means at his disposal.

West German Bundestag passed by a vote of 384–100 the controversial emergency laws.

Arnulfo Arias was declared the winner of the Panamanian presidential election, which had been held on May 12.

31

French Premier Pompidou revised his Cabinet amid signs of an emerging back-to-work trend among France's ten million striking workers and civil servants.

North Vietnamese negotiators, at the sixth session of the talks in Paris, rejected the U.S. demand for reciprocity in exchange for a halt to U.S. bombing of North Vietnam.

U.S. and the U.S.S.R., bowing to pressure from smaller nations, announced changes in their proposed nuclear nonproliferation treaty.

Biafra withdrew from peace talks with Nigeria at Kampala.

JUNE

1

Viet Cong infiltrators clung to positions in the heart of Cholon, Saigon's Chinese quarter, and at the northeastern edges of the city despite heavy pounding by allied forces.

2

José Velasco Ibarra won election as president of Ecuador by a narrow margin.

3

U.S. Supreme Court held that persons expressing general conscientious scruples against the death penalty could not automatically be kept off juries in capital cases.

4

Israeli and Jordanian forces engaged in a day-long battle along the northern sector of the Jordan River.

France drew $745 million from the International Monetary Fund to protect the value of the franc.

Pres. Johnson signed a bill authorizing a U.S. contribution of $412 million toward a $1 billion increase in the ordinary capital of the Inter-American Development Bank.

5

Sen. Robert Kennedy was shot in Los Angeles shortly after he had claimed victory in the California Democratic presidential primary held the preceding day; Sirhan B. Sirhan, a Jordanian Arab, was seized by Kennedy aides at the scene of the shooting.

Robert F. Kennedy assassinated . . . June 5

Pres. Johnson appointed a commission of distinguished citizens to investigate the phenomenon of physical violence in the U.S.; Johnson also ordered Secret Service protection for all major presidential candidates.

Aldo Moro resigned as premier of Italy.

Demonstrations, marked by some violence, were held by Arabs in Israeli-occupied territory to commemorate the beginning of the June 1967 Arab-Israeli war.

6

Pres. Johnson proclaimed June 9 as a national day of mourning following the death of Sen. Robert Kennedy.

Indonesian Pres. Suharto dismissed five generals and three civilians and named eight new ministers in a major Cabinet shake-up.

7

U.S. Federal Reserve Board ordered an increase in stock margins to 80 from 70%.

Violent clashes between French workers and police took place at the nationalized Renault automobile assembly plant at Flins, 25 mi. W of Paris.

8

James Earl Ray, alleged assassin of the Rev. Martin Luther King, Jr., was arrested by Scotland Yard detectives at Heathrow Airport in London.

Police removed students who had occupied the buildings of several institutions of higher education in Milan during the latest wave of student demonstrations in Italy.

Former French Premier Georges Bidault returned to Paris after six years in Brazil and Belgium, where he had fled to avoid prosecution for alleged involvement with a terrorist organization during the Algerian war.

9

King Faisal of Saudi Arabia was reported to have pledged $36 million to buy arms for the Jordanian Army.

Nigerian government announced that all Biafran troops had been driven from Port Harcourt, the principal port city of Biafra.

10

U.S. administration sent to Congress its proposals to ban the mail-order sale of rifles, shotguns, and ammunition.

U.S. Supreme Court upheld, by a vote of 6–3, a New York law requiring public school systems to lend textbooks to students in private and parochial schools.

Gen. Westmoreland turned over command of U.S. forces in Vietnam to Gen. Abrams.

11

East Germany announced a number of regulations governing travel by West German citizens between West Germany and West Berlin.

Pledge to maintain the defense of Southeast Asia was reaffirmed in a joint communiqué issued in Kuala Lumpur, Malaysia, by representatives of the U.K., Australia, New Zealand, Singapore, and Malaysia.

12

UN General Assembly adopted, by a vote of 95–4, a resolution commending the draft nuclear nonproliferation treaty.

U.S., the U.K., and France issued a joint statement denouncing as invalid East Germany's newly imposed restrictions on travel to and from West Berlin.

French government banned all protest demonstrations during the election campaign and dissolved 11 extremist student organizations.

13

Pres. Johnson renewed his plea for Soviet cooperation at White House ceremonies marking the exchange of ratifications of the U.S.-Soviet consular treaty.

14

Viet Cong fired about 20 mortar shells into southwestern Saigon.

West German Bundesrat unanimously approved the government's emergency powers bill.

Benjamin Spock and three others were convicted in a federal district court in Boston of conspiring to aid, abet, and counsel draft registrants to violate the Selective Service Act.

WIDE WORLD

Benjamin Spock . . . June 14

Israeli and U.A.R. units fought a 2½-hour artillery and tank battle in the Suez-Bur Tawfiq area at the southern end of the Suez Canal

15

Joint session of the South Vietnamese National Assembly approved Pres. Thieu's general mobilization bill.

Raoul Salan, former general commander of a terrorist organization that tried to block Algerian independence, and 13 others were released from prison on orders from Pres. de Gaulle.

16

Paris police surrounded and

cleared the Sorbonne of some 200 occupying students.

17

Gaston Eyskens ended Belgium's 132-day political crisis with the formation of a new two-party coalition government.

U.S. Supreme Court held, by a vote of 7–2, that an 1866 law prohibited racial discrimination in all sales and rentals of property.

Queen Elizabeth II invested her oldest son, Prince Charles, with the Order of the Garter in ceremonies at Windsor Castle.

18

British House of Lords voted, 193–184, to oppose stricter sanctions against Rhodesia.

West German Foreign Minister Willy Brandt declared that the new East German rules governing traffic between West Germany and West Berlin did not pose an immediate crisis over access to Berlin.

Sen. McCarthy made an unexpectedly good showing in the New York Democratic presidential primary.

19

Pres. Johnson signed a bill authorizing U.S. participation in the international "paper gold" plan to supplement the world's gold and foreign exchange resources.

More than 50,000 persons, about half of them white, took part in the Solidarity Day March in Washington, D.C., climaxing the Poor People's Campaign.

Pres. Johnson signed an omnibus anticrime bill barring the interstate shipment and out-of-state purchase of handguns, but expressed objections to some other provisions of the bill dealing with wiretapping and rules of evidence in federal criminal trials.

20

U.S. command in Saigon reported that U.S. combat deaths in Vietnam had passed 25,000.

Warsaw Pact military exercises, in which a large number of Soviet troops were participating, began in Czechoslovakia.

Brazilian students clashed with police during antigovernment demonstrations in Rio de Janeiro.

21

U.S. Secretary of the Army Stanley R. Resor announced that the Army had reduced its support of civilian marksmanship clubs.

22

East Germany complained against West German travel restrictions under which the Bavarian border police barred entry of a delegation of 700 East Germans.

23

Israeli and U.A.R. forces clashed for 85 minutes in the Ismailia region of the Suez Canal.

Gaullist candidates showed great strength in the first round of elections for the French National Assembly.

24

Washington, D.C., police closed Resurrection City, the Poor People's Campaign encampment.

Pres. Johnson asked Congress to require the national registration of every firearm and a license for every gun owner.

Christian Democrat Giovanni Leone announced the formation of a minority Italian Cabinet, ending an 18-day political crisis.

25

Canadian Liberal Party of Prime Minister Trudeau won a majority of 154 seats in national elections for the House of Commons.

North Atlantic Council, in a communiqué issued after its semiannual meeting in Reykjavik, Ice., appealed to the U.S.S.R. and its Eastern European allies for a mutual and balanced reduction of forces to promote East-West détente in Europe.

U.S. House of Representatives passed and cleared for the White House a bill making it a federal crime to desecrate the U.S. flag.

Czechoslovak National Assembly passed a law providing for the rehabilitation of persons unjustly persecuted, jailed, and tortured on political grounds.

26

The Bonin Islands, including Iwo Jima, were returned to Japan by the U.S.

U.S. and North Vietnamese negotiators held their tenth session in Paris with no outward signs of progress toward substantive talks on ending the war in Vietnam.

Resignation of Earl Warren as U.S. chief justice was announced by Pres. Johnson, who nominated Justice Abe Fortas to be chief justice and Judge Homer Thornberry of Texas to be an associate justice.

27

U.S. command in Saigon confirmed that U.S. Marines had begun to withdraw from the military base at Khe Sanh.

Pres. Johnson in a special message asked Congress to approve a constitutional amendment to lower the voting age to 18.

28

Pres. Johnson signed into law a bill combining a 10% income tax surcharge with a $6 billion cut in government expenditure.

30

Candidates supporting the de Gaulle regime won a landslide victory in the second and final round of elections for the National Assembly.

JULY

1

Last tariff barriers between the member states of the EEC were eliminated.

Sixty-two nations, including the U.S., the U.K., and the U.S.S.R., signed the nuclear nonproliferation treaty when it was opened for signature in Washington, D.C., London, and Moscow.

Bank of Canada reduced its discount rate from 7½ to 7%.

Pres. Johnson announced that the U.S. and the U.S.S.R. had agreed to begin talks in the "nearest future" on means of limiting and reducing their arsenals of offensive and defensive nuclear weapons.

Kristian Eldjarn was elected president of Iceland.

2

London court ordered James Earl Ray returned to the U.S. to stand trial as the accused assassin of the Rev. Martin Luther King, Jr.

U.S. airliner that was forced to land with its 231 passengers and crew on a Soviet island in the Kuriles chain was released by the Soviet government.

3

French government raised the basic interest rate from 3½ to 5% to combat inflationary pressures.

U.S., the U.K., and France protested to the U.S.S.R. over travel restrictions imposed by East Germany on West Berlin transit traffic.

4

Soviet Union announced the conclusion of a new military and economic agreement with North Vietnam.

Protestant and Orthodox leaders from more than 80 countries opened the fourth assembly of the World Council of Churches in Uppsala, Swed.

U.S. command in Saigon announced that U.S. combat deaths in the first six months of 1968 had exceeded those in all of 1967.

5

Prime Minister Trudeau named a 29-man Cabinet, the largest in Canadian history.

Allied ground forces found three major caches of enemy munitions as they swept the provinces around Saigon.

Nigerian federal government warned against outside efforts to airlift supplies directly to Biafra.

6

U.S. Defense Department announced that the U.S. had agreed to sell additional batteries of Hawk antiaircraft missiles to Israel.

Pres. Johnson met in San Salvador with five Central American presidents and announced new loans totaling $65 million for regional and national development in the area.

U.S. Atty. Gen. Clark announced that the Department of Justice had begun to implement in a broad way throughout the South a U.S. Supreme Court decision calling for more effective school desegregation.

7

France resumed its nuclear testing program with the explosion of a "moderate strength" atomic fission device in the South Pacific.

8

U.S. Federal Trade Commission announced an investigation of the causes, effects, and implications of conglomerate corporate mergers.

Romania agreed to broaden its contacts with the U.S. in science and technology.

10

Pres. de Gaulle named Maurice Couve de Murville to succeed Pompidou as premier of France.

Soviet leaders and U.A.R. Pres. Nasser announced after talks in Moscow that they had agreed on further joint steps in the Arab conflict with Israel.

UN Secretary-General U Thant appealed to the leaders of Biafra to permit international relief supplies to reach its starving population.

British House of Commons passed, by a vote of 182–44, a government bill to outlaw racial discrimination.

11

Deputy premiers of North Vietnam and Communist China reaffirmed continued solidarity between their two countries.

Soviet Premier Kosygin arrived in Stockholm on an official visit to Sweden.

Italian Premier Leone won a vote of confidence in the Chamber of Deputies by a narrow margin.

Greek junta made public a 138-article draft constitution that would remove many of the king's powers and enhance the authority of the executive.

12

U.S. Postmaster General Watson announced an immediate ban on the extension of service to new residential developments as part of a plan to conserve postal manpower.

13

Pres. de Gaulle told his new Cabinet and the French nation that public order must be assured thenceforth.

14

Withdrawal of Soviet troops from Czechoslovakia, where they had participated in Warsaw Pact maneuvers, was halted without explanation.

15

First direct airline service between the Soviet Union and the U.S. was opened by Aeroflot, the Soviet airline, and Pan American World Airways.

Malaysia rejected the Philippine claim to the North Borneo state of Sabah.

British House of Commons voted stricter sanctions against Rhodesia, overruling an earlier veto by the House of Lords.

16

U.S.S.R., East Germany, Hungary, Bulgaria, and Poland in a joint letter warned Czechoslovakia that its liberalization program was completely unacceptable.

Eighteen-nation UN Disarmament Committee reconvened in Geneva.

17

Iraqi government of Abdul Rahman Arif was overthrown by a coup d'etat led by Maj. Gen. Ahmed Hassan al-Bakr.

Rhodesian Front Party announced constitutional proposals for the declaration of a republic with a Rhodesian chief of state.

Dahomey returned to civilian rule, following 2½ years of military government, with the inauguration of Émile Derlin Zinsou as president.

U.S. and North Vietnamese negotiators held their 13th meeting in Paris without any sign of progress.

18

Yugoslav Communist Party declared unconditional support for Czechoslovakia's liberalization policies.

U.S. B-52 bombers were used for the first time in raids on suspected missile sites in North Vietnam.

Canadian postal services were completely stopped by a strike of carriers and postal workers.

North Vietnam released three U.S. airmen captured after they had been shot down over North Vietnam.

19

U.S. House of Representatives killed proposals for federal registration of guns.

Leadership of the Czechoslovak Communist Party won the unanimous endorsement of the Central Committee for its policy of resisting pressure from the U.S.S.R.

Nigeria and Biafra agreed to resume peace negotiations in Addis Ababa.

20

Pres. Johnson and South Vietnamese Pres. Thieu completed two days of talks in Hawaii.

21

Chilean government announced that Bolivian Interior Minister Antonio Arguedas, who had fled to Chile two days earlier, had admitted giving copies of "Che" Guevara's diary to Cuban agents; the diary was published in Cuba July 1 and in the U.S. the following day.

23

U.S. House of Representatives refused, by a vote of 179–84, to require state licensing of gun owners.

Soviet Union announced that large-scale maneuvers of support and supply troops were under way in the western part of the country, including areas near the Slovak region of Czechoslovakia.

Israeli commercial airliner was hijacked over Italy by members of an Arab commando group and landed in Algeria.

24

Mayor Carl B. Stokes of Cleveland, O., ordered all national guardsmen and white police withdrawn from a six-square-mile area on the city's East Side; the move was made as community leaders attempted to quiet disorders that had followed a gun battle between black nationalists and police.

25

Mayor Stokes ordered white police and national guardsmen to return to Cleveland's turbulent East Side and announced a curfew in the area.

26

About 20 guerrillas attacked the U.S. air base at Udon Thani, Thailand.

27

First Secretary Dubcek of the Czechoslovak Communist Party vowed in a radio and TV address that Czechoslovakia would continue to the end on the road it had chosen and would not retreat one step.

Bolivian Pres. René Barrientos Ortuño appointed an all-military Cabinet as an emergency measure; his civilian Cabinet had resigned July 25 in the aftermath of the scandal over "Che" Guevara's diary.

29

Pope Paul VI in an encyclical, *Humanae Vitae,* upheld the Roman Catholic Church's prohibition against all artificial means of contraception.

Bank of Canada reduced its discount rate from 7 to 6½%.

Virtually the entire governing bodies of the Soviet and Czechoslovak Communist parties met in Cierna, Czech., to try to bridge the divisions between them.

30

U.S. steel industry and the United Steelworkers of America agreed on a new three-year contract.

Final U.S. budget results for the

fiscal year ended June 30, 1968, showed revenue of $153.5 billion and expenditure of $178.9 billion.

Federal troops and police fought students and other youths during massive demonstrations in Mexico City.

31

Pres. Johnson assailed Bethlehem Steel Corp. for making a 5% across-the-board price increase.

AUGUST

1

U.S. Defense Department ordered military buyers not to buy steel from several companies announcing general steel price increases of 5%.

Pres. Johnson signed an omnibus housing bill providing $5.3 billion for 1.7 million low-cost housing units.

U.S. command in Saigon reported the arrival of 4,500 additional U.S. troops, bringing the total to 541,-000 men.

Communiqué issued at the close of the meeting of the U.S.S.R. Politburo and the Czechoslovak party Presidium gave no details of the nearly four days of talks.

2

World Bank raised the loan rate for less developed countries from 6¼ to 6½%, the second raise in less than a year.

UN Secretary-General U Thant charged Israel had imposed conditions that prevented a UN fact-finding mission from operating in the Middle East.

3

Summit meeting of leaders of the U.S.S.R., Czechoslovakia, and four other Eastern European countries was held in Bratislava, Czech., as the last of the Soviet troops reportedly left Czechoslovakia, more than a month after finishing Warsaw Pact maneuvers.

4

First Secretary Dubcek of the Czechoslovak Communist Party declared in a TV address that no secret deals had been made at the Cierna and Bratislava talks with Soviet and Eastern European leaders and that Czechoslovakia's sovereignty was not threatened.

Pres. Barrientos authorized the August 6 opening of Parliament as the Bolivian political crisis appeared to be over.

Pres. Alphonse Massamba-Debat of the Congo (Brazzaville) resumed his office one day after having been ousted by a military coup.

Allied forces began a sweep of the A Shau Valley as the June-July lull in fighting in South Vietnam ended.

5

Spain declared a state of emergency in the Basque province of Guipúzcoa.

International Committee of the

Red Cross resumed relief flights to Biafra as new Nigeria-Biafra peace talks began in Addis Ababa.

Republican national convention opened in Miami Beach, Fla.

6

Former U.S. Pres. Dwight D. Eisenhower suffered his sixth heart attack a few hours after addressing the Republican national convention by television.

7

Steel price controversy between the U.S. government and the steel industry ended in a compromise under which prices would rise by 2½%, about half as much as the industry had planned.

8

National Guard troops were called into Miami after three Negroes were killed in rioting that reportedly began at a black "vote power" rally.

U.S. river patrol unit accidentally killed 72 civilians while repelling Viet Cong attacks in the Mekong Delta.

Richard M. Nixon won the Republican presidential nomination on the first ballot; his surprise choice for the vice-presidential nomination was Gov. Spiro T. Agnew of Maryland.

9

Yugoslav Pres. Tito arrived in Prague on an official visit to show his support of the Czechoslovak liberalization drive.

Biafran delegates to peace talks in Addis Ababa rejected a Nigerian nine-point peace plan and submitted their own seven-point plan.

Canada's postal workers ended their three-week strike.

Detroit newspapers resumed publication after a 267-day strike, the longest newspaper strike in U.S. history.

Southern Yemen announced that government forces had captured the last of the mountain tribesmen who had been engaged in two weeks of armed uprising.

10

Soviet news agency Tass announced the start of new Warsaw Pact military exercises along the Czechoslovak border.

Relief flights to Biafra were canceled after Nigerians fired on relief planes.

13

Nigeria rejected a Biafran peace proposal.

U.S. imposed temporary duties on French goods to counteract new French tariff restrictions.

15

U.S. Federal Reserve Board approved a reduction in the discount rate from 5½ to 5¼%.

Nigerian government rejected a plan by which the International

---

Committee of the Red Cross would fly relief supplies to starving Biafrans using a neutralized airstrip.

South Vietnamese and U.S. troops engaged in heavy fighting as they pursued a North Vietnamese battalion into the Demilitarized Zone.

16

U.S. Commerce Department reported that the U.S. balance of payments deficit fell to its lowest level in two years in the second quarter of 1968.

Soviet press resumed its attacks on Czechoslovakia after a three-week letup.

Czechoslovakia and Romania renewed their 20-year treaty of friendship during a state visit to Prague by Romanian Pres. Nicolae Ceausescu.

18

Grenade explosions by Arab saboteurs in Jerusalem led to rioting by Israeli youths in the Arab section of the city.

Heaviest fighting in three months broke out as North Vietnamese and Viet Cong troops staged 19 separate attacks throughout South Vietnam.

19

Pres. Johnson ruled out any change in Vietnam policy until Hanoi made a serious move.

20

Czechoslovakia was invaded late

---

at night by troops of the U.S.S.R., East Germany, Poland, Hungary, and Bulgaria; several government leaders were arrested including Communist Party First Secretary Dubcek.

Argentine Pres. Juan Carlos Onganía dismissed the army, navy, and air force chiefs in a purge of the liberal opposition.

21

Czechoslovak Communist Party Congress met secretly, reelecting Dubcek as first secretary, and the Czechoslovak National Assembly convened, pledging not to adjourn until the Warsaw Pact troops had left the country.

U.S.S.R. justified its invasion of Czechoslovakia, claiming that Czechoslovak "government and party" leaders had requested assistance.

World leaders and Communist parties in Western countries issued statements critical of the U.S.S.R.-led invasion of Czechoslovakia.

Sen. Edward M. Kennedy (Mass.), in his first speech since the funeral of his brother Robert, proposed a four-point plan to end the Vietnam war.

22

Pope Paul VI arrived in Bogotá, Colombia, to attend the International Eucharistic Congress.

Czechoslovakia invaded . . . August 20

UPI (UK) LTD.

Saigon came under Communist rocket fire for the first time in two months.

23

U.S.S.R. cast its 105th veto in the UN Security Council to defeat a resolution condemning its invasion of Czechoslovakia.

Heavy rocket and mortar attacks were carried out by Communist forces against South Vietnamese cities, provincial capitals, and military installations.

Czechoslovak Pres. Svoboda and other Czechoslovak officials flew to Moscow for talks with Soviet leaders.

Yippies, members of the Youth International Party, and their presidential candidate, a pig, were arrested in the Chicago Civic Center.

24

France exploded its first hydrogen bomb in the South Pacific and became the world's fifth thermonuclear power.

25

Representatives of the invading countries joined in the Soviet-Czechoslovak talks in Moscow.

26

Democratic national convention opened in Chicago and settled 14 of 15 credentials disputes.

27

Pres. Svoboda and First Secretary Dubcek returned to Czechoslovakia from Moscow talks; a communiqué issued in Moscow indicated that occupation troops would leave Czechoslovakia when the situation normalized.

Israel reported that two Israeli

Lincoln Park, Chicago . . . August 27

RICHARD H. HOOSIN

soldiers had been killed by U.A.R. troops in an ambush near Ismailia.

Compromise vote settled the seating dispute of the two delegations from Georgia to the Democratic national convention.

Demonstrators were chased from Chicago's Lincoln Park by police.

28

U.S. Vice-Pres. Hubert H. Humphrey won the Democratic presidential nomination on the first ballot after forces led by Sen. McCarthy failed to modify a tough platform statement endorsing the Johnson administration's Vietnam policy.

Violence erupted in clashes between police and demonstrators in front of Chicago's Conrad Hilton Hotel, Democratic convention headquarters, leading to charges of police brutality.

U.S. Ambassador to Guatemala John Gordon Mein was assassinated by terrorists trying to kidnap him in Guatemala City.

Czechoslovak National Assembly declared the country's invasion "illegal" and demanded a specific date for the withdrawal of Warsaw Pact forces.

29

Democratic vice-presidential nomination went to Sen. Edmund S. Muskie of Maine.

30

Viet Cong announced that it had begun a new general offensive.

Pres. Johnson warned the U.S.S.R. against further aggression in Eastern Europe as rumours of an imminent invasion of Romania grew.

31

Romanians began paramilitary training amid reports of new Soviet troop movements.

U.S. State Department indicated that the NATO allies were reviewing the changes in the balance

of power in Europe caused by the Soviet invasion of Czechoslovakia.

Algeria released the last five passengers and seven crewmen of the Israeli airliner hijacked on July 23.

SEPTEMBER

1

Czechoslovak Communist Party Central Committee elected a new party Presidium including many liberals.

Arab League meeting opened in Cairo and adjourned when an anti-U.A.R. speech by the Tunisian delegate caused an uproar.

2

Prague radio reported that three journals were to be barred from publishing because they were considered "counterrevolutionary" by the U.S.S.R.

U.S.S.R. warned West Germany to alter its course toward Eastern Europe or "face the consequences."

3

Arab League ended three days of stormy meetings by urging members to aid Jordan against Israeli attacks.

Ota Sik, deputy premier of Czechoslovakia and architect of the economic reforms, resigned under pressure from the U.S.S.R.

4

UN Security Council began an emergency session to consider Israeli charges against the U.A.R.

Pres. Massamba-Debat was forced to resign as president of the Congo (Brazzaville); Capt. Alfred Raoul was named interim president.

NATO Defense Planning Committee said prospects for a NATO-Warsaw Pact mutual force reduction had dimmed.

France lifted currency exchange controls imposed during the economic crisis of the previous May.

5

U.S. Secretary of Defense Clifford ordered the proposed Sentinel missile defense system exempted from congressionally-ordered budget cuts.

National Commission on the Causes and Prevention of Violence announced plans to investigate the disorders in Chicago during the Democratic national convention.

6

Chicago Mayor Richard J. Daley issued a report supporting the actions of the police during Chicago's convention-week disturbances.

Vasily V. Kuznetsov, U.S.S.R. first deputy foreign minister, arrived in Prague apparently to work out difficulties between Czechoslovakia and the U.S.S.R. in the fulfillment of the Moscow agreement.

Swaziland became independent,

ending Britain's colonial links with Africa.

8

Israeli and U.A.R. forces shelled each other across the Suez Canal.

9

Plan for $2 billion in credit to support the pound was concluded in Basel, Switz., by 12 central banks.

French Pres. de Gaulle, in a news conference, criticized the Soviet invasion of Czechoslovakia but said he would continue to press for an East-West détente.

Arthur Ashe won the U.S. Open tennis title at Forest Hills, N.Y., in the first tournament open to professionals and amateurs.

10

Czechoslovak government issued a proclamation guaranteeing all its people "personal security and freedom."

Czechoslovak Premier Cernik, in Moscow talks, signed two economic protocols.

U.S. Secretary of State Dean Rusk discounted reports from South Korea that the U.S. planned to apologize for the alleged intrusion of the "Pueblo" into North Korean waters.

Pres. Johnson defended his Vietnam policy in a speech and attacked isolationism in the U.S. and Europe.

11

Soviet tanks and military units began to be withdrawn from Prague.

12

Trudeau government called for a "just society" at the opening of the Canadian Parliament.

13

Czechoslovak National Assembly approved the reestablishment of direct press censorship.

U.S. and South Vietnamese forces penetrated the Demilitarized Zone to prevent an expected enemy influx.

Rhodesian High Court upheld the legality of the government of Prime Minister Smith.

Albania announced its formal withdrawal from the Warsaw Pact.

14

U.A.R. Pres. Nasser announced that his country had completed rebuilding its armed forces.

Dennis McLain became the first baseball pitcher since 1934 to win 30 games in one season as the Detroit Tigers defeated the Oakland Athletics 5–4.

First Secretary Dubcek of the Czechoslovak Communist Party appealed to his nation on TV not to provoke occupying forces.

15

Summit meeting of the Organiza-

GAMMA—PIX FROM PUBLIX

Student unrest in Mexico City . . . September 18

tion of African Unity in Algiers appealed to Biafra to abandon its struggle for independence.

16

Allied forces repulsed a sustained attack on Tay Ninh by North Vietnamese and Viet Cong forces, the second in a month.

Nigeria claimed it had captured the Biafran city of Owerri, leaving only one more city in Biafran hands.

17

U.S., the U.K., and France warned the U.S.S.R. that any effort to use military force against West Germany would bring an "immediate" allied response.

Two thousand U.S. Marines were airlifted into the Demilitarized Zone to cut North Vietnamese supply lines.

18

UN Security Council passed a resolution asking Israel and the Arab states to observe the cease-fire and cooperate with UN envoy Jarring.

Pravda, Soviet Communist Party newspaper, repeated assertions of the U.S.S.R.'s right to intervene militarily in West Germany under terms of the UN Charter.

Mexican federal troops occupied the National University in Mexico City after seven weeks of student unrest.

19

Jiri Hajek, Czechoslovak foreign minister, was removed from office as a result of Soviet pressure.

Mickey Mouse celebrated his 40th "birthday."

Malaysia suspended diplomatic ties with the Philippines because the Philippines had declared its sovereignty over the state of Sabah.

Bank of England reduced its bank rate from 7½ to 7%.

20

U.S. officials in Saigon asserted that defoliation in South Vietnam had produced no harmful results.

21

Zond 5, an unmanned Soviet spacecraft, splashed down in the Indian Ocean after a successful flight around the moon.

22

United Auto Workers' Pres. Walter P. Reuther warned that former Alabama Gov. George Wallace was increasing the danger of a police state in the U.S. amid reports that large numbers of union members were supporting Wallace for the U.S. presidency.

23

UN Secretary-General U Thant speculated that a majority of General Assembly members would support a resolution urging a halt to U.S. bombing of North Vietnam.

King Husain of Jordan was reportedly seeking indirect peace negotiations with Israel.

24

Scheduled trip to Moscow by Czechoslovak Communist Party First Secretary Dubcek was canceled, reportedly because of failure to agree on an agenda for talks.

Guatemalan Foreign Minister Emilio Arenales Catalan was elected president of the UN General Assembly at the opening of its 23rd session; Swaziland became the 125th UN member.

Fighting between police and students in Mexico City resulted in 15 deaths in 24 hours.

25

Four-point Soviet peace plan for the Middle East was made public by the U.S.

26

Israeli Prime Minister Eshkol warned that continued Arab attacks on Israel's borders could produce a new war; Foreign Minister Abba Eban rejected the Soviet peace plan.

George W. Ball resigned as U.S. ambassador to the UN to help Vice-Pres. Humphrey's presidential campaign; James R. Wiggins succeeded him.

Pravda advanced an ideological doctrine to justify the U.S.S.R. invasion of Czechoslovakia, citing the "necessity" of protecting any fraternal socialist country from outside attack.

UN Secretary-General U Thant proposed a Big Four summit meeting to counteract the worldwide sense of insecurity.

Quebec Premier Daniel Johnson was found dead in Manicouagan, Que., presumably of a heart attack.

27

France vetoed an interim commercial arrangement that would have led ultimately to Britain's admission to the EEC.

Marcelo Caetano was sworn in as premier of Portugal to replace ailing António de Oliveira Salazar.

Pincer action to trap a North Vietnamese division was begun by 4,000 U.S. Marines in the Demilitarized Zone.

28

UN Conference of Non-Nuclear-Weapon States adjourned in Geneva, having failed to reach any firm positions.

29

Greek voters gave overwhelming approval to the new constitution drawn up by the ruling military junta.

30

U.S. lost its 900th aircraft over North Vietnam.

British Labour Party urged the repeal of wage and price controls in the U.K. at its annual conference.

OCTOBER

1

Malaysian Prime Minister Abdul Rahman ruled out any summit conference with the Philippines to discuss sovereignty over Sabah.

2

U.S. Secretary of State Rusk in a speech at the opening of general debate in the UN General Assembly denounced the invasion of Czechoslovakia, warned the U.S.S.R. against similar action in West Germany, and reported that North Vietnam had rejected all U.S. peace proposals.

Pres. Johnson withdrew his nomination of Justice Abe Fortas as chief justice of the United States after the Senate failed to end a filibuster against the nomination.

Bloodiest clash of troops and students in the nine-week student strike occurred in Mexico City.

3

George Wallace, American Independent Party presidential nominee, named Gen. Curtis E. LeMay, retired air force chief of staff, as his vice-presidential running mate.

Peruvian Pres. Fernando Belaúnde Terry was ousted; Maj. Gen. Juan Velasco Alvarado headed the new military government.

International observers reported finding no evidence of genocide being committed by the Nigerian government against Biafrans.

4

World Bank and the International Monetary Fund ended their annual meetings in Washington without reaching agreement on the disposal of newly mined South African gold.

Czechoslovak leaders acceded in Moscow to Soviet demands that they dismantle the remnants of their liberal policies and agreed to the indefinite stationing of foreign troops in their country.

U.S. officials said that Cambodia had indirectly conceded for the first time that North Vietnam and the Viet Cong had been using Cambodian territory for attacks against South Vietnam.

5

U.A.R. government was reported to have barred the departure of the 1,000 Jews still in the country.

6

U.S. forces were reported to have launched a drive to relieve North Vietnamese pressure on the An Duc and Thuong Duc outposts.

Survey report in the *New York Times* indicated that the consensus of several hundred political leaders was that Richard Nixon was leading in the U.S. presidential race with third-party candidate George Wallace carrying more states than Vice-Pres. Humphrey.

Londonderry police clashed with Roman Catholics who were demonstrating against discrimination by the Protestant majority.

7

Agreement granting British university students a say in the operation and curricula of their schools was announced.

8

Israeli Foreign Minister Eban presented a nine-point peace plan for the Middle East to the UN General Assembly.

Canadian Prime Minister Trudeau announced the Nigerian government's approval of the use of a Canadian Hercules air transport

for relief flights anywhere in Nigeria.

9

René Cassin, French jurist, was awarded the Nobel Peace Prize for 1968.

Pres. Johnson directed the State Department to begin negotiations with Israel on its request to buy supersonic fighter-bombers.

Soviet Premier Kosygin and Finnish Pres. Kekkonen completed three days of secret talks aboard a fishing vessel in the Gulf of Finland.

10

Detroit Tigers won the World Series by taking their third straight game from the St. Louis Cardinals, 4–1.

South Vietnamese Pres. Thieu denied reports that his regime had suppressed an attempted coup d'etat.

U.A.R. Foreign Minister Mahmoud Riad reaffirmed his government's support of the UN peace plan of Nov. 22, 1967.

Pres. Johnson made his first major political speech on behalf of the presidential candidacy of Vice-Pres. Humphrey.

11

French National Assembly adopted sweeping educational reforms, the first since Napoleon.

Five Soviet citizens were sentenced to exile or hard labour for demonstrating against the Soviet invasion of Czechoslovakia.

Apollo 7 spacecraft with three astronauts aboard was successfully launched from Cape Kennedy, Fla.

Panamanian Pres. Arnulfo Arias

Black Power at Olympic Games . . . October 12

UPI COMPIX

was ousted by a coup d'etat 11 days after taking office.

12

Equatorial Guinea achieved its independence from Spain.

Mexican Pres. Gustavo Díaz Ordaz proclaimed the opening of the Olympic Games in Mexico City.

British Conservative Party ended its annual conference issuing criticisms of both the Labour government and its own right wing.

13

Conference between British Prime Minister Wilson and Rhodesian Prime Minister Smith aboard the British warship "Fearless," anchored at Gibraltar, broke up without agreement.

14

Second session of the 90th U.S. Congress adjourned after House liberals failed to pass a law permitting televised debate by the three major presidential candidates.

West German Pres. Heinrich Lübke announced he would retire in June 1969.

Parti Québecois, a new Canadian separatist party, was formed.

16

White House statement denied any basic change in the U.S. position on Vietnam as hints of a breakthrough in Paris negotiations grew.

Soviet Premier Kosygin flew to Prague to sign a treaty authorizing the temporary stay of Soviet troops in Czechoslovakia.

17

Pres. Johnson signed two appropriation bills for fiscal 1969: the largest ever—$71.9 billion—for defense and the smallest foreign aid bill, $1.8 billion.

Prime Minister Wilson announced a number of changes in the British Cabinet.

18

U.S. Undersecretary of State Nicholas deB. Katzenbach and Yugoslav Pres. Tito conferred in Belgrade.

20

Mrs. Jacqueline Kennedy and Aristotle S. Onassis, Greek shipowner, were married on the Greek island of Skorpios.

Yugoslav Pres. Tito said that any attack on Yugoslavia would be "sharply received."

Five-year trade agreement between Romania and the U.K. was reported.

21

Fourteen North Vietnamese prisoners were freed by U.S. military authorities.

U.S. announced it would resume the supply of major military equipment to Greece.

22

Apollo 7 astronauts brought their 11-day earth-orbiting flight to a successful conclusion with a splashdown in the Atlantic Ocean.

Pres. Johnson signed a bill banning the interstate mail-order sale of rifles, shotguns, and ammunition.

Canadian Finance Minister Edgar J. Benson proposed a deficit budget for fiscal 1969 and called for increased taxes.

23

U.A.R. claimed its planes had shot down three Israeli jets near the Suez Canal.

Nine Cuban exiles were arrested in New York on charges of bombing six offices of countries that traded with Cuba.

Arab demonstrations against Israeli rule of the West Bank erupted into violence.

24

Pres. Johnson announced that he had received no reply to the most recent U.S. bombing halt offer.

25

Hanoi radio said that Pres. Johnson's statement that North Vietnam had not replied to his peace offer showed his unwillingness to stop the bombing.

U.S. Secretary of Defense Clifford said that Pres. Johnson had ordered no reduction of military pressure in Vietnam.

Pres. de Gaulle arrived in Ankara on the first visit of a French chief of state to Turkey.

26

U.S.S.R. launched Soyuz 3, its first manned spacecraft since April 1967.

Communist troops began their first major ground assault in a month in South Vietnam.

Israeli and U.A.R. forces exchanged heavy artillery fire along

the Suez Canal for the first time in a month.

27

Approximately 50,000 persons protesting the Vietnam war marched through London with minor violence.

28

Anti-Soviet demonstrations marked the celebration of the 50th anniversary of the Czechoslovak republic.

Italian United Socialist Party congress disbanded without deciding whether to renew its coalition with the Christian Democrats.

29

Israeli Defense Minister Moshe Dayan warned the U.A.R. that if it continued to violate the cease-fire it "must be prepared for severe military blows."

30

Czechoslovak Pres. Svoboda signed a constitutional law providing for Czech and Slovak autonomy within a two-state federation.

31

Pres. Johnson announced a complete halt to all U.S. air, naval, and artillery bombardment of North Vietnam and said that in return North Vietnam had agreed to include representatives of South Vietnam and the U.S. had agreed to let the National Liberation Front take part in the Paris peace talks.

Israeli commandos attacked a Soviet-built transformer station and two Nile River bridges deep inside U.A.R. territory.

Chinese Communist Party Central Committee announced that Chief of State Liu Shao-ch'i had been expelled from all posts "once and for all."

NOVEMBER

1

Colombia, Finland, Nepal, Spain, and Zambia were elected to two-year terms on the UN Security Council.

British government White Paper announced a plan for the drastic reform of the House of Lords.

2

South Vietnamese Pres. Thieu said his government would not attend the Paris peace talks if the National Liberation Front participated as a separate delegation.

U.A.R. Pres. Nasser announced formation of a home guard to ward off Israeli attacks on civilian installations.

3

National Liberation Front issued a communiqué agreeing to participate in expanded Vietnam peace talks.

Funeral of former Greek Prime Minister Georgios 'Papandreou in Athens turned into a demonstration against the military government.

5

Richard M. Nixon was elected the 37th president of the U.S., taking 32 states with 302 electoral votes in a close popular vote; Democrats retained control of both houses of Congress.

Queen Elizabeth II arrived in Brasília on start of state visits to Brazil and Chile.

First meeting of the expanded Paris peace talks was postponed indefinitely because of South Vietnam's refusal to participate.

Israeli Prime Minister Eshkol declared that no Arab troops could be stationed on the West Bank of the Jordan River under any peace arrangement.

Arab commando groups accused Jordan of attempting to break them up and to negotiate peace with Israel.

French Foreign Minister Michel Debré introduced a nine-point plan for increased intra-European trade to the Council of Ministers of the EEC.

6

Anti-Soviet demonstrations broke out in Prague on the eve of the 51st anniversary of the Russian Revolution.

7

UN General Assembly adopted resolution condemning Britain for failing to bring down the Rhodesian government.

Cambodian Chief of State Prince Sihanouk said he would free 11 captured U.S. servicemen if the U.S. promised not to bomb Cambodian villages.

Antigovernment student rioting began in Pakistan.

8

North Korean patrol boats seized ten South Korean fishing boats off the demilitarized zone.

South Vietnamese Pres. Thieu proposed a two-sided peace conference formula; North Vietnam rejected the plan.

9

Pres.-elect Nixon announced that he would give Vice-Pres.-elect Agnew new policy-making responsibilities and an office in the White House.

South Vietnam protested the Communist shelling of populated areas since the bombing halt.

Czechoslovak Defense Ministry announced that Soviet occupation troops scheduled to return to the U.S.S.R. would complete their withdrawal by Dec. 15, 1968.

10

Communist forces shelled U.S. Marine positions from within the Demilitarized Zone for the first time since the bombing halt.

11

British Union Jack was replaced by a new flag in Rhodesia.

Pres.-elect Nixon visited the White House for briefings with Pres. Johnson and sessions with top officials.

Israeli Foreign Minister Eban accused the foreign ministers of the U.A.R. and Jordan of breaking off peace discussions with UN envoy Jarring.

12

French Finance Ministry announced an increase in the key lending rate from 5 to 6% and other severe measures aimed at restricting the flow of credit.

U.S. Secretary of Defense Clifford warned South Vietnam that if it persisted in boycotting the expanded Paris peace talks, the U.S. might proceed without South Vietnam.

Canadian Prime Minister Trudeau announced that Canada would make no new contributions to NATO before completing a review of its foreign and defense policies.

13

U.S. charged that North Vietnamese activity in the Demilitarized Zone failed to live up to the terms of the bombing halt agreement.

UN announced an agreement with the Nigerian government allowing the World Food Program to supply war victims.

14

NATO Defense Planning Committee announced a program to bolster its conventional military strength in Europe.

Pres.-elect Nixon indicated that Pres. Johnson had agreed to reach no major foreign policy decisions without Nixon's concurrence.

15

Pres. Johnson clarified the extent of his agreement with Pres.-elect Nixon on foreign policy by declaring he would make whatever decisions the president was called on to make until inauguration day.

Canadian Trade and Commerce Minister Jean-Luc Pepin announced the sale of 58.5 million bu. of wheat to Communist China.

16

North Atlantic Council warned the U.S.S.R. against any direct or indirect intervention affecting Europe or the Mediterranean.

Communiqué issued in Salisbury following British-Rhodesian talks said that major differences remained unresolved.

17

Cambodian government charged that U.S. and South Vietnamese patrol boats had shelled a Cambodian village.

Unmanned Soviet spacecraft Zond 6 completed its circumlunar flight.

South Korean government reported having killed 33 North Korean infiltrators and captured two others.

18

Czechoslovak Communist Party published excerpts from a Central Committee policy resolution that stressed the need to prevent the "errors" that had occurred in the liberalization process.

19

Mali's socialist president, Modibo Keita, was overthrown by junior army officers in a bloodless coup.

UN General Assembly, by vote of 44–58, rejected a resolution for the seating of Communist China.

Teachers' strikes that had closed New York City schools for two months ended.

Italian Premier Giovanni Leone and his minority government resigned in the midst of a wave of major strikes.

20

European foreign exchange markets closed in an effort to halt speculation against the French franc and in favour of the West German Deutsche Mark.

Lieut. Moussa Traore was named the new president of Mali.

21

U.S.S.R. overrode the objections made in Budapest by Western Communist parties and won agreement for a meeting of world Communist leaders in Moscow in May 1969.

22

Bomb exploded in a marketplace in the Jewish section of Jerusalem, apparently set off by Arab terrorists.

Emergency meeting of the International Monetary Fund ended with an announcement that France, West Germany, and the U.K. had agreed to measures that should stabilize the monetary situation.

23

Pres. de Gaulle refused to devalue the franc.

24

Pres. de Gaulle, in a radio address, proclaimed a policy of political and economic retrenchment,

---

63

Chronology of Events

including a wage-price freeze and new budget cuts.

U.A.R. government shut down all universities to prevent the spread of student rioting.

25

Czechoslovakia announced restrictions on travel to the West.

26

South Vietnamese government announced that it was prepared to participate in expanded Vietnam peace talks.

Communist China called for a meeting with the U.S. in Warsaw on Feb. 20, 1969, and asked the U.S. to join in an agreement on the five principles of peaceful coexistence.

Mariano Rumor was designated to form a new Italian centre-left coalition government, ending an eight-day crisis.

ROMA'S PRESS PHOTO—PIX FROM PUBLIX

Mariano Rumor (right) . . . November 26

27

South Vietnamese Pres. Thieu announced the appointment of Vice-Pres. Ky to oversee South Vietnam's delegation to the Paris peace talks.

U.S.S.R. and North Vietnam announced an aid agreement under which the U.S.S.R. would provide large supplies of military equipment and civilian goods to North Vietnam.

29

UN General Assembly resolution condemned Portugal's colonial policy in Africa.

30

Czechoslovak government announced that it had requested the U.S.S.R. to ban the distribution of a Soviet Czech-language newspaper.

Japanese Prime Minister Sato announced a completely reshuffled Cabinet three days after being reelected president of the Liberal-Democratic Party.

Laotian army intelligence chief reported that four North Vietnamese regiments were operating in Laos.

DECEMBER

1

Israeli commandos, striking targets 37 mi. within Jordan, destroyed two bridges.

Special panel of the National Commission on the Causes and Prevention of Violence issued a report sharply criticizing members of the Chicago police force for their conduct during the 1968 Democratic convention.

Venezuelans elected as president Rafael Caldera, leader of the Social Christian Party.

2

Soviet Foreign Minister Andrei Gromyko accused the U.K. of using the invasion of Czechoslovakia as an excuse for hardening its policy toward the U.S.S.R.

UN General Assembly voted to condemn South Africa for its apartheid policy.

U.S. and North Vietnamese delegates at procedural talks in Paris exchanged protests over alleged military activity since the bombing halt.

3

Laotian Army chief of staff reported Communist Chinese troops had entered Laos.

4

William Scranton, former governor of Pennsylvania, arrived in Iran at the start of a Middle East fact-finding tour on behalf of Pres.-elect Nixon.

New wave of speculation began on European foreign exchange markets.

Pres. Johnson warned Pres.-elect Nixon not to risk a recession by trying to end inflation in the U.S. economy too sharply.

Israeli planes carried out the third air strike against Jordan in three days.

5

Six nations, led by Italy, called for a reconvening of the UN Disarmament Commission in a resolution placed with the UN General Assembly's Political Committee.

6

U.S. Defense Department announced that 12,000 troops, and supporting aircraft, would be sent to Europe for NATO exercises in early 1969.

French Communist Party asserted that, in developing a socialist program for France, it intended to pursue an independent course.

U.S. administration sources announced willingness to resume plans for summit talks with the U.S.S.R., broken off after the invasion of Czechoslovakia by Warsaw Pact forces.

7

Jordan called for unified Arab action to liberate Israeli-held Arab territories.

8

Czechoslovak and Soviet leaders ended a summit meeting held secretly in Kiev.

Vice-Pres. Ky arrived in Paris to lead South Vietnam's negotiating team in the expanded peace talks.

9

Second report of the Royal Commission on Bilingualism and Biculturism recommended reform of the Canadian school system to require opportunities for students to study their own language and learn the other—French or English.

William Scranton stirred controversy by saying in Israeli-occupied Jordan that the U.S. should conduct a "more evenhanded" policy toward the Middle East.

Two U.S. destroyers began a cruise in the Black Sea despite Soviet protests.

10

U.S.S.R. budget presented to the Supreme Soviet contained increased defense and consumer outlays.

11

Pres.-elect Nixon introduced all 12 of his Cabinet appointees in a single televised announcement; William P. Rogers was to be secretary of state, Rep. Melvin R. Laird (Wis.), secretary of defense, and David M. Kennedy, secretary of the treasury.

Swiss Federal Assembly elected Ludwig von Moos confederation president for 1969.

Prime Minister Terence O'Neill of Northern Ireland dismissed Home Affairs Minister William Craig for opposing moderation in the Catholic-Protestant dispute.

Spokesman for Pres.-elect Nixon stated that William Scranton's remarks on the Middle East were his own and not Nixon's.

12

French government announced it would shut down one-third of the national railroad system in the next five years.

Malaysia and the Philippines agreed to resume diplomatic relations and to defer for at least one year their dispute over the sovereignty of Sabah.

13

Brazilian Pres. Artur da Costa e Silva suspended the Congress and assumed emergency dictatorial powers.

14

Israeli Defense Minister Dayan met with Pres.-elect Nixon in New York City.

New outbreaks of student disturbances in France prompted the issuance of a government decree threatening the expulsion of student agitators.

U.S. and South Vietnamese forces in Saigon were put on alert in anticipation of a possible Communist attack.

15

U.S. Secretary of Defense Clifford blamed Saigon for delaying procedural talks in Paris.

16

Kings of Thailand and Laos met midway across the Mekong River to inaugurate a power link between the two countries.

U.S. Navy released seven North Vietnamese civilian seamen captured in October 1967.

Italian Premier Rumor outlined to Parliament a reform program that touched every section of Italy's economic, political, and social life.

Spanish government declared void a 1492 decree expelling the Jews from Spain.

17

U.S. Federal Reserve Board raised the discount rate from 5¼ to 5½%.

U.S. Treasury Secretary-designate Kennedy refused to commit himself to maintaining the price of gold at $35 an ounce.

18

Intelsat 3A, first in a new series of communications satellites, was launched from Cape Kennedy.

Major U.S. banks joined the program to restrain inflation by raising interest rates to 6¾%.

19

U.S. warned North Vietnam that an attack on Saigon might have serious consequences for the Paris peace talks.

Cambodian Chief of State Prince Sihanouk announced the release of 11 captured U.S. servicemen as "a gift to the United States."

20

Pope Paul VI's annual Christmas message betrayed deep pessimism.

U.S. government lifted its ban on cultural exchanges with the U.S.S.R.

21

Apollo 8, with three astronauts aboard, was launched from Cape Kennedy on a flight to the moon.

Soviet Foreign Minister Gromyko flew to Cairo for urgent talks with U.A.R. leaders.

UN General Assembly Pres. Arenales criticized the "unrealistic and emotional" attitudes among the delegates at the closing meeting of the 1968 session.

22

Eighty-two crewmen of the "Pueblo" were released by North Korea after the U.S. signed a document, previously denounced as false, admitting the ship had violated North Korean waters.

Julie Nixon, daughter of Pres.-elect Nixon, and Dwight David Eisenhower II, grandson of the former president, were married in New York City.

Vice-Pres. Ky left Paris for Saigon amid hints of a new South Vietnamese position toward the National Liberation Front.

23

U.S. proposed to return to Japan, relocate, or share control of 50 of its military installations in Japan.

Pope Paul VI called the first extraordinary session of the Synod of Bishops to meet in Rome in October 1969.

24

White House announced there would be an "urgent investigation" of reports that members of the "Pueblo" crew had been beaten.

Apollo 8 crew became the first men to orbit the moon.

Nigerian government turned down an appeal by Ethiopian Emperor Haile Selassie for a one-week Christmas truce in the war with Biafra.

25

Queen Elizabeth II made a call for racial tolerance in her annual Christmas message to Britain and the Commonwealth.

26

Two Arab terrorists attacked an Israeli jetliner in Athens.

27

Apollo 8 splashed down in the Pacific Ocean.

Communist China was thought to have resumed nuclear testing after a one-year lapse with an above-ground explosion with a force of about three megatons.

Several members of the South Vietnamese delegation to the Paris peace talks were dismissed.

28

Israeli commandos staged a helicopter raid on the Beirut airport, destroying or damaging 13 Lebanese airliners.

Pres.-elect Nixon ordered his foreign policy advisers to survey all options open to the U.S. in Vietnam.

29

Cunard Line refused to take delivery of the luxury liner "Queen Elizabeth II" until its defects were corrected.

30

New Soviet initiative for Middle East peace, calling for big-power pressure, was reported.

31

UN Security Council unanimously censured Israel for its attack on the Beirut airport.

U.S.S.R. conducted the world's first test of a commercial supersonic jetliner.

(D. K. WI.; J. W. MW.)

PRAGUE

CHICAGO

PARIS

Advertising

No one new campaign could be singled out as of particular interest during 1968. In the U.K. motorists were being reminded constantly through TV, press, and poster campaigns of the need for safety on the roads. The 1967 "breathalyser" law, providing for on-the-spot testing of motorists suspected of drunken driving, had been painstakingly explained to the public through mass-media advertising. The success of the campaign encouraged the government to invest even greater funds in road safety advertising, which in 1968 cost approximately £700,000. The importance of the campaign lay in demonstrating that advertising could have a community function as well as a commercial role.

Europe. Expenditure in the U.K. was estimated at £447 million for 1967, only 8% above the previous year and the smallest increase in any year since sta-

Example of the humorous commercials created for Excedrin by Young & Rubicam is titled "Headache No. 39. The Shoe Store." Dialogue—Harried clerk: "Well, now as I read this, this is a 7-D." Lady: "Well, that must be the . . . somebody else's foot, not mine. I've always had a 4-AAA." Clerk: "Well, it's growing on the end of your leg; it must be your foot . . . ."

DAVID GAHR

tistics had been available. However, expenditure for the first nine months of 1968 showed a 12% increase over the corresponding period a year earlier. In an article in *Advertising Quarterly*, D. S. Dunbar of the J. Walter Thompson Co. observed that, although there had been an increase in monetary terms, it was probable that the volume of activity declined somewhat in 1967. National newspapers and magazines and periodicals suffered most. Newspaper revenue from advertising dropped from £87 million in 1966 to £82 million in 1967, and that for magazines and periodicals from £50 million to £46 million. Television advertising, on the other hand, increased both its revenue and its share. Income went up from £109 million to £124 million and the percentage of total expenditure going to TV rose from 25 to 28%. *Advertising Quarterly* pointed out that much of the growth in TV expenditure resulted from the fact that TV rates had increased, while other types of media maintained their charges at 1966 levels.

These figures changed the advertising investment picture considerably. In terms of advertising expenditure as related to national income, the U.K. had always been estimated as one of the top four countries in the world. In 1966, however, the Rome Research Co. of New York placed the U.K. eighth. Of the countries reporting, the highest rates occurred in the U.S. and in Switzerland, where the ratio was 2.6%. Next were Finland and West Germany (2%), Austria (1.78%), Canada (1.7%), Sweden (1.6%), the U.K. and Australia (1.5%), Denmark (1.4%), the Nether-

Aden: *see* Southern Yemen

lands (1.39%), Spain (1.37%), Japan (1.36%), Portugal (1.3%), Italy (1.15%), Belgium (1.1%), Mexico (1.05%), and Argentina and Venezuela (1%). Figures lower than 1% were reported by 19 countries.

West Germany led Europe in advertising expenditure with a total of DM. 7,410,000,000 in 1967, some DM. 4 million greater than in 1966. Taking gross national product as the yardstick (as opposed to national income), the percentage spent on advertising rose from 1.3 to 1.53%. Newspapers accounted for DM. 2,191,000,000, magazines for DM. 1,718,000,000, and TV for DM. 558 million. Colour TV was introduced in West Germany in September 1967, and it was estimated that 100,000 colour sets were operative by the beginning of 1968. Total time available to advertisers continued to be limited to 20 minutes a day in two continuous transmissions.

The growth in TV advertising throughout Europe continued. By 1968, 29 European countries plus Cyprus and Iceland had television, and 25 of these permitted TV advertising. Only Norway, Sweden, Belgium, and Denmark did not. Even Albania, Yugoslavia, and all the Eastern European countries had "commercial" television, and France at last relented and agreed to commercial TV, though on a very limited basis, starting in the autumn of 1968.

France lagged behind other Western European countries in its approach to advertising. However, serious attempts to catch up were being made; for example, the Centre d'Étude des Supports de Publicité renewed its extensive research program on newspaper and magazine readership and radio audiences. For the first time, research was carried out on cinema attendance.

It had been reported in 1967 that the Office de Radiodiffusion-Télévision Française (ORTF) had required a government subsidy of Fr. 250 million and that the government would propose commercial TV on both channels, limited to ten minutes daily. The arrival of international advertising agencies in Paris was attributed more to the anticipation of commercial TV than to current profits. The way France introduced commercial TV disappointed the agencies, however. It was permitted on only one channel for only two minutes a day. (*See* TELEVISION AND RADIO.) Only 15- and 30-second spot lengths were allowed, and advertisers were subject to a quota of four 30-second or six 15-second spots from October to December 1968. The tight restrictions were attributed to pressure from the French daily press, which had been in a poor state of health for many years. Furthermore, a list of authorized commodities was issued with the objective of bolstering some sectors of French industry. Only food, textile, shoe, and household appliance ads would be permitted on TV. No new products would be allowed, and no foreign advertisers, even from within the EEC, would be able to book time.

Advertising expenditure in Italy continued to grow, but regulations still prevented the use of films and artwork unless they were produced in Italy by Italians. Furthermore, the advertisers' association signed an agreement with the Federation of Editors and the Italian radio and television authority that limited advertisers to spending not more than 20% of their total media expenditure on TV time.

The commission set up by the Swedish government in 1966 to investigate the possible introduction of TV advertising had not yet reported. Norway and Den-

mark were awaiting the results and would almost certainly follow Sweden's lead. One of the main features of advertising in Sweden in 1967 was the growing importance placed on advertising by government departments. This advertising was designed to increase consumer knowledge in the selection of goods and services and to improve the image of the department concerned. To handle it a special agency was set up, owned partly by the Swedish cooperative society and partly by a private agency. Despite the lack of commercial TV, Sweden had the highest per capita advertising expenditure in Europe. Much of the total expenditure of 1,850,000,000 kronor did not go through the 102 recognized agencies.

Denmark was openly opposed to commercial TV, but the feeling among the major international agencies established there was that it must come soon, and that it certainly would if the Swedish committee reported favourably. In 1967 these agencies accounted for one-third of all Danish agency turnover. Total turnover in Denmark increased by 8%, reaching a new peak of 556 million kroner. However, the advertising agencies' association expressed disappointment, since the increase in the first half of 1967 corresponded with a general price rise and the second half showed a downward trend.

Norway had 43 recognized agencies in 1967, as opposed to 40 in 1965 and 42 in 1966. Turnover through these agencies was 324 million kroner.

As the headquarters for European activities, Brussels continued to appeal to international agencies. Advertising expenditure in Belgium continued to rise, and agency turnover began to emerge from a static position. Advertising agencies agreed to be audited by the accountants of their association to ensure that all were charging the agreed commission fee. Pressure from major business interests for the introduction of commercial TV continued. Since both France and the Netherlands were permitting commercial TV and since both had a transmission overlap into Belgium, it was thought likely that Belgium would decide to have two commercial TV channels, one in French and one in Flemish.

It was difficult to estimate total advertising expenditure in Switzerland. In 1967 the International Advertising Association's eighth biennial report put it at SFr. 1,351,000,000, a staggering increase over a 1966 estimate of SFr. 918 million. Furthermore, Switzerland ranked among the highest in the world in both per capita expenditure and expenditure related to GNP or national income. As expected, TV time was increased to 15 minutes a day, but this made little difference in the enormous excess of demand over supply. Selection of other media was made more effective by the completion of a comprehensive media survey giving national readership data on all magazines and the major dailies. There was no advertising on radio in Switzerland, and no change was expected.

The use of advertising to sell goods and services and to inform people of government action in the social field seemed to be widely accepted in the Communist countries as well as in the West. Such acceptance did not appear to have brought the two sides any closer together in power terms, nor did it indicate willingness to allow the free expression of ideas in Eastern Europe. Nonetheless, it was partly a consumer revolution in Czechoslovakia (a desire for the attainment of better material standards) that sparked the desire for greater political freedom.

(Mu. L.)

North America. Although 1968 went into the record books as the eighth consecutive year of prosperity for the U.S., the gains recorded during the year had to be classified as modest. Until 1967 advertising had been racking up increases that averaged in excess of 5% per year; in 1967 the gain in ad volume slackened off to 3%, and indications were that expenditures for 1968 would be up about 3 to 4%. In dollars, this meant an increase from the 1967 figure of $17.3 billion to a new high of more than $17.8 billion.

Each of the seven major advertising media in the U.S. estimated an increase in ad expenditures in 1968 as compared with 1967. The seven—TV, radio, newspapers, magazines, business publications, outdoor, and direct mail—expected an aggregate national advertising volume for the year of about $8.9 billion, representing about a 6% increase over the actual aggregate total posted in 1967. Newspapers expected a gain of about 6.8% in national advertising volume, which would give them a final figure of about $1 billion. Network TV predicted a 5% rise, from $1,455,000,000 in 1967 to $1,525,000,000 in 1968; spot TV estimated the greatest percentage increase, 10%, from $968 million to $1,065,000,000. Network radio anticipated a very slight increase in national ad volume, from $46.9 million to $47 million; spot radio painted a much rosier picture, predicting a 7% rise from $286.5 million to $306.5 million. Consumer magazines expected a $1,175,000,000 year, up 1.5% from the 1967 total of $1,161,000,000. Business publications expected a 4% rise, from $760 million to $792 million. Outdoor anticipated an increase of more than 5%, up from $140.6 million to $148,392,000. Direct mail looked for the second largest percentage increase, 9.5%, which would take it from $2,580,000,000 to a new high of $2,830,000,000.

The 90th Congress did much to protect the consumer. "Truth in packaging" and auto safety laws, a tough new flammable fabrics law, and a meat inspection measure were passed in the first session, and the second session added measures on "truth in lending," poultry inspection, mail fraud, deceptive land sales, auto liability insurance, and a number of product safety problems. Congress also passed laws giving state officials more say in establishing billboard control standards on the interstate and federal highway systems, authorized formation of a nationwide organization to develop noncommercial

COURTESY. STAN FREBERG, LTD.

Television commercial for Jeno's frozen pizza rolls starring the Lone Ranger and Tonto was written, produced, and directed by Stan Freberg. It won Clios in two categories at the American Television and Radio Commercials Festival, June 1968.

Two of a series of gun control ads prepared by North Advertising following the assassination of Robert F. Kennedy. The ads were made available to all interested publications as a public service.

television, and approved a tax deduction for ads on programs covering political conventions.

In a presidential year, the amount of money spent on political advertising reached new highs. It was estimated that between $17 million and $20 million was spent on behalf of Richard Nixon, about $12 million for Hubert Humphrey, and about $6 million for George Wallace. Thus some $35 million–$38 million was spent on these three candidates, compared with about $25 million on the Johnson-Goldwater campaigns of 1964 and about $20 million on the Kennedy-Nixon campaigns of 1960. Much of the rising cost was attributable to the extensive use of TV. Most of the political advertising was hard-hitting, but only one ad brought objections from the opposition—a TV spot that showed scenes of riot and war and photos of a laughing Hubert Humphrey. The spot ran once on the NBC-TV network and at least once on a local TV station, but it was subsequently withdrawn.

The American Association of Advertising Agencies' annual report on agency profits was not particularly cheery. Net profits of incorporated agencies, figured as a percentage of gross income, dropped from 4.98% in 1966 to 3.57% in 1967, and net profits calculated as a percentage of agency billings slipped from 0.98% to 0.69%. The decline was attributed to substantial increases in payroll costs and small increases in almost all overhead costs. An informal poll by *Advertising Age* indicated that virtually all agencies felt the biggest cost problem facing them was rising salaries.

According to *Advertising Age*, 564 agencies in the U.S. billed $8.3 billion in 1967, and 55 agencies topped the $25 million mark. Once again the largest agency was J. Walter Thompson Co., with $590.6 million in billings in the U.S. and overseas. It was followed by McCann-Erickson Inc. ($476 million), Young & Rubicam ($430.3 million), Batten, Barton, Durstine & Osborn ($313.5 million), Ted Bates & Co. ($301 million), Foote, Cone & Belding ($268.6 million), Leo Burnett Co. ($261.3 million), Doyle Dane Bernbach ($245.4 million), Grey Advertising ($200 million), and Ogilvy & Mather International ($183.2 million). These top ten combined to bill $3,269,900,000 in 1967, 6% more than in 1966. Nevertheless, 1967 was a difficult year for many agencies and overseas billings often saved the day. Although only one agency in the top ten—Batten, Barton, Durstine & Osborn—showed a drop in worldwide billings, BBDO and two others, J. Walter Thompson and McCann-Erickson, lost ground in the U.S.

The biggest agency story of the year involved the Interpublic Group of Companies, whose agency units had combined billings in 1967 of $721.5 million. Overextended financially, the giant complex was reorganized and the man who conceived Interpublic and put it together, Marion Harper, Jr., resigned. Wells, Rich, Greene went public in October by selling 28% of its outstanding shares to the public. The shares opened at $17.50 each and all 409,000 were quickly sold out.

The country's 125 leading national advertisers poured a record $4,540,000,000 into advertising in 1967, according to *Advertising Age*'s annual compilation; this was only 1.6% more than in 1966. The leading advertiser was again Procter & Gamble, which increased its advertising investment from $265 million to an estimated $280 million. General Motors was second with $184 million, a sharp drop from $208 million in the previous year. Following GM in decreasing order were General Foods, Bristol-Myers, Ford Motor, Colgate-Palmolive, Sears, Roebuck & Co., American Home Products, R. J. Reynolds, and Warner-Lambert.

Following the assassination of Sen. Robert Kennedy, *Advertising Age,* Chicago's North Advertising agency, and others in the advertising industry embarked on a campaign designed to get as many people as possible to write their congressmen asking for strong gun control legislation. These efforts—plus the efforts of many others—led to passage of a law that substantially tightened control over gun and ammunition sales but did not provide for gun registration.

Canadian advertising expenditures were expected to reach Can$978 million in 1968, or 6% more than in 1967, according to estimates made by the research bureau of Maclean-Hunter. The bureau predicted that ad expenditures in Canada would surpass Can$1 billion for the first time in 1969, and that in 1970 the total would be Can$1,110,000,000.

Canada's top 100 national advertisers increased their television, radio, and print spending 2.1% in 1967 to Can$155 million, according to an annual survey made by the Television Bureau of Canada. Expenditures in TV increased 5.4% to Can$78.2 million and represented 50.3% of total expenditures. In the fall the Department of Consumer and Corporate Affairs announced that it was preparing a code on misleading advertising. The department also announced the introduction of a national consumer information service in the form of a newsletter-style bulletin, called "Consumer Communiqué," to be published 10 or 12 times a year.   (J. J. GM.)

See also Industrial Review; Merchandising; Telecommunications; Television and Radio.

Aerospace Industry: *see* Astronautics; Defense; Industrial Review; Transportation

Afars and Issas, French Territory of: *see* Dependent States

Afghanistan

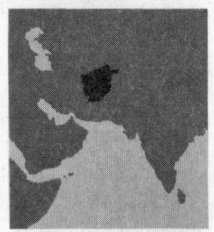

A constitutional monarchy in central Asia, Afghanistan is bordered by the U.S.S.R., China, West Pakistan, and Iran. Area: about 251,000 sq. mi. (650,000 sq.km.). Pop. (1966 est.): 15,909,000, including Pathans, Tadzhiks, Uzbeks, Hazaras. Cap. and largest city: Kabul (pop., 1966 est., 441,147). Language: Persian and Pashto. Religion: Muslim. King, Mohammad Zahir Shah; prime minister in 1968, Noor Ahmad Etemadi.

The resignation for health reasons of the prime minister, Mohammad Hashim Maiwandwal, in October 1967 was widely regretted, since he was looked upon as one of the main architects of the new Afghanistan. He had successfully concluded the second five-year development plan and launched the third; he had won national confidence in the 1964 constitution, which liberalized the political structure of the country; his visits abroad had strengthened Afghanistan's international position and its traditional policy of friendship without involvement. He had eased relations with Pakistan and given a new impetus to the growth of trade between the two countries. Only a few days after Maiwandwal's resignation, the king took the final step to complete the structure of the government as contemplated in the 1964 constitution by inaugurating the Supreme Court. This body, consisting of eight judges presided over by Abdul Hakim Ziayee, a prominent jurist with experience in diplomacy, completed the separation of powers among the executive, the legislature, and the judiciary.

Maiwandwal was succeeded, after a short period of interim government, by his foreign minister, Noor Ahmad Etemadi, a firm believer in his predecessor's domestic and foreign policies. Etemadi retained the portfolio of external affairs and otherwise made few changes in the personnel of the Cabinet. In domestic affairs the year was marked by a thorough overhaul of the judicial system by the new Supreme Court; this involved reorganizing the powers and functions of the lower courts in line with the requirements of the constitution. In economic affairs the policies laid down in 1967 for encouraging investors in the private sector by substantial inducements—tax holidays, free import of capital goods, and protective tariffs—were continued. Government investment was again directed to

the completion of projects begun under the second development plan and to the encouragement of heavy industry. The emphasis was again on consolidation rather than on beginning new projects, and on the gradual replacement of foreign aid by increased exploitation of national resources.

In foreign affairs the country maintained its traditional determination not to permit external aid from either the Western or the Communist bloc to interfere with its complete mastery over its own policies. At the end of January the Soviet premier, Aleksei N. Kosygin, visited Kabul. The visit was brief, and appeared to imply no more than a continuation of the already substantial Soviet aid to heavy industry and communications. In the spring Georges Pompidou, then French premier, paid a somewhat longer visit, from May 7 to May 11. (L. F. R. W.)

Africa

In comparison with the frenetic events of the previous decade, the pace of change in Africa slowed somewhat during 1968. World attention focused most notably on the tragic consequences of the Nigerian civil war.

Independence. Three small states achieved their independence during the year. On March 12, after 154 years of British rule, the tiny Indian Ocean island of Mauritius was granted its freedom and immediately signed a defense pact with Great Britain. On September 6 the British protectorate of Swaziland in southern Africa became independent and was approved for United Nations membership. Although small in size (6,704 sq.mi.) and population (398,400), its economic prospects were enhanced by sugar, timber, iron ore, and asbestos resources. King Sobhuza II proclaimed his intention of trying to obtain the best of the white and black worlds.

On October 12 the republic of Equatorial Guinea, consisting of Río Muni, the island of Fernando Po, and several smaller islands, was granted its freedom from Spain. Equatorial Guinea became the 38th African country to gain its independence since World War II. The economy of the 10,830-sq.mi. country, based on tropical products, provided its inhabitants with a per capita annual income of about $250, one of the highest in Africa. In Spanish Sahara the voters decided to keep their connection with Spain.

Nigerian-Biafran War. On May 30, 1967, the Eastern Region of Nigeria proclaimed itself the Republic of Biafra, culminating years of intermittent regional friction. Fighting broke out in July 1967. During 1967 and 1968 Nigerian federal government troops occupied much of Biafra. But in spite of the contraction of Biafran territory, which by mid-October had been reduced to about one-fifteenth of its original size, the struggle continued. Fifteen months after the war began, it was estimated that at least $840 million had been spent in the efforts to suppress Biafra. Biafrans charged that Soviet planes flown by pilots from the United Arab Republic and British-supplied equipment were instrumental in the federal government's success.

During the autumn, as Biafra's last city of consequence, Umuahia, was under attack, Biafran head of state Lieut. Col. Odumegwu Ojukwu called the situation "difficult but not hopeless." What angered the Nigerian government and encouraged the Biafrans was diplomatic recognition given the secessionist state by Tanzania, the Ivory Coast, Gabon, and Zambia. More substantial in terms of potential material aid

AFGHANISTAN

Education. Public schools only (1965–66): primary, pupils 397,155, teachers 7,852; secondary, pupils 43,-874, teachers 1,444; vocational, pupils 5,775, teachers (1964–65) 538; teacher training, students 8,334, teachers 329; higher (including Universities of Kabul and Nangrahar), students 3,426, teaching staff 557.

Finance. Monetary unit: afghani, with a par value of 45 afghanis to U.S. $1 (126 afghanis = £1 sterling) and a free rate (end August 1968) of 72 afghanis to U.S. $1 (172 afghanis = £1). Budget (1965–66 est.): revenue 3,579,000,000 afghanis; expenditure 2,364,-900,000 afghanis (excluding 5,390,800,000 afghanis development expenditure). Money supply: (March 1968) 5,529,000,000 afghanis; (March 1967) 5,194,-000,000 afghanis.

Foreign Trade. (1966–67) Imports (commercial) U.S. $55,310,000, (financed by aid; 1965–66) U.S. $74,470,000; exports U.S. $72,880,000. Import sources: U.S.S.R. 15%; Japan 6%; India 5%. Export destinations: U.S.S.R. 34%; U.K. 16%; India 13%; Pakistan 8%; U.S. 8%; West Germany 5%. Main exports: fruit and nuts 30%; cotton 23%; karakul (Persian lamb) skins 17%; wool 10%; carpets 9%.

Transport and Communications. Roads (motorable; 1966) c. 6,700 km. Motor vehicles in use (1966): passenger 18,400; commercial (including buses) 16,-300. Telephones (Jan. 1967) 9,400. Radio receivers (Dec. 1965) 40,000.

Agriculture. Production (in 000; metric tons; 1967; 1966 in parentheses): cottonseed c. 44 (c. 40); cotton, lint c. 22 (c. 20); sugar, raw value (1965–66) c. 10, (1964–65) c. 4; wool, greasy (1962) c. 24; rice (1965) 380, (1964) 380; wheat (1965) 2,282, (1964) 2,250; corn (1965) 720, (1964) 720; barley (1965) 380, (1964) 380. Livestock (in 000; 1966–67): cattle c. 3,700; sheep 20,600 (including c. 5,600 karakul); horses 300; asses 1,200; goats 3,200; camels 300; chickens (1954) 40,000.

Industry. Production (in 000; metric tons; 1966–67): coal 141; electricity 350,000 kw-hr.; cement 175; salt 39; cotton yarn (1962–63) 0.3; cotton fabrics (1965–66) 55,000 m.

was the French government's announcement on July 31 that the war should end on the basis of "self-determination." Indeed, Biafra was accused of re-cruiting 180 mercenaries, most of them French. The difficulty, however, of seeing the conflict in simple ideological or economic terms was illustrated by Ojukwu's call on September 29 for Communist Chinese aid.

In spite of growing irritation in some African quarters at external meddling in Nigerian affairs, there was acknowledgment of worldwide humanitarian concern for the fate of millions of refugees and peripheral victims of the war. More than 100,000 lives may have been lost during the first year of the war. Charges by the Biafran Ibos of genocide by Nigerian forces were denied in October by an international observing team invited by the federal government to investigate them.

Aside from the military casualties, international concern was also aroused by reports throughout the summer of tens of thousands of civilian deaths due to malnutrition and disease. The International Committee of the Red Cross reported late in September that 8,000 to 10,000 persons were dying every day in Biafra; despite its shipment of 1,015 tons of supplies during that month by air, the Red Cross noted that only a land corridor would give adequate access to those in need. Relief activities were hampered not by the unavailability of food and medicine but by the suspicion on both sides that the other would abuse its position. The Biafrans insisted that if supplies were checked by the federal forces, the food permitted to pass would be poisoned. The federal government feared that if supplies were flown in unexamined, they would contain guns and munitions. Under these conditions, attempts at arranging a cease-fire were futile. Meetings at Kampala, Uganda, in May and at Addis Ababa, Eth., in August brought no agreement. As the war continued there were numerous appeals to save the Biafran children from kwashiorkor, a disease resulting from protein deficiency.

Although the Nigerian war was by no means a war between the Muslim north and the pagan or Christian south, it was occasionally seen in those terms. Farther to the east, in Chad, the government called upon the French to assist them in suppressing a rebellion in the Muslim north. And in the Sudan, the 13-year-old war between the northern Muslims and the pagan southerners dragged on; casualties had run into the hundreds of thousands.

Coups d'Etat and Internal Dissension. While attempted coups were fewer in number than in 1967, several African regimes were toppled or shaken during 1968. In Sierra Leone, on April 18, Col. Andrew Juxon-Smith was deposed by soldiers rebelling for higher pay. His austerity measures had also caused increased unemployment. A 14-member Anti-Corruption Revolutionary Movement was installed. On April 26, Siaka Stevens was reappointed prime minister; Stevens had been deposed in March 1967, after having held the position for only a few minutes. In Dahomey the military regime which had seized power on Dec. 17, 1967, voided the election of early May 1968 which had been boycotted by three-fourths of the registered voters. On June 27 the regime appointed Émile Zinsou to the presidency. In the Congo (Brazzaville) Pres. Alphonse Massamba-Debat, who had come to power in 1963 with a leftist orientation, began early in 1968 to seek aid from the West. In May a coup to depose him failed, but in late summer another coup, led by Capt. Marien Ngouabi, succeeded in gaining control and forcing his resignation.

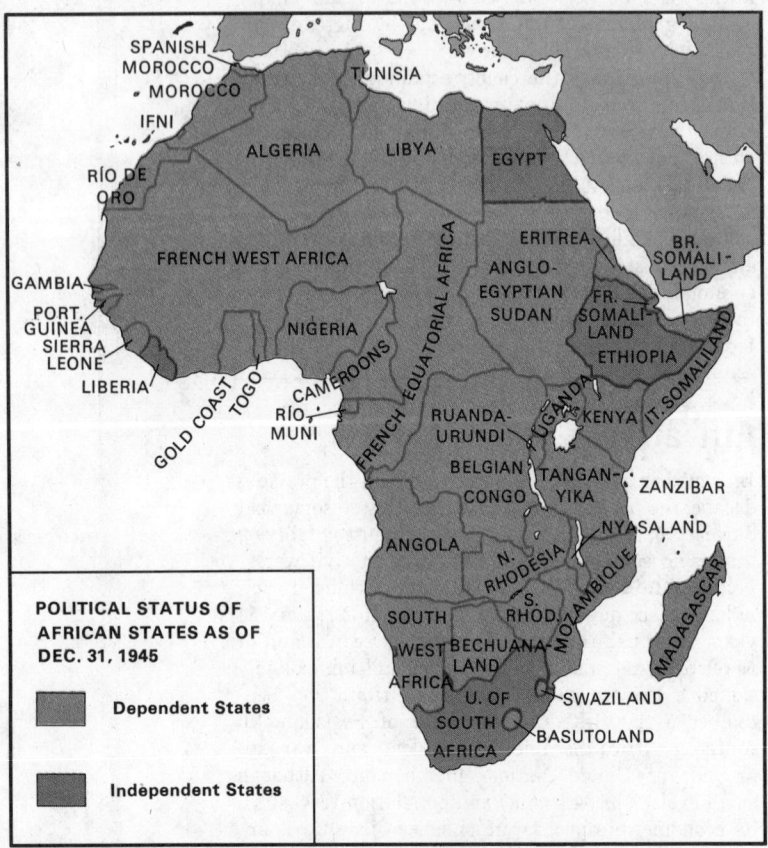
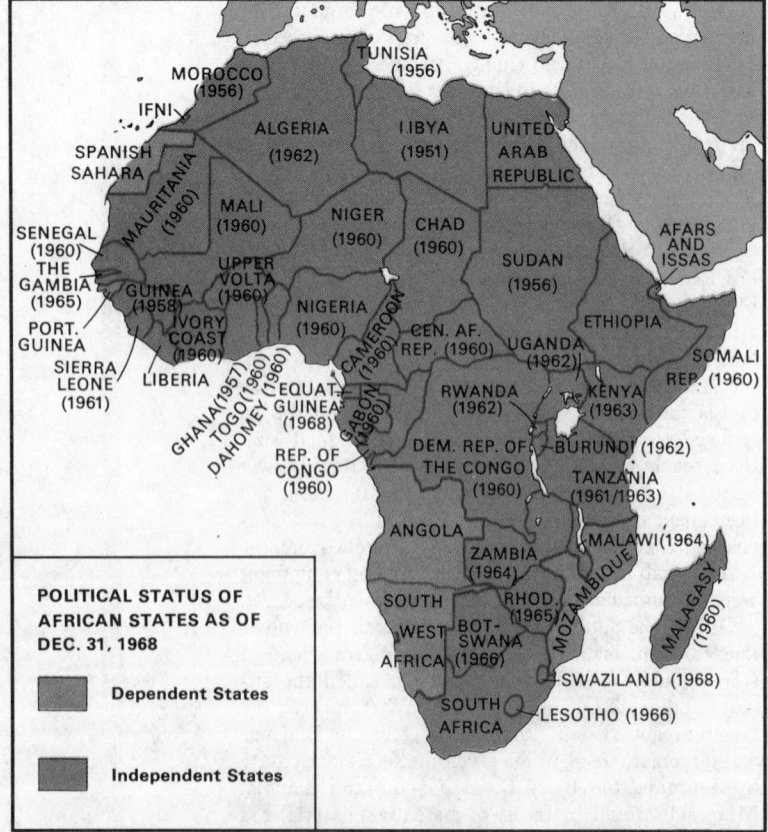

Political status of African states on Dec. 31, 1945, and Dec. 31, 1968, shows the decline of the colonial system on that continent. Dates in parentheses on the 1968 map indicate the year in which each country achieved independence.

continued on page 74

AFRICA: A DIVIDED CONTINENT

By Colin Legum

Once it was thought the Sahara Desert divided Africa into two natural parts: to the north, the Arab Muslim countries; to the south, "black Africa" with, here and there, settled white communities. With the passing of colonialism in the mid-20th century, it soon appeared that the Sahara was not only a movable political barrier but that there were other, wider and deeper divisions. These divisions will determine not only the future shape of Africa, but could affect world political alignments.

The Rise and Moderation of Pan-Africanism. Like other continents, Africa is full of quarrelsome leaders and countries, all primarily concerned with their own national interests, which have the familiar habit of cutting across each other's interests. Africa, however, is unique in having successfully spawned a pan-continental movement. The Organization of African Unity (OAU) included 40 independent states at the end of 1968, only those countries still under white rule being excluded; Equatorial Guinea, newly independent, had not yet asked for membership.

The OAU's creation in May 1963 was the apogee of Pan-Africanism, but it was a false dawn. For although the OAU remains, its authority has been corroded by three factors. First, the political divisions between its members have prevented its machinery from working effectively. Second, internal troubles have overwhelmed a large number of African countries—there have been a dozen military coups in less than a decade—and this has resulted in shifting the focus of interest from continental involvement to greater concentration on domestic affairs. Third, the OAU has proved unable to make any serious progress in fulfilling its commitment "to liquidate the remnants of colonialism in the white supremacist parts of the continent," viz., South Africa, South West Africa, Rhodesia, and the Portuguese territories of Angola, Mozambique, and Guinea (Bissau).

The provision in the OAU charter banning member states from combining in separate political groups has been ineffectual. Although the radical Casablanca group—once led by Algeria's Ahmed ben Bella, Ghana's Kwame Nkrumah, Guinea's Sékou Touré, and the U.A.R.'s Gamal Abd-al-Nasser—has disappeared, the Francophone group of 14 states—the African and Malagasy Common Organization (OCAM)—remains active. Disagreements between the Arab nations in Africa have divided allegiances. Thus the Maghreb countries (Morocco, Algeria, and Tunisia) defend themselves against the pull of Cairo; Tunisia's moderating role in Arab politics has isolated it from both Algeria and the U.A.R., while the U.A.R. and Algeria have latterly become rivals for the leadership of the struggle against Israel.

On the other hand, the disruptive disputes that raged over centres of subversion in Nkrumah's Ghana, Sékou Touré's Guinea, and Cairo largely died away after 1965; and with the consolidation of Gen. Joseph Mobutu's power over a subdued Congo, the rivalries that once so bitterly divided African leaders in their competing allegiances to Patrice Lumumba, Joseph Kasavubu, and Moise Tshombe have disappeared. Nigeria's civil war, however, opened up a new source of division, while the start of a violent struggle by a Muslim-conscious "national liberation" movement in Eritrea worsened Ethiopia's relations with its Muslim neighbours.

Frontier disputes, too, have been a cause of angry divisions—especially Somalia's irredentist movements against Ethiopia and Kenya in the Horn of Africa. But these conflicts show signs of diminishing, especially since the beginning of a détente between Somalia and Kenya in late 1967.

While much of the heat of the early 1960s has gone out of the conflicts between the so-called "moderate" and "radical" African states (especially since the downfall of Nkrumah and Ben Bella, and with the mellowing of Sékou Touré), Africa has been left bruised and uncertain by the shattering experiences of its first decade of independence. There is now much more caution in advancing ideas of Pan-Africanism. Nevertheless, there have been encouraging signs of regional cooperation, reflected in economic agreements over multinational projects such as the development of Lake Chad and the Niger and Senegal River basins. The outstanding achievement, though, was the agreement in 1966 to establish an East African Economic Community embracing Kenya, Uganda, and Tanzania. Less publicized, but ultimately of considerable significance, was the success of the UN Economic Commission for Africa in winning active support for the creation of five regional economic groupings to cover the entire continent.

The picture that emerges from this survey of relations between African states is of a process of "fission and fusion"; of sharp divisions, followed by a period of reconciliation and consolidation. It is a dynamic process that is likely to characterize developments in the continent for a long time to come.

The Southern Frontier. If the divisions between black African states are fluid and subject to sudden change, this cannot be said of the racial division of the continent between "black Africa" and the "white redoubt." Between them stretches a frontier that has become as bitter as the Mason-Dixon Line in its worst period. It runs from the Atlantic Ocean on the west to the Indian Ocean on the east, and is marked by the borders of the Congo (Kinshasa) and Zambia with Angola, the Zambezi River between Zambia and Rhodesia, and the frontiers of Zambia, Malawi, and Tanzania with Mozambique. North of this border lie almost all of Africa's black independent states. To the south lie all the countries (except for tiny Portuguese Guinea, the French Territory of Afars and Issas, and the small Spanish possessions) still under white rule, as well as a few of the weakest of the independent black states: Lesotho, Botswana, and Swaziland, all of them economic hostages to South Africa.

It was along this troubled frontier that the "African revolution" came to a dead stop in 1962. Unlike the British, French, Belgian, and Spanish colonial empires, the Portuguese refused to bend to "the wind of change." (Southern) Rhodesia, a self-governing British colony, finally went into open rebellion in November 1965 rather than yield to the demand for majority—i.e., black—rule. South Africa, a white supremacist society of three centuries' duration, defiantly stood its ground in defense of its policy of racial separation (apartheid), and chose to defy the world community by its refusal to allow the mandated territory of South West Africa to be brought under United Nations supervision and control.

As far as these white-ruled societies were concerned, the African revolution was over. For black Africa these territories represented a defiant challenge to their demand that majority rule must be the guiding principle by which the whole continent was to be governed in the post-colonial era. Between these two diametrically opposed viewpoints there was to be no room for compromise.

In 1963, at the founding conference of the OAU, Africa's leaders spoke with one voice, calling on the world community to help them overthrow the white supremacist regimes by collective action through the UN and by a program of persuasion and economic pressure. They established a National Liberation Committee to give support to "liberation movements," com-

Heads of state conference held in Kampala, Uganda, Dec. 1, 1967, inaugurated the newly formed East African Economic Community. Kenya, Uganda, and Tanzania, the charter members, accepted applications for association from a number of other nations, including Ethiopia and Zambia.

mitting member states to provide financial, technical, and military assistance. The Portuguese, Rhodesians, and South Africans met this challenge by strengthening their military capacity, by formally recognizing their alliance of interest, and by engaging in skillful and energetic diplomacy. Because they are the main trading partners of these white-ruled states, the Western nations (and Japan) found themselves caught in a cross fire between the opposing sides.

Guerrilla warfare developed slowly and, at first, amateurishly, justifying the earlier refusal by Portugal, Rhodesia, and South Africa to treat this threat seriously. The first assaults were launched in Angola at the beginning of 1961 and in Guinea in 1962. Four years later the Angolan revolt had been blunted; it seemed as though the Portuguese had won, although their position in Guinea was far less satisfactory. During the following three years, however, the outlook was transformed, resulting, by 1968, in the Portuguese having to keep an estimated 120,000 troops in Africa: 15,000–20,000 in Guinea, 50,000–60,000 in Angola, and possibly 45,000 in Mozambique. About 40% of Portugal's budget was absorbed in military expenditure, and on Jan. 4, 1968, the then Portuguese premier, António de Oliveira Salazar, was reported as saying: "If the troubles there [in Africa] continue very much longer, they will diminish and destroy our ability to carry on."

Instead of having to deal with simply local insurgent attacks, the Portuguese found they had a colonial war on their hands in Africa. The most skillful attacks were those pressed against Portuguese Guinea across the frontier of Sékou Touré's Guinea. Because Portuguese Guinea is largely developed by the Companhia União Fabril (CUF), critics in Portugal have dubbed it "the company war." Four fronts were activated in Angola: in the north along the Congo (Kinshasa) frontier; in the southeast along the Zambian and South West African frontiers; around the capital of Luanda; and in the Cabinda enclave along the Congo (Brazzaville) frontier. In September 1964 guerrillas moved into action against Mozambique for the first time, operating across the Tanzania frontier. They concentrated on the two northern districts, Cabo Delgado and Niassa, and later began to show signs of activity farther south in the Tete area, where the Portuguese have recently embarked on an ambitious U.S. $315 million hydroelectric industrial complex at Cahorabassa.

In Rhodesia the guerrilla movement mounted slowly after the unilateral declaration of independence by the Ian Smith

regime on Nov. 11, 1965, and was at first unable to make much impression. In July 1967 the whole picture changed dramatically when about 100 guerrillas, armed with modern Soviet and Czech weapons and mostly well trained, crossed the Zambezi River from Zambia. This marked the start of cooperation between black South African and Rhodesian guerrillas which has since continued on an expanding scale. The immediate result was to bring white South African police and security forces into Rhodesia in defiance of a protest by Britain.

Thus, from Sept. 8, 1967, when the South African prime minister, B. J. Vorster, publicly announced that South African police were assisting the Rhodesian government, the whole of the "white redoubt" in southern Africa had become actively engaged in fighting guerrillas. Vorster stated that South Africa was willing to help fight guerrillas wherever it was invited to do so. Meanwhile, too, guerrillas had made their first appearance in South West Africa, the territory South Africa refuses to hand over to the UN despite the latter's resolution rescinding a mandate conferred by the League of Nations. The guerrillas began to infiltrate from Zambia, through Botswana, Angola, and the Caprivi Strip (South Africa's northern military base area) in September 1965; they went into action a year later. On Dec. 4, 1966, the first white South African was attacked by guerrillas in his own home on a farm in the north of South West Africa.

The Guerrillas. Most of the guerrilla movements act independently of each other, and some are bitter rivals. The more important movements that accept the notion of armed struggle as part of a philosophy of national liberation are listed below.

In Portuguese Guinea the leading group is the Partido Africano da Independencia da Guinée e Cabo Verde (PAIGC), formed in 1965; effective leader, Amilcar Cabral; main training and supply bases in Sékou Touré's Guinea; main support from the OAU and from Guinea, Algeria, and Communist countries; claims to control half of Guinea. The Portuguese insist the rebels hold no ground, merely operating as a terrorist group in remoter parts of the territory.

In Angola there are three rival groups. The União dos Populações de Angola (UPA), the oldest, was established in 1954; it combined in 1962 with the Partido Democratico Angolano to form the Revolutionary Government of Angola-in-Exile (GRAE); leader, Holden Roberto; main areas of operation in northern territory; training and supply bases in the Congo (Kinshasa); leadership maintains contact with both Western and Communist countries; main support from the OAU. The Movimento Popular de Libertação de Angola (MPLA) was established in 1957; leader, Antonio Augustinho Neto, a poet; operates mainly in the eastern and southern parts of the country, around Luanda, and in the Cabinda enclave; headquarters in Zambia; support comes from the OAU and Communist countries (both the U.S.S.R. and China). The União Nacional para a Independência Total de Angola (UNITA) was established as a splinter group of the UPA in 1964; leader, Joseph Savimbi; appears to have little outside help; operates mainly in the eastern part of the country.

In Mozambique there is only one effective movement, the Front for the Liberation of Mozambique (FRELIMO), but an insignificant faction, the Revolutionary Committee for Mozambique (COREMO), is encouraged by Peking. FRELIMO was formed in 1962 through the fusion of three nationalist groups—the Mozambique African National Union, the União Nacional Africana de Moçambique Independente, and the União Nacional Africana de Moçambique; leader, Eduardo Mondlane (see BIOGRAPHY), sociology graduate of Northwestern University and a former UN staff member; military operations began Sept. 25, 1964; external bases in Tanzania; support comes from the OAU and from Communist countries, with some aid for educational, social, and health programs coming from Western countries.

In Rhodesia there are two rival organizations. The Zimbabwe African Peoples Union (ZAPU), established in 1968, grew out

of earlier nationalist groups; leader, Joshua Nkomo, in political detention in Rhodesia; external headquarters in Zambia; since 1967 its operations have been carried out jointly with the African National Congress of South Africa; military support comes from the OAU and from Eastern European countries, while Western sources provide limited help for educational programs. The Zimbabwe African National Union (ZANU) was established in 1963 in a breakaway from ZAPU; leader, the Rev. N. Sithole, in political detention in Rhodesia; external headquarters and training centres in Tanzania; support comes from the OAU.

In South Africa there are two movements. The African National Congress (ANC) was established in 1912; leader (from 1952 until his death in 1967), Chief Albert Luthuli; now its two most prominent leaders are Nelson Mandela (serving a life sentence on Robben Island, South Africa) and Oliver Tambo; external headquarters in Tanzania; military training centre in Algeria; support from the OAU, Algeria, the U.A.R., and from Eastern European countries. Since 1967 its forces have collaborated with ZAPU in Rhodesia; so far they have not engaged in military activities on the republic's soil. South African official sources put its trained military strength at 800 officers and men. The Pan-African Congress (PAC) was established in a breakaway from the ANC in 1959; leader, Robert Maugatiso Sobukwe, in indefinite detention on Robben Island; external headquarters in Tanzania; effectiveness severely limited due to fissions in the exile leadership.

Of the two movements in South West Africa, the South West Africa People's Organization (SWAPO) was established in 1958; leader, Sam Nujoma; external headquarters and military training centre in Tanzania; main support lies among the Ovambo people in the north of the territory; outside aid from the OAU and Eastern European countries; began active guerrilla operations in 1966. The South West Africa National Union (SWANU) was formed in 1956; main support from the Herero people and urban workers in the capital, Windhoek; recently ceased functioning effectively in exile; so far has made no contribution to guerrilla activities.

The southern African guerrilla movements have several features in common. They look primarily to the OAU for their political, economic, and military support; they accept the OAU rule that all foreign-supplied arms, from whatever source, must be channeled through its Liberation Committee; all describe

themselves as nonaligned; all have sought and continue to seek support from Western countries, but few have received any, and as a result their arms are mainly Communist supplied.

Drift to War. The official attitude of South Africa, Portugal, and Rhodesia is that all the "liberation movements" are, in fact, terrorist groups "inspired, financed and executed from outside sources—by Communists and Communist lackeys." That the guerrillas are mainly armed with Communist weapons is undeniable, but hardly surprising in view of Western governments' refusal of assistance. Despite Western policies, guerrilla leaders still lobby in Western countries for support to balance Communist aid. They insist that while they are grateful for help from Communist sources, they are determined not to compromise their independence by entanglements with Communist countries. "Gratitude is one thing," they say, "subservience is another."

Considerable rivalry exists between Moscow and Peking for influence with the guerrilla movements—a tendency that causes much concern to most guerrilla leaders and to the OAU. So far, the Soviets have been more successful in establishing close relations with the guerrilla movements than the Chinese.

The three African countries most directly involved with the guerrilla movements are Algeria, Tanzania, and Zambia. The latter two, as border countries on Africa's Mason-Dixon Line, are strategically vulnerable to reprisals. This danger has opened up a new dimension in the confrontation between white and black Africa. The Portuguese, South Africans, and Rhodesians declare that they may be forced to act in their own defense if Zambia and Tanzania continue to allow the guerrillas to use their countries as bases for attacks. In a warning to Zambia, South Africa's prime minister has said: "If you want to try violence we will hit you so hard, you won't forget it." Reacting to such warnings, Pres. Kenneth Kaunda sought the help of Britain in 1968 in providing Zambia with an effective missile-defense system.

Both sides take the drift to war seriously. President Kaunda, in a statement made during his state visit to Britain in July 1968, warned that: "Race war is coming; there is a grave danger that the world will split up on colour lines." Two months before, Vorster had warned South Africans that "slowly but surely" an army would be built up in certain Central African states for an eventual "now or never" attack on the republic. His military leader, Lieut. Gen. J. P. Verster, forecast that "terrorism is a prelude to war." In August 1968 South Africa's army, the most effective in the continent, staged its first massive anti-guerrilla tactical operations on its northern frontier. The escalation of war preparations has progressed yearly, but never faster than in 1968.

Meanwhile, South Africa has not rested its strategy on military tactics alone. It pursues a vigorous diplomatic offensive to encourage a "good neighbour policy" with black African states, mainly by offering substantial trade and economic advantages to those states willing both to establish diplomatic relations with the republic and to repudiate the guerrillas. Predictably, its first successes have been with the former British High Commission Territories—Lesotho, Botswana, and Swaziland—all of which lie wholly or partially within South Africa's territorial frontiers and are largely dependent on trade and communications with the republic.

More surprising was the decision of Malawi's president, H. K. Banda, to open diplomatic relations with the republic, thereby breaking the boycott imposed in 1963 by the OAU, of which Malawi is a member. Banda neither resigned nor was expelled from the organization. In this way, another new division opened up in Africa, between those black states that refuse to have any dealings with South Africa and those that, because of their own national interest, see some advantage in doing so. Banda has justified his action by claiming that more could be done to change South Africa's racial policies through cooperation than by implacable hostility, which only hardens white attitudes. Banda's policy has not so far found support in black Africa across the Zambezi—Africa's most dangerous frontier.

Southern Africa includes almost all the countries still under white rule and three independent black states—Lesotho, Botswana, and Swaziland.

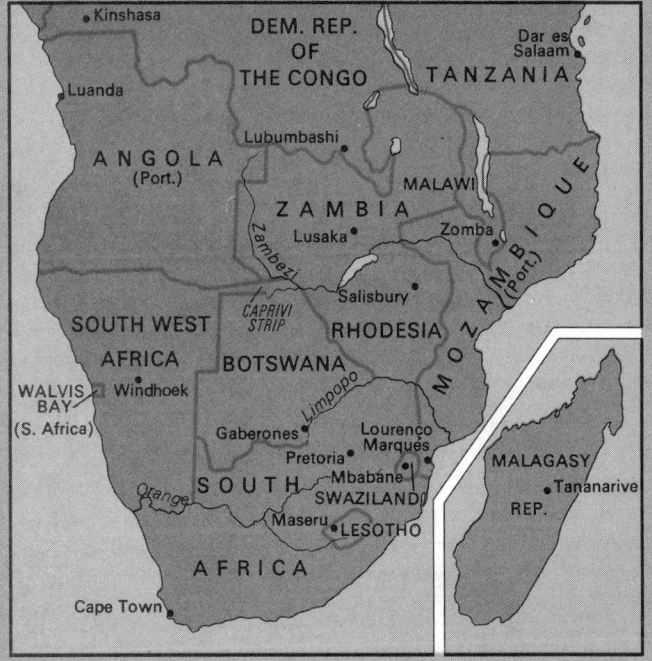

WIDE WORLD

Rhodesian security forces capturing two guerrillas who had infiltrated from Zambia. The terrorist attacks were largely ineffective and several dozen guerrillas were reported killed during the spring and summer months of 1968.

continued from page 70

Other states, too, felt the turmoil of discontent. In Senegal the government had to declare a state of emergency in the face of student riots during late May. Thousands of students in Ethiopia fought police in riots sparked by the question of miniskirts. In Liberia, Pres. W. V. S. Tubman permitted criticism of his regime to be aired at a public trial of a diplomat, Henry Fahnbulleth, accused of conspiring with Chinese Communists. In the U.A.R. reports circulated of unsuccessful plots in June and July to overthrow Pres. Gamal Abd-al-Nasser. In Mali, Pres. Modibo Keita was overthrown by army officers in a bloodless coup in November; it was announced that a referendum on a new constitution would be held in 1969. An attempted military coup in Algeria failed in December 1967 as did an attempt on April 25 on the life of Pres. Houari Boumédienne. After months of tension and violence in the copper belt of Zambia, Pres. Kenneth Kaunda banned one of the opposition parties.

In the midst of such turmoil it was noteworthy that the Congo (Kinshasa), after seven years of turbulent independence, experienced a year of relative calm in 1968. The 120 mercenaries who had left Bukavu in November 1967 for Rwanda were flown to Europe in late April.

The Southern Tier. The whites who controlled southern Africa evidently felt sufficiently confident about their military and economic position to maintain their defiance of African and world public opinion. The raiding efforts of hundreds of Rhodesian African guerrillas (about 3,000 were reported to be in training abroad) were limited and scarcely successful. British efforts at applying economic pressure against Rhodesia also proved ineffective. On September 13 the Rhodesian High Court, in defiance of the Privy Council, Britain's highest court, asserted that ultimate sovereignty lay with Rhodesia. At a four-day meeting at Gibraltar ending October 13, Prime Ministers Harold Wilson of the U.K. and Ian Smith of Rhodesia were unable to agree on any accommodation of their positions. Wilson wanted the inclusion of black Africans in the Rhodesian government, while Smith balked at Wilson's insistence that the Privy Council held ultimate judicial power. On October 25 the UN General Assembly voted 92–2 to have all members refuse to recognize Rhodesia's independence.

In the face of South Africa's repeated flouting of UN condemnations and requests concerning South West Africa, the world body was incapable of enforcing its termination (1966) of the League of Nations mandate which gave South Africa governing power over the territory. Nor was it able to secure the release of 30 South West Africans held by South

Africa for terrorist activities. A General Assembly resolution of June 12 gave the territory the name of Namibia, but it had no practical effect. Earlier, in April, a UN mission was denied entrance into the territory.

Portugal, which had approximately 120,000 men combating guerrillas in the territories of Angola, Mozambique, and Portuguese Guinea, was sufficiently secure to give the first contract to an international concern to build the Cahorabassa Dam in Mozambique. Scheduled for completion in 1974, the complex would cost $315 million.   (W. So.)

French-Speaking Africa. For most of the French-speaking African states 1968 was a relatively untroubled year. On some occasions, however, the general calm was disturbed. The proposed formation in February (confirmed in April) of the Union of Central African States (UEAC) was feared to be harmful to the existing Central African Customs and Economic Union (UDEAC). The UEAC, however, attracted only three members, Congo (Kinshasa), the Central African Republic, and Chad, and never became an effective organization. After conflicts between the member countries the UEAC was dissolved in December.

In May Gabon and the Ivory Coast recognized Biafra's independence, unlike their partners in the African and Malagasy Common Organization (OCAM) who held to the charter of the Organization of African Unity and refused to acknowledge the sovereignty of Ojukwu's separatist government.

In September, the same month in which Massamba-Debat formally resigned as president of the Congo (Brazzaville), French troops were called in by Pres. François Tombalbaye of Chad to help government forces restore order near the frontier with Libya. These few disturbances in French-speaking Africa were in direct contrast to the unanimity expressed in the January conference of OCAM, at which the prestige of Hamani Diori, Niger's chief of state, was further enhanced. Indeed, he was retained by his colleagues in his presidential functions and elected to negotiate the renewal of the association's convention with the European Economic Community, due to expire on May 31, 1969.   (Ph. D.)

Economic Matters. The fundamental factors affecting the African economic condition did not change

"It's not our business to interfere—we're just here to see fair play." ©"Punch"

BEN ROTH AGENCY

very much during the year. A revolution of rising expectations, a growing population which, according to one estimate would number more than 600 million by the end of the century, limited capital, nationally oriented economies, the need for skilled personnel—all these factors influenced the fiscal picture.

Financial news of importance included: the opening on September 2 of the $38 million, 1,060-mi. oil pipeline from Dar es Salaam, Tanzania, to Ndola, Zambia; the announcement that the Soviet Union would aid the U.A.R. in the building of an $800 million industrial complex south of Cairo; the activating of the first two generators of the U.A.R.'s Aswan High Dam, now 85% complete; and the announcement by Prime Minister Muhammad Egal of Somalia that UN geologists had discovered major reserves of uranium ore in his country. The deepwater port of Lomé, Togo, built with West German loans of $16.8 million, was opened, and the Italian government granted a loan of $20 million, which was to help build the Inga Dam on the Congo River.

Organization of African Unity (OAU). The OAU meeting in Algiers in September reelected Diallo Telli as secretary-general for a second term. The OAU reiterated its support for the territorial integrity of Nigeria. Two-thirds of its small budget of $3 million was earmarked to aid the freedom fighters of southern Africa.

Several steps were taken toward achieving regional unity and cooperation. In December 1967, Kenya, Tanzania, and Uganda, which had been at odds in recent years, joined to inaugurate the East African Community. Its prospects were good enough so that Somalia and Zambia expressed interest in joining. In May 1968 leaders of 14 East and Central African states met at Dar es Salaam for two days of discussions on closer economic cooperation. Nine African nations, Guinea, The Gambia, Liberia, Mali, Mauritania, Senegal, Upper Volta, Ghana, and Nigeria, signed an agreement in Monrovia, Liberia, in April creating a West African Regional Group. It remained to be seen how far they would be willing to go to reduce tariffs and plan joint ventures. In March, Senegal, Mali, Guinea, and Mauritania formed the Organization of States Bordering the Senegal River.

Other Developments. The first gold medal won at the Olympic Games in Mexico City went to a Kenyan, Naftali Temu, in the 10,000-m. run. Mamo Wolde of Ethiopia and Kipchoge Keino of Kenya won the marathon and 1,500-m. races, respectively.

In March the U.K. limited the number of British citizens of Asian ancestry living in East Africa that could emigrate to Britain. Only 1,500 heads of families and their dependents could enter Britain per year. In the weeks before the new law was passed, 20,000 Asians left East Africa.

A UNESCO study of 35 African countries showed that although there was an enrollment increase of 150% in higher education, enrollment in primary schools was not keeping pace with the rapidly rising number of children. The report forecast that more than half of the children who were six years old in 1960 would still be illiterate in 1969.   (W. So.)

See also **Dependent States; Refugees;** articles on the various political units.

ENCYCLOPÆDIA BRITANNICA FILMS. *Mediterranean Africa* (1952); *Life in the Sahara* (1953); *Egypt and the Nile* (1954); *East Africa (Kenya, Tanganyika, Uganda)* (1962); *The Suez Canal* (1962); *Continent of Africa (Lands Below the Sahara)* (1963); *The Republic of South Africa* (1963); *West Africa (Nigeria)* (1963); *The Nile Valley and Its People* (1964); *Oasis* (1965).

Agriculture

Record-large production of several major crops in important sectors of the agricultural world during 1968 reinforced the improved situation of 1967. Through a combination of fortunate circumstances, principally abundant rains at the right time, large populations were rescued from the threat of famine that had followed two years of drought—a situation described by some as the "disaster that never was." A battle had been won, temporarily; necessary time had been purchased for agricultural development and, it was hoped, for downward adjustments in population growth rates. World food supplies increased significantly in 1968 from the high levels established in 1967, when the world total had risen by 3%.

Not only favourable weather but the effect of accumulated planning and investment in agriculture and, more especially, the fruition of pertinent technology were factors in the success story. Early prospects were for another very good world wheat crop in 1968–69 in both developed and less developed countries. Fats and oils, dairy products, and sugar as well as grains would be abundant and under price pressure.

In 1968, as in 1967, the value of agricultural trade declined; both the quantity and the average price of exports were lower. The total in 1967 was $21,335,000,000, down about 5% from 1966; developed countries earned $9,854,000,000, less developed countries $10,123,000,000. The less developed countries were hardest hit by price declines, although cocoa and rice were outstanding exceptions. There was growing promise that further large-scale use of new improved crop varieties would reduce the aid requirements of the less developed areas, with a possible leveling off of grain requirements except in years of unfavourable weather.

The new director-general of the UN Food and Agriculture Organization (FAO), A. H. Boerma of the Netherlands, announced five priority areas for the work of that organization: high-yielding varieties of cereals; the protein gap; reduction of waste in agricultural production and marketing; institutional and other measures needed for the development of rural populations; and the acute problem of agricultural export earnings of less developed countries.

NORTH AMERICA

United States. With weather generally favourable in 1968, U.S. agricultural production reached new record levels, despite official programs designed to limit output. Stocks again accumulated, and prices for some grains declined to the lowest levels since World War II. Farmers earned about 2% more from the sale of a larger volume of products at lower prices, but sharply advancing prices for most production and capital items continued to restrict farmers' incomes. Foreign competition and overseas restrictions increased; exports declined. Government farm programs were widely attacked; yet Congress extended their major features through 1970. And although the affluent society was better fed than ever, hunger in some sectors was much discussed and appropriations for remedial programs were increased.

Crops. Official efforts to hold down production of some major crops were unavailing in 1968; favourable weather supported a record-high yield index of 128,

4% higher than in 1967 and 28% above the 1957–59 average. Indicated total crop production stood at an index of 120 (1957–59 = 100), compared with 117 a year earlier. Planted acreage of 59 major crops was indicated at 309,569,000, down 2% from 1967 but the second highest since 1960. Acreages planted to rice, cotton, flaxseed, and sugar beets were up sharply and soybean acreage was moderately larger. Feed-grain, tobacco, potato, and wheat acreages were lower. Some 297,589,000 ac. were harvested, compared with 300,851,000 ac. in 1967.

The index of total food-grain production was 144, compared with 134 in 1967 and an average of 110 for 1962–66. Included were a record 1,597,858,000 bu. of wheat from 56,039,000 ac., 5% above 1967 and 30% above average. The average yield of 28.5 bu. per ac. was one bushel higher than the 1958 record. As usual, winter wheat provided a large part of the total, with 1,251,537,000 bu. The spring wheat crop, other than durum, was 244,827,000 bu., compared with 249,225,000 bu. in 1967, but the durum crop was a record-large 101,494,000 bu., compared with 63,013,000 bu. a year earlier. Because of the accumulating surplus, the national acreage allotment for all wheats in 1969 was reduced by 13% to 51.6 million ac. With acreage allotments increased by 20%, the rice crop rose 19% to 106,903,000 cwt. Both production and yield per acre set records for the seventh consecutive year. The rye crop of 24,124,000 bu. was about the same as in 1967, but 26% below average.

Production of the four feed grains totaled about 171 million tons, 3% below the 1967 record but 15% above average. Some 116 million ac. were planted to feed grains, 4 million less than in 1967, but growing and harvesting conditions over much of the country were good to excellent and yields were amazingly high. Corn provided 4,439,758,000 bu., compared with 4,722,164,000 bu. in 1967; yields averaged a record-high 79.4 bu. per ac. against 78.2 bu. a year earlier. Sorghum grain production, at 755,085,000 bu., was one-third above average, and per-acre yield was estimated at 55.7 bu., compared with 50.7 in 1967. Oat production, which had shown a declining trend in recent years, totaled 934,424,000 bu., compared with 781,867,000 bu. in 1967; the average yield was a record 52.6 bu. per ac. Barley rose to 424,563,000 bu. from 370,246,000 bu., and the yield was 42.5 bu. per ac. against 40.3.

Hay of all kinds was forecast at 126,261,000 tons, slightly less than the 1967 record crop and 4% above average. Alfalfa accounted for 73,831,000 tons. The total oilseed crop was a fabulous 39 million tons, 14% more than in 1967 and a fourth above average. Soybeans, exceeding one billion bushels for the first time,

rose 14% to 1,079,490,000 bu. Indicated cottonseed production was up 46% and flaxseed was forecast at 26,909,000 bu., 35% above 1967. The 1968 peanut crop of 2,476,905,000 lb., only slightly larger than in 1967, was well above the 1962–66 average. The per-acre yield of 1,738 lb. was below the 1967 record.

The 1968 U.S. cotton crop was 10,912,000 bales, 46% above 1967 but well below the 1962–66 average. Acreage rose 29% and lint yield was 508 lb. per ac., compared with 447 lb. in 1967. World cotton production in 1968 was estimated at 52,214,000 bales, but preliminary forecasts for non-Communist countries other than the U.S. indicated 1968–69 production at a record 25,120,000 bales.

The U.S. sugar production index was 165 (1957–59 = 100), against 136 in 1967. Sugar-beet production was forecast at a record 25,688,000 tons, 33% above a year earlier. A small decline in sugarcane production in Louisiana and Florida was countered by an increase in Hawaii, giving an indicated total of 26,681,000 tons. The maple sugaring season was unusually short, and production of maple syrup, estimated at 979,000 gal., was 29% below the 1962–66 average.

Combined production of all types of tobacco was indicated at 1,720,004,000 lb., 13% less than in 1967 and far below the 1962–66 average. Estimated acreage of the important flue-cured type was down 10%, and production was 991,309,000 lb., compared with 1,263,-159,000 lb. a year earlier. The Burley crop totaled 559,040,000 lb., 3% above 1967.

Vegetable production was indicated at an index of 115 (1957–59 = 100), 3% more than in 1967. Fresh vegetables remained in below-average supply through early spring. Summer supplies were more abundant than a year earlier, but fall vegetables (excluding melons) were down 2%. Production of nine principal vegetable crops grown for processing was up 20%, but harvesting in some areas was disrupted by strikes. The total potato crop was about 292,962,000 cwt., compared with 305,412,000 cwt. in 1967. The sweet-potato harvest of 13,570,000 cwt. was about the same as a year earlier. Dry-bean production was indicated at 17,688,000 cwt., up 14%. Production of dry field peas, at 3,803,000 cwt., was up slightly.

Total output of deciduous fruits was indicated as 12% above 1967. The apple crop was down 1%, but peaches were up 34% and the pear crop, though average, was 34% above 1967. Grape production was forecast at 3,478,000 tons; marketing of the table types was carried on in the face of an attempted union boycott. Production of edible tree nuts was indicated at 3% below 1967. Early reports on the 1968–69 citrus crop were almost uniformly favourable. The 1968–69 orange crop, excluding California Valencias, was forecast at 156.2 million boxes, 36% above the preceding season. Grapefruit production, excluding a portion of the California crop, was forecast at 55.3 million boxes, 31% more than in 1967–68. Lemon production in California and Arizona was estimated at 19.2 million boxes, up 16%.

Livestock. After increasing about 4% in 1967, production of all livestock and products rose only 1% in 1968. Meat-animal products increased by 3%, but dairy products declined 1% and poultry and eggs were off 4%. The Jan. 1, 1968, inventory of livestock and poultry numbers on U.S. farms and ranches held steady at the 1967 level. The value was estimated at $18.7 billion, down from $19 billion a year earlier.

Table I. Index Numbers of Volume of Agricultural Production

Average 1952–56 = 100

Region	Total agricultural production			Per capita food production		
	1967*	1966	1948–52	1967*	1966	1948–52
Western Europe	141	133	84	126	120	86
North America	122	120	93	106	104	99
Latin America	145	140	88	103	101	98
Oceania	140	151	90	106	122	102
Far East (excl. Communist China)	143	135	87	108	104	94
Near East	154	149	84	108	107	93
Africa	143	135	87	100	97	95
Eastern Europe and U.S.S.R.	164	165	82	140	142	87
All above regions	142	138	87	112	111	93

*Preliminary.

Source: United Nations Food and Agriculture Organization, *The State of Food and Agriculture, 1968* (1968).

All cattle and calves totaled 108,813,000 head, only slightly less than the record 109 million head at the beginning of 1965. Beef cattle represented 80% of the total, compared with only 65% ten years earlier. Some 49,962,000 cows and heifers two years old or older (including dairy stock) produced a calf crop of about 43.9 million head, 1% more than in 1967. The upward trend in marketing of fed cattle continued. Cattle processed through feed lots approximated 18 million head per year, with a record 9.3 million head of cattle and calves "on feed" as of July 1. Though federally inspected slaughter continued to run as much as 8% above a year earlier, beef demand was strong and price weakness did not develop.

The total dairy herd declined to 22,231,000 head as of Jan. 1, 1968, 3% less than in 1967 and only 69% of the 1957–59 average. Of the total, 14,662,000 were cows two years and older kept for milk, 4% fewer than a year earlier. Improved milk prices, lower feed costs, and good pasture conditions slowed the decline in cow numbers during the year. Milk production for all of 1968 was indicated as more than 1% below the 119.3 billion lb. of 1967.

Official warnings late in 1967, calling on hog producers not to respond to the record-large corn crop and lower feed prices by overproducing pork, apparently had considerable effect. All hogs on farms at the beginning of 1968 totaled 54,264,000 head, 2% more than a year earlier, but the spring pig crop of 1968 was down 1%. Though hog prices were moderately lower than in 1967, corn prices declined even more, resulting in a very favourable hog-corn price ratio of about 20 after midyear. The fall pig crop was indicated at more than 44 million head, so that the total 1968 crop was about the same as that of 1967. The January inventory of all sheep and lambs, at 22.1 million head, was 7% under 1967 and the smallest since records were started in 1867. Value per head averaged $19.20, down 50 cents from a year earlier. The 1968 lamb crop of 14.5 million head was 4% below 1967.

There were 424,550,000 chickens on farms as of Jan. 1, 1968, only 1% less than a year earlier. Value per bird averaged $1.10, down from $1.20. As the egg-feed price ratio improved after midyear, more egg-type pullets were started for replacements; nevertheless, it was estimated that the nation's flock would be about 4% smaller at the end of 1968 than a year earlier. Egg production, January through October, totaled 58,093,000,000, compared with 58,474,000,000 for the same period of 1967. Turkeys on farms as of Jan. 1, 1968, totaled 7,289,000, down 17% from a year earlier, and production in 1968 was cut sharply. Futures trading on whole, ready-to-cook, ice-packed USDA grade A broilers was opened in August for the first time by the Chicago Board of Trade.

Colonies of bees in the contiguous United States totaled 4,771,000 on July 1, a decline of 1% from the 1967 level. Early indications were for a honey crop significantly below the 223 million lb. of the preceding year.

Farm Prices, Costs, Income, and Finances. Prices received by U.S. farmers in September 1968 stood at a composite index of 267 (1910–14 = 100), compared with 253 in September 1967. The price index for all crops was 230, against 218 a year earlier. Food and feed grains and oil-bearing crops were substantially lower, but cotton, tobacco, vegetables (except potatoes), and fruits were up. Livestock and products, at 299, were up from 283.

LARRY S. WIGGINS

A Wichita, Kan., farmer demonstrated his disgust with falling wheat prices by plowing protest sign in his fields. Prices fell to $1.19 a bushel in August 1968, the lowest price in a quarter of a century.

The parity index of production costs paid by farmers for commodities and services, interest, taxes, and wages reached a new high of 356 in September 1968, compared with 343 a year earlier. The rapid rise in costs involved chiefly taxes, wage rates, and interest; most other items were also higher, but feed and fertilizer prices had declined.

The parity ratio, an overall composite measure of the purchasing power of farm products in terms of the things farmers buy, stood at 81 in September, compared with 79 a year earlier; this was the "adjusted" ratio reflecting government payments. The farmer's share of the retail "market basket" was about 39%, up from 38% in 1967. In August 1968 the index of retail food costs was 120.5 (1957–59 = 100), against 116.6 a year earlier; meanwhile the more inclusive consumer price index had moved up from 116.9 to 121.9.

Cash receipts from farm marketings during the first half of 1968 were estimated at $18.5 billion, $300 million above the corresponding period of 1967. Receipts for livestock and livestock products, at $12.3 billion, accounted for all of the increase; crop receipts were $5.2 billion in both periods. Through May 1968, direct government payments to participating farmers under all programs totaled $568 million, down from $640 million a year earlier; for all of 1968 such payments were expected to be around $3.4 billion, compared with $3.1 billion in 1967. Realized net farm income for 1968 was not expected to be much above the $14.2 billion of 1967. Total income per average farm operator family was $8,978 in 1967, against $9,176 in 1966. For 1968, it was indicated that off-farm income per farm operator family would equal or exceed realized net farm income.

The estimated value of U.S. farm assets on Jan. 1, 1968, exceeded $273 billion, up $269.5 billion from a year earlier. Farm real estate accounted for about two-thirds of the total. Farm real estate values climbed higher in 1968; the value of farmland and buildings on March 1, 1968, was 6% above March 1, 1967. At the beginning of 1968 farm debt totaled about $48.6 billion; farm mortgage debt of $25 billion was up from $23,283,000,000 a year earlier and short-term debt, excluding Commodity Credit Corpo-

ration (CCC) loans, was $23.6 billion, against $21,-249,000,000 in 1967. Necessary interest payments were approaching $3 billion, roughly one-fifth of realized net farm income.

Trade and Stocks. U.S. agricultural exports in 1967–68 totaled $6,315,000,000, 7% below the record $6,772,000,000 in 1966–67 but 16% above the 1961–65 average. In part the decline reflected the lower price levels of the principal U.S. agricultural trade items. Commercial sales (including barter) for dollars totaled $5.1 billion, against $5.5 billion in 1966–67. Exports under the Food for Peace program, at $1.5 billion, were down slightly.

U.S. imports of agricultural commodities in 1967–68 increased to $4,657,000,000, up 5% from 1966–67. Supplementary (competitive) farm products, which made up 61% of the total, rose by 6.7% to $2,846,-000,000; complementary (noncompetitive) agricultural items rose 1.4% to $1,811,000,000. Most commodity groups registered lower values, but green coffee was up 5%.

U.S. carry-over stocks of some major commodities began to pile up again after a major reduction. Wheat stocks on July 1, 1968, totaled 537 million bu., up from 425 million bu. a year earlier but down from the 1,229,000,000-bu. average for 1959–63. In view of the world supply-demand situation, it appeared that they would rise to more than 700 million bu. as of July 1, 1969. The estimated Oct. 1, 1968, carry-over of 49 million tons of feed grains was up from 37.1 million tons the previous year but below the 1962–66 average of 60.7 million tons. Cotton carry-over on Aug. 1, 1968, had been reduced to about 6.4 million bales, compared with 12.5 million a year earlier. As of March 31, 1968, the CCC inventory totaled only $920,382,000 for all programs, compared with $1,950,-447,925 on March 31, 1967.

Legislation and Administration. Agricultural legislation of 1968 was highlighted by the one-year extension of the Food and Agriculture Act of 1965, which otherwise was due to expire at the end of 1969. The extension would give Congress time to consider alternatives, amendment, or further extension of the price support programs for dairy products, feed grains, cotton, wheat, tobacco, and wool, as well as the cropland adjustment program. The Wholesome Poultry Products Act of 1968, patterned after the Wholesome

Meat Act of 1967, gave the states two years to establish poultry inspection standards at least equal to those in the federal program. The Agricultural Producers Marketing Act, which became law in April, prohibited discrimination against, or interference with, an agricultural producer concerning his right to belong to an association of producers.

Public Law 480—the Food for Peace program—was extended for two years through December 1970; an amendment required that at least 5% of total proceeds from sales be made available for voluntary population-control programs. The Food Stamp program was renewed through Dec. 31, 1970, and the secretary of agriculture extended it to all counties. The National School Lunch Act was amended to extend the pilot school breakfast program through 1969 and 1970. The Senate consented to the ratification of a new International Coffee Agreement and the International Grains Arrangement.

Canada. Canadian agricultural production in 1968 recovered moderately from the sharp setback of the previous year, but farm income improved only slightly. Prime Minister Pierre Elliott Trudeau, in a farm-policy statement in June, recognized that the real problems of agriculture were neither simple nor temporary and that the ability of the Canadian farmer to meet the cost-price squeeze through increased productivity had been impaired. Among other aspects of the problem discussed was income protection for grain producers, which assumed uncommon importance as a supply glut developed in world wheat markets.

Wheat planting intentions were down 2% compared with 1967, and soil moisture reserves were below normal over wide areas. Nevertheless, the crop was estimated at 627.9 million bu., compared with 592.9 million bu. in 1967. Supplies available from previous crops at midyear amounted to about 725 million bu., up 115 million bu. from a year earlier. Increasingly refractory overseas markets and reduced world wheat prices rather than drought constituted the major problems. Basic to the developing oversupply was a near-record world wheat crop of 10.8 billion bu., 6% above 1967 and 30% above the 1966 record. Moreover, crops were excellent in some countries that only recently had required large imports. Several wheat-exporting countries reported excess accumulation of stocks and new countries entered the export market.

Table II. Tobacco Production of the Principal Producing Countries

In 000 lb.

Country	Indicated 1968	1967	Average 1955–59	Average 1935–39
Argentina	130,733	138,890	106,262	...
Brazil	330,500	323,635	336,211	202,703
Bulgaria	...	255,735	211,393	...
Burma	93,000	93,184	88,212	...
Canada	219,250	213,096	196,295	76,556
China, Com.	...	...	1,399,820	1,254,539
Colombia	91,490	93,696	76,950	...
Dom. Rep.	25,000	41,887	61,729	...
France	105,270	107,565	92,090	...
Greece	229,378	253,803	218,741	132,819
Hungary	...	48,500	48,192	...
India	738,541	771,610	736,399	761,600
Indonesia	242,500	209,400	159,569	238,685
Italy	153,325	191,657	125,595	95,511
Japan	450,000	462,696	333,382	148,680
Korea, South	143,000	143,299	76,291	...
Mexico	98,766	98,766	96,364	...
Pakistan	451,200	392,000	212,912	324,053
Philippines	165,345	142,197	152,708	...
Rhodesia	137,500	206,500	226,233	...
Thailand	89,660	81,759	64,750	...
Turkey	355,084	402,763	278,771	128,505
U.S.S.R.	540,130	573,195	368,206	525,000
United States	1,720,004	1,972,147	2,178,400	1,460,054
Yugoslavia	119,048	119,710	88,261	...

Source: U.S. Department of Agriculture.

Table III. Cotton Production of the Principal Producing Countries

In 000 500-lb. bales

Country	Indicated 1968	1967	1966	Average 1960–64	Average 1935–39
Argentina	...	335	400	552	289
Brazil	3,000	2,700	2,050	2,235	1,956
China, Communist	6,400	7,000	6,500	5,040	2,855
Colombia	600	465	400	335	23
Greece	450	441	404	377	77
India	5,200	5,300	4,600	4,741	5,348*
Iran	650	528	519	494	171
Mexico	2,250	2,000	2,250	2,206	334
Pakistan	2,400	2,305	2,100	1,656	...
Peru	425	460	475	632	379
Spain	260	297	410	427	10
Sudan	900	850	890	675	248
Syria	650	580	650	656	28
Turkey	1,800	1,800	1,750	1,091	249
U.S.S.R.	9,500	9,350	9,300	7,370	3,430
U.A.R.	2,000	2,005	2,090	2,037	1,893
United States	11,071	7,455	9,575	14,795	13,149

*Includes Pakistan.
Source: U.S. Department of Agriculture.

Table IV. Orange (Including Tangerine) Production in Principal Producing Countries

In 000 boxes

Country	1967*	1966	Average 1960–64
Algeria	11,800	12,000	11,647
Argentina	23,772	24,849	21,540
Brazil	46,800	40,100	27,020
Greece	10,250	12,777	7,646
Israel	28,250	25,123	16,536
Italy	44,864	43,131	30,650
Japan	60,255	65,600	38,314
Mexico	30,000	27,715	23,478
Morocco	20,330	21,295	15,493
South Africa	15,481	14,849	13,939
Spain	65,390	73,882	51,191
Turkey	12,157	11,584	8,522
U.A.R.	12,950	12,775	10,336
United States	165,597	242,091	145,937

*Preliminary.
Source: U.S. Department of Agriculture.

The International Grains Arrangement, adopted in 1968 and in part a replacement for the expired International Wheat Agreement, was designed to stabilize the market and to raise prices about 20 cents per bushel above the minimum of the old agreement. As late as October, efforts in this direction had been frustrated, however. Canadian wheat exports, including flour equivalent, during fiscal 1968 were only 327 million bu., compared with the previous year's total of 544 million bu. Smaller shipments to Communist countries accounted for 50% of the decline. Parliament doubled, to $6,000 a year, interest-free cash advances to wheat farmers.

Increased farm capital inputs were basic to the developing distress. Estimated 1967 expenditures for machinery and equipment amounted to $695 million, nearly double those for 1961. As farm costs continued to rise in the face of lowered returns, western Canadian wheat farmers urged positive steps to develop new export markets, a base price of $2.12 per bushel for no. 1 wheat at Lakehead, and an extra $1 per bushel for wheat used in Canada, the additional payment to come from millers when they purchased wheat from the Wheat Board. The price was set at $1.95½ per bushel at Lakehead from August 1967 to June 1968, pending implementation of the International Grains Arrangement.

Feed-grain production in 1968 recovered significantly from the drought levels of 1967. The barley crop totaled 316.2 million bu., compared with 248.7 million bu. a year earlier, and oats were 357.6 million bu., compared with 304.2 million bu. Acreage of most oilseeds was expanded, the major exception being rapeseed. Following a record rapeseed crop of 26.5 million bu. in 1967, prices stood at a disappointing $2.31 per bushel in February 1968. Trade missions were sent abroad to promote its use.

Livestock and products were a generally flourishing aspect of the agricultural economy. Cattle increased only slightly to 11,775,000 head at the beginning of the year, but hogs were up more strongly to 6,058,000 head. Total output of red meats in 1967 was estimated at 1.4 million tons. The number of dairy cows tended to stabilize in response to higher dairy price supports and subsidies.

A complex new method of grading and pricing market hogs, effective Jan. 1, 1969, would provide a price advantage for production of high quality hogs with large proportions of lean pork. Some 8.2 million head of hogs were sold in 1967, and exports of pork and pork products amounted to about $35 million. Price support programs for lamb and wool were continued in 1968–69.

LATIN AMERICA

Agricultural progress in Latin America in 1967–68 was set back by widespread drought, particularly in the Pacific coast region, the Caribbean area, and, to a lesser extent, the Río de la Plata. The FAO's estimate of a 5% increase in food production in 1967, while encouraging, had been mitigated by a continuation of rapid population growth. The official view of the Alliance for Progress was one of optimism, stressing advances in food production, increased investment in planning and development, and progress toward regional economic integration. There was, however, general recognition of the tenacity of old problems, including widespread illiteracy, low productivity and income, shortages of capital for investment, and resistance to land reform. In May the establish-

COURTESY, "FOREIGN AGRICULTURE"

ment of an international organization to coordinate efforts to combat hunger and malnutrition in Latin America occasioned a statement by the U.S. delegate that, in spite of all efforts, "we are gradually losing ground." Added to these long-standing problems, the 1968 drought was a cruel blow.

Mexico. The outlook for Mexico's agriculture in 1968 was optimistic. Moisture levels were higher, and productivity increases were expected to result from increased irrigation and use of fertilizers and pesticides.

Early in 1968, the minister of agriculture reported exportable supplies of cotton, coffee, sugar, corn, and rice from a good agricultural year in 1967. Crop production in 1967 included 8.5 million tons of corn, 2,057,000 tons of wheat, 1 million tons of beans, 435,000 tons of rice, and a record 1.6 million tons of sorghum. Drought in some areas reduced the output of potatoes and sugarcane, although increased sucrose content of the cane raised sugar output to 2,679,000 short tons from 2,320,000 in 1965–66. Sugar production for 1967–68 was indicated at 2,542,000 tons. Unfavourable weather and insect damage reduced the cotton crop for the second year in a row; the 1967–68 crop was estimated at 2 million bales (480 lb. net), the smallest since 1961–62. The early outlook was for a 5% improvement in 1968–69. A slowdown in the livestock industry and exports continued to plague Mexico in 1967, though cattle numbers showed a slight increase over 1966. Coffee production of 2.8 million bags in 1967–68 was nearly 6% above a year earlier, and early estimates placed the 1968–69 crop at 2.9 million bags.

Central America. All the Central American countries registered gains in total agricultural output in 1967; the index of total production rose 5% to 148 (1957–59 = 100), but output of food rose less than 2%, to 137. Corn production was slightly below 1966, chiefly because of a 6% decline in Guatemala. Rice production rose 8% in response to favourable prices, although yields in Honduras and Nicaragua were reduced by dry weather. Production of centrifugal sugar was estimated at 745,000 short tons, compared with 769,000 in 1966–67.

The 1967 coffee harvest of 6.4 million bags was nearly 18% above average; El Salvador's production rose to 2.3 million bags from 1,960,000 a year earlier. Early estimates for the 1968–69 crop were for a regional production of 6 million bags. The important Nicaraguan cotton crop was estimated at 450,000 bales for 1967, compared with 525,000 a year earlier; higher production costs, adverse weather, and damage from pests were blamed for the decline. Livestock

Workers planting rice at the rice breeding station at Prins Bernhard Polder in Surinam. New varieties developed here were grown on a large scale at the new Wageningen Polder, which produces one-third of Surinam's annual rice crop.

production weakened as a result of poor pasture conditions in some areas, and cattle exports were 19% below 1966. Coffee exports were also off, and cotton exports declined to their lowest levels in recent years. In Costa Rica, a banana "boom" was expected to raise acreage from 49,000 in 1969 to 59,000 in 1970.

South America. Brazil's agriculture recovered in 1967 from the adverse conditions of 1966. Total agricultural production rose an estimated 7%, with the principal gains being made in food and livestock products. The area planted to principal crops increased 5% in 1967, and an additional 8% gain was anticipated for 1968. Drought lowered coffee yields, however, and early estimates placed 1968–69 production at 18.5 million bags, 20% below a year earlier. Reduced yields partly offset a 30% increase in rice acreage, so that the 1968 crop was only 10% above the estimated 6.5 million tons of 1967. The 1968 corn crop was estimated at a record 13.1 million metric tons, compared with 12 million a year earlier. Brazil's 1968 cotton production, at 2.6 million bales, exceeded 1967 in both quantity and quality.

The U.S. Department of Agriculture's first estimate of the 1968–69 world coffee crop placed production at 62,640,000 bags of 132.3 lb. each, 7% less than the 67,777,000 bags of a year earlier. Exportable production was tentatively set at 45,599,000 bags, some 5.7 million less than a year earlier and 13% below import requirements. The smaller Brazilian crop and decreased production in Colombia, El Salvador, and the Asian nations were only somewhat offset by a slightly larger output in Africa. By late summer indications pointed to a reduction of the world's coffee surplus; stocks were expected to decline by September 30 to 75 million bags from 78 million in the previous coffee year. Renegotiation of the 60-nation International Coffee Agreement, due to expire Sept. 30, 1968, was accomplished in February, after resolution of a heated controversy between U.S. and Brazilian negotiators over the production of soluble coffee by Brazil under conditions that U.S. negotiators charged were preferential to Brazilian producers. A compromise was reached under which Brazil agreed to an export tax on soluble coffee sent to the U.S. and which provided for creation of a board of arbitration to rule on future disputes. Under the new agreement, Brazil's share of the 47.9 million-bag world export quota for 1968–69 was set at 20.9 million bags, or 38%.

The 1967–68 Argentine grain crop was, on the whole, disappointing. Record acreages were planted, but adverse weather reduced prospects for wheat and corn below average levels. Wheat production, estimated at about 7.4 million tons, was below the most recent five-year average of 7,670,000 tons, although better than the year before. Exports of 1967–68 wheat were expected to be slightly higher than in 1966–67. However, some of Argentina's traditional Latin-American wheat markets appeared to be threatened by U.S. traders, who were in a position to offer attractive credit terms. Prospects for the 1968–69 wheat crop were uncertain as moisture levels continued low over large areas. The important corn crop was estimated at 6.6 million tons, compared with 8 million tons in 1966–67. Through the end of June 1968, export sales of new-crop corn were around 1,870,000 tons, with Italy the principal buyer; 1968 exports were sharply lower than a year earlier. Argentina's livestock industry suffered, both from poor pasture conditions and from sharply decreased exports. Meat shipments

of 164,402 metric tons in the first half of 1968 were 50% below a year earlier, in large measure because of the ban on Argentine meat imposed by the U.K. during the foot-and-mouth disease epidemic there. The ban on beef and pork was lifted in mid-April 1968, but the ban on lamb was continued and the Argentine National Meat Board refused to issue permits for beef exports to the U.K. Reports in October indicated that Argentina, instead of returning to the old carcass sale system, would increase exports of meat cuts and cooked-and-frozen meats. Export problems were further aggravated by Peru and Chile's ban on beef imports (later removed), as well as EEC meat-import restrictions.

Uruguay's 1967 agricultural output index declined about 11% below a year earlier, chiefly because of adverse weather, and agricultural exports fell nearly one-fifth. Wheat production was down by 55% and corn by 35%. Livestock production was the lowest in nine years, but prospects brightened somewhat in 1968 as Uruguay's meat exporters sought to take advantage of Argentina's refusal to ship beef to the U.K.

Chile, Peru, Ecuador, and Colombia suffered from severe drought in 1968. Rainfall was off by an estimated 80% in Chile's northern region and the 700-mi.-long Central Valley, and agricultural production was down at least 50% along the Pacific coast and in the province of Loja in Ecuador. Peru's cotton, rice, and sugarcane crops were nearly wiped out. In August the FAO approved emergency measures to assist well-drilling and the dredging of canals in Chile. Emergency food supplies from commodities pledged to the World Food Program were ordered, and U.S. food aid shipments were planned.

Chile's agrarian reform corporation (CORA) continued its land-redistribution program; 286,000 ha., of which 61,000 were irrigated, had been expropriated by mid-1968, raising total expropriations to 1,236,000 ha. A total of 8,427 families were reported to have been resettled on 248 *asentamientos*. In his fourth annual message to Congress on May 21, Pres. Eduardo Frei announced that the government's policy of expropriating estates in excess of 80 basic irrigated hectares (197.7 ac.) would not apply to owners who demonstrated highly efficient agricultural operations and acceptable standards of employment.

New commercial accords reached in late 1967 called for shipments of Ecuadoran bananas, cocoa, rice, and coffee to Eastern European nations in return for heavy equipment and machinery; under the agreements, Ecuador shipped some 7,150 metric tons of cocoa beans to the U.S.S.R. in early 1968. Peru's Agricultural Development Law went into effect on April 1, 1968; it was designed to exempt food-processing firms from some taxes and to reduce others on condition that profits be reinvested in such projects as rural electrification, reforestation, and rural housing. The budget for Colombia's land reform program was tripled in 1968, and a new law subjected all farms worked by tenants or sharecroppers to confiscation.

Venezuela's agricultural output increased 6.6% in 1967 to an index of 161 (1957–59 = 100); the per capita increase was 2.4%. The minister of agriculture and livestock stated that 83% of domestic demand had been satisfied by the country's agriculture by the end of 1967, against 72% ten years earlier, and that self-sufficiency had been reached in such commodities as rice, poultry, eggs, and, to a large extent, milk. Government policies continued to aim at improving yields; a $1.3 million UN Development Programme

Table V. Honey Production in Specified Countries In 000,000 lb.		
Country	1967*	Average 1960–64
Argentina	77	47
Australia†	35	41
Austria	11	10
Brazil	15	17
Canada	46	35
Chile	12	14
France	31	32
Germany, West	21	26
Guatemala	6	5
Italy	15	15
Japan	18	15
Mexico	63	60
New Zealand	10	12
Spain	22	20
United States	223	253
Yugoslavia	7	8

*Preliminary.
†Crop year beginning July of previous year.
Source: U.S. Department of Agriculture.

loan, to which Venezuela would add $5.5 million, was to be used to increase productivity.

An initial step toward economic unification of the six Andean countries, Colombia, Venezuela, Chile, Peru, Ecuador, and Bolivia, was taken with the signing, in February, of an agreement to form the Andean Development Corporation. The organization, designed to finance some of the larger projects needed to increase agricultural and industrial production in the region, had an authorized capital of U.S. $100 million, and an initial subscription of $25 million was planned.

The Caribbean Area. Agriculture throughout the Caribbean countries suffered as continuing drought reduced output of sugar, cocoa beans, tubers, and other early crops, and severely affected pasture conditions. In the Dominican Republic, drought in the early months of 1968 lowered production of sugarcane, plantains, milk, sweet potatoes, and cocoa, although production of rice, corn, sorghums, and tomatoes was expected to rise. Production overall was estimated at about 1967 levels. A development project, involving an international consortium of industrial and financial concerns in cooperation with the Dominican government, was reported to be in the early stages.

Cuba's agriculture, already severely affected by large world sugar supplies and low prices in the world market, received a heavy blow as drought reduced both sugar and food crops and forced increasingly stringent restrictions on food distribution. The government's sugar-production target of 8 million tons was not realized; estimated production of 5.5 million tons was 8% below a year earlier and short of Cuba's export commitments to Communist China, Eastern Europe, and other markets. Nevertheless, the government continued to pursue its goal of a 10 million-ton sugar crop by 1970. In April Prime Minister Fidel Castro ordered construction of 1,000 Cuban-designed cane-cutting combines, and plans were being implemented to increase cane-producing land by almost 30%.

Despite the Cuban shortfall, world sugar production for 1967–68 was estimated at a record 73,126,000 short tons (raw equivalent), 5% above a year earlier and more than 20% above the average for the 1960/61–1964/65 period. Production was up 14% in the U.S.S.R., 9% in Western Europe, 6% in Africa, and 8% in Asia. World sugar reserves totaled 11,738,000 tons at the beginning of the 1967–68 sugar year, a slight increase over a year earlier and more than 45% greater than average, and world prices fell, in some periods, well below 2 cents per pound (estimated to be less than half the probable cost of production). Negotiations aimed at concluding a new International Sugar Agreement, suspended on June 1, were resumed in late September. By late October an accord was reached by representatives of 72 nations on a new five-year sugar agreement; neither the U.S. nor the EEC countries were represented. Conferees agreed on a price range of from 3.25 to 5.25 cents per pound. U.S. abstention was explained in terms of its purchases of sugar under its quota system, which sets prices above the world level.

WESTERN EUROPE

Agricultural problems in 1968 related more directly to marketing and prices than to production. Some 10,374,000,000 ac. were sown to grains, 400,000 more than in 1967. Before the uncommonly heavy autumn rains, it appeared that the grain crops would equal the record 118 million tons of 1967; even so, the damp

harvest probably damaged quality more than quantity. The wheat crop was estimated at 1,704,900,000 bu., down from 1,730,800,000 bu. in 1967. It seemed likely that wheat imports into Western Europe in 1968–69 might exceed those of the previous year by as much as 2.5 million tons, with some offsetting decline in imports of feed grains. The area seeded to barley was up 1,400,000 ac. to a total of 30,190,000 ac., which yielded about 1,713,200,000 bu. The corn crop was larger than in 1967; the rye and oats crops were somewhat smaller; and the potato crop was indicated as 4 million tons below the 65 million-ton crop of 1967. A record-large sugarbeet crop appeared probable. Cattle numbers, at 88 million head, were comparatively stable. Hog numbers were up to 75 million head from 70 million a year earlier.

United Kingdom and Ireland. Devaluation did

French farmers demonstrating against the de Gaulle government. Farmers joined students and other workers in demanding higher income, fair taxation, full employment, and a larger voice in government.

not bring any basic changes in the U.K.'s agricultural policy. The 1968 Farm Price Review, setting broad policies for crops until July 1969 and for livestock until April of that year, provided £52.5 million more in guaranteed prices, subsidies, and grants than in the previous year. Farmers' costs of producing the commodities covered in the review were expected to rise £68.5 million. The total budget cost of all provisions of the review was estimated at £286 million. Guaranteed prices were higher or unchanged for all review commodities except eggs.

The U.K. grain trade showed mixed trends in the first nine months of fiscal 1968. Imports of wheat were little changed; corn purchases increased 26%; sorghum imports declined sharply; oats imports declined by 82% because of a larger home crop (which supplied some exports); and barley exports were off 36%. The U.S. was the major supplier of corn, but heavy shipments were resumed from South Africa. New minimum import price levels for cereals entering the U.K., set in August, included increases of about 13% for wheat and 9% for most feed grains. Heavy rains and flooding in early autumn made the harvest season of 1968 the worst in 12 years.

The foot-and-mouth disease epidemic that lasted from Oct. 25, 1967, to June 25, 1968 (when the quarantine was lifted), resulted in the slaughter of 210,539 cattle, 104,285 sheep, 114,819 pigs, and 39 goats. Direct and indirect monetary losses were estimated at £150 million, with direct compensation to farmers

exceeding £26,250,000. With the epidemic overcome, attention was shifted to restocking, and it was anticipated that exports of breeding stock would be reduced for some time to come. Beef prices increased from an average 2s. 8d. to as high as 3s. 4d.

In Ireland, a Small Farm Incentive Bonus Scheme came into effect in May. Its purpose was to assist potentially viable farmers, who over a four-year period would carry out a development plan designed to raise the yearly gross margin (value of farm output less direct expenses) to at least £700. Higher farm supports were announced in April for mountain lambs and finished hogs of top quality; increased grants were set for piggeries; and a floor price for oats and further tax rebates to small farmers were instituted. Even so, the farm revolt of 1966 and 1967 continued, as farmers united to demand higher prices for milk, rural development, more cooperatives, and social security.

EEC Countries. The current farming year brought a 10 to 15% reduction in EEC grain prices and a drastic cut in adjustment aid, as well as unusual price declines for other farm products resulting from cyclical surpluses and lower demand. West German officials and economists expressed concern over the rising costs of EEC farm policies, especially in relation to the large surplus of dairy products.

The Western European barley crop of 37.3 million tons was slightly smaller than the record crop of 1967; the French crop, at 8,890,000 tons, was down sharply from 1967, but the West German crop was 4,915,000 tons, up from 4,734,000 a year earlier. With grain acreage for 1968–69 at the highest level since 1965 and beginning stocks larger, it seemed doubtful that grain imports into the EEC would be increased much above the 17.9 million tons of 1967–68.

The EEC established a single market for beef on July 1, 1968, unifying the import prices of its six members. The primary purposes were to encourage domestic production, to free trade within the Community, and to regulate imports as a means of maintaining producer prices. All the EEC countries would use identical factors to determine when domestic cattle prices should be raised through government intervention and when additional levies should be applied on imports from third countries. Also in July new dairy regulations fixed common export subsidy rates on a large number of dairy products. It was resolved to liquidate about half the Community's butter stocks, which in October amounted to 350,000 tons, partly by gifts to developing countries. With a record-large world production of fats and oils looming in 1968, the EEC in October increased its import levy on sunflower oil from Eastern Europe and the U.S.S.R. to $40 per ton. A more protective but complex EEC sugar policy was implemented July 1.

The large French grain crops in 1968 included about 14,340,000 tons of wheat, of which about 4 million tons would be available for export. This, coming on top of record crops in 1967, left the EEC with the difficult and expensive problem of finding markets for French surplus grains outside the Community in a period of grain glut, and of financing such exports as prices declined. Most of the increase resulted from higher per-acre yields rather than expansion of the planted area. French milk production rose about 5% in 1968 to a record-high level; overabundant stocks accumulated, particularly of butter and nonfat dry milk. In June an import tax of about 2 cents per pound, in addition to the regular import levy and a 6% added value import tax, was applied to imports of

live hogs and pork. Strikes and civil disturbances occurred as farmers protested lower prices for hogs and cattle.

Following record-high yields in 1967, Belgium's farmers increased winter grain plantings by 29%. Higher agricultural production in the Netherlands also was indicated; there was a further decline in wheat imports but increased purchases of feed grains were forecast.

In West Germany, 1966–67 agricultural production totaled a record 45.2 million tons, 9% more than in the previous year. West German production had risen 60% in two decades, while the agricultural labour force had been reduced by more than half. Cash receipts for 1966–67 amounted to $6,820,000,000, and a further gain of 4% was indicated for 1967–68. Domestic food production as a share of total consumption ranged from 100% for fresh milk down to 5% for vegetable oils. Grain imports ran at a high level of about 6.7 million tons, however, and grain prices dropped at least 10%. With about 14 million cattle, 19 million hogs, and over 91 million head of poultry on German farms, the mixed feed industry had increased its output to 7.6 million tons in 1967; even so, requirements had to be met largely from imported feed and feedstuffs. The 1968 budget for agriculture, primarily to satisfy EEC commitments, called for total expenditures of $1,350,000,000, compared with about $1.2 billion in the previous year. As spelled out by the minister of agriculture, the new farm policy called for a sweeping program to integrate farm and rural communities into the national economy, establish a market promotion organization, and improve the country's financial position.

Italy was midway through the second (1965–70) Green Plan for development and modernization of agriculture to serve future market needs. It appeared that the $40 million provided for the plan would be insufficient. Nearly half the total would be used to expand grape and wine production; dairy and fruits and vegetables would each receive about 15% and livestock about 7½%. Wheat acreage in 1968 was up 7% but the harvested crop was only 338 million bu., compared with the record 351.4 million bu. in 1967. Torrential rains following drought damaged some areas. The almond crop was forecast at 55,000 tons, the largest since 1961, and anticipated filbert production was one-third above 1967.

Other Countries. Agricultural problems in several areas were related more or less directly to nonmembership in the EEC. Denmark estimated that full membership might increase Danish farmers' income by $200 million and that prices would rise for all products except pork. In an effort to hold down prices after the devaluation of November 1967, Denmark froze home market prices of agricultural products, while at the same time enacting several farm aid programs. Overall, agricultural exports continued to fall, with the greatest declines occurring in the EEC—and especially the West German—market. The growing of winter barley was prohibited for five years in order to control a mildew fungus that used winter barley as a host and then spread to the important spring barley crop; spring barley accounted for about 70% of all grain produced in Denmark.

Sweden continued to implement its policy, approved in 1967, of seeking rural-urban balance by shifting to lower levels of self-sufficiency in farm production, with food supplies to be supplemented by lower-cost imports. Farmers were encouraged to develop efficient

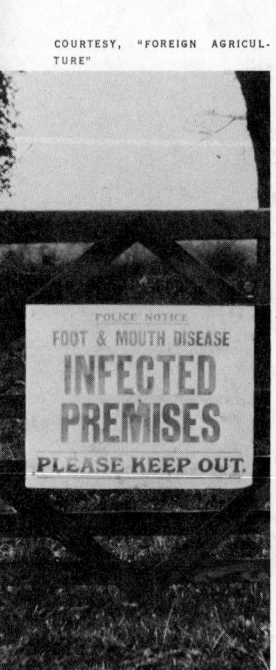

COURTESY, "FOREIGN AGRICULTURE"

Quarantine sign on a British farm during the 1967–68 outbreak of foot-and-mouth disease. Despite prompt emergency measures, the epidemic claimed over 400,000 animals, more than any other outbreak in British history.

World Production and Trade of Principal Grains
In 000 metric tons

	Wheat Production 1948-52 average	Wheat Production 1967	Wheat Imports− Exports+ 1964-67 average	Barley Production 1948-52 average	Barley Production 1967	Barley Imports− Exports+ 1964-67 average	Oats Production 1948-52 average	Oats Production 1967	Oats Imports− Exports+ 1964-67 average	Rye Production 1948-52 average	Rye Production 1967	Rye Imports− Exports+ 1964-67 average	Corn (Maize) Production 1948-52 average	Corn (Maize) Production 1967	Corn Imports− Exports+ 1964-67 average	Rice Production 1948-52 average	Rice Production 1967	Rice Imports− Exports+ 1964-67 average
World total	170,900	295,610	−c.51,000* / +c.51,300*	58,900	121,000	−c.7,800* / +c.8,100*	62,039	46,783	−c.1,450* / +c.1,480*	36,966	31,425	−c.590* / +c.550*	139,410	259,920	−c.24,060* / +c.24,750*	167,239	278,552	−7,234 / +7,157
Europe																		
Austria	348	1,045	−67	210	772	−239	274	336	−27	343	377	−41	120	316	−333 / +2†	—	—	−37*
Belgium	525	842	−515‡ / +213†	244	623	−381‡ / +32†‡	483	361	−77‡ / +1†‡	221	90	−28‡	3	3§	−851‡ / +90‡	—	—	−39† / +7*‡
Bulgaria	1,776	3,254	−278† / +8†	332	985	−148† / +1†	148	169	−5†	240	38	−13†	720	1,971	−68† / +144†	37	57	−39† / +26†
Czechoslovakia	1,493	2,247§	−1,156*	1,046	1,608§	−519† / +28†	961	c.760	—	1,110	c.690	−36†	316	c.423	−294* / +8†	—	—	−81† / +4†
Denmark	285	420	−18 / +42†	1,709	4,385	−394 / +217	922	928	−67 / +17	365	118	−25 / +1	—	—	−183	—	—	−6†
Finland	203	507	−62	201	681	−25†	718	840	−8	201	163	−39	—	—	−37	—	—	−14*
France	7,791	14,383	−696 / +3,170	1,534	9,725	+2,130	3,392	2,758	−5 / +50	573	362	+21 / −51†	452	3,679	−570 / +1,098	46	116	−86 / +15
Germany, East	1,243	1,521§	−1,264* / +2†	593	c.1,440	−254†	1,188	c.760	—	2,516	c.1,700	+4† / −50	5	2§	−246†	—	—	−34†
Germany, West	2,669	5,819	−1,677 / +129†	1,402	4,734	−1,445 / +34	2,523	2,719	−464 / +38	3,066	3,159	+9	20	127§	−2,322 / +195	—	—	−129 / −3†
Greece	894	1,850	−20	211	848	−33	119	c.165	—	47	c.14	—	225	331	−207	39	c.90	−3† / +3†
Hungary	1,909	2,349§	−256† / +55†	654	927	−241†	218	95	−1†	732	226	−2†	2,068	3,573	−106† / +78†	40	43	−16† / +1†
Ireland	327	185§	−249	163	666	−24	616	294	−21	4	1§	—	—	—	−116	—	—	−2†
Italy	7,170	9,564	−872 / +15	258	295	−821 / +2†	495	556	−194	123	82	−2	2,306	3,830	−4,356 / +275	723	756	−2† / +97
Netherlands	324	739	−666 / +218	201	447	−231 / +146	419	365	−110 / +102	455	239	−109 / +10	26	—	−2,000 / +49	—	—	−50 / +17*
Norway	58	4§	−369	109	493	−50	170	123	−9	2	2	−42	—	—	−98	—	—	−6†
Poland	1,833	3,934	−1,628	1,061	1,420	−332 / +66	2,238	2,802	−24†	6,374	7,691	—	24	13§	−496†	—	—	−63
Portugal	499	560	−320	96	87	−7†	124	124	—	162	204	—	421	426	−182	114	147	−21 / +2†
Romania	2,778	5,820	−201† / +89†	412	531	—	369	170§	—	177‖	71	+20†	2,495‖	6,858	+810†	35‖	56§	−33†
Spain	3,625	5,602	−74	1,909	2,632	−585	519	492	−1	482	336	−1†	520	1,178	−1,928	280	366	+78
Sweden	677	1,095	−85 / +242	231	1,677	−7 / +108†	804	1,425	−1 / +124	258	193	−61 / +9	—	—	−44	—	—	−11†
Switzerland	260	c.330	−408	55	107§	−324	68	30	−151	34	47§	−1	6	19§	−198	—	—	−22*
United Kingdom	2,397	3,898	−4,040 / +5†	2,061	9,391	−245 / +554	2,852	1,362	−24 / +2†	52	12	−6†	—	—	−3,430 / +5†	—	—	−111
U.S.S.R.	35,759¶	77,300	−6,828† / +1,846†	6,354♀	24,600	+1,367†	13,005♀	11,500	+20†	17,961♀	13,000	+94†	5,751‖	8,416§	+595†	202♀	890	−277 / +4†
Yugoslavia	2,171	4,870	−893	323	606	−33† / +25†	286	364	+1	248	171	—	3,078	7,200	−58† / +303	5	20	−32†
Asia																		
Burma	4	97§	−2†	—	—	—	—	—	—	—	—	—	30‖	61§	+16*	5,481	c.8,052	+1,123
Cambodia	—	—	...	—	—	—	—	—	—	—	—	—	57	150	+121‖ / −195§	1,635‖	2,457	+337
China	15,913‖	25,700§	−5,396† / +55†	12,360	c.16,000	−296†	1,540	c.1,900§	−88†	—	—	—	14,082	c.25,000	+207†	58,188‖	88,000§	+948
India	6,087	11,528	−6,625*	2,384	2,449	—	—	—	—	—	—	−1†	2,165	c.5,500	−116	33,383	c.60,000	−667 / +3†
Indonesia	—	—	—	—	—	—	—	—	—	—	—	—	1,535¶	2,874§	—	9,441¶	14,800	−563
Iran	c.1,879‖	c.3,800	−100§	c.767	c.1,000§	+1δ	—	—	—	—	—	—	6¶	c.15§	−2δ	424	c.925	−4† / +9†
Iraq	448	866	−117* / +1†	722	860	+101*	—	—	—	—	—	—	14	4§	—	203	309	−25
Japan	1,375	997	−3,821	2,020	1,032	−539	119	101	−14	6	1§	−41*	57	61	−3,555	12,736	18,768	−659
Korea, South	139	315§	−426*	573	1,100§	−150†	4	—	—	36	41§	−6†	14	34§	—	3,385	4,869	−37 / +19
Lebanon	51	70§	−222*	25	13§	−59† / +5†	2	2§	—	—	—	—	12	9§	−38† / −52*	1	—	−18†
Malaysia, West	—	—	−139† / +3†	—	—	—	—	—	−1†	—	—	—	6□	c.7§	+5†	532□	913§	−440 / +50*
Pakistan	3,685	4,393	−1,349	150	104	—	—	—	—	—	—	—	384	795	—	12,399	c.18,000	−109 / +150
Philippines	—	—	−390†	—	—	—	—	—	−1†	—	—	—	695	1,483	−1† / −4†	2,767	4,341	−289
Syria	761	1,060	−90† / +74*	321	599	+157*	6	2§	—	—	—	—	31	8§	+2†	13	2§	−32†
Thailand	—	—	−11†	—	—	—	—	—	−1†	—	—	—	31	c.1,000	+1,065*	6,846	9,595	+1,685
Turkey	4,770	10,940	−170	2,270	4,500	−5† / +47δ	326	510	—	500	980	+48*	747	1,000	−8†	109	250§	+1†
Vietnam, South	—	—	...	—	—	...	—	—	...	...	...	...	30¶	35§	—	2,395□	4,688	−361 / +12
Africa																		
Algeria	996	c.1,350	−340† / +4†	808	138§	+33δ	137	6§	—	1¶	—	—	6	3§	−42† / +20	—	6§	...
Kenya	101◇	128◇	+3†	8◇	14◇	—	5	1§	—	—	—	—	93◇	54§◇	−5† / +33	c.6	14§	−1†
Morocco	786	1,090	−329* / +1†	1,481	1,100	−1† / +20	51	11	+1	4	1	—	302	255	—	8	27§	+4†
South Africa	555◇	1,023◇	−271*	41◇	31§◇	−1δ / +3†	79‖	184	−12†	10‖	13	−1†	2,400◇	9,299◇	+593*	c.6	c.2▲	−59*
Tunisia	452	c.370	−195 / +49	218	c.80	−34 / +11	14	11▲	−1†	—	—	—	4+	c.4+	−8†	—	—	—
United Arab Republic	1,113	c.1,500	−1,313 / +1†	123	c.110	−2† / +1†	—	—	—	—	—	—	1,378	c.2,200	−232	971	c.2,300	+401
North and Central America																		
Canada	13,443	16,137	+12,402	4,245	5,414	+884	6,220	4,691	+198	469	334	+179	388	1,882	−567 / +7†	—	—	−43*
Mexico	534	c.2,240	−5† / +398	160	228§	−40	47	20§	−4† / +1†	—	—	—	3,090	8,161	−14 / +934	173	463	−8†
United States	31,065	41,486	−36 / +19,559⊕	5,843	8,061	−170 / +1,278	18,970	11,349	−47 / +230	524	612	−44* / +103*	74,308	119,948	−23 / +13,957⊕	1,925	4,066	−15† / +1,523
South America																		
Argentina	5,175	7,400	+4,371	656	700	+254	743	590	+281	526	352	+54	2,839	8,510	+3,553	137	217	+25†
Bolivia	37□	c.70§	−12†	39	95§	—	2	11▲	—	17	17§	—	163□	271§	—	20¶	47§	—
Brazil	498	640	−2,327	15	35§	−35† / +1†	9	23§	−12	17	15§	—	5,841	12,401	−1† / +311†	2,921	6,555	+142
Chile	928	c.1,174	−318*	79	140§	+1†	80	123§	+2†	5	15§	—	68	c.250	−6†	75	71§	−16†
Colombia	124	c.125	−194*	50	c.115	—	—	—	−6†	—	—	—	733	940§	−10† / +1†	248	700	—
Peru	146	c.140	−452	208	c.180	−16 / −2†	2	c.9§	−6†	—	—	—	275	c.550§	−10† / +1†	191	458	−47
Uruguay	469	329§	−2† / +41†	23	c.30	−2† / +1†	44	72§	−6†	—	—	−11*	141	c.117	−30†	41	116§	+29*
Venezuela	5¶	1§	−543*	—	—	—	—	—	—	—	—	—	303	630	−102†	41	210§	−1†
Oceania																		
Australia	5,161	7,548	+6,302	531	794	+363	560	733	+339	12	16§	—	126	175	—	63	182§	+78
New Zealand	139	322	−133	49	124	—	49	35	—	2‖	1▲	—	10	19§	—	—	—	−4†

Note: (—) indicates quantity nil or negligible; (. . .) indicates quantity not known; (c.) indicates provisional or estimated.

*1964-66 average. †1964-65 average. ‡Belgium-Luxembourg economic union. §1966. ‖Average of 4 years. ¶Average of 3 years. ♀1950. δ1963-64 average. □Average of 2 years. ◇Farms and estates only. ▲1965. +Incl. sorghum. ⊕Incl. foreign aid shipments.

Sources: FAO Production Yearbook 1967; FAO Trade Yearbook 1966; FAO Monthly Bulletin of Agricultural Economics and Statistics.

(M.C. Mac D.)

production units, supplement farming with other occupations, or enter new fields. Sweden's 1968 wheat crop was one-fourth smaller than the unusually large 1967 harvest.

Spanish farmers continued to divert land from cotton; about 300,000 ac. were planted, compared with 355,000 in 1967–68 and an average 680,000 ac. for 1960–64. The harvest of 260,000 bales was the smallest since 1958–59. Little change in citrus production was anticipated, and wheat, at 206 million bu., was about the same as the large crop of 1967. Large acreage and favourable weather resulted in a record almond crop of 52,000 tons (kernel basis), 73% more than in 1967. Export equalization fees on almonds and filberts were eliminated in the first half of 1968. Portugal began its third development plan (1968–73), in which nearly 12% of the funds, or about $511 million, were allocated to agriculture; this was 8% more than in the second plan. Nearly 25% of the agricultural funds would go to developing livestock and forage. Irrigation was to be increased, particularly in the Alentejo area southeast of Lisbon.

Switzerland, which imported about 1 million tons of feed grains, increased subsidies paid to growers for diverting land from dairy production; a premium rate was paid for land over 3,250 ft. in elevation. The so-called chicken war was resumed in April when the U.S. Department of Agriculture announced subsidies on chicken exported to Switzerland. Austria, which had dairy surplus problems, enacted measures aimed at discouraging factory output of milk products and subsidizing dairy product exports. Guaranteed prices to producers were reduced 3% for wheat and increased $2\frac{1}{2}$% for rye as an incentive for farmers to grow more rye and feed grains in 1968–69. Greece was probably taken out of the wheat export market when drought reduced the 1968 crop to about 56 million bu., compared with 68 million bu. in 1967. Cotton production of 450,000 bales equaled the record of 1961; 1967–68 exports of 304,000 bales were the largest on record. As part of an effort to stop the drift of farmers to the cities, farmers' debts amounting to about 20 million drachmas, mostly owed to the Agricultural Bank, were canceled.

AFRICA

Africa's agriculture recorded a significant rise in 1967 over the previous year; food production overall increased 6.2% over 1966 and per capita output went up as much as 3.7%. Good weather in northwest Africa resulted in improved crops of wheat and barley, and in South Africa record crops of corn and sorghum were harvested. Coffee output increased, mainly because of a recovery of production in Ivory Coast. Drought reduced some crops in East Africa, and the U.A.R. suffered insect damage. Efforts to expand agricultural production were continued by nearly all governments, but shortages of capital and technology, as well as environmental and social diversities, continued to delay development.

North Africa. Agriculture throughout most of North Africa performed in a rewarding fashion in 1967–68, and prospects were for a continuation of high productivity in 1968–69. Algeria's production of an estimated 1.9 million tons of cereal grains was double the 874,000 tons of a year earlier; the index of total agricultural production rose 20%, from 79 in 1966 to 96 in 1967 (1957–59 = 100). The wheat harvest was 1,350,000 tons, compared with 722,000 tons in 1966; the barley crop, at 500,000 tons, was

COURTESY, "FOREIGN AGRICULTURE"

Men working at the edge of an irrigated grove of young banana trees in the Ivory Coast. Production of bananas, one of the country's major exports, was expected to climb as the new groves began producing.

far in excess of 1966 output of 136,000 tons; and other cereal production was well above 1966 levels.

Tunisia's 1967 output fell below average as drought reduced grain crops; citrus production dropped 30% to 77,000 tons and wine production fell 36%. Production of olive oil was more than double the 1966 level of 20,000 tons but still below normal. Wheat production, at 330,000 tons, was 5% below a year earlier, and imports of cereals totaled over 350,000 tons. With favourable weather, the outlook was for an average wheat crop in 1968, on the order of 450,000 tons, and a larger olive crop than in 1967 appeared likely. After several years of poor agricultural production, Tunisia decided to give high priority to agriculture in its next four-year plan, scheduled to begin in 1969.

With recovered wheat production and an excellent rice crop, Morocco's agricultural output rose above the 1967 index to 112. Estimated cereal production for 1968 showed a further improvement, and it was expected that the need for imports would be reduced. King Hassan II announced plans to increase irrigated acreage from the current 370,000 to 2,470,000. A new five-year plan (1968–72), announced in March, called for an investment of $1 billion, about half of which would be spent on agriculture and dam building.

The agricultural production index in the U.A.R. in 1967 was unchanged at 114, and population growth lowered per capita output from 92 to 90. Grain production in 1967 was estimated at almost 7 million tons, and the government imported over 2 million tons to meet domestic demand. It was expected that large imports would be needed again in 1968–69. The cotton crop was a disappointing 435,000 tons or less, the smallest since 1961 and about 5% below 1966; 80 to 85% was shipped by June 1967 and the remainder was committed. The cotton crop was again attacked by the cotton leafworm and pink boll weevils, and thousands of boys and girls went into the fields to pick them off the plants. In March, Pres. Gamal Abd-al-Nasser arranged for a squadron of Polish aviators to spray the crops.

Agricultural production in the Sudan rose 11% in 1967–68. The important cotton crop was only 2,000 tons above 1966–67, but sorghum grain output dou-

bled and wheat and millet were both up. Per capita food production rose from 111 in 1966 to 120 in 1967.

West Africa. Moderate overall gains were shown for agriculture in West Africa in 1967–68. Production of cocoa for the area as a whole was little changed from a year earlier, but the crop in Ghana, the leading cocoa bean producer, rose 12% to an estimated 430,-000 tons. Ghana increased its output of staples; the index of agricultural production rose 9 points to 125 (1957–59 = 100) and the per capita index rose six points to 110. A 4% increase in production was registered in Cameroon. The 1967 cocoa crop, at 91,100 tons, was up by 5,000 tons, coffee production rose 10% to 66,000 tons, and most food crops showed increases. Ivory Coast production of 4 million bags of coffee (240,000 tons) was nearly twice the size of the 1966 crop, and cocoa beans were estimated at 146,600 tons, the third largest crop on record. Diversification efforts continued: cotton production rose to 22,000 tons in 1966–67 from 9,921 tons a year earlier, and progress was reported in the planting of oil and coconut palms in two large projects.

Senegal's 1967–68 peanut production was estimated at about 15% above the drought-reduced crop in 1966–67 but far below early estimates of a 1.4 million-ton crop. Poor weather and unofficial sales over the Gambian border were blamed. Marketings of more than 840,000 tons were reported, compared with 730,-000 tons a year earlier. With the ending of the French guaranteed price of U.S. $200 per ton, prices fell to $155 per ton, c.i.f., Europe. Nigeria, in the throes of civil war, experienced some reductions in agricultural production; the index of total output fell 8% and the per capita index fell from 104 to 93. The 1967–68 cocoa crop, grown mostly in Western and Mid-West Nigeria, was estimated at 236,000 tons, 14% smaller than a year earlier. The 1967–68 cotton crop, estimated at 125,000 bales (480 lb. net), was the smallest since 1952–53. Production of major food crops was generally adequate, though extremely severe shortages and famine developed in areas where fighting occurred.

World production of cocoa in 1968–69 was estimated by the FAO Cocoa Study Group at 1,287,000 metric tons, 4% less than revised estimates for the preceding year's crop and, for the fourth successive year, more than 300,000 tons below the record crop of 1964–65. The reduction was attributed to a sharp fall in West African production caused by extremely heavy rains and black pod disease. Ghana's production was reduced to 405,000 tons and Nigeria's to 224,000 tons, although newly planted trees coming into production in Cameroon raised that country's output to 95,-000 tons. An estimated 240,200 tons came from South America. Consumption in calendar 1969 was forecast at 1,367,000 metric tons, a 6,000-ton decrease from the 1968 estimate. The imbalance between production and consumption was made up by stocks from the 1964–65 crop. The outlook for a poor 1968–69 African crop, coupled with the probability of a considerably smaller Brazilian crop, made it likely that the tight demand-supply situation would continue through 1969.

The UN Conference on Trade and Development (UNCTAD) Cocoa Conference, which met at Geneva in late 1967, had adjourned without arriving at an international cocoa agreement. Discussions were resumed in mid-June 1968, but again the conference ended without reaching full agreement. At issue were technical differences between consuming and producing countries on estimates of demand as a basis for annual sales quotas, and some other unsolved problems including the sales quota mechanism.

East Africa. Generally favourable weather and the implementation of development plans raised overall agricultural output to new levels throughout much of East Africa in 1967. The index of total agricultural production in Ethiopia rose from 116 in 1966 to 125 in 1967 (1957–59 = 100) as a result of good crops of grains, sugar, teff, sorghum, and millet. Kenya's agriculture recorded moderate improvement; a 7% increase in the corn crop reflected expanded acreage and wider use of improved seed. In Tanzania production was set back 3 to 4% by unfavourable weather. Locusts in crop-destroying concentrations swarmed over East Africa in 1968; damage was heaviest in Ethiopia, and an active antilocust campaign was mounted, with the aid of the FAO, the U.S., and the U.S.S.R. In October it was reported that the infestation had spread all the way across Africa to Mauritania.

The 1967–68 East African cotton crop, estimated at 675,000 bales (480 lb. net), was 8% below the record 735,000 bales produced a year earlier but far ahead of the 1960–64 average. Tanzanian production fell to 300,000 bales from 360,000 in 1966–67 as a result of heavy rains and insect attacks; Kenya's production

Table VI. Poultry Meat Production in Selected Countries*

In 000,000 lb.

Country	1967†	1966	1965	Average 1955–59
Belgium-Luxembourg	232	217	207	95
France	1,058	1,076	1,035	511
Germany, West	450	388	332	172
Italy	783	769	811	215
Netherlands	437	389	332	96
Total EEC	2,960	2,839	2,720	1,089
Austria	74	73	63	4
Canada	818	790	697	428
Denmark	146	149	146	58
Greece	97	79	74	36
Japan	463	411	350	...
Poland	251	229	196	109
Switzerland	32	30	27	7
United Kingdom	1,019	950	898	455
United States	9,418	8,994	8,170	5,480

*On ready-to-cook basis (70% of live weight).
†Preliminary.
Source: U.S. Department of Agriculture, Foreign Agricultural Service.

Table VII. Egg Production in Specified Countries

In 000,000

Country	1967*	1966	1965
Argentina	2,640	2,520	2,880
Australia†	2,554	2,328	2,676
Belgium-Luxembourg	3,083	2,932	2,888
Brazil	9,036	8,604	8,119
Canada	5,306	5,002	5,194
Czechoslovakia	3,113	3,080	3,007
France	10,000	9,700	9,220
Germany, East	3,968	3,894	3,935
Germany, West	13,802	12,901	11,194
Hungary	2,630	2,436	2,393
Italy	11,000	10,570	9,990
Japan	21,746	18,756	18,625
Mexico	5,356	5,200	5,000
Netherlands	3,655	4,144	4,213
Poland	6,300	6,253	6,264
Romania	2,900	2,814	2,630
U.S.S.R.	33,700	31,700	29,000
United Kingdom‡	14,736	14,760	14,520
United States	70,161	66,484	65,692

*Preliminary.
†Year ending June 30 of year shown.
‡Excludes Northern Ireland production consumed locally; year ending May 31.
Source: U.S. Department of Agriculture, Foreign Agricultural Service.

Table VIII. Milk Cows and Milk Production in Specified Countries

	Number of milk cows in 000			Milk production in 000,000 lb.		
Country	1967*	1966	Average 1961–65	1967*	1966	Average 1961–65
Australia	3,060	3,094	3,190	16,157	16,172	15,244
Austria	1,109	1,103	1,122	7,341	7,090	6,743
Belgium	1,026	1,016	1,024	8,934	8,823	8,664
Canada	2,668	2,674	2,930	18,304	18,380	18,404
Denmark	1,328	1,350	1,428	11,499	11,704	11,713
Finland	1,041	1,078	1,171	7,847	8,133	8,207
France	8,572	8,458	9,409	57,775	55,422	54,162
Germany, West	5,858	5,854	5,852	47,872	47,084	45,368
Greece	493	450	434	1,353	1,325	1,159
Ireland	1,568	1,582	1,373	7,614	7,125	6,458
Italy	3,500	3,420	3,448	23,046	22,826	21,872
Netherlands	1,783	1,764	1,701	16,634	15,952	15,597
New Zealand	2,141	2,088	2,007	13,930	13,680	12,302
Norway	478	503	568	3,820	3,763	3,666
Sweden	877	954	1,180	7,352	7,813	8,446
Switzerland	928	917	926	7,202	6,951	6,837
United Kingdom	4,364	4,269	4,203	25,779	24,900	24,791
United States	13,524	14,093	16,195	119,294	119,892	125,660

*Preliminary.
Source: U.S. Department of Agriculture, Foreign Agricultural Service.

Workers in Northern
Nigeria stacking sacks
of peanuts into large
pyramid-shaped piles
for storage.

of 25,000 bales was about equal to a year earlier; and the Ugandan crop was no more than 300,000 bales, compared with 350,000 a year earlier. Exports from the three countries were estimated at 600,000 bales.

After two years of shortages, grain production in Ethiopia increased significantly in 1967; production of teff, sorghum, and millet rose 16% above 1966, and barley, corn, and wheat were up about 15%. Coffee production declined slightly, but raw sugar rose 5,000 tons to 85,000. Corn production in Kenya was estimated at 1,750,000 tons in 1967, and the wheat crop, at 205,000 tons, was far above the 1960–62 average of 125,000 tons. Kenya's 1967–68 coffee crop of 700,000 bags reflected losses suffered from fungus attack, but early forecasts were for an improved crop of 935,000 bags in 1968–69. Tanzania produced an estimated 700,000 tons of corn, compared with 750,-000 in 1966 and an average of 508,000 in 1960–62. Sorghum and millet production rose slightly, to 1,145,-000 tons. Output of sisal, at 220,000 tons, was somewhat below 1966. Zanzibar's clove production, in an "off year," was 4,000 tons, compared with 15,000 tons in 1966. Total agricultural production in Uganda increased a moderate 3% in 1967. Production of coffee, estimated at 153,000 tons, was 12,000 tons above a year earlier and a large crop was forecast for 1968–69. Sugar production was reported to have reached an all-time high.

Total world production of the major hard fibres (sisal, abaca, and henequen) in 1967 was estimated at 1,941,000,000 lb., 5% below a year earlier. Reduction in sisal to 1,391,700,000 lb. accounted for more than half of the decline; of the major producers, only Tanzania and Brazil remained above 1960–64 levels. Production of an estimated 208.5 million lb. of abaca or "manila hemp" was 13% below a year earlier, and henequen production, at an estimated 341.1 million lb., was slightly below the 345 million lb. of 1966. The decline reflected lower world prices and increasing competition from synthetics. An FAO study group in September 1967 had suggested regulation of exports and prices of hard fibres through an informal agreement, but this appeared to be unsuccessful. Prices in 1968 continued at the lowest levels since the 1930s, and import demand remained extremely weak.

Central and Southern Africa. With minor exceptions, agriculture in this region was more productive in 1967 than a year earlier; modest offsetting changes among most countries were eclipsed by unprecedented output in South Africa.

Total agricultural output in the Congo (Kinshasa) was reduced slightly below 1966 levels, the result of disturbances in the eastern part of the country that caused many European plantation owners to leave. An estimated 9,000 tons of cotton represented an improvement over the previous year, but was far short of the preindependence level. Sugar production rose nearly a third, to 45,000 tons.

After several years of growth, Cameroon's agriculture in 1966–67 was set back somewhat by unfavourable weather. Sales of cocoa rose from 73,000 tons in 1966 to 80,000 tons in 1967, despite a slight decline in production. The Price Stabilization Board ended the 1967 season with a positive balance of $6 million. The Portuguese government's plan to turn Angola's highland plateau into an important meat-producing area continued, in conjunction with the joint Portuguese-South African hydroelectric and irrigation scheme on the Cune River.

In Rhodesia the effects of the tobacco embargo were compounded in early 1968 by a severe drought, which also took a heavy toll of corn and other crops. In an effort to reduce dependence on tobacco and sugar, the government sought to raise output of beef, wheat, corn, and cotton. Tobacco production for 1968 was estimated at 66,000 tons, compared with 90,000 in 1967 and 113,000 in 1966, and the number of tobacco growers had reportedly fallen to 1,700 from 3,000. Sugar production in 1967 declined more than 50%, exports were down, and a large stockpile remained on hand. Prospects for 1968 crops, particularly corn and tobacco, were poor.

The outlook for Malawi in 1968 was fair; rains in January and February partly compensated for an earlier dry period. The 1967 tea crop was a record 37.1 million lb., 9% higher than in 1966. Expansion of the cashew nut industry in Mozambique was expected to double revenues within a few years; the 1966 crop of 140,000 tons represented 52% of world production. The Malagasy Republic, which accounted for 65% of the world's supply of vanilla, produced 1,500 tons in 1967, compared with 1,050 tons in 1966.

Record production of several crops raised the index of total agricultural output in South Africa to 154 (1957–59 = 100) in 1967 from 123 a year earlier. The minister of finance announced the 26% increase, which compared with an average 2.1% increase in the previous five years. Corn production rose 94% to 9.9 million tons, and sorghum (kaffir corn) rose 177% to 932,000 tons. Wheat production of an estimated 1,270,000 metric tons was large enough to exceed domestic consumption for the first time. Sugar production for the 1966–67 season was a record 1,794,100 tons. The increase resulted from extremely favourable weather, larger acreages, and wider use of fertilizer and hybrid seed. The 1968 crop was expected to show a decline from these record levels as drought in April was reported over large areas; however, this reduced production would be offset by surpluses from the 1967 crop.

EASTERN EUROPE AND THE U.S.S.R.

Eastern Europe. Diversity in the condition of agriculture again prevailed in 1968. Following the rather good year of 1967, in which net agricultural output

fell only moderately below the record growth rates of 1966, weather again was unfavourable. Spring drought, centring in the southern part of Eastern Europe, was reported as the worst in 50 years, resulting in decreased wheat and rye production, smaller crops of corn and sunflower seed, and poor pasture conditions that probably would bring some reduction in milk, meat, and eggs. On the other hand, prospects appeared favourable for root crops. Sugar beets and potatoes, grown principally in Czechoslovakia, Poland, and East Germany, were expected to hold at the high levels of 1967.

The total wheat crop for Eastern Europe was indicated at 849 million bu., against 922 million bu. in 1967. Rye production, at 417 million bu., was down from 430 million bu. in 1967. The southern countries—Bulgaria, Hungary, Romania, and Yugoslavia—all had larger numbers of livestock at the beginning of 1968 than a year earlier. Continued gains in meat and milk output were forecast for Poland, Czechoslovakia, and East Germany, and imports of feed grains were expected to remain at 1967 levels.

Several of the Eastern European countries gave increased attention to planning, organizing, and managing agricultural production. In Bulgaria, major decisions defined the territorial specialization of farms and introduced a five-year contract for state purchase of commodities. District associations were formed in Czechoslovakia to integrate the production and purchasing functions of agriculture and small ancillary industries. Management reforms were extended further in East Germany, and thousands of workers were given specialized training. Land reclamation and soil improvement continued to have priority in agricultural investment. In Hungary, higher product prices for agricultural products, fuller integration of agriculture into the industrial system, more competition between farms, and further limitation on the privilege of cultivating household plots were among the changes in 1968. Farm incomes, disproportionately low for many years because the collective farm system discouraged productivity, were reported to have risen 20% after permission was granted to market vegetables and poultry privately. Policy in Poland continued to focus on the 1966–70 plan, which called for a 17% rise in crop production and an 11% rise in livestock output. Investment in mechanization, land reclamation, fertilization, and the livestock sector were being increased in Romania.

A major upward shift in Yugoslavia's farm prices, intended to stimulate farm output in the large private sector as well as to generate investment capital in both the private and the collective sectors, was to a degree frustrated by unfavourable weather. Market surpluses of sugar, tobacco, wool, and hides did develop, however. Efforts to increase hard currency earnings were reported to have led to a direct confrontation with the EEC as concessions were sought in the Community market. As of mid-1968, exports of farm products (mainly corn) were reported to be off by 35% and exports of livestock by 28%, the latter reportedly as a result of the high EEC variable levies, which particularly affected sales in Italy. Farm production in 1968 was expected to be down as much as 10%. The important corn crop suffered more severely, and the late forecast of 6.2 million tons was about 1 million tons below earlier expectations. A prospective bumper wheat crop was reduced to a good one of 4.2 million tons.

U.S.S.R. With reports of good if not excellent major crops in important areas in 1968, it appeared that the U.S.S.R. would not need to increase wheat imports above the 1.5 million tons of 1967–68. The area sown to grains was 1.4 million ha. larger than in 1967, and the preliminary estimate was a near record 167 million tons. A dry fall in 1967 lowered winter wheat production below the previous year, but conditions at mid-1968 suggested that the spring wheat crop might be larger.

The U.S.S.R. produced 472.4 million bu. of rye in 1967, more than one-third of the world crop; another one-third was produced in Eastern Europe. The 1968 Soviet crop was 416.5 million bu. Rice production continued to expand; the 1967 crop was estimated at

Table IX. Cattle and Buffalo Numbers in Major Producing Areas

In 000

Area	Estimated 1968	1967	Average 1961–65
North America	158,700	158,500	149,400
Canada	11,775	11,749	11,257
Mexico	23,627	...	20,396
United States	108,813	108,645	103,892
South America	190,600	187,700	168,200
Argentina	...	...	42,983
Brazil	91,093	90,244	78,715
Colombia	18,830	17,932	15,780
Venezuela	6,911	6,822	6,510
Western Europe	87,400	87,400	83,400
France	21,417	21,184	20,020
Germany, West	13,981	13,973	13,115
Italy	9,750	9,700	9,292
United Kingdom	12,018	12,171	11,610
Eastern Europe	36,000	35,200	33,000
Poland	...	10,768	9,697
Yugoslavia	...	5,770	5,506
U.S.S.R.	97,100	97,100	83,500
Africa	134,000	133,500	127,400
South Africa	12,145	11,920	12,514
Tanzania	...	...	8,550
Asia	422,400	418,800	395,500
Iran	5,750	5,640	4,782
Japan	3,050	2,928	3,327
Philippines	5,805	5,620	4,849
Turkey	15,175	15,022	13,783
Oceania	27,000	26,300	25,300
Australia	18,500	18,250	18,357
New Zealand	8,200	7,767	6,648
World total*	1,153,200	1,144,500	1,065,500

*Includes allowance for any missing data for countries shown and for other producing countries not shown.
Source: U.S. Department of Agriculture.

Table X. Hog Numbers in Major Producing Areas

In 000

Area	Estimated 1968	1967	Average 1961–65
North America	77,400	76,000	76,600
Canada	6,058	5,783	5,211
Mexico	9,978	...	9,438
United States	54,263	53,249	55,544
South America	77,900	76,500	66,700
Argentina	...	...	3,388
Brazil	63,000	61,728	53,126
Western Europe	75,000	70,400	66,700
Denmark	8,061	8,081	7,284
France	9,746	9,239	8,908
Germany, West	19,032	17,682	16,930
Italy	5,000	5,370	4,787
Spain	6,700	5,858	5,870
United Kingdom	7,636	7,284	7,099
Eastern Europe	49,500	48,900	46,800
Germany, East	...	9,312	8,654
Hungary	...	...	6,216
Poland	...	14,233	12,880
Yugoslavia	...	5,525	5,815
U.S.S.R.	51,000	58,000	57,800
Africa	5,500	5,500	5,200
South Africa	1,290	1,272	...
Asia	171,800	160,600	122,400
Japan	5,400	5,975	3,474
Philippines	11,500	11,200	9,236
Taiwan	...	3,110	2,917
Oceania	2,800	2,700	2,500
Australia	1,950	1,813	1,567
World total*	510,900	498,600	444,700

*Includes allowance for any missing data for countries shown and for other producing countries not shown.
Source: U.S. Department of Agriculture, Foreign Agricultural Service.

Table XI. Sheep Numbers in Major Producing Areas

In 000

Area	Estimated 1968	1967	Average 1961–65
North America	30,900	32,700	37,500
Canada	653	682	920
Mexico	6,705	...	6,259
United States	22,122	23,898	29,023
South America	124,800	125,000	122,200
Argentina	...	48,000	48,127
Brazil	22,000	22,102	19,997
Peru	...	15,600	14,454
Uruguay	...	21,400	21,860
Western Europe	75,700	76,500	80,100
France	9,248	9,186	8,876
Greece	8,200	9,117	9,458
Italy	8,576	8,150	7,956
Spain	16,610	16,671	20,574
United Kingdom	20,446	21,053	20,689
Eastern Europe	45,400	45,300	42,800
Bulgaria	...	9,998	10,070
Romania	14,369	14,109	12,217
Yugoslavia	10,345	10,329	10,232
U.S.S.R.	138,300	135,500	133,900
Africa	129,400	129,000	128,400
Morocco	...	12,000	14,710
South Africa	42,172	41,755	39,759
Asia	237,300	234,000	218,600
Iran	22,000	21,500	21,445
Turkey	35,000	34,663	32,863
Oceania	226,000	224,500	211,500
Australia	165,000	164,407	160,924
New Zealand	...	60,100	50,536
World total*	1,007,800	1,002,500	975,000

*Includes allowance for any missing data for countries shown and for other producing countries not shown.
Source: U.S. Department of Agriculture, Foreign Agricultural Service.

780,000 tons, up 22% from the previous year. Sugar-beet plantings were off 5% from 1967, but early indications were that the 1968 crop might equal the 86.9 million tons of 1967. Area sown to sunflower was slightly smaller than in 1967, when 6.1 million tons were produced. Despite weather trouble, the cotton crop was expected to approximate the 1967 level of 6 million tons (unginned).

Cattle numbers on Jan. 1, 1968, stood at 97 million head, the same as a year earlier, but hog numbers declined 12%, from 58 million to 51 million. Sheep and goat numbers totaled 144 million, compared with 141 million in 1967. The 1967 output of meat, milk, and eggs increased 5.7, 4.6, and 6.3%, respectively. Exports of most major agricultural commodities rose in 1967—wool was the main exception. Exports of wheat (mostly to Eastern European countries) and sunflower seed oil (mostly to Western Europe) were nearly doubled.

As in 1967, efforts to carry economic reforms to the countryside were being continued. The budget for 1968 reportedly anticipated an investment in agriculture of 12.4 billion rubles, an increase of perhaps 7.6% over 1967.

MIDDLE EAST AND INDIA

Middle East. Swarms of locusts in crop-destroying concentrations appeared in most of the area, with the most serious infestations in Saudi Arabia and southern Iran. By mid-1968 it was apparent that the crop year would not provide the bonanzas of 1967. With more acreage in wheat, Turkey reported a harvest of 316 million bu., compared with 330.7 million bu. in 1967. The 1967–68 cotton crop was a record 1.8 million bales and exports were about 1.1 million bales. The 1968–69 acreage was reported to be slightly smaller, but higher yields resulted in another 1.8 million-bale crop. With stocks building up, the Turkish Tobacco Monopoly moved to cut back production.

The value of agricultural output in Israel had increased sixfold in 20 years, to $480 million in 1967. Near self-sufficiency had been reached in citrus and

Indian merchant measuring out a portion of wheat flour. Although India harvested a record grain crop in 1967–68, lack of storage facilities slowed the movement of grain from farmer to consumer.

COURTESY, "FOREIGN AGRICULTURE"

other fruits, vegetables, milk, eggs, and poultry, but the country was still far short of supplying its needs for feed grains, food grains, and fats and oils. The 1968 wheat crop was only 6.2 million bu., against 8.1 million bu. a year earlier. Citrus exports in 1968–69 were forecast at 21 million cases, up from 19.5 million in the preceding season. A new dryland wheat was announced in Lebanon as a first step toward doubling wheat production in the Middle East. In Syria the Ministry of Agriculture and the Ministry of Agrarian Reform, which since 1958 had distributed land to some 20,000 families, were merged.

The Iranian Agricultural Ministry was divided into three parts, relating to production, irrigation, and marketing. The World Bank approved a $22 million loan to assist the development of water resources and agriculture in the Ghazain Plain, some 90 mi. W of Teheran. Cotton production totaled about 528,000 bales, up from 519,000 in 1966–67, and exports were around 325,000 bales, 290,000 higher than in the previous year. The wheat crop was a large one of 161.7 million bu., compared with 147 million bu. in 1967; barley, rice, and pulse crops were also larger.

Pakistan. Pakistan overhauled its third five-year plan to emphasize agriculture, which accounted for nearly half of the gross national product and most of the foreign exchange earnings. Particular attention was given to fertilizers, irrigation, drainage, better seeds, and the movement toward self-sufficiency in food grains by 1970.

The weather remained favourable in 1968. The wheat crop, at 233.6 million bu., was considerably above the 161.4 million bu. of 1967. The supply of grain available in 1967–68 was indicated at 23 million tons, of which wheat imports accounted for 2.2 million tons. The record large 1967–68 wheat crop resulted in part from the rapid adoption of new high-yielding varieties. A 21% increase in acreage, additional inputs of fertilizers, and favourable weather resulted in a cotton crop of 2,305,000 bales in 1967–68, compared with 2.1 million bales a year earlier. The 1968 crop was 2.4 million bales. Exports totaled 420,000 bales in the first seven months of the 1967–68 season, compared with 192,000 bales in the corresponding period of 1966–67. Inadequate rains during May, which delayed the planting of jute, were followed by severe monsoon rains and floods, and the jute and kenaf crops in India and Pakistan were perhaps 1 million bales below the 7.6 bales of a year earlier. The 1968 tea crop, forecast at 62 million lb., was moderately smaller than in 1967 and 1966.

India. Agricultural recovery highlighted the year. The wheat crop of 1967–68 was an outstanding 624.6 million bu., compared with 423.6 million bu. in 1966–67. Some 8 million ac. were planted to the new high-yielding Mexican wheats, compared with 3.5 million ac. the previous year—a development that was described as a "wheat revolution." The 1967–68 rice crop was indicated at a record 61.5 million tons, compared with a crop of only 45.7 million tons in 1966–67.

Drought in some areas and floods in others after mid-1968 aroused old fears and reduced the autumn rice harvest by perhaps 5%; prices rose, and there was clamour for release of government stocks. The Food Ministry, with stocks of about 4 million tons and storage space for about 6 million tons, appeared to have control over market prices. Also, the very abundance of the crop discouraged hoarding and caused some producers to dump their grain at the minimum support

price offered by government buying agencies. Deficiencies in India's transportation and grain storage system, long recognized, became acute with the record harvest. The Army was ordered to help protect grain from water and rodent damage. A major battle against locusts was won for the time being, with antilocust teams using planes, ground vehicles, and hand sprayers. Cereal imports in 1968–69 were indicated at about 6.5 million tons, of which 3.5 million tons were already contracted for with the U.S. Imports of grains had declined from about 10.2 million tons in 1966 to about 8.9 million tons in 1967; wheat imports fell from 7.8 million tons to 6.4 million.

After four difficult years, the vegetable oils situation improved considerably in 1967–68. The total harvest of all major oilseeds was a near-record 11.2 million tons, compared with 9.2 million tons in the previous year. Per capita availability of edible oils rose to 12 lb. from 10.7 lb. in 1966–67, but because of population increases it was below the 12.9 lb. per person available in 1964–65. Production of jute and mesta in 1967–68, at 7.6 million bales, was 16.6% above 1966–67. The 1967–68 cotton crop was 5.2 million bales, compared with 5.3 million bales a year earlier. Preliminary 1968–69 indications were for a crop approximating that of the previous year. Sugarcane acreage was estimated to be down 8.8%, reflecting the greater profitability of grains. Domestic consumption utilized about half the 1967 tea output of 841.3 million lb.; the 1968 crop was forecast at a new record 865 million lb. Exports of 213,700 tons in 1967 were higher than in any of the preceding two years. Black pepper exports during the first four months of 1968 totaled 31.5 million lb., up 61%.

After standing on the brink of famine in 1966–67, India had come far enough to speak of self-sufficiency at the "earliest possible moment." The budget for agricultural development was reported to be up 42% from the previous year, and the equivalent of 20% of India's foreign exchange earnings were being used to import fertilizers and fertilizer materials. Something over $1 billion would be spent on planned fertilizer imports in the next three years. In May 1968 a new five-year plan was announced, designed to raise agricultural production by 5% per year.

FAR EAST

Early indications were for a comparatively good agricultural year in 1968. Production in 1967 was about 11% above that of 1966.

Though few firm data on Communist China were available, scattered reports in the earlier part of the year mentioned drought, a fertilizer shortage, disruptive internal strife, and floods. Later items, however, suggested that 1968 was a good crop year. In 1967 production of wheat, rice, and other grains probably reached about 200 million tons, the highest output since 1958. Weather appeared to have been moderately favourable. Imports of wheat, at 4 million tons, were the lowest in over six years, while rice exports were estimated at about 1 million tons, 13% less than in the previous year. A missing but major factor in any appraisal of probable production in 1968 was the unknown degree to which the Cultural Revolution had penetrated and disrupted the countryside.

Taiwan's agricultural production in 1967 was about 10% higher than in 1966, and early indications were that 1968 was again favourable. Rice accounted for

Table XII. Sugar Production of the Principal Producing Countries
In 000 short tons, raw value

Country	Forecast 1968–69	1967–68	Average 1960–61 to 1964–65	Average 1936–40
Argentina	1,005	855	950	510
Australia	2,857	2,556	1,806	...
Brazil	5,076	4,922	3,815	830
China, Communist	2,200	2,000	1,026	100
Colombia	818	743	421	...
Cuba	6,000	5,500	5,596	3,183
Czechoslovakia	1,000	1,000	1,160	715
Denmark	359	363	341	...
Dominican Republic	850	730	852	490
France	2,576	1,904	2,309	1,078
Germany, East	825	820	869	979
Germany, West	2,193	2,271	1,980	610
India	4,089	3,083	3,694	1,303
Indonesia	750	716	708	1,206
Iran	593	508	185	...
Italy	1,362	1,805	1,082	414
Jamaica	504	530	524	...
Mauritius	690	700	559	320
Mexico	2,576	2,542	1,899	359
Netherlands	761	829	620	...
Peru	716	827	878	444
Philippines	1,821	1,745	1,704	1,058
Poland	1,850	2,100	1,693	990
South Africa	1,800	2,009	1,233	...
Spain	730	690	560	...
Taiwan	1,000	950	991	1,240
Turkey	719	872	639	...
United Kingdom	1,103	1,075	988	...
U.S.S.R.	11,300	11,500	7,623	2,761
United States	6,210	5,381	4,830	1,991*
U.S. dependencies†	800	645	1,011	...
Yugoslavia	420	540	323	...
World total	76,414	73,126	60,914	...

*Excluding Hawaii.
†Puerto Rico and Virgin Islands of the U.S.
Source: U.S. Department of Agriculture, Foreign Agricultural Service.

Table XIII. Coffee Production (Green) in Principal Producing Countries
In 000 bags, 132.3 lb. each

Country	1968–69*	1967–68	1966–67	Average 1960–61 to 1964–65
Angola	3,300	3,200	3,300	2,910
Brazil	18,500	23,000	20,000	25,840
Cameroon	1,030	1,100	1,000	801
Colombia	7,700	7,900	7,600	7,760
Congo (Kinshasa)	850	900	900	990
Costa Rica	1,300	1,280	1,215	1,056
Ecuador	1,100	1,175	975	696
El Salvador	2,000	2,300	1,960	1,812
Ethiopia	2,045	1,750	1,750	1,490
Guatemala	1,750	1,800	1,670	1,704
India	1,435	1,260	1,395	1,045
Indonesia	2,150	2,500	1,850	2,016
Ivory Coast	3,500	4,300	2,200	3,185
Kenya	935	700	935	624
Malagasy Republic	925	925	900	923
Mexico	2,900	2,800	2,650	2,431
Peru	900	860	900	700
Philippines	735	725	740	631
Tanzania	900	740	990	497
Uganda	2,850	2,475	2,450	2,429
Venezuela	750	750	725	821
World total	62,640	67,777	60,642	65,284

*First estimate.
Source: U.S. Department of Agriculture, Foreign Agricultural Service.

Table XIV. World Cocoa Production in Leading Areas*
In 000 metric tons

Area	Forecast 1968–69	1967–68	1966–67	Average 1960–61 to 1964–65
North and Central America	84.0	75.2	73.2	84.8
Dominican Republic	33.0	29.0	28.5	35.4
Mexico	22.0	21.0	20.5	20.3
South America	240.2	250.3	267.3	195.6
Brazil	141.0	144.7	173.3	118.1
Ecuador	50.0	60.0	53.0	41.3
Venezuela	24.7	24.1	21.0	16.7
Africa	848.6	971.6	965.0	929.2
Ghana	405.0	430.0	381.4	458.4
Nigeria	224.0	236.0	267.3	217.8
Ivory Coast	140.0	146.6	149.6	104.7
Cameroon	95.0	91.1	86.0	79.9
Equatorial Guinea	34.0	34.0	38.5	30.2
Asia and Oceania	37.1	33.4	31.5	25.7
New Guinea and Papua	28.0	25.0	21.2	14.2
World total	1,330.5	1,209.9	1,337.0	1,235.3

*Crop year, October 1 to September 30.
Source: U.S. Department of Agriculture, Foreign Agricultural Service.

Table XV. Tea Production in Principal Producing Areas
In 000,000 lb.

Area	Forecast 1968	1967	1966	1965	Average 1960–64
World*	2,230	2,184	2,165	2,070	1,909
Asia	1,975	1,953	1,930	1,874	1,753
Ceylon	487	487	490	503	465
India	865	841	826	808	768
Indonesia	90	90	88	104	98
Japan	192	188	183	171	177
Pakistan	62	65	62	59	54
Taiwan	52	54	47	46	42
U.S.S.R.	122	121	124	102	92
Africa	202	183	181	146	122
South America	54	49	53	51	33

*Excluding Communist China.
Source: U.S. Department of Agriculture, Foreign Agricultural Service.

about 40% of total farm output in 1967; paddy production totaled 3.2 million tons. Total production and yield per unit area of the first rice crop of 1968 reached a record high. Large exports of sugar, bananas, canned fruits and vegetables, rice, and tea went predominantly to Japan and the U.S.

Reductions in Japan's 1968 grain and oilseed plantings suggested a possible increase in imports. The 1967 rice crop of 18,064,000 tons (rough) had been by far the largest in Japan's history and quite enough to meet requirements. Preliminary estimates for 1968 were for a tonnage second only to that of 1967, and carry-over stocks were at record high levels. Acreage and production of barley declined very slightly as compared with 1967. Livestock, especially cattle, were more abundant, with milk production up about 5% from the 3,660,000 tons of 1967. New stress being placed on beef production would probably result in larger feed-grain imports. The mixed feed industry experienced a 10% growth in fiscal 1968. The rapidly growing pork industry produced 619,000 tons in 1967, against 565,-000 tons the previous year. Reduced marketings were forecast for 1968. Japan continued to be the best market for U.S. soybeans, though imports of Soviet sunflower seed made some inroads. Wheat imports totaled about 4.2 million tons in fiscal 1967, and cotton imports reached 3,466,000 bales.

Self-sufficiency in agriculture, one of the basic aims of South Korea's second five-year plan (1967–71), received a setback in 1967 as output of food grains decreased about 6%. Rice production in 1967 was indicated at 5 million tons paddy, or about 66% of total grain production. Seed varieties had been improved and the use of fertilizers was second only to that in Japan and Taiwan. Imports of wheat, rice, and barley, mostly from the U.S., totaled 788,000 tons, compared with only 451,000 tons in 1966; the increase was largely the result of severe drought in four southern provinces.

The Philippine rice crop suffered severe typhoon damage in 1967, but the 1967–68 harvest was officially estimated at 4.3 million tons, up 4% from 1966–67. Supplies of new high-yielding seed varieties were more than adequate to meet planned production for 1968–69. Production had approached self-sufficiency, but inadequate marketing channels, poor warehousing and drying facilities, and insufficient funds for the government's price support program appeared to be major unsolved problems. Copra production also suffered

typhoon damage; exports of copra for January–July 1968 totaled 295,261 tons, compared with 417,714 in the corresponding period a year earlier. Coconut oil and desiccated coconut exports rose slightly. The 1967–68 tobacco harvest was estimated at 165 million lb., up 16% from the previous year; all of the increase was in native dark air-cured types.

An unusually dry summer in 1967 reduced the Indonesian rice crop, and the resulting price rise in 1967–68 renewed the galloping inflation that had been slowed down under an austerity program. Rubber, tobacco, and peanut production set new records, and a strong comeback was made in pepper exports to world markets. Expanding agricultural production was assigned top priority, with emphasis on adapted seeds, heavy application of fertilizers, and careful use of insecticides and fungicides. Agreements with the U.S. called for substantial import supplies of rice, bulgur, wheat flour, and cotton.

In Malaysia sagging rubber prices and rising prices for rice imports tightened the economic situation. Poultry and swine production showed steady growth. Smallholders increased both acreage and production of pineapples, but the large plantations also maintained output; Malaysia had become the second-ranking exporter of canned pineapples, after Taiwan. Agrarian reform was still a key issue in South Vietnam. Only 667,000 ac. of the 2,470,000 ac. acquired by the government in 1954 had been distributed. Some 600,000 tons of U.S. rice were supplied to this former rice-exporting area, and it was suggested that prices on American rice be increased as much as 15% to counteract the effects of its sale on local production incentives. Production of most crops declined; a major exception was vegetables, which were usually profitable because of military procurement and increased local consumption.

Thailand, formerly the leading exporter of rice, dropped to second place after the U.S. in 1967. With more favourable weather, crop production was expected to resume its upward trend in 1968, but no export target for rice was set. Double cropping, more irrigation, higher-yielding varieties, pest control, and improved cultural practices were officially encouraged. Under the second national development plan (1967–71), development expenditures on agriculture were increased to 20% of the total, compared with 14% in the first plan. Major emphasis would be placed on irrigation projects. Although it was one of the very few food surplus countries in Asia, Thailand imported $25 million worth of U.S. farm products in 1967, mostly cotton, tobacco, wheat, and packaged foods.

OCEANIA

Early estimates indicated that Australia's 1967–68 farm output would be down by 12%, the result of widespread and persistent drought in many areas throughout much of the crop year. The loss to farmers in 1967–68 was placed at $500 million. However, drought conditions eased in April and May and the outlook for the 1968–69 crop year brightened.

Australia's 1968–69 wheat crop was off to a good start by August; the year-long drought had ended, and good rains, in many places the best in 20 years, raised prospects for a crop of as much as 500 million bu. Acreage was up an estimated 10%, despite fears that disposal problems could result in the event of a good crop. The 1967–68 crop was a disappointing 277.4 million bu., 199 million bu. less than in 1966–67. Total deliveries to the Wheat Board were estimated at 245.6

Table XVI. Production of Meats in Principal Producing Countries

In 000,000 lb., carcass-meat basis

Country	Beef and veal 1967*	Beef and veal 1966	Beef and veal Average 1961–65	Pork (excluding lard) 1967*	Pork (excluding lard) 1966	Pork (excluding lard) Average 1961–65	Mutton, lamb, and goat meat 1967*	Mutton, lamb, and goat meat 1966	Mutton, lamb, and goat meat Average 1961–65
Argentina	5,732	5,262	4,913	474	494	384	381	419	345
Australia	1,937	2,086	1,941	313	298	257	1,314	1,341	1,310
Belgium-Luxembourg	534	509	482	665	591	506	4	4	6
Brazil	3,113	3,201	3,095	1,218	1,200	1,022	122	123	106
Canada	1,858	1,865	1,588	1,195	1,027	1,003	23	23	30
Colombia	818	805	837	88	87	95	4	4	4
Denmark	401	393	354	1,622	1,605	1,459	5	4	3
France	4,040	3,786	3,576	3,170	3,028	2,824	316	312	282
Germany, West	2,641	2,632	2,541	4,332	4,176	3,982	24	24	30
Italy	1,565	1,485	1,388	914	897	887	95	90	88
Japan	308	340	403	1,364	1,245	668	5	4	6
Mexico	1,058	1,124	1,046	557	509	453	134	135	129
Netherlands	653	620	617	1,193	1,110	928	19	20	18
New Zealand	661	644	614	80	90	94	1,145	1,035	1,039
Poland	...	929	878	...	2,046	1,826	...	...	58
South Africa	...	1,058	998	...	137	115	...	295	281
Spain	463	436	404	957	829	632	296	293	268
U.S.S.R.	7,900	7,870	6,520	7,300	7,280	6,250	1,950	1,940	1,870
United Kingdom	2,035	1,912	1,978	1,815	1,972	1,796	576	596	559
United States	21,010	20,635	17,860	12,550	11,337	11,863	650	650	755
Yugoslavia	520	476	415	683	633	648	106	101	102

*Preliminary.
Source: U.S Department of Agriculture.

million bu., or 220 million bu. less than a year earlier. A carry-over of only 20 million bu. was reported at the end of November 1967, but total supplies available in the 1967–68 marketing year were estimated at 317 million bu., a quantity exceeded in only three previous years.

Wheat exports in July–December 1967 were estimated at 139 million bu., an increase of 77% over the corresponding period a year earlier. Communist China took 52 million bu., or 38% of total exports. Observers saw a change in direction of Australia's wheat exports, however. Shipments to Communist China and Pakistan were expected to decline while an increase in the quality of Australian wheat raised prospects of heavier trade with Japan. Wheat quality continued to be emphasized by industry leaders and by the Wheat Board. Innovations in shipment, specifically the development of bulk wheat carriers with their own unloading equipment, permitted transshipment from Amsterdam and Rotterdam at lower cost than would be possible with cargo lots.

Record plantings of oats and barley for the 1968–69 crop year were reported. The 1967–68 barley crop yielded only 36.9 million bu., compared with 64.2 million bu. a year earlier, and production of 50.5 million bu. of oats was far below the 1966–67 outturn of 133.8 million bu. Early prospects were for a sorghum crop close to the 12.5 million bu. of 1966–67, and corn production appeared to be near year-earlier levels. The 1967–68 rice harvest was estimated at 217,000 metric tons, the seventh record in as many years, in spite of shortages of irrigation water. Exports of Australian rice in the last half of 1967 totaled 65,503 long tons, and the export potential for 1968–69 was reported as excellent.

Australia's livestock industry suffered from the effects of prolonged drought, and smallholders in western New South Wales and Victoria were reported to have been forced to sell sheep for extremely low prices. A bright spot was noted, however, in the development of livestock outside the traditional areas in Queensland and New South Wales, particularly in Western Australia. Wool production for 1968–69 was forecast at 1,832,000,000 lb., 3.6% more than the previous season's output of 1,768,300,000 lb. Sheep numbers on farms on March 31, 1968, totaled 167 million head, an increase of 1.7% over 1967; net losses caused by drought in Victoria and New South Wales were more than offset by larger numbers in other states.

With increased livestock slaughter in drought areas, Australian meat production, except lamb, was expected to be up 2% or more in 1967–68. Beef cattle numbers were reported to be rising but still below the 19 million head enumerated in the census of 1964. Milk production in 1967–68 was down from the record 7.5 million tons of 1966–67; butter production fell substantially, making it impossible for Australia to fulfill its 75,000-ton export quota to the U.K.

The 1967–68 outlook for New Zealand's farm production was good, although unfavourable export prices for wool, butter, skins, and tallow spelled lowered farm income. The country was still heavily dependent on agricultural exports for its foreign exchange earnings. The 1967 trade balance was unfavourable, and the continued slump in export receipts was expected to result in a greater deficit in 1968.

A new record for wheat production was set in 1967–68 with an estimated harvest of 14,897,000 bu. Bad weather at harvest time reduced the quantity of mill-

ing wheat, and diversion to cattle feeding consumed what might otherwise have been a worrisome surplus. Reduction of the guaranteed wheat price for 1968–69 by 10 cents per bushel was announced, but was strongly protested by farmers; upon renegotiation, the price was continued at the levels in effect a year earlier. Production of oats fell slightly from the previous year; barley production rose 500,000 bu.; and the corn crop surpassed the record of a year earlier. Meat exports in 1967 were reported at $251 million, or $13 million more than in 1966. Production of butterfat in 1967–68 totaled 564.3 million lb., a drop of 2.7%.

Wool production for 1968–69 was forecast at 760 million lb., compared with 728.3 million lb. for the previous season. Sheep numbers on June 30, 1968, estimated at 60 million head, were up 5%. Responding to lower wool prices, the government in late 1967 instituted a temporary stabilization program for wool growers, under which repayment of debts incurred by farmers on expanding farms was guaranteed. Government wool purchases from 1966–67 production amounted to 645,786 tons, raising total commission holdings as of December 1967 to 704,000 bales. The Wool Commission's policy for 1967–68 wool was not to sell at less than the purchase cost; a change in that policy lowered the floor price on two occasions, and at midyear 1968 the commission decided to put some 100,000 bales from the stockpile up for auction. The commission also departed from its practice of maintaining fixed prices through floor purchases in the auction market and began to make deficiency payments to growers for sales below established minimums; the floor price was reduced to about 18 cents per pound.

World wool production in 1968 was estimated at 6,162,000,000 lb., an increase of 1.1% from the 6,094,000,000 lb. produced in 1967 and 7.2% more than average. The 3.6% increase in Australia's production, plus lesser gains in the U.S.S.R. and Africa, offset reduced production in the Western Hemisphere and Europe. The world wool market continued in a depressed state; stocks—especially of the coarser grades—were high; prices, although exhibiting firmness, were low; and the competition from man-made fibres continued unabated. Carry-over stocks at the beginning of the 1967–68 marketing season were estimated at 320 million lb., more than three times the carry-over of a year earlier and the highest since 1949–50. New Zealand's decision to begin liquidation of its large stocks and to reduce floor prices and support wool through deficiency payments added to price uncertainty in the world market. In August Australia approved a statutory marketing authority, a step that appeared to spell the end of the free-market auctioning system of wool in that country. The Australian and New Zealand actions were both criticized by the International Wool Federation, which viewed them as an impediment to the laws of supply and demand.

(J. K. R.; H. R. SH.)

See also Commercial Policies; Commodities, Primary; Conservation; Cooperatives; European Unity; Fisheries; Food; Gardening; Industrial Review; Prices; Tobacco.

ENCYCLOPÆDIA BRITANNICA FILMS. *Antibiotics* (1952); *The Story of Rice* (1952); *The Story of Sugar* (1953); *The Truck Farmer* (1954); *The Middle States* (1955); *Milk* (1955); *Meat—From Range to Market* (1956); *The Wheat Farmer* (1956); *The Corn Farmer* (1960); *DNA: Molecule of Heredity* (1960); *Seed Germination* (1960); *Wheat Country* (1960); *Wheat Rust* (1960); *The Cotton Farmer* (1963); *Cattleman—A Rancher's Story* (1964); *The Dairy Farmer* (1965); *Interior West: The Land Nobody Wanted* (1966); *The Great Plains—Land of Risk* (1966); *The Orange Grower* (1967); *The Sheep Rancher* (1967); *Midwest—Heartland of the Nation* (1968); *Produce—From Farm to Market* (1968).

Albania

A people's republic in the western part of the Balkan Peninsula, Europe, Albania is on the Adriatic Sea, bordered by Greece and Yugoslavia. Area: 11,100 sq.mi. (28,748 sq.km.). Pop. (1967 est.): 2 million. Cap. and largest city: Tirane (pop., 1964 est., 156,950). Language: literary Albanian and two spoken dialects, Gheg in the north, Tosk in the south. Religion: Muslim, Orthodox, Roman Catholic. First secretary of the Albanian (Communist) Party of Labour in 1968, Enver Hoxha; president of the Presidium of the People's Assembly, Haxhi Leshi; chairman of the Council of Ministers (premier), Mehmet Shehu.

The year 1968 brought no change in the awkward international position of Albania: it remained pro-Chinese and anti-Soviet, pro-Romanian and anti-Yugoslav; it had no diplomatic relations with Greece (which did not renounce its claims to the Albanian districts of Korce and Gjinokaster). On July 22, D. Balili, Albanian ambassador in Sofia, was ordered to leave Bulgaria with his staff of five, and the next day the Albanian government asked the Bulgarian diplomatic mission in Tirane to leave Albania immediately.

On September 12 Premier Shehu asked the People's Assembly to approve the withdrawal of Albania from the Warsaw Treaty Organization. Although an original member of the 1955 treaty, Albania had been virtually excluded from it since 1961. Shehu accused the Soviet Union of aggression against Czechoslovakia, adding that Albania had no wish to be a member of an organization created as a defense against imperialist aggres-

EASTFOTO

First Secretary of the Albanian Party of Labour Enver Hoxha and other state leaders attending the celebration of the 25th anniversary of the Albanian People's Army, July 10, 1968.

ALBANIA

Education. (1965–66) Primary, pupils 361,241, teachers 12,980; secondary, pupils 31,270, teachers 1,189; vocational, pupils 18,574, teachers 718; teacher training, students 5,417, teachers 209; higher (at University of Tirane and 7 other institutions), students 12,761, teachers 517.

Finance. Monetary unit: new lek, with an official exchange rate of 5 leks to U.S. $1 (12 leks = £1 sterling) and a tourist rate of 12.5 leks to U.S. $1 (30 leks = £1). Budget (1966 est.): revenue 3,580,000,000 leks; expenditure 3,520,000,000 leks.

Foreign Trade. (1964) Imports U.S. $98 million; exports U.S. $66 million. Import sources: China 63%; Czechoslovakia 10%; Poland 8%; East Germany 5%. Export destinations: China 40%; Czechoslovakia 19%; East Germany 10%; Poland 10%. Main exports: fuels, minerals, and metals 54%; foodstuffs 21%; timber, wool.

Transport and Communications. Roads (motorable; 1960) 3,100 km. Motor vehicles in use (1960 est.): passenger 1,900; commercial (including buses) 3,400. Railways: (1965) 151 km.; traffic (1961) 82 million passenger-km., freight (1962) 76 million net ton-km. Telephones (Dec. 1963) 10,150. Radio receivers (Dec. 1965) 130,000. Television receivers (Dec. 1965) c. 1,000.

Agriculture. Production (in 000; metric tons; 1965; 1964 in parentheses): wheat c. 100 (124); corn 158 (188); rye c. 7 (c. 6); oats c. 16 (15); barley (1966) c. 9, (1965) 8; cottonseed (1967) c. 16, (1966) c. 16; sugar, raw value (1967–68) c. 14, (1966–67) c. 15; potatoes c. 33 (34); tobacco 13 (13); wool, greasy (1961) 2.8, (1960) 2.7; sawn timber (1964) 142 cu.m., (1963) 156 cu.m. Livestock (in 000; Dec. 1966): sheep c. 1,700; cattle c. 435; goats (Dec. 1964) 1,199; pigs (Dec. 1964) 147; horses (Dec. 1964) 44; asses (Dec. 1964) 60; poultry (Oct. 1964) 1,730.

Industry. Production (in 000; metric tons; 1966): lignite c. 310; crude oil 920; electricity (1965) 341,-000 kw-hr.; chrome ore c. 315; iron ore c. 370; copper ore (metal content) c. 2.6; cement 135.

sion but which "had been turned by the Kremlin into an enslaving instrument against the Socialist countries themselves." Broadcasting from Tirane, Kazimierz Mijal, the leader of the pro-Chinese "Communist Party of Poland," condemned Poland's part in the occupation of Czechoslovakia.

In January Albania solemnly commemorated the 500th anniversary of Skanderbeg (George Kastrioti). On January 11 a huge monument was unveiled in Tirane to the memory of this national hero, who had resisted the Turkish invaders for 24 years in the 15th century. Its erection in Skanderbeg Square necessitated the relocation of Stalin's statue. Speaking at the main commemorative celebration, Shehu laid stress on the notion of self-reliance. "Just as the Albanians then dared to stand alone under Skanderbeg, so they would now under Hoxha," he said. The absence of the Chinese at the celebrations was unusual, but there were other guests. Albania invited 43 persons from ten countries for the occasion, including nine Americans of Albanian descent.

Reporting to the People's Assembly on the 1967 economic plan fulfillment, Deputy Premier Haki Toska said that industrial production exceeded the 1966 record by 11%, while agricultural production topped the 1966 output by 12%. During 1967 a cement factory was completed at Fush-Kruje, a nitrogenous fertilizer plant at Fier, and a soda factory at Vlore. The 1968 plan called for increases of 20.7% in industrial output and of 12% in agricultural production. A visit to Albania by Chinese military chiefs in November gave rise to reports of a defense agreement.   (K. SM.)

Alcoholic Beverages

Beer. World production of beer in 1967 reached nearly 550 million hl. (hectolitres), an increase of about 3.4% over the 1966 figure. Nearly 90% of the production was again accounted for by Europe (in 1967 about 300 million hl.) and the Americas (about 190 million hl.; 125 million hl. by the U.S.). The percentage increase, however, was most noticeable in Asia, with a 13% rise to 35 million hl., including the 14.4% increase to 23.4 million hl. in Japan. Political disturbances in some African countries and other negative influences, such as increases in the beer tax in South Africa, resulted in only a slight rise in production in Africa of 3.3% to about 10 million hl. In Australia and New Zealand production stagnated at around 16 million hl.

In other countries with high beer consumption a certain saturation of the market was noticeable. West Germany had a growth rate of only 1.5%, which was, nevertheless, higher than that of Belgium, Luxembourg, the U.S.S.R., and the U.K. Austria's growth rate was slightly better (+4%), and in Denmark production rose by nearly 8%. Denmark also was able to increase its already substantial beer exports to 1,150,-000 hl. (about 20% of total production) and displaced West Germany (1,120,000 hl.) as the leading beer-exporting country. Over a million hectolitres were also exported by the Netherlands. In comparison, the world's largest brewery, Anheuser Busch Inc. (headquarters at St. Louis, Mo.), produced more than 18 million hl. in 1967, which was almost equal to the total beer production of the Benelux countries.

The trend toward mergers and international cooperation in the brewing industry continued. Allied Breweries Ltd. (U.K.) acquired the Dutch firms Oranjeboom (Rotterdam) and Drie Hoefijzers (Breda), which between them produced 20% of the Dutch beer; thus the merger created the second largest brewery group in the Netherlands, behind Heineken (about 38% of the market) and ahead of Amstel (about 18%). Prompted in part by the British action, Heineken and Amstel announced in August 1968 that they would merge, forming the largest brewery association in Europe.

In Great Britain, Allied Breweries also acquired the Showerings group of companies, leading producers of wines, cider, and nonalcoholic drinks. The annual turnover of the two companies amounted to about £350 million. Another U.K. firm, Watney Mann, Ltd., acquired the Belgian brewery Vandenheuvel (Brussels).

Research in brewing methods continued to make progress, but most breweries proceeded cautiously in the application of new techniques. In one major English brewery, for example, about 40% of the output was being produced by the continuous fermentation process and was then blended with the remaining 60%, fermented in the traditional way. Another innovation was the development of syruplike wort extracts that made mashing and lautering unnecessary. The wort extract, produced with the help of enzyme preparations from barley, was dissolved in water, which was then boiled with hops and fermented. This new method, however, restricted the brewer's ability to give an individual character to his beer.

A further development of the conventional hop extract began to win wider recognition among brewers. "Pre-isomerized" extracts already converted into products soluble in water could be added to the beer after fermentation or even just before bottling, thus avoiding the loss of bitterness ordinarily incurred during the various brewing processes. (T. Sc.)

Spirits. During 1967–68 overall consumption of spirits throughout the world continued to increase. Some markets were particularly affected by increases in revenue duties, excessive markups, import restrictions, and similar causes, but others expanded.

Production in Great Britain of Scotch whiskey was cut back for the second year in succession, maturing stocks having increased by about 30 million proof gallons (one proof gallon = about $8\frac{1}{2}$ bottles at the standard strength of 70 proof) to some 640 million proof gallons; annual production (about 103 million proof gallons) was in excess of demand by about 60 million proof gallons. Three-year-old grain whiskey (the earliest age at which it can be put into consumption) suffered heavily and was freely available below the original selling price. Home consumption fell to about 8.5 million proof gallons of Scotch whiskey and 9.5 million proof gallons of all other spirits.

During 1967, the U.K. exported 43,150,000 proof gallons of Scotch whiskey, 4.7 million proof gallons of gin and other British compounds, and 1.7 million proof gallons of other spirits for a total of 49,550,000 proof gallons. Over half went to the U.S.; the next best customers were France, West Germany, and Italy. Exports from Great Britain increased further during 1968, but home consumption was low, owing to a further duty increase in March.

Production of brandies throughout the world also showed an increase. The tendency toward lighter and less pungent spirits, spearheaded by the U.S., continued and hit particularly the heavier rums of the Jamaica type, the malt whiskies, and the full-bodied fruit brandies. Lighter rums, particularly the white rums, made further headway. A big marketing program was initiated for Irish whiskey.

Under the Kennedy Round trade agreements, spirits were treated as an industrial product and gained tariff advantages. Moves toward freedom of trade in spirits were seen in the European Economic Community. Protective tariffs against spirits were abolished within the European Free Trade Association, but revenue duties were retained and in some instances increased. The subcommittee of the Council of Europe made no progress on its draft convention on spirits. International bodies called for prohibitions on the use of synthetic alcohol.

Excluding the U.S.S.R. and other major countries from which figures were not available, production of potable spirits in 1967 in 33 major countries was in the region of 18,000,000,000 hl. of absolute alcohol. The U.S., U.K., and West Germany accounted for more than half of this. Spain remained in top place with the biggest consumption of spirits per capita per annum. (J. W. MA.)

Apparent consumption of distilled spirits in the U.S. in 1967 reached a record high of 325 million gal., 5.2% above 1966. Per capita consumption rose 3.8% to 1.64 gal. Consumption per drinker remained at 3.8 gal. Prohibition was eliminated in 1967 by local option in 59 areas in 17 states, adding 410,000 people to the area where the sale of distilled spirits was legal.

Consumer expenditure for alcoholic beverages for 1967 was $18.3 billion, compared with $17.4 billion in 1966. Federal excise taxes on alcoholic beverages totaled $4,225,078,000 in 1967, or 29.1% of all excise

English brewery official disposing of spoiled beer. Strike by 1,000 workers at Ansells Brewery in Birmingham during February 1968 caused the spoilage of 500,000 pints of beer.

taxes collected; 74.3% of the beverage tax was accounted for by distilled spirits. During fiscal 1968, U.S. agents seized 5,899 stills producing illicit spirits —709 less than in 1967—and 2,697,345 gal. of mash.

A total of 905,459,342 gal. of distilled spirits was produced in the U.S. in fiscal 1968, 3.7% more than in 1967. This included some alcohol not used for beverages. Whiskey production was up 24% to 163,878,-152 tax gallons; the increase included 17,175,790 tax gallons of light whiskey distilled at higher than 160 proof authorized for production on Jan. 26, 1968. Brandy decreased 14.5% to 15,412,123 tax gallons, and rum decreased 41.5% to 1,006,216 tax gallons. Total bottlings rose 5%. Vodka exceeded gin bottlings by 21.5%, and production of bottled cocktails continued to rise significantly. Bourbon was the largest selling whiskey in the U.S. (and, by virtue of this fact, in the world), accounting for about 88% of total U.S. whiskey withdrawals in 1967. The 86 proof and lighter-bodied bourbons outsold the higher-proof bottled in bond bourbons by 9 to 1.

Total imports of spirits into the U.S., at 72,130,000 tax gallons, were up 8% in 1967. The percentage of bulk to total whiskey rose from 21.6 to 36.2% for Canadian whiskey and from 23.2 to 24.9% for Scotch. Rum imports increased 13.5%. Tequila imports rose 27% to 581,589 gal. in 1967. Total U.S. distilled spirits exports rose 6% to 2,290,000 gal. in 1967; whiskey exports, at 1,683,000 gal., increased 15.5%.

In Canada public revenue from liquor taxes rose 6.6% to Can$714,933,000 in 1967. Consumption of spirits in the same year was up 5.2%. Production rose 13.7% to 62,389,000 imperial tax gallons, imports rose 35%, and exports increased 5.7%.　　　(Ju. W.)

Wine. World production of wine in 1968 fell by nearly 12.5 million hl. (4–5%) from the 1967 figure of 281.8 million hl. Total production failed to reach 270 million hl. The three largest producers—France, Italy, and Spain—had poorer harvests than in 1967 because of bad weather. The quality of the wines also was inferior in most cases.

In France 63.5 million hl. were produced in 1968,

compared with 65 million hl. in 1967. The quality showed a slight falling off. Bordeaux wines, however, were satisfactory in both quality and quantity. The red wines were light, having less alcoholic content than those of 1967, but were still agreeable. In Burgundy the quality of the wines was better than had been thought possible at the beginning of the season. In the Beaujolais region quantity was normal and the new wines were good, of fine colour, and with sufficient alcoholic content. In the Rhône Valley, at Châteauneuf-du-Pape and Tavel, the harvest was slightly smaller than in the past. In the Champagne district, spring frosts caused some serious damage and, later, heavy rains brought on a plague of insects; the 1968 harvest was down by 20% but the quality was on the whole good.

In Italy the reduction was even greater than in France; the harvest fell from 75 million hl. in 1967 to 67 million hl. in 1968. In Piedmont, as in Emilia-Romagna, production was lower by 25 to 30% and the wines were of uneven quality. In Veneto the harvest was 30 to 40% smaller, but the quality was good. In Puglia production was higher. In Sicily quantity and quality were far above the 1967 average.

In Portugal, in the Douro Litoral, the production of port was 10% less than in 1967. Quality was satisfactory in both red and white wines. The Spanish harvest was down by about 3 million hl. compared with that of 1967. In fact, the 1968 production of about 19.5 million hl. was distinctly less than the average figure (28.4 million hl.) for the previous five years.

In Australia wine production in 1968 was estimated at 1,950,200 hl., an increase over the 1967 figure (1,-895,670 hl.) and well above the average for the previous five years (1,659,300 hl.).　　　(R. Pn.)

The 1968 vintage in the U.S. was generally rated as average to low in quantity and good to excellent in quality. The harvest was from 10 to 25% below normal expectations. Spring frosts damaged some of the vines, and wind and rain at blossom time cut down on the berry set. In California, which traditionally

UPI COMPIX

New York pub owner Joe Carroll dumping his entire French wine stock as a personal protest against the policies of Pres. Charles de Gaulle of France.

Table I. Estimated Consumption of Beer in Selected Countries				
In litres* per capita of total population				
Country	1963	1964	1965	1966
Belgium†	140.0	140.0	140.0	140.0
Czechoslovakia	115.7	124.7	130.0	132.1
Luxembourg	122.8	130.8	125.7	128.7
Germany, West	113.5	122.3	122.0	125.8
Australia‡	103.3	106.8	109.1	113.7
New Zealand	100.9	101.8	103.7	107.3
Austria	85.2	89.9	92.1	98.8
United Kingdom	87.7	89.6	91.5	90.4
Denmark	78.5	83.7	78.5	88.7
Germany, East	76.5	80.3	80.6	81.7
Switzerland	72.8	79.3	74.0	74.8
Canada§	65.9	67.5	67.7	67.7
United States‡	57.4	60.2	60.2	62.1
Ireland	59.6	62.2	66.3	61.7
Hungary	41.1	42.5	44.2	46.4
Sweden	39.4	40.4	40.4	43.3
France	36.0	40.7	39.2	40.4
Netherlands‖	31.2	35.0	37.2	39.0
Colombia	43.2	48.6	37.0	...
Venezuela	31.0	31.0	32.0	...
Mexico	22.5	26.3	30.0	...
Norway	26.6	26.5	27.8	28.8
Finland	24.4	24.5	25.1	27.8
Spain	18.4	21.6	23.4	26.4
Poland	23.5	23.9	24.0	25.6

*One litre = 1.0567 U.S. quarts = 0.8799 imperial quart.
†Including so-called "household beer."
‡Years ending June 30.
§Years ending March 31.
‖Excluding ships' supplies.

Table II. Estimated Consumption of Potable Distilled Spirits in Selected Countries				
In litres* of 100% pure spirit per capita of population				
Country	1963	1964	1965	1966
Spain	1.80	2.10	2.50	3.21
Yugoslavia	...	...	2.60	2.80
Poland	2.50	2.40	2.60	2.80
Sweden	2.35	2.60	2.70	2.65
United States†	2.24	2.36	2.47	2.55
Germany, West	2.52	2.40	2.72	2.35
Germany, East	1.70	1.80	1.90	2.09
Canada‡§	1.68	1.71	1.79	2.03
Austria	2.30	2.00	2.20	2.00
Switzerland	1.70‖	...	1.80	...
Hungary	1.65	1.90	1.50	1.75
Romania	1.43	1.50	1.67	...
Ireland	1.37	1.37	1.76	1.66
Italy	1.40	1.50	1.48	1.60
France‖	1.75	...	...	1.60
Netherlands	1.44	1.48	1.89	1.44
Finland	1.40	1.30	1.40	1.40
Norway	1.34	1.29	1.33	1.36
Czechoslovakia	1.00	0.96	1.08	1.24
New Zealand	1.09	1.17	1.22	1.22
South Africa¶	0.90	1.00	1.11	1.14
Belgium	0.94	0.93	1.12	0.95
United Kingdom	0.84	0.90	0.83	0.84
Australia†	0.81	0.78	0.90	0.78

†Years ending June 30.
‡Years ending March 31.
§Reported annual consumption for the years 1961–63.
‖Including alcohol-based aperitifs but excluding liqueur wines.
¶Consumption per capita of whole population, irrespective of colour.

Table III. Estimated Consumption of Wine in Selected Countries				
In litres* per capita of total population				
Country	1963	1964	1965	1966
France†	127.1	124.0	121.1	119.0
Italy	109.0	105.4	111.0	117.0
Portugal	114.0	104.0	108.6	114.5
Argentina	82.9	87.2	85.1	80.2
Spain	64.8	62.8	57.6	68.0
Chile	57.6	54.0	42.4	...
Switzerland‡	38.1	41.0	38.3	39.1
Greece	34.2	37.9	39.2	38.7
Luxembourg	41.7	40.6	30.1	34.9
Hungary	29.3	34.3	32.8	30.1
Austria§	22.5	26.0	29.8	30.0
Romania§	35.0	...	29.0	...
Yugoslavia	25.0	25.0	24.8	25.0
Uruguay	26.0	...	25.0	...
Bulgaria	14.1	16.7	17.6	20.0
Germany, West	15.4	18.0	16.8	17.4
Czechoslovakia	10.8	12.3	11.9	17.1
Cyprus	12.0	...	12.0	12.0
Belgium	7.0	9.2	11.2	9.7
South Africa	7.8	9.1	8.7	8.4
Australia	5.3	5.5	6.1	6.8‖
U.S.S.R.	4.1	5.6	5.8	6.0‖
Sweden	3.9	4.2	4.3	4.6
Poland	4.7	4.9	4.8	4.5
Israel	4.6	4.7	4.8	4.4

†Excluding cider (23.3 litres per capita in 1963).
‡Excluding cider (11.8 litres per capita annually, 1961–63).
§Estimates based on production of wine.
‖Year ending June 30, 1967.

Source: Produktschap voor Gedistilleerde Dranken, *Hoeveel Alcoholhoudende Dranken Worden er in de Wereld Gedronken?*

produces some four-fifths of U.S. wines, the vintners in 1968 crushed 1.5 million tons of grapes, only slightly above the previous year and far below the record of 2,054,968 tons in 1965. A gross wine production of 160–170 million gal. was expected. (A ton of grapes can produce roughly 180 gal. of table wine, 86 gal. of dessert wine, or 42 gal. of brandy.) New York State, which ranks second in wine production in the U.S., was expected to produce some 18 million gal. of wine from its 1968 vintage.

The U.S. public continued its now firmly established trend of consuming more table wine, sparkling wine, vermouth, and "special natural wines" (the wines with the dramatic brand names), while giving the traditional dessert wines rather cool treatment. The sale of 11.4 million gal. of sparkling wines (of which 9.4 million gal. were U.S. produced) topped the mark of the previous year by 16% and established a new high for the tenth year in a row. Table wine sales moved ahead a substantial 9.5 million gal. to reach 92 million gal. (of which 80 million gal. were domestic), setting a new record for the 16th consecutive year. Vermouth sales in fiscal 1968 hit 9.9 million gal., of which 5.3 million gal. were domestic.   (I. H. M.)

Algeria

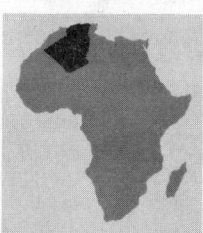

A republic on the north coast of Africa, Algeria is bounded by Morocco, Mauritania, Mali, Niger, Libya, and Tunisia. Area: 919,591 sq.mi. (2,-381,743 sq.km.). Pop. (1966): 12,093,203. Cap. and largest city: Algiers (pop., 1966, 903,530). Language: Arabic, Berber, French. Religion: Muslim. President in 1968, Col. Houari Boumédienne.

After the failure in December 1967 of the coup d'etat attempted by Col. Tahar Zbiri, former chief of staff of the Algerian Army, Houari Boumédienne emerged as the undisputed leader of the country. When they seized power in 1965, Boumédienne and his supporters had denounced the "cult of personality" adopted by the former president, Ahmed ben Bella. They agreed to rule the country through a "collegiate" body known as the Revolutionary Council, which originally had 26 members. There followed a period of weak leadership marred by internal personal feuds. Zbiri's attempted coup was therefore considered as a blessing in disguise since it gave Boumédienne a chance to assume strong leadership and act decisively. The revolt, which involved a few army units led by Zbiri and some of his relatives, was smashed.

Boumédienne's status as an unproclaimed head of state was enhanced internationally when Algeria played host to the fifth summit conference of the Organization of African Unity (OAU) in September. Boumédienne personally welcomed the African heads of state and was elected chairman of the conference. With his customary revolutionary fervour, he delivered a fiery speech to the opening summit session. Instead of limiting himself to the usual welcoming niceties, he made a strong attack on the imperialists and denounced those who were supporting Biafra in the Nigerian civil war. Zambia's president, Kenneth Kaunda, whose country was one of the four African countries that recognized Biafra, felt that Zambia was included in Boumédienne's strictures; he therefore declined to accept election as vice-president of the con-

Barrels of Algerian wines awaiting shipment to overseas markets including the Soviet Union. France restricted imports of Algerian wine after customs duties on luxury goods were increased by Algeria.

ference. This did not provoke a major incident, but it underlined Algeria's uncompromising attitude.

Algeria's foreign policy remained strongly anti-imperialist or, to be more exact, anti-United States. In April diplomatic relations were resumed with Britain after a nearly three-year break over Rhodesia, but Algiers still had no diplomatic ties with the U.S. or West Germany.

The Czechoslovak crisis took place shortly after Moscow had promised a substantial increase in trade with Algeria, but it was impossible to say whether this had a direct bearing on the Algerian press and radio expressing only the Soviet view of the situation. Relations with France remained good on the whole but were sometimes strained over trade issues.

The strengthening of the leadership of the country was coupled with a major move to reinforce Algeria's single party, the National Liberation Front (FLN), in

ALGERIA

Education. (1966–67) Primary, pupils 1,350,518, teachers 30,586; secondary, pupils 96,845, teachers 4,430; vocational, pupils 34,439, teachers 2,618; teacher training, students 4,052, teachers 255; higher (including 3 universities), students 9,272, teaching staff 682.

Finance. Monetary unit: dinar, at par with French franc (4.94 dinars = U.S. $1; 11.85 dinars = £1 sterling). Budget (1967 est.) balanced at 3,332,000,-000 dinars.

Foreign Trade. (1966) Imports 3,341,000,000 dinars; exports 3,746,000,000 dinars. Import sources: France 71%; U.S. 11%. Export destinations: France 67%; West Germany 11%; U.K. 8%. Main exports (1963): crude oil 61%; wine 13%; citrus fruits 5%.

Transport and Communications. Roads (1965) 35,541 km. Motor vehicles in use (1965): passenger 210,000; commercial (including buses) 95,000. Railways (1964): 3,843 km.; traffic 556 million passenger-km., freight 960 million net ton-km. Telephones (Dec. 1966) 143,116. Radio receivers (Dec. 1963) 1.5 million. Television receivers (Dec. 1965) c. 150,000.

Agriculture. Production (in 000; metric tons; 1967; 1966 in parentheses): wheat c. 1,350 (627); barley (1966) 138, (1965) 379; oats (1966) 6, (1965) 23; potatoes (1966) 175, (1965) 232; dates (1965) c. 110, (1964) 110; figs (1965) c. 60, (1964) 58; oranges (1966) 382, (1965) 395; tomatoes (1965) c. 110, (1964) 113; onions (1965) c. 68, (1964) c. 68; tobacco (1966) c. 12.5, (1965) c. 6; olive oil c. 20 (c. 15); wine (1966) 682, (1965) 1,403. Livestock (in 000; Nov. 1966): sheep c. 6,000; goats (Nov. 1965) c. 1,700; cattle 720; asses (Nov. 1964) 248; mules (Nov. 1964) 147; horses (Nov. 1964) 117; camels (Nov. 1964) c. 225.

Industry. Production (in 000; metric tons; 1967): crude oil 38,378; natural gas 2,197,000 cu.m.; coal (1966) 44; electricity (excluding most industrial production) 1,189,000 kw-hr.; iron ore (52% metal content; 1966) 1,740; phosphate rock (1966) 80.

order to make it an effective instrument for the control of the masses. Kaid Ahmed, a trusted aid of Boumédienne, was appointed head of the party and was given the task of reorganizing it. His harsh measures sometimes created problems. He managed to control the once-powerful trade unions (UGTA) but failed to tame the university students. An inevitable clash occurred when his men tried to encroach on the authority of local administrators. This brought strong opposition from Ahmed Medeghri, the minister of the interior, who was reported to have resigned in protest.

The enemies of the regime did not relax after the failure of the December 1967 coup. In January the authorities uncovered a plot to assassinate the country's leaders and in April Boumédienne escaped injury when two Algerians dressed as security guards sprayed his limousine with submachine gun bullets.

Socialism was still the proclaimed goal of the Boumédienne regime, a favourite motto of which was "there can be no real independence without economic independence." The effects of this policy were felt strongly in 1968 when more than 60 French companies were nationalized. In May the government nationalized oil and gas marketing operations. The facilities of the former foreign oil companies, which were promised compensation, were turned over to the state oil concern, Sonatrach (National Society for the Transport and Commercialization of Hydrocarbons). This measure increased the fear in foreign oil circles that the government would one day also nationalize the production of oil, which was mainly undertaken by French companies. In 1967 oil production totaled 40 million tons, of which 38.5 million were exported. Revenue to Algeria from these exports amounted to $200 million.

A major step to encourage industry was taken in midyear. Customs duties were increased on imported luxury goods, sometimes in excess of 300%, while they were lowered on imports of machinery. But despite these steps three out of five Algerian workers remained unemployed.

The national census released in midyear came as a shock to many Algerians; it revealed a yearly population increase of 3% and showed that 74% of the population was illiterate. Serious consideration was being given to education, however. For the second consecutive year, education topped the budget with an allocation of 20% of total government expenditure, but shortages of teachers and schools were among the obstacles facing the planners.   (A. R. Y.)

ENCYCLOPÆDIA BRITANNICA FILMS. *Mediterranean Africa* (1952).

Andorra

An autonomous principality of Europe, Andorra is in the Pyrenees Mountains between Spain and France. Area: 175 sq.mi. (453 sq.km.). Pop. (1967 est.): 15,000. Cap.: Andorra la Vella (Catalan) or Andorra la Vieja (Spanish) (pop., 1967 parish est., 3,000). Language: chiefly Catalan. Religion: predominantly Roman Catholic. Co-princes: the president of the French Republic and the bishop of Urgel, Spain, represented by their *vegeurs* (provosts) and *batlles* (prosecutors). An elected Council General of 24 members elects the first syndic (*sindic procurador general de les valls d'Andorra*); in 1968, Francesc Escudé-Ferrero.

Andorra continued its active program to increase

PORTERFIELD-CHICKERING FROM NANCY PALMER AGENCY

Andorran farmer harvesting his 1968 tobacco crop. Tobacco continued to be one of Andorra's most important agricultural commodities.

the revenues gained from tourism, which accounted for approximately 80–90% of the gross national product. Emphasis was placed on the construction of hotels and improving the facilities for winter sports. Such facilities allowed the skiing season to be lengthened so that it would extend from November 15 through May 15.

The governmental reorganization begun in 1967 led to the establishment of eight departments or boards. Each comprised a permanent staff under the direction of six of the councillors. The first syndic chaired the general board (junta) and the Department of Organization and Personnel. The subsyndic directed the plans and policies of the Tobacco Commission. Each of the remaining five departments or boards was directed by an elected councillor. The reorganization was expected to eliminate much of the inefficiency of the former system while preserving the pure democracy of traditional Andorra.

No progress was made on the proposed road tunnel through the Pas de la Casa, a project pledged by France's Pres. Charles de Gaulle on a state visit in 1967. Andorra considered the tunnel necessary to end the five-month isolation from France during the winter. The tunnel would also contribute handsomely to the earnings from tourism.   (R. D. Ho.)

ANDORRA

Education. (1965–66) Primary, pupils 963, teachers 34; secondary, pupils 168, teachers 11.

Finance. Monetary units: French franc and Spanish peseta. No budget and taxes; public treasury is funded by small import, gasoline, and liquor levies and frontier tolls. Exchange and deposit banking is important.

Foreign Trade. (1967) Imports from France, Fr. 111,593,000 (U.S. $22,603,000), from Spain, 479,611,-000 pesetas (U.S. $7,830,000). Tourism (1967): *c.* 1 million visitors; *c.* 160 hotels.

Communications. Radio receivers (Dec. 1966) 5,000. Television receivers (Dec. 1966) *c.* 1,000.

Agriculture and Industry. Production: cereals, potatoes, tobacco, wool; hydroelectric generation and export. Livestock (in 000; 1965): sheep *c.* 25; cattle *c.* 3; horses *c.* 1.

Antarctica

The tenth plenary session of the Scientific Committee on Antarctic Research (SCAR) of the International Council of Scientific Unions (ICSU) was held in Tokyo, June 10–15, 1968. Of the 12 Antarctic Treaty nations, only Chile was not represented. Delegates from Argentina, Australia, Belgium, France, Japan, New Zealand, Norway, South Africa, the U.K., the U.S., and the U.S.S.R., along with delegates from affiliated international scientific organizations, took part in the meeting.

In December 1967 earthquakes and a volcanic eruption occurred on Deception Island near the north end of the Antarctic Peninsula, forcing the evacuation of 52 members of Argentine, British, and Chilean research stations located nearby. During the eruption, columns of steam and ash rose to around 40,000 ft. and a small new island was formed in the bay.

Scientific Programs. The Antarctic Treaty provides that the continent of Antarctica will be used for peaceful purposes only. Cooperative scientific research and exchange of scientists and data are carried on under its provisions. Ten of the 12 Antarctic Treaty nations maintained stations in Antarctica and the surrounding islands.

Argentina. The Argentines carried on research at eight permanent bases, two on the continent and six in the Antarctic Peninsula and nearby islands. The stations were resupplied by the icebreaker "General San Martín" and the transports "Bahia Aguirre" and "Martin Karlsen." An emergency hut at Groussac Base was reconditioned to accommodate summer investigators.

Australia. The Australian program was centred at three main bases: Mawson, Wilkes, and Macquarie Island. A new station was established on the Amery Ice Shelf, 300 mi. from Mawson. The Australian National Antarctic Research Expedition again chartered the ships "Nella Dan" and "Thala Dan" to resupply their Antarctic stations.

Four men made a dogsled trip to the edge of Vanderford Glacier, 35 mi. S of Wilkes, where a small field support station was established. A field party using radio-echo sounding techniques mapped the rock profile beneath the nearby icecap and made a topographical survey from Wilkes to Cape Poinsett. A four-man party wintered over at the Amery Ice Shelf Station.

Belgium. Although Roi Baudouin Base remained temporarily closed, the Belgians participated with the South Africans in an expedition to a mountainous region south of the South African Sanae Base.

Chile. Chile continued its investigations from three main bases in the Antarctic Peninsula and nearby islands. Annual resupply was accomplished by the "Piloto Pardo" and "Yelcho." Helicopters from the "Piloto Pardo" were used to take a census of marine mammals. A new seismograph station was erected at the Bernardo O'Higgins Base.

France. French activities in Antarctica were centred in and around their main base, Dumont d'Urville, in Adélie Coast. A 46-man summer party was transported to the base on the "Thala Dan," and 26 members remained for the 1968 winter. A cosmic ray laboratory and a seawater distillation plant were installed during the summer of 1967–68. Fieldwork included a survey of Astrolabe Glacier and biological work at Cape Denison.

Japan. The icebreaker "Fuji" arrived at Showa Station on January 13 to initiate the Japanese Antarctic Research Expedition; of the 40 members, 29 wintered over. A party of nine men participated in an oversnow traverse from Showa Station to Plateau Station (U.S.) and back in preparation for the proposed 1,800-mi. journey to the South Pole by a 12-man party during the 1968–69 summer season. On February 10 the body of a Japanese cosmic-ray geophysicist, lost during a blizzard in 1960, was recovered about 4 mi. W of Showa Station.

New Zealand. Scott Station, Ross Island, was relieved by U.S. ships and aircraft and by HMNZS "Endeavour," and was manned in 1968 by a wintering party of 11. A subsidiary station at Lake Vanda in the Wright Valley was also occupied. Geologists and surveyors worked in the mountains between the upper Rennick and Lillie glaciers in northern Victoria Land. Another party, led by Sir Edmund Hillary, mapped the Moubray Bay–Robertson Bay area and made the first ascent of Mt. Herschel (11,745 ft.). A party also climbed Mt. Erebus (13,200 ft.) to check ablation markers. Combined U.S.-New Zealand parties measured ablation and collected ice cores at Byrd, South Pole, and Plateau stations; an intensive study of the ice shelf north of Ross Island was continued. Biologists continued a survey of penguin rookeries along the entire Ross Sea Coast.

Norway. Norway did not maintain permanent stations, but Norwegian scientists participated in the Weddell Sea Oceanographic Expedition and in the South Pole–Queen Maud Land Traverse.

South Africa. South Africa maintained three stations in Antarctica: Sanae, Marion Island, and Gough Island. The South African ship "RSA" arrived at Sanae on January 17. The South Africans and Belgians joined in an expedition to a mountainous region 248 mi. S of Sanae. Unfortunately, much of the work was frustrated by unusually bad weather.

United Kingdom. Six main stations were relieved in the summer of 1967–68 by the RRS "John Biscoe," RRS "Shackleton," and the "Perla Dan." Three bases in the Antarctic Peninsula area, one in the South Orkneys, and one at Halley Bay, Coats Land, were occupied. During 1966 the Halley Bay Base was completely rebuilt two miles farther inland. A light aircraft assisted summer field parties in the Palmer Land–Alexander Island area until it crashed in February, making it necessary for five men (including the pilot) to winter at the Fossil Bluff advance base in George VI Sound. Biological work at Signy Island, South Orkneys, included a study of sea-floor fauna by divers. Seals, penguins, skuas, and fish collected in the South Orkneys and elsewhere were found to contain up to 25 parts per million of DDE (from DDT) in their fat. The wintering parties totaled 84.

United States. The U.S. Antarctic Research program was conducted at seven main bases, remote field sites, and at several foreign stations. Stations operating throughout the year were Byrd, Plateau, McMurdo, Palmer, and South Pole. Hallett Station, the site of a joint New Zealand-U.S. scientific program, was open from October through February. With Argentina, Norway, and West Germany, the U.S. participated in the International Weddell Sea Oceanographic Expedition, February 18 to March 20, the primary objective of which was to measure deep currents in the Weddell Sea associated with the formation of Antarctic bottom waters.

The Marie Byrd Land Survey was the largest scien-

COURTESY, AMERICAN MUSEUM OF NATURAL HISTORY

Jaw fragment of a giant salamander-like animal is the first land vertebrate fossil ever found in the Antarctic. Its discovery lends support to the continental drift theory.

tific field operation conducted by the U.S. In January the South Pole–Queen Maud Land Traverse, including representatives from Belgium, Norway, and the U.S., crossed central Queen Maud Land, the largest remaining unexplored region of Antarctica. On January 29 the first drill hole to penetrate to the bottom of the Antarctic Ice Sheet was completed at Byrd Station; it was drilled to a depth of 7,098 ft.

Geologists uncovered a jawbone of a land vertebrate, believed to have resembled a giant salamander about four feet long. The fossil, found in rocks of early Triassic Age, was the first indication that land vertebrates once inhabited Antarctica.

U.S.S.R. The U.S.S.R. conducted its research program at four main stations in Antarctica—Novolazarevskaya, Molodezhnaya, Mirnyy, and Vostok—and at remote sites. A new station, Bellingshausen, was established on King George Island in the South Shetland Islands group. Altogether, 181 personnel wintered over in Soviet bases.

Work continued on moving the main Soviet Antarctic headquarters from Mirnyy to Molodezhnaya, made necessary by the strong winds and poor weather that hampered operations at Mirnyy. The icebreaker "Ob," which provided annual support of the Soviet Antarctic bases, circumnavigated the Antarctic continent.

Tourism. Two tourist parties visited Ross Island and Cape Hallett from New Zealand, on board the "Magga Dan." Their itinerary included the New Zealand and U.S. stations and huts built by the Scott and Shackleton expeditions. A third party visited the South Shetland Islands and the northwest coast of the Antarctic Peninsula on the Chilean ship "Navarino."

(L. M. Gd.; E. To.)

See also Geography.

Elwyn L. Simons of Yale University displaying the 28 million-year-old skull of an ape found in the Fayyum region of the U.A.R. The skull is 8 to 10 million years older than any previously discovered, according to Simons.

Anthropology

Several issues that claimed front-page attention in 1968, including poverty, Black Power, student unrest, and social deviance, also attracted notice from a number of anthropologists. Some wrote or acted on those topics in the role of concerned citizen, while others approached them as professional anthropologists. Among the latter was Charles A. Valentine, who intended his book, *Culture and Poverty,* to repair what he called serious shortcomings in social science research done on lower-class life. Never, he maintained, had the "entire" way of life of the poor been reported in ethnographic fashion. Consequently, knowledge of the so-called "culture of poverty" remained partial.

Contrary to some opinions, Valentine questioned whether any empirical evidence actually showed that lower-class values and socialization practices were responsible for a lower-class subculture. Is it not equally or even more plausible, he argued, that conditions within the larger society, against which the poor are powerless, produce the distinctive patterns of lower-class behaviour for which we blame the poor? Countering the claim that special lower-class values encourage crime and delinquency in low-income neighbourhoods, Valentine maintained that the poor in the U.S. share many of the same values and concerns that the more affluent citizens endorse; however, he determined that the poor tend to express those values differently in word and deed. He urged that in order to reduce inequalities between rich and

poor the United States commit itself to "positive discrimination" in favour of lower-class employment or other forms of advancement. Valentine repudiated antipoverty measures that attempt to deal with poverty and its attendant problems simply by inculcating middle-class standards of achievement in the children of the poor.

A second U.S. anthropologist, Ronald Cohen, offered a similar plea for social change accomplished without imposing middle-class ways of doing things on everyone. Writing in the *New York Times,* Cohen called for "faith not in our own way of doing things— the white-middle-class way, which has failed to help the black man—but faith in the ghetto and its people to find their own solution, even if some of their ways and means transgress our canons of respectability." Further support of popular initiative came from two Columbia University anthropologists, Morton Fried and Marvin Harris, who joined other faculty members at that institution to affirm confidence in dissident Columbia students, whose demands they held justified in view of administrators' insensitivity and other shortcomings.

Contemporary problems influenced work done by the Tri-Ethnic Research Project and reported in *Society, Personality, and Deviant Behavior,* a book written by Richard Jessor, Theodore D. Graves, and others. The interdisciplinary project studied the roots of delinquency and adult deviance, especially heavy drinking, among American Indians, Spanish-Americans, and Anglo-Americans in southwestern Colorado. Results supported the theory that people such as the Indians, Spanish-Americans, and other minority groups, who are ill-prepared to employ legitimate means to achieve goals generally valued in U.S. culture, use deviant or illegitimate means in order to cope with their deprivation. The evidence also indicated that the persons who are especially likely to commit illegitimate acts are those who, in addition to being prevented from attaining culturally valued goals, belong to groups in which only fairly mild social controls are directed against deviant behaviour. Another finding showed that minority groups relatively high in deviance do indeed share the same basic values held in Anglo-American culture, a point that conforms to Valentine's contention mentioned earlier.

G. Alexander Moore, Jr., applied anthropological methods to U.S. educational problems. In *Realities of the Urban Classroom* he reported on observations he had carried out in urban elementary schools with the aim of giving new teachers "the strength to meet the culture shock awaiting any newcomer to these classrooms." Meanwhile, an analysis prepared for the National Council for the Social Studies reviewed gains achieved in introducing anthropology itself into the secondary school curriculum and expressed fear that anthropologists writing for an educational market might abandon the rigorous standards they maintain when addressing colleagues. Good teaching of anthropology in secondary schools, the report also said, demands adequately prepared teachers who have progressed beyond the doctrine of cultural relativity and are familiar with more than popular anthropological works.

Most of what appeared in professional anthropological sources remained considerably more removed from current social issues. Marvin Harris' *The Rise of Anthropological Theory,* for instance, revived several classic academic questions concerning the best way to explain culture. Harris extolled cultural ma-

terialism as the scientific strategy most capable of satisfactorily explaining supraindividual adaptation. Reviewing the history of cultural theory, he pointed to the shortcomings of anthropologists who failed to acknowledge cultural causality, who overemphasized particular cultures rather than pursuing generalization, who overstressed the role of the individual in history, and who sought to account for cultural facts exclusively in mentalistic terms or by reference to psychological motives. Harris stressed the importance of studying real behaviour rather than being content to elucidate underlying mental states and symbols. Nevertheless, a symbolist position continued to be enthusiastically supported by a number of anthropologists in the United States and Great Britain. It was conspicuously revealed in David Schneider's *American Kinship: A Cultural Account,* wherein the author deliberately turned his back on actual, observable behaviour and focused instead on its definitions and rules, which he defined as culture. Claude Lévi-Strauss, distinguished by intense preoccupation with cultural symbols, continued to enjoy international prominence. However, a number of frank demurrals were heard in evaluations of his contributions.

Several international meetings of anthropologists marked 1968, including the 38th International Congress of Americanists in Stuttgart and Munich, W.Ger., the eighth International Congress of Anthropological and Ethnological Sciences in Tokyo and Kyoto, Jap., and the first Conference on Algonquian Studies in St. Pierre de Wakefield, Que. In Detroit the American Association of Physical Anthropologists joined with the British Society for the Study of Human Biology in a meeting that symbolized the strong identification linking physical anthropologists with the biological rather than the social sciences.

(J. J. Ho.)

See also Archaeology.

ENCYCLOPÆDIA BRITANNICA FILMS. *Remnants of a Race* (1955); *American Indians of Today* (1957); *Indian Family of Long Ago* (1957); *Indians of Early America* (1957); *Eskimo Family* (1959); *Eskimo in Life and Legend (The Living Stone)* (1960); *The Egyptologists* (1967).

Archaeology

Eastern Hemisphere. So far as reports were available, no highly spectacular archaeological finds were made in the Eastern Hemisphere during 1968. At the same time, allowing for the more or less disturbed political situations in several regions and the increasing necessity of devoting time to archaeological salvage efforts, it was a year in which much was learned of man's past.

There were renewed signs of concern on the part of professional archaeologists over the irreparable loss of contextual information resulting from the increase in illicit excavations being done commercially for the antiquities market. In April 1968 the members of the International Congress of Iranian Art and Archeology in Teheran forwarded a resolution to UNESCO and to individual countries urging stronger controls on the importation of antiquities from clandestine excavations.

The archaeological year was also marked by the appearance of more detailed studies on the degree to which radioactive carbon age determinations conform to true calendrical reality. Since its development soon after World War II, carbon-14 age determination had become a standard archaeological tool for assessing the ages of materials from *c.* 50,000 years ago down to the range of chronologies known through written historical records. For about a dozen years, however, some discrepancy had been apparent between the chronologies established by tree rings and by the dynastic Egyptian materials on the one hand, and by carbon-14 on the other. Recent studies, by—among others—C. W. Ferguson, M. Stuiver, and Hans E. Suess, were based on the radiocarbon checking of ten-year unit samples of bristlecone pine rings back to *c.* 5000 B.C. It was now clear that for the period 3000 to 4000 B.C., for example, carbon-14 "dates" are about 800 years more recent than the annual ring-date counts of the bristlecone pine.

As the new High Dam at Aswan, U.A.R., neared completion, most of the recent salvage archaeology in the area had been completed save far south in Nubian Sudan. The finishing touches were given to the Abu Simbel monuments, which had been moved onto the Nile cliff above their original site. Undoubtedly the increase in the number of archaeological salvage efforts in other parts of the Old World was due in large part to the success and popular appeal of the Nubian salvage project.

Examples of the year's salvage efforts included work on a Phoenician town encountered during road building in Israel, more of the wall of the Second Temple, and some ossuaries exposed by a bulldozer in a Jerusalem housing-project clearance; excavations of sites in the pool area above a new dam on the Peneios River in Greece; and the appearance of an original early church under the basilica of Santa Croce in Florence during flood-damage restoration work. In France more fortifications of the original Greek settlement appeared during urban-renewal efforts in Marseilles, and an impressive portion of a Roman town was discovered during clearance of a site for a new school in Vienne. In the summer of 1968, a large-scale three-year international salvage effort began in central Turkey, where a dam was being built just below the confluence of two major branches of the Euphrates River at Keban. The most remarkable results of salvage activity concerned the early settlement of Lepenski Vir in Yugoslavia, on the banks of the Danube River at the Iron Gate. The exposure indicated a community of hunters and fishermen who lived in trapezoidal planned houses, probably around 7000 B.C. The finds, which included curious life-size human faces carved on sandstone boulders, were so far unique in late European prehistory.

British Navy diver swimming toward shattered amphorae from the wreck of a Greek vessel dated about 400 B.C. The Greek ship was discovered under another wreck, that of a man o' war from A.D. 1700, near the volcanic island of Filicudi.

Sacred hearth and carved stone face unearthed at Lepenski Vir, an early Neolithic settlement in Yugoslavia. Ruins have been found in eight different layers representing three distinct cultures.

COURTESY, DR. DRAGOSLAV SREJOVIĆ

Pleistocene Prehistory. Few new paleolithic sites were reported during the year, although most of the established field programs in Western Europe and the Near East were continued. The year was marked by the appearance of several useful new studies of paleolithic materials. François Bordes's *The Old Stone Age* indicated one of the current directions of French prehistoric thinking away from that of the late H. Breuil, and also something of the impressive variety of open-air encampment sites that "cavemen" were now known to have inhabited. The magnificently illustrated *Treasures of Prehistoric Art* by A. Leroi-Gourhan—whose interpretations had been sharply disputed—became available in an English edition.

The Near East. Archaeological activity in the Arab lands of the Near East had not yet returned to normal following the Arab-Israeli war of June 1967. Only a few of the old and well-known archaeological enterprises had resumed work in the U.A.R. In Iraq, British, French, and German work was continued, but in Syria only the French were reported to have worked again. There was some activity in Jordan, including that of the American Schools of Oriental Research, and very considerable local and foreign archaeological effort in Israel. The various activities of the Hebrew Union College Biblical and Archaeological School included the establishment of a "Middle Bronze Age" date for the stones of the Gezer "High Place." A University of Missouri expedition under Saul S. Weinberg excavated at an important new Hellenistic site, Tel Anafa, in upper Galilee. A rich yield of information on late classical Greek pottery and decorated architectural stucco and mosaics resulted.

The year's closest approach to the spectacular came with the continued clearances in the royal tombs area of Salamis, an ancient capital of Cyprus. The tombs consist of stone-built underground chambers with a wide sloping approach (*dromos*). Although in most cases the central chambers had been robbed in ancient times, the *dromos* of these tombs sometimes contained chariot burials and in one case yielded an inlaid wooden throne and a magnificent collection of Phoenician carved-ivory plaques.

A new site complex near Mandali, Iraq, at the Iranian frontier east of Baghdad, was brought under examination by Joan Oates of the British School in Iraq. Excavations at one of these sites, Choga Mami, promised to clarify, at last, understanding of the interrelationships between the earliest agricultural communities of northern, central, and southern Mesopotamia. Two important Canadian expeditions, from the Royal Ontario Museum and the Université de Montréal, resumed work at Godin Tepe and Ganj Dareh, near Kermanshah. Ganj Dareh showed promise of being a key site for understanding of the appearance of agriculture.

In Turkey the joint prehistoric project of Istanbul and Chicago universities was about to resume work near Diyarbakir. More Hellenistic sculpture was recovered at Aphrodisias by a New York University team. At Sardis a joint Harvard-Cornell expedition identified a number of crucible-like depressions in which gold ores had been reduced; these were in a level attributed to the age of the proverbially rich Sardian king Croesus.

Greece and Rome. In Greece there was a trend toward further prehistoric studies. T. W. Jacobsen encountered preceramic remains rich in flint and obsidian in the Frangthi Cave on the east coast of the Peloponnesus. Details became available on the British work at

WIDE WORLD

Bone needle discovered at the Marmes rock-shelter in Washington is believed to be more than 11,000 years old. Scientists working at the site considered the needle a feat of engineering comparable to the wheel.

Saliagos, a thriving island settlement of fisherfolk (who also farmed and kept livestock). In eastern Greek Macedonia, Jean Deshayes reopened the early village site of Dikili Tash, which promised to provide links between the Karanovo materials of Romania and those of Troy I type.

For the classical range of time, detailed excavations in the Athenian Agora, under H. A. Thompson, cleared offices of civil officials, and a newly found sanctuary was identified. In the Corinth region, work on a Roman bath and on various workshops including a dye works, a glass blower's shop, and a foundry went forward. Greek archaeologists identified a shrine dedicated to Zeus near the top of Mount Olympus.

Late Prehistoric and Historic Europe. Aside from Lepenski Vir, one of the more impressive late prehistoric monuments of Europe to be cleared was the "passage-grave" tumulus of Knowth, Ire. Dating to about 2500 B.C., the tumulus was about 300 ft. in diameter and 36 ft. high, being built up in ordered layers of sod, clay, and stones within a circular curbing of large decorated stones. There was evidence of cremated bone from the chamber area, but detailed clearance was not yet complete.

In England the "ghost" (impression of an original form of now decomposed material in the earth) of the royal Anglo-Saxon burial ship at Sutton Hoo was cast in plaster, after the remaining bolts and rivets were removed. The ship "ghost," some 75 ft. long, contained the royal treasure when it was found and cleared in 1939.

Africa and Asia. Archaeological news from these troubled continents was scarce. The important excavation of a mound of successive debris layers (the common "tell" of the Near East but very rare in Africa) was reported from the Dikwa region of northeastern Nigeria. The occupation appeared to have persisted from *c.* 500 B.C. to early in this millennium, and to have been a community of cattle-rearing people.

Two new groups of rock engravings were reported by Soviet archaeologists from Uzbekistan and Kazakhstan, respectively. Neither group could be precisely dated. Rayed circular symbols appear in both groups, as well as figures suggesting hunting, plowing, and wheeled vehicles. (R. J. B.)

Western Hemisphere. The Museum of New Mexico, the University of New Mexico, the School of American Research, the Museum of Navajo Ceremonial Art, the National Park Service (Southwest Region), and the Institute of American Indian Arts were the host institutions for the 33rd annual meeting of the Society for American Archaeology. The meeting was held in Santa Fe, N.M., May 9–11, 1968. Featured were sessions on archaeological method, symposia on the problems of pre-Columbian New World contacts, and archaeology of the eastern and southwestern United States.

Alaska. An unusual Arctic archaeological site was recorded by Douglas D. Anderson, Brown University, at Onion Portage, on the bank of the Kobuk River in northwestern Alaska. The deeply stratified site had been intensively excavated from 1964 through 1967, and the evidence suggested that man was present in Alaska as long ago as 13000 B.C. It clearly showed that men with strong Asian affinities were there by 6500 B.C. Because the tradition, of which this complex—the Akmak—is the earliest, appears to have been an indigenous development arising from earlier Arctic-adapted cultures, it was named the American Paleo-Arctic tra-

continued on page 103

NEW EVIDENCE ON THE EARLY PEOPLING OF THE NEW WORLD

By Charles E. Borden

It is now fairly well known at what times in the past animals and men could range freely over the more than 1,000-mi.-wide land bridge that during periods of low sea level linked Asia with America. New research by D. M. Hopkins and others on the recent geological history of the Chukchi-Bering region has clearly dated that period. What needs to be determined more precisely is when and where game animals and hunters passed from permanently unglaciated areas of central Alaska to and through parts of North America that were repeatedly buried under continental glaciers. In past discussions and speculations concerning the early peopling of the New World, the postulated migration corridor between the Cordilleran (western) and Keewatin (eastern) ice sheets, which periodically opened and closed, has figured prominently. By contrast with this much-mooted route east of the Rocky Mountains, little consideration has been given to possible population movements through the intermontane corridor of British Columbia.

Flanked by the towering Coast Mountains in the west and by the Rockies in the east, the high plateaus of British Columbia's intermontane interior form part of a continuous belt of similar plateau country in southwestern Yukon Territory and central Alaska. Moreover, from central Alaska natural pathways lead via the Tanana River valley and Teslin River directly toward and deeply into the interior of Canada's westernmost province.

During the Fraser (Wisconsin) glaciation, British Columbia was completely blanketed by Cordilleran ice which attained a thickness of more than 2,000 m. (6,560 ft.) over wide areas. Beginning around 23000 B.C., the glaciation lasted for more than 13,000 years. Radiocarbon dates on peat from recessional lakes suggest the ice did not vanish from the interior until around 7500 B.C. The province thus represents a natural laboratory for the tracing of population movements during early Holocene time. We start with a clean slate, as it were.

The Early Boreal Cultural Tradition. During the Upper Paleolithic, blade technology became the basis for many of the great technological and artistic achievements of that period. The term "blade" denotes parallel-edged, razor-sharp slivers of flint or similar stone that were detached by highly skilled flint knappers from specially prepared stone cores. Blades could be used directly without modification, but they also formed the starting point for many other tools. Among the important implements based on blades were burins, narrow chisel-edged cutting tools for grooving, sectioning, gouging, and carving. Tools to make other tools, burins made possible the manufacture from bone, antler, and ivory of awls, needles, fishhooks, barbed harpoons, and a great variety of other devices essential for satisfying the needs of peoples living in subarctic and Arctic environments. Late in the Upper Paleolithic and during the ensuing Mesolithic, it became the fashion to make smaller and smaller bladelettes. Commonly inserted as "side blades" into lateral grooves in antler and bone projectile points, such "microblades" lacerated the flesh of wounded game animals and thus promoted free bleeding and rapid death. Microblades are found in quantity

at virtually all late Upper Paleolithic and Mesolithic sites in Europe and most of Siberia. The discovery of these distinctive artifacts and the microcores from which they were derived also at sites in North America was, therefore, highly significant.

Eight years ago, this author utilized the then rather sparse data on the distribution of microblades in space and time to demonstrate that cultural influences emanating from Asia could reach the northwest coast of North America by traveling interior routes through Alaska, Yukon Territory, and British Columbia. Since then, thanks to the researches of many scholars, the data have proliferated enormously, and they now carry implications far beyond those envisaged in 1960.

Of particular significance is a new series of early radiocarbon dates on archaeological cultures, all of which evince a strong reliance on microblade technology. A charcoal sample associated with microblades and side-slotted projectile points of antler collected at the important Trail Creek Cave site in western Alaska was recently dated at 7000 B.C. Farther north, on Kobuk River in western interior Alaska, D. D. Anderson of Brown University, Providence, R.I., is excavating the deeply stratified Onion Portage site. Here Anderson uncovered the Kobuk complex, an assemblage of microblades and other artifacts dated at 6500 B.C. Beneath the latter, Anderson and his crew came upon the Akmak complex, an even earlier microblade culture, whose bearers may have been using the locality from as far back as 13000 B.C. Anderson recognized relationships between this complex and Siberian cultures far to the west.

Recent Soviet discoveries are of importance in this context, especially the late Upper Paleolithic culture uncovered by N. N. Dikov at sites on Ushki Lake, Kamchatka. Dated at 8500 B.C., this culture, according to Dikov, is related to late Pleistocene cultures at south Siberian sites on the Angara River and Yenisei River west of Lake Baikal. But Dikov also discerned affinities with the microcore and blade technology of the Denali culture recently defined at Donnelly Ridge and other sites in the lower Tanana River drainage area of central Alaska. Afontova Gora II, one of the sites west of Lake Baikal, dates to a time earlier than 9400 B.C. In view of the similarities with the distant Siberian sites, it seems probable that the Denali culture of central Alaska is at least as old as the Ushki culture, dated at 8500 B.C. The bearers of the Denali culture should, therefore, have crossed the Bering land bridge prior to that time. Further new discoveries lend support to this conclusion.

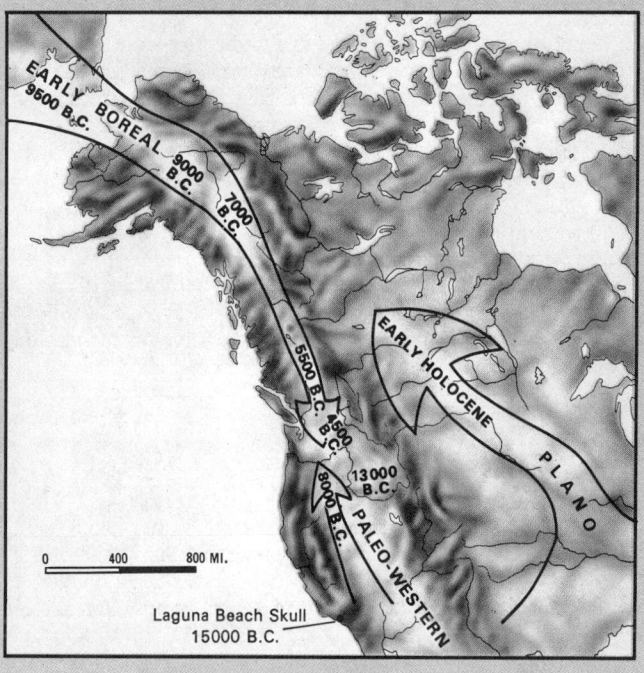

EARLY BOREAL 9500 B.C.
9000 B.C.
7000 B.C.
EARLY HOLOCENE
5500 B.C.
4500 B.C.
13000 B.C.
8000 B.C.
PLANO
PALEO-WESTERN

0 400 800 MI.

Laguna Beach Skull 15000 B.C.

Early microblade components, radiocarbon-dated at 7000 B.C. and 9150 B.C., have recently been uncovered farther up Tanana River at Healy Lake, some 125 mi. SE of Fairbanks. Still farther to the southeast in southwestern Yukon Territory sites have revealed microblade components that have been arranged chronologically into three phases, estimated to span the period from the 6th millennium B.C. to shortly before A.D. 300. The initial date is probably too conservative. A carbon-14 date of 8000 ($\pm$ 900) B.C. has been obtained on a microblade site on Icy Strait on the northwest coast of southeastern Alaska. This date suggests the presence of microblade-using groups in the adjacent Yukon interior by at least 71000 B.C., because the only possible route to the site locality at that time was one that passed through southwesternmost Yukon Territory.

While Asian immigrants could move into the permanently unglaciated areas of central Alaska before the end of the Wisconsin glaciation, the apparent presence of microblade groups in the southern Yukon around 7000 B.C. suggests that these groups were advancing into newly deglaciated territory hard upon the retreating Cordilleran ice. That microblade-using groups continued to press onward into newly opened territory is revealed by the findings in the south-central interior of British Columbia. Thus, the date of 5500 B.C. on the Drynoch Slide site on the Thompson River shows that by then microblade bands had passed through virtually the full length of British Columbia's intermontane corridor. The southernmost penetration of early microblade groups, according to present evidence, is the Vantage region of western interior Washington, where the earliest date obtained at the Ryegrass Coulee site indicates their presence by about 4500 B.C.

Various technological specializations in the production and use of microblades, as well as recurrent traits in the composition of associated assemblages, make it possible to recognize a number of distinct traditions. However, all these local and regional traditions are clearly manifestations of that great Upper Paleolithic cultural tradition that was belatedly carried from Asia to the New World at the very end of the Pleistocene.

Another core and blade culture, on Anangula Island in the eastern Aleutians, has been dated at 6500 B.C. The later bearers of this Anangula culture seem to have favoured the southern coastal region of the broad Bering land bridge. By contrast the bearers of the more northerly tradition were inland hunters adapted to the Siberian tundra. Their chief game animal no doubt was the reindeer, but like all late Upper Paleolithic peoples of southern Siberia they also exploited the fish resources of lakes and rivers. These immigrants to the New World brought with them microblade technology and refined techniques for fashioning a multitude of artifacts from bone and antler with the aid of burins. In addition, they brought many other Upper Paleolithic refinements and innovations. It is the New World manifestations of this northerly inland culture that this author proposes to call the Early Boreal tradition.

It is important to emphasize that we are not concerned here with cultural diffusion, but with a migration-borne spread of a cultural tradition, as is demonstrated by the fact that in southeastern Alaska, in southwestern Yukon, and in the interior of British Columbia these groups were moving into newly deglaciated, still uninhabited regions. As suggested by the newly available radiocarbon dates, the time gradient of this population movement may have been approximately as follows (*see* map):

Lake Baikal	10500 B.C.
Bering land bridge	9500 B.C.
Central Alaska	9000 B.C.
Southwestern Yukon	7000 B.C.
Northern interior British Columbia	6500 B.C.
South central British Columbia	5500 B.C.
Western interior Washington	4500 B.C.

There is no more likely ethnolinguistic stock that could have been involved in this population movement and the spread of the Early Boreal tradition than the Athapaskans who still inhabit much of the same area, although their present distribution shows that they both gained and lost territory in later periods. Already

during their early Holocene expansion in the New World, Athapaskans must have occasionally encountered Paleo-Indian hunters from the plains who, upon the northward shift of biotic zones in the postglacial period, were following game herds into the western Canadian provinces east of the Rockies, the Northwest Territories, and into the Yukon and Alaska. Cultural exchange with such hunting groups, who made the beautifully fashioned stone projectile points of the Plano tradition, was inevitable. When, somewhat later in their expansion, Athapaskans spread into the plateaus of southern British Columbia and adjacent Washington, they probably came in contact with other ethnic groups who, according to still tenuous archaeological evidence, were moving into these parts from the Columbia River valley and Great Basin areas to the south. Thus the stage was set for further cultural interaction. Some of the Early Boreal culture elements acquired by southern groups evidently diffused rapidly far beyond the areas occupied by the Athapaskans. It is significant, for instance, that the Five-Mile-Rapids site on the Columbia River, radiocarbon-dated at 5700 B.C., included burins, sectioned bone and antler, cylinders, and splitting wedges of antler, barbed antler points, components for spear throwers, fishhooks and fish spears of antler, and several hundred thousand salmon bones.

In assessing the advent and spread of the Early Boreal culture in western North America, two significant facts stand out: (1) While there are rare occurrences of microblades east of the Rocky Mountains, none of these has been shown to have an antiquity comparable to that of the early complexes in the west. There seems no doubt that the early thrust of the Athapaskans and of their Early Boreal culture passed west of the Rockies through the intermontane corridor of British Columbia. (2) Aside from the arrival of the ancestral Eskimo-Aleuts, which is assumed to be documented by the Anangula culture, and the advent and early spread of the Athapaskans, traceable in space and time through the remains of the Early Boreal culture, there is no convincing evidence for the passage from Asia to the New World of any other major cultural tradition or ethnic stock in terminal Pleistocene or early Holocene time. Indications are that all other late Pleistocene and early Holocene cultures in the Americas are derivatives of cultures brought to the New World during a much earlier period.

The Paleowestern Cultural Tradition. South of British Columbia, in the vast intermontane and Great Basin areas as well as on the coast, are found some of the earliest dated human remains in America. These include human skeletal material uncovered in the summer of 1968 at Marmes rock-shelter in southeastern Washington, well beneath occupational levels radiocarbon-dated at 9000 B.C., and a skull from Laguna Beach, Calif., for which a carbon-14 date of 15000 B.C. was obtained. Widely spread in the same areas are assemblages of stone artifacts that are distinct both from those of the Early Boreal tradition to the north and from Paleo-Indian traditions on the Great Plains east of the Rocky Mountains. Among such assemblages were some in the area from Puget Sound southward to the northern Great Basin and eastward to southeastern Idaho. Also included must be various assemblages farther south in Nevada, California, and Mexico, especially those subsumed under the name San Dieguito complex. Though regional and local specializations are often apparent, such assemblages commonly feature large bifacially worked stone knives and laurel-leaf-shaped projectile heads, scrapers in a wide range of size and type, occasionally crude blades, and usually varying quantities of heavy tools made of pebbles and cobbles. One example of such an assemblage is that of the Milliken culture (7100–6200 B.C.), excavated by this author in the Fraser Canyon of southwestern British Columbia.

Undoubtedly of earlier, more southerly origin, the Milliken culture is at present the northernmost exponent of these cultural manifestations. Farther south a component at Five-Mile-Rapids, dated at 7800 B.C., and the material from the lower levels of Fort Rock Cave (south-central Oregon), for which a date of

11200 B.C. has been obtained, probably represent earlier manifestations of this tradition. Highly significant also is the small but important early component excavated at Wilson Butte Cave in Idaho. Included in this assemblage, which was dated at 12600 B.C., is a bifacially worked laurel-leaf-shaped projectile point. An underlying occupation level in the same cave has a carbon-14 date of 13150 B.C. The antiquity of the San Dieguito complex is in dispute, but geological evidence indicated that the San Dieguito occupations date from earlier than 9000–7000 B.C.

The San Dieguito complex and the similar, in part seemingly earlier artifact complexes in Oregon, Idaho, Washington, and southwestern British Columbia appear to be manifestations of a distinctive and widespread tradition in western North America that can be aptly termed the Paleowestern cultural tradition. In assessing the significance of this tradition to New World prehistory, it should be noted that it was in existence in areas south of British Columbia and west of the Rocky Mountains at a time when Canada was still buried under coalesced continental glaciers. We must conclude, therefore, that the population movement that brought the parent culture across the Bering land bridge to Alaska and then to areas south of the ice front occurred prior to the Fraser (Wisconsin) glaciation, probably toward the end of the preceding interstadial, around 23000 B.C. The absence in the Great Plains of archaeological remains from periods earlier than the 10th millennium B.C. and accumulating indications for man's much earlier presence in areas west of the Rocky Mountains hint that this early population movement, like that of the Athapaskans many millennia later, passed through the intermontane corridor of British Columbia.

A strong case can be built in support of the proposition that the simple, bifacially worked laurel-leaf projectile head was the progenitor not only of the well-known fluted points (Clovis and Folsom) but of virtually all early stone projectile point traditions in both North and South America. This probability enhances the importance of the simple laurel-leaf form. The findings at Ust'-Kanskaia Cave in the Altai Mountains of western Siberia indicate the occurrence of biface laurel-leaf projectile points in Paleolithic contexts of Siberia predating the Fraser (Wisconsin) glaciation. These findings raise expectations that Soviet archaeologists will eventually discover comparable assemblages of the right age at Siberian sites nearer the Bering Strait.

The Pebble Tool Tradition. Finally, it is necessary to mention, at least briefly, the pebble tool tradition as a likely additional basic cultural tradition that may have been brought to America in pre-Wisconsin time and that may have contributed substantially to early cultural development in the New World. As most American archaeologists know, virtually all early assemblages of stone artifacts contain quantities of rather heavy, crudely percussion-flaked tools, commonly based on whole or split pebbles and cobbles. At present, we do not know when or where the bearers of these early cultures acquired such implements. The great usefulness of these tools is demonstrated by the fact that they persisted in many areas until quite recent times. Ironically, it is perhaps because of this very fact that when pebble tools do turn up they are often dismissed as unimportant, as "probably recent," even when they occur in great numbers and are unaccompanied by artifacts of thin biface form. This author and a few other New World archaeologists suspect that there once existed in the Americas an ancient stone-working tradition that lacked bifacially worked projectile points and knives. Some investigators do not share this view. The problem is far from settled. Pure pebble tool sites occur in the lower Fraser River valley of southwestern British Columbia. Similar and seemingly older pebble tool sites exist along the lower Amur River and along other river valleys on the opposite side of the Pacific. Hence, we still cannot discount the possibility of a separate movement from the Pacific coastal zone of northeast Asia of folk who brought with them the tenaciously persisting pebble tool tradition and contributed it as a significant component to early American stone technology.

continued from page 100

dition. A change in climate around 4000 B.C., from a tundra to a forested environment, coincided with the advance of the forest-adapted Archaic tradition that had its origins in the eastern woodlands of the U.S. When tundra conditions were reestablished at the end of the post-glacial warm period (about 2200 B.C.), Arctic cultures returned.

Canada. J. V. Wright, National Museum of Canada, made a brief survey of God's Lake in northeastern Manitoba. Of the 16 sites recorded, one produced examples of the entire recognized occupation of the region, consisting of the Shield Archaic Laurel tradition (Middle Woodland period), Selkirk focus (Late Woodland period), and historic Cree.

William C. Noble, under the auspices of the National Museum of Canada, directed an archaeological survey of the coniferous Boreal Forest and adjacent Barren Lands in central District of MacKenzie, N.W.T. A mapping program of the raised beaches around Great Slave Lake offered a relative cultural-chronological sequence in which radiocarbon dates were helping to clarify specific details. Agate Basin remains appeared to be earliest in the area. A late Arctic Small Tool complex, the Tundra complex, was defined in the region between Dubawnt and Great Slave Lake. The Tundra complex exhibited a blend of quartzite bifaces and small Denbigh-like tools in a culture adapted to caribou–musk-ox hunting around 1500–1000 B.C. The Taltheilei Shale complex persisted from at least A.D. 500 to the historic Yellowknife Indian period.

Eastern United States. William A. Ritchie, State University of New York, reported that several additional radiocarbon determinations had been made for the various strata at the Peterson site on Squibnucket Pond, Martha's Vineyard. The earliest, relating to Late Archaic Stratum 3, was 2070 B.C. ± 115 years. The next overlying stratum, 2B, initiating the Early Woodland horizon at this site, was dated at 590 B.C. ± 105 years, which is the earliest ceramic date for New England. Stratum 1, at A.D. 1565 ± 90 years, was the most recent dated Late Woodland stratum found in the Martha's Vineyard excavations.

Don W. Dragoo and Donald P. Tanner, Carnegie Museum, investigated a series of Middle Woodland (Hopewellian) sites recently discovered in the Chartiers Valley in eastern Pennsylvania. The work, supported by a grant from the National Park Service, concentrated on the finding of village patterns to add new knowledge to the study of late Hopewellian settlements. These settlements must have been an important early stage in the development of the sizable and well-defined village life seen in the Late Prehistoric cultures of the upper Ohio Valley.

Human skull unearthed at Laguna Beach, Calif., has been dated at approximately 17,150 years by the carbon-14 method. It is the oldest example of human remains unearthed in the Western Hemisphere.

RANIER BERGER, UNIVERSITY OF CALIFORNIA AT LOS ANGELES

The marine archaeologist for the Florida Board of Archives and History, Carl J. Clausen, reported on investigations of the campsite of the survivors and salvagers of a Spanish fleet that sank off the lower Florida east coast in a 1715 hurricane. In addition to the data developed on the European occupation, some useful information was recovered on what was probably the terminal phase of the local aboriginal ceramic tradition. Additional reports were prepared by Clausen on the many thousands of artifacts recovered from two of the Spanish ships wrecked in the 1715 storm. The recoveries, which ranged from complete muskets to copper pots, crucifixes, and ship's gear, provided a startlingly detailed look at early 18th-century material shipboard culture.

Plains. The department of anthropology of the University of Kansas conducted archaeological salvage excavations at the Sutter site situated on a minor tributary of the West Fork of Muddy Creek north of Topeka. The site, buried from eight to ten metres below the surface, was exposed by reservoir construction. Camp refuse occurred in an ochre-stained, gray clay terrace remnant estimated by geologists to be dated from 8000 to 3000 B.C. Included on the occupation level were burned-rock hearths and bone deposits composed mostly of bison remains. Artifacts recovered included projectile points, knives, and scrapers.

Western United States. In 1933 a human skull was dug out of a sandy loam deposit in a vacant lot at Laguna Beach, Calif., by Howard Wilson, and, over the years, was sent to numerous specialists who were impressed by its apparent antiquity. After seeing the skull in 1967, Louis S. B. Leakey asked Rainer Berger of the Isotopes Laboratory of the Institute of Geophysics at the University of California, Los Angeles, to test it by the carbon-14 method. The test returned a minimal date of $17,150 \pm 1470$ years ago, making the skull the oldest dated human remains so far discovered in the Western Hemisphere.

Roald Fryxell, Tadeusz Bielicki, R. D. Daugherty, C. B. Gustafson, H. T. Irwin, and B. C. Keel, Washington State University, recovered human skeletal remains from sediments of mid-Pinedàle (classical Wisconsin) age at the Marmes rock-shelter in southeastern Washington. Radiocarbon dates, obtained from sediments overlying the buried floodplain surface on which these bones occurred, showed them to be older than 11,000 years, while geomorphic relationships showed the site to be younger than about 13,000 years. Artifacts recovered included one or more fragmentary pointed bone implements, a stone scraper and two stone flakes that have been retouched and used, several other stone tools, and a finely made bone needle. The site would be flooded when the Lower Monumental Reservoir was filled.

Middle America. Claude F. Baudy, Centre National de la Récherche Scientifique, Paris, published a report on excavations in Cholulteca and at Lo de Vaca, near Camayagua, Honduras. Five cultural phases were found at the former and three at the latter. The earliest Cholulteca phase, Chismuyo, is thought to have ended about A.D. 550. The latest, the Malalaca, is a Late Postclassic phase ending about A.D. 1500.

South America. A field study was carried out in 1967–68 in Carchi, northern Ecuador, by Alice E. Francisco, University of California, Berkeley. Carchi lacked a reliable sequence based on archaeological associations, and earlier attempts to classify the pottery of the area relied on an oversimplified typology. Mrs. Francisco's studies permitted the distinction of three major pottery style units in Carchi: Tuza, Piartal, and Capuli (the latter being the earliest).

Rogger Ravines of the National Museum of Anthropology and Archaeology of Peru discovered and excavated part of a Middle Horizon offering deposit in Huancavelica. He also discovered the first obsidian mine reported for Peru, a very large one that probably supplied a considerable area. Hermilio Rosas, also of the National Museum of Anthropology, excavating at the Chavín site of Pacopampa in the extreme north of the known area of Chavín influence, found the remains of a large temple and important refuse deposits.

A large party from the University of California at Berkeley, under the direction of John H. Rowe, spent the summer of 1968 doing archaeological reconnaissance and studies of museum collections in southern Peru and northern Bolivia. Systematic survey work was undertaken around Ayacucho, Cuzco, Siguani, and Puno, leading to the recording of many new sites and the discovery of at least two previously unknown pottery styles.

A National Program of Archeological Research had been under way for three years in Brazil, under the cosponsorship of the Brazilian Conselho Nacional de Pesquisas and the Smithsonian Institution of the U.S. During July 1968 the investigators met for a two-week seminar at the Museu Paraense Emilio Goeldi in Belém in order to correlate their results and attempt some general interpretations of the prehistory of coastal Brazil.

Hunters and gatherers had settled in southern Brazil by 7000 B.C., and by 6000 B.C. were exploiting food resources both in the interior and along the seacoast. The earliest pottery appears in 9th century B.C. shell middens on the Bahia coast. The next earliest date is A.D. 570 for the Taquara tradition in Rio Grande do Sul, associated with pit dwellings and beautifully made ceramics decorated with intricate patterns executed principally with the fingernail. Between the 6th and 8th centuries A.D., a ceramic tradition featuring polychrome painting and corrugation, and associated with secondary burial in large urns, spread over most of the coast. The origins of all of the coastal cultures were still unknown. There was nothing to suggest that the ceramic complexes developed locally, but in the absence of information from adjacent portions of the South American continent, no inferences could be made about their possible derivations.   (F. A. Ri.)

See also Anthropology; Biological Sciences.

ENCYCLOPÆDIA BRITANNICA FILMS. *Carbon Fourteen* (1953); *The Egyptologists* (1967).

Architecture

Unlike the previous year when Montreal's Expo 67 provided a testing ground for new architectural ideas, 1968 was a year of more modest activity. However, it had its notable events and produced some outstanding architectural monuments. Again the problem of integrating new buildings with existing environments was uppermost in the minds of many designers, and the fields of architecture and city planning continued to grow closer together.

In the spring the Royal Institute of British Architects (RIBA) awarded its Gold Medal for architecture to the dynamic U.S. engineer-philosopher R. Buckminster Fuller. Highly original and experimental, his geodesic domes had become well known in the preceding decade, and one formed the structure for the U.S.

pavilion at Expo 67. Fuller, it was generally agreed, well deserved the Gold Medal. Many of his most influential ideas were developed in the 1920s and only received attention 30 years later.

Later in the year RIBA made its annual awards, on a regional basis, for outstanding buildings of the year in Great Britain. The Glasgow architectural firm of Gillespie, Kidd and Coia became the first company to receive a RIBA award for three years in succession, winning in 1968 for two halls of residence at the University of Hull, Yorkshire. The winners in the northern region were Yorke Rosenberg Mardall, architects of the North East Regional Airport, Woolsington, Newcastle upon Tyne, praised by the judges as "a splendid group of buildings generously handled in a simple and direct manner." In the northwest, Wallasey Grammar School, Wirral, by Richard Sheppard, Robson and Partners was similarly commended as a functional success. Cavendish and Ancaster Hall of Residence at Nottingham University by architects Williamson, Faulkner Brown won the award for the East Midlands, and in the eastern region the winning project was Churchill College, Cambridge, again by Richard Sheppard, Robson and Partners. Architect Hubert Bennett's Andover Town Development, Hampshire, Area 11, a highly successful community comprising approximately 350 houses, was the award winner for the southeastern region. In London the jury honoured the new St. Paul's Choir School by the Architects' Co-Partnership, and winner for Scotland was the outstanding Edinburgh University Library designed by Sir Basil Spence, Glover and Ferguson.

Another St. Paul's School, this time the public school in Hammersmith, West London, moved into new quarters in the autumn of 1968. In great contrast to the aggressively Victorian red brick and terra-cotta buildings by the 19th-century master Alfred Waterhouse, which had been the school's home for many years, the new modern rectangular blocks employed a system of prefabricated construction, with a light steel framework. The architect was Bernard Feilden of Feilden and Mawson of Norwich, and the cost of the new school, including the 44-ac. riverside site, was £3.3 million.

In June the American Institute of Architects awarded its Gold Medal for 1968 to Marcel Breuer at its annual convention in Portland, Ore. Breuer, whose recent work included New York City's almost windowless, brutalist Whitney Museum of American Art, was involved with plans for a monumental new wing for the Cleveland (O.) Museum of Art. The wing, again brutalist and faced in granite, was planned to harmonize with the museum's older existing premises and to provide space for the educational and social functions of a great museum, including a 740-seat auditorium. Also on Breuer's drawing board were plans for a skyscraper to sit atop Grand Central Terminal at the foot of New York's Park Avenue in front of the recent Pan American Building. And, on a different note, some of Breuer's formative early designs could be seen during the year in Stuttgart and London as part of the large Bauhaus exhibition. (*See* ART EXHIBITIONS.)

The coveted R. S. Reynolds Memorial Award worth $25,000 was given in June to the designers of the Netherlands pavilion at Expo 67: Walter Eÿkelenboom and Abraham Middelhoek of Rotterdam and associate architect George F. Eber of Montreal.

One of the most highly praised and original of the year's new buildings was the Ford Foundation's headquarters in New York City. Designed by architects Kevin Roche, John Dinkeloo and Associates, it provided office space for 350 people involved in the administration of Ford funds. The offices were contained on two and a half sides of an enclosed and landscaped court which provided a transitional space between office and street and a new alternative to the street-level or raised plaza solution offered by many of New York's recent buildings. The architects, according to Roche, attempted to establish "a sense of the individual identifying with the aims and intentions of the group."

Another important new office building to rise in New York was the Marine Midland Building on 52nd Street by the firm Skidmore, Owings and Merrill. A dramatic tower of black anodized aluminum and bronze glass, it formed the backdrop for a red cube sculpture by Isamu Noguchi, who collaborated with the architects in the design and placement of his sculpture.

One of the most significant and progressive designs in the underdeveloped field of public housing in the U.S. was that produced by the firm of Wells and Koetter of Ithaca, N.Y., for a development of middle-income apartments to be built on a site in Brooklyn's Brighton Beach. The plan won first prize in New York's first open international design competition. The winning design, to be executed at a cost of $6 mil-

St. Paul's Choir School designed by the Architects' Co-Partnership won the 1968 Royal Institute of British Architects award for the London area.

lion, featured one 25-story tower, one 6-story tower, and two 8-story buildings, all grouped around a multi-level court partly open to the sea.

Also in the U.S., at Boulder, Colo., the National Center for Atmospheric Research by architect I. M. Pei was completed. It comprised an imposing group of abstract towerlike concrete slabs of great complexity. And a not entirely dissimilar design nearing completion was architect Louis Kahn's Salk Laboratory Buildings at La Jolla on the coast of southern California. The composition consisted of two long blocks facing each other with a series of attached staircase towers.

In Montreal, a city which boasts many excellent new buildings, the Trade Centre, Place Bonaventure, was completed. The architects were Affleck, Desbarats, Dimakopoulous, Lebensold and Sise. The structure, with an exterior of ribbed, sandblasted concrete, housed an exhibition hall, merchandise mart, and hotel.

Also in Canada, the first two phases of the new Simon Fraser University, Vancouver, B.C., were completed. The university occupies a dramatic site on the crest of Burnaby Mountain. It was the subject of a competition held in 1963, the winning architects being

continued on page 109

NEW SPACE AND
NEW STRUCTURES
FOR MODERN MAN

By Kenzo Tange

Some call this the Space Age, some call it the Atomic Era. The economists tell us we have entered the second Industrial Revolution or, alternatively, that we have arrived at some barely defined state of "post-maturity." Mass consumption, mass communication, and mass organization are reaching unheard-of levels. In the midst of dealing with the complicated, troubling political divisions between East and West, North and South, we are trying at the same time to create out of this explosive change a new epoch in civilization.

The very rapidity of our efforts suggests a crisis that has arisen in the human condition. Because of the speed of man's changes, conditions to which we have only recently adjusted must now be regarded as outmoded; solutions that we have only now put into practice must be regarded as obsolescent. Functions that have barely been defined are already seen to overlap and explode one upon the other. The waves of change sweep repeatedly over the realms of painting, music, drama, and literature.

The Challenge for Architects. It has fallen to the architects and urban planners to be in the forefront of this revolution of thought and method. The reason is an obvious one. As organization advances and the whole shape of society undergoes large-scale metamorphosis, new demands and new conditions must receive immediate concrete form. The design for a political solution may perhaps be pondered. The effort of change in art or the drama may be allowed time for debate and reflection. But a changing city cannot be left as it is. It must be worked on, reconstructed, planned, and conceptualized—even as it is being used. Nor can this be thought of simply in terms of "housing" or "construction." For, among other things, the revolution in thought and communication has forced us to think of the city in terms of art and symbol as well.

There was a time, very recently, when an architect could comfortably call himself a functionalist—that is, architects employed a static and deterministic approach to the relations between function and space. Each function, they thought, must have its own particular space. For example, people relax on a sofa, eat at a table, sleep in bed, work before a desk, take exercise in a playground, and use walls and corridors to link these places. This way of thinking was applied to cities as well as to individual houses. People must have a living place for living, a working place for working, a recreational place for recreation, a street for transportation. So a city as a whole, in the time-honoured tradition, was considered as a comprehensive unit including all such places.

The idea in this functional approach was not wrong. In fact, it produced great architectural advances from 1920 to 1960. It was simply made obsolescent by the developments of the contemporary age. Two pivotal phenomena, in particular, caused this obsolescence. The first was the revolution in energy: the extension of the Industrial Revolution to maturity and to a time of mass production and consumption and rapid scientific innovation. The Industrial Revolution was a revolution of production, in which progress was made by increasing the supply of things in a quantitative way. The current revolution in science brings with

it constant qualitative as well as quantitative change. It is a revolution in communication, in information. For the second phenomenon of this era is the lightning development of modern communication methods.

The confluence of these two phenomena has given our age its special character. The rapid consumption, quick obsolescence, high population, and economic growth they have engendered are inexorably stepping up the whole metabolism of life on this planet. And to house—not merely to house but to channel, encourage, and act on this new metabolism, man needs a new physical environment.

The Superhuman Scale in Modern Civilization v. the Eternally Human. The order in modern civilized society, notably that of the city with ten million inhabitants, is now being disarranged by the speed and scale of man's new technology. The medieval plazas, churches, or government offices were built on a scale adequate to the numbers of people who gathered there. They had orderly, harmonious, and uniform composition befitting the human-scaled streets that spread radially from the central plazas.

Now huge-scale highways have intruded into these streets. These highways, of superhuman scale, have never been in harmony with the human-scaled architecture of the 19th and preceding centuries. Nevertheless, the accumulation of capital in modern economies accelerates construction and increases its size. In this way man has revolutionized the old order and system in urban spaces. These huge-scale constructions will frame cities and become the elements of new systems of urban spaces. And, indeed, their hugeness is not so huge to human eyes that are moving in vehicles at speeds of more than 100 km. per hr. [60 mph].

On the other hand, man still walks less than a metre each step, and in this context he is still made aware of the eternal human scale of things. Individuality, man's eternal urge toward freedom and spontaneous action, becomes stronger out of sheer opposition to the domination of technology. Man insists on moving freely, using his spontaneous choice in selecting and planning spaces such as houses, gardens, streets, and plazas.

Thus, there are two conflicting pressures. There is the major force (*i.e.*, the march of technology) which controls and restricts the free choice of individuals and determines the trend of the times, over the long term. Then there is the minor force (*i.e.*, the persistence of personal choice) which permits individuals some spontaneity and freedom of their own, but makes its changes

Left, Kenzo Tange standing before the mock-up of his Tokyo Bay plan. Buildings designed by Tange include (above and right) St. Mary's Cathedral in Tokyo, stainless steel and stone exterior and top-lighted interior, and (below) the National Gymnasium for the 1964 Olympic Games, concrete with a hanging roof.

in a short cycle. The gulf between these extremes is doubtless deepening. The major scale of things will be metamorphosed through the progress of technology. On the other hand, those things of a minor order, although they replace themselves within short cycles, are regulated and conditioned by human nature and the unchangeable human dimension. It is the vital problem of our time to establish an organic relationship between these two orders, in our search for a new design in urban space.

This relationship is vital to the modern architect. Space can no longer be a static thing to him: something to be filled and neatly parceled out through competent design. Space, itself, has become a type of communication. That is, when we design a space, we must think not merely of its function but also of how it can be used as an active, living channel of communication. A work of architecture must be likened to the leaves of a great tree, with transportation and communication facilities forming the trunk.

Obvious examples of this approach include the house and the street. Until the dawn of modern times there was nothing in cities but streets and houses. The houses were simply lined up along the streets. When the railroads came, everybody realized that it was senseless to have houses built along the railroad tracks, and so stations were erected at important points. A new urban relationship developed between the station and nearby architectural groups.

When people began to drive about the streets in automobiles, however, no one seems to have noticed at first what an unnatural situation the new vehicles created. It took quite a long time to realize that without parking space it would be impossible to preserve the connection between streets and buildings. It was not until the appearance of throughways that the impossibility of building houses along roads was discovered. Now, however, we have come to see the need for an ordered progression from housing to parking space to low-speed highway to high-speed highway.

Parking spaces have been made basic parts of buildings. Even highways are finding their way into buildings. In large-scale

building the elevators have taken on the characteristics of public roads, albeit vertical ones. The need has arisen for a direct link between, say, the 20th floor of one building and the 20th floor of the neighbouring building. As a result we now see signs of vertical traffic grids developing in the air. All of this signifies that we are faced with the necessity of working out completely new means of keeping the infrastructure linked with the element structure— the trunk of the tree with its leaves.

Man has a tendency to cling to the ground, but there are limits to the compactness that can be achieved when he actually lives on the ground. Natural ground tends to hinder rather than promote the construction of the facilities needed in contemporary buildings. Planners, therefore, have developed the concept of man-made ground. They are in the process of creating methods whereby such land, replete with "topographical" variety, can serve as an infrastructure within or upon which people can construct high-density element structures.

"Land" must be created in the air as it has in many high-rise building designs. Alternatively, land can be projected out over the sea, as I suggested in my Tokyo plan. There, we projected a network of elevated lattices with perpendicular roads. The roads gave structure to the forms of the buildings to be built above that axis.

This Tokyo plan, still under development, was based on the premise that the centripetal radiating pattern (a series of concentric circles fanning out from the centre of the city) had already reached a dead end as a structure for the contemporary city. This is true, whether the city be Tokyo, London, Paris, or Moscow. This pattern was a reflection of the closed, rigid society of the Middle Ages. In contemporary cities that developed according to this pattern, the central section of the city has already reached the point of suffocation because communications between it and the outlying rings have grown so overworked. A new system of communication has become necessary for the wide-open, fluid organization of contemporary society. The structural reorganization of the city system has, therefore, become a necessity.

Taking Tokyo as our subject, our architectural team made a proposal involving structural reorganization. We suggested that Tokyo change its design from a centripetal radiating pattern to one of linear development, thus substituting the extendable line for the concentric circle. This line would be called the civic axis. Each of the elements along the axis could contact the others in the most comprehensible manner, and there could also be a free choice of contacts.

The nucleus of the total city activity would lie in this civic axis. The physical system of communication possessed by this axis, as well as the movement that unfolds there, would in itself represent the organization of the contemporary city and also would become a symbol of the mobility of the city. It could permit constant urban expansion along straight lines, both horizontally and vertically.

We believe that we can readily develop new urban design ideas through buildings constructed on such an axis, even in Tokyo, where the axis was extended over the waters of Tokyo Bay. In such buildings intensified vertical cores would carry people, information, and energy upward. As necessity demanded, these cores could be built one after another, and large-span, bridgelike buildings could be suspended between them, forming a three-dimensional lattice pattern.

In some existing buildings I have already endeavoured to put this latticelike network into operating practice. One structure in Yamanashi Prefecture is a unity made up of facilities for the *Yamanashi Nichinichi* newspaper, the Yamanashi Broadcasting Company, and a commercial printing company. The building also plays a part in promoting the development of the north side of the local railroad station by including shopping spaces on the side facing the station. Its functions demand four kinds of space: space for shops, office space for the newspaper and the broadcasting company, printing space for the newspaper and the commercial printing company, and studio space for the broadcasting company. Each of the occupants makes different demands on the building. For instance, in the case of vertical transportation the office spaces require passenger elevators and staircases to handle employees and guests, the printing plant requires heavy-duty freight elevators for massive loads, and the newspaper requires both passenger and freight elevators.

To meet these needs we erected a number of vertical communications shafts so that each had a different function. We then put the various spaces among the cores in places best suited to their functions. The result was that the vertical "roads" were built but with unoccupied voids in various places. These would provide the extra space needed for expansion. In this sense the building was both a single spatial type capable of change and growth and also a space established within a three-dimensional communications grid. Thus, it was, at once, a proposal for a single building and for urban design. Of course, there was a problem of scale in this type of construction. Such a design would probably be meaningless in a very small building but would become progressively more relevant as the building became larger.

The principle behind all urban planning is to keep the historical city alive, while at the same time building new structures corresponding to new speeds and scales in the sky above the city. In future cities, the two extremes of new and old, of the superhuman and the human scale, of high speed and human step, will coexist. Thus, in the plan for Tokyo several multistoried shopping centres, auditoriums, etc., have been built on a human scale, close to the lowest artificial ground. Similarly, there are many walkways for pedestrians and plazas of various sizes for circulating masses of people. This is the same as in the old historical cities. Nevertheless, this type of spatial coexistence cannot have a continuous hierarchy of centripetal streets and quarters as medieval cities had. Medieval cities were organized on the basis of the speed of human walking, a speed for which the centripetal arrangement was well suited. But in modern cities walking speed and automobile speed mix together. Thus, the modern city cannot be closed and centripetal; it must be open and circulating.

The Formation of the Tokaido Megalopolis. The actual situation in Japan today is that people and capital are flowing in landslide proportions into areas along the Tokaido, the coastal trunk line that links Tokyo, Nagoya, and Osaka. Of the country's 40 million urban residents, no less than 28 million, or 70%, live along this highly developed strip of land. When the urban population has increased to 110 million, as predicted for the year 2000, what will be the pattern of distribution? In my opinion, the reduction of the farming population in the undeveloped sections of the country will only lessen the chances for the development of cities in those districts, and the result will be that about 80% of the newly urbanized population will move to the Tokaido strip, forming a great urban belt with a population of about 90 million.

There then arises the question of what parts of the Tokyo-Nagoya-Osaka belt will be preferred by the inflowing population. There is little question but that the bulk of the newcomers will aim at Tokyo. If this happens, there will develop a hierarchy of satellite cities in the vicinity of the capital, forming a megalopolis of 60 million to 70 million people. This would mean a fantastic centripetal force pressing on the centre of the system, and it is difficult to imagine a structural transformation that would enable Tokyo to stand up under such pressure.

If, however, we could work along the lines of my Tokyo plan, we would replace the present circular nucleus of the city with a civic axis that could be lengthened at either end as necessary. This axial construction could break into open territory—even across Tokyo Bay, if need be—freeing the metropolis from the confining circle of centre-seeking suburbs.

It would appear, however, that in the natural course of development, the lines of connection along the Tokyo-Nagoya-Osaka strip are gradually breaking through administrative divisions and overcoming the traditional atmosphere of competition that has divided the three great cities. I have, therefore, come to believe that the strengthening of links along the Tokaido strip could become a vital factor in the conversion of the Japanese nation as a whole into a higher organic entity.

The Tokaido megalopolis would form Japan's central nervous system, while Hokkaido, northeast Honshu, and northwest Honshu on the north and Shikoku, southwest Honshu, and Kyushu on the south would form the arms and legs. The entire archipelago would then have a single coordinated structure.

To achieve this goal, it will be necessary to reorganize the pattern of traffic within the urban centres in such a way as to ensure smooth interchange with the great arteries. A basic revision of the land system is also foreseen, not so much because such a revision would be morally proper as because it will probably result inevitably from the increasing scale of investment. Finally, more compactness must be achieved in the planning and distribution of the various buildings and facilities needed for urban life.

The construction of compact urban environments will make it possible to leave much of the natural setting as it is. Mountains and seashores will no longer have to be marred by straggling urban or semiurban developments. This will make it much easier to preserve that which is good in Japanese history and culture—to a much greater extent than a system of dispersed cities, in which there is no clear distinction between city and nature. The faster Japan ends the dispersion of urban complexes, the safer will be its natural surroundings and historical heritage.

Conclusion. Such efforts point up the modern architect's challenge. Can modern technology restore humanity? Can modern civilization rediscover the core of humanity in its machines and edifices? Can architecture and the use of space uplift the human soul, where its predecessors have deadened the soul?

I would answer yes to these questions. Furthermore, I would say that this is the central part of any architect's task. For architects have the responsibility to create a channel between man's physical environment and the metaphysical world—to build a bridge between technology and humanity and to restore human significance to the human environment.

continued from page 105

Erickson and Massey. Eventually to house 18,000 students, the university featured a covered mall between the residences at the west end of the ridge and the academic quadrangle at the east end. The mall was designed to be a focus of student life.

Other new university buildings of more than routine interest were the lecture theatres for the University of Essex, Colchester, Eng., by H. T. Cadbury Brown and Partners and the halls of residence at the University of East Anglia, Norwich, by architect Denys Lasdun. At the University of Newcastle, the new Claremont Complex of science and arts buildings, designed by architects Richard Sheppard, Robson and Partners, was the largest single building project undertaken by the university since its completion in 1834.

At Cambridge, Eng., architects Howell, Killick, Partridge and Amis' University Centre was completed. The building, on the banks of the Cam River, provided common rooms, dining rooms, and general club facilities for senior members of the university. It featured a precast reinforced concrete frame and prominent concrete staircase towers. The characteristic external effect was produced by cladding the exteriors of the common room bays with slabs of portland stone which were fixed to the frame with exposed stainless-steel bolts, giving an almost armoured effect. The dining room, two stories high, was covered by a spectacular open-timber and tie-rod roof.

At the University of Malaya, Kuala Lumpur, James Cubitt and Partners were the architects for the new Medical Centre, which consisted of a 750-bed teaching hospital and was built along a linear plan.

In preparation for the XIX Olympic Games held in the autumn, Mexico City erected two new structures. The Sports Palace, an enclosed single-span steel structure on three levels, was designed by the internationally known Mexican architect F. Candela in collaboration with E. Casteneda and A. Peyri. Designed principally for basketball, the building could also be used for boxing and wrestling. The Olympic Swimming Pool and Gymnasium, actually two buildings side by side, were designed by Rosen Morrison, Recamier Montes, Guitierrez Bringas, and Valverde Garces. They were catenary structures supported on three parallel rows of concrete pillars.

Ford Foundation headquarters in New York City designed by Kevin Roche, John Dinkeloo and Associates. The 11-story building occupies a one-acre site and encloses an interior garden with office wings and glass curtain walls.

© EZRA STOLLER (ESTO)

Marine Midland Building by Skidmore, Owings and Merrill, a black aluminum and bronze glass tower. The cube sculpture in front of the building is by Isamu Noguchi.

© EZRA STOLLER (ESTO)

In Brazil the extension to the De La Rue factory in Rio de Janeiro by architect Brian Bogue was cited by the Brazilian Institute of Architects. The structure was of concrete poured in situ.

In London's Leicester Square the Swiss Centre opened in 1968. Designed by architect Justus Dahinden, the elegant open-plan building, housing shops and four restaurants, quickly became a popular West End rendezvous. Across the Thames the new Hayward Gallery, part of the South Bank Arts Centre which already included the Royal Festival Hall, Queen Elizabeth Hall, and Purcell Room, opened with a colourful and exciting Matisse exhibition. The gallery, designed by Greater London Council architect Hubert Bennett, was of windowless concrete with prismatic skylights and was integrated closely with the existing buildings to form an extensive arts complex.

Work began on the National Museum of Modern Art in Tokyo, Jap., designed by Yoshiro Taniguchi and situated just opposite the historic Imperial Palace. The new museum was being donated to the country by industrialist Shojiro Ishibashi.

In Israel, A. Riskin and G. Aneckstein were chosen from 87 competitors to design the Harry S. Truman Center for the Advancement of Peace in Jerusalem. Construction began in the spring on the centre. It would house teaching and research staffs whose purpose would be to study means of achieving international cooperation and amity. The building, sited atop Mt. Scopus, was to be clad in Jerusalem stone in an attempt to integrate it with the historic older buildings surrounding the mount.

Work proceeded on the new terminal at Helsinki Airport, Fin. The architects Ström and Tuomisto were responsible for the concrete structure with a cable-suspended roof and aluminum-clad walls.

Finally, in Berlin, Ludwig Mies van der Rohe's new National Gallery opened, an elegant steel and glass box that underlined once again Mies's position as one of the great architects of the century. Plans were also proceeding for a prominent office block to be designed by Mies for the City of London, a building that would be England's first by this great man.   (SA. B.)

See also Cities and Urban Affairs; Engineering Projects; Housing; Industrial Review.

ENCYCLOPÆDIA BRITANNICA FILMS. *The Living City* (1953); *Art of the Middle Ages* (Humanities Course) (1962); *Athens: The Golden Age* (Humanities Course) (1962); *Chartres Cathedral* (Humanities Course) (1962).

Arctic Regions

Exploration—both adventurous and resource oriented—highlighted the list of events in the circumpolar regions during 1968. The four-man expedition organized by Ralph S. Plaisted of St. Paul, Minn., reached the North Pole in April after a 44-day journey from Ward Hund Island. The four were the first men to reach the pole by an overland route since 1909. The expedition traveled 825 mi. through the ice ridges of the frozen Arctic Ocean in order to cover a straight-line distance of 474 mi.

In August a five-man expedition to Polaris Promontory examined the remains of C. F. Hall to determine whether he had been poisoned. In 1871, Hall had attempted an expedition to the North Pole using a converted U.S. Navy tugboat, the "Polaris." The vessel became locked in by frozen ice and, at the height of the dissension that developed during the winter, Hall had died mysteriously after drinking a cup of coffee.

In October the U.S. Department of Labor announced that a $72,000 grant had been made to the Kodiak Community College to train Eskimos, Aleuts, and Indians to repair refrigeration equipment used in the fishing industry. Under a grant from the Central Mortgage and Housing Corporation, the Canadian Department of Indian Affairs and Northern Development continued its program of training Eskimo families in the operation and management of modern housing facilities.

A report submitted to the Canadian Department of Indian Affairs and Northern Development late in 1968 indicated that longer-term investments in the Yukon had been discouraged because of a lack of adequate transportation and other basic services. Given the right economic climate and capital investments of $1.4 billion from both private and public sources, it was predicted that the gross value of the Yukon's annual mineral output could expand at least eight or nine times by 1985.

On February 21, a four-man British expedition headed by W. Herbert left Point Barrow, Alaska, on a 16-month trek of 3,800 mi. across the Arctic Ocean to the Spitsbergen Archipelago. The team hoped to conduct snow and ice and physiological studies. In October one member of the party was reported seriously injured and was evacuated by aircraft from Ellesmere Island, Canada. A four-man group led by David Humphreys of Australia visited Cape Morris Jesup, Greenland, in late May and proved that the earth's northernmost tip of land had been incorrectly located on all maps. Moreover, the cape was found to be an island and not a peninsula.

It was reported in June that the U.S.S.R. had begun the construction of a number of new atomic-powered icebreakers and that they would be used to keep the northern sea-lanes open for longer periods each year. In April the Soviet newspaper *Trud* reported that construction had begun on a new town, Aykhal, located at the very edge of the Arctic Circle.

Resources. The discovery of an oil field at Prudhoe Bay, Alaska, estimated to contain five to ten billion barrels of low-sulfur crude oil was the most momentous resource event in 1968. (*See* FUEL AND POWER.) During the 1968–69 winter, up to ten oil drilling rigs were expected to be operated on the Arctic coastal plain by major Canadian and American companies. Panarctic Oils, Ltd., a consortium of Ca-

© TOPIX

Wally Herbert, leader of a British trans-Arctic expedition conducting snow and ice and physiological studies. The team left Point Barrow, Alaska, in 1968 and planned to cover the 3,800 mi. to Spitsbergen Archipelago in 16 months.

nadian mining and oil companies, conducted over 700 mi. of seismic surveys in the Melville Island area. Panarctic also was testing a new icebreaker bow, the Alexbow, which was expected to be the crucial factor in opening up sea transportation in the event oil was found in the Arctic Islands. The Soviet newspaper *Sovetskaya Sibir* reported in April that 106 oil and gas deposits had been discovered in western Siberia during the 15-year period ending in 1968.

The Fish and Wildlife Service of the U.S. Department of the Interior reported that the estimated 700 musk-oxen on Nunivak Island off the Alaska coast were being endangered because of inadequate forage. In order to reduce the herd the department was considering reestablishing herds on the Alaska mainland or donating musk-oxen to research institutions or museums. On April 1, the management of 2,700 reindeer in the Mackenzie River Delta, Northwest Territories, was taken over by the Canadian Wildlife Service from private contractors. The herd was an important source of meat for the people in the area, and the Wildlife Service was to study the animals and their range to determine the level of sustained yield that was technically possible. In April the U.S., Canada, Japan, and the U.S.S.R. agreed to extend an 11-year-old curb on the hunting of fur seals in the Pacific Ocean. It was agreed by the four countries that the fur seal population in the northern Pacific was still too low to permit unrestricted hunting. Under the agreed conditions fur seals could be caught only in summer when they come ashore.

In January 1968 the Canadian government announced a number of changes in regulations governing the conditions and eligibility clauses of the Northern Mineral Exploration Program. Under this development incentive program, up to 40% of the costs of mineral exploration in either the Yukon or Northwest Territories would be provided by the Department of Indian Affairs and Northern Development.

In March the U.S.S.R. newspaper *Morskoy Flot* reported a radical reorganization of the hydro-meteorological service in the Soviet Arctic. Various computer centres were being established at locations in the Arctic including Dixon Island in the port of Tiksi and at the town of Tebek. The data collected by automatic stations eventually would be supplemented

Areas:
see Populations and Areas; *see also the individual country articles*

by data received from satellites and from high-altitude aircraft.

Research. In July the U.S., Canada, Denmark, and France began the largest study of Eskimos ever undertaken, under the auspices of the International Biological Program. The objective was to gain an insight into the general patterns of human adaptability and evolution in the very harsh northern environment. In the summer the U.S. Coast Guard icebreaker "Staten Island" conducted a two-month oceanographic survey of the Chukchi Sea, the Bering Sea, and the Bering Strait, off the Siberian coast.

During February and March, a field party from the Frozen Sea Research Group of the Canadian Marine Sciences Branch took measurements in the water below a growing ice sheet at Cambridge Bay to determine the mechanism by which salt released from frozen surfaces leads to convective processes in the water. The major activities of the Canadian Polar Continental Shelf Project during 1968 included aeromagnetic surveys, marine and glacial geology, geomagnetic studies, glaciology, gravity, and hydrographic surveys, sea-ice studies, and topographic control surveys. The U.S.S.R. established two new ice drift stations, one about 500 mi. to the northeast of the Novosibirsk Islands, to carry out oceanographic, hydrophysical, ice, and other studies related to shipping along the northern sea route.   (K. DE LA B.)

See also Archaeology; Geography.

ENCYCLOPÆDIA BRITANNICA FILMS. *The Arctic—Islands of the Frozen Sea* (1959); *The Face of the High Arctic* (1959); *High Arctic—Life on the Land* (1959); *The High Arctic Biome* (1961); *Life on the Tundra* (1965).

Argentina

The republic of Argentina, occupying the southeastern section of South America, is bounded by Bolivia, Paraguay, Brazil, Uruguay, Chile, and the Atlantic Ocean. It is the second largest Latin-American country, after Brazil, with an area of 1,072,156 sq.mi. (2,776,884 sq.km.), excluding 481,177 sq.mi. of Antarctic and South Atlantic island areas. Pop. (1968 est.): 23,707,000. Cap. and largest city: Buenos Aires (pop., 1966, 3.3 million). Language: Spanish. Religion: mainly Roman Catholic. President in 1968, Juan Carlos Onganía.

After more than 20 years of severe inflation and frequent devaluations in the exchange market, the degree of monetary stability achieved in 1968 was without doubt one of the most notable features of the Argentine economy. The cost of living, which recently had shown an annual increase of 20–30%, remained virtually unchanged for several months, while the international strength of the peso, supported by exchange reserves of about U.S. $1 billion, was sufficient to induce the Argentine government to subscribe to art. 8 of the Articles of Agreement of the International Monetary Fund (IMF). By the terms of this article Argentina undertook to impose no restrictions on international transfers on current account.

The stability and strength of the currency resulted from the measures introduced in 1967 by the minister of economy and labour, Adalbert Krieger Vasena, to abolish exchange control, to attract international credit and foreign capital, and to contain inflation. A complete wage freeze was maintained in 1968 with only minor resistance from the labour union movement, which was seriously weakened by internal strife.

Although the international reputation of the peso was enhanced during the year, there were several reverses to the country's export trade, which since 1962 had been a creditable feature of the balance of payments. Foremost among the setbacks was the deterioration in trade relations with the U.K. The British government's decision to ban all imports of meat between early December 1967 and mid-April 1968 as a precautionary measure in its fight to end the disastrous epidemic of foot-and-mouth disease then affecting cattle in England and Wales dealt a severe blow to the Argentine chilled beef trade. The value of exports of chilled beef to all destinations in the first half of the year was only $18.8 million, compared with $81.6 million in the same period of 1967. Britain's subsequent allegation that infected Argentine lamb had been the probable source of its epidemic caused great resentment in Argentina, and negotiations for important trade contracts between the two countries were jeopardized. Even after the British import embargo had been lifted, the Argentine government forbade the resumption of the former system of shipping chilled beef quarters to the U.K. on a consignment basis and insisted that a firm f.o.b. price should be established before shipment—a condition that, for technical reasons alone, was not conducive to the restoration of this important trade.

Anglo-Argentine relations were further aggravated by a revival of interest in the long-standing dispute over the ownership of the Falkland Islands (Islas

OAS Secretary-General Galo Plaza (left) and Ambassador Carlos Holguin of Colombia attending the opening of a Pan American Union show of carpets designed by Argentine artists.

ARGENTINA

Education. (1965) Primary, pupils 3,124,870, teachers 153,685; secondary, pupils 184,955, teachers 29,287; vocational, pupils 425,588, teachers 59,775; teacher training, students 184,934, teachers 22,066; higher (including 13 universities), students 243,303, teaching staff 15,361.

Finance. Monetary unit: peso, with exchange rates of 350 pesos to U.S. $1 and 840 pesos to £1 sterling. Gold and convertible foreign exchange, central bank: (March 1968) U.S. $641 million; (March 1967) U.S. $256 million. Budget (1968 est.): revenue 639,870,000,000 pesos; expenditure 688.4 billion pesos. Gross national product: (1966) 4,012,000,000,000 pesos; (1965) 3,232,000,000,000 pesos. Money supply: (March 1968) 1,125,000,000,000 pesos; (March 1967) 815 billion pesos. Cost of living (Buenos Aires; 1963 = 100): (May 1968) 305; (May 1967) 252.

Foreign Trade. (1967) Imports 364,450,000,000 pesos; exports 462,870,000,000 pesos. Import sources: U.S. 22%; Brazil 11%; West Germany 10%; Italy 7%; U.K. 6%. Export destinations: Italy 16%; Netherlands 13%; U.K. 9%; Brazil 7%; Spain 7%; West Germany 5%; Chile 5%. Main exports: meat 26%; corn 15%; wheat 7%; wool 7%; hides and skins 5%.

Transport and Communications. Roads (1965) 135,200 km. Motor vehicles in use (1965): passenger 925,258; commercial 542,139. Railways (1966): *c.* 41,840 km.; traffic 14,076,000,000 passenger-km., freight 13,464,000,000 net ton-km. Shipping (1967): merchant vessels 100 gross tons and over 315; gross tonnage 1,240,372. Air traffic (1966): 1,140,790,000 passenger-km.; freight 15,804,000 net ton-km. Telephones (Dec. 1966) 1,526,767. Radio receivers (Dec. 1966) 7 million. Television receivers (Dec. 1966) 1,850,000.

Agriculture. Production (in 000; metric tons; 1967; 1966 in parentheses): wheat 7,400 (6,247); corn 9,054 (7,040); barley 700 (438); oats 575 (540); potatoes 1,794 (1,484); linseed 430 (577); cotton, lint 90 (116); peanuts 354 (411); oranges 935 (789); apples 516 (414); sunflower seed 1,120 (782); tobacco (1966) 42, (1965) 52; beef and veal (1966) 2,412, (1965) 2,018; butter (1966) 46, (1965) 42; cheese (1966) 170, (1965) 151; wool, greasy (1966) 198, (1965) 186; quebracho extract (1966) 113, (1965) 109; wine 2,817 (2,192). Livestock (in 000; June 1967): cattle *c.* 48,800; sheep (June 1965) *c.* 48,500; pigs (June 1966) *c.* 4,000; poultry (1964–65) 34,200.

Industry. Fuel and power (in 000; 1967): crude oil 16,409 metric tons; coal 410 metric tons; natural gas 4,793,000 cu.m.; electricity (excluding most industrial production) 12,417,000 kw-hr. Production (in 000; metric tons; 1967): cement 3,552; crude steel 1,326; cotton yarn 84; passenger cars (including assembly) 134 units; commercial vehicles (including assembly) 41 units. Index of manufacturing (1963 = 100): (1966) 129; (1965) 129.

Malvinas) in the South Atlantic; the delicate nature of the situation was underlined by the rather obvious omission of Argentina from the itinerary of the South American tour of Queen Elizabeth II in November.

In its meat trade Argentina also had trouble with another important customer, Spain, which, having agreed to receive a total of 60,000 tons of beef in 1968, suddenly suspended imports in April, ostensibly because of plentiful local supplies. The underlying reason, however, appeared to be Spain's dissatisfaction with its large adverse trade balance with Argentina; after talks between the two governments shipments were resumed in August. Similar difficulties were encountered in trade with Brazil. After several months of negotiations agreement was reached for the sale of one million tons of wheat to that country.

The marked improvement in Argentina's international credit status was well demonstrated by two successful bond issues, each of DM. 100 million, in West Germany in December 1967 and September 1968, and also—for the first time since 1938—one of $25 million in the U.S. in June. These funds were raised to assist in financing the government's huge 1968 investment program, costing 319 billion pesos (more than $900 million). The program paid particular attention to the improvement of road communications, especially between La Plata and Buenos Aires and northwestward along and across the Paraná River to provide better links with the provinces of Entre Ríos and Corrientes.

During the year further preliminary arrangements were made concerning work on the hydroelectric and irrigation project of El Chocón–Cerros Colorados, which was expected to cost more than $500 million. The World Bank indicated its willingness to lend $70 million for this scheme, and offers of suppliers' credits, also totaling $70 million, were received from the U.S., Canada, and several Western European countries. Calls for bids to perform the civil engineering work and to supply the electrical equipment for the project aroused considerable international interest.

The question of private foreign investment in Argentina caused much controversy. It was alleged, particularly in nationalist circles, that foreign (mainly U.S.) interests were gaining a dominant position in some activities. In reply, the government repeatedly emphasized that it sought foreign investment only to finance new developments or expansion programs; significantly, protection for foreign interests acquiring shares in existing local companies was excluded from the investment guarantees agreement with the U.S., which became effective in July.

Nationalists and liberals in the administration were divided on the political aims of the regime. The experiment conducted during the year in the province of Córdoba for the establishment of an economic and social council to represent community interests led many liberals, both within and outside the government, to fear that the regime might embrace the principles of a corporate state rather than restore the traditional system of political parties. The resignation during the summer of Alvaro Alsogaray as Argentine ambassador in the U.S., followed shortly afterward by the dismissal of his brother Gen. Julio Alsogaray as commander in chief of the Army (together with the dismissal of the other military service chiefs), was regarded by some observers as an indication of growing nationalist influence.　　　　(I. C. C.)

ENCYCLOPÆDIA BRITANNICA FILMS. *Argentina (People of the Pampa)* (1957).

Art Exhibitions

In 1968, as in the preceding few years, many of the major art exhibitions mounted throughout the world concentrated on the works of a single artist. Centenaries and birthdays were sometimes the excuse for a retrospective—an opportunity for the gallery-goer to see, in one place, a representative selection of an important artist's work. Often such shows resulted in new insights and evaluations of the artist and his place in the history of art.

A large exhibition of the paintings of Jean-Édouard Vuillard (1868–1940), celebrating the centenary of his birth, was held at the Orangerie in Paris. It revealed him as a more complex artistic personality than hitherto had been thought. The intimacy of his early works contrasted with the increasing classicism of the portraits that began to occupy him after 1914.

KEYSTONE

Sculptor Barbara Hepworth looking through one of her works on exhibit at the Tate Gallery, London. The retrospective, held April 4 through May 19, covered her 40-year career.

Joan Miró's 75th birthday was celebrated by a week of festivities on France's Côte d'Azur, culminating in the opening of an important exhibition of works by this colourful artist at the Maeght Foundation in Saint-Paul-de-Vence.

In London the Tate Gallery celebrated the 70th birthday of the great English sculptor Henry Moore (*see* BIOGRAPHY) with a magnificent retrospective. An outdoor sculpture park was especially set up to display the larger works. Both the traditionalism of Moore, whose sources of inspiration ranged from Mexican sculpture to natural forms in the landscape, and his dominant role in English sculpture in the 20th century, were well brought out in this fitting tribute. In May, Moore was awarded the prestigious Erasmus Prize by Prince Bernhard of the Netherlands. The Erasmus award, worth 100,000 guilders ($27,624), part of which must be given to a cultural organization of the recipient's choice, was founded by the prince in 1958. Concurrently, an exhibition of Moore's work was mounted at the Kröller-Müller Museum in Otterlo. It later moved on to Düsseldorf, Rotterdam, and Stuttgart.

Two other sculptors whose work reflects in some ways the influence of Moore were shown in London. The Tate Gallery organized an exhibition of the work of Barbara Hepworth, covering 40 years and showing how she had progressed from the small carved animal

figures of the late 1920s to the sensuous and beautiful abstract stone carvings, with which she is usually identified, and to her most recent works: large geometrical bronzes. In contrast to Moore, who always used the human figure as a basis for his sculptural forms, Hepworth's pieces rely primarily on the natural forms of rocks and landscape. Isamu Noguchi had his first one-man show in London since 1934 at the Gimpel Fils Gallery. As with Moore and Hepworth, his work displayed a sure feeling for materials and a brilliant sense of pure form.

One of the Tate Gallery's most popular shows of the year was an exhibition of the work of the American pop artist Roy Lichtenstein, illustrating his use of comic strip imagery and the techniques of commercial art. Lichtenstein's work was also shown in Switzerland at the Kunsthalle, Bern. Eighty-four paintings by the Surrealist André Masson were exhibited at the Musée Cantini in Marseilles, France. Masson's work had a strong influence on American painting, but this was the first time that many of his important works had been seen in France. In West Germany the Stuttgart Art Gallery paid tribute to Oskar Schlemmer, one of the most important German artists of the 20th century, with an exhibition of his work which showed both the influence of his disciplined Bauhaus teaching and his own mystical romantic vision.

Other large one-man shows included the works of the Norwegian Expressionist Edvard Munch in Schaffhausen, W.Ger.; paintings by the abstractionist Max Bill at the Kunsthalle, Bern; a Jean Lurçat retrospective at the Arras Museum, France; and an Arts Council show in London of paintings and drawings by Gwen John, the sister of Augustus John. The Holburne Museum, Bath, Eng., mounted a retrospective of the work of James Wilson Morrice (1865–1924), one of the first Canadian artists to attract international attention, as part of the Bath Festival. The exhibition was organized by the National Gallery of Canada.

Many large and unusual group shows were also mounted during 1968, one of the most important being the Documenta 4 exhibition in Kassel, W.Ger. The Documenta exhibitions, quadrennial compendiums of contemporary art, are financed mainly by industries in the Kassel area. There was an enormous predominance of work by American artists in the 1968 Documenta, revealing the extent of invention prevalent in the U.S. art world. Artists shown included Barnett Newman, Kenneth Noland, Donald Judd, Robert Morris, and Philip King. Motorized objects and objects with lights were among the more experimental works on display.

The 1968 Venice Biennale, also an international

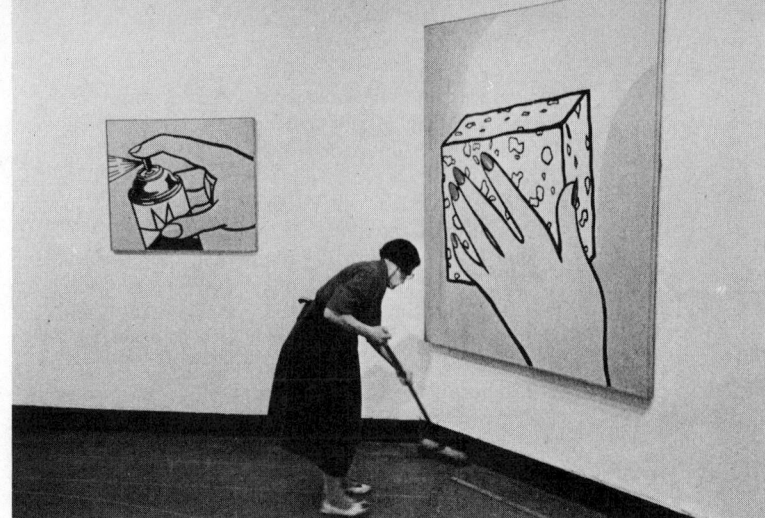
Cleaning lady at Tate Gallery, London, between works of pop artist Roy Lichtenstein.

"THE GUARDIAN"

barometer of contemporary art, was marred by riots and student sit-ins so serious that they left the future of these major exhibitions in doubt. On view were paintings by Guido Molinari of Canada, Kumi Sugai of Japan, Paul Delvaux of Belgium, and the Venezuelan New Yorker Marisol. The British restricted themselves to the work of two artists: the painter Bridget Riley and the sculptor Philip King.

The Institute of Contemporary Arts, installed in its new headquarters in London's Carlton House Terrace, staged two unusual exhibitions of contemporary art. "The Obsessive Image" featured works in which the human figure formed the central image. "Cybernetic Serendipity," illustrating the use of machines and computers in art, demonstrated a bewildering variety of possibilities. Many of the exhibits allowed viewers to participate by touching, talking into microphones, or listening to speakers.

Very different but attracting at least equal attention was the magnificent exhibition of Gothic art in Europe from the 12th to the 14th century, organized by the Council of Europe and held at the newly reopened Pavillion de Flore of the Louvre in Paris. This very comprehensive and enormously impressive exhibition included sculpture, paintings, illuminated manuscripts, stained glass windows, church plate, reliquaries, and other small objects. The National Museum of Copenhagen lent a gold altar from Jutland, one of many interesting items of the lesser-known Scandinavian Gothic. From England came the Ormsby Psalter, the Psalter of Robert de Lisle, and Lord Bute's Bannatyne cup. There was sculpture from the Benedictine cloister of Notre-Dame-en-Vaux, Châlons-sur-Marne, France, and from Chartres. The contrast between Italian and French sculpture of the period was well illustrated by such works as "Henry VII" by Tino di Camaino and Giovanni Pisano's "Justice."

The Royal Academy in London staged "France in the Eighteenth Century" as its big winter exhibition in 1968. It was a gargantuan show featuring paintings, drawings, sculpture, architectural drawings, furniture, and objets d'art. Many of the pictures were familiar to enthusiasts of the *dix-huitième siècle*, including François Boucher's famous nude "Miss O'Murphy," Fragonard's "Le Billet Doux" from the Metropolitan Museum in New York City, and a splendid series of Chardins and Watteaus. Jacques-Louis David's small "Oath of the Horatii" from the Toledo (O.) Museum and his painting of Marat dead in his bath from the Louvre were chosen to represent the neoclassicism of the Revolutionary period.

Lifelike sculpture entitled "Young Lady" exhibited by Frank Gallo at the Venice Biennale.
UPI COMPIX

Sculpture titled "Mitosis" by Isamu Noguchi. Noguchi's 1968 show was his first in London since 1934.
HANNA SCHREIBER FROM RAPHO GUILLUMETTE

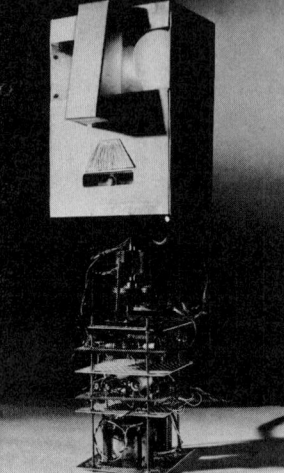

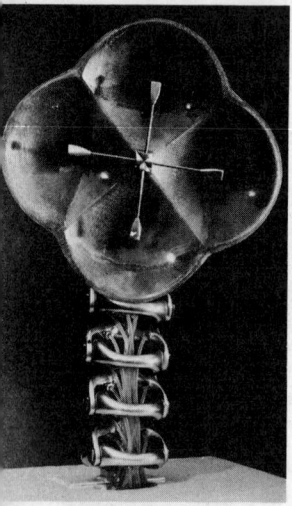

Top, "Albert" by John
Billingsley exhibited
in the "Cybernetic
Serendipity" show
at the Institute
of Contemporary Arts,
London. Below, "Sound
Activated Mobile 1968"
by Edward Ihnatowicz
at the same exhibit. Both
works have electrically
operated moving parts
that respond to light.

An exhibition celebrating the 50th anniversary of the founding of the Bauhaus, the German school of design that flourished first in Weimar (1919–25), then in Dessau, and finally briefly in Berlin before it was closed by the Nazis in 1933, opened in May in Stuttgart and moved to the Royal Academy in London in September. The exhibition, designed by Herbert Bayer who was himself a Bauhaus master, included specimens of the school's many industrial products and textiles as well as works by the artists and designers who taught there and who continued to promote the Bauhaus theory of design after the school closed. These included the architects Walter Gropius (the school's first director), Marcel Breuer, and Ludwig Mies van der Rohe and the painters Wassily Kandinsky, Paul Klee, Lyonel Feininger, Oskar Schlemmer, and Laszlo Moholy-Nagy. The exhibition emphasized the lasting contribution made by the Bauhaus in the field of design.

The Albright-Knox Gallery in Buffalo, N.Y., staged a highly significant modern exhibition in the spring. Organized for the second Buffalo Festival of the Arts Today, it was entitled "Plus by Minus: Today's Half-Century" and presented geometric abstraction in painting and sculpture from 1913 to the present. It attempted to show that there exists a mainstream of 20th-century art that owes absolutely nothing to tradition. A large number of Russian works by such artists as K. Malevich, El Lissitzky, and A. Pevsner were included and there were over 100 sculptures, paintings, and drawings by Naum Gabo. Works from the Bauhaus, de Stijl, and Circle groups were also shown.

American naïve paintings from the Garbisch Collection were shown first in Paris and then later in the year in London. The charming primitivism of Edward Hicks's "The Cornell Farm" contrasted with the smoky "City of Fantasy" by an unknown Massachusetts artist and illustrated the variety and depth of expression to be found in this little-known type of American painting.

The Metropolitan Museum of Art in New York City was the scene of the highly unusual "The Great Age of the Fresco," sent to the United States from Italy in the fall in recognition of the American contribution toward restoring the art works of Florence following the 1966 flood. The frescoes—some of which had become detached during the flood, others by the passage of time—were seen there for the first time away from the buildings where they were originally painted. The exhibition provided an unprecedented opportunity to study these masterpieces, many of which had been in awkward and poorly lit locations.

Many smaller exhibitions throughout the world attracted attention. The Musée Rodin in Paris held a show of "Czech Sculpture from Myslbek to Today" as its summer exhibition. The first half of the show was devoted to earlier works of modern classical sculpture, including pieces by Josef Myslbek, the acknowledged father of modern Czech sculpture and himself strongly influenced by Rodin. The second half was contemporary work by artists such as Otto Gutfreund and Jiri Novak.

The Museum of Modern Art in New York City mounted a show of realistic art titled "The Art of the Real." It included works by Georgia O'Keefe, Ellsworth Kelly, and Tony Smith. Also in New York City, the Brooklyn Museum staged "The Triumph of Realism," featuring the works of the German W. Leibl (1844–1900) and his circle, influenced by

Gustave Courbet. Their related contemporaries outside Germany included Whistler, Thomas Eakins, and Winslow Homer. The exhibition moved on to the Virginia Museum of Fine Arts and to the California Palace of the Legion of Honor in San Francisco.

Admirers of French art in the U.S. had the opportunity to see a traveling exhibition called "French Paintings from French Museums—XVII–XVIII Centuries." The Louvre lent paintings by S. Vouet, N. Poussin, Claude Lorrain, Philippe de Champaigne, Watteau, and others. The museums at Le Mans, Auxerre, and Nîmes also lent works.

The Nottingham (Eng.) University Art Gallery held an exhibition of "Pictures from Locko Park, Derbyshire," the collection of Capt. P. J. B. Drury-Lowe, many of which had never before been seen outside Locko. The collection, formed by William Drury-Lowe (1803–77) between 1840 and 1855, consisted of fine 13th- and 14th-century Italian pictures including a St. Catherine of Alexandria from the Daddi workshop and the delicately drawn "Head of a Youth" by Andrea del Sarto.

Also in London, Roland, Browse and Delbanco exhibited an important set of 37 recently discovered sheets of drawings by the Swiss romantic artist Henry Fuseli, lent by the Auckland (N.Z.) City Art Gallery. The Arts Council mounted a show of "Italian Old Masters Drawings from the Janos Scholz Collection," and there was a retrospective at the Tate Gallery of the work of the 20th-century Polish painter Balthus. The Victoria and Albert Museum displayed 147 German drawings of the 19th century lent by the Düsseldorf and Hamburg museums and including work by Hans von Marées and Adolf Menzel.

The new Hayward Gallery, part of London's South Bank Arts Centre, opened in the spring with a splendid Matisse retrospective that included many important works from foreign museums and collections. In the autumn the gallery housed a large show of the work of the Expressionist Emil Nolde.

Lovers of art nouveau were treated to a beautiful centenary exhibition of the work of Charles Rennie Mackintosh, first shown in the summer at the Edinburgh Festival and then moved to the Victoria and Albert Museum. The exhibition included drawings, furniture, and household objects by this highly original architect and designer. (SA. B.)

See also Museums and Galleries; Photography.

ENCYCLOPÆDIA BRITANNICA FILMS. *Michelangelo* (1965); *The Louvre* (1965); *Meaning in Modern Painting* (1967); *The Artist at Work—Jacques Lipchitz Master Sculptor* (1968).

Art Sales

The fall in the value of money accounted for part of the steep increase in prices for works of art at auction, but the rise was exceptional during the 1967–68 sales season. Vast numbers of pictures changed hands at a profit, and there was a big rise in the number of modern pictures sold at high prices. Sotheby's of London alone sold 400 Impressionist and modern pictures in three days in April 1968 at an average price of about £6,000 each. On the first day of this sale a small oil painting on paper by Paul Klee fetched £36,000, and an oil called "Il flûte sur la Bosse," painted by Jean Dubuffet in 1947, went for £20,000; the highest price was £125,000, paid by the New York dealer Stephen Hahn for a Cubist painting by Picasso called "La Pointe de la Cité."

Sotheby's London turnover for the season was £20,-592,764, 50% more than the record figure of the previous year. Christie's of London also had a large increase of business, with a total of £11.7 million. In New York, Sotheby's Parke-Bernet branch totaled $22,694,419, nearly one-quarter more than the year before.

In October 1968 Renoir's "Le Pont des Arts, Paris" was sold at Parke-Bernet for $1,550,000, beating the previous year's record for an Impressionist or modern painting of £588,000 ($1,411,200) for Monet's "La Terrasse à Sainte-Adresse" from the Rev. Theodore Pitcairn's collection. Another painting from the Pitcairn collection reached a high price in London, however, when Hahn paid £115,500 at Christie's for van Gogh's portrait of his mother, painted in 1888. In New York $310,000—a world record price for a painting by J. B. C. Corot—was paid at Parke-Bernet's for "Jeune Femme au Corsage rouge tenant une mandoline."

Increasing interest in Rembrandt etchings was shown when Parke-Bernet held a sale of the well-documented Nowell-Usticke collection; the finest of these marvellous etchings, "Six's Bridge" (Hind 209, second state of three), went for $45,000.

Record-breaking prices of the year included $85,000 paid in Paris at the Palais Galliéra for a Louis XV lacquer commode. This was the highest price ever paid for a piece of lacquer furniture, but fine French furniture had always been expensive and prices in general did not rise much during the year.

Prices for English and American 18th-century silver made by the most respected silversmiths shot up spectacularly. An early American silver teapot, stand, and creamer made by Paul Revere in Boston in 1793 were sold at Parke-Bernet's for $70,000, while a single creamer by the same maker went for $16,500. In England, Christie's sold a George I silver coffeepot with the mark of Anthony Nelme, 1720, for £5,500, and Henry Spencer and Sons of Retford, Nottinghamshire, sold a silver salver with the monogram of Queen Victoria, by Storr and Mortimer, for £1,250. The world record price for a single lot of English silver was beaten at Sotheby's on July 4 when a pair of Elizabeth I silver-gilt livery pots went for £36,000. At the end of the season, Christie's silver sales totaled £1,431,299, a 77% increase over the previous year.

The big London auctioneers caused some resentment by opening branches elsewhere. On June 7, Christie's first sale in Geneva was boycotted by nearly all the members of the Swiss Antique Dealers' Association.

Some of the most interesting sales were of African art: £11,000 was paid at Sotheby's for a Benin plaque of a warrior and attendants; and £10,000 for a splendid Benin bronze head of an Oba. Elizabeth Taylor Burton paid a world record price for a diamond ring, $305,000, at Parke-Bernet's when she bought a platinum ring set with an emerald-cut diamond weighing 33.19 carats. Although most of the best glass paperweights are French, London appeared to have become the centre for their sale. In May a weight well known among fanciers—the Maba liver-red Salamander—was sold at Sotheby's for £6,000.

In spite of the record prices noted above, however, 67% of the 85,000 lots sold at Sotheby's during the year went for £100 or less and 18% for £20 or less.

(WA. Ls.)

Book Sales. The season was an active one in London, where 45 sales brought in over £2 million, and

continued on page 118

ART AS A GROWTH STOCK

By Geraldine Keen

The collection of works of art has flourished among devoted connoisseurs and princes since Greek and Roman times. It has provided the livelihood of artists and craftsmen, from Praxiteles to Michelangelo, from Joshua Reynolds to Picasso. Thus the connection between money and art has always existed. Today it is underlined as salesroom prices make headline news, and an investment in Rembrandt, Canaletto, or Chagall makes stock market appreciation look insignificant.

The Artist as Moneymaker. In every age the work of the artist or craftsman has borne a different relation to society, and the scale of money values relating to art has shifted accordingly. In the building of Pompeii the fresco artists were no more highly considered than the carpenters or the plumbers, and the rate of remuneration was minimal. The Renaissance saw the birth of the "artist" as a superbeing, whose genius was virtually priceless. Raphael or Benvenuto Cellini would probably rank as millionaires if money values could be properly converted to present-day terms.

This change in the artist's status coincided with a reappraisal of the Greek achievement. The unearthing of Greek marbles, or even the burial and subsequent "discovery" of contemporary fakes, brought massive financial rewards—an early form of the antique trade. In 18th-century France fine furniture, silver, and porcelain were as highly valued as pictures. Thus the value of works of art today is no new phenomenon; it reflects the changing values and interests of our society.

The years since World War II have seen a fabulous increase in the prices paid for works of art. This can be demonstrated from salesroom records. A painting by Chagall, "La Mariée à double face," passed through the salesroom at $1,000 in 1950; it was sold again in 1967 for $25,000. In 1952 a colour-twist candlestick, dating from around 1760, was sold for £110; in March 1968 it was sold for £1,350. A 15th-century Ming blue and white dish, sold for £775 in 1954, was bid up to £18,000 in June 1968.

Collectors and dealers have watched art prices spiraling upward with amazement—and in many cases with satisfaction. Until recently no general measure of the order of magnitude of these price increases existed. At the end of 1967 *The Times*

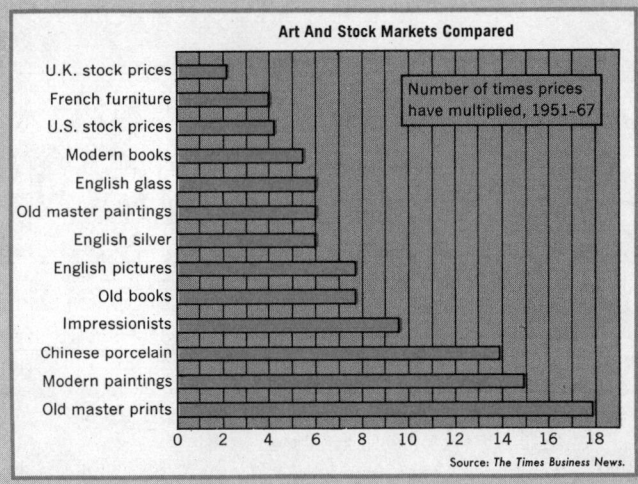

Art And Stock Markets Compared

Number of times prices have multiplied, 1951–67

- U.K. stock prices
- French furniture
- U.S. stock prices
- Modern books
- English glass
- Old master paintings
- English silver
- English pictures
- Old books
- Impressionists
- Chinese porcelain
- Modern paintings
- Old master prints

0 2 4 6 8 10 12 14 16 18

Source: The Times Business News.

(London), in cooperation with Sotheby's auction house, began to publish a series of statistical price indices measuring the record of appreciation in various fields of the art market since the early 1950s. These indices measure no more than the average movement of salesroom prices, and are frequently affected by the exceptional and erratic nature of bidding at particular sales. However, for the first time they provide a basis for assessing the comparative record of different sectors of the art market, and the way in which the forces at work in contemporary society add a price tag to works of art that are in themselves priceless.

The most rapid increases in price have come on the one hand among the most expensive works of art passing through the salesroom—Impressionist and modern pictures—and on the other hand among the cheapest, the most striking example being old master etchings and engravings. On the rare occasions when important paintings by old masters appear in the salesroom, very high prices can be paid—such as the $2.3 million given by the Metropolitan Museum of Art, New York, in 1961 for Rembrandt's "Aristotle Contemplating the Bust of Homer," the highest salesroom price on record for any work of art. It must be noted, however, that

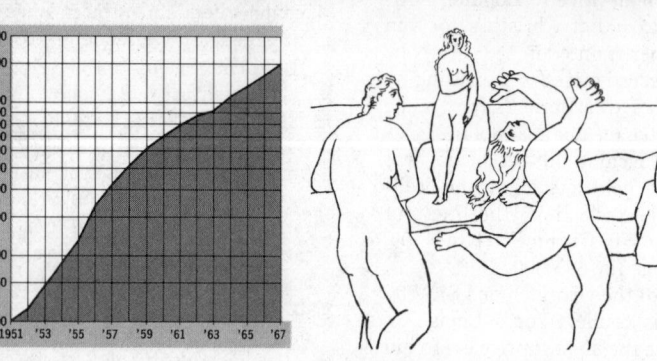

OLD MASTER PRINTS

up 18 times 1951–67.*
Detail from "Christ Healing the Sick" by Rembrandt, an impression of which sold for £13,542 in May 1968.

COURTESY, SOTHEBY & CO.

20TH-CENTURY PAINTINGS

up 15 times 1951–67.*
Detail from Picasso's "Les Baigneuses" which sold for £9,000 in April 1968.

COURTESY, GRAWZ COLLECTION

IMPRESSIONIST PAINTINGS

up 9½ times 1951–67.*
Detail from "Le Pont des Arts, Paris" by Renoir which sold for $1,550,000 in October 1968.

WIDE WORLD

prices of this order are in the main lonely exceptions and cannot properly be compared with earlier ones to obtain a meaningful "rise in price."

The types of old pictures that are seen regularly in the salesroom—Dutch and Flemish works of the 16th and 17th centuries, Italian and French of the 18th century, and a number of earlier, often anonymous works by Italian and Northern artists—are, quality for quality, much cheaper than Impressionist pictures or the works of well-established 20th-century artists. Their increase in price has been much less spectacular—about 6-fold since 1951, compared with 9½ times for the Impressionists and 15 times for 20th-century artists.

Leaving 1968 aside for the moment (it was an unusual year in the salesroom in many fields), the increase in price for old master pictures is typical of most traditional fields of collecting, where no exceptional forces are at work. Very much the same record of appreciation was achieved between 1951 and 1967 for English silver, English glass, European porcelain, and British 18th- and 19th-century pictures.

The record for the Impressionists and for the bigger names among 20th-century artists is exceptional in that their paintings are in the forefront of modern taste. A considerable share of the work of these artists remains in private hands, while museums are still building up their collections—factors making for an active market in which the monied collectors of today tend to concentrate. *The Times*-Sotheby index is based on six Impressionist and seven important modern artists. In each case a number of relatively minor as well as major names were chosen in

order to give a representative picture. The record of appreciation is impressive. (*See* Table.)

At the other end of the scale, old master prints are also exceptional, with an average 18-fold price increase between 1951 and 1967. In this case it has been intense competition among a growing band of collectors of modest means that has pushed prices dramatically higher. This is the same general trend that has started "antique" shops mushrooming and sent the price of junk escalating. In the case of old master prints, however, considerable scholarship and expertise is required by the collector. It is vital to be able to distinguish between early valuable impressions and later ones that are worth very little. For instance, recent prices paid for Rembrandt's famous "Christ Healing the Sick" (the "Hundred Guilder Print") range from £30 to £26,000, according to the rarity of the impression.

The most striking records of appreciation have been for prints by Rembrandt, Canaletto, and those made by contemporary engravers after drawings by Pieter Brueghel the Elder. According to the index, prices multiplied 24, 21, and 25 times, respectively, between 1951 and 1967. The reasons behind these rises are probably substantially different.

Rembrandt provides the best example of sheer quality making for high salesroom prices. His engravings are superb. In addition, he has been continually brought to the public's mind and eye over the last decade as a number of very fine paintings from his hand have come up for auction—two of them fetching the highest salesroom prices ever recorded (his "Aristotle" mentioned above, and his "Portrait of the Artist's Son Titus," sold

OLD MASTER PAINTINGS

up 6 times 1951–67.*
Detail from "A Regatta
on the Grand Canal,
Venice" by Canaletto
which sold for £100,000
in 1967.

SOTHEBY & CO.

BRITISH 18TH- AND 19TH-CENTURY PAINTINGS

up 7½ times 1951–67.*
Detail from "A Huntsman
in a Long Green Coat"
by George Stubbs which
sold for £37,000
in June 1968.

SOTHEBY & CO.

ENGLISH SILVER

up 6 times 1951–67.*
The Westwell Livery pots
which sold
for £36,000 in July 1968.

SOTHEBY & CO.

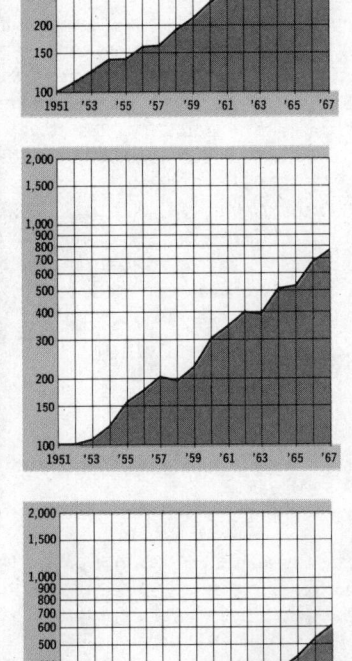

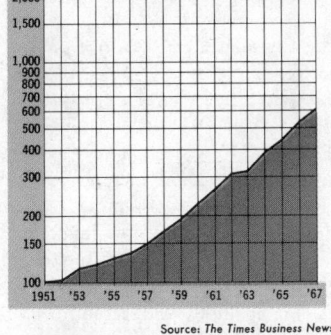

Source: The Times Business News.

for £798,000 in 1965). This has undoubtedly enhanced his reputation and boosted the value of his engravings, which are much easier to find and far cheaper. Canaletto, on the other hand, has been subject to a major reappraisal both as artist and as engraver. His "pretty" views of Venice have achieved a completely new standing and popularity, mainly on account of their decorative qualities. Finally, Brueghel has ridden up in price on the wave of a fashion for the weird and fantastic.

Hedging Against Devaluation. The exceptional nature of price increases in 1968 points up some further characteristics of the art market today. Prices have bounded higher in three fields in particular: Impressionist and modern pictures; silver; and old English glass. The first two can be linked directly to the sterling devaluation and the fear of a general upset among the world's leading currencies. More than in any other field, collectors of modern pictures tend to be those with large self-made fortunes. This implies considerable financial acumen. The knowledge that an important picture can be a good investment has undoubtedly helped to loosen purse strings for many years; in 1968 a further attraction has been that the market in important modern pictures is truly international and that a Picasso, Braque, Chagall, or Monet can be expected to hold its value along with the strongest currency.

There is no doubt that a considerable number of Impressionist and modern pictures were purchased in 1968 with currency hedging in the back if not the front of the mind. With a large vol-

ume of trade at very high prices, these markets are particularly well adapted to absorb a flight from currency. In three days at Sotheby's in April, 400 Impressionist and modern pictures and drawings were sold at an average price of £6,000. Prices in the first half of 1968 were, on average, one-third higher than the 1967 level.

In the case of silver, the effect of the continuing monetary crisis has been even more dramatic—although the connection with currency is perhaps more psychological than real. By the end of the 1967–68 season the value of 18th-century silver was roughly 70 to 100% above its level a year earlier. This was presumably linked to the rise in price of silver bullion, which doubled over the same period. However, for good 18th-century silver the bullion value is only 1 or 2% of the salesroom price —although it can be much higher for Victorian silver. While family silver is still in use in many homes, of course, new purchasers of fine old silver are often investors. During 1968 there were vast speculative purchases of silver bullion—at mid-year, dealers were said to be holding £200 million worth of silver against the speculation of their clients—and the purchase of old silver for the same reason makes very good sense. Tucked away in the vaults, a Queen Anne coffeepot can be expected to appreciate in value not only in line with silver bullion, but also on account of its beauty and rarity. It is thus an even better bet than silver bars.

The rise in value of English glass, on the other hand, is probably not directly linked to devaluation. Because of its fragility, the amount of good 17th- and 18th-century glass that has survived to our day is limited. An enthusiastic collector will probably know, at least by hearsay, most of the important pieces that appear in the salesroom. At the same time, the vogue for collecting glass is only beginning to get under way. Compared with those in other fields, prices have been low enough to attract an increasing number of young, educated collectors of modest means, whose effect has begun to be felt on a major scale in recent years. During late 1967 and through 1968 the collection of English glass belonging to Walter J. Smith, Jr., of New Jersey was sold by Sotheby's in a series of four sales. A collection of this quality and range had not been on the market for several years. The result was a rush to obtain pieces from the famous collection, with prices building up from sale to sale as the opportunity for future purchases diminished. During 1960–67 prices had tripled; but between the first Smith sale in December 1967 and the second in March 1968, *The Times*-Sotheby index measured a 50% price increase.

The Art Market. The major difficulty in trying to assess the record of appreciation in different sectors of the art market lies in the range of purchasers and their motivation. There are, in essence, a number of different markets catered for by the same

*Between 1951 and 1961 the charts are based on three-year moving averages, between 1961 and 1967 on annual figures. 1950–52 = 100.

117

auction houses and dealers. In very simplified terms, these may be distinguished by price ranges. At the top of the market—say £25,000 ($60,000) upward to £1 million ($2.4 million) and potentially beyond—museums, American universities, and the millionaire collector are in charge. American purchasers in this range frequently have endowment policies in mind, since the U.S. tax system allows the value of a bequest to a museum or university to be set against current tax liabilities. In this range there is a huge amount of both public and private money available for investment. As important works of art go to museums and are thus removed from the market for good, less important works have to be upgraded to museum standard to meet the purchasing power available. This can lead to astonishing increases in price. Canaletto is a case in point. His "A Regatta on the Grand Canal, Venice" was sold for £100,000 in 1967, having been bought for £12,000 in 1953.

The market range of £5,000 to £25,000 ($12,000 to $60,000) is largely the domain of rich private investors. The money available for purchases in this range has not increased so dramatically and the record of appreciation is comparatively modest. There

Number of Times Prices Have Multiplied, 1951–67

Impressionists		Moderns	
Sisley	12½	Chagall	28
Monet	12	Bonnard	15
Boudin	9½	Picasso	15
Pissarro	9½	Vlaminck	15
Fantin-Latour	9	Braque	14
Renoir	5	Utrillo	10
		Rouault	8

are a few exceptions where the top auction prices in a particular field fall in this range. The best example is early Ming porcelain: a major scholarly reappraisal of its rarity and importance has sent prices rocketing to 25 times their 1951 level.

Prices between £200 and £5,000 ($500–$12,000) are generally paid by the cultured middle class with good incomes or small fortunes. Internationally this is a rapidly expanding class. Thus prices in this range have come up steeply from low levels in the early 1950s. Included in this group are minor old masters, the majority of old master prints, and a large proportion of British 18th- and 19th-century art. This includes watercolours, whose prices rose 9-fold between 1951 and 1967, Pre-Raphaelites (12-fold), and Victoriana (8-fold).

In general, the index does not cover pictures and works of art in the price range below £200, which virtually anyone who likes things that are old or vaguely artistic can afford. With the spread of education the number of such buyers has multiplied many times over, and prices for quaint junk have boomed. Compared with other sectors of the market, this area tends to give poor value for money.

Finally, one key characteristic of the contemporary art market should be noted. This is the higher standing accorded to artistic "genius" than to craftsmanship. Thus it seems perfectly acceptable that a rough sketch by Picasso would bring several thousand pounds—the price of genius—while many people are astonished at the thought of a pair of simple Queen Anne candlesticks selling for £3,000. This is reflected in the index record over the last 17 years.

The smallest increases have come for French furniture, 4½ times its 1951 level; porcelain (excluding Chinese), in general 5 or 6 times higher; glass before the 1968 boom and silver before the bullion craze, both 6 times higher. Old master pictures, a traditional and rather unfashionable market, have done marginally better, for here genius is at work. British 19th-century pictures have come back into fashion and shown a strongly rising price trend. Impressionists are fashionable and there has been a rapid increase in prices; 20th-century artists have done even better. But in both these cases prices were high to begin with and it is now difficult to find anything worthwhile below £10,000. Thus old master prints, comparatively cheap multiple originals of artistic genius, have been the market leaders.

118

continued from page 115

in Paris, where two anonymous Rothschild sales attracted conspicuous bids. In New York, however, turnover was only about two-thirds that of the previous year, Americana from the Streeter collection being mainly in evidence.

At a sale of manuscripts and rare books at Geneva, the first volume out of two of *Biblia latina* (Mainz, 1462), of which the last complete copy had been sold in London in 1948 for £15,400, brought SFr. 89,700, and Copernicus' *De revolutionibus orbium coelestium* (1543), in contemporary vellum, SFr. 104,075.

Flower books maintained their high prices. In Paris a copy of Redouté's *Les Roses* (3 vol. quarto, with 170 plates) reached Fr. 52,820, while a large paper copy of the same book with a double set of the plates was purchased at Christie's for £10,000 by the trustees of the Chatsworth Settlement. At the same sale, an exceptional Persian manuscript of Firdausi's *Shah-Nama*, written in Shiraz *c.* 1436–40 and illustrated with 58 miniatures, was put up by the marquis of Dufferin and Ava and fetched £50,000. At the sale of Enrique Garcia Merou's books at Parke-Bernet's, Goya's *Los Caprichos* (1799) fetched $15,000; J. Renard's *Histoires naturelles* (1899), with original lithographs by Toulouse-Lautrec, $11,000; and Paul Verlaine's *Parallèlement* (1902), illustrated by Pierre Bonnard, $4,800.

Sotheby's sold material from the Sergei P. Diaghilev collection, including books, drawings, and documents. Their June sale of atlases and travel books included the first atlas of sea charts for sailors, L. J. Waghenaer's *Speculum nauticum* (Leiden, 1586), which went for £8,500, and a series of Ptolemy atlases of which the Ulm edition of 1486 brought £6,800. At the same sale a collection of 137 engraved plates of maps by V. M. Coronelli (Venice, 1691–99) fetched £5,400. At a sale of books on angling in October, a set of the first five editions of Izaak Walton's *The Compleat Angler,* dating from 1653 to 1676, went for £4,600.

Further sales of the Bibliotheca Phillippica took place at Sotheby's, the third part (medieval manuscripts) reaching the peak of the season with £155,660 for a single sale. Many Italian manuscripts found their way back home; *e.g.,* a Tuscan 15th-century illuminated manuscript of Philippo di Vadi's *De arte gladiatoria* dedicated to Guidobaldo da Montefeltro, duke of Urbino (£15,000). The Pierpont Morgan Library of New York secured a 15th-century northern French manuscript of *Le Roman de Renart* at £6,800;

Vincent van Gogh's portrait of his mother, being removed from Christie's in London after purchase by a New York buyer for £115,500.

fragments of a papyrus codex (Egypt? 6th–7th century) listing the tenants of the Abbey of Saint-Martin of Tours (£7,800) and a Bavarian 11th-century manuscript including Bede's *De natura Rerum*, Plato, Timeus, and other works (£27,000) also went to American buyers.

The first issue of the first edition of Isaac Newton's *Philosophiae naturalis principia mathematica* (1687) was sold in Hamburg for DM. 26,450. In Paris a collection of 2,334 political pamphlets of *c.* 1648, *Mazarinades,* brought Fr. 25,320. Twelve poems from *Les Fleurs du mal* by Baudelaire sold for Fr. 168,870 at the (Rothschild) sale of manuscripts held in Paris in May, and the Bibliothèque Nationale bought a number of items—*e.g.,* Diderot's *Le Salon de 1767* for Fr. 40,170. Illuminated manuscripts from the same source were sold at the Palais Galliéra on June 24. A 15th-century manuscript of Christine de Pisan's *Le Livre des trois vertus* brought Fr. 396,570, and a 14th-century *Apocalypse,* with 72 large paintings, Fr. 1,100,570.   (P. Bs.)

Astronautics

As 1967 brought to a close the first decade of the Space Age, 1,291 of the 3,088 man-made objects that had been launched were reported to be orbiting in space. Among them were 294 U.S. satellites and 14 deep-space probes, 54 Soviet satellites and 14 deep-space probes, 5 French satellites, 2 British satellites, 2 Canadian satellites, and 1 Australian satellite.

In commenting on the tenth anniversary of the Space Age, Anatoli Blagonravov, chairman of the Soviet Commission for Space Research and Uses, strongly stressed the role of man in space, indicating that future Soviet space flights would rely heavily on manned missions. He stated: "No matter how great the possibilities of modern automatic and cybernetic devices, they are still very far from the variegated, primarily creative, possibilities of man. . . . An automatic device cannot investigate things that are not known in principle. . . . Man alone can efficiently study the unknown, make correct decisions in unforeseen circumstances, and make full use of the opportunities opening for the investigation of the world surrounding us."

The year was generally a poor one for space research in Europe and the U.S. Civil disorders, war, and demands for funds from competing governmental agencies resulted in reduced space budgets for the U.S. and most Western European nations. The fiscal 1969 budget for the U.S. National Aeronautics and Space Administration (NASA) was $3,850,000,000. It had requested $4,370,000,000.

The European Launcher Development Organization (ELDO) seemed doomed to disintegration. Britain decided to withdraw from the organization in 1971 as a part of a general retrenchment in space expenditures. ELDO, an organization suggested by the British, had had an existence marked by one crisis after another since its inception. In 1965 France had wanted to cancel the Europa I vehicle and proceed to more advanced boosters. In the following year the British reduced contributions to the organization from 38.8 to 27%. As a result of the British announcement to withdraw, France began a reassessment of its participation. A meeting of ELDO was scheduled for November to discuss means of sustaining the venture.

Italy withdrew its support from the TD 1 and TD 2 satellites planned by the European Space Research

BEN ROTH AGENCY

Organization (ESRO), a move that caused both scientific projects to be canceled. This organization had been informed by Spain, in December 1967, that it was withdrawing from membership. By late 1968 it was apparent that ESRO was in as serious straits as ELDO. On December 5, however, ESRO launched a satellite from Cape Kennedy, Fla., to study solar radiation; the booster was a Delta bought from the U.S.

In other European developments Belgium announced that it would join France and West Germany in the Symphonie communications satellite project. Italy announced a San Marco C as a follow-up program to be undertaken jointly with the U.S. France revealed that its Laboratoire de Recherches Ballistiques et Aerodynamiques, at Vernon, was studying the problems involved in military satellites, which when solved would permit France to develop photographic reconnaissance satellites similar to those of the U.S. and U.S.S.R.

Elsewhere in the world, Japan announced a plan for launching 13 scientific satellites and 12 applications satellites between 1971 and 1975. Some confusion seemed to exist over the future direction of space technology in Japan. The Science and Technology Agency backed a five-year plan for the development of a new family of launch vehicles, while the University of Tokyo's Institute of Space and Aeronautical Science favoured an advanced satellite development program using U.S. space boosters.

A more promising international note occurred on April 22, when representatives of 42 nations signed a space-rescue treaty at separate ceremonies in Washington, D.C., Moscow, and London. It was to become effective when ratified by the U.S., U.S.S.R., U.K., and any two other countries. The treaty had been unanimously approved by the UN General Assembly in December 1967.

Astronauts and cosmonauts of the U.S. and Soviet Union made news in 1968. On March 27 Yuri Gagarin, the Soviet Air Force colonel who was the first man to orbit the earth, was killed when his jet aircraft crashed near Moscow. In February, 16 scientist-astronauts from groups selected by NASA in 1965 and 1967 complained of dimming prospects for scientific space work because of the slowdown in the space flight schedule caused by the U.S. Congress' reduction in NASA's funds. The scientists claimed that they

Association Football: *see* Football

would fall behind in their professional fields because their required flight training left little time for the scientific research needed to maintain their professional competence. Wilmot N. Hess, director of science for the Manned Spacecraft Center, Houston, Tex., was appointed to work out a means for relieving the complaints.

NASA lost the services of astronaut Michael Collins for at least a year. On July 23 he underwent surgery to remove a bone spur from a vertebra in his neck. A member of the flight crew training for the third manned Apollo flight, Collins was replaced by James Lovell, who had flown on Gemini 12. Astronaut trainee John A. Llewellyn resigned from training in August because he was having trouble learning to fly jet aircraft. A chemist by profession, he had been selected as an astronaut in August 1967. Earlier, on April 23, Brian T. O'Leary, who had been selected at the same time, withdrew from the program because he disliked flying aircraft. On May 15 trainee Robert A. Parker suffered a fractured spine during parachute training. During the same month John Bull was also deleted from the ranks of American astronauts because he contracted a rare disease about which little is known. Sometimes known as "aspirin asthma," it generally strikes young men between the ages of 20 and 30. It is marked by asthmatic attacks and a marked sensitivity to and intolerance of aspirin.

On September 16 James E. Webb, administrator of NASA since his appointment to that post by Pres. John F. Kennedy in February 1961, announced his resignation effective October 7. In so doing he clearly expressed his disappointment with the way in which NASA had been used as "a sort of whipping boy" for other agencies and organizations competing for federal funds. Appointed as acting administrator until January 1969 was Thomas O. Paine, the deputy administrator.

Space Carrier Vehicles. As 1968 opened preparations were made at Cape Kennedy, Fla., for launching Saturn IB Vehicle 204, the booster that had been scheduled to launch the first manned Apollo spacecraft in January 1967. On this occasion, however, it had an unmanned payload. On January 22 the Saturn IB was launched with the first Apollo lunar module as its payload. The mission was to check out the 31,-

700-lb. lunar module in space for the first time. The spacecraft was placed into an orbit with a perigee of 101 mi. and an apogee of 138 mi., at an inclination angle of 31.6° and a period of 89.5 min. The module separated from the S-IVB stage of the Saturn IB and entered an orbit with a slightly higher perigee.

Both the descent and the ascent stage engines of the lunar module were tested in space for the first time. Both performed successfully, although the first 39-sec. burn of the descent engine was prematurely shut down by "overly conservative computer programming."

The second Saturn V was launched on April 4, but unlike the eminently successful first flight, this one was marred by a series of malfunctions that caused the mission to be officially classified as a failure. The first stage of the vehicle performed satisfactorily from the point of view of required thrust; however, a phenomenon known as the "pogo" effect, marked by excessive oscillations of the vehicle, occurred. The situation was later remedied when engineers introduced helium accumulators into the pre-valves of the liquid oxygen system.

Additional complications in the missions arose when two of the Saturn V's second stage J-2 engines cut off prematurely. This action caused the remaining three engines and the single J-2 engine of the third stage to burn longer than planned. As a result the spacecraft went into an elliptical instead of a circular orbit. To compound the troubles further the single J-2 engine of the third stage failed to reignite in orbit on command. Later studies found the causes of these problems, and solutions were immediately applied to prevent future occurrences.

On May 20 the Soviet Union announced a series of reentry and recovery test flights into the South Pacific Ocean. Two locations were asked to be cleared of shipping near Christmas Island, one for the reentering spacecraft and one for the last stage of its booster. The tests were completed eight days later.

August 16 saw two significant occasions in booster-vehicle technology. One was a success and one a failure. NASA for the first time used a "long tank" Thor-Delta to boost the Essa 7 weather satellite into orbit. The modified Thor vehicle had been lengthened by 15 ft. to provide 25% more propellant capacity. Less successful was the first attempt to orbit a payload with an Atlas-Burner II. While the Atlas first stage functioned perfectly, the Burner II stage did not. Apparently a shroud failed to separate from the Burner II stage, preventing it from igniting properly. Had it performed as planned, the vehicle would have orbited ten small satellites. Previously, the Burner II stage had performed successfully with a Thor booster.

A second long-tank Thor-Delta failed at Cape Kennedy on September 18. The vehicle was to have boosted the Atlantic 3 (Intelsat 3) communications satellite into orbit. The lift-off appeared normal, but the Thor then began to deviate from its planned trajectory after 20 sec. of flight. It tilted back toward the coast of Florida, and the severe structural stresses began tearing it apart. Pieces fell into the ocean about ten miles offshore.

Space-vehicle launchings resumed at Japan's Kagoshima Space Centre on September 10 after a lapse of almost 17 months. A Lambda 3H was fired vertically for test purposes in preparation for the launching of the country's first satellite, scheduled between Jan. 1 and Feb. 14, 1969. Launchings had been delayed because Japanese fishermen objected to the loss of fish-

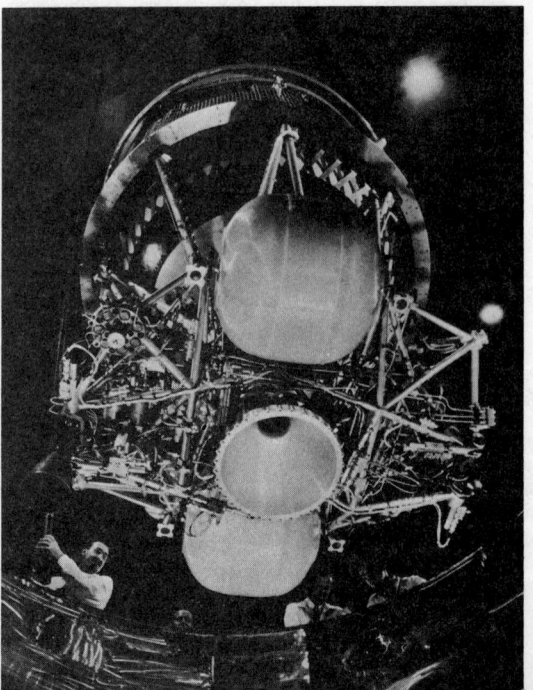

Third stage of launch vehicle Europa I being prepared for testing in West Germany as part of the European Launcher Development Organization program. The fate of ELDO remained uncertain in 1968.

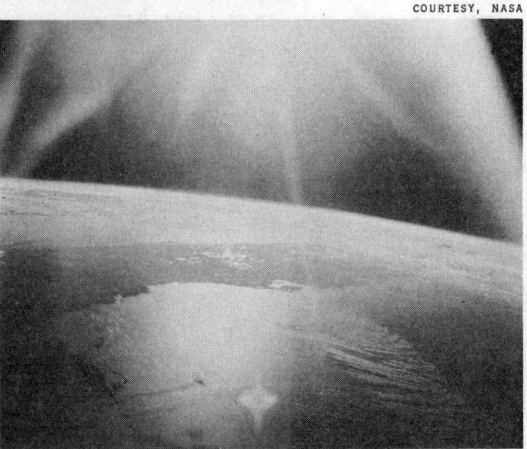

ing grounds near Tanegashima Island, a part of the space centre.

A Titan III-C orbited four satellites from Cape Kennedy in September. The versatile transstage of the booster ejected one radiation-measuring satellite into a highly eccentric orbit with a perigee of 113 mi. and an apogee of 22,300 mi. Four hours later it ejected an LES-6 communications satellite and a scientific satellite into a synchronous orbit at 22,300 mi. over the Equator west of South America. A final scientific satellite to measure radiation was placed into an orbit that ranged between 21,000 and 22,300 mi., so that it would slowly cruise around the earth.

Manned Spacecraft. Manned space flight returned to the U.S. in 1968 after a two-year interval following the launching of the final Gemini spacecraft on Nov. 11, 1966. On October 11, a Saturn IB flawlessly launched Apollo 7 into orbit. Crew commander of the three-man spacecraft was the veteran astronaut Walter M. Schirra, Jr. Accompanying him were Donn Eisele and Walter Cunningham, neither of whom had flown in space before.

The purpose of the mission was a thorough test of the Apollo and its systems, as well as the performance of the astronauts in it. The mission marked the first manned flight of the craft, which had been under development for approximately seven years. Among the things accomplished by Apollo 7 was a station-keeping exercise with the orbiting second stage of the Saturn IB booster. It demonstrated the ability of the Apollo to locate another spacecraft in orbit. The guidance and control system of the Apollo also received a checkout to ensure that the position of the Apollo could be determined from observation of well-known features on the earth. Several restarts of the rocket engine of the craft's service module also proved its reliability.

During the 11-day mission, Schirra did most of the piloting, astronaut Eisele acted as navigator, and Cunningham was systems engineer, monitoring the electrical communications and life-support systems. From the viewpoint of space medicine, the flight provided a first when a cold spread quickly among the three crewmen. However, medications in the first-aid kit kept the illness under control.

Fearing that reentering the atmosphere in spacesuits would rupture the astronauts' eardrums, because of the head colds, Schirra overruled the mission control centre and stated that the crew would reenter without the helmets. The spacecraft landed safely on October 22 in the Atlantic Ocean about $7\frac{1}{2}$ mi. from the recovery ship, the USS "Essex."

The most impressive and far-reaching achievement in manned space flight took place in late December

Above left, readying the Apollo 7 command module for shipment to Cape Kennedy. During the flight the three astronauts photographed the expended Saturn IVB stage, above, during docking maneuvers, and, right, the morning sun reflecting on the Atlantic Ocean and the Gulf of Mexico (the dark silhouette in the centre of the picture is the Florida peninsula).

when the U.S. spacecraft Apollo 8, with three astronauts aboard, made a successful round-trip journey from the earth to the moon. On December 21 a Saturn V rocket launched the spacecraft into earth orbit from Cape Kennedy, Fla. The three-man crew included Frank Borman, command pilot of the mission, James Lovell, Jr., and William Anders; for Anders it was the first flight in space, while it was the second for Borman and the third for Lovell. After making $1\frac{3}{4}$ revolutions around the earth, the Apollo was thrust on its way toward the moon at an initial speed of 24,200 mph by the still-attached third stage of the Saturn. Borman, Lovell, and Anders thus became the first human beings to venture to another body in the solar system. En route to the moon the astronauts suffered briefly from nausea, but it was not serious enough to hamper their flight plan. They transmitted television pictures showing views of the receding earth and scenes inside the Apollo.

On December 23 Apollo 8 entered the moon's "sphere of gravitational influence," 214,000 mi. from the earth. The next day the astronauts twice fired a thrust rocket in their attached service module to slow the spacecraft from 5,758 mph to 3,551 mph and place it in a circular orbit 69.8 mi. above the moon's surface and 231,000 mi. from the earth. Apollo 8 then made ten revolutions around the moon, during which time the astronauts photographed the lunar surface and performed various tests of the spacecraft's systems. They also transmitted a Christmas Eve telecast to the earth. On December 25 the astronauts again fired their thrust rocket, which sent the Apollo on its journey back to the earth. The incredible flight ended safely with a landing in the South Pacific Ocean on December 27.

continued on page 124

Major Satellites and Space Probes Launched Oct. 20, 1967—Oct. 30, 1968

Name/country/ launch vehicle/ scientific designation	Launch date, lifetime*	Weight (kg.)†	Shape	Diameter	Length or height	Experiments	Perigee (km.)†	Apogee (km.)†	Period (min.)	Inclination to Equator (degrees)
ATS-3/U.S./Atlas-Agena D/1967-111A	11/5/67	326.3 (805)	Cylinder	1.5 m. (5 ft.)	1.8 m. (6 ft.)	Nine major experiments in communications, meteorology, navigation, and earth resources management	35,564.8 (22,228)	35,606.4 (22,254)	1,436.4	0.4
Surveyor 6/U.S./Atlas-Centaur/1967-112A	11/7/67	277.7 (617)	Tetrahedral frame with tripod landing gear and two solar panels	4.3 m. (14 ft.)	3 m. (10 ft.)	Photographed surface of the moon after soft landing	Flight time: 65.4 hr.; soft-landed on moon			
Essa 6/U.S./Thor-Delta/ 1967-114A	11/10/67	141 (290)	Cylinder	107 cm. (42 in.)	56 cm. (22 in.)	Weather satellite	1,401.6 (876)	1,480 (925)	114.8	102.1
WRESAT 1/Australia/Redstone/1967-118A	11/29/67 12/11/67	45 (100)	Cone			Effects of solar radiation on the earth's upper atmosphere	169.6 (106)	1,243.2 (777)	95.7	83.2
Pioneer 8/U.S./Thor-Delta/ 1967-123A	12/13/67	19.8 (44)	Cylinder	93.98 cm. (37 in.)	88.9 cm. (35 in.)	Studied effects of solar wind, magnetic fields, cosmic rays; small TTS-1 satellite for testing Apollo unified S-band communications launched piggy-back at same time	Solar orbit			
Surveyor 7/U.S./Atlas-Centaur/1968-01A	1/7/68 1/10/68	281.3 (625)	Tetrahedral frame with tripod landing gear and two solar panels	4.3 m. (14 ft.)	3 m. (10 ft.)	Last in series of lunar exploration vehicles	Flight time: 66.5 hr.; soft-landed on moon			
Explorer 36/U.S./Thor-Delta 1968-02A	1/11/68	207 (460)	Octagonal body with truncated, eight-sided pyramid top	121.9 cm. (48 in.)	81.3 cm. (32 in.)	Experiments in geodesy and measurements of the earth's gravitational field	203.2 (127)	384 (240)	112.2	105.8
Apollo 5/U.S./Saturn IB/ 1968-07A	1/22/68	14,265 (31,700)	Two-man spacecraft on octagonal base with four legs	4.2 m. (14 ft.)	6.9 m. (23 ft.)	Test the lunar module of the Apollo spacecraft in space environment	161.6 (101)	120.8 (138)	89.5	31.6
Zond 4/U.S.S.R./not available/ 1968-13A	3/2/68	‡	‡	‡	‡	Probable test of Soyuz lunar mission spacecraft launched from parking orbit at an imaginary moon	209.6 (131)	288 (180)	89.5	51.6
OGO-5/U.S./Atlas-Agena D/1968-14A	3/4/68	606.2 (1,347)	Rectangular body with six instrumentation booms	⌐1 m. (3 ft.)	⌐2 m. (6 ft.)	Conduct measurements within the earth's trapped radiation belts, magnetosphere, and interplanetary space	288 (180)	146,016 (91,260)	1,347	31
Explorer 37/U.S./Scout/ 1968-17A	3/5/68	89.1 (198)	12-sided body	76.2 cm. (30 in.)	18.6 cm. (27 in.)	Measure and monitor selected solar X-rays and ultraviolet emissions	518.4 (324)	872 (545)	98.7	59.4
Cosmos 206/U.S.S.R./ not available/1968-19A	3/14/68	‡	Cylinder with two solar panels	1 m. (3.3 ft.)	2 m. (6.6 ft.)	Weather satellite	625.6 (391)	625.6 (391)	97	81
Apollo 6/U.S./Saturn V/ 1968-25A	4/4/68 4/4/68	38,205 (84,900)	Cone	4 m. (12 ft.)	3.8 m. (12.8 ft.)	Test of Saturn V booster and Apollo spacecraft	177.6 (111)	361.6 (226)	88.2	32.5
Luna 14/U.S.S.R./not available/ 1968-27A	4/7/68	‡	‡	‡	‡	Photographic reconnaissance; radiation and micrometeorite measurements of space near moon	Lunar orbit			
Cosmos 212/U.S.S.R./ not available/1968-29A	4/14/68 4/19/68	⌐7,200 (⌐16,000)	Cylindrical body with spherical Soyuz spacecraft in forward end and two solar cell panels	⌐3.4 m. (⌐11.25 ft.)	‡	Demonstrate rendezvous and docking of unmanned Soyuz spacecraft; docked with Cosmos 213	208 (130)	238.4 (149)	88.75	51.7
Cosmos 213/U.S.S.R./ not available/1968-30A	4/15/68 4/20/68	⌐7,200 (⌐16,000)	Cylindrical body with spherical Soyuz spacecraft in forward end and two solar cell panels	⌐3.4 m. (⌐11.25 ft.)	‡	Passive docking target for Cosmos 212	203.2 (127)	289.6 (181)	89.16	51.4
Molniya 1H/U.S.S.R./ not available/1968-35A	4/21/68	⌐1,100 (⌐2,200)	Cylinder with conical top, six solar panels	⌐1.2 m. (⌐4 ft.)	⌐3.6 m. (⌐12 ft.)	Communications satellite	457.6 (286)	39,468.8 (24,668)	713	65
ESRO 2B/ESRO/Scout/ 1968-41A	5/17/68	73.8 (164)	12-sided body	76.2 cm. (30 in.)	85.1 cm. (33.5 in.)	Make studies of solar and cosmic radiation in lower layer of Van Allen belt for six months	328 (205)	1,083.2 (677)	101.2	97.2
Cosmos 226/U.S.S.R./ not available/1968-49A	6/12/68	‡	Cylinder with two solar panels	⌐1 m. (⌐3.3 ft.)	⌐2 m. (⌐6.6 ft.)	Weather satellite	600 (375)	646.4 (404)	96.9	81.2
Explorer 38/U.S./Thor-Delta/1968-55A	7/4/68	‡	Cylinder with two 1,500-ft. antennas			Make studies of low frequencies in space	5,830 (3,499)	5,873 (3,522.8)	224.3	120.8
Molniya 1 (9)/U.S.S.R./ not available/1968-57A	7/6/68	‡	Cylinder with conical ends and six solar panels	⌐1.2 m. (⌐4 ft.)	⌐3.6 m. (⌐12 ft.)	Communications satellite	492 (295.2)	39,870 (23,932)	717.9	65
Explorer 39/U.S./Scout/ 1968-66A	8/8/68	‡	Sphere	3.6 m. (12 ft.)		Study air density	685 (411)	2,515 (1,509)	118.1	80.6
Explorer 40/U.S./Scout/ 1968-66B	8/8/68	‡	Cylinder	‡	‡	Study bombardment of the atmosphere by charged particles	677 (406.2)	2,536 (1,521.6)	118.3	80.6
Essa 7/U.S./Thor-Delta/ 1968-76A	8/16/68	192 (320)	18-sided polygon	107 cm. (42 in.)	56 cm. (22 in.)	Weather satellite	1,432 (859.2)	1,475 (885)	114.9	101.7
Zond 5/U.S.S.R./not available/ 1968-76A	9/14/68 9/21/68	‡	Cylinder	‡	‡	Test of the Soyuz spacecraft systems in cislunar and translunar flight	Circled moon and returned to the earth			
ESRO 1/ESRO/Scout/ 1968-84A	10/3/68	73.8 (164)	12-sided polygon	76.2 cm. (30 in.)	85.1 cm. (33.5 in.)	Study Aurora Borealis and related phenomena in the northern ionosphere	259 (155.4)	1,528 (916.8)	102.8	93.7
Molniya 1 (10)/U.S.S.R./ not available/1968-85A	10/5/68	1,100 (2,200)	Cylinder with conical top, six solar panels	1.2 m. (4 ft.)	3.6 m. (12 ft.)	Communications satellite	480 (300)	39,360 (24,600)	714	65
Apollo 7/U.S./Saturn IB/ 1968-89A	10/11/68 10/22/68	5,696 (12,659)	Truncated cone	3.8 m. (12.8 ft.)	3.6 m. (12 ft.)	Test all systems of Apollo spacecraft in first manned flight	233.4 (138.4)	284.6 (177.9)	89.6	31.6

*All dates are in universal time (UT).
†English units in parentheses: weight in pounds, perigee and apogee in statute miles.
‡Not available.

Selection of photographs taken by the three astronauts aboard the Apollo 8 spacecraft which orbited the moon in December 1968. Right, view of the earth showing nearly the entire Western Hemisphere. Below, rising earth as it appeared to the astronauts as they emerged from the far side of the moon during the course of their first lunar orbit. Width of the photographed portion of the lunar horizon is approximately 110 mi. Bottom left, oblique view of the Sea of Tranquillity, a possible landing site for future astronauts. Bottom centre, brightly rayed crater on the far side of the moon at the point where the sun was directly overhead in relation to the spacecraft. Botton right, large crater Goclenius in the foreground is about 40 mi. in diameter. The three clustered craters behind it are Magelhaens, Magelhaens A, and Colombo A.

COURTESY, NASA; BOTTOM RIGHT, KEYSTONE

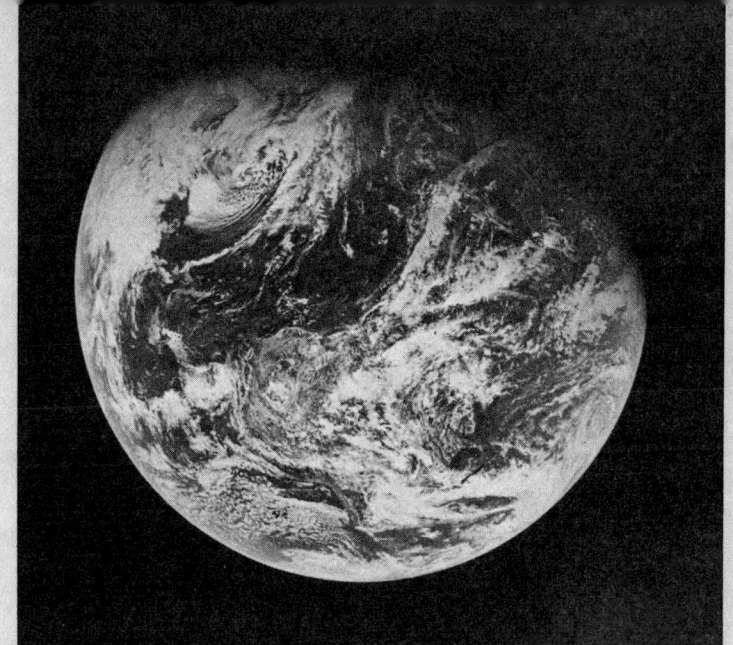

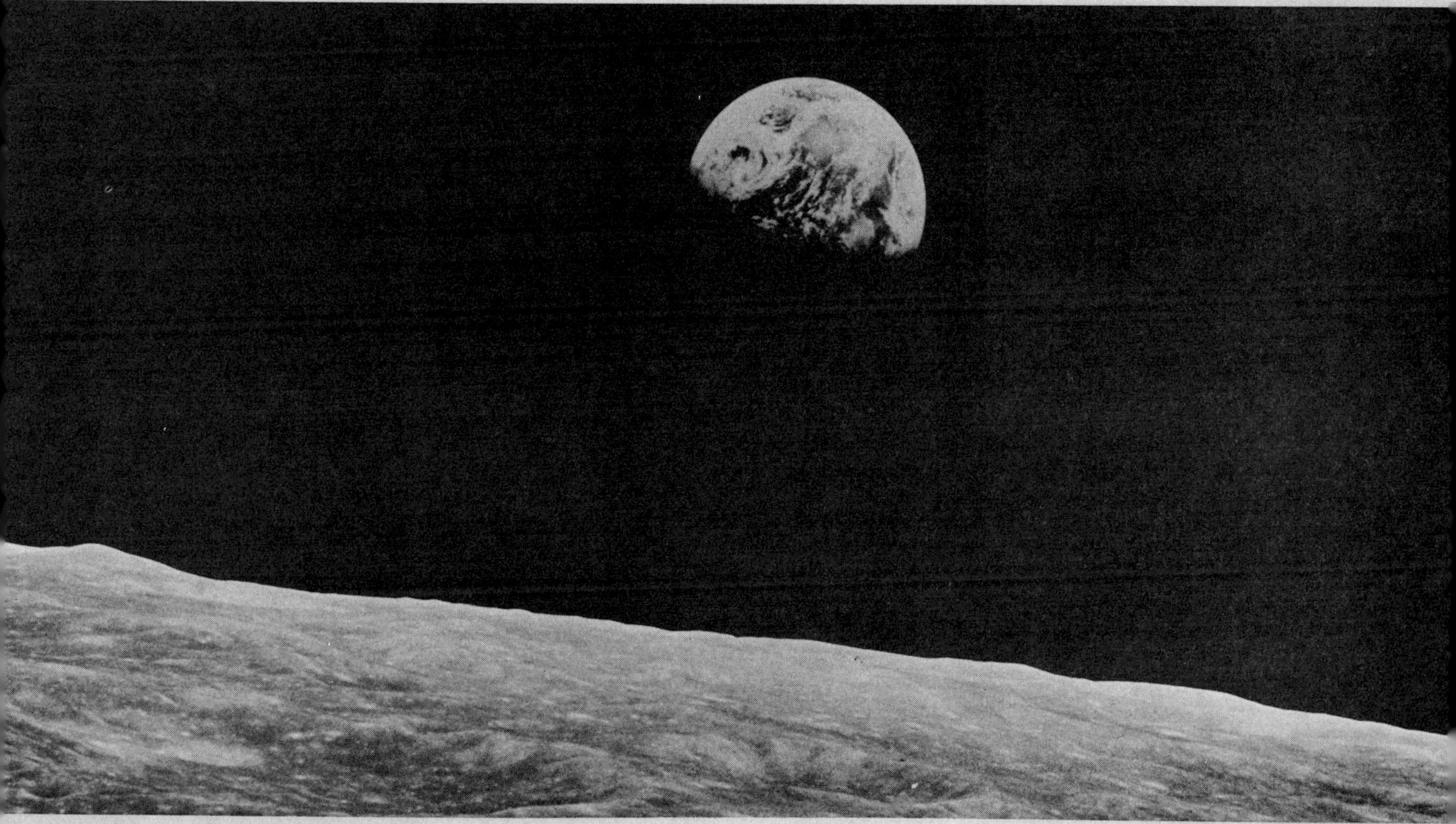

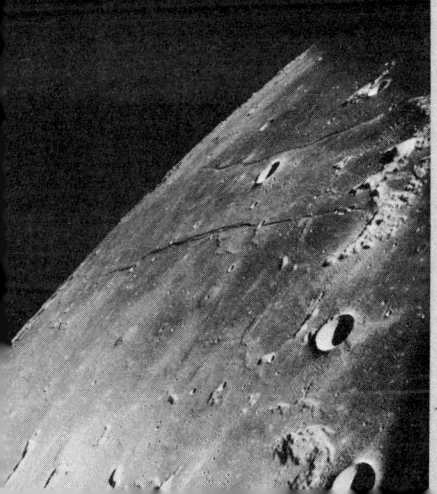

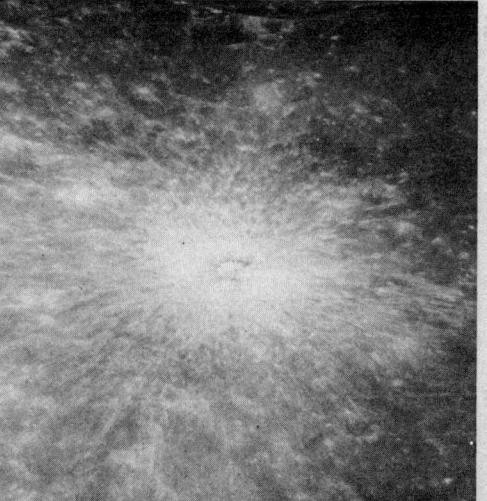

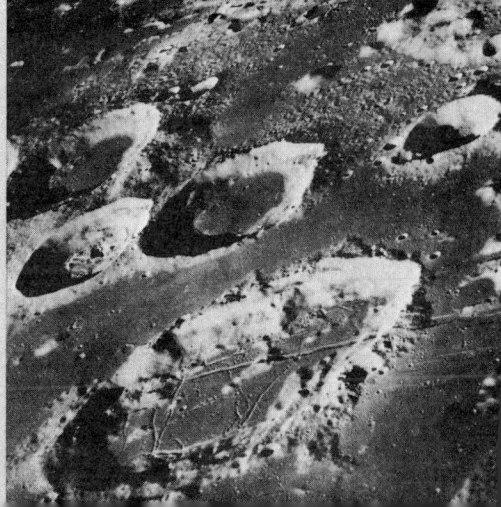

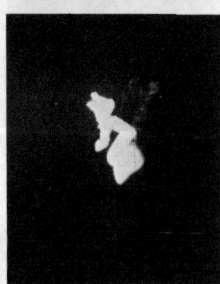

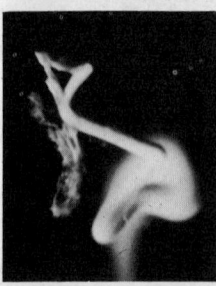

Series of sequential pictures of sodium cloud configuration launched from Wallops Island, Va., in February 1968. The test was part of a study using three chemicals, triethylborane, trimethylaluminum, and sodium to ascertain short-term and seasonal variations in the wind structure in the upper atmosphere.

COURTESY, NASA

continued from page 121

Late in October the Soviet Union staged its first manned space mission since April 1967, when Vladimir Komarov was killed descending from his flight. Georgi Beregovoi piloted the Soyuz 3 spacecraft for 64 orbits around the earth on a four-day solo mission. Among the achievements of the flight was a soft landing of the spacecraft by parachute at a prearranged spot on dry land. The U.S.S.R. reported that Beregovoi performed extensive maneuvers near the previously launched unmanned Soyuz 2 and that the two spacecraft rendezvoused twice by the use of automatic ground controls. Although the mission did not appear to be a great breakthrough for the Soviet Union, observers believed that the Soyuz spacecraft proved itself to be maneuverable and reliable.

Scientific Satellites. The orbital behaviour of a Soviet satellite launched in December 1967 caused speculation in the West that it might be a prototype of an orbital glide bomb from which nuclear weapons could be launched to the earth. On December 27 Cosmos 198 was launched into a near-circular orbit at 160 mi. On the following day it was maneuvered into an orbit with a perigee of 535.8 mi. and an apogee of 571.8 mi. A similar maneuver was performed on March 22, 1968, by Cosmos 209.

The new year opened with the launching of the 460-lb. Explorer 36 (Geos B) on January 11. It was a geodetic satellite with flashing lights and corner reflectors for radar as well as tracking beacons and radio transponders. Its estimated lifetime in orbit with a perigee of 127 mi. and apogee of 240 mi. was about 5,000 years. It was followed shortly by the 200th satellite to be launched in the Cosmos series by the U.S.S.R.; it appeared to be a scientific satellite, possibly of an applications or navigation nature.

January 31 marked the tenth anniversary in orbit of the first U.S. satellite, Explorer 1. Despite a predicted orbital lifetime of three to five years, the 30.8-lb. satellite was still circling the earth every 100 min. in an orbit with a perigee of 215 mi. and an apogee of 771 mi. Its radio voice, however, was silent, having gone dead on Feb. 28, 1958.

France's minister of state for scientific research, Maurice Schumann, announced on January 10 that his nation would orbit a French satellite using a Soviet booster in late 1971 or early 1972. He also revealed that French instrumentation would be aboard a Soviet lunar orbiter to be launched later in 1968. However, he denied that Soviet space scientists or technicians would use the French launching site in French Guiana.

Pakistan on February 20 announced that its newly installed satellite tracking station at Dacca was operational. The station was capable of receiving cloud-cover photographs from the U.S. Essa and Nimbus satellites. Such information was expected to be particularly helpful in a region where cyclones are frequent.

At a joint symposium sponsored by the National Science Foundation and NASA, in Washington, D.C., on February 23–24, the results of 13 experiments conducted aboard Biosatellite 2, launched Sept. 7, 1967, were discussed. The experimenters indicated that radiation caused greater damage to plants and animal organisms when combined with weightlessness than radiation does alone on the earth. The most affected

cells, they reported, were the young and multiplying ones or those with a high rate of metabolic activity. However, the scientists all emphasized that the results of their experiments with lower forms of life could not be transferred directly to human beings.

OGO-5 (Orbiting Geophysical Observatory 5) was launched in March by an Atlas-Agena D into a highly elliptical orbit with an apogee of 91,260 mi. and a perigee of 180 mi. The fifth in a series of such satellites, it was designed to study electrical and shock-wave phenomena in the Van Allen radiation belt and in the ionosphere.

On April 21 the eighth Molniya 1 communications satellite was launched by the Soviets. The 2,200-lb. satellite was expected to have a useful lifetime of about five years. Initially placed into a low earth orbit, the satellite was later fired into a highly elliptical orbit with a perigee of 286 mi. and an apogee of 24,668 mi.

In May, Canada revealed a joint governmental-industrial program to establish a $100 million domestic communications satellite system for the early 1970s. It would be capable of handling both telephone and television channels. Proposed capacity would be between 4 and 12 channels, each carrying one television broadcast or 600 two-way telephone conversations. The system would consist of two satellites in synchronous orbits above the Equator.

Iris 1 (ESRO 2B), the first successful ESRO satellite, was launched on May 17 by a Scout. The 164-lb. satellite was placed into a polar, sun-synchronous orbit to make scientific measurements of solar and cosmic radiation in the lower layer of the Van Allen belt. Instrumentation was supplied by French, Dutch, and British institutions. The satellite was expected to have a lifetime of five years.

On May 23 Echo 1, one of the earliest communications satellite experiments, reentered the earth's atmosphere and burned up off the coast of South America. Launched from Cape Canaveral (Cape Kennedy) on Aug. 12, 1960, the 100-ft.-diameter balloon made of aluminized Mylar plastic weighed only 167.4 lb. During its eight-year lifetime it performed many useful experiments as a passive relay station and made 36,000 orbits of the earth.

One of the oddest looking satellites ever to be launched was orbited by the U.S. on July 4 by a thrust-augmented Thor-Delta. Explorer 38 was placed into a parking orbit for three days while it was checked out. A small rocket motor then ignited to thrust it into a nearly circular orbit with a perigee of 3,499 mi. and an apogee of 3,522.8 mi. The spacecraft traveled in a direction opposite to the earth's rotation. By so doing, it remained in the sunlight for six months before going into the earth's shadow for a similar period. Designed to study low-frequency radiowaves, many of which had never been heard before, in space, Explorer 38 featured two V-shaped antennas, each 750 ft. long. When both were fully extended, the spacecraft was taller than the Empire State Building. The antennas were rolled into a drum only seven inches in diameter and could be deployed at a rate of seven inches per minute. Both were fully extended on October 9.

Intelsat, the International Telecommunications Satellite Consortium, suffered a setback on September 18 when its Atlantic 3 satellite was launched from Cape Kennedy. The satellite was destroyed when its Thor booster malfunctioned 108 sec. after launch and had to be destroyed. It was to have been placed in a synchronous orbit over the Equator off the coast of

Brazil. Approximately five times more powerful than the other satellites in the system, Atlantic 3 would have been able to relay 1,200 two-way telephone conversations per day or four colour television broadcasts.

In August OGO-4, launched July 28, 1967, was pressed into service in a three-way scientific investigation of the Aurora Borealis, together with a Convair 990 jet airplane and sounding rockets launched from Fort Churchill, Man. As the aircraft cruised at 31,000 ft., making photographs and recording other data in 13 different experiments, sounding rockets launched from the Canadian range probed the lower fringes of the aurora. Also simultaneously, OGO-4, as it passed over the range, made certain measurements that could be correlated in time with the findings of the aircraft and the sounding rockets.

Space Probes. The first scientific probe of 1968 was Surveyor 7, the last in the scheduled series of highly successful instruments to study the lunar surface prior to man's first landing on it. It was launched on January 7 by an Atlas-Centaur. Landing on the moon 66.5 hr. later, it began to perform as the others in the series had. Analysis of the data it sent back to earth revealed that the crater Tycho probably was made by the impact of a meteorite about two miles in diameter. Some of the rocks in the crater exhibited eroded surfaces even though there was no atmosphere or running water on the moon. Surveyor 7 also found that the iron content of the lunar soil was significantly less than that reported by earlier probes examining the maria. The spacecraft also turned its 200-line-scan television camera toward the earth and detected two laser beams fired at the moon from observatories in California.

On March 2 the Soviet Union launched Zond 4 but gave no indication of its mission. After three and a half days, it reached its apogee, a distance from the earth comparable to that of the moon, and then returned toward the earth. Speculation arose that it had been fired toward an "imaginary" moon in a test of the Soyuz spacecraft to be used on the Soviets' manned lunar landing mission.

The U.S.S.R. on April 7 launched Luna 14 into a parking orbit and then into a translunar trajectory. It went into orbit around the moon on April 10. The purpose of the probe, as given by the Soviet press, included collection of data on the moon's motion in space, study of the relation of the masses of the earth and moon and the moon's gravitational field, measurement of solar particle streams in the vicinity of the moon, and study of the propagation and stability of radio waves between the earth and the moon; all of this information would be vital to a later manned mission.

Analysis of data in 1968 from Pioneer 8, launched in 1967, produced information that indicated the earth's magnetic field may be far smaller than at first suspected by scientists. When the space probe passed through the tail region at a distance of 1,750,000 mi., its sensors indicated that this region might be one of turbulence rather than of a relatively smooth, cylindrical, laminar structure. Corroboration of the phenomenon probably would have to depend upon findings from Soviet probes. No additional missions were planned through this region of space by U.S. probes because of budgetary restrictions.

A Soviet space probe launched on September 14 caused some harsh words between the Soviet Union and Britain. Zond 5 was launched with no indication as to its mission or possible target. It was immediately tracked by Britain's Jodrell Bank Experimental Station antenna, and Sir Bernard Lovell, director of the station, announced two days later that the probe had passed around the moon and was returning toward the earth. The Soviets immediately branded this statement as "a canard" but offered no other information. Several days later they blandly confirmed that Zond 5 had, indeed, circled the far side of the moon at 1,250 mi. and was returning for a soft landing on the earth. The mission appeared to be a test of the Soyuz spacecraft's guidance, communications, control, life-support, and recovery systems. In November Zond 6 made a similar mission.

Rocket-Powered Research Vehicle (X-15) and Lifting Bodies. Heavy slashes in NASA's budget left the nation's space agency with no alternative but cancellation of the X-15 research program. Cancellation of the program meant that Phase III of the Hypersonic Research Engine program, flight test of the engine on an X-15, could no longer be conducted. On January 21, NASA's Flight Research Center, at Edwards Air Force Base, California, announced that the program would be closed in the fall. Relatively little activity took place during the year as a result of the cancellation. On April 4 a flight with X-15 No. 1 was made to an altitude of 40 mi. During the mission the craft reached a velocity five times the speed of sound in a test of spray-on insulating material for the second stage of the Saturn V launch vehicle. X-15 No. 1 was flown to test secret U.S. Air Force instruments to be used with its manned orbiting laboratory. Maj. William J. Knight piloted the X-15 No. 1 to 207,000 ft. at a velocity five times the speed of sound in April to check instrumentation to be used on the Saturn V launch vehicle. Earlier, William H. Dana flew the plane to 105,000 ft. at about 4½ times the speed of sound to check out its electrical systems.

Lifting body activity also slowed during the year. The HL-10 lifting body made its second flight on March 15, being dropped from 45,000 ft. at 400 mph. The rocket engine was not fired, and the craft was flown through a "U" pattern and landed at 220 mph. On June 11, it made another unpowered, gliding drop from its mother ship at Edwards Air Force Base. While it was successful, another such unpowered drop was planned before the first powered flight.

Sounding Rockets. A new launching system was revealed for the U.S. Arcas sounding rocket. A modified Arcas launcher with a new plenum chamber at the breech end used compressed air instead of an aircraft ejection seat cartridge to boost the Arcas from the tube. An air compressor supplied air at a pressure of 800 psi to the plenum chamber. This force drove the Arcas from the launcher at a velocity of 220 fps, instead of the original velocity of 120 fps. obtained with the cartridge. Not only did this make the launcher more reliable and less costly, but it resulted in a maximum height of 225,000 ft. for the Arcas.

On February 2 Prime Minister Indira Gandhi dedicated India's Equatorial Rocket Launching Station at Thumba to the UN, thus making it the world's first international rocket range. Mrs. Gandhi said that the range was "an umbrella under which international collaboration in the peaceful uses of outer space could be pursued most vigorously."

Also during February, developmental work on the British Petrel ended, with a successful test flight, the fifth, from the rocket range at South Uist, in the Outer Hebrides. The same month saw the beginning of a series of coordinated sounding rocket launches by

France from the Kerguelen Islands and by the U.S.S.R. from Franz Josef Land to study the auroras and associated phenomena. The French used Dragon 2B's, but the Soviets did not specify the rockets they used.

A Canadian Black Brant IV was launched by NASA from the Wallops Station at Wallops Island, Va., on May 7. It was conducted to check out some of the instrumentation to be carried in Canada's third ionospheric research satellite, scheduled to be launched later in the year. A transmitter in the nose cone of the rocket produced artificial whistlers, electromagnetic waves that occur naturally in lightning discharges. These same waves are also generated by an unexplained mechanism in the ionosphere. The launch was made at the same time that Canada's *Alouette 2* satellite was passing 500 mi. over the Wallops Island range. Tracking stations at Wallops Island and Bermuda received telemetered signals from both the rocket and the satellite for comparison.

On June 8, at White Sands Missile Range, New Mexico, 12 high-resolution X-ray photographs were taken of the sun which showed for the first time the inner structure of an X-ray flare in progress. The special 9-in. X-ray camera was mounted in an Aerobee 150A, which was launched within 3 min. after the flare was announced. Detailed X-ray structures in the flare as small as a few seconds of arc were recorded.

(M. R. S.)

See also Astronomy; Defense; Industrial Review; Meteorology; Photography; Telecommunications; Television and Radio.

ENCYCLOPÆDIA BRITANNICA FILMS. *Earth Satellites: Explorers of Outer Space* (1958); *Rockets: How They Work* (1958); *First Men into Space* (1962); *Frontiers in Space* (1962); *A Trip to the Planets* (1963); *The Van Allen Radiation Belts* (1963); *Space Probes—Exploring Our Solar System* (1964); *You and the Aerospace Age* (1966).

Astronomy

Pulsars. The most outstanding event of 1968 was the announcement of the discovery of pulsating radio sources by A. Hewish and his associates at the Mullard Radio Astronomy Observatory, Cambridge, Eng. These objects, which acquired the name "pulsars," caused much excitement both among observers, who scrambled to discover all they could, and among theoreticians, who began speculating on what pulsars may be. This attention is merited, for the radiations from pulsars will reveal much to us about the galaxy, and the physical laws governing the universe.

Hewish for many years interested himself in the design of very powerful radio telescopes and in their use for studying the sparse wind that flows radially from the sun throughout interplanetary space. His technique was to observe a radio source as the solar wind appeared to pass it by. From the type of twinkling produced by the source, he was able to discover both the fine structure and speed of the solar wind and a little about the nature of the radio source observed. Sources of very small angular diameter appear to twinkle more than larger objects. This phenomenon is familiar in our atmosphere to anyone who looks at a star and then at a planet. A star appears to twinkle but a planet, being much closer to the earth, has a larger angular diameter and thus seems to shine steadily. This phenomenon occurs to radio waves not in our atmosphere but as they traverse the solar wind, and on this basis Hewish developed a method for discovering the angular size of a small radio source. He did

this by determining the amount of the source's twinkling when it was observed at different apparent distances from the sun.

This method can be applied to determine the angular sizes of quasi-stellar radio sources (quasars) at low radio frequencies, something very difficult to do by other means. To produce many such observations a large fixed aerial was built. Instead of averaging the signal over many seconds, a procedure normal in radio astronomy to make the weakest signals stand out clearly above the noise, a short averaging time was used so that the twinkling of the not-so-weak sources could be studied. As the earth turned, different parts of the sky swept overhead and the twinkling of different objects was observed. However, in 1967 a strange source of interference occurred on the records. Not very strong and occurring for only four minutes a day, it consisted of a series of "pips" (brief radio pulses), each separated by $1\frac{1}{3}$ seconds from its neighbours. The strength of the pips was variable and sometimes they almost disappeared, but their timing was apparently perfect. It was also discovered that the pips did not occur at exactly the same time each day but rather at the time that a certain patch of sky lay overhead.

The time between pips at first seemed constant, but this period slowly changed a little in a manner that indicated the changing velocity of the earth in its orbit around the sun. This observation both yielded proof that the pips were not terrestrial in origin and also enabled Hewish to determine a very rough position for their source. With this information Sir Martin Ryle, director of the Mullard Radio Astronomy Observatory, was able to use the fully steerable Cambridge one-mile radio telescope to follow the pulsating source and to determine a precise position in the sky. Hewish had determined the period of the pulsar to great accuracy to ensure that it really was constant once the effect of the earth's rotation was removed. This proved that the pulsar was not a radio transmitter on some planet circling around another star, for in that case the changing velocity of that planet should have shown up as small extra changes in the apparent period between pips.

Ryle and Judith A. Bailey, looking at the Palomar Observatory photographic sky survey, saw that there was a faint star in the direction of the pulsar. This could have been a coincidence, but because the star was bluer than its neighbours the two astronomers requested the astronomer royal to find out whether the light from that star was pulsing with the same frequency as the pulsar. The new Isaac Newton 98-in. telescope at Herstmonceux, Eng., was completing its acceptance trials, and at first it was hoped that it might immediately identify the pulsar. Observers hoped that they might see the star visibly brighten and dim every $1\frac{1}{3}$ seconds, but they were disappointed; in the original estimate the brightness of the star had been exaggerated and so, in fact, it could not be seen. However, a month later workers at Herstmonceux, using more sophisticated equipment attached to a 36-in. telescope, showed that the star did not vary in brightness. Many other optical observers confirmed and refined this result. Thus, it seemed likely that the faint star had nothing to do with the pulsar but merely lay approximately in the same direction.

With no optical identification there was no normal method of finding out how far away the pulsar was. However, the shortness of its pulses provided Hewish

with a completely new way by which he determined its distance. All light in empty space travels at a speed of nearly 300,000 km/sec. (186,000 mi/sec.). In glass, water, air, or any other transparent medium, however, light interacts with the atoms of the particular substance. This causes the light to travel more slowly. The interaction is particularly strong for light of colours corresponding to the natural vibration frequencies of the atoms of which the medium is made. Therefore, within a particular medium, light of different colours (or frequencies) travels at slightly different speeds. Interstellar space, though a far better vacuum than anything that can be attained on the earth, is filled with sparse interstellar gas. It is the free electrons in this gas, those unattached to atoms, that produce the most reaction on radio waves as they travel through. Although the slowing effect is very slight, the small change in speed accumulates over the years that it takes the radio waves from a pulsar to reach the earth. Because it is the low frequencies that are most delayed, the pip from a pulsar arrives first at high frequencies, later at intermediate frequencies, and later still at low frequencies. Several other pips will have arrived at the high frequency end before the last is heard of the first pip at the lowest frequency. The total delay between high and low frequencies depends on how many free electrons the radio wave has passed over on its way to the earth from the pulsar. Because other astronomical techniques have indicated roughly how many free electrons there are in interstellar space, Hewish was able to find out approximately how far the radio pip had traveled from the number of electrons it had passed over. His estimate was 200 light-years.

Soon after the discovery and pinpointing of the first pulsar, called Cambridge Pulsator (CP) 1919, came the announcement of the discovery of three others. Two had periods of just over one second, while the third indicated only one quarter of a second between pips. Again, immediately after the first announcement of the discovery, F. G. Smith used the Jodrell Bank, Eng., telescope to study the structure of the individual pip or pulse. It was found to be quite complicated and somewhat variable, but Smith discovered that individual pulses are highly polarized, the electric field of the radio pulse vibrating in just one plane.

The Cambridge group next began to search for new pulsars beyond the four they announced initially. About 30 possibilities were found, but only two of those were confirmed when they were recorded in more detail. Meanwhile, a group from Harvard University had independently discovered and confirmed another of the 30 suspects and had put the nomenclature in disarray by calling it HP, for Harvard Pulsator. This made a total of seven known pulsars, but then two Southern Hemisphere objects were added by A. J. Turtle and A. E. Vaughan of the University of Sydney, working with the Molongo Mills Cross radio telescope in Australia. One of those two could prove to be very important because L. V. Morrison of the Nautical Almanac Office, Herstmonceux, predicted that it would soon be occulted as the moon passed in front of it. This would happen not once but on a number of separate occasions. The timing of such occultations provides the most accurate positions achievable in radio astronomy. By using two occultations several years apart, it may be possible to measure in considerable detail the motion of this pulsar across the sky. This will indicate how fast the pulsars move in the galaxy and help determine what they are. The distance estimates show that the pulsars that have been discovered

to date are within our galaxy, but there is conflicting evidence as to how close they are. The nine discovered so far are not concentrated toward the galactic plane as seen from the earth, which indicates that they are nearby. This is reasonable if the distance estimates are correct and if the pulsars are distributed in a manner similar to the stars of the Milky Way. However, such an idea suggests that as more distant pulsars are discovered the distribution of the fainter ones should be concentrated more toward the galactic plane.

Late in the year a tenth pulsar, notable for the very rapid rate of its pulses, which occurred every 0.033 sec., was discovered by astronomers at the National Radio Astronomy Observatory, Green Bank, W.Va. The pulsar was located in the region of the Crab Nebula.

In discussing theories it is apparent that the observations require a powerful and very regular basic mechanism to produce the period of the pulses and also an irregular mechanism for turning the regular pulse into radio pips with quite variable intensities. Other known, very regular periods that could be responsible for the basic mechanism are stellar rotation and vibration. In normal stars these have periods of days or hours, and high densities are required to make such periods shorter. White dwarf stars with densities of one ton per cubic inch are not dense enough to accomplish this unless some mechanism picks out a rather complicated form of vibration of the star rather than the natural breathing in and out of ordinary variable stars. Some theories seek such a mechanism. There are very strong theoretical reasons why no stable spherical stars with densities of a hundred tons per cubic inch should exist. However, J. P. Ostriker of Princeton University suggested that the basic pe-

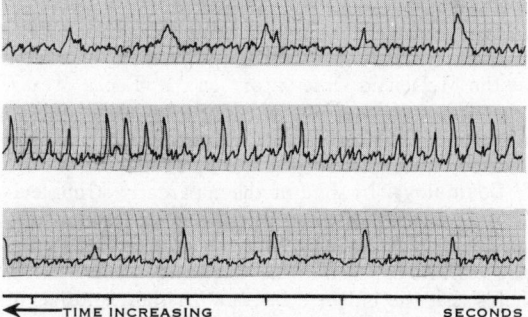

TIME INCREASING   SECONDS

The uniform intervals between the repeating signals from each pulsar were displayed in traces made on March 21 at Mullard Radio Astronomy Observatory, Cambridge, Eng. From top to bottom are signals of pulsar CP 0834 with intervals of 1.27 sec.; CP 0950, 0.25 sec.; and CP 1133, 1.19 sec. The Isaac Newton 98-in. telescope (photo) was put into service during the year at the Royal Greenwich Observatory at Herstmonceux, Eng., and was used in an attempt to observe a faint star in the direction of a pulsar.

riod is rotation and that rotation is capable of stabilizing what would otherwise be an unstable star. Thomas Gold of Cornell University pointed out that in the surroundings of any such star there must be strong electromagnetic phenomena because if the magnetic field rotated uniformly, as in the earth's magnetosphere, the outer parts would exceed the speed of light. The resulting "electrosphere" of a rapidly rotating superdense star seems to be a likely model for a pulsar. Alternatively, F. Hoyle and G. Narlikar of the Institute of Theoretical Astronomy at Cambridge University pointed out that the remnant core of a large star that has exploded as a supernova will vibrate violently and have no easy mechanism for getting rid of this vibrational energy.

No description of pulsars would be complete without pointing out that probably within a year they would help to solve an outstanding cosmological question. There are slender but plausible theoretical reasons for believing that the force of gravity may change as the universe expands. If this is so, then the general theory of relativity will have to be revised and a great deal of astronomical thinking about the remote past has been wrong. Since the universe is about 10^{10} years old, such theories that gravity varies predict that G, Newton's constant of gravitation, should change by about one part in 10^{10} per year. In 1968 it already seemed quite likely that the pulsar periods are constant to better than one part in 10^{10}, and in all the theories of pulsars their periods would depend on gravity. It was likely, therefore, that pulsars would provide the first good proof that gravity does not change its strength.

New Giant Telescopes. On Dec. 1, 1967, Queen Elizabeth II inaugurated the 98-in. Isaac Newton telescope at the Royal Greenwich Observatory, Herstmonceux. This was the fifth largest optical telescope in the world and the largest in Western Europe. The world's third largest optical telescope, a 107-in. mirror at the McDonald Observatory on Mt. Locke, Texas, was dedicated on Nov. 26, 1968. According to the director of the observatory, astronomers had already booked the new telescope for a year in advance.

Cosmology. In spite of the apparently strong evidence against the steady-state theory of the universe, its proponents received some encouragement during the year. As opposed to the "big bang" theory, which holds that the universe began with the explosion of a superdense ball of matter and is continuing to expand, the steady-state theory holds that the universe, in its overall aspects, remains unchanged in time. By using the Parkes radio telescope in Australia at a high radio frequency, astronomers showed that the counts of numbers of radio sources at each apparent brightness were in agreement with the predictions of the steady-state theory. However, at almost the same time G. G. Poolley and Ryle completed a survey into very deep space that showed a disagreement for the faintest sources at their lower frequencies. As of 1968, Poolley had had the last word in this controversy by pointing out that had his group studied as small a region of sky as did the Australian survey and had they restricted themselves to sources within the reach of the Australian survey, then they would have obtained the same apparent result as the Australians. Poolley claimed that the point of the Cambridge results was that there were too few bright sources and too few very faint sources when these were compared with the numbers of fairly faint sources. To detect these discrepancies, Poolley maintained that one needed either

a large patch of sky so that the number of bright sources could be reliably estimated or a survey into very deep space so that the discrepancy concerning the very faint sources would appear. The Australian survey, he claimed, did not meet those requirements.

The other stumbling block of the steady-state theory, the fact that the universe seems to be filled with faint radiation coming from all directions, continued to resist all attempts to explain it away. The explanation by P. J. E. Peebles and R. H. Dicke of Princeton University that it is the radiation from the original big bang that started the universe seemed to be the only good one so far. However, there was one disquieting sign. This radiation should destroy the cosmic rays of the very highest energies; nevertheless, both in the U.S. and in the U.K. the numbers of such cosmic rays recorded was not unexpectedly low.

Quasars and Compact Galaxies. Controversy still raged about the distance to the quasi-stellar radio sources (quasars) and the interpretation of the red shifts of the spectral lines found in them. G. R. Burbidge of the University of California had pointed out in 1967 that red shifts of 1.95 occurred in almost all those quasars that showed absorption lines. This observation was modified somewhat by the reinterpretation of some of the lines, but it remained a fact that there were an abnormally large number of quasars that showed emission red shifts of 1.95. This is not very easy to explain by means of the expanding universe theory, although it is possible that the expansion of the universe slowed down and then accelerated again and that red shifts of 1.95 correspond to looking back to the time when the expansion was very slow. Burbidge believed that the data probably indicate a red shift that arises from within some quasars.

F. Zwicky of the California Institute of Technology circulated a number of lists of compact galaxies, objects that look almost stellar but with a faintly discernible fuzz around the image. Some of these objects vary in brightness as do the quasars. A number of them have large red shifts, and some were grouped in large clusters. As yet, no one knew how these objects may relate to the evolution of galaxies.

Venus Probes. Some controversy continued over the findings obtained as a result of the soft (intact) landing on Venus of the Soviet spacecraft Venera 4 and the flight past Venus of the U.S. Mariner 5 in October 1967. Venera 4 measured the composition of the Venusian atmosphere and found it to be dominated by carbon dioxide, with less nitrogen present than had been expected. However, the more unexpected discovery was the great depth of the atmosphere. The pressure at the surface of Venus is at least 15 earth atmospheres, and some U.S. scientists claimed that even this pressure is really achieved some distance above ground level. In several ways the two spacecraft confirmed each other's findings, but there were considerable differences of interpretation.   (D. L.-BE.)

Ammonia in Space. In December astronomers at the University of California's new radio telescope at Hat Creek, Calif., detected molecules of ammonia gas in interstellar space near the centre of our galaxy. It marked the first time that such a complex molecule had been found in the regions between stars.

See also **Astronautics.**

ENCYCLOPÆDIA BRITANNICA FILMS. *Energy from the Sun* (1955); *Jupiter, Saturn, and Mars in Motion* (1960); *Planets in Orbit—The Laws of Kepler* (1960); *Stars and Star Systems* (1960); *The Story of Palomar* (1960); *Charting the Universe with Optical and Radio Telescopes* (1963); *A Trip to the Planets* (1963); *The Van Allen Radiation Belts* (1963).

Eclipses, 1969

March 18 Sun, annular (begins 02:07.1 E.T.*), visible in Indian O., S.E. Asia, Australia, Antarctica

April 2 Moon, penumbral (begins 16:39 E.T.*), visible in Pacific O., Asia, Europe, Africa, Indian O., Australia, New Zealand, Antarctica

Aug. 27 Moon, penumbral (begins 10:21.6 E.T.*), visible in N. and S. America, Pacific O., Asia, Australia, New Zealand, Antarctica

Sept. 11 Sun, annular (begins 17:02.1 E.T.*), visible in Asia, N. and S. America

Sept. 25 Moon, penumbral (begins 18:05.6 E.T.*), visible in Asia, Pacific O., Australia, New Zealand, Indian O., Africa, Europe, Atlantic O., S. America, Arctic region

Equinoxes and Solstices, 1969

March 20 Vernal equinox (19:08 E.T.*)

June 21 Summer solstice (13:55 E.T.*)

Sept. 23 Autumnal equinox (05:07 E.T.*)

Dec. 22 Winter solstice (00:44 E.T.*)

*Ephemeris Time.
Source: *American Ephemeris and Nautical Almanac, 1969.*

Athletics:
see Baseball; Basketball; Bowling and Lawn Bowls; Boxing; Cricket; Cycling; Football; Golf; Hockey; Ice Skating; Rowing; Skiing; Sporting Record; Swimming; Tennis; Track and Field Sports

Atomic Energy:
see Nuclear Energy

Australia

A federal parliamentary state and a realm of the Commonwealth of Nations, Australia occupies the smallest continent and, with the island state of Tasmania, is the sixth largest country in the world. Area: 2,967,877 sq.mi. (7,-686,810 sq.km.). Pop. (1968 est.): 11,990,787. Cap.: Canberra (pop., 1967 est., 100,900). Largest city: Sydney (pop. of metropolitan area, 1966, 2,444,735). Queen, Elizabeth II; governor-general in 1968, Lord Casey; interim prime minister to January 10, John McEwen; prime minister from January 10, John Grey Gorton.

Domestic Affairs. On Dec. 19, 1967, following the death of the prime minister, Harold Holt, John McEwen, leader of the Country Party, had been sworn in as prime minister of a caretaker government until the Liberal Party could elect a new leader. Immediately after taking office McEwen had told William McMahon, the deputy leader of the Liberal Party and federal treasurer, and other senior Liberals that he would not serve in a coalition of the Liberal and Country parties that was led by McMahon. When the parliamentary Liberal Party met on January 9, there were four candidates for the leadership post: Paul Hasluck, minister of external affairs; L. H. E. Bury, minister of labour and national service; B. M. Snedden, the minister for immigration; and John Grey Gorton (*see* BIOGRAPHY), minister for education and science and government leader in the Senate. McMahon presided at the meeting and declined to be a candidate. Gorton was elected on the second ballot and was sworn in as prime minister by Lord Casey, the governor-general, the next day (January 10).

On April 19, E. G. Whitlam, leader of the federal opposition, announced he was resigning his position and called for an election meeting to test his strength in the parliamentary Labor Party. His move had followed a stormy meeting of the federal executive of the Australian Labor Party (ALP) in Sydney in which Whitlam had received strong opposition on several major voting issues. Whitlam retained his leadership on April 30 by a vote of 38–32, defeating James Cairns of Victoria, the left-wing opponent of Whitlam's demands for reform in the Victorian branch of the party.

Further evidence of disruption within the ALP was obvious after the new plan for federal electoral redistribution was announced in July. In all, ten electorates were to disappear under sweeping changes in the electoral map of Australia that reflected the changes in population since the last redistribution in 1955. Conflict developed between Cairns and Arthur Calwell over which of them was to gain preselection for the Victorian federal seat of Melbourne. Cairns was proposed as a nominee for the seat, which was presumed to be Calwell's property, after Cairns's seat, Yarra, was abolished under the new allocation. As Calwell had been the member for Melbourne since 1940, he had no intention of standing down, and finally in September Cairns decided to stand for a

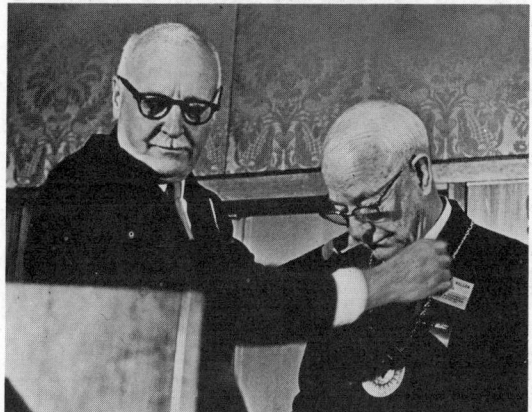

"LONDON DAILY EXPRESS" FROM PICTORIAL PARADE

Sir Leonard Mallen, new president of the World Medical Association, accepting the chain of office from Gerald Dorman of the U.S., chairman of the World Medical Assembly held in Sydney. A general practitioner from Adelaide, S.Austr., Sir Leonard was the first Australian to head the organization.

new Victorian seat, Lalor. General elections, however, were not due until November 1969.

The Liberal-Country Party (LCP) government faced strong criticism over the control of the VIP aircraft used for transporting senior politicians and visitors in Australia. The auditor-general reported that new aircraft for the VIP flight (two BAC-III twin jets, three Dassault Mystère twin jets, and two Hawker Siddeley HS-748 twin turboprop planes) would cost A$21.6 million instead of the anticipated A$11.4 million. The squadron's two BAC-III twin jets were said to be the only ones of their type in the Southern Hemisphere and, therefore, were expensive to service. The main issue was over the avail-

---

AUSTRALIA

Education. (1965) Primary, pupils 1,666,631, teachers 61,000; secondary, pupils 771,046, teachers 39,400; vocational, pupils 138,000; higher (including teacher training), students 131,703, teaching staff (at universities and teacher-training colleges only) 6,362.

Finance. Monetary unit: Australian dollar, with a par value of A$0.89 to U.S. $1 (A$2.14 = £1 sterling). Gold and foreign exchange, official and banks: (June 1968) U.S. $1,223,000,000; (June 1967) U.S. $1,342,000,000. Commonwealth budget (1967–68 est.): revenue A$5,686,000,000; expenditure A$6,124,000,000. Gross national product: (1966–67) A$22.5 billion; (1965–66) A$20,560,000,000. Money supply: (May 1968) A$4,379,000,000; (May 1967) A$4,106,000,000. Cost of living (1963 = 100): (Jan.–March 1968) 115; (Jan.–March 1967) 111.

Foreign Trade. (1967) Imports A$3,130,700,-000; exports A$3,105,200,000. Import sources: U.S. 26%; U.K. 22%; Japan 10%; West Ger-

many 6%. Export destinations: Japan 20%; U.K. 13%; U.S. 12%; New Zealand 5%. Main exports: wool 25%; wheat 15%.

Transport and Communications. Roads (1966) 896,943 km. (including 383,000 km. with improved surface). Motor vehicles in use (1967): passenger 3,193,485; commercial (including buses) 893,323. Railways: (government; 1967) 40,327 km.; traffic (excluding New South Wales and Queensland; 1965) 3,504,000,000 passenger-km., freight 18,850,000,000 net ton-km. Shipping (1967): merchant vessels 100 gross tons and over 307; gross tonnage 803,027. Air traffic (1966): 5,614,000,000 passenger-km.; freight 181,640,000 net ton-km. Telephones (June 1966) 2,978,336. Radio receivers (Dec. 1967) 2,558,-000. Television receivers (Dec. 1967) 2,430,000.

Agriculture. Production (in 000; metric tons; 1967; 1966 in parentheses): wheat 7,548 (12,-570); oats 733 (1,905); barley 794 (1,322),-corn 175 (203); potatoes 623 (653); apples 370

(377); oranges c. 150 (248); wool, greasy 803 (798); milk (1966–67) 7,512, (1965–66) 7,128; butter (1966–67) 222, (1965–66) 209; cheese (1966–67) 70, (1965–66) 59; beef and veal 899 (948); mutton and lamb 637 (613); sugar, raw value (1967–68) 2,372, (1966–67) 2,380; wine 189 (154). Livestock (in 000; March 1967): sheep 164,237; cattle 18,219; pigs 1,804; horses 479.

Industry. Fuel and power (in 000; metric tons; 1967): coal 35,345; lignite 23,762; crude oil 966; manufactured gas (1966) 3,144,000 cu.m.; electricity 42,937,000 kw-hr. Production (in 000; metric tons; 1967): iron ore (65% metal content) 18,760; bauxite 4,236; pig iron 5,056; crude steel 6,289; zinc 198; copper 67; lead 193; tin 3.6; aluminum 92; cement 3,718; cotton yarn 28; wool yarn 24; gold 800 troy oz.; passenger cars (including assembly) 314 units; commercial vehicles (including assembly) 76 units. Dwelling units completed (1967) 116,000.

Soldiers of the 3rd Battalion, Royal Australian Regiment, leading a captured Viet Cong guerrilla in the Long Hai Hills of South Vietnam. Viet Cong strongholds in the area's granite caves have been practically impregnable, even to heavy bombing.

ability of information about passengers' names and places to which the VIP craft had taken passengers. The government first said in May 1966 that no detailed records were available. But flight authorization books and passenger manifests were tabled in the Senate on Oct. 25, 1967. Charges that patently false information had been given to the national Parliament called into question the vital issue of ministerial responsibility.

On July, 1, 1968, the Democratic Labor Party (DLP) Senate team doubled from two to four, following the November 1967 Senate elections in which both the LCP and the ALP yielded one seat.

National service legislation proved to be a controversial issue. The government introduced a national service bill containing a clause requiring universities to provide the Department of Labour and National Service with the names, addresses, and birth dates of all male students for the purpose of catching draft dodgers. The DLP, which held the balance of power in the federal upper house, opposed this clause as "pimping," and said that it would use its power in the Senate to block the bill. The government withdrew the objectionable clause after a stormy debate during which the ALP members were described as "defenders of shirkers" and the government was said to be comprised of "jingoists and fascists."

The Gurindji tribes land issue in the Northern Territory was a controversial feature of aboriginal affairs in 1968. The Gurindji tribe petitioned W. C. Wentworth, minister for aboriginal affairs, for 500 sq.mi. of land. They wanted to develop their own cattle ranch and claimed that since this was their tribal land they had the right to it. The Cabinet ruled that integration was the accepted policy for aboriginals and a land grant would be inconsistent with this because it would create an aboriginal enclave. The government responded to the claim of the Gurindji aboriginals by granting them 900 ac. comprising a residential area, paddock, and orchards. The decision was described in the press as a shameful farce. Aboriginals in Darwin talked of leaving the mission and settlements, rejecting education and assimilation, and returning to the bush to live by hunting. On Aug. 13, 1968, the treasurer, McMahon, observed that as citizens of Australia, the aboriginal people had a right to share in the educational and other community and welfare services provided by public authorities.

In 1968 special provision was made for aboriginal people in the fields of health, education, housing, and productive enterprises. Of the A$10 million that was set aside in an Aboriginal Advancement Trust Fund, half was to be used for assistance in the fields of housing, education, and health. The other half was to constitute a fund for assisting enterprises carried on by aboriginal citizens.

Foreign Affairs. The government passed controversial legislation to prevent Australians from sending assistance to North Vietnam and the National Liberation Front of South Vietnam. The prime minister also had announced on Oct. 17, 1967, that an extra 1,700 men would be sent to Vietnam, together with a tank squadron and helicopters, bringing the Australian commitment up to 8,000 men in 1968.

Australia had to adjust its thinking on regional security in Southeast Asia in January 1968 when the U.K. government announced the decisions it had taken to hasten the withdrawal of its forces east of Suez. In March, Paul Hasluck, as minister for external affairs, stressed the need for regional cooperation between Australia, Malaysia, Singapore, and Indonesia. Australia, said Hasluck, had to face the fact that the strength of nonregional powers was needed to meet regional threats and to maintain global security.

The guaranteed security provided by the U.S. to a number of Asian states under a range of bilateral treaties, and by the ANZUS pact between the U.S., Australia, and New Zealand, did more than any other factor to give Australia a sense of security in the East. So long as the situation in Vietnam was unresolved, however, the future of Southeast Asia as a whole was uncertain. The Australian government did not regard the bombing of targets in North Vietnam as a substitute for sustained military and political effort in the South, but it did maintain that the bombing achieved important military objectives.

On Jan. 31, 1968, the UN Trust Territory of Nauru became independent. The island had been administered by Australia on behalf of the joint administering authority of Australia, New Zealand, and the U.K. Nauru had come under the trusteeship of the UN on Nov. 1, 1947. (*See* NAURU.)

Soviet-Australian friendship was strained in June 1968 when Soviet prawn-fishing fleets attracted notice for fishing in the Gulf of Carpentaria. One Australian company claimed that the largest Soviet prawn-fishing vessel in the area intimidated the smaller Australian vessels, scattering them by sounding its warning siren. Sometimes the Soviet ship with its radar equipment located prawns first and when it moved to a new area the Australians followed. At other times, the Australian spotter plane had located catches that were fished by the Soviets. HMAS "Attack" was sent from Darwin to keep order. The Soviet embassy in Canberra described the prawn-fishing incidents as small matters that should not be allowed to harm Soviet-Australian relations. Although the Soviets did not condemn the sending of a gunboat, they thought that there were cheaper and easier ways of investigating the affair.

In February 1968 foreign fishermen operating within 12 mi. (19 km.) of the Australian coast became liable to a fine of A$10,000, a year in jail, and confiscation of boat, catch, and gear. The prime minister disclosed in July 1968 that legislation was to be

introduced to give the Australian government control over the taking of sedentary fish life from inside the continental shelf. This new move was taken after the prime minister of Queensland, J. C. A. Pizzey, had reported that one Soviet fishing boat had been seen taking clams from the Barrier Reef within the 12 mi. zone off Cairns.

The Economy. On Nov. 21, 1967, following the devaluation of British sterling by 14.3% to £1 = U.S. $2.40, the prime minister announced that Australia had taken a historical decision not to devalue. Australia ranked among the 12 leading trading nations of the world. At the time Australia made its decision, ten of the other 11 trading nations had already decided to maintain their currency values undisturbed. The decision to hold the Australian dollar at the 1967 level avoided any addition to Australia's budgetary burdens. Indebtedness to the U.S. was approaching A$800 million. If Australia had devalued to the same degree as Britain, it would have added, in effect, A$100 million to this debt immediately.

In Australia there was a boom in the stock market. In the first three months of 1968 about A$100 million of British portfolio funds came into Australia. This had followed the A$150 million of the previous six months and made an annual rate of about A$330 million. Minerals attracted most British investment, especially in two stocks: Broken Hill Proprietary Ltd. and Western Mining Corporation Ltd. Western Mining claimed that its nickel fields at Kambalda might turn out to be the world's largest.

In July 1968 Australian wool growers received an average 31.75 cents a pound for their product, the lowest return in nine years. Wool revenues were A$639 million, down 10% from 1966–67. Australia ended the financial year with total reserves of A$1,-092,000,000; the decline of A$106 million reflected the devaluation of sterling in November 1967. On Aug. 13, 1968, the Liberal-Country Party treasurer introduced the 19th budget of three successive Conservative governments. McMahon labeled his budget "a social welfare budget" that aimed to help those most in need while at the same time not discouraging thrift, self-help, and self-reliance.

Throughout 1967–68 consumer spending continued to grow at a rate of 8%. Demand for consumer durable goods was particularly strong, most markedly in the sale of motor vehicles. New registrations totaled 443,000 in 1967–68, a rise of 14% over the 1966–67 figure. Gross national expenditure, or the sum total of public and private spending, increased by 8% to A$24,832,000,000. This was A$618 million more than the gross national product, which increased by 6% at 1968 prices to A$24,214,000,000. Drought had cut farm output and poor export prices had reduced earnings from exports of farm products. On the other hand, imports and payments abroad for defense increased. Consequently, the external deficit on current account widened to about A$1 billion. This was more than covered, however, by a surplus of over A$1,100,-000,000 on capital account. Bigger government loan raising abroad and the exceptionally large inflow of portfolio investment produced the means by which a record addition to the supply of resources from abroad could be financed.

The leader of the federal parliamentary Labor Party opposition, Whitlam, argued that the question the treasurer had neglected to ask was who should own, develop, and use Australian resources. To rely on overseas investment to buy up and own Australian

industries to solve a balance of payments problem in 1968 was simply to store up a massive problem for later years when dividends exceeded new capital inflow. Whitlam concluded that since Australian companies had been slow to grasp the development opportunities presented by the mineral discoveries, there was a case for direct participation by the public sector. (A. R. G. G.)

See also Dependent States.

ENCYCLOPÆDIA BRITANNICA FILMS. *Australia* (1959); *Australia, the Changing Matilda* (1965).

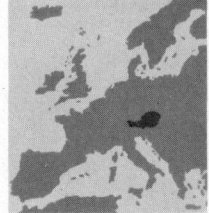

Austria

A republic of central Europe, Austria is bounded by Germany, Czechoslovakia, Hungary, Yugoslavia, Italy, Switzerland, and Liechtenstein. Area: 32,374 sq.mi. (83,849 sq.km.). Pop. (1967 est.): 7,322,800. Cap. and largest city: Vienna (pop., 1967 est., 1,636,-600). Language: predominantly German. Religion: 89% Roman Catholic. President in 1968, Franz Jonas; chancellor, Josef Klaus.

For Austria, the military occupation of its neighbour Czechoslovakia by Communist troops in August 1968 had far-reaching repercussions. The policy of détente which Austria had for some years been pur-

AUSTRIA

Education. (1965–66) Primary, pupils 772,153, teachers 35,197; secondary, pupils 95,334, teachers 6,298; vocational, pupils 213,791, teachers 12,974; teacher training, students 6,194, teachers 1,272; higher (including 6 universities), students 49,382, teaching staff 4,775.

Finance. Monetary unit: schilling, with a par value of 26 schillings to U.S. $1 (62.40 schillings = £1 sterling). Gold and foreign exchange, central bank: (June 1968) U.S. $1,336,000,000; (June 1967) U.S. $1,264,000,000. Budget (1967 rev. est.): revenue 74,-992,000,000 schillings; expenditure 78,590,000,000 schillings. Gross national product: (1967) 276.5 billion schillings; (1966) 260.5 billion schillings. Money supply: (May 1968) 59,080,000,000 schillings; (May 1967) 54,910,000,000 schillings. Cost of living (1963 = 100): (June 1968) 119; (June 1967) 115.

Foreign Trade. (1967) Imports 60,046,000,000 schillings; exports 47,029,000,000 schillings; net foreign exchange receipts from tourism 10.3 billion schillings. Import sources: EEC 59% (West Germany 42%, Italy 8%); Switzerland 7%; U.K. 6%. Export destinations: EEC 41% (West Germany 22%, Italy 12%); Switzerland 9%. Main exports: machinery 18%; iron and steel 13%; textile yarns and fabrics 8%; timber 7%; chemicals 6%.

Transport and Communications. Roads (1967) 92,976 km. Motor vehicles in use (1967): passenger 966,570; commercial 103,602. Federal railways (1966): 5,933 km.; traffic 6,540,000,000 passenger-km., freight (1967) 8,044,000,000 net ton-km. Air traffic (international only; 1967): 301,426,000 passenger-km.; freight 3,539,000 net ton-km. Telephones (Dec. 1966) 1,087,007. Radio receivers (Dec. 1966) 2,171,000. Television receivers (Dec. 1966) 853,000.

Agriculture. Production (in 000; metric tons; 1967; 1966 in parentheses): wheat 1,045 (897); rye 377 (363); barley 772 (706); oats 336 (325); corn 316 (275); potatoes 3,049 (3,007); sugar, raw value (1967–68) 300, (1966–67) 355; apples 361 (367); wine 259 (131); timber (1966) 11,600 cu.m., (1965) 10,900 cu.m. Livestock (in 000; Dec. 1966): cattle 2,497; sheep 138; pigs 2,786; horses 75; goats 94; chickens 10,777.

Industry. Fuel and power (in 000; 1967): coal 14 metric tons; lignite 4,605 metric tons; crude oil 2,684 metric tons; natural gas 1,797,000 cu.m.; electricity (73% hydroelectric in 1966) 24,419,000 kw-hr.; manufactured gas (Vienna only) 608,000 cu.m. Production (in 000; metric tons; 1967): iron ore (30% metal content) 3,473; pig iron 2,141; crude steel 3,022; magnesite (1966) 1,615; aluminum 108; copper 18; cement 4,616; paper (1966) 737; nitrogenous fertilizers (N content; 1966–67) 234; cotton yarn 20; woven cotton fabrics 19; wool yarn 12; rayon fibres (1966) 56.

suing vis-à-vis the Communist nations and which during the summer of 1968 had led to hopes of a general improvement in relations received a great setback.

After the Soviet occupation the Austrian government ordered the reinforcement of its frontiers by the Army, police, and customs guards. Strong protests were made to Moscow against numerous infringements of Austrian frontiers, particularly by Soviet planes. All soldiers due for release on September 15 had their national service extended until early October. Statements in the Soviet press that Austria had actively helped the Czechoslovak "counterrevolution" were emphatically denied by Austria.

Austrian private and official sources immediately began a program of aid for Czechoslovak refugees and for tourists whose return home was delayed. Many thousands received free shelter, food, clothing, gasoline, and free railway passes. By mid-September, 12 million schillings had been spent on relief. At that time more than 1,200 Czechoslovaks had asked for political asylum in Austria.

Several Cabinet changes were made by the Austrian People's Party (ÖVP). Stephan Koren became minister of finance, Kurt Waldheim, foreign minister, and other ministerial changes included new appointments to the vice-chancellorship and to the Ministry of Trade, formerly combined (since 1966) under one minister. A state secretariat for information was created. Wolfgang Schmitz, the finance minister in the previous Cabinet, was appointed president of the Austrian National Bank in February.

In all provincial elections in Salzburg, Klagenfurt, and Graz, and in the state assemblies in Upper Austria (October 1967) and in Burgenland (March 1968), the Socialist Party of Austria (SPÖ) gained seats from the ÖVP and from the small Austrian Freedom Party (FPÖ). In the Burgenland legislative assembly the Socialists gained an absolute majority. In Upper Austria, for the first time ever, the Socialists received the majority of votes, although the seats in the legislature were equally divided with the ÖVP. An agreement between the ÖVP and the FPÖ finally enabled the former to retain the state governorship.

The trial of Viktor Müllner, a former high official of the ÖVP, began in May. Convicted of corrupt practices, he was sentenced to four years' imprisonment and ordered to pay 20 million schillings compensation to Lower Austria, where he had been deputy state governor and financial adviser, and to the electricity corporation of Lower Austria, in which he had held the post of director general. In July the public prosecutor of Vienna brought a charge of embezzlement against the former president of the Austrian Federation of Trade Unions and minister of the interior, Franz Olah, also a former high official of the ÖVP. Damages of 8.5 million schillings were asked for. In May and June, in Austria as elsewhere, left-wing students demonstrated and were involved in clashes with the police.

In October 1967 there had been a revival of terrorism in South Tirol, an area in Italy on the Austrian border that had about 250,000 inhabitants of Austrian descent. Austro-Italian negotiations for the solution of the problem made little progress during 1968. In retaliation for the unrest, which it blamed in large part on Austria, Italy continued to veto negotiations for Austria's admission to the European Economic Community.

In July 1968 Austria signed the nuclear nonproliferation treaty. This was of special significance to Aus-

tria since through it, Vienna, as the headquarters of the International Atomic Energy Agency (IAEA), could become the centre of a worldwide nuclear security control. In March ground was broken in Vienna's Donaupark for the building of an international centre which was to house IAEA, UNIDO (UN Industrial Development Organization), already based in Vienna, and other international organizations.

Important international congresses were held in Vienna during 1968, notably the UN Conference on the Law of Treaties in May and the UN Conference on the Exploration and Peaceful Uses of Outer Space in August. Also in August the Austrian foreign minister appointed a special representative to assist in peacemaking and relief work in the Nigerian-Biafran conflict. Austria sent several medical teams into Biafra, and public as well as private collections of money and materials were started.

The doldrums into which Austria's economy had drifted in 1967 were replaced in the spring of 1968 by an upward trend. At the beginning of the year the ÖVP introduced the Koren Plan, a comprehensive concept for economic growth and budgetary reform. To counter the threatened 16 billion schilling deficit in the 1969 budget, stiff tax increases were to take effect beginning January 1969.

A treaty with the U.S.S.R. in which the Soviet Union agreed to supply natural gas to Austria was of great importance to future Austrian energy supplies. Through a lengthened pipeline running from the Czechoslovak frontier to Vienna three million cubic metres of natural gas would flow into Austria daily within a few years. Work was also started on the Adria-Vienna pipeline which would on completion carry ten million tons of petroleum a year.   (E. DI.)

Barbados

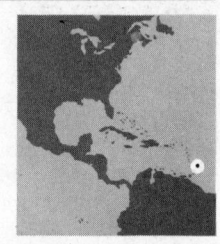

The parliamentary state of Barbados is a member of the Commonwealth of Nations and occupies the most easterly island in the southern Caribbean Sea. Area: 166 sq.mi. (430 sq.km.). Pop. (1967 est.): 248,166, predominantly Negro. Cap. and largest city: Bridgetown (pop., 1960, 11,452). Language: English. Religion: Christian, with Anglicans in the majority. Queen, Elizabeth II; governor-general in 1968, Sir John Stow; prime minister, Errol Walton Barrow.

During 1968, Barbados, whose prime minister, Errol Barrow, could take credit for being an initiator of the scheme, continued to be active in the development of the Caribbean Free Trade Area (CARIFTA). The

BARBADOS
Education. (1964–65) Primary, pupils 39,173, teachers 1,241; secondary, pupils 15,431, teachers 497; higher, students 407, teaching staff 57.
Finance and Trade. Monetary unit: East Caribbean dollar, with a par value of ECar$2 to U.S. $1 (ECar$4.80 = £1 sterling). Budget (1967–68 actual): revenue ECar$44.9 million; expenditure ECar$62.2 million. Foreign trade (1966): imports ECar$128 million (31% from U.K., 19% from U.S., 12% from Canada, 7% from Venezuela, 6% from Trinidad and Tobago); exports ECar$69 million (45% to U.K., 9% to U.S., 8% to Windward Islands, 7% to Canada). Main exports: sugar 67%; rum 7%; molasses 7%.
Agriculture. Production (in 000; metric tons) sugar, raw value (1967–68) 173, (1966–67) 204.

agreement on free trade involving Barbados, Guyana, Trinidad and Tobago, and Antigua came into force on May 1. This group was joined in July by Dominica, Grenada, St. Kitts-Nevis-Anguilla, St. Lucia, and St. Vincent, and in August by Jamaica and Montserrat, the total comprising a larger group than the defunct West Indian Federation. Barbados was selected as the site for the Regional Development Bank, whose membership included all the CARIFTA countries, together with the Bahamas and British Honduras. Barbados continued to expand contacts in the Western Hemisphere.

Barbados took part during the year in the Geneva World Sugar Conference; sugar, its main crop in 1967, reached a peak annual sale that year of ECar$37.3 million. During May, the deputy prime minister, J. Cameron Tudor, led a delegation to the U.S. for discussions on the Barbadian economy, which resulted in a promise of aid for specific purposes. An agreement with the Texas Crude Oil Co. was signed, providing for offshore oil prospecting, and the first U.S. bank to operate in Barbados opened in October. In July the prime minister (also minister of finance) presented his 1968–69 budget. During 1967–68, though a deficit had been anticipated, a surplus of ECar$1.6 million was achieved. It was hoped, despite expanded expenditure estimates, that a similar result would be achieved for 1968–69. Estimated current expenditure for 1968–69 was ECar$56.1 million, and capital expenditure, ECar$9.3 million, with a deficit of ECar$2.1 million on current expenditure alone and an urgent need for increased loans to cover the capital estimate. Proposed taxation was geared to the problems raised by devaluation, CARIFTA duty-free goods, and the difficulty of raising external loans. The emphasis was on taxing luxury imports and consumption. To promote the development of the economy the government also set up in July a National Agricultural Research Committee to examine the possibilities of diversification in food and export crops. In particular the question of mechanizing the sugar industry was to be examined, because of rising costs and a labour shortage. The average age of Barbadian sugarcane cutters was over 50, and though the 1968 crop stood at 173,000 metric tons (204,000 metric tons in 1967) 753 labourers had to be imported in 1968, as compared with 368 in 1967. The tourist industry continued to expand during the year. A total of five new hotels and apartment buildings were built, and further extensions were made to existing hotels.

Social security benefits were introduced at the end of 1967, and educational developments included the opening of a community college and a Canadian gift of $63,000 for books. In April the prime minister opened the new Centre for Multi-Racial Studies, as part of the University of the West Indies, a joint venture undertaken with the University of Sussex in Great Britain. (M. MR.)

Baseball

The Detroit Tigers defied prohibitive odds to win the world championship of baseball in 1968. They dethroned the St. Louis Cardinals in the World Series, four games to three, after trailing three games to one. Only two other teams in Series history had overcome such a deficit. Detroit's Mickey Lolich pitched and won three complete games, including the decisive seventh, a 4–1 verdict over Bob Gibson.

WIDE WORLD

Lou Brock of the St. Louis Cardinals sliding safely into second with a stolen base as ball bounces from glove of Detroit Tiger shortstop Mickey Stanley during the third game of the World Series.

It was the Year of the Pitcher in the major leagues. Punctuating that fact were the following accomplishments: Denny McLain (see BIOGRAPHY) of the Tigers posted a 31–6 record, the first man to win 30 or more games in one season since Dizzy Dean's 30–7 in 1934. Don Drysdale of the Los Angeles Dodgers pitched a record six consecutive shutouts en route to erasing Walter Johnson's long-standing mark for consecutive scoreless innings. Johnson threw 56 shutout innings in a row in 1913, Drysdale $58\frac{2}{3}$ in 1968. Gibson, the St. Louis standout, totaled 13 shutouts, including 5 in a row and one string of $47\frac{2}{3}$ successive scoreless innings. His 22–9 record also included a 15-game winning streak.

Jim ("Catfish") Hunter of the Oakland Athletics pitched a perfect game in May, 4–0 over Minnesota, the first regular-season masterpiece in the American League in 46 years. Other no-hitters were registered by Baltimore's Tom Phoebus, Cincinnati's George Culver, San Francisco's Gaylord Perry, and St. Louis' Ray Washburn, the last two on successive days during a San Francisco-St. Louis series.

Houston's Don Wilson tied two records in one game, striking out eight Cincinnati batters in a row and a total of 18. Luis Tiant of Cleveland smashed the strikeout record for ten-inning games when he cut down 19 against Minnesota. Veteran Hoyt Wilhelm of the Chicago White Sox made 72 pitching appearances for a career total of 937, surpassing Cy Young's 57-year-old record of 906. Pittsburgh's Roy Face made his 802nd pitching appearance with one

Table I. Final Major League Standings, 1968

American League

Club	W	L	Pct.	G.B.	Det. W-L	Balt. W-L	Cleve. W-L	Bos. W-L	N.Y. W-L	Oak. W-L	Minn. W-L	Calif. W-L	Chi. W-L	Wash. W-L
Detroit	103	59	.636	—	—	10-8	12-6	12-6	10-8	13-5	10-8	13-5	13-5	10-8
Balt.	91	71	.562	12	8-10	—	7-11	9-9	13-5	9-9	10-8	10-8	11-7	14-4
Cleve.	86	75	.534	16½	6-12	11-7	—	8-10	10-8	6-12	14-4	11-7	13-5	7-10
Boston	86	76	.531	17	6-12	9-9	10-8	—	10-8	8-10	9-9	9-9	14-4	11-7
N. Y.	83	79	.512	20	8-10	5-13	8-10	8-10	—	10-8	6-12	12-6	12-6	14-4
Oakland	82	80	.506	21	5-13	9-9	12-6	10-8	8-10	—	10-8	13-5	8-10	7-11
Minn.	79	83	.488	24	8-10	8-10	4-14	9-9	12-6	8-10	—	11-7	8-10	11-7
Calif.	67	95	.414	36	5-13	8-10	7-11	9-9	6-12	5-13	7-11	—	8-10	12-6
Chicago	67	95	.414	36	5-13	7-11	5-13	4-14	6-12	10-8	10-8	10-8	—	10-8
Wash.	65	96	.404	37½	8-10	4-14	10-7	7-11	4-14	11-7	7-11	6-12	8-10	—

Ties: New York 2, Detroit 2, Oakland 1, Cleveland 1.

National League

Club	W	L	Pct.	G.B.	St.L. W-L	S.F. W-L	Chi. W-L	Cinn. W-L	Atl. W-L	Pitt. W-L	L.A. W-L	Phil. W-L	N.Y. W-L	Hous. W-L
St. L.	97	65	.599	—	—	8-10	9-9	11-7	13-5	12-6	9-9	10-8	12-6	13-5
S. F.	88	74	.543	9	10-8	—	9-9	10-8	9-9	9-9	9-9	9-9	11-7	10-8
Chicago	84	78	.519	13	9-9	9-9	—	7-11	10-8	10-8	12-6	9-9	8-10	10-8
Cinn.	83	79	.512	14	7-11	8-10	11-7	—	8-10	10-8	9-9	11-7	10-8	9-9
Atlanta	81	81	.500	16	5-13	9-9	8-10	10-8	—	6-12	9-9	11-7	12-6	11-7
Pitt.	80	82	.494	17	6-12	7-11	8-10	8-10	12-6	—	8-10	9-9	9-9	13-5
L. A.	76	86	.469	21	9-9	9-9	6-12	9-9	9-9	10-8	—	10-8	7-11	7-11
Phil.	76	86	.469	21	8-10	9-9	9-9	7-11	7-11	9-9	8-10	—	10-8	9-9
N. Y.	73	89	.451	24	6-12	7-11	10-8	8-10	6-12	9-9	11-7	8-10	—	8-10
Hous.	72	90	.444	25	5-13	8-10	8-10	9-9	7-11	5-13	11-7	9-9	10-8	—

Ties: Pittsburgh 1, Cincinnati 1, Chicago 1, San Francisco 1, Atlanta 1, New York 1.
Source: The Sporting News.

Don Drysdale pitching against the Giants in his fifth consecutive shutout. In 1968 he set two new major league records with six consecutive shutout games and 58⅔ scoreless innings.

club to tie a record, but then was traded to Detroit. Wilbur Wood of the White Sox pitched in 88 games, another major league record.

It was the Year of the Pitcher despite baseball's efforts to put teeth in legislation forbidding use of the spitball. The rules committee had at first threatened pitchers with expulsion after a second warning for putting hand to mouth. Subsequent revisions dictated that umpires call the pitch a ball should a pitcher bring his pitching hand in contact with his mouth while in the 18-ft. circle surrounding the pitching rubber. In a further attempt to curtail pitcher dominance, the baseball rules committee in December reduced the strike zone to between the armpits and the tops of the knees; it had been between the shoulders and the knees. Also, the height of the pitcher's mound was lowered to 10 in. from the previous 15 in., and the mound was required to slope gradually.

The National League decided to join the American League in expanding from 10 to 12 teams in 1969. The National League awarded franchises to San Diego and Montreal. Each league would contain two six-team divisions, with divisional playoffs determining World Series berths.

The American League's Eastern Division would include Boston, New York, Baltimore, Washington, Cleveland, and Detroit, with the Western Division featuring Chicago, Minnesota, Kansas City, Oakland, Seattle, and California. In the National League, the Eastern Division would embrace Chicago, New York, Philadelphia, Pittsburgh, St. Louis, and Montreal. In the West, it would be San Francisco, Los Angeles, San Diego, Houston, Cincinnati, and Atlanta.

Hank Aaron of the Atlanta Braves hit the 500th home run of his career on July 14. Aaron became the eighth man in the major leagues to gain this milestone.

Early in December the owners of the major league teams held their annual winter meeting. At its conclusion, baseball commissioner William D. Eckert resigned his post, reportedly under pressure from the owners. In late December the owners met in Chicago

to select a new commissioner. The meeting lasted for some 14 hours, but no agreement was reached and further efforts were postponed until early in 1969.

The Baseball Hall of Fame at Cooperstown, N.Y., enshrined the names of three great outfielders of the past: Joe Medwick, Leon ("Goose") Goslin, and Hazen ("Kiki") Cuyler. The minimum salary in the major leagues was raised from $7,000 to $10,000.

Major Leagues. The Detroit Tigers, managed by Mayo Smith, and the St. Louis Cardinals, managed by Red Schoendienst, won their respective pennant races by convincing margins. The Tigers outdistanced Baltimore by 12 games. Cleveland was third, 16½ games out, and defending champion Boston finished fourth, 17 games behind. Detroit had not won a pennant since 1945.

St. Louis grabbed National League honours for the second year in a row. The Cardinals finished nine games in front of runner-up San Francisco. The Chicago Cubs were third, 13 games out.

The World Series opened in St. Louis and set the stage for one of the most talked-about pitching confrontations in baseball history: Bob Gibson of St. Louis versus Denny McLain of Detroit. It was Gibson who survived the showdown. He struck out a record 17 batters, scattered five hits, and beat the Tigers and McLain, 4–0. A three-run Cardinal fourth, featured by Julian Javier's two-run single, broke open the game. Lou Brock homered for the final St. Louis run.

Mickey Lolich launched his campaign for the role of Series hero in the second game. Lolich stopped the Cardinals and pitcher Nelson Briles, 8–1, and he hit a home run to help matters along. Willie Horton and Norm Cash also homered for the Tigers.

The Series moved to Detroit for the next three games, and St. Louis, with Ray Washburn pitching, rolled over the Tigers and Earl Wilson, 7–3. Three-run homers by Tim McCarver and Orlando Cepeda paced the Cardinals after Al Kaline's two-run blast had given Detroit a 2–0 lead. Brock got three hits and stole three bases. Washburn received excellent relief help from Joe Hoerner for the final 3⅔ innings.

Gibson prevailed over McLain again in the fourth game as the Cardinals won, 10–1, to take an imposing lead of three games to one. Gibson struck out ten while allowing only five hits. He also hit a home run. Brock led off the game with a home run, later added a triple and double, and stole his seventh base to tie his own World Series record. It was his 14th stolen base in World Series competition, also tying a record. The game was played despite two lengthy delays because of rain.

With their backs to the wall the Tigers again looked to Lolich in the fifth game. He delivered handsomely, checking the Cardinals 5–3, and chipping in with a key single in a three-run Detroit seventh that wiped out a 3–2 deficit. Kaline's two-run single put the Tigers in front to stay.

The teams returned to St. Louis for the sixth game, and McLain evened the Series at three games apiece, 13–1. Detroit pushed over ten runs in the third inning to tie a Series record. Highlight of the outburst was a grand-slam home run by Jim Northrup. The losing pitcher was Washburn.

Lolich and Gibson, both in quest of a third win, were matched in the seventh and final game, played in St. Louis. After six scoreless innings Detroit exploded with three runs in the seventh, the first two scored after centerfielder Curt Flood misjudged a

Denny McLain, Detroit Tigers' pitcher, received the Cy Young award and was named the American League's most valuable player after winning 31 games and losing only 6 during the 1968 season.

long fly by Northrup that went for a triple. Thereafter, Lolich was home free. His shutout was ruined by Mike Shannon's home run in the ninth. Lolich gave up five hits, while Detroit got eight hits off Gibson. Total attendance at the seven games of the Series was 379,670.

Pete Rose of Cincinnati won the National League batting championship after a torrid duel with Pittsburgh's Matty Alou. Rose hit .335 and Alou, .332. Willie McCovey of San Francisco led the league in home runs with 36 and in runs batted in with 105. Brock stole 62 bases for leadership in that category.

The league's 20-game winners were Juan Marichal of San Francisco, with 26–9; Gibson, with 22–9; and Ferguson Jenkins of the Chicago Cubs, with 20–15. Gibson's earned run average was an outstanding 1.12. He also led in strikeouts with 268. After the season Gibson won the Cy Young award for the outstanding pitcher in the National League.

Boston's Carl Yastrzemski captured the American League batting title for the second year in a row. His .301 was the lowest mark ever to lead the league. Yastrzemski was the league's only .300 hitter. Washington's Frank Howard topped home run hitters with 44. Boston's Ken Harrelson led in runs batted in with 109. Bert Campaneris of Oakland led base-stealers with 62.

McLain pitched 28 complete games in compiling his spectacular 31–6 record, and at the season's end won the Cy Young award for the outstanding American League pitcher. The 20-game winners were Baltimore's Dave McNally, with 22–10; Cleveland's Luis Tiant, with 21–9; and New York's Mel Stottlemyre, with 21–12. Sam McDowell of Cleveland collected 283 strikeouts, and McLain had 280.

That it was the Year of the Pitcher was again emphasized when McLain and Gibson were voted the most valuable players in their respective leagues; it was the first time a pitcher had won in the American League. Rookies of the year were Stan Bahnsen, a New York pitcher, in the American League, and Johnny Bench, a Cincinnati catcher, in the National.

The National League beat the American League, 1–0, in the 39th annual All-Star game in Houston's Astrodome. Willie Mays of San Francisco singled in the first inning and eventually scored on a double play to give Don Drysdale of Los Angeles the win over Cleveland's Luis Tiant. A crowd of 48,321 watched the National League score its 6th win in a row and 21st in the series, against 17 losses and one tie.

Philadelphia fired manager Gene Mauch and hired Bob Skinner, and Houston replaced Grady Hatton with Harry Walker in a pair of managerial changes during June. In July Baltimore dismissed Hank Bauer in favour of Earl Weaver, and the Chicago White Sox parted company with Eddie Stanky and called back Al Lopez. The new San Diego entry named Preston Gomez as manager, while Seattle picked Joe Schultz. At the end of the season Minnesota dismissed Cal Ermer and brought in Billy Martin, while Oakland replaced Bob Kennedy with Hank Bauer. Herman Franks resigned as San Francisco's pilot, and the job went to Clyde King.   (J. Be.)

Other Leagues. It was a successful year for the National Association of Professional Baseball Leagues (NAPBL), the organization that works in concert with the major leagues and operates the minor leagues. The NAPBL in 1968 numbered 21 leagues consisting of 152 clubs, the largest number of clubs in ten years. The total attendance was in excess of ten million, a healthy figure for an organization often characterized as moribund.

Part of the increase resulted from expanding interest in Mexico, where two new four-club leagues sought and were granted NAPBL membership in 1968. The 152 clubs ranged from Vancouver, B.C., and Pittsfield, Mass., to Merida, Mex., and Honolulu.

Table II. Minor League Standings, 1968

Pacific Coast League
Eastern Division

Club	W	L	Pct.	G.B.
Tulsa	95	53	.642	—
San Diego	76	70	.521	18
Phoenix	76	71	.517	18½
Denver	73	72	.503	20½
Indianapolis	66	78	.458	27
Oklahoma City	61	84	.421	32½

Western Division

Club	W	L	Pct.	G.B.
Spokane	85	60	.586	—
Hawaii	78	69	.531	8½
Portland	72	72	.500	12½
Seattle	71	76	.483	15
Tacoma	65	83	.439	21½
Vancouver	58	88	.397	27½

Tulsa defeated Spokane four games to one in best-of-seven play-off.

International League

Club	W	L	Pct.	G.B.
Toledo	83	64	.565	—
Columbus (O.)	82	64	.562	½
Rochester (N.Y.)	77	69	.527	5½
Jacksonville (Fla.)	75	71	.514	7½
Syracuse	72	75	.490	11
Louisville	72	75	.490	11
Buffalo	66	81	.449	17
Richmond	59	87	.404	23½

Play-offs
Semifinals (best of five): Jacksonville defeated Toledo three games to one; Columbus defeated Rochester three games to two. Finals (best of seven): Jacksonville defeated Columbus four games to none.

Mexican League

Club	W	L	Pct.	G.B.
Mexico City Reds	82	58	.586	—
Veracruz	79	60	.568	2½
Jalisco	77	63	.550	5
Puebla	72	68	.514	10
Reynosa	69	71	.493	13
Mexico City Tigers	62	78	.443	20
Poza Rica	60	79	.432	21½
Monterrey	58	82	.414	24

The Pacific Coast League (PCL), classified as a Triple A league, had 12 teams split into Eastern and Western divisions. Tulsa, managed by Warren Spahn, a one-time star major league pitcher, won the Eastern Division title by 18 games. Spokane was the Western Division winner, finishing 8½ games ahead of Hawaii. Tulsa then won the league title by defeating Spokane four games to one in a best-of-seven play-off series.

Outfielder Jim Hicks of Tulsa won the PCL batting title with a .366 average. Chuck Taylor, also of Tulsa, tied Rich Robertson of Phoenix for the most pitching victories, 18. Taylor, who had never won more than nine games in one season, was 18–7 under Spahn's tutelage. Pete Mikkelsen, a veteran right-hander, also responded to Spahn's handling and had a 16–4 record with a 1.91 earned run average, lowest of any pitcher who worked more than 80 innings.

The International League (IL), also Triple A, had another extremely close pennant race. For the third year in a row the pennant was decided on the final day. The Toledo Mud Hens, managed by Jack Tighe, captured the league's regular season title, finishing ½ game ahead of the Columbus Jets. It was the first pennant for Toledo since 1953.

Rain forced a postponement in a season-ending eight-game series between Columbus and Jacksonville; this cost Columbus a possible tie for the title. The second game of a September 5 doubleheader was rained out and could not be made up since both clubs had doubleheaders on each of the next three days. The IL has no provision for postseason make-up games and thus Columbus played one less game.

The Mud Hens trailed Columbus by one percentage point on September 8, the final day; Toledo needed a victory and help from Jacksonville, which was playing a doubleheader in Columbus. Les Cain, a 20-year-old southpaw, pitched a three-hitter as the Mud Hens whipped Rochester, 17–0. In addition, Cain also hit a grand-slam home run and drove in six runs. Jacksonville, in the meantime, beat Columbus in the first game of the doubleheader, thus assuring the Mud Hens of the title.

Jacksonville, fourth in the regular season standings, won the postseason play-offs. Jacksonville eliminated Toledo, and Columbus ousted Rochester in the semifinals, contested in a best-of-five series. Jacksonville then met Columbus in the best-of-seven finals and concluded with a four-game sweep.

The championship in the Mexican League, designated as Triple A for the first time, was won by the Mexico City Reds, who finished 2½ games ahead of runner-up Veracruz. Individual stars were pitcher Aurelio Lopez of the Mexico City Reds, named rookie of the year; outfielder Ramón Montoya, also of the Reds, selected as the most valuable player; and pitcher Jim Horsford of Reynosa, who led in victories with 20, in innings pitched with 278, and in earned run average with 1.59. Tom Herrera of the Reds was chosen manager of the year. (JE. HO.)

Amateur. The University of Southern California Trojans won the National Collegiate Athletic Association (NCAA) baseball championship in the college play-offs at Omaha, Neb. They beat Southern Illinois, 4–3, in the finals of the double elimination tournament on a two-run triple by Pat Kuehner with two out in the ninth inning. The Trojans captured five straight games in the tournament in winning their fifth NCAA title, their fourth under coach Rod Dedeaux. Bill Seinsoth hit a two-run homer for Southern California's other two runs. Seinsoth was named most valuable player of the tournament. The winning pitcher was Brent Strom. (J. BE.)

Basketball

United States. *Intercollegiate.* The University of California at Los Angeles (UCLA) continued its domination of U.S. college basketball. Paced by Lew Alcindor (*see* BIOGRAPHY), a 7-ft. 1⅜-in. centre, the Bruins were a somewhat surprise winner in the National Collegiate Athletic Association (NCAA) tournament. En route to the title, their fourth in the last five years, UCLA whipped Houston 101–69 in a game so highly publicized that many fans later thought it was the championship game. But it was a semifinal, and UCLA won the title the next night with a 78–55 victory over North Carolina. The 23-point spread in this triumph was the widest ever in an NCAA final.

It was the second successive NCAA championship for the Bruins, who, in addition to Alcindor, had a well-balanced team that was strong at every position. Lucius Allen and Mike Warren were the starting guards, and Mike Lynn and Lynn Shackelford the starting forwards. The team was expertly coached by John Wooden, the first coach to twice have teams win back-to-back NCAA titles.

UCLA and Houston played each other twice, and these two games highlighted the collegiate season. The first match, played at mid-season (on January 20) in Houston, drew 52,693, the largest crowd ever to see a basketball game in the United States. Seldom had a game attracted such interest. First, there was the individual contest between the rival centres, Alcindor and 6-ft. 8-in. Elvin Hayes of Houston.

Houston won this first game, 71–69, on a pair of

Table I. Major College Champions, 1968

League	Team and location	League record	All games
Eastern (Ivy)	*Columbia (New York, N.Y.)	12–2	23–5
	Princeton (N.J.)	12–2	20–6
Yankee	Rhode Island (Kingston)	8–2	15–11
	Massachusetts (Amherst)	8–2	14–11
Atlantic Coast	North Carolina (Chapel Hill)	12–2	28–4
Southeastern	Kentucky (Lexington)	15–3	22–5
Southern	Davidson (N.C.)	9–1	24–5
Ohio Valley	*East Tennessee State (Johnson City)	10–4	19–8
	Murray State (Ky.)	10–4	16–8
Intercollegiate	*Ohio State (Columbus)	10–4	16–8
(Big Ten)	Iowa (Iowa City)	10–4	16–9
Mid-American	Bowling Green (O.)	10–2	18–7
Big Eight	Kansas State (Manhattan)	11–3	19–9
Missouri Valley	Louisville (Ky.)	14–2	21–7
Southwest	Texas Christian (Fort Worth)	9–5	15–11
Western A.C.	New Mexico (Albuquerque)	8–2	23–5
AAWU	UCLA (Los Angeles, Calif.)	14–0	29–1
West Coast	Santa Clara (Calif.)	13–1	22–4

*Won play-off for NCAA tournament berth.

Table II. NBA Final Standings and Play-offs, 1968

Eastern Division				Western Division			
Team	W	L	Pct.	Team	W	L	Pct.
Philadelphia	62	20	.756	St. Louis	56	26	.683
Boston	54	28	.659	Los Angeles	52	30	.634
New York	43	39	.524	San Francisco	43	39	.524
Detroit	40	42	.488	Chicago	29	53	.354
Cincinnati	39	43	.476	Seattle	23	59	.280
Baltimore	36	46	.439	San Diego	15	67	.183

Play-offs

Eastern semifinals	Western semifinals
Philadelphia 4, New York 2	San Francisco 4, St. Louis 2
Boston 4, Detroit 2	Los Angeles 4, Chicago 1
Eastern finals	**Western finals**
Boston 4, Philadelphia 3	Los Angeles 4, San Francisco 0

Championship series

Boston defeated Los Angeles 4 games to 2
Boston 107, Los Angeles 101
Los Angeles 123, Boston 113
Boston 127, Los Angeles 119
Los Angeles 118, Boston 105
Boston 120, Los Angeles 117 (overtime)
Boston 124, Los Angeles 109

free throws by Hayes with 28 seconds left to play. Hayes outshot and outrebounded Alcindor, who was playing despite an injured eye which apparently impaired his vision. Hayes scored 39 points, 29 in the first half, sank 17 of 25 attempts from the field, and grabbed 15 rebounds. It was one of Alcindor's worst games. He was held to four baskets (in 18 attempts) and took only five rebounds.

The loss snapped UCLA's winning streak at 47 games, and Houston was then ranked as the best U.S. college team. But in the NCAA tournament the experts were proved wrong. In the semifinal game, held in late March in Los Angeles, UCLA turned on a blitz offensive attack and whipped Houston by a 32-point margin. Coach Wooden devised a special zone defense to stop Hayes, who was limited to ten shots from the floor and sank only four of those. Alcindor outscored Hayes 19–10 in this game and outrebounded him 19–5.

Eliminated from the title round, Houston suffered its second and final loss of the season the following night when the Cougars were beaten 89–85 by Ohio State in the third place consolation game. Hayes, however, scored 34 points. UCLA then took the floor and won its record-breaking victory over North Carolina for the title. Alcindor was UCLA's top scorer in the championship game with 34 points.

Though almost all of the national attention was focused on the Alcindor-Hayes confrontations, neither won the NCAA scoring championship. This title was not computed on total points but on the per-game average, and, according to this standard, the top scorer was Pete Maravich of Louisiana State University, a 6-ft. 5-in. sophomore. Maravich pumped in 1,138 points in 26 games, a record 43.8 average. The previous highest game average had been 41.7, set by Frank Selvy of Furman in 1953–54.

Calvin Murphy of Niagara, a 5-ft. 10-in. guard, was second to Maravich in scoring with a 38.2 average. Hayes was third with a 36.8 average. Hayes played in 33 games and scored 1,214 points, the most ever by a player from a major college in one season. This increased Hayes's three-year college total to 2,884, lifting him to second place behind the record set by Oscar Robertson. Alcindor, who was in 28 games, scored 734 points for a 26.2 average.

Players chosen on the first team All-America, as published in the *Official NCAA Basketball Guide*, were Wes Unseld, Louisville; Alcindor, UCLA; Hayes, Houston; Larry Miller, North Carolina; and Maravich, LSU. The second team consisted of Murphy, Niagara; Bob Lanier, St. Bonaventure; Lucius Allen, UCLA; Don May, Dayton; and Jojo White, Kansas.

Kentucky Wesleyan (Owensboro) won the NCAA's college division title by defeating Indiana State (Terre Haute) 63–52, only the second time in the last eight years that the title was decided by a margin of more than four points. Kentucky Wesleyan finished its season with a record of 28 wins against 3 losses. Mike Davis of Virginia Union (Richmond) won the college division scoring title with a 36.3 average, narrowly beating Willie Scott of Alabama State, 35.6.

The new and controversial anti-dunk rule, which outlawed the practice of ramming the ball directly downward through the basket, had virtually no effect in stopping extremely tall players. These players made the necessary adjustments and released the ball before their hand was extended over the basket.

Professional. The National Basketball Association (NBA) continued to expand in 1968 by adding two franchises, both to become operative for the 1969 sea-

JAMES DRAKE, "SPORTS ILLUS-TRATED" © TIME INC.

UCLA's Mike Warren driving for a lay-up against North Carolina in the NCAA tournament finals. UCLA defeated North Carolina 78–55 for their second consecutive national title.

son and thereby bringing the league membership to 14. New teams were placed in Milwaukee and Phoenix at a price (per club) of $2 million, which was then divided equally among the 12 existing teams. In return, the new teams were each allowed to select 18 players placed in a special expansion pool by the other clubs, which lost three players apiece.

The 1968 NBA title was won by the Boston Celtics who, though finishing second in the Eastern Division, defeated the Los Angeles Lakers four games to two in the best-of-seven play-off finals. It was the tenth time in the last 12 years that the Celtics had won the league championship, all achieved after the arrival of star centre Bill Russell, who was also their player-coach. Russell again was among the NBA's leading rebounders, averaging 18.6 rebounds a game during the regular season. The Celtics' scoring stars were John Havlicek, Bailey Howell, and Sam Jones, all of whom averaged about 20 points per game.

The Philadelphia 76ers, led by Wilt Chamberlain, were the most effective team prior to the championship play-offs. The 76ers won the Eastern Division title with a 62–20 record, eight games ahead of Boston, but then were upset by Boston in the play-off round. The St. Louis Hawks, the Western Division winners, were also eliminated in the play-offs, losing to San Francisco, which, in turn, was eliminated by Los Angeles.

Chamberlain set one and extended two of his other NBA records. He led in assists with 702, becoming the first centre in NBA history to lead in playmaking. He also extended his record of consecutive games played without fouling out to 706 and increased his all-time record league scoring total to 25,434 points. For the regular 82-game season, Chamberlain was third in scoring with 1,992 points. Dave Bing of Detroit led with 2,142, a 27.1 average.

Four months after the completion of the season, the 76ers traded Chamberlain to Los Angeles, sending him to the Lakers in exchange for Archie Clark, Darrall Imhoff, and Jerry Chambers. The trade apparently was made because of a salary impasse. Chamberlain was believed to have asked for a three-year, $1 million contract.

The NBA total attendance was 3,649,511, an increase of 17% over the previous season. That the NBA was financially successful became evident when Boston signed player-coach Russell to a three-year

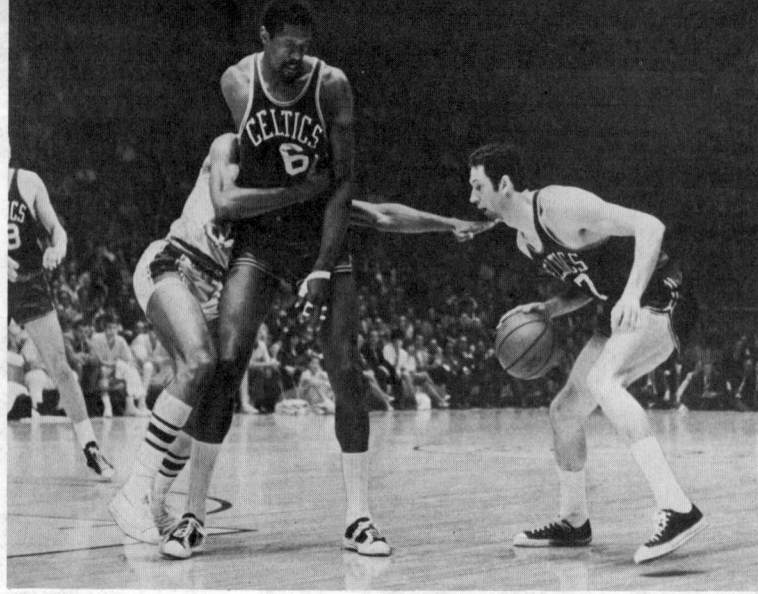

Boston Celtics' player-coach Bill Russell screening for John Havlicek in the final game of the NBA championship play-off against the Los Angeles Lakers. Boston won 124–109.

Lew Alcindor of UCLA outjumping Houston's Elvin Hayes in the season's first meeting between the two top-ranked teams, Jan. 20, 1968. Houston defeated UCLA 71–69.

contract calling for $200,000 a year. The NBA also outdid the rival American Basketball Association (ABA) in the competition for most of the prize rookie talent. San Diego, which entered the NBA in 1968, landed Elvin Hayes of Houston with a four-year contract for a reported $440,000.

Pittsburgh won the championship in the newly created ABA, which played its first year of competition. Eleven teams started and finished the season, with Pittsburgh winning the Eastern Division title and New Orleans winning the Western Division. At the season's end, there was considerable franchise shifting. Minneapolis moved to Miama, Fla.; Pittsburgh shifted to Minneapolis; Anaheim, Calif., moved to Los Angeles; and Teaneck, N.J., regarded as the league's New York franchise, was transferred to Commack, N.Y. Connie Hawkins won the league's scoring title with 1,875 points, a 26.8 average. (JE. HO.)

World Amateur. The ambition of most national teams affiliated with the International Basketball Federation was to take part in the Olympic Games in Mexico City. During the season tournaments took place throughout the world to determine the ten teams that would join the first five from the previous Olympics in Tokyo, plus the sixth place reserved for the host nation, Mexico. The teams already qualified by their performance at the Tokyo Olympics were the U.S., the U.S.S.R., Brazil, Puerto Rico, and Italy.

The European Olympic qualifying tournament took place in Sofia, Bulg., and it resulted in triumphs for Yugoslavia and Bulgaria. A surprise nonentry for this tournament was Spain. The Spaniards decided to take their chance in the pre-Olympic qualifying tournament held in Monterrey, Mex., two weeks prior to the Olympic Games. There they were successful, along with Poland, in qualifying for the Olympics. In the Pan-American Games, Panama and Cuba finished third and fourth to the U.S. and Mexico and, in so doing, qualified for the Olympics because the U.S. and Mexico were already assured of places.

In the Asian championships in Seoul, South Korea, the Philippines and South Korea finished first and second and so gained a place in Mexico City. The African championships were held in Casablanca, Mor., early in the year and were won by Senegal with Morocco as runner-up. Thus, these two nations qualified as the African entries for the Olympics.

In the Olympic Games the U.S. defeated Yugoslavia in the final game. For a discussion of Olympic competition, *see* SPORTING RECORD: *Special Report*.

The finals of the European championships for women took place in Sicily in August, and, as expected, the U.S.S.R. retained its championship, going through the whole series undefeated. In the final game they beat Poland 92–55.

In the third International Cup, played in Philadelphia in January, the Akron-Goodyear team was successful. Real Madrid of Spain gained second place and S. P. Simmenthal of Milan, Italy, finished third.

(K. K. MI.)

ENCYCLOPÆDIA BRITANNICA FILMS. *Basic Elementary Basketball Skills* (1967); *Playing Better Basketball* (1967).

Belgium

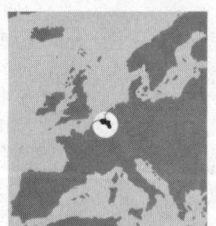

A constitutional monarchy on the North Sea coast of Europe, Belgium is bordered by the Netherlands, Germany, Luxembourg, and France. Area: 11,781 sq.mi. (30,513 sq.km.). Pop. (1968 est.): 9,605,601. Cap.: Brussels (commune pop., 1968 est., 168,632). Largest city: Antwerp (commune pop., 1968 est., 239,848). Language: French and Flemish. Religion: predominantly Roman Catholic. King, Baudouin I; prime ministers in 1968, Paul Vanden Boeynants and, from June 12, Gaston Eyskens.

Hopes that a special commission would succeed in finding a solution for the problems causing conflicts between the two language communities in Belgium were dashed early in 1968, a year marked by a serious crisis over whether to keep the French section of the Catholic University of Louvain (Leuven) in that Flemish city or to transfer it to the French-speaking area of the country (Wallonia). This crisis eventually brought about the downfall of the coalition government of Social Christians and Liberals, led by Paul Vanden Boeynants.

At a mass demonstration held in Antwerp on Nov. 5, 1967, all of the Flemish cultural organizations had stressed their determination to safeguard the cultural integrity of Flanders. They insisted that the French section of Louvain University be established in Wallonia, but the Academic Council of Louvain-French refused to consider such a move, as was obvious from the details of the expansion program revealed early in 1968. This caused immediate and violent reactions from the Flemish students at Louvain, and the trouble soon spread to other cities in Flanders.

Noting the persistent refusal of Louvain-French, the Academic Council of Louvain-Flemish asked the prime minister and the political parties to impose a political solution. The government, however, felt that the decision should be left to the Belgian episcopate, the body responsible for the university's policies. The bishops were divided on the issue. With no decision forthcoming, the Flemish wing of the Social Christians raised the subject in Parliament, where it expected to force a vote on a motion laying down the principles of the transfer of the French section.

On the day of the debate the Flemish Social Christian ministers resigned from the government. Protracted efforts to solve the government crisis failed. Parliament was therefore dissolved on March 1, and new elections were scheduled for March 31. The two major parties, the Social Christians and the Socialists, were rent by internal divisions; the former over the

Louvain University question, the latter because Flemish candidates in the Brussels voting district felt wronged by their place on the party's official election list and decided to go to the polls on a separate list. The French and Flemish wings of the Social Christians remained at odds over the Louvain issue and presented different election programs. However, Vanden Boeynants managed to reconcile the Social Christians in Brussels, and both French- and Flemish-speaking candidates were listed on the same slate, led by the prime minister.

The three traditional parties all lost seats in the election, and only the parties claiming to speak for language groups and termed "extremists" made progress. The results of the election were: Social Christians, 69 seats (77 in 1965); Socialists, 59 (64); Liberals, 47 (48); Communists, 5 (6); Volksunie (Flemish Nationalist Party), 20 (12); Front Démocratique des Francophones, 5 (3); Rassemblement Walloon (French Language Federalist Party), 7 (2). Vanden Boeynants scored a personal success, polling 116,000 preference votes.

The election results left only two possibilities for a new coalition government: a tripartite coalition, rejected by the Socialists, or a coalition of Social Christians and Socialists. After arduous negotiations two prime ministers designate, a Social Christian and the

Police using fire hoses to quell a riot by more than 2,000 students at the Catholic University of Louvain (Leuven). The demonstration was part of the continuing controversy between the French and Flemish factions and resulted in more than 300 arrests.

Socialist party leader, Léo Collard, failed to form a new Cabinet, so King Baudouin once more called on Vanden Boeynants. Agreement was eventually reached on a government program containing no less than 150 points and providing on the one hand for cultural autonomy for the two language communities, as requested by the Flemish, and on the other for the economic decentralization about which the Walloon Socialists had been particularly insistent. That part of the program dealing with cultural autonomy required a two-thirds majority, which the coalition parties could not muster in Parliament. Legislation providing for cultural autonomy and economic decentralization would have to be passed simultaneously, which became the source of the first friction between the two government parties. Once the agreement was approved by a special congress of both parties, Vanden Boeynants withdrew and on June 12 Gaston Eyskens (see Biography) was invited by the king to form the new government.

Awaited with considerable apprehension by Flemish public opinion was a judgment by the International Court for Human Rights in Strasbourg, concerning a plea from Belgian French-speaking citizens. Most of those involved were living in the Flemish area of the country, and as a result of the new linguistic legislation their children could not get a French education in their home towns. Only one of six complaints was declared contrary to the Convention on Human Rights.

Industrial production, which had begun to increase in September 1967, continued its upward trend throughout the first months of 1968, mostly as the result of the start of new production units but also because of a revival of foreign demand. Instead of an expected 3% increase in the gross national product for 1968, a 3.5 to 4% increase seemed more likely. Unemployment figures nevertheless dropped much more slowly, and among workers under 25 they assumed alarming proportions in some areas. There was a continuing decline in the amount of private investment.

Among the last measures passed by the outgoing Social Christian and Liberal government was a program for aid to the developing countries. It provided for a gradual increase in Belgian participation, rising to a target of 1% of the national income. Priority would continue to be given to the Congo (Kinshasa).

Belgium's relations with the Congo improved and almost fully returned to normal in August following a visit by the Congolese foreign affairs minister, Justin Bomboko. (JA. R. E.)

See also Congo, Democratic Republic of the.

BELGIUM
Education. (1964–65) Primary, pupils 967,124, teachers 38,220; secondary, pupils 300,406, teachers 35,348; vocational, pupils 443,766, teachers 39,439; teacher training, students 24,840; higher (including 5 universities), students 75,489.

Finance. Monetary unit: Belgian franc, with a par value of BFr. 50 to U.S. $1 (BFr. 120 = £1 sterling). Gold and foreign exchange, central bank: (June 1968) U.S. $2,056,000,000; (June 1967) U.S. $2,120,000,000. Budget (1968 est.): revenue BFr. 241,189,000,000; expenditure BFr. 271,934,000,000. Gross national product: (1966) BFr. 906 billion; (1965) BFr. 847 billion. Money supply: (May 1968) BFr. 362.3 billion; (May 1967) BFr. 335.2 billion. Cost of living (1963 = 100): (June 1968) 119; (June 1967) 116.

Foreign Trade. (Belgium-Luxembourg economic union; 1967) Imports BFr. 358.8 billion; exports BFr. 351.6 billion. Import sources: EEC 56% (West Germany 21%, France 15%, Netherlands 15%, Italy 5%); U.S. 8%; U.K. 7%. Export destinations: EEC 63% (Netherlands 21%, West Germany 20%, France 18%); U.S. 8%; U.K. 5%. Main exports: iron and steel 17%; machinery 10%; textile yarns and fabrics 9%; nonferrous metals 9%; motor vehicles 8%; chemicals 7%.

Transport and Communications. Roads (1967) 91,718 km. (including 335 km. expressways). Motor vehicles in use (1967): passenger 1,667,054; commercial 262,065. Railways: (state only; 1966) 4,364 km.; traffic (1967) 8,531,000,000 passenger-km., freight 6,070,000,000 net ton-km. Navigable inland waterways in regular use (1966) 1,595 km. Shipping (1967): merchant vessels 100 gross tons and over 218; gross tonnage 940,426. Air traffic (international only; 1967): 1,953,857,000 passenger-km.; freight 98,308,000 net ton-km. Telephones (Dec. 1966) 1,658,355. Radio receivers (Dec. 1966) 3,047,000. Television receivers (Dec. 1966) 1,660,000.

Agriculture. Production (in 000; metric tons; 1967; 1966 in parentheses): wheat 842 (660); oats 361 (293); barley 623 (486); rye 90 (76); potatoes 1,943 (1,474); flax fibre (1966) 26, (1965) 31; sugar beets, raw value (1967–68) 578, (1966–67) 421; meat 568 (481). Livestock (in 000; Dec. 1966): cattle 2,597; pigs 2,117; sheep 68; horses 87; chickens (May 1966) 32,192. Fish catch (in 000; metric tons) (1966) 63, (1965) 60.

Industry. Fuel and power (in 000; 1967): coal 16,430 metric tons; manufactured gas 4,194,000 cu.m.; electricity 23,929,000 kw-hr. Production (in 000; metric tons; 1967): pig iron 8,901; crude steel 9,717; copper 318; lead 108; zinc 227; tin 4.3; cement 5,819; cotton yarn 71; cotton fabrics 68; wool yarn 61; woolen fabrics 38; rayon and acetate yarn 18; rayon and acetate fibres 21.

ABERNATHY, RALPH DAVID

The death of the Rev. Martin Luther King, Jr., by an assassin's bullet on April 4, 1968, in Memphis, Tenn., shifted the burden of leadership in his nonviolent movement to his closest friend, the Rev. Ralph David Abernathy. Although King had prepared for such an eventuality two years earlier by handpicking Abernathy as his successor in the Southern Christian Leadership Conference, Abernathy was sorely tried in 1968 as its new president.

Lacking King's intellectual grasp and personal magnetism, Abernathy sought to make up for this by militancy. He pushed ahead with plans for a Poor People's Campaign in Washington, D.C., and presented Congress with several broad demands for jobs and a guaranteed annual income for persons unable to work.

Abernathy did not lack resourcefulness. It was he who coined the name "Resurrection City" for the improvised poor people's camp near the Lincoln Memorial in Washington. He kept lawmakers in a state of apprehension and managed to dominate the news for months. But the Poor People's Campaign faced major problems. The public showed little of the enthusiasm it had evinced for the civil rights march on Washington in 1963. Bickering broke out within SCLC ranks. The weather turned the camp into a quagmire. And Abernathy's demands for federal aid to the poor came at a time when Congress was busy cutting back numerous domestic programs to offset the spiraling cost of the war in Vietnam.

In a final gesture, Abernathy led a march on Capitol Hill in June and was sentenced to 20 days in jail. He fasted while serving the sentence, losing 12 lb. By the time he was released, on July 13, Resurrection City had been torn down and most demonstrators had gone home. Nevertheless, he promised to take the Poor People's Campaign into marginal congressional districts to help candidates sympathetic to his goals.

Born March 11, 1926, in Linden, Ala., Abernathy was ordained in the Baptist ministry in 1948 and received a B.S. degree in mathematics at Alabama State College in 1950. From 1951 to 1961 he served as pastor of First Baptist Church in Montgomery, Ala., where he met King and helped organize the Montgomery Improvement Association, precursor of the SCLC. He served in a number of posts in the SCLC from 1957 onward.
(T. R. T.)

ABRAMS, CREIGHTON WILLIAMS, JR.

When Gen. Creighton Abrams took over as commander, United States Military Assistance Command, Vietnam (MACV), on July 2, 1968, it must have seemed a dubious honour at best. Of the three wars he had been in—World War II, the Korean War, and Vietnam—the last was proving the most unpopular and controversial.

In April 1967 the four-star general had been named deputy commander in Vietnam, second in command to Gen. William C. Westmoreland. A year later, on April 10, 1968, Pres. Lyndon B. Johnson announced that Abrams would be the top commander. It was no surprise; most people had assumed he would be moved up when, just prior to this announcement, the president had named Westmoreland as army chief of staff.

The change in command gave observers a chance to cite comparisons between Abrams and Westmoreland—as men and as commanders. Abrams was usually abrupt and blunt-spoken, cutting through preliminaries in briefings and conversations, demanding the meat without garnishing. He was considered more casual in his dress and in the symbols of command—his quarters and the vehicle he rode in. His cigars were as much a part of his image as pistols were for his World War II commander, Gen. George Patton.

A tactical commander—meeting the problems of war on a day-to-day basis—Abrams told his troops that they were to "hound and harass" the enemy from the land. The capability and possibility of doing this, however, seemed to be hampered by political restraints, national and international. Abrams accepted the limitation on the bombing of North Vietnam announced by President Johnson on March 31, and later concurred with the complete bombing halt ordered by Johnson on October 31. While the United States agonized through its presidential campaign and the deadlocked Paris peace talks, Abrams concentrated on initiating aggressive ground tactics for finding, encircling, and destroying the enemy; providing intensive training and greater use of South Vietnamese forces; and improving the use of strategic bombing.

Abrams was born Sept. 15, 1914, in Springfield, Mass., and graduated from West Point in 1936. During World War II he commanded the 37th Tank Battalion, which went into action in Normandy in July 1944 and was in the vanguard of Patton's 3rd Army as it swept across Europe. After the war, Abrams held a number of assignments and attended various military command schools. He went to Korea in 1953, serving successively as chief of staff for the I, X, and IX Corps.
(B. S. KA.)

AGNEW, SPIRO THEODORE

Rarely had a politician risen so rapidly. In 1968 Spiro T. Agnew was elected vice-president of the United States to serve under Richard M. Nixon. Just eight years earlier he had finished last in a five-man contest for a judgeship in Baltimore County, Md.

Agnew's luck had begun to change in 1962. He was elected county executive of Baltimore County, primarily because local Democrats, who outnumbered Republicans four to one (Agnew himself was a Democrat until 1946), were divided and tarnished by scandal. Four years later a similar situation occurred. Division in the state Democratic Party resulted in the nomination of George P. Mahoney for governor. A bumbling campaigner, Mahoney acquired a reputation as a racist because of his opposition to fair housing and his slogan, "Your home is your castle—protect it." Agnew defeated Mahoney with the help of numerous Democrats, though he failed to carry his own county. In his first year as governor Agnew showed skill, and during this period Maryland adopted the first state open housing law south of the Mason-Dixon Line. Later, however, there was criticism, especially of his handling of racial disorders.

As the Republican national convention opened, Agnew was considered a very outside possibility for the vice-presidential nomination. Few politicians took the possibility seriously, however, even when Nixon selected Agnew to place his name in nomination. But Nixon wanted a running mate whom both the South and the North could live with. A handful of Republicans sought to block Agnew's nomination but failed.

During the campaign, Agnew displayed a tendency to put his foot in his mouth.

He charged the Democratic presidential candidate, Vice-Pres. Hubert Humphrey, with being "squishy soft on Communism," and he was quoted as having used the terms "Polacks" and "fat Jap" (he later apologized). As election day neared, the Democrats seemed to be concentrating on him rather than on Nixon. Yet many reporters who covered his campaign noted that audiences responded to him with warmth and approval.

Agnew was born Nov. 9, 1918, the son of a Greek immigrant whose name was originally Anagnostopoulos. He attended Johns Hopkins and received a law degree from the University of Baltimore.
(RI. T. S.)

ALCINDOR, FERDINAND LEWIS, JR.

To basketball fans in the Los Angeles Sports Arena on March 23, 1968, and to the thousands watching on television, the sight was somewhat incongruous—7-ft. 1⅜-in. Lew Alcindor teetering on a chair beneath the backboard as he calmly unhooked the net of the basket—emblematic of the conqueror's reward—and draped it around his neck. In the game just ended, 20-year-old Ferdinand Lewis Alcindor, Jr., had been gracefully soaring above and around the net as he scored 34 points, secured 16 rebounds, and blocked seven of his opponents' shots before they could reach the basket. Alcindor was the main reason the University of California at Los Angeles defeated the University of North Carolina, 78-55, for UCLA's second straight National Collegiate Athletic Association (NCAA) national championship.

Alcindor was born April 16, 1947, in New York City, the son of an officer in the New York City Transit Authority police. During his four years at Power Memorial Academy in upper Manhattan his team lost only once and he scored 2,067 points. He became the most sought-after high-school basketball player since Wilt Chamberlain and was offered 150 scholarships. The interest was so high in his choice of colleges that it was announced at a televised press conference.

During Alcindor's 1965–66 season at UCLA his freshman team defeated the UCLA varsity and won every game on its schedule. As a sophomore Alcindor led UCLA to an undefeated season, conquering the University of Dayton, 79-64, in the NCAA final. Only a midseason loss to the University of Houston marred a near perfect 1967–68 season for the Bruins. Revenge for that loss came in the NCAA semifinals. With Alcindor making half his 14 shots, grabbing 18 rebounds, scoring 19 points, and blocking many Houston shots, UCLA won easily, 101–69.

Twice an all-American, Alcindor was expected to make it three in a row in his senior year (1968–69 season). And a huge professional contract—possibly more than $1 million—would await him after the season. Many experts believed that Alcindor, with his size, reach, long legs with whipcord muscles, and ability on offense and defense, might become basketball's greatest attraction.
(R. CA.)

ALVAREZ, LUIS W.

Luis W. Alvarez, senior physicist at the University of California's Lawrence Radiation Laboratory in Berkeley, was awarded the 1968 Nobel Prize for Physics. He was one of the seven U.S. scientists who swept the scientific awards for the year. This marked the second such monopoly for Americans and only the third time in the 67-year history of the prizes that they had all gone to scientists from one nation.

Alvarez was cited "for his decisive contributions to elementary particle physics, in particular the discovery of a large number of resonance states, made possible through his development of the technique of using a hydrogen bubble chamber and data analysis."

More specifically, he developed methods of studying transitory subatomic particles with lifetimes on the order of 10^{-22} sec.—1,000 times shorter than the lifetimes of the most short-lived particles (or resonances) known before. Alvarez' approach was based on passing electrical charges through liquid hydrogen and observing the formation of the resulting bubbles—an experimental technique analogous to studying a speedboat by the wake it creates. His major contributions related to developing ever larger bubble chambers, finding methods of recording data instantaneously through stereophotography, and introducing high-speed computer data analysis. His work was largely responsible for the "population explosion" of subatomic particles from a family of about 30 to well over 100.

While he was most famous for this basic research, Alvarez had been active in a variety of fields. He developed a way to X-ray the Pyramids, floated spark chambers into the upper atmosphere, produced nuclear reactions without uranium, invented a colour television system, discovered radioactive helium, and built an electric indoor golf-training device that was used by Pres. Dwight Eisenhower.

The son of the well-known physician Walter C. Alvarez, Luis Alvarez was born in San Francisco, June 13, 1911. He took undergraduate and advanced degrees at the University of Chicago and joined the faculty of the University of California in 1936. During World War II he invented microwave beacons and performed research in the field of radar. He was also involved in the development of the atomic bomb. He attended the first atomic explosion at Alamogordo, N.M., in 1945 and, weeks later, flew over Hiroshima as a scientific observer. His awards included aviation's Collier Trophy, for his contributions to ground-controlled approach systems, and the National Medal of Science.   (PH. K.)

ARENALES CATALAN, EMILIO

In assuming the presidency of the 23rd session of the UN General Assembly, Emilio Arenales noted the upsurge of disorders in many parts of the world and declared that "violence emerges on the national or international scene when peoples, communities, nations or governments lose hope." Since the founding of the UN, he said, hope has been withering, slowly but surely, while young people are increasingly calling for deeds, justice, and the righting of wrongs. He urged his fellow delegates to make it their primary task to infuse new hope, faith, and dynamism in the UN in an effort to restore its waning prestige. "It is my hope," he asserted, "that this Assembly may be remembered as the Assembly of reconsideration and rectification."

Arenales reminded the delegates that the UN was not a superstate, but rather a parliament with many limitations, and said it could not be asked to solve the problems of war and peace by itself. "The weaknesses or limitations of the United Nations," he stated, "are not those of a body with an independent life of its own, but are the direct and unavoidable responsibility of the states which founded the United Nations, of the governments which now belong to it, and of those who make up those governments and their delegations." Paraphrasing the late Pres. John F. Kennedy, he said: "We must

WIDE WORLD

Spiro Theodore Agnew

DENNIS BRACK FROM BLACK STAR

Ralph David Abernathy

COURTESY, UNIVERSITY OF CALIFORNIA,
LAWRENCE RADIATION LABORATORY

Luis W. Alvarez

WIDE WORLD

Creighton Williams Abrams, Jr.

not ask the United Nations, as a body isolated from us, what it can do for member states, but rather we must ask the member states what they can do for the United Nations and its principles."

On October 15 Arenales entered Lenox Hill Hospital in New York City and on October 22 he underwent surgery. A statement from the hospital said "a tumor of the brain was completely and successfully removed." In his absence the assembly's vice-presidents took turns in the chair.

Arenales was born in Guatemala City, Guatemala, on May 10, 1922. He was educated at the Instituto Modelo in Guatemala City and took his law degree at the University of San Carlos. His connection with the UN began in 1946 when he became legal counselor to the preparatory commission for the Educational, Scientific, and Cultural Organization (UNESCO). From 1955 to 1958 he was permanent representative of Guatemala at UN headquarters. After eight years of private law practice, he became Guatemala's foreign minister.   (Mx. H.)

ARGUEDAS MENDIETA, ANTONIO

A former minister of the interior of Bolivia, Antonio Arguedas Mendieta, became a mystery man in the strange aftermath of the capture and execution of guerrilla leader "Che" Guevara. Arguedas fled Bolivia in July 1968 but returned voluntarily a month later to await trial on charges of releasing a classified document without authorization.

The document in question was no ordinary one: it was Guevara's guerrilla diary, which Arguedas admitted sending to Fidel Castro. Not only did this gesture permit Cuba to rush the diary into print before

the Bolivian government could sell its version to a publisher but it also precipitated rioting and a state of siege in the Bolivian capital of La Paz.

Arguedas' motive in handing the document over to Castro agents was not known. There was speculation he had been either a long-time secret agent of Castro or that he had sent Castro the diary as documentary proof that foreign-fomented, violent revolution in Latin America was destined for failure.

The deed was even more mysterious because of Arguedas' long-time friendship with Bolivian Pres. René Barrientos Ortuño as a fellow air force officer and his role in promoting Barrientos' successful candidacy in 1966. As the country's top police official, Arguedas also played an important part in Bolivia's successful campaign to wipe out the Guevara band in the mountainous jungles in the south of the Andean nation.

Arguedas was born in 1928. As a young man he was active in the Party of the Leftist Revolution, a Marxist-oriented group. But in 1964, while serving in the Air Force, he joined the socialist Movement of the National Revolution (MNR) and was elected to the national Chamber of Deputies on that ticket.

The MNR government of Pres. Víctor Paz Estenssoro was overthrown in November 1964, in a coup in which Barrientos and Gen. Alfredo Ovando Candía played leading parts. Arguedas emerged as an undersecretary in the Ministry of Government when Barrientos and Ovando served as co-presidents. Later, Arguedas took part in the Frente de la Revolución Boliviana, the political coalition that successfully promoted the 1966 candidacy of Barrientos as sole president.   (J. A. O'L.)

ARIAS, ARNULFO

Arnulfo Arias, a longtime Panamanian political leader, in 1968 endured another stormy episode in his turbulent career. He campaigned for the presidency of Panama against David Samudio, the candidate backed by the incumbent government. In the election, held in May, Arias was declared the winner by a margin of 41,545 votes. At first it appeared that he would not be allowed to take office, but Panama's national police force supported him and he assumed the presidency on October 1.

Arias served as president for only 11 days, however, and then was deposed in a coup led by Col. José M. Pinilla of the national police force. Arias fled to the U.S.-controlled Panama Canal Zone, where he called for U.S. military assistance to overthrow the coup leaders. The U.S. refused, and Arias remained out of office as the year ended. It was the third time that he had been deposed while serving as president.

Arias was born Aug. 15, 1901, the youngest of six children of a plantation owner in Penonomé, about 75 mi. W of Panama City. He was educated at the University of Chicago and Harvard University medical school, partly financed by his elder brother, Harmodio, who was Panama's president in 1932. Arias became interested in politics in the late 1920s and was elected president of Panama in 1940. During the following year he scrapped the constitution to extend his term for six years and was then overthrown and exiled. He again was elected president in 1948 but the results were thrown out. After a year and a half of turmoil his election was recognized but, in 1951, he once more tried to throw out the constitution and was again deposed. After his second expulsion from the presidency, Arias went into obscurity for more than a decade. In 1964 he tried for the presidency again and was beaten by what he and many others have consistently claimed was fraud at the ballot box.

(J. A. O'L.)

ASHE, ARTHUR ROBERT, JR.

In 1951, at the age of eight, Arthur Ashe started playing tennis with a borrowed racket on a segregated public playground in Richmond, Va. In 1968, at the West Side Tennis Club in Forest Hills, N.Y.—which once barred Negro Ralph Bunche from membership—25-year-old Army Lieut. Arthur Robert Ashe, Jr., became the first Negro man to win a major tennis championship.

Ashe captured the U.S. National Men's Singles Championship (the first American in 13 years to win), and then, overcoming the greatest field ever to compete in a U.S. tennis tournament, won the first U.S. Open. In December he teamed with Clark Graebner, Bob Lutz, and Stan Smith to win back the Davis Cup from Australia. Ashe won his first match in Davis Cup competition from Ray Ruffels, but lost his second to Bill Bowrey.

Ashe faced many obstacles in his rise to the top ranks of tennis. He was born on July 10, 1943, in Richmond, Va. His father, a playground guard for Richmond's recreation department, could not afford to buy new rackets for Arthur or pay his way to tournaments. R. Walter Johnson of Lynchburg, Va., a Negro physician, backed Ashe financially. Johnson had backed Althea Gibson, also a Negro tennis champion, a decade earlier.

On the strength of wins at the 1960 and 1961 U.S. national junior indoor tournaments, Ashe received a scholarship to the University of California at Los Angeles and also a job tending the tennis courts. He became national collegiate champion in 1965 and was ranked second among men players in the U.S. in 1965, 1966, and 1967.

In the 1968 finals of the U.S. Open against Tom Okker of the Netherlands, Ashe displayed his remarkable composure when things get toughest. After Okker had rallied to tie the match at two sets apiece, Ashe poured in service aces, volleyed brilliantly, and made strong backhand passing shots down the line to win the set and the match, 14–12, 5–7, 6–3, 3–6, 6–3.

Ashe was expected to sign a professional contract in 1969 after completing his army duties. In 1968 he was assigned to the U.S. Military Academy at West Point, N.Y., as a computer specialist, but was allowed leave time for Davis Cup and other major tennis competition.

(R. Ca.)

BAKR, AHMED HASSAN AL-

Maj. Gen. Ahmed Hassan al-Bakr, who engineered the July 17, 1968, coup d'etat in Iraq, was an old hand at this kind of undertaking. On Feb. 8, 1963, he had played a major part in overthrowing and killing Brig. Abdul Karim Kassem, the dictator who had seized power in 1958. Al-Bakr emerged as prime minister of Iraq under Col. Abdul Salam Arif, who became president of the republic. The legislature of the new government was dominated by the right wing of the Baath (Socialist) Party, of which al-Bakr was a member. On Nov. 18, 1963, the moderate Arif succeeded in overthrowing the Baathist government, and, as a result, al-Bakr faded into the background as vice-president. He was dismissed from that post in January 1964.

On April 13, 1966, President Arif was killed in a helicopter crash. He was succeeded by his brother, Maj. Gen. Abdul Rahman Arif. Not a strong leader, he appointed and dismissed in quick succession two prime ministers, assumed the premiership himself, and finally, on July 10, 1967, asked Lieut. Gen. Taher Yahya to form a government composed of generals and representatives of the left-wing Arab Nationalist Movement.

This was the government that al-Bakr overthrew in 1968 with the help of armed forces officers and his Baath Party friends. He appointed himself president of Iraq and commander in chief of the armed forces, sent President Arif to London in exile, and retired three senior armed forces officers on pension. Yahya was arrested and charged with corruption.

Al-Bakr's relations with the United Arab Republic and Syria were rather cool, in spite of his statement that "Israel must disappear." Mullah Mustafa al-Barzani, the leader of the minority Kurds in Iraq, described al-Bakr as a mortal enemy of the Kurds, while the Iraqi Communist Party, one of the strongest in the Arab world, called in November for the overthrow of the al-Bakr regime.

Ahmed Hassan al-Bakr was born in Baghdad in 1916. He joined the Iraqi Army shortly before World War II; as a colonel of infantry he became a member of the Baath Party in 1958. The following year he was retired from the Army by Kassem.

(K. Sm.)

BARNARD, CHRISTIAAN (NEETHLING)

A successful heart transplant operation on Jan. 2, 1968, by Christiaan Barnard at Groote Schuur Hospital in Cape Town, S.Af., made medical history but also raised a number of puzzling legal and ethical questions.

The patient, a retired dentist named Philip Blaiberg, received the heart of a 24-year-old mulatto who had died of a stroke only hours earlier. Two other human heart transplant operations had been performed the preceding month—one of them by Barnard—but the patients had died. Blaiberg fought off liver and lung complications and was living at home at year's end.

In the ensuing months Barnard was accused of seeking publicity and his radical surgery was described as "premature." Others criticized the large sum of money paid for the physician's autobiography. The doctor had many defenders, however. He answered critics by insisting the public had a right to know details of the operation. The money, in fact, went to his research foundation.

Although Barnard was personally congratulated by both Pres. Lyndon B. Johnson and Pope Paul VI, the implications of transplanting a heart from one human body to another disturbed the legal and medical professions. In March a commission of the American Heart Association launched a study of the legal and moral aspects of heart transplants. A U.S. Senate subcommittee held hearings on a proposed National Commission on Health, Science, and Society that would evaluate medical research. Barnard testified against the proposal, warning that heart surgery would be impeded by such outside regulation.

Whatever the inquiries might conclude, it was obvious that Barnard's feat had given a tremendous impetus to the whole subject of heart surgery. By the end of the year, more than 100 human hearts had been transplanted in various countries around the world.

Barnard was born in 1923 in Beaufort West, S.Af., the son of a Dutch Reformed Church minister. He received his M.D. in 1953 from the University of Cape Town Medical School and a Ph.D. in surgery from the University of Minnesota Medical School in 1955. He directed surgical research at the Groote Schuur Hospital from 1958.

(T. R. T.)

BAUNSGAARD, HILMAR TORMOD INGOLF

It was not surprising that Denmark's new prime minister following the January 1968 general election should be a Radical Liberal—no more surprising than that the choice should fall on Hilmar Baunsgaard. It had been expected that the election would result in big gains for the Radical Liberals, but scarcely that the party's 13 seats in the Folketing would be more than doubled to 28. Both Conservatives and Liberal Agrarians—the other partners in the "bourgeois" coalition that was formed after some days of negotiation—favoured Baunsgaard as leader of the new government, and this was an indication of a popularity that extended well beyond his own party.

The first non-Social Democratic prime minister the country had had since 1953—but one whose motto was "welfare for all"—Baunsgaard faced the task of persuading the Danes to swallow some bitter economic medicine if order was to be brought into the hard-pressed Danish economy and inflation curbed. He was well equipped for the job in hand, being an effective cooperator, unfettered by orthodox party dogmas and therefore capable of finding unifying, supra-party solutions. Furthermore, he had a first-rate television presence, an inestimable advantage for any politician.

The son of a provincial warehouse keeper, Baunsgaard was born in Slagelse on Feb. 26, 1920. He went to business school and at the

age of 22 became chief clerk at a big country store. A year later he was manager of a wholesale grocery business. Meanwhile, attracted by the policies of the Radical Liberals, he joined the party's youth organization and served as its national chairman from 1948 to 1950. In 1957 he was elected to the Folketing and was returned with increasing majorities at subsequent elections. In 1961 he was appointed minister of trade, an office he held until 1964, when he became director of an advertising and market-research firm. (S. M. Aa.)

BENTON, WILLIAM

William Benton received high honours both at home and abroad in 1968 as *Encyclopædia Britannica* observed its 200th anniversary and Benton marked his 25th year as publisher and board chairman. The former U.S. senator, who had been proprietor of the Britannica longer than any other individual, was presented with the newly created William Benton Distinguished Service Medal by the University of Chicago, the Human Relations Award by the American Jewish Committee, and honorary doctorates by Brandeis University, Dartmouth College, and the University of Notre Dame.

In May, Benton went to Edinburgh, Scot., birthplace of the Britannica, where he and the encyclopaedia were honoured at special ceremonies sponsored by the university and the city. In October the Britannica bicentennial and Benton's own 25th anniversary were celebrated at a dinner in London's historic Guildhall. Earlier, Prime Minister Harold Wilson was host to Benton and some 200 other distinguished guests at 10 Downing Street. At the Guildhall, Benton announced publicly for the first time his long-standing intention to leave his own and Mrs. Benton's stock in the Britannica to the William Benton Foundation.

In August Benton was a delegate from Connecticut to the Democratic national convention, and for the fourth time served on the convention's platform committee and its drafting subcommittee. He was one of the delegates selected to escort presidential nominee Hubert H. Humphrey to the speaker's platform. Another significant event was a trip to Paris in October to do his final stint as U.S. ambassador to UNESCO. His six-year term expired at the end of the UNESCO General Conference in November.

Benton was born in Minneapolis, Minn., April 1, 1900. He was graduated from Yale in 1921 and, with Chester Bowles, founded the advertising agency of Benton and Bowles in 1929. He retired from the advertising business in 1936 and became vice-president of the University of Chicago in 1937. In 1943, in partnership with the university, he became publisher and chairman of *Encyclopædia Britannica*. He served as assistant secretary of state under Pres. Harry S. Truman, was appointed to the U.S. Senate in 1949 and reelected for a two-year term in 1950. He traveled widely and wrote extensively; his books include *The Voice of the Kremlin, This Is the Challenge,* and *The Voice of Latin America.* (Mx. H.)

BONGO, ALBERT BERNARD

When he became president of Gabon in November 1967, Albert Bernard Bongo, at 32, was one of the youngest chiefs of state in the world. He succeeded Gabon's first and only previous president, Léon M'ba, who died in November 1967 and under whom Bongo had served as vice-president.

Bongo was expected to continue the policies of his predecessor in large part, particularly the maintenance of close relations with France. In domestic politics, however, he was expected to adopt a more conciliatory

approach toward the opposition than had M'ba.

Bongo was born in 1935 in the region of Franceville in what was then French Equatorial Africa. He was a member of a Gabonese ethnic minority group, the Bateke. After receiving his education in Brazzaville, he served from 1958 to 1960 in the French Air Force. He then entered government as a civil servant in Gabon's Ministry of Foreign Affairs. In 1960 he was named assistant director of the ministry and then was appointed director of the Office of the President.

Bongo was appointed vice-president of Gabon in November 1966 and was elected to that office in March 1967. As M'ba's health declined during 1967, he entrusted an increasing amount of responsibility to Bongo. (Ph. D.)

BOYD, MALCOLM

The Rev. Malcolm Boyd, Episcopal chaplain-at-large to American colleges, was an irreverent reverend, an ex-adman, a self-styled Christian existentialist who wrote secular plays and theological books, worked coffeehouses and nightclubs, and cut records of musical prayers.

Something of a swinger, even in an unorthodox age, Father Boyd began attracting attention in 1959, when he served as Protestant chaplain at Colorado State University. He ministered to his flock where he found them and became known as the "espresso priest." His bishop denounced him. Later he served at Wayne State University, Detroit, and began turning out dramas that used less-than-genteel language. They were denounced as profane by the bishop of Detroit. He finally found "friendly shelter" with Suffragan Bishop Paul Moore, Jr., of the diocese

of Washington, D.C., where he held an assistant pastorship.

In 1965, in the belief that "there's something phony about praying to God in Old English," he wrote a book of contemporary prayers, *Are You Running with Me, Jesus?*, which sold 60,000 copies the first year. (A sequel, *Book of Days,* appeared in 1968.) In 1966 he appeared at San Francisco's hungry i where, he suggested, Jesus and the Apostles would be found if they were alive today and "if they could get out of jail." At an Ivy League university, where he was in residence during the fall of 1968, he moderated a seminar on "Men and Sex at Yale." So it went for the pop evangelist ministering to "the alienated generation."

The son of an investment banker, Malcolm Boyd was born in Buffalo, N.Y., June 8, 1923. After graduating from the University of Arizona, he was a radio announcer, a Hollywood adman, and executive of a production agency. He was the first president of the Television Producers' Association of Hollywood. After entering the Episcopal priesthood in 1955, he served as a missionary in an English slum, studied with Reinhold Niebuhr at Union Theological Seminary, and joined the worker-priest movement in France. *Variety* called him "hippier than thou," but perhaps a better characterization comes from his introduction to *Are You Running with Me, Jesus?* Explaining that his prayers spring from an awareness of God's love, he says, "Thus I am able to live in a kind of Christian nonchalance rooted in a trust of God." (Ph. K.)

CAMERA PRESS—PIX FROM PUBLIX
Ahmed Hassan al-Bakr

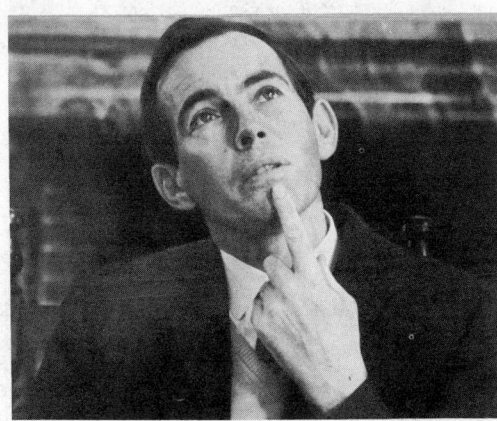

"LONDON DAILY EXPRESS" FROM PICTORIAL PARADE
Christiaan Barnard

Malcolm Boyd

RAY ROSS FROM NANCY PALMER AGENCY

SARRA, INC.
William Benton

BREZHNEV, LEONID ILYICH

Despite indecision in handling "fraternal" relations with Czechoslovakia, and the ultimate embarrassment of the Soviet invasion of that wayward ally, Leonid I. Brezhnev, general secretary of the Communist Party of the Soviet Union, remained first in rank in the Soviet hierarchy in 1968. As in past years, he stayed mainly out of the limelight. He attempted to ease increasingly tense relations with Communist Party leaders in other countries, launched a new campaign for ideological purity at home, and left diplomacy with the West and with the uncommitted world—plus domestic economic administration—to Premier Aleksei N. Kosygin.

Early in the year Brezhnev moved to stop the spread of the rebellious Czechoslovak spirit among the Soviet intelligentsia. In April he personally served notice that "hypocrites" and "renegades" among Soviet intellectuals would be punished. On the international level Brezhnev concentrated on bringing the new Czechoslovak leadership into line. He led his own Politburo at the three-day meeting with Czechoslovak party leaders on July 29–31 in the Slovak town of Cierna nad Tisou. Despite Czechoslovak pledges of continued membership in the Warsaw Pact and an ostensible Soviet agreement to let the Czechoslovaks handle their own affairs, the Soviet leadership under Brezhnev subsequently decided to stop the reforms by armed intervention.

Brezhnev was born Dec. 19, 1906, in the steel city of Kamenskoye (now Dneprodzerzhinsk) in the Ukraine. His career centred on the bureaucracy of the Communist Party. His first breakthrough came in 1954 when Nikita S. Khrushchev put him in charge of the scheme to grow wheat on the virgin lands of Kazakhstan. With Khrushchev firmly in power, Brezhnev became titular head of the Soviet state in May 1960. He stepped down in favour of Anastas I. Mikoyan in early 1964, and on October 15 of that year he succeeded Khrushchev as first secretary (later changed to general secretary) of the party.   (G. F. Sh.)

BRUNDAGE, AVERY

Despite a year full of controversy, Avery Brundage, the 81-year-old multimillionaire champion of amateurism in sports, oversaw a successful XIX Olympiad at Mexico City, after which he was reelected president of the International Olympic Committee. The first major problem facing him during the year was whether or not South Africa should be allowed to participate in the Olympic Games. Brundage, who always maintained that sports should be free from politics, believed that the invitation to South Africa should not be withdrawn because of that nation's controversial racial separation policy. The Executive Committee, which Brundage headed, felt otherwise, however, and Brundage had to inform South Africa that it could not compete.

Controversy erupted again when some U.S. black athletes first threatened to boycott the Olympics in protest against racial problems within the U.S. and then declared they would wear "Black Nationalist" insignias on their Olympic uniforms. In a speech before the National Press Club in Washington, D.C., on September 17, Brundage declared that if any such demonstrations were held, "the boys will be sent home." Subsequently, 21 black athletes signed a petition demanding that Brundage be removed from his position.

Capping the Olympic troubles were a series of violent student riots in Mexico City shortly before the Games were to open. More than 50 persons were killed. Brundage held an emergency meeting and decided that the Olympics would be held on schedule.

Brundage was born in Detroit on Sept. 28, 1887. He studied civil engineering at the University of Illinois and was graduated in 1909. He had his first contact with the Olympics as a member of the U.S. team at the 1912 Games, held in Stockholm, where he specialized in the decathlon and pentathlon. In 1914, 1916, and 1918 he won the title of Amateur All-Around Champion of America, which required winning ten events all contested in a single day.

In 1935, while in London for a meeting on the Olympic Games, Brundage began his collection of Oriental art, which was reportedly valued at over $30 million. Through the construction business he achieved the wealth that enabled him to acquire such a collection.   (J. F. Ba.)

BUÑUEL, LUIS

"The cinema seems to have been invented for the expression of the subconscious, so profoundly is it rooted in poetry." So said Luis Buñuel, the Spanish film director whose works, long the objects of critical acclaim, were at last emerging from the art houses to reach a wider audience. In his late 60s, Buñuel was recognized as a master—albeit a disturbing and difficult one—of his craft.

Buñuel was born in Calanda, Spain, on Feb. 22, 1900, and was educated at a Jesuit school and at Madrid University. In 1923 he went to Paris, where he worked as assistant to the French director Jean Epstein. It was there that he and Salvador Dali made their two Surrealist films, *Un Chien Andalou* (1929) and *L'Age d'Or* (1930), in which their uninhibited use of religious and sexual symbols caused a scandal.

In the years that followed, Buñuel worked in Spain and France. He remained in exile after the Spanish Civil War, and in 1946 made his home in Mexico. It was in 1951 that one of his Mexican films, *Los Olvidados* —a violent study of juvenile delinquency—

"fell," as one critic put it, "like a thunderbolt into the Cannes Festival." Much of his routine work in Mexico was never exported, but his versions of *Wuthering Heights* and *Robinson Crusoe* (1953) were appreciated in Europe, as were two highly idiosyncratic and darkly comic films, *El* (1952) and *The Criminal Life of Archibaldo de la Cruz* (1955). But it was probably *Nazarin* (1958), a deceptively simple story of a peasant priest who sincerely tries to live a Christ-like life only to be rejected and misunderstood, that brought Buñuel to the art houses of the world.

Many of the same preoccupations—the fierce anticlericalism, the exploration of conventional Christianity—appeared again in *Viridiana* (1961)—made, ironically enough, in Spain—and *The Exterminating Angel* (1962). Two culminating masterpieces— *Diary of a Chambermaid* (1964) and *Belle de Jour* (1966)—both made in France— brought together all the obsessions, fetishes, symbols, and attitudes that had been central to Buñuel's work from the beginning. His contempt for conventional values, his tolerance for human weakness, his sudden vivid violence shocked the timid only because they failed to appreciate his concern for the individual, his wit, and his dazzling skill.
(B. D.)

BUSBY, SIR MATTHEW

Long-serving manager of the English soccer team Manchester United, soft-spoken Sir Matt Busby realized an 11-year dream when he steered his club to victory in the final game of the European Cup tournament at Wembley, London, on May 29.

Busby was born in Orbiston, Scot., on May 26, 1909. His father, a coal miner, was killed in World War I. The boy was educated at local schools and was soon playing soccer for the team in his village.

After leaving school Busby became a professional soccer player for Denny Hibs and was recommended to Manchester City, which signed him in 1929 after one trial game. As an inside forward he was far from a success and almost quit the game. But a chance match at right-half led to a regular

Barbara Castle

Leonid Ilyich Brezhnev

first-team spot and two appearances at Wembley in the Football Association (FA) Cup final, losing in 1933 but winning the next year against Portsmouth. Busby played for Scotland against Wales in 1934.

Busby was transferred to Liverpool in March 1936 and played there for three years. He joined the British Army at the start of World War II in 1939 and served for six years. After the war, despite an offer to return as coach to Liverpool, he accepted the post of manager at Manchester United in October 1945. He took the club from debt and virtual obscurity to a profit of £60,000 two years later and to the position of runner-up in the English League for the first three postwar seasons. Under his guidance United moved on to take five league titles and two FA Cups, as well as to win the European Cup. He also managed the British Olympic soccer team in 1948.

Busby was a victim of the Munich air disaster in 1958. The aircraft in which his team was returning from a European Cup match in Yugoslavia crashed on takeoff. Seven players and three club officials were among those who died in the accident. Busby sustained severe injuries that kept him in the hospital for many weeks. He was knighted by the queen in 1968.   (T. W.)

CASSIN, RENÉ

The winner of the 1968 Nobel Peace Prize was René Cassin, president of the European Court of Human Rights and principal author of the UN Declaration of the Rights of Man. In announcing the award, the Nobel Committee said the international jurist was the prime mover of the declaration and "has tirelessly worked for the carrying out of its rules, both universally and on the European level," for two decades. The award was conferred in Oslo on December 20, the 20th anniversary of the declaration's ratification.

The selection of France's foremost expert on international law as the Peace Prize laureate marked the first time an individual had been so honoured since 1964, when the Rev. Martin Luther King, Jr., won the award. In 1965 UNICEF was the recipient, and in the two succeeding years the prize

was not conferred. Cassin, who received a $70,000 honorarium with the award, was the 9th Frenchman to be so honoured since the prize was established in 1901.

Born in Bayonne, Oct. 5, 1887, the son of a Jewish merchant, Cassin studied law before entering the French Army in World War I. During the war he sustained a severe abdominal wound, from which he continued to suffer. He later became a professor of international law in Paris and, in 1924, joined the French delegation to the League of Nations. After the fall of France in World War II, he joined Gen. Charles de Gaulle in London and served as a key member of the French government in exile.

In 1946 he became a member of the UN Human Rights Commission, which he later chaired, and he was a founder of UNESCO. He served on the European Court of Human Rights, an agency of the Council of Europe, from 1959 and as its president from 1965.

Acknowledging that the international organizations he had served had been unable to prevent war, Cassin said, "That is because unfortunately there are forces in all countries that favour war. I am not a moralist who believes that man must change before peace will reign. I think we must work to change the conditions that result from the fact that men are not always good."
     (Ph. K.)

CASTLE, BARBARA

After more than two years as British minister of transport, Mrs. Barbara Castle was moved to become head of the newly named Department of Employment and Productivity (formed out of the old Ministry of Labour) at the beginning of April 1968. As minister of transport she had won a reputation for being tough and spirited and not afraid of controversy. She had introduced breath tests as a check on driving under the influence of alcohol, established a permanent speed limit of 70 mph on the roads, and imposed more stringent regulations for the mechanical safety of vehicles. Shortly before she left the Ministry of Transport she launched a massive and hotly contested road transport bill.

behind him. He had won contracts with nine growers in the San Joaquin Valley of California, mostly producers of wine grapes, by employing boycotts plus a unique mixture of Mexican-American ethnic ties and religious fervour to unite his followers.

His most celebrated battle in 1968 was against the Guimarra Vineyards Corp., a producer of table grapes, with vineyards near Delano, Calif. When Guimarra began using other growers' labels to frustrate Chavez' boycott of its own brand, the union broadened the boycott to include all California grapes. Chavez, a devout Roman Catholic, underwent a voluntary fast from February 14 to March 10, losing 35 lb. in an effort to dramatize his union's cause. Shortly before he was assassinated, Sen. Robert F. Kennedy flew to Delano to participate, beside Chavez, in an open-air mass and called the labour leader "one of the greatest living Americans."

Chavez failed to keep a tight rein on events, however, and in July he announced he would urge strikers to halt picketing and demonstrations because of incidents of violence. Meanwhile, more than 100 California growers and shippers filed a $25 million damage suit, charging the union and five New York City labour groups with illegal boycott.

A few days prior to the Democratic convention in August, Sen. George S. McGovern of South Dakota, who was seeking the presidential nomination, joined a picket line of grape workers in New York City and publicly praised Chavez. Vice-Pres. Hubert Humphrey also endorsed the boycott, a move that drew fire from the Republican nominee, Richard Nixon.

Chavez was born March 31, 1927, on a farm near Yuma, Ariz., and knew firsthand the life of a migrant worker from the age of ten onward. His apprenticeship in organizing the poor was served in California with the Community Service Organization (CSO), a group providing legal aid to Mexican-Americans. Chavez became national director of the CSO in 1958. In 1965 he put together the National Farm Workers Association, which later merged with the Agricultural Workers Organizing Committee. (T. R. T.)

CLIFFORD, CLARK McADAMS

The room in the Pentagon—3E880—occupied by the secretary of defense was slightly refurbished to reflect the tastes of its new occupant, Clark Clifford, soon after he replaced the outgoing Robert S. McNamara in March 1968. But the complex and awesome problems inherent in running the defense establishment remained—a sword over the head of anyone sitting behind the massive walnut desk once used by Gen. John J. Pershing.

On Jan. 19, 1968, about one and a half months after McNamara's pending resignation was revealed, Pres. Lyndon Johnson announced that Clifford was his choice to manage Defense. The Senate unanimously confirmed the appointment on January 30, and Clifford was sworn in on March 1. He had enjoyed a good working relationship with the Congress in the past, and military men felt he was more willing to lend them a sympathetic ear than McNamara had been. The transition was smooth, partly because of Clifford's own personality and partly because of the understanding that a new president would probably be appointing a new secretary in 1969.

There were too many problems facing

Clifford to allow him to dwell on such thoughts, however. Vietnam was first priority, but his attention also had to be directed toward a variety of other problems—the U.S. intelligence ship "Pueblo," captured by North Korea in January 1968; the accidents befalling the F-111 swing-wing plane; the efforts to get the Congress to accept a "thin" antiballistic missile system. In October Clifford journeyed to Bonn, W.Ger., to meet with Western defense ministers regarding the tactical use of nuclear weapons by members of NATO.

Clifford was born Dec. 25, 1906, in Fort Scott, Kan. Soon afterward his family moved to St. Louis, Mo., where he attended school. He earned his LL.B. from Washington University in 1928 and was admitted to the bar the same year. During World War II he served as a Navy officer and became naval aide to Pres. Harry S. Truman in 1946. Later, after discharge from the service, he was special counsel to the president until 1950.
(B. S. KA.)

COHN-BENDIT, DANIEL

Out of the disturbances in France in May and June 1968, there emerged the figure of a young revolutionary, with a freckled, doll-like face and a wild laugh, whose tactical and political gifts were at once fully confirmed in the heat of action, a figure to whom no hitherto accepted political category could be applied. Daniel Cohn-Bendit was thrown into the political limelight by the very means he condemned. He appeared to his allies, his opponents, and the public as the leader and driving force behind the disturbances, while his own principles forbade him to be anything other than an activist among other activists, or, at most and according to circumstances, a spokesman.

The "Twenty-second of March Movement," under Cohn-Bendit's leadership, was the crystallization and spearhead of the contentious students, the *enragés* (hotheads) at the Faculty of Letters at Nanterre, a branch of the University of Paris. It took its name from the day on which it first occupied the administration building at Nanterre.

Cohn-Bendit described himself as an anarchist who was also "a Marxist as Bakunin was a Marxist." He especially retained the anarchist's criticism of the oppressive nature of all forms of authority.

He owed his political education to his brother Gaby, with whom he wrote, after the events of May–June, a book called *Le Gauchisme, remède á la maladie sénile du communisme* ("Leftism, a Cure for the Senile Disorder of Communism"), a play on Lenin's *Left-wing Communism, an Infantile Disorder*. His critical theory attempted a synthesis of the programs worked out by tiny factions in the obscurity of the periods of recession in revolutionary activity. These programs call, in varying degrees, for autonomy of and spontaneous action by the masses.

Born in Montauban in 1945, the son of German-Jewish parents who left Germany with the triumph of Nazism (up to that time his father had been a celebrated political lawyer), Daniel Cohn-Bendit returned with his parents to West Germany in 1958. He took German nationality and finished his secondary education there. Returning to France in 1964, he became a sociology student at the Faculty at Nanterre until his expulsion from France and return to West Germany in June.
(B. EL.)

COUVE DE MURVILLE, MAURICE

In 1968 Maurice Couve de Murville satisfied a long-felt ambition: after considering abandoning the diplomatic service for poli-

tics since 1945, after serving as Pres. Charles de Gaulle's foreign minister for ten years, and after having made one unsuccessful attempt, in March 1967, to enter the French National Assembly, he at last managed on June 23 to be returned as a deputy for the 8th *arrondissement* of Paris. Less than three weeks later, de Gaulle chose him as the third premier of the Fifth Republic.

Couve de Murville, who had been a follower of de Gaulle since 1943, an ambassador under the Fourth Republic to Rome, Cairo, NATO, Washington, and Bonn, had been described as the most "British" of French diplomats. A son of the Protestant upper class who preferred to express himself in understatements, he bought his clothes in London, played golf, and spoke in a slow and considered manner. No one had ever seen him lose his self-control or depart from his somewhat disdainful good manners. For ten years he had presented the Gaullist point of view with loyalty and tact, impenetrability and confidence.

After taking over as premier, he had to search uneasily for another image, to humanize himself, and to find the gifts of repartee and decisiveness. This quest was not without difficulties—or without surprises for those who watched it. Gone were the cautious maneuvers, the veiled allusions and subtleties. Admittedly he had not become a popular leader, but his savoir faire and flexibility, as well as the aura of mystery behind which he hid from the public gaze, all helped to give him a promising start in his new office.

Maurice Couve de Murville was born in 1907 and received an education in law and political science. In 1930 he became a treasury inspector and by 1940 was director of external finance. In that capacity he was a member of the French delegation to the armistice negotiations with Germany at Wiesbaden. He rallied to Algiers in 1943 and soon joined the French National Liberation Committee. After World War II he began a diplomatic career, and when de Gaulle returned to power in June 1958 he was given the post of foreign minister. (P. V.-P.)

CURRAN, CHARLES

The appointment of Charles Curran to succeed Sir Hugh Greene as director general of the British Broadcasting Corporation (BBC) in April 1969 was announced in August. Though he was not well known outside the BBC, his appointment did not come as a surprise. Within the BBC he was considered an administrator of great ability, and this evidently outweighed his lack of experience in television. His appointment came at a time when the BBC was somewhat out of favour with politicians and when attacks on the BBC's handling of politics were being made by some members of the Labour government. This brought the traditional independence of the BBC into public debate. Curran was expected to be a diplomatic but tough director general, ready to take a stand on principle against political pressures should the situation arise.

The youngest director general since Lord Reith (the first man to hold that office), Curran was born Oct. 13, 1921, in Dublin, the son of a schoolmaster. He was brought up in Yorkshire, and from the local grammar school went to Cambridge University where he received honours in history. Following wartime service in the Indian Army, he joined the BBC in 1947 and became a producer. After a brief and unsuccessful venture in magazine journalism, he returned to the BBC in 1951 and was chosen to be one of its first administrative trainees. He then worked up quickly into responsible administrative posts, spending a good deal of time

in the BBC External Service, from 1967 as its head.

From 1963 to 1967 Curran served as secretary of the BBC, a position that gave him an insight into the workings of the whole corporation as well as experience in dealing with public criticism. During that period the BBC became a centre of controversy because of the freedom given to producers—in particular to producers of political satire programs. The departure of Sir Hugh Greene inevitably led to speculation that there might be a reaction against the license that had been allowed to producers during his term of office, but Curran disclaimed any intention to interfere. "Programs are the business of program creators," he said.   (W. H. Ts.)

Clark McAdams Clifford

Maurice Couve de Murville

DAY-LEWIS, CECIL

Long before it was announced (on Jan. 1, 1968) that C. Day-Lewis was to succeed John Masefield as Britain's poet laureate, he had been thought the most likely candidate. A respected member of the literary Establishment, a pleasantly traditional "modern" poet, perceptive critic, and felicitous translator, he was widely known, partly for broadcast works and poetry readings. Thirty years earlier the appointment would have been thought outrageous, for in 1938 Day-Lewis, a member of the Communist Party and one of the Auden group that had brought poetry into the battle for social justice, had called for "Revolution . . . [as] the one correct solution."

Born at Ballintogher, southern Ireland, on April 27, 1904, the son of a Church of Ireland clergyman, Day-Lewis was taken to England at an early age and was educated at Sherborne and at Wadham College, Oxford. He became a schoolmaster and while at Summerfields, an Oxford preparatory school (1927–28), met Auden, then an undergraduate. Later, at Cheltenham (1930–35), his political and poetic affiliations began to alarm parents. Many also thought his detective story, *A Question of Proof* (1935; the first of many published under the pseudonym of "Nicholas Blake"), in poor taste, but its success set him free to become a full-time poet.

Two early volumes (1925 and 1928) were little noticed, but in the poetry of his next period—*Transitional Poem* (1929), *From Feathers to Iron* (1931), *The Magnetic Mountain* (1933), *A Time to Dance . . .* (1935), and *Overtures to Death* (1938)—he developed a distinctive voice within the Auden "poetic collective." World War II (spent at the Ministry of Information) brought a change, discernible in *Poems in Wartime* (1940) and *Word Over All* (1943); and in *An Italian Visit* (1953) and three collections following *Collected Poems* (1954), he returned to themes that had often provided a starting point or setting—nature, love, birth, death. A Socialist after 1939, he played no part in postwar political life. His most creative work was critical—in the Cambridge Clark lectures (1946; *The Poetic Image,* 1947) and as professor of poetry at Oxford (1951–56) and Harvard (1964–65). He was a member of the Arts Council and the Royal Society of Literature, was made commander of the Order of the British Empire in 1950 and an honorary fellow of the American Academy of Arts and Letters in 1966.   (D. M. PA.)

DE GAULLE, CHARLES ANDRÉ JOSEPH MARIE

For the president of the French Republic, 1968 brought the most serious threat since his return to power in 1958 and his greatest electoral success.

The first four months were what de Gaulle

Charles de Gaulle

Charles Curran

Daniel Cohn-Bendit

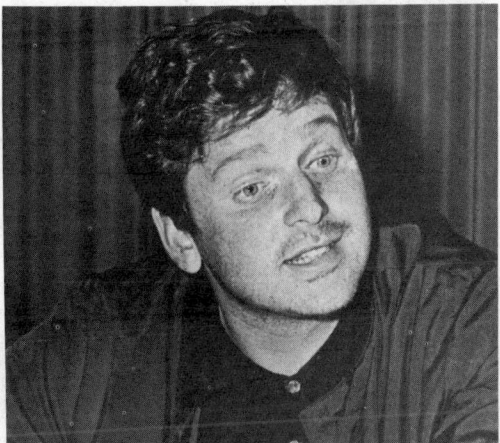

called "ordinary days." There were some satisfying moments, especially the prestigious success of seeing U.S.-North Vietnamese negotiations open in Paris. There were also some worries—a working class disturbed at the rise in unemployment and a political class made uneasy by the advances of the left-wing opposition in the previous year. Then, in a matter of days, everything changed. Rebellious students set up barricades in the Latin Quarter; striking workers paralyzed the country; the mechanism of command no longer obeyed the authorities. At first de Gaulle refused to believe what was happening: he made no change in his plans for a trip to Romania, and on his return merely promised France a referendum on "participation." In a few days disorder gave way to anarchy, and the regime seemed on the point of collapse.

Finally, de Gaulle took action. In a spectacular secret journey he ensured the support of the Army. The next day, in a four-minute broadcast on radio and television, he managed to reverse the situation completely. From then on he was the representative of order, and as such he achieved a return to calm and to work. He went on to hold legislative elections in June in which his supporters gained a considerably increased majority in the National Assembly.

The feverish outburst of May had revealed a deep feeling of disillusionment. It marked a major turning point and, for de Gaulle, a great disappointment. Nevertheless, in November he withstood yet a new challenge to his prestige when, with the franc under seemingly overwhelming pressure, he rejected devaluation as "the worst of absurdities."

Born Nov. 22, 1890, de Gaulle graduated from the École Spéciale Militaire at Saint-Cyr. After the fall of France in World War II, he rallied continued French resistance to Germany from England and formed the first provisional government in France after liberation. He retired from public life in 1953 but returned in 1958 to become president under a new constitution. (P. V.-P.)

DENEUVE, CATHÉRINE

It was a testing year for this coolly beautiful French screen star, in her personal life as well as in her professional career. *Mayerling,* her big 1968 film release, showed her for the first time in a heavily romantic role, in a picture based on the true-life love affair—ending in an apparent suicide pact in 1889—between a minor Austrian countess and Habsburg Crown Prince Rudolf. Film critics, impressed by earlier Deneuve films, particularly by her performance as a homicidal schizophrenic in Roman Polanski's *Repulsion* and in the title part of Luis Buñuel's *Belle de Jour,* received *Mayerling* rather coolly. All were interested, but most were unconvinced by her attempt to convey deep passion.

These cold comments were preceded in 1968 by a personal problem. Undenied press statements at the beginning of the year announced that her 1965 marriage to leading British fashion photographer David Bailey was breaking up. Meanwhile, her next scheduled productions were to be *La Chamade,* based on a Françoise Sagan novel, and a François Truffaut film, in which she would be costarred with Jean-Paul Belmondo.

Born in German-occupied Paris on Oct. 22, 1943, daughter of actor Maurice Dorléac, she attracted the attention of French film

PIERLUIGI FROM RAPHO-GUILLUMETTE
Cathérine Deneuve

director Roger Vadim in 1961. Having steered his two previous wives, Brigitte Bardot and Annette Strøyberg, to stardom, he made it a threesome with Cathérine Deneuve, giving her a plum part in *Vice and Virtue* (1962). No marriage blessed this alliance, however. When she bore him a son in 1963, she would not marry him, commenting: "Why marry and risk divorcing? Marriage is a rope around the neck. It does not help love."

Cathérine Deneuve's earlier films included *Les Demoiselles de Rochefort,* in which she starred with her sister, Françoise Dorléac, killed in a 1967 car crash, and *Les Parapluies de Cherbourg* (which was awarded the Grand Prix at Cannes and gave Miss Deneuve the "best actress of 1964" title). (B. HI.)

DUBCEK, ALEXANDER

A man little known in his own country and not at all abroad began a fantastic career as first secretary of the Communist Party of Czechoslovakia on Jan. 5, 1968. Alexander Dubcek succeeded Antonin Novotny and quickly became the most popular party leader any Communist country ever had. He promised "socialism with a humane face," and one of his first acts was the relaxation of censorship, opening the floodgates of free speech in a country where this freedom had disappeared two decades earlier. The leaders of the other Warsaw Treaty countries became alarmed, but Dubcek gave assurances that Czechoslovakia would remain a socialist country. That was not enough. On March 23, at Dresden, the Warsaw Pact members (minus Romania) proclaimed their determination to strengthen Soviet leadership of the socialist camp.

In the following months, as the Czechoslovaks asserted their new freedom, the warnings grew. Between a meeting of the Soviet Politburo and its Czechoslovak counterpart at Cierna nad Tisou on July 29–August 1 and a six-party meeting at Bratislava on August 3, Dubcek told his nation that he would stand firm on the post-January policy. This stand was the main reason why, on the night of August 20–21, forces of the five Warsaw Pact coun-

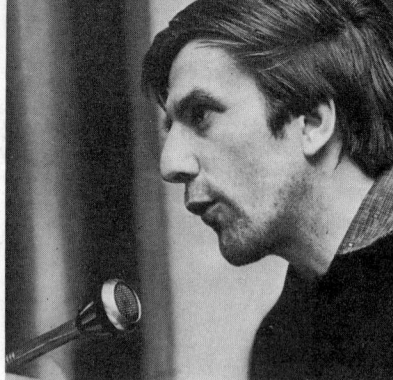

Rudi Dutschke

Alexander Dubcek

tries invaded Czechoslovakia. Dubcek was arrested and taken to Moscow. Pres. Ludvik Svoboda, however, refused to negotiate without Dubcek, whose moral authority was such that without his acquiescence no agreement would be valid to the Czechoslovak people.

After the dramatic Moscow meeting, Dubcek returned to Prague—still as party secretary. Although he retained his post for the rest of the year, negotiated the treaty on the "temporary" stationing of Soviet troops in Czechoslovakia, and was present at all major conferences, it was apparent that he was being carefully isolated from the positions of power in the new federated republic that was to be established in Czechoslovakia on Jan. 1, 1969.

Dubcek was born on Nov. 27, 1921, at Uhrovec, Slovakia, the son of a cabinetmaker who had just returned from ten years in the U.S. He was educated in the U.S.S.R. and was active in the Slovak underground during World War II. In 1958 he was elected to the central committees of both the Slovak and Czechoslovak Communist parties and to their presidiums in 1962. He became first secretary of the Slovak party's Central Committee in 1963. (K. SM.)

DUTSCHKE, RUDI

Until April 1968, when he was seriously wounded by a bullet fired by a youth in the Kurfürstendamm, West Berlin, Rudi Dutschke was the most prominent leader of West Germany's student protest movement. He was often described as the chief ideologist of the Socialist Students' League (SDS), the most militant of the student organizations, and his revolutionary élan struck terror into the hearts of the establishment and the bourgeoisie.

Dutschke was born in 1940 in the province of Brandenburg, in what later became East Germany, and went to school at Luckenwalde, south of Berlin. Although he passed his university entrance examination, he was not permitted to study in East Germany because he refused to join the National People's Army. He took a job in the sales department of a factory, but then began to commute to and from West Berlin,

Harry Edwards
JESSE ALEXANDER FROM NANCY PALMER AGENCY

Gaston Eyskens
PHOTO NEWS SERVICE—PIX FROM PUBLIX

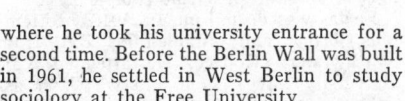
"PARIS MATCH" FROM PICTORIAL PARADE
El Cordobés

where he took his university entrance for a second time. Before the Berlin Wall was built in 1961, he settled in West Berlin to study sociology at the Free University.

Although he joined the SDS soon afterward, he was regarded as an outsider until 1966. Dismayed by the formation of the coalition government of Christian Democrats and Social Democrats in November of that year, he set about organizing an extra-parliamentary opposition. From then on, Dutschke was in the vanguard of student demonstrations throughout the country.

Many of Dutschke's views were vague. He had said that his goal was "self-organization of all people. Democracy at the bottom —councils of people everywhere, discussing and deciding." He insisted that he advocated the use of violence only against objects and property, not against people.

Dutschke made an almost complete recovery from the attempt on his life, but there was no sign that he would return to his former tempestuous role. Some of his colleagues even said that they did not want him back, because the SDS had abandoned the "cult of personality."   (N. Cr.)

EDWARDS, HARRY

Declaring that black athletes should refuse to be "utilized as performing animals for a little extra dog food," Harry Edwards kept a proposed Negro boycott of the Olympic Games in the news during much of 1968. In a year when the myth of racial equality in athletics seemed to be evaporating, he emerged for a time as an imaginative spokesman for black power in sports.

Edwards had first attracted attention the preceding year at San Jose State College in California, where he was an instructor in sociology and anthropology. The 6-ft. 8-in. leader, bearded and wearing a black leather beret, had presented a list of grievances to the college on behalf of Negro students, warning that unless racial discrimination was halted, the opening football game would be disrupted. Alarmed authorities canceled the game and later took the unprecedented step of hiring an ombudsman to help bring racial harmony.

But it was the Olympics issue that kept Edwards in public view. Early in 1968 some 40 nations were threatening to withdraw from the Olympics unless South Africa was excluded, and although the International Olympics Committee later barred that country, Edwards continued to urge a boycott. In February he led a demonstration against the New York Athletic Club at its Madison Square Garden track meet. By May, 20 of the nation's top collegiate basketball players, both white and black, had refused to attend Olympic tryouts.

As the months passed, however, there were signs that Edwards' influence had waned. Lee Evans, a San Jose track star, told a reporter that athletes at the Los Angeles tryouts in June had voted almost unanimously to compete in the Olympics. They made a protest gesture, however, when Tommie Smith and John Carlos, both from San Jose State, raised black-gloved fists while receiving their 200-m. dash medals. Meanwhile, Edwards left San Jose and resumed work on a Ph.D. at Cornell.

Born in poverty on Nov. 22, 1942, in East St. Louis, Ill., Edwards borrowed money to attend Fresno City College in California and later graduated from San Jose State. He was an outstanding athlete at both institutions. He received an M.A. from Cornell in 1966.   (T. R. T.)

EL CORDOBÉS

El Cordobés was the paradox of the Spanish bullring. His artistry was disputed by critics, but fans thronged to the box office. Born in abject poverty, he was worth some $11 million in 1968. The son of a doomed Loyalist, he was often Francisco Franco's hunting partner. A friend of the Kennedy family, he only recently learned that the world is round.

He was born Manuel Benítez Pérez in May 1936, in the Andalusian town of Palma del Río. His father, a farmhand who earned 5½ pesetas a day, joined the Loyalists during the Spanish Civil War, was imprisoned, and barely predeceased his widow, who died in the family's one-room slum flat. Manuel, raised by a sister, became a petty thief and

panhandler. His first experience with bulls was bootlegged—he slipped past night watchmen on the breeding ranches to challenge fighting bulls in the moonlight. Then he began to appear in *capeas,* casual corridas in small towns.

In his provincial debut he was tossed by the bull so often that one observer "got airsick just from watching." Still, he had a certain flair. "Right away I knew this kid was worth gold," recalled El Pipo, a professional manager who arranged the novice's Madrid debut in 1960. "Art you can get at the Prado . . . you want . . . a kid who can excite a crowd."

El Cordobés (meaning the man from Córdoba) could certainly do that, and the people loved his unorthodox, daredevil style. Critics remained unimpressed, however, and he drew continual criticism for refusing to fight particularly large or ferocious animals. One rival matador, Miguelín, became so infuriated that he leaped into the Madrid ring where El Cordobés was fighting and fondled the bull's head.

El Cordobés continued to draw the biggest crowds in the history of bullfighting and to earn the highest fees. He had killed more than 1,000 bulls and been gored by more than a score of them. Larry Collins and Dominique Lapierre, whose biography of El Cordobés, *Or I'll Dress You in Mourning,* was a best seller in 1968, called him "a symbol of the Spain of tourists and television, the miniskirt . . . he represents to many of his countrymen a reflection of their own hopes for a better life."   (Ph. K.)

EYSKENS, GASTON

When King Baudouin called on Gaston Eyskens to head the new Belgian coalition government of Social Christians and Socialists in June 1968, the 63-year-old ex-prime minister and former dean of the Flemish Faculty of Economic and Social Sciences at the Catholic University of Louvain was hoping for a less hectic life.

The circumstances in which he started his third term as prime minister were hardly propitious. Relations between the Dutch-speaking Flemish majority and the French-

speaking Walloon minority in the country had been severely strained following the demand by the former that the French section of Louvain University be transferred to the Walloon area of the country, the reluctance of the local administrations of the Brussels agglomeration to apply the linguistic legislation of 1963, and the Flemish opposition to any extension of the bilingual Brussels agglomeration. Undaunted, Eyskens planned to carry out the program, elaborated by his predecessor, Paul Vanden Boeynants, calling essentially for cultural autonomy (a Flemish demand) and economic decentralization (a Walloon demand).

Many Socialists resented Eyskens' appointment, however. Memories of the *Loi Unique* of 1961 still rankled. This law provided for a rationalization of the administration, as well as new taxation. The Socialists, then in opposition, called a general strike against the austerity measures included in the bill, but strike action remained largely limited to the Walloons and it contributed to the animosity between the two communities. Nevertheless, Eyskens, who early in life adopted the slogan: "In politics as in love, neither never, nor always," formed his Cabinet with the Socialists.

Eyskens' reputation was that of a cold, calculating politician and financier. He was probably one of Belgium's, if not the world's, top financial experts. Born at Lier on April 1, 1905, he studied at Louvain, London, Geneva, Chicago, and Columbia. In 1931 he was appointed to the chair of public finance, banking, and political economy at Louvain and was elected to the Chamber of Representatives in the same year. He was prime minister (the youngest in Belgium's history) from August 1949 until March 1950 and from June 1958 to March 1961. (JA. R. E.)

FAURE, EDGAR

If, in the autumn of 1968, the French had been asked to name the most able politician active in their country, Edgar Faure might well have come ahead of all others—perhaps even Pres. Charles de Gaulle. This reputation was not new; it was acquired under the Fourth Republic, of which he was twice *président du conseil,* and it was confirmed under the Fifth Republic with the success of several diplomatic missions, most notably the preparation for recognition of Communist China. As de Gaulle's minister of agriculture, Faure won back the support of the farmers, who had gone over to the opposition in 1965. But his popularity was never as great as when, after taking over the difficult post of minister of education in July 1968, he supervised the beginning of the academic year following the student revolt of May, and the passage through Parliament of a radical reform of higher education.

Faure was a man who liked power and who did not hide the fact he felt uneasy in opposition. He was a ready and brilliant speaker and perhaps the regime's most formidable political charmer. It had been said that, after de Gaulle, he might become the champion of conciliation between the Gaullists and the non-Communist left. When asked if he had any ambition to become president, he replied epigrammatically: "Grace is accepted with that movement of recoil which Botticelli expresses so well in his *Annunciation*. It is never refused."

Born in 1908, the son of a military doctor, Faure was a brilliant scholar and became a barrister at the Paris bar. After reaching Algiers in 1943, he collaborated successively with Louis Joxe and Pierre Mendès-France, and in 1946 became deputy for the Jura. He held several important government posts and, as *président du conseil* in 1955, pronounced the only dissolution of the Assembly under the Fourth Republic. He was beaten in the first Gaullist elections in 1958, but soon became a senator. While carrying on his practice at the bar and his historical writing, he still found time to sit for the difficult competitive examination for the law *agrégation,* which allowed him to add to his qualifications that of professor at the University of Dijon. He became minister of agriculture in 1966. (P. V.-P.)

FORMAN, MILOS

Until the early 1960s the postwar Czechoslovak cinema was known in the West chiefly through the puppet films of Jiri Trnka and the magical trick effects of Karel Zeman. Then came a surge of younger talent that gained for the Czechoslovak film industry recognition as one of the most innovative in the world. One of the first of the new directors to make an impact was Milos Forman, whose *Peter and Pavla* took the Grand Prix at the Locarno Festival in 1964.

Forman was born in Caslav, Bohemia, on Feb. 18, 1932. He studied at the Prague Film Faculty, worked as a scriptwriter and assistant director, and was deputy to Alfred Radok on the stage-film spectacle *Laterna Magica,* which was an outstanding success at the 1958 Brussels World's Fair. His debut as a film director came in 1963 with a short semidocumentary film, *Talent Competition.*

His first feature was *Cerny Petr,* literally "Black Peter" but generally known in the West as *Peter and Pavla.* Its gently humorous view of a not very bright boy facing the problems of growing up struck a universal chord. Forman's second feature, *A Blonde in Love* (U.S. title: *Loves of a Blonde*), looked at similar problems from the point of view of a young girl factory worker, and his first colour film, *A House on Fire* (U.S. title: *The Firemen's Ball*), which was seen and praised at the abortive 1968 Cannes Festival, was set almost entirely in a dance hall where a country fire brigade is holding its annual ball.

The great charm of Forman's work and the source of its strength was his affectionate concern for ordinary people whose comic foibles he exposed without holding them up to ridicule. To achieve this difficult balance, he used mostly amateur actors; he did not allow them to see the complete script and sometimes incorporated their spontaneous reactions into it. The resulting films, seemingly almost plotless, actually contained sophisticated patterns of deceptive depth.

The Soviet intervention of August 1968 left the future freedom of the Czechoslovak film industry in question. Earlier in the year Forman had written a script about runaway girls in New York, and there was at least a possibility that he might make his next film in the United States. (B. D.)

FORTAS, ABE

U.S. Supreme Court Justice Abe Fortas, after a long and acrimonious Senate controversy over his nomination as chief justice, in 1968 became the first nominee for that post since 1795 to fail to receive Senate approval.

The dispute began shortly after June 26, when Pres. Lyndon B. Johnson nominated Fortas, an old and trusted friend whom he had chosen as his first appointee to the court in 1965. Fortas was to replace the retiring Earl Warren, chief justice since 1953, and Homer Thornberry, a federal district judge from Texas, was named to replace Fortas as associate justice.

The nomination of Fortas, who generally sided with the liberal court majority as an associate justice, was quickly assailed from many quarters. Republicans saw it as a maneuver to deprive the next president—who might well be a Republican—of the chance to appoint the chief justice. Southerners and other conservatives were angered by recent court liberalism on civil rights and criminal law. The choice was also decried as "cronyism" because of Fortas' close friendship with the president.

In July the Senate Judiciary Committee subjected Fortas to an unprecedented four-day grilling by hostile members. Fortas refused to comment on questions concerning Supreme Court decisions, and he balked at discussing his association with the president. Opponents charged that this association violated the traditional separation between the executive and judiciary. They brought out that Fortas had received $15,000 to teach summer university seminars, and that these funds had been raised by a former law partner from friends and clients of the Fortas law firm. Much time was also spent on films that had figured in Supreme Court decisions on obscenity.

The nomination was finally cleared by an 11–6 vote of the committee on September 17, but when the nomination came to the Senate floor its opponents began a filibuster. On October 1 supporters of the nomination failed to close the debate. Shortly afterward Fortas requested that his name be withdrawn, and the president complied.

Fortas was born June 19, 1910, in Memphis, Tenn., and obtained his B.A. from Southwestern College. He attended Yale University Law School and was later assistant professor of law there under William O. Douglas. He remained at Yale until 1937, when he accepted an appointment with the Securities and Exchange Commission. He held a number of government posts before entering private law practice in 1946. (D. Fo.)

FOUCHÉ, JACOBUS JOHANNES

On April 10 Jacobus Johannes Fouché became South Africa's second president. His election crowned a lifetime of political activity combined with successful farming in his home province, the Orange Free State.

Fouché was born June 6, 1898, in South Africa. His family spoke Afrikaans, a language derived from the Dutch spoken by 17th-century settlers. He was educated at the Afrikaans-speaking Victoria College. After finishing his education he became active in the Nationalist Party, made up primarily of Afrikaners (South Africans of Dutch descent). He was one of a small band of Afrikaner politicians who refused to follow their leader, Gen. J. B. M. Hertzog, into a coalition with Gen. J. C. Smuts to form the United Party government; in the 1930s this coalition tried to sink the differences between English-speaking and Afrikaans-speaking South Africans. Instead, Fouché went into the political wilderness with D. F. Malan, choosing to work for the victory of Afrikaner nationalism. Elected to the South African Parliament in 1941, he was made administrator of the Orange Free State in 1951, two years after Malan's regime came to power.

In 1959, with the Nationalists still in power, Fouché became minister of defense under Prime Minister Hendrik Verwoerd. During this time international opinion was turning strongly against South Africa because of its policy of racial separation. In response, Fouché developed South Africa's Army into one of the world's strongest for that size nation; defense expenditures rose more than sixfold. Fouché was often re-

membered for his warning to world opinion that "white South Africans will defend their fatherland until blood rises to their horses' bits." After seven years in charge of defense, he was transferred in 1966 to the post of minister for agriculture, technical services, and water affairs. (Co. L.)

FRANKLIN, ARETHA

Aretha Franklin was Lady Soul, and in some circles that said it all. But for those who needed further explanation, her records had earned more than $1.2 million; she had won two Grammy awards; she was *Billboard* magazine's top female vocalist in 1967; and she had toured in Europe and had been hailed in England as the new Bessie Smith. Four of her records had sold a million copies each. She was on the cover of *Time* and she had been honoured by the Southern Christian Leadership Conference. She sang the national anthem in gospel style (though she botched the lyrics) at the Democratic national convention in Chicago.

In 1966 she had been virtually unknown. Atlantic Records' Jerry Wexler, who managed her rise to stardom, explained the phenomenon: "There's nothing new in what she is singing. Negro music has always been at the core of our music, but always manicured and sanitized. Now there has been a breakthrough."

Her songs were not simple, atavistic derivatives of spirituals, however. Soul was something more complex and contemporary, more on the order of musical Black Power, combining a sense of personal pain or purpose with new tonal and rhythmic patterns built around the one-to-one communication that was the heart of gospel music's particular intensity.

Aretha Franklin was born in Memphis, Tenn., in 1942 and brought up on Detroit's East Side in a household where the best gospel singers came and went. Her father, the Rev. C. L. Franklin, was a successful evangelist and pastor of the New Bethel Baptist Church.

When Aretha was a child she heard a family friend, Clara Ward, sing "Peace in the Valley" at her aunt's funeral, and decided to become a singer. She sang her first church solo at 12 and two years later was featured with her father's gospel caravan. At 18 she tried popular music in New York, but nothing happened until she switched to the Atlantic label and her original repertoire.

One striking aspect of her music was the ensemble effect. While the finished disc sounded like a solo singer and chorus, it was, in fact, only the electronically compounded voices of Aretha and her two sisters, Erma and Carolyn. Other elements in the musical recipe were the explicit lyrics, written by Carolyn, and Aretha's direct, pained, spiritualistic delivery. "I sing to people about what matters," she said. "I sing to the realists, people who accept it like it is."

(Ph. K.)

FROST, DAVID PARADINE

In 1968, with a reputed annual income of £100,000 ($240,000) and a chauffeur-driven golden Mercedes, David Frost, at 29, was Britain's highest-paid television personality and was well known in Australia and North America as well. Nevertheless, the year brought its setbacks. Following the 1967 reallocation of contracts among independent program companies by the U.K. Independent Television Authority, London Weekend Television Ltd. was launched in July 1968, with Frost, its brightest star (and a large shareholder), spearheading the attack with "Frost on Friday," "Frost on Saturday," and "Frost on Sunday." So much exposure inevitably brought criticism, and a sharp

CAMERA PRESS—PIX FROM PUBLIX
Jacobus Johannes Fouché

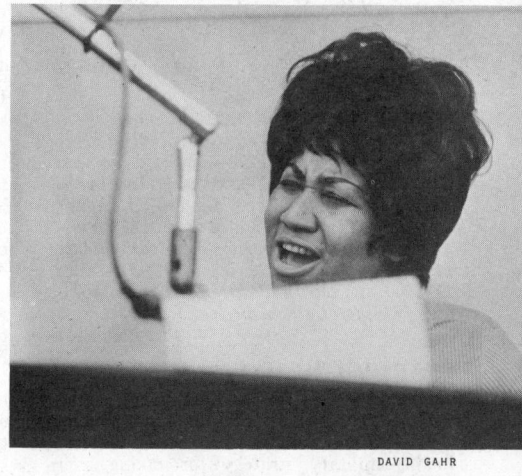

DAVID GAHR
Aretha Franklin

TERRENCE SPENCER,
"LIFE" © TIME INC.
David Frost

"THE NEW YORK TIMES" FROM WIDE WORLD
Abe Fortas

drop in ITV audience ratings led to the rescheduling of Frost's programs outside peak viewing periods.

He also continued to disgruntle members of the government. In 1967 the minister of defense had fallen afoul of his professional skill. In 1968 Frost's program on the Ronan Point disaster (involving the partial collapse of a system-built high-rise apartment building) was called "alarmist" by the minister of housing, who nevertheless hastened official action to avoid a repetition of the disaster.

The son of a Methodist minister, Frost was born at Tenterden, Kent, on April 7, 1939. At 18 he won a state scholarship to Cambridge University. After graduating with a second-class honours degree, he spent a year teaching, then became a trainee researcher for an ITV weekly news program. He earned extra money by appearing in nightclubs, and his act was seen by BBC producer Ned Sherrin, who offered him the star spot in "That Was the Week That Was" (TWTWTW, or TW3). Frost's relaxed adaptability, which enabled him to switch from current affairs to humorous sketches, immediately registered with viewers, and his rise was meteoric. TW3 was successfully adapted for NBC, and other "satirical" programs followed ("Not so Much a Programme, More a Way of Life," "The Frost Report," etc.). In 1967 "Frost over England" won the Golden Rose of Montreux; he was nominated by the Variety Club of Great Britain as "Personality of the Year" and awarded the Royal Television Society's Silver Medal. He also acquired his own film company and published several books, including (with Antony Jay) *To England with Love* (1967; U.S. title, *The English*). (P. Os.)

FUENTES, CARLOS

A Change of Skin, the most recent novel by the socially concerned Mexican author and intellectual Carlos Fuentes, was awarded the Biblioteca Breve prize by the Spanish publishing house of Seiz Barral in 1968. Then, less than one month after its publication, Spanish authorities banned it. In a letter from Barcelona, Fuentes said the Spanish authorities claimed the book was "pornographic, communistic, anti-Christian, anti-German, and pro-Jewish."

Like Fuentes' other novels, *A Change of Skin* is a perceptive examination of current Mexican social attitudes, written in an involved and difficult style. The novel is filled with his philosophy. An example:

"Earth is not the dwelling place of truth; truth wanders among men, lost and unrecognized. What if fair-haired J. C., our era's first hippie, had made his peace with Rome and the Pharisees and sat down to a few quiet hands of gin rummy with Iscariot.

"Or what if he had joined the soap business of Pilate, Procter and Gamble. What our gentried holy don't dig about the Holy Ghost being nailed to his cross is that in reality he was history's first psychopath, the first son of Man way out in grassy left."

Born in 1928, Fuentes was educated at the University of Mexico and remained closely associated with that institution. He held several government positions, the highest being head of the Department of Cultural Relations in the Ministry of Foreign Affairs in 1957–59.

He also served as assistant head of the press section of the Ministry of Foreign Affairs in 1954, and was a member of the Mexican delegation to the International La-

bour Organization (ILO) in Geneva in 1950–52. Fuentes was editor of *Revista Mexicana de Literatura* (1954–58) and *Siempra* and *Política* (1960), and co-editor of *El Espectador* (1959–61). Besides *A Change of Skin*, his books included *Los días enmascarados* (1954), *La región mas transparente* (1958), *Las buenas conciencias* (1959), *Aura* (1962), *The Death of Artemio Cruz* (1962), and *Whither Latin America?* (1963).

(J. F. Ba.)

GIAP, VO NGUYEN

In 1968 Gen. Vo Nguyen Giap, vice-premier, defense minister, and commander in chief of North Vietnam, suffered a rare defeat in his military strategy for taking over South Vietnam. U.S. and South Vietnamese forces frustrated the massive guerrilla offensive against all major South Vietnamese cities and towns, which began January 30 on the Tet (lunar new year) holiday and which Giap personally organized and directed.

The eight-week onslaught was traced to Giap through captured documents and personnel. This "Tet offensive" was the carefully planned culmination of a major winter-spring offensive throughout South Vietnam, aimed at severing communications, isolating cities from one another and from the countryside, opening up the two northern provinces to Communist occupation, and forcing the collapse of the South Vietnamese government and eventual U.S. withdrawal from South Vietnam. When it and later, weaker offensives failed, Giap withdrew up to 40,000 North Vietnamese troops from the South. The subsequent falling off of violence in South Vietnam set the stage for the complete halt of all U.S. bombing of North Vietnam on November 1.

Giap had not previously suffered many setbacks in his brilliant military career. His greatest triumph was the defeat of the French at Dien Bien Phu in 1954. His two books, *People's War, People's Army* and *Big Victory, Great Task,* are virtually textbooks in guerrilla warfare.

Giap often boasted that his military talent was not learned in formal military school. He was born in 1912 in Quang Binh Province, just north of the line now dividing North and South Vietnam. His father, a poor landholder, sent his son south to a French college in Hue. At 18 Giap was jailed by the French for student agitation, and at 24 he was already a militant Communist leader. After the collapse of the Japanese occupation of Vietnam in 1945, Giap became minister of the interior in the provisional government formed before the French could return to Hanoi. In the war against France that followed, Giap emerged as a ruthless, single-minded general, able to exploit every weakness of conventional French tactics.

(G. F. Sh.)

GORTON, JOHN GREY

On Jan. 10, 1968, John Grey Gorton became prime minister of Australia, having succeeded Harold Holt as leader of the parliamentary Liberal Party after Holt's death in a swimming accident late in 1967. On February 24 the prime minister won the by-election for the Victoria seat of Higgins in the House of Representatives, Holt's former constituency.

From the time he assumed office, Gorton—like Holt before him—was preoccupied with problems of defense and threats to Australia's security. Also like Holt, he emerged as a firm supporter of the U.S.

position in Southeast Asia. Shaken by the Viet Cong's Tet offensive and Pres. Lyndon Johnson's decision not to run again, he described Australia as relatively defenseless. Later he spoke of the need to take the first shock of any attack on Australia and made analogies with Israel. At a government parties' meeting on May 8, Gorton said that the "forward defense" policy, though legitimate, had to be reexamined. It was necessary, he added, to get absolutely ironclad guarantees of the American backup for Australian troops in Southeast Asia.

In mid-1968, Gorton visited the United States and Southeast Asia, where he had talks with national leaders. At an Australian base near Nui Dat in Vietnam, Gorton assured the Australian troops that for every "nut" who waved placards and sat on the roadway, there were a hundred Australians behind the troops. His hawkish speeches left the South Vietnamese government in no doubt that Australia would stand firm to its commitment. In Parliament, where Gorton's style improved as the year progressed, he hit hard at the Australian Labor Party opposition for its attempt to draw an analogy between the Soviet suppression of Czechoslovakia and U.S. policy in Vietnam.

Gorton was born at Melbourne on Sept. 9, 1911, and was educated at Geelong Grammar School and at Brasenose College, Oxford. He was senator for Victoria from 1950; minister for the navy, 1958–63; minister assisting the minister for external affairs, 1960–63; minister for the interior, 1963–64; minister for works, minister assisting the prime minister, and minister in charge of Commonwealth activities in education and research, 1963–68. (A. R. G. G.)

HARRIMAN, W(ILLIAM) AVERELL

In 1968 W. Averell Harriman, chief U.S. negotiator at the Vietnam peace talks in Paris, proved himself the most durable of diplomats. At age 76, with a lifetime of politics, business, and diplomatic service behind him, he tenaciously fought verbal battles week after week with North Vietnamese negotiator Xuan Thuy.

Pres. Lyndon B. Johnson, in his March 31 speech ordering a partial halt in the bombing of North Vietnam, named Harriman as his personal representative for opening the talks. Up to that time Harriman had been a roving diplomatic troubleshooter, with the title ambassador at large. When the talks with Hanoi finally began on May 13, Harriman's first speech laid down the central U.S. position: the U.S. would not stop all bombing of the North until Hanoi gave assurances that it would not take military advantage and would move promptly to substantive negotiations.

By summer Harriman was convinced that the North Vietnamese would not talk seriously until the bombing was stopped, and on September 17 he and Johnson agreed on a formula for achieving this. Hanoi must give firm assurances not to abuse the Demilitarized Zone and not to shell South Vietnamese cities. If the Saigon government were permitted to join the subsequent peace talks, the National Liberation Front could join also. Although vague and open to different interpretations later, the formula was accepted by the North and led to the bombing halt of November 1. Controversy over such issues as the seating arrangement around the conference table delayed the start of the expanded peace talks, which by the year's end had not begun.

Harriman's whole life prepared him for this arduous test of diplomacy. He was born in New York City on Nov. 15, 1891,

and when he was 17 he and his brother inherited more than $100 million. By 1932, having graduated from Yale, he was chairman of the board of the Union Pacific Railroad. Pres. Franklin Roosevelt first tapped his energy for government service, making him a member of the National Recovery Administration and, during World War II, ambassador to the Soviet Union. After the war he served as Pres. Harry S. Truman's secretary of commerce. After one term as governor of New York, he returned to federal service under Pres. John F. Kennedy.

(G. F. Sh.)

HOFFMAN, DUSTIN

Dustin Hoffman was "The Graduate," the title character in one of the most popular movies of 1968 and one that took on the importance of gospel among students and young people. His performance as Benjamin Braddock won him great acclaim.

Named by his mother for Western film star Dustin Farnum, Hoffman began an acting career that looked for a time like that of a saddle-bum prototype—everything was dismal until Mike Nichols, a leading Broadway and Hollywood director, summoned Hoffman to California to do a screen test for *The Graduate* after he had won an Obie award for a part in an off-Broadway play.

Hoffman, frazzled from doing eight shows a week in the play *The Journey of the Fifth Horse* and from the flight to California on his day off, was scared. Nichols tried him out in a love scene with ingenue Katherine Ross. "I'd never asked a girl in acting class to do a love scene," Hoffman said later. He added, "No girl asked me either." As for Miss Ross, she thought, "He looks about 3 feet tall [he was all of 5 ft. 6 in.] . . . so dead serious, so humorless, so unkempt. This is going to be a disaster."

But Nichols decided Hoffman had what he wanted for the film. According to Nichols, Hoffman "had a kind of pole-axed quality with life, but great vitality underneath." Nichols' instinct was right. Hoffman gave a sterling performance in the part, which deals with what worshipers of the film called "alienation from the established norms of the suburban ethic." Many people, mostly young, saw the movie several times and threatened to make it one of the biggest money-makers of all time.

Hoffman was born in 1937 in Los Angeles, Calif. Other than *The Graduate*, he had little acting experience except for off-Broadway character parts and a stint at the Pasadena Community Playhouse. This was not to say, however, that Hoffman was a one-character actor—he was well received off-Broadway as a middle-aged Russian clerk, a cockney hippie, and a hunchbacked Nazi. For the future, his success in *The Graduate* brought him many offers. He starred in a movie, *Midnight Cowboy*, and also prepared to open in a Broadway comedy. (Ph. K.)

HOLLEY, ROBERT W.

For his work in deciphering the genetic code, Robert W. Holley of Cornell University and the Salk Institute was one of the three U.S. scientists who received the 1968 Nobel Prize in Medicine or Physiology. He shared the award—and its accompanying $70,000 stipend—with Marshall W. Nirenberg and Har Gobind Khorana (qq.v.).

The work of the three men combined to shed the first real light on the genetic mechanisms through which individual cells (and, hence, all organisms) copy the qualities of their ancestors. Working independently, they examined the nature of basic biochemical substances in the cell's chromo-

somes—proteins, amino acids, and the primary vehicles of heredity, deoxyribonucleic acid (DNA) and ribonucleic acid (RNA).

Holley's contribution related principally to transfer-RNA. After six years of research with yeast he determined the chainlike structure of the RNA molecule, and then he showed how, in one form, it picks up individual amino acids within a cell in a predetermined order and transports and combines them into specific proteins according to the cell's master plan, as dictated by the DNA molecule. His work constituted a major step toward the understanding of the life process.

Born in Urbana, Ill., Jan. 28, 1922, Holley studied chemistry at the University of Illinois and took his doctorate in organic chemistry at Cornell University. He won a fellowship from the American Chemical Society to Washington State College. Having worked at Cornell Medical School in New York City with the team that synthesized penicillin during World War II, he returned to another branch of Cornell in 1948—the New York State Agricultural Experiment Station at Geneva, N.Y.

He was later a research chemist at the Plant, Soil, and Nutrition Lab at Cornell in Ithaca and became a professor of biochemistry in 1964. Shortly before his Nobel citation he became permanent resident fellow at the Salk Institute in La Jolla, Calif., though maintaining an affiliation with Cornell. Holley also won the Albert Lasker Award for medical research and the U.S. Department of Agriculture's Distinguished Service Award.   (PH. K.)

HUMPHREY, HUBERT HORATIO

For over three years, Vice-Pres. Hubert Humphrey had lived in the shadow of Pres. Lyndon Johnson, with no expectation of leaving it in the near future. Then, on March 31, 1968, Johnson announced he would not seek reelection, and on April 27 Humphrey declared his candidacy for the Democratic nomination for president. Despite a valiant campaign in which he almost overcame tremendous odds, Humphrey could not completely escape the Johnson administration's unpopularity. On November 5 he lost to Republican Richard Nixon by about 300,000 votes.

That he came so close was something of a political miracle. When he entered the race, the Democratic Party was bitterly divided over the war in Vietnam, and the primary fight between Eugene McCarthy and Robert Kennedy was the centre of attention. But Kennedy was assassinated and McCarthy was anathema to the party regulars. Humphrey coasted to the nomination at the Democratic national convention in Chicago in August.

The convention itself was a major setback. Security precautions against threatened antiwar demonstrations had turned Chicago into an armed camp, and the bloody battle between police and demonstrators on nomination night was carried around the world by television.

For weeks Humphrey was greeted by hecklers bearing placards recalling Chicago. He was also clearly hampered by his long defense of administration policies. It was not until September 30 that he moved slightly away from the Johnson position by promising to seek an end to the bombing of North Vietnam and a quick end to the war.

In the final three weeks his campaign came alive. He began to shave away Nixon's once comfortable margin and to win back northern Democrats who had wandered to third-party candidate George Wallace.

John Grey Gorton

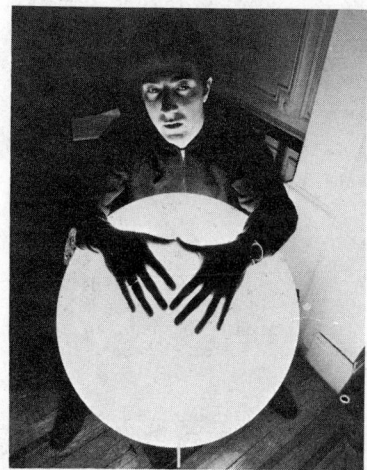

Dustin Hoffman

McCarthy at long last endorsed him. And on October 31, after weeks of rumours, Johnson announced a total halt to the bombing of North Vietnam. The polls showed Nixon and Humphrey in a virtual dead heat, and in the event they were right.

Humphrey was born May 27, 1911, in Wallace, S.D. He became mayor of Minneapolis in 1945, and in 1948 was elected to the Senate, where he gained a reputation as an outspoken liberal.   (RI. T. S.)

JACKSON, JESSE L.

A young, dynamic former college athlete, the Rev. Jesse L. Jackson, emerged in 1968 as one of the new leaders of the U.S. civil rights movement following the assassination of the Rev. Martin Luther King, Jr. The 26-year-old Baptist minister, who was ordained during the year, gained prominence as "city manager" of Resurrection City, the makeshift shantytown that housed the participants in the Poor People's Campaign march on Washington.

A close associate of King and a leader in the Southern Christian Leadership Conference (SCLC), Jackson was one of the planners of the march, the purpose of which was to dramatize the plight of the poor and apply pressure to Congress. Marchers from all over the country converged on Washington in late May, with Jackson as coordinator of their temporary encampment.

Jackson repeatedly displayed aggressiveness and eloquence in controlling and calming the demonstrators, while maintaining their dedication in the face of arrests, frustration, and almost constant downpours that turned the camp into a quagmire. Nevertheless, on May 25 he was forced to plan the evacuation of about half the inhabitants because of a threatened influenza epidemic.

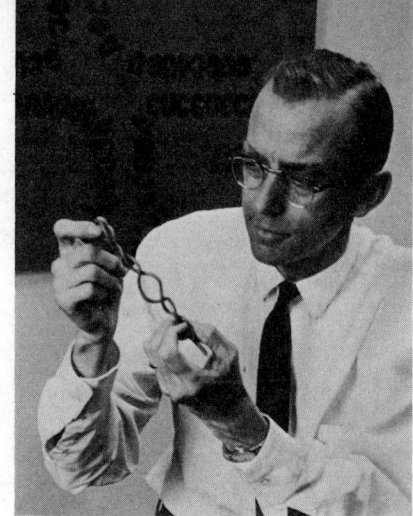

Robert W. Holley

Vo Nguyen Giap

On May 31 Jackson was replaced as city manager by Hosea Williams and was sent to organize support for the campaign in other cities. There were reports, denied by Jackson and other SCLC officials, that his departure was the result of a dispute over a "cult of personality" building up around him.

He returned to Washington just before Resurrection City was closed by local authorities. Again assuming a leadership role on June 23, he ordered the camp evacuated following a skirmish between the residents and the Washington police. A day later he announced a new phase of the Poor People's Campaign—a plan to organize economic boycotts in 40 U.S. cities. The year's end found him in Chicago promoting a "black Christmas" campaign in support of black merchants.

Jackson was born Oct. 8, 1941, in Greenville, S.C., and attended the University of Illinois and North Carolina Agricultural and Technical College. In 1964 and 1965, while attending Chicago Theological Seminary, he became active in open-housing demonstrations and attracted the attention of King. He joined the SCLC and subsequently became national director of Operation Breadbasket, designed to promote economic development among blacks.   (D. Fo.)

JARRING, GUNNAR VALFRID

On Nov. 23, 1967, Gunnar Jarring, a prominent Swedish diplomat, was appointed a special representative of the UN Security Council with the unenvied mission to proceed to the Middle East "to establish and maintain contacts with the states concerned in order to promote agreement and assist efforts to achieve a peaceful and accepted settlement." The fragile basis of this desired

settlement between Israel and the Arab states was a British-sponsored resolution, unanimously adopted the previous day by the Security Council.

During the following year Jarring was constantly commuting between Cairo, Amman (Jordan), Beirut, Jerusalem, New York City, and his Cyprus headquarters discussing the situation with Arab and Israeli statesmen. He did not visit Damascus because his mission was boycotted by the Syrian left-wing Baath government. Jarring's task was made difficult by the conflicting demands of the opposing parties. The Arabs were only interested in that passage of the UN resolution that spoke of the "withdrawal of Israeli armed forces from territories occupied in the recent conflict," while the Israelis kept insisting on "termination of all claims of belligerency," "territorial integrity and political independence of every State in the area," and "their right to live in peace within secure and recognized boundaries free from threats or acts of force." After a year of skillful persistence, Jarring had been unable to bring Arabs and Israelis together at the conference table, but he did not renounce his mission.

Gunnar Valfrid Jarring was born at Malmö, Swed., on Oct. 12, 1907, and graduated from the University of Lund. Called to the Swedish diplomatic service in 1940, he was sent first to Turkey and a year later went to the Swedish legation in Teheran, Iran. In 1945 Jarring became chargé d'affaires at the Swedish embassy in Baghdad, Iraq, and the next year he was appointed chargé in Ethiopia. He assumed the post of ambassador to India two years later. From 1953 to 1956 he served as director of the political department of the Swedish Ministry of Foreign Affairs, and afterward as Sweden's permanent envoy to the UN. From 1958 to 1964 he was Sweden's ambassador to the U.S. and in the latter year became ambassador to the Soviet Union.   (K. Sm.)

JENKINS, ROY

Roy Jenkins took charge of British economic policy immediately after the devaluation of sterling in November 1967, when he was appointed chancellor of the exchequer. To make room for additional exports by imposing severe restrictions on demand at home was his main purpose, and through 1968 he persisted with this policy with great tenacity. He forecast "two years' hard slog" followed by "a very great breakthrough in the '70s." The benefits of devaluation were, in fact, rather slow to take effect, and though exports were doing exceptionally well in the latter part of 1968, imports remained persistently high.

Jenkins was criticized for allowing a domestic boom to develop in the weeks before submitting the new budget in March. In the budget he imposed higher taxes, which were estimated to bring in an additional £923 million and to reduce domestic demand by about £500 million. Jenkins resisted pressure by trade unions to allow a faster rate of economic growth. While this was unpopular in the labour movement, he commanded respect by his firmness, and he began to be talked of as a likely future prime minister.

Though Jenkins was only 47 when he became chancellor, he had been in Parliament for nearly 20 years, being elected in 1948, when he was the youngest M.P. in the House of Commons. Born Nov. 11, 1920, in Abersychan, Wales, he was the son of an M.P. who became parliamentary pri-

vate secretary to Clement Attlee, the Labour Party prime minister from 1945 to 1951. Jenkins, who had a brilliant academic career at Oxford University, made a name for himself as a biographer and historian, specializing in the period 1870 to 1914, and shortly before the election of 1964 he briefly considered retiring from politics to devote himself entirely to writing. Instead, however, he became minister of aviation in 1964 and then, in 1965, home secretary. His interest in law reform was demonstrated by the Criminal Justice Act, which he steered through Parliament in 1966–67. In 1959 he had been responsible for the Obscene Publications Act, which opened the way to a more tolerant atmosphere for book publishing.

(W. H. Ts.)

JOHNSON, LYNDON BAINES

U.S. Pres. Lyndon B. Johnson surprised the world on March 31, 1968, by announcing that he would not seek reelection. In the same nationwide telecast he disclosed a reduction in the bombing of North Vietnam and plans for preliminary peace negotiations.

Johnson said his decision was based on his desire to take the search for peace in Vietnam out of politics, but observers felt there were political reasons as well. The announcement came at a time when public approval of his performance as president had dropped to 38%, as reflected in the Louis Harris poll. It also came two days before the Wisconsin primary, in which he faced certain defeat by Sen. Eugene McCarthy.

As it had for more than two years, Vietnam dominated Johnson's final year in office. In July he flew to Honolulu for his fifth visit with South Vietnamese Pres. Nguyen Van Thieu. The talks with Hanoi dragged on inconclusively through the summer and fall, but Washington was filled with rumours of behind-the-scenes negotiations, and on October 31 Johnson announced a halt to all bombing of the North. He also indicated that broadened talks—including South Vietnam and the National Liberation Front—would begin shortly, but his hopes of achieving peace before he left office met an obstacle in Thieu's refusal to sit down with the NLF.

Johnson maintained a studied neutrality in the presidential race until mid-October, when he made the first of several statements in support of the Democratic nominee, Vice-Pres. Hubert Humphrey. The White House denied that the October 31 announcement had been timed to help Humphrey, but many felt that it had narrowed Republican Richard Nixon's margin of victory.

Johnson's other travels included an April visit to Honolulu for a meeting of the Pacific allies and a July trip to San Salvador to meet with the Central American presidents. He continued to seek improved U.S.-Soviet relations, but his planned announcement of a summit meeting with Soviet leaders was postponed indefinitely after the Warsaw Pact invasion of Czechoslovakia. His relations with Congress remained strained. He won a year-old fight for a temporary 10% tax surcharge, though Congress ordered a $6 billion budget cut along with it, and his anticrime bill was amended to the point where he signed it with reluctance. He obtained laws on fair housing and gun control and received a blistering defeat when the Senate refused to confirm Abe Fortas as U.S. chief justice.

Johnson watchers wondered how this longtime activist would adapt himself to retirement, but they were assured that his time would be filled. His plans included writing and teaching, supervising the large

Johnson interests in Texas, and being with his family. He acquired a second grandchild in 1968 when his daughter Lynda Bird Robb gave birth to a daughter, Lucinda Desha.

Born Aug. 27, 1908, in Stonewall, Tex., Johnson served from 1937 to 1948 in the House and from 1949 to 1961 in the Senate, where he made his reputation as majority leader. He took office as vice-president in 1961, succeeded to the presidency after John F. Kennedy's assassination in 1963, and was elected to a full term in 1964.   (Ri. T. S.)

KAUNDA, KENNETH

Kenneth Kaunda, president of Zambia, was emerging as a leading challenger of British and Portuguese policies toward the white-ruled parts of southern Africa. His republic, which produces more than $300 million of copper annually, was the largest black state along the frontiers of Rhodesia, South Africa, Angola, and Mozambique. From the time that Zambia gained its independence in October 1964, Kaunda faced the dilemma of reconciling his country's national interests with his political principles. Zambia's economy depended almost wholly on the communications systems of its white-ruled neighbours; but, in opposition to that, Kaunda was committed by principle to help eradicate those minority-dominated regimes. To fight them was to invite economic troubles and possible military reprisals; not to fight them was to submit to coexistence with regimes Kaunda regarded as intolerable.

In an effort to end his country's dependence on the railway systems of Rhodesia, South Africa, and Portugal, Kaunda sought to find new outlets to the sea through East Africa. He obtained Italian help to build a new oil pipeline to Dar es Salaam and obtained U.S. and British help to build an all-weather road to Tanzania. When Western countries refused to help finance a new Tanzania–Zambia railway line, he agreed with Tanzanian Pres. Julius Nyerere to accept a Communist Chinese offer to build it. Meanwhile, his Zambezi River frontier with Rhodesia increasingly became a place of violence.

Born to mission teachers of the Church of Scotland at Lubwa in Northern Rhodesia (now Zambia) on April 28, 1924, Kaunda started life as a teacher. Reacting to the colour-bar policies practiced under colonial rule in Northern Rhodesia, he gave up teaching to become a full-time nationalist political organizer. He was several times imprisoned and exiled, but emerged in 1958 as the leader of the United National Independence Party, which became the effective movement of independence. When Zambia became independent in 1964, Kaunda was elected its first president.   (Co. L.)

KAWABATA, YASUNARI

"Japan's most eminent man of letters" and a "human treasure" in his own country, Yasunari Kawabata was Nobel laureate for literature in 1968. He was the first Japanese and only the second Asian to win the literary prize since it was established in 1901. In its citation, the Swedish Academy of Letters described Kawabata's work as a "spiritual bridge spanning between East and West." Kawabata responded modestly to the award, which carried a stipend of $70,000. "I feel I am very lucky. It is a great honour," he said, adding that "for authors, honours can sometimes become unbearable burdens."

The author was born June 11, 1899, in Osaka. His parents died when he was an infant, and he was raised by his grandfather. He studied English and Japanese literature at Tokyo Imperial University, and by the time of his graduation was a leader of the Neosensualists, a group of young

writers who rejected social themes for pure lyricism.

His work remained lyrical and was frequently compared to the *haiku,* the traditional Japanese 17-syllable poetic form that relates seeming incongruities in a mystical motif. His most widely read works, which had been translated into English and seven other languages, were *Snow Country* and *The Thousand Cranes.* The former, according to an American critic, is "a bittersweet, erotic story of the doomed affair of a deteriorating geisha and a Tokyo dilettante." The latter dwells on the ancient ritual of the tea ceremony.

Kawabata's translator, Edward Seidensticker, said, "His best writing is episodic and wanting in grand climaxes, a stringing together of tiny lyrical episodes. He sometimes takes upwards of a decade in completing a short novel, and even then one cannot be sure that it is complete, or indeed that it needs completion."

Despite Kawabata's study of Western literature, he remained a quintessentially Japanese writer. Indeed, a Buddhistic anti-temporality was a primary facet of his work. He had won all the major Japanese literary prizes, and had served as president of the Japanese PEN Club and as vice-president of International PEN. (Ph. K.)

KENNEDY, EDWARD MOORE

Following the assassination of his brother Robert in June 1968, Sen. Edward M. ("Ted") Kennedy (Dem., Mass.) became the last surviving son of the illustrious Kennedy family and the leader of the political following he and his brothers had acquired.

Robert Kennedy, who had begun his campaign for the Democratic presidential nomination on March 16, had just won in the California Democratic primary when he was murdered in a Los Angeles hotel. After delivering a moving eulogy at his brother's funeral in New York City, Edward spent ten weeks mourning in seclusion with his family and the families of Robert and Pres. John F. Kennedy, who had been assassinated five years earlier. He went on a trip overseas with Robert's oldest son and discussed his future with his family and friends.

For the next few weeks that future became the subject of intense speculation. Vice-Pres. Hubert H. Humphrey and others strongly hinted that Kennedy could assure victory for the Democratic Party in 1968 by becoming the vice-presidential candidate on a ticket headed by Humphrey. However, on July 26 Kennedy said personal reasons made it "impossible" for him to run.

On August 21, in his first public appearance since his brother's funeral, he again renounced any plans for public office in 1968, but he said he was picking up his brothers' fallen standard because "there is no safety in hiding." A substantial but undetermined number of delegates to the Democratic national convention were reportedly ready to back him for the presidency, but he failed to give a clear indication of his desires and the movement never surfaced. Kennedy later endorsed Humphrey despite differences between the two over Vietnam.

Edward M. Kennedy was born Feb. 22, 1932, in Brookline, Mass., and was educated at Harvard and the University of Virginia Law School. In 1962, in a contest that was widely publicized because of his inexperience and because then Pres. John Kennedy was his brother, he was elected senator from Massachusetts. In the Senate he became a quiet, diligent, and amiable spokesman for unglamorous causes. He was reelected by a wide margin in 1964 while hospitalized following a serious back injury suffered in an airplane crash. (D. Fo.)

KHORANA, HAR GOBIND

One of the three U.S. scientists who shared the 1968 Nobel Prize in Medicine or Physiology for deciphering the genetic code was Har Gobind Khorana of the University of Wisconsin. Working independently, Khorana, Marshall W. Nirenberg, and Robert W. Holley (*qq.v.*) determined how cells transmit genetic messages so that their offspring inherit their chemical composition and functions. The three men would share the $70,000 stipend.

Using a new approach that employed synthetic materials, Khorana confirmed Nirenberg's findings that genetic material comprises four basic substances and that the way these substances are linked in large molecules of deoxyribonucleic acid (DNA) determines the chemical composition and function of a new cell. Holley, working with yeast, discovered the manner in which amino acids are produced by transfer-RNA (ribonucleic acid) in the cells.

Khorana added details about what serial combinations of basic substances form which specific amino acids. He also proved that the key combinations always come in groups of three, called codons, and that each group is separate. The 64 possible combinations are read off along a strand of DNA, as required to produce the desired amino acid. Further research showed that some of the codons prompt a cell to start or stop the manufacturing of protein and that some amino acids are precipitated by more than one three-letter combination.

Khorana was born in Raipur, India, Jan. 9, 1922, and earned two chemistry degrees from the University of Panjab, was awarded a Ph.D. by the University of Liverpool in 1948, and did post-doctoral work at the Federal Institute of Technology in Zürich and with an earlier Nobel Prize winner, A. Todd. He was appointed head of the Organic Chemistry Group of the British Columbia Research Council before becoming a professor and group leader at the Institute of Enzyme Research at the University of Wisconsin in 1960 and Conrad A. Elvejhem professor of life sciences four years later.

A naturalized U.S. citizen and tireless researcher who had published some 300 papers, he suggested, "I work all the time, but then I guess we all do." (Ph. K.)

KIM IL SUNG

North Korea's chief of state, Kim Il Sung, one of the least known of the Communist rulers, caused the biggest single foreign-policy crisis for the U.S. in 1968. On January 23 four of his patrol boats seized the U.S. Navy intelligence ship USS "Pueblo" off the coast of North Korea and took it into the North Korean port of Wonsan. The 82 surviving members of the 83-man crew were not released until late December, after almost a year of difficult negotiations. The ship remained in North Korean hands.

The North Korean Radio had broadcast what it claimed were confessions of Comdr. Lloyd Mark Bucher and his crew that the "Pueblo" was caught within the 12-mi. territorial limit of North Korea, and Kim demanded that the U.S. apologize for this intrusion. Eventually the U.S. did sign such an apology, which was accepted by Kim even though Secretary of State Dean Rusk and other U.S. spokesmen repudiated it publicly. The whole affair strained relations between the U.S. and South Korea, which resented the fact that the U.S. had undertaken the negotiations unilaterally.

The seizure of the "Pueblo" coincided with a sudden rise in tensions between North and South Korea. On January 22,

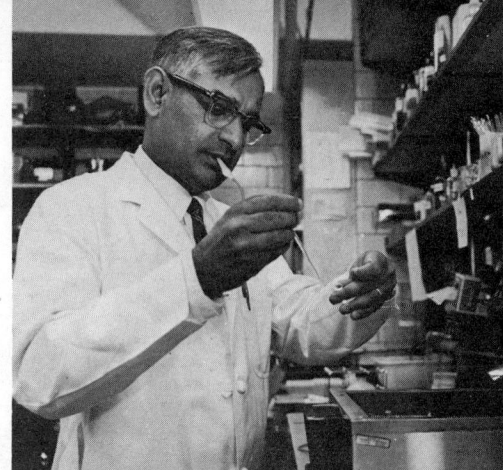
COURTESY, THE UNIVERSITY OF WISCONSIN
Har Gobind Khorana

COURTESY, CONSULATE GENERAL OF JAPAN
Yasunari Kawabata

CARL PURCELL—PIX FROM PUBLIX
Edward Moore Kennedy

Kenneth Kaunda
NORDFOTO FROM PICTORIAL PARADE

the day before the seizure, a group of North Koreans sought to kill South Korean Pres. Pak Chung Hi in a guerrilla raid on Seoul, South Korea. U.S. Pres. Lyndon Johnson then dispatched the aircraft carrier "Enterprise" to Korea, added 400 jet fighters to U.S. forces in Korea, and warned against a reopening of the Korean War. But Kim Il Sung carefully kept the crisis within limits, manipulating the tensions with South Korea and the U.S. to rally North Korea behind his regime and put the country on a war footing.

The tactics followed closely those he had employed to maintain his undisputed rule of North Korea for 20 years. In 1946, he obtained control of the local Communist Party; during the following year he absorbed a potential rival organized by Chinese-trained cadres, and in 1948 he emerged as the sole leader of North Korea.

Kim was born April 15, 1912, in the northern town of Mangyongdae, the son of a middle class schoolmaster. His original name was Kim Sung Chu. In 1945 he took the name Kim Il Sung, after a legendary anti-Japanese guerrilla fighter.   (G. F. Sh.)

KOIVISTO, MAUNO

Mauno Koivisto, a onetime dock worker, became prime minister of Finland in March 1968. He enjoyed confidence beyond his own party in spite of the unpopular methods he took to stabilize Finland's economy. During the year he continued to defend that policy, which he had helped formulate as minister of finance in the coalition government formed by Social Democratic Party leader Rafael Paasio in 1966.

A carpenter's son, born on Nov. 25, 1923, Koivisto worked in the 1940s as a docker at Turku in southwest Finland. But at the same time he continued his studies and at the age of 25 received his undergraduate degree, advanced to a post as head of the harbour office in Turku, and entered graduate school. He helped finance his graduate education by working also as a temporary teacher at an elementary school. In 1953 he received a master of arts degree and began working in the office for professional guidance in Turku. His paper on the social conditions in the harbour of Turku gained him a doctorate in 1956.

In 1958 Koivisto was appointed a member of the board of the Workers Savings Bank in Helsinki, and a year later he became the bank's managing director. He was elected to leading posts within the Social Democratic cooperative movement, and in 1966 became chairman of the board of administration of the large cooperative Elanto.

But he was still unknown both to the public in general and to the rank and file of the Social Democratic Party when he became minister of finance in 1966. Then, however, he became a front-page personality, and in spite of unpopular tax increases, which he defended as necessary for the nation's economy, he gained support and popularity. He was the man behind the 31% devaluation of the Finnish currency in October 1967, and later, for a short period, he acted as governor of the Bank of Finland before becoming his party's choice for the post of prime minister. In that office he faced the problem of keeping together a five-party coalition, in which the leading groups—Social Democratic Party, Centre (former Agrarian) Party, and Peoples Democratic League (Communists)—often disagreed on vital matters.   (C. F. Sa.)

KOLLEK, THEODORE

Elected mayor of Jerusalem in November 1965 as essentially an independent, and against the opposition of the majority party, Teddy Kollek had adopted the well-being of Jerusalem as his policy, as in earlier years he had devoted himself to his kibbutz Ein Gev on the Sea of Galilee and to Prime Minister David Ben-Gurion, whom he served for 11 years as director general.

Both at the prime minister's office and as mayor of Jerusalem, Kollek had done much to restore the ancient beauties of the country and of the Holy City. He initiated and supervised the building of the Israel Museum and began the process of cleaning up Jerusalem, which had been neglected by previous local administrations and governments. Following the June 1967 war, he became mayor of the united Jerusalem and sought almost immediately to introduce reforms and improvements in East Jerusalem (as the former Jordanian section was now called), despite the difficulties of its unsettled state and the operations of conflicting governmental authorities.

With characteristic energy, imagination, and enthusiasm, in 1968 he worked to unite, physically as well as psychologically, the Arab and Israeli communities within the city. "If we can prove that it works," he said, "this will be a breakthrough in Jewish-Arab relations which politics and propaganda will not be able to undermine."

Born in Vienna in 1911, Kollek went to Israel in 1934 and was a founder of the Ein Gev kibbutz. He was active in the Zionist Youth Movement, in the organization of illegal immigration into Palestine, and in the rescue of young people from Germany and German-occupied countries during World War II. He was a staff member of the Political Department of the Jewish Agency, closely connected with the work of the underground Haganah, and was placed in charge of contact with the European Jewish underground movements in 1942. In the U.S. after the war, he engaged in soliciting aid for the Israeli fight for independence.   (J. K.)

KOSYGIN, ALEKSEI NIKOLAYEVICH

Soviet Premier Aleksei N. Kosygin's diplomatic talents as number two man in the

LEIF ERIK NYGARDS KERS FROM BLACK STAR

John Vliet Lindsay

SHEL HERSHORN FROM BLACK STAR

James Joseph Ling

DALMAS—PIX FROM PUBLIX

Aleksei Nikolayevich Kosygin

Eugene Joseph McCarthy

WIDE WORLD

RALPH CRANE, "LIFE" © TIME INC.

Rod McKuen

Soviet hierarchy were sorely tried in 1968 by Czechoslovakia. Prior to the Soviet invasion of August 20–21, he tried and failed to dissuade the new Czechoslovak leaders from their liberalization course. The Soviet invasion, in turn, postponed indefinitely Soviet-U.S. talks on mutual limitation of nuclear missile systems.

On May 18 Kosygin met with Czechoslovak leaders, mainly about a $400 million Soviet loan for the ailing Czechoslovak economy. No agreement was reached. At the same time, he helped get Czechoslovak consent to Warsaw Pact maneuvers on Czechoslovak territory. At the talks between the Soviet and Czechoslovak party leaders in July and at the August 3 Bratislava conference of Warsaw Pact members, Kosygin helped arrange an agreement to end the feud over Czechoslovak reforms. When the invasion exploded that understanding, the Soviet Foreign Ministry, on August 21, officially denied rumours that Kosygin had resigned in protest.

As chief Soviet diplomatic troubleshooter, Kosygin attempted to keep crises elsewhere below the boiling point. On February 18 he publicly assured the U.S. that North Korean seizure of the U.S. intelligence ship "Pueblo" was not meant to spark off a new confrontation in Asia, and in October he became the main Soviet channel for reassuring Pres. Lyndon Johnson that North Vietnam would not take military advantage of a bombing halt. He also visited India, Pakistan, Sweden, and Finland.

Born in St. Petersburg (now Leningrad) on Feb. 20, 1904, and a volunteer in the infant Red Army for three years in his teens, Kosygin spent his adult career in Soviet industry. Although rising rapidly in the technical bureaucracy, he did not gain a place in the Communist hierarchy until 1939, as commissar for textiles. That same year he became a member of the party Central Committee and in 1948 moved up to the Politburo. Dismissed by Stalin in 1952, Kosygin returned to his party posts in 1960. He became premier after Nikita S. Khrushchev's downfall in October 1964.   (G. F. SH.)

LINDSAY, JOHN VLIET

Problems multiplied in 1968 for John Lindsay, the handsome, progressive mayor of New York City, and seriously placed his promising political career in jeopardy.

In February sanitation workers went on strike, and for nine days the city faced a health crisis as tons of garbage accumulated; the situation was aggravated by feuding between Lindsay and New York Gov. Nelson A. Rockefeller over who should take the lead in settling the dispute. Welfare rolls continued to spiral upward. The perennial housing crisis became more serious. In the fall strikes by firemen, policemen, and, again, the garbagemen were narrowly averted. A teachers' strike kept a million pupils out of classes for weeks. Fuel deliverymen struck in the midst of a flu epidemic, and there was even a three-day strike of actors on Broadway.

Lindsay had called his New York "Fun City," and for a time it had seemed just that, with Parks Commissioner Thomas Hoving staging "happenings" in Central Park and movie companies making films in Greenwich Village. No New York mayor had ever been elected to higher office, but Lindsay's political lieutenants began plotting a possible course to the White House in 1972 or 1976 or to the governor's mansion in 1970. Before the Republican national convention, Lindsay was frequently mentioned as a potential vice-presidential nominee and, though he denied aspirations, he began to speak more frequently in other parts of the country. He was vice-chairman of the President's Advisory (Kerner) Commission on Civil Disturbances.

But as troubles piled up at home, increasingly disenchanted New Yorkers began to feel his attentions were drifting elsewhere. Lindsay kept the peace in New York during the summer, partly by walking through ghetto areas when trouble threatened to show the people he understood their problems. By fall the teachers were shouting "Lindsay must go!" and it was becoming apparent that he might find reelection difficult in 1969.

Lindsay was born Nov. 24, 1921, in New York City, received a law degree from Yale, and was elected to the U.S. House of Representatives from New York's 17th ("Silk-Stocking") district in 1958. In 1965, running on a fusion ticket, he became the first Republican mayor of New York City since Fiorello La Guardia had left office 20 years earlier.   (RI. T. S.)

LING, JAMES JOSEPH

Hailed as the "Merger King" by a national magazine, Jimmy Ling continued his reign into 1968 with additional acquisitions for Ling-Temco-Vought, Inc. (LTV), a conglomerate in which he was chairman of the board and chief executive officer. Jones & Laughlin Steel Corp., National Car Rental System, and Braniff International (part of the Greatamerica Corp. acquisition) came into the fold, bringing to ten the number of subsidiaries that flourished under the parent LTV, headquartered in a 33-story Dallas, Tex., office building.

Ling, who started his career with $3,000 in 1946 after being discharged from the Navy, envisioned the day when LTV would be doing a $10 billion annual business. Sales for 1968 were estimated to be near the $3 billion mark, compared with the previous year's sales figure of $1.8 billion.

Ling's ability was recognized in 1968 when U.S. Pres. Lyndon B. Johnson named him in September to be a member of the National Housing Partnership, formed to create "an adequately capitalized, professionally managed corporation" that would serve to link together American industry and labour in the production of housing for people of moderate and low incomes.

Ling, whose name is of Bavarian origin, was born in Hugo, Okla., Dec. 31, 1922. He left school at 14 and journeyed around the country for four years, working at odd jobs. He was 19 when he went to Dallas and began working for an electrical contractor. In July 1944 he enlisted in the U.S. Navy. Discharged in 1946, he returned to Dallas and electrical contracting.

Ling placed his foot on the first rung of the ladder to affluence in 1946 when he began his own electrical contracting business. By 1955 the firm was handling sales of $1.7 million. He decided to go public with Ling Electric Co., and almost single-handedly raised over $700,000 after having prepared his own stock prospectus. In 1960 he merged Ling-Altec Electronics, Inc., with Temco Electronics & Missiles Co. and in 1961 gained control of Chance Vought Corp. after a bruising struggle with the company's management.   (B. S. KA.)

McCARTHY, EUGENE JOSEPH

With an army of volunteers made up largely of professors, suburban housewives, and college students, Sen. Eugene McCarthy of Minnesota drastically changed the politics of 1968 with his surprising campaign for the Democratic presidential nomination. Though given absolutely no chance on Nov. 30, 1967, when he announced he would challenge Pres. Lyndon B. Johnson, McCarthy put together a string of primary successes that for a time seemed to bring him within reach of the nomination. But in the end the delegates to the Democratic national convention overwhelmingly chose Vice-Pres. Hubert Humphrey.

Running in opposition to the administration's Vietnam policies, McCarthy scored his first success on March 12, when he polled almost as many votes as the president in the New Hampshire primary. After Johnson withdrew from the race and Humphrey entered it too late to run in the remaining primaries, McCarthy and Sen. Robert Kennedy of New York were pitted against each other and, in some states, against local candidates representing the administration point of view. Kennedy won in Indiana and Nebraska, but McCarthy came back in Oregon. Kennedy won narrowly in California and was assassinated moments after acknowledging victory. Political observers believed that, had Kennedy lived, his and McCarthy's combined strength might have denied Humphrey the nomination.

McCarthy brought a low-key, urbane style to the campaign, and the "McCarthy kids," who left their campuses and shaved their beards in order to work for him, gave a new, fresh look to the political scene. He provided a political focus to widespread dissatisfaction with the war and, his supporters maintained, was in large measure responsible for Johnson's moves toward peace and his decision not to seek reelection. In an effort to force Humphrey closer to his views, McCarthy withheld his support until late in the campaign. This brought recriminations from party regulars, who felt his hesitancy had helped elect Republican Richard Nixon.

McCarthy was born March 29, 1916, in Watkins, Minn. After a year as a novice in a Benedictine monastery, he studied at St. John's University, Collegeville, Minn., and the University of Minnesota. He was a college economics professor until his election to the U.S. House of Representatives in 1948. Ten years later he won a seat in the Senate.   (RI. T. S.)

McKUEN, ROD

A case could be made for calling Rod McKuen the world's most successful poet. Certainly he was the only poet to earn a projected $500,000 in 1968.

But it was not always thus. For a time he was a songwriter, arranger, and lyricist whose commercial output totaled some 40 million records. He was also a performer who toured from San Francisco's Purple Onion to New York City's Copacabana and "ruined" his voice by belting out a rock 'n' roll song called "Oliver Twist."

McKuen was born in 1933 and grew up in a poor part of Oakland, Calif., around the street named in his first book's title, *Stanyan Street & Other Sorrows*. As an adolescent he had a local newspaper column and spun records for KROW, where comedienne Phyllis Diller was then a copywriter. After his discharge from military service, he appeared in "beach ball and bikini" films. Meanwhile, Miss Diller got him a job singing at the Purple Onion.

Unable to find enough folk songs he liked, McKuen started writing his own. With no more training than the perusal of a couple of music theory texts, he composed and conducted for the old "CBS Workshop."

His bout with "Oliver Twist" ended when he lost his voice. When he started singing

Edmund Sixtus Muskie

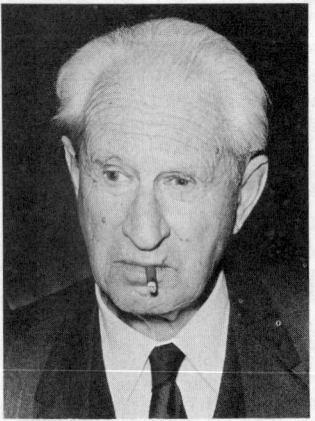

Herbert Marcuse

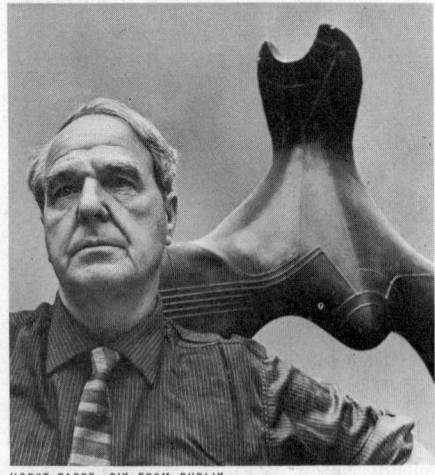

Henry Moore

Huey P. Newton

again, he discovered that "it sounds like I gargle with Dutch Cleanser." But he turned his hoarseness to gold by switching from rock to a more sublime and soulful repertoire. California loved it. So did the French; he won the Grand Prix du Disque in 1966.

Branching out again, McKuen wrote and published *Stanyan Street & Other Sorrows,* which, when it had sold 65,000 copies, became the biggest poetry hit in two decades. Random House picked up his work, releasing *Listen to the Warm,* and the combined circulation of the two books soon grew to 250,000. A third slim volume was released in 1968. Explaining his poetic success, McKuen said, "It just happens I've said something at a time when people need to be talked to. . . . I'm convinced we're on the verge of another Romantic era." But until we get there this sort of thing will have to suffice:

Someday some old familiar rain
will come along and know my name.
And then my shelter will be gone
and I'll have to move along.
But till I do I'll stay awhile
and track the hidden country of your smile.

(*Listen to the Warm,* p. 80)

(PH. K.)

McLAIN, DENNIS DALE

On the pitcher's mound, a scowling Denny McLain tilts his cap down almost over his eyes, squints toward the catcher, contorts his face into a sneer, and fires the ball toward home plate. More often than not, it is either a strike or the batter hits into an out.

Detroit Tiger Denny McLain, 24-year-old right hander, did this routine so well in 1968 that he won 31 games while losing only 6, joining the select group of pitchers who have won 30 or more games in one major league season. He became the first 30-game winner since Dizzy Dean accomplished the feat in 1934.

Off the mound, McLain also made headlines with his musical ability, oddball antics, and brash statements. He played the electric organ well enough to give recitals and make nightclub and television appearances. Newspaper reporters at various times quoted his derogatory remarks about Detroit baseball fans, other players on the team, and even the manager.

For all his cockiness, McLain in 1968 had the ability to match it. He was big (5 ft. 11 in., 185 lb.) and had speed and control. Although his best pitch was a fast ball, he also threw curves, change-ups, and sliders and could deliver the ball overhand or sidearm. His earned run average for the 1968 season was 1.96. After the season he was voted the most valuable player in the American League and also won the Cy Young Award as the league's best pitcher.

Dennis Dale McLain was born March 29, 1944, in Chicago. He received his start in both baseball and organ playing from his father, an insurance adjuster, who had played semiprofessional baseball in his youth, and who also gave electric organ lessons on the side. Having made a brilliant pitching record at Chicago's Mount Carmel High School, McLain signed with the Chicago White Sox for $17,000 immediately after graduating in 1962. He had only a 4–7 record with Chicago's minor-league farm club at Clinton, Ia., in 1962, and Chicago let him go to Detroit in 1963 for the waiver price of $8,000.

In 1965 he had his first good year, tying an American League record with seven strikeouts in a row and posting a 16–6 record. He won 20 and lost 14 in 1966, and the next season won 17 and lost 16.

In the 1968 World Series, McLain was

hit freely in his first two appearances, losing the first and fourth games against the St. Louis Cardinals. But he won the sixth game, 13–1, keeping the Detroit chances alive and enabling the Tigers to go on to win the Series. (R. CA.)

MARCUSE, HERBERT

From being a teacher and essayist known only to a small academic circle, Herbert Marcuse in 1968 was becoming the prophet of the New Left. As *Ramparts* magazine put it, "When the improbable student rebellions of West Berlin, Morningside Heights, and the Sorbonne broke out this spring, all agreed that Herbert Marcuse was the Marx of the children of the new bourgeoisie."

A frank exponent of resistance to the established order, Marcuse did not applaud the campus demonstrations. "I still consider the American University an oasis of free speech and real critical thinking in the society," he said. "Any student movement should try to protect this citadel . . . [but] try to radicalize the departments inside the university."

A Hegelian/Freudian/Marxist, Marcuse was wedded to the ideas of radicalization, vociferous dissent, and "resistance to the point of subversion." He believed that Western society is unfree and repressive by its very nature; that its technology has bought the complacency of the masses with material goods, robbed them of their traditional reasons to revolt, and kept them intellectually and spiritually captive. Contemporary Western civilization, then, is essentially tyrannical; to support tyranny is immoral; to subvert it in the name of a better world is a moral imperative.

Marcuse, nearing 70 in 1968, was born in Germany. He earned a doctorate at Freiburg in 1922 and was Martin Heidegger's assistant at the Frankfurt Institute of Social Research. He emigrated to the U.S. in the 1930s to escape the Hitler regime, and worked for the Office of Strategic Services and the State Department during and after World War II. He returned to academic life in 1954 at Brandeis University, where he was so popular that a newly endowed chair was named for him. He retained his popularity at the University of California in San Diego, not only with leftists but with all students. Columnist Drew Pearson checked him out and found him "very proper . . . sometimes described as being as homey as an old shoe." About the same time the Ku Klux Klan threatened his life. His major books were *Eros and Civilization* and *One-Dimensional Man.* (PH. K.)

MONDLANE, EDUARDO CHIVAMBO

One of the most effective guerrilla leaders engaged in fighting "wars of liberation" in southern Africa, Eduardo Mondlane headed FRELIMO—the Front for the Liberation of Mozambique, the Portuguese territory wedged between Tanzania, Rhodesia, and South Africa. Yet there was little in his manner that would lead one to suppose that he was a formidable challenger to Portugal's colonial rule in Africa. With his soft U.S. accent and his white American wife, he more closely resembled a U.S. college professor—which he had been at one time—than a guerrilla leader.

Mondlane was born to a peasant family in a southern province of Mozambique in 1920. Educated by missionaries, he then went to South Africa for his higher education but was expelled from the University of the Witwatersrand under a government edict prohibiting "foreign natives" from studying there. His subsequent experiences as a student in Portugal were equally un-

satisfactory except that he was able to establish contact with many of the younger intellectuals from Portuguese African territories, who, in the early 1950s, were beginning to dream of African liberation. Mondlane went to the U.S. as a refugee and, through scholarships, achieved a degree from Oberlin (O.) College and, subsequently, a Ph.D. in sociology from Northwestern University. After teaching for a time he joined the staff of the UN Trusteeship Council, but he resigned at the age of 41 to work for the liberation movement in Mozambique.

Mondlane made an immediate impact on the badly splintered liberation movement. Within a year he succeeded in unifying three opposition groups and emerged as the most effective nationalist leader. Announcing his willingness to accept help from any source, he set about creating a trained guerrilla army, a military headquarters in Tanzania, and an institute in Dar es Salaam, Tanzania, to train future political leaders, technicians, and administrators.

In September 1964, to the surprise of the authorities, Mondlane's forces launched their military campaign. Progress was slow but methodical. Mondlane refused to predict an early victory, but was confident that his tactics would succeed in the long run.

(Co. L.)

MOORE, HENRY

The greatest English sculptor of the 20th century and a figure of international importance in the world of art, Henry Moore was honoured in many countries in 1968 on the occasion of his 70th birthday. The most imposing tribute was probably the magnificent retrospective exhibition held at the Tate Gallery, London, to which, the previous year, Moore had presented a collection of his major works.

Born in the bleak industrial north of England, at Castleford, Yorkshire, on July 30, 1898, Moore was the seventh child of a coal miner. When he was still a child, his sculptural sensitivity and natural aptitude for design began to be recognized and encouraged by his more perceptive teachers. At the insistence of his father he trained to be a teacher, but service in World War I intervened. After the war, more determined than ever to be a sculptor, he entered the Leeds School of Art, where one of his contemporaries was the sculptor Barbara Hepworth. After two years at Leeds, Moore won a scholarship to the Royal College of Art, London, where he later became a sculpture instructor. In 1932 he was made head of the sculpture department at Chelsea School of Art, remaining there until the outbreak of World War II.

The influences on Moore were many and varied, beginning with the medieval sculpture in his native Yorkshire. Historical influences included Mexican and Negro sculpture, Masaccio, Michelangelo, and Rodin. Of contemporary artists, probably Gaudier Brzeska, A. Modigliani, J. Epstein, and C. Brancusi were most important. Certain themes preoccupied Moore, although his work constantly evolved and changed. The reclining female figure, family group, and mother and child recur in his sculpture, and his preference for direct carving in wood or stone and his sensitivity to the nature of materials are evident. All his work partakes of a monumentality and abstraction that is characteristic of Moore alone. His many public monuments include the "Madonna and Child" for the Church of St. Matthew, Northampton (1943–44), the screen for the Time-Life Building, London (1952), and a reclining figure for Lincoln Center, New York (1962–65). (Sa. B.)

MUSKIE, EDMUND SIXTUS

One of the bright new faces to appear on the national political horizon in 1968 was that of Sen. Edmund Muskie of Maine, Democratic presidential nominee Hubert Humphrey's choice as a running mate.

A tall (6-ft. 4-in.), craggy-featured man with a faint resemblance to Abraham Lincoln, Muskie appealed to the voter's power to reason rather than to his emotions. Early in the campaign, Democrats who were unhappy with the choice of Humphrey responded to Muskie, many even suggesting it was too bad he was not running for the top spot. The son of a Polish immigrant whose original name was Marciszewski, Muskie campaigned heavily in Polish-American and other ethnic areas, seeking to counteract the influence of third-party candidate George Wallace, who found responsive audiences among many ethnic groups. Despite the ultimate Democratic loss, speculation immediately began that Muskie would move into a new position of leadership in the Senate and perhaps be a prime contender for the Democratic presidential nomination in 1972.

After serving in the Navy in World War II, Muskie ran for election to the Maine House of Representatives in 1946. He served there for six years, becoming minority leader of the few House Democrats. In 1952 he became Democratic national committeeman from Maine and in 1954 announced his candidacy for governor. Although Republicans far outnumbered Democrats in the state, Muskie was elected the first Democratic governor Maine had had in 20 years. The state legislature was controlled by Republicans, but he steered a nonpartisan course and succeeded in passing most of his program of educational and economic reforms. In 1958 he became the first popularly elected Democratic senator in Maine's history. In the Senate, he was the author of groundbreaking legislation dealing with federal-state-local relations and air and water pollution.

Muskie was born March 28, 1914. He attended Bates College, Lewiston, Me., and received a degree from Cornell Law School in 1939. Before entering the Navy he engaged in private law practice. (Ri. T. S.)

MYRDAL, (KARL) GUNNAR

In a monumental study published in March 1968, Swedish economist Gunnar Myrdal concluded that the abysmally low level of living in South Asia was caused by irrational attitudes and outmoded institutions rather than by a shortage of capital. The study, a three-volume, 2,284-page work financed by the Twentieth Century Fund at a cost of $250,000, took a decade to complete. Its title, *Asian Drama: An Inquiry into the Poverty of Nations,* was reminiscent of Adam Smith's *Inquiry into the Nature and Causes of the Wealth of Nations.*

The study deals chiefly with eight countries—India, Pakistan, Ceylon, Burma, Thailand, Malaysia, Indonesia, and the Philippines. Pointing out that four have parliamentary governments and four have authoritarian regimes, he stated that "it is impossible to say that one form of government has proved more conducive to the application of policies of economic and social reform than the other."

The Western concept of unemployment has little meaning in a society where many persons of working age are disinclined to engage in physical labour and where standards of performance are very low, he said. What is needed "is not the creation of job opportunities but an attempt to increase the number of persons who respond to existing opportunities." For agriculture, he suggested that South Asians might do well to make a deliberate policy choice in favour of capitalistic farming. Another conclusion was that economic development in South Asia cannot be realized unless the rate of population growth is checked.

Myrdal had established his reputation abroad with two other major works. The first, *Crisis in the Population Question* (1934), was written in collaboration with his wife, the former Alva Reimer, and dealt with Sweden's declining birthrate. The other was his classic study of the American Negro, financed by the Carnegie Corporation and published in 1944 under the title *An American Dilemma: The Negro Problem and Modern Democracy.*

Born on Dec. 6, 1898, in Gustaf Parish, Dalecarlia, Swed., Myrdal studied law and economics at the University of Stockholm. He served in the Swedish Senate in 1936–38, was minister of commerce from 1945 to 1947 and executive secretary of the UN Economic Commission for Europe from 1947 to 1957. (Mx. H.)

NEWTON, HUEY P.

A founder of the Black Panther Party in California, Huey Newton in 1968 almost became a martyr to the militant black cause. Involved in the death of an Oakland policeman, he was convicted of manslaughter. In discussing the possible consequences of a murder conviction for Newton, black activist James Forman told followers if he himself were killed, anti-establishment reprisal should be limited to "10 war factories, 15 power plants, 30 police stations, one southern governor, two mayors and 50 cops . . . But for Huey Newton, the sky's the limit."

The incident that brought Newton to trial began in September 1967, when he was stopped by Patrolman John Frey for a traffic check. According to another policeman's testimony, Newton was ordered from the car and as he walked away with Frey shooting started. The second officer, Herbert Hearnes, drew his pistol and was shot in the arm before he shot Newton in the stomach. Frey died; Newton pleaded not guilty. A jury deliberated the verdict for four days before returning the manslaughter finding. Newton was sentenced to 2 to 15 years in prison.

The case became a political issue, as it capped animosity between left-wing activists and the Oakland police. One result was to give the Black Panther Party a national prominence it would not otherwise have enjoyed, as Newton became a rallying point for anticonservatives of all stripes. Another result was the prisoner's nomination for Congress while his trial was in progress. The Black Panthers were able to extract this gesture from the radical Peace and Freedom Party in return for support in the black ghettos around San Francisco Bay.

Newton, who was 26, was born in New Orleans, La., and raised in Oakland. He attended junior college in Oakland and night school in San Francisco before devoting his time to the Black Panther Party, which he served as minister of defense. He first made headlines by carrying guns into the state legislature in Sacramento as part of a protest demonstration. Regarding his party, Newton said, "The Black Panther Party is against racism . . . It believes that the only culture worth holding on to is revolutionary culture." (Ph. K.)

BURT GLINN FROM MAGNUM
Richard Milhous Nixon

Lars Onsager
COURTESY, YALE UNIVERSITY

COURTESY, U.S. PUBLIC HEALTH SERVICE
Marshall W. Nirenberg

UPI COMPIX
Paul VI

NIRENBERG, MARSHALL W.

In recognition for his trailblazing research into the chemistry of genes, Marshall W. Nirenberg shared the 1968 Nobel Prize in Medicine or Physiology with two other U.S. scientists. He was specifically credited with the nonpareil accomplishment of cracking the genetic code.

Nirenberg first attracted attention in 1961 at the fifth International Congress of Biochemistry in Moscow when he delivered a ten-minute paper that has been called "the biological Rosetta stone." He had started from the previously proved premise that cells carry hereditary messages through the deoxyribonucleic acid (DNA) in the chromosomes. DNA is made up of four major large molecules, or nucleotides, shaped like a double spiral (helix) and containing simpler chemicals, purines and pyrimidines. The configuration of a helix, and hence its genetic message, is determined by the order in which its nucleotides are linked in combinations of threes.

Nirenberg first demonstrated that DNA does not work directly, but uses an intermediary, ribonucleic acid (RNA). In a criti-

cal experiment, he discovered that synthetic RNA containing only one pyrimidine served as a model for creating a protein with only one amino acid. He had decoded one three-letter combination. In repeated experiments he discovered the codes for virtually all 20 amino acids, the basic biochemical building blocks.

While Nirenberg "provided the very key" to nature's code for new cell generations, his thesis was confirmed and fleshed out by the independent research of Robert W. Holley and Har Gobind Khorana (qq.v.), with whom he shared the $70,000 Nobel stipend.

Nirenberg was born in New York City on April 10, 1927. He studied zoology at the University of Florida and received his Ph.D. in biochemistry from the University of Michigan. He joined the staff of the National Institute of Arthritis and Metabolic Diseases and performed genetic research under the auspices of the American Cancer Society and the U.S. Public Health Service. In 1962 he was named head of the biochemical genetics section of the National Heart Institute.   (Ph. K.)

NIXON, RICHARD MILHOUS

Former U.S. Vice-Pres. Richard M. Nixon, who just six years earlier had said he was through with politics, was elected as the country's 37th president on Nov. 5, 1968, in perhaps the most amazing political comeback in U.S. history. Nixon narrowly defeated Vice-Pres. Hubert Humphrey with 43.4% of the popular vote to Humphrey's 43% (third-party candidate George Wallace got 13.5%). Thus Nixon's share of the popular vote was the lowest for a winning candidate since Woodrow Wilson's 41.9% in 1912.

Republican Nixon ran on the tried and true theme that it was time for a change. He promised an "honorable end" to the war in Vietnam, though he declined to make specific proposals on the ground that it might interfere with the Paris peace talks. Less permissive law enforcement was another Nixon talking point. He directed his message to what he called the "forgotten Americans"—the often silent middle class. To attract youth there were his daughters, Tricia and Julie, and Julie's fiance, David Eisenhower, grandson of the former president (they were married in December).

Nixon had only token opposition for the Republican nomination. Gov. George Romney of Michigan dropped out of the race after the New Hampshire primary, and New York Gov. Nelson Rockefeller, who had considerable support among Eastern liberals, waited too long to announce his candidacy. A last-minute effort by California Gov. Ronald Reagan at the Republican national convention never got off the ground, though Nixon's choice of the little-known Spiro Agnew as his running mate was interpreted by some as the price he paid the Southern delegations for holding against Reagan.

Nixon entered politics in 1946 as a congressman from California. Four years later he won a seat in the Senate, and in 1952 he was selected to run for vice-president on the ticket headed by Dwight Eisenhower. His hard-hitting campaign tactics and his use of the "soft on Communism" theme earned him something of a reputation as "Tricky Dicky."

In 1960 Nixon lost the presidency to John F. Kennedy almost as narrowly as he won in 1968. Badly beaten in the 1962 race for California governor, he retired from politics at an emotional news conference and entered private law practice. But he reappeared to campaign for Republican candidates in 1964 and 1966 and gradually came to dominate the field of GOP presidential hopefuls. By 1968 he had emerged as a much smoother, more mature man, and his campaign, if it lacked the spark that some candidates ignite, was one of the most expensive and highly professional ever mounted.

Nixon was born Jan. 9, 1913, in Yorba Linda, Calif., and graduated from Whittier (Calif.) College and Duke University School of Law, Durham, N.C. He worked briefly for the Office for Emergency Management before entering the Navy in World War II.
(Ri. T. S.)

O'HORGAN, TOM

Theatrical director Tom O'Horgan "brought total nudity to Broadway"—which is to say his productions enjoyed audiences swelled by some who did not come to look at art. Nonetheless, his plays attracted serious theatregoers as well as voyeurs; Howard Junker, writing in Newsweek, pronounced that "his highly individual style has emerged as a major vision of the possibilities for American theater."

The play in question, Hair, moved to Broadway on April 29, 1968, after playing in

Greenwich Village, the neighbourhood of off-Broadway and off-off-Broadway where O'Horgan had been most active. It was at the Café La Mama, a mecca for theatrical experimenters, that O'Horgan directed some 30 plays written by unknowns. Ellen Stewart, manager of the theatre-coffeehouse, called him "the beautiful person who would always help the young playwrights no other director would touch."

This may have been a mixed blessing for the writers, since O'Horgan took great liberties with scripts. *Life*'s Tom Prideaux suggested, "He may change the theater from a writer's to a director's medium"—a development that would not be universally applauded. But "whatever O'Horgan invents for his actors to do—whether it is aisle-hopping, swinging on a rope above the audience, doing calisthenics or facing the audience totally nude—is a victory over theatrical dullness." This is to say he could smother a vapid script in original sauce.

A play with substance, as some thought *Futz!* to be, was obscured by the O'Horgan technique—though it still won him an Obie award. This perverse epic, which played at La Mama before moving to the off-Broadway Theatre de Lys in June 1968, concerned the malevolent reaction of witless hillbillies to a neighbour who loved a sow in his sty.

What O'Horgan seemed to be aiming at was a new sort of freedom for everyone connected with theatre—especially for the actor. It was noteworthy that the nude scene in *Hair* was gratuitous, and actors could appear on stage clothed or naked as they chose.

Forty-year-old O'Horgan went to New York from Chicago, where he had been a member of the noted Second City Company. After a quixotic early career, he performed in a seriocomic harp act and later directed Jean Genét's *The Maids*. He led the La Mama Troupe on three European tours and participated in the International Theatre Institute in Prague. Of his newfound notoriety, he said, "Obviously it means something if people are bothered, but it's sad after trying so long to evolve a personal style to be called the Minsky of our time." (Ph. K.)

ONSAGER, LARS

The 1968 winner of the Nobel Prize in Chemistry, Lars Onsager, a research chemist at Yale, was the man who added a "fourth law of thermodynamics" to the classic three principles of the science of heat. His complex theory involves the relationships of temperature and electricity, especially as they behave dynamically. Theoretical mysteries to laymen, the "reciprocity relations of Onsager" can be used to determine how heat and voltage relate to each other in an electrical conductor. Practical applications of his studies are found in such diverse fields as the synthesis of uranium-235 and the desalting of seawater.

As his Nobel citation noted, "the strange thing is that Onsager presented his law in 1931, but it was not until after the second World War that it attracted great attention." One manifestation of the belated attention, of course, was the Nobel Prize itself.

Onsager was born in Oslo, Nov. 27, 1903, and studied at the Norwegian Technical University and the Swiss Federal Technical University before joining the staff of Johns Hopkins University in Baltimore in 1928. The following year he was at Brown University, Providence, R.I., where he published his primary paper comprising the "fourth law" and his theories on irreversible chemical processes. He earned his Ph.D. at Yale in 1935, became an associate professor there in

1940, and was installed in the J. Willard Gibbs chair for theoretical chemistry in 1945, the year he was naturalized.

Perhaps the most startling application of his theoretical research relates to atomic energy. Shortly before World War II, when scientists were theorizing on the possibilities of thermonuclear weaponry, Onsager calculated how to create uranium-235, the basic fuel for nuclear reactors, from the more common uranium-238. He told a blue-ribbon conference of dubious scientists in Washington, D.C., that the two isotopes could be separated in gaseous form from tubes superheated on one side and cooled on the other. His theory was applied at Oak Ridge, Tenn., where the first gaseous-diffusion plant began operation in 1943, and the technique remained the primary method of acquiring uranium-235 in the 1960s.

(Ph. K.)

OSBORNE, JOHN

British dramatist John Osborne won recognition on three fronts in 1968: two of his plays, *Time Present* and *The Hotel in Amsterdam,* were being presented in London; his epoch-making earlier play, *Look Back in Anger,* was revived; and he married Jill Bennett, the leading actress in *Time Present.*

Osborne was born Dec. 12, 1929, the son of working-class parents. He left school at 15, tried his hand at journalism, and then became an actor at the age of 19. Soon afterward he began writing plays, and his fourth effort, *Look Back in Anger* (1956), brought him worldwide fame. It ushered in the so-called "new wave" of British drama, and, with its hero, Jimmy Porter, introduced the concept of the "angry young man." As with many of Osborne's later protagonists, Jimmy Porter was a bitter failure in a cruel and unjust society. The heroine of 1968's *Time Present* was, in effect, a female Jimmy Porter. (*See* Theatre.)

After *Look Back in Anger,* Osborne wrote *The Entertainer* (1957), starring Sir Laurence Olivier and inspired by Bertolt Brecht. *Epitaph for George Dillon,* written earlier, was staged in 1958. Then followed a musical, *The World of Paul Slickey* (1959); the historical *Luther* (1961); *Inadmissible Evidence* (1964); *A Patriot for Me* (1965); and *A Bond Honoured* (1966), adapted from a drama by Lope de Vega. Osborne's plays were performed in many parts of the world.

Woodfall Films, which Osborne co-founded with Tony Richardson, produced *Look Back in Anger,* the prizewinning *Tom Jones,* and *The Charge of the Light Brigade.* Osborne also wrote a play for television, *A Subject for Scandal and Concern,* later presented on stage. (O. Tr.)

PACHECO ARECO, JORGE

Jorge Pacheco Areco, elected vice-president of Uruguay in 1966, became president of that troubled South American republic when Pres. Oscar D. Gestido died in December 1967. The ensuing year was one of considerable trouble for Pacheco in his attempts to guide the destiny of his small nation. By training and education he was not well equipped to handle the complex economic problems facing him, but he was remarkably responsive to the advice of experts who realized that Uruguay could not be permitted to sink into financial chaos.

In June Pacheco took two steps that contributed largely in preserving the government from possible downfall: he froze prices and wages in the face of runaway inflation, and he declared a state of siege that remained in force. The first move was prompted by the 136% inflation spiral of

1967, and it slowed down the surge of 67% in the first six months of 1968. The second step involved a limited suspension of the constitutional process and was designed mainly to give Pacheco the right to ban strikes and public assemblies. The state of siege, however, did not prevent the government from finding itself repeatedly in confrontations with leftist students and other elements. The Communists dominated unions controlling half of the work force including the government employees, and strikes were called frequently throughout the year.

In spite of these setbacks Pacheco continued to work to achieve economic stability for his country. He negotiated a $40 million loan from the United States and worked out new trade deals with the Soviet Union, Bulgaria, Hungary, and Romania.

A member of one of the oldest families in Uruguay, Pacheco was born in 1920. He was a direct descendant of Capt. Jorge Pacheco, who fought beside Uruguay's national hero, José Artigas. For many years Pacheco worked as a newspaperman, becoming editor of a large daily paper in Montevideo. His political career had been relatively undistinguished when he was elected vice-president, but President Gestido increased his prestige by using him to negotiate with other factions of the ruling Colorado Party. (J. A. O'L.)

PAUL VI

During the fifth year of his reign, Pope Paul VI continued to make historic trips and to streamline the administration of the Roman Catholic Church, but his encyclicals and credos reemphasized basic conservative dogma that liberals had hoped would be changed. Following the trend set by his reorganization of the powerful Roman Curia, the pope reformed the papal court by eliminating many of the worldly trappings of splendour and creating instead a purely functional, strictly religious body. The Swiss Guard was retained, but many of the prestigious "black retinue" were dismissed; 30 laymen were chosen to advise the Vatican in specialized fields.

Although observers regarded the reforms as the most significant moves made by the pope during his reign, his encyclical *Humanae Vitae* ("Of Human Life") proved the most controversial development of the year, and possibly of his rule. The long-awaited document, issued July 28, reaffirmed the Vatican's opposition to any use of artificial birth control methods. It declared that the rhythm method, which was approved by the church, should not be employed as a regular practice. Abortion and direct sterilization of either sex also were banned. Widespread criticism was almost immediate. Liberal Catholics expressed belief that many would not follow the encyclical, and charged it had created an authority crisis within the church. The pope made frequent appeals for understanding and acceptance of the prohibition.

The first reigning pontiff to visit Latin America, Pope Paul traveled to Bogotá, Colombia, on August 22 to attend the 39th International Eucharistic Congress. While urging that the Latin-American church become more active in meeting the social needs of the continent, he stressed that *Humanae Vitae* "does not hinder any lawful therapy or the progress of scientific research," but rather excludes methods "which aim at resolving the

great problems of population with over-facile expedients."

On June 30 Pope Paul issued a 3,000-word "Credo of the People of God," stressing acceptance of church dogma. In other messages he reaffirmed the importance of clerical celibacy and deplored extremism among youth. On September 1 he conferred with Archbishop Makarios, president of Cyprus, on ways to strengthen cooperation between the Catholic and Orthodox churches. His quiet efforts to end the Vietnam war continued throughout the year.

Pope Paul, born Giovanni Battista Montini on Sept. 26, 1897, in Concesio, Italy, was crowned as pontiff on June 30, 1963. (*See* RELIGION: *Roman Catholic Church.*)

(J. F. BA.)

PLAZA LASSO, GALO

Election of Ecuador's Galo Plaza Lasso to be secretary-general of the Organization of American States (OAS) was regarded as the first major step by the Western Hemisphere nations to elevate the OAS from an ineffective debating society to a vital influence on the political, social, and economic future of the New World. When first approached to be a candidate for the secretary-generalship in the 1968 election, Plaza laid down the condition that he would only accept the nomination if his role would be executive and dynamic as well as ceremonial.

The 62-year-old Plaza brought to his new post vast experience not only in the government of his own small South American nation but in international affairs as well. As president of Ecuador from 1948 to 1952, he was regarded by many as the greatest chief executive that turbulent land had ever had. For the UN he performed highly successful missions as an observer and mediator in such trouble spots as the Congo, Cyprus, and Lebanon.

Plaza became secretary-general in May after winning a sixth-ballot victory in February, and it became his public policy to make the Pan American Union a more efficient organization as well as to upgrade the role of the OAS in terms of hemisphere relationships. He immediately launched on a series of trips to every member nation except the pariah, Communist Cuba, to reacquaint himself with the problems, aspirations, and conditions of each.

Plaza was born Feb. 17, 1906, in New York City, where his father, Gen. Leonidas Plaza Gutiérrez, twice a president of Ecuador, was on a diplomatic mission. The young Galo was educated at the universities of California and Maryland and later at the Georgetown University School of Foreign Service. Before his election as its president he served Ecuador as a senator and as minister of defense. Although he was friendly to the U.S. and was suspected by some Latins of being "pro-Yanqui," Plaza was strongly opposed to the 1965 intervention by the U.S. in the Dominican Republic. (J. A. O'L.)

POMPIDOU, GEORGES JEAN RAYMOND

A stroke of the pen, on July 10, 1968, was enough to send Georges Pompidou from the second highest office in France to the humble situation of deputy for the second constituency of the *département* of Cantal. For six years he had been the key figure of Gaullist rule, and leader of the majority. Now he was nothing—or almost nothing.

At the beginning of May, Pompidou could still see himself as the number one

candidate to succeed Charles de Gaulle as president of the republic. During the May–June crisis, he was almost the only member of the government who never lost his nerve. Indeed, it was thanks to his clearheadedness and daring that he was able, on May 12, to obtain from de Gaulle in five minutes everything that had been so obstinately refused since the first disturbances at the Sorbonne—the freeing of the imprisoned demonstrators and the promised university reform. Again, it was thanks to his obstinacy and skill that, on May 26–27, after 30 hours of negotiations with representatives of management and the trade unions, an agreement was concluded that eventually put an end to the strikes. Finally, it was thanks to his political acumen that de Gaulle agreed on May 30 to pronounce the dissolution of the National Assembly, and thanks to his skillful management that the legislative elections on June 23 and June 30 confirmed the triumph of the regime.

Nonetheless, ten days later he was dismissed, with a bouquet that was not without thorns. Observers noted that he had been right where de Gaulle had been wrong; he was no longer a servant, but almost a rival. Henceforth he would be hoping for a reversal of fortune—not in the favour of the sovereign but in the hearts of the public. Significantly, in a poll published on December 31, Pompidou headed the list as France's "man of the year."

Pompidou was born in 1911 into a family of schoolteachers in the Cantal. At the end of 1944 he held a post in de Gaulle's Cabinet, and later he became a member of the general's personal staff, while continuing his career in the Conseil d'État and then as a director of the Rothschild Bank. When de Gaulle returned to power in 1958, he made Pompidou director of his Cabinet during the transition between the Fourth and Fifth Republics. He was appointed as premier in April 1962. (P. V.-P.)

POWELL, (JOHN) ENOCH

Racism in Great Britain, which had become a growing problem as the number of coloured Commonwealth immigrants settling there increased, found a spokesman in 1968 in Enoch Powell, a Conservative politician who began to say publicly the sort of thing heretofore associated with Southern politicians in the U.S.

Though Powell had served in several Conservative governments, it was not until the Conservatives found themselves out of office after the 1964 general elections that he began to play a prominent part in British politics. He had established a reputation for independence by resigning from the Cabinet on an issue of financial economy in 1958 and by refusing to serve in the government of Sir Alec Douglas-Home. He had also given a hint of his political ambition when he unsuccessfully contested the election for leadership of the party in July 1965.

In 1968 Powell began to gain wider support by means of a series of provocative speeches. He had already set himself apart from the official Conservative economic policy by advocating the virtues of an unfettered free market economy. But it was when he drew attention to immigration policy that he became the centre of national controversy. Following a particularly outspoken attack in Birmingham on April 20, he was dismissed from the Conservative shadow cabinet by party leader Edward Heath, who said that the speech was "racist in tone and liable to exacerbate racial tensions." Opinion polls showed that Powell was winning an increasing measure of popular support. At the annual Conservative conference,

Mark Rudd

Nelson Aldrich Rockefeller

however, Heath was confirmed in his leadership and Powell's policies were rejected.

Powell was born in Birmingham June 16, 1912, the son of schoolteachers. He studied on scholarships at Cambridge University, where he was a brilliant classics scholar and became a fellow of Trinity College at the age of 22. At 25 he was professor of Greek at the University of Sydney, Austr. Serving in India during World War II, he became at 32 the Army's youngest brigadier. He entered politics after the war and was elected to Parliament from Wolverhampton South West in 1950. After holding junior ministerial posts, he served as minister of health from 1960 to 1963. (W. H. Ts.)

PREBISCH, RAÚL

Raúl Prebisch, a distinguished Argentine economist and government official, was elected in 1963 secretary-general of the United Nations Conference on Trade and Development (UNCTAD). This agency, formed under pressure from the less developed nations, held its second major conference in 1968. Meeting in New Delhi, India, from February 1 to March 29, the conference tried to narrow the gap between the views and desires of the less developed countries and those of the industrial nations. Success seemed unlikely, and Prebisch warned the conference that to avoid failure "patience, energy, determination, and imagination" were needed. He returned from New

Georges Pompidou

Enoch Powell

Galo Plaza Lasso

Delhi disillusioned and at the end of the year decided to give up his post of secretary-general, ostensibly on grounds of health and age.

The first UNCTAD had assembled in Geneva from March 23 to June 16, 1964, with 120 states represented. It recommended that the UN's role in international trade be enlarged and that new conciliation procedures aimed at changing the existing international division of labour be developed. That conference decided to establish in Geneva a permanent secretariat, with Prebisch as secretary-general.

Raúl Prebisch was born in Tucumán, Arg., on April 17, 1901. After graduating from the University of Buenos Aires, he was appointed first as a lecturer there and later as professor of political economy (1925–48). At the same time, he served in succession as deputy director of the Argentine Department of Statistics (1925–27), director of economic research at the National Bank of Argentina (1927–30), undersecretary at the Ministry of Finance (1930–32), and director general of the Central Bank of the Argentine Republic (1935–43). From 1950 to 1963 he was executive secretary of the UN Economic Commission for Latin America. (K. Sм.)

PROTOPOPOV, OLEG ALEKSEEVICH and LUDMILA EVGENIEVNA

One of the most outstanding figure skating teams the world has known, Soviet husband and wife Oleg and Ludmila Protopopov, in 1968 climaxed a triumphant career. At Grenoble, France, they won a second Olympic Games title, retaining the honour first gained at Innsbruck, Aus., in 1964. Eight of the panel of nine judges at Grenoble gave them 5.9 out of a possible 6 marks for artistic presentation, and six judges awarded them the same score for technical merit. More than 11,000 spectators breathlessly admired their skillfully timed split lutz lift and characteristic one-handed death spiral. Their smooth, ballet-like movements throughout a memorably efficient display included an extra long, superbly held forward spiral in commendable unison.

During the same season they also won both the world and European titles, each for the fourth consecutive time, at Geneva and at Västerås, Swed., respectively. Their achievements were all the more noteworthy, not only because they remained foremost international performers at the ages of 35 and 32, but also because neither took up the

sport until 16, much later than most championship skaters.

Protopopov began skating in Leningrad in 1948. Three years later he joined the Soviet Navy and in 1953 finished third in the U.S.S.R. pairs championships, partnered by Margarita Bogoyavlenskaya. Possibly unaware that there were only three entrants, his impressed naval commanders permitted him training time at a Moscow rink, where in 1954 he met Ludmila Belousova. They quickly teamed together, off the ice as well as on it, living first in Leningrad and then in Moscow where they trained under a former Soviet skating champion, Igor Moskvin.

At 5 ft. 9 in. and 152 lb., Protopopov was 50 lb. heavier and 6 in. taller than his wife. He was born in Leningrad on July 16, 1932. She was born at Ul'yanovsk on Nov. 22, 1935. Son of a ballerina, Protopopov loved music from childhood, and this background undoubtedly contributed to the artistic finesse of their skating. Now Honoured Masters of Soviet Sport, both were still students—Protopopov in the Hertzen Teachers Institute and his wife in the Railway Engineers Institute. (H. B.)

ROCKEFELLER, NELSON ALDRICH

New York Gov. Nelson Rockefeller conducted an intense on-again, off-again campaign in 1968, but the psychological moment slipped by, and he lost the Republican presidential nomination to Richard Nixon. As in 1960 and 1964, Rockefeller insisted early in 1968 that he would not be a candidate for the nomination under any circumstances, despite the urging of liberal elements of the Republican Party. He publicly supported the candidacy of Michigan Gov. George Romney.

Then the political situation changed: Romney withdrew and Pres. Lyndon Johnson announced he would not seek another term. Rockefeller changed his mind and declared his candidacy in late April. Once the decision was made, Rockefeller waged a strong campaign. Believing that Nixon was the choice of the party leaders, he took his campaign to the public through television, radio, and newspaper appeals. He called for an honourable end to the war in Vietnam, and declared he would avoid "future Vietnams" if elected. He promised to revamp U.S. foreign policy, placing greater importance on relations with Latin-American nations, and to adopt policies that would strengthen the U.S. economy.

But, again as in 1960 and 1964, the conservative elements in the party were too strong for him. In 1959 he had opposed Nixon, but withdrew in December of that year. In 1964 he won several primaries, but withdrew late in the campaign to support then Pennsylvania Gov. William Scranton. Attempting to speak at the '64 national convention, he was all but drowned out by Barry Goldwater's supporters. The Republicans at Miami Beach in '68 were politer, but Nixon won on the first ballot.

Born July 8, 1908, at Bar Harbor, Me., Rockefeller graduated from Dartmouth College in 1930. He helped manage several family enterprises before entering government service as an appointed official. He was elected governor of New York in 1958 and reelected in 1962 and 1966. (J. F. Ba.)

RUDD, MARK

A 20-year-old onetime Boy Scout leader, Mark Rudd, was the instigator of student demonstrations that closed Columbia University for two periods of several days each in spring 1968. The uprisings were symptomatic in the extreme of what was happening on large campuses everywhere: radical, politically aware students were making their presence known.

With energy undergraduates used to reserve for fraternal hazing and panty raids, Rudd and his New Left group at Columbia had attacked "the establishment" of the university. It was unlikely that their effort would have gone very far without a local cause célèbre that led campus moderates into joining with the radicals. Rudd's organization, Students for a Democratic Society (SDS), was a very loose confederation of campus groups noted for its absence of real structure and effectiveness.

The rallying point at Columbia was the apparent callousness of Pres. Grayson Kirk's administration in taking over part of a neighbourhood park to build a gymnasium. Essentially peaceful demonstrations were organized and escalated. New York City police overreacted, putting down the demonstrations with what a fact-finding commission determined was unnecessary force. In their course demonstrators took over a number of university buildings, including Kirk's office, for days. The upshot was that the university acceded to several SDS demands, work on the gym was halted, and Kirk, whose administration was widely regarded as dictatorial, resigned. Rudd, with several dozen others, was suspended, and a tenuous peace returned to the campus.

What had became clear was that a radical minority could impose radical demands on the total community. It was typical of the New Left, however, that Rudd and company were content to strike out against the status quo; they offered no concrete, positive proposals or solutions to problems.

Rudd exemplified the New Left leader. He was a bright European history major earning a B+ average. He became enamoured of radical political thought through reading Marx and contemporary leftist writer Herbert Marcuse. In Maplewood, N.J., his father said, "We're glad Mark has time to spend on activities like politics." The elder Rudds, children of immigrants, had not enjoyed such luxuries.   (Ph. K.)

SERVAN-SCHREIBER, JEAN-JACQUES

Having sold 500,000 copies in France in 19 weeks and a million in Europe, and having run to 16 foreign editions, Jean-Jacques Servan-Schreiber's *Le Défi Américain* (*The American Challenge*) was more than an outstanding best seller in 1968. It was a dramatic warning to Europe that had taken on the importance of a political event. The facts were not new, nor the ideas. But they had never been brought together and synthesized so that the public was brutally confronted with them in all their simplicity and force: In 15 years the third industrial power in the world, after the U.S. and the U.S.S.R., might well be U.S. industry in Europe. In 30 years four countries—the U.S., Canada, Japan, and Sweden—would advance to the stage of post-industrial societies. Without an immediate mobilization Europe would no longer belong to the same world.

Jean-Jacques Servan-Schreiber refused to believe in the inevitability of this sensational historical development. He analyzed the subtle mechanism of the U.S. conquest and declared that there was still time to fight back—not with dollars, machines, or oil but with creative imagination and organizing talent. The 150 pages he devoted to a review of Europe's resources for counterattack might be, in his words, "not a history book, but, with a little luck, a handbook for action."

This program was consistent with the political beliefs of the man who in 1953 founded the weekly *L'Express,* who from 1952 to 1955 collaborated with Pierre Mendès-France, and who in 1963–65 supported the candidacy of Gaston Deferre for the presidency of the French Republic. Born on Feb. 13, 1924, and graduated from the École Polytechnique in 1943, Servan-Schreiber joined the Free French as a fighter pilot. Called up as a lieutenant for Algeria in 1956, he published *Lieutenant d'Algérie* on his return and was prosecuted on a charge of undermining the morale of the Army. The trial ended with the prosecution unable to prove its case. In 1968 he was chief director of a press group that controlled Presse-Union (*L'Express*), Technic-Union (specialized magazines), and Liste-Union (computer card-indexing).   (S. Ls.)

SHAABI, QAHTAN MUHAMMAD AL-

On Nov. 30, 1967, the British colony and protectorate of Aden and South Arabia became an independent nation, the People's Republic of Southern Yemen. Qahtan Muhammad al-Shaabi, leader of the National Liberation Front (NLF) of Southern Yemen, became both first president and prime minister of the new Arab country.

The NLF, composed of young nationalists, had been created in January 1963 to oppose the British-sponsored Federation of South Arabia, which was dominated by conservative sultans and sheikhs and which the British planned to make the nucleus of an independent South Arabian state. The U.A.R., however, hoped to dominate South Arabia after the British had left. When U.A.R. Pres. Gamal Abd-al-Nasser discovered that al-Shaabi, as head of the NLF, would not be his obedient tool, he ordered the formation of the Front for the Liberation of South Yemen (FLOSY), headed by Abdul Qawi Mackawi. In January 1966 Nasser invited al-Shaabi and Mackawi to Cairo and advised them to join forces. Al-Shaabi refused. His goal was a unified republic of South Arabia comprising both the British territories and Yemen proper, while Cairo wanted the British territories incorporated within an aggrandized republican Yemen under U.A.R. domination. Al-Shaabi was placed under house arrest in Cairo and was not permitted to return to South Arabia until 1967, two months after the U.A.R. military disaster in the Arab-Israeli war. That defeat had reduced U.A.R. influence in Yemen and had led to the eclipse of FLOSY.

The British took the opportunity to abandon the Federation of South Arabia and to negotiate with the NLF, which by October 1967 had gained control of all the states in the federation. As a result of a conference in November 1967 between a British delegation led by Lord Shackleton and an NLF delegation led by al-Shaabi, the British agreed to grant immediate independence to the People's Republic of Southern Yemen.

Al-Shaabi was born about 1925 at Lahij, which was to become the western province of the new republic. He was educated in Aden and at the University of Khartoum, Sudan, where he was graduated. While working in Lahij as an agricultural officer in the 1950s, he joined the South Arabian League, proved himself an able organizer, and settled in Cairo when the league was banned in Aden in 1957.   (K. Sm.)

SHAFFER, PETER LEVIN

One of Britain's leading dramatists, Peter Shaffer returned to the London stage in 1968 after a four-year absence with a twin bill of plays, *The White Liars* and the hilarious, prizewinning *Black Comedy*. Both were well received though they did not gain the critical and popular acclaim of Shaffer's last offering, *The Royal Hunt of the Sun,*

Peter Shaffer
CAMERA PRESS—PIX FROM PUBLIX

Jean-Jacques Servan-Schreiber

Aleksandr I. Solzhenitsyn
CAMERA PRESS—PIX FROM PUBLIX

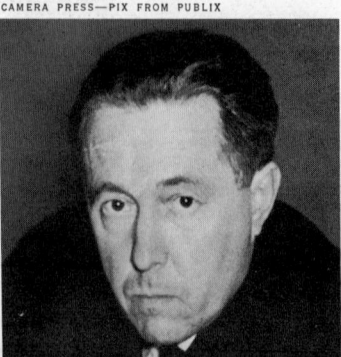

D.P.A. FROM PICTORIAL PARADE

Axel Springer

a historical drama about the treacherous European conquest of Peru.

Shaffer, unlike many of his contemporaries among British playwrights, was born of well-to-do parents, in Liverpool on May 15, 1926. He attended St. Paul's School and Cambridge University. This background may have contributed to his aversion for the school of "kitchen-sink drama" and his preference for middle-class settings in his plays.

After graduation from Cambridge, Shaffer went to the U.S., where he worked in the New York City Public Library and wrote his first play, a "modern" classical tragedy set in Israel called *The Salt Land*. Never performed on the stage, it was presented on British television in 1955. BBC radio broadcast Shaffer's *The Prodigal Father*, written when he was working for a London music publisher.

Shaffer first gained prominence in 1958 when Sir John Gielgud directed his first play to be staged in London, *Five Finger Exercise*. A study of the nature of violence and abnormality in personal relations, it ran for 609 performances in London, won various critics' awards, and later was successful on the Broadway stage and as a film. Shaffer's other works include *The Private Ear* and *The Public Eye* (1962), a comic double bill, and the filmscript of William Golding's novel *Lord of the Flies* (1963).   (O. TR.)

SOLZHENITSYN, ALEKSANDR ISAEVICH

A onetime Soviet Army officer, a victim of Stalinist forced labour camps rehabilitated in the Khrushchev era, and a novelist of genius, Aleksandr Isaevich Solzhenitsyn marked his 50th birthday in 1968 without the honours usually accorded to public figures in the U.S.S.R. Although his two major novels, *Cancer Ward* and *The First Circle*, were being translated and read throughout the rest of the world, at home Solzhenitsyn was the centre of an extraordinarily bold attack on literary censorship.

Three short stories and his first novel, *One Day in the Life of Ivan Denisovich*, were published in the U.S.S.R. in 1962, but after that nothing by him appeared. Early in 1967 he called for the abolition of censorship, asking the Soviet Writers' Union to defend wronged writers instead of hounding them. The letter remained a clandestine document in the U.S.S.R., but its publication in Paris by *Le Monde* led to charges that he was "providing material help to the capitalist world." Solzhenitsyn received support, particularly from Aleksandr T. Tvardovski, the editor of the journal *Novy Mir*.

At a hearing before the Writers' Union in September 1967, he was told that if he wished to be helped by the union he must first publish a declaration protesting "against the dirty way his name was being made use of in the West." Solzhenitsyn replied that he could not make such a declaration because, as neither *Cancer Ward* nor *The First Circle* had been published in the U.S.S.R., no Russian reader would understand what it was all about. No official sanctions were taken against him, and he continued to teach in provincial Ryazan as an "unperson" whose name did not appear in public print in the U.S.S.R.

Solzhenitsyn was born on Dec. 11, 1918, at Kislovodsk in the south of Russia and graduated in physics and mathematics from the University of Rostov-on-Don. He was decorated for bravery several times during World War II, but in 1945 was arrested and sent to a labour camp for making obliquely critical remarks on Stalin in letters to a friend. After Stalin's death he was released from the labour camp and exiled to Central Asia where he developed and was cured of

cancer. In 1957, a year after Nikita S. Khrushchev had denounced Stalinism, he was declared innocent.   (K. SM.)

SOYINKA, WOLE

Wole Soyinka, a leading Nigerian author and an outspoken critic of the Nigerian-Biafran war, was several times reported to have been killed in 1968, but at the year's end he was still alive, though a prisoner of the Nigerian federal government. At 34, Soyinka had become one of Africa's outstanding writers and had involved himself closely with the political storms that had rocked his country since its independence in 1960. In 1965 he was arrested for holding up a radio announcer at the point of a gun and forcing him to switch a tape that announced an election result against the party supported by Soyinka. He was later acquitted on a technicality. Two years later he was arrested and detained without trial while acting as a liaison agent between Nigerian federal leaders and the Biafrans in an effort to halt the civil war. Although he was a Yoruba and not an Ibo (the predominant people of Biafra), Soyinka was an outspoken opponent of continuing the bitter civil war.

Born in 1934, Soyinka was educated at Ibadan University (Nigeria) and Leeds University (England). After working as a lecturer and as head of the department of English at Lagos University in Nigeria, he was appointed director of the School of Drama at Ibadan University; he was, however, arrested before taking up that post.

A writer of great versatility, Soyinka also had considerable success as a producer and manager of his own theatre company. *The Strong Breed* was performed in London in 1968, and other plays include *The Lion and the Jewel*, *The Trials of Brother Jero*, *Kongi's Harvest*, and *The Road*. The last play won first prize at the Dakar Festival of Negro Arts (1960) and was staged in London in 1965. He received a British Arts Council award for 1966–67 as a playwright. As a poet, Soyinka became known chiefly for *Idanre and Other Poems* (1965).

Soyinka's literary specialty was political satire; in the years before the collapse of the Nigerian federation he won a wide following for the sharpness of his attacks on the politicians of the day and on the social life of Nigeria.   (Co. L.)

SPRINGER, AXEL

The largest newspaper publishing organization on the European continent was owned by Axel Springer. His concern accounted for nearly 40% of the total circulation of West German daily newspapers. It produced five dailies, *Die Welt, Bild Zeitung* (circulation about 4.5 million), *Hamburger Abendblatt, Berliner Morgenpost,* and *BZ;* two Sunday papers, *Welt am Sonntag* and *Bild am Sonntag;* and two radio and television weeklies, *Hör Zu* (4.3 million) and *Funk Uhr.* The size of the Springer business was largely responsible for the concern about growing concentration in the West German newspaper industry. Indeed, if the circulation of *Bild Zeitung* was taken into account, Springer's share of the national— as distinct from the regional or local—press was as high as 88%.

Springer had adopted four guiding principles by which all his publications were supposed to abide: support for the reunification of Germany; reconciliation of Germans and Jews; rejection of every form of totalitarianism; and promotion of the social market economy. Within "these four compass points of a tolerant outlook on the world," every Springer man was entitled to express his own views. In fact, the Springer Press mainly projected a political

view that was far to the right and highly intolerant of dissenting minorities.

After the attempted assassination of the left-wing student leader Rudi Dutschke at Easter, students attacked Springer offices in a number of cities. Springer said the campaign was directed from several sources —extreme left-wingers who were displeased because his newspapers refused to submit to Communist demands; competitors who had jumped on the bandwagon in the hope of making life difficult for him; and those people who attacked the establishment with the same kind of hatred that the Nazis had felt for the Weimar Republic.

Springer was born on May 2, 1912, in Altona, a suburb of Hamburg. His father owned a printing plant and a local newspaper, where he acquired his knowledge of the business. Because of his clean record during the Nazi period, he received a publishing license from the occupying forces soon after the end of World War II.   (N. CR.)

STEVENS, SIAKA PROBYN

When Sierra Leone's short-lived military regime decided to return the soldiers to the barracks, it entrusted 63-year-old Siaka Probyn Stevens with the task of setting up a new civilian government with himself as prime minister. This action brought to a full circle a political upheaval that started in 1967 when Siaka Stevens' party was denied an electoral victory by the defeated prime minister, Sir Albert Margai. Thus, late in life, Sierra Leone's most turbulent politician finally achieved power.

Siaka Stevens was born on Aug. 24, 1905, in Sierra Leone, then a British colony. He became a policeman when he was 18, but after rising to the rank of sergeant he decided to become a railwayman instead; this led him into labour politics. He helped to form the United Mineworkers' Union in 1943 and was soon embroiled in labour disputes that marked him as a militant orator of considerable power and a menace to the colonial authorities. When he was 42, he obtained a scholarship to study industrial relations at Ruskin College, Oxford. After his return to Sierra Leone, he was elected to the colonial legislature; and after internal self-government was granted to Sierra Leone, he became minister of lands, mines, and labour in 1953. But he continued to be a controversial figure and soon quarreled with the ruling party. As a stormy opposition leader, Stevens refused to accept all the conditions for independence negotiated with Britain, and he proceeded to build up his own political party. By 1967 his forces were strong enough to win an electoral majority.

A tall, well-built, quiet-spoken man, Siaka Stevens had lost little of the fire that marked his turbulent life; but with a country almost bankrupt and disrupted by military coups, he appeared to be facing his biggest challenges.   (Co. L.)

STYRON, WILLIAM

An astonishing historical novel, *The Confessions of Nat Turner,* earned the Pulitzer Prize for fiction—and some brickbats—for William Styron in 1968.

The book is a fictional exploration into the experience and surroundings of the Negro who organized the most famous slave rebellion in American history, inspiring a band of blacks who killed about 50 whites around Southampton County, Va., in 1831.

Using a document the real Turner dictated in jail before his execution, Styron sought to get inside the slave's mind through the daring use of first-person narrative.

The novel was guaranteed to cause controversy. James Baldwin, the eminent Negro writer and a personal friend of Styron, predicted that "Bill's going to catch it from black and white," and he did. Some whites undoubtedly used the book's superficial specifics to reinforce their own simplistic bigotry, while several prominent black writers accused Styron of perpetuating white misunderstanding and bolstering essentially racist mythology. Still, many people felt they had gained an understanding of the Negro psyche and agreed with Baldwin's verdict that it was "a very courageous book that attempts to fuse the two points of view, the master's and the slave's. . . . He has begun the common history—ours."

Financially, the effort was an unalloyed success. *Harper's Magazine* paid $7,500 for an excerpt, the highest fee in the magazine's 117-year history. The Book-of-the-Month Club paid $150,000, setting another precedent. Paperback rights brought $100,000 and film rights sold for over $600,000.

Styron was born near the scene of his subject, in Newport News, Va., June 11, 1925. He encountered the history of Nat Turner's rebellion as a boy and, after attending Davidson College and Duke University, discussed it with a writing teacher and editor as early as 1947. His first book, *Lie Down in Darkness* (1951), won the Prix de Rome. The next year brought *The Long March,* an account of brutality in the Marines which he wrote in Paris. He may have borrowed on his own experience as an expatriate for *Set This House on Fire* (1960), which portrayed Americans in Rome after World War II.　　(PH. K.)

SVOBODA, LUDVIK

When Ludvik Svoboda was made "Hero of the Czechoslovak Socialist Republic" and also "Hero of the Soviet Union" in 1965, the old man could certainly have expected nothing more than a quiet life in retirement. On March 30, 1968, however, the National Assembly elected him sixth president of the Czechoslovak Republic. It was Alexander Dubcek, the new first secretary of the Communist Party of Czechoslovakia, who successfully recommended Svoboda's candidature to the three parties of the National Front as the man most agreeable to the U.S.S.R.

Svoboda's first months in office were, for a man of 72, very exhausting indeed. No mere titular head of state in the mold of other Communist chairmen of presidiums or legislative assemblies, Svoboda showed himself as a man of courage and character. After the occupation of Czechoslovakia on August 20–21 by the armies of the Warsaw Treaty Organization, Svoboda stood firmly by Dubcek, whom the Soviets wanted to disgrace and dismiss from office.

Svoboda was born on Nov. 25, 1895, at Hroznatin, in Moravia. He was studying agronomy when World War I broke out. Mobilized in the Austro-Hungarian Army, he deserted to the Russians to fight against the Central Powers. After the war he managed his father's farm before joining the Czechoslovak Army in 1922. After the German occupation of Prague in 1939 he took refuge in Poland and later the U.S.S.R., where he formed the first battalion of the Czechoslovak Army in Russia. On Oct. 6,

1944, he was back on Czechoslovak soil with the Soviet Army.

When Edvard Benes formed his government in 1945, he appointed Svoboda, under Soviet pressure, minister of defense. In 1948, when Benes surrendered to Klement Gottwald, the Communist leader, Svoboda, then 53, joined the Communist Party. Two years later Stalin told Gottwald that he did not trust Svoboda, and the general was dismissed forthwith. He held a minor administrative post on a collective farm until 1955, when Nikita S. Khrushchev inquired what "his friend Svoboda" was doing. Pres. Antonin Novotny of Czechoslovakia then appointed him commandant of the Czechoslovak Military Academy, a job from which he retired in 1959 with the rank of army general.　　　　(K. SM.)

THADDEN, ADOLF VON

Adolf von Thadden, chairman of the National Democratic Party—frequently characterized as neo-Nazi—had been at the forefront of right-wing extremist politics in West Germany since shortly after World War II. He was elected to the first federal parliament in 1949 as a member of the Deutsche Reichspartei (DRP), but lost his seat four years later when a new electoral law limited representation in the Bundestag to parties with at least 5% of the total vote.

The NPD was formed in Lower Saxony in November 1964, as the result of a fusion of the DRP with the Deutsche Partei and other conservative groups. From the start, Thadden dominated the party, but he was not elected chairman until 1967, when he won a struggle for power against the more moderate Fritz Thielen.

Born on July 7, 1921, in Pomerania, where his family owned extensive estates, Thadden joined the Army soon after passing his university entrance examination and served throughout World War II on the eastern front. As an officer commanding an assault battery, he was wounded several times. He was taken prisoner by the U.S. forces and released from a camp in Austria in the summer of 1945. He was an obligatory member of the Hitler Youth, but contended that he was never in the Nazi Party. Indeed, his sister was executed by the Nazis after the 1944 bomb plot against Hitler.

His party had a primitive nationalistic appeal, and much of its ideology and language were reminiscent of the Third Reich. Thadden, a tireless worker and an accomplished mob orator, displayed a remarkable capacity for exploiting national sentiments, and was largely responsible for developing the NPD into a movement to be reckoned with. Within four years, the party had succeeded in winning 60 seats in seven state parliaments—although state elections in the fall of 1968 reversed this trend.　　(N. CR.)

THUY, XUAN

In 1968 Xuan Thuy (pronounced Swan Twee), chief North Vietnamese negotiator in the Paris peace talks, showed the United States what it meant to negotiate Hanoi-style. Week after week, he confronted U.S. negotiators W. Averell Harriman and Cyrus Vance with unyielding propaganda in public, while in private conducting delicate negotiations that yielded some small progress by the end of the year.

Thuy's careful tactic began at the opening of the talks on May 13, when he announced that an "essential precondition" for negotiations on a peace settlement must be a total halt in U.S. bombing of North Vietnam. U.S. Pres. Lyndon B. Johnson had already ordered a partial halt on March 31 and refused to go further until the North Vietnamese promised some gesture of reci-

procity. For the next 5½ months Harriman and Thuy did not move beyond this basic deadlock in public.

But by late June it had become clear that the informal discussions that occurred during the 45-minute coffee or tea breaks at the conferences were more productive. The first real break came on October 19, when the North Vietnamese privately told Harriman that they accepted the U.S. formula for stopping all bombing of the North. North Vietnam would not abuse the Demilitarized Zone between North and South Vietnam, nor shell cities in the South. The government of South Vietnam could join the talks on the U.S. side, while the Viet Cong's political front would join North Vietnam. The U.S. stopped its bombing on November 1. But the vagueness of the formula did not suit the South Vietnamese government, which resented being equated with the Viet Cong. Xuan Thuy took advantage of the subsequent quarrel between the U.S. and South Vietnam by insisting that the resumed peace talks would be among four equal parties, thereby giving legitimacy to the Viet Cong.

Xuan Thuy was born in the outskirts of Hanoi on Sept. 2, 1912. As a young man he fought against French rule in Indochina. For six years after the outbreak of World War II he was in prison, where he ran an underground Communist newspaper. He first worked as a diplomat during the long Indochina war (1947–54) against the French. After that war ended he served as North Vietnam's representative at various left-wing peace meetings.　　(G. F. SH.)

TINY TIM

The musical curiosity of 1968 was Tiny Tim, an almost middle-aged boy soprano with shoulder-length hair and a left-handed ukulele. With an astonishing falsetto he rose to the top of "the charts" with the sort of songs Rudy Vallee and Al Jolson made famous; he made an album of these, dedicated it to his septuagenarian parents, and sold 150,000 copies in the first 15 weeks.

Why the sudden interest in an atavistic balladeer? The press tried manfully to explain, but usually was forced to settle for describing the phenomenon. According to the *Washington Post,* he appeared a "sartorial blunder," wearing a black raincoat, checked sports jacket, wide brown tie, and green socks. *Newsweek* dutifully described "the face of a teen-age vampire and the mannerisms of a music hall diva" before trying to fathom the genesis of the whole business: "His origins are shrouded in mystery, but apparently he was born some 45 years ago on West 81st Street in Manhattan, the son of a Lebanese textile worker and a Yiddish momma." Since coming into the world as Herbert Khaury, he had been known by various aliases, among them Emmett Swink, Rollie Dell, Darry Dover, and Larry Love, the Singing Canary.

Earlier in his musical career "I went from dive to dive and bar to bar all over New York and New Jersey," he recalled. One memorable place he appeared was Hubert's Museum (cum Flea Circus) on Times Square. He was on the Greenwich Village bôite circuit for a time until he improvised a gig at The Scene, a Manhattan nightery that adopted him as the darling of the disco-set and launched his rise to broader public acclaim.

What did it all mean? He was called "the Douanier Rousseau of pop music" and "one of the last true innocents." Few successfully explained the why of "the most bizarre entertainer this side of Barnum & Bailey's side show." The performer himself said that the spirits of singers whose songs he sings live within him.

Tiny Tim was a fastidious man who claimed he took a 90-minute shower every day and brushed his teeth six times daily, with toothpaste and papaya powder. His diet consisted of pumpkin seeds, sunflower seeds, honey, and wheat germ. He made his home with his parents (when he was in New York) or in a California motel. "I really believe I'm 19," he said, "and I try to stay that way." (PH. K.)

TRUDEAU, PIERRE ELLIOTT

A comparative newcomer to national politics, wealthy bachelor Pierre Elliott Trudeau, was elected head of Canada's Liberal Party on April 6, 1968, and became the nation's 15th prime minister April 20 when Lester B. Pearson retired at the age of 70. Two months later, on June 25, Trudeau led his party to a decisive victory in the national elections, ending the precarious minority rule under which Pearson and his Conservative predecessor, John G. Diefenbaker, had governed since 1962.

The secret of Trudeau's success appeared to be mainly a matter of his unconventional personality and his unorthodox approach to politics. As an unconventional thinker he appealed to intellectuals and as a "swinger" and bon vivant he attracted an enthusiastic following among the younger set. He was better known for his sports cars, miniskirted girl friends, and offbeat attire than for his views on political issues. On the serious side, Trudeau was unusual as a French-Canadian who spoke out against special status for Quebec.

Trudeau built his campaign around a commitment to create a "Just Society." This was the central theme of the speech from the throne, read by Gov.-Gen. Roland Michener when Parliament met September 12. The government said it wanted Parliament to begin dealing at once with the pressing problems of youth, poverty, regional disparities, unemployment, urban growth, and housing.

Trudeau was born in Montreal on Oct. 18, 1919, the son of a Scottish mother and a French-Canadian father, and was equally at home in French and English. As a young man he traveled widely, studying at Harvard, the University of Paris, and the London School of Economics and visiting the U.S.S.R. at Soviet government expense. Before entering politics, he taught constitutional law and wrote on social and political affairs. He was sharply critical of the Liberal Party's stand in 1963 in favour of accepting U.S. nuclear weapons on Canadian soil, but in 1965 he was induced to become a Liberal candidate for a seat in the House of Commons. He won easily and soon became a part of the Pearson government as parliamentary secretary to the prime minister and later as minister of justice. (Mx. H.)

UPDIKE, JOHN

John Updike, probably America's most steadily prolific young writer, eclipsed his rather quiet critical success in 1968 with *Couples,* a best seller describing the socio-sexual goings-on behind the traditional facade of a quiet New England town; movie rights sold for $500,000. The novel, his fifth, marked a distinct and perhaps welcome departure from his habitual literary concern: themes and situations borrowed from his own impecunious youth in Pennsylvania. Though the place names might have been changed, *The Poorhouse Fair* (1959), *Rabbit Run* (1960), *The Centaur* (1963); and *Of the Farm* (1965) were read as quasi-autobiographical extrapolations.

The author, whose father was a phone company worker turned teacher and Lu-

IVAN MASSAR FROM BLACK STAR
John Updike

WIDE WORLD
Ludvik Svoboda

UPI COMPIX
Tiny Tim

WIDE WORLD
Pierre Elliott Trudeau

Adolf von Thadden
PIERRE BOULAT, "LIFE" MAGAZINE © TIME INC.

theran deacon during the depression of the 1930s, was born March 18, 1932, in West Reading, Pa., and raised in the village of Shillington, Pa. He attended public schools until he won a full scholarship to Harvard, where he was president of the *Lampoon* and was cited for writing the best undergraduate short story. He graduated summa cum laude in 1954, studied fine arts at Oxford on a year's fellowship, and joined the staff of *The New Yorker* magazine.

Influenced by James Thurber, Robert Benchley, and Wolcott Gibbs, Updike contributed essays to the *New Yorker*'s celebrated weekly column "The Talk of the Town." About the same time the magazine began to carry his often whimsical poetry and well-turned short stories. Many of these were collected in *The Same Door* (1959) and *Pigeon Feathers* (1962); the poems were anthologized in *The Carpentered Hen* (1958) and *Telephone Poles and Other Poems* (1963). *Assorted Prose* (1965) contained many of his nonfiction pieces.

Updike had been quite widely read, but there seemed to be a healthy lack of unanimity among the critics. Fellow novelist John Barth called him "The Andrew Wyeth of literature"; John W. Aldridge declared he "has nothing to say." While the release of *Couples*, with its more ambitious scope, might lead some to temper their remarks, Updike would probably remain "kind of elegiacally concerned with the Protestant middle class." He received the National Book Award for *The Centaur* and the Rosenthal Award of the National Institute of Arts and Letters, which, in 1964, elected him a member of its department of literature. (Ph. K.)

VANCE, CYRUS R.

The Johnson administration's top domestic and international peacemaker, Cyrus R. Vance, in 1968 undertook his most demanding and important assignment to date—the task of trying to bring an end to the war in Vietnam through negotiations in Paris between the U.S. and North Vietnam.

Enlarging the reputation he had acquired as Pres. Lyndon B. Johnson's leading troubleshooter, Vance applied his talent to other delicate problems during the year. On February 9 he was dispatched by the president to Seoul, South Korea, for discussions with South Korean Pres. Pak Chung Hi, who felt that the U.S. should take a harder line on North Korean terrorist activities and the capture by that country of the U.S. intelligence ship "Pueblo." Following a week of talks, Vance emerged with a compromise agreement.

Before President Johnson curtailed U.S. bombing of North Vietnam, in March, Vance reportedly was one of nine informal advisers who told the president that the increasing military efforts in Vietnam had not accomplished their purpose. He was pressed into domestic service in April during the rioting in Washington, D.C., following the murder of the Rev. Martin Luther King, Jr., and spent six days coordinating antiriot strategy between the White House and the Washington authorities. Hardly had that assignment ended when he was named by the president to be deputy to Ambassador W. Averell Harriman in the negotiations with North Vietnam. These discussions began on May 10 and lasted through the rest of the year. Vance periodically took over the talks when Harriman was absent and met with North Vietnamese participants to supplement Harriman's efforts.

Vance began undertaking such missions for President Johnson after resigning as deputy secretary of defense in 1967. In that year he served as presidential representative during the Detroit riots and was also named as a mediator in the dispute between Greece and Turkey in Cyprus.

A lawyer by profession, Vance was born March 27, 1917, in Clarksburg, W.Va. He received a B.A. in economics from Yale in 1939 and an LL.B. from Yale Law School in 1942. He joined the Department of Defense in 1961 as its general counsel, subsequently becoming secretary of the army and deputy secretary of defense. (D. Fo.)

WALLACE, GEORGE CORLEY

The U.S. is accustomed to the two-party system, especially in presidential years, and a strong third-party candidate drives politicians frantic and sends constitutional lawyers scurrying for their precedents. Such a candidate appeared in 1968 in the person of George Wallace, the fiery former governor of Alabama. He received a larger percentage of the popular vote (13.5) than any third-party candidate since Robert La Follette in 1924, won more electoral votes (46) than any since Teddy Roosevelt in 1912, and almost sent the election into the House of Representatives.

In the last analysis, however, his candidacy proved to be sectional. The five states he won were in the South, and the white Northern factory workers, though they provided him with enthusiastic audiences, failed to vote for him in large numbers. Most observers felt Wallace damaged his chances when he named as his running mate former Air Force Gen. Curtis LeMay, whose outspoken support for a military solution in Vietnam may have frightened otherwise sympathetic voters.

Wallace's campaign actually began in 1966 when, barred from a second consecutive term as governor by the Alabama constitution, he successfully ran his wife, Lurleen, for the office, thus retaining his base of power. Mrs. Wallace died in May 1968, but after a period of mourning Wallace continued his campaign. By election day his name was on the ballot in all 50 states and was backed by a large volunteer organization.

Wallace drew larger crowds than either Democrat Hubert Humphrey or Republican Richard Nixon. He also drew swarms of hecklers, but he soon learned to use them to whip up his supporters. Much of his appeal was implicitly racist. Yet he also spoke to the problems facing the country—the breakdown of law and order, the frustrating war in Vietnam, growing disrespect for long-accepted institutions and attitudes. Wallace on the right and Eugene McCarthy on the left demonstrated that millions of Americans were ready to leave the old political patterns.

Wallace was born Aug. 25, 1919, in Clio, Ala., and received a law degree from the University of Alabama. Elected governor in 1962, he first achieved national prominence in June 1963 when he "stood in the schoolhouse door" in an attempt to bar blacks from the University of Alabama. (Ri. T. S.)

WILSON, (JAMES) HAROLD

Harold Wilson, British prime minister since October 1964, played a deliberately inconspicuous role in British politics in 1968, but even so he became the scapegoat for disenchantment within his own Labour Party and for the frustrations of the opposition parties. In the early months of the year some members of his own party called for his resignation; he was mobbed by demonstrators on a number of occasions when he

undertook engagements outside London; and the opinion polls registered the lowest popularity ratings for a prime minister in office ever recorded. Meanwhile, his party suffered catastrophic defeats at by-elections and in local government elections. Later in the year, however, Wilson made something of a comeback with a successful speech at the annual Labour Party conference in October.

Wilson's unpopularity could be attributed to two main causes. He had assumed personal responsibility for the direction of the economy in August 1967, only to have devaluation become necessary in November. Second, British foreign policy had also proved ineffectual, with Wilson making fruitless visits to the U.S.S.R. in January and to the U.S. in February in the hope of helping resolve the war in Vietnam. Nor did his continuing efforts to reach a settlement in Rhodesia win much sympathy from many in his own party. The appearance in the autumn of a highly polemic attack on his pragmatism by Paul Foot in the book *The Politics of Harold Wilson* was symptomatic of the public mood. Yet in the later months of the year there was some evidence that he was quietly reestablishing his position as a prime minister who had every intention of leading his party in the next general election.

Wilson was born at Huddersfield, Yorkshire, on March 11, 1916. After a brilliant scholastic career at Oxford University, he entered Parliament in 1945 and at the age of 31 was president of the Board of Trade. He was elected leader of the Labour Party in 1963, following the death of Hugh Gaitskell. As prime minister, he contrived to stay in office with a majority of only three until March 1966. A shrewdly timed election campaign then increased his majority to 97.
(W. H. Ts.)

ZINSOU, ÉMILE DERLIN

One of the year's most unexpected appointments took place in Dahomey in June when the Dahomean Army designated Émile Derlin Zinsou, a physician and political leader, as president of the nation. Dahomey had been caught in a political deadlock since May, when a large majority of the electorate boycotted the presidential elections held under the auspices of the military regime. The boycott took place among the supporters of former presidents Hubert Maga, Sourou Migan Apithy, and Justin Timotin Ahomadegbé, all of whom had been exiled by the Army. As a result of the boycott the Army nullified the election and then surprised many by appointing Zinsou as head of state.

The new president was born March 23, 1918, in Ouidah, a religious and cultural centre of Dahomey, which was then part of French West Africa. He studied to be a physician and received his degree from the Dakar Medical School. After continuing his studies in France, he practiced medicine in the Ivory Coast and in Dahomey.

Zinsou began his political career in 1947 as a counselor in the French Union, an organization of French overseas territories. He later became a senator, representing Dahomey in the French National Assembly, and in 1955 joined a group of leaders known as the Overseas Independents. In Dahomean internal politics, he was a founder of the Dahomean Progressive Union and served as secretary-general of the Dahomean Progressive Party, formed in 1958.

After Dahomey achieved independence in 1960, Zinsou held various government positions, including minister of foreign affairs and president of the Supreme Court. For a time he also served as ambassador to France.
(Ph. D.)

Biological Sciences

Vigorous advances in almost all of the innumerable branches of biology continued in 1968. The spectacular progress being made in molecular biology, however, was providing the long-desired link by which such disparate sciences as physiology, morphology, genetics, evolution, and taxonomy could be brought together into a unified science of biology.

With the publication of the *Atlas of Protein Sequence and Structure,* the full amino acid sequences of some 250 proteins were made available. Among other things, knowledge of the sequences, especially for hemoglobins and cytochromes, provided a powerful new tool for the elucidation of phylogenetic relationships, including a reexamination of the relationships between the apes and man. Progress in the hitherto intractable problem of the relation between cell chemistry and cell morphology was made in two independent lines of research. R. S. Edgar and his associates gave a detailed account of the ways in which the morphologically distinct components of the complex bacteriophage T4 are formed and assembled. Work in various laboratories successfully related the structure and behaviour of ribosomes, under control of ribonucleic acid (RNA), with particular stages in the synthesis of proteins.

Unlike the senses that depend upon physical stimuli, knowledge of the chemical senses had previously eluded the experimentalist. Significant progress was made when J. E. Amoore produced attractive evidence in support of a hypothesis that smell depends upon molecular shape. He postulated seven types of receptor cells, each specific for molecules of a particular shape. Other investigators, however, stressed the importance of the distribution of electric charges on the molecules and their infrared vibrational frequencies.

A link between chemistry and the more traditional interests of biologists appeared in the search for a theory of the origin of life on the earth. The syntheses, under conditions presumed to resemble those of the pre-biotic earth, of the sulfur-containing amino acid methionine and of porphyrin (the most characteristic component of hemoglobin and chlorophyll) completed the list of basic biochemical materials whose synthesis under such conditions is essential for any such theory. C. Ponnamperuma showed that the key biochemical process of phosphorylation, normally dependent upon specific enzymes, could have been carried out under pre-biotic conditions through the condensation of naturally occurring phosphates. The nonbiological origin of adenine had already been shown to be possible and when adenine and these condensed phosphates are mixed, adenosine monophosphate (essential for all cellular energy transfers) is formed. There was still no plausible theory to explain how all these materials could have been assembled into workable living units. Meanwhile, information gathered by American and Soviet spacecraft about conditions on Mars and Venus destroyed popular myths that life exists on these planets.

Concern about the social aspects of biology, especially the problems of the population explosion and the pollution and exploitation of the natural environment, was enhanced by publication of information on the use of biological agents in war and on the extensive research associated with this, and by the public interest in issues involving life and death (organ trans-

plants, the contraceptive pill, the use of drugs, gerontology, etc.). A symposium organized by the British Institute of Biology on biology and ethics was typical of many discussions, and while the International Biological Program, devoted broadly to the investigation of every aspect of man's relation to his environment, entered the second year of its operational phase, a major international conference on the same subjects was organized in Paris by UNESCO.   (H. Sa.)

Botany. Since the discovery in 1955 of the first of the cytokinins, many other adenine derivatives with similar properties had been synthesized artificially or isolated from plants. Their effects on plants are multiple and profound; they regulate protein and nucleic acid metabolism, morphogenesis, food transport, and may retard senescence. In 1968 certain cytokinins were found to be incorporated into transfer-RNA, a type of nucleic acid that has a key role in protein synthesis. Whether this presence was the key to the biological activity of the RNA was still uncertain, even though the position of incorporated cytokinins in the RNA molecule was constant and such that it might be expected to prevent the RNA from functioning properly. In another experiment, however, a synthetic radioactive cytokinin was prepared that was biologically active, but its presence could not be detected in transfer-RNA. This suggested that the observed incorporation was not related to biological activity.

Studies of the digestive glands of five species of opisthobranch mollusks showed that the animal cells retained whole plastids from their algal food. In *Elysia viridis,* which feeds on the alga *Codium tomentosum,* the plastids were found to be capable of an independent functional existence within the digestive cells of the animal. This was the first report of plastids surviving for any length of time outside plant cells, and might be of importance in the understanding of the nutritional requirements of these organelles.

A new class of subcellular organelle was described and characterized in 1968. Termed glyoxysomes by the authors, they were found in plant tissues that are largely concerned in the breakdown of fats, such as the endosperm of germinating castor beans. Physical separation of glyoxysomes was possible on a sucrose gradient, since they had a greater density than either mitochondria or proplastids. With the electron microscope, glyoxysomes were shown to be spherical organelles surrounded by a single unit membrane and having a fine granular matrix. Biochemically, they contained certain enzymes characteristic of the glyoxylate cycle, a metabolic chain that brings about the partial oxidation of glyoxylate in tissues active in fat degradation.

From Czechoslovakia, a technique was reported for the test-tube fertilization of *Nicotiana tabacum* ovules by means of an artificial pollen-tube culture. Ovules taken from mature flowers were incubated on a nutrient medium before being brought into contact with a culture of pollen tubes growing in a sugar solution. By this method, which might have a number of applications, up to 70% of ovules were fertilized and produced viable seeds.

A study of toxic substances liberated in water by certain blue-green algae and known to cause deaths in farm animals and dysenteric symptoms in man produced some surprising results. Soviet scientists tested various blue-green algae on *Daphnia,* and found that *Anabaena* produced toxic effects but only when the alga were present in large quantities, over one million

cells per millilitre, when the medium was about pH 8, and when no other blue-green algae were present. When *Phormidium* and *Nodularia* were added to the *Anabaena*, the toxic effect was markedly reduced.

Phytochrome, a blue-green biliprotein, had been known to exist in two forms, one of which absorbed red light, and one far-red light. When illuminated with far-red light the far-red-absorbing form was converted to the red form, and similarly, the red-absorbing form was converted to the far-red form by red light. The nature of these photoconversions was shown to be complex, involving a number of intermediate stages. Also, experiments using intact tissues instead of phytochrome extracts demonstrated the presence of two or more phytochrome populations that differed with respect to the kinetics of their induced conversions. The primary action whereby phytochrome controls photoperiodism and photomorphogenesis within the plant remained unsolved.

Akebia quinata from the Berberidales was shown to possess a primitive open conduplicate type of carpel. This type of megasporophyll had been known only among the Ranales, most of the Berberidales having more advanced flowers. Although *A. quinata* was native only to Chile and Asia, it was cultivated throughout the eastern and central U.S. and promised to be of value to students of primitive angiosperm flowers.

Advances in techniques for locating specific regions for electron microscopy enabled many short-lived processes and obscure areas to be examined. Egg formation, fertilization, and embryo development in flowering plants were studied in *Capsella bursa-pastoris,* and portions of the reproductive cycle described in *Gossypium hirsutum, Zea mays,* and *Myosurus minimus.* In the development of the pollen tube and sperm of *G. hirsutum,* the sperm cells were found to contain very poorly developed organelles, and no plastids could be recognized. The vegetative nucleus was large and dense, containing numerous whorls of membrane. (C. L. F. W.)

Zoology. The first record of tetrapod vertebrate life was reported from the Antarctic land mass in 1968. A fossil fragment some 200 million years old of an amphibian left lower jaw was discovered in the bed of an ancient stream near the upper Beardmore Glacier, about 325 mi. from the South Pole. The tropical habitat of the salamander-like animal, a labyrinthodont amphibian, suggested that Antarctica was once at a more tropical latitude. Since animals of this type also existed in Africa, Australia, and Mada-

gascar, the find provided further evidence for the theory that these regions had once been joined in a single land mass, Gondwanaland, and had later separated, due to continental drift. The discovery was made by P. J. Barrett and R. J. Baillie of Ohio State University's Institute of Polar Studies and identified by E. H. Colbert of Columbia University and the American Museum of Natural History.

A cause of mass extinctions of animals that are known to have taken place during the earth's history was suggested by K. D. Terry and W. H. Tucker. Calculations showed that every 50 million years the earth should receive a dose of at least 500 roentgens of radiation released from the explosion of nearby type II supernovae. Mass extinctions are known to have occurred approximately once every 60 million years since the Cambrian Period. Because doses of 200 to 700 roentgens kill laboratory animals 50% of the time, this estimated radiation would have been sufficient to sterilize or eliminate animal populations, such as the dinosaurs. This concept also explained why plants generally had been spared in known extinctions. The acute lethal dose for most plants is on the order of 2,000 roentgens.

Findings in animal behaviour included the report by D. Grant, O. Anderson, and the late Victor Twitty of Stanford University that homing ability in newts of the California species *Taricha rivularis* was greatly reduced by cutting the olfactory nerves or destroying olfactory tissue with formaldehyde. Previous work had shown that blinding did not significantly reduce homing ability. Another phenomenon was described by T. Eisner of Cornell University and J. A. Davis of the New York Zoological Park. They found that the African banded mongoose *Mungos mungo* consumes coiled millipedes after throwing them backward between its legs to smash them against rocks. Glomerid millipedes usually coil up into tight spheres when disturbed, making them invulnerable to predators. The mongoose's behaviour was observed in the zoo and presumed to occur in nature, since the habitats of the two animals overlap in Central and South Africa.

Among developmental findings was the announcement by Merle Mizell of Tulane University of the first case of induced limb regeneration in a mammal. Replacement of the foot and three toes took place in newborn opossums (*Didelphis marsupialis*). As previously known, when brain tissue is implanted prior to forelimb amputation, successful regeneration can occur. Success in grafting the nervous tissue in this case was attributed to the relatively poorly developed immune mechanism of the newborn opossum. It was also presumed that the primitive nature of marsupials contributed to the success.

Findings in comparative physiology included the report by T. Bauchop and R. W. Martucci of the University of California, Davis, of a case of significant ruminant-like digestion occurring outside of the group of animals in which it is normally found. Old World langur monkeys of the subfamily Colobinae were found to have larger and more complex stomachs than other primates. This feature was attributed to their diet, which consists mainly of leaves. Although the langur does not chew its cud, fermentative or ruminant-like digestion occurs in its stomach. The stomach contents of related monkeys were known to contain high concentrations of short-chain volatile fatty acids similar to the fermentation products found in the rumens of true ruminants. Fatty acids of this type and cellulose-digesting bacteria were found in the

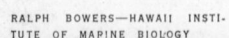

Female boxfish, from which the repellent substance pahutoxin was isolated.

stomach contents of both species of langur examined. The anatomy of the langur stomach resembles superficially that of the rumen of herbivorous animals; it has a large capacity and makes up a large percentage of the body weight when filled. This causes the delayed flow of digesting food known to be necessary for extensive fermentation.

Freshwater rays from the Amazon Basin (genus *Potamotrygon*) were found by T. B. Thorson, C. M. Cowan, and D. E. Watson to have an almost complete lack of urea in their blood and tissues. All previously studied elasmobranchs (sharks and rays) had blood urea concentrations of from 300 to 1,300 mg. per 100 ml. of blood. This high level is part of a mechanism whereby enough urea is reabsorbed into the ray's blood to keep its osmotic concentration at the same overall level as the seawater that it inhabits. Since the urea concentrations of two freshwater species were only two or three milligrams per 100 ml. of blood, it was assumed that the absence was related to their freshwater habitat. Other freshwater elasmobranchs studied had blood urea concentrations only 25 to 35% lower than those of marine forms and could be assumed to have had marine or brackish-water origins, or access to the sea. The Amazon rays were caught some 2,500 mi. from the ocean, had no ready access to it, and may even have had freshwater ancestors. They were expected to serve as useful controls in studies of the phenomenon of urea retention.

Fish toxicology had attracted much attention ever since the successful identification of the potent neurotoxin of the puffer fish, the tetrodotoxin of James Bond fame. D. B. Boylan and P. J. Scheuer achieved the chemical identification of pahutoxin, the poison of the Hawaiian boxfish (*Ostracion lentiginosus*) of the trunkfish family (Ostraciontidae), and claimed the first such identification in a marine organism of an alarming or repellent substance thought to protect slow-moving animals. Pahutoxin turned out to be the choline chloride ester of 3-acetoxyhexadecanoic acid. Its fish-killing potency closely paralleled its ability to cause the rupture of fish red blood cells (hemolysis). The work thus far showed that pahutoxin has a different mode of action than tetrodotoxin, as was to be expected from its different chemical structure.

(R. R. No.)

Entomology. Insects continued to be a major threat to man's food supplies throughout the world, despite the efforts of economic entomologists and the productiveness of insecticide chemists. In 1967 and early 1968, the Anti-Locust Research Centre in London warned that swarms of the desert locust *Schistocerca gregaria* were building up in Saudi Arabia, south and west of the Red Sea, and in Mali and Niger in West Africa. Control measures· proved only partially effective and there was a serious danger that a major plague cycle would redevelop in these areas after years of comparatively low populations of the insect.

Organic insecticides remained the most effective means of controlling the majority of insect pests; but the effects of the widespread use of these compounds on nontarget organisms and, ultimately, on man himself were receiving ever more critical examination. In addition to research on the possibilities for nonchemical control of insects, refinements in the use of insecticides and new forms of chemical control were the subjects of active research. M. J. Whitten and K. R. Norris suggested a novel means of making use of the resistance built up by some strains of blowflies in Australia to the insecticide dieldrin. Female flies bred from a resistant strain could be used as "booby traps" for susceptible males. A single female treated with the insecticide could kill over 100 males that attempt to mate with her, yet the amount of insecticide released into the environment would remain minute.

Resistant male blowflies treated with insecticide did not prove as effective as "booby traps" for females as the females did for males. The technique recalled the method of insect control known as "sterile male release," in which a very large number of males are reared and sterilized with ionizing radiation before release into the natural population. The mating of females with the sterile males reduces the fecundity of the population as a whole. This method of control was strikingly successful in Curaçao, where it had been used over a decade before to rid the island of the screw-worm fly, and it had since been highly successful against the same pest in the southern part of the U.S. Sterile male release had not been particularly effective against many other insects, especially those in which multiple matings take place. One mating with a fertile male tended to undo the effect of previous matings with sterile males. Nevertheless, the use of males as carriers, not of defective sperm but of physiologically active chemicals, had added a new dimension to the method and one in which multiple matings were actually an advantage.

Another possible pest control came out of work on the growth-controlling hormones of insects. The growth and development of insects is under the control of two major hormones—one that initiates molting and another, the juvenile hormone, that determines whether the insect will remain immature or not after it molts. Treatment of insects with the juvenile hormone at the time they were about to become adults prevented them from becoming sexually competent; while treatment of eggs with the hormone—or treatment of the mature female before the eggs were laid—could render the embryos nonviable. Moreover, several terpenes with activity similar to natural juvenile hormone had been recognized and synthesized. P. Masner and co-workers showed that the dihydrochloride of methyl farnesoate could be applied externally to adult males of *Pyrrhocoris apterus* in quantities that caused the male during subsequent matings to transfer sufficient amounts of the compound to females to prevent the development of all their eggs.

Compounds that mimicked juvenile hormone tended to be selective in the insects they affected; but it was argued that as more of the compounds were discovered, their application to pest control would become increasingly possible. Several compounds that could act as the molting hormone had also been found. The insect "hormones" discovered thus far appeared to cause no deleterious effects to mammals and it seemed inconceivable that insects could develop genetic resistance to their own hormones. Compounds that mimicked insect hormones had thus been hailed by C. M. Williams as the "third generation" of insecticides—following the inorganic "first generation" and the "second generation" of the organic insecticides that were currently in use.

The natural transfer of other hormones from male to female during mating had also been investigated. Mating triggers egg production in the females of various insects, and the cause had been traced in some flies to a hormone secreted by the accessory glands of the male sexual apparatus. The function of these glands had hitherto been mainly unknown, but Sister M. G. Leahy showed that the glands will stimulate ovulation

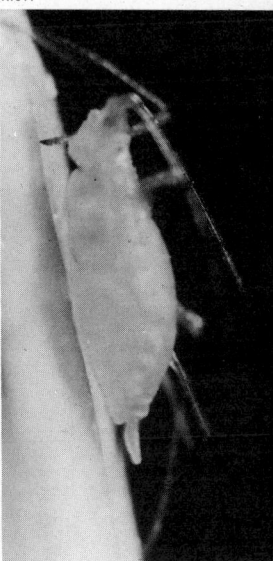

Aphid thrusting its sucking tube into a leaf. Intensive studies of these insects were taking place because they transmit viral diseases to plant life.

and oviposition when implanted into virgin females of a number of species.

The nutrition of insects was under intensive study in many countries. Some investigations were concerned with the natural resistance of certain plants to attack by insects, while others were concentrated on the choice exercised by insects between different edible plants. Central to these studies was the development of artificial diets, the composition of which could be rigorously controlled. One result of such studies was the provision of experimental evidence for the long-suspected nutritional value of the microbial symbionts that were known to occur in the cells of many insect species. R. H. Dadd and D. L. Krieger showed that the aphid *Myzus persicae* has a requirement for only three amino acids—methionine, histidine, and isoleucine—while it is in possession of its normal intracellular symbionts, but appears to require at least ten amino acids when freed from its symbionts with antibiotics. (P. W. Mɪ.)

Ornithology. A review of the changes in status among breeding birds in Britain and Ireland was concluded in June 1968 by J. L. F. Parslow. Of the 216 species known to have nested in the area since 1800, 19 never established themselves as regular breeders,

MALCOLM PENNY

Brush warbler, unique
to Seychelles,
and surviving only
on Cousin Island
in the Indian Ocean.
The International
Council for Bird
Preservation
in conjunction with
the World Wildlife Fund
planned to raise
funds to buy the island.

11 voluntarily colonized the archipelago (*e.g.*, little ringed plover and collared dove), 3 were deliberately introduced by man (*e.g.*, little owl), and 12 had become extinct (*e.g.*, great auk and Kentish plover). Five species, however, had subsequently reestablished themselves, including the famous avocets and ospreys. Thus, 190 species were currently regarded as regular nesters.

A study of the food of the tawny owl undertaken in three very different areas of London reported that the proportions of birds to small mammals preyed upon by the owls was 93% in a central park, 45% in a suburb, and 10% in an oak wood on the outskirts. Clearly the tawny owl takes mammals where available, but can successfully turn its talons to birds in central London where mice, voles, and shrews are very scarce.

In a report on the seabirds killed following the 1967 wreck of the tanker "Torrey Canyon" and subsequent pollution of nearby beaches, marine ornithologists stated that the absolute minimum total kill from oiling was about 10,000 birds and the full total was

likely to have been at least two or three times greater. Of 1,223 dead birds from southwest Britain, 78% were guillemots and 19% razorbills.

A considerable stir among British bird watchers was caused from May to August 1967 and again in April 1968 when a black-browed albatross, a species normally confined to the Southern Hemisphere, took up residence among the gannets of the Bass Rock in Scotland. There was speculation as to how long the bird would continue to return. A bird of this species had lived in a Faeroese gannetry on Myggenaes Holm from 1860 until it was shot there in 1894.

A study of the movements of albatrosses showed that young of the black-browed species ringed in the Falkland Islands and on South Georgia in the South Atlantic regularly turned up off the eastern coast of South America, on the seaboard of South Africa, and occasionally in Australia. Young gray-headed albatrosses from South Georgia had flown to South Africa, Australia, and New Zealand.

A report on the ornithology of the Aldabra coral atoll, the only Indian Ocean island still largely unaffected by man, noted that, as with many insular populations, many of the birds were very tame. The white-throated rail—the only flightless bird remaining in an area that once held the dodo and the solitaire—could be lured in the direction of the observer by any unusual noise. The local race of the sacred ibis was still very confiding though it no longer probed in people's shoes for food as early seafarers had described. Of the 14 species of land birds cited, one was a full species unique to Aldabra and 10 were endemic at the subspecies level. Another dozen sea- and shorebird nesters were also noted. Early in 1968 a full species new to Aldabra and to science was discovered on North Island by Malcolm Penney. It was a kind of brush warbler and was named *Bebrornis aldabranus.*

Phonograph recordings issued during the year included the last five of Sture Palmér's set of 40 *Radio Bird Records,* which carried songs and cries of 292 north European birds. *Sound-Guide to the Birds of Southern Europe* by Jean-Claude Roché was the first album to be issued by ECHO, the newly formed French institute for the recording and study of birds' songs and calls. Under the title *The Voices of Wild Nature: Birds of the Far East,* the All-Union Studio of Disc Recording in Moscow presented songs from Ussuriland and Amurland recorded by Boris N. Veprintsev and Irene Neufeldt. Tapes from Japan included *100 Singing Birds,* recorded by Reiji Nakatsubo of the Japan Broadcasting Corporation. A list of all records of African bird songs ever issued was prepared by Jeffery H. R. Boswall and Myles E. W. North.

Volumes on ornithology published in 1967 included Derek Goodwin's *Pigeons and Doves of the World,* a definitive work on the Columbidae. Folio 14 of the American Geographical Society's *Serial Atlas of the Marine Environment* was devoted to the "Distribution of North Atlantic Pelagic Birds" by Robert Cushman Murphy. Maps detailed the breeding sites and oceanic ranges of the North Atlantic's oceangoing birds. *Radar Ornithology* by Eric Eastwood traced the history of radar's unique contribution to the study of the mysteries of migration. Reference books included *The Birds of Canada* by W. E. Godfrey and one of the very few works in English on the birds of the neotropics, A. W. Johnson's *The Birds of Chile and Adjacent Regions of Argentina, Bolivia, and Peru.*

(J. H. Bo.)

Marine Biology. The habits of fish, especially the phenomenon of schooling, were much studied in 1968. Schooling is common in fish that migrate. Such fish—e.g., herring, cod, tuna—have large geographic ranges and produce great numbers of young. Because they are migratory they are very abundant. They assemble in vast shoals to common spawning areas, and the younger and older stages spread out to widely separated feeding grounds, thus ensuring provision of sufficient food for a large population. Formation of schools may also give protection against predation and exercise a regulatory role in the gene flow of the species.

Large bluefin tuna, *Thunnus thynnus*, migrate across the Atlantic from the American coast to Europe. It was shown that young tuna, tagged on the American side, had migrated to the Bay of Biscay in under a year.

Nonschooling fish, with more restricted ranges, may also migrate to spawning areas. It was found that sole in the North Sea appear at the surface at night in spring and lie passively, heading generally in an easterly or northeasterly direction, when the surface tidal streams are flowing toward the spawning areas.

A remarkable example of schooling was observed from a deep-sea submarine in slope water off the east coast of America. Dense shoals of a widely distributed small oceanic myctophid fish, *Ceratoscopelus madarensis*, up to 100 m. in diameter and 10 m. deep, separated from each other by about 100 m., were encountered. The schools migrated daily from about 330 m. at midday to within about 20 m. of the surface in the evening. These fish are only about 65 mm. long and the reason for schooling was unknown, unless it be a defense from predation.

Of special interest was the finding of two freshwater eels in the stomachs of the deep-sea fish *Mora mora* and *Aphanops carbo* caught at 720 m. in 59° 21′ N, 10° 22′ W. These were in the "Blankaal" stage and must have been on their way to the spawning area.

Surface-living fish have lenses in their eyes that absorb ultraviolet light strongly, whereas fishes living deep down during the day have lenses usually transparent to ultraviolet down to about 310 mμ. A squid *Calliteuthis meleagroteuthis* has a large and a small eye. The small eye transmits ultraviolet, but the large eye does not. Absorbing pigment, however, is only present in the outer layer of lens, so that at first both eyes are transparent to ultraviolet. The addition later of a filter in the large eye probably indicates an adaptation to change in habit to enable the animal to come near the surface in daytime.

In a study of the vertical diurnal migration of plankton evidence was found of vertical movements below the photic zone at about 1,000 m. A downward movement was shown by certain species from 1,000 m. at night to 1,400 m. during the day, and two species of chaetognath, most abundant around 1,700 m. at midnight, appeared even to descend below this depth in the daytime.

Experiments with the chaetognath *Spadella cephaloptera* showed that they were sensitive to a certain range of vibrations. Accurate feeding movements were made toward a source vibrating at 9–20 Hz (hertz) with an amplitude of 100–500 mμ. at a distance of 1–3 m. Other vibrations were ignored or resulted in escape movements. Within the correct range *Spadella* would seize and chew a vibrating wire.

It was shown that the flatworm *Convoluta roscoffensis* would select its normal symbiont flagellate *Platymonas convolutae* in preference to other flagellates. But if presented with other flagellates in the absence of *P. convolutae* it would accept them, but again showed a preferential selection. In "chimaera" specimens in which both *P. convolutae* and another flagellate were present the latter was eliminated.

As in corals, the algal symbiont found in the temperate zone sea anemone *Anemonia sulcata* was shown to be a dinoflagellate. It is remarkable that it is apparently the same species as that symbiotic in corals and *Tridacna*. Several kinds of hermit crabs carry sea anemones on their shells. For one species it is known that the anemone seeks out the crab, but it was found that in Hawaii the anemone *Calliactis polypus* is sought by the crab. The anemone is gently stroked by the crab with the result that it becomes relaxed. The crab can thus easily remove the anemone from the rock and it then places it on its shell.

Pogonophora can take up amino acids and macromolecules directly from solution in seawater. The cuticle, particularly over the forepart of the body and the tentacle, is very active and a number of enzymes have been demonstrated there. Since concentrations of amino acids of up to 125 μg/1 have been found in seawater with a mean value of about 25 μg/1 total amino acid near the sediment, it is possible that in Pogonophora this may be one of the principal means of obtaining nutrition.

A factor of great importance in the ecology of intertidal plants and animals is the extent of wave action. This can cause abrasion, pressure, and drag, the last of which is probably most significant. The first objective study of this factor was made possible by the production of a dynamometer designed to record the maximum drag produced in the period during which the instrument is exposed on the shore. Another limiting factor in shore ecology is temperature. It was found that the echinoids *Lytechnis variegatus* and *Tripneustes ventricosus* suffered mortalities of up to 64 and 86%, respectively, during extreme midday low water in spring and summer on reefs around Puerto Rico.

The mangrove tree crab *Aratus pisoni* breeds throughout the year at full and new moon. It was found that females with eggs about to hatch migrate to the seaward margin of the swamp. The newly hatched larvae are then washed off into the water in a minimum of time, reducing the chances of predation on the adult.

A specimen of the rare hydroid *Pelagohydra mirabilis* was found floating in the sea off New Zealand. Only two specimens have ever been seen before, both damaged and washed ashore in this same locality in New Zealand, in 1901 and 1929, respectively. Medusae were liberated by this specimen. Another unusual find was a new species of ascidian, *Pyrosoma benthica*. Having structural characters typical of the pelagic *Pyrosoma*, this is the first species of a thaliacean ascidian to be found with a benthic habit.　(F. S. RL.)

See also Antarctica; Conservation; Gardening; Medicine; Molecular Biology.

ENCYCLOPÆDIA BRITANNICA FILMS. *Life Along the Waterways* (1952); *The Atom and Biological Sciences* (1953); *The Strands Grow* (Part I, "Web of Life Series") (1953); *Insects* (1953); *Marine Life* (1953); *Life in the Desert* (1954); *Life in the Grasslands (North America)* (1954); *Flowers at Work* (1955); *Life in the Forest* (1955); *Mollusks (Snails, Mussels, Octopuses, and Their Relatives)* (1955); *Plant Traps—Insect Catchers of the Bog Jungle* (1955); *Reptiles* (1955); *Worms—The Annelida* (1955); *Crustaceans (Lobsters, Barnacles, Shrimp, and Their Relatives)* (1956); *Seed Dispersal* (1956); *Spiders* (1956); *The Frog* (1957); *Growth of Seeds* (1957); *Protozoa (One-Celled Animals)* (1957); *Roots of Plants* (1957);

Life in the Sea (1958); *Microscopic Life: The World of the Invisible* (1958); *Osmosis* (1958); *The EBF Biology Program* (a basic series of 50 films and 51 filmstrips divided into five major units: ecology; plant life; animal life; physiology; and heredity and adaptive change) (1960–63); *Beginnings of Vertebrate Life* (1963); *How Pine Trees Reproduce—Pine Cone Biology* (1963); *Life Between Tides* (1963); *Life Story of the Hummingbird* (1963); *Life Story of the Oyster* (1963); *Life Story of the Sea Star* (1963); *The Marine Biologist* (1963); *Metamorphosis—Life Story of the Wasp* (1963); *Life Story of a Water Flea (Daphnia)* (1965); *Life Story of the Ladybird Beetle* (1965); *Message from a Dinosaur* (1965); *A Plant Through the Seasons (Apple Tree)* (1966); *Army Ants: Study In Social Behavior* (1966); *Discovering the Forest* (1966); *Experimenting with Animals (White Rats)* (1966); *Flowering Plants* (1966); *Food from the Sun* (1966); *Green Plants and Sunlight* (1966); *Life Story of a Grasshopper* (1966); *The Fish in a Changing Environment* (1966); *The Marsh Community* (1966); *Trees and Their Importance* (1966); *Chromosomes of Man* (1967); *Life Story of a Social Insect: The Ant* (1967); *Looking at Mammals* (1967); *Monarch Butterfly Story* (2nd ed., 1967); *Photosynthesis* (2nd ed., 1967); *Water for Living Things* (1967); *Insect Parasitism—The Alder Woodwasp and Its Enemies* (1968).

Bolivia

A landlocked republic in central South America, Bolivia is bordered by Brazil, Paraguay, Argentina, Chile, and Peru. Area: 424,162 sq.mi. (1,098,581 sq.km.). Pop. (1968 est.): 3,852,000, of whom more than 50% were Indian. Language: officially Spanish. Religion: Roman Catholic. Legal cap.: Sucre (pop., 1966 est., 59,701). Seat of government and largest city: La Paz (pop., 1966 est., 362,298). President in 1968, Gen. René Barrientos Ortuño.

In 1968 Bolivia experienced economic difficulties and political instability. A severe crisis in July and August followed the flight (July 19) of a former minister of the interior, Antonio Arguedas Mendieta (*see* BIOGRAPHY), who was discovered to have passed the campaign diary of the slain guerrilla leader "Che" Guevara to Cuban agents; the affair nearly caused the overthrow of President Barrientos. Arguedas, who fled to Chile, Britain, the U.S., and Peru, later returned to Bolivia where he was to be tried for treason by a military tribunal.

President Barrientos had passed the diary to Arguedas for 24 hours, on his own responsibility and against the advice of the army high command; the former minister had been his close friend and principal lieutenant for many years. On his return to Bolivia (August 17), Arguedas alleged at a press conference that he had been an agent of the U.S. Central Intelligence Agency for three years and gave the names of CIA operatives in the country; at the same time, however, he proclaimed his left-wing sympathies.

Violent demonstrations in principal cities followed the announcement of Arguedas' flight, and some legislators and prominent opposition members were arrested. On July 22, Barrientos proclaimed a state of siege, suspended Congress, and assumed full powers. The vice-president, Luis Adolfo Siles Salinas, withdrew his support from the government, mainly because of the arrests of politicians; and the ministers of foreign affairs and of culture, information, and tourism resigned from their posts. Relations with the armed forces were strained, as many officers resented the loss of potential profits from the publication of the diary. However, on July 27 President Barrientos restored a more harmonious atmosphere by the appointment of an all-military Cabinet, consisting mainly of personal friends, with the collaboration of the commander in chief of the armed forces, Gen. Alfredo Ovando Candía.

JOSEPH FABRY; PHOTO, COURTESY "TIME" MAGAZINE

President René Barrientos Ortuño survived a government crisis in Bolivia after a former minister of the interior turned over the diaries of "Che" Guevara to Cuban officials who published them.

By September political conditions had become more normal, although the five small parties backing the government in Congress, who had agreed in June to combine their activities, were once more in disarray. An attempted coup on August 21, led by a former army chief of staff, Gen. Vázquez Sempertegui, was easily suppressed, and relations with the military improved. Agreement was reached with students, who had demonstrated throughout the year, on the release of arrested leaders and on university autonomy.

A renewal of guerrilla activity was reported in August in Bolivian-Peruvian frontier areas, near Lake Titicaca. The guerrillas were believed to be led by

BOLIVIA

Education. (1965) Primary, pupils 526,833, teachers 17,661; secondary, pupils 78,380, teachers 2,739; vocational, pupils 8,391, teachers 1,448; teacher training, students 6,109, teachers 454; higher (at 7 universities), students 11,090.

Finance. Monetary unit: peso boliviano (11.88 pesos = U.S. $1; 28.51 pesos = £1 sterling). Gold and foreign exchange, central bank: (April 1968) U.S. $35.9 million; (April 1967) U.S. $34.3 million. Budget (1967 est.) balanced at 3,427,000,000 pesos. Money supply: (April 1968) 1,115,500,000 pesos; (April 1967) 1,053,800,000 pesos. Cost of living (La Paz; 1963 = 100): (Jan. 1967) 129; (Jan. 1966) 117.

Foreign Trade. Imports (1966) U.S. $138.4 million; exports (1967) U.S. $171.4 million. Import sources: U.S. 41%; West Germany 12%; Japan 11%; Argentina 6%; U.K. 5%. Export destinations (1966): U.K. 45%; U.S. 39%; West Germany 5%. Main exports: tin 53%; tungsten 5%; silver 4%.

Transport and Communications. Roads (1966) c. 28,000 km. (including c. 5,600 km. all-weather). Motor vehicles in use (1966): passenger 17,200; commercial 6,200. Railways (1967) 3,560 km. Telephones (Jan. 1967) 27,418. Radio receivers (Dec. 1965) 525,000.

Agriculture. Production (in 000; metric tons; 1966; 1965 in parentheses): corn 271 (239); barley c. 95 (c. 95); wheat c. 70 (c. 70); potatoes 635 (650); cassava c. 170 (174); sugar, raw value (1967–68) c. 108, (1966–67) 88; rubber, exports (1966) c. 2.5, (1965) 2.6. Livestock (in 000; Oct. 1965): sheep c. 6,150; cattle c. 2,700; pigs c. 705; horses c. 214; asses 550; goats c. 1,200; llamas c. 1,500; chickens 2,950.

Industry. Production (in 000; metric tons; 1966): crude oil 416; electricity (79% hydroelectric in 1965) 584,000 kw-hr.; cement 65; tin concentrates (metal content) 26; other metal ores (exports; metal content): lead 21.3, antimony 10.7, zinc 16.7, tungsten 1.6, copper 5.7, silver 0.15.

Guido Peredo, formerly one of "Che" Guevara's chief lieutenants; troops were dispatched to the region and several arrests made.

Little economic progress was made during the year and a decline of revenue from tin, the country's principal export, adversely affected the foreign exchange position. Credit was also extremely tight, and there was a sharp recession in business activity.

In April import controls were introduced, and stringent controls were imposed on the operations of state-owned enterprises; tax collection methods were overhauled and public expenditure reduced. The government obtained a special U.S. loan of $12 million to help support the budget.

In February Yacimientos Petrolíferos Fiscales Bolivianos (YPFB) reached agreement with Bolivian Gulf Oil on the ownership of natural gas reserves in southern Bolivia, and a jointly owned company was formed to sell the gas. The two organizations were building a pipeline from Santa Cruz to the Argentine border to facilitate exports of natural gas to Argentina. Petroleum production began at the Montegudo deposits in the department of Chuquisaca.

In February it became clear that a fundamental change had been made in foreign policy. Emphasis was to be placed on assisting Latin-American economic integration, rather than on the traditional objective of acquiring a trade outlet on the Pacific.   (Rn. C.)

Botswana

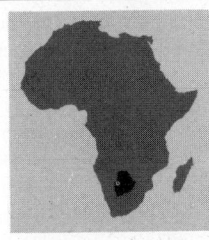

A landlocked republic of southern Africa, Botswana is bounded by South Africa, South West Africa, and Rhodesia. Area: 220,000 sq.mi. (569,797 sq.km.). Pop. (1968 est.): 611,000, almost 99% African. Capital: Gaberones (pop., 1968 est., 18,000). Largest city: Serowe (pop., 1966, 37,350). Languages: English (official) and Tswana. Religion: about 85% pagan. President in 1968, Sir Seretse Khama.

The well-being of Botswana continued to depend on political neutrality and beef. About 90% of the people remained dependent on farming, and cattle products constituted more than 90% of total exports (about £5 million annually in recent years). Though the disastrous years of famine from drought, to which Botswana is peculiarly vulnerable, ended, relief was still needed in some areas; but the corn crop was a good one, and the national cattle herd increased to more than 1.1 million head by 1968, with a potential of more than 2 million head—given adequate water supply.

Botswana remained dependent on outside aid, British grants balancing budgetary deficits (1967–68, £4.5 million; 1968–69, £4.2 million) and providing for de-

BOTSWANA
Education. (1966) Primary, pupils 71,546, teachers 1,673; secondary, pupils 1,531, teachers 89; vocational, pupils 43, teachers 3; teacher training, students 293, teachers 20.
Finance and Trade. Monetary unit: South African rand (R 1 = U.S. $1.40; R 1.714 = £1 sterling). Budget (1967–68 est.): revenue R 15,400,483; expenditure R 15,092,244. Foreign trade (1965): imports R 16,591,000; exports R 11,385,000. Main exports: meat 51%; live cattle 7%; canned meat 7%; hides and skins 6%.
Agriculture. Livestock (in 000; 1966–67): cattle 1,050; sheep 151; goats 398; poultry 59.

velopment programs of up to £13 million over the next three years. Although tourism and big-game hunting already earned revenue in the Chobe National Park area, Seretse Khama pointed out in April that a major breakthrough to economic viability must be based on mining and private investment, themselves dependent on political stability. Asbestos, gold, silver, and manganese were already mined in small amounts; and in 1968 the Roan Selection Trust established the existence of more than 33 million tons of copper and nickel in the Matsitama and Selibe-Philwe areas. The trust also showed interest in developing brine resources in the Makarikari region. De Beers Consolidated Mines reported considerable diamond potential at Lethlakane and at Orapa, where a major new mine was discovered. Coal deposits were investigated at Morupule.

Activities of terrorist bands continued to embarrass the government, and the British Francistown Radio, beamed at Rhodesia, closed down after two ineffectual years and a cost of more than £1 million. In May Seretse Khama moderated the tone of certain statements by Pres. Kenneth Kaunda of Zambia during the latter's state visit, by pointing out that Botswana could not accept unrealistic UN resolutions regardless of the consequences nor the UN's attempts to interfere in the internal affairs of other countries, particularly in southern Africa. In August it was announced that John Dendy Young, former High Court judge in Rhodesia, had become chief justice of Botswana. In spite of criticism from other African nations relations with South Africa remained close, with more than 30,000 inhabitants of Botswana annually remitting more than £500,000 from their work in South Africa, while South African technical and economic aid continued to flow into Botswana. South Africa flew in medical teams to work and to provide equipment in Botswana, while some patients were flown to South Africa. During August and September Seretse Khama received medical treatment in Johannesburg.   (M. Mr.)

Bowling and Lawn Bowls

The year 1968 was awaited by the bowling world with great expectations. The Olympic Games would once again take place, and this time in Mexico—one of the strongest amateur bowling countries in the world. A chance was seen to secure recognition of tenpin bowling by the International Olympic Committee and have it included in the Olympic program as one of the three exhibition sports. However, recognition was denied, and the biggest indoor participant sport still lacked Olympic status.

The biggest and most interesting amateur tournament of the year was the International Masters Championships. It began with thousands of bowlers participating in local, national, and area eliminations. Qualified representatives of 29 countries then met in the international finals at Paris in December 1967. The 29-man field was first divided into three divisions. Each division bowled its own round-robin elimination. The top-ranking four bowlers of each division advanced to the 12-man semifinals, at which time they bowled another round-robin tournament. The four best in this competition qualified for the final field. In the finals each man bowled a one-game match against each other finalist. Through the whole tournament each match had consisted of two games, and a

bowler was credited with 50 bonus pins for each game won. Twenty-one-year-old Jack Connaughton, the 1967 U.S. intercollegiate champion, was the hero of a fine tournament; runner-up was Kazuo Hayashi of Japan; third, Lino Braghieri of Italy; and fourth, René Ferrié of France.

The sixth annual Tournament of the Americas took place in July in Miami, Fla. This annual tournament had been sponsored and conducted from its founding by the city of Miami, and in 1968 it drew 70 bowlers from 20 countries and territories on the American continents. The winners were: men's singles, B. Corona, Mexico, 3,180; men's all events, Corona, Mexico, 7,513; men's doubles, Canada, 3,619; women's singles, Susie Reicheley, U.S., 3,127; women's all events, Susie Reicheley, U.S., 7,209; women's doubles, United States, 3,512; mixed doubles, Mexico, 2,417; mixed foursome, United States, 4,818.

The fifth Central American Tournament was conducted in May in San Salvador, El Salvador. The following were the winners: men's division: teams of five, Panama; doubles, Panama; teams of six, Guatemala; singles, B. Morales, Guatemala; all events, J. de la Guardia, Panama. Women's division: teams of five, doubles, and teams of six, Panama; singles, B. Viggiano, Panama; all events, A. Cardozo, Panama.

By the end of 1968, two new members, Israel and Hong Kong, had affiliated with the Fédération Internationale des Quilleurs (FIQ)—the world governing organization of the sport of bowling—increasing the number of its members from 39 to 41. Of the estimated 40 million bowlers throughout the world, about 8 million belonged, through their own national organizations, to the FIQ.   (Y. S.)

United States. Professional bowling continued its pattern of a hero a year, with the standout of the previous campaign slipping into comparative obscurity. In 1968 the dominant figure clearly was Jim Stefanich of Joliet, Ill. Stefanich, a 26-year-old righthander, reintroduced the slow ball to major competition, a technique that no bowler had been able to adopt successfully since Don Carter used it early in the decade. With several tournaments remaining on the 1968 schedule, Stefanich had won the All-Star Tournament, five Professional Bowlers Association (PBA) meets, and two American Bowling Congress (ABC) tournament titles. In addition, Stefanich established a record for money winning in PBA competition as he brought his year's total to better than $63,000.

Dave Davis, the slim lefthander from Phoenix, Ariz., won bowler-of-the-year honours in 1967 by making the PBA National in December his sixth tournament triumph that year. He also won the $25,-000 first prize at the 1968 Tournament of Champions.

In the All-Star meet, conducted by the Bowling Proprietors' Association of America at Garden City, L.I., N.Y., Stefanich set a record by averaging better than 222 for his 48 games of match play. The previous mark was 220, set by Dick Weber in 1963. Stefanich won 34 games, lost 13, and tied one. Billy Hardwick, San Mateo, Calif., was second, and Wayne Zahn, Atlanta, Ga., finished third. In the women's division of the All-Star, lefthander Dorothy Fothergill of North Attleboro, Mass., was the winner.

The only double winner at the 65th annual ABC Tournament, held at the Convention-Exposition Center in Cincinnati, O., was Stefanich. Competing in the Classic Division, for professionals, Stefanich won the all-events crown with 1,983 for his nine games. He also was a member of the Bowl-Rite quintet from

First prize winner Dave Davis at the 1968 Tournament of Champions. Davis defeated Don Johnson 213–205 in the finals.

Joliet, Ill., that took the Classic team title with a six-game score of 6,285. Dave Davis topped the singles entrants with 741, while Bill Tucker of Los Angeles and Don Johnson of Kokomo, Ind., rolled 1,329 to win the doubles championship.

In the ABC's Regular Division the winners were: team, Dave's Auto Supply, Philadelphia, 3,084; doubles, Richard Stark and Walt Roy, Glenwood Springs, Colo., 1,325; singles, Wayne Kowalski, Revere, Mass., 738; all-events, Vince Mazzanti, Philadelphia, 1,971. The Masters Tournament which was held in conjunction with the ABC meet, was won by Greek-born Pete Tountas.

The 49th annual Woman's International Bowling Congress (WIBC) Tournament was held at Wonder Bowl in San Antonio, Tex. The winners in Division I (for better bowlers) were: team, Hudepohl Beer, Cincinnati, O., 2,923; doubles, Mary Lou Graham and Pauline Stickler, Miami, Fla., 1,250; singles, Norma Parks, Raytown, Mo., 691; all-events, Susie Reicheley, Waco, Tex., 1,889. Division II: team, Just Made It, Westport, Conn., 2,448; doubles, Lamar Wars and Betty Beamon, Alice, Tex., 1,105; singles, Beatrice Harm, Enola, Pa., 610; all-events, May Monroe, Childress, Tex., 1,626. The Queens Tournament, a match-game event staged on the same lanes used for the WIBC meet, was won by Phyllis Massey of Alameda, Calif., who had been the runner-up in the previous year.

The winners of the 1968 National Duckpin Championships in the men's division were: team, Valley Oilers, Portland, Conn., 2,085; doubles, George Haugh-Robert Cleary, Baltimore, Md., 919; singles, Andy Constantinople, New Haven, Conn., 489; all-events, Lindsey Hammonds, Washington, D.C., 1,324. The women's winners were: team, Johnny's New & Used Cars, Baltimore, Md., 1,849; doubles, Doris Shortt-Jean Stewart, Baltimore, Md., 780; singles, Mary Ann Mitchell, Manchester, Conn., 447; all-events, Mary Ann Mitchell, 1,202. In the mixed competition the team champion was Mixed Masters, Baltimore, Md., 1,842, and the doubles winners were Beverly Conner and Randy Tull, Baltimore, Md., 859.
                    (J. J. A.)

Lawn Bowls. Administrative differences arose in 1968 because of the divergent ideas on the place of bowls in society; Australia and South Africa considered the game to be a competitive, international sport, while the British Isles believed it should be primarily a recreation, though with some competition. These differences came to a head in June when England, Ireland, Scotland, and Wales simultaneously forwarded letters of resignation to the International Bowling Board (IBB), the resignations to become effective at the end of the year. The ostensible reason was a proposal to base affiliation fees on a capitation tax of one penny per member of affiliated clubs. This would have involved England and Scotland in a fee of £600 per annum each; Australia's obligation would have been almost £1,000. Those advocating the proposal aimed at more frequent meetings of national officials rather than of their proxies. The British countries disputed the need for this. Britain's standpoint was accepted at the meeting in Sydney, Austr., on September 2 when affiliation fees of £50 per annum for full members and £25 for associate members were agreed for the next two years up to the next IBB meeting in Edinburgh, Scot., during the 1970 Commonwealth Games. The British resignations were then withdrawn.

The United States finally realized that it could not stage a world championships meeting, and New Zealand came forward with a request to hold the successor to Sydney, 1966, during 1971. Fittingly, New Zealand's G. N. Boulton succeeded N. Benjamin as IBB president, and R. Thompson was elected vice-president. C. G. Smart of Sydney was reelected secretary.

David Bryant continued to show that he was the leading lawn bowler of the world by qualifying for three of the four English Championship events and by winning one of them, the fours. The English singles title went to Norman Groves. N. Jackson and A. Barrett won the pairs. J. Lamont won the Scottish Championship and, subsequently, the British Isles title.

In the U.S. George Dunn became singles champion at Buck Hill Falls, Pa., and in two respects the U.S. set the world pace. Only in that country was there an official national mixed doubles event and this was won by Alex and Dorothy Veitch. Veitch also captured the Vitalite, world drawing-to-the-jack title.

Australia appeared about to become the first country to follow Britain in introducing full-scale indoor play, with a proposed hall in Melbourne. (C. M. Jo.)

Boxing

The world heavyweight championship was in dispute throughout 1968. This was due to the fact that Muhammad Ali, who had refused on conscientious grounds in 1967 to be drafted into the U.S. armed forces, was not allowed to take part in any contest after successfully defending his title against Zora Folley in March 1967. Though his appeal against induction had not yet been heard, the World Boxing Association (WBA) and the New York State Athletic Commission declared his championship vacant.

As a result, the WBA began a series of elimination contests for the title in 1967. Jimmy Ellis (Louisville, Ky.), a former sparring partner of Muhammad Ali, won this version of the championship after outpointing Jerry Quarry of Los Angeles in April. Ellis defended his title in September by outpointing former world heavyweight champion Floyd Patterson in Stockholm. Ellis, however, was not recognized in all states. The new Madison Square Garden staged a New York championship version, matching Joe Frazier, 1964 Olympic heavyweight champion, against Buster Mathis. Frazier stopped Mathis in 11 rounds and was accepted as champion by New York State.

Curtis Cokes sends contender Willie Ludick to the canvas in Dallas, Tex., during championship bout April 16, 1968. Cokes retained his welterweight title with a TKO in the fifth round.

With the U.S. recognizing both Frazier and Ellis as heavyweight champions, Europe had little to offer in opposition throughout the year. Karl Mildenberger of West Germany, who had failed in the WBA elimination series, defended his European title by outpointing another German, Gerhard Zech, but later lost the title to Henry Cooper, the British champion. Mildenberger was disqualified in the eighth round when he knocked his head against Cooper's, resulting in the British champion's sustaining a cut around the eye. Cooper thus regained the title he had won in 1964. The European Boxing Union (EBU) had declared the title vacant later that same year when Cooper announced he was not fit to meet Mildenberger.

The reign of Dick Tiger as world light heavyweight champion ended in May when Bob Foster (U.S.) stopped the veteran Nigerian champion in four rounds in New York. Tiger had won the world middleweight title at the age of 33 in 1962. When he lost this championship to Emile Griffith in 1966, he surprised boxing fans by going on to take the light heavyweight crown from José Torres of Puerto Rico at the age of 37.

Nino Benvenuti (Italy) recaptured the world middleweight title, outpointing Emile Griffith (U.S.). He then successfully defended it against Don Fullmer (U.S.) in December. Curtis Cokes (U.S.) was most active of world champions, successfully defending the welterweight championship he had won in 1966 by beating Willie Ludick of South Africa in five rounds

			Boxing Champions			
			as of Dec. 31, 1968			
Division	World	Europe	Commonwealth	Britain	Canada	Orient
Heavyweight	Jimmy Ellis, U.S.* Joe Frazier, U.S.*	Henry Cooper, Eng.	Henry Cooper, Eng.	Henry Cooper, Eng.	George Chuvalo, Ont.	...
Light heavyweight	Bob Foster, U.S.	Tom Bogs, Denmark	Bobby Dunlop, Austr.	Young McCormack, Eng.	Al Sparks, Man.	...
Middleweight	Nino Benvenuti, Italy	Carlos Duran, Italy	Johnny Pritchett, Eng.	Johnny Pritchett, Eng.	Dave Downey, N.S.	Ki Soo Kim, S. Korea
Junior middleweight	vacant	vacant†	...	...	...	Ansano Lee, S. Korea
Welterweight	Curtis Cokes, U.S.	Edwin Mack, Neth.	Ralph Charles, Eng.	Ralph Charles, Eng.	Joey Durelle, Que.	Musashi Nakano, Japan
Junior welterweight	Paul Fujii, Hawaii, U.S.	Bruno Arcari, Italy†	Des Rea, Eng.	Des Rea, Eng.	...	Larry Flaviano, Phil.
Lightweight	Carlos Cruz, Dom. Rep.	Pedro Carrasco, Spain	Percy Hayles, Jamaica	Ken Buchanan, Scot.	Al Ford, Alta.	Pedro Adigue, Phil.
Junior lightweight	Hiroshi Kobayashi, Jap.	...	Jimmy Anderson, Eng.	Jimmy Anderson, Eng.	Les Gillis, N.S.	Yoshiaki Numata, Japan
Featherweight	José Legra, Spain‡	vacant	Johnny Famechon, Austr.	...	...	Herbert Kang, S. Korea
Junior featherweight	...	...	...	...	...	Sulfredo Basco, Phil.
Bantamweight	Lionel Rose, Austr.	Salvatore Burruni, Italy	Alan Rudkin, Eng.	Alan Rudkin, Eng.	Jack Burke, N.B.	Won Suk Lee, S. Korea
Flyweight	Chartchai Chionoi, Thailand	Fernando Atzori, Italy	Walter McGowan, Scot.	John McCluskey, Scot.	Alex Martin, N.S.	Takeshi Nakamura, Japan

*Ellis recognized by World Boxing Association; Frazier, by New York State.
†Under European Boxing Union rules these divisions are classed light middleweight and light welterweight. There is a slight difference in the actual weight.
‡Legra not accepted as champion throughout U.S.

at Dallas, Tex. Cokes also won several nontitle contests.

The world lightweight championship, which had been dominated by Carlos Ortiz of Puerto Rico for six years, changed hands when Carlos Cruz of the Dominican Republic outpointed Ortiz at Santo Domingo in June. Cruz defended this title three months later, beating Mando Ramos (U.S.) at Los Angeles.

With world featherweight champion Vicente Saldivar (Mex.) retiring after his third title fight victory over Howard Winstone (Wales) at the end of 1967, this division remained vacant for some months. Winstone was matched in London against Japan's Mitsunori Seki and was declared world champion when the referee stopped the fight because of an injury to Seki's eye. Most states in the U.S. declined to recognize Winstone as official champion, and the EBU agreed to recognize the Welshman as champion only

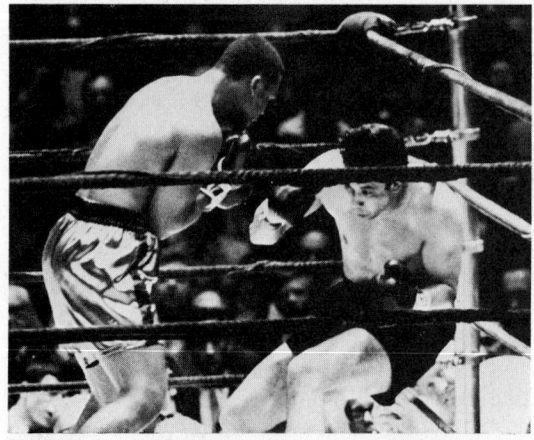

Challenger Manuel Ramos goes down under the blows of champion Joe Frazier in a heavyweight title fight June 24 in New York City. Frazier retained the title in two rounds.

Jimmy Ellis jabbing Jerry Quarry during their heavyweight title match in Oakland, Calif., on April 27. Ellis won in a split decision.

WIDE WORLD

if he met and defeated José Legra, an exiled Cuban living in Spain. This fight took place at Porthcawl, Wales, in July and Legra won in five rounds. He was recognized as champion throughout much of the world, but not by all states of the U.S. or by the EBU.

The world bantamweight championship was won by Lionel Rose of Australia, who beat the Japanese champion, Masahiko Harada, in Tokyo, and then successfully defended it against Chucho Castillo of Mexico. In the flyweight division Chartchai Chionoi (Thailand) continued to be recognized as champion.

As in the United States, there were fewer title fights in Europe than in the previous year. In addition to the heavyweight defeat of Mildenberger, the light heavyweight title changed hands when Tom Bogs (Denmark) stopped Lothar Stengel (W.Ger.) in the first

round. Carlos Duran (Italy) retained his European middleweight title against Wally Swift (Eng.), who was disqualified in the tenth round of the contest in Birmingham, Eng. Duran later defended his title again, beating Jupp Elze (W.Ger.) in Cologne, W.Ger. The welterweight championship changed when Edwin Mack (Neth.) stopped the champion, Carmelo Bossi (Italy), in nine rounds in Milan, Italy. The most active European champion was Pedro Carrasco (Spain), who retained the lightweight title, beating Kid Tano (Spain) in eight rounds in Madrid and stopping Bruno Melisano (Italy) in three at Barcelona, Spain. The European featherweight title, which had become vacant when Winstone fought Seki, was won by José Legra who beat Yves Desmarets (France) in three rounds, but after Legra beat Winstone, the European championship was again declared vacant. Salvatore Burruni (Italy), a former world flyweight champion, won the European bantamweight title, beating Mimun ben Ali (Spain) in Naples. Italy continued to hold the flyweight crown as Fernando Atzori easily beat off the challenge of John McCluskey (Scot.), winning in four rounds in Naples.

The big boxing events in the amateur world were the Olympic Games championships in Mexico City. The Soviet Union had the best results, winning three gold medals, two silver, and one bronze, while the United States was not far behind with two gold, one silver, and four bronze. Poland collected one gold, two silver, and two bronze.

Much interest was shown in George Foreman, a 19-year-old Negro from the U.S., who followed the footsteps of Floyd Patterson, Muhammad Ali, and Joe Frazier by winning an Olympic gold medal. They had all gone on to win the world professional heavyweight championship (in Frazier's case only the New York version so far), and it was speculated that Foreman would turn professional. Foreman, who stood 6 ft. 3 in. and scaled 218 lb., showed great strength in stopping a big Soviet miner, 29-year-old Jonas Chapulis, in two rounds. One of the best Olympic champions was Boris Lagutin (U.S.S.R.), who had won a gold medal in Tokyo and repeated this performance with a devastating display against Roland Garbey (Cuba) in the light middleweight final. Britain's Chris Finnegan won the middleweight title by a narrow decision from Aleksei Kiselev (U.S.S.R.). A new category—the light flyweight—produced a Venezuelan Olympic champion for the first time in Francisco Rodriguez, who outpointed Jung-Ju Jee (S. Korea) in the final. For a listing of the Olympic winners, see SPORTING RECORD: Special Report. (F. BR.)

Brazil

A federal republic in eastern and central South America, Brazil is bounded by the Atlantic Ocean and all the countries of South America except Ecuador and Chile. Area: 3,286,470 sq.mi. (8,511,965 sq.km.). Pop. (1968 est.): 89,376,000, including (1960 census) Caucasians 60%; mulattoes 26%; Negroes 11%; Amerindians 2%; Asians 1%. Principal cities (metropolitan area pop., 1968 est.): Brasília (cap.) 390,000; Rio de Janeiro 4,207,000; São Paulo 5,685,000. Language: Portuguese. Religion: 93% Roman Catholic. President in 1968, Artur da Costa e Silva.

At the time President Costa e Silva was inaugurated, the country was going through a period of serious political unrest and economic recession, the latter due mainly to the severe anti-inflationary measures taken by the previous administration. The provision in the 1967 constitution for indirect election of the president and vice-president was bitterly criticized by many as antidemocratic and tending to keep the country under a regime of dictatorship; the decrees signed by former Pres. Humberto Castelo Branco suspending for ten years the political rights of so-called corrupt politicians and enemies of the 1964 revolution were resented not only by those affected but also by a great many people who wanted to see their country returned to its traditional political freedom.

Despite repeated assurances on the part of the administration that there were no Brazilian exiles or persons banished by act of the government, the fact remained that a large number of prominent political leaders—including three former presidents of the re-

LISL STEINER—KEYSTONE

Brazilian Air Force officers and diplomatic officials watching the flight of a de Haviland C-5 Buffalo at Ontario, Can. Brazil purchased 12 of the aircraft in 1968 to transport mail and medical aid and for emergency services in the Amazon Basin and other remote areas.

BRAZIL

Education. (1965) Primary, pupils 9,923,183, teachers 351,466; secondary, pupils 1,553,699, teachers (1964) 81,230; vocational, pupils 380,459, teachers (1964) 30,272; teacher training, students 220,272, teachers (1964) 20,782; higher (at 1,304 institutions, including 45 universities; 1966), students 180,109, teaching staff 36,109.

Finance. Monetary unit: new cruzeiro, with an exchange rate (as devalued Sept. 23, 1968) of 3.70 cruzeiros to U.S. $1 (8.88 cruzeiros = £1 sterling). Gold and foreign exchange, monetary authorities: (May 1968) U.S. $268 million; (May 1967) U.S. $321 million. Budget (1967 est.): revenue 11,098,000,000 cruzeiros; expenditure 13,591,000,000 cruzeiros. Gross domestic product: (1966) 43,844,000,000 cruzeiros; (1965) 30,405,000,000 cruzeiros. Money supply: (Dec. 1967) 15,055,000,000 cruzeiros; (Dec. 1966) 10,586,-000,000 cruzeiros. Cost of living (São Paulo; 1963 = 100): (May 1968) 704; (May 1967) 566.

Foreign Trade. (1967) Imports U.S. $1,667,000,-000; exports U.S. $1,654,000,000. Import sources: U.S. 34%; West Germany 10%; Argentina 7%. Export destinations: U.S. 33%; West Germany 8%; Netherlands 7%; Italy 7%; Argentina 6%. Main exports: coffee 43%; iron ore 6%; raw cotton 6%.

Transport and Communications. Roads (1965) 803,068 km. (including 36,170 km. main roads). Motor vehicles in use (1966): passenger 1,337,000; commercial (including buses) 1,059,900. Railways (1966): 31,961 km.; traffic 13,724,000,000 passenger-km., freight 19,253,000,000 net ton-km. Shipping (1967): merchant vessels 100 gross tons and over 394; gross tonnage 1,304,848. Air traffic (1966): 3,-124,170,000 passenger-km.; freight 97,765,000 net ton-km. Telephones (Jan. 1967) 1,431,653. Radio receivers (Dec. 1964) c. 7.5 million. Television receivers (Dec. 1966) c. 2.5 million.

Agriculture. Production (in 000; metric tons; 1967; 1966 in parentheses): cotton, lint 608 (622); coffee (1966) 1,366, (1965) 1,832; cocoa (1966–67) 173, (1965–66) 171; wheat (1966) 615, (1965) 585; corn 12,401 (11,371); rice 6,555 (5,802); cassava 26,646 (24,710); potatoes (1966) 1,329, (1965) 1,-246; sweet potatoes (1966) 1,913, (1965) 1,721; bananas (1965) 4,531, (1964) 4,397; sisal 315 (287); tobacco (1966) 228, (1965) 248; peanuts 711 (895); sugar, raw value (1966–67) 4,390, (1965–66) 4,851; dry beans 2,309 (2,148); soybeans 674 (595); rubber (1966) 24, (1965) 29; timber (1966) c. 161,100 cu.m., (1965) c. 156,400 cu.m. Livestock (in 000; Dec. 1966): cattle 90,153; horses 9,082; pigs 61,728; sheep 22,102; goats 13,957; chickens (Dec. 1965) 254,434. Fish catch (in 000; metric tons) (1966) 436, (1965) 422.

Industry. Fuel and power (in 000; 1966): coal 1,734 metric tons; crude oil (1967) 6,978 metric tons; natural gas 788,000 cu.m.; electricity (85% hydroelectric) 32,654,000 kw-hr. Production (in 000; metric tons; 1966): pig iron 2,960; crude steel (1967) 3,-673; bauxite 250; iron ore (65–70% metal content) 23,260; manganese ore (metal content) 640; gold 208 troy oz.; cement (1967) 6,286; wood pulp (1965) 683; paper (1965) 627; passenger cars (including assembly; 1967) 141 units; commercial vehicles (including assembly; 1967) 85 units.

public—were either living abroad or, if allowed to live in the country, were barred from exercising the constitutional rights granted to ordinary citizens. The political opposition grouping known as Frente Ampla (Broad Front) remained active; but in April the minister of justice issued an ordinance declaring that Frente Ampla did not conform with the legal provisions regarding political parties. For that reason it could not, as such, engage in any public political activities. The federal authorities were instructed to arrest and bring to trial any persons who, though their political rights had been suspended, still insisted on taking part in political activities. In addition, any publications issued by such persons were to be seized.

This, apparently, was brought about by the serious disorderly conduct of groups, allegedly of students, who, in disregard of the authorities' prohibition, had carried on public demonstrations in Rio de Janeiro. The demonstrators destroyed property, shouted slogans offensive to the authorities, and threw missiles of all kinds at the police officers. There was also some shooting. Unable to control the demonstrators, the authorities of Guanabara state (Rio de Janeiro) requested the help of the federal authorities. The regular armed forces were ordered to reestablish and maintain public order in the city.

Similar outbreaks occurred in other cities throughout the nation. During the disturbances of March 29 in Rio de Janeiro one student was killed. A few days later, during the religious ceremonies connected with his funeral, there were again demonstrations that provoked violent reaction from the soldiers. President Costa e Silva, returning from a visit to the south of the country, declared at this time that no extraordinary measures would be taken by his government despite the provocations from extremists who, he declared, were trying to overthrow the government. However, he added, law and order would be maintained at any cost. At the same time, he assured the nation that valid complaints from the students would be considered.

The demonstrations continued. The army barracks in the city of São Paulo were bombed and one soldier was killed. On June 26 in Rio de Janeiro about 60,000 persons, including students, workers, Roman Catholic priests and nuns, teachers, and writers, marched through the central streets of the city in a peaceful and authorized protest against the administration's policies and alleged police brutalities. New demon-

strations by students occurred in São Paulo and other cities, and the outbreaks continued sporadically throughout the nation into July.

Alarmed at the proportions of the students' protests, the Cabinet met with President Costa e Silva and requested that immediate measures be taken to revamp the national educational system. As a consequence, the president decided to request the planning minister to formulate plans for new educational policies to be adopted by the administration. A project sent to the president early in July called for the revision of the universities' curricula, better pay for teachers, broader autonomy for the university authorities, compulsory retirement of teachers appointed for life, and admission of a larger number of students. The administration released funds for immediate improvements in the federally supported institutions. At the end of the month the administration announced that a program to offer new school facilities to more than 600,000 children would be carried out in 1969 and that an additional one million children would be provided for in 1970.

At about the same time the National Security Council also met to study the general situation and to suggest measures to be taken to preserve law and order. It was officially announced that the council was convinced that there was a concerted plan of action among subversive and antiadministration elements to disturb public order for the ultimate purpose of overthrowing the government.

Recognizing that the country was going through a stage of rapid growth, the council suggested that the president take the following measures: (1) back fully the state and local authorities in their determination to prohibit political rallies and any action in disregard of their authority; (2) take the exceptional measures allowed under the constitution; (3) appeal to the mass information media not to condone disorderly conduct; and (4) continue to promote the principles of the 1964 revolution with the backing of the armed forces.

Apparently, some religious leaders and members of the clergy sided with the critics of the government. Although at the end of 1967, 21 bishops, after a three-day meeting in Rio de Janeiro, had published a manifesto condemning subversive activities, in April 1968 the hierarchy allowed priests and nuns to participate in the students' demonstrations. In July, during the 19th meeting of the National Bishops Assembly, President Costa e Silva met with the archbishop of São Paulo to hear the church's points of view in regard to national problems. In a letter addressed to the president, the bishops repudiated the declarations of some religious leaders and laymen criticizing the government.

Finally, in mid-December, President Costa e Silva deemed the situation so threatening that he dissolved Congress and placed Brazil under martial law. Former President Juscelino Kubitschek was reported to be under arrest.

Despite the social unrest, the administration persevered in its determination to keep inflation at a level compatible with national development. As announced by the Getúlio Vargas Foundation, the inflationary rate was estimated at 1.5% a month during the first quarter of 1968. It had been 45% for the whole of 1966 and 30% for 1967. By the middle of 1968 the administration claimed that there were good reasons for optimism insofar as economic conditions were concerned. There had been, it was announced, a 14%

increase in industrial production; exports had increased perceptibly; crops were good; credit facilities had become easier; and the gross national product rose 5% in 1967, compared with 3.5% in 1966. It was expected that the rate of growth would attain 6% during 1968.   (R. d'E.)

ENCYCLOPÆDIA BRITANNICA FILMS. *The Amazon—People and Resources of Northern Brazil* (1957); *Brazil—People of the Highlands* (1957).

Bulgaria

A people's republic of Europe, Bulgaria is situated on the eastern Balkan Peninsula along the Black Sea, bordered by Romania, Yugoslavia, Greece, and Turkey. Area: 42,823 sq.mi. (110,912 sq.km.). Pop. (1967 est.): 8,310,200. Cap. and largest city: Sofia (pop., 1967 est., 825,200). Language: chiefly Bulgarian. First secretary of the Bulgarian Communist Party and chairman of the Council of Ministers (premier) in 1968, Todor Zhivkov; chairman of the Presidium of the National Assembly, Georgi Traikov.

Faithfully pro-Soviet in foreign policy, Bulgaria continued in 1968 to be reluctant to deviate from "orthodox" Marxism-Leninism. Following the re-

---

BULGARIA

Education. (1965–66) Primary, pupils 1,129,315, teachers 49,442; secondary, pupils 125,333, teachers 6,969; vocational, pupils 174,910, teachers 8,761; teacher training, students 157, teachers 2; higher (at 47 institutions, including Sofia University), students 100,102, teaching staff 6,538.

Finance. Monetary unit: lev, with an official exchange rate of 1.17 leva to U.S. $1 (2.81 leva = £1 sterling) and a tourist rate of 2 leva to U.S. $1 (4.80 leva =£1 sterling). Budget (1968 est.): revenue 4,420,000,000 leva; expenditure 4,480,000,000 leva.

Foreign Trade. (1967) Imports U.S. $1,572,000,-000; exports U.S. $1,458,000,000. Main import sources (1966): U.S.S.R. 48%; West Germany 9%; East Germany 7%; Czechoslovakia 5%. Main export destinations (1966): U.S.S.R. 51%; East Germany 8%; Czechoslovakia 5%. Main exports (1966): tobacco and cigarettes 14%; clothing 7%; metals 6%; fruit and vegetables 6%.

Transport and Communications. State roads (1965) 28,914 km. (including 2,374 first-class motor roads). Motor vehicles in use (1961): passenger *c.* 9,300; commercial *c.* 20,400. Railways: (1966) 4,094 km.; traffic (1967) 5,393,000,000 passenger-km., freight 11,710,000,000 net ton-km. Shipping (1967): merchant vessels 100 gross tons and over 97; gross tonnage 470,814. Air traffic (1966): 506,677,000 passenger-km.; freight 8,678,000 net ton-km. Telephones (Dec. 1966) 306,361. Radio receivers (Dec. 1966) 2,144,000. Television receivers (Dec. 1966) 288,000.

Agriculture. Production (in 000; metric tons; 1967; 1966 in parentheses): wheat 3,254 (3,193); corn 1,971 (2,207); barley 985 (1,064); oats 169 (182); sunflower seed (1966) 423, (1965) 357; cottonseed (1966) 45, (1965) 25; sugar, raw value (1967–68) *c.* 220, (1966–67) *c.* 220; tomatoes (1966) 751, (1965) 775; grapes 923 (1,081); tobacco (1966) 132, (1965) 123; eggs (1966) 1,438,000 units, (1965) 1,402,000 units. Livestock (in 000; Jan. 1967): sheep 9,998; cattle 1,385; goats 409; pigs 2,276; horses 229; asses 291; poultry 23,637.

Industry. Production (in 000; metric tons; 1967): coal 467; lignite 26,723; crude oil 499; electricity 13,600,000 kw-hr.; iron ore (32% metal content) 2,496; manganese ore (metal content; 1966) 8; copper concentrates (metal content) 29; lead concentrates (metal content) 87; pig iron 1,028; crude steel 1,240; copper (1966) 26; lead 97; zinc (1966) 77; cement 3,356; sulfuric acid 360; soda ash (1966) 226; cotton fabrics 306,000 m.; woolen fabrics 24,000 m. Index of industrial production (1963 = 100): (1967) 162; (1966) 143.

newal in 1967 for another 20 years of its alliances with the Soviet Union (May 13) and Poland (April 6), and the conclusion, for the first time, of a Bulgarian-East German treaty of mutual assistance on September 7, Bulgaria signed in Prague on April 26, 1968, a new 20-year treaty with Czechoslovakia. A new clause of this treaty proclaimed that the two countries would assist each other against "the forces of West German militarism and revanchism that are threatening peace." When Bulgaria participated in the military occupation of Czechoslovakia August 20–21, it was alleged that it was acting in accordance with the above-mentioned clause. (*See* CZECHOSLOVAKIA.)

The old Bulgarian-Yugoslav conflict over the national character of Macedonia (dating back to 1878) was revived significantly for another round of polemics at a time of new coolness between the Soviet Union and Yugoslavia. Christo Christov, director of the Institute of History of the Bulgarian Academy of Sciences, published in *Istoricheski Pregled* (no. 2, 1968) an article in which he accused the Yugoslavs of "falsifying Bulgarian history." Commenting on the 90th anniversary of the Russo-Turkish treaty of San Stefano (March 3, 1878), which had created an ephemeral Greater Bulgaria covering all modern Yugoslav Macedonia, Christov spoke of "the Bulgarian population" of this member republic of the Yugoslav Federation. Replying, the Belgrade *Borba* (July 5) sharply criticized this "very persistent and unusually broadly organized campaign to deny Macedonian national independence." Some observers believed that Bulgaria's move was prompted by the Soviet Union in order to put pressure on Yugoslavia and discourage pro-Western tendencies there. In October it was reported that two Soviet airborne divisions had been stationed in Bulgaria.

At the end of March, Todor Zhivkov paid an official visit to Turkey. He signed with Suleyman Demirel, the Turkish prime minister, an agreement providing for the repatriation of approximately 15,000 Bulgarian citizens of Turkish origin to their true homeland.

The 11th congress of the Dimitrov Communist Youth Union was held in Sofia January 10–13. The main point on the agenda was the "Theses on Youth" submitted by Todor Zhivkov in his position as first secretary of the Bulgarian Communist Party. He stated in this document that "national nihilism" and "admiration for everything foreign" by young people was "insufferable and must be eradicated with a red-hot iron." The newly elected Central Committee appointed Ivan D. Panev as first secretary of the Youth Union, replacing Georgi Atanasov.

The ninth World Youth Festival was held in Sofia from July 28 to August 6 and was attended by 18,800 youths and students from 142 countries. The festival was not the success its organizers had hoped for, mainly because the delegations from Czechoslovakia, Yugoslavia, Great Britain, France, and West Germany were not handpicked and screened in advance. As a result criticism and dissension began on the first day, illustrating the disarray in the Communist world between the radicals of the New Left and members of the orthodox Old Left.

Industrial production in 1967 climbed 13.4% above that of 1966, while agricultural output only slightly exceeded the preceding year's figures. Total foreign trade rose between 1960 and 1967 from U.S. $1,149,-000,000 to $3,030,000,000; exports rose during the same period from $571 million to $1,458,000,000.

(K. SM.)

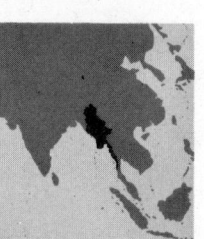

Burma

A republic of southeast Asia, Burma is on the Indochinese Peninsula, bordered by East Pakistan, India, Tibet, China, Laos, and Thailand. Area: 261,789 sq.mi. (678,034 sq.km.). Pop. (1967 est.): 25,811,000. Cap. and largest city: Rangoon (pop., 1966 est., 1,-358,000). Language: Burmese 66%. Religion: Buddhist 84%. Chairman of the Revolutionary Council and prime minister in 1968, Gen. Ne Win.

Gen. Ne Win's Revolutionary Council continued in 1968 to place its major emphasis on building up a nation of healthy, literate citizens, trained to make the fullest use of their own natural resources. Development of medical services was a top priority, and a continuous expansion of rural health centres was designed to give Burma the first nationwide health service in its history. With the growth of health consciousness among the people the demand for medical personnel increased rapidly. New medical schools in Mandalay and Mingaladon and a paramedical institute in Rangoon were gradually supplying the personnel needs. Specialized training was mainly acquired from the U.K. through the Colombo Plan and other organizations, and the U.K., Japan, and West Germany provided modern medical equipment.

The wide area over which general research was being carried out was indicated during the third Research Congress held in Rangoon in March. It heard reports dealing with the excavation of old cities prominent in

BURMA
Education. (1965–66) Primary, pupils 1,886,335, teachers 36,975; secondary (1964–65), pupils 497,-275, teachers 15,631; vocational (1964–65), pupils 2,846, teachers 99; teacher training (1964–65), students 3,138, teachers 145; higher (at 24 institutions, including Universities of Rangoon and Mandalay), students 31,190, teaching staff 3,264.
Finance and Banking. Monetary unit: kyat, with a par value of 4.76 kyats to U.S. $1 (1 kyat = 1s. 9d. sterling). Gold and foreign exchange, official: (June 1968) U.S. $151.7 million; (June 1967) U.S. $160.2 million. Budget (1967–68 est.): revenue 9,253,000,000 kyats; expenditure 9,195,000,000 kyats. Money supply: (March 1968) 2,522,000,000 kyats; (March 1967) 2.4 billion kyats. Gross national product: (1963–64) 7,731,000,000 kyats; (1962–63) 8,115,-000,000 kyats.
Foreign Trade. (1967) Imports 674.5 million kyats; exports 588.3 million kyats. Import sources (1966): Japan 24%; U.K. 12%; U.S. 11%; China 7%; Pakistan 6%. Export destinations (1966): India 25%; Ceylon 10%; China 9%; Japan 7%; U.K. 6%; Indonesia 5%. Main exports: rice 53%; teak 21%; oil cakes 6%.
Transport and Communications. Roads (1965) *c.* 25,000 km. (including *c.* 11,000 all-weather). Motor vehicles in use (1965): passenger 25,200; commercial (including buses) 24,800. Railways: (1966) 4,295 km.; traffic (1967) 2,405,000,000 passenger-km., freight 785 million net ton-km. Air traffic (1966): 74,938,000 passenger-km.; freight 1,276,000 net ton-km. Telephones (Dec. 1966) 20,198. Radio receivers (Dec. 1966) 335,000.
Agriculture. Production (in 000; metric tons; 1967; 1966 in parentheses): rice *c.* 8,052 (6,636); rubber, exports (1966) *c.* 8, (1965) 8; sesame (1966) 57, (1965) 62; peanuts (1966) 278, (1965) 288; dry beans (1966) 141, (1965) 114; cotton, lint (1966) 15, (1965) 15; jute (1966) 13, (1965) 15; tobacco *c.* 38 (52); sugar, raw value (1967–68) *c.* 223, (1966–67) *c.* 216; timber (1963–64) 919, (1962–63) 1,094. Livestock (in 000; June 1966): cattle 6,096; sheep 181; buffaloes 1,259; pigs 1,032; goats 607.
Industry. Production (in 000; metric tons; 1966): cement 141; crude oil (1967) 587; electricity (excluding most industrial production) 396 kw-hr.; lead ore and concentrates (metal content; 1965) 17; zinc concentrates (metal content) 6; tin concentrates (metal content) 0.4.

182

Burundi

Burmese history, the production of newsprint paper from bamboo, and the scientific use of raw materials for medical supplies and of fertilizers.

Intensive oil prospecting in the Irrawaddy Delta, helped by a modern drilling rig from the U.S., promised a high yield close to the main refinery at Syriam, thus avoiding the long, expensive journey from the oil fields at Chauk. In any event, the latter area was becoming depleted.

The nine-man board set up under the Iron and Steel Industry Implementation Board Order of 1966 issued its report in August 1968 stating that there were more than 63 million tons of iron ore deposits in the Taunggyi region and 128 million tons of coal in the Kalewa area. Together, they made the establishment of a steel industry a feasible proposition.

Considerable progress was made during the year in the construction of roads, and the amount of irrigated land also increased as large-scale projects matured. The largest of these projects was the Kyetmauktaung Dam in Myitkyina District, built with Soviet aid. Fieldwork on the Mu River survey undertaken by the UN Development Programme jointly with the Burmese government was completed. It was carried out by 14 Italian technicians and 12 Burmese engineers. The Sittang Valley project made progress; when complete it would control floods and irrigate 2.4 million ac. (972,000 ha.) in the Toungoo, Pegu, and Hanthawaddy districts.

Agricultural production remained the most intractable problem of the Revolutionary Council. The peasants still lacked incentive in spite of lavish loans. To this was added the threat of insurgents who, in varying degrees according to the area, engaged in acts of sabotage. The spasmodic mining of bridges and explosions on the railroad lines from Mandalay and Moulmein to Rangoon had a great nuisance value in keeping a large army continuously on the alert.

The outlines of Burma's road to socialism had become clear by the end of the year. The parliamentary system had been abandoned as unsuitable. In its place, workers and peasants, who constituted the main forces in the country, were organized by means of the People's Workers Council and the People's Peasants Council. National solidarity was built on this worker-peasant alliance. The only recognized political party, the Burmese Way to Socialism Program (*Lanzin*), was growing slowly but had not yet achieved any widespread popularity. Gradually, cadres of political workers were being trained (1,000 at a time) in the School of Political Science in Rangoon. In February 1968 practically all the political prisoners arrested during the coup of 1962 were released. Their future and potential influence remained obscure.

In its foreign policy Burma remained neutral, unprovoked by the violent riots of Chinese students in June 1967 or by the vicious propaganda onslaughts of Communist China; however, it took the precaution of tightening up its frontiers with Thailand and with India. A new and serious problem developed on the border with India, along a stretch of which rebel Nagas crossed over through Burmese territory into China. That part of the border was later sealed. However, Chinese infiltration into Kachin State, where the local Communists were openly supported by Peking, continued. By the end of the year this northern part of Kachin State had become the most dangerously unsettled region in Burma. (D. Wn.)

ENCYCLOPÆDIA BRITANNICA FILMS. *Burma, People of the River* (1957).

Business Management:
see Employment, Wages, and Hours; Industrial Review; Merchandising

Business Review:
see Economy, World

Butter:
see Agriculture

Burundi

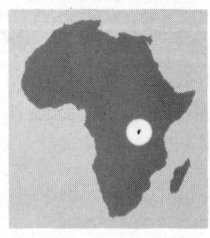

A republic of eastern Africa, Burundi is bordered by the Congo, Rwanda, and Tanzania. Area: 10,707 sq.mi. (27,731 sq.km.). Pop. (1967 est.): 3,340,000, mainly Hutu, Tutsi, and Twa. Cap. and largest city: Bujumbura (pop., 1965 est., 71,390). Language: Kirundi and French. Religion: Roman Catholic 40%; Protestant 5%; animist 55%. President in 1968, Michel Micombero.

In August Col. Michel Micombero reorganized his government, ridding himself of five members of the Cabinet (including the secretary-general of the ruling Uprona Party) to ensure "a dynamic and authentically republican government." Close relations with Tanzania and the Congo (Kinshasa) were maintained. On April 24, after talks with Pres. Julius Nyerere of Tanzania, the foreign minister of Burundi stated that Biafra must be recognized if the present situation in Nigeria continued, and that the civil war there was "not political and should be viewed from humanitarian grounds." Following the Burundi commander in chief's visit to the Congo (Kinshasa); a March communiqué stated that the Congolese National Army (itself Israeli-trained) would train Burundi parachutists, in return for Burundi's help against white mercenaries at Bukavu in 1967.

On February 4 Pres. Joseph Mobutu of the Congo (Kinshasa) announced the formation of the Union of Central African States (UEAC), which Burundi and several other nations were invited to join. Burundi refused, and the UEAC, which attracted only three nations, was dissolved in December.

External aid continued to shore up the economy, with the European Economic Community providing $91,000 toward the Burundi College of Administration, and awards to 153 scholars. Belgium continued to supply considerable aid under the Brussels Convention. For 1968 this was estimated at BFr. 92.5 million (comprising a loan of BFr. 64.5 million, an endowment of BFr. 6 million, and supplementary aid), which was to be spent on the Institute of Agronomy, medical supplies, and other public works. Belgium also supplied about 300 technical personnel. (M. Mr.)

BURUNDI

Education. (1965–66) Primary, pupils 146,920, teachers 3,633; secondary, pupils 2,469, teachers 217; vocational, pupils 1,658, teachers (1964–65) 115; teacher training, students 1,698, teachers 180; higher (including University of Bujumbura), students 188, teaching staff 66.

Finance. Monetary unit: Burundi franc, with a par value of BurFr. 175 to Belgian Fr. 100 (BurFr. 87.50 = U.S. $1; BurFr. 210 = £1 sterling). Gold and foreign exchange, central bank: (March 1968) U.S. $2,590,000; (March 1967) U.S. $2,560,000. Budget (1965 est.): revenue BurFr. 1,273,000,000; expenditure BurFr. 1,158,000,000.

Foreign Trade. (1966) Imports BurFr. 1,698,000,000; exports BurFr. 1,213,000,000. Import sources: Belgium-Luxembourg 25%; U.S. 20%; Tanzania 14%; West Germany 8%; France 7%. Export destinations: U.S. 84%; Belgium-Luxembourg 6%. Main exports: coffee 83%; cotton 8%.

Transport and Communications. Roads (1966) c. 6,000 km. (including 45 km. with improved surface). Telephones (Jan. 1964) c. 2,300.

Agriculture. Production (in 000; metric tons; 1966; 1965 in parentheses): sweet potatoes 743 (714); dry beans 155 (141); coffee 15 (15). Livestock (in 000; Dec. 1965): cattle 583; sheep 195.

Cambodia

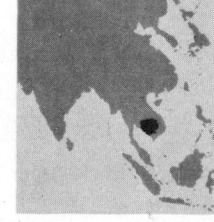

A constitutional monarchy (without a ruling monarch in 1968) of Southeast Asia, Cambodia is the southwest part of the Indochinese Peninsula. Area: 69,898 sq.mi. (181,035 sq.km.). Pop. (1968 est.): 6,557,000, including (est.) Cambodian 85%; Vietnamese 8%; Chinese 6%. Cap.: Phnom Penh (pop., 1962, 393,995). Language: Khmer and French. Religion: Buddhism. Chief of state in 1968, Prince Norodom Sihanouk; premier, Son Sann.

The period from late 1967 to late 1968 was considerably quieter than the preceding 12 months had been for Cambodia. The quarrel with Communist China was patched up in a manner that represented a clear victory for Prince Sihanouk, who had observed that Cambodia was China's only friend in Southeast Asia. In January 1968 the prince reported that China, together with certain leftist French advisers in Cambodia, was dissatisfied with his decision that the poorly equipped Cambodian Army of 35,000 men would not oppose U.S. forces who might pursue Viet Cong or North Vietnamese troops into Cambodian border areas. This decision was, in fact, in line with the prince's consistent policy, which was to spare Cambodia damage and suffering.

A few weeks later Prince Sihanouk again had to face a Communist threat, in the west and southwest. The Army was ordered to recover the rifles recently distributed to the villagers and to paramilitary units in that region in order, Sihanouk said, to prevent their capture by Communists operating on the Viet Cong pattern. At the same time, a sampan manned by North Vietnamese and Khmer rebels was caught smuggling arms into the country. Incidents such as these, said Sihanouk, made him "wonder if the Chinese were not trying to force him to turn the country over to the Americans."

On March 1 Sihanouk also threatened to hand the government back to Lieut. Gen. Lon Nol, commander in chief of the armed forces and a former premier, who had previously had close ties with the U.S. military advisers in the country. One result would be that the Viet Cong would no longer be able to use Cambodia as a sanctuary, apparently the prince's first admission that they were doing so.

Thereafter, the local Communists confined their activity largely to the distribution of antigovernment leaflets. China ceased its overt support for the Cambodian leftists, allowing Sino-Cambodian relations to revert to normal. In April the *People's Daily* of Communist China issued an emphatic declaration of support for Cambodia against U.S. imperialism, and a delegation of the Cambodian Royal Council visited Peking in August as a gesture of friendship.

Meanwhile yet another danger appeared, in the north, the prince stating in April and May that the pro-Communist Pathet Lao had established in southern Laos a headquarters for subversion in Cambodia and had begun infiltrating agitators among the hill peoples of northeastern Cambodia. China and North Vietnam, he observed, had declared their respect for Cambodia's frontiers, but the Pathet Lao and the Thai Patriotic Front had always refused to do so; in fact, the Pathet Lao had claimed part of Stung Treng province two years earlier. Hence, it appeared possible that Cambodia might be overrun by Communists from other countries, even if China and North Vietnam kept their promises.

Despite these difficulties, relations with the anti-Communist governments of Thailand and South Vietnam and with the U.S. showed no improvement. To the U.S., indeed, Sihanouk used the exact converse of the language he had used to the Chinese, suggesting that U.S. and South Vietnamese attacks on Cambodian border regions might drive him into the arms of Peking. Two Americans and eight Filipinos on board a tug captured on May 25 after straying into Cambodian waters on the Mekong River were released on June 10. On July 17, however, a landing craft with 11 Americans on board was captured in similar circumstances; the prince suggested that he would release the prisoners only if he received a "ransom" in the form of tractors or bulldozers or of an indemnity for Cambodians killed in a border village that had been shelled.

(P. H. M. J.)

Yugoslavian President Tito being welcomed to Cambodia by Prince Sihanouk during Tito's state visit in January 1968.

Cameroon

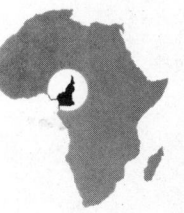

A federal republic of west equatorial Africa on the Gulf of Guinea, Cameroon borders on Nigeria, Chad, the Central African Republic, the Congo (Brazzaville), Gabon, and Equatorial Guinea. Area: 183,591 sq.mi. (475,500 sq.km.). Pop. (1965 est.): 5,229,000, mainly Negro. Cap.: Yaoundé (pop., 1964 est., 103,015). Largest city: Douala (pop., 1964 est., 159,000). Language: Bantu, Sudanic, French, and English. Religion: mainly animism or tribal beliefs; some Christian and Muslim. President in 1968, Ahmadou Ahidjo.

In January and August 1968 two minor government reshuffles mildly disturbed the generally even tenor of Cameroon's internal politics. In foreign affairs, however, two significant aspects of President Ahidjo's policy emerged during the year: the attitude toward the newly formed Union of Central African States (UEAC), and governmental reaction to the Nigerian conflict.

CAMEROON

Education. (1965–66) Primary, pupils 713,603, teachers (including preprimary) 15,719; secondary, pupils 28,529, teachers 1,080; vocational, pupils 10,279; teacher training, students 2,045; higher (at 7 institutions, including University of Cameroon), students 1,567, teaching staff 134.

Finance. Monetary unit: CFA franc, with a parity of CFA Fr. 50 to the French franc (CFA Fr. 246.85 = U.S. \$1; CFA Fr. 592.45 = £1 sterling). Federal budget (1965–66 est.) balanced at CFA Fr. 30.9 billion (including capital expenditure of CFA Fr. 4.3 billion).

Foreign Trade. (East Cameroon; 1967) Imports CFA Fr. 43,780,000,000; exports CFA Fr. 30,130,-000,000. Import sources (1966): France 59%; West Germany 6%; U.S. 5%. Export destinations (1966): France 36%; U.S. 19%; Netherlands 14%; West Germany 8%. Main exports (1966): coffee 29%; cocoa 20%; aluminum 16%; cotton 8%; timber 7%. West Cameroon accounted for 13% of total Cameroon trade in 1965.

Transport and Communications. Roads (East Cameroon only; 1967) 32,558 km. (including 4,182 km. main roads). Railways: (1966) 520 km.; traffic (1967) 134 million passenger-km., freight 198 million net ton-km. Telephones (Jan. 1967) c. 4,500. Radio receivers (1966) c. 200,000.

Agriculture. Production (in 000; metric tons; 1966; 1965 in parentheses): sweet potatoes c. 260 (c. 270); cassava c. 700 (c. 696); coffee c. 60 (55); cocoa c. 86 (c. 79); bananas c. 120 (c. 135); peanuts 132 (c. 130); rubber, exports 12.9 (11.2); cotton, lint (1967) c. 17, (1966) c. 19; corn (East Cameroon only; 1965) 170, (1964) 216; dry beans (1965) 26, (1964) 94; millet and sorghum c. 490 (484); palm kernels c. 21 (c. 25); palm oil c. 35 (c. 34); timber (1966) c. 5,800 cu.m., (1965) c. 5,800 cu.m. Livestock (in 000; East Cameroon only; Dec. 1966): cattle 1,900; pigs 300; sheep (Dec. 1965) c. 1,150; goats 3,500; poultry 5,000.

Industry. Production (1967) aluminum 48,000 metric tons.

The February announcement by the Central African Republic, Chad, and the Congo (Kinshasa) that they intended to secede from the Central African Customs and Economic Union in favour of the UEAC in no way affected Cameroon's decision to remain loyal to the former institution, which had proved a considerable source of benefit to it. The UEAC proved ineffective and was dissolved in December.

Although the government refused to recognize the breakaway Nigerian state of Biafra, both out of respect for the charter of the Organization of African Unity (OAU) and out of the need to maintain internal order, in July Cameroon did send a representative to the OAU Consultation Committee on Nigeria. This envoy, together with the representative from Ghana, offered to provide shipping facilities for conveying relief supplies to victims of the civil strife.

Friendly relations with France were further cemented by the opening of a French cultural centre by the French ambassador in Bueà on February 27. An agreement on cultural exchanges with the U.S.S.R. during 1968–69 was also concluded.

On May 4 additional evidence of governmental interest in cultural pursuits was provided when President Ahidjo opened the first international exhibition of African books in Yaoundé. The themes of the exhibition were concerned with the history, ethnology, and literature of both modern and traditional Africa.

In June a governmental decree was passed approving the creation of a Ministry of State to be in charge of territorial administration. The central secretariat of the new ministry would include departments of territorial organization and political affairs and would be responsible for discussing matters in dispute.

On June 17 Cameroon attended the fifth session of the OAU ad hoc commission on refugees at Addis Ababa, Eth. (PH. D.; X.)

Canada

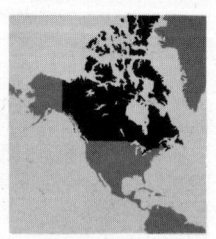

Canada is a federal parliamentary state and member of the Commonwealth of Nations covering North America north of conterminous United States and east of Alaska. Area: 3,-851,809 sq.mi. (9,976,196 sq.km.). Pop. (1968 est.): 20,744,000, including (1961) British 43.8%; French 30.4%; other European 22.6%; Indian and Eskimo 1.2%. Cap.: Ottawa (metro. pop., 1967, 508,000). Largest city: Montreal (metro. pop., 1967, 2,489,000). Language (1961): English only 67.4%; French only 19.1%; both 12.2%; neither 1.3%. Religion: Roman Catholic 45.7%; Protestant 47.7%. Queen, Elizabeth II; governor-general in 1968, D. Roland Michener; prime ministers, Lester B. Pearson and, from April 20, Pierre Elliott Trudeau.

The success of Canada's centennial celebrations in 1967 and the wide acclaim accorded to Expo 67 contributed to the mood of renewed confidence in the prospects of their country that Canadians experienced during 1968. The new spirit was reflected in the change in the leadership of the Canadian federal government in April.

Lester Bowles Pearson, 71, a career diplomat and Cabinet minister since 1928, retired from the post of prime minister, to be succeeded by Pierre Elliott Trudeau (*see* BIOGRAPHY), 48, who had obtained his first elective office as recently as 1965. Trudeau won a decisive victory at the polls for the Liberal Party in June and made himself the master of a youthful administration that was backed by the first parliamentary majority in Canada within a decade. At the year's end it was apparent that the new government planned a number of innovations in legislation and public policy.

Domestic Affairs. Lester Pearson had announced on Dec. 14, 1967, that he planned to resign as prime minister and leader of the Liberal Party as soon as a party convention could be held to choose his successor. The convention was later arranged to take place in Ottawa, April 4–6, 1968, and eight Cabinet members

A 1968 cartoon by Yardley Jones, "Toronto Telegram."

BEN ROTH AGENCY

announced themselves as candidates to succeed Pearson. Inevitably the frequent absences of these ministers from their posts in Ottawa hampered the operations of the Pearson administration in its last months.

A dramatic demonstration of this weakness occurred on February 19, when the government was defeated in the House of Commons on the third reading of a bill to impose a 5% surcharge on the personal income tax. Several ministers, including Pearson, who was in the West Indies, were absent when the vote occurred. The opposition parties combined to defeat the minority government 84–82, producing a crisis that could have led to the resignation of the government. The Cabinet took the position that the defeat had occurred on a technical point, since the principle of the tax increase had been approved on the second reading of the measure. It sought a formal motion of confidence from the House of Commons. The opposition parties failed to remain united to defeat the motion; the Quebec Créditiste Party of eight members voted with the government and the motion was approved on February 28 by a vote of 138–119.

The emergence of Trudeau as the leading contender for Pearson's mantle was the most remarkable political phenomenon of 1968. At the beginning of the year he had been regarded by many as a dilettante in politics, a critic and theorist whose lack of acquaintance with practical politics made him an unlikely prospect for the leadership. He had, however, played a major role in determining the Pearson government's response to the challenge posed by Quebec's claim for separate status in the Canadian federal system. Trudeau's plain speaking on constitutional issues came to the fore on the weekend of Jan. 27, 1968, at a convention of the federal Liberal Party in Quebec. He criticized the idea of a particular status for Quebec and proclaimed instead the need to provide "equal status for all French-speaking Canadians in all of Canada."

Trudeau's speech was well received by the Quebec Liberals and in English-speaking Canada and catapulted him into a strong position to succeed Pearson. He also improved his standing at the federal-provincial conference of February 5–7. Here he clashed with Quebec Premier Daniel Johnson, who made a powerful claim for special powers for Quebec as the solution for Canada's national dualism. Trudeau countered with the view that language rights for the individual, guaranteed in all sections of Canada, would eliminate the need for special powers for Quebec. Trudeau announced his definite decision to try for the Liberal leadership on February 16 and set out to make himself known across Canada. He attracted great popular attention, both by his relaxed and witty manner and unconventional behaviour and by his undoubted intellectual capacity and moral courage.

At the April convention Trudeau emerged as winner after a tumultuous session of balloting. His opponents included six leading members of the Pearson Cabinet, the most formidable being Trade and Commerce Minister Robert H. Winters, who was defeated on the fourth ballot by a vote of 1,203–954. Two weeks later (April 20) Pearson resigned his office, and Trudeau was sworn in by the governor-general, Roland Michener, as the 15th prime minister of Canada. Pending the general election called for June, he named an interim cabinet, composed largely of members of the Pearson administration. The most important change concerned Paul Martin, formerly secretary of state for external affairs, who moved to the Senate as government leader and was succeeded by Mitchell Sharp, formerly minister of finance.

Trudeau led a revived Liberal Party into the general election on June 25, seeking a firm mandate from the people. He made few campaign pledges but asked for an end to the minority government that had existed in Ottawa since 1962. His appeal was successful, for in the voting the Liberal Party increased its representation in the House of Commons from 127 seats to 155 seats. In Ontario the Liberals won 64 out of 88 seats, many in urban ridings, and in Quebec the party maintained its hold on 56 of the province's 74 seats. In the prairie provinces the Liberals increased their strength from one representative in 1965 to 11 seats; they more than doubled their number of members from British Columbia.

The election was a bitter defeat for the Progressive Conservative Party and for Robert Stanfield, the former premier of Nova Scotia who had taken the party into its first general election since his assumption of its leadership in September 1967. Although the Conservatives had captured most of the seats in the Atlantic provinces, they fared badly in Quebec and Ontario and lost ground in the west. From 94 seats at dissolution the Conservatives had dropped to 72. The New Democratic Party emerged from the contest with the same number of seats, 22, as it possessed when Parliament was dissolved; it suffered a blow, however, in the defeat of its leader, T. C. Douglas, in a British Columbia riding. The Créditistes, under Réal Caouette, gained ground in several Quebec ridings, increasing their numbers from 8 to 14 members. The English-speaking section of the party, once strong in Alberta and British Columbia, was eliminated. One independent, sitting for an Ontario seat, was elected.

About 75% of the Canadian electorate had voted in the election, representing an estimated total popular vote of 8,295,000. The Liberal Party secured 45% of the vote, an increase of 5% over the 1965 election; the Conservatives dropped from 32 to 31%. The election was the sixth in Canada since 1957 and the first to produce a government with an overall majority since John Diefenbaker's victory for the Conservative Party in 1958.

The new Trudeau Cabinet was sworn in on July 6.

Canadian Prime Minister Trudeau being pursued by youthful admirers. Trudeau's youthfulness, intelligence, and unconventional attitudes made him a popular hero to the young.

CANADIAN PRESS

Newly designed trademarks representing beaver skins stretched out to dry were instituted in 1968 to protect authentic Indian art. Similar bilingual trademarks had been used in the past to protect the Eskimo crafts industry.

It consisted of 29 members, the largest in Canadian history. It was also the youngest Cabinet on record, with an average age of 47 years. All provinces were represented except Prince Edward Island, which had returned no Liberals. E. J. Benson, a member of the Pearson ministry, became minister of finance; Paul Hellyer, who had contested the leadership race, became minister of transport; A. J. MacEachen, another of Trudeau's former rivals, took over the expanded Department of Manpower and Immigration; John Turner was appointed minister of justice; and Jean Marchand, former Quebec labour leader and a close friend of Trudeau, was made responsible for Forestry and Rural Development. Mitchell Sharp continued as external affairs minister.

During its last month in office the Pearson government continued to apply a flexible policy to the problems of Canadian unity while endeavouring to promote a climate of bilingualism that would meet the cultural interests of French-speaking Canadians. Its efforts were complemented by the working alliance between Premier John Robarts of Ontario and Premier Johnson of Quebec, leaders of the two largest provinces. An interprovincial conference that Robarts had called in Toronto in November 1967 had discussed the problems that were taken up on Feb. 5–7, 1968, at a full-scale federal-provincial conference in Ottawa. The ground for this discussion had been laid down in the first book of the Final Report of the Royal Commission on Bilingualism and Biculturalism, which Pearson had tabled in the House of Commons on Dec. 5, 1967. The report had recommended that both English and French be used as official languages in bodies under federal jurisdiction and in local government and, where possible, in the system of education in any area where an official language minority reached or exceeded 10% of the population.

In addition to the royal commission's report, the provincial premiers were asked to study two working papers prepared by the federal government. One paper proposed a charter of individual rights to be entrenched in the Canadian constitution; the other was a scheme for a modified division of authority in the Canadian federation.

The Pearson government had hoped to obtain agreement on the principle of the equality of the French and English languages, and on the proposal to entrench linguistic rights in the constitution. It also had wished to secure approval for the concept that the charter of individual political and legal rights should be built into the constitution. The last plan did not win general support from the provinces and, together with the question of entrenching language rights, was sent to a committee for further study. The conference, however, did agree that French-speaking Canadians living outside Quebec should possess the same rights as English-speaking Canadians living in Quebec. Each province was urged to proceed as speedily as possible toward the implementation of the changes suggested by the royal commission, and a special joint committee was set up to propose steps to bring the constitution into conformity with it.

Action on the provincial level followed the conference. Premier Robarts sponsored a resolution in the Ontario legislature in July establishing the right to address the chamber in either English or French. He announced that task forces had been created to look into bilingualism in the Ontario provincial courts, in the public service, and in municipal governments. School legislation provided for greater use of French

as a teaching language in Ontario high schools and made the traditional use of French in some elementary schools a legal right. The use of both official languages in the legislature was sanctioned in Newfoundland, Prince Edward Island, and New Brunswick. In the latter province, which had a French minority of 40%, Premier Louis Robichaud set official bilingualism as an early goal. Changes to expand language rights were made in provincial school legislation across Canada.

In October, Trudeau introduced an Official Languages Act into Parliament to implement the federal provisions of the royal commission's report. The measure contained a provision opening the door to the use of either language in criminal court proceedings but leaving discretion over its implementation to the courts.

The second session of Canada's 27th Parliament, begun on May 8, 1967, ended on April 23, 1968, in order to allow preparations for the general election on June 25. Important measures enacted during this period included the outlawing of capital punishment for a five-year trial period for all cases except those in which the victims were police officers or prison guards and a measure extending the grounds for divorce, especially by adding a new principle of matrimonial breakdown. A special division of the Exchequer Court was created to hear divorce petitions from Quebec that had formerly gone to the Senate. In the other nine provinces, divorce proceedings would be heard by provincial supreme courts. A sweeping modification of Canada's criminal code was given extensive debate but not passed. It would have altered the law relating to homosexual activities, sanctioned government-licensed lotteries, legalized abortions in cases where the mother's health was in jeopardy, and provided rigorous controls over the ownership of firearms. The bill was reintroduced in the first session after the election.

Benefits payable under the Unemployment Insurance Act were increased by act of Parliament and the federal medical care insurance plan became effective on July 1. Only two provinces, British Columbia and Saskatchewan, entered the program in which the federal government offered to pay half the operating costs of approved plans. It was expected, however, that other provinces would come into the arrangement in 1969.

The legislative program of the new Trudeau administration was unveiled when the first session of the 28th Parliament opened on September 12. It contained few measures that had not been anticipated, including proposals for the reform of the rules of Parliament to provide for a more rapid passage of legislation. The government announced its plan to establish a Department of Regional Development, which would incorporate the old Department of Forestry and Rural Development, to correct some of the disparities in income levels between the different regions of the country, an objective that recalled Trudeau's campaign emphasis on achieving a "just society."

Quebec politics were disrupted on September 26 with the death of Premier Daniel Johnson (*see* OBITUARIES), who had been a leading exponent of the demand for greater authority for the province of Quebec. Johnson was succeeded by the minister of justice in his Union Nationale government, Jean-Jacques Bertrand. René Levesque, a prominent member of the Liberal administration that had been ousted by the Union Nationale Party two years before, continued

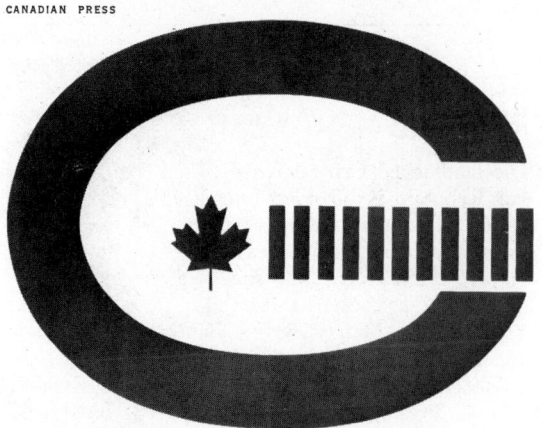

Official emblem adopted for the Canadian summer games to be held in Halifax and Dartmouth in August 1969.

to rally separatist opinion in Quebec behind a new organization, the Parti Québecois.

Manitoba had gained a new premier on Nov. 27, 1967, when Walter Weir, 38, succeeded Dufferin Roblin as the head of a Conservative administration. Roblin had made an unsuccessful bid for leadership of the national Conservative Party in September 1967 but gained a seat in the House of Commons in June 1968. Weir had been Roblin's minister of highways.

Foreign Affairs. The French government, under Pres. Charles de Gaulle, continued to give his tacit encouragement in 1968 to movements aimed at strengthening a French cultural and political consciousness in Canada. On several occasions de Gaulle spoke of the solidarity he hoped to see develop between French communities on both sides of the Atlantic. Quebec was invited to send a representative to an educational conference of the Francophone nations to be held in Gabon in February. The failure of Gabon to recognize the federal government's jurisdiction in external affairs brought a protest from Ottawa and led to a decision not to proceed with the appointment of a Canadian ambassador to Gabon. Canadian external aid to Gabon also was cut off. When the conference was resumed in Paris on April 22, a Quebec representative was again invited, suggesting that France had inspired Gabon's earlier action. The Canadian ambassador in Paris was recalled for discussions in Ottawa, and later the Canadian government issued a White Paper setting out the claim for exclusive federal authority in the conduct of external affairs. The

document indicated that a Canadian delegation to an international conference would include provincial representatives if the subject of discussion was one that fell under provincial jurisdiction.

Another incident occurred at the end of August, this time involving the visit to the French-speaking community of Manitoba of Philippe Rossillon, an official of a French government committee charged with promoting the use of the French language in countries outside France. Rossillon had entered Canada without informing Ottawa. At Daniel Johnson's funeral in Montreal, Prime Minister Trudeau met privately with French Premier Maurice Couve de Murville, but no statement concerning the Rossillon visit was issued.

An exchange problem developed in Canadian-U.S. relations in the first few months of 1968. The problem had resulted from a lack of confidence in the soundness of the Canadian dollar and had led to heavy purchases of gold by private speculators and a fall in the exchange value of the dollar. The pressure had been accentuated by the devaluation of the British pound on Nov. 18, 1967, but it became much greater after January 1 when the U.S. stiffened controls on capital exports in order to improve its balance of payments. The U.S. restrictions directly affected Canada, which depended on large amounts of U.S. capital in order to finance its deficit on current account. The Canadian government raised the bank rate from 6 to 7% in order to attract more foreign funds and borrowed from the International Monetary Fund to strengthen its reserves, but the pressures on the dollar continued to increase.

Finally, on March 7, it was announced that the U.S. would exempt Canada from the restrictions in exchange for an agreement not to allow Canadian financial institutions to be used to circumvent the U.S. regulations. Canada also promised to invest a high proportion of its U.S. dollar reserves in nonmarket obligations of the American government, an action that helped to ease the pressure on U.S. financial reserves. The currency crisis was surmounted by mid-March as a consequence of these measures, together with the establishment of the two-price system for international transactions in gold. By the end of the summer the Bank of Canada was able to return its lending rate to 6% and to terminate the special credit arrangements it had made with foreign countries.

An extradition case concerning Harold Banks, the former head of the Seafarers' International Union of

---

CANADA

Education. (1965–66) Primary, pupils 3,566,-019, teachers 134,136; secondary and vocational, pupils, 1,332,415, teachers 76,189; higher (including 42 universities), students 323,625, teaching staff 29,324.

Finance. Monetary unit: Canadian dollar, with a par value of Can$1.08 to U.S. $1 (Can$2.595 = £1 sterling). Gold and foreign exchange, official: (June 1968) U.S. $2,582,000,000; (June 1967) U.S. $2,178,000,000. Budget (1966–67 actual): revenue Can$8,376,181,844; expenditure Can$8,-797,648,457. Gross national product: (1967) Can$62,070,000,000; (1966) Can$58,120,000,-000. Money supply: (May 1968) Can$11,990,-000,000; (May 1967) Can$10,850,000,000. Cost of living (1963 = 100): (June 1968) 116; (June 1967) 112.

Foreign Trade. (1967) Imports Can$10,877,-000,000; exports Can$11,413,000,000. Import sources: U.S. 72%; U.K. 6%; EEC 6%. Export destinations: U.S. 64%; U.K. 10%; EEC 6%. Main exports: newsprint 8%; wheat 7%; timber 7%; wood pulp 5%.

Transport and Communications. Roads (1967) 557,865 km. Motor vehicles in use (1966): passenger 5,499,500; commercial (including buses) 1,427,800. Railways: (1966) 69,-205 km.; traffic (1967) 5.1 million passenger-km., freight 135,070,000,000 net ton-km. Shipping (1967): oceangoing merchant vessels 100 gross tons and over 948, gross tonnage 825,984; Great Lakes merchant vessels 288, gross tonnage 1,479,-518. Air traffic (1967): 10,938,650,000 passenger-km.; freight 217.8 million net ton-km. Telephones (Dec. 1965) 7,440,000. Radio receivers (Dec. 1966) c. 12 million. Television receivers (Dec. 1966) c. 5.7 million.

Agriculture. Production (in 000; metric tons; 1967; 1966 in parentheses): wheat 16,137 (22,-516); oats 4,691 (5,778); barley 5,414 (6,597); rye 334 (437); corn 1,882 (1,685); mixed grains (1966) 1,478, (1965) 1,346; potatoes 2,035 (2,490); sugar, raw value (1967–68) 135, (1966–67) 154; linseed 259 (559); tobacco (1966) 106, (1965) 77; butter 154 (154); cheese 86 (88); timber (1966) c. 114,100 cu.m., (1965)

c. 114,000 cu.m. Livestock (in 000; June 1966): cattle 12,546; sheep 1,094; horses 389; pigs 5,443; poultry 71,738. Fish catch (in 000; metric tons) (1966) 1,349, (1965) 1,262.

Industry. Fuel and power (in 000; metric tons; 1967): coal 8,515; lignite 1,821; crude oil 47,-395; natural gas 48,082,000 cu.m.; electricity (82% hydroelectric in 1966) 167,000,000 kw-hr. Mineral and metal production (in 000; metric tons; 1967): crude steel 8,793; iron ore (shipments; 55% metal content) 37,248; copper ore (metal content) 547; nickel ore (metal content; 1966) 212; asbestos (1966) 1,353; zinc ore (metal content) 1,133; lead ore (metal content) 308; aluminum (1966) 823; gold 3,000 troy oz.; silver 37,000 troy oz.; uranium oxide (1966) 3.5. Other production (in 000; metric tons; 1967): wood pulp 14,021; newsprint 7,304; synthetic rubber 200; passenger cars 721 units; commercial vehicles 236 units. Unemployment: (June 1968) 4.8%; (June 1967) 3.7%. Index of industrial production (1963 = 100): (1967) 131; (1966) 128.

188

Central African Republic

Canada, was one of the rare occasions on which a Canadian request for extradition was turned down by the U.S. In March the U.S. State Department refused to accept a federal court ruling that Banks be returned to Canada to face perjury charges. A Canadian request that the decision be reconsidered was refused.

The North American Air Defense Command (NORAD) was renewed for a third five-year term by an exchange of notes between Canada and the U.S. on March 30.

Economy. The Canadian economy showed reasonable strength in 1968, recording a gross national product that was expected to reach $67,033,000,000 for the year. This figure represented an increase of 8% over 1967 and included a real increase in the output of goods and services of 4.5%. A spectacular export performance, led by sales of automobiles and auto parts to the U.S. and foreign sales of metals and ores, contributed to the favourable trend. It was expected that the pace of exports to the U.S. would slacken in 1969 when the tax increase of 1968 and reduced federal spending began to affect the U.S. economy.

The economy was stimulated by an unanticipated increase of 6% in capital spending and a record pace of construction during the first seven months of 1968. It was apparent, however, that the labour force was growing more rapidly than the number of jobs being created. The rate of unemployment in June reached 5.5% of the labour force, a four-year high. The jobless rate had been 4.2% in June 1967.

Exports for January–September 1968 amounted to $9,882,200,000, a gain of 18% over the comparable period in 1967. Imports for the first three quarters of the year stood at $8,904,500,000, an increase of 10%. The trade surplus produced was $977.7 million, compared with $251.3 million in 1967. It was expected that the normal interest and dividend charges on foreign investments, as well as the costs of Canadians travelling abroad, would mean that the overall international payments deficit for 1968 would run to about $1 billion.

The federal budget was not presented to Parliament until October 22, the normal spring date being delayed by the onset of the general election. In an effort to balance the budget, Finance Minister E. J. Benson imposed limits on federal expenditures and proposed measures to increase federal revenues. A 3% surcharge had been added to the personal income tax in March by Benson's predecessor, Mitchell Sharp, and Benson imposed an additional 2% social development tax. The new tax was limited to a maximum of $120 a year for each taxpayer. Insurance companies were required to pay corporation income taxes for the first time, and part of their investment incomes were to be taxed at a rate of 15%. Means for accelerating corporation tax payments in order to produce additional revenues were also proposed. The first installment of long-range reforms in the structure of estate and gift taxes abolished tax levies on transactions between husbands and wives. Benson estimated an increased yield of $845 million from the new taxes, the largest annual increase to result from new federal taxes in Canadian history. The October budget estimated revenues for the fiscal year 1968–69 at $10,105,000,000 and expenditures at $10,780,000,000, leaving a deficit of $675 million.   (D. M. L. F.)

ENCYCLOPÆDIA BRITANNICA FILMS. *Canada: The Atlantic Provinces* (1958); *Canada: The Industrial Provinces* (1958); *Canada: The Pacific Provinces* (1958); *Canada: The Prairie Provinces* (1958); *The St. Lawrence Seaway* (1959); *Canada's Royal Canadian Mounted Police* (1963).

Central African Republic

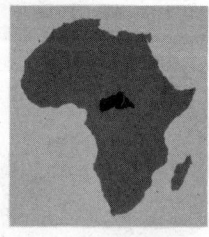

The landlocked Central African Republic is bounded by Chad, Sudan, the Congo republics, and Cameroon. Area: 240,540 sq.mi. (663,000 sq. km.). Pop. (1968 est.): 1,488,000, chiefly Mandja-Baya, Banda, Mbaka, and Azande. Cap. and largest city: Bangui (pop., 1966, 150,000). Official language: French. Religion: mainly animist. President and premier in 1968, Jean Bedel Bokassa.

President Bokassa declined to attend the January 1968 conference of the African and Malagasy Com-

Central African Republic President Bokassa and the secretary-general of the French Presidency for African and Malagasy affairs, Jacques Foccart, touring a cotton mill opened in 1968 in Bangui.

mon Organization (OCAM) because of "political tensions." However, relations with France remained good, and in February economic and defense ties were established with the Congo (Kinshasa) and Chad to form a Union of Central African States (UEAC), which was officially confirmed in April. With the proposed association of Rwanda, Burundi, and Congo (Brazzaville), the union would affect the economy, trade, transport, telecommunications, security, and cultural relations of

CENTRAL AFRICAN REPUBLIC
Education. (1965–66) Primary, pupils 128,436, teachers 2,302; secondary, pupils 3,866, teachers 185; vocational, pupils 849, teachers 108; teacher training, students 465, teachers 39.
Finance. Monetary unit: CFA franc, with a parity of CFA Fr. 50 to the French franc (CFA Fr. 246.85 = U.S. $1; CFA Fr. 592.45 = £1 sterling). Budget (1968 est.) balanced at CFA Fr. 9.6 billion.
Foreign Trade. (1967) Imports CFA Fr. 10,909,000,000; exports CFA Fr. 7,166,000,000. Import sources: France 61%; West Germany 9%. Export destinations: France 42%; U.S. 30%; Israel 14%. Main exports: diamonds 47%; cotton 23%; coffee 20%.
Agriculture. Production (in 000; metric tons; 1966; 1965 in parentheses): sweet potatoes 40 (40); cassava 1,000 (1,000); cotton, lint 15 (9); peanuts 60 (58); coffee 9 (11). Livestock (in 000; 1965–66): cattle 450; pigs 21; sheep c. 112; goats 500; chickens 900.
Industry. Production (1966) diamonds 541,000 metric carats.

all six member states and would comprise approximately 1.8 million sq.mi. populated by about 28 million people. Within the association, the headquarters of which were to be established in the Central African capital, Bangui, the free traffic of goods and people would be formally guaranteed. Rwanda, Burundi, and Congo (Brazzaville) refused to join the UEAC, however, and the organization proved ineffective. Conflicts between Congo (Kinshasa) and the Central African Republic led to the dissolution of the UEAC in December.

On February 12 and April 11 two minor ministerial reshuffles took place, but these had much less effect on the government than the growing concern, formally acknowledged in March, which arose from the number of refugees in the eastern region. About 27,000 Sudanese, who had fled into the region to escape the incursions into Sudan of Simba rebels from Congo (Kinshasa), began to present the danger of compromising Central African-Sudanese relations.

Returning from Kinshasa in May, Bokassa revealed at Bangui airport his discovery of an attempted coup d'etat planned against him by a minority who, he alleged, wished to establish a new system of colonization at the instigation of an unspecified foreign power. Bokassa also denied rumours that the Central African Republic wished to attack a neighbouring unnamed state. In that same month relations with Nationalist China (Taiwan), first established in April 1962 and then broken off in November 1964, were resumed.

In June plans for a University of Bangui were outlined. The university, to be opened in October 1970, was to have faculties of law, science, and medicine.

In July a French-Central African agreement on the exploitation of uranium deposits in the Bakouma region was signed. As with Niger and Gabon, the Central African Republic hoped to establish itself as one of the main suppliers of uranium to the French nuclear industry. (PH. D.; X.)

Ceylon

An Asian parliamentary state of the Commonwealth of Nations, Ceylon occupies an island off the southeast coast of peninsular India. Area: 25,332 sq.mi. (65,610 sq.km.). Pop. (1967 est.): 11,701,000, including Sinhalese about 70%; Tamils 22%; Moors 6%. Cap. and largest city: Colombo (pop., 1966, 546,-000). Language: Sinhalese (official), Tamil, and English. Religion: mainly Buddhism, with Hindu, Christian, and Muslim minorities. Queen, Elizabeth II; governor-general in 1968, William Gopallawa; prime minister, Dudley Senanayake.

Ceylon in 1968 once again faced the adverse trend in its balance of payments that has been a main feature of the country's economy in recent years. Devaluation of the Ceylonese rupee by 20% in November 1967 provided a measure of relief for exports. Nevertheless, the declining trend of export prices and the rising prices of imports caused concern. Introducing the budget on August 2, U. B. Wanninayake, minister of finance, explained that the 1967 terms of trade had declined by 9%, reflecting a fall in export prices of 6% and a rise of 3% in import prices. Export earnings reached their lowest level since 1953, while import payments were only slightly below the

record total of 1966. However, improved export figures were expected in 1968 for tea, rubber, and coconuts, the three main agricultural products.

Growth prospects for the domestic economy were also favourable, and in August Prime Minister Senanayake expressed his confidence that Ceylon's economy was turning the corner. An encouraging feature, which favourably impressed a World Bank mission to the island, was the progress achieved with the national policy of replacing imports with the products of home-grown crops. The 1967 rice production, for instance, reached a record level of 55 million bu., compared with 36 million bu. in 1965, and this enabled payments on rice imports during the year to be reduced by CRs. 43 million. The country was expected to become 75% self-sufficient in rice in 1969.

Progress was made with government projects to stimulate the efforts of the small farmers. Fertilizer subsidies were expanded, rice prices were guaranteed, and a marked increase was planned for 1967–68 in irrigation facilities and in the number of families settled on land set aside under colonization schemes. In industry there was an improvement in the output of public corporations, which employed 25,942 persons in 1968 and manufactured goods valued at CRs. 196 million, nearly double the output of the previous year. Five new state factories produced goods valued at CRs. 66 million during their first year of operation. The output of the steel rolling mill and the tire and tube factories, new projects started with the help of U.S.S.R. experts, exceeded the targets laid down for them. The opening of a second factory enabled the Ceylon ceramics industry to meet the entire local demand.

The Colombo International Airport, financed in part by the government of Canada and developed at a cost of CRs. 66 million to provide facilities for the operation of jet airliners, came into service on July 1.

In pursuit of government policy to increase the number of visitors to Ceylon, the Tourist Development Act of 1968 provided for the establishment of national holiday resorts and the development of various facilities for tourists, including the building of new hotels. After a five-year period of little growth in tourism the number of foreign visitors in 1967 reached more than 23,000, an increase of 25% over 1966.

The most important of Ceylon's foreign relations, those with India, were strengthened by arrangements for senior officials of the two countries to meet every year to discuss matters of common interest. Trade delegations from the two countries discussed economic and commercial cooperation, particularly the launching of joint measures to arrest the decline of world tea prices and secure a better return for growers. Against this background of closer association Ceylon began to repatriate a proportion of its Indian inhabitants, mainly labourers on the tea and rubber estates, whose status had aroused long-standing controversy. This process, to be spread over 15 years, was agreed on the basis of Ceylon granting citizenship to four Indians for every seven who chose to return to their homeland. The first 80 Indians were granted Ceylon citizenship in September. More than 800,000 were affected, many of them descendants of labourers brought over from southern India during the 19th century.

(Jo. HN.)

Chad

A landlocked republic of central Africa, Chad is bounded by Libya, Sudan, the Central African Republic, Cameroon, Nigeria, and Niger. Area: 490,733 sq.mi. (1,271,000 sq.km.). Pop. (1967): 3,410,000, including Saras, Arabs, and other Africans. Cap. and largest city: Fort-Lamy (pop., 1967 est., 118,000). Official language: French. Religion: Muslim and animist. President and premier in 1968, François Tombalbaye.

In August the government requested French military support for Chadian troops besieged at Aozou near the Libyan border by rebels from the northern regions. Air cover was provided, but it was stated in Paris that no French troops were directly involved. To justify its action the government of Chad recalled previous disturbances in the same area in March and drew attention to the traffic in areas through Chad from Khartoum and the U.A.R. to Nigeria.

The announcement in January that Chad's two labour unions, the National Union of Chadian Workers and the Confederation of Chadian Workers, were to unite into a single National Union of Chadian Work-

ers was followed in February by the arrest at Fort-Lamy of union leaders for distributing antigovernmental leaflets which had been printed in Paris. Similar disturbances occurring throughout the year provoked continued accusations by the government of antigovernment plots.

Internal unrest was to some extent reflected in a changing foreign policy. In February Chad joined with the Central African Republic and Congo (Kinshasa) in the economic and political Union of Central African States. The union was not successful, however, and was dissolved in December. In early April it was announced that the Chad ambassador to the UN was to be appointed secretary-general of the new organization.

In May Chad participated in the East and Central African summit conference at Dar es Salaam, where problems relating to South Africa, mercenary soldiers, and the UN Conference on Trade and Development were discussed. In June President Tombalbaye, on an official visit to the U.S.S.R., expressed his gratitude for Soviet technical and scientific aid and reiterated his wish to consolidate Soviet-Chadian cooperation still further.

Efforts to improve agriculture, Chad's main economic activity, were aided in August by an International Development Association grant which was to be used mainly for the education of an increasing number of agricultural technicians. The grant also was to be used to improve primary teacher training.

(PH. D.; X.)

Chemistry

Physical and Inorganic. *Chemical Accelerators and High Energy Reactions.* R. L. Wolfgang and his collaborators at Yale University developed two types of chemical accelerators for studying reaction mechanisms over the energy range 1 to 25 ev. One apparatus, EVA (short for Evatron), made possible the first complete cross-beam studies of the energy dependence of reactions of positive argon and nitrogen ions with deuterium molecules. A beam of ions was crossed at an angle of 90° with a beam of thermal molecules. The angular distributions and kinetic energies of product and reactant ions were measured with a mass spectrometer and a stopping-potential analyzer. Low beam energies (0.7 ev) led to relative energies of collision as low as 0.1 ev and enabled comparison with data obtained under thermal conditions. For the reactions, $Ar^+ + D_2 \rightarrow ArD^+ + D$ and $N_2^+ + D_2 \rightarrow N_2D^+ + D$, it was shown that even at the lowest energies the contribution of any long-lived intermediate complex was negligible, and the interactions occurred in roughly the same time as a molecular vibration. At higher energies (25 ev) the reactions were adequately described by the "spectator-stripping" model previously postulated by A. Henglein (Hahn-Meitner Institute, West Berlin) whereby the free D atom proceeded with a velocity vector unchanged from the D_2 reactant, thus playing the part of a spectator to the reaction. The product ion (ArD^+ or N_2D^+) carried the momentum of both the ionic reactant and half that of the D_2 reactant.

Reactions of hot tritium atoms with molecules were studied in a second apparatus, called ADAM, where a beam of monoenergetic tritium ions (T_2^+ or T^+), with energies from 1 to 200 ev, was directed at a solid hydrocarbon target, such as cyclohexane at −196° C.

Cheese:
see Agriculture

Chemical Industry:
see Industrial Review

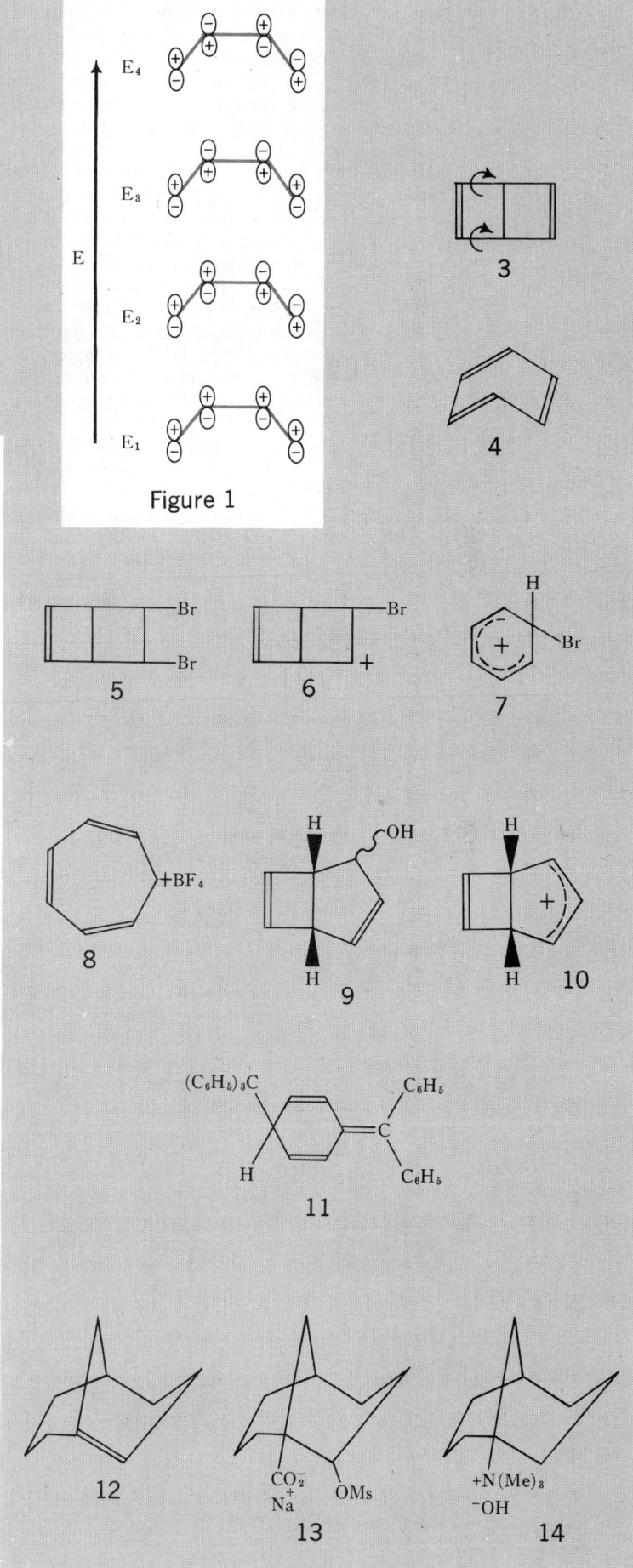

Figure 1

The tritium ions were converted to hot tritium atoms on the surface of the target by charge transfer, and the subsequent reactions of the hot tritium atoms and hydrocarbon yielded labeled products by normal hot abstraction and displacement mechanisms. Threshold energies were determined for several types of reactions and the results agreed well with hot-atom reactions studied previously by nuclear recoil techniques.

Hard and Soft Acids and Bases. Considerable interest was focused on the concept of hard and soft acids and bases, first suggested in 1963 by R. G. Pearson of Northwestern University, Evanston, Ill., and used extensively to interpret a wide variety of chemical phenomena. The underlying principles involved the G. N. Lewis definition of generalized acids and bases: in the reaction, $A + :B \rightarrow A:B$, the acid (A) accepted electrons donated by the base (:B) forming an acid-base complex (A:B). Soft bases were defined as those in which the valence electrons were easily distorted, polarized, or removed, whereas hard bases had the opposite properties, retaining their valence electrons more firmly. Hard acids were defined as having acceptor atoms of small size with high positive charge and no valence electrons that were easily distorted or removed. Conversely, soft acids had large acceptor atoms, small or zero positive charges, and valence electrons capable of being distorted or removed. Thus, Lewis acids and bases were classified as follows—hard acids: H^+, Li^+, Be^{2+}, Al^{3+}, Si^{4+}, $BeMe_2$, $AlMe_3$, RPO; soft acids: Cu^+, Hg^{2+}, Tl^{3+}, $GaCl_3$, I^+, I_2, bulk metals; hard bases: H_2O, OH^-, F^-, CH_3CO_2, ROH, NH_3; and soft bases: R_2S, I^-, R_3P, C_2H_4, R^-.

The general principle of hard and soft acids and bases states that "hard acids prefer to coordinate with hard bases and soft acids prefer to coordinate with soft bases." Unfortunately it had not been possible thus far to draw up a quantitative scale of hardness or softness based on a physical property such as polarizability, electronegativity, or oxidation potential, and there appeared to exist a continuous range of softness or hardness such that intermediate cases arose.

The wide scope of the principle was illustrated by its prediction of the rates of electrophilic and nucleophilic substitution reactions. In both types of processes the reaction rate was determined by the hard or soft character of the acid and base centres. Thus in electrophilic substitution, $B' + A:B \rightarrow A:B' + B$, if A is a hard centre, then hard bases B' reacted fast. On the other hand, if A is a soft centre then soft centres B'

reacted faster, as in the substitution reactions of methyl chloride, where the carbonium ion $CH_3{}^+$ was moderately soft and reacted very rapidly with soft bases such as RS^-, R_3P, $S_2O_3{}^{2-}$, and I^-.

Although the theories underlying the principle of hard and soft acids remained obscure, some general points had emerged: hard acids and hard bases contained ionic bonds whereas most soft acid-base combinations involved largely covalent bonds; π-bonding was also involved, with hard acids being π-bond acceptors and soft acids π-bond donors; van der Waals forces exerted a stabilizing influence in the case of larger atoms in close proximity, as occurred in soft acid-base combinations.

Carbon-Fibre Reinforced Plastics. Research workers at the Royal Aircraft Establishment, Farnborough, Eng., achieved a notable breakthrough in the production of carbon fibres bonded in resin matrices. The final material is two or three times as strong as steel, twice as stiff but only one quarter as dense, and, of course, is extremely corrosion resistant. It had been recognized for some time that single crystals of refractory nonmetals and covalent and ionic compounds exhibit remarkable strength, owing to the absence of defects and flaws in their structures that limit the strength of most bulk materials. Hitherto the difficulty had been in producing the fibres in a form suitable for commercial application at an economical price. The new fibre-forming process involved the carbonization of polyacrylonitrile fibres in a two-stage pyrolysis process under carefully controlled conditions.

(J. A. Kr.)

Organic. Aspects of stereochemistry were much discussed in 1968, and lectures by C. A. Coulson and V. Prelog in particular drew attention to the power of a formal mathematical approach to symmetry properties in interpreting experimental results and in suggesting new synthetic work.

There is a striking stereospecificity in electrocyclic reactions involving the interconversion of a polyene with its cyclic isomer by bonding between the terminal carbon atoms. Thus, *cis*-dimethylcyclobutene **1a** gave the hexadiene **2a** on heating to 175° C, whereas *trans*-dimethylcyclobutene **1b** gave the geometrical isomer **2b**. In 1965 R. B. Woodward and R. Hoffmann rationalized these results in generalizations (Woodward-Hoffmann rules) that correlated the stereochemistry of such reactions with the symmetry of the occupied molecular orbital of highest energy. To explain the example given above, the set of π-molecular orbitals for a conjugated diene are shown in figure 1: only the lower two orbitals (E_1 and E_2) are occupied in the ground state of the diene, each by a pair of electrons. Bonding between the terminal carbon atoms involves the electron pair in the higher of the occupied orbitals, provided that the wave functions of the electrons overlapping to form the new bond have the same sign. Thus, in thermal reactions that involved the ground state, the terminal carbon atoms and their associated orbitals in E_2 must rotate through 90° in the same, *e.g.*, clockwise, sense to form the new bond. This mode of cyclization is known as conrotatory. The reverse of this reaction follows similar rules so that the conversions **1a → 2a** and **1b → 2b** proceeded stereospecifically.

However, a photochemically induced reaction proceeds with the opposite stereochemistry because in the photochemically excited state an electron is promoted to E_3 (fig. 1), making this the occupied orbital of highest energy. Again, bond formation involves an overlap of wave functions having the same sign but now this demands that the terminal carbon atoms rotate in the opposite sense. Such a process, called disrotatory, should thus be preferred for the photochemical reaction of butadiene.

These generalizations provided an explanation of the unexpectedly high stability of some strained bicyclic systems, such as [2.2.0]bicyclohexadiene (Dewar benzene, **3**). This compound aromatized relatively slowly, since the preferred thermal conrotatory ring opening would lead to the even more highly strained *trans*-benzene, **4**. Similar considerations apply also to the reactions of charged species, for example, in electrophilic addition reactions to Dewar benzene: addition of bromine gave the dibromide **5** and no bromobenzene, so isomerization of the carbonium ion **6** to the Wheland intermediate **7** cannot be significant.

Irradiation of tropylium fluoroborate **8** in aqueous sulfuric acid solution produced the bicyclic alcohol **9**: disrotatory ring closure of the photochemically excited tropylium ion gave preferentially the intermediary bicyclic cation **10**.

At the beginning of the 20th century M. Gomberg prepared the triphenylmethyl radical, $(C_6H_5)_3C\cdot$, by the action of silver powder on chlorotriphenylmethane. It had been widely accepted that the radical dimerized reversibly to hexaphenylethane $(C_6H_5)_3C - C(C_6H_5)_3$ but new spectroscopic evidence suggested structure **11** for the dimer. This conclusion was supported by the synthesis of new diarylmethyl radicals, $ArCH\cdot$, that gave two distinct types of dimer: stable tetraarylethanes $Ar_2CH - CHAr_2$ and products analogous to **11** that readily dissociated to free radicals in solution.

Also controverted, having stood the test of more than 60 years, was Bredt's rule, which states that in a bridged cyclic system a double bond cannot terminate at the bridgehead unless the rings are large enough to accommodate this double bond without strain. Two independent syntheses of bicyclo[3.3.1]non-1-ene **12** were announced in which the final introduction of the double bond was achieved by standard elimination reactions from compounds **13** and **14**.

Some reactions of alkanes with the very strongly acidic $FSO_3H - SbF_5$ solvent mixture are so remarkable as to have prompted the name "magic acid" for the reagent. At room temperature neopentane Me_4C gave the *t*-butyl cation Me_3C^+ and methane; at lower temperatures hydrogen was evolved, and the ion Me_2EtC^+ resulted from rearrangement of $Me_3CCH_2{}^+$. Methane itself also evolved hydrogen on solution in the acid, but the carbonium ion $(CH_3{}^+)$ presumably formed is so reactive that further rapid reactions gave rise to carbonium ions of higher molecular weight such as the *t*-butyl ion. It was suggested that the initial protonation of methane gave the ion $CH_5{}^+$; the exact nature of this ion remained to be elucidated.

The precision of synthesis by organometallic reagents continued to improve. Lithium dimethylcopper $(Li^+CuMe_2{}^-)$, prepared from methyllithium and cuprous iodide in ethereal solution, proved to be an excellent reagent for the substitution of bromine or iodine in organic compounds by a methyl group and in this respect showed quite different reactivity from methyllithium.

(J. C. Y.)

See also Industrial Review; Molecular Biology; Physics.

Encyclopædia Britannica Films. *Chemistry and a Changing World* (1953); *Preface to Chemistry* (1954).

Chess

In August 1967 Pal Benko won the U.S. Open Championship at Atlanta, Ga. The fifth Rubinstein Memorial Tournament was held at Polanica Zdroj, Pol., and was won by S. Furman (U.S.S.R.).

At a big international tournament in Havana in August and September, Bent Larsen (Denmark) scored a great success, finishing first with 15 points out of 19. The woman world champion, Nona Gaprindashvili (U.S.S.R.), won two women's international tourna-

ments, at Havering and Paignton, Eng. At Varna, Bulg., there was a triple tie for first place between L. Kavalek (Czech.), V. Sergievski (U.S.S.R.), and A. Minic (Yugos.). There was a quadruple tie for first place at the Tschigorin Memorial Tournament at Sochi, U.S.S.R., between N. Krogius, L. Shamkovich, B. Spassky, and I. Zaitsev (all U.S.S.R.). Bobby Fischer (U.S.) won first prize at Skopje, Yugos., with 13½ points. A match between Soviet and U.S. computers ended in a Soviet victory, 3–1. The fourth Zinnowitz, E.Ger., international tournament ended in a tie for first place between Vladimir Liberson (U.S.S.R.) and Wolfgang Uhlmann (E.Ger.). Wolfgang Unzicker (W.Ger.) was first with 9½ points at Krems, Aus. Larsen added to his list of successes by tying K. Darga (W.Ger.) at Winnipeg, Man., with 6 points.

At Venice, Italy, in late October and early November the Dutch grand master J. H. Donner finished ahead of the world champion, Tigran Petrosian (U.S.S.R.), scoring 11 to Petrosian's and Larry Evans' (U.S.) 10 points.

The most important tournament of the year was the Interzonal at Sousse, Tunisia. The first five, who qualified for the Candidates' matches, the next stage in the World Championship, were Larsen 15½, V. Korchnoi and E. Geller (both U.S.S.R.) and S. Gligoric (Yugos.) 14, and L. Portisch (Hung.) 13½. Fischer was leading at almost the halfway stage, but he withdrew twice from the event and was excluded by the organizers. The tie for the remaining sixth qualifying place between S. Reshevsky (U.S.), V. Hort (Czech.), and L. Stein (U.S.S.R.) was played off at Los Angeles and, this play-off also ending in a triple tie, the qualifying place went to Reshevsky who had the superior opponents' point count at Sousse. Shortly after the Sousse event, Larsen won first prize in another big tournament, at Palma in Majorca, Spain, in November and December, where he was first with 13 points.

Two international tournaments were held over the turn of the year: at Hastings, Eng., where there was a quadruple tie for the first place between Hort, F. Gheorghiu (Rom.), Stein, and A. Suetin (both U.S.S.R.); and at Göteborg, Swed., won by Geller. Korchnoi achieved a triumph at the Beverwijk, Neth., international tournament where he was first with 12 points out of 15. An international tournament in Moscow in January 1968 ended in a quadruple tie for first place between V. Bagirov, A. Chasin, and I. Zaitsev (all U.S.S.R.), and B. Soos (Rom.) with 7 points out of 11. In March Gligoric beat Donner in a match at Eersel, Neth., 6½–3½. Bruno Parma (Yugos.) won first prize in an international tournament at Bucharest, Rom. The fifth World Correspondence Championship was won by H. Berliner (U.S.).

In April the series of matches that go to make up the Candidates' event began. In the quarterfinals Spassky beat Geller 5½–2½, Tal beat Gligoric 5½–3½, Larsen beat Portisch 5½–4½, and Korchnoi beat Reshevsky 5½–2½. In the semifinals Spassky beat Larsen 5½–2½ and Korchnoi beat Tal 5½–4½. Spassky beat Korchnoi in the final 6½–3½ and thus became the official challenger for the World Championship.

In April an Olympiad for the blind at Weymouth, Eng., was won by the Soviet team. An international tournament at Bamberg, W.Ger., was won easily by Paul Keres (U.S.S.R.) with 12 points. A strong international tournament at Monaco was won by Larsen with 9½ points. The Clare Benedict European Team Tournament was again won by West Germany.

First prize at the Sarajevo international tournament

French defense (Interzonal Tournament at Sousse, October 1967)

White R. Fischer	Black Mjagmarsuren	White R. Fischer	Black Mjagmarsuren
1 P — K4	P — K3	17 Kt — B1	Kt — K3
2 P — Q3 (a)	P — Q4	18 Kt — Kt5	Kt — Q4
3 Kt — Q2	Kt — KB3	19 B — Q2	B X Kt (f)
4 P — KKt3	P — B4	20 B X B	Q — Q2
5 B — Kt 2	Kt — B3	21 Q — R5	KR — B1
6 KKt — B3	B — K2 (b)	22 Kt — Q2	Kt — B6
7 O — O	O — O	23 B — B6	Q — K1 (g)
8 P — K5	Kt — Q2	24 Kt — K4	Kt — K3
9 R — K1	P — QKt4 (c)	25 Kt — Kt5	Kt X Kt
10 Kt — B1	P — Kt5	26 R X Kt	P — B5
11 P — KR4 (d)	P — QR4	27 P — R5	P X P
12 B — B4	P — R5	28 R — R4 (h)	R — R2
13 P — R3	P X P (e)	29 R — Kt2	P X P
14 P X P	Kt — R4	30 Q — R6	Q — B1 (i)
15 Kt — K3	B — R3	31 Q X RPch	resigns (j)
16 B — R3	P — Q5		

(a) A rather unusual method of treating the French defense that has the virtue of being comparatively uncharted. (b) Overpassive; instead he should fight for the control of his K4 square by, for instance, 6 . . . , B — Q3; 7 O — O, O — O; 8 R — K1, Q — B2; 9 Q — K2, P X P; 10 P X P, P — K4; 11 Kt — B4, Kt — Q5; 12 Kt X Kt, BP X Kt; 13 P — KB4, B — KKt5. (c) Instead of this ineffectual attempt at counterattack, he should strike at the centre by 9 . . . , P — B3; 10 P X P, Kt X P; 11 Kt — Kt5, P — K4. (d) A move with a twofold purpose: aggressive, so as to undermine Black's king side by an eventual P — R6, and defensive, so as to safeguard the development of the QB on B4. (e) A little more attacking here would have been 13 . . . , R — Kt1. (f) Wrongly yielding Fischer the advantage of two bishops; he is, however, already quite outplayed and there is little to be done. If, for example, 19 . . . , P — R3; then 20 Kt — K4, followed by Q — R5 with the threat of B X RP. (g) If 23 . . . , P X B; 24 P X P, K — R1; 25 B — B5, P X B; 26 R — K7, Q — Q1; 27 R X P, Q — Kt1; 28 Kt — B3, Q — Kt3; 29 Q X Q, P X Q; 30 Kt — Kt5, followed by R — R7ch, P — B7ch and Kt — K6ch. (h) Threatening 29 P X P, BP X P; 30 R X P, K X R; 31 Q — R4ch, and mate in two moves. (i) This loses at once; the only way of prolonging the fight was by giving up his passed pawn, though after 30 . . . , P — B8 = Qch; 31 R X Q, R X Rch; 32. Q X R, White should still win in the end. (j) It is mate in two by either 31 . . . , K X Q; 32 P X Pdb/ch, K X P; 33 B — K4, or 32 . . . , K — Kt1; 33 R — R8 mate.

Queen's pawn, king's Indian defense (7th match game, Candidates' final at Kiev, September 1968)

White B. Spassky	Black V. Korchnoi	White B. Spassky	Black V. Korchnoi
1 P — Q4	Kt — KB3	19 Q X B	B — B1
2 P — QB4	P — KKt3	20 P — R5	QP X P (e)
3 Kt — QB3	B — Kt2	21 P X P	P X P
4 P — K4	P — Q3	22 Q — K6	R — Q1 (f)
5 P — B3	O — O	23 R X R	Q X R
6 B — K3	Kt — B3	24 R — Q1	Q — K2
7 KKt — K2	P — QR3	25 Q X QBP	Kt — B2
8 Kt — B1	P — K4	26 Q — Kt6 (g)	K — Kt2
9 P — Q5	Kt — Q5	27 Kt — Q5	Q — K3
10 Kt — Kt3	Kt X Kt	28 B X P	B X B
11 Q X Kt	P — B4 (a)	29 Q X B	Kt — Kt4
12 P X Pep	P X P	30 Q — K3	Q — B3ch
13 O — O — O	B — K3 (b)	31 K — Kt1	Kt — Q5
14 Q — R3	Kt — K1	32 R — QB1	Q — Kt4 (h)
15 P — R4	P — B3 (c)	33 Kt — B7	Q — K7 (i)
16 P — B5	R — B2 (d)	34 Kt — K6ch	K — R2
17 Q — R4	Q — B2	35 Q — R6ch (j)	resigns
18 B — QB4	B X B		

(a) He does not want to allow White to play P — B5; but in this line Black should go all out for a king-side counterattack by 11 . . . , Kt — R4 followed by P — KB4. (b) Here it was essential to remove his queen from the indirect attack of the enemy rook by 13 . . . , Q — K2. (c) Weakening his king-side position gravely; K — R1 and B — B3 have been suggested as preferable here, but best seems 15 . . . , Q — B2. (d) If 16 . . . , P — Q4; 17 B — Q84; 18 P X P, Kt X P; 19 Kt X Kt, P X Kt; 20 B X P, B X B; 21 R — Q2, followed by 22 KR — Q1. (e) Too risky; 20 . . . , P — KKt4, though leaving Black positionally worse off, would at any rate stem the attack. (f) A better defense was 22 . . . , Kt — Q3 with R — K1 to follow. (g) Stronger than 26 Kt — Q5, against which Black has the defense 26 . . . , Q — K3. (h) After 32 . . . , Q — Q3; White can force Black to make further holes in his position by 33 R — R1, P — Kt4. (i) Losing offhand; a little better was 33 . . . , Q — K3, though White would still have had a won game after 34 Kt — K8ch, K — B1; 35 R — B8, K — K2; 36 Q — R3ch. (j) This very pretty finish forces mate.

Leonid Stein of the U.S.S.R., who shared in a quadruple tie with V. Hort, F. Gheorghiu, and A. Suetin at the Hastings International Tournament.

in May was shared by D. Ciric (Yugos.) and A. Lein (U.S.S.R.). An international tournament at Busum, W.Ger., was won by a 19-year-old West German, Robert Hubner. Stein easily won first prize at Kecskemet, Hung.

In June an international tournament at Reykjavik, Iceland, was won by the Soviet grand masters Taimanov and E. Vasiukov. Bobby Fischer was an easy first at Nathanya, Israel. The annual match between the U.S.S.R. and Yugoslavia was played at Sochi and was won by the Soviet team 17–11. An international tournament at Solingen, W.Ger., was won by the Hungarian L. Lengyel. In the absence of Fischer, Evans won the U.S. championship with 8½. The World Students Team Championship was played at Ybbs, Aus., and was won by the U.S.S.R. after a tie with West Germany.

The IBM international tournament at Amsterdam in July and August was won by Kavalek. At Skopje, Portisch was first with 14½. The English Counties Championship was won for the third consecutive year by Lancashire and J. Penrose won the British Championship for the ninth time. (H. Go.)

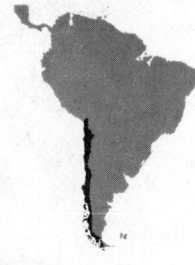

Chile

A republic extending along the southern Pacific coast of South America, Chile has an area of 292,257 sq.mi. (756,946 sq.km.), not including its Antarctic claim between 53° and 90° W. It is bounded by Argentina, Bolivia, and Peru. Pop. (1967 est.): 9 million. Cap. and largest city: Santiago (pop. of greater Santiago, 1966 est., 2,346,781). Language: Spanish. Religion: predominantly Roman Catholic. President in 1968, Eduardo Frei Montalva.

A continuation of traditional party politics and the

CHILE
Education. (1965) Primary, pupils 1,524,979; secondary, pupils 218,305; vocational, pupils 125,344; teacher training, students 6,896, teachers 525; higher (including 8 universities), students 43,608, teaching staff 8,835.
Finance. Monetary unit: escudo, with (end August 1968) a banks' free market exchange rate (for trade and some invisible operations) of 7.07 escudos to U.S. $1 (16.85 escudos = £1 sterling) and a brokers' market rate (for most other transactions) of 8.12 escudos to U.S. $1 (19.35 escudos = £1 sterling). Gold and foreign exchange, central bank: (June 1968) U.S. $125.4 million; (June 1967) U.S. $142 million. Budget (1968 est.): revenue 7,557,000,000 escudos; expenditure 7,947,000,000 escudos. Gross national product: (1966) 24,336,000,000 escudos; (1965) 17,547,000,000 escudos. Money supply: (Dec. 1967) 3,239,000,000 escudos; (Dec. 1966) 2,594,000,000 escudos. Cost of living (Santiago; 1963 = 100): (June 1968) 346; (June 1967) 274.
Foreign Trade. (1966) Imports U.S. $755.3 million; exports U.S. $877.5 million. Import sources: U.S. 39%; West Germany 13%; Argentina 9%; U.K. 5%. Export destinations: U.S. 25%; U.K. 15%; Netherlands 13%; Japan 10%; West Germany 10%. Main exports: copper bars, ore, and concentrates 73%; iron ore 9%; nitrates 3%.
Transport and Communications. Roads (1966) c. 60,000 km. Motor vehicles in use (1966): passenger 108,200; commercial (including buses) 96,900. Railways: (1965) 8,408 km.; traffic (principal railways; 1967) 2,039,000,000 passenger-km., freight 2,505,000,000 net ton-km. Shipping (1967): merchant vessels 100 gross tons and over 134; gross tonnage 279,087. Air traffic (1966): 529,285,000 passenger-km.; freight 26,479,000 net ton-km. Telephones (Dec. 1966) 269,516. Radio receivers (Dec. 1962) 1.5 million. Television receivers (Dec. 1966) c. 55,000.
Agriculture. Production (in 000; metric tons; 1967; 1966 in parentheses): wheat c. 1,174 (1,167); barley (1966) 140, (1965) 138; oats (1966) 123, (1965) 117; corn c. 250 (246); sugar, raw value (1967–68) c. 169, (1966–67) 119; rice (1966) 71, (1965) 80; potatoes (1966) 705, (1965) 735; dry beans (1966) 93, (1965) 74; wine (1966) c. 474, (1965) 365; wool, greasy 23 (23); timber (1966) 6,900 cu.m., (1965) 7,100 cu.m. Livestock (in 000; 1965–66): cattle c. 2,900; sheep c. 6,600; pigs 1,007; horses c. 534. Fish catch (in 000; metric tons) (1966) 1,383, (1965) 709. Whale catch (1965–66) 1,099, (1964–65) 1,348.
Industry. Production (in 000; metric tons; 1967): coal 1,447; crude oil 1,612; electricity 6,766,000 kw-hr.; iron ore (65% metal content) 9,840; pig iron 498; crude steel 596; copper (1966) 343; nitrate of soda (1966) 1,062; iodine (1966) 2.9; molybdenum (metal content; 1966) 4.7; silver (1966) 0.12; gold (1966) 75 troy oz.; woven cotton fabrics c. 110,000 m.; fish meal (1966) 220.

initial jockeying for position prior to the 1970 presidential elections dominated the Chilean political scene during 1968. President Frei and the ruling Christian Democratic Party were unable to form an alliance with any of the major opposition parties in order to obtain a working majority in the Senate. Much of the politicking resulted directly or indirectly from the unexpected victory of Radical Party Sen. Alberto Baltra Cortés in a by-election held in December 1967 in the provinces of Bío-Bío, Malleco, and Cautín. Senator Baltra's victory over the favoured Christian Democratic candidate, Jorge Lavandero, had two important consequences. First, it gave the combined opposition forces in the Senate a two-thirds majority, just enough to block any legislation the administration wanted to introduce in the Christian Democratic-controlled Chamber of Deputies. Second, it expanded the range of potential political alliances among the country's six major parties, thereby throwing open the list of possible presidential candidates for 1970.

By dominating the Senate, the opposition succeeded in blocking most major legislation proposed by the administration. A major confrontation began early in 1968 when the administration introduced the annual wage bill to compensate workers for the previous year's inflation. The bill proposed a full readjustment of wages but part of it was to be in readjustable government bonds rather than in cash. The bonds were to be used to create a National Capitalization Fund to finance public investment programs. The opposition parties in the Senate defeated the measure, which led to the resignation of two finance ministers and a consequent reshuffling of the Cabinet. The measure as it was finally passed called for a 21.9% wage increase in private industry and 20% for public employees.

Although the next presidential elections were not scheduled until 1970, candidates began behind-the-scenes campaigning. Senator Baltra's victory effectively prevented what might have become another confrontation between the Christian Democratic Party and the leftist Popular Action Front (FRAP), as happened in 1964. The leading candidates included Radomiro Tomic, former ambassador to the United States, for the Christian Democratic Party; Felipe Herrera, president of the Inter-American Development Bank; Salvador Allende, the three-time losing candidate of the FRAP; Jorge Alessandri, a former president of Chile and popular among independent voters; and Baltra himself. Baltra's strategy seemed based on a re-creation of the FRAP-Radical Party alliance that won in the 1938 presidential elections.

The hierarchy of the Roman Catholic Church was pressured to take a stronger stand on social reform. In a move unprecedented in Chilean history, approximately 200 Catholic priests, nuns, students, and laymen occupied the cathedral in Santiago for several days in August to publicize their demands. Also, students continued to pressure for reform both in and out of the universities, and isolated cases of violence and bombings took place. But, despite these publicized actions on the part of reformist and revolutionary groups, occasional by-elections and public opinion polls suggested that the mass of independent voters was switching to a more conservative position.

The government pressed ahead with its economic and social reforms despite opposition from the Senate. The application of the agrarian reform law, passed the previous year, was extended and accelerated although not without opposition from the landholders. The program was frequently attacked for poor management,

WIDE WORLD

Clotario Blest, one of a group of 200 Catholics including eight priests, talking to newsmen from behind the barred gates of Santiago's cathedral during a sit-in intended to dramatize the group's demands for social reform.

and several expropriations of land led to violence and to legal suits.

Among the more important economic events of the year were the opening of a $100 million, 350,000-kw. hydroelectric station at Rapel; the formation of a joint venture between the government and the privately owned Anglo-Lautaro nitrate mining company, which was expected to lead to a $25 million investment in a diversified chemical complex based on the country's vast resources of nitrate; and the inauguration of the $6 million Longovilo station for telecommunications by satellite, the first to be completed in Latin America.

Despite a high level of investments, particularly in mining, the economy stagnated during the year. During the first months of the year this perhaps was caused by the unusually long delay in passing the wage readjustment bill. In midyear a drought that affected 11 central provinces from Coquimbo to Ñuble severely damaged the economy. The drought, the worst in 110 years, caused losses estimated at nearly $100 million. The lack of rain reduced the level of water reserves so that electric power, mostly from hydroelectric sources, had to be rationed. This adversely affected industrial output.

Chile made medical history during 1968 when two heart transplants were successfully made at the Admiral Neff Naval Hospital in Valparaíso under the direction of Jorge Kaplan. The first of these operations, in June, was carried out on a woman, María Elena Peñaloza, the first woman in the world to survive a heart transplant. (R. L. Ro.)

China

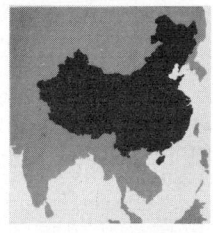

The most populous country in the world and the third largest in area, China is bounded by the U.S.S.R., Mongolia, North Korea, North Vietnam, Laos, Burma, India, Bhutan, Sikkim, Nepal, Pakistan, and Afghanistan. From 1949 the country has been divided into the People's Republic of China (Communist) on the mainland and on Hainan and other islands, and the Republic of China (Nationalist) on Taiwan (*see* TAIWAN). Area: 3,691,-

502 sq.mi. (9,561,001 sq.km.), including Tibet but excluding Taiwan. Pop. of the People's Republic (1968 est.): 850 million, of which about 94% are Han. Cap.: Peking (pop., 1964 est., 7 million). Largest city: Shanghai (pop., 1964 est., 10.4 million). Language: Chinese (Mandarin dialect). Chairman of the Communist Party in 1968, Mao Tse-tung; chief of state until October 15, Liu Shao-ch'i; premier, Chou En-lai.

The Great Proletarian Cultural Revolution, which began in September 1965 by attacking intellectuals and led to disputes in political ideology and in internal and foreign affairs, became a tense struggle for personal power in early 1966 with the purge of P'eng Chen, mayor of Peking and a senior Politburo member. The next stage began on Aug. 18, 1966, when the Red Guards were inaugurated as the instrument to liquidate Chairman Mao Tse-tung's political opponents and when Marshal Lin Piao emerged as Mao's heir apparent, replacing Pres. Liu Shao-ch'i, who had been number two man in the Chinese Communist Party for decades. The Red Guards' attack centred on four "olds" (old ideas, old culture, old customs, and old habits), bureaucratic tendencies, and the leadership of President Liu and Teng Hsiao-p'ing, party secretary-general and member of the Politburo.

The rampage of the Red Guards shattered Communist Party machinery; weakened the governmental system; strengthened the position of militarists; undermined economic operations and production; and created confusion, disorder, and chaos throughout the country. In those circumstances and under pressure from the Army and moderates, Mao and Lin decided in October–December 1967 to call for an end to factional strife between rival groups of Red Guards, the reopening of schools and universities, and the speeding up of the formation of revolutionary committees based on a three-way alliance among the Army, Communist Party officials, and leaders of mass organizations, including Red Guards. Such committees would serve as organs of government at provincial and local levels. It was then revealed by Hsieh Fu-chih, minister of security and chairman of the Peking Municipal Revolutionary Committee, that the ninth Communist Party Congress would be held not later than October 1, to regain the control of the party and to formally dismiss Liu as chief of state. The Central Committee of the party met in October in an "enlarged" session in which nonmembers were allowed to attend and vote. The committee announced that Liu had been stripped of all his official functions.

Before the Cultural Revolution, the highly organized Chinese Communist Party was the main instrument for implementing national policies at the central and local levels. However, after two years of political strife and turmoil the majority of the Politburo and of the Central Committee elected by the eighth party congress in 1956 had been either purged, disgraced, or denounced; the central party secretariat, which controlled party committees at provincial, municipal, and county levels, had been virtually destroyed. At the traditional May Day rally a list of members of the Politburo of the party's Central Committee was made public for the first time in more than two years. According to this list, seven Politburo members including Liu Shao-ch'i, Teng Hsiao-p'ing, and P'eng Chen had been purged; the new Politburo was composed of eight active members: Mao Tse-tung, Lin Piao, Chou En-lai; two new members (Chen Po-ta and K'ang Sheng); and three persons (Chen Yi, Li Fu-chun, and Li Hsien-nien) of administrative ex-

Child Welfare:
see Education; Social Services

perience. Mao's wife, Chiang Ch'ing, who headed the Cultural Revolution Group, was regarded as a de facto member of the Politburo and one of the five leaders in the innermost policy-making circle around Chairman Mao. In order of their official party ranking, this circle included Lin Piao, Chou En-lai, Chiang Ch'ing, Chen Po-ta, and K'ang Sheng.

On the 19th anniversary of the People's Republic on October 1 a celebration rally was held. Such rallies usually provided a list of high-ranking leaders by means of noting those who mounted the rostrum at T'ien-an Men (Gate of Heavenly Peace) in Peking; but for the first time the official Chinese press agency, Hsinhua, failed to distribute the usual account of prominent leaders present at the rally. However, the toll of the Cultural Revolution was not hard to detect as only a few of the once-supreme Politburo and State Council members were even reported present at the rally. Following Chairman Mao, Lin Piao,

KEYSTONE

Writing lessons in a Peking primary school include making posters of the quotations of Chairman Mao Tse-tung.

vice-chairman and defense minister, who had retained second rank, delivered a relatively brief and mild main speech. Chou En-lai remained the third ranking leader, but, in addition to Chiang Ch'ing, Chen Po-ta, and K'ang Sheng, several top-ranking leaders whose names only became known to the people during the Cultural Revolution, were proclaimed. These included Yeh Chun (Mrs. Lin Piao) and Wang Tung-hsing, the captain of Mao's bodyguard.

Perhaps the most significant and notable event at the rally was the subordinate position accorded to the Red Guards, who had occupied a prominent and influential place in the 1966 and 1967 rallies. Instead, urban labourers and peasants were honoured as the most important segments of Chinese society.

The demotion of the Red Guards at the ceremony was taken as an indication that Mao had been persuaded to abandon them in order to bring order out of chaos. At the rally Peking's diplomatic isolation became apparent, as none of the important Communist countries sent a delegation to participate in the celebration. North Vietnam sent a message expressing its gratitude to Communist China for its support and assistance in the war against the U.S., while the Soviet Union sent merely a curt, frigid message of congratulations. However, Peking's staunch ally, Albania, was represented at the celebration by a delegation headed by the Albanian deputy premier.

Domestic Affairs. As the People's Republic began its 20th year, the Cultural Revolution, which created such convulsion and turmoil, subsided if it did not entirely disappear. The three-year revolution had succeeded in purging the upper ranks of the Communist Party and shattering the party apparatus, but it failed to meet the target date for convening the ninth party congress. The recent decision to restore order and strengthen authority at the expense of the revolutionary Red Guards, with the Army providing the muscle, seemed to indicate that Chairman Mao's efforts to build an egalitarian society on the foundation of mass activists had been at least temporarily abandoned. The continuing struggle in Communist China centred more on personal power than policies, and it seemed that Mao had come to value loyalty more than ability in his close associates.

Mao demonstrated genius in destroying the old but failed to construct a viable new society. Nevertheless, the glorification and apotheosizing of Mao's person and thought became a common feature in Communist China during 1968. His statue and portraits, as well as quotations from his writings, were everywhere in public and private buildings. The book *Quotations from Chairman Mao Tse-tung* was made required reading in the Army and in the schools. The expanded cult of Mao might partly reflect the respect for his advanced age (75 on December 26) and partly might indicate the divisions among his top-ranking associates, who were rivals for his confidence.

Each of the highest leaders in the innermost policy-making circle around Mao headed a ruling body in addition to holding membership in the Politburo. These leaders included: Lin Piao, actual head of the Military Affairs Committee of seven active members; Chou En-lai, premier of the State Council with six deputy premiers; and Chiang Ch'ing, director of the Cultural Revolution Group, which virtually displaced the party secretariat and directed Red Guard activities outside the party. As party chairman, Mao served as ex officio chairman of the Military Affairs Committee, which coordinated internal and external security matters. These ruling bodies sometimes pursued different policies and competed for authority. Since the Army wielded the actual power, the Military Affairs Committee was regarded as the most effective.

The membership of the Military Affairs Committee, including invariably the defense minister, the chief of the Army, and the minister of security, was in constant shift during the Cultural Revolution. At a big rally in Peking on March 26 Chiang Ch'ing attacked Yang Cheng-wu, acting chief of the Army, and two of his colleagues for trying to establish absolute authority and plot against Chairman Mao. A few days later the three officers were dismissed, and Gen. Huang Yung-sheng, former military commander of Canton, was appointed to succeed Yang. As chairman of the Revolutionary Committee of Kwangtung Province in late 1967, General Huang had been a target of radical Red Guard criticism. Thus, contrary to Chiang Ch'ing's wishes, Huang's appointment was interpreted generally as strengthening the authority of moderate factions led by Chou En-lai. The open attack on the Army by the extreme left wing and the appointment of General Huang as the chief of the Army appeared to mark a shift toward the ascendancy of the militarists and moderates.

The Revolutionary Committees. These committees were to be made up of representatives of three components—the armed forces, the Red Guards, and the

remnants of the party hierarchy. They provided a mechanism for provincial and local government, replacing the old structure of local government. Because the composition of these committees was subject to the approval of the central authority in Peking, factional leaders around Mao tried to exert their influence in order to enhance their power. Political rivalry and disputes, personality clashes, and factional fights of the Red Guards made it impossible to meet the target date, May 1, as the goal for the establishment of revolutionary committees in all 26 administrative areas and 3 self-governing municipalities (Peking, Tientsin, and Shanghai). At the end of 1967 only nine revolutionary committees had been established. Between January and the end of May one municipal and 14 provincial committees were established, making a total of 24.

The five provinces and regions that had not formed revolutionary committees by October 1 were Tibet, Yunnan, and Kwangsi Chuang in the southwest, Fukien on the east coast, and the large western region of Sinkiang Uighur. In Kwangtung and Kwangsi Chuang intensive and brutal clashes were reported. The Red Flag and East Wind factions, two major organizations in Kwangtung with student and worker affiliations and both calling themselves Maoists, had been constantly feuding, with the loss of many lives, until Peking early in August authorized the Army to launch a drive to curb factional fighting and halt the extreme leftists' militant struggle for power. Battles between Maoist rival factions in Kwangsi continued to rage from April to July, and it was reported that during the first half of 1968 the fighting cost nearly 100,000 lives and that the city of Wuchow, about 125 mi. W of Canton, was devastated. The fighting in Kwangsi seriously affected the supply of weapons, food, and other materials by rail from China to North Vietnam. According to the press in Hong Kong, Mao had to use the Army to stop the fighting.

According to press reports, 21 of the 29 revolutionary committees were under the chairmanship of military leaders, and only 8 were controlled by genuine Maoists. This situation made the task of organizing a new party structure for convening the ninth party congress more difficult. Obviously, the Peking leadership wanted to ensure that delegates to the congress and officials to be elected would be loyal to Maoism.

Worker-Peasant Teams and the New Educational System. The Cultural Revolution created confusion and havoc in the schools. High-school and college students, who joined Red Guards to spearhead the revolution, did not want to settle down to an academic routine again. In early 1967 the government had called upon students and teachers to return to their institutions and homes, but the response was poor. In the spring of 1968 the Army was given a free hand to persuade students to return to their schools and to enforce peace between rival Red Guard groups. Many Red Guards were sent to remote areas to do hard labour.

An innovation in 1968 was the formation of Worker-Peasant-Soldier Propaganda Teams in August in accordance with Mao's directives to take control of schools, colleges, universities, research institutes, and other educational institutions as well as newspapers and other press organs throughout the country. According to the official news agency, 49 colleges and universities in Peking, 26 institutions in Shanghai, 6 in Tientsin, and 38 in Nanchang had been taken over by these newly formed teams by the end of August. Intellectuals were told to accept subordination to workers, soldiers, and peasants and also to a new check on their thoughts, loyalties, and actions. In September Worker-Soldier and Peasant-Soldier Teams began to take over primary and secondary schools in cities and rural areas, respectively.

These actions were in line with the ideology of Chairman Mao, who regarded the old academic system of education as too Western since it emphasized intellectual training and individual accomplishments. The new educational system, according to official sources in September, would reduce primary and secondary education from 12 to 9 years, and college education to 2 years. In the meantime, the campaign continued to urge college students who would have been in the classes of 1966 and 1967 to leave school for assignments on farms and in reclamation projects, mines, factories, and other enterprises.

Nuclear Development. On December 27 Communist China was reported to have exploded a three-megaton device, presumably thermonuclear, in the atmosphere, in the Lop Nor region of Sinkiang Province. It marked the first successful nuclear test for China since June 17, 1967. A test in December 1967, reported by the U.S. and Japan, was believed a failure because Peking never made any mention of it.

In June Peking denounced the draft treaty to halt the spread of nuclear weapons, which had been approved by the UN General Assembly, calling it a plot to preserve the nuclear monopoly of the U.S. and the Soviet Union. Consequently, China declined an invitation to attend the conference of nonnuclear states held in August–September.

Economy. A shortage of food and goods in 1968

CHINA

Education. Primary (1959–60), pupils 90 million; secondary (1958–59), pupils 8,520,000; vocational (1958–59), pupils 850,000; teacher training, students (1958–59) 620,000; higher (1962–63), students 820,000.

Finance. Monetary unit: jen min piao or people's bank dollar, also called the yuan, with an official exchange rate of 2.46 yuan to U.S. $1 (5.85 yuan = £1 sterling). Budget (1960 draft est.; no later figures published) balanced at 70,-020,000,000 yuan. Net aggregate product (1959 at 1952 prices; 1952 in parentheses) 152 billion yuan (61.1 billion yuan).

Foreign Trade. (1966) Imports c. U.S. $1,-750,000,000; exports c. U.S. $1.7 billion. Import sources: Japan c. 20%; Canada 11%; U.S.S.R. c. 10%. Export destinations: Hong Kong c. 26%; Japan c. 17%; U.S.S.R. c. 9%. Main exports: textiles and clothing; metals and ores; meat; rice; tea.

Transport and Communications. Roads (1966) c. 550,000 km. (including c. 200,000 km. with improved surface). Motor vehicles in use (1965): passenger c. 40,000; commercial c. 250,-000. Railways: (1966) c. 32,000 km.; traffic (1959) 45,670,000,000 passenger-km., freight 265,260,000,000 net ton-km. Shipping (1967): merchant vessels 100 gross tons and over 247; gross tonnage 772,125. Air traffic (1960): 63,-882,000 passenger-km.; freight 1,967,000 net ton-km. Telephones (1951) 255,000. Radio receivers (Dec. 1963) c. 8 million. Television receivers (Dec. 1965) c. 100,000.

Agriculture. Production (in 000; metric tons; 1966; 1965 in parentheses): rice c. 88,000 (c. 89,000); wheat c. 25,700 (c. 26,000); soybeans c. 10,970 (c. 10,970); peanuts c. 2,360 (c. 2,300); cotton, lint c. 1,301 (c. 1,258); jute c. 450 (c. 430); sesame c. 370 (c. 370); rapeseed c. 1,120 (c. 1,120); sugar, raw value c. 3,055

(c. 2,885); tobacco c. 450 (c. 450); tea c. 159 (c. 159); oranges, tangerines, and clementines c. 600 (c. 570); wool, clean c. 47 (c. 46); timber (1965) c. 135,000 cu.m., (1964) 134,000 cu.m. Livestock (in 000; 1965–66): cattle 62,800; sheep 68,400; pigs 206,000; goats 55,000; buffaloes 28,608; camels 15; horses 7,600; asses 11,100.

Industry. Fuel and power (in 000; 1966): coal (including lignite) c. 325,000 metric tons; coke c. 17,000 metric tons; crude oil c. 10,000 metric tons; electricity (1960) c. 58,500,000 kw-hr. Production (in 000; metric tons; 1966): iron ore c. 40,000; pig iron c. 20,000; crude steel c. 16,-000; tin concentrates (metal content) c. 22; bauxite c. 400; tungsten (1964) c. 20; cement c. 11,000; sulfuric acid (1959) 1,100; chemical fertilizers c. 1,260,000; aluminum c. 100; cotton yarn (1960) 1,633; woven cotton fabrics 5,900,-000 m.; paper (1965) 2,800.

was reported as a result of the disruptive effect of the Cultural Revolution. However, the 1967 grain crop was considered the best in recent years. The report of the UN Food and Agriculture Organization estimated Communist China's 1967 grain production at 215 million tons, compared with 206 million in 1966 and 208 million in 1965.

Foreign Relations. Deeply embroiled in its ideology, which claimed an inevitable political and economic crisis in the imperialist system, and greatly preoccupied with the problems created by the Cultural Revolution, Communist China remained more or less isolated from the world of international reality. During the year only 45 countries maintained diplomatic relations with Peking.

In 1968 the U.S. government made overtures to Communist China to accept new contacts and exchanges with the United States. Early in May the director of the United States Information Agency invited China to send journalists to the U.S. to cover the 1968 presidential election campaign. This invitation was followed by statements from two leading U.S. foreign-policy spokesmen (Undersecretary of State Nicholas Katzenbach and Eugene V. Rostow, undersecretary of state for political affairs) concerning an invitation to Chinese scientists, scholars, and journalists to visit the U.S. and a relaxation of restrictions on travel to Communist China. However, at Peking's insistence, it was agreed toward the end of May that the infrequent U.S.-Chinese ambassadorial talks in Warsaw should be postponed until after the U.S. presidential election. Late in November China proposed that a meeting be held in Warsaw in February 1969.

North Vietnam's decision to enter negotiations with the U.S. on the Vietnam war in response to U.S. Pres. Lyndon Johnson's appeal did not please Communist China. Shortly before the opening of the peace talks in Paris on May 13, Peking withdrew its press attaché and news agency from North Vietnam as a sign of disapproval. However, it was believed that the disruption of the flow of military supplies by rail through Communist China to North Vietnam in the summer was primarily caused by fighting between Red Guard factions in provinces bordering North Vietnam. In July North Vietnam's deputy premier visited Peking, and the two countries reaffirmed their solidarity.

Despite ideological differences between the U.S.S.R. and China and their rivalry for leadership in the Communist movement, regular air and rail connections and services were maintained between the two nations. In early April the Soviet government sent two protests to Peking concerning China's detention of a Soviet tanker carrying cargo to North Vietnam. At a reception in Peking on August 1 to mark China's Army Day, the diplomatic representatives of the Soviet Union, Czechoslovakia, Mongolia, and India walked out of a banquet when the Army chief of staff referred to China's role in the struggle against "U.S. imperialism, Soviet revisionism, and Indian reactionaries." In August and September Peking strongly attacked the Soviet invasion of Czechoslovakia. In 1968 the Soviet Union and India ceased to be sponsors of the perennial resolution in the General Assembly for seating Communist China at the United Nations. In November only 44 (including the U.S.S.R. and India) of 126 members voted for the resolution, which was sponsored by Albania and 14 other countries.

In Southeast Asia the insurgent movements in Thailand and Burma inspired by Peking proved to be disappointing. Communist China and Burma were re-

portedly ready to move toward restoration of their once-cordial relations, shattered by anti-Chinese violence in Rangoon in 1967. China continued to show interest in developing a foothold in Africa. Following the conclusion of an agreement in September 1967 with Tanzania and Zambia for the construction of a 1,000-mi. railway between those two countries, approximately 300 Chinese engineers and technicians arrived in Dar es Salaam, Tanzania, in April to start survey work. After a visit to Peking by a joint delegation from Guinea and Mali, it was announced in May that an agreement had been signed whereby China would help build a railroad giving Mali access to the sea through Guinea.   (H. T. CH.)

See also **Propaganda; Taiwan.**

ENCYCLOPÆDIA BRITANNICA FILMS. *China Under Communism* (1962); *China: A Portrait of the Land* (1967); *China's Industrial Revolution* (1967); *China's Villages in Change* (1967).

Cinema

English-Language Films. The year 1968 was not a vintage year for Hollywood. Too few "old masters" were active, and there was little sign of a rising younger generation. Westerns, thrillers, and comedies continued to appear, along with a couple of important musicals. As these types of films were, perhaps because of their very lack of ambition, Hollywood's most satisfying, they deserve to be considered before the so-called "important" new films.

Thrillers fell into two groups, plain and fancy. To the first belonged *Tony Rome,* in which Frank Sinatra satisfyingly played the role of a tough, terse detective; Donald Siegel's *Madigan* began in his best tough simple style, but unfortunately the scenario soon got bogged down in an excessive number of subplots and brooding on ethics. *No Way to Treat a Lady* could be classified either as thriller or as comedy: as a psychopathic murderer Rod Steiger had a field day, impersonating, in the course of his slaughters, a host of characters. The "fancy" thrillers were John Boorman's *Point Blank* and Norman Jewison's *The Thomas Crown Affair,* the latter an entertaining duel between Boston-banker-turned-criminal Steve McQueen and insurance inspector Faye Dunaway. *Point Blank*'s portrait of a crime syndicate constituted an indictment of contemporary U.S. society, and was extremely impressive stylistically. Moreover, the acting (by Lee Marvin, Keenan Wynn, and Angie Dickinson) was absolutely right.

Chimpanzee scientists defending American astronaut (Charlton Heston) in "Planet of the Apes," a satirical science-fiction film directed by Franklin Schaffner for 20th Century-Fox.

Except for *Star!* the musicals were less satisfying. Most found *Camelot* inflated and lacking in charm; and though some hailed *Finian's Rainbow* as a welcome return to the old days, others maintained that it proved that the old days were gone. But *Star!* (directed by Robert Wise, with Julie Andrews as Gertrude Lawrence) seemed to many the most engaging musical in years. *Funny Girl* featured Barbra Streisand playing Fanny Brice, and the star generally received better notices than the movie as a whole.

Among Westerns, John Sturgis' *Hour of the Gun* and Jerry Thorpe's *Day of the Evil Gun* stood out for acting, tight construction, and ingenious screenplays. The year's most popular comedy was *The Odd Couple*, a straight version of the stage hit, starring Jack Lemmon and Walter Matthau. More interesting was an unusual fantastic satire, *The President's Analyst*. Starring James Coburn and directed by Theodore J. Flicker, it was a successful incursion of comedy into the angst-ridden world of political intrigue and violence.

The "important" films included John Huston's *Reflections in a Golden Eye*, Franklin Schaffner's *Planet of the Apes*, Mike Nichols' *The Graduate*, Roman Polanski's *Rosemary's Baby*, Richard Brooks's *In Cold Blood*, Paul Newman's *Rachel, Rachel*, and Stanley Kramer's *Guess Who's Coming to Dinner*. The first, an adaptation of Carson McCullers' novel, starred Elizabeth Taylor, Marlon Brando, and Julie Harris. Somewhat airless, it was well acted and directed, though the original monochrome colour effects Huston had wanted were not widely shown. *Planet of the Apes* adapted a Pierre Boulle science-fiction novel about a society in which, to restrain man's killer instincts, the apes have taken over. In the U.S. *The Graduate* was the year's most popular film: it turned its "hero," Dustin Hoffman (*see* BIOGRAPHY), into a star. Some had doubts about its profundity, finding it merely an engaging comedy, but many hailed it as the first Hollywood film to speak for contemporary youth.

Rosemary's Baby ran *The Graduate* a close second

in popularity. It was a horror story based on a best-selling novel about a young woman (Mia Farrow) who bears a child to the Devil. Many thought it most successful in its wryer moments, but that it built up tremendous tension to culminate in an impressive final scene was undeniable. *Rachel, Rachel*, Newman's first film as director, starred his wife, Joanne Woodward, in a magnificent performance as a frustrated 35-year-old schoolteacher. *Guess Who's Coming to Dinner* starred Katharine Hepburn, Spencer Tracy (who died soon after it was completed: *see* OBITUARIES), and Sidney Poitier in a sentimental drama about racial intermarriage.

Another "important" film was John Cassavetes' *Faces*, his first really independent film since *Shadows* (1960). Generally hailed as a triumph of social realism, it disappointed some by disjointedness, particularly in the acting.

In April the U.S. Academy of Motion Picture Arts and Sciences presented its annual Academy Awards. *In the Heat of the Night*, a detective drama with a racial theme, was voted the best movie of 1967. Rod Steiger was named best actor for his performance in that film, while Katharine Hepburn won best actress for her role in *Guess Who's Coming to Dinner*. Mike Nichols received the best director award for *The Graduate*, while Estelle Parsons in *Bonnie and Clyde* and George Kennedy in *Cool Hand Luke* were voted best supporting actress and actor.

There were a number of "mid-Atlantic" films during the year: either official co-productions or those combining U.S. and British talents. One was almost literally mid-Atlantic: Peter Glenville's *The Comedians*, a British-French-Bermudan co-production. An adaptation of Graham Greene's novel, it boasted star performances by Elizabeth Taylor, Richard Burton, and Sir Alec Guiness. The most important mid-Atlantic movies were Stanley Kubrick's *2001: A Space Odyssey* and two Joseph Losey productions, *Boom* and *Secret Ceremony*. The Kubrick film was hailed as the most visually convincing science-fiction movie ever made. Opinion was divided about its content, however.

Both the Losey films starred Elizabeth Taylor. *Boom*, in which she was accompanied by Richard Burton, was a stylish adaptation of Tennessee Williams' play *The Milk Train Doesn't Stop Here Anymore*, but many thought that the material was not very interesting. *Secret Ceremony*, in which Elizabeth Taylor gave an outstanding performance, was much more successful. Losey's handling of a plot involving a bereft woman whose daughter has died and a girl (Mia Farrow) who had lost her mother was dramatically and visually impressive.

The Lion in Winter, directed by Anthony Harvey, was an adaptation of James Goldman's play about Eleanor of Aquitaine and Henry Plantagenet (Henry II). It wallowed in anachronism, but Katharine Hepburn's performance as Eleanor was, perhaps, the best of her career: she made one forget that the dialogue belonged more to the New York suburbs than to medieval France. Peter O'Toole played Henry. Other co-productions included the musical *Half a Sixpence* and Franco Zeffirelli's *Romeo and Juliet*; the latter was disappointing, while the former, a musical version of H. G. Wells's novel *Kipps*, was diverting, partly because of the ingratiating performance of Tommy Steele.

Native British products included Tony Richardson's *The Charge of the Light Brigade*, a controversial but generally well-received treatment of the famous Cri-

Keir Dullea as commander of the space ship "Discovery" in "2001: A Space Odyssey," directed by Stanley Kubrick from a screen play by Kubrick and noted science fiction author Arthur C. Clarke.

Mia Farrow in a scene from the nightmarish film "Rosemary's Baby," adapted from the best-selling novel by Ira Levin and directed by Roman Polanski.

Katharine Hepburn
as Queen Eleanor
of Aquitaine during
the filming of a scene
from "The Lion in Winter,"
directed by Anthony
Harvey.

mean War episode. A remarkable feature film debut was that of Jack Gold, who, in *The Bofors Gun,* succeeded in making a powerful film about army life, rooted in documentary realism; it starred Nicol Williamson, Ian Holm, and David Warner. Another successful debut was that of actor Albert Finney as director of *Charlie Bubbles.* Purporting to be autobiographical, this study of the perils of success had some remarkable and telling sequences. Finney starred, along with Liza Minnelli. Another first feature film, Don Levy's *Herostratus,* produced independently on a small budget, displayed its director's remarkable visual talent, though many felt the scenario overblown.

Western Europe. *France.* Though the so-called "new wave" in France was ten years old, French cinema continued to be dominated by directors who sprang up at the end of the 1950s: Alain Resnais, Jean-Luc Godard, François Truffaut, and Claude Chabrol. The year's most successful film was Godard's *Weekend,* a tough, hard-hitting denunciation of contemporary French society. Using that idol of French sex films, Mireille Darc, as a typically depraved young bourgeoise, Godard mixed documentary, fiction, and fantasy to present an apocalyptic picture of the present and near future.

Resnais' *Je t'aime, je t'aime* was in some respects disappointing. Based on a script by Jacques Sternberg, the film concerned a scientific experiment to enable a man to relive a moment of his life. The greater part of the film consisted, therefore, of an unchronological montage of its hero's life, and in this Resnais succeeded brilliantly. Reservations focused on the acting and on the script.

Chabrol's *Les Biches* was generally regarded as his best film in some years. A sensual triangle story, it involved a Lesbian photographer, an undecided young Bohemian waif, and a seductive young architect. Mixing humour with tragedy, it was beautifully acted by Stéphane Audran, Jacqueline Sassard, and Jean-Louis Trintignant and was a gripping dramatic experience.

Truffaut made two films, *La Mariée était en noir* (*The Bride Wore Black*) and *Baisers volés.* The first, starring Jeanne Moreau in an adaptation of a U.S. thriller, failed to carry conviction despite its ingenious plot. *Baisers volés* was much more successful. A continuation of Truffaut's first film, *Les Quatre Cents Coups,* it carried on Antoine Doisnel's life story, with Antoine again played by Jean-Pierre Léaud.

With "new wave" films should be included *Loin du Vietnam:* a collectively directed film made as a protest against the war in Vietnam. With Chris Marker as organizer and editor, it included sections by Godard, Resnais, and William Klein. Making no claim to objectivity, it was marked by considerable passion.

Estelle Parsons
and Joanne Woodward
(right) as schoolteachers
in "Rachel, Rachel,"
which was directed
by Paul Newman.

There were three interesting debuts in France: by Maurice Pialat, with *L'Enfance nue* (*Naked Childhood*); Dominique Delouche, with *24 Heures de la vie d'une femme;* and Jean-Daniel Simon, with *Adélaïde,* his second film but the first to attract critical attention. Pialat, known for short films, attracted attention at the Venice Festival with *L'Enfance nue,* about a boy who is deserted by his mother and farmed out to prospective adoptive families. This potentially sentimental plot was treated with warm austerity and succeeded in being moving without becoming mawkish.

Delouche was also known for "shorts." His first long film, based on a novella by Stefan Zweig, was about a woman who suddenly discovers the reality of physical passion. Danielle Darrieux gave perhaps one of her best performances as the widow who finds her life's real meaning in a Swiss casino, only to learn that for her it is too late.

In *Adélaïde,* Simon transposed a 19th-century story by Pierre Gobineau about a mother and daughter in love with the same man to modern times, and gave it a solid provincial French setting. In the principal roles Ingrid Thulin and Jean Sorel were excellent, as was Sylvia Fennec, a newcomer.

Another outstanding film was Orson Welles's *L'Histoire immortelle* (*The Immortal Story*). Welles played the principal role, opposite Jeanne Moreau, in an adaptation of an Isak Dinesen story about a merchant in 19th-century Macao who presumes to play God, with predictably fatal results.

No survey of the French cinema in 1968 can overlook the extraordinary series of events that began at the film festival at Cannes in May, at the same time as the general wave of industrial and political troubles. To cut a long and complex story short, young directors made a bid for freedom from the governmental apparatus of license and censorship surrounding the film industry in France. In a sense the French cinema suffered a crisis of "politicalization"; it was still too soon late in 1968 to say what results this might produce. In some cases it could affect methods of financing, production, and distribution; in others— as with Godard, all of whose films after May were almost entirely political—the change could be more profound and far-reaching.

Italy. The Italian cinema continued to produce a profitable, and increasingly violent, series of so-called "spaghetti Westerns"; but there were no new films from such major directors as Luigi Visconti, Michelangelo Antonioni, Federico Fellini, or Roberto Rossellini. The year was dominated by three directors: Bernardo Bertolucci, Pier Paolo Pasolini, and a newcomer, Gianni Amico.

Bertolucci's *Partner* was the long-awaited successor to *Before the Revolution.* In it the audience was bombarded for nearly two hours with some of the most exciting imagery ever seen. Freely inspired by Dostoevski's *The Double,* the plot concerned a young drama teacher—quiet, unassuming—who suddenly discovers the existence of an alter ego, a wild revolutionary. Both parts were played by the Frenchman Pierre Clementi, and in a cameo role Stefania Sandrelli was excellent. With this film Bertolucci became, perhaps, the most important young director of the post-Godard generation.

Pasolini's *Teorema* created scandal, first, because its director sent it to Venice, then withdrew, and finally reinstated it. Second, its subject caused offense. A Christian allegory, it concerned a young man who

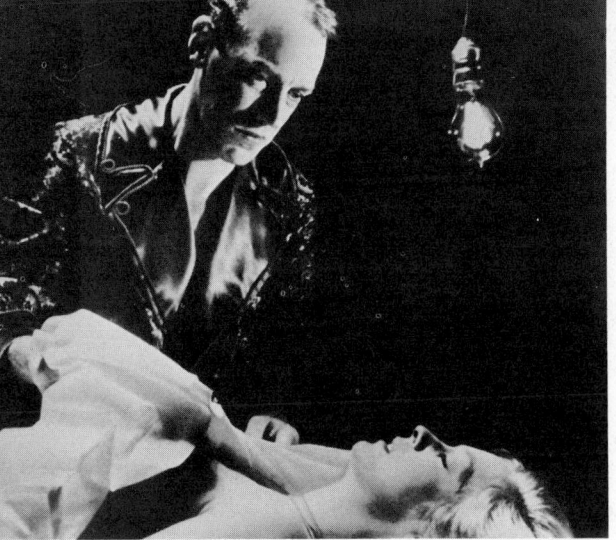
COURTESY, UNITED ARTISTS

Max von Sydow in a scene from "Hour of the Wolf," a chilling fantasy written and directed by Ingmar Bergman.

seduces all the members of a household in which he is a visitor—husband, wife, sister, brother. Though receiving the prize of the Catholic Office of Cinema, it was subsequently banned for a time throughout Italy. It was, however, an extremely powerful work.

Amico, who had made several short films, in *Tropici* presented a fictional documentary about Brazil. His masters were Rossellini and Godard, and with this, his first feature film, he scored a small triumph. Its basic plot, following a family on the road from the dust bowl of Brazil to São Paulo, was opened up by inserts that lifted it onto another level, both higher and more conventionally entertaining.

West Germany. The long-awaited renaissance of the German cinema seemed to have arrived in 1968. The Berlin Festival saw the debut of Werner Herzog, whose *Lebenszeichen* (*Signs of Life*) won the Silver Bear prize for best first film. Set on a Greek island during the German occupation, it was about three convalescent soldiers detailed to guard a munitions depot. The hero, a rebel who puts up a hopeless fight against the universe, suddenly threatens to blow up the town. The style of this allegory was simple, realistic, pure; and the bright Mediterranean sunshine emphasized the work's demonic intensity.

Another outstanding film shown at Berlin was French refugee Jean-Marie Straub's *Chronik der Anna-Magdalena Bach.* A film about Bach as seen by his second wife, it could be more precisely described as a film that *is* music, not as one *about* music. It consists mainly of performances of sections of Bach cantatas, suites, preludes, etc.; the "plot" is limited to a kind of liturgical reading of the basic facts of Bach's life. At first sight visual elements seem unimportant, but a closer second look shows that, after all, visuals play an important part. The camera did not move often, but when it did, it moved with tremendous effect.

The third German "renaissance" film was Alexander Kluge's *Die Artisten in der Zirkuskuppel: Ratlos* (*Artistes at the Top of the Big Top: Disorientated*), which won the Venice Festival's Golden Lion *grand prix.* An allegory, it described the efforts of a young woman who has inherited her father's bankrupt circus not only to bring it back to life but to give it new meaning. Ultimately she fails because, as the narrator tells us, she loves the circus too much, and that which we greatly love we can seldom change.

Scandinavia. Four Scandinavian films deserve mention: Ingmar Bergman's *Hour of the Wolf,* Kjell Grede's *Hugo and Josefin,* Jan Troell's *Ole Dole Doff,* and Vilgot Sjöman's *I Am Curious—Yellow* and *I Am Curious—Blue.* Some thought the Bergman film a brilliant Gothic fantasy and saw in it strong affinities with *Sawdust and Tinsel* and *The Face.* A strange relationship with Bergman's recent *Persona* was also noticed; *Hour of the Wolf* could be interpreted as an attempt to portray the state of mind that made *Persona*'s heroine retreat into despairing silence. It starred Max von Sydow, Liv Ullmann, and Gertrud Fridh.

Hugo and Josefin, marking Kjell Grede's debut as director, nominally a children's film, was actually more like a kind of prepubescent *Elvira Madigan.* The main characters were two lonely children, but the real stars were the luscious Swedish summer and the magnificent colour photography. The treatment of the characters was psychologically subtle and spiritually liberating, but the film depended on a charm as difficult to describe as it was impossible to resist.

Ole Dole Doff won the Berlin Festival's Golden Bear *grand prix.* Jan Troell's second film, it starred Per Oscarsson. Shot in a grammar school in Malmö, it purported to study the problem of authority in a democracy, as exemplified in the "new approach" to education. The interest lay mainly in Oscarsson's performance as that most fatally unsuccessful kind of teacher—the one who doesn't really like children and for that very reason has too idealistic a view of them.

Vilgot Sjöman's *I Am Curious—Yellow* and *I Am Curious—Blue* was a mixture of *cinema verité* and Pirandello that caused censorship scandals all over the world. It seemed to many, however, nothing more than a boring curiosity unsuccessfully mixing social comment and semipornography.

Eastern Europe. Czechoslovakia continued to dominate Eastern European cinema. Before August and the Soviet invasion, it seemed indeed that the Czechoslovak cinema was moving toward a new freedom. After August, with some film makers having left Prague, the future was uncertain. Earlier in the year three important Czechoslovak films were released. Milos Forman's (*see* BIOGRAPHY) *The Firemen's Ball,* shown at Cannes, might well have won the *grand prix* had the festival not been interrupted. In one sense an allegory of the Czechoslovak situation, it could be enjoyed equally well simply as a story. The setting was a small town where the firemen were giving a ball for a retired colleague. The Flaubertian nastiness of Forman's observation of small-town life was countered by a kind of affection; and as a result, in spite of the film's biting humour, the final effect was of a heartwarming sadness.

Also shown at Cannes was the long-awaited *Report on the Party and the Guests,* made by Jan Nemec in 1965 but banned for export. This Czechoslovakian movie existed only on an allegorical level, and some found it unsatisfactory. It could be praised for its courage, but a lack of cinematic vitality tended to nullify even that quality. Many, however, found it both moving and meaningful.

At the Karlovy Vary (Czech.) Festival the *grand prix* went to Jiri Menzel's *Capricious Summer.* Less obviously attractive than the Czechoslovak director's *Closely Watched Trains,* it seemed to some even better. About three men whose lives were disturbed by the arrival in their tiny town of a tightrope walker (played with wry humour by Menzel) and his beautiful assistant, its end-of-summer mood was painfully

Annual Cinema Attendance

Country	Total in 000	Per capita
Albania	7,800	4
Algeria	26,900	2.4
Andorra	200	18
Argentina	145,000	7
Australia	210,000	21
Austria	72,100	10
Bahrain	1,300	7
Barbados	1,600	7
Belgium	46,900	6
Bolivia	3,200	0.9
Brazil	314,500	4
Brunei	2,200	22
Bulgaria	126,400	15
Burma	218,000	9
Cambodia	10,000	2
Canada	101,700	5
Ceylon	35,000	3
Chile	55,800	7
China, Communist	4,000,000	6
Colombia	78,500	5
Congo (Brazzaville)	1,700	2
Cuba	49,900	7
Cyprus	8,600	15
Czechoslovakia	128,400	9
Denmark	33,600	7
Dominican Republic	5,300	2
Ecuador	15,100	3
El Salvador	15,100	6
Finland	28,000	6
France	257,800	5
Germany, East	119,000	7
Germany, West	320,000	5
Ghana	15,900	2
Greece	61,200	7
Guatemala	9,700	2
Guyana	4,400	7
Hong Kong	93,700	25
Hungary	106,000	10
India	1,825,000	4
Indonesia	259,600	3
Iran	52,000	3
Iraq	8,300	1
Ireland	38,000	13
Israel	50,300	2
Italy	697,500	14
Japan	372,700	4
Jordan	6,100	3
Kenya	7,300	0.8
Korea, South	127,700	5
Kuwait	200	0.9
Lebanon	32,100	14
Liberia	1,400	1.4
Libya	3,400	3
Liechtenstein	70	4
Luxembourg	3,000	9
Macao	4,600	26
Mali	3,700	0.8
Malta	3,300	10
Mauritius	8,500	11
Mexico	346,500	9
Monaco	200	9
Mongolia	1,500	1.5
Morocco	19,400	1.5
Netherlands	36,400	3
New Zealand	26,000	10
Nicaragua	7,500	5
Norway	35,200	10
Peru	67,000	7
Poland	173,100	6
Portugal	27,900	3
Romania	193,100	10
San Marino	220	13
Senegal	5,200	1.5
Singapore	25,100	14
Somali Republic	3,200	1
Spain	435,200	14
Sudan	10,100	0.8
Sweden	52,000	7
Switzerland	48,000	8
Syria	9,000	2
Taiwan	67,000	7
Trinidad and Tobago	6,700	8
Turkey	30,000	1
U.S.S.R.	4,300,000	19
U.A.R.	63,300	2
United Kingdom	327,000	6
United States	2,288,000	12
Uruguay	16,500	6
Venezuela	60,000	8
Vietnam, South	14,500	0.9
Western Samoa	300	2
Yugoslavia	121,200	6

Note: Figures given are most recent available.
Source: *UNESCO Statistical Yearbook* (1966).

Battle scene from
Tony Richardson's
"The Charge of the Light
Brigade," a controversial
treatment of the famous
Crimean War episode.

COURTESY, UNITED ARTISTS

nostalgic. The colour photography was rich, and Menzel seemed to have a genius for acquiring evocative musical scores.

From Yugoslavia came an extraordinary film by Vatroslav Mimica, known previously for animated cartoons. *Kaya, I'll Kill You* was an unusually beautiful colour film. The action takes place in an ancient, quiet Dalmatian seaside town to which war comes overnight. Though set during the Italian World War II occupation, the theme—that Fascism symbolizes the destructive impulses in man—is universal. Mimica brought to a live-action film the invention, brilliance, and freedom of his work in animation.

Also shown at Cannes before the festival closed was Miklos Jancso's *The Red and the White*. Some found this adaptation of Isaac Babel's stories about foreign troops in the Soviet Union immediately after the Bolshevik Revolution disappointing; others acclaimed its austerity and portrayal of the chaos of civil war.

Cuba. *Memories of Underdevelopment*, directed by Tomás Gutiérrez Alea and shown at Karlovy Vary, where it shared second prize, was the best Cuban film seen in Europe. The protagonist was a landowner in his 30s, cultured and europeanized, whose property has been nationalized, and whose wife has run off to Miami. He has decided to stay on in Havana and is not without sympathy for Castro's Cuba. Throughout the film, fragments from his past—the nation's pre-Castro past—well up, filling out the picture of Cuba and of the man himself. The title is deliberately ambiguous: is it Cuba that is "underdeveloped" or the "hero"? (RD. R.)

Nontheatrical. Among outstanding international events in nontheatrical motion pictures was the European-organized International Film Festival held in Vienna from September 23 to 28. In this competition approximately 400 industrialists and film makers from 14 countries of Western Europe, plus the United States and Japan, participated in the showing of 135 motion pictures. Though most of these productions were by and for private industry, films were also shown by two international agencies, the Organization for Economic Cooperation and Development and the European Launcher Development Organization. Most of the entries were top prizewinners from industrial film competitions in the participating countries.

The showings were distinguished for the wide use of the new techniques of the film maker's art as applied to the industrial field. The range of styles was perhaps most clearly revealed in the two grand prize-winners of the show. These were the Italian film *Itinerario Industriale*, sponsored and produced by the Society Montecatini Edison of Milan, and the U.S. film *Memento*, sponsored by American Telephone and Telegraph Co. and produced by the Center for Mass Communication, Columbia University Press, New York. The Italian film was a superbly done, but typically industrial, survey of the work of a large chemical firm. The AT & T entry made a strong emotional impact with its imaginative handling of the subject of automobile safety. Though it won only third prize in its class, one of the most notable films shown was that entered by the International Organization for Economic Development. Titled *Pas Assez*, this film provided a dramatic review of the vital tasks and problems of less developed countries. In the competition, films from West Germany won the most prizes, followed by those from the U.S. and Italy.

Trends in U.S. nontheatrical films indicated that this field had become firmly established as a billion-dollar industry, despite a slump in the educational film and audiovisual materials market. Having reached the billion-dollar mark in 1966, the industry in 1967 enjoyed total expenditures by customers of an estimated $1,107,000,000, an increase of $27 million.

Though many new producers had entered the field in recent years, this was not reflected in 1968 in any increase in the number of nontheatrical film productions. The number of films released was only 4% higher than the previous year, with an estimated 12,-570 titles. However, the number of productions for classroom and educational use rose 13% to an estimated 1,700. Significantly, about 40% of these were released by colleges, universities, and school systems, disclosing an important new movement of such institutions toward the production of educational materials.

Probably one of the fastest-growing areas of new film production was in the field of the independent, avant-garde, or underground film, which, according to available figures, increased from an estimated 250 titles in 1966 to a probable 300 or more in 1967. Though no firm statistics were possible for this type of film, it was estimated that if all underground films were reported, the number of releases would be considerably higher. A related area, for which data was likewise not available, was that of films produced by youth groups and students, which was growing rapidly.

The increasing interest among youth and students in film study and film production was indicated by a *New York Times* report in April that 60,000 graduate and undergraduate students were enrolled in 1,500 film courses at 120 colleges and universities.

The newest technological area of film production, the 8-mm. loop, or short film, continued to show the greatest promise for innovative use in education and industrial training. The striking expansion in this field, begun in 1966, continued in 1967 with the number of films produced reaching an estimated 1,600 titles, double the output of the previous year. (J. T. B.)

See also Photography; Television and Radio.

ENCYCLOPÆDIA BRITANNICA FILMS. *New Tools for Learning* (1952); *The Unique Contribution* (1959); *Project Discovery: A Demonstration in Education* (1965); *Let Them Learn* (1967).

Cities and Urban Affairs

In 1968 political instability and disorders in many countries led to financial crises, cuts in government spending, and riots in the cities. Many planners continued to concentrate on quantification and the collection of data, techniques of management and organization, and critical path analysis and comparative costing. Some, however—stimulated perhaps by a massive revolt against monolithic public authorities that take little account of what individual people think or want—showed an interest in the sociological aspects and the attitudes of those planned for. With strikes and student riots in France, the "routine" riots in U.S. cities, and the defeat in Britain of the government's proposals for a third London airport at Stansted, the people seemed to have begun to take a hand in their own affairs. If "public participation in planning" had become the official catchphrase, it was simply an attempt to channel this massive concerted public anger into less destructive directions.

Trends in Urban Planning. As was emphasized at a world conference on "People and Cities" at Coventry, Eng., in June 1968, the basic problems of cities, at least in the more developed countries, were the same the world over. The plight of the suburban housewife was much the same in Tokyo or Buenos Aires, Arg., as in Paris or New York, and the citizens in all these cities were just as alienated from the forces that controlled them. The problems of cities were also seen to be much more complex than had been assumed, and some important new trends in planning began to emerge.

"Twilight Areas" and Ghettos. In the past renewal had been largely concerned with the physical decay of buildings rather than with underlying social and economic issues. It was increasingly realized, however, that nothing would be gained if the middle classes moved into the new buildings and the poor, unable to pay the new rents, moved off to "blight" another area. A total attack was needed at all levels of the problem, including, if necessary, such programs as rent subsidies, increased job opportunities, national assistance, and government mortgage facilities.

Rehabilitation. The indiscriminate tearing down of complete areas often destroyed an essential network of social relationships that had rarely been appreciated by planners and city councillors, who themselves tended to live in white-collar suburbia. Often the only tangible result of vast public expenditure had been isolation of the residents and the doubling of the crime

rate. The British study of the Deeplish "twilight area" of Rochdale, Lancashire, found that 60% of those questioned were basically satisfied with their environment. In an increasingly mobile society with its attendant psychological problems, there would be no point in tearing people unnecessarily from their "roots," and a policy of rehabilitating and converting old houses, as outlined in the 1968 British White Paper *Old Houses into New Homes,* was thought preferable to the comprehensive redevelopment of large areas. It was also believed that a central area should have a variety of activities, and that this would be possible only if it contained buildings of varied ages and, therefore, varied rents. The substitution of a new bank for the "little shop next door that stays open late" was to be regretted.

Flexibility in Planning. With technology and society changing rapidly, it was likely that many predictions would be inaccurate. Therefore, much greater flexibility—particularly in decision procedures and land-use planning—was needed. Thus many of the city plans in the late 1960s were "open-ended," a prime example being the *Comprehensive Plan of Chicago* published in December 1966, which did not recommend one course of action so much as it presented a set of possible alternatives.

Environmental Planning and Conservation. The new awareness of environmental factors noted in 1967 continued, with an increased interest in such topics as air pollution, noise, traffic, and the conservation of historic and attractive houses and streets. Many city plans included proposals for complete pedestrian and vehicular separation and—in some cases—preservation of the complete central historic core as a pedestrian area.

Traffic and Transportation. It was generally agreed that adequate roads for unrestricted use of the automobile could not be provided without destroying many of the most worthwhile features of a city centre. The emphasis, therefore, shifted to traffic management and imposing curbs on central traffic, the construction of new expressways on the city's fringes, and the development and improvement of urban rapid transit systems.

Regional Planning. Since the problems of the city could not be isolated from those of the surrounding areas, planners were increasingly thinking in terms of "city regions" and were trying to set up the necessary administrative machinery. There was considerable disagreement, however, over whether regional planning should be primarily a study of how best to use the resources of a region, as in most of the U.S., or whether it should be a mechanism for subsidizing the poorer regions at the expense of the richer ones, as had been attempted somewhat unsuccessfully in Britain.

The old distinctions between town and country no longer held. The U.S. president's National Advisory Commission on Rural Poverty asserted in a report in December 1967 that "a high proportion of the people crowded into city slums come there from rural slums" and that "the only solution is a coordinated attack on both urban and rural poverty." For the first time in Britain, the Countryside Act, 1968, gave legal recognition to the fact that the countryside had a role to play in providing leisure and recreation to the townspeople.

The countries with the most advanced regional planning were France and the Netherlands, and their regional plans (to judge at least from the spectacular Languedoc coastal development) seemed to be progressing well. (L. C. Br.)

Left, garbage piled up on New York City sidewalks at the rate of 10,000 tons a day as sanitation workers struck for higher wages. Right, quays along the Seine in Paris were used as garbage dumps during a massive general strike directed against the de Gaulle government. Below, Vancouver couple cope with a civic employees' strike by hauling their own rubbish.

United States. Urban and especially metropolitan America continued to reveal both acute and chronic problems, as it was likely to do for many years to come. Overshadowing the other manifestations of confusion and disorder was the black rebellion—the overt display by Afro-Americans of disillusionment, frustration, alienation, and hostility in forms ranging from picketing, boycotts, and demonstrations to riots and guerrilla warfare. Urban disorder was by no means restricted to the blacks, however. It was evident in the increasing "white backlash," revealing ugly ethnic and racial bigotries; the rising rate of delinquency and crime; the revolt of youth, including the "hippies," the "Yippies," and the "New Left" containing hard-core revolutionaries, anarchists, and nihilists; the mounting disaffection and strikes of public employees including teachers, policemen, firemen, and sanitation workers; the increasing indications of municipal financial strain and inadequate or deteriorating public services; and the flourishing of organized crime, which continued to provide the consuming public with such illegal services as gambling, vice, and loans at exorbitant interest.

The increasing chaos characterizing metropolitanism as a way of life in the U.S. was the product of the convergence of four developments that were reaching climactic proportions in the last third of the 20th century: (1) the population explosion; (2) the population implosion; (3) population diversification; and (4) the accelerating tempo of technological and social change. These developments were apparent in many countries, but the U.S. was the world's most dramatic example.

The population explosion refers to the remarkably rapid growth of the nation, from a population of fewer than four million in 1790 to more than 200 million in 1968 and probably to more than 300 million by the century's end. The population implosion refers to the increasing concentration of people in urban and metropolitan areas. In 1790, 95% of the American people lived in rural places—on farms or in centres of fewer than 2,500 persons. By 1960, 70% of the population

was urban and 63% was metropolitan, and the trend toward increased concentration continued. Population diversification refers to the diversity of peoples that were coming to share not only the same geographic area but also the same life space—social, economic, and political activities. To the "melting pot" of diverse ethnic groups in American urban and metropolitan centres, Afro-Americans flooded in great numbers during and after World War II. The population explosion fed the population implosion; both fed population diversification; and the accelerated tempo of technological and social change was both antecedent to and consequent of the other developments.

The net product of these developments was an urban America characterized by 20th-century population agglomerations together with an admixture of 19th- and 20th-century physical urban plant, residential and nonresidential; an admixture of 19th- and 20th-century attitudes, values, institutions, and ideologies; and a system of 18th- and 19th-century local government. The U.S. did not become an urban nation until 1920, when for the first time a majority (51%) lived in cities, and it would be 1970 before it completed its first half century as an urban nation. It was little wonder, therefore, that metropolitan America was characterized by tension and conflict on many fronts.

Within the framework of the developments outlined above, a combination of physical, demographic, social, and political forces was converting metropolitan areas into black central cities and white suburbias. Central cities continued to lose white population as the black population increased, and, although some recent census evidence suggested that this trend might have slackened or even reversed, it was still too tenuous a finding to be accepted as indicative of fundamental change. Should the trend continue, it was possible that by 1985, 75% of all blacks would live in the central cities and 70% of all whites in the suburbs. Thus, the formation of an "apartheid society" was likely to continue, with important implications for the future.

U.S. Justice Department statistics indicated that there were fewer "disturbances" for the three-month period June–August 1968 (120) than during the corresponding period in 1967 (138). "Major" disturbances (*e.g.*, Detroit) diminished to 7 in 1968 from 11 in 1967. These data, however, could not be interpreted as indicating that tensions in the "ghettos" were abating. It might well be that riots, which had proved more costly to Negroes than to "the Establishment," would be displaced by other forms of violence, such as guerrilla warfare on the Cleveland pattern—the shooting of policemen. Certainly there was no evidence that the conditions of life in the ghettos—segregation, substandard housing, high unemployment, inadequate education—had improved.

The mass violence of Afro-Americans rebelling against ghetto life had been accompanied by growing mass violence on the part of "backlash" groups, anti-Vietnam war "peacenik" groups, and rebellious students spearheaded by the extremist Students for a Democratic Society. "Backlash" elements, fearing for the integrity of their neighbourhoods and the maintenance of their property values and opposing integrated schooling, increasingly demonstrated against transfer or bussing of Negro children to white schools with sporadic episodes of violence.

"Peace" movements, reflecting emotional objection to the U.S. involvement in Vietnam, led to violent incidents as well as to peaceful demonstrations and tried the patience of many police and security forces. The demonstrations for peace peaked in the disorders in Chicago during the Democratic national convention, when television showed excesses by both demonstrators and police that shocked the nation.

Overt physical violence disrupted college and university campuses throughout the land, as well as abroad, with the most violent domestic examples being Columbia University and the University of California at Berkeley. The hard-core New Left students openly espoused "revolution" and "disruption" as means of undermining "the Establishment." College and university administrations were groping for ways to deal with increasing student unrest—trying to separate and meet legitimate requests while resisting extreme and impossible "demands."

Police departments had been sorely tried by mass demonstrations and disruptions from these several directions, and were increasingly accused of "police brutality" by the dissident and demonstrating groups. The growing climate of disruption and violence would require greater public attention to the problems of adequate policing and safety. It raised questions about the adequacy of resources allocated for police and security functions, including specific questions about salary rates, recruiting, training, and methods of "mob control."

Cities were faced with many other problems, as well. The rising tide of teacher strikes shut down schools in many areas, including New York City. The strikes, although aimed primarily at improving teachers' salaries and other emoluments, symbolized the inadequacy of resources allocated for education. Primary and secondary school education in the U.S., and especially in inner-city black ghetto areas, fell far short of providing children with the basic skills, the salable skills, and the citizenship skills that would enable them to assume the obligations and responsibilities as well as the rights of American citizenship. Thus the conditions of the slums and ghettos of America were being recycled into the next and possibly succeeding generations.

Other public employees, including police, firemen, and sanitation workers, also used the strike as a threat or as a weapon to win their objectives.

Finally, it could be observed that the cities, as creatures of the state legislatures, continued to be afflicted with inadequate sources of revenue and inadequate authority to deal with their problems, even as their problems were exacerbated. Thus the trend toward increased federal-municipal relationships continued and could be expected to grow further as cities turned to the federal government for resolution of their problems.   (P. M. Ha.)

The administration could not be accused of inaction. In his "Crisis of the Cities" message in February 1968, Pres. Lyndon Johnson announced total current financial commitments of $22 billion and a national goal of 26 million new housing units over a ten-year period. In April he announced the setting up of an Urban Institute, on the same day that a Riot Control Center was formed at the Pentagon, and after the assassination of Sen. Robert Kennedy in June the president appointed a Commission on Violence. New legislation in 1968 included the Air Quality Act, which provided a three-year, $429 million program to combat air pollution; the Civil Rights Act, providing a three-stage reduction of racial barriers for 53 million housing units; the Anti-Crime Act, which restricted the sale of handguns, though not rifles, shotguns, or ammunition (to be followed by restrictions on the purchase of rifles by mail order later in the year); and the Housing and Urban Development Act of 1968, which contained new programs to reduce mortgage interest for low-income families, established a special high risk insurance fund within the Federal Housing Authority, raised the maximum rehabilitation grant from $1,500 to $3,000, and required that a majority of the housing in urban renewal schemes should be for low- and moderate-income families. Most of the necessary legislation had already passed in the mid-1960s, however, and the administration's chief difficulty was in obtaining adequate funding. Almost all congressional appropriations for the cities were much less than requested.

Great Britain. In Britain the only legislation in the planning field in 1968 was the Countryside Act, though with the Transport and Planning Bills going through

World's 25 Most Populous Cities

Rank	City and country	City proper Most recent census	City proper Estimate	City proper Year	Metropolitan estimate	Metropolitan Year
1	Tokyo, Japan	8,893,094*	8,998,000	1968	...	...
2	New York, U.S.	7,781,984	8,125,000	1968	11,679,858	1968
3	London, U.K.†	7,671,220§	7,880,760	1967	—	—
4	Shanghai, China (Communist)	6,204,417‡	6,977,000	1958	9,600,000	1958
5	Moscow, U.S.S.R.	5,049,905	6,507,000	1967	8,500,000	1966
6	São Paulo, Brazil	3,164,804	5,000,000	1966	5,685,000	1968
7	Cairo, U.A.R.	4,219,853§	4,585,000	1968	4,904,000	1966
8	Peking, China (Communist)	2,768,149‡	4,148,000	1958	6,800,000	1962
9	Leningrad, U.S.S.R.	2,899,955	3,706,000	1967	4,050,000	1965
10	Rio de Janeiro, Brazil	3,223,408	...	...	4,207,000	1968
11	Chicago, U.S.	3,550,404	3,500,000	1968	6,810,000	1968
12	Seoul, Korea	3,805,261§	...	...	...	...
13	Mexico City, Mexico	2,832,133	3,418,471	1968	6,815,000	1967
14	Buenos Aires, Argentina	2,966,634	3,350,000	1967	7,866,000	1967
15	Tientsin, China (Communist)	2,693,831‡	3,278,000	1958	3,800,000	1958
16	Osaka, Japan	3,156,222*	3,091,000	1968	...	...
17	Bombay, India	2,771,933	3,077,000	1967	5,368,000	1968
18	Jakarta, Indonesia	2,973,053			4,349,950	1967
19	Calcutta, India	2,927,289	3,044,000	1967	3,109,000	1968
20	Los Angeles, U.S.	2,481,595	2,935,000	1968	7,120,000	1968
21	Teheran, Iran	2,719,730§	2,840,494	1967	3,114,950	1965
22	Delhi-New Delhi, India	2,359,408	2,760,000	1966	3,470,000	1968
23	Madrid, Spain	2,259,931	2,680,769	1967	2,926,374	1965
24	Rome, Italy	2,188,160	2,630,535	1968	3,150,900	1966
25	Paris, France	2,790,091‖	2,581,794	1968	8,182,241	1968

*1965. †Greater London. ‡1953. §1966. ‖1962.
Rankings based on latest estimates of city proper population. Most recent census refers to 1959, 1960, or 1961, except as footnoted. Berlin, both sectors combined 1968 population 3,231,697, is excluded due to the political as well as physical division of the city. Cities of China reflect urban area populations as city proper.

Parliament and with publication of the Fulton and Maud committee reports, much more was to be expected in 1969. In April the government published a White Paper, *Old Houses into New Homes,* which contained proposals for the improvement of older neighbourhoods on a scale never before attempted. To deal with an estimated 1.8 million unfit homes in England and Wales, plus a further 4.5 million that needed repairs, increases were proposed in the "discretionary" grants for new bathrooms, etc.; the "standard" grants for new amenities; the improvement grants for converting houses into flats; and the grants to housing societies (and, for the first time, to local authorities) for buying up and converting old property. Also proposed was a new Exchequer grant of 50% for environmental improvements costing up to £100 in "general improvement areas" designated by the local authorities; and, from April, owner occupiers faced with slum clearance and compulsory purchase orders would be given the market value of their houses through supplementary payments.

Stansted. In February, after a concentrated campaign backed by remarkably unanimous public opinion, the government abandoned its £55 million proposal to build London's third airport at Stansted, Essex, and promised a new inquiry with far wider terms of reference. The main points of the opposition were that the locating of a third London airport involved broad regional decisions that had not been considered; that the cost estimates were slanted so as to avoid a dispute with the Ministry of Defence over the artillery range at Shoeburyness, Essex; and that, just as historic towns were being destroyed to accommodate traffic, so large areas of valuable agricultural land and attractive countryside were being sacrificed to air traffic. It was possible, of course, that Stansted would again be chosen, but noise and safety arguments favoured an estuary airport. The favourite proposed site was Foulness—north of Southend-on-Sea, Essex, and by the sea—where the draining of the Mappin sands and the reclamation of new land was envisaged, combined with new port facilities. The site was 15 mi. farther from central London than Stansted, but new transport links would have to be developed in any case and a company had been formed to raise between £50 million and £70 million for the project.

Historic Towns. In April a historic towns conference was held at York, primarily for local authorities. The discussion naturally centred on the cost of conservation and the need to combine the designation of conservation areas with schemes to reduce central area traffic. In contrast to the local authorities and their request to "give us the tools and we will do the job," there was a strong dissident element from the civic societies which emphasized the destructive capabilities of road "improvement" schemes. The case was cited of Canterbury, Kent, which had elaborate and expensive proposals for the destruction of most of its historic core to further its development as a shopping centre. The planners were also reminded that the current dogmas of zoning and densities were inapplicable to historic towns, whose character depended on their mixed land use and compactness. It was agreed that the sociological aspects had been underrepresented at the conference, and one delegate suggested that historic towns served an important social and psychological function by helping people feel that they mattered and belonged. The conference was concluded by Lord Kennet, joint parliamentary secretary to the Ministry of Housing and Local Government, who announced new

steps to preserve historic buildings and further controls on new buildings in conservation areas.

One of the main problems of historic towns had always been the elimination of vehicular traffic from the streets in the face of opposition from shopkeepers convinced that they would lose money. After the successful transformation of London Street, Norwich, Norfolk, however, three more streets in Norwich were to be made into pedestrian streets and the conversion of a fifth was being discussed. Alfred Wood, the Norwich planning officer, believed that similar closures could be carried out in towns all over Britain without waiting for new roads or rear access ways to be built. "When we closed London Street," he said, "60% of the traffic just vanished, as it did when they closed a street in Copenhagen. It is Parkinson's Law in reverse." Meanwhile, the number of pedestrians using the street trebled.

Vertical Living. The partial collapse, attributed to a gas explosion, of a 23-story block of council flats in London on May 16, 1968, killing five people, triggered a reappraisal not only of the safety of the many similar system-built towers all over the country, but of the whole principle of local authorities building tall blocks at all. Unofficially, the Ministry of Housing had been against high flats for the previous four years, and it was planned that from January 1969 the grant subsidies for high-rise flats would be discontinued. Tall blocks, supposedly vertical accents in the urban landscape, might look attractive in the models presented to town planning committees, but they were expensive and unpopular. The much publicized stay by the architect Erno Goldfinger—scarcely a typical council tenant—at the top of a recently completed one in February emphasized how little professional interest there had been in the feelings of those who live in them. With the development, particularly in Lambeth, of high-density low-rise schemes, even the old argument that towers were needed to prevent urban sprawl was no longer valid.

As an editorial in *The Times* of May 18 pointed out, however, the strongest argument against high blocks was the quality of life they imposed. "Children with nowhere to play unless out of sight and sound of their parents; no private open space, not even the tiny yard that the lately condemned houses provided; public open space sterile and hard-surfaced, often restricted, usually a collection of wind-blown corners where rubbish accumulates, the objections are general and vehement. Moreover the high block cannot offer the sense of community that a street can. The familiar neighbour passing a front door becomes a barely recognized face in the lift. If a community takes shape in such a block it does so against all the constraints of the building and its surroundings."

New Towns. In February 1968, to celebrate the 21st anniversary of the British New Towns, the Town and Country Planning Association published a special booklet, *The New Towns Come of Age,* containing much useful information. By December 1967, the first 21 New Towns had a total population of 800,243, an employment of 355,000, and capital expenditure of £574.3 million, including £374.1 million on housing. By the end of the century, with five others designated, the total population would be more than 2 million. The more recent New Towns included Peterborough, Warrington-Risley, Buckinghamshire, and Ipswich, Suffolk. Other developments were a revision of the Basildon, Essex, target population figure from 106,000 to 140,000; the doubling of the size of Dawley, Shrop-

Londoners walking
on the Mall in front
of Buckingham Palace.
As an experiment the area
was reserved
for pedestrians
on Sundays during
the summer of 1968.

shire, to take 100,000 Midlanders; the decision, following a report by Colin Buchanan and Partners, not to designate Ashford, Kent, as a New Town; and the publication of a second report in April by Robert Matthew, Johnson-Marshall and Partners on the effects of the proposed central Lancashire New Town of 500,-000.

The New Towns booklet contained a heated controversy about densities (the average being about 18 persons per acre, compared with more than 2,100 for Hong Kong's most recent housing scheme). Various contributors criticized the New Towns on the grounds that they had not allowed for high car ownership; that they had inadequate housing either for the rich and successful or for the retired and elderly; that they had been too rigidly planned; that there had not been enough houses to buy; and that architecturally they were rather dull and uniform. All these points were considered in the design of the later New Towns, which tended to be centred on existing towns, to have target populations of the order of 250,000, and to be more open-ended in form.　　　　(L. C. Br.)

Municipal Government. The year 1968 again demonstrated the need for reform in local government. Local authorities in many countries had to assume new tasks and provide more services than ever before, and the conditions under which they were functioning were changing rapidly. The structure of local government in many cases proved inadequate to meet these conditions.

First of all, new tasks were being imposed on municipalities in the field of planning, education, social welfare, and other services. Second, many of the new services, particularly those of a technical nature, could be provided effectively only on a rather large scale, considerably larger than the areas normally covered by local authorities. Third, improved communications enabled many citizens to make use of distant services and to feel at home in more than one community of interest. Finally, and perhaps most important of all, there was a growing awareness that a coherent public policy of social and economic development could only be set up on the basis of some form of medium-term and long-term planning, especially in view of the enormous investments to be made. Such plans and investments had to be made for areas considerably larger than those covered by the usual municipalities, towns, and cities.

It was not surprising, therefore, that in 1968 two large international congresses, organized by the International Institute of Administrative Sciences and the International Union of Local Authorities (IULA), concentrated, respectively, on the adaptation of the administration to changes in society and on the theme of amalgamation of or cooperation among local authorities.

At one time or another, many municipalities had felt the need to undertake some action on a larger scale, and a maze of single and multipurpose authorities, joint boards, *syndicats de communes, Zweckverbände,* and the like covered the territories of many countries. The result was often a complex and fragmented structure of government, which became increasingly difficult to manage and very difficult for the citizen to understand. To cope with this situation, drastic proposals for reform were being worked out in several countries.

In Great Britain a Royal Commission on Local Government was appointed in May 1966, to prepare recommendations for changing the territorial division of

units of local government and reviewing the distribution of functions between local and central government. In the course of 1968, a wealth of evidence was submitted to the commission, provoking a vivid and interesting debate on the future of local government in England and Wales. Generally speaking, two alternatives were proposed. The first suggested the creation of between eight and ten large regions, which would more or less comprise areas previously covered by the regional planning councils and regional economic planning boards. These units of government would be charged with large-scale functions, such as regional economic planning, major highways, land use planning, technical education, water and energy supply, public health, and air pollution. The other tasks of government would be accomplished by a second tier, consisting of units of 300,000 to one million inhabitants. Such a solution was backed by a number of representatives of the academic world and such professional groups as the National Association of Local Government Officers (NALGO) and the Town Planning Institute.

A second solution, supported by the County Councils Association and many government departments, favoured the creation of a first tier of some 35 to 40 city-regions, fairly large areas consisting of central cities with a large hinterland and comprising populations of 300,000 to three million inhabitants. A second tier of government might be created in some areas but would generally have a more representative character. The regional economic planning councils and boards might be maintained as coordinating and advisory bodies.

Much the same problems were under consideration in France, with the difference that separate solutions were envisaged for municipal and regional reform. A draft bill proposed by the French government, which was intended to rationalize the fragmented structure of French local government (some 38,000 communes for a total population of not quite 50 million, of which 8 to 9 million were in Paris alone), drew much criticism from representatives of local government associations.

Obviously, the local government structure was ill-adapted to meet the demands of the modern society, especially in the metropolitan areas. A noteworthy innovation in this respect was the introduction in four French metropolitan areas (Lille, Bordeaux, Lyons, and Strasbourg) of the so-called *communautés urbaines,* a metropolitan-wide level of government with an indirectly elected council and board, which was to assume a large number of functions previously undertaken on a voluntary cooperative basis.

The excessive degree of centralization that characterized the French system of administration led, partly under the impetus of the May "revolution," to the elaboration of proposals for a regional reform. At the congress of the Conseil National des Économies Régionales, held in Lyons, much of the debate centred around the question of whether or not the territories covered by the 21 "regions" could provide an adequate framework for viable units of government with a directly elected assembly, or whether much larger regions were to be preferred.

In Italy a similar development took place, and a law approved by Parliament entrusted the *regioni* with more powers. However, the implementation of this law would depend on the acceptance of a financial reform bill that was still to be introduced.

Some of the smaller European countries were under-

"THE VANCOUVER SUN"
FROM CANADIAN PRESS

Vancouver's town fool Joachim Foikis jumping for joy after being awarded a Canada Council grant of $3,500 to continue in his role. A majority of the council believed the jester made a serious contribution to the self-awareness of the community.

taking far-reaching reforms. Denmark, to a certain extent following the Swedish example, was planning to reduce the number of local authorities from 1,350 to some 700.

In the United States the need for reform was most pressing in the great metropolitan areas. Many of these urban areas witnessed the creation of organizations of local government that were attempting to meet common challenges on an area-wide basis. These organizations, of which there were some 350 by September 1968, included councils of government, regional planning commissions, economic development districts, and transportation study groups. Of these, some 100 councils of government, composed of local government elected officials, offered the most promise. The activities of the National Service to Regional Councils, an organization sponsored by the National Association of Counties and the National League of Cities, were greatly expanded as a result of grants provided by the U.S. Department of Housing and Urban Development (HUD) and the Ford Foundation. The concern of the federal government for the cities was also apparent in the creation of a nonprofit Institute for Urban Development, a "think-tank" designed to provide HUD with research capability in the urban field. President-elect Richard Nixon demonstrated that he would continue this concern by creating a Cabinet-level Council on Urban Affairs and appointing as its head Daniel P. Moynihan, a widely acclaimed sociologist.

Financial Reform. There had long been a demand for a financial reform in West Germany, but it was not until May 1968 that the first reading of a relevant bill took place in the Parliament. The basic problem with respect to municipal finances was the central position of the business tax, which provided almost 80% of total municipal tax revenue. While the main municipal associations were agreed on a partial reduction of the business tax, there was considerable controversy over the way in which the resulting reductions in income should be offset. The federal government proposed to give local authorities a share in income tax, but the municipal associations flatly rejected the possibility of federal or state subsidies. Instead, they favoured the suggestions of a governmental committee of experts, which recommended that local authorities be given the authority to impose, in addition to the income tax, a variable levy of between 80 and 120%. It was clear that the financial power of local authorities would have to be increased—probably through stronger measures than the existing ones, which consisted of raising land taxes and obtaining concessions for municipal road improvements out of gasoline taxes.

Proposals for financial reform were also prepared in France and Italy. In this connection, it was expected that the IULA congress on local government finance, scheduled to convene in Vienna in June 1969, would provide a worldwide forum for a substantial debate on this problem.

Technical Facilities. The new role of municipalities in the modern world was also reflected in the increasing use that local authorities made of modern means of technology and communication. During 1968 an international conference discussed various aspects of cooperation for the use of computers between local authorities. In most cases, computers were used as accounting tools and for record-keeping. In a few countries, such as the U.K. and the U.S., more advanced use of computers was made in the field of planning and the management of housing schemes, public utilities, and

the like. In 1968 there was a great need for cooperation among local authorities in this respect, particularly in those European countries where the municipalities were comparatively small and weak financially.

Participation. The changing role of local government in Western society had an important bearing on the ways and means provided for citizen participation. One such method involved the introduction of local radio stations, which could provide citizens with direct information about the local authority, the community, and available services. In Britain eight experimental stations were set up, under the combined sponsorship of local government and industries. (*See* TELEVISION AND RADIO.)

It seemed likely that 1968 would be recorded as the year in which the idea of popular participation made an important breakthrough. The events in France and the "Czech spring" were the most obvious manifestations of this development, but in fact many countries were experiencing a consistent demand for participation, particularly at the local level. One area in which such participation was immediately applicable was the field of planning. In this respect, the establishment in Britain of the Skeffington Committee on public participation in planning was a hopeful sign of change. The evidence made available to this committee by professional organizations provided some significant examples of the evolution of thinking in this field. While it was agreed that final responsibility for planning proposals rested with the elected representatives, it was also emphasized that citizens should be consulted and involved at all stages of the planning process.

Training for Local Government. A serious effort in the field of public participation would imply additional training in the various sectors of municipal activity, not only of public officials but also of elected representatives. In Scandinavia, existing local government schools in Sweden and Denmark were to be supplemented by a municipal training centre in Norway to be run by the local government associations. An important development in Britain during 1968 was the establishment of a Local Government Training Board.

Training public officials and elected councillors at the local level was probably the foremost problem of local government in less developed countries. In this connection, the publication by the UN Public Administration Division of a handbook entitled *Local Government Training* provided a very useful and solid basis for further action. (EI. K.)

See also Architecture; Crime; Historic Buildings; Housing; Parks; Police; Transportation.

ENCYCLOPÆDIA BRITANNICA FILMS. *The Living City* (1953); *Health in Our Community* (1959); *Megalopolis—Cradle of the Future* (1962); *Chicago—Midland Metropolis* (1963); *Operation Bootstrap* (1968).

Colombia

A republic in northwestern South America, Colombia is bordered by Panama, Venezuela, Brazil, Peru, and Ecuador and has coasts on both the Caribbean Sea and the Pacific Ocean. Area: 439,734 sq.mi.

(1,138,914 sq.km.). Pop. (1968 est.): 19,829,185. Cap.: Bogotá (pop., 1968, 1,984,599). Language: Spanish. State religion: Roman Catholic (90%). President in 1968, Carlos Lleras Restrepo.

Pope Paul VI (right) greeting crowds in Bogotá where he attended the 39th International Eucharistic Congress (above) in August 1968.

The government coalition (National Transformation Front) won a clear victory in the midterm congressional elections held on March 17. The coalition, consisting of "Ospinista" Conservatives (followers of former Pres. Mariano Ospina Pérez) and the unified Liberal Party, obtained more than two-thirds of the seats (141 out of 204) in the Chamber of Representatives and registered similar successes in the municipal elections held at the same time. The government success was to some extent due to the reunification of the Liberal Party in August 1967 when the left-wing Movimiento Revolucionario Liberal agreed to rejoin the National Front Liberal Party. The principal opposition came from the Alianza Nacional Popular (supporters of Gustavo Rojas Pinilla, who was deposed as president in 1957) and the Conservatives following former Pres. Laureano Gómez, who won 38 seats and 23 seats, respectively.

In June President Lleras triumphantly survived a serious constitutional crisis. He had threatened to resign (June 7) because the Senate defeated reform proposals already passed by the Chamber of Representatives and the appropriate Senate committee. The reforms sought to give the government increased powers to regulate the economy and to ensure a smooth transition to more representative democracy when the existing National Front arrangement would expire, in 1974. The president was widely supported, and several labour unions appealed to him not to resign. Popular demonstrations were organized, and the armed forces assured the president of their total support. When, nevertheless, the president did submit his resignation (June 11), it was overwhelmingly rejected and subsequently withdrawn; the Senate later passed most of

the requested reforms. On December 16, as Congress recessed for three months, President Lleras ended the state of siege that had been imposed on May 21, 1965, by his predecessor.

The Colombian economy continued to improve. With a national accounts surplus of 1,464,000,000 pesos on June 30, it seemed likely that in 1968 the government would achieve its third successive fiscal surplus. Severe credit restrictions and other monetary restraints helped restrict the rise in the cost of living to 7% in 1967 (in contrast to 13% in 1966) and to 4% in the first six months of 1968. In the 18 months ended June 1968 the gross gold and foreign exchange reserves of the Banco de la República increased from $144 million to $163 million, and the bank's net reserves improved from a negative balance of $94 million to one of $10 million.

Attempts to attract foreign loans met with considerable success. In January a Colombian finance mission negotiated credits of $33.5 million and $73 million from the International Monetary Fund and the Agency for International Development, and several important loans were secured from the International Bank for Reconstruction and Development (World Bank).

The Credit Consulting Group for Colombia, headed by the World Bank, was scheduled late to consider loan requests for projects costing $500 million. In view of the improved exchange position and the early prospect of substantial foreign loans, the Foreign

COLOMBIA

Education. (1965) Primary, pupils 2,274,014, teachers 63,250; secondary, pupils 266,140, teachers 19,527; vocational, pupils 110,875, teachers 8,626; teacher training, students 43,729, teachers 4,467; higher (at 287 institutions, including 34 universities), students 43,254, teaching staff 6,844.

Finance. Monetary unit: peso, with a free rate (end August 1968) of 16.30 pesos to U.S. $1 (39.12 pesos = £1 sterling). Gold and foreign exchange, central bank: (June 1968) U.S. $117 million; (June 1967) U.S. $73 million. Budget (1968 est.) balanced at 8,097,000,000 pesos. Gross national product: (1966) 70,780,000,000 pesos; (1965) 57,940,000,000 pesos. Money supply: (March 1968) 13,228,000,000 pesos; (March 1967) 10,996,000,000 pesos. Cost of living (Bogotá; 1963 = 100): (June 1968) 168; (June 1967) 162.

Foreign Trade. (1967) Imports 6,987,000,000 pesos; exports 6,009,000,000 pesos. Import sources (1966): U.S. 48%; West Germany 11%; U.K. 5%. Export destinations (1966): U.S. 43%; West Germany 14%; Spain 5%. Main exports: coffee 59%; crude oil 10%.

Transport and Communications. Roads (1964) 41,409 km. (including 7,200 km. with improved surface). Motor vehicles in use (1966): passenger 135,300; commercial (including buses) 115,800. Railways: (1965) 3,435 km.; traffic (1967) 419 million passenger-km., freight 996 million net ton-km. Shipping (1967): merchant vessels 100 gross tons and over 42; gross tonnage 195,535. Air traffic (1967): 1,491,232,000 passenger-km.; freight 53,576,000 net ton-km. Telephones (Dec. 1966) c. 500,000. Radio receivers (Dec. 1966) c. 2.2 million. Television receivers (Dec. 1966) c. 400,000.

Agriculture. Production (in 000; metric tons; 1967; 1966 in parentheses): rice 700 (621); wheat c. 125 (94); corn (1966) 940, (1965) 972; barley c. 115 (62); potatoes (1966) 762, (1965) 816; cassava (1966) 1,625, (1965) 2,213; coffee (1966) c. 468, (1965) c. 492; bananas (1966) 962, (1965) c. 965; cotton, lint (1966) 82, (1965) 65; cane sugar, raw value (1967–68) c. 636, (1966–67) 604; sugar, panela (1967–68) c. 671, (1966–67) c. 680. Livestock (in 000; Dec. 1965): sheep 1,702; pigs 1,788; cattle (Dec. 1966) c. 16,000; goats 688; horses 951; chickens 20,765.

Industry. Fuel and power (in 000; 1967): crude oil 9,602 metric tons; natural gas 1,151,000 cu.m.; coal (1966) c. 3,000 metric tons; electricity (excluding industrial production) c. 5,840,000 kw-hr. Production (in 000; metric tons; 1967): crude steel ingots 208; magnesite (1966) 0.2; gold (1966) 275 troy oz.; salt (1966) 391; cement 2,113.

Trade Board transferred (May 9) to the freely permitted list a wide range of essential goods accounting for about 20% of the country's total imports. The country's exchange structure was simplified on June 1 with the elimination of the capital exchange market and the transfer of all transactions previously handled through it to the exchange certificate market. Exports improved following a rise in the volume and value of coffee exports and a marked increase in minor exports, and the government estimated (September) that 1968 exports would reach $670 million, compared with only $510 million in 1967. It decided to proceed with plans for a three-year (1969–71) investment program, to be partly financed by foreign loans totaling $350 million.

In May a new oil field was discovered in the Putumayo region. An official announcement that the new deposit was completely separate from the Orito and other important nearby fields gave some weight to the theory that one of the world's largest oil reservoirs exists in the Putumayo region.

In contrast to 1967, when reduced production schedules led to the dismissal of workers in several firms, business activity increased in 1968. This was partly the result of increased public capital expenditure and the higher permitted level of essential imports. The apparent restoration of confidence to the private business community was reflected in a remarkable increase in stock exchange transactions, the total value of which reached 321 million pesos in the first half of 1968, about 30% higher than in the comparable 1967 period. In April business on the Bogotá Stock Exchange reached an unprecedented level of 103 million pesos.

Pope Paul VI visited Bogotá in August to attend the International Eucharistic Congress, the first visit to Latin America of a reigning pope.   (R. B. LE.)

ENCYCLOPÆDIA BRITANNICA FILMS. *Colombia and Venezuela* (1961).

Commercial Policies

International trade at the beginning of 1968 was influenced by the economic slowing-down that had begun in industrial Europe in mid-1966, by the precarious exchange positions of the U.K. and the U.S., by a weakening of import demand in deficit countries, and by sagging trends for primary products in many markets. The rate of increase in world trade in 1967 was much lower than in preceding years; a little more than 5%, against 9% in 1966. The most dynamic flow was again the exchange of goods among industrialized countries. Trade inside the Eastern trading area increased nearly 9% whereas trade between industrialized countries increased 6.4%. Trade was sluggish between industrialized and less developed areas, among the less developed countries themselves, and with the Eastern trading area.

Shrinking opportunities for export expansion sharpened competition in world markets and strengthened protectionist forces. Most governments, however, lived up to the commitments of the Kennedy Round tariff negotiations, which had been concluded in May 1967 under the auspices of the General Agreement on Tariffs and Trade (GATT). With a few minor exceptions, all the reductions bargained for had been put into force by July 1968. Pressure to restrict trade in sensitive items did not ease and the danger that the drive toward freer trade might be halted or even reversed remained.

In many respects, 1968 was a year of transition; no fresh initiative of significance was launched. The program of studies adopted by the GATT Council of Ministers in 1967 was in progress and was expected to pave the way for future action. The U.S. limited its trade program to an extension of the residual powers embodied in the Trade Expansion Act, which lapsed in mid-1968; avoidance of new restrictive measures; and elimination of the American Selling Price.

Commercial Policies of Industrial Countries.
The parties to the Geneva Protocol had agreed to carry out the Kennedy Round tariff reductions in five yearly installments until 1972. They could begin gradually by making a one-fifth reduction as of Jan. 1, 1968, or wait until July 1, 1968, to reduce rates by two-fifths. Some signatories, such as Canada and the U.S., adopted the former procedure; others, such as the EEC and U.K., opted for the latter. The industrial states generally acceded to the wishes of the less developed countries and applied in full the reductions on many items instead of spreading them over the five years.

To assist the U.S. in solving its balance of payments problems, the industrial countries indicated their readiness to apply in 1969 the reductions contemplated for 1970 while allowing the U.S. to stick to the original schedule. This offer, however, was dependent on an agreement by the U.S. not to introduce any new restrictive measures and to refrain from subsidizing exports. Some governments also insisted on the prompt removal of the American Selling Price (ASP) system of levying duty on the U.S. wholesale prices of some chemical products rather than on the cost to the importer. In the meantime, attempts in the U.S. Congress to impose quantitative restrictions on a large number of imported goods, including steel products, were successfully warded off. Only temporary restrictions were established.

Following strikes in May and June, on July 1 the French government applied a series of safeguards to be in force until the end of 1968. Import ceilings were established for some textiles and clothing, a number of iron and steel products, automobiles and tractors, and some household goods. The ceilings were at or slightly above the actual level of imports in the preceding period. To offset wage increases, a 6% export subsidy was adopted until the end of October, and was to be reduced to 3% from November through January 1969. These measures applied equally to EEC partners and third countries. The U.S. government set a countervailing duty on the subsidized French goods. At the 25th annual session of GATT in late November, France assured the members that its austerity program, undertaken in response to the November franc crisis, would not result in any new trade restrictions. However, there was evident concern among many members over possible repercussions of the French action.

Changes in tariff rates were also applied to a few individual items. The EEC reduced duties on a few products of interest to Iran and Israel when it renewed trade agreements with these countries. Together with the U.K., the EEC extended until June 30, 1969, the suspension of duties on tea, maté, and tropical timber; it also suspended duties on spices and sporting goods of interest to India. In the agricultural sector, the EEC granted its associated states preferential reductions in the special levy on some products including rice but did not extend the privilege to sugar. In return, Norway eliminated its 8% duty on jute

manufactures. As in previous years, the EEC suspended the collection of import duties on a number of raw materials and semimanufactures and extended the measure to other agricultural or industrial products. In some cases, the suspension replaced tariff quotas. The individual states were authorized to suspend duties on some items or to grant duty-free quotas for specific agricultural or industrial products.

As a result of their accession to GATT, Iceland and Ireland reduced or eliminated import duties on individual items. For Ireland, further tariff reductions were made possible by devaluation of the currency. In Finland, Iceland, and Spain, readjustment of overvalued currencies led to reductions in the tariff levels or relaxed import restrictions. The Spanish government used import subsidies to cushion the effect of devaluation on the prices of essential commodities. In a few cases, new or increased taxes were levied for revenue purposes; Austria increased taxes on spirits, tobacco, and imported cars.

With tariff protection losing much of its importance, governments were anxious to prevent increased use of nontariff techniques. The GATT was surveying the actual situation and examining the "border adjustment taxes" that were alleged to distort the trade patterns and to discriminate against imports. The Benelux countries, Denmark, and France, however, eliminated residual import restrictions on a number of items, and the U.K. eased import conditions for cotton textiles and increased import quotas for apples.

Policies of the Less Developed Countries. Slow progress in the less developed countries did not encourage liberal policies. Pakistan, East Africa, Mauritius, and Upper Volta raised duties for revenue purposes or to protect their local industries. Brazil and Argentina, however, continued to encourage the importation of raw materials, components, and equipment needed by their industries, and Pakistan granted duty-free treatment to herbicides and pesticides. The Indian government required would-be importers to advertise in the local press to get domestic supplies. Tariffs were reduced to offset the price increases resulting from devaluation in Ghana, the Democratic Republic of the Congo, Nepal, and Uruguay. These countries and Finland also raised export duties to wipe out the windfall profits that would have accrued to exporters. The Israeli customs tariff underwent a general reduction; maximum rates came down from 270 to 220%.

While New Zealand considered replacing import controls by additional tariff measures and a reduction in the imperial preference margins, and while relaxation measures were undertaken by Morocco, Israel, South Korea, Nigeria, Turkey, and Argentina, most less developed countries continued to rely on import restrictions and prohibitions to protect local industries. New controls were introduced in countries such as Malawi and Malaysia, which before had resorted mainly to tariff measures. In many countries, restrictions became more drastic as local industries supplied larger parts of their markets. Where import substitution had been pursued energetically, however, governments were becoming aware of its adverse effect on price structures and considered relaxing controls to permit some competition with foreign supplies.

The financial situation induced less developed countries to cut import bills again and to rely on local producers to supply the domestic market without heeding the cost of excessive protection. In addition to, or as substitution for, restrictions and prohibitions, some

A 1968 cartoon by Waite, "The Sun," London.

governments required prior deposits, which sometimes exceeded considerably the price of the imported product. Dual exchange rates were applied in Ceylon; Pakistan innovated an equalization tax that had the effect of a "variable levy"; and Bolivia resorted to the technique of minimum values and fixed values for assessing import duties. In the maze it was not easy to detect a trend. The number of absolute import prohibitions, however, seemed to increase from year to year.

Planned Economy Countries. Greater reliance on market forces to determine the allocation of resources to the different sectors of production affected, in varying degrees, the commercial policies of the planned economy countries. In the U.S.S.R., where international trade accounted for a small part of the gross national product, the internal price system continued to be insulated against price movements abroad. Some foreign firms, however, were authorized to establish agencies in the Soviet Union. The foreign trade corporations continued to prevent world prices from disturbing the domestic price structure.

In other Eastern European countries, which were more dependent on foreign trade, commercial practices were being reappraised. In some cases, it was considered that the monopoly granted to foreign trade corporations should be made more flexible; industrial undertakings were authorized to contact directly would-be purchasers or suppliers abroad and to make their own decisions within the general framework of production and/or import-export plans. Attempts were made to price foreign components on the basis of actual cost at world prices and to reflect that cost in the domestic product price.

The most coherent policy was probably that of Hungary, which, on Jan. 1, 1968, introduced a new customs tariff as a part of a general economic reform and readjusted and unified its exchange rate. The aim was to let foreign prices, corrected by import duties, influence the whole range of internal prices. For the time being, however, the impact of such prices was limited. Whereas the emphasis in other Eastern European countries was on increased imports of equipment goods, the Hungarian reform would also facilitate imports of consumer goods.

There was also some relaxation of controls in West European countries, especially in Sweden, which eliminated all import controls on goods originating in Eastern Europe except on arms and ships. In addition, new bilateral agreements with less developed countries

continued on page 214

ATLANTIC FREE TRADE ASSOCIATION

By H. Edward English

The General Agreement on Tariffs and Trade (GATT), signed in 1947, is the legal basis on which the majority of the world's trading nations have carried on efforts to liberate international trade from the tangle of restrictions that developed during the interwar years and as a consequence of the unequal burden of wartime destruction. By 1968 there were 76 contracting parties to the agreement and approximately a dozen other countries had associated themselves with it in various ways.

Trade negotiations carried on under GATT auspices have generally adhered to the most-favoured-nation principle according to which each concession granted in a bilateral or multilateral negotiation between members is automatically passed on to all other members. The belief that some countries might more effectively work toward the dismantling of trade barriers by regional groupings encouraged the authors of GATT to include article 24, under which customs unions and free trade associations might be formed as an exception to the most-favoured-nation principle. While it was recognized that any such grouping would inevitably be discriminatory against nonmembers, it was felt that the contribution to the improved efficiency of national economies through the specialization of production and trade would more than outweigh the discrimination effects.

Many of those who supported article 24 expected it would be used by less developed countries that were reluctant to become signatories of GATT but that might be willing to promote specialization and trade among themselves. In fact, while there have been efforts to form free trade groups in Latin America and Africa, the customs union and free trade association concepts have been applied mainly in Europe. The European Economic Community (EEC), founded under the Rome Treaty of 1957, and the European Free Trade Association (EFTA), established under the Stockholm Convention of 1959, were motivated in part by an interest in potential economic benefits, but also, and especially in the EEC case, by the political interest in so integrating the economies of France, West Germany, Italy, and the Benelux countries that the kind of conflict that had broken out in Western Europe twice in the century would never again be possible. The need for restoring European economic strength in the face of the challenge from Eastern Europe provided perhaps an even more important incentive to success in the EEC.

It was out of this latter motivation that the urge to Atlantic community also gained strength in the postwar years. While the idealist Clarence Streit had proposed Atlantic union during the 1930s, it was only in the face of threat of conflict with the U.S.S.R. that substance was given to Atlantic community in the formation of the North Atlantic Treaty Organization in 1949. From the beginning, certain countries (notably Canada) insisted that the central defense purposes of the alliance should be accompanied by economic arrangements, but these were never specified.

Need for Integration. Various U.S. spokesmen, including some who had been government officials, proposed more active U.S. involvement in transatlantic political and economic integration but no steps were taken in this direction. By the early 1960s it was recognized that European recovery was changing the relationship of Western Europe to the United States. There came a shift from a concept of Atlantic *community* in which the European countries had been implicitly assumed to be relatively weak and dependent upon the U.S. to a concept of *partnership* in which the EEC, hopefully to be expanded through inclusion of most of the EFTA countries (Great Britain, Denmark, Norway, Sweden, Switzerland, Austria, and Portugal), would be a true equal to the U.S., except in nuclear power. But it became difficult to define the basic or continuing motive for such a partnership, especially given the relaxation of East-West tensions and the probability of independent policy positions on the part of Western European leaders, especially the French.

It was hoped in 1962 that the union of Western Europe that would follow British entry into the EEC would increase the stability of the Community and foster a cooperative transatlantic partnership, but the hope was dashed by French Pres. Charles de Gaulle. The Kennedy Round of GATT negotiations was delayed in the aftermath of the disappointment over the failure of Britain's application and the partial breakdown of cooperation among the EEC countries. Although considerable success was finally achieved just before the expiry of the negotiating authority in 1967, the more ambitious aims of the U.S. government to achieve a large measure of free trade between Atlantic countries had long since been abandoned. Meanwhile, the involvement of the U.S. in Vietnam, a conflict unpopular in European capitals, had caused a further divergence of the Atlantic partners' views and interests. Even their erstwhile close cooperation in the monetary sphere had been disrupted by the French gold policy, though Atlantic cooperation excluding France had, for the time being, stabilized the situation.

Atlantic Trade Area Proposals. It is in these circumstances that the idea of an Atlantic free trade association has been gaining support. The definition of the concept has taken many specific forms, but there are essentially two distinguishable ideas that command support from overlapping but not identical groups. One is strictly Atlantic—with the membership of the group limited to the U.S., Canada, the U.K., any other members of EFTA who would care to join, and the EEC. Since the proposal is for a free trade area in which each individual country maintains its own commercial policy vis-à-vis nonmembers, the members of EFTA could join as individual members and the effect would be to extend the size of EFTA to include the North American countries. For the EEC, which is a customs union and common market, common external commercial policy would make it necessary for the Community to join any larger free trade association as a unit. One of the principal advantages of the free trade association idea is that, provided that it is open to all applicants, it is possible to begin operation with a group of countries when it serves their purposes and to extend association to include other countries or customs unions when they are ready to join.

There is also a much broader concept identified with the expression of an Atlantic free trade association. According to this definition, the association would be open to all developed countries with market economies and would unilaterally offer access to the members' markets to exports from the less developed countries. The essential differences between this version and the narrower one are (1) that Japan, Australia, New Zealand, and perhaps some of the more advanced among the less developed countries could become full members, and (2) that arrangements would have to be worked out respecting the form of relationship between the less developed countries and the association. This broad and open-ended concept has been variously labeled an "industrial," or "general," or even "world" free trade association, but it remains Atlantic in the sense that without the support of the U.S., Canada, and some of the European countries it is most unlikely to become operative.

One other definitional question of major significance is the commodity scope of any free trade association. GATT article 24 indicates that substantially all the trade of member countries

should be covered by the arrangement. Most of the discussion about the Atlantic-based association has assumed that all industrial raw materials and manufactures would be covered, but that agricultural products would be excluded. In this respect, the association would be following the practice of EFTA. One of the most compelling reasons for treating agricultural products by arrangements outside the association would be to enable the EEC to join the industrial free trade group. The complex common agricultural policy of the EEC would make it very difficult for the Community to join any wider association that covered agricultural as well as other products.

A less important question is how much institutional superstructure the free trade association would require. In general, because there are few common policies in such an association, supranational institutions of the kind established for the EEC at Brussels are considered unnecessary. The main needs are for statistical and other information centres and for facilities for consultation between member governments to ensure that the aims of the agreement are not frustrated by the actions of individual governments.

Implications of Atlantic Association. There remains a difference of view about the implications of a free trade association between those believing that supranational institutions will inevitably be required and those who consider that national policy independence will be largely preserved in a free trade association except for an intensification of the discipline imposed by international competition. Any assessment of the prospects for the free trade association in either of the forms described will depend on analysis of the economic and political merits of the proposals for the principal countries involved, and on a judgment concerning the probable political attractiveness of the arrangements to the governments likely to be in power in the next few years.

Economic studies on the implications of free trade undertaken by groups in the U.S., Britain, and Canada indicated that the economic benefits to each country varied markedly in importance. Even without empirical studies, there is little doubt that the general effect of substantial and broadly based trade liberalization among the more developed countries helps to achieve greater economies of specialization. But the distribution of the benefits depends on the extent to which the productive potentials of each country have been realized already and on the contribution that the removal of barriers can make to their fuller realization. For the U.S., the studies generally showed the economic benefits that can be captured by free trade to be limited, amounting perhaps to a small fraction of 1% of the gross national product (GNP). While many industries might be stimulated by heightened international competition, it was not expected that direct economic benefits alone would ensure U.S. sponsorship of a free trade association.

For the U.K., the economic benefits were larger, though the British studies stressed the prospect of greater competitiveness in British industry as a consequence of import pressures rather than any fundamental changes in the pattern of production. Since the U.K. was already committed to seeking entry to the EEC, it was interesting to note that a study of the economic effects for Britain of membership in a community including the U.S. and Canada indicated that such an arrangement would be more favourable for Britain than participation in the EEC as presently constituted. The main reason for this was the cost of food associated with British adherence to the Community's protectionist common agricultural policy.

For Canada, estimates of the economic benefit of the removal of Canadian-U.S. trade barriers ran as high as 10% of GNP. It was stressed, however, that the achievement of such benefits would require an adequate transitional period and appropriate adjustment policies to minimize transitional costs.

The political benefits of an Atlantic free trade association in the narrower of the two suggested arrangements would consist primarily in a new initiative for Britain and the U.S. Among the most important of these advantages would be an improvement in Britain's bargaining position vis-à-vis the EEC and an end to the persistent uncertainty concerning the future direction of Britain's international economic commitments. The increased stability of Britain's sterling position would further improve its prospects for an effective role in the world. Against these considerations is the fear on the part of some in Britain that the country's best hope, as a leader among Western European nations, might necessarily be sacrificed by participation in any economic group involving the U.S. In any Atlantic or wider association, all others might be cast in satellite roles vis-à-vis the U.S.

Ironically, the traditional postwar view of the U.S. State Department has been to prefer British membership in the EEC, as a force on the side of political stability and democracy among countries with a record of lapses into autocracy. This assumes a close association between membership in trading communities and political influence.

Of greater importance, particularly in Washington, is the relevance of transatlantic relationships for U.S. policy in the rest of the world. In recent years, while U.S. policy toward Western Europe has been largely at a standstill, major U.S. diplomatic preoccupations have been with Far Eastern and Western Hemisphere problems and there has been singularly little success in involving European countries in situations where the U.S. would have welcomed a sharing of its responsibilities. It is in this context that the larger concept of an industrial free trade association becomes important. If Britain, its EFTA partners, and Japan were to join the U.S. and Canada in the first stage of a larger trade grouping, they might constitute a force for efficiency and growth that would not only contribute to the economic strength of Britain and Canada, but also would avoid that discrimination against Japan (and perhaps Australia and New Zealand) that U.S. leaders have sometimes regarded as one of the drawbacks of the narrower conception of an Atlantic trade area.

U.S. interests in the less developed countries also make the wider concept of a free trade association desirable. Any grouping of developed countries only would be likely to raise the familiar cry against "a rich man's club." If substantial unilateral concessions to the less developed countries were introduced, however, the scheme could become the basis of a new approach to development policy. Groups of less developed countries (*e.g.*, within Latin America, Southeast Asia, South Asia) might be encouraged to form their own regional trade groups as a condition for receiving unilateral free access to the markets of the industrial free trade association. The crucial role of the Atlantic-based free trade grouping in these circumstances would arise out of the economic strength that all member countries would derive from the new association and, conceivably, they would be willing to share in aid programs as well as in the offer of unilateral market access.

These far-reaching development problems might well reduce the short-term political acceptability of a wider free trade association but they might ultimately provide one of the most compelling reasons for serious consideration of the free trade association approach. The epicentre of so many of the world's political earthquakes nowadays is outside Europe, and the importance of dealing with the underlying problems of economic development, and of involving both Europe and Japan in this enormous task, could make the wider concept both essential and practical.

Clearly, in 1969 and beyond, the political prospects for any ambitious new trade proposal will depend on political attitudes in the leading nations suggested as probable "charter" members. Many observers have questioned whether the new administration in Washington will find it advisable even to resist the protectionist forces that appear to have been gaining strength since the end of the Kennedy Round. Only a conviction that a liberal trade policy might serve the wider political interests of the United States would be likely to encourage the new administration to espouse the free trade association in either of its tentative forms. It is evident, however, that in certain of the developed countries that are the main trading partners of the U.S., there is increasing interest in encouraging a U.S. initiative in this direction.

continued from page 211

were concluded or former ones renewed. Ecuador negotiated agreements with a number of Eastern European countries to increase its exports of tropical products.

Trade Policies of Regional Groups. On July 1, 1968, the EEC followed EFTA and removed entirely tariffs on industrial products for trade among the Six. The common external tariff also entered into force. With a few exceptions, the common agricultural policy was extended to all staple products. For the EFTA countries, the few remaining exceptions in their tariff-free trade in industrial products were being removed gradually and Portugal was accelerating its liberalization process. During the international monetary crisis in November, Britain imposed a requirement that importers make a six-month, interest-free deposit with the government amounting to half the value of imported goods. The British government refused to exempt imports from other EFTA countries from this restriction, but its EFTA partners indicated that there would be no recriminations.

As a first step toward economic union, the EEC adopted a uniform system of consumption taxes levied on the basis of value added (TVA) at each stage of processing and marketing. This reform led to some readjustments in rates, and some countries regarded the changes as discouraging for their exports. In another significant move, workers were allowed the full right to get employment in any EEC country or to receive all the social benefits of that country. Capital could also move more freely. Governments were also prepared to exchange views on medium-term trends in economic life and to harmonize their general economic policies in an effort to establish a common commercial policy before 1970. On the other hand, the cleavage between member states over accession to the EEC of the U.K. and other European countries did not narrow substantially.

The EEC faced serious problems resulting from the weak competitive positions of some of its major economic sectors. It tried to safeguard the interests of producers while reconciling conflicting views of members and avoiding antagonizing other trading nations. The common price and support system, which allowed the free movement of staple agricultural products, resulted in a certain amount of competition between member countries. The domestic sugar market continued to be protected by quota arrangements, special support measures were authorized for pork and some vegetables and fruits, and butter surpluses were sold at bargain prices to stimulate domestic consumption.

In spite of proposals by the European Parliament, no change was made in the EEC common price for wheat for the crop year 1968–69. Prices for barley, corn, and rye were raised, and oilseed and olive oil prices remained practically the same. Beef became more expensive in an attempt to discourage milk production by offering more attractive prices to breeders and fatteners.

One of the baffling problems created by the insulation of staples from world market forces was how to regulate competition in processed foodstuffs. The EEC applied a dual variable levy on eggs and poultry. A fixed element protected the processor, and a mobile element equalized the price differential affecting feed grains. Within EFTA, as an interim measure Switzerland and Austria were allowed to postpone the elimination of the import duties on confectionery, biscuits, and chocolate products.

The weakening competitive position of the Community industry was due not so much to the higher efficiency of suppliers from other countries as to a structural shift in fuels from coal to oil and gas. No new protective measures were introduced and, while long-term solutions were being considered, local industry was sheltered by subsidies coordinated at the Community level. For iron and steel, the EEC extended the protective measures taken in 1963 and 1964. These measures had raised import duties to the Italian levels, established ceilings for imports from state trading countries, and prohibited attempts to bring down prices to the levels offered by such countries. Some flexibility was introduced as a result of the Kennedy Round and of individual relaxation measures taken by EEC authorities.

The EEC's association agreements with Greece and Turkey were carried out according to plan. The Greek government began annual tariff reductions and obtained additional advantages including the elimination of duties on Greek tobacco. Turkey secured preferences in the form of tariff quotas on which import duties were halved. The East African Community (Kenya, Tanzania, and Uganda) concluded an agreement with the EEC whereby it granted preferences on 60 Community products while its products enjoyed duty-free treatment.

The Yaoundé Convention, by which the African and Malagasy Common Organization (OCAM) had acquired associate status with the EEC, was to come up for renewal in 1969. The EEC member states had not yet defined their positions, but the Commission indicated that it favoured the renewal of the convention with associated states while keeping separate the agreements concluded with Nigeria and East Africa. Apart from the renewal of commercial arrangements with Iran and Israel, negotiations with other countries had not made significant progress.

Agreements and Projects for Less Developed Areas. The proposed merger of the Latin American Free Trade Association (LAFTA) and the Central American Common Market was still in its initial stages. The meeting of the coordinating committee was delayed and its agenda enlarged to include monetary problems. The subregional group of the Andean countries contemplated accelerating trade through concessions that would not be extended to the more advanced LAFTA members. The annual LAFTA negotiating conference resulted in tariff reductions in the sectors in which industrialists had agreed in advance to coordinate their production programs, but expansion of the common liberalization list still faced serious opposition from vested interests.

The Central American Common Market faced balance of payments difficulties as a result of fallen export prices, accelerated development, and high social budgetary charges. A protocol agreed upon at San José, Costa Rica, raised import duties by 30% on a wide range of products and allowed members to introduce internal taxes on several products produced in the area but not in the importing country. These decisions, designed mainly to assist Costa Rica and Nicaragua, were resented by other countries, especially El Salvador.

In other areas, only moderate progress toward regional integration was achieved. The East African Customs Union and the Common Services arrangement, which entered into force in December 1967, made the East African Community an attractive nucleus group. Ethiopia, Somalia, and Zambia were

contemplating accession to or association with it. Its approach might prove more successful than that of the wider Economic Community of Eastern Africa set up under the auspices of the UN Economic Commission for Africa. The establishment of a West African Community along similar lines had not led to any commercial rapprochement. The Union of Central African States, formed in April by the Central African Republic, Chad, and the Congo (Kinshasa) in an effort to promote free circulation of goods and factors of production among the participants, collapsed in December when the Central African Republic withdrew.

The Common Market of the West Caribbean, which was to enter into force during 1968, was replaced on May 1 by the Caribbean Free Trade Area (CARIFTA), a wider association covering 12 English-speaking states and territories. The Regional Co-operation for Development Scheme between Turkey, Iran, and Pakistan was supplemented by additional coordinated planning and investment measures.

Among the few preferential arrangements negotiated between less developed countries was one between India and Mongolia. A tariff agreement between the U.A.R., India, and Yugoslavia, which entered into force on April 1, 1968, and provided for preferential tariff reductions of up to 50% on some 250 items, was the first significant trade arrangement between less developed countries from different areas.

The second conference of the UN Conference on Trade and Development (UNCTAD), held at New Delhi in February, did not produce a breakthrough in the move toward a new trade policy adjusted to the commercial interests of less developed countries. Although industrial countries no longer opposed the tenets of the UNCTAD dogma and were prepared to accept the principle of nonreciprocal preferences in favour of less developed countries, they were not ready to commit themselves to any practical formula. Australia was the only country granting preferences. The notion that advanced countries should contribute at least 1% of national income to development was restated in a slightly different form, but most countries were unwilling to accept a target date. The project for supplementary financing to assist less developed countries facing shortfalls in their export earnings was sent back to the working party that examined the World Bank proposals. Rapid action on commodity agreements was urged, but the meetings dealing with cocoa and sugar were disappointing. The coffee agreement, however, was renewed for five years. The countries producing sisal and henequen agreed in Rome on a world target price and quotas. The African peanut-producing countries met at Bamako, Mali, with a view to coordinating their marketing policies.

(J. E. Ro.)

See also Agriculture; Commodities, Primary; Development, Economic; Payments and Reserves, International; Trade, International.

Commodities, Primary

Despite increased emphasis by developing countries in expanding their exports of manufactured goods, primary commodities continued to account for 88% of their export trade. Also, the number of developing countries that benefited materially from the increasing average rate of growth of manufactured goods was relatively small. Of the approximately 100 less developed countries in the world, only in 6—Hong Kong, Singapore, India, Taiwan, South Korea, and Israel—did exports of manufactured goods amount to as much as 10% of total exports in 1963–65. Among primary commodities, exports of fuel (mainly petroleum) rose at a much faster rate (7.1% between 1953–55 and 1963–65) than the average. Developing countries' exports of primary commodities other than fuels (food and raw materials) showed a comparatively low average rate of increase of 2.6% a year between 1953–55 and 1963–65.

Trends in World Trade and Production. World trade in food and raw materials grew at a faster rate (5.7% a year on the average) during the first half of the 1960s than in the late 1950s (4.5% a year). Although the developing countries' share of this trade continued to decline, their exports of food and raw materials showed an acceleration in the recent period, to 3.9% in 1963–65 from a 2.6% level in 1953–55. Concurrently, the rate of growth of the total exports of developing countries approached 6% a year. This was the minimum rate, according to world experts, at which the purchasing power of these exports must grow if the modest target rate of growth of 5% per year in the real incomes of developing countries was to be reached by the end of the United Nations Development Decade.

The UN Food and Agriculture Organization (FAO) estimated that combined world output of agricultural, fishery, and forestry products rose nearly 3% in 1967, about the same as in 1966 (*see* Table I). Breaking down this combination, the rapid expansion of fishery production continued with a rise of 5% over 1966. Agricultural output moved up about 3% in 1967, while production of forestry products remained unchanged for the second consecutive year.

Food production in the world as a whole during 1967 rose by about 3%. But in the developing regions, after two years of poor harvests, food output increased by almost 6%. Thus, on a per capita basis, much, but not all, of the ground lost in 1965 and 1966 was made up. While much of the increase in food production in 1967 was the result of improved weather, other factors were also important. These included increased use of fertilizers and other improved practices and techniques, including the introduction into a number of Asian countries of high-yielding varieties of rice and other cereals.

Looking at the individual developing regions, food production in both Africa and the Far East (excluding Communist China) rose about 6%; in the Middle East, output was up 4%. A significant feature in all those areas was the increase in cereal crops. FAO estimates indicated that food production in China may have fallen a bit in 1966 but was up sharply in 1967.

In the developed regions, the picture was mixed. Food production increased about 6% in Western Europe and about 3% in North America. In both regions (except in Canada) grain crops were larger than during the previous year. In Eastern Europe and in the Soviet Union production fell slightly. In Australia drought reduced 1967 food output sharply from the record 1966 level. Grain crops were especially hard hit, but livestock also suffered.

Among other primary commodities—excluding agricultural, fishery, and forestry products—crude petroleum, pig iron, crude steel, and cement continued to be beset with problems of surpluses and excess capacity, brought about by sharp increases in world production of those items (*see* Table II). Likewise, sizable increases in world output occurred for nonferrous

metals, particularly aluminum, zinc, and tin. On the other hand, production of lead fell moderately, while copper output, notwithstanding large increases in production capacity, was held down by strikes in the U.S., Chile, and Africa. Natural rubber production, benefiting by increasing world requirements, continued to move upward in the face of intense competition from lower-priced synthetic rubber. In the U.S. the synthetic product provided more than three-fourths of total new rubber requirements.

Prices and Terms of Trade. Table III shows trends in primary commodity prices during recent years. While there was considerable variation among the various products, declines and rises were about equal. Declines were noticeable for butter, peanuts, jute, rubber, sugar, tea, and hides. The prices of beef, newsprint, rice, tin, copper, cotton, and tobacco showed the largest advances.

Factors behind the commodity price declines were overexpansion of production in relation to domestic and export demand, the growth of agricultural protectionism in importing countries, the increasing substitution of synthetic products, and the continued upturn in materials-saving methods of industrial production. Erratic economic growth in some industrial countries, along with slow demand for some industrial raw materials, also contributed to price declines for primary commodities.

The terms of trade in 1967 generally continued to be against countries that were deficient in grain supplies and that were exporters of commodities whose prices fell, such as rubber, sisal, coarse wools, arabica coffee, some oilseeds and vegetable oils, meat, and jute. Specifically, the terms of trade seemed to have deteriorated for Ceylon, India, Pakistan, Malaysia, and New Zealand. Exporters of cereals, tropical beverages, and cotton probably improved their terms of trade. The terms of trade of meat exporters, such as Argentina and Uruguay, appeared to have worsened.

In 1968 there were sharp price advances for cocoa

beans (because of reduced production) and for copper. Prices for the latter rose because production, following the 8½-month-long strike in the U.S. copper industry, was slow in catching up with demand. World sugar prices also moved up sharply in the expectation that the new International Sugar Agreement would be successful in reducing the market offerings. Cotton production was less than expected, and tin offerings were restricted in the last quarter of 1968 by the International Tin Council's imposition of export quotas for producing members of the International Tin Agreement. Overall, prices for commodity exports of industrial countries continued to be more favourable than for those of less developed countries. However, as is shown in the accompanying chart, the spread narrowed considerably during 1967 and 1968.

Commodity Policies. *National Policies.* Policies relative to agricultural and other commodities in the various countries during 1967–68 generally continued along the lines of recent years, though in some cases important changes in emphasis were made. In new plans for the Ivory Coast, Rwanda, and Upper Volta, as well as in most Latin-American countries, there were significant increases in investment in agriculture, both in absolute terms and in relation to total investment. Another major trend in developing countries was toward increased emphasis on the use of improved seeds, fertilizers, and crop-protection chemicals. India, for example, foresaw about 32 million ac. planted to high-yielding varieties of cereals by 1970–71, and in Pakistan the target was 7.4 million ac. for 1969–70. These goals amounted to 14% of the cereal area in India and 15% in Pakistan, and both countries expected to be nearly self-sufficient in food grains in a few years.

Targets for agricultural production in the five-year plan for 1966–70 in the Soviet Union were adjusted upward in 1967. The average annual production target for meat was raised from 11 million to 11.6 million tons, for milk from 78 million to 81 million, and for eggs from 34 million to 35 million. In both the Soviet Union and Eastern Europe planning methods were under revision, and attempts were being made to bring prices of agricultural commodities more closely into line with their costs of production. An 18% increase over 1967 was planned in 1968 in national investment in agriculture in the U.S.S.R.

In Western Europe the continued accumulation of butter stocks, both inside the EEC and elsewhere, led several governments to introduce measures to discourage milk production or to encourage meat production. The common market for milk and dairy products, which came into being in the EEC countries on July 1, 1968, did not involve an immediate price reduction. However, a ceiling was placed on the amount that could be spent by the European Commission on price support operations for dairy products. Although the common market for both agricultural and industrial commodities became virtually complete for the EEC, other regional economic cooperation plans in other parts of the world reported little or no progress.

There were no major changes in U.S. food and agricultural policies in 1968. The Food for Peace Act (Public Law 480) was extended through Dec. 31, 1970, with no changes in its basic provisions except that suppliers of export sales commodities under Title I of the act had to certify that they were not trading and had not traded in the preceding six-month period with North Vietnam, either directly or indirectly. Despite various acreage reduction programs, the U.S. crop

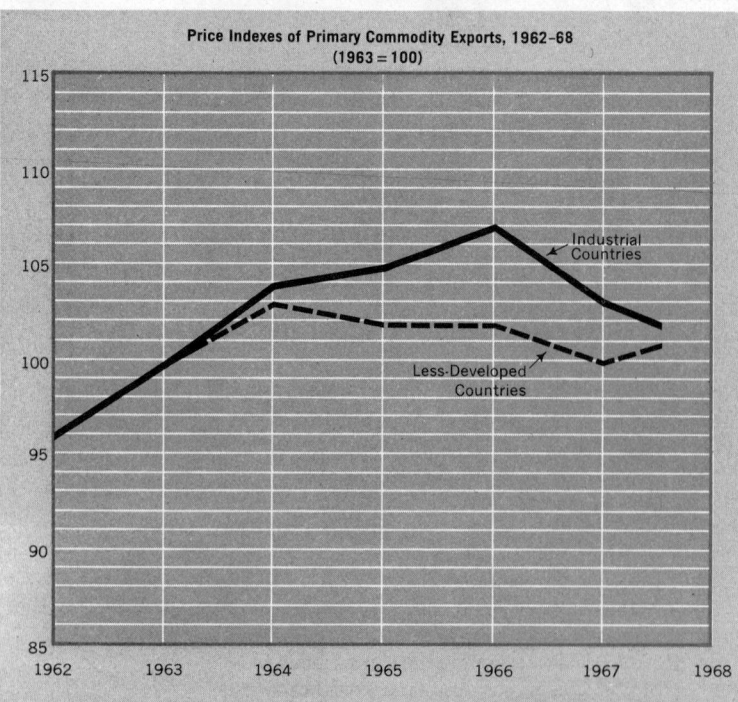

Price Indexes of Primary Commodity Exports, 1962–68
(1963 = 100)

Industrial
Countries

Less-Developed
Countries

NOTE: Industrial Countries: North America, Western Europe, Australia, New Zealand, Japan, South Africa.
Less-Developed Countries: Latin America, rest of Africa, rest of Asia, rest of Oceania.

Source: United Nations, *Monthly Bulletin of Statistics*

harvest in 1968 was the largest ever. Benefiting from favourable weather and the increased use of technology, the 1968 U.S. wheat crop, notwithstanding a 15% cut in the authorized acreage, was record large; this dropped prices of that cereal for a time to 26-year lows. The U.S. secretary of agriculture, in an attempt to keep future wheat stocks down, announced an additional 13% reduction in the wheat acreage allotment for the 1969 crop. While overall farm prices in 1968 were moderately above 1967 levels, record production costs kept the parity index—the ratio of prices received by farmers to prices of things they buy—close to levels prevailing in the depression of the 1930s. This situation led to continued dissatisfaction among farmers. The federal administration requested a four-year extension of the Food and Agriculture Act of 1965, which was scheduled to expire at the end of 1969 and which authorized the federal programs for production control and price support of wheat, feed grains, cotton, and wool. Congress, however, extended the legislation for only one year, through 1970. Thus, U.S. farmers had definite programs only for 1969 and 1970, and the new administration of President-elect Richard Nixon would have time to devise its own farm policies.

International Policies. Major international commodity agreements were successfully concluded in 1968 for two important commodities, coffee and sugar. In addition, the International Grains Arrangement (IGA), which was formulated in 1967, became effective July 1, 1968, for a three-year period. It provided for continued international cooperation in world wheat trade. The IGA was formulated during the Kennedy Round tariff negotiations in 1967 to stabilize and strengthen world wheat prices and to broaden worldwide food assistance efforts. The first part of the arrangement was a Wheat Trade Convention which set minimum and maximum prices for 14 major wheat varieties in world trade (the basic reference price for No. 2 hard winter wheat, ordinary protein, f.o.b. Gulf ports, was set at a minimum of $1.73 and a maximum of $2.13 per bushel). The new minimums were about 20 cents per bushel higher than under the old wheat agreement, with maximums of 40 cents per bushel above the minimums. Importing members of the IGA were obligated to take specified minimum percentages of their import requirements from member exporting countries and to purchase a maximum possible share of their total commercial needs from other member countries. When prices reached their maximum, importing countries were to be assured specific quantities of wheat based on average imports during a recent period. Because of the record world wheat harvest in 1968 and the resultant rise in supplies, some producers reportedly offered wheat to customers at prices below the IGA minimums. As a result, the effectiveness of the IGA remained in question.

The second part of the IGA was a Convention on Food Aid, which set up a program in which participating developed countries, importers and exporters alike, agreed to contribute 4.5 million tons of food grain annually to developing countries. Of that amount, the U.S. offered to supply 42%; the EEC, 23%; Canada, 11%; and Australia, the U.K., and Japan, each 5%. Other countries contributed smaller amounts. Contributions were made in the form of wheat, coarse grains suitable for human consumption, or the cash equivalent to purchase grains.

The new International Coffee Agreement (ICA), which went into effect Oct. 1, 1968, was essentially a

Table I. Indexes of World Production of Agricultural, Fishery, and Forestry Products

1952–56 average = 100

Item	1958	1961	1965	1966	1967
Total production	113	121	133	137	141
Agriculture	114	121	133	138	142
Fisheries	112	127	152	159	167
Forestry	106	111	123	123	123
Population	108	114	124	126	129
Per capita production	105	106	107	109	109
Agriculture	106	106	107	109	109
Fisheries	104	111	123	126	129
Forestry	98	97	97	97	95

Source: Food and Agriculture Organization of the United Nations, *The State of Food and Agriculture, 1968.*

Table II. Indexes of World Production of Certain Raw Materials

1963 average = 100

Raw material	1958	1961	1965	1966	1967
Coal*	93	94	105	106	105
Crude petroleum	69	85	115	125	134
Cement	69	88	115	123	128
Pig iron†	71	91	120	124	130
Crude steel	70	91	118	122	129
Copper (smelter)‡	74	95	109	112	101
Zinc‡	82	93	113	119	119
Lead‡	94	96	105	108	107
Tin§	84	95	104	109	121
Aluminum‡	66	83	120	130	140
Natural rubber	94	101	113	116	119

*Including coal equivalent of brown coal and lignite.
†Including ferroalloys.
‡Excluding the U.S.S.R., East Germany, North Korea, Czechoslovakia, and Romania.
§Excluding the U.S.S.R. and Eastern Europe.
Source: United Nations, *Monthly Bulletin of Statistics.*

continuation of its 1962 predecessor. Its objectives were: (1) to achieve a reasonable, long-term balance between supply and demand so as to assure adequate supplies of coffee to consumers and markets for coffee to producers at equitable prices; (2) to alleviate the hardship caused by burdensome surpluses and excessive price fluctuations; (3) to encourage coffee consumption; (4) to bring about fair wages, higher living standards, and better working conditions in coffee-producing nations; and (5) to promote increased international cooperation in connection with world coffee problems.

Two new provisions were included in the 1968 ICA, which had a membership of 60 nations, 40 exporting and 20 importing, covering more than 98% of world trade in coffee. One new provision was that specific national production goals were to be established for each exporting country so that by 1973 production in each country would be approximately in line with requirements for export quotas and for working stocks.

Table III. Changes in International Prices of Selected Major Primary Commodities

Commodity, unit, country of origin, and market	Wholesale price in U.S. dollars				
	1960	1965	1966	1967	July 1968
Beef (100 lb.) U.K. (London)	29.82	36.72	34.39	32.74	35.00
Butter (100 lb.) New Zealand (London)	38.12	41.66	37.66	36.60	32.14
Newsprint (short tons) Canada (Quebec)	117.30	116.40	119.50	122.40	123.80
Wheat (bu.) Canada (Ft. William, Can.)	1.71	1.80	1.92	1.90	1.85
Wool (100 lb.) Australia (Sydney)	49.10	52.30	57.20	51.00	50.50
Cocoa (100 lb.) Ghana (N.Y.)	28.40	17.28	24.43	29.07	29.65
Coffee (100 lb.) Brazil (N.Y.)	36.60	44.78	40.79	37.93	32.72
Peanuts (100 lb.) Nigeria (London)	8.95	9.45	8.46	8.11	7.25
Jute (short tons) Pakistan (London)	330	317	343	310	270
Petroleum (bbl.) Venezuela (La Cruz)	2.80	2.80	2.80	2.80	2.80
Rice (100 lb.) Thailand (Bangkok)	5.60	6.15	7.11	9.78	9.04
Rubber (100 lb.) Malaysia (Singapore)	35.31	22.90	21.35	17.70	17.68
Sugar (100 lb.) Caribbean (N.Y. for exp.)	3.10	2.12	1.92	2.06	1.71
Tea (100 lb.) Ceylon-India (N.Y.)	58.40	54.00	48.20	45.93	46.10
Tin (100 lb.) Malaysia (Penang)	96.50	172.20	158.40	147.10	136.30
Copper (100 lb.) U.K. (London)	30.70	58.72	69.22	51.10	47.78
Cotton (100 lb.) U.A.R. (Liverpool)	49.04	51.17	49.96	53.24	56.80
Hides (100 lb.) Argentina (London)	31.38	22.00	32.59	25.26	19.59
Lead (100 lb.) U.K. (London)	8.95	14.39	11.69	10.28	11.20
Tobacco (100 lb.) U.S. (U.S.)	58.20	59.40	64.50	65.00	65.90*
Zinc (100 lb.) U.K. (London)	11.09	14.12	12.75	12.34	12.04
Copra (100 lb.) Philippines (London)	9.26	10.34	8.71	9.28	9.33

*June.
Source: International Monetary Fund, *International Financial Statistics.*

Penalties were established for noncompliance, and importing countries were to cooperate by refusing to provide financial assistance for the pursuit of policies contrary to the established goals. New basic export quotas were determined for each member producing country to replace those in effect since 1962. The new quotas totaled 55,838,000 bags, up from 45,587,183 in the former coffee pact. This substantial increase and numerous individual country adjustments eliminated some of the inequities of previous quota levels. The export quotas for the 1968–69 coffee marketing year, beginning Oct. 1, 1968, were set at 47.9 million bags, with a possible upward adjustment of 1.5 million bags depending on the composite price. The new ICA also included a requirement that coffee beans used in the domestic production of instant or other processed coffee for export be valued at the same price as exported beans.

The other major new provision in the 1968 coffee agreement was the creation of a diversification fund to provide technical and financial assistance to member countries in production-control programs. It was also to assist farmers wishing to diversify from coffee to other agricultural commodities. If successful, this provision in the agreement could serve as a model for other pacts dealing with other commodities burdened with supply-demand problems. Mandatory payments from exporting countries and contributions from importing nations would finance the fund. The U.S. offered to lend up to $15 million to the fund and to match assistance up to an additional $15 million.

The 1968 ICA continued the selectivity system for adjusting the export quotas of countries producing the four principal types of coffee, in response to fluctuations in the price of each variety. This system, designed to assure adequate quotas of the various types of coffee at reasonable price levels, went into effect whenever the daily price of any type of coffee averaged below its respective floor or above its respective ceiling for a period of 15 consecutive market days. The quota of each member producing that type of coffee would then be adjusted—decreased if the price was below the floor and increased if the price was above the ceiling—by an amount equal to 3% of the member's annual quotas as of October 1 of the year in question. There was no limit on upward adjustments, but downward adjustments were limited to 5% of the member's annual quota plus any net increase therein resulting from previous upward adjustments.

As the leading importing member of the ICA, the U.S. was required to limit its imports from nonmembers of the pact, to comply with import control procedures in shipments from quota countries, and to furnish statistics and other information pertinent to coffee trade. Implementing legislation limited U.S. participation in the ICA to a period of two years rather than the full five-year term of the pact.

The UN Sugar Conference, meeting in Geneva, reached accord on the adoption of a new International Sugar Agreement (ISA) on Oct. 24, 1968. Conclusion of the pact by delegates from 73 nations represented a victory for the United Nations Conference on Trade and Development (UNCTAD) and particularly for its secretary-general, Raúl Prebisch (*see* BIOGRAPHY), who had laboured long and hard on its behalf. The agreement was designed to bring world production and consumption of sugar into closer balance at prices above the low levels prevailing in 1967 and 1968. It aimed to maintain stable prices for sugar that would be reasonably remunerative to producers but that would not encourage additional expansion of production in developed countries. The new five-year ISA was scheduled to become effective Jan. 1, 1969. Importers and exporters each were to have 1,000 votes on the International Sugar Council, which was to administer the pact. The EEC was not a member of the pact, but a quota was provided in the hope that it would participate at a later date.

The new agreement set up an export quota of 8.6 million tons for the "world market." This represented about half of the total world sugar trade; the other half moved under preferential arrangements. Sugar imported into the U.S. under the U.S. Sugar Act was not subject to the new agreement.

The new sugar pact sought to stabilize the world free market price of sugar between a minimum of 3.25 cents per pound (f.o.b. Caribbean port basis) and a maximum of 5.25 cents a pound. If the price should drop to 3.5 cents, basic export quotas of producing countries would be reduced by 10%. A further cut of 5% in the quotas would be made if the price should dip below 3.25 cents, the lowest price at which ISA-member countries might buy from nonmembers. Should prices rise above 5.25 cents, export quotas would be suspended in an attempt to prevent runaway prices. However, in the case of such a rise, exporting nations would agree to supply importing countries at the average price and quantity of the previous year up to a maximum of 6.5 cents per pound. Another feature of the new ISA provided a special hardship fund of 150,000 tons for developing countries. Particular attention was to be given to the needs of small developing countries whose export earnings were heavily dependent upon the export of sugar, of countries whose economies were becoming increasingly dependent upon sugar, and of countries burdened with excessive stocks.

After several years of deficit production, world tin production in 1967 surpassed world tin consumption. This situation worsened in 1968, and prices declined to their lowest levels in some time. As a result, the buffer stock manager of the International Tin Council was forced to make heavy purchases of metal. The International Tin Council on September 18 declared the period from September 19 to December 31 as one of export control. Thus, permissible export quotas for the six producing members of the International Tin Agreement—Bolivia, Congo (Kinshasa), Indonesia, Malaysia, Nigeria, and Thailand—during that period were set at 42,950 long tons, equivalent to 38,000 per quarter. After the imposition of the quotas, tin prices strengthened noticeably.

Several cocoa conferences were held in 1966 and 1967 under UNCTAD auspices, at which the text of an International Cocoa Agreement was formulated. However, agreement was not reached on some issues, and the conference suspended its meetings on Dec. 19, 1967. Afterward world cocoa crops did not come up to expectations, particularly in West Africa and Brazil. As a result, it appeared that world cocoa production in the 1968–69 season (October 1–September 30) would fall behind world consumption for the fourth consecutive year. With demand continuing high, prices soared to ten-year peaks. Little interest in an international cocoa agreement was expected until supplies and prices returned to more normal levels.

(N. R. U.)

Common Market:
see Commercial Policies; European Unity; *see also* Index *for information on specific common markets*

See also Agriculture; Commercial Policies; Development, Economic; Food; Payments and Reserves, International; Trade, International.

Commonwealth of Nations

The number of independent members of the Commonwealth increased to 28 in 1968, with Mauritius joining in March and Swaziland in September. Nauru, a tiny island with only 6,000 inhabitants, became independent in March. Under a bill pending in Parliament, it would be given a special status: it would not be represented at meetings of Commonwealth heads of state but could participate in Commonwealth activities having to do with such matters as education and health.

The Commonwealth Office and Foreign Office were merged on October 17 under one secretary of state, and it was announced in July that after a lapse of two and a half years, a Commonwealth Prime Ministers' Conference would be held in London, in January 1969.

Africa. In July Tanzania resumed diplomatic relations with Britain; it was the last of the nine countries who broke with Britain over Rhodesia in 1965 to do so. The Nigerian civil war replaced Rhodesia and Kashmir as the most urgent Commonwealth problem. Despite sympathy for Biafra and its virtual recognition by Zambia, Tanzania, Gabon, and the Ivory Coast, the Organization of African Unity (OAU) at its various 1968 meetings was acutely aware of the danger of the creeping internationalization of the dispute and of the fact that many other African states faced similar tribal conflicts. Ghana made progress toward civil government, promised for September 1969. In Sierra Leone, a coup (April 18) put Siaka Stevens (see BIOGRAPHY) into power.

Biafrans demonstrating in London against British government aid to the federal government of Nigeria, January 1968. The demonstration ended in a battle with police and four were arrested.

In Rhodesia the main events of the year were increased guerrilla activity from neighbouring African territories; the execution of three Africans in March in defiance of the exercise of the queen's prerogative of mercy; the recognition by the Rhodesian High Court of the Rhodesian government as the de facto government of the country; the stiffening of UN sanctions; the report of the Rhodesian Constitutional Commission in favour of eventual "race parity"; and, finally, the meetings between the British and Rhodesian prime ministers, Harold Wilson and Ian Smith, at Gibraltar October 10–13. At the meetings it was found impossible to bridge the gap between the British and Rhodesian official viewpoints.

Botswana, Lesotho, and Swaziland, though politically independent, remained economically and strategically dependent upon the Republic of South Africa for development and security. Malawi became the first

Commonwealth of Nations

Country	Area (sq.mi.)	Pop. (1966–68 estimate)	Capital	Status	Chief of state and head of government* (as of Dec. 31, 1968)
United Kingdom	94,213	54,744,100	London	Constitutional monarchy	Queen, Elizabeth II
					Prime minister, Harold Wilson
Australia	2,967,877	11,990,787	Canberra	Federal parliamentary state	Governor-general, Lord Casey
					Prime minister, John Grey Gorton
Barbados	166	248,166	Bridgetown	Parliamentary state	Governor-general, Sir John Stow
					Prime minister, Errol Walton Barrow
Botswana	220,000	611,000	Gaberones	Republic	President, Sir Seretse Khama
Canada	3,851,809	20,744,000	Ottawa	Federal parliamentary state	Governor-general, D. Roland Michener
					Prime minister, Pierre Elliott Trudeau
Ceylon	25,332	11,701,000	Colombo	Parliamentary state	Governor-general, William Gopallawa
					Prime minister, Dudley Senanayake
Cyprus	3,572	618,000	Nicosia	Republic	President, Archbishop Makarios III
Gambia, The	4,000	343,000	Bathurst	Parliamentary state	Governor-general, Alhaji Sir Farimang Singhateh
					Prime minister, Sir Dawda Jawara
Ghana	92,100	8,376,000	Accra	Republic	Chairman of National Liberation Council, Gen. Joseph Ankrah
Guyana	83,000	676,521	Georgetown	Parliamentary state	Governor-general, Sir David J. E. Rose
					Prime minister, Forbes Burnham
India	1,232,560	524,080,000	New Delhi	Federal republic	President, Zakir Husain
					Prime minister, Mrs. Indira Gandhi
Jamaica	4,232	1,890,000	Kingston	Parliamentary state	Governor-general, Sir Clifford Campbell
					Prime minister, Hugh L. Shearer
Kenya	224,960	10,209,000	Nairobi	Republic	President, Jomo Kenyatta
Lesotho	11,716	852,459	Maseru	Constitutional monarchy	Chief of state, Moshoeshoe II
					Prime minister, Leabua Jonathan
Malawi	48,623	4,130,000	Zomba	Republic	President, H. Kamuzu Banda
Malaysia	127,672	9,675,000	Kuala Lumpur	Federal constitutional monarchy	Yang di-pertuan agong, Tuanku Ismail Nasiruddin Shah ibni al-Marhum Sultan Zainal Abidin
					Prime minister, Tunku Abdul Rahman
Malta	122	319,000	Valletta	Parliamentary state	Governor-general, Sir Maurice Dorman
					Prime minister, George Borg Olivier
Mauritius	720	787,400	Port Louis	Parliamentary state	Governor-general, Sir John Rennie
					Prime minister, Sir Seewoosagur Ramgoolam
New Zealand	103,736	2,755,092	Wellington	Parliamentary state	Governor-general, Sir Arthur Porritt
					Prime minister, Keith J. Holyoake
Nigeria	356,669	61,450,000	Lagos	Federal republic	Head of provisional military government, Yakubu Gowon
Pakistan	365,529	109,519,831	Rawalpindi†	Federal republic	President, Field Marshal Muhammad Ayub Khan
Sierra Leone	27,699	2,475,000	Freetown	Parliamentary state	Acting governor-general, Banja Tejansie
					Prime minister, Siaka Stevens
Singapore	225	1,974,600	Singapore	Republic	President, Inche Yusof bin Ishak
					Prime minister, Lee Kuan Yew
Swaziland	6,704	398,400	Mbabane	Constitutional monarchy (protected state)	King, Sobhuza II
					Prime minister, Prince Makhosini Dhlamini
Tanzania	361,800	12,231,342	Dar es Salaam	Republic	President, Julius Nyerere
Trinidad and Tobago	1,980	994,850	Port-of-Spain	Parliamentary state	Governor-general, Sir Solomon Hochoy
					Prime minister, Eric Williams
Uganda	91,076	7,934,000	Kampala	Federal parliamentary state	President and prime minister, Milton Obote
Zambia	290,587	4,014,000	Lusaka	Republic	President, Kenneth Kaunda

*Where Queen Elizabeth II serves as chief of state, her representative (governor-general) is listed.
†Provisional.

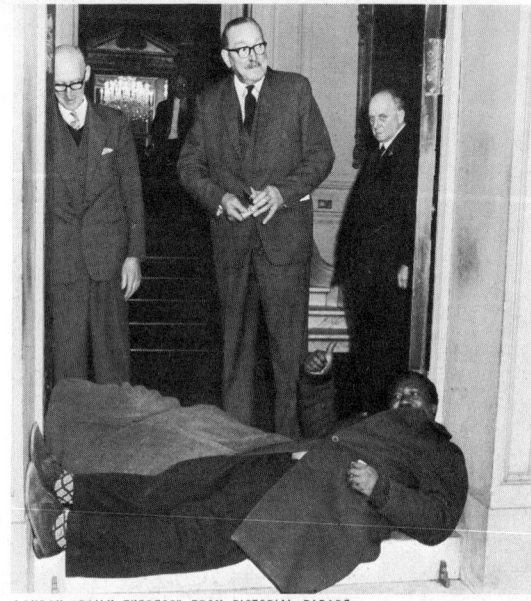

Above, Prince Makhosini Dlamini (right) of Swaziland attending a conference in London in February 1968 where planning for his country's independence was completed. Right, A. F. Zwane and K. T. Samketi, leaders of a nationalist group, blocking the door of Marlborough House after being excluded from the conference.

independent African state openly to avow cooperation with South Africa and established diplomatic relations with the republic on January 1. South Africa in return supported Malawi's sugar complex and provided a loan of R 8 million toward Malawi's future capital at Lilongwe.

Zambia remained painfully poised between Rhodesia and Tanzania. Though sympathetic to the guerrillas aimed at southern Africa and offering them "moral and material aid," Zambia remained aware that too overt aid could result in a preemptive strike against itself. Closer economic ties with the U.S.S.R. and Communist China developed in Zambia and Tanzania, in connection with road and rail building, though the oil pipeline from Ndola to Dar es Salaam completed in July, was undertaken by Italian enterprise. Tanzania remained the guerrilla camp centre, with the OAU Committee of Liberation sitting in Dar es Salaam, and was responsible for arms supply.

Kenya remained troubled by problems of the succession and of race. The latter flared to a crisis in February and March, when Asians, who had not and could not become citizens, attempted to emigrate to Britain and India following stringent economic measures against them. Race riots marred the achievement of independence by Mauritius on March 12, and British troops were flown in to restore order.

Other Countries. Following a royal visit to Malta in November 1967 and a British pledge to see Malta through to viability, a transfer of the dry docks to the Maltese government was made in April. In Cyprus, Greece and Turkey had reached the edge of war after incidents that culminated in an armed conflict at Kophinou in November 1967; diplomatic activity and

UN troops, mainly British, eased the situation during 1968.

The heavy burden of defense and expanding populations still retarded development in India and Pakistan. Their proposed nonaggression pact again foundered on the problem of Kashmir. Indian suspicion of Chinese support to Pakistan was not helped by Peking support of the Naga minority and their rebellion in the northeast frontier area of India. The opening of the Mangla Dam at the end of 1967, part of the Indus Basin Scheme, augured better for economic cooperation between Pakistan and India. During the year there was spectacular economic development in Australia, which was emerging as a major Pacific power.

Canada, through its new prime minister, Pierre Elliott Trudeau, emphasized its role as a Pacific power and its intention of recognizing Communist China and acting as a political go-between for China and the U.S. As a leading member of the Caribbean Free Trade Area, Canada also expanded its economic interests in the West Indies and in Latin America, replacing British power in the Western Hemisphere.

Economic Affairs. Commonwealth trade continued to grow (as did intra-Commonwealth trade, with Britain as the most important component). The total value of Commonwealth trade increased by 6% in 1967, faster than the world total and above the 1966 increase. Commonwealth exports rose from £13,822 million to £14,260 million; imports into the Commonwealth from £15,151 million to £16,417 million, totaling 22% of world trade. The Commonwealth as a whole remained a net world aid contributor, with Britain by far the largest in absolute terms. In 1967 Britain disbursed £207.9 million in economic aid to less developed areas, the biggest single recipient being India. Under the Colombo Plan, British contributions in 1966 totaled £66.1 million (an increase from £47.4 million in 1965, bringing the total since 1951 to £420 million). (M. Mr.)

See also articles on the various political units.

Communist Movement

The breakup of the formerly monolithic Communist movement, which started in 1948 with Yugoslavia's "heresy," reached a new height during 1968. Reversing the trend followed under former Soviet Premier Nikita S. Khrushchev, who had recognized the new doctrine of "different roads to socialism," the collective leadership of the Soviet Union tried to reassert its leading position, at least among the European Communist countries. The rift between China and the U.S.S.R., the two Communist "giants," continued, but the main attention shifted to the struggle in central Europe between the desire for full national sovereignty on the part of the smaller Communist nations and the Soviet claim to leadership of the whole movement.

Fragmentation Within the Bloc. This Soviet claim was motivated less by ideological reasons than by the U.S.S.R.'s determination to hold firm to the strategic great power position that it had achieved at such great cost during World War II. East Germany, Poland, and Czechoslovakia represented for the Soviet Union a shield against future aggressions from the West, similar to those the U.S.S.R. had suffered in 1915 and 1941. In addition, the highly developed industrial capacity of Czechoslovakia and East Germany and the efficiency of their skilled workers strengthened

Communications:
see
Telecommunications;
Television and Radio

"Quo vadis, little party member?"—Bahrendt, "Het Parool," Amsterdam.

economic progress in the Soviet Union and bolstered its program of aid to less developed countries.

Beyond this, the Soviet leaders were also afraid that the emphasis on true national sovereignty in a growing number of Communist countries and the intellectual revolt against the dogmatic and authoritarian party line in artistic and cultural affairs might affect the U.S.S.R. and create troubles there. The many non-Russian nationalities within the Soviet Union might claim independence, and the party hierarchy and bureaucracy might lose their formerly undisputed control over all aspects of political, economic, and intellectual life. For the heirs of the czarist regime and of Stalin's autocracy, this seemed to undermine the very foundations of the Soviet government.

In 1968 one could no longer speak of a pluralism of Communist regimes and parties, but rather of a fragmentation of the Communist movement. The Cultural Revolution, which had shaken China to its very foundations, seemed to be ebbing. Mao Tse-tung's main goal of purging revisionist leaders and renovating the Communist system appeared to have succeeded, and consolidation was now being demanded. The Army had apparently regained a position of prominence, and the Military Affairs Committee was headed by Lin Piao, Mao's presumptive successor and second in the Politburo. This change in emphasis had no influence on China's attitude toward the Soviet Union, however. "Soviet revisionism" remained linked with "American imperialism" as the chief enemy of the "true" revolution. This was true even after the invasion of Czechoslovakia by Warsaw Pact forces. Chinese official utterances concerning the Czechoslovak affair were far more violently anti-Soviet than Western comments. China was seconded in this by Albania, its only close ally.

There was as little unity in what was sometimes called "Asian Communism" as there was in European Communism. None of the other Asian Communist countries supported China. North Korea and North Vietnam followed a neutral policy between China and the U.S.S.R., whereas Mongolia, the oldest Communist state in Asia, followed the U.S.S.R. In Europe the situation was even more complex. East Germany under Walter Ulbricht followed a most faithful pro-Soviet line. In Poland Wladyslaw Gomulka, who had been imprisoned by his Stalinist predecessors for his "nationalism," had become more and more dependent on Moscow. The same policy of dependence was followed by Antonin Novotny during his almost 15 years in power in Czechoslovakia. Janos Kadar, who came

to power in Hungary with Soviet help, had been asserting a mild form of independence from the Kremlin. These countries, together with Bulgaria, which under Todor Zhivkov had followed a strictly pro-Soviet line, formed part of the Warsaw Pact, an organization conceived as a countermeasure to NATO.

For more than two years Romania, also a part of the Warsaw Pact, had played the role that Pres. Charles de Gaulle's France was playing in NATO. The Romanian leader Nicolae Ceausescu stressed the full sovereignty and independence of Romania from Soviet foreign and economic policy, while maintaining the strictest Communist Party control over all aspects of life inside the country. Unexpectedly, in 1968 he accused his predecessor, Gheorghe Gheorghiu-Dej, and Gheorghiu-Dej's colleague, Deputy Premier Alexandru Draghici, of crimes against "socialist democracy" and "socialist legality." The most important personality of the past to be rehabilitated was Lucretiu Patrascanu, Romania's first postwar minister of justice, who had been arrested in 1948 and tried and executed in 1954. Always insisting on its own independence, Romania tried to reestablish unity among the Communist countries, but this did not mean any deviation from Marxism-Leninism. When a study group published a proposal to limit compulsory courses in Marxism-Leninism to students of philosophy, political economy, history, and law, Ceausescu asserted that higher education should become "a centre fighting against all backward and obsolete elements, against all idealistic, mystical and reactionary views."

Whereas Romania participated only nominally in the Warsaw Pact but stressed its loyalty to dialectical and historical materialism, Yugoslavia, which had never been a member of the Warsaw Pact, allowed the progressive liberalization of its economic policy and stressed independence in its relationships with all countries, especially the so-called "third world." The last European Communist country, Albania, followed an extremely dogmatic and aggressive policy in close cooperation with China.

Czechoslovakia. In 1968 a further split in the Communist movement attracted the attention of the whole world and led to criticism of the Soviet Union even by many of its usual supporters. In 1967 Czechoslovakia had witnessed a mounting rebellion of writers against the dogmatic attitudes of the Communist Party leadership. This opposition was strongly expressed at the fourth congress of the Czechoslovak Writers' Union in Prague in June 1967.

The liberalizing faction gained the upper hand in January 1968. On January 5, Antonin Novotny was replaced as the first secretary of the Communist Party of Czechoslovakia by Alexander Dubcek, who had been the first secretary of the Communist Party of Slovakia. The Central Committee of the Czechoslovak party dismissed Novotny from his party post in an orderly, almost democratic fashion, leaving him for the time being the purely honorary office of president of the republic. Economic mismanagement as well as political and cultural repression had led to this step, and the liberalizers' hand was strengthened by the economic deterioration.

Dubcek was the first Slovak to achieve a leading position in the Czechoslovak party. He was himself a faithful Communist, raised and educated in the Soviet Union, and he wished to preserve the pro-Soviet orientation of Czechoslovak foreign policy and trade. But the suddenly released groundswell went further than was originally intended. In early March

censorship was lifted and the Communist regime was subjected to public criticism. On March 22 Novotny resigned as president and Ludvik Svoboda, a general in the Soviet Army during World War II, was elected in his place. A memorandum of "2000 Words" signed by the novelist Ludvik Vaculik and 70 others, which appeared on June 27, stated that "the Communist party betrayed the great trust that people put in it after the war. It preferred the glories of office until it had those and nothing more." In the U.S.S.R. and Poland this manifesto was condemned as a "counter-revolutionary program."

On July 15 five members of the Warsaw Pact—the Soviet Union, Poland, East Germany, Bulgaria, and Hungary—demanded the end of Czechoslovak "liberalism." The Czechoslovak government rejected this demand, and Czechoslovak and Soviet leaders met in the Czechoslovak village of Cierna near the border of the Soviet Ukraine on July 29 to discuss the situation. Five days later Czechoslovakia and the five Warsaw Pact members signed an agreement at Bratislava, the capital of Slovakia. Meanwhile, the leaders of Yugoslavia and Romania had met in Belgrade, where they expressed their condemnation of "acts of aggression and pressure, threats and interference in the internal affairs of other states" and their support for "democratic development" in the building of socialism, and called for the disbanding of NATO and of the Warsaw Pact. In August they visited Prague and received enthusiastic welcomes.

All this seemed to confirm the fears of the Soviet Union. After a meeting in Warsaw, the five Warsaw Pact countries sent a message to the Czechoslovak leadership affirming that "antisocialist and revisionist forces have laid hands on the press, radio and television, making of them a rostrum for attacking the Communist Party, disorienting the working class and all working folk, spewing forth uncurbed antisocialist demagogy and undermining the friendly relations between the Czechoslovak Socialist Republic and the other socialist countries."

The Czechoslovak reply of July 18 tried to remove these fears.

> We do not see any realistic reasons for our present situation to be called counterrevolution, for statements about an immediate danger to the basis of the socialist system, for statements that Czechoslovakia is preparing a change in the orientation of its socialist foreign policy. Our alliances and friendships with the U.S.S.R. and other socialist countries are deeply rooted in the social system, in the historical traditions and the experience of our peoples, and in their interests, their thoughts and feelings.

But in the opinion of the other Warsaw Pact members, these reassuring words were contradicted by facts. On July 19 *Pravda*, the official organ of the Communist Party of the Soviet Union, wrote in an editorial that "the key question now at issue is whether Czechoslovakia is to be socialist or not." The compromise reached at Bratislava seemed to be differently interpreted by Czechoslovakia and by its Communist partners.

The ambiguities of the situation led the Soviet Union and its four Warsaw Pact partners to try a military solution. About 200,000 Soviet soldiers invaded Czechoslovakia on August 20–21, but if the Soviets had hoped to find any Czechoslovak collaborators, they were thoroughly disappointed. The Czechoslovak leaders, returning from Moscow where they had negotiated with Soviet leaders, assured the people that there would be no return to the pre-January 1968 situation, that the road entered in January would be continued, and that the personal freedom and safety of all citizens would be ensured. The Soviet Union continued to deliver the oil and wheat that Czechoslovakia desperately needed, and the Soviet tanks withdrew from Prague to the countryside.

If the Soviets refrained from an overtly brutal crackdown, however, it soon became apparent that their control over major policy decisions within Czechoslovakia was tightening. Press censorship was reimposed in September, and in October a Soviet-Czechoslovak treaty was signed providing for the continued stationing of Soviet troops on Czechoslovak soil. As the year came to an end, power within the Czechoslovak leadership seemed to be gravitating toward those who favoured accommodation with the U.S.S.R. Something of the reforms initiated in January and March 1968 might still be saved, but it was clear that the heady freedom of the spring would no longer be permitted. At least for the time being, the hopes of establishing Czechoslovakia as a country of democratic socialism had vanished. (*See* CZECHOSLOVAKIA; DEFENSE.)

Above, Soviet Army units leaving Czechoslovakian territory in July 1968 after completing what were termed Warsaw Pact maneuvers which were held despite Czechoslovak protests. Right, Soviet soldiers occupying Prague following the August 20–21 invasion.

Nevertheless, the assertion of military superiority by the Soviet Union had not been without its costs in terms of Communist unity. Many Western European Communists disapproved of the invasion. The Italian Communist leader Luigi Longo had insisted in the Communist weekly *Rinascita* in October 1967 on "relationships, which strictly preserve the autonomy of each single [Communist] party and do not try to impose any compulsory lines of action or orientation of thought. . . . A return to the monolithic structure can and must not be attempted, to a commanding state or party, as the 20th Congress of the Communist Party of the Soviet Union made it clear." As the *New York Times* put it, "the reality today is of many independent communist parties and almost hopeless difficulties for Moscow or any other center that tries to re-introduce the old monolithic unanimity of Stalinist days."

Further Disagreements. The extent to which the Communist movement had been split was shown by the attitude of Cuba, which depended entirely on the Soviet Union for its economic survival. Not only did Cuba not participate in the various movements started by Moscow to emphasize common unity, but it also made unmistakably clear that it disagreed with the Soviet Union on fundamental questions. Cuban propaganda painted the Soviet Union as being in league with the U.S. because the Soviet Union opposed guerrilla tactics in Latin America and wished instead to develop its economic and cultural relations with the existing Latin-American governments. Veteran Cuban Communist leaders, among them Aníbal Escalante, were expelled from the Cuban Communist Party in January 1968. Nor did Cuba participate in preparations for the world Communist meeting which the Communist Party of the Soviet Union had planned for the end of 1968.

This meeting, to promote Communist unity and to condemn China, was first envisaged by Khrushchev, but the Soviet leaders, fearing that it might turn into a fiasco, had delayed calling it. In April 1968, 54 parties met in Budapest for a preparatory conference. Of the 14 ruling parties, 7 were absent—China, North Korea, North Vietnam, Albania, Yugoslavia, Romania, and Cuba. The burning issues of China, Czechoslovakia, and Romania were not discussed officially at all; "respect for the equality and independence of all parties" was proclaimed and no condemnation of China was attempted. The conference reconvened in June and again in October, but when the October meeting was adjourned for six weeks it became clear that the summit meeting, tentatively scheduled for November 25, would not be held before the end of the year. At the next meeting of the conference, in late November, the summit meeting was set for May 1969. A number of Western parties had opposed the meeting, but only those of the U.K., Switzerland, and Réunion actually voted against it. All Communist parties, including those that had not taken part in the preparatory conference, were to be invited. Meanwhile, there were signs that the five powers that had participated in the invasion of Czechoslovakia might group themselves together into some kind of community within the Communist movement; the leading spirit behind this move appeared to be the Soviet theoretician Mikhail Suslov.

Meanwhile, the first steps toward a rapprochement between the Roman Catholic Church and certain Communist governments were taken. In June 1968 Eugène Cardinal Tisserant paid a 12-day visit to Yugo-slavia, where he was received by President Tito and had talks with the head of the Serbian Orthodox Church. Franz Cardinal König, archbishop of Vienna, was the head of a Vatican secretariat working for dialogue between the Roman Catholic Church and nonbelievers, and such dialogues did develop, especially in Austria and France. Of historical importance also was the meeting in June between the patriarch of the Serbian Orthodox Church and the archbishop of Zagreb, the Roman Catholic primate of Yugoslavia. A relaxation of the antichurch attitude of the Prague government was noticeable before the invasion, but it was not clear whether this attitude would continue.

At the end of 1968, the future of the Communist bloc—or rather what had been the Communist bloc—was unpredictable. It was of interest to note that when students of the University of Belgrade conducted the nation's first sit-in in June 1968, President Tito refused to apply the old police methods, called the student revolt spontaneous, and said its root was the party leadership's failure to carry out long-delayed reforms. In Poland the opposite happened, and student demonstrations were suppressed by the police. As much as anything, this illustrated the great differences existing among parties and countries professing themselves to be guided by Marxism-Leninism.

(H. Ko.)

See also China; Intelligence Operations; and articles on the various countries.

ENCYCLOPÆDIA BRITANNICA FILMS. *Poland: Land Under Communism* (1960); *Poland and the Soviet Power* (1961); *Berlin: Test for the West* (1962); *China Under Communism* (1962); *The Soviet Challenge* (*The Industrial Revolution in Russia*) (1962); *Hungary and Communism: Eastern Europe in Change* (1964).

Congo, Democratic Republic of the

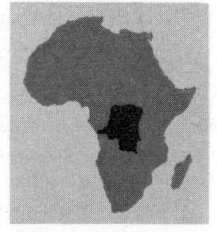

A country of equatorial Africa, the Congo is bounded by the Central African Republic, Sudan, Uganda, Rwanda, Burundi, Tanzania, Zambia, Angola, the Congo (Brazzaville), and the Atlantic Ocean. Area: 905,063 sq.mi. (2,344,116 sq.km.). Pop. (1967 est.): 15,917,000. Cap. and largest city: Kinshasa (Léopoldville; pop., 1967, 901,520). Language: French; Bantu dialects, mainly Swahili and Lingala. Religion: mainly fetishism. President in 1968, Joseph Mobutu.

The problem of the white mercenaries, which had created so much trouble in the Congo until they took refuge in Rwanda toward the end of 1967, was solved in April 1968. The Katangese gendarmes who had accompanied the mercenaries were repatriated to the Congo in December 1967, but on January 11 President Mobutu broke off relations with Rwanda when it would not surrender the refugee mercenaries. In April, however, he agreed that they should be evacuated to Europe on the understanding that they would never be allowed by their home countries to return to Africa. On April 24–25 the mercenaries were flown to Europe. A few days later, their Belgian leader, Jean Schramme, stated in Brussels that in the latter part of 1967 he had planned to overthrow Mobutu who, he claimed, was detested by the Congolese people. He had then hoped that elections would be held and democracy restored.

Mobutu did, indeed, appear to have enemies within

Comoro Islands: *see* Dependent States

Mercenary troops under the command of Robert Denard surrendering their arms to Portuguese soldiers as they leave Katanga Province for Angola. Their withdrawal along with that of troops led by Jean Schramme marked the end of open rebellion against President Mobutu.

the Congo, though their activities were firmly restricted. Toward the end of February the executive committee of the Congo students' union was dissolved because it was allegedly involved in a Marxist-Leninist plot to eliminate the president and his chief ministers and to seize control of the government. In April Mobutu himself stated in the course of a visit to Kasai-Occidental that yet another plot to assassinate him had been foiled. Behind it had been three politicians from Kasai-Occidental who had hoped that by arranging for the murder of the president while he was in Luluabourg they would strengthen their position in preparation for the forthcoming elections to the legislature.

Other problems arose out of the conduct of the mining industry. On February 9 the prosecutor general ordered the arrest on a charge of embezzlement of 12 directors of Générale Congolaise des Minérais (GECOMIN), the company that had taken over mining operations from the Union Minière du Haut-Katanga in 1967. A week later, on February 16, six Swiss technicians of GECOMIN were also arrested while trying to leave for Zambia.

How serious these issues were or to what extent the speedy intervention of the government indicated a firm control of events by Mobutu was difficult to say. In August the president reshuffled his Cabinet, two ministers leaving the government and several others exchanging portfolios. Mobutu himself retained responsibility for defense, while the Foreign Ministry, under Justin Bomboko, was strengthened by the creation of a second assistant minister. Simultaneously, and as part of the plan to reform the judicial system, an ordinance was promulgated setting up a new Supreme Court to be presided over by Marcel Lihau, professor of law at the University of Louvanium. Early in September all political prisoners, including Godefroid Munongo, former minister in the secessionist government of Katanga and also in Moise Tshombe's central government, were released. At this time the Congo government informed Algeria that they would not object to the release of Tshombe himself, who had been detained in Algiers for 14 months. However, in October Mobutu executed Pierre Mulele, one of the leaders of the 1963–64 rebellion in the Congo. Mulele had returned from the neighbouring Congo Republic, believing that the September amnesty would guarantee his safety. In explaining Mulele's trial and subsequent execution, Mobutu stated that the pardons applied only to political prisoners and not to war criminals.

Earlier in the year Mobutu had achieved what ap-

peared to be a limited success in external affairs when, on April 2, he and the presidents of Chad and the Central African Republic signed the charter of the Union of Central African States. By the provisions of the charter the three nations agreed to a common market and, to promote this aim, stated that they would endeavour to harmonize their plans for development, industrialization, transport, and communications. There was also provision for mutual military assistance in the event of foreign aggression. It was decided that Mobutu would be president.

The strength of the union lay in its practical attempt to improve the economic development prospects of the countries involved rather than endeavouring to achieve the more difficult goal of political union. Its shortcomings lay in the failure to extend its scope, as Mobutu had hoped, to include other neighbouring states and in the fear of some of those states that the new group would undermine the Central African Customs and Economic Union, of which Chad and the Central African Republic were formerly members. Nor was the development of the new association helped by conflicting rumours of, on the one hand, French displeasure at a possible threat to France's influence over Chad and the Central African Republic and, on the other, French or even U.S. approval in the hope of extending foreign control over the economy of tropical Africa. Late in the year a dispute between the Congo and the Central African Republic over the latter's failure to pay for equipment sold to it by the Congo led to a series of retaliatory moves by the two countries, culminating in the action by Mobutu barring all flights of Air Afrique from Congolese airspace. The Central African Republic thereupon withdrew from the union, effectively killing it and leaving Mobutu more isolated than ever from the French-speaking African states.   (K. I.)

CONGO, DEMOCRATIC REPUBLIC OF THE
Education. (1964–65) Primary, pupils 1,592,225; teachers 43,499; secondary, pupils 52,309, teachers (1962–63) 1,875; vocational, pupils 17,334, teachers (1962–63) 863; teacher training, students 19,248, teachers (1962–63) 943; higher (including 3 universities), students 3,136, teaching staff 443.
Finance. Monetary unit: zaire, with an official exchange rate of 0.50 zaires to U.S. $1 (1.20 zaires = £1 sterling). Gold and foreign exchange, central bank: (March 1968) U.S. $93,240,000; (March 1967) U.S. $20,170,000. Budget (1967 est.) balanced at 59.9 million zaires.
Foreign Trade. (1966) Imports 168.2 million zaires; exports 232.4 million zaires. Import sources: Belgium-Luxembourg 34%; U.S. 22%; West Germany 5%. Export destinations: Belgium-Luxembourg 25%; Italy 10%; France 8%; U.K. 6%. Main exports: copper 57%; tin 6%; diamonds 6%; coffee 6%.
Transport and Communications. Roads (1962) 147,000 km. Motor vehicles in use (1964): passenger 42,500; commercial (including buses) 32,900. Railways: (1964) 5,164 km.; traffic (1966) 532 million passenger-km., freight 1,969,000,000 net ton-km. Waterways (1965) 13,744 km. (including Congo River). Telephones (Jan. 1967) c. 21,000. Radio receivers (Dec. 1964) c. 200,000.
Agriculture. Production (in 000; metric tons; 1966; 1965 in parentheses): palm oil c. 168 (c. 162); palm kernels c. 102 (c. 96); rubber, exports 28 (21); cotton, lint c. 8 (c. 7); coffee c. 57 (c. 60); peanuts c. 112 (c. 112); rice 122 (109); corn c. 241 (c. 237); sweet potatoes and yams c. 306 (c. 298); cassava 8,116 (7,247); sugar, raw (1967–68) 34, (1966–67) 32; timber (1964) c. 10,900 cu.m., (1963) c. 11.000 cu.m. Livestock (in 000; Dec. 1965): cattle c. 1,230; sheep c. 701; goats c. 2,409; pigs c. 395.
Industry. Production (in 000; metric tons; 1966): copper 156; coal (1967) 116; zinc 61; tin (1967) 1.8; cobalt ore (metal content) 11.3; manganese ore (metal content) 119; gold 159 troy oz.; diamonds 12,432 metric carats.

Congo, Republic of

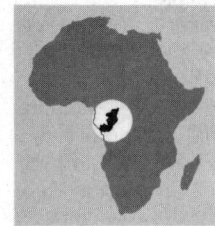

A republic of equatorial Africa, the Congo Republic is bounded by Gabon, Cameroon, the Central African Republic, the Congo (Kinshasa), Angola, and the Atlantic Ocean. Area: 134,749 sq.mi. (349,000 sq.km.). Pop. (1966 est.): 850,000, mainly Bantu Negroes; Europeans 11,000. Cap. and largest city: Brazzaville (pop., 1962 est., 135,632). Language: French and Bantu dialects. Religion: mostly pagan, with a strong Christian minority. President to Sept. 4, 1968, Alphonse Massamba-Debat; premier to January 12, Ambroise Noumazalay; premier from August 21 and interim president from September 5, Alfred Raoul.

In a government reshuffle on January 12, President Massamba-Debat eliminated the post of premier and excluded Premier Ambroise Noumazalay from Cabinet responsibility. On January 17, in a radio and television broadcast, he combined an explanation that in his view the post was superfluous with a warning that elements within his regime were trying to subvert the Army, the youth movement, and the police in order to bring down the government.

Massamba-Debat in May attended the fourth East and Central African summit conference at Dar es Salaam, Tanzania. During his absence, an attempted coup took place and failed. It was allegedly inspired by "high finance and international reaction, and led by a European."

On July 22, in an attempt to counteract extreme left-wing activity, the president invited anyone with presidential ambitions to come forward, but there was no response. On July 31, however, Cuban-trained Civic Guards attempted to blockade Brazzaville despite massive opposition by Congolese workers who marched to the town hall shouting their support for the president. Later, joined by members of the only political party, the National Movement for the Revolution (MNR), the Civic Guards called for the dissolution of Parliament, the suspension of the party's

Central Committee and Political Bureau, and the establishment of a revolutionary council under Massamba-Debat.

Following these disturbances, on August 1 the president dissolved the National Assembly, suspended the activities of the Political Bureau, and announced that until new elections were held he would rule personally by decree. Four days later he released the names of the members of a new Cabinet and announced the creation of a National Council of the Revolution (CNR). The situation at the time was confused, with the president apparently protected by the Army. On August 17, however, Radio Brazzaville announced the diminution of certain presidential responsibilities, and this was followed on August 21 by the appointment of Army Capt. Alfred Raoul to the position of premier of the provisional government. Raoul, together with Capt. Marien Ngouabi, principal instigator of the coup and president of the Bureau of the CNR, took over the dual responsibilities of government. Fighting followed between the Army and the Civic Guards (recruited from the Marxist youth league of the MNR), and on August 30 a state of siege was declared in Brazzaville. On September 4 the resignation of Massamba-Debat was announced, and the following day Raoul assumed the office of interim president.   (PH. D.; X.)

Conservation

The year 1968 was marked by the growing realization that man is a creature capable of fouling his own environment. The David Davies Memorial Institute of International Studies, London, issued a bulletin entitled *Principles Governing Certain Changes in the Environment of Man,* which detailed the activities of 45 international organizations that play a part in safeguarding the surroundings on which we all depend for survival.

Cecil H. Wadleigh, director of the Soil and Water Conservation Research Division, U.S. Agricultural Research Service, published a comprehensive survey entitled *Wastes in Relation to Agriculture and Forestry.* Agriculture and forestry produce their own wastes and are also affected by the waste products of industry and urban life. Research was under way into all aspects of these problems, from the origin of the waste substance through its effects on crops and livestock to its ultimate disposal.

Waste products of industry and commerce continued to pollute the air at alarming rates. Sulfur dioxide, present in the fumes from burning coal and hydrocarbon oils, built up to damaging concentrations even where the emission of "black smoke," holding carbon particles, was checked by clean-air laws. In England the Forestry Commission was obliged to cut back, to an experimental scale, its conifer afforestation in the industrial zones of Lancashire and Yorkshire because sulfur dioxide stunted all tree species tried.

Airborne dusts arising from soil erosion formed a major waste, damaging both the land where they originated and that on which they fell. They could travel great distances—a freak storm on July 1, 1968, deposited red sand from the Sahara Desert on the roofs of houses and cars over a large area around London. Another exceptional storm on March 17 turned the fertile eastern counties of England into a short-lived but costly dust bowl. After weeks of dry

Congregational
Churches:
see Religion

CONGO, REPUBLIC OF
Education. (1965–66) Primary, pupils 186,544, teachers 3,115; secondary, pupils 12,778, teachers 460; vocational, pupils 2,755, teachers 132; teacher training, students 486; higher, students 840, teaching staff 84.
   Finance. Monetary unit: CFA franc, with a parity of CFA Fr. 50 to the French franc (CFA Fr. 246.85 = U.S. $1; CFA Fr. 592.45 = £1 sterling). Budget (1968 est.) balanced at CFA Fr. 13,260,000,000.
   Foreign Trade. (1967) Imports CFA Fr. 20,240,-000,000; exports CFA Fr. 11,730,000,000. Import sources: France 54%; West Germany 13%. Export destinations: Netherlands 21%; West Germany 18%; U.K. 16%; France 15%; Israel 5%; Congo (Kinshasa) 5%. Main exports: timber 42%; diamonds 34%.
   Transport and Communications. Roads (1965) 10,842 km. (including 243 km. with improved surface). Motor vehicles in use (1965): passenger 9,028; commercial 6,830. Railways: (1966) 785 km.; traffic 117 million passenger-km., freight 351 million net ton-km. Telephones (Dec. 1966) 8,467. Radio receivers (Dec. 1960) 11,000. Television receivers (Dec. 1966) 500.
   Agriculture. Production (in 000; metric tons; 1966; 1965 in parentheses): cassava *c.* 700 (*c.* 700); coffee *c.* 0.8 (*c.* 0.8); peanuts *c.* 11 (*c.* 11); palm kernels 6 (5.6); palm oil *c.* 7.1 (*c.* 7.1). Livestock (in 000; 1965–66): cattle 28; sheep *c.* 54; pigs 35.

weather, an easterly wind removed both topsoil and newly sown seed from thousands of acres. The blown soil filled drainage ditches in the treeless Fens, and they had to be reexcavated at great expense. Both Soviet and U.S. investigators believed that windbreak plantings provided the best long-term solution.

Waterborne sediments made up the most serious form of waste, however. The loss was twofold—valuable topsoil was carried away by storm water, and rivers were silted up, causing floods. The total amount of sediment produced annually in the U.S. was estimated at four billion tons. One quarter of this reached the oceans, while three-quarters remained in floodplains and watercourses.

Land and Forests. C. P. Bhimaya and R. N. Kaul, writing on "Land Use in the Arid Zone of Rajasthan" for the ninth Commonwealth Forestry Conference, held in India in January, presented an alarming picture of the imbalance of natural equilibrium resulting from population pressures in the semidesert regions of western India. They reported that large-scale cereal farming on natural grasslands had brought about major changes in the vegetation cover. Recurrent cultivation, without conservation methods, of submarginal lands formerly cropped only once in five years, together with overgrazing and wood removal, was causing massive deterioration of resources. Around such cities as Jodhpur and Bikaner there were wide belts from which fuel gatherers had removed every stick of woody vegetation. In an area where rainfall is as low as four inches a year, the raising of cereal crops depends heavily on dewfall. Dust from bare soil reduces this, because it alters the daily rhythm of rise and fall in air temperature. With less dew, still less grass grows and more dust enters the atmosphere, intensifying the problem. Conservation methods advocated by the authors included contour plowing, the raising of grain crops amid high stubble of the previous crop, the sowing of improved crop varieties, and the planting of windbreaks.

In Vietnam, U.S. experts in scientific warfare used chemical defoliation on a massive scale to harass Viet Cong and North Vietnamese raiders. During 1968 an estimated 1.5 million ac. were treated, at a cost of $500 million. Though effective, defoliation created major conservation problems. Grass and weeds returned within six months of treatment, but forest trees were killed outright and fish were poisoned in polluted streams. A major task when peace returned would be the replanting of the destroyed woodlands. Most had been poor and commercially unproductive, and an opportunity would arise for replacement by high-yielding timber crops.

Japan emerged as a major operator on the world timber scene. Purchases of softwood timber were made in western North America on a scale that caused the U.S. authorities to ban further sales of round logs from national forests in order to safeguard the domestic sawmilling industry. Japan also drew heavily on the Siberian coniferous forests, through trade agreements with the U.S.S.R., and stepped up traditional imports of tropical hardwoods from the Philippines, Indonesia, and Malaysia. To help feed expanding wood-using industries, the management of Japan's indigenous forests was intensified. These forests cover 70% of the land area and, because of Japan's mountainous character, they are vital for the conservation of soil and water supplies. Past neglect had left 750,000 ac. of landslips and bare land, each losing around 200 cu.yd. of soil and sand a year. Erosion control projects began with the terracing of affected hillsides, followed by the planting of timber trees to establish permanent protective cover.

In a special issue of the *Allgemeine Forstzeitung,* April 1968, Austrian foresters reported extraordinary engineering works designed to conserve alpine soils and water supplies. These works were needed in order to prevent avalanche damage to valley lands, as well as to check normal water erosion of torrents coursing down steep slopes after summer storms. Concrete, masonry, steel, and timber were all employed to hold watercourses firmly in place, and complex mathematics were applied to rates of streamflow, silt deposition, and strength of foundations. The main protective measure, however, continued to be the maintenance of tree cover on steep hillsides vulnerable to erosion. Trees break the impact of rain, regulate downflow by holding moisture in the surface layers of the soil, delay snowmelt in the spring, and resist all but the worst avalanches.

Scottish foresters faced a major conservation problem following the hurricane that swept across the Central Lowlands on the night of Jan. 16, 1968. The storm affected a belt of country 50 mi. wide and brought down 50 million cu.ft. of timber. This could be harvested, but it was equivalent to two years' normal felling for the whole country, all thrown on the market in one night. Reorganization of felling plans and expansion of industrial intake, with accelerated exports to England, were begun promptly. A dramatic feature of this gale was the collapse of sturdy oaks and other broad-leaved trees that had braved the winds for 200 years in fully exposed situations.

Reports to the ninth Commonwealth Forestry Conference showed that hurricane and cyclone damage was something that must be considered in every for-

Serpentine gashes and mounds of rubble left by strip miners in the Cumberland Mountains of eastern Kentucky. Mining operations for coal lying near the surface destroyed forests and small farms.

ester's conservation plans, rather than regarded as an exceptional act of God. N. R. Brouard of Mauritius, which lies near the main Indian Ocean cyclone tracks, reported that every plantation that grew for 20 years would experience at least one violent storm. Economic damage could be restricted by planting quick-growing trees, such as tropical pines and *Eucalyptus robusta*, which yield useful timber on a 20-year rotation. Such crops suffer little harm during their younger, flexible stages, and a premature blowing down a few years before maturity causes relatively slight losses. From British Honduras, S. Lindo reported 15 hurricanes between 1787 and 1961, averaging one every 13 years. As a result, timber harvesting tended to take place wherever the last storm had struck, rather than in the best place for sustained forest management. The quick growth of the native Caribbean pine lessens economic loss, but the slower-maturing mahogany, the country's most valuable hardwood for export, suffers severely.

Reviewing fire-prevention measures throughout Canada, W. T. Foster, supervisor of the Forest Protection Section of the Ontario Department of Lands and Forests, reported that Canada still loses 1 million ac. each year, out of 900 million ac. at risk, through uncontrolled forest fires. This amounts to over 0.1% of a crop that takes 100 years to mature, and wastes 10% of all effective growth. The forest was being exposed to ever increasing risk by the rapidly developing use of forest lands for recreation, but on the credit side there was a welcome growth of support for fire-prevention programs.

Aircraft had become the major weapon in the fire fighter's armoury. Across North America they were gradually superseding lookout towers for rapid detection of outbreaks. They need only fly when hazards are high and can quickly move closer to any suspicious source of smoke, which a tower-based observer cannot do. Trials with the infrared sensing of heat from forest fires too remote for ordinary visibility proved promising.

"Water bombing"—the release of large quantities of water from the air onto the advancing front of a forest fire—was being developed rapidly. In 1968 there were 150 aircraft in Canada equipped for this purpose, carrying loads of from 100 to 6,000 imperial gallons of water. Small aircraft with capacities of 600 gal. were proving very effective in situations where they could make repeated short trips from a lake to the fire, dropping each load where it was most needed. Specially equipped Otter float planes could load water without landing; they skimmed the surface of the lakes, using a pickup probe to drive water into their pontoons, which were designed for quick release of the load.

The publication in 1968 of an English translation of *Fundamentals of Forest Biogeocoenology* brought to the West a new insight into Soviet conservation activities. Written by two Soviet ecologists, V. Sukachev and N. Dylis, this comprehensive study set forth the viewpoint that every natural community results from the interaction of natural and biological forces. The Soviet Union had 2,700,000,000 ac., or half its territory, under forest and had 75,000,000,000 cu.m. of standing timber, or 40% of the world's resources. Despite these vast reserves, the U.S.S.R. found it necessary, in 1968, to draft a new forest law, making it clear that forests cannot be regarded merely as a source of wood to the detriment of the country's land and rivers. The national reafforestation program was

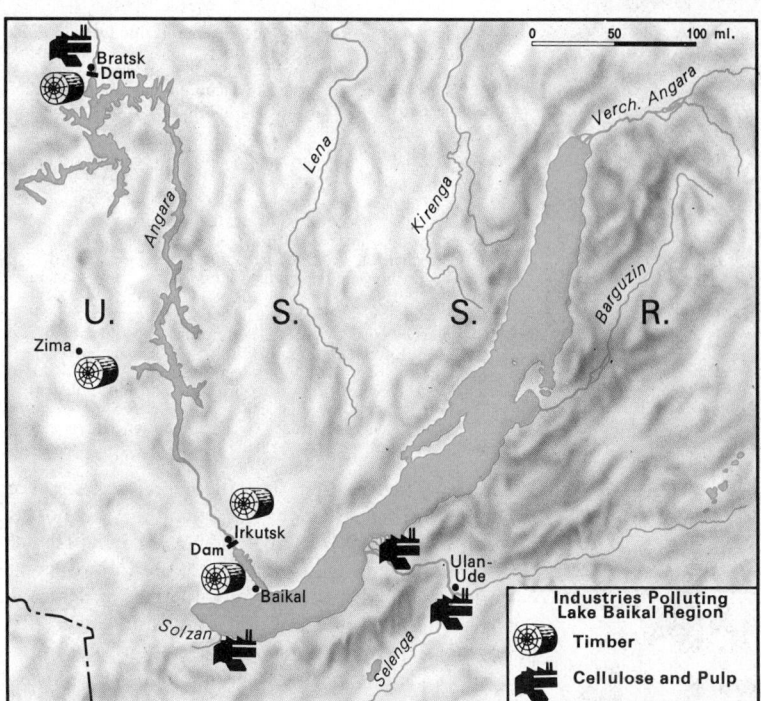

Several industrial complexes are producing waste products which conservationists fear will destroy the unique plant and animal life in Lake Baikal, the world's largest body of fresh water by volume. Purification facilities included in the complexes proved to be defective in design and inadequate in capacity. As a result, 2.5 million rubles was allocated to build additional sedimentation pools.

expanded to 5.2 million ac., but logging removed 7.5 million ac., usually of the best and most accessible timber stands.

The Soviets regarded two long tons per acre (dry weight) as a high figure for spruce forests, but on the western seaboard of North America and in the west of Britain, twice that productivity was recorded for the Alaskan Sitka spruce, *Picea sitchensis*. In this context, it was not surprising that the British Forestry Commission restricted still further its planting of relatively slow-growing European conifers, including the Norway spruce, *Picea abies*. Two-thirds of its planting in 1968 was done with "Pacific-slope" conifers from Oregon and British Columbia, notably Sitka spruce, lodgepole pine, Douglas fir, western hemlock, and western red cedar.

In New Zealand, A. L. Poole, director general of the Forest Service, outlined similar differences between the yields of contrasting types of forest. Native rimu, *Dacrydium undulatum*, yields only half a ton of timber per acre each year, and the southern beeches, *Nothofagus* species, only one ton. On the other hand, Monterey pine, *Pinus radiata*, introduced from California, will give five tons (dry weight) of timber per year indefinitely. Nevertheless, for scientific and scenic reasons it was considered imperative to conserve substantial areas of indigenous New Zealand forests, despite their low economic return.

(H. L. EN.)

Water. The European Information Centre for Nature Conservation published a simple but convincing *European Water Charter,* which merits quotation in its entirety:

1. There is no life without water. It is a treasure indispensable to all human activity.
2. Water resources are not inexhaustible. It is essential to conserve, control, and wherever possible, to increase them.
3. To pollute water is to harm man and other living creatures which are dependent on water.

Esso scientist sprays a beach with Corexit, a new product developed to disperse seaborne oil slicks and clean oil-fouled beaches without harming marine life.

4. The quality of water must be maintained at levels suitable for the use to be made of it and, in particular, must meet appropriate public health standards.

5. When water is returned to a common source it must not impair further uses, both public and private, to which the common source will be put.

6. The maintenance of an adequate vegetation cover, preferably forest land, is imperative for the conservation of water resources.

7. Water resources must be assessed.

8. The wise husbandry of water resources must be planned by appropriate authorities.

9. Conservation of water calls for intensified scientific research, training of specialists and public information services.

10. Water is a common heritage, the values of which must be recognized by all. Everyone has the duty to use water carefully and economically.

11. The management of water resources should be based on their natural basins rather than on political and administrative boundaries.

12. Water knows no frontiers; as a common resource it demands international cooperation.

In 1968, for the first time in several years, there were no deficiencies in winter runoff in the northeastern U.S., except on a small portion of Long Island. Precipitation and runoff elsewhere in the U.S. resumed a normal checkerboard pattern, with areas of deficient or below normal water supplies about in balance with areas of above normal supply. Heavy winter rains caused flooding in parts of the mountain states. Excessive precipitation and runoff in the Atlantic provinces and the eastern Great Lakes region of Canada during the first part of the year was followed by drought during the summer. Elsewhere in the Western Hemisphere, severe drought was experienced in western South America. The driest winter in more than 100 years was recorded in Chile, and lack of snow in the high Andes suggested that drought conditions would continue. The drought in Australia eased somewhat in 1968, and inhabitants of that continent were cheered by the discovery of vast reserves of groundwater in the desert heart of the country.

Seasonal fluctuations in groundwater levels in the U.S. were reaching greater magnitude, in line with the increased use of groundwater for new water supplies as well as to supplement existing surface supplies. Studies by the U.S. Geological Survey showed that 8,100,000,000 gal. a day, or more than one-third of total public water supplies in the U.S., were obtained from groundwater sources. Overuse of groundwater in several parts of the country, notably central Arizona, the San Joaquin Valley in California, and the high plains of the Texas Panhandle, had led to drastic lowering of the water table. The high and increasing cost of pumping would eventually lead to a decline in the agricultural economy of those areas unless surface water supplies were developed.

One effort along this line led to authorization of the Central Arizona Project in September 1968, climaxing a 20-year struggle in Congress. The project provided for pumping and conveying water from Lake Havasu on the Colorado River to the vicinity of Phoenix and Tucson, Ariz., together with construction of a large number of ancillary water-control projects and structures that would cost over $1.3 billion. The authorizing legislation guaranteed California the use of 4.4 million ac-ft. of water from the Colorado in perpetuity. A ten-year moratorium was placed on studies of any plan to import water into the Colorado basin, largely to protect the Columbia River basin states. Further dams on the Colorado between Hoover Dam and Glen Canyon Dam were also prohibited, a stricture that was hailed as a major victory by conservationists who had opposed the construction of Bridge Canyon and Marble Canyon dams in the Grand Canyon.

While progress continued on the huge California water project, which would bring relief to southern California by importing water supplies from the northern part of the state, hopes for a breakthrough into an economical means of desalting ocean water were dashed by a 70% increase in the estimated cost of the huge combined nuclear power plant and 150 million-gal.-per-day desalting project being planned for construction on an island off the coast. With the cost now estimated at $765 million, the consortium of power companies and the Los Angeles Department of Water and Power, which had agreed to finance the power costs, decided that the project could not be economically developed. The secretary of the interior and the chairman of the Atomic Energy Commission called for a restudy of the project.

Legislation creating a National Water Commission was signed by Pres. Lyndon B. Johnson late in September. The new seven-man commission would be given five years to review present and anticipated water resources problems, consider the economic and social consequences of water resources development, and make recommendations on these and other water resources matters.

In Scotland, work began on the Loch Lomond Barrage Scheme, designed to use the largest lake in Great Britain as a reservoir for drinking water. In its unregulated state, the water level of the loch fluctuates between 23 ft. above sea level in summer and 31 ft. in winter. A short barrage across the River Leven, the loch's outlet to the Clyde estuary, would stabilize the level at 26 ft., regulating outflow all year round. This would provide, at low cost, 100 million gal. of water daily, to be pumped to the rapidly developing, water-hungry Central Scottish Lowlands.

Hungary produced a comprehensive survey of its water resources and their utilization, which approached 80% of the potential. Hungary's situation was uniquely difficult because its great rivers rise beyond its frontiers—the Danube in Germany, the Tisza in the U.S.S.R., and the Drava in Austria—while the whole country is virtually a landlocked plain with low rainfall. Control measures included 4,000 km. of flood prevention embankments, mainly along the Danube, with a further 400 km. under construction. To provide irrigation, 100 reservoirs had been built, holding 54 million cu.m., and 50 more were planned.

Soviet experts, equipment, and finance were being directed toward construction of the Al Tabqa Dam across the Euphrates River in northern Syria. The completed dam would provide irrigation water for 1.5 million ac. of land, supporting 60,000 families, and 800,000 kw. of hydroelectric power. International complications arose because the Turks planned to harness the Euphrates with their Keban Dam upstream on Turkish territory, while the Iraqis wished to control this same river with their El Hadithah Barrage downstream in mid-Iraq.

Progress was made on planning the great Tonle Sap Dam in the Mekong River delta. The Mekong, which flows down from Laos and Thailand, ends in a huge delta that lies partly in Cambodia and partly in South Vietnam. Monsoon rains cause annual floods in both countries, but these are relieved by a reversible flow in and out of a great natural reservoir called the Grand Lac. The object of the dam would be to delay the filling of the Grand Lac until the delta floods approached a critical level, then to fill it rapidly and so lower the flood peak. Once the lake was filled, water would be stored until needed for dry-season irrigation.

A mathematical simulation study at the Société Grenobloise d'Études et d'Applications Hydrauliques of Grenoble, France, showed that a dam only 600 m. long, costing only £5.5 million, would regulate a river carrying 450,000,000,000 cu.m. a year over a delta area of 50,000 sq.km.

The largest dam construction contract ever reported, for $623 million, was awarded in March to a group of French and Italian contractors for construction of the Tarbela Dam on the Indus River, 40 mi. NW of Rawalpindi in West Pakistan. The project was being financed through a development fund set up with contributions from the World Bank and nine Western industrial nations. It would cost about $827 million and, together with the huge Mangla Dam which was completed in November 1967, would form a part of the works required to implement the Indus Waters Treaty of 1960.

In British Columbia the Peace River was harnessed by the closing of the 6,700-ft.-long Bennett (Portage Mountain) Dam, and began to form a reservoir covering 640 sq.mi. The Peace River flows north to the Arctic, and it was estimated that approximately one-third of the world's total supply of fresh water was held in Canada's cold northern wastes. Diversion of

stretching from the Urals to the Altai Mountains and from western Siberia to the Tien Shan Range. In Italy the government approved a law banning all spring hunting and trapping of wild birds. In France there were public outcries against the netting of wild birds, which had reached a huge annual total in the *départements* of Gironde, Landes, and Basses-Pyrénées.

In Ceylon the Fauna Preservation Society and the World Wildlife Fund combined to give a Land Rover to the local Wildlife Protection Society, to be used in the Smithsonian Institution's ecological survey of the Ceylon elephant. A new wildcat was discovered in the Ryukyu Islands; it was named *Mayailurus iriomotensis* and given legal protection.

In January a group of eight scientists from four countries bordering the Arctic Ocean—the U.S.S.R., the U.S., Canada, and Norway—met at the International Union for Conservation of Nature and Natural Resources (IUCN) at Morges, Switz., to consider conservation of the polar bear. A polar bear research group was formed within the Survival Service Commission, IUCN, under the chairmanship of S. M. Uspensky of the U.S.S.R. The number of wild reindeer in the Kola Peninsula, U.S.S.R., was reported to have increased to 20,000 from about 100 in the 1930s.

A black rhinoceros calf, a species threatened with extinction, flees Kenyan game department workers who are moving the rhinos to protected areas. The conservation project was directed by John King of Cambridge University.

northern waters to the prairie provinces or even to the Midwestern U.S. was seriously considered.

Adaptation of an old and well-known concept into a new method for obtaining fresh water from moist tropical air was advanced by Columbia University scientists at the annual meeting of the National Research Council in Washington, D.C. The plan, which could be placed into effect under conditions such as those found in the Virgin Islands, would involve pumping water from ocean depths of 3,000 ft. or more, where water temperatures are near freezing, through a giant condenser located in the path of the trade winds. Some 90 million gal. of water per day would have to be moved through the condenser to produce about 1 million gal. per day of fresh water. Costs of such a project had not been estimated, but there was speculation that it might be cheaper than existing desalting techniques. (T. M. Sc.; H. L. En.)

Wildlife. In June the Royal Society for the Protection of Birds started its plan to reintroduce the sea eagle into Scotland by moving four young eagles from Norway to Fair Isle. In *Acta Theriologica*, vol. xii, no. 1–3, the Swedish zoologist Kai Curry-Lindahl described how the beaver, which had become extinct in Sweden about 1871 but had been reintroduced from Norway, had built up a thriving population. Its numbers had also greatly increased in the U.S.S.R.

To protect migratory birds nesting in northern Siberia, the U.S.S.R. prohibited temporarily the capture and killing of all birds throughout Kazakhstan,

In March the U.S. Bureau of Sport Fisheries and Wildlife issued a list of wildlife imported into the United States in 1967, including 74,304 mammals (62,526 of them primates) and 203,189 wild birds. This was the first attempt by a major importer to keep records of all animal importations. In July the British committee of the Animals Restriction of Importation Act, 1964, issued its summary of statistics for 1967. Though giving much greater detail than the U.S. statistics, the summary was concerned only with families of mammals and reptiles containing endangered species. In Alaska the use of poison for predator control was made illegal and the payment of bounties for predators was restricted.

In Canada the use of the snowmobile or skidoo, prohibited for hunting in Canada and the U.S., became a menace to wildlife, mainly because of the disturbance it caused. The barren-ground caribou, which had decreased to about 279,000 in 1955 from about 1,750,000 in 1900, had increased to some 350,000 by 1968 (A. W. F. Banfield, "The Plight of the Barren-Ground Caribou," *Oryx*, vol. iv, no. 1). In the joint U.S.-Canadian whooping crane survival project, 10 chicks were successfully reared, making a captive flock of 15 and bringing the world total of whooping cranes to 63.

At the regional conference of the IUCN held in Argentina in March, the mass destruction of bats in Central America was discussed. Their roosting places had been dynamited in an attempt to eliminate vam-

pire bats, which were carriers of rabies, and these indiscriminate—and largely ineffectual—measures had resulted in the destruction of many harmless and/or useful bats, as well as of more than 700 caves in Brazil and the beautiful Chilibrillo Caves in Panama. At the International Council for Bird Preservation (ICBP) meeting in Venezuela, C. Lehman said that one shipment from Colombia to New York contained 28,000 wild birds and that ten times that many died before shipment.

Following the establishment of the Pampas Galeras Reserve for the vicuña in 1967, the Peruvian government set aside the basin of the Río Manú as a reserved area, within which the Manú National Park would be defined. Though threatened by hunters and timbermen, who had devastated the wildlife along the neighbouring rivers, the area still abounded in animals. A grant of $2,400 toward this project was made jointly by the World Wildlife Fund and the Fauna Preservation Society.

An investigation by Hugh Cott, completed in April, confirmed fears for the preservation of the Nile crocodile in the Murchison Falls National Park, Uganda, and its probable extinction in many other parts of Africa. Poaching for skins and disturbance by visitors during the breeding season deprived the young crocodiles of the maternal care essential to protect them from predators. Cott's recommendations included the establishment of a closed season against river launches and a reduction in the number of baboons, monitors, and maribou storks.

In Australia, following the rediscovery in May 1967 of the dibbler, *Antechinus apicalis*, a carnivorous marsupial which had not been seen for 83 years, another "extinct" mammal, the New Holland mouse, *Pseudomys novaehollandiae*, was found living in Kuring-gai Chase National Park, New South Wales, and to be abundant at Port Stephens within 25 mi. of the industrial city of Newcastle. H. J. Frith, chief of the Commonwealth Scientific and Industrial Research Organization, demonstrated that kangaroos help the sheep farmer by eating grasses unpalatable to sheep and increasing the land's protein potential without damaging the range.   (C. L. BE.)

See also Arctic Regions; Biological Sciences; Disasters; Engineering Projects; Fuel and Power; Historic Buildings; Medicine; Mining; Parks; Timber.

ENCYCLOPÆDIA BRITANNICA FILMS. *Nature's Plan* (1953); *Look to the Land* (1954); *Succession—From Sand Dune to Forest* (1960); *The Cave Community* (1961); *The High Arctic Biome* (1961); *The Community* (1962); *The Grasslands* (1962); *The Temperate Deciduous Forest* (1962); *The Tropical Rain Forest* (1962); *What Is Ecology?* (1962); *The Pond and the City* (1964); *The House of Man: Our Changing Environment* (1965); *Waterfowl: A Resource in Danger* (1965); *Trees and Their Importance* (1966); *Water for Living Things* (1967); *The Everglades: Conserving a Balanced Community* (1968); *Problems of Conservation—Air* (1968).

Consumer Expenditures

Following the marked slowdown in the rate of growth of consumer spending in many countries in 1967, a sharp recovery took place in 1968. Consumer spending changed direction in different ways during the course of the year, however. Spending was buoyant, if not excessive, in both the U.S. and the U.K. in the first part of the year, whereas in West Germany and France it was sluggish. By the end of the year these roles had been exactly reversed.

The Western world's personal spending on consumer goods and services rose by around 7% in cur-

Construction Industry:
see Engineering
  Projects; Housing;
  Industrial Review

Consumer Credit:
see Money and
  Banking

rent prices in 1968, and by more than $3\frac{1}{2}\%$ in volume. This rate of growth matched the long-run average of recent years and was remarkable when viewed against the background of a difficult international monetary situation. The severe balance of payments problems of both the U.S. and the U.K. might have been expected to result in restrictions that would damp down demand and lead to a slowdown in world trade. The worst fears were certainly not fulfilled and, although the shortage of world liquidity grew more acute, personal incomes and spending in most countries continued to expand.

The slowdown in spending on consumer goods that lasted from mid-1966 to mid-1967 was due in large measure to a fall in the sales of motor vehicles in the U.S., West Germany, and the U.K. Recovery began in the second half of 1967 and was particularly strong in the U.S. and the U.K. In the U.S. inflationary conditions began to develop during 1967, and to counter this situation the administration sought a tax increase. Congress, however, deferred action on the president's request until June 1968. Thus for the first half of 1968 personal incomes and spending rose rapidly. Moreover, although a slackening of the rate of growth was apparent in the second half of the year, by that time an expansionary monetary policy was tending to offset the potential effects of both the tax increase and the cuts in government spending. The secondary effects of these developments in the U.S. were a rapid rise in American imports, a strong increase in other countries' exports, a good recovery in world trade, and a revival in internal consumer spending.

Another major influence stemmed from the British devaluation of November 1967. Although the purpose of devaluation was to damp down imports and to expand British exports through improved price competitiveness, little effort was made to restrict U.K. home demand until March 1968. Forewarned of the impending cutbacks, consumers increased their spending at an annual rate of 9% in the last quarter of 1967 and the first quarter of 1968. Indeed, in the early months of 1968 British consumer spending rose at an annual rate of more than 12% in volume and 14% in value. This spurt in Britain's consumer spending contributed to the rise in world trade through a large increase in U.K. imports. The subsequent cutback in British de-

Table I. Consumer Expenditure, 1967 and 1968

| Region | Percent change over previous year | | | |
| | In current prices | | In fixed prices | |
	1967	1968	1967	1968
EEC	+4	+6	+1½	+3½
North America	+6	+8	+3	+4
Other OECD countries	+6	+7	+2½	+3

Table II. Consumer Expenditure in OECD Countries, 1966

Item	Percent	Percent increase over previous year
Food	25.3	7.8
Clothing	10.2	9.3
Rent	12.1	7.6
Durables	10.5	5.2
Other	41.9	8.6
Total	100.0	8.0

Table III. Expenditure on Various Consumer Items as a Proportion of Total Consumer Expenditure, 1966

| Region | In percent | | | |
	Food	Clothing	Rent	Durables
EEC	32.2	11.4	9.1	9.9
North America	19.8	9.2	14.4	11.9
Other OECD (Europe)	30.4	10.9	9.7	8.7

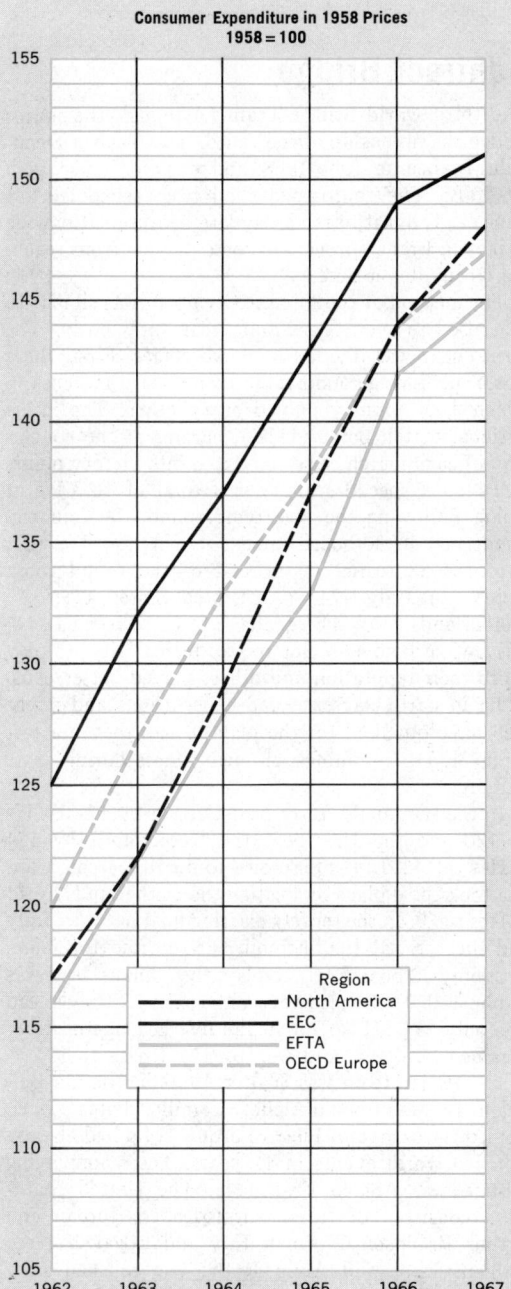

Consumer Expenditure in 1958 Prices
1958 = 100

Region
- North America
- EEC
- EFTA
- OECD Europe

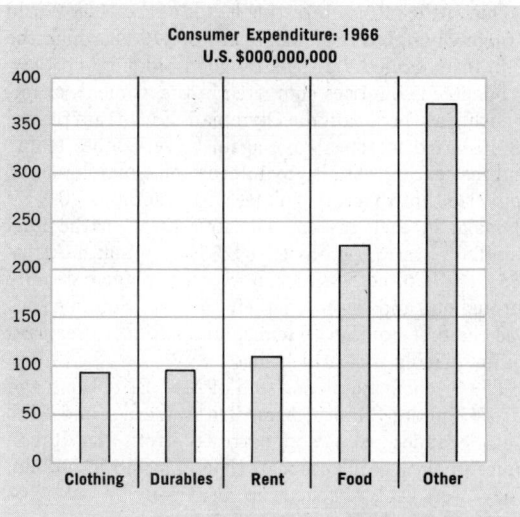

Consumer Expenditure: 1966
U.S. $000,000,000

Clothing | Durables | Rent | Food | Other

mand, however, occurred at a time when other countries were beginning to expand demand more forcibly. West Germany and Japan in particular exerted an important influence on activity and demand.

In addition, the disturbances in France contributed to the change in trend. The riots and strikes in the late spring disrupted output and retarded consumer spending, but the resulting concessions and very substantial increase in wage rates led to greater spending, an increased rate of growth of output, and an exceptional rate of growth in incomes and prices. These influences could be seen in the enhanced value of retail sales later in the year; it was expected, however, that this process would be reversed by the imposition of the austerity program following the international monetary crisis in November. During 1968 Italy experienced continued good growth in output, incomes, and consumer spending. Consumer spending in real terms increased by nearly 4% while prices rose by less than the world average.

Since a number of other countries devalued at the same time as the U.K., prices rose unevenly around the world. Devaluation inevitably leads to price rises, and the rate of price inflation in the countries that devalued was greater than elsewhere. North America, by contrast, experienced a substantial price increase without devaluation, and it was surprising to find consumer prices rising faster in the U.S. than in Britain in the first part of 1968.

The revival in growth of output in the industrialized nations in 1967–68 benefited the primary producing countries. Although commodity prices on the average were largely unchanged, experience was mixed. Sugar prices were extremely poor, whereas cocoa prices rose sharply. On balance, however, the primary producing areas enjoyed a more profitable year, and this began to show in higher levels of incomes and spending toward the year's end. Australia had a boom year, South Africa showed a good increase in consumer spending, and New Zealand recovered from its poor balance of payments position. India experienced a timely and much needed improvement in agricultural output. The Indian subcontinent produced record grain crops in 1968, partly because of favourable weather conditions but also because of the introduction of improved, high-yield varieties. Consumer spending rose as a result of the good harvests and higher farm incomes.

A substantial rise in spending was also recorded in the U.S.S.R. and Eastern Europe. It was not certain to what extent the invasion by Warsaw Pact troops in August and the subsequent occupation interfered with output and spending in Czechoslovakia. Any repercussions in terms of higher defense spending in various countries as a result of increased international tensions were unlikely to be reflected in higher production and spending until 1969.

Comparisons between countries were still difficult to make in view of the inadequacies of official statistics. Some countries do not estimate consumer spending. In others there are serious delays in reporting and differences in timing. Only in a handful of countries are the figures produced for quarterly intervals with a time lag of three to six months. In the majority of cases only annual statistics are available, and only long after the fact.

Reasonably complete data for 1966 and provisional figures for 1967 were available. In Table I the increase in consumer spending is given in both fixed and current prices for 1967 and 1968 for the major coun-

try groupings. The improvement of 1968 compared with 1967 was common to all groupings, but it is striking that the highest rates of growth—in both current prices and volume—were recorded by North America, the richest region. In fact, the fastest growing and most important countries within the Organization for Economic Cooperation and Development (OECD) were the U.S. and Japan. Substantial population growth in the U.S. helped to sustain the growth in output, incomes, and spending. In Japan, which did not have a significant element of population growth, the extremely high rate of savings and investment was responsible for the strong growth rate and the resultant rise in living standards. This trend appeared to be a soundly based and continuing feature of the Japanese economy.

Consumer prices rose more in 1968 than in 1967. Devaluations were responsible for part of the process, but the contribution of wage inflation in the U.S. to the rise in the level of world prices was highly significant. Since the U.S. contributed more than half the OECD total of consumer spending, any change in the U.S. must have a disproportionate effect on the OECD total.

Table II shows the breakdown on the main items of consumer spending in the OECD countries in 1966, the last year for which complete information was available. Food accounted for a quarter of the total. Clothing, rent (including the national value of owner-occupied houses), and durable goods accounted for roughly similar proportions. Services, including electricity, gas, water, transport, distribution, and finance, accounted for nearly two-fifths.

Spending on durable goods, in current prices, rose by 5%, compared with an 8% increase in total spending. This unusual performance was due to the recession in spending on cars in the U.S., the U.K., and West Germany in the last half of 1966. The long-run trend was for spending on durables to rise at an above average rate.

The contrast between regions in the pattern of consumer spending is shown in Table III. In the richest continent, North America, a comparatively small proportion of spending was accounted for by food and clothing—both necessities—illustrating the obvious change that takes place in spending patterns as wealth increases. On the other hand, spending on housing, another necessity, accounted for a larger share of spending in North America than elsewhere. This is because consumers demand more space and more amenities as incomes rise.

Broadly speaking, spending patterns fall into three national groupings. The advanced industrial nations divide between the U.S. and Canada (the rich countries) on the one hand and the other OECD countries of Western Europe and Japan on the other. Countries such as Australia, South Africa, and New Zealand have standards of consumption similar to those of the second group.

The third group of countries consists of the poor primary producing areas. As of 1968, there was no evidence of any leveling of standards of consumption among the three groupings.

A factor bearing on spending in 1968 was the cost of credit. Interest rates rose to high levels again in the first half of 1968 and, after a time lag of several months, this tended to check the growth in demand for housing in some countries. Interest rates began to decline in the second half of the year, following the lead set by the U.S.   (J. G. M.)

Contract Bridge

The third world bridge Team Olympiad, the major bridge championship of the world, took place at Deauville, France, in June 1968, and was won once again by Italy. The tournament had been scheduled for June 6–21, but it began a day late because nationwide strikes in France prevented some players from reaching Deauville on time.

The method of running the Olympiad was similar to that used in New York four years previously. The open event was divided into two stages. First, there was a qualifying round robin of 20-board matches in which each country played every other. The international match point (IMP) margins at the conclusion of each match were converted into victory points (VP) on a special scale with a total of 20 VP's at stake. Following the qualifying round, the four top teams met in 80-board knockout matches. The first 6 of the 33 teams at the end of the round robin were: (1) Italy 474; (2) United States 473; (3) Netherlands 460; (4) Canada 451; (5) Australia 444; (6) Switzerland 434. One or two teams failed to play up to their reputation and others played better. Australia in particular exceeded expectations and might well have qualified for the play-off had they not lost a player, D. Cummings, through illness during some matches.

In the semifinals, Italy beat Canada by 171 IMP's to 120 and the U.S. beat the Netherlands by 174 IMP's to 142. In the play-off (40-board match), Canada took third place by beating the Netherlands by 74 IMP's to 59. In the tensely exciting final between Italy and the U.S., at the beginning of the fourth session, with only 20 boards left to play, the Italians' lead was a robust 39 IMP's. However, at board 75 Italy's lead was only 11 IMP's. But in the five last boards Italy regained 38 points and won by 172 IMP's to 123.

The Italian team was Walter Avarelli, Giorgio Belladonna, Massimo d'Alelio, Camillo Pabis Ticci, Benito Garozzo, and Pietro Forquet, who had already won ten world events in 11 years. Their nonplaying captain was Angelo Tracanella. The United States team consisted of three pairs: Robert Jordan and Arthur Robinson, Norman Kay and Edgar Kaplan, William Root and Alvin Roth, who finished first, second, and fourth in the American trials at Montreal. The nonplaying captain was Julius Rosenblum.

One of the most interesting hands of the 1968 World Bridge Olympiad final was board no. 70 on which the U.S. team gained 7 IMP's by good bidding and play.

Nineteen countries competed in the women's championship at the Deauville Olympiad. Each team played 18 40-board matches (one against every other team) and the scoring was also by international match points, converted into victory points, with a total of 20 VP's at stake in each match. The first three in the final standings were: (1) Sweden 295; (2) South Africa 275; (3) United States 266. Sweden played steadily throughout and deserved their victory. South Africa was the first Southern Hemisphere nation to secure a major placing in world bridge.

The Swedish team consisted of Mrs. Britt Blom and Mrs. Gunborg Silborn, Mrs. Britta Werner and Mrs. Rut Segander, who won narrowly from the Italian ladies in the 1967 European championship in Dublin. They were ably backed up in Deauville by Mrs. Martensson and Mrs. Karin Eriksson.

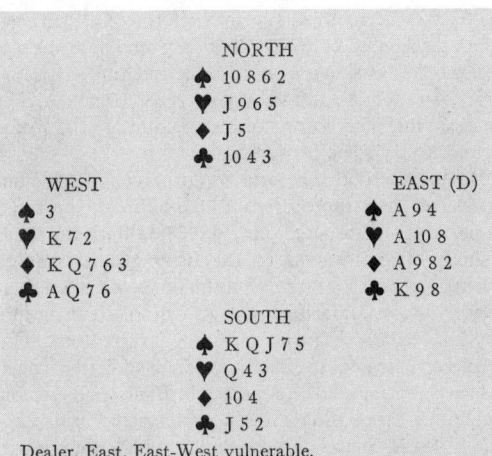

```
              NORTH
          ♠ 10 8 6 2
          ♥ J 9 6 5
          ♦ J 5
          ♣ 10 4 3
WEST                        EAST (D)
♠ 3                         ♠ A 9 4
♥ K 7 2                     ♥ A 10 8
♦ K Q 7 6 3                 ♦ A 9 8 2
♣ A Q 7 6                   ♣ K 9 8
              SOUTH
          ♠ K Q J 7 5
          ♥ Q 4 3
          ♦ 10 4
          ♣ J 5 2
```

Dealer, East. East-West vulnerable.

Playing in a closed room, Kaplan and Kay reached the excellent contract of six diamonds:

East Kaplan	South Garozzo	West Kay	North Forquet
1 NT	Pass	2 ♣	Pass
2 ♦	Pass	3 ♦	Pass
3 ♥	Pass	6 ♦	Pass
Pass	Pass	—	—

The one no-trump opening showed 15–18 points and two clubs was the Stayman convention. Three hearts was an encouraging bid for slam. The lead was the king of spades and declarer made 13 tricks easily by discarding one heart on dummy's fourth club.

In the open room, Robinson and Jordan put up a powerful barrage and brought the contract for the same hand in five spades doubled:

East Pabis Ticci	South Jordan	West d'Alelio	North Robinson
1 ♣	2 ♠	3 ♣	5 ♠
Double	Pass	Pass	Pass

The overcall of two spades was a weak bid and three spades was a cue bid to show a strong hand. The raise to five spades was preemptive and the bidding was too high for East to find the best suit and try for the slam. The defense started with two rounds of trump and Jordan was able to draw the last trump and exit with a diamond to wait for a heart trick. He made five tricks and was six down. Although Jordan went down on the hand, the team as a whole gained 7 IMP's because of the successful bidding of the other U.S. team. (After the spade lead the best defense to get three heart tricks is to cash the spade ace, three clubs, two diamonds, and return a spade.)

Spectators follow tournament play on the Bridge-O-Rama, an electrically operated board.

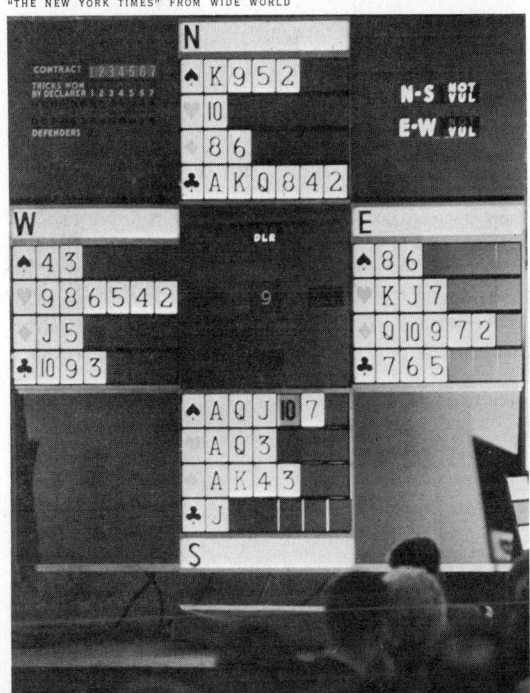

Before embarking on trials for the 1968 Olympiad, the British Bridge League (BBL) requested the World Bridge Federation (WBF) to advise as to its position in the event that Terence Reese or Boris Schapiro were selected as members of the British team. Reese and Schapiro had been banned from WBF events when they were accused of cheating in the world championship play in Buenos Aires in 1965. The WBF consulted their credentials committee and duly advised the BBL that this committee would find the names unacceptable. In view of the Foster Report of the BBL, which exonerated Reese and Schapiro, the consequent withdrawal by the BBL of its teams from the Olympiads was automatic and no British team was sent to Deauville, in spite of the fact that the British women's team had been the winners in the 1964 Women's Olympiad. However, on June 6, 1968, the executive committee of the WBF announced that it felt that the ban already imposed constituted a sufficient penalty and removed the ban against Reese and Schapiro's participation in future contests.

The first-ever European Junior Championship, staged in Prague during August 5–10, was won convincingly by Sweden. The final placings were: (1) Sweden with 74 VP's; (2) Portugal 56; (3) Great Britain 55; (4) Poland 53; (5) Netherlands; (6) Finland; (7) Denmark; (8) Austria; (9) Hungary; (10) Czechoslovakia; (11) Ireland. Sweden thus became the first winner of the David Pigot Trophy.

(J. E. E. Le D.)

Cooperatives

During 1968 the trend toward reorganization and rationalization continued in many cooperative movements as they sought to bring their activities into line with present-day demands. Structural reforms were being implemented in some countries but were only discussed in others.

In Austria a Reform Commission, set up to investigate structural changes, was expected to report its findings in 1969. The Cooperative Union of Canada sponsored a committee to study the structure of consumer cooperatives. In March 1968 the committee issued an interim report, which was to be the basis for further discussions rather than a program of implementation. At the first congress of the Federation of German Consumers' Cooperatives, established in 1967 to serve as a supreme policy-making body, three major structural developments were discussed: regional warehousing, rationalization of shopping facilities, and a new approach to management. The Committee on Structural Changes set up by the Norwegian Cooperative Movement reported its findings. The proposals put forward were: closer collaboration between retail and wholesale societies, the expansion of non-food sales, and the rationalization of retail outlets. The Polish Consumer Movement recognized the need for concentration of trading activities and was proceeding with the establishment of integrated regional societies. A plan for amalgamating smaller and medium-size societies into larger units was reported on at the annual meeting of the Swiss Cooperative Union. It was hoped that a completely new organizational structure based on 30 to 40 regional societies would be achieved.

In the U.K. the number of consumer societies had been reduced from 680 to 625 by the end of 1967, the largest reduction in any one year. A £3,250,000

computer-controlled grocery distribution centre with an area of 4,240,000 cu.ft. and a capacity for handling £40 million worth of groceries and related commodities was under construction at Birtley in County Durham. A grant of £150,000 toward the cost had been given by the Ministry of Technology to the Cooperative Wholesale Society (CWS); the grant was the first of its kind made by the ministry. The success of the national marketing campaign organized by the CWS and of the new cooperative symbol was reflected in the increased share in the retail market obtained by cooperatives. However, the campaign suffered a serious blow in April 1968 when Philip Thomas, the chief executive of the CWS and initiator of the campaign, was killed in an airplane crash in South Africa. The Swedish cooperative society, Kooperativa Förbundet, was said to be the largest commercial organization in the country in terms of total sales, which in 1967 increased by 10% to 4,623,000,000 kronor (U.S. $894 million). It accounted for 17% of all retail sales and 24% of all food sales and its manufacturing interests included some 30 companies, covering a wide range of products from detergents to fork-lift trucks. Goods valued at 414 million kronor were exported in 1967. A new national warehouse to serve Swedish consumer societies was under construction on a 583-ac. site at Nygård, near Stockholm, at a cost of $15.6 million; when completed in 1970, it would be the largest of its kind in northern Europe.

Problems and achievements arising from structural changes were discussed at the 38th International Cooperative Seminar, organized by the International Cooperative Alliance (ICA) and held at Søhus, Denmark, at the end of September 1968. The Consumer Working Party of the ICA, at its conference in Vienna in October, discussed "European Cooperation in the Service of Consumers."

The International Cooperative Alliance. The appointment in 1968 of a non-European (S. K. Saxena, formerly regional officer of the ICA in Southeast Asia) as director of the ICA for the first time in its 73-year history was a clear indication of the growing importance of the work of the alliance throughout the world.

In collaboration with the cooperative movements of Kenya, Tanzania, and Uganda, an office of the ICA—the first in East Africa—was set up in Moshi, Tanzania, and began operations on Oct. 1, 1968. The Organization of Cooperatives of America (OCA), through which the ICA was extending its activities into Latin America, had 188 member organizations by the end of 1967. The OCA was promoting trade between cooperatives in Latin America and those in the U.S.

In the course of 1968, four new cooperative federations joined the ICA, while the Hutt Valley Cooperative Society of New Zealand ceased operations. The ICA had a membership of 142 cooperative organizations in 60 countries. According to the latest available statistics, the total number of societies in membership with the ICA was 611,523 at the end of 1966, compared with 603,326 in 1965; membership within these societies had reached 230,547,925, compared with 222,897,389. The largest increase in the number of societies took place in the U.S. (22.1%), while membership grew most rapidly in Africa (41.1%). The highest membership was still found in the U.S.S.R. (over 54 million), followed by India (47 million). The total membership consisted mainly of consumers' societies (48.53%), followed by credit societies

(28.04%), agricultural societies (16.03%), miscellaneous societies (2.67%), building and housing societies (2.37%), workers' productive and artisanal societies (1.72%), and fishery societies (0.64%). The greatest increase in membership during 1966 was within fishery societies (18.61%).

Trade. In 1966 the total trade of cooperative societies reached more than $110 billion; consumer cooperatives transacted nearly $78 billion worth of business. The turnover of the international trading federations, such as the Scandinavian wholesale society, Nordisk Andelsforbund, its export organization, Nordisk Andels Export, and the International Cooperative Petroleum Association, showed little change.

The International Cooperative Bank had 32 organizations from 16 countries participating in its capital in 1967. Shareholdings and assets amounted to SFr. 276.1 million, an increase of SFr. 74.6 million over the previous year. The dividend remained at 5%. Cooperative insurance societies in 20 countries received premiums to the value of approximately $1,620,000,000 in 1966, an increase of about 18% over 1965. The total assets of 38 cooperative banks and unions of credit societies amounted to nearly $10.5 billion in 1966. CUNA International Inc., the international organization of credit unions, reported at the end of 1967 that there were 53,059 credit unions in the world serving 33.3 million members, with savings of $14.6 billion and loans outstanding of $12.6 billion.

During 1968 progress was made in promoting trade between cooperatives in various countries. The first trade agreement between the Scottish Cooperative Wholesale Society (SCWS) and the Polish Cooperative Movement was concluded, under which the SCWS supplied sportswear in exchange for Polish agricultural produce. SCWS also contracted to supply Centrosoyus, U.S.S.R., with clothing and knitwear. The Norwegian Cooperative Wholesale Society supplied the Swiss Cooperative Wholesale Society with toilet soap, and Centrosoyus, U.S.S.R., with textiles and footwear. The Cooperative Wholesale Committee of the ICA, composed of European wholesale societies, reported progress in joint purchasing of coffee, tea, canned fruit, vegetables, and fish. EURO-COOP, set up by the EEC countries to promote trading and joint production, established a baked-goods factory at Utrecht, Neth.

A conference on international cooperative trade in Southeast Asia, organized by the ICA regional office, took place in Tokyo in June 1968. In May an inter-cooperative food conference was held under the auspices of the ICA's Committee on Retail Distribution; it dealt with stock control, assortment policy, brand names, price policy, efficiency, and trends in modern food distribution. Also during May, a group of experts studied problems of packaging and handling at a meeting in Malmö, Swed., organized by the ICA Agricultural Committee.

Investment planning and financing methods were discussed at the first International Cooperative Top Management Conference, organized by the Cooperative Wholesale Committee of the ICA and held in Paris in April; it was attended by high-level representatives from wholesale consumers' societies of ten European countries.

Other Activities. Further progress was made in the collaboration between the ICA and the UN and its specialized agencies and other nongovernmental organizations in an attempt to coordinate activities.

In February 1968 an International Conference on Cooperative Education, organized by the ICA and supported by UNESCO and the National Cooperative Union of India, was held in New Delhi. The conference, attended by 43 delegates and representatives from the International Labour Organization (ILO), the Food and Agriculture Organization (FAO), and UNESCO, brought together cooperative education specialists and heads of cooperative institutes engaged in training in Southeast Asia to discuss the coordination of educational programs.

Problems of agricultural cooperation in Africa were discussed at a meeting sponsored by the FAO, the ILO, and the International Federation of Agricultural Producers (IFAP), which was held in Niger at the end of 1967. A joint part-time secretariat of the FAO, ILO, ICA, and IFAP was set up in Rome to collaborate in a program for the promotion of agricultural cooperatives in less developed countries.

The third General Conference of the Afro-Asian Rural Reconstruction Organization, attended by delegates from 15 countries and representatives of nongovernmental organizations, was held at Seoul, South Korea, in April 1968. Rural cooperatives were among the main topics of discussion.

A program on agricultural credit and related services through cooperatives in Afghanistan was launched by the Freedom from Hunger Campaign and financed by the Swedish International Development Authority. The main purpose of the program was to demonstrate in pilot areas how a coordinated and integrated approach to agricultural credit and cooperatives could lead to the development of agriculture. The Indian Farmers' Fertilizer Cooperative, established with the help of fertilizer cooperatives of the U.S. and the U.S. Agency for International Development, was inaugurated in April 1968. The government of India decided to set up rural electric cooperatives on a pilot basis in the states of Maharashtra, Mysore, Gujarat, Andhra Pradesh, and Uttar Pradesh. The Governing Council of the UN Development Programme agreed to assist in training cooperative personnel in the Ivory Coast, Cameroon, and Tunisia.

The importance of cooperative housing was being recognized by both national cooperative movements and nongovernmental organizations. The International Cooperative Housing Development Association, set up in 1967, received a contract under the UN Development Programme to study sources and methods of financing for cooperatives and nonprofit housing societies in certain selected countries. In Canada a foundation was established to promote all forms of cooperative housing, and a similar body was set up in India to deal with the technical and financial problems involved.   (L. KE.)

Cosmetics

The 1967 trend toward a "healthier" look in makeup continued into 1968. Darkly outlined, heavily shaded oriental eyes, pallid cheeks, and ashy lips continued to give way to out-of-doors freshness or to what Harriet Hubbard Ayer described as "the wet, dewy look."

Encouraged by new ranges of pinkly transparent lipsticks and by fashion's return to a 1930s style, lips assumed a new rosebud curviness. "We begin to look really 'girlie' again," reported one well-known American fashion writer.

In her handout for spring 1968, "The Modern Transparencies," New York's Estée Lauder spoke of lips "shaped round with Coral Gold or Coral Peach" and of "the final mouth . . . rich in colour and texture." In Paris, Orlane advocated a pink lipstick that would give the mouth the look of a rosebud or of "a full stop."

"Soft Shell Pink," "Fresh Water-Melon," "Wedgwood Rose," and "Dresden Peach" were among the shades favoured by leading international beauty specialists. Once more, the mouth had come into its own. "Blushing Powder" and the "precious pallor of porcelain" accompanied these enticing lips.

Although eyes were of secondary importance, they were nevertheless solicitously cared for. Revlon International brought out "The Enlightened Eye," the "serendipity" of which was inspired, so it was declared, by the "dew-drenched sky colours of a rainwashed May morning." Lilac, pink, peach, yellow, palest green-gray, and the "butterfly-blue" of noon made up the eye harmonies. The upper lashes were freed from eyeliner, and the brows were finely plucked in the 1930s tradition. All this was far from the femme fatale eye of the very recent past.

Similarly reminiscent of the 1930s were the softly waved hair styles that began to appear in the fall of 1967 and continued well into 1968, and which caused some leading beauty salons to revert to finger waving. Conversely, in Paris, Alexandre encouraged ultrashort "garçonne" cuts. In the fall of 1968 he launched the "Apple Look" of neat, round, glossy heads, tridentshaped side locks, and irregular fringes. "Intercoiffure America is thumbs down on teasing (backcombing)," Patricia Shelton reported in the *Christian Science Monitor* in May 1968, continuing "they are doing big, bouncy waves, big, big bouncy curls." To achieve this bouncy effect, Harold Chalef of Beverly Hills rejected the permanent wave in favour of the curling rod, which, he claimed, enabled him to complete a set in five minutes.

Continued and determined efforts to persuade men to use cosmetics were very evident. Lotions and perfumes, already long accepted, were joined by male beauty preparations. Revlon International, for example, extended its 1967 "That Man" line of lotions (including an after-shave cream for which they claimed antiwrinkle properties) by introducing "That Man Bronzer," guaranteed by the makers to be "absolutely undetectable."   (P. W. HE.)

See also Fashion and Dress.

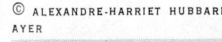
© ALEXANDRE-HARRIET HUBBARD AYER

Harriet Hubbard Ayer's "wet, dewy look"—natural lipsticks, eyes smudged with gray and mauve, and transparent powder for a soft, matte finish. Hairdo is the "Apple Look" by Alexandre.

Costa Rica

A Central American republic, Costa Rica lies between Nicaragua and Panama and has coastlines on the Caribbean Sea and the Pacific Ocean. Area: 19,652 sq.mi. (50,900 sq.km.). Pop. (1967 est.): 1,567,230, including white and mestizo 97.6%. Cap. and largest city: San José (pop., 1966 est., 180,717). Language: Spanish. Religion: predominantly Roman Catholic. President in 1968, José Joaquín Tréjos Fernández.

Throughout 1968 the government persisted in its efforts to stabilize the economy and to avoid devaluation. In March it approved a plan presented by the Banco Central, with the declared aim of reestablishing a simple rate of exchange at 6.65 colones to one U.S. dollar. The free exchange rate appreciated regularly throughout the year; in March it was 8.25 colones per U.S. dollar, but by September 30 it had been re-

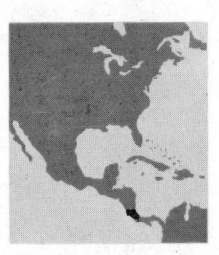

Copper:
see Mining

Corn:
see Agriculture

Deserted village of Pueblo Nuevo following the eruption of Mt. Arenal (background), July 1968. Over 100 persons died. Damage to nearby villages and rich plains was placed in the millions of dollars.

duced to 7.35 colones per U.S. dollar. The dual exchange system remained, but the country's financial position was strengthened enough for the International Monetary Fund to give temporary approval in August to the dual exchange rate system for an indefinite period and to extend the existing standby agreement for an additional year.

President Tréjos gave an optimistic survey of the economy in his annual address to the National Assembly. He stated that the foreign trade position was promising because the volume of coffee and banana exports had risen to compensate for low prices. He predicted that banana exports would rise by $12 million in 1968 and by double that amount in 1969, making the crop more significant in foreign exchange than coffee. Tréjos forecast that Costa Rica's gross national product would rise by 8.2% in 1968, compared with a rise of 8.1% in 1967.

The volcano Arenal, situated about 60 mi. NW of San José and believed to be totally extinct, erupted in July. Besides bringing about the deaths of over 100 persons, it caused damage amounting to about $44.8 million. To alleviate the situation the banks made

loans to farmers for restocking their farms; also, the Inter-American Development Bank agreed to allow an undrawn balance of $680,000, originally earmarked for the development of cattle farming, to be used to repair some of the damage.

Costa Rica received a substantial loan to build an extension to the San José–El Coco highway as far as San Ramón. Construction of a water supply system for the metropolitan area of San José was started in October. To deal with the expected increase in volume of banana exports, a pier to handle banana shipments was begun at Limón. The entire electrical network of the country was brought under public ownership, with the transfer of shares from private companies to the Instituto Costarricense de Electricidad. Two new hospitals were under construction, at Nicoya and at San Isidro de El General. A new airport designed to accommodate large jet aircraft was planned for construction at Puntarenas.

Despite the fact that the banking reforms proposed in 1967 were not passed by the National Assembly, foreign banks maintained their interest in Costa Rica. A branch of the Bank of America opened in San José in July. The manager of the Corporación Costarricense de Financimiento Industrial stated that his company intended to establish a stock exchange in the near future in Costa Rica, the first in Central America.

Progress continued to be made in industrial development. New proposals and plans included the installation of factories to produce steel tubes, petrochemicals, veterinary products, and perfumes. A new oil company was expected to begin exploration at the end of the year, subject to approval by the Ministry of Economy and Industry, over an area of 2,907 sq.mi. in the Bay of Coronado.   (J. C. Bd.)

COSTA RICA

Education. (1965–66) Primary, pupils 283,210, teachers 10,176; secondary, pupils 41,118, teachers 1,931; vocational, pupils 7,485; teachers 284; teacher training, students 2,108, teachers 22; higher (including University of Costa Rica), students 7,229, teaching staff 617.

Finance. Monetary unit: colón, with a par value of 6.625 colones to U.S. $1 (15.9 colones = £1 sterling). Gold and foreign exchange, central bank: (June 1968) U.S. $22,020,000; (June 1967) U.S. $17.8 million. Budget (1968 est.) balanced at 680.3 million colones. Gross national product: (1966) 4,194,000,000 colones; (1965) 3,940,000,000 colones. Money supply: (March 1968) 808.1 million colones; (March 1967) 652.4 million colones. Cost of living (San José; 1963 = 100): (June 1968) 108; (June 1967) 103.

Foreign Trade. (1967) Imports 1,263,400,000 colones; exports 949.8 million colones. Import sources (1966): U.S. 39%; West Germany 10%; Japan 9%; Guatemala 5%; U.K. 5%. Export destinations (1966): U.S. 46%; West Germany 11%; Nicaragua 7%; Netherlands 5%. Main exports: coffee 38%; bananas 22%.

Transport and Communications. Roads (1966) c. 10,000 km. (including c. 5,800 km. all-weather and 660 km. of Pan-American Highway). Motor vehicles in use (1966): passenger 27,200; commercial (including buses) 14,300. Railways (1966) 703 km. Air traffic (1967): 104,630,000 passenger-km.; freight 8,040,000 net ton-km. Telephones (Jan. 1967) 23,935. Radio receivers (Dec. 1965) 130,000. Television receivers (Dec. 1966) c. 65,000.

Agriculture. Production (in 000; metric tons; 1966; 1965 in parentheses): coffee c. 71 (c. 61); bananas c. 680 (c. 567); sugar, raw value (1967–68) c. 118, (1966–67) c. 116; dry beans c. 14 (22); cocoa (1966–67) 9, (1965–66) 7. Livestock (in 000): cattle (1966–67) c. 1,110; pigs (1965–66) c. 146.

Industry. Electricity production (84% hydroelectric; 1966) 697 million kw-hr.

Cricket

During 1967–68 international cricket was played between West Indies and England, Australia and India, New Zealand and India, and England and Australia.

West Indies v. England. England under M. C. Cowdrey won an exciting series in the West Indies. Cowdrey, taking over the captaincy under inauspicious circumstances, was an outstanding success as captain and batsman, making 534 runs, including two centuries and four fifties. G. Boycott and J. B. Edrich were efficient openers, and the veterans T. W. Graveney and K. F. Barrington each made one century. The bowling was based on three fast men: J. A. Snow (27 wickets) and D. J. Brown and I. J. Jones (14 each). G. S. Sobers, captain of West Indies, had another brilliant season, scoring 545 runs, including two centuries and two fifties. Other centuries were scored by R. B. Kanhai (2), S. M. Nurse (1), and a

newcomer, C. H. Lloyd (2). Fast bowlers W. W. Hall and C. C. Griffith were not the powers of old, and the chief wicket-takers were L. R. Gibbs (20) and Sobers (13).

In the first test, at Port-of-Spain, Trinidad and Tobago, England made 568 (Barrington 143, Graveney 118) to which West Indies replied with 363 (Lloyd 118, Kanhai 85) and, following on, had lost eight wickets for 180 before Sobers and Hall saved the side (243 for 8).

In the second test, at Kingston, Jamaica, England scored 376 (Cowdrey 101, Edrich 96) and West Indies 143 (Snow 7 for 49). Again following on, West Indies had lost five for 204 when spectators rioted and play was held up. Afterward West Indies recovered to 391 for 9 declared, Sobers making a remarkable 113 not out, and England (68 for 8) achieved a draw.

In the third test, at Bridgetown, Barbados, West Indies made 349 (B. F. Butcher 86, Snow 5 for 86) and England 449 (Edrich 146, Boycott 90). West Indies then made 284 for 6 (Lloyd 113 not out). England won the fourth test, at Port-of-Spain, by 7 wickets after West Indies had declared at 526 for 7 (Kanhai 153, Nurse 136). England replied with 404 (Cowdrey 148, Butcher 5 for 34). West Indies then declared at 92 for 2 and, thanks to Boycott (not out 80) and Cowdrey (71), England scored 215 for 3. In the fifth match, at Georgetown, Guyana, West Indies made 414 (Kanhai 150, Sobers 152), and England replied with 371 (Boycott 116, G. A. R. Lock 89). Fine bowling by Snow (6 for 60) helped England to dismiss West Indies in their second innings for 264 (Sobers 95 not out), and England saved the match and won the rubber by scoring 206 for 9 (Cowdrey 82, A. Knott 73 not out, Gibbs 6 for 60).

Australia v. India. Australia easily won a four-match series against India 4–0. India, upset by injury to its captain, the nawab of Pataudi, and consequent psychological worries, lacked concentration in batting and fielding and, with no fast bowler available, relied on medium pace and spin. After missing the first test, Pataudi scored 339 in six innings, and R. F. Surti, a fine all-rounder, scored 367 runs and took 15 wickets.

R. B. Simpson captained Australia in the first two tests and then retired in favour of W. M. Lawry, but returned under him in the fourth test. K. D. Walters returned from national service to score 254 in four innings, twice not out.

Australia won the first test, at Adelaide, Austr., by

W. F. Severn of the U.S. plays a ball from J. D. Piachaud of the Marylebone Cricket Club for 4 runs. The U.S. team, making its first world tour, was beaten easily by the British club at Lord's, July 27, 1968.

146 runs, making 335 (A. P. Sheahan 81, R. W. Cowper 92, Abid Ali 6 for 55) and 469 (Simpson 103, Cowper 108, Surti 5 for 74). India replied with 304 (F. M. Engineer 89, Surti 70, C. G. Borde 69) and 251 (V. Subramanyar 75, D. A. Renneberg 5 for 39). At Melbourne, Austr., the margin was an innings and four runs. India made 173 (Pataudi 75, G. D. McKenzie 7 for 66) and 352 (A. A. Wadekar 99, Pataudi 85), and Australia, for whom Simpson (109) and Lawry (100) put on 191 for the first wicket, made 529 (I. M. Chappell 151). The best match was at Brisbane, Austr., where Australia won by 39. They made 379 (Walters 93) and 294 (I. R. Redpath 79, Walters not out 62, E. A. S. Prasanna 6 for 104). India made 279 (Pataudi 74, M. L. Jaisimha 74) and 355 (Jaisimha 101, Surti 64, Borde 63).

Australia won the fourth match, at Sydney, Austr., by 144, making 317 (Walters not out 94, Sheahan 72, Lawry 66) and 292 (Cowper 165). India made 268 (Abid Ali 78) and 197 (Abid Ali 81, Simpson 5 for 59).

New Zealand v. India. India then won three test matches out of four against New Zealand. At Dunedin, N.Z., India won by five wickets. New Zealand made 350 (G. R. Dowling 143) and 208 (Prasanna 6 for 94); India 359 (Wadekar 80, Engineer 63, R. C. Motz 5 for 86) and 200 for 5 (Wadekar 71). New Zealand turned the tables at Christchurch, N.Z., with a 6-wicket victory. Dowling made 239 out of 502 (B. S. Bedi 6 for 127). India then made 288 (Surti 67, Borde 57, Pataudi 52, Motz 6 for 63) and 301 (Engineer 63, G. A. Bartlett 6 for 38). New Zealand made 88 for 4 to win the match (B. E. Congdon 61 not out). India easily won the third test, at Wellington, N.Z., by 8 wickets. New Zealand made 186 (M. G. Burgess 66, Prasanna 5 for 32) and 199 (Burgess 60, R. G. Nadkarni 6 for 43). India made 327 (Wadekar 143) and 61 for 2. India also won the fourth test, at Auckland, N.Z., making 252 (Pataudi 51) and 261 for 5 declared (Surti 99, Borde not out 65). New Zealand was then bowled out for 140 and 101 (Prasanna 4 for 44 and 4 for 40).

England v. Australia. The Anglo-Australian series was drawn, Australia winning the first test, England the fifth, with three drawn, two strongly in England's favour. In an unusually wet summer Australia, with an inexperienced side under Lawry, was fortunate to draw the series. The batting was inconsistent, Lawry making the only century, and the bowling lacked penetration, but the fielding was superb, with Sheahan outstanding. For England, Cowdrey made 100 at Edgbaston, Eng., in his 100th test. Edrich (564 runs) was the leading batsman, and D. L. Underwood took the most wickets (20). For Australia, Chappell, Walters, and Redpath were the best batsmen, and A. N. Connolly (23 wickets) was the chief bowler.

Australia won the first test, at Old Trafford, Eng., by 159 runs. They made 357 (Sheahan 88, Lawry 81, Walters 81, Chappell 73). England replied with 165. Australia then made 220 (Walters 86, P. I. Pocock 6 for 79), and England was bowled out for 253 (B. D'Oliveira 87 not out).

The second test, at Lord's, London, was drawn in England's favour. England made 351 for 7 declared (C. Milburn 83, Barrington 75) and bowled out Australia for 78 (Brown 5 for 42). Australia, following on, made 127 for 4. England was similarly thwarted in the third test, at Edgbaston. Having made 409 (Cowdrey 104, Graveney 96), England bowled Australia out for 222 (Chappell 71), declared its second

innings at 142 for 3 (Edrich 64), but took only one wicket for 68 in Australia's second innings.

With the Ashes at stake in the fourth test, at Headingley, Leeds, Eng., the Australians achieved a keenly fought draw. Making 315 (Redpath 92, Chappell 65), they bowled England out for 302 (Edrich 62, R. M. Prideaux 64, Connolly 5 for 72). Australia then made 312 (Chappell 81, R. Illingworth 6 for 87), and at stumps England was 230 for 4 (Edrich 65).

England won a thrilling final test, at the Oval, London, by 226 runs only five minutes from time. Again rain nearly saved Australia. England made 494 (Edrich 164, D'Oliveira 158) to which Australia replied with 324 (Lawry 135, Redpath 67). England then made 181 and bowled Australia out for 125 (R. J. Inverarity 56, Underwood 7 for 50).

County and National Cricket. Yorkshire won the English County Championship for the third successive year. Kent finished second, Glamorgan surprisingly placed third, and Nottinghamshire, captained by Sobers, was fourth. The one-day competition for the Gillette Cup was won by Warwickshire, which beat Sussex in a thrilling finish by 4 wickets.

Overseas players, who by a new regulation were permitted to play in county cricket, made a big impact. Sobers (1,590 runs and 84 wickets) transformed Nottinghamshire, the South African B. A. Richards (Hampshire) scored the most runs in England (2,-395), and his compatriot M. J. Procter was a great success for Gloucestershire. For Warwickshire, Kanhai scored 1,819 runs, but his fellow West Indian Gibbs took only 72 wickets. Majid Jehangir (Pakistan) made 1,372 runs for Glamorgan, and Asif Iqbal scored 1,236 for Kent. The best all-rounder was J. Shepherd of Barbados (Kent), with 1,157 runs and 96 wickets.

Two famous test cricketers, F. J. Titmus (Middlesex) and J. H. Parks (Sussex), resigned county captaincy during the season, and the Cape Coloured South African D'Oliveira (Worcestershire) was the centre of a political storm when included in the MCC England team for South Africa for 1968-69. His inclusion resulted in the banning of the team by the South African government and the cancellation of the tour by the MCC. (*See* RACE RELATIONS.)

Well-known players to retire from English cricket were J. B. Statham (Lancashire, 252 wickets in 70 test matches), D. Shackleton (Hampshire, 100 wickets in 20 consecutive seasons), and the Australian W. E. Alley (Somerset, 3,000 runs in 1961). Simpson retired after a career in which he captained Australia against all the major countries.

Western Australia, captained by the Englishman Tony Lock, won the Sheffield Shield for the first time in 20 years. In New Zealand the Plunket Shield was retained by Central Districts, and in South Africa, Natal retained the Currie Cup. In India the Duleep Trophy was won by South Zone, the Ranji Trophy by Bombay for the tenth successive year, and the Moin-ud-Dowlah Tournament Gold Cup was retained by the State Bank of India. In Pakistan, Karachi Blues won the Ayub Trophy, and Karachi won the Qaid-i-Azam Trophy.   (A. R. A.)

Crime

International collaboration in criminological research, the prevention and control of juvenile delinquency and adult crime, and the treatment of offenders continued and developed further in 1967-68. To strengthen international action a UN Social Defence Research Institute was established in Rome in January 1968 in cooperation with the Italian government. The institute was to advance the policies and practices of crime prevention and control on a worldwide basis. The UN secretary-general, U Thant, designated Edward Galway of the U.S. to be the director.

Among recent UN reports was the 1967 publication, *Capital Punishment, Developments 1961-65*, produced through the Economic and Social Council, which reported that there was an overall tendency toward less frequent use of the death penalty in states whose statutes provided for it and a steady movement toward legislative abolition of capital punishment. Where it was used, capital punishment was increasingly a discretionary rather than a mandatory sanction. All available data suggested that the presence of or absence of capital punishment did not appear to affect murder rates.

The Council of Europe published in 1967-68 the fourth and fifth volumes of the bulletin *International Exchange of Information on Current Criminological Research Projects in Member States* and continued publication of a bulletin on *International Exchange of Information on Bills and Draft Regulations on Penal Matters*. The European Committee on Crime Problems published the second volume of *Collected Studies in Criminological Research*. In November 1967 the Council of Europe held the fifth Conference of Directors of Criminological Research Institutes in Strasbourg.

Other work continued to be done on international, regional, and national levels. The Scandinavian Research Council for Criminology, which holds official status as a consultative body to the five Scandinavian governments, arranged a "contact seminar" in Denmark (March 1967) for members of the different Scandinavian police forces and their criminologists. In October 1967 a meeting held in Melbourne, and attended by representatives from all the Australian states and from New Zealand, resulted in the formation of the Australian and New Zealand Society of Criminology. The American National Council on Crime and Delinquency provided a bibliography on *The Young Adult Offender*.

For many reasons it was misleading to compare crime statistics from different years in the same country and especially to make international comparisons. International efforts were being made to find improved methods of measurement.   (V. GR.; S. G. J.)

Major Crimes. *United States.* Crimes of violence in the U.S. had increased 57% since 1960 and, in 1968, had a shocking impact on the American public. Negro civil rights leader the Rev. Martin Luther King, Jr., was assassinated just outside his motel room in Memphis, Tenn., on April 4. James Earl Ray, 40, an escaped convict accused of the murder, fled to Canada, obtained a passport under the name of Ramon George Sneyd, and on May 6 proceeded to England and a day later to Lisbon. He returned to England on May 17 and was arrested at Heathrow Airport, London, on June 8. On July 19 Ray was returned to Memphis to stand trial. Immediately following King's assassination, violence erupted in many parts of the nation. Several persons were killed and arson, looting, and vandalism in 100 cities caused property damage estimated in excess of $45 million.

U.S. Sen. Robert F. Kennedy of New York was fatally shot on June 5, just after he had claimed victory in the California primary for the Democratic

presidential nomination. Seized at the scene of the shooting was Sirhan Bishara Sirhan, 24, a Jerusalem-born Jordanian. On June 7 Sirhan was indicted for the murder of Senator Kennedy and assault with intent to kill five other persons who had been injured. He pleaded not guilty to all charges in a later hearing.

In the aftermath of Kennedy's assassination, there was renewed agitation for strict gun controls. The FBI reported that in 1967 firearms were used to commit over 7,600 murders, 52,000 aggravated assaults, and 73,000 robberies. Pres. Lyndon B. Johnson asserted that of 15 countries reporting on homicide by gunfire, the U.S. ranked the worst—2.7 gun murders per 100,000 population, as compared with 0.03 in the Netherlands, 0.04 in Japan, and 0.05 in England and Wales. The Safe Streets Act, signed by the president in June, curbed the interstate traffic in hand guns and prohibited their sale to minors.

The American Bankers Association reported that losses from bank holdups and burglaries, as well as the number of such attacks, reached a record high in 1967. Bank holdups jumped from 865 in 1966 to 1,318 in 1967; bank burglaries increased from 223 to 273. Losses totaled $8.7 million, as compared with $4.8 million in 1966.

On Dec. 19, 1968, a man with a toy pistol forced the pilot of an Eastern Airlines Philadelphia-to-Miami flight with 151 persons aboard to fly to Cuba. This was the 21st occasion during the year on which a U.S. commercial airliner had been commandeered in flight and had been taken to Cuba. Two attempts had failed. A Railway Express Agency truck containing 500 sacks, each holding 10,000 dimes, was hijacked on May 29 near Fort Lee, N.J. Subsequently $300,000 in dimes was found under a platform of a sportswear company in Patchogue, N.Y. The firm's proprietor, Raymond C. Curiole, was arrested.

On March 18 Winston Moseley escaped from the Meyer Memorial Hospital in Buffalo, N.Y. Moseley had been convicted in 1964 of stabbing Catherine Genovese 15 times while 38 neighbours listened to her screams without calling police. He had entered the hospital for minor surgery four days before his escape. On March 21 Moseley was recaptured.

Barbara Jane Mackle, daughter of a Florida land developer, was kidnapped December 17 from an Atlanta motel and released unharmed after $500,000 ransom was paid. An early ransom attempt had failed when Miami police had chased two men retrieving a suitcase from Biscayne Bay. An escaped convict, Gary Steven Krist, was arrested. A woman and another man were also charged.

A celebrated criminal trial in 1968 involved as defendants Benjamin Spock, noted author of *Baby and Child Care*, the Rev. William Sloane Coffin, Jr., chaplain of Yale University, Michael Ferber, a Harvard University graduate student, Mitchell Goodman, novelist and travel writer, and Marcus Raskin, co-director of a private research organization. Indicted on charges of conspiring to counsel young men to evade the draft, Spock, Coffin, Ferber, and Goodman were found guilty and sentenced to two years in prison; Raskin was acquitted.

National interest focused on a federal trial in New York City involving James L. Marcus, former commissioner of water supply, gas, and electricity, an appointee of New York Mayor John V. Lindsay. Others indicted with Marcus included Antonio ("Tony Ducks") Corallo, well-known underworld chieftain, Daniel J. Motto, president of Local 350, Bakers and

JERRY HAYNES

New York City police close in on a sniper who killed one and wounded three in Central Park in July 1968.

Confectionery Workers Union, and Henry Fried, millionaire contractor. Marcus had awarded an $840,000 emergency contract, without bids, to Fried and the company he headed to refurbish the Jerome Park Reservoir in the Bronx. A $40,000 kickback was paid to Marcus, Corallo, Motto, and others.

In a federal criminal conspiracy trial in Chicago, government testimony revealed that when four men were arrested following a bank robbery in 1963, crime syndicate chieftain William ("Willie Potatoes") Daddano had arranged through Richard Cain (Richard Scalzetti), then chief investigator for the Cook County sheriff's office, to have lie detector tests given to men suspected of being police informers.

On July 15 Huey P. Newton (*see* BIOGRAPHY), a co-founder of the militant Black Panther Party Negro group, was placed on trial in Oakland, Calif., charged with shooting to death patrolman John Frey during a wild street gun battle on Oct. 28, 1967. As the trial opened, 2,500 chanting, sign-carrying demonstrators ringed the Alameda County Courthouse; the Black Panthers threatened vengeance if Newton were convicted. Almost two months later, Newton was found guilty and given a 2–15 year prison sentence.

Mexico. In 1968 Tijuana had become a marijuana mecca. Official U.S. customs statistics at neighbouring San Ysidro, Calif., revealed that during the first four months of 1968 seizures and arrests surpassed those for all of 1967. U.S. Narcotics Bureau agents were operating in Mexico in cooperation with the Mexican federal judicial police. On April 12, 1968, Dorothy Sandra Futterman, a New York designer, was found fatally beaten on the beach of Puerto Escondido. A Canadian student, François Lavalle, was charged with the murder. The Mexico City Better Business Bureau warned in June that a man posing as a Mexican lawyer had been bilking persons in numerous U.S. cities. In letters to intended victims he said that a long-lost relative or friend had left them rich legacies and requested money to process the necessary papers.

Guatemala. In January two members of a U.S. military mission in Guatemala, Lieut. Comdr. Ernest A. Munro and Col. John D. Webber, were shot to death and two other persons were injured. On August 28 the U.S. ambassador, John Gordon Mein, was machine-gunned to death as he was returning to the embassy following a lunch he had given for the foreign press.

Argentina. Burglars rented a store next to a bank in Buenos Aires and had spent two months tunneling toward the bank's vaults when a bank employee smelled the odor from acetylene torches and called the police. In May Bahía Blanca police passed a search warrant through the mail slot to a man charged with operating the numbers racket. When the suspect refused to open the door the police forced entry and found that the man had swallowed the warrant.

Brazil. During the first seven months of 1968, 15 taxi drivers were murdered in Rio de Janeiro. On July 31, to press their demands for better police protection, taxi drivers caused traffic snarls in the city by mass-parking their cars. In July it was announced that a gang, headed by Ulysses Azevedo and known as "Ulysses and his 80 thieves," had swindled a charity out of $1 million by forging the signature of Brazil's first lady, Yolanda da Costa e Silva.

In June, 11 prisoners, led by a visiting state legislator, Geraldo Qumtao, broke out of an old prison at Belo Horizonte and installed themselves in a new one. Qumtao said the prisoners could not remain in the old filthy jail. On March 18 prison authorities in the state of Guanabara, which covers Rio de Janeiro, put into effect a system whereby inmates with good behaviour records could spend one weekend a month with their families.

Venezuela. In Caracas, in February, three men robbed a cab driver, José Vicente Gomez, stripped his cab, and locked him in its trunk where the police found him three days later. A Venezuelan airliner was hijacked over the Caribbean on June 19, and forced to fly to Cuba.

Uruguay. On August 12 about 300 university students clashed with the police in Montevideo. The disturbances broke out a few hours after Ulises Pereira Reverbel, president of the state power and telephone monopoly, was released by a pro-Peking Communist terrorist organization that had abducted him on August 7. The students were angered when the police raided the University of the Republic during their search for Reverbel.

Colombia. On April 26 a gang using walkie-talkies, limousines, and an elaborate series of lookouts stole $200,000 from the international airport vaults in Bogotá. By May 10 ten persons had been arrested and about 20% of the loot recovered.

Canada. Charles Frederick Wilson, a member of Britain's Great Train Robbery gang who had escaped from a Birmingham, Eng., prison in 1964, was captured in Rigaud, Que., on January 25 and returned to England to complete his 30-year prison sentence.

The largest jewelry theft in Toronto history occurred in June, when jewelry valued at $750,000 was stolen from the home of John David Eaton, head of the T. Eaton department store chain, while the Eaton family was hosting a Queen's Plate reception following the 105th running of Canada's richest Thoroughbred race.

On March 8, after a riot call from the Lagune Bleu Discotheque, Montreal police took 68 members of the Devil's Disciples motorcycle gang to the police station. The group went on a rampage, smashed a cell divider, jammed door locks with gum and paper, smashed chairs against the walls, and tore the arrest book. In 1967 the Canadian national penitentiary system added four new minimum-security penal institutions designed to emphasize correctional training.

United Kingdom. Throughout England and Wales crime increased 0.6% in 1967, the lowest rise for more than ten years. In London crime declined (3.3%) for the first time since 1954. Nevertheless, crimes of violence increased 7.6% over 1966, robberies were on the increase, and prosecutions for drug offenses doubled. In Liverpool the most intensive local anticrime drive in Britain was launched in March. The number of shotguns used in robberies had risen from 107 in 1961 to 500 in 1967. During a three-month amnesty period ending May 1, 1968, Britons turned in weapons to police stations without fear of prosecution. Over 2,000 weapons and 74,000 rounds of ammunition were surrendered.

In August a woman dashed into a London antique shop shouting that a travel agency next door was being robbed. Maj. John Wilkinson-Lathrop, a descendant of a famous sword-making family, and his two sons grabbed ancient swords from the walls. An off-duty policeman grabbed an 1854 musket. Led by the major who yelled "Charge!" the four men raced into the travel agency as six robbers fled through a back door, clutching $9,600 and firing sawed-off shotguns. On the night of February 24, five masked men burst into a post office in the London Paddington District and fled with bank notes worth $312,000.

On the night of March 15, chalices and altarpieces valued at $40,000, including a 15th-century silver altar cross and a 300-year-old flagon, were stolen from Canterbury Cathedral. The Ecclesiastical Insurance Office, which insures the contents of Church of England buildings, reported that a church was being looted almost every week. On June 3 thieves stole 40 paintings insured for $1.2 million from the North London home of Ronald Lee, an antique dealer. Jewels and furs belonging to actress Natalie Wood and valued at $72,000 were stolen on August 14 from the London home of Richard Gregson.

West Germany. On August 1 the criminal court of Weiden convicted two U.S. soldiers, Privates Thomas Overko of New Jersey and Larry Miller of Kansas, of killing a taxicab driver during an attempted robbery on Dec. 17, 1967. Police reported on August 2 that jewels valued at more than $12,000 had been stolen from the home of Princess Ann-Marie von Bismarck near Hamburg. The victim was the wife of a grandson of Germany's Iron Chancellor. A report of a parliamentary inquiry made public in April revealed that brutal beatings had taken place in Cologne's Klingelputz prison and at least one inmate may have died from maltreatment. It was West Germany's biggest prison scandal since World War II.

On April 11 Rudi Dutschke (*see* BIOGRAPHY), leading figure in West Germany's student protests, was shot three times.

British police placed signs at this roundabout in Chessington requesting information regarding a 14-year-old boy, murdered after getting off a bus at this spot.

"LONDON DAILY EXPRESS" FROM PICTORIAL PARADE

Police captured his assailant after a gun battle. In street violence that followed, Peter Brandt, son of Foreign Minister Willy Brandt, was arrested for violating the antiriot law. He received a six-week suspended jail term.

Austria. The crime rate in Austria had increased 21.6% over the past two years; the number of prison inmates rose 36.8%. Police reported that the murder rate in Vienna in 1967 doubled that of 1966.

France. Although huge seizures of narcotics were being made in France, police asserted that most of the drugs passed through France to the U.S. and presented only a minor problem in France. The crown of King Behanzin of Dahomey was stolen from a museum in August. The gilded crown had historical value only.

Greece. A bombing attempt against Prime Minister Georgios Papadopoulos on August 13 resulted in a wave of arrests in Athens. Charged with the attempted assassination was Georgios Panagoulis, an army deserter who had a police record dating back to 1959.

Poland. The juvenile division of the Polish police reported it had investigated 66,100 juvenile crimes in 1967, an increase of 4,500 over 1966. The official Polish press agency reported in June that a district military court in Warsaw had sentenced to death Adam Henryk Kaczmarzyk for having sold military defense secrets to British intelligence agents.

Italy. Graziano Mesina, a Sardinian bandit, was captured on March 26 in northern Sardinia. He confessed that his gang was responsible for two recent kidnappings and he called upon his associates to release the victims unharmed. In Turin on July 31, about 15 persons watched as a man drowned his wife in the Dora Baltea River. Giuseppe Ebonon had found his wife in the car of another man and was holding her head under water when police arrived.

In Taurisano three teen-age cousins and a friend gagged and bound their 99-year-old great-great grandmother and robbed her of her savings. On July 25 a Palermo, Sicily, court cleared 17 Sicilians and Italian-Americans accused of running narcotics and currency rackets for the Italian Mafia and U.S. Cosa Nostra crime syndicates.

U.S.S.R. Two employees of the Ministry for the Grain Product and Fodder Industry were murdered on July 26. Evgeni A. Filatov, a habitual criminal, was captured after a nationwide manhunt. The murders had followed the denial of his request to the ministry for a job. In March a dog found in a Ul'yanovsk store following a burglary was turned loose and followed home to its master who was surrounded by the loot from the burglary. The U.S. embassy reported on August 7 that Stephen F. Abney of Milwaukee, Wis., had received a three-year sentence on a charge of smuggling hashish into the U.S.S.R. He was one of 11 Westerners arrested in Tashkent for smuggling narcotics during the year.

India. In 1967 the Indian Customs and Central Excise offices confiscated $15 million in gold from smugglers. Equipped with a few small launches, the understaffed Central Excise Department was trying to stem the flow of gold, diamonds, watches, and textiles, estimated at $300 million in 1967, that were being smuggled into India from the Persian Gulf. In April provincial administrations expressed concern over the wave of lawlessness that had been sweeping some states for over 14 months. The crime wave was attributed in part to "goondas" who took advantage of political movements to engage in antisocial activities. The term "goonda" included extortionists, protection racketeers, bootleggers, gamblers, paramours or prostitutes, truck looters, pickpockets, and burglars. Officials estimated that 25,000 goondas infested the cities of Bombay, Calcutta, Madras, New Delhi, and Kampur. In May it was announced that police departments in many provinces were supporting a campaign against films, asserting that gangs copy the gangster tactics portrayed in them.

Japan. Police reported in January that the number of crimes committed in Japan in 1967 (1,446,229 up to December 25) was about the same as in 1966. In April 1968 an Osaka real estate dealer was beaten by eight men who charged that he had swindled them out of $278,000. He escaped and ran to the nearest police station to report the beating and confess the swindling.

Philippines. In August the nation's anticrime drive was stepped up as public alarm grew over the waves of violence that included the killing of 43 persons in one week. Among those killed were the vice-governor of Tarlac Province, a judge, and a popular screen actor. There were 3,500 crimes committed with guns in 1967. Pres. Ferdinand Marcos announced the provision of $10 million to acquire modern crime fighting weapons and ordered all law enforcement agencies to check on the licenses of persons who were carrying guns.

In April, when the offices of two judges and two city councilmen were found to have been ransacked, police confiscated 60 weapons, including knives and daggers made of scrap metal and wire, from city hall jail inmates. Two miniskirted girls and a male escort held up a bus in Nueva Ecija Province in May after the girls had asked the driver to take them to a party nearby.

Rhodesia. Three black Africans convicted of murder were hanged behind the walls of the top-security prison in Salisbury on March 6, despite a commutation of their sentences to life imprisonment by Queen Elizabeth II. The executions were considered the most serious act of defiance against Britain since Prime Minister Ian D. Smith had declared Rhodesia's independence in 1965. The government later announced a commutation of sentence for 35 other prisoners who had been condemned to death.   (V. W. P.)

See also Law; Police; Prisons and Penology.

Scotland Yard detectives return Charles Frederick Wilson, a member of Britain's Great Train Robbery gang, to London after he was recaptured in Canada. He escaped from Birmingham prison in 1964.

Cuba

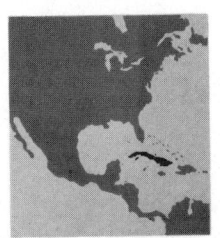

The socialist republic of Cuba occupies the largest island in the Greater Antilles of the West Indies. Area: 44,218 sq.mi. (114,524 sq.km.), including several thousand small islands and cays. Pop. (1967 est.): 7,799,600, including (1953) white 72.8%; mestizo 14.5%; Negro 12.4%. Cap. and largest city: Havana (pop., 1966 est., 990,050). Language: Spanish. Religion: predominantly Roman Catholic. President in 1968, Osvaldo Dorticós Torrado; prime minister, Fidel Castro.

Cuba made little economic progress in 1968; political conditions, however, continued to be stable. The government strengthened its position in the country and, despite some discontent over falling living standards, the majority of the population continued to support it.

On January 28 the government announced the arrest of a group of nine prominent Communists, including Aníbal Escalante, a veteran of the old Cuban Communist Party. At the same time two members

Cuban Prime Minister
Fidel Castro denounces
Bolivian Gen. Alfredo
Ovando Candía whom
Castro held responsible
for the death
of "Che" Guevara,
leader of the revolutionary
guerrilla movement
in Bolivia.

of the party's Central Committee, José Matar and Ramón Calcines Gordillo, were dismissed from high party posts. Escalante was sentenced by a revolutionary tribunal to 15 years' imprisonment and the eight others to terms of 12 years. The group was accused of offering "false information" to foreign officials and of removing secret documents from government departments. The deputy prime minister, Raúl Castro, accused the Soviet Union of plotting against the government with the assistance of the group, and it was alleged that some of the conspirators had contacted leading Soviet officials while traveling in Eastern Europe.

The purge was an attempt to remove from the government and the local Communist Party leadership opponents of the official policy of fomenting violent revolution throughout Latin America. Relations with the Soviet Union became increasingly strained during the year, owing to the Soviet policy of improving commercial relations with regimes which the Cuban government wished to overthrow. The death (October 1967) of "Che" Guevara, leader of the guerrillas in Bolivia, was a severe blow to Cuba. The complicity of Fidel Castro and other prominent Cuban leaders in the Bolivian revolt was clearly proved in Guevara's campaign diary, which was published during the year. (See BOLIVIA.)

Late in August Castro officially expressed guarded support for the Soviet invasion of Czechoslovakia August 20–21. He stated that the occupation could be justified on political but not on legal grounds; Czecho-

slovak territory had been "flagrantly violated," but the Czechoslovak leadership had been pursuing a course "which would have led to capitalism and imperialism." Conflicting reasons lay behind the statement. Relations with Czechoslovakia had not been friendly in recent years; the Czechoslovaks resented having to purchase unwanted Cuban sugar, and Cuba had protested that the Czechoslovaks could have supplied more aid to them. Castro's main motive, however, was his desire to avoid any action that might induce the Soviet Union to curtail economic aid.

During the year a number of U.S. airliners were hijacked at gunpoint and forced to land at Havana, where the hijackers sought sanctuary. Cuba in every case released the passengers and planes. (See CRIME.)

The Cuban government intensified its policy of increasing state control over the economy at a faster rate than had been attempted in any other Communist-oriented country; it was proposed to set up a "pure" form of Communist society that would render money unnecessary. In March a campaign was launched "finally to eradicate bourgeois values"; it included the nationalization of all privately owned business, with the exception of a small part of agriculture; by mid-May about 60,000 small businesses had been expropriated.

The measure was considered to be an attempt to counter increasing protests about the deteriorating economic conditions. Severe rationing of clothing and foodstuffs was introduced; on at least one occasion the government had to call in security forces to suppress demonstrations against food shortages.

The 1968 sugar crop was 5 million tons, compared with 6.1 million tons in 1967; this low total was due mainly to a severe drought. It was originally planned to raise production to 10 million tons annually by 1970 and then to resume the emphasis on industrialization. The government tacitly recognized this target as unattainable and directed that the area sown to sugar and other food crops be increased at a faster rate. In an attempt to speed up the harvesting of the sugar crop, a million people were mobilized for emergency agricultural labour, including, for the first time, schoolchildren.

In January Castro announced that severe controls were to be imposed on fuel consumption, as the Soviet Union would be unable to supply enough oil to meet local demand. However, petroleum deposits were discovered at Playa Santa Maria, near Havana.

A trade agreement for 1968 between Cuba and the Soviet Union was signed in March after prolonged negotiations. The agreement provided for an increase in trade of 10%, compared with 23% in 1967. The Soviet Union had refused to negotiate a three-year agreement; it was estimated that by 1967 Cuba had accumulated a deficit of $1 billion in its trade with the Soviet Union, compared with a 1961 surplus.

Despite its economic difficulties the government continued to pursue a deliberate program of long-term investment with regard to industry, agriculture and livestock, roads and dams, cement, and power. Investment in 1968 was forecast at 31% of the gross national product, compared with 27% in 1967. Production of some agricultural commodities, including beef, cattle, and citrus fruits, increased and this output was exported; the resulting foreign exchange was used to purchase fertilizers and agricultural and industrial machinery and equipment. (RN. C.)

ENCYCLOPÆDIA BRITANNICA FILMS. *The West Indies* (1965).

CUBA

Education. (1965–66) Primary, pupils 1,321,768, teachers 41,922; secondary, pupils 148,991, teachers 9,584; vocational, pupils 40,541, teachers 3,339; teacher training, students 30,640, teachers 1,429; higher (at 3 universities), students 30,536, teaching staff 3,032.

Finance. Monetary unit: peso, officially at parity with the U.S. dollar (2.40 pesos = £1 sterling). Budget (1965) balanced at 2,536,000,000 pesos.

Foreign Trade. (1966) Imports 926 million pesos; exports 592 million pesos. Import sources: U.S.S.R. 56%; China 9%; Spain 8%. Export destinations: U.S.S.R. 46%; China 15%; Czechoslovakia 8%; Spain 6%; East Germany 5%. Main exports sugar and products 85%.

Transport and Communications. Roads (1965) 13,340 km. (including 1,144 km. of the Central Highway). Motor vehicles in use (1965): passenger 162,000; commercial (including buses) 103,700. Railways (1965): public 5,977 km.; plantation (carrying some public-revenue traffic) 12,137 km. Shipping (1967): merchant vessels 100 gross tons and over 101; gross tonnage 235,253. Telephones (Dec. 1966) 234,456. Radio receivers (Dec. 1964) 1,345,000. Television receivers (Dec. 1966) c. 555,000.

Agriculture. Production (in 000; metric tons): rice (1967) 93, (1966) 51; sugar, raw value (1967–68) c. 4,800, (1966–67) c. 6,128; coffee (1966) c. 27, (1965) c. 28; tobacco (1966) 51, (1965) 44. Livestock (in 000; 1965–66): cattle 6,700; pigs c. 1,850; sheep c. 229.

Industry. Production (in 000; metric tons; 1966): electricity 4,100,000 kw-hr.; crude oil 30; copper ore (metal content; 1965) 6; nickel ore (metal content) c. 27; manganese ore (metal content) c. 33; chrome ore (oxide content; 1965) c. 15; cement 800; petroleum products (1964) 3,496.

Cycling

While the governing bodies of most sports in the Olympic Games at Mexico City were concerned with the problems of competition at high altitude, cyclists were among the few exceptions. For many years European and American riders had raced the 1,700-mi. Tour of Mexico with no ill effects, and in October 1967 at the "Little Olympics" in Mexico City a dozen world amateur track records were beaten at distances from 200 to 5,000 m.

A few days before the 1968 Olympic Games started a professional rider, Ole Ritter of Denmark, broke the world hour unpaced record on the Olympic track at Mexico City, covering 30.214 mi., as against the 1967 distance of 29.866 mi. by Ferdinand Bracke of Belgium. While the high altitude of Mexico City affected cyclists' oxygen intake, it more than compensated for this drawback by greatly reducing the air resistance.

In the Olympics at Mexico City all records were broken, with French riders dominating the track events. Daniel Morelon won the sprint from Giordano Turrini (Italy) and Pierre Trentin (France). Trentin took the one-kilometre time trial in 1 min. 3.91 sec., followed by Niels Fredborg (Den.), 1 min. 4.61 sec., and Janusz Kierzkowski (Pol.), 1 min. 4.63 sec. Morelon and Trentin combined forces to win the tandem sprint from Jan Janssen-Leijn Loevesijn (Neth.) and Daniel Goens-Robert Van Lancker (Belg.). West Germany (4 min. 18.94 sec.) finished clearly ahead of Denmark (4 min. 22.44 sec.) in the 4,000-m. team pursuit, but was disqualified for a technical infringement, the Danes being awarded the gold medals and Italy the bronze. Winner of the 4,000-m. individual pursuit race was Daniel Rebillard (France) with 4 min. 41.71 sec., second being Mogens Frey-Jensen (Den.), 4 min. 42.43 sec.

Individually on the road, Pierfranco Vianelli (Italy) won the 122-mi. race in 4 hr. 41 min. 25 sec. from Leif Mortensen (Den.) and Gösta Pettersen (Swed.). Partnered by his three brothers, Pettersen finished second in the 100-km. team time trial in 2 hr. 9 min. 26.6 sec., the winners being the Netherlands, 2 hr. 7 min. 49.06 sec.

Two months earlier in Rome, the professional world titles were contested. Inspired by vocal home supporters, Giuseppe Beghetto scored a surprising victory over defending champion Patrick Sercu (Belg.) in the sprint event, but noise could not help Italy's 5,000-m. pursuit riders Leandro Faggin and Pietro Guerra, who were beaten in the semifinals by Hugh Porter (U.K.) and Ritter. Porter brilliantly won the final, the first British rider to take this title. Leo Proost (Belg.) won the 100-km. motor-paced race.

In the world amateur championships in November in Uruguay, Mogens Frey-Jensen (Den.) won the 4,000-m. pursuit, and Luigi Borghetti (Italy) the sprint. Because the Uruguayan track was not suitable for all events, the 100-km. amateur motor-paced race was contested in Rome. The winner was Giuseppe Grassi (Italy). Originally also allocated to Uruguay, the women's amateur championships were held in Rome also, where Soviet riders won both gold medals. Alla Baguiniantz took the sprint test from compatriot Irina Kirichenko, and Raisa Obodovskaya narrowly defeated Britain's Beryl Burton—five times winner of the title—in the final of the 3,000-m. pursuit.

The track championships were followed by the pro-

fessional men's and women's road races at Imola, Italy. Katie Hage of the Netherlands won the 34-mi. event without much public interest, but on the next day 300,000 enthusiastic Italians cheered their countryman, Vittorio Adorni, as he finished ten minutes ahead of the next man in the 173-mi. race. The previous champion, Eddy Merckx (Belg.), placed eighth.

Despite the loss of his title, Merckx had an excellent season, starting with a win in the six-day Tour of Sardinia in February, followed shortly by victory in the most coveted of all one-day classic road races, the approximately 165-mi. test between Paris and Roubaix. Efforts failed to get Merckx to ride the June–July Tour de France, though his Italian sponsors had persuaded him to take part in the equally long (3,000 mi.) Tour of Italy a month earlier. Merckx dominated this competition, taking the points and mountain awards as well as the individual classification.

Because of strikes and civil unrest, the Tour de France was almost canceled, but it started on schedule on June 27. Following the retirement, due to an accident, of favourite Raymond Poulidor (France), there was the closest finish on record when Jan Janssen (Neth.) snatched victory in the last 20 min. to win by 38 sec. from Hermann Van Springel (Belg.). Two riders were disqualified following tests that indicated they had been doped. The two other major professional tours included one in Switzerland, won by home rider Louis Pffeninger, and one in Spain, in which the victor was Felice Gimondi (Italy).

Whereas there were several one-day "classic" races for professionals apart from Paris–Roubaix, such as Milan–San Remo (won by Rudi Altig, W.Ger.), Flèche Wallonne (Rik Van Looy, Belg.), and Liège–Bastogne–Liège (Valère Van Sweefelt, Belg.), there were few equivalent amateur events. An important exception was the 113-mi. Manx International over three laps of an Isle of Man motorcycle course. The 1968 winner was John Bettinson (Eng.).

British riders, however, took a sound beating in their 1,400-mi. Tour of Britain in June. The event was dominated by the four Pettersen brothers of Sweden. Gösta Pettersen won the first stage and kept the yellow jersey of leadership for all 14 days, helped in a masterly display of teamwork by brothers Tomas, Erik, and Sture. Vladimir Sokolov of the U.S.S.R. finished second, and the third man, Peter Doyle (Ire.), won the points and King of the Mountains prizes.

Despite the growing importance of the Tour of Britain, the biggest international amateur competition remained the Eastern European marathon known as the Peace Race. In 1968 this was run off on the 1,500-mi. Berlin–Prague–Warsaw triangle. Victory seemed assured for Vladimir Cherkassov (U.S.S.R.), still ahead with two days to go after holding the lead for 10 stages, but he fell back and retired. Axel Peschel (E.Ger.) took the race by only 16 sec. from Karel Vavra (Czech.). Canada, too, had its 1,200-mi. stage race, the Tour de Nouvelle France, won by Siegi Koch of West Germany from John Allis (U.S.).

Cyclo-cross—a mixture of cycling and cross-country running—continued to gain in popularity in 1968. In the world championships in Luxembourg the amateur and professional titles were won by the Belgian brothers Roger and Eric de Vlaeminck, respectively.

As in 1967, Beryl Burton continued to register remarkable road time trial performances. Now 31, Mrs. Burton rode 100 mi. "out and home" (with and against any wind blowing) in 3 hr. 55 min. 5 sec. Only three men had beaten this time.   (Jo. B. W.)

Hugh Porter, Great Britain, winning the world professional track pursuit cycling championship in Rome, Aug. 28, 1968. Porter's winning time was 6 min. 5.93 sec., a margin of 8 sec. over Ole Ritter of Denmark.

Curling:
see Sporting Record
Currency:
see Money and Banking
Cybernetics:
see Information Science and Technology

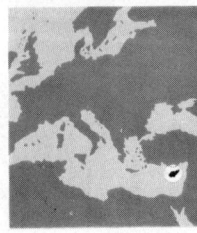

Cyprus

An island republic and a member of the Common-wealth of Nations, Cyprus is in the eastern Mediterranean. Area: 3,572 sq.mi. (9,251 sq.km.). Pop. (1968 est.): 618,000, including Greeks 77%; Turks 18%. Cap. and largest city: Nicosia (pop., 1967 est., 109,000). Language: Greek and Turkish. Religion: Greek Orthodox 77%; Muslim 18.3%. President in 1968, Archbishop Makarios III.

President Makarios announced in January that a presidential election would be held in Cyprus in February. He underlined his need of a fresh mandate from the people, since he was planning the establishment of a new constitution which would give Cyprus full sovereign independence under a presidential regime and would also include a charter of guaranteed rights for the Turkish Cypriots.

Among the Greek Cypriots there existed a political front ranged in opposition to the president. This front, led by Themistocles Dervis, a former mayor of Nicosia, was critical of the new policies which Makarios was formulating and insisted that *enosis* (union with Greece) should be asserted once more as the ultimate aim of Cyprus. It was thought that the opposition front could hope for the approval of the "Association of Greek Cypriot Fighters," an extremist group, but that there was little prospect of its securing an appreciable measure of support among the Greek Cypriots as a whole. The opposition group put forward Takis Evdokas as its candidate for the presidency. In the election, held on February 25, Makarios was reelected with more than 95% of the votes.

At the same time, Makarios was moving forward with his proposals for constitutional reform. He made it clear that his aim was to seek a solution for the Cyprus troubles on the basis of what was attainable in practice rather than desirable in theory, a view that might be interpreted to indicate a renunciation, at least for some considerable time, of the long-expressed wish of the Greek Cypriots for *enosis*. By March he had placed before the secretary-general of the UN proposals for a new constitution. It ensured the Turkish Cypriots, within a unitary state of Cyprus, of equal rights with the Greek Cypriots but also granted special privileges endowing them with reli-

gious, cultural, and educational autonomy, together with unrestricted freedom of movement.

During the first months of 1968 Makarios, striving to facilitate agreement between the rival communities, began to remove various restrictions hitherto imposed on the Turkish Cypriots. All Greek police and roadblocks in the Nicosia area were removed in March. Among the other measures that the president had enforced was a relaxation of the embargo on the transmission to the Turkish Cypriots of essential materials such as cement, iron, and timber.

In March Makarios formally opened a new terminal building at the Nicosia international airport. The building, erected in accordance with plans prepared by a West German company, was made by two Cypriot firms, which had begun the work in October 1967. The terminal building cost £1.1 million, of which the British government contributed £500,000. It was stated at the opening ceremony that the main runway would be lengthened at a later date in order to allow larger jet aircraft to land and take off at Nicosia.

The groundwork was being prepared for a renewal of formal negotiations between the Greek Cypriot and the Turkish Cypriot leaders. Initial contact to examine methods of procedure was achieved in May. At that time Glafkos Clerides, the president of the Cyprus House of Representatives, met with Rauf Denktash, former chairman of the Turkish Cypriot Communal Chamber.

An official resumption of talks between delegates of the two communities was delayed because of a dispute over the choice of a meeting place. It was agreed eventually, with the good offices of Bibiano Osorio-Tafall, the special representative of U Thant in Cyprus, that the negotiations would begin at Beirut, Lebanon, and continue later at Nicosia. The first series of talks involving the Greek Cypriot and the Turkish Cypriot delegates ended in July. It was reported that, while agreement had been reached on a number of issues, there were other problems that would demand further examination. The UN Security Council voted in December to maintain the UN peace-keeping force in Cyprus for six more months.

There was also discussion of the Cyprus question at London in June among representatives of Greece, Turkey, and the two Cypriot communities. President Makarios went to Athens in September for consultation with the Greek prime minister, Georgios Papadopoulos. Reports from Athens suggested that among the matters under review were the course, thus far, of the negotiations between the Greek Cypriots and the Turkish Cypriots and also the relations existing between Athens and Ankara.   (V. J. P.)

CYPRUS
Education. (1965–66) Primary, pupils 72,191, teachers 2,077; secondary, pupils 28,584, teachers 1,138; vocational, pupils 3,807, teachers 222; higher, students 154, teaching staff 54.
Finance. Monetary unit: pound, at par with the pound sterling (C£1 = U.S. $2.40). Budget (1967 rev. est.): revenue C£22,750,000; expenditure C£19,880,-000. Gold and foreign exchange, monetary authorities: (May 1968) U.S. $129 million; (May 1967) U.S. $93.9 million.
Foreign Trade. (1966) Imports C£60,390,000; exports C£29.9 million. Import sources: U.K. 56%; Italy 10%; West Germany 9%; U.S. 5%; France 5%. Export destinations: U.K. 40%; West Germany 10%; U.S.S.R. 6%; Spain 5%; Netherlands 5%. Main exports: copper concentrates 19%; citrus fruit 19%; iron pyrites 8%.
Transport and Communications. Roads (1967) 8,150 km. Motor vehicles in use (1967): passenger 37,330; commercial 12,795. Shipping (1967): merchant vessels 100 gross tons and over 60; gross tonnage 360,615. Air traffic (1967): 57,383,000 passenger-km.; freight 1,430,000 net ton-km. Telephones (Dec. 1966) 30,432. Radio receivers (Dec. 1966) 139,000. Television receivers (Dec. 1966) 21,000.
Agriculture. Production (in 000; metric tons; 1966; 1965 in parentheses): grapes 142 (127); oranges 62 (56); grapefruit *c.* 36 (*c.* 27); wheat 56 (91); potatoes 134 (139). Livestock (in 000): sheep (1965–66) 400; cattle (1966–67) 36.
Production (in 000; metric tons; 1966): asbestos 26; copper ore (exports; metal content) 25; chromium ore (oxide content) 5; electricity (excluding most industrial production; 1967) 412,000 kw-hr.

Czechoslovakia

A socialist republic of central Europe, Czechoslovakia lies between Poland, the U.S.S.R., Hungary, Austria, and Germany. Area: 49,371 sq.mi. (127,870 sq.km.), including Slovakia 18,922 sq.mi. Pop. (1968 est.): 14.5 million (Slovakia 4.5 million), including (1966) Czech 66%; Slovak 29%. Cap. and largest city: Prague (pop., 1968 est., 1.1 million). First secretaries of the Communist Party of Czechoslovakia in 1968, Antonin Novotny and, from January 5, Alexander Dubcek; presidents, Novotny and, from March 30, Ludvik

Above, Soviet officer threatening citizens with his pistol. Right, Czechoslovak patriot standing in the path of a Soviet tank. Below right, road signs in the centre of Prague were defaced except the one showing the way to Moscow. These photographs appeared in clandestine newspapers.

Svoboda; premiers, Josef Lenart and, from April 4, Oldrich Cernik.

Late in the evening of Aug. 20, 1968, while the ruling Presidium of the Czechoslovak Communist Party was holding a routine meeting, troops from the Soviet Union, East Germany, Poland, Hungary, and Bulgaria—Warsaw Pact allies of Czechoslovakia—secretly crossed its borders and seized control of the country. The invasion stunned the world.

CZECHOSLOVAKIA

Education. (1965–66) Primary, pupils 2,221,160, teachers 95,950; secondary, pupils 112,153, teachers 7,393; vocational, pupils 287,325, teachers 18,485; teacher training, students 10,303, teachers 561; higher (including 9 universities), students 141,687, teaching staff 18,576.

Finance. Monetary unit: koruna, with an official exchange rate of 7.20 koruny to U.S. \$1 (17.28 koruny = £1 sterling) and a tourist rate of 16 koruny to U.S. \$1 (38.74 koruny = £1). Budget (1968 est.) balanced at 144.8 billion koruny.

Foreign Trade. (1967) Imports U.S. \$2,768,000,-000; exports U.S. \$3,013,000,000. Import sources (1966): U.S.S.R. 33%; East Germany 12%; Poland 7%; Hungary 6%. Export destinations (1966): U.S.S.R. 34%; East Germany 11%; Poland 9%; Hungary 5%. Main exports (1966): machines and equipment 50%; metals and fuels 19%; consumer goods 17%.

Transport and Communications. Highways (1965) c. 133,000 km. (including 72,974 km. main roads). Motor vehicles in use: passenger (1959) 156,-000; commercial (including buses; 1966) 151,500. Railways (1966) 13,330 km. (including 1,891 km. electrified); traffic (1967) 19,740,000,000 passenger-km., freight 55,782,000,000 net ton-km. Shipping (1967): merchant vessels 100 gross tons and over 8; gross tonnage 78,199. Air traffic (1966): 751,949,000 passenger-km.; freight 15,283,000 net ton-km. Telephones (Dec. 1966) 1,582,852. Radio receivers (Dec. 1966) 3,829,000. Television receivers (Dec. 1966) 2,375,000.

Agriculture. Production (in 000; metric tons; 1966; 1965 in parentheses): wheat 2,247 (1,992); barley 1,608 (1,399); oats (1967) c. 760, (1966) 746; rye c. 690 (770); potatoes 5,846 (3,678); sugar, raw value (1967–68) c. 822, (1966–67) c. 834. Livestock (in 000; Jan. 1967): cattle 4,462; pigs 5,305; sheep 670; chickens (Jan. 1966) 26,408.

Industry. Production (in 000; metric tons; 1967): coal 26,076; brown coal 71,363; electricity 38,590,000 kw.-hr.; crude oil (1966) 190; iron ore (30% metal content) 1,913; pig iron 6,822; steel 10,002; cement 6,460; sulfuric acid 1,012; nitrogenous fertilizers (1966) 248; superphosphates (1966) 1,277; cotton fabrics 514,000 m.; woolen fabrics 50,000 m.; silk fabrics (1966) 963 m.; linen and semilinen yarn (1966) 28; passenger cars 112 units; commercial vehicles 53 units. Index of industrial production (1963 = 100): (1967) 129; (1966) 120.

In the past few years, the Czechoslovak leadership had permitted a substantial degree of liberalization to take place. Under Novotny, cultural life was vibrant, and extensive experimentation was going on in the economic sphere. Nevertheless, Czechoslovak intellectuals and journalists chafed under the limitations that remained, and it was generally felt that the economy was not achieving its potential. Moreover, Novotny, a Czech, was distrusted by the Slovaks.

On January 5, the Communist Party leadership decided to replace the veteran Novotny as first secretary with Alexander Dubcek (*see* BIOGRAPHY), the head of the Slovak branch of the party (Novotny retained the presidency until March). At first the Soviet and other Communist parties welcomed the change, but apprehension grew in Poland and East Germany over the Dubcek regime's liberalization measures. Controls over the press were relaxed; public rallies were held at which young people spoke their minds freely; heroes of the pre-Communist era, such as Thomas Masaryk and his son Jan, were resurrected; and the more "Stalinist" of the Czechoslovak Communists were removed from office. Josef Smrkovsky, later to become head of the National Assembly, began agitating publicly for a complete break with the past.

The first signs of Soviet apprehension occurred in late February following the defection of Maj. Gen. Jan Sejna to the U.S. The supreme Warsaw Pact commander, Marshal Ivan Yakubovsky, flew to Prague on February 28 to investigate whether Sejna had taken secrets with him. The Sejna case led to the resignation of Bohumir Lomsky as defense minister and the eventual retirement of Novotny as president. Others who fell by the wayside were such friends of the U.S.S.R. as Foreign Minister Václav David and party ideologist Jiri Hendrych. On April 9, following the election of Ludvik Svoboda (*see* BIOGRAPHY) as president, a new Cabinet was sworn in, led by Oldrich Cernik, a liberal. An "action program" was adopted that allowed for freedom of expression for minority interests and groups.

In a more calm atmosphere, the changes in Czechoslovakia might have attracted little notice, but March and April were not calm months. Students had demonstrated in Poland; intellectuals in the U.S.S.R. were criticizing the trials of liberal writers; and East Germany was afraid that the unrest might infect its

people. On March 23, Dubcek went to Dresden, E. Ger., for a one-day meeting of Warsaw Pact members (minus Romania). When he returned, Dubcek told his people that "a certain concern was shown . . . that antisocialist elements should not take advantage of the process of democratization in our country." Moscow, however, kept silent until May 7, when Tass, the Soviet news agency, strongly protested a story in *Rude Pravo,* the newspaper of the Czechoslovak Communist Party, that said Soviet agents had been involved in the death of Jan Masaryk in 1948.

In early May the leaders of the U.S.S.R., East Germany, Poland, Bulgaria, and Hungary held a meeting in Moscow to discuss Czechoslovak developments. This was followed by Warsaw Pact maneuvers on May 9 along Czechoslovakia's borders. On May 31, maneuvers also began on Czechoslovak soil. Thousands of Soviet combat forces entered Czechoslovakia and stayed until August 3—one month more than originally announced. Nevertheless, plans went ahead to hold the 14th Czechoslovak Communist Party Congress on September 9. New party statutes were drawn up to allow complete freedom of debate in the press. Moreover, there were hints of improved relations between Prague and Bonn. A commission was established to make Czechoslovakia a federated republic, with greater rights given to Slovakia.

On July 4 Dubcek received letters from his Warsaw Pact allies (except Romania) calling for joint talks, but Dubcek replied that he would be willing to take part only in bilateral discussions. Tensions increased dramatically during July 14–15 when the five nations that later were to take part in the invasion met in Warsaw, and signed a letter to Czechoslovakia claiming that the liberalization there had led to an "absolutely unacceptable" situation. They demanded that all non-Communist political groups be banned, that the press and radio be tightly controlled, that dissent be forbidden publicly, and that the Czechoslovak Army be strengthened. On nationwide television, Dubcek said, "We do not wish to yield anything at all on our principles."

From July 29 to August 1, the Soviet Politburo, en masse, met with the Czechoslovak leadership at the border town of Cierna. The results of that meeting were confirmed on August 3 by the other Warsaw Pact nations, except Romania, in Bratislava. The communiqués were loosely written but gave the impression that pressure would be eased on Czechoslovakia in return for a somewhat tighter control over the press. Soviet troops were finally pulled out of Czechoslovakia and there was a general feeling of relief.

Very shortly, however, anti-Czechoslovak polemics began to reappear, and on August 11 new Warsaw Pact maneuvers were started along Czechoslovakia's borders. On August 17, Dubcek held a secret meeting with Hungarian leader Janos Kadar, who reportedly warned him of possible intervention. On August 20 the invasion took place. At first, the Soviet justification was an alleged appeal from Czechoslovak party and state leaders to save Communism, but when no leader stood up publicly to welcome the invasion, this line was dropped in favour of a more doctrinaire one—that Czechoslovakia was showing signs of turning away from socialism and therefore presented a security risk to the Warsaw Pact. Later, the Soviets asserted a right to intervene in socialist countries.

At the time of the invasion, Dubcek, Cernik, Smrkovsky, and some others were arrested by the Soviets and taken to Moscow. They were released after Svoboda announced that he would not negotiate with the Soviets until the leadership had been restored, and after it had become clear that an alternative leadership could not be imposed without bloodshed. Until Dubcek's return from Moscow, the people carried on a remarkable campaign of passive resistance, which included such activities as removing road signs so that the invasion troops would become lost.

The retention of the Dubcek leadership was purchased, however, at the cost of many of its liberalizing policies. On August 26, before returning to Prague, the Czechoslovak leaders signed a pact with the Soviets in which they agreed to tighter controls over political and cultural activities and a cutback in economic cooperation with the West. Dubcek urged his people to support the compromise and warned them that sacrifices would be necessary. Three weeks after the invasion, the Soviet tanks had withdrawn from Prague into the countryside.

There followed a series of meetings between Czechoslovak and Soviet leaders at which it became apparent that the Soviets were dissatisfied with the pace of Czechoslovak compliance with the August 26 pact. Under Soviet pressure, press censorship was reimposed in September. A further agreement, reiterating the promises of August 26, was signed in Moscow on October 4. On October 18 the National Assembly approved a treaty permitting some Soviet troops to remain in the country indefinitely. A number of leaders unacceptable to Moscow—including Foreign Minister Jiri Hajek, who had protested the invasion to the UN—left the government. The plan to give greater autonomy to Slovakia went forward, however, and the new Czecho-Slovak federal state was to be formally inaugurated on Jan. 1, 1969. Foreign observers reported that most Czechoslovaks seemed resigned to the end of their liberalizing experiment, but there were still some signs of resistance. Students turned the celebrations of the Czechoslovak national day on October 28 and the anniversary of the Russian Revolution into anti-Soviet demonstrations.　　(B. M. G.)

See also Communist Movement; Defense; Economic Planning; Propaganda.

Dahomey

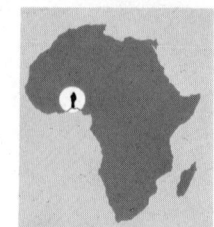

A republic of West Africa, Dahomey is located north of the Gulf of Guinea and is bounded by Togo, Upper Volta, Niger, and Nigeria. Area: 43,483 sq.mi. (112,622 sq.km.). Pop. (1968 est.): 2,576,600, mainly Dahomean and allied tribes. Cap.: Porto-Novo (pop., 1968, 81,412). Largest city: Cotonou (pop., 1968 est., 129,140). Language: French and local dialects. Religion: animist, with Christian and Muslim minorities. Head of state to July 31, 1968, Lieut. Col. Alphonse Alley; president from July 17 and head of state from Aug. 1, 1968, Émile Derlin Zinsou.

The designation in June 1968 of Émile Derlin Zinsou (*see* BIOGRAPHY) as president by the military junta that had seized power in December 1967 seemed likely to put an end to the instability that had characterized Dahomey's political life in recent years.

In February a Constitution Committee appointed by the then head of state, Lieut. Col. Alphonse Alley

DAHOMEY
Education. (1965–66) Primary, pupils 130,774, teachers 3,136; secondary, pupils 11,206, teachers 372; vocational, pupils 439, teachers 72; teacher training, students 322, teachers 27; higher, students 39, teaching staff 5.
Finance. Monetary unit: CFA franc, with a parity of CFA Fr. 50 to the French franc (CFA Fr. 246.85 = U.S. $1; CFA Fr. 592.45 = £1 sterling). Budget (1968 est.): receipts CFA Fr. 8,258,000,000 (including CFA Fr. 600 million French aid); expenditure CFA Fr. 7,757,000,000.
Foreign Trade. (1967) Imports CFA Fr. 10,730,-000,000; exports CFA Fr. 3,750,000,000. Import sources (1966): France 53%; Netherlands 5%; U.S. 5%; Senegal 5%. Export destinations (1966): France 53%; U.S. 10%; Netherlands 8%; West Germany 5%; Nigeria 5%. Main exports: palm oil 40%; cotton 10%; palm nuts and kernels 9%.
Agriculture. Production (in 000; metric tons; 1966; 1965 in parentheses): palm oil 43 (43); palm kernels, exports c. 49 (c. 54); cassava c. 1,200 (c. 1,200); peanuts c. 27 (c. 25); cottonseed c. 6 (c. 4); sweet potatoes c. 570 (c. 570); corn c. 250 (243); coffee c. 1.4 (c. 1.4). Livestock (in 000; 1965–66): cattle 449; pigs 353; sheep c. 460.

(who had replaced Maj. Maurice Kouandete at the end of 1967), and under the supervision of the president of the Supreme Court, Ignacio Pinto, was given one month in which to draw up a new constitution, based on a single-party democratic state, prior to presidential elections. The consequent constitutional proposals were overwhelmingly approved by 846,521 votes to 71,695 in a national referendum on March 31.

In April, despite protests that such measures were unconstitutional, the military government published decrees stipulating that the new constitution would not come into force until after the government's formation and that presidents, vice-presidents, and ministers of former constitutional governments would be debarred from seeking presidential office. In an endeavour to bridge the transition to civilian rule the junta reshuffled the Cabinet in May in order to absorb younger and more active military personnel.

The presidential elections of May 5 resulted in an overwhelming majority for Basile Adjou, one of five candidates. However, they were annulled on May 11 because of a massive boycott by supporters of the former presidents Hubert Maga, Justin Timotin Ahomadegbé, and Sourou Migan Apithy, and the term of military control was extended. In June the junta designated Zinsou president and head of state, these offices to be assumed no later than August 1. On July 17, Zinsou was inaugurated president. He was confirmed in that office by a referendum, followed by the dissolution on July 31 of the Military Revolutionary Committee and by the public announcement of the new government officials. (PH. D.)

Dance

The key to the 1968 dance scene in the U.S. was decentralization. The movement away from the paramountcy of Broadway was not new. It had been happening as regional ballet increased in vigour, in size, in choreographic creativity, and, of great importance, in local support. With 80 or more groups functioning in the four regional associations of the U.S.—Southeast, Northeast, Southwest, and Pacific Northwest—further manifestations of dance decentralization occurred. Approaching its 40th year, the Atlanta (Ga.) Civic Ballet, the oldest regional ballet in the country,

dropped "civic" from its title and became a professional, rather than a semiprofessional, company.

In 1968, under its new name, the Atlanta Ballet joined the Atlanta Opera and the Atlanta Repertory Theater to form the Atlanta Municipal Theater. For its opening production in the new $13 million Atlanta Memorial Arts Center it selected the 17th-century English masque *King Arthur*, written by John Dryden, with music by Henry Purcell. Joyce Trisler was the choreographer for a lavish production (which attracted celebrities from the theatre and dignitaries from Great Britain and other lands) that gave equal accent to dancing, music, and acting. Subsequently, the three constituent companies embarked on separate repertory seasons in an overall program that guaranteed the performers 40 weeks of employment a year.

In 1966 the Rockefeller Foundation had made a grant of $370,000 for the establishment of a modern dance repertory company in the Rocky Mountain

JACK MITCHELL

Robert Blankshine, Maximiliano Zomosa, and Erika Goodman in "The Clowns," a new ballet presented by the City Center Joffrey Ballet company in 1968.

area with headquarters at the University of Utah campus in Salt Lake City. In 1967 the new company, the Repertory Dance Theatre, had begun its choreographic workshop enterprises under the artistic direction of Joan Woodbury. In 1968 reorganization took place, and the young dancers themselves took charge of the project with a manager (Wayne Richardson) and a board of directors to serve as a consulting unit. In an ambitious, and highly successful, fall repertory season in Salt Lake City, the youthful dancers offered new works created especially for them by John Butler and Anna Sokolow, a new staging of José Limon's *Concerto Grosso* (Vivaldi), and dances choreographed by the group's members. The students were required to choreograph for workshop performances, and the best were selected for the repertory.

The University of Utah also maintained a modern dance department of long standing, a more recent ballet department, and a division of creative dance for children that had more than 600 pupils a year. The Utah Civic Ballet, now five years old and headed by Willam Christensen, drew many of its dancers from the university's ballet department. It boasted a repertory of 25 ballets and toured extensively in the Rocky Mountain states and as far as the West Coast.

Dairy Products: *see* Agriculture

Dams: *see* Engineering Projects

Late in 1968, an expansion program changed the Utah Civic Ballet into Ballet West, promising extended dance training and performing facilities in an eight-state area.

The decentralization theme was mirrored elsewhere, in theatres and on campuses. Indeed, the linking of professional dance with departments of dance education on college campuses also represented a swiftly developing trend.

Decentralization of a sort took place within greater New York when Festival of Dance 68–69 was launched late in October at the Brooklyn Academy of Music. The schedule, to run to February 1969, called for the presentation of some 80 works, including several new creations, in more than 100 performances by 12 modern dance companies and one ballet company. The event was cosponsored by the Brooklyn Academy of Music (Harvey Lichtenstein, director) and Theater 1969, headed by Richard Barr and Edward Albee.

MARTHA SWOPE

Suzanne Farrell and Arthur Mitchell in the New York City Ballet's "Slaughter on Tenth Avenue," revived in 1968 by George Balanchine.

Martha Graham and her company opened the festival with a two-week engagement. The other groups were those of Anna Sokolow, Erick Hawkins, Paul Taylor, Alwin Nikolais, Merce Cunningham, José Limon, Alvin Ailey, Twyla Tharp, Meredith Monk, Yvonne Rainer, and Don Redlich and the American Ballet Theatre. The concluding events in the festival were scheduled to be held in the Billy Rose Theatre, a Broadway house.

In July the American Ballet Theatre became the first U.S. ballet troupe to play in repertory in the new Metropolitan Opera House. A revival of Leonide Massine's *Aleko*, with scenery and costumes by Marc Chagall, was among the novelties of the season. In addition to a U.S. tour, the company danced in Japan and traveled to Spain to make a feature-length movie of its new production of *Giselle*, staged by David Blair. Italy's Carla Fracci and Denmark's Erik Bruhn were Giselle and Albrecht; Toni Lander, Bruce Marks, Eleanor D'Antuono, and Ted Kivitt also starred.

continued on page 251

THE AVANT-GARDE TRADITION

By Walter Terry

Ballet, since its earliest and barely recognizable beginnings in the Italian ducal courts of five centuries ago, has gone through many cycles of change in every era. When it did not engage in change or even aesthetic rebellion, it stagnated, became moribund. Today, we are inclined to look upon "modern" ballet, as distinct from "traditional" ballet, as a mid-20th-century phenomenon. True, the ingredients of contemporary ballets are very much of our age, but each ballet age has introduced its own innovations, and what was avant-garde once has now become traditional.

Le Ballet comique de la royne (*reine*, in modern French), for example, represented a considerable advancement over the dances and pageantry used in the earlier banquet-fêtes of Italy, for, although a banquet was an important ingredient in this sumptuous affair presided over by Catherine de Médicis, the queen mother of France, it was put together by a choreographer, and it had a theme to present in terms of dancing, mime, poetry, music, scenic effects, and, of course, food. The year was 1581 and the place was Paris. So impressive and novel was this extravaganza, performed by royalty (the queen herself danced) and courtiers, that the ambassadors and foreign envoys among the 10,000 guests hastened to tell their monarchs of this fabulous event. Before long, other royal courts began to foster ballet. Yet, as new as this seemed in 1581, it would seem quaint and totally unclassical, except in deportment, by ballet standards today.

In the beginning, the five positions of the feet, now fundamental to classical ballet training (along with equivalent positions of the arms), were just starting to evolve, and as for dancing on pointe—something we consider essential to classical ballet—it was unknown in the time of Queen Catherine and would not become a part of classical ballet for more than 200 years. The fundamentals of classical ballet technique may be said to have been founded in 1661 when Louis XIV, himself an accomplished amateur dancer, ordered the establishment in Paris of the Académie Royale de Danse (a Royal Academy of Music was formed eight years later). It was here that the five positions became incorporated into ballet technique along with the exaggerated turnout of the limbs. (When Nijinsky used turned-in stances in his *Afternoon of a Faun* in 1912, he shocked the world of ballet.)

Although ladies of the court performed in court ballets, in the public theatre female roles were played by boys. The Royal Academy, however, accepted girls as students, and in 1681 the world's first professional ballerina, Lafontaine, made her debut. This startling innovation made her the object of vilification, and she subsequently sought haven in a convent. But her admirers at the Paris Opéra were many, and they hailed her as "queen of the dance." Lafontaine was a classical dancer, yet she wore high heels, hoopskirted (or panniered) dresses that swept the floor, cumbersome wigs, and headdresses. More than a quarter of a century was to pass before the premiere danseuse at the Opéra would begin to look like a ballerina as we know her. Marie Camargo, in the early 1700s, took off her heels so that she could spring into the air like the male dancer, thus trans-

forming the ballerina from a terre à terre dancer to an aerial one. She also shocked Europe by cutting off her skirts to some point between ankle and calf so that she could show the public (and her rivals) that she had mastered—perhaps invented—the entrechat.

Camargo's most famous rival, Marie Sallé, was also an innovator. She not only rid herself of cumbersome panniers but also let her hair fall loose in her *Pygmalion* ballet in order to come closer to classical Greek dress. She was also an adventurer in that she choreographed *Pygmalion* herself, thus becoming ballet's first female choreographer. She became too "modern" for a London audience when she donned doublet and hose to play a male part, the title role in a dance treatment of *Hamlet*, and she was run out of town.

In the mid-1700s, a modern-minded choreographer took the ballet world to task for being concerned primarily with muscular prowess, with tricks, for he believed in meaningful movement. Jean-Georges Noverre removed the masks that dancers wore and added facial expressivity to ballet's mime; he exploited the drama of movement in ballets d'action (ballets with plots expressed in movement terms); and he wrote one of the most famous books in dance literature, *Lettres sur la danse et sur les ballets*. At first he was considered much too advanced for the Opéra in Paris, but ultimately, due to the influence of Marie Antoinette, who, as a child, had studied with him in Vienna, he was appointed ballet master at the Opéra.

In a few decades, there were advancements that made Noverre's reforms seem old fashioned. Sometime close to the end of the 1700s, a ballerina with very strong feet (very possibly a Mlle Millerd) rose onto the tips of her toes. Others imitated her, but it remained for Marie Taglioni to make dancing on pointe essential to the art of ballet. The year was 1832, and the ballet created for her by her father, Filippo Taglioni, was *La Sylphide* (not *Les Sylphides*). It ushered in a whole new age of ballet, the Romantic Ballet.

Where does classicism end and modernism begin? In the 1830s the new romantic ballets, with dancing on pointe, were modern and, quite literally, the classical line came to an end. There had been exceptions, of course, such as the extravaganza *Les Indes galantes*, but favoured subjects had always been Jason and Medea, or Circe, or Eros, or any of an endless list of classical characters. All of these are lost to us. Just about the only balletic survivors from the late 18th century are two comedies: *La Fille mal gardée*, which, in its current stagings, probably resembles the original only in story line and not in step, and the Danish *The Whims of Cupid and the Ballet Master*, which is presumed to be done today as it was in 1786.

So although 20th-century ballet classicism has its roots in the academy established by Louis XIV, we now look upon the surviving ballets of the romantic age, such as *Giselle* and *La Sylphide*, as classical. There is an admitted contradiction in terms here: the ballet scholar and follower know that such works belong to the Romantic Age of Ballet, yet they recognize them as superb examples of the technique of classical ballet, which reached a major peak during the reign of Marius Petipa, the choreographic genius of the Russian Imperial Ballet. It was Petipa who created *The Sleeping Beauty*, who conceived *Swan Lake* and choreographed two of its four acts, who dictated to Tchaikovsky the musical form *The Nutcracker* was to have, and who created scores of other ballets, among them *Don Quixote*, *Le Corsaire*, and *La Bayadère*. Petipa was the supreme classicist, and it is his line that today George Balanchine carries ahead and goes beyond. Balanchine, of course, creates ballets that are completely contemporary—some are even avant-garde—but most of today's choreographers who work outside the Petipa tradition owe much of their freedom, or direction, to a rebel against Petipa, Michel Fokine.

The popular dances of a given period—folk, court, ballroom—have always found their way into ballet, feeding it, influencing it, modernizing it. Indeed, ballet itself was born of a combination of ceremony, spectacle, and social dances—the pavane, the galliard, the saraband, and all the other preclassic dance forms.

The Romantic Ballet brought along with it not only the toe shoe but also national dances of the day. Fanny Elssler, Taglioni's greatest rival, had her most popular successes in those adapted national dances, which she performed with earthiness and fire. In fact, her *La Cachucha*, a Spanish dance, almost served as her trademark. Even the ethereal *La Sylphide* contains some hearty Scottish dances. When *Giselle* was first done (1841), the second act, which we now look upon as the epitome of classical-romantic ballet, included in its band of wilis (ghosts of affianced maidens who had died before their wedding day) a Turkish wili and an East Indian one, and they had suitable solo dances. It is not much of a change then, except in time, for Agnes de Mille to create a ballet that includes a Kentucky running set or for Jerome Robbins to make entrechats and snakehips, tours en l'air and cartwheels go side by side.

Fokine, however, did not settle for incorporating national dances into his ballets, as did Coralli, or Bournonville, or Perrot, or Petipa, simply as divertissements in an otherwise classical ballet. He went further, and it was his statement of principles of choreography that introduced modern ballet as we see it today. In a now-historic letter written to *The Times* of London in 1914, he stated that the new ballet should (1) "create in each case a new form of movement corresponding to the subject matter, period and character of the music"; (2) use conventional

Merce Cunningham with members of his company, Barbara Lloyd and Albert Reid, in "Rain Forest," choreographed by Cunningham with an electronic score by David Tudor.

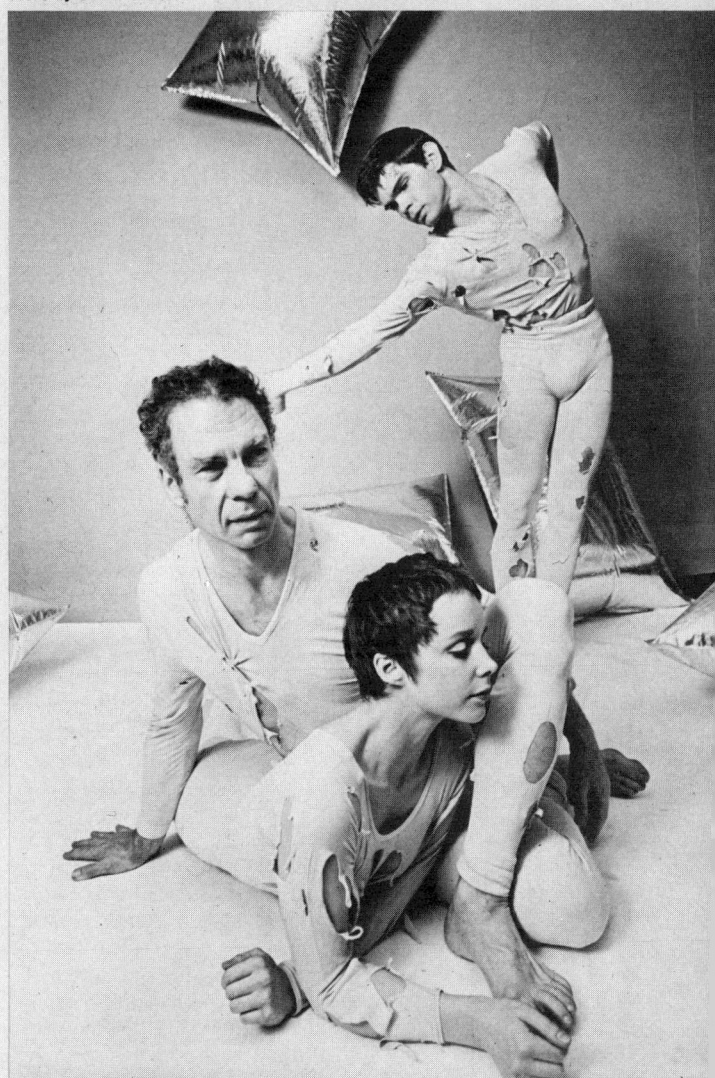

JACK MITCHELL

Carla Fracci and Erik Bruhn in the American Ballet Theatre's presentation of "Giselle."

gestures only to "serve as an expression of dramatic action"; (3) "replace the gestures of the hands by movements of the whole body"; (4) advance "from the expressiveness . . . of the individual body to groups of bodies and the expressiveness of the combined dancing of a crowd"; and (5) recognize "the alliance of arts only on the condition of complete equality."

The fruits of these tenets were such diversified ballets as *Les Sylphides,* perhaps the first abstract ballet as well as a tribute to the romantic style of *La Sylphide; Petrouchka,* a drama-fantasy surrounded by Russian folklore and folkways; and, in fact, a total of 81 ballets including *The Firebird, Prince Igor, Le Spectre de la rose,* and *Daphnis and Chloë.*

As the new century came in, ballet was in desperate need of reform. In central Europe and the U.S., Isadora Duncan, Ruth St. Denis, Ted Shawn, Mary Wigman, Rudolf von Laban, Martha Graham, Doris Humphrey, Charles Weidman, and Helen Tamiris —with Hanya Holm as a link between the new German and American modern dance—elected to dance, choreograph, and build techniques outside the confines of ballet. Fokine chose to make his reforms within the framework of ballet, as his successors have continued to do in most instances.

Fokine disapproved highly of modern dance; and modern dancers, in their turn, scoffed at ballet. It was said that these two dance art forms were separate and distinct and that they could never be successfully wedded. But they have been. Leonide Massine, a product of Russian ballet, in *Choreartium* (1933) used free dance forms closely related to modern dance set to music of Brahms. Agnes de Mille, with some training at Denishawn and a great deal of ballet study, created works in both the classical and the new dance idioms. In her *Three Virgins and a Devil,* which was presented in 1934 in a London revue and as a ballet, revised, in 1941, only the Devil occasionally engaged in balletic steps (tours à la seconde), while the three virgins and a passing youth were given expressions of acting in terms of movement and gesture. Her famous *Rodeo* was a translating of folk measures and mores into theatrical dancing and danceacting. In her *Fall River Legend,* based on the Lizzie Borden murder case, Lizzie danced on pointe, romantic ballet passages were used in a dream sequence, and there was an almost continual interweaving of classical-ballet-rooted actions with freely devised dramatic dance.

The chief distinction between these modern dramatic ballets and the old classics is that in almost all of the old ballets the story was conveyed in mime to be followed by and alternated with dancing. The Mad Scene in *Giselle,* although it contains echoes of dancing, is conceived and considered as a mime scene. When Lizzie, however, is driven to madness by her stepmother, her desperation is expressed wholly in dance, and the toe shoe,

which can accomplish exciting balances and vertiginous turns, becomes not a tool for physical prowess or elegance of movement, but rather an instrument of drama.

Antony Tudor, in his great dramatic ballets, also uses the pointe, along with many classical ballet steps, as expressional dance. In a classical ballet divertissement, the ballerina would get up onto pointe in order to start dancing. Tudor uses the act of rising not as a preparation but as a dramatic culmination. In *Lilac Garden* the tragic heroine, waiting in the garden, feels a hand on her shoulder, and for her it is the only touch in the world. In ecstatic response, she rises onto pointes not merely physically but because she has moved to a new emotional plane.

Today's ballet repertories frequently include not only classical ballet and modern ballet but also modern dance. Indeed, the ballet field has been borrowing choreographers from the world of modern dance. John Butler, a product of Martha Graham, choreographs not only for modern dance troupes but also for ballet companies, both U.S. and European, for opera ballet, and other theatre outlets. Norman Walker, one of the most versatile of the modern dance choreographers, creates not only for his own modern dance group but for ballet companies as well.

In 1966 Merce Cunningham took his *Summerspace* out of his own modern dance repertory and put it on pointe for the New York City Ballet, and in 1968 Paul Taylor, of the U.S. avantgarde, produced his modern dance work *Aureole* (to music of Handel) for the Royal Danish Ballet, Europe's oldest royal ballet company. Eliot Feld, one of the newest and most admired ballet choreographers, used no pointe work and very little classical movement in his first big success, *Harbinger,* for the American Ballet Theatre. Some classical movement, including pointe, was to be found in Feld's second success, *At Midnight,* and his third ballet, *Meadow Lark,* created for the Royal Winnipeg Ballet, was not only wholly classical but evoked the ballet aura of the days of royal courts. George Balanchine and Sir Frederick Ashton, perhaps the most celebrated senior choreographers in classical ballet, step over the frontiers on many occasions to create pieces that are closer to free dance than to the ballet d'école. Jerome Robbins' monumental staging of Stravinsky's *Les Noces* for the American Ballet Theatre does not have one traditional ballet step in it— it is a danced ceremony performed by a ballet company.

So what is ballet today? It is certainly still *Giselle* and *La Sylphide,* and *The Nutcracker* and *Swan Lake* (the most popular ballet in the world), a grand pas de deux and brand new ballets in the classical idiom. It is also *Billy the Kid, Rodeo, Dark Elegies, Monument for a Dead Boy,* and Robert Joffrey's *Astarte,* in which a comparatively classical pas de deux mates with modern dance effects in a psychedelic setting that overwhelms dancers and onlookers.

Tomorrow, this will become part of tradition.

Martha Graham and Bertram Ross in "A Time of Snow."

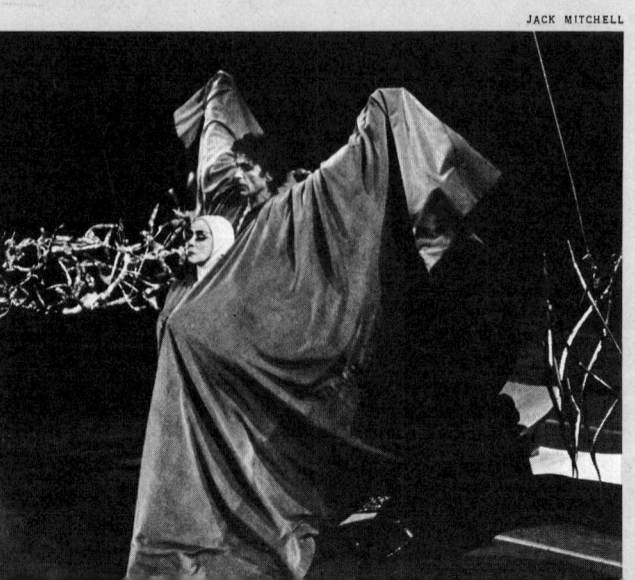

continued from page 248

"Stars of the Bolshoi," a unit from the Bolshoi Ballet, also played the new Met and toured the U.S. The repertory consisted mainly of divertissements, short ballets, and ballet extracts. Maya Plisetskaya was the prima ballerina. Of particular interest in a repertory closely resembling dance vaudeville was a production of Michel Fokine's *Le Spectre de la rose,* staged by the Bolshoi's Maris Liepa. Liepa had consulted with Western ballet experts in order to re-create the Fokine style, a style with which Soviet dancers are not closely familiar.

For the performances of Britain's Royal Ballet at the Met, Dame Margot Fonteyn and Rudolf Nureyev were the guest superstars. Nureyev was also represented by his restaging of Act IV of Petipa's *La Bayadère* and his almost completely new choreography for *The Nutcracker.* Sir Frederick Ashton's new comedy ballet, *Jazz Calendar* (with music by Richard Bennett), was presented in London. A revival of his *La Fille mal gardée* was featured during the engagement at Lincoln Center.

Activities of other royal companies included gala performances in London by the Royal Danish Ballet; King Frederick IX of Denmark and Queen Elizabeth II of Great Britain were present at the opening. In Stockholm, Erik Bruhn, director of the Royal Swedish Ballet, staged a new production of Bournonville's *La Sylphide,* the Danish classic. In Canada, the oldest royal ballet in the British Commonwealth, the Royal Winnipeg Ballet, set a new record for itself by presenting a bill composed of new productions only, including the world premieres of Eliot Feld's *Meadow Lark* (Haydn's flute quartet) and John Butler's *Labyrinth* (music by Harry Somers) and two new stagings, Anna Sokolow's *Opus '65* (Teo Macero) and Todd Bolender's *Donezettiana.* Later, the company toured Europe and the U.S.S.R.

Among the many companies touring during the year were the Netherlands Dance Theatre, troupes from Spain (Ballets de Madrid), India (Uday Shankar), and Korea, and the Compagnie Nationale de Danses Françaises, directed by the singer Jacques Douai.

The New York City Ballet celebrated its 20th anniversary as resident ballet company at the New York City Center of Music and Drama. In 1968 it remained as a constituent member of the City Center, although it was now the resident company of the New York State Theater at Lincoln Center where it performed approximately 22 weeks out of the year.

To its already large repertory, the New York City Ballet in 1968 added *Metastaseis & Pithoprakta,* a new ballet by George Balanchine to music by Iannis Xenakis; *Pas de deux: La Source* (Balanchine-Delibes); and a revival-reworking of Balanchine's famous *Slaughter on Tenth Avenue* from the old Broadway musical *On Your Toes.*

One of the company's principal artists, Edward Villella, was the subject of a one-hour television special, "Man Who Dances," presented by Bell Telephone. The documentary was focused upon Villella on stage and off—in rehearsal, in lecture-demonstration, and in interview. Some of the scenes showed him in performance on stage at the State Theater in such Balanchine works as *Jewels* and *Tarantella.*

Robert Joffrey, whose company had changed its name to the City Center Joffrey Ballet when it became the resident ballet group at the City Center, led his dancers through both spring and fall seasons in a repertory including works by Joffrey himself, Gerald

George Balanchine's tribute to the Rev. Martin Luther King, Jr., "Requiem Canticles," performed May 2 by the New York City Ballet to a score of the same name by Igor Stravinsky.

Arpino (the troupe's chief choreographer), Balanchine, and others. Among the novelties were Arpino's *The Clowns* (music by Hershy Kay), *Secret Places* (Mozart), *A Light Fantastic* (Britten), *Fanfarita* (Ruperto Chapi), and a production of Lew Christensen's *Distractions* (Haydn).

John Butler, who staged ten of his choreographies (eight of them premieres) within a year's period, not only created for the Royal Winnipeg Ballet and the Repertory Dance Theater in Utah, but also fashioned a work involving a dancer and an actress for Carmen de Lavallade and her Theater of Dance. *Touch of Loss,* originally performed on television, used the poetry of François Villon with Miss de Lavallade and Mildred Dunnock as its performers.

Martha Graham, in addition to opening the Festival of Dance 68–69 in Brooklyn, appeared earlier in the year in a Broadway engagement. The repertory included two new works, *The Plain of Prayer,* with music by Eugene Lester, and *A Time of Snow* (Norman Dello Joio); Miss Graham performed in the latter. Increasingly, the veteran dancer was turning over to members of her company the roles she had first performed. In 1968, in revivals of *Errand into the Maze* (Menotti) and *Dark Meadow,* younger principal dancers took over the physically demanding assignments.

Limon, in performances in New York, at the American Dance Festival in New London, Conn., and else-

Robert Mead, Merle Park, and Anthony Dowell in the Royal Ballet's production of "Jazz Calendar."

ANTHONY CRICKMAY

where, offered a repertory including two new creations which he had choreographed: *Comedy,* with music by Josef Wittman, and *Legend,* with a score utilizing words, sounds, and music selected for tape by Simon Sadoff. For the Juilliard Dance Ensemble, Limon revived his Mexican ballet, *Tonantzintla* (with music by Antonio Soler and decor and costumes designed by the late Miguel Covarrubias) and *La Malinche,* with music by Norman Lloyd.

The ten-week summertime Jacob's Pillow Dance Festival in Lee, Mass., founded and directed by Ted Shawn, continued to include ballet, modern dance, many ethnic dance forms (Spanish, Indian, etc.), American folk, mime, and experimental dance. Norman Walker, head of the Pillow's modern dance department, created *Songs* (to music of Tadeusz Baird) for his own company and *Evocation* (Hovhaness) for the Jacob's Pillow Dancers, which was composed mainly of students. The Pillow also presided over the U.S. debut of one of India's major dancers, Ritha Devi. Among the many featured performers at the Pillow were Louis Falco, Ivan Nagy, Eleanor D'Antuono, Niels Kehlet and Solveig Øestergaard of the Royal Danish Ballet, Jean Cébron from France, the Pennsylvania Ballet, and the Boston Ballet with Edward Villella and Patricia McBride of the New York City Ballet as guest stars. Nagy had defected to the West from Hungary in 1968 while dancing with the National Ballet of Washington, D.C. Subsequently he joined the New York City Ballet as guest and was then engaged by the American Ballet Theatre.

The annual festival sponsored by the Rebekah Harkness Foundation in the Delacorte Theater in New York City's Central Park featured a variety of artists. Lucette Aldous of British ballet fame and Karl Musil from Austria were participants along with ballet principal Patricia Neary of the U.S., David and Anna Marie Holmes from Canada, and the Harkness Youth Company. The Harkness Ballet itself directed its attention to tours abroad, including appearances in the Festival of Two Worlds at Spoleto, Italy.

The avant-garde, headed by Merce Cunningham, Paul Taylor, Alwin Nikolais, Yvonne Rainer, Jeff Duncan and his Dance Theater Workshop, and others less well known, flourished in big theatres and small, at home and on tour, in churches and in studios.

The focus on dance glitter shifted from New York to Kansas City, Mo., for a one-night gala which cost approximately $31,000. The stars included Antoinette Sibley and Anthony Dowell of the Royal Ballet; Kirsten Simone and Henning Kronstam of the Royal Danish Ballet; Lupe Serrano and Royes Fernandez of the American Ballet Theatre; Melissa Hayden and Jacques d'Amboise of the New York City Ballet; stars of Canada's National Ballet, the Alvin Ailey Dance Theater, the City Center Joffrey Ballet; and Tamara Toumanova, one of the Ballet Russe de Monte Carlo's "Baby Ballerinas" of the 1930s.

During the year death came to the great American dance pioneer Ruth St. Denis, a professional dancer for 75 years, and to Europe's internationally celebrated Harald Kreutzberg. Dame Marie Rambert, founder of Ballet Rambert, celebrated her 80th birthday; Dame Adeline Genée, a contemporary of Miss St. Denis, turned 90; and Mathilde Kchessinska, one-time prima ballerina assoluta of the Russian Imperial Ballet, became 96 years old.   (W. Te.)

See also Music; Theatre.

Encyclopædia Britannica Films. *Steps of the Ballet* (1950).

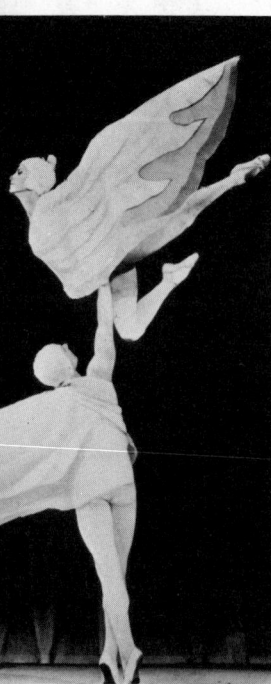

Stanislav and Liudmilla Vlasov danced the spectacular extravaganza "The Doves" during the Bolshoi Ballet's 11-week tour of the U.S. in 1968.

Danish Literature:
see Literature

Deaths:
see Vital Statistics;
see also biographies of prominent persons who died in 1968, listed under Obituaries

Debts, National:
see Government Finance

Defense

The Soviet invasion of Czechoslovakia in August overshadowed all other events in the military field in Europe during 1968. For the rest of the year, NATO countries were preoccupied with assessing its consequences and implications. The immediate reaction in many nonofficial circles was that it invalidated the Western policy of seeking a détente with the Soviet Union and that the West would have to rebuild its European defenses, which had been allowed to run down as the détente developed. Reaction among the Western governments was more restrained. Both the U.S. and the U.K. refrained from acting in any way that might be considered provocative by the Soviet Union, and France pressed its determination to continue with its policy of détente. The reaction in West Germany, however, was more forceful. Chancellor Kurt Kiesinger was among the most insistent advocates of an overhaul of NATO strategy and organization. (*See* Czechoslovakia.)

The liberal Czechoslovak leaders who came to power early in the year insisted that they remained loyal to the Warsaw Pact, but some among them added their voices to that of Pres. Nicolae Ceausescu of Romania in criticizing its organizational structure. Alexander Dubcek (*see* Biography), first secretary of the Communist Party of Czechoslovakia, called for new joint command arrangements to give member countries a share with the Soviet Union in policy making. Gen. Vaclav Prchlik, head of the Security and Defense Department of the party's Central Committee, went further in urging that the top command posts, hitherto reserved for Soviet officers, be rotated among member nations, and he recommended amendment of the Warsaw Treaty to prevent its being used for political ends. The general also insisted that Czechoslovak officers should not feel bound to accept Soviet military doctrine uncritically. On February 28 the Warsaw Pact commander in chief, Marshal Ivan Yakubovsky, visited Prague. The subsequent cancellation of Warsaw Pact maneuvers, scheduled to take place in Czechoslovakia in the spring, was seen as a triumph for the Dubcek regime. Soviet troop movements were reported in southern Poland in early May, but Prague calmed the fears they aroused by claiming to have been officially informed.

Nevertheless, Soviet pressure continued. The Soviet defense minister, Marshal Andrei A. Grechko, visited Prague on May 20 with a demand that at least one Soviet division be stationed in Czechoslovakia, as Soviet troops were stationed under the Warsaw Pact in East Germany, Poland, and Hungary. Although this demand was successfully resisted, Prague had to make a concession on May 24, when it was announced that the Warsaw Pact would hold staff exercises in Czechoslovakia in June.

The main reason behind the Soviet Union's wish to have its troops in Czechoslovakia was doubtless to ensure Soviet control over internal Czechoslovak politics, but specifically strategic motives may have played a part. Despite Czechoslovak disclaimers, the Soviet Union said that it feared Dubcek's regime would take Czechoslovakia out of the Warsaw Pact into neutrality, causing a breach in the buffer zone that had been erected across Europe after World War II. Another possible reason for the Soviet Union's strategic interest in Czechoslovakia lay in the fact that

Soviet military doctrine had moved away from the "massive retaliation" strategy favoured by N. S. Khrushchev toward a strategy of "flexible response," much like that urged on NATO after 1960 by U.S. Secretary of Defense Robert McNamara. This strategy demanded that the Warsaw Pact be able to fight on the East-West borders, using highly sophisticated weapons and tactics. It was suggested that Warsaw Pact maneuvers held in 1966 to test this strategy had revealed the Czechoslovak Army's inability to carry out its allotted role of fighting a holding action on the German border for 72 hours before the introduction of nuclear weapons.

On June 4, despite assurances from the Czechoslovak defense minister, Gen. Martin Dzur, that the June maneuvers were to be staff exercises only, Soviet troops and tanks began to enter Czechoslovakia. By the end of June about 16,000 Soviet soldiers with 4,500 vehicles and 100 tanks were reported to be inside the country. After the official end of the maneuvers on June 30, the departure of the troops was delayed until mid-July, often on such flimsy pretexts as that abnormal traffic conditions prevented large-scale military movements. On August 11 the Soviet Union announced that new maneuvers would take place in Poland, the Ukraine, East Germany, and Hungary.

The invasion of Czechoslovakia began at 11 P.M. on the night of August 20. It was executed by Soviet troops supported by Polish, Hungarian, East German, and Bulgarian units. Between 150,000 and 200,000 Warsaw Pact troops, composed of elements of 20 Soviet, 2 Polish, 2 Hungarian, and 2 East German divisions, were reported to have entered Czechoslovakia by the evening of August 21 in the biggest military movement in Europe since World War II. The troops occupying Prague were accompanied by an estimated 500 tanks and a quantity of heavy artillery, including antiaircraft guns. The 170,000-man Czechoslovak Army offered no resistance. In line with its Warsaw Pact role, it was deployed in defensive positions in the south of the country. In any case, the Czechoslovak Army was composed largely of national service men, and its military efficiency was rated as low, at least by the Soviet high command. Consistent with Prague's official policy of offering no resistance to the Soviet invasion, General Dzur restricted himself to issuing orders that Czechoslovak soldiers were to obey no one but Pres. Ludvik Svoboda (see BIOGRAPHY). As a result, most of them became virtual prisoners in their own camps and barracks, surrounded and guarded by Soviet troops.

From a military point of view, the Soviet invasion was an outstanding success. Prague was secure less than four hours after the first troops crossed the border. The speed of the take-over suggested to some Western observers that the Soviet Union had not withdrawn all its troops from Czechoslovakia following the summer maneuvers. It seemed likely, at least, that the maneuvers had been used as camouflage for planning the invasion.

A striking feature of the Soviet occupation was the moral resistance of the Czechoslovak people against the invaders. Although they obeyed the official call not to resist the invasion forcibly, thousands of Czechoslovaks demonstrated their opposition in the streets. Soviet troops were jeered and insulted; a few tanks were burned out after demonstrators pushed burning rags into their fuel pipes; and some demonstrators attempted to block the tanks by sitting on the road in

continued on page 257

CHEMICAL AND BIOLOGICAL WARFARE

By Robin H. Clarke
and Robert E. Hunter

The Weapons. The idea of using toxic materials, poisonous or asphyxiating chemicals, or the microorganisms that produce disease in man as military agents in war is not new. Such practices were proposed and used by the ancient Greeks as long ago as 600 B.C., and the poisoning of water supplies has been used as a military strategy for almost as long as wars have been waged. It was not until the 19th century, however, that modern technology provided really effective toxic weapons. The use of poisonous chemicals was first suggested to the British War Department in 1855, and in 1862 the use of chlorine gas was proposed for use in the U.S. Civil War. Chemical weapons were not to make their real debut, however, until World War I, when they were used on a massive scale. Since then, all countries have lived under the threat of chemical or biological attack.

Advances in knowledge of the nature of toxic materials and the organisms that produce disease have now made the threat a much more serious one. Today many countries possess stockpiles of these weapons, or the knowledge of how to make them, and the problem of their control has come to the fore once again at the disarmament table. Indeed, with the prospect of lasting and binding agreements to control the use of nuclear devices now in sight, similar and even more widespread control of chemical and biological weaponry is likely to become a major concern of many governments. The problem is particularly pressing because, although these weapons have a killing capacity that almost rivals that of nuclear weapons, they are much cheaper to manufacture and somewhat cheaper to deliver. They are thus within the financial reach of even very small countries, whereas nuclear stockpiles are likely to remain in the hands of the financial elite for many years to come.

History. Chemical weapons were first used in earnest on April 22, 1915, near Ypres, Belg., by the German forces. They released 168 tons of pressurized chlorine gas from 500 cylinders and let it drift with the wind toward the opposing forces. The result was devastating: more than 15,000 casualties were produced and about 5,000 people died from the attack. Chlorine is a poisonous chemical and was to be used many times during World War I. By comparison with the other chemicals that were soon used on the battlefield, however, it was not very effective. Phosgene, which is about ten times more toxic, was soon introduced, and it penetrated the hastily developed gas masks that had been found effective against chlorine. Gas masks were again improved, and for the duration of the war there was a perpetual race to produce better masks and more effective chemicals. This trend culminated in July 1917, when the Germans first used mustard gas, which in liquid form produces large and painful blisters on the skin, while the vapour produces intense respiratory irritation, vomiting, nausea, fever, and eventually death if a large enough dose is inhaled. During the last year of the war mustard gas caused 16% of British and nearly 27% of U.S. casualties.

Between 1915 and 1918 more than 3,000 possible chemicals were screened for military use. Of these, 12 tear gases, 15 choking agents, 3 blood poisons, 4 blister agents, and 4 vomiting gases were actually used. They produced between 800,000 and 1.3 million casualties on all sides, of which more than 400,000 were attributed to mustard gas.

After the war, the major nations were concerned to ban the use of these devastating weapons, and in Geneva in 1925 a protocol was drafted and signed that prohibited the use in war of asphyxiating, poisonous, or other gases, as well as of bacteriological methods of warfare. At the time, 46 nations signed the protocol and many more have since signed and ratified it (*see* below).

Only 11 years later, however, the protocol was broken by the Italians, who used mustard gas against the Ethiopians in 1935–36. The Japanese made repeated but minor chemical attacks against the Chinese between 1937 and 1942, but chemical weapons were not used in World War II on anything like the scale of World War I. This was particularly fortunate, for in the late 1930s the Germans had discovered a new class of chemical weapon, based on organophosphorous compounds, that was far more effective than any previously known. Although some of these gases were extensively stockpiled during the war by the Germans, they were never used. These chemicals were the forerunners of the nerve gases currently stockpiled by both the Soviet Union and the U.S.

The Chemical Weapons. Three nerve gases were developed by the Germans in the late 1930s and early 1940s. In order of increasing toxicity, they were Tabun, Sarin, and Soman, and all had similar chemical constitutions. Their formulas and their methods of manufacture were taken back to the U.S., where they were code-named GA, GB, and GD, respectively. The Soviets captured one of the Tabun manufacturing plants and had it shipped to the Soviet Union and reassembled. All the nerve gases are colourless and relatively odourless and will kill when used in very small quantities; 40 drops of liquid Sarin deposited on the clothing will penetrate both clothing and skin, producing a fifty-fifty chance of death. They act by interfering with the mechanism by which the nerves control the muscles, producing intense muscle fibrillation that ultimately leads to death by asphyxiation as the respiratory muscles become paralyzed.

In the early 1950s, British chemists discovered another group of closely related but even more toxic chemicals. They were investigated at the Ministry of Defence Chemical Defence Experimental Establishment at Porton Down, Wiltshire, and their properties were revealed to the U.S. under the quadripartite agreement by which Canada, Australia, the U.K., and the U.S. exchange information relating to defense. The Americans code-named them VE and VX and produced stockpiles of them. They are today the most toxic chemicals stockpiled and standardized for military use. They differ from earlier nerve gases mainly in their increased toxicity and increased ability to penetrate the skin

Over 5,000 sheep were killed near Skull Valley, Utah, when deadly nerve gas was blown onto a ranch from a U.S. Army chemical and biological warfare proving ground.

and in their lower volatility. This means that they can be used to deny territory to an enemy for long periods of time because, once sprayed on the ground, they will take some time to evaporate completely.

Almost none of the World War I chemical weapons remain operational. In the U.S. the mustard gases have been further developed, and several new forms are now standardized for military use. Along with this concern for the development of more lethal chemicals, there has been a large research effort into both harassing agents and incapacitating ones. The object of this research is to discover chemicals that could be used to render an enemy temporarily incapable but that would allow him to return to normality within a few hours or days. The U.S. Army Chemical Corps made much of this possibility in the late 1950s, claiming that such developments could make possible "war without death." In fact, the research has proved more difficult than originally supposed. So far only one incapacitating agent has been standardized for military use. Code-named BZ, it has a hallucinatory effect, producing giddiness, disorientation, and occasionally maniacal behaviour. In view of its somewhat unpredictable effects, it, and other agents based on the psychochemical LSD, are not thought to be of great military value. The main emphasis of this part of the research program is now believed to be directed toward the discovery of a satisfactory "knockdown" agent, which would render an enemy temporarily unconscious but would allow him to return to perfectly normal health within a few hours. No such chemical capable of being used on the battlefield has so far been discovered.

The third major area of current interest is in harassing agents, a class that includes the tear gases used by police in riot control. Their military use is on a small scale—to allow the capture, for example, of a house, tunnel, or small fort. The chemicals code-named CN and DM, both discovered in 1918, have been used for this purpose. Their main disadvantage, however, is that they can cause death if inhaled in large but not enormous doses; at the same time, quite large doses are needed to render the enemy quite incapable of offering any resistance. Accordingly, scientists at Porton were asked in the 1950s to find an alternative chemical. After screening some 90 possibilities, they rediscovered CS, very small doses of which will disperse crowds and which has a much lower toxicity than either DM or CN. It causes the sensations of an acute and very painful cold, but its effects wear off within minutes. It is now a standardized military chemical used by the U.S.

The Biological Weapons. Unlike the chemicals, biological weapons have never been used on a large scale in war. They are thus untried and unproved, although a number of major powers have invested large research funds in their development. The object of this research is to learn how to grow the organism that causes a disease such as plague or smallpox in such a way that existing vaccines or antibiotics would not be effective against it. The organisms would be grown much as are the organisms currently used in live vaccines. They would then be packaged into a delivery system and sprayed as an aerosol of very fine particles over enemy territory. As the aerosol cloud settled, these particles would be inhaled by the enemy who, after the relevant incubation period, would contract the disease. The reason that such weapons have not been used so far is mainly that their development is much more difficult than would appear. Living organisms are difficult things to handle and there are few known disease-producing organisms that can survive the process of dispersion as an aerosol, plus the combined effects of wind, rain, and ultraviolet radiation from the sun while floating in the atmosphere, and still remain effective when they finally come in contact with the enemy. The only kinds of organisms that can be considered are those that when inhaled in very small quantities will produce disease. For instance, Q fever will ensue if only a dozen or so of the organisms are inhaled. Organisms that must be inhaled by the thousands in order to produce disease are less effective.

Some diseases are caused by bacteria that are capable of forming extremely hardy spores. Undoubtedly such spores could survive the rigours of dissemination as a weapon, but their very stability poses another problem. If sprayed onto enemy territory, they might survive there for years, making the territory virtually uninhabitable to both sides. One example is the organism that causes anthrax. During the 1940s the British government decided to test the feasibility of biological warfare by spraying the island of Gruinard off northwest Scotland with anthrax spores. The sheep chosen as the victims for this experiment certainly died, but the organisms lingered much longer than would be militarily desirable. The island is still out of bounds and is inspected yearly by a team from the Microbiological Research Establishment at Porton. During a recent visit to the island, the director of this establishment stated that he suspected the island would remain infected for another hundred years.

Nevertheless, it seems likely that, with the large research effort being made into biological weapons, the technical problems will one day be solved. When this happens, the threat from biological warfare will become very real indeed. In theory so little material is needed to cause so many deaths that these weapons might even become more powerful than the nuclear devices now stockpiled. Furthermore, they could be manufactured by small teams of microbiologists and engineers whose services could be afforded by even small and poor countries.

Research Establishments and National Policies. Research and development programs on chemical and biological weapons exist in many countries, but only in the U.S. and the U.K. is much publicly known about their scale and objectives. In the U.S. the main biological research centre is at Ft. Detrick, near Frederick, Md. It is a large centre, occupying 1,300 ac. and employing nearly 700 scientifically trained personnel. The Edgewood Arsenal, also in Maryland, is responsible both for the manufacture of the raw material for chemical weapons and for filling the munitions to be stockpiled. Other plants that have been or are being used for the manufacture of chemicals include the Rocky Mountain Arsenal in Denver and a plant at Muscle Shoals in Alabama. At an estimated annual cost of $3.5 million, a plant in Newport, Ind., produces the nerve gas code-named VE and fills rockets, mines, and shells with it. Both chemical and biological weapons are tested at the Dugway Proving Ground, 60 mi. SW of Salt Lake City, Utah, where a field trial of a nerve gas in early 1968 killed about 5,000 sheep on neighbouring farmland. About 900 people work at Dugway. The Pine Bluff Arsenal in Arkansas has responsibilities for the manufacture of both chemical and biological weapons. In 1964 the total cost of the U.S. program—research, development, and production—had reached nearly $300 million a year. Since then the figures have not been made public but are thought to have increased.

In Britain, the situation is different, since British policy is to investigate defense only; there is currently no requirement for the stockpiling of either chemical or biological weapons, and no such stockpiles exist. The Chemical Defence Experimental Establishment and the Microbiological Research Establishment, both at Porton Down, are the two main research centres, run at an official cost of £1.6 million and £900,000 each year, respectively. Small quantities of likely weapons are produced so that defensive research shall be realistic, but there is no manufacturing plant at Porton and no British munitions have been developed for the delivery of either chemical or biological warheads. The only exception concerns riot control agents such as CS, which is manufactured at Nancekuke in Cornwall. The plant there has an annual capacity of four–five tons of CS. Other plants are in existence for the pilot-scale production of chemicals of military interest. Although Britain stockpiled chemicals extensively during World War II, most of these have now been destroyed and those that remain are no longer considered operational. The only country other than the U.S. known to have stockpiles of chemical weapons is the Soviet Union, which also operates an elaborate civil defense program against chemical warfare.

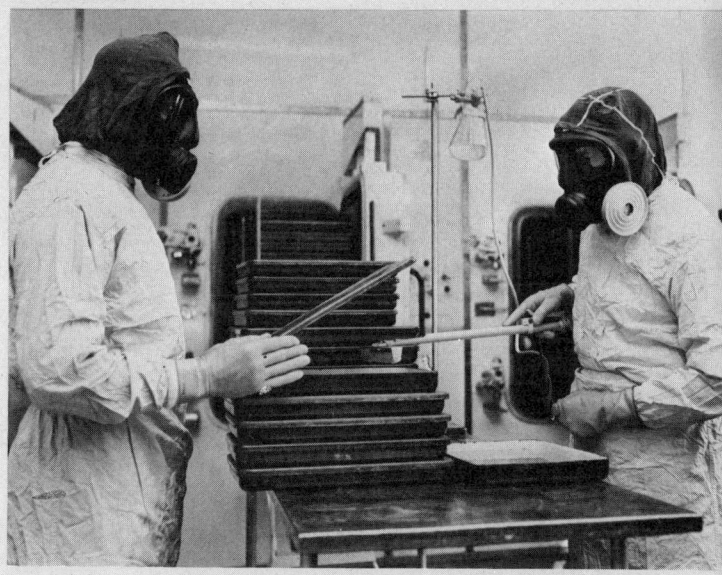

Researchers handling virulent biological material at the Microbiological Research Establishment at Porton Down near Salisbury, U.K. The laboratory is attempting to develop defenses against chemical and biological warfare.

Recent Uses of Chemical Weapons. There have been two recent uses of chemicals that appear to infringe the Geneva Protocol. One was in Yemen, where throughout 1966 and 1967 claims were made that chemicals had been used by U.A.R. forces. Several hundred casualties were said to have been caused, including more than 200 deaths. Eventually, the International Red Cross was called in to investigate and these claims were substantiated. Both mustard gas and phosgene are thought to have been used.

In Vietnam in 1965, U.S. forces began to use the three harassing agents, DM, CN, and CS, against Viet Cong forces. Department of Defense officials repeatedly argued that the use of these chemicals did not infringe the Geneva Protocol (the United States is not, in fact, bound by that treaty since the Senate has refused to ratify it). The official argument was that the Geneva Protocol did not apply to nonlethal gases of the type being used. This view has been disputed by international lawyers, since the wording of the protocol is not specific here. However, the declassification of Porton Technical Paper No. 651 in June 1968 threw some light on the point. The paper states that DM was ruled out as a riot-control agent by the legal branch of the U.K. War Office because, in view of its poisonous nature, "the use of DM must be proscribed in accordance with the provisions of the Geneva Gas Protocol." Chemicals were also being used in Vietnam by U.S. forces to defoliate the jungle on a very large scale and to destroy crops. Five million gallons of defoliants and herbicides were purchased at a cost of $32 million for this purpose during fiscal 1967. By the end of 1966 rice crops on 150,000 ac. of paddy field had been destroyed in this way, and 500,000 ac. of jungle had been defoliated.

These actions in Vietnam brought renewed activity from those seeking to control the use of chemical and biological weapons more effectively. Two shortcomings of the 1925 protocol are its lack of specificity about the so-called "nonlethal" agents and the fact that it does not preclude the use of either type of weapon against domestic animals or plants. The argument has been raised, therefore, that the protocol should be reworded to take care of these points and then re-presented for signature. Against this is the argument that the existing protocol has stood the test of time reasonably well and has been both signed and ratified by nearly all major countries (the United States, Japan, and Brazil being the most important exceptions). (R. H. CL.)

The Strategic View. Chemical and biological warfare is now an advanced science. Hundreds of millions of dollars have been spent on these weapons, and great quantities of lethal agents have been stockpiled by the U.S. and the Soviet Union. But there

is still no clear understanding of the actual strategic value of preparing, either offensively or defensively, for gas and germ warfare. In fact, there are no real strategic arguments for this kind of warfare, or even for the major powers' developing the weapons needed for it. Quite the reverse is true. The strategic arguments all militate strongly against any such efforts.

To begin with, there is simply no case for any of the five nuclear powers having offensive gases and germs. Not only are there technical arguments against their use—in the macabre phrase, they are not "efficient"—but there is no need for any country with vast quantities of nuclear weapons to go in for other devices to accomplish roughly the same purpose—namely, deterrence. By some miracle the world is learning to live with the Bomb, so let us leave well enough alone.

But what about preparing active defenses against chemical and biological weapons—against the mad act of some small country with a grievance? This is the position in Britain today, where none of these weapons is prepared for offensive use. But the strategic argument here is hardly less clear: no defense is ever going to be effective enough to afford real protection. Look, for example, at the dismal failure in Britain and the U.S. of plans to create civil defenses against a nuclear attack—a much easier task.

Of course, there would always seem to be some value in building defenses, however meagre. But in the process, what effect would researches into chemical and biological warfare have on the small nations of the world? We are now faced with the prospect that these gases and germs could become the "poor man's atom bomb"; they would be far easier to build and conceal, though less easy to use, than nuclear weapons.

Therefore, from a strategic point of view, every precaution should be taken to prevent the technology for making chemical and biological weapons from falling into the wrong hands; and the psychological barriers against these weapons should not be eroded. There is a simple standard: how much are defenses worth to a major power if, in the building, they only make it more likely that poison gases and germs will actually be made and used in some other part of the world?

First, there is the need to prevent information about making and using chemical and biological weapons from spreading around the world. It is a truism of modern industrial research that the initial developments are the hardest; after the first discoveries, the technical processes tend to become rather more simple. This has been true even of nuclear weapons. Therefore, everything that goes on in this field, in terms of technical details, should be kept secret.

Of course, there is some chemical and biological warfare research that is of value in the study of disease. But here the argument for transferring such work to ministries of health is overpowering. It is not so much that defense ministries would always be interested in the "dirty tricks" that could follow from basic research; it is a question of preserving the psychological and moral barriers that alone will dissuade many countries from acquiring—and using—gases and germs. It is far easier to convince another country to keep away from chemical and biological warfare if the research is undertaken, not by a ministry connected with war, but rather by one connected with health.

Second, there are the psychological and moral restraints themselves. This is not just a fantasy of the pacifist left. Indeed, much of Soviet-U.S. understanding, as well as the crude limits imposed on the war in Vietnam, derives from just such barriers in men's minds. With regard to gas, we have already seen the negative effect of not taking the psychological barriers seriously enough: the U.S. began using nonlethal gases in Vietnam, after which the U.A.R. used a more lethal variety in Yemen. There was very little outcry in the world against this act, a poor precedent from a strategic as well as a moral point of view.

There may seem little to choose between one horrible means of killing and another. Is bubonic plague any worse than napalm for those directly attacked? The real problem is the nature of

war, and the actual weapons used give one very little choice from a moral point of view. But there is a strategic difference that lies, basically, in the nature of indiscriminate weapons that do not spare civilians. Nuclear weapons, gases, and germs are all of a piece here, and their spread around the world actually makes conflict more likely. Two small countries may not have to match one another's ability to make and use napalm, but it will be to their peril to stand aloof from a race in nuclear weapons, gases, or germs.

Therefore, whenever one nation engaged in a squabble starts stockpiling these weapons, its neighbour must do the same. The arguments against the spread of nuclear weapons apply to gases and germs with even stronger force: what happens if there is an accident? Can less politically "sophisticated" nations learn rapidly enough the demands of caution and restraint in a dangerous world?

There is one more argument that must be met. Could not workable nonlethal gases—such as LSD, perhaps—give us a world in which wars would be fought without death? This may seem an attractive notion, but it is basically nonsense. It neglects the reasons wars are fought in the first place—namely, to gain or preserve something of political value. Would any leader surrender a position just because all or part of his army had been put to sleep? Or would he search for some means of raising his enemy's price of victory? It is inconceivable that something thought "worth dying for" would be given up without fatalities.

Nonlethal gas or germ warfare makes sense only in an incidental way. Putting enemy soldiers to sleep might delay the start of the killing—and save lives—where a war had begun by error or excess of élan. And using tear gas or defoliants in guerrilla wars does enable separation of civilian sheep from enemy goats without harming the former. Unfortunately, these benefits of nonlethal gas and germ warfare are purchased at a stiff price. A few countries might be able to control the kinds of gases and germs they use, but at little profit if this encourages countries elsewhere in the world to use deadly varieties of the same weapons. For the major powers, then, there is a choice: either they will forswear all their offensive chemical and biological weapons—and even a low level of defense preparedness—or they will help to bring about a spread of such weapons to smaller countries that would be more likely to use them, not against the major powers but against one another. This hardly seems a price worth paying for "defenses" of little value to anyone.

But would the total abstinence of any major power really help, or would it only seem as meaningless as proposals for unilateral nuclear disarmament? It would probably help. After all, the Geneva Protocol of 1925 has been a surprising success. Indeed, the weapons barred by it were the only ones not used with abandon during World War II, partly because of deterrence, but also because of the existence of a convention that encouraged every country to refrain from using these weapons, with a high degree of expectation that its enemies would do likewise. Today, as we have seen, the issue is not one of great powers deterring one another with gases and germs, but of their convincing small powers to be bound by the same restraints. To this end, at a meeting of the 18-Nation Disarmament Committee in August 1968 the British delegation proposed a new convention, to extend restraints to include the barring of manufacture and use for hostile purposes of "microbiological agents." This new convention could strengthen the 1925 protocol and reinforce psychological barriers against anyone manufacturing or using gases and germs in warfare.

Therefore, there is here a rare event in the study and practice of warfare: a correspondence between moral values and the most hardheaded strategic arguments—arguments that are particularly forceful because they concern the possibility of preventing strategic warfare in parts of the world where the attractions of the "poor man's atom bomb" might otherwise prove all too powerful.

(R. E. Hu.)

continued from page 253

front of them. In reacting to these provocations, Soviet soldiers killed an estimated 30 civilians in Prague during the first week of the occupation. Czechoslovaks also operated clandestine printing presses, radio stations, and even a television station.

Unable to find an alternative leadership with sufficient public support, the Kremlin was forced into negotiations with Dubcek. On August 27, a communiqué issued in Moscow said that Soviet troops would be withdrawn as the situation was "normalized," and that meanwhile they would not interfere in Czechoslovakia's internal affairs. However, it was not until September 11–12 that tanks withdrew from Prague, and then it was simply to regroup in the countryside. In the strategically sensitive area of southwest Czechoslovakia, on the border with West Germany, five Soviet divisions were reported to have replaced Czechoslovak divisions in permanent positions. Airfields were reportedly being built to accommodate 500 Soviet aircraft. Thirty miles outside Prague, the Milovice military barracks, capable of housing 20,000 soldiers, were said to have been taken over by Soviet troops. At the beginning of December it was uncertain just how many of the 250,000 (some estimates claimed 600,000) invading troops had been withdrawn, but one estimate was that at least 70,000 remained.

NATO and the Czech Crisis. The Western reaction to the invasion was deliberately muted. NATO governments were anxious to avoid any action, such as extensive troop movements, general alerts, or even tough statements, that might appear to justify the Soviet claim that the Czechoslovak liberals were serving NATO's interests, or that might lead the Soviet leaders to the conclusion that the West had decided on war. As late as September 20, land maneuvers under way in Germany were drawn back from the border area. A call by Kiesinger for an immediate summit meeting was turned down by other Western leaders, and the U.S. made it clear that the Soviet action would not be allowed to obstruct the search for a détente.

Nevertheless, the Soviet occupation raised some important questions for the NATO governments. In December 1967 NATO had officially abandoned the strategy of massive retaliation in favour of a strategy of flexible response, which required that a Soviet attack be contained in the first instance by conventional troops, with tactical nuclear weapons held in reserve. The entry of Soviet troops into Czechoslovakia raised in a more acute form the familiar question of whether NATO's strength in central Europe was adequate to the requirements of the new strategy. Before the invasion, the Warsaw Pact forces had a slight superiority in manpower (960,000 as against NATO's 900,000), which was balanced by NATO's superior air strength. The invasion was estimated to have increased Soviet strength in Eastern Europe by as much as 100,000, including a substantial addition to its forward air strength. In addition, some critics argued that the Soviet action had revealed serious deficiencies in NATO's intelligence system. On the other hand, the Warsaw Pact command could no longer rely on the Czechoslovak armed forces.

Delegates to the NATO defense ministers' conference at Brussels in November promised only modest force increases. The U.S. earmarked an additional 14 squadrons of the Tactical Air Force based in the U.S. for a NATO role and advanced to early in 1969 the return of two infantry brigades and four air squadrons

to Germany for exercises. The U.K. agreed to supply 20 additional Harrier vertical take-off fighter aircraft at a cost of £25 million for use in Germany and to assign an additional infantry battalion and signals troop to NATO. West Germany announced a defense budget increase of DM. 2.8 billion and Italy promised a 7% increase in defense spending. Belgium agreed to defer the projected withdrawal from Germany of two infantry brigades. Meeting at the same time, the NATO foreign ministers warned the Soviet Union that their governments would feel obliged to take collective action—of an unspecified nature—in the event of Soviet aggression in such "gray areas" as Yugoslavia and Austria.

Disarmament. On January 18, at the 18-Nation Disarmament Committee meeting at Geneva, the Soviet Union and the U.S. tabled a complete joint draft of a treaty to prevent the proliferation of nuclear weapons. The draft bound nuclear states party to the treaty not to transfer nuclear weapons to any nonnuclear state, and nonnuclear states not to receive nuclear weapons. The U.K. pledged its support for the treaty, but the two other nuclear powers, France and China, did not attend the negotiations.

The draft was extensively criticized by the nonnuclear states at Geneva. Their reservations centred on the lack of reciprocal restraints in the nuclear development of the nuclear states, the consequences for the development of civil nuclear technology by the nonnuclear states, and the broader political-strategic implications of dividing international society into nuclear "haves" and "have-nots." Sweden and India, particularly, expressed concern about the treaty's failure to prevent "vertical proliferation"—that is, an increase in the number of nuclear weapons held by the nuclear states. They pointed to the decisions taken by the U.S. and the Soviet Union in 1967 to build antiballistic missile (ABM) systems, the U.S. development of a multiple independently targeted reentry vehicle (MIRV), and the Soviet Union's development of the fractional orbital bombardment system (FOBS). India, with Chinese developments in mind, criticized the absence of any guarantee to the nonnuclear states against aggression by a nuclear power.

In an attempt to satisfy the nonnuclear states' fear of aggression, the Soviet Union, the U.S., and the U.K. offered to table a resolution in the UN Security Council recognizing that aggression with nuclear weapons, or the threat of nuclear weapons, against a nonnuclear state would create a situation in which the Security Council would feel bound to act in accordance with its obligations under the UN Charter. The strength of this guarantee was limited by its vagueness and by the fact that any Security Council action would be subject to the permanent members' power of veto. India rejected the proposal in March. Three days earlier, the U.S. and the Soviet Union had tabled an amended draft embodying some concessions to the other criticisms. On July 1 the treaty was signed in Washington, Moscow, and London. By the end of August, 68 nonnuclear nations had signed, but the absentees included such potential nuclear states as India, Israel, Japan, and West Germany.

When the Disarmament Committee reconvened at Geneva on July 16, hopes of a U.S.-Soviet agreement to limit the deployment of antiballistic missile systems were revived by a U.S. statement that a time and place were to be arranged for talks on the limitation and reduction of offensive and defensive weapons systems. However, at least partly because of the

Czechoslovak crisis, no meeting took place during the year. The U.K. contributed a proposal to extend the test-ban treaty to cover underground tests. To meet Soviet fears that on-site inspections would be used as a cover for espionage, the U.K. suggested that a committee, composed of the three nuclear states that were signatories to the test-ban treaty, three non-aligned countries, and a nominee of the UN secretary-general, be established to decide by a majority of not less than 5–2 whether a prima facie case for inspection existed. The Soviet Union rejected the proposal on the ground that developments in seismological technology made on-site inspection unnecessary. On August 6 the U.K., in response to a campaign waged in Britain by leading scientists and others, proposed a new convention on the use of microbiological weapons to supplement the Geneva Protocol of 1925 on the use of asphyxiating, poisonous, and other gases. It was noted that the proposals did not cover chemical weapons, perhaps from a concern with U.S. susceptibilities over Vietnam. (*See* Special Report.)

NATO

In January, in response to an increase in Soviet naval strength in the Atlantic, NATO set up a Standing Naval Force Atlantic, consisting of four to six frigates provided by the U.S., the U.K., Canada, and West Germany. At least in the first seven months of 1968, however, NATO was more concerned about establishing a new raison d'être in a period of apparent détente than about making new force dispositions.

The Harmel report of the previous December, calling for extension of the political détente to the military field through mutual and balanced force reductions, provided the main themes of both the defense ministers' meeting in Brussels in May and the foreign ministers' meeting in Reykjavik, Ice., in June.

The May meeting reaffirmed the importance of achieving balanced military cutbacks on both sides of the iron curtain, as called for in the Harmel report. At the same time, it acknowledged that the Soviet Union had not shown any interest in cutting back its own forces in Eastern Europe. The U.K., as an expression of support for the strategy of "flexible response," undertook to assign to the supreme allied commander, Europe (SACEUR), a mobile task force of 20,000 men for use in emergencies. An amphibious force consisting of two commando carriers, two assault ships, and antisubmarine frigates was to be made available in the Mediterranean, where growing Soviet naval strength was causing concern.

The British decision came at a time when other members of NATO were showing signs of reducing their contributions. The U.S. obtained the agreement of the May council to withdraw 35,000 men from Europe by the end of September, a decision that was carried through in spite of the Soviet invasion of Czechoslovakia. An attempt was made in the U.S. Senate to examine more closely the role of the U.S. forces in Europe, but the Senate majority leader, Mike Mansfield, canceled the debate following the Soviet invasion.

Troop strengths and air and missile bases in central European member nations of the North Atlantic Treaty Organization and the Warsaw Treaty Organization. Inset map shows NATO and WTO participation throughout Europe. The U.S.S.R. was expected to maintain 70,000–75,000 occupation troops in Czechoslovakia on a permanent basis following the invasion of that country on Aug. 20–21, 1968.

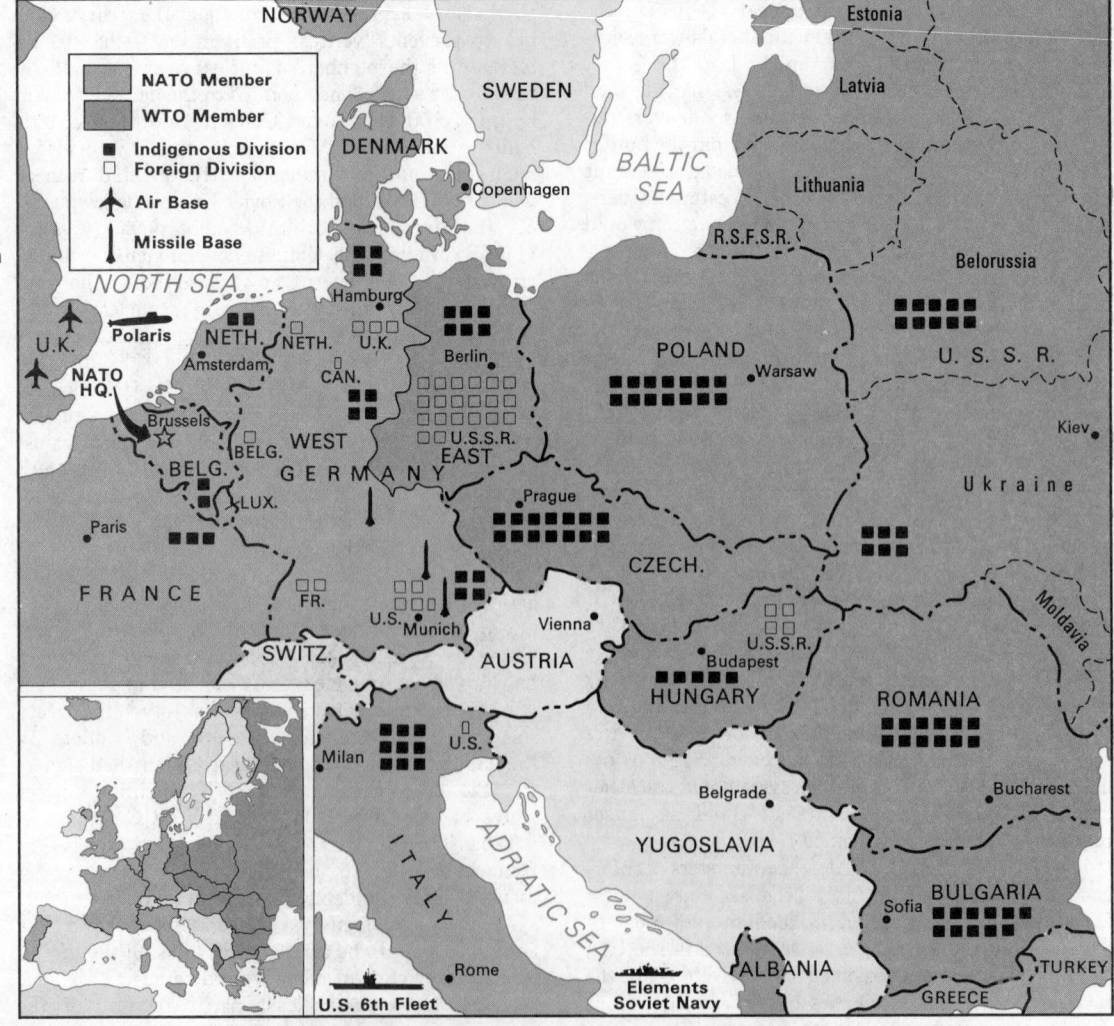

Belgium was in the process of withdrawing two out of the six Belgian brigades assigned to NATO, a force of some 12,000 men. The Liberal government of Pierre Elliott Trudeau, which came to power in Canada in June, promised a thorough review of Canada's role in NATO. The U.K., even as it assigned a mobile task force for use in Europe in an emergency, won the agreement of the council to redeploy 5,000 men and four tactical fighter squadrons out of Germany. The May meeting also considered and rejected the idea of a European ABM system.

In March the East German government imposed restrictions on access to East Berlin, following Soviet accusations that, by holding meetings of the Cabinet and Bundestag in West Berlin, the West German government was contravening Berlin's status under the interallied agreements. On March 10 members of the neo-Fascist West German party, the National Democratic Party of Germany (NPD), were banned from crossing East Germany to attend meetings in West Berlin, and on April 13 the ban was extended to ministers and officials of the West German government. Protests by the Western governments did not stop the East German government from imposing, on June 11, further restrictions on the transit of West German citizens and goods to and from West Berlin. At the spring meeting of the NATO foreign ministers in Reykjavik, the Western governments retaliated by imposing restrictions on the movement of East German citizens and goods, and reemphasized their determination to maintain free access to West Berlin. At the same time, however, the foreign ministers instructed the allied permanent representatives in Berlin to intensify their search for mutual East-West force reductions. The ministers' persistence in the face of the Soviet Union's complete lack of interest gave rise to suggestions that the talk of bilateral force reductions was intended principally as a rationalization of NATO's unilateral reductions.

In a different field, the meeting expressed concern at the growth of the Soviet Union's naval strength in the Mediterranean, but reportedly it was agreed that the threat was political rather than military. Nevertheless, it was announced in October that a new NATO group, Maritime Air Forces Mediterranean, was to be established to ensure improved air surveillance of surface ships and submarines in the area.

On July 17 the governments of the U.K., West Germany, Italy, and the Netherlands signed an agreement for the development of an advanced supersonic strike aircraft, to be capable of flying under radar defenses. This new aircraft was to be a replacement for the widely used American F-104 Starfighter. A long-term requirement of 1,000 aircraft was envisaged, and the total cost of development and production was estimated at £2,000 million. At the beginning of the year France and the U.K. had signed an order for 400 Jaguar supersonic strike trainer aircraft. Development had been in progress since 1965 by a joint company formed by the British Aircraft Corp. and Avions Louis Breguet. The first prototype made its maiden flight on September 8. The total estimated cost of the 400 aircraft, including development, was £200 million.

UNITED STATES

In a presidential year, U.S. policy in Vietnam and "law and order" at home were the two principal political issues. Liberal opposition to Pres. Lyndon B. Johnson's Vietnam policy found a champion in Sen. Eugene J. McCarthy of Minnesota, who announced on Nov. 30, 1967, that he would seek the Democratic nomination for the presidency. The evidence of widespread support for McCarthy's position provided by the New Hampshire and Wisconsin primaries persuaded Sen. Robert F. Kennedy of New York to declare his own candidacy for the Democratic nomination in a speech on March 16. On March 31, President Johnson announced his decision not to seek a second term in the White House, putting the presidency and the immediate direction of U.S. policy in Vietnam above "divisive partisanship." In the same speech, he announced a partial cessation of U.S. bombing of North Vietnam.

Vietnam dominated the Democratic national convention, both outside the convention hall, where peace demonstrators battled police, and inside, where a floor debate on the issue ended in adoption of the more "hawkish" of two proposed platform planks. In the campaign, however, the stands of the two principal candidates were not sufficiently clear-cut to offer a sharp choice. The Democratic nominee, Vice-Pres. Hubert H. Humphrey, did not diverge from official policy until fairly late, and then it was not so much to criticize as to indicate that, if elected, he would devise his own policy. Richard Nixon, the Republican nominee, called for a quick end to the war, but refused to make concrete proposals on the ground that it might interfere with the preliminary peace talks between the U.S. and North Vietnam, which had begun in Paris after the partial bombing halt. The American Independent Party candidate, George C. Wallace, campaigned largely on domestic issues, although he chose as his running mate Gen. Curtis E. LeMay, former chief of staff of the Air Force and an outspoken critic of U.S. defense policy as being too "soft."

Five days before the election, President Johnson announced that he was calling a halt to all bombing and shelling of North Vietnam and that expanded peace talks, including representatives of South Vietnam and the National Liberation Front, would begin shortly. It was not clear what effect this had on the election, which Nixon won by an extremely narrow popular margin. As president-elect, Nixon continued to hold back from making any strong pronouncements on the war. During the campaign, however, he had called for increased defense spending.

There were some indications that Hanoi might have become more conciliatory because it felt better terms could be obtained from the outgoing administration, and that Saigon was hesitant about participating in peace talks because it felt Nixon would be more sympathetic.

On January 21 a B-52 bomber carrying nuclear weapons crashed on the ice of North Star Bay in Greenland while attempting an emergency landing at Thule, seven miles away. In spite of U.S. assurances that the four nuclear weapons carried by the plane had not been primed and that there was no danger of an explosion or of radiation, the Danish government asked for a guarantee against nuclear flights over Greenland. On February 28, the U.S. suspended all nuclear-armed airborne alert flights by B-52 bombers, thus discontinuing a measure introduced by Pres. John F. Kennedy in 1961.

Meanwhile, the U.S. had become involved in an inconclusive wrangle with North Korea over the fate of 82 surviving officers and crew of the Navy intelligence ship USS "Pueblo," which had been seized off the North Korean coast on January 23 by four North Korean patrol boats and taken to the port of Wonsan,

Above, tank and soldier as seen at night through the starlight scope developed by the Night Vision Laboratory of the U.S. Army Electronics Command. The device intensifies faint moonlight, starlight, or skyglow in the observer's target area and, mounted on a weapon, right, was used successfully in Vietnam during 1968.

where one crewman died of injuries. North Korea claimed that the "Pueblo" had been engaged in espionage activities in North Korean territorial waters at the time of its capture. The U.S. denied this, and demanded the release of the crew. When North Korea refused, President Johnson ordered the call-up of about 15,000 air force and naval reservists and sent two squadrons of fighters to South Korea. The world's largest warship, the USS "Enterprise," moved up the North Korean coast to a station 200 mi. off Wonsan. The North Korean action, which followed a number of border clashes between South Korean and U.S. patrols and North Korean infiltrators and an unsuccessful attempt by a North Korean commando group to assassinate South Korean Pres. Pak Chung Hi, was seen in the U.S. as part of a new militant North Korean policy. Following a visit to Seoul on February 11–15, Cyrus R. Vance, President Johnson's personal representative, issued a U.S.-South Korean joint communiqué expressing U.S. determination to resist North Korean aggression and promising an extra $100 million of military aid to South Korea. In December the crew was released. The U.S. signed an apology which it repudiated in advance but which North Korea apparently accepted for its propaganda value.

The U.S. defense budget for fiscal 1969, presented to Congress on January 29, totaled $76.7 billion—$3.3 billion above the preceding year—of which $25.8 billion was earmarked for Vietnam. Although this was $1.3 billion above the previous year's Vietnam expenditure, it marked a slowing down in the rate of increase. The budget assumed a leveling-off of U.S. forces in Vietnam at about 525,000, a number that had been exceeded by the end of the year. One new item was the allocation of $1.2 billion to start production of the Sentinel antiballistic missile system, designed primarily as a defense against a future Communist Chinese nuclear force. The total cost of the system, which was expected to take five or six years to deploy, was estimated at $5 billion. Complementary to the ABM program was a $250 million increase in the Atomic Energy Commission's allocation ($1.2 billion) for the production of nuclear weapons. An attempt to block the ABM program, led by Sen. Stuart Symington (Dem., Mo.), a former air force secretary, was finally defeated in August. Symington felt that it would appear provocative to Peking, would be impossible to test because of the test-ban treaty and the danger of fouling the atmosphere, and would not provide protection in any case. The Air Force's Manned

Orbiting Laboratory, aimed at exploring the military uses of space, was allocated $600 million. The Poseidon missile, replacement for the Polaris submarine missile, and the land-based Minuteman missile were to be fitted with MIRV warheads and other devices to increase their penetration capability. All in all, it was a disappointing budget for the advocates of arms control.

In its passage through Congress, the budget was reduced by $7.9 billion, though Vietnam spending and most of the big hardware items emerged unscathed. One congressional casualty, however, was the much criticized naval version of the F-111 aircraft. The air force version, of which about 100 were in service, was itself encountering difficulties. After a series of crashes and other mishaps, it was grounded for three weeks in the fall, and there was some question as to how many would actually be produced.

On March 1 Clark Clifford (*see* BIOGRAPHY) was sworn in as secretary of defense in succession to Robert S. McNamara. During his seven years as defense secretary, McNamara had been responsible for many reforms. He introduced the concept of program packaging by which military requirements are assessed in terms of strategic function—strategic retaliatory forces, general purpose forces, and so on—rather than by individual service criteria; and also the five-year defense budget. In the field of strategy, his first actions had been to cancel the development of the B-70 bomber and increase the number of B-52 bombers on airborne alert. He accelerated the expansion of an invulnerable retaliatory force based on Polaris and Minuteman missiles, increased U.S. airlift capability, and merged the Strategic Air Command and the Tactical Air Command to form the Strike Command. NATO finally accepted his strategy of flexible response in 1967, though it was doubtful whether it had the will to implement it. Three issues clouded his concluding year: the controversy over the F-111; escalation of the war in Vietnam; and the decision to deploy an antiballistic missile system, which he had accepted with evident reluctance.

UNITED KINGDOM

As a follow-up to the devaluation of the pound in November 1967, on Jan. 16, 1968, Harold Wilson's Labour government announced cuts in both civil and military expenditure to effect estimated savings of £325 million in 1968–69 and £441 million in 1969–70. Because of cancellation charges and the time lag in expenditure cuts taking effect, there would be no reduction in defense expenditure in 1968–69, but in 1969–70 there would be an estimated saving of £110

million. By 1972–73 the defense budget was expected to be between £1,600 million and £1,650 million at 1964 prices. Assuming a 3% annual growth in GNP, this would represent 5% of GNP, compared with the 1968 level of nearly 5.6%.

The dates of Britain's withdrawal from the Far East and the Persian Gulf, excluding a small garrison in Hong Kong, were brought forward from the mid-1970s to the end of 1971. The aircraft carrier force was to be phased out in step with the withdrawal. The planned reduction of 75,000 in service manpower was also brought forward to 1971, and a planned cut of 80,000 in the number of civilians employed by the services was to be accelerated. The order for 50 F-111 aircraft was canceled, yielding a total saving of £400 million between 1968 and 1977–78.

There were strong reactions to the cuts from Commonwealth members in the Far East and the Pacific. The Australian prime minister, John Grey Gorton, described the cuts as involving "drastic alterations of previously understood arrangements as to the continuing availability of British forces in the region," and Keith Holyoake, the New Zealand prime minister, described them as a "great disappointment to New Zealand." Prior to the January 16 announcement, Lee Kuan Yew, prime minister of Singapore, had said that it was open to Singapore to withdraw its sterling balances from London and to transfer its shipping, banking, and other business to countries other than Britain in retaliation for British withdrawal. However, after discussions with Wilson and other leaders from January 13, Yew announced that Britain had offered air defense equipment and a squadron of Lightning fighters and that he was considering the purchase of a missile defense system. On May 30 it was announced that Britain would give Singapore and Malaysia £75 million in military aid over the next five years to offset the effects of the British withdrawal. On June 10–11, representatives of Malaysia, Singapore, Australia, New Zealand, and the U.K. met in Kuala Lumpur, Malaysia, for joint discussions on common defense problems arising from the British decision. The U.K. agreed to make facilities and technical personnel available for a joint Malaysia-Singapore air defense system, and Singapore announced a decision to buy Hunter Mark 9 fighters.

In the Persian Gulf, the announcement of the British withdrawal produced a proposal from the ruler of Abu Dhabi that the Gulf States should themselves pay the cost—variously estimated at between £12 million and £25 million a year—of keeping the British forces in the area. The offer was rejected, and on February 24 the rulers of the seven Trucial States, plus Bahrain and Qatar, met at Dubai to form a federation to deal with foreign, defense, and economic policy.

In the Defence White Paper published on February 22, it was revealed that estimated expenditure for the financial year 1968–69 would be £2,271,190,000, an increase of £66,070,000 over the previous year. A brigade of the British Army of the Rhine and a helicopter squadron were to be brought home from West Germany, but would be held ready to return on short notice. Civil defense preparations were to be reduced to a care and maintenance basis, and March 31 was designated as the date for the official disbandment of the Civil Defence Corps and the Auxiliary Fire Service.

On March 28 the U.K. and West Germany agreed that about 80% of the foreign exchange costs of British troops in Germany should be offset by German purchases of British military and civilian goods to the value of £53 million—a modest £4 million increase over the previous year—and by the purchase by the Bundesbank of £21 million of medium-term U.K. government bonds.

FRANCE

The French Army took no active part in the political crisis that endangered Pres. Charles de Gaulle's regime in May. (*See* FRANCE.) On May 29, after de Gaulle's May 24 broadcast had failed to end the disturbances, the president left Paris by helicopter, officially to return to his home at Colombey-les-deux-Églises. It was subsequently revealed, however, that he traveled first to Baden-Baden in West Germany, the headquarters of the French forces in Germany, for talks with Gen. Jacques Massu, the French commander in chief. It was assumed that his purpose was to ensure the support of the two French divisions in Germany. Subsequently, troop and tank maneuvers were reported around Paris and other main centres. However, the massive pro-Gaullist demonstration that followed de Gaulle's second broadcast on May 30 meant that the troops were not needed.

The emphasis in French defense planning continued to be on the development of a French nuclear striking force. In 1967–68 expenditure on the *force de frappe* accounted for more than 25% of the defense budget of Fr. 25 billion. Although this represented a lower proportion both of overall state spending and of GNP than in preceding years, it nevertheless exerted pressure on some areas of nonnuclear military spending, notably the development program for the tactical nuclear weapon Pluton. As a result, the transformation of the French Army into a small mobile force trained to use tactical nuclear weapons was expected to be delayed until 1974.

The defense budget for 1968–69 was increased by 5.27% to Fr. 26 billion, but the rise in industrial costs resulting from the settlement of the general strike in May meant that there was no room for increased capital spending on the *force de frappe*, and the government warned that the timetable for its development would have to be revised. The November financial crisis forced the government to cut military spending by Fr. 399,024,000, of which Fr. 222,984,000 was to come from the cancellation of a nuclear test in the Pacific planned for 1969, thus increasing the likelihood of serious delays in the nuclear program. The deployment of the second stage of the French striking force, the twenty-seven 2,500-km.-range ballistic missiles in the Vaucluse, originally scheduled to be operational by 1971, was expected to be delayed into the mid-1970s. This necessitated an extension to 1975 of the operational lives of the 50 Mirage IV bombers that constituted the first stage of the force, to be achieved by fitting them with ground-to-air nuclear missiles in 1970. For a time the future of the swing-wing replacement for the Mirage in its tactical role was in doubt, but in October the government, which had withdrawn from a joint Anglo-French swing-wing project the previous year for financial reasons, placed an order for two Dassault G4 prototypes. In September, Dassault had announced an agreement with a U.S. firm for the further joint development of their aircraft. The plane, which was to be able to fly at supersonic speeds at ground level and at $2\frac{1}{2}$ times the speed of sound at altitude, was expected to be ready in 1971.

The third stage in the French nuclear program, which had envisaged four missile submarines to be operational by the mid-1970s, was also expected to be delayed. The development of an intercontinental ballistic missile, to be the instrument of de Gaulle's *tous azimuts* strategy, looked more than ever like the *aventure des années 1990.*

Because of technical difficulties, it had been expected that the explosion of the first French thermonuclear device would be delayed until 1969. However, in spite of the May crisis, the difficulties were overcome, and the explosion took place on August 24 at Fangataufa atoll in the South Pacific. The French defense minister, Pierre Messmer, revealed that the device had had an explosive power of two megatons, and that it was intended to fit miniaturized thermonuclear warheads to the medium-range ballistic missiles being developed for the French missile submarines. There were also reports that France was working on an MIRV.

At the beginning of the year France completed its withdrawal from the naval base at Mers-el-Kébir in Algeria, retaining in Algeria only two airfields for staging purposes. The French government announced the withdrawal from West Germany of two tank regiments, comprising 5,000 men, and the reorganization of the two French divisions remaining in Germany.

WEST GERMANY

It was an anxious year for West Germany. Beginning in March, East Germany imposed progressively tighter restrictions on overland access to Berlin. With the rise of the NPD, the Soviet Union claimed the right to intervene in West Germany to prevent a resurgence of German imperialism. Finally, the Soviet invasion of Czechoslovakia brought at least five highly trained Soviet divisions to Germany's southeastern border. Despite these alarums, West Germany's original defense budget of $4.7 billion for 1968–69 represented only a small increase over the previous year's $4.5 billion, and the difference was almost all accounted for by increased costs. The 1969 defense budget represented 4.7% of West Germany's GNP, a lower proportion than the defense budgets of the U.S., the U.K., and France. As a proportion of total budget expenditure, the cost of West Germany's defense had decreased from 32% in 1964 to 22.4% in 1968.

Following the invasion, West Germany came under pressure from its NATO allies to bring its army of 454,000 up to the NATO goal of 508,000. Its reluctance to do so was only partly financial. The fact was that West Germany had never fully accepted the doctrine of flexible response because it conceded the possibility of a conventional, but immensely destructive, war on German soil; West Germany would have preferred the full emphasis of NATO strategy to be placed on the nuclear deterrent. The second reason for the shortfall in the Bundeswehr's numbers was the lack of suitable candidates for noncommissioned officer and technical posts, about 30,000 of which would have to be filled if the force target was to be achieved. It was reported that plans to create a new class of specialists somewhere between NCO's and commissioned officers were before the Cabinet. By the offer of suitable financial inducements, holders of these posts were to be persuaded to serve more than the conscripts' 18 months. The West German forces suffered shortages of equipment as well as personnel, reflecting the Bundestag's reluctance to

KEYSTONE

Belgian Army officers observing the performance of the German "Leopard" tank which was chosen over the French AMX-30 for purchase by the Belgian Army in 1968.

increase defense expenditure. The Defense Ministry's plan to buy a large number of U.S. Phantom aircraft was blocked by the Bundestag Defense Committee until the end of November when, as a result of the NATO defense ministers' meeting earlier in the month, the Bundestag agreed to a $624 million allocation to cover the cost of 88 Phantoms, 135 helicopters, a substantial number of multiple rocket launchers, and 50 Starfighters as a partial replacement for the 94 that had been lost in accidents by the end of September 1968.

VIETNAM

The war in Vietnam reached a new peak of intensity during 1968, even as some hope appeared for meaningful negotiations. Starting on January 30, Communist forces launched a series of attacks on 30 of South Vietnam's 45 provincial capitals. Saigon, the capital, and Hue, a key northern city, came under particularly determined attack, and both were penetrated by Communist commando-type groups. Concurrently, 40,000 North Vietnamese troops besieged 5,000 U.S. Marines in their northern outpost at Khe Sanh near the Laotian border in the largest conventional battle of the war to date. Many observers believed that the long-drawn-out war was reaching its climax, and interpreted the Communist offensive as the first stage of a "fight-and-talk" policy directed at negotiating an end to the war on terms favourable to the National Liberation Front (NLF), the Viet Cong's political organization. This interpretation was supported by North Vietnam's acceptance of President Johnson's offer to negotiate, contained in his March 31 broadcast. Talks opened in Paris on May 13, but it quickly became apparent that the road to peace would be long and arduous. Johnson's October 31 announcement of a complete halt to bombing in the North had apparently been preceded by an understanding that Hanoi would not take advantage of it to intensify the war in the South. However, hopes that broadened peace talks would lead to immediate progress were dampened by the unwillingness of the South Vietnamese to take part in negotiations that included the NLF as a separate entity.

In November 1967 the NLF had announced that its forces would observe a seven-day truce over Tet, the lunar new year, at the end of January and the beginning of February. It had also suggested a three-day truce for the calendar new year, but the South Vietnamese authorities only conceded 36 hours. In the event, a large number of violations by the Viet

Cong were reported, and on January 3 North Vietnamese troops attacked the U.S. air base at Da Nang with 120-mm. rockets, destroying about 30 aircraft. Attacks on airfields at Kon Tum and Ban Me Thuot followed on the 10th. Throughout January the rate of Viet Cong activity was high, especially in the Dak To area in Kon Tum Province.

The siege of Khe Sanh began on January 21 with a North Vietnamese artillery bombardment of the Khe Sanh airstrip and the fortifications surrounding it. Khe Sanh was less than 20 mi. S of the Demilitarized Zone (DMZ) separating North and South Vietnam, and within 7 mi. of the Laotian border. It was used by U.S. troops as a base for operations against the Communist supply lines along the Ho Chi Minh Trail in Laos and as a barrier to the infiltration of North Vietnamese troops across the DMZ. It also protected the flank of the important Route Nine running from the Laotian border to Dong Ha on the coast. Five thousand U.S. Marines, supported by a thousand South Vietnamese Marines and irregulars, held the main camp and the airstrip and some of the overlooking hills.

The outstanding feature of the siege was the weight of artillery deployed by the North Vietnamese. An estimated 100–150 guns, ranging from 100 mm. to 152 mm.—heavier than any previously used by Communist forces—subjected the U.S. garrison to a heavy if spasmodic bombardment. On January 24 the North Vietnamese shelled the airstrip with small mortars with a range of three-quarters of a mile and they subsequently forced the U.S. garrison into reliance on airdropped supplies. On January 26 the U.S. retaliated with a massive air offensive that was to set the pattern for American tactics. Canceling missions over North Vietnam, U.S. fighter-bombers flew more than 480 sorties against the North Vietnamese positions, without, however, causing any great diminution in the rate of fire. The next day the U.S. artillery base at Camp Carrol, 15 mi. NE of Khe Sanh, was the scene of a clash between North Vietnamese and U.S. forces in which 20 Marines and 150 North Vietnamese were reported killed. In response to the North Vietnamese offensive, the South Vietnamese government canceled the Tet truce.

The circumstances of the siege of Khe Sanh, particularly the tactical artillery surprise achieved by the Communists and the garrison's dependence on an exposed airstrip for supplies, strongly reminded some observers of the siege of Dien Bien Phu in 1954, when a French garrison had surrendered to Viet Minh besiegers under Gen. Vo Nguyen Giap (*see* BIOGRAPHY). The parallel was reinforced when it was reported that General Giap was in command of the Khe Sanh operations. Unlike the French at Dien Bien Phu, however, the garrison in Khe Sanh was strongly supported. The allies had about 55,000 troops in the three northernmost provinces, and Khe Sanh lay within range of the 175-mm. guns at Camp Carrol and at Rockpile 12 mi. NE. Most important, weather conditions permitting, the U.S. and its allies were capable of mounting up to 600 bombing missions a day, including B-52 bomber raids from Guam, in support of the garrison. It was reported that in the month ending February 15, 120 million lb. of bombs had been dropped on the besiegers.

Although U.S. sources subsequently claimed that 5,000 North Vietnamese soldiers had been killed by the bombing, its ultimate effectiveness was difficult to determine. The North Vietnamese artillery fire did not slacken noticeably during the two months in which the siege was most intensively pressed. The North Vietnamese, like their Viet Minh predecessors, were adept at tunneling. Their artillery was dug into the thickly wooded hillsides and often mounted on rails so that it could be run to the mouth of the tunnel for firing and then drawn back into relative safety. The North Vietnamese infantry built an elaborate system of trenches, tunnels, and bunkers, often 10 to 12 ft. underground, in some places coming to within 100 yd. of the U.S. lines. In spite of these protective measures, however, U.S. Air Force spokesmen were probably correct in claiming that U.S. airpower was the decisive factor in the successful defense of Khe Sanh. Certainly, the siege provided an awesome example of the tactical use of a strategic weapon such as the B-52.

On January 30, without relaxing their pressure on Khe Sanh, the Communist forces broke the Tet truce to launch the biggest offensive of the war, directed principally against provincial capitals. Saigon and Hue were the scenes of particularly heavy fighting. In Saigon the fighting started in the early hours of January 31 when 5,000 Viet Cong infiltrators attacked selected objectives in the centre of the city, including the presidential palace, the Saigon Radio building, and the U.S. embassy, part of which they occupied and held for six hours. The airport on the outskirts of the city was also attacked, causing the cancellation of civilian flights. The attackers won their most substantial success in the Chinese suburb of Cholon, large areas of which they controlled for several days and which was not completely pacified until the third week of February.

In Hue, Communist forces won their most striking propaganda success by capturing part of the French-built Citadel in the Old City and holding it for three weeks, during which they received reinforcements and supplies through tunnels dug under the walls. Bombing and gas attacks failed to dislodge them, and it was only after days of bitter fighting by U.S. Marines that Hue was cleared. The allied, and especially the U.S., use of superior firepower in the fighting in the cities was heavily criticized. Areas in which Communist groups were believed to be hiding were frequently attacked by fighter-bombers or strafed by helicopter gunships. The result was widespread destruction of property and the killing of many noncombatants. Large parts of Cholon were devastated, and an estimated 100,000 of Hue's 150,000 inhabitants were made homeless.

Estimates of the total casualties involved in the Tet offensive varied widely. One U.S. source claimed that in the cities offensive the Viet Cong had lost 10,000 killed, against U.S. losses of 249 and South Vietnamese losses of 553. The U.S. Information Service claimed that in all of January and February the Communists had lost 60,000 killed (compared with 85,000 for the whole of 1967) and the U.S. had lost 2,600 (9,400 for 1967). The accuracy of these and other official figures was challenged by many observers, who pointed out that an accurate body count under battlefield conditions was impossible.

The official American view was that the U.S. had won an important victory in the Tet fighting. The Communist attacks had failed to trigger the general uprising and mass defections from the South Vietnamese Army that captured Communist documents showed to have been the aim of the offensive. Only in Hue, where some students and teachers were re-

North Vietnamese woman clearing rubble from ruins of what was once Haiphong's largest market area.

264

Defense

GAMMA—PIX FROM PUBLIX

Ruins at Hue, the ancient
imperial capital
of Vietnam. The battle
to take Hue from the Viet
Cong lasted for nearly
the whole month
of February 1968.

ported to have joined the fighting, and perhaps in Cholon had the local population given the Communist attackers any active support. It was claimed that the executions of Vietnamese civilians by the Viet Cong— most noticeably at Hue where, according to official South Vietnamese sources, more than 1,000 bodies were found in mass graves—had shocked and alienated the Vietnamese public. It was also claimed that the South Vietnamese public held the Communists responsible for the destruction of property and life caused by the U.S. and South Vietnamese response.

On the other hand, it was noted that large numbers of Viet Cong guerrillas had infiltrated Saigon and other towns without the government having been warned by civilian sympathizers. The U.S. commander in South Vietnam, Gen. William C. Westmoreland, conceded that the Communists had achieved a "tactical surprise." By demonstrating the vulnerability of even the most important towns, the offensive had weakened confidence in the Saigon government, at the same time that it imposed on that government the problem of caring for many thousands of refugees. Strategically, the allies were thrown on the defensive, as units that had been engaged in search-and-destroy operations in the countryside were drawn back to defend the towns.

The siege of Khe Sanh continued during the Tet fighting. On February 7 a U.S. Special Forces camp at Lang Vei, a few miles from Khe Sanh, was overrun by a North Vietnamese force using light Soviet tanks, the first time that tanks had been used by the Communist forces. The next day a strong North Vietnamese attack was launched against Khe Sanh, but it was defeated after hard fighting lasting for three days. Subsequently, the siege took the form of a duel between the North Vietnamese artillery, which fired an average of 100 rocket and mortar shells onto the base every day, and the U.S. long-range guns, at Rockpile and Camp Carrol, and U.S. aircraft. On February 13, in response to a request from General Westmoreland, President Johnson ordered 10,500 more troops to South Vietnam.

Meanwhile, peace efforts had been in progress. On Dec. 29, 1967, North Vietnamese Foreign Minister Nguyen Duy Trinh announced his government's readiness to begin talks with the U.S. if bombing of North Vietnam and "all other acts of war" were ended unconditionally, a statement that appeared to go further in committing North Vietnam to negotiations than previous North Vietnamese statements. On January 21 the U.S. replied with a demand for reciprocal action— or at least the exercise of restraint—by North Vietnam following a bombing pause. Four days later the U.S. defense secretary-designate, Clark Clifford, said that holding North Vietnamese infiltration to the South at the current level would come within the meaning of "restraint." Pressure on the U.S. government to halt the bombing increased with the statement by the UN secretary-general on January 18 that talks could begin within four weeks of a halt.

In the spring the issue of U.S. bombing of the North was introduced directly into the presidential campaign by the candidacies of McCarthy and Robert Kennedy. Despite the evidence of growing public dissatisfaction with U.S. Vietnam policy, President Johnson was under pressure from other directions to continue the bombing. South Vietnamese Pres. Nguyen Van Thieu had demanded in February that bombing should continue until the Viet Cong ceased guerrilla warfare in the South. The U.S. military command in

South Vietnam, while admitting that the bombing had not stopped infiltration from the North, argued that without it the number of infiltrators would have been much higher. The Defense Department estimated that since bombing began in 1965 it had cost North Vietnam $430 million, and that 83% of North Vietnam's oil-storage facilities, 62% of its electric generating capacity, 47% of its rail repair shops, and 100% of its steel manufacturing capacity had been destroyed or made inactive. Domestic pressures proved too strong, however, and on March 31 President Johnson announced that bombing would cease over North Vietnam except for an area north of the DMZ and certain other vital strategic areas. The offer was less generous than it appeared. On April 1 it was explained that bombing would continue up to the 19th parallel, 200 mi. N of the DMZ. The U.S. claim that this would leave 90% of North Vietnam's population untouched was challenged by the North Vietnamese, who nevertheless offered to negotiate on the question of a complete cessation of bombing. Paris was eventually agreed on as the site and the talks opened there on May 13.

During March and April, the allied forces in Vietnam began to return to the offensive. Khe Sanh was relieved on March 31 after the anticipated all-out offensive had failed to materialize. The opposition to the relieving forces proved much weaker than expected, and it was concluded that the larger part of the North Vietnamese forces in the area had withdrawn across the Laotian border. Between January and March, 199 American Marines had been killed and 1,000 wounded in the Khe Sanh area. North Vietnamese killed were estimated at between 6,000 and 10,000. However, on May 5 the Viet Cong launched a second offensive against South Vietnamese towns, similar to the Tet offensive but on a smaller scale. Saigon was again a chief target, and division-scale fighting took place in the A Shau valley around Hue. In the week ended May 11, 562 U.S. deaths were reported, a figure higher than any reported during the Tet fighting, and in the two weeks beginning May 15, 13,000 Communists were said to have been killed. The high rate of fighting continued into June. On the 11th, Viet Cong guerrillas launched the largest in a series of rocket attacks against Saigon, killing an estimated 130 civilians. The upsurge in the fighting was not due solely to Communist attacks, however. It was subsequently disclosed that the U.S. military command in South Vietnam had ordered an all-out effort on the eve of the Paris talks. In spite of the partial cessation of bombing, the number of missions flown over North Vietnam reached 3,593 in May and 3,792 in June, compared with 2,648 in March, before the pause was announced.

At the Paris talks the North Vietnamese representative, Xuan Thuy, continued to press for the complete cessation of bombing and all other acts of war against the North, while Averell Harriman, the U.S. representative, continued to press for some sign that the North Vietnamese were prepared to reciprocate U.S. concessions. By mid-July, some observers were claiming to have discovered the reciprocation the U.S. was seeking. They argued that the rate of infiltration had dropped; that one-third to one-half of the 80,000 North Vietnamese troops in the South had been withdrawn; that, on the admission of the U.S., the Communist forces were avoiding combat, and that consequently U.S. casualties were the lowest since Tet; that terrorist attacks had dropped off sharply;

that rocket and mortar attacks against Saigon had ceased; and that enemy forces around the capital had been withdrawn.

In August, however, there was another of the periodic upsurges in the fighting when Viet Cong forces attacked Saigon, Duc Lap, Tay Ninh, and other towns with 120-mm. rockets. In the week ended August 24, 308 U.S. servicemen were killed, bringing the total of U.S. combat deaths in Vietnam to more than 25,000. The August fighting was interpreted by some as the long-awaited third offensive. Its lack of success was attributed to the aggressive strategy pursued by the new U.S. commander, Gen. Creighton Abrams (*see* BIOGRAPHY), who had taken up his command in July following the appointment of General Westmoreland as army chief of staff. Until forced onto the defensive by the Tet offensive, Westmoreland had favoured massive search-and-destroy operations, in which thousands of troops made wide sweeps through areas where the presence of Communist units and bases was suspected. In contrast, General Abrams concentrated on first locating the enemy by small reconnaissance patrols and the use of electronic sensing devices and then exploiting U.S. mobility and firepower to cordon off the area and subject it to intensive bombing.

Following President Johnson's announcement of October 31, all bombing of the North ceased on November 1, although fighting continued in the South. Despite some reports to the contrary, official U.S. sources insisted that there had been no step-up in the infiltration of men and supplies into the South. Indeed, on December 10, U.S. Defense Secretary Clifford expressed hope that bilateral force reductions would begin within 40 days. A delegation representing the NLF arrived in Paris to take part in expanded negotiations, but the beginning of talks was delayed by President Thieu's insistence that South Vietnamese participation in four-sided talks would constitute recognition of the NLF—a step that his government was unwilling to take.

The manpower demands of the war continued to grow during 1968. By mid-September the U.S. had 535,000 troops in Vietnam, 14,000 below the revised ceiling of 549,000. This compared with a total of 470,000 in the previous November. Of these, 209,000 were combat troops. General Abrams initiated a policy of cutting down the number of support troops by placing foreign nationals in some rear-echelon jobs. South Vietnamese forces were increased by 18% to 770,000 in the seven months following the Tet offensive and were expected to reach 800,000 by the end of the year. Also by the end of the year, all South Vietnamese Army units were to be equipped with the M-16 rifle, and M-60 machine guns, M-79 grenade launchers, and more artillery were to be provided. Official U.S. policy envisaged a transfer of combat tasks to the South Vietnamese forces as their battlefield capabilities increased.

There were small increases in some of the allied contingents in South Vietnam. Australia added another 2,000 troops, including a squadron of Centurion tanks, to the 6,000 already there. Thailand announced a decision to increase its 2,500 men by another 5,000. South Korea's contribution rose by about 3,000 to 49,000. The Philippines maintained 2,200 troops, chiefly engaged in civil engineering work, and New Zealand maintained 200 men in two infantry companies and an artillery battery.

The Communist forces were variously estimated at between 220,000 and 230,000, approximately the same as in 1967 despite the heavy fighting. Of these, about 80,000 were regular North Vietnamese troops—out of a total North Vietnamese Army of 440,000—though some sources claimed that 70% of the Viet Cong regular units were composed of North Vietnamese-trained soldiers. There were wide variations in estimates of the rate of infiltration of North Vietnamese troops to the South. U.S. sources claimed 30,000 a month in May, June, and July, dropping to 20,000 in August, compared with a monthly average of 6,000–7,000 in 1967. South Vietnamese sources claimed much lower figures—2,500 in July, for instance. A further 40,000 North Vietnamese troops guarded the supply trail through Laos. Communist China was believed to have as many as 70,000 air defense and engineer technicians in North Vietnam. Late in 1968 there was an unconfirmed report that three Chinese infantry divisions and supporting elements were in northernmost North Vietnam.

Since 1961 more than 30,000 U.S. and other allied troops had been killed and 192,000 wounded. South Vietnamese troops had suffered more than 70,000 fatal casualties. Over the same period, 30,000 civilians were estimated to have been killed and 50,000 were reported missing. The Communist forces in South Vietnam were estimated to have suffered more than 400,000 dead. By September 1968 the U.S. had lost more than 4,000 aircraft in the war. Of these, 873 were fixed-wing aircraft destroyed over North Vietnam and 1,400 were fixed-wing aircraft destroyed by enemy action or technical mishap in the South. About 1,900 helicopters had been lost.

SOVIET UNION

The Soviet defense budget for 1968 was 16.7 billion rubles ($39,780,000), a 15% increase over the 1967 defense budget of 14.5 billion rubles. The increase was thought to be partly due to the inclusion, for the first time, of Soviet military aid—principally to North Vietnam—in declared defense expenditure. A large part of the increase, however, was almost certainly due to the expansion during the year of the Soviet Union's land-based strategic missile forces, from an estimated 500 at the beginning of 1968 to an estimated 1,000 at the beginning of 1969. Even so, the total cost of this expansion was not recorded in the declared defense expenditure. The cost of nuclear warheads, research and development on advanced weapons systems, and some items of capital expenditure were believed to be included under the budget expenditures of other ministries. Taking these costs into account, Soviet defense expenditure in 1968 may have been as high as $50 billion.

The strategic rationale behind the doubling of Soviet land-based strategic missile strength, which gave it numerical equality with the U.S. in these weapons, was thought to lie in a downgrading of the effectiveness of antiballistic missile defense systems. During 1966 and 1967 it was believed in the West that the Soviet Union was in the process of deploying the Galosh ABM system in considerable strength around important Soviet centres, particularly Moscow and Leningrad. The Soviet move was considered to be consistent with the traditional Soviet preference for defensive rather than offensive deployment. Thus, in 1966–67 the Soviet Union possessed only an estimated 300 intercontinental ballistic missiles against 800 for the U.S. Under political pressure, the U.S. government responded to the deployment of the

Soviet ABM systems by announcing a decision to build its own $5 billion system, officially directed against China but widely interpreted as the first stage of a system effective against the Soviet Union.

It became clear during 1967 that opinion in the Soviet Union had been divided on the question of missile defense. In January 1967 the Soviet minister of defense, Marshal Rodion Malinovski, ignored ABM's when listing Soviet military capabilities, while Marshal Grechko, commander in chief of the Warsaw Pact and shortly to succeed Malinovski as defense minister, and Marshal Vasili Chuikov, the head of civil defense, were noticeably lacking in enthusiasm. Also, during the year the expansion of Soviet missile forces and the testing of the FOBS, which reduces the warning time for ABM defenses, suggested that the leadership in the Soviet Union agreed with McNamara's view that the best answer to an ABM system is to increase offensive capabilities.

Apart from the action in Czechoslovakia, the other striking feature of Soviet military policy during 1968 was the continued emphasis on increasing Soviet naval strength. This was consistent with the policy of flexible response that the Soviet Union was believed to have adopted after Khrushchev's departure. The Soviet naval presence in the Mediterranean was considerably strengthened during the year. The number of Soviet ships in the Mediterranean in September was thought to be 40, including 1 missile cruiser, 3 escort vessels armed with rockets, 4 fast escort vessels, 1 atomic submarine, and 6 conventional submarines. Perhaps of greatest interest to Western observers were the two 15,000–20,000-ton helicopter carriers, each carrying 30–35 helicopters and about 1,000 Soviet Marines. These ships gave the Soviet Union, for the first time, the capability of intervening directly in Middle Eastern affairs on the model of the U.S. intervention in Lebanon in 1958.

Nonetheless, Soviet naval strength in the Mediterranean remained far inferior to U.S. and NATO strength. The U.S. 6th Fleet consisted of between 50 and 60 ships, including two aircraft carriers, and NATO's total Mediterranean strength was about 300 ships. The Soviet naval presence was interpreted as complementing the Soviet Union's political interest in the Middle East. In an attempt to extend its influence westward, the Soviet Union was reported to have approached the Algerian government about using the naval base at Mers-el-Kébir and to be interested in acquiring a base in Malta.

CHINA

The situation in China remained confused. Reports reaching the West, however, suggested that the 2.6 million-strong People's Liberation Army (PLA), which had been the target of Red Guard criticism for its alleged "bourgeois" tendencies, was in the process of being rehabilitated. Chairman Mao Tse-tung was coming to rely increasingly on the Army to maintain at least a semblance of order in the country following the breakdown of the Communist Party and the administrative machinery during the Cultural Revolution. Yang Cheng-wu, chief of staff of the Army, who throughout the Cultural Revolution had supported Mao against provincial military commanders impatient with Red Guard excesses, was dismissed from his post toward the end of 1967. Other victims of the purge were thought to include Fu Ching-pi, commander of the Peking garrison and the man responsible for maintaining order in the capital, and the air

KEYSTONE

Demonstration in Prague, August 24, against Warsaw Pact troop occupation of Czechoslovakia.

force commissar, Yu Li-chin. Significantly, the new chief of staff was reported to be Huang Yung-sheng, commander of Kwangtung, who had taken a firm line with Red Guard extremists in his own area.

Since the spring of 1967, units of the Army had reportedly been taking over the administration of many of China's 29 major political divisions—running public utilities and transport, supervising industry and agriculture, and even teaching in schools, editing newspapers, and running radio stations. This political involvement brought its own strains and a renewal of warnings about "warlordism." Serious fighting was reported between units of the Chinese 14th Army in Yünnan Province, where political factionalism was rife. In Kwangsi Chuang Region, bordering on North Vietnam, army units had resisted Red Guard attempts to disrupt the rail links with North Vietnam through Liuchou and Nanning. Troops were also reported to have been sent to such key strategic areas as Fuchien, facing Taiwan; Sinkiang, which contained China's nuclear installations; and Szechwan. All this led some observers to wonder whether Mao's principle that the party should control the gun had not been reversed.

The size of the PLA was reported to have increased substantially during 1968, following the reintroduction of the draft for the first time since the Cultural Revolution began in 1965. The new draft embraced between 500,000 and 800,000 young people, including women. It was thought that a large number of these might be Red Guard activists, another sign that Mao Tse-tung was concerned to restore order and discipline. With the new draftees, the Army was expected to exceed three million by 1969.

China's development of a nuclear bomb at first appeared to have encountered serious obstacles during 1968. Its failure to acknowledge a nuclear test carried out at Lop Nor in Sinkiang on Dec. 24, 1967, was interpreted by some observers as meaning that it had been unsuccessful. It was also noted that so far China had not deployed any of the anticipated medium-range ballistic missiles. The reason for the slowdown in the rate of China's nuclear development was thought to lie in a combination of Red Guard disruption of China's scientific establishment and technical troubles. Late in December, however, China was reported to have exploded a three-megaton device, presumably thermonuclear. The test, which took place at Lop Nor, appeared to have been successful.

INDIA AND PAKISTAN

The Indian defense budget for 1968–69 was announced as $1,353,000,000, an increase of 4.5% over the previous year. Despite the absolute increase, the figure represented a decrease in the proportion of GNP devoted to defense to below 3%. The greater part of the budget, $923 million, was to be devoted to the continuing modernization of the Indian Army. The Navy was allocated $50 million and the Air Force, $220 million. Capital expenditure of $161 million made up the total.

The significance of India's developing military links with the Soviet Union was a subject of some concern and considerable speculation among Western observers. On January 26, in a military parade before the visiting Soviet premier, Aleksei N. Kosygin, India displayed a number of Soviet ground-to-air missiles. In February a visit by the Soviet naval chief of staff, Adm. Sergei Gorshkov, was followed by reports that the Indian Navy was to acquire at least three Petya-class destroyers. Two Indian crews were reported to

be training in the Soviet Union. In March an aircraft-manufacturing plant built near Bombay with Soviet aid started production of MiG-19s and MiG-21s. Two other Soviet-built plants were expected to be open by the end of the year, joining the British-built plant already producing the Folland Gnat fighter-trainer. In the same month a Soviet naval squadron paid a visit to India. Delivery of the first of four Soviet submarines was expected in April but did not actually take place until July. There were also reports that India was to purchase 100 Su-7 fighters from the Soviet Union in addition to the 6 it already possessed. Approximately 400 Soviet military advisers were reported to be in India.

All this caused particular concern in Washington, and in July a U.S. team led by Undersecretary of State Nicholas Katzenbach visited New Delhi. The visit came at an auspicious moment for the U.S., following reports that the Soviet Union had concluded an arms agreement with Pakistan. However, the U.S. envoy had to work hard to persuade his hosts that the 100 refurbished Patton tanks Italy had agreed to sell Pakistan would only replace those destroyed in the Indo-Pakistani war of 1965.

In August India's prime minister, Mrs. Indira Gandhi, offered Pakistan a "no war" pact but, like previous Indian offers, it was rejected by Pakistan on the ground that it would be meaningless as long as the status of Kashmir remained in dispute. In Kashmir the formation of a National Liberation Front to wage guerrilla warfare was reported, but the situation remained quiet. There was a resurgence of fighting in Nagaland on India's northeastern frontier, however. Major clashes were reported in May and June, in which the Indian government claimed 300 Naga rebels had been killed. In the June battle Indian troops captured a rebel camp near Kohima, where they claimed to have found 60-mm. Chinese mortars, 7.62 rifles with Chinese markings, AK-47 rifles, and rocket launchers. Reports suggested that as many as 4,000 Nagas were in Yünnan in China undergoing military training. In Assam, Mizo tribesmen were also reported to have clashed with Indian troops. In an attempt to contain the trouble, India kept 36,000 troops in the northeastern area.

Official policy remained opposed to the acquisition of nuclear weapons. At the same time, India showed itself determined to keep its nuclear option open. At the Disarmament Committee meeting in Geneva, India criticized the draft nonproliferation treaty presented by the U.S. and the Soviet Union on a number of grounds. On January 23 it was announced that in the future India intended to build nuclear power stations without foreign aid, thus avoiding inspection requirements. Both the right-wing nationalist party, the Jan Sangh, and powerful elements in the ruling Congress Party called for an Indian response to China's developing nuclear capability.

Pakistan announced a defense budget for 1968–69 of PakRs. 2,450,000,000 ($514 million), an increase of PakRs. 220 million over 1967–68. In introducing the defense budget, which comprised 35% of Pakistan's total budget, the finance minister regretted the increase, but claimed it was necessary following India's failure to reciprocate the token $14.7 million cut in defense spending made by Pakistan the previous year.

In July it was reported that Pakistan had concluded an arms agreement with the Soviet Union. Since the 1965 Indo-Pakistani war, when U.S. supplies had

Approximate Strengths of Regular Armed Forces of the World

Country	Army	Navy	Air Force	Total aircraft	Defense expenditure as % of GNP
I. NATO					
Belgium	75.0	4.0	20.0	140	2.8
Canada	41.5	16.6	43.5	300	2.7
Denmark	28.0	7.2	10.3	115	2.6
Germany, West	326.0	32.0	98.0	600*	4.3
Greece	118.0	20.0	23.0	250	4.5
Italy	265.0	40.0	60.0	450	2.9
Luxembourg	.56	—	—	—	1.2
Netherlands	83.5	21.5	23.5	145*	4.0
Norway	19.0	7.0	9.0	130	3.7
Portugal	150.0	15.0	17.5	100	6.7
Turkey	425.0	39.0	50.0	500	4.6
United Kingdom	210.0	96.0	121.0	600	5.7
United States	1,535.0	1,005.0†	900.0	12,500*	9.8
II. OTHER EUROPEAN					
Austria	45.0	—	5.0	21	1.3
Finland	31.4	2.0	3.0	50	1.6
France	328.0	69.0	108.0	475*	5.3
Ireland	13.0	1.0	.6	15	1.4
Spain	225.0	42.0	38.0	225	2.3
Sweden	50.0	4.6	24.0	650	3.9
Switzerland	1.0	—	7.0	400	2.4
Yugoslavia	180.0	20.0	20.0	335	4.7
III. WARSAW PACT					
Albania	30.0	3.0	5.0	60	3.4
Bulgaria	125.0	6.0	22.0	250	3.0
Czechoslovakia	175.0	—	50.0	600	5.7
Germany, East	85.0	16.0	25.0	270	3.7
Hungary	95.0	—	7.0	140	2.6
Poland	185.0	19.0	70.0	750	5.4
Romania	150.0	8.0	15.0	240	3.1
U.S.S.R.	2,000.0	465.0	735.0‡	11,000*	9.6
IV. FAR EAST AND OCEANIA					
Australia	45.4	17.2	21.7	200	4.9
Burma	125.0	6.0	6.5	26	6.4
Cambodia	45.0	1.5	2.5	55	6.6
China (Communist)	2,500.0	141.0	120.0	2,500	9.2
Indonesia	275.0	40.0	25.0	200	2.3
Japan	174.0	36.0	40.0	570	0.9
Korea, North	345.0	9.0	30.0	370	17.3
Korea, South	550.0	47.0§	23.0	195	3.9
Laos	60.0	.4	1.5	40	19.4
Malaysia	28.0	2.8	3.0	20	4.1
New Zealand	5.8	2.9	4.4	28	1.7
Philippines	15.5	5.5	9.0	60	1.7
Taiwan	372.0	71.0‖	85.0	370	7.9
Thailand	95.0	21.5	25.0	150	2.5
Vietnam, North	440.0	2.5	4.5	128	25.0
Vietnam, South	370.0	24.0	16.0	125	8.8
V. MIDDLE EAST, NORTH AFRICA, AND SOUTH ASIA					
Afghanistan	80.0	—	4.5	100	1.1
Algeria	45.0	1.5	2.0	150	4.9
India	950.0	25.0	58.0	500	3.3
Iran	200.0	6.0	15.0	200	5.5
Iraq	70.0	2.0	10.0	215	10.3
Israel	29.0	3.0	8.0	270	13.8
Jordan	53.0	.25	1.7	30	12.8
Lebanon	10.0	.2	.6	20	4.2
Libya	5.3	.1	.2	8	3.6
Morocco	50.0	1.0	3.0	40	3.6
Pakistan	300.0	9.0	15.0	250	3.6
Saudi Arabia	30.0	1.0	5.0	40	11.9
Sudan	17.5	.5	.4	20	4.4
Syria	50.0	1.5	9.0	150	11.9
Tunisia	16.0	.5	.5	15	11.5
U.A.R.	180.0	12.0	15.0	400	12.7
VI. AFRICA SOUTH OF SAHARA					
Cameroon	3.0	.2	.3	3	4.2
Congo (Kinshasa)	30.0	—	2.0	125	1.7
Congo (Brazzaville)	1.4	—	2.0	3	10.9
Ethiopia	35.0	1.1	2.0	60	2.3
Ghana	14.0	1.0	1.0	50	2.5
Guinea	4.8	—	—	—	3.1
Liberia	4.0	.2	—	—	1.8
Malawi	.8	—	—	—	1.8
Nigeria (excl. Biafra)	50.0	2.0	2.0	60	...
Rhodesia	3.4	—	1.0	60	...
Somali Rep.	4.0	—	1.5	20	4.8
South Africa	17.0	3.0	8.0	200	3.5
Tanzania	1.7	—	.1	10	.3
Zambia	3.0	—	.3	18	2.5
VII. CENTRAL AND SOUTH AMERICA					
Argentina	80.0	30.0	15.0	120*	2.1
Bolivia	20.0	—	1.8	70	2.0
Brazil	120.0	50.0	30.0	650	3.2
Chile	38.0	15.0	8.0	270	2.5
Colombia	15.0	7.1	6.0	60	1.3
Cuba	90.0	6.0	25.0	200	7.2
Dominican Republic	12.0	4.0	3.5	90	3.9
Ecuador	12.8	4.0	3.5	40	2.0
El Salvador	4.5	.1	1.0	20	1.2
Guatemala	7.8	.2	1.0	30	0.9
Guyana	1.0	—	—	—	2.1
Haiti	5.0	.25	.25	15	2.1
Honduras	3.5	—	1.2	25	1.2
Jamaica	1.0	.25	.25	—	0.6
Mexico	54.0	8.5	6.0	300	0.8
Nicaragua	5.4	.2	1.5	40	1.6
Paraguay	17.5	1.9	.8	10	2.1
Peru	35.0	8.0	9.0	150	3.1
Uruguay	12.0	1.8	1.6	30	1.5
Venezuela	15.0	6.5	9.0	150	2.2

Note: The total figure for aircraft includes noncombat aircraft such as transport, training, and reconnaissance aircraft.
*Includes naval aircraft and helicopters. †Includes 302,000 Marine Corps. ‡Includes 250,000 Strategic Rocket Forces.
§Includes 30,000 Marine Corps. ‖Includes 36,000 Marine Corps.
Source: Institute for Strategic Studies, London, *The Military Balance, 1968–69.*

been cut off, Pakistan had obtained the bulk of its military supplies from China, but the Soviet agreement suggested that China had not been able to satisfy all its requirements. Details of the Soviet agreement were not available, but it was thought that it might include 200 135-mm. guns and 200 tanks. Earlier in the year, Pakistan had received the first 6 Mirage III's out of a total order of 18. In August the delivery of 3 out of 12 TF-104G Starfighters purchased from Belgium added further to the variety of planes in the Pakistani Air Force, which already included Mirages, MiG-15s and MiG-19s, Canadian-manufactured Mark 6s, Martin B-57B's, and Lockheed T-33A's. To replace its tank losses in the 1965 war, Pakistan concluded an agreement with Italy for the purchase of 100 refurbished Patton tanks.

MIDDLE EAST

The year in the Middle East opened violently. In Yemen there was heavy fighting between royalists and republicans around the capital of San'a' and its airport and along the Hodeida road. Between 500 and 600 deaths were reported, many of them civilian. Although the last U.A.R. forces had been withdrawn from the country by the end of 1967, Soviet technicians continued to assist the republican forces.

Arab-Israeli relations, however, remained the main focus of attention. Although the six-day war in June 1967 had left Israel better placed strategically than ever before, it still faced serious defense problems. The land area to be defended had increased fourfold to 80,000 sq.km., with a hostile population of 600,-000 West Bank Arabs and 300,000 refugees in the Gaza Strip. Israel had quickly overcome the threat of guerrilla warfare in the occupied territories by a brutally efficient policy of retaliation, but it proved more difficult to stop the infiltration of Al Fatah guerrillas across the Jordan River and harassing attacks by Jordanian artillery.

On January 8 a six-hour tank, artillery, and air battle erupted along the Jordan River when Israeli aircraft attacked Jordanian artillery positions that had been shelling Israeli settlements in the Beisan Valley. On February 18, 18 Jordanian civilians were killed in another artillery and air battle in the Beisan Valley. On March 21, following the deaths of two Israeli children when their school bus was blown up, Israel launched an attack against Jordan on a 200-mi. front. The attack, executed by 12,000 Israeli troops supported by tanks and planes, centred on the village of Karameh, which was being used by the guerrillas as a training camp. In a fierce engagement, 150 Arab guerrillas were killed. The intervention of Jordanian Army units was chiefly responsible for the unusually high Israeli casualties— 23 according to official Israeli sources, 200 according to Jordanian sources.

The high casualties and widespread condemnation of the attack on Karameh led Israel to adopt new tactics. Small commando groups, sometimes helicopter borne, were sent into Jordanian territory to harass the guerrillas in their base areas. However, minor clashes continued to escalate into artillery duels. On June 4, 35 Jordanians were reported killed in an Israeli artillery and air attack. In the same incident, Jordanians claimed 45 Israelis killed or wounded and four Mystère jets destroyed. In the last week of October Israeli commandos sabotaged a dam and hydroelectric power station on the Nile in retaliation for U.A.R. shelling along the Suez Canal that had killed 15 Israeli soldiers and wounded 34, and on December 1

two bridges 40 mi. inside Jordan were blown up in retaliation for an estimated 50 Al Fatah actions in Israeli-occupied territory since November 16. On December 26 an Israeli airliner was attacked at the Athens airport by two Arab terrorists who had traveled to Greece from Lebanon. In reprisal, Israeli helicopters attacked Beirut airport, destroying 13 civil aircraft estimated to be worth $43.8 million.

Since the June war, the Soviet Union had been rebuilding the military strength of the Arab countries. About 80% of the U.A.R.'s air strength had been replaced, principally by 125 MiG-21s and 50 MiG-19 interceptors. Special attention was given to U.A.R. artillery strength along the Suez Canal facing Israeli-occupied Sinai; 3,000 Soviet engineers and technicians were reported to be helping the U.A.R. build a strong defensive line of fortifications and gun emplacements, housing 130-mm., 152-mm., and 160-mm. guns. In addition, 150,000 of the 180,000-man U.A.R. Army was concentrated in the area. On September 8 attention was switched to Suez when U.A.R. and Israeli artillery fought an intense four-hour duel.

The U.A.R. defense budget for 1968-69 was about $690 million, compared with the previous year's expenditure, including the emergency war budget, of $655 million. The Army was increased by 40,000 to 180,000, and the tank force was augmented by the purchase of 300 T-54/55 Soviet tanks. The Navy acquired six Soviet Osa missile patrol boats carrying the Styx short-range cruise missile, making a total force of 18 missile boats of the Komar and Osa types.

Syria's 1968–69 defense budget rose to $137 million from the previous year's $125 million. Although Army strength remained constant at 50,000, the tank force was increased by about 100 Soviet T-54/55 tanks and the Air Force, reduced to 25 combat aircraft following the June war, was built up to a strength of 150, including 60 MiG-21 interceptors and 70 MiG-15 and MiG-17 fighter-bombers. Syria was also believed to have obtained six Komar-class missile patrol boats, possibly with Styx missiles.

Jordan's defense expenditure during 1968 was estimated at $81 million, compared with $64 million in 1967. This figure represented nearly 40% of the total budget, a ratio of defense expenditure to total government expenditure even higher than Israel's. The Army was increased from its post-June war strength of 30,000 to 53,000, and the armour was strengthened by the purchase of 50 M-47 and M-48 Patton tanks from the U.S., part of a $100 million agreement that included 30 Starfighters ordered before the war but not delivered until July 1968.

Israel's defense budget for 1968–69 rose by $165 million to $628 million, representing one-third of total government expenditure and 20% of Israel's GNP, the highest proportion of GNP devoted to defense by any country in the world. The increase was made necessary by the purchase of new military equipment; the replenishment of ammunition stocks; the construction of fortifications and the erection of detector devices along the Jordan cease-fire line; the extension of regular army service by three months; the lengthened supply lines through occupied territory; and measures to meet the security problems. In January, Israel bought 25 A-4 Skyhawk light bombers from the U.S. and, in July, 32 additional Hawk surface-to-air missiles. France continued to refuse to sell Mirage V strike aircraft, but arrangements for the purchase of 50 F-4 Phantom reconnaissance fighters from the U.S. were completed in late December.

AFRICA SOUTH OF THE SAHARA

The African scene was dominated throughout the year by the civil war between the Nigerian federal government and the secessionist state of Biafra, largely made up of Ibo tribesmen. Although the Biafran Army, led by Col. Odumegwu Ojukwu, had enjoyed some initial success in 1967, by the end of that year it was fighting an increasingly desperate defensive action. The Biafran capital, Enugu, had fallen to federal troops in October 1967, and in the second week of December the oil town of Port Harcourt came under attack. However, it was not until the middle of May 1968 that Port Harcourt fell to the federal troops, and even then fighting continued in and around the town for several weeks. The loss of the airfield at Port Harcourt considerably increased the Biafrans' difficulties in obtaining military supplies. The aging Super Constellations which, in the presence of a federal naval blockade, were Biafra's main source of supplies had to be diverted to airstrips deeper in the Ibo heartland, often improvised out of a strip of road or cut out of the bush. As the federal Air Force strengthened its command of the air, the landing strips could be used only at night. Federal antiaircraft artillery added to the hazards. Nevertheless, 14 Constellations were still reported to be flying in and out of Biafra in June.

In the northwest, Onitsha was the centre of fighting from January until April, when it was reported that 1,000 federal troops, who had fought their way into the town, were besieged by 15,000 Biafrans. By June the Biafrans, although winning occasional local victories and displaying considerable skill at disruptive guerrilla fighting behind the federal lines, retained only the towns of Aba, Umuahia, and Owerri in an area of 9,000 sq.mi.

A succession of unsuccessful peace efforts took place during the year. (See NIGERIA.) Meanwhile, international attention had been increasingly drawn to the Nigerian war by the plight of the large numbers of Ibo refugees concentrated in the ever diminishing area held by Biafran forces.

In July the British government sent Lord Hunt with a small mission to assess the needs of the refugees, but the Biafran government refused to admit him to its territory, alleging that the British were in collusion with the federal government. Lord Hunt reported that one million people were desperately in need, and other reports claimed that 3,000 were dying of starvation every day. In spite of Lord Hunt's report, the two sides remained intransigent on the question of the transport of supplies. Following reports that a British organization was planning to airdrop supplies into Biafra, the federal government threatened in July to destroy any unauthorized aircraft. Notwithstanding, a Roman Catholic relief agency claimed that during July it had delivered 30 planeloads of supplies to Biafra, and the Scandinavian Lutheran Church's organization reported up to 22 flights a night during October. Each side accused the other of exploiting the refugees for political ends.

During July and August the federal commander, Gen. Yakubu Gowon, had resisted the demand of field commanders for a final push into the Ibo heartland. International opinion was fearful that the federal offensive would be accompanied by the indiscriminate killing of Biafrans. Some hoped that Gowon would follow a strategy of bottling up the Biafrans in their heartland territory and waiting for internal opposition to arise to Ojukwu's policy of fighting to the last.

However, in the face of the Biafrans' intransigence and of their continued success in obtaining at least a minimum of supplies, Gowon surrendered to the demands of his field commanders and took the offensive in the third week of August. Like previous federal offensives, this one failed to achieve immediate and decisive results. Owerri was reportedly in federal hands on September 17, but Gowon admitted that the war might drag on. Reports of a Biafran plan for a government in exile in Libreville, Gabon, confirmed the prospect of a long guerrilla war.

The federal government enjoyed superiority in both manpower and firepower. Between July 1967 and October 1968, the federal Army grew from 12,000 to 75,000 men, armed with modern light weapons, mainly of British and Belgian manufacture, including mortars, recoilless rifles, and bazookas. Its artillery consisted of British 25-pounder field guns and Bofors 40-mm. antiaircraft guns. The Air Force consisted of about 12 MiG-15 and MiG-17 fighter-bombers, a number of Czechoslovakian Delfin jet fighter-trainers, and 4 Il-28 light bombers. The pilots were believed to be from South Africa and the U.A.R.

The Biafran Army numbered about 30,000, equipped with light arms, recoilless rifles, and mortars from a variety of sources. It possessed no armour and

WIDE WORLD

Volunteers for the Biafran Army drill with sticks at Owerri in August 1968. Arms were only available to troops fighting the Nigerian Army. By September the Ibo town of Owerri was in the hands of the federal Army.

very little artillery and, except for six Alouette helicopters and four light transport aircraft, had no strength in the air. Although the Biafran Army was outnumbered, its morale was generally excellent, though by autumn the federal superiority in firepower was believed to be having a damaging effect on its battlefield performance. The Biafran Army was particularly well officered, about half of the officer corps of the Nigerian Army having been Ibos.

The indecisive course of the war in 1968 reflected weaknesses in federal planning and logistics. Advances were limited by lack of transport and by logistical failures that produced frequent shortages of ammunition and fuel. The federal strategy of fighting on several widely separated fronts—in February federal forces were active around Onitsha in the northwest, Ogoja in the northeast, Calabar in the

Denmark

"I think it was our
simple firing mechanism
that hooked them. . . ."
—Myers, "Evening News,"
London.

southeast, Bonny in the south, and Nsukka in the north—dissipated federal strength and exacerbated the logistical weaknesses. The federals were unable to exploit their command of the air to any serious effect.

The issue of arms sales to the federal government became politically controversial in some of the supplier countries. In May Czechoslovakia, which had provided the federal government with jet aircraft, ceased all arms supplies. The Netherlands followed suit in June and Belgium stopped in July. The U.K., the traditional supplier of the Nigerian Army, continued to permit the sale of ammunition. As the plight of the refugees received more publicity, the British government came under heavy criticism. Government spokesmen defended the policy on the ground that it gave Britain influence with the federal government. The Soviet Union was also reportedly continuing to supply the federal government. France, on the other hand, not only put a total embargo on arms shipments to the federal government but, while stopping short of recognition, associated itself with the Biafran struggle for independence. In August it was reported that France had provided Biafra with foreign currency for arms purchases, and rumours persisted that it was even supplying Biafra with arms.

No official casualty figures for the war had been published, but it was believed that the federal Army had lost more than 30,000 killed and the Biafran Army, 15,000. A report in April spoke of a total of 100,000 deaths, combatant and noncombatant. In October reports spoke of as many as 10,000 Biafrans dying of starvation daily.

During 1968 there was spasmodic guerrilla fighting in Rhodesia. In March planes of the Rhodesian Air Force went into action in the Zambezi Valley against a group of 200–300 guerrillas who had crossed from Zambia. In a running battle that lasted for more than two weeks, the group penetrated to within 100 mi. of Salisbury before being finally broken up. In April another large group was reported to have crossed into Rhodesia, and in July guerrillas were said to be active around Makuti in the east and Wankie in the west. Over 100 guerrillas were reported to have been killed between the beginning of the year and the end of July, while about 20 members of the Rhodesian forces had been lost.

In spite of the guerrillas' lack of success, the Rhodesian minister of justice, Desmond Lardner-Burke, admitted in April that they were better trained and armed than the force that had entered the country the previous August. Many had passed through training camps in Cuba, China, Algeria, or the Soviet Union. They were equipped with a wide range of weapons, many of which—like the highly regarded Chinese Kalashnikov 47 automatic rifle—were of Communist manufacture. Base facilities and training camps were located in Tanzania and in Zambia, which shares a 400-mi. border with Rhodesia, much of it thickly wooded and providing excellent cover. Western sources estimated that as many as 2,500 trained guerrillas were waiting their turn to infiltrate into Rhodesia. Zambia's support of the guerrillas prompted South Africa's defense minister to threaten retaliation. Some circles in Rhodesia were known to favour air strikes against Zambian bases before Zambia built effective antiaircraft defenses.

The Rhodesian forces, comprising an army of 4,000 and a 7,000-man police force, backed up by territorial units, were aided by about 300 men of the South African police, especially trained for anti-guerrilla warfare and equipped with helicopters. Rhodesian leaders, although confident of their ability to defeat any guerrilla force entering the country, acknowledged that the problem was likely to increase. The guerrillas in Rhodesia faced two problems: lack of suitable guerrilla country outside the Zambezi Valley, and apparent lack of support among the African population.

Guerrilla fighting continued in Portugal's African territories, imposing upon one of Europe's poorest countries an annual defense expenditure of $216 million, representing 40% of the total budget. One-fifth of the area of Mozambique was reported to be controlled by the Front for the Liberation of Mozambique. In Angola the nationalist movement continued to be split between the Popular Movement for the Liberation of Angola, which was active in the eastern areas, and the Revolutionary Government of Angola-in-Exile, which was reported to hold an area 300 mi. N of Luanda. There were also reports of guerrilla successes in Portuguese Guinea. Against the guerrilla forces, Portugal maintained an estimated 120,000 troops in Africa. (*See* AFRICA: *Special Report*.)

(J. S. M.)

See also Astronautics; Nuclear Energy; Vietnam.

Denmark

A constitutional monarchy of north central Europe lying between the North and Baltic seas, Denmark includes the Jutland Peninsula and 100 inhabited islands in the Kattegat and Skagerrak straits, the largest being Sjaelland (Zealand) and Fyn. Area (excluding Faeroe Islands and Greenland): 16,629 sq.mi. (43,068 sq.km.). Pop. (1968 est.): 4,854,721. Cap. and largest city: Copenhagen (pop., 1968 est., 842,649). Language: Danish. Religion: the Danish Lutheran Church is the established church. King, Frederick IX; prime ministers in 1968, Jens Otto Krag and, from February 2, Hilmar Baunsgaard.

The year began with a general election necessitated by the fall of Jens Otto Krag's Social Democratic minority government in December 1967; the government fell when support from the Socialist People's Party, upon which the Social Democrats depended, was withheld in a vote on a post-devaluation deflationary measure. To counter the effects of the 7.9% devaluation of the krone that followed the sterling devalua-

U.S. team hunt for lost H-Bombs

"Found anything yet, Hank? . . . Hank? . . ."
—Franklin, "London Daily Mirror."

Workers searching for four nuclear bombs lost when a U.S. B-52 bomber crashed near Thule Air Force Base, in Greenland.

tion, the Social Democrats had proposed the freezing of hitherto automatic wage increases linked to rises in the price index; the left wing of the Socialist People's Party opposed this, and so brought the government down.

In the election (January 23) the Social Democrats lost 7 seats in the Folketing, and the Socialist People's Party (which had meanwhile split into two parliamentary groups) lost 9; the Conservatives won 3, the Liberal Agrarians lost 1, and the Radical Liberals won

14 seats. The new government, a Conservative-Liberal coalition led by Radical Liberal Hilmar Baunsgaard (*see* BIOGRAPHY), took office on February 2. Its strength was 98 seats out of 175. (The Folketing has 179 members in all, but by tradition 2 representing Greenland and 2 the Faeroes stand apart from the parliamentary party groups.) The government seats were divided as follows: Conservative 37; Liberal Agrarian 34; Radical Liberal 27.

Political feelings on the day of the election were heightened by the report that a U.S. Air Force B-52 bomber had crashed at North Star Bay, Greenland, on the evening of January 21, while attempting a forced landing at a U.S. Air Force base at Thule, 7 mi. NE. It was revealed that the bomber had carried four nuclear bombs. Although these were not primed, thus eliminating any chance of an explosion, and although danger from radioactivity was also estimated to be small, the crash suggested that nuclear-armed U.S. planes had been flying over Danish territory and caused considerable resentment in Denmark. Eventually (January 28) parts of all four bombs were found. On February 6 the new prime minister reaffirmed Denmark's policy of forbidding such flights over any of its territory.

The government's program for economic stabilization was built on legislation already introduced by its predecessor. A wages and prices freeze was imposed, but because prices showed a remarkable stability in spite of devaluation their regulation was eased in the autumn. The 10% added-value tax introduced in July 1967 was increased to $12\frac{1}{2}\%$, and the taxpayer's right to reduce declared income by the amount of tax paid in the previous year was withdrawn. The pay-as-you-earn income tax system, due to be introduced at the beginning of 1969, was postponed because of administrative difficulties until—provisionally—Jan. 1, 1970.

Because of its dependence on foreign trade the Danish economy was very susceptible to outside influences. During recent years the balance of payments deficit had caused concern. In mid-1967 it stood at 1.3 billion kroner and by the end of the year had reached 2 billion kroner; during the first half of 1968 it remained at almost the same level and showed only slight improvement in the latter part of the year. A continuing deficit of more than 10% of the annual value of imports was considered unacceptable, especially when gold and foreign exchange reserves only approximated to a single month's import bill.

The deflationary measure caused unemployment to rise to about 5%, more than double the rate for 1967.

The traditional Danish export of agricultural products continued to face difficulties, especially from the countries of the European Economic Community

DENMARK
Education. (1965–66) Primary, pupils 519,279, teachers (1963–64) 20,548; secondary, pupils 158,931, teachers (1963–64) 11,657; vocational, pupils 154,-826; teacher training, students 114; higher (including 4 universities), students 47,825, teaching staff 6,423.

Finance. Monetary unit: Danish krone, with a par value of 7.50 kroner to U.S. $1 (18 kroner = £1 sterling). Gold and foreign exchange, central bank: (June 1968) U.S. $388.1 million; (June 1967) U.S. $475.9 million. Budget (1968–69 est.): revenue 22,588,000,-000 kroner; expenditure 21,392,000,000 kroner. Gross national product: (1966) 76.9 billion kroner; (1965) 69,970,000,000 kroner. Money supply: (May 1968) 23,340,000,000 kroner; (May 1967) 20,950,000,000 kroner. Cost of living (1963 = 100): (April 1968) 132; (April 1967) 118.

Foreign Trade. (1967) Imports 21,928,000,000 kroner; exports 17,651,000,000 kroner. Import sources: EEC 33% (West Germany 19%); U.K. 14%; Sweden 14%; U.S. 9%. Export destinations: U.K. 23%; EEC 22% (West Germany 12%); Sweden 14%; Norway 7%; U.S. 7%. Main exports: meat and meat preparations 23% (bacon 10%); machinery 18%; dairy products 9%.

Transport and Communications. Roads (1965) 61,302 km. (including 102 km. expressways). Motor vehicles in use (1967): passenger 878,800; commercial 250,200. Railways: state (1966) 2,354 km., private (1965) 1,451 km.; traffic (state only; 1967) 3,085,-000,000 passenger-km., freight 1,405,000,000 net ton-km. Shipping (1967): merchant vessels 100 gross tons and over 1,072; gross tonnage 3,014,094. Air traffic (including Danish part of international operations of Scandinavian Airlines System; 1967): 1,058,105,000 passenger-km.; freight 40,845,000 net ton-km. Telephones (including Faeroe Islands; Dec. 1966) 1,411,-040. Radio licenses (including combined radio-television; Dec. 1966) 1,561,000. Television licenses (Dec. 1966) 1,140,000.

Agriculture. Production (in 000; metric tons; 1967; 1966 in parentheses): wheat 420 (390); barley 4,385 (4,159); oats 928 (864); rye 118 (136); potatoes 859 (972); sugar, raw value (1967–68) *c.* 329, (1966–67) 319; butter 154 (160); cheese 124 (125); pork 791 (792); beef and veal 263 (258). Livestock (in 000; July 1966): pigs 8,127; sheep 112; cattle (July 1967) 3,293; horses 46; chickens 20,270. Fish catch (in 000; metric tons) (1966) 851, (1965) 841.

Industry. Production (in 000; metric tons; 1967): pig iron 76; crude steel 401; cement 2,150; superphosphates (1965) 799; nitrogenous fertilizers (1966–67) 45; manufactured gas 384,000 cu.m.; electricity (net, excluding most industrial production) 9,123,000 kw-hr. Merchant vessels launched (100 gross tons and over; 1967) 483,000 gross tons.

Royal wedding of Princess Benedikte Astrid Ingeborg Ingrid to Prince Richard Casmir Karl August Robert Konstantin zu Sayen-Wittgenstein-Berleburg at Fredensborg Castle, February 3.

(EEC), and industrial exports, mainly machinery and electronic equipment, which had already overtaken agricultural goods, further increased their share of total exports. Denmark continued to benefit considerably from trade liberalization within the European Free Trade Association—and particularly from increased trade with its Scandinavian co-members—but it also sought the greatest possible degree of European economic integration. Membership in the EEC was desired, provided the United Kingdom, Danish agriculture's biggest customer, also gained entry.

In April, on Baunsgaard's initiative, the Scandinavian leaders met in Copenhagen to discuss intensified economic cooperation, with the possible formation of a customs union. This was opposed by Danish industry and to some extent by agriculture, too, on the ground that the consequent common external tariff would affect a number of raw materials that were freely imported under the current systems.

Thus, the main problems facing Denmark at the year's end were the balance of payments deficit, export market difficulties, and the possibility of further inflation resulting from wage negotiations due to begin early in 1969. The excellence of the 1968 harvest met with less than general satisfaction in view of the prevailing conditions for agricultural exports.

On May 26 Crown Princess Margrethe gave birth to a son, Prince Frederick, who thus became second in succession to the throne.　　　　　　　(S. M. Aa.)

ENCYCLOPÆDIA BRITANNICA FILMS. *Scandinavia—Norway, Sweden, Denmark* (1962).

Dentistry

The 46th general meeting of the International Association for Dental Research was held in March 1968 in San Francisco. John B. Macdonald, of Toronto, was installed as president. The International Dental Federation (FDI) met in Varna, Bulg., in September. In the U.S. a direct outgrowth of the increases in dental research was the establishment, in two years' time, of dental research institutes at six universities.

Studies on bacterial plaques had increased because it was found that the capacity of bacteria to produce large amounts of extracellular polysaccharides (primarily the 1,6 linked dextrans) was one of the major differences between bacteria that caused dental caries in gnotobiotic (germ-free) experimental animals and those bacteria that did not. Furthermore, it had been found that the dextrans are produced in greatest quantities when sucrose (ordinary white table sugar) is available to the bacteria. Dextrans produced in the mouth by bacteria (principally by anaerobic streptococci) have several characteristics of importance in the plaque, namely, adherence to saliva-coated teeth, insolubility in saliva, and relative resistance to breakdown by other bacteria. Studies with immunodiffusion tests indicated that plaque material was very similar to the bacterial dextrans produced in the test tube. These data were helpful also in studies on periodontal disease, because bacterial plaques may extend below the margin of the gum and serve as centres for the formation of dental calculus. Most recent work demonstrated that it was possible to prevent plaque formation on tooth surfaces, experimentally, by applying a dextranase, an enzyme produced by a fungus, *Penicillium funiculosum.*

The most recent data indicated, almost uniformly, that continuous use of fluoridated water to at least 1 part per million resulted in a 50% reduction in the frequency of carious lesions. Many people, however, did not have access to a public water supply and studies were continuing on applying fluorides to teeth by other methods such as inclusion in table salt, milk, or tablets. But the reduction in new carious lesions seemed to be less stable than it was when the water supply was fluoridated. The problem seemed to be in controlling dosage and discontinuance of use by patients.

The alkyl cyanoacrylates, which had offered great promise as a prototype of a new restorative (filling) material, were shown to be unstable and to have little resistance to shearing forces. Biological cements, such as those produced by marine plants and animals, were being studied to determine the nature of their chemical bonds. Experience with the alkyl cyanoacrylates did show that the material could be sprayed on the tissues to protect from the excessive bleeding and pain of the exposed tissue. The bacteriostatic qualities of the plastic prevented bacterial breakdown of the tissue.

The usefulness of specimens from the surfaces of oral tissues in the diagnosis of oral cancer was difficult to define clearly, depriving dentists of an additional method for preventing or diagnosing oral cancer. Recent epidemiologic studies showed that exfoliative cytology techniques were best applied when it was not possible to perform a biopsy, when the lesion was in a site in which biopsy was undesirable, or when it was possible to repeat the cytology study frequently.

Cleft lip or cleft palate appeared in about one of every 800 births and in only about one-fifth of the instances could genetic transfer be implicated. That inheritance was not always accountable was supported by the fact that when a cleft appeared in one identical twin, there was only a 40% chance of the other being affected. Studies on experimental teratology using agents such as chlorcyclizine, on palatal closure in the fetus, and on the effects of physical phenomena on the fetus in utero were being followed closely.

　　　　　　　　　　　　　　　　　　　(N. B. Wi.)

Dependent States

Four dependent territories became fully independent nations in the course of 1968: Nauru (January 31); Mauritius (March 12); Swaziland (September 6); and Equatorial Guinea (October 12). (*See* separate articles.) Some of the remaining dependencies, however, were prevented from pursuing a peaceful course toward autonomy or some other self-determined status as they developed into hotly disputed points of conflict for new imperialisms. This was true of British Honduras and, in particular, of Gibraltar, where, despite the overwhelming desire of Gibraltarians to remain British (as evidenced by the referendum of 1967), the UN, by denying the principle of self-determination, prolonged an uneasy confrontation between Britain and Spain. In the British colony of the Falkland Islands, to which claims were pressed by both Argentina and Chile, the 2,000-odd inhabitants of British stock, who wished to remain under British sovereignty, expressed fears that talks between the U.K. and Argentina would deny them the right to self-determination. (*See* also UNITED NATIONS.)

Africa. Excluding the special case of Rhodesia, which the U.K. still ruled officially, the independence of the former High Commission Territory (protected state) of Swaziland marked the end of British colonial rule on the African continent. British influence continued, however, just as French influence did in French-speaking Africa.

French Africa. After an official visit to France by the prime minister of the Somali Republic, Muhammad Haji Ibrahim Egal, political tensions in the French Territory of Afars and Issas (formerly French Somaliland) were somewhat relaxed, with Egal recognizing the colonial status of the territory. In November, the first-ever legislative elections did much to combat nationalistic feeling, aggravated by the 75% fall in shipping at Djibouti, caused by the closing of the Suez Canal.

Portuguese Africa. In August a movement in support of the peoples of Angola and the other Portuguese dependencies announced its start in Geneva. Its founders argued that the struggle for independence was growing stronger but that the world knew little of it, and that in spite of condemnation by the UN, Portuguese authorities still pursued a policy of repression. Eduardo Mondlane (*see* BIOGRAPHY), Dar es Salaam-based leader of the Front for the Liberation of Mozambique (FRELIMO), stated during a visit to England in March that 8,000 guerrillas were active over about one-third of Mozambique and that they actually controlled one-fifth of the country.

In Angola the guerrillas were most active along the frontier with Zambia, where the Benguela railway was a frequent target. In the northern parts of the country the Portuguese authorities were able to maintain effective control in spite of the presence of guerrilla forces. They drew the African inhabitants together into large, new villages, which were more readily defensible, and issued a few rifles to the villagers, enabling them to take part in their own protection. A similar regrouping policy in Guinea also allowed the Portuguese to introduce a wider range of social services. Marcello Caetano, who succeeded António de Oliveira Salazar as Portuguese premier, reaffirmed Portugal's intention to maintain its position in Africa. (*See* AFRICA: Special Report.)

"LONDON DAILY EXPRESS"
FROM PICTORIAL PARADE

Mob turning over a bus on Gibraltar where violence erupted when a group calling themselves the Doves openly suggested a negotiated settlement between the U.K. and Spain over the dependency's future.

Economic prospects were enhanced by reported important oil strikes in Angola (in the Cabinda enclave and south of Luanda). Plans also went ahead for the vast Cahorabassa hydroelectric project in Mozambique.

Spanish Africa. Announcing that its influence in Africa had always been civilizing rather than colonialist, Spain continued its dispute with Morocco over the possession of the coastal "plazas" (Ceuta, Mellila, Alhucemas, Chafarinas, and Peñón de Vélez) and Ifni. In the face of rival claims to Spanish Sahara by Morocco and Mauritania, Spain continued to control the 100,000-sq.mi. territory with the help of 10,000 administrators. Spanish Sahara, together with the Canary Islands, remained vital to Spanish interests, particularly since vast phosphate deposits had been discovered at Bu-Craa. Negotiations to find partners who would help exploit the deposits and at the same time provide security against Moroccan claims continued. However, as a gesture of good faith and no doubt to provide a lever in its dispute with Britain over Gibraltar, on October 12 Spain granted independence to Río Muni and Fernando Po (Equatorial Guinea).

Caribbean. In some British dependent territories there were suspicions that the British government would disown its Commonwealth commitments. The merger of the Foreign Office and the Commonwealth Office, with which the Colonial Office had already been combined, and the abolition of Cabinet status for the minister of overseas development did little to allay such fears. In the April elections in the Bahamas the government increased its majority and at the September constitutional conference in London made demands for full self-government. General elections in Bermuda in May resulted in the return to office of the conservative multiracial United Bermuda Party. These were the first elections to be held under the 1966 constitution, which had granted the islands a larger measure of autonomy. The five island states of the Windward and Leeward Islands remained in their new status of association with Britain. Following the state of emergency proclaimed in 1967 when Anguilla attempted secession from St. Kitts, a senior civil servant was sent to the islands in 1968 to negotiate a political solution.

The U.S. mediator's report on the Guatemalan claim to British Honduras was published in April and rejected by all concerned. Guatemala regarded its claim to "Belize" as unsatisfied; British Honduras saw the proposed treaty as a betrayal of the sovereign independence due to it as a member of the Commonwealth. The treaty would establish a close relationship between Guatemala and British Honduras in matters

continued on page 276

DEPENDENT STATES

Territory	Political status	Area (sq.mi.)	Population (1966–68)	Capital	Population of capital*	Government officials
AFRICA						
Afars and Issas	French overseas territory	8,880	126,700	Djibouti	65,000	Governor, Louis Saget
Angola	Portuguese overseas province	481,135	5,293,000	Luanda	300,000	Governor-general, Lieut. Col. Silvino Silvério Marques
British Indian Ocean Territory	British colony	29	2,000	—	—	Commissioner, the earl of Oxford and Asquith
Cape Verde Islands	Portuguese overseas province	1,557	228,000	Praia (São Tiago)	13,142	Governor, Cmdr. Rosado do Sacramento Monteiro
Comoro Islands	French overseas territory	878	243,876	Moroni (Grande Comore)	11,515	High commissioner, Henri Bernard
Ifni	Spanish African province	579	53,000	Sidi Ifni	13,770	Governor-general, Gen. Adolfo Artalejo Campos
Mozambique	Portuguese overseas province	302,328	7,040,000	Lourenço Marques	183,798	Governor-general, Gen. José Augusto da Costa Almeida
Portuguese Guinea	Portuguese overseas province	13,948	529,000	Bissau	55,958	Governor, Brig. Arnaldo Schulz
Réunion	French overseas département	969	408,000	Saint-Denis	72,500	Prefect, Alfred Diefenbacher
Saint Helena	British colony	156	4,707	Jamestown	1,475	Governor, Sir John Field; Administrators, Maj. J. M. E. Wainright (Ascension), B. Watkins (Tristan da Cunha)
São Tomé and Príncipe	Portuguese overseas province	372	59,000	São Tomé (São Tomé)	5,714	Governor, Maj. A. da Silva Sebastião
Seychelles	British colony	89	47,612	Port Victoria (Mahé)	12,000	Governor, the earl of Oxford and Asquith
South West Africa†	South African League of Nations mandate§	317,827	610,000	Windhoek	66,810	Administrator, W. C. du Plessis
Spanish Sahara	Spanish African province	102,703	48,607	Aaiún	9,812	Governor-general, Gen. Joaquín Agulla Jiménez-Coronado
ANTARCTICA						
Australian Antarctic Territory	Australian external territory	2,472,000	—	—	—	—
Bouvet Island	Norwegian dependency	23	—	—	—	—
British Antarctic Territory‡	British colony	650,000	86	—	—	High commissioner, Sir Cosmo Haskard
French Southern and Antarctic Lands	French overseas territory	157,874	132	—	—	Administrator, Pierre Rolland
Heard and McDonald Islands	Australian external territory	113	—	—	—	—
Peter I Island	Norwegian dependency	96	—	—	—	—
Prince Edward and Marion Islands	South African dependency	110	—	—	—	—
Queen Maud Land	Norwegian dependency	—	—	—	—	—
Ross Dependency	New Zealand dependency	160,000	42	—	—	—
ASIA						
Bahrain	British-protected sheikhdom	256	200,800	Manama	89,500	Sheikh, Isa bin Sulman al-Khalifah British political agent, A. D. Parsons
Bhutan	Indian-protected kingdom	16,000	750,000	Thimphu		Druk Gyalpo (king), Jigme Dorji Wangchuk
Brunei	British-protected sultanate	2,226	104,000	Brunei	17,000	Sultan, Pengiran Muda Mahkota Hassanal Bolkiah
Christmas Island	Australian external territory	52	3,381	—	—	Official representative, J. W. Stokes
Cocos (Keeling) Islands	Australian external territory	5.5	684	—	—	Official representative, C. I. Buffet
Hong Kong	British colony	398	3,926,500	Victoria	621,200	Governor, Sir David Trench
Macao	Portuguese overseas province	6	280,000	Macao	153,630	Governor, Lieut. Col. António Lopez dos Santos
Muscat and Oman	British-protected sultanate	82,000	750,000	Muscat	6,200	Sultan, Sa'id bin Taimur
Neutral Zone	Area jointly governed by Kuwait and Saudi Arabia	2,500	...			
Neutral Zone	Disputed area claimed by Iraq and Saudi Arabia	7,000	...	—	—	—
Portuguese Timor	Portuguese overseas province	5,763	560,000	Dili	10,753	Governor, Lieut. Col. José Alberty Correia
Qatar	British-protected sheikhdom	4,000	80,000	Doha	22,500	Sheikh, Ahmad bin Ali bin Abdullah al-Thani British political agent, R. H. M. Boyle
Ryukyu Islands	U.S. civil administration	848	969,000	Naha City (Okinawa)	269,000	High commissioner, Lieut. Gen. Ferdinand T. Unger
Sikkim	Indian-protected state	2,744	180,000	Gangtok	9,000	Chogyal (king), Palden Thondup Namgyal Principal administrative officer, R. N. Haldipur
Trucial States	7 Arab sheikhdoms under British protection	32,278	180,184	Dubaið / Abu Dhabið	55,000 / 6,500	Sheikh for each state British political agent, H. G. Balfour-Paul British political agent, A. T. Lamb
EUROPE						
Faeroe Islands	Self-governing integral part of the kingdom of Denmark	540	37,310	Thorshavn	9,796	Head of local government, Hakun Djurhuus
Gibraltar	British colony (self-governing)	2.25	25,281	—	—	Governor, Sir Gerald Lathbury; Chief minister, Sir Joshua Hassan
Guernsey	British crown dependency	30	47,879	St. Peter Port	15,706	Lieutenant governor, Sir Charles Coleman; Bailiff, Sir William Arnold
Isle of Man	British crown possession	227	50,423	Douglas	19,269	Lieutenant governor, Sir Ronald Garvey
Jan Mayen	Part of kingdom of Norway	144	36	—	—	—
Jersey	British crown dependency	45	63,000	St. Helier	26,594	Lieutenant governor, Sir Michael Villiers; Bailiff, R. H. Le Masurier
Svalbard	Part of kingdom of Norway	23,957	2,808	Longyearbyen	857	Administrator, Tollef Landsverk
NORTH AMERICA						
Antigua	British associated state (self-governing)	108	61,000	St. John's	14,000	Governor, Sir Wilfred E. Jacobs; Premier, Vere Cornwall Bird
Bahama Islands	British colony (self-governing)	4,404	142,846	Nassau (New Providence)	89,354	Governor, Sir Ralph Grey; Prime minister, Lynden O. Pindling
Bermuda	British colony (self-governing)	21	51,000	Hamilton (Great Bermuda)	3,000	Governor, Lord Martonmere
British Honduras	British colony (self-governing)	8,866	113,000	Belize	36,677	Governor, Sir John Paul; Prime minister, George C. Price
British Virgin Islands	British colony	59	8,650	Road Town (Tortola)	1,950	Administrator, M. S. Stavely

Territory	Political status	Area (sq.mi.)	Population (1966–68)	Capital	Population of capital*	Government officials
Canal Zone	U.S. leased territory	553	49,430	Balboa Heights	—	Governor, Brig. Gen. Walter P. Leber
Cayman Islands	British colony	100	9,010	Georgetown (Grand Cayman)	2,573	Administrator, J. A. Cumber
Corn Islands	U.S. leased territory	4	1,872‖	—	—	Administrator, U.S. State Department
Dominica	British associated state (self-governing)	290	70,000	Roseau	15,880	Governor, Louis Cools-Lartigue; Premier, E. O. Le Blanc
Greenland	Self-governing integral part of the kingdom of Denmark	840,000	43,600	Godthaab	5,586	Official representative, N. O. Christenson
Grenada	British associated state (self-governing)	133	99,000	St. George's	8,099	Governor, I. G. Turbott; Premier, E. M. Gairy
Guadeloupe	French overseas département	685	317,000	Basse-Terre	15,360	Prefect, Pierre Bolotte
Martinique	French overseas département	421	327,000	Fort-de-France	95,000	Prefect, Raphael Petit
Montserrat	British colony	38	14,056	Plymouth	1,950	Administrator, D. R. Gibbs; Chief minister, W. H. Bramble
Netherlands Antilles	Self-governing integral part of the kingdom of the Netherlands	394	210,521	Willemstad (Curaçao)	43,547	Governor, N. Debrot; Prime minister, E. Jonckheer
Puerto Rico	U.S. commonwealth	3,421	2,749,000	San Juan	504,400	Governor, Roberto Sánchez Vilella
Saint Kitts	British associated state (self-governing)	138	60,000	Basseterre	15,742	Governor, Sir Frederick Phillips; Premier, R. L. Bradshaw
Saint Lucia	British associated state (self-governing)	238	105,000	Castries	24,587	Governor, Sir Frederick J. Clarke; Premier, John G. M. Compton
Saint-Pierre and Miquelon	French overseas territory	93	5,129†	Saint-Pierre (Saint-Pierre)	4,501	Governor, Georges Poulet
St. Vincent	British colony	150	90,000	Kingstown	20,688	Administrator, Hywel George; Chief minister, E. T. Joshua
Swan Islands	U.S. unincorporated territory	1	28‖	—	—	Administrator, Federal Aviation Administration
Turks and Caicos Islands	British colony	166	6,272	Grand Turk	2,339	Governor, Sir Ralph Grey; Administrator, R. E. Wainwright
Virgin Islands of the U.S.	U.S. organized unincorporated territory	133	49,742	Charlotte Amalie (St. Thomas)	13,914	Governor, Ralph Paiewonsky
OCEANIA						
American Samoa	U.S. organized unincorporated territory	79	28,000	Pago Pago (Tutuila)	1,608	Governor, Owen S. Aspinall
British Solomon Islands	British protectorate	11,500	139,730	Honiara (Guadalcanal)	6,684	High commissioner for the Western Pacific, Sir Robert Foster
Canton and Enderbury Islands	British/U.S. condominium	27	370	—	—	British high commissioner for the Western Pacific, Sir Robert Foster; U.S. administrator, Federal Aviation Administration
Central and Southern Line Islands	British dependency	36	—	—	—	High commissioner for the Western Pacific, Sir Robert Foster
Cook Islands	Self-governing territory of New Zealand	88	19,777	Avarua (Rarotonga)	—	High commissioner, R. G. Davis; Prime minister, Albert Henry
Fiji	British colony	7,055	503,000	Suva (Viti Levu)	55,000	Governor, Sir Francis Derek Jakeway
French Polynesia	French overseas territory	1,543	90,000	Papeete (Tahiti)	30,000	Governor, Jean Sicurani
Gilbert and Ellice Islands	British colony	342	56,139	Tarawa	7,911	High commissioner for the Western Pacific, Sir Robert Foster; Resident commissioner, V. J. Andersen
Guam	U.S. organized unincorporated territory	212	53,744	Agaña	2,200	Governor, Manuel F. S. Guerrero
Howland, Baker, and Jarvis Islands	U.S. unincorporated territory	3	—	—	—	Administrator, U.S. Department of the Interior
Johnston and Sand Islands	U.S. unincorporated territory	1	156‖	—	—	Administrator, U.S. Department of the Navy
Kingman Reef	U.S. unincorporated territory	9	—	—	—	Administrator, U.S. Department of the Navy
Midway Islands	U.S. unincorporated territory	2	2,356‖	—	—	Administrator, U.S. Department of the Navy
New Caledonia	French overseas territory	7,335	100,500	Nouméa	43,100	Governor, Jean Risterrucci
New Guinea	Australian trust territory	92,160	1,578,650	Port Moresby (on Papua)	22,243	Administrator, Sir Donald Cleland
New Hebrides	British/French condominium	5,700	76,500	Vila	3,100	British high commissioner, Sir Robert Foster; French high commissioner, Jean Risterrucci; Resident commissioner, L. A. Shanks
Niue Island	New Zealand island territory	100	5,232	—	—	Administrator, Roger B. Nott
Norfolk Island	Australian external territory	13	1,152	—	—	Administrator, U.S. Department of the Interior
Palmyra Island	U.S. unincorporated territory	4	—	—	—	Administrator, Sir Donald Cleland
Papua	Australian external territory	86,100	606,336	Port Moresby	41,848	Governor, Sir Francis Derek Jakeway
Pitcairn Island	British colony	19	87	Adamstown	—	Administrator (high commissioner in Western Samoa), J. B. Wright
Tokelau Islands	New Zealand island territory	4	1,900	—	—	King, Tupou IV; Premier, Prince Tu'ipelehake; British commissioner, A. C. Reid
Tonga	British-protected kingdom	270	77,429	Nuku'alofa	15,545	High commissioner, W. R. Norwood
Trust Territory of the Pacific Islands (Marshall, Caroline, and Mariana Islands)	United States trust territory	687	92,373	Saipan	8,664	Administrator, Federal Aviation Administration
Wake Island	U.S. unincorporated territory	3	1,400¶	—	—	Administrator, André Duc Dufayard
Wallis and Futuna	French overseas territory	93	8,611†	Matautu (Uvea)	…	
SOUTH AMERICA						
Falkland Islands	British colony	6,270	2,079	Stanley	1,073	Governor, Sir Cosmo Haskard
French Guiana	French overseas département	35,135	36,008	Cayenne	20,310	Prefect, René Letellier
Surinam	Self-governing part of the kingdom of the Netherlands	63,251	345,000	Paramaribo	110,867	Governor, H. de Vries; Prime minister, J. A. Pengel

*Most recent available figure.
†1965.
‡Includes some territory claimed by Argentina and Chile.
§On Oct. 27, 1966, the UN General Assembly adopted a resolution to terminate South Africa's mandate and put South West Africa under the direct responsibility of the UN.
‖1960.
¶1963.
9Less than 0.5 sq.mi.
ᵟDubai and Abu Dhabi are the residences of the two British agents to the Trucial States.
A dash (—) indicates none or negligible; three dots (…) indicate not available.

Survey party of Bikinians approaching the atoll which they were forced to leave in 1946 when the area was used for atomic tests. Radioactivity had decreased to normal levels, and a program for resettlement was under way.

continued from p. 273

of trade, foreign affairs, security, travel, and work, and also provided for British Honduras joining the Central American Common Market. By late 1968 British Honduras was the only one of 12 participants in the setting up of the Caribbean Free Trade Area not to have ratified the trade agreement. The rebuilding of Belize, the capital, some miles from its present site was expected to be completed by 1970.

The existence of an active separatist movement in Guadeloupe—a French *département* and therefore legally an integral part of France—was publicized when the trials of alleged members took place in Paris and at Pointe-à-Pitre, Grande-Terre, during 1968.

Puerto Rico. The long-standing controversy over whether Puerto Rico should remain an autonomous commonwealth bound to the U.S. or seek another status was revived in 1968. The Popular Democratic Party, which had dominated the island's politics for 28 years and had championed continuation of the commonwealth, lost its control of the governorship, the House of Representatives, and several mayoralties in the November elections. The Progressive Party candidate, Luis Ferré, led in the balloting for the governorship by 390,964 votes to 367,355 for the Popular Democratic candidate, Sen. Luis Negrón López. Gov. Roberto Sánchez-Vilella, who had run as an independent after failing to be renominated by the Popular Democrats, obtained 81,800 votes.

Ferre announced he would work toward U.S. statehood and hold a new referendum on the issue in about two years. Supporters of the commonwealth idea maintained that Puerto Rico would suffer economically if it lost its exemption from U.S. federal taxes or was forced to establish higher local taxes.

Middle East. Despite British promises of technical and other assistance after 1971, rival powers rushed into the vacuum caused by the announcement of British withdrawal from the Persian Gulf. Aden, South Arabia, Perim, and Kamaran became independent as the People's Republic of Southern Yemen on Nov. 30, 1967. British proposals to transfer Kuria Muria to Muscat and Oman, at the unanimous request of its 78 inhabitants, were opposed by Yemen and were followed in May 1968 by the termination of the 1961 Anglo-Kuwaiti agreement to which residual defense obligations attached. Iran refused to recognize the British-supported Federation of Arab Amirates, in view of its territorial claim to Bahrain. Iraq and Saudi Arabia also made claims in these areas.

Far East. Increased instability was expected in Southeast Asia in the wake of British withdrawal from Singapore and other stations east of Suez. In Hong Kong, where the remnants of the British forces were to be based, Peking-inspired incidents continued until late 1967; deliberately created shortages and the influx of refugees further demonstrated that Hong Kong owed its existence to the suffrance of Peking. Progress to self-government continued to be hampered by Chinese accusations that Britain was attempting to create a "third China." Trade, however, increased by about £70 million in 1967 to over £1,100 million.

In the British-protected sultanate of Brunei the new sultan, Hassanal Bolkiah Mu'izuddin Waddaulah, was installed on August 1, following the abdication of his father in October 1967. In September the sultan visited London for talks on Brunei's future status.

Indian Ocean. In the Comoro Islands students clashed with authorities at the Said Mohammed Cheickh de Moroni Institute in February and March. Propaganda by the National Liberation Movement (MOLINACO) based in Tanzania continued to grow, and demands to the French government for independence increased.

In the British colony of Seychelles, the first elections under the November 1967 constitution, which had provided for a new form of government for small administrations, took place in December 1967. The government opted for continuing close ties with Britain, but the conference of the Association of the French-Speaking World, which the majority party leader attended in Paris in 1968, issued maps marking the islands as part of the French cultural area.

Pacific. *British Pacific Territories.* Britain continued to be responsible for numerous Pacific territories as well as for the sea-lanes of New Zealand and of Australia. The Anglo-Tongan Treaty of Friendship of May 30, 1968, which replaced a 1958 treaty, gave Tonga greater independence within the Commonwealth, but reserved Britain's continuing responsibility for defense, aid, and the five-year plan.

In Fiji racial issues took a grave turn as native Fijians, increasingly outnumbered by immigrant Indians, feared a political take-over. The opposition party of A. D. Patel, largely representing immigrants and supported by the UN, boycotted the legislature and forfeited its 9 seats out of 36, only to regain them in the September by-elections. Patel's party fought for a "one man, one vote" republican status within the Commonwealth. When he threatened further boycotts, the Fijian Association demanded the deportation of Patel and "his people." Dissidence was in no way diminished by Patel's support of the demand of the Banabans of Ocean Island (now settled on Rabi in the Fijian group) to the UN for resettlement on Ocean Island with independence on the Nauru model and with similar phosphate compensation claims. On the Gilbert and Ellice Islands (GEIC), of which Ocean Island formed part, R. K. Uatioa, the locally elected leader, refuted the right of Patel and the UN to interfere in GEIC affairs.

Australian External Territories. In January 1968 Nauru achieved independence. A treaty of friendship was signed with Australia, and direction of the island's economy was taken over from the British Phosphate Company. (*See* NAURU.)

Indigenous leaders in Papua-New Guinea continued to affirm their preference for association with Australia and its concomitant economic aid despite the 1967 statement by C. E. Barnes, minister for external

AUSTRALIAN EXTERNAL TERRITORY

PAPUA

Education. (1965) Primary, pupils 64,369, teachers 2,151; secondary, pupils 3,020, teachers 148; vocational, pupils 984, teachers 90; teacher training, students 367, teaching staff (1963) 17; higher (at 3 institutions), students 506.

Finance and Trade. Monetary unit: Australian dollar (A$0.89 = U.S. $1; A$2.14 = £1 sterling). Budget (1965–66): revenue A$21,460,-134 (excluding A$19,804,167 grant by Australian government); expenditure A$43,267,675. Foreign trade (1965–66): imports A$42,864,957 (61% from Australia, 7% from Japan, 7% from U.K., 7% from U.S.); exports A$8,940,268 (76% to Australia, 13% to U.K.). Main exports: rubber 29%; copra 29%.

Agriculture. Production (in 000; metric tons): copra (1966) 15, (1965) 17; rubber (1965–66) 6, (1964–65) 5.

Industry. Gold production (1966) 38 troy oz.

AUSTRALIAN TRUST TERRITORY

NEW GUINEA

Education. (1965) Primary, pupils 168,377, teachers 5,347; secondary, pupils 4,509, teachers 236; vocational, pupils 1,622, teachers 101; teacher training, students 660, teachers 107; higher, students 36.

Finance and Trade. Monetary unit: Australian dollar. Budget (1965–66): revenue A$22,-730,076 (excluding A$49,979,402 grant by Australian government); expenditure A$76,762,308. Foreign trade (1965–66): imports A$67,566,246; exports A$40,889,317. Import sources: Australia 54%; Japan 10%; U.K. 8%; U.S. 7%. Export destinations: Australia 40%; U.K. 38%; West Germany 6%; U.S. 5%. Main exports: copra 29%; coffee beans 21%; coconut oil 14%; cocoa beans 11%; plywood 5%.

Agriculture. Production (in 000; metric tons; 1966; 1965 in parentheses): copra 93 (107); coconut oil, exports (1965) 22, (1964) 26; cocoa 22 (19); coffee c. 3.4 (3.4); timber (1965–66) c. 4,200 cu.m., (1964–65) c. 4,100 cu.m. Livestock (in 000; March 1966): cattle c. 27; pigs c. 4; horses 1.

Industry. Gold production (1966) 28,068 troy oz.

BRITISH COLONIES AND PROTECTORATES

ANTIGUA

Education. (1963–64) Primary, pupils 11,052; secondary, pupils 6,073; primary and secondary, teachers 470; teacher training, students 50, teachers 3.

Finance and Trade. Monetary unit: East Caribbean dollar (ECar$2 = U.S. $1; ECar$4.80 = £1 sterling). Budget (1967 est.): revenue ECar$13,759,496; expenditure ECar$12,632,803. Foreign trade (1966): imports ECar$43,913,-958; exports ECar$2,369,710. Main exports: sugar, cotton, molasses.

BAHAMA ISLANDS

Education. (1965–66) Primary, pupils 21,000, teachers 471; secondary, pupils 7,512, teachers 167; vocational, pupils 525, teachers 17; higher, students 28, teaching staff 3.

Finance and Trade. Monetary unit: Bahamian dollar, with a par value of B$1.02 = U.S. $1 (B$2.45 = £1 sterling). Budget (1967 est.): revenue B$51,679,524; expenditure B$53,374,-994. Foreign trade (1966): imports B$142,634,-703 (64% from U.S., 14% from U.K., 7% from Canada); exports B$23,720,026 (76% to U.S., 6% to U.K.). Main exports: cement 27%; pulpwood 17%; rum 13%; salt 8%. Tourism: visitors (1966) 531,200; gross receipts (1965) U.S. $60 million.

Transport and Communications. Shipping (1967): merchant vessels 100 gross tons and over 106; gross tonnage 281,584. Telephones (Jan. 1967) 25,136. Radio receivers (Dec. 1966) 47,000. Television receivers (Dec. 1964) c. 4,500.

BERMUDA

Education. (1965–66) Primary, pupils 9,402, teachers 355; secondary, pupils 2,790, teachers 193; vocational, pupils 916, teachers 28.

Finance and Trade. Monetary unit: Bermuda pound, at par with the pound sterling (Ber£1 = U.S. $2.40); British coin (legal tender) and U.S. currency circulate freely. Budget (1967 est.): revenue £7,008,449; expenditure £7,469,836. For-

eign trade: imports (1967) U.S. $114.5 million; exports (1966) U.S. $53.5 million. Import sources: U.S. 29%; U.K. 12%; Canada 6%. Export destinations: Australia 22%; U.K. 18%; U.S. 12%; Netherlands 10%; France 9%; Japan 7%. Main exports: concentrated essences 24%; beauty preparations 4%. Tourism (1966): visitors 210,600; gross receipts U.S. $40.5 million.

Transport and Communications. Shipping (1967): merchant vessels 100 gross tons and over 27; gross tonnage 346,338. Telephones (Jan. 1967) 23,018. Radio receivers (Dec. 1966) c. 23,000. Television receivers (Dec. 1966) 12,000.

BRITISH HONDURAS

Education. (1965–66) Primary, pupils 27,292, teachers 1,030; secondary, pupils 2,669, teachers 165; vocational, pupils 283, teachers 16; teacher training, students 146, teachers 12.

Finance and Trade. Monetary unit: British Honduras dollar (BH$1.67 = U.S. $1; BH$4 = £1 sterling). Budget (1967 est.): revenue BH$18,700,653; expenditure BH$18,628,942. Foreign trade (1966): imports BH$38,762,000; exports BH$19,239,000. Import sources: U.K. 38%; U.S. 34%; Jamaica 5%; Netherlands 5%. Export destinations: U.K. 47%; U.S. 25%; Mexico 10%; Canada 7%; Jamaica 5%. Main exports: sugar 34%; citrus fruit and products 24%; mahogany 9%.

BRITISH SOLOMON ISLANDS

Education. (1966) Primary, pupils 23,348, teachers 1,046; secondary, pupils 430, teachers 19; teacher training, students 108, teaching staff 8.

Finance and Trade. Monetary unit: Australian dollar. Budget (1967 est.): revenue A$6,484,-500; grant-in-aid A$1,624,125; expenditure A$7,-759,469. Foreign trade (1967): imports A$8,-198,347; exports A$5,104,740. Main exports: copra 74%; timber 22%.

BRITISH VIRGIN ISLANDS

Education. (1964–65) Primary, pupils 1,959; secondary, pupils 551; primary and secondary, teacher 88.

Finance and Trade. Monetary unit: U.S. dollar (U.S. $2.40 = £1 sterling). Budget (1965 est.): revenue U.S. $993,011; expenditure U.S. $1,365,109. Foreign trade (1967): imports U.S. $4,178,296; exports U.S. $264,262. Main exports: livestock, fish, fruit and vegetables.

CAYMAN ISLANDS

Education. (1965–66) Primary, pupils 1,491, teachers (1964–65) 53; secondary, pupils 585.

Finance and Trade. Monetary unit: Jamaica pound, at par with the pound sterling; U.K. cupronickel coinage is also legal tender. Budget (1966 actual): revenue Jam£436,720; expenditure Jam£359,532. Foreign trade (1966): imports Jam£1,490,914; exports Jam£23,716. Main exports: rope 34%; turtle shell 15%; turtle skins 14%; turtles 9%. Invisible income derives mainly from employment of Caymanians in U.S. ships (c. 1,100 in 1960).

DOMINICA

Education. (1963–64) Primary, pupils 15,439, teachers 459; secondary, pupils 1,561, teachers 83; vocational, pupils 350, teachers 16. .

Finance and Trade. Monetary unit: East Caribbean dollar. Budget (1966 actual): revenue ECar$8,762,164; expenditure ECar$8,574,732. Foreign trade (1965): imports ECar$17,273,000; exports ECar$9,546,000 (90% to U.K.). Main export bananas 78%.

FALKLAND ISLANDS

Education. (1966) Primary and secondary, pupils 330, teachers 37.

Finance and Trade. Monetary unit: Falkland Island pound, at par with the pound sterling; British currency also circulates. Budgets: (colony; 1967–68 est.) revenue FI£376,733, expenditure FI£409,646; (dependencies; 1967–68 est.) revenue FI£52,531, expenditure FI£52,531. Foreign trade: (colony; 1966) imports FI£697,000, exports FI£1,037,890 (mainly wool); (dependencies; 1966) imports FI£74,916, exports FI£1,-368,361 (mainly whale and seal oil).

FIJI

Education. (1966) Primary, pupils 99,138; secondary, pupils 8,466; vocational, pupils 733; teacher training, students 280; teachers, all grades (1963) 2,891; higher (medical school), students 155. The South Pacific University at Suva opened in 1968.

Finance and Trade. Monetary unit: Fiji pound (F£0.435 = U.S. $1; F£1.045 = £1 sterling). Budget (1966 actual): revenue F£12,503,-590; expenditure F£12,584,806. Foreign trade (1967): imports U.S. $68.8 million (26% from Australia, 18% from U.K., 16% from Japan, 8% from New Zealand); exports U.S. $52.4 million (41% to U.K., 13% to U.S., 13% to Australia, 6% to Canada, 6% to New Zealand). Main exports (1966): sugar 54%; gold 8%; coconut oil 7%.

Transport and Communications. Ships entered (1966) vessels totaling 1,607,000 net registered tons; goods loaded (1966) 444,000 metric tons, unloaded 399,000 metric tons. Telephones (Dec. 1966) 12,109. Radio receivers (Dec. 1966) c. 36,000.

Agriculture and Industry. Production (in 000; metric tons): sugar, raw value (1967–68) c. 315, (1966–67) 308; copra (1966) 26, (1965) 30; cement (1966) 41; gold (1966) 113 troy oz.

GIBRALTAR

Education. (1965–66) Primary, pupils 3,404, teachers 171; secondary, pupils 1,595, teachers 101; vocational, pupils 117, teachers 12.

Finance and Trade. Monetary unit: Gibraltar pound, at par with the pound sterling; British currency also circulates. Budget (1967 rev. est.): revenue Gib£2,190,600; expenditure Gib£2,105,-600. Foreign trade (1966): imports Gib£8,367,-990; exports Gib£1,749,570. Tourism (1966) arrivals 500,211.

Transport. Ships entered (1966) vessels totaling 13,737,000 net registered tons; goods loaded (1966) 3,000 metric tons, unloaded 256,000 metric tons.

GILBERT AND ELLICE ISLANDS

Education. (1966) Primary, pupils 12,393; secondary, pupils 707; primary and secondary, teachers 582; vocational, pupils 15, teachers 1; teacher training, students 63, teachers 7.

Finance and Trade. Monetary unit: Australian dollar. Budget (1966 actual): revenue A$2,-708,691; expenditure A$2,834,121. Foreign trade (1966): imports A$2,694,569; exports A$4,802,-090. Main exports: phosphates 64%; copra 26%.

GRENADA

Education. (1965–66) Primary, pupils 28,449, teachers 691; secondary, pupils 2,703, teachers 117; teacher training, students 33, teachers 5.

Finance and Trade. Monetary unit: Trinidad and Tobago dollar (TT$2 = U.S. $1; TT$4.80 = £1 sterling). Budget (1966 est.) balanced at TT$12,758,559 (including TT$4,377,000 aid and grants). Foreign trade (1966): imports TT$21,-724,661; exports c. TT$10 million. Import sources (1965): U.K. 31%; Canada 12%; U.S. 10%. Export destinations (1965): U.K. 40%; U.S. 21%. Main exports: nutmegs 40%; bananas 26%; cocoa beans 23%; mace 7%.

GUERNSEY

Education. (1966) Primary and secondary, pupils 8,066.

Finance and Trade. Monetary unit: pound sterling. Budget (1966): revenue £4,357,767 (including £111,496 for Alderney); expenditure £4,167,222 (including £124,251 for Alderney). Foreign trade included with U.K. Main exports (1966): tomatoes, flowers, stone. Tourism (1966) arrivals 202,720.

HONG KONG

Education. (1965–66) Primary, pupils 636,455, teachers 20,339; secondary, pupils 184,365; vocational, pupils 11,437; secondary and vocational, teachers 7,564; higher (including University of Hong Kong and Chinese University of Hong Kong with 4,103 students in 1966–67), students 8,994, teaching staff 1,127.

Finance and Trade. Monetary unit: Hong Kong dollar (HK$6.06 = U.S. $1; HK$14.55 = £1 sterling). Budget (1967–68 est.): revenue HK$1,885,639,000; expenditure HK$1,992,600,-110. Foreign trade (1967): imports U.S. $1,-829,000,000 (22% from China, 19% from Japan, 13% from U.S., 9% from U.K.); exports U.S. $1,537,000,000 (30% to U.S., 13% to U.K., 7% to Indonesia, 6% to Japan). Main export (1966) textiles 52%.

Transport and Communications. Roads (1967) 948 km. Shipping (1967): merchant vessels 100 gross tons and over 142; gross tonnage 795,971. Ships entered (1966) vessels totaling 28,010,000 net registered tons; goods loaded (1967) 2,613,000 metric tons, unloaded 8,579,-

territories, that Australia would encourage self-determination. The UN also pressed for independence, as evidenced by the presence of a UN visiting mission in 1968. In the February and March elections for an increased House of Assembly on an interracial basis, a relatively greater number of candidates of every racial variety stood for election. About 50% of the old House were returned and of the total 84 seats, 65 were held by members of indigenous or mixed race. The mood remained moderate and pro-Australian but not pro-Indonesian. Pressure for a united New Guinea

grew as the date grew nearer for the 1969 plebiscite to decide whether West New Guinea (Irian Barat) should remain part of Indonesia. Economic deterioration in Irian Barat continued to contrast with the expanding economy of New Guinea, which received A$120 million in aid from Australia in 1967–68.

French Pacific Territories. Pressure grew in the French Pacific for a territorial assembly and internal self-government. The French minister for overseas territories was asked to lay the question before the French Assembly. In July the reelection of Francis

---

000 metric tons. Telephones (Dec. 1966) 301,673. Radio receivers (Dec. 1966) 589,000. Television receivers (Dec. 1966) 58,000.

ISLE OF MAN
Education. (1965–66) Primary, pupils 3,830; secondary, pupils 3,849; vocational, pupils 340.

Finance and Trade. Monetary unit: pound sterling. Budget (1965–66): revenue £5,116,275; expenditure £4,331,654. Foreign trade included with U.K.

Transport. Roads (1967) 660 km. Motor vehicles in use (1967): passenger 13,227; motorcycles 2,135; tractors 1,341. Railways (1967) 100 km.

Agriculture. Livestock (in 000; 1966): cattle 32; sheep 123; pigs 4.

JERSEY
Education. (1967) Primary and secondary, pupils 9,280.

Finance and Trade. Monetary unit: Jersey pound, at par with the pound sterling. Budget (1966–67): revenue £10,251,346; expenditure £9,591,593. Foreign trade included with U.K. Main exports (1966): potatoes, tomatoes, cattle. Tourism (1966) arrivals 836,688.

MONTSERRAT
Education. (1964–65) Primary, pupils 3,001; teachers 89; secondary, pupils 238, teachers 16.

Finance and Trade. Monetary unit: East Caribbean dollar. Budget (1967 est.) balanced at ECar$2,958,229. Foreign trade (1965): imports ECar$4,887,839; exports ECar$324,015. Main exports: cotton 51%; vegetables 11%; bananas 7%.

ST. HELENA
Education. (1965–66) Primary, pupils 773, teachers 31; secondary, pupils 401, teachers 30; teacher training (1964–65), students 31, teachers 6.

Finance and Trade. Monetary unit: pound sterling. Budget (1966 actual): revenue £498,358, expenditure £509,909. Foreign trade (1967): imports £410,037 (56% from U.K., 30% from South Africa); exports £19,234 (44% to South Africa, 44% to U.K.). Main export (1966) hemp 75%.

Agriculture. Livestock (1966): cattle 658; sheep 1,059; goats 1,113; pigs 333; poultry 9,611; donkeys 887; horses 25.

ST. KITTS-NEVIS-ANGUILLA
Education. (1964–65) Primary, pupils 16,345, teachers 453; secondary, pupils 1,538, teachers 68; vocational, pupils 300, teachers 4.

Finance and Trade. Monetary unit: East Caribbean dollar. Budget (1966 actual): revenue ECar$6,820,617; expenditure ECar$6,530,756. Foreign trade (1964): imports ECar$13,557,000; exports ECar$9,965,000. Main export sugar 89%.

ST. LUCIA
Education. (1964–65) Primary, pupils 23,417, teachers 688; secondary, pupils 1,032, teachers 56; teacher training, students 40, teachers 7.

Finance and Trade. Monetary unit: East Caribbean dollar. Budget (1965 est.): revenue ECar$9,690,096; expenditure ECar$8,030,866. Foreign trade (1964): imports ECar$20,408,831 (33% from U.K.); exports ECar$9,827,276 (83% to U.K.). Main exports: bananas 83%; copra 8%; coconut oil 5%.

ST. VINCENT
Education. (1965–66) Primary, pupils 26,262, teachers 896; secondary, pupils 2,871, teachers 89; teacher training, students 100, teachers 8.

Finance and Trade. Monetary unit: East Caribbean dollar. Budget (1967 est.) balanced at ECar$9,727,599. Foreign trade (1965): imports ECar$14,808,502 (31% from U.K., 16% from Trinidad and Tobago, 11% from U.S.); exports ECar$6,422,137 (56% to U.K., 13% to U.S., 13% to Trinidad and Tobago, 8% to Barbados). Main exports: bananas 49%; arrowroot flour 20%; copra 13%.

SEYCHELLES
Education. (1965) Primary, pupils 7,341, teachers 291; secondary, pupils 1,234, teachers 59; vocational, pupils 175, teachers 10; higher, students 48, teaching staff 5.

Finance and Trade. Monetary unit: Seychelles rupee, valued at SRs. 5.55 = U.S. $1 (SRs. 13.33 = £1 sterling). Budget (1967 est.): revenue SRs. 10,415,966; expenditure SRs. 12,017,098. Foreign trade (1966): imports SRs. 19,957,802 (33% from U.K., 7% from Hong Kong, 7% from Burma, 7% from India); exports SRs. 8,610,410 (61% to India, 10% to U.K., 6% to France). Main exports: copra 58%; cinnamon bark 15%; cinnamon oil 5%.

TURKS AND CAICOS ISLANDS
Education. (1966) Government primary, pupils 1,688.

Finance and Trade. Monetary unit: Jamaica pound; U.K. cupronickel coinage is also legal tender. Ordinary budget (1966 actual): revenue Jam£303,827; expenditure Jam£267,205. Foreign trade (1966): imports Jam£422,795; exports Jam£44,953. Main exports: crayfish 66%; salt 22%.

BRITISH-FRENCH CONDOMINIUM
NEW HEBRIDES
Education. (1964–65) Primary, pupils 12,521, teachers 570; secondary, pupils 1,734, teachers 80; vocational, pupils 104, teachers 7; teacher training, students 70, teachers 5.

Finance. Monetary units: Australian dollar and CFP franc (CFP Fr. 89.76 = U.S. $1; CFP Fr. 215.44 = £1 sterling; CFP Fr. 100.54 = A$1). Condominium budget (1967 est.) balanced at A$2,380,000. British administration budget (1966–67 est.): revenue A$351,194; expenditure A$1,963,799. French administration budget (1967 est.): revenue CFP Fr. 122,122,000; expenditure CFP Fr. 129,372,000.

Foreign Trade. (1966) Imports A$7,056,802; exports A$9,302,750. Import sources: Australia 44%; France 18%; Japan 8%; Hong Kong 6%. Export destinations: France 47%; U.S. 20%; Japan 19%; Venezuela 7%. Main exports: copra 48%; fish 26%; manganese ore 20%.

Agriculture and Industry. Production (in 000; metric tons): copra (1966) 34, (1965) 29; manganese ore (metal content; 1966) 37.

BRITISH-PROTECTED STATES
BAHRAIN
Education. (1965–66) Primary, pupils 31,579, teachers (including preprimary) 1,215; secondary, pupils 5,995; vocational, pupils 333; teacher training, students 497; secondary, vocational, and teacher training, teachers 479.

Finance and Trade. Monetary unit: Bahrain dinar, with a par value of 0.48 dinars to U.S. $1 (1.14 dinars = £1 sterling). Budget (1966 est.) balanced at 9 million dinars. Foreign trade (excluding oil; 1966): imports £31,525,523 (mainly from U.K., India, U.S., Japan); reexports £9,446,610 (16% to Saudi Arabia, 15% to Qatar, 12% to Iran, 6% to Abu Dhabi, 6% to Kuwait).

Exports to U.K. (including oil) £5,636,000. Main export petroleum products.

Industry. Production (in 000; metric tons): crude oil (1967) 3,443; petroleum products (1966) c. 9,700.

BRUNEI
Education. (1966–67) Primary, pupils 24,693, teachers 1,020; secondary, pupils 5,121, teachers 291; vocational, pupils 81, teachers 8; teacher training, students 390, teachers 22.

Finance and Trade. Monetary unit: Brunei dollar, with a par value of Br$3.06 to U.S. $1 (Br$7.35 = £1 sterling); Malayan and Singapore dollars are freely interchangeable with the Brunei dollar. Budget (1967 est.): revenue Br$143,371,090; expenditure Br$154 million. Foreign trade (1967): imports Br$137,662,898; exports Br $248,264,287. Import sources: U.K. 28%; Singapore 17%; U.S. 9%; Japan 7%; China 6%; Thailand 5%. Export destination Sarawak 98%. Main export crude oil 95%.

Agriculture. Production (in 000; metric tons): rice (1966) c. 3, (1965) 3; rubber, exports (1966) 0.7, (1965) 0.8.

Industry. Production (1966): crude oil 4,693,000 metric tons; natural gas 201 million cu.m.

MUSCAT AND OMAN
Finance and Trade. Monetary units: Persian Gulf rupee (official), valued at 1s. 9d. sterling (21 cents U.S.); Maria Theresa dollar or thaler (common medium of exchange; value varies between Rs. 3.45 and Rs. 3.75); and (in Dhofar province) half dollar; in interior generally, baiza (64 baizas = Rs. 1). Foreign trade (1966): imports (excluding government and oil company imports of c. £2.5 million) £3,388,831 (mainly from India and U.K.); exports c. £800,000. Main exports (1961–62): dates 48%; fruit and vegetables 24%; fish and fish products 9%.

Industry. Crude oil production (1967) 2,556,000 metric tons.

QATAR
Education. (1965–66) Primary, pupils 11,188, teachers 574; secondary, pupils 1,236, teachers 109; vocational, pupils 169, teachers 28; teacher training, students 43, teachers 6.

Finance and Trade. Monetary unit: Qatar/Dubai riyal, with a par value of 4.75 riyals to U.S. $1 (11.40 riyals = £1 sterling). Foreign trade: imports (1966) 162,747,821 riyals (15% from U.K., 11% from U.S.); exports (1963) 290 million riyals. Main export crude oil.

Industry. Crude oil production (1966) 15,479,000 metric tons.

TONGA
Education. (1966) Primary, pupils 16,173, teachers 609; secondary, pupils 7,473, teachers 309; teacher training, students 66, teachers 5.

Finance and Trade. Monetary unit: pa'anga, at par with the Australian dollar. Budget (1967–68 est.) balanced at 2,084,260 pa'angas. Foreign trade (1966): imports 4,141,000 pa'angas; exports 3,617,500 pa'angas. Main exports: copra 51%; bananas 37%.

TRUCIAL STATES
Education. Primary-intermediate (1958), pupils c. 2,000; limited secondary and vocational.

Finance and Trade. Monetary units: Abu Dhabi, Bahrain dinar; other states, Qatar/Dubai riyal. Budgets (1965 est.): Abu Dhabi £11 million; other states £2.5 million. Foreign trade, Dubai only (1966): imports 311,319,152 riyals; exports 56,092,197 riyals. Import sources: Switzerland 22%; Japan 13%; U.K. 12%; India 6%; U.S. 5%. Export destinations: Persian Gulf

Sanford, spokesman of Tahitian nationalism and an antinuclear candidate, underlined Tahiti's demands for autonomy and its complaints that the economy was geared too much to the prosperity derived from atomic experiments. There were demands for an international commission to control radiation pollution, and the French thermonuclear test in August aroused opposition in Tahiti and in the Cook Islands, which persuaded New Zealand to protest to the UN. Establishment of a second Canada-U.S. company in New Caledonia for mining nickel and reform of the communal and mining statutes revived old arguments between local and central governments. The June elections in the Wallis and Futuna Islands increased the governmental majority by a single Gaullist deputy.

U.S. Pacific Territories. In 1968 the UN urged the U.S. Trusteeship of Micronesia to speed self-government. The scattered nature of the islands and their lack of resources, however, still required the U.S. to provide 95% of the territorial budget. In November the people of Okinawa, electing their own chief executive for the first time since World War II, chose a

states 63%; Ceylon 10%; Saudi Arabia 8%; Muscat and Oman 7%. Main export dry fish 8%; reexports (entrepôt trade) account for 92% of total. Foreign trade, Abu Dhabi (with U.K. only; 1967): imports £5,905,000; exports £6,- 755,000.

Industry. Crude oil production (1967) 18,- 976,000 metric tons.

DANISH REALM
FAEROE ISLANDS
Education. (1965–66) Primary, pupils 5,488; secondary, pupils 878; primary and secondary, teachers 283; vocational, pupils 994, teachers 83; teacher training, students 70, teachers 14; higher, students 6, teaching staff 5.

Finance and Trade. Monetary unit: Danish krone (7.50 kroner = U.S. $1; 18 kroner = £1 sterling). Foreign trade (1966): imports 195,- 302,000 kroner; exports 152,652,000 kroner. Import sources: Denmark 70%; U.K. 9%; Norway 6%; Sweden 5%. Export destinations: Italy 16%; Denmark 12%; Spain 12%; U.K. 12%; U.S. 10%; Norway 9%; Sweden 9%. Main exports fish and products 83%.

Agriculture and Industry. Fish catch (1966) 165,400 metric tons. Electricity production (82% hydroelectric; 1966–67) 55 million kw-hr.

GREENLAND
Education. (1965–66) Primary, pupils 7,186; secondary, pupils 553; primary and secondary, teachers 435; teacher training, students 26, teachers 4.

Finance and Trade. Monetary unit: Danish krone. Foreign trade (1966): imports 263,381,- 000 kroner; exports 102,773,000 kroner. Import source Denmark 94%. Export destinations: Denmark 62%; U.S. 32%. Main exports: fish and products 69%; minerals 23%.

Agriculture. Livestock (in 000): sheep (Nov. 1965) 40; reindeer (1961) 2.8; sledge dogs (1959) 12.5. Fish catch (in 000; metric tons) (1966) 44, (1965) 41.

Industry. Production (in 000; metric tons): coal (1966) 34; cryolite (exports; 1965) 57.

FRENCH OVERSEAS DÉPARTEMENTS AND TERRITORIES
COMORO ISLANDS
Education. (1966) Primary, pupils 8,648; secondary, pupils 564; primary and secondary, teachers 218.

Finance and Trade. Monetary unit: CFA franc, with a parity of CFA Fr. 50 to the French franc (CFA Fr. 246.85 = U.S. $1; CFA Fr. 592.45 = £1 sterling). Budget (1967 est.) balanced at CFA Fr. 1,150,110,000. Foreign trade (1966): imports CFA Fr. 1,777,000,000; exports CFA Fr. 963 million. Import sources (1965): France 47%; Malagasy Republic 17%; Cambodia 10%; Thailand 7%; Argentina 6%. Export destinations (1965): France 47%; U.S. 28%; Malagasy Republic 6%. Main exports (1965): vanilla 43%; essential oils 35%; copra 13%.

FRENCH GUIANA
Education. (1965–66) Primary, pupils 6,572, teachers (including preprimary) 223; secondary (1966–67), pupils 1,192, teachers 48; vocational, pupils 591, teachers 27; higher (1966–67), students 46, teaching staff 8.

Finance and Trade. Monetary unit: franc, at par with the French (metropolitan) franc (Fr. 4.94 = U.S. $1; Fr. 11.85 = £1 sterling). Budget (1966 est.) balanced at Fr. 50,266,345. Foreign trade (1967): imports Fr. 207.9 million (72% from France, 13% from U.S.); exports Fr. 18.4 million. (78% to U.S., 11% to France, 5% to Martinique). Main exports: shrimps 76%; timber 5%.

FRENCH POLYNESIA
Education. (1965) Primary, pupils 24,046, teachers 782; secondary, pupils 3,526, teachers 204; vocational, pupils 1,170, teachers 65; teacher training, students 27, teachers 3.

Finance. Monetary unit: CFP franc. Budget (1967) balanced at CFP Fr. 2,332,000,000.

Foreign Trade. (1966) Imports CFP Fr. 15,- 596,000,000 (80% from France, 8% from U.S.); exports CFP Fr. 1,547,000,000 (52% to France, 23% to South Vietnam, 9% to New Zealand, 6% to Japan). Main exports: phosphates 16%; copra 15%; vanilla 7%.

Industry. Phosphate rock production (1966) 200,000 metric tons.

FRENCH TERRITORY OF AFARS AND ISSAS
Education. (1965–66) Primary, pupils 4,082, teachers 117; secondary, pupils 596, teachers 40; vocational, pupils 145, teachers 9; teacher training, students 9, teaching staff 2.

Finance. Monetary unit: Djibouti franc, with a par value of DjFr. 214.39 to U.S. $1 (DjFr. 514.54 = £1 sterling; DjFr. 43.43 = 1 French franc). Budget (1966 est.) balanced at DjFr. 2,108,000,000.

Foreign Trade. (1966) Imports DjFr. 4,954,- 000,000; exports DjFr. 566 million. Import sources: France 50%; U.K. 11%; Netherlands 5%. Export destinations: France 66%; Aden 5%. Main exports: manufactures, hides. There is a considerable transit trade through Djibouti for Ethiopia.

Transport. Ships entered (1965) vessels totaling 14,834,000 net registered tons; goods loaded (1965) 139,000 metric tons, unloaded 2,140,000 metric tons.

GUADELOUPE
Education. (1965–66) Primary, pupils 64,009, teachers 1,450; secondary, pupils 15,187, teachers 588; vocational, pupils 2,352, teachers 51; teacher training, students 108, teaching staff 8.

Finance and Trade. Monetary unit: local franc, at par with the French (metropolitan) franc. Budget (1966 est.) balanced at Fr. 228,- 262,936. Foreign trade (1967): imports Fr. 491.8 million (72% from France, 10% from U.S.); exports Fr. 160.1 million (74% to France, 19% to U.S.). Main exports: sugar 50%; bananas 35%; rum 8%.

MARTINIQUE
Education. (1965) Primary, pupils 66,528, teachers 2,963; secondary, pupils 22,043, teachers 1,019; vocational, pupils 1,910, teachers 100; teacher training, students 72, teachers 7; higher (at Institut Henri Vizioz), students 623, teaching staff (1964) 19.

Finance and Trade. Monetary unit: local franc, at par with the French (metropolitan) franc. Budget (1965 est.) balanced at Fr. 178 million. Foreign trade (1967): imports Fr. 521 million (73% from France, 6% from U.S.); exports Fr. 177.9 million (91% to France). Main exports: bananas 57%; sugar 16%; rum 11%; canned fruit 9%.

NEW CALEDONIA
Education. (1966) Primary, pupils 20,575, teachers 819; secondary, pupils 2,519, teachers 151; vocational, pupils 1,005, teachers 80; teacher training, students 33, teachers 12.

Finance. Monetary unit: CFP franc. Budget (1968 est.) balanced at CFP Fr. 2,556,451,- 000.

Foreign Trade. (1967) Imports CFP Fr. 7,- 060,000,000; exports CFP Fr. 7.1 billion. Import sources (1966): France 51%; Australia 19%; Japan 8%. Export destinations (1966): France 51%; Japan 26%; Canada 14%; U.S. 6%. Main export (1966) nickel (ore, matte, and smelter) 99%.

Transport and Communications. Ships entered (1965) vessels totaling 1,351,000 net registered tons; goods loaded (1966) 1,425,000 metric tons, unloaded (1966) 821,000 metric tons. Telephones (Dec. 1966) 5,192. Radio receivers (Dec. 1966) 15,000.

Industry. Production (in 000; metric tons; 1966): nickel ore (metal content) 87; iron ore (metal content) 121; electricity 606,000 kw-hr.

RÉUNION
Education. (1965) Primary, pupils 83,127, teachers 2,325; secondary, pupils 19,008, teachers 686; vocational, pupils 696, teachers 54; teacher training, students 286, teachers 20; higher, students 405, teaching staff 65.

Finance and Trade. Monetary unit: CFA franc. Budget (1966): revenue CFA Fr. 9,753,- 000,000; French aid (1968) CFA Fr. 1,912,000,- 000. Foreign trade (1967): imports CFA Fr. 28,- 720,000,000; exports CFA Fr. 8,990,000,000. Import sources: France 66%; Malagasy Republic 9%. Export destination France 90%. Main exports: sugar 81%; essential oils 11%.

SAINT-PIERRE AND MIQUELON
Education. (1965–66) Primary, pupils 842, teachers 53; secondary, pupils 235, teachers 33; vocational, pupils 142, teachers 14.

Finance. Monetary unit: CFA franc. Ordinary budget (1967 est.) balanced at CFA Fr. 590,075,- 000.

Foreign Trade. (1966) Imports CFA Fr. 1,- 616,000,000; exports CFA Fr. 556 million. Import sources: Canada 50%; France 32%; U.S. 8%. Export destinations: U.S. 51%; France 16%. Main exports: frozen and dried fish 61%; fish meal 6%.

INDIAN-PROTECTED STATES
BHUTAN
Education. (1965–66) Primary, pupils 9,986, teachers 242; secondary, pupils 3,314, teachers 118.

Finance and Trade. Monetary unit: Indian rupee (Rs. 7.50 = U.S. $1; Rs. 18 = £1 sterling). Budget (1962 est) balanced at Rs. 4.2 million (including Rs. 500,000 subsidy from India). Five-year development plan (1961–66): total expenditure (revised est.) Rs. 153 million, all granted or guaranteed by India; plan expenditure (1962–63 actual) Rs. 11,046,000. About 95% of external trade, including unrecorded barter, is with India. Main exports (1963–64): timber Rs. 1,250,000; coal Rs. 220,000.

SIKKIM
Education. (1963) Pupils (est. all schools) 11,- 620.

Finance and Trade. Monetary unit: Indian rupee. Public revenue (1965–66 est.) c. Rs. 10.5 million. Five-year development plan (1961–66) Rs. 81,330,000, all granted or guaranteed by India. Foreign trade mainly with India. Main exports (excluding barter; 1960 est.): cardamom Rs. 5 million; oranges Rs. 1.4 million; potatoes Rs. 400,000.

candidate who favoured immediate reversion of the island to Japanese control.

Indian Protected States. *Bhutan*. The king's desire to take his mountain country out of its isolation was advanced partly because Bhutan's strategic position made it important to its neighbours but also because the king's close cooperation with India, which was responsible for its defense, provided him with the initial financial, technical, and economic means. In March 1968 Morarji Desai, India's deputy prime minister, inaugurated Bhutan's first airfield in high mountains at Paro. In May, Indian Prime Minister Indira Gandhi inaugurated the 180-km. Thimbu-Phuntsholing highway. Both had been built by the Indian Border Roads Organization. As a step toward democratization, the king appointed a three-man Cabinet.

Membership in the Colombo Plan provided Bhutan with facilities for the education and training that would make it less dependent on India. The central theme of the meeting between the king and Desai in March was that Bhutan should become self-reliant as early as possible. There were 700 Indians serving the

NETHERLANDS OVERSEAS TERRITORIES

NETHERLANDS ANTILLES

Education. (1965–66) Primary, pupils 40,127, teachers 1,113; secondary, pupils 8,612, teachers 354; vocational, pupils 3,246, teachers 156.

Finance. Monetary unit: Netherlands Antilles guilder or florin, with a parity of 0.52 Netherlands Antilles guilders to the Netherlands guilder (1.89 Netherlands Antilles guilders = U.S. $1; 4.53 Netherlands Antilles guilders = £1 sterling). Budgets: central (1966 est.), revenue 66,689,603 Netherlands Antilles guilders, expenditure 66,593,089 Netherlands Antilles guilders; Curaçao (1965), revenue 57,195,006 Netherlands Antilles guilders, expenditure 57,697,423 Netherlands Antilles guilders; Aruba (1965), revenue 34,091,426 Netherlands Antilles guilders, expenditure 32,954,275 Netherlands Antilles guilders. Cost of living (Curaçao; 1963 = 100): (April 1968) 105; (April 1967) 103.

Foreign Trade. (1966) Imports 1,164,000,000 Netherlands Antilles guilders; exports 1,116,000,000 Netherlands Antilles guilders. Import sources: Venezuela 76%; U.S. 9%. Export destinations: U.S. 46%; Canada 7%; U.K. 7%. Main export refined petroleum products 94% (crude oil imported from Venezuela).

Transport and Communications. Roads (1963) 971 km. (Curaçao 445 km., Aruba 325 km., Bonaire 158 km.). Motor vehicles in use (Aruba and Curaçao; 1966): passenger 23,700; commercial 3,800. Ships entered (Aruba and Curaçao; 1965) vessels totaling 47,083,000 net registered tons; goods loaded (Aruba and Curaçao; 1966) c. 36.3 million metric tons, unloaded c. 42.2 million metric tons. Telephones (Dec. 1966) 23,318. Radio receivers (Dec. 1966) 121,000. Television receivers (Dec. 1966) c. 25,000.

Industry. Production (in 000; metric tons; 1966): petroleum products 35,378; phosphates (exports) 148; electricity (1965) 1,080,000 kw-hr.

SURINAM

Education. (1964–65) Primary, pupils 71,397, teachers 2,052; secondary, pupils 10,252, teachers 463; vocational, pupils 1,430, teachers 78; teacher training, students 1,583, teachers 150; higher, students 667, teaching staff 74.

Finance. Monetary unit: Surinam guilder or florin, with a parity of 0.52 Surinam guilders to the Netherlands guilder (1.89 Surinam guilders = U.S. $1; 4.53 Surinam guilders = £1 sterling). Budget (1968 est.): revenue 134,671,000 Surinam guilders; expenditure 137,216,000 Surinam guilders.

Foreign Trade. (1966) Imports 169.2 million Surinam guilders; exports 164.9 million Surinam guilders. Import sources: U.S. 41%; Netherlands 22%; Trinidad and Tobago 7%; U.K. 7%; West Germany 7%. Export destinations: U.S. 81%; Netherlands 7%; Canada 5%. Main exports bauxite and aluminum 91%.

Transport and Communications. Roads (1965) 1,335 km. Motor vehicles in use (1966): passenger 8,100; commercial 2,122. Most internal transport is by water. Telephones (Dec. 1966) 9,227. Radio receivers (Dec. 1966) c. 50,000. Television receivers (Dec. 1966) 16,000.

Agriculture. Production (in 000; metric tons; 1966; 1965 in parentheses): rice 112 (101); sugar, raw value 18 (19); oranges 10 (9); grapefruit 6 (5); bananas 25 (16). Livestock (in 000; Jan. 1966): cattle 43; goats 8; sheep 4; pigs 11.

Industry. Production (in 000; 1966): bauxite 5,563 metric tons; crushed stone 47 metric tons;

gold 5.2 troy oz.; rum 2,523 l.; electricity 681,000 kw-hr.

NEW ZEALAND TERRITORIES

COOK ISLANDS

Education. (1965) Primary, pupils 4,873, teachers 273; secondary, pupils 683, teachers 41; teacher training, students 167, teachers 8.

Finance and Trade. Monetary unit: New Zealand dollar (NZ$0.89 = U.S. $1; NZ$2.14 = £1 sterling). Budget (1965–66): revenue NZ$1,582,130 (excluding NZ$1,743,000 grant-in-aid); expenditure NZ$3,229,860. Foreign trade (1965): imports NZ$3,067,026; exports NZ$1,992,942. Main exports: fruit juice 40%; clothing 24%; copra 13%; tomatoes 9%.

NIUE ISLAND

Education. (1964) Primary, pupils 1,551, teachers 64; secondary, pupils 154, teachers 8; teacher training, students 32, teachers 5.

Finance and Trade. Monetary unit: New Zealand dollar. Budget (1966–67): revenue NZ $576,852 (excluding NZ$729,000 grants); expenditure NZ$1,387,924. Foreign trade (1966): imports NZ$516,772; exports NZ$109,554. Main exports: copra, bananas.

PORTUGUESE OVERSEAS TERRITORIES

ANGOLA

Education. (1964) Primary, pupils 199,307, teachers 4,434; secondary, pupils 13,158, teachers 639; vocational, pupils 11,220, teachers 630; teacher training, students 550, teachers 39; higher, students 537, teaching staff 86.

Finance and Trade. Monetary unit: Angola escudo, at par with the Portuguese escudo (28.75 escudos = U.S. $1; 69 escudos = £1 sterling). Budget (1967 est.): revenue 4,247,462,000 escudos; expenditure 4,247,462,000 escudos. Foreign trade (1966): imports 5,947,606,000 escudos (43% from Portugal, 11% from West Germany, 11% from U.K., 8% from U.S.); exports 6,359,390,000 escudos (35% to Portugal, 23% to U.S., 13% to Netherlands, 5% to West Germany). Main exports: coffee 48%; diamonds 18%; sisal 5%.

Transport. Roads (1967) c. 48,000 km. Motor vehicles in use (1966): passenger 48,200; commercial (including buses) 19,700. Railways (1966) 3,110 km. Ships entered (1966) vessels totaling 3,672,000 net registered tons.

Agriculture. Production (in 000; metric tons; 1967; 1966 in parentheses): cottonseed c. 14 (c. 14); sisal c. 60 (61); sugar, raw value (1967–68) c. 80, (1966–67) 71; coffee (1966) 226, (1965) 205; palm kernels, exports (1966) 14, (1965) 14. Livestock (in 000; Dec. 1965): sheep c. 135; goats c. 478; cattle (1966–67) 1,550; pigs c. 312. Fish catch (in 000; metric tons) (1966) 327, (1965) 257.

Industry. Production (in 000; metric tons; 1966): crude oil 631; diamonds (76% gem grades) 1,268 metric carats; iron ore (60–65% metal content; 1967) 1,154; salt 61; fish meal 48.

CAPE VERDE ISLANDS

Education. (1964–65) Primary, pupils 22,319, teachers 388; secondary, pupils 1,212, teachers 53; vocational, pupils 643, teachers 58.

Finance and Trade. Monetary unit: Cape Verde escudo, at par with the Portuguese escudo. Budget (1966 est.) balanced at 85,838,000 escudos. Foreign trade (1966): imports 244,203,000 escudos; exports 32,926,000 escudos.

Transport. Ships entered (1965) vessels totaling 6,115,000 net registered tons; goods loaded (1965) 37,000 metric tons, unloaded (1964) 336,000 metric tons.

GUINEA

Education. (1965–66) Primary, pupils 13,449, teachers 245; secondary, pupils 434, teachers 24; vocational, pupils 623, teachers 32.

Finance and Trade. Monetary unit: Guinea escudo, at par with the Portuguese escudo. Budget (1966 est.) balanced at 152,590,000 escudos. Foreign trade (1966): imports 507,348,000 escudos; exports 85,095,000 escudos.

Agriculture. Production (in 000; metric tons; 1966; 1965 in parentheses): peanuts c. 65 (c. 65); palm kernels, exports c. 9 (c. 8). Livestock (in 000; 1965–66): cattle c. 235; pigs c. 102; sheep c. 61; goats c. 162.

MACAO

Education. (1965–66) Primary, pupils 35,774, teachers 971; secondary, pupils 8,657, teachers 440; vocational, pupils 1,577, teachers 91; teacher training, students 91, teachers 18.

Finance and Trade. Monetary unit: patacá (1 patacá = 4.75 escudos; 6.05 patacás = U.S. $1; 14.53 patacás = £1 sterling). Budget (1967 est.) balanced at 46,677,000 patacás. Foreign trade (1966): imports 1,463,000,000 escudos (54% from Hong Kong, 42% from China); exports 684 million escudos (27% to Hong Kong, 15% to West Germany, 13% to U.S., 13% to Mozambique, 7% to Angola).

Transport. Ships entered (1966) vessels totaling 5,279,462 gross tons; goods loaded and unloaded (1965) 288,175 metric tons.

MOZAMBIQUE

Education. (1963–64) Primary, pupils 44,725, teachers 1,471; secondary (1964–65), pupils 8,290, teachers 598; vocational pupils 10,388, teachers 597; teacher training (1964–65), students 841, teachers 65; higher (1964–65), students 388, teaching staff 81.

Finance and Trade. Monetary unit: Mozambique escudo, at par with the Portuguese escudo. Budget (1967 est.) balanced at 5,253,000,000 escudos. Foreign trade (1966): imports 5,971,411,000 escudos (31% from Portugal, 11% from U.K., 11% from South Africa, 7% from U.S., 6% from West Germany, 5% from Iraq); exports 3,216,321,000 escudos (38% to Portugal, 14% to India, 11% to South Africa, 6% to U.S.). Main exports (1965): cotton 19%; vegetable oils and nuts 15%; sugar 11%; timber 7%; tea 6%; sisal 6%; copra 5%.

Transport. Roads (1966) 38,090 km. Motor vehicles in use (1966): passenger 52,700; commercial (including buses) 11,600. Railways (1966) 3,670 km. Ships entered (1965) vessels totaling 15,017,000 net registered tons; goods loaded (1966) 7,327,000 metric tons, unloaded 3,766,000 metric tons.

Agriculture. Production (in 000; metric tons; 1967; 1966 in parentheses): cotton, lint c. 39 (c. 39); agaves c. 31 (31); sugarcane (1967–68) c. 175, (1966–67) 179; copra, exports equivalent (1966) 38, (1965) 39; bananas (1966) c. 25, (1965) c. 25; tea (1966) 14, (1965) 11. Livestock (in 000; Dec. 1965): goats 497; sheep 101; cattle (Dec. 1966) 1,120; pigs 128, asses 15.

SÃO TOMÉ AND PRÍNCIPE ISLANDS

Education. (1964–65) Primary, pupils 6,500, teachers 150; secondary, pupils 398, teachers 19; vocational, pupils 110, teachers 5.

Finance and Trade. Monetary unit: Guinea

Bhutanese government and they were to be superseded in time by trained Bhutanese. An officer of the Indian Ministry of External Affairs was accepted at Thimbu (the capital) for the purposes of liaison.

Sikkim. The chogyal, while recognizing Sikkim's role in Indian defense strategy, wanted increased economic aid for small industries. Visits by both the Indian prime minister and the deputy prime minister in 1968 were welcomed by the chogyal and the Sikkim Durbar. One result was that for the first time Sikkimese officials agreed to explore foreign markets for the sale of cardamom. Another was increased aid for the Mining Corporation at Rangpo, a joint venture of the two governments.

Sikkim's membership in UN agencies provided additional financial and technical support. A malaria eradication program began slowly. The Namgyal Institute of Tibetology, financed from the Durbar revenues and a matching grant from the Indian government, became firmly established as a world centre of Tibetan studies.

Economic Aid. CARIFTA, established in 1968

---

escudo, at par with the Portuguese escudo. Budget (1966 est.) balanced at 74,887,000 escudos. Foreign trade (1966): imports 158,360,000 escudos; exports 176,581,000 escudos.

Agriculture. Production (in 000; metric tons; 1966; 1965 in parentheses): cocoa 9.6 (9); copra 5.5 (6.3); bananas *c.* 5 (3); palm kernels, exports *c.* 3.5 (*c.* 3.5); palm oil *c.* 1.4 (*c.* 1.4).

TIMOR

Education. Primary (1963–64), pupils 7,674, teachers 194; secondary (1962–63), pupils 272, teachers 20; vocational (1961–62), pupils 49, teachers 6.

Finance and Trade. Monetary unit: Timor escudo, at par with the Portuguese escudo. Budget (1966 est.) balanced at 77,904,000 escudos. Foreign trade (1966): imports 141,468,000 escudos; exports 35,416,000 escudos.

Agriculture. Production (in 000; metric tons; 1966; 1965 in parentheses): copra *c.* 1 (*c.* 1); coffee 2.1 (2.8). Livestock (in 000; 1965–66): goats *c.* 232; pigs *c.* 227; buffaloes *c.* 120; horses *c.* 94; cattle *c.* 37; sheep *c.* 54.

SOUTH AFRICAN LEAGUE OF NATIONS MANDATE

SOUTH WEST AFRICA

Education. (1962) Primary and secondary, pupils 71,691, teachers 2,111.

Finance and Trade. Monetary unit: South African rand, with a par value of R 0.71 to U.S. $1 (R 1.71 = £1 sterling). Budget (1966–67): revenue R 115,370,000; expenditure R 113,047,000. Foreign trade included in the South African customs union.

Agriculture. Production (in 000; metric tons; 1966; 1965 in parentheses): corn *c.* 10 (*c.* 10); millet *c.* 13 (*c.* 13); sorghum *c.* 2 (*c.* 2); butter *c.* 4 (*c.* 4); wool (1962) 2, (1961) 1.9. Livestock (in 000; 1965–66): cattle *c.* 2,330; sheep *c.* 3,760; pigs *c.* 20; goats *c.* 1,595; poultry *c.* 339. Fish catch (in 000; metric tons) (1966) 650, (1965) 678.

Industry. Production (in 000; metric tons; 1966): copper ore 37; lead ore (metal content) 102; zinc ore (metal content) 28; tin concentrates (metal content) 0.7; silver (1965) 0.05; diamonds 1,759 metric carats; electricity (1963) 188,000 kw-hr.

SPANISH OVERSEAS PROVINCES

IFNI

Education. Primary (1965–66), pupils 1,143, teachers 37; secondary, pupils 333, teachers 24; vocational, pupils 329, teachers 19.

Finance. Monetary unit: Spanish peseta (70 pesetas = U.S. $1; 168 pesetas = £1 sterling). Budget (1966) balanced at 129,390,000 pesetas (Spanish subsidy amounted to 99,108,855 pesetas in 1964).

Foreign Trade. Imports (1966) 221,112,000 pesetas; exports (1963) 127,310 pesetas.

Agriculture. Production (in 000; metric tons): barley (1966) 2, (1965) 2; wheat (1963) 0.9, (1962) 0.9. Livestock (in 000; 1965–66): goats *c.* 85; sheep *c.* 44; cattle *c.* 25; asses *c.* 7; camels *c.* 6.

Industry. Electricity production (1966) 1,841,170 kw-hr.

SPANISH SAHARA

Education. Primary (1965–66), pupils 1,923, teachers 50; secondary, pupils (1964–65) 332, teachers (1959–60) 24.

Finance. Monetary unit: Spanish peseta. Budget (1966) balanced at 216 million pesetas.

Foreign Trade. Imports (1966) 156,683,000 pesetas; exports negligible.

Agriculture. Livestock (in 000; 1965–66): camels *c.* 52; goats 52; sheep *c.* 46.

Industry. Electricity production (1966) 2,735,000 kw-hr. Phosphate mining is being developed; estimated annual production 10 million metric tons.

UNITED STATES DEPENDENCIES

AMERICAN SAMOA

Education. (1965–66) Primary, pupils 6,502, teachers 294; secondary and vocational, pupils 2,019, teachers 59.

Finance. Monetary unit: U.S. dollar. Budget: revenue (1967 est.) $13,149,000 (including $9,149,000 U.S. grant); expenditure (1965) $13,010,350.

Foreign Trade. (1966–67) Imports $9,437,481 (64% from U.S.); exports $27,180,978. Main export (1964–65) fish (mostly canned tuna) 98%.

Agriculture. Production (in 000; metric tons; 1966; 1965 in parentheses): copra *c.* 0.7 (0.7); bananas 1 (1). Livestock (in 000): pigs (April 1966) *c.* 20; chickens (July 1966) *c.* 20.

GUAM

Education. (1965) Primary (including preprimary), pupils 13,488, teachers 392; secondary and vocational, pupils 8,198, teachers 302; higher, students 1,624, teaching staff 110.

Finance. Monetary unit: U.S. dollar. Budget (1965 actual): revenue $28,615,091 (including $3,097,543 U.S. grant); expenditure $30,189,542.

Foreign Trade. (1965–66) Imports $63,682,432 (60% from U.S.); exports $7,616,788 (49% to U.S.). Main exports transshipped foodstuffs and scrap metal.

Agriculture. Main crops: corn, sweet potatoes, taro, and cassava. Livestock (in 000; 1966–67): pigs 7; cattle 6; buffaloes 1; chickens (June 1966) 72.

Industry. Production (1966): crushed stone 820,000 metric tons; electricity (excluding most industrial production) 486 million kw-hr.

PANAMA CANAL ZONE

Finance. Monetary unit: U.S. dollar.

Traffic. (1966–67) Total number of oceangoing vessels passing through the canal 12,412; total cargo tonnage 86,193,430; total tolls collected U.S. $76,768,605. Nationality and number of commercial vessels using the canal: U.S. 1,725; Norwegian 1,542; Liberian 1,380; British 1,317; West German 1,231; Japanese 864; Netherlands 491; Panamanian 474; Greek 469; Danish 439. Imports (1964) U.S. $64.7 million; exports (1964) U.S. $9.1 million.

PUERTO RICO

Education. (1965–66) Primary, pupils 453,725, teachers 11,706; secondary and vocational, pupils 241,626, teachers 8,216; higher (including 3 universities), students 40,294, teaching staff 3,200.

Finance. Monetary unit: U.S. dollar. Central government budget (1966–67): revenue $795,425,023; expenditure $783,460,977 (U.S. total payments in Puerto Rico, $336.1 million). Gross national product: (1965–66) $3,037,900,000; (1964–65) $2,720,500,000. Cost of living (1963 = 100): (Feb. 1968) 115; (Feb. 1967) 111.

Foreign Trade. (1966–67) Imports $1,811,491,432 (81% from U.S.); exports $1,320,753,754 (89% to U.S.). Main exports (1963–64): textiles 24%; sugar 14%. Tourism (1964–65)

visitors 1,254,300; gross receipts U.S. $119.3 million.

Transport and Communications. Roads (1967) *c.* 8,000 km. Motor vehicles in use (1966): passenger 304,700; commercial (including buses) 60,000. Shipping (1966–67) goods unloaded 28,028,759 tons. Telephones (Jan. 1967) 218,658.

Agriculture. Production (in 000; metric tons; 1966; 1965 in parentheses): bananas 112 (118); coffee 13 (14); sugar, raw value (1967–68) *c.* 658, (1966–67) *c.* 742; tobacco 7 (17); pineapples 66 (73); oranges 37 (34); grapefruit 12 (15); sweet potatoes 27 (28); milk 354 (350). Livestock (in 000; Jan. 1967): cattle 485; pigs 180; chickens (Jan. 1966) 3,619.

Industry. Production (in 000; metric tons; 1966): sand and gravel 8,962; stone 5,200; cement (1967) 1,614; electricity 4,730,000 kw-hr.

RYUKYU ISLANDS

Education. (1965–66) Primary, pupils 151,798, teachers 4,173; secondary, pupils 114,724, teachers 4,068; vocational, pupils 10,956, teachers 595; higher (including 3 universities), students 4,954, teaching staff 418.

Finance. Monetary unit: U.S. dollar. Budget (1967): revenue $95,960,230 (including $9,267,604 U.S. grant and $17,225,000 Japanese grant); expenditure $95,960,230.

Foreign Trade. (1966–67) Imports $338,717,000; exports $77,503,000. Import sources (1965–66): Japan 79%; U.S. 15%. Export destinations (1965–66): Japan 89%; U.S. 10%. Main exports: sugar 52%; canned pineapple 20%.

Agriculture. Production (in 000; metric tons; 1966; 1965 in parentheses): rice 12 (10); pineapples 88 (68); sweet potatoes *c.* 68 (*c.* 70); sugarcane (1967–68) *c.* 210, (1966–67) 199. Livestock (in 000; Oct. 1966): cattle 20; horses 12; pigs 190; goats 39; chickens 1,390. Fish catch (1965–66) 26,000 metric tons.

VIRGIN ISLANDS, U.S.

Education. (1965–66) Primary, pupils 8,856, teachers 393; secondary and vocational, pupils 3,899, teachers 288; higher, students 714, teaching staff 40.

Finance and Trade. Monetary unit: U.S. dollar. Budget (1966–67) revenue (including grant-in-aid) $61,504,681. Foreign trade (1966): imports $137,720,755 (68% from U.S.); exports $56,145,017 (94% to U.S. in 1964). Tourism (1967): visitors 554,434; gross receipts *c.* $75 million.

Industry. Crushed stone production (1966) 80,000 metric tons.

UNITED STATES TRUST TERRITORY

CAROLINE, MARIANA, AND MARSHALL ISLANDS

Education. (1965–66) Primary, pupils 23,605, teachers 997; secondary, pupils 2,300, teachers 209; vocational, pupils 106, teachers 21; teacher training, students 605.

Finance. Monetary unit: U.S. dollar. Budget (1967 est.) balanced at $18,530,000 (including $17,022,000 U.S. grant).

Foreign Trade. (1967) Imports $9.8 million (66% from U.S., 22% from Japan); exports $2.3 million (87% to Japan). Main exports: copra 74%; scrap metal 17%.

Agriculture. Production (in 000; metric tons; 1966; 1965 in parentheses): copra *c.* 12.5 (12.5); bananas *c.* 3 (*c.* 3); pineapples 110 (93). Livestock (in 000; June 1966): cattle 6; pigs 21; chickens 117; goats 4.

among Antigua, Barbados, Guyana, Trinidad and Tobago, the Windward and Leeward Islands, Jamaica, and Montserrat, under the auspices of Canada and Britain, was indicative of the integration in economic cooperation between dependent territories and other members of the Commonwealth. Britain approved grants totaling £8.3 million for over 300 development schemes in 26 dependent territories for the year ending March 31, 1968.

Private investment continued to thrive, particularly in connection with engineering and construction projects. British firms were awarded large contracts for water development in Muscat and Oman and Abu Dhabi, while Australian firms spread in the Pacific. The total net flow from Britain to less developed countries was estimated at £135 million; Britain's own dependent territories were considerable participants.

Available figures of economic and military expenditure in the territories of Spain, Portugal, France, and the U.S. for 1967–68 indicated that disbursements everywhere outweighed income.

(Pii. D.; K. I.; M. Mr.; Ra. R.; D. Wn.; X.)

See also Africa; South Africa; United Nations.

Development, Economic

According to provisional indicators, the gross domestic product (GDP; equals gross national product minus net factor payments on foreign investments) of the developing countries increased during 1967 at a faster rate than in the period 1960–66, when their combined GDP grew at about 4.8% per year. Per capita income growth during the same period was much lower— only about 2.3% per year—because of the increase in population (2.5% annually). (Unless otherwise indicated, the term "developing countries" refers to all Asian countries except Japan and the Sino-Soviet countries, all African countries except South Africa, all of Latin America, and Cyprus, Greece, Malta, Portugal, Spain, Turkey, and Yugoslavia. The group covers 1,720,000,000 people, or more than 70% of the world's population outside the Sino-Soviet countries.)

The average income growth rate of 2.3% per capita for developing countries conceals wide differences among regions. South Asia had a per capita growth rate of about 0.5% during 1960–66, Africa had only 1%, Latin America only 1.7%, and East Asia about 2.1%. On the other hand, the Middle East and the developing countries of southern Europe achieved 4.2 and 6.2%, respectively.

Financial Position of Developing Countries. Export earnings of developing countries increased by about 3.5% in 1967, compared with an average growth of 6.5% during 1960–66. If exports of major petroleum-producing countries and the developing countries of southern Europe are excluded, moreover, the increase in 1967 amounted to only $200 million, a fraction of 1%. This stagnation was in part a result of the slow economic growth in industrialized countries, which affected their import demand and reduced the average price level of primary products. Rapid supply expansion in some commodities also contributed to the decline in average prices.

Developing countries in all regions were affected by the slow growth of world trade in 1967, although in varying degrees: South Asia and Latin America actually experienced a small absolute reduction in export earnings. The World Bank primary commodity price index for low- and medium-income countries, which from 1960 had fluctuated within narrow margins, fell by 0.7% in 1967; if petroleum prices are excluded, the decline amounted to about 1.5%.

Imports into developing countries, which had increased at an annual rate of 7% between 1961 and 1966, rose only 3% in 1967. The combined trade deficit of the developing countries in 1967 was estimated at around $6 billion, approximately the same as in 1966. If southern Europe and the major oil exporters are excluded, however, the figures are nearly $8 billion in 1967, compared with $7.1 billion in the preceding year. (*See* Table II.) Although the foreign exchange reserves of the developing countries rose by approximately $800 million in 1967, only a few countries benefited from the increase (*e.g.*, major oil exporters, Argentina, Portugal, South Korea, Israel, Jordan, Taiwan, and Thailand).

The major source of finance for investment in the developing countries is their own domestic savings. A study of 45 developing countries in various regions during 1960–66 showed that the contribution of domestic savings to investment was 94% in Latin America, 90% in East Asia, 88% in southern Europe, 80% in South Asia, and nearly 75% in the Middle East and Africa. Data on savings are often unreliable and become available only after a considerable time lag, but the available evidence suggested that the developing countries were endeavouring to increase the ratio of savings to income. During the period 1960–66, for the 45 developing countries, average savings as a ratio of GNP amounted to over 15%; in some countries the proportion was considerably higher (*e.g.*, Argen-

Flow of net official and private financial resources from the industrial countries to the less developed countries and the multilateral agencies, 1961–67. The industrial countries included are Australia, Austria, Belgium, Canada, Denmark, France, West Germany, Italy, Japan, Netherlands, Norway, Portugal, Sweden, U.K., and U.S.

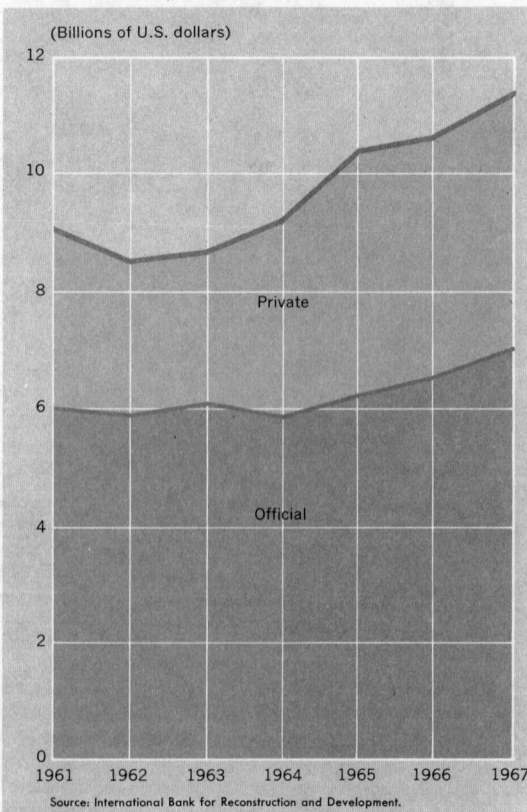

(Billions of U.S. dollars)

Private

Official

1961   1962   1963   1964   1965   1966   1967

Source: International Bank for Reconstruction and Development.

Dermatology:
see Medicine

tina, Ivory Coast, Malaysia, Peru, and Trinidad and Tobago). Also, for a large number of developing countries the proportion of savings out of additional income (usually called the marginal savings ratio) was higher than the average savings/income ratio, suggesting that the average savings ratio over time was also rising. For a majority of developing countries, however, partial data suggested a savings rate considerably below 15%. Very few industrialized countries, in contrast, saved less than 20%.

Helped by the inflow of foreign resources, gross investment in most developing countries was higher than domestic savings. For the 45 developing countries studied, gross investment was roughly 17.4% of GNP during 1960–66. In some of these countries a dramatic improvement in the rate of investment had taken place in the 1960s; for example, Korea's investment as a proportion of GDP rose from 12.5% in 1953–59 to 21.6% in 1966, and Thailand's rose from 15.3% in 1952–59 to 23.1% in 1966. As with savings, however, the investment rate in a large number of developing countries continued to be considerably lower than the average.

Official Financial Assistance. This brief record of recent economic trends in the developing countries must be viewed within the context of the international efforts being made to quicken their pace of growth. National aid agencies and international organizations continued to study the problems of development and to endeavour to improve the means by which financial assistance was made available. Meanwhile, the need for development finance continued to rise, chiefly as a result of population growth, efforts to achieve higher growth in per capita income, and the increase in repayment obligations and debt service charges.

Naturally enough, external capital tends to seek out those investment projects that meet high technical, economic, and financial standards. In the past, however, the lack of managerial, organizational, and technical expertise in developing countries often hampered the preparation of projects. Individual developed countries as well as international organizations have provided technical assistance to developing countries in order to increase their portfolio of projects and facilitate the inflow of foreign capital. In 1967 technical assistance disbursements by members of the Development Assistance Committee (DAC) of the Organization for Economic Cooperation and Development reached a record $1.3 billion, an increase of 9% over 1966.

As a result of the development experience of the past, developing countries with reasonably satisfactory economic policies did have enough economically sound programs to justify considerably higher levels of capital inflow. The World Bank estimated that these countries could utilize effectively some $4 billion more per year in development finance than had been available in the recent past.

According to preliminary estimates of the DAC, the flow of official capital from DAC member countries to developing countries and to multilateral institutions, net of amortization, amounted to nearly $7 billion in 1967. (*See* Table III.) Official assistance thus increased by some $500 million from 1966 and was about $800 million higher than in 1965. The flow of official aid from France rose from $745 million in 1966 to $831 million in 1967; official assistance from West Germany increased from $490 million to $549 million; and the flow of official aid from Japan amounted to $391 million, compared with $285 mil-

lion. However, official assistance from the U.S. rose only slightly in 1967, and assistance from the U.K. actually decreased.

While the volume of official assistance registered a welcome increase in 1967, the terms of this assistance, according to preliminary DAC data, showed some deterioration compared with 1966. Average interest rates on loans extended by DAC members rose by nearly 20% to 3.7%. The average maturity period of loans in 1967 was roughly the same as in 1966, but there had been a substantial hardening between 1964 and 1966, when the average maturity of bilateral loans declined from 28.4 to 23.4 years. At the same time, the share of grants in total flows of official as-

Table I. Economic Indicators for Developing Countries— Regional Summary*

| Region | Average annual rates of growth (%) 1960–66 | | | | | | Percent of GNP average 1960–66 | | |
	Population	Total GDP	GDP per capita	Exports†	Imports†	Total gross investment	Gross investment	Savings	Current account deficit
Total	2.5	4.8	2.3	7.4	7.8	8.6	17.4	15.2	2.2
Africa	2.3	3.3	1.0	5.3	4.8	5.7	13.7	10.1	3.6
South Asia	2.5	3.4	0.5	2.2	2.8	7.5	13.8	11.0	2.8
East Asia	2.7	4.9	2.1	7.2	6.6	9.3	13.4	12.0	1.4
Southern Europe	1.4	7.7	6.2	14.7	18.4	17.2	23.8	21.0	2.8
Latin America	2.9	4.7	1.7	5.3	4.3	3.7	18.0	16.9	1.1
Middle East	2.9	7.2	4.2	10.1	9.5	5.7	19.3	14.4	4.9

*Data are for 56 developing countries covering approximately 90% of the GDP of all developing countries. Countries included under each region are as follows:
Africa—Algeria, Congo (Brazzaville), Ethiopia, Ghana, Kenya, Malawi, Morocco, Nigeria, Rhodesia, Sudan, Tanzania, Tunisia, Uganda, U.A.R., and Zambia. (These countries account for 76% of the aggregate GDP of the region); South Asia—Burma, Ceylon, India, and Pakistan (100% of regional GDP); East Asia—Communist China, Malaysia, Philippines, Thailand, Indonesia (68% of regional GDP); southern Europe—Cyprus, Greece, Portugal, Spain, Turkey, Yugoslavia (100% of regional GDP); Latin America—Argentina, Bolivia, Brazil, Chile, Colombia, Costa Rica, Dominican Republic, El Salvador, Ecuador, Guatemala, Haiti, Honduras, Jamaica, Mexico, Nicaragua, Panama, Paraguay, Peru, Trinidad and Tobago, Uruguay, Venezuela (99% of regional GDP); Middle East—Iran, Iraq, Israel, Jordan, Syria (73% of regional GDP). (Columns 4 through 9 exclude Algeria, Congo (Brazzaville), Malawi, Rhodesia, U.A.R., Zambia, Bolivia, Costa Rica, Haiti, Trinidad and Tobago, and Syria.)

†Goods and services at current prices.

Source: International Bank for Reconstruction and Development.

Table II. Trade Balance of Developing Countries
In U.S. $000,000,000

Item	1961	1962	1963	1964	1965	1966	1967*
Developing countries							
Exports (f.o.b.)	29.3	31.0	33.8	37.1	39.3	42.4	43.8
Imports (c.i.f.)	−34.4	−35.5	−37.2	−41.0	−44.2	−48.3	−49.8
Trade balance	−5.1	−4.5	−3.4	−3.9	−4.9	−5.9	−6.0
Excluding developing countries of Southern Europe†							
Exports (f.o.b.)	27.1	28.6	31.2	34.0	35.9	38.4	39.5
Imports (c.i.f.)	−30.5	−31.1	−32.0	−35.2	−37.3	−40.2	−41.7
Trade balance	−3.4	−2.5	−0.8	−1.2	−1.4	−1.8	−2.2
Excluding southern Europe and major petroleum exporters‡							
Exports (f.o.b.)	21.3	22.2	24.4	26.2	27.5	29.5	29.7
Imports (c.i.f.)	−27.7	−28.3	−29.3	−31.8	−33.3	−36.6	−37.6
Trade balance	−6.4	−6.1	−4.9	−5.6	−5.8	−7.1	−7.9

*Preliminary.

†Greece, Portugal, Spain, Turkey, Yugoslavia.

‡Iran, Iraq, Kuwait, Libya, Saudi Arabia, Venezuela.

Source: International Monetary Fund, *International Financial Statistics* (June 1968).

Table III. Total Official and Private Flow of Long-Term Financial Resources (Net)* from DAC Countries to Less Developed Countries and Multilateral Agencies by Country
In U.S. $000,000

| | Official flows | | | | Private flows | | | | Total flows | | | |
	1961	1965	1966	1967	1961	1965	1966	1967	1961	1965	1966	1967
Australia	71†	122	128	171	...	15	8	15†	71†	137	136	186
Austria	2	34	37	39	18	14	13	9	20	47	49	48
Belgium	92	102	81	99	72	120	97	55	164	221	178	153
Canada	62	124	212	213	26	45	55	40	87	169	267	253
Denmark	8	13	26	28	25	2	−2†	−3†	33	15	24	25
France	943	752	745	831	463	547	575	513	1,406	1,299	1,320	1,344
Germany, West	618	472	490	549	221	255	248	594	839	727	738	1,142
Italy	80	88	122	203	177	178	510	82	258	266	632	285
Japan	107	244	285	391	275	242	384	465	381	486	669	855
Netherlands	56	70	94	114	144	169	160	114	200	239	254	227
Norway	9	12	13	16	18	27	4	15	27	38	17	30
Portugal	44	21	24	...	...	9	15	...	44†	31	40	...
Sweden	8	38	57	60	44	35	51	61	52	73	108	121
Switzerland	23	4	7	4	187	159	116	117	211	163	123	121
United Kingdom	457	481	526	500	444	518	500	480	899	999	1,026	980
United States	3,447	3,627	3,660	3,723	1,102	1,892	1,323	1,844†	4,549	5,520	4,983	5,567†
Total	6,029	6,202	6,506	6,971†	3,213	4,227	4,056	4,411†	9,241	10,429	10,563	11,382

*Net of loan repayments and private capital repatriation.   †Estimate.

Source: Organization for Economic Cooperation and Development, *Statistical Tables for the 1968 Annual Aid Review*, (July 1968).

sistance continued to decline—in 1967 it was about 59%, as compared with 64% in 1966 and 76% in 1961. (*See* Table IV.)

In 1967 grant and loan disbursements of the multilateral organizations concerned with providing financial assistance to developing countries (chiefly the World Bank, the International Development Association [IDA], the European Development Fund, the Inter-American Development Bank, the European Investment Bank, and various UN agencies) were slightly higher than in 1966—about $1 billion compared with a little over $900 million (net of capital subscriptions, bond purchases, and repayments by less developed countries). Loan commitments, on the other hand, declined from nearly $1.6 billion to $1.2 billion. Because of tighter financial conditions in the capital markets, multilateral organizations that borrow in these markets found it necessary to raise their lending rates; the World Bank, for example, raised its rate from 6 to 6¼% in January 1968 and to 6½% in August. In March 1968 the economically advanced member countries of the IDA, an affiliate of the World Bank that makes low-interest loans (0.75%) with a maturity period of 50 years, reached agreement on a second general replenishment of the association's resources at the rate of $160 million annually for three years, beginning November 1968. However, the U.S. Congress did not complete action on this agreement during the 1968 session, and it did not go into effect.

By mid-1967 the total outstanding debt of 92 developing countries for which data were available

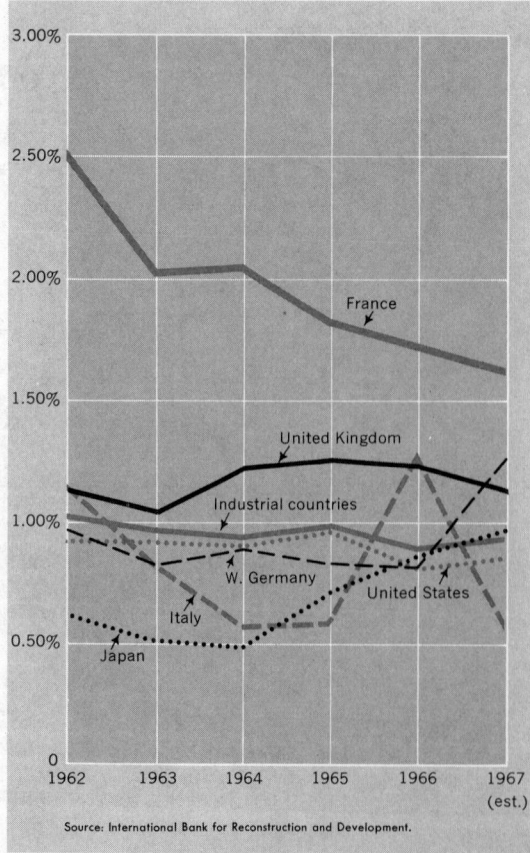

Flow of net official and private financial resources from the industrial countries as a group and the principal industrial countries separately as a percentage of their national incomes, 1962–67. The industrial countries included are Australia, Austria, Belgium, Canada, Denmark, France, West Germany, Italy, Japan, Netherlands, Norway, Portugal, Sweden, U.K., and U.S.

Source: International Bank for Reconstruction and Development.

reached $43.6 billion, representing an increase of 10% over the end of 1965 and of 45% over 1963. The increase in total indebtedness had been accompanied by a sharp rise in total debt service payments. (*See* Table VI.) Debt service payments on public and publicly guaranteed external debt of the 92 developing countries increased by about $400 million in 1966 and by about $185 million in 1967. In percentage terms, the most rapid increases occurred in Africa, East Asia, and South Asia.

In a number of countries, the rapid expansion of debt service obligations in recent years had imposed severe difficulties. The experience of India was a case in point. As a result of the relatively large volume of past loans on rather hard terms, combined with slow export growth, India's service payments on foreign debt (including suppliers' credits) rose from about 15% of merchandise exports in 1961 to about 28% in 1967. In May 1968 the creditor countries, under the leadership of the World Bank, agreed in principle to provide debt relief of about $100 million (or roughly 25%) of debt service payments for three years beginning April 1968.

Unless the terms of aid became more appropriate and commensurate with the debt-servicing capacity of the developing countries, there was a danger that debt crises would become more frequent and more persistent in the future. The short-term solution to the problem for countries already in difficulty might lie in rescheduling or refinancing arrangements for debt service payments due in the next few years, but the longer-term and more basic solution depended on increasing the magnitude and liberalizing the terms of future aid, together with achieving implementation of economic policies that would strengthen the ability of countries to service foreign debt and ensure the effectiveness of all borrowed funds.

Private Capital Flows. The flow of private capital from DAC countries to developing countries and multilateral institutions, net of amortization, was tentatively estimated at $4.4 billion in 1967, an increase of more than $350 million over 1966. Bilateral private capital flows remained at roughly the same level, but the sales of bonds net of redemptions by multilateral institutions in capital markets (other than to official institutions) rose. (*See* INVESTMENT, INTERNATIONAL.)

New Initiatives. The most dramatic change in the field of economic development was in the area of food production. In contrast to 1965 and 1966, when the less developed countries experienced alarming declines in food production per capita, 1967 showed a marked improvement. Moreover, there were signs that this recovery was not merely the result of more favourable weather, but was influenced also by widespread application of agricultural inputs, thus reflecting a permanent technological change. Nonetheless, at least for the next few years there would still be need for imports of food into the less developed countries.

The second session of the United Nations Conference on Trade and Development (UNCTAD) took place in New Delhi, India, in early 1968. The discussions were mainly centred around four topics: the need for a higher level of development assistance; the provision of stable and satisfactory income to the producers of primary products; ways in which the developing countries can improve the mobilization of their domestic resources; and a scheme for extending preferences to exports of manufactures and semimanu-

Table IV. Net Flow of Official Bilateral Capital to Less Developed Countries by Type
In U.S. $000,000

Item	1961	1966	1967
Total official bilateral,* net	5,277	5,971	6,203
Bilateral grants and grant-like contributions	4,034	3,802	3,677
Grants as a percent of total bilateral	76.4	63.7	59.3

*Disbursements.
Source: OECD

Table V. Average Financial Terms of Official Bilateral Loan Commitments

	Weighted average maturity years			Weighted average interest rates (%)		
	1965	1966	1967	1965	1966	1967
Total bilateral loans*	22.2	23.5	23.4	3.6	3.1	3.7
United States	27.9	29.3	28.2	3.3	3.0	3.6
United Kingdom	22.2	23.9	24.1	3.3	1.0	1.1
France	16.8	15.3	15.1	3.7	3.5	3.7
Germany, West	16.9	21.2	19.0	4.2	3.3	4.3
Italy	6.3	8.0	9.3	4.3	3.7	4.0
Japan	12.0	14.1	16.6	4.4	5.2	4.8

*Countries covered are members of the Development Assistance Committee of the OECD, listed in Table I.
Source: OECD, *Statistical Tables for 1968 Annual Aid Review* (July 1968).

Table VI. External Public Debt Service Payments of Developing Countries
In U.S. $000,000,000

Region	1963	1964	1965	1966	1967*
71 countries†					
Africa	0.192	0.242	0.252	0.320	0.413
Southern Europe	0.266	0.325	0.414	0.437	0.432
East Asia	0.076	0.080	0.123	0.167	0.200
Middle East	0.186	0.213	0.184	0.196	0.161‡
South Asia	0.280	0.406	0.352	0.426	0.539
Latin America	1.333	1.686	1.820	2.004	2.007
Total	2.332	2.951	3.146	3.552	3.753
92 countries					
Total	2.583	3.295	3.477	3.890	4.075

*Projected.

†The 71 countries are as follows: Africa—Algeria, Botswana, Central African Republic, Chad, East African Common Services Organization (EACSO), Ethiopia, Federation of Rhodesia and Nyasaland, Gabon, Ghana, Ivory Coast, Kenya, Lesotho, Liberia, Malagasy, Malawi, Mali, Mauritania, Mauritius, Morocco, Nigeria, Rhodesia, Senegal, Sierra Leone, Somalia, Sudan, Swaziland, Tanzania, Tunisia, Uganda, and Zambia; southern Europe—Cyprus, Greece, Malta, Spain, Turkey, Yugoslavia; East Asia—Korea, Malaysia, Philippines, Singapore, Taiwan, Thailand; Middle East—Iran, Israel, Jordan, Lebanon; South Asia—Afghanistan, Ceylon, India, Pakistan; Latin America—Argentina, Bolivia, Brazil, Chile, Colombia, Costa Rica, Dominican Republic, Ecuador, El Salvador, Guatemala, Guyana, Honduras, Jamaica, Mexico, Nicaragua, Panama, Paraguay, Peru, Trinidad and Tobago, Uruguay, Venezuela.

‡Understated because data on Israel are not up to date. Actual figures are probably not less than for 1966.
Source: International Bank for Reconstruction and Development.

factures from the developing countries. The conference did not take any concrete action on these issues, but it adopted a number of resolutions that, if acted upon, would be of considerable benefit to the developing countries. Of special importance was the decision to continue negotiations for a general nondiscriminatory, nonreciprocal scheme of preferences for exports of manufactures from the developing countries. A new target that would call on each economically advanced country to provide annually to developing countries net financial resources amounting to at least 1% of GNP (rather than 1% of national income as approved by the first session of UNCTAD in 1964) was also adopted, although no date was set for its achievement.

The conference also decided to continue consideration of the scheme for supplementary financial measures, proposed by the staff of the World Bank. The scheme was designed to protect development programs from the disruptive effects of unexpected export shortfalls by providing supplemental resources to countries that pursue sound economic and financial policies. The scheme had secured widespread support from the developing countries and from a number of developed ones. The Intergovernmental Group on Supplementary Financing, set up earlier by UNCTAD to examine the scheme, was to be expanded; it would discuss some unresolved issues and report to the UN Trade and Development Board.

In the fall of 1967 the boards of governors of the International Monetary Fund and the World Bank had adopted a resolution that the staffs of the two institutions should prepare a special study concerning possible solutions to the problem of stabilizing prices of primary products. The draft of the first part of the study, completed in August 1968, examined postwar price fluctuations, trends in commodity trade, and their causes; considered measures to improve the level and trend of export earnings; and analyzed measures to deal with fluctuations around the trend. The study attempted to view the commodity problem in the perspective of development efforts and policies.

An international commission was appointed in August 1968 to examine the past and future of world development. The commission, originally proposed by George D. Woods, former president of the World Bank, and endorsed by his successor, Robert S. McNamara, was headed by Lester Pearson, former prime minister of Canada. The commission would examine the effect of external assistance on development and measures that the less developed countries themselves needed to take to facilitate their economic growth.

(I. S. F.)

See also Agriculture; Commodities, Primary; Economic Planning; Industrial Review; Inter-American Affairs; Nuclear Energy; Payments and Reserves, International; Trade, International.

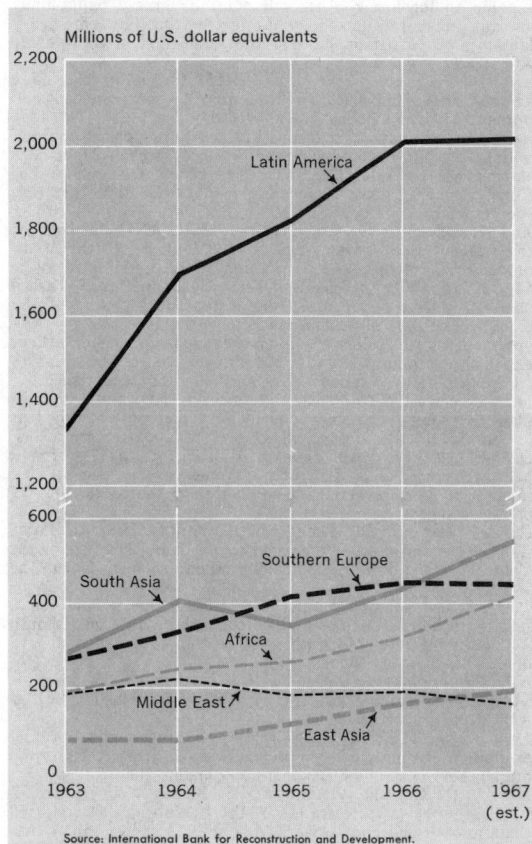

Growth of service payments on external debt of selected developing countries, 1963–67.

Millions of U.S. dollar equivalents

Source: International Bank for Reconstruction and Development.

Diamonds:
see Mining

Disasters

The loss of life and property in disasters during 1968 included the following. (*See also* METEOROLOGY.)

AVIATION

Jan. 10 Near Battle Mountain, Nev. U.S. Marine Corps C-54 transport plane, caught in a blizzard, crashed into 9,978-ft. Mt. Tobin; all 19 Marines aboard were killed.
Feb. 7 In the Himalayas, India. Indian Air Force AN-12 transport plane was lost in the mountains; all 98 persons aboard were presumed dead.
Feb. 8 Amazon Region, Braz. Brazilian Air Force Catalina seaplane went down in dense jungle; all 27 men aboard were missing and presumed dead.
Feb. 16 T'ai-pei, Taiwan. Nationalist Chinese Boeing 727 transport jet failed to make a proper landing at T'ai-pei International Airport and fell into a tea plantation; 21 of the 63 passengers were killed, as well as a villager on the ground.
March 5 Saint-Claude, Guadeloupe. French Boeing 707 jetliner en route from Santiago, Chile, to Paris slammed into a mountainside and burst into flames; all 63 persons aboard perished.
March 9 Réunion Island. French DC-6 taking off in a rainstorm veered to the right and plowed into a hill; 19 persons died, 1 survived.
March 24 Off southwest Wales. Irish Viscount turboprop en route from Cork to London plunged into the Irish Sea after going into a spin; all 61 persons aboard were killed.
April 8 Southern Chile. Chilean DC-3 airliner flying from Santiago to Chihaigue dived into a mountainside and burst into flames; all 36 persons aboard were killed.
April 20 Windhoek, South West Africa. South African Boeing 707 bound for London from Johannesburg, S.Af., crashed on takeoff from J. G. Strijdom Airport; 122 passengers and crewmen were killed, 6 persons survived.
April 30 West Pakistan. Pakistani Air Force transport crashed in the northern hills, killing all 22 crewmen aboard.
May 3 Dawson, Tex. U.S. Electra turboprop exploded while heading through a rainstorm; all 85 passengers and crewmen perished.
May 23 Paramount, Calif. U.S. S-61L passenger helicopter loaded with Disneyland visitors disintegrated in flight, fell, and burst into flames; all 23 persons aboard were killed.
June 25 Near Saigon, South Vietnam. Two U.S. Army helicopters collided in midair and exploded, knocking down a third copter; 29 men were killed.
Aug. 9 Pfaffenhofen, W.Ger. British Viscount en route from London to Innsbruck, Aus., fell onto the grassy bank along an autobahn, presumably while attempting an emergency landing; all 48 persons aboard the plane died in the blazing wreckage.
Aug. 10 Charleston, W.Va. U.S. FH-227 turboprop in making an instrument approach to Kanawha Airport crashed and burned; 35 of the 37 persons aboard died.
Aug. 14 Compton, Calif. U.S. S-61L helicopter broke apart in midair, fell into a playground, and caught fire; all 21 persons aboard were killed. (This was the second Disneyland–Los Angeles shuttle copter to go down in less than three months; see May 23.)
Aug. 18 Off south coast of Cyprus. U.A.R. AN-20 airliner en route from Cairo to Damascus, Syria, plunged into the Mediterranean; all 40 passengers and crew were presumed dead.
Sept. 3 Near Burgas, Bulg. Bulgarian Il-18 turboprop crashed on its way from Dresden, E.Ger., to the Black Sea coast; 50 of the 89 persons aboard were killed.
Sept. 11 Off the French Riviera. French Caravelle jetliner caught fire in midair and plunged into the sea just ten minutes from Nice, its destination; all 95 persons aboard perished.
Sept. 28 Lagos, Nigeria. Red Cross-chartered DC-4 transport plane, ferrying Nigerian troops to Port Harcourt, crashed as it approached the runway; all 57 persons aboard were killed.
Oct. 4 Near Hue, South Vietnam. U.S. Army CH-47 Chinook helicopter and a U.S. Air Force Caribou cargo plane collided in midair; 24 men were killed (11 aboard the copter and 13 on the plane).
Oct. 21 Near Ban Me Thout, South Vietnam. U.S. Air Force C-47 plane en route from Saigon to Da Nang crashed in the Central Highlands when one engine failed; 24 men died in the wreckage.
Oct. 25 Near Hanover, N.H. U.S. twin-engine propjet on a scheduled flight from Boston to Lebanon, N.H., rammed into fog-covered Moose Mountain; 32 of the 42 persons aboard died in the burning plane.
Nov. 25 Savannakhet, Laos. U.S. C-46 transport, chartered for a flight to Vientiane, cracked up when an engine failed; at least 20 persons were killed.
Dec. 2 Near Iliamna, Alaska. U.S. F-27 twin-engine propjet en route to Anchorage in fog and sub-zero weather fell onto the marshy shore of Spotsy Lake; all 39 persons aboard died.
Dec. 12 Off Caracas, Venezuela. U.S. Boeing 707 jetliner fell into the shark-infested waters of the Caribbean as it started the approach one minute from Maiquetía Airport; all 51 persons aboard the plane perished.

KEYSTONE

Wreckage of the British Viscount that crashed on the Munich–Nürnburg Autobahn at Pfaffenhofen, W.Ger., on Aug. 9, 1968, taking 48 lives.

Dec. 24 Bradford, Pa. U.S. twin-engine Convair 580 on a routine flight from Detroit to Washington, D.C., made a too-short landing approach at the snow-obscured Bradford-McKean Airport and crashed into wooded, marshy terrain; of the 47 persons aboard 20 were killed and the other 27 hospitalized.
Dec. 27 Chicago, Ill. U.S. turboprop Convair 580 about to touch down on a fog-covered runway at O'Hare Airport veered suddenly to the left, ripped through the closed door of a hangar, and burst into flames; 27 of the 53 persons aboard the plane were killed, as was one of eight young members of a drum and bugle corps practicing in the hangar.
Dec. 31 Port Hedland, Austr. Australian Viscount propjet ending a flight from Perth and coming in for an apparently normal landing suddenly burst into flames and crashed; all 26 persons aboard perished.

FIRES AND EXPLOSIONS

Jan. 9 Brooklyn, N.Y. A four-story tenement and factory building blazed for five hours in the sub-zero cold; 13 persons, including 9 children, perished in the flames.
Feb. 11 Franklin, Pa. Becoming confused in their blazing home as their mother attempted to lead the way to safety, ten children burned to death; a man was also a victim.
Feb. 12 Kowloon, Hong Kong. A five-story building caught fire and burned to death 18 persons; 8 others were injured.
Feb. 16 Moberly, Mo. Fire in a downtown tavern entrapped and killed 12 persons.
Feb. 26 Shrewsbury, Eng. Several floors of a 100-year-old mental hospital were consumed by flames that killed 22 elderly patients; 13 others were seriously injured.
April 6 Richmond, Ind. An explosion in a sporting goods store rocked the city's business district, destroyed eight buildings, and killed 43 persons; 15 others were missing and 91 injured.
May 11 Vijayawada, India. A photographer's gasoline lamp ignited a fire in a wedding pavilion; in the ensuing panic at least 58 persons were burned or crushed to death and more than 200 others were injured.
Aug. 16 Alicante, Spain. An explosion in a toy-pistol factory killed at least 21 workers.
Oct. 9 Zürich, Switz. A downtown hotel was swept by flames from a fire started by a disgruntled employee; 10 persons died and 20 others were injured.
Nov. 1 Near Algiers, Alg. A forest fire in the Miliana Forest brought death to 22 persons.
Nov. 9 Iloilo, Phil. Children ignited leaking gasoline which caused an explosion of a nearby fuel storage tank; 14 persons burned to death and 56 others were injured.
Nov. 18 Glasgow, Scot. Fire in a window-barred furniture factory engulfed and burned to death at least 24 trapped workers; 3 others escaped.
Nov. 25 Froissy, France. Flames swept through the dormitory floor of a home for the retarded and brought death to 14 adolescents.
Dec. 29 Rio de Janeiro, Braz. Loosened by nearby blasting, a slum hillside slid down into the valley below carrying along 20 shacks with 40 to 70 occupants, all of whom were buried beneath tons of rock.

MARINE

Jan. 25 Eastern Mediterranean Sea. Israeli submarine, the 1,280-ton "Dakar," was reported missing and presumed lost with 69 men aboard.
Jan. 27 Mediterranean Sea. French 850-ton submarine "Minerve," on maneuvers southeast of Toulon, France, suddenly disappeared and was presumed sunken with a crew of 52 men.
March 8 Persian Gulf. Arab dhow, overloaded with 400 Paki-

Rescue column approaching the wreckage of Boeing 707 jetliner which crashed near Saint-Claude, Guadeloupe, on March 5, 1968, killing 63 persons.

A.F.P. FROM PICTORIAL PARADE

stanis en route home from a pilgrimage to Mecca, Saudi Arabia, struck a sandbar in Dubai Harbour and sank; 200 passengers were missing and at least 90 were known dead.

March 28 Near Chapra, India. Strong winds upset a boat crossing the Gogra River; all 60 persons aboard drowned.

April 4 Persian Gulf. Motor launch carrying Pakistani pilgrims capsized off Dibal, Trucial Oman; at least 75 persons drowned.

April 10 Wellington Harbour, N.Z. New Zealand's worst marine disaster occurred when the 8,994-ton interisland ferry "Wahine," labouring in a 123-mph gale, was ripped open on Barrett's Reef, then, taking water, went aground and capsized; of the 727 persons on board an estimated 52 perished.

May 21 Near the Azores. U.S. 3,075-ton nuclear submarine "Scorpion," making a submerged crossing of the Atlantic to its home base in Norfolk, Va., failed to report; all 99 officers and crewmen were presumed dead.

June 14 Indian Ocean. Liberian-registered "World Glory," a 28,323-ton storm-tossed vessel, broke in two and caught fire about 90 mi. NE of Durban, S.Af.; 21 men were missing and presumed drowned, 10 others were rescued.

Oct. 11 Off Mindanao Island, Phil. Philippine ferryboat "Dumaguete," heavily loaded with passengers on their way to participate in a religious festival in Zamboanga, foundered after springing a leak and went down in a shark-infested strait of the Sulu Sea; 300 to 500 persons perished.

Oct. 19 Rourkela, India. Local riverboat capsized as it crossed the Koel River; 40 persons were missing and presumed drowned.

Oct. 31 North Atlantic Ocean. Fire and explosions aboard the Norwegian tanker "Etnefjell" forced abandonment by the crew; the 25 missing seamen were presumed dead after a 19-day search by the U.S. Coast Guard; the captain and two officers who remained aboard the "Etnefjell" were rescued by a salvage vessel.

Nov. 18 Cebu, Phil. Philippine interisland boat "Iruna," pulling away from the dock in the rainy dusk, collided with an incoming British freighter, the 5,338-ton "Eastern Moon," split in two, and sank; 40 passengers were rescued, 200 others were missing and presumed dead.

Dec. 7 Off White Castle, La. U.S. Coast Guard buoy tender "White Alder" was sheared in half by 400-ft. Taiwan freighter "Helena" when the vessels collided in midstream; 17 of the Coast Guard crew drowned, 3 were rescued.

Dec. 21 Grenadine Islands, West Indies. British interisland schooner "Federal Queen" capsized for some unknown reason; 41 persons drowned, 37 others were rescued.

MINING

Jan. 26 Lengede, W.Ger. Explosion in a 300-ft.-deep shaft in an iron mine killed 12 miners.

Column of smoke rising from the burning Llewellyn portal of the no. 9 mine near Mannington, W.Va., where explosions trapped 78 miners on Nov. 20, 1968.

WIDE WORLD

March 6 Belle Isle, La. Fire in the 1,200-ft. shaft of the Belle Isle salt mine destroyed the entrance and suffocated all 21 men trapped at the bottom of the shaft.

May 6 Hominy Falls, W.Va. Water pouring into a soft-coal mine cut off the crew about a mile from the entrance; all 28 men in the mine died.

Oct. 4 Luenen, W.Ger. Ruhr Valley coal mine caved in causing the deaths of 17 miners.

Nov. 20 Mannington, W.Va. Series of explosions set off fires that raged through no. 9 mine and trapped 78 men; recovery of the entombed bodies was deemed impossible and the mine was sealed.

MISCELLANEOUS

Jan. 1–4 Guadalajara, Mex. Continuing round of New Year's celebrations resulted in the deaths of 22 persons, mostly from drinking industrial alcohol.

Feb. 25–28 Rio de Janeiro, Braz. Four-day pre-Lenten Carnival brought death to 89 persons.

June 24 Buenos Aires, Arg. During a stampede of 90,000 spectators fighting to get out of El Estadio Monumental following a soccer game, at least 70 persons were trampled to death, 67 others were hospitalized.

July 12 Mexicali, Mex. A heat wave with temperatures of up to 114° F left at least 40 persons dead.

Aug. 1 Sutur Khana, India. Food eaten during a Muslim religious festival poisoned and killed at least 46 participants.

Dec. 1–16 São Paulo, Braz. City temperatures of around 100° F brought death from dehydration to at least 113 children.

NATURAL

Jan. 7 Johore State, Malaysia. Week-long monsoon rains falling on the southern lowlands drove almost 10,000 residents from their homes and brought death to 21 persons.

Jan. 14 Eastern U.S. Weekend snow, sleet, and icy rain falling along the Atlantic coastline caused the deaths of 55 persons.

Jan. 14–15 Scotland. Winds of 125 mph raged through most of the country damaging buildings and farmlands; 20 persons died, at least 700 others were homeless with damage amounting to about $2.5 million. Elsewhere in Europe, storms, avalanches, and high seas caused the deaths of more than 21 persons.

Jan. 15–16 Sicily. Series of earthquakes struck the western tip of the island, destroyed the towns of Gibellina, Partanna, Salaparuta, and Montevago, as well as many villages; 235 bodies were recovered, 1,500 persons were missing, 1,500 others injured, and more than 83,000 left homeless with damage estimated at $320 million.

Jan. 16 Mindanao Island, Phil. Floods and landslides caused by nine days of heavy rain brought death to at least 29 persons.

Jan. 28 Swiss Alps. Avalanches occurring over the weekend accounted for the deaths of 20 persons; 2 others were missing.

Feb. 20 Aegean Sea. Severe earthquake rocked several small Greek islands killing 19 persons on Ayios Efstratios and Lemnos; 39 others were injured, and many left homeless when more than 500 houses collapsed.

March 8 Eastern Congo (Kinshasa). Earth tremors caused a landslide on the slopes of Mandwe Mountain that swept away the village of Luhonga and killed about 150 persons.

April 4 Central states, U.S. Freezing temperatures, snow, and tornadoes hit the Midwest bringing death to 18 persons.

April 12 East Pakistan. A cyclone ripped through Faridpur District, ruined numerous towns and killed at least 100 persons; more than 1,000 were injured and hundreds left homeless.

April 23 Midwest U.S. Four-state area of Ohio, Kentucky, Michigan, and Tennessee bore the brunt of a chain of tornadoes; 12 persons died and 200 were injured.

April 29 Western Iran. An earthquake jolted the area between Maku and Rizaiyeh killing more than 50 persons; 250 were injured and many left homeless.

May 16 Northern Japan. Northern Honshu Island and southern Hokkaido Island were severely damaged by an earthquake that left 47 persons dead and 281 others injured; damage amounted to at least $131 million.

May 16 Midwest and lower Mississippi Valley, U.S. Twisters snaked through an 11-state area bringing great damage to Arkansas, Iowa, Illinois, and Indiana; known dead stood at 70 with more than 1,000 injured and thousands homeless.

June 19 Northern Peru. An earthquake extensively damaged the town of Moyobamba; 16 persons were killed and at least 100 others injured.

July 15 Northwestern and southeastern India. Monsoon floods swirled through six states and caused the deaths of 80 persons.

July 28 Southern Japan. A typhoon swept across the land and piled up floodwaters that killed 22 persons.

July 29–31 San José, Costa Rica. Eruption of 5,249-ft. Mt. Arenal, the first in about 500 years, hurled rocks and lava over a 30-mi. area and killed 52 persons; 112 others were missing; damage amounted to millions of dollars.

Aug. 2 Manila, Phil. A sharp earthquake hit the city at dawn and toppled a five-story apartment building; more than 300 died, most of them residents of the apartment building.

Aug. 7–14 Gujarat and Rajasthan states, India. Week-long flooding claimed the lives of more than 1,000 persons.

Aug. 10–24 Celebes I., Indonesia. Earthquakes in the Donggala area and resultant tidal waves caused the disappearance of Tuguan Island and killed 293 persons; 23 others were missing.

Team of rescue workers digging to recover the bodies of a family from their house, which was crushed by an avalanche in the Swiss Alps on Jan. 28, 1968.

Aug. 31–Sept. 4 Northeastern Iran. A series of devastating earthquakes struck 11 populous areas in the province of Khurasan and centred upon the village of Kakhk; official disaster figures stood at 30,000 dead, 17,000 injured, and 100,000 homeless.
Sept. 25 Chiapas State, Mex. A 26-second earth tremor brought death to 15 persons; more than 500 others were injured.
Oct. 2–5 Sikkim. Three-day, 30-in. rainfall caused flooding of the Tiesta River that washed out villages, roads, and bridges and brought death to at least 267 persons.
Oct. 7 Sub-Himalayan region, India. Four days of torrential rain caused floods and landslides around the Darjeeling and Jalpaiguri areas; at least 560 persons died, many others were homeless.
Oct. 24 South Korea. Rainstorms and heavy snowfall swept the east coast, bringing death to at least 18 persons; landslides caused an estimated $3 million damage.
Oct. 28 Caspian Sea coast, Iran. Weekend floods along the coastal regions killed at least 30 persons.
Nov. 2–3 Northeastern Italy. Floods and landslides wrought great destruction to the Piedmont countryside; at least 113 persons died or were missing.
Nov. 12 New England and Eastern Canada. High winds, tides, and snow struck the east coast of North America as far south as Long Island, N.Y.; at least 25 persons perished.

RAILROAD

Jan. 1 Northeastern Transvaal, S.Af. Collison of two trains brought death to at least 13 persons; 25 others were injured.
Jan. 6 Hixon, Eng. Manchester-to-London express traveling at 70 mph over a grade crossing struck a truck loaded with a 125-ton transformer; 13 train passengers were killed, 50 others injured.
Jan. 27 Fanfa, Braz. Combined passenger-freight train and an all-freight crashed into one another at the station; at least 40 persons were killed and 60 others injured.
Feb. 16 New Delhi, India. Crack New Delhi–Calcutta express plowed into a group of pilgrims on the way to bathe in the sacred waters of the Ganges River; 16 persons were killed.
March 18 Hubli, India. Speeding express crashed into a standing passenger train and killed 52 persons.
Sept. 30 Corinth, Greece. Stationary passenger train was rammed by another crowded express; 10 persons died, and at least 100 others were injured.
Dec. 22 Near Budapest, Hung. Head-on collision between a heavy freight and a fast passenger train caused the deaths or injuries of over 100 persons.

TRAFFIC

Jan. 21 Cuernavaca, Mex. Brake failure caused an overloaded bus to ram into a wall, killing 18 persons and injuring 45 others.
Jan. 26 Near Conquista, Braz. En route from Ilhéus to São Paulo a bus skidded off the highway and into a lake; 13 passengers drowned.
Feb. 22 Bogotá, Colombia. A bus carrying more than 80 persons went out of control on a steep incline and crashed into a house; 11 persons were killed and 32 others injured.
March 7 Near Baker, Calif. Las Vegas-bound Greyhound bus collided with an automobile, overturned on the rain-slick high-

way, and burst into flames; 19 bus passengers and the driver of the car were killed.
March 16 North of Lagos, Nigeria. Collision between a bus and an oil truck brought death to 19 persons; 12 others were injured.
March 17 West of Istanbul. Two passenger buses collided on the Istanbul–Edirne highway, killing 35 persons and injuring 45 others.
March 18 Near Rampur, India. A bus ran off the road and slid into the Jhelum River, drowning 27 persons.
April 30 Benares, India. Transporting a wedding party of about 50, a truck hit a tree and careened into a ravine; 19 persons died and at least 25 others were injured.
May 4 Northern Colombia. Pamplona-to-Cucuta bus skidded over a 1,200-ft. cliff and killed more than 20 persons.
May 17 Bercha, India. Passing over a grade crossing, a heavily loaded bus was struck by an express train; 27 bus passengers were killed and the other 38 were injured.
May 18 Near Manipur, India. Plunging into a ravine, a bus overturned, killing 10 persons and injuring 33.
June 21 Colombia-Venezuela border. A bus transporting 60 schoolgirls plunged over a precipice, reportedly killing between 20 and 25 of the girls.
Aug. 18 Gifu, Jap. Earth loosened by the torrential rains of Typhoon Polly slid down over the highway and swept two sight-seeing buses into the churning Hida River; at least 102 women and children perished in the muddy waters.
Oct. 14 Northern Kashmir. Plunging off the road, a bus fell 1,000 ft. into a ravine, killing 21 persons and injuring 20.
Nov. 11 Accra, Ghana. Collision of a bus and a tank truck brought death to 22 persons, most of them children.

Frogmen searching for victims in one of the two sight-seeing buses swept by a landslide into the Hida River in Gifu, Jap. At least 102 persons were killed.

Domestic Arts and Sciences

Home Economics. The 11th congress of the International Federation of Home Economics, which was held in Bristol, Eng., in July, dominated the thoughts and actions of home economists throughout the world in 1968. The congress was attended by 1,200 delegates from 58 countries.

In anticipation of the congress and its theme of "Home Economics in the Service of International Cooperation," the United Kingdom Federation for Education in Home Management sent a questionnaire to all participating countries, asking what problems they faced relating to the family and the community and what part the home economist played in these spheres. The replies, which came from 35 countries, were collated into book form and used by delegates as background information for the talks and discussion groups at the congress.

One striking conclusion arose from this document: the developed countries of the West and the emergent countries in other parts of the world had many social problems in common, including those arising from an aging population, the movements of people from rural to urban areas, and the education, leisure-time activities, and employment of young people. The immensity of this last problem was highlighted by the report from Burundi, where there were only 500 jobs to be shared among 18,000 18-year olds.

In the developed countries, home economists were widely employed as teachers, food consultants, and journalists, while in the less developed countries, aided in many cases by the UN Food and Agriculture Organization, they were actively working to educate women, especially those in rural communities, in health and hygiene, child care, agricultural work, and family living. In some countries in Africa, where facilities for home economics education were almost nonexistent, they often held their homecraft classes under the largest village tree. In others, where the literacy rate among women over 20 was low, they helped write textbooks that could teach a woman to cook at the same time that they taught her to read.

At the three plenary sessions of the congress, speakers from Finland, France, and the U.S. gave papers that treated the theme of the congress from three points of view—the sociological, the scientific, and the economic and educational. For the 12 subplenary sessions, the delegates divided into four "interest groups": catering, institutional management, and dietetics; professional training, teacher training, and technical education; education up to statutory school-leaving age; and informal education, including industry, public relations, social services, community development, and the service of youth.

From these sessions, which covered such subjects as "the means by which international cooperation could reduce the time between scientific discovery and its application to the training of home economists" and "the place of consumer education and market research in informal home economics education," arose the material for the 60 discussion groups, organized by a committee under the chairmanship of Mrs. Joan Robins of the Association of Home Economists of Great Britain. These groups eventually reported back to the assembled congress, under its chairman, Fraülein Leny Voellmy of Switzerland, the president of the IFHE.

Four resolutions passed by the congress summed up the major questions on which immediate action was felt to be needed: (1) establishment of an International Institute of Home Economics; (2) acceptance by member nations of UNESCO of an international code of practice to regulate exchange visits of students and young people; (3) that home economics teaching in each country should be consistent with that country's philosophy, culture, and practical resources, and that the practices of more highly developed areas should not be imposed on countries in the process of development; and (4) a request to the UN to ensure that member governments establish and enforce international standards for the nutrient content of foods, for food hygiene, and for the safety and performance of industrial products, whether for home use or export.

While these resolutions accurately represented the mood of the congress, many delegates looked to the implementation by home economists themselves of a series of "points for action" as the best means of deriving lasting benefit from the congress. These "points for action," which arose from face-to-face discussions among the delegates, proposed ways in which the member organizations of the IFHE could best direct their energies toward solving the problems that had been revealed by the questionnaire, through the more effective deployment of their individual members.

It was hoped that progress made would be reported back at the next international congress, to be held in Helsinki, Fin., in 1973. Members were asked to assess the role of the home economist in relation to mass communication, consumer education, the social services, and international agencies. Further areas for investigation included the position of the home economist in relation to population control and economic problems at both the national and the international level.

Food Preparation. As food preparation, on both the commercial and the domestic scale, became increasingly a matter for the boardroom rather than the marketplace in 1968, news of food products appeared with growing regularity in the financial rather than the women's pages of the daily press.

Manufacturers produced even more sophisticated convenience foods, many of which (such as Checkerboard Farms' solid breast turkey roast with the pan to cook it in) aimed at simplifying cooking for the housewife rather than taking it completely out of her hands.

In Great Britain, where the yearly market for prepared potato products was estimated by *The Times* of London at £360 million (£58 million in potato chips alone), a battle for the £70 million instant mashed potato market was joined between the two giant firms of Cadbury and Mars. McCain Foods of Canada announced the opening of a £1 million production line (said to be the largest in Europe) solely for the production of frozen french fries.

Despite the increasing number of "multipack" foods, such as Chef Boy-ar-Dee's lasagna with canned meat sauce, canned grated cheese, and packeted pasta, frozen foods continued to be eaten in the U.S. at the rate of 68 lb. per person per year. In Britain, where consumption was about 12 lb. per person (an increase of 11% over the previous year), Birds Eye Foods Ltd. announced plans to invest a minimum of £30 million in the industry during the next five years. The rival Swiss-controlled Findus group announced plans for a £1 million advertising and promotional campaign

aimed at increasing its present 20% share of the market.

Sugar and sugar substitutes became an explosive issue in Britain when the Consumer Council, following an adverse report on cyclamates by Austrian research workers, spearheaded an attack on the use of the sugar substitutes in factory-prepared foods. Several leading food retailers announced that they would sell no more foods containing cyclamate artificial sweeteners until further research had been done by the British Industrial Biological Research Association. A British government family-expenditure survey showed that the weekly consumption of sugar had fallen by 0.32s. per person in the previous three years. In Japan it was expected to rise by at least 50,000 tons a year when the ban on the artificial sweetener "Dulcin" came into effect at the end of the year.

The search for new sources of protein engaged scientists throughout the world. In the U.S. a Minneapolis manufacturer marketed a new textured vegetable protein called TVP which he claimed could be produced in granular, chunk, diced, strip, or chip form, and with meaty, nutty, tangy, or fruity flavouring. At Leeds (Eng.) University a Nigerian scientist from the Federal Institute of Industrial Research at Oshodi led a team in research to improve the protein content of ogi, the baby food and breakfast cereal which is the exclusive food of the majority of Nigerian infants.

A preoccupation with "diet" foods continued to absorb Americans, who were offered new products that promised to make dieting even easier. Carnation's Slender milk diet food was promoted as a "diet for the weakwilled," while Coffee-mate, a nondairy "creamer" with only 11 calories per spoonful, promised to "take the edge off black coffee." In London, Weight Watchers International was launched at a meeting in July.

Though U.S. housewives continued to be offered "soft" margarines that were low in saturated fats and a "buttery flavour oil" that its makers (Wesson) claimed was so good it had been banned in the dairy state of Minnesota, real butter from the cow was still the choice of the European consumer. In Switzerland, as a result of a consumer boycott launched in May of the previous year, the price of table butter came down from SFr. 14 to SFr. 12 50 centimes a kilo. In Britain, where imported Danish butter was selling at less than the production price, the deputy director of the Danish Butter Export Council called for a tightening of the quota and the introduction by Great Britain of

an antidumping levy in the form of a minimum price.

Pans and casseroles were noteworthy for the variety of materials used and for originality of colour and decoration. Nontraditional finishes included aluminum with a porcelain finish, steel with a ceramic finish, enamel on iron, and solid copper lined with stainless steel. Nonstick finishes were more durable and could be obtained in a number of colours. For the gourmet, there was a proliferation of luxury aids to food preparation. In the U.S., Sylvania offered a home ripener for fruit and vegetables, while Nieman Marcus' Christmas customers could buy a French coffeemaker that simultaneously produced six separate cups of espresso coffee.

Looking to the future, the marketing director of Batchelors Foods (a subsidiary of the giant Unilever group) claimed that, before too long, instant coffee might be expected to eliminate ground coffee. Instant coffee that had been brewed and then freeze dried made its appearance on the U.S. market.

Household Appliances. Practicality rather than gimmickry was the outstanding feature of household appliance design in 1968. While few completely new trends were apparent, many proven features, previously available in luxury models only, were being incorporated in appliances designed for the mass market. An increasing number of refrigerators, for example, were fitted with automatic defrosting and ice-cube makers, while stoves with automated oven controls could be purchased in every price range.

Even external design was rethought in terms of greater efficiency. Frigidaire, for example, introduced a range of taller, slimmer appliances that ingeniously utilized previously wasted space. By moving control panels from counter height to eye level, they made space for storage cupboards and automatic dispensers on their laundry equipment and for "keep hot" infrared lamps on their freestanding ranges. There was still room for frivolity in decor, however, and refrigerator door panels sported pop art, still life decorations, and even—in line with the patriotic fervour that gripped so many British kitchenware designers during the year—Union Jacks.

Responding to a widespread consumer demand for larger capacity refrigerators, more American companies imported refrigerators to Great Britain, ranging from the monster Admiral freezer refrigerator (with a 409-lb. frozen food capacity) to the 12-cu.ft. Monogram. British refrigerators were strongly competitive in price, however—a 4-cu.ft. refrigerator that sold for £70 in 1959 cost only £40 in 1968.

As automatic washing machines took an increasingly larger share of the market, their programming was improved to deal with a wider variety of laundry loads. Many machines, for example, were operated by solid state controls that enabled agitation and spin speeds to be varied according to the kind of materials in the washload. Several new British models had their control panels correlated with the program wording recommendations of the Home Laundering Consultative Council. In a related field, the introduction in the U.S. of the "enzyme action" presoak washing products— some of which were being incorporated into detergents —promised yet another cutthroat round among the highly competitive washing products manufacturers.

Dryers were becoming standard equipment in more and more homes, and compact models (such as the Parnall) were designed to fit into even the smallest kitchen. Flexibility in use was extended by new features such as Whirlpool's "gentle" setting for very

COURTESY, LINK INFORMATION SERVICES LTD.

Left, range top of glossy white glass-
ceramic material with all electric units
sealed out of sight, developed
by Corning Glass Works. Above, shelves
of this English Rose kitchen cabinet
roll forward as the door opens.

COURTESY, CORNING GLASS WORKS

delicate clothing and cool-down cycles expressly designed to deal with garments having a "permanent press" finish.

While better dishwasher performance was being sought in the U.S. through the use of improved detergents, European makers concentrated on enlarged capacity and more flexible programming. Bosch produced a 12 place setting-capacity model incorporating three programs—"intensive," "standard," and "glass."

A growing number of "unit kitchens" were marketed, especially in Europe, comprising variable arrangements of units and appliances. Some of these were joint endeavours of appliance and unit manufacturers, such as Hygena/Creda and Wrighton/Moffat; others were produced, as with the Italian "cucina companibile," by a single firm. Bosch introduced a teak-faced "apartment kitchen" which incorporated a stainless steel sink unit, a 5-cu.ft. refrigerator, and a folding hot plate. Scholtes made a wide range of "slot in" cooking rings (in both electricity and gas) that could be located anywhere in the kitchen.

In Britain, the changeover to the metric system due in the 1970s was anticipated by Wrighton, which marketed a range of kitchen units designed on a 10-cm. (almost exactly 4-in.) module. The redesigned Hi-power Blender by Sunbeam was marked in both pints and litres.

Small appliances became increasingly sophisticated, though no radically new ideas appeared. Electric frypans were universally nonstick and incorporated such practical refinements as multiposition ratchets that enabled the lid to be converted into an antisplash shield. The "second refrigerator" was joined by the "second vacuum cleaner" for "in between" floor and carpet cleaning. Pioneered a few years earlier by such products as the Electric Broom, this slim, lightweight type of cleaner was now being offered by virtually all the manufacturers in the field.

Interior Decoration. Heralding an interest in "decoration" greater than at any period since the days of the Prince Regent, an exuberant use of colour, texture, and pattern in interiors of widely varying mood dominated interior decor throughout the world in 1968. To offset this growing trend toward the mannered display of objets d'art, room settings themselves became simpler and less cluttered, with "space" increasingly treated as an essential part of room design.

While on the one hand the desire for more decorative interiors manifested itself in renewed appreciation of the craftsmanship of the past (and a consequent boom in Victoriana and other antiques), on the other it found expression in a huge variety of furnishings made by young designers to meet the needs of youthful customers. Cheap and practical, if often less than durable, these pieces could be inflated, knocked down, folded up, and eventually thrown away.

Inspired by the Olympic Games in Mexico City, the bold colourings of Latin America were everywhere. In a modern living room, a single, if violent, colour accent might be used in carpeting or wall hangings to offset an all-white or chalky pastel-shaded scheme of vinyl-upholstered plexiglass furniture. In these settings, furniture in the Bauhaus style of the 1920s was reinterpreted in the mood of the '60s by such designers as Platner and Knolle, using the most advanced products of modern technology. In more traditional interiors the Mexican influence was seen in "cottage" living rooms, where bursts of primary colour in rugs, upholstery, or curtains were used to offset simple pine furniture and natural-textured walls and floors.

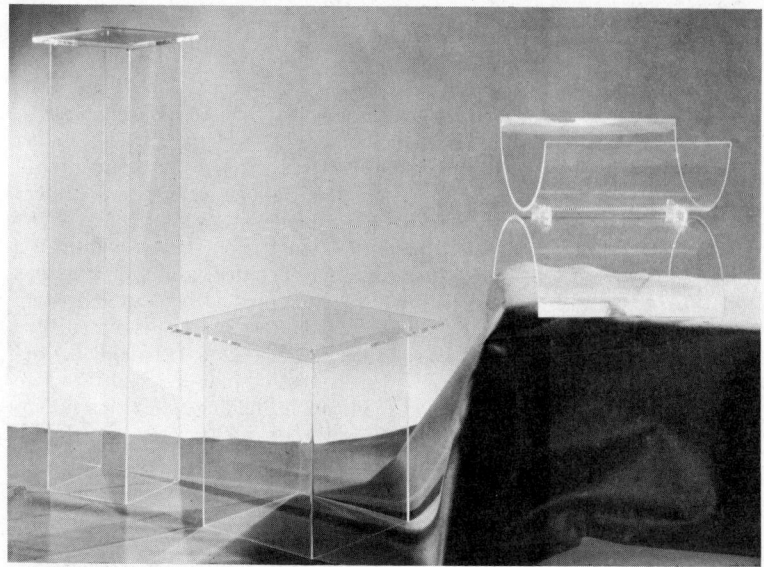

Urn stand, table, and magazine rack are among the pieces of furniture constructed entirely of lucite introduced by M.G. Inc. of Pennsylvania.

The conventional furniture materials of wood and metal were increasingly challenged by plastics. Polyester was used by Swedish industrial design students to upholster an expensive slot-together chair. Brilliant-coloured vinyl was used by Terence Conran for his blow-up range of furniture, while laminated paper was used by designers in Italy and Great Britain to make paper furniture with special appeal to the young. For more sophisticated interiors, plastics were used to make bulky, though light, low-backed chairs and couches that would have been impractical to manufacture in conventional materials. Thus fibre-glass reinforced with polyester resin was used for the framework of an armchair by Bartoli, while molded polyester was used for the white chair by Joe Colombo that was a feature of the Exhibition of Italian Industrial Design held during the year in London.

It became easier to buy carpets custom-designed by leading free-lance American and British designers (such as Jacqueline Groag) which were actually woven by native craftsmen using the traditional skills of such countries as Ireland and Portugal. At the same time, the year saw dramatic growth in the popularity of tufted carpets, mass produced to meet the growing demand for wall-to-wall carpeting at popular prices. In Britain 50% of the market was claimed for these nonwoven carpets, which—with improved methods of manufacture—were beginning to rival woven carpets in both texture and variety of design.

Lighting continued to be more functional than decorative, with industrial systems of spotlights and electrical tracking widely used in domestic interiors. Where lighting fixtures were used for decorative effect, shapes were essentially simple, often using enlarged light bulbs set in Venetian glass or molded plastic holders.

The "total" look in bedroom decor grew in popularity. In Sweden low-cost coordinated cottons and wallpapers were produced for the "young married" market; in America chintz designs were printed on vinyl for both curtaining and wall covering; and in Great Britain ready-made curtains and bedspreads were teamed by Sanderson's with wallpapers printed in the widely popular Persian and Islamic designs. Wall coverings of all kinds were often vinyl coated,

ranging from stained wood effects to textured designs such as Nairnflock's classic brocade design welded in solid vinyl. Kimberley Steven's silver-paper fabric wall covering was especially effective in setting off the new glass and plastic pedestal-based dining tables.

In kitchen design, there were signs of fresh thinking for the first time in several years. A prototype kitchen by Alberto Mambriani, in which bending and stretching were reduced to a minimum, was evidence of the preoccupation with ergonomics of many avant-garde designers, in both Europe and the U.S. In Mambriani's kitchen, an electrically operated hydraulic system brought both top and bottom units to waist or eye level at the touch of a switch. Similar thinking lay behind the new English Rose custom-designed furniture (previewed at the London Building Exhibition in November 1967), in which all cabinets were fitted with forward sliding "filing cabinet" drawers and racks. In more conventionally planned kitchens, the streamlined "clinical" look that had been dominant for so long was softened, by patterns in tiled surrounds, by "Tiffany" lampshades, or by displays of kitchen "bygones" in copper, china, and wood.   (Ev. R.)

See also Fashion and Dress; Food; Industrial Design.

ENCYCLOPÆDIA BRITANNICA FILMS. *Cloth—Fiber to Fabric* (1968).

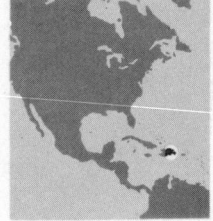

Dominican Republic

Covering the eastern two-thirds of the Caribbean island of Hispaniola, the Dominican Republic is separated from Haiti, which occupies the western third, by a rugged mountain range. Area: 18,703 sq.mi. (48,442 sq.km.). Pop. (1968 est.): 4,029,000, including European 28%; mestizo and mulatto 60%; Negro 11%. Cap. and largest city: Santo Domingo (pop., 1967 est., 577,371). Language: Spanish. Religion: Roman Catholic. President in 1968, Joaquín Balaguer.

DOMINICAN REPUBLIC
Education. (1966–67) Primary, pupils 584,529, teachers (1964–65) 9,774; secondary, pupils 63,512, teachers 2,734; vocational, pupils 25,272, teachers (1964–65) 814; teacher training, students 397, teachers 49; higher (1965–66), students 6,606, teaching staff 414.
   Finance. Monetary unit: peso, at parity with the U.S. dollar (2.40 pesos = £1 sterling). Gold and foreign exchange, central bank: (June 1968) U.S. $34.7 million; (June 1967) U.S. $38.1 million. Budget (1967 est.) balanced at 178.2 million pesos. Gross national product: (1966) 996 million pesos; (1965) 899 million pesos. Money supply: (June 1968) 106.5 million pesos; (June 1967) 109.7 million pesos. Cost of living (Santo Domingo; 1963 = 100): (June 1968) 105; (June 1967) 100.
   Foreign Trade. (1967) Imports 174.7 million pesos; exports 156.2 million pesos. Import sources (1966): U.S. 47%; Japan 9%; West Germany 6%. Export destination U.S. 89%. Main exports: sugar 58%; coffee 11%; bauxite 8%; cocoa 8%; tobacco 7%.
   Transport and Communications. Roads (1963) 6,250 km. (including 4,250 km. first class). Motor vehicles (1966): passenger 31,600; commercial (including buses) 10,700. Railways (1965) 220 km. (excluding c. 1,600 km. on sugar estates). Telephones (Jan. 1967) 31,524. Radio receivers (Dec. 1966) c. 150,000. Television receivers (Dec. 1966) 65,000.
   Agriculture. Production (in 000; metric tons; 1966; 1965 in parentheses): coffee c. 30 (c. 37); sugar, raw value (1967) c. 819, (1966) 691; corn c. 95 (c. 90); cassava c. 150 (c. 150); peanuts c. 54 (c. 45); sweet potatoes c. 80 (c. 80); rice (1967) c. 155, (1966) 147; cocoa (1966–67) 27, (1965–66) 28; tobacco c. 28 (c. 14). Livestock (in 000; June 1966): cattle c. 1,025; pigs c. 1,200; horses c. 255; mules c. 85; asses c. 145; sheep c. 79.
   Industry. Production (in 000; metric tons; 1966): bauxite 818; cement 278; electricity 617,000 kw-hr.

Political tension mounted in early 1968 as the Dominican Republic prepared for nationwide municipal elections on May 16. At stake were 77 mayoralties and 488 city council seats, plus the prestige of President Balaguer and his Reformist Party, in power since 1966. The left-leaning Dominican Revolutionary Party of former Pres. Juan Bosch resolved to abstain from the elections, charging a lack of sufficient guarantees of security for its candidates, and it was followed by the National Civic Union, the Quisqueyano Democratic Party, and the Communists. Remaining to contend with the government party were the Revolutionary Social Christian Party and independents of varied political hues.

Intense rivalry on the domestic scene was augmented by political maneuvering abroad. From self-exile in Spain, Bosch proclaimed a doctrine of "popular dictatorship" and the need for a revolution to achieve it. Col. Francisco Caamaño Deñó, leader of the 1965 revolution that had led to U.S. intervention, was reported missing from his London diplomatic post and was variously rumoured to be in Cuba plotting against the Dominican government or in South America following in the footsteps of the slain guerrilla leader "Che" Guevara. Brig. Gen. Elías Wessin y Wessin, from exile in Miami, announced his candidacy for the presidential elections of 1970.

A sweeping election victory was gained by the Reformists, and greater stability prevailed during the remainder of the year. President Balaguer followed moderate policies, and, despite periodic clashes with university students, traditionally strained relations with Haiti, and threats of subversion emanating from Cuba, the government could claim progress on the political scene.

Despite a year-long drought, lasting through June, crop production was steady or slightly improved. Sugar production for the 1968 crop year was set at 907,400 short tons, of which 85% was for export. The Dominican quota in the U.S. preferential market was increased by 19,402 short tons over 1967, and these sales were supplemented by expanded exports of coffee, tobacco, and cacao. Basic food commodities such as corn, wheat, and milk were imported, contributing to a balance of payments deficit of about $18 million.

Agriculture received highest priority in development plans, and diversification was given particular emphasis. An international consortium was formed to promote cattle raising and the cultivation of such crops as peanuts, winter vegetables, melons, and rice on land eventually to be sold to Dominican peasants on easy terms. A project was also undertaken to settle 90 farm families on the Azua plains in the southwest, but the total needs of the Dominican rural population far exceeded land reform and resettlement efforts.

Industry was still little developed, but investment of both foreign and domestic capital increased in 1968. Food processing expanded, and a new container factory with a capacity of 100 million food cans daily was planned. Mining also showed substantial gains. Falconbridge Dominicana, a Canadian company, announced plans for the commercial production of nickel by 1971, while a U.S. company and the Dominican government developed joint plans for the exploitation of salt deposits.

Of great significance was the formal agreement with the U.S. and the Inter-American Development Bank on April 30, 1968, for partial financing of a $57.1 million project to expand the nation's irrigation system

and electric power capacity. The Tavera Dam, to be constructed by 1971 on the Río Yaque del Norte, would supply water to 93,000 ac. of agricultural land in the fertile Cibao Valley. Related power facilities would generate 80,000 kw. of electricity, a 24% increase over the existing national total.   (C. W. MI.)

ENCYCLOPÆDIA BRITANNICA FILMS. *The West Indies* (1965).

Economic Planning

Economic planning in the industrialized countries tends to have somewhat less precise connotations than in the less developed countries. In the former, planning means the bringing together of programs in furtherance of a coherent economic policy. In some of the industrialized countries, including the U.K., the main objective was to secure a faster rate of economic growth. In Spain the first priority was faster industrialization and in Portugal, an increased rate of exports. In the less developed countries economic planning is the embodiment of official initiatives to bring about specific changes in the economy within a designated period.

Even when a development plan contains no explicit reference to the private sector, its rationale must rest on various assumptions regarding the private decisions and actions of those who will be supplying the necessary inputs. No effective planning can be carried out where decisions are based only on a series of public investments in infrastructure. In recent years development plans have tended to extend beyond mapping out a program of public-sector projects into the area of target setting for the economy as a whole. In the less developed countries the strategic elements in the economy about which specific arrangements need to be made include the production of selected goods vital for investment or consumption, of major export commodities, and of transport and power facilities, particularly where these are privately owned. Agriculture, which provides much of the foreign exchange earning capacity in the majority of less developed countries, is generally the most difficult element in the private sector to integrate into a development plan.

Industrialized Countries. In Western Europe—notably in Great Britain but also in West Germany, and to a lesser extent in Italy—planning in 1968 was concerned with the control of price inflation. In the two latter countries investment was directed toward raising the supply of exports and increasing market penetration, especially within the EEC. The Italian government actively encouraged foreign investment as a means of promoting the manufacture of new products.

The events of May–June 1968, when strikes effectively paralyzed the French economy, caused a considerable setback to the current plan. The suddenness of the crisis indicated the strength of the tension that had been building behind the imposing façade of the Gaullist regime. It had always been difficult to understand how a country with so manifestly weak an industrial structure as France could afford to build up vast gold reserves while undertaking prestige expenditure programs. The strikes revealed the social price in terms of backwardness and poverty in certain areas of the economy.

It was not easy to assess the economic damage done by the May "revolution." What seemed clear was that the stoppage would eliminate the increase of 5% in industrial production forecast for 1968 and cut back the hoped-for growth in gross national product (GNP) from about 5.4 to 3.5%. In addition, the French gold reserves were reduced by at least one-third. The Grenelle Protocol, containing the wage increases that French industrialists were forced to concede in order to get their staffs back to work, provided for rises of about 10% in wages in 1968, to be increased later, as well as a reduction in the work week of between one and two hours. A feature of the agreement was an increase of 35% in the guaranteed industrial minimum wage and alignment with it of the minimum agricultural wage, involving a rise of 56%. The twin dangers facing the French economy in 1968–69 were rising prices and mounting unemployment. Between them these could produce a situation in which the govern-

Workers seized control of the Usinor factory at Denain, France, in May 1968 during the general strike against the de Gaulle regime.

ment would have to choose between further drastic losses of its gold reserves and an increasingly difficult political situation, a point that was underscored by the franc crisis in November.

In the U.K. the severely deflationary budget of March 19, 1968 (*see* GOVERNMENT FINANCE), inevitably increased the pressures on the prices-and-incomes policy. The government's new policy was set out in a White Paper, *Productivity, Prices and Incomes Policy for 1968 and 1969*, which was published April 3. The implementation of this policy was the responsibility of the new Department of Employment and Productivity. The most important of the proposals in the White Paper was for a ceiling of $3\frac{1}{2}\%$ on wage, salary, and dividend increases. However, the government intended to encourage agreements that raised productivity and efficiency. Price increases, including those in the public sector, were to be allowed only in certain defined circumstances. Discussions were held in the National Economic Development Council and the Department of Economic Affairs on the content and scope of a new national plan.

In Spain a draft of the second *Plan de Desarrollo* (1968–71) was submitted to Gen. Francisco Franco in May. The new plan envisaged a growth rate of 5.5%, and its main objectives included the modernization of agriculture and the improvement of the industrial and commercial structure. In addition, the plan contained measures to extend educational facilities.

The main event in the Spanish economy in 1967–68 was the devaluation of the peseta following that of the pound in November 1967. This was followed

within a week by a program of measures intended to stabilize the economy. The discount rate of the Banco de España was raised from 5 to $5\frac{1}{8}\%$; wages, including those in the public service, were frozen until 1968 at the level of Nov. 18, 1967; prices were fixed for the same period; rents and dividends in 1968 were not to exceed the levels of 1967; the luxury tax was raised by up to 50% for some products and the profits tax by 10%. Imports of certain foods, raw materials, and other commodities having a direct effect on the cost-of-living index were assisted by reductions in customs tariffs and by subsidies.

After devaluation, exports increased sufficiently to raise hopes of a substantial expansion, but greater diversification of products was thought necessary. In retrospect, 1967 might prove to have been a turning point in the industrial progress of Spain. The favourable factors that emerged after the 1959 stabilization plan, particularly the inflow in invisibles that allowed imports to outpace exports without unduly affecting the balance of payments, were still operating. Since 1960 a growth rate of 7.4% had been achieved—a rate that, as the second plan recognized, could not be maintained without creating severe strains on the economy. De-

BEN ROTH AGENCY

—Lone, "Sunday Times,"
London.

valuation helped the export position, and the subsequent measures made it possible to maintain living standards in spite of the increased cost of imports.

Less Developed Countries. Economic planning in the less developed countries was concerned for the most part with the attainment of specific objectives through the control of the allocation of resources and the regulation of overseas trade. Although conditions in the less developed countries varied in different parts of the world, three broad areas of deficiency were common to them all in some degree: shortage of foreign exchange; shortage of qualified manpower; and lack of the means to deal with the increasing pressure of population. In the face of these problems development plans had a tendency to fall short of their objectives, due to both faulty planning techniques and failure to take account of the facts of economic life.

If levels of unemployment and underemployment were to be reduced, jobs had to be made available faster than the current annual growth rates of the labour forces. Recognition of this fact lay behind a continuing shift in emphasis from infrastructure investment to human resources planning. One example of this trend was the social and economic development plan of Peru (1967–70), which gave special attention to urban employment and the consequences

for the labour force of planned improvements in agricultural productivity. In Argentina the economic plan introduced by Adalbert Krieger Vasena, the minister of economy and labour, combined measures for strengthening the infrastructure through expanded public works with the promotion of competition in the private sector. Measures to curb inflation, particularly the stringent wages policy, met with unusual success, indicated by a fall of 3.4% in the cost-of-living index over the first half of 1968.

Among the less developed countries, the economic planning activities of India attracted the most interest in the 1950s and 1960s, because of the extent to which the Western nations and some Communist countries had become involved in the successive Indian plans. The fourth five-year plan was due to start, after a three-year delay, in April 1969. The Planning Commission, in its statement, *Approach to the Fourth Five-Year Plan,* had suggested an overall compound rate of growth of 5 to 6% per year. This assumed a growth of 5% in the agricultural sector and 8 to 10% in industry. The commission stated that, to attain this faster growth, domestic savings must be increased from the current 8% to a level of 12% a year. In the public sector additional resources were to be mobilized to the extent of Rs. 2 billion during each year of the plan. The means to be employed to secure these objectives were the familiar ones of loans, utilization of profits of state enterprises, additional taxation, and the more effective mobilization of small savings. Indications at year's end were that the plan's objectives might have to be modified.

Compared with many developing countries, India had a head start in industrialization. On the export front the intention was to get away from reliance on traditional commodities and raise the proportion of such items as iron ore, iron and steel, engineering goods, and chemicals. However, due attention was to be given to maintaining output in the jute industry, an important traditional asset that had been allowed to deteriorate. The major weakness of the statement by the Planning Commission was that it failed to indicate, except in very broad terms, the amount of foreign aid that would be available.

In Kenya, GNP grew by approximately 5% in 1967–68, a figure well below the target of 6.3% in the national development plan. Even so, the prospects for 1968 were regarded as not unfavourable. Legislation had been introduced to provide for the licensing of banks and to restrict the field within which commercial banks could lend money. Local savings were to be encouraged and utilized through a "dynamic" banking policy.

In Zambia, Pres. Kenneth Kaunda announced, on April 19, sweeping measures to control foreign interests operating in the country. Some 26 key companies were invited to sell 51% of their enterprises to the state. The mining companies were not included in the list, but, in common with other foreign-owned companies, they were forbidden to remit more than 50% of their profits. Other measures provided for a change in the mining royalty tax, the encouragement of small Zambian businesses by limiting the areas in which expatriate firms could operate, the spread of cooperative or company ownership rather than that of single entrepreneurs, and the establishment of a stock exchange. The development plan met with considerable difficulties as a result of the application of sanctions against Rhodesia and the interruption of

continued on page 297

ECONOMIC REFORM IN THE SOVIET UNION

By Yevsei Grigorievich Liberman

About three years have passed since the decision was made in the U.S.S.R. to carry out an economic reform. The reform was to be implemented in a number of successive stages over a period of five years.

The reform is essentially designed to strengthen centralized planned management by combining it with broader initiative and material incentives for the individual enterprises. What is profitable for society, as a whole, should be profitable for each enterprise as well. With this in mind, a set of measures is being introduced into the U.S.S.R.'s national economy, including: improvement and optimization of planning and greater managerial independence for enterprises; appraisal of the efficiency of enterprises by measuring the scope of goods marketed and the profit derived; introduction of payment for production assets; enlargement of bonuses and premiums to the personnel out of profits, according to their efficiency; intensification of direct contractual relations with reference to deliveries of goods; and establishment of economically substantiated prices. A total of 704 enterprises, employing more than 10% of Soviet industry's manpower —*i.e.*, more than 2.5 million people—changed over to the new managerial methods in 1966.

Meaning and Scope of the Reform. Overall, Soviet industry in 1966 showed an 8.6% increment in gross output, a 10% growth in profits, and a 5.2% rise in labour productivity, whereas the 704 enterprises operating under the new managerial system as of 1966 showed an increase in sales of more than 10%, a growth in profits of approximately 25%, and a rise in labour productivity of 8%. These are average data; some enterprises produced even better results. This means that the economic reform, even though it has not yet demonstrated its full potential, is bringing vast reserves of productivity into more effective use.

By the end of September 1968, over 25,000 industrial enterprises, including all the plants and factories of the instrument-making and chemical- and petroleum-equipment industries, numerous light-industry factories, enterprises of the iron-and-steel and nonferrous-metals industries, and others, were already operating under the new system. These enterprises account for about half the entire industrial output of the U.S.S.R., but they produce approximately 60% of the total profit.

From an enterprise director's viewpoint, the reform has done much good, but it has also given him many new worries. The advantages are that it has freed him from unwarranted tutelage by higher-level bodies and given him more opportunities for showing initiative. A director needs practical, competent supervision from higher-level bodies only in coordinating and endorsing the basic plan targets, in obtaining timely information on the latest technological and economic developments, in drafting technical policy, and—what is most important—in providing materials and equipment. In principle, under the new system the director manages all current business himself, including all transactions with suppliers, consumers, transport agencies, the bank, and financial bodies. Formerly, a manager showing less initiative actually had an easier time, because almost all activities were regulated by higher-level bodies. Today, however, directors must seek, experiment, and sometimes even take risks.

As for the worker, his working conditions have improved greatly. He has many more opportunities to affect the whole course of production, since most problems are now solved at the enterprise itself with the large-scale participation of the workers. The opportunities for introducing innovations have become greater, because the enterprise creates its own fund for production development out of profits. Last but not least, earnings and bonuses have become much larger. Data for 1966 show that in many cases bonuses to workers had risen by 30 to 40% of their wage scales. The subsequent rapid growth of labour productivity (6.1% in 1966–67) has led to a still larger increase in bonuses and in the working people's personal incomes as a whole.

Planning and Profit. Prior to the reform, the issue of profit was extensively discussed, not because there was no such category in the Soviet economy before, but because profit was not used as a principal generalizing criterion of an enterprise's efficiency. An enterprise used to receive a large number of obligatory indicators: gross output, an extremely wide range of goods, cutting of production costs, numerical strength of personnel, output per worker, average wages, etc. Such a wide range of indicators inhibited initiative. More often than not, the enterprise was chiefly concerned with putting out more goods, because efficiency was measured, first and foremost, by gross output rather than by the amount of goods marketed (sold). Moreover, enterprises were not greatly concerned about the efficient utilization of their production assets.

Much of this is explained by the fact that, for a long time, the Soviet Union was the only socialist country in the world. It was confronted with the task of building up its industry and its defense potential, and the quality and attractiveness of goods and even their production cost and profitableness did not matter so much. That policy justified itself, because in the war of 1941–45 the Soviet Union not only survived, but played a decisive part in ridding the world of Fascism.

Everything in the Soviet Union is done with the aim of steadily raising the people's standards of living and enriching their spiritual life. After the war, however, it became apparent that this could not be accomplished by rigidly centralized planning alone. It was essential to provide the enterprises with incentives for making more efficient use of their capacities and for servicing their customers in the best possible way.

Profit generalizes all the aspects of an enterprise's operation, including the quality of goods, since more efficient implements of labour and better quality manufactured goods will be priced correspondingly higher. It is extremely important, however, to point out that in the U.S.S.R. profit is neither the sole nor the principal aim of production. The primary aim is the output of goods to meet the needs of the population and of production. Profit is used as a mechanism for appraising and stimulating the enterprise's performance and as an essential source of accumulation and investments.

Bonuses and premiums out of profits are aimed at encouraging the enterprises themselves to draft adequate plans, profitable both for society and for the enterprise, and to carry them out. This is not a question of slackening or giving up planning. On the contrary, the reform envisions the intensification and improvement of planning by including the enterprises themselves in the planning process.

Contractual relations with consumers or customers, which are now being introduced in a number of branches of both light and heavy industry in the U.S.S.R., do not by any means involve a changeover to spontaneous regulation of production by the market. In the Soviet Union the effective demand of consumers can be predicted much more easily than in the West because the wage bills of the urban population and the revenues of collective farmers are known exactly, and well-substantiated balance sheets of the population's income and outlay can be drafted. Effective demand on a nationwide scale is quite predictable. But just how this demand is to be met—*i.e.*, what colour jackets and what kind of suits should be manufactured and how de-

liveries should be planned—is not the business of centralized planning. Rather, it is an issue for coordination between factories and trade outlets.

Profit: the Western and the Soviet View. There are fundamental differences between profit in the West and in the U.S.S.R. From the viewpoint of private enterprise, all profit belongs to the capitalists alone. In his *Theory of Economic Development*, the American economist Joseph A. Schumpeter wrote that everything in excess of cost is profit. But this "cost" includes the enterprise owner's "salary," land rent, and interest on capital, as well as a premium for "risk." In addition, profits must reward the enterprise owner if, by resorting to a new combination of production elements, he succeeds in lowering this "cost" below the existing average cost level.

The nature of this "combination of elements" can be gauged by the fact that the bulk of profit in the private enterprise system is now derived through the redistribution of profits on the market, in the process of exchange. Large profits, for instance, are known to be derived most easily through profitable purchases of raw materials, monopolistic raising of retail prices, nonequivalent exchange with developing countries, export of capital to countries with low wage levels, systems of preferential duty and customs tariffs, boosting of prices on the stock exchange by capitalizing superprofits, and, last but not least, by fulfillment of military orders—*i.e.*, at the expense of pumping taxpayers' money into the pockets of monopolies through the state budget.

All these sources of profit are ruled out in the U.S.S.R. by the very essence of socialism, which knows no private ownership of the means of production, no stock capital, and, consequently, no stock exchange. The labour remuneration level depends on productivity and is regulated by legislation. Raw material prices are planned. It is impossible to take advantage of market conditions in buying raw materials or hiring labour, or in pricing manufactured goods. Exchange with other countries (mainly socialist states) is effected under equitable and long-term agreements.

Profit in the Soviet Union indicates only the efficiency level of production; it is the difference between the selling price and the cost price of goods. But since in the U.S.S.R. the price expresses, in principle, the input of socially necessary labour, a growth in profit actually reflects relative savings in production. Profits resulting from accidental circumstances—overly high prices, for instance—are looked upon as the result of insufficiently flexible price-formation practices.

Let us now look at the purposes for which profits are used in the U.S.S.R. In the first place, no individual, no group of individuals, and no enterprise can appropriate profits or invest them for the purpose of deriving private income. In the U.S.S.R. profit belongs to those who own the means of production, that is, to all the working people. First and foremost, profit is used for the planned expansion and improvement of social production (49.9 billion rubles out of 114.5 billion rubles in the 1967 state budget) and for free social services such as education and science, health services, pensions, and scholarships (43.4 billion rubles). A certain portion is spent on administration (1.5 billion rubles) and, unfortunately, a rather large share (12–13%) on defense (14.5 billion rubles). The U.S.S.R. would gladly give up this last expenditure if a general disarmament program were attained.

Profit in the Soviet Union lost some of its significance before the economic reform due to a certain neglect of the law of value. This law had been incorrectly treated by some Soviet authors as a sort of unpleasant relic of capitalism which, allegedly, had to be gotten rid of as soon as possible. Disregard of the law of value led to arbitrary fixing of planned prices and, moreover, of prices that operated for a rather long period of time. That was why prices were divorced from the real value of goods, while profits fluctuated greatly from enterprise to enterprise and even from product to product within the same range of commodities. Under these conditions profit only feebly reflected the actual achievements of an enterprise. Thus many economists and executives came to regard profit as being entirely independent of the enterprise and, hence, a poor guide in managerial affairs. It was precisely to correct this mistake that the economic reform was conceived. Centralized planning is quite compatible with the enterprise's initiative as far as profitable management is concerned. This is just as far from private enterprise as the latter is from feudalism.

Initial Difficulties and Successes. The initial stage of the economic reform involved some apparently inevitable difficulties. The transition of the first group of enterprises to the new system was not followed immediately by profound changes in relations among those enterprises, their superiors, other enterprises, transport organizations, banks, and material-and-equipment supply bodies.

The necessary changes in production planning methods on the level of ministries and industrial administration boards and, above all, in the procedure for substantiating the plan assignments to enterprises have not been fully carried out. Because of lack of experience, in some cases old plan indicators were merely converted into new ones. For instance, all marketable goods were considered as marketed goods, while the range of these goods was not always coordinated with the consumers or customers on the basis of direct contractual relations. Nor has the changeover to planned trade in supplies been fully completed. There are other examples of the deviation of practice from theory, but all these difficulties are being successfully surmounted.

The experience gained in operating along the new lines in 1966 and 1967 showed graphically that, on the one hand, the process of planning and the economic activity of enterprises have been growing increasingly dynamic and imaginative. The ever growing influence of enterprises on the development of production as a whole is among the most important consequences of the economic reform. On the other hand, the higher-level organizations and the enterprises themselves have not always been capable of promptly getting rid of their old habits and practices, and many enterprises still lack experience in making responsible decisions. This came out at the May 1968 All-Union Conference, where a number of recommendations were advanced for eliminating shortcomings and improving managerial methods.

So far the reform does not adequately cover top-level economic management. This is a complex process involving a wide range of factors, but complaints and mutual reproaches will not help to get things running. The reform demands, first of all, a great deal of competence and efficiency on the part of the executives themselves. If the economic and organizational efficiency of the management is low, then the economic efficiency and profitableness of the enterprise will also be inadequate. The basic aim of the reform is to enhance the efficiency of production, boost the productivity of labour, and pave the way for rapid technological improvement. In the course of its implementation, it is bound to help in the selection and promotion of the most competent men and women to leading positions. The reform will not tolerate the obsolete and useless in managerial practice.

Industrial Enterprises Operating Under the New System of Planning and Economic Incentive					
Period	Number of enterprises operating under the new system	Percent of total industry			
		Number of enterprises	Output	Industrial capacity	Profits
1966					
First quarter	43	0.1	1	1	2
First half	232	0.5	4	4	7
Jan.–Sept.	659	1.4	8	8	13
Jan.–Dec.	704	1.5	8	8	16
1967					
First quarter	2,249	5	19	16	35
First half	3,490	7	26	22	41
Jan.–Sept.	5,316	11	34	28	47
Jan.–Dec.	7,069	14	38	32	50

communications with that country. However, hopeful developments included the provision of World Bank loans for the modernization of roads, the first issue of Zambian-registered development bonds, and the opening in May of the Nakambala sugar estates, the biggest commercial and industrial project to be inaugurated since independence.

The bulk of project equipment for the less developed countries was purchased in Western Europe and North America. Among the few examples of an economic plan focusing attention on the manufacture of equipment for sale to other less developed countries was the production of railway rolling stock in India for East African Railways. With industrial projects proliferating, there was increased need for regional planning coordination through bodies such as the Latin American Free Trade Association (LAFTA), the East African Common Market, the regional organs of the United Nations such as the Economic Commission for Asia and the Far East (ECAFE), or by agreements between governments.   (Rɪ. B.)

Centrally Planned Economies. The huge, Y-shaped, 32-story building on the Krasnaya Presnya Embankment in Moscow, that was to serve as headquarters for the Council for Mutual Economic Assistance (CMEA, or Comecon), was nearing completion by the end of 1968. The 950-seat hall for plenary sessions was ready, and the hotel section was also in service. In 1969, on the 20th anniversary of the foundation of Comecon, its general secretariat and specialized committees, as well as the International Bank for Economic Cooperation, would be housed in the blue skyscraper (which the Soviets—officially not too fond of Americanisms—preferred to call "the high building").

Notwithstanding a common one-party political system and a mutual conviction that a centrally planned economy was possible only in a socialist state, 20 years of economic cooperation between the six Eastern European "people's democracies" and the U.S.S.R. had not created a coherent economic body. To achieve economic interdependence between the U.S.S.R. and Eastern Europe, Moscow had only one means at its disposal: a barter foreign trade based on bilateral agreements. After 20 years this was still the main basis of Comecon's activities. The 1966–70 development plans had two more years to run, but in September 1968 the Executive Committee of Comecon had already started the extremely complicated task of coordinating and dovetailing the 1971–75 national plans. This was a difficult task not only because of the discrepancies between the respective national economies, but also because every country had a different, more or less artificial, system of prices and wages; because customs walls between the member countries were still in existence; and because their respective currencies were not transferable, even within the socialist bloc.

When the International Bank for Economic Cooperation (IBEC) started its operations in 1964, with an initial capital of 300 million "conversion" (*perevodny*) rubles, it was hoped that it would ensure multilateral clearing of economic transactions. The IBEC continued, however, to use the conversion ruble mainly in bilateral trade agreements based on the quota system. Henryk Kisiel, undersecretary of state in the Polish Ministry of Finance, criticized this on May 26, 1968, in an article in *Zycie Gospodarcze* ("Economic Life"). He pointed out that it was essential to create a really convertible currency, which the *perevodny* ruble was not.

The U.S.S.R. By September 1968 (three years after the Communist Party Central Committee recommended the introduction of a new system of planning and economic stimulation) there were in the Soviet Union more than 25,000 industrial enterprises (out of some 200,000) working under the general supervision of their respective ministries but enjoying a measure of autonomy in applying, however cautiously, the principles of a market economy. These enterprises, chosen from among the largest and best equipped, manufactured roughly half of the country's industrial output and obtained about 60% of industry's total profits.

At an All-Union Economic Conference held in Moscow in May, Nikolai Baibakov, deputy chairman of the Council of Ministers and chairman of the State Planning Committee, reported that the reform was progressing satisfactorily. It created, he said, new possibilities to accelerate the growth of industrial production. The current five-year (1966–70) plan provided for a yearly increase of between 8 and 8.4%, but the success of the new system authorized the government to raise the target to 8.9%. Commenting in *Pravda,* however, in September, Baibakov admitted that application of the reform's provisions was far from complete, and that the new economic (as distinguished from administrative) methods of management were being introduced too slowly. Furthermore, earnings were increasing more rapidly than productivity. Baibakov announced that the 1971–75 plan would lay down only the broad lines of development and fewer details, thereby providing for greater initiative on the part of both the ministries and the managers of enterprises. (*See* Special Report.)

The rate of growth of Soviet industry slowed down during the first nine months of 1968. It was 9.3% during the first quarter, 9% during the first six months, and 8.2% during the first nine months. The crisis over Czechoslovakia was believed to be mainly responsible. Meanwhile, Soviet agricultural output was marking time. The grain crop rose from 147.6 million metric tons in 1967 to about 167 million in 1968, but this was still short of the record 1966 crop.

East Germany. In June 1968, five years had elapsed since the new system of economic planning and management had been introduced by East Germany, the first among the Comecon countries to do so. In the course of the 1960s, East Germany became a powerful industrial state, second only to the U.S.S.R. in the socialist bloc. East German prosperity was not yet on the West German level, but the gap was being reduced. The total value of East German industrial production in 1968 was estimated at MDN. 100 billion or $24 billion (MDN. 2.22 = $1). This placed East Germany fifth in Europe and ninth in the world in

Rates of Industrial Growth in Eastern Europe

Yearly averages in percentages

Country	1956–60 actual	1961–65 actual	1966–70 plan	1966* actual	1967 actual	1968 actual
U.S.S.R.	10.4	8.6	8.3	8.7	10.0	8.2†
Germany, East	9.2	5.9	...	6.7	8.0	...
Czechoslovakia	10.5	5.2	5.5	8.0	7.1	6.0‡
Poland	9.9	8.6	7.6	7.4	7.5	9.0‡
Hungary	7.5	8.1	6.0	6.7	9.0	6.0‡
Romania	10.9	13.0	11.6	13.5	13.5	...
Bulgaria	15.9	11.7	11.5	12.5	13.4	...

*Increases over 1965.
†First nine months.
‡First six months.

Sources: Reports of National Central Statistical Offices.

terms of output—and that with a population of 17 million. Calculated per capita, East German industrial production amounted to 85% of that of West Germany.

Czechoslovakia. The far-reaching reforms introduced on Jan. 1, 1967, were aimed at a radical improvement of the national economy, which for many years had been marked by a series of interlocking difficulties: from shortages of consumer goods, lack of services, and transport breakdowns to low productivity and poor quality of products. That this should happen in the most industrialized country of the socialist bloc was the result of a number of factors. Czechoslovak industry, which had escaped wartime destruction, badly needed modernization. The investments in heavy industry laid down in the third (1961–65) plan resulted in too many mining, ore-processing, iron and steel, and heavy engineering projects. Between 1947 and 1967, the U.S.S.R. and other Comecon countries were importing from Czechoslovakia more than they were exporting to it, so that accumulated Czechoslovak credit in nonconvertible rubles at the IBEC reached an estimated $500 million.

The economic reforms of 1967 had been prepared by a team of experts under the chairmanship of Ota Sik, director of the Economic Institute of the Czechoslovak Academy of Sciences and member of the Communist Party Central Committee. Sik's principal supporters were Alexander Dubcek (*see* BIOGRAPHY) and Oldrich Cernik. When, on April 8, 1968, Cernik formed a new government (*see* CZECHOSLOVAKIA), Sik was appointed deputy premier and one of the eight members of the newly created Supreme Economic Council. On April 24 Cernik, presenting his government's program to the National Assembly, criticized the "rigid priority" previously given to heavy industry, put forward the necessity of a convertible Czechoslovak koruna, and alluded to the probability of foreign loans.

On April 29 Sik stated publicly that Czechoslovakia needed a foreign loan of $500 million. As the Soviets declined to grant such a loan (which, in their opinion, would mean subsidizing an attempt to escape from the Comecon trading circuit), news began to leak in the Prague press, now free from censorship, that the Czechoslovak government was considering massive loans from the U.S. or West Germany. This no doubt influenced Moscow's decision to occupy Czechoslovakia on the night of August 20–21. In any case, that date marked the end of the economic reform conceived by Sik. On September 3 he resigned from the government and went to Switzerland, and the Moscow-Prague agreements included the proviso that Czechoslovakia stop trying to increase economic relations with the West. (K. SM.)

See also Development, Economic; Government Finance.

Economics

Economics is a discipline that has thrived on controversy, and 1968 held firmly to this tradition. A major new work on economic development raised questions of the most fundamental type in methodology for economics generally; and the issue of whether monetary or fiscal policy is the key to stability and growth in the United States was debated in connection with economic conditions leading to the 1968 surtax on incomes.

Asian Drama: An Inquiry into the Poverty of Nations, a three-volume work by Gunnar Myrdal (*see* BIOGRAPHY), was an outstanding contribution to economics in 1968. This monumental 2,284-page study provides a theory of economic development of South Asia, with India as the centrepiece of the analysis. Because Myrdal finds traditional economics thoroughly inadequate, he devotes much attention to methodology, a subject to which he had previously made important contributions. He pleads for an institutional approach to a theory of economic development. Institutional economic theory views the economic system as part of a total culture. Many things that are taken as given in traditional economic theory become variables in the broadly based institutional approach.

Western economics abstracts from many of the conditions that are responsible for the underdevelopment of South Asian nations. For example, Myrdal finds language, literacy, health, population, class structure, and climate essential variables in a realistic theory of the development of South Asia. He is not opposed to model building, which he views as the universal method of scientific research. He does strongly oppose models based on unrealistic assumptions and irrelevant concepts. Many such models come "near to being intellectual frauds" (p. 31).

Theory and policy are closely linked in institutional economics. Myrdal's policy is economic planning. In part iv, "A Third World of Planning," he deals with a type of policy that avoids the extremes of Communist planning, on the one hand, and of the laissez-faire policies associated with capitalist nations on the other. Myrdal's methodology takes explicit account of the influence of ideology (value premises) on theories and concepts, including his own. He appeals for an understanding of the relationship of the sociology of knowledge to economic theory. The sociology of knowledge brings an awareness of the ideological blinders that traditional economists wear in their claims to be "neutral" theorists forging and using conceptual tools of "universal" validity.

Myrdal severely criticizes economists who apply Western concepts and theories uncritically to Asian problems. For example, the concepts of unemployment and, more particularly, underemployment have been used widely to explain the low utilization of the Asian labour force. Underemployment means that workers, although employed, would be more productive if employed elsewhere. One major suggestion has been that workers be transferred from agriculture, where their marginal productivity is said to be zero (they are underemployed), to nonagricultural employment. In several hundred pages of text on labour utilization and population prospects, plus a special appendix on the concept of underemployment, Myrdal shows how unrealistic this proposal is for Asia. Alternative sources of employment and the motivation to move to them do not exist. He insists that the poverty of Asia emanates from its total culture and not from special characteristics of agriculture. Since the assumptions of Western economic theory do not correspond to the characteristics of Asian society, attempts to apply policies based on this theory may prove disastrous.

The Asian "drama" of Myrdal's title refers to the unfolding of conflicts between the lofty aspirations of the leading actors and the harsh realities of life for hundreds of millions of Asians. The outcome of the drama, however, is not predetermined. It will not

necessarily be a tragedy, although it tends in that direction. Hope for avoiding a tragedy rests with Asians through reforms in agriculture, education, health, and population; but the world as a whole will feel the effect of whatever happens, and the outcome can be influenced within narrow limits by outside aid in the form of capital, new markets for Asian products, and technical assistance. Correct analysis itself can influence the outcome of the drama. In this sense there is an urgency about Myrdal's work, which may prove no less prophetic than his earlier *An American Dilemma: The Negro Problem and Modern Democracy* (1944), in which he pointed to rising tensions related to the conflict between American ideals and the plight of the American Negro. Myrdal, who has been called the greatest living social scientist, was an economist, but one who broadened the traditionally narrow confines of this discipline in order to render it more useful in solving real world problems.

Another major work published in 1968 was the first British edition of Max Weber's *Economy and Society* (translated in three volumes from the German *Wirtschaft und Gesellschaft*). Like Myrdal, Weber took a broad cultural approach to economics. His contributions to methodology and model building were immense, and he has been called the greatest social theorist of the first half of the 20th century.

A trend toward greater attention to monetary policy and theory was highlighted by Milton Friedman's presidential address to the American Economic Association on "The Role of Monetary Policy" (*American Economic Review,* March 1968). Friedman reiterated his recommendation for a steady increase in the quantity of money as the policy best designed to create price stability, high employment, and steady growth. The precise rate of increase is less important, according to Friedman, than adherence to a rule that the stock of money change at some publicly announced fixed rate, such as 3% annually. He would not permit central bankers to exercise discretion in changing the quantity of money because history shows they will be wrong more frequently than they are right. He attributes the "great contraction" (1929–33), as well as most post-World War II inflation, to wrong monetary policy. Mismanagement of money is, in Friedman's view, responsible for nearly all serious economic disturbances. In the absence of bad monetary management, he believes that the market system is the best guarantee that the major goals of economic policy will be realized. This comes close to laissez-faire.

Friedman's advocacy of monetary policy is associated with his version of the quantity theory of money. In the new 1968 *International Encyclopedia of the Social Sciences* he writes, "Acceptance of the quantity theory clearly means that the stock of money is a key variable in policies directed at the control of the level of prices or of money income" (article on "Money: Quantity Theory," vol. x, p. 445). An important supplement to this view is relative stability in the velocity of circulation of money, a view that Friedman accepts. In another sense, the issue is whether money has a causal impact on the quantity of real output, or whether money adapts to changing levels of real output.

Since the great depression of the 1930s, fiscal policy has been favoured over monetary policy for promoting high employment, price stability, and steady growth. Automatic stabilizers, discretionary tax changes, and discretionary governmental expenditures were the chief tools of the Kennedy-Johnson adminis-

"It can happen here."—Liederman, "Long Island Press," New York.

tration in guiding the record-breaking U.S. economic expansion from 1961 through 1968. Nevertheless, the propriety and effectiveness of fiscal policy have been seriously questioned by critics such as Friedman. During 1967, when the U.S. economy became excessively buoyant, the Johnson administration recommended a tax increase and, after much delay in Congress, a 10% surtax on incomes was passed in June 1968. The effectiveness of the surtax as a brake on excessive expansion and inflation was a subject of much debate in the second half of the year. The economy responded slowly to fiscal restraint. Output continued to grow at unsustainable rates, prices continued to rise at inflationary rates, and the stock market boomed. Did this mean that fiscal policy was, after all, not such an effective device for curbing booms, or did it mean only that the restraints worked with a considerable lag? The president's Council of Economic Advisers took the latter position, but the question was not subject to a definitive answer at the end of 1968.

The effectiveness of tax reductions as a stimulant to economic activity seemed to be verified by two studies published during 1968 by the Brookings Institution. George Katona and Eva Mueller found that the U.S. federal income tax cuts of 1964 and 1965 did stimulate consumers to increase their spending out of larger after-tax incomes. Their sample showed that consumers do not distinguish between income increases resulting from lower taxes and increases resulting from higher wages and salaries (George Katona and Eva Mueller, *Consumer Response to Income Increases,* 1968). This result was confirmed in a study by Albert Ando and E. Cary Brown on the effect of the 1964 tax reduction. Consumer responses to income changes resulting from the tax reductions in 1964 and 1965 were consistent with responses to income changes for the period from 1947 to 1963 (Albert Ando, E. Cary Brown, and Ann F. Fridelander [eds.], *Studies in Economic Stabilization,* 1968).

A serious shortcoming of discretionary fiscal policy, either by changes in taxation or by changes in expenditures, is the delay between the time that the

need for a change is recognized and enactment of the necessary legislation. Greater flexibility could be introduced by means of legislation that would permit changes in tax rates and/or expenditures according to an agreed-upon formula. Formula flexibility has been discussed for many years by economists, but recent attention to fiscal drag during upswings and the damaging congressional delay in raising tax rates in 1968 lent new urgency to tax and expenditure flexibility if fiscal policy was to continue as a major policy weapon for attaining national economic goals.

The American Economic Association awarded its highest honour, the Francis A. Walker Medal, given at approximately five-year intervals to the outstanding senior economist in the U.S., to Alvin H. Hansen, professor emeritus of Harvard. Hansen (born 1887) was known as the leading American Keynesian for expanding and modifying the ideas of John Maynard Keynes, the famous British economist. Hansen developed the stagnation thesis implicit in Keynes's *General Theory* in a book entitled *Full Recovery or Stagnation?* (1938). Other important books by Hansen included *Monetary Theory and Fiscal Policy* (1949), *Business Cycles and National Income* (1951), and *A Guide to Keynes* (1953).

The John Bates Clark Medal for the outstanding American economist under 40 years of age was awarded to Columbia University's Gary S. Becker, whose major work was on the economics of discrimination and on investment in human capital. In 1968 he published an article on "Crime and Punishment: An Economic Approach" (*Journal of Political Economy*, March/April 1968). This article attempts to answer the question: How many resources and how much punishment should be used to enforce different kinds of legislation? Policemen, judges, and special equipment cost money; therefore they are never available in unlimited quantities. Hence, decisions concerning the size of expenditures to combat crime also involve decisions as to how many offenses should be permitted and how many offenders should go unpunished.   (D. D.)

See also Economy, World; Government Finance; Income, National; Merchandising; Money and Banking; Payments and Reserves, International; Trade, International.

Economy, World

The world economy, which during the past two decades had at least doubled the output of goods and services, once again showed notable growth in 1968, following some slowdown in the rate of expansion dur-

Gold and precious metals market in the Paris Bourse on March 15, 1968, when the price of gold jumped from Fr. 5,700 to Fr. 7,000 per kilogram; i.e., from roughly $36 to $44 an ounce.

ing the previous year. Nevertheless, it was not able to produce enough to meet all of the demands on it—demands that became all the more pervasive and exacting as new aspirations and expectations arose throughout the world. Political and social unrest became more acute. Amid unprecedented abundance, the awareness of poverty spread painfully but unmistakably.

The renewed momentum in the world economy virtually ignored the three international monetary crises of confidence in a 12-month period—November 1967, March 1968, and November 1968—described in companion articles. Failing a real remedy, however, such crises—by sapping confidence and creating violent tensions in exchange, gold, and money markets—could endanger world prosperity.

Most continental European countries—except France—restored growth and stability to their economies. This stands out clearly from the charts illustrating year-to-year percentage increases in gross national product and trends in industrial production; the first chart also shows changes in money supplies, which may be regarded as an indication of the degree of monetary expansiveness in each country. The good economic performance in this group of countries is also evidenced from the table showing the depreciation of money. West Germany's accomplishment in this regard was particularly noteworthy. The principal factor sustaining the business expansion in countries such as West Germany, Italy, and Switzerland was export demand—with rising demands from the United States, the United Kingdom, and, later in the year, France having become especially important elements. With

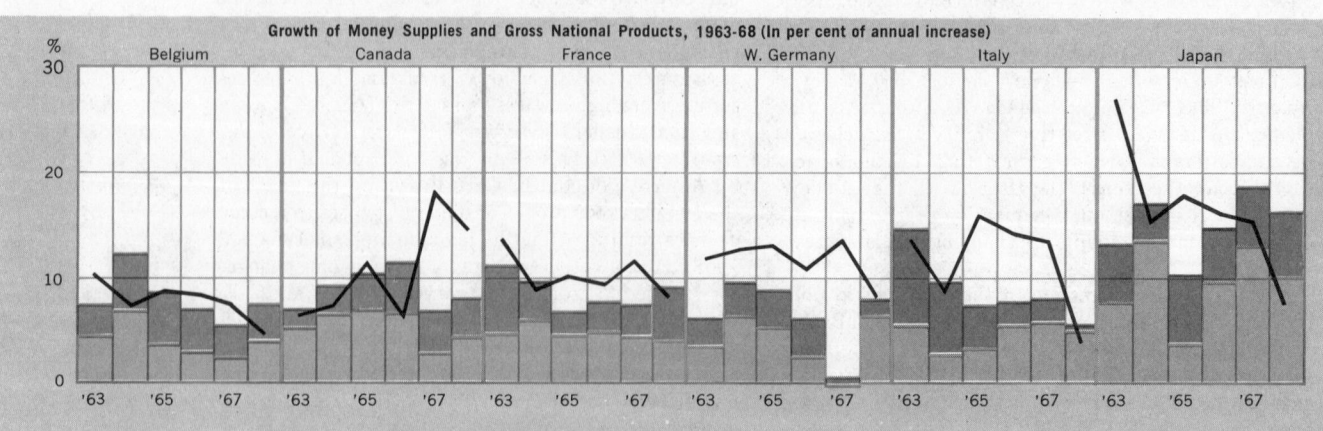

Growth of Money Supplies and Gross National Products, 1963-68 (In per cent of annual increase)

a few exceptions, personal consumption remained the least dynamic component of aggregate demand in most of the continental countries.

In France, the political and social unrest that sprang up in May and June virtually without notice in support of demands of a political and cultural nature was met by unusually large and sudden increases in wage payments and, hence, in production costs and budgetary expenditures. Subsequently, industrial production rose, but the price exacted for allowing the nation to return to work was bound to take an inflationary toll, which led in November to a franc crisis.

Beginning with late 1967, the United Kingdom gradually took a succession of steps to curb internal demand in order to make the sterling devaluation work. Because of the delays, but also because of a continuing expansion in money supplies to shore up government bond prices, because of weaknesses in resisting wage pressure, and because of expectations of further taxation and price inflation, consumer spending remained very strong; saving was depressed. Devaluation did not produce a favourable balance of payments, although some improvement was recorded. Among the positive signs was a sharp increase in industrial output. The crucial test remained Britain's readiness to accept transitory unemployment and a slowdown in the improvement of living standards in order to break through into faster economic growth and to reduce the foreign trade deficit.

Following a period from early 1961 to early 1965 of substantial economic growth coupled with price stability, the U.S. economy was unable to absorb the mounting demands on it stemming from Vietnam and the increasing costs of government programs at home. The nation could not have both guns and butter simultaneously. By 1966, in the absence of government fiscal action and in an environment of an expansive monetary policy, a classic wage-price inflationary spiral got under way. In early 1967, the administration proposed a tax increase but made no effort to achieve it. It was only in mid-1967 that the effort for a surcharge was really launched and it took until June 1968 to get the needed action from the Congress. But consumers refused to cut spending and, by year's end, there were only the barest signs of a slowdown in the economy. Unemployment fell to a 15-year low.

The U.S. dollar during 1967–68 suffered a more rapid rate of loss in buying power than in earlier years. At the 4.4% rate of annual depreciation recorded during the 12 months ended November 1968, the dollar would lose half of its purchasing power in 15 years.

In many parts of the world, people—uneasily aware that the longer they held money, the less they would

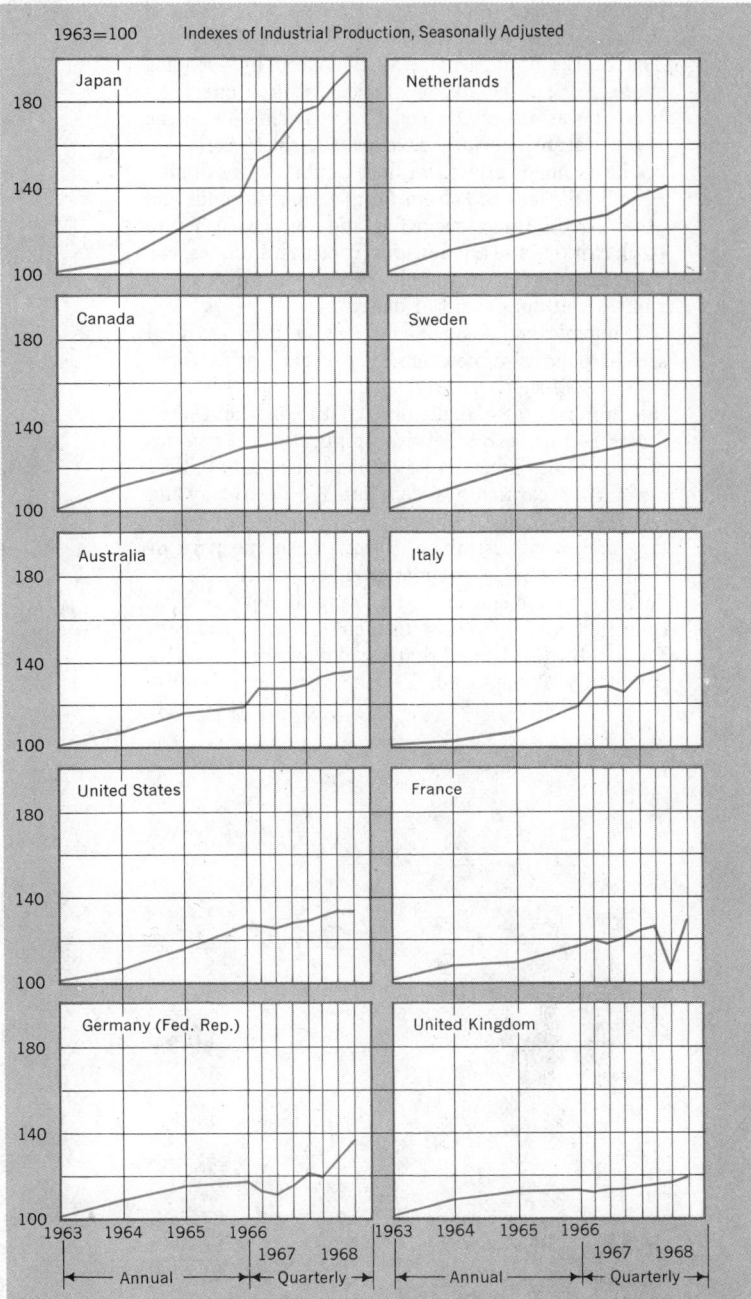

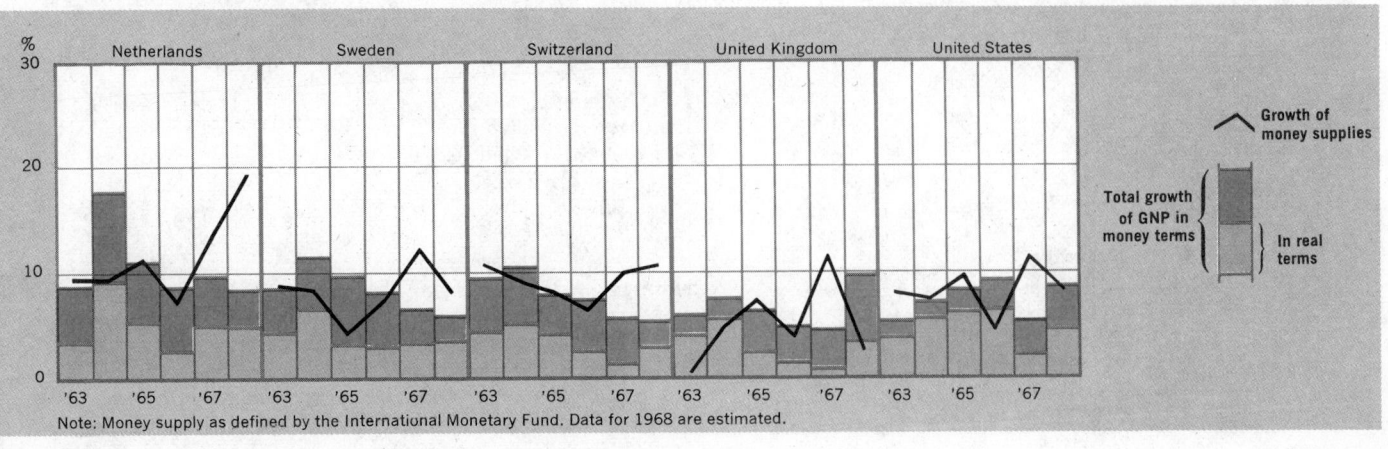

Note: Money supply as defined by the International Monetary Fund. Data for 1968 are estimated.

get for it—tried to protect themselves by buying real values even more forcefully than in preceding years. The cancer of inflation was evidenced by spending sprees to beat the gun on further inflation and taxation. It was also evidenced by the decline in saving habits—a most serious development since there cannot be economic growth without capital. It was dramatized by the lack of esteem for government bonds and other fixed-interest securities and by the rush into stock markets and auctions for paintings, antiques, etc. To learn to live with monetary crises became a new cult—a cult not devoid of dangers.

Economic and financial matters in 1968 assumed serious political dimensions. The French crisis, Britain's lack of success in restraining wage increases, and the problems of the disturbed cities in the United States had explosive political implications. Processes of balance of payments adjustment also had political aspects of great significance. Thus, West Germany and Switzerland could in 1966 and 1967 implement monetary and fiscal restraints to slow down the pace of their overheated economies even at the cost of reducing employment because many of the unemployed could temporarily return to their homes in southern Europe. But the United States had nowhere to send its potentially unemployed. Yet the very fact that ex-

continued on page 307

Depreciation of Money

Country	Indexes of value of money 1957=100 1962	Indexes of value of money 1957=100 1967	Annual rates of depreciation '57-'67*	Annual rates of depreciation '66-'67	Annual rates of depreciation '67-'68†
Pakistan	92	72	3.3%	6.5%	−2.3%
Honduras	96	82	2.0	2.5	−0.1
Guatemala	99	99	0.1	0.5	0.1
Italy	89	71	3.4	3.1	0.3
Philippines	88	67	4.0	5.4	0.8
Sweden	86	69	3.7	4.1	0.8
Greece	93	82	2.0	1.7	0.9
Thailand	96	85	1.6	3.8	0.9
India	86	54	6.0	11.5	1.3
Germany, West	91	79	2.2	1.4	1.4
South Africa	91	79	2.3	3.3	1.7
Switzerland	92	76	2.6	3.8	1.8
Australia	91	80	2.2	3.1	1.8
Luxembourg	97	84	1.8	2.1	1.8
Venezuela	91	88	1.2	−0.9	1.9
Belgium	95	80	2.2	2.8	2.3
Israel	80	60	4.9	1.6	2.4
Austria	88	74	3.0	3.8	2.5
El Salvador	98	94	0.6	1.4	2.5
Iran	79	73	3.1	1.6	2.8
Netherlands	92	73	3.1	2.8	3.2
Portugal	91	75	2.9	5.6	3.2
Norway	86	71	3.4	4.3	3.2
New Zealand	88	74	3.0	5.8	3.3
Mexico	81	71	3.4	2.9	3.4
Spain	75	50	6.6	6.1	3.5
Canada	93	82	2.0	3.4	3.7
Ireland	89	73	3.1	3.1	4.3
United States	93	84	1.7	2.7	4.4
France	73	62	4.7	2.6	4.8
Ecuador	92	74	2.9	3.5	4.9
Denmark	87	65	4.2	7.6	5.0
Colombia	70	34	10.2	7.5	5.4
United Kingdom	89	75	2.8	2.4	5.6
Japan	85	66	4.1	3.8	6.1
Turkey	62	45	7.7	12.3	7.1
Bolivia	63	49	6.9	7.4	7.1
Finland	85	63	4.4	5.5	7.9
China (Taiwan)	67	62	4.6	3.3	9.1
Korea	81	36	9.6	9.8	9.6
Argentina	19	6	24.8	22.5	10.3
Peru	68	41	8.4	9.3	12.7
Vietnam	92	31	11.1	30.4	18.8
Brazil	22	2	31.6	22.8	19.5
Chile	42	11	20.1	15.4	20.9

Note: Depreciation computed from official data. Value of money is measured by reciprocals of official cost of living or consumer price indexes. The quality of official measurement of overall price levels varies greatly from country to country.
*Compounded annually.
†Latest 12-month period available.
Source: First National City Bank, New York, N.Y.

THE GOLD CRISIS AND ITS AFTERMATH

By Miroslav A. Kriz

The world found itself during 1968 in greater stress and strain in its international monetary affairs than at any time since the 1930s. In the wake of sterling devaluation in November 1967, reviewed in the 1968 *Book of the Year*, two other international crises of confidence shook the world—the gold crisis in March 1968 and the crisis of November 1968 that revolved principally around the French franc and the pound sterling.

During the gold crisis, the U.S. dollar, the world's principal trading and reserve currency, was in the centre of intense heat; but the crisis was, basically, one of confidence in all currencies. During the November currency turmoil, the heat on the dollar, and on gold itself, was largely radiation, not a direct flame. The dollar was involved mainly as the vehicle for massive movements of funds out of the French franc and other currencies into the German Deutsche Mark. It was much less exposed because, as described elsewhere in these pages, the U.S. balance of payments, although still heavily in deficit, was relieved partly by large capital inflows from abroad and partly by a substantial improvement in the U.S. fiscal position and by a measure of monetary restraint. This led to expectations that the very rapid business expansion accompanied by price inflation of the order of 5% a year was coming gradually, if slowly, under control.

Nevertheless, given all the circumstances—Vietnam, the problems of the cities, and the seemingly intractable inflation in the United States, as well as the overabundance of dollars outside the United States and the attrition of the U.S. gold stock over the past decade—the dollar appeared less impregnable than many Americans tended to take for granted on the strength of the resources and productivity of the American economy. Beyond this —for reasons that are set forth later in this essay—there was the fundamental question of the relation between the dollar and gold.

Several meetings of finance ministers and central bankers were convened hastily, and bulletins were repeatedly broadcast to reassure people. These and other trappings did not fully restore confidence and stability; for, like Aristotle's Magnificent Man, a banker should never be seen to hurry or talk too much. Nevertheless, international monetary cooperation, evidenced principally in rescue operations to help the currencies in trouble, prevented cracks in the international monetary structure.

In the midst of the gold crisis, and as a consequence of it, the governments and central banks of the United States and six other countries abandoned in mid-March the support, at close to the official price of $35 an ounce, of the London gold market price. Private and official transactions in gold were thus separated into two circuits—after a decade and a half of official intervention at costs to monetary reserves that had proved prohibitive. The abandonment of the official price support eliminated one source of weakness in the international monetary system, but heavy clouds continued to obscure the international monetary horizons.

For the first time in a generation, the solidity of the world's exchange rate structure—based on the assured convertibility of

dollars into gold at the U.S. Treasury's fixed gold price of $35 an ounce and on a meaningful convertibility among the principal currencies at fixed exchange rates—could not be taken for granted. These links had led to the widespread use of the dollar as a world trading currency and, gradually and organically, as the principal currency held, along with gold, in the reserves of other nations. Within this framework, and also because of basically free, multilateral, and nondiscriminatory trade, the world had experienced, over the past decade, the most rapid, varied, and widely distributed economic advance in history.

The Chronicle of the Gold Crisis. The tensions in the international monetary system that came to a head in the devaluation of the pound sterling in November 1967 gave rise to widespread doubts about the general level of all currencies in terms of gold. The doubts also stemmed from a further weakening in the U.S. balance of payments and from the persistent decline in the domestic buying power of practically all currencies, as evidenced in the table accompanying the article ECONOMY, WORLD. Not unnaturally, the private demand for gold by individuals and corporations for investment, saving, and hedging against the depreciation of currencies literally exploded. Private ownership of gold is legal in much of the world outside the United States and the United Kingdom (and, of course, the Communist countries).

World gold output, after having reached an all-time high in 1965 and having remained stationary in 1966, declined by 2% in 1967—for the first time in 14 years. Even though it rose moderately in 1968, production in coming years is expected to decline from the plateau of recent years—about 40 million oz. a year, worth $1.4 billion. In this picture, South Africa, which accounts for somewhat over three-fourths of world output, was a decisive factor. The Soviet Union, which had previously disposed of large amounts of gold, sold little during 1966–68. Nevertheless, supplies from new output remained, in historical perspective, substantial (*see* Chart I).

The pressures on the gold price in 1967 and early 1968 thus did not stem from the failure of physical production. They came from an upsurge in private demand (*see* Chart II).

Private demand for gold is surrounded by mystery. Some of it goes into industrial uses (including jewelry); some of it is added to private holdings. In reality, of course, the dividing line is not as clear-cut as it seems statistically. Broadly speaking, something like $750 million worth of gold, or one-half of the annual output, was consumed during 1968 in the electrical, electronic, and aerospace industries—uses as new as the umbilical cords of space-walking astronauts—and in fabrication of gold articles of all sorts. Uses in industry and jewelry had been stimulated by general prosperity, with incomes at record levels, and by factors like population growth. But the fact that gold, at the $35 price, had become cheap relative to other products was also important.

Most of the privately absorbed gold that does not go into uses in industry and jewelry is added to private holdings—customary savings, as in Asia and the Middle East, or investments made, hopefully, as protection against the depreciation of currencies, inheritance taxes, and political and social upheavals, as in Europe and Latin America. On top of these investments, there was in late 1967 and early 1968 hedging against possible worldwide devaluation of currencies in terms of the established dollar price of gold as their common denominator. Some of the gold that was statistically regarded as absorbed privately may have gone into unpublished central bank holdings, including those of Eastern European countries and Communist China.

The private buying of gold is frequently labeled speculation. If so, it is speculation in the sense Bernard Baruch used when, questioned by a congressional committee about his vocation, he answered: "Speculator!" As he recalled, "I was perfectly willing . . . to say I was a speculator. I defined a speculator as a man who observes the future and acts before it occurs." Corporate treasurers and others who administer large amounts of cash are continuously compelled to take a view of the future values of currencies, for these will determine the future amount of their

Changes in World Gold Reserves*

In U.S. $000,000

Country	Change Oct. 1967– March 1968	April 1968– Sept. 1968	Stock as of Sept. 1968	% of gold in total re- serves† Sept. 1968
United States	−2,374	+ 52	10,755	78%
United Kingdom	− 338	− 7	1,486	55
Germany, West	− 312	+ 484	4,456	58
France	+ 1	−1,069	4,166	95
Switzerland	− 238	+ 25	2,628	90
Italy	− 25	+ 408	2,784	64
Netherlands	− 77	+ 43	1,697	88
Belgium	− 96	+ 106	1,524	78
Portugal	+ 21	+ 142	853	66
Canada	− 123	− 113	863	34
All other	+ 781	+ 774	7,458	...
International institutions‡	+ 56	− 353	2,055	...
Total	−2,720	+ 490	40,725	...

Note: (...) indicates not applicable.
*Excluding the U.S.S.R., other Eastern European countries, Communist China, etc.
†Total gold and foreign exchange reserves.
‡International Monetary Fund, Bank for International Settlements, European Payments Union, etc.

profits or losses. Speculation in this sense is a normal precautionary activity—given all the circumstances in the world in 1968, including the occurrence of three monetary crises in 12 months.

By 1965, the rise in industrial and savings demand—influenced by the decline in the U.S. Treasury gold stock and by the cheapness of the metal—had come to absorb almost all of world output outside the U.S.S.R. When hedging demand skyrocketed in late 1967 and early 1968, all of it had to be met out of the reserves of the monetary authorities of the seven countries participating, after France's withdrawal in June 1967, in the so-called London Gold Pool—Belgium, Italy, West Germany, the Netherlands, Switzerland, the United Kingdom, and the United States. While continuing to provide gold to the market, they reiterated on several occasions their intention to stabilize the market around the official price and to maintain the existing market arrangements. But after they had supplied, from mid-November 1967 through mid-March 1968, close to $3 billion to individual and corporate buyers without having succeeded in

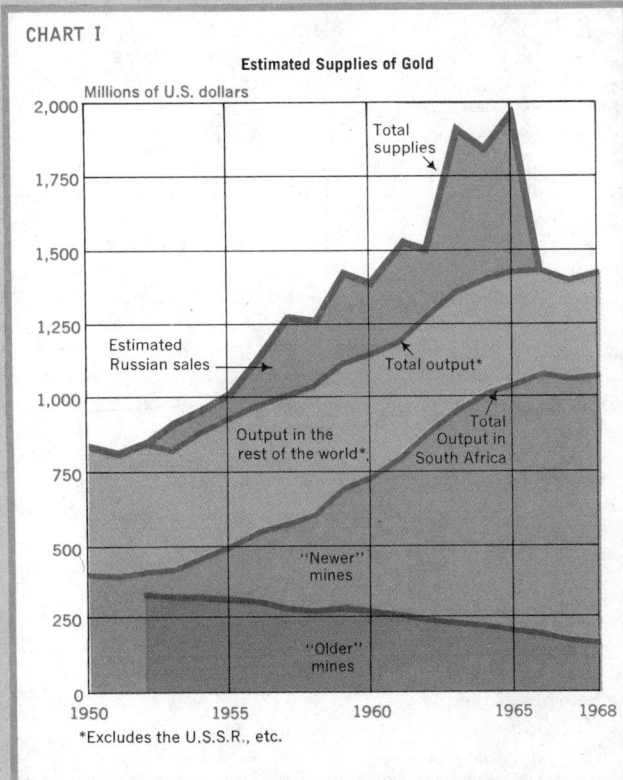

CHART I

Estimated Supplies of Gold

Millions of U.S. dollars

Total supplies

Estimated Russian sales

Total output*

Output in the rest of the world*

Total Output in South Africa

"Newer" mines

"Older" mines

*Excludes the U.S.S.R., etc.

stemming the tide, they decided, at a meeting in Washington on March 16–17, to bring to a halt their support of the market price of gold. The $3 billion cost to official reserves equaled roughly 10% of the $28 billion gold stock that these seven countries held in September 1967; the United States met 59% of the total. The decision to stop putting a ceiling on the London gold market price was inevitable as a means of conserving the stock of monetary gold, especially since the citizens of the United States had long been forbidden to own gold.

Gold as the Key Element in the World Monetary System. Among all the options open in the circumstances, the governments chose the smallest possible change in the world's gold arrangements—separation of private and official transactions in gold into two circuits. Gold remained, at its established price of $35 an ounce, the key element of international liquidity—the element in the form of which the governments of most of the leading countries keep 60–90% of their international reserves (see Table) and to which all other forms of reserves are tied.

The monetary authorities of the seven nations represented at the Washington meeting expressed the belief that, henceforth, gold held by governments and central banks should be used only to effect transactions among monetary authorities. The world thus found itself in a state where official transfers of gold continued to be effected at the fixed price of $35, while the private market was left free to find a price that equated demand and supply. This state of things, generally called the "two-tier price system," was neither a two-tier price—since the official $35 parity was an act of the U.S. government embodied in law, not a market price—nor a system, since the world merely returned to an arrangement that existed from the end of World War II to 1961 but was regarded as so unsystematic that it was changed to enable the governments to intervene in the London gold market to support the price.

The representatives of the seven nations also announced that they no longer felt it necessary to buy gold from the market on the ground that the growth of monetary reserves in the future would be assured by the creation of a new monetary facility based on the so-called Special Drawing Rights (SDR's). To these ends, they invited the cooperation of other countries. The accord to create the SDR's—summarily baptized "instant" or "paper" gold—was presented in May 1968 for approval by national legislatures. But while the new international money might, as discussed later, be created in 1969, it was to be issued, as and when needed, to supplement, not to supplant, gold and foreign exchange; its value was to be guaranteed "in terms of a weight of gold"—a clause that, unlike a similar provision in the International Monetary Fund (IMF) charter, could not be rescinded by the Fund's board of directors in the event of a uniform change in the price of gold.

Along with these announcements, the U.S. government reaffirmed its policy—going back to 1934—of buying and selling gold at the existing price of $35 in transactions with monetary authorities. The representatives of other nations expressed support for this policy as a contribution to the maintenance of stability of the world's exchange rate structure. The decision, of course, merely confirmed what is the cornerstone of the international monetary system today. To remove it would be tantamount to fracturing the international exchange structure and world trade.

The Shortage of Monetary Gold. The decline of $3 billion in the gold stocks of governments and central banks in the wake of the explosion of private demand in late 1967 and early 1968 was the sharpest in world monetary history. It contrasted strikingly with the steady annual increases, averaging about $500 million a year, in monetary gold stocks during 1946–65; there was a small decline in 1966. In March 1968, world monetary gold stocks stood at about $40 billion. Had it not been for private gold hoarding over the previous ten years, they would have exceeded $49 billion.

Following the March 1968 crisis, official gold stocks in the world as a whole rose (see Table). Practically the entire increase came from new South African output. Although a tussle arose regarding the disposal of newly mined gold, a conviction was developing that an increase in monetary gold stocks outside the United States without denuding the U.S. stock would be a stabilizing development.

As a matter of fact, the price of gold in international private markets like London and Zürich fluctuated during April–December 1968 at levels that were, for the most part, 10–20% higher than the official $35 price. At year's end, the price in London stood at $41.90. This behaviour, among other things, reflected the uncertainties regarding the disposal of South African gold. It was also greatly affected by the fact that, especially during the early months following the crisis, gold purchased in the expectation of a near-term rise in the official gold price was sold and gradually found its way into industrial uses and stocks and into firm private holdings. The overhang weighing on the gold market in the wake of the crisis was large, for the sales by the "pool" from November 1967 through mid-March 1968 were equivalent to twice the amount of the world's annual output.

While the new arrangements proved workable in 1968, their future workability depended on the spread between the official and the market prices of gold. The spread in turn depended on supply-demand conditions in the gold markets, on the course of the balances of payments of the major industrial countries, and on confidence that international monetary problems could be dealt with through cooperation among governments, including moral suasion to restrain official demands for gold in order to avoid massive conversions of dollars into gold. Convertibility becomes nominal when governments and central banks have little choice but to refrain—for nonmonetary reasons—from exercising it.

In practice, gold moves from the reserves of one country to those of another whenever settlements have to be made that cannot otherwise be financed. Understandably, therefore, in the wake of the disturbances in its economy and its balance of payments, France not only used the dollars it had in its reserves or secured from the IMF and the central banks of other countries but also sold $1,424,000,000 of gold from June through November. The demand for gold by governments was also evidenced by the arrangements in June 1968 providing that the IMF would—apart from its own resources and borrowings—raise $547 million by selling gold to 14 countries other than the United States to obtain the currencies it needed to finance the drawings by the United Kingdom and France. West Germany, Italy, and other continental countries added appreciable amounts to their already substantial gold reserves. (See Chart III.) Although the United States had bought about two-fifths of the gold sold by France, its reserve showed but a moderate rise.

France thus disposed of a large part of the gold reserve it had built up during 1959–67 mainly through purchases from the United States, to which it had sold substantial amounts of gold during the prolonged period of its balance of payments deficits from 1935 to 1958. Even so, it had the third largest gold reserve in the world, though mortgaged by borrowings from central banks. Germany and Italy, which had little gold before World War II, were the second and the fourth largest gold-holding countries; Switzerland was the fifth. The U.S. was, of course, the first.

The U.S. gold stock, which had fallen by $1.2 billion in 1967 and $1.4 billion during the first three months of 1968, subsequently increased to $10.9 billion at the end of December. At this level, it was $13.9 billion below December 1949, before its depletion had begun (see Chart IV). At $10.9 billion in December —the lowest level since 1936—the U.S. gold stock represented about one-fourth of the world monetary stock, compared with somewhat more than two-thirds in 1949.

The ratio of gold to Federal Reserve notes in early 1968 fell close to the legal minimum of 25%; and, at the administration's urging, the House and the Senate—by 9- and 2-vote majorities—passed legislation eliminating the gold cover requirement on domestic currency. This measure made the entire U.S. gold stock available for sale to support the dollar internationally. At the

same time, however, the thought of last-ditch selling raised searching questions. The United States needs a gold reserve commensurate with its far-flung financial and political responsibilities.

The preference for gold—evidenced in the table—basically reflects deeply anchored views that there are times and circumstances where no other money will do because gold alone is universally acceptable, without any questions being asked, as the means of payment of last resort. These views rest in part on the thought that governments cannot print it at their whim and that gold is beyond the control of any one nation—especially as it was redistributed in late 1968, with the United States holding only slightly more than one-quarter of the world's monetary stock. As a result, gold makes it easier than any alternative arrangement—whether an inconvertible dollar standard controlled by the United States or money controlled by an international board—for governments and central banks to safeguard a substantial measure of autonomy and independence in their own monetary and fiscal matters. For acceptance of an inconvertible dollar exchange standard or of money controlled by an international board would be like having two central banks—one of them at home and the other outside the country—sometimes working at cross purposes.

The preference for gold also reflects the desire to protect reserves against the hazards of depreciation. In many countries, especially on the continent of Europe, the attachment of governments and central banks to gold is also motivated by the desire to display respectably large gold stocks to people who, having lived through the inflation of the past half century, tend to keep an eye on the state of their country's gold reserve as a vital indicator of the soundness of its domestic finances.

Gold, of course, is not the only reserve asset usable internationally. Over the past half century, governments and central banks chose to hold sterling and, after World War II, dollars in monetary reserves because they found it safe, profitable, and convenient to do so and because they were confident that they could at any time, without having to give any explanation, shift from one currency to another or into gold.

The dollar reserves of governments and central banks outside the United States increased substantially during the past two decades. Until about 1958, foreign governments were eager to build up dollar reserves. They took for granted, and regarded as eminently desirable, that a nation endowed with rich national resources, high productivity, large savings, and efficient money and capital markets should run a deficit on capital account as a result of which the rest of the world could build up dollar reserves.

The rub is that the U.S. deficits have year in and year out been much larger than the governments of the surplus nations have wanted to finance willingly by building up their dollar reserves in amounts they have judged to be in their own national interest. An inherently good thing has thus been overdone—in part because of Vietnam. The dollar assets of foreign governments—which are, of course, liabilities of the United States—now exceed the U.S. gold stock (*see* Charts IV and V).

The U.S. balance of payments deficit thus came to be regarded as an increasingly unsatisfactory way of providing international reserves. Any further increase in foreign official holdings of dollars relative to the U.S. gold stock would itself weaken the international monetary system. Ways were thus prepared for a new international monetary facility to ensure that, if need be, there would be enough international reserves.

The New International Facility. Following debates and negotiations over the previous five years, a contingency plan to establish a new international monetary facility was submitted in May 1968 to governments for their consideration and approval. The United States was the first of the major industrial nations to complete, in July 1968, the governmental action needed to approve the plan; the United Kingdom was second. In the aggregate, only 27 countries, with 47% of total IMF voting power, had ratified by the end of 1968; for the scheme to become effective, ratification must come from 67 of the Fund's 111 mem-

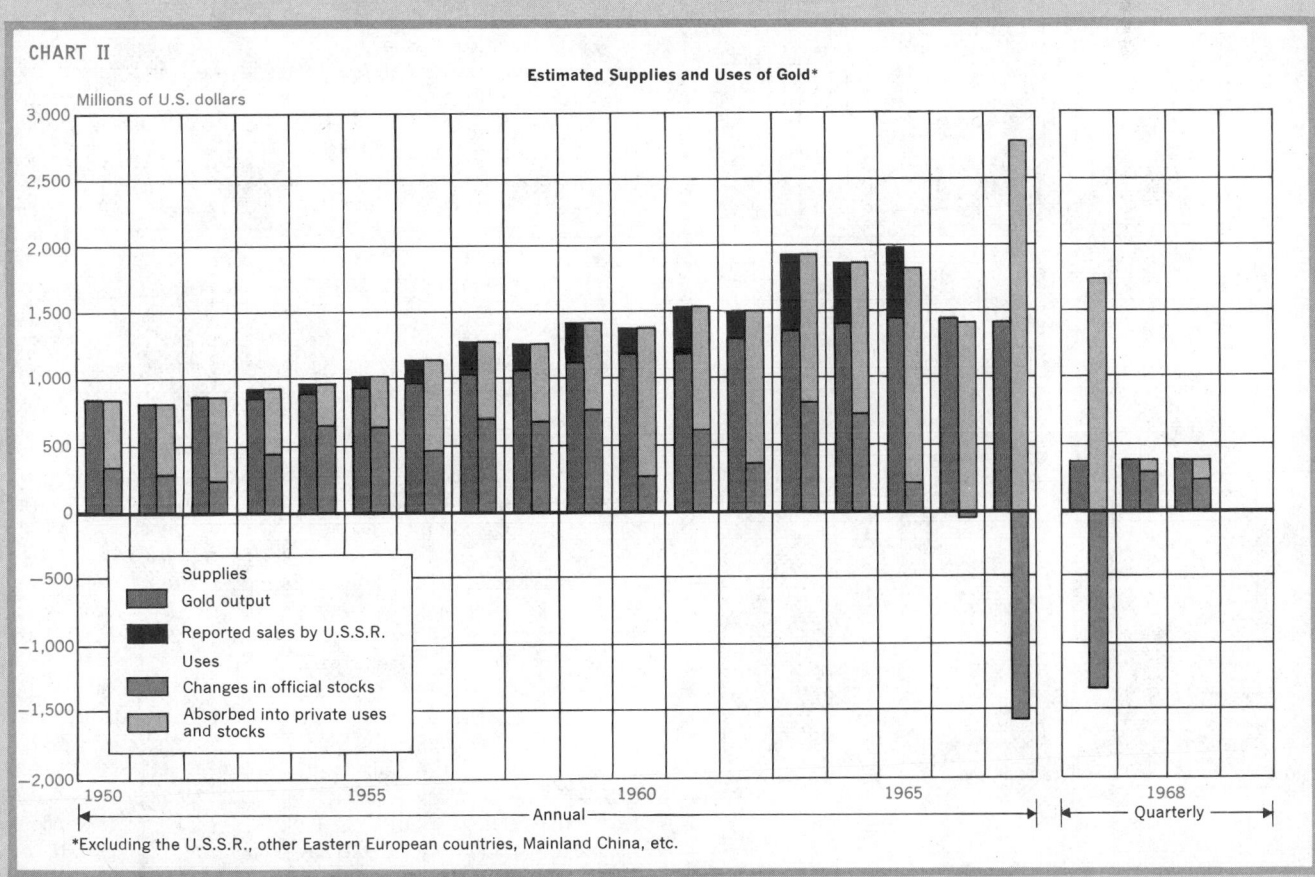

CHART II

Estimated Supplies and Uses of Gold*

Millions of U.S. dollars

*Excluding the U.S.S.R., other Eastern European countries, Mainland China, etc.

Supplies
Gold output
Reported sales by U.S.S.R.
Uses
Changes in official stocks
Absorbed into private uses and stocks

bers, with at least 80% of the vote. At year's end, the process of ratification was expected to be completed by mid-1969.

The establishment of the new facility, described in the 1968 *Book of the Year*, was designed to create and allocate special drawing rights that the participating governments were to accept from one another up to specified limits. The SDR's were thus reserve assets that would not have to be "earned" through balance of payments surpluses but would be distributed freely. The holdings of these rights were, in effect, to be internationally acceptable assets that, like gold, would be a claim on the world's resources.

Like gold, the SDR's were to be transferable directly among central banks or used by monetary authorities to acquire any international currencies actively traded in exchange markets. The absolute gold guarantee with which the SDR's were endowed would protect the potential surplus countries as long as there was any probability of a rise in the official gold price; for potential deficit countries, the guarantee implied the possibility of a future increase in the burden of their SDR indebtedness.

The establishment of the facility set up the mechanism whereby governments would proceed to supplement reserves as and when they reached a collective decision that it was appropriate to do so. This decision was subject to strong safeguards of a procedural as well as substantive nature.

Some students of international finance had expressed the thought that an international monetary system containing more than one kind of international asset—gold, dollars, reserve positions in the IMF, and SDR's—would be difficult to operate. The difficulty was that so long as there were several assets in which

monetary authorities could keep reserves and so long as the composition might be freely changed by shifting from one kind to another, instability could result. The SDR's might help meet the need for more reserves, but they could not deal with matters of confidence.

Rules were devised to prevent switches from SDR's into gold, but switches from dollars to gold were not banned. To prevent conversions of dollars into gold, schemes were suggested to blend gold, dollars, and SDR's in fixed proportions; to, take dollars out of official reserves by having them turned into deposits on the books of an international institution; or to crown SDR's as the only reserve asset. Schemes like these, however, found little echo outside narrow circles. Governments and central banks were not ready to relinquish freedom of choice with regard to the composition and administration of their nations' monetary reserves.

It appeared that the buildup of the new international reserve assets would be cautious and gradual, for they involved a surrender of present goods, services, and capital assets for claims on the resources of other nations in an indefinite future—for periods short or long, or even "for good." As the old fable goes, the thrifty ant refuses, when the winter comes, to give food to the improvident grasshopper who sings all summer long. Much would, therefore, depend on the confidence of markets as well as of governments in the intrinsic strength and usefulness of the new international monetary facility—confidence that presupposed a degree of orderliness and responsibility in the financial affairs of nations, domestically as well as internationally, that could not be taken for granted.

The Stately Mysteries of the Gold Price. The SDR's—a gold supplement linked to gold—were designed to provide a gradual increase in international reserves on the basis of the $35 gold price. With the basic structure of the international monetary system unchanged except for the divorce of the monetary from the market gold price, the advent of SDR's did not, however, give an answer to the question of whether the present price of gold was appropriate to enable gold to function properly as the keystone of the international monetary system.

The argument is economic—whether or not a rise in the dollar price of gold is in the interest of world trade and growth and, specifically, in the interest of the United States. It is also political, for there is no neat solution to international monetary problems that will not bring about political repercussions. In the ultimate analysis, it is philosophical: some are unwilling to give gold another lease on life through a price rise, on the ground that this would narrow the room for "monetary management" (and this includes fiscal policy). Others are deeply concerned lest people's monetary fortunes come to be entirely dominated by governments.

1. Gold as the Yardstick of Values. Gold, the common yardstick of monetary values, should have an immutable value. A gold price rise would invalidate the role of gold as a fixed point of reference.

There are some counterarguments. The price of gold is an act of government. It is right that governments be unwilling to raise it—aware as they are of, and sharing in, the aversion of a large body of public opinion to the depreciation of money in terms of gold. But much water has flowed under the bridges of the Potomac since Pres. Franklin D. Roosevelt raised the price of gold from $20.67 to $35 an ounce in the early 1930s—as arbitrarily as Henry I chose the distance from the tip of his nose to the tip of his thumb as the measure of a yard.

As a result, the 1968 dollar was worth, in its actual buying power, only 39 cents of the 1934 dollar. A gold upvaluation must not, therefore, be confused with a dollar devaluation. In terms of what it bought, the dollar had already been devalued. This dichotomy between an unchanged monetary gold price and the depreciated buying power of the dollar—so concludes this school of thought—should be remedied by recognizing frankly that the $35 price has become inappropriate and should be raised in an

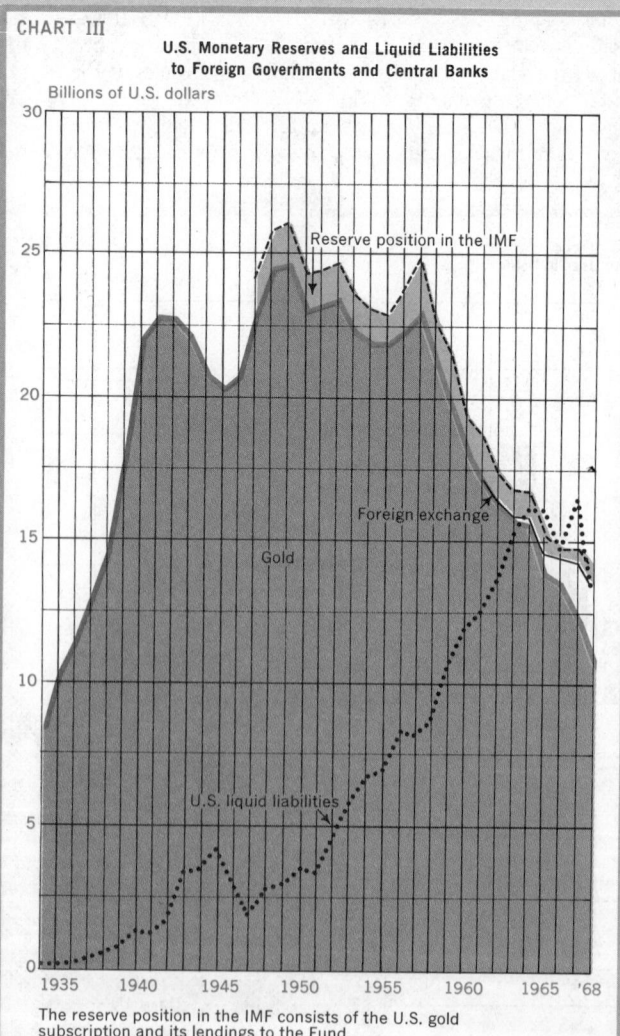

CHART III

U.S. Monetary Reserves and Liquid Liabilities to Foreign Governments and Central Banks

Billions of U.S. dollars

The reserve position in the IMF consists of the U.S. gold subscription and its lendings to the Fund.

orderly manner so that gold could function properly as the most important single form of international reserves.

These considerations in turn raise the question of how large an adjustment in the gold price would be indicated. A small adjustment—10–20%—would not change matters very much. It would arouse expectations that, sooner or later, yet another adjustment would take place. Those who regarded an increase in the gold price as desirable for essential monetary reasons had almost unanimously concluded that any adjustment made should be large.

2. Matter of Politics or Essential Monetary Techniques? A gold price rise would bring about a sudden surge in the purchasing power of current gold output and accumulated reserves. Gold-producing nations (South Africa, the U.S.S.R., etc.), those holding the largest gold reserves and maintaining the highest proportion of gold in their total international reserves (continental Western Europe), and those whose private gold holdings were large (France) would benefit most. Politically speaking, an increase in the dollar price of gold would reward those who had been the least cooperative in international monetary matters and would breach solemn U.S. promises to those who have believed the assurances and held substantial amounts of dollars. What is needed, the argument concludes, is not a sudden surge in international liquidity, arbitrarily distributed, but a gradual expansion, fairly shared—as under the SDR's.

This argument is in turn countered by pointing out that the gold price is not a matter of politics but a matter of essential monetary techniques. A particularly crucial point concerns the increment in the value of current gold output. An expanding world economy requires some gradual increase in world monetary reserves (even if it is evident that the desirable increase does not have to be proportionate to the rate of growth of world trade, since trade is not "financed" by government reserves but by commercial bank credit). In the past, governments built up reserves either by acquiring them from other countries (by transfers of existing gold reserves, but mainly—from 1950 on—as a result of U.S. balance of payments deficits) or, prior to 1965, by obtaining a share in new gold supplies from current output (see Chart II).

As things stood in 1968, the balance of payments targets of all governments taken together—targets exemplified by efforts to bring about steady increases in net monetary reserves—were much larger than the average annual supply of newly mined gold even during those years of the preceding decade when private absorption was relatively small. With a higher gold price, however, there would once again be an appreciable supply from new output available for acquisition by governments—provided, of course, that private demand was kept within bounds in an environment of reasonable monetary stability.

It is often said that the hazards, vagaries, and caprices of gold production are one of the principal reasons why the flows of new gold into official reserves cannot be relied upon to meet fully the world's liquidity needs. Surely, it was to economize on gold that there developed—gradually and organically—the use of internationally acceptable currencies and of international credit. However, despite the fears expressed in recent years—fears that were also voiced in the 1920s and the early 1930s—gold output has made a steady and large contribution to international reserves. Of the total amount of gold ever mined—something like the equivalent of $80 billion at the $35 price—more than three-fourths has been mined during the 20th century; more than half of the total has been mined since sterling was devalued in 1931; and almost one-third has been mined since 1948.

The shortage of monetary gold is, therefore, due to factors other than the failure of physical production: it is due to the cheapness of gold, which is stimulating uses in industry and jewelry—like that of silver until very recently—and makes savings and investment in gold attractive. Fundamentally, the

continued in the article PAYMENTS AND RESERVES, INTERNATIONAL, *on page 591*

continued from page 302

pansionist governments presiding over high employment with inflation coexisted with governments committed to price stability was a crucial factor in international monetary tensions.

Looking forward to 1969, the best that could be hoped for was that the strains and stresses in the world economy would remain within the limits of tolerance.

(M. A. K.)

See also Advertising; Agriculture; Economics; Employment, Wages, and Hours; Housing; Income, National; Industrial Review; Labour Unions; Merchandising; Money and Banking; Payments and Reserves, International; Prices; Stock Exchanges; Trade, International; United States; also articles on various industries.

Ecuador

A republic on the west coast of South America, Ecuador is bounded by Colombia, Peru, and the Pacific Ocean. Area: 109,483 sq.mi. (283,561 sq. km.), including the Galápagos Islands (a dependency of 3,-075 sq.mi.) and excluding claimed territory. Pop. (1967 est.): 5,508,000. Cap.: Quito (pop., 1966 est., 421,600). Largest city: Guayaquil (pop., 1966 est., 645,430). Language: Spanish, but Indians speak Quechuan and Jíbaro. Religion: mainly Roman Catholic. Interim constitutional president until Aug. 31, 1968, Otto Arosemena Gómez; president from September 1, José María Velasco Ibarra.

Elections for the presidency, vice-presidency, and Congress were held on June 2. The presidential elec-

ECUADOR

Education. (1965–66) Primary, pupils 800,507, teachers 21,418; secondary, pupils 62,956, teachers 6,004; vocational, pupils 40,588, teachers 2,446; teacher training, students 13,724, teachers 780; higher (including 9 universities), students 15,395, teaching staff 1,756.

Finance. Monetary unit: sucre, with a par value of 18 sucres to U.S. \$1 (43.20 sucres = £1 sterling) and a free rate (Oct. 14, 1968) of 23.20 sucres to U.S. \$1 (55.50 sucres = £1). Gold and foreign exchange, central bank: (June 1968) U.S. \$60.7 million; (June 1967) U.S. \$65.6 million. Budget (1968 est.) balanced at 4,944,000,000 sucres. Gross national product: (1967) 24.3 billion sucres; (1966) 22,280,000,000 sucres. Money supply: (June 1968) 3,373,000,000 sucres; (June 1967) 3,012,000,000 sucres. Cost of living (Quito; 1963 = 100): (May 1968) 122; (May 1967) 116.

Foreign Trade. (1966) Imports 3,126,000,000 sucres; exports 2,682,000,000 sucres. Import sources: U.S. 39%; West Germany 16%; U.K. 7%; Japan 7%. Export destinations: U.S. 51%; West Germany 14%; Belgium-Luxembourg 6%; Italy 5%. Main exports: bananas 47%; coffee 22%; cocoa 12%.

Transport and Communications: Roads (1965) 16,726 km. Motor vehicles in use (1966): passenger 19,400; commercial (including buses) 21,900. Railways: (1965) 1,340 km.; traffic (1966) 53 million passenger-km., freight 72 million net ton-km. Air traffic (1966): 160,685,000 passenger-km.; freight 2,822,000 net ton-km. Telephones (Jan. 1967) c. 44,000. Radio receivers (Dec. 1966) 650,000. Television receivers (Dec. 1966) 55,000.

Agriculture. Production (in 000; metric tons; 1966; 1965 in parentheses): corn 200 (191); barley c. 95 (93); coffee 58 (66); cocoa 49 (36); bananas 2,954 (3,304); rice c. 200 (157); cassava c. 250 (254); oranges c. 150 (188); sugar, raw value (1967–68) c. 172, (1966–67) 193. Livestock: (in 000; 1965–66): cattle c. 2,100; sheep c. 2,000; pigs 1,650; horses c. 227; chickens c. 5,350.

Industry. Production (in 000; metric tons; 1966): petroleum products 761; crude oil (1967) 294; electricity c. 700,000 kw-hr.; cement 342; gold 10.9 troy oz.; silver 2.4 kg.

tion resulted in a narrow victory for independent candidate José María Velasco Ibarra (with 280,350 votes), closely followed by Andrés Córdova (264,-312 votes), representing centre-left groups, and Camilo Ponce Enríquez (259,833 votes), representing the Movimiento Social Cristiano and centre-right groups. Already four times president of Ecuador, Velasco had long been the dominant politician in his country, but his individualistic policies often failed to attract the major parties. In the elections for the vice-presidency and for Congress the centre-left candidates outpolled their centre-right rivals. After his victory Velasco said he would work with any group that was prepared to support his program of social justice, national progress, and efforts to stimulate the economy.

Ecuador maintained its position as the world's principal banana exporter but, with a further reduction in banana shipments to the U.S. expected in 1968, the country had to continue to diversify its outlets in Europe and Asia. In 1966 Europe had replaced the U.S. as Ecuador's principal market, a trend confirmed in 1967 when exports to the U.S. fell substantially to less than 480,000 tons. The Dirección Nacional de Banano (DNB) estimated that banana exports in 1968 would amount to 1,340,000 tons, compared with 1,270,000 tons in 1967. The DNB forecast that sales to Japan between August 1968 and March 1969 would be double those of the comparable 1967–68 period. In the meantime several Ecuadorean banana exporting firms opened aggressive publicity campaigns in Europe. The first ship built for the Flota Bananera Ecuatoriana (FBE) arrived in Guayaquil in February. Built at Breda, Italy, at a cost equivalent to 90 million sucres, it delivered its first shipment of 200,000 boxes of bananas to Kopek, Yugos., for sale in Italian, Polish, and Yugoslav markets. The president of the FBE announced that Czechoslovakia had agreed to purchase 20,000 tons of Ecuadorean bananas in the 12 months to March 1969. The FBE hoped to reach similar agreements with Yugoslavia, Hungary, Bulgaria, Greece, East Germany, Poland, and the U.S.S.R.

The dramatic development of the oil industry in eastern Ecuador (El Oriente), which began in 1967, continued in 1968 with the drilling of additional exploratory wells and the granting of concessions to eight oil companies; it was estimated that the government would receive about $60 million from the concessions. The government also granted a contract to Cia Petrolera de la Costa to survey the Gulf of Guayaquil for petroleum resources; technical assistance was to be provided by U.S. and U.K. firms. The daily capacity of the first eight wells drilled in El Oriente was estimated at 10,000 bbl., compared with 6,500 bbl. from nearly 900 wells in the Santa Elena Peninsula, formerly the country's principal oil region. By September the Texaco and Gulf Oil companies had begun the drilling of two further exploratory wells in that area. After the minister of industries and trade had denied reports that oil discovered in El Oriente would be carried by a Colombian pipeline, the Texaco-Gulf group contracted with a U.S. company to study a route for a pipeline linking the deposits in El Oriente with the Pacific coast. The pipeline would be about 190–250 mi. in length, and would cost more than $50 million. The government submitted a bill to Congress calling for reforms to the oil law, including increased payments for both exploration and production rights.

Ecumenical Movement:
see Religion

After the sound economic progress achieved in 1967, some less favourable economic trends became apparent in 1968. The international reserves of the Banco Central del Ecuador fell from the record level of $55.9 million reached on Sept. 30, 1967, to $41.1 million on July 31, 1968. A 17.5% rise in bank credit in 1967 helped to precipitate a renewed rise in imports in 1968: the value of import permits liquidated in the first six months of 1968, at $93.8 million, exceeded the previous year's comparable figure by $13.2 million. Fortunately a rise of nearly $8.6 million in the value of export permits granted helped to prevent a dangerous fall in exchange reserves. Since the government faced the prospect of a national accounts deficit of more than 1 billion sucres in 1968 and also had to find 400 million for the repayment of state bonds, a special committee was instructed to study the country's finances and submit proposals to the new Congress that had begun its sessions in September.

In the early summer a serious drought affecting much of the lowlands and inland valleys in the south of Ecuador destroyed or endangered a large portion of the country's cotton, sugar, and rice crops. The combination of these adverse trends, together with doubts about the new government's policies, posed serious problems for Velasco when he began his four-year term of office on September 1. President Velasco subsequently proposed new direct taxes on personal incomes and company profits, and also on certain free-market exchange operations and foreign travel. Furthermore, he stated that he intended to curb the powers of the autonomous state agencies and to reduce their allocations from the national budget. The new president's Cabinet included eight Velasquistas (supporters of Velasco), one Liberal, one Conservative, and two Socialists.   (R. B. Le.)

Education

Student unrest in many parts of the world continued to make news during 1968, and public attention was largely concentrated on the troubles. One reaction to the unrest, however, was significant for the future. Partly to obviate further disturbances and partly because the unrest often did disclose legitimate grievances, those in charge of education began to show a new determination to understand their pupils and to reach agreement with them. In particular, there was some movement away from authoritarian attitudes. At the university level this was seen in a new readiness to accord to undergraduates a measure of self-determination in their courses and their college life. Proposals to bring them in one way or another into the counsels of the universities were common. Below the college level the new spirit was manifested in revision of school organization and curricula to meet the social and vocational demands of the modern age. (*See* Special Report.)

The mood of reappraisal evident in 1968 had been foreshadowed by the International Conference on the World Crisis in Education, which Pres. Lyndon B. Johnson convened at Williamsburg, Va., in late 1967. It was attended by 150 educational leaders from 52 countries and had as joint hosts John W. Gardner, then U.S. secretary of health, education, and welfare, and James A. Perkins, president of Cornell University. Regional reports compiled for the conference and the basic working papers prepared for it by the International Institute for Educational Planning in Paris

brought out the depressing facts of how achievements in education throughout the world fell short of aspirations. There were disturbing statistics of staff shortages and college dropouts, of universities poorly geared to the manpower needs of their nations and of teachers poorly equipped to manage the modern methods of instruction. In his address to the conference, President Johnson pointed squarely to the fundamental gravity of the world situation:

> In the world in which we live today four adults in ten cannot read and write—that is one of the reasons you are here. There are whole regions of the world where eight out of ten people are illiterate; even now, most people end their lives unable to write "cat" or "dog." These are most disturbing facts in the 20th century, in this the richest age that man has ever known. They are facts which, I think, cry out "Shame on the world and shame on its leaders!"

President Johnson noted that when it came to education every nation, including the U.S., was a developing country. In this context, he put the following questions to the conference:

> How can we use what we already know about educational television to accelerate the pace of basic education for all the children of the world? How can we use modern technology to economize on that most essential and most needed educational resource—the good teacher? How can we make the good teacher available to the maximum number of students in the world through television? How can we make the best scholars and teachers in the world available to all the universities wherever they may be, through satellite communications?

His final questions, however, were deeper:

> How can we persuade the governments of one hundred and thirty-one other nations to make it their primary objective to give every boy and girl born anywhere in the world as much education as he or she wants and needs and can absorb? How can we get the world's leaders to convert man's tragic will to destroy into a determination to build? How can we shape a world in which men employ their minds in projects of peace—instead of sacrificing their all, their bodies and their lives, on the field of battle? Can we train a young man's eyes to absorb learning as eagerly as we train his finger to pull a trigger?

The Williamsburg conference considered education from many angles, including its management, its aims and contents, its technologies, resources, and productivity. Central to the conference's conclusions was the proposition "that education is now a central preoccupation of every nation in the world and, further, that educational plans can be carried out with maximum success only if they are made in relation to educational systems and plans in other countries." Education, in short, is a global enterprise. Up-to-date statistics are essential. Every educational system should establish effective machinery to evaluate its own performance on a continuing basis, to seek specific ways for increasing the quantity and quality of educational services within the limits of available resources, and to point the way to needed and promising innovations of every kind.

The uneven spread of education in the world, which was brought home by the Williamsburg conference, was underlined as far as Africa was concerned by a UNESCO conference on education and scientific and technical training in relation to development in that continent, held in Nairobi, Kenya, in July 1968. Reports made there showed that while higher education in some places was expanding at a faster rate than had been expected, expansion of primary and secondary education was falling short of estimates. In particular, African primary schools were losing the battle against illiteracy because they were not keeping up with the growth of population. Figures suggested that of the 5,350,000 African children aged six in 1960, at least 71% would have to be classed as adult illiterates when

they reached the age of 15 in 1969. Nor was the failure merely quantitative. At the 1968 University of East Africa conference on teacher education, held at Mombasa, Kenya, in October and attended by regional officials and overseas experts, it was agreed that the greatest overall need in East Africa was for the qualitative improvement of primary education.

Proposals for Change. In view of all this, it was ironic that by the autumn of 1968 the Soviet Union was announcing plans to introduce elementary military training into the senior classes of secondary schools and the teacher-training colleges. The military training was to be linked with a more complete ideological preparation of the students, and a new textbook published for them included such matters as the role of the Communist Party in relation to the Army. The students were to acquire proficiency in some technical branch of the Army and were to take part in tactical exercises. Instruction was to be provided by officers of the reserve and the schools were to set up storerooms for rifles and other instructional equipment. Girls in the appropriate classes were to be taught ambulance and similar duties. The Ministry of Education maintained that the program would improve discipline and good order in the schools, but it also held that the ideological and psychological training of the pupils to defend the motherland was part of the school curriculum, and that it was the duty of every teacher to foster the interest of his charges in the romance of military service.

Ideology of a different sort was a source of controversy in Britain, where the year brought the long-awaited report of the Public School Commission. This commission, led by Sir John Newsom, had been set up by the government to consider ways of integrating with the state system the independent fee-paying schools, long denounced by progressives as socially divisive. In its first report the commission was concerned with the leading boarding schools, including such famous institutions as Eton, Winchester, and

Columbia University students playing "Trustees," a Monopoly-like game involving real estate owned by the university. The game was a part of the student protests that occurred during the spring of 1968.

A.F.P. FROM PICTORIAL PARADE

UNESCO volunteer
conducting a literacy
class in a village
in India. Only 30%
of the population
of the country age 11
and over could read and
write.

Harrow. Chief among its recommendations was the proposal that suitable schools should offer at least half their places to pupils assisted from public funds. To facilitate this, the schools should relax their entrance standards so that they could take pupils of a wider range of ability than hitherto.

Reactions to the commission's report were lukewarm. The public schools, though anxious to rid themselves of the charge of social divisiveness, saw more clearly perhaps than they had before the practical difficulties of integration, particularly as it would affect their academic standards, and there was some resistance to the commission's suggestion that a Boarding Schools Corporation be set up to administer the integration scheme. On the other side, the local education authorities, already hard pressed for money, looked askance at the cost of the proposals, estimated at £12 million a year when the scheme became fully operational. It was clear that many of them wanted to continue and, if necessary, expand their own arrangements for boarding education, which did in fact often involve sending pupils to independent boarding schools. At its October conference the Labour Party rejected the Newsom report out of hand, and the year ended with renewed fears among the independent schools that the government would seek to weaken their position by taxation, rationing of teachers, and other measures.

There was further progress in Britain away from the principle of selective secondary education and toward a national system of comprehensive schools taking all pupils without regard to ability. There remained, however, some areas of resistance which were encouraged by Conservative victories at the local council elections. The reluctance of some local education authorities to produce reorganization schemes that satisfied the government led to hints at the Labour Party conference that new legislation would compel them to adopt the comprehensive principle. At their own annual conference, the Conservatives condemned suggestions of compulsion and pledged their determination to support Conservative local authorities that sought to preserve their grammar schools.

In Canada, 1968 was remarkable for the publication of a revolutionary report on education, commissioned by the Ontario legislature and prepared over a three-year period by a 21-member commission under the joint chairmanship of Emmett Hall and Lloyd A. Dennis. Starting from the proposition that the underlying aim of education is to further man's unending search for truth, the Hall-Dennis report saw school

life as a unified and continuous process of discovery, beginning with kindergarten and embracing an optional year at the university level at public expense. Any demarcation within the continuum was to be conceived in stages of growth rather than types of school. Activities at the kindergarten stage would be carried over to the primary years, where the emphasis would be on the skills of communication. The junior years (9 to 11) would extend these skills to include environmental interests involving the humanities. An intermediate period (12 to 14 years) would take the pupils on to more direct contact with mathematics, science, and social studies, and in their final years the pupils would select courses of their own choice within the limits of their ability. The curriculum was to be couched in broad statements rather than detailed directives, with the interpretation left to the individual school. The report further proposed the total abolition of all crude punishments and rewards, competitive ratings, marks, examinations, report cards, tracking, and compulsory homework.

While Ontario considered this radical blueprint, the U.S. recorded a further step in the process of racial integration. In September Berkeley, Calif., became the first American city with more than 100,000 inhabitants to desegregate its schools entirely. The city had desegregated its secondary schools four years earlier, and in preparation for the final step teachers had been given special training in the techniques of running classes containing children at widely different stages of educational development. Complete desegregation involved the movement of about 3,500 elementary school children from one district to another by bus, so that the schools might correctly reflect the city's racial balance—about 50% white, 41% black, and 9% Asian and other minorities. The change was not achieved without much continuing resentment on the part of many white citizens, who blamed liberal elements from the Berkeley campus of the University of California for forcing it upon them.

Nor was the movement toward desegregation uniformly smooth elsewhere. One complicating factor, which drew much attention during the year, was the increasing difficulty of providing equal educational opportunities for all American children under the existing arrangements for financing the schools. Since the principal source of support for U.S. schools was local taxation, a child's chances were largely determined by the wealth or poverty of the community in which he lived. These arrangements often put the big cities at a disadvantage. In 1968 the Detroit Board of Education, drawing on precedents in which the U.S. Supreme Court had placed the responsibility for ensuring equal educational opportunities on the state governments, decided to file suit against the State of Michigan for failing to fulfill its obligations.

In the continuing controversy over the relevance of the education being provided in ghetto schools, investigators for the Michigan Board of Education found that 12 American history textbooks widely used in Midwestern schools were seriously deficient in their treatment of minorities in general and blacks in particular. On the constructive side, much educational work was done on television concerning the contributions of blacks to American history. A number of big-city school systems began to provide courses in Afro-American history and culture (and in a few cases in Swahili), although a boycott by black high school students in Chicago was triggered because the students felt that too many of the teachers of these

World Education

Most recent official data

Country	1st level (primary)			General 2nd level (secondary)			Vocational 2nd level			3rd level (higher)			Literacy	
	Students (full-time)	Teachers (full-time)	Total schools	Students (full-time)	Teachers (full-time)	Total schools	Students (full-time)	Teachers (full-time)	Total schools	Students (full-time)	Teachers (full-time)	Total schools	% of population	Over age
Afghanistan	393,276	7,803	2,017	43,925	1,453	240	14,515	713	58	...	...	...	17.7	7–12
Algeria	1,439,268	30,666	4,380	96,337	8,719	329	34,308	4,009	212	4,052	225	19	...	...
Australia	1,740,521	58,300	11,204*	847,818	43,200	...	172,000	...	200	202,000	...	220	...	...
Austria	647,810	28,236	4,896	353,145	21,013	1,204	54,438	5,152	397	55,483	6,369	16	100.	...
Barbados	40,712	1,226	144	22,600	922	99	555	21	3	439	40	2	98.1	5
Belgium	979,626	45,591	9,007	282,629	40,350	1,140	359,396	51,799	2,622	84,000	...	413	99.36	20
Botswana	71,546	1,673	251	1,531	91	9	336	23	3	—	—	—	33.9	10
Brazil	10,695,391	393,001	127,355	2,483,212	157,643	6,698	677,965	57,978	2,897	180,109	36,109	609	66.	11
Burundi	171,870	4,308	945	3,297	...	18	4,268	...	47	258	...	2	...	...
Canada	4,153,250	154,660	17,480	1,043,282	94,050	2,540	303,876	...	1,221	325,832	25,319	468	98.4	10
Central African Republic	148,845	2,650	736	4,645	130	15	972	83	17	—	—	—	39.6	10
Chad	178,699	2,406	740	8,222	284	27	1,126	41	8	188	...	4	12.4	10
Chile	1,853,701	31,145	7,040	128,186	...	593	57,842	...	284	51,153	...	8	16.2	15
Congo (Brazzaville)	194,968	3,264	922	15,939	512	53	3,255	287	35	1,404	137	2	82.33	6–16
Congo (Kinshasa)	2,338,895	61,264	9,230	110,301	2,691	604	36,462	1,261	350	5,827	811	24	...	...
Costa Rica	296,058	11,165	2,235	47,823	3,104	49	4,145	285	92	1,759	533	1	85.69	10
Cuba	1,205,566	35,788	13,999	135,745	8,399	338	80,328	4,483	149	23,284	2,520	27	76.4	...
Cyprus	75,051	2,241	594	30,039	1,170	54	4,071	263	15	168	18	3	81.9	7
Czechoslovakia	2,109,183	97,505	10,966	97,865	6,409	347	189,616	13,796	573	95,872	15,878	35	...	...
Dahomey	132,690	3,302	787	11,961	469	312	...	...	...	53	4	1	22.	12
Denmark	506,014	38,172	2,462	193,041	3,478	75	115,261	...	139	38,218	4,690	13	99.2	8
Dominican Republic	649,073	11,681	4,770	76,079	...	178	2,475	...	10	10,224	612	8	...	...
El Salvador	473,449	12,736	2,936	48,378	2,096	501	21,095	826	307	6,769	633	15	50.8	10
Ethiopia	452,457	9,525	1,712	71,467	3,062	328	8,067	648	68	3,234	464	9	...	...
Finland	508,633	23,070	5,799	294,576	14,838	625	72,531	6,577	270	45,333	4,276	15	100.	8
France	7,460,065	257,558	79,484	2,598,644	188,413	9,942	833,492	20,519	2,682	458,409	19,905	518	100.	7
Gabon	85,328	2,130	647	5,712	246	39	2,172	139	22	70	16	2	20.	13
Gambia, The	15,386	465	94	3,860	148	16	109	10	1	136	11	1	...	...
Germany, East	2,393,617*	...	8,107*	...	...	...	565,470	...	1,334	74,777	...	44	100.	...
Germany, West	5,373,002	155,205	28,452	1,976,742	89,156	4,355	2,132,350	43,493	6,884	330,399	20,838	165	...	...
Ghana	1,423,076	49,092	10,647	50,843	2,985	165	21,796	1,926	188	5,437	714	5	23.4	16
Greece	952,829	26,639	10,256	294,200	9,145	833	7,191	6,035	434	53,305	1,161	27	82.	10
Guatemala	474,919	12,313	4,735	43,570	...	342	15,591	...	388	11,161	129	4	39.8	7
Guinea	164,119	3,990	1,637	17,520	619	35	5,791	345	15	470	115	3	40.	7
Guyana	163,344	5,105	378	20,829	572	57	1,299	54	5	515	45	1	85.	...
Haiti	286,187	5,696	1,654	21,010	1,289	71	6,105	364	27	1,527	...	12	78.	18
Honduras	366,907	10,322	4,087	19,974	29,828	102	1,039	144	9	2,467	...	1	47.3	10
Hungary	1,331,079	62,340	5,866	129,110	8,170	362	98,549	4,413	230	52,407	8,996	91	96.6	7
Iceland	26,979	950	208	11,818	733	113	13,312	310	100	1,180	76	1	99.	8
India	37,357,556	914,120	387,976	28,286,574	929,034	97,321	2,593,862	45,565	262,721	1,735,135	114,092	5,664	30.	11
Indonesia	12,516,159	308,718	51,340	721,244	30,346	1,700	312,188	28,874	1,909	278,000	10,000	355	43.	10
Iran	2,575,667	81,127	15,429	674,058	22,441	1,867	22,966	2,075	231	46,700	3,100	67	30.	7
Iraq	1,019,246	52,380	5,332	254,033	8,663	757	24,941	1,379	72	34,926	1,619	6	38.	14
Israel	557,676	28,212	4,465	68,861	6,470	332	49,678	4,909	326	33,215	5,227	65	...	...
Italy	4,646,024	207,053	40,758	2,239,602	174,346	9,963	1,025,840	77,584	4,224	457,703	12,302	58	91.6	6
Japan	9,452,071	351,416	25,487	10,051,482†	432,018†	16,511†	...	...	...	1,430,775	82,856	888	...	...
Jordan	334,653	8,534	1,249	103,791	4,318	776	3,357	237	16	4,409	242	18	42.	15
Kenya	1,043,416	33,522	5,699	63,193	3,004	400	6,820	527	41	1,147	...	1	35.	15
Korea, South	5,548,577	92,530	5,601	1,286,780	33,012	1,856	207,700	8,201	429	172,410	8,896	222	93.8	11
Kuwait	86,151	10,156	155	694	612	8	2,622	399	5	418	30	1	48.	10
Laos	197,805	5,527	2,959	5,652	352	21	3,739	588	15	483	58	3	66.	6
Lebanon	499,217	23,879	2,504	103,822	2,517	236	14,800	911	206	30,782	1,171	11	87.	14
Lesotho	167,803	3,065	1,077	3,201	170	26	1,014	94	12	301	...	1	...	...
Liberia	110,635	3,137	933	11,324	521	85	1,270	95	3	797	98	3	8.9	10
Libya	224,085	7,530	948	28,167	1,827	157	6,382	553	27	2,737	287	2	24.5	6
Liechtenstein	2,298	77	14	871	51	5	—	—	—	110	26	1	100.	...
Luxembourg	36,700	1,584	444	8,977	415	17	4,700	221	28	...	...	...	99.	7
Malagasy Republic	633,039	8,408	3,478	50,147	1,945	262	...	535	155	4,288	...	8	61.	15
Malawi	300,467	8,104	1,687	7,974	424	51	1,818	187	21	720	93	5	42.	15
Malaysia	1,628,583	52,667	6,330	549,334	20,328	1,063	9,925	342	51	15,813	1,375	28	...	...
Mauritius	136,960	4,110	293	38,293	1,637	141	741	33	6	634	37	2	62.	13
Mexico	6,916,204	148,273	39,057	889,260†	3,984†	...	...	...	...	133,374	...	275	...	...
Monaco	2,065	87	7	1,864	127	5	410	30	7	—	—	—	100.	7
Morocco	1,115,672	31,673	5,910	267,631†	14,267†	332†	...	...	...	7,986	489	15	...	...
Nauru	1,624	95	8	347	25	2	9	1	1	—	—	—	100.	7
Nepal	394,700	13,960	6,319	69,100	3,500	741	...	...	...	10,230	730	35	10.	10
Netherlands	1,495,562	50,579	8,770	547,990	29,788	2,017	341,902	34,000	1,740	144,139	8,000	313	100.	7
New Zealand	500,898	17,983	2,610	168,534	8,356	380	1,355	633	6	23,338	2,031	20	...	...
Nicaragua	251,621	7,269	2,255	26,885	1,397	112	6,496	463	48	5,144	592	5	50.8	10
Nigeria	2,911,742	87,074	14,967	209,645	10,855	1,383	43,572	2,885	258	7,697	1,209	5	...	...
Norway	497,611	22,973	4,246	98,300	5,176	312	71,044	4,977	659	29,300	2,843	25	100.	...
Pakistan	7,050,741	172,953	61,496	2,585,986	94,511	8,953	65,139	3,287	273	277,271	11,392	386	19.2	5
Panama	218,475	6,980	1,618	39,264	1,970	58	21,415	864	122	11,531	427	2	78.3	...
Paraguay	373,230	12,379	2,734	39,422	...	423	...	...	...	6,746	847	36	25.	10
Philippines	5,815,675	185,086	37,581	1,040,814	32,299†	1,884	131,881	...	17	527,047	23,278	527	72.	10
Poland	5,706,270	201,368	26,563	306,135	15,044	862	871,897	50,287	6,799	178,145	25,565	76	97.3	7
Rhodesia	724,395	20,159	3,351	42,484	3,665	165	3,634	266	48	1,433	236	4	...	...
Romania	1,444,558	55,412	7,267	1,833,277	92,816	8,309	340,997	18,769	954	141,589	13,792	47	...	...
Rwanda	345,654	5,281	2,017	6,199	595†	49	2,316	...	34	162	51	2	...	...
San Marino	2,041	129	33	1,480	41	3	—	—	—	—	—	—	...	...
Sierra Leone	136,570	4,300	939	22,119	1,107	66	1,851	120	13	818	191	2	10.	10
Singapore	379,828	12,705	498	129,743	5,268	115	21,894	1,311	23	8,028	700	5	80.	7
Somali Republic	30,154	1,004	237	10,454	311	94	1,752	187	16	622	21	1	60.	7
Spain	4,025,244	117,067	113,790	969,898	33,872	3,175	330,614	18,884	1,148	143,560	9,659	34	97.5	15
Sudan	518,261	10,612	3,430	128,057	5,741	810	6,350	595	47	9,474	787	8	17.1	10
Swaziland	59,287	1,539	349	3,792	232	31	294	42	3	...	...	...	29.4	15
Sweden	643,900	27,700	4,900	378,700	32,600	330	152,000	15,300	800	97,592	...	35	...	...
Switzerland	577,055	21,762	...	142,987	6,583	...	15,806	...	...	33,430	1,069	10	100.	16
Syria	723,153	20,119	4,810	193,597	8,025	633	6,616	841	43	31,770	827	3	44.	10
Taiwan	2,348,218	55,683	2,208	640,447	23,706	458	144,866	7,153	142	138,613	7,564	79	6.64	13
Tanzania	790,468	15,879	4,484	32,276†	275†	116†	...	...	...	740	...	3	...	...
Thailand	4,648,142	154,449*	27,579*	316,238	...	...	67,975	7,320	229	34,781	3,788	7	70.8	10
Togo	157,548	3,031	811	12,589	488	58	1,062	102	10	85	8	...	30.	8
Trinidad and Tobago	225,433	...	608	37,533	...	115	2,943	...	39	286	...	6	61.	5
Turkey	6,509,633	102,061	33,369	757,883	27,363	1,567	203,512	12,887	881	126,039	6,727	89	68.72	6
Uganda	641,639	19,257	2,648	35,617	1,471	116	7,250	640	52	1,860	216	1	...	...
U.S.S.R.	37,581,000	1,417,000	218,000	4,182,000	231,000	...	3,326,000	...	3,717	3,608,000	...	754	...	...
United Arab Republic	3,459,496	88,095	7,958	821,121	34,925	1,475	177,313	14,470	291	143,024	6,205	60	35.	10
United Kingdom	5,483,764	190,974	28,315	3,420,843	184,248	7,256	237,476	46,310	937	260,702	46,310	9	...	...
United States	32,327,475	1,152,451	92,584	17,227,580†	848,894†	30,882†	...	...	...	4,438,606	334,000	2,329	97.6	14
Upper Volta	97,360	1,862	587	8,728	363	37	1,231	108	10	58	8	1	...	...
Venezuela	1,559,633	45,637	10,700	230,371	9,941	628	119,643	5,806	342	54,540	5,692	11	73.	18
Vietnam, South	1,785,841	30,880	5,937	429,638	10,811	644	10,279	513	32	31,643	807	26	...	...
Western Samoa	25,596	790	154	8,609	323	38	61	17	1	277	27	3	95.	16
Yugoslavia	2,945,520	101,478	14,146	177,237	7,863	388	434,034	19,006	1,342	121,824	10,094	7	80.3	10
Zambia	608,893	11,986	2,517	42,388	1,917	110	4,293	284	14	844	198	2	33.	21

Note: Third level may include individual faculties within a university.
*Primary and secondary combined.
†General and vocational combined.

Fifteen thousand New York City teachers and parents marching around City Hall on Sept. 16, 1968, in a mass rally supporting the strike by the teachers.

WIDE WORLD

courses were white. Mrs. Elizabeth D. Koontz, a teacher of educable mentally retarded children at Salisbury, N.C., was installed as the first Negro president of the National Education Association (NEA), the major union of the American teaching profession.

By contrast, the Rhodesian government in 1968 disclosed rules for multiracial sporting events under which a school had to seek permission from the Ministry of Education for any games against teams with

nonwhite players, and had to allow any of its pupils who so wished to refrain from participating. In Britain the opening of the 1968–69 school year in September was marked by several sensational reports, particularly from the Midlands, of friction when white parents found that their children had been put into classes with heavy concentrations of coloured pupils.

Another educational controversy in Britain related to corporal punishment. There was another report of allegedly excessive caning in a school for juvenile delinquents, and the headmaster in question was dismissed after a Home Office inquiry. The case reinforced the arguments of those who were demanding that corporal punishment be abolished throughout the British educational system. In Cardiff, Wales, a ban on the use of the cane in primary schools was introduced, but it was lifted after protests from the teachers. Edward Short, former headmaster, who succeeded Patrick Gordon Walker as secretary of state for education and science, made it clear that in his view this was a matter for the teaching profession itself.

By contrast, corporal punishment was banned in all Greek schools by the Greek government in 1968 as being an anachronism and contrary to modern educational practice. With the 1967–68 school year Denmark, too, had instituted new regulations removing the last traces of corporal punishment from its schools, thus making the ban on caning complete throughout Scandinavia. Pres. H. Kamuzu Banda of Malawi had a different view. He declared that young people overseas were pampered too much. "In Malawi," he said, "a child must be taught respect for his elders. If he does not listen, whip him. It doesn't do him any harm."

Teachers. Another controversy that embroiled British teachers in 1968 concerned school meals. In the autumn of 1967 the National Union of Teachers emphasized its dissatisfaction over a recent pay award by instructing its members in selected areas to resist the regulations by which teachers could be required to supervise school meals. This led to the breakdown of the meals service in some places and to some ac-

Increase in Student Population Since 1950			
COUNTRY	YEARS	STUDENTS	PERCENT INCREASE
United States	1950	2,296,592	240
	1965	5,526,325	
U.S.S.R.	1950	1,247,382	289
	1964	3,608,400	
Japan	1950	390,817	252
	1964	985,077	
China (Communist)	1950	138,731	591
	1962	820,000	
France	1950	139,593	326
	1964	455,111	
W. Germany	1950	134,700	208
	1964	281,332	
Italy	1950	145,170	180
	1964	261,358	
United Kingdom	1950	133,756	168
	1964	225,960	
Czechoslovakia	1950	43,809	323
	1965	141,687	
E. Germany	1951	27,822	271
	1964	75,578	

Source: *UNESCO Statistical Yearbook* (1966).

tual closures of schools. Subsequently, agreement was reached between the teachers and the local education authorities that compulsory supervision should be ended, though it was clear that the voluntary help of many teachers would still be required if the meals service was to be maintained. The amended regulations operated from the beginning of the 1968–69 school year, and it became clear at once that unexpectedly large numbers of teachers were refusing to undertake any duties connected with the meals service.

The school meals controversy illustrated the continuing concern of teachers with their status, salaries, and conditions of work. In South Africa J. R. Dick, president of the Transvaal Teachers' Association, called for a teachers' register similar to that of the medical and other professions. In Japan the teachers' union, estimated to be the largest union in the country, was opposing government proposals to pay teachers a lump sum for overtime rather than the hourly rate and to place head teachers on an administrative level that would in effect take them out of the union. In France teachers in secondary and technical schools staged token strikes in February to protest against overcrowded classes and the employment of underpaid part-time teachers and teachers without proper qualifications. The teachers, backed by many parents, demanded an increased number of teaching posts and the introduction of a rule that no one should teach more than 15 hours a week. The parents in their turn protested against government plans for tracking children toward particular subjects and careers.

Dissatisfaction among teachers and parents was also rife in the U.S. Some of the militancy among the teachers reflected the power struggle between the two rival unions, the NEA and the American Federation of Teachers. In February nearly half the public school teachers in Florida struck, in protest against poor salaries and the low spending on education in general. Pittsburgh, Pa., San Francisco, Oklahoma, South Dakota, and Albuquerque, N.M., also experienced teachers' strikes in the early part of the year. In the autumn New York City was the scene of a complicated dispute involving an experiment in community control of the predominantly nonwhite Ocean Hill-Brownsville school district. The community organization in charge of the district attempted to remove several white teachers, and the union, fearing for the safety of teachers' tenure should the community control movement spread, struck the entire city school system for five weeks. Since many of the teachers were Jewish, the controversy developed unpleasant racial and religious overtones. Community control of local schools within big-city systems was being supported in some quarters as a possible way to meet the criticism that ghetto schools were neglected.

The agitation sometimes brought results. In France Edgar Faure (see BIOGRAPHY), the minister of education, took advice from a commission that included representatives of teachers, parents, and educational bodies as well as 12 boys and girls attending lycées. The outcome was a new system for the governing bodies of schools under which the governors were to be composed of three groups, roughly equal in size, covering the administration and distinguished people; employees of the school, including the teachers; and pupils and parents. Florida Gov. Claude Kirk abandoned an undertaking not to raise taxes and signed a $254 million appropriation for schools.

continued on page 316

YOUTH IN REVOLT

By John R. Seeley

Aspectre is stalking America.

It is the more fearsome because, unlike the spectre of Communism that Marx saw stalking Europe in 1848, it has no single name, form, or seeming unity. It is sighted now here, now there, now in this guise, now in that. It eludes or defies precise description. To call it the "revolt of youth" or the "rebellion of the young" or the "generation gap" is simply to stretch old terms to cover new events. What we see lends itself as uneasily to traditional thoughtways as insurgency and guerrilla warfare do to traditional military analysis. Bob Dylan's haunting, mocking "Something is happening here/ But you don't know what it is/ Do you, Mr. Jones?" sends shivers of appreciation down the backs of the young and chills of fear down the spines of the old.

Not only America is thus haunted. Similar spectres appear almost everywhere, shaking the security of states and testing the strength of societies. Everywhere some considerable part of the young is aligned against some considerable part of the old, in struggles increasingly sensed to be life and death matters. What is manifest in America is at least latent elsewhere. The degree of similarity turns on the degree to which other nations also possess a technological society and mounting material affluence, ostensibly "beyond ideology" because the ideology of technology is the unquestioned criterion for all action. We may consider America as providing the clearest case in hand.

War on Youth. The weightiest testimony to the emergence of something among the young that commands the overwhelming preoccupation of the old is evident in the actions of the state. The state massively mobilizes itself only against something that is assumed to be a serious enemy of the going order. Increasingly, the most dramatic and widespread use of authorized force and fraud at home is against youth. Age warfare has seemingly superseded class warfare and race warfare and the earlier petty warfares on organized crime and dissident ideas. The young have thus succeeded to the title of "public enemy number one."

All wars have been, in a sense, wars on youth, since the young furnish the soldiery that the old require. But formerly the two counterposed youthful armies were largely commanded and partly manned by the elders. What is now emergent is an array of the young, self-commanded or uncommanded, thrown against the mobilized, organized forces of official society. Even in the ghetto wars, where the picture is most blurred, increasingly the elders lose their hold and the action and its direction pass primarily to the young.

The assaults against this array of youth are coming more and more to resemble those against an external enemy. They range from large-scale armed action to the subtlest psychological warfare. The armed assaults of 1968 include Columbia University, the city of Berkeley, San Francisco State College, Haight-Ashbury (over and over again), Tompkins Square in New York City, Chicago during the Democratic convention—a long roster of cities large and small, campuses famous and unrememberable, and the little hippie communes and hiding places in the Western mountain gaps and eastward across the land. The engagements—sometimes small military set pieces, sometimes fluid guerrilla warfare—involve now military forces (not excluding elite formations) and now the new police forces transformed into para-

military organizations, making use of tanks, helicopters, gas masks, plastic personnel shields, and bullet-resistant vests.

As with an external enemy, the tactics move toward those of terror—massive, gratuitous, sometimes permanently injurious beating of the already captured and wholly subdued or of innocent bystanders and reporters. A whole new technology and industry are being developed and employed, and a literature, both theoretical and practical, flourishes. Cattle prods, which but a few short years ago served Southern sheriffs well enough, are succeeded by gases, foams, dyes, sound generators, and sophisticated arrays of firepower. Even the strategies come to resemble the external ones: the search-and-destroy operations against Haight-Ashbury, for instance; the hit-and-run bombing directed indifferently at all abroad on the streets from speeding police vehicles in Berkeley; and the "hammer and anvil" operations, now virtually standard.

The wanton brutality and its visitation on the wholly innocent is no accident; it is, in intent and effect, a strategy of terror. Mere proximity to a protest action is sufficient to bring down the direst consequences. As in German-occupied Europe in World War II, or in Algeria later, the object is to isolate and separate the enemy so that his destruction by the state can be more efficiently accomplished.

But violence and battle aside, the hostile designs of the state upon the young are evident in the connected series of state schemes labeled "Selective Service," "channeling," and "Universal Voluntary National Service." The first two are in operation; the last, in design. Each scheme is more general and embracing than the one before. Taken together, they assert the right and intent of the state to place, use, and dispose of the manpower that youth is to furnish for ends that the state may deem fit. Formal studies continue in an attempt to determine what stick-and-carrot combination would be least likely to provoke massive resistance until too late.

Nor are the planned and unplanned operations of state-dominated institutions limited to acts so overt. More and more, institutions give the young the sense of being "processed"—readied, shaped, and trimmed for conventional uses—of being prepared for a slot into which each must fit, and this pressure is felt earlier in life every year. The feel of the "total institution," common to boot camp, prison, and asylum, comes more and more

noticeably to mark the high school and even the earlier grades. Diffuse resentment is followed by widespread discussion, and then the first faint beginnings of counterorganization: underground newspapers and resistance cells. Self-identification with other oppressed minorities and resistance begin to show themselves at ever and ever younger ages and at a logistically increasing rate.

Who Is the "Enemy"? It is time to turn from the mobilization to that which is mobilized against. Is it a unitary enemy? Or is there only a set of unrelated wars: against hippies, ghetto blacks, seekers of student power, peace advocates, civil-rights protagonists, blowers of pot and droppers of acid, those whose sole distinction is sex-atypical hair length, and self-conscious young politicians of a more or less traditional stamp?

The answer is that the whole movement does have important common properties, but it is not fully a unity, even in the loose sense in which the major political parties are unities. When the range at a given age level extends from "hippies," Free People, and Diggers, through "hippie politicos," to "politicos" with universal or restricted, cosmopolitan or parochial reform programs, radical or otherwise, the difficulty of perceiving the unity in diversity is critically increased.

The level at which the unity lies cannot be ideological or programmatic or organizational. Only when the whole is viewed as a social movement can one see the similarity below the differences.

Clearly the most universal common characteristic is the sense of being outside and in opposition to the mainstream society. Closely associated is the conclusion that the differences involved are radical and irreconcilable. The other society is held to be alien—as well as alienated and alienating: alien, *their* society; alienated, divorced from its own once-high ethic; alienating, severing those who remain "in" it from their most vital selves, from each other, from nature, and from life. Thus the moral judgment that anything "out" is better than anything "in." And hence, in part, the sense of loose alliance. Equally widespread is the belief that this society is doomed, and that its being doomed demands that those who so see it prepare the successor society. Equally pervasive is the belief that the society in its death throes will eschew no measures, even to the mass devouring of its own, to extend its survival span. The anticipations of

hippies seeking only to build and preserve tiny communes of love in the dry niches of the ecological net in no wise differ on this point from the premonitions of those activists who have blown power lines, torn telephone cables, or thrown Molotov cocktails at police.

Again, in common, all hold to a tremendous sense of urgency: "Freedom Now!" (1960) yields to "Power Now!" (1964) which in turn gives way to "Revolution Now!" (1968). The meanings of the three key words remain fudged and fleeting, but the "Now!" retains its insistence and force. Also universal are identification with and action on behalf of others oppressed, at home or abroad. There is a tremendous feeling of responsibility for procuring the "needed" changes personally; a belief that this can only be done by active, first-hand participation in "the revolution." And universal is the belief that the human and humane potential, the possibilities of individuation and growth, the capacities for creation and joy have been so untapped and unappreciated in Western society—indeed have been so markedly "cabin'd, cribb'd, confin'd"—that a joyous explosion into a full humanity is possible and imminent for the first time in the history of the West.

Beyond this point, what has been viewed thus far as one social movement begins, characteristically, to divide deeply—without, however, losing the capacity to act as an alliance (as in the Pentagon affair of October 1967 or the Berkeley street affair of June–July 1968). "Affinity groups" permit persons or groups differing in many respects to act together upon a fellow feeling transcending differences.

Paramount among the divisions—again classic for a social movement with essentially redemptive or religious overtones—is that between the quietist and the activist wings. The underlying doctrinal issue is a familiar one in Western thought.

Broadly speaking, the quietists—the hippies and their numerous next-of-kin—take the doctrinal stand that insists that good institutions cannot be built by bad or unenlightened men; that personal reconstruction must accompany, if not precede, political or social reconstruction; that the lines of policy appropriate for secondary groups cannot be determined before better ways of living in primary groups (pads, communes, "tribes") are found; that the test of social life must be its effect on personal and primary group life; that the goodness of primary group life must be judged by the degree to which it favours love, spontaneity, and wisdom—as against, say, justice, order, and competence; and that these aims are assisted by access to extraordinary states, horrific or ecstatic, produced by any means from ancient religious practices to modern chemicals, light shows, highly amplified music, or nude dancing. Their rejection of ideology, organization, "leadership," conventional discussion, "spiritually unsuitable jobs," argument, agitation, enduring or relatively permanent association, and their espousal of voluntary poverty, propertylessness, harmlessness, nonviolence, an endless inner search (more on the model of the East than of the West) are corollaries of their primary theorems.

On the other wing of the movement—the activists—we have almost the opposite of these views: preoccupation with the realities of power; more inclination to let the reform of men follow the reform of institutions; more emphasis on intellectual clarification first; more reliance on modern technology to use persuasion to procure power over events; more willingness to attempt the organization and discipline traditionally held necessary for large-scale action directed toward a more traditional kind of revolution: the supersession of one elite by another.

Much of the movement's energy is consumed in attempts to integrate or reconcile these differences and their associated implications for ways of being and doing in the world. Those most concerned with the maintenance of the going order may properly take as little comfort from these divisions as responsible Romans should have taken from the endless squabbles among pre-Constantine bishops. Those squabbles did not prevent the church from becoming the successor to the Romans' glory.

The Conditions of Revolt. No one can state exactly what circumstances give rise to a movement such as this. Some of the conditions leading to it have been cataloged often enough: sufficient affluence to assure the nonstarvation even of "outlaws"; elaborate and virtually instant communications facilities; widespread knowledge of an analytic and critical literature "exposing" men and society, especially American; literacy and, despite criticisms against the school system, sufficient education to make such a literature comprehensible; the spread of child-raising methods that foster independence in the young.

But these conditions alone do not account for the depth and force of the movement: the emergence of a different society and culture, a counterposed moral order among the young. Nor do such relatively short-term exacerbations as the war in Vietnam, the draft, military service, the nuclear threat, or even the surfacing of the black-white conflict explain the situation. They add their weight, but only as they are seen—as type-products of the society.

The thrust of the movement's critique, and that which lends force to the action and the sense of irreconcilability to the issues, is that these—and larger matters such as the drift of war toward biocide; the mindless spoliation of nature and probable poisoning of the environment; the total corruption of men's minds by mass propaganda in small matters and large; the progressive alienation, constriction, and truncation of the human being in such a society; the dominance of technological thought-ways in which means float free of or determine ends—are the climactic, characteristic, and inseparable results (and, in a sense, aims) of the existing order. The indictment is drawn not in terms of reversible deviations from a right path, but in terms of persistence to a path so patently bound for hell on earth that a fresh beginning by new men, based on entirely new assumptions and with entirely different aims, is required—and inescapable.

The Shape of the Future. The terms "revolution," "revolt," "rebellion" fit the facts but poorly, though the movement—like the 16th-century religious movements, particularly the "minor" Protestant sects—may well result in all of these. What we witness, if it survives—if it is not extinguished, as is entirely possible, in fire and blood—may be the beginning of a transformation of society, more closely analogous to the Reformation or the Renaissance or the spread of Hellenistic culture or Christianity than to a revolution on the French, American, or Russian models. The catholic, apocalyptic, and chiliastic overtones and undertones are evident. The message is not alone for Americans, let alone Americans of any one class, colour, or condition, but for all men in the Western cultural sphere.

It is this that makes assimilable under a common rubric the anti-Communist movements in those countries where Communism is paramount and the anticapitalist movements in those areas where capitalism holds sway. The two systems are essentially identical with respect to that which the movement opposes most determinedly: mass, technological, "rationalized," bureaucratized, centrally controlled, conquest- and control-oriented, militarized, order-obsessed society, society that dehumanizes its subjects, reducing them to mindless, soulless serfs and servants of things or of plans having the impersonal force of things. The challenge of the movement to Communism and capitalism alike reaches far beyond their challenges to each other.

Only a prophet of incredible imprudence would extrapolate from this to the future. At most, one might allow oneself a compound contingency statement: if lovers of "continuity" and "evolution" continue to meet the new movement with the hitherto standard intellectual incomprehension and politically dictated distortion, if they continue to believe that they can rely principally on force and fraud to crush it, they will soon be faced with the ugly choice between complete regression to a military state for the sake of containment or an equally unwelcome massive disjunctive break in the social, moral, political, and cultural orders. The moments in which choice is possible tick by relentlessly—if they have not already ticked away.

continued from page 313

In South Africa a memorandum to the minister of education from the National Council of Women complained that married women were paid as junior teachers even when they held senior posts, could not receive promotion, and were ineligible for pensions. In Canada the machinery by which exchange teachers were brought from Britain came under criticism, particularly because differences of salary, in spite of some adjustments, put the British visitor at a great disadvantage. On a brighter note in Canada, the Prince Edward Island Department of Education introduced a scheme of one-year sabbatical leave on half-pay.

Curricula. But what of the content of education in 1968? Chief among the curricular matters claiming attention during the year was the position of science in schools. In Britain a working party under F. S. Dainton, vice-chancellor of Nottingham University, reported in February that there was a swing away from science in the schools of England and Wales— a situation that obtained in several other European countries as well. It was estimated that the number of sixth-form pupils taking science would fall from 40,000 in 1964 to 30,000 in 1971 while total enrollment in the sixth form increased from 107,000 to 130,-000. The working party warned that this was a serious threat to science and technology. Chief cause of the drift was the number of pupils who dropped mathematics at or before they were 16, thus barring themselves from science at the university. The working party recommended that all pupils should study mathematics until they left school, that school science courses should be made more up-to-date and relevant, that strong incentives should be offered to science graduates to encourage them to enter teaching, and that extra pay should be given to teachers who completed refresher courses.

The Dainton report found an echo in South Africa. There were complaints at a meeting of the National Association of Scientists in Johannesburg that because of poor science teaching in the schools the country was in danger of losing a great part of its scientific potential in the coming decade. In the Land of Hesse, W.Ger., where over 250 posts for science teachers remained unfilled, it was agreed that the existing science teachers should be allowed to do a limited amount of paid overtime.

Teaching aids of all sorts continued to be developed during 1968. In Australia the school of the air at Alice Springs, which provided radio lessons for children isolated on remote farming stations, was enlarged and improved by an anonymous gift of A$23,000. September saw the start of ETV London, an educational television service that was expected to become the largest closed circuit network in the world by 1969. Nearly 200 programs were scheduled for the

first year of operation, including a series for eight-year-old beginners in French.

Handicapped children were not neglected. Representatives of special teachers from 13 European countries, meeting at Norrköping, Swed., in September, called on UNESCO to inquire into the needs of such children and their teachers. The meeting brought out a number of issues. While most delegates saw the special teacher as one of a team working for the benefit of all the children, there was some feeling that where special education was part of the general system it tended to suffer under any economic squeeze. There was also much discussion about the age of entry to teacher training, and whether or not it should be undertaken only after considerable experience with normal children. An Interim Committee for European Special Education was formed at the conference.

Meanwhile, two significant announcements were made elsewhere in the world. In July Leonid Brezhnev, first secretary of the Communist Party of the Soviet Union, told a national congress of Soviet teachers that the school could not stand aloof from politics and the class struggle. The Communist outlook, he said, had to be inherent in a Soviet citizen, and teachers were responsible for the graduation of politically versed, ideologically convinced fighters for the Communist cause. In China in August Chairman Mao Tse-tung instructed workers and peasants to take over and run the schools and universities. Demonstrations throughout China marked the announcement, which was designed to end the domination of Chinese education by intellectuals of bourgeois origin.

Universities. These announcements were perhaps exceptional. But beyond the confused picture of world university affairs in 1968, created by student unrest and the varying moves to allow greater student participation, there could be discerned a definite preoccupation of politicians and academics with their relationship and with the relevance of the university to the state. At one extreme, the military regime in Greece dismissed 49 university professors in January in what it described as a move to modernize the educational system and to eliminate elements hostile to the social and political regime and its basic institutions. At the other extreme was the increasing concern of the politicians that the university should give value for money, a concern heightened in some places by reports critical of university efficiency. Thus in May it was revealed that a special mission of the Organization for Economic Cooperation and Development had described the Italian university system as out of date and faulty.

Vision control room of ETV London which began broadcasting on Sept. 16, 1968. Three hundred schools, colleges, and institutes in east and northeast London received the station's educational programs on seven channels.

In Britain a study published by the Department of Education and Science, prepared by M. C. McCarthy of the petrochemical and polymer laboratory at Imperial Chemical Industries Ltd., suggested that the training of five out of six science and technology graduates from British universities was likely to be out of date within a few years of graduation. The education of a student, it was pointed out, had to fit him for work in areas of science and technology that might be unknown when he took his degree. Unlike scientific education in the U.S., where specialization generally occurred only during postgraduate work, scientific education in Britain often involved specialization at both the undergraduate and postgraduate academic levels.

In Africa there were complaints from the press and from local politicians that the universities were not playing their full part in nation building. In particular, the constituent colleges of the University of East Africa faced criticism—which they rebutted—for ivory-tower attitudes and for their high proportions of expatriate staff. Relevant here perhaps was an opinion expressed by V. E. King, dean of the faculty of education at Njala University College, Sierra Leone, at the Commonwealth universities congress in Sydney, Austr., in August. Academics, he said, tended to think that politicians were fools and politicians tended to regard academics as highbrow theorists. As a remedy he suggested that universities should place more emphasis on research projects designed to help governments solve pressing problems.

Some governments did initiate improvements. In Italy a University Reform Bill was passed in September, which among other things increased the number of state awards at the universities, though it was admitted by the government to be inadequate. In France, against much opposition from the Paris bureaucracy and some conservative academics, Edgar Faure introduced a university bill based on the principles of academic autonomy, student-teacher participation, and educational diversity, in contrast to the state-controlled, uniform system that existed. In South Africa in September the government appointed a commission of general inquiry into the country's universities. Earlier, the Canadian government had announced a commission to study the role of the university in society.

Meanwhile, university development continued. The Norwegian Storting (parliament) agreed that there should be new universities at Tromsø and Trondheim and that Oslo University should establish a professorship of peace and conflict research. In Madagascar the University of Tananarive was inaugurated. The University of Bombay, with a grant of over Rs. 9 million from the University Grants Committee, made plans to set up new departments for Marathi, Gujarati, Hindi, history, education, biology, and journalism and to introduce a new bachelor's degree in journalism and a master's degree in chemical engineering. In South Africa the University of Pretoria planned a medical course for the general practitioner leading to a master's degree in family medicine, while the University of Port Elizabeth announced the launching of a fund to set up a chair of aviation. The South African prime minister announced that the five segregated colleges for African, Coloured, and Asian students were to be given full university status. In France the University of Paris set about accommodating 35,000 extra students by the end of the year, with eight new university campuses in the Paris area and extensions to the existing campuses at Orsay and Nanterre. The University of Guyana at Georgetown, founded in 1963, awarded its first degrees to 31 students.

In Northern Ireland the new University of Ulster at Coleraine, County Londonderry, enrolled its first 400 students. It would accommodate 5,000 to 6,000 students when its three-stage building program was completed. Argument continued over the allocation of studies between Trinity College and University College, Dublin, initiated by the Irish government's proposal to associate the two colleges in a newly constituted University of Dublin. Contracts were signed for the construction of a new University of Libya. Designed by a London firm of architects, it was to be built just outside Bengasi by a Yugoslav consortium. With the capture of the Old City of Jerusalem by the Israelis in June 1967, the Hebrew University of Jerusalem regained its original home on Mount Scopus, from which it had been cut off for 20 years. Plans were being made to establish the Truman Foundation for the Advancement of Peace and an institute of adult education dedicated to the memory of Martin Buber. In February it was announced that Britain was to give £575,000 toward the cost of a new science building at the University of Ife in Western Nigeria and another £50,000 for its equipment. Ironically, a six-month moratorium on university building in Britain was imposed by the Treasury in August because of the country's economic difficulties. The University of Cape Town, S.Af., established an Institute for Inter-Racial Studies, while Latin-American specialists meeting at the University of Guelph, Ont., took the first steps toward setting up an Ontario Institute for Latin American Research.

The relationship between higher education and the military made news during the year. The University of Maryland celebrated the 20th anniversary of the program by which it offers courses carrying college credits to American servicemen stationed abroad. Since 1948 the program had attracted 500,000 students at over 130 centres in Western Europe, Africa, and the Middle East. In Vietnam it was reported that the war had forced Hanoi to abandon a project for a university at a Viet Cong base in the jungle near Saigon, said to have been planned over some years and to have involved the sending to South Vietnam of a staff of 300 intellectuals. In the U.S., Columbia and Yale said that they would consider for readmission graduate students who went to jail in protest against the draft laws on the same basis as those who had finished their military service. Harvard left the matter to the individual deans. In Australia the universities were disturbed over sections of the new National Service Act under which they could be required to give information about students who might be liable for service. The Australian Vice-Chancellors Committee issued a statement saying that disclosure of such information might seriously prejudice good relations between the universities and their students.

Problems and Developments. The choice of a language for instruction continued to be a source of controversy in various parts of the world. In India the argument as to whether English or some local tongue should be used went on unabated and was a frequent cause of student disturbances. A similar controversy continued in Ceylon. In Canada, French-speaking and English-speaking students demonstrated and counterdemonstrated in New Brunswick, while in Ontario the government promised that state-supported secondary schools would be opened in areas with large

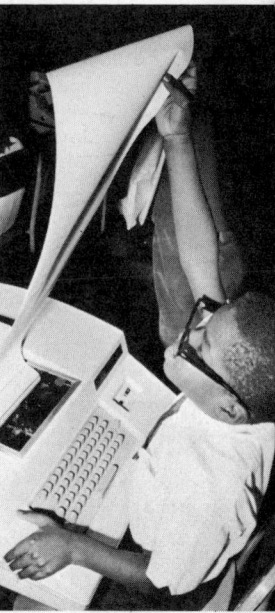

UPI COMPIX

Pupil at P.S. 244 in New York City using a new desk computer system introduced in March 1968. The system provided drill and practice at a level appropriate to each student's capabilities.

Students of the Guildford School of Art in London demonstrating for increased student representation in the formation of school policies.

UPI (UK) LTD.

French-speaking populations. At Pontypridd, Wales, a centre was opened, financed by the education authorities, to supply Welsh-language teaching materials throughout the principality. The new Rand Afrikaans University was opened at Johannesburg, S.Af., as a counterpart to the nearby English-speaking University of the Witwatersrand.

The major news about language, however, came from Belgium. In February the government of Paul Vanden Boeynants resigned after it had failed to resolve a bitter controversy over the Roman Catholic University of Louvain. The Flemish members of Vanden Boeynants' Social Christian Party—resisted by the French-speaking Walloons—were exerting pressure to remove the French-speaking section of the university from the Flemish-speaking section of the country. In July the Court of Human Rights in Strasbourg ruled that the Convention on Human Rights was not infringed by the Belgian language laws, which divided the country into two unilingual sections plus bilingual Brussels and refused any state subsidy to French-speaking schools in the Flemish-speaking area.

In the field of technical education it became more and more difficult to detect and define boundaries. The growing interdependence of education and national economies tended to blur the lines of demarcation between different sorts of educational institutions, and because of the growing prestige of technical education it was claimed by them all. The Latin-American countries provided an instance of this. In 1968 the Union of Latin American Universities, covering over 80 major institutions of higher learning, was giving special attention to the establishment of short courses designed to train students as nongraduate, semiprofessional, and technical assistants. The Mexican National University was already giving such courses, offering a technical diploma, under certain conditions, to students who could not complete a degree course.

Britain provided further instances of this trend. With the colleges of advanced technology already promoted to university status, the government went ahead with its plans to form a series of major technical institutions or polytechnics out of some existing colleges or groups of colleges. Individual industries were setting up machinery for training their employees, as required by the Industrial Training Act. And the Council for National Academic Awards was busy examining and approving courses leading to its university-standard degrees at institutions outside the universities. Meanwhile, the universities themselves were busy providing technical courses. Thus at the start of the year the new University of Bradford, itself originally a college of advanced technology, announced what was said to be Britain's first course for senior business executives on business strategy and policy forming. There was some argument, however, about the siting and the constitution of the new polytechnics and about the effect they would have on the work and prestige of smaller institutions, as well as about the content of studies. Nor was everything satisfactory with the Industrial Training Act. Many of the training boards showed large surpluses of income over expenditure, suggesting either that the compulsory levy on firms was too high or that many firms were paying the levy but not bothering to provide the training.

Things were different in the U.A.R., judging by a report issued in the spring by the International Labour Organization concerning the Vocational Instructor Training Institute in Cairo. The institute had been

Four-year-old Jonathan Pierce knocking on the door of Prime Minister Harold Wilson's official residence in London. The children, led by a member of Parliament, delivered a letter protesting the shortage of nursery schools in Britain.

planned ten years before, when less than 5% of the population was engaged in industry and such technical training as existed was in no way coordinated with national needs. The Cairo institute, it was reported, had remedied this situation, and it was estimated that by 1970 the U.A.R. would have over 60 training centres, with a total capacity of 14,000 apprentices a year.

Things also appeared to be different in the Soviet Union. According to a survey prepared by Soviet educators for the International Institute for Educational Planning and published in July, the system of "vocational-technical" education was training 800,000 to 900,000 workers annually for 700 occupations and specialties, while 9 million to 10 million workers were learning new occupations or improving their qualifications. One striking paragraph in the survey, however, showed how completely the educational system was coordinated with the manpower needs of the country:

> Certificates of direction to employment and cash funds are handed to the young specialists not later than five days after they complete their studies. In this way everyone graduating from a higher or secondary specialized educational establishment in the U.S.S.R. immediately obtains employment corresponding to the specialized training received, the necessary funds for a month's leave, travel costs to the place of employment for himself and members of his family, and an installation grant. The Soviet State does everything to see that all young specialists, as soon as they graduate from training, are incorporated into the general labour force of the Soviet people.

Other educational concerns lay outside the schools, the universities, and the technical colleges. In Britain there were signs that the long standstill in the development of nursery schools, imposed by the government for financial reasons, was coming to an end, and in Australia the federal government was able to earmark large sums for this purpose. Sweden reported a surge of interest in aesthetic subjects and "do-it-yourself" courses on such subjects as "oil-heating for home-owners." In an Olympic year, the International Council of Sport and Physical Education proposed a school textbook that would give outstanding examples of fair play. In the U.S. the Committee for Economic Development, representing the nation's business, political, and cultural interests, questioned the ability of the existing American system of education to produce rational, responsible, and effective citizens. And at the Williamsburg conference René Maheu, director general of UNESCO, emphasized the neglect of education in rural areas.

These were worldwide concerns. At the individual level, however, 1968 provided some striking examples of people already fulfilling President Johnson's Williamsburg objective of as much education for everyone as he or she wanted and could absorb. In the U.S.S.R. a 12-year-old boy was advanced enough to enroll for mathematics at Kiev University; in the U.S. a 16-year-old girl became a lecturer in the same subject at Michigan State University; and in Britain a woman passed the examination for the General Certificate of Education in Italian at the age of 89.

(L. R. Bu.)

See also Cinema; France; Libraries; Medicine; Museums and Galleries; Police.

ENCYCLOPÆDIA BRITANNICA FILMS. *New Tools for Learning* (1952); *Should I Go to College?* (1957); *The Unique Contribution* (1959); *You Can Go a Long Way!* (1961); *George W. Beadle* ("Dialogue for This Decade") (1962); *Sterling McMurrin* ("Dialogue for This Decade") (1962); *Project Discovery: A Demonstration in Education* (1965); *How a Scientist Works* (1967); *The Humanities Films: Their Aims and Uses* (1967); *Project Discovery II: Let Them Learn* (1967); *Teaching French with Films,* Parts I and II (1967).

Electronics

In a year that included man's first flight around the moon, electronics seemed to become more and more earthbound. The U.S. government, the U.S. National Aeronautics and Space Administration (NASA), and the electronics industry started to apply, in 1968, the vast technology derived from the huge space expenditures of recent years in an effort to confront the major urban upheaval resulting from inadequate jobs, housing, and education; the growing menace of air and water pollution; and the need for better public air and ground transportation.

At the year's end an eight-company consortium had been formed and was already examining ways of applying systems analysis to specific problems of urban renewal; NASA had begun to think in terms of practical, near-earth projects; and the federal budget to support industry training programs was more than doubled.

Communications. The year was one of decisions: the U.S. Federal Communications Commission (FCC) ruled that electronic devices, for such purposes as expanding services or saving costs, could be directly connected to telephones; the U.S. Congress passed a "safe streets" bill that prevented eavesdropping devices from being sold to the public; the U.S. Supreme Court contributed to the expansion of cable television by ruling that copyright fees need not be paid; and the U.S. government's Communications Satellite Corporation (Comsat) approved plans to build the world's largest communications satellite (Intelsat 4), with a total capacity of 6,000 channels.

The problem of electromagnetic spectrum "overcrowding" was alleviated by an airborne system that processed 280,000 voice channels in the same bandwidth that previously contained only 28,000. Overcrowding was also a problem for the massive internal communications systems of the new supersonic jet transports and airbuses. To deal with this a 2,400-channel multiplexing system was proposed that would eliminate most of the 150 mi. and 5,400 lb. of wiring currently required.

A new generation of airborne radar systems was tested; it replaced the familiar mechanically rotated antennas with an electronic scanning system consisting of radiating elements that are phase shifted to shape and position the beam in space. These "phased-

General Electric scientist displaying a compound electron lens composed of 1,024 smaller lenses. Similar in function to a fly's eye, seen projected on the background, the new electron lens would be capable of recording the contents of 3,000 pages in an area the size of a postage stamp.

KEYSTONE

array" radars, however, were soon expected to employ a beam-steering technique using gallium arsenide (GaAs) devices; this method would eliminate even the phase shifters.

The effective range of the data link between space vehicles and earth stations, long enhanced by the use of digital communications, was expected to be extended by 40% with a technique introduced by NASA called "convolutional coding." Also, a remarkable test of the theory of relativity might result from U.S. Air Force plans to develop the most powerful radar in existence. It would use 700 Mw. of power with nanosecond (one-billionth of a second) pulses to hurl electrons at velocities approaching the speed of light. According to the theory of relativity, the electrons should then take on enormous mass.

Solid-State Components. Although the greater reliability and lower cost of the integrated circuit (IC) continued to appeal to manufacturers, applications requiring high power or precision remained dependent upon such discrete semiconductor devices as silicon-controlled rectifiers, triacs, thyristors, unijunction transistors, field-effect transistors, and metal-film and wire-wound power resistors. As a result, hybrid IC's (those combining monolithic circuits with discrete components) continued to remain popular. Plastic became a dominant packaging material for IC's, although military users questioned its ruggedness. Large-scale integration (LSI), arbitrarily defined as IC's having 100 or more gates on a chip, became a common reality as the largest producers offered their first off-the-shelf computer-aided versions of this most promising of solid-state technologies.

One of the greatest breakthroughs in electronics occurred when scientists from the General Electric Corp. succeeded in linking four of the powerful limited space charge accumulation diodes in series. This led to the possibility of further linkages which could generate thousands of watts of power. Another considerable achievement took place when International Business Machines Corp. (IBM) was able to operate four Gunn oscillators in phase for the first time, providing a necessary tool for building phased-array radars.

Other accomplishments during the year included the first solid-state equivalent of the conventional television camera. It required 10,000 silicon phototransistors and 10,000 field-effect transistors on a $\frac{1}{2}$-in. chip and, including power pack and lens system, was capable of being put into a 4-cu.in. package. The feasibility of a wristwatch-size computer was brought closer when U.S. scientists were able to jam 12 million unconnected transistors onto a 1-sq.in. wafer.

The most significant advance in photomultiplier tubes in 35 years was created by a device that detected the light produced from a single electron; this gave such tubes a potential for mapping the deoxyribonucleic acid (DNA) molecule, gathering light from radio stars, or probing nuclear activity. One company produced a power transistor that operated even after an overload by "opening" up rather than "shorting" out; this provided police and ambulance mobile radios with a means of preventing disastrous malfunctions.

Displays. Although vacuum-tube displays of the cathode-ray and Nixie type continued to dominate the field, solid-state displays represented the major areas of advancement. Disenchantment with early electroluminescent phosphor-type devices—which proved to be dim and short-lived, and required high voltages—led to a major examination of semiconductor replace-

ments. Matrix-type arrays of light-emitting diodes, which had the advantages of long life, small size, adjustable brightness, low cost, and compatibility with integrated circuits, were developed in the U.S. for alphanumeric displays. A GaAs display was even made that contained its own logic and memory.

Perhaps the most exciting prospect for making inexpensive, flat display screens came with the discovery of a new electrooptic effect in nematic (first state of a substance after cooling from a liquid melt) liquid crystals. Called "dynamic scattering," this reflective phenomenon enabled displays using it to change from transparent to opaque with a simple application of voltage, and also offered the remarkable quality of being brightest in direct sunlight.

Computers. As the computer industry readied itself for new developments—characterized by LSI components, nanosecond speeds, and billion-bit memories —many problems arose with the machines already in operation. The increasing speed of computers created demands either to increase the speeds of peripheral equipment or to provide more direct access to computer memories. As an answer, machines were developed that transcribed data directly from the keyboard to magnetic tape. The punched card, used to

KEYSTONE

Technician at the Tokyo Shibaura Electric Co. Ltd. of Japan Central Research Laboratory in Tokyo operating a newly developed long-life, high-output argon and krypton laser which has the ability to produce intense, multicoloured beams of light. Future applications could include three-dimensional colour movies and television.

move data in and out of automatic equipment for 81 years, was seriously threatened by a plastic card with a storage potential 100 times greater than punched cards; it could be reused indefinitely and even be stapled.

Of the several memories destined to replace the ferrite core, plated and woven wires held the most promise for achieving higher speed and lower cost. They were used in areas where core arrays were not able to penetrate.

Lasers. The furor following the first demonstration of laser action by Hughes Aircraft in 1960 had by 1968 given way to more sober applications of this source of coherent light. The development of more than 50 different types of lasers, as well as gradual increases in their power and efficiency, created a device that was primarily being used either to do a better job than other methods or to accomplish tasks that could not be done any other way.

The newest and most powerful member of the laser family was the carbon dioxide gas laser, which one firm produced with an output of 8.8 kw. at 15% efficiency. Other developments included a laser that aided pollution control by detecting minute particles and a television-laser system that enabled oceanographers to see objects under water at eight times the distance perceived by the eye.

Holographic techniques improved during the year: a laser used ordinary photographs to create a "holographic stereogram" of three-dimensional panoramic pictures; a "flat" hologram gave the appearance of viewing an object through a 360° angle as the viewer moved from side to side; and a technique gave structures a life-size appearance by producing three-dimensional colour images with unlimited depth. The technique of holographic interferometry was first used in 1968 to determine when a material would crack under strain; this could be done by analyzing the material's fracture patterns.

Instrumentation. The greatest demand in this field was for digital readout meters that could combine the advantages of nonambiguity and high resolution with that of accuracy and computer compatibility and thus minimize human error. Automobile makers benefited from an ultrasonic meter that measured the thickness of cylinder heads and blocks up to 3 in. thick within an accuracy of 1%. One firm successfully demonstrated a probeless nucleonic fuel-measuring system that measured fuel mass rather than level, and another proposed a new "mass sensor" to be used to map the mass distribution of the moon by detecting changes in the gravitational field.

A submarine navigation system for finding range and bearing without using triangulation also was developed during the year, and a West German firm built a test track ten miles long that electronically checked out automobile drift, steering, acceleration, braking characteristics, and tire expansion at high speeds. The best prospect for detecting the gun of an assassin or a bomb on a plane seemed to lie in a low-priced portable magnetometer for measuring low-level magnetic fields.

Industrial and Consumer Electronics. As the price of semiconductors continued to drop, newer uses were found for them. A quartz-controlled electronic wristwatch, similar to one introduced by the Swiss in 1967, was built by the Japanese that contained 60 transistors, 80 resistors, and 50 capacitors on three IC's; it had an error of one second per month. Entirely solid-state 23-in. colour television sets were offered for the first time.

Although much concern arose during the year over all types of potential radiation hazards, from military radars to microwave ovens, the most publicity was accorded X rays found to be emitted from a small percentage of colour television sets. One firm proposed to eliminate such radiation, which resulted from high voltages in vacuum tubes, by replacing the involved tubes with inexpensive solid-state equivalents.

Traffic control received a boost from a French analyzer that detected highway bottlenecks and either informed police or controlled the traffic lights, and the Japanese invented a traffic-light system that was controlled by the "roar" level of passing cars.

A 23-in. colour television set was used by one company to project colour slides on its screen, and a second firm developed a combination camera and video tape recorder that played back on black-and-white TV by connecting it to the antenna. The declassification of a U.S. Army starlight night-vision scope that intensified light 40,000 times was destined to find many applications in such fields as astronomy and nuclear research.   (M. E.)

See also Industrial Review; Information Science and Technology; Medicine; Photography; Telecommunications; Television and Radio.

ENCYCLOPÆDIA BRITANNICA FILMS. *Electrons at Work* (1961).

El Salvador

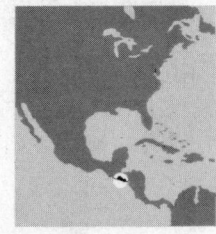

A republic on the Pacific coast of Central America and the smallest country on the isthmus, El Salvador is bounded on the west by Guatemala and on the north and east by Honduras. Area: 8,056 sq.mi. (20,865 sq.km.). Pop. (1968 est.): 3,250,000. Cap. and largest city: San Salvador (pop., 1968 est., 375,000). Language: Spanish. Religion: Roman Catholic. President in 1968, Col. Fidel Sánchez Hernández.

El Salvador was in the international spotlight briefly, July 6–8, when U.S. Pres. Lyndon B. Johnson met in San Salvador with the presidents of the five Central American republics. It was the first visit that a U.S. president had ever made to El Salvador. The meeting was an acknowledged effort "to dramatize the Central American Common Market," but it also brought substantial new U.S. funds (about $65 million) into development programs in the isthmus, including money for educational television in El Salvador. Although there was a protest by 2,000 Salvadoran students against United States policy in Vietnam, President Johnson's visit was otherwise considered a success.

Coincident with the meeting of the presidents, El Salvador and Honduras announced that they had taken additional steps toward a solution of their boundary dispute. The two governments agreed to exchange nationals who had been detained during the dispute. Tension between the two countries was thus considerably eased, but a precise definition of the boundary was delayed pending further negotiations.

Otherwise, the year in El Salvador was marked by modest social and economic progress. Improved prices for coffee and a better cotton crop strengthened the economy. The cotton farmers began to overcome the pests that had plagued recent crops. At the same time, the trend toward increased manufacturing continued as industry began to account for about one-fifth of the gross domestic product.

Politically, Pres. Fidel Sánchez Hernández sought to maintain a balance between conservative pressures and the demands of the people for reform. Sánchez' Party of National Conciliation barely maintained a majority in the 52-seat National Legislative Assembly in the elections of March 1968. The fast-growing Christian Democratic Party won nearly 50% of the popular vote and increased its representation in the Assembly from 15 to 19, while the president's party dropped from 31 members to 27. The Christian Democratic Party also won control of the municipal governments in almost every major city of El Salvador. After only three electoral campaigns, it was a strong contender for national power.

There were significant Cabinet changes during 1968, notably the departure of Rafael Glower Valdivieso, the reform-minded minister of economy, who left office protesting that President Sánchez had abandoned his reformist goals under pressure from conservative business and landowning interests. Glower was replaced by Alfonso Rochac, a Salvadoran economist of international reputation.

Under conflicting political pressures from both the left and right wings, the Sánchez administration was not able to achieve the enactment of any significant new legislation. An important new law to introduce regulations of banking institutions failed to be passed. Given the intensity of the forces to his left and to his right, it appeared that President Sánchez might have to make survival rather than reform his principal goal.   (M. W. Wı.)

EL SALVADOR

Education. (1965–66) Primary, pupils 397,810, teachers 11,537; secondary, pupils 38,619, teachers 1,848; vocational, pupils 9,929, teachers 908; teacher training, students 6,288, teachers 368; higher (including 2 universities), students 3,627, teaching staff 619.

Finance. Monetary unit: colón, with a par value of 2.50 colones to U.S. $1 (6 colones = £1 sterling). Gold and foreign exchange, central bank: (June 1968) U.S. $64.7 million; (June 1967) U.S. $77.1 million. Budget (1968 est.) balanced at 247.3 million colones. Gross national product: (1967) 2,205,000,000 colones; (1966) 2,093,000,000 colones. Cost of living (1963 = 100): (May 1968) 105; (May 1967) 101.

Foreign Trade. (1967) Imports 558.8 million colones; exports 517.7 million colones. Import sources: U.S. 31%; Guatemala 13%; Japan 8%; West Germany 7%; U.K. 6%; Honduras 6%. Export destinations: U.S. 27%; West Germany 22%; Guatemala 16%; Honduras 10%; Japan 8%; Nicaragua 7%; Costa Rica 6%. Main exports: coffee 48%; cotton 8%.

Transport and Communications. Roads (1966) 8,394 km. (including 625 km. part of Pan-American Highway). Motor vehicles in use (1966): passenger 27,600; commercial (including buses) 12,900. Railways (1966) c. 720 km. Telephones (Jan. 1967) 30,061. Radio receivers (Dec. 1965) 396,000. Television receivers (Dec. 1965) 35,000.

Agriculture. Production (in 000; metric tons; 1966; 1965 in parentheses): rice 50 (35); corn 266 (203); coffee 117 (106); cotton, lint 39 (52); sugar, raw value (1966–67) 130, (1965–66) 120. Livestock (in 000; 1965–66): cattle c. 922; pigs c. 322; horses c. 74; chickens c. 2,000.

Industry. Production (1967): cement 149,000 metric tons; electricity (excluding most industrial production) 490 million kw-hr.

Employment, Wages, and Hours

Analysis of the trends in employment, wages, and hours throughout the world in 1968 was based on information available in such publications as the International Labour Office's *Year Book of Labour Statistics*, 1967, the Organization for Economic Cooperation and Development's *Main Economic Indicators* and its annual economic surveys of member countries, and various United Nations publications. Also available in 1968 were two new studies prepared by the UN Economic Commission for Europe, *Economic Survey of Europe in 1967* and *Incomes in Postwar Europe*. Because of the differences in scope and in the methods of compilation used in these reports and because the significance of the statistics varied from country to country according to the degree of economic and social development, conclusions had to be drawn carefully.

Employment and Unemployment. The contrast between the developed, or industrialized, economies and the less developed, or predominantly agricultural, economies with regard to their rates of population growth and the proportion of the economically active population in agriculture is of significance for explaining trends in employment and unemployment up to early 1968. (*See* Table I.) The industrialized economies in 1965–66 had an average rate of population growth of 0.7% and an average proportion of only 13% of their economically active population

Emigration:
see Immigration and Emigration

in agriculture; the less developed economies had averages of 1.7 and 53%, respectively.

Agriculture in the less developed economies tended to be a backward sector offering little future, so that in addition to the natural increase in the labour force resulting from population growth there tended to be an exodus of workers from the agricultural sector to other sectors of the economy, which were not fully capable of absorbing them. Thus there was a general increase in unemployment and in the underemployment of labour.

By contrast, in most of the industrialized market economies the rates of growth of population were lower and their reserves of labour were smaller than in the less developed economies. In the industrialized economies changes in unemployment were due mainly to attempts to achieve price stability and balance of payments surpluses.

Less Developed Economies. The average increase in employment in the less developed economies in 1966 over the previous year was 3.2%, with employment in the manufacturing sector expanding fastest at an average of 8.4%. Employment in agriculture was expanding slowly at an average of 1%. Although unemployment statistics were not very meaningful for these countries, they tended to show high rates of increase for 1965, 1966, and 1967. (*See* Table II.) To these official statistics on unemployment must be added the unquantified problem of underemployed labour in these countries. Estimates of underemployed labour for some less developed countries ran from 10 to 30% of the employed civilian labour force.

Industrial Market Economies. The rates of employment growth in the industrialized market economies were much lower than in the less developed countries, and all countries showed a decline in agricultural employment. From the beginning of 1965 the

Table II. Unemployment in Less Developed Economies

Country	Change over previous year (%)		
	1965	1966	1967
Barbados	0.6	−5.8	—
Burma	9.8	—	—
Ceylon	13.8	24.3	10.7
Chile	8.6	2.0	—
Cyprus	−28.6	−13.6	−17.8
Fiji	0	38.5	—
Ghana	−16.9	2.7	45.2
Greece	−0.8	0.8	28.9
Guatemala	−20.0	137.6	—
Guyana	142.4	−2.3	—
India	−0.6	3.4	3.7
Iraq	−21.0	—	—
Korea, South	−0.9	−1.6	—
Malaysia	5.9	13.8	—
Malta	15.5	−5.2	−26.4
Mauritius	29.5	69.6	—
Morocco	9.4	27.4	—
Niger	14.3	37.5	—
Nigeria	0.5	27.3	—
Pakistan	2.2	−1.6	2.2
Philippines	11.1	4.0	—
Puerto Rico	12.3	5.5	0
Sierra Leone	28.7	17.0	6.6
Singapore	15.7	20.2	17.7
Taiwan	−19.7	−16.0	—
Zambia	57.9	−6.6	—
Average	18.7	20.2	15.9

Source: United Nations, *Monthly Bulletin of Statistics* (August 1968).

related problems of rising prices and balance of payments deficits had beset most of the industrialized economies. The use of monetary and fiscal policies to combat adverse trends meant slower rates of economic growth and increases in unemployment levels. (*See* Tables I and III.) Table III shows that the increase in manufacturing employment for 1965 over 1964 averaged 1.4%; in 1966 the increase over 1965 averaged 0.7%, a reduction by half; and in 1967 the average decrease was 1.1%. The converse of this was the changes recorded in unemployment: an average decrease of 1% in 1965 over 1964, followed by an average increase of 6.1% in 1966, and a very large increase of 35% in 1967. From the first quarter of 1967 to the first quarter of 1968, the increase in unemployment averaged 23.4%, but the UN Economic Commission for Europe considered that the unemployment situation would show improvement rather than continued deterioration during the rest of 1968.

In the U.S. and Canada employment in manufacturing was expanding rapidly up to 1966. Unemployment was falling in the U.S. because of the expansion of economic activity consequent upon the tax cuts of 1964 and the continuing rise in military expenditures. In response to rising prices and a worsening balance of payments, U.S. authorities took steps in 1966 to reduce the expansion of output. As a result the rate of increase of manufacturing employment dropped sharply from 6.4% in 1965–66 to 1.2% in 1966–67 and, following a 14.5% fall in unemployment in 1965–66, unemployment rose by 3.5% in 1966–67. Fiscal restraint continued in the U.S. into 1968 and it was likely that unemployment would continue to rise.

In Western Europe many countries adopted various measures of economic restraint from 1965 onward as governments countered rising wages and prices and balance of payments deficits. After a deficit on current account in 1965, West Germany adopted certain restrictive fiscal measures; by 1966 monetary restraint had begun to take effect. The result was a trebling of unemployment in 1966–67 and a decline of 6.1% in the manufacturing labour force, which caused many immigrant workers to return home. The government acted quickly to correct its previous over-correction, particularly as the deficit had been eliminated, and unemployment fell from the first quarter

Table I. Employment, Unemployment, and Population

Country	Changes for 1966 over 1965 (%)					
	Employment					
	General	agriculture*	Manu-facturing	Unemploy-ment	Popula-tion	Labour force in agriculture (%)
Less developed:						
British Honduras	4.3	−0.8	11.1	—	2.9	45
Cameroon	3.7	3.2	22.2	87.5	0.9	84
Cyprus	2.0	−0.2	—	−13.7	1.2	39
Gabon	4.3	3.5	−7.4	—	0.9	84
Kenya	1.6	1.2	0.3	−4.9	2.9	88
Philippines	4.7	5.0	−1.1	6.1	3.4	59
Puerto Rico	3.5	−1.4	6.9	4.5	1.9	19
Singapore	9.6	0.4	15.1	20.2	2.5	7
Syria	4.3	4.7	—	—	−3.5	50
Taiwan	−0.3	−3.9	—	−16.0	3.0	47
Tanzania	0.8	0.4	16.0	—	1.9	95
Trinidad and Tobago	−0.2	−0.1	12.1	—	2.7	19
Average	3.2	1.0	8.4	12.0	1.7	53
Industrialized:						
Austria	0.2	−0.2	−0.4	−6.3	0.6	20
Belgium	0.5	−0.5	−0.2	11.0	0.9	6
Canada	4.2	−0.8	5.4	9.4	1.9	9
Germany, West	−0.4	−0.3	0	10.9	−2.5	11
Italy	−1.7	−1.6	0	6.7	1.0	24
Japan	2.1	−0.8	2.0	12.8	1.1	27
Netherlands	0.9	−0.5	0	31.6	1.4	9
Norway	1.2	−0.1	1.8	−11.2	0.8	18
Sweden	0.8	−1.3	−2.0	33.7	1.0	12
United Kingdom	0.2	−0.5	−0.2	4.0	0.7	4
United States	2.5	−0.7	6.2	−14.6	1.3	6
Average	1.0	−0.7	1.2	8.0	0.7	13
Planned economies:						
Bulgaria	8.4	6.0	9.1	—	0.7	59
Czechoslovakia	2.0	−0.3	2.8	—	0.7	16
Germany, East	1.0	0	1.0	—	—	19
Hungary	0.4	−0.2	1.3	—	0.3	31
Romania	3.7	1.6	3.7	—	1.1	42
Yugoslavia	4.5	2.7	3.5	—	0.5	59
Poland	−2.7	−1.7	−1.4	—	1.2	53
Average	2.5	1.2	2.9	—	0.8	40

*The change in agricultural employment was calculated as the change in overall employment *minus* the change in nonagricultural employment *times* the proportion of the economically active labour force outside agriculture.
Sources: International Labour Office, *Year Book of Labour Statistics* (1967) and United Nations Food and Agriculture Organization, *Production Yearbook* (1966).

LONDON "DAILY EXPRESS" FROM PICTORIAL PARADE

Delegates of the All-India State Government Employees Federation marching through the streets of New Delhi to Parliament House where they presented demands for better wages and working conditions.

of 1967 to the first quarter of 1968 and continued to fall.

In France exports and consumer demand hardly increased from mid-1966 onward and the rise in investment was insufficient to expand employment. Because of the natural increase in the working age population unemployment increased, rising steeply in 1967 and increasing by 40.2% from the first quarter of 1967 to the first quarter of 1968. In the U.K. restraints were introduced in mid-1966 in response to a deteriorating current balance of payments. This increased unemployment by 8.6% in 1966. For the first half of 1967 unemployment continued to rise but there was a slight fall in the second half of the year. Further measures of fiscal restraint were introduced and unemployment again took an upward trend.

Centrally Planned Economies. The growth rates of employment in the Eastern European countries tended to be greater than those in the industrialized market economies. (*See* Table I.) Most of these countries had low rates of population growth, but they also had larger labour forces in agriculture from which they could draw to expand the manufacturing labour forces. Most of these countries were undergoing economic reforms to increase efficiency in general and labour productivity in particular. Thus, as seen in Table IV, although the rate of growth of output in 1967 was on an average slightly higher than in 1966, employment growth tended to be slower and productivity growth faster.

In the U.S.S.R. economic reforms seemed to be having a considerable effect on labour productivity and, despite a faster rate of increase of output, the rate of growth of employment was slower in 1967 than in 1966. A fast increase in labour productivity was planned for 1968. In East Germany employment actually declined, partly as a result of the shortening of the work week, but output expansion continued along a steady path.

The highest rates of output growth were in Bulgaria and Romania, which had the highest proportions of the labour force in agriculture and, hence, the most plentiful labour reserves. But this expansion of output was achieved mainly through increased productivity. Both countries had fairly stringent limits on

the expansion of industrial employment because too rapid an intake of labour from agriculture tended to depress standards of quality.

In Hungary in 1965 and 1966 economic growth was restrained in order to achieve a balance of payments surplus. In 1967 investment activity was high and a rapid expansion, particularly of industry, was permitted at the expense of the balance of payments. This restraint and expansion were reflected in employment changes. In Czechoslovakia expansion was deliberately restrained in the second half of 1967 as an investment boom threatened to disrupt the economy. Added to this were economic reforms that boosted productivity growth. The combined effect was to slow employment growth considerably. In Poland in 1967 much of the increase in output was concentrated in the producer goods sector and this imbalance in expansion resulted in a higher than planned increase in employment.

Wages. Table V gives the rates of increase for money and real wages for manufacturing and consumer prices in the industrialized market economies. The average rate of increase of money wages was 7.9% in both 1964–65 and 1965–66; it was 6.7% in 1966–67. Thus in 1967 the rate of growth of money wages slowed by a little over one percentage point. The corresponding rates of growth of real wages were 3.5, 3.6, and 3.3%, all very similar. The average rise in consumer prices was a little slower in each succeeding year, 4.3, 4, and 3.5%. This gradual decline of a little under one percentage point in the rate of price increase was associated with the policies of restraint adopted increasingly from 1965 onward. From the first quarter of 1967 to the first quarter of 1968 the average rate of growth of money wages slowed a little further to 6.4%, the average rate of growth of real wages was down to 2.8%, and the rate of price increase was unchanged.

In the U.S. restrictive policies from 1966 on reduced the rate of growth of money wages but had little effect on consumer prices. Thus, the rate of growth of real wages was reduced to 0.8% in 1967. From the first quarter of 1967 to the first quarter of 1968 the

Table III. Employment in Manufacturing in Industrialized Countries

Country	Employment 1965	1966	1967	Unemployment 1965	1966	1967	1968*
Canada	5.5	5.3	−0.3	−13.6	−4.6	18.0	22.2
United States	4.6	6.4	1.2	−11.1	−14.5	3.5	0
Japan	1.9	0.9	1.9	5.4	12.8	—	—
Austria	0.2	−0.7	−3.3	0	−6.0	4.8	23.2
France	−1.5	0.1	−1.2	—	4.2	32.4	40.2
Germany, West	2.3	−0.5	−6.1	−13.0	9.5	185.7	−9.3
Ireland	1.2	0.6	1.1	0	10.3	12.5	2.9
Italy	−1.9	−0.3	3.5	31.3	6.7	−10.4	—
Netherlands	0.9	−0.9	−4.4	17.9	30.3	95.4	10.7
Norway	1.7	2.0	1.1	−13.6	−11.2	−4.2	36.4
Sweden	4.1	−3.0	−3.1	−2.4	33.7	29.7	24.0
Switzerland	−2.0	−2.0	−1.0	0	0	0	—
United Kingdom	1.3	1.5	−3.1	−12.8	8.6	53.2	3.2
Average	1.4	0.7	−1.1	−1.0	6.1	35.0	23.4

*First quarter over first quarter 1967.
Source: Organization for Economic Cooperation and Development, *Main Economic Indicators* (August 1968).

Table IV. Output, Employment, and Productivity in the Planned Economies

Country	Output 1965	1966	1967	Employment 1965	1966	1967	Productivity 1965	1966	1967
Bulgaria	13.7	12.2	13.4	6.9	9.2	4.9	6.4	2.8	8.1
Czechoslovakia	7.9	7.4	7.1	2.0	2.5	1.1	5.8	4.8	5.9
Germany, East	6.2	6.4	6.5	0.1	0.1	−0.3	6.1	6.3	6.2
Hungary	4.8	6.6	9.1	0.4	0.9	2.1	4.4	5.6	6.9
Poland	9.0	7.4	7.5	4.9	3.5	3.8	3.9	3.7	3.5
Romania	13.1	11.7	13.5	5.5	3.3	3.7	7.2	8.1	9.4
U.S.S.R.	8.7	8.6	10.0	4.3	3.9	3.0	4.2	4.5	7.0
Average	9.1	8.6	9.6	3.4	3.3	2.7	5.4	5.1	6.7

Source: United Nations Economic Commission for Europe, *Economic Survey of Europe in 1967.*

Table V. Money and Real Wages in Manufacturing and Consumer Prices: Industrialized Countries

	Money wages				Real wages				Prices			
Country	1965	1966	1967	1968*	1965	1966	1967	1968*	1965	1966	1967	1968*
Canada	4.8	5.5	7.0	5.8	2.3	1.7	3.3	1.2	2.4	3.7	3.5	4.6
United States	2.9	4.7	3.6	6.2	1.2	1.8	0.8	2.4	1.7	2.9	2.8	3.7
Japan	8.7	11.6	13.6	14.3	2.1	6.1	9.3	8.5	6.5	5.2	4.0	5.3
Austria	10.8	8.1	6.4	5.2	5.7	6.2	1.8	2.6	4.8	1.8	4.5	2.6
Belgium	9.9	9.8	6.7	—	5.6	5.5	3.7	—	4.0	4.2	2.9	—
Denmark	11.9	11.5	—	—	4.9	4.9	—	—	6.7	6.3	6.8	10.7
France	5.8	5.9	6.0	6.3	3.2	3.1	3.3	2.3	2.5	2.7	2.7	3.9
Germany, West	9.4	7.3	3.9	2.2	5.8	3.7	2.5	0.9	3.4	3.5	1.5	1.3
Ireland	3.5	9.4	7.0	6.7	−1.4	6.2	3.7	2.0	5.1	2.9	3.2	4.6
Netherlands	10.3	10.2	6.4	6.1	5.4	3.6	3.8	1.9	4.7	6.3	2.5	4.2
Norway	9.4	6.9	8.1	6.2	5.5	3.1	3.5	1.8	3.8	3.6	4.4	4.3
Sweden	11.3	7.6	9.5	6.6	5.3	1.1	4.9	4.0	5.8	6.4	4.3	2.5
Switzerland	4.7	6.3	5.1	4.1	1.3	1.4	1.1	0.6	3.4	4.8	3.9	3.5
United Kingdom	6.9	6.2	3.3	9.7	2.0	2.2	0.8	6.5	4.7	3.9	2.5	3.0
Average	7.9	7.9	6.7	6.4	3.5	3.6	3.3	2.8	4.3	4.0	3.5	3.5

*First quarter over first quarter 1967.
Source: Organization for Economic Cooperation and Development, *Main Economic Indicators* (August 1968).

rise in money wages accelerated more than the rise in consumer prices so that the rate of increase of real wages was faster than in previous years. Increased taxes in 1968 and the consequent reduction in consumption were expected to restrain the increase.

In West Germany deflation had a marked impact upon the rate of increase of money wages, which was 9.4% in 1964–65 and 3.9% in 1966–67. The rate of consumer price increase also declined between 1966 and 1967 but not as fast as the decline in the rate of growth of money wages so that the rate of growth of real wages fell between 1965–66 and 1966–67. This trend continued into 1968. In France the rates of growth of money wages and retail prices, and thus of real wages, tended to be steady in all three years. But from the first quarter of 1967 to the first quarter of 1968, the rate of increase of money wages accelerated and price inflation increased considerably more with the result that real wages increased at a lower rate. Wage settlements after the strikes in May meant that the rate of increase in money wages would be considerable in 1968.

In the U.K. economic restraint had a considerable impact—the rate of increase of money wages fell from 6.9% in 1964–65 to 3.3% in 1966–67. The rate of price increase also fell, but not as rapidly, so the rate of increase of real wages declined between 1965–66 and 1966–67. In 1967 real wages were only 0.8% above the 1966 level. From the first quarter of 1967 to the first quarter of 1968, however, money wages increased dramatically by 9.7% and real wages by 6.5% as a backlog of wage increases was made up.

As shown in Table VI, the average rate of growth of money wages in the centrally planned economies was lower than that for the industrialized market economies. The figures were not strictly comparable: the former were economy-wide, the latter referred to manufacturing only. Since the rate of increase of the cost of living was also lower in the centrally planned economies, the rate of increase of real wages was similar to or slightly lower than that for the industrialized economies. The rate of growth of money wages showed a slight tendency to increase, especially in those countries (Czechoslovakia, Hungary) trying to carry out economic reforms.

There were few reliable figures on average earnings in the less developed countries and, given the instability of these economies, year to year movements in wages were liable to considerable fluctuations. Table VII presents available data on the long-term annual rate of growth of wages in manufacturing from 1957 to 1965 for 13 less developed countries together with comparable data for the developed economies. In the less developed economies the rate of growth of money wages varied considerably, from 2.4 to 18% (excluding from consideration an exceptional 48.7% increase in Brazil) and the average, 8.6%, was somewhat higher than that for the developed economies. The average rate of increase in prices was 3.7%, only slightly higher than that for the industrialized economies. Thus, rates of increase in real wages in the less developed economies, although ranging from −0.7% to 12.6%, averaged 4.7%—somewhat higher than the 3.1% average for the developed economies. This might be tentatively generalized into a pattern where workers in manufacturing were becoming a privileged group in the less developed economies, while those outside the (small) manufacturing sector had barely any increase in their living standards.

Hours. In 1957 the average number of hours worked per week in manufacturing was 44.4 in the developed industrialized economies and 45.2 in the less developed economies. (*See* Table VIII.) By 1965 the respective averages were 43.4 and 45.5. There had been a fall of 2% in hours worked in the industrialized economies and a slight increase of 0.8% in the less developed economies. Most of the developed economies had managed to shorten the length of the working week by an hour or so.

One of the effects of deflationary policies is to shorten the average length of the working week by providing less overtime work and putting workers on short time. Thus, while in 1965 the average of hours worked was only 0.3% down from 1964, in 1967 the working week had shortened by 1.3% from 1966, reflecting the impact of deflationary policies. (*See* Table IX.)

Incomes Policies. The basic problem for most economies, and the one most often reflected in employment patterns in 1968, grew out of the fact that in periods of expansion (when labour may become

Table VI. Wages and Cost of Living: Planned Economies

	Money wages			Real wages			Cost of living		
Country	1965	1966	1967	1965	1966	1967	1965	1966	1967
Bulgaria	2	5	8	3	5	—	−1	*	—
Czechoslovakia	2.3	2.6	5.5	1.2	2.3	3.9	1.2	0.3	1.5
Hungary	1	3	3.5–4†	*	2	3–3.5†	1	1	0.5–0.7†
Germany, East	3.8	2	—	3.9	2.0	—	0.1	*	—
Poland	2.6	4.5	4‡	*	3.3	2.5‡	2.6	1.2	1.5
Romania	7	6	3	6	6	—	1	*	—
U.S.S.R.	6.1	3.6	4.1	4	2	—	—	—	—
Average	3.5	3.8	4.7§	2.6	3.2	3.2§	.8	.8	1.2

*Negligible.
†Figures given as ranges have been taken at midpoint.
‡Approximate.
§Average of available statistics.
Source: United Nations Economic Commission for Europe, *Economic Survey of Europe in 1967*.

scarce) earnings tend to rise faster than output per employee. Thus, the labour cost of each unit of output increases and, conversely, each person has slightly more to spend than there are goods and services available. Because of the increased unit costs employers will tend to increase prices in order to protect their profits. In overall terms, the increase in individual

spending ability means that the volume of purchasing power in the economy is rising faster than the volume of domestic output. The excess tends to spill over into a demand for imports and for goods that might otherwise have been exported. This means that the balance of trade tends to become adverse.

Given that international currency reserves, which should cushion such essentially temporary deficits, are in very short supply, as they often were in 1968, it is imperative if currency crises are to be avoided that such deficits be corrected with all possible speed. This is done by reducing the volume (slowing down the rate of growth) of purchasing power or expenditure in the economy by making it more difficult and/or expensive to purchase goods on credit (monetary policy), by raising taxes to reduce disposable income (fiscal policy), and by direct reduction of government expenditure.

The fall in expenditure (or in the rate of growth of expenditure) will entail cutbacks in output and in employment. The consequent increase in unemployment will not reflect the whole of the change in the employment situation: temporary immigrant workers will return home (as they did in West Germany in 1967) and working wives will return to domestic life. Increased unemployment means that the volume of purchases will decline still further and it is hoped that the purchases of imports will fall, thus correcting the deficit in the balance of trade.

This "stop-go" solution means not only reduced purchases of consumer goods but also reduced purchases of capital goods, which are of importance to modernization and efficiency. In this case, deflation jeopardizes the long-run security of the economy. Thus, it was being suggested that it would be preferable to bring the rate of growth of purchasing power under control by some less damaging means, such as an incomes policy. If the overall increase in earnings were linked to the overall increase in the volume of output, there would be less of a tendency for unit labour costs in general to rise and less excess purchasing power to spill over into imports. Thus, an incomes policy has two aims: limiting the increase in earnings to the increase in productivity, and stimulating increases in productivity.

The first aim, if achieved, should both slow down the rate of increase of prices as unit labour costs are stabilized and reduce the rate of growth of imports. In practice it was not usually being achieved because of powerful economic and institutional forces that pushed up both rates of pay and actual earnings. Furthermore, as productivity measurement is not a very precise matter, the amount of the increase might become a matter for negotiation between the employers and the workers, as it had in the Netherlands. What was more practicable and effective, and therefore highly unpopular, was a complete, and perhaps statutory, freeze on all wage and salary increases. This, however, could lead to a backlog of wage demands and result in a wage explosion, as it had in the U.K. by the first quarter of 1968.

The second aim is, in the long run, the more effective one. It is upon continuing advances in productivity that the maintenance and increase in standards of living must depend. (D. A. S. J.)

See also Economics; Economy, World; Income, National; Industrial Review; Labour Unions; Prices.

ENCYCLOPÆDIA BRITANNICA FILMS. *Working Together* (1952); *Walter P. Reuther* ("Dialogue for This Decade") (1963); *The Industrial Revolution—Beginnings in the United States* (1968); *The Rise of Labor* (1968).

Table VII. Prices and Wages: Long-Term Annual Growth Rate (%), 1957–65

Country	Manufacturing Money wages	Manufacturing Real wages	Prices
Developed economies:			
Belgium	5.8	3.7	1.9
Canada	3.5	1.9	1.6
Denmark	8.7	4.9	3.6
Finland	7.4	2.6	4.7
France	7.8	2.3	5.4
Italy	7.8	4.0	3.6
Netherlands	7.8	4.5	3.2
New Zealand	3.1	0.4	2.8
Norway	6.7	3.2	3.5
Sweden	7.6	4.0	3.4
Switzerland	6.1	3.6	2.3
United Kingdom	6.1	3.3	2.8
United States	3.1	1.6	1.4
Average	6.4	3.1	3.1
Less developed economies:			
Brazil	48.7	0.2	48.4
Ceylon	6.2	5.0	1.1
Colombia	18.0	6.5	10.9
Dominican Republic	10.3	9.2	0.9
Ecuador	3.3	0.5	2.8
Ghana	7.0	−0.7	7.7
Kenya	7.7	5.6	1.9
Korea, South	11.1	0.6	10.4
Pakistan	4.6	2.1	2.4
Puerto Rico	6.3	3.9	2.3
Singapore	2.4	2.0	0.4
Tanzania	13.9	12.6	1.1
Zambia	11.9	9.5	2.2
Average (excl. Brazil)	8.6	4.7	3.7

Source: International Labour Office, *Year Book of Labour Statistics* (1967).

Table VIII. Hours of Work per Week in Manufacturing

Country	1957	1965	Rate of change 1957–65 (%)
Developed economies:			
Austria	44.9	43.4	−3.34
Canada	40.4	41.0	1.49
France	46.1	45.6	−1.08
Germany, West	46.4	44.1	−4.96
Japan	46.9	44.3	−5.54
Netherlands	48.6	46.1	−5.14
New Zealand	39.9	40.7	2.01
Norway	40.6	38.3	−5.67
Switzerland	47.4	44.9	−5.27
United Kingdom	48.0	46.1	−3.96
United States	39.8	41.2	3.52
Ireland	44.7	43.9	−1.79
Finland	43.2	43.9	1.85
Average	44.4	43.4	−2.14
Less developed economies:			
Colombia	52.0	50.0	−3.85
Cyprus	45.0	46.0	2.22
Ecuador	46.0	44.0	−4.35
Guatemala	46.3	46.1	−.43
Mexico	46.7	45.5	−2.57
Peru	44.5	48.4	8.76
Philippines	43.0	45.6	6.05
Puerto Rico	35.9	36.9	2.79
El Salvador	45.7	45.1	−1.31
Singapore	46.7	47.2	1.07
Average	45.2	45.5	0.84

Source: International Labour Office, *Year Book of Labour Statistics* (1967).

Table IX. Hours Worked in Manufacturing

Country	Change over previous year (%) 1965	1966	1967	1968*
Canada	0	−0.5	−1.2	0.3
United States	1.2	0.2	−1.7	0
Japan	−2.0	0.6	−1.6	−0.6
Denmark	1.0	−5.8	−4.1	−6.1
France	−0.6	0.4	−1.1	−1.5
Germany, West	1.1	−0.9	−2.3	—
Ireland	−0.9	0	−0.5	−0.5
Switzerland	−1.1	−0.2	−0.2	−0.2
United Kingdom	−1.7	−2.4	0.7	—
Average	−0.3	−0.9	−1.3	−1.2

*First quarter over first quarter 1967.
Source: Organization for Economic Cooperation and Development, *Main Economic Indicators* (August 1968).

Endocrinology: see Medicine

Engineering Projects

Bridges. *Suspension Bridges.* While the construction of a traditional type of steel suspension bridge at Quebec City (spans of 617 ft., 2,800 ft., and 617 ft.) continued, work began on a suspension bridge of smaller span but of more original design, which would cross the Zambezi River in Mozambique. It was to have two outer spans of 296 ft. and three central spans of 592 ft. with a width of 38 ft. This bridge was to have no stiffening girders, these being replaced by a system of triangles of cables (stretched by external weights or else prestressed). Each triangle would comprise the carrying cable (continuous between the anchorings at the extremities), the stiffening cable, situated at the level of the deck, and oblique slings. The deck was to be made up of a series of plates in prestressed concrete, providing transversal wind-bracing, and it would rest on the two stiffening cables.

Cable-Stayed Girder Bridges. To cross great distances, the cable-stayed girder bridge often proved the most economical. This was particularly true of two bridges built across the Rhine River in West Germany: the Friedrich Ebert Bridge in Bonn (395 ft., 921 ft., and 395 ft.) and the Maxau Bridge (576 ft. and 384 ft.). In spite of their width (115 ft.), the decks of these two bridges could be formed by a single caisson, covered by an orthotropic plate; they were carried by an axial row of cables which hung from pylons consisting of a single steel pole about 150 ft. high. The heights of the decks were about 10 ft. for the Maxau Bridge and 14 ft. for that in Bonn.

When the deck is not in caisson form, that is to say when it does not have independent torsional rigidity, it is essential that it should be given sufficient stability to withstand the wind, the builders of the Onomichi Bridge, in the Inland Sea of Sato (Japan), discovered. This continuous bridge consisted of three spans of 280 ft., 692 ft., and 280 ft.; its 35½-ft.-wide deck consisted of two full web girders, 105 ft. deck, covered by an orthotropic plate. Tests carried out during construction showed that the stability of the bridge under local wind conditions was only just sufficient and that it would be advisable to pierce the deck with a lengthwise slit in order to lessen its resistance to the wind.

Among notable designs for cable-stayed girder bridges was a project to cross the Danube River at Bratislava in Czechoslovakia with a span of 1,000 ft., supported by three cables carried by a V-shaped pylon inclined toward the land and anchored into the abutments. In the international competition organized by Denmark for a bridge about 3¾ mi. long and 100 ft. wide to cross the Store Baelt (Great Belt) channel, among the four best projects, which were awarded prizes, three were cable-stayed girder bridges in steel. Two of them were mixed traffic (road-rail) bridges, with triangulated bracing girders and orthotropic plates (maximum spans of 1,480 ft. and 1,973 ft., respectively), and the third was a road bridge consisting of a caisson girder (maximum span 1,591 ft.) carried by an axial sheet of cables. But in October the U.S.S.R. criticized the idea of a Great Belt bridge because, if it were destroyed, it might trap the Soviet fleet in the Baltic.

Classic Metal Bridges. Canada saw the completion of its longest bridge (nearly 2 mi.), crossing the St. Lawrence River between Quebec City and Montreal, with a maximum span of 1,000 ft. It consisted of triangulated girders of variable height supporting a low-level deck. The longest continuous bridge in Germany was built at Mintard across the Rhun Valley. Consisting of a caisson girder with orthotropic plate, 1⅛ mi. long, it was curved and comprised 19 spans. In Czechoslovakia the Moldau was crossed, south of Prague, by an arch of 1,085-ft. span and 43-ft. width. In California a bridge more than 2 mi. long across San Diego Bay was built with three spans decked with orthotropic plates. In France the Bono River was crossed by a gantry on inclined props of 485-ft. span and 75-ft. height, the 32-ft.-wide deck consisting of a caisson topped by an orthotropic plate.

Prestressed Concrete Bridges. In spite of the availability of improved forms of centring, a notable feature in the construction of large prestressed concrete bridges was the increasing use of prefabricated elements. Many bridges were constructed in the form of a series of independent spans of prefabricated girders, which were then assembled by means of transversal prestressing. Thus, the longest bridge in the world (24 mi.), crossing Lake Pontchartrain in Louisiana, was doubled by placing a series of independent spans of 84 ft. each above those of the old bridge (56-ft. spans). In Ghana the Lower Volta River was crossed by 17 spans 125 ft. in length. In India 41 spans of 100 to 115 ft. were placed across the Gangolli River. A viaduct in Sicily 1,770 ft. long was made up of spans of 171 ft., resting on piles constructed between sliding frames (cofferings) 430 ft. high. Finally, a bridge 12½ mi. long was being built near Orléans, France, as a roadway for the "aerotrain" (a vehicle carried on an air cushion): it consisted of prefabricated

The 100-story John Hancock Center in Chicago, world's tallest residential-office building, during topping-out ceremonies, May 6, 1968. The trussed walls form a rigid truncated pyramid which carries all principal stresses.

WIDE WORLD

girders 65 ft. long, in continuous sections of 390 ft. In section it comprised a plate with two lower ribs and an upper one which served as a rail for the vehicle.

But the most striking development in 1968 was in cantilever construction by means of prefabricated voussoirs (tapering wedge-shaped pieces forming arches or vaults). This development was made possible by the perfecting of glued joints, achieved by a thin layer of epoxy resins or of polyesters. It allowed builders to take advantage of all the benefits of prefabrication: precision, speed of assembly, reduction of strains. It was used for the first time in France, in constructing in 1968 the two bridges by which the ring road around Paris crossed the Seine River (maximum span 303 ft.), as well as the Bonpas Bridge on the Durance River (in seven spans of 253 ft.). It was also used in the U.S.S.R. in the construction of the Yaroslav Bridge over the Volga River, half a mile long. Lightweight concrete emerged from the laboratory and was used in the construction of numerous full-size experimental bridges in the U.S., the Netherlands, and West Germany.

In conclusion, it should be mentioned that the collapse, on Dec. 15, 1967, of the suspension bridge spanning the Ohio River at Point Pleasant, W.Va., which led to the death of 46 people, was a reminder to all engineers of the importance which they should accord to the durability of their constructions. While technical progress allowed for genuine economies, false economizing on the upkeep of constructions could only lead to much higher ultimate expense. For this reason it was hoped that all engineers would follow the example of their U.S. colleagues, who, after this tragic accident, decided to undertake a thorough annual inspection of typical sections of roadway networks. (J. FA.)

Buildings. The influence of the greater mobility of people on the design and location of buildings continued to manifest itself in interesting ways in 1968. For example, the significant movement of people into and out of urban areas made the effective utilization of space a matter of paramount importance and continued the trend toward unique combinations of land use in urban areas. An interestingly designed hotel and convention centre was scheduled to be the first of six buildings to be erected on a six-block area in the centre of Philadelphia. This hotel was described in *Buildings* as being in the form of two hyperbolic paraboloids and terraced like a Mayan temple. Conforming to developments in some other cities in the multiple purpose use of land, it was to be built over the Penn-Central railroad track which traversed the building site. This was one of six buildings that would eventually make up a $200 million complex designated as Century 21. Accompanying the report on this project was another about the plan for a future Florida city to be called Rotonda. It also reflected the impact of the greater mobility of people and the developments in construction technology that allowed mass construction projects to be completed within a comparatively short period of time. This not only influenced the design of buildings but also the detailed design of the entire residential community. The unusual aspect about the plans for this community was the careful attention given to a functionally efficient layout so that all residents could be located in a convenient relationship to schools, churches, business and professional offices, and shops.

In 1968, as in preceding years, there was ample evidence that plastics were being used extensively to meet new maintenance and construction cost demands imposed upon builders. In reporting on the use of plastics in building construction, *Buildings* reported that in Expo 67, the Montreal world's fair, a dozen pavilions used reinforced plastics as a major building material. The report further indicated that even before Expo 67, the use of fibre-glass-reinforced plastic had demonstrated its worth as an economical material in large building projects. A related concern to the owners of buildings was the cost of maintenance, and reinforced plastic offered economies in this regard as well. In construction, the economies emerging from the use of plastics were reported to be manyfold. Using plastics allowed a reduction in the overall weight of a building, thereby making it possible to reduce the size of the steel frame and foundations and to introduce the utilization of prefabricated parts that could be quickly put into place with the use of modern construction machinery. Furthermore, fabricated reinforced plastic was reputed to have high strength, was easy to shape and resisted corrosion. It was believed that the use of this material in self-contained prefabricated shells would offer a significant advantage in reduced inside construction work and would make possible the construction of buildings that could be dismantled easily and moved to other locations if necessary or desirable.

Technology likewise brought about the extensive use of glass in the construction of buildings. The appropriate design of buildings greatly reduced the costs that had been involved in the use of glass in the past. Various types of techniques were utilized to overcome the problems created by the use of glass such as the amount of heat caused by the sun on glass, which led to the need for more air conditioning. It was reported that the trend in 1968 was toward a more extensive use of larger panes of glass and a greater use of heat-absorbing and solar-reflecting glass. The use of glass as a facing material for buildings was expected to continue to increase, mainly because it allowed more floor space and was considered desirable as a design feature. One of the most significant innovations had been the float process for producing structural glass. This method eliminated the need for grinding and polishing and resulted in a smooth, distortion-free glass that could be used in the same way as plate glass. A new

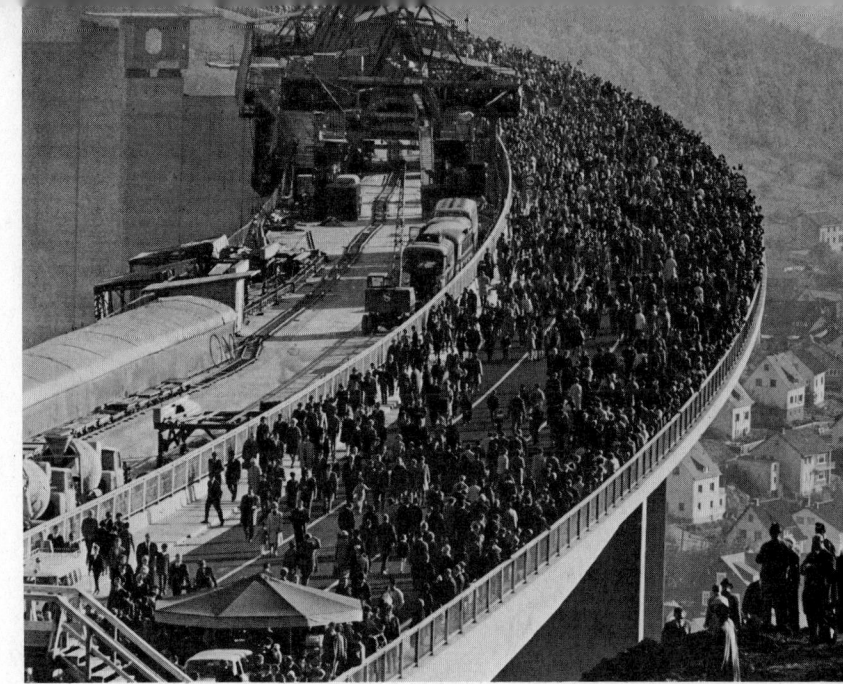

Crowd of thousands inspecting the Siegtal highway bridge prior to its official opening in 1968. Located in Siegen, W.Ger., the bridge was part of the new Dortmund–Giessen Autobahn.

method of glazing allowed large panels to be hung free of stress and strain. (C. C. O.)

Dams. *Europe.* At the beginning of 1967 there were 107 large dams under construction on Spanish territory—95 on the mainland and 12 on the Canary Islands. Construction continued in 1968 on the Almendra Dam on the Tormes River. The main structure was of the cupola type and would provide the storage for one of Spain's most important hydroelectric developments. The dam (663 ft. high) was designed to have a right-hand embankment and a left-hand buttress section, giving a total crest length of about 1,860 ft. The Atazar arch dam on the Lozoya River (height 430 ft., crest length 1,607 ft., volume 900,000 cu.yd.) and the Gran Suarna arch dam on the Navia River (height 499 ft., crest length 1,148 ft., volume 884,200 cu.yd.) were also among the more important of those under construction.

In France the Vouglans arch dam on the Ain River, 426 ft. high, was completed early in 1968. The project would create 478,313 ac.-ft. of water storage, the second largest capacity in France. In Switzerland the Punt dal Gall double-curvature arch dam on the Spöl River was inaugurated at the end of May. This structure (volume 910,000 cu.yd.) was remarkable for its crest length (1,771 ft.) and height (426 ft.). The Santa Maria double-curvature arch dam (height 389

ft., crest length 1,848 ft., volume 837,000 cu.yd.) and the Gebiden double-curvature arch dam (height 406 ft., crest length 1,072 ft., volume 275,000 cu.yd.) were completed at the end of 1967, as was the Austrian Durlassboden rockfill dam with a symmetrical earth central core (height 249 ft., volume 2,970,000 cu.yd., storage capacity 45,833 ac.-ft.). Under construction in Austria was the Schlegeis arch dam (height 425 ft., crest length 2,380 ft., volume 1,250,000 cu.yd., storage capacity 105,833 ac.-ft.).

In Romania the Izvorul-Muntelung concrete gravity dam, 417 ft. high (volume 2,150,000 cu.yd., storage capacity 745,000 ac.-ft.), was being built, and in Turkey work began on the Oymapinar arch dam on the Manavgat River (height 607 ft., volume 916,000 cu.-yd., storage capacity 227,000 ac.-ft.). Construction also continued on the Gokcekaya arch dam (height 518 ft., crest length 1,201 ft., volume 790,000 cu.yd., storage capacity 746,000 ac.-ft.). The 1,017-ft.-high Nurek rockfill dam with a loam core was nearing completion in the Soviet Union. The project comprised a surface-type powerhouse with nine vertical power units. The dam would be the highest of any earth or rockfill dam in the world.

Asia. In Pakistan the huge Mangla earthfill dam on the Jhelum River, a tributary of the Indus River, was inaugurated on Nov. 23, 1967. This 380-ft.-high dam

Major World Dams Under Construction in 1968*

Name of dam	River	Country	Type†	Height (ft.)	Length of crest (ft.)	Volume content (cu.yd. in 000)	Gross capacity of reservoir (ac-ft. in 000)
Almendra	Tormes	Spain	AG	663	1,860	3,275	2,005
Aswan, High (Sadd-el Aali)	Nile	U.A.R.	ER	364	11,808	56,287	127,281
Auburn	N.F. American	U.S.	A	680	3,500	6,000	2,500
Ayvacik	Yesil Irmak	Turkey	A	551	1,362	1,465	689
Bakovica Klisura	Tara	Yugoslavia	E	495	1,410	7,940	1,120
Beas	Beas	India	E	380	5,000	44,200	6,600
Bennett (Portage Mt.)	Peace	Canada	E	600	6,700	56,680	57,000
Bullards Bar‡	North Yuba	U.S.	A	645	1,800	19,930	930
Cahorabassa	Zambezi	Mozambique	MA	508	750	...	54,000
Castaic	Castaic	U.S.	E	335	5,200	44,000	350
Charvak	Chirchik	U.S.S.R.	ER	551	2,500	24,994	1,626
Chirkey	Sulak	U.S.S.R.	A	764	1,109	1,604	2,250
Cochiti	Rio Grande	U.S.	E	255	28,050	53,000	602
Don Pedro‡	Tuolumne	U.S.	R	580	1,900	16,535	2,030
Dworshak	Clearwater	U.S.	G	593	3,302	6,000	3,453
Emosson	Barberine	Switzerland	A	584	1,736	1,400	180
Gokcekaya	Sakarya	Turkey	A	518	1,201	790	746
Gran Suarna	Navia	Spain	A	499	1,148	884	567
Guri	Caroni	Venezuela	ER	348	2,264	3,894	14,350
Idikki	Periyar	India	A	560	1,100	740	1,375
Ilha Solteira	Paraná	Brazil	EG	262	20,293	32,914	17,187
Inguri	Inguri	U.S.S.R.	A	886	2,240	3,920	1,261
Kanev	Dnieper	U.S.S.R.	E	82	52,950	49,520	2,125
Keban	Euphrates	Turkey	RG	679	3,590	19,620	25,132
Kishau	Tons	India	A	700	940	1,500	1,630
Kolnbrein	Malta	Austria	A	610	1,810	1,800	130
Krasnoyarsk	Yenisei	U.S.S.R.	G	390	3,428	4,970	59,425
Melones‡	Stanislaus	U.S.	ER	608	1,500	17,860	2,400
Mica	Columbia	Canada	R	800	2,550	40,000	19,800
Montanejos	Mijares	Spain	A	554	820	164	203
Mossyrock	Cowlitz	U.S.	A	605	1,750	1,270	1,586
Mratinje	Piva	Yugoslavia	A	721	938	770	722
Nagawado	Azusa	Japan	A	509	1,204	865	100
Nurek	Vakhsh	U.S.S.R.	ER	1,040	2,395	58,860	8,512
Portas	Cambia	Spain	A	499	1,588	979	609
Saratov	Volga	U.S.S.R.	E	131	4,130	34,500	10,860
Sayansk	Yenisei	U.S.S.R.	A	774	3,500	11,925	12,400
Talbingo	Tumut	Australia	R	530	2,300	19,000	700
Taktogul	Naryn	U.S.S.R.	A	705	1,352	3,480	15,800
Tarbela	Indus	Pakistan	E	485	9,000	159,000	11,100
Ukai	Tapti	India	EG	225	16,164	33,370	6,900
Ust-Ilim	Angara	U.S.S.R.	G	344	4,085	5,760	48,100
Viliuy	Viliuy	U.S.S.R.	ER	213	1,968	2,008	12,400
Zeya	Zeya	U.S.S.R.	E	371	2,313	17,580	26,000
MAJOR WORLD DAMS COMPLETED IN 1967 AND 1968							
Curnera	Rein de Curnera	Switzerland	A	499	1,115	824	32
Jari	Jari-Jhelum	Pakistan	E	234	7,050	43,000	8
Mangla	Jhelum	Pakistan	E	380	11,000	84,000	5,900§
Manicouagan No. 5	Manicouagan	Canada	MA	704	4,200	2,600	115,000
Oroville	Feather	U.S.	ER	770	7,600	80,325	3,484
San Luis	San Luis	U.S.	E	384	18,500	78,000	2,095
Vidraru	Arges	Romania	A	545	1,000	654	377
Yellowtail	Bighorn	U.S.	A	525	1,450	1,460	1,375

*Having a height exceeding 492 ft. (150 m.); or having a total volume content exceeding 20 million cu.yd. (15 million cu.m.); or forming a reservoir exceeding 12 million ac-ft. capacity.
†Type: E=earthfill; R=rockfill; A=arch; G=gravity; MA=multiple arch.
‡Replacement of present dam.
§Formed jointly by Jari and Mangla dams.

(T. W. Me.)

was completed a year ahead of schedule. Its spillway, containing 1.2 million cu.yd. of concrete, was the world's largest. Construction was started on the Tarbela earth and rockfill dam on the Indus River (height 485 ft., crest length 9,000 ft., volume 160 million cu.yd., storage capacity 11.1 million ac.-ft.). It would be one of the largest of the rockfill type.

In India the Nagarjunasagar stone masonry dam, 411 ft. high, due to be completed in 1971, would have one of the world's biggest masonry sections (4,756 ft. long). It would impound 9.4 million ac.-ft. and irrigate 3.2 million ac. of semiarid land. At the beginning of 1967 there were about 160 dams under construction in India.

Construction continued in Japan on the Nagawado arch dam on the Azusa River (height 509 ft., crest length 1,204 ft., volume 865,000 cu.yd.). This imposing structure, scheduled for completion in 1969, was the largest of the three arch dams being built as part of the Azusa hydroelectric project. In 1967–68 approximately 65 dams were being built in Japan.

North and South America. About 240 dams of various types were under construction in North America in 1967. The Amistad earthfill and concrete gravity dam on the Rio Grande, a joint project of the U.S. and Mexico, was nearing completion and started storing water in the spring of 1968. The Morrow Point double-curvature arch dam, on the Gunnison River, Colorado, 465 ft. high, was topped in September 1967. In January 1968, gates were lowered to begin storage in the reservoir. The dam was the first large one of that type built in the U.S. and was characterized by a unique free-fall spillway in the crest of the dam and a 60-ft.-deep stilling basin at the foot. The Boundary arch dam on the Pend Oreille River (height 400 ft., storage capacity 95,000 cu.yd.) was inaugurated in January. This thin-arch dam was only 32 ft. thick at the base and 8 ft. thick at the crest. Under construction were: the New Bullards Bar double-curvature arch dam on the North Yuba River, due to be the highest in California and one of the longest arch dams in the world (height 645 ft., crest length 1,800 ft.); and the Melones earth- and rockfill dam on the Stanislaus River, California (height 608 ft.), which would be the second highest earthfill structure in the U.S. The Portage Mountain earthfill dam on the Peace River, British Columbia (height 600 ft., volume 60 million cu.yd., crest length 6,700 ft., storage capacity 62 million ac.-ft.), was completed at the end of 1967.

In Brazil the Ilha Solteira earth and gravity dam on the Paraná River (height 262 ft., storage 17,187,000 ac.-ft.) was under construction.

Oceania. In Australia the Geehi earth- and rockfill dam was inaugurated at the end of 1967; the Blowering earthfill dam (height 368 ft., volume 14 million cu.yd., storage 846,000 ac.-ft.) and the Talbingo rockfill dam (height 530 ft., volume 19 million cu.yd.) were under construction in 1968. All these projects were part of the Snowy Mountains Scheme. In New Zealand the Aviemore combined concrete and earth dam across the Waitaki River neared completion.

Africa. The Pongolapoort arch dam (height 293 ft., crest length 1,580 ft., volume 750,000 cu.yd., storage capacity 2 million ac.-ft.) and the Hendrik Verwoerd arch dam on the Orange River, with the exceptional crest length of 3,000 ft., were under construction in South Africa. The latter would create the main storage reservoir of the Orange River Project. In Mozambique the Cahorabassa double-curvature arch dam being built on the Zambezi River (height 508 ft.) would bestow benefits not only in Mozambique but also in Malawi, Rhodesia, South Africa, and Zambia. (CL. M.)

Roads. At the Second International Conference on the Structural Design of Asphalt Pavements, held at the University of Michigan, Ann Arbor, in August 1967, the theme, "Fundamental Concepts of Design and Their Correlation with Field Performance," threw into prominence a basic weakness in current road pavement design methods. Whereas in almost all other branches of engineering the design of structures and machines was based on generally accepted theory, there was no such theoretical basis for the pavement design methods used in different parts of the world. All were based almost entirely on judgments resulting from actual experience. Theories of pavement design were being developed using the concept that the road structure could be represented by a series of layers with different elastic properties. Although at the end of this conference it was clear that no such theory had yet been developed for full practical use, the stage seemed set for rapid advances in the application of theory to practical advantage in the next few years. In November 1967, the 13th World Road Congress of the Permanent International Association of Road Congresses was held in Tokyo. Delegates from 55 countries considered reports on general highway matters, flexible pavements, rigid pavements, the road in relation to traffic requirements, and urban road networks.

Europe. It was announced in 1968 that the U.S.S.R. was planning to increase its road network by about 40,000 mi., that is, by one-fifth, over the next five years. About 600 mi. of the highway linking Leningrad and Murmansk had been completed. Ring roads had also been completed in Podolsk, Serpukhov, Tula, and Kursk.

In Italy a 196-mi. section of expressway in Valle d'Aosta, linking Quincinetto and Verrès, was opened to traffic. A 90-mi. section between Salerno and Reggio di Calabria was also opened; this expressway would be 275 mi. long when completed.

In Switzerland a 7.5-mi. expressway section, linking Mendrisio and Grancia, was opened to the south of Lugano. Another 7.5-mi. section, this one between St. Margrethen and Castione, on national road N.13, was also completed. The Innsbruck–East Matrei section of Austria's Brenner Expressway was opened to traffic in December 1967.

With the opening during 1968 of 16 mi. of the French Autoroute du Nord, north of Bapaume, there were 134 mi. of continuous expressway between Paris and Lille, close to the Belgian border. In West Germany the North-South Expressway was opened throughout its entire length from Hamburg to Würzburg.

An important Norwegian road, linking the eastern valleys in the region of Haukeligrend with the western fjords, was opened early in the year for all-year-round traffic (it was formerly closed in winter). An 8-mi. expressway section opened near Helsinki was an extension of another expressway, which, with a total length of 16.8 mi., provided the longest dual road of its kind in Finland. During the year, Greece opened the Lamia–Velestinon–Larisa highway section (89 mi. long) of the E92 European road artery.

The £7,470,000 Townhead interchange in Glasgow, Scot., was officially opened in April. It formed a part of the first section of the Glasgow inner ring road

<small>MARION KAPLAN</small>

Paving of the main highway linking Kenya's capital, Nairobi, and the country's main port, Mombasa, was completed in mid-1968.

designed to reduce traffic congestion in the city. About 90 mi. of new expressway were built in Great Britain during 1967–68.

North and South America. During the year Peru announced the completion of the first express highway ever built there, running between Lima and Pucusana. The first 124 mi. of the marginal highway between Tabalosos and Juanjui were also completed. A 10.6-mi. section of that highway extended from Satipo across the Satipo River to just outside the village of Mazamari. The new route was designed to open up extensive lands suitable for colonization.

The opening of the Rama Road bridge in Nicaragua in January completed this important Central American link between the Atlantic and the Pacific oceans. The road, gravel-packed and partially paved, extended 160 mi. from the river port of Rama, near Bluefields on the Atlantic coast, through Nicaragua's underdeveloped eastern region to Managua, the capital, and then to the principal ports on the Pacific.

In November 1967, two new lanes on the 253-mi. President Dutra Highway in Brazil were opened. As a result, the journey between Rio de Janeiro and São Paulo was reduced from about ten hours to six or seven hours.

By the end of 1967, more than 25,000 mi. of the United States 41,000-mi. national system of interstate highways were open to traffic and another 6,000 mi. were under construction. This interstate system would be the key highway network in the U.S. and was expected to carry more than 20% of all traffic. The projects were planned to accommodate the traffic expected 20 years after the time they were designed.

Africa. A new road across the Sahara Desert was opened during the year. Making use of old caravan routes, it extended through Nefta, an important oasis in southern Tunisia, through El Oued in Algeria, and across the Sahara in eastern Mali to Niger. A modern highway, 307 mi. long, between Nairobi, the capital, and Mombasa, the major port of Kenya, was completed in June. Other roads of importance completed during the year were: in Algeria, the road from Adrar to Bechar (454 mi.) and on to Tindouf (435 mi.); in Nigeria, from Maiduguri to Lake Chad; and in Tanzania, from Mkumbara to Kisangiro.

Asia and Oceania. Japan's new Tokyo–Nagoya

expressway was partly opened to traffic in May. The 216-mi. route would link up with the 118-mi. Nagoya–Kobe expressway at Komaki, near Nagoya, and would provide a modern road system through the main island of Honshu. The Tokyo–Nagoya expressway was a fully controlled, asphaltic concrete, limited-access highway, costing an estimated $951 million. Three sections of the 214-mi. Tomei Expressway, from Tokyo to Komaki, were also opened to traffic.

It was announced during the year that, of the 7,381 mi. of road in Papua and New Guinea, 338 mi. were now paved; 985 mi. had surfaces of gravel, crushed stone, or stabilized soil; 4,149 mi. were earth roads; and 1,909 were unimproved. The annual expenditure on road improvement and development there stood at $8.5 million.

The first section of the Warringah Expressway at Sydney, Austr., was opened in June. More than a quarter of a million explanatory sketches and leaflets were distributed before the opening to help motorists understand the complexities of the 1½-mi. section, which cost A$28.3 million to build. In New Zealand extensive expressways were under construction at Auckland, Wellington, and Christchurch.

(R. S. Mɪ.)

Tunnels. During 1968 the development of new machines to make tunneling safer continued. In Japan a digger shield 23 ft. in diameter was designed for use in compressed air working; it maintained the pressure at the cutting face only, enabling the operators to work under atmospheric pressure.

Throughout the world many road tunnels were either under consideration or being built. At Antwerp, Belg., the world's largest sunken tube tunnel, forming part of the E3 European road link, was under construction across the Scheldt River. Five precast, prestressed concrete units were floated out on the river to the required positions. Each section weighed 47,000 tons and was 328 ft. long, 157 ft. wide, and 27.8 ft. high. The tunnel was designed to accommodate six lanes of roadway, two railway tracks, and a motorcycle lane. Also part of the same road link was the Limfjord Tunnel at Aalborg in Denmark. This tunnel, built in the same way as that across the Scheldt, though only containing six lanes and a sidewalk, was to be complete by the summer of 1969. The submerged section was 1,670 ft. in length, and it comprised five prefabricated concrete units, each 334 ft. long, 92 ft. wide, 27.8 ft. high, and weighing 25,000 tons.

A two-lane highway tunnel between France and Spain, through the Pyrenees Mountains, was under construction. The completed tunnel would be 24 ft. wide, 18 ft. high, and 9,900 ft. long, and would shorten the route between the two countries by 20 mi. A six-lane sunken tube tunnel under the Elbe River at Hamburg, W.Ger., was completed in June. It was 3,450 ft. long and constructed from eight prefabricated units, each 136 ft. wide and 27.5 ft. high. At Kiesberg, W.Ger., construction started on Europe's only double-decker tunnel. It would be 3,200 ft. long and 43 ft. high with a floor built halfway up to provide a roadway on each deck for traffic to travel in either direction. The ventilation would be produced by the suction caused by the movement of the vehicles.

In Britain enlargement of the pilot heading for the second Mersey Tunnel began, using the boring machine previously used for the Mangla Dam tunnels in Pakistan. This tunnel, 7,300 ft. long and 31 ft. 7 in. in diameter, was driven through weakly cemented sandstone. The section under the river was to be lined

with flexible reinforced concrete segments with an inner steel skin to prevent the entry of water through the fissured rock. Where the tunnel emerged from rock at the Liverpool end for 640 ft., the lining would be orthodox cast iron. The Great Charles Street tunnel in Birmingham, Eng., was being constructed as part of that city's inner ring road scheme. The tunnel was 1,900 ft. long through sandstone and was constructed as double horseshoe sections, each 30 ft. wide and 25 ft. high, sharing a common concrete spine wall. Before excavation of the roof in arched heading, the spine and sidewalls were excavated by a mechanical digger, and the concrete walls were cast. Ventilation would be by injection of air at high velocity from a central fan house to induce longitudinal airflow from the portals. At Heathrow Airport, London, a vehicular tunnel connecting the central terminal area and the new cargo terminal, begun in the autumn of 1967, was completed. The driven tunnel was 2,048 ft. long with extensions in cut-and-cover construction. The internal diameter of 33 ft. 9 in. made it the largest tunnel in Britain to be shield-driven in soft ground. The primary lining was formed from boltless precision precast concrete segments stressed by hydraulic jacks to form a tunnel ring.

Many tunnels were built in 1968 for new, or for extensions to existing, underground railway systems throughout the world. At San Francisco construction of the tunnels for the Bay Area Rapid Transit System railway continued and, by July, of the total of 57 tube sections for the 3.6-mi. Trans-Bay Tube, 37 had been floated out and sunk into position. The tube sections were constructed of a structural steel shell acting compositely with a 2-ft. internal concrete lining; they housed two separate tracks and a duct for ventilation and services. Because of earthquake considerations, the tube was designed as a 3.5-mi. continuous pipe floating on the soft alluvial soils of the bay. Sliding universal joints were provided at each end of the tube where it joined the relatively rigid underground subway.

In Japan an investigatory pilot heading 14 mi. long was started for the Seikan Tunnel, which would be the world's longest undersea crossing, connecting Japan's main island of Honshu with the island of Hokkaido. This tunnel would be built through tufa and andesite, and three major faults were identified on the route. The decision whether to construct a twin- or single-track main tunnel would depend on the information on the ground conditions provided by the pilot heading. Near Kobe work started on six access tunnels for a 10-mi. twin-track railway tunnel through Rokko-Zan Mountain for the Sanyo line. The tunnel was designed to be a concrete-lined horseshoe section 27.2 ft. wide and 26.7 ft. high and would be driven through badly faulted granite containing water-filled seams of·broken rock.

The first 5½-mi. section of the Victoria Line underground railway in London was opened in September, and the remainder was due to be opened by the spring of 1969. Civil engineering work for the extension to Brixton was under way. It was hoped that the extension would be completed in the early 1970s.

It was announced in November that the cost of an Anglo-French tunnel across the English Channel could be as high as £350 million by the time it was built.

(H. D. M.)

ENCYCLOPÆDIA BRITANNICA FILMS. *St. Lawrence Seaway* (1959); *The Panama Canal* (1961); *The Suez Canal* (1962); *Holland: Hold Back the Sea* (1967).

Equatorial Guinea

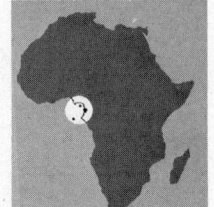

The African republic of Equatorial Guinea consists of Río Muni, which is bordered by Cameroon on the north, Gabon on the east and south, and the Atlantic Ocean on the west; and the offshore islands of Fernando Po and Annobón. Area: 10,830 sq.mi. (28,050 sq.km.). Pop. (1968 est.) 281,000. Cap. and largest city: Santa Isabel, or Fernando Po (pop., 1965 est., 37,152). President in 1968, Francisco Macias Nguema.

A Spanish possession since 1778, with the status of an autonomous region of Spain from 1963, Equatorial Guinea became an independent republic on Oct. 12, 1968. In elections held the previous month Francisco Macias Nguema, candidate of a tripartite electoral coalition, was chosen as the republic's first president.

In spite of opposition to independence within the colony itself—mainly by the indigenous Bubi people on Fernando Po, who feared possible domination by the more populous, less developed mainland territory of Río Muni—it had been promised by the Spanish chief of state, Gen. Francisco Franco, in a decree of February 19. Rejecting a UN proposal that independence should be granted by mid-July, the Spanish Cortes on July 24 approved a draft constitution embodying certain guarantees for the future rights of the Fernando Po inhabitants in relation to the state as a whole. This constitution was accepted by 63.1% of the participants in a national referendum held on August 11, in which 93.7% of the electorate took part.

Elections to the presidency, to the new 35-seat National Assembly, and to local councils took place on September 22. As none of the four presidential candidates then achieved a clear majority, a runoff between the two leaders was held on September 29, resulting in victory for Macias, the candidate of IPGE (Popular Idea of Equatorial Guinea—his own party) and dissident wings of MUNGE (National Union Movement of Equatorial Guinea) and MONALIGE (National Liberation Movement of Equatorial Guinea). The runner-up was Bonifacio Ondó Edu, representing the main wing of MUNGE and formerly prime minister of the autonomous government.

(PH. D.; X.)

See also Dependent States.

EQUATORIAL GUINEA
Education. (1965–66) Primary, pupils 37,373, teachers 599; secondary, pupils 1,688, teachers 51; vocational, pupils 464, teachers 35; teacher training, students 178, teachers 49.
Finance. Monetary unit: Spanish peseta with a par value of 70 pesetas to U.S. $1 (168 pesetas = £1 sterling). Budget (1966) balanced at 1,650,623,000 pesetas.
Foreign Trade. (1965) Imports 1,284,000,000 pesetas (62% from Spain and provinces in 1961); exports 1,635,000,000 pesetas (97% to Spain and provinces in 1961). Main exports (1964): cocoa 45%; timber 16%; coffee 15%.
Transport and Communications. Length of bus routes (1962) 5,002 km.; buses in use 124. Ships entered (1964) 582; cargo unloaded (1962) 158,100 metric tons, loaded 455,400 metric tons. Telephones (Jan. 1965) 1,249. Radio receivers (1966) 27,650.
Agriculture. Production (in 000; metric tons; 1966; 1965 in parentheses): cocoa (1966–67) 39, (1965–66) 32; coffee 6.4 (6.7); palm kernels, exports *c.* 2 (2.3); palm oil *c.* 3.8 (3.8); timber, exports (1965) 331. Livestock (in 000; 1965–66): sheep *c.* 26; cattle 3; pigs *c.* 4; goats *c.* 5.
Industry. Electricity production (1964) 10,212,336 kw-hr.

Ethiopia

A constitutional monarchy of northeastern Africa, including the formerly autonomous federated state of Eritrea, Ethiopia is bordered by the Somali Republic, the French Territory of Afars and Issas, Kenya, the Sudan, and the Red Sea. Area: 471,776 sq.mi. (1,221,-900 sq.km.). Pop. (1967 est.): 23,644,300. Cap. and largest city: Addis Ababa (pop., 1968, 644,100). Language: Amharic (official) and English. Religion: Ethiopian Orthodox (Coptic) Christian 65%; Muslim 30%. Emperor, Haile Selassie I; prime minister in 1968, Aklilu Habte Wold.

Ethiopia's long-standing quarrel with neighbouring Somalia was patched up in a series of high-level talks between the two countries, culminating in the visit of the Somali prime minister, Muhammad Haji Ibrahim Egal, to Addis Ababa in September. Ethiopia also considerably improved relations with its western neighbour, the Sudan. On the wider international scene, 1968 was significant for the strenuous peacemaking efforts of Emperor Haile Selassie as chairman of the Organization of African Unity (OAU) Six Nation Consultative Committee on Nigeria. Although unsuccessful in bringing about a cease-fire, these talks undoubtedly hastened the provision of relief missions to Nigeria.

Ethiopia also participated in events marking aspects of development on the continent. In April the foundation stone was laid in Addis Ababa for the All-Africa Leprosy and Rehabilitation Training Centre, supported by aid from the U.S., the U.K., Norway, Sweden, and the World Council of Churches.

The third five-year economic and social development plan was launched, with a government budget for the fiscal year 1961 (Ethiopian calendar) exceeding Eth$600 million, the largest in its history. The development plan incorporated a number of large aid agreements signed during the year, notably for Eth$64 million with the Swedish International Development Association (SIDA) for a five-year primary school-building program and for assistance totaling Eth$44 million from the World Bank, SIDA, and the West German government for highway development.

Nature's contribution was, however, negative, for the country experienced what were probably the heaviest rains of the century, resulting in considerable damage to crops and in disastrous floods in the middle Webi Shebeli at Kelafo. There were also serious locust infestations. Both the U.S. and the U.S.S.R. contributed large quantities of insecticide in efforts to control the locust swarms.

In common with universities elsewhere, the Haile Selassie I University (Addis Ababa) was disrupted during March by student demonstrations which originated in a protest against the wearing of miniskirts but developed into a wider conflict with the authorities. Other developments in the university included the graduation of the first physicians from the medical faculty and the phasing out of contract support by the University of Utah for the faculty of education and the University of Oklahoma for the faculty of agriculture, as those programs had produced a full complement of local, trained staff.

A spectacularly unsuccessful attempt by a British expedition in March to navigate the Blue Nile (Abbai) River from Lake Tana to the Sudan border was followed by a second British expedition in September. This larger expedition, totaling 70 members and in-

TERRENCE SPENCER FOR WORLD BANK

Camel caravan resting near the Awash River at the junction of an old camel trail and the new highway linking Wonde and Adola.

cluding Ethiopian personnel, employed aircraft to supply the teams in the gorge and succeeded in navigating the 425 mi. of river in two stages. This was regarded as a considerable feat because it is only feasible to navigate the Blue Nile during the flood season when it has sufficient water, and at that time cataracts, whirlpools, and huge waves, sometimes as high as 12 ft., are frequently encountered.

During the year, Ethiopia received visits from Vice-Pres. Hubert Humphrey of the U.S., Marshal Tito of Yugoslavia, and the shah of Iran. The year was also

ETHIOPIA

Education. (1965–66) Primary, pupils 378,750, teachers 9,137; secondary, pupils 50,438, teachers 1,603; vocational, pupils 3,461, teachers 271; teacher training, students 1,680, teachers 93; higher (at 2 universities; 1966–67), students 3,096, teaching staff 469.

Finance. Monetary unit: Ethiopian dollar, with a par value of Eth$2.50 to U.S. $1 (Eth$6 = £1 sterling). Gold and foreign exchange, central bank: (June 1968) U.S. $69 million; (June 1967) U.S. $78.6 million. Budget (1967–68 est.): revenue Eth$547.3 million; expenditure Eth$581.6 million. Money supply: (June 1968) Eth$385.3 million; (June 1967) Eth$375.7 million.

Foreign Trade. (1967) Imports Eth$357.7 million; exports Eth$252.7 million. Import sources (1966): Italy 19%; Japan 13%; West Germany 11%; Netherlands 9%; U.K. 9%; U.S. 8%. Export destinations (1966): U.S. 44%; Italy 9%; West Germany 6%; Saudi Arabia 5%; U.K. 5%. Main exports: coffee 55%; hides and skins 12%; oilseeds 9%; cereals 8%.

Transport and Communications. Roads (1965) c. 26,000 km. (including 6,300 km. all-weather). Motor vehicles in use: passenger (1966) 26,700; commercial (including buses; 1965) 8,900. Railways (1966) 1,087 km. Air traffic (1967): 284.7 million passenger-km.; freight 15.2 million net ton-km. Telephones (Dec. 1966) 28,610. Radio receivers (Dec. 1964) c. 325,000. Television receivers (Dec. 1966) 5,000.

Agriculture. Production (in 000; metric tons; 1966; 1965 in parentheses): corn 740 (730); teff and sorghum 3,128 (3,060); barley 820 (803); wheat 313 (294); linseed 59 (56); sunflower seed 34 (31); sugar, raw value (1967–68) c. 76, (1966–67) c. 84; chickpeas (1967) 173, (1966) 170; lentils 100 (97); sweet potatoes c. 70 (69); potatoes 146 (142); coffee c. 150 (138). Livestock (in 000; 1965–66): cattle 25,-490; sheep 25,275; goats 17,888; horses 1,352; mules 1,352; asses 3,775; camels 952; poultry 42,600.

Industry. Production (in 000; metric tons; 1965–66): cotton yarn 7.9; cotton fabrics (1964–65) 8; shoes 648 pairs; cement c. 100; electricity (1964–65) 238,000 kw-hr.

notable for a series of overseas visits made by the emperor, who toured Southeast Asia, participated in the OAU meeting on Nigeria in Niamey, Niger, and took part in ceremonies in Cairo marking the dedication of a new cathedral of St. Mark.   (G. C. L.)

European Unity

Even the briefest sketch of the efforts toward unity among European nations in 1968 would take note of the realization of the customs union for manufactured goods for the six states associated in the European Communities. France, West Germany, Italy, Belgium, the Netherlands, and Luxembourg constituted the membership of the three Communities: the European Economic Community (EEC or Common Market), by far the most important; the European Coal and Steel Community (Schuman Pool); and the European Atomic Energy Community (Euratom). As originally projected by the Treaty of Rome, which inaugurated the EEC, annual incremental reductions of tariffs among the six states would have brought the customs union into existence in 1970. Its achievement by July 1, 1968, was, therefore, cause for some elation among the champions of European unity.

Those who witnessed the Brussels ceremonies marking the achievement quite understood that the event was being celebrated at a time when the climate of policy and opinion was distinctly less than propitious for the ambitions of the dyed-in-the-wool Europeans. They knew full well that if these hurdles were to be overcome, and if the customs union were to become a way station toward more intimate collaboration among European states, formidable political obstacles and conventional concepts of national interest would have to be overcome.

The other two institutional expressions of the concept of a united Europe were the 18-nation Council of Europe at Strasbourg, France, and the European Free Trade Association (EFTA), headquartered at Geneva. In 1968, the Council continued, with increasing effectiveness, to serve as an intergovernmental forum. EFTA was hampered by the lack of resolution of the obstacles to membership in the EEC, which at least three of its member states were seeking.

EEC. A major hurdle for the new customs union came during the summer when France, suffering from the economic decline caused by strikes in the spring, sought relief, in part, through special import quotas and subsidies to its exporters. In defense of these measures France pleaded justification under the Treaty of Rome. The measures applied equally to the Community partners and to the rest of the trading world and were a distinct shock to the EEC partners since they came so soon after the customs union had been proclaimed. France had, moreover, acted arbitrarily and without prior consultation with the European Commission at Brussels.

These circumstances suggested to many that the new customs union would continue to experience surprises in the way of nationalistic economic tendencies as it sought to move toward adolescence and adulthood. Apprehension among the EEC partners was by no means wholly allayed when France sought and secured, retrospectively, approval of its actions from the Community and the General Agreement on Tariffs and Trade (GATT) and assured its associates that the special economic measures would be temporary and short-lived.

In addition to this special difficulty with France, rather acrimonious debates continued within the Community on agricultural policy. Farm, dairy, and related products were outside the customs union plan and subject to special arrangements. For grains and staples, to be sure, a single policy had been adopted and was probably irreversible. Indeed, it represented as great an advance toward a common Community policy for agriculture as the customs union already provided for manufactures. How centralized this agricultural policy had become was indicated in rather startling fashion in May, when half of the estimated 5,000 farmers and dairy producers who demonstrated before the European Commission headquarters in Brussels consisted of French farmers. Nevertheless, despite these advances in central control, there were products, particularly dairy products, on which a definitive Community support policy had not yet been agreed. Discussion on this subject reached an impasse more than once. Debate also persisted on the question of the distribution of the cost of agricultural subsidies among national partners. Both West Germany and Italy insisted that France was getting the better of the bargain, and progress toward a greater degree of union in the economic field awaited a favourable decision on these matters.

Those who applauded the completion of the customs union also realized, all too soon, that the elimination of duties and quotas among the Six did not eliminate the frontiers or customs checkpoints. National customs officials would not soon have to seek job protection from their unions. Their professional penchant for filling out documents in quintuplicate could still be satisfied by existing regulations on traffic and inventory control, the latter being applied mostly for the administration of internal taxes and subsidies on goods moving across borders. The claim to survival by customs officers would be ably seconded by others in the various national civil services charged with the enforcement of immigration and public sanitary regulations and of a host of other national regulations that find a focal enforcement point at any national frontier station. The EEC customs union was still a far cry from a community where national economic borders have been razed.

Although considerations of caution tempered enthusiasm, the attainment of the complete customs union was rightly regarded as an event of historic significance. It was a major constitutional achievement. Without it, all other fundamental Community goals would founder and the hope of eventually substituting federal economic policy for purely national policies would have become academic. The customs union was also a great political achievement. Leaders in the six states and in the European Commission had demonstrated the political art of patient and constructive compromise in the interests of a goal that transcended national and particularistic interests. Some of these leaders had not balked at sacrificing certain nationally vested interests, despite threats of voter retaliation that, in a few cases, proved to be quite real. Finally, the customs union was a major contribution toward more orderly world trade.

Accomplishments such as these illustrated graphically the advance of the EEC over EFTA. Although EFTA had achieved free trade among its seven members in 1966, it had no common customs frontier and scarcely any institutional urge to seek a common commercial policy. As the customs union was being unveiled in July, the Community also initiated the first

of the GATT trade reductions that its members had negotiated as a unit in the Kennedy Round. To be sure, these reductions in favour of the rest of the world had been scheduled; but, coming just as the union took effect, they symbolized for the outside world, which might continue to question the EEC's economic liberalism, a desire to prevent the customs union from degenerating into a protectionist club.

While, on balance, 1968 saw considerable advances toward European economic union, steps to advance the broader economic aims of the EEC were also undertaken in various subject areas. Illustrative was the intra-Community agreement to recommend harmonization of the rates and types of taxation by 1970, chiefly by the adoption, by each of the six states, of a value-added turnover or transactions tax modeled on a French tax of this type. Another step was the preparation of rules for the establishment of "European" corporations, that is, corporations whose charters would be registered with the Court of Justice of the EEC and would be formally valid throughout the Community. Still a third illustration was the step taken to secure agreement among national transport ministers on Community licenses for freight haulers and on the substitution of Community freight rates for existing national rates.

Yet another suggestion that the EEC was becoming a more solid economic entity was the activity of the European Investment Bank, an institution operating under a Community charter. A review of the ten years since it had begun operations stated that the bank had extended loans approximating $1 billion, 60% of which had gone to governments or private borrowers for transportation facilities and agricultural resources and 40% to a variety of private industries. Of the total funds committed, about five-sixths went to the six Community states, chiefly for use in less developed regions such as the south of Italy. The other one-sixth went to associate members—Greece, Turkey, and certain African states. Not more than 2% was earmarked for Africa, suggesting that the bank shared the general current hesitation over increasing commitments to the less developed nations.

The bank's loanable funds were derived from the sale of its obligations to investment banking consortia within the Six and in other Western European countries. American underwriting was considerable. The bank's first decade suggested that, in a very limited way, a Community institution was contributing to the establishment of a Western European capital market.

There were also broader issues that engaged the concern of Community leadership. Jean Rey, president of the European Commission and the most articulate recent spokesman of the six states, expressed the fear that progress within the Communities actually complicated the problem of adjusting the economies of potential new members to the integrated economy of the Six. Hence the longer the United Kingdom and other states were kept out, the more difficult it would be to harmonize their economies with the Community economy. He was fearful that it might already be too late to combine policies affecting some of the newer technologies (especially the computer and space technologies), energy (particularly nuclear energy), and the economics of armament and disarmament.

The long-term concern of Rey and of the majority of his associates on the Commission was that if "little Europe" persisted long enough in being "little Europe," hopes of a continent-wide union would never be realized. He condemned the reiterated opposition of

France to membership in the Communities for Britain and other European states, and deplored the fact that France vetoed such membership for a second time in December 1967 and reiterated that veto in September 1968.

Rey also wanted to strengthen Community institutions. Apparently speaking for the great majority of the European Commission, he advocated gradual elimination of the national veto and increasing use of majority or qualified majority voting in decision-making, a change that would augment the managerial powers, and hence the prestige, of the 14-member Commission. At the same time, he wanted to have the European Parliament elected directly and become more intimately involved in making and influencing policy, thus justifying its rather grandiose title. He also recommended steps to overcome the relative indifference of the general public toward European institutions and their purposes. He advocated study groups among farmers, trade unions, and youth, so that such constituencies might begin to understand the stake they had in the political and economic integration of the continent.

EFTA. Following the French veto of its second application to join the Communities, Britain, the leading EFTA state, acknowledged that the issue of EEC membership was not limited to the U.K. but that it affected other EFTA states. "We are," said a British spokesman, "by no means the only country whose hopes of progress towards a genuine European unity have been temporarily disappointed." The membership of EFTA, or the "Outer Seven," consisted of the U.K., Portugal, Switzerland, Sweden, Norway, Denmark, and Austria, with Finland as an associate member. Apparently French Pres. Charles de Gaulle's vetoes had not disheartened those EFTA states that felt that the ambitious concept of unity mirrored in the Communities held more promise for them than the limited goal of EFTA.

Even so, the repeated disappointments administered by the EEC to such EFTA member states as Denmark and Norway, as well as to the U.K., caused more than one EFTA spokesman to raise the same questions that President Rey had posed. Attainment of the Community customs and agricultural unions—and of internal free trade among EFTA members—were successes that might become liabilities if the eventual aim in Europe was to abolish blocs and establish a continent-wide union.

Meanwhile, in its eighth year EFTA boasted quite properly that since December 1966 it had provided a free trade area with an internal market for 100 million persons. During the first year for which tariffs and quotas had been abolished (1967), intra-EFTA trade had increased by some $10\frac{1}{2}\%$ in terms of relatively stable prices. During that year, moreover, the free trade area was extended to include the Faeroes, a commercially autonomous Danish island area. Finland was also firmly integrated into the free trade area. These were modest achievements, but they suggested that, while EFTA members might still be awaiting admission bids to the EEC, they were not just marking time but were building up a respectable record as a liberal trade bloc, at least among themselves.

Council of Europe. The oldest of the European agencies, the Council of Europe, continued to air problems and possible solutions in such broad areas as education, social welfare, civil rights, science and technology, public health, and medicine. The fact that the membership of the Consultative Assembly of the

Council consisted of persons who were members of their own national legislatures and who often represented both governing coalition and opposition ensured a direct relationship among national lawmakers in an international forum and greatly enhanced the usefulness of their discussions. In 1968 the Council's Consultative Assembly considered 31 reports of its own committees and outside authorities and adopted some 15 recommendations for action by member states.

Although the Council's agenda supported the observation that since its founding in 1948 it has changed from a "diplomatic alliance" to an agency for technical cooperation, the Council had by no means lost its symbolic political significance as the most comprehensive expression of united Europe.

Nor was "high policy" entirely outside the Council's orbit. In September it took the initiative in seeking the views of Western European states on the Soviet invasion of Czechoslovakia. Earlier it had made recommendations on a peace formula for the Middle East and on the trials of intellectuals in the Soviet Union. On still another occasion the Council threatened to use cancellation or suspension of Greece's membership as a sanction for its demand that Greece restore an acceptable form of parliamentary democracy by the spring of 1969 at the latest.   (A. J. Z.)

See also Commercial Policies; Defense; Payments and Reserves, International; Trade, International.

Fairs and Shows

Undaunted by soaring inflation, domestic strife, and general unrest around the world, more than one billion persons flocked to an estimated 14,000 indoor and outdoor public fairs, exhibitions, and shows during 1968; nearly twice that number attended the better than 16,000 amusement parks. At least three-fourths of the facilities and events showed gains in business returns of 15–20%. Over 110 million North Americans attended approximately 4,000 state, county, district, and provincial fairs in the U.S. and Canada, while three times that number patronized the amusement parks, zoos, and aquariums. The majority of the events in North America recorded the highest grosses in their history.

HemisFair was the only world's fair in 1968. Held at San Antonio, Tex., on 92.6 ac. in the heart of the business district, the U.S. Southwest's first world's fair drew 6,384,482 visitors from April 6 to October 6. Closing short of its predicted 7.2 million attendance, the $156 million fair suffered a deficit of more than $6 million. The fair had been sanctioned as a special category, controlled-theme world's fair by the Bureau of International Expositions, and 35 nations participated. Its Tower of the Americas, standing 622 ft. high with a revolving restaurant at the 550-ft. level, was the tallest permanent world's fair structure since the Eiffel Tower. In the industrial and institutional exhibits sector, 19 major U.S. industrial firms were represented by pavilions and exhibits. The three other areas were the International sector, complete with pavilions, shops, and restaurants; Fiesta Island, with games, rides, and souvenir stands; and the Theme exhibits and structures sector, which collectively endeavoured to illustrate the theme of the fair, "The Confluence of Civilizations in the Americas."

HemisFair's layout was considered ideal for pedestrians. Every pavilion, exhibit, shop, or food stand could be reached easily on foot via elevated walkways

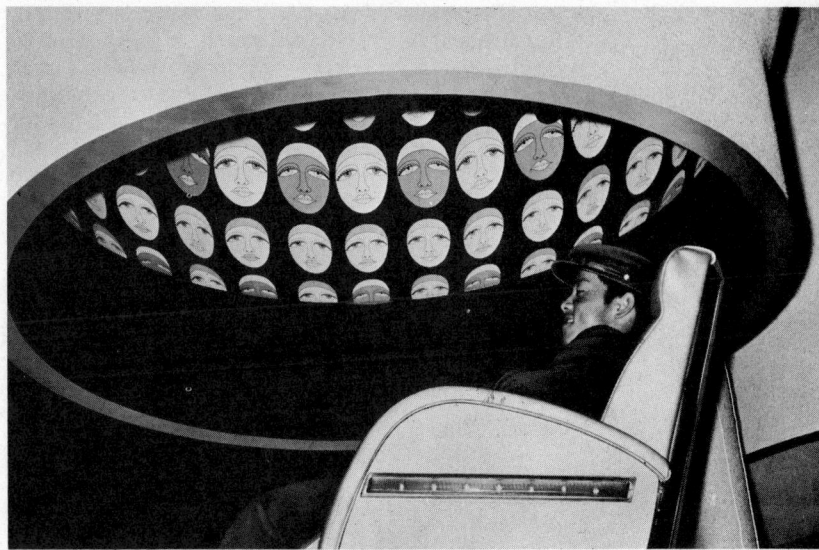

Chair rising into a dome where fluorescent faces and electronic music provide the viewer with a "psychedelic" experience at the eighth International Trade Fair in Osaka, Jap., April 9–29, 1968.

and footbridges. The blending of modern architectural techniques with the old, ranging from Victorian and Greek styles to the adobe and caliche units built by the Spanish settlers and their descendants, won the approval of exhibitors and visitors alike.

Over $10 million worth of Spanish art treasures, including the works of masters such as Goya and El Greco and the only existing portrait of Amerigo Vespucci, were shown in the Theme gallery. "Project Y" was unique for world's fair facilities in that it provided a special area for the youth of many lands to convene. A Woman's Pavilion was claimed to be the "first pavilion of its kind in the history of world expositions." The first such structure, however, had been hailed with equal enthusiasm by the Philadelphia Centennial Exposition in 1876.

Admission to HemisFair was $2 for adults and $1 for children. In late May, however, new management instituted sweeping changes in the face of lagging attendance, and admission prices were greatly reduced. Stellar attractions were brought in to bolster attendance.

Elsewhere in world's fair activities, ground-breaking ceremonies early in the year for the Japan World Exposition in Osaka were marked by some trepidation over international participation. Only 29 nations were committed after 88 invitations to participate had been sent by the fair's patron, Prime Minister Eisaku Sato. More were expected during the year, even as rumours circulated over a possible postponement from March 15, 1970, to 1971. By the year's end, however, a $220 million budget had been approved and ticket sales for Asia's first world's fair had been announced. Observers suggested that the slowness of acceptances by foreign nations was due largely to the fair's lack of emotional magnetism.

International Trade Fairs. Competition among the great European fair centres was increasingly fierce in the course of the year. The trend toward internationalization had caused marked changes in some of the commercial fairs. Greater promotional efforts were mounted overseas; exhibit halls were being modernized and refurbished to accommodate the needs of buyers. In many instances, the leading trade fairs were slowly evolving as instruments of foreign trade policy of their governments.

Despite declining exports, uncertainty of monetary valuations, and tariff restrictions and quotas, most of the world's 800 international trade fairs showed gains of from 11 to 25% in foreign buyer attendance. A few, however, experienced marked reversals as the result of the increased specialization of nearby fairs in other countries. Of 70 nations hosting trade fairs in 1968, 80% reported generally oversubscribed exhibit space sales months before opening. West German trade fairs continued to maintain their popularity, with one-third of the total number occurring at Co-logne. All reported substantial rises in attendance and exhibitors.

Afghanistan celebrated its 50th year of independence with the "1968 Jeshyn" (fair) at Kabul. The 20th Trieste International Samples Fair commemorated the 50th anniversary of the transfer of Trieste to Italy.

Fairs. The key news item about the fair world in 1968 was the passing of the three million attendance mark for the first time at any U.S. state fair. The State Fair of Texas, Dallas, rolled up a 3,014,114 gate October 5–20, up 64,205 from 1967. The fair maintained its lead in the U.S. as the top attendance fair, second only in North America to the Canadian National Exhibition, Toronto. Attendance at the Canadian fair was 3,239,500 in 1968, up 222,500 from 1967.

Gate admissions were higher at a number of U.S. and Canadian fairs, with a few opening their grand-stand shows free. This was a reversal of the trend, initiated a few years before, of boosting ailing grosses by lowering or eliminating front gate fees while charging high fees for grandstand shows that featured top-name talent. European and South American fairs held to comparatively low admission charges. Attendance and grosses ran to all-time highs at U.S. and Canadian fairs with gains of from 17 to 22%. Talent and show bookings were budgeted at over $22 million. Overall costs were generally higher than in 1967.

A number of the million-attendance fairs held or surpassed their previous record gates. These included the Feria Del Hogar, Mexico City; Royal Easter Show, Sydney, Austr.; Pacific National Exhibition, Vancouver, B.C.; Illinois State Fair, Springfield; Minnesota State Fair, St. Paul; and the Ohio State Fair, Columbus.

Industrial Shows. Appropriations for new convention and exposition facilities continued to mount in 1968 as this multibillion dollar business began to feel the pinch of lack of space. Record crowds were noted at most shows, and trade activity was reported to be at its highest level in all sectors. Typical of the shows held exclusively for trade people were the International Exhibition of Plumbing, Heating, and Air Conditioning held at Zürich, and the National Hardware Show at New York City's Coliseum. Typical public shows included the International Salon of Household Equipment and Furnishings at Puteaux, France; the International Flower Show, New York City; and the Ideal Homes Exhibition, Dublin, Ire.

Despite exhibit shortages around the world, some facilities, notably New York City's new Madison Square Garden and Montreal's Place des Arts, reported downturns due to booking problems. The new Madison Square Garden announced a $1.8 million loss for its fiscal quarter ending August 31, compared with a $1 million net profit for the same period in 1967. An estimated 17,000 trade shows and 16,000 conventions were held throughout the world during 1968. By year's end, over $62 billion had been committed for the construction of new facilities for exhibitions.

Amusement Parks. Fun and recreation parks, numbering over 16,400 around the globe, emerged at the year's end with spectacular gains in attendance and grosses as operators continued to invest millions of dollars in new equipment, facilities, and attractions. Over 1.8 billion people jammed amusement parks. Over 1,500 public parks, zoos, and aquariums, and 980 theme parks, kiddielands, and general amusement parks throughout North America attracted a record

Selected Major National and International Fairs, 1968

Country and date	Event and place	Attendance
Afghanistan		
Aug. 24–Sept. 6	International Trade Fair, Kabul	300,000
Australia		
Aug. 8–17	Royal National Show, Brisbane	220,000
Sept. 19–26	Royal Agricultural Show, Perth	270,000
Austria		
Sept. 8–15	International Trade Fair, Vienna	690,000
Belgium		
Sept. 14–29	International Trade Fair, Ghent	525,000
Oct. 26–Nov. 11	International Household Exhibition, Charleroi	700,000
Bulgaria		
Sept. 24–Oct. 1	International Trade Fair, Plovdiv	800,000
Canada		
July 4–13	Calgary Exhibition & Stampede, Alta.	853,620
July 18–27	Klondike Days Fair, Edmonton, Alta.	502,273
Aug. 15–Sept. 2	Canadian National Exhibition, Toronto	3,240,000
Aug. 17–Sept. 2	Pacific National Exhibition, Vancouver, B.C.	1,038,700
Aug. 24–31	Central Canada Exhibition, Ottawa	681,334
Aug. 30–Sept. 8	Provincial Exhibition, Quebec	492,943
Sept. 6–14	Western Fair, London, Ontario	445,942
Chile		
Oct. 7–24	International Fair, Santiago	650,000
Czechoslovakia		
Sept. 8–17	International Trade Fair, Brno	1,000,000
Finland		
Sept. 19–29	International Trade Fair, Helsinki	317,541
France		
Feb. 22–March 3	International Salon of Household Equipment & Furnishings, Puteaux	1,146,792
March 5–10	International Agricultural Machinery Exhibition, Paris	650,000
Sept. 19–30	International Fair, Marseilles	1,500,000
Germany, West		
Sept. 28–Oct. 6	World's Fair of Photography, Cologne	220,000
Greece		
Sept. 1–22	International Fair, Thessaloniki	1,250,000
Hong Kong		
Dec. 5–Jan. 9 '69	Exhibition of Hong Kong Products	1,500,000
Hungary		
May 17–27	International Trade Fair, Budapest	950,000
Iraq		
Oct. 1–30	Baghdad Fair	500,000
Italy		
Feb. 1–11	International Boat Show, Genoa	350,000
Aug. 4–19	International Trade Fair, Messina, Sicily	240,000
Libya		
Feb. 28–March 20	International Trade Fair, Tripoli	525,000
Malta		
July 1–15	International Malta Trade Fair, Naxxar	90,000
Mexico		
March	La Feria Del Hogar, Mexico City	1,550,000
Portugal		
June 9–23	International Trade Fair, Lisbon	253,725
South Africa		
April 5–12	Rand Easter Show, Johannesburg	550,000
Spain		
March 31–April 9	International Agricultural Machinery Fair, Zaragosa	200,000
May 23–June 23	Feria Del Campo, Madrid	2,500,000
Sudan		
December	Khartoum Fair	1,000,000
Switzerland		
Sept. 7–22	Swiss Fall Fair, Lausanne	225,000
Syria		
Aug. 25–Sept. 20	International Fair, Damascus	1,000,000
United Kingdom		
Oct. 16–26	International Motor Exhibition, London	375,000
United States		
Sept. 26–Oct. 5	Alabama State Fair, Birmingham	482,000
Sept. 13–22	Eastern States Exposition, West Springfield, Mass.	703,034
June 28–July 7	50th State Fair, Honolulu, Hawaii	437,000
Aug. 9–18	Illinois State Fair, Springfield	1,099,577
Aug. 23–Sept. 2	Indiana State Fair, Indianapolis	850,000
Oct. 18–27	Louisiana State Fair, Shreveport	564,000
Sept. 20–28	Mid-South Fair, Memphis, Tenn.	704,920
Aug. 24–Sept. 2	Minnesota State Fair, St. Paul	1,457,829
Sept. 12–22	New Mexico State Fair, Albuquerque	642,298
Aug. 30–Sept. 5	Nebraska State Fair, Lincoln	457,000
Sept. 14–22	New Jersey State Fair, Trenton	565,550
Aug. 27–Sept. 2	New York State Fair, Syracuse	563,815
Aug. 22–Sept. 2	Ohio State Fair, Columbus	1,652,074
Sept. 21–29	Oklahoma State Fair, Oklahoma City	925,106
Oct. 5–20	Texas State Fair, Dallas	3,014,114
Sept. 20–29	Virginia State Fair, Richmond	624,325
U.S.S.R.		
Aug. 6–20	International Fishing Equipment Exhibition, Leningrad	200,000
Yugoslavia		
Sept. 12–22	International Autumn Fair, Zagreb	2,000,000
Sept. 22–Oct. 5	International Hunting & Fishing Exhibition, Novi Sad	500,000

Source: Frederick P. Pittera, *Fairs of the World* (1968).

355 million visitors, with grosses well over $500 million.

Carnivals, Rodeos, and Circuses. More fairs in the U.S. and Canada booked carnival shows, rodeos, and circuses than ever before in their history. The public image of carnivals had improved, circuses were fast becoming production extravaganzas, and rodeos emerged with a greater flair for showmanship than their competition. Grosses and attendance jumped sharply around the world. With the exception of smaller, undercapitalized units, virtually all shows reported gains of from 15 to 25% over the last season with some going as high as 60 to 70%.

Circuses enjoyed their best year in 1968 with over 295 tented and indoor shows touring Europe, Africa, Asia, and South America, and over 50 touring North America. Lavish costuming, colourful props, and impressive production numbers replaced the traditional circus acts in a number of North American units. Europe's venerable Circus Williams was purchased by the Ringling Bros. and Barnum & Bailey Circus, whose successful season included its first appearance at the new Madison Square Garden in New York. The Rudy Bros. International Circus in Germany played to capacity audiences, with its 45-car train and 3,000-seat tent, in its second year of operation. Among the circuses reporting bigger years than ever were the Clyde Beatty-Cole Bros. Circus, the ranking tent show in the U.S., Circus Knie of Switzerland, Hamid-Morton Circus, Tom Packs Circus, and Circo Dumbar of Mexico.

Over 3,200 cowboys and some cowgirls competed for nearly $4 million in prize money at more than 2,000 rodeo shows in the U.S. and Canada. Approximately 400 were events sanctioned by the U.S.-based Rodeo Cowboys Association and 150 by the Cowboys Protective Association of Canada. Some of the more gripping aspects of this wild and woolly sport had disappeared in the U.S. as the result of the constant efforts of local humane societies to outlaw rodeos because of the alleged inhumane treatment of animals. Despite such action, more rodeos were held in 1968 than ever before. The annual Texas Prison Rodeo, held in the Huntsville, Ala., prison stadium, drew 64,713 patrons for a gross take of $237,862. At New York's Madison Square Garden, 70,000 rodeo fans paid $300,000 to see the National Mexican Festival and Rodeo.

Livestock and Horse Shows. Great Britain's oldest livestock shows continued to flourish as Europe's key shows in 1968. Attendance by overseas visitors was the highest ever recorded. Breed and market entries also broke previous records with sales bringing top money to registrants. Most annual fairs on the North American continent featured livestock and horse shows, as did the thousands of agricultural fairs around the world.

A number of horse shows were held during the year in conjunction with fairs and livestock shows. In North America, the Pin Oak Charity Horse Show, Houston, Tex., continued to reign as the largest horse show, while Europe's most prominent event was held at Aachen, Ger. Over 4,000 unrecognized horse shows took place in the U.S. and Canada alone during the year, while thousands more were held on the other continents. The American Horse Show Association sanctioned more than 750 shows with cash and plate prizes reported at over $2 million. Quarter Horse and Appaloosa shows increased in the U.S. (F. P. P.)

See also Architecture; Art Exhibitions.

Fashion and Dress

The year 1968 was marked by the individualist in fashion, and by lawlessness. Anything went! Writing in the *Christian Science Monitor* in September, fashion reporter Patricia Shelton said: "Any genius can put a wardrobe together—all it takes is an artist's eye for color, line, and rhythm; confidence; a little common sense and a good credit rating. Prices," she added, "are going up." At about the same time, English *Vogue* wrote: "Fashion is self-consciously sociological and frankly feather-brained. It's classic and immediate. Nostalgic and now. Worldly and other-worldly. Whatever's happening you are part of it and at last you can be yourself and look as you choose."

In this mood of worldwide fashion permissiveness, what could be pinpointed as typical for 1968? The hemline as news had ceased to be. Youthful Londoners still wore their skirts to mid-thigh, but the general trend, insofar as the fashion establishment went—and this included the woman in the street—was to just short of the knees. (Mary Quant, one of the promoters of the mini, had declared, "It is now a classic and therefore boring.") The mid-calf-length midi had, according to one fashion expert, "become merely an extra, whether as coat, cape, pants, or late-day dress." U.S. designer Anne Klein had shown midi coats in her fall collection but cut them shorter "after getting the message from the stores' buyers."

The maxi length (with hemlines often extending to the ankles), which was launched in 1967, did not make any significant progress, despite sporadic boosting by leading designers in most of the fashion-producing countries. Norman Norell showed minis and maxis in his spring 1968 collection but ignored both in the fall collection.

Reviewing *The Why of Fashion* by Karlyne Anspach in the *Guardian*, Alison Adburgham wrote: "No one at this confusing point in fashion history would make predictions with any confidence. But I will hazard that when all the minis and maxis, the neo-1930s and the Victorian revivals have had their day, it may well be the casual yet well-groomed American way of dressing so fitted to modern life that will bridge the great divide now existing between young clothes and the rest." This forecast was already showing signs of being justified by the sportswear influence that permeated the Paris and New York shows in the fall for formal as well as for informal wear. "The tennis sweater gathers sequins and goes to the Opera. The riding habit takes a skirt and goes to lunch at Le Pavillion," wrote a New York fashion reporter.

The 1968 silhouette lay considerably closer to the body. Suit jackets were long, skinny looking, and, typically, belted. They were worn over skirts that were slightly flared or kilted. The London suit was in either plain shetland, overcheck, or flannel, or again in classical Harris or Donegal tweed. Blazer jackets went over the all-round pleated skirt of the print silk dress underneath. Closely belted wraparound "happi" jackets went over shorts or trousers.

The film *Bonnie and Clyde,* set in the gangster days of the 1930s, and later the Gertrude Lawrence musical *Star* with Julie Andrews in the title role, brought with them a nostalgic return to the late 1920s and early 1930s: cardigan jackets, berets worn low over the brow, soft curls, knotted silk scarves, jumper dresses and suits, and a general look of feminine softness. The

Falkland Islands:
see Dependent States

Farming:
see Agriculture

Left, black velvet evening skirt with long-sleeved transparent top from Yves St. Laurent's fall-winter collection. Above, high-necked and long-sleeved top totally separated from the skirt (left) by Donald Brooks and halter-necked design (right) by Jacques Tiffeau. Right, midi-length white dress with attached jeweled belt by Mollie Parnis. Far right, "mini-medievals" inspired by nun's and monk's habits were created exclusively for Paraphernalia by Walter Holmes.

trouser suit, after tentative efforts over the past few seasons to secure a foothold in fashion, appeared at last to be gaining ground. The wide-legged trouser suit launched by Yves St. Laurent, featuring a tunic top, loosely belted, topped by a long, clinging, button-through jacket, went some way toward reconciling the dual demands of practical comfort and femininity for the average woman. Of his "city pants," St. Laurent was reported to have said: "I am convinced that trouser fashions are truly the incoming way to dress." Despite an unenthusiastic reception from the press and initial hesitation among buyers, the final orders for trouser suits and culotte suits were reported to represent two-thirds of the total buying at St. Laurent's fall-winter collection.

The unacceptability of trouser suits in many elegant restaurants continued to put off the press. The story went around of a trousered client who was regretfully refused admittance by the headwaiter of a well-known London restaurant and who, by way of reply, retired to the ladies' room, removed her trousers, presented herself anew in her mini-length suit jacket, and was smilingly led to her table. Apocryphal or not, the story mirrored faithfully enough the crazy incoherence that was inherent in fashion at the time.

Wide belts were an essential feature of the new close-to-the-body silhouette. It was the "fit and fling" line and was to be found in dresses and suits as well as in coats. The firmly belted waistline tended to stress the natural turn of the hip. Geoffrey Beene created suit jackets with padded hips, the first to be used in dressmaking since "figures" went out of fashion. Was it a straw in the wind or the dawn of a new trend?

The new dandyism apparent at this time was expressed in romantic velvet trouser suits worn with frilly silk shirts; by Victorian braiding, jeweled and embroidered waistcoats, Byronic collars, swirling capes, cavalier hats, gold chains, and extravagant baroque costume jewelry. St. Laurent's "George Sand" suits were held responsible for this fashion phenomenon, but its initial inspiration came no doubt from the passion of young Londoners for old clothes from street markets. Panne velvet was a case in point. "The kids have been wearing it in tenth-hand dresses to Chelsea parties and now it's abundant in both couture shows and in our manufactured clothing," wrote London fashion journalist Serena Sinclair. In 1968 Mary Quant put her mini shapes over trousers to create romantic silky ensembles trimmed at waist and neck with rows and rows of gilt chains. Sequin trimmings abounded in the Paris collections.

The flashback to the 1930s produced a feeling for supple, smooth knitwear characterized by long, belted jumper tops over flaring skirts. Or it was the hug-me-tight, casually belted knit dress. Turtleneck collars continued to be popular, but "V" necklines borrowed from the 1930s made their appearance. Wool jersey proved to be one of fashion's favourite fabrics.

After a burst of frank flag colours in the spring, colours quieted in the fall to ladylike neutrals with beige and gray in the lead. Black staged a dramatic comeback and the "little black dress" tentatively returned to sophisticated favour.

Ireland continued to progress in the field of fashion. By 1967 clothing manufacture had grown to be one of the country's leading industries, and Ireland's first Fashion Fair was held in Dublin in April 1968. Donald Davies, whose shirtwaist dresses were already appreciated throughout the world, opened a shop in Paris' West End. A newcomer to the Irish fashion scene was Thomas Wolfangel, winner of the Couture Class gold medal in the London Tailor and Cutter Exhibition for

ARTHUR GREENSPOON AND WILLIAM E. SAURO, "THE NEW YORK TIMES" FROM WIDE WORLD

Left, tunic and pants ensemble made of du Pont's new fabric "Qiana" with jewel trim and feather tassels by Marc Bohan of Christian Dior. Above, tawny guanaco cape from Fur & Sport. Right, Jacques Heim's fall-winter collection included this dark fur tunic with chestnut-coloured leather pants. Far right, fur-trimmed coat over pants won Coty Award for Luba of Elite.

COURTESY, DUPONT COMPANY

AGIP FROM PICTORIAL PARADE

both 1966 and 1967, who opened his own salon in Dublin during the year.

The closing in 1968 of such well-known houses as Balenciaga and Castillo in Paris and Worth in London was symptomatic of the changing pattern of the industry since World War II. In the 1960s the old concept of haute couture was proving to be no longer valid, and younger, more resilient firms such as Dior, Venet, Courrèges, Ungaro, and finally Givenchy, following the lead given by Cardin, were opening ready-to-wear shops and boutiques in many Western capitals and in leading provincial towns.

After a short-lived interest in curls and moplike hair styles in the early part of the year, smoother, smaller heads were proposed by leading Paris stylists for the fall. Alexandre's "apple head"—round and smoothly shining as its name suggests—was accepted as the significant trend by hairdressers in New York, London, and Rome. The general vogue in the fall for helmets, hoods, and snoods was no doubt the cause of this volte-face and the success of the "small, contained" style of hair dressing.

"The stretchiest stockings and panti-hose yet, resulting from a new concept of hosiery manufacture," were announced by the British firm Pretty Polly. These articles were marketed in one standard size and were guaranteed to fit all normal dimensions. Bear Brand, one of Britain's largest hosiery firms, explained its £207,000 group loss in 1967 by the massive swing in consumer preference to stretch stockings, tights, and the popular new "self-support" hose, and a subsequent worldwide shortage of stretch yarn.

Boots continued to be extremely popular, especially with younger women. The latest style to be reported from New York was a two-tone, two-material model either knee or hip high. Shoes, however, appeared to be returning to general favour. Influenced by Italy's lead in styling, the most fashionable shape in Paris, London, and New York was cut well-up on the foot, had a chunky heel that was higher than in the preceding year, and was "piled high with decoration." Toes were still broad but squares were rounded off. Heels continued to climb as the hour grew later.

Meanwhile, the world of men's fashions continued to make news—the more so, perhaps, because of its long quiescence. Even among the more conservative, combinations of colours and patterns that would have been unthinkable a few years earlier were becoming commonplace, and such styles as the turtleneck and pendant were accepted, at least for casual wear. The high-collared Nehru jacket—which even at the height of its popularity had been confined largely to the young and flamboyant—appeared to be losing favour. Symptomatically, one large U.S. formal-wear establishment offered to exchange Nehru suits that it had sold for more conventional evening wear. On the other hand, the closely fitted Edwardian look was apparent, in varying degrees, in both "high-style" clothes and in the pervasive business suit.   (P. W. He.)

See also Cosmetics; Furs; Industrial Review.

Finland

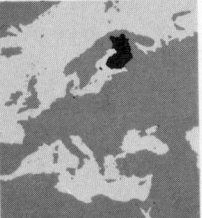

The republic of Finland is bordered on the north by Norway, on the west by Sweden and the Gulf of Bothnia, on the south by the Gulf of Finland, and on the east by the U.S.S.R. Area: 139,128 sq.mi. (337,032 sq.km.). Pop. (1968 est.): 4,675,569. Cap. and largest city: Helsinki (pop., 1968 est., 529,286). Language (1960): Finnish 92.4%; Swedish 7.4%. Religion: Lutheran 92.5%; Orthodox 1.3%. President in 1968, Urho Kaleva Kekkonen; prime ministers, Rafael Paasio and, from March 22, Mauno Koivisto.

Pres. Urho Kaleva Kekkonen was reelected for a third six-year period as head of state in February. He received 201 votes against 66 for the Conservative candidate, Matti Virkkunen, and 33 for Veikko Vennamo. Kekkonen, aged 68, was supported by the Social Democratic Party, the Centre Party, the People's Democratic League, the Liberal People's Party, the Socialist League, and by a fraction of the Swedish Party. He officially began his third term of office on March 1, and on that day, in accordance with Finnish tradition, Prime Minister Paasio resigned. He did not seek reappointment and so the Social Democratic executive group designated as its candidate for prime minister Mauno Koivisto (*see* BIOGRAPHY), governor of the Bank of Finland and formerly finance minister in Paasio's government. Koivisto was asked by the president to form a broadly based coalition government, and his Cabinet, announced on March 22, included six members of the Centre Party, three People's Democrats, one member of the Swedish Party, and one from the Socialist League. Ahti Karjalainen (Centre Party) continued as foreign minister. A new post for economic planning was created, and the new government saw the political comeback (as deputy minister of trade and industry) of Väinö Leskinen, a Social Democrat who in the 1950s was regarded by the U.S.S.R. as a foe of Finnish-Soviet friendship.

The coalition introduced wage and price controls to stabilize the economy, but efforts were hampered by increasing unemployment (numbers had reached about 60,000 at the end of the year). New investment capital was granted to private and state-run enterprises, and the budget for 1969 was planned in an atmosphere of cautious optimism. Exports were improving, and the Finns hoped to achieve a favourable balance of trade by the year's end. However, an 18-day harbour strike, ending in a wage agreement reached on March 8, adversely affected the export of paper and cellulose. Another wage conflict involved about 10,000 nurses and midwives, who went on strike in hospitals in 33 cities and 6 market towns. Their action was much criticized, but because a skeleton staff remained at work no deaths or mistreatment resulted.

The municipal elections held October 6–7 were won by the non-Socialist parties, which during the four-year period 1969–72 would hold about 7,360 seats in local councils as against 4,245 for Socialist deputies. The Socialist parties lost nearly 900 seats. Out of a total 2.2 million votes cast, the Social Democratic Party received 24% (−0.8% compared with 1964), the Centre Party 19.3% (−1.3%), the Peoples' Democratic League 17.1% (−4.9%), the Conservatives 17.4% (+2.9%), the Rural Party 7.3% (+5.8%), the Liberal People's Party 5.8% (−1%), the Swedish Peoples' Party 5.8% (+0.1%), the Socialist League 1.8% (−1.1%), and others 1.5% (+0.1%).

In early October Kekkonen met the Soviet premier, Aleksei N. Kosygin, for unofficial talks near Hangö in southwest Finland. Kosygin came at Kekkonen's invitation to discuss European and worldwide security, international cooperation, and Soviet-Finnish relations in the light of the Warsaw Pact intervention in Czechoslovakia. The atmosphere was friendly, and the outcome of the talks was seen as positive. In August the Finns had voiced their sympathy for the Czechoslovaks.

Kekkonen had already met Soviet leaders in June during a holiday in the Soviet Union, and another example of Finnish-Soviet cooperation was seen on August 5, when the reconstructed Saimaa Canal was in-

augurated. The canal, originally built in 1856 and partly located on territory surrendered to the Soviet Union in 1944, linked the southeast lake district with the Gulf of Finland. It covered 15.2 mi. on Finnish and 12.1 mi. on Soviet territory, and was constructed for vessels of up to 1,600 tons. Although there had been doubts about the wisdom of this project, it was hoped that the waterway would serve to promote the economy of southeast Finland.

The government decided on July 25 that Finland, at least until 1975, would continue to rely on conventional power for industry and domestic use, because the construction of the proposed first nuclear power station involved political matters of great delicacy. The U.K. Atomic Energy Authority, ASEA of Sweden, and the Soviet Techknopromexport had been the final competitors for the order for the 500-Mw. station. One of the reasons for the government's decision was the Soviet announcement that the U.S.S.R. would not provide fuel if the reactor were bought elsewhere.

The first Finnish Peace Corps, consisting of 23 persons, left in August for two years of work in Tanzania, where Finland was already participating in projects in cooperation with the Scandinavian countries.

Besides Kosygin, foreign visitors included Romanian Premier Ion Gheorghe Maurer and Foreign Minister Corneliu Manescu (March 31–April 5), the Soviet first deputy premier, Kirill Mazurov (attend-

FINLAND
Education. (1965–66) Primary, pupils 460,012, teachers 19,899; secondary, pupils 352,049, teachers 18,055; vocational, pupils 75,823, teachers 6,985; teacher training, students 2,478, teachers 372; higher (including 7 universities), students 38,775, teaching staff 3,905.
Finance. Monetary unit: markka, with a par value of 4.20 markkaa to U.S. $1 (10.08 markkaa = £1 sterling). Gold and foreign exchange, central bank: (June 1968) U.S. $322.8 million; (June 1967) U.S. $188.5 million. Budget (1968 est.): revenue 9,250,000,000 markkaa; expenditure 9,249,500,000 markkaa. Gross national product: (1966) 27,530,000,000 markkaa; (1965) 25,760,000,000 markkaa. Money supply: (June 1968) 2,308,000,000 markkaa; (June 1967) 2,105,000,000 markkaa. Cost of living (1963 = 100): (June 1968) 138; (June 1967) 126.
Foreign Trade. (1967) Imports 5,794,000,000 markkaa; exports 5,230,000,000 markkaa. Import sources: West Germany 16%; U.S.S.R. 16%; Sweden 14%; U.K. 13%; U.S. 5%. Export destinations: U.K. 20%; U.S.S.R. 17%; Sweden 9%; West Germany 9%; U.S. 6%; Netherlands 5%. Main exports: paper 31%; timber 16%; wood pulp 16%.
Transport and Communications. Roads (1967) 70,094 km. (including 86 km. expressways). Motor vehicles in use (1967): passenger 551,445; commercial 97,134. Railways: (1966) 5,994 km. (excluding 74 km. private in 1965); traffic (state only; 1966) 2,131,000,000 passenger-km., freight (1967) 5,597,000,000 net ton-km. Navigable inland waterways (1962) 6,679 km. Shipping (1967): merchant vessels 100 gross tons and over 415; gross tonnage 1,063,810. Air traffic (1967): 455,086,000 passenger-km.; freight 7,480,000 net ton-km. Telephones (Dec. 1966) 892,300. Radio receivers (Dec. 1966) 1,605,000. Television receivers (Dec. 1966) 822,000.
Agriculture. Production (in 000; metric tons; 1967; 1966 in parentheses): wheat 507 (369); rye 163 (119); barley 681 (597); oats 840 (881); potatoes 881 (1,066); sugar, raw value (1967–68) *c.* 62, (1966–67) 66; timber (1966) 41,600 cu.m., (1965) 42,900 cu.m.; butter 96 (101). Livestock (in 000; June 1967): cattle 2,036; sheep (June 1966) 175; pigs 653; horses (June 1966) 165; chickens (June 1966) 6,960; reindeer (June 1962) 188. Fish catch (in 000; metric tons) (1966) 71, (1965) 73.
Industry. Production (in 000; metric tons; 1967): iron ore (65% metal content) 643; pig iron 1,038; crude steel 395; copper 34; cement 1,514; plywood (1966) 546 cu.m.; cellulose (1966) 3,737; mechanical wood pulp (1966) 1,743; chemical wood pulp (1966) 3,963; cardboard (1966) 1,064; newsprint 1,217; other paper (1966) 1,020; electricity 16,747,000 kwhr.; manufactured gas 72,480 cu.m.

ing on April 6 the 20th anniversary of the signing of the Finnish-Soviet treaty of friendship, cooperation, and mutual assistance), Israeli Foreign Minister Abba Eban (May 13–14), Bulgarian head of state Georgi Traikov and Foreign Minister Ivan Bashev (June 6–11), U.A.R. Foreign Minister Mahmoud Riad (June 30–31), Pres. Kenneth Kaunda of Zambia (July 12–16), and the president of Cyprus, Archbishop Makarios (August 19–21).

On November 1 Finland was elected a member of the UN Security Council for a two-year period, in succession to Denmark.   (C. F. Sa.)

Fisheries

Among the North Atlantic fishing nations, 1968 followed the previous year's pattern of supply exceeding demand in frozen fish and, for some species, in fresh fish as well. In West Germany, Britain, and France, trawlers were laid up because of poor markets or in an effort to regularize the situation by cutting down landings. The British trawling industry came near disaster, and £4 million of government aid was provided, only to be criticized as being "too little too late." Britain's easygoing import policy was blamed for bringing in excessive foreign landings.

France's problem was aggravated by a further lowering of tariff barriers among Common Market countries. Boulogne and other Channel ports were the scene of disturbances, including attempts to turn back trucks carrying foreign fish. At Lorient, in Brittany, a strike of fishermen grew into a six-month lay-up, which added to the effects of the nationwide student and labour disturbances.

The herring purse seining fishery in Norway and Iceland failed once more to get into high gear, at one time operating a limited, self-imposed quota system with the overloaded meal and oil plants and later suffering from an almost complete failure of the winter herring. Possibly seeing the writing on the wall, a number of owners took delivery of herring seiners with refrigerated tanks, from which they could land herring for sale, brined for human consumption.

Peru continued to dominate the world fish meal market with a landing for the year of nearly 10 million tons—almost one-fifth of the world total. This was achieved despite the fact that the number of fish meal operators had been cut drastically—a sign, perhaps, of increased efficiency ashore and productivity afloat.

In Chile the policy of diversified fishing continued, with shipbuilding and shrimp (*langostino*) doing well. There were signs that other South American countries were planning to exploit their fisheries more fully. Exploratory programs and projects were announced for Colombia, Ecuador, Brazil, and Argentina. The indication was that South America would be the next major expansion area—and a promising market for U.S. equipment. The 200-mi. limits claimed by some nations were already a cause of trouble, however.

The U.S. vessel-building subsidy program showed no signs of gaining momentum. Long delays in completing administrative paperwork and excessively strict control of specifications were blamed. Many fishermen bypassed the subsidy, claiming that a better deal could be negotiated privately and that, if a man needed a new boat, early delivery paid bigger, quicker dividends than a building subsidy.

A subject of controversy in Canada and the U.S.

MICHAEL WOOD

Fishing boats lying idle in the harbour of Concarneau, France, during a fishermen's strike in 1968.

was FPC (fish protein concentrate), legalized in 1967 for human consumption by the U.S. Food and Drug Administration. The product was seen not merely as a protein supplement for the undernourished, but as an alternative to skim milk powder and soybean flour. However, the regulations called for one-pound packs, labeled in a way that was not conducive to sales.

Australia found itself with a prawn bonanza so big that it lacked the boats and men to exploit it. Prawns had been found in the Gulf of Carpentaria on a scale that attracted Japanese and Soviet trawlers and factory vessels. Lacking the boats, Australia made deals with the Japanese for joint enterprise. It also extended its fishing limits to 12 mi.

New Zealand's efforts to expand and modernize its fisheries suffered a severe blow in the near failure of the newly formed New Zealand Sea Products Export, Ltd. Poor catches and insufficient throughput sent turnover below the break-even line—due, it was said, to time needed to "work up" the new Norwegian-built stern trawlers. During the summer, a report on the future of the fisheries, prepared by the late W. F. Hampton, was released. It called mainly for a strengthening of the fisheries administration.

Japan, with the second-highest catch in the world, was still faced by a fish deficit; annual landings of 7 million tons were 1½ million tons below the country's needs. One of Japan's troubles was a falling off in the tuna long-line catch. Significantly, perhaps, one company built two giant tuna purse seiners fitted with U.S. equipment, opening up a new export field for the U.S.

The buildup of fishing potential in Eastern Euro-

Area and country	Blue whale	Fin whale	Humpback whale	Sei whale	Sperm whale	Others	Percentage assigned under quota agreement*
Antarctic: pelagic (open sea)							
Japan	3	374	...	8,695	357	...	47
Norway	1	857	...	2,232	595	...	23
U.S.S.R.	...	1,662	...	1,441	4,008	...	30
Total	4	2,893	...	12,368	4,960	...	...
Outside the Antarctic†	242	4,346	58	5,480	22,823	262	...

Table I. Whaling: 1966-67 Season
Number of whales caught

Note: No whaling operations from South Georgia during the season 1966–67.
*Antarctic only.
†1966.
Source: Committee for Whaling Statistics, *International Whaling Statistics.*

pean countries continued, with the U.S.S.R. placing orders for large new factory vessels in Denmark, East Germany, Poland, and France. Catches were disappointing, however. The big event of the year for the U.S.S.R. was the Leningrad Fisheries Exhibition Inrybpron-68, where, for the first time, the Soviet Union invited the fishing nations of the Western world to trade and to exchange technical knowledge. The U.S.S.R. had shown an increasing willingness to work with the West in regulating and promoting the world's fisheries.

In the field of technical achievement, the general trend was toward developments that would improve productivity and ease the fisherman's job. One major contribution was the successful design—by a Shetland farmer-inventor—of a fish-gutting machine. Most European countries removed the viscera of groundfish before icing down, and the need for a gang of men to perform this unpleasant task had inhibited mechanization in other areas. If the machine would, in fact, do the work of three men, then the way would be clear to make mechanization pay for itself. The U.S. also had developed a gutting machine, which operated as a vacuum cleaner/washer.

Research continued during the year on the hatching and rearing of shrimp and the more valuable types of sea fish. In Japan shrimp cultivation was already a productive commercial undertaking, but the breeding of groundfish was more an insurance policy against shrinking natural stocks. The ever widening interest in shrimp rearing was apparent at the Food and Agriculture Organization Shrimp Conference, held in Mexico during June, and at the London Shellfish Conference which preceded it.　　　　(H. S. N.)

See also Food.

Table II. World Fisheries, by Country, Catch, and Value of Catch, 1966*

Country	Catch in 000 metric tons	Value in U.S. $000
Argentina	251	16,428
Australia	89	47,405
Belgium	63	15,868
Burma	360	63,819
Cambodia	163	38,384
Canada	1,349	160,197
Chile	1,384	32,198
Colombia	57	8,626
Cuba	43	20,055
Denmark	851	19,303
Faeroe Is.	165	...
Finland	71	20,212
France	805	249,044
Germany, East	231†	...
Germany, West	657	92,527
Hong Kong	83	11,264
Hungary	26	33,739
Iceland	1,240	...
India	1,368	...
Israel	25	15,667
Italy	334	162,770
Japan	7,077	...
Korea, South	701	89,515
Malaysia	296	78,699
Mexico	286	66,263
Morocco	303	15,341
Netherlands	353	61,386
Norway	2,849	183,293
Panama	72	22,683
Peru	8,789	113,649
Philippines	726	237,138
Poland	335	...
Portugal	502	67,429
South Africa	532	22,692
South West Africa	650	...
Spain	1,357	282,757
Sweden	314	46,019
Taiwan	425	96,404
Thailand	708	122,578
United Kingdom	1,067	177,511
United States	2,514	...
Venezuela	117	22,047
Vietnam, South	381	122,238

*Excludes whaling.
†1965.
Sources: United Nations Food and Agriculture Organization, *Yearbook of Fishery Statistics.*

Fishing:
see Sporting Record

Floods:
see Conservation; Disasters; Engineering Projects

Folk Music:
see Music

Food

Food Supplies. After two discouraging years, food production in 1967 rose 3% in the world as a whole and almost 6% in the less developed nations of Latin America, the Near and Far East, and Africa. Favourable weather in most of the important producing areas and vigorous efforts by governments in support of agriculture coincided with "payoffs" of some long-term research and development programs, reversing—at least temporarily—the disheartening record of 1965 and 1966.

There were indications that food production would also be at a more comfortable level in 1968, but the year was not without disturbing reminders of mankind's oldest scourges. Drought struck over wide areas of Latin America, as well as in India and Pakistan; famine stalked the secessionist state of Biafra as a result of the Nigerian civil war; and locusts swarmed across East Africa and the Middle East. Even in the well-fed U.S., congressional and citizens' committees reported widespread hunger and malnutrition. Representatives of international organizations warned that, in the face of continued rapid population growth, the longer-term problem of the adequacy of agriculture in less developed nations remained unsolved.

Food Production. The UN Food and Agriculture Organization (FAO) reported the index of total food production for 1967 as 144 (1952–56 = 100), compared with 140 in 1966. For the less developed regions, the index rose to a new high of 145 from 137 a year earlier, while in the developed regions, chiefly in the Northern Hemisphere, the index rose 2% to 144. Production was more evenly distributed in 1967 than a year earlier, when recovery from the low levels of 1964 and 1965 was confined largely to the developed countries. The most striking advances in 1967 were made in the Far East and Africa, where production rose 6% or more.

Much improved weather and higher-yielding varieties of cereals raised 1967 production of food grains in India to nearly 100 million metric tons, as against requirements of about 106.5 million tons. Pakistan also reported a substantial increase in food-grain output. In the Far East overall, rice production rose 12% to nearly 104 million metric tons, about 3% above the 1964 record. For Communist China, an excellent harvest of 215 million tons of food grains and potatoes was estimated by the FAO. Africa's agricultural output increased 6% above 1966; total production of six principal grains rose 24% to 41,150,000 metric tons. The Near Eastern nations continued their steady improvement, with 1967 output 4% better than a year earlier. Latin-American food production rose about 5%.

Food production in the developed nations rose moderately in 1967. A 6% expansion in overall food output in Western European countries included a 12% increase in grain. Production in Eastern Europe and the U.S.S.R. was down slightly from 1966, when a 12% increase over 1965 was registered. The U.S.S.R. cereal grain harvest of 147.6 million tons was sharply below the 171.2 million tons of 1966 but still 7% above the 1962–66 average. Grain production rose in the Eastern European countries except for Bulgaria and Romania. The estimated 2% increase in total agricultural production in North America in 1967 was largely the result of a large feed-grain crop, including an 11%

increase for corn. The wheat harvest, totaling 57,-620,000 tons, was 600,000 tons below a year earlier, reflecting a 28% reduction in Canadian output. Severe drought in southeastern Australia reduced Oceania's total output by 11%.

Early indications pointed to generally good crops in 1968, although serious droughts in parts of Latin America, Eastern Europe, and Central and Southern Africa were expected to check further gains. Wheat acreage in Western Europe was 6% above 1967 and, with normal weather, production of some 30 million tons might be expected. Conditions in the U.S.S.R. were favourable for a harvest equal to that of 1967. Somewhat reduced acreages of wheat and feed grains in the U.S. and Canada would probably be offset by favourable weather, and in Oceania the wheat crop was expected to be of record dimensions. The outlook for Latin America was dimmed by severe drought in widespread areas. Intensive use of new cereal varieties in the Far East improved prospects for increased production there. Abundant rainfall in northwest Africa was expected to bring good wheat harvests, but drought in portions of Central and Southern Africa threatened production in those regions.

Food Balance. Because of population growth, the 3% increase in world food production in 1967 resulted in an increase of less than 1% in available per capita supplies. The index of world population stood at 129 (1952–56 = 100), 2.4% higher than a year earlier. In the developed regions the index rose one point to 117, while in the less developed regions it rose 3 points to 136. Thus, in the less developed regions, the 6% increase in food production, when shared by 2.3% more people, raised per capita production about 3%. In the developed countries per capita supplies rose 0.8%.

In the absence of more accurate statistics and a fuller knowledge of nutrition, the exact magnitude of the world food problem continued to be controversial. Nevertheless, there was general agreement that a significant percentage of the world's population was undernourished and that, over a period of years, improvement in the food situation in the less developed areas had been slow. The FAO reported that much of the increase in per capita food production since World War II had taken place in the early postwar period, as agriculture recovered from the effects of the war. For 33 less developed countries on which the FAO kept detailed statistics, per capita food production had risen about 15% between 1952–56 and 1963–65 (compared with a 25% increase in the developed regions), and in 11 of these countries food production had failed to keep pace with population growth. In May, Paul G. Hoffman, administrator of the UN Development Programme, warned that the world food balance was still perilous, and that because of population increases "some regions had less food available per capita in 1967 than in the early 1960s."

Another dimension of the food balance lay in the reduced stocks of surplus food in developed nations. At the second UN Conference on Trade and Development, held in New Delhi, India, in February, the U.S. representative, Eugene Rostow, said that "the era of vast food surpluses is over" and that future food aid would depend to a large extent on production programmed for that purpose. Recognizing the critical role of agriculture in development, the conference approved a declaration on the world food problem. It urged the development of human and technological resources and the promotion of stabilization measures and trade policies aimed at the rapid development of agriculture; recognized the joint responsibility of both the developed and the less developed countries; and agreed on the need for a coordinated approach to the problem. The developed countries were also urged to continue food aid.

The UN viewed the next 10 to 20 years as particularly critical, since it would take this long for population-control measures to have an appreciable effect and for the agricultural revolution in the less developed nations to get fully under way. To provide a framework for a coordinated approach to agricultural development, the FAO issued a preliminary Indicative World Plan for Agricultural Development. The purpose of the plan was to identify the optimum combination of aid needed for each country at various stages of development, and to indicate to both donor and recipient nations needed food aid, development, and trade policies. A more complete version of the plan was scheduled for submission in November 1969. In contrast to the UN view, six development specialists testified before a U.S. congressional committee to the effect that some parts of the less developed world were already on the verge of an agricultural revolution and that for many countries self-sufficiency within a few years was a realizable goal.

The most dramatic example of food shortage in 1968 occurred in Biafra, where a Red Cross representative estimated that 100,000 persons died from malnutrition in July alone. Other estimates put the death toll from starvation at 3,000 per day in late summer. The problem in this case was not lack of food supplies. Rather, a combination of political and diplomatic maneuvering by leaders of Biafra, Nigeria, and other nations frustrated attempts by relief organizations to move food into the area. In Latin America, where the worst drought on record threatened to produce water and food shortages and, possibly, starvation in some areas, food relief efforts were mounted by national and international organizations.

In the U.S. a citizens' group report, "Hunger, U.S.A.," and a television documentary program, "Hunger in America," reported that as many as ten million Americans were suffering from malnutrition. The reports, which were sharply challenged by U.S. Secretary of Agriculture Orville Freeman, raised debate among nutritionists over whether emphasis should be placed on increasing food supplies or on attacking deficiency diseases, as well as over technical questions relating to the nutritive value of some foods. The question of food distribution in the U.S. also became entwined with racial issues. Members of the largely black Poor People's Campaign picketed the Department of Agriculture, charging it with unwillingness to distribute surplus food. A study reported that only about one-third of U.S. schoolchildren participated in the national School Lunch Program, and that large numbers of children existed on grossly deficient diets. A Washington, D.C., hospital official testified before a congressional committee that the average low-income black baby in the District of Columbia was not getting a healthy diet. Another congressional committee reported that shoppers in poverty areas of Washington, D.C., New York City, and St. Louis paid higher prices at food chains for items of lower quality than shoppers in middle- and upper-income neighbourhoods—a finding that was disputed by the industry in the face of conflicting evidence.

Per capita food consumption in the U.S. in 1968 was little changed from a year earlier; there were indications of some changes in the patterns of food use—

New York City residents donating food in response to an appeal by the American Committee to Keep Biafra Alive. Food was collected on the sidewalk across the street from UN headquarters to protest lack of aid to Biafra from world leaders.

UPI COMPIX

Elderly Mexican-American woman in San Antonio, Tex., was part of the CBS television documentary "Hunger in America," criticizing the federal surplus-food program. The television report was criticized in turn by Agriculture Secretary Orville Freeman.

EUGENE GARRY—COURTESY, CBS

higher consumption of beef, pork, broilers, cheese, noncitrus fruits, and vegetables, and reductions in use of veal, lamb, eggs, citrus fruits, wheat flour, and some dairy products. Per capita consumption of red meats was estimated at 1% above the 177.5 lb. of a year earlier. Spending on food was forecast at $101 billion, compared with $94.9 billion in 1967. While this represented a 6.4% increase, it was nevertheless only 17.2% of estimated disposable income.

A comparison of consumer food prices among 50 nations by the U.S. Department of Agriculture indicated that in a five-year period (1963–67), prices in the U.S., Canada, and several European countries, including France, the U.K., West Germany, and Hungary, had risen about 10%. In Latin America price increases ranged from 6% in Venezuela to over 40% in Brazil. For six African countries, prices rose in a range of from 5% in Morocco to 45% in the U.A.R. Information on eight Asian nations indicated price rises of 10 to 20% for most countries, but in India food prices had increased 64%.

Aid Programs. Food aid programs in 1967 were strengthened by ratification of the International Grains Arrangement, which included a Food Aid Convention providing for annual shipments of 4.5 million metric tons of food grains by 12 participants as aid to less developed countries. Under the convention, the U.S. pledged a minimum of 1.9 million tons (42%); the EEC promised 1,035,000 tons (23%); and Canada, 495,000 tons (11%). Australia, Sweden, and the U.K. indicated they would make all or part of their contributions through the UN.

The UN World Food Program provided $24.7 million worth of food aid in 1967. As of mid-1968, pledges to the program for the 1969–70 period amounted to $168 million in cash, food, and services; a goal of $200 million had been set. The U.S. pledge of cash, food, and services was $100 million, of which $70 million was for food commodities pledged on the condition that U.S. commodities would not exceed 50% of total contributions from all countries.

U.S. Food for Peace (Public Law 480) exports in 1967 totaled $1,504,000,000, a slight reduction from 1966 and about 12% below 1964. Government-financed shipments under the U.S. Agency for International Development Program were $33 million, compared with $47 million in 1966. On July 29, 1968, Pres. Lyndon Johnson approved legislation extending Public Law 480 through Dec. 31, 1970; authorizations under the extended program were continued at $2.5 billion.

Foreign assistance for agricultural development appeared to have increased in 1967. The Organization for Economic Cooperation and Development reported a total of $11,360,000,000 in net flows of foreign assistance to developing countries under a variety of programs. On the basis of an OECD estimate that 9% of official commitments for development aid in recent years had been for agricultural development, some $627 million may have been devoted to this purpose in 1967. Data from the World Bank and the International Development Association indicated that, for 1967–68, loans for agricultural development totaled $134.4 million. This compared with World Bank loans and IDA credits of $87 million in 1966–67 and $152.4 million in 1965–66. The Inter-American Development Bank placed $154 million in loans to the agricultural sector in 1967, representing 30% of IDB loans for the year.

In late May an international organization to coordinate and intensify public and private effort to combat hunger and malnutrition in Latin America was inaugurated: the Inter-American Council for Action Against Malnutrition was organized by government representatives from 14 Latin-American countries, Guyana, and the U.S. A new Food Bank of New Zealand, a private enterprise effort, was formed by the New Zealand Dairy Research Institute to distribute a unique whole-milk biscuit to protein-deficient children in India, Africa, and Fiji; New Zealand business firms and the Dairy Board guaranteed consignment of the biscuit for an experimental program in 12 coun-

tries. In April the Ford and Rockefeller foundations announced grants of nearly $5 million for support of specialized agricultural research and training centres; two centres were operating in Mexico and the Philippines and two were planned for Colombia and Nigeria.

Responding to increased criticism of domestic food distribution programs, the U.S. Congress appropriated more funds for fiscal 1969 operations of the Food Stamp Program ($225 million), the new Special Child Feeding Program ($45 million), the Special Milk Program ($104 million), and the School Lunch Program ($242,799,000). In addition, Congress extended the Food Stamp Program through 1970 with increased appropriations. Secretary of Agriculture Freeman said in late August that the School Lunch Program was reaching nearly 20 million children, of whom some 2.5 million were being provided with free, or nearly free, lunches. The Food Stamp and Commodity Distribution programs were reaching over 6 million people in 2,400 counties and all except 40 of the 1,000 lowest-income counties had begun or were in the process of developing food assistance programs. In those 40 counties, the initiative for opening food programs was being taken by the Department of Agriculture. The secretary also stated that the department had reduced the minimum amount required of very poor participants in the Food Stamp Program from $2 per person per month to 50 cents.

Trade and Stocks. Preliminary data for 1967 indicated that world trade in agricultural commodities was slightly lower than a year earlier; the FAO index of total volume, at 135 (1957–59 = 100), was down one point. Prices of agricultural exports overall were estimated to have been 1% less than a year earlier. The decline in volume was attributed to reduced exports of wheat and feed grains by the U.S. and Canada, which offset the increased volume of shipments of wheat flour, coarse grains, and rice from Western Europe. Among the less developed countries, a decline of 2% was indicated in export earnings for agricultural exports, attributable chiefly to lower prices.

The overall level of stocks of agricultural commodities changed little in 1967–68. Slightly increased wheat stocks were offset by reductions in cotton. Expected carry-over into the 1968–69 season of wheat stocks in the five major exporting countries was expected to be about 38 million tons, some 10 million tons less than the 1960–65 average. An increase of about 3 million tons was predicted for the U.S. Canadian carry-over was large, and constituted about half of the total for the five leading nations. Australian stocks were expected to be drawn down to low levels, and stocks in the U.S.S.R. were thought to have been reduced. Rice supplies were short during 1967 and, although a record production level was reached, most of the increases would be consumed domestically. Coarse-grain stocks in five major exporting countries in 1967–68 were estimated to have increased by about 5%; anticipated carry-over into the 1968–69 season of about 44 million tons was nearly the same as a year earlier. Stocks of dairy products increased in 1967 as production continued to outpace consumption. World sugar stocks were reduced only fractionally.   (H. R. SH.)

Food Processing and Technology. *Legislation and Control.* Following passage of the Trade Descriptions Act, 1968, which made it an offense to apply false trade descriptions to goods or advertisements, Britain introduced new regulations governing the labeling of food. Draft regulations were also issued following the report of the Food Standards Committee

on claims and misleading descriptions. There was much controversy in the technical and daily press concerning the regulations made the previous year permitting the use of cyclamate sweeteners. Japanese scientists had discovered that cyclamates are metabolized by certain individuals, and the British government ordered further long-term toxicological investigations.

Spain introduced a food regulation code for the first time and established a series of guiding principles for future legislation under this code. Belgium carried out a wide-ranging review of its food regulation codes. Japan followed the example of many other countries and banned the use of Dulcin as an artificial sweetener.

The U.S. Food and Drug Administration rescinded a previous decision and placed new restrictions on the distribution of irradiated foods. According to the FDA, animal tests carried out by the Army had failed to establish that the use of gamma-irradiation was safe. The U.S. armed forces had planned to use irradiation-sterilized meat packs for feeding troops, but an application to the FDA for approval of the process for treating smoked canned hams was rejected. Subsequently, the FDA withdrew its previous approval of irradiated bacon and also expressed misgivings about irradiated pork products, potatoes, and wheat.

Food Dehydration. Freeze-drying technology continued to make rather slow progress, but work at the Commonwealth Scientific and Industrial Research Organization Division of Food Preservation in Australia on the fundamental physics of heat and vapour transfer in freeze-dried products resulted in the development of a new cyclic-pressure process that was said to reduce costs. Many new freeze-dried products were introduced. Freeze-dried egg became an established commercial product in Britain, where a new plant was installed to increase output to 50 tons daily. In West Germany a new plant was installed to freeze-dry coffee and cottage cheese, and a large plant was commissioned in Arequipa, Peru, to freeze-dry garlic and onions.

The relatively new technique of reverse osmosis, which had already been applied to the desalting of brackish waters, underwent an ingenious development at the Western Regional Research Laboratory of the U.S. Department of Agriculture, where it was applied to the osmotic dehydration of various foods. The process utilized semipermeable membranes which were deposited on the surface of the food. The coated products were then immersed in a concentrated invert sugar syrup, which withdrew water from the food. Various edible membranes were developed comprising, for example, calcium pectate, aluminum carboxymethylcellulose, and starch derivatives. Preliminary investigations indicated that very good dehydrated products could be obtained by this process, which eliminated the heating or freezing needed in other dehydration procedures. A salt-rejecting membrane, such as cellulose acetate, was used to dehydrate ground fish, and it was suggested that this procedure could be used as an inexpensive means of drying fish against brine immediately after catch.

Dehydrofreezing and Dehydrocanning. Considerable attention was given to dehydrofreezing and dehydrocanning, whereby about 50% of the moisture is removed prior to either canning or freezing. Such foods differed little in quality from normally frozen or canned products, and they had the advantage of being cheaper to handle and distribute. The U.S. Navy found that dehydrofrozen peas were superior to canned peas for use on board ship.

Food

Treatment of foods with certain liquids such as ethyl acetate, which form lower boiling point admixtures with water—so-called azeotropic mixtures—was developed as a means of dehydrating such products as strawberries, bananas, and hamburger chunks. Drying rates under vacuum eight times faster than freeze-drying were achieved at lower cost.

Dairy Industry. Rising costs hastened the trend toward automation in the dairy industry, especially the introduction of high-speed milk-bottling lines that filled more than 500 bottles per minute. At these speeds visual inspection of bottles for foreign bodies was impracticable, and much attention was devoted to the development of automatic scanning equipment that would reject contaminated bottles before filling. The need for more advanced systems of in-line cleaning also became imperative, and some completely automated systems involving prerinsing, detergent cleaning, final rinse, and sterilization were introduced.

Such procedures, together with improvements in aseptic packaging, made possible the export of substantial quantities of ultraheat treated (UHT) milk, with a shelf life of some six months, to tropical and semitropical countries. Such long-life milk also made its appearance in supermarkets in a number of European countries and it was predicted that its use would become widespread as a means of counteracting labour difficulties and mounting distribution costs in the industry. An Italian company developed a completely packaged and fully automated unit for the production of UHT milk, and several packaging-machine manufacturers developed rectangular cartons as alternatives to the usual tetrahedral pack.

Fishing Industry. The decline in yields of British vessels fishing Arctic waters led to the building of more stern trawlers equipped to freeze the whole gutted fish at sea. Factory trawlers were proving uneconomical because of their requirements for specialized staff and costly machinery.

Further important developments in fish culture were made in many countries, and it seemed probable that in the future greater emphasis would be placed on "fish farming" than on the traditional and precarious "fish hunting." In Britain improved procedures for raising plaice, Dover sole, and prawns were developed. The decimation of young plaice by crabs in sea loch hatcheries was overcome by the use of floating cages. A synthetic diet of redworm was developed consisting of cast seaweed or queen scallop made into a paste with alginate and mechanically formed into wormlike lengths for feeding. Interesting work was begun in the U.S. on the culture of the saltwater pompano, which is normally an Atlantic surf feeder. This investigation was double edged, since the high price of pompano made a contribution to research costs while valuable information was acquired on the culture of fin fish.

With trout culture well established, other freshwater fish began to receive attention. It was reported from West Germany that "bottle fed" carp weighing up to 14 lb. had been raised in tanks on a diet of fish meal, crushed soybeans, and vitamins fed through a nippled feeding bottle at the tank's surface. Some 60 million lb. of catfish were raised in ponds in the U.S. on pellets resembling dog food. In Louisiana the culture of crayfish was successfully begun in rotation with the rice crops.

Canning and Packaging. The chrome-treated steel developed in Japan for food cans went into production there, in the U.S., and in Europe. High-speed pressure or forge welding of the side seams was developed in the U.S. as an alternative to the use of thermoplastic adhesives that did not withstand retort temperatures. An interesting development, still in the pilot-plant stage, was the coating of steel strip with aluminum vaporized under a very high vacuum. The treated strip had a bright, smooth surface with no intermetallic layer, but it required chemical conversion and treatment to achieve satisfactory lacquer adhesion. The potential applications were reported to be for crown seals and beer cans.

Although more expensive than steel-based bodies, cans made from extruded aluminum found further acceptance in the U.S.; 4.6% of the cans on the U.S. market were reported to be of this type. Consumer appeal was based on easy opening and an attractive, hygienic appearance. Corrosion remained a problem, but spraying techniques to repair the lacquer damaged at the score line improved shelf life. Containers consisting of a fibreboard-plastic laminate with tinned-steel or aluminum ends were introduced for a variety of liquid products, including fruit juices and fresh dairy cream. Boxes of such laminates with a capacity of 600–1,400 lb. were developed for the bulk shipment of farm products.

Natural Toxic Agents in Foods. The discovery of the toxicity of peanuts contaminated with aflatoxin led food technologists throughout the world to give careful consideration to the occurrence of other toxicants in foods, including those naturally present as well as those resulting from microbiological deterioration. Benzpyrene and other polynuclear hydrocarbons are deposited in the soil from smoky atmospheres, and workers in several countries showed that they may become concentrated to a measurable extent in some vegetable products. The nitrosamines, which may be formed when certain foods—especially fish and cheese—are smoked, received much attention in Britain, West Germany, and the U.S. in view of their cancer-inducing properties.

Concern was expressed in various countries concerning the high nitrate content of some vegetables—especially spinach—as a result of excessive use of nitrate fertilizers. Nitrate in these products may be reduced to nitrite by bacteria prior to processing or by intestinal bacteria, and this caused some cases of nitrite poisoning in infants. There was an acute outbreak of mussel poisoning in Britain resulting from ingestion by the mussels of a poisonous dinoflagellate, *Gonyaulax,* which contains a potent neurotoxin. Normally these dinoflagellates are not found in any numbers in British waters, and their presence was attributed to abnormal climatic conditions.

Food Technology in Relation to Nutritional Requirements. The problem of providing protein for a rapidly increasing world population and especially to supplement the protein deficit of less developed countries attracted much attention from food technologists. Interest turned increasingly to the protein resources of oilseeds and of biological fermentations. The British Ministry of Overseas Technology announced the development of a process to increase the protein content of cassava by fermentation with a strain of *Rhizopus,* and a commercial organization developed a process for producing protein by growing a strain of *Penicillium* on enzyme-digested cellulose and hemicelluloses. A petroleum company announced the commissioning of a plant to produce 50 tons of microbial protein daily and a factory was built in the U.S.S.R. to produce 15 tons of microbial protein daily from paraffin.

Food and Agriculture Organization, United Nations:
see Food

Food Preparation:
see Domestic Arts and Sciences

Nevertheless, some disillusionment was voiced by food technologists because even protein-hungry peoples do not take readily to bland powders, however nutritious they may be. Such preparations cannot be adapted readily for use in simple dietaries and in countries where food is prepared under primitive conditions. Consequently, there was a tendency for these supplements to find their way into sophisticated processed foods, where they could be utilized technically but not in the alleviation of malnutrition. Costs of production, isolation and purification, and subsequent processing made many preparations almost as costly as more conventional foods.

For these reasons, efforts were being directed toward the production of protein-enriched beverages and toward the exploitation of the explosive puffing and texturing procedure whereby defatted soy flour and other vegetable protein preparations could be given meatlike textures. Such products, manufactured in a variety of suitably coloured and flavoured forms, proved readily acceptable as ingredients of stews, as meat replacements in prepared dishes, and as meat substitutes in Chinese-, Indonesian-, and Japanese-style foods. One advantage of these products was that amino acid, vitamin, and mineral supplements could be included to confer any desired nutritional characteristics. Much progress along these lines had been made in the U.S. and Japan.

Amino acid supplementation likewise attracted increasing attention, since many proteins could be upgraded by the incorporation of essential amino acids with only trivial alterations to the customary dietary. Development work was begun in India by the U.S. AID mission, and in Thailand through U.S. and Japanese collaboration on the production of lysine- and threonine-supplemented cereal grains for addition to rice. This new approach involved a minimum of interference with customary foods, thereby obviating resistance to "unnatural" foods or supplements.

(HE. B. H.)

See also Agriculture; Commercial Policies; Commodities, Primary; Domestic Arts and Sciences; Fisheries; Prices.

ENCYCLOPÆDIA BRITANNICA FILMS. *Food and People* (1956); *Why Foods Spoil (Molds, Yeasts, Bacteria)* (1957); *Food from the Sun* (1965); *Plankton: Pastures of the Ocean* (1965); *Produce—From Farm to Market* (1968).

Football

Association Football (Soccer). The Olympic year of 1968 gave the major soccer nations twin aims: to qualify for the XIX Olympic Games in Mexico and to set out on the long trail to the World Cup finals scheduled for the same country in 1970. Because soccer in the Olympic Games is restricted to amateurs, many of the world's top countries did not qualify for the finals (*see* SPORTING RECORD: *Special Report*) simply because their best players were professionals.

The trend away from the blanket defense system continued, with tangible evidence in the European Cup where Benfica, of Portugal, and Manchester United, of England—both attacking teams—contested the final at Wembley, London, on May 29, 1968, thus following the trend set by Celtic 12 months previously. But in South America and Italy the system of using the type of rear guard with a sweeper at the back still largely prevailed.

In Europe the European championship was settled in Italy during the early summer with the host nation

GERRY CRANHAM, "SPORTS ILLUSTRATED" © TIME INC.

Celtic goalkeeper John Fallon making a save against the Rangers as the two Glasgow clubs played to a 2–2 tie in their annual New Year's match.

coming out on top, although it had to win its semi-final game with the toss of a coin. Argentina again provided the winners of the Copa Libertadores de America (South American Club Championship Cup) in Estudiantes de la Plata.

Violence continued both off and on the field, and international and national associations stepped up the penalties for transgressions. A novel idea was tried out in Bulgaria: before the start of the Levski-CSKA game in Sofia—a traditional "blood match"—a table was carried out and set down just off the pitch. A robed judge and clerks followed and sat round it. An official warned over the public address system in the stadium that anyone, player or spectator, causing a disturbance would be tried and sentenced on the spot. There was no trouble, and players accidentally fouling opponents apologized profusely.

Because of the political upheaval in Czechoslovakia evoked in August by the invasion there of Warsaw Pact troops, the Union of European Football Associations (UEFA) rescheduled the European Cup and European Cup-winners' Cup tournaments with the intention of avoiding any confrontation between Communist bloc countries and those from the rest of Europe. But the plan misfired because Hungary, Poland, Bulgaria, the U.S.S.R., and East Germany all withdrew their teams from the competition, and at the same time the Soviet Union threatened to pull out of UEFA. The Fairs' Cup committee wisely decided to let the draw stand although Union Sportive (Luxembourg) and KB Copenhagen (Denmark) both withdrew from their first-round matches, in which they

Everton goalie Gordon West punching the ball away from Clive Clark of West Bromwich Albion. Albion defeated Everton 1–0 to win the Football Association Cup at Wembley, May 18, 1968.

KEYSTONE

were opposed by Eastern European teams, on "political grounds."

Inter-Continental Club Championship Cup. This competition, between the winners of the European Cup and the South American Club Championship Cup, needed three games before it was decided and in the third degenerated into a bruising, kicking, hacking brawl. In the first contest Celtic of Scotland, the European champions, beat Racing of Buenos Aires, at Hampden Park, Glasgow, on Oct. 18, 1967, when their centre back and captain, W. McNeill, scored in the second half of a game that was played hard from the first whistle.

When Celtic flew to South America for the second match on November 1, the scene was already set for a tough encounter and the trouble started before the kickoff. Ronnie Simpson, the Celtic goalkeeper, was knocked out by a stone hurled by a spectator. John Fallon took over in goal and the start was delayed 20 minutes. When the incident-packed match did get under way, J. Johnstone had the ball in the net for Celtic, but the goal was disallowed; then Tommy Gemmell scored from a penalty midway through the first half. S. Chalmers had a shot hit a post five minutes later, before Racing got to grips with the game and tied the score with a goal by N. Raffo. The interval was extended to nearly half an hour because of a

Final match of the season's international Rugby championship, at Cardiff. France beat Wales 14–9, retaining its title and remaining undefeated in the series.

plumbing fault in the Celtic dressing room, but within three minutes of the restart J. C. Cardenas scored the winning goal for the South Americans.

In the play-off, on the following Saturday in the Centenarios Stadium, Montevideo, trouble was expected but not on the scale that developed. Weak refereeing helped fan it, and five players (R. Lennox, Johnstone, and W. Hughes of Celtic and Racing's A. Basile and J. C. Rulli) were ejected from the game. The referee, R. P. Osorio of Paraguay, afterward said he ordered off a fourth Scot, Bertie Auld, but did not make him go "as it was so late in the game." Fouls, kicks, and hacks flowed more freely than the nearby Río de la Plata, and several times some of the 2,000 riot police provided by the Uruguayan authorities for crowd control went onto the field to separate the scuffling players. The vital goal which won the trophy for Racing was scored by Cardenas in the 56th minute. After the game Celtic fined all their players and Racing also disciplined theirs, and world reaction to the game was almost universally hostile.

European Championship. Formerly called the Nations Cup, this competition, spread over two years, was won by Italy when they defeated Yugoslavia in a play-off in Rome on June 10 with goals by L. Riva and P. Anastasi. The two countries had played to a 1–1 tie two days earlier in the same stadium.

The eight nations to qualify in their groups were Yugoslavia and France; England and Spain; Hungary and the U.S.S.R.; and Bulgaria and Italy. The quarter-finals were settled on a home-and-away basis during April and May. In the semifinals, held in Italy, Yugoslavia beat England 1–0 in Florence, while Italy qualified at the expense of the U.S.S.R. on the toss of a coin, in Naples.

In the third place play-off in Rome, England, in their familiar attacking style, beat the U.S.S.R. 2–0 with goals by Bobby Charlton and Geoff Hurst. In the evening the Italy-Yugoslavia final was played in the same stadium, and almost from the kickoff the crowd of 100,000 realized that it was going to be a great defensive struggle. The Yugoslavs dominated play for most of the game and D. Dzajic scored first. So predominant were the Yugoslavs that it was only fine goalkeeping by D. Zof that gave his country the chance of staying in the game and eventually tying it with only six minutes left, when a free kick by A. Domenghini crashed through the defensive wall of Yugoslavia.

In the play-off the tables were turned, and it was I. Pantelic's chance to shine as Yugoslavia's goalkeeper with a series of brilliant saves that prevented a rout. The Italians reveled in the gaps left by the visiting defense, and Riva and Anastasi, the world's most costly footballer at a transfer fee of nearly £442,000, fired in goals within half an hour to win the championship.

European Cup. For the second year in succession a British club took this prize, when Manchester United beat Benfica 4–1 after extra time at Wembley. Though the game was a little disappointing for the purist, it supplied plenty of drama and excitement. Bobby Charlton's header—a rarity for this England forward—was answered late in the game by a shot from Jaime Graca but then, inspired by two masterly saves by Alex Stepney from Portugal's ace marksman, Eusébio, United held on until overtime. The men from Manchester then hauled themselves back in the final 30 minutes to become a team worthy of the title of Europe's champions. George Best of Northern Ireland scored to make it 2–1 from a pass by Brian Kidd; then Manchester added two more goals to their total to win 4–1 and so realize the ambition of Sir Matt Busby (*see* BIOGRAPHY), the Manchester club's long-time manager. Even the brilliance of Eusébio could not wrest the trophy in the closing minutes, for he was playing almost a lone hand.

Shocks of the first round were the defeat of Celtic, the defending champions, by Dynamo Kiev (U.S.S.R.) and the fact that Benfica only won their match with Glentoran, the Northern Ireland club and one of the weaker teams of the competition, on the away goals rule by 2–1. (Under this rule goals scored on opponents' ground count double, and it was applied to the early rounds of the competition to avoid play-offs.)

Francisco Gento, captain of Real Madrid, set a record of playing in every one of the 13 competitions held. He had taken part in 82 of his club's 87 matches in the competition, appearing in eight finals and taking six winner's medals.

European Cup-winners' Cup. AC Milan brought

back the European Cup-winners' trophy to Italy for the first time since the opening competition when Fiorentina triumphed in 1961. Milan defeated SV Hamburg with two goals by Kurt Hamrin, their Swedish international, in the first half of the final game in Rotterdam on May 23. His first came after three minutes and the second a quarter hour later; the Hamburg team never recovered from this swift double blow and so the chances of a West German hat trick—Borussia Dortmund won in 1966 and Bayern Munich in 1967—were shattered.

There were some surprises in this tournament, especially when Cardiff, a Welsh club playing in the English second division and operating near the bottom of it, reached the semifinals. At that stage they held Hamburg in West Germany to a 1–1 draw, but then lost in the second match in Cardiff.

Inter-Cities Fairs' Cup. Leeds United made it two out of three in Europe for England when they became that country's first club to win the Inter-Cities Fairs' Cup in a two-leg final that was held over until the start of the 1968–69 season. They defeated the Hungarian champions, Ferencvaros, by the narrow margin of 1–0 at Leeds and then held them to a goalless draw in Budapest.

In the first leg in Yorkshire the English club did most of the attacking, and the vital goal was scored by Mick Jones, their centre forward. In the return match, a fortnight later, in Budapest on September 11, Leeds adopted defensive tactics, though they went out for a quick goal to lengthen their lead. Though they failed in that effort and the contest ended in a 0–0 draw, it was far from as dull as the score might suggest, and the Hungarians, Florian Albert in particular, were always on the attack.

The playing of matches in this competition continually lagged behind schedule; even so, the organizers, the Inter-Cities Fairs' Cup committee, increased the size of the event to 48 clubs during the 1968–69 season.

British Isles Championship. This tournament also comprised Group 8 of the European championship, and so far more importance was attached to the matches. Scotland held a one-point halfway stage lead over England at the start of the season. As the new season began England beat Wales 3–0 in Cardiff on Oct. 21, 1967, and were given a helping hand in their quest for the top spot and the quarterfinals of the European championship by Northern Ireland, who, inspired by Best, beat the Scots 1–0 in Belfast the same day.

England defeated Northern Ireland 2–0 the following month at Wembley, while Scotland beat Wales 3–2 in Glasgow to leave the whole thing hinging on the penultimate match of the series at Hampden Park, Glasgow, on February 24. Watched by 134,000 fans, England gained the draw they needed to win the championship outright for the 24th time despite a tremendous effort by the Scots to beat them. Four days later, Wales beat Northern Ireland 2–0 at Wrexham to leave the latter in last place.

Administration. Experiments were carried out in Britain using a system of double control with two referees; each controlled half the field of play. Another scheme involving one referee and four linesmen was tried, but neither plan was adopted. In the European Cup and Cup-winners' Cup two substitutes would be allowed at any stage of the game in the 1968–69 competitions, and if a side should be reduced to seven men then the match must be stopped. The UEFA de-

cided that a player ejected by the referee from a game would be automatically banned from the next one in the competition. (T. W.)

U.S. Professional Leagues. The two U.S. professional soccer leagues, which played their first seasons in 1967, merged in January 1968 to form the North American Soccer League (NASL). Both of the former leagues had suffered financial losses in 1967. The new organization did not fare much better, however, as attendance remained generally poor in 1968. The 17-team league was reduced to 14 at the season's end when the Detroit, Boston, and Vancouver clubs announced that financial difficulties were forcing them to disband. In the two-game championship series Atlanta and San Diego played to a 0–0 tie in the first match, and then Atlanta scored a 3–0 triumph in the second game to win the NASL title.

In November the NASL club owners met and decided that audience support was not sufficient to maintain the league in its present state. They then submitted a proposal to the governing bodies of North American soccer, the U.S. Soccer Football Association and the Canadian Soccer Football Association. The proposal stated that the NASL should be temporarily disbanded and its leading players concentrated into one all-star team, which would play outstanding opponents from throughout the world. In December the U.S. association refused to allow the NASL to disband unless it guaranteed that the association would not be responsible for claims made by dissident league members. (X.)

Rugby. *Rugby Union.* The 1967–68 period was a time of much touring. The British Isles Lions made a major tour of South Africa, the New Zealand All-Blacks toured Britain and France, and the French toured New Zealand and Australia. In addition, the All-Blacks made a short tour of Australia, and England played five matches in Canada.

The first of these tours was England's to Canada in September 1967. The Canadians proved no match for the English in games played at Calgary, Victoria, Vancouver, Toronto, and Ottawa. In winning all the matches comfortably, England, captained by Phil Judd, scored 164 points and had only 9 points (three penalty goals) scored against them. But in spite of the uneven contest it was hoped that the visit would do much to encourage the development of Rugby in Canada.

The All-Blacks played 15 matches in Britain and France in October–December 1967, and their record was won 14, drawn 1, lost 0, points for 294, against 129. Just as impressive as their record was the way in which they played open attacking Rugby. The basis of this was an experienced team, with such fine forwards as Brian Lochore (captain), Colin Meads, Kel Tremain, and Ken Gray. On the foundation of this forward work Fred Allen, the coach, was able to build the creative play on which he and Charles Saxton, the manager, had set their hearts. In the international matches the All-Blacks beat England 23–11, Wales 13–6, France 21–15, and Scotland 14–3. The two matches due to be played in Ireland had to be canceled because livestock foot-and-mouth disease there restricted all movement, and in their place a final game was arranged against the Barbarians at Twickenham, the All-Blacks winning 11–6. In the match against Scotland Colin Meads was sent off the field for dangerous play. He was subsequently suspended for two matches. On their way to Europe the All-Blacks played two matches in Canada, beating British Columbia

36–3 at Vancouver and Eastern Canada 40–3 at Montreal.

The home countries international championship was retained by France, who for the first time in their history defeated all four British Isles teams in one season. They beat Scotland 8–6 at Murrayfield, Ireland 16–6 in Paris, England 14–9 in Paris, and Wales 14–9 at Cardiff. Ireland, recovering from defeat by France in their first match, managed to finish second by drawing with England 9–9 at Twickenham and then beating Scotland 14–6 and Wales 9–6, both in Dublin. England started by drawing with Wales 11–11 at Twickenham, but then, after their draw with Ireland and their defeat by France, they managed to gain third place by beating Scotland 8–6 at Murrayfield. Wales also beat Scotland, 5–0 at Cardiff, so that Scotland finished without a win or even a draw.

The International Board, at its annual meeting in Edinburgh in March, made two important decisions regarding laws. First, it decided to experiment, for the 1968–69 season in the Northern Hemisphere and the 1969 season in the Southern Hemisphere, with the full application of the Australian dispensation, which aimed to cut out kicking directly to touch except from within the kicker's 25; second, it agreed that substitutes should be allowed for players injured in matches in which a national representative team is involved.

The first substitute brought on under the second rule was Barry Bresnihan, an Irish centre three-quarter, during the first of the 20 matches played by the British Isles (the Lions) in South Africa in May–July 1968. The Lions, captained from fullback by Tom Kiernan of Ireland, won all their matches against provincial opponents except one, against Transvaal, but were defeated in the four-match international series 3–0 with one drawn. South Africa won the first international 25–20 at Pretoria, the third 11–6 at Cape Town, and the fourth 19–6 at Johannesburg. The second was drawn 6–6 at Port Elizabeth. Kiernan's goal kicking accounted for 35 of the 38 points the Lions scored in the internationals. South Africa fielded a strong team, with such outstanding forwards as Tommy Bedford, Jan Ellis, Frik du Preez, and Gys Pitzer, and these largely controlled the first two matches. Under the coaching of A. R. Dawson the Lions' forwards improved by the third game, but in this their backs were found wanting. The Lions scored 53 tries in 20 matches and had 20 scored against them, 8 in the internationals. The Lions' final record was played 20, won 15, drawn 1, lost 4, points for 377, against 181.

In the first match of the New Zealanders' visit to Australia, against Sydney in May, Colin Meads, the New Zealand lock forward, played his 100th game in a New Zealand jersey. The tour included 11 games, some of them against weak opposition, and the final record was played 11, won 11, points for 427, against 60. New Zealand won the first international 27–11 at Sydney and the second (there were only two) 19–18 at Brisbane.

The French, after their successes in the home international championship, were expected to do well in New Zealand in July and August even though they had to travel without some of the best players. But they made a poor start, losing 19–24 to Marlborough, one of the weaker provincial teams in New Zealand. The French improved, however, and did not lose another provincial match. New Zealand won the three-match international series 3–0, the scores being 12–9 at

Christchurch, 9–3 at Wellington, and 19–12 at Auckland. The French captain, Christian Carrere, missed the first two internationals because of injury, but in the third he led his men in a gallant rally after they had been down 0–16 at half time. In the second half they scored three splendid tries and added to their reputation for dashing back play. The French then carried on in the same style in Australia, beating Queensland 31–11 but losing to Australia 10–11 in Sydney, where their brilliant attacking game was met by a determined defense. France's record in New Zealand and Australia was played 14, won 9, drawn 0, lost 5, points for 195, against 142.

Rugby League. A period of international activity began in October 1967 with a tour of England by Australia. Three test matches were played, Great Britain beating Australia 16–11 in the first at Leeds, Australia winning the second 17–11 in London, and Australia clinching the series by triumphing in the third 11–3 at Swinton. The Australians thus became the first team from their nation to win three successive series. But their glory was short-lived, for they moved on into France and were beaten 2–0 with one drawn in the three-match test series. The first test was drawn 7–7, but France won the second 10–3 and the third 16–13. This was the first time Australia had failed to win a match in a series against France. Form was reversed again soon afterward when Great Britain beat France 22–13 in Paris and followed this by a victory over the same opponents 19–8 at Bradford. Then in May and June the World Championship matches were held in Australia and New Zealand. In this competition Australia reasserted their authority, beating France 20–2 in the final in Sydney. This was Australia's second success in the competition, which was started in 1954. In the match that decided third place behind Australia and France, Great Britain outplayed New Zealand 38–14.   (D. B. J. F.)

U.S. Football. Ohio State won the mythical national collegiate championship for the fourth time, having first achieved it in 1942. The Buckeyes, undefeated in nine regular-season games, were rated no. 1 in both the Associated Press (AP) and United Press International (UPI) final polls after marching to the Big Ten title and earning a trip to the Rose Bowl. There, led by sophomore quarterback Rex Kern, they climaxed the year by defeating second-ranked University of Southern California (USC) 27–16.

USC just missed retaining the national title won the previous season, finishing second in both polls. The Trojans, led again by halfback O. J. Simpson, winner of the Heisman Trophy, won nine straight games en route to the Pacific Eight Conference title. But in their final regular-season contest they were tied 21–21 by Notre Dame, which held Simpson to 55 yd. gained in 21 rushes. The Trojans then lost to Ohio State in the Rose Bowl.

Penn State was ranked third and Georgia fourth in both polls. Penn State (10–0) won the Lambert Trophy as the outstanding team in the East and then went on to defeat Kansas 15–14 in the Orange Bowl. Georgia (8–0–2) won the Southeastern Conference title, beating Auburn 17–3 in the next to last game of the season to break a tie for the league lead. The Bulldogs, however, were upset 16–2 by Arkansas in the Sugar Bowl. Texas, fifth-ranked in both polls, and Arkansas, ninth-ranked, tied for the Southwest Conference championship. Texas went on to defeat Tennessee 36–13 in the Cotton Bowl. Kansas, sixth-ranked, finished in a tie for the Big Eight Conference title

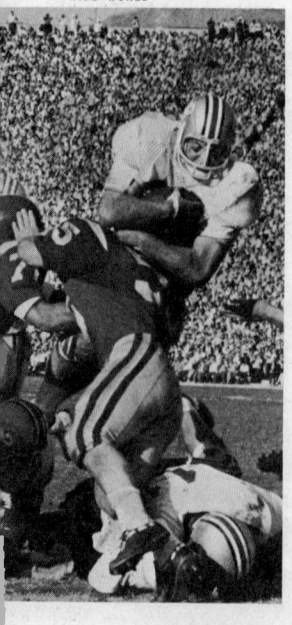

Ohio State fullback Jim Otis scores against Southern California in the second quarter of the Rose Bowl game, Jan. 1, 1969. Ohio State won 27–16.

with Oklahoma, rated tenth. Notre Dame was ranked seventh in the AP poll and Tennessee eighth, with the order reversed in the UPI ratings.

Two major teams that experienced disappointing seasons were Purdue and Notre Dame, both early favourites for the national title. Purdue, led by Leroy Keyes, Simpson's chief challenger for the Heisman Trophy, lost its fourth game of the season to Ohio State 13–0 and finished with an 8–2 record. Notre Dame lost to Purdue in its second game of the year and later was upset 21–17 by Michigan State.

High scoring was characteristic of the entire season, with the peak being reached in major college play by Houston University when it defeated Tulsa 100–6. The scoring outburst was general, the 615 major college games of 1968 producing an all-time record of 42.4 points per game (both teams combined), exceeding the previous record of 38.8 set in 1951. Other statistics per game reflected this with new records being set in the following categories: total yards gained on offense (657); total offense plays (150.1); rushing plays (99.4); pass attempts (50.7); pass completions (24.1); yards gained passing (315.4); and percentage of passes completed (47.4).

This opening up of the offense was the result of several changes in the game, including a rules change requiring that the clock be stopped after each first down. This produced an average of almost ten plays more per game than in previous years. Another change dealt with punt returns. The controversial 1967 punt coverage rule was repealed. It had required all interior linemen on the kicking team to hold their position until the ball was booted. The repeal allowed the linemen to move up field with the kicker.

Spectators reacted favourably to the increased offensive nature of the game. Attendance continued to rise, as it had every year since 1953. According to the National Collegiate Sports Services, a record 27,-025,846 spectators watched 2,786 college football games in 1968. This represented an increase of 595,207 in college football attendance over 1967. The total did not include the large crowds at the bowl games and other postseason events.

USC halfback Simpson captured 855 of a possible 1,042 votes to win the Heisman Trophy as college football's player of the year. Simpson, a senior, gained 1,709 yd. rushing, an NCAA record, and scored the most touchdowns (22) although finishing second in total points to Jim O'Brien of the University of Cincinnati. O'Brien led the country in scoring with 142 points, including 12 touchdowns, 13 field goals, and 31 extra points. Both Simpson and Eugene ("Mercury") Morris of West Texas State, who gained 1,571 yd. rushing, topped the former season rushing record of 1,570 yd., set in 1948. Morris set an all-time major college career rushing record with 3,388 yd. Steve Owens of Oklahoma became the hardest-working rusher in history with 357 carries, 2 more than Simpson and 61 more than the old mark of 296.

Simpson and Keyes were unanimous All-America choices, with Terry Hanratty of Notre Dame being selected as quarterback on virtually all teams. The fourth member of the All-American backfield generally was Chris Gilbert, University of Texas running back. Keyes, although injured much of the season, scored 14 touchdowns and finished 16th in the nation in rushing, gaining 1,003 yd. He was second to Simpson in the balloting for the Heisman Trophy, with Hanratty placing third.

East. Led by Ted Kwalick, tight end, Penn State

New York Jets' Pete Lammons (87) is tackled by Rodger Bird of the Oakland Raiders after gaining 15 yd. on a pass from quarterback Joe Namath. New York won the AFL championship by defeating Oakland 27–23, Dec. 29, 1968.

WIDE WORLD

swept to ten straight victories in regular-season play and retained the Lambert Trophy, emblematic of Eastern supremacy. Kwalick, a pass catcher and blocker, was selected to most All-America teams. Penn State's greatest challenge came from Army, which it edged 28–24. Army recovered from that defeat to round out a 7–3 season by winning its traditional game with Navy 21–14 in Philadelphia. Navy had its worst season in years with a 2–8 record.

Traditional rivals Harvard and Yale each went into their annual game unbeaten for the first time since 1909 and remained that way, tying 29–29 to share the Ivy League title with 6–0–1 records. Harvard trailed Yale 22–0 at one point in the game and was behind 29–13 with 42 seconds remaining. Then Frank Champi, a substitute quarterback, threw two touchdown passes and a two-point-conversion pass—the other two-point conversion coming on a run—to gain a tie for Harvard. Both teams finished with overall season records of 8–0–1. The universities of Connecticut and New Hampshire shared the Yankee Conference championship with 4–1 league records.

Midwest. Ohio State won the Big Ten championship by defeating Michigan 50–14 in the final league game. In that game Jim Otis, Ohio State junior fullback, scored four touchdowns, gaining 143 yd. in 34 carries. Both teams went into the game at Columbus, O., with 6–0 conference records, Michigan thus finishing second in the Big Ten. Purdue and Minnesota shared third place with 5–2 records.

Kansas, with a 9–1 overall record, tied Oklahoma

Tom Matte of the Baltimore Colts gains yardage against the Cleveland Browns in the NFL championship game at Cleveland, Dec. 29, 1968. Baltimore defeated Cleveland 34–0.

WIDE WORLD

WIDE WORLD

New York Jets quarterback Broadway Joe Namath hands off the ball to Matt Snell during the fourth quarter of the Super Bowl Jan. 12, 1969, in Miami. The AFL Jets scored a stunning upset 16–7 victory over the favoured NFL Baltimore Colts.

for the Big Eight Conference championship with 6–1 league marks. Oklahoma's major victory was 27–23 over Kansas, which had a 7–0 record going into that showdown contest. Kansas was rated among the nation's top teams all season, with Bobby Douglass, a fine quarterback, providing the leadership. Owens, running back, led Oklahoma by finishing fourth in the nation in rushing with 1,536 yd. Ohio University of Athens, won all of its ten games and took the Mid-American Conference championship.

Far West. USC was almost upset on its march to the Pacific Eight Conference title, which it eventually won with a 6–0 record. In the next to last game of the regular season Oregon State, which had defeated USC in 1967, led the Trojans 7–0 in the third period before falling 17–13. Oregon State placed second in the conference with a 5–1 record. Wyoming won the Western Athletic Association title with a 6–1 record.

South. Georgia was the power of the area, winning the Southeastern Conference title with a 5–0–1 record. It was, even so, the closest conference race in many years as Tennessee finished second with 4–1–1 and Alabama, Auburn, and Louisiana State tied for third with 4–2. Georgia won the title with the best defense in the country, permitting an average of only 9.8 points per game.

North Carolina State won the Atlantic Coast Conference title with a 6–1 record, but needed help. This was provided by South Carolina in the last game of the season against Clemson, which was undefeated with a 4–0–1 conference record and could have won the title. South Carolina defeated Clemson 7–3 to assure North Carolina State of the championship.

Southwest. Texas started off the season poorly but won its last eight games to win the Southwest Conference championship behind the quarterbacking of Jimmy Street and the running of All-American Gilbert. Texas was tied by Houston in the season opener and lost the second game to Texas Tech, but then won its next eight games, including a 39–29 victory over Arkansas. Since Texas and Arkansas finished with identical 6–1 conference records, the Texas victory in the game between the two teams gave it the conference crown. Memphis State, a newcomer to the Missouri Valley Conference, ran up a 5–0 league record to win the title.

Bowl Games. Ohio State, the Big Ten champion, reaffirmed its top national rating by defeating USC 27–16 in the Rose Bowl. Kern, sophomore quarterback, starred for Ohio State and broke the game open with two fourth-quarter touchdown passes. Penn State defeated Kansas 15–14 in the Orange Bowl, scoring its

tying and winning points in the final 15 seconds when Bob Campbell plunged over from the 1-yd. line for a 2-point conversion. Kicking specialist Bob White booted three field goals, of 34, 24, and 31 yd., to lead Arkansas to a 16–2 triumph over Georgia in the Sugar Bowl, and Texas defeated Tennessee 36–13 in the Cotton Bowl.

Professional. Sport's first major strike almost disrupted the beginning of the 1968 National Football League (NFL) season, but an agreement between the players and owners salvaged the exhibition and regular seasons. The major subject of dispute was the financing of the players' pension fund. Agreement was finally reached when the owners almost doubled their contributions to the fund. The averting of the strike by the increased share of money given the players was part of the continuing prosperity of professional football. According to the owners, the average professional salary reached a new high of $25,000 in 1968.

The Green Bay Packers, who had won three successive NFL titles under Coach Vince Lombardi, could not even capture a divisional title under his successor, Phil Bengtson, in 1968. Divisional winners were Cleveland (Century), Dallas (Capitol), Baltimore (Coastal), and Minnesota (Central). In the play-offs Cleveland defeated Dallas 31–20 for the Eastern title, and Baltimore triumphed over Minnesota 24–14 for the Western title. In the NFL title game Baltimore decisively defeated Cleveland 34–0 as halfback Tom Matte ran for three touchdowns. Baltimore quarterback Earl Morrall, substituting for the injured Johnny Unitas, was voted the NFL player of the year.

The ten-team American Football League (AFL), with a new club in Cincinnati, had to go into a play-off game to determine the Western Division winner, while the New York Jets ran away with the Eastern Division title. The Oakland Raiders, the 1967 AFL champions, and the Kansas City Chiefs tied for the Western title with 12–2 records. Veteran quarterback Daryle Lamonica then led the Raiders to a 41–6 victory over the Chiefs with five touchdown passes to capture the Western Division crown and move Oakland into the league championship game. In that contest the Jets won 27–23 as New York quarterback Joe Namath threw three touchdown passes.

Defying the forecasts that had made them three-touchdown underdogs, the Jets became the first AFL team to win the Super Bowl by upsetting the Baltimore Colts 16–7. The Jets were led by Namath, who completed 17 of 28 passes and was voted the game's most valuable player. Other outstanding Jet players were fullback Matt Snell, end George Sauer, and defenseman Johnny Sample.

The year was marked by the retirement from coaching of Lombardi, who remained as general manager of the Green Bay team. Even more notable was the retirement from coaching of George Halas, owner of the Chicago Bears and one of the founders of the NFL.

Canadian Football. The Ottawa Rough Riders, led by two speedy players from the U.S. and by Russ Jackson, a Canadian quarterback, defeated the Calgary Stampeders 24–21 to win the Grey Cup and Canada's professional football championship. Halfback Vic Washington of Plainfield, N.J., and end Margene Adkins of Tyler, Tex., each scored a touchdown for the Rough Riders in the fourth quarter. Terry Evanshen, who played college football at Utah State, scored two of the Calgary touchdowns on passes from Peter Liske, a quarterback who once played for the New York Jets.   (JE. HO.)

France

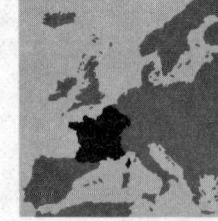

A republic of western Europe and head of the French Community, France is bounded by the English Channel, Belgium, Luxembourg, Germany, Switzerland, Italy, the Mediterranean Sea, Monaco, Spain, Andorra, and the Atlantic Ocean. Area: 211,209 sq.mi. (547,033 sq.km.), including Corsica. Pop. (1967 est.): 49,650,200. Cap. and largest city: Paris (pop., 1967 est., 2,823,800). Language: French. President in 1968, Charles de Gaulle; premiers, Georges Pompidou and, from July 11, Maurice Couve de Murville.

Two events overshadowed all others in France in 1968: the student revolt and the workers' strike of May and June. On the surface everything returned to normal following President de Gaulle's decision to remain in power. However, it was not possible to say that the storm had completely passed. Fresh signs of unrest began to appear among students and workers late in the year, after de Gaulle had introduced his austerity program designed to stabilize the franc.

Admittedly the government had a remarkable success when, on the night of October 10–11, the National Assembly passed by 441–0, with only the Communists and six Gaullist deputies abstaining, the bill on the development of higher education which was designed to pacify the students. Many amendments to the government bill, which was defended by the minister of education, Edgar Faure (*see* BIOGRAPHY), were tabled, but these did not alter the two principles of autonomy and participation which were the basis of the reforms.

It was intended that other government measures dealing with new administrative and political structures, designed to give more life to the regions and to reform the Senate, would be submitted to a referendum in the spring of 1969. The participation of workers in management appeared to be one of the major concerns of Gaullism in its search for a social doctrine that would end the class struggle and reconcile capital and labour, but this had not yet been presented in the form of a bill by the end of 1968.

Domestic Affairs. *The May–June Crisis.* Student opposition had begun with the start of the 1967–68 academic year in the Faculty of Letters at Nanterre, a subsidiary of the Sorbonne, and from there it spread to the whole of France. A one-week strike occurred in November 1967 over the introduction of a new system of literary studies and interchangeability of courses and diplomas. There was an argument between Daniel Cohn-Bendit (*see* BIOGRAPHY), a sociology student who rejected traditional higher education entirely, and François Missoffe, at that time minister of youth and sports, on the occasion of the opening of the campus swimming pool in January 1968. During the preceding winter the student residence had been the site of opposition to the hostel system and to hostel regulations, especially those restricting the right of men and women students to visit each other in their rooms.

The "hard" revolt began on March 22. On that day, as a protest against the arrest of several of their comrades—members of the Vietnam Solidarity Committee (Comité Vietnam-national)—following attacks against the premises of U.S. organizations in Paris, the students occupied the administrative building of the Faculty, including the staff common room. The intransigence of these students earned them the name *enragés* (hotheads). Also on that day, Cohn-Bendit's "Twenty-second of March Movement" was born.

The factions that took part in the "Twenty-second of March Movement" consisted of two groups of the Federation of Revolutionary Students (Fédération des Étudiants Révolutionnaires; FER), one of Trotskyite persuasion, the other pro-Chinese (Maoist). Tired of debating the advantages and disadvantages of their rival ideologies, they suddenly decided, on Cohn-Bendit's initiative, to make a concrete demonstration of power by "occupying." The subsequent unrest reached such a pitch that the doyen was obliged to close the Faculty, first on March 28 for two days before the Easter vacation, and then a second time on May 3, at the request of the teaching staff. It was then that the revolutionary agitators, hounded from their strongholds, took refuge in the Sorbonne. On that day they held a political meeting in the venerable Parisian university to denounce the established university system as a product of bourgeois society. At the request of the rector the police intervened to expel them, and the scuffles that followed were the starting point of the "cultural revolution" in France. With the help of the National Union of Students (Union Nationale des Étudiants de France; UNEF) and the National Union for Higher Education (Syndicat National de l'Enseignement Supérieur, SNE-Sup.), led by Jacques Sauvageot and Alain Geismar, respectively, violent riots erupted in Paris during the whole of the month of May. Students and police fought in the streets of the Latin Quarter while almost every university, both in Paris and in the provinces, ceased to function.

At the same time, a movement of industrial protest developed, accompanied by strikes and the occupation of factories. Premier Pompidou (*see* BIOGRAPHY) cut short his trip to Afghanistan. In the National Assembly an opposition censure motion received only 233 votes and was not adopted. Negotiations opened between the government, unions, and management, which culminated in the "Grenelle agreement." At first rejected by the strikers, this agreement was later to provide the basis for a return to work, in exchange for substantial increases in the workers' pay and the promise that unions would have adequate representation on management committees. (*See* LABOUR UNIONS.)

However, May 29–30 was the period of most dramatic suspense. De Gaulle left the Elysée late on the morning of May 29 for Baden-Baden, W.Ger., and Colombey-les-deux-Églises, and did not return to the capital until the early afternoon of May 30. Then, in a broadcast speech, he told the nation of his intention to remain in power and to dissolve the National Assembly. A few moments later a Gaullist demonstration in the Place de la Concorde developed into a huge procession along the Champs-Élysées in which hundreds of thousands of Frenchmen reaffirmed their personal devotion to the head of state. This outburst was a reaction of fear, resulting from the riots and from the inability of the left to offer alternative policies, and was to be translated in the legislative elections into a veritable Gaullist landslide.

The Legislative Elections. On June 23 the first round of the elections resulted in a marked Gaullist advance throughout the country, while at the same time the Communist Party and François Mitterrand's Federation of the Left suffered definite losses. This

Student at the Sorbonne, Paris, attacking police with slingshot during the June demonstrations.

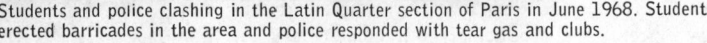
Students and police clashing in the Latin Quarter section of Paris in June 1968. Students erected barricades in the area and police responded with tear gas and clubs.

tendency was accentuated in the second round (June 30), which gave the Democratic Union of the Fifth Republic (Union Démocratique pour la Cinquième République)—the Gaullists—a gain of nearly 100 seats. The left was in disarray, and the government could henceforth rely on an absolute majority of a size rarely achieved in France. It had the support of more than 350 deputies, since most of the Independent Republicans voted with the Gaullist group. In terms of the different parliamentary groups, the 487 seats in the new National Assembly were distributed as follows: UDR (Union des Démocrates pour la République, which replaced the Democratic Union for the Fifth Republic), 292 (+92); Independent Republicans led by Valéry Giscard d'Estaing, 61 (+18); Progrès et Démocratie moderne (PDM) of Jacques Duhamel, 33 (−10); Federation of the Left (FGDS), 57 (−61); Communist Party (PCF), 34 (−39). The remainder was made up by ten independent deputies.

Significant though it was, the Gaullist landslide did not obscure the fact that the majority poll system (as opposed to a system of proportional representation) had amplified the swing of seats, since the proportions

of the total vote remained more stable. In the first round, 9 million went to the left, compared with 10.5 million for the "majority" (Gaullists); in the second round, 6.1 million went to the left and 6.7 million to the majority. Nonetheless, the group of Independent Republicans and the PDM group had to give up the balance of power, which they held in the preceding assembly. François Mitterrand took advantage of the conference of Institutions Républicaines, when it met in October at Levallois-Perret, to stand aside both from the FGDS and from a proposed new socialist party that would reunite the left on a new basis.

The Government of Maurice Couve de Murville. While much of the Gaullist success in the legislative elections could be attributed to de Gaulle's prestige, the part played by Pompidou and his personal performance contributed in large part to the victory. So his replacement in mid-July by Couve de Murville (*see* BIOGRAPHY) caused a sensation, despite the flattering terms in which the head of state addressed the man who had been generally thought of as his successor at the head of the regime: "I hope that you will remain in readiness to carry out any mission and to take up any office which the nation may one day

---

FRANCE

Education. (1965–66) Primary, pupils 5,523,827, teachers (including preprimary) 263,025; secondary, pupils 2,455,209; vocational, pupils 772,160; secondary and vocational, teachers 189,448; teacher training, students 31,907, teachers 2,033; higher (including 23 universities), students 509,764, teaching staff (universities only; 1964–65) 16,904.

Finance. Monetary unit: franc, with a par value of Fr. 4.94 to U.S. $1 (Fr. 11.85 = £1 sterling). Gold and convertible currencies, official: (June 1968) U.S. $5,517,000,000; (June 1967) U.S. $5,772,000,000. Budget (1968 est.): revenue Fr. 117,625,000,000; expenditure Fr. 117,622,000,000. Gross national product: (1966) Fr. 500.5 billion; (1965) Fr. 464.7 billion. Money supply: (April 1968) Fr. 191,580,000,000; (April 1967) Fr. 191,660,000,000. Cost of living (1963 = 100): (June 1968) 116; (June 1967) 111.

Foreign Trade. (1967) Imports Fr. 61,110,000,000; exports Fr. 56,180,000,000. Import sources: EEC 44% (West Germany 20%, Belgium-Luxembourg 9%, Italy 9%); U.S. 10%; U.K. 5%. Export destinations: EEC 41% (West Germany 17%; Belgium-Luxembourg 10%, Italy 9%, Netherlands 5%); U.S. 6%; Switzerland 5%; U.K. 5%. Main exports: machinery 18%; chemicals 9%; iron and steel 8%; motor vehicles 8%; textile yarn and fabric 6%; cereals 5%.

Transport and Communications. Roads (1966) 784,030 km. (including 774 km. expressways). Motor vehicles in use (1967): passenger 10,565,000; commercial 1,756,000. Railways: (1966) 37,670 km.; traffic (1967) 38,380,000,000 passenger-km., freight 62,907,000,000 net ton-km. Navigable inland waterways: (1965) 10,325 km. (of which 7,677 km. in regular use); freight traffic (1966) 12,652,000,000 ton-km. Shipping (1967): merchant vessels 100 gross tons and over 1,538; gross tonnage 5,576,500. Air traffic (1966): 8,986,688,000 passenger-km.; freight 273,146,000 net ton-km. Telephones (Dec. 1966) 6,554,441. Radio licenses (including combined radio-television; Dec. 1966) 15,861,000. Television licenses (Dec. 1966) 7,471,000.

Agriculture. Production (in 000; metric tons; 1967; 1966 in parentheses): wheat 14,383 (11,297); rye 362 (357); barley 9,725 (7,421); oats 2,758 (2,543); corn 3,697 (4,340); potatoes 10,632 (10,270); broad beans 42 (37); dry beans 50 (65); tomatoes 563 (613); onions 205 (204); apples 3,886 (3,095); flax fibre 63 (66); sugar, raw value (1967–68) 1,727, (1966–67) 1,786; wine 6,164 (6,225); beef and veal (1966) c. 1,650, (1965) 1,636; pork (1966) c. 1,350, (1965) 1,320; milk (1966) 28,980, (1965) 27,733; butter 530 (492); cheese (1966) 651, (1965) 618. Livestock (in 000; Oct. 1966): cattle 20,800; sheep 9,186; horses 1,044; pigs 9,840; chickens (laying hens) c. 75,000. Fish catch (in 000; metric tons) (1966) 805, (1965) 768.

Industry. Fuel and power (in 000; 1967): coal 47,623 metric tons; electricity 111,640,000 kw-hr.; manufactured gas (1966) 7,893,000 cu.m. Production (in 000; metric tons; 1967): iron ore (35% metal content) 49,220; bauxite 2,771; pig iron 15,970; crude steel 19,655; aluminum 421; lead 135; zinc 186; cement 24,790; cotton yarn 259; cotton fabrics 210; wool yarn 127; wool fabrics 63; rayon filament yarn 50; rayon staple fibre 59; sulfuric acid 3,220; superphosphates (1966–67) 1,438; passenger cars 1,752 units; commercial vehicles 258 units; petroleum products (1966) 61,260. Merchant shipping launched (100 gross tons and over; 1967) 578,000 gross tons. Index of production (1963 = 100): (1967) 120; (1966) 116.

Student attacking police with rocks during June demonstrations. Right, workers at the Renault factory listen to government proposals to end nationwide strike. Workers later joined students in mass rally to enforce their demands.

Georges Bidault, who opposed de Gaulle on the Algerian question, looks out his hotel window in Paris upon his return from six years of exile in Brazil and Belgium.

call on you to assume." As de Gaulle stated in his press conference on September 9, Pompidou had been put "in reserve for the republic." He had been premier since April 15, 1962, and during that time had formed five successive governments. Couve de Murville had been foreign minister since June 1958.

The seventh government of the Fifth Republic (after that of Michel Debré and the five Pompidou governments) officially came into being on July 13. Debré moved to the Foreign Ministry, François Ortoli to the Ministry of Finance, and Edgar Faure to the Ministry of Education. Two new ministers came into the government: Roger Frey (responsible for relations with Parliament) and Jean-Marcel Jeanneney (minister without portfolio). Others remained in their previous posts, notably André Malraux (Cultural Affairs), Maurice Schumann (Social Affairs), René Capitant (Justice), and Raymond Marcellin (Interior).

Senatorial Elections. On September 22 elections were held for the renewal of about one-third of the seats in the Senate. From the political point of view the composition of the Senate changed only slightly, showing a mild fall in the number of representatives of the non-Communist left and of the centre left.

These were probably the last elections to the Senate in its existing form, since, in theory at least, the country was to vote by referendum in the spring of 1969 on a proposal to unite the second house with the Economic Council and to transform it into a consultative (and no longer legislative) assembly. At most, the new members would occupy their seats until 1969, since the Senate was due to be dissolved the following summer.

On October 3, Alain Poher, senator from Val-de-Marne, a Centre Democrat and former chairman of the European Parliament, was elected president of the Senate on the third ballot. He succeeded Gaston Monnerville, who refused to stand for reelection in order to give himself greater freedom to fight against the reform of the Senate. Poher received 135 votes, against 107 for Pierre Garet (Independent) and 22 for Georges Cogniot (Communist). Poher was a convinced supporter of a supranational Europe, and he had said that he would be "a man of unity and conciliation."

The Economy. The events of May–June dealt a very serious blow to France in the economic field, as Couve de Murville admitted shortly after he took office at the head of the government. At the beginning of September the premier and Ortoli presented the budget proposals for 1969, and they made no secret of the fact that there was no possible policy for France other than a rapid return to work so that there might be a steady return to balance and prosperity. However, it was expected that budgetary expenditure in 1969 would exceed Fr. 152 billion, some 18.4% above that under the previous financial law and nearly 30% above the Fr. 117.6 billion of the initial budget for 1967.

The state was faced with a heavy bill as a result of the Grenelle agreement: Fr. 7.5 billion of additional expenses, the main beneficiaries of which would be state employees and farmers. Couve de Murville had to reduce credits for expansion and to increase certain taxes in order to prevent the deficit from exceeding Fr. 11.6 billion. Finally, by ending the exchange control introduced on May 29, the government hoped to reinforce the international standing of the franc and to put a stop to the outflow of currency.

Despite these measures, strong pressure on the franc developed in the fall, reaching crisis proportions by November. The expectation within the international monetary community was that devaluation was inevitable, but de Gaulle stunned the experts by refusing to make any such move. On November 24 he once again addressed the nation by radio, announcing in general terms (later made explicit) the austerity program deemed necessary to forestall devaluation: severe exchange restrictions, wage and price controls, a cut of about one half in the budget deficit (necessitating, among other things, a cutback in the nuclear program), measures to discourage imports and promote exports. By mid-December reserves were flowing back into France and the immediate crisis appeared to have subsided, although monetary experts expressed doubts that confidence in the franc had truly been restored. More ominously, perhaps, students and workers again appeared restive, as the austerity program affected both the educational reform and wages.

In October the government refused to approve a

Barricades in Paris streets during the demonstrations included overturned automobiles. Below, antiwar demonstrators rename the Boulevard St. Michel the Boulevard of Heroic Vietnam as a protest against the U.S. position in Vietnam.

GAMMA—PIX FROM PUBLIX

proposed merger between Citroën and Fiat of Italy on the ground that it wished to "maintain independence of a very vital French company." Fiat subsequently acquired a 15% share in the French automobile manufacturer.

Foreign Affairs. While the events of May and June had a profound effect on life in France, the invasion of Czechoslovakia by the U.S.S.R. somewhat upset de Gaulle's foreign policy of relaxing tension with the East and building a Europe "from the Atlantic to the Urals." During his September 9 press conference he unreservedly condemned Moscow's power-bloc policies, but he drew from them the conclusion that France's policy was correct.

Later, Debré, now foreign minister, was to give a more explicit definition of the four great principles on which, in the French view, peace must be founded —first in his address to the French association of the diplomatic press and later before the General Assembly of the United Nations in New York. The first of these principles was the right of nations to self-determination, and Debré illustrated his remarks by referring to the war in Vietnam, the Nigerian conflict, and the Czechoslovak crisis. The second was respect for international law, particularly in the Middle East. Aid to the less developed countries was the third principle necessary for the preservation of peace, and finally he mentioned the fourth aim, disarmament, which should be accompanied by precise and efficient methods of control.

During the first part of the year, de Gaulle had been continuing his policy of personal contacts with the leaders of the central European countries. At the end of March the visit of the Hungarian premier, Jeno Fock, to Paris confirmed the reality of the relaxation of tension between the two countries. After King Husain of Jordan, Pres. Arif of Iraq, and Premier Yussef Zayen of Syria, the Libyan prime minister, Abdul Hamid Bakkush, was the fourth leading Arab personality to visit France since the six-day war of June 1967.

Pompidou visited Iran from May 2 to 7, went on to Afghanistan, and returned home May 11. Following this there was a state visit of de Gaulle to Romania, May 14 to 18, which ended, as it had begun, in an atmosphere of euphoria. Pompidou, who was accompanying the head of state, was obliged to return in haste to Paris because of the crisis there, but de Gaulle cut short by only a few hours a journey during which he gave great encouragement to emotional

ties of "latinity." This was the third time he had been to Eastern Europe but the first time he had visited the country that was sometimes considered the stronghold of a sort of "Eastern Gaullism."

While continuing to preserve firm ties with French-speaking Africa, de Gaulle did not forget the English-speaking African states. In September he welcomed, on an official visit, Pres. Kenneth Kaunda of Zambia, whose policy of nonalignment in East Africa met with de Gaulle's approval. From October 25 to 30, de Gaulle and his wife visited Turkey to return the visit of Pres. Cevdet Sunay to France in 1967.

The traditional Franco-German "summit" meetings, which took place in Bonn on September 27 and 28, did not result in the confrontation over the question of widening the EEC that might have been expected. It appeared that there was no alternative to a policy of Franco-German cooperation, since only relaxation of tension in Europe could lead to the reunification of Germany. From another point of view, the Franco-German entente was perhaps the main obstacle in the way of British entry into the EEC. In 1968 nothing indicated that de Gaulle was likely to relax his opposition to this. (J. KN.)

See also Propaganda.

Fuel and Power

The oil industry was startled in July by an announcement of an oil discovery in Alaska that was unusual in two respects: it was the largest discovery ever made in the Western Hemisphere, and the estimate of its size was based on only two wells, drilled seven miles apart. Described as potentially "one of the largest petroleum accumulations known to the world today," the new field was estimated to contain recoverable reserves of from 5 billion to 10 billion bbl. of oil, together with large quantities of natural gas. Discovered by two U.S. oil companies exploring jointly, it was located at Prudhoe Bay on the Arctic Ocean coast of Alaska about 390 mi. N of Fairbanks. Because of its size (at 10 billion bbl. it was equivalent to one-third of the total current proved reserves of crude oil in the U.S.), the discovery had profound implications for the future oil supply of North America.

Elsewhere in the world, there were other notable discoveries of crude oil. The Soviet Union revealed that the newly found Samotlorskoye field, along the middle reaches of the Ob River in Tyumen Province, was one of the major fields of the world, with 2.9 billion bbl. of reserves. An exploratory well encountered the first petroleum hydrocarbons found in the Norwegian portion of the North Sea. In September it was announced that a U.S. oceanographic expedition had encountered petroleum hydrocarbons on the Sigsbee Knolls on the floor of the Gulf of Mexico. This discovery, made in water 11,753 ft. deep, was the first indication that oil and gas may occur in the sediments of the deep ocean floor.

Offshore exploration in more conventional areas continued to make news. Two sales of offshore leases by the U.S. government during the year were noteworthy because of the enormous sums involved. In February a lease sale in the Santa Barbara Channel off the coast of southern California yielded $602 million to the government, the largest total ever recorded for such a sale. This was followed in May by a sale of leases in an area offshore from Texas, which resulted in $594 million in accepted bids. Be-

fore the end of the year significant discoveries had been made in both areas.

The effects of the Arab-Israeli war of 1967 continued to be felt. New discoveries in the U.A.R. enabled that country to produce more oil than before it lost its Sinai oil fields, while Israel proceeded with the construction of a 42-in. oil pipeline to bypass the closed Suez Canal by taking oil from its southern port of Elath on the Red Sea to Ascalon, on the Mediterranean. Delays in putting the first generation of "supertankers" into operation, together with an increased pace of growth in oil consumption in Europe, brought about a shortage of tankers during the summer.

That this shortage was only temporary was made clear by the delivery of the "Universe Ireland," the first 312,000-ton-deadweight tanker. This ship, and the five scheduled to follow it, could each carry a full cargo of 2.5 million bbl. of oil. With approximately 25 other tankers of 150,000 tons or more scheduled for early delivery, the Suez Canal, even if it were reopened, was being relegated to the status of a minor convenience.

The world's first tar sands project, in Alberta, encountered difficulties during its first year of operation. These difficulties were in the power plant, however, and did not concern the pioneer process for converting the tar into synthetic crude oil. Government approval of a second tar sands project was requested during the year.

A long-standing controversy over the role of the federal government in the development of a shale-oil industry in the U.S. was finally resolved. In May the U.S. Department of the Interior issued a report suggesting that it modify its existing policy of refusing to lease public lands for shale-oil development and experimentation and offer a limited number of "test leases" for commercial shale-oil ventures. In September the department, having received generally favourable comments from industry, offered for lease three tracts in northwest Colorado containing an estimated total of 2.3 billion bbl. of shale oil. Two bidders responded and began testing.

Encouraging tests were obtained from Project Gasbuggy, which involved the explosion of a nuclear device (in December 1967) in an underground natural gas reservoir in New Mexico in an attempt to make a commercial gas field out of a noncommercial one. Radioactivity in the produced gas was low, and fracturing of the rock occurred as predicted. It was still too early, however, to determine whether this method of creating gas reserves would be economic. Planning proceeded for additional similar experiments to take place in Colorado in 1969.

Continued exploration and development in the rich Tyumen Province of the U.S.S.R. revealed a new claimant for the title of world's largest gas field. The Urengoiskoye field was estimated to contain 91.8 trillion cu.ft. of known reserves and possibly more than 100 trillion cu.ft. This compared with the 58.2 trillion cu.ft. of reserves in the previous record holder, the Slochteren field of the Netherlands.

In the field of power, the Hell's Canyon Dam on the Snake River in Oregon was dedicated in May. Also dedicated in the same month was the Oroville Dam on the Feather River in California. Fifth largest in the world, Oroville was part of a $2.8 billion project designed to supply water from northern to southern California.

Responding to continuing public pressure to put high-voltage transmission lines underground, the electrical utility industry of the U.S. instituted an investigation of the technical and economic feasibility of "cryogenic transmission." This technique would take advantage of the fact that the conductivity of metals is greatly increased at very low temperatures. It was estimated that a cable 18 in. in diameter, immersed in liquid nitrogen or hydrogen to make it extremely cold, could carry one-third the power needs of New York City.

The first high-voltage, direct-current interconnection line in the Western Hemisphere was placed in service in Canada between the mainland of British Columbia and Vancouver Island; the line spanned a distance of 42 mi., involving 19 mi. of underwater cable. Initial contracts were awarded in the construction of the El Chocon-Cerros Colorados hydroelectric project in Argentina and the Cahorabassa hydroelectric project on the Zambezi River in Mozambique.

Orders for nuclear power plants in the U.S. slackened off from the boom level of the preceding year. This was due partly to the large backlog of orders. It was also due in part, however, to a more cautious attitude toward nuclear power generation, engendered by difficulties in the construction and initial operation of large plants previously ordered. The Bolsa Island project, calling for a combined power generating and seawater desalting operation off the southern California coast, was abandoned when estimated costs rose from $444 million to $765 million.

The first commercial application of nuclear power to the production of oil and gas went into operation in February. A valve assembly operated by nuclear-generated electricity was installed on a wellhead on the bottom of the Gulf of Mexico in 92 ft. of water, 55 mi. off the Louisiana coast. The installation was used to control the flow of oil from the well and was operated remotely by means of coded sound waves transmitted through the water.

An important step was taken toward the long-range goal of fusion, or thermonuclear power, with the attainment of a continuous stable plasma in a ring-shaped magnetic field at the Max Planck Institute in West Berlin. Even with this achievement the possibility of commercial fusion power remained dubious, however.   (B. C. N.)

Main deck of the "Universe Ireland," a tanker completed in 1968 capable of carrying 2.5 million bbl. of oil. The ship was purchased by the American Gulf Oil Co.

COAL

Despite a decreasing proportional importance in the world energy market, it was considered that in 1968 the tonnage of coal mined would show an increase over the preceding year. During 1967 there had been a reversal of the gradual upward trend in world coal output and the estimated production of coal of all grades fell by 106 million metric tons to 2,721,000,000 tons. This marked the first decline since 1961 and was almost wholly due to an estimated 100-million-ton drop in production in China. Production cuts in Western Europe were severe, but were counterbalanced by gains in Eastern Europe, the U.S., and Australia.

U.S.S.R. In 1967 the total production of coal of all grades rose to 595 million metric tons, which represented an increase of 10 million tons over the previous year. Of the total output, 151 million tons were lignite. As in previous years, emphasis was on the development of opencut mines, although considerable attention was also given to the mechanization of underground operations. By the autumn of 1968 it was estimated that, including hydraulic mining, about 26% of total coal production came from surface mining operations. By late 1968 mining authorities confidently expected that more than 600 million metric tons of coal would be produced.

United States. The U.S. coal industry entered 1968 with a record 70 new large mines under development or planned. These proj-

ects had a cumulative annual production capacity of 150 million short tons. During 1967 bituminous coal output rose for the sixth successive year and reached 545.5 million tons, which represented a rise of 3% over 1966. However, anthracite production dropped by 5% to 12.2 million tons. An additional 4.4 million tons of lignite were mined, giving a total coal production of 562 million tons.

A significant feature of the resurgence of coal during the late 1960s was the development of the unit train concept and the trend toward bigger haulage units. By such measures the coal operators were able to trim surface freight charges and make coal economically competitive with other fuels. Exports of bituminous coal in 1967 totaled 49.5 million tons, of which about 15 million tons went to Canada and 12 million to Japan. By the fall of 1968 output of bituminous coal was much the same as for the comparable period in 1967, but anthracite lagged by almost 5%.

European Economic Community (EEC). Coal production in the six EEC countries continued the downward path of the past decade and in 1967 fell to 190.1 million metric tons. Thirty-three collieries with a cumulative annual capacity of 13.5 million tons were closed in 1967, and the average number of underground workers fell by 16% to slightly more than 320,000. However, the premature closure of the more difficult pits along with increasing mechanization resulted in an 8% rise in productivity. Average underground output per manshift in 1967 was 2.83 tons. In addition to the 190 million tons of hard coal mined, 104 million tons of lignite were produced, all but 6 million tons in West Germany.

In the first six months of 1968 production of hard coal in the Community was 90 million tons, 5 million below the comparable figure in the previous year. The number of underground workers fell to approximately 290,000, but despite these reductions the coal stocks at the mines stood at nearly 32 million tons in mid-1968.

United Kingdom. During the financial year ending March 30, 1968, the total tonnage of deep-mined coal from National Coal Board collieries declined by 1.9 million long tons to 162.7 million tons. Including 7.1 million tons from opencut operations and the production from small private mines, total output for the year 1967–68 dropped to 170.9 million tons, compared with 173 million tons in the previous year.

The capacity of the industry was reduced in accordance with the government's White Paper on fuel policy published in November 1967, and 62 collieries were closed or merged in 1967–68. Sales of coal were down by 6.8 million tons in 1967–68, largely due to the introduction of new nuclear generating capacity, a reduction in the tonnage of coal for gas making, the displacement of coal on the railways by diesel fuel, and the low level of industrial activity generally.

Overall productivity rose by 6.6% to an average of 1.95 tons per manshift and by autumn 1968 had reached 2.15 tons. This was achieved by increased mechanization and the closing of unproductive collieries. Manpower fell by approximately 43,000 men to 365,000 by the end of the financial year, and by September 1968 had decreased to 335,000.

Poland. During 1967 there was a steady expansion in both the bituminous coal and lignite sectors of the industry. Almost 124 million metric tons of bituminous coal were produced and 24 million tons of lignite. Exports topped 24 million tons, so that Poland ranked second only to the U.S. as a coal exporter. During the first nine months of 1968 hard coal output rose 3.5% and lignite production by almost 10%, compared with a year earlier.

There was a considerable increase in mechanized mining in 1968, the objective being 75% mechanical loading underground by 1970. Tests were carried out at the Yan experimental mine on coal faces that had been designed for a completely automated operation.

India. Production of coal in 1967 amounted to 70,250,000 metric tons, a decline of approximately a quarter of a million tons from the previous year. The overall rate of growth of the Indian economy was considerably below the target fixed by the current five-year plan, and reduced demand for coal from industry was responsible for a 5-million-ton cut in home sales. On the basis of data available in mid-1968 there appeared to be little change in this pattern of production and demand.

Japan. Despite the tremendous upsurge in general industrial activity in Japan during the 1960s the position of coal in the national economy steadily worsened. In 1967 only 47.5 million metric tons of coal of all types were mined, compared with 51.4 million tons during the previous year. At the same time as this drop in local production, imports soared by 7 million tons to reach 25 million tons in 1967, of which total the iron and steel industry took 22 million tons. Preliminary figures released in mid-1968 placed requirements for imported coking coal in the year under review at 30 million tons at an estimated cost of nearly $400 million. By mid-1968, production of coal in Japan had dropped by 3%, and more high-cost mines were closed during the year. Substantial long-term contracts were signed with the

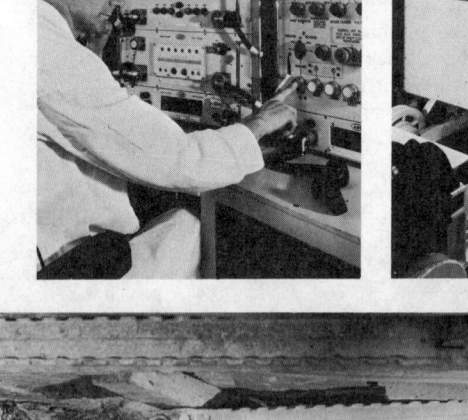

COURTESY, NATIONAL COAL BOARD, U.K.

Increased mechanization was credited with rise in manshift productivity of coal in the U.K. during 1968. At the Bevercotes Colliery a man at electronic controls at the head of the pit (above) operates the shearer loader (left).

U.S. and Australia to ensure adequate supplies of coking coal.

Australia. Production of black coal during the financial year 1967–68 (ending June 30) reached a record total of 36.8 million long tons, which represented an increase of 7% over the previous year. The brown coal industry also enjoyed a record year with 23.2 million tons being produced. Exports rose to 10.8 million tons, of which New South Wales supplied 8 million tons and Queensland 2.4 million tons. The value of exports during the fiscal year was provisionally given as A$110 million. The industry expected a production increase to 50 million tons over the next five years, which would necessitate considerable investment in modern mining equipment.

South Africa. The total production of coal in South Africa during 1967 comprised 52.9 and 1.4 million short tons of bituminous coal and anthracite, respectively. This represented an overall increase of approximately 3% over the previous year. The Transvaal accounted for the major portion of the total output, mining 31.5 million tons of coal in 1967. During the early months of 1968 production of both bituminous coal and anthracite continued at a level higher than during the preceding year.

Canada. Total production of coal and lignite was 11.4 million short tons in 1967, compared with 11.3 million tons in 1966. High production costs together with remoteness from major consumer centres continued to put coal at a considerable disadvantage compared with alternative fuels, but many mining engineers were confident that the long-term future for coal was brighter. Much of their optimism was based on a projected significant improvement in exports. A contract was signed with Japan for delivery of 45 million tons of coking coal in a 15-year period beginning in 1970, and other major contracts were under discussion.

China. Social and political disturbances were believed to have retarded coal output in 1967. Estimates published by the U.S. Bureau of Mines placed output during 1967 at 225 million metric tons. This compared with the total of 325 million tons believed to have been mined in 1966.   (AL. GR.)

ELECTRICITY

The decline in the growth rate of electricity consumption, which began in 1966, continued and became more marked during 1967. Of the major industrial countries only Japan (11.7% as compared with 8.6%) and the U.S.S.R. (8.1% as compared with 7.6%) showed a higher growth rate than in the previous year. This was not the case in Europe (5.8% instead of 6.2%), in the U.S. (5.5% instead of 7.8%), or in Canada (4.3% instead of 9.3%).

Nuclear-Electric Power. On Jan. 1, 1968, the number of reactors in service in the world was 70, representing a total capacity of 10,195 Mw. (gas-graphite, 6,700 Mw.; light water, 2,950 Mw.; heavy water, 450 Mw.; advanced gas-cooled reactor [AGR], 40 Mw.; high-temperature gas-cooled reactor [HTGR], 55 Mw.). The total electric power produced by all these reactors (excepting the Eastern bloc) was 38.7 billion kw-hr. in 1967, less than 1% of world electric power production. The number of power reactors under construction or on order in the world reached 118, with a total capacity of 71,105 Mw. (gas-graphite, 4,700; light water, 58,435; heavy water, 3,680; AGR, 3,960; HTGR, 330).

On June 30, 1968, the situation in the U.S. was the following: 15 nuclear power stations were in operation (2,798 Mw.), 31 under construction (22,500 Mw.), and 42 on order (34,980 Mw.). By far the greater number of these reactors were light-water reactors,

and the two principal types, pressurized-water reactors (PWR; Westinghouse) and boiling-water reactors (BWR; General Electric), represented almost equal quantities in the U.S. nuclear program.

In the U.K., operational nuclear capacity, together with capacity under construction or on order, reached 10,185 Mw. The program of magnox-type reactors was being completed with the power stations at Oldbury, Gloucestershire (two groups of 312 Mw. each), and at Wylfa, Anglesey (four groups of 327 Mw. each). The construction of power stations of the AGR type at Dungeness B, Kent (1,200 Mw.), at Hinckley Point B, Somerset (1,300 Mw.), and at Hunsterton B, Scotland (1,250 Mw.), continued, and it was decided to construct a fourth AGR-type station at Hartlepool, Durham (1,250 Mw.).

The U.S.S.R. was perfecting a series of superheating uranium-graphite reactors of 100 and 200 Mw., and was also developing two fast breeders of 350 and 600 Mw., respectively. Nuclear stations in operation or under construction in the U.S.S.R. represented a capacity of about 6,000 Mw. This comparatively low figure might be explained by the amount of the country's alternative fuel resources and by its hydroelectric potential.

With the first stages of the construction of the Fessenheim station (two twin reactors of 750 Mw. each), France remained faithful to the natural uranium graphite-gas series. Nevertheless, it shared in the project for the Franco-Belgian station at Thiange (a PWR reactor of 750 Mw.) and participated in a Franco-Swiss study for a light-water reactor of 700 Mw. to be built at Kaiseraugst, near Basel.

In West Germany, where 2,210 Mw. were in operation or on order, the most important electric concern, Rheinisch Westfälisches Elektrizitätswerk (REW), announced that it would begin construction in 1968, at Biblis, near Worms, of a nuclear power station of 1,000 Mw.

Two reactors of 200 and 400 Mw., respectively, were under construction in Sweden, and the State Power Board signed contracts in July for the provision of two reactors of 750 Mw. each, a BWR by the Swedish concern Allmänna Svenska Elektriska AB (ASEA) and a PWR by Westinghouse.

In Japan three stations (one PWR and two BWR) with a total capacity of 1,100 Mw. were under construction in 1968, and a decision had been made to build three others, also made up of two BWR and one PWR, with a total capacity of 1,780 Mw. Spain had a capacity of 1,093 Mw. under construction and on July 17 it brought into service at Zorita, near Madrid, its first nuclear power station, with a PWR type reactor of 153 Mw. Argentina ordered a 313-Mw. reactor from West Germany.

Thermoelectricity. For a long time a considerable part of the progress accomplished by thermoelectric power stations concerned raising the pressure and temperature of the steam provided by the boilers to the turbines in order to reduce the cost of the electricity produced. But it seemed that, in this quest, an economic ceiling had been reached (3,500 psi for pressure and 1,000° F for temperature). Thus, more recently the most noticeable progress has been obtained by increasing the unitary power of the groups, which results in a decrease in the cost of the equipment per unit of power installed.

In the U.S. the maximum power for groups (200 Mw. in 1950) reached 1,300 Mw. in 1967, and it was hoped that it would increase to 2,000–2,500 Mw. by 1980. In the U.S.S.R., the Uglegorsk (Ukraine) plant would have a total capacity of 3,600 Mw. (four groups of 300 Mw. and three of 800 Mw., all in

Political division	Hydroelectric power		Total electric power	
	Operating plants			
	Installed capacity (000 kw.)	Production (000,000 kw-hr.)	Installed capacity (000 kw.)	Production (000,000 kw-hr.)
World	...	...	...	3,602,200
Afghanistan	58†	169‡	89†	350
Albania	...	203§	...	341†
Algeria	228†	355	500†	1,119
Argentina	392	1,223†	5,363†	15,400
Australia	2,377	7,105	9,396	38,279
Austria	4,132	17,331	6,060	23,817
Belgium	65	299	5,823	22,881
Bolivia	92†	426†	213	584
Brazil	5,524	27,905	7,566	32,654
Bulgaria	767	2,010	2,641	11,757
Burma	84§	280§	252§	570§
Cambodia	—	—	33†	82
Cameroon	152†	1,069†	170†	1,008
Canada	22,428	129,834	30,775	158,135
Central African Republic	6.6†	24.5	8.3†	24.6
Ceylon	110	365†	220†	522
Chad	—	—	9.8†	22
Chile	710	4,168	1,493	6,662
China (Communist)	...	...	...	58,500‖
Colombia	843†	3,721§	1,546†	6,350
Congo (Kinshasa)	576¶	2,419¶	659¶	2,926
Costa Rica	142.6	586	196.1	697
Cuba	—	—	1,100	4,100
Czechoslovakia	1,545	4,256	9,149	36,528
Denmark	—	—	2,916	9,309
Ecuador	67†	249†	255	700
El Salvador	87§	409	141	477
Ethiopia	73§	136§	292	238†
Finland	1,996	10,381	4,317	15,877
France	13,292	51,695	30,217	106,111
Gabon	—	—	22.2	49.2
Germany, East	630	1,050	11,067	56,866
Germany, West	4,181	16,647	36,160§	172,938
Ghana	512	480	681.6	807
Greece	268†	759†	1,170†	4,432†
Guatemala	31‖	117‡	135	520
Guyana	—	—	98.1§	212§
Honduras	33	129	77	204
Hong Kong	—	—	894†	3,120
Hungary	21	100	2,007	11,855
Iceland	123	624	188	678
India	3,854†	15,405†	9,745†	37,437†
Indonesia	282	...	658†	1,520
Iran	250†	...	791†	907ᵠ
Ireland	219†	939†	1,070†	3,856
Israel	—	—	720	4,561
Italy	14,472	44,321	26,756	89,993
Jamaica	19§	133†	260	870
Japan	16,888	79,965	44,991	214,955
Kenya	27.9†	198†	100.1†	346
Korea, South	215	985	947	4,186
Kuwait	—	—	163§	983
Laos	—	—	6.8‖	12.8‖
Lebanon	198	556	374	864
Liberia	4†	17†	115.7†	339
Libya	—	—	71.1	182
Luxembourg	923†	970	1,174†	2,279
Malagasy Rep.	28.7†	84	82.4†	152†
Malawi	0.6†	4.1†	14.3†	67
Malaysia:				
Malaya	139†	692	491†	2,387
Sabah	—	—	21.4	56
Sarawak	—	—	27.9	79
Mexico	2,292†	8,609†	5,684	19,024
Morocco	301	1,055	388	1,431
Netherlands	—	—	8,425	27,869
New Zealand	2,089	9,297	2,522	11,311
Nicaragua	59.3†	204†	135	335
Nigeria	21	144	432	1,279
Norway	10,140	48,188	10,272	48,348
Pakistan	353	1,753	1,175	3,903
Panama	—	—	86.1§	472
Paraguay	—	—	61	205
Peru	680†	2,625†	1,148†	4,080
Philippines	291	1,479	1,222	5,567
Poland	350	929	9,920	47,385
Portugal	1,801	5,306	2,314	5,591
Rhodesia	705	3,874	1,191	4,217
Romania	777	1,035	4,471	20,806
Rwanda	21.3	46.8	22.5	48.1
Singapore	—	—	464	1,236
South Africa	14‡	40†	5,970†	33,558
Spain	7,370	27,176	10,650	37,466
Surinam	...	464	232.5†	681
Sweden	9,460	45,508	12,300	50,640
Switzerland	8,440	27,444	8,950	27,962
Syria	—	—	243†	658
Taiwan	718	2,661	1,574	7,527
Tanzania	41.2	178†	71.6	267
Thailand	41.2	178	71.6	267
Trinidad	—	—	280	1,007
Tunisia	27.9	27	210.8	574
Turkey	510†	2,318	1,768	5,535
Uganda	136	634	167	635
U.S.S.R.	23,077	91,823	123,007	544,566
U.A.R.	345	1,837	1,681	5,895
United Kingdom	2,061	4,560	51,814	202,568
United States	45,690	197,632	266,768	1,248,232
Uruguay	236	1,399	488	1,841
Venezuela	387δ	1,405	1,977δ	8,735
Vietnam, South	163	58†	439	602
Yugoslavia	2,592	9,880	4,268	17,174
Zambia	50	276†	262	602

*Preliminary. †1965. ‡1963. §1964. ‖1960. ¶1958. ᵠ1959. δ1962.
Source: *United Nations Statistical Yearbook, 1967.* (B.B.M.)

line) when completed, and in Japan the first group of the new Anegasaki plant went into operation in September 1967, with a capacity of 600 Mw., the most powerful in that country.

The U.K. Central Electricity Generating Board continued to bring into operation groups of its 500-Mw. series, which would eventually total 47 single-shaft units. Construction began on a 660-Mw. unit at Dran, Yorkshire, where final capacity would total nearly 4,000 Mw.

France continued building its 250-Mw. series, of which 13 groups were in service and 15 under construction in July 1968. The next series would be of 600 Mw., of which three groups were under construction.

Hydroelectricity. In the U.S., out of the 145,000 Mw. of power on order for all plants on Jan. 1, 1968, only 7% was to be supplied by hydroelectric stations, as against 47.8% by power stations and 45.2% by nuclear power stations. This decrease in the use of hydroelectric equipment was not typical. The U.S.S.R., for example, continued the construction of its large Siberian plants; it intended to harness the Yenisei River by means of three plants, providing a total of 20,000 Mw.

The World Bank agreed to finance 50% of a $440 million hydroelectric complex at El Chocon-Cerros Colorados in Argentina. When completed, this project would supply the province of Buenos Aires with electric power and would facilitate the development of part of Patagonia. Another World Bank loan, of $17.5 million was extended to Empresas Electricas Asociadas of Peru, to construct the Matucana hydroelectric station, which would have a capacity of 120 Mw.

The Portuguese government decided in July 1968 to develop Cahorabassa on the Zambezi River in Mozambique, constructing a dam supplying a power station of 2,250 Mw. and a 220,000-v. direct current trans-

Site of the Churchill Falls hydroelectric plant in Labrador. When completed in 1972, the $1 billion development should produce twice as much power as the Grand Coulee Dam.

ROBERT O. BOYD

mission line to allow the power to be transported as far as Irene, near Pretoria in South Africa. Also in Africa, the government of Congo (Kinshasa) decided to carry out a development at Inga, which would have an eventual capacity of 300 Mw. Hydroelectric projects were also under way in Pakistan and in Albania, where a 225-Mw. station was being built on the Drin River with Chinese aid.

In 1968, France began the development of the Strasbourg station (147 Mw.), probably the last power station to be built on the Rhine. It also brought into operation the 124-Mw. station at Vouglans and conducted trials on the two groups of the Mont Cenis plant (381 Mw.).

Considerable activity also took place in the field of pumped storage stations, even in countries such as Belgium which possess hardly any hydroelectric resources. Such a station involved using excess electrical power at times of low demand to pump water into higher level reservoirs, which could be used to power hydroelectric plants at times of high demand or as an emergency supply. The North of Scotland Hydro-Electric Board asked for permission to carry out a development at Foyers which would comprise a normal hydroelectric station and a pumped storage station operating between Loch Ness and Loch Mohr. The capacity of the project would be 300 Mw. and its mean annual production capability 400 million kw-hr. Ireland decided on the construction in the Wicklow Mountains, about 40 mi. from Dublin, of its first pumped storage plant, which would have a capacity of 280 Mw. In 1967, on the slopes of Mt. Kisen, Japan began the construction of an underground pumped storage plant at Kinsenyama, which was to have a capacity of 466 Mw. Finally, in the U.S. a plant was being constructed at Ludington, Mich., on the shores of Lake Michigan, which was expected to have a capacity of up to 1,872 Mw.

(L. CH.)

GAS

U.S. natural gas supplies remained plentiful and were expected to satisfy growing needs for at least a dozen years. Reserves were well over 200 trillion cu.ft., and more than 12 trillion cu.ft. were produced and purchased

per year. However, supply was increasing by less than 2% while demand was rising by 7%, and so efforts to obtain more gas were under way. Among these efforts was Project Gasbuggy, a $5 million experiment aimed at increasing the flow of natural gas by a nuclear explosion beneath the earth's surface. Other attempts included Project Ketch, deferred in 1968 but aimed at eventually creating off-season storage of natural gas, and Project Dragon Trail, an effort to stimulate the recovery of gas from a rock structure so tight that it otherwise might remain untapped.

Development in the U.S. of offshore gas reserves advanced rapidly in the Gulf Coast offshore area. While offshore activities in the U.S. had begun about 40 years earlier, only in recent years had major interest turned to exploitation of the energy beneath the sea. Full benefits remained to be seen, but with the prospects of a diminishing supply of gas, the industry was beginning to search in earnest for all productive areas.

U.S. industry in 1968 spent a record $3 billion for construction, a third more than in 1967, as part of a $10.3 billion four-year construction program through 1971. Included in the amount were $196 million for production and storage; $1.7 billion for transmission; $110 million for distribution; and $117 million for general purposes.

After three years in the courts, the nation's first permanent uniform gas pricing system for producers was effected. The U.S. government's Federal Power Commission (FPC) handed down a series of rate decisions aimed at pricing for producers over a wide geographic area. The FPC action followed a decision by the U.S. Supreme Court in the Permian Basin case upholding the philosophy of basing the price structure on a geographic area. The general effect of the decision was that producers would have to lower their rates and refund approximately $68 million, including interest to pipeline purchasers for the above-ceiling rates charged between 1965 and 1968.

The high court also agreed to review a dispute between the U.S. Department of the Treasury and the industry, involving almost $25 million in federal taxes. The issue centred on the tax treatment companies were to be given when they refunded overcharges to their customers. Skelly Oil Co. in 1958 refunded $505,536 in overcharges to its customers and then claimed the full amount as a deduction on its tax return. The Treasury then stated that Skelly had not actually paid taxes on the full amount when it was earned because Skelly had taken $139,022 in deductions against its depletion allowance.

Existing oil and gas depletion allowances stood at 27.5% of the gross income at the wellhead, providing that figure did not total more than half of the taxable income. The allowance helped provide impetus for high-risk investment toward uncovering energy needed by the country; it also gave some taxpayers an argument that they were paying taxes for many of the services enjoyed by those under the shelter of the depletion allowance. The regulations provided that net operating losses that were carried over must be taken into account when computing taxable income for the property in order to ascertain the amount of depletion allowance. Industry representatives maintained that one year's losses should not be charged against depletion allowances in another year.

Codification of law as to the safety of gas pipelines was undertaken by the U.S. government for the first time. While the industry generally maintained high standards of safety in 1968, the U.S. Congress and the president in 1968 accepted responsibility in this area. As a result, the Office of Pipeline

Safety was established as a part of the U.S. Department of Transportation and given the task of establishing and enforcing federal safety standards covering the transportation of natural gas or other flammable, toxic, or corrosive gases. Although the office was set up, funds for the implementation of its work were slow in being appropriated, and its effectiveness was, therefore, somewhat limited in its first year.

Still basic to the needs of the U.S., however, remained the availability of gas, which accounted for about one-third of the U.S. total energy consumption through more than 800,000 mi. of gas pipeline. The use of gas increased three times after World War II and in 1968 was two-thirds the amount expected by 1980. Thus, when the New England area, which received its gas from sources halfway across the U.S., felt the harshest winter in half a century, greater political pressure was brought to bear on providing for the needs of the citizens of New England. However, the response was slow to come. While industry and government bolstered their provisions in New England against the possibility of another harsh winter, Project Ketch, involving a gas storage area in Pennsylvania for use in the New England states, ran into local opposition and was deferred. FPC approval of the Great Lakes gas pipeline extending from Canada down through the U.S. Midwest and back to eastern Canada was sidetracked by a court decision. Involved in the decision was the ownership of the pipeline, particularly with regard to possible violations of the Sherman Anti-Trust Act. The FPC planned to hold further hearings on the case. The pipeline was completed in 1968.

Canada's natural gas reserves were estimated at 46 trillion cu.ft., enough to supply its needs for about 37½ years. Production in 1967 totaled almost 1.7 trillion cu.ft., an increase of 8.9% over 1966. Beginning in 1959 Canada's gas industry had grown annually by at least 10% in volume and value of gas consumed. In 1967 the growth rate was 12%, and revenues reached $470 million. More than 85% of the gas was produced in Alberta and another 13% or more in British Columbia.

Mexico added 16 billion cu.ft. to natural gas production in North America. Its success in gas exploration was increasing. In South America five countries accounted for more than 90% of proven reserves: Venezuela, 27 trillion cu.ft.; Argentina, 8 trillion; Colombia, 4 trillion; and Bolivia and Chile, 3 trillion each. The quantity of reserves appeared to be declining. Venezuela, whose gas production is keyed to its oil production by law, produced almost 1 billion cu.ft. per year directly, and 25 billion cu.ft. annually as part of its oil production. (J. J. Ac.)

The first long-term contracts for large quantities of British North Sea gas were concluded during 1968 between the producing companies and the Gas Council, after two years of negotiations. The agreements were seen to be especially important at this stage in the development of European markets for natural gas, because many countries were in the course of negotiations for supplies.

First of the British agreements was between the Gas Council and the Phillips group of companies. It stipulated a price of 2.879d. a therm for an average supply of 350 million cu.ft. of natural gas a day for a period of 25 years. The gas was to come from the Hewett field about 20 mi. off the Norfolk coast. This agreement was followed by a similar one with the Arpet group, which shared the Hewett field with Phillips. Altogether, approximately 600 million cu.ft. a day (roughly equivalent to half of Britain's 1968 gas demand) was to flow from the

Drilling platform "Constellation" arriving at gas bubble in the North Sea. The leak was caused by the drifting of the drilling rig "Sea Quest" during February storms in the area.

Hewett field, starting from October 1969.

The biggest gas field discovered in the North Sea, the Leman Bank, about 30 mi. off the Norfolk coast, began production in August 1968. This was under an interim agreement between the producer and the Gas Council, and contract quantities were expected to rise to 250 million cu.ft. a day by winter.

Exploration work continued actively during the year in the North Sea, but in British waters the emphasis was more on drilling development wells for fields already discovered. There were additional fresh discoveries, however, and the evaluation of these in terms of reserves was awaited. The four major fields in the U.K. part of the North Sea contained about 25 trillion cu.ft. of natural gas, about half of which was in the Leman field, one of the largest offshore discoveries in the world.

During 1968 the British gas industry announced its ambitious marketing targets of doubling sales of gas by 1971–72 and doubling them again by the mid-1970s, the latter target presupposing additional finds in the North Sea. To get the gas to market involved laying pipelines on a scale unprecedented in the U.K. Approximately 300 mi. of large-diameter transmission lines had been laid for the national system in 1967–68 and the 1968–69 program would be half again as large. It was expected that by 1972–73 the transmission network, computer controlled and using a complex system of microwave radio communications, would total about 2,500 mi. of large-diameter pipelines.

Large-diameter gas pipelines generally meant, in the U.K. and elsewhere, pipe with diameters up to 36 in. In the U.S.S.R., however, the Soviets were thinking in terms of 72-in. diameters for the immediate future and up to 100-in. diameters by 1970. Meanwhile, they completed the first 125-mi. section of their 48-in. pipeline running westward from the Vuktylskoye field near the Pechora River to Ukhta in the Komi Republic. Work was continuing on the remaining 860 mi., which would take the line from Ukhta southwest to Cherepovets and Torzhok, where it would link up with the twin

mains connecting Moscow and Leningrad. This section was scheduled for completion by November 1968.

Altogether at the end of 1967, gas distribution lines in the Soviet Union totaled 32,500 mi. and an additional 11,250 mi. were planned by 1970. Gas accounted for almost 20% of all fuel used in the Soviet Union. Production rose 10% in 1967, and an eightfold increase was planned for the subsequent ten years. Proved gas reserves, including the mammoth fields in western Siberia, were put at 325 trillion cu.ft. at the end of 1967.

Exploration for natural gas in Australia continued in 1968. New discoveries were made in the Bass Strait in May, and development work progressed on the Marlin and Barracouta fields discovered there earlier. The reserves in those two fields were estimated at three trillion cu.ft., just below the requirements of Sydney and Melbourne for 20 years. Elsewhere in Australia, pipelining work was going on during the year. Adelaide was to be linked to a field 500 mi. away, and Brisbane to one 260 mi. distant. The country's reserves totaled eight trillion cu.ft.

Offshore exploration for natural gas began during 1968 in the Dutch part of the North Sea. Licenses, after a four-year wait, were issued in March by the government, and by the end of the year 20 exploratory drillings were expected to have been carried out, though there were no finds reported after six months of drilling. The Netherlands, with its huge Groningen gas field, doubled its sales of natural gas as forecast during 1967, and expected to double them again in 1968. About 240 billion cu.ft. were sold. Exports of natural gas to France, Belgium, and Germany rose steeply in 1967, totaling 39.4 billion cu.ft. (4.7 billion in 1966). In 1968 it was expected they would rise to 141.2 billion cu.ft.

Norway, Sweden, and Denmark were all continuing work in the North Sea, while Italy was successful in the Adriatic Sea, where two new gas fields were discovered with reserves estimated at 700 billion cu.ft. The Italians continued their negotiations with the U.S.S.R. and Algeria for natural gas supplies, and their plan to import 235 million

cu.ft. a day from Libya was scheduled to start by the end of 1968. It was intended that the gas would be shipped in liquid form to Italy (a relatively new form of world trade). Another similar project was that between Alaska and Japan, which represented the longest chain for such shipments in the world. Japan was expected to start receiving the liquid gas in 1969 and had also agreed to take supplies by tanker from Brunei. (X.)

PETROLEUM

An important feature of 1968 was a rise of about 10% in the amount of newly discovered oil. This exceeded growth in both production and consumption, which remained well balanced, both increasing at a rate of about 7.5% a year. Proved and probable world crude oil reserves increased by 3.3% from the estimated figure at the end of 1966 (479,681,000,000 bbl.) to 495,677,000,000 bbl. in 1967. At the current rate of consumption reserves were assessed as being sufficient to last until 2001. Middle East reserves accounted for about 57% of the total; North America and the Communist countries had about 12% each. It was forecast that, as discovery is usually followed by rapid exploitation, the volume produced would rise rapidly, regardless of the existing demand. Politically, one of the most significant trends of the period was the ever increasing share that oil-producing countries demanded from the exploiters. Indeed, it was declared at the conference of the Organization of Petroleum Exporting Countries meeting in Vienna during June that "the smallest government is stronger than the biggest company," and experience had proved this to be a correct assumption. Another interesting feature was the increasing participation of the smaller oil companies. The seven major concerns (Esso, Royal Dutch-Shell, British Petroleum, Texaco, Standard Oil of California, Gulf, and Mobil) retained the lead, but their share had fallen from about 90% of world production in 1952 (excluding the North American area) to about 75% in 1965; product sales and refining showed the same

World petroleum needs and supply sources showed continuing growth during the years 1960–69.

trend. While it was certain that the oil industry would continue to grow in line with the primary energy needs, the major producing firms would be faced with more challengers.

Exploration. The largest single oil find ever made was the well discovered in 1967 by the Occidental Oil Company in the Libyan desert. From this single source a yield of approximately 25 million tons a year had been maintained, and it was estimated that the potential buildup could amount to double that figure.

Nigerian oil activity was held up by the Biafran war, but the U.A.R. appeared to have a sound possibility of entering the ranks of the oil-exporting countries. Discoveries by the Atlantic Richfield group in Alaska seemed to have influenced British Petroleum to make a major exploration of its concessions in that region, and many experts appeared to be convinced that Alaska might hold one of the world's largest oil reserves; figures from 5 to 10 billion bbl. were prophesied. But, on the whole, drilling continued to decline, as it had done for several years, and even fewer wells were predicted for 1968. The estimated total of new wells for 1967 was 36,732, 12% fewer than the 1966 total. Almost all of this decrease was contributed by a 13.5% drop in U.S. activity, for although the U.S. remained the world's largest oil producer it appeared certain that future major finds would be made elsewhere. It was estimated that a total of 750,000 wells were producing in the U.S., compared with the much smaller number (approximately 1,200) in the whole of the Middle East, though it should be noted that some of the U.S. wells had an output of only a few barrels a day. Percentage changes for the major geographical areas were: Africa, down 25%; South America and Europe, down 6.2% and 38%, respectively; the Middle East, up 3.7%; and the Far East and Asia, up 13%.

Production. A significant factor in 1967 was the Arab-Israeli war with the consequent closure of the Suez Canal, a temporary stoppage of crude oil production in the Arab countries, the embargo of exports to the U.K. and the U.S., and the shutdown of the major pipeline from the Middle East to the Mediterranean. Oil-consuming countries began to pay attention to more reliable producing sources, including Australia, Alaska, Europe,

and the North Sea. Total world production of crude oil in 1967 increased on the average to 35 million bbl. a day. As had been the case for a number of years, most of the gain came from the Eastern Hemisphere. In Great Britain pressure on the government to form a Hydrocarbons Corporation to exploit the North Sea gas finds and so develop a nationalized oil company—including, as some surmised, British Petroleum—naturally produced an unfavourable reaction in established oil circles; such a development appeared to be unlikely under the existing economic and political conditions. A substantial rate of gain was shown by the U.S., almost 500,000 bbl. a day; Mexico and Canada showed positive increases, while Venezuela overcame the previous year's drop and achieved a growth of 5%, thus retaining third place among the world's producing countries (behind the U.S. and the U.S.S.R.) with almost one million barrels a day more than Iran or Saudi Arabia. The large Middle Eastern increase recorded over recent years was not repeated due to political factors. Production in the U.S.S.R. grew at a rate higher than the world average, reaching 5,760,000 bbl. a day, a gain of 8.7%, and Western oil combines estimated that with associated East European countries, the U.S.S.R. would become, by reason of its fast-growing oil consumption, a major importer by the mid-1970s. It is a truism of the industry that oil is nearly always discovered in the least accessible area of a country. In the U.S.S.R. the major fields were discovered in Asia, far from the main industrial zones, and it was considered possible that a satisfactory solution of the problem might be to import oil from the West while at the same time exporting it from the Pacific seaboard to Asian users such as Japan.

Consumption. World demand for petroleum increased during 1967 to approximately 35,744,000 bbl. a day (nearly 7%). In the Western Hemisphere it approached 15.8 million bbl. a day, while the corresponding figure for the Eastern Hemisphere was about 20 million bbl. a day. Excluding the U.S., U.S.S.R., and Japan, five countries consumed more than one million barrels a day. They were: West Germany 1,950,000; U.K. 1,782,-000; France 1,290,000; Canada 1,280,000; and Italy 1,260,000.

Processing. World crude refining capacity increased to 37,706,300 bbl. a day during 1967, about 3 million bbl. a day over the preceding 12-month period. The number of countries with refining capacity of one million barrels a day or more remained at nine, totaling 73.5% of world capacity. These countries, with their capacities in barrels a day, were: U.S. 10,952,500; U.S.S.R. 4,736,-000; Japan 2,182,300; Italy 2,085,700; West Germany 1,964,500; U.K. 1,750,700; France 1,682,000; Venezuela 1,190,500; Canada 1,-166,800. The total number of petrochemical plants increased to 1,119 in 1967; 400 in the Eastern Hemisphere and 719 in the Western.

Transportation. The closing of the Suez Canal was responsible for a massive construction program for giant tankers. By the end of 1970 it was expected that one company alone would have 29 ships of 200,000 tons deadweight in service. The economics of transport were heavily in favour of the larger vessel, and oil company planners were said to be preparing to scrap prematurely many ships of less than 100,000 tons. (E. G. Es.)

See also Conservation; Engineering Projects; Industrial Review; Mining; Nuclear Energy; Transportation.

ENCYCLOPÆDIA BRITANNICA FILMS. *Jet Propulsion* (1952); *Light and Power* (1955); *Fuels—Their Nature and Use* (1958); *Rockets: How They Work* (1958); *The Steam Engine: How It Works* (1961); *Industrial Revolution —Beginnings in the United States* (1968).

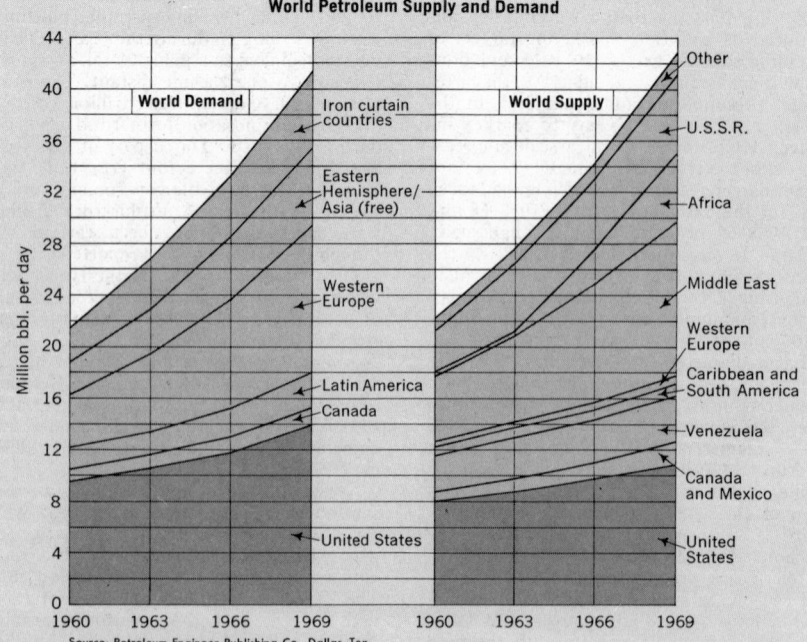

World Petroleum Supply and Demand

World Demand — Iron curtain countries — Eastern Hemisphere/Asia (free) — Western Europe — Latin America — Canada — United States

World Supply — Other — U.S.S.R. — Africa — Middle East — Western Europe — Caribbean and South America — Venezuela — Canada and Mexico — United States

Million bbl. per day

44 40 36 32 28 24 20 16 12 8 4 0

1960 1963 1966 1969   1960 1963 1966 1969

Source: Petroleum Engineer Publishing Co., Dallas, Tex.

Furs

Continued prosperity throughout most of the Western world in 1968 had a beneficial effect on the fur industry. The steady comeback from the low point reached in mid-1967 continued and, despite some hesitancy, the final tallies for the year were expected to be slightly above those for 1967. Again, the fur market's fortunes appeared to be a direct reflection of both the general economy and the fortunes of the investment community.

To be sure, fashion also exerted a strong influence. There was a resurgence of demand for furs by younger women and students, as well as a new awareness of furs as a status symbol on the part of men. The latter development was ironic in that, historically, furs were first worn by men and were not adopted by women until relatively recently. Of particular significance was the sharp increase in the diversity of the furs sold. In the U.S. there were indications that the dominance of mink was about to be challenged for the first time in a generation. Mink was in no danger of losing its prestige position, but other furs were taking a bigger share of the consumer dollar.

Prices of nearly all fur skins rebounded from the depths to which they had dropped the previous year. Mink made a dramatic recovery, as did Alaska seal, Persian lamb, fox, and beaver. The other important furs also showed considerable improvement. However, the 1967 plunge had taken its toll. About a thousand mink ranchers in the U.S. alone had gone out of business, beleaguered by labour shortages, rising costs, declining prices, and tight credit.

This situation constituted an important part of the presentation made by U.S. ranchers in pleading their case for the imposition of quotas on imports of mink from such areas as Scandinavia. Import interests, on the other hand, argued that the mink market is international and is uniformly affected by supply and demand. By the end of the year, Congress had taken no action on the subject, but the issue did result in an independent investigation of the U.S. ranch mink industry by the Tariff Commission. One of its findings was that the National Board of Fur Farm Organizations, because of faulty statistical methods, was overestimating U.S. ranched mink production by about one-third. The commission estimated the U.S. crop for 1968 at about 6.7 million mink.

Imports of mink into the U.S. from all sources during the 1968 crop year amounted to 4,075,000 pelts, at an average price of $11.46. This compared with 4,573,000 at an average of $10.72 for 1967. At the same time, exports rose to 1,283,000 pelts from 1,188,-000. The import drop, according to industry sources, was due to the fact that U.S. buyers were outbid by Germans and Italians at the auctions overseas. Preliminary information indicated that for the auction season of December 1968 through June 1969, the world mink crop would be about 25 million pelts, slightly smaller than in the preceding year.

Alaska sealskin prices rose 30% at the first of the semiannual sales, but slipped back some 23% at the second sale. An interesting development in this connection was the indictment of 20 sealskin dealers and manufacturers on a charge of conspiracy to rig bids at the auctions and thereby defraud the U.S. government, which owned the skins. The 20 pleaded not guilty and the case was still pending at year's end.

News was made in 1968 by the reappearance of a fur that had not been seen since 1911. Sea otter, protected by the U.S. government because it was in danger of extinction, was allowed to be taken in limited quantities for the first time in 57 years. The approximately 1,000 pelts offered at auction in Seattle, Wash., brought a top price of $2,300 per pelt, paid by Neiman-Marcus of Dallas, Tex., and an average price of $170.

Meanwhile, humane societies, wildlife and naturalist groups around the world strongly protested the indiscriminate killing of African leopards and cheetahs on the ground that these species were becoming extinct. Measures were introduced in the U.S. Congress to prohibit the importation or interstate shipment of the skins or products of animals or reptiles proclaimed by the secretary of the interior to be in danger of extinction.

Subsequently, statistics gathered by the International Union for the Conservation of Nature and Natural Resources, based in Switzerland, indicated that neither the leopard nor the cheetah was in danger. One important New York furrier announced that he would no longer sell cheetah coats and ran newspaper ads urging women to forgo such coats so that "in twenty years . . . your daughters will again wear them." There were no signs that the rest of the industry would follow his lead, however.   (S. PA.)

See also Fashion and Dress.

Gabon

A republic of western equatorial Africa and a member of the French Community, Gabon is bounded by Río Muni, Cameroon, the Congo (Brazzaville), and the Atlantic Ocean. Area: 102,317 sq.mi. (265,000 sq. km.). Pop. (1967 est.): 474,000. Cap. and largest city: Libreville (pop., 1964, 45,909). Language: French and Bantu dialects. Religion: traditional tribal beliefs; Christian minority. President in 1968, Albert Bernard Bongo.

Albert Bernard Bongo (*see* BIOGRAPHY), who had succeeded to the presidency in November 1967 following the death of Léon M'ba, reshuffled his Cabinet in

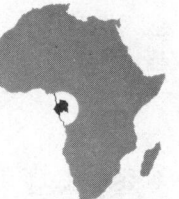

GABON
Education. (1967) Primary, pupils 81,125, teachers 2,314; secondary, pupils 5,203, teachers 336; vocational, pupils 1,504, teachers 92; teacher training (1966), students 418, teachers 27; higher, students 364 (students abroad 376).
Finance. Monetary unit: CFA franc, with a parity of CFA Fr. 50 to the French franc (CFA Fr. 246.85 = U.S. $1; CFA Fr. 592.45 = £1 sterling). Budget (1967 est.) balanced at CFA Fr. 11.5 billion.
Foreign Trade. (1967) Imports CFA Fr. 16,650,-000,000 (60% from France, 7% from West Germany); exports CFA Fr. 29,520,000,000 (36% to France, 19% to U.S., 11% to West Germany, 6% to Netherlands). Main exports: crude oil 30%; manganese 27%; timber 22%; uranium 7%.
Transport and Communications. Roads (1962) 5,104 km. (of which *c.* 4,000 km. all-weather). Motor vehicles in use (1965): passenger 3,200; commercial 5,800. Railways (1966) 566 km. Telephones (Jan. 1967) *c.* 3,900. Radio receivers (Dec. 1966) 40,000. Television receivers (Dec. 1964) 1,200.
Agriculture. Production (in 000; metric tons; 1966; 1965 in parentheses): corn *c.* 2 (*c.* 2); coffee *c.* 2.5 (*c.* 2.5); cocoa (1966–67) 4, (1965–66) 1.7; bananas *c.* 10 (*c.* 10); timber (1965) *c.* 2,600 cu.m., (1964) *c.* 2,400 cu.m. Livestock (in 000; 1965–66): cattle 4; pigs 5; sheep *c.* 50; goats *c.* 57.
Industry. Production (in 000; metric tons): crude oil (1967) 3,415; manganese ore (metal content; 1966) 637.

Furniture:
see Domestic Arts and Sciences

January 1968 to take personal control of foreign affairs, defense, and information. He then relinquished the last two posts in a second governmental reorganization in July.

In February the government announced that it had no intention of joining the Congo (Kinshasa), the Central African Republic, and Chad in the newly formed economic and political Union of Central African States (which broke up in December) and reaffirmed Gabon's loyalty to the Central African Customs and Economic Union (UDEAC) already in existence.

The invitation to the minister of education for the province of Quebec to attend the meeting of ministers of education of French-speaking countries at Libreville in February provoked the federal Canadian government's displeasure. The altercation that ensued from the precedence given to an essentially provincial government resulted February 19 in the breaking off of Ottawa-Libreville relations.

A government communiqué in March announced the creation of a new single Gabonese Democratic Party, the policy of which would be to improve relations with neighbouring states and to encourage a more nationalistic trend, while at the same time maintaining strong ties with France.

On May 8, in a broadcast by Radio Libreville, the government, in advance of support by most other African states, declared its recognition of Biafran sovereignty. As a consequence, in July Gabon was invited by the Consultation Committee on Nigeria, meeting under the aegis of the Organization of African Unity (OAU) at Niamey (Niger), to use its influence to persuade the Biafran delegation to resume negotiations to end the war.   (PH. D.)

COURTESY, JOHN DARBYSHIRE & CO. LTD.

Farmer in The Gambia using a plow manufactured in the U.K. as part of an international program to provide developing countries with inexpensive agricultural implements.

Gambia, The

A small independent parliamentary state and member of the Commonwealth of Nations, The Gambia extends from the Atlantic Ocean along the lower reaches of the Gambia River in West Africa, and is completely surrounded by Senegal. Area: 4,361 sq.mi. (11,295 sq.km.), including 358 sq.mi. of estuarine water. Pop. (1967 est.): 343,000, including (1963) Mandingoes 40.8%; Fulas 13.5%; Woloffs 12.9%; Jolas 6.9%; Sarahulis 6.8%; non-Africans 1.9%. Cap. and largest city: Bathurst (pop., 1967 est., 31,833). Language: English (official). Religion: predominantly Muslim. Queen, Elizabeth II; governor-general in 1968, Alhaji Sir Farimang Singhateh; prime minister, Sir Dawda Jawara.

During 1968 The Gambia showed an increasing interest in external economic relations. In September 1967 it had become a member of the International Monetary Fund (IMF), and in October of the In-

THE GAMBIA
Education. (1965–66) Primary, pupils 14,218, teachers 460; secondary, pupils 3,689, teachers 145; vocational, pupils 184, teachers 29; teacher training, students 129, teachers 10.
  Finance and Trade. Monetary unit: Gambian pound, at par with the pound sterling (Gam£1 = U.S. $2.40). Budget (1967–68 est.): revenue Gam£2.5 million; expenditure Gam£2.3 million. Foreign trade (1966–67): imports Gam£7.125,000; exports Gam£6.313,000. Import sources: U.K. 36%; Japan 19%; China 5%; Burma 5%. Export destinations: U.K. 61%; Portugal 21%; Italy 7%; Switzerland 6%. Main exports: peanut oil, peanuts, and peanut cake.

ternational Bank for Reconstruction and Development and the International Development Association (IDA). Its quota in the IMF was $5 million and its subscription to the capital stock of the World Bank 53 shares, with a par value of $5.3 million. Its subscription to the IDA was $267,000.

The prime minister, Sir Dawda Jawara, reshuffled his Cabinet on Dec. 30, 1967. S. S. Sisay, the finance minister, was appointed foreign minister, and S. M. Dibba became finance minister. Sisay resigned after his appointment, and Andrew Kamara, previously minister of education, was appointed foreign minister.

In February, Dibba addressed the second UN Conference on Trade and Development (UNCTAD) at New Delhi and fully associated his government with the Algiers Charter, although The Gambia had been unable to attend the Algiers meeting of the "Group of 77" less developed countries in October 1967.

The Gambia's closer West African relationships were strengthened by the visit that Pres. Moktar Ould Daddah of Mauritania paid in 1967, in the course of his tour to discuss the proposal for a summit conference on setting up a West African Economic Community. The president and Sir Dawda agreed on strengthening contacts between their two countries. Sir Dawda also paid a visit to Dakar, Senegal, for talks with Pres. L. S. Senghor about establishing closer relations between Senegal and The Gambia. They set up the Inter-Ministerial Committee, which was to have its headquarters at Bathurst. Senegal was to pay three-quarters of the cost of the secretariat.

Among the projects made possible by the loan granted by Britain in 1967 were the surfacing of the two main roads linking The Gambia and Senegal, and the improvement of other roads at a total cost of £930,000. In addition to the loan, Britain was expected to provide technical assistance valued at about £250,000 a year. A similar sum was expected to be provided in 1968–69.   (W. H. Is.)

Gardening

A deep lavender rose named Angel Face, with a spicy, old-fashioned fragrance, and a cucumber named Spartan Valor, which produces almost double the normal amount of cucumbers, were among the 1968 introductions for gardeners and farmers. Scientists were accomplishing, or attempting to accomplish, the seem-

ingly impossible in their research with chemicals to regulate plant behaviour, protect plants from insects and diseases, develop plants with insect and disease resistance, and to develop methods of improving the environment for plant growth.

For more than ten years scientists at the University of Michigan worked on the concept of underground barriers, using clay and plastic to hold moisture in sandy soils. Later they tried using layers of asphalt placed at varying depths below the soil surface to prevent leaching. By 1968 the project showed real promise. Yields from asphalt-paved plots watered only by natural rainfall had been increased 33% over unpaved plots for cucumbers, 43% for cabbage, and 51% for potatoes. In all tests, plant development had been faster above asphalt barriers and vegetative growth more dense, with crops maturing earlier. The cost of asphalting was estimated at $250 to $350 an acre, which compares favourably with the cost of tiling wet soils to bring them into profitable production.

U.S. Department of Agriculture (USDA) researchers produced improved, larger azalea plants and flowers by treating the plants with colchicine, a solution extracted from fall-flowering crocus bulbs that doubles the number of chromosomes within the plant cells. Flowers were not only larger but lasted longer on plants and, since doubling the chromosomes doubled the size of each plant cell, leaves and stems were thicker and tougher. The improved azaleas also showed promise for adding new colour and toughness to the species.

Angel Face was the first lavender rose to win an All-America rose award. A floribunda with four-inch or larger blooms borne in clusters, it has a low and broad growth habit. The flowers last for several days even after fully opened. The other 1969 All-America award winners were: Gene Boerner, a pink floribunda; Comanche, a scarlet floribunda; and Pascali, a white hybrid tea. Gene Boerner was named for the late Eugene S. Boerner, long-time plant research director for Jackson & Perkins of Rochester, N.Y. Pascali, probably the whitest of the existing hybrid tea varieties, has high resistance to the powdery mildew disease of roses.

The trial of new roses carried out in the U.K. by the National Rose Society of Great Britain in 1968 had to assess 200 varieties in one of the worst summers on record. Only 20 varieties received any kind of award. Molly McGredy (S. McGredy) won the President's International Trophy. This is an upright, shapely floribunda producing hybrid tea-shaped blooms. The petals are cherry-red with a silver reverse. The Harry Edland Trophy, awarded to the best new fragrant rose, went to Duke of Windsor, raised in Germany and distributed in Britain by H. Wheatcroft & Sons. It is a hybrid tea with orange-vermillion coloured blooms. Blessings (C. Gregory) and Glengarry (J. Cocker) were the only two varieties to receive a Certificate of Merit. Both are floribundas of the hybrid-tea type; the former is coral-pink and fragrant and the latter carries scarlet blooms, with some fragrance, on compact, bushy plants.

Eight flowers and one vegetable were 1968 All-America selections. The flowers were Carefree Scarlet, an orange-red geranium; Carefree Deep Salmon and Carefree Bright Pink, geraniums; First Lady, a hybrid bright-yellow marigold; Orange Jubilee, a marigold; Wild Cherry, a cherry-rose zinnia; Blaze, a scarlet verbena; and Golden Triumph, a celosia. Spartan

Valor, the winning cucumber, produces fruit eight to nine inches long with a diameter of about two inches. It is highly resistant to mosaic and scab and produces much more fruit in less space than ordinary varieties.

The second Technology in Horticulture Exhibition was held in Karlsruhe, W.Ger., in September and October. Flower novelties presented there included Borntaler, a dwarf, free-flowering, and fragrant cyclamen in shades of pink, cream, and red; fragrant cyclamen to be marketed internationally under the names of Rose-Marie, Kate, and Anali; a pure blue saintpaulia shown under the name of Magdeburg Blue; new strains of Gerbera resistant to *Fusarium* root rot; Enzett Dag, an azalea grown on its own roots for home decoration in October and November; and a new selection of Chabaud carnations from Bulgaria. The British Flower Industry Association decided to begin marketing flowers in spring 1969 in multiples of five and ten as a step toward decimalization.

Water was the latest mulching material being tried to reduce soil temperature fluctuations, conserve soil moisture, and provide frost protection for vegetable crops. At the University of Idaho, large plastic bags with about four inches of water in them were placed between the crop rows. An early, more vigorous growth of heat-sensitive plants was noted; the lead was maintained throughout the season and yields were higher than with regular plastic mulches.

About 400 different kinds of insects were found on apple trees but most were harmless, according to the Canadian Department of Agriculture. It was found, however, that a heavy, uncontrolled outbreak of the European red spider mite, numbering as high as 20 million mites per tree, could cause considerable damage on a tree bearing a heavy apple crop. Even more serious losses could be caused by only 400 codling moths, the cause of wormy apples, on a tree. Codling moths were virtually eliminated from a 93-ac. Yakima, Wash., orchard by releasing 1 million male codling moths that had been sterilized by exposure to radioactive cobalt. The released moths retained their normal mating instincts, but eggs produced from their matings were infertile.

USDA scientists investigating flower colours produced some blue pigments chemically. These might be instrumental in developing unusual flowers, such as the cornflower-blue rose that gardeners had sought for years. Blue colours in flowers derive chiefly from anthocyanin compounds. Stable anthocyanins can be produced only by manipulating the metallic and chemical substances in the plant. A tiny nematode, a small parasitic worm, killed up to 80% of early spring pond mosquitoes in some areas of Michigan. The nematode was being studied at Michigan State University to see if it could provide an effective control method. In the U.K. loamless composts were becoming increasingly accepted. In the Netherlands the Dutch Flower Research Station at Aalsmeer was selling a standard compost under its label subject to chemical and growing tests.

Gardeners might soon tip, prune, or pinch the stem tips of outdoor chrysanthemums, azaleas, rhododendrons, yews, pyracanthas, and cotoneasters with chemical sprays, according to the USDA. The plants would be bushier and, in the case of chrysanthemums, have more flowers. Phosfon, one of the new retardants, was used with spectacular success on chrysanthemums. B-Nine, a formulation of Alar acid, could be applied to foliage of most species without causing injury.

Cycocel was being used successfully on poinsettias and azaleas.

Researchers at the USDA found that antibiotics that cure pneumonia in human beings will suppress aster yellows, a fatal disease of this species. Work done in Japan on a mulberry disease led scientists to suspect that aster yellows was really caused not by a virus, as had been suspected, but by Mycoplasmalike organisms. It could indeed be successfully treated with the same antibiotic drugs used to treat certain diseases of man. In the U.K., the National Vegetable Research Station showed that rhubarb was susceptible to at least five viruses. Propagation by apical tissue resulted in the production of virus-free clones with a potential yield 20–30% greater than those from infected stocks. Growth was quicker and less time was required to obtain crowns of forcing size.

A new breeding technique at the Arizona Agricultural Experiment Station produced the first commercial hybrid of a small grain, hybrid barley. Since many major crops have a genetic makeup similar to barley, the breakthrough might succeed with them also. The technique produces two types of seeds; 70% are male sterile and 30% are fertile and BTT (balanced tertiary trisomic), that is, they contain the extra chromosome. When grown and pollinated by BTT plants, these seeds produce two kinds of plants, 70% of which are male sterile, normal, and white-seeded, and 30% of which are fertile, BTT, and black-seeded. The black seeds can be used to repeat the BTT cycle; the white seeds can be planted between rows of a male parent having good combining qualities to give a vigorous hybrid. (Tm. S.; J. G. S. M.)

See also Agriculture; Biological Sciences; Zoos and Botanical Gardens.

Encyclopædia Britannica Films. *Plant Through the Seasons (Apple Tree)* (1965); *Flowering Plants and Their Parts* (1966); *Green Plants and Sunlight* (1966); *Gardens for Everyone* (1967).

Geography

A special panel on geography, in the National Academy of Sciences' Behavioral Sciences Survey, selected in 1968 a group of studies to illustrate contemporary geographical research. The selected themes were: "Spatial Distributions and Interrelationships," "Network Analysis," "Regionalization," "Central Place Systems," "Diffusion Models," and "Environmental Perception." To carry out research in such fields, contemporary geographers had to use new tools and techniques. Among them were a variety of remote sensors, including multilens cameras and infrared, radar, and other imaging and detecting devices, to gather data from aircraft and satellite overflights. Many geographers utilized electronic scanning devices for pattern recognition and enhancement in photographs, and they programmed computers for an automated print-out of graphics. They found that such techniques greatly accelerated production and improved the validity of maps, graphs, charts, and tables for synthesizing and displaying research results.

Geographers began to participate more effectively in government programs for land evaluation, for multiple use of floodplains and coastal zones, and for the long-distance transfer of water in the western United States. They also studied the environmental stress areas that resulted from the tremendous growth of urban agglomerations. The U.S. Geological Survey established a position for a chief geographer in the

Director's Office to manage production of a *National Atlas of the United States,* to coordinate a Geographic Applications Program for research on the use of remote sensor data from aircraft and spacecraft, and to maintain close liaison with national and international developments in the profession.

Meanwhile, the Office of Education sponsored institutes in geography to update geographic instruction at all levels and to help meet the demand for competent geography teachers. The National Science Foundation renewed grants to the Association of American Geographers to prepare new textbooks, packaged lesson plans, and mechanical aids for high school geography courses, and to redirect the trend of geographic instruction in colleges toward a better understanding of man-environment interactions. The National Council for Geographic Education met in Kansas City, Mo., November 1–3, and focused on the theme of "Media Development and Curriculum Change"; special sessions were concerned with the classroom use of satellite photography and with restructuring the council's educational periodical, *The Journal of Geography,* to make more effective use of new techniques and concepts.

The Association of American Geographers, whose membership had increased from 1,800 in 1963 to 5,600, concerned itself during the year with the role of professional geographers in business, industry, planning, and government. The fully matured research of the association's members was reported in its *Annals,* whereas progress reports and short articles on topics of broad interest appeared in its *Professional Geographer.*

The American Geographical Society of New York continued to publish the *Geographical Review* as well as area studies in a small monthly journal, *Focus,* and a monthly bibliographical list of *Current Geographical Publications.* The National Geographic Society, with more than six million members, remained an effective channel between professional geographers and the general public through its maps and *National Geographic* magazine.

The International Geographical Union and its affiliate, the International Cartographic Association, held a joint congress at New Delhi, India, December 1–8, with sectional meetings on specialized aspects of physical, economic, historical, and demographic geography plus thematic mapping. Commissions of the union reported on research and planned new programs to deal with land-use analysis, medical geography, eco-

Children at the Middlestown Primary School in Yorkshire, Eng., study geography by placing dolls dressed in national costumes on a world map painted on their playground.

"LONDON DAILY EXPRESS" FROM PICTORIAL PARADE

nomic regionalization, quantitative methods, agricultural typology, interpretation of aerial and space photography, automation in cartography, and national and regional atlas production.

The other international organization in the field of geography, the Pan American Institute of Geography and History, planned during the year for its ninth General Assembly, May 30–June 18, 1969. The agenda stressed multinational cooperation on projects for economic development, the restructuring of educational programs, and on plans for an Inter-American Data Bank.

By means of such a data bank, imagery and other forms of remote sensing data from earth-orbiting satellites could be applied throughout the Americas to studies of land use; changes in the area and functional structure of cities; transportation networks and traffic flows; inventory and management of resources; monitoring of disasters such as floods, fires, earthquakes, and landslides; and the production of maps and other graphics to display effectively the results of such studies.

Through international meetings and national programs, such as those described above, the change of geography from its traditional role of exploring and describing the earth to one of interpreting man-environment interactions was becoming increasingly apparent. The use of masses of data from remote sensors in satellites yielded large-scale coverage of broad areas, repetitive coverage of time-lapse phenomena, and an almost infinite expansion of potential research studies for better understanding the earth as the home of man. (A. C. Ge.)

See also Antarctica; Arctic Regions.

ENCYCLOPÆDIA BRITANNICA FILMS. *Maps for a Changing World* (1960); *The Earth in Change: The Earth's Crust* (1961); *The Language of Maps* (1964); *If You Could See the Earth* (1967).

Geology

Recent criticisms of the validity of the principle of uniformitarianism (the principle that processes now acting on the earth have operated continuously and rather uniformly through long ages) received statistical support by P. E. Gretener (*Bull. Am. Ass. Petrol. Geol.*, 1967). He pointed out that an event of low probability has an ever increasing probability of occurrence if the number of trials increases to the number possible within geologic time, and may, indeed, even become a certainty. Several types of geologic events are applicable, including dispersal of floras and faunas; the origin(s) of life; spacing of planets of a star; meteor impacts; major faunal breaks in earth history (there are fewer than ten in 6×10^8 years, they recur at irregular intervals, and are probably random); the frozen mammoths (their extreme rarity indicates that they are freaks and do not deserve attention from the statistical point of view); and the roles of major storms, earthquakes, landslides, and flash floods in erosion and sedimentation.

In addition to supporting the retirement of the principle of uniformitarianism, the significance of the rare event introduces an element of uncertainty in geologic interpretation. What may be an example of a rare event was postulated by D. L. Lamar and P. M. Merifield (*Bull. Geol. Soc. Am.*, 1967), who based the appearance of many fossils in Lower Cambrian strata on the origin of the earth-moon system in late Precambrian time. They linked the gradually de-

Above, helicopter lifting a projectile for a terradynamics test; below, a projectile partially buried after a low-velocity drop from 2,000 ft. Engineers can determine subsurface structure by measuring the deceleration of the projectile as it penetrates the earth.

creasing number of days in the year (shown by daily coral growth lines) to the origin of lunar tides, which caused rapid evolution of hard-shelled organisms in the variable and more severe environment of tides.

Information from more than 3,000 wells and outcrops, plus geophysical data and isotopic ages, provided evidence for an interpretation of basement rocks (firm, underlying rocks) of North America by W. R. Muehlberger, R. E. Denison, and E. G. Lidiak (*Bull. Am. Ass. Petrol. Geol.*, 1967). It appeared that continental accretion is less important than was once thought, as at least half of the continent existed 2.5 billion years ago. Crustal stabilization occurred 2.5, 1.7, 1.35, and 1 billion years ago.

Fifty-four concordant intrusions, most in the western U.S., were analyzed by M. R. Mudge (*Bull. Geol. Soc. Am.*, 1968). He found that they intruded nearly flat-lying sediments along well-defined parting surfaces (unconformities or bedding planes) in a depth range of 3,000 to 7,500 ft. The lower limit was proposed because it is the greatest depth at which overburden pressures are less than pressures from magma (molten matter in the earth's interior); the shallower limit exists because at depths less than 3,000 ft. the overlying rock is brittle, allowing steam and magma to escape. A capping fluid barrier, usually mudstone, was always present.

Conventional geosynclinal sequence was not followed in the structural development of the Iranian mountain ranges. Jovan Stöcklin (*Bull. Am. Ass. Petrol. Geol.*, 1968) stated that a complete Alpine orogeny occurred in areas of thin platform sediments there. More typical geosynclinal events occurred in peripheral ranges.

SANDIA CORP.

Magnetic, seismic subbottom, and gravity (from an ice island) profiles were made in the Greenland Sea by N. A. Ostenso (*Bull. Geol. Soc. Am.*, 1968). This study determined that the Mid-Atlantic Ridge extends northward in subdued form from the Jan Mayen fracture zone, with a lessened rift valley anomaly. Crustal thickness under the Greenland continental shelf was found to be 22 mi., apparently an abrupt increase from the 11-mi. thickness under the Greenland Sea.

Marginal basin faulting was studied in widely separated areas. Peter G. Temple (*Bull. Geol. Soc. Am.*, 1968) reported large-scale gravity faulting in the

Greek Peloponnese. The deep basin was first uplifted at the east, propelling pelagic sediments westward and on neritic sediments. The complex-to-chaotic overlapping thrust sheets of the central Greece allochthonous spine were presumed to have moved by gravity. J. W. Shelton also reported on faulting during basin subsidence in the Los Angeles, Hanna, Ardmore, and Gulf of Mexico basins (*Bull. Am. Ass. Petrol. Geol.*, 1968). Faulting was independent of the depositional framework (turbidites in Los Angeles, alluvial in Hanna, shallow marine in Ardmore, and in brittle sediments overlying ductile sediments in the Gulf Coast geosyncline) and thus was presumed to have originated in the basement layer. Robert E. Carver (*Bull. Am. Ass. Petrol. Geol.*, 1968) concluded that the faults of the Gulf Coast resulted from differential compaction, the maximum settlement occurring some distance seaward of the faults.

The first of a series of reports on the geochemistry of the Amazon River was issued by R. J. Gibbs (*Bull. Geol. Soc. Am.*, 1967). Using water samples, measurements at the site, and regression analysis, he concluded: (1) 86% of dissolved salts and 82% of the suspended solids came from the mountainous 12% of the basin; (2) physical weathering in the mountainous area, chemical weathering in the plains, and the amount of calcic rocks in the upper parts of the tributary basins control various of the mineral species in the clastic (made up of preexisting rock) sediments.

Origins of sedimentary iron minerals continued to be the subject of investigations. Theoretical and field relationships were explored by C. D. Curtis and D. A. Spears (*Econ. Geol.*, 1968). Their theoretical calculations indicated that ferric compounds are the only stable ones in normal marine waters; ferrous minerals can be stable only in interstitial waters; and that siderite, magnetite, and silicates will be relatively mobile. Field observations in the Coal Measures of Yorkshire, Eng., showed that pyrite and siderite grains are diagenetic; that is, they were altered immediately after their disposition by such forces as the weight of overlying strata or hot waters. Jurassic iron deposits of England confirmed this finding.

Reef morphology on sheltered coasts was described by M. S. Lewis (*J. Geol.*, 1968) as being substantially different from conventional reefs on windward coasts. Sheltered reefs were broken into segments by low-salinity exits and were paralleled by numerous steep-sloped subsea ridges, most two to ten metres high. The ridges were asymmetrical, with the steeper side landward.

J. N. Jennings and J. A. Mabbutt (*Landform Studies from Australia and New Guinea*) collected 17 essays by as many authors on various aspects of landforms in the areas titled. Of the papers, seven were descriptive and four were concerned with local physiography; other subjects included denudation chronology, evolution of the Western Australia coastline, coastal lagoons and coral reefs, slopewash, and the relation of soil to landform development.   (L. ON.) .

See also Antarctica; Mining; Oceanography; Seismology; Speleology.

ENCYCLOPÆDIA BRITANNICA FILMS. *Geological Work of Ice* (1960); *The Earth in Change: The Earth's Crust* (1961); *Erosion—Leveling the Land* (1964); *Evidence for the Ice Age* (1964); *Rocks that Form on the Earth's Surface* (1964); *Waves on Water* (1964); *What Makes Clouds?* (1964); *What Makes the Wind Blow?* (1964); *Why Do We Still Have Mountains?* (1964); *The Beach—A River of Sand* (1965); *Rocks that Originate Underground* (1966); *How Solid Is Rock?* (1968).

German Literature:
see Literature

Germany

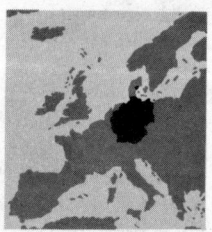

A country of central Europe, Germany was partitioned after World War II into the Federal Republic of Germany (Bundesrepublik Deutschland; West Germany) and the German Democratic Republic (Deutsche Demokratische Republik; East Germany), with a special provisional regime for Berlin. Germany is bordered by Denmark, the Netherlands, Belgium, Luxembourg, France, Switzerland, Austria, Czechoslovakia, and Poland and the North and Baltic seas.

Federal Republic of Germany. Area: 95,964 sq.mi. (248,548 sq.km.). Pop. (1968 est.): 60,165,100. Provisional cap.: Bonn (pop., 1968 est., 138,090). Largest city: Hamburg (pop., 1968 est., 1,826,411). (West Berlin, which is an enclave within East Germany, had a population of 2,149,678 in 1968.) Language: German. Religion: Protestant 50.6%; Roman Catholic 46.3%; Jewish 0.04%. President in 1968, Heinrich Lübke; chancellor, Kurt Georg Kiesinger.

Apart from relatively minor squabbles, the "grand coalition" government of the Christian Democratic Union (Christlich-Demokratische Union, or CDU) and the Social Democratic Party (Sozialdemokratische Partei Deutschlands, or SPD) worked successfully. Measures taken to stabilize the economy were effective. The recession was overcome, and unemployment fell to a point of insignificance. In November West Germany's position of economic strength was demonstrated when the "Group of Ten" central bankers met in Bonn to discuss means of supporting the French franc. (*See* MONEY AND BANKING.) But in foreign affairs there was a rapid deterioration in the relations between Bonn and Moscow, especially since the U.S.S.R. claimed it had a right of military intervention in West Germany under the enemy states clauses of the United Nations Charter.

Domestic Affairs. The attempted assassination of the left-wing student leader Rudi Dutschke (*see* BIOGRAPHY) in West Berlin on April 11 caused a violent wave of student demonstrations throughout the country. The brunt of the students' wrath was borne by the offices of the Axel Springer (*see* BIOGRAPHY) newspaper concern, which had been extremely hostile to the students. Student unrest had grown from a campaign for university reform into a demand for a reform of society generally.

In many cases the demonstrations were brutally suppressed by the police, and there was a clamour in Bonn for much sterner measures against the students. The progress made by the extreme right-wing National Democratic Party of Germany (Nationaldemokratische Partei Deutschlands, or NPD) in the state elections in Baden-Württemberg on April 28 was thought to be partly a reaction to the student unrest. The NPD, contesting a state election there for the first time, polled 9.8% and was allocated 12 seats in the Landtag in Stuttgart. In less than four years the party had won 60 seats in seven state parliaments. However, in the municipal elections in the Saarland, Hesse, and Baden-Württemberg on October 20, support for the NPD dropped substantially to about 5%. (*See* BIOGRAPHY: *Thadden, Alfred von.*)

A new Communist Party was formed in West Germany in September. For some years the Communists

Student leader "Red" Rudi Dutschke of the left-wing Socialist Students' League. The attempted assassination of Dutschke set off demonstrations in April 1968.

Speaker at a mass rally in Munich wearing a placard of a saluting skeleton to express his opposition to the proposed Emergency Powers Bill.

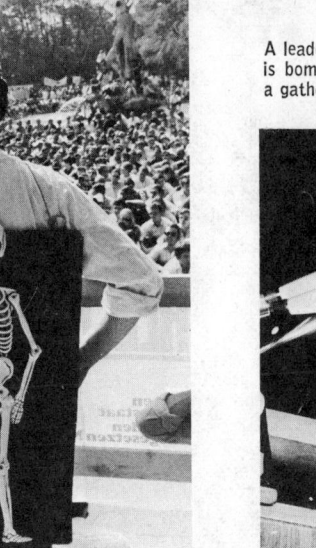

A leader of the National Democratic Party is bombarded with confetti during a gathering of the party at Essen in May.

Foreign Minister Willy Brandt among protesters at the Nürnberg convention of the (West) German Socialist Party in March.

West Berlin students are hosed by police while demonstrating in April against the shooting of student leader Rudi Dutschke.

had been demanding that the ban on their party, imposed by the Federal Constitutional Court in 1956, should be lifted. As there was no appeal against a decision of the Constitutional Court, the federal government said the only remedy was for the Communists to form a new party that would undertake to abide by the constitution. The founding members of the new party agreed to this, but like the NPD they were under the constant scrutiny of the Office for the Protection of the Constitution.

The first policy statement of the grand coalition government had contained a proposal to amend the electoral law to introduce majority voting on the British pattern. The principle aim was to secure the return of comfortable majorities, thus avoiding the need to form coalitions, but another motive was to keep extremist parties out of the Bundestag. The SPD, which had more to fear from the change, postponed its decision on whether to support the amendment, and therefore the legislation could not be passed in the life of the current Parliament. The way was open for the NPD to enter the Bundestag.

The controversial Emergency Powers Bill was approved by the Bundestag on May 29; 384 members voted for it and 100 against. In the fourth attempt in ten years, Parliament believed it had hammered out a compromise which, while safeguarding the state in

time of emergency, did not invest the executive with uncontrolled authority. An emergency Parliament consisting of 33 members, 22 from the Bundestag and 11 from the second chamber, the Bundesrat, which represents the Länder, would take over the country's affairs if the Bundestag was not able to meet when the country was under attack or when an attack was thought to be imminent. There was also a provision for the use of the armed forces to assist the police when it was thought that the "free democratic order of the Federation or of a state is threatened." The legislation canceled out the Allies' reserve rights in West Germany, removing the last obstacle to complete sovereignty.

The federal president, Heinrich Lübke, announced on October 14 that he would retire from office at the end of June 1969, ten weeks before his second five-year term would expire. He said he had decided to step down to make it possible for the Federal Assembly to elect his successor well ahead of the federal elections in September.

The East German government imposed a number of regulations restricting the rights of West Germans and West Berliners to use the overland routes to and from West Berlin. Members of the NPD were banned altogether from using the surface routes across East Germany from March 10, and so were West German ministers and senior officials from April 13. Finally, on

GERMANY: Federal Republic

June 11, the East German government ordered that West Germans and West Berliners crossing East Germany must obtain transit visas, for which a fee was charged at the border.

Foreign Affairs. West Germany and Yugoslavia resumed diplomatic relations on January 31 after a break of more than ten years. Diplomatic relations had already been taken up with Romania. Elsewhere in Eastern Europe, Bonn's attitude continued to get a hostile reception and the invasion of Czechoslovakia by the Soviet Union and its allies in August made further progress impossible. Nonetheless, the federal government said that its policy of détente would be maintained. The presence of Soviet troops on the Czechoslovak border with Bavaria resulted in demands in Bonn for a strengthening of NATO, and the government increased its defense budget.

Allegations by the Soviet government that Bonn had been meddling in Czechoslovak affairs and supporting a counterrevolution took on an increasingly menacing tone. The U.S.S.R. claimed that it retained the right under the enemy states clauses of the UN Charter to intervene in the Federal Republic under certain circumstances. Moscow indicated that a resurgence of Nazism would be an adequate reason for intervention. The Western allies denied that the Soviets had a unilateral right of intervention and the governments of the U.S., U.K., and France reiterated their guarantees of the security of West Berlin and the Federal Republic.

Bonn had initiated a correspondence with Moscow at the end of 1967 with a view to opening discussions on an exchange of nonaggression declarations. The correspondence was broken off halfway through 1968 after the U.S.S.R. had said that such declarations would have to be accompanied by Bonn's acceptance of the existence of two German states. After the invasion of Czechoslovakia the federal government announced that it would defer its decision whether to sign the nuclear nonproliferation treaty.

In West European affairs, the federal chancellor continued to give priority to fostering the special relationship between West Germany and France. He refused to apply pressure on Pres. Charles de Gaulle to drop his veto on U.K. membership in the EEC. Instead, the West German government submitted proposals for an economic arrangement between Britain and the Six. This was acceptable to France as long as the undertaking was not regarded as a step on the road

to full membership. The other Community members would have preferred to have gone much further than the German proposals.

Talks between the chancellor and President de Gaulle in Bonn in September under the Franco-German treaty of friendship revealed wide differences of opinion on defense matters as well as on the problems of enlarging the EEC. But Kiesinger rejected the advice of some German politicians to seek ways of extending European cooperation without French participation. (N. Cr.)

West Berlin. The view of *The Times* (London) on Jan. 20, 1968, that Berlin was "still an exposed nerve in the middle of Europe" found ample confirmation throughout 1968. The Soviet-East German combined operation of warnings, threats, and pinpricks of varying intensity was an attempt to bolster up the Ulbricht regime in the German Democratic Republic and gradually to isolate West Berlin from the Federal Republic. On January 6 Semyon Tsarapkin, Soviet ambassador to West Germany, warned Willy Brandt, West German foreign minister, not to pursue activities in West Berlin. On January 18 Klaus Schütz, governing mayor of West Berlin, met P. A. Abrassimov, Soviet ambassador to East Germany, at the latter's residence in East Berlin for a three-hour talk about the Soviet view on the status of West Berlin.

In March the East German authorities began their series of travel restrictions on West Germans, but things began to take a far more serious turn on June 11 with the announcement of comprehensive new restrictions which the East Germans began to implement two days later. Basically, the restrictions fell into two groups: those that introduced as of July 15 passport and/or visa requirements for West Germans and West Berliners desirous of traveling through East Germany; and those levying transit taxes on goods transported through East Germany by West German and West Berlin carriers.

The government of the Federal Republic at once announced its willingness to assume the financial burden, estimated at DM. 80 million, which the new visa fees and transit taxes were expected to impose on the West Berlin economy. The Bundestag also passed a new Berlin Aid Law which provided for tax concessions. It was expected to stimulate further investment in industry, research and development, and housing. Subsidies for air travel were also increased.

On October 28 several West German parliamentary

committees opened the customary working week of the Bundestag in West Berlin, ignoring Communist warnings that they were meeting there illegally. The Christian Democratic Party, similarly warned, held its first full congress in West Berlin since 1953 at the beginning of November. Concurrent with these events the three Western allies were holding air exercises over Berlin and, for the first time, also over the three air corridors linking West Berlin with the Federal Republic.

German Democratic Republic. Area: 41,766 sq.mi. (108,174 sq.km.). Pop. (1968 est.): 17,089,884. Cap. and largest city: East Berlin (pop., 1968 est., 1,082,019). Language: German. Religion (1950): Protestant 81.3%; Roman Catholic 11%. First secretary of the Socialist Unity (Communist) Party (SED) and president in 1968, Walter Ulbricht; minister president (premier), Willi Stoph.

The people of Czechoslovakia had good reason to regard Walter Ulbricht as the principal instigator of the Soviet-led invasion of their country. He was the first to call for concerted action to check the course of events in Czechoslovakia. In addition, the first hastily summoned meeting of the Soviet, Bulgarian, Hungarian, Polish, and East German Communist Party leaders with the new Czechoslovak leadership on March 23 was held in East Germany at Dresden. Although Alexander Dubcek appeared to have won a vote of confidence at this meeting, only three days later Kurt Hager, head of the SED's Ideological Commission, complained in East Berlin that "West German propaganda centres" were using the situation in Czechoslovakia in their campaign against East Germany.

Ulbricht's hand was again evident in the communiqué and the joint letter to the Czechoslovak Party Central Committee issued after the Warsaw meeting on July 14. Once again there were references to the threat to European security from what was alleged to be "increasing militarist and neo-Nazi activity in the Federal Republic." After the issuance of the joint letter, the East German propaganda campaign against Czechoslovakia was stepped up. The most sinister threat—in the light of subsequent events—appeared in a commentary in *Neues Deutschland* on July 23: "If the imperialists are hoping to make a breach in the status quo in their favour and gain an important position in Central Europe, then it is no longer an internal affair of Czechoslovakia." Of the five party leaders who signed the joint letter only Ulbricht visited Czechoslovakia after the meetings at Cierna and Bratislava. After meeting Dubcek in Karlovy Vary on August 12 he remained behind "for a cure."

Members of the East German National People's Army patrolling the border between the two Germanys.

On August 20 (the day of the invasion) *Neues Deutschland* carried an article that said, "Socialist internationalism also means readiness of the Marxist-Leninist Party in a Socialist state to call upon the help and support of the fraternal Socialist states." The SED Central Committee statement published in *Neues Deutschland* on August 21 was the first statement from the parties after the invasion to attack Dubcek by name. On August 25 the paper carried a lengthy article that tried to justify the invasion by alleging that the Czechoslovak Party's Action Program was "riddled with revisionist concepts." This, however, even contradicted the anonymous letter from the group in the Czechoslovak Central Committee inviting the five Warsaw Pact members to intervene, which explicitly supported the Action Program.

On April 22 the State Council approved new directives for economic planning the main emphasis of which was on "perspective" (longer term) as against annual plans. In its report to the sixth plenary session of the SED Central Committee (June 6–8), the Politburo spoke of agreements reached by a party and government delegation in Moscow (May 29–31) that were of "fundamental importance for the economic and social perspectives" of East Germany. The negotiations had led to the "most far-reaching results so far" in the course of relations between East Germany and the U.S.S.R. After the invasion of Czechoslovakia, East Germany's interest in the closest possible economic relations with the U.S.S.R. and the intensified economic integration of the entire Soviet bloc was expressed with mounting fervour. When he addressed the ninth plenary session of the Central Committee on October 24, Ulbricht insisted that the existing economic links were not enough; more economic integra-

---

GERMANY: Democratic Republic

Education. (1965–66) Primary, pupils 2,273,-597, teachers (1963–64) 102,017; secondary, pupils 85,279, teachers (1963–64) 5,441; vocational (including teacher training), pupils 530,-700, teachers (1962–63) 20,095; higher (including 7 universities), students 74,418.

Finance. Monetary unit: "Mark of the German Bank of Issue" (Ostmark), with an official exchange rate of MDN. 2.22 to U.S. $1 (MDN. 5.33 = £1 sterling) and a general rate (Oct. 1968) of MDN. 4.20 to U.S. $1 (MDN. 10.01 = £1). Budget (1966): revenue MDN. 66,473,000,-000; expenditure MDN. 66,387,000,000. National income (net material product): (1966) MDN. 87.2 billion; (1965) MDN. 82.8 billion.

Foreign Trade. (1966) Imports MDN. 13,-503,000,000; exports MDN. 13,460,800,000. Import sources: U.S.S.R. 43%; Czechoslovakia 9%; West Germany 9%; Poland 5%; Hungary 5%. Export destinations: U.S.S.R. 39%; Czecho-slovakia 10%; Poland 9%; West Germany 7%. Main exports: lignite; chemicals; machinery; motor vehicles.

Transport and Communications. Roads (1966) *c.* 160,000 km. (of which 47,276 km. main roads, 1,390 km. autobahns). Motor vehicles (1966): passenger 721,031; commercial 172,564. Railways: (1966) 15,730 km. (of which 1,095 km. electrified); traffic (1967) 17,462,000,000 passenger-km., freight 38,473,000,000 net ton-km. Navigable inland waterways in regular use (1965) 2,519 km.; freight traffic 2,556,000,000 ton-km. Shipping (1967): merchant vessels 100 gross tons and over 347; gross tonnage 755,960. Telephones (Dec. 1966) 1,723,814. Radio receivers (Dec. 1966) 5,812,000. Television receivers (Dec. 1966) 3,559,000.

Agriculture. Production (in 000; metric tons; 1967; 1966 in parentheses): rye *c.* 1,700 (1,642); wheat (1966) 1,521, (1965) 1,802; barley *c.* 1,440 (1,525); oats *c.* 760 (703); potatoes (1966) 12,823, (1965) 12,857; sugar, raw value (1967–68) *c.* 734, (1966–67) *c.* 672. Livestock (in 000; Dec. 1966): sheep 1,928; cattle 4,918; pigs 9,312; goats 279; horses used in agriculture 250; poultry (Dec. 1965) 37,988.

Industry. Production (in 000; metric tons; 1967): lignite 242,400; coal (1966) 1,987; petroleum products (1966) 4,332; manufactured gas 3,816,000 cu.m.; electricity 59,693,000 kw-hr.; iron ore (metal content; 1966) 430; pig iron 2,523; steel (ingots only) 4,243; copper ore (metal content; 1966) 19; potash (oxide content; 1966) 2,006; cement 7,182; sulfuric acid 990; nitrogenous fertilizers (1966) 344; superphosphates (1966) 157; synthetic rubber (1966) 101; passenger cars (1966) 107 units; commercial vehicles (1966) 20 units; cotton fabrics 245,-000 sq.m. Index of production (1963 = 100): (1967) 127; (1966) 119.

tion should lead to some kind of Communist Common Market.

Of the 12,202,130 people entitled to vote on April 6, 11,536,265 (94.54%) signified their assent to the new constitution, but 409,329 (5.46%) voted against, while another 28,843 votes were said to be spoiled. The constitution, which came into force at midnight on April 8, proclaimed East Germany a "Socialist State of German nationality" and abandoned the first principle of the 1949 constitution that "Germany is an indivisible democratic republic." The right to strike and to emigrate were omitted. Although it emphasized the separate statehood of East Germany, even to the extent of asserting responsibility for its airspace—which might foreshadow a claim to control traffic in the air corridors between the Federal Republic and West Berlin—the constitution was clearly intended to apply eventually to the whole of Germany. Article eight envisaged the "step-by-step rapprochement of the two German states up to the time of their unification on the basis of democracy and Socialism."

At the same time as the Soviet government restated its views on the existence of "two independent German states with equal rights," the East German government intensified its efforts to achieve recognition. At the 11th annual Baltic Week in Rostock in July, Ulbricht again appealed to non-Communist countries to recognize the sovereignty of East Germany.

In its session on June 26 the Council of Ministers decided to appoint Alfred Neumann, hitherto one of the 11 deputy chairmen, first deputy chairman and to relieve him of his duties as minister for materials supply. On August 9 Erich Haase was appointed in Neumann's place. The post of first deputy chairman had remained unfilled since the death of Otto Grotewohl in September 1964. Gerhart Eisler, chairman of the State Broadcasting Committee and member of the SED Central Committee, died on March 21 (*see* OBITUARIES).

According to Western sources special prayers for the Czechoslovak people were said in churches on August 25. Meetings of the East German section of the all-German Evangelical Church Council, which were to have been held in East Berlin September 27–29, were canceled by the East German authorities because of the "very strained political situation in Berlin." (The churches in East and West Germany had been unable to meet jointly since the Berlin Wall was built by the Communists in 1961.)   (S. E. S.)

ENCYCLOPÆDIA BRITANNICA FILMS. *Germany—People of the Industrial West* (1957); *Berlin: Test for the West* (1962).

Ghana

A republic of West Africa, Ghana is on the Gulf of Guinea and is bordered by Ivory Coast, Upper Volta, and Togo. Area: 92,100 sq.mi. (238,539 sq.km.). Pop. (1968 est.): 8,376,000. Cap. and largest city: Accra (pop., 1968 est., 615,800). Language: English (official); local Sudanic dialects. Religion: traditional tribal beliefs; Christian and Muslim minorities. Chairman of the National Liberation Council and of the Executive Council in 1968, Lieut. Gen. Joseph A. Ankrah.

During 1968 Ghana continued its progress toward a resumption of civilian government and a balanced economy. On May 22 General Ankrah fixed Sept. 30, 1969, as the latest date for return to civilian rule. Draft proposals of a constitutional commission, pub-

lished in January, provided for a nonexecutive president, a National Assembly of 140 chosen by universal adult suffrage, and an independent judiciary. Certain departments and organs of government would come under presidential control together with the Council of State. The possibility of appointing Cabinet ministers from outside the Assembly was also provided for. Following these proposals Ankrah announced the formation of a nonparty political Constituent Assembly of 140 to discuss and establish the final form of the new constitution. The government decided that the Assembly should be partially elected from administrative districts and partially selected by various organizations and by the government. Also established exemptions commission, to which officials of the former Convention People's Party (the party of deposed Pres. Kwame Nkrumah) could appeal against disenfranchisement. An electoral commissioner was appointed to deal with constituency demarcation and other preparations for the 1969 elections.

The Mills Odoi commission on the structure and remuneration of public services reported its findings in May, and provided both for a salary increase over a two-year period and for the establishment of regional authorities by July to decentralize the power of such departments as health, education, and agriculture. Also in May General Ankrah announced that following the selection of the Constituent Assembly the ban on political parties would be lifted for elections to the National Assembly. Meetings of a political nature already were taking place in 1968, and in August Ankrah denied rumours that a party was being formed on his behalf.

In March a defense council was established under Ankrah's chairmanship, to be responsible for the defense and security of the country and for the preserva-

GHANA
Education. (1965–66) Primary, pupils 1,145,488, teachers 35,998; secondary, pupils 316,197, teachers 10,539; vocational, pupils 14,950, teachers 670; teacher training, students 15,144, teachers 955; higher (at 3 universities), students 4,267, teaching staff 600.
 Finance. Monetary unit: new cedi, with a par value of 1.02 cedis to U.S. $1 (2.45 cedis = £1 sterling). Gold and foreign exchange: (June 1968) U.S. $111 million; (June 1967) U.S. $109.5 million. Budget (1967–68 est.): revenue 288,718,000 cedis; expenditure 303,824,000 cedis. Gross national product: (1966) 779 million cedis; (1965) 1,571,000,000 cedis. Money supply: (May 1968) 226.3 million cedis; (May 1967) 226.5 million cedis. Cost of living (Accra; 1963 = 100): (March 1968) 144; (March 1967) 131.
 Foreign Trade. (1967) Imports 261,520,000 cedis; exports 224,160,000 cedis. Import sources: U.K. 31%; U.S. 17%; West Germany 10%; Japan 6%; Netherlands 5%. Export destinations: U.K. 28%; U.S. 17%; U.S.S.R. 9%; Netherlands 7%; West Germany 7%; Japan 7%. Main exports: cocoa 58%; timber 10%; diamonds 6%.
 Transport and Communications. Roads (1967) c. 33,000 km. (including 8,970 km. government maintained). Motor vehicles in use (1966): passenger 30,300; commercial (including buses) 18,600. Railways: (1967) 953 km.; traffic (1966) 417 million passenger-km., freight 310 million net ton-km. Shipping (1967): merchant vessels 100 gross tons and over 58; gross tonnage 131,571. Telephones (Dec. 1966) 35,930. Radio receivers (Dec. 1964) 555,000. Television receivers (Dec. 1966) 4,000.
 Agriculture. Production (in 000; metric tons; 1966; 1965 in parentheses): cassava c. 1,250 (c. 1,250); sweet potatoes c. 1,200 (c. 1,200); corn c. 180 (c. 180); rice c. 42 (43); peanuts c. 50 (c. 50); cocoa, exports (1966–67) 381, (1965–66) 416; timber 7,200 cu.m. (9,800 cu.m.). Livestock (in 000; 1965–66): cattle c. 510; sheep c. 660; pigs c. 255.
 Industry. Production (in 000; 1966): gold 684 troy oz.; diamonds 2,819 metric carats; manganese ore (metal content) 277 metric tons; bauxite 352 metric tons; electricity 807,000 kw-hr.

tion of public order. An agreement with Britain provided for an exchange of army training units.

Although Ghana's external debts still rose (by April the total was $651.9 million against $520.3 million in 1966), longer-term repayments lessened the annual burden. Two new types of loan from the International Monetary Fund (IMF), of $73.7 million and $58.9 million, were undertaken at a very low repayment rate, as well as a standby credit loan in May of $12 million. Additional loans were also made by the U.K. (£2,860,000) and by West Germany, whose total loan now equaled 23 million new cedis. In September a $15 million loan was negotiated with the U.S., bringing total U.S. aid since 1966 to $66 million. A trade protocol for the exchange of goods was signed with the U.S.S.R. in June; it followed the lines of previous agreements. In 1968 Ghana's debt to the U.S.S.R. was more than $48 million, mainly for projects begun under the Nkrumah regime.

Economic progress was reflected in trade and budget figures. A combination of higher cocoa earnings and strict import controls reduced the adverse trade balance from 59.8 million new cedis in 1966 to 16.4 million in 1967, and a small surplus was seen for the first six months of 1968. Total exports for 1967 were 245.1 million new cedis, an increase of 53.7 million, largely due to cocoa, though timber and gold also rose. Chemical imports rose steeply, but manufactured goods declined. The U.K. provided nearly 30% of Ghana's trade in 1967, and following devaluation the proportion increased. Imports from the countries of the European Economic Community and the U.S.S.R. declined.

Brig. A. A. Afrifa, commissioner for finance, introduced a hopeful note in his 1968 budget by announcing that a small surplus had been earned in the financial year 1967–68, and that the estimates for a balanced 1968–69 budget allowed for an expansion of recurrent and development expenditure. The gross national product rose by 3% in 1967–68 as against 1% in the two preceding years. Manufacturing jumped 15%, and despite devaluation, price increases were kept to a minimum. Afrifa, however, warned of the need to reduce recurrent expenditure and dependence on foreign aid. Education and defense continued to be major budget burdens, though the University of Ghana received much foreign aid.

The 221.6 million new cedis development plan of 1968–70, details of which were published early in 1968 and which was designed to take the country from "stabilization" to "development," was confronted by a current situation of acute shortage in foreign exchange, heavy debt, a downward trend in domestic savings, stagnant agriculture, unused productive capacity, and high unemployment. An additional problem was the difficulty in estimating future income because of uncertainty in cocoa earnings and foreign aid.

Following a September 1967 decree dissolving Ghana State Enterprises, the new Ghana Industrial Holding Corporation came into being in July. This would control the 19 state corporations, and although none was immediately sold to the private sector, provision was made for outright sale or for joint public-private operation. The Volta Aluminum Company reached full production in November 1967, a year ahead of schedule. Agriculture, employing more than 60% of the labour force, remained the most important item in the development plan. Food marketing corporations to aid in price stabilization were established during the year.   (M. MR.)

Golf

The golfing year of 1968 was highlighted by many unusual incidents. In the Masters Tournament at Augusta, Ga., Roberto de Vicenzo of Argentina signed an incorrect scorecard for the last round, which barred him from a play-off for the title with Bob Goalby. Lee Trevino, a comparative newcomer to first-class golf, won the U.S. Open and became the first man to break 70 in all four rounds. His total of 275 tied the record set the previous year by Jack Nicklaus, who placed second. Julius Boros, winner of the Professional Golfers' Association (PGA) championship, was at 48 the oldest major tournament champion of modern times. In the fall of the year, after months of argument and discussion had culminated in a court case, the leading U.S. tournament professionals broke away from the control of the PGA. In December, however, the tournament professionals and the PGA agreed to settle their differences. They set up a ten-man policy board that would have final authority over the tournament schedule. On the international front, the U.S. won the Eisenhower Cup in the world team championship in Melbourne, Austr., by one stroke from Great Britain. The U.S. women golfers retained the Curtis Cup, defeating the U.K. $10\frac{1}{2}$–$7\frac{1}{2}$ at Newcastle in Ireland. In November, 43 countries competed for the World Cup at Olgiata, near Rome. Canada was the winner, with the United States and Italy finishing second and third.

The conflict between the leading U.S. professionals and the PGA had been simmering for years. The players considered that they should be entirely responsible for all matters concerning tournaments, relations with sponsors, contracts, television, and so on, but the PGA executive committee had always retained the right to veto decisions made by the players' tournament committee and refused to yield it. Had they done so, the affair might have been resolved and solutions found to various other points of difference concerning the management of tournaments, but neither side would give in. Eventually the PGA obtained a court order restraining the APG's activities. The case was then appealed, and in October U.S. District Judge Caleb M. Wright set aside the restraining order. The APG, whose members included all the leading players

Lee Trevino (left) exulting after sinking a 20-ft. birdie putt on his way to winning the U.S. Open in June. Bob Goalby (right) blasting from a sand trap during the second round of the Masters Tournament in April. Goalby won by a stroke and default after Roberto de Vicenzo signed an incorrect scorecard and lost the chance for a play-off.

UPI COMPIX   WIDE WORLD

**Government
Finance**

Carol Mann digging out
of a sand trap at the
Atlanta Lady's Gold
Tournament which she
won by 10 strokes.
Miss Mann in 1968 became
the first woman to earn
over $50,000 in one year
on the LPGA tour.

WIDE WORLD

almost without exception, therefore was free to negotiate its own tournament circuit. It had the support of
the sponsors, who had little choice; they could not
promote successful events without the leading players
that the public and television demanded.

The Masters ended sadly for Vicenzo. The Argentine player began his final round by holing his second
shot for an eagle; he then proceeded to play one of
the greatest last rounds in the history of golf. When
he came to the 18th hole, he needed a par four for a
64, which would have meant that Goalby, his nearest
challenger, would have to finish with two pars to
tie. Unfortunately, Vicenzo pulled his second shot
and took five. He thought that he had lost the tournament, not knowing then that Goalby had taken three
putts on the 17th. In his disappointment and weari-
ness, Vicenzo failed to notice that Tommy Aaron, his
playing partner, had entered a four instead of a three
for the 17th on Vicenzo's scorecard. Vicenzo signed the
card and left the scorer's table. Under Rule 38 (3)
the score for the 17th had to stand, and the Masters
tournament committee had no course but to rule that
his round was 66, not 65. Because Goalby finished
with a four on the 18th, it meant that he had won
by one stroke. Vicenzo bore his anguish without complaint, but there was little doubt that improved arrangements for the checking and signing of cards
would have to be instituted.

Trevino, a colourful, extroverted personality with
a highly individual style, scored magnificently in the
U.S. Open at Rochester, N.Y., which became a two-
man duel between himself and Bert Yancey. In the
end Yancey faltered, and Nicklaus came charging
from behind, playing superb golf but failing in his
putting. The same was true in the British Open at
Carnoustie, Scot., one of the severest tests ever for the
championship. Again Nicklaus could not hole the telling putts, and a great contest between him and Gary
Player went to the South African, who won his first
major title in three years. Player triumphed by virtue
of splendidly controlled golf; he did not have a six
in the entire tournament. He beat Nicklaus by two
strokes with a total of 289, one over par. Player later
won the $50,000 World Series of Golf tournament
at Akron, O., defeating Goalby in a sudden-death
play-off.

Billy Casper was the leading money winner on the
U.S. circuit with $203,769, and he maintained his po-
sition as second on the all-time money-winning list
to Arnold Palmer, whose victory in the Kemper Open
took his official PGA winnings past the $1 million
mark. The richest prize in any tournament, £23,000
($55,200) for the Alcan Golfer of the Year, was won

WIDE WORLD

Sandy Post of Ontario,
Can., adds some body
English to aid a long putt.
Miss Post defeated
defending champion Kathy
Whitworth in an 18-hole
play-off for the Ladies'
Professional Golf
Association title
on June 24.

by Gay Brewer for the second time in succession.
He finished three strokes ahead of Peter Townsend,
easily the outstanding golfer of the year in the U.K.,
who went on to success in Australia. The British
image was further strengthened by Tony Jacklin, who
won almost $60,000 in the United States, including
a victory in the Jacksonville Open, the first by a
U.K. golfer in a major event since Ted Ray won the
Open in 1920. The Australian Open was won by
Nicklaus, the South African by Player, and the French
by Peter Butler (U.K.). In the World Cup tournament
Al Balding and George Knudson of Canada won by
two strokes over Boros and Trevino.

Youth was strongly served in the amateur world.
Bruce Fleischer, aged 19, won the U.S. amateur championship at Columbus, O., where Marvin Giles, for
the second straight year, was runner-up, one stroke
behind. Giles played a major part in the U.S. victory
in the world team event, returning the lowest individual score together with Michael Bonallack, the
British captain. Bonallack proved himself the finest
British amateur of the generation. He gained his third
victory in the Amateur Championship and, in winning
the English title for the fifth time in seven years,
played Ganton (Scarborough, Yorkshire) in 61, 10
under par. The U.S. Women's Open was won by Mrs.
Susie Berning; Mickey Wright placed second. The
British women's championship was won by Brigitte
Varangot of France. Carol Mann became the first
player on the Ladies' PGA tour to earn more than
$50,000 in one season.

Certain rules changes came into force at the beginning of the year, including the banning of croquet-
type putting. Continuous putting in stroke play and
cleaning only once on the green were introduced in
an attempt to speed up play.   (P. A. W.-T.)

Government Finance

The background of government finance in 1968 was
characterized by an unusual combination of international problems affecting most industrial economies,
together with, in many instances, special and severe
political and economic problems at home. Many countries faced the readjustment problems arising out of
emergence from the recession of 1966–67, though
Italy, Norway, and the U.S. were prominent exceptions. The problem was—using a combination of monetary and fiscal measures, together with an incomes
policy or wage-price controls—to ensure a healthy recovery without excessive inflation. One challenge was
how to accomplish this without too much recourse to
government spending. Thus, in the Netherlands, for
example, the question arose in 1968 as to how to convert economic recovery from the excessive reliance on
public investment that characterized 1967 to more
balanced public- and private-sector growth.

Special Problems. It proved difficult to integrate
policies aimed at an orderly recovery because of the
special—and in some instances very severe—economic
disequilibriums confronted by various countries. Thus,
Great Britain stood in constant fear of a worsening
balance of payments and ever greater pressure on the
pound. In West Germany the problem of allocation of
fiscal functions among the central, state, and local governments moved to a climax, raising issues as to the
efficiency of Germany's federal form of government.
The Kiesinger government took a new look at the traditional desire of Germans for a balanced budget.

There was a general feeling that the events of 1966–67 had demonstrated Germany's vulnerability to recession and, therefore, the need to use spending and tax policy to reverse a downswing.

In France public finance, like most other political and economic areas in 1968, was dominated by the May riots and their aftermath. On two major counts these events necessitated a marked change of course. To divide the workers from the students, the government was forced to accede to substantial wage increases. At the same time, because of financial problems it was under pressure to rescind the social security reform and to move to an austerity budget characterized by substantially higher tax rates on the working classes. The second serious effect of riots was the damage done to the fifth plan. It was necessary to cut back on targets, and this, in turn, meant a smaller growth in gross domestic product and in tax receipts.

The experience of the U.S. was severely affected by the war in Vietnam, which continued to produce an uncontrollable rise in federal government expenditures. The inflationary pressure generated by war spending, coupled with expanded civilian programs, finally compelled Congress in June to enact the 10% surcharge on personal and corporate income taxes requested by the administration in 1967. Congress coupled the tax rise with the requirement that $6 billion be cut from federal spending. Another special aspect of U.S. government finance during 1968 was the relation of the balance of payments problem to fiscal policy. Unlike many smaller countries, especially those heavily dependent on trade, the U.S. could not hope to effect substantial relief by way of tax and spending changes aimed at reducing aggregate demand and, thus, demand for imports.

Government finance in Japan was conditioned by the weakening of the investment boom in the early months of 1968. Private consumption and residential construction showed no signs of weakening, however. The balance of payments position evidenced a marked improvement in the first part of the year, though it was still regarded as disturbing. Restrictive monetary and fiscal measures had been introduced during 1967, partly because of balance of payments difficulties, but the boom was strong enough to sustain fears of inflation and to foreshadow an even worse balance of payments position. Government spending in the first half of 1968 was affected by the supplementary budget introduced in late 1967, and there was an acceleration of government expenditures for purchases of rice under the price support program. The result was an increase in the size of the government deficit. The principle of running a deficit to stimulate recovery had been introduced in 1966 to counteract recession, but restrictive measures were necessary by the fall of 1967. The result was what Finance Minister Mikio Mizuta, in his budget message, called a very severe budget for 1968.

One of the major lessons learned by the Japanese government, and one that has had to be learned in all countries, was the difficulty of using Keynesian recipes for full employment in the face of national welfare objectives unrelated to stable growth. The combination of increased interest by workers in durable consumer goods, high employment, and rising real income, together with a system of escalators operating by way of the price support system for rice (practically synonymous with "cost of living"), carried the threat of inflation as well as foreshadowing a decline in the rate of saving and in the very rapid rate of growth. The complaint also arose that rising government expenditures, however efficacious in eliminating recession, had not resulted in provision of the public goods needed to provide an infrastructure adequate for an industrial nation of Japan's stature. Government financial policy, coupled with a rapid rate of growth, was doing an excellent job of generalizing the power to purchase commodities to all income groups. But though poverty was being rapidly eliminated, inadequate output capacity was translating some of the rise in nominal purchasing power into higher prices.

Italy did not participate in the 1966–67 recession, and could be said to have had an economic and fiscal experience all its own in 1968. Italy was in the rather special position of having a tax system generally regarded as growth inhibiting, but because of its recent freedom from recession it had nevertheless enjoyed rapid growth. Of major importance to government finance in Sweden was the success of the Social Democratic government in the September election and the determination of Economics Minister Krister Wickman to pursue an "energetic economic policy." Despite the fact that incomes were more equally distributed among the income groups in Sweden than in any other country, it was announced that still greater equality must be achieved. It was denied that the government wished to increase the proportion of nationalized industry substantially, but it would have to assume an aggressive role in state—or joint state and private—ownership in order to combat the unemployment problem.

The inflationary factors operating in Canada in the previous year continued during 1968. Rising government expenditures in 1967 had led to the issuance of large amounts of new debt, and to the decision of the government at the end of the year to propose increases in the personal income surtax, higher excise taxes on liquor and tobacco, and an acceleration by two months of tax payments by corporations. At the same time, restrictions were introduced on government spending. From the social welfare standpoint, it was of interest to note that the government considered a reduction in existing government spending programs in the event that the planned expansion of the medicare program took place. Rising interest rates, which were deplored for their adverse effect on building construction, also posed problems for debt management. Many millions of dollars worth of Canada Savings Bonds were offered to the government for redemption. Generally buoyant economic conditions were making for a tight capital market, providing impetus to the government to strive for a more than 50% reduction in borrowing during the fiscal year ending in March 1969.

Four Major Economies. Because of their effect on other economies, developments in Great Britain, West Germany, France, and the U.S. were of special interest. A key element in British government finance during the year was the devaluation of the pound in November 1967, together with the legislation passed to ensure that the British balance of payments would benefit from it. On Jan. 16, 1968, Prime Minister Harold Wilson announced that in order "to make devaluation work" it would be necessary to cut domestic spending drastically. The most severe reductions were made in national defense, the intention being to eliminate virtually all military bases east of Suez by 1971. Fiscal measures were aimed at curtailing national consumption by 2% in order to reduce demand for imports and to release productive agents for the export industry.

Some of the measures undertaken could hardly appeal to the lower income groups. For example, charges

for prescriptions and dental work were increased, although family allowances were to rise (this subsidy to be financed by a rise in the standard rate of income tax along with other minor tax increases). The seriousness with which the government went about deflating aggregate spending was illustrated by the postponement from 1971 to 1973 of the increase in the school-leaving age from 15 to 16. Free milk was to be discontinued at secondary schools. In a country that would benefit economically from a more efficient system of roads, the road-building program was to be reduced, as well as expenditure by localities on construction.

The relation between Britain's fiscal measures and its balance of payments problems may be summarized in the following way: In a comparatively high-consumption economy, the British were importing too many goods, including consumer goods. Yet tax and spending measures aimed at reducing aggregate demand and improving the import-export ratio could not be aimed solely at consumption. They affected adversely both the infrastructure of government investment and private investment spending. Thus, the badly needed relief for the balance of payments was partly at the cost of a retardation of the rate of growth, which would have the long-run effect of slowing down technological progress and cost reduction. This worked against a needed improvement in the balance of trade.

Despite the unwanted by-products of the above policies, by September 1968 consumption spending had declined sharply from the high levels attained earlier in the year. The problem remained of redirecting the released production factors into investment and exports. As in 1966, when the government imposed a payroll tax to finance a subsidy for industries contributing relatively heavily to exports, the problem would be how to deal with transitional unemployment. Indeed, the chancellor of the exchequer imposed a 50% increase in the selective employment tax, effective on September 2, thus adding further to the transitional unemployment problem.

The government expected to benefit from the tax increases to the extent of £5,280 million a year, or about 8.5% of total government tax revenue during 1968. Rates were increased on cigarettes, whiskey, gasoline, and candy, as well as on automobiles and many other commodities. To help offset this increased burden on the lower income groups, a special one-year tax was imposed on investors, in some cases at very high rates. Measures lying outside the scope of government finance, but aimed in the same direction, were restrictions on consumer credit and a proposal to limit wage and dividend increases to 3.5% a year.

Developments in government finance in the U.S. during 1968 can best be appreciated in light of the state of the economy at the beginning of the year. At that time the prospects for continued prosperity were somewhat mixed, and there was considerable disagreement as to whether fiscal measures should be aimed at slowing down the boom or assuring its continuance. In the private sector, while the rise in investment spending by business firms was substantially down from 1966, housing activity experienced a marked recovery. But the high level of government spending and the resulting federal budget deficit provided much support for the view that inflation, not recession, was the prospect that had to be dealt with. In fighting for an income tax increase, the administration indicated concern that the large tax reductions of 1962–65, introduced when aggregate spending needed stimulation, could not be reversed as easily

when there was reason to believe that aggregate spending ought to be cut back.

Congress ultimately accepted a 10% across-the-board increase in personal and corporate income tax rates, but at the insistence of Rep. Wilbur Mills (Dem., Ark.), chairman of the House Ways and Means Committee, the tax rise was coupled with a $6 billion cut in federal government spending. It was hoped that this would reduce the federal budget deficit to under $5 billion for fiscal 1969 from a previously expected $24 billion. Even so, this did not mean a reduction in federal spending, but rather a significant reduction in the rate of increase in federal spending.

Anxiety was felt throughout 1967 and 1968 at the very rapid increase in the federal debt. Not only would this raise substantially the interest cost of financing the debt, and thus divert to bondholders tax revenues that could be better used for social welfare programs, but the marketing of so much debt kept constant upward pressure on interest rates. In turn, high interest rates were beginning to have an adverse effect on residential construction. Another effect of the rising debt was the shortening of its maturity, and this complicated the task of the Treasury in refinancing maturing issues. Finally, to the extent that the rising debt was financed by the banks, the effect was a rise in the money supply and, thus, inflationary pressure.

The great expansion in the U.S. social security program had had major implications for the structure of the federal tax system. Since there were no exemptions or deductions with respect to social security taxes, and since there was a ceiling ($7,800 in 1968) on the base to which the tax applied, the effect was very regressive. Moreover, the rates had been increasing sharply in recent years. That labour unions had not been moved to a strong protest was probably due to the fact that any alternative method of financing social security would likewise have to be based on a mass tax. However, it was perhaps evidence of the delicate balance of political forces in the U.S. that the unions had not taken a stronger stand for the elimination of some of the more egregious tax dodges in the federal income tax law that favoured those whose incomes were largely in some form other than wages and salaries.

An issue that was much debated throughout the earlier part of 1968 was the negative income tax, a means of subsidizing those with incomes below subsistence (say $3,000 a year) by means of payments based on the deficiency of family income below that amount. Largely because of its alleged disincentive effects on willingness to work, this proposal, though appealing to many academic economists, did not receive much public support.

State and local expenditures continued the steady rise that had characterized them since World War II, a phenomenon observable in many countries. During 1968 the trend toward greater use of the income tax and the general sales tax continued, as the states and localities strove to hold down a rise in debt that, in percentage terms, was as great as the rise in tax receipts during the previous decade (both had more than doubled). Despite the perennial problems relating to property taxation, and although rates had not risen comparably to those of other taxes at the disposal of the states and localities, property tax receipts had gone up substantially as a result of new construction and higher land values.

Prominent among the problems in West Germany

during 1968 was the relationship between the federal government and the states. As in Canada and the U.S., the constitution gave the states substantial financial powers without, perhaps, giving them enough. In Germany one result of this was a greater rise in combined state and local debt than in federal debt. The latter, incidentally, had occurred mainly as a result of the not insignificant recession of 1966–67, and had given rise to much discussion. Credit financing by the federal government assumed a considerable role in 1968, however, and promised to rise further. It was given a boost by the Stable Growth Law of June 1967, which emphasized middle-term planning and growth.

A financial reform law received its second round of discussion in the financial committee of the Bundestag in September 1968, and on September 13 the government proposed that as from Jan. 1, 1969, the proceeds of individual and corporate income taxes be divided in the ratio of 35% to the central government and 65% to the states, a change from the existing 37 and 63%. The idea was that, by assuring the states and localities of a larger share in projected tax receipts in future years, expansion would be made possible in the kind of growth-creating public investment for which the states and localities were responsible. These considerations were summed up in the concept of "co-operative federalism." At the political level, cooperative federalism involved the appropriate vertical distribution of political power. At the level of governmental finance it was particularly concerned with sharing the economic power of financially strong states with the weaker ones and with measures for enhancing the financial powers of the localities.

The tax on value added adopted by West Germany on Jan. 1, 1968, in connection with its membership in the EEC was raised from 10 to 11% as of July 1, 1968 (from 5 to 5.5% for food). The substitution of the value-added tax for the traditional turnover tax would remove some of the impetus for vertical integration and monopoly that had been a characteristic of German industry for many years. Another aspect of German public finance was the debate over the role that Germany should play in covering the costs of U.S. troops stationed within its borders. A dispatch from Washington on June 10, 1968, indicated that an agreement had been reached on the allocation of the $800 million-a-year cost of maintaining 210,000 U.S. troops and 160,000 dependents in West Germany. The agreement involved the purchase by West Germany of medium-term U.S. Treasury bonds and military equipment in the reported amount of $700 million a year.

Two special tax measures were of interest. It was announced on June 26 that the Leber Plan had finally been adopted by the Bonn government. This was a surtax on truck transportation, the proceeds to be used to reduce the heavy deficit of the railroads. Minister of Transport Georg Leber, who had long fought for this measure, was primarily interested in discouraging excessive traffic on the autobahns. Finally, an interesting recommendation announced on June 28 was a special tax of 3% of taxable income for 20 years on those men between the ages of 25 and 45 who escaped induction into the Bundeswehr. This tax was strangely reminiscent of the "Saladin tithe," levied in the late 12th century to provide an incentive for joining the Crusade, and to help finance it.

In France the May disturbances so disorganized production that gross domestic product for 1968 was anticipated to be about Fr. 29,340,000,000—or 6%—lower than original estimates. The balance of payments was seriously upset, and tourist receipts were adversely affected. Finance Minister Maurice Couve de Murville's emergency tax law, announced on July 11, 1968, provided for a tax increase of 10% on wines and liquor. Moreover, it was planned to impose a surcharge on higher incomes amounting to as much as 25%. The complexity of the French financial situation was indicated by the fact that the tax rises were not only to help restore budgetary balance after the disturbances, but also to siphon off purchasing power resulting from the agreed-upon wage increases. Another effect of the revolt was the imposition of temporary trade restrictions, although under the EEC timetable France's average tariffs would have dropped from 14.4 to 10.7% on July 1, 1968.

In the area of social security, a 1967 measure had been aimed at reducing certain benefits in order to improve the financial position of the government, as well as to cause some shift from consumption to saving and investment. This was, in fact, one of the many incidents leading to the revolt; and the response to the latter, which included substantial wage increases but higher tax rates on the working classes, resulted in a very complex situation so far as the government's budget and the impact on the consumption-savings ratio were concerned.

Near the close of 1968, severe currency disturbances compelled the enactment of draconian measures that included fiscal action in France, West Germany, and Britain. Late in November great pressure on the franc, coupled with the refusal of Pres. Charles de Gaulle to devalue, necessitated a number of tax rises and a sharp curtailment of government expenditures (including even the nuclear program) as the only alternative to outright devaluation. The British pound, for the second time during 1968 coming under similar (though not so severe) pressure, required support in a further series of deflationary measures. Among other tax moves was an increase in the purchase tax of 10%. In West Germany the situation was the reverse. The Kiesinger government did not feel politically strong enough to revalue the Deutsche Mark, but instead plumped for a partial revaluation in the form of a reduction of about 3% in the tax imports and a tax rebate of the same amount on exports. In effect, this amounted to an unofficial revaluation of the Deutsche Mark. Only time would tell whether the measures adopted by the three countries would suffice to reduce balance of payments problems to manageable proportions. (K. E. P.)

See also Economic Planning; Economics; Economy, World; Money and Banking; Payments and Reserves, International.

Greece

A constitutional monarchy of Europe, Greece occupies the southern part of the Balkan Peninsula. Area: 50,-944 sq.mi. (131,944 sq.km.), of which the mainland accounts for 41,227 sq.mi. Pop. (1967 est.): 8,716,-000. Cap. and largest city: Athens (pop., 1961, 627,-564). Language: Greek. Religion: Orthodox. King, Constantine II, in exile since Dec. 14, 1967; regent in 1968, Lieut. Gen. Georgios Zoitakis; prime minister, Georgios Papadopoulos.

Domestic Affairs. The Greek Army officers who seized power on April 21, 1967, in order to forestall what they claimed was an impending Communist coup

Great Britain: *see* United Kingdom

Left, ministers of the new Greek government are sworn in by Archbishop Hieronymos of Athens in June 1968. Right, 70,000 spectators crowd the sports stadium to celebrate the military revolution that overthrew civilian government. A replica of Mt. Olympus occupies the centre of the stadium.

d'etat, consolidated their control of the country throughout 1968 after defeating the military counter-coup staged by King Constantine (Dec. 13, 1967) which led to his fleeing abroad. The Greek rulers reiterated their promise to restore parliamentary democracy as soon as the comprehensive reforms planned by the "revolution" had been carried out.

As a first step, they organized for September 29 a national referendum to obtain popular approval for a new constitution. The referendum was held under martial law and had been preceded by a vigorous, one-sided campaign in the censored press in favour of a "yes" vote. The final results were: "yes," 4,638,543; "no," 391,923; invalid ballots, 18,515. Registered voters totaled 6,516,285, so that the rate of abstention stood at 22.51%, despite the fact that voting had been made compulsory. Opponents of the regime

denounced the results as the product of widespread coercion. The prime minister claimed the referendum had given the "revolution" a popular vote of confidence.

The new constitution thus approved was due to be put immediately into effect, except for 12 of its 138 articles, those safeguarding individual and political rights. Under article 138 of the constitution the regime was empowered to activate those provisions whenever it thought fit. The 1968 constitution, which replaced the one introduced in 1952, qualified and curtailed the prerogatives of the king, limited the powers of Parliament, and broadened those of the Cabinet (which, except for the prime minister and his two deputies, was made up of extraparliamentary members). It established a Council of the Nation to advise the king and a Constitutional Court with wide-ranging authority to protect democracy from abuses of individual and political freedoms and from subversion, in the broadest sense. The armed forces, which henceforth would owe allegiance to the "national ideals and national traditions," stood out as a separate, supraconstitutional entity.

The regime's draft, originally prepared in December 1967 by a commission of 20 jurists, led to arduous and often heated Cabinet sessions punctuated by disagreement and the subsequent resignation of the minister of justice. The final text was released by the prime minister on July 11. A few modifications were announced on September 16 and, following the referendum, the new constitution went into effect on November 15. In December it was confirmed that the powers of the Revolutionary Council, which had, in effect, ruled Greece since the coup, had been transferred to the Cabinet. The membership of the Revolutionary Council had not been made public, but it was believed to have been composed largely of military officers.

Under the new constitution King Constantine could not return to his throne before the first parliamentary elections, unless the government decided to recall him at an earlier date. But the regime firmly refused to set a date for elections, which, it stated, would be held only after the "revolution" had succeeded in reforming "Greek mentality," the nation's social structure, political ethics, and the country's economy.

Andreas Papandreou, politician son of the former Prime Minister Georgios Papandreou (who died November 1), had received amnesty over Christmas 1967 and was allowed to leave the country with his

GREECE

Education. (1965–66) Primary, pupils 963,846, teachers 27,872; secondary, pupils 368,884, teachers 14,140; vocational, pupils 53,252; teacher training, students 4,350, teachers 261; higher (including 4 universities), students 55,334, teaching staff 1,826.

Finance. Monetary unit: drachma, with a par value of 30 drachmas to U.S. $1 (72 drachmas = £1 sterling). Gold and foreign exchange, central bank: (June 1968) U.S. $228 million; (June 1967) U.S. $235 million. Budget (1967 est.): revenue 40,417,000,000 drachmas; expenditure 40,604,000,000 drachmas. Gross national product: (1966) 197.4 billion drachmas; (1965) 177.4 billion drachmas. Money supply: (May 1968) 41,330,000,000 drachmas; (May 1967) 37,580,000,-000 drachmas. Cost of living (1963 = 100): (June 1968) 111; (June 1967) 111.

Foreign Trade. (1967) Imports 35,559,000,000 drachmas; exports 14,856,-000,000 drachmas. Import sources: EEC 44% (West Germany 19%, Italy 10%, France 8%); U.K. 9%; U.S. 8%. Export destinations: EEC 40% (West Germany 16%, Italy 10%, France 9%); U.S. 13%; U.S.S.R. 6%; Yugoslavia 5%; U.K. 5%. Main exports: tobacco 28%; cotton 8%; dried fruit (raisins, currants) 8%; cereals 6%; fresh fruit 6%; aluminum 6%; vegetable oils 5%.

Transport and Communications. Roads (1967) 34,050 km. (including 11 km. expressways). Motor vehicles in use (1966): passenger 122,479; commercial 72,-382. Railways: (1965) 2,581 km.; traffic (1967) 1,151,000,000 passenger-km., freight 563 million net ton-km. Shipping (1967): merchant vessels 100 gross tons and over 1,600; gross tonnage 7,432,793. Air traffic (1967): 1,145,465,000 passenger-km.; freight 24,733,000 net ton-km. Telephones (Dec. 1966) 579,076. Radio receivers (Dec. 1966) c. 936,000.

Agriculture. Production (in 000; metric tons; 1967; 1966 in parentheses): wheat 1,850 (1,959); barley 848 (639); oats c. 165 (174); corn 331 (320); potatoes (1966) 579, (1965) 589; rice 91 (86); tomatoes (1966) 610, (1965) 470; tobacco (1966) 92, (1965) 126; oranges (1966) 407, (1965) 408; lemons (1966) 109, (1965) 162; cotton, lint c. 98 (88); olive oil 225 (180); wine (1966) 384, (1965) 406; raisins (1966) 179, (1965) 176; currants and sultanas (1965) 177, (1964) 163; figs (1966) c. 110, (1965) 114. Livestock (in 000; Dec. 1965): sheep 7,848; goats 3,895; cattle (Dec. 1966) 1,092; horses 294; mules 213; asses 441; pigs 558; poultry 21,808.

Industry. Production (in 000; metric tons; 1967): lignite 5,162; manufactured gas 10,320 cu.m.; electricity (excluding most industrial production) 6,310,-000 kw.-hr.; bauxite 1,687; magnesite (1965) 314; cement 3,696; cotton yarn 37.

family (January 16). On arrival in Paris he denounced the Greek junta, and one month later set up the Pan-Hellenic Liberation Movement (PAK) with headquarters in Stockholm, where he had been offered a chair in political science at the university.

Resistance to the regime in Greece was haphazard and amateurish throughout most of 1968. It included an abortive attempt (August 13) to assassinate Prime Minister Papadopoulos. An explosive charge placed in a gully under the highway was detonated by remote control a few seconds after his car had driven near it. In the wake of this episode came a wave of arrests, mainly of retired Greek officers and former deputies. Later, the authorities arrested all 20 persons involved in the assassination plot.

Other resistance episodes involved the scattering of leaflets and the detonation of a few bombs in Athens, which caused neither serious damage nor personal injury. The regime discouraged such activities by inflicting heavy penalties on those apprehended. Several members of such underground organizations as the Democratic Defense and the Patriotic Front were sentenced to long terms of imprisonment, but there were no death sentences or executions.

Attention was focused on Greece in October when Aristotle Onassis, a wealthy Greek shipping magnate, married Jacqueline Kennedy, widow of U.S. Pres. John F. Kennedy. The ceremony took place on the island of Skorpios off the coast of Greece.

Foreign Relations. After the initial diplomatic embarrassment caused to Greek foreign relations by the king's flight abroad and the assumption of the regency by Lieut. Gen. Georgios Zoitakis, diplomatic contacts between foreign embassies and the government were resumed in January, particularly after the regime made it clear that it did not intend to depose King Constantine.

Relations between Greece and the Scandinavian countries, particularly Sweden and Denmark, continued to be strained as a result of the hostility shown by those governments toward the Greek regime and their open support of Andreas Papandreou's organization. The U.S., which had imposed a selective suspension of shipments of heavy military equipment to Greece after the coup, until tangible proof of the intention to restore democratic rule was given, continued diplomatic efforts to induce the regime to produce such evidence. However, the Soviet invasion of Czechoslovakia in August, with its repercussions in the Balkans and the Mediterranean (where the Soviet Union was building up an impressive naval force), enhanced the regime's position among the military leaders of NATO. The Greek rulers had missed no opportunity to reaffirm their loyalty to the West.

The Economy. Throughout 1968 the Greek economy continued to suffer from the impact of the coup, which had undermined confidence abroad. At the beginning of the year the government announced an ambitious five-year economic development plan costing $12,720,000,000. Overall prospects for 1968 seemed poor, however, in view of a scarcity of foreign capital, which traditionally bridged the gap in the Greek balance of payments. The generous credit policy introduced during the year to end domestic recession resulted in higher imports without a corresponding growth in exports. Tourist revenue declined and so did emigrant remittances.   (Mo. M.)

ENCYCLOPÆDIA BRITANNICA FILMS. *People of Greece* (1955); *The Mediterranean World* (1961).

Guatemala

A republic of Central America, Guatemala is bounded by Mexico, British Honduras, Honduras, El Salvador, the Caribbean Sea, and the Pacific Ocean. Area: 42,042 sq.mi. (108,889 sq.km.). Pop. (1968 est.): 4,863,520. Cap. and largest city: Guatemala City (pop., 1967 est., 652,934). Language: Spanish, with some Indian dialects. Religion: predominantly Roman Catholic. President in 1968, Julio César Méndez Montenegro.

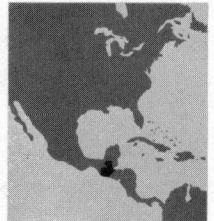

Although the advent of 1968 was attended by political and economic uncertainties, a measure of improvement was evident by midyear. President Méndez Montenegro, moving toward the midpoint of his term in office, continued to walk a delicate balance between warring extremist political factions.

GUATEMALA

Education. (1965–66) Primary, pupils 421,446, teachers 12,251; secondary, pupils 35,541, teachers 4,216; vocational, pupils 6,794, teachers 985; teacher training, students 6,798, teachers 1,197; higher (at 3 universities), students 8,171, teaching staff 705.

Finance. Monetary unit: quetzal, at par with the U.S. dollar (2.40 quetzales = £1 sterling). Gold and foreign exchange, central bank: (June 1968) U.S. $84.5 million; (June 1967) U.S. $69.1 million. Budget (1967 est.) balanced at 190.6 million quetzals. Gross national product: (1966) 1,379,000,000 quetzales; (1965) 1,316,000,000 quetzales. Money supply: (June 1968) 154 million quetzales; (June 1967) 146 million quetzales. Cost of living (Guatemala City; 1963 = 100): (June 1968) 107; (June 1967) 101.

Foreign Trade. (1967) Imports 247.3 million quetzales; exports 199.1 million quetzales. Import sources (1966): U.S. 42%; El Salvador 11%; West Germany 9%; Japan 7%; U.K. 5%. Export destinations (1966): U.S. 31%; West Germany 13%; El Salvador 13%; Japan 9%. Main exports: coffee 34%; cotton 16%.

Transport and Communications. Roads (1965) 11,230 km. (including 830 km. of Pan-American Highway). Motor vehicles in use (1966): passenger 33,300; commercial (including buses) 18,300. Railways (1966): 1,160 km.; freight 133 million net ton-km. Air traffic (1967): 78,456,000 passenger-km.; freight (1966) 3,570,000 net ton-km. Telephones (Jan. 1967) 32,526. Radio receivers (Dec. 1961) *c.* 210,000. Television receivers (Dec. 1966) *c.* 60,000.

Agriculture. Production (in 000; metric tons; 1967; 1966 in parentheses): corn *c.* 782 (722); cotton, lint *c.* 75 (*c.* 63); cane sugar, raw value (1967–68) *c.* 149, (1966–67) *c.* 181; sugar, panela (1967–68) *c.* 27, (1966–67) *c.* 29; coffee (1966) *c.* 100, (1965) *c.* 123; bananas (1966) *c.* 100, (1965) *c.* 90. Livestock (in 000; March 1966): cattle *c.* 1,170; sheep *c.* 818; pigs *c.* 543.

Industry. Production (in 000; metric tons; 1966): cement 204; lead ore (metal content) *c.* 0.6; zinc ore (metal content) *c.* 0.5; electricity (excluding most industrial production) *c.* 520,000 kw-hr.

Terrorist action, inaugurated early in the 1960s by leftist elements, was countered by the rise of counterinsurgency in 1967. During 1968 the peace of Guatemala City and regions to the northeast and east was broken by a series of disturbances for which opposing radical elements were held responsible. In mid-January two U.S. military attachés were assassinated in the capital city, presumably in revenge for the suspected involvement of ultraconservatives in the murder of a member of the rebel movement. A "state of alarm" was declared at that time. Continuing disturbances and retaliatory actions culminated in the kidnapping of Archbishop Mario Casariego in mid-March by right-wing terrorists. Although he was released unharmed several days later, a "state of siege" was declared which remained in effect until June 20, when it was lifted because of a substantial drop in terrorist activity.

By midyear, as a consequence of military pressure, the arena of major rebel activity, although reduced, appeared to have switched from the region of the Motagua Valley and Guatemala's eastern uplands to the capital city. For the most part, an uneasy peace came to reign except for occasional flare-ups and murders, provoked by extremists and possibly by gangster-like elements.

Greek Orthodox Church: *see* Religion

Greenland: *see* Dependent States

Grenada: *see* Dependent States

Gross National Product: *see* Economy, World; Income, National

Guadeloupe: *see* Dependent States

Guam: *see* Dependent States

The rebel leader César Montes was reportedly killed by military forces in June. The arrest of guerrilla leader Camilo Sánchez in August was countered by the assassination of the U.S. ambassador, J. Gordon Mein, at which time the "state of alarm" suspending certain constitutional rights was reestablished for the second time during 1968.

Throughout 1968 the Guatemalan economy recovered gradually from the sluggish performance of the previous year in spite of the fact that the nation was beset by a series of problems that slowed the rate of economic progress. The flow of trade and industrial production was hampered considerably by a 72-day strike that halted all operations of the International Railways of Central America between the first week of January and mid-March. Shortly after the turn of the year the government was also beset by public protests that forced the cancellation of a previously scheduled 5% general sales and a 20% luxury tax. Consequent budget reductions cut anticipated government capital expenditures to near their 1967 level.

HOLMES-LEBEL—PIX FROM PUBLIX

Children in Guatemala City playing their game version of the terrorism they have witnessed.

The initial effect of this was a sharp reduction in the operational funds for the government's agrarian reform program. At the same time, expenditures in the public sector began to show an upturn during 1968 as the government began to draw upon almost $54 million in loans for economic development programs secured by the Méndez administration from international agencies.

A serious imbalance of trade in 1967 was continued into 1968. However, generally improved agricultural production and a moderate recovery of export earnings from the sale of coffee and cotton, combined with a program of federal austerity and a lower level of deficit financing, was expected to stabilize financial reserves.

Within the realm of Central American affairs attention continued to be focused upon a pending move toward independence in neighbouring British Honduras and upon the activities of the Central American Common Market (CACM), of which Guatemala, El Salvador, Honduras, Nicaragua, and Costa Rica were members. At midyear, British Honduras rejected an attempted plan of arbitration between the U.K. and Guatemala concerning the political future of its post-independence relations with Guatemala. (*See* DEPENDENT STATES.) (O. H. H.)

ENCYCLOPÆDIA BRITANNICA FILMS. *Guatemala—Nation of Central America* (1961).

Guiana:
see Dependent States; Guyana

Guided Missiles:
see Defense

Guinea, Portuguese:
see Dependent States

Gymnastics:
see Sporting Record

Gynecology and Obstetrics:
see Medicine

Guinea

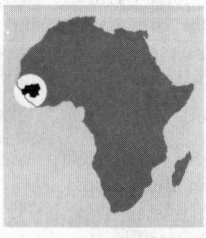

A republic on the west coast of Africa, Guinea is bounded by Portuguese Guinea, Senegal, Mali, Ivory Coast, Liberia, and Sierra Leone. Area: 94,925 sq.mi. (245,856 sq.km.). Pop. (1966 est.): 3,608,000, chiefly Fulani, Malinké, and Susu. Cap. and largest city: Conakry (pop., over 100,000). Language: French (official). Religion: mostly Muslim. President in 1968, Sékou Touré.

Sékou Touré, sole candidate for election and unanimous choice of the executive council of the Guinea Democratic Party (PDG), was reelected president on Jan. 1, 1968. Later in the same month he reshuffled his government, and in accordance with the decision at the PDG's eighth congress, restructured the existing ministries into seven *domaines*.

Efforts toward the resumption of closer relations with France continued in January, and in February diplomatic relations with the U.K., severed in December 1965 as a result of Britain's Rhodesia policy, were resumed. In February, also, the arrest was announced of about 500 insurgents. Officials claimed the force had infiltrated Guinea after training in an unnamed African state.

Although elected president of the newly formed Organization of Senegal River States in March, Sékou Touré did little to improve his relations with the rest of French-speaking Africa. Furthermore, relations with Portuguese Guinea deteriorated in March when, after a forced landing at Aldeia Formosa, Guinean pilots were detained as hostages for the return of five Portuguese soldiers allegedly kidnapped and forced into Guinean territory. Relations with the Ivory Coast, already markedly cool, were futher impaired in April when Sékou Touré reaffirmed his government's resolve to continue support for the federal government of Nigeria against the separatist Biafran regime.

On May 16 Radio Conakry, reiterating the policy of africanization of the clergy, warned white priests who were "now trying to return through the back door" and had been reported in the Nimba district on the Guinea-Liberia border that they would be summarily dealt with.

After the return from Communist China of a joint Guinea-Mali delegation, the three governments issued a communiqué in May which promised further political, economic, and cultural cooperation. The communiqué also approved an agreement, signed May 24, for the continuation of the Guinea–Mali railway

GUINEA
Education. (1965–66) Primary, pupils 164,119, teachers 3,990; secondary, pupils 16,698, teachers 567; vocational, pupils 5,018, teachers 261; teacher training, students 822, teachers 52; higher, students 1,243, teachers 199.
Finance. Monetary unit: Guinea franc, at par with the CFA franc (GFr. 246.85 = U.S. $1; GFr. 592.45 = £1 sterling). Budget (1967–68 est.) balanced at GFr. 20.7 billion.
Foreign Trade. (1964) Imports GFr. 11,201,000,-000; exports GFr. 16.1 billion. Import sources: U.S. 22%; U.S.S.R. 12%; China 10%. Export destinations: France 16%; U.S. 11%; Cameroon 10%; Poland 8%. Main exports (1962): aluminum 60%; bananas 10%; palm products 7%; coffee 6%; iron ore 6%.

to Bamako. Financial support was being provided by China.

At a meeting of the PDG's Central Committee, July 29–August 3, a decision was made to intensify Guinea's "cultural revolution" by modifying the existing syllabi of schools; by establishing regional revolutionary councils; and by the compulsory teaching of the national languages—Malinké, Susu, Guerzé, and Konyagui. In September a decision was made to exploit vast reserves of bauxite near Boké, with U.S. aid. (PH. D.)

Guyana

A parliamentary state and a realm of the Commonwealth of Nations, Guyana is situated between Venezuela, Brazil, and Surinam (Netherlands Guiana) on the Atlantic Ocean. Area: 83,000 sq.mi. (214,970 sq.km.). Pop. (1967 est.): 676,521, including (1964) East Indian 50.2%; Negro 31.3%; mestizo and mulatto 11.9%; Amerindian 4.6%. Cap. and largest city: Georgetown (pop., 1965 est., 85,994). Language: English (official). Religion: Protestant and Roman Catholic. Queen, Elizabeth II; governor-general in 1968, Sir David Rose; prime minister, Forbes Burnham.

Border disputes with Venezuela and Surinam seriously engaged Guyanan attention in 1968. At the end of 1967 Gen. Ramón Florencio Gómez of Venezuela issued statements about Venezuelan-occupied Ankoko Island to which Guyana took exception. Shortly thereafter Surinam laid claim to approximately 6,000 sq.mi. of land along the Courantyne River in what Guyana had always considered its own territory. The subsequent appointment of a new Venezuelan ambassador to Georgetown had a conciliatory effect, but in June a Venezuelan government advertisement in *The Times* (London) warned investors of the possible illegality of holdings in the disputed area. Guyana's protest was followed by the withdrawal of Venezuelans from the subcommittee of the mixed Boundary Commission. In July Venezuela laid claim to several square miles of coastal waters off the disputed area, which prompted the Guyanan prime minister, Forbes Burnham, to visit the U.S. and the U.K., while Guyanan ambassadors sought to arouse fa-

GUYANA
Education. (1965–66) Primary, pupils 163,344, teachers 5,021; secondary, pupils 15,486, teachers 583; vocational, pupils 2,197, teachers (1962–63) 56; higher, students 255, teaching staff 61.
Finance. Monetary unit: Guyanan dollar (Guy$2 = U.S. $1; Guy$4.80 = £1 sterling). Budget (1968 est.): revenue Guy$98,354,000; expenditure Guy$95,865,000.
Foreign Trade. (1967) Imports Guy$227.7 million; exports Guy$193.9 million. Import sources (1966): U.K. 33%; U.S. 23%; Trinidad and Tobago 10%; Canada 9%. Export destinations (1966): U.K. 22%; U.S. 22%; Canada 22%; Trinidad and Tobago 8%; Norway 6%. Main exports (1966): sugar 30%; bauxite 23%; alumina 17%; rice 13%.
Agriculture. Production (in 000; metric tons): sugar, raw value (1967–68) 361, (1966–67) 349; rice (1967) 198, (1966) 249; timber (1967) 2,449 cu.m., (1966) 2,552 cu.m. Livestock (in 000; 1965–66): cattle 350; sheep 87; pigs 65.
Industry. Production (in 000; metric tons; 1966): manganese ore (metal content) 64; bauxite (1965) 4,302; diamonds 99 metric carats; electricity (1964) 212,000 kw-hr.

vourable world opinion. By the end of the year Guyana was entering into close relations with Brazil following a Brazilian statement of support in the Venezuelan dispute; a commission led by the deputy prime minister, Ptolemy Reid, visited Brazil.

Major progress was noted on the Caribbean front. In May Guyana was a signatory to the agreement setting up the Caribbean Free Trade Association (CARIFTA), the secretariat of which was situated in Georgetown.

In April the government began to make special arrangements for registering Guyanan residents aboard and for granting them voting rights. At the annual party convention in April of the People's National Congress, its leader, Prime Minister Burnham, asserted that no coalition government would be formed and that his party had recruited certain dissidents from Cheddi Jagan's opposition People's Progressive Party. Burnham further stated that a republic would be proclaimed early in 1969 following the general elections. The elections, held December 16, resulted in a victory for the People's National Congress.

A commission under B. A. N. Collins of the University of Guyana investigated the organization of and salaries in public service. A state-controlled radio service was introduced. The defense force came under Guyanan command and the nucleus of a small navy was launched.

The 1968 budget provided for the expenditure of Guy$141 million, including Guy$45 million for capital development; small tax increases were announced, but the budget was supported by the labour unions. In an independence day speech Burnham pointed to various signs of economic advances: the balance of payments surplus; rising currency reserves; the favourable effect of the Guyanan devaluation on the bauxite and sugar industries; extensive plans under way for development of the rice industry; and a record sugar crop. (RA. R.)

Haiti

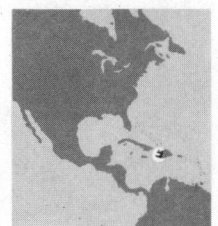

The Republic of Haiti occupies the western one-third of the Caribbean island of Hispaniola, which it shares with the Dominican Republic. Area: 10,714 sq.mi. (27,750 sq.km.). Pop. (1967 est.): 4,577,000, of whom 95% are Negro. Cap. and largest city: Port-au-Prince (pop., 1961 est., 239,000). Language: French and Creole. Religion: Roman Catholic; Voodooism practiced in rural areas. President in 1968, François Duvalier.

During 1968 the position of the Duvalier government continued to deteriorate, and economic development was almost at a standstill. There were unconfirmed reports that President Duvalier was suffering from cancer, and the government experienced increasing difficulty in paying the wages of the Tonton Macoute, the secret police. Foreign interests began to refuse to advance loans and donations to the state, and many were considering withdrawing from the country.

The most publicized event of the year was the trial on espionage charges of South African-born David Knox, an information officer employed by the Bahamian government. He was tried in August by a military tribunal. In July the same tribunal had tried ten Haitians accused of participating in an invasion of the country by exiles in May; 20–30 persons had landed by plane at Cap-Haïtien but practically all

PRESS ASSOCIATION LTD.
Guyana Prime Minister Forbes Burnham arriving at Heathrow Airport, London, for a visit to obtain British backing for the Guyana position in a boundary dispute with Venezuela.

were immediately arrested. Knox, who conducted his own defense, was sentenced to death despite a lack of evidence, but he was later deported. The trial was used by the government as a publicity stunt, and Duvalier in one of his rare press conferences announced that he would grant clemency to the invaders.

Several prominent businessmen and lawyers were arrested, accused of financing the abortive invasion; these included Oswald Brandt, Jamaican consul in Port-au-Prince and an important local factory owner. These prisoners, however, were permitted to live in comfort, and some were released after they had advanced loans to the government.

The policy of commuting death sentences was part of an attempt by the regime to establish a more moderate image abroad. Clemency was granted by Duvalier to his son-in-law, Col. Max Dominique, who had been sentenced to death for plotting against him early in 1967 and had fled to exile in Switzerland. In October a new attempt on Duvalier's life was made, and a number of people were arrested.

In August the government of the Bahamas deported illegal Haitian immigrants; about 200 of these, however, mutinied, and in the ensuing violence one person was killed and several were wounded. The ship returned to the Bahamas to disembark casualties, but later the immigrants were returned to Haiti. One of the last possibilities for emigration from Haiti was the Bahamas, as the Dominican Republic had closed its borders and Cuba was no longer available.

In a message to the National Assembly in August, Duvalier announced that defense needs perpetually absorbed funds allocated to promote economic development; positive measures were, however, to be taken to remedy the situation. The public finances gave growing cause for concern; total revenue and expenditure amounted to $19 million and $26 million, respectively, in 1967, and a large part of revenue was required to pay the Army and the secret police. The only flour mill in the country closed down because wheat imports could not be paid for, and the govern-

ment remained unsuccessful in obtaining badly needed foreign loans. There was a further decline in the tourist trade.

In an attempt to attract industry, a contract was signed in May with an unidentified Italian concern to build generators for a hydroelectric plant at the Peligré Dam in the central Artibonite Valley. A first payment of $550,000 was made when the contract was signed; a second payment of $517,000, due in January 1969, was expected to be difficult to achieve.

(RN. C.)

ENCYCLOPÆDIA BRITANNICA FILMS. *The West Indies* (1965).

Heads of State

The following is a list of the names of those holding chief positions in their countries as of Dec. 31, 1968.

Country	Name and office	Accession
Afghanistan	Mohammad Zahir Shah, king	1933
	Noor Ahmad Etemadi, prime minister	1967
Albania	Enver Hoxha, first secretary of the Albanian (Communist) Party of Labour	1954
	Haxhi Leshi, president of the Presidium	1953
	Mehmet Shehu, chairman of the Council of Ministers	1954
Algeria	Houari Boumédienne, president	1965
Andorra	Francesc Escudé-Ferrero, sindic procurador general de les valls d'Andorra	1967
Argentina	Juan Carlos Onganía, president	1966
Australia	Elizabeth II, queen	1952
	Lord Casey, governor-general	1965
	John Grey Gorton, prime minister	1968
Austria	Franz Jonas, president	1965
	Josef Klaus, chancellor	1964
Barbados	Elizabeth II, queen	1952
	Sir John Stow, governor-general	1966
	Errol Walton Barrow, prime minister	1966
Belgium	Baudouin I, king	1951
	Gaston Eyskens, prime minister	1968
Bolivia	Gen. René Barrientos Ortuño, president	1966
Botswana	Sir Seretse Khama, president	1966
Brazil	Artur da Costa e Silva, president	1967
Bulgaria	Todor Zhivkov, first secretary of the Bulgarian Communist Party (1954) and chairman of the Council of Ministers	1962
	Georgi Traikov, chairman of the Presidium	1964
Burma	Gen. Ne Win, chairman of the Revolutionary Council and prime minister	1962
Burundi	Michel Micombero, president	1966
Cambodia	Prince Norodom Sihanouk, chief of state	1960
	Son Sann, premier	1967
Cameroon	Ahmadou Ahidjo, president	1960
Canada	Elizabeth II, queen	1952
	D. Roland Michener, governor-general	1967
	Pierre Elliott Trudeau, prime minister	1968
Central African Rep.	Jean Bedel Bokassa, president and premier	1966
Ceylon	Elizabeth II, queen	1952
	William Gopallawa, governor-general	1962
	Dudley Senanayake, prime minister	1965
Chad	François Tombalbaye, president (1960) and premier	1968
Chile	Eduardo Frei Montalva, president	1964
China — People's Rep.	Mao Tse-tung, chairman of the Communist Party	1949
	Chou En-lai, premier	1949
China — Rep. of (Taiwan)	Chiang Kai-shek, president	1943
	C. K. Yen, president of the Executive Yuan	1963
Colombia	Carlos Lleras Restrepo, president	1966
Congo, Dem. Rep.	Joseph Mobutu, president	1965
Congo Rep.	Alfred Raoul, interim president	1968
Costa Rica	José Joaquín Tréjos Fernández, president	1966
Cuba	Osvaldo Dorticós Torrado, president	1959
	Fidel Castro, prime minister	1959
Cyprus	Archbishop Makarios III, president	1960
Czechoslovakia	Alexander Dubcek, first secretary of the Communist Party of Czechoslovakia	1968
	Ludvik Svoboda, president	1968
	Oldrich Cernik, premier	1968
Dahomey	Émile Zinsou, president	1968
Denmark	Frederick IX, king	1947
	Hilmar Baunsgaard, prime minister	1968
Dominican Rep.	Joaquín Balaguer, president	1966
Ecuador	José María Velasco Ibarra, president	1968
El Salvador	Col. Fidel Sánchez Hernández, president	1967
Equatorial Guinea	Francisco Macias Nguema, president	1968
Ethiopia	Haile Selassie I, emperor	1930
	Aklilu Habte Wold, prime minister	1961
Finland	Urho Kaleva Kekkonen, president	1956
	Mauno Koivisto, prime minister	1968

HAITI

Education. (1965) Primary, pupils 283,799, teachers 6,210; secondary, pupils 20,128, teachers 1,259; vocational, pupils 4,173, teachers 337; teacher training, students 213, teachers 46; higher (at University of Haiti), students 1,822, teaching staff 135.

Finance. Monetary unit: gourde, with a par value of 5 gourdes to U.S. $1 (12 gourdes = £1 sterling). Gold and foreign exchange, central bank: (June 1968) U.S. $3.1 million; (June 1967) U.S. $2.4 million. Budget (1967–68 est.) balanced at 140.2 million gourdes. Money supply: (Feb. 1968) 144.1 million gourdes; (Feb. 1967) 121 million gourdes. Cost of living (Port-au-Prince; 1963 = 100): (March 1968) 114; (March 1967) 125.

Foreign Trade. Imports (1966) 194 million gourdes; exports (1967) 166.9 million gourdes. Import sources: U.S. 61%; Japan 6%; U.K. 5%; France 5%. Export destinations (1966): U.S. 47%; France 12%; Italy 10%; Japan 8%; Belgium-Luxembourg 7%. Main exports: coffee 43%; sisal 4%.

Transport and Communications. Roads (1965) 3,107 km. (including 348 km. with improved surface). Motor vehicles in use (1966): passenger 4,900; commercial 1,100. Railways (1966) 354 km. (used mainly for transporting sugar cane). Telephones (Jan. 1967) c. 4,400. Radio receivers (Dec. 1966) c. 64,000. Television receivers (Dec. 1966) c. 10,000.

Agriculture. Production (in 000; metric tons; 1966; 1965 in parentheses): coffee c. 28 (c. 34); sugar, raw value (1967–68) c. 63, (1966–67) c. 61; sisal c. 27 (27). Livestock (in 000; 1965–66): cattle 699; pigs 1,367; goats 1,070; sheep 62.

Industry. Production (in 000; metric tons; 1966): cement 38; bauxite (exports) 412; electricity 73,000 kw.-hr.

Country	Name and office	Accession
France	Charles de Gaulle, president	1959
	Maurice Couve de Murville, premier	1968
Gabon	Albert Bernard Bongo, president	1967
Gambia, The	Elizabeth II, queen	1952
	Alhaji Sir Farimang Singhateh, governor-general	1966
	Sir Dawda Jawara, prime minister	1965
Germany {Federal Rep.	Heinrich Lübke, president	1959
	Kurt Kiesinger, chancellor	1966
Germany {Dem. Rep.	Walter Ulbricht, first secretary of the Socialist Unity (Communist) Party of Germany (1946) and president	1960
	Willi Stoph, minister president	1964
Ghana	Gen. Joseph Ankrah, chairman of the National Liberation Council (1966) and of the Executive Council	1967
Greece	Constantine II, king	1964
	Georgios Papadopoulos, prime minister	1967
Guatemala	Julio César Méndez Montenegro, president	1966
Guinea	Sékou Touré, president	1958
Guyana	Elizabeth II, queen	1952
	Sir David J. E. Rose, governor-general	1966
	Forbes Burnham, prime minister	1966
Haiti	François Duvalier, president	1957
Honduras	Osvaldo López Arellano, president	1963
Hungary	Janos Kadar, first secretary of the Hungarian Socialist Workers' (Communist) Party	1956
	Pal Losonczi, president of the Presidential Council	1967
	Jeno Fock, president of the Council of Ministers	1967
Iceland	Kristjan Eldjarn, president	1968
	Bjarni Benediktsson, prime minister	1963
India	Zakir Husain, president	1967
	Mrs. Indira Gandhi, prime minister	1966
Indonesia	Suharto, president and prime minister	1968
Iran	Mohammad Reza Pahlavi, shah-in-shah	1941
	Amir Abbas Hoveida, prime minister	1965
Iraq	Ahmed Hassan al-Bakr, president and prime minister	1968
Ireland	Eamon de Valera, president	1959
	John Lynch, prime minister	1966
Israel	Schneor Zalman Shazar, president	1963
	Levi Eshkol, prime minister	1963
Italy	Giuseppe Saragat, president	1964
	Mariano Rumor, premier	1968
Ivory Coast	Félix Houphouët-Boigny, president and premier	1960
Jamaica	Elizabeth II, queen	1952
	Sir Clifford Campbell, governor-general	1962
	Hugh L. Shearer, prime minister	1967
Japan	Hirohito, emperor	1926
	Eisaku Sato, prime minister	1964
Jordan	Husain I, king	1952
	Bahjat al-Talhouni, prime minister	1967
Kenya	Jomo Kenyatta, president	1964
Korea {Rep.	Gen. Pak Chung Hi, president	1963
	Gen. Chung Il Kwon, prime minister	1964
Korea {Dem. People's Rep.	Marshal Kim Il Sung, secretary-general of the Korean Workers' (Communist) Party and chairman of the Council of Ministers	1948
	Choi Yong Kun, president	1964
Kuwait	Sheikh Sabah as-Salim as-Sabah, amir	1965
	Crown Prince Sheikh Jabir as-Ahmed as-Jabir as-Sabah, prime minister	1965
Laos	Savang Vatthana, king	1959
	Prince Souvanna Phouma, premier	1962
Lebanon	Charles Helou, president	1964
	Abdullah Yafi, prime minister	1968
Lesotho	Moshoeshoe II, chief of state	1966
	Leabua Jonathan, prime minister	1966
Liberia	William V. S. Tubman, president	1944
Libya	Idris I, king	1951
	Wanis al Gaddafi, prime minister	1968
Liechtenstein	Francis Joseph II, sovereign prince	1938
	Gerard Batliner, chief of government	1962
Luxembourg	Jean, grand duke	1964
	(no prime minister as of December 31)	
Malagasy Rep.	Philibert Tsiranana, president	1960
Malawi	H. Kamuzu Banda, president	1966
Malaysia	Tuanku Ismail Nasiruddin Shah ibni al-Marhum Sultan Zainal Abidin, yang di-pertuan agong	1965
	Tunku Abdul Rahman, prime minister	1963
Maldive Islands	Amir Muhammad Farid Didi, sultan	1948
	Ibrahim Nassir, president	1968
Mali	Capt. Yoro Diakité, head of military government	1968
Malta	Elizabeth II, queen	1952
	Sir Maurice Dorman, governor-general	1964
	George Borg Olivier, prime minister	1964
Mauritania	Mokhtar Ould Daddah, president and premier	1960
Mauritius	Elizabeth II, queen	1952
	Sir John Rennie, governor-general	1968
	Sir Seewoosagur Ramgoolam, prime minister	1968
Mexico	Gustavo Díaz Ordaz, president	1964
Monaco	Rainier III, prince	1949
	Jean Émile Reymond, minister of state	1963
Mongolia	Yumzhagiyin Tsedenbal, first secretary of the Mongolian People's Revolutionary (Communist) Party (1958) and chairman of the Council of Ministers	1952
	Zhamsarangibin Sambuu, chairman of the Presidium of the Great People's Khural	1962
Morocco	Hassan II, king	1961
	Muhammad Benhima, prime minister	1967
Nauru	Hammer de Roburt, president	1968
Nepal	Mahendra Bir Bikram Shah Deva, king	1955
	Surya Bahadur Thapa, chairman of the Council of Ministers (prime minister)	1965
Netherlands	Juliana, queen	1948
	Piet J. S. de Jong, prime minister	1967
New Zealand	Elizabeth II, queen	1952
	Sir Arthur Porritt, governor-general	1967
	Keith J. Holyoake, prime minister	1960
Nicaragua	Anastasio Somoza Debayle, president	1967
Niger	Hamani Diori, president and premier	1960
Nigeria	Yakubu Gowon, head of provisional military government	1966
Norway	Olav V, king	1957
	Per Borten, prime minister	1965
Pakistan	Field Marshal Muhammad Ayub Khan, president	1958
Panama	José Pinilla, provisional president	1968
Paraguay	Gen. Alfredo Stroessner, president	1954
Peru	Gen. Juan Velasco Alvarado, president of the military government	1968
Philippines	Ferdinand Marcos, president	1965
Poland	Wladyslaw Gomulka, first secretary of the Polish United Workers' (Communist) Party	1956
	Marian Spychalski, chairman of the Council of State	1968
	Jozef Cyrankiewicz, chairman of the Council of Ministers	1954
Portugal	Rear Adm. Américo Deus Rodrigues Tomás, president	1958
	Marcello José das Neves Alves Caetano, premier	1968
Rhodesia	Elizabeth II, queen	1952
	Sir Humphrey Gibbs, governor-general	1959
	Ian D. Smith, prime minister	1964
Romania	Nicolae Ceausescu, general secretary of the Romanian Communist Party (1965) and chairman of the State Council	1967
	Ion Gheorghe Maurer, chairman of the Council of Ministers	1961
Rwanda	Grégoire Kayibanda, president	1961
Saudi Arabia	Faisal ibn 'Abd al-'Aziz ibn 'Abd al-Rahman Al Sa'ud, king and prime minister	1964
Senegal	Léopold Sédar Senghor, president	1960
Sierra Leone	Elizabeth II, queen	1952
	Banja Tejan-Sie, acting governor-general	1968
	Siaka Stevens, prime minister	1968
Singapore	Inche Yusof bin Ishak, president	1965
	Lee Kuan Yew, prime minister	1965
Somali Rep.	Abd-i-Rashid Ali Shermarke, president	1967
	Muhammad Haji Ibrahim Egal, prime minister	1967
South Africa	Jacobus J. Fouché, president	1968
	Balthazar J. Vorster, prime minister	1966
Southern Yemen	Qahtan Muhammad al-Shaabi, president (1967) and prime minister	1968
Spain	Gen. Francisco Franco Bahamonde, chief of state and premier	1939
Sudan	Ismail al-Azhari, president of the Supreme Council	1965
	Muhammad Ahmed Mahgoub, prime minister	1967
Swaziland	Sobhuza II, king	1921
	Prince Makhosini Dlamini, prime minister	1968
Sweden	Gustaf VI Adolf, king	1950
	Tage Fritiof Erlander, prime minister	1946
Switzerland	Willy Spühler, president of the confederation	1967
Syria	Nureddin al-Attassi, chairman of the Presidency Council (1966) and premier	1968
Tanzania	Julius Nyerere, president	1964
Thailand	Bhumibol Adulyadej, king	1946
	Field Marshal Thanom Kittikachorn, prime minister	1963
Togo	Gen. Étienne Eyadema, president	1967
Trinidad and Tobago	Elizabeth II, queen	1952
	Sir Solomon Hochoy, governor-general	1962
	Eric Williams, prime minister	1962
Tunisia	Habib Bourguiba, president	1957
Turkey	Gen. Cevdet Sunay, president	1966
	Suleyman Demirel, prime minister	1965
Uganda	Milton Obote, president (1966) and prime minister	1962
U.S.S.R.	Leonid I. Brezhnev, general secretary of the Communist Party of the Soviet Union	1964
	Nikolai V. Podgorny, chairman of the Presidium of the Supreme Soviet	1965
	Aleksei N. Kosygin, chairman of the Council of Ministers	1964
United Arab Rep.	Gamal Abd-al-Nasser, president (1958) and prime minister	1967

Country	Name and office	Accession
United Kingdom	Elizabeth II, queen	1952
	Harold Wilson, prime minister	1964
United States	Lyndon B. Johnson, president	1963
Upper Volta	Gen. Sangoulé Lamizana,	
	president and premier	1966
Uruguay	Jorge Pacheco Areco, president	1967
Vatican City State	Paul VI, pope	1963
Venezuela	Rafael Caldera, president	1968
Vietnam Rep.	Nguyen Van Thieu, president	1967
	Tran Van Huong, premier	1968
Vietnam Dem. Rep.	Ho Chi Minh, president	1945
	Pham Van Dong, premier	1955
Western Samoa	Malietoa Tanumafili II, head of state	1965
	Fiame Mata'afa Faumuina Mulinu'u II,	
	prime minister	1962
Yemen Rep.	Qadi Abdul Rahman al-Iryani, president	1967
	Maj. Gen. Hassan al-Amri, premier	1967
Yemen Royalist	Muhammad al-Badr, imam	1962
	Sayf al-Islam al-Hassan, premier	1964
Yugoslavia	Marshal Tito, president of the republic	
	and secretary-general of the League	
	of Communists	1953
	Mika Spiljak, president of the	
	Federal Executive Council	1967
Zambia	Kenneth Kaunda, president	1964

Historical Studies

Congresses held during 1968 ranged from those concerned with wide areas and periods to highly specialized ones, such as the Colloque sur l'histoire de la Méditerranée de 1919 à 1939 at Nice, France, in March. Perhaps the most significant of these smaller gatherings was the first Anglo-Czechoslovak Conference of Historians, which contrived to meet in London and Oxford during September, despite the political crisis in Czechoslovakia. The steady increase in the output of books and articles was illustrated at the annual Anglo-American Conference in July, when more than 800 historical works issued during the previous 12 months in Great Britain alone were exhibited.

All the more welcome were selective guides such as *A Bibliography of Modern History*, prepared by J. Roach for the *New Cambridge Modern History*, and comprehensive bibliographies such as those provided by the Royal Historical Society for *Writings on British History, 1901–1933* (6 vol.). A big gap was filled by the complementary *Guide to the Historical and Archaeological Publications of the Societies of England and Wales, 1901–1933*, a massive volume compiled by E. L. C. Mullins.

A brilliant synthesis of many monographs on the Greek world from Mycenaean to Roman times was supplied by the French scholar Pierre Lévêque; it appeared in English under the title *The Greek Adventure*. An Italian scholar, Sabatino Moscati, contributed a volume on *The World of the Phoenicians* to an English series. Another series started with *Ancient Sicily to the Arab Conquest* by M. I. Finlay and *Medieval Sicily, 800–1713* by D. Mack Smith. The newest Cambridge series was *The Cambridge History of Iran*, vol. i and v of which appeared during the year. A valuable contribution on Byzantium was made by L.-P. Raybaud in *Le Gouvernement et l'Administration centrale de l'empire byzantin sous les premiers Paléologues*.

A useful French synthesis was provided by Jean Chélini, on *Histoire religieuse de l'Occident médiéval*. An English translation of a definitive work by Robert Latouche on the beginnings of France appeared under the title *Caesar to Charlemagne*. Marjorie Chibnall's edition of *The Ecclesiastical History of Orderic Vitalis* appeared in the new series of Oxford Medieval Texts. Other essential documents for the period were printed in the final volume of *Regesta Regum Anglo-Norman-*

norum, 1066–1154, edited by R. H. C. Davis and H. A. Cronne.

A well-known British politician, J. Enoch Powell, published *The House of Lords in the Middle Ages*, in collaboration with Keith Wallis. The best *History of Medieval Ireland* for many years was produced by A. Jocelyn Otway-Ruthven. A study in depth entitled *Barcelone, centre économique 1380–1462* (2 vol.) by Claude Carrère was an example of the new demographic approach. An important monograph, Ramón Carande's *Carlos V y sus Banqueros*, investigated the Spanish external debt, the function of the treasure ships from the New World, and the emperor's financial policy. For England during the same period the most significant publication was undoubtedly J. J. Scarisbrick's full-scale biography of *Henry VIII*.

Computers were successfully used by an American, Theodore K. Rabb, in his analysis of *Enterprise and Empire: Merchant and Gentry Investment in the Expansion of England, 1575–1630*. Using older methods, another American scholar, Carl Bridenbaugh, unearthed much hidden evidence on contemporary conditions in his *Vexed and Troubled Englishmen, 1590–1642*. An English publication on *The Enserfment of the Russian Peasantry* consisted of translated documents, ably edited by R. E. F. Smith.

Crane Brinton (*see* OBITUARIES) added to his numerous works a general study of *The Americans and the French*. D. T. Miller suggested that the Northern States exhibited growing social cleavages rather than egalitarian tendencies in his *Jacksonian Aristocracy: Class and Democracy in New England 1830–1860*. Woodrow Wilson continued to attract much attention; publications included further volumes of his *Papers*, edited by Arthur S. Link.

The first two volumes of a huge new edition of the works of the utilitarian philosopher contained *The Correspondence of Jeremy Bentham, 1752–1780*, edited by T. L. S. Sprigge. The youth and early career of another great Englishman were covered in *The Gladstone Diaries*, vol. i and ii, 1825–1839, edited by M. R. D. Foot, but these turned out to be disappointingly concise memoranda. A Canadian scholar, J. B. Conacher, skillfully handled *The Aberdeen Coalition, 1852–1855*.

A much more promising approach than had appeared in previous publications was shown in *The Oxford History of South Africa*, vol. i (to 1870), edited by M. Wilson and L. Thompson. Two first-rate monographs in this field were C. F. Goodfellow, *Great Britain and South African Confederation, 1820–1881*, and T. R. H. Davenport, *The Afrikaner Bond*.

A History of the World in the Twentieth Century by D. C. Watt, F. Spencer, and N. Brown had more bite than vol. xii of the *New Cambridge Modern History*, which dealt with *The Shifting Balance of World Forces, 1898–1945*. German scholars were still concentrating on the recent past. In *Das NS-Geschichtsbild und die Geschichtswissenschaft*, K. F. Werner examined the records of German historians confronted by Nazi doctrines. The various official series on World War II continued to appear, including a newcomer from the Vatican archives. (A. T. M.)

See also Literature.

ENCYCLOPÆDIA BRITANNICA FILMS. *India: Introduction to Its History* (1957); *Egypt: Cradle of Civilization* (1962); *The Mediterranean World* (1962); *Athens: The Golden Age* (Humanities Course) (1963); *Julius Caesar: Rise of the Roman Empire* (1964); *Life in Ancient Rome* (1964); *Middle Ages: Culture of Medieval Europe* (1965); *Middle Ages: Rise of Feudalism* (1965); *The Spirit of Rome* (1965).

Heart and Circulatory Diseases:
see Medicine

Hebrew Literature:
see Literature

Hematology:
see Medicine

Highways:
see Engineering Projects; Transportation

Hinduism:
see Religion

Historic Buildings

During 1968 increased anxiety was expressed in many parts of the world on the deterioration and loss of historic buildings and sites. Ironically, this was caused largely by the rise in the standard of living, particularly among urban populations. As the cost of land and labour rose, old, low structures were replaced by high-rise buildings. Furthermore, increased pollution of the atmosphere and water supplies accelerated the effects of weathering, particularly in older structures.

Worldwide interest in this problem was manifested in a number of ways. In March 1968, at the invitation of the director general of UNESCO, 55 member states sent experts and observers to take part in a meeting to review the Draft Recommendation on the Preservation of Cultural Property Endangered by Public and Private Works. It was felt that the greatest current threat to cultural property was posed by urban expansion and renewal, but highways, parking lots, and other forms of construction were also cited. Particular attention was drawn to the necessity of protecting historic quarters in urban or rural centres and groups of traditional structures by zoning, and it was agreed that this should be made an absolute requirement of any well-designed plan for urban redevelopment. The Draft Recommendation was submitted to the 15th session (October 1968) of the General Conference of UNESCO.

Among the outstanding monuments that were attracting interest as a result of problems involved in their preservation was the Parthenon. The dangers to which it had been exposed were cumulative in their effect. The foundation of tufa upon which it rests is of poor quality and had suffered some erosion. Constant exposure to diurnal and seasonal variations in temperature had caused the marble to spall in many places, and the effects of weathering had been accelerated by the growth of industrialization and resultant atmospheric pollution.

A great Buddhist monument, the Borobudur in Central Java, was also threatened. Its foundations had been weakened by infiltrating rain, and the carvings on andesite stone had been weathered by water and the growth of moss and lichens. In India anxiety was expressed about the state of the Taj Mahal, the foundations of which were gradually shifting toward the Jumna River. Recent checks had shown that the tilt of the four minarets had increased and that the cracks in the upper reaches of the dome were widening.

In Tokyo, the Imperial Hotel, designed by Frank Lloyd Wright, was dismantled during the winter of 1967-68, despite many protests. The decision was taken partly because of subsidence of the foundations and the poor condition of the building, but chiefly because restoration would have been expensive and because the hotel, situated on expensive urban land, had a low capacity for guests. However, its façade was being transferred to Meiji Village, an open-air museum near the city of Nagoya. One result of the campaign for its preservation was the decision to create a legal organization empowered to protect other notable buildings in Japan.

Some progress was recorded, however. UNESCO's International Campaign for Nubia was continued during 1967–68. Formal ceremonies on Sept. 22, 1968, marked the successful transfer of the temples of Abu Simbel, threatened by flooding from the Aswan High

Workers demolishing the Imperial Hotel in Tokyo during January 1968. The famed landmark was designed by Frank Lloyd Wright and construction began in 1916.

Dam, to cliffs above the Nile River. The salvage operations had cost $36 million, of which $15.5 million was budgeted by the U.A.R. The largest foreign contribution ($12 million from the government, $1 million from private sources) came from the U.S. Still remaining to be salvaged in the Nile Valley were the temples of Philae.

The City of London Corporation, faced with having to replace London Bridge because it was too narrow and was slowly sinking into the Thames mud, sold the historic structure to the McCulloch Oil Corp. of Los Angeles. The bridge, built in 1831, was being dismantled brick by brick and brought to the U.S., where it would be reassembled at Lake Havasu City, Ariz., a resort and retirement community developed by McCulloch.

In connection with the International Campaign for Florence and Venice, UNESCO began a study of the different problems involved in saving the monuments of the latter city. These included changes taking place in the lagoon, overall dampness of monuments resulting from subsidence and penetration of water through capillary action, weathering of stone and masonry, and the necessity of finding a satisfactory role for the ancient island city.

As part of the overall development of tourism, the Brazilian government, with the cooperation of

Columns of the Parthenon in Athens are in danger of collapsing as a result of weathering and erosion of the foundation.

UNESCO, was planning a program for the conservation of some of its cities with historically interesting quarters. Among these were Salvador da Bahia, with its hundreds of churches built in the Baroque style of the early 18th century, and Ouro Preto, formerly a wealthy mining town. The historic quarters of these cities, which once contained the homes of the upper classes, had turned into run-down, overcrowded slums. The program was designed to ensure their restoration and revitalization.

In Vienne, France, archaeologists discovered an important Roman site including villas, a tannery, a dyeing factory, and fragments of a highway. The site was classified and would be protected by the government. Also in France, the great Baroque château of Vaux-le-Vicomte was opened to the public. The architect of the château was Louis le Vau, the interior had been decorated by Charles le Brun, and the gardens designed by André le Nôtre. In disrepair for decades, the château had been carefully restored by the family that was its current proprietor.

In England, as in France, a Roman site attracted particular attention. Excavations were largely completed at Fishbourne, Chichester, of a large villa, believed to have been built for a British king—probably Cogidumnus—by the Romans. With the aid of a substantial grant from *The Sunday Times,* a museum was created on the site, containing models of the villa and its appurtenances and giving a picture of life among the aristocracy of Roman Britain.

Under the sponsorship of UNESCO, a meeting of experts was held at Pistoia, Italy, during September to examine the problem of training the architect/restorers and technicians responsible for conservation. The experts deplored the general tendency among architectural schools to reduce training in historical architecture and the lack of current information on old building practices and techniques.

Other aspects of the problem of preservation were discussed in a series of meetings organized by the International Council of Monuments and Sites (ICOMOS). Among these were the preservation of historic quarters and their adaptation to contemporary requirements, the problems of controlling humidity in old buildings, and the development of worldwide inventory standards. (H. Du.)

See also Museums and Galleries.

Hockey

Field Hockey. Talk and attention, action and assessment in 1968 in each country were of and for and about its team for the Olympic Games. This preoccupation was intensified in Great Britain by the upheaval that put a new manager, G. M. Cutter, and a new trainer, S. J. Wigmore, in charge of the team. Under their direction the British team began to make rapid improvement and won two of its last three international contests before leaving for the Olympics.

Pakistan repeated its 1960 performance by triumphing in the hockey competition at the Olympics; the Pakistanis achieved nine consecutive victories and scored 26 goals to their opponents' 5. In the final match they defeated second-place Australia 2–1. India, which had won the Olympic gold medal in the 1964 Games, finished third with a record of seven wins and two losses. They won third place by defeating West Germany 2–1. The latter country placed fourth and was followed, in order, by the Netherlands, Spain, New Zealand, Kenya, Belgium, and France. The U.K. team did not live up to advance expectations and finished with a disappointing two victories against five losses and one tie.

The international championship of the four Home Countries was won by Ireland, which beat Scotland and Wales and tied England. Scotland's only win was against Wales, and England had the remarkably undistinguished record of playing three goalless draws.

The International Hockey Federation, which was strongly represented on the International Hockey Rules Board, appointed a subcommittee to study ways and means of improving the rules so as to make the game "more clear, more interesting and more enjoyable." This subcommittee made suggestions which the federation asked member countries to experiment with and report on. One of these experimental rules involved re-marking the pitch with two 35-yd. lines and a centre spot, replacing the current 25-yd. and centre lines.

The Hockey Association, controlling body of the game in England, had in 1968 to wrestle with the problems of an expanding game in a world of rising prices and the effect of intensified international competition. Instead of cutting costs by restricting activity, the association decided to increase income by increasing the annual subscription payable to it by affiliated clubs. At the same time, improved organization enabled the association to cut losses without sacrificing efficiency, and this was especially the case in the expensive field of international match promotion. Arising out of this was the decision to plan an international contest on the second to last Saturday

Above, Hautefort castle, built in 1644 in Périgord, France, as restored by the widow of its last owner, Baron de Bastard. Five days before its dedication was scheduled in 1968, the castle was destroyed by fire, right.

of March each year at Lord's Cricket Ground. A match between Great Britain (which won 1–0) and Belgium was staged there in April and produced a net profit of more than £1,000.

Rising world standards and intensified competition created a demand that England should fall into line and make its hockey more competitive. The response from the Hockey Association was positive, if not enthusiastic. It did not launch any competitions itself but left the way open for others by relaxing Rule 14, which banned all challenge cups and prize competitions without the consent of its council. The rule still stood but the consent which made it inoperative could be had virtually for the asking. As a result, more counties began to arrange championships for their clubs.

The England women's team continued their winning record in 1968. In the Home Countries' international championship they won three matches out of three by an aggregate of 9 goals to 1, and in the annual match at Wembley Stadium they defeated the Netherlands 1–0. At the end of the 1968 season they had played 15 successive international matches without defeat.

In June the code of rules sanctioned by the Women's International Hockey Rules Board was adopted by women's hockey associations throughout the world. Previously the game in the Home Countries had been played under the rules of the Women's Hockey Board of Great Britain and Ireland. The change to the new code involved relatively minor adjustments and had the great advantage that it enjoyed worldwide acceptance.   (R. L. Hs.)

Amateur Ice Hockey. The world and European titles were retained by the U.S.S.R. at Grenoble, France, on February 6–17. The championships were decided concurrently with the Olympic Games competition. It was the sixth successive Soviet victory, a feat only equaled by Canada in 1932, and it was the tenth European title for a Soviet team, five more than the next highest number of wins, by Sweden. Czechoslovakia finished second, and Canada third.

The championships were contested by eight nations, each playing the other seven once. The new stadium had an official capacity of 11,500, but this figure was appreciably exceeded at many of the games. After first trouncing Finland 8–0 and East Germany 9–0, the Soviet players appeared to be invincible supermen until Don Ross of the U.S. achieved the distinction of scoring the first goal against them, though the U.S.S.R. still won 10–2. When Sweden lost only 2–3 to them, it seemed that the Soviet team might be fallible after all—and so it proved when Czechoslovakia beat them 5–4. The U.S.S.R. won the title as a result of Canada's 3–2 victory over Czechoslovakia.

A.F.P. FROM PICTORIAL PARADE

Czechoslovak hockey team forming a defensive wall in front of their goal during their 5–4 upset victory over the Soviet Union in the 1968 Winter Olympics.

The Soviets conceded 10 goals while scoring 48 in their seven matches.

The six outstanding players in Grenoble were goalkeeper Ken Broderick (Can.), defensemen Jan Suchy (Czech.) and Lennart Svedberg (Swed.), and forwards Frantisek Sevcik (Czech.), Francis Huck (Can.), and Anatoli Firsov (U.S.S.R.).

A secondary competition, comprising another six nations, was won by Yugoslavia during the same period at Grenoble. As runner-up, Japan continued to reflect its rapid improvement of recent years.

A proposed intercontinental league tournament was discussed at a meeting of the International Ice Hockey Federation in Geneva. The Canadians suggested that the league be formed by the national teams of Sweden, Czechoslovakia, the U.S.S.R., Canada, and the United States, but A. H. Ahearne, British president of the federation's European section, insisted that the league should comprise the club champions from each nation.
                                    (H. B.)

Professional Ice Hockey. The Montreal Canadiens won their third Stanley Cup in four seasons in a runaway dominance of the National Hockey League (NHL). The Canadiens lost only 1 of their 13 playoff games, successively dismissing the Boston Bruins, the Chicago Black Hawks, and the St. Louis Blues. Montreal's championship was the first in the expanded NHL. The Canadiens finished first in the Eastern Division, and then beat the Bruins in four games and the Black Hawks in five.

St. Louis finished third in the Western Division, three points behind the first-place Philadelphia Flyers. The Blues, strongly supported by goalkeeper Glenn Hall, qualified for the Stanley Cup final by winning post-season series against Philadelphia and the Minnesota North Stars.

Each game in the Stanley Cup final was close, but the Canadiens won four in a row—3–2, 1–0, 4–3, and 3–2. Hall, a 15-year NHL veteran, was awarded the Conn Smythe Trophy as the outstanding performer in the play-offs.

Stan Mikita, the nimble Chicago centre, was the outstanding player of the season, winning the Art Ross Trophy, the Lady Byng Trophy, and the Hart Trophy, all three for the second consecutive year. Mikita won the Ross as the NHL's leading scorer with 40 goals and 47 assists. He was voted the Byng as the player best uniting playing skill with exemplary behaviour, and he won the Hart as the league's most valuable athlete.

Mikita was also picked by NHL coaches as the

NHL Final Standings

	Won	Lost	Tied	Goals	Goals against	Pts.
EASTERN DIVISION						
Montreal Canadiens	42	22	10	236	167	94
New York Rangers	39	23	12	226	183	90
Boston Bruins	37	27	10	259	216	84
Chicago Black Hawks	32	26	16	212	222	80
Toronto Maple Leafs	33	31	10	209	176	76
Detroit Red Wings	27	35	12	245	257	66
WESTERN DIVISION						
Philadelphia Flyers	31	32	11	173	179	73
Los Angeles Kings	31	33	10	200	224	72
St. Louis Blues	27	31	16	177	191	70
Minnesota North Stars	27	32	15	191	226	69
Pittsburgh Penguins	27	34	13	195	216	67
Oakland Seals	15	42	17	153	219	47

all-star centre for the sixth time. The all-star vote indicated a preference for players in the older division, not one man from the expansion section being named to either the first or second team. The first team included: goalie, Lorne ("Gump") Worsley (Montreal); defense, Bobby Orr (Boston) and Tim Horton (Toronto); centre, Mikita; right wing, Gordie Howe (Detroit); left wing, Bobby Hull (Chicago). On the second team were: goalie, Ed Giacomin (New York); defense, Jim Neilson (New York) and J. C.

WIDE WORLD

Dick Duff (8) of the Montreal Canadiens firing puck into net as St. Louis Blues goalie Glenn Hall watches. Montreal won 3–2, taking their third Stanley Cup in four seasons.

Tremblay (Montreal); centre, Phil Esposito (Boston); right wing, Rod Gilbert (New York); left wing, John Bucyk (Boston).

Orr, the precocious Boston sophomore, won the James Norris Trophy as the commanding defenseman in hockey. Worsley, a long-time veteran, and young Rogatien Vachon of Montreal shared the Vezina Trophy as goalies for the team allowing the fewest number of goals. Derek Sanderson, a combative Boston centre, received the Calder Trophy as rookie of the year.

The league expansion program was a success everywhere except in Pittsburgh and Oakland, where attendance fluctuated from modest to poor. Both clubs required a transfusion of fresh money from new owners to guarantee their stability for the 1968–69 season.

The NHL was sobered by the first death of a player in a game in the league's 51-year history. Bill Masterton, a 29-year-old centre with the Minnesota North Stars, died after striking his head on the ice during a match against Oakland.

The Rochester Americans won the Calder Cup as champions of the American Hockey League, beating the Quebec Aces four games to two in the final. The Seattle Totems easily subdued the Portland (Ore.) Buckaroos four games to one for the championship of the Western League. By winning four straight games from the Fort Worth Wings, the Tulsa Oilers captured the Jack Adams Trophy, symbolic of supremacy in the Central Pro League.   (R. H. BE.)

Hogs:
see Agriculture

Holland:
see Netherlands

Home Economics:
see Domestic Arts and Sciences

Honduras

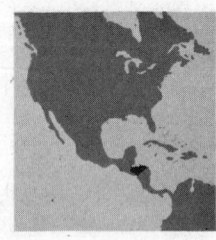

A republic of Central America, Honduras is bounded by Nicaragua, El Salvador, Guatemala, the Caribbean Sea, and the Pacific Ocean. Area: 43,277 sq.mi. (112,088 sq.km.). Pop. (1968 est.): 2,532,042, of which 87% is mestizo. Cap. and largest city: Tegucigalpa (pop., 1968 est., 205,829). Language: Spanish; some Indian dialects. Religion: Roman Catholic. President in 1968, Osvaldo López Arellano.

The incumbent conservative Nationalist Party continued in power, and Osvaldo López Arellano entered his sixth year as chief of state and his fourth as the nation's elected president. In March, amid charges of widespread fraud, personal threats, and some reports of persons killed, the first nationwide elections since the new constitution of 1965 were held. At stake were 281 municipal offices, in which the principal opposition party, the Liberals, hoped to make considerable gains. The Nationalists, however, won 246 posts. The Liberals won 35, primarily in the large towns of the north coast including San Pedro Sula, the nation's second city.

Relations with neighbouring republics were relatively stable except for disputes with El Salvador. Again, as in past years, the unresolved border demarcation between the two countries was the source of friction. In July at the El Salvador meeting of the Organization of Central American States (ODECA) the presidents of Honduras and El Salvador agreed,

HONDURAS

Education. (1965) Primary, pupils 283,606, teachers 9,862; secondary, pupils 17,980; vocational, pupils 2,450; teacher training, students 3,554; secondary, vocational, and teacher training, teachers (1964) 2,079; higher, students 2,578, teaching staff (1963) 302.

Finance. Monetary unit: lempira, with a par value of 2 lempiras to U.S. $1 (4.80 lempiras = £1 sterling). Gold and foreign exchange, central bank: (June 1968) U.S. $33,390,000; (June 1967) U.S. $31,670,000. Budget (1968 est.) balanced at 196.1 million lempiras. Gross national product: (1967) 1,152,000,000 lempiras; (1966) 1,090,000,000 lempiras. Money supply: (June 1968) 131,890,000 lempiras; (June 1967) 115.4 million lempiras. Cost of living (Tegucigalpa; 1963 = 100): (May 1968) 120; (May 1967) 112.

Foreign Trade. Imports (1967) 328.9 million lempiras; exports 310.5 million lempiras. Import sources (1966): U.S. 49%; El Salvador 11%; Guatemala 7%; West Germany 5%. Export destinations (1966): U.S. 56%; West Germany 15%; El Salvador 7%. Main exports (1966): bananas 51%; coffee 14%; timber 7%.

Transport and Communications. Roads (1964) 3,347 km. (including 367 km. paved). Motor vehicles in use (1966): passenger 11,800; commercial (including buses) 8,700. Railways (1963) 1,152 km. (confined to northern plantation area). Shipping (1967): merchant vessels 100 gross tons and over 45; gross tonnage 74,586. Air traffic (1966): 79,187,000 passenger-km.; freight 6,877,000 net ton-km. Telephones (Jan. 1967) 9,859. Radio receivers (Dec. 1965) 135,000. Television receivers (Dec. 1966) c. 10,000.

Agriculture. Production (in 000; metric tons; 1966; 1965 in parentheses): corn c. 285 (356); rice c. 28 (27); coffee c. 20 (35); sugar, raw value (1967–68) c. 53, (1966–67) 49; dry beans c. 51 (49); bananas 1,000 (1,090); cottonseed 19 (20); timber (1965) 3,800 cu.m., (1964) 3,700 cu.m. Livestock (in 000; 1965–66): cattle 1,720; pigs c. 901; chickens 5,850.

Industry. Production (in 000; metric tons; 1966): lead ore (metal content; exports) 8.6; zinc ore (metal content; exports) 10.8; silver (exports) 0.12; gold (exports) 3.9 troy oz.; electricity 204,000 kw-hr.

reluctantly, to an exchange of nationals each had been holding because of alleged border violations.

Honduras began to recover slowly from the adverse economic conditions of 1967, when economic indicators showed a growth rate at or below zero. This rate—lowest of any of the Central American republics—combined with a highly critical public report on government inefficiencies, forced the government to initiate or increase efforts in the realms of planning, agrarian reform, and transportation, and to make administrative changes in the government agencies involved in those three realms. As an outgrowth of these 1967 events, efforts were being made to build a proposed industrial complex on the Aguán River in northern Honduras, 30 mi. inland from the port of La Ceiba. The investment funds for the complex, estimated at $72.5 million, were to be used for enlargement of port facilities at La Ceiba, road construction, and the building of an integrated lumber and paper mill. Operation of the latter was to be by Pulpapel, a company organization in Honduras set up for that purpose. Adela, a consortium formed by many nations for investment throughout Latin America, committed itself for a $3.5 million share in Pulpapel. Pulpapel was regarded as an important venture in the greater development of the substantial and varied forest resources of Honduras, which remained largely unsurveyed and often difficult to reach.

The National Agrarian Institute, in conjunction with the National Planning Council, promised substantive action in agrarian reform activities, which had been largely stagnant. This action was to involve both the acquisition of unexploited large landholdings for distribution either through expropriated or negotiated sale and the colonization of new lands in the public domain. The Aguán Valley was designated as the site of one such effort, which involved the settlement of approximately 3,000 families organized into farmer cooperatives on banana lands.

Efforts to extend and improve Honduran transportation continued, aided indirectly by the United States' $30 million loan to the Central American Fund for Economic Integration, which was to be used specifically for the development of regional transport and telecommunications systems. Other financing for road construction was obtained through a loan in 1967 from the World Bank. These funds were used in 1968 to continue paving the 154-mi. Western Highway from Puerto Cortés on the north coast via San Pedro Sula and Santa Rosa de Copán to the Salvadorean border. By the end of 1968 only the portion between Puerto Cortés and a point a few miles south of San Pedro Sula had been paved.

(A. D. Bu.)

Horse Racing

Thoroughbred Racing. *U.S.* Scandal and suspicion struck at the heart of U.S. Thoroughbred racing in 1968 when urine samples from Dancer's Image, taken minutes after the Peter Fuller-owned colt had won the Kentucky Derby, were found to contain traces of the drug phenylbutazone, an anti-inflammatory agent. Upon receiving the report from the Kentucky Racing Commission chemist, the track stewards made the first disqualification in the 94 years the Kentucky Derby had been run as the country's number one horse race.

Dancer's Image, a son of Native Dancer, won the Derby by 1½ lengths from Calumet Farm's Forward Pass, a Kentucky-bred colt, on May 4. Then, on May 7, the track officials announced the results of the urine tests and disqualified Dancer's Image; Forward Pass, which had placed second, thus became the winner. Fuller, a millionaire Boston auto dealer, appealed the track stewards' ruling to the Kentucky Racing Commission, which opened a hearing on the case on November 19. After 3½ weeks of testimony the commission decided that Dancer's Image was the official Derby winner but withheld the first-place purse money. As the year ended Fuller appealed to civil court for the purse money, which was being held in escrow pending the outcome of the case.

In U.S. racing 1968 was also the year of the girl jockeys despite the fact that neither Kathy Kusner nor Penny Ann Early, granted jockey's licenses in Maryland and Kentucky, respectively, got to the post in actual competition. Miss Kusner, a member of the U.S. Olympic Games equestrian team for several years, established a precedent when she became the first woman to receive a jockey's license. She was, however, injured in a horse show in Madison Square Garden and would not be able to start her racing career until she recovered from a broken leg.

The state of Kentucky licensed Miss Early, who had had experience as an exercise girl, to ride professionally. Her plans to ride in several races at Churchill Downs were foiled, however, when male jockeys boycotted the races in which she was scheduled to ride.

That Pennsylvania would become the 28th state in the U.S. to present Thoroughbred racing with parimutuel wagering was assured for 1969. The newly appointed state racing commission granted franchises to four associations hopeful of building tracks.

Perhaps vindicating the Churchill Downs stewards, who had moved him into the win position in the Kentucky Derby by disqualifying Dancer's Image, Forward Pass galloped to victory by six lengths in the Preakness Stakes, second race of the U.S. "Triple Crown" for three-year-olds, held in Baltimore two weeks later. Dancer's Image, under heavy guard to prevent a second dose of illegal medication, finished third in the race.

The Preakness was the final start for Dancer's Image. The horse was moved to New York for the Belmont Stakes, but the weak foreankles that had plagued him throughout his career gave way three days before that final classic of the Triple Crown, and he was retired to stud.

A new face in the competition for three-year-old supremacy appeared in the Belmont Stakes, when Greentree Stable's Stage Door Johnny upset Forward Pass with a 1¼-length victory. Stage Door Johnny made only two starts after the Belmont, the Saranac and Dwyer Handicaps, but won both of them, and that was enough to earn the colt the three-year-old championship in all year-end polls. Trained by John Gaver, Stage Door Johnny won five of six starts and earned $221,765 before suffering a bowed tendon at Saratoga in late July. He, too, was then retired to stud in Kentucky.

While the leading three-year-old colts were taking turns defeating each other, Dr. Fager, owned by the Tartan Stable, steadily worked his way to the 1968 horse-of-the-year title, far in front of Mrs. Edith Bancroft's Damascus, which had beaten him in the previous year's poll. Capturing the handicap, grass, and sprint championships in addition to the horse-of-the-year title, Florida-bred Dr. Fager was the odds-on favourite in seven of his eight races. He never carried

UPI COMPIX

Dancer's Image crossing the finish line first in the 1968 Kentucky Derby. Dancer's Image was disqualified when a urinalysis revealed the presence of the drug phenylbutazone, but the Kentucky Racing Commission later ruled him the winner.

Honduras, British: *see* Dependent States
Hong Kong: *see* Dependent States

"Harness Horse
of the Year" Nevele
Pride, driven by Stanley
Dancer, leading
in the first heat
of the Hambletonian
at Du Quoin, Ill.,
Aug. 26, 1968.

less than 130 lb. and ran all the distances from 7 furlongs to 1¼ mi. in all kinds of weather. Only once during the year did Dr. Fager let down his loyal legions, his lone reversal coming in the Brooklyn Handicap at Aqueduct. In that race he carried 135 lb. and placed second to Damascus, which carried five pounds less.

Although as sound at the end of the year as he was at the beginning, Dr. Fager was retired to stud after being syndicated for a projected value of $3.2 million. In his three seasons of racing, he started 22 times, won 18, was second twice and third once. His track earnings at retirement amounted to $1,002,642.

Damascus, which also earned more than $1 million, bowed a tendon in November and was retired to stud.

Dr. Fager and Damascus were invited to represent the U.S. as a team in the $150,000 Washington, D.C., International turf classic at Laurel (Md.) Race Course on November 11, but neither appeared. Sir Ivor, champion three-year-old of Europe, owned by Raymond Guest, former U.S. ambassador to Ireland, was flown from Ireland to become the first winner of the English Derby to win the International.

In the combined poll of the *Morning Telegraph* and *Daily Racing Form,* the other U.S. champion horses of 1968 were: best two-year-old colt or gelding, Top Knight, owned by Steven B. Wilson and winner of 5 of 9 races and $325,954; best two-year-old filly, Gallant Bloom, owned by Robert J. Kleberg, Jr.'s King Ranch and winner of 6 of 10 starts and $231,400; best three-year-old filly, Dark Mirage, owned by Lloyd L. Miller, winner of 9 of 10 starts and $322,432; best handicap filly or mare, Gamely, owned by William Haggin Perry, winner of 7 of 14 starts and $282,742; and best steeplechase horse, Bon Nouvel, owned by Mrs. T. A. Randolph, winner of 5 of 15 races and $41,869.

Among turf personnel three veteran titleholders and two newcomers to championship status topped the 1968 North American racing statistics. One of the new champions was jockey Angel Cordero, Jr., of Puerto Rico, who took race-winning honours with a total of 345 victories. The other first-time titleholder was Jack Berg, the leading trainer in number of races won with 256. Championships were, however, far from new to the other three divisional leaders: Marion Van Berg, who swept honours among owners in both money and races won (338 wins and $1,106,503); Eddie Neloy, top money-winning trainer with $1,233,101; and Braulio Baeza, leading jockey in money won ($2,835,108).   (W. B.)

Canada. Two notable occurrences highlighted the 1968 Thoroughbred season in Canada: Sunday racing was legalized in Ontario, and Northern Dancer's first crop of two-year-old runners appeared on the race courses.

Northern Dancer, bred and owned by Mr. and Mrs. E. P. Taylor of Toronto, became one of Canada's "folk heroes" in 1964 when he invaded the United States and won both the Kentucky Derby and the Preakness Stakes. He was the first Canadian-bred horse to capture any of the U.S. Triple Crown events. When Northern Dancer was retired to breeding duty at the National Stud Farm, Oshawa, Ont., in 1964, Canadian Thoroughbred fanciers eagerly awaited the public appearance of his progeny. Northern Dancer's first offspring became two-year-olds in 1968, and some of their successes verged on the spectacular.

Viceregal, the most outstanding son of Northern Dancer, racked up a record of eight consecutive wins against no defeats. His purse winnings totaled $117,-649, a single-season record for Canadian tracks. Seldom in the history of Canadian racing had a two-year-old dominated the scene with such complete authority.

Canada's three-year-olds were plagued by injuries, and there was no clearly established champion in that division. Merger, a western-bred colt, owned by Max Bell of Calgary, Alta., and Frank M. McMahon of Vancouver, B.C., won the 109th running of the Queen's Plate at Toronto's Woodbine in June. This was only the second time that an invader from western Canada had won North America's oldest annually contested Thoroughbred fixture.

Merger began to bow a tendon after his Queen's Plate triumph, and he was retired. With Merger out of the way, Rouletabille, owned by Jean-Louis Levesque of Montreal, won the Prince of Wales Stakes at Fort Erie, Ont. Rouletabille also suffered an injury, however, and, when the third of Canada's three-year-old "Triple Crown" events, the Breeders' Stakes, was raced at Woodbine in October, it was won by No Parando, owned by Frank Sherman of Hamilton, Ont.   (JA. Co.)

Europe and Australia. National Hunt racing in England in 1967–68 was halted in midseason when competition in Britain was canceled on Nov. 28, 1967, as a result of an unusually severe foot-and-mouth disease epidemic. Officials did not begin to lift the ban until January, and in the meantime the King George VI Steeplechase had to be given up. The day before the ban came into force Rondetto won the Hennessy Gold Cup at Newbury, from Stalbridge Colonist. In spite of encouraging reports, the great Irish steeplechaser Arkle, who had broken a bone in his hoof the previous season, did not race, and it was finally announced in October 1968 that he would be retired. Among his triumphs Arkle had won the Cheltenham Gold Cup three times. At Cheltenham in March the Champion Hurdle was won by Persian War (who had narrowly beaten Major Rose in the Schweppes Gold Trophy at Newbury in February), and the Gold Cup by the Irish horse Fort Leney. At

Sandown Park in April, Larbawn won the Whitbread Gold Cup from Fort Leney; and the Grand National Steeplechase at Aintree was won by Red Alligator by 20 lengths from Moidore's Token and Different Class. In Paris Haroué won the Grand Steeplechase de Paris at Auteuil, while Orvilliers won the Grande Course de Haies d'Auteuil from Biriatu and Persian War.

In flat racing in England the name of Sir Ivor, voted the nation's horse of the year, was on everyone's tongue. U.S.-bred (by Sir Gaylord out of a Hyperion mare), trained in Ireland by Vincent O'Brien, and ridden by Lester Piggott, he took the Two Thousand Guineas (from Petingo and Jimmy Reppin) and the English Derby (from Connaught and Mount Athos) almost effortlessly. In July, however, Sir Ivor lost the Irish Derby to Ribero, ridden by Piggott, and a week later was again defeated in a terrific battle for the Eclipse Stakes at Sandown Park by Royal Palace. Beaten by U.S.-owned, English-bred, and French-trained Vaguely Noble, who proved himself to be clearly the best colt in Europe, Sir Ivor was nevertheless well clear of the rest of the big field in the Prix de l'Arc de Triomphe at Longchamp, Paris, in October. A fortnight later he turned out at Newmarket to win the 1¼-mi. Champion Stakes, and he climaxed the season by triumphing in the Washington, D.C., International in November.

Another outstanding British horse during the year was H. Joel's Royal Palace. After a setback late in the previous season, he won all his 1968 races, including the Coronation Stakes at Sandown, the Coronation Cup at Epsom, the Eclipse Stakes, and the King George VI and Queen Elizabeth Stakes at Ascot. At Ascot he broke down in the final furlong and was retired after that victory.

In the Gold Cup at Ascot French horses, Pardallo II, Samos III, and Petrone, finished first, second, and third, respectively. Because of the strikes and unrest in France at the end of May, the French equivalent of the Gold Cup, the Prix du Cadran, could not be run. A French filly, La Lagune, took the Oaks, and the One Thousand Guineas, which went to Caergwrle, was the only English classic won by an English-bred horse. U.S.-bred Ribero gave Charles Engelhard the pleasure of seeing a colt of his win the St. Leger for the third time.

In France Zeddaan won the Poule d'Essai des Poulains, and Pola Bella, the Poule d'Essai des Pouliches (French Two Thousand and One Thousand Guineas, respectively); Tapalque won the Prix du Jockey Club (Derby); Roselière, the Prix de Diane (Oaks) and later the Prix Vermeille; and Dhaudevi, the Prix Royal Oak (St. Leger) as well as the Grand Prix de Paris; Yelapa won the Grand Criterium for two-year-olds. There were two notable English successes in France: Queen Elizabeth II's Hopeful Venture in the Grand Prix de Saint-Cloud and Folle Rousse in the Prix Robert Papin. In Ireland the Two Thousand and One Thousand Guineas went to Mistigo and the English filly Front Row, respectively, the Oaks to Celina, and the St. Leger to Giolla Mear. The Italian Derby was won by Hogarth, and the Gran Premio del Jockey Club and the Premio Roma both by the English horse Chicago. The German Derby went to Elviro. In Australia the 2-mi. Melbourne Cup was won by the four-year-old South Australian horse Rain Lover, in the record time of 3 min. 18.6 sec.

Piggott was champion jockey in Britain for the sixth time, with 139 winners. At the end of the season there, the 81-year-old trainer Capt. Cecil Boyd-Rochfort, who had won every classic including six St. Legers, and the Australian jockey A. Breasley retired after outstanding careers. (R. M. GN.)

Harness Racing. Record-shattering horses—and the men who trained and drove them—made 1968 an exciting and eventful harness-racing year. Both horses and men rewrote the standards of the sport.

Nevele Pride, harness horse of the year, swept the "Triple Crown" and "Big Five" for trotting three-year-olds and won more money in a single season—almost $500,000—than any other harness horse in history. His "Triple Crown" victories in the $116,190 Hambletonian, $150,000 Yonkers Futurity, and $57,398 Kentucky Futurity, and triumphs in the additional $100,000 Colonial and $166,746 Dexter Cup to make up the Big Five, were the most rewarding financially; however, Nevele Pride's most outstanding performance came in the $34,738 Horseman Futurity at Indianapolis, Ind., where he set a double world record with miles in 1 min. 56⅗ sec. and 1 min. 57⅖ sec. They were the fastest one and two heats ever trotted by a three-year-old. He also set a world mark for the mile on half-mile tracks, winning in 2 min. 1 sec. at Saratoga, N.Y. Trainer Stanley Dancer drove him in all of his victories.

Cardigan Bay, the 12-year-old pacing star from New Zealand, also trained and driven by Dancer, became the first harness horse ever to win $1 million. He reached that amount by winning a $15,000 special at Freehold Raceway in New Jersey on September 14 and was promptly retired by Dancer.

Best of All, a four-year-old pacer, moved up to third in all-time standings behind Bret Hanover and the immortal Dan Patch on the measuring stick of extreme speed production, the total number of miles paced in 2 min. or faster. Best of All boosted his total to 25, just 6 short of the record.

Laverne Hanover, a brilliant two-year-old pacer, won 22 of 23 races and was hailed as the coming superstar of the sport. His victories included a mile in 1 min. 59⅘ sec. over the half-mile track at Saratoga—the first time a juvenile of either gait ever ran that distance in less than 2 min. on that size track.

Bill Haughton, the driving champion who raced Laverne Hanover, also campaigned the sport's best three-year-old pacer, Rum Customer. This colt, modestly regarded when the season began, swept the "Triple Crown" of pacing, the $150,000 Cane Futurity, $104,226 Little Brown Jug, and $189,018 Messenger Stakes (richest race in the history of harness racing). He ran the fastest pacing mile at 1 min. 56 sec.

Haughton and Dancer, as usual, were the national leaders among drivers in money won, finishing as the top pair in the U.S. for the seventh consecutive year. Haughton, in leading all world drivers for the 12th time in this department, personally accounted for purses totaling approximately $1.5 million, eclipsing his own record set in 1957. Dancer, meanwhile, won an incredible 40% of all races in which he drove.

International competition again added zest to the U.S. scene. Yonkers Raceway's three-race international pacing series in the spring was swept by Cardinal King, a New Zealand import, but Yonkers' international trotting events went to U.S. horses, Carlisle and Earl Laird. The $100,000 Roosevelt International for trotters was captured for the second straight year by the French mare Roquépine. (ST. F. B.)

Glamour horse of the Australian season was the pacer Halwes (by U.S. sire Nephew Hal), winner of the Miracle Mile in Sydney and a host of valuable

Forward Pass leading on his way to winning the Preakness at Pimlico on May 18. Second was Out of the Way, left.

races. He collected more than $48,000 in prize money for the season. Top trotting horse was Intangible Command, the leading trotter money winner and Trotting Cup winner. The Sydney Pacers' Derby was won by visiting New Zealand colt Cardinal Garrison, while Adios Bear won both the Victoria and New South Wales trotting derbys.

The Inter-Dominion Championships for Australian and New Zealand horses were held in Auckland. The pacers' final was won by the Australian First Lee, while the trotters' section was taken by the New Zealand horse Stylish Major. The New Zealand Pacers' Derby was won by Good Chase, while Great Adios won the New Zealand Cup of 2 mi.

In Britain the National Pacing Derby was won by Eastwood from Royal Gem and Thunderbolt, all being British-bred. The Trotters' Derby went to Miss Hodgen and the Prestatyn Futurity to Red Sails. The Trotters' Futurity was won by the filly Zia Verna. The U.K. Trotting Association's two-year-old classic was taken by Thunder's Boy.

Top Scandinavian horse was Kentucky Fibber, winner of the Scandinavian Championship at Charlottenlund, Denmark, and second to Roquépine in the Roosevelt International World Trotting Championship. The $54,885 (richest ever) Swedish Derby at Malmö was won by Björn. The Danish Trotting Derby of $15,000 produced a season's "find" in Karina Axworthy, which won with ease in race record time of 2 min. 11.4 sec. The 1968 Norwegian Trotters' Derby, raced at Oslo, went to Prima Royal, a colt by the French sire Jasimo Royal. At Helsinki, Fin., in July the trotting stallion Fredrik created a new national record for four-year-olds by winning a mile race in 2 min. 7 sec. The gray Soviet stallion Palenjat won several races in the U.S.S.R. He also defeated an international field for the Swedish Åby Prize of $14,000.

In France the Criterium for five-year-olds, raced over 3,000 m. for a purse of $51,000, was won by Ténébreuse M at a record mile rate of 2 min. 8.8 sec. The Prix de l'Étoile went to Vat, a three-year-old, also in record time (2 min. 6.4 sec.). Roquépine brought her total earnings to $890,040.

The Trotting Derby in Berlin saw a purse of $38,000 won by Manzanares. In West Germany the filly Violine won both the Max-Herz Stakes of $25,000 and the Youth Prize of $7,500 in one week.

Horseshoe Pitching:
see Sporting Record

Horticulture:
see Gardening

Hospitals:
see Medicine

Household Appliances:
see Domestic Arts and Sciences

In Italy the four-year-old classic Premio Presidente della Republica ($25,000) at Trieste was won by Quesco. The $35,000 Gran Premio Nazionale for three-year-olds went to Flegias. U.S.-bred Eileen Eden won the coveted $80,000 Lottery Prize raced in Naples, beating Roquépine, but in the Fiera-Fair prize of $48,000 in Milan the French mare turned the tables.
(N. Sɪ.)

Housing

In 1968, some progress was made in housing in the U.S. and other more developed countries even though there were grave factors offsetting efforts for improved housing: the rise in urban land costs and wage increases in building industries. On the other hand, in the less developed countries very little improvement was made in the housing situation.

One of the crucial factors was the imbalance between demand and supply of houses. The types of demand and supply of housing differed according to the social, economic, and physical conditions of each country, region, district, or community. In the U.K. (Great Britain only) 3.9 million dwellings were needed in 1966–70, of which 80.8% would fill the replacement requirement and 19.2% the natural increase in households. In contrast, in West Germany, the housing requirement in 1968–75 was 3.9 million units, of which only 18.9% would be needed for replacement and 70.3% for natural increase in households. The U.S.S.R. showed more or less the same trend as West Germany. Total future requirement in 1966–80 was 26.7 million dwellings: 12.2% for replacement, 81.4% for natural increase in households, and 6.4% for a reserve of vacant dwellings.

The rate of annual housing production in 1966 was 8.2 dwellings per 1,000 inhabitants for all of Europe, 8.6 for Western Europe, 9.7 for the U.S.S.R. The highest production rate occurred in Sweden with 12.4 dwellings per 1,000 inhabitants, followed by West Germany (10.1) and the Netherlands (9.8). In other developed countries the rate of housebuilding was not so high: *e.g.*, 7.3 per 1,000 population in the U.K., 5.6 in Italy, and 6.4 in the U.S.

In the less developed countries of Africa, Asia, and Latin America, the rate of housing production was still very low, less than three dwelling units per 1,000 population in most countries, and the dwelling capital formation constituted 2–4% of the gross national product (GNP), which was below the UN recommendation (5–6% of GNP).

Again in 1968 there were many types of investors in housing. In Western Europe and the U.S. the private sector was most active. In 1966, 97.5% of the total dwellings built in the U.S. were built privately; 72.3% in West Germany; 52.1% in the U.K.; 92.3% in Spain; 68% in France; and 65.6% in Denmark. In Eastern Europe, housing financed through governments, work councils, and cooperatives was predominant. In 1966, in East Germany, 59% of the housing was built by the state and 28.5% by cooperatives; in Poland, 44.1% by the state, 29.2% by cooperatives; and in the U.S.S.R., 68.7% by the state and cooperatives together.

As for basic equipment in houses, there also existed considerable differences between countries and between urban and rural areas. According to the UN *Statistical Yearbook 1967*, the percentage of dwellings with piped water in urban areas was over 70 in Eastern

Europe and over 98 in the U.S. Even in the developed countries, fixed baths or showers were not sufficiently provided, except in Sweden (73%), Switzerland (81.8%), the U.K. (78.7%), and the U.S. (96.3%). A relatively high percentage had been reached in Denmark (56.1%), Ireland (59.8%), Norway (61%), and Portugal (53.1%). In urban areas, provision of electricity was almost sufficient in most European countries, though in the rural areas of some southern European countries it was still inadequate. In Greece only 13.5% of the dwellings had electricity; in Portugal, 27.4%; and in Yugoslavia, 36.1%. A high percentage of toilet installations in urban areas was found in Denmark (99.9%), Ireland (98.3%), Sweden (99.9%), Switzerland (99.9%), the U.K. (95.8%), and the U.S. (98.1%).

According to country monographs submitted by participants in the UN Seminar on Industrialization of Housing for Asia and the Far East in 1968, actual construction during the five years ending in 1966 was, in Ceylon, 75,000 houses (8.9% of the target number for the period); in India, 1,135,000 (57.3%); in Iran, 417,500 (94.1%); and in Japan, 3,995,000 (99.9%). Private investors were predominant in most countries during this period: Ceylon, 80%; Iran, 70.4%; Japan, 63.5%; and South Korea, 81.9%. Considering the enormous housing shortages in most of these countries, more intensive efforts were needed in both private and public sectors.

For the next five-year period, ending in 1971, Ceylon aimed to maintain more or less the same target for construction as the previous figure of 900,000 houses. India planned to raise the projected number of dwellings from 1,980,000 to 2,336,000 (up 18%). Iran's plans called for a 9% decrease, 443,500 to 405,300 units. Japan was to increase planned construction by 68%, from four million to 6.7 million units. Comparisons of the targets with actual housebuilding in the countries covered by the seminar showed wide differences in accomplishment.

Ceylon was suffering from a lack of funds for development schemes. The Special Committee on Housing had estimated in 1963 that the number of dwellings required by the end of 1972 would be 352,336 in the urban areas and 1,334,702 in the rural areas. Of these 1,687,038 units, 30% would be required for lower income housing. It was also suggested that the public sector should bear one-third of the total outlay for this housing.

The rate of investment in housing in Taiwan was a very low 1.73% of the GNP, and the annual ratio of new housing units to population, about two per 1,000, was also far from satisfactory. The total demand for urban housing had been estimated at 80,000 to 90,000 units per year but the actual construction rate was approximately 15,000 units per year.

In Hong Kong, housing construction activity in the public sector was divided into three categories: government resettlement housing, government low cost housing, and housing by the Hong Kong Housing Authority. The Resettlement Department had housed about 1,016,000 people by the end of 1967 (over a quarter of the total population). Its target was to accommodate 1.4 million people by 1972.

In India, the housing shortage was estimated at nearly 74 million units, 11.4 million in the rural areas. To cope with the vast problem, the government was planning to set up a Central Housing Finance Corporation that would undertake mortgage financing and mortgage guarantee schemes. In Laos, the ratio of

housing investment to the total planned investment in overall development in 1961–66 was 27% for the private sector, 4% for the public sector, and 19% for social housing. According to the target in the plan for 1967–71, the ratios were to change to 40% for the private sector, 2.7% for the public, and 5.4% for social housing.

In Malaysia, the Ministry of Local Government and Housing allocated M$150 million for the five-year period from 1966 to 1970 to build 30,000–35,000 low cost housing units. There were other types of housing planned, such as housing for government employees, land settlers, and industrial workers. As to the actual construction, the Federal Land Development Authority built 4,624 houses of the timber type (one bedroom) in 1966–67 and wanted to built 11,500 settler houses in 1968–70. The Japanese government established a housing construction program of 6.7 million dwellings in 1966–70, of which public aid would provide only 2.7 million dwellings, or 40% of the total. The rest would be dependent upon private funds.

Generally speaking, the housing supply in the Latin-American countries was considerably limited. The private sector predominated over the public sector in providing new housing. Incompatibility between housing costs and the purchasing power of low income groups was a serious problem, and costs were still going up. In Argentina, the annual housing shortage in 1960 had been estimated at 128,500 units in urban areas and 33,600 units in rural areas; about 55,000 units were actually built in the urban areas that year. In Chile, the annual housing deficit in 1960 was 39,600 urban units and 5,900 rural, and the annual housing construction target for 1961–70 was set at 44,500 urban units and 9,400 rural ones. The actual construction figure for 1959–62 was 33,500 units annually.

The housing shortage in Mexico had remained quite acute since 1960 when the required minimum annual

Balfron Tower, a 26-story apartment building in London's East End designed for the Greater London Council by Erno Goldfinger. Goldfinger lived in one of the apartments for several weeks in order to study the living conditions he had created.

BEN ROTH AGENCY

"As shop steward of Local 1, Union of Tenants Against Paying Unwarranted and Exorbitant Rent Increases . . . now what?"
—Len Norris, "Vancouver Sun."

number of new housing units was 227,700 units and actual construction was only 2,400 units annually. In Peru, the annual housing shortage was 60,711 units, and an ambitious plan for 1962 called for 79,000 units annually for the whole country. The actual construction in urban areas in 1962 was 5,400 units. Venezuela's housing target had been 65,000 units annually for 1963–66, or about 10,200 units more than the total requirement in 1960 and 24,000 units over the actual number constructed.

In the U.K., the current government policy was to balance housing activities between public and private sectors, to increase slum clearance, and to help private individuals, housing associations, and local authorities improve substandard but still serviceable houses. The government housing program proposed the production of over 400,000 new houses a year. As the actual construction had been 402,500 dwellings in 1966 and 415,400 in 1967, this target remained attainable even under hard economic conditions.

A new Housing Subsidies Act provided special financial assistance to local authorities, New Town corporations, and subsidized housing associations for extra building costs, such as construction of multi-storied flats or acquisition of expensive land. In addition, the difference between the current borrowing rate (around 7% in 1968) and the rate set by the government (4%) was to be paid by the government.

Furthermore, by the Leasehold Reform Act, tenants of houses held on long leases were entitled to acquire them outright at fair compensation or to extend their leases to 50 years. Also, under the Option Mortgage Scheme, persons in the low income groups, with houses valued at less than £5,000, could obtain mortgages of up to 100% of the valuation of the houses. The government also provided grants to local authorities and housing associations for slum clearance and modernization of houses, especially in areas designated as General Improvement Areas.

In the U.S., changing economic and social conditions aggravated the housing problem so that many urban areas, especially in the central parts of the cities, deteriorated at a faster rate than ever before. Furthermore, according to a Census Bureau prediction, the number of U.S. households would rise by 1.3 million a year from 1970 to 1975. The crucial housing problems were the need for slum clearance and a shortage of mortgage money; the average interest rate on a conventional home mortgage in September 1968 was 7.23%.

To cope with the vast problems, the Housing and Urban Development Act, which was enacted in August

1968, authorized a massive three-year, $5.3 billion housing package. It contained several new programs for homeownership assistance, new rent subsidies, assistance to developers of new towns, reinsurance for companies insuring riot-prone properties through the National Insurance Development Corp., flood insurance for homeowners, assistance for college housing, protection for purchases of subdivided undeveloped land made on an interstate basis or through the mail, and a neighbourhood development program under which short-term urban renewal projects could be carried out.

Highlights of the act were the homeownership and rental housing aid sections. The homeownership assistance program aimed to help families with annual incomes of $3,000–$6,500 purchase their own homes by providing a federal subsidy on the mortgage interest. The plan was programmed to aid 500,000 families over three years. Under the rental housing assistance program, federal subsidies would cover the difference between the market rate mortgage and the amount required on a mortgage bearing an interest rate of 1%. The same income limits were to be placed on the future tenants of units built under this program.

In contrast to the unfruitful attempt to pass a $20 million rat-control bill in 1967, discussions on this act reflected the change in the opinion of the legislature and the public. The only vigorous debate on the bill in Congress concerned the eligibility requirements of low income groups. The riots in 1967 had apparently pointed up the importance of helping the lower income groups build decent homes. The target set by the Housing and Urban Development Act was 1.7 million housing units built or renovated in three years.

Considerable progress was made in the research field. The Urban Institute was set up in 1968 to carry out and coordinate research on solutions to urban problems. The institute was expected to be supported by contracts and grants from several federal agencies as well as from private foundations. The first-year budget was expected to be about $5 million, with support increasing to $10 million–$15 million annually as the institute developed. There was also a trend in big cities to use systems analysis in order to analyze complicated urban phenomena and form comprehensive housing programs. The community analysis program for Los Angeles was assisted by a $1,420,000 grant under the Community Renewal Program of the Department of Housing and Urban Development.

(HI. S.)

See also Architecture; Cities and Urban Affairs; Economy, World; Industrial Review; Money and Banking; Race Relations.

ENCYCLOPÆDIA BRITANNICA FILMS. *The Living City* (1953); *Megalopolis: Cradle of the Future* (1962).

Hungary

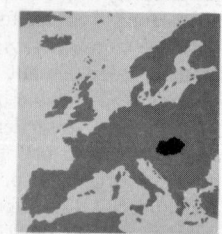

A people's republic of central Europe, Hungary is bordered by Czechoslovakia, the U.S.S.R., Romania, Yugoslavia, and Austria. Area: 35,919 sq.mi. (93,030 sq.km.). Pop. (1968 est.): 10,240,000, including (1956) Hungarian 97%; German 2.2%. Cap. and largest city: Budapest (pop., 1968 est., 2 million). Language (1960): Hungarian 98.2%. Religion (1956): Roman Catholic 67%; Protestant 27.3%; Orthodox 2.5%;

Jewish 1.5%. First secretary of the Hungarian Socialist Workers' (Communist) Party in 1968, Janos Kadar; president of the Presidential Council (head of state), Pal Losonczi; president of the Council of Ministers (premier), Jeno Fock.

Throughout 1968, Hungarian leaders sought to concentrate their country's energies on making the New Economic Model a success. Efforts to avoid outside distractions failed in late summer, however, when Hungarian troops joined with Soviet, East German, Polish, and Bulgarian forces to invade and occupy Czechoslovakia.

The Czechoslovak crisis caused concern in Hungary, where the leadership had been following liberal policies in the economy and the arts that were not dissimilar from those under attack in Czechoslovakia. The chief difference seemed to be that Kadar enjoyed the confidence of Moscow while Alexander Dubcek, the first secretary of the Czechoslovak Communist Party, did not.

The New Economic Model, known by its initials NEM, officially came into effect on Jan. 1, 1968. Not unexpectedly, it ran into bureaucratic difficulties. In principle, the NEM should bring needed life to the rather sluggish Hungarian economy. The general features of the NEM were: (1) shifting enterprises to a profit rather than a production basis by giving them independence in production and marketing decisions, the purpose being to encourage the efficient use of capital; (2) introduction of a limited free market and price reform so that economic factors could come into play; (3) easing of labour laws to allow more flexible use of manpower; (4) liberalization of foreign trade so that domestic producers would be encouraged to export under threat of competition from imports; (5) raising of agricultural income to promote rural development and end the migration to the cities; and (6) currency reform to increase Hungary's participation in the world market.

The reforms were handicapped by the reluctance of enterprise managers to take the necessary initiatives. In addition, a long drought threatened Hungary's farm production. Most economists, however, believed at year's end that Hungary would achieve significant growth rates.

In the arts, Hungarian writers and playwrights, as well as artists and musicians, appeared to be working under an informal agreement with Kadar: namely, they would be permitted to produce without direct restraints as long as they did not attack the Communist leadership, the government, or the country's foreign policy. The press, unlike that in Czechoslovakia prior to the occupation, remained tightly controlled.

At first the liberal trends in Czechoslovakia were treated with sympathy by Hungarian leaders, but Kadar and others warned Prague not to make the same mistakes that Hungary had made in 1956, which had led to Soviet intervention. Kadar and Dubcek signed a treaty of friendship in June and met at other times, including a secret meeting that reportedly took place three days before the August 20–21 invasion.

In general, Hungary tried to steer a moderate course in world Communist councils. It served as the host nation for the meetings of a commission composed of representatives of more than 60 Communist parties, held in February, September, and November to prepare for the long-delayed summit meeting of world Communist parties. Sharp disagreements broke out at the Budapest meetings, including a walkout by the Romanians in February, but in November it was finally agreed that the world meeting—which earlier in the year had been scheduled for November—would be held in Moscow in May 1969.

Although Hungary participated in the invasion of Czechoslovakia, its press was fairly moderate in its justification for the affair. Unlike East Germany and Poland, which virulently attacked the Czechoslovaks, the Hungarians acted as if they virtually had been forced to take part. Kadar did not speak to the nation on the reasons behind the action, although he did talk to party leaders at a special meeting in late August.   (B. M. G.)

ENCYCLOPÆDIA BRITANNICA FILMS. *Hungary and Communism—Eastern Europe in Change* (1964).

HUNGARY

Education. (1966–67) Primary, pupils 1,380,300, teachers 62,241; secondary and vocational, pupils 375,734, teachers 12,317; higher (including 15 universities), students 89,544, teaching staff 8,889.

Finance. Monetary unit: forint, with an official exchange rate of 11.74 forints to U.S. $1 (28.18 forints = £1 sterling) and a tourist rate (Oct. 1968) of 30 forints to U.S. $1 (72 forints = £1). Budget (1967 est.) balanced at 104.7 billion forints. National income (net material product): (1966) 186 billion forints; (1965) 167 billion forints.

Foreign Trade. (1966) Imports 18,378,000,000 forints; exports 18,705,000,000 forints. Import sources: U.S.S.R. 33%; East Germany 10%; Czechoslovakia 8%; West Germany 6%; Poland 6%. Export destinations: U.S.S.R. 33%; Czechoslovakia 11%; East Germany 10%; Poland 7%; West Germany 5%. Main exports: machinery 19%; transport equipment 12%; chemicals 8%; fruit and vegetables 7%; iron and steel 6%; meat and products 5%; textiles 5%.

Transport and Communications. Roads (1967) 29,352 km. (including 1,366 km. unmetaled roads). Passenger vehicles in use (1967) 144,601. Railways: (1966) 8,801 km.; traffic (1967) 13,740,000,000 passenger-km., freight 18,061,000,000 net ton-km. Air traffic (1961): 2,355,000 passenger-km.; freight 1,311,-000 net ton-km. Telephones (Dec. 1966) 597,376. Radio receivers (Dec. 1966) 2,485,000. Television receivers (Dec. 1966) 996,000.

Agriculture. Production (in 000; metric tons; 1967; 1966 in parentheses): corn 3,573 (3,958); wheat (1966) 2,349, (1965) 2,453; rye 226 (242); barley 927 (916); potatoes 1,670 (2,433); sugar, raw value (1967–68) c. 441, (1966–67) 464; tobacco (1966) 20, (1965) 18; sunflower seed (1966) 102, (1965) 75; wine (1966) 337, (1965) 242; beef and veal (1966) 144, (1965) 140; pork (1966) 310, (1965) 320. Livestock (in 000; March 1967): cattle 2,014; pigs 6,005; sheep 3,274; horses 287; chickens (March 1966) 47,556.

Industry. Production (in 000; metric tons; 1967): coal 4,054; lignite and brown coal 22,974; crude oil 1,686; natural gas 2,044,000 cu.m.; electricity 12,-474,000 kw-hr.; iron ore (25% metal content) 715; pig iron 1,670; crude steel 2,738; bauxite 1,650; cement 2,656; sulfuric acid 425; nitrogenous fertilizers (nitrogen content; 1966) 167; superphosphates (1966) 711; cotton fabrics 324,000 sq.m.; woolen fabrics 33,-000 sq.m.; pure silk fabrics (1966) 196 sq.m. New dwellings completed (1966) 53,200. Index of production (1963 = 100): (1967) 125; (1966) 118.

Iceland

Iceland is an island republic in the North Atlantic Ocean. Area: 39,800 sq.mi. (103,000 sq.km.). Pop. (1967): 199,-920. Cap. and largest city: Reykjavik (pop., 1967, 80,-090). Language: Icelandic (similar to old Norse). Religion: 98% Lutheran. Presidents in 1968, Asgeir Asgeirsson and, from July 30, Kristjan Eldjarn; prime minister, Bjarni Benediktsson.

The presidential elections (July 1) brought a surprise victory for 51-year-old Kristjan Eldjarn, director since 1947 of the National Museum at Reykja-

Hurricanes:
see Disasters; Meteorology

Hydroelectric Power:
see Engineering Projects; Fuel and Power

Ice Hockey:
see Hockey

vik and virtually unknown until he appeared in an archaeological series on television. He won 64.9% of the votes cast, defeating his only rival, Gunnar Thoroddsen, Iceland's ambassador to Denmark.

The year—which marked the 50th anniversary of Iceland's independence—was one of great economic difficulty. The deterioration of the economic situation in 1967 and the devaluation of the pound sterling had led to the announcement of a new par value for the Icelandic króna of 57 krónur to the U.S. dollar. This was a devaluation of 24.6%. Loss of purchasing power caused the labour unions to call a general strike in March; after two weeks agreement was reached, the workers on the whole gaining their demands. To compensate for devaluation, an immediate 3% salary raise was granted to the lowest-paid workers, and this was to be increased to 5% in 1969.

On September 5 the finance minister, Magnus Jonsson, announced the imposition of a 20% sur-

---

ICELAND

Education. (1966–67) Primary, pupils 26,976, teachers 950; secondary, pupils 11,818, teachers 596; vocational, pupils 3,196, teachers 119; teacher training, students 514, teachers 27; higher (at Reykjavik University), students 1,180, teaching staff 76.

Finance. Monetary unit: króna, with a par value of 88 krónur to U.S. $1 (211.20 krónur = £1 sterling). Gold and foreign exchange, central bank: (June 1968) U.S. $27.2 million; (June 1967) U.S. $45.1 million. Budget (1968 est.): revenue 6,195,296,000 krónur; expenditure 6,120,431,000 krónur. Gross national product: (1966) 23,920,000,000 krónur; (1965) 20,420,-000,000 krónur. Money supply: (June 1968) 2,822,-000,000 krónur; (June 1967) 2,836,000,000 krónur. Cost of living (Reykjavik; 1963 = 100): (May 1968) 166; (May 1967) 145.

Foreign Trade. (1967) Imports 6,944,000,000 krónur; exports 4,137,000,000 krónur. Import sources: U.S. 16%; U.K. 13%; West Germany 13%; Denmark 9%; Norway 8%; Sweden 7%; U.S.S.R. 6%; Netherlands 6%. Export destinations: U.K. 21%; U.S. 15%; U.S.S.R. 12%; Sweden 8%; West Germany 6%; Denmark 5%; Portugal 5%. Main exports: fish 57%; fish meal 20%; fish oil 11%.

Transport and Communications. Roads (1967) c. 11,100 km. Motor vehicles in use (1967): passenger 35,491; commercial 6,126. There are no railways. Shipping (1967): merchant vessels 100 gross tons and over 283; gross tonnage 133,178. Air traffic (1967): 1,102,946,000 passenger-km.; freight 6,352,000 net ton-km. Telephones (Dec. 1966) 57,615. Radio receivers (Dec. 1966) 57,000.

Agriculture. Production (in 000; metric tons; 1966; 1965 in parentheses): hay 342 (376); potatoes 5 (13); sheepskins 2.6 (2.5); mutton and lamb 13 (12). Livestock (in 000; Dec. 1966): cattle 55; sheep 847; horses 35; poultry 120. Fish catch (in 000; metric tons) (1966) 1,240, (1965) 1,199.

Industry. Electricity (public supply only; 1967) 695 million kw-hr.

---

charge on imports and on purchases of foreign currency. Imports between January and July had totaled 4,439,000 krónur as against export earnings of 2,509,-000 krónur. The deficit was attributed partly to a general reduction in world prices, but in large measure to a vast reduction of the 1968 fishing catch. As of November 12 the króna was once again devalued—this time by 35.2%—to a par value of 88 krónur to the U.S. dollar. Also at this time Iceland submitted an application (November 14) for membership in EFTA.

A new national park was established at Skatftafell (near the highest mountain in Iceland, Oraefajokull, 6,952 ft.) in a magnificent landscape, where the area between the white caps of the Vatnajokull and the black sand of Skeidhara is thickly vegetated. The road traffic in Iceland changed from left to right on May 26. The change was preceded and accompanied by a widespread publicity campaign.   (VA. K.)

Ifni:
see Dependent States

Ice Skating

In 1968 increasing numbers of electrically refrigerated ice rinks throughout the world reflected the sport's expanding popularity and caused skaters generally to become less dependent on natural ice. Many mountain resorts in the Swiss Alps adopted such facilities so that they would be less reliant on weather conditions. Numerous Japanese rinks were inaugurated. In the U.S. three new rinks in Boston increased the city's artificially frozen surfaces to 21. In Canada the number in Toronto's metropolitan area rose to 70, including 28 indoors. The U.K.'s 38th indoor ice rink opened at Inverness, Scot.

The farewell appearance of several top-ranking amateurs was a sentimental feature of the world ice figure and dance skating championships, held at Geneva from February 27 to March 2, less than a fortnight after the Winter Olympic Games. (*See* SPORTING RECORD: *Special Report*.)

Emmerich Danzer ended a great amateur career with a third consecutive men's title for Austria, which silenced most critics of his surprising Olympic defeat. Neatly landed double lutz jumps on each foot were his spectacular highlights, but Danzer also emphasized a rare versatility in his fast, smooth spins and clever linking footwork. Tim Wood, the U.S. runner-up hitherto noted more for his figures, challenged Danzer with a freestyle display well above his previous best. Patrick Pera of France gained third place by a hairline decision; with Scott Allen and Gary Visconti close behind Pera, the United States filled three of the top five places.

Peggy Fleming (U.S.) bowed gracefully out of amateur championships with a third consecutive women's title. Her best, effortless-looking performances were a double axel sandwiched between two outside spread eagles, a delayed-rotation axel jump, a split to double flip combination jump, and the best flying sit-spin on view. Her big winning margin of 89.9 points over Gabriele Seyfert, the East German runner-up, stressed how clearly Miss Fleming had reached a class of her own. Hana Maskova (Czech.) finished third.

For the fourth consecutive year, the U.S.S.R.'s Oleg and Ludmila Protopopov (*see* BIOGRAPHY) took the world pairs title with one of the finest performances of their long and distinguished career. They left a capacity crowd of 6,000 gasping in admiration for their

Oleg and Ludmila Protopopov of the U.S.S.R. during their gold medal winning performance in the pairs figure skating competition at the 1968 Winter Olympics.

UPI (UK) LTD.

Peggy Fleming during her fifth straight win of the U.S. women's figure skating championship in January. After winning her third world championship and an Olympic gold medal, she left amateur competition.

perfectly timed split jumps and delayed takeoff double loop jumps. The Soviet runners-up, Alex Gorelik and Tatiana Zhuk, though marked deservedly high, found the Protopopovs just too good to catch. A great finish by Ronald and Cynthia Kauffman of the U.S. prevented a Soviet grand slam.

British couples swept the board by taking the first three places in the ice dance championship. A similar feat had last happened in 1956. Displaying masterly technique, Bernard Ford and Diane Towler majestically retained their title, followed by Malcolm Cannon with Yvonne Suddick and Jon Lane with Janet Sawbridge.

The International Skating Union confirmed that a 50–50 marking system would be adopted for the 1969 championships. This meant that the maximum points possible for free skating would equal those for the compulsory figures, replacing the ratio of 60 for figures and 40 for free skating. An adjustment of pair skating rules limited the future means by which partners would be able to assist each other in overhead lifts.

In speed skating, the outstanding male racer was the Norwegian Fred Anton Maier, who regained the world overall title for Norway at Göteborg, Swed., February 24–25. Another Norwegian, Magne Thomassen, finished second, with the Dutchman Ard Schenk third. Stien Kaiser (Neth.) retained her women's overall title at Helsinki, Fin., on January 27–28, while her compatriots Ans Schut and Carry Geijssen finished second and third, respectively.

During the season world records were bettered 11 times by men and 3 times by women. The year's most prominent sprinter, Erhard Keller (W.Ger.), covered 500 m. in 39.2 sec. on home ice at Inzell. All the other best men's times were finally established by Norwegians, all at Inzell, except the 1,500 m., reduced by Thomassen to 2 min. 2.5 sec. at Davos, Switz. Ivar Eriksen clipped the 1,000-m. time to 1 min. 20.5 sec.; Maier's lowest figure for the 5,000 m. became 7 min. 16.7 sec.; and Per Willy Guttormsen brought down the grueling 10,000-m. time to 15 min. 16.1 sec.

Tatiana Sidorova kept Soviet racing in the picture by clocking the women's 500-m. sprint in 44.7 sec. at Davos. Miss Kaiser set the other two women's world

records, in 1 min. 31.0 sec. for the 1,000 m. at Inzell and 4 min. 54.6 sec. for the 3,000 m. at Davos.

Europeans were joined by competitors from the United States and Japan for the 12th world professional championships, at Wembley, Eng., on April 19. Cash prizes totaling £4,500 were contested by more than 40 entrants. The free-skating singles went to Miwa Fukuhara (Jap.) and Emmerich Danzer (Aus.), the latter making his professional debut. Wolfgang Danne and Margot Glockshuber (W.Ger.) became pairs champions, and the ice dance title was taken again by a British couple, Michael Webster and Iris Lloyd-Webb. (H. B.)

Immigration and Emigration

Human Rights Year, celebrated in 1968 to mark the 20th anniversary of the adoption of the UN Universal Declaration of Human Rights, provided the occasion for a searching look at human rights as they were affected by the immigration laws and practices of various countries. In 1968 the problem appeared to have two parts: the right of a person to maximize his opportunities by choosing his place of residence and work as against the attempts of governments to regulate the inflow of immigration and to protect the working and living conditions of their own nationals; and the human rights of immigrants within the receiving country. The latter problem, since it involved both governmental regulation of immigrants and their reception by the host society, was both a legal and a social one.

A number of developments during the year exemplified these problems or foreshadowed greater difficulties to come. For most of the modern period, the principal migratory movement had been from Europe to other parts of the world. This out-migration was still significant, and Canada and Australia, in particular, continued active recruiting programs. After World War II, however, it had been rivaled in importance by migration within Europe itself, principally from the labour-surplus countries of the south to the more industrialized areas. By the mid-1960s this movement had begun to show signs of slackening, partly because of economic recession in some of the northern European countries—notably West Germany—but also because the governments of the receiving countries had become alarmed over the large number of nonnationals within

Relatives of Asians emigrating from Kenya waiting behind bars at the Nairobi airport. When Britain imposed strict immigration quotas effective March 1, the Nairobi airport was so jammed with people hoping to beat the deadline that police had to bar all nontravelers from the concourse.

BEN ROTH AGENCY

"Now do you believe I'm the local chimney sweep?". —Myers, "Evening News," London.

their work forces and had begun to set up restrictions. In June 1968, for example, the Dutch government announced its intention to limit the immigration of foreign workers from non-EEC countries because of domestic labour unrest. It remained to be seen whether economic recovery in Europe would again reverse the trend.

Much the same conditions that had caused the—largely unplanned—movement in Western Europe lay behind what was apparently the first large-scale planned transfer of labour in Eastern Europe. Early in 1968 it was reported that some 3,000 Hungarian workers had taken jobs in East Germany, which suffered from a severe labour shortage. According to authoritative sources, their numbers would eventually be raised to 30,000, under an agreement signed in 1967 by the labour ministers of the two countries.

Migrants within Europe and from Europe to predominantly ethnically European countries such as the U.S. and Canada faced problems of social distance resulting from differences in language, culture, and religion. The difficulties multiplied drastically, however, when the differences between the immigrant and receiving populations were highly visible, involving, for example, colour. The inability of the United States to accommodate a black minority that had been in North America for some 300 years and that retained almost no trace of its original African culture was not encouraging. Yet all the signs indicated that the next great wave of migration would be not from East to West, as in the past, but from South to North—from the less developed areas to the developed countries, with their promise of jobs and improved living conditions. In 1968 the minister of labour of Norway, which traditionally had had a very open labour market, reported an increase in the number of Arabs and Latin Americans coming to his country to work. This was only one small sign among many.

In the U.K., where the immigration of Commonwealth citizens, chiefly from India, Pakistan, and the West Indies, had been a political and social issue for several years, further restrictions on immigration and severe penalties for aiding Commonwealth citizens to enter the country illegally were introduced in February 1968 under the new Commonwealth Immigrants Act. A particularly touchy issue involved Asians (chiefly Indians) in Kenya, who were suffering increasing discrimination as a result of the Kenyatta government's attempts to africanize the country. Despite considerable opposition from political, re-

Immunology: see Medicine

ligious, and immigrant circles, legislation was introduced to limit the influx of Kenyans possessing Commonwealth citizenship into the U.K. A report published in March showed that, over the four years 1963–66, more people had left the U.K. than had entered it. The net outflow had risen every year, from 58,000 in 1963 to 83,000 in 1966 (and 84,000 in 1967). Nevertheless, 1968 saw growing agitation for drastic reduction—or even a complete ban—on what some described as "the flood of immigrants," and the favourable reaction from large sections of the population to the appeal by Enoch Powell (see BIOGRAPHY) to "keep England white" showed the strength of the underlying sentiment.

This same shift in the pattern of international immigration was apparent in the U.S., where the Immigration and Nationality Act Amendments of 1965 came into force on July 1, 1968, after a two-year transition period. The 1965 act, the first thoroughgoing revision of the U.S. immigration regulations in 40 years, replaced laws enacted in 1924 and 1952, under which immigrants were admitted according to a quota system based on the national origins of the American population as of 1920, and non-Europeans from outside the Western Hemisphere were virtually excluded.

The 1965 act set a limit of 170,000—exclusive of spouses, parents, and children of citizens—on the number of persons entering the country from outside the Western Hemisphere, and a limit of 20,000 on the number from any one country. Within these limits, the old national-origin quota arrangement was replaced by an elaborate system of preferences based on family relations with U.S. citizens, the possession of skills needed in the U.S., and the need for asylum. The new law also imposed, for the first time, a limit—120,000—on persons born in the Western Hemisphere.

A combination of the two systems had been in force during the transition period, under which unused numbers from high-quota countries had been distributed among other nations. Even this modified arrangement had produced startling changes in the pattern of immigration into the U.S., the most apparent being an increase in the number of immigrants from southern Europe and Asia as compared with the number from traditionally favoured countries of northern and western Europe. Cuba replaced Canada as the chief supplier, as many of the refugees who had fled the Castro regime became settled in the U.S. and changed their status to that of permanent immigrant. Estimated totals for fiscal 1968 showed that Cuba had provided 110,000 immigrants, followed by Mexico (43,000), Great Britain (34,166), Canada (29,300), and Italy (23,113). In fiscal 1965, the last full year under the old system, the order had been Canada (39,896), Mexico (37,393), Great Britain (29,056), Germany (22,899), and Cuba (20,031). The State Department predicted that in 1969 the five leading countries would be

Mobility of Labour Within the EEC

Number of permits issued annually to workers moving within the Community

Year	All EEC	Italy
1961	292,494	233,249
1962	281,549	221,173
1963	231,701	177,572
1964	240,390	180,137
1965	317,927	254,185
1966	260,619	216,357
1967	129,138	91,647
Total, 1961–67	1,753,818	1,374,320
Annual average	250,000	200,000

Italy, Greece, Portugal, Taiwan, and the Philippines.

Not all government officials and congressmen were satisfied with the new arrangement; a number of suggestions were made for changes, although none was adopted during the year. An unsuccessful effort was made in Congress to delay imposition of the limit on Western Hemisphere immigration on the ground that the American nations enjoyed a special relationship with the U.S. Barring that, it was suggested that Cubans resident in the U.S. not be included in the Western Hemisphere quota, since they would use up so many of the places.

The 1965 act provided that, before an immigrant could enter the country to perform skilled or unskilled labour, the secretary of labour must certify that there were insufficient U.S. workers available at the immigrant's destination or that his entry would not adversely affect the wages and working conditions of U.S. workers in similar occupations. This significantly affected immigration from northern Europe, which in former years had supplied a high number of labourers without close relatives in the U.S. Ireland was especially hard hit—one source said that immigration from Ireland had fallen by almost three-fourths—and congressmen from Irish-American constituencies began to show concern. A bill—introduced in the House by 24 members—provided that if immigration from any nation fell more than 75% below its 1956–65 average, that nation would be allotted extra places to bring the total back up to the original number. Another problem involving labour certification was that of immigrants who entered the U.S. as domestic servants; a survey showed that only a few of these were still in their original jobs after two months.

Perhaps more significant in its international implications was a congressional committee report pointing out that between 1956 and 1967 the number of scientists, engineers, physicians, and other trained personnel emigrating to the U.S. from less developed countries had risen from 1,769 to 7,912, although the less developed countries could ill afford to lose such persons. One proposed remedy was that foreign graduate students studying in the U.S. be given a status that would ensure their return home.

(G. O. K. B.; D. Fo.)

See also Race Relations; Refugees.

Income, National

The rate of growth of real gross national product (GNP) in the industrial countries was about 3.5% in 1967, well below the 5% registered in both 1966 and 1965. There was a great diversity of experience, however. Growth rates fell by more than half in both the U.S. and Canada but rose in Japan. In Western Europe real GNP fell slightly in West Germany and the growth rate was slightly lower in France, but the growth rate rose somewhat in the other EEC countries. It remained low in the U.K. but rose in the three industrialized countries of Scandinavia. Official estimates suggested faster growth for the industrialized countries in 1968, possibly averaging about 4.5% but slackening during the year. The prospects for 1969 were dominated by the attempts of the U.S. and the U.K. to improve their balance of payments positions.

In the less industrialized developed countries, the rate of growth fell sharply in Spain and slackened in Greece and Turkey. The Yugoslav recession resulted from the restrictive measures taken to counteract in-

flationary tendencies following the economic reforms. On the other hand, the growth rate in Ireland improved considerably. GNP rose less than in the previous year in Australia and New Zealand, but slightly more in South Africa.

In the less developed countries experience varied considerably in 1967. The closing of the Suez Canal led to a large increase in petroleum exports from Libya, raising its GNP by about 18%. Iran also achieved a very rapid rate of growth. The steady increase of recent years continued in Taiwan, and the growth rate in South Korea, although down from 13% in the previous year, was still high. Output rose in Argentina, Ceylon, and Rhodesia, where real GNP had fallen in 1966, but for the Philippines 1967 was a year of recession.

Comparisons between Eastern European and other countries are made difficult by their exclusion from national income accounts of certain "nonproductive services" such as public administration. On the basis of the definitions used elsewhere, the growth rates in these countries would probably be somewhat lower

Table I. Gross National Products, 1965–67

Country	Currency	At current prices 1965	At current prices 1966	At current prices 1967	Percentage real increase* 1967 over 1966	Percentage real increase* Average 1958–67
Industrial countries						
Austria	(billion schillings)	240.2	260.5	276.5	3	4.3
Belgium	(BFr. billion)	852.8	916.3	977.1	3½	4.5
Canada	(Can$billion)	52.20	58.12	62.07	3	4.8
Denmark	(billion kroner)	69.94	76.83	84.03	3½	4.9
France	(Fr. billion)	464.7	500.5	537.7	4½	5.1
Germany, West	(DM. billion)	450.6	478.3	479.5	−½	4.7
Italy	(billion lire)	35.65	38.49	41.85	6	5.6
Japan	(billion yen)	30.50	35.09	41.64	13	10.9
Luxembourg	(LFr. billion)	33.12	35.18	36.61	2	3.2
Netherlands	(billion guilders)	69.24	74.81	82.27	5½	5.1
Norway	(billion kroner)	50.21	54.27	59.46	5	4.8
Sweden	(billion kronor)	102.5	111.4	120.9	3	4.6
Switzerland	(SFr. million)	59.99	64.48	67.98	2½	4.8
United Kingdom	(£000 million)	35.63	37.74	39.32	1½	3.3
United States	($billion)	696.3	760.5	803.9	2½	4.6
Other developed areas						
Australia†	(A$billion)	20.58	22.45	24.21	4	4.6
Finland	(billion markkaa)	25.70	27.62	29.81	2½	6.2
Greece	(billion drachmas)	177.4	197.4	212.8	6	6.7
Ireland	(£million)	996	1,046	1,131	4½	3.8
New Zealand†	(NZ$million)	3,736	3,937	4,060‡	1½	4.5
South Africa	(R million)	7,839	8,545	9,343	7	5.7
Spain§	(billion pesetas)	1,288	1,482	1,622	3	6.5
Turkey	(billion lire)	73.21	84.22	95.37	6½	5.0
Yugoslavia‖	(billion new dinars)	79.5	98.9	103.4	½	7.6
Less developed areas						
Argentina	(billion pesos)	3,232	4,012	5,200‡	2	2.3
Ceylon	(Crs. million)	7,906	8,217	8,791	4½	4.5
Costa Rica	(million colones)	3,867	4,149	4,465	6	4.9
Ecuador	(billion sucres)	20.23	22.28	24.30	5½	4.8
El Salvador	(million colones)	1,975	2,093	2,205	4	5.3
Guatemala	(million quetzales)	1,316	1,375	1,417	3½	4.3
Guyana	(Guy$million)	338.2	365.0	396.5	5½	5.9
Honduras	(million lempiras)	1,027	1,090	1,152	2	2.9
India¶♀	(Rs. billion)	204	211	242	2	4.5
Iran†	(billion rials)	467.6	503.4	563.5	12½	7.8δ
Israel	(I£000 million)	10.82	11.77	12.17	3½	8.0
Ivory Coast§	(CFA Fr. billion)	236.8	257.7	276.0	4½	5.6δ
Kenya§	(£ million)	359	410	433	3½	3.8
Korea, South	(billion won)	806	1,032	1,245	8	6.7
Kuwait♀	(million dinars)	542	565	607	..	..
Libya§	(Lib.£million)	427	539	660	18	..
Malagasy Rep.§	(MalFr. billion)	166.2	174.6	185.0	5	..
Mexico	(billion pesos)	242.7	272.1	301.4	6½	6.1
Morocco	(billion dirhams)	13.25	12.88	13.73	7	2.5
Netherlands Antilles	(million Netherlands Antilles guilders)	449	458	472	2½	−0.1
Pakistan♀	(PakRs. billion)	48.62	53.04	62.41	4½	5.3
Panama§	(million balboas)	646	711	734	2	6.7
Paraguay	(billion guaranies)	54.98	57.80	61.43	7	3.7
Peru§	(million soles)	127.9	152.1	176.2	6	6.3
Philippines	(billion pesos)	20.74	22.86	24.93	½	5.0
Puerto Rico♀	(U.S. $million)	2,721	3,038	3,360	5½	8.0
Rhodesia	(£million)	364.3	356.2	386.8	2½	4.1
Taiwan	(NT$billion)	113.1	125.5	141.6	9	9.2
Thailand	(billion baht)	81.5	96.2	105.3	4½	7.8
Venezuela	(billion bolivares)	34.09	35.72	38.32	5	4.7

*Allowing for price changes.
†Financial year beginning in year shown.
‡Nonofficial estimate.
§Gross domestic product.
‖Gross material product (*i.e.*, excluding "unproductive" services).
¶National income.
♀Financial year ending in year shown.
δIran 1959–60 to 1967–68; Ivory Coast 1960 to 1967.
Sources: Publications of United Nations; International Monetary Fund; Organization for Economic
Cooperation and Development; official national sources.

than those recorded. Table III indicates that output rose less in 1967 than in 1966 throughout the Soviet bloc.

Expenditure of GNP is analyzed for a number of countries in Table II. While the share of private consumption expenditure had fallen since the late 1950s in virtually all countries, private consumption rose noticeably faster than GNP in 1967 in West Germany, Canada, New Zealand, the Philippines, Thailand, and several Latin-American countries. Government current expenditure generally took a higher share in 1967 than in 1966, important exceptions being Italy and Japan. A large increase occurred in the U.K. despite cutbacks in expenditure plans.

The share of fixed investment fell in many of the advanced countries experiencing slower growth, but rose in the U.K., the increase coming entirely within the public sector. The faster rates of growth in Italy, Japan, and Scandinavia were associated with more rapid increases in fixed capital formation. Among the less developed countries, as well as in most of the advanced ones, investment's share in GNP had generally risen over the preceding decade.

Inventory building was modest in most advanced countries. Inventory levels fell in Belgium, West Germany, and Norway, but inventory building represented over 5% of GNP in Japan and South Africa. There was little increase in inventories in most of the less developed countries.

During the preceding decade the distribution of na-

Table II. Disposal of Gross National Product (%)

Country	Year	Private con- sumption	Public con- sumption	Gross fixed capital formation	Change in inven- tory	Export surplus	Country	Year	Private con- sumption	Public con- sumption	Gross fixed capital formation	Change in inven- tory	Export surplus
Industrial countries							New Zealand	1958-59	64.4	13.3	22.2	1.4	−1.3
Austria	1958	61.2	13.7	21.8	1.5	1.9		1966-67	62.0	14.2	23.6	3.7	−3.5
	1966	59.5	13.9	26.1	3.1	−2.6		1967-68	62.6	14.8	21.9	3.0	−2.2
	1967	59.7	14.8	25.4	1.8	−1.7	South Africa	1958	70.1	10.5	23.8	1.3	−3.9
Belgium	1958	68.3	11.9	16.5	0.0	3.2		1966	63.9	12.6	24.4	0.6	−1.5
	1966	65.0	13.0	21.5	0.8	−0.4		1967	62.7	12.2	23.7	5.3	−3.8
	1967	64.3	13.6	21.7	−0.3	0.7	Turkey	1958	76.5	11.6	12.7	...	−0.9
Canada	1958	64.6	14.6	25.4	−1.0	−3.3		1966	72.3	11.6	18.0	...	−1.8
	1966	60.0	15.0	26.0	1.6	−2.1		1967	71.3	12.6	17.5	...	−1.5
	1967	60.8	15.4	24.4	0.4	−0.9	Less developed areas						
Denmark	1958	67.4	13.1	17.2	0.5	2.6	Ceylon	1958	73.3	14.7	16.0	−1.8	−2.2
	1966	62.9	16.1	21.3	1.1	−2.2		1966	73.7	14.1	13.6	−0.8	−0.6
	1967	63.3	16.8	21.6	0.7	−2.3		1967	73.4	14.0	14.3	−0.2	−1.5
France	1958	65.8	13.3	19.2	2.2	−0.6	Costa Rica	1958	76.6	10.8	15.5	1.1	−3.9
	1966	63.7	13.3	21.8	0.9	0.3		1966	71.6	13.6	20.8	2.4	−8.3
	1967	63.7	13.5	21.9	0.7	0.3		1967	73.5	13.8	21.3	2.1	−10.7
Germany, West	1958	59.4	13.2	21.8	1.6	3.7	El Salvador	1958	75.3	12.2	12.7	...	−0.2
	1966	57.1	15.8	25.5	0.3	1.4		1966	80.0	8.8	15.6	1.7	−6.0
	1967	58.1	16.8	22.6	−0.8	3.4		1967	80.2	9.4	15.0	...	−4.6
Italy	1958	65.6	12.3	20.5	0.7	0.9	Guatemala	1958	80.4	12.4	15.3	...	−8.0
	1966	63.2	14.4	18.4	1.2	2.8		1966	82.4	7.6	13.4	−1.2	−2.2
	1967	63.5	13.9	19.1	1.5	2.0		1967	81.3	8.0	13.9	2.2	−5.5
Japan	1958	60.8	9.9	26.3	1.6	1.4	Guyana	1958	72.8	13.2	28.5	2.3	−16.8
	1966	54.8	9.7	31.4	2.6	1.4		1966	72.1	16.4	23.4	1.8	−13.8
	1967	52.5	9.1	32.8	5.5	0.0		1967	70.4	16.0	27.0	1.3	−14.7
Luxembourg	1958	60.2	12.8	24.0	1.8	1.1	Honduras	1958	79.0	10.0	12.9	0.6	−2.5
	1966	61.0	11.6	27.4	0.0	0.0		1966	77.7	9.5	15.6	1.5	−4.2
	1967	59.9	11.6	22.7	1.4	4.5		1967	78.3	9.2	17.4	1.4	−6.3
Netherlands	1958	58.6	14.4	22.4	0.2	4.3	Israel	1958	73.1	19.9	27.2	2.6	−22.8
	1966	58.0	16.2	25.3	1.2	−0.7		1966	67.1	22.4	20.3	0.9	−10.9
	1967	57.2	16.2	25.5	1.3	−0.3		1967	67.1	28.0	15.9	−0.5	−10.5
Norway	1958	58.5	13.9	32.4	−1.0	−3.6	Korea, South	1958	81.0	14.6	12.7	0.6	−9.0
	1966	54.8	16.7	29.1	1.6	−2.2		1966	78.1	10.2	20.0	1.7	−8.5
	1967	54.4	16.9	31.0	−0.1	−2.3		1967	78.2	10.6	21.2	0.7	−9.1
Sweden	1958	61.8	17.9	20.8	−0.1	−0.4	Mexico	1958	82.8	4.7	14.9	...	−2.4
	1966	55.7	20.5	23.3	1.3	−0.8		1966	79.1	5.9	16.7	...	−1.7
	1967	54.8	21.3	23.8	0.4	−0.3		1967	79.2	5.9	17.6	...	−2.6
Switzerland	1958	65.5	12.2	19.7	−0.9	3.5	Morocco	1958	72.4	12.1	9.6	3.5	2.4
	1966	58.3	11.9	26.5	0.7	2.6		1966	74.8	14.6	11.8	−1.2	−0.1
	1967	58.7	12.1	25.3	0.7	3.1		1967	73.3	14.1	13.9	0.2	−1.5
United Kingdom	1958	66.7	15.9	15.1	0.5	1.8	Paraguay	1958	85.3	10.2	13.1	...	−8.5
	1966	63.9	17.1	17.1	0.6	0.8		1966	79.9	7.3	15.6	0.3	−3.2
	1967	63.9	18.1	18.1	0.3	−0.4		1967	81.1	7.3	16.3	0.3	−4.9
United States	1958	64.6	18.8	16.2	−0.1	0.5	Philippines	1958	84.1	8.5	8.2	0.8	−1.6
	1966	61.5	19.2	17.1	1.6	0.7		1966	69.6	9.6	20.0	1.3	1.2
	1967	61.5	20.8	16.6	0.6	0.6		1967	70.2	9.7	20.4	1.6	−3.7
Other developed areas							Puerto Rico	1957-58	83.4	13.7	20.2	1.6	−19.0
Australia	1958-59	66.6	9.9	24.3	2.7	−2.8		1965-66	80.3	14.1	24.8	3.4	−22.6
	1966-67	61.6	12.0	26.0	2.1	−2.5		1966-67	76.8	14.8	26.3	1.8	−19.8
	1967-68	61.7	12.5	25.9	1.3	−2.6	Taiwan	1958	69.2	19.9	15.3	2.9	−7.3
Finland	1958	59.6	12.5	24.8	0.9	1.5		1966	61.3	17.2	18.6	4.5	−1.0
	1966	58.4	15.2	25.6	3.2	−2.3		1967	59.7	17.2	21.8	2.2	−1.1
	1967	58.6	15.8	24.4	2.9	−1.7	Thailand	1958	77.1	9.5	15.6	0.9	−3.1
Greece	1958	77.7	10.7	19.1	0.5	−8.1		1966	64.1	9.0	24.0	3.1	−0.4
	1966	69.3	12.5	24.7	1.0	−7.5		1967	66.1	9.4	25.3	0.1	−1.0
	1967	68.2	14.3	22.5	1.3	−6.3	Venezuela	1958	60.5	15.9	26.5	1.6	−4.5
Ireland	1958	77.9	12.1	13.6	−1.4	−2.2		1966	64.2	14.7	20.4	1.3	−0.6
	1966	70.6	13.0	18.5	0.9	−3.0		1967	64.0	14.5	20.2	1.8	−0.4
	1967	69.0	12.7	18.7	0.0	−0.4							

Note: Components do not always add to 100% because of statistical discrepancies.
Sources: UN, IMF, and OECD publications; official national sources.

Table III. Eastern Europe and U.S.S.R.: Growth of Real Net Material Product, 1965–68
Percentage change over preceding year

Country	1965	1966	1967*	(Plan) 1968
Albania	3	9	7.5	...
Bulgaria	7.1	11.1	9	10.5
Czechoslovakia	3.4	10.8	8	...
Germany, East	4.4	5.3	5.0	5.4
Hungary	1.1	8.4	7	5.6
Poland	7.0	7.2	6.0	4.8
Romania	9.7	9.8	7.5	8.6
U.S.S.R.	6.9	7.5	6.7*	6.8†

Note: The concept of net material product includes only the production of goods and "productive" services.

*Provisional figures.
†Net material product distributed.
Source: UN, Economic Survey of Europe 1967.

tional output had undergone some general shifts in its sectoral pattern. The primary industries, and particularly agriculture, declined in importance relative to the total production of most economies. In the advanced countries the growth of the service industries was increasing their share of total output, at least in current prices.

Table IV shows levels of total and per capita national income in over 50 countries. The national figures at current prices have been converted to U.S. dollars at current exchange rates. This procedure does not adequately reflect differences in the purchasing power of the various national currencies, and the effect of devaluation results in several reductions in dollar incomes in 1967. Nevertheless, it is still possible to draw worthwhile conclusions from the data presented.

Over four-fifths of the aggregate income of the countries listed was accounted for by the 15 industrial countries, while the 30 less developed countries represented under 10% of the total. The U.S. economy was roughly seven times the size of the two next largest, Japan and West Germany. However, a more sophisticated analysis that allowed for differences in the internal purchasing power of national currencies would probably show a somewhat different picture. The available evidence suggests that, in comparison with the U.S., real output in several Western European countries was relatively higher than is suggested by the 1967 figures, particularly in West Germany, Italy, and the U.K. Similarly, the gap in living standards between the advanced and the less developed countries was generally less than that suggested when current exchange rates are used to derive per capita income figures.

Table IV. National Income and Income per Head

Country	National income in U.S. $000,000,000 1967	National income per head in U.S. $ 1958	1966	1967
Industrial countries				
Austria	8.0	590	1,035	1,095
Belgium	15.3	935	1,520	1,600
Canada	42.8	1,505	1,980	2,095
Denmark*	8.7	890	1,810	1,795
France	82.1	1,005	1,540	1,645
Germany, West	90.4	840	1,530	1,510
Italy	53.4	480	950	1,020
Japan	92.1	285	790	920
Luxembourg	0.6	1,080	1,595	1,655
Netherlands	18.5	695	1,350	1,465
Norway	6.4	870	1,545	1,675
Sweden	18.1	1,200	2,150	2,300
Switzerland	13.0	1,195	2,055	2,155
United Kingdom*	74.7	1,015	1,530	1,360
United States	652.9	2,115	3,155	3,280
Other developed areas				
Australia†	22.3	1,125	1,770	1,900
Finland*	5.6	725	1,475	1,205
Greece	5.7	325	620	655
Ireland*	2.1	465	795	735
New Zealand*†	3.9	1,170	1,765	1,430
South Africa	11.1	315	490	520
Spain*	19.8	300	665	620
Turkey	9.7	180	275	300
Less developed areas				
Ceylon*	1.3	120	130	110
Costa Rica	0.6	360	340	355
Ecuador	1.1	165	190	200
El Salvador	0.8	205	240	245
Guatemala	1.2	235	265	265
Guyana*	0.2	210	265	240
Honduras	0.5	170	200	210
India*‡	39.4	60	90	80
Iran†	6.4	150§	225	245
Israel*	2.7	455	1,160	1,010
Ivory Coast	0.8	125	205	210
Kenya	1.0	80	95	100
Korea, South	4.0	160	115	130
Kuwait‡	1.6	1,825§	3,130	3,260
Libya	1.4	110	680	800
Malagasy Rep.	0.6	90	95	100
Mexico	21.8	270	445	480
Morocco	2.4	160	165	170
Nepal‡	1.0	45	85	90
Netherlands Antilles	0.2	1,075	975	995
Pakistan‡	11.8	65	95	110
Panama	0.6	320	450	455
Paraguay	0.4	120	190	195
Peru*	3.6	175	375	290
Philippines	5.2	180	145	150
Puerto Rico‡	2.8	505	945	1,030
Rhodesia	0.9	180	195	205
Taiwan	2.9	100	200	220
Thailand	4.2	80	125	125
Venezuela	7.1	630§	745	760

*Countries which devalued in the course of latest year shown; new exchange rate is used for that year.
†Financial year beginning in year shown.
‡Financial year ending in year shown.
§1959.
Sources: UN; IMF; official national sources.

Table V. Distribution of National Income (%)
Main types of income

Country	Year	Wages and salaries	Interest, dividends, and rent	Income from self-employment*	Corporate profits*†
Austria	1958	60.1	32.2		7.9
	1966	67.0	26.5		7.1
	1967	67.5	32.6		
Belgium	1958	57.3	14.6	26.1	3.5
	1966	62.8	12.5	23.7	4.2
	1967	63.5	12.6	23.1	4.0
Canada	1958	68.0	8.4	13.3	12.3
	1966	69.9	8.9	11.9	11.9
	1967	71.5	9.4	10.5	10.8
France	1958	58.3	5.9	30.0	6.8
	1966	65.1	6.2	24.7	4.7
	1967	65.3	6.5	24.3	4.8
Germany, West	1958	60.5	31.4		6.3
	1966	66.6	27.4		4.4
	1967	67.2	27.6		3.8
Italy	1958	52.2	48.9		
	1966	58.8	8.5	32.5	
	1967	59.2	8.6	32.1	
Japan	1958	51.9	7.3	31.8	8.2
	1966	56.1	10.8	22.6	9.8
	1967	55.3	10.7	22.5	11.4
Netherlands	1958	57.8	33.4		9.6
	1966	66.7	26.4		7.6
	1967	65.9	26.8		8.0
New Zealand	1958–59	58.0	16.6‡	13.0§	11.4
	1966–67	61.7	22.4‡	8.9§	13.5
	1967–68	63.0	22.3‡	8.8§	12.7
South Africa	1960	63.5	25.4		10.0
	1966	62.5	24.4		11.8
	1967	60.8	26.0		11.6
United Kingdom	1958	72.1	9.7	8.3	11.3
	1966	75.8	12.2	7.1	7.1
	1967	75.4	12.4	7.9	7.0
United States	1958	69.9	12.4	12.6	8.0
	1966	70.2	13.6	9.8	10.0
	1967	71.1	13.8	9.3	8.8

Note: The totals may exceed 100% in cases where the remaining items (consisting mainly of government income from property and entrepreneurship less interest on the public debt) are negative.
*Allowing for depreciation of fixed capital.
†Profits before tax but after dividend payments.
‡Includes nonfarm self-employment income.
§Farm income.
‖For 1966 and 1967, figures are estimates based on data of national sources to conform with concepts used in this table.
Sources: OECD, National Accounts Statistics, and official national sources.

In many countries much of the increase in per capita money income during the preceding decade represented a rising price level. Allowing for price changes, per capita income probably rose by some 3.5–4% in both groups of developed countries and by about 1.5–2% in low-income countries.

The distribution of national income by major categories of revenue is shown for a number of countries in Table V. Wages and salaries represented the major source of income in all the countries shown. In some less developed countries income from self-employment represented the largest proportion of income, reflecting the importance of small-scale agriculture, but even there the relative importance of wages and salaries had tended to grow. (M. F .F.)

See also Economy, World.

India

A federal republic of southern Asia and a member of the Commonwealth of Nations, India is situated on a peninsula extending into the Indian Ocean with the Arabian Sea to the west and the Bay of Bengal to the east. Area: 1,232,560 sq.mi. (13,192,330 sq.km.). Pop. (1968 est.): 524,080,000; Indo-Aryans and Dravidians are dominant, with Mongoloid, Negroid, and Australoid admixtures. Cap.: New Delhi (pop., 1968 est., 3,470,000). Largest city: Bombay (metro. pop., 1968 est., 5,368,000). Language falls into two main groups: Indo-Aryan, or northern, includes Hindi 30%; Dravidian, or southern, includes Telugu 10% and Tamil 8%. Hindi in the Devnagari script is the official language; English, an associate language, continued to be used. Religion (1961): Hindu 83.5%; Muslim 10.7%; Christian 2.4%; Sikh 1.8%; Jain 0.5%; Buddhist 0.7%; others 0.4%. President in 1968, Zakir Husain; prime minister, Mrs. Indira Gandhi.

Domestic Affairs. There was a return to comparative stability, both politically and economically, in 1968. The Union (national) government withstood opposition challenges despite its small parliamentary majority and reached important decisions; *e.g.*, on the reorganization of the state of Assam. Under article 307 of the constitution the president took over the administration of four states—West Bengal in February, Uttar Pradesh in April, Bihar in June, and Punjab in August. In West Bengal, a government supported by the Congress Party had taken office after the governor had ousted the non-Congress coalition in November 1967; the new government, however, found itself unable to function owing to the decision of the speaker of the State Assembly that a session should not be convened. In Bihar the non-Congress coalition made way for a Congress-backed government in February. This regime survived for only 45 days. Another non-Congress government was formed in March, and it resigned two months later. A Congress-supported minority government, which had replaced a united front government in Punjab, vacated office on August 21.

Midterm elections for the State Assembly of West Bengal were due to be held in November, but owing to serious floods and landslides that occurred in the autumn in the northern part of the state (causing a death toll of 1,000), the elections were postponed to February 1969. The chief election commissioner announced in October that elections for the state assemblies of Uttar Pradesh, Bihar, and Punjab and

for the Assembly of Nagaland would also be held in February 1969. In Hariana, which had come under president's rule in 1967, elections in May resulted in a Congress victory. In December, however, the state government again collapsed when a third of the Congress members of the Assembly joined the opposition.

At the end of the year, of the 17 states of India only four had non-Congress governments. In Madhya Pradesh the non-Congress united front government hung onto power precariously. Relations between the Communist-led government of Kerala and the Union government were subject to numerous stresses, with a major conflict occurring in September over a strike by employees of the Union government. In November and December there were outbursts of violence in Kerala and other parts of the country, said to be fomented by Peking-inspired Communists.

The year began with the release (on January 2) of Sheikh Abdullah, the Kashmiri leader, from detention without trial. Sheikh Abdullah met leaders of the government and the political parties and also called a convention in October to seek new moves toward a settlement of the dispute between India and Pakistan over Kashmir.

In September the government announced its decision to give the people of the districts of the Assam Hills Division a large measure of autonomy in recognition of their long-standing demand for it. The proposal provided for the creation within Assam of an autonomous state with its own Legislative Assembly and Council of Ministers having control over a wide range of subjects. The hill areas would continue to be represented in the legislature of Assam, and the government of the larger state would continue to be responsible for maintenance of law and order. Another feature envisaged in this novel constitutional experiment was the creation of an Advisory Council to ensure a coordinated approach to the security and development of a northeastern region consisting of Assam, the autonomous state within Assam, Nagaland, Manipur, and Tripura. The Assam question had at one stage threatened to split the Congress Party.

Earlier in the year, there were language riots in various parts of the country following the adoption by Parliament in December 1967 of the Official Languages Amendment Bill. This bill provided for the continued use of English in addition to Hindi for all the official purposes of the national government and for transaction of business in Parliament. Hindi enthusiasts regarded the bill as a concession to anti-Hindi elements, while anti-Hindi groups regarded a government resolution accompanying the bill as a repudiation of solemn promises; *e.g.*, it made the knowledge of English optional for recruitment to Union services. The government of Madras announced its decision not to give effect to the legislation.

Hindu-Muslim riots occurred during the year in Meerut, Karimganj, Aurangabad, and Nagpur. In order to check their spread the prime minister revived the National Integration Council, on which were represented all the political parties (except the Swatantra and Samyukta Socialist parties). At a meeting held in Srinagar in June the council decided that persons fomenting religious riots should receive exemplary punishment.

Among the other events of the year persistent attacks were made in Parliament on the deputy prime minister, Morarji Desai, on the ground that his son had business interests while being his private secretary. The president of the Bharatiya Jan Sangh, Din

Dayal Upadhyaya, was murdered in a train in February. The state of emergency that had been proclaimed in 1962 after the invasion by Communist China was ended in January. Workers on some of the leading newspapers went on strike in July, forcing a two-month closure.

The Economy. There were clear signs of a recovery in the economy, with agricultural and industrial production and exports registering improvement. The output of food grains in the agricultural year 1967–68 (ending on June 30, 1968) was estimated at 95,580,000 metric tons, an all-time record; it represented an increase of 21,350,000 metric tons over the previous year and was regarded as evidence of a breakthrough in Indian agriculture. The Agricultural Prices Commission estimated that the increase resulting from the intensive agricultural program was 7.7 million metric tons. The government announced plans to supply 1.7 million metric tons of nitrogenous fertilizer in 1968–69, compared with 1,070,000 metric tons in 1967–68, and to bring 16 million ac. (6,480,000 ha.) for the *kharif*, or summer crop, under high-yielding seed varieties, compared with 7.6 million ac. (3,090,000 ha.) during the previous summer. Predictions about the size of the 1968–69 harvest were rendered difficult by the onset of drought in Andhra Pradesh and Rajasthan and floods in Assam and West Bengal.

With the revival of demand, industrial production also rose. There was an impressive improvement in the machinery, chemical, and durable consumer goods industries. Jute manufacture, steel, caustic soda, cement, coal, iron, and the fertilizer industries also showed a better performance. Exports were expected to increase by 8% in 1968 as compared with 1967, despite a decline in tea, chemicals, and hides and skins. With a marked reduction in imports, the level of foreign exchange reserves was virtually unchanged. First estimates of the national income in 1967–68 indicated a 9.1% increase in real terms, compared with a gain of only 1% during the previous year.

Prices were generally under control. The monthly general index of wholesale prices in September 1968 was only 0.5% above the level of September 1967 (compared with a 17% rise between 1966 and 1967). Wholesale prices of food grains were in fact 10.3% lower than during the previous year. The decline in prices was particularly noticeable in wheat, pulses, and edible oils. Prices of industrial raw materials rose, however.

Morarji Desai presented his annual budget for the Union government on February 29, estimating revenue

UPI COMPIX

Camel caravan moving through India's Thar Desert near the Pakistan border. During 1968 many people were forced to abandon their homes in this region as the rainfall dropped from the annual average of 7 in. to 1.87 in.

at Rs. 27,284,900,000 and expenditure at Rs. 26,225,700,000 for 1968–69. He proposed new levies, chiefly on postal articles and tobacco, to bring in Rs. 657.3 million. With capital receipts of Rs. 16,569,700,000 and capital expenditure of Rs. 20,778,900,000, and allowing for losses due to some tax concessions, an overall deficit of Rs. 2.9 billion was estimated, which was to be left uncovered. The allocation for defense (revenue and capital budgets together) was Rs. 10,152,600,000, compared with Rs. 9,706,400,000 in 1967–68.

The reconstituted Planning Commission (deputy chairman, D. R. Gadgil) presented a preliminary outline of the revised fourth five-year plan, which was to be launched in April 1969. As a measure of enhanced social control over financial institutions, a Central Credit Council was constituted. Registered shipping tonnage passed the two million mark. The first Indian-built frigate, "Nilgiri," was launched in October. Work began on the Soviet-aided steel plant at Bokaro.

Foreign Affairs. Some strain developed in Indo-Soviet relations when the U.S.S.R. decided to supply military equipment to Pakistan. But India appeared to wish not to do anything to affect the basic friendship between the two countries. In a statement to Parliament on July 22, Mrs. Gandhi said that India "cannot but view with concern this further accretion of armed strength to Pakistan" which would not pro-

mote peace or stability in the subcontinent but would add instead to India's defense responsibilities.

The president, Zakir Husain, personally conveyed India's misgivings to the Soviet leaders during his visit to Moscow in July. Earlier in the year the Soviet premier, Aleksei N. Kosygin, paid an official visit to India. He visited New Delhi again in April for a day on his way back from Pakistan.

Within hours of the entry of the armed forces of the Warsaw Pact countries into Czechoslovakia, Mrs. Gandhi told the House of the People on August 21 that India viewed the action with anguish. She urged the withdrawal of the forces and expressed the hope that the people of Czechoslovakia "will be able to determine their future according to their own wishes and interests" and without outside interference. While reiterating this position in the UN Security Council, the Indian representative abstained from voting on the Anglo-U.S. resolution seeking to condemn the U.S.S.R.

The minister of petroleum and chemicals, Asoka Mehta, resigned from the Cabinet in protest against the government's policy in the Czechoslovak affair. Later, the House of the People adopted a nonofficial

Indian officials at the New Delhi railroad station signaling for the departure of the first train to carry an advertisement encouraging family planning.

"LONDON DAILY EXPRESS" FROM PICTORIAL PARADE

resolution expressing sympathy and support for the people of Czechoslovakia.

In February national tempers were frayed when an international tribunal gave its award on the Indo-Pakistan dispute over the Rann of Cutch (which had led to fighting between the two countries in April 1965). By a majority decision the tribunal held that about 300 sq.mi. (777 sq.km.), representing about one-tenth of the whole area, was Pakistani territory. Mrs. Gandhi told Parliament on February 20 that, although the tribunal had not wholly upheld India's position, India would honour the international commitment. In August Mrs. Gandhi made an offer of a no-war pact to Pakistan.

India declined to sign the nuclear weapons nonproliferation treaty on the ground that it perpetuated the division between nuclear "haves" and "have-nots." The second UN Conference on Trade and Development was held February 1–March 29 in New Delhi. Mrs. Gandhi paid visits to Australia, New Zealand, Malaysia, and Singapore in May and to eight South American countries in September–October.

(H. Y. S. P.)

ENCYCLOPÆDIA BRITANNICA FILMS. *Hindu Family* (1952); *India (Pakistan and the Union of India)* (1952); *Mahatma Gandhi* (1955); *Animals of the Indian Jungle* (1957); *India (Customs in the Village)* (1957); *India (Introduction to Its History)* (1957); *Ganges: Sacred River* (1965).

Indonesia

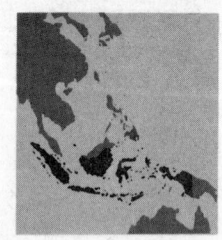

A republic of Southeast Asia, Indonesia consists of the major islands of Sumatra, Java, Kalimantan (Indonesian Borneo), Celebes, and Irian Barat (West New Guinea) and approximately 3,000 smaller islands and islets. Area: 735,268 sq.mi. (1,904,345 sq.km.). Pop. (1967 est.): 110 million. Cap. and largest city: Jakarta (pop., 1966 est., 4 million). Language: Bahasa Indonesia (official); Javanese; Sundanese; Madurese. Religion: mainly Muslim; some Christian, Buddhist, and Hindu. President and prime minister in 1968, General Suharto.

For the first time since the collapse of the Sukarno regime in 1966–67 Indonesia appeared to be on the mend in 1968. The nation was still confronted, however, with the legacies inherited from the Sukarno government: a ruined economy, widespread graft and corruption, an overstaffed and lethargic bureaucracy, and the breakdown of constitutional democracy. Nonetheless, during the year Indonesia displayed remarkable recuperative powers. Parliament bestowed the full powers of the presidency on General Suharto, who had filled the role of acting president following the demise of President Sukarno's regime, and gave the new Suharto government a five-year term in office. Suharto announced plans to launch the country's first five-year plan in 1969 and promised to hold general elections in 1971. The new president's Cabinet gave Indonesia a new air of political stability and immediately concentrated on the problem of economic recovery. During the year Indonesia made dramatic strides in checking inflation, and the government was buoyed by the visit of a World Bank mission which expressed an interest in assisting Indonesia's rehabilitation.

The twin problems of Sukarno and the Communists, who in 1965 jointly engineered the abortive coup against the Indonesian general staff, remained, however. But neither fared well in 1968. A Communist insurgency on Borneo collapsed, and an effort by the regrouped Communists to develop a "liberated area" in East Java also foundered. Sukarno's continuing liaison with the Communists was detected and ended. The former dictator was removed from his palace in Bogor, West Java, and was placed under house arrest.

Domestic Affairs. A new era opened for Indonesia on March 27, when the fifth session of the Provisional People's Consultative Congress (MPRS) unanimously elected General Suharto to a five-year term as president. Thus, he became only the second man to hold the office since the proclamation of Indonesian independence on Aug. 17, 1945. In his inaugural address, the new president pledged "to give meaning to [our] independence by rehabilitating the shattered economy. He also declared that he would dedicate himself "to bringing the country back to constitutional democracy."

As a result of Indonesia's economic and political disarray, the MPRS postponed for three years the general elections scheduled for 1968. A bill was adopted that fixed the election for July 1971 and authorized the elected MPRS to choose a president in February 1973.

While choosing Suharto, Congress did not elect a vice-president, although the issue was debated during the ten-day session that adjourned on March 31. Significantly, however, when Suharto left for Japan in quest of economic aid shortly after his inauguration, the sultan of Jogjakarta, Hamengku Buwono IX, assumed the powers of the presidency in Suharto's absence. The sultan appeared to command the respect of both the Javanese majority and the non-Javanese minority of Indonesia's diverse ethnic population.

Indicative of Indonesia's deepening interest in economic affairs, the MPRS before its adjournment instructed Suharto to revamp his government and install a "development Cabinet." In June Suharto complied and named a new Cabinet of 18 ministers, 17 of whom were civilians, including 7 professors. The Cabinet was heavily weighted with economic and technical experts. The appointment of academicians to the Cabinet damped the charges of "creeping militarism" previously made against the Suharto government by students and intellectuals. The Suharto Cabinet's stature thus rose at home and abroad.

The Communist setbacks on Java and Borneo during the year also strengthened the government's prestige. The most serious Communist debacle occurred on Java, where the Indonesian Communist Party (PKI) laboured to regroup its shattered forces. It set about to reorganize itself into a "free zone" or liberated area in the vicinity of Blitar, East Java. A reformed underground Politburo, headed by Oloan Hutapea, a Sumatran, pledged to "avenge the death" of those who had been massacred in the 1966–67 reprisals against the PKI.

In the spring several terrorist acts were reported in the Blitar area, including the ambushing of a jeepload of army officers. These incidents led to massive security enforcement by the Army. The Communist militants lacked a popular following, and the Army's operations were, therefore, successful. Several members of the underground Politburo were slain, including Hutapea. The Army took 850 prisoners, and subsequent interrogation led to the disclosure of an underground Communist network still operating within the government and maintaining contact with the deposed Sukarno. As a consequence about 350 army personnel, including senior officers, were arrested, and Sukarno was summoned to Jakarta for five days of intensive questioning. He was warned against further political activities amid a renewal of public demands that he be brought to trial for his role in the attempted coup

President Suharto receiving greetings from Indonesian women at the state palace during the celebration of the Islamic new year.

of 1965 and for his mismanagement of the economy during his tenure in office. However, it seemed unlikely that such a trial would take place. Suharto preferred to keep the former dictator under house arrest rather than jeopardize Indonesia's new-found political stability by a sensational trial.

The Communists also lost ground in Borneo. Between 1963 and 1965, youth from Sarawak, a Malaysian state in Borneo, slipped into the Indonesian part of Borneo for arms and training during the period of the Sukarno regime's "confrontation" against Malaysia, an undeclared war that was enthusiastically supported by the Communists in Indonesia, Vietnam, and China.

Following the fall from power of Sukarno and the PKI, these youth, largely Communists of Chinese racial ancestry, were trapped in a jungle no-man's-land between Malaysian and Indonesian Borneo. In a desperate maneuver, they sought to establish a "free zone." Combined Malaysian-Indonesian military operations, however, scored impressively against them during 1968. Once again the Communist loss was traceable to a lack of popular support.

Foreign Affairs. Under the stewardship of Foreign Minister Adam Malik, Indonesia continued to play a modest role in international affairs. Indonesia vigorously denounced the Soviet military occupation of Czechoslovakia and criticized the Philippines for its revival of a territorial claim to Sabah, the Malaysian state in northeast Borneo. The otherwise general improvement of relations with its immediate neighbours, however, was marred by tension with Singapore. Indonesian students sacked the Singapore embassy in

---

INDONESIA
Education. (1964–65) Primary, pupils 11,482,-647, teachers 281,894; secondary, pupils 1,011,-786, teachers 44,731; vocational, pupils 381,483, teachers 20,648; teacher training, students 75,871, teachers 6,856; higher, students (universities only; 1961–62) 65,635, teaching staff 3,940.
Finance. Monetary unit: rupiah, with a free rate (Oct. 1968) of 460 rupiah to U.S. $1 (1,102 rupiah = £1 sterling). The province of West Irian has its own bank notes, the Irian Barat rupiah, at par with the metropolitan rupiah. Gold and foreign exchange, central bank: (Dec. 1963) U.S. $51 million; (Dec. 1962) $135 million. Budget (1968 est.) balanced at 97,186,000,000 rupiah. Net national product (at 1960 values): (1965) 429.7 billion rupiah; (1964) 406.6 billion rupiah. Money supply: (Dec. 1963) 265.3 billion rupiah; (Dec. 1962) 135.3 billion rupiah. Cost of living (Jakarta; 1963 = 100): (April 1968) 52,145; (April 1967) 22,581.

Foreign Trade. Imports (1966) 30,987,000,-000 rupiah; exports (1965) 31,798,000,000 rupiah. Import sources (1964): Japan 23%; U.S. 13%; West Germany 10%; Thailand 9%; Hong Kong 9%; Burma 7%. Export destinations (1964): U.S. 25%; Japan 17%; Netherlands 13%; Australia 10%. Main exports: petroleum and products 38%; rubber 32%.
Transport and Communications. Roads (1960) 81,000 km. Motor vehicles in use (1966): passenger c. 162,000; commercial (including buses) c. 110,000. Railways: (1966) 6,785 km.; traffic (1963) 6,262,000,000 passenger-km., freight 951 million net ton-km. Shipping (1967): merchant vessels 100 gross tons and over 458; gross tonnage 624,202. Air traffic (1966): 509,-556,000 passenger-km.; freight 10,760,000 net ton-km. Telephones (Dec. 1966) 166,332. Radio receivers (Dec. 1966) c. 1,250,000. Television receivers (Dec. 1966) 46,000.

Agriculture. Production (in 000; metric tons; 1967; 1966 in parentheses): rice 14,800 (14,-503); corn (1966) 2,874, (1965) 2,283; cassava (1966) 10,845, (1965) 10,273; sweet potatoes and yams (1966) 2,308, (1965) 2,723; sugar, raw value (1967–68) c. 600, (1966–67) 605; tea (1966) c. 86, (1965) 89; copra (1966) c. 528, (1965) c. 483; soybeans c. 365 (353); palm oil (1966) 353, (1965) 356; peanuts c. 500 (488); coffee (1966) c. 117, (1965) 105; tobacco (1966) 137, (1965) 121; pepper, exports (1966) 20, (1965) 12; rubber (1966) 716, (1965) 717. Livestock (in 000; Sept. 1965): cattle 6,638; sheep c. 2,360; horses 852; buffaloes c. 3,000; pigs 3,040; goats c. 5,050. Fish catch (in 000; metric tons) (1966) 1,001, (1965) 955.
Industry. Production (in 000; metric tons; 1967): crude oil 25,260; coal (1966) 320; tin concentrates (metal content) 14; bauxite 912; electricity (1966) 1,520,000 kw-hr.

Jakarta and staged an anti-Chinese riot in Surabaja in retaliation for the hanging in Singapore of two Indonesians convicted as saboteurs. The two were sentenced to death for planting a bomb, during the "confrontation" conflict in 1965, that claimed 3 lives and injured about 30 persons. Indonesia urged Singapore to commute their death sentences on the ground that both men were marines who had acted under the orders of the former Sukarno regime. In the wake of the executions, Malik said that Indonesia would review its relations with Singapore, but he rejected suggestions of a new "confrontation."

At the UN, Indonesia was preoccupied with the question of West Irian, formerly Netherlands New Guinea. Sukarno had waged an undeclared war against the Dutch in West Irian, and under the terms of an agreement signed by Indonesia and the Netherlands at the UN in 1962 the Dutch withdrew from the disputed territory and Indonesia administered it, pending a final solution. The solution provided for in the accord pledged the native Papuan people the right of self-determination through an "act of free choice" before the end of 1969. UN Secretary-General U Thant in 1968 appointed Fernando Ortiz-Sanz of Bolivia as his representative in the region and instructed him to make arrangements for the 1969 vote. Meanwhile, in December a major military drive, involving some 6,000 troops, was begun against nationalist rebels in West Irian's mountainous northwestern section.

The Economy. During 1968 the economy, wrecked by the Sukarno regime, showed signs of recovery. The government's stabilization program continued to make progress despite a rice crisis in early 1968 that temporarily increased rice prices, depreciated foreign exchange rates, and jeopardized budget planning. In the following months, however, the price of rice held firm and the rise in the cost of living slowed to a bare 3% per month, compared with a rise of 10% monthly in 1967 and 50% monthly in 1966. If rice prices could be held in line into 1969, as most economists believed they could, Indonesia would approach a balanced budget for the first time after more than a decade of economic chaos. To increase revenues the Suharto government increased the price of numerous public services, raised import levies, and improved the tax structure.

Indonesia was especially heartened by the visit of Robert S. McNamara, the newly appointed president of the World Bank. Impressed with Indonesia's potential and the qualities of its new leadership, McNamara raised hopes for an enlarged World Bank role in the rehabilitation of the economy, including financial support. As a portent of things to come, the bank established a permanent overseas office in Jakarta and dispatched a staff of economists and others to Indonesia to assist the government. In addition, Indonesia received encouragement from the Inter-Governmental Group (IGG), composed of non-Communist countries.

Many economists believed that Indonesia's immediate problems stemmed largely from a chronic rice shortage of about 600,000 tons per year. If the Suharto government could narrow that deficit by expanding food production and curbing the country's population growth, observers believed that Indonesia might recover its economic health in three or four years.

(AR. C. B.)

ENCYCLOPÆDIA BRITANNICA FILMS. *Indonesia* (*New Nation of Asia*) (1959).

Industrial Design

Early in 1968, the U.S. magazine *Fortune* carried a report titled "The Decline of Industrial Designers." "Industrial design," it said, "is a 40-year-old profession, slowing down as it reaches middle age. . . . Radical innovation in design is now the exception rather than the rule." Once upon a time, said *Fortune,* design was founded on "practical product design," but "today's industrial designer, even when he does reach into the package and redesign the product, is likely to apply timid if wasteful talents, a plastic tidiness, a simplification of shape, and a 'recognition factor'. . . . Discretion has replaced daring."

Similar misgivings had been whispered more or less clandestinely within the profession for some time, but the irony of *Fortune*'s report was that it came in a year when it was sometimes almost embarrassingly obvious that the young, at any rate, were determined not to see design enjoy a quiescent middle age.

Education and Demonstration. One instance where argument did not do any good was the closing of the Hochschule für Gestaltung at Ulm, W.Ger., which for some years had been regarded as the most important design school in Europe because of its fundamental and influential work. When the foundation that had set up and partly sustained the school got into difficulties and decided to withdraw its contributions, the school became involved in an unhappy political quarrel with its state parliament. Demonstrations on its behalf merely hardened the hostility of the local politicians who, according to Britain's *Design* magazine, had "always been jealous of Ulm's independence and radicalism." The school was dissolved in September, not long after the opening of a major international exhibition devoted to a retrospective look at the work of the Bauhaus—another, even more famous, German school, which also dissolved itself after encountering political and financial difficulties. (*See* ART EXHIBITIONS.)

Students and their supporters had more success in Italy and Britain during the summer. The 14th Milan Triennale, one of the most prestigious regular exhibitions for industrial designers, had been open for a little over an hour when a small group of demonstrators occupied the exhibition hall and succeeded in closing it. The demonstrators—artists, designers, architects, and students—were protesting against the way the Triennale was run, demanding a more democratic administration and greater influence for a larger number of artists and designers on how the exhibition was set up.

A few weeks later, Britain's pattern of higher design and art education, thoroughly reorganized only some five years previously, was thrown into confusion by a series of student protests. These ranged from token strikes and brief periods of noncooperation with the authorities to a few sit-ins involving protracted occupation of college premises by student groups eager to debate, in considerable detail, the shortcomings and failures of the educational system of which they were a part. As a result of these actions, which aroused nationwide debate concerning the effectiveness of the system, it seemed likely that in the future British design education would be characterized by a much more informal and flexible organizational structure.

A Broader View of Function.

A desire to break down existing views of design as an essentially autocratic discipline was by no means confined to the students and their allies. The English designer and writer Ken Baynes, in an important book published toward the end of 1967 and significantly entitled *Industrial Design and the Community*, claimed that: "It is the designer's responsibility to look more deeply at the needs of society than is suggested by the idea simply of solving material problems by rational engineering. The environment is the home of men's hopes, aspirations and fears, just as much as it is the home of their physical bodies. The 'function' of an object is a complex thing, and as a society we are not yet good at seeing the wider implication of innovation in technology or design." And in fact it did seem as if this advice was being heeded from time to time during 1968.

The marked division between "functional" and "emotional" design seemed to grow at least a little blurred, especially among design critics. Two examples came early in the year in *Design* magazine. One article, by Hilary Haywood, took a long—and sympathetic—look at coal-effect electric fires, usually the subject of massive sneers from anyone associated with the design world. Miss Haywood enlisted the aid of a clinical psychologist to explain how such products filled a genuine need: "The time-honoured family patterns are being increasingly disrupted by shifting industrial demands and disturbing rootlessness, and lack of familiar family cohesion results. In these unreliable circumstances, there is a real place for anything that provides a central focus, a sense of continuity, a link with the more solid past and a shared memory of happier human comforts. It may only be a 'dummy,' but it is valid as such and, times being what they are, it does no psychological harm. . . . Even an imitation of what's good and sound may prove helpful."

Clothes design, on the other hand, has been viewed as an area in which common sense and functionalism are entirely sacrificed to aesthetic and emotional appeal. Yet in the very next issue of *Design* another woman journalist, Claire Rayner, was looking at clothes with a wholly objective eye, and felt able to conclude that "Clothes at present only satisfy some of the needs of the people who wear them, often at the expense of other needs that are equally important. If the principles of industrial design were applied to clothing it could be made more ergonomically sound, possibly more aesthetically pleasing, cheaper, and above all more comfortable. If any reader. . .can claim that he or she has never worn an uncomfortable garment, I will be extremely surprised—or suspect that he or she is a nudist."

Further evidence of this tendency to rethink traditional functions came in more whimsical fashion from the United States, where designer Sherle Wagner described himself as "the first to upgrade the bathroom from a utility room in a dark corner of the house to a sumptuous lounge worthy of Cleopatra." He went on to point out that "now some people even entertain in this once neglected area in the house." Many other, perhaps more serious, designers were also prepared to question the previously accepted limitations of a number of products, from exhibition pavilions and transportation systems to sink units and furniture.

One of the most ingenious pieces of problem solving of 1968 had yet to reach the construction stage. The Canadian architects Melvin Charney and Harry Parnass, with engineers Janos Baracs and Marcel Pageau, designed a project for the Canadian pavilion at the 1970 World's Fair to be held in Osaka, Jap. The ingenuity lay in the idea of making the constructional equipment, and even the process of construction, become the pavilion itself. Prefabricated, prewelded steel modules would be bolted together on the site and post-tensioned. Eleven masts would rest on exposed caisson pods, and the main roofs would be triodetic two-way space frames suspended on cables radiating from the masts. The cranes used for construction would remain as part of the pavilion, and could be used to change and reassemble the display as well as to install the exhibition areas. The exhibition areas themselves were designed as containers for easy transporting, and would fold out when they were set up. At the end of the show, the building would dismantle itself, and the cranes would be left as readily marketable construction equipment.

Another method of integrating construction method with the object constructed involved a frame tent and automobile roof rack by the British designer Ivor Pollard. After removing all luggage from the roof rack, the camper releases the automatic rack clips, presses buttons to release spring-loaded arms built into the rack, attaches a telescopic leg to each corner, and drives the car out. After the frame legs have been stretched to their maximum, the canvas is dropped to the ground and pegged, and finally the canopy fittings are inserted. The maker claimed that one person could erect the tent "in less time than it takes to smoke a cigarette," no matter what the weather conditions.

Two Functions in One.

The theme of a number of the more interesting new products of 1968 was the combining of two functions (performed by separate products in more conventional designs) in the same device. The most far-reaching examples of this kind of design came from the United States and from Switzerland.

A three-way project involving the U.S. Department of Housing and Urban Development, the city of Los Angeles, and a number of commercial firms produced for the Los Angeles Department of Airports a combined ground-air transportation plan. The result was a 40-passenger vehicle designed to pick up passengers at various points in business areas and carry them to the central pickup station. From there, a flying

Fibreglass chairs and table designed by Eero Aarnio for the Swedish firm Asko were available in white, yellow, red, green, and brown.

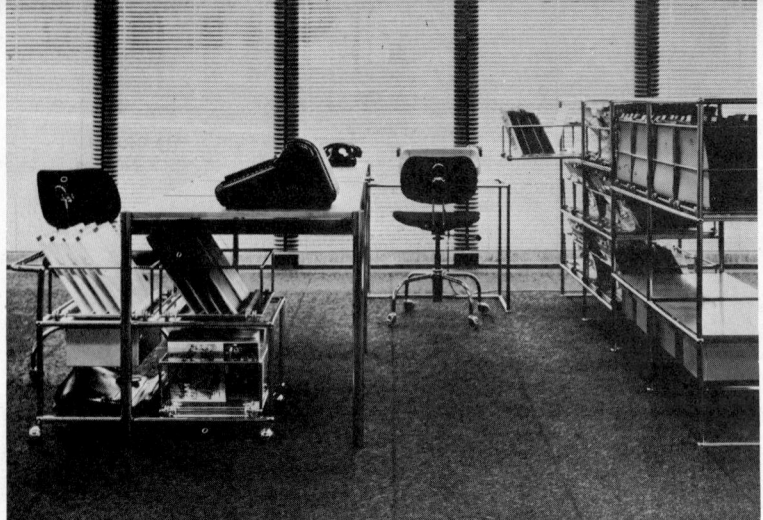

Office furniture designed by Bruno and Fritz Haller includes interchangeable parts and mobile units.

crane helicopter would lift vehicle, passengers, and luggage directly to the International Airport, cutting the time of the journey from one hour to around eight minutes. Nor was the adaptability of the plan confined to the vehicle. The project itself was planned in such a way as to be capable of use in other urban areas. Indeed, various alternative plans were being tried out as the initial project neared completion; some possibilities included operating the vehicle—named the Skylounge—only from a central point or only from outlying districts, as well as testing it for freight-carrying during off-peak hours.

In Switzerland the designer-architects Bruno and Fritz Haller produced, for the firm of Schärer Söhne in Münsingen, an intriguingly flexible office building. The offices were arranged on an open plan, with a central conference area as the only enclosed space. To make it possible for the flexibility of the open-plan scheme to be followed through in the furnishings, the designers and their client cooperated to produce a new range of furniture and office equipment. Without individual offices that would have had to be fitted with separate heating systems, doors, and windows, there was a chance to provide working areas that could be rearranged if necessary to meet a changing pattern of office work. The furniture system was designed on a modular basis so that, from a minimum of interchangeable components, it was possible to produce variations for specialist jobs at no extra cost.

Futuristic Finnish house displayed at Finnfocus-68 trade fair in London. The house, designed by Matti Suuronen, is made of polyester plastic and fibreglass.

All main elements of the furniture—particularly the desks, cabinets, and partitions—could be moved easily, while the document files were easy to push around and retrieve. Most of the equipment, moreover, could be used for several purposes; the mobile typing table, for instance, could serve as a tea trolley.

A new device from the West German firm of Hermann Zanker KG brought this theme of dual functionalism into the home—in a sink unit that incorporated an automatic dishwasher, intended for small kitchens with little room for separate machines. The unit consisted of a stainless steel sink and drainboard, a five-litre hot water cylinder, a controllable hand spray with mixer, a rubbish bin with plastic bag, a cleaning materials drawer, and, under the drainboard, the dishwasher. Known as the Zanker Spulcenter, the unit was designed to conform to standard German kitchen measurements.

Other designers concentrated on finding new solutions to existing single-function problems. Two new British designs brought fresh thinking to bear on the important fields of safety and leisure. In the first design, the small engineering firm of Elliot and Garrood cooperated with the Life Spheres Co. of California in the development of a revolutionary lifeboat. In the form of a capsule with a fibreglass, pumpkin-shaped shell, the craft holds up to 28 men, who enter through two sliding doors. Once the men are inside, the craft is automatically dropped into the sea from its parent ship and rights itself from any angle up to 125°. With the doors shut, it cannot be swamped or dragged underwater by a sinking ship. It offers a number of advantages over the conventional lifeboat. Besides preventing exposure, it can withstand severe impact and is able to survive an oil-slick fire for up to one hour (water jets spray the hull to keep it cool). The capsule's diesel engine gives a speed of 3.2 knots for 24 hours; the engine also provides heat and uses a snorkel system to draw in air. To enhance its occupants' chances of rescue, the capsule is fitted with a radar-reflecting skin and with various homing devices.

The second design was John Walker's prototype 24-ft. trimaran, which offered some new handling characteristics: it can sail either forward or backward and will not capsize. The yacht—the "Planesail"—has a self-trimming, rigid sail rig of four plywood and fibre-glass–reinforced polyester resin sails mounted on a needle-bearing assembly that is secured to the gunwales and the keel of the main hull. The whole sail unit is trimmed continuously to the wind by a tail vane mounted on booms extending aft from the main sails. By adjusting the vane angle from a lever in the cockpit, the helmsman can decide whether the boat will move forward or backward and can control its speed. This control represented a major advance for sailing vessels in that it was independent of both the boat's course and the direction of the wind. Stability is provided by adjustable hydrofoils.

Blowups. The most interesting single exhibition of the year was the display of blowup structures at the Musée National d'Art Moderne in Paris. Designs for transparent inflatable furniture had appeared in several cities in Europe, but this exhibition showed some major extensions of the blowup concept. Among the exhibits were large-scale structures and exhibition halls, a temporary hospital, Hovercraft and boats, barrages for canals and reservoirs, storage units and vehicle support cushions, packaging for crated instruments, medical isolation systems, and supports for

damaged or broken limbs. There was also, of course, a large and varied collection of leisure objects (balls, animals, mattresses, canoes) and even advertisements (in the form of, for example, blowup bottles and bananas). The most ambitious project shown was a design for a transportable theatre by Bruno Schneider-Manoury. The internal structures would be independent of the pneumatic shell, which would be made of fabric panels joined by zip-type fasteners.

The practicability of projects such as this, and some of their potential advantages over more permanent forms of building, were hinted at by some of the completed designs in the exhibition, shown in photographic form. A sports centre at Montfleury, Cannes, in France (designed by Roger Taillibert and made by L. Stromeyer and Co. of West Germany), had a winter swimming pool, the cover of which was supported by internal pressure. The cover, 157 ft. by 79 ft. by 30 ft. and made of polyester fabric coated with polyvinyl chloride, could be erected in two days by eight men. Some airhouses in the show, notably one made by Gourock Ropeware Co. Ltd. and used by Vauxhall Motors of Britain for storage purposes, were said to withstand severe weather, to be easily removable, and to provide very dry storage space. The houses were inflated by electric or motor-driven fan units. (DE. C.)

See also Industrial Review.

Industrial Review

Following an uninterrupted period of high rate of growth, world industrial activity slowed down considerably in 1967: the annual expansion was just under 2%, as compared with an average of well over 6% for each year from 1960 to 1966. Italy and Japan were the only major industrial countries that were able to achieve significantly faster growth. During 1968 production in most countries recovered again, and growth was about twice as fast as in 1967, although still below that reached in earlier years.

The decline in the rate of industrial growth was mainly due to economic stagnation in major countries, notably the United States, West Germany, and the United Kingdom; this depressed industrial activity in most other countries as well. The revival was rather

fast in the early part of 1968, but was slowed toward the middle of the year under the impact of measures taken in the U.S. to reduce its budgetary deficit and the political events in France, which disrupted productive activity there for several weeks. In the second half of the year significant production capacity remained idle as reflected by the considerable industrial unemployment in a number of countries.

According to new calculations of the United Nations, the less industrialized countries accounted for about one-eighth (12½%) of the world's manufacturing production (excluding the Soviet Union, Eastern Europe, and Communist China) in 1963. In 1958 the share of the less industrialized nations was not more than 9%.

In the U.S., which in the late 1960s produced almost half of the world's manufactures, the increase of manufacturing activity in 1967 was only marginal. Two factors were mainly responsible for the slack demand: a dramatic fall in the rate of building stock inventories, and a major strike at the Ford Motor Co. plants in the autumn which had a wide-ranging depressing effect. Monetary and fiscal policies to stimulate the economy resulted in accelerated growth which continued into the first half of 1968. Trends were similar in Canada, although production was somewhat livelier in 1967 than in the U.S.

The Japanese manufacturing industry grew faster than in earlier years in spite of various restrictive measures taken in the second half of 1967. The rate of growth was, however, much reduced during 1968, both because of tighter monetary conditions and because the rise in investment had been exceptionally high in 1967.

West German industry produced less in 1967 than the year before. The recession, due to many factors but mainly to a serious decline in investment activity, was rather rapid until midyear; expansionary measures introduced in two contingency budgets succeeded in halting it and in starting an upturn. The loss of production in France probably contributed to the upward trend in West German production in 1968.

French industry also suffered a mild recession early in 1967; reacting to reflationary measures (supplementary public spending and fiscal incentives), manufacturing production started to rise in the second half of the year. This upward trend was accelerated in

Italian workers carrying protest signs past the Colosseum during a 24-hour general strike in Italy Dec. 5, 1968.

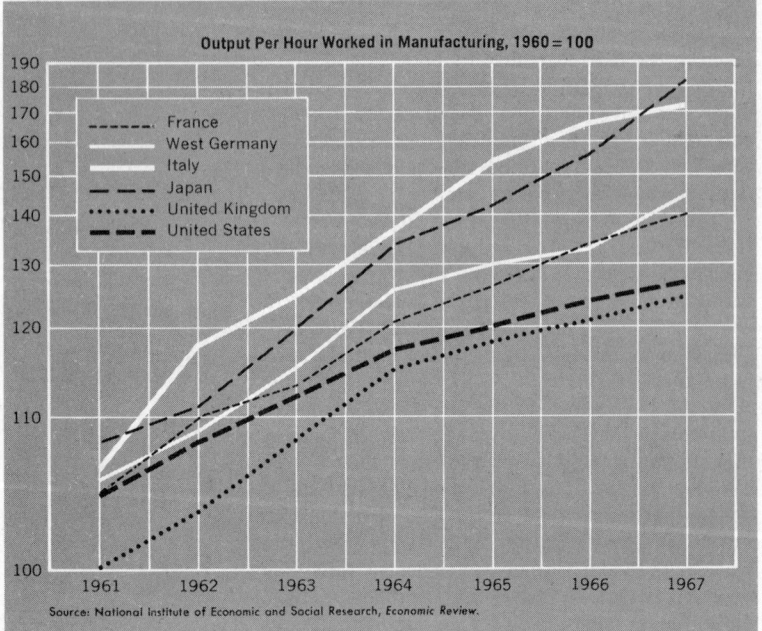

Output Per Hour Worked in Manufacturing, 1960 = 100

France
West Germany
Italy
Japan
United Kingdom
United States

190
180
170
160
150
140
130
120
110
100

1961 1962 1963 1964 1965 1966 1967

Source: National Institute of Economic and Social Research, *Economic Review*.

The European recession hit Belgian industry fairly severely toward the middle of 1967, but recovery was rapid until mid-1968. Manufacturers in the Netherlands avoided a recession, though growth decelerated there as well in 1967; toward the end of the year output started to rise quickly until it reached a new plateau, at a higher level, in 1968.

The output of the British manufacturing industry fell in 1967. An upturn came in the last months of the year, mainly as a result of higher current private and public expenditure, and continued into 1968, helped by the devaluation of the pound sterling in November 1967. During early 1968 the incentive for higher production came from consumption, followed toward the middle of the year by exports and investment as the main generators of demand.

The stagnation in the major industrial countries affected manufacturing in the smaller European countries as well. Their output either advanced in 1967 at a rate below that in earlier years (as in Finland, Greece, Norway, and Sweden) or fell (Austria and Yugoslavia). The exception was Ireland, where manufacturing output rose 8% in 1967. A modest revival in most of the smaller European countries occurred in 1968.

A somewhat new feature of 1967 was that, despite the slow advance or even decline of manufacturing activity, productivity, as measured by output per hour worked in manufacturing, rose quite considerably in all major industrial countries. (*See* Table III.)

Among the less industrialized countries manufacturing output rose quickly in many areas. The increase in 1967 in the output of the less developed countries was, however, not more than about half of that in 1966. Two of the main reasons for the slower growth were the decline of output in Pakistan and the slow progress made by India.

Industrial production in the U.S.S.R. continued to rise in 1967 at a rate of about 9%, similar to the gains of the preceding years. Among the other Eastern European countries industrial output rose at a steady pace in Czechoslovakia, East Germany, and Hungary, and accelerated somewhat in Bulgaria, Poland, and Romania. The Soviet intervention in Czechoslovakia brought output in the latter country to a brief temporary halt in the summer of 1968. (G. F. R.)

1968 until nationwide strikes, following general unrest, dislocated industry in May and June. Although recovery was fairly rapid, the rate of growth in 1968 was below the already depressed 3½% achieved in 1967.

In Italy manufacturing output rose more than 9% in 1967, the highest rate in Europe. In the first half of 1968 industry was affected by strikes, though much less severely than in France. The strikes and a resulting loss of business confidence, however, slowed down further industrial growth in 1968.

Table I. Index Numbers of World Production, Employment, and Productivity in Manufacturing Industries
1963 = 100

Area	Relative importance 1963	Relative importance 1967	Production 1965	Production 1966	Production 1967	Employment 1965	Employment 1966	Employment 1967	Productivity* 1965	Productivity* 1966	Productivity* 1967
World†	1,000	1,000	115	123	126	...	...	...	...	...	...
Industrialized countries	876	873	115	123	126	...	...	...	...	...	...
Less industrialized countries	124	127	117	125	129	...	...	...	...	...	...
North America‡	480	488	116	127	128	...	...	...	...	...	...
Canada	28	29	119	127	129	110	116	116	108	109	111
United States	452	459	116	127	128	106	113	114	109	112	112
Latin America§	49	49	115	123	127	...	...	...	...	...	...
Mexico	8	9	122	135	147	...	...	...	...	...	...
East and Southeast Asia‖	88	105	119	132	151	...	...	...	...	...	...
India	16	15	112	114	116	...	...	...	...	...	...
Japan	55	72	121	137	164	105	107	112	115	128	146
Pakistan	3	3	118	151	144	...	...	...	...	...	...
Europe¶	350	325	112	116	117	...	...	...	...	...	...
Austria	7	6	111	115	113	100	99	96	111	116	118
Belgium	11	10	110	113	114	103	103	...	107	110	...
Finland	4	4	115	120	123	109	111	111	106	108	111
France	51	49	108	117	121	99	99	98	109	118	123
Germany, West	89	81	115	117	115	102	102	97	113	115	119
Greece	2	2	120	138	142	106	110	108	113	125	131
Ireland	1	1	113	116	125	102	103	103	111	113	121
Italy	36	37	106	118	128	95	95	99	112	124	129
Netherlands	12	12	116	122	126	101	101	98	115	121	129
Norway	4	4	115	122	126	103	105	106	112	116	119
Portugal	2	2	119	127	...	...	...	...	...	...	...
Sweden	14	14	119	124	126	105	103	98	113	120	129
United Kingdom	73	65	111	113	112	103	103	101	108	110	111
Yugoslavia	13	14	128	135	134	113	111	111	113	122	121
Rest of the world⁹	33	33	...	...	...	...	...	...	...	...	...
Australia	14	14	112	115	127	109	109	111	103	106	...
South Africa	5	5	122	130	138	123	129	134	99	101	103

*This is 100 times the production index divided by the employment index, giving a rough indication of changes in output per person employed.
†Excluding Albania, Bulgaria, China (Communist), Czechoslovakia, East Germany, Hungary, Mongolia, North Korea, North Vietnam, Poland, Romania, and the U.S.S.R.
‡Canada and the United States.
§South and Central America (including Mexico) and the Caribbean islands.
‖Afghanistan, Brunei, Burma, Ceylon, China (Taiwan), Hong Kong, India, Indonesia, Iran, Japan, Malaysia, Pakistan, Philippines, South Korea, South Vietnam, Thailand, and Singapore.
¶Excluding Albania, Bulgaria, Czechoslovakia, East Germany, Hungary, Poland, Romania, and the U.S.S.R.
⁹Africa, the Middle East, and Oceania.
Sources: UN *Monthly Bulletin of Statistics;* National Institute of Economic and Social Research, *Economic Review*.

Table II. Industrial Production in the U.S.S.R. and Eastern Europe
1963 = 100

Country	1965	1966	1967
Bulgaria	127	143	162
Czechoslovakia	112	120	129
Germany, East	112	119	127
Hungary	111	118	125
Poland	119	128	140
Romania	129	143	163
U.S.S.R.	116	127	139

Source: UN *Monthly Bulletin of Statistics*.

Table III. Output per Hour Worked in Manufacturing in Selected Countries
1960 = 100

Country	1965	1966	1967
France	126	134	140
Germany, West	130	133	145
Italy	154	166	172
Japan	142	156	182
United Kingdom	118	121	125
United States	120	124	127

Source: National Institute of Economic and Social Research, *Economic Review*.

AEROSPACE

There were no signs of any decrease in aerospace-industry activity during the year, although there was a much greater emphasis on civil aircraft programs and an increasing amount of activity in space. The Vietnam war, although slowing down perceptibly from a political standpoint, continued to make heavy demands on the U.S. aerospace industry's military suppliers. Military aircraft manufacturers in the U.K., France, and the Soviet Union, as well as U.S. firms, also began supplying aircraft and missiles to Middle East countries that had been involved in the six-day war of June 1967. Britain's aerospace industry secured a large export order for aircraft, missile systems, and air defense facilities from Libya.

In the U.S. the industry settled down into its recently changed corporation alignment following the merger of the McDonnell and Douglas companies. In Europe there were signs of much wider collaboration agreements than those that had previously been in existence, and the predominantly Anglo-French pattern began to disintegrate when the French government decided to break the agreement with Britain to produce a swing-wing fighter aircraft—but then went ahead on its own to develop a design for such a plane.

Swing-wing aircraft (those in which the wings can be spread out and retracted) lost much of their former attraction in the U.S. The F-111, a controversial swing-wing fighter designed and made by General Dynamics, saw combat duty in Vietnam for the first time but had to be withdrawn after several accidents. Boeing's winning design for a U.S. supersonic airliner, the 2707 (also a swing-wing design), was canceled during the year because, it was said, the problems of designing hinges and operating mechanisms for the movable wings, within the weight limits laid down, were too great to make the aircraft a commercial proposition at the time. The U.S. government allowed Boeing to change its design to one similar to those being produced in Britain, France, and the Soviet Union.

Concorde, the Anglo-French supersonic airliner, was unable to meet its first flight deadline during the year although the first two prototypes were rolled out and underwent ground testing at Toulouse and Bristol. The Concorde program was put back two months by the strikes of May-June in France; technical and supply problems led to further delays; and in November

ber France announced a $12 million cutback in the program as one of the austerity measures designed to bolster the franc. Other Anglo-French programs which continued during the year were the helicopter-building agreements between Sud-Aviation Corporation and Westland, and the British Aircraft Corporation-Breguet program to build the Jaguar supersonic strike/trainer aircraft. The Jaguar made its maiden flight during the year.

Because the U.S. aerospace industry had completely full order books throughout the year, pressure on the two main aircraft engine manufacturers, Pratt & Whitney and General Electric, was great. It was so great, in fact, that a major order, worth $445 million, for the 250-seat, medium-range civil "airbus," Lockheed's L-1011, was won by a

UPI COMPIX

Air Force C-5 Galaxy on the runway at the Lockheed-Georgia Company. The first Galaxy C-5, capable of carrying 900 troops, flew successfully on June 30, 1968.

British manufacturer, Rolls-Royce. Rolls planned to make the RB.211 engines for the airbus in Britain and then send them to the U.S. together with pods made by the Northern Ireland-based firm of Short Bros.

The airbus project—one of the world's biggest potential civil aircraft markets in the early 1970s—occupied much of the efforts of both Lockheed and McDonnell Douglas during the year. Nearly one hundred 1011s and a similar number of McDonnell Douglas DC-10s had been ordered before the year's end. Progress with the European airbus, a collective project between Britain, France, and West Germany, was slow, however, and the aircraft remained firmly in the paper stage throughout the year. In December a revised version was announced, with the seating capacity lowered from 300 to 250. Boeing also developed an airbus design.

But Boeing's greatest effort was being thrown into the 500-seat 747, popularly known as the "Jumbo Jet." The roll-out

of the first of these giant aircraft took place in the autumn. More than 160 had been ordered by the end of the year, and with the first aircraft expected to be in service by the end of 1969, a growing auxiliary industry was beginning to emerge in order to satisfy a demand from airlines and airport authorities for radically new passenger, freight, and servicing equipment to handle aircraft of this size.

At the other end of the civil airliner scale, the first Boeing 737 (101 passengers) went into passenger service during the year, but throughout the world a great deal of interest was beginning to be shown in V/STOL (vertical/short takeoff and landing) aircraft which would carry fewer than 100 passengers over medium ranges. The concept of V/STOL aircraft gained considerable support in military circles during 1967, after the Arab-Israeli conflict, and this in turn seemed to generate interest on the civil side.

The prime advantages of a V/STOL aircraft are that it does not need long runways and that it can make steep approaches and climbs. Both features mean that it can be used at airports much nearer to city centres than is possible with conventional airliners. Severe helicopter reliability problems in Vietnam, coupled with their noise and uneconomic features, brought home to civil operators the impracticability of using helicopters for this task. Breguet of France collaborated with McDonnell Douglas to produce a civil version of the Breguet 941 STOL aircraft. With a capacity of 60 passengers, it was used by Eastern Airlines on highly successful trials during the autumn between New York City, Washington, D.C., and Boston. Vereinigte Flugtechnische Werke GmbH (VFW) of West Germany announced a military tilt-wing transport with possible applications in the civil field.

In the military aerospace industry the trend once again was toward greater simplicity. Ling-Temco-Vought A-7 Corsairs went into action in Vietnam, supplementing the supersonic Phantoms with subsonic performance in a strike role. Little was known of progress on military aircraft in the U.S.S.R., although it was thought that a new interceptor (a large twin-finned aircraft code-named Foxbat) and a swing-wing fighter (code-named Flogger) had gone into production. Certainly manufacture of conventional Soviet aircraft continued unabated, many being exported to Eastern European countries and to the Middle East. On the civil side, the Tu-144 supersonic airliner made its first flight December 31.

The Soviet Union's other great race, this time with the U.S., was toward the moon. Both countries suffered setbacks in their

Left, technicians at NASA's Wallops Station research centre icing specially grooved runway with slush during tests (below) to curb skidding. Pilots claimed that experimental grooved runways in use supplied a safety margin equivalent to 2,000 additional feet of runway.

COURTESY, NASA

moon programs during 1967 when one Soviet cosmonaut and three U.S. astronauts were killed in accidents, but in the autumn of 1968 both countries resumed manned flights, culminating with that of Apollo 8. Launchings of both Soviet and U.S. unmanned space vehicles took place at an average frequency of more than two per week. Many of these were military space vehicles placed in earth orbit for a variety of reasons, from reconnaissance to communications. An increasing number of civilian spacecraft were being launched, also mainly for communications purposes, although several weather and navigation satellites were placed in orbit.

A significant event in the aerospace industry was the first flight of the giant Lockheed C-5A Galaxy, designed to carry 900 troops, in late summer at Burbank, Calif. More than 200 of these aircraft were ordered for the U.S. Air Force so that men and vehicles could be moved to any part of the world in large numbers at short notice. A significant feature of this great aircraft was that many of its parts were made by subcontracting companies across the U.S. and then shipped to California for assembly. Such collaboration in one form or another had become definitely established in the Western world as the only way in which the aerospace industry could forge ahead, on time, with the widest possible diversity of products. (J. B. Be.)

AUTOMOBILES

All the automobile manufacturing countries of the Western world except for France recorded increases in motor vehicle production for the first half of 1968 in spite of many adverse political and economic factors. The setback suffered by the French motor industry during the strikes of May and June was severe, and as a result car production for the first half of 1968 fell by nearly 10%. In contrast, the gain in Italy was 3.2%; in West Germany, 30%; in Sweden, 17.4%; and in the U.K., 13.6%. Helped by the devaluation of the pound sterling in November 1967, British automobile exports increased by 20% during the same period.

The decline in automobile production in the United States during the two years following the record high of 1965 ended with a gain of 19% in the first half of 1968. In Canada an even greater increase occurred (27%), helped by a trade agreement with the U.S. The growth of the motor vehicle industry in Japan continued to be spectacular, and the interest shown by Japanese manufacturers in the British car market was stimulated by the reduction in the import duty on cars entering the U.K. (from 25.2% to 17.5%), which occurred in July.

Automobiles imported into the U.S. from Europe and Japan increased to an annual sales volume approaching one million, or about 10% of total U.S. sales. To meet this challenge, Ford and General Motors announced plans for engineering and building new, low-priced small cars in their U.S. plants. These automobiles were expected to be larger than the small Volkswagen "Beetle" but probably somewhat smaller than the original "compacts" of 1960.

The proliferation of models continued in the U.S. and in Europe. Computerized controls for factory scheduling and assembly operations enabled plants to handle a variety of specifications that would have been unmanageable with earlier systems. The objective was to present the customer with a range of choice never previously associated with automobiles manufactured in large numbers.

Research and development related to safety continued to challenge the engineering resources of the motor vehicle industries of all automobile manufacturing countries, although there was a lull in the enactment of new legislative measures. Consultative meetings were held among ministers of transport in Europe in an attempt to coordinate safety regulations based on U.S. standards, but there was a tendency in most countries to evolve local requirements; this created difficult problems for exporters anxious to build vehicles to a uniform safety specification. A similar situation developed in relation to the control of exhaust gas pollution.

Information gained from the full-scale crash testing of automobiles was applied to the structural improvement of car bodies and frames by many manufacturers. An interesting example was a new reinforcement for the doors adopted for the majority of the 1969 passenger cars; it had been introduced by General Motors in September. By welding a strong, though light, steel beam across the width of each door, within the paneling, resistance to penetration by a vehicle striking the car from the side was greatly increased. General Motors also introduced energy-absorbent instrument panels and an improved version of a collapsible steering column.

A new and successful Ford marketing decision was to offer front disc brakes as a package in association with optional power braking. The Ford engineers also developed, with Kelsey-Hayes, a highly sophisticated system that automatically modulated hydraulic line pressures to prevent the rear brakes from locking the wheels when a car was being braked on a slippery surface. Concurrent developments with a similar objective occurred in Europe, notably in the

Table IV. Production and Exports of Motor Vehicles by the Principal Producing Countries
In 000 units

Country	1965 Passenger cars	1965 Commercial vehicles	1966 Passenger cars	1966 Commercial vehicles	1967 Passenger cars	1967 Commercial vehicles
Production						
United States	9,335.2	1,802.2	8,598.3	1,731.1	7,436.7	1,539.4
Germany, West	2,733.7	242.7	2,830.0	220.7	2,295.7	186.6
France	1,423.1	218.6	1,785.9	238.6	1,776.5	233.2
United Kingdom	1,722.0	455.2	1,603.7	438.7	1,552.1	385.1
Japan	696.2	1,179.4	877.7	1,408.7	1,375.8	1,770.7
Italy	1,103.9	71.6	1,282.4	81.5	1,439.2	103.5
Canada	710.7	144.7	701.5	200.5	720.8	226.4
Australia	335.0	72.6	280.1	64.0	313.6	76.5
Sweden	181.8	23.8	173.5	26.4	194.0	20.6
U.S.S.R.*	972.0		675.0		728.8	
Other countries*	1,020.4		1,306.7		1,310.5	
World total	24,444.8		24,453.0		23,688.7	
Exports						
Germany, West	1,419.1	108.1	1,475.5	105.7	1,350.8	104.8
United Kingdom	627.6	166.2	556.0	165.9	502.6	153.2
France	487.2	37.0	501.0	41.6	547.0	42.7
Italy	307.5	19.2	371.6	21.9	404.4	22.5
United States	106.0†	61.7†	177.5†	78.9†	280.6†	82.6†
Sweden	84.2	13.8	104.7	16.6	123.0	15.4
Japan	100.7	93.4	153.0	102.6	223.5	138.8
Canada	77.9	10.9	189.5	63.5	342.4	111.8

*In the case of U.S.S.R. and "Other countries," a reliable breakdown between cars and commercial vehicles was not available.
†Excludes unassembled vehicles recorded only by value.
Source: British Society of Motor Manufacturers and Traders, *The Motor Industry of Great Britain.*

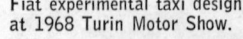
Fiat experimental taxi design at 1968 Turin Motor Show.

1969 Pontiac Grand Prix.

1969 Jaguar XJ6 sedan.

1969 Volkswagen 411, the company's first four-door sedan.

1969 Opel GT two-seater sportscar.

redesign of the Dunlop Maxaret braking system.

The Dodge Division of Chrysler Corp. introduced another kind of safety feature in its 1969 model line: a new headlight designed to meet the requirements of high-speed night driving on busy highways. As an alternative to the familiar short-range low beam and very bright high beam, the driver was given the option of using intense "long-throw" illumination from an offset lamp with a tungsten-halogen bulb, the beam being rigidly controlled to avoid glare on oncoming traffic. Other Chrysler innovations for 1969 were a new body with more sharply curved side windows, a simpler form of front disc brake with improved cooling, and warning lights to remind car occupants to lock the doors and fasten their seat belts.

Illustrative of some advanced styling trends noticeable in the many new U.S. cars were the Pontiac Grand Prix J and SJ models, with a bold central "radiator," long hood, and curved instrument panel, and Ford's Mustang Mach 1 coupé, which carried the fastback principle to a new extreme of tapering elegance. Another notable trend-setter, introduced in the spring of 1968 by American Motors, was the AMX two-place sports coupé.

With the development of more effective ventilation systems, featuring extractor vents toward the back of the car to encourage air circulation, the long-familiar hinged windows (wing-mounts) in the front doors were discarded from many of the new models introduced in 1968 in both America and Europe. Better vision, reduced wind roar, and greater security against theft were the principal gains.

In France Renault extended the policy of providing both sedan and station wagon features in a single five-door body by launching a new scaled-down version of the "16" called the "Six"; it was a practical, all-purpose, low-priced car but had an angular appearance that lacked style appeal. Another and outwardly more attractive new model to appear in France was the medium-sized Peugeot 504 sedan. An independent rear suspension was one of several departures from the more conservative engineering specifications of the older model 404.

Volkswagen announced its largest car to date in the new VW411 (overall length, 178 in.), which was also its first four-door sedan. The new model had the characteristic rear-mounted, four-cylinder, air-cooled engine, but the coil-spring suspension and unitized body structure were entirely new for Volkswagen. Another interesting break with a long-standing design feature was the independent rear suspension introduced in a new range of medium-priced Mercedes-Benz models early in the year. It had semitrailing arms in place of the traditional swing-axle arrangement.

Opel, the General Motors subsidiary in West Germany, staged a surprise offering at the Paris Motor Show: an advanced two-passenger GT sports model, based on an experimental vehicle which had originally been developed for engineering experiments at Opel's proving ground. A striking appearance and high performance were attractive features. Optional 1.1-litre and 1.9-litre engines were offered. In the U.K., Vauxhall Motors (the other European subsidiary of General Motors) announced a Viva four-door sedan to supplement the highly successful range of two-door Viva models.

Ford (Britain) launched a new competitor in the low-priced field to supersede their best-selling Anglia line. Named the Escort, it appeared early in the year as a two-door sedan and a station wagon with a choice of three engines and automatic or manual

transmissions. A similar car was featured in the West German Ford line for 1969, announced in the fall. This was the first major indication of closer cooperation between the British and West German Ford organizations.

An outstanding British introduction in a year not notable for new models was the Jaguar XJ6 sedan. It represented a further development of traditional Jaguar chassis and body engineering with advances in performance, safety, handling, ride, and seating comfort as major objectives. It was 12 in. shorter and 6 in. narrower than the 420 G model.

British Leyland Motor Corp. was formed in May by the merging of the Leyland and British Motor Holdings groups of car and commercial-vehicle companies. The integration of selling organizations overseas was one of many operating developments that followed the merger. In September Leyland announced the first gas-turbine-powered truck to be developed by any European organization. The probable production date was forecast for the late 1970s.

Prolonged negotiations between Fiat and Citroën became public knowledge in October, but the initial plan, which would have placed Fiat in a controlling position, was opposed by the French government. Eventually Fiat acquired a 15% interest in Citroën, and cooperation was forecast in various areas, such as engineering research and development.   (M. PL.)

BUILDING AND CONSTRUCTION

In October the U.S. Department of Commerce reported that the total value of new construction in the United States during the first eight months of 1968 amounted to $54.3 billion. Thus, on a seasonally adjusted basis, construction during that period was at an annual rate of $83.6 billion. If such a level of activity continued during the remainder of 1968, as appeared likely, there would be a gain of almost 10% over the $76.2 billion value reported for 1967. Although the total value of new construction in the U.S. had moved up in 1966 and 1967, the gains were comparatively small, largely because of a sharp downturn in private housing starts during 1966. For 1967 as a whole, housing starts numbered 1,321,900, compared with 1,196,200 in 1966; the prospect for 1968 was that the upward trend would be maintained and that total starts for the year would exceed 1.5 million.

In the contract construction industry in the U.S. wage negotiations in 1968 brought requests for sizable increases in basic wage rates in some local areas of the nation. This matter attracted considerable public notice and directed attention to the role of the construction industry in terms of price stability. There was clear evidence that construction price increases were providing a strong stimulus to inflation. For example, from 1961 to 1965, while the price deflators used in the

gross national product were increasing 1.5% annually, construction costs were increasing almost 3% per year. With the continuing price increase pressures in 1968, there was fear that the physical volume of future construction would be curtailed because of excessively high costs. To avoid such curtailment, the president urged restraint on the part of both management and labour.

In Canada the official survey in early 1968 revealed that investment intentions by businesses did not point to an early revival in fixed-asset formation. It was expected also that home building would continue at a lower rate than in 1967 because of the tighter monetary conditions created by an increase in the discount rate from 5 to 6% and an increase in taxation.

In Western Europe the outlook for construction activity in 1968 was somewhat mixed, reflecting in part differences in governmental policies. In France the national output in 1967 increased over the preceding year by only 4%, and the forecast for 1968 was for an increase of 4.5% over 1967. Part of the government's program to increase output was to step up the construction of houses. The average number of new dwelling units constructed monthly in France dropped from 49,505 in 1965 to 41,311 in 1967. The government, which subsidized about 90% of the housing construction, favoured a greater use of prefabricated housing and components. In West Germany the upturn in the economy that began in late 1967 was expected to continue in 1968, but the outlook for investment indicated an increase of only about 1% over the low level of activity in 1967. The output of the building and construction industry in West Germany stood at 160 in 1967 (1958 = 100), compared with 166 in the preceding year. This drop was due in large part to a decline in the construction of new dwelling units.

Investment in Italy was expected to increase in 1968, and the forecast was that the national output would be above the 1967 level by as much as 5%. The average number of new dwelling units being built each month had declined from 31,985 in 1965 to 21,782 in 1967. However, fixed investment in 1967 had risen almost 10% over that in 1966, and the expectation was that the increase in 1968 would be 7% over 1967. In the U.K. fixed investment was expected to continue to rise. The increase in 1968 was projected to be about

Town house unit being lowered into position at the Fairways housing development near Rochester, N.Y. The Fairways consists of 412 such houses, all models being constructed at the Stirling Homex Corp. four miles away and transported by truck to the site.

Table V. Output of the Building and Construction Industries in Selected Countries
1958 = 100

Country	1966	1967
Belgium	174	115
France	159	176
Germany, West	166	160
Hungary	185	225
Luxembourg	82	78
Mexico	182	205
Romania	264	n.a.*
Taiwan	605	794
United Kingdom	139	145

*Not available.
Source: UN *Monthly Bulletin of Statistics.*

5%, the same as in 1967. Surveys in 1968 of current business trends indicated an upturn in private nonresidential investment. Private residential construction rose in the first half of 1968 as a result of the strong increase in housing starts in 1967. The forecast for fixed investment was that the first half of 1968 would be up 4% and the last half of 1968 up 8.5% compared with the corresponding periods of 1967.

In Belgium construction declined sharply in 1966, and although the rate of decline lessened in 1967, an additional small decline was expected in 1968. In Sweden and Denmark the monthly average number of new dwelling units constructed continued to decline through 1967. The average in Denmark reached 5,867 units and in Sweden, 5,268 units.

Construction statistics for many parts of the world were meagre. In Australia the national output rose by 5% in 1967, and the outlook for construction was good. Governmental policies to control inflationary measures produced a continuing decline in activity in New Zealand during 1967; however, an economic expansion was expected by the end of 1968.

In the Far East, Japan continued to enjoy a record period of prosperity in 1968. Estimates were that investment in plant and equipment would be up 28%, and residential building was also expected to accelerate. The average number of new dwelling units started in 1967 was 85,929, a substantial increase over the average of 71,382 in 1966. In Taiwan also the construction industry achieved a significant gain in output.

(C. C. O.)

CHEMICALS

Chemical industries in industrialized countries throughout the world continued their growth during 1967 and 1968, in general performing considerably better than industry as a whole. In the U.S. chemical consumption per capita had been at a relatively high level. Growth rates as a result were not so great as in countries that had younger industries and where chemical growth potential was greater. The Organization for Economic Cooperation and Development (OECD) reported in 1968 that the chemical industry sales for the U.S. in 1966 had grown 8.5% per year since 1958. The comparable percentage for the European member countries of OECD combined (excluding Finland) was 10.5%, and for Japan, 16%.

The Office of Business Economics of the U.S. Department of Commerce tabulated the value of shipments of chemicals and allied products during 1966 at $38,676,000,-000. In 1967 shipments were up 3.6% to $40,058,000,000. For the first half of 1968 they amounted to $21,883,000,000, a figure 7.2% higher than the total for the corresponding period for 1967. The higher sales reflected increased chemical production and stable prices. The Federal Reserve Index of Chemical Production, which was 203.8 (1957–59 = 100) in 1967, rose to 216.8 (seasonally adjusted) in June 1968 and to 217.5 in July.

The U.S. Department of Labor Index of Wholesale Prices climbed from 97.8 (1957–59 = 100) in 1966 to 98.4 in 1967 and continued at approximately that level for the first seven months of 1968, varying from a low of 98.1 in February to a high of 98.8 in April.

Expenditures for new plant and equip-

ment by U.S. chemical companies fell off in 1967 but continued at a high level. In 1966 expenditures were $2,990,000,000 and in 1967, $2,880,000,000, according to official figures. Government estimates, based on a survey in July and August 1968, indicated another drop in 1968 to $2,780,000,000.

Organizationally, U.S. chemical companies were realigning to permit themselves greater participation in the growth outside the U.S. A number of variations were employed but the concept put into effect by several companies was the same: to establish a global chemical company in which, eventually, the U.S. would be only one of several regions served. Financially, plant and equipment expenditures by foreign manufacturing affiliates of U.S. chemical companies were being increased sharply.

There was no dearth, of course, of new chemical opportunities within the U.S. One potential area was in new improved synthetic fibres. Du Pont, for example, after a big research and development effort, introduced a new fibre, Qiana, said to combine the highest level of aesthetics and performance of any fibre developed to that time. Chemically similar to nylon, it was designed to combine the look, feel, and other characteristics of silk with the wash-and-wear characteristics of polyesters such as Dacron. The fibre was introduced to the public in June. Allied Chemical Corp. also brought out a new fibre called Source; it was a biconstituent (a polyamide and a polyester) intended as a silk substitute. In Japan several companies were bringing silk-like fibres to the market. Nippon Rayon introduced A-Tell, a generically new type of fibre containing alternate ester and ether linkages; Toyo Rayon had two new polyesters, Sillook and Siltop; Toyobo had plans for a casein/acrylic designated K-6; and Teijin was making and selling Silpearl, a modified polyester.

The West German chemical industry ranked behind those of the U.S. and the Soviet Union in size. Sales in 1966 rose to $8,215,000,000 from $7,680,000,000 in 1965. The price index for the period fell off slightly from 96.9 (1958 = 100) in 1965 to 96.5 in 1966. The drop-off was considerably higher in some key areas, however, such as organic and inorganic chemicals. The increase in sales, therefore, was not so high as the increase in production, which rose from 214 (1958 = 100) in 1965 to 255 during the first half of 1967.

West Germany continued as the biggest chemical trader in Europe, leading during 1966 in both chemical exports ($2,414,000,-000) and in imports ($876.6 million). The

basic soundness of the West German chemical industry was illustrated by the fact that while the production index for chemicals rose 8% in the January–June period in 1967, the overall index of industrial production during the same time fell by 8%. The increase in new investment for plant and equipment was not so great as it had been in preceding years, however. The total for 1966 was up 15% to $925 million. In the two earlier years, the increases had been 25 and 23%, respectively.

With few indigenous raw materials and depending for the most part upon imported technology, Japan's chemical industry recorded remarkable progress. In terms of chemical sales it surpassed the United Kingdom in 1966, posting $7,055,000,000. This represented a 16% increase over the $6,055,000,000 registered in 1965. The rise continued only slightly abated during the first half of 1967.

The Japanese index of chemical production grew at a 16% annual rate from 246 (1958 = 100) in 1964 to 286 in 1965, and to 333 in 1966. Particularly impressive was the increase in production of synthetic organic chemicals, where the production index shot from 501 in 1964 to 636 in 1965 and to 854 in 1966. Productivity had been climbing swiftly in that period too because the labour force had been declining steadily. The net drop in plant operating force from 1965 to 1966 amounted to 6,000. Investment in the chemical industry, which had fallen 7% in 1965 to $655 million, dropped an additional 13% to $570 million in 1966. A strong business recovery and generally high demand for chemicals was causing the figure to rebound sharply in 1967, however. OECD's provisional figure, $944 million, indicated a 60% increase over 1966.

The chemical industry in the United Kingdom had not grown so fast in 1965 as it had in earlier years. The same trend continued into 1966, when chemical sales rose 5% and production increased only 4%. That represented a significant improvement over industry as a whole, however, and the signs for 1967 were more encouraging. Chemical production in the first six months was up 6% over the same period in 1966.

The OECD estimated the value of chemical sales in 1966 in the U.K. at $6,720,-000,000, up from $6,385,000,000 in 1965. The index of chemical production, which was 155 (1958 = 100) in 1964, rose to 163 in 1965, 169 in 1966, and 180 for the first half of 1967. Prices for chemicals rose slightly. Investment for new plant and equipment had increased 19% in 1965 and 12% in 1966 (to $703 million). In the first half of 1967, however, expenditures were down 9% from the first half of 1966.

Sales of the French chemical industry rose in 1966 by approximately 7%, reaching $5,950,000,000. Early indications were that this figure would be easily surpassed in 1967. Production in 1966 increased 9%, as the production index averaged 213 (1958 = 100). This represented a substantial increase over the production index for industry as a whole, which increased only 5%. The same trend was evidenced in the first half of 1967, when the overall production index was only 3% higher than in the corresponding period of 1965 while that for the chemical industry was up 11%. Investment was rising at a faster rate. In 1966 approximately $500 million was spent on new plant and equipment, 21% more than the $417 million spent in 1965.

A perhaps portentous move for the French and, in fact, for the entire European chemical industry occurred in October 1968, when Farbwerke Hoechst, one of West Germany's largest chemical companies, made

Table VI. Chemical Sales, Exports, and Imports, 1966

In $000,000

Country	Sales	Imports	Exports
Austria	425	204.5	90.1
Belgium	965	467.4†	422.3†
Denmark	...	265.5	126
Finland	...	172.9	31
France	5,950	840.5	1,133.8
Germany, West	8,215	876.6	2,414
Ireland	...	93.7	19.2
Italy	5,230	578	656.7
Netherlands	1,535	590.9	763.4
Norway	...	189.8	137
Spain	1,725	312.8	77.4
Sweden	695	361.8	160.5
Switzerland	855*	367.3	650
United Kingdom	6,720	825.1	1,312.8
Canada	1,975	513.9	346
United States	38,700	957	2,675.9
Japan	7,055	497	669.4

*Estimated.
†Figures for Belgium-Luxembourg Economic Union.
Source: Organization for Economic Cooperation and Development, *The Chemical Industry—1966–1967.*

an agreement with Roussel-Uclaf, a French pharmaceutical firm. The agreement called for cooperation between the two on research, production, and marketing of ethical and veterinary drugs and animal feed additives. Hoechst also obtained a minority interest (about 22%) in the French concern. The combination, it was expected, would prove a formidable force in the industry.

Italy's chemical industry bounded back from a 1965 slowdown in growth, chemical production rising by more than 16% in 1966. The index of chemical production averaged 287 (1958 = 100) in 1966, up from 247 in 1965. Sales increased almost as much, rising from $4,520,000,000 in 1965 to $5,230,000,000 in 1966. Capital investment in Italian chemical plant and equipment started to rebound also.

In the fourth quarter of 1968, two Italian state corporations acquired working control of Montecatini-Edison, the country's giant chemical combine. The government said that the move was necessary for the economic health of the nation and that other private companies might be taken over also if they did not gear their activities to the government's economic plans.   (D. P. B.)

ELECTRICAL

The overall average annual growth rate in sales of electrical machinery and apparatus declined slightly in 1968 from the 8% levels recorded in 1967. The decline reflected the fluctuations in interest rates and controls following the pressures on the reserve currencies and the devaluation of the pound sterling in November 1967.

The number of mergers and acquisitions in the U.S. in 1967 rose 25% from 1966. The Continental Telephone Corp. of St. Louis, Mo. ($184 million revenue) led the field, acquiring Superior Cable Corp. ($28 million sales in 1966) and 106 other companies. The English Electric–General Electric Co. (GEC) of England merger was probably the largest single change in the industry's structure proposed in 1968. The combined company would be Europe's biggest electrical group.

In the developing countries there was a rapid expansion in the range of equipment produced and in the overall output of the electrical manufacturing industries. In India, for example, the output of electrical goods increased by 82% from 1961 to 1966. Viewed as export markets, the developing countries had become more discriminating and the industrialized countries of Europe and North America had to provide a higher technical excellence in their products to satisfy those markets. Therefore, additional

Table VII. Deliveries and Exports of Electrical Machinery and Apparatus in 1966

Country	Total deliveries Value in U.S. $000,000	Percent increase over 1965	Exports Value in U.S. $000,000	Percent increase over 1965
Germany, West	5,867	1.4	1,619*	10
Belgium	578	0.7	256*	−1
France	3,119	5.3	556	4
Italy	1,208†	3.0	494	15
Netherlands	1,179	2.9	623	0
Austria	295	4.7	110	10
Denmark	303†	2.0	109	6
United Kingdom	5,024	1.4	969	5
Switzerland	516†	7.7	229	8
Spain	575	11.8	15	0
Japan	7,244	11.3	1,055	36
United States	n.a.‡	...	1,899§	14

*Including Luxembourg.
†Provisional.
‡Not available; 34,430 in 1965.
§Excluding special category goods.
Source: Organization for Economic Cooperation and Development.

spending on research became necessary. Annual expenditure on research and development in electrical machinery and communications in the U.S. was about $4.3 billion in 1968, accounting for more than a quarter of the total U.S. research and development bill, although the electrical industry produced only 10% of the total U.S. industrial output. In Britain research and development expenditure in electrical and electronic engineering was about $230 million, or 4% of the annual net output of the industry. About two-thirds of electrical engineering research and development in the United States was government supported, and about one-third in Britain. In West Germany, only about 4% of the electrical research and development bill of about $210 million was government supported, while in Japan government support accounted for less than 1% of the total.

The problems of international standardization in the electrical industry in Europe were considerably eased by Britain's scheduled changeover to the metric system. Attention was directed to safety regulations, and the International Electrotechnical Commission at its general meeting in London in September decided to attempt to reconcile the differences in the safety requirements of household electrical appliances in Europe, Britain, and the United States. A common colour code for flexible cables for domestic appliances was agreed upon and was to come into operation in 1969 in Europe (including Britain). The new colours were a brown "live" core, a blue neutral core, and yellow/striped green for the grounding wire.

The application of plastics as the insulating material in cables made remarkable progress. In June French manufacturers announced the development of a 225,000-v. cable with solid extruded polythene insulation. Much interest was shown in gas-insulated cables, which have considerable potential technical and economic advantages. In July the Reynolds Metals Co., the second largest producer of aluminum in the United States, and the High Voltage Engineering Corp. of Burlington, Mass., agreed to form a partnership to develop, produce, and sell gas-insulated systems.

The most novel development announced during 1968 was probably the 50-hp. homopolar motor with superconducting windings, built by the International Research and Development Co. in England. The machine operated at −268.6° C (only 4.4° C above absolute zero) using liquid helium as a refrigerant. An 8,000-hp. version would be only half the price of a conventional electric motor, and would have an efficiency of 97% and weigh 40 tons as against the 94% efficiency and 370 tons of the conventional motor.

In April the development of air-cooled, cast-resin foil transformers was announced. Electrically and mechanically strong and compact, they caused a new approach to methods of supplying domestic consumers in the United States. Each house was furnished with its own cast foil transformer, fed by a small high-voltage cable, instead of the previous system in which one large transformer served several houses through expensive low-voltage cables.

The prospects of a lucrative market in high-voltage, direct-current transmission caused many manufacturers to embark on the development of high-power, solid-state (thyristor) converters. This development was expected to be very expensive, and in West Germany, Allgemeine Elektricitäts-Gesellschaft (AEG) and Siemens, together with the Swiss-based Brown Boveri, were sharing costs. Other manufacturers working

Sulfur-hexafluoride gas-insulated cable sectionizing made by Delle-Alsthom, recently installed in a Parisian substation.

on thyristor converters included General Electric and Westinghouse in the U.S. and English Electric in Britain. In Sweden successful experience with experimental thyristor stacks led the Swedish State Power Board to order six additional units for commercial operation in the link to Gotland Island. These units would enable an extra 10 Mw. of power to be supplied from the mainland to the island.   (T. C. J. C.)

GLASS

The principal international event of the year was the eighth International Congress on Glass, held in the United Kingdom. Under the patronage of Prince Philip, the congress was attended by more than 700 delegates from 30 countries; it was supported by special displays of historical glass at the British and the Victoria and Albert museums in London, and the U.K. glass industry installed a permanent gallery on glass at the Science Museum, also in London.

Despite several reports of excess productive capacity in the flat glass industry, development continued. New production facilities were reported under construction or in operation in Burma, the United Arab Republic, Iran, Turkey, and Ceylon. Float glass continued to grow in importance, and the major flat glass producers throughout the world were given licenses to produce it. Pilkington Brothers, Ltd., the original developers, announced an additional process whereby float glass could be tinted without the necessity of changing the colour in the glass melting tank.

The use of lightweight, nonreturnable bottles for beverages, already achieving a remarkable growth rate in the U.S., spread to Europe; most countries reported success in using this new product. The Owens-Illinois Glass Co. announced that it was developing a glass-bottle-making process that would revolutionize manufacturing methods. The process, based on that used for manufacturing electric light bulbs, would be used for making lightweight, nonreturnable bottles at a speed of 600 a minute (as compared with the conventional speed of about 200 a minute). The plant was expected to be in commercial operation by 1973. Despite widespread strikes during the early part of the year, the U.S. container industry reported that shipments during 1968 would achieve a record level. Production of all types of glass received a setback in France, but strikers maintained the furnaces during the May–June shutdown.

Studies to improve the efficiency of the

glass container industry in the U.K. continued; the monopoly in the flat glass industry was not considered in any way to be against the public interest. All sectors of the industry began concerning themselves with the impending change to metric weights and measures.

Producers throughout the world studied the U.S. development of using glass fibres in the manufacture of automobile tires; considerably increased demand for this product was expected. A more unusual development occurred when Corning Glass Works reported the use of glass spheres for acoustic navigation systems. These hold electronic underwater communications devices safely regardless of deep-sea currents, slope of ocean floor, and high compression loads expected in hydrospace. (Cy. W.)

IRON AND STEEL

Despite a progressive strengthening in market trends, 1968 was an uncomfortable year on the whole for the steel industry. In the U.S. steel industry, the period was dominated by lengthy negotiations over the new three-year wage settlement. The agreement finally reached at the end of July averted, at the cost of a 6% rise in basic wages, the much-feared threat of a nationwide strike; in anticipation of such a strike U.S. consumers had built up stocks of steel to an unprecedentedly high level of 36 million tons. This stockbuilding exacerbated an existing irritant to U.S. steelmakers, the rate of imports. These rose to a new annual record of about 15 million tons, or just short of 15% of U.S. domestic consumption. U.S. producers redoubled their efforts to secure government regulation of the inflow, but a resolution calling for quotas failed in both the U.S. Senate and the House of Representatives. The rise in prices of domestically produced steel after the wage settlement promised continued competition from imports.

Foreign sales in the U.S. market merely reflected, however, the continuing world oversupply of steel, apparent since the end of the 1950s. Foreign steel inflows into West Germany, for instance, amounted to nearly 30% of that nation's total consumption in 1968. Despite the broad improvement in demand noted above, the fundamental worldwide position of the industry remained little changed, and prices, particularly in the international market, failed to rise to levels adequate to cover costs. Returns on capital in the U.S. steel industry, at about 7%, stood at half the level applying for the remainder of the economy; at the same time, these returns were twice the rate common in Europe. At the beginning of July the entry into force of the first stage of the tariff reductions agreed to in the Kennedy Round of negotiations contributed an ill-timed adverse effect.

Apart from underselling and protective endeavours, steel companies sought in other ways to strengthen their economic position. In the U.S. a wave of diversification into other industries began. Capital investments were made in plastics, aluminum, and chemicals. In Europe the trend to larger and fewer companies, begun in 1966 and 1967, was continued. The merger of Sidelor, de Wendel, and the Société Mosellane de Siderurgie, completed at the beginning of the year, together with a close association in the closing months among the special steel producers of the Loire River region, virtually reduced France's steel industry to three enterprises. In West Germany, where all steel sales were already concentrated in four nationwide selling agencies, August Thyssen-Hütte merged with Oberhausen, creating a combine with more than 10 million tons of annual capacity; the Hoesch/Dortmund-Hörder Hüttenunion group, already tied to the Hoogovens undertaking in the Netherlands, entered into a joint rolling mill venture with Mannesmann, and a study was commissioned on the feasibility of a merger between Klöckner, Salzgitter, and Ilseder Hütte. In Belgium, Cockerill-Ougree, which had combined with the partly French-owned Providence in the previous year, coalesced with the only other major producer,

Espérance-Longdoz. In Japan a proposed merger between Yawata and Fuji, entailing a combined productive potential of 20 million tons, was under consideration by the nation's Fair Trade Commission.

A further unhappy note in the world steel situation was struck by the introduction of steel import quotas by the French government; these quotas, stated to be short-term in intention, were accompanied by various export aids.

World steel production as a whole increased 6.7% over the year, an improvement on the small increment registered in 1967. However, the increase was largely confined to the U.S. and its supplier countries and was a reflection, no doubt, of the steel strike threat in that country. U.S. production rose from 115 million tons in 1967 to just under 128 million tons in 1968. France, in contrast to the general European trend, lost 500,000 tons of output as a result of the spring strikes. (W. A. P. M.)

MACHINERY AND MACHINE TOOLS

Competition for international markets in the machine tool industry intensified in 1968. European and Japanese tool builders continued to improve their equipment so that it competed favourably with most of that made in the U.S. Sales and service techniques developed by companies in Europe and Japan made inroads into foreign and domestic markets of U.S. manufacturers.

The import-export situation caused concern among U.S. machine tool builders. A continuation of the recent sales trend would cause the balance of trade in machine tools to become unfavourable for U.S. manufacturers in the near future. More than 80% of the imports of machine tools into the U.S. came from four European countries (West Germany, the United Kingdom, Italy, and Switzerland) and Japan.

Factors that contributed to the rise of imports from Europe and Japan included improved engineering of machine tools; lower labour costs; intensive promotional and selling efforts; satisfactory inventories of replacement parts; availability of factory-

Table VIII. World Production of Pig Iron and Blast Furnace Ferroalloys

In 000 metric tons

Country	1963	1964	1965	1966	1967
World	270,957	306,471	324,985	335,853	352,963
U.S.	65,658	78,210	80,612	83,594	79,501
U.S.S.R.	58,691	62,377	66,200	70,264	74,930
Japan*	19,936	23,778	27,502	32,018	40,095
Germany, West	22,909	27,182	26,990	25,413	27,366
France	14,307	15,863	15,770	15,590	15,711
United Kingdom	14,826	17,551	17,740	15,962	15,394
China, Communist†	11,000	12,000	14,000	14,000	15,000
Belgium	6,899	8,047	8,366	8,230	8,902
Italy*	3,741	3,498	5,490	6,259	7,294
India	6,603	6,593	6,952	7,041	6,867
Czechoslovakia	5,254	5,716	5,869	6,269	6,822
Poland	4,993	5,268	5,375	5,611	6,581
Canada‡	5,383	5,943	6,422	6,547	6,297
Australia*§	3,456	3,824	3,999	4,450	5,058
Luxembourg	3,587	4,191	4,145	3,963	3,961
South Africa	2,252	2,669	3,322	3,464	3,421
Brazil	2,323	2,487	2,538	2,889	2,963
Spain	1,911	1,901	2,328	2,095	2,685
Netherlands	1,708	1,947	2,364	2,209	2,579
Germany, East	2,150	2,262	2,338	2,448	2,523
Romania	1,706	1,924	2,019	2,198	2,456
Sweden	1,888	2,173	2,286	2,229	2,353
Austria	2,106	2,204	2,200	2,195	2,140
Korea, North	1,158	1,206	1,600	1,800	1,799
Hungary	1,395	1,494	1,583	1,635	1,671
Mexico*	833	926	946	1,137	1,286
Yugoslavia	996	1,026	1,115	1,143	1,177
Finland	336	592	934	934	1,039
Bulgaria	261	449	696	875	992
Norway	407	437	524	631	644

*Pig iron only.
†Estimated.
‡Includes remelt iron produced in the smelting of titanium ores.
§Years ended May 31.
Source: British Iron and Steel Federation, Statistics Department.

Table IX. World Production of Crude Steel

In 000 metric tons

Country	1963	1964	1965	1966	1967	1968 Year to date	1968 No. of months	1968 Annual rate	Percent change 1967-68
World	383,200	433,356	456,461	473,039	495,291	...	...	530,913	+ 6.7
U.S.*	99,121	115,282	119,261	121,655	115,135	85,271	8	127,906	+10.0
U.S.S.R.	80,226	85,034	91,000	96,907	102,129	44,323	5	106,380	+ 4.0
Japan	31,501	39,799	41,161	47,784	62,154	32,502	6	65,004	+ 4.4
Germany, West	31,597	37,339	36,821	35,316	36,744	27,181	8	40,772	+ 9.9
United Kingdom	22,882	26,651	27,440	24,706	24,278	17,174	8	25,761	+ 5.8
France	17,557	19,780	19,604	19,585	19,659	12,722	8	19,083	− 3.0
Italy	10,157	9,793	12,681	13,639	15,890	9,928	7	17,020	+ 6.6
China, Communist†	8,000	9,000	12,000	13,000	14,000	...	...	...	...
Poland	8,004	8,573	9,088	9,850	10,450	5,500	6	11,000	+ 5.0
Czechoslovakia	7,598	8,377	8,598	9,128	10,002	4,456	5	10,694	+ 6.5
Belgium	7,524	8,726	9,162	8,911	9,714	5,690	6	11,380	+14.6
Canada	7,436	8,281	9,134	9,090	8,796	5,115	6	10,230	+14.0
Australia‡	4,373	4,889	5,274	5,716	6,289	3,190	6	6,380	+ 1.4
India	5,969	6,033	6,413	6,608	5,933	1,082	2	6,492	+ 8.6
Sweden	3,899	4,444	4,727	4,764	4,757	2,578	6	5,156	+ 7.7
Spain	2,765	3,150	3,515	3,847	4,520	1,533	4	4,599	+ 1.7
Luxembourg	4,032	4,559	4,585	4,390	4,481	3,550	9	4,733	+ 5.3
Germany, East	4,092	4,310	4,366	4,541	4,246	1,094	3	4,376	+ 2.9
Romania	2,704	3,039	3,425	3,670	4,088	1,824	5	4,368	+ 6.4
Brazil	2,832	3,073	3,017	3,713	3,665	655	2	3,930	+ 6.7
South Africa§	2,751	3,002	3,287	3,291	3,631	1,293	4	3,879	+ 6.4
Netherlands	2,342	2,646	3,138	3,268	3,407	1,787	6	3,574	+ 4.7
Mexico	2,026	2,327	2,455	2,788	3,025	832	3	3,328	+ 9.1
Austria	2,947	3,194	3,221	3,193	3,023	1,972	7	3,377	+10.5
Hungary	2,374	2,364	2,520	2,646	2,738	1,220	5	2,928	+ 6.5
Yugoslavia	1,588	1,677	1,769	1,867	1,832	814	5	1,954	+ 6.2
Argentina	895	1,265	1,368	1,267	1,326	844	7	1,447	+ 8.4
Bulgaria	448	471	588	700	1,240	713	6	1,426	+13.0

*Excludes production of independent foundries.
†Estimated.
‡Years ended May 31.
§Up to 1964 steel ingots only.
Source: British Iron and Steel Federation, Statistics Department.

COURTESY, THE ENGLISH ELECTRIC CO., LTD.

Shaft lathe installed at the Stafford works of English Electric for machining the largest turboalternator shafts envisaged in the future. It would accept forgings 60 ft. long and 6 ft. in diameter.

trained servicemen to install and maintain equipment of U.S. customers; and shorter delivery schedules.

Competition to U.S. manufacturers formerly occurred mainly in the lower priced standard machines, but by 1968 competitors began cutting into U.S. markets at home and abroad in the more sophisticated, numerically controlled (NC) machines. European and Japanese companies competed favourably with the U.S. in NC equipment in many sizes and types.

Machine tool production in the U.S. continued to remain high, however, and shipments in 1968 were expected to approximate the projections of $2,750,000,000, which would be 4.8% above the total shipment of the industry for 1967. The dollar value of new orders for equipment had been unsatisfactory since early 1967. Machine tool orders for September 1968 reached a five-year low, but industry spokesmen hoped for an increase in orders during the fourth quarter of the year.

The backlog of orders built up in 1966 and 1967 was reduced in 1968. Delays in shipment that ranged from 12 to 24 months in previous years were reduced by many months. As the backlogs were lowered, companies adjusted by reducing the amount of overtime work, eliminating the third shift, doing work that was formerly subcontracted, and, in many cases, reducing the work force by means of attrition. The industry did not anticipate the need for any drastic cutbacks in the number of employees in the fourth quarter, even though some companies had found it necessary to lay off a substantial number of employees.

Orders were slower for standard machines than for NC machines, which were purchased to help reduce production costs. It was estimated by leaders in the industry that in six to seven years NC machines would produce 80% of all machine parts.

The largest user of NC machines was the aerospace industry. The demands of this industry for improved methods of machining were contributing much to the improvement of machine design. Requirements for machining newer alloys of intricate shapes necessitated more rigid equipment. This equipment was designed to employ sensor devices, which would relay information to a computer. The computer would then adjust the NC machine for the proper cutter speed and feed rate of the workpiece, as specified by the requirements of the material to be cut. These adaptive control systems were expected to reduce tool wear drastically and increase productivity.

Material handling and transfer machinery continued to be in heavy demand in 1968. These machines did much to increase productivity rates and to eliminate hazardous and monotonous jobs.

World production of all types of machinery and machine tools was highly favourable in 1968. Western European manufacturers were expanding sales to Communist countries, and Japan was also active on the world market. The Soviet Union and Czechoslovakia continued to be the leaders in Eastern Europe.

In the U.S. representatives of the National Machine Tool Builders' Association appeared before the House of Representatives Ways and Means Committee in June for hearings on the balance of trade in the industry. Their recommendations concerning imports urged that the U.S. make no further tariff concessions on machine tools beyond those already agreed to in the Kennedy Round, and that consideration be given to the adoption of a system of selective import surcharges to be imposed on specific categories of machine tools when those imports reached levels considered inimical to the best long-term interests of the U.S. Their recommendations to increase exports included: (1) pressing for the elimination of preferential and discriminatory tariffs and nontariff trade barriers abroad; (2) expansion of trade with Eastern Europe to increase the export of U.S. machine tools there and prevent competitors from preempting those markets; (3) continuing the development of export programs; (4) extending tax advantages that accrue under the Western Hemisphere trading corporation provisions of the Internal Revenue Code; and (5) liberalizing capital recovery allowances of U.S. industry and assuring that those allowances would continue.   (O. K.)

PAINTS AND VARNISHES

Paint production in 1968 continued to expand throughout the world, and this expansion was expected to continue. One authority in the U.S. suggested that production there would increase by about 50% in less than ten years, in spite of the competition from plastics. Eastern European countries were likely to be increasing at an even higher rate, with the Soviet Union not yet able to satisfy its own requirements in either quality or quantity.

No outstanding new developments in production machinery occurred; however, by 1968 most modern paint factories in the U.S., Oceania, and Europe were probably largely equipped with modern cavitation dispersers and sand mills. In Eastern Europe a large new factory began operation in Romania. Designed on an in-line production layout, it was reputed to be equipped with the latest dispersion and handling equipment. Methods in East Germany were probably also well up-to-date, and at least one East German manufacturer began offering a type of sand mill for sale in Western Europe. Sand mills of various designs were being used in increasing numbers, particularly in Italy, France, West Germany, Belgium, and Denmark; the first British-made sand mills also became available.

Most of the larger producers of paint in Western Europe, the U.S., and Oceania equipped themselves with computer colour matching to improve their standards of shade continuity, to reduce the chance of human error, and especially to make the most economical use of tinting pigments. The application of paint by electrophoresis, originally developed in Europe, was being in-

creasingly employed in U.S. industry. At least one U.S. automobile plant began installing a new production line for applying the primer coat by electrophoresis, followed up by electron beam cure.

The development of automatic devices for the combined surface preparation and painting of large steel surfaces, such as sides of ships, was being energetically pursued, particularly in the U.K. Paints for ship bottoms that could be applied underwater became available in the U.K. and France.

The use of shop primers, or temporary protectives, continued to increase, and more were being applied at steel mills in Sweden, West Germany, and the U.K. Reinforced wash primers were the most popular in Europe, with a second preference for primers pigmented with metallic zinc with epoxy and other binders. Demand also increased for a third type of primer, restricted in its use to the tank interiors of tankers designed to carry a variety of solvent cargoes. This specialized shop primer was usually of the red-oxide-cured epoxy type.

Because modern shipping practices involved considerably longer intervals between maintenance operations, the shipping industry increased its use of high-performance coatings. Chlorinated rubber, by itself or combined with other resins, was preferred in northern Europe, where weather conditions in winter and low temperatures did not favour epoxy or other chemically cured coatings. Vinyl acrylics were also popular and, where weather permitted their use, cured epoxies.

Organic and inorganic silicate coatings pigmented with metallic zinc increased in popularity, principally in the U.S., for both marine and land steel structures. Where such coatings were used as a primer and a decorative finish was required, vinyls and chlorinated rubbers were most often used to overcoat them.

The considerable increase in the output of natural gas led to a demand for pipe linings, principally to increase gas flow. Polyamide-cured epoxies were widely used as linings in the U.S., Canada, and the U.K. A special epoxy powder coating was developed in the U.S. for external coating. Claimed to be more economical, it was expected to supersede the more traditional wrapping and bitumen coating.

Coil coatings grew steadily in use in Europe, principally in Sweden, West Germany, the U.K., and, more recently, Spain; such coatings were already well established in the U.S. The coil coatings preferred in the U.S. were silicone alkyds, acrylics, and vinyls, while in Europe coatings were mostly restricted to vinyls.

A number of corrosion inhibitors and additives appeared during the year, but they were still largely in the proving stage. They included chromic fluoride from Israel, organic dichromates from the U.S. and West Germany, and zinc chromium phosphate from the U.K. Organic dichromates showed promise for use in clear lacquers.

New developments in vinyl resins included polyvinyldene fluoride for high-temperature stoving coatings and vinyl urethanes for plywood lacquers. Fire-retardant additives of the pentabromotoluene type were tested with favourable results in the U.K. With demand continuing to increase for emulsion paints, new types of emulsion continued to appear. Vinyl acetate/ethylene copolymers and silicone emulsions were reported to be promising.   (A. D. C. H.)

PAPER AND PULP

World output of paper and paperboard again increased in 1967, although not as rapidly as in the immediately preceding years. The total was approximately 120 million short tons, as against 118 million in 1966. The increase of 2 million tons compared unfavourably with the gain of 8.2 million in 1966. The smaller rise in 1967 reflected a slowdown in the rate of economic growth in several of the largest paper-using countries. It followed a period of unusually rapid expansion and appeared to be one of those pauses that occur from time to time, usually lasting for only a short period. Through the early months of 1968, it seemed that growth in world paper production had once again quickened, although there was still a substantial surplus of manufacturing capacity for some products.

Of the total production in 1967, 48% was in North America, 22% in Western Europe, 5% in the Soviet Union, and 8% in Japan. These advanced industrial areas thus accounted for 83% of the total world production and roughly a similar share of consumption. Among the countries producing pulp and paper, the U.S. ranked first, followed by Canada, Sweden, Japan, Finland, and the U.S.S.R.

World trade in pulp and paper, consisting chiefly of newsprint and wood pulp, showed little change from 1966, with exports totaling approximately 31 million tons. As in the past, Canada was by far the largest exporter, accounting for more than one-third of the total.

New trading agreements reached during 1967 through the General Agreement on Tariffs and Trade (GATT), following lengthy negotiations, provided for a lowering of tariffs on pulp and paper products among the leading industrial nations. As the reductions come into effect in stages over the five years 1968–72, they were expected to stimulate trade. The reductions applied to a broad range of products that in the past comprised only a small portion of the pulp and paper trade. The products included paperboard, book and writing paper, and wrapping papers.

The rapid growth of world demand for paper and paperboard in recent years stimulated the construction of new paper mills throughout the world. In most countries, including the U.S., these mills were designed chiefly to fill domestic needs. But the great exporting areas, especially Canada and Scandinavia, also enlarged their facilities.

In Canada, whose vast forests were expected to be of increasing significance in serving future world demand, several new mills began production in 1967, and others were under construction. Growth was most rapid in British Columbia. In the U.S. the South continued to lead in pulp and paper expansion. Within Scandinavia, the Swedish industry was growing the most rapidly. In Japan the pulp and paper industry had tripled in size within ten years.

The expansion of paper manufacture in many of the less developed nations also continued in 1968. A number of raw materials other than the traditional softwoods and hardwoods were being utilized in some of those areas. They included not only bagasse, or sugarcane waste, now well established as a raw material for paper, but also bamboo, rice straw, and esparto grass.

In pulp and paper manufacture, important developments in technology were occurring.

As always, there was a trend toward wider and faster paper machines, and experimental work continued into the use of computers for machine control. Among the more interesting and significant developments were new methods for forming the sheet on the paper machine, a procedure little changed during the past 150 years. The new techniques, which involved using a vertical rather than a horizontal plane, seemed likely to make the paper machine of the future more compact and less costly.

As competition for markets among the various industrial materials grew more intense, paper and paperboard continued to appear in novel forms. Often these involved their use in combination with plastics, metals, and even wood itself, especially for packaging. Paper furniture was being designed; paper clothes and jewelry created a flurry in the world of fashion; and paper was being formed into an increasing variety of disposable soft goods, such as hospital sheets and pillowcases and surgical gowns.

New forecasts of future world pulp production, made in 1968 by the UN Food and Agriculture Organization (FAO), reflected this versatility. They also reflected the impact that rising standards of living and literacy were constantly exerting on demand for paper and paperboard. FAO forecast that by 1971 world pulp production would reach nearly 135 million tons, as compared with an expected 120 million tons in 1968.   (Go. M.)

PETROLEUM

In spite of political and military conflicts throughout the world, and in spite of a Suez Canal blocked for more than a year, the international petroleum industry continued to surge ahead. The flexibility and resurgence of the industry, led mostly by private enterprise working closely with national petroleum agencies, brought about a vigorous period following the Arab-Israeli war of June 1967. In one month after that conflict, production of crude oil from the Middle East and North Africa plunged almost 4.5 million bbl. per day. Much of what was supplied went to Europe, which had to draw upon its oil storage and imports from the U.S. and South America to meet its minimum demands. By the spring of 1968, however, much of the production was reestablished, and an expanded world tanker fleet began to move crude oil and petroleum products to normal markets once again.

The search for oil and gas continued throughout much of the world, with almost complete disregard for changing and sometimes explosive political climates. At the beginning of 1968, total world reserves of crude oil and natural gas liquids amounted to an estimated 423,650,000,000 bbl. Significant discoveries in North and West Africa, the Middle East, and northern Alaska indicated that continued substantial increases in reserves would be recorded for 1968.

Table X. World Petroleum Statistics for 1967

Area	Production of petroleum liquids (000,000 bbl. daily)	Estimated proved reserves		Refining capacity (000,000 bbl. daily)
		Oil and gas liquids (000,000,-000 bbl.)	Natural gas (000,000,-000 cu.ft.)	
North America	11.74	52.88	352.66	13.17
South America	4.54	23.40	57.21	2.96
Western Europe	0.40	2.06	112.30	11.15
Africa	3.13	45.09	162.89	0.72
Middle East	10.05	248.52	207.96	2.16
Asia	0.78	13.99	41.79	4.22
Eastern Europe (Communist bloc)	6.33	37.71	361.35	6.20
World total	36.97	423.65	1,296.16	40.58

Source: Petroleum Engineer Publishing Co.

Saudi Arabia possessed the largest reserves of petroleum liquids of any country in the world, with proved reserves of 76 billion bbl. Second was the tiny amirate of Kuwait on the Persian Gulf with proved reserves at the beginning of 1968 of 68.7 billion bbl. Next was Iran with 44.2 billion bbl., followed by the United States with 40 billion, the Soviet Union with an estimated 35 billion, and Libya with 31 billion.

North America, principally the U.S., ranked as the world's largest consumer of crude oil, using 41% of the world's production, yet North America had only 11% of the reserves and produced 29% of the world's oil. At the other end of the spectrum was the Middle East, which possessed 60% of the world's crude reserves and produced 28% of the oil, but consumed only 2% of the total. Western Europe had about 1% of the reserves, produced about 1%, and consumed 26%. The Communist bloc countries accounted for about 9% of the reserves, produced 17%, and consumed about 15%.

Total world demand for oil at the beginning of 1968 averaged about 33 million bbl. per day, including an estimated 5.3 million bbl. daily by the Communist bloc countries. The U.S., world's largest consumer of liquid petroleum, opened 1968 with a demand of 12.3 million bbl. per day, and an increase of 4% was expected by year's end.

Japan, consuming about 2.1 million bbl. daily, was the world's fastest growing market for crude oil and gas liquids. It had sustained annual increases of more than 23% for the last several years and expected a similar rise for 1968.

World production of crude oil and natural gas liquids increased by 7% during 1967 over the previous year, averaging 40 million bbl. per day. A similar increase was expected for 1968. The U.S. ranked as the world's largest producer of crude oil and gas liquids, averaging about 10.2 million bbl. daily in 1967, with an anticipated gain of 3½% for 1968. The Soviet Union was credited with a 1967 average daily production of 5.7 million bbl., representing most of the Communist bloc nations' production of 6,330,000 bbl. per day. Venezuela continued to dominate South America, with daily production of 3.5 million bbl. of petroleum liquids.

The year 1967 had seen upsurges in world petroleum activity, and the first half of 1968 indicated an equally strong pace. Consumption rose just under 8%, and oil production rose about 7.4%. Natural gas output grew by 16% in the Eastern Hemisphere, including 38% in Europe. Worldwide gas production rose 8%. Refining capacity passed the 15 billion-bbl.-per-year mark in 1967, a 10% increase over the previous year.   (J. E. Ka.)

PLASTICS

The production of plastics continued to grow at a high rate, achieving in 1968 a total of more than 22 million metric tons, compared with 19 million in 1967. The major producing countries remained in the same order: still in front by a large lead was the U.S., which reached an estimated 7.4 million metric tons, a substantial increase over the 1967 revised figure of 6.4 million. West Germany followed one good year with another and finished 1968 with a figure of just under 3 million metric tons, having maintained a growth rate of nearly 15%. In third place was Japan, whose production climbed to 2.1 million metric tons. Italy continued to maintain the highest expansion rate of the larger producers and followed its outstanding achievements of 1967, during which it had produced 1,266,000 metric tons, with a total of more than 1.4 million in 1968. Official Soviet production in 1967 was 1.1 million metric tons, and it seemed likely that in

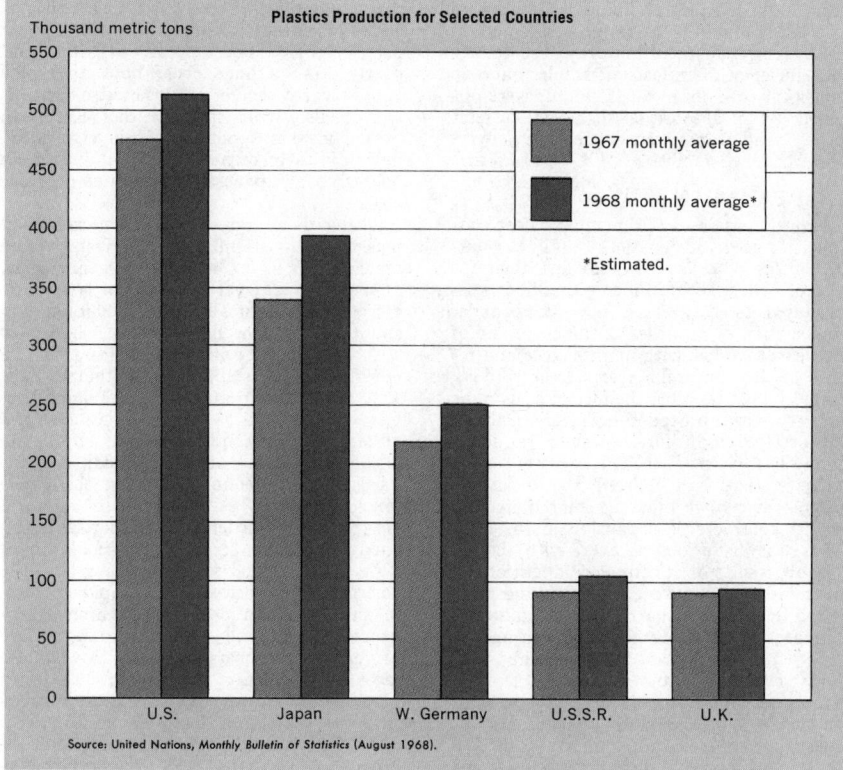

Plastics Production for Selected Countries

Thousand metric tons

Legend: 1967 monthly average / 1968 monthly average*

*Estimated.

Countries: U.S., Japan, W. Germany, U.S.S.R., U.K.

Source: United Nations, *Monthly Bulletin of Statistics* (August 1968).

meet new demands. Companies in the U.S. and Europe announced plans for larger injection machines, and work continued on the mechanical problems accompanying such equipment. Computer control was applied to the injection process in a machine manufactured by the Fellows Gear Shaper Co. of the U.S. The control system, which was included in the machine package, received information from dimensional measurements on the product: if variations exceeded a predetermined value, the machine functions were automatically adjusted to correct them.

In attempts to speed up production new techniques stemming from metalworking methods were developed. The introduction during 1967 of ABS sheets that could be stamped to shape was followed by forging techniques in which hot billets of plastics were fed to a press and stamped, either between matched metal molds or by the use of one formed tool and a rubber block.

(C. I.)

PRINTING

The consumption of printed matter increased in 1968 as did the momentum of change toward an automated industry. The development of expensive, high-speed, automated equipment gave an impetus to the merging of companies both in printing itself and in industries supplying it with equipment, processes, and materials. The need for such equipment provided an opportunity for companies outside the industry to invest the considerable amounts of required capital. For example, computer manufacturers were taking over printing businesses to ensure an outlet for their computerized products. Growth in in-plant printing in the U.K. and most of the other industrialized countries was encouraged by the availability of IBM's MT Composer, a machine that automatically set and justified text matter from a magnetic tape, and also by the availability of new offset plates and easily controlled automatic plate-making equipment. Thus, a pattern was emerging of an industry with automated machinery and equipment and standardized materials and processing. Copying equipment became more sophisticated, with the quality of reproduction improving and output speeds increasing. There was a trend toward installing such equipment in larger organizations and academic institutions to produce limited-edition textbooks and theses.

The United States held one of its largest international printing exhibitions, Print 68, in Chicago in June. Although it was not so large as some European exhibitions such as the German DRUPA and British IPEX, it had some 500 exhibitors (mainly U.S., but also British, East and West German, Italian, and Japanese) and approximately 50,000 visitors.

In lithographic printing the quality of reproduction of business forms and general commercial work improved, due in large part to improvements in paper and ink supplies. The use of web-fed offset machines in the production of newspapers, magazines, and books increased. The use of four-colour, sheet-fed lithograph presses increased for general work, but they were still being used primarily for newspaper, magazine, and directory printing. In the U.S. it was estimated that in less than three years more than half the daily newspapers would be printed by the offset method. In 1968, 46% of U.S. newspapers were printed by offset, including 400 dailies; in the U.K. 90 news-

1968 this figure had risen to 1,250,000. The French production tonnage was 920,000, and no other country exceeded half a million metric tons.

The year 1968 represented the 100th anniversary of the U.S. plastics industry. Almost all materials had a good year, but the polyolefins rated special mention—polypropylene, as in other major countries, experienced tremendous growth. A significant result of this performance was that the prices of commodity plastics finally stopped their long decline and showed signs of hardening. This was particularly marked in the U.S., where polyethylene prices especially became much more firm in the second half of the year.

Plans for increasing production to meet these growing demands were being made not only in the U.S. but also in Europe, where Imperial Chemical Industries announced plans to double its capacity by 1980, and in Japan, where proposed plans would double the output of polyvinyl chloride (PVC) within five years. Growth was also notable in Italy, one of the liveliest of the large producing countries, which was host to the 1968 International Plastics Exhibition in Milan. Not only was Italian production rising rapidly but so was home consumption, while exporting performance was outstanding.

The pattern of plastics utilization seemed likely to remain stable for the next few years, although opportunities for growth seemed greater in some fields than in others. The building industry was expected to increase its usage of plastics by steady escalation rather than by a massive replacement of conventional materials. In the U.K. a building system was announced that was based on large-area panels injection-molded from rigid PVC.

In the automobile industry, consumption of plastics per car continued to increase, on an average, by a figure of a few pounds per year. The introduction by a Japanese firm, Honda, of a small car that featured injection-molded ABS (acrylonitrile-butadiene-styrene) trunk lid and hood, extensive use of large components made of plastics, and, on some models, doors with external panels of ABS undoubtedly caused manufacturers throughout the world to look anew at their designs. A major plastics company in the U.K. announced the installation of a press for thermosetting laminates that was described as being large enough for automobile panels.

Also in the transport field, the Royal Navy reported that since 1960 it had equipped 20 Oberon-class conventional submarines with glass-reinforced polyester casings weighing 20 tons each. It was claimed that the casings would have a maintenance-free life of 20 years, while their aluminum predecessors required servicing every 3 years. In a related area of transportation, plastics materials, especially rigid polyurethane and glass-reinforced polyester materials, were finding use in the construction of containers for shipping and rail freight.

In packaging the major story was from Sweden, where a plastics-based beer bottle was announced. A competitive price was achieved by the use of a thin-walled, thermoformed PVC/PVDC (polyvinylidene chloride) container which was held rigidly in a card tube.

On the materials front the most noteworthy item was the remarkable growth of polypropylene, which had enjoyed an increase in consumption at a rate of about 50% per year beginning in 1966. New materials were mainly of the exotic variety, often the result of work in the aerospace industry. Of greater interest were additions to the polyphenylene resins, which began in 1966 with polyphenylene oxide, followed by a modified version, and then joined commercially by polyphenylene sulfide.

As the sizes of plastics articles became larger and the competition with other materials grew more intense, it became necessary for production methods to be developed to

papers were printed web-offset, 6 of these being dailies. For the production of large-circulation letterpress newspapers, there was a trend toward the installation of letterpress/offset machines as a transition stage for a future changeover to offset.

The development of computers and film-setting machines for typesetting continued, and their use was increasing. High-output cathode-ray-tube filmsetting machines of new design were developed in the U.S. by Harris-Intertype Corp., IBM, Mergenthaler Linotype Co., and RCA. They produced text matter at speeds of up to 10,000 characters a second.

The Harris-Intertype Lithotronic 78 sheet-fed offset machine, which could produce 7,500 sheets per hour, was in operation in the U.S. This was an integrated machine, the operation of which was controlled by a digital logic system computer that automatically controlled ink flow, ink/water balance, register, and paper misfeed. The Goss Co. produced a web-offset press that also used an integrated electronic control system.

Letterpress printing gained a new foothold in Britain, where there was a steady increase in the use of single-, two-, and four-colour sheet-fed rotary presses. Costs of long runs of colour work compared favourably with those of sheet-fed offset presses and were expected to be improved further when the cost of plate making was reduced by the introduction of methods now being developed by plate manufacturers. One of these methods involved presensitized letterpress plates, which were becoming available in the U.S., the U.K., and West Germany.

In New Jersey a book-printing company installed automatic equipment, originally devised in Canada, for the production of books from a reel. A reel of paper was fed into a machine and brought into contact with an endless belt bearing rubber blocks of each page in sequence. The paper was passed through two such units so that it was printed on both sides, with the pages in sequential order. This method eliminated the need for folding and gathering sections, and subsequent binding operations could be conveniently carried out in the same production line. Using this procedure, production of up to 260 books a minute was claimed.

In the field of photogravure printing a new cylinder etching system was produced in West Germany and Finland. The etching process was controlled by a computer into which was fed information concerning the characteristics of the pigmented paper and gelatin to be used. In Italy the Acigraph process, an economical method of making gravure cylinders in about 30 minutes, became available. No carbon tissue or other carrier was required, the cylinders being sensitized and a special magenta screen laid down directly on the metal. Exposure, using xenon light, was made in a special machine, and the cylinders were then developed in the usual way. In Britain and the U.S., equipment was developed to improve the quality of gravure printing by adding to the printing unit an electrostatically charged roller to assist in the transfer of ink from the printing cylinder to the paper. It did this by placing an electrical charge behind the web to draw the ink from the gravure cells.

As a follow-up to an act of Parliament passed in 1964, the British government set up industrial training boards for the printing and publishing and the paper and paperboard industries. The aims of the act were to provide a supply of trained personnel at all levels in industry, to improve the quality and efficiency of industrial training, and to apportion costs more fairly. Funds were obtained by the imposition of a levy on employers, and grants were made to employers with approved facilities.   (J. WHI.)

SHIPBUILDING

As world trade and the merchant fleet continued to grow during 1968, so did the output of the world's shipyards and their intake of orders. With about 40 million gross registered tons (grt) of new ships under construction or on order at the beginning of the year, together with maintenance and repairs on the 200 million grt already afloat, shipbuilding presented the face of a booming industry with an expanding future. One did not need to look far, however, to detect the fly in the ointment. The persistent over-capacity that had marred the industry's progress ever since Japanese shipbuilding began its considerable expansion in the mid-1950s was as serious as ever, with the inevitable results of cutthroat competition for orders, low or nonexistent profits, and competing measures of artificial assistance to shipyards by their respective governments.

The most significant shift, perhaps, was the first sign, if not of distress at least of nervousness, on the part of Japanese shipbuilders about the latest trends. Having hoisted themselves during the previous decade, by brilliant technical achievement and strong home support, to the position of building about half the entire world's new shipping, and having brought into being a new generation of highly advanced shipyards to match their highly trained labour force, they found themselves losing the initiative for the first time since their expansionist era began. Japanese quotes for new orders were found to be uncompetitive with those from Europe on both price and delivery. This most unaccustomed situation elicited from the Japanese builders requests for additional help from their government and an appeal for "stabilization" of prices and capacity by world shipyards. It was an appeal that, when a Japanese delegation put it to European shipbuilders at a meeting in Rome during the summer, met with a somewhat reserved response. For while recent Japanese uncompetitiveness sprang partly from domestic cost inflation and partly from a huge order book that prevented early delivery for new business, it sprang also from the fact that European yards were responding more vigorously, both by their own efforts and with state help, to the Japanese initiatives of previous years.

Although no agreements on international measures to stabilize the industry were reached, much was being done in this regard at the national level by means of large-scale mergers in almost all the main shipbuilding countries. Britain, which by 1967 had been reduced from its historic position as the world's leading shipbuilder to fourth place (exceeded in output by Sweden and West Germany as well as Japan), was the most outstanding example. Spurred by state grants, loans, and attractive credit, famous yards such as John Brown on the Clyde joined up with erstwhile rivals to form groupings of sufficient size to match the big Japanese combines.

On the technical side, disturbing evidence emerged to suggest that the rapid advance in ship design and construction in recent years had, in fact, been too rapid in the case of very large tankers. In about 15 years the most extraordinary development had taken place in the size of standard crude oil carriers, as they grew from about 30,000 to 300,000 tons deadweight. The first series of leaps—to 45,000 tons, then 65,000, then 80,000, then 100,000 tons deadweight—were made without great technical difficulty. But the big advances of the last two years (spurred on by the second closing of the Suez Canal) to 150,000, 200,000, and 250,000 tons deadweight had not been achieved so easily. There were a number of cases of large tankers buckling either on launching or on entry into service, and at one time in 1967 the great majority of big tankers under construction throughout the world had to be modified, with consequent delayed deliveries.

The trend toward specialization continued. Large numbers of container ships were under construction, particularly in West Germany, and novel types of craft such as Hovercraft, hydrofoils, and catamarans were attracting increasing interest.   (M. BY.)

Right, "American Lancer," the first of the United States Lines' container ships arriving at Tilbury, Eng., where the Port of London Authority had invested nearly £30 million for container handling facilities. Below, unloading the ship's 1,200 land-sea containers.

CENTRAL PRESS FROM PICTORIAL PARADE

TEXTILES AND FIBRES

Textile Industry. Great structural changes continued in the world textile situation during 1968. In total activities textile industries collectively still ranked second in comparison with all other industries in terms of increased consumption and production. Nationally and internationally, textiles had become a multifibre, multiprocess industry. The range of raw materials continued to widen, due to the many new man-made fibres. In many textile-producing countries exports continued as a major source of foreign exchange earnings.

In the U.K. several more mergers were arranged to economize in labour and machine utilization. Imbalance of labour was often a problem, and management became more involved with training. By more efficient study of the problems involved, it was realized that an enormous potential existed for increasing productivity from 30 to 50%, using existing equipment. More use was made of computer technology to improve considerably the degree of control over all the resources of large companies and mill groups.

In the U.K. manufacturing activities were expanded and new machinery developments introduced. Imperial Chemical Industries announced plans to build a £5 million dyestuffs plant at Grangemouth, Scot., and Klinger Manufacturing Co., Ltd., completed an impressive expansion program at Ballymena, N.Ire. A new British finishing plant, claimed to be the only one of its kind in Europe, allowed cotton polyester blended sheetings to be continuously bleached and finished, and dyed when required.

In continental Europe production of yarns and cloths was maintained at previous levels, but new machinery developments were fewer. Certain modifications appeared on ring spinning machinery and on conventional winding, warping, and weaving machinery, including rapier and air- and water-jet-operated looms.

A new method for improving flax fibre processing methods on a modified automatic scutcher was announced by a Polish research institute. Designed to handle short lengths of yarn (6 to 9 yd.), a German warp-sampling machine enabled manufacturers to assess speedily the potential in new fabric constructions. Prominent among research activities in the U.S. was the construction of a novel fabric with which to make "fuel-proof" safety suits for astronauts. (A. Dr.)

Natural Fibres. *Cotton.* For the second successive season world cotton production was severely curtailed. The action on the part of the U.S. was deliberate, the aim being to eliminate what was described as the most burdensome surplus of raw cotton in history. As a result, world cotton stocks in two seasons were reduced by about one-third, representing almost 10 million bales, so that at the beginning of the season (August 1968) the supplies held were lower than they had been for many years.

With the disposal of this accumulation of unsold stocks, the foundation was laid for a new approach toward the maintenance of a balanced cotton economy. The adjustment was almost entirely in the U.S., where virtually the whole surplus had built up, but other producers and exporting countries, by restraining their acreage planted, made important contributions toward reestablishing a better statistical position.

The cotton crop in the U.S. during the 1967–68 season was the lowest since the end of the 19th century, being only 7.4 million bales, while other non-Communist countries provided 23.5 million bales, and the Communist areas produced an estimated output of nearly 16 million bales. The world total

of 46.8 million bales was more than 6 million bales smaller than in 1965–66, and the total supply was 73.2 million bales, compared with 78.5 million bales in 1966–67.

World cotton consumption continued to rise, but this tendency leveled off. The use of cotton rose substantially in Asia, but increases elsewhere were modest. Continuation of the strong competition from man-made fibres was again a feature, but more use of blended yarns, particularly those incorporating polyester fibres with cotton, offered fresh scope for future business.

The substantial reduction in output during a period when demand was rising resulted in rising prices. Although shortages were not pronounced, some difficulties were encountered in securing adequate supplies of particular grades and these commanded premium rates. (A. Tl.)

Silk. Although no longer a supplier of raw silk to the main consuming countries, Japan still held the key to the world market. The year 1967 witnessed the unprecedented situation of Japan changing from a large exporter to a hungry buyer of silk from all over the world, in direct competition with those who had been its traditional customers. Throughout the early part of 1968 this position continued unabated. In the period January–June, Japan's consumption of its own production increased by 5%, to 10,400 tons. Meanwhile, imports of silk, both yarns and fabrics, amounted during the same period to the equivalent of about 1,500 tons, and by the middle of the year stocks at last began to accumulate. In markets as sensitive as those of Yokohama and Kobe, this brought about a sharp reaction in prices, which fell in July to a level 20% below the peak and came for a short spell within reach of U.S. and European buyers. Then the tide turned; the Japanese government's tight-money policies were eased and a record consumption spree was expected. Prices rose rapidly.

Meanwhile, the plight of those who, attracted by its cheaper prices, had become dependent upon Communist China was pitiable indeed. In 1967 China was already beginning to fall behind in fulfilling its previous commitments, and in 1968 it became apparent that it was either unable or unwilling to maintain supplies. A bumper crop of cocoons was said to have been harvested in 1967 and again in 1968, and it was difficult to explain why China should not have been a willing or even an anxious seller. There were several contributory factors. China had considerably augmented its capacity for the conversion of raw silk into fabric and into garments, and its policy seemed to be turning toward the export of silk in this form, thus earning a larger slice of foreign currency. Whether or not internal strife disrupted production could not be known, but it was possible that the activities of the Red Guards hampered production and transport.

The difficulty of obtaining supplies had a disastrous effect upon the industry. Orders for silk goods could not be accepted so long as raw material could not be secured with any certainty of being received on time. Coupled with a scarcity of skilled labour, it was not surprising that many traditional silk manufacturers were forced to look to other fibres. (P. W. Ga.)

Wool. World wool consumption declined in the latter half of 1967, but rates were showing signs of improvement toward the end of the year and the overall picture was one of a rising trend during 1968. Prices declined along with consumption in the closing months of 1967, but here too there were signs of recovery by the end of that year. Indeed, world demand for finer merino wool kept prices very firm from the beginning of

the Australian selling season in August, and firmer conditions spread down the quality range to affect coarser crossbreds by the beginning of 1968. Price trends during this period were confused by sterling devaluation, and the New Zealand situation in particular went through a spell of sharp and erratic price movements.

Throughout the first half of 1968 the wool situation was affected by currency uncertainties. The trend of prices turned upward, and in March the gold crisis was closely associated with a peak in wool prices. The rise in prices at that time was only partially lost when the crisis subsided, and subsequent currency nervousness helped to create a firmer movement during May and June.

By mid-1968 wool consumption estimates published quarterly by the Commonwealth Secretariat showed an advance of about 3% in the first half of 1968, compared with the same period in 1967. These estimates referred to nine consuming countries including the major ones in the West.

World production of wool in the 1967–68 season amounted to 5,912,000,000 lb., greasy basis. Production in the 1968–69 season would be about 5,950,000,000 lb. greasy, according to preliminary estimates by the Commonwealth Secretariat. This would represent a new record. (H. M. F. M.)

Man-Made Fibres. In 1968 man-made fibres shared in the expanding demand for textiles and, because of the stabilizing of prices at lower levels in 1967, tended to lead demand in most countries. In the U.K. the effects of devaluation of sterling favoured man-made fibres, as natural fibres became more expensive and as leaders among the man-made fibre producers adopted a restrained policy and kept price increases resulting from more expensive raw materials down to a minimum. Thus consumption of man-made fibres in the U.K. probably rose faster than in most other countries relative to the size of the market. Shortages of various types of fibres led to some firming of prices in various countries. Much interest was shown in a new polyamide-based fibre by du Pont known as Qiana and in Allied Chemical Corp.'s promising biconstituent fibre called Source. (See *Chemicals*, above.)

Interest in carbon fibres for industrial purposes continued to broaden, and a major breakthrough was a carbon fibre developed by Rolls-Royce, Ltd. It was made by carbonizing an acrylic fibre at temperatures approaching 3,000° C.

In most Western countries increasing attention was given to developing fibres from film, and the ability to fibrilate a film to form the warp of a woven fabric without the need for a creel was a notable technical advance. This was applied to polypropylene and polyethylene tape yarns, which appeared to be capable of replacing jute for carpet backing and hessians. (P. M. Re.)

See also Advertising; Alcoholic Beverages; Cooperatives; Economy, World; Electronics; Employment, Wages, and Hours; Fisheries; Food; Fuel and Power; Housing; Industrial Design; Labour Unions; Merchandising; Metallurgy; Mining; Nuclear Energy; Prices; Rubber; Television and Radio; Timber; Tobacco; Tourism; Toys and Games; Trade, International.

ENCYCLOPÆDIA BRITANNICA FILMS. *Chemistry and a Changing World* (1953); *The Living City* (1953); *The Basic Elements of Production* (1954); *Glass—From the Old to the New Through Research* (1954); *You and the Aerospace Future* (1966); *Midwest—Heartland of the Nation* (1968).

Information Science and Technology

Information science and technology is concerned with the structure and properties of scientific information, the techniques for information handling, the characteristics of information processing devices, and the design and operation of information handling systems. Information processing systems are normally expected to collect, identify, and store information items, and to make them available upon demand to a given user population.

In 1968, as in the immediately preceding years, the principal effort in information technology concerned the development of a computer utility that would allow large classes of individual users to have access, more or less simultaneously, to a great variety of services. Such services would be based on the storage of extensive and varied data and program libraries in centralized locations, but, at the same time, would provide information services to users dispersed over large geographical areas.

In working to achieve such a facility, scientists and engineers have developed and improved many types of information processing equipment. They have generated computer storage devices ranging from small so-called associative stores, which provide very fast access to a few stored items, to larger tape-strip stores, which can be used to gain access to many millions of stored items in a second or two. Intermediate-size swapping devices were also increasingly being used to transfer data from large slow-access stores to small fast-access devices.

The terminal equipment (devices used to introduce search requests and display answers) available in 1968 ranged from teletypewriters costing a few hundred dollars to complex cathode-ray-tube graphic art displays valued at more than $200,000 each. Devices providing intermediate facilities included cathode-ray-tube alpha-numeric displays that, when coupled with input keyboard devices, could be used to introduce and display written information.

Data communications equipment was being developed to transmit information at rates ranging from 150 to more than 1.5 million bits (binary digits) per second. This equipment provides links from one computer to another and from the terminals to the computer. To render a service that is really accessible to large groups of users such equipment should be simple, reliable, and inexpensive. Unfortunately, the dynamic, interactive capability needed in a multi-user environment was not currently attainable with simple telephonelike equipment. Considerable work thus remained to be done before fast, sophisticated information facilities could be made universally available.

A computer utility providing long-distance information facilities to many different types of users lends itself to a great variety of applications. Chief among them are the following: automated inquiry systems, including, for example, those used to provide a nationwide airline reservation network; data collection systems, such as those used to handle instantaneous stock quotations; conversational computing systems, in which individual users are provided with personalized computational facilities and which have the capability of defining and storing their own file structures; information distribution systems, which can disseminate information to customers on a selective basis; and interactive graphic systems, such as computer-assisted instruction, where individual students are introduced to new subject matter more or less at their own speed.

While some of the aforementioned applications were not yet in widespread use, in part for technological and in part for economic reasons, there was general agreement that large sections of the population can be provided with personalized interactive information and computing facilities within a few years. There also existed the realization that such a development may bring with it not only considerable benefits but also many social and political problems. On the beneficial side, the timely access to various information facilities can lead to a better informed public and to a faster solution of many problems; some of the technological developments might, in fact, lead to the formulation and solution of new problem areas that could not previously even be considered. On the other hand, there were uncertainties about the facilities as to which of them would lead to desirable progress as opposed to useless, although novel, button-pushing. Furthermore, many people were becoming increasingly aware of the fact that information, thoughtlessly dispersed and used, can create social problems of considerable magnitude. The issues relating to the protection of privacy and ownership of stored information are more complex and more difficult to solve than the technological questions and could be expected to require increasing attention on the part of growing numbers of people in the immediate future.   (GD. SN.)

See also Electronics.

Insurance

The English-speaking nations, especially the U.S., Britain, and Canada, continued in 1968 to lead the world in private insurance. Other nations, however, also increased their sales more rapidly than their growth in national income; percentage gains were high in Germany, Italy, and Japan. Compared with the spectacular disasters of the previous year, 1968 seemed relatively free from exceptional losses. The largest natural catastrophes, earthquakes in Iran and Central America, involved only minor insured losses. Automobile insurance continued to be the major headache for insurers everywhere; increased emphasis on safety and law enforcement hardly slowed the death and damage rates.

U.S. federal government activity in regard to insurance increased in 1968. The Senate inaugurated a federal reinsurance plan for state and industry programs that insure property in riot-prone urban areas; a two-year study of automobile insurance began in the Department of Transportation; and numerous hearings on automobile insurance were held by the Senate Anti-Trust and Monopoly Subcommittee.

Life and Health Insurance. In the U.S. life insurance companies continued an approximate 8% annual growth rate during 1968 and started on the second trillion dollars ($1,000 billion) of life insurance in force. Income from this business was approximately $40 billion; three-fourths came from the premiums from policyholders and one-fourth from investments. Of the $30 billion paid in premiums, slightly less than two-thirds was for life insurance, about one-fourth for health insurance, and less than 10% for annuities. Assets exceeded $182 billion by mid-1968 and investments provided 10% of the increase in U.S. financial capital. A net rate of return of more than 4.8% (be-

fore U.S. income taxes) was expected for the year. Mergers to combine life insurers, mutual funds, and other financial institutions and the formation of holding companies were notable in 1968.

The average U.S. family had approximately two years of its disposable income, or more than $17,000, insured through life insurance, yet it spent less than 4% of its income for this insurance. Purchases of group and credit life insurance increased more rapidly than individual expenditures and accounted for about 40% of all life insurance in force. Benefit payments were estimated at more than $15 billion in 1968; death payments were more than $6 billion, the remainder going to living policyholders and annuitants.

U.S. insurance companies and organizations such as Blue Cross-Blue Shield were each responsible for about one-half the $12 billion in health insurance benefits paid in 1968. More than 165 million persons were insured. Group health insurance sales increased substantially, with employers paying the entire cost in nearly two-thirds of the new contracts. Part B Medicare payments made through private insurers serving as agents for the U.S. government rose sharply. Basic Medicare payments were paid directly by the government.

The life insurance industry in the U.K. again produced record new business totals in 1967, due mainly to a rise in single premiums and an upsurge in the purchase of immediate annuities. New ordinary and industrial (home service) life sums written by members of the Life Offices' Association totaled £7,131 million, an increase of 10%, compared with a 17% increase in 1966. Of the new business total, £6,435 million, against £5,838 million in 1966, was written in the ordinary branch, and £696 million, against £652 million, in the industrial section. New premiums necessary to secure the new benefits were £346 million, compared with £305 million in the previous year. A gross investment yield of 7% was general and bonus distributions to participating policyholders were at or above previous levels.

A growing number of life offices opened up new possibilities for the equity investor by investing premiums under special "equity" life insurance policies and the unit trust movement furthered its appeal as a savings medium through a number of new schemes. New rulings on tax relief involved fundamental changes in general insurance practice designed to close tax loopholes.

Property and Liability Insurance. U.S. property and liability insurers expected a break-even result for underwriting during 1968. Comparisons with 1967 figures were close, indicating approximately a 100% loss and expense ratio for 1968. The loss ratio appeared to be up about 1% and the expense ratio down 1%.

A booming automobile industry and higher automobile insurance rates in some areas were significant factors in an expected 9% overall sales increase for 1968. The total property and liability premium income approached $27 billion. Riots were more widespread in 1968 than in 1967. Fortunately, however, property damage in the more than 170 cities that experienced disorders within the month following the assassination of the Rev. Martin Luther King was less severe than that resulting from the Newark and Detroit riots of the previous year. The summer months brought less trouble than had been predicted.

Fire losses increased about 5% over the previous year's $2 billion record. Windstorms were less spectacular but total extended coverage losses for the year

ending August 1968 were very close to the $1.3 billion losses for the year ending August 1967. Innovations included the formation of a National Flood Insurers Association to write flood insurance on residential property; this insurance was to be backed up by a federal reinsurance plan.

There were experimental programs in several states to guarantee benefits, regardless of liability, for automobile injuries and several new attempts to merchandise automobile insurance through group contracts. Changes based on the first comprehensive revision of the homeowners' multiple-peril insurance program since 1959 were adopted in many states during the last quarter of 1968.

The combined worldwide fire, motor, and miscellaneous accident insurance business of member companies of the British Insurance Association (BIA) rose 9% to an all-time high of £1,372 million in 1967. The premium total included motor insurance of £543 million, fire business of £425 million, and accident (nonmotor) of £404 million. The 1% underwriting profit of £13.1 million compared with £900,000 for 1966 and a loss of £9.3 million for 1965. Devaluation was considered to have played an insignificant part in the improvement. The biggest factor was the virtual elimination of motor insurance losses in both U.K. and overseas business.

The trading accounts of Lloyd's Underwriters on a three-year basis reflected the closure of the 1965 account, a year in which Lloyd's sustained the heaviest underwriting loss in its history, 8.2% or £38 million. The open accounts for 1966 and 1967 indicated improved underwriting in both marine and nonmarine sections.

Although worldwide losses to marine insurers in 1967 were down from the two preceding years, the number of vessels totally lost was the highest ever recorded. The increasing size of tankers and the container revolution presented underwriters with the need to strengthen marine funds against the prospect of heavier claims. Increased liabilities under aviation insurance expected when the "jumbo jets" began operation were also being given serious consideration.

Premiums for fire, motor, and other accident business transacted overseas reached a record £865 million, an increase of £71 million, due in part to the effects of devaluation. Claims were affected by two major disasters—bush fires in Tasmania and the l'Innovation store fire in Brussels—and by the loss of the tanker "Torrey Canyon," U.S. riots, a Louisiana oil fire, Hurricane Beulah, storms and floods in northern Europe, Italy, India, Pakistan, and Australia, and earthquakes in South America, Turkey, and Iran.

Fire damage in the U.K. was £90 million, 10% higher than in 1966. The rising cost of individual large fires continued during 1968; six fires cost over £1 million each, the biggest being the Blackpool store fire, at £1.8 million. Hurricane damage in Scotland early in 1968 was estimated at £25 million–£30 million. BIA member companies paid out £15.9 million in crime losses, compared with £16.7 million in 1966. The total crime haul of £46.7 million, only £9.4 million of which was recovered, included the £711,000 Rothschild bullion robbery.

Problems caused by new insurance legislation around the world were in no way abated. In Tanzania and the Congo (Kinshasa), nationalization of insurance forced out private insurers. Cyprus established new deposit and technical reserve requirements that

Gas works of the Société des Hydrocarbures burning at St. Denis, France, on Feb. 17, 1968. Damage from the fire, set by an arsonist, was estimated at Fr. 20 million.

"PARIS MATCH" FROM PICTORIAL PARADE

could force insurers to withdraw. Singapore introduced an insurance act calling for deposits and returns separate from those formerly required under the Malaysian act. Financial and other controls curbed foreign insurance operations in Uganda, Kuwait, Zambia, Thailand, Pakistan, India, and Brazil. In contrast, the Indonesian government began favouring foreign insurers. (D. L. Bi.; P. Ss.)

See also Cooperatives; Disasters; Industrial Review; Social Services.

ENCYCLOPÆDIA BRITANNICA FILMS. *Casualty Insurance* (1954).

Intelligence Operations

Although no major espionage activity came to public attention in 1968, there was the usual sporadic crop of arrests concerning petty agents and superficial breaches of security. Most notable was the number of disturbing incidents in West Germany, pointing to weaknesses in the security of NATO.

A mysterious wave of suspected suicides among senior Bundeswehr officers and West German government officials started on October 8, when Rear Adm. Hermann Lüdke was found shot dead in a friend's hunting preserve in the Eifel Mountains of West Germany. From early 1966 to mid-1967 he had been deputy chief of the logistic section of SHAPE (Supreme Headquarters, Allied Powers Europe), then located at Rocquencourt near Versailles in France. He had held a CTS (cosmic top secret) clearance, and he knew the capacities of European ports, transport, defense industries, the location of some 16,000 tactical nuclear war-

South Korean Supreme Court in July 1968 reduced sentences imposed earlier against Ung-no Yi (below), a painter, and more than 30 other Koreans charged with spying for North Korea. Left, children of the defendants weeping in the Seoul District Criminal Court when sentences were pronounced.

CAMERA PRESS—PIX FROM PUBLIX

heads, ordnance stockpiles of the allied armed forces, and perhaps also the details of "Strike Plan," the overall contingency plan against a Soviet attack on the West.

On September 27 Gerhard Schröder, the West German minister of defense, had presided over a luncheon given in honour of Lüdke, who was due to retire from the Bundesmarine three days later. After the luncheon Vice-Adm. Gert Jeschonnek, the navy chief and an officer of the Military Counterespionage Service (MAD or Militärische Abschirmdienst der Bundeswehr), took Lüdke aside for questioning. Lüdke was presented with a film made with his own miniature camera and developed at a Bonn photographic shop—containing a few photos of NATO documents marked "Secret." At first he pretended that somebody must have stolen his camera, but later (as the film also contained a few pictures of his family at a seaside resort) he admitted that he wanted the documents for his memoirs. He was allowed to go home, but the following day was again interrogated for six hours by MAD officers. However, he was neither arrested nor shadowed. Before the West German prosecutor general took over the investigation, Lüdke was dead. Since he had a fist-sized wound in his chest, the suspicion was that he was shot from behind.

On the day of Lüdke's death, his close friend, Maj. Gen. Horst Wendland, deputy chief of the Federal Intelligence Service (BND or Bundesnachrichtendienst), shot himself in his office. On October 14 Hans Heinrich Schenk, civil servant in the Ministry of Economics, hanged himself in his Cologne apartment. On October 16 Edeltraud Grapentin, a librarian in the Federal Press and Information Office, took a fatal overdose of sleeping tablets. On October 18 Lieut. Col. Johannes Grimm, working in the Alarm and Mobilization Section of the Ministry of Defense, shot himself in his Bonn office. On October 21 the Ministry of Defense announced that a senior clerk, Gerhard Böhm, had been missing for six days, and on October 31 his body was found in the Rhine near Cologne. In Bonn it was officially explained that all these suicides (Lüdke's suicide or murder excepted) had nothing to do with security matters.

On October 25 Konrad Ahlers, the official government spokesman, confirmed press reports that six East German spies, all scientists who had come to West Germany from East Germany as "political refugees," had succeeded in escaping to East Berlin.

The prosecutor general, speaking on October 29 at a press conference in his Karlsruhe office, revealed the extraordinary story of the theft by three Soviet spies of a Sidewinder air-to-air rocket, as used by the West German Starfighter jets. It was stolen in October 1967 from a NATO base at Zell, near Neuburg on the Danube, by Master Sergeant Wolf Diethard Knope, a Starfighter pilot, Manfred Ramminger, a Krefeld architect, and Josef Linowski, a Polish-born master locksmith. They loaded the rocket into a car, smashing the rear window to allow the missile's nose (covered with a carpet) to project. Ramminger took the Sidewinder to Krefeld, where it was dismantled, packed into previously prepared crates, and sent by air freight to Moscow via Paris.

On September 12 Nihat Imre, a Turkish official at NATO headquarters in Brussels, was caught redhanded in his office photographing secret documents. As chief financial controller responsible for the administrative budget, he had complete access to

Evidence exhibited at trial of convicted spy Douglas Britten included a Soviet spy-kit camera that works in total darkness. Camera was found inside a wallet in Britten's car with a miniature code book for decoding messages from Moscow.
KEYSTONE

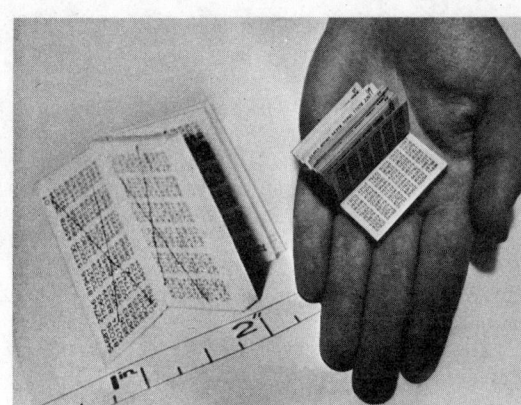

BEN ROTH AGENCY

NATO's military and infrastructures budgets and probably more secrets than Lüdke, Wendland, or Grimm. Deported by the Belgian government, Imre left for Turkey on September 18, shadowed en route by Turkish security men. He was arrested in Ankara after allegations of espionage for the U.S.S.R. and was to be tried by a military court.

A Royal Air Force chief technician, Douglas Ronald Britten, who for six years sold defense secrets to Soviet agents, was sentenced at Old Bailey, London, on November 4, to 21 years' imprisonment. After four years' service at a British air base in Cyprus, Britten was employed from October 1966 at RAF Digby, a secret communications centre in Lincolnshire. His contact was "Yuri," actually Aleksandr Ivanovich Borisenko, first secretary in the cultural department of the Soviet embassy. Borisenko left Great Britain on Sept. 20, 1968, six days after Britten made his first appearance at Bow Street Magistrates' Court, London.

In this connection Michael Stewart, the British secretary of state for foreign affairs, ordered an investigation into the number of staff employed by the Soviet embassy in London. On November 11, Sir Paul Gore-Booth, permanent undersecretary at the Foreign Office, told Mikhail Smirnovsky, the Soviet ambassador, that there were 69 Soviet diplomats and 10 service attachés in London, compared with 31 diplomats and 9 service attachés in the British embassy in Moscow. There were also in London about 180 members of trade missions, Moscow Narodny Bank and Aeroflot officials, as well as journalists. Sir Paul expressed the hope that the size of the Soviet embassy personnel would be limited.

On October 6 Gennadi Roskov, a member of the economic section of the Soviet embassy in Rome, was ordered by the Italian government to leave Italy immediately. On the same day it became known that police had arrested four Italians, including two employees of the Ministry of Foreign Affairs. The last two were Ardens Polastri, a duplicating machine operator, and Aurelio Pasquali, an archivist. Italian counterespionage officers alleged that Polastri and Pasquali had been selling secret documents to Soviet agents.

In March and April 1968 the London *Sunday Express* published, in four installments, the memoirs of "Kim" Philby (Harold Adrian Russell Philby), a Soviet agent within the British intelligence for more than 20 years. Each installment was accompanied by a critical analysis by Chapman Pincher, a defense correspondent. In September Philby's memoirs, under the title *My Silent War*, appeared in London in book form, with an introduction by Graham Greene. Also published in 1968 was an investigation entitled *Philby*

—the Spy Who Betrayed a Generation by Bruce Page, David Leitch, and Philip Knightley, with an introduction by a thriller writer and former diplomat, David Cornwell (pseudonym, John Le Carré). Hugh Trevor-Roper, professor of modern history at Oxford, devoted a book to *The Philby Affair*, in which he described his wartime colleague as a Hamlet figure, a divided soul. "How," he asked, "can anybody claim to have known him, since he deceived us all?" Trevor-Roper did not put Philby in the class of the Soviet Oleg Penkovski or the German master spy Richard Sorge, but rated him as an operator of remarkable ability and nerve. Le Carré, in his introduction, pointed out an intriguing coincidence: Gen. Wladyslaw Sikorski, the Polish prime minister, perished at Gibraltar on July 4, 1943, in an aircraft accident, at a time when Philby was in charge of British counterintelligence operations in Spain. "If Sikorski was assassinated," asked Le Carré, "is it conceivable that Philby planned the operation on behalf of his Russian masters . . . ?"   (K. Sм.)

Inter-American Affairs

The hopeful tone in inter-American relations that had been set by the conference of American presidents in Punta del Este, Uruguay, in 1967 was hardly maintained in 1968. Economic realities limited the ability of the U.S. government to maintain the financing of Latin-American development at former levels; the Latin Americans were forced by hard facts to reconsider the direction of their own efforts toward economic integration; the influence of Cuba began to wane despite the Havana government's continuing efforts to promote guerrilla activities.

Alliance for Progress. The U.S. balance of payments and domestic fiscal position made cuts in the aid program inevitable; for the fiscal year beginning July 1 the U.S. House of Representatives reduced appropriations for the Alliance for Progress from $765 million, which had been requested by the administration, to $420 million. The reactions of prominent Latin Americans were predictable, but the decision did no more than underline the evident fact that the concepts on which the Alliance for Progress was based were of little interest to either the administration or Congress in the U.S. It seemed likely that the Alliance, like previous attempts by Washington to promote political stability and economic growth in Latin America, would soon cease to have any meaning.

It became clear in 1968, as the good intentions expressed at the 1967 meeting of presidents faded, that the Latin Americans expected little from the U.S.

"Launching of the first German rocket to Moscow."—Wolf, Osnabruck, Germany.

and were on the whole more prepared than in the past to seek their own solutions to the problems of reform and growth.

Regional Integration. The seventh annual conference of the Latin American Free Trade Association (LAFTA) closed at the end of 1967 without reaching agreement on the important question of adding a further 25% in value of the region's trade to the common list for duty-free treatment by 1973. It was found that the requirements of the Treaty of Montevideo (1960), which had brought LAFTA into existence, could not be met without adding petroleum (15% of total intraregional trade) and wheat (12.5%), both sensitive subjects in which the Latin-American republics were deeply involved, either as producers with exportable surpluses or as reluctant net importers. The meeting was adjourned until July, when another attempt was made to reach agreement; by September it seemed that an easier way out of the difficulty would have been to modify the treaty.

Besides the specific obstacles to integration that discussions failed to remove in 1968, it became clear that as trade liberalization progressed it was necessary to include in the duty-free group a growing number of industrial goods, a step for which the highly protected manufacturing enterprises of many Latin-American countries were by no means prepared. Another difficulty built into LAFTA was the complexity of the adjustments and concessions needed in the simplest trade liberalization. It was feared that profound market disturbances would occur in the economies of smaller member states such as Chile, Colombia, or Uruguay, when required to lower their tariff barriers toward countries, such as Argentina or Brazil, having more developed industrial structures and lower production costs.

An appreciation of these problems was a factor in the energy with which the Andean countries pursued the goal of a subregional form of economic integration. As a consequence of earlier meetings in Bogotá, Colombia, in 1966 and in Quito, Ecuador, in 1967, the Corporación Andina de Fomento (Andean Development Corporation) was established by Bolivia, Chile, Colombia, Ecuador, Peru, and Venezuela; its authorized capital was $100 million and its head office was set up in Caracas, Venezuela.

The Andean group also drew up in February a framework for the regional development of petrochemical industries, designed to avoid duplication and to utilize resources most efficiently; all the member states were petroleum producers. The allocation of investment and production programs within the group was seen as a good response to the frequent recommendations of the Inter-American Development Bank and other economic experts that the basic development of Latin America should be conceived and planned on a regional basis, with geographic rather than political boundaries as the guiding factor.

The Andean group also attempted, without great success, to reach agreement on the creation of an Andean common market. Although the levels of development of the six countries differed less than those of the LAFTA countries as a whole, there were, nevertheless, problems related to the high cost structure in Venezuela. A meeting planned for May was postponed until the beginning of August, and held in Cartagena, Colombia, but no agreement was reached after ten days of talks.

Another move toward the integration of the interests and resources of a geographic subregion was the setting up of an intergovernmental committee by the foreign ministers of the countries of the Río de la Plata Basin, or, more correctly, the countries with territories in the Paraná-Paraguay river system. These countries (Argentina, Brazil, Bolivia, Paraguay, and Uruguay) had refrained from considering the possibility of creating a common market, for which economic conditions were hardly propitious, and concentrated their attention on drawing up priorities for joint development. At a meeting held in May in Santa Cruz, Bolivia, a treaty was drawn up for subsequent ratification. The development of the very large hydraulic and navigational resources of the Río de la Plata Basin was of great potential importance to all the countries concerned; one particularly important result might be a modification of Paraguay's economic isolation.

The harmonious development of the region was not encouraged, however, by argument between Argentina and Brazil over fishing rights in the Río de la Plata estuary and allegations by Argentina that the construction of dams and irrigation projects in the upper reaches of the Paraná River in Brazil was interfering with the water level downstream.

Integration in the Central American Common Market (CACM) progressed modestly; the more nearly equal levels of economic development of the member countries enabled them to achieve a closer harmonization of their trade policies than was possible elsewhere in Latin America. In July U.S. Pres. Lyndon Johnson announced additional aid from the U.S. for the CACM countries. A meeting of Central American congresses was held early in the year, at which the integration of financial policies was discussed. At a meeting of the Central American Monetary Council it was agreed to set up a joint fund for monetary stabilization and policy coordination. Ambitious discussions on the question of political unity not surprisingly foundered on the deeply rooted differences of regime among the member states.

A difficulty that had not been fully foreseen became evident in 1968; the encouragement of industry by offering "regional" status—that is, free access to the combined market of the five Central American countries for the products of a plant of economic size—resulted in the setting up of large modern establishments, many foreign-owned, which were driving small local concerns out of business. The small industrialist in Central America could not be said to have a strong political lobby, but the collective resentment against foreign encroachment to which integration had opened the door was, nevertheless, becoming a matter for concern.

Foreign Capital. There had been for some years in Latin America a growing apprehension over the acquisition of locally constituted businesses by foreign, especially U.S., interests. The Latin-American economies required the contribution to their development that foreign capital could make, but a distinction was seen between the introduction of new industrial activities by means of an investment of foreign capital, and the practice, increasingly followed by foreign interests, of acquiring the control of domestic businesses. The former was regarded as a positive contribution to the economy—provided that it did not conflict with national interests—and the latter was seen as a threat to economic autonomy and even to national sovereignty.

A further distinction was sometimes drawn between

continued on page 430

TOWARD
A SOUND ECONOMY
IN LATIN AMERICA

By Ludwig Erhard

Ludwig Erhard, minister of economics after World War II and later chancellor of West Germany. German economic recovery after the war was credited in large part to his policies. In this article he examines Latin America's economy and offers solutions to its problems.

The Latin-American world, despite its size and diversity, could still be comprehended as a whole in 1968 so far as its culture and spirit were concerned. But, in contrast, different socioeconomic philosophies and, here and there, doubts about political stability distinguished the economies of the individual nations. The transformation in living conditions that became manifest everywhere after World War II brought about radical shifts bordering on upheaval in the Latin-American states, which were moving "between the times" in their evolution. Such considerations of the historical evolution and present political shape of Latin America give a definite cast to its sociological, economic, and cultural phenomena. This distinctiveness must be kept in mind in any consideration of this relatively young continent still trying to find and develop its place in both world politics and the world economy and seeking to give itself a new look in a changed world.

What a Communist calls "socialism" is by no means identical —apart, perhaps, from individual judgments—with the political concepts prevailing in Latin America. There, "socialism" is considered to mean social progress and more social justice and its features are, therefore, evolutionary rather than revolutionary. In a similar way a "dictatorship" is not simply tantamount to terror and rule by force, but often presents itself as the guardian of outward order. Political parties that call themselves "Christian" hold convictions that are quite different from those maintained by their alleged brother parties in Europe, especially on economic matters. The same can be said of the religious content of the prevailing Catholic faith. And in Latin America liberalism is certainly not understood to mean "progressive" as it does in the U.S., nor does it signify, as yet, a forward-looking neoliberalism of the European kind. The term "liberal" is used rather in the sense of Manchester liberalism, the classical notion of laissez-faire and free trade.

Yet, considering that in the rest of the world, and especially in Europe, sociological and sociopolitical ideas seem to be getting more and more blurred and tempered by a feeling that modern times could dispense with clearly defined concepts of order, it is only natural that the younger Latin-American nations should not think in terms of rigid order when contemplating economic buildups. At the same time, it is not surprising that while ideological allegiances are being regarded as old-fashioned or outdated in Europe, they should still have relatively major significance in Latin America.

Supranationalism. Advances in technology, science, and transport tend to cause economic areas and human beings to move ever closer together, and, at the same time, new interest groups assume shape on a higher than national level. One might be tempted to say that while the world has widened, it has also become narrower. Nobody, to be sure, would speak up for national autarchy any longer, but neither can anyone deny that national protectionism has merely given way to group selfishness on a wider basis. The scene has changed, but the mischief has not been removed.

Despite their success in intraregional trade the new units that

have arisen in Europe, the European Economic Community (EEC) and the European Free Trade Association (EFTA), are unable to overcome the weaknesses inherent in their constitutional division and will, therefore, run up against the limits of their "common" policies over and over again. It is also more and more clearly recognizable that the supranational principle as a possible interim solution has not, at least up to the present, been able to supersede, let alone replace, either the national economies or the free play of economic forces on a worldwide scale. Hence, it may be assumed that a supranational Europe cannot and will not be the ultimate form of the continent, either economically or politically.

This criticism must not be understood to be a downright condemnation; for the nearly explosive technological development, with ever newer and farther-reaching discoveries in natural science, makes it plausible to ignore national frontiers and to call for wider and wider common markets. And it is certainly true that only countries in more or less the same stage of development can combine in economic unions that will enable them, by their very unity, to hold their own in the modern world. Even so, the world must not once again, albeit by different means, become divided into wealthy and powerful countries and peoples on the one hand, and poor and weak ones on the other.

Major economic blocs become culpable when they abuse their economic power to create a new kind of dependence, which can only be understood as reminiscent of the old colonial system. One may well ask, for example, for what compelling or intelligible reasons (for the standards of productivity are obviously not the yardstick) certain countries, especially in Africa, are regarded as eligible for association in the EEC while the demands for a closer relationship of other economies, more similar to those of Europe, are flatly refused. An unbiased observer would find it hard to accept, as appropriate for an "economic community," the argument that such decisions have been based on purely economic considerations.

The resort to economic association without a constitutional framework, in the hope that it will provide a new political and socioeconomic order that might prove to be a genuine synthesis, is an undertaking that will keep people excited and engaged for some time to come. Also, apropos of Latin America, people have not only given thought to the question of how to pull that continent, or parts of it, into closer economic coordination, they have also established the framework for it. The results obtained so far from commercial interrelationship certainly justify higher expectations, but the Latin-American continent, thinly populated as it still is despite high local birthrates, will ultimately be less able than Europe to solve its problems in isolation.

The structural features of the Latin-American economies are especially significant with regard to their sociological foundations and do not readily permit a comparison with Europe. A continent, still rather at the beginning of its industrialization and with pronounced agrarian monocultures in some of its regions, can neither attain industrial self-sufficiency nor hold its own in international competition if the highly developed industrial countries maintain sharply rising agricultural outputs that

render them less and less dependent on external supplies. Moreover, the practice (demonstrated by the EEC) of selling one's own produce on the world markets by means of high subsidies while shielding domestic production by a preference system is bound to lead to dislocations not only in the home markets but in the world market as well. Under the pretense of putting things "in order," any genuine, organic order is systematically disrupted.

Preferential treatment is all the more disastrous when not just industrial products of other countries are favoured, or disfavoured, but when agriculture is also affected. It remains unintelligible what logic is involved in reeducating consumers to buy African coffee, cocoa, or bananas if they really prefer the same products from Latin America, unless political reasons that do not really fit into the contemporary landscape are invoked. Once colonial domination has declined, it must not be permitted to go on under a different name. Desirable though the development of economic relations between Europe and Africa may be, Africa cannot readily be bracketed together with Europe as far as economic and trade policies are concerned. Nor should the countries of Latin America be regarded and treated as a domain of the U.S. Anyone who seeks to justify and praise the advantages of large economic areas is, therefore, credible only if and when he points at the same time to the dangers to which they give rise.

Agrarian Reform. There seems to be general agreement that a more intense development of the industrial sector is indispensable to the building of a sound economy in Latin America; overproduction of agricultural and animal products can no longer be overlooked. In view of the sociological structure of Latin America, writers all over the world advocate a land reform: breaking up of the large estates in order to overcome the threatening poverty and to prevent the emergence of an industrial proletariat. Their arguments are irrefutable on both moral and sociopolitical grounds. But other problems are involved. The creation of new farmsteads will, more often than not, result in a higher agricultural output, which is certainly a social benefit to the extent to which it helps to feed the hungry. Where such additional output comes on an already saturated market, however, and

either remains unsold or endangers the viability of the new farms, evil will merely assume a different shape.

Many inadequacies in this field may yet be remedied by education and training, but the countries concerned are engaged not only in a struggle for economic and social progress but also in a race against time. It must not be forgotten that educational and training facilities may be more readily available in the cities and towns than in rural areas, since developed rural communities have not yet evolved or have been hampered in their development by the redistribution of land. As land reform progresses, even viable farmsteads may operate for some time with lower productivity and less profit than large estates did, because the expanding farming sector lacks markets for the part of its output that exceeds mere self-sufficiency. Owing to the vastness of the area, it is hard to organize cooperative societies that would aid production and distribution. The high birthrate, however, warrants expectations of a more rapid and intense exploitation of the land as well as more harmony in the coordination of country and town. Considering these aspects, one should not yield to premature resignation when viewing the difficulties that stand in the way of a more balanced sociological structure.

In Latin America, with its strong element of monoculture, one should not try to resort to a regional or even worldwide manipulation of production and distribution; this is merely a handy technique that does not get at the roots of the problem. Half a century ago, Brazil's practice of dumping coffee into the sea rather than letting the price fall below cost was severely criticized and pointed out to students as a strange phenomenon. At least the Brazilians were attempting, though with questionable results, to avoid overproduction, whereas Europeans have since developed a downright perfect system that encourages overproduction almost without risk to producers but at the expense of consumers and taxpayers. It seems to me that we thus forfeit any right to hand out advice to other countries faced with similar problems.

The fact that such manipulations are classified as "order" is just one symptom of degeneration in a world that subscribes to the illusionary belief that life can be brought into conformity with calculation. It would seem that economic planners have erred once more at the taxpayer's expense.

Inflation Problems. In Latin America the progress of industrialization is in part appreciable and always recognizable. In most countries, however, the opinion prevails that a collectivist economic system should have precedence over liberal tenets and that it is incumbent upon the authorities to provide economic planning with regard to both principles and targets. It is true that liberal voices are heard increasingly, but their philosophy is still quite frequently, and unfortunately, associated with the exploitation of the poor.

Most Latin-American countries are ridden with inflation, although in different degrees, and efforts at stabilization fail only too often. This would seem to indicate a general lack of confidence in a stable economic and political order, which, apart from all other handicaps, provides little incentive for the investment of foreign capital. As a rule, industrial activity is subject to official authorization and control and is tied, directly or indirectly, to national targets. Foreign exchange allocations for the purchase of capital goods, spare parts, or even raw and auxiliary materials are granted or refused according to the balance of payments situation. Only the businessman who adjusts his activity to the government's plan and gets the necessary licenses can count on regular supplies and an orderly flow of production. He can also be sure of nearly absolute protection from any, and especially foreign, competition.

Since such a procedure tends to impair productivity rather than promote it, new industries can be developed only behind high tariff walls and without exposure to constant pressure for greater efficiency. As a result output is seldom competitive in the world market. Excessive tariffs lose their character as a temporary assistance to infant industries and tend to become

Organizations formed to establish economic cooperation among countries of Central and South America. The Andean Development Corporation and the Río de la Plata Development Group were set up in 1968 to promote economic development on a regular basis.

REGIONAL ECONOMIC COOPERATION IN LATIN AMERICA

Nations participating in:
Latin American Free Trade Assn.

Central American Common Market

Regions benefiting from multinational participation in:
Andean Development Corporation

Río de la Plata Development Group

permanent institutions, keeping countries away from the world market instead of permitting them to be more integrated with it. Thus, by means of excessive protectionism, many Latin-American governments, though committed to social progress and to overcoming revolutionary tendencies, make it easy for the rich or otherwise privileged to earn more and more money without making an appropriate effort while keeping down the already low living standard of the masses.

This, in the last analysis, is also at the root of inflation. People who do not live with the market do not realize the nature of inflation. They are unable to judge how much they stand to gain from sound conditions or through a more efficient national economy and/or a wealthier state. Those with capital are, however, hesitant to put it to productive use. It does not seem to pay to invest or to step up production for a stagnant market. This behaviour seems surprising, as entrepreneurs (and there *are* entrepreneurs in Latin America) still have at their disposal local raw materials and cheap labour, which, with the application of the most recent production methods, can promote both economic and social progress and political stability. Entrepreneurs feel handicapped by the all too frequent interference with their freedom of decision. They shy away from ventures, with the result that the planning authorities become ever more ambitious.

A protectionist policy that encourages local investment or curbs the outflow of capital cannot remove the general suspicion that a government might resort once more to an expansion of credit and deficit spending. Moreover, the questionable merits of foreign exchange controls have been seen too often to inspire confidence. This instrument can help overcome a temporary balance of payments deficit but, when used for purposes of trade policy, it is bound to paralyze the dynamic forces of an economy and deprive it of all flexibility.

Foreign Investments. As a rule, the countries of Latin America are in need of foreign capital of one kind or another, although the causes of the need vary widely. Capital, however, is not attracted by easy profit but by a sound basis for investment. It need not be feared, except in special cases, that foreign capital will assume a controlling position. One cannot really expect foreign investors to have more confidence in the domestic order of a country than national owners of capital who try to place their money abroad. A more liberal policy vis-à-vis foreign investors would help to keep national capital at home.

Another danger in the industrialization of Latin America is that efforts may be concentrated in the cities and larger towns while the rural areas are allowed to stagnate or decline. A modern development, however, is not compatible with such a material and cultural division, which would tend to give rise to social unrest. No solution is to be found in mere "self-sufficiency" for more human beings, although that would be a lot better than desperate poverty. The aim must be to absorb more and more people and ever wider strata of the population into the economic process. In no other continent has it become so clear that the division of city and country creates stark social contrasts and causes deep-seated unrest as it has in Latin America, rich in natural resources though it is. Social backwardness on the one hand and an undeniable will to progress on the other give rise to those tensions that move Latin America more and more into the centre of world politics. It is, therefore, by no means odd to subscribe to the opinion that the last big struggle between a free way of life and totalitarian coercion may well be waged in that region.

Finally, the capital-possessing countries should reconsider the forms and techniques of their development aid. The fact that schools and training centres are highly appreciated shows the urge of these developing nations to make headway by their own means and abilities. There must, however, be room for the practical application of newly acquired knowledge. This calls for modern plants, which might best be provided by foreign investors.

More and more economies, especially those of the industrial countries of Europe, resort to deficit spending as an easy way to cover budget deficits or to ensure full employment. Ignoring the dangers inherent in such a practice, policy makers do not hesitate to use short-term loans to finance long-term investments, the productivity of which may even be highly questionable. This is done in the expectation that the economic recovery so sparked may produce higher yields and rising tax revenues and thus allow for a consolidation of the economic situation. While this may work out, it is by no means a foregone conclusion.

Those economists who demand low interest rates or additional money or credit facilities as an integral part of a policy mix should consider whether it might not be appropriate to put such anticyclical expenditure, in the form of tied loans, at the disposal of countries in the course of industrial development. Such a policy would require careful consideration and continuous review. It would also be necessary to ensure that funds were not applied in a one-sided way to develop state-owned industries but were made available on an increasing scale to private enterprise. Where such a policy also succeeds in encouraging the activation of local capital, optimum results might be expected.

Such a policy would be a convincing manifestation of solidarity. If it is asked whether social expenditure of one kind or another will ultimately serve the local population better than an effort to overcome the poverty of other peoples and ease international tension, then there can only be one honest response: allegiance to a free world committed to mutual solidarity. All nations should come to realize that a further accentuation of the existing social contrasts, or just the spread of hopelessness, will divide the world to the disadvantage of everybody.

Economic Prospects. Another problem is indissolubly connected with this. When an entire continent, admittedly in different ways, is faced with the responsibility to spread and promote industrialization, then excessive external protection is the worst possible means of attaining world market standards. While it is advisable to specialize, it would certainly not be a good thing to concentrate on items too far out of the ordinary.

The industry of Latin America must be competitive in the world market, or at least it must consistently strive toward that end. Governments should, therefore, afford a maximum of liberty and competition. Particularly at the beginning, domestic demand will not be large enough to allow for a rational scale of operations. Higher productivity and reasonable prices can ensure not only better chances in the world market, but also increasing domestic demand, which will in turn allow a country to continue its liberal policy. The "rich" in Latin America probably do not fully appreciate how much their fate depends on whether or not the "poor" will be turned into consumers. If this breakthrough succeeds, all conditions for a wealthy, progressive, and politically stable continent will be satisfied.

It is my conviction, gained by personal experience, that Latin-American statesmen show, on the whole, an impressive open-mindedness and sobriety. They are knowledgeable and responsible enough to know what is sound and what is not and to realize, moreover, how inadequate are many of the methods that the people still tolerate. On my last tour of Central America, in the spring of 1968, I had talks with heads of states and governments, Cabinet members, central bank presidents, and other bankers. I spoke to students at universities, and also to businessmen and trade unionists. All the time I tried to arrive at a fair and balanced opinion.

It is my own conclusion that Latin America will win the race if it sticks to the principles of freedom and is also courageous enough to counter those political influences not based on economic achievement and to check the power of monopolies. Genuine entrepreneurs of the kind I met desire not protection but freedom, not dependence upon the authorities but free enterprise and their own responsibility. I am deeply convinced that an economic policy designed to give room to free enterprise and efficiency will also produce the best social result. Latin America is faced with a fundamental decision.

continued from page 426

manufacturing (or industries with a physical end product to be added to national supplies) and activities that exploited national physical resources (the extractive industries) or made profits out of the nation's savings (banking and insurance). In Mexico, for instance, foreign ownership of or even participation in certain "sensitive" activities was limited or proscribed in accordance with the principle of "mexicanization."

This issue had not been clearly defined, since there were many different shades of opinion all over Latin America. It was, however, extensively discussed in 1968 and, virtually for the first time, brought fully into the open. The almost traditional resentment of foreign control of national resources, such as petroleum, shifted to other fields and was unequivocally manifested in connection with, for example, banking and finance, the automobile industry, and pharmaceuticals.

A factor that exacerbated a difficult situation was the support given to private business interests in Latin America by the U.S. Congress and administration. Many Latin Americans believed, not without some justification, that the U.S. corporations in Latin America were the instruments through which U.S. foreign policy was carried out. In comparison with the U.S., the private sector in Latin America was weak and was rarely or never able to defy the government; the influence of government officials in the business world had long conditioned Latin-American thinking.

Attempts were made in 1968 to achieve more precise definitions of the acceptable roles of foreign capital, though little progress was made in removing this source of friction.

Guerrillas. The guerrilla movement that the 1967 conference of the Organization of Latin-American Solidarity sought to promote throughout Latin America made virtually no progress in 1968. Militia forces gained experience in tackling guerrilla bands, and the few exploits of kidnapping or more serious activity that the subversive groups could claim were not such as to do them much credit. The capture and death of "Che" Guevara in Bolivia in October 1967 deprived the guerrilla movement of its most romantic figure; no one appeared to take Guevara's place.

A major crisis occurred in July when the Cuban press published excerpts from a document claimed to be Guevara's campaign diary, which had fallen into the hands of the Bolivian Army when he was captured. The Bolivian minister of the interior, Antonio Arguedas Mendieta (*see* BIOGRAPHY), who had obtained the diary from Bolivian Pres. René Barrientos Ortuño, admitted giving a copy to Cuban agents; he fled the country when the facts became known in Bolivia, but later returned. The diary was of little intrinsic value, but its publication in Cuba was generally regarded as a minor tactical victory for Havana.

Student Unrest. The rapid spread throughout Latin America of demonstrations of differing degrees of violence among university and even secondary school students reached alarming proportions in 1968, erupting into extremes in Mexico City on the eve of the Olympic Games (October). This unrest was variously attributed to Cuban subversion, to genuine dissatisfaction with scholastic conditions and the quality of teaching, and to resentment at attempts by governments to deprive universities of their traditional autonomy and immunity from police intervention.

Some governments accentuated the bitterness of the students' mood by excessively harsh repression, and there was little doubt that police methods were in many cases more brutal than the situation required. Some Latin Americans drew cold comfort from the observation that student violence was occurring elsewhere in the world and appeared to have become a very widespread phenomenon. There was little evidence to support the contention that student demonstrations throughout the world were planned and guided from a single centre of subversion; a more generally accepted hypothesis was that a taste for demonstrations is contagious, that there are legitimate reasons for discontent in most universities, and that inflammatory personalities are to be found in every student body.

Organization of American States (OAS). After long debate and argument among member states, Galo Plaza Lasso (*see* BIOGRAPHY), a former president of Ecuador, was elected secretary-general of the OAS to replace José A. Mora, who retired in May 1968 after 12 years in office. Although the policy decisions of the OAS were made by its permanent council, the personality of the secretary-general could be important as an influence for urgency or restraint. Plaza was not only Ecuador's most admired statesman, but had become known outside his country as UN mediator in Cyprus.

The main criticism leveled at the OAS had been that it was not sufficiently independent of U.S. foreign policy. This had been brought out clearly in 1965 when the OAS tamely acquiesced to U.S. intervention in the Dominican Republic, which was widely condemned even by Latin Americans normally well disposed toward the U.S. There must inevitably be doubts on the future of an organization attempting to promote the political cohesion of 21 independent states with dissimilar historical antecedents, diverse societies and cultures, and political institutions that had no more than superficial resemblances. The feeling that appeared to have become prevalent in the U.S. in 1968 could be described as a reversion to the pre-Kennedy period, when Latin America was regarded as a "safe" region and was not given a high priority for economic aid. The Cuban crisis of 1962, which raised many doubts over the political reliability of the other republics, had now receded from the forefront of U.S. thinking; the failure of guerrilla subversion to make significant headway and the evident preference of the Latin Americans themselves for political stability combined to remove all sense of urgency from the attitude of the U.S.

This was variously commented on, according to shades of opinion, as a neglect of Latin America's pressing economic needs or as a healthy avoidance of the many pitfalls inherent in "special relationships" between nations. Since it has at all times been doubtful whether direct economic aid can achieve the political purposes for which it is given, many policy makers believed that the slight cooling off of relations between the U.S. and the Latin-American republics was not necessarily to be regretted. (DD. H.)

ENCYCLOPÆDIA BRITANNICA FILMS. *The Amazon—People and Resources of Northern Brazil* (1957); *Argentina—People of the Pampa* (1957); *Brazil—People of the Highlands* (1957); *Peru: People of the Andes* (1959); *Colombia and Venezuela* (1961); *Guatemala—Nation of Central America* (1961); *Puerto Rico: Past, Present, and Promise* (1965); *The West Indies* (1965).

International Organizations

The accompanying table shows the membership of the world's sovereign states in various international organizations as of Sept. 30, 1968. The growing realization that political and economic problems transcended international boundaries led to a proliferation of international organizations after World War II. Of these, the UN and its specialized agencies (some of which, such as the ILO and the UPU, antedated the

Membership in International Organizations

As of Sept. 30, 1968

SEE KEY ON PAGE 432

Country	UN 1	FAO 2	IMCO 3	IAEA 4	ICAO 5	ILO 6	IBRD 7	IDA 8	IFC 9	IMF 10	ITU 11	UNESCO 12	UPU 13	WHO 14	WMO 15	GATT 16	CE 17	AL 18	OAS 19	WEU 20	OCAS 21	C-Plan 22	Comecon 23	Euratom 24	ECSC 25	EEC 26	EFTA 27	IDB 28	LAFTA 29	OECD 30	ANZUS 31	CENTO 32	NATO 33	SEATO 34	WTO 35	Antarctic treaty 36	OAU 37	SPC 38
Afghanistan																						●																
Albania																							●															
Algeria																		●											●								●	
Argentina																												●	●								●	
Australia																						●								●	●					●		●
Austria																											●			●								
Barbados																						●																
Belgium																				●				●	●	●				●			●					
Belorussia																																			●			
Bolivia																												●	●									
Botswana																																					●	
Brazil																												●	●									
Bulgaria																							●												●	●		
Burma																																						
Burundi																																					●	
Cambodia																																						
Cameroon																																					●	
Canada																						●								●			●					
Central African Rep.																																					●	
Ceylon																						●																
Chad																																					●	
Chile																												●	●									
Colombia																												●	●									
Congo (Brazzaville)																																					●	
Congo (Kinshasa)																																					●	
Costa Rica																			●		●																	
Cuba																			●																			
Cyprus																	●					●																
Czechoslovakia																							●												●	●		
Dahomey																																					●	
Denmark																											●			●			●					
Dominican Rep.																			●									●										
Ecuador																			●									●	●									
El Salvador																			●		●																	
Equatorial Guinea																																						
Ethiopia																																					●	
Finland																											●			●								
France																				●				●	●	●				●			●			●		●
Gabon																																					●	
Gambia																																						
Germany, East																							●												●	●		
Germany, West																				●				●	●	●				●			●					
Ghana																						●																●	
Greece																											●			●			●					
Guatemala																			●		●																	
Guinea																																					●	
Guyana																						●																
Haiti																			●																			
Honduras																			●		●																	
Hungary																							●												●	●		
Iceland																														●			●					
India																						●																
Indonesia																						●																
Iran																																	●					
Iraq																		●																				
Ireland																	●													●								
Israel																																						
Italy																				●				●	●	●				●			●					
Ivory Coast																																					●	
Jamaica																						●																
Japan																													●									
Jordan																		●																				
Kenya																																					●	
Korea, South																																						
Kuwait																		●				●																
Laos																																						
Lebanon																		●																				
Lesotho																																					●	
Liberia																																					●	
Libya																		●																			●	
Liechtenstein																																						
Luxembourg																				●				●	●	●				●			●					
Malagasy Rep.																																					●	
Malawi																																					●	
Malaysia																						●																
Maldive Islands																																						
Mali																																					●	
Malta																																						

war) aimed at least theoretically at universality. The World Bank, originally established to provide help to war-devastated nations, turned more and more in succeeding years toward concentration on the problems of economic development. Organizations with more restricted membership included regional political groupings (OAS, OAU), military alliances (NATO, the Warsaw Pact), and organizations with a primarily economic orientation (EEC, Comecon). Such groupings as the Colombo Pact and the Alliance for Progress were chiefly vehicles for channeling aid from the developed to the less developed countries.

Membership in International Organizations
As of Sept. 30, 1968

Country	UN 1	FAO 2	IMCO 3	IAEA 4	ICAO 5	ILO 6	IBRD 7	IDA 8	IFC 9	IMF 10	ITU 11	UNESCO 12	UPU 13	WHO 14	WMO 15	GATT 16	CE 17	AL 18	OAS 19	WEU 20	OCAS 21	C-Plan 22	Comecon 23	Euratom 24	ECSC 25	EEC 26	EFTA 27	IDB 28	LAFTA 29	OECD 30	ANZUS 31	CENTO 32	NATO 33	SEATO 34	WTO 35	Antarctic treaty 36	OAU 37	SPC 38
Mauritania	●	●		●	●	●	●	●		●	●	●	●	●	●	●																					●	
Mauritius		●			●	●	●	●	●	●	●	●	●	●																							●	
Mexico	●	●	●		●	●	●	●	●	●	●	●	●	●	●				●									●	●									
Monaco				●							●		●	●																								
Mongolia	●										●	●	●	●	●								●															
Morocco	●	●	●	●	●	●	●	●	●	●	●	●	●	●	●	●		●																			●	
Nepal	●	●			●	●	●	●		●	●	●	●	●	●							●																
Netherlands	●	●	●	●	●	●	●	●	●	●	●	●	●	●	●	●	●			●				●	●	●				●			●					
New Zealand	●	●	●	●	●	●	●	●	●	●	●	●	●	●	●	●						●									●			●				●
Nicaragua	●	●	●	●	●	●	●	●	●	●	●	●	●	●	●				●		●							●										
Niger	●	●			●	●	●	●		●	●	●	●	●	●																						●	
Nigeria	●	●	●		●	●	●	●	●	●	●	●	●	●	●																						●	
Norway	●	●	●	●	●	●	●	●	●	●	●	●	●	●	●	●	●										●			●			●					
Pakistan	●	●	●	●	●	●	●	●	●	●	●	●	●	●	●	●						●										●		●				
Panama	●	●	●		●	●	●	●	●	●	●	●	●	●	●				●									●										
Paraguay	●	●			●	●	●	●	●	●	●	●	●	●	●				●									●	●									
Peru	●	●	●		●	●	●	●	●	●	●	●	●	●	●	●			●									●	●									
Philippines	●	●	●	●	●	●	●	●	●	●	●	●	●	●	●							●												●				
Poland	●	●	●	●	●	●					●	●	●	●	●	●							●												●			
Portugal	●	●	●	●	●	●	●		●	●	●	●	●	●	●	●											●			●			●					
Rhodesia																●																						
Romania	●	●		●	●	●					●	●	●	●	●								●												●			
Rwanda	●	●			●	●	●	●		●	●	●	●	●	●																						●	
San Marino											●		●																									
Saudi Arabia	●	●	●	●	●	●	●	●	●	●	●	●	●	●	●			●																				
Senegal	●	●	●		●	●	●	●	●	●	●	●	●	●	●																						●	
Sierra Leone	●	●	●		●	●	●	●	●	●	●	●	●	●	●																						●	
Singapore	●	●	●		●	●	●	●	●	●	●	●	●	●								●																
Somalia	●	●			●	●	●	●		●	●	●	●	●	●			●																			●	
South Africa	●	●	●	●	●	●	●	●	●	●	●		●	●	●	●																				●		
Southern Yemen	●										●		●	●				●																				
Spain	●	●	●	●	●	●	●	●	●	●	●	●	●	●	●	●														●								
Sudan	●	●		●	●	●	●	●		●	●	●	●	●	●			●																			●	
Swaziland																																					●	
Sweden	●	●	●	●	●	●	●	●	●	●	●	●	●	●	●	●	●										●			●						●		
Switzerland		●	●	●	●	●					●	●	●	●	●	●	●										●			●						●		
Syria	●	●	●	●	●	●	●	●		●	●	●	●	●	●			●																				
Taiwan	●	●	●	●	●	●	●	●	●	●	●	●	●	●	●																							
Tanzania	●	●	●		●	●	●	●	●	●	●	●	●	●	●																						●	
Thailand	●	●	●	●	●	●	●	●	●	●	●	●	●	●	●							●												●				
Togo	●	●			●	●	●	●		●	●	●	●	●	●																						●	
Trinidad and Tobago	●	●	●		●	●	●	●	●	●	●	●	●	●	●				●									●										
Tunisia	●	●		●	●	●	●	●	●	●	●	●	●	●	●			●																			●	
Turkey	●	●	●	●	●	●	●	●	●	●	●	●	●	●	●	●	●													●		●	●					
Uganda	●	●			●	●	●	●	●	●	●	●	●	●	●																						●	
Ukraine	●					●					●	●	●	●	●																							
United Arab Republic	●	●	●	●	●	●	●	●	●	●	●	●	●	●	●			●																			●	
United Kingdom	●	●	●	●	●	●	●	●	●	●	●	●	●	●	●	●	●					●					●			●		●	●	●		●		●
United States	●	●	●	●	●	●	●	●	●	●	●	●	●	●	●	●			●									●		●	●	●	●	●		●		
Upper Volta	●	●			●	●	●	●		●	●	●	●	●	●																						●	
Uruguay	●	●	●		●	●	●	●	●	●	●	●	●	●	●				●									●	●									
U.S.S.R.	●			●	●	●					●	●	●	●	●								●												●	●		
Vatican City				●							●		●																									
Venezuela	●	●	●		●	●	●	●	●	●	●	●	●	●	●				●									●	●									
Vietnam, South		●	●	●	●	●	●	●	●	●	●	●	●	●	●							●												●				
Western Samoa													●																									
Yemen	●	●			●	●	●			●	●	●	●	●	●			●																				
Yugoslavia	●	●	●	●	●	●	●	●	●	●	●	●	●	●	●	●																						
Zambia	●	●	●		●	●	●	●	●	●	●	●	●	●	●																						●	

KEY

UN	1	United Nations.
FAO	2	Food and Agriculture Organization of the United Nations.
IMCO	3	Intergovernmental Maritime Consultative Organization.
IAEA	4	International Atomic Energy Agency.
ICAO	5	International Civil Aviation Organization.
ILO	6	International Labour Organization.
IBRD	7	International Bank for Reconstruction and Development.
IDA	8	International Development Association.
IFC	9	International Finance Corporation.
IMF	10	International Monetary Fund.
ITU	11	International Telecommunication Union.
UNESCO	12	United Nations Educational, Scientific and Cultural Organization.
UPU	13	Universal Postal Union.
WHO	14	World Health Organization.
WMO	15	World Meteorological Organization.
GATT	16	General Agreement on Tariffs and Trade.
CE	17	Council of Europe.
AL	18	Arab League.
OAS	19	Organization of American States.
WEU	20	Western European Union.
OCAS	21	Organization of Central American States.
C-Plan	22	Colombo Plan for Co-operative Economic Development in South and South-East Asia.
Comecon	23	Council for Mutual Economic Assistance.
Euratom	24	European Atomic Energy Community.
ECSC	25	European Coal and Steel Community.
EEC	26	European Economic Community.
EFTA	27	European Free Trade Association.
IDB	28	Inter-American Development Bank.
LAFTA	29	Latin American Free Trade Association.
OECD	30	Organization for Economic Cooperation and Development.
ANZUS	31	Security treaty between Australia, New Zealand, and the United States.
CENTO	32	Central Treaty Organization.
NATO	33	North Atlantic Treaty Organization.
SEATO	34	Southeast Asia Treaty Organization.
WTO	35	Warsaw Treaty Organization.
	36	Antarctic Treaty.
OAU	37	Organization of African Unity.
SPC	38	South Pacific Commission.

Investment, International

The main factor affecting international investment in 1968 was the introduction by the U.S. government of measures to restrict the overseas investment activities of U.S. companies. The aim of these measures was to reduce U.S. direct investment to almost 2.5% below its 1967 level in an attempt to reduce the deficit on the U.S. balance of payments. As a result, the steady increase in the worldwide flow of investment capital was halted in 1968. In the previous year nearly all the major lending countries had recorded higher levels of international investment than in 1966.

In 1967 and 1968 progress was made in dismantling restraints on international capital transfers by certain industrial countries although the U.S. increased controls (see *United States*, below) and few were removed in the U.K. Exchange control was removed in France in 1967 although direct investment transactions still had to receive official approval. Controls were temporarily restored in 1968. In July 1967 the Japanese government liberalized the procedures by which foreign investments could be made in Japan by raising the limits for automatic approval on stock purchased by foreigners and by introducing an automatic approval system for certain direct investment projects.

United States. Although the growth in the value of assets held overseas by U.S. residents continued in 1967, the rate of investment was sharply curtailed in 1968 by controls announced by the U.S. government on January 1. At the end of 1967 the total value of U.S. foreign assets was $81.4 billion, a growth of about 80% since 1960. Direct investments (*i.e.*, assets

Table I. U.S. Foreign Assets
In $000,000,000 at end of year

Item	1950	1960	1965	1966	1967
Book value of direct investments	11.3	32.8	49.4	54.7	59.3
Portfolio investments*	5.7	12.6	21.6	21.0	22.1
Total	17.0	45.4	71.0	75.7	81.4

*Book value of foreign bonds and shares held by U.S. residents and U.S. banking claims.
Source: U.S. Department of Commerce, *Survey of Current Business.*

Table II. U.S. Investment Abroad
In $000,000

Item	1964	1965	1966	1967	1st half 1968*
Direct investment					
New funds	2,416	3,418	3,543	3,020	2,820
Reinvested profits	1,431	1,542	1,739	1,578	...
Total	3,847	4,960	5,282	4,598	...
Portfolio investment	1,961	1,078	261	1,270	390
Total	5,808	6,038	5,543	5,868	...

*Seasonally adjusted; at annual rate.
Source: U.S. Department of Commerce, *Survey of Current Business.*

Table III. U.S. Investment Earnings
In $000,000

Item	1960	1965	1966	1967	1st half 1968*
Direct investment					
Repatriated profits	2,355	3,918	3,963	4,439	4,560
Reinvested profits	1,266	1,542	1,739	1,578	...
Total	3,621	5,460	5,702	6,017	...
Portfolio investment					
Total income	646	1,428	1,605	1,717	1,856
Total earnings	4,267	6,888	7,307	7,734	...

*Seasonally adjusted; at annual rate.
Source: U.S. Department of Commerce, *Survey of Current Business.*

Table IV. U.S. Direct Investment and Earnings by Region, 1967
In $000,000

Area	Total value of assets at end of year	Net investment — Reinvested profits	Net investment — New funds	Net investment — Total	Earnings — Repatriated profits	Earnings — Total*
Canada	18,069	644	392	1,036	683	1,327
Latin America	10,213	172	191	363	1,031	1,203
Other Western Hemisphere	1,708	39	26	65	161	200
EEC	8,405	41	816	857	407	448
United Kingdom	6,101	81	342	423	297	378
Other European countries	3,376	144	284	428	169	313
Africa	2,277	44	176	220	374	418
Asia	4,282	128	318	446	1,214	1,342
Oceania	2,515	117	326	443	54	171
International	2,321	168	149	317	49	217
Total	59,267	1,578	3,020	4,598	4,439	6,017

*Total earnings equals reinvested profits plus repatriated profits.
Source: U.S. Department of Commerce, *Survey of Current Business.*

of U.S. companies) comprised more than 70% of the total, the remainder being securities and stocks held by U.S. residents. (*See* Table I.)

The regional distribution of U.S. direct investments abroad at the end of 1967 is shown in Table IV. Assets in Canada and in Europe each accounted for 30% of the total; much of the growth in recent years took place in assets in Europe. The importance of manufacturing in the total continued to increase and accounted for more than half the total growth since 1960. In recent years a number of large-scale projects in mining were developed. The most important of those were iron ore, copper, and bauxite mining and processing, particularly in Australia, Canada, Peru, and West Africa. In addition, projects for processing of raw materials for the chemical industry were developed in Asia and Latin America.

Direct investment in 1967, at $4.6 billion, was almost $700 million lower than in the previous year. (*See* Table II.) This decrease reflected partly the lower rate of economic activity in many countries in 1967 and partly the results of the voluntary program of restraint adopted in 1965. Under this program U.S. firms attempted to finance overseas operations by raising capital abroad, thus reducing the net capital outflow from the U.S. Both the outflow of new funds and the level of reinvested earnings fell in 1967, although the drop was greatest in the case of new funds. Manufacturing industry was primarily responsible for the lower level in 1967, recording $500 million less in outflow than in 1966. Much of this decline was in Canada, with smaller decreases in Europe and Latin America. Investment by oil companies rose by $200 million, declines in Europe and Canada being offset by large increases elsewhere.

About 37% of U.S. direct investment in 1967 was directed to Europe (half of this to the EEC) and 22% to Canada. (*See* Table IV.) Compared with 1966, the major change in capital flow was to Canada, which received $750 million less in 1967 although reinvested earnings increased by $100 million. Europe received $370 million less in U.S. funds in 1967, and the level of reinvested earnings there was $170 million lower. The decline was concentrated in the EEC countries and was greatest in the petroleum, chemicals, and nonelectrical machinery industries. The outflow to Asia and Africa increased by $200 million, and there was an increase of $120 million in investment in primary metal industries in Australia.

The aim of the measures announced at the start of 1968 was to cut direct investment in 1968 to a level

Table V. U.K. Investment Abroad
In £000,000

Item	1963	1964	1965	1966	1967	1968*
Direct investment†						
New funds	118	116	142	93	87	...
Reinvested profits	118	147	166	183	180	...
Total	236	263	308	276	267	300
Portfolio Investment‡	5	0	95	−83	33	140
Oil and miscellaneous§	79	133	140	110	124	120
Total	320	396	353	303	424	560

*Estimate based on first half of year.
†Excluding oil.
‡Net disinvestment in 1965, 1966, and 1967.
§Includes purchase of real estate abroad and investment by the Commonwealth Development Finance Co.
Sources: U.K. Balance of Payments 1968; Economic Trends.

Table VI. U.K. Investment Earnings
In £000,000

Item	1963	1964	1965	1966	1967	1968*
Direct investment†						
Repatriated profits	212	223	234	246	258	...
Reinvested profits	118	147	166	183	180	...
Total	330	370	400	429	438	530
Portfolio investment	137	143	157	153	145	165
Oil and miscellaneous‡	371	391	468	408	430	440
Total	838	904	1,025	990	1,013	1,135

*Estimate based on first half of year.
†Excluding oil.
‡Includes purchases of real estate abroad and investment by the Commonwealth Development Finance Co.
Sources: U.K. Balance of Payments, 1968; Economic Trends.

$1 billion lower than in 1967. To achieve this, recipient countries were classified into three groups. Restrictions were most severe in Class C countries, which included Western Europe and South Africa; there new investment in 1968 was limited to reinvested earnings and could not exceed 35% of the average level of direct investment in 1965 and 1966. In Class B countries and in the less developed countries—Class A—an outflow of new funds was permitted, but the total investment could not exceed 65 and 110%, respectively, of the 1965–66 average. Canada was exempted from the restrictions in March. Direct investment in the first half of 1968 was running at a rate approximately $250 million below that of 1967, and there were signs of a sharper cutback in the second half of the year.

U.S. portfolio investment in 1967 increased to $1,270,000,000 from the very low level of $200 million in the previous year. This was due largely to record U.S. purchases of newly issued foreign securities, which amounted to $1.6 billion and greatly exceeded the $500 million in sales of foreign dollar securities.

Table VII. U.K. Direct Investment and Earnings by Region, 1964–67*
In £000,000

Area	Investment				Earnings			
	1964	1965	1966	1967	1964	1965	1966	1967
North America	34	41	61	...	74	85	108	...
Latin America	18	18	11	...	19	20	25	...
EFTA	5	15	11	...	9	8	8	...
EEC	37	32	51	...	13	19	25	...
Other nonsterling areas	8	16	23	...	6	17	26	...
Total nonsterling areas	102	122	157	125	121	149	192	184
India and Pakistan	18	20	3	...	25	29	23	...
Australia and New Zealand	84	67	57	...	66	73	67	...
South Africa	33	45	35	...	62	57	60	...
Other African states	−14	16	1	...	38	30	25	...
Other	40	38	23	...	58	62	62	...
Total sterling area	161	186	119	142	249	251	237	254
Total	263	308	276	267	370	400	429	438
Of which developing countries (included above)	65	95	61	58				

*Excluding oil companies.
Sources: U.K. Board of Trade Journal; U.K. Balance of Payments, 1968.

The World Bank borrowed $250 million in the U.S. in 1967, and Canadian borrowing increased by 10% to a record $1 billion. Israel doubled its recent rate of borrowing to $200 million. Small net purchases (about $100 million) of other foreign stocks were recorded for the first time since the interest equalization tax was enforced in 1963.

The 6% increase in earnings on U.S. investments in 1967 was similar to the increase recorded in 1966 but less than in any other year since 1958. Direct investment earnings increased by 5% and earnings on portfolio investments by 7%. (See Table III.) The small increase in direct investment earnings occurred despite a 14% increase in earnings by the petroleum industry.

Earnings in the first half of 1968 were approximately 10% higher than in the first half of 1967, the major increase being in earnings on direct investments. Earnings from the EEC and Latin America both increased by $70 million and from Canada by $60 million.

United Kingdom. The outflow of investment capital from the U.K. showed a sharp increase in 1967 after falling considerably in the previous two years. (See Table V.) Preliminary figures for 1968 suggested a further sharp increase, bringing the level to a value about 80% higher than in 1966. A conservative estimate based on information relating to the first six months suggested a total outflow in 1968 of £560 million, an amount equal to the outflow in the years 1962 and 1963 combined.

There was little change in 1967 in the level of direct investment, but there was a sharp turnaround in portfolio investment from considerable net sales in 1966 to moderate net purchases in 1967. Direct investment in 1968 increased by about 10% to reach the record 1965 level. Purchases of overseas shares continued at a very high rate in the first half of 1968, and, although the rate slackened later in the year, the total outflow in portfolio investment was £140 million, by far the highest recorded in recent years.

The regional pattern of U.K. direct investment, using the latest available data, is shown in Table VII. The importance of the nonsterling area for British investment declined sharply in 1967, although the share (about 45%) of the total was more in line with the years before 1966 when the nonsterling area share was particularly high (approaching 60%). The available regional information shows sharply increasing investment in North America, with flows in 1966 exceeding the previous high levels of £40–£45 million in 1960–61. Over this period investment in the U.S. recorded most of the increase. Investment in EEC countries continued to grow as the advantages of producing within the EEC increased with the final removal of internal industrial tariffs by that organization. Investment in Australasia continued at a higher level.

The amount of U.K. direct investment in less developed countries is shown at the foot of Table VII. Apart from a high value in 1965, this figure averaged between 20–25% of total U.K. investment. There was a decline in the proportion of this investment financed by new funds. Slightly more than half the total of U.K. investment in recent years was in manufacturing; about 25% was in distribution and transport; 15% in banking, insurance, and other services; and somewhat under 10% in agriculture and mining.

There were some considerable changes in portfolio investment in 1967 and 1968. In the years 1960–62 U.K. residents were reducing their holdings of overseas stocks and shares at the rate of £35 million per year.

In 1963–64 there was slight positive investment, but a reduction was renewed in 1965–66 with sales exceeding purchases by £80–£90 million. This disinvestment slowed down considerably during 1967 and in the fourth quarter of the year changed into a positive figure of £58 million. This was inspired by the possibility of capital gains to be achieved from the expected devaluation of the pound and also by the tremendous potential of the Australian economy, which received much of these funds. This outflow of investment funds continued virtually unchecked in the first half of 1968 but slackened somewhat later in the year.

Earnings on U.K. overseas investments showed a slight increase in 1967 after a small decline in the previous year and then increased again by 10–12% in 1968. In part, this gain reflected increased profitability and in part the effects of devaluation, which raised the sterling value of profits earned abroad. (*See* Table VI.) Provisional figures for 1968 showed a sharp increase in direct investment earnings from £438 million to £530 million.

An analysis of the effect of U.K. direct investment overseas on the U.K. balance of payments showed that overseas investment had a less favourable effect on the balance of payments than had previously been imagined: direct investment overseas of £100 could be expected to have an initial effect of increasing exports (mostly capital goods) by only £11.

Other Industrial Countries. *Canada.* As in previous years Canada was a net receiver of international investment capital on quite a considerable scale. The inflow of direct investment, much of it U.S. capital, declined in 1967 from the high level of the previous year. This reflected in large part U.S. government measures to curtail the outflow of capital. There was a modest increase in Canadian investment abroad, and the inflow of funds on portfolio account increased by $180 million. The total net inflow of capital in 1967, at $980 million, was approximately $70 million greater than in the previous year.

France. In 1967 both French investment abroad and foreign investment in France increased considerably. This growth applied to both direct and portfolio investment. The outflow of funds, at $390 million, was more than double the rate of 1965. A large part of this increase was due to the increased purchases of foreign securities, but there was also a moderately large increase in direct investment. The inflow pattern was similar. The net figures changed relatively little between the two years, a net inflow of $155 million in 1966 giving way to a figure of $120 million in 1967.

West Germany. There was a major shift in the West German international investment position in 1967. A net inflow of more than $400 million in the previous two years shifted in 1967 to a net outflow of $550 million. The biggest reason for this was a reduction of $750 million in foreign investment in West Germany in 1967. The main change was on portfolio account, where the easing of domestic monetary conditions, along with falling interest rates and bond yields, had a considerable impact. West German banks, which had borrowed $100 million in 1966, repaid $175 million in 1967; holdings by foreigners of West German securities, which had been reduced by $85 million in 1966, were further liquidated by $180 million in 1967. Direct investment in West Germany fell by $225 million from the level of 1966. At the same time, the outflow of West German capital increased, largely on portfolio account.

Italy. There was little change in the overall capital

| | | 1966 | | | 1967 | |
Country	Direct	Port-folio	Total	Direct	Port-folio	Total
Canada						
Outflow	20	390	410	45	320	365
Inflow	655	665	1,320	500	845	1,345
Net*	−635	−275	−910	−455	−525	−980
France						
Outflow	185	30	215	225	165	390
Inflow	310	60	370	340	170	510
Net*	−125	−30	−155	−115	−5	−120
West Germany						
Outflow	330	300	630	390	460	850
Inflow	835	220	1,055	610	−310	300
Net*	−505	80	−425	−220	770	550
Italy						
Outflow	100	150	250	235	75	310
Inflow	315	−70	245	260	80	340
Net*	−215	220	5	−25	−5	−30
Netherlands						
Outflow	330	−55	275	415	45	460
Inflow	255	95	350	340	40	380
Net*	75	−150	−75	75	5	80

Table VIII. Other Developed Countries' Investment Abroad, 1966–67
In $000,000

*Net outflow of funds is shown by a (+); net receipts of funds by a (−).
Sources: Annual Reports of International Monetary Fund, Bank for International Settlements, and Banca d'Italia.

outflow from Italy in 1967 compared with the previous year; a negligible net outflow in 1966 moved into a small net inflow in 1967. Both the outflow and the inflow of capital increased, but there were marked changes in the composition between direct and portfolio investment. Overall, the net inflow of direct investment was reduced from $215 million to $25 million while the net outflow of portfolio capital of $220 million became in 1967 a net inflow of $5 million. Italian direct investment abroad, which had been decreasing since 1963, rose by $135 million in 1967. Portfolio investment, negligible until recently, amounted to $75 million in 1967, though this was only half the 1966 value.

Australia. One of the largest single flows of investment capital during the past decade was the inflow of private capital to Australia associated with the development of the vast mineral resources discovered in the north and west of the country. It was estimated that in 1967 almost one-quarter of the assets in Australia were foreign owned, a much larger proportion than in most advanced countries. Some industries were completely dominated by foreign capital; foreign-owned assets accounted for 97% of the pharmaceuticals industry and 95% of the motor industry.

(A. G. A.)

See also Development, Economic; Payment and Reserves, International; Trade, International.

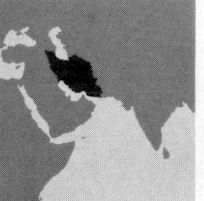

Iran

A constitutional monarchy of western Asia, Iran is bounded by the U.S.S.R., Afghanistan, Pakistan, Iraq, and Turkey and the Caspian Sea, the Arabian Sea, and the Persian Gulf. Area: 636,292 sq.mi. (1,648,-000 sq.km.). Pop. (1967): 26,315,000. Cap. and largest city: Teheran (pop., 1967 est., 2,840,494). Language: Farsi (Persian). Religion: Muslim; Christian, Jewish, and Zoroastrian minorities. Shah-in-shah, Mohammad Reza Pahlavi; prime minister in 1968, Amir Abbas Hoveida.

The third five-year plan, which ended in March, closed with a growth rate of 10%, the gross national product having risen from 503.4 billion rials in 1966 to 563.5 billion rials in 1967. The bill providing for the fourth five-year plan (March 1968–March 1973)

Iranian woman
in the village of Kakhk
weeping over members
of her family killed
in the twin earthquakes
that occurred
on Aug. 31 and Sept. 1,
1968. About 12,000
persons died as a result
of the quakes.

UPI (UK) LTD.

was passed by Parliament in February; it called for a total investment of 810 billion rials, of which 480 billion would be from the government and 330 billion from the private sector, with attractive prospects for local and foreign investment in a wide variety of fields. The Plan Organization, a corporate body directly responsible to the prime minister, had control over all matters connected with foreign assistance; it kept in touch with the parliamentary planning committees, approved projects, and delegated authority to implement them. The High Planning Council was responsible for coordinating the activities of the various government departments concerned with planning, for making recommendations on economic, financial, and social policies, and for deciding on the extent of the annual operations.

In accordance with the shah's successful insistence upon decentralization, local responsibility, and provincial initiative, the development programs for the provinces were drawn up by the provincial governors and submitted to the Plan Organization. The latter then decided the priorities of the various public utilities and announced that attention first must be given to drinking water, power, and communications.

The success of the third plan and the preparations for the execution of the fourth plan seemed certain to ensure that Iran would soon become a new industrial centre in the Middle East. During the year under review, Iran's partnership with Pakistan and Turkey in the Regional Cooperation for Development (RCD) prospered. Projects approved in 1967 all made satisfactory progress. Iran's geographic position, as well as its natural wealth, ensured for it a key function in RCD, and it was significant that Teheran was chosen as the site of the second Asian International Trade Fair, to be held in October 1969.

Throughout 1968 Iran continued to maintain its traditional policy of cultivating friendly relations both with the Western democracies—whose political institutions it seemed gradually to be adopting, with the variations that suited its circumstances—and with the Communist powers. In April Soviet Premier Aleksei N. Kosygin paid a friendly visit, in the course of which he went to the site of the new steel mill that was being set up with Soviet help at Isfahan. He also had talks with the shah and the prime minister, Amir Abbas Hoveida, on political and economic questions. In May Georges Pompidou, then premier of France, accompanied by the foreign minister, Maurice Couve de Murville, paid a state visit, during which arrangements were made for closer cultural and economic ties between the two countries. Later in the year France pledged assistance for the fourth development plan in the shape of loans to be devoted to expenditure on railways, electric power, and radio and television.

In February the United Kingdom granted Iran a loan of £18 million to assist in the construction of a natural gas trunk line which was to be completed in 1970. This would lead from the oil fields of southern Iran to Saveh, 80 mi. SW of Teheran. The U.S.S.R. was constructing the northern portion of this line, from Saveh to Rasht on the Caspian Sea to the Soviet border town of Astara.

In spite of the traditionally friendly relations between Iran and the United Kingdom, however, a shadow was cast upon the old cordiality by the aftermath of the decision of the British government to withdraw from its long-established control over the Persian Gulf by 1971. In preparation for this event, the seven Trucial States of the Gulf, along with Bahrain and Qatar, decided to federate for mutual protection and development. Iran maintained certain traditional claims—not acknowledged by the British government—to suzerainty over Bahrain, and thus viewed this development unfavourably. The United Kingdom, arguing that the move to federation was both natural and spontaneous, showed little sympathy with Iran's attitude, and a certain coolness resulted.

IRAN
Education. (1966–67) Primary, pupils 2,378,082, teachers (1964–65) 56,696; secondary, pupils 579,716, teachers (including vocational and teacher training; 1964–65) 17,158; vocational, pupils 15,840; teacher training, students 5,679; higher (including 8 universities), students 36,250, teaching staff (1961–62) 1,752.
Finance. Monetary unit: rial, with a par value of 75.75 rials to U.S. $1 (181.80 rials = £1 sterling). Gold and foreign exchange, central bank: (June 1968) U.S. $310 million; (June 1967) U.S. $260 million. Budget (1966–67) balanced at 217,232,000,000 rials. Money supply: (June 1968) 76,080,000,000 rials; (June 1967) 65,770,000,000 rials. Cost of living (1963 = 100): (June 1968) 108; (June 1967) 108.
Foreign Trade. (1967) Imports 85,340,000,000 rials; exports 146,170,000,000 rials. Import sources: West Germany 22%; U.S. 19%; U.K. 12%; Japan 7%; France 5%; Italy 5%. Export destinations: Japan 28%; U.K. 22%. Main export petroleum 91%.
Transport and Communications. Roads (1965) 34,459 km. (including c. 20,000 km. all-weather). Motor vehicles in use (1966): passenger c. 142,000; commercial (including buses) c. 49,400. Railways: (1966) 3,480 km.; traffic (1967) 1,152,000,000 passenger-km., freight 1,881,000,000 net ton-km. Shipping (1967): merchant vessels 100 gross tons and over 29; gross tonnage 73,040. Air traffic (1966): 306,-934,000 passenger-km.; freight 2,847,000 net ton-km. Telephones (Jan. 1967) 213,420. Radio receivers (Dec. 1966) c. 1.7 million. Television receivers (Dec. 1966) c. 130,000.
Agriculture. Production (in 000; metric tons; 1967; 1966 in parentheses): wheat c. 3,800 (c. 3,190); barley (1966) c. 1,000, (1965) c. 1,000; cotton, lint c. 119 (c. 113); rice c. 925 (c. 875); sugar, raw value (1967–68) c. 372, (1966–67) c. 243; dates (1966) c. 308, (1965) c. 285; grapes (1966) c. 265, (1965) c. 250; tobacco (1966) c. 20, (1965) c. 25; tea (1966) c. 18, (1965) c. 15. Livestock (in 000; Oct. 1965): cattle c. 6,065; sheep c. 26,000; goats c. 18,000; asses c. 2,000.
Industry. Production (in 000; metric tons): crude oil (1967) 128,760; coal c. 300; iron ore (metal content; 1966–67) c. 30; lead concentrates (metal content; 1966–67) c. 20; chrome ore (oxide content; 1964–65) c. 56; cement (1966) 1,393; electricity (excluding most industrial production; 1965–66) 2,139,-000 kw-hr.

But when the terrible earthquake disaster struck Khurasan in the late summer (*see* DISASTERS), British relief for the sufferers was prompt and generous.

(L. F. R. W.)

ENCYCLOPÆDIA BRITANNICA FILMS. *The Middle East* (1955); *The Mediterranean World* (1961).

Iraq

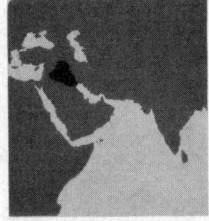

A republic of western Asia, Iraq is bounded by Turkey, Iran, Kuwait, Saudi Arabia, Jordan, Syria, and the Persian Gulf. Area: 169,284 sq.mi. (438,446 sq.km.). Pop. (1968 est.): 8,547,149, including Arabs, Kurds, Turks, Assyrians, Iranians, and others. Cap. and largest city: Baghdad (pop., 1965 est., 1,745,328). Language: Arabic. Religion: mainly Muslim, some Christian. Presidents in 1968, Abdul Rahman Arif to July 17 and Gen. Ahmed Hassan al-Bakr; prime ministers, Taher Yahya to July 17, Col. Abdel Razak al-Nayef to July 30, and General al-Bakr.

Iraq in 1968 saw the ousting of Pres. Abdul Rahman Arif's regime by moderate Baathists in a bloodless coup. The country was not deeply affected, and there were no dramatic changes in government policy.

The Arif regime had had some success in improving Iraq's relations with its neighbours. In May the Turkish president paid a state visit to Iraq and in the same month Iraq's prime minister, Taher Yahya, went to Iran for the main purpose of settling problems of frontier demarcation in the Persian Gulf area. During the year Iraq also established a new relationship with France, which could take advantage of its high prestige in the Arab world since the Arab-Israeli war of June 1967. In January a high-ranking French military delegation visited Iraq, and in February President Arif paid a four-day state visit to France. Although he offended some French opinion by his vehement attacks on Israel, he succeeded in obtaining a joint French-Iraqi communiqué that demanded Israel's withdrawal from occupied Arab territories. Shortly before his visit an agreement had been signed in Baghdad between the French oil company ERAP and the Iraq National Oil Company (INOC). ERAP agreed to act as contractors for INOC in the exploration, drilling, and marketing of oil in Iraq in areas where no oil had yet been discovered. INOC would take over the management of the project in cooperation with ERAP after five years.

France also hoped to receive a concession for the rich, proven North Rumaylah oil field in southern Iraq, and President Arif promised that French bids would have favourable consideration. But on April 10 INOC announced that it would undertake the development of the field itself with the aim of producing five million tons a year within three years. INOC hoped to barter some of the North Rumaylah oil for oil drilling equipment.

The agreement with France and the decision on North Rumaylah were seen by the Iraqi government as expressions of independence against the major oil companies represented in the Western-owned Iraq Petroleum Company (IPC). However, a partial agreement on problems outstanding with IPC was reached in June whereby the company agreed to pay the equivalent of seven U.S. cents a barrel for oil pumped through the Kirkuk pipeline since the Arab-Israeli war, which, in closing the Suez Canal, had made Iraqi oil more valuable. IPC paid Iraq £10 million immediately, and the country's total oil revenues for the first half of 1968 amounted to £94 million.

In the first half of the year there were numerous signs of public impatience with the Yahya government, which was widely accused of corruption and inertia. In January there was student unrest in Baghdad, and on January 13 six ministers (of generally pro-United Arab Republic tendencies) resigned and were replaced by men loyal to President Arif. On April 16 prominent army officers (including three ex-prime ministers) published an open letter to the president asking for a coalition government and the election of a legislative assembly. The government responded in May by announcing that elections could probably be held before 1970 and that a legislative assembly would be appointed to draft a permanent constitution during the interim period. But this concession was insufficient to preserve the Arif regime; it was overthrown in a bloodless coup on July 17 by a coalition

CAMERA PRESS

WIDE WORLD

Gen. Ahmed Hassan al-Bakr (top) became president after overthrowing Abdul Rahman Arif (above). Below, tank patrolling the streets of Baghdad following the coup d'etat on July 17, 1968.

GAMMA—PIX FROM PUBLIX

IRAQ

Education. (1965–66) Primary, pupils 964,327, teachers 42,878; secondary, pupils 241,065, teachers 6,935; vocational, students 7,626, teachers 729; teacher training, students 5,760, teachers 328; higher (including Baghdad University and Al-Hikma University), students 28,410, teaching staff 1,002.

Finance. Monetary unit: Iraqi dinar, with a par value of 0.36 dinars to U.S. $1 (0.86 dinars = £1 sterling). Gold and foreign exchange, central bank: (June 1968) U.S. $440.9 million; (June 1967) U.S. $279.7 million. Budget (1966–67 est.) balanced at 170 million dinars. Money supply: (June 1968) 174 million dinars; (June 1967) 160.1 million dinars. Cost of living (Baghdad; 1963 = 100): (March 1968) 104; (March 1967) 102.

Foreign Trade. (1967) Imports 152 million dinars; exports 298.3 million dinars. Import sources (1966): U.K. 14%; West Germany 12%; U.S. 10%; Japan 6%; Taiwan 6%; U.S.S.R. 5%; Italy 5%. Export destinations: U.K. 15%; France 15%; Italy 13%; Netherlands 8%; Japan 7%; West Germany 5%. Main export petroleum 92%.

Transport and Communications. Roads (1967) 17,480 km. (including 4,210 km. main roads). Motor vehicles in use (1967): passenger 74,700; commercial 44,600. Railways: (1965) 1,630 km.; traffic (1964–65) 431 million passenger-km., freight 818 million net ton-km. Air traffic (1967): 72,140,000 passenger-km.; freight 1,012,000 net ton-km. Telephones (Dec. 1966) c. 76,000. Radio receivers (Dec. 1965) 2.5 million. Television receivers (Dec. 1966) 180,000.

Agriculture. Production (in 000; metric tons; 1967; 1966 in parentheses): wheat 866 (826); barley 860 (832); rice 309 (182); dates (1966) 380, (1965) c. 280; oranges (1966) c. 44, (1965) c. 45; cotton, lint (1966) c. 10, (1965) c. 10. Livestock (in 000; 1965–66): sheep 11,040; cattle (1966–67) 1,455; horses 122; asses 542.

Industry. Production (in 000): crude oil (1967) 60,165 metric tons; electricity (1965) 1,207,000 kw-hr.

438

Ireland

of independent right-wing army officers and moderate Baathists led by Gen. Ahmed Hassan al-Bakr (*see* BIOGRAPHY), who became president. The coup was masterminded by Col. Abdel Razak al-Nayef, who became prime minister, and Lieut. Gen. Ibrahim Abdul Rahman al-Daoud, who became defense minister. However, on July 30 Daoud and Nayef were ousted by the Baathists and the next day President Bakr was also named prime minister at the head of a government dominated by Baathists. The new government reaffirmed its belief in socialism and made friendly overtures to the United Arab Republic. The resurgence of Baathism caused less dismay in the U.A.R. than in Syria, where the moderate Baathists had been ousted in 1966 by leftists opposed to the party's international leadership.

The new government pledged itself to solve the Kurdish problem on the basis of the 12-point plan formulated by the government of then Prime Minister Abdul Rahman al-Bazzaz in 1966. It reinstated civil servants and Kurdish nationalists dismissed from government service for political reasons. It arrested and sequestered the property of senior government officials responsible for oil policy under the Arif regime, but reports that it intended to rescind the French oil agreement proved unfounded.

On September 22 a new provisional constitution was published. It concentrated almost all executive and legislative power in the hands of the Baathist-dominated Revolutionary Command Council, all members of which became vice-presidents. It defined the Iraqi republic as a popular democratic state with Islam as the state's religion.   (P. MD.)

ENCYCLOPÆDIA BRITANNICA FILMS. *The Middle East* (1955).

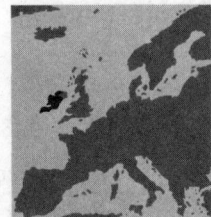

Ireland

Separated from Great Britain by the North Channel, the Irish Sea, and St. George's Channel, the Republic of Ireland shares its island with Northern Ireland to the northeast. Area: 27,136 sq.mi. (70,283 sq.km.), or 83% of the island. Pop. (1968): 2,910,000. Cap. and largest city: Dublin (pop., 1967, 568,772). Language: English (80%) and Gaelic. Religion: predominantly Roman Catholic (95%). President in 1968, Eamon de Valera; prime minister, John Lynch.

The major constitutional issue of a proposed reform of the Irish electoral system dominated political life in the country throughout 1968. The government party, Fianna Fail, decided at the end of January to introduce a referendum to amend the constitution in

order to replace the proportional representation (PR) system of election to the Dail with a straight-vote system. It also proposed a rearrangement of constituencies to allow for a variation in the proportion of electors to each member of the Dail.

A similar attempt, made in 1959 by the same party, had been only narrowly defeated, and there had been other, earlier attempts to change the PR voting system with which the state had been equipped at the time of independence. The proposed changes were strongly challenged by the two opposition parties, Fine Gael and the Labour Party, and vigorous campaigning went on throughout the summer and autumn. The country went to the polls on October 16, when 63% of the electorate voted, and the result was a crushing defeat for the government on both the abolition of PR and the changes in constituency boundaries.

The voting figures were as follows: out of a total electorate of 1,717,000, the valid poll was 1,080,000. The majority against the constituency amendment to the constitution was 232,000, and against the PR amendment, 234,000, a ratio of 40% for and 60% against on both issues. In 1959 the poll had been 940,-000 and the ratio was 48% for and 51% against.

In spite of the defeat, the government insisted that the issue was a nonparty one, and that there was no question of going to the country. Prime Minister Lynch said that his administration would stay in office for the full term—that is, until the spring of 1970—but it was widely rumoured that Fianna Fail was considering an election early in 1969.

The government party suffered another serious setback when the popular and dynamic minister for education, Donagh O'Malley, died suddenly on March 10. He was succeeded temporarily by the prime minister. Lynch subsequently reshuffled his Cabinet, moving Brian Lenihan from the Department of Justice to that of Education, making Michael O Morain minister for justice, and promoting Patrick Faulkner to O Morain's post of minister for lands and the *gaeltacht*.

At by-elections held during the year, Fianna Fail retained its seat for East Limerick (May 22) and won the seat for Clare from Fine Gael (March 14). Fine Gael won Wicklow from Labour (March 14). As a result, the government held 75 seats in the Dail; Fine Gael had 46; and Labour, 19. There were also 4 independent members.

Education was much in the public mind throughout the year. The proposed merger of the two universities in Dublin—the predominantly Protestant Trinity College, founded by Queen Elizabeth I in 1591, and University College, its Roman Catholic counterpart—to create a new University of Dublin caused particular

IRELAND
Education. (1965–66) Primary, pupils 506,134, teachers 14,614; secondary, pupils 98,667, teachers 6,795; vocational, pupils 105,742, teachers 4,626; teacher training, students 1,736; higher, students 21,280, teaching staff (1962–63) 1,208.
Finance. Monetary unit: Irish pound, at par with the pound sterling (£1 = U.S. $2.40). Gold and foreign exchange, official: (June 1968) U.S. $342 million; (June 1967) U.S. $469 million. Budget (1967–68 est.) balanced at £295,222,-000. Gross national product: (1967) £1,131 million; (1966) £1,046 million. Money supply: (May 1968) £330,709,000; (May 1967) £314.1 million. Cost of living (1963 = 100): (May 1968) 125; (May 1967) 119.
Foreign Trade. (1967) Imports £390.5 million; exports £284.4 million. Import sources: U.K. 50%; U.S. 8%; West Germany 6%. Export destinations: U.K. 72%; U.S. 9%. Main

exports: meat 21%; livestock 18%; textiles and clothing 8%; dairy produce 7%. Tourism (1966): visitors 1,696,000; gross receipts £65 million.
Transport and Communications. Roads (1966) 52,987 km. Motor vehicles in use (1967): passenger 314,434; commercial 45,575. Railways: (1965) 2,346 km.; traffic (1967) 527 million passenger-km., freight 410 million net ton-km. Shipping (1967): merchant vessels 100 gross tons and over 79; gross tonnage 143,466. Air traffic (1967): 1,224,128,000 passenger-km.; freight 30,176,000 net ton-km. Telephones (Dec. 1966) 230,000. Radio licenses (including combined radio-television; Dec. 1966) 816,000. Television licenses (March 1966) 371,000.
Agriculture. Production (in 000; metric tons; 1967; 1966 in parentheses): oats 294 (283);

barley 666 (638); wheat (1966) 185, (1965) 233; potatoes (1966) 1,678, (1965) 1,648; sugar, raw value (1967–68) c. 145, (1966–67) 111; milk (1966) 3,232, (1965) 3,142; butter 74 (68); meat (1966) 473, (1965) 451. Livestock (in 000; June 1967): sheep 4,239; cattle 5,586; horses 143; pigs 985; poultry 10,593. Fish catch (in 000; metric tons) (1966) 40, (1965) 36.
Industry. Production (in 000; metric tons; 1967): coal 190; cement 1,126; electricity (excluding most industrial production) 4,162,000 kw-hr.; manufactured gas 196,000 cu.m.; beer (1965–66) 3,424 hl.; wool fabrics 7,900 sq.m.; rayon and acetate fabrics 7,700 sq.m. Index of industrial production (excluding power; 1963 = 100): (1967) 129; (1966) 119. Unemployment: (1967) 6.7%; (1966) 6.1%.

anxiety and growing opposition. Specific plans for the future of Ireland's universities were announced on July 5. The National University of Ireland was to be dissolved and the existing University Colleges of Cork and Galway were to become separate universities in their own right. A Conference of Irish Universities was also to be established. It was announced that in the Dublin merger each college would retain its separate identity, and that they would be equally represented on the governing body of the new university. St. Patrick's College, Maynooth, would become an associate college of the university, and in the future lay students and members of religious orders would be able to study there as well as those preparing for the secular priesthood. The adoption of a steamroller approach to the delicate Dublin merger talks by the new minister for education aggravated the situation, and by the end of the year it was still unresolved.

There were numerous industrial disputes and strikes, the worst being an unofficial strike by employees of the Electricity Supply Board at the end of March. In this crisis the government invoked special powers under the Electricity (Special Provisions) Act, which had made it illegal to strike or encourage a strike in the industry, but pickets continued to be posted at the board's main generating stations. Some were arrested, and they stiffened the attitude of their colleagues by choosing imprisonment rather than the payment of fines. A total industrial standstill was brought about, which lasted for almost a week. A further wave of strikes took place at the end of July, involving Dublin bus crews, barmen, corporation workers, and dockers. The unhappy industrial climate was to some extent alleviated by wage increases in a number of sectors, but in many cases these increases outstripped productivity. In October the prime minister issued a fairly severe warning of growing restrictions on expansion and credit unless productivity increases could be more closely related to wage demands. Despite a good export record for 1966–67, a further drive to encourage manufacturers to seek export markets was planned. On January 12 the government announced that the metric system would be introduced, but no dates were given.

The prime minister and his wife traveled to India and to Japan, where Mrs. Lynch launched the world's largest tanker, the "Universe Ireland." The first royal visit to the Republic of Ireland, that of the king and queen of Belgium, took place in May. On January 8 the prime minister of Northern Ireland, Capt. Terence O'Neill, and his wife paid a visit to Dublin, returning that of Prime Minister Lynch to Belfast in December 1967. Lynch met British Prime Minister Harold Wilson for talks on EFTA/EEC progress in February.

The year was one of the warmest and driest in living memory, with droughts in many parts of the west. Many tourism records were broken.　　(B. Ar.)

ENCYCLOPÆDIA BRITANNICA FILMS. *British Isles—The Land and the People* (1962).

Israel

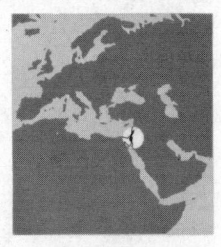

A republic of the Middle East, Israel is bounded by Lebanon, Syria, Jordan, the U.A.R., and the Mediterranean Sea. Area (not including territory occupied in the June 1967 war): 7,993 sq.mi. (20,700 sq.km.). Pop. (1968 est.): 2,827,-

000. Cap.: Jerusalem (pop., 1968 est., 200,300). Largest city: Tel Aviv-Jaffa (pop., 1968 est., 388,-000). Language: Hebrew and Arabic. Religion: predominantly Jewish. President in 1968, Schneor Zalman Shazar; prime minister, Levi Eshkol.

There was no ease in Zion as the year that had witnessed the six-day victory in June 1967 drew to its close. The prime minister, Levi Eshkol, had given his assessment of the immediate future to the Knesset on Nov. 13, 1967. It was an uncompromising speech offering little prospect of an early peace. Speaking of the reputedly moderate Arab leaders, King Husain of Jordan and Pres. Gamal Abd-al-Nasser of the United Arab Republic, the prime minister said that the real purpose "of the hypocritical talk of the Arabs and their supporters" was to achieve the withdrawal of the Israeli forces to the borders existing before the June war. The prime minister took the unusual course of quoting from reports presented to him by the

Israel Intelligence Service. These claimed to quote President Nasser at the Khartoum summit conference of the Arab heads of state in August–September 1967 as saying that the U.A.R.'s military strength must be restored speedily so that "it will be possible for us to attack Israel with the certainty of victory." King Husain was cited in similar vein.

The prime minister's words were evidently addressed to the UN Security Council as much as to the Israeli public and the Arab leaders. The Security Council, again seeking to take charge of events had two resolutions before it. One, submitted by a group of Afro-Asian countries, proposed drastic action against Israel; the other, by a number of Latin-American countries, also condemned Israel but in a more restrained manner. Neither resolution appeared to have the support of a valid majority, though the Israeli government was becoming greatly concerned at the possibility of some mandatory action by the council. It was therefore with some relief that the Israeli government received the passing of a British-sponsored compromise resolution on Nov. 22, 1967, by unanimous vote. The foreign minister, Abba Eban, said on his return to Tel Aviv after the UN vote that the adoption of the British resolution had shown that Israel had succeeded in its objective "of getting the understanding of the world community for our

Thirty jet fighters flying over Jerusalem in a Star of David formation during a military parade for Israel's 20th anniversary celebration, May 2, 1968.

Ireland, Northern: *see* United Kingdom

Iron and Steel: *see* Industrial Review; Mining

Islam: *see* Religion

KEYSTONE

Arabs watching Israel's 20th anniversary parade. It had been feared that Arab terrorists would attempt to disrupt the celebration, but Israeli security measures prevented any incidents.

Italian Literature:
see Literature

basic views," and that the world community did not believe that Israel should move from the cease-fire lines except as a result of properly negotiated peace treaties with its neighbours. These attitudes expressed by Israel's prime minister and foreign minister, were to dictate Israel's foreign policy for the whole of 1968: distrust of Arab undertakings and insistence on negotiations as the first step toward the settlement proposed by the Security Council.

But it soon became evident that the Israeli foreign minister's reading of the Security Council resolution was not identical with that of a good many other members of the "world community." Spokesmen for the U.S.S.R. at the UN and in the Soviet press insisted that before there could be any negotiations, Israel must "in the first place" withdraw from all the territories it had occupied during the June war. France, the Arab countries, and a number of African countries took similar stands.

The appointment of Gunnar Jarring (see BIOGRAPHY) as the UN secretary-general's special representative to promote agreement in the Middle East was at first coolly received. Israel continued to insist on direct negotiations with the Arab governments. But as the year wore on, the initial Israeli position underwent considerable modification from the hard line taken by the prime minister and the foreign minister at the outset. Jarring's function as a mediator was increasingly accepted though the term was never employed. In the peace plan presented by Eban at the UN in October (and later rejected by the U.A.R.), the question of direct negotiations was muted and greater emphasis was placed on Israeli insistence on recognized and secure frontiers. The Cabinet, however, still opposed any precise definition of what Israel considered to be "recognized and secure frontiers," the one question that now appeared to matter more than any other.

The reasons for this attitude were partly, if not largely, rooted in domestic policy, and partly in a reassessment of future relations with Israel's Arab neighbours based on the activities of the Palestinian fedayeen (guerrillas) and their political organizations. That the de facto security situation, and the political state of the occupied territories, had greatly improved since the six-day war was principally a result of the personal policy of the defense minister, Moshe Dayan, who had virtually complete control over the occupied territories and exercised it with imagination and a degree of liberalism that surprised his opponents and encouraged his friends.

Dayan made it no secret that he did not believe that there was any hope of an early settlement ac-

ceptable to Israel with either the U.A.R. or Jordan. He advocated acceptance of things as they were and making the best of them until such a time as the Arab countries were prepared to negotiate a peace settlement. In his opinion, and in that of such leading Palestinian nationalists as Aziz Shihade and his circle, there was an opportunity for a settlement with the Palestinian Arabs on a basis of absolute equality. This view sparked off one of the most significant public debates in Israel, about its own future and its relationship to its Palestinian citizens and neighbours. Powerful politicians were aligned against Dayan and his views, especially Pinhas Sapir, the former finance minister.

These were the real issues of 1968. The fedayeen clashes, although they made the headlines at times, were of comparatively minor importance; even the larger engagements across the Suez Canal were significant only insofar as they reflected the attitudes of the U.A.R. and future Soviet intentions. Both of these were of great concern to the Israelis and remained shrouded in uncertainty. Again the principal Israeli reaction came as a result of the defense minister's initiative. The armed forces were built up to a point where the Israeli military authorities felt that they were a match for any combination of Arab countries as long as the U.S.S.R. did not intervene either directly or indirectly.

It was against this confident background that the defense minister reported to the Knesset on October 29, three days after the bombardment of Israel's Suez Canal positions by some 600 U.A.R. guns and

ISRAEL

Education. (1965–66) Primary, pupils 449,837, teachers 22,507; secondary, pupils 66,048, teachers 6,155; vocational, pupils 38,113, teachers 3,750; teacher training, students 4,291, teachers 423; higher (including 4 universities), students 35,878, teaching staff 4,269.

Finance. Monetary unit: Israeli pound, with a par value of I£3.5 to U.S. $1 (I£8.40 = £1 sterling). Gold and foreign exchange, central bank: (June 1968) U.S. $722.1 million; (April 1967) U.S. $590.8 million. Budget (1967–68 est.) balanced at I£5,130 million. Gross national product: (1966) I£11,862 million; (1965) I£10,934 million. Money supply: (May 1968) I£2,824 million; (May 1967) I£2,329 million. Cost of living (1963 = 100): (June 1968) 127; (June 1967) 125.

Foreign Trade. (1967) Imports I£2,340.1 million; exports I£1,691.8 million. Import sources: U.S. 26%; U.K. 19%; West Germany 8%; Netherlands 5%. Export destinations: U.S. 16%; U.K. 13%; West Germany 11%; Belgium-Luxembourg 7%; Netherlands 6%; Switzerland 5%. Main exports: diamonds 32%; citrus fruit 18%; textiles and clothing 10%.

Transport and Communications. Roads (1967) 8,303 km. (including 2,387 km. main roads). Motor vehicles in use (1967): passenger 97,408; commercial 47,900. Railways (1967): 746 km.; traffic 337 million passenger-km., freight 278 million net ton-km. Shipping (1967): merchant vessels 100 gross tons and over 109; gross tonnage 688,053. Air traffic (1966): 1,452,-812,000 passenger-km.; freight 37,181,000 net ton-km. Telephones (Dec. 1966) 302,946. Radio receivers (Dec. 1965) 743,000. Television receivers (Dec. 1966) 20,-000.

Agriculture. Production (in 000; metric tons; 1967; 1966 in parentheses): oranges c. 790 (682); grapefruit c. 226 (185); grapes (1966) 76, (1965) 80; wheat (1966) 101, (1965) 150; sorghum (1966) 13, (1965) 67; cotton, lint c. 28 (25); tomatoes (1966) 112, (1965) 100; olives (1966) c. 11, (1965) 11; bananas (1966) 54, (1965) 44. Livestock (in 000; Dec. 1966): cattle 209; sheep and goats 355; poultry 8,200. Fish catch (in 000; metric tons) (1966) 24, (1965) 19.

Industry. Production (in 000; metric tons; 1967; cement 712; electricity 4,727,000 kw-hr.; salt (1966) 58; potash (oxide content; 1966–67) 314. New dwellings completed (1966) 37,150.

missile launchers. Since the cease-fire in June 1967, U.A.R. forces had opened fire 119 times on the Israeli forces in the Suez Canal zone. In these incidents 110 Israeli soldiers had been killed and 300 wounded; these figures included the casualties in the sinking of the "Elath." Fedayeen operations against civilians by Al Fatah and other organizations since the June war had caused about 20 deaths and 200 wounded, while Israel held more than 1,000 fedayeen prisoners.

The three most significant counteractions by Israel during the year were an attack on the Al Fatah centre at Karameh in Jordan on March 21, a raid by an Israeli commando unit on October 31 against an electric transformer station north of the Aswan Dam, and the December 28 helicopter attack on the Beirut, Lebanon, airport, in which civil aircraft worth an estimated $43.8 million were destroyed.

The economy made a rapid recovery during 1968. The gross national product was expected to rise by 13%, compared with 2.2% in 1967. Employment increased by 8% and unemployment, which had reached the unprecedented height of 10.4% in the early months of 1967, had largely disappeared except for some special pockets. Immigration, which had been practically canceled out by emigration during the previous two years, rose to an estimated 30,000, with a higher proportion coming from Western Europe and the U.S. Investment, which had been on the decline for the previous three years, was increasing at a substantial rate; 199 projects costing in all $160 million had been approved during the first half year.

But some of the economic weaknesses remained. A report by the director of the Manpower Division of the Ministry of Labour pointed out on November 7 that the economic slowdown of 1966 had failed in one of its main objectives: the labour force in productive employment had decreased while the percentage of those employed in the services, already higher in Israel than anywhere else in the world, had increased from 51 to 55% of the labour force. Government and public services had also increased from 22 to 24%. The report also pointed out a major weakness in Israel's educational system: only 15% of the children had matriculated, a figure that had become dangerously constant. (J. K.)

ENCYCLOPÆDIA BRITANNICA FILMS. *Major Religions of the World* (*Development and Rituals*) (1954); *The Middle East* (1955); *Planning Our Foreign Policy* (*Problems of the Middle East*) (1955); *The Mediterranean World* (1961).

Italy

A republic of southern Europe, Italy occupies the Apennine Peninsula, Sicily, Sardinia, and a number of smaller islands. On the north it borders France, Switzerland, Austria, and Yugoslavia. Area: 116,316 sq.mi. (301,257 sq.km.). Pop. (1968 est.): 53,656,042. Cap. and largest city: Rome (pop., 1968 est., 2,630,535). Language: Italian. Religion: predominantly Roman Catholic. President in 1968, Giuseppe Saragat; premiers, Aldo Moro to June 5, Giovanni Leone from June 25 to December 12, and Mariano Rumor.

Domestic Affairs. The year 1968 saw the end of the centre-left coalition government of Aldo Moro when the Socialists refused to take an active part in the administration of the country after the general

election of May 19–20. Giovanni Leone was chosen interim premier while the country waited for the United Socialist Party to decide whether or not it should be part of a new coalition. Finally, on December 12, following a 23-day crisis precipitated by Leone's resignation and accentuated by strikes, civil unrest, and intra-party struggles, a new coalition government formed by Mariano Rumor, secretary of the Christian Democrats, was sworn in.

Parliament had been dissolved on March 11, and on May 19–20, 35 million persons voted to elect the 315 senators and 630 deputies that comprised Italy's legislative power. The Christian Democratic Party had confirmed its strength by increasing its percentage of the votes from 38.3 to 39.1%, or 12,429,030 votes as against 11,773,182 in the previous general election. Of the other parties of the centre-left coalition, the Republican Party made a slight gain (from 1.4 to 2%) while the United Socialist Party, which contained the former Socialist and Social Democrat parties, collected only 14.5% of the votes. This compared with the total 19.9% achieved by the two parties while still independent (13.8% to the Socialists and 6.1% to the Social Democrats).

The main opposition party, the Communists, received 8,555,477 votes, a narrow improvement over the previous election (from 25.3 to 26.9%); 4.5% of the votes went to the PSIUP (Socialist Party of Proletarian Unity), formed since the previous general election by 24 dissident Socialist deputies. In the right-wing opposition, the Liberal Party saw its share of the vote reduced from 7 to 5.8%; the neo-fascist Italian Social Movement (MSI) dropped from 5.1 to 4.5%; and the Monarchist Party (PDIUM) lost some votes (from 1.8 to 1.2%).

On June 5, when the new Parliament took office, Premier Aldo Moro officially handed in his resignation and Pres. Giuseppe Saragat started consultations with representatives of the leading parties in order to form a new government. On June 10 Rumor had been asked to form a new government, but a few days later he had to report his failure: the United Socialist Party had withdrawn its support of the centre-left coalition. To carry out the most immediate needs of the country while waiting for the autumn conference of the Socialist Party, on June 19 Giovanni Leone was given the task of forming a government acceptable to the Socialists. Premier Leone announced the formation of

Residents of the village of Gibellina in Sicily warming themselves around a fire following an earthquake that left thousands homeless, Jan. 15–16, 1968.

Italian students rioting in Rome in April 1968. Both left-wing and right-wing students clashed with police during demonstrations for better physical facilities at the universities, modern educational standards, and an end to what the students termed tyrannical professorial rule.

a minority government on June 24, and he and his Cabinet were sworn in on June 25. A Christian Democrat, Leone for a few months had led a similar government in 1963 just before the centre-left "experiment." On July 11 the Chamber gave its vote of confidence and on July 17 the Senate confirmed it.

On November 14, 12 million workers, supported by all the major Roman Catholic, Communist, and anti-Communist unions, staged a 24-hour, nationwide strike to urge major social security reforms. They were joined by high school and university students seeking liberalization of the educational system. The Leone government had attempted to establish a university reform plan but had lacked the strong parliamentary position required to pass any reform legislation. To help hasten formation of a coalition that could cope with these domestic problems, Leone resigned on November 19, agreeing to administer only routine affairs until a new government could be formed.

In the next several days, while strikes and demonstrations continued, leaders of the Christian Democratic Party tried to resolve internal rivalries and arrive at a new majority position that could be used to negotiate a coalition plan with the Socialist and Republican parties. A Socialist, Alessandro Pertini, was designated on November 24 by President Saragat to make an "exploratory" attempt to form a government.

On November 26, after the Christian Democrats had put off party reform until their national congress in the spring of 1969, Rumor was given the assignment to form a government for the second time in the year.

On December 12, Rumor presented the new Cabinet —16 Christian Democrats, 9 Socialists, and 1 Republican. The new government's program was to give maximum priority to reforms, including delegation of some federal authority to regional governments, efforts to combat unemployment and establish higher wages and pensions, and democratization of education.

In February both the Chamber and Senate had given final approval to the controversial bill fixing regional elections for the end of 1969. In the same month the Moro government had received a vote of confidence after the left-wing opposition had requested a parliamentary inquiry into the activities of SIFAR (Service of Information of the Armed Forces) during the summer of 1964. Accusations brought by a Rome magazine, *L'Espresso*, had implied that Gen. Giovanni de Lorenzo, as head of SIFAR, had taken anticonstitutional steps in planning a coup d'etat. A military commission reported to the Parliament in July, however, denying the charges.

A series of earthquakes hit Sicily January 15–25. More than 200 people died, 500 were injured, and many villages completely destroyed, leaving thousands homeless. The rebuilding was a long and difficult task, and by the end of the year many still lived in tents and provisional homes built by the military and by the Red Cross. On November 3, after a weekend of

ITALY

Education. (1965–66) Primary, pupils 4,480,207, teachers 202,803; secondary, pupils 2,082,878, teachers 171,091; vocational, pupils 764,540, teachers 61,217; teacher training, students 210,631, teachers 14,675; higher (including 30 universities), students 300,940, teaching staff 26,053.

Finance. Monetary unit: lira, with a par value of 625 lire to U.S. $1 (1,500 lire = £1 sterling). Gold and foreign exchange, official: (June 1968) U.S. $4,177,000,000; (June 1967) U.S. $4,069,000,000. Budget (1967 est.): revenue 7,786,100,000,000 lire; expenditure 8,952,200,000,000 lire. Gross national product: (1967) 41,849,000,000,000 lire; (1966) 38,493,000,000,000 lire. Money supply: (May 1968) 18,389,000,000,000 lire; (May 1967) 16,367,000,000,000 lire. Cost of living (1963 = 100): (June 1968) 119; (June 1967) 117.

Foreign Trade. (1967) Imports 6,060,000,000,000 lire; exports 5,439,000,000,000 lire. Import sources: EEC 35% (West Germany 17%, France 11%); U.S. 11%. Export destinations: EEC 39% (West Germany 18%, France 12%); U.S. 10%; U.K. 5%; Switzerland 5%. Main exports: machinery 24%; motor

vehicles 8%; chemicals 8%; fruit and vegetables 7%; petroleum products 6%; clothing 6%.

Transport and Communications. Roads (1967) 282,001 km. (including 2,377 km. expressways). Motor vehicles in use (1967): passenger 7,311,385; commercial 693,134. Railways: state (1966) 15,897 km.; private (1965) 4,963 km.; traffic (1967) 29,643,000,000 passenger-km., freight 17,106,000,000 net ton-km. Shipping (1967): merchant vessels 100 gross tons and over 1,445; gross tonnage 6,219,041. Air traffic (1967): 5,247,006,000 passenger-km.; freight 148,601,000 net ton-km. Telephones (Dec. 1966) 6,467,597. Radio licenses (including combined radio-television; Dec. 1966) 11,163,000. Television licenses (Dec. 1966) 6,855,000.

Agriculture. Production (in 000; metric tons; 1967; 1966 in parentheses): wheat 9,564 (9,406); corn 3,830 (3,510); barley 295 (253); oats 556 (477); potatoes 4,040 (3,860); rice 730 (616); broad beans 408 (397); onions 479 (436); sugar, raw value (1967–68) c. 1,637, (1966–67) 1,370; tomatoes 3,459 (3,469); tobacco (1966) 73, (1965) 73; olives 2,450 (1,802); oranges 1,425 (1,370); lemons 722

(654); wine 7,503 (6,471); apples 1,932 (2,584); peaches (1966) 1,423, (1965) 1,300; figs (1966) 241, (1965) 247; hemp 7 (11); cheese (1966) 437, (1965) 411; hen eggs (1966) 477, (1965) 458; beef and veal (1966) 551, (1965) 467; pork (1966) 327, (1965) 366. Livestock (in 000; Jan. 1966): sheep 7,900; cattle (Jan. 1967) 9,821; pigs 5,450; goats 1,225; horses, mules, and asses 1,018; poultry 110,000.

Industry. Fuel and power (in 000; metric tons; 1967): lignite 2,201; coal 410; crude oil 1,690; natural gas 9,353,000 cu.m.; manufactured gas 2,833,000 cu.m.; electricity 97,200,000 kw-hr. Production (in 000; metric tons; 1967): iron ore (50% metal content) 737; pig iron 7,462; crude steel 15,880; zinc 89; lead 60; aluminum 128; cement 26,272; cotton yarn 196; rayon filament yarn 90; rayon staple fibre 91; nitrogenous fertilizers (1966–67) 950; sulfuric acid 3,515; passenger cars 1,439 units; commercial vehicles 103 units. Merchant vessels launched (100 gross tons and over; 1967) 505,000 gross tons. New dwelling units completed (1967) 268,000.

heavy rain, gales, and floods in northern Italy, over 102 persons were reported to have lost their lives. Piedmont was the worst hit area, and 79 died at Valle Mosso near the Alps when a dam burst.

Foreign Affairs. After forming his new government, Leone stressed Italy's belief in the United Nations, the Atlantic alliance, and the Common Market. During the year Italy expressed its wishes for the formation of a wider European Parliament, and the new foreign minister, Giuseppe Medici, declared repeatedly that the entry of the United Kingdom, Ireland, Norway, Denmark, and other countries in the EEC "would be a firm step toward a political cooperation that can be the only outcome of the process of unification that has already given us economic integration."

Great hope was repeatedly expressed in the outcome of the Paris talks between representatives of the U.S. and North Vietnam. Foreign Minister Medici rejected the Italian Communist Party's demand of official recognition of the Hanoi government, feeling it would endanger Italy's potential role as a mediator. The civil war in Nigeria caused great concern in Italy. A sum of $600,000 was given to the International Red Cross and to UNICEF for their struggle against starvation in the worst-hit areas of the region, and the Italian government intervened with the Nigerian authorities, urging the necessity of a peaceful settlement.

When Czechoslovakia was occupied by Warsaw Pact troops, President Saragat interrupted his summer vacation and Parliament met in extraordinary assembly. The occupation was condemned by the Leone government as a "violation of the natural rights of all people," and the Soviet Union was warned that this action would have repercussions on East-West relationships. Medici reaffirmed Italy's faith in the Atlantic alliance as the only guarantee of common defense and safety. The Italian Communist Party, along with the Communist parties of other Western countries, approved after three days of silence a document condemning the Soviet military intervention in Czechoslovakia, and urged the Communist parties of the Warsaw Pact countries to recall their troops and restore freedom to the government in Prague.

When he took office, Rumor asserted that Italian foreign policy efforts would be limited to actions within the Atlantic alliance, in deference to left-wing elements in his government that objected to an Italian endorsement of U.S. policy in Vietnam. He named as foreign minister Pietro Nenni, an opponent of Italian membership in NATO.

The full text presented by the U.S. and the U.S.S.R. of the treaty for the nonproliferation of nuclear weapons was accepted as a realistic attempt at solving a long-standing problem. On July 19 the Senate voted for the acceptance of the treaty, and the Chamber followed suit on July 26. It was pointed out that the supply of nuclear materials for peaceful purposes to nonnuclear powers should be clearly guaranteed.

The Economy. The favourable trend of the Italian economy continued into its fourth year in 1968. The balance of payments after the first six months showed a surplus of $42.4 million, compared with a deficit of $221.2 million in the first six months of 1967. This improvement was due mainly to a reduction in the trade deficit ($223.9 million in the first six months of 1968, compared with $637.2 million a year earlier). There were also remarkable surpluses of $235 million from shipping and of $443.7 million from tourism. Of all Italian imports, 35% were from other EEC countries, 12.2% from EFTA countries, and 6.7% from

Eastern Europe. Exports followed a similar pattern: 39.2% within the EEC, 15.5% to EFTA, 5.3% to Eastern Europe.

The retail price index in the first half of 1968 showed an increase of 1.8% over the first six months in 1967, but the general average index only showed an increase of 1%. The index of industrial production rose 4.7% in the first half of 1968. Particularly encouraging was the output in the mining industry, up 11.2%. In manufacturing the increase was 4.4%.

In the automobile industry, Fiat kept well ahead of its nearest European competitors and in October acquired a 15% share of the French Citroën firm. A previous deal that would have amounted to a takeover was vetoed by the French government. A new Fiat assembly plant was begun in Sicily in May and was expected to be ready to put out 50,000 cars a year by the end of 1969. Another Italian car manufacturer, Alfa Romeo, went ahead with plans for a modern factory near Naples that would produce a new, small-capacity car. (F. G.)

Encyclopædia Britannica Films. *Italy—Peninsula of Contrasts* (1952); *The Mediterranean World* (1961).

Ivory Coast

A republic on the Gulf of Guinea, West Africa, the Ivory Coast is bounded by Liberia, Guinea, Mali, Upper Volta, and Ghana. Area: 123,485 sq.mi. (319,-822 sq.km.). Pop. (1967 est.): 4,010,000, including about 15,000 Europeans. Cap. and largest city: Abidjan (pop., 1963 est., 285,000). Language: French and local dialects. Religion: pagan 65%; Muslim 25%; Christian 10%. President and premier in 1968, Félix Houphouët-Boigny.

At the January conference of the African and Malagasy Common Organization (OCAM) at Niamey, Niger, President Houphouët-Boigny was largely responsible for persuading Pres. Joseph Mobutu of the Congo (Kinshasa) and Pres. Grégoire Kayibanda of Rwanda to reconcile their differences and to take part together in formal negotiations. In February Pres. Julius Nyerere of Tanzania paid a state visit to Abidjan, where he was given the freedom of the city. In February, also, the Ivorean foreign minister, Arsène Usher Assouan, urged African nations to seek

---

IVORY COAST

Education. (1965–66) Primary, pupils 353,745, teachers 7,478; secondary, pupils 28,166, teachers 1,087; vocational, pupils 2,826, teachers 415; teacher training (1962–63), pupils 2,328, teachers 190; higher, students (1964–65) 1,566.

Finance. Monetary unit: CFA franc, with a parity of CFA Fr. 50 to the French franc (CFA Fr. 246.85 = U.S. $1; CFA Fr. 592.45 = £1 sterling). Gold and foreign exchange, central bank: (May 1968) U.S. $66 million; (May 1967) U.S. $71 million. Budget (1967 est.) balanced at CFA Fr. 39.8 billion. Money supply: (March 1968) CFA Fr. 59,390,000,000; (March 1967) CFA. Fr. 47,570,000,000.

Foreign Trade. (1967) Imports CFA Fr. 63,570,-000,000 (54% from France, 7% from West Germany, 6% from U.S., 5% from Netherlands); exports CFA Fr. 80,260,000,000 (38% to France, 13% to U.S., 9% to Italy, 9% to West Germany, 7% to Netherlands). Main exports: coffee 32%; timber 17%; cocoa 15%.

Agriculture. Production (in 000; metric tons; 1966; 1965 in parentheses): corn 194 (179); sweet potatoes 1,916 (1,896); cassava 1,044 (1,230); coffee 130 (273); cocoa 145 (113); bananas 179 (184); peanuts 29 (31); cottonseed 17 (9); timber c. 8,300 cu.m. (c. 8,200 cu.m.). Livestock (in 000; 1965–66): cattle 322; pigs 120; sheep 714; goats 790.

some kind of rapprochement with South Africa despite its "abominable doctrine" of apartheid.

Rioting at Abidjan in March by sympathizers with Biafra and the looting of hundreds of Nigerian-owned shops demonstrated the feelings of many in the Ivory Coast about the Nigeria-Biafra conflict. On April 3 Radio Biafra reported that the Ivory Coast, with other nations, had been asked to intercede with the Nigerian federal government to end the war. This was followed on May 14 by the Ivory Coast's recognition of Biafra as a sovereign and independent state.

The unrest among students and workers in France during May was reflected in student and labour disturbances in the Ivory Coast. Continuing unrest based on wage claims was, however, forestalled in July when, following the example of Senegal, the president introduced a general restraint on prices and raised minimum salaries by 10%. Austerity measures adopted in 1967 to counter stagnation in agricultural production were relaxed, and economic development and cooperation plans were begun as a result of an August meeting in Abidjan between President Houphouët-Boigny and Pres. William Tubman of Liberia. Work began on a new deepwater port at San Pedro, with French, West German, and Italian financial aid. (PH. D.)

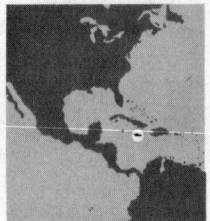

Jamaica

A parliamentary state within the Commonwealth of Nations, Jamaica is an island in the Caribbean Sea about 90 mi. S of Cuba. Area: 4,244 sq.mi. (10,992 sq.km.). Pop. (1967 est.): 1,893,077, predominantly Negro, but including Europeans, Chinese, Indians, and persons of mixed race. Cap. and largest city: Kingston (pop., 1967 est., 204,449). Language: English. Religion: Christian, with Anglicans and Baptists in the majority. Queen, Elizabeth II; governor-general in 1968, Sir Clifford Campbell; prime minister, Hugh Lawson Shearer.

A curious mixture of boom and crisis, long-term planning for development and short-term setbacks characterized 1968, which was a testing time for the government of Prime Minister Hugh Shearer. Overseas borrowing for development projects reached a new high, necessitating legislative revision of the debt

JAMAICA
Education. (1965–66) Primary (including prepri-mary), pupils 333,000, teachers 5,831; secondary, pu-pils 34,594, teachers 1,429; vocational, pupils 3,524, teachers 218; teacher training, students 212, teachers 10; higher (at University College of Mona), stu-dents 1,902.
Finance. Monetary unit: Jamaica pound, at par with the pound sterling (Jam£1 = U.S. $2.40). Bud-get (1967–68 est.): revenue Jam£77,931,751; expendi-ture Jam£77,351,751.
Foreign Trade. (1967) Imports Jam£126,340,000; exports Jam£81,472,000. Import sources: U.S. 39%; U.K. 20%; Canada 11%; Venezuela 5%. Export destinations: U.S. 40%; U.K. 26%; Canada 14%; Norway 8%. Main exports: alumina 26%; bauxite 23%; sugar 19%; bananas 8%.
Agriculture. Production (in 000; metric tons; 1966; 1965 in parentheses): sweet potatoes c. 220 (c. 220); sugar, raw value (1967–68) c. 476, (1966–67) 456; bananas c. 330 (327); oranges 87 (66); grapefruit c. 35 (34); copra 16 (16). Livestock (in 000; 1965–66): horses, mules, and asses 56; cattle 240; pigs 150; sheep 10.
Industry. Production (in 000; metric tons; 1967): bauxite 9,395; gypsum 187; cement 391; electricity (public service only) 607,000 kw-hr.

ceiling, newly set at £75 million. The government decided to raise money locally by issuing National Development Bonds, and a law was passed setting up a national lottery.

In addition to the plans for waterfront development in Kingston, Montego Bay, and Ocho Rios, an Urban Development Corporation was set up to undertake the long-term redevelopment of such areas as might be specified. The building trade enjoyed a boom, and there was much activity in public as well as private housing projects for a variety of income groups, along with office and hotel accommodations.

Throughout the year there were strikes, affecting at one time or another all the essential services. The rising cost of living, resulting from devaluation and a general rise in world prices, was the source of much unrest.

The prime minister undertook a series of overseas tours to make the personal acquaintance of the leaders of countries with whom Jamaica had, or expected to develop, relationships of importance. Jamaica joined the Caribbean Free Trade Association. A decision was taken to change over to decimal currency by September 1969. (G. C. Cu.)

ENCYCLOPÆDIA BRITANNICA FILMS. *The West Indies* (1965).

Japan

A constitutional monarchy in the northwestern Pacific Ocean, Japan is an archipelago composed of four major islands (Hokkaido, Honshu, Kyushu, and Shikoku) and minor adjacent islands. Area: 142,799 sq.mi. (369,-850 sq.km.). Pop. (1968 est.): 100,510,000. Cap. and largest city: Tokyo (pop., 1968 est., 8,998,000). Language: Japanese. Religion: primarily Shinto and Buddhist; Christianity 1.6%. Emperor, Hirohito; prime minister in 1968, Eisaku Sato.

Domestic Affairs. For fiscal 1967 (April 1, 1967–March 31, 1968), according to the Economic Planning Agency, Japan's gross national product (GNP) totaled 41,637,000,000,000 yen. This GNP ($115.7 billion) allowed Japan to enter the ranks of major economies, which included the U.S., U.S.S.R., Britain, France, and West Germany. In the field of shipbuilding Japan far surpassed all other nations. It ranked first in the world in tonnage of merchant vessels and production of radio sets; second in output of television sets, automobiles, and synthetic fibres; and third in production of crude steel, nitrogenous fertilizer, and plastics.

During the second half of 1967 the growth rate in nominal terms was 18% (in real terms, 13.2%). The per capita national income was, however, still $955, ranking Japan 20th in the world. Moreover, living standards and expenditure on social welfare lagged. In housing, Japan had only ten rooms available for every 14 people. Consumer prices were rising faster than those in other developed countries, while the average wage per hour was only 50 cents, less than one-fifth the U.S. average. Japan's annual per capita expenditure for social security averaged 19,000 yen, less than one-fourth the U.S. figure.

In late June all five major parties and leaders began campaigning for the upper house election on July 7. Rising prices, the presence of U.S. military bases in

Japan, and the U.S.-Japan security treaty were the main issues touched on by party leaders in the campaign. As final returns were announced July 9, the Liberal-Democrats succeeded in obtaining a working majority in the 250-seat House of Councillors. Of the 125 seats at stake (plus one vacancy) the Liberal-Democrats won 69. The Socialists suffered a serious setback, taking only 28 seats. Other opposition parties—the Komeito, Democratic Socialists, and Communists—all made large gains. The resultant lineup of the House of Councillors was as follows: Liberal-Democrats, 137; Socialists, 65; Komeito, 24; Democratic Socialists, 10; Communists, 7; independents, 7 (total, 250).

Japan did not escape the effects of the wave of student unrest that swept the world in 1968. Approximately 90 university disputes resulted in the arrests of more than 3,000 students. Causes of the disputes varied widely. At the University of Tokyo a strike started with students of the Faculty of Medicine protesting the laws governing medical practitioners. On June 17 the university president, Kazuo Okochi, called for police help to evict students barricaded in Yasuda Auditorium, which housed the administration. On June 20 about 5,000 students boycotted all classes, claiming that the university's autonomy had been violated by the entry of 1,200 riot police into the Hongo campus. Other university students protested tuition increase plans (Kansai University, Tohoku Gakuin University); demanded "democratization" of management (Kanagawa University, Beppu University); and even demanded participation in presidential elections (Waseda University, Doshisha University).

On June 15 approximately 25,000 demonstrators marked the eighth anniversary of the accidental death of a woman student, Michiko Kamba, who had been a victim of the massive 1960 demonstrations. Students used the occasion to protest U.S. involvement in the Vietnam war and demanded nullification of the U.S.-Japan security treaty. The bloodiest clash occurred in Osaka, where 2,000 riot police tried to prevent 3,000 students from engaging in an unauthorized demonstra-

tion; 141 police and 70 students were seriously injured.

On May 16 a violent earthquake struck an extensive area in northern Japan, affecting more than 200 settled places in Hokkaido, Aomori, Iwate, Miyagi, and Akita prefectures. The first quake, followed ten hours later by an equally violent but less destructive tremor and giant tsunami waves, resulted in at least 44 deaths, 33 vessels sunk, and 250 houses flooded. (*See* DISASTERS.)

Foreign Affairs. During World War II, in a fierce battle for the island of Iwo Jima, approximately 22,000 Japanese and more than 4,500 U.S. troops had been killed. On June 26 the Japanese national flag replaced the U.S. flag flying over a building on Chichi-shima, symbolizing reversion of the Bonin Islands to Japanese administration after 23 years of U.S. control. The largest islands—including Iwo Jima and Marcus—plus smaller, uninhabited islets became a village under jurisdiction of the Tokyo metropolitan government. Arrangements for the reversion had been worked out during a visit to Washington, D.C., by Prime Minister Sato late in 1967.

Earlier, on April 28, "Okinawa Reversion Day," an estimated 25,000 workers and students gathered from throughout Japan to demand from the U.S. the immediate and unconditional return of Okinawa. Following his 1967 visit to Washington, Prime Minister Sato had maintained that he had received assurances from U.S. Pres. Lyndon B. Johnson that Okinawa would be returned to Japan "within two or three years." This was apparently contradicted on July 14, when testimony in the U.S. Congress by Richard L. Sneider, director of Japan affairs in the U.S. State Department, was released. In the testimony, originally delivered in March, Sneider was reported to have said that President Johnson had made no commitment on the return of Okinawa. Rather, from the text of the communiqué issued following the Sato-Johnson meeting, it was clear that the status of Okinawa would be kept under continuous and joint review, with the aim of eventually returning administrative rights over the

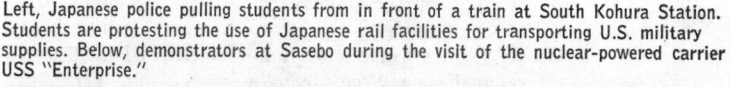
Left, Japanese police pulling students from in front of a train at South Kohura Station. Students are protesting the use of Japanese rail facilities for transporting U.S. military supplies. Below, demonstrators at Sasebo during the visit of the nuclear-powered carrier USS "Enterprise."
ASAHI SHIMBUN

JAPAN

Education. (1965–66) Primary, pupils 9,775,-532, teachers 347,326; secondary, pupils 8,964,-354; vocational, pupils 2,060,158; secondary and vocational, teachers 473,026; higher (including 69 universities), students 1,116,430, teaching staff 106,412.

Finance. Monetary unit: yen, with a par value of 360 yen to U.S. $1 (864 yen = £1 sterling). Gold and foreign exchange, official: (June 1968) U.S. $1,730,000,000; (June 1967) U.S. $1,837,000,000. Budget (1967–68 est.) balanced at 4,998,401,000,000 yen. Gross national product: (1967) 41,638,000,000,000 yen; (1966) 35,092,000,000,000 yen. Money supply: (June 1968) 13,442,000,000,000 yen; (June 1967) 11,485,000,000,000 yen. Cost of living (1963 = 100): (June 1968) 127; (June 1967) 119.

Foreign Trade. (1967) Imports: 4,198,700,-000,000 yen; exports 3,759,000,000,000 yen. Import sources: U.S. 28%; Australia 7%; Canada 5%; Iran 5%. Export destinations: U.S. 29%; South Korea 4%; Liberia 4%. Main exports:

machinery 20%; iron and steel 12%; textile yarns and fabrics 12%; ships 9%; chemicals 7%; motor vehicles 6%.

Transport and Communications. Roads (1967) 996,819 km. (including 416 km. expressways and 150,285 km. main roads). Motor vehicles in use (1967): passenger 3,836,415; commercial 6,531,836. Railways: (1965) 27,882 km.; traffic (1967) 265,986,000,000 passenger-km., freight 58,936,000,000 net ton-km. Shipping (1967): merchant vessels 100 gross tons and over 6,409; gross tonnage 16,883,353. Air traffic (1966): 5,371,006,000 passenger-km.; freight 157,628,000 net ton-km. Telephones (Dec. 1966) 16,011,745. Radio receivers (Dec. 1966) 24,787,000. Television receivers (Dec. 1966) 19,002,000.

Agriculture. Production (in 000; metric tons; 1967; 1966 in parentheses): rice 18,768 (16,-552); wheat 997 (1,024); barley 1,022 (1,105); sweet potatoes 4,031 (4,810); potatoes 3,686 (3,383); tea (1966) 83, (1965) 77; dry onions

(1966) 1,032, (1965) 860; oranges 1,993 (2,000); timber (1966) 59,600 cu.m., (1965) 59,300 cu.m. Livestock (in 000; Feb. 1967): cattle 2,928; sheep 113; pigs 5,975; horses 240; goats 246; chickens 150,616. Fish catch (in 000; metric tons) (1966) 7,077, (1965) 6,908. Whale and sperm oil (in 000; metric tons) (1965–66) 89, (1964–65) 136.

Industry. Fuel and power (in 000; metric tons; 1967): coal 47,482; crude oil 787; natural gas 2,158,000 cu.m.; electricity 237,550,000 kw-hr. Production (in 000; metric tons; 1967): iron ore (55% metal content) 2,210; pig iron 41,044; crude steel 62,152; cement (portland only) 43,256; cameras 3,632 units; cotton yarn 518; woven cotton fabrics 2,820,000 sq.m.; rayon staple fibres 386; sulfuric acid 6,280; radio receivers 28,180 units; television receivers 7,038 units; passenger cars 1,376 units; commercial vehicles 1,798 units; motorcycles 2,207 units. Merchant vessels launched (100 gross tons and over; 1967) 7,548,000 gross tons.

island to Japan. (In line with this, the first Japan-U.S. consultation on Okinawa's status had been held on May 27 between Foreign Minister Takeo Miki and U.S. Ambassador U. Alexis Johnson.) The day after the release of Sneider's testimony, Chief Cabinet Secretary Toshio Kimura reemphasized Prime Minister Sato's confidence in the timetable of "two or three years." However, opposition parties—Socialist, Democratic Socialist, and Komeito—claimed that Sato had misled the nation in implying that reversion would be effected within that time.

On September 2 Sato announced that he hoped to visit the U.S. in January, after the inauguration of the new U.S. president, to seek an early return of Okinawa to Japanese administration. The continued presence of a U.S. base with nuclear capability, after reversion, was an important issue that would have to be dealt with in negotiations.

Meanwhile, Japan had begun to face the difficult problem of its own security posture, a problem immensely complicated by the continued "American presence" in Japan itself. Under the Japan-U.S. security treaty, Japan provided the U.S. with 146 military bases and facilities (total area, 96,000 ac.) scattered throughout the country; played host to about 40,000 U.S. personnel; and, in return, was placed under the U.S. defensive nuclear umbrella. Leased facilities included such large air bases as Yokota, Tachikawa, Atsugi, and Itazuke, and giant naval bases at Yokosuka and Sasebo.

On January 19, by arrangement with the government of Japan, the 75,700-ton nuclear-powered carrier USS "Enterprise" anchored off Cape Iorizaki at the mouth of Sasebo Bay. Opposition parties charged that the ship might carry nuclear arms, despite assurances to the contrary by the government. Students of the Three Faction Alliance (Sampa Rengo) of the left-wing group Zengakuren fought with riot police for three days in an attempt to storm the U.S. base.

The situation was made more serious on June 2 when a U.S. Air Force F-4C Phantom jet crashed into the Kyushu University computer centre, then under construction. Flying debris narrowly missed crowded dormitories. Mayor Genzo Abe of Fukuoka and Gov. Hikaru Kamei of Fukuoka Prefecture made immediate and strong protests to Maj. Gen. Benjamin Matlick, commander of the Itazuke air base. The Fukuoka city assembly unanimously passed a resolution calling for immediate relocation of the Itazuke base.

Japanese police estimated that approximately 15,-

000 students participated in nationwide demonstrations on June 7, in protest over the Itazuke incident. Rear Adm. Eugene P. Wilkinson, chief of staff of U.S. forces in Japan, then announced suspension of night flights by U.S. aircraft "except when absolutely necessary."

Transport Minister Yasuhiro Nakasone inspected both Kyushu University and the Itazuke base for the Japanese government. On June 11, following his suggestion, the Cabinet decided to take steps to have the U.S. remove the base. On June 27 in Tokyo, at a meeting of a Japan-U.S. joint committee, U.S. authorities agreed to relocate the base; the Japanese government agreed to seek a new site. Meanwhile, on June 3 Ambassador Johnson had disclosed that the U.S. would not send nuclear-powered vessels into either Sasebo or Yokosuka until an adequate radioactivity monitoring system had been established in both ports.

Despite these tensions, on June 17 Naka Funada, chairman of the ruling party's Security Affairs Council, announced the Liberal-Democratic policy on national security. The U.S.-Japan security treaty would remain in effect until such time as Japan and the U.S. became convinced that the UN was capable of effective measures to ensure international peace and security. In August Prime Minister Sato, in a letter to President Johnson, stated that the Liberal-Democrats' victory in the upper house election was a clear manifestation of national sentiment in favour of cooperation between Japan and the U.S., and that government policy would be to retain the security treaty beyond 1970. On November 30, three days after his reelection as party leader, Sato reshuffled his Cabinet, naming as foreign minister the strongly pro-U.S. Kiichi Aichi.

On July 30 in Tokyo, a long-range contract was signed calling for export of Japanese lumbering machinery and equipment in return for Soviet lumber. This marked the start of a Japan-U.S.S.R. joint project for the economic development of Siberia.

On June 29 in Fukuoka, Prime Minister Sato stated that private one-year trade agreements with Communist China should be replaced by a long-term trade pact. The Japanese government, Sato said, had followed a policy of approving credits for such trade on a case-by-case basis. The implication by the prime minister was that Communist China would have to create conditions for stable trade relations.

(A. W. Bs.)

ENCYCLOPÆDIA BRITANNICA FILMS. *Japan—Harvesting the Land and the Sea* (1963); *Japan—Miracle in Asia* (1963).

Jordan

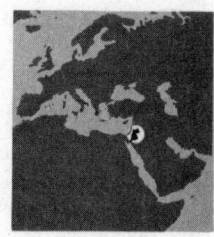

A constitutional monarchy in southwest Asia, Jordan is bounded north by Syria, northeast by Iraq, east and south by Saudi Arabia, and west by Israel. Area (including territory occupied by Israel in the June 1967 war): 37,737 sq.mi. (97,740 sq.km.). Pop. (1967 est.): 2,145,000. Cap. and largest city: Amman (pop., 1967 est., 330,000). Language: Arabic. Religion: Muslim 88%; Christian 12%. King, Husain I; prime minister in 1968, Bahjat al-Talhouni.

With half its territory occupied by Israel, Jordan continued in 1968 to cling to survival as an independent state with the help of substantial aid from other Arab countries. But the very real possibility remained of an open conflict between the Palestinian refugee commando organizations and King Husain and his government, with the threat of the partition of the country or the downfall of the monarchy.

Throughout the year there were almost daily artillery duels with Israel across the cease-fire line in the Jordan Valley, and on five occasions, in February, March, June, August, and December, Israel launched heavy air and rocket attacks on Jordanian territory in reprisal for commando raids. After the February incident King Husain strongly denounced the commandos for provoking the attacks, but the government was divided over the issue and a former prime minister, Wasfi al-Tal, called for the utmost support for the commandos. Eventually the government compromised by taking the line that Jordan could not be held responsible for attacks on Israelis inside occupied Arab

"THE NEW YORK TIMES" FROM WIDE WORLD

Suspected and convicted members of Arab terrorist organizations, most of them associated with Al Fatah, taking one of their two daily walks in the courtyard of the Nablus Prison in Israeli-occupied Jordan.

territory. In March, when Israel attacked with tanks as well as planes across a 30-mi. front, the Jordanian Army and the commandos joined hands in a resistance which inflicted heavier losses on the Israelis than on any similar occasion. An understanding was reached whereby the government allowed the commandos independent control of their own bases in the Jordan Valley, but relations between the government and the commandos remained uneasy as the commandos suspected King Husain of preparing to reach a direct settlement with Israel at their expense.

Throughout 1968 the Jordan government kept up a propaganda barrage accusing Israel of terrorizing the Arab inhabitants of the occupied lands in order to force them to leave. In July Jordan closed the Allenby Bridge over the Jordan River to Palestinian Arab refugees from Gaza.

King Husain pursued his customary vigorous diplomatic campaigning throughout the year. He continued to press for the holding of an Arab summit meeting, implying that without it Jordan might have to act alone, but he failed to gain the support of King Faisal of Saudi Arabia and the summit was not held. Refusing to turn to the Communist countries for arms, Husain continued to rely on the U.S. to make up the losses of the June 1967 war. (P. Md.)

ENCYCLOPÆDIA BRITANNICA FILMS. *The Middle East* (1955).

JORDAN

Education. (1965–66) Primary, pupils 295,177, teachers 7,692; secondary, pupils 99,076, teachers 4,216; vocational, pupils 3,267, teachers 278; teacher training, students 98, teachers (1964–65) 26; higher (including University of Jordan), students 2,023, teaching staff 124.

Finance. Monetary unit: Jordan dinar, with a par value of 0.36 dinars to U.S. $1 (0.86 dinars = £1 sterling). Gold and foreign exchange: (June 1968) U.S. $246.3 million; (June 1967) U.S. $232.5 million. Budget (1967 est.): revenue 67,043,840 dinars; expenditure 69,030,150 dinars. Gross national product: (1966) 185.8 million dinars; (1965) 180.5 million dinars. Money supply: (June 1968) 84,690,000 dinars; (June 1967) 66,910,000 dinars.

Foreign Trade. (1967) Imports 54,760,000 dinars; exports 11,330,000 dinars. Import sources: U.K. 12%; West Germany 12%; U.S. 12%; Lebanon 7%; Syria 5%. Export destinations: Kuwait 15%; India 13%; Lebanon 12%; Syria 11%; Iraq 10%; Saudi Arabia 10%; Italy 7%; Yugoslavia 5%. Main exports: phosphates 31%; tomatoes 18%; vegetables 12%.

Transport and Communications. Roads (1967) 3,055 km. (excluding local roads). Motor vehicles in use (1966): passenger 12,046; commercial 5,160. Railways (1965) 366 km. Air traffic (1967): 97,912,000 passenger-km.; freight 660,000 net ton-km. Telephones (Jan. 1967) 32,000. Radio receivers (Dec. 1965) *c.* 269,000.

Agriculture. Production (in 000; metric tons; 1966; 1965 in parentheses): barley 23 (95); wheat (1967) *c.* 248, (1966) 101; cucumbers 40 (61); lentils 11 (29); onions and garlic 22 (19); tomatoes 145 (189); olives 33 (37); oranges *c.* 45 (36); grapefruit *c.* 12 (11); figs 16 (19); grapes 62 (80); bananas 17 (15). Livestock (in 000; 1965–66): sheep 987; cattle 73; goats 759; camels 19; asses 94; chickens *c.* 2,100.

Industry. Production (in 000; metric tons; 1966): phosphate rock 1,036; cement 375; electricity 176,000 kw-hr.

Kenya

A republic and a member of the Commonwealth of Nations, Kenya is bordered on the north by Sudan and Ethiopia, east by the Somali Republic, south by Tanzania, and west by Uganda. Area: 224,960 sq.mi. (582,647 sq.km.), including 5,171 sq.mi. of inland water. Pop. (1968 est.): 10,209,000, including (1962) African and Somali 96.9%; Asian 2%. Cap. and largest city: Nairobi (pop., 1968 est., 389,000). Language:

English (official); Bantu, especially Swahili; Nilotic. Religion: pagan; Christian and Muslim minorities. President in 1968, Jomo Kenyatta.

During 1967 there had been a substantial increase in the number of Asians leaving Kenya to take up permanent residence in the United Kingdom. Toward the end of the year the publication of a new Immigration Bill which stated that no work permits would be issued to non-Kenyans if unemployed citizens could be found to do the work led to a still greater increase in emigration. The Kenya government's policy resulted from its difficulties over African unemployment, but early in 1968 it threatened to give rise to serious difficulties of another character when thousands of Asians, fearing that the U.K. government might enact legislation to restrict the number of Asian immigrants, tried to beat the ban by leaving at once.

The background to the problem was to be found in the arrangements made at the time that Kenya achieved independence, when second- and later-generation Kenya Asians by birth automatically became Kenya citizens. First-generation Kenya Asians were already citizens of the United Kingdom and colonies because they were born in a British colony, but they were given two years in which to take up Kenyan nationality if they wished to do so. Uncertain about their future in an independent Kenya, only a small number availed themselves of the opportunity, leaving more than 100,000 still claiming British nationality. If anything approaching that number of Asians had left Kenya within a short space of time, it would have been a serious blow to the country's economy, which still relied heavily upon the skills possessed by the Asian community.

The enactment of a new and more restrictive Commonwealth Immigration law by the U.K. government early in March aroused heavy criticism in Britain as well as in Kenya and India, in spite of the eventual introduction of a clause setting up machinery to hear appeals from U.K. passport holders liable to suffer hardship as a result of the new legislation. Pakistan offered some amelioration of the position of Asians in danger of expulsion by agreeing in April to grant permanent residence to Asian Muslims from Kenya or to other Kenya Asians who had their origins in Pakistan. India, after first tightening its control on the immigration of Kenya Asians, later agreed to some relaxation after negotiations with Britain.

Constitutional issues had also given rise to some problems. In March a bill was published in which it was proposed that the next president should be elected by a popular vote at the time of the parliamentary elections. Only candidates supported by registered political parties would be eligible, and each party would nominate only one candidate. Candidates for parliamentary seats would also have to be nominated by the leader of a registered political party, and the same arrangement would hold good in local government elections.

Dissatisfaction at the elimination of independent members from future parliaments was considerable, but very much more vigorous were the protests of Oginga Odinga and his party, the Kenya People's Union (KPU), in August when all the candidates of the governing Kenya African National Union (KANU) were returned unopposed in the local government elections. KPU candidates had been disqualified throughout the country for allegedly having filled in their nomination papers incorrectly. Oginga Odinga also claimed that other prospective KPU can-

didates had been forced to withdraw owing to various technicalities, such as the sudden increase of a candidate's deposit from £5 to £10 or the unexpected moving forward of the nomination date.

The KPU had already suffered many setbacks, due in many cases to the fact that its members were not permitted to hold public meetings. Some had transferred to the KANU in the hope of improving their political opportunities; others had looked to the local government elections to provide them with an opportunity to show their strength, but the disqualifications had frustrated their hopes. Oginga Odinga himself had been ordered to get off an airplane, which he had boarded in Nairobi prior to its takeoff for Tanzania, and had been informed by immigration officers that he was not permitted to leave the country.

In the economic sphere Kenya's main preoccupation was with the implementation of the plans made in 1967 for the creation of the East African Community. This involved moving a number of the headquarters of the self-contained services from their former Kenya locations to other centres in Uganda and Tanzania and considering the changes that would be necessary if other states that had shown an interest in the Community were to be admitted.

Kenya won its first Olympic Games gold medals during the competition at Mexico City in October. Kipchoge Keino won the 1,500-m. run, while Naftali Temu captured the 10,000 m. and Amos Biwott triumphed in the steeplechase. In addition, Kenyans placed second in the 800-m. and 5,000-m. runs, the steeplechase, and the 1,600-m. relay.   (K. I.)

ENCYCLOPÆDIA BRITANNICA FILMS. *East Africa (Kenya, Tanganyika, Uganda)* (1962).

KENYA
Education. (1965–66) Primary, pupils 1,010,889, teachers 30,592; secondary and vocational, pupils 49,-223, teachers 2,629; teacher training, students 5,115, teachers 366; higher, students 2,795.
Finance. Monetary unit: Kenyan shilling, with a par value of 7.14 Kenyan shillings to U.S. $1 (17.14 Kenyan shillings = £1 sterling). Budget (1966–67 est.): revenue £50 million; expenditure £52.8 million. Gross domestic product: (1967) 8,660,000,000 Kenyan shillings; (1966) 8.2 billion Kenyan shillings. Cost of living (Nairobi; 1963 = 100): (June 1968) 110; (June 1967) 112.
Foreign Trade. (Excluding trade with Tanganyika and Uganda; 1967) Imports 2,130,000,000 Kenyan shillings; exports 1,186,000,000 Kenyan shillings. Import sources: U.K. 33%; West Germany 10%; Iran 8%; U.S. 7%; Japan 5%. Export destinations: U.K. 22%; West Germany 8%; U.S. 6%. Main exports: coffee 26%; tea 12%; petroleum products 12%; meat and meat products 5%.
Transport and Communications. Roads (1965) 41,900 km. (including 1,940 km. with improved surface). Motor vehicles in use (1966): passenger *c.* 75,000; commercial (including buses) *c.* 14,000. Railways: (1966) 2,053 km. (operated under East African Railways Corporation, serving Kenya, Tanzania, and Uganda with a total of 5,880 km.); traffic (total East African, including road and lake services; 1963) 4,004,000,000 passenger-km., freight (1966) 3,936,-000,000 net ton-km. Ships entered (1966) vessels totaling 5,235,000 net registered tons; goods loaded (Mombasa only; 1967) 2,103,000 metric tons, unloaded 2,882,000 metric tons. Telephones (Dec. 1966) 57,123. Radio receivers (Dec. 1965) 359,000. Television receivers (Dec. 1966) *c.* 10,500.
Agriculture. Production (in 000; metric tons; 1966; 1965 in parentheses): corn, farms and estates 54 (58); wheat, farms and estates (1967) 128, (1966) 127; coffee *c.* 56 (*c.* 52); tea 25 (25); sugar *c.* 76 (39); sisal 57 (64); cottonseed 9 (9). Livestock (in 000; 1965–66): cattle 7,242; sheep *c.* 5,375; pigs 31; goats, farms and estates *c.* 6,400; camels *c.* 178; poultry, farms and estates 202. Fish catch (in 000; metric tons) (1966) 28, (1965) 23.
Industry. Production (in 000; metric tons; 1966): salt 32; copper ore (metal content) 0.8; soda ash 112; gold 12 troy oz.; limestone 17; cement (1967) 493; electricity (1967) 340,000 kw-hr.

Korea

A country of eastern Asia, Korea is bounded by China, the Sea of Japan, the Straits of Korea, and the Yellow Sea. It is divided into two parts at the 38th parallel.

Republic of Korea (South Korea). Area: 38,022 sq.mi. (98,477 sq.km.). Pop. (1968 est.): 30,469,000. Cap. and largest city: Seoul (pop., 1967 est., 3,972,-000). Language: Korean. Religion: Buddhist; Confucian; Tonghak (Chutokyo). President in 1968, Gen. Pak Chung Hi; prime minister, Gen. Chung Il Kwon.

North Korean infiltration into South Korea had increased greatly in 1967, about 120 South Koreans and U.S. troops being killed in clashes with the infiltrators, most of whom landed from small boats along the islands of western Korea. On the night of Jan. 21, 1968, a band of 31 Communist infiltrators slipped into Seoul with the mission of assassinating Pres. Pak Chung Hi. Almost all were killed in a battle with the police near Pak's residence or within the next few days as they fled northward; 32 South Koreans were also killed and 42 wounded. North Korea was said to have 18,000 men under training for guerrilla activities.

On January 22 the U.S. electronic intelligence ship "Pueblo," carrying 83 men, was captured by North Korean patrol boats off the east coast of North Korea. Shortly afterward the North Korean radio broadcast an alleged "confession" by the "Pueblo's" commander stating that he had been in North Korean waters and promising, if released, to continue to admit the "crimes" he had committed "on orders from my superiors." Clashes involving U.S. troops also occurred in the western sector of the demilitarized zone during the following few days.

South Korea was greatly annoyed at being excluded from the North Korean-U.S. negotiations for the return of the "Pueblo" and its crew, an official complaint about this being made on February 6. In Seoul's view, the U.S. was showing excessive concern for its own

UPI COMPIX

South Korean troops searching for North Korean infiltrators in Seoul on Jan. 24, 1968, following an attempt to assassinate South Korean Pres. Pak Chung Hi.

interests and insufficient concern for the growing threat to South Korea. This tension gave rise on February 6 and 7 to the first anti-U.S. demonstrations in South Korea in five years, as groups of university students urged the U.S. to stop its "appeasement" of North Korea and demanded the withdrawal of the 49,000 South Korean troops in Vietnam.

On February 8, U.S. Pres. Lyndon Johnson announced the grant of an additional $100 million in military aid to South Korea, and on February 11 he sent Cyrus R. Vance (see BIOGRAPHY) to Seoul in an effort to restore good relations. As a result South Korea acquiesced in the "Pueblo" talks, obtaining some minor concessions to its demand that the U.S. should give "immediate" support to South Korea under the mutual security agreement in case of additional attacks from the North. Such intervention was subject to "constitutional processes," but the resistance in the U.S. Congress to the U.S. involvement in Vietnam

---

KOREA, Republic

Education. (1965–66) Primary, pupils 4,941,-345, teachers 79,164; secondary, pupils 1,005,-436, teachers 26,961; vocational, students 195,-512, teachers 7,388; higher (including 16 universities), students 141,635, teaching staff (1964–65) 9,486.

Finance. Monetary unit: won, with an official exchange rate (July 1968) of 274 won to U.S. $1 (658 won = £1 sterling). Gold and foreign exchange, central bank: (June 1968) U.S. $367 million; (June 1967) U.S. $300,209,000. Budget (1967 est.): revenue 164,346,000,000 won (including foreign aid 27,068,000,000 won); expenditure 164,346,000,000 won (including defense 48,001,000,000 won). Gross national product: (1967) 1,249,200,000,000 won; (1966) 1,032,-000,000,000 won. Money supply: (March 1968) 145,350,000,000 won; (March 1967) 73,860,-000,000 won. Cost of living (Seoul; 1963 = 100): (May 1968) 135; (May 1967) 124.

Foreign Trade. (1967) Imports 245,910,000,-000 won (including 10,020,000,000 won official aid); exports 86,070,000,000 won. Import sources: Japan 44%; U.S. 31%. Export destinations: U.S. 43%; Japan 26%; Hong Kong 5%. Main exports (1966): textiles 14%; clothing 13%; wood products 12%; fish and fish products 9%; silk 5%.

Transport and Communications. Roads (1966) 34,709 km. Motor vehicles in use (1966): passenger 17,500; commercial (including buses) 31,600. Railways: (1966) 3,063 km.; traffic (1967) 9,578,000,000 passenger-km., freight 5,959,000,000 net ton-km. Shipping (1967): merchant vessels 100 gross tons and over 196; gross tonnage 305,905. Air traffic (1966): 56,-850,000 passenger-km.; freight 185,000 net ton-km. Telephones (Jan. 1967) 324,049. Radio receivers (Dec. 1966) 2,632,000. Television receivers (Dec. 1966) 55,000.

Agriculture. Production (in 000; metric tons; 1966; 1965 in parentheses): wheat 315 (300); potatoes 688 (581); rice (1967) 4,869, (1966) 5,296; barley c. 1,100 (1,135); sweet potatoes and yams 2,997 (2,690); soybeans 161 (174). Livestock (in 000; Dec. 1966): cattle 1,299; pigs 1,437; horses 27; goats (Dec. 1965) 177; poultry 14,007. Fish catch (in 000; metric tons) (1966) 701, (1965) 640.

Industry. Production (in 000; metric tons; 1967): coal 12,360; iron ore (c. 50% metal content) 698; tungsten concentrate (oxide content; 1966) 2.9; graphite (1966) 129; kaolin (1966) 112; fluorspar (1966) 32; limestone (1966) 2,926; gold (1966) 61 troy oz.; silver (1966) 0.016; electricity (excluding most industrial production) 4,911,000 kw-hr.

KOREA, People's Democratic Republic

Education. (1964–65) Primary, pupils 1,113,-000, teachers 25,221; secondary, pupils 704,000, teachers 27,162; vocational, pupils 441,000, teachers 17,176; higher (including 3 universities), students 186,000, teaching staff 9,013.

Finance and Trade. Monetary unit: won, with an official exchange rate of 2.57 won to U.S. $1 (6.17 won = £1 sterling). Budget (1967 est.) balanced at 3,960,000,000 won. Trade is almost entirely with China and the U.S.S.R. Main exports (1964): metals 50%; minerals 12%; farm produce 11%.

Transport. Motor vehicles in use (1961): passenger 3,226; commercial 1,600. Railways: (1966) c. 10,000 km.; freight (1961) 9,823,-000,000 net ton-km.

Agriculture. Production (in 000; metric tons; 1966; 1965 in parentheses): rice c. 2,500 (c. 2,500); corn c. 1,600 (c. 1,640); barley c. 250 (c. 250); potatoes c. 955 (c. 955). Livestock (in 000; Dec. 1965): cattle c. 685; pigs c. 1,200; sheep c. 156; goats c. 165. Fish catch (in 000; metric tons) (1964) 770, (1963) 640.

Industry. Production (in 000; metric tons; 1966): coal c. 15,500; iron ore 6,000; pig iron c. 1,500; steel c. 1,300; lead c. 50; zinc c. 75; cement c. 2,500; tungsten concentrate (oxide content) c. 2.6; fertilizers (1963) 853; electricity (1965) 13,300,000 kw-hr.

Confessions

I am CDR Lloyd Mark Bucher, captain of USS Pueblo belonging to the US Pacific Fleet, US Navy, who was captured while carrying out espionage activities after intruding deep into the territorial waters of the Democratic People's Republic of Korea.

My serial Number is 582540. I was born in Pocatello Idaho, USA. I am 38 years old.

Three photographs released by official North Korean sources following the capture of the U.S. intelligence ship "Pueblo" in the Sea of Japan on Jan. 22, 1968. Above, the crew of the ship being led into captivity; below left, the ship's captain, Cmdr. Lloyd Bucher, writing his "confession"; left, a portion of the alleged "confession."

without a declaration of war was believed to throw doubt on the U.S. commitment in Korea.

An additional 200 U.S. planes were brought to South Korea after the "Pueblo" incident, which had demonstrated the inadequacy of U.S. air strength in Korea. South Korea wanted these aircraft to remain in Korea, and the demand was apparently granted. Meanwhile, the "Pueblo" talks continued throughout most of the year. On December 22 the 82 surviving crew members were finally released. In exchange, the U.S. signed an apology for the intrusion of the ship into North Korean waters—which, however, it repudiated in advance.

President Johnson's offer to negotiate with North Vietnam caused further dismay, on the ground that if Vietnam were allowed to go Communist the threat to South Korea would greatly increase. Seoul also felt that it should be included in any such negotiations, having provided by far the largest of the smaller allied contingents fighting in Vietnam, and one of acknowledged effectiveness. In mid-April President Pak met President Johnson at Honolulu, where these questions were discussed without apparent result.

A lull ensued until early July, when a clash between North and South Korean troops occurred in the western sector of the demilitarized zone, followed by two more clashes on August 13. On August 21, 14 North Koreans attempted to land on Cheju Island, apparently in an effort to rescue a leader of a subversive "United Revolutionary Party." All the invaders were apparently killed or captured. Four days later the South Korean Central Intelligence Agency (CIA) announced that 158 South Koreans, mostly intellectuals, had been found to be members of the subversive organization; 73 were referred to the authorities for possible indictment.

In mid-1967 the South Korean CIA had abducted 17 South Korean students from West Germany, and others from France, the U.S., and Austria. Some of the students were among 34 persons brought to trial on Nov. 9, 1967, on charges of being connected with a North Korean spy ring operating out of East Berlin. On December 13 all but three were found guilty and sentenced to death or imprisonment. The sentences caused considerable indignation in West Germany, and relations with South Korea came close to the breaking point. At the end of July 1968 the Supreme Court quashed the three death sentences conferred, but two were reimposed following a retrial.

On May 21 President Pak reshuffled his Cabinet, retaining as prime minister Chung Il Kwon, who had

led it for four years. Ten days later Kim Chong Pil, Pak's "heir apparent," announced his intention of retiring from politics, apparently owing to Pak's expulsion from the ruling Democratic Republican Party, a few days earlier, of one of his senior aides for having led a factionalist group. Then, on August 5, the defense minister, Choi Yung Hi, resigned because he was "morally responsible" for the disclosure of secret military information in the course of a parliamentary investigation, held in the presence of the press.

Democratic People's Republic of Korea (North Korea). Area: 46,540 sq.mi. (120,538 sq.km.). Pop. (1967 est.): 12.8 million. Cap.: P'yongyang (pop., 1960 est., 653,100). Language: Korean. Religion: Buddhist; Confucian, Tonghak (Chutokyo). Secretary-general of the Korean Workers' (Communist) Party and chairman of the Council of Ministers (premier) in 1968, Marshal Kim Il Sung; president, Choi Yong Kun.

Addressing the Supreme People's Assembly on Dec. 16, 1967, Kim Il Sung, the leader of the Korean Democratic People's Republic (KDPR), emphasized the need for a spirit of independence, self-sufficiency, and self-defense. Industrial production was later stated to have risen by 17% and food production by 16% during the year. The warlike note first sounded by the capture of the U.S. intelligence ship "Pueblo" in January (see *South Korea,* above) was struck still more vigorously in the following April, when the armed forces were said to have been entirely modernized, the whole people armed, and the whole country fortified. The 1968 budget was 33% higher than that of the previous year and defense allocations were increased proportionately.

In foreign affairs North Korea seemed closer to the U.S.S.R. than to China in 1967–68. Kim Il Sung in December 1967 made a speech dwelling on the necessity for a united anti-U.S. front, a concept that China had rejected since the outbreak of the Sino-Soviet dispute. But Kim Il Sung also showed signs of annoyance with the U.S.S.R. as insufficiently belligerent. In August P'yongyang confined its comments on the Czechoslovak crisis to criticism of Alexander Dubcek's regime.

Chou En-lai and other Chinese leaders were reported in December 1967 as condemning North Korea for "revisionism," and Communist China tended to play down the "Pueblo" incident. The Chinese also stayed away from the celebration of the 20th anniversary of the KDPR on September 8, as did the Czechoslovaks.   (P. H. M. J.)

Kuwait

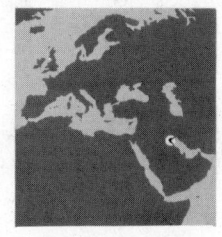

An independent Arab sheikhdom, Kuwait is on the northwestern coast of the Persian Gulf between Iraq and Saudi Arabia. Area: 7,450 sq.mi. (18,850 sq.km.). Pop. (1967 est.): 520,000. Cap. and largest city: Kuwait (pop., 1965, 99,633). Language: Arabic. Religion: Muslim. Amir in 1968, Sheikh Sabah as-Salim as-Sabah; prime minister, Crown Prince Sheikh Jabir as-Ahmed as-Jabir as-Sabah.

In 1968 Kuwait pursued its role as a moderating and mediatory force among the Arab states. It also played a part in normalizing relations between the United Arab Republic and Iran. In April King Faisal of Saudi Arabia paid a state visit to Kuwait, and the Kuwaiti

KUWAIT
Education. (1965–66) Primary, pupils 49,562, teachers 2,316; secondary, pupils 29,494, teachers 1,783; vocational, pupils 1,033, teachers 155; teacher training, students 1,144, teachers 163.
Finance and Trade. Monetary unit: Kuwaiti dinar, with a par value of 0.36 dinars to U.S. $1 (0.86 dinars = £1 sterling). Gold and foreign exchange: Currency Board (June 1968) U.S. $167.7 million, (June 1967) U.S. $187.8 million; government (March 1968) U.S. $950.3 million, (March 1967) U.S. $953.4 million. Budget (1967–68 est.): revenue 285.2 million dinars; expenditure 193.4 million dinars. Foreign trade (1967): imports 211,893,000 dinars; exports 469 million dinars. Import sources: U.S. 22%; U.K. 12%; West Germany 9%; Italy 5%. Export destinations (1966): Italy 23%; Japan 20%; U.K. 18%; France 10%; Netherlands 7%. Main exports petroleum and products 97%.
Industry. Crude oil production (1967) 115,215,000 metric tons.

foreign minister toured the Persian Gulf to express Kuwait's support for the proposed new federation of Arab sheikhdoms.

Kuwait also continued to be the chief supplier of capital to the Arab states. By June it had already paid out 73.5 million dinars, partly from state reserves and partly from the general budget, to Arab countries that had suffered from the June 1967 war. Oil revenues for the 1968–69 financial year were estimated at 239 million dinars, compared with 242 million dinars in the previous year. In May a new oil agreement was signed with the Spanish state-sponsored Hispanoil. Government spokesmen in September expressed confidence in sterling. At the same time the finance minister denied reports that Kuwaiti deposits in London amounted to more than £400 million.

On May 13 the defense agreement with the United Kingdom, concluded after Kuwaiti independence in 1961, was canceled by mutual agreement. A provision of the defense agreement had been that it would remain effective for three years after the announcement of its cancellation; Britain had already announced the withdrawal of all its forces from the Persian Gulf area by 1971.   (P. MD.)

Labour Unions

There was a general intensification of labour union activity in many areas of the world during 1968, particularly in Western and Central Europe. Labour unions tended to be more militant in their dealings with both governments and employers. The net general effect was an increase in strike action and a growing concern about union solidarity. Insofar as labour activity was concerned, the world fell into three broad categories. In Western industrial countries the economic pressures on workers increased during the year and produced, in some cases, spontaneous reactions from workers followed by official union action; in other cases the unions reacted more quickly and were in control of the situation. Within this category, union activity was greatest in France, followed by Britain and Japan. In the second category, the less developed areas of the world, the main question was that of trade union rights. Governments in those areas frequently sought to impose greater restrictions on unions in order to achieve political stability for themselves or conformity with their economic aims. The third category included those Communist countries where liberalizing forces were present.

Western Industrial Countries. In some countries labour unrest that began in 1967 was carried over into 1968. The United Automobile Workers of America, which had conducted a 45-day strike against the Ford Motor Co. in September and October 1967, still had not agreed on new contracts with all of the remaining U.S. automobile manufacturers by the new year. In the case of General Motors, national terms had been ratified but many local issues were unresolved, and the union imposed a deadline, January 9, when strike action would be considered if issues remained unsettled. The copper strike in the U.S., which started on July 15, 1967, continued for eight months. At the beginning it involved 37,000 workers, but by January 1968, 60,000 workers were on strike, halting 97% of domestic copper-smelter production. Agreements between the employers and 26 unions were reached late in March on three-year contracts covering a wage increase and improved retirement, sickness, vacation, and unemployment benefits. A strike of New York City public transportation workers was averted almost on the strike deadline of January 1, after 39 hours of continuous bargaining between the union leaders and the city authorities. A newspaper strike in Los Angeles, which began on Dec. 15, 1967, continued into January and spread to newspapers in San Francisco. The newspaper proprietors in Los Angeles imported blackleg labour (scabs) from as far away as Hawaii and Florida, and there was violence between strikers and strikebreakers. A strike against Detroit's two major newspapers lasted from midnight, Nov. 15, 1967, to Aug. 9, 1968. The U.S. Department of Labor reported more man-days were lost through strikes in 1967 than in any other year since 1959, and forecast a further increase for 1968. Wage bargaining for four million workers was anticipated.

In Italy a strike movement began in November 1967. First there was a general strike in Naples on November 23, the biggest since 1948. A national general strike was called by the three principal labour federations for December 15, but was suspended when the government, against whom the demands were made, agreed to consider the unions' terms. A series of one-day bank strikes was staged between December 4 and January 5 to create the maximum effect during the holidays. In Britain, the National Union of Bank Employees engaged in its first big strike late in November when it called a two-day strike to support its demand for full recognition and negotiating rights from the Committee of London Clearing Banks. The

union suspended subsequent strikes to allow negotiations to continue, but on January 15 it delivered an ultimatum to the banks. On February 2, nine clearing banks agreed to set up national negotiating machinery. The strike at the U.S.-owned Roberts-Arundel factory in Stockport, Eng., which had started in November 1966 over management's refusal to consult the unions on the employment of women in place of men (at lower wage rates), ended, after 16 months, on April 29, 1968.

In Japan the Ministry of Postal Services disciplined 3,061 postal employees on January 13 for protesting against the rationalization of the postal services between July and December of the previous year. Thirty-nine employees were suspended, 1,182 received wage cuts, and the remainder were either reprimanded or warned. In Spain a number of workers were put on trial in January and February for their participation in illegal May Day demonstrations in 1967 and were subsequently imprisoned. The Spanish Supreme Court had declared on Dec. 7, 1967, that all strikes in Spain were illegal in principle. Amendments to the labour law two years earlier had led to the belief that strikes for economic motives were permissible, but the rejection of two appeals under the law by 560 dismissed Basque steelworkers dispelled this impression.

Fresh movements were soon under way. The *Shunto* or "Spring Wage Offensive" in Japan started before the year began. Nikkeireu (the Japan Federation of Employers' Associations) urged at its meeting in October 1967 that the *Shunto* should end and that the government should prescribe guidelines for wage negotiations. In response to this appeal the trade unions issued three white papers outlining their policies and their spring demands, and made no concessions to the employers' requests. At its convention on March 6, Sohyo (the General Council of Trade Unions) decided to launch its spring offensive with strikes of undisclosed duration from March 26 to early April. Key unions in private industry were to provide the strike leadership. Another national organization, Domei, decided to use the All Japan Seamen's Union and the Federation of Electrical Workers' Unions of Japan to establish the wage pattern. Disputes involving the private railway systems were settled by April 21, and this marked the climax of the "Offensive." Wage settlements were reached that averted what had threatened to be the largest strikes of public service employees since 1945. In almost all industries except iron and steel, the wage rises were higher than in 1967. On the average, the unions gained a wage increase of 13.2% from 204 major firms, and also checked the government's intention to introduce wage controls. The two main railway workers' unions resisted a rationalization plan for the railways by working to rule, and on April 15 Tanro, the coal miners' union, staged a 48-hour strike for the nationalization of the coal industry.

Three issues began to crystallize in Britain early in the year. The engineering unions had submitted a pay claim before Christmas. On March 27 the employers turned down the whole of the general claim and on April 18 submitted counterproposals which the unions, in turn, rejected. The employers wanted an arrangement based on productivity. On May 15 the unions staged a one-day strike, after which the employers stated they were prepared to consider a general wage increase within the context of a three-year productivity agreement.

Meanwhile, union resistance to the British govern-

ment's incomes policy was increasing. A special conference of trade union executives, which met on February 28 to discuss the matter, endorsed the Trades Union Congress (TUC) policy of voluntary restraint by a margin of only 536,000 votes out of a total of 8,704,000. Even so, the government in May introduced a new Prices and Incomes Bill, which gave it stronger powers to regulate incomes than before.

The third issue concerned the bargaining rights of white collar unions in the steel industry. Manual workers' unions which organized some white collar workers, supported by the TUC, opposed the granting of national recognition to the Clerical and Administrative Workers' Union and the Association of Scientific, Technical, and Managerial Staffs, and these two unions staged a series of strikes in various steelworks from the end of May. The government set up a court of inquiry which generally supported the white collar unions' claim, but the issue remained unsettled. The Royal Commission on Trade Unions and Employers' Associations, set up in 1965, published its report on June 13. Its main recommendations were aimed at extending and consolidating a voluntary local bargaining system. Except in limited ways, it rejected the use of legislation to regulate industrial relations further and suggested instead that a Commission for Industrial Relations be established to deal with particularly difficult issues. The Confederation of British Industry and the TUC issued a joint statement in October urging the government to establish such a commission as soon as possible. At the end of October the government announced its intention to introduce proposals for action on the report. The context for these issues in Britain was one of intense industrial militancy by workers in the automobile industry, road haulage, shipbuilding, and building construction. Up to the end of August, 13 out of the 25 groups into which British industry was divided for statistical purposes had lost more than double the number of working days through strikes than in the first eight months of 1967.

In Australia during February, the Commonwealth Industrial Court imposed a strike ban on 100,000 metalworkers and on employees from seven trade unions in about 3,000 plants. The unions had called for a nationwide campaign of action in support of wage claims. Shortly afterward, the Australian Commonwealth Arbitration Commission decided that a wages award, which was opposed by the employers, should stand. A controversy flared up in the early part of the year in South Africa over the Trade Union Council's advocacy of the unionization of African workers. The council had been attacked for its attitude by the minister of labour in December 1967, and it had responded by excluding African trade unions from its membership. However, at its annual conference in April the Trade Union Council reversed its earlier decision by a large majority, thus putting itself into a position where its registration as a trade union federation was in jeopardy.

The labour situation in the U.S. was slow to develop strike characteristics, largely because the procedure for ending and renewing contracts had first to be exhausted and this took time. The Uniformed Sanitationmen's Association of New York City, however, was early in the field for a wage increase. Despite a strike ban and the imprisonment of its president, the union successfully conducted a nine-day strike, which ended on February 11, and obtained a wage increase. In Spain the annual May Day demonstra-

tions were met by the equally annual countermeasures of the government. A number of the workers' leaders were arrested before the demonstration, and Madrid radio warned that anyone taking part in the demonstrations organized by the illegal Workers' Commission would be arrested and punished. An inquiry among Spanish workers, conducted by the clandestine Unión Sindical Obrera, showed that 97% were opposed to the existing union structure which linked workers, employers, and the state into a corporate unity. The Icelandic Federation of Labour called a nationwide strike on March 4 to obtain the reintroduction of the law, abolished the previous autumn, adjusting wages to the cost-of-living index. After two weeks the union's demand was met. In Turin, Italy, there were clashes between workers and the police during strikes at the Fiat automobile works in March and April. About 50 workers were injured and a number were arrested.

There was little forewarning in France of the outbreak of the strikes in May and June that virtually brought the country to a standstill. The situation began with student demonstrations in Paris during the week ending May 4. Trade unions displayed their sympathy for the students and supported demands for changes in the educational system by calling a general strike on May 13. On the following day the workers of Sud-Aviation in Nantes voted against returning to work. On May 16 workers at the Renault factories at Rouen and the Paris suburb of Flins occupied their factories and declared unlimited strikes. By May 17 all the Renault factories were occupied, along with the heavy vehicles firm of Berliet, the Rhodiacéta textile firm in Lyons, and a number of others. Strikes spread to all sections of the French economy including the transport, postal, and banking services. Coal miners in northern France occupied their pits. The number of strikers on May 26 was estimated to be about ten million.

French workmen at the Renault factory in Boulogne-Billancourt returning to work on the morning of June 18, 1968, following a vote to end their month-long strike.

Before long, the strikers' demands became distinct from those of the students; they included wage increases, a reduction in working hours, guaranteed jobs, and an extension of union rights in industry. Premier Georges Pompidou invited representatives of all trade union organizations and employers' federations to meet with him to discuss solutions to the crisis, and the three leading union organizations, the Confédération Générale du Travail, the Confédération Française Democratique du Travail, and the Force Ouvrière, immediately accepted. Tentative agreements reached during the weekend of May 25–26, which included an offer of a 10% pay rise, a 35% increase in the guaranteed minimum wage, shorter hours and longer vacations, and half pay for the time on strike, were rejected by the strikers. The strike continued into June, when the government announced a general election for June 23 and 30. The Confédération Générale du Travail (CGT) stated it would not disrupt the elections. The police began to clear strikers from communications centres and factories, but the return to work was slow. There were still approximately one million on strike on June 11, and violence between strikers, students, and police continued. After the Renault workers voted to return to work on June 17, however, most of the strikes were terminated relatively quickly.

A number of labour movements began at about the time of the French strikes. Thirty thousand Dutch workers demonstrated in Utrecht on May 25 at a union-organized rally against a government proposal to impose a six-month wage freeze. Building workers in Belgium conducted a nine-day nationwide strike from May 1 for a new, improved collective agreement, and on May 11 West German workers joined students in demonstrating against the Emergency Powers Bill introduced by the federal government. Against the background of the workers' occupation of French automobile factories, a conference of national trade unions representing automobile workers from various parts of the world met in Turin, Italy, May 16–19, to discuss common problems.

Postal operations came to a complete standstill in Canada when postal workers struck for a wage increase on July 18 and stayed out for three weeks. British airline pilots took the unusual step of striking for a salary increase in June. This brief but effective strike was followed by dislocation on the British railways when a work-to-rule decision was applied by the National Union of Railwaymen on June 23. The decision was rescinded on July 7. Transport in Canada was affected by a 23-day strike of the St. Lawrence Seaway workers beginning June 21, affecting about 200 Great Lakes ships and 5,000 seamen. The strikers obtained a 19% wage increase in the final settlement. Industrial unrest spread to Italy in July when about 250,000 workers in the city and district of Rome held a 24-hour general strike for an improvement in working and living conditions.

A nationwide strike by U.S. telephone workers, which lasted from April 18 to May 5, caused comparatively little disruption of service because of the high degree of automation in the U.S. telephone system. It was immediately followed, however, by a strike of telephone installers in Illinois, which dragged on until fall and threatened to curtail television coverage of the Democratic national convention, scheduled to be held in Chicago in August. A special agreement was finally reached with the union whereby communications facilities were installed inside the convention

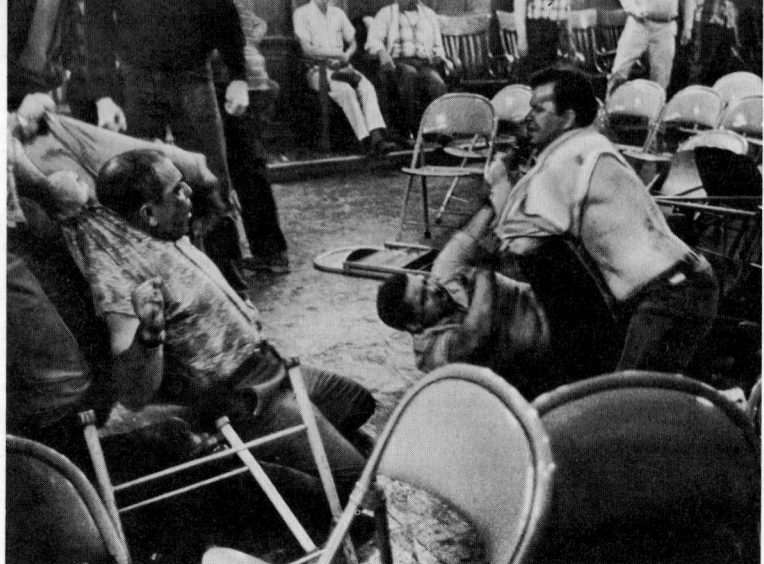

Members of Boilermakers Union Local No. 10 in Oakland, Calif., fighting at a meeting on March 29, 1968. The conflict erupted over 600 members of the local who were to be transferred to locals in Sacramento and Stockton.

hall itself, but there was no live telecasting of events outside.

The U.S. continued to experience an increasing number of strikes by teachers and other government employees, although such strikes were forbidden by law in many states. In New York City in the fall, a teachers' strike was accompanied by slowdowns by police and firemen and a threat on the part of the sanitation workers to reexamine their contract. Another group that had been largely outside the mainstream of the U.S. labour movement, the migrant farm workers, was being organized with some success in California. A prolonged strike among grape pickers, led by César Chavez (see BIOGRAPHY), resulted in the calling of a nationwide boycott of California table grapes.

In both the U.S. and Britain there were discussions about union mergers, and in Britain some actually occurred. In the principal U.S. labour organization, the AFL-CIO, there was fission. On May 16 the United Automobile Workers was suspended for nonpayment of dues. This caused the first major change in the membership of the AFL-CIO since 1957, when the International Brotherhood of Teamsters was expelled. In December four of the five railway operating unions (excluding the locomotive engineers) announced they would merge Jan. 1, 1969. The racial turmoil in the U.S. was reflected in the labour movement, as blacks charged that some unions refused to admit them, and even unions with an open membership were accused of deliberately excluding blacks from the union power structure. In Chicago, for example, black members of the transit union, who constituted a majority of the active membership but were outvoted because retired members were permitted to retain their voting rights, called a strike and subsequently attempted to obtain recognition as a separate bargaining unit.

At its congress in October, the International Federation of Christian Trade Unions deleted the word Christian from its title and also renounced any reference to the social principles of Christianity in its constitution. The general secretary of the International Confederation of Free Trade Unions commented that no real obstacle now stood in the way of a merger between the two bodies.

Less Developed Countries. There was extensive governmental action against unions. Legislation to make strikes illegal was proposed in Tanzania toward the end of 1967. Action of a different kind occurred in Rhodesia where, at the end of 1967, it was estimated that 168 union leaders were under arrest. The Rhodesia African Teachers' Association alone was said to have 38 of its leading members in detention. When members of the Kenya Electrical Trade Workers' Union went on strike in November 1967, the union president and general secretary were arrested for allegedly calling out workers on an unlawful strike in breach of their contracts of service. In the same month the governing body of the International Labour Organization (ILO) considered complaints against Liberia, Argentina, and Libya for the violation of trade union rights. The complaint against Argentina, raised again in 1968, was that the general secretary of the port workers' union had been arrested and detained for more than a year without trial and that several unions had been suspended. It was discovered that the port workers' leader, Eustraquio Tolosa, had been sentenced to five years' imprisonment in March 1968 because in November 1966 he had voted in favour of a decision of the International Transport Workers' Federation to boycott Argentine ships and aircraft in protest against that government's antilabour campaign. Trade union freedom was curtailed in Malaysia by revisions in the Industrial Relations Act.

There was extensive industrial unrest in South Vietnam from the beginning of the year. A wave of strikes by electrical workers, water supply workers, dockers, and busmen started on January 11. Under a governmental emergency decree prohibiting strikes and demonstrations, the police arrested six leaders of the electrical workers' trade union while they were actually at the negotiating table in the appropriate government department. They were held for seven days, then released because of protests by workers and the Vietnamese Confederation of Labour.

Industrial unrest also occurred in several African countries during the year, and in each case the government concerned took repressive action. Seven officials of the National Union of Workers in Chad were arrested on February 9 and detained in custody. This union had been formed on January 10 by a merger between two national labour organizations; its principal aim was to improve the living and working conditions of the workers and to extend the literacy campaign among the people. Workers' demonstrations in Dakar, Senegal, at the end of May resulted in the arrest of 36 officials of the National Union of Senegalese Workers. The arrests provoked a general strike on May 31, involving widespread violence. On Saturday, June 1, Pres. Léopold Sédar Senghor issued an ultimatum that all workers who had not returned to work by Tuesday would be dismissed without compensation. However, by that day all the union leaders had been released and negotiations had begun. An odd situation developed in Togo in May. The Togo Trade Union Federation held its congress on May 10 and elected its leaders. The newly elected general secretary was arrested almost immediately, whereupon the congress was suspended on May 12, and on May 13 and 14 a general strike was held. The union leader was then released, the strike was called off, and the congress resumed its deliberations on May 25.

There was a wave of strikes in Chile late in February over the steep rise in the cost of living. University professors and grammar school teachers were among the most militant of the many groups involved. The teachers resented the fact that they had re-

ceived only 12.5% of their cost-of-living increase in cash and the rest in bonds to help poor people's public housing. The inflation of the peso was the cause of a series of large-scale strikes in Uruguay in April and May. On May 16 about 200,000 public employees began a 48-hour strike to demand compensation for the 20% devaluation of the peso, the fifth adjustment against the U.S. dollar in 15 months. The strike was led by the Uruguayan TUC and was the third of its kind in less than a month. A 24-hour strike was called on July 2 by the country's largest labour federation, the National Workers Convention, representing most of the nation's civil servants. On this occasion both the police and the national reserve were mobilized. Inflation also produced wage disputes in Honduras. After a strike had been called for September 22 by the trade union federation of northern Honduras, the government took over control of the press and radio, suppressed the unions involved, and put the executive council of the federation into custody.

Communist Countries. Labour disputes and concern about the organization of trade unions were present in both Yugoslavia and Czechoslovakia. The causes of the 85 work stoppages during the first nine months of 1967 were examined at a meeting of the Central Council of the Yugoslav Trade Union Federation late in 1967. It was found that in 23 cases the workers were dissatisfied with their personal incomes, in 51 cases they claimed that their work had not been acknowledged in any way, and the remainder had occurred for a variety of reasons. In general, it was said that the basic cause was the slowness and inconsistency in the development of self-management relations. When the sixth congress of Yugoslav trade unions met in June there was a protest from delegates about inequalities in the distribution of income and the restrictions of bureaucracy.

In Czechoslovakia criticisms of trade union organization and strikes were a consequence of the liberalizing process that began early in the year. Following various criticisms of the labour organizations, the new chairman of the Central Council of Trade Unions, Karel Polacek, described in March a freshly formulated trade union program that would give greater autonomy to individual unions and branches of unions. A protest strike of about 1,000 workers in an electrical instruments plant in Bohemia was announced on March 26 because of dissatisfaction with the quality of management. A similar strike was held by railway workers in northern Slovakia early in June. Also in June, workers' councils were formed in two plants of the Ceskomoravska Kolben Danek works, Sokolov and Smíchov, near Prague. The question of establishing workers' councils was discussed at a three-day conference of about 1,200 delegates later in June, and on June 30 the government issued basic regulations for the establishment of workers' councils which would have controlling and auditing functions in factories. Several protest strikes were called in Czechoslovakia following the country's occupation by Warsaw Pact troops in August. A general strike of one hour took place on August 23 and was followed by sectional strikes of coal miners, uranium miners, and railway workers. A further general protest strike took place for a short period on August 26.   (V. L. A.)

See also Education; Employment, Wages, and Hours; Race Relations.

ENCYCLOPÆDIA BRITANNICA FILMS. *Working Together* (1952); *Walter P. Reuther* ("Dialogue for This Decade") (1962); *The Rise of Labor* (1968).

Laos

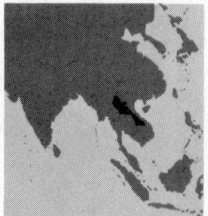

A constitutional monarchy of southeast Asia, Laos is bounded by China, North and South Vietnam, Cambodia, Thailand, and Burma. Area: 91,428 sq.mi. (236,800 sq.km.). Pop. (1967 est.): 2,440,000. Administrative cap. and largest city: Vientiane (pop., 1967 est., 140,000). Royal cap.: Luang Prabang (pop., 1967 est., 22,000). Language: Lao (official); French and English. Religion: Buddhist; tribal. King, Savang Vatthana; premier in 1968, Prince Souvanna Phouma.

In 1968, the royal government in Vientiane controlled about one-third of the country and two-thirds of its population; the Neo Lao Hak Sat (or Pathet Lao, a pro-Communist dissident movement dating from 1963) controlled the rest. Generally speaking, the regions under the control of the Vientiane government lay in the west of the country, along the Mekong River and the frontier with Thailand. The influence of the Neo Lao Hak Sat extended through the north and east, in the regions close to China and the two Vietnams. Passing through its territory was the "Ho Chi Minh Trail" (in actual fact, a whole network of trails), used for several years by the North Vietnamese to convey men and equipment from North to South Vietnam. That the two divisions were not always clear-cut was indicated by the presence of several military bases of the royal armed forces in the Neo Lao Hak Sat regions, and Communist attacks in the areas controlled by the Vientiane government.

The only outstanding political events of 1968 were the setting up, in March, of a "parliamentary group for the application of the Geneva agreements of 1962 on Laos," which numbered 38 out of the 59 deputies, and, in September, the vote on the budget for 1968–69. The latter allowed for an expenditure of 15.9 billion kips, of which 8,218,000,000 were allocated to the Army, against receipts of 7.4 billion kips. The foreign aid necessary to balance this budget was expected to come principally from the U.S. The year was also marked by the opening in Vientiane of a large radio station financed chiefly by Great Britain under the Colombo Plan, and by the beginning of work on the Nam Ngum Dam, an important complex costing $30 million and financed by nine countries (the U.S., Canada, Australia, Denmark, the Netherlands, New Zealand, France, Japan, and Thailand). This complex, designed to irrigate the plain of Vien-

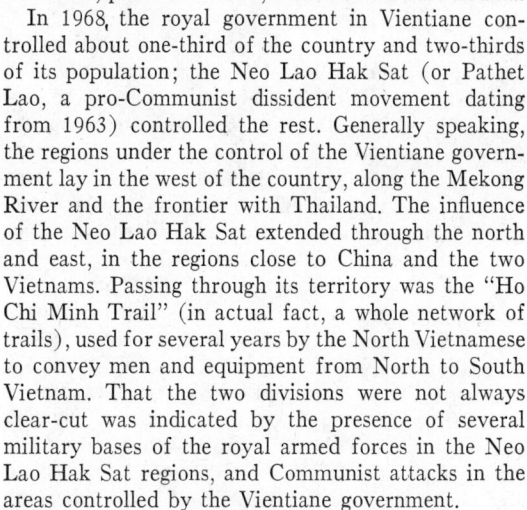

LAOS
Education. (1965–66) Primary, pupils 161,455, teachers 4,333; secondary, pupils 4,467, teachers 178; vocational, pupils 870, teachers 42; teacher training, students 1,625, teachers 197; higher, students 145, teaching staff 18.
  Finance and Trade. Monetary unit: kip, with an official exchange rate of 240 kips = U.S. $1 (576 kips = £1 sterling) and an unofficial buying rate (Oct. 1968) of 625 kips = U.S. $1 (1,500 kips = £1). Budget (1967 est.): revenue (excluding foreign aid) 6,377,800,000 kips; expenditure 15,994,000,000 kips (including military expenditure 8,345,000,000 kips). Foreign trade (1966): imports 10,037,159,000 kips (44% from Thailand, 10% from Japan, 10% from U.S., 8% from Hong Kong, 7% from U.K.); exports (excluding gold reexports) 357,725,000 kips (61% to Malaysia, 16% to Singapore, 16% to Thailand). Main exports: tin ore 61%; coffee 15%; timber 11%.
  Transport. Roads (1966) 5,623 km. (including 2,941 km. main roads). Motor vehicles in use (1966): passenger 6,800; commercial (including buses) 2,200. Inland waterways (main Mekong River routes only; 1966) 1,614 km.

Lacrosse:
see Sporting Record

tiane and to provide electric power for Laos and Thailand, was due to be finished in 1971.

The military situation in general worsened for the royal armed forces, which in January lost more than 2,000 men during a violent battle at Nam Bac, 62 mi. N of Luang Prabang. This defeat was followed by the evacuation of Houei Sane, the last place held by the royal forces immediately bordering on the South Vietnamese frontier. Following this, the Pathet Lao put strong pressure on two southern towns, Saravane and Attopeu, which it had surrounded for some years, and it committed numerous acts of sabotage in the Mekong Valley, which was occupied by the royal forces.

While continuing to denounce the violations of his country's neutrality and sovereignty committed by North Vietnam, Prince Souvanna Phouma gradually modified his attitude toward reaching an agreement with the Pathet Lao. In January his government declared its opposition to the extension through Laos of the "McNamara line," the purpose of which was to stop Communist infiltration into Vietnam. In July the prince came out in favour of a halt to U.S. bombing of North Vietnam and of the establishment of a coalition government in Saigon. He stated in October that he was prepared if necessary to go and meet the leaders of the Neo Lao Hak Sat in order to find a solution to the Laotian problem that would permit a return to national unity. Meanwhile, Prince Souvanna Vong, president of the Neo Lao Hak Sat and a half-brother of Prince Souvanna Phouma, appealed to him in April to "join the Pathet Lao" and to "become aware of the development of the situation in Laos and throughout Indochina, where conditions are becoming less and less favourable to American imperialism." The Neo Lao Hak Sat made the opening of direct discussions conditional on the ending of the activities of the U.S. Air Force in the area that it controlled. These activities were described in the U.S. and Vientiane as reconnaissance flights over the North Vietnamese supply routes, but Communist capitals denounced them as massive bombing attacks.

(M. Cт.)

Law

Court Decisions and Related Developments. The invasion of Czechoslovakia by Warsaw Pact forces in 1968 triggered reactions in the Soviet Union that led to important legal decisions regarding the right of free speech. In many other countries significant developments in this area also were occurring, not the least of which was a decision by the U.S. Supreme Court concerning obscenity. Noteworthy judicial activity, however, was not limited to matters of speech. A number of cases, many remarkable in terms of quality and effect, were handed down on a variety of subjects by courts throughout the world.

Freedom of Speech. Open criticism of the invasion of Czechoslovakia resulted in the imprisonment of several Soviet citizens for violation of public order, including Pavel M. Litvinov, grandson of former Foreign Minister Maxim M. Litvinov; Mrs. Larisa Bogoraz-Daniel, wife of Yuli M. Daniel, who had been sentenced in 1966 to four years in prison for publishing writings abroad that were allegedly critical of the Soviet Union; Konstantin Babitsky, professor at the Russian Language Institute; and Vadim Delone, a 23-year-old student and poet.

After being sentenced to three years in prison, Delone told the court that "For three minutes on Red Square I felt free. I am glad to take your three years for that." Some of the other defendants also made statements in court that championed freedom of speech. The fact that these statements were allowed gave some civil libertarians a glimmer of hope that freedom of expression in some modified form might yet prevail in the U.S.S.R. This hope also was sustained by the fact that the court had invoked an article in the penal code giving it discretion to hand down lighter penalties in cases where there were special circumstances. Most scholars, however, took the view that the prosecutions terminated all present hope for freedom of expression in the U.S.S.R., pointing out that the invasion of Czechoslovakia was prompted in no small measure by the fact that the Presidium of the Czechoslovak Communist Party had "deviated" from "true Communism"—in the Soviet view—by deciding to abolish press censorship.

The U.S. Supreme Court, in *Ginsberg* v. *State of New York* (88 S. Ct. 1274), sustained the constitutionality of a New York criminal obscenity statute prohibiting the sale to minors under 17 of materials defined as obscene on the basis of its appeal to them, whether or not the materials would be obscene to adults. The case involved the sale of "girlie" picture magazines to a 16-year-old boy. The court found that these magazines were not obscene for adults, and the defendant contended that the constitutional freedom of expression secured to a citizen to read or see material concerned with sex cannot be made to depend upon whether he is an adult or a minor. A majority of the court, through a decision written by Justice William J. Brennan, Jr., disagreed with this contention, holding that a state may accord minors under 17 a more restricted right than that assured to adults to judge for themselves what material concerning sex they may read or see. Justices William O. Douglas, Hugo L. Black, and Abe Fortas dissented.

The dissent by Justice Fortas (*see* BIOGRAPHY) in the Ginsberg case was widely discussed in the U.S. Senate during confirmation hearings on his nomination for the position of chief justice. Though this opinion was used against him with telling effect, most U.S. legal scholars concluded that political factors, rather than the quality of Justice Fortas' work on the court, caused the defeat of his nomination.

There were many other developments in the area of free speech. In Italy, for the first time in 20 years, a journalist and a publisher were jailed under an accusation of obscene publication. The Italian police also announced that they intended to urge prosecutions under a 1962 law prohibiting tobacco advertisements.

Perhaps the most surprising development in this field was the report by a Danish committee in December 1967 recommending abolition of film censorship for adults. The report was adopted by the government, and a bill was introduced into the Folketing to implement it. This was believed to be the first time that a state had ever abolished film censorship as a deliberate act of policy, and it followed the abolition in 1967 of the offense of written pornography. It was expected that visual pornography would also be taken out of the criminal law before long, and the minister of justice hinted at further prospective liberalization in the field of "private morals."

Almost as unexpected was the abolition from September 1968 of the well-established theatrical censorship in Britain, in implementation of the report of a

joint select committee of both houses of Parliament. The repealing act did, however, set out a special procedure for prosecution of obscene stage performances.

In Australia uniform treatment of obscene literature was promoted by the creation of a National Literature Board of Review. The board would advise both state and federal governments on the acceptability of imported and domestic literature.

Denmark's courts handled two interesting speech cases during the year. In one a clergyman had asked the attorney general to prosecute the Danish Broadcasting Corporation for blasphemy. This case, still pending at year's end, was of particular interest to legal scholars because only one blasphemy prosecution has been brought in Denmark since 1930. In the other case, the Frederiksberg Birkeret dismissed an action brought by a prostitute against the Danish Broadcasting Corporation that alleged invasion of privacy by reason of a telecast of a street scene in which she appeared "on duty."

In France and Great Britain developments occurred relating freedom of expression to the right to a fair trial. The French Cour de Cassation, holding that secrecy of jury deliberations must remain sacrosanct, affirmed a decision of the Cour d'Appel de Paris fining two writers for their description of the jury deliberations that culminated in condemning Marshal Philippe Pétain to death. In Great Britain, *Regina* v. *Malik* dealt with the rights of an accused in a situation where an inflammatory newspaper article seemed likely to prejudice his right to a fair trial. The court held that it would not set aside the conviction of the accused unless in fact the article did prevent a fair trial. In *Ex Parte Blackburn*, the court held that freedom of speech includes the freedom to comment vigorously on court decisions and that, even where the comment is inaccurate, it cannot be punished as contempt of court.

Eavesdropping and Wiretapping. In *Katz* v. *United States* (88 S. Ct. 507), the U.S. Supreme Court greatly clarified the use of eavesdropping devices in criminal prosecutions. On the basis of past decisions, criminal lawyers had assumed that eavesdropping devices could be used validly only after a warrant had been served on the person to be "bugged." While this assumed limitation seemed to make eavesdropping impractical in most cases, its effect was mitigated by another assumption, based on Supreme Court decisions and widely held by the criminal bar, that no limitations applied to eavesdropping done without physical penetration of "constitutionally protected areas," presumably limited to a person's home, office, automobile, or other private premise. The Katz case, in effect, held that both of these assumptions were incorrect.

Katz had been convicted of transmitting wagering information by telephone from Los Angeles to Miami, Fla., and Boston in violation of a federal statute. At the trial the government was permitted to introduce evidence of Katz's end of telephone conversations, overheard by FBI agents who had attached an electronic listening and recording device outside the public telephone booth from which he placed the calls. Even though the FBI agents had no warrant, the trial court permitted this testimony on the ground that a public telephone booth is not a constitutionally protected area. The Supreme Court, through Justice Potter Stewart, rejected this contention and the assumption upon which it was based. "The Fourth Amendment," said Justice Stewart, "protects people—and not simply 'areas'—against unreasonable searches." Once this

New York City detectives searching youths whom they found shooting dice. In 1968 the Supreme Court upheld laws permitting police to "stop-and-frisk" persons suspected of criminal activity.

fact is recognized, he said, "it becomes clear that the reach of that amendment cannot turn upon the presence or absence of a physical intrusion into any given enclosure." The court then said that if a warrant had been obtained in this case, the conviction of Katz would be allowed to stand, notwithstanding the fact that Katz had not been notified. This destroyed the other assumption of the criminal bar, that the warrant must be served on the person being investigated.

In Great Britain a court held that recordings of conversations made by private individuals are admissible in criminal proceedings. The point had been in doubt because of assurances given by the crown to Parliament limiting electronic surveillance by the police and security services. The court held that the assurances bound only these bodies and did not prevent the court from using in evidence recordings obtained from others. In Switzerland the Federal Council published a bill that would have the effect of reducing substantially the number of instances in which information obtained by wiretapping would be permitted in evidence. In a related development, the Bundesrat enacted an amendment to the Swiss Penal Code providing that the sale and use of ultrasensitive electronic and optical devices should be subject to prior authorization. Apparently the police were not exempted. In West Germany a law was enacted to permit certain authorized bodies to wiretap and examine mail under limited circumstances. (See *International Law*, below.)

International Relations. The decision in *Madzimbamuto* v. *Lardner-Burke*, handed down by the Privy Council in Great Britain, brought to a head the judicial struggle between the U.K. and Rhodesia. The case arose when the Rhodesian Appellate Division of the High Court refused to restrain the government of Rhodesia from executing three Africans, sentenced to death but subsequently given a reprieve by the queen. The court held that the 1965 Rhodesian constitution, adopted after the Rhodesian declaration of independence in that year, had divested the crown of its prerogative of mercy and vested it in the Rhodesian Executive Council. The condemned men sought leave to appeal this decision to the Privy Council under a provision of the 1961 constitution, but the Rhodesian Appellate Division refused on the ground that the Ian Smith government, in any event, would ignore any judgment of the Privy Council. The High Court of Rhodesia affirmed this decision, although one judge resigned in protest.

Below, German children learning to swim were crippled before birth when their mothers during pregnancy used the tranquilizer Contergan containing thalidomide. Above, a session of the trial against seven top executives of Chemie Grünenthal, the producer of Contergan.

Despite this, the Privy Council granted leave to appeal to one of the condemned men in order to test the constitutionality of the decision. It then held that all the legislation of the Smith regime had no force or effect, and ruled that the three condemned men were entitled to the reprieve. As was expected, the General Division of the High Court of Rhodesia rejected the judgment of the Privy Council. Justice Harold E. Davies, speaking for the court, held that the Smith regime had acquired an "internal de jure status," and that this fact gave validity to the 1965 constitution. Thus, the Rhodesian courts in the Madzimbamuto case were not sitting in accordance with the 1961 constitution and were not in the same "hierarchy of courts" as the Privy Council. Another judge resigned from the High Court in protest, and the three condemned men were executed.

Medical and Biological Developments. A new theory to explain criminal behaviour, advanced by some biologists, was that males with a chromosomic make-up of "XYY," rather than the usual XY, were prone to crime. A French court appeared to have been the first to take note of this new theory. A routine medical examination of a man accused of murdering a prostitute revealed that he had an XYY chromosomic makeup. The court agreed to refer the case to three specialists in heredity, indicating that it would follow their recommendation as to whether the defendant should stand criminal trial or be placed under psychiatric or other medical treatment.

Fear of tort and possibly criminal liability arising out of the transplantation of human organs caused a number of doctors throughout the world to prepare legislation that would give them certain guidelines. In France new regulations were promulgated by the National Assembly defining "death" in terms of cessation of brain rather than heart activity. Under these regulations, "death" must be pronounced by two doctors, neither of whom may be concerned with any subsequent transplant surgery. Once this certification is given, there is no need for consent by the deceased's family if the deceased has given consent during his lifetime. The Dutch government was reported to be willing to introduce a similar bill, except that the Dutch act would presume consent in all cases where the donor had not expressly provided to the contrary

or where there was not opposition by a close relative. A bill pending in the British House of Commons would permit the removal of kidneys from a dead body for medical purposes unless there was reason to believe that the deceased, during his lifetime, had given contrary instructions.

A Harvard University committee, made up of members of the faculties of law, medicine, public health, divinity, and arts and sciences, recommended that the definition of "death" be based on brain activity. The International Medical Society adopted a statement to the effect that the determination of death is a basic responsibility that remains with the physician, aided by medical devices such as the electroencephalograph (EEG). The specific reference to the EEG was interpreted by many to mean that the society had adopted a "brain death" test.

In Great Britain 62 cases claiming damages caused to unborn infants by the drug thalidomide were settled on a basis whereby the drug companies agreed to pay 40% of all claims plus costs. The settlement left in doubt the English position on the question: Is an infant in utero owed a duty of care by a manufacturer of drugs who knew of its existence and that it could be damaged by thalidomide? Similarly, an out-of-court settlement in Canada with respect to claims of eight children against an American pharmaceutical company did not settle the Canadian position with regard to infants in utero.

Other Developments. In Great Britain an important judgment was delivered in the House of Lords in *Warner* v. *Metropolitan Police Commissioner.* Following a discussion of the metaphysical subtleties of the concept of "possession" in the context of an absolute offense of possessing certain substances under the Drugs (Prevention of Misuse) Act, 1964, it was held that, even though the offense was an absolute one, a person who had in his possession a box, which unknown to him and against his intention contained the prohibited substance, was not thereby in possession of such contents.

In *Conway* v. *Rimmer* (1968), the House of Lords at last overruled part of its previous judgment in *Duncan* v. *Cammell Laird & Co.* (1942) and held that where the production of public documents is required in the course of civil legal proceedings, the crown may no longer claim absolute privilege not to produce them. The courts would be entitled to compel production unless they (the courts) decided otherwise, after balancing the public interest in withholding the documents (as expressed by the minister) against the other public interest that justice should be done between litigants.

In addition to the Katz and Ginsberg cases, the U.S. Supreme Court handed down at least four other noteworthy decisions. In *United States* v. *O'Brien* (88 S. Ct. 1673), it held that the statute prohibiting knowing destruction or mutilation of draft cards did not abridge the free speech guarantees of the Constitution. Justice Douglas filed the lone dissent, asserting that the U.S. has no right to conscript for the military in the absence of a declaration of war. From this premise he argued that the U.S. cannot regulate draft cards issued pursuant to an undeclared war.

In *Terry* v. *State of Ohio* (88 S. Ct. 1868), the court sustained a state "stop-and-frisk" law. Under such a law, police are permitted to stop a person and detain him briefly for questioning upon suspicion that he may be connected with criminal activity. Upon suspicion that the person may be armed, the police

also are given permission to "frisk" him for weapons. The court held that these laws do not violate the Fourth Amendment to the Constitution, which prohibits unreasonable searches and seizures, because the search and detention is reasonable in cases where the police officer can point to specific and articulable facts that, taken together with rational inferences from those facts, make the intrusion appropriate.

In *Jones* v. *Alfred H. Mayer Co.* (88 S. Ct. 2186), the court resurrected the Civil Rights Law of 1866 to protect a Negro in his right to purchase a house. The court held that the statute means that a Negro citizen who wants to buy or rent a home cannot be turned away simply because he is not white. Although many newspaper accounts of the Jones case credited the Supreme Court with converting the 1866 statute into a fair housing law, the court was careful to point out, through Justice Stewart, that:

> Whatever else it may be, [the 1866 law] is not a comprehensive open housing law. . . . [T]he statute deals only with racial discrimination and does not address itself to discrimination on grounds of religion or national origin. It does not deal specifically with discrimination in the provision of services or facilities in connection with the sale or rental of a dwelling. It does not prohibit advertising or other representations that indicate discriminatory preferences. It does not refer explicitly to discrimination in financing arrangements or in the provision of brokerage services. It does not empower a federal administrative agency to assist aggrieved parties.

In *Board of Education* v. *Allen* (88 S. Ct. 1923), the court sustained the constitutionality of a New York statute requiring school districts to lend textbooks to students enrolled in parochial and private as well as in public schools. The statute had been attacked as an effort to "establish" a religion or "prohibit the free exercise" thereof in violation of the First and Fourteenth Amendments. The Allen case was also important in that it seemed to broaden the class of individuals said to have a sufficient stake in the outcome of litigation to be given "standing to sue" in the federal courts.   (W. D. Hd.)

International Law. *United Nations.* The third amendment to the UN Charter came into force in June 1968 after the 83rd instrument of ratification had been deposited. This relates to art. 109, and increases from seven to nine the number of Security Council votes needed to convene a general conference to review the Charter.

In December 1967 the General Assembly adopted the Agreement on the Rescue and Return of Astronauts and the Return of Objects Launched into Outer Space. It also created an ad hoc committee to study the question of the reservation exclusively for peaceful purposes of the seabed and ocean floor, and the subsoil thereof, beyond the limits of present national jurisdiction. The first session of the diplomatic conference to consider an international convention on the law of treaties, based on the 75 draft articles prepared by the International Law Commission, was held in Vienna (March–May). The definitive text of the convention would be adopted in 1969.

International Adjudication. The International Court of Justice remained underemployed, with only two causes on its list, neither being new. The interminable case between Spain and Belgium, *Concerning the Barcelona Traction, Light and Power Company Ltd.*, continued, the time limits for pleadings again being extended. The other cause involved twin cases brought by Denmark and the Netherlands, respectively, against West Germany. These two cases related to the delimitation of the boundaries of the West German sector of the North Sea continental shelf.

European Convention on Human Rights. The European Court of Human Rights delivered judgment in three cases during 1968. In *Neumeister* v. *Austria* (June 27), the court for the first time gave judgment against a member state, holding that Neumeister had been detained pending trial for an excessive length of time (about $2\frac{1}{2}$ years in all) in violation of art. 5(3) of the Convention. On the other hand, in *Wemhoff* v. *Germany* (also June 27), the court held that Wemhoff's pretrial detention for three years, plus a further five months between opening of the trial and delivery of the verdict, was justified by the exceptional complexity of the case.

The court's final judgment in the Belgian linguistics case (July 23) supported the Belgian government on all counts except one. The case concerned the linguistic laws that divide Belgium into three parts (Flemish, French, and bilingual Brussels) and provide that education shall be given in the area language, irrespective of the maternal language of the schoolchildren. French-speaking parents living in Flemish-speaking areas had complained that this prevented their children from being taught in French, even in out-of-school hours, in state-supported schools.

The most important case before the European Commission of Human Rights was the application brought by Denmark, Norway, and Sweden alleging wholesale violation of the Convention by the new military government of Greece; this was only the fourth application brought under the Convention by a government against another state. The commission held the application admissible, and it was being argued on the merits before the usual subcommission.

European Economic Community. Freedom of establishment throughout the Community was completed, so that Community citizens now had equal status in seeking and keeping employment in all six member states. The Six also signed a Convention on the Mutual Recognition of Firms and Companies and Legal Persons, which provided private international law rules applicable to the recognition of companies whose incorporation, seat of business, and business activity took place in different member states. The first step was taken toward harmonizing company law within the EEC—a directive relating to the protection of shareholders and third parties. Other aspects of company law were being studied for similar harmonization.

Important advances were made in the field of restrictive practices law. After the "group exemption" regulation of 1967, the EEC Commission issued guidelines that amounted in practice to a "group negative clearance," and also issued four more individual decisions further clarifying what constitutes permissible agreements. For the first time, in the guidelines, the restrictive practices law of the EEC was linked to that of the European Coal and Steel Community (one result of the fusion of the Community executives in 1967); further linkage was to be expected in the future, as EEC policy moved toward larger units and company mergers, a policy followed for some years by the ECSC High Authority in coal and steel matters.

Two 1968 decisions of the Court of Justice of the European Communities clarified important aspects of restrictive practices law. In *Brasserie de Haecht* v. *Wilkin,* the practice of "tied houses" in the sale of beer was held not to be prohibited per se, the ultimate decision depending upon the facts. In *Parke, Davis & Co.* v. *Probel,* the court held that the mere

existence of a patent right was not a violation of art. 85(1) or art. 86 of the EEC treaty; the exercise of the right would only be prohibited if it were the subject of a prohibited agreement under art. 85(1) or of an abuse of a dominant position under art. 86. In this, the court was following its line laid down in *Grundig & Consten* v. *EEC Commission* (1966) in the field of trademarks.

Nordic Council. Apart from the unsuccessful attempt to create a Nordic customs union, the major development within the Nordic Council was the report of the Nordic Committees on Patent Procedure. The report recommended the establishment of a joint Nordic Patent Appeal Tribunal to hear appeals in patent matters from Denmark, Norway, Sweden, and Finland (Iceland did not take part).

Boundaries and Territorial Disputes. The government of Chile decided to seek the arbitration of the U.K. in its boundary dispute with Argentina, relating to the Beagle Canal Zone, under the Chile-Argentine Treaty of 1902. Algeria and Tunisia concluded an agreement concerning the southern part of their common border. Norway and the U.S.S.R., through a mixed boundary commission, completed the marking of a 20-km. stretch of their common border in Pasvikdalen.

The Philippines renewed its claim to sovereignty over Sabah (previously British North Borneo, and now part of Malaysia) by specifically including it within the jurisdiction of a domestic law. The president of the Philippines subsequently offered to place the claim before the International Court of Justice, but Malaysia rejected the claim and refused to cooperate in bringing it before the court.

The Guatemalan claim to sovereignty over British Honduras was investigated by a U.S. mediator, who proposed a treaty to be adhered to by British Honduras when it should become independent (probably in 1970) that would give Guatemala important economic privileges and provide for joint consultation on defense and foreign affairs. Subsequently, Guatemala claimed certain territorial waters off the British Honduras coast.

The Spanish claim to sovereignty over Gibraltar was the subject of fitful talks, of no consequence. General talks on the Argentine claim to the Falkland Islands were held between the Argentine and British governments. Spokesmen for the latter were evasive in the House of Commons and refused to give an undertaking that sovereignty over the islands would not be transferred without the consent of the islanders. The Rann of Cutch Arbitral Tribunal issued its award in February, giving 10% of the disputed territory to Pakistan and the remainder to India.

Wars and the Laws of War. The exact status of the war in Vietnam continued to evade legal analysis. Discussions were opened in Paris in May between representatives of North Vietnam and the U.S.

In the civil war between the Nigerian federal forces and the secessionist Biafrans, accusations of genocide were made but not substantiated. The laws of neutrality were blatantly infringed, both by those countries (including the U.K.) that supplied arms to the federal government exclusively and by those (*e.g.,* the Scandinavian countries) that tried to break the federal blockade and organize airlifts to relieve the suffering of the besieged Biafrans. Attempts at mediation by the Organization of African Unity failed.

The invasion of Czechoslovakia by troops of the U.S.S.R., Poland, Hungary, East Germany, and Bul-

garia took place without any ultimatum or declaration of war. The country came under military occupation, although the civilian government remained in office. The U.S.S.R. justified the invasion as being in the interest of the collective security of the Warsaw Pact.

Two judgments clarifying the status of prisoners of war were delivered in Britain in 1968 by the Judicial Committee of the Privy Council; both arose out of the recent "confrontation" between Indonesia and Malaysia. In *The Public Prosecutor* v. *Oie Hee Koi,* Malaysian members of the Indonesian armed forces were held not to be entitled to protection as prisoners of war; nevertheless, convictions under domestic legislation (the Malaysian Internal Security Act) for consorting with persons possessing unlawful arms were bad where the persons in question were Indonesian troops, for the criminal law did not apply to regular enemy forces. In *Osman Bin Haji Mohamed Ali* v. *The Public Prosecutor* (May 21), the court held that regular soldiers of the Indonesian Army who engaged in acts of sabotage in Malaysia while wearing civilian clothes, and who were still in mufti when arrested, were not entitled to protection as prisoners of war; they were "unprivileged belligerents," a term that applies to spies, saboteurs, and irregular guerrillas. Consequently, they were rightly convicted of the civilian crime of murder.

Administrative Law. The major changes predicated in British administrative law related to entry and expulsion of aliens and Commonwealth citizens. A report by a departmental committee in August 1967 had recommended a right of appeal against decisions of immigration officers (who enjoyed complete discretion, the exercise of which did not have to be supported by grounds and which was not subject to any form of judicial supervision). The government accepted the report, but no implementing legislation followed. However, under the stricter sanctions policy against Rhodesia, which involved in certain cases withdrawal of British passports from persons too closely identified with the secessionist policy, provision was made for an administrative advisory body to hear appeals. The Commonwealth Immigrants Act (1968), which further impeded the entry of Commonwealth citizens into Britain, went a long way toward abolishing U.K. citizenship by descent.

In India, also, the movement across the national border was closely restricted. After the Supreme Court, in *Satwant Singh Sawhney* v. *Assistant Passport Officer, New Delhi* (1967), held that a purported withdrawal of a citizen's passport by an administrative official was an unconstitutional infringement of the right to personal liberty, Parliament passed the Passports Act (1967), which regulated in detail departure from India (the previous Indian Passport Act, 1920, which remained in force, dealt only with entry). Departure might now take place only with a valid passport or travel document.

Criminal Law. East Germany brought into force on July 1 a comprehensive criminal law reform, consisting of a new Criminal Code (replacing that of 1871), Criminal Procedure Code, Execution of Sentences Law, and *Ordnungswidrigkeit* (*i.e.,* infringements of public discipline) Law.

West Germany, where the 1871 Criminal Code remained in force, continued discussions over two rival (one official and one unofficial) reform drafts. The 17th amendment to the constitution, which came into force on June 25, 1968, provided for extensive re-

Lawn Bowls:
see Bowling and Lawn Bowls

Lawn Tennis:
see Tennis

Lead:
see Mining

distribution of powers in cases of emergency, including the formation of a special supplementary parliament and derogation from some of the constitutional provisions guaranteeing civil liberties. The amendment was followed by other emergency laws to regulate the economy, supplies, trade, traffic, and labour during an emergency. The occasion was taken to revise that part of the Criminal Code relating to political criminal law.

In Britain the substantial reforms contained in the Criminal Justice Act, 1967 (which, among other things, introduced majority instead of unanimous jury verdicts and provided for prohibition of press reporting of committal proceedings), and the Criminal Law Act, 1967 (which included replacement of the classification of felonies and misdeameanours by that of "arrestable" and "nonarrestable" offenses), were followed by the Theft Act, 1968, which totally reformed and codified the crimes relating to theft and provided a new definition of theft itself.

Torts. The report of the New Zealand Royal Commission on Compensation for Personal Injury (December 1967) recommended the total abolition of the tort action based on fault in all cases of personal injury, no matter how they occurred. Instead, the injured person, or his survivors if death resulted, would be compensated by a state-run fund at a rate equivalent to 80% of previous tax-paid income for total incapacity, up to a maximum of NZ$120 per week.

Shortly afterward the (U.K.) report of the Winn Committee on Personal Injuries Litigation appeared. However, because the committee had been debarred from questioning the principle of fault liability at all, the report merely concentrated on procedural matters.

In March 1968 the Organization for Economic Cooperation and Development Convention on Third Party Liability for Nuclear Damage entered into force upon the deposit of its fifth instrument of ratification.

Commercial Law. Major reforms of patent law were enacted in West Germany and Israel. The German act, of Sept. 4, 1967, basically followed the Dutch act of 1964. The earlier requirement of a full novelty and patentability examination (which had resulted in a backlog of about 300,000 applications, with a normal six-year waiting period) was replaced by a system of provisional protection, with a full examination only on request. The Israeli statute, which applied to agriculture but excluded breeds of plants and animals, introduced a change in the concept of novelty, so that previous description or public use anywhere in the world would disqualify the invention from patent protection. Apart from the procedural changes proposed in the Nordic Council and the continuing discussion on a universal patent registry, the principal international action was completion by the Council of Europe of an International Classification of Patents for Invention, which came into force in September 1968. In Switzerland a total revision of the Trade Marks Law of 1890 was embodied in a bill that provided for protection by registration for a continuous period of ten years.

Maritime Law. On May 31, 1968, the Brussels Convention on the Limitation of Liability of the Owners of Sea-going Ships, 1957, came into force. A major conference was held in Rome in October to discuss problems of pollution of the seas. The Assembly of the Intergovernmental Maritime Consultative Organization unanimously adopted an amendment to the Safety of Life at Sea Convention requiring ships to be fitted with VHF radio-telephone equipment for use in waters where a marine traffic control network was in operation. The 12th Brussels Maritime Law Conference prepared for signature on Feb. 23, 1968, a supplementary protocol to the 1924 Hague Rules on Bills of Lading.

(N. M. H.)

See also Crime; Merchandising; Police; Race Relations.

ENCYCLOPÆDIA BRITANNICA FILMS. *Understanding the Law —Equal Justice for All* (1953); *The Congress* (1954); *The Supreme Court* (1954); *The Bill of Rights of the United States* (1956); *The Constitution of the United States* (1956); *Magna Carta, Part I (Rise of the English Monarchy)* (1959); *Magna Carta, Part II (Revolt of the Nobles and the Signing of the Charter)* (1959); *Justice Under Law (Gideon Case)* (1966); *Equality Under Law* (1967); *Freedom to Speak (N.Y. v. Feiner)* (1967).

Lebanon

A republic of the Middle East, Lebanon is bounded by Syria, Israel, and the Mediterranean Sea. Area: 4,015 sq.mi. (10,400 sq.km.). Pop. (1966 est.): 2,460,-000. Cap. and largest city: Beirut (pop., 1961 est., 298,129). Language: Arabic. Religion: approximately 50% Christian, 34% Muslim. President in 1968, Charles Helou: prime ministers, Rashid Karame and, after February 8, Abdullah Yafi.

In the three-stage parliamentary elections which ended on April 8, the right-wing and pro-Western Triple Alliance of Pierre Gemayel's Kata'eb Party, ex-Pres. Camille Chamoun's National Liberals, and Raymond Eddé's National Bloc had some success, bringing its strength in the 99-member Chamber of Deputies to about 30. This was equal to the Democratic bloc led by ex-Prime Minister Rashid Karame, the remaining members being mainly independents. The Alliance demanded a change of government but the prime minister, Abdullah Yafi, reshuffled his Cabinet and stayed in office.

Sharp tension and the fear of Muslim-Christian conflicts were caused by the attempted assassination of ex-President Chamoun on May 31 by a young Muslim; the government, however, succeeded in sur-

LEBANON
Education. (1965–66) Primary, pupils 354,270, teachers 14,786; secondary, pupils 82,073, teachers 4,878; vocational, pupils 1,394, teachers 317; teacher training, students 1,714, teachers 267; higher (including 4 universities), students, 20,304, teaching staff 1,434.
Finance. Monetary unit: Lebanese pound, with an official rate of L£3.08 to U.S. $1 (L£7.39 = £1 sterling). Gold and foreign exchange, central bank: (June 1968) U.S. $318.2 million; (June 1967) U.S. $343.9 million. Budget (1969 est.) balanced at L£564 million. National income: (1965) L£2,500 million; (1964) L£2,038 million. Money supply: (June 1968) L£1,685 million; (June 1967) L£1,660 million.
Foreign Trade. (1966) Imports L£1,641 million; exports L£316 million; transit trade (through free port of Beirut) L£1,050,015,000. Import sources: U.S. 14%; Syria 12%; West Germany 10%; France 8%; Italy 8%; U.K. 7%. Export destinations: Saudi Arabia 15%; Jordan 10%; Iraq 9%; Syria 8%; Kuwait 7%; Libya 5%; U.K. 5%. Main exports: fruit and vegetables 24%; precious metals 15%; livestock and meat 8%; textiles and clothing 7%.
Transport and Communications. Roads (1967) 7,108 km. (including 1,990 km. main roads). Motor vehicles in use (1967): passenger 114,242; commercial 12,763. Railways: (1966) 417 km.; traffic (1967) 6 million passenger-km., freight 38 million net ton-km. Shipping (1967): vessels 100 gross tons and over 139; gross tonnage 598,282. Air traffic (1966): 615,073,000 passenger-km.; freight 44,341,000 net ton-km. Telephones (Jan. 1967) 120,323. Radio receivers (Dec. 1966) 450,000. Television receivers (Dec. 1966) 150,000.
Agriculture. Production (in 000; metric tons; 1967; 1966 in parentheses): grapes 88 (76); wheat (1966) 70, (1965) 55; dry onions (1966) 32, (1965) 26; olive oil c. 8 (c. 6); figs (1966) c. 25, (1965) 22; bananas (1966) 30, (1965) 25; oranges, tangerines, and clementines 68 (181); lemons 51 (69); apples 157 (104). Livestock (in 000; 1965–66): cattle 105; asses 37; goats 442; sheep (1964–65) 220; poultry 14,793.
Industry. Production (in 000): cement (1967) 1,014 metric tons; petroleum products (1966) 1,602 metric tons; cotton fabrics (1961) 11,634 m.; electricity (1966) 864,000 kw-hr.

mounting the trouble. There was a political crisis in October when the president, unable to form a government, resigned. He withdrew his resignation only when the warring parliamentary factions agreed to serve in a government headed again by Yafi. In November Yafi resigned following student demonstrations in support of the Palestinian commandos, but he was persuaded to remain.

In May and June there were two major incidents on the southern border when the Israelis shelled Lebanese villages which Israel said had been harbouring Arab commando raiders. Lebanon managed to stay fairly well apart from the Arab-Israeli conflict, however, until December 28, when an Israeli helicopter raid on the airport in Beirut resulted in the destruction of 13 civil aircraft. The raid was in reprisal for an earlier attack on an Israeli airliner at Athens, carried out by two Arab terrorists from Beirut. Lebanon, which immediately appealed to the UN Security Council, disclaimed responsibility for commandos that were active on its territory. As the year ended, however, there was considerable agitation within the country, especially among students, for the adoption of a more overt anti-Israeli policy. (P. Mᴅ.)

ENCYCLOPÆDIA BRITANNICA FILMS. *The Middle East* (1955); *The Mediterranean World* (1961).

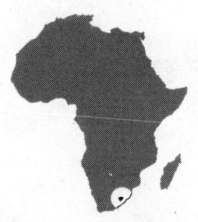

Lesotho

A constitutional monarchy of southern Africa, Lesotho is completely surrounded by South Africa. Area: 11,716 sq.mi. (30,344 sq.km.). Pop. (1968): 1,018,135, almost 99% African. Cap. and largest city: Maseru (pop., 1966, 14,000). Language: English (official) and Sesotho. Religion: about 70% Christian. Chief of state in 1968, Paramount Chief Moshoeshoe II; prime minister, Chief Leabua Jonathan.

Lesotho steadily developed potential political and economic viability during 1968. Farming methods improved and the establishment of small industries seemed more likely following the creation in 1967, under South African guidance, of the National Development Corporation. The minister of finance, introducing the 1968–69 budget in March, estimated revenue at R 5,223,945 and expenditures at R 9,106,040. The deficit was made up by the U.K.

Following the reorganization of mining development in July 1967, and the subsequent Mining Rights Act to regulate exploitation in the national interest, a 25-year diamond concession was granted to the Rio Tinto Zinc Corporation, with prospecting rights in the

MARION KAPLAN

Leabua Jonathan, prime minister of Lesotho, who continued a policy of close cooperation with South Africa during 1968.

LESOTHO
Education. (1966) Primary, pupils 167,169, teachers 2,799; secondary, pupils 2,825, teachers 120; vocational, pupils 173, teachers 29; teacher training, students 530, teachers 57; higher (University of Lesotho, Botswana, and Swaziland), students 344, teaching staff (1964) 38.
Finance and Trade. Monetary unit: South African rand, with a par value of R 0.71 to U.S. $1 (R 1.71 = £1 sterling). Budget (1967–68 est.) balanced at R 11,200,851 (including R 6 million U.K. grant). Foreign trade (1966): imports R 22,917,000; exports R 4,387,000. Main exports: wool 42%; mohair 21%; diamonds 16%. The adverse trade balance is partly offset by receipts from labour working in South Africa (R 4.4 million in 1966).
Agriculture. Production (in 000; metric tons; 1966; 1965 in parentheses): corn *c.* 110 (*c.* 110); wheat *c.* 40 (*c.* 40); sorghum (1963) *c.* 55; wool *c.* 2.2 (*c.* 2.2); meat *c.* 22 (*c.* 22). Livestock (in 000; 1965–66): cattle *c.* 370; sheep *c.* 1,490; goats *c.* 890.

Mokhotlong area. For the first time, diamond exports exceeded R 1 million in 1967, helped by the discovery of the Lesotho Diamond, sixth largest in the world, which was sold for R 216,360.

Scheduled air services between Lesotho and South Africa were inaugurated in October 1967, and work on a R 20,000 passenger terminal at Maseru was begun; rail service between South Africa and Maseru was resumed in May. About half the Basuto male working population continued to send remittances home from their labour in South Africa.

Close cooperation with South Africa developed in other spheres. In June, for example, a justice of the South African Supreme Court was loaned to Lesotho, as was a regional magistrate from Durban, who was to act as attorney general for a period of two years. Two other South African government officials were sent to help Lesotho as chief electoral officer and in post office development. Beginning in February a team of South African medical experts were regularly flown to Lesotho to perform operations and supply medical equipment. Addressing a large National Party convention, the prime minister, Chief Leabua Jonathan, said that Lesotho's economic future was inseparably linked with South Africa, and that those who criticized Lesotho for cooperating with South Africa offered no constructive alternative. (M. Mʀ.)

Liberia

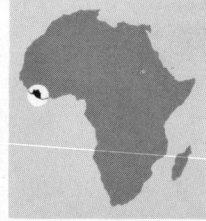

A republic on the west coast of Africa, Liberia is bordered by Sierra Leone, Guinea, and Ivory Coast. Area: 43,000 sq. mi. (111,370 sq.km.). Pop. (1967 est.): 1,098,000. Cap. and largest city: Monrovia (pop., 1962, 80,992). Language: English and tribal dialects. President in 1968, William V. S. Tubman.

President Tubman was inaugurated for the sixth time on January 1, in a ceremony attended by U.S.

LIBERIA
Education. (1966–67) Primary, pupils 110,251, teachers 3,137; secondary, pupils 11,324, teachers 521; vocational, students 856, teachers (1964–65) 39; teacher training, pupils 279, teachers 31; higher, students 797, teaching staff 129.
Finance. Monetary unit: Liberian dollar, at par with the U.S. dollar (L$2.40 = £1 sterling). Budget (1968 est.): revenue L$51.4 million; expenditure L$55.9 million.
Foreign Trade. (1966) Imports L$113,664,000; exports L$150,458,000. Import sources: U.S. 45%; West Germany 13%; U.K. 9%. Export destinations: U.S. 35%; West Germany 28%; U.K. 8%; Italy 8%; Netherlands 6%; Belgium-Luxembourg 5%. Main exports: iron ore 71%; rubber 18%.
Transport and Communications. Roads (1965) *c.* 3,200 km. (including 2,000 km. state roads). Motor vehicles in use (1961): passenger 4,240; commercial (including buses) 3,670. Railways (1965) 420 km. Shipping (1967): merchant vessels 100 gross tons and over 1,513 (mostly owned by U.S. and other foreign interests); gross tonnage 22,597,808. Telephones (Jan. 1965) *c.* 3,000. Radio receivers (Dec. 1966) 175,000. Television receivers (Dec. 1966) 3,500.
Agriculture. Production (in 000; metric tons; 1966; 1965 in parentheses): rice *c.* 180 (*c.* 180); cassava *c.* 430 (*c.* 425); rubber, exports 53 (49); palm kernels, exports 13 (12); cocoa 1.5 (1.2); coffee 3 (3.4). Livestock (in 000; August 1966): cattle *c.* 29; pigs *c.* 33; sheep *c.* 12; goats *c.* 56.
Industry. Production (in 000; 1966): electricity 339 million kw-hr.; iron ore (metal content; exports) 11,255 metric tons; diamonds (exports) 555 metric carats.

Vice-Pres. Hubert H. Humphrey, U.S. Associate Justice Thurgood Marshall, and officials of various African countries. In his inaugural address, Tubman called on the "superpowers" and other permanent members of the UN Security Council to exercise their responsibility to mankind and to regard themselves as guardians of world peace. Tubman also called on the "developing and nonnuclear" nations to settle their disputes without risking intervention by the great powers.

A major scandal erupted in February when Atty. Gen. James Pierre announced that Henry Fahnbulleth, former ambassador to Kenya and Tanzania, had been arrested for seditious activities. Fahnbulleth was indicted on charges of treason by a grand jury in Monrovia on March 7. He was charged specifically with heading a secret movement aimed at forcibly overthrowing the government.

Evidence against the former ambassador included a letter he had allegedly written to the Israeli embassy in Monrovia asserting that "African states which maintain ties with your Zionist government are colonial stooges and lackeys, especially so our own Liberian government." In a letter to the Nigerian embassy, Fahnbulleth claimed that "one day the aborigines, like our counterpart gallant Ibos, will rise up against their reactionary minority clique to regain our fatherland." A "secret memo" was said to outline plans to bring in "Chinese experts to mastermind the local government and its activities," and to place agents in three radio stations "to enable take-over and seizure at the proper time."

Shaken by the Fahnbulleth case, Tubman lashed out in late April at "subversive elements" at work in the country. He warned certain unnamed non-Liberian students and faculty members at the University of Liberia and at Cuttington College that they would be deported unless they ceased their "underground movements" immediately.

In a major economic development, a $52 million iron-ore washing and treatment plant was opened at Buchanan on April 27. Hailed as the only one of its kind in Africa, the plant was built by the Liberian American-Swedish Minerals Co. (LAMCO).

Liberia played host in April to a conference which approved in principle the establishment of a West African Regional Group to promote economic, social, and cultural cooperation. Although the group had been originally conceived as an association of 14 countries, only 9 were represented at Monrovia.   (Ri. W.)

Libraries

"Books and Libraries in an Industrial Society" was the theme of the 1968 annual session of the International Federation of Library Associations (IFLA), held at Frankfurt am Main, W.Ger. The theme covered two topical library problems: the urgent need for libraries to provide an efficient technical information service to industry, and the mechanization of library and indexing processes. In presenting it to the 400 librarians from 33 countries who attended the session, W. Rüegg, sociologist and rector of Frankfurt University, set it within a wider controversy: between the increased importance of books and libraries resulting from the bureaucratization of industrial society and the suggestion that new methods of communication might make books—and traditional libraries—superfluous. The same theme was developed by J. E.

Morpurgo, director of the National Book League, London, who pointed out that over some 50 years books and libraries had survived the silent film, the sound film, radio, television, and cybernetics.

UNESCO Department of Documentation, Libraries, and Archives. A meeting of experts on national planning of library services in Asia was sponsored by UNESCO at Colombo, Ceylon, in December 1967; it was agreed that UNESCO should establish a model project for public and school libraries in Ceylon. Two meetings on the International Council of Scientific Unions-UNESCO Scientific Information Project, held in Paris in December 1967 and July 1968, proposed international agreement on a world science information system, bibliographical descriptions, the sharing of translations, and the microcopying of books and documents. A UNESCO meeting of experts on school libraries in Central America was held in Guatemala at the end of July. UNESCO continued to support the English-language school of librarianship at Makerere College, Kampala, Uganda, and a course for African librarians was held at the Danmarks Biblioteksskole, Copenhagen.

Europe. *Belgium.* At its 1967 conference, the Flemish Association of Librarians and Archivists had sharply criticized the aims and organization of Belgian public libraries, and demanded a single network of libraries to replace the existing uncoordinated systems dominated by religious or political interests. The long-expected law on libraries, prepared some years earlier, remained unpassed, and a trend toward consolidation of existing libraries into a single public library was apparent in only a few towns. In Antwerp, however, construction continued on a central library, designed to serve the whole Flemish population of Belgium. At Mechelen (Malines) the reconstruction of the central public library, burned down in 1962, was already completed. Good progress was made in the field of hospital library service, largely as a result of the activity of the Conseil National des Bibliothèques d'Hôpitaux; in 1968 this organization was responsible for 110 hospital libraries. With the completion of the general reading rooms and the catalog hall, the new building for the Royal (national) Library in Brussels was at last finished; the official opening was scheduled for February 1969.

Bulgaria. A survey of district libraries was being made to provide a basis for improvement of the public library service. The Cyril and Methodius National Library in Sofia held an exhibition of British scientific books, organized by the British Council, and an exhibition to celebrate the centenary of the death of the revolutionary and poet Georgi S. Rakovski.

Finland. The outstanding event was the opening in May 1968 of the magnificent new building for the public library at Kuopio, a town of about 53,000. The library had a total floor area of 4,500 sq.m. (48,600 sq.ft.). The Finnish Library Association published *A Handbook on Finnish Libraries* by K. Ranta and a "who's who" of Finnish librarians.

France. The library for the Faculty of Letters at the University of Nancy, completely recataloged and reclassified, was installed in a new building. At Saint-Étienne a modern traveling library ("bibliobus") began serving a scattered rural population of some 200,-000. A report on the state of public libraries and reading in France appeared in the March issue of the *Bulletin des bibliothèques de France.* The percentage of readers in the population of France was found to be only 4.6% (compared with 40% for Canada, 31%

for Denmark and the U.S.S.R., and 30% for Great Britain), and the number of loans per capita was only 0.74 (Denmark 7; Canada 5.8; U.S. 5.4; U.S.S.R. 4.5).

West Germany. A conference of the two associations for public libraries, the Deutscher Büchereiverband (Association of German Libraries) and the Verein Deutscher Volksbibliothekare (Association of German People's Libraries), took place at Duisburg in May. Resolutions were passed demanding a national network of public libraries, which should be the joint responsibility of the federal government, the states, and the municipalities. The building of new libraries continued: the Mannheim University library had been completed at the end of 1967, and the new university library at Marburg was completed in 1968.

East Germany. The (East) German Library Association held its third annual conference in 1968 at Rostock; during the year it took an active part in an analysis of the library situation in East Germany, and published the only account in German of the 1967 session of the IFLA at Toronto. The state library in Berlin continued its international activities, including exchanges of publications with 72 countries. The Zentralbibliothek der deutschen Klassik in Weimar, with its 135,000 volumes on German literature from 1750 to 1850, was housed in a new building.

Hungary. In November 1967 the heads of government library departments of seven East European countries had met in Budapest to discuss closer collaboration with the IFLA in the fields of theory of libraries, exchange of publications, and library work in general. The Hungarian Centre for Library Science and Methodology elaborated programs for cooperative acquisition and for the training and payment of librarians.

Italy. The annual conference of the Italian Library Association, held in Venice at the end of May, coincided with the 500th anniversary of the Biblioteca Marciana on the Piazzetta San Marco. Reports of the Commission on University Libraries in Italy and on the recently published cumulative catalog of Italian publications from 1886 to 1957 were presented. At the Biblioteca Nazionale Centrale, Florence, damaged by the floods of November 1966, experts from the U.S. and elsewhere were consulted on the modernization of some of the library's processes.

Poland. On April 9, 1968, the Sejm passed a new law on libraries, which had been prepared in collaboration with the Association of Polish Librarians. The law prescribed the tasks of a national network of all types of libraries and cooperation in the acquisition, storage, and use of books.

Sweden. The inadequacy of university libraries in Sweden had caused much concern, especially to the Council of Research Libraries. In 1968 the council published a study of the international exchanges of publications, addressed to the government and to the Office of University Vice-Chancellors. The latter, after studying the supply of students' textbooks, produced a report recommending that libraries should provide more textbooks and more seats for students. Toward the end of 1968 the university library at Umeå moved into a new building, and the foundation of a fifth Swedish university library at Linköping was announced.

United Kingdom. The Office of Scientific and Technical Information (OSTI) played an increasingly important part in library organization: in January a grant of over £5,000 by OSTI to the Library Association and

the Royal Statistical Society was announced, to support a two-year survey of library resources for statisticians and economists. OSTI also administered grants to support projects concerned with the mechanization of cataloging and indexing at Cambridge, the Bodleian Library at Oxford, Newcastle, and the British National Bibliography (BNB) in London, and operated a survey of loan and information requests passing between organizations in selected areas. The BNB was using its grant to set up a computer system to produce its bibliographical records of British book production on magnetic tape. This was to be coordinated with the U.S. Library of Congress MARC (machine-readable cataloging) project to form an international MARC network. The problems of a new building for the British Museum library and its organization as the national library were not yet settled.

Yugoslavia. Two new buildings for national libraries were under construction: for the National Library of Serbia at Belgrade and for the National and University Library of Macedonia at Skopje, which was destroyed by the earthquake of July 1963. The new Yugoslav cataloging rules, based on the principles set forth at the IFLA Conference at Paris in 1961, were prepared for printing. Three governmental bodies to promote the development of libraries were set up.

Other Countries. *Canada.* At the conference of the Canadian Library Association in June an important interim report was given on "The Study of Canadian Libraries: Their Resources, Performance and Future Development." In May, W. Kaye Lamb, for many years national librarian at Ottawa, retired and was succeeded by G. Sylvestre of the Library of Parliament. Lamb had been responsible for building up the national library service and for the new building housing the National Library.

United States. For the 1968–69 fiscal year, Congress appropriated nearly $50 million for public library services and construction, interlibrary cooperation, and the specialized state library service. A similar amount was granted for school library resources, textbooks, and other instructional materials. Assuring these federal grants had been the special concern of the American Library Association (ALA) during the first half of 1968. The association's International Relations Committee was active in sponsoring advisory committees and consultants to Japanese libraries and to the Biblioteca Nazionale Centrale in Florence, and its Library Education Division held a conference in April on the bibliographic control of the literature on libraries. ALA publications issued during the year included *Costs of Public Library Service, 1968* and *Standards for Library Services for the Blind and Visually Handicapped.* The first Mildred L. Batchelder Award, which is given to the American publisher of the most outstanding children's book originally published in a foreign language, was presented to A. A. Knopf for Erich Kästner's *The Little Man,* translated by James Kirkup and illustrated by R. Schreiter.

Australia and New Zealand. The new building for the national library in Canberra, Austr., was officially opened in August by Sir Frank Francis, director and principal librarian of the British Museum. In New Zealand the National Library Act was passed, whereby the three major state libraries, the Alexander Turnbull Library, the General Assembly Library, and the National Library Service, were combined to form the National Library of New Zealand.   (A. Th.)

Encyclopædia Britannica Films. *The Library Story* (1952); *The Library: A Place for Discovery* (1965).

Libya

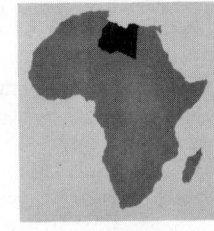

A constitutional monarchy on the north coast of Africa, Libya is bounded by the United Arab Republic, Sudan, Tunisia, Algeria, Niger, and Chad. Area: 679,536 sq.mi. (1,760,000 sq.km.). Pop. (1967 est.): 1,743,367. Co-capitals and largest cities: Tripoli (pop., 1967 est., 236,718) and Bengasi (pop., 1967 est., 152,221). Language: Arabic. Religion: predominantly Muslim. King, Idris I; prime ministers in 1968, Abdul Hamid Bakkush and, after September 4, Wanis al-Gaddafi.

Libya managed during 1968 to recover almost completely from the repercussions of the 1967 Arab-Israeli war, which had deeply affected the internal situation. A series of violent demonstrations by students and workers and threats of sabotage in the oil fields had led to massive arrests in the second half of 1967. But by February 1968, when out of 106 persons tried only 12 had been acquitted, popular reaction to the trials was not as intense as had been expected, even though the secretary-general of the Libyan Workers' Union and the chairman of the Libyan Students' Union were among those who received sentences.

Much of the lessening of internal unrest came from the presence of Prime Minister Abdul Hamid Bakkush. Bakkush, in his mid-30s, undertook the task of trying to bridge the gap between the conservative older generation, grouped around a handful of rich and powerful families, and an impatient younger generation led by have-not intellectuals increasingly conscious of their growing importance in a country swiftly moving from a rural nomadic community to an oil-rich modern state. He alleviated the frustration and discontent of the younger generation by arousing in them a "Libya first" nationalism, by modernizing and developing the Army, by substituting conscription for voluntary military service, and by expanding and diversifying foreign relations.

The nation's economic situation continued to develop favourably, though the rate of increase in oil production relaxed slightly and financial difficulties threatened to hamper further expansion seriously. Companies' estimated revenue from oil operations accruing to the government in 1968 exceeded Lib£200 million ($560 million), compared with Lib£170 million for 1967. Bakkush, having served his purpose well, resigned as prime minister in September. Wanis al-Gaddafi, the foreign minister, succeeded him.

(M. B. A.)

Encyclopædia Britannica Films. *Oasis* (1965).

Liechtenstein

An independent principality between Switzerland and Austria, Liechtenstein is united with Switzerland by a customs and monetary union. Area: 62 sq.mi. (160 sq.km.). Pop. (1967 est.): 19,500. Cap. and largest city: Vaduz (pop., 1966 est., 3,957). Language: German. Religion: 92.3% Roman Catholic. Sovereign prince, Francis Joseph II; chief of government in 1968, Gerard Batliner.

In February 1968 the U.S. government revealed that an intensive investigation was being made of more than 50 U.S. firms that had established holding companies in Liechtenstein. The federal check was for possible tax evasion and was related to the balance of payments problem. A Liechtenstein attorney was cited for contempt of court when he fled the country to avoid testifying in the case. The actions of the firms were legal under Liechtenstein law but they might be in violation of U.S. law.

On July 4, women joined men at the polls for the first time in the long history of the principality to help the government determine whether the nation should give women the vote. The special election was a consultative poll and its results were not binding on the parliament. Of 8,203 eligible voters, 4,765 cast ballots, and the proposal was "defeated" by 2,582–2,152, with 31 ballots left blank.

The principal bills taken up by the parliament concerned voting rights for women, the exhibition of art belonging to the state, the protection of highland and mountain regions, and regulations concerning the profession of lawyers and trustees.

On March 10 the prince and princess celebrated their silver wedding anniversary and on July 26 Francis Joseph commemorated his 30th year of rule. Earlier, on June 11, Prince Alois was born to Crown Prince Hans Adam and Crown Princess Marie Aglae. Prince Heinrich wed Countess Amalie Podstatzki-Lichtenstein on March 23. (R. D. Ho.)

Life Insurance: *see* Insurance

Liquors, Alcoholic: *see* Alcoholic Beverages

Yasunari Kawabata of Japan, recipient of the 1968 Nobel Prize for literature.

Literature

The 1968 Nobel Prize for Literature went to Yasunari Kawabata of Japan—the first Asian to win the award. (*See* BIOGRAPHY.)

AMERICAN

Fiction. More well-written, delightfully readable books were published in the United States in 1968 than had appeared in many a year. Changes for the better were most apparent in nonfiction, but storytelling also took a welcome turn. *Red Sky at Morning,* a first novel by Richard Bradford (son of the late Roark Bradford), reminded reviewers of another superb first of almost a decade ago, Harper Lee's *To Kill a Mockingbird,* because of the quality of the writing and the attractiveness of most of the book's characters. The story, told by 17-year-old Josh Arnold, dealt with life in a Spanish-speaking community in New Mexico. It had humour, great sensitiveness, and enough spice to season without repelling. A veteran novelist, Anton Myrer, who served as a Marine corporal in the South Pacific before completing his studies at Harvard, turned out a war story that overcame many critics' aversion to that genre for the first time since Robert Crichton's memorable *Secret of Santa Vittoria.* In *Once an Eagle,* Myrer traced the career of Sam Damon, a youngster out of Nebraska, from his enlistment during World War I to Vietnam and the rank of lieutenant general. While the novel was antiwar in tone, its hero came off as a thoroughly admirable combat commander, and the battle scenes had an unforgettable authenticity. *Paradise Falls* by Don Robertson, a Cleveland newsman, took more than 1,000 pages (about 200 more than Myrer's book) to explore a fictional Ohio town and its inhabitants between the year 1865 and midnight of Dec. 31, 1899. The regular publisher, Putnam, issued this massive work in one volume, but the Literary Guild thoughtfully sent it to subscribers in two-volume form. Robertson, who promised two more books about the same community (bringing it up to 1970), dealt with so many persons—more than 500—that he kept not only a map of Paradise Falls but a chart showing eye colour, birth dates, relationships, and other data about his principal characters.

For sheer charm it would be hard to surpass *The Last Unicorn* by Peter Beagle, a not-yet-30 author whose *A Fine and Private Place* was acclaimed several years earlier, even before Beagle had reached voting age. His new book pleased those who could be captivated by a fairy tale involving a unicorn, a bumbling but friendly magician, a king, a prince, and a host of other entrancing characters both human and animal. It was filled with haunting phrases: "Outside, the night lay coiled in the street, cobra-cold and scaled with stars. . . ." And there were other repeaters who found eager audiences: Arthur Hailey with *Airport,* a fast-moving drama about "Lincoln International Airport" (for which read Chicago's O'Hare) and the people working there or just passing, frantically, through. Rabbi Herbert Tarr, remembered for *The Conversion of Chaplain Cohen,* scored once more with *Heaven Help Us!* It painted so engaging a picture of Rabbi Gideon Abel's experiences at Hillendale Temple that the book was to become a Broadway musical by the same group that put together *Fiddler on the Roof.* Rabbi Tarr, a bachelor like his fictional counterpart,

John Updike, whose novel "Couples" was published April 5, 1968.

takes his religion seriously, but little else; the result has twice been great fun for the reader.

Meyer Levin, a proven professional, came up with a surprising change of pace in *Gore and Igor,* in which an American folk singer and a Russian poet follow great extent, it was one of the year's most amusing paths that converge in Israel during the Arab-Israeli war. Though it failed to catch the public fancy to any books, with overtones of seriousness that removed it from the thistledown class. In the picaresque vein, a best seller was *True Grit* by Charles Portis. In it, 14-year-old Mattie Ross of Arkansas seeks the renegade who shot her father and stole his horse. She persuades Rooster Cogburn, a United States marshal (he's the one with "true grit") to accompany her—though she thinks the $100 he demands for his services is a mite high, since he will also collect a bounty. But Cogburn, whose past includes riding with Quantrill and Bloody Bill Anderson, and a couple of holdups, reassures her: "I am giving you," he says, "my children's rate."

Other fiction worth mentioning included Elie Wiesel's *Legends of Our Time,* a moving examination of the fate of the Jew in the modern (Nazi and post-Nazi) world; *The Innocent* by Richard Kim, set in the author's native Korea and dealing with the conflict between love and hate; *The Burning Glass* by S. N. Behrman, telling of gentle people and their fate in the years before World War II; and *The Hurricane Years,* a study of stress by Cameron Hawley.

Three works by well-known authors reached best-sellerdom despite critics' disapproval: *Myra Breckinridge* by Gore Vidal, which was intended as a spoof on sex but was thoroughly unpleasant reading; *Couples* by John Updike (*see* BIOGRAPHY)—the title tells it all; and *Preserve and Protect* by Allen Drury, a potentially lively sequel to *Advise and Consent* and his two subsequent books, slowed down annoyingly by Drury's lecturing the reader on ideological matters.

Outstanding short-story collections of the year were Saul Bellow's *Mosby's Memoirs and Other Stories* and John O'Hara's *And Other Stories.*

Poetry. One of the poetic highlights was *In the Mecca,* the first collection of completely new poems by Gwendolyn Brooks, Chicago's 1950 Pulitzer Prize winner, in almost a decade. The title poem told of murder in a slum building in the South Side ghetto where Miss Brooks once worked for a purveyor of love potions; the shorter poems dealt with such subjects as the Blackstone Rangers (a Chicago gang), Malcolm X, Medgar Evers, and a winter squirrel. *Selected Poems* by Karl Shapiro contained more than 200 poems, of which 25 were previously unpublished in book form. Fifty-four poets, many of them unknowns, were represented in *The Young American Poets,* edited by Paul Carroll, himself a poet and fairly young. James Dickey, a not-so-young poet, said of the volume: "These young American poets are with and *in* human experience as poets have not been for a very long time."

That polished writer of light (and weighty) verse, Phyllis McGinley, was responsible for *Wonders and Surprises,* an anthology intended for juveniles but too good to be wasted on the young. The book contained pieces by Elinor Wylie, E. B. White, Langston Hughes, T. S. Eliot, and dozens more. Another giant in his own corner of the poetic world, Ogden Nash, was represented by *There's Always Another Windmill.* The maestro still had his touch: to quote only one title, "All Good Americans Go to Larousse, or, I Don't Pretend to be Molière than Thou."

Other noteworthy books of verse were *The Harvesters' Vase* by Ned O'Gorman, which, said Chad Walsh, possessed "sheer linguistic fireworks"; *T.V. Baby Poems* by Allen Ginsberg, who, a reviewer observed, "can be, in the same poem, the most powerful poet of his age and one of the most banal"; *The Collected Poems of James Agee,* a posthumous collection of 60 poems never before between covers, plus others; *The Wild Wicked Old Man and Other Poems* by Archibald MacLeish; *Once* by Alice Walker, a 24-year-old Mississippian; and *The Day of the Parrot and Other Poems* by Stanley Cooperman, a master of technique.

Biography. One of the year's finest biographies was *Stephen Crane* by R. W. Stallman, a study of the late-19th-century figure who wrote with doomed haste until his death at age 28. Stallman, the editor of five books of Crane's writings, had turned up an amazing amount of material and had woven it into an absorbing portrait of a truly remarkable man.

The Last Hero: Charles A. Lindbergh by Walter S. Ross was unauthorized by its shy subject but was nonetheless adequately researched. Despite Lindbergh's refusal to cooperate with Ross in any way, the biographer managed to search out a vast amount of information, including many revealing anecdotes. A virtue of this interesting work was that it set in proper perspective Lindbergh's activities before World War II that brought him criticism from some quarters.

Thomas Wolfe by Andrew Turnbull described the tempestuous life of the Carolina author who is now, perhaps, more talked about than read. John Kobler produced a well-written biography with one of the best punning titles ever invented: *Luce: His Time, Life, and Fortune.* This dealt with the co-founder of Time, Inc., and was based in part on personal knowledge—Kobler worked briefly for that publication—and in part on the magazine's files and on interviews with the Luces. An earthy collection was *The Letters of Carl Sandburg,* edited by Herbert Mitgang. *Gambling Secrets of Nick the Greek* by Ted Thackrey, Jr., was part biography, part advice to the gambling addict. *Broken Cigars* by Myron Cope presented a gallery of sports screwballs.

The Literary Life: A Scrapbook Almanac of the Anglo-American Literary Scene from 1900 to 1950 by Robert Phelps and Peter Deane was a book too good to carry so pedestrian a title. *Memoirs: Sixty Years on the Firing Line* by Arthur Krock, Pulitzer Prize-winning *New York Times* correspondent, covered politics and much else. From the world of theatre came Marc Connelly's unpretentious but absorbing *Voices Offstage: A Book of Memoirs* and Helen Hayes's autobiography, *On Reflection.*

Other Nonfiction. What promised to become one of the year's most widely discussed works, Jim Bishop's *The Day Kennedy Was Shot,* appeared late in November and was inevitably (and in some cases favourably) compared with its 1967 counterpart, William Manchester's *The Death of a President.*

Peter Farb was responsible for what was not only one of the most enthusiastically reviewed books of 1968 but the one with the longest and dullest title: *Man's Rise to Civilization as Shown by the Indians of North America from Primeval Times to the Coming of the Industrial State.* It was admired by, among others, the anthropologist Laura Bohannon, who said: "He knows what he is talking about and has an attention-holding fluency of style which reveals the inherent fascination of a story too often buried in scholarship." Another of the year's standouts in nonfiction was

Lawrence and Oppenheimer by Nuel Pharr Davis, an engrossing study of the two famous physicists in relation to each other and to the Manhattan Project. It told of the anguished self-dissection and sometimes savage infighting among the men who developed the atomic bomb. If it still left many questions unanswered, this might well be because they were unanswerable.

Norman Mailer contributed a pair of worthwhile books: *The Armies of the Night,* about the march on the Pentagon (October 1967) by Vietnam war protesters, and *Miami and the Siege of Chicago,* in which he set down his picture of the Republican and Democratic conventions. Both books represented superb reporting by—like him or not—one of America's most vital men of letters.

It was a fine year, too, for collections of columns and magazine articles: *Slouching Towards Bethlehem* by Joan Didion, which covered Haight-Ashbury, Hawaii, John Wayne, Howard Hughes, Joan Baez, and other phenomena; *Do You Sleep in the Nude?* by Rex Reed, which offered 23 outspoken interviews (Barbra Streisand, Lester Maddox, Buster Keaton, *et al.*) plus a description of a stranded American theatrical troupe in Berlin; *Best Magazine Articles: 1968,* which ran a gauntlet from *Ramparts* to the *National Review;* and George E. Condon's *Laughter from the Rafters,* the work of a funny man on the staff of the *Cleveland Plain Dealer. The Pump House Gang,* a collection of short pieces, was one of two books published by Tom Wolfe, the other being *The Electric Kool-Aid Acid Test,* a portrait of the novelist Ken Kesey and a group of companions in their search for the ultimate experience. Sports books included *Seven Days to Sunday: Crisis Week with the New York Giants* by Eliot Asinof (who wrote *Eight Men Out*), a self-confessed Giants' idolator; *The Third Fireside Book of Baseball,* edited by Charles Einstein, which was every bit as good as its two predecessors; and *Instant Replay: The Green Bay Diary of Jerry Kramer,* edited by Dick Schaap—another inside look at pro football, this time by one of the players.

John Hersey wrote *The Algiers Motel Incident,* a horrifying account of the wanton slaying of three Negroes during the Detroit riots—a crime for which three white policemen were indicted. Hersey refused all royalties from the book, ordering the money used to promote race relations. In the same general area were *Violence in the Streets,* Shalom Endlemen's anthology of articles dealing with cause and prevention as viewed by writers as far apart as Norman Mailer and William Buckley; and *Black Rage* by two Negro psychiatrists, William Grier and Price M. Cobbs, who cited case histories and declared that information is the most necessary ingredient in abating racial hostility.

A truly gorgeous art book, *Andrew Wyeth* by Richard Meryman, sold for $55 before Christmas (1968) to the 50,000 purchasers lucky enough to obtain it and for $75 afterward, when it was virtually unavailable. Wyeth himself had supervised the making of the plates —more than 100 of them—and their quality was beyond reproach.

The scope of the year's nonfiction, and something of its general tone, can perhaps be summarized with closing mention of two delightful works: *The Bogey Man,* George Plimpton's account of his latest venture in playing with the champs—this time on the golf course; and Leo Rosten's warm tribute to a marvelous language, *The Joys of Yiddish.*   (R. A. Cr.)

Peter Beagle, whose adult fairy tale "The Last Unicorn" was published in 1968.

Will and Ariel Durant, authors of the 10-vol. "The Story of Civilization" and "The Lessons of History," received the Pulitzer Prize for general nonfiction in 1968.

CANADIAN

English Language. In 1968 fresh gloom settled over Canadian fiction. Its general quality reached a new low; and although many first novels were published, not one gave exceptional promise. However, two volumes of short stories by new writers showed considerable originality and competence. *The Miracle at Indian River* by Alden Nowlan, although narrowly Maritime in setting, was versatile in characterization and subject matter: the pathos of a teen-age lumberjack eager to show his strength, and the fanaticism of a preacher determined to marry off, by fair means or foul, the single members of his congregation regardless of their age, are examples of themes from this collection. Alice Munro's *Dance of the Happy Shades* portrayed with great sensitiveness a childhood and adolescence in rural Ontario.

Footsteps on Old Stairs, the last collection of short stories by the late Thomas Raddall, proved disappointing. Also falling short of expectations was an eagerly awaited novel by Ernest Buckler, *Ox Bells and Fireflies;* it turned out to be a rambling and effusive reminiscence of a boyhood in Nova Scotia. Jack Ludwig's latest novel, *Above Ground,* depicted a Canadian who moves from a sickly childhood in Winnipeg through a series of irresolute junkets around America in his later years. Neither the hero nor other characters who drift through the haze elicited much response from readers.

Cocksure by Mordecai Richler, an established writer living in England, was the year's only critically acclaimed and controversial novel by a Canadian. A wickedly entertaining satire on the London scene, it centred on a handsome, middle-aged, middle-class citizen whose encounters with bizarre individuals cause him to doubt his sanity and manhood.

The author-illustrator James Houston produced another of his Eskimo stories. In *Akavak* he described a journey undertaken by a 14-year-old boy and his grandfather so that the old man, who is dying, may see his brother once more. This tale of endurance, told in easy-flowing prose, was stark, vivid, and ennobling. Similarly, Kerry Wood in *Samson's Long Ride* achieved a creditable re-creation of a true story from Canadian history: the odyssey of a ten-year-old Assiniboin boy who runs away from a mission to find his family and survives the vicissitudes of a winding and treacherous trail home.

In keeping with the growing acknowledgment of the value of Canada's native legends, 18 Eskimo folktales were retold by Helen Caswell in *Shadows from the Singing House.* Her prose was simple and direct; and the illustrator, Robert Mayokok, who is an Eskimo, added intriguing detail.

Unlike the situation in fiction, a surge of creativity and interest in poetry was sustained in Canada in 1968. First prize in the Canadian Centennial Commission's poetry competition went to Margaret Atwood for *The Animals in That Country.* Tense, delicate, technically fine, her poems search for harmony between inner and outer worlds. Joe Rosenblatt in *Winter of the Luna Moon* showed imagination of phrase, image, and thought, based on a sound technique. Irving Layton in *The Shattered Plinths* presented 60 new poems, many of them deriving from the heated atmosphere preceding the Arab-Israeli crisis of June 1967. A social and political poet, he speaks out angrily, with strength, against misery and indifference. The versatile Leonard Cohen brought out *Selected Poems, 1956–1968.* The edition was sold out almost immediately,

for his writing establishes instant rapport with many young readers. Most of the book consisted of selections from his earlier collections; the new poems in it were disappointing departures from his line of development.

Younger poets have found support from the newer small publishers of Canada. The House of Anansi, started by W. D. Godfrey of Toronto, and the Coach House Press were particularly active. *T. O. Now,* edited by Dennis Lee, introduced 13 apprentice poets living in Toronto. Alfred Purdy's vigorous *Wild Grape Wine* demonstrated his adeptness in sardonic comicality. In sharp contrast was *The Documentaries* by Dorothy Livesay—poems from the 1930s and '40s, reflecting the mood and social outlook of those years, and followed by a long poem, "Roots," written in Winnipeg especially for the conclusion.

The Wind Has Wings, a stunning collection of 77 Canadian poems for children, compiled by Mary Alice Downie and Barbara Robertson, afforded a sense of pride and distinction. The anthology contained modern and old-time poems, nonsense verse, Eskimo chants, and translations of French-Canadian folk songs —all brilliantly illustrated by Elizabeth Cleaver.

Excellent books of history, travel, and biography appeared in 1968. In *The Distemper of Our Times,* Peter C. Newman presented an account that was partly a biographical study of former Prime Minister Lester B. Pearson and partly a dissection of Canadian politics from 1963 to 1968—the years in which Pearson, for the Liberal Party, and John Diefenbaker, for the Conservatives, conducted a full-fledged political feud. Many considered this the most perceptive book available on near-contemporary Canadian affairs. A companion volume was Patrick Nicholson's *Vision and Indecision,* which recorded the 1956–67 period when Diefenbaker occupied posts as leader of the government and of the opposition. In *Smallwood: The Unlikely Revolutionary,* Richard Gwyn expertly examined the paradox that is Joseph Smallwood, premier of Newfoundland. The author's exciting analysis made clear the background politics of an emerging province and the personality of its leader, who almost single-handedly carved out a place for Newfoundland in the 20th century. With a less flamboyant but equally impressive subject, John Swettenham presented *McNaughton: 1887–1939*—the first volume of the definitive biography of Gen. Andrew McNaughton (1887–1966), one of Canada's most distinguished leaders in both World Wars and in the many and varied posts he filled in the public service.

ASHLEY AND CRIPPEN

Peter C. Newman, author of the political study "The Distemper of Our Times," published in 1968.

Blair Fraser, who wrote "The Search for Identity: Canada, 1945–1967," a political history of Canada.

Margaret Atwood, first prize winner in the Canadian Centennial Commission's poetry competition for "The Animals in That Country."

COURTESY, OXFORD UNIVERSITY PRESS

Confederation at the Crossroads: The Canadian Constitution by E. Russell Hopkins was a scholarly discussion of the constitution. The author's satisfaction with its inherited British characteristics, at least from a juridical point of view, generally seemed to preclude attempts at reevaluation.

The late Blair Fraser's *The Search for Identity: Canada, 1945–1967* was an entertaining political history that benefited greatly from the author's personal knowledge of many of the people he described. Concentrating on political highlights, he provided a lucid and balanced discussion of Canada's attempts to develop an independent personality. Some of Canada's best thinkers presented papers of high quality in *An Independent Foreign Policy for Canada?*—an examination of Canada's role in foreign affairs, edited by Stephen Clarkson.

George Woodcock and Ivan Avakumovic, in *The Doukhobors*, offered a well-researched and eminently readable history of the sect and its dramatic search for religious freedom. *Bluenose Magic* by Luella Creighton examined the lore of the supernatural in the Atlantic provinces. She reported that belief in omens and portents is as prevalent today, among all classes of people there, as it was a century ago.

In *War and Peace in the Global Village* Marshall McLuhan and Quentin Fiore insisted that electronic media have created a new, worldwide environment to which everyone must adjust. The authors adroitly used marginal quotations (including some from *Finnegans Wake*) to embellish their stimulating but undisciplined prose.

Naomi Jackson Groves wrote *A. Y.'s Canada* to accompany more than 100 pencil drawings of A. Y. Jackson. These depict his travels, from the Arctic to the Gaspé, during a period of 40 years in which the artist interpreted the spirit of Canada in the manner the country then seemed to demand. The text supplemented Jackson's pictures with a wealth of historical and aesthetic information.

Expo '67 was the sumptuous memorial album of the international exhibition held in Montreal from April to October 1967. Two-thirds of the book consisted of close description of the national pavilions. *This Was Expo* by Robert Fulford (editor of *Saturday Night*) was a popular rendition of the sights and sounds of the fair, together with a critique by the author. *The History of Stratford, 1958–68* was a pictorial record of the Stratford, Ont., Shakespeare festival performances during the past ten years. (H. C. CL.)

French Language. The most noteworthy books of 1968 were not to be found in the realm of belles lettres but in such categories as political science, sociology, and history. It was an exceptionally poor year for poetry, and good novels and short stories were few.

The only important book of verse was *Pays sans parole* by Yves Préfontaine, a collection of poems lamenting the poet's inability to express the true aspirations of the French-Canadian community. Similarly, Hubert Aquin's second novel, *Trou de mémoire*, described a highly sophisticated and unsuccessful search for the self on the part of the author-hero. In *Mater Europa*, Jean-Ethier Blais, on the contrary, achieved self-discovery through reminiscing over his experiences as a child, a youth, and a man both at home and in Europe. Other works of fiction were *La Saison des artichauts* by Réal Benoit and *La Chèvre d'or* by Anne Bernard. The only plays of the year worth mentioning were *L'Exécution* by Marie-Claire Blais and *Les Beaux Dimanches* by Marcel Dubé.

Le Dix-huitième Siècle canadien by Guy Frégault portrayed Canadian society before and after the British conquest. *Québec-Canada anglais* by Michel Brunet was a series of studies of the more recent evolution of, and clashes between, the two Canadian peoples. Political and economic problems facing the nation today were discussed in *Le Fédéralisme et la Société canadienne française* by Pierre Elliott Trudeau, a collection of essays written and published before the author became prime minister of Canada, as well as in *Vers une nouvelle constitution* by Marcel Faribault. The outstanding book of the year probably was *Le Lieu de l'homme* by Fernand Dumont, a study of the factors—both personal and social—that contribute to the development, flourishing, and decay of cultures.

Two major French-Canadian authors were the subjects of authoritative critical essays: *Félix-Antoine Savard* by André Major and *Alain Grandbois* by Jacques Brault.

Canada du temps qui passe, a collection of photographs of Canadian scenery with a short text by Jean Sarrazin, was possibly the most beautiful achievement in Canadian publishing history. (G. SR.)

Guy Frégault, author of "Le Dix-huitième Siècle canadien."

DANISH

Student revolt, radical liberalism, and the questioning of established systems were as much a feature of life in Denmark during 1968 as in many other countries. Literature reflected this in various ways, though without the emergence of any militantly engaged writing. Nevertheless, that a landslide was under way could be discerned partly in choice of themes, partly in demolition of accepted ideas of art by a group of young authors. Klaus Rifbjerg's *Lonni og Karl*—the title carried undertones of *Bonnie and Clyde*—was about a revolt that never takes place. In daydreams (their alternation with his middle-class waking existence is conveyed in masterly fashion) Karl experiences Denmark in the middle of a revolution. This was an entertaining, humorous novel in the "angry young man" tradition, but with Rifbjerg's poetic, intense imagery—grotesque yet tender. The somewhat younger Sven Holm's *Min elskede: En skabelonroman,* consisting of a series of brief, precise, ironic situations, was a fable in modern terms, describing an attempt by a couple of foreign agents to assassinate the Danish foreign minister, with resultant disintegration of national institutions and the establishment of the population as one big happy family in a flexible urban society.

Anders Bodelsen, of the same generation, took a different direction. With two realistic psychological thrillers, *Tænk på et tal* and *Hændeligt uheld*, both about the individual in the welfare state, he skillfully introduced a genre based on the American-English crime novel, analyzing the equivocal morality of the consumer society. At the end of 1968 both were being translated into several languages.

Other novelists made impressive reappearances in 1968—*e.g.,* Tove Ditlevsen, Willy-August Linnemann, Peter Ronild, Dorrit Willumsen—but perhaps Svend Åge Madsen's experimental *Liget og Cysten* presented the most interesting perspectives. The young author, originally influenced by Kafka and, even more, by Beckett, showed further development in his use of language, inspired to some extent by Wittgenstein. His new novel was a clever amalgam of models from popular literature—a stimulating synthesis of clichés culled from pornographic and detective novels, from romantic love stories and science fiction.

Klaus Rifbjerg, author of the novel "Lonni og Karl."

Madsen could best be considered in relation to the latest developments in Danish poetry. A generation whose starting point had been Concretism was developing what might be called a "systematic" poetry, their poems being "linguistic examples." The title of Per Højholt's collection, *Turbo*, indicated the method: to put words into turbulent motion, creating poems on a purely linguistic framework and so conveying a new, existential experience. This was also true of two books published during the year by the movement's philosophical "father," Hans Jørgen Nielsen: *Fra luften i munden* and *Nielsen og den hvide verden* (essays). Nielsen also attracted attention by demonstrating against the Danish literary academy and what he called its anachronistic, bourgeois structure. Other interesting "system" poets were Charlotte Strandgaard and Per Kirkeby. In contrast was the academician Thorkild Bjørnvig's classical-modernistic cycle, *Ravnen*, describing, in monumental verse, a great personal crisis. (Ni. B.)

ENGLISH

Prose. There was little of the "new and wonderful" in 1968, although the growing fashion for multidecker memoirs and cyclic works of fiction perhaps heightened the sense of déjä vu. The year brought more autobiographical chapters from Bertrand Russell, Kingsley Martin, Han Suyin, and (in translation) Konstantin Paustovski; the last of Frank O'Connor's memoirs, Sir Harold Nicolson's *Diaries and Letters*, and Michael Holroyd's massive biography of Lytton Strachey; and the beginning of yet another literary autobiography, V. S. Pritchett's. From novelists came more of C. P. (Lord) Snow's "Strangers and Brothers" sequence, of Anthony Powell's "Music of Time," of serial works by Philip Toynbee, Simon Raven, and Paul Scott. Anthony Burgess' *Enderby Outside*—"off the Loo and into the Bar," to some of his fans—proved to be a single-shot sequel to *Inside Mr. Enderby* (1963), not the second length of a larger design on that memorably rebarbative poet.

Biography, Letters, Diaries, Criticism. All this work in progress, though including several of the year's best performances, made for predictability. "The feast continues," wrote one reviewer of vol. ii of *The Autobiography of Bertrand Russell*, which carried his complex, absorbing story from the beginning of World War I to almost the end of World War II, showing him in strenuous pursuit of truth and love, as well as providing a rare anthology of correspondence with his peers—Conrad, Wittgenstein, T. S. Eliot, Malinowski, *et al.* Han Suyin's *Birdless Summer* and Paustovski's *Years of Hope* were the latest phases of longer autobiographies also unfolding as vistas of the histories of the two great countries—China and Russia—to which their authors belonged, and both works showed clearly that, when finished, they would have the character and stamina of major modern examples of the genre. Paustovski's death (*see* OBITUARIES) did not mean that his would be incomplete: vol. v was to appear in English in 1969.

Along with this cumulation of retrospective writing, literary prose was dominated by gatherings of the work of two writers long dead: D. H. Lawrence and George Orwell. *Phoenix II* (editors, Harry T. Moore and Warren Roberts) was described on its title pages as consisting of "uncollected, unpublished and other prose works" by Lawrence. That the "other" made up the bulk of the volume did not detract from its value: many had long been unobtainable. Of "new" pieces

COURTESY, HOLT, RINEHART AND WINSTON, INC.

Michael Holroyd, author of a biography of Lytton Strachey published in 1968.

JONATHAN GREEN-ARMYTAGE, COURTESY, MACMILLAN

Arthur Koestler, whose collection of essays, "Drinkers of Infinity," was published in 1968.

the best were "A Prelude," an early story; sketches of Lawrence's years of teaching; and two disturbing accounts of homecomings. But even of the casual late journalism one might say, with Raymond Williams, that it was "some mark of a creative writer that these pieces from the twenties read like a man alive now, and that the things he's attacking—still busily current—fade back into the commercial scum of that dead period." (Late in the year more unpublished Lawrence formed a personal appendix to this collection: *Lawrence in Love: Letters to Louie Burrows*, edited by J. J. Boulton.) Similar vitality was seen in the four-volume *Collected Essays, Journalism and Letters of George Orwell*, edited by his widow and Ian Angus (and providing, incidentally, the biography that Orwell had wanted not to be written). "The most offhand or ephemeral bit of *Tribune*-fodder," wrote Dennis Potter in his *Times* review, "can suddenly be jolted on to a different level by a lethal sentence buzzing angrily out of long-since faded columns."

A challenge of this kind was rarely encountered in contemporary writing, though there were flashes of something like it in A. Alvarez' *Beyond All This Fiddle: Essays 1955–67*, chiefly on the dilemmas of modern poets in America and Eastern Europe. These essays, indeed, reminded Frank Kermode specifically of Orwell: in them could be heard the accents of "a harsh diagnostician, issuing from time to time his unillusioned commentaries on our violence and our cosiness."

During 1968 it was mostly "our cosiness," sometimes of a rather curious kind. Most curious was the ambience of J. R. Ackerley's *My Father and Myself*. "I was born in 1896 and my parents were married in 1919," began this posthumously published "family memoir" by a central, if backroom, figure of the literary Establishment of the 1930s and '40s. When his father died Ackerley discovered that this respected king of the banana trade had a flourishing second family in an adjacent suburb, and that the father's progress from obscurity to modest fortune had been founded on homosexual adventures rather more successful than those in which the son had been engaged. In a candid, delicate analysis of this relationship and its consequences, Ackerley has left us a small confessional classic. Another remarkable father—a Micawberish bankrupt and a Christian Scientist—bulked large in V. S. Pritchett's *A Cab at the Door*, which included characteristically vivid pictures of Edwardian lower-middle-class life but left a sense of strain: its author had been remembering too hard, forcing the pace of his style. "Can life have been quite such relentless knockabout?" one ruffled reviewer asked.

With vol. ii of his Lytton Strachey biography, *The Years of Achievement, 1910–1932*, Michael Holroyd completed a 1,200-page study of this "legendary" essayist and lover—leaving no story untold, no scrap of his writing unexamined. He completed too an unnervingly candid description of just what the famous code of "personal relationships" could mean in practice in the Bloomsbury inner circle. "Who would have guessed from G. E. Moore's *Principia Ethica*," Frank Kermode reflected, "that they required so much spite and sodomy?" A cooler view of the coterie was offered in *Bloomsbury*, a short, well-illustrated study by art historian Quentin Bell, Virginia Woolf's nephew. And perhaps the perturbed spirit of a famous Bloomsbury "cousin" will rest more easily for the final dispersal, with Sir Geoffrey Keynes's edition of *The Letters of*

Rupert Brooke, of the more facile myths about his life and work. Harold Nicolson's *Diaries and Letters, 1945–62,* last of three volumes (i, 1966; ii, 1967), was a sad appendix to the record of a Bloomsbury (and more) life, drawn out distressfully in the alien years of postwar Britain. The work was ended by Nigel Nicolson, its editor, not with the father's death (*see* OBITUARIES), but with the death of his mother, Victoria Sackville-West. Their deepening relationship was eventually seen as the loosely held chain running through life and book; and many readers finally found this the work's most rewarding aspect. *The White-Garnett Letters,* edited by and involving David Garnett, another sprig of the many-tentacled Bloomsbury cousinage, put on public view his long friendship with that sad suicide, the swashbuckling T. H. White; and this book, in its different way, also was distressing.

But for cousins and eccentricity, Maurice Collis' composite biography *Somerville and Ross,* of the two half-forgotten, indivisible writers of Irish pastoral comedy, was the book to turn to. Drawing heavily on their copious diaries and letters, it showed "Ross" (Violet Martin) as a creative artist of quality and perception. Lady Cynthia Asquith's *Diaries, 1915–18* was a self-portrait, almost too revealing, of another intelligent, original woman who, despite her gifts, lacked the energy to break the bonds of period and class.

Two autobiographical essays by famous left-wing publicists claimed attention. Kingsley Martin's *Editor: A Second Volume of Autobiography, 1931–45* covered the more controversial years of his direction of the *New Statesman.* He was "the gayest of Jeremiahs," to quote the review by his one-time literary editor, Raymond Mortimer. Others were less charitable in treating the political oscillations produced by his mixture of aggressiveness and defeatism—notably during the Munich crisis. The verdict seemed to be that Martin, though a brilliant journalist, was a dangerous counselor for the British left. *Reminiscences of Affection,* the last book from Martin's old ally Victor Gollancz (d. 1967), publisher and winner of belligerently conducted battles for unpopular causes, was a gathering of people, places, and things that had meant much to its author; it was compiled by his daughter Livia from unfinished manuscripts. More polished and substantial, *My Father's Son* by Frank O'Connor (d. 1966) contained fine portrayals of Yeats and Æ in and past their prime, reporting astringently on the squabbling shoal of literary minnows that swam in that great wake in the Liffey in the 1920s and '30s; it too was a labour of editorial piety, by a Dublin professor. Two accomplished, vivid autobiographies by young Indians described the sharp discomforts of a "passage to England"—to Western, mid-20th-century culture. Dom Moraes, in *My Son's Father,* showed "the elegance of the poet and the poet's hard core," as V. S. Pritchett observed; Sasthi Brata's *My God Died Young* was more vigorous, rhetorical, and sociologically interesting.

By general consent the year's best literary biography was Robert Gittings' massive *John Keats.* "Mr. Gittings makes no pretension to critical insights," wrote John Bayley in his *Guardian* review; but "a work of such detailed and sensitive recording hardly needs them—it helps to put us in a position where we can find and feel them for ourselves." Two useful critical works were Denis Donoghue's *The Ordinary Universe: Soundings in Modern Literature,* which resisted the idea that the only experience relevant to

IRVIN KERSHNER · CAMERA PRESS—PIX FROM PUBLIX · ROGER HENDRIX

Left, Brian Moore, author of the novel "I Am Mary Dunne." Centre, Muriel Spark, whose short novel "The Public Image" was published in 1968. Right, James D. Watson, who wrote "The Double Helix," an account of the cracking of the genetic code.

"art in our time" is the experience of extremity; and *Innovations,* essays edited by Bernard Bergonzi, in which contributors considered what has been happening in the arts since the end of the "classical phase" in the modern movement. Interesting writings on music were Igor Stravinsky and Robert Craft's *Dialogues and a Diary,* and Wilfrid Mellers' *Caliban Reborn,* a stimulating piece of aesthetic theorizing.

Science. Arthur Koestler's *Drinkers of Infinity: Essays 1955–67* gathered fugitive pieces, mainly on scientific subjects; and Sir Bernard Lovell's *The Story of Jodrell Bank* was a well-written account of the scientific and political background to the building of his giant radio telescope. But understanding of creative science was most deeply enriched by James D. Watson's *The Double Helix,* a record of the work at Cambridge that culminated in the cracking of the genetic code, by a Nobel Prize-winning scientist and a born writer. It was one of the year's successes: tactless, remarkable, full of sharp gossip and the excitement of the quest. By its skill in depicting "the true diversity of minds in a scientific project," wrote Alex Comfort, "this book marks the final interment of current nonsense about two cultures."

Fiction. Now in plump, if scarcely placid, middle age, the novelists of the Angry Generation of the 1950s (the crude label seems indelible) were on parade in force in 1968. One novelist not to be included in this category was Iris Murdoch, "present" with a new novel in the roll call of every season's parades and, moreover, already elevated out of her generation (class of Amis and Wain) to the rank of "Modern Novelist," *tout court.* Her 11th novel, *The Nice and the Good,* was another hectic set in the game of pairings familiar to her readers—as improbable in skeleton as an opera buffa plot but given flesh with a wayward skill and fantasy thought by some almost Mozartian, though others found this an unnatural use of the novel form.

Of the Angries "proper," Kingsley Amis remained the natural leader. *I Want It Now,* the first "really Amisy" Amis since *Take a Girl Like You* (1960), as several reviewers pointed out, took a somewhat sordid "telly" intellectual and his world of make-it-quick, and through characteristic retchings and hilarities proceeded to "one of those mild reformations on both sides that makes Amis into a kind of contemporary Jane Austen," as Malcolm Bradbury put it in the *New Statesman.* Robert Nye, however, thought that Amis had done this turn before, "and though the doing gets cleverer all the time, it still stinks of sentimentality, like a rake's conversion." John Braine's *The Crying Game* attacked a similar world in a not dissimilar way, but less acutely; and David Knight,

Cecil Day-Lewis, the new poet laureate of Great Britain, succeeded John Masefield who died in 1967.

in *The Man Who Invented Tomorrow,* produced the most subtle and penetrating of several attempts to get under the skin of "television man."

Alan Sillitoe, in *Guzman, Go Home,* his new book of stories, was thought better on home than foreign ground, the latter seeming always to tempt him to overwrought effects. Stanley Middleton—among the provincial realist tradition's most assured and substantial writers—gave us *The Golden Evening,* a study of a family at breaking point as the mother lies dying; his book was rightly praised for its "exact emotional honesty." Philip Callow's *Going to the Moon,* rather too much of a baggy monster for some critics, was, nevertheless, one of the richest re-creations of a working-class boyhood since Lawrence.

Among other novelists of roughly the same generation, Brian Moore notably consolidated his achievement with *I Am Mary Dunne,* a painful, harshly funny account of a day of self-discovery in the life of a much-married Canadian in New York City. Mordecai Richler (who, settling in London, made some return for Moore's emigration to Canada) in *Cocksure* satirically attacked contemporary horrors. Everything was there: the corruption of liberal institutions and standards, racial prejudice and racial paranoia, organ transplants, and, above all, the prevalent "sex-in-the-head" disease and the strenuous self-deception it involves. Critical reaction divided fairly smartly between those who thought it a Good Thing, and the rest, who found it too ambiguously much of a good thing. A native satirist, Michael Frayn, projected some of the same horrors into a fairy tale of the future, *A Very Private Life*—a modest but intelligent fantasy-to-some-purpose which the *Times Literary Supplement* reviewer thought should be placed beside Orwell's *Animal Farm.*

Simon Raven continued as most gifted of the small group of dandies (still youngish) who in the 1950s had defended an outpost or two against the provincial eruption. *The Judas Boy,* continuing his "Alms for Oblivion" chronicle in a series of attractions and repulsions, confirmed more than one reviewer in the opinion that Raven remained "about the pick of all the writers content . . . to be unextended." *The Indian Summer of Gabriel Murray* by Hugh Charteris, another bright descendant of Evelyn Waugh, was much admired by Malcolm Muggeridge, though some thought its social fantasy a little overextended. Waugh's most direct descendant, Auberon Waugh, produced in *Consider the Lilies* a cruel, sometimes comic assault on the confusions of liberal Anglicanism. Julian Mitchell's serious and complex novel of a novel within a novel, *The Undiscovered Country,* was treated with more general critical respect.

To return to the long-distance cyclists: *The Sleep of Reason,* penultimate installment (we are told) of C. P. Snow's "Strangers and Brothers" sequence, was

not among its most compelling, despite intriguing autobiographical traces. Lawrence Durrell, from the silence following his *Alexandria Quartet* (1957–60), returned with *Tunc,* first part of a duo; set in Athens, Istanbul, and London, it glittered with the richest local colour, the boldest allegory, the loftiest speculations on the largest subjects. Some thought these were old games tiresome before the end of *Clea* (1960); others were willing to suspend judgment until the promised *Nunquam* shows how it will all turn out. There was, perhaps, more genuine respect for *Views from a Lake,* book iv of Philip Toynbee's waywardly clever, idiosyncratic novel in verse; and for J. B. Priestley's *Out of Town,* first shot of *The Image Men,* a two-barreled assault on various kinds of modern conmanship. Here, Priestley recovered his robust old form; and the second part, *London End,* following before the end of the year, was thought by many even better. There was approval, too, for the solid, sensitive realization of a past world in *The Day of the Scorpion,* vol. ii of Paul Scott's large-scale work about the end of the British raj. But the sequence no one would willingly have missed, to judge by the chorus of affectionate praise that greeted it, was the ninth movement of Anthony Powell's "Dance to the Music of Time," *The Military Philosophers.* It was a prime example of this delectably serious comedy, phrased so discreetly, in a style that has, as Norman Shrapnel observed, "the echoes, hesitations, and evasions of real speech and thought."

Several established women writers published new books. Muriel Spark followed *Collected Stories* with *The Public Image,* a story stretched into a short novel, with the familiar whiff of brimstone rising like smoke about the willful games. Elizabeth Taylor's *The Wedding Group* was another of her deceptively mild moral tales. Edna O'Brien with *The Love Object,* Christina Stead with *The Puzzleheaded Girl,* and Jean Rhys with *Tigers Are Better Looking* strengthened their reviving reputations.

Melvyn Bragg's *Without a City Wall,* W. J. Weatherby's *One of Our Priests Is Missing,* Rosemary Tonks's *The Bloater,* and Piers Paul Read's *The Junkers* all showed advance in skill and depth over first novels; and there were five interesting newcomers. Walter Hamilton's fable *All the Little Animals* and Lois Lang-Sims's disturbing romance *A Contrite Heart* had the look of things that might prove unrepeatable. Others showed more than promise. Paul Strathern's *Pass by the Sea,* for all its debt to Malcolm Lowry, was the work of a gifted, serious writer; P. J. Kavanagh's first novel, *A Song and Dance,* translated into fiction the unusual yea-saying talents admired in his poems and his essay in autobiography (1966); and Barry England, in *Figures in a Landscape,* produced a novel of such assurance and accomplishment that many found it hard to believe that it was indeed his first.   (W. L. WE.)

Poetry. Though 1968 failed to produce any outstanding new talent (much less anyone who could be hailed as a "discovery"), the variety, depth, and development of work by poets with established reputations made it a satisfying year for serious readers of verse.

Stewart Conn's *Stoats in Sunlight,* Maureen Duffy's *Lyrics for the Dog Hour,* and Norman Jackson's *Beyond the Habit of Sense* were among first volumes that attracted attention. Although Conn seemed to be working much the same vein of violence as Ted Hughes, his celebration of his native Scottish land-

Kingsley Amis (left) published a collection of poetry, "A Look Round the Estate," and a novel, "I Want It Now." Other poetry collections were published by Edwin Morgan (centre), his first, "The Second Life," and by Charles Causley (right), "Underneath the Water."

MARK GERSON

Roy Fuller, recipient of the 1968 Duff Memorial Prize, elected professor of poetry at Oxford on Nov. 23, 1968.

scape and traditions, character sketches of northern eccentrics, and way of observing life enabled him to achieve a distinctive style. Miss Duffy's reflections on a literary pilgrimage to Dublin made less impact than her love poems, addressed to women. Jackson (poet-in-residence at Keele University), more concerned with ideas and attitudes, showed that he was a poet of intelligence and honesty, even if inclined to let his poems slip out of control.

Easily the most impressive first collection, however, was Edwin Morgan's *The Second Life*, though its author, a leading exponent of Concretism, could not be called a "new poet": his work had been appearing in magazines for some years. This elegant volume, the first in Britain to be typeset by computer, contained Concrete poems on fawn paper and conventional free verse on white. At his best, as in "Message Clear" and "Starryveldt," Morgan contrived ingenious and witty structures going far beyond the wordplay and expressionistic typography associated with Concrete poetry; in more orthodox style, he wrote fine poems on space travel, Marilyn Monroe, and life in Glasgow.

The year was notable for good, somewhat unused anthologies: among them *Music and Sweet Poetry*, poems about music, selected by John Bishop; *Without Adam: The Femina Anthology of Poetry*, poems by women, edited by Joan Murray Simpson; and *Poems from Hospital*, collected by Jean and Howard Sergeant, which portrayed the hospital as not only a mirror of human emotions but an embodiment of life itself. *Poetry from Africa*, also edited by Sergeant, featured the work of Gabriel Okara (Nigeria), Gaston Bart-Williams (Sierra Leone), Kwesi Brew (Ghana), and David Rubadiri (Malawi).

With *Underneath the Water*, Charles Causley substantially increased his reputation for delight in language and liveliness in approach to such varied subjects as childhood in Cornwall, treatment in hospital, life as a teacher, and wartime experiences in the Navy. Equally competent but more restricted in range was Dannie Abse's *A Small Desperation*, which threw new light on the suburban scene. In *A Look Round the Estate*, Kingsley Amis took readers on a personally conducted tour. Adrian Mitchell indulged his warm-hearted humanitarianism, perhaps a little too indignantly, in his collection of poems for speaking, *Out Loud*; and George MacBeth again demonstrated his virtuosity in *The Night of Stones*. But the year's most accomplished volume was Roy Fuller's *New Poems*: experimenting with new ideas and forms,

Fuller confirmed his reputation as one of the finest poets currently writing in Britain. Also worth attention were Edward Brathwaite's second collection, *Masks*; Tony Connor's *Kon in Springtime*; Richard Murphy's *The Battle of Aughrim*; D. J. Enright's *Unlawful Assembly*; Zulfikar Ghose's *Jets from Orange*; Muriel Spark's *Collected Poems*, vol. i; and an anthology edited by Rodney Hall and Thomas Shapcott, *New Impulses in Australian Poetry*.

Poets were in the news, with the announcement on January 1, after seven months' speculation, that Cecil Day-Lewis had succeeded John Masefield as poet laureate (*see* BIOGRAPHY), and the usual tussle for the chair of poetry at Oxford, unexpectedly vacated in the summer by Edmund Blunden. After a slow start, nominations came fast, and Kathleen Raine (an early nominee) was joined by (among others) Roy Fuller, Enid Starkie, and Evgeni Yevtushenko. Fuller, with 385 votes, obtained the post.   (Ho. S.)

FRENCH

Nonfiction. The events of May–June 1968 were a serious blow to publishing in France. "Regular" nonfiction was the first victim because, when they reopened, all publishers gave rush priority to accounts of the disorders. Four such topical books, by experienced writers, were well received by critics. In *La Révolution introuvable*, R. Aron tried to produce a "deconsecration of the delirium." His essay was ironical and at the same time anguished, and in its breadth of vision it deserved to be compared to the thought of de Tocqueville. *La Mort d'une révolution* by J. Ferniot was a critical history of the crisis by a great journalist who lamented the ideological bankruptcy of the left. *Le Pape est mort* by J. Cau was a devastating satire on the events. *L'Avenir en désarroi* by M. Druon expressed tragic unease. These four books long remained on best-seller lists.

Less heated works did, of course, appear. Among biographies, *Molière génial et familier* by G. Bordonove was outstanding. The monumental length of this readable study prevented it from reaching, widely, a public preoccupied with politics. Taking account of all that is known about Molière, Bordonove also discovered new aspects of the actor's troubled life in the literary, social, and religious world of 17th-century France. Of even greater length (1,000 pages), A. Castelot's *Napoléon* (complementing his *Bonaparte*) was an objective and easily understood work that followed the emperor through the stages of his career—from cabaret to château, from coronation to death.

Several titles had a more contemporary flavour. Hardly had M. Butor published *Répertoire III* (a collection of criticism) and *Essais sur les "Essais"* (essays on the *Essays* of Montaigne) than a new study of Butor himself appeared, by G. Raillard. Its biographical element was particularly fascinating because, contrary to current fashion, Butor had revealed nothing of his life in his works. His life was here examined in relation to his work, from the first poems to the novels and then the essays; and the study as a whole was at times brilliant, sometimes obscure, but always subtle. Paul Morand, who had at last been elected to the French Academy, published *Monplaisir*, consisting of literary reflections in a very different style: the most eclectic taste, covering the 16th century to the present day, was expressed in his own precise and robust manner. In *Le Monde est intérieur*, Pierre Emmanuel, also a new member of

the Academy, affirmed his faith in the supremacy of spiritual things and revealed his fervour in his meditations on d'Aubigné, Villon, and Péguy. A similar trend of thought was found in *Vers l'invisible,* a journal in which J. Green carried on the struggle between grace and sin—an enriching spiritual quest in which a trace of narcissism could be found. At the opposite pole from these two writers, M. Jouhandeau continued, in his *Journaliers,* the story of his marital entanglements—with particular ferocity—in *Le Gourdin d'Élise.* F. Marceau, a novelist who had become an outstanding playwright, in *Les Années courtes* revealed secrets of his childhood and youth, of the maturing of his work, and of the emergence of an unostentatious personality. This engaging autobiography was marked with the gift for understatement, spiced with the humour, of his plays.

Yambo Ouologuem, a writer from Mali, who won the 1968 Prix Renaudot for "Le Devoir de violence."

Fiction. Until age 70 ignored by the public despite four works of considerable quality, A. Cohen suddenly achieved success with his fifth, *Belle du seigneur.* Awarded the Grand Prix du Roman by the French Academy, this swarming, torrential novel of appalling density opened with a satire on the League of Nations and of Genevan society before 1939, but soon turned to the Jew Solal, who experiences, with a Frenchwoman, the most romantic of love affairs: carried away by their passion or torn by jealousy, they advance toward death. The excesses and the implausible details were acceptable, thanks to the power of the style. Something of the same uninhibited romanticism was found in *Mélusine,* a first novel by M. Dard, which was greatly admired by the critics. It was soon followed by *Années profondes,* in which all-powerful love was extolled by a writer who is a thinker and a scholar.

The Prix Goncourt and the Prix de la Ville de Paris were both awarded to the peasant novel, represented by B. Clavel: with *Les Fruits de l'hiver* he completed the series "La Grande Patience." Writing about the people without sentimentality, Clavel offered a partly autobiographical panorama of rural life in which minute everyday details illuminated the inmost being of his characters. Much more strictly autobiographical was F. Nourissier's *Le Maître de maison,* the story of the purchase and furnishing of an old Provençal cottage, told partly as the author experienced it and partly through the eyes of the estate agent. This description of the joys and sorrows of a man and a house was valued chiefly for the extreme facility of the writing. J. Giono, painter of the Mediterranean world, produced in *Ennemonde et autres caractères* a pure, brief masterpiece, bursting with the life of primitive but attractive characters isolated in the Provençal soil, where light and animals are as important as men.

Simone de Beauvoir published *La Femme rompue,* depicting the pain suffered by a betrayed woman. Other subtle psychological studies were *L'Été d'une vie* by Andrée Martinerie, in which a woman confronts the difficulties of the growing up of her children, and *Les Choses de la vie* by P. Guimard, conveying the semiconscious thoughts of a man dying after a car accident.

A number of novelists explored religious themes: for example, Luc Estang in *L'Apostat,* a fictional biography of the Emperor Julian; J. Sulivan in his short-story collection *Bonheur des rebelles;* R. Bésus in *Le Maître* (the last two could be compared to Bernanos); and G. Cesbron in *C'est Mozart qu'on assassine* (although here the moral and social themes

Simone de Beauvoir, whose novel "La Femme rompue" was published in 1967.

were more important). Others dealt on the highest level with problems of conscience. In order to serve a great cause, should one disobey orders in a career in which discipline is a major virtue? This question confronts the hero of Louis Casamayor's *La Désobéissance,* set in France in 1940. A similar problem, also treated in a masterly fashion, was at the centre of G. Buis' *La Barque,* which takes place in Lebanon during the same period. And the Prix Médicis was awarded to Elie Wiesel for *Mendiant de Jérusalem,* a testimony of the Jewish soul, inspired by the six-day war of 1967: the author implanted the oldest traditions of his religion upon present-day events.

In satire, R. Peyrefitte's *Les Américains* remained at the top of best-seller lists despite a systematic campaign of denigration. Although overextended, the novel had a farcical side that was amusing. This element also appeared, though more subtly (and again with reference to the Americans), in R. Merle's *Un Animal doué de raison.* F. Sagan's *Le Garde du coeur,* set in Hollywood, was similarly comic, with a light macabre touch. Geneviève Dormann's *La Passion selon Saint Jules* described the antics of a most ludicrous Parisian family—a family related to those portrayed by Christine de Rivoyre in *Le Petit Matin* (awarded the Prix Interallié), about a young French girl who is the mistress of a German officer.

In *L'Oeuvre au noir,* Marguerite Yourcenar painted a panorama of 16th-century Flanders, swarming with characters and facts and centring on Zénon, a fictitious hero who is an apprentice alchemist and, as the contemporary of Paracelsus and Copernicus, is deeply troubled by freedom of thought. This scholarly work was awarded the Prix Fémina. Another woman writer, Françoise Mallet-Joris, was also attracted by Flanders and witchcraft: *Trois Âges de la nuit* retold authentic stories in a forceful, concise style.

Outstanding among first novels was *La Petite Marche du Télengana* by M. Larneuil. Presenting an English journalist in India as the central character, the author told the tale with as much penetration, economy, and reserve as E. M. Forster (*A Passage to India*). Quite different was *Le Devoir de violence* by a writer from Mali, Y. Ouologuem. Bursting with life, sexuality, humour, and horror, this book, which was awarded the Prix Renaudot, differed from others by erstwhile colonials in that it attacked with savage force both black and white.

Since Céline, and in the genre created by him, no young writer had caused so powerful a stir as D. Apruz with *La Baleine:* shocking, vulgar, and derisive, it mingled delirious lyricism with the crudest realism. In a similar picaresque vein, *Max et les ferrailleurs* by C. Néron enchanted those who understood the argot, introducing them to the life of a small gang in the Parisian suburbs.

La Rose de sable, which H. Montherlant wrote more than 30 years earlier but withheld from publication until 1968, was one of the outstanding works of the season—indeed, of the age. Set in Morocco, it had two main characters: a lieutenant who is moved by certain ideals, but who allows himself to be made a fool of and ends by being killed; and a painter, a proudly cynical modern Don Juan. The novel contained implicit but subtle criticism of the colonial system, and the love story was told with polished eroticism. Throughout, there was deep feeling for humanity and its contrasts—Arab with European—together with descriptions of haunting beauty.

Inspired by Algeria, Jules Roy published two monu-

"PARIS MATCH" FROM PICTORIAL PARADE

Françoise Sagan discussing her latest work, "Le Garde du coeur," during a 1968 press interview.

mental historical novels, *Les Chevaux du soleil* and *Une Femme au nom d'Étoile;* they were well received by critics and public alike. Another historical novel was *Le Cahier,* in which Henri Troyat, telling the story through the eyes of a serf, evoked Russia at the time of Alexander II. Other experienced writers demonstrated the continuing strength of their talent: in *Jardin sans murs,* M. Genevoix described his wondrous memories of childhood gardens; with *Le Temps d'aimer,* P. Hériat completed his series on the Boussardel, a Parisian upper-middle-class family, ending in the town of Aix; and H. Bazin in *Le Matrimoine* used a more ordinary middle-class setting for a savage analysis of how a married man is devoured by his wife.

The French literary world in 1968 mourned the deaths of J. Schlumberger and J. Paulhan. (*See* Obituaries.)

Poetry. The most striking collection of poems was *E* by J. Roubaud, a first-rate mathematician as well as a scholar. His poems crystallized around mathematical signs, the moves in the Japanese game of Go, or an extract from *Encyclopædia Britannica.* Despite this somewhat artificial technique, certain passages were clearly the work of a born poet, the heir of Cummings and Mallarmé.

Marc Alyn's *La Nuit majeure* expressed the disintegration of the dark side of the soul in poetry whose obscurity often disguised its magnificent lyricism. A. Bosquet's *Quatre Testaments et autres poèmes* contained all his poetic work, supported by "testaments" reflecting research into existential problems. Denis Roche in *Eros énergumène* (a tag from Valéry) wrote strangely fragmented poetry that was difficult to understand. L. Foucher's *Argyne et les Gypaètes,* third part of a trilogy, confirmed his taste for fantasy and eroticism. Easier to understand, *Feux contre feux* by Armel Lubin expressed the arguments of a man against the pain that is leading him to death.

R. Queneau continued to offer bantering, rhythmical, lucid outpourings in *Battre la campagne,* peopled with a gamekeeper and animals reminiscent of La Fontaine's. G. Puel's *La Lumière du jour* reflected the brilliance of the southern sun. *Poésiepures* and *Quelconqueries* by J. Berthet enchanted readers both by their vivacity and by their melancholy humour reminiscent of Verlaine. In *De Lumière et de nuit,* C. Fourcade achieved a charming clarity in classical poetry—like that of F. Millepierres in *Cheval noir et cheval blanc,* with its firm, agreeable rhythms. J. Bancal's *L'Épreuve du feu* fervently expressed his Roman Catholic faith.

In the important collection *Poètes d'aujourd'hui,*

J. Follain introduced the recently dead P. Albert-Birot, author of *Grabinoulor.* The editor emphasized the "linguistic ardour" of this friend of Apollinaire. In the same series J. de La Ville de Mirmont, author of *L'Horizon chimérique,* who died in battle in the flower of a youth obsessed with dreams and hopes, was recalled by M. Suffren. P. Seghers, publisher of this collection, had agreed to appear in it, and himself introduced his work and his life as a struggling, politically engaged poet. (Ae. B.)

GERMAN

Despite continued failure to produce the long-awaited great work, and, in 1968, lack of any exceptional or even exciting new writing, German literature had still not reached a point of stagnation or crisis. For this some younger novelists were mainly responsible.

Among them was Hubert Fichte, with *Die Palette.* Its focal point is a Hamburg beer cellar, meeting place of a group of social outcasts, all more or less perverts, presented as the unfortunate end products of a perverted society. Though their behaviour is brutal, and their outlook seems wholly cynical, they long for love—for which, however, they are as unready as for any other aspect of adult life: no longer boys, they remain, in their inability to take hold of life, essentially adolescents. Their sullen retreat into an underworld symbolized by the beer cellar in the heart of the big city is not so much a protest against society as it is a flight, resolving nothing and achieving only greater suffering for themselves. In a novel made up of disconnected scenes and episodes—the technique of the snapshot, not the film sequence—and of scraps of conversation interspersed with random observations, Fichte's prose ranged from a style plain to the point of brusqueness to one of masterly virtuosity.

Rolf Dieter Brinkmann's *Keiner weiss mehr* was another critical and psychological analysis of society. Superficially the story of the crisis point of marriage, it unfolds as a portrait of the young intellectual whose insecurity, disorganization, impatience, and fatigue all have their origin in his inability to understand or cope with his own sexual impulses. He struggles to control his animal nature: it ends up controlling him. Brinkmann showed unusual ability to infuse life into inanimate objects, so giving them their own place in the action. This feature of his narrative style was particularly apparent in his description of the power of the material world (symbolized by the life of a big West German city) to create a tension between the alternating poles of horrified aversion and fascination.

Concentration on one character also distinguished Horst Bienek's novel *Die Zelle.* In it an elderly man, deported from East Berlin in 1951 for political reasons and already having spent some years in solitary confinement, broods on his own character and his sufferings. The author sought to create from the multitudinous confusion of the old man's memories and dreams a psychological portrait of a particular personality, against a critical analysis of the contemporary background and, at the same time, to provide a parable for our times. Bienek failed because his treatment, falling short of the potential greatness of his theme, declined into sentimentality and a fatal tendency to be poetic in approach and style.

A young Hungarian, Mario Szenessy, who had lived in West Germany since 1964 and wrote in German, made a notable contribution to the novel of Germany with *Verwandlungskünste.* Against a variety of settings

in the Hungary of 1942–56, it dealt with the sufferings of those who, by intention or through circumstance, are drawn into the whirlpool of politics. Made up of several different shorter forms—stories and parables, set pieces exemplifying particular genres, and informal sketches—the novel yet achieved unusual unity by its treatment and style, which blended the realistic with the fantastic, and sobriety and clarity with an unusually poetic vision.

Of established older writers the only one to publish a new novel in 1968 was Hans Erich Nossack. In *Fall d'Arthez* he tells the farcical story of a painter who, turning his back on society, is suspected—wrongly—by the police of being a member of a dangerous international organization. Nossack's view of life, obscured by romantic images, is distorted into oversimplification of character and events, presented as either wholly black or wholly white. But in the sketches and single episodes in the second part of the book, this writer of unusual talent revealed once more his deep insight into human nature and his acute powers of observation.

Farce of a very different kind was seen in *Maulwürfe,* a small collection of the first prose writings by the outstanding lyric poet Günter Eich. They were essentially a poet's work: jottings of impressions caught on the wing, marginalia made in passing, at their best embodying Eich's lightly expressed wisdom and regal powers of lamentation, his serenity in sorrow, and his essential sensitiveness to the comic. Many of the pieces taken as a whole, however, maintained precariously a vigorous, somewhat forced gaiety that threatened to topple over into absurdity; and the way he strained to drive each joke home, to make every point plain, and his constant puns and wordplay seemed more the result of a painful exercise than the natural overflow of high spirits. His flights of fancy were too anxious to please, too deliberate, to be convincing: Eich here allowed his imagination too free a rein and so evaded responsibility.

A more ambitious prose was that of Jürgen Becker's *Ränder,* which aimed at interpreting contemporary consciousness. He restricted himself to diary entries and annotations lyrical in style, of which the most surprising feature was a consistent use of the idioms of everyday speech. It became clear that his prose belonged less to the future than to the German avant-garde of the early 1960s.

Like 1967, the year brought worthwhile collections of short stories by younger writers: *Ländliches Fest,* Gabriele Wohmann's crisp new collection; *Fremdkörper* by the Swiss Adolf Muschg, collected stories of a pleasing elegance, in which humour put events into their proper perspective; and Reinhard Lettau's *Feinde,* in which the grotesque was used to express his strong antimilitarism and intensified the reality at the heart of the fantastic in order to reveal its absurdity. The year's outstanding work in short prose forms, however, proved to be Günter Kunert's collection *Die Beerdigung findet in aller Stille stadt.* Kunert, an East Berliner best known as a lyric poet, had, however, already shown himself to be a master of the ironic short story and the parable.

In drama the outstanding event was the Swiss Max Frisch's new play, *Biografie: Ein Spiel,* in which a Swiss scientist, given the chance to live his life over again, in doing so only succeeds, despite all his efforts to correct his mistakes, in making two comparatively minor changes. Though lacking in any great depth, this was an unusually attractive and amusing play

Poet Günter Eich, whose "Maulwürfe," his first collection of prose, appeared in 1968.

that reached its height in some brilliantly written erotic scenes. Martin Walser's duologue *Die Zimmerschlacht,* on the other hand, was a disappointing mixture of elements very dissimilar in quality, ranging from subtle psychological drama that, after a good beginning, failed to develop to a primitive form of slapstick farce full of the jokes and catchwords of a group of close friends. More interest was aroused by *Kaspar,* a radical, extremely experimental play by the young Austrian Peter Handke, in which the only character to appear on stage is constantly hectored and threatened by the voices of four unseen protagonists.

Among many diaries, recollections, and more or less informal collected reflections, mainly from older writers, two deserve special mention: Marie Luise Kaschnitz' *Tage, Tage, Jahre,* a diary both profound and witty; and *Die Stimmen von Marrakesch* by Elias Canetti, a Londoner by adoption.

(M. R.-R.)

ITALIAN

Prose writing in 1968 ranged from old-fashioned storytelling to nonrepresentational avant-garde experiment. At the more traditional end came vol. iii of *L'autobiografia di Giuliano di Sansevero* by Andrea Giovene, which seemed like yet another attempt to fill the gap caused by the scarcity of great Italian 19th-century novels. Roberto Ridolfi's *I ghiribizzi* and Tommaso Landolfi's *Un paniere di chiocciole,* collections of literary essays and divertissements first published in newspapers, contained perfect examples of *elzeviri* (a kind of occasional essay), a genre very fashionable in the 1930s. Some "new" books were only apparently new. Thus, the title story of Luigi Incoronato's *Le pareti bianche* appeared posthumously, with a reissue of his first novel, *Scala a San Potito* (1950). Also a reissue was Goffredo Parise's *La grande vacanza,* which reads like a kind of *Alice in Wonderland,* but without the funny bits, and of which only 38 copies were sold when it was first published in 1953—a good reason, one might think, for not reprinting it. Better, but still dated, was *Racconto militare,* a revised edition of a story by Alessandro Bonsanti first published in 1937. Some well-known novelists could be relied upon to produce annually examples of their standard work: from Carlo Cassola came another colourless novel in which scarcely anything happens, *Ferrovia locale;* and Italo Calvino brought back from the space-time continuum of 1965's *Le cosmicomiche* his hero Qfwfq to tell more weird tales in *Ti con zero.* Echoes of science fiction with a keen sense of the absurd and uncanny could be heard too in Giovanni Arpino's short stories in *La babbuina.* Carlo Monterosso tried the detective story, a genre not favoured by Italian writers, but his attempt to combine judicial inquiry with moral satire, in *Il caso T.,* was unconvincing. In *La cupidigia,* a robust satirical tale in an archaic setting, Armando Meoni drew a parable of modern revolution. Anna Maria Ortese delicately poised her stories in *La luna sul muro* between pathos and bathos, lyricism and realism. A promising first novel was *La poltrona,* in which Carlo Sgorlon etched with acid humour the life of a middle-aged teacher trapped in his bed-sitting-room by his own foibles and fears.

Modern neuroses also fascinated Giuseppe Cassieri, whose novel *Andare a Liverpool* was an unusual combination of the themes of brontophobia, psychoanalysis, incestuous sex, and linguistics. Indeed, writers seemed much preoccupied with sex, language, or both.

In Carlo Castellaneta's *Gli incantesimi,* sex heightens the protagonist's perceptive and imaginative powers: through focusing his desires on his mysterious and elusive mistress, he relives experiences or conjures up new ones by projecting himself as a protagonist into past events. Sex was placed in wider perspective in Alberto Bevilacqua's *L'occhio del gatto,* in which echoes of distant wars and blind violence counterpointed a tale of conjugal dissension and mental cruelty. Language ran riot in Vittorio Sermonti's *Novella storica,* strongly influenced by Carlo Emilio Gadda, but at least it here took recognizable forms. Gaetano Testa, however, succeeded in writing a "novel," *Cinque,* beyond the grasp of grammarians, semanticists—or reviewers. Perhaps the most successful attempt to use a mastery of language and understanding of sexual life to expand artistic resources was Fabrizio Onofri's *In nome del padre,* superficially the story of the meeting at the seaside of a middle-aged intellectual and a young girl, but on a deeper level the analysis of a man's psychic continuum from conscious to subliminal self.

Some works belonged to more than one genre. Pier Paolo Pasolini's *Teorema* was the somewhat naïve translation into literary terms of his film of the same title: the longish fragments of bad verse between the prose scenes made the whole affair seem rather futile and pretentious. Elsa Morante combined prose, verse, and comedy in a hybrid full of humour and humanity, *Il mondo salvato dai ragazzini.* Ignazio Silone told, in a book half-essay, half-drama, *L'avventura d'un povero cristiano,* the story of the resignation from the papacy of Celestine V; Silone's religious and social vision, however, was not matched by equally high literary qualities.

In poetry, many of the year's notable offerings were reprints, with few additions, of previously published works. In *La luce ricorda,* Giorgio Vigolo collected most of his poems from 1923 onward. Sergio Solmi's *Dal balcone* contained verse written in the last 20 years. Aldo Palazzeschi's poems in *Cuor mio,* though recent, were reminiscent of his early work. Poets seemed on the whole more successful than prose writers in renewing their language without clouding its meaning. Giovanni Testori revitalized worn-out images in his forceful love poems in *L'amore,* as he had done in his earlier prose. Both Giuseppe Guglielmi in *Panglosse blandimentis oramentis coeteris meretriciis* and Andrea Zanzotto in *La beltà* founded their poetic inventiveness on free, etymological association, erudite quotation, linguistic borrowings, and literary pastiche, while remaining within the field of literary experience. Franco Fortini's poems in *Una volta per sempre,* on the other hand, made the reader aware of a world of extraliterary experience, not because they were political pamphlets or social tirades, but because they were good poems. Angela Giannitrapani's *Professione di poesia* resembled a newborn child, in all its fresh innocence brought forth with pain and love.

In the essay, Armanda Guiducci's outstanding *Il mito Pavese* contained both a penetrating analysis of Pavese and an exhaustive treatment of American influence on Italian literature and thought in the 1930s and '40s. Salvatore Battaglia studied, in *Mitografia del personaggio,* the evolution of the concept of protagonist; examples were drawn from the whole range of Western tradition. In *Semiotica ed estetica,* Emilio Garroni attempted to lay the foundation of a semeiology of cinema. A mixture of literary criticism, histori-cal document, essay, and creative writing, Stelio Crise's *Epiphanies e phadographs* gave a fascinating and imaginative account of James Joyce's impact on the intellectual life of Trieste and Italy.   (G. C.)

JEWISH

Hebrew. Literature in Israel in 1968 again demonstrated its vitality. Of intense topical interest were many volumes on the Arab-Israeli war of 1967. In this category, special note must be made of *Hasufim ba-tsariah* ("Exposed in the Turret") by S. Tevet; *Yaldut Baah Ba-Esh* ("Children Under Fire"), edited by A. Kovner; and *Siah Lohamin* ("Soldiers' Talk"), collected by A. Shapiro.

The complete works, in 12 volumes, of a leading elder novelist, H. Hazaz, were published. Old Jerusalem was recreated in E. Hamenahem's *Sippurai ha-Ir Haatika* ("Stories of the Old City") and Y. Haezrahi's *Ir Ewen ve-Shamaim* ("City of Stone and Sky"). A. B. Yehoshua's *Mul ha-Yearot* (translated by the author as "Over Against the Woods") and *Michael Sheli* ("My Michael") by Amos Oz were books by young novelists who won increased attention. Y. Oren's nightmarish stories and *Nemalim* ("Ants") by Y. Orpaz were noteworthy. Charming evocations of the past were *Bain ha-Armon veha-Lilah* ("Between the Chestnut Tree and the Lilacs") by Y. Kesheth and *Ad Sof ha-Kayitz ha-Indiani* ("To the End of Indian Summer") by N. Yonatan. Mati Meged's *Yomo ha-Aharon Shel Dany* ("Danny's Last Day") was a stirring war story.

Sh. Kremer's *ha-Realism U-Shevirato* ("Realism and Its Decline"), E. Shavid's *ha-Erga le-Melaut ha-Havaya* ("The Longing for Fulfillment"), and the late M. Tuchner's *Pesher Agnon* ("The Meaning of Agnon") were incisive volumes of literary criticism. Of some interest were A. Ukhmani's and G. Katzenelson's studies, as well as the late Z. Woislawski's essays in *Rishonot ve-Acharonot* ("The Early and the Late"). A. Bendavid's disquisitions on the styles employed in the Bible and the writings of the Sages were enlightening, and Y. Avineri contributed a fine volume on lexicography.

Shirai Levi Ibn Altabban was a historic-literary evaluation by D. Pagis of the poems of a medieval Hebrew poet. A. Shlonsky's *Mishiai ha-Perozdor ha-Aroch* ("From the Poems of the Long Corridor") was the fully matured work of an older poet. *Lichtov Siftai Yeshainim* ("To Write from the Lips of the Sleepers") was A. Gilboa's volume. Different in manner were H. Guri's *Tenua le-Maga* ("A Move to Touch") and A. Halfi's *Mivhar Shirimx* ("Selected Poems"). The dramatic *Ahot Ketana* ("Little Sister") by A. Kovner and the satirical *Massa Zafonah* ("Northward Journey") by B. Galai also appeared during the year.

In the U.S., Hebrew literature was at low ebb. Three volumes by authors living there were published: Sh. Federbush's *ha-Lashon ha-Ivrit be-Yisrael u-Vaamim* ("The Hebrew Language in Israel and Abroad"); *Hasipporet ha-Ivrit Mehapeset Gibbor* ("Hebrew Fiction in Search of a Hero") by Y. Rabinovich; and G. Preil's collection of poems, *ha-Esh veha-Demama* ("The Fire and the Silence").   (G. P.)

Yiddish. The second volume of *Reb Tsemakh Atlas* by Khayim Grade concluded this monumental novel, which portrayed a self-contained Jewish world of Eastern Europe in the prewar era. The hero, whose strivings and ideals suffer an ultimate defeat, symbolized a transitional period when the traditional foundations of Jewish life started to crumble. Grade's

novel was written in the lucid, precise manner of Jewish classical realism, whereas Leyb Rokhman's *With Blind Steps over the Earth* (all titles are given here in English translation) was Kafkaesque and surrealistic. The hero is in constant confrontation with the tragic legacy of the six million dead, who obsess his mind and prevent him from being his normal self.

Rokhman's novel was a new approach to a subject that had defied Yiddish fiction since the fateful years 1939–45. Other contributions to the field of fiction included Shloyme Bikl's chronicle *The Family Orchik;* ghetto stories by Rakhmiel Bryks and a promising newcomer, Volf Karmiol; lyrical narratives of new beginnings in the land of Israel by Shloyme Varzoger and Rikude Potash; and M. Tsanin's symbolic novel about the return of the "Wandering Jew."

Since World War II, poetry has dominated the field of creative Yiddish writing, and in 1968 all the great names of American-Yiddish poetry appeared in print —notably Yaykev Glatshteyn, Aron Tseytlin, Efroyim Oyerbakh, I. J. Shvarts, Itsik Manger, Eliezer Grinberg, Rokhl Korn, and the late A. Glants-Leyeles. The selections by Glatshteyn in *I Do Remember* and Tseytlin in *Poems of the Holocaust and Poems of Faith* constituted, each in its unique way, the poetic lament of a generation that saw more than a third of its people slaughtered. The Israeli group of poets included Malke Loker, Leyb Olitski, Avrom Lev, I. Manik, Binem Heler, Rivke Basman, and Abraham Sutzkever (whose *Square Letters and Miracles* revealed new facets of this great master of poetic image and association). The Soviet-Yiddish poets—Itsik Fefer, a victim of Stalinist purges, and two survivors, Zyame Telesin and Mendl Lifshits—represented a different poetic tradition. Close to their native Russian soil, they still managed to be warmly Jewish. The shrinking territory of Yiddish letters in Poland yielded two volumes of poetry, by Eliyohu Reyzman and the late P. Tsibulski, and a collection of stories by Kalman Segal. (D. Az.)

LATIN-AMERICAN

João Guimarães Rosa, who is to literature in Portuguese what James Joyce is to literature in the English language, died in November 1967. João Cabral de Melo Neto (Brazilian consul in Barcelona, Spain, in 1968), perhaps the greatest living Brazilian poet, published his "Complete Works."

The year 1968 was a good one for criticism in Brazil. Luiz Costa Lima wrote *Lira e Antilira,* essays on modern Brazilian poetry. In *Informação, Linguagem, Comunicação,* Décio Pignatari, poet and professor of the theory of communication, delved into the problem of vanguardist art and mass culture with the verve and imagination of a Marshall McLuhan of the tropics. Otto Maria Carpeaux, a naturalized Brazilian, celebrated his 25 years of literary endeavour in his adopted country by publishing a volume of his best essays.

Brazil boasts the emergence of a new generation of poets who are not, properly speaking, in the literary field but in that of popular music or art for the masses. These young poets, called *tropicalistas,* include Caetano Veloso, Gilberto Gil, Torquato Neto, and others. Their main idea is to carry over the text of vanguardist poetic experimentation into popular songs; and their selection of lyrics ranges from Oswald de Andrade to Concretism. Their concurrent goal is to attain a "universal sound" in music. The poet Augusto de Campos dedicated a book, *O balanço*

da Bossa, to this matter. His work was a serious study of the evolution of Brazilian popular music in its relation to the new poetry, from the *bossa nova* to the *tropicalista* movement.

An anthology of modern Russian poetry, compiled by Augusto and Haroldo de Campos in collaboration with Boris Schnaiderman, presented for the first time in the Portuguese language a panoramic view of Russian poetry from Symbolism to the most recent poets. The Poundian idea of a critical and creative translation was applied in this noteworthy effort. In the same vein, and also by the de Campos fraternity, was the anthology *Traduzir e Trovar,* dedicated to *il miglior fabbro* Ezra Pound; it contained versions of Provençal poets, Cavalcanti, Dante, English metaphysical poets, and the Italians of the Baroque.

In general, 1968 was not marked by the production of significant imaginative works in Spanish America. However, two of the best novels of the year before, *Cien años de soledad* by the Colombian Gabriel García Márquez and *Paradiso* by the Cuban José Lezama Lima, continued to enjoy unparalleled popularity, with numerous editions in Spanish and several foreign languages. These two works were in many ways a summation of the art of novelizing as evolved in Europe: *Cien años de soledad* was the masterful application of the "linear" narrative established by Miguel de Cervantes, and *Paradiso* was the best example in Spanish of the collage, acrostic, Baroque, stream-of-consciousness techniques of James Joyce. Lezama Lima applied Joyce's esoteric and lyrical treatment to the conjuration of a hermetic world consisting of himself and his national circumstance; thus, like Julio Cortázar in *Hopscotch,* the Cuban writer was catching up with the furthest reaches of the novel in English, a half century later.

The Latin-American Community of Writers together with *Ecuador 0°0'0",* a periodical devoted to world poetry, and in conjunction with Mexico's Cultural Olympics, offered a prize in poetry and also sponsored a festival of new Latin-American theatre. More than 800 poets in 15 Latin-American countries, Spain, the United States, and France participated. Octavio Amórtegui Rojas, a Colombian, won the 50,-000 (Mexican) peso prize. Amórtegui was affiliated with the group called *los nuevos.* His work, and that of 24 winners of honourable mention, was to be published. Of special note among the latter were the Guatemalan Otto Raúl González, with *Oratorio del maíz;* Mexico's Eduardo Lizalde, with *El tigre en la casa;* and Paraguay's Elvio Romero, with *Los innombrables.*

Mexico, usually a great producer of all kinds of literary material, was lacking in creative works in 1968. Significantly, Mexico's major productions recently had been in criticism and in cataloging. Aurora M. Ocampo de Gómez and Ernesto Prado Velázquez compiled a massive and indispensable work on Mexican writers from pre-Hispanic times to the present, *Diccionario de escritores mexicanos.* Emma Godoy wrote an excellent interpretation of José Gorostiza's "Muerte sin fin"; the compass she provided for navigation within this unique poem was its relationship to German idealism. This explanation of a great Mexican poem and the concurrent one relating Humberto Díaz Casanueva's "El Blasfemo Coronado" to Martin Heidegger's philosophy were signs of a radically different orientation in the assessment of the poetry of Spanish America; hitherto, the constant reference in Spanish-American letters, especially poetry, had been to France. Another book on Gorostiza was Emma

Godoy's *Sombras de Magia. Agua bajo el puente* by the novelist Mauricio Magdaleno was the other prose work from Mexico that deserves mention; it contained highly belletristic studies of the nefarious Antonio López de Santa Anna (self-styled "Serene Highness" and "Napoleon of the West"), Manuel Lozada (precursor of the famed Zapata), Federico Gamboa (Mexico's finest representative of naturalism), and others.

The centennial celebration of the birth of Rubén Darío (1867–1916) yielded thousands of articles and panegyrics throughout the Spanish-speaking world. *Rubén Darío y el Modernismo en España* by the Mexican Carlos Lozano easily ranked as the most scholarly, useful, and complete work on the influence of the Nicaraguan master who transformed literature in Spanish as no other writer before or since.

A welcome addition to the gathering throng of women now cultivating the novel in Spanish America was Argentina's Alicia Jurado. In *En soledad vivía* she made use of the botanical to amplify amorous situations in a manner reminiscent of W. H. Hudson's *Green Mansions*—though the locale was Buenos Aires, not the jungle. There was novelty, too, in her book: for the first time in a South American narrative of a liaison, the woman engages in unabashed voyeurism of the man's physical charms.

Manuel Mujica Láinez of Argentina brought out *Crónicas reales.* These "chronicles" were fantastic tales of "dynasties of the eternal, which is ancient and future world history."

The most abundant contribution to the Latin-American novel came from Chile. In *El compadre,* depicting the life of a drunken labourer, Carlos Droguett skillfully mingled memory, reality, and fantasy in stream-of-consciousness style to present a man caught in tragic circumstances that alienate him from his fellows. *El compadre* reaffirmed Droguett's place as one of Chile's best contemporary writers. Rodrigo Quijada and Rodrigo Baño, co-authors of *Tiempo de arañas,* had some fun at the expense of those who had thought they must be foreigners—for here they wrote convincingly about happenings in a native setting. The two male protagonists of the novel plunge into the jungle and are followed there by the woman of one of them, in a manner strongly reminiscent of José Eustasio Rivera's *La vorágine.* The style of these two novelists caused critics to compare them with Julio Cortázar, Mario Vargas Llosa, and Juan Rulfo, masters of the genre in Latin America.

Jorge Edwards' *El peso de la noche* was an abbreviated *Forsyte Saga* of a Chilean family. A suitable coda to the predominant Chilean production of the year was Nicanor Parra's *Canciones rusas,* in which the poet's barbed humour evinced a philosophical perspective and, perhaps, a degree of disenchantment that his earlier writings had not foreshadowed.

(J. F. V. A.)

NORWEGIAN

Outstanding in 1968's literary output in Norway was *Båten om kvelden* by Tarjei Vesaas, the leading writer of the older generation. A loosely linked collection of fragments presenting the key incidents and moods in a long life, it contained the quintessential Vesaas: subtle simplicity and visionary insight. The lyrical element was strong and two themes predominated: a feeling of close relationship between man and the animal world, and the essential solitude of the individual.

Among novelists, Odd Winger in *Nattegjest* treated, with considerable elegance, the theme of a grass wid-

ow's conquest by a gay Don Juan, whose reminiscences of past conquests counterpoint the story. In contrast, Karin Bang's *Blues* presented with stark, concentrated realism the twilight jazz world of young drug addicts from well-to-do homes. A promising newcomer, Kåre Prytz, told in *Jegernes kvinne* the story of a girl, sole survivor of the destruction by pirates of a medieval Norse settlement in Greenland, who falls in love with a young Eskimo; the author handled the clash of Norse and Eskimo values with insight and unusual command of language. Terje Stigen's *De tente lys* was an attempt at a medieval Norse "family saga," but its rambling, essentially trivial dialogue bore little relation to the taut, pithy saga style. Also medieval in setting was Alfred Hauge's *Legenden om Svein og Maria,* second part of a cycle centred in the Utstein monastery in southwestern Norway and stylistically much influenced by folktale and legend. In Hauge's opening volume, *Mysterium* (1967)—a somewhat uneasy blend of mysticism, Freud, and Jung—dreams had played a prominent part, and the narrative had been too often interrupted by the author's comments and reflections. Hauge also published in 1968 *Cleng Peerson: Utvandring,* a dramatization of his trilogy (1961–65); but its many short scenes, overloaded with action, conveyed little inner drama or psychological insight. Another recasting—of a radio play as a novel—was Finn Carling's *Tilfluktsrommet,* which failed because in the longer narrative version the claustrophobic intensity of the play's presentation of a group of people in an air-raid shelter was lost.

The 23-year-old Gunnar Lunde made his debut with an unusually mature collection of short stories, *Flukten fra en flukt,* combining a keen sense of the grotesque with a spare, tense style. Another first work, *Dyvekes grav,* by a dentist, Johan Fredrik Grøgaard, showed great promise in its keen sense of the humorous and generally showed considerable talent, as yet undisciplined.

Publication of Hallvard Lie's monumental scholarly study on Norwegian prosody, *Norsk verslære,* was an event of great importance to poetics. The central position achieved in Norwegian poetry by Arnulf Øverland (1889–1968) was confirmed by *De hundrede fioliner: Dikt i utvalg,* a representative and impressive selection from his works made by Øverland not long before his death (see OBITUARIES). Two "new poets" to publish collections were Tor Obrestad, whose *Vårt daglige brød* was a biting, ironic attack on modern materialism, and Arnljot Eggen, who in *Roller og røynd,* a survey of the contemporary scene, tempered his irony with humour.

Critical works included Edvard Beyer's *Utsyn over norsk litteratur,* a brief survey; Torbjørn Støverud's *Milestones of Norwegian Literature,* concentrating on key works; Harald Noreng's *Bjørnsons skuespill på svensk scene,* valuable for its comment on particular plays; Leif Longum's *Et speil for oss selv,* a thematic analysis of postwar Norwegian fiction; and Leif Mæhle's *Frå bygda til verda,* devoted to *nynorsk* 20th-century literature and containing detailed accounts of the poetry of Tore Ørjasæter (who died on February 29) and Aslaug Vaa. Vol. iii of the *Norsk litterær årbok,* an annual survey, mainly of contemporary Norwegian and other Scandinavian literature, as usual contained a comprehensive critical bibliography of the year's writings on Norwegian literature.

A contribution to contemporary history was *Operasjon Oleander,* Asbjørn Øksendal's detailed account of the often successful activities in the Trøndheim region

of Nazi agents provocateurs; although uneven in quality, the book contained chapters of great intensity. *London svarer ikke* by Sverre Midtskau, founder and first head of the Norwegian intelligence service in London during World War II, gave a thrilling, unusually well-written account of his wartime experiences. Aslaug Rein's *Kirsten Flagstad* was a full portrayal of the life, long career, and unassuming character of the great Norwegian mezzo-soprano.   (To. S.)

SOVIET

Increasing interest in translated Soviet literature in the West and such evidence of respect for Soviet writers as the nomination (October 1968) of Evgeni Yevtushenko for the chair of poetry at the University of Oxford and the discussion of Konstantin Paustovski's autobiography as "one of the great modern examples of the genre" (see *English,* above) make a survey of the Soviet literature almost as relevant for Western readers who must await translations as for those who can read Russian. (That titles are here given in English does not mean, however, that translations are available.)

Much of Soviet literature published in 1967–68 contributed to the celebration of the 50th anniversary of the Revolution (October 1917). In an outstanding novel, *Incidence Angle,* Vsevolod Kochetov presented the Red Army's campaign against the White Guard in 1919 as a death struggle between two opposing worlds; an interesting feature of his technique was the intermingling of history and fiction. V. Ardamataski's *Retribution* carried the story of the newborn U.S.S.R. into the 1920s, treating in fascinating detail and with full documentation the discovery and liquidation of an anti-Soviet political group; like Kochetov, he combined real and fictional people and situations. Further installments of work begun earlier had as subject the eve of the Revolution: the second part of vol. iii of D. Smirnov's "Discovery of the World" sequence and the third volume of the trilogy *Ordeals* by the Kazakh novelist Aleksei Nurpeisov.

Lenin again inspired creative as well as scholarly works. Two anthologies, *Poems About Lenin* and *V. I. Lenin,* collected a variety of works in his honour; the documentary novel *Tomorrow Will Be Too Late* by P. Kapitsa dealt with his part in preparing for the Revolution; and Marietta Shaginian continued her conducted tour through the byways of his life with *Lenin in the British Museum Reading Room.* Anthologies of verse with the Revolution as theme were *Soviet Poetry on the October Revolution* ("Library of Poets" series), which included more than 200 pieces by 120 authors of different nationalities, and *The Song That Became a Book,* poems translated into Russian from more than 40 languages of peoples incorporated into the U.S.S.R.

Vsevolod Kochetov, author of "Incidence Angle," a historical novel portraying the Red Army campaign against the White Guard in 1919.

NOVOSTI PRESS AGENCY

who before the Revolution had no written language. Collections by writers abroad, on the same subject, were *Comrades: October Is Enshrined in Bulgarian Hearts,* contemporary Bulgarian poetry and prose; and *Friends of the October Revolution and of Peace,* containing works by 60 modern writers of many nationalities and successive generations, together with reproductions of paintings; authors and artists represented included John Reed, Henri Barbusse, Rabindranath Tagore, Theodore Dreiser, Anna Seghers, Lu Shin, Louis Aragon, Bertolt Brecht, A. R. Williams, Pablo Neruda, and José Rivera. Among novels about the immediate postwar period were Vladimir Dimedov's impressive *The Last to Leave,* the story of a pyrotechnist working against time to remove mines, often from historic architectural monuments; and the Latvian E. Liv's *Devil's Mountain Ridge,* about life in German-occupied countries after their liberation.

Novels of contemporary Soviet life, in its spiritual and ethical rather than its material aspects, included D. Pavlova's outstanding *A Particular Case;* and, perhaps most interesting, several that continued a tendency previously discernible: descriptive analysis of the experiences and characters of men engaged in struggle against the elements, disease, or the complex world created by modern technology. Among novels of this kind were Vladimir Semenikhin's continuation, in *Stellar Variations,* of *Cosmonauts Live on the Earth* (1966); Andrei Perventsev's *Island of Hope,* showing sailors aboard atomic submarines grappling with a new art of navigation; Yuri Shovkoplya's *Man Lives Twice,* about a surgeon who performs complex organ transplants; and A. Tekemchuk's *Bare Continent,* the heroes of which are oil prospectors—a geologist, the regional party committee chairman, and a foreman—whose hard lives in the far north are made endurable by a sense of shared purpose. Another contemporary novel of a very different kind was the first large-scale work by the short-story writer I. Iroshnikova, who in *How Are You, Mrs. Katerina?* offered the moving story of two women whose lives are brought together by love for a child: when the real mother, from whom the child was separated in the concentration camp at Auschwitz, and the foster mother meet 20 years later they are faced with the question, "To which of us does she really 'belong'?" Another writer publishing his first work on a larger scale was Gyorgy Semenov, who in the long title story of the collection *Who Is He? Whence Comes He?* portrayed with idealistic realism the everyday life of a keen young flier. *Kaleidoscope,* a collection by the Moldavian writer E. Bukov, presented a medley of impressions and sketches that included satiric portraits of bureaucrats, sycophants, and arrogant local authorities, as well as love stories in a poetic style. Eduard Vilks, a Latvian master of the short story, in *Tales, 1955–65* (1968), collected stories

Evgeni Yevtushenko, a nominee in 1968 for the Oxford professorship of poetry, reading his new poetry at a Pushkin poetry recital.

NOVOSTI PRESS AGENCY

of contemporary life that were notable for freshness and sincerity. A new writer, Vasilii Belov, attracted attention with his story "The Usual Thing," later included in *Beyond the Third Haulage*, a collection treating with originality the familiar themes of love of nature, homeland, and fellow countrymen. In Vasilii Ivanov's collection *The Empress Fike*, each story has its basis in a crucial event of Russian 16th-, 17th-, or 18th-century history. Vera Panova's latest play, *Trediakovski and Volynski*, was also historical, the main characters being the Empress Anna Ivanovna, the scholar-poet Trediakovski, the Cabinet minister Volynski, and the empress' powerful favourite, Biron.

Poetry included A. Tvardovski's *Selected Lyrics, 1959–67; Horseshoe* by A. Mezhov, known for wartime poetry but here treating the more positive themes of life, love, and happiness; and Robert Rozhdestvenski's *Poem from Various Points of View*, reaffirming life's essential beauty and ultimate value. New poems by Yarlov Smelyakov (who won a state prize with *The Russian Day*, 1966), collectively entitled *December*, were published serially in the periodical *Friendship Between the Peoples* in 1967–68.

Regional autobiographical work continued to flourish, with the outstanding *My Daghistan* by the well-known poet Rasul Gamsatov, in which he made effective use of his expressive native folk idiom to give an account of Daghistan's life and of his own.

Interesting memoirs, autobiographies, and collections of letters were V. Inber's *Turning the Pages of the Day*, Paustovski's *Near and Far* (trans. 1969; the last volume of his autobiography), and the collected letters of Aleksandr Aleksandrovich Fadeev (1901–56).

One of the year's most important literary events, the centenary of the birth of Maksim Gorki (1868–1936), was celebrated with conferences of scholars in many of the cities where he had lived: Gorki, his birthplace, renamed in his honour in 1932; Kazan, where he lived as a young man; Leningrad (formerly St. Petersburg), where his first important story (*Chelkash*, 1895) appeared; and Moscow, where Soviet scholars were joined by many from abroad (including, from Britain, M. I. Budberg, Gorki's secretary) at the Gorki Institute of World Literature. Also in Moscow, the opening in March, at the A. M. Gorki Museum, of a big new exhibition was attended by foreign scholars, critics, and journalists. The year was notable for discovery of much unpublished Gorki correspondence. The largest collection, already lodged in the Gorki Archives, Moscow, was found in Paris; the art critic I. Zilbergstein gave an account of its discovery. It consisted of letters from Gorki to Z. A. Peshkov (a relative; Gorki's real name was Peshkov), who in his will had asked that they be returned to Russia.

Publications forming part of the celebrations included *Gorki and the Soviet Press*, two volumes of letters from Gorki to publishers and journalists; *Gorki the Journalist*, a monograph by V. D. Pelt; *The Fate of Gorki* by B. A. Bialik, foremost Soviet Gorki scholar; and *Gorki in Moscow*, containing much new material, by L. Byukovtseva of the Gorki Institute. Critical works on other great Russian writers included *The Creative Path of Pushkin* by D. D. Blagoi, the internationally known Pushkin scholar (and author of the article on Pushkin in the *Encyclopædia Britannica*); K. Chukovski's *Chekhov;* and A. Baborenko's *I. A. Bunin*. I. Maisky's *Bernard Shaw and Others* was founded on reminiscences of his years as Soviet ambassador in London. The playwright N. Pavlova wrote

a study of the Swiss-German dramatist Friedrich Dürrenmatt. Popular in translation was a collection of American folksongs, *Guitar in Battle*.

General critical works showed the influence of the 50th anniversary of the Revolution: B. Varanov's *Revolution and the Fate of the Artist* and his *Tolstoi: The Road to Socialist-Realism;* V. Ozerov's *Half a Century of Soviet Literature;* and, less directly, B. Bursov's brilliantly interpretative *Realism Today and As It Has Always Been*. Essays collected in *The Great October Revolution and World Literature* discussed the relationship between the development in the last half century of the literatures of the Soviet Union and those of Czechoslovakia, Mexico, the U.S., India, China, Japan, and Turkey. And in *The October Revolution and the National Literatures of the U.S.S.R.* K. Zelinski brought the year's two celebrations together, in a masterly survey and analysis of the development within the Soviet Union of the literatures of many nations, with particular emphasis on the significance in Soviet literary development of Gorki's works. (*See* also UNION OF SOVIET SOCIALIST REPUBLICS.) (X.)

SPANISH

During 1968 one of Spain's newest publishing houses, the Alianza Editorial—which had already introduced new editions of many of the lesser-known Spanish classics, besides publishing modern books likely to become classics—brought out its 100th title. Among its outstanding new titles was Julio Caro Baroja's *El señor inquisidor y otras vidas por oficio*, a valuable historical study of the "style" of the Inquisitors. It also attempted to "place" the two principal Basque conquistadores—Pedro de Ursúa and Lope de Aguirre "the traitor"—in relation to the era and their regional background, by way of explaining their loyalty, and disloyalty in America, to Philip II. A notable new edition, also from Alianza, was a well-annotated collection of amorous writings by the little-known Golden Age novelist, María de Zayas y Sotomayor (1590–1661?). Entitled *Novelas ejemplares y amorosas, o Decamerón español*, with a prologue and notes by Eduardo Rincón, it contained six racy, satirical *novelas*, popular for 200 years but virtually lost when prohibited by the Inquisition. A worthwhile reissue was Ramón Sender's novel *Mr. Witt en el cantón* (1935), about the end of the first Spanish Republic. No edition of this, perhaps his best work, had appeared in Spain for more than 30 years. From exile in Los Angeles, Sender contributed a delightful, humorous prologue. From the same publisher came Pedro Salinas' *El defensor*, also written in exile in the U.S., "the world of the machines"; in it Salinas (d. 1951) vigorously defended (at the risk of "being characterized as a fascist") literary minorities against the masses, who, he declared, would be better off if they did not read. Salinas also put forward, as some compensation for a nation of nonreaders, a Spaniard, the book-mad Don Quixote, who made his reading his life.

From Camilo José Cela came the tour de force of the year, vol. i of his *Diccionario secreto*—a study of a single Spanish word, *testículo* ("testicle"), with its various synonyms and euphemisms as found in writings and popular usage throughout the Spanish-speaking world. The first edition was quickly sold out. He also produced a book of verse, *María Sabina*, evoking the hallucinations of an American Indian woman drugged with "magic mushrooms."

Ramón Carande's *Carlos V y sus banqueros*, a two-volume history of the ruinous relations between the

Poet Rasul Gamsatov, whose autobiography, "My Daghistan," was published in 1968.

Julio Caro Baroja, author of "El señor inquisidor y otras vidas por oficio," a historical analysis of the Inquisitors.

Holy Roman Emperor Charles V (Charles I of Spain) and his creditors, principally the banking houses of Fugger and Welsen, gave documentary evidence of 491 credit transactions that resulted in the undermining of the foundations of the Spanish economy, including the treasures then flowing in from the Indies. Another historical work, *El arte de matar* by the novelist Daniel Sueiro, was· an illustrated, discursive account of the practice of killing in its more or less legal forms: historical and present-day methods of torture; the six legal ways of carrying out the death penalty; the "ceremony" itself; and the executioners.

Art books of interest included Eduardo Westerdhal's study of the Spanish Surrealist Óscar Domínguez, a painter of the School of Paris who committed suicide in despair of a world that had become a mechanism; an unusual collection of texts and illustrations on Antoni Tàpies, with an essay in four languages by Francesco Vicens, an "oracle" by Joan Brossa (one of the founders of Surrealism), and 128 photographs of the objects, real or created by the artist, in Tàpies' world; and *1900 en Barcelona,* an evocation of Catalan *modernismo,* of which the text, "La Barcelona de las mariposas de oro," was by Cirici Pellicer.　　(AY. K.)

SWEDISH

A preoccupation with political and social themes was again noticeable in Swedish literature in 1968. Two of the year's most discussed books, Per Olof Enquist's *Legionärerna* and Sara Lidman's *Gruva,* were both documentary in form. Enquist, an intellectual and sophisticated experimentalist previously much concerned with problems of individual freedom, dealt in his new book with a controversial chapter of contemporary Swedish history: the extradition to the Soviet Union in 1945 of Baltic refugees who had served in the German Army during World War II. Enquist, whose researches included visits to some of the extradited Balts, contended that conservative opinion in Sweden had presented the event, and the refugees' subsequent fate, in a false light.

Sara Lidman began her literary career as a chronicler of provincial life, but her writing had become progressively more international and political in tone. Having written a book about North Vietnam, in 1968 she returned to Sweden, to its remotest and most sparsely populated region, for her theme—the life of the hardrock miners in Lapland. Based on interviews with workers at the state-owned mines there, her book was an indictment of inhuman working conditions and the breakdown of democratic processes.

Lars Gyllensten, one of the country's leading prose writers, published a novel about the process of authorship, *Diarium spirituale,* in which he developed his views on the significance of character creation and of inanimate objects in all realistic descriptive writing. Sven Fagerberg, in his essay collection *Dialog i det fria,* carried further the criticism of capitalism that he had previously propounded in a number of novels; his alternative was not socialism, for he expressed his belief in private enterprise while considering that it had failed in a system based on power concentration and monopolistic commodity production. Eyvind Johnson's first novel in four years, *Favel ensam,* another book touching on matters of current debate, was mainly a discussion of utopias.

Also noteworthy were a new novel by Pär Wästberg, *Vattenslottet;* articles by Jan Myrdal, a leading writer of the left; and collections of poetry by Lars Forssell, Johannes Edfelt, Petter Bergman, and Lars Gustafs-

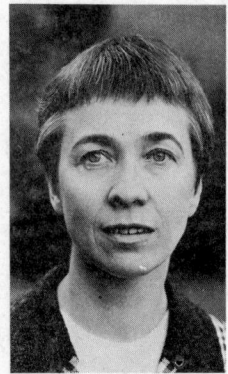

LENNART NILSSON

Sara Lidman, who criticizes the inhuman working conditions of the Lapland miners in "Gruva."

son. Sweden's two leading poets of the 20th century, Gunnar Ekelöf and Erik Lindegren, both died during the year (*see* OBITUARIES). Ekelöf's seat in the Swedish Academy was taken by Artur Lundkvist, who published a book of aphorisms, *Brottställen,* and a historical novel, *Snapphanens liv och död,* during the year.

The Nordic Council's 1968 literature prize, worth about $6,700, went to Per Olof Sundman for his documentary novel *Ingenjör Andrées luftfärd* (1967).

(L. ZE.)

See also Libraries; Philosophy; Theatre.

ENCYCLOPÆDIA BRITANNICA FILMS. *Chaucer's England—With a Special Presentation of The Pardoner's Tale* (1958); *The Theater—One of the Humanities* (Humanities Course) (1959); *Early Victorian England and Charles Dickens* (Humanities Course) (1962); *Great Expectations I: The Story* (Humanities Course) (1962); *Great Expectations II: The Story Interpreted* (Humanities Course) (1962); *The Novel: What It Is, What It's About, What It Does* (Humanities Course) (1962); *Morning on the Lièvre* (1964); *Huckleberry Finn I* (1965); *Huckleberry Finn II* (1965); *Huckleberry Finn III* (1965); *The Odyssey I—The Structure of the Epic* (1965); *The Odyssey II—Return of Odysseus* (1965); *The Odyssey III—Central Themes* (1965).

Luxembourg

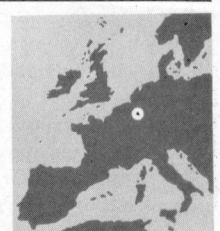

A constitutional monarchy, the Benelux country of Luxembourg is bounded on the east by Germany, on the south by France, and on the west and north by Belgium. Area: 999 sq.mi. (2,587 sq.km.). Pop. (1968 est.): 335,234. Cap. and largest city: Luxembourg (pop., 1968 est., 77,-105). Language: French and German. Religion: 97% Roman Catholic. Grand duke, Jean; prime minister until Oct. 30, 1968, Pierre Werner.

The Christian Socialist-Socialist coalition government of Pierre Werner fell on October 30, following pressure from Socialist trade union leaders for higher wages and greater welfare benefits than the government (including the Socialists) was willing to support. Grand Duke Jean ordered new general elections for December 15, which resulted in gains for both opposi-

LUXEMBOURG

Education. (1965–66) Primary, pupils 36,546, teachers 1,519; secondary, pupils 7,417, teachers 498; vocational, pupils 5,542, teachers (1964–65) 210; higher, students 616.

Finance. Monetary unit: Luxembourg franc, at par with the Belgian franc (LFr. 50 = U.S. $1; LFr. 120 = £1 sterling). Dollar assets reported by U.S.: (Dec. 1967) U.S. $32 million; (Dec. 1966) U.S. $25 million. Budget (1968 est.): revenue LFr. 10,647,431,000; expenditure LFr. 10,905,378,000. Gross domestic product: (1967) LFr. 36,606,000,000; (1966) LFr. 35,-184,000,000. Money supply: *see* BELGIUM. Cost of living (1963 = 100): (June 1968) 115; (June 1967) 112.

Foreign Trade. *See* BELGIUM.

Transport and Communications. Roads (1967) 4,440 km. Motor vehicles in use (1967): passenger 69,-949; commercial 10,870. Railways: (1965) 337 km.; traffic (1967) 263 million passenger-km., freight 572 million net ton-km. Air traffic (1967): 32,610,000 passenger-km.; freight 204,000 net ton-km. Telephones (Dec. 1966) 87,040. Radio receivers (Dec. 1966) 126,-000. Television receivers (Dec. 1966) 38,000.

Agriculture. Production (in 000; metric tons; 1967; 1966 in parentheses): oats 30 (31); wheat (1966) 34, (1965) 38; rye *c.* 8 (5); potatoes (1966) 65, (1965) 74. Livestock (in 000; May 1967): cattle 183; sheep 3; pigs 116; horses 2; poultry 409.

Industry. Production (in 000; metric tons; 1967): iron ore (30% metal content) 6,303; pig iron 3,963; crude steel 4,481; electricity 2,222,000 kw-hr.; manufactured gas 25,680 cu.m.

tion parties—the Liberals (+5 seats) and the Communists (+1). The Christian Socialists lost 1 seat and the Socialists 3. Negotiations to form a new government were expected to be protracted.

Provisional statistics released in January 1968 showed that Luxembourg's economy continued to gain slightly in 1967, but at a lower rate than in 1966. The gross national product increased LFr. 1.4 billion in 1967 to a total of LFr. 36.6 billion, the national income rose to LFr. 28.9 billion, and per capita income (based on national income rather than GNP) was approximately LFr. 86,000 ($1,720). The growth rate of 2.5% was the lowest of the six EEC states. Prospects for 1968 were for a continued general softening of the economy. U.K. restrictions on imports, programs introduced by the U.S. to offset its balance of payments problems and to stem the outflow of gold, and the general weakening of the French economy were all expected to affect the economy unfavourably.

The 20th International Fair of Luxembourg opened on May 23 in the presence of the grand duke and duchess; 1,818 exhibitors from 43 countries took part.

Luxembourg, with the other Benelux states and West Germany, continued its active support for Britain's admission to the EEC, and Werner, with Foreign Minister Pierre Gregoire, visited London to discuss ways to soften French Pres. Charles de Gaulle's opposition.   (R. D. Ho.)

Malagasy Republic

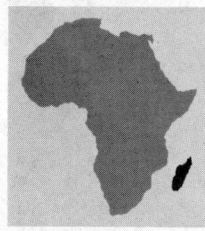

The Malagasy Republic occupies the island of Madagascar and minor adjacent islands in the Indian Ocean off the southeast coast of Africa. Area: 226,657 sq.mi. (587,041 sq.km.). Pop. (1966 est.): 6,562,041. Cap. and largest city: Tananarive (pop., 1966 est., 335,149). Language: French and Malagasy. Religion: Christian (approximately 50%) and traditional tribal beliefs. President in 1968, Philibert Tsiranana.

MALAGASY REPUBLIC
Education. (1965–66) Primary, pupils 672,100, teachers 9,475; secondary, pupils 55,439, teachers 2,404; vocational, pupils 7,715, teachers 539; teacher training, students 2,079, teachers (1964–65) 118; higher (including University of Madagascar), students 3,082.
Finance. Monetary unit: Malagasy franc, at par with the CFA franc (MalFr. 246.85 = U.S. $1; MalFr. 592.45 = £1 sterling). Budget (1967 rev. est.): revenue MalFr. 30 billion; expenditure MalFr. 42,395,000,-000.
Foreign Trade. (1967) Imports MalFr. 35,890,000,-000 (65% from France, 7% from U.S., 5% from West Germany); exports MalFr. 25,710,000,000 (37% to France, 25% to U.S., 11% to Réunion, 5% to Senegal). Main exports: coffee 32%; sugar 8%; rice 7%; vanilla 6%.
Transport and Communications. Roads (1965) c. 40,000 km. (including 8,191 km. all-weather). Motor vehicles in use (1966): passenger 35,000; commercial (including buses) 28,600. Railways: (1966) 864 km.; traffic (1967) 172 million passenger-km., freight 179 million net ton-km. Air traffic (1967): 179,191,000 passenger-km.; freight 7,301,000 net ton-km. Telephones (Dec. 1966) 21,573. Radio receivers (Dec. 1966) 300,000.
Agriculture. Production (in 000; metric tons; 1966; 1965 in parentheses): cassava 870 (836); rice (1967) 1,464, (1966) 1,418; corn 100 (96); sweet potatoes 264 (280); peanuts c. 45 (36); sugar, raw value (1967–68) c. 112, (1966–67) 111; coffee 58 (55); tobacco 5.8 (5.5); pepper 2.2 (1.8); sisal 30 (28). Livestock (in 000; Dec. 1966): cattle 9,500; sheep c. 300; pigs 560; goats (Dec. 1965) 460; chickens 14,000.

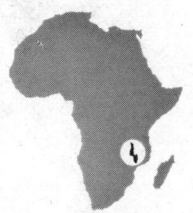

At the tenth session of the Council of Ministers of the Organization of African Unity (OAU), held at Addis Ababa, Eth., in February, the Malagasy Republic, together with Ghana and the Ivory Coast, combined to forestall the passing of a resolution demanding Israel's immediate withdrawal from occupied Arab territories. Later in February, following the decision (subsequently rescinded) to permit South Africa's admittance to the Olympic Games, the Malagasy Republic—as a member of the Executive Committee of the Supreme Council for Sports in Africa—joined with the nine other member states to condemn the admission and "to support the African countries in the fight against racial discrimination in sport."

In April President Tsiranana condemned Tanzania's recognition of the breakaway Biafran regime, a policy that he resumed in September at the OAU summit meeting at Addis Ababa.

The Malagasy Republic, together with nine other French-speaking countries, attended a UN-organized seminar on the employment of youth and national development at Niamey, Niger, in May. A representative of Malagasy also attended an educational conference in Nairobi, Kenya, jointly organized by the OAU and the UN, in July.

The 12th annual conference of the ruling Democratic Party was held in Tananarive late in August. At the conference President Tsiranana took pains to reassure French investors that he was violently opposed to nationalism. Indeed, of all the nations dependent on French investments, the Malagasy Republic most feared the eventual reduction in French aid. Efforts to diversify the sources of foreign aid continued throughout the year, and in July a series of cooperation agreements were signed between the Malagasy Republic and West Germany.   (Ph. D.; X.)

Malawi

A republic in east central Africa, Malawi is bounded by Tanzania, Mozambique, and Zambia. Area: 45,725 sq.mi. (118,428 sq.km.). Pop. (1966): 4,042,412, nearly all of whom are Africans. Cap.: Zomba (pop., 1963, 12,000). Largest city: Blantyre-Limbe (pop., 120,000). Language: English and Nyanja. Religion: predominantly traditional beliefs. President in 1968, H. Kamuzu Banda.

In the latter part of 1967 President Banda announced plans to open up and develop Malawi's fertile northern province. A canal was to be dredged to make the Shire River navigable between Fort Johnson and Lilongwe. This would make it possible for cargoes to be loaded onto ships at northern lake shore ports and transported direct to Lilongwe, the new railhead, and thence by rail to the port of Nacala in Mozambique. The £3 million construction costs of the 90-mi. stretch of railway from Lilongwe to Nova Freiza in Mozambique were to be provided by a Japanese consortium.

During 1968 Banda continued to denounce the African nationalist policies of other independent African states and to stress the importance of Malawi's maintaining strong diplomatic and economic links with white-dominated South Africa, Rhodesia, and Portuguese Africa. In May he publicly thanked the government of South Africa for its loan of £4.7 million for the first phase of the building of the new capital at Lilongwe, while in October he appealed to African leaders to adopt a more realistic policy over racial matters and called upon the UN and the Common-

wealth to face facts and not to live in an atmosphere of self-deception and unreality.

Banda's attitude did not escape criticism by members of the Organization of African Unity (OAU), and there were additional lively reactions when Hilgard Muller, South African minister for foreign affairs, paid an official visit to Malawi in August. Banda, however, met denunciation with denunciation, while critics within Malawi were summarily dealt with. Two British subjects and a South African were declared prohibited immigrants in January, while another Briton had his work permit withdrawn in July and was ordered to leave the country. However, seven Asians who had been declared prohibited immigrants in 1967 were permitted to return to Malawi.

On June 14 Sir Peter Watkin Williams, judge of the high court, sentenced to death eight of the men captured in October 1967 after entering Malawi from Tanzania under the leadership of former Foreign Minister Yatuta Chisiza, with the alleged intention of killing President Banda and overthrowing the government. Chisiza had been killed by security forces. Those who were captured, having been convicted of treason, were subject to the mandatory death penalty.

President Banda's policy undoubtedly had the support of the vast majority of the people of Malawi, although his autocratic manner sometimes imposed a strain upon his more senior officials. The basic issue, however, was one of finance. Malawi needed approximately £7 million annually to balance its budget, and by the end of 1968 South African investment would have amounted to approximately £10 million.

By contrast, no financial help had been forthcoming from Malawi's critics. Thus, Banda could ignore accusations of being a traitor to the African cause and was able to demonstrate his independence by refraining from sending a representative to the conference of African leaders held in Algiers in September. To a charge that he was sending mercenaries to aid Israel in its struggle against the Arabs, he proffered only a contemptuous denial and, in typically aggressive fashion, added that if Malawi were to send mercenaries anywhere it would be to the Sudan, where Arabs and black Africans had been in actual conflict for a considerable period.   (K. I.)

MALAWI

Education. (1966) Primary, pupils 286,753, teachers 8,778; secondary, pupils 6,718, teachers 416; vocational, pupils 886, teachers 109; teacher training, students 1,350, teachers 141; higher, students 326, teaching staff 54.

Finance. Monetary unit: Malawi pound, at par with the pound sterling (Mal£1 = U.S. $2.40). Budget (1968 est.): revenue Mal£19,750,000; expenditure Mal£20.5 million. U.K. aid: (1967) Mal£4.6 million; (1966) Mal£5.3 million.

Foreign Trade. (1967) Imports Mal£25,554,000 (28% from U.K., 21% from Rhodesia, 8% from Japan, 8% from South Africa, 7% from Zambia); exports Mal£20,518,000 (55% to U.K., 5% to Netherlands). Main exports: tea 22%; tobacco 21%; peanuts 17%.

Transport and Communications. Roads (1967) 10,558 km. Motor vehicles in use (1967): passenger 8,367; commercial 5,934. Railways: (1966) 509 km.; traffic (1963) 49 million passenger-km., freight (1966) 135 million net ton-km. Telephones (Dec. 1966) 8,201. Radio receivers (Dec. 1961) 12,000.

Agriculture. Production (in 000; metric tons; 1966; 1965 in parentheses): corn c. 920 (c. 915); tobacco 19 (23); cottonseed c. 9 (c. 9); peanuts 65 (35); tea 15 (13). Livestock (in 000; 1965–66): sheep 81; cattle 455; goats 500; pigs 143; poultry, farms and estates c. 2,600.

Industry. Electricity (public supply; 1966) 67 million kw-hr.

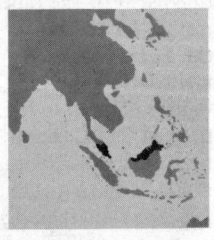

Malaysia

A federation within the Commonwealth of Nations comprising the 11 states of the former Federation of Malaya (known as West Malaysia), Sabah (formerly North Borneo), and Sarawak (together known as East Malaysia), Malaysia is an elective constitutional monarchy situated in Southeast Asia at the southern end of the Malay Peninsula (excluding Singapore) and on the northern part of the island of Borneo. Area: 127,672 sq.mi. (330,671 sq.km.). Pop. (1967 est.): 10,020,801. Cap. and largest city: Kuala Lumpur (pop., 1968 est., 592,785). Official language: Malay. Religion: Malays are Muslim; Indians mainly Hindu; Chinese mainly Buddhist, Confucian, and Taoist. Supreme head of state in 1968, with the title of *yang di-pertuan agong*, Tuanku Ismail Nasiruddin Shah ibni al-Marhum Sultan Zainal Abidin; prime minister, Tunku Abdul Rahman.

"THE TIMES," LONDON, FROM PICTORIAL PARADE

Prime Minister Tunku Abdul Rahman of Malaysia (right) receiving the freedom of the City of London from the lord chamberlain on June 18, 1968, in London's Guildhall.

The British government's decision to withdraw its forces from the country by the end of 1971 made it necessary for Malaysia to increase its defense capability. The British withdrawal also was expected to create a new military and political situation in the region. Britain offered £25 million (M$200 million) to offset the effects of the withdrawal, but the finance minister, Tun Tan Siew Sin, said that Malaysia would need at least M$600 million in investments to fully offset the effects.

The Philippines continued to press its territorial claim to Sabah, and after four weeks of fruitless talks, during which Malaysia rejected the claim, the Philippine Congress passed a bill in September that in effect annexed Sabah. Malaysia withdrew its diplomatic staff from Manila except for an assistant to handle administrative matters and rejected a Philippine offer to submit the matter to the International Court of Justice. In December, however, the foreign ministers of the two countries, meeting in Bangkok, agreed to restore diplomatic relations and to set aside the dispute over Sabah for at least a year.

Education. *West Malaysia.* (1965) Primary, pupils 1,215,020, teachers 45,037; secondary, pupils 346,046, teachers 14,434; vocational, pupils 9,-143, teachers 315; higher (including University of Malaya), students 12,704, teaching staff 1,400. *East Malaysia: Sabah.* (1965) Primary, pupils 86,413, teachers 2,955; secondary, pupils 11,380, teachers 478; vocational, pupils 151, teachers 10; teacher training, students 413, teachers 47. *East Malaysia: Sarawak.* (1966) Primary, pupils 135,-114, teachers 4,151; secondary, pupils 30,197, teachers 1,194; vocational, pupils 177, teachers 20; teacher training, students 314, teachers 39; higher (1965), students 89, teaching staff 11.

Finance. Monetary unit: Malaysian dollar, with a par value of M$3.06 to U.S. $1 (M$7.35 = £1 sterling). Gold and foreign exchange, official: (May 1968) U.S. $433 million; (May 1967) U.S. $515 million. Budget (1967 est.): revenue M$1.8 billion; expenditure M$1,829,000,000. Gross national product: (1966) M$9,344,000,-000; (1965) M$8,776,000,000. Money supply: (March 1968) M$1,454,000,000; (March 1967) M$1,597,000,000. Cost of living (West Malaysia; 1963 = 100): (March 1968) 108; (March 1967) 104.

Foreign Trade. (1967) Imports M$3,327,000,-000; exports M$3,723,000,000. Import sources (West Malaysia only): U.K. 16%; Japan 14%; Singapore 8%; Australia 8%; China 7%; Thailand 7%; U.S. 6%; West Germany 5%. Export destinations (West Malaysia only): U.S. 24%; Singapore 18%; Japan 15%; U.K. 7%. Main exports: rubber 34%; tin 20%; timber 16%.

Transport and Communications. Roads (1966) 19,846 km. (including 4,020 km. in East Malaysia). Motor vehicles in use (1966): passenger 192,800; commercial (including buses) 54,000. Railways (1966): 1,809 km. (including 154 km. in Sabah); traffic (including Singapore) 610 million passenger-km., freight 983 million net ton-km. Shipping (1967): merchant vessels 100 gross tons and over 110; gross tonnage 64,172. Ships entered (1966) vessels totaling 38,566,000 net registered tons; cargo loaded (1966) 17,868,-000 metric tons, unloaded 8,085,000 metric tons. Air traffic (Malaysia-Singapore Airlines; 1967): 510,052,000 passenger-km.; freight 5,896,000 net ton-km. Telephones (Jan. 1967) 137,726. Radio receivers (Dec. 1966) c. 454,000. Television receivers (Dec. 1966) 67,000.

Agriculture. Production (in 000; metric tons; 1966; 1965 in parentheses): rice 1,105 (1,090); rubber 1,001 (949); copra 176 (167); palm oil, West Malaysia estates only 181 (149); tea, West Malaysia only 3.5 (3.3); bananas, West Malaysia only c. 330 (332); pineapples, West Malaysia only c. 355 (c. 355); pepper, Sarawak only 15 (18); timber 12,700 cu.m. (10,500 cu.m.). Livestock (in 000; 1965–66): cattle c. 334; pigs 783; goats c. 346; sheep, West Malaysia only c. 40; buffaloes c. 360; poultry, West Malaysia only c. 22,000. Fish catch (in 000; metric tons) (1966) 296, (1965) 253.

Industry. Production (in 000; metric tons; 1967): tin concentrates (metal content) 73; bauxite 906; cement (West Malaysia only; 1966) 784; iron ore (West Malaysia only; 60% metal content) 5,436; crude oil (Sarawak only) 44; gold (1966) 5.1 troy oz.; electricity (West Malaysia only) 2,720,000 kw-hr.

In view of the security threat posed by the Philippine move, Malaysia transferred more armed forces to Sabah and Sarawak, revived the Vigilante and Local Defense Corps, making them as strong as during the period of the threat from Indonesia, and introduced national service training and registration.

On the international front Malaysia continued to pursue an independent foreign policy, maintaining cordial relations with all friendly countries regardless of their economic and social systems. During the year Malaysia strengthened its diplomatic links with many countries, including the U.S.S.R. and Yugoslavia.

Vice-Pres. Hubert H. Humphrey of the United States; Pres. Ferdinand Marcos of the Philippines; Mohammad Reza Pahlavi, shah of Iran; the chairman of the Revolutionary Council of Burma, Gen. Ne Win; Emperor Haile Selassie of Ethiopia; Mrs. Indira Gandhi, prime minister of India; John Gorton, prime minister of Australia; and Keith Holyoake, prime minister of New Zealand, paid official visits to Malaysia during the year. Tunku Abdul Rahman paid an official visit to Indonesia.

Internally, Communism and subversion, though under control, remained a threat to the security of the country. It was, therefore, necessary for the government to retain the Internal Security Act to deal with the small number of Communists in Sarawak and on the Malaysian-Thai border, who were active, dedicated, well organized, and well indoctrinated. Following a Communist ambush at Kroh on the Malaysian-Thai border on June 17 in which 15 members of the Malaysian Police Field Force were killed and 18 wounded, the Malaysian and Thai governments agreed that their troops could move into each other's territory when chasing terrorists along the border.

The Malaysian economy continued to expand, although the rate of growth was less than during the previous year. The country at the end of 1967 had an overall balance of payments deficit of M$247 million and gold and foreign exchange reserves of M$1,963,-000,000. The currency interchangeability arrangements between the monetary authorities of Malaysia, Singapore, and Brunei operated satisfactorily during the year.

The 1968 budget provided for ordinary expenditure of M$1,932,000,000 and revenue of M$1,867,000,000. With development expenditure estimated at M$680 million and allowing for special receipts of M$62 million, an overall deficit of M$683 million was anticipated, compared with an overall deficit of M$634 million in 1967. This would be partly financed by foreign loans of M$200 million and domestic borrowing of M$400 million.

To induce a greater and more rapid inflow of investment in Malaysian industry and to encourage the expansion of exports of Malaysian manufactured goods, the Malaysian Parliament passed the Investment Incentives Bill. It provided a variety of incentives, including relief from income and payroll taxes, investment tax credits, and export and accelerated depreciation allowances.

Parliament also passed the Employment Restriction Bill, which for the first time in the history of the country required noncitizens to register and obtain work permits. (M. S. R.)

ENCYCLOPÆDIA BRITANNICA FILMS. *Malaya, Land of Tin and Rubber* (1957).

Maldive Islands

The Republic of Maldive Islands lies in the Indian Ocean southwest of the southern tip of India. Area: 115 sq.mi. (298 sq.km.). Pop. (1966): 100,883. Cap. and largest city: Male (pop., 1966, 11,561). Language: Divehi. Religion: Muslim. Sultan, Amir Muhammad Farid Didi; president in 1968, Ibrahim Nassir.

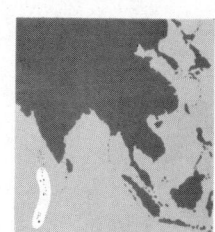

A plebiscite held in March 1968 resulted in a decision in favour of a republican constitution. In September 1967 a bilateral agreement with Ceylon, the only country outside the U.S. where the Maldives had an embassy, allowed Air Ceylon to fly a regular monthly

MALDIVE ISLANDS

Education. (1964–65) Primary, pupils 4,864, teachers 315; secondary, pupils 762, teachers 32.

Finance. Monetary unit: Maldivian rupee, with a par value of MRs. 5.95 to U.S. $1 (MRs. 14.29 = £1 sterling). Budget (1965): expenditure MRs. 19,646,-830; U.K. grant for development from 1960 £850,000, of which c. £300,000 paid by mid-1965.

Foreign Trade. Mainly with Ceylon. Main exports (metric tons; 1967): fish 3,400; cowrie shells 7; copra 18. Fishing accounts for c. 95% of exports.

Agriculture. Main crops are copra, papaya, pineapples, citrus fruits, and yams.

schedule to the islands with reciprocal rights when the Maldives developed their own airline. Extensions to Hulele Airport, to enable jet landings, were planned, and the government also declared Male a free port. Trade, almost entirely with Ceylon, to which Maldive fish and fish products were exported in return for most of the islands' daily needs, rose considerably in 1967 to MRs. 14 million with an even balance of trade.

As a member of the UN, the Maldive Islands received medical aid through the World Health Organization, particularly in connection with a polio outbreak during 1967. On Gan Island the Royal Air Force treated a typhoid outbreak successfully, its laboratory staff carrying out thousands of typhoid tests and running an isolation hospital for the islanders. The British defense minister stated in January that the Gan and Masirah airfields would be used as a staging post for some time. (M. Mr.)

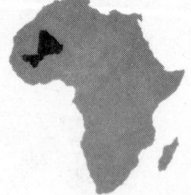

Mali

A republic of West Africa, Mali is bordered by Algeria, Niger, Upper Volta, Ivory Coast, Guinea, Senegal, and Mauritania. Area: 479,000 sq.mi. (1,240,000 sq.km.). Pop. (1967 est.): 4,740,800. Cap. and largest city: Bamako (metro. pop., 1967 est., 175,000). Language: French (official); Hamito-Semitic and various tribal dialects. Religion: Muslim 63%; animist 36%. President and prime minister until November 19, 1968, Modibo Keita; head of military government, from November 19, Capt. Yoro Diakité.

A group of army officers staged a bloodless coup on November 19 and overthrew President Keita, the only chief of state Mali had known since achieving its independence in 1960. A week after the coup Capt. Yoro Diakité, the leader of the new military regime, announced that a referendum on a new national constitution would be held in 1969 and that this would be followed by elections to the National Assembly and the eventual designation of a new president. Diakité stated that the goals of the military government would include restoration of individual liberties, budgetary reform, and increased agricultural production. Keita was arrested and reportedly imprisoned to face trial at a later date. Whether the new regime would be more pro-Western in its political orientation than had been Keita remained uncertain at the year's end. One indication that it might be was Diakité's order ending collectivization and restoring free trade in farm produce.

Earlier in the year moves toward closer ties between Mali and Guinea were approved by President Keita and Pres. Sékou Touré of Guinea when they decided

to strengthen bilateral relations in regard to people's democratic organizations in the two countries. In April President Keita refused to recognize the Biafran breakaway regime in Nigeria on the ground that it would encourage the disintegration of Africa and support the formation of tribal states. April 10 marked the resumption of diplomatic relations with the U.K., broken off in December 1965 in protest against the U.K. policy toward Rhodesia. Following a visit to Communist China in May by a joint delegation, a communiqué from Mali and Guinea acknowledged a trend toward future cooperation among the three governments. (Ph. D.; X.)

Malta

An island in the Mediterranean Sea, between Sicily and Tunisia, Malta is a parliamentary state and a member of the Commonwealth of Nations. Area: 122 sq.mi. (316 sq.km.), including Malta, Gozo, and Comino. Pop. (1967 est.): 319,000. Cap.: Valletta (pop., 1968 est., 15,430). Largest city: Sliema (pop., 1968 est., 21,572). Language: English and Maltese. Religion: mainly Roman Catholic. Queen, Elizabeth II; governor-general in 1968, Sir Maurice Dorman; prime minister, George Borg Olivier.

Although trade disputes and a series of strikes in the most important industries bedeviled labour relations, the year 1968 registered a buoyant home economy. The rapid increase of tourism led to a high level of activity in hotel building. An intensified factory construction program and the considerable upsurge in residential housing development contributed to pressures on the building industry.

The budget for 1968–69 provided for a capital investment program of M£10.7 million, while ordinary expenditure was expected to be M£20 million. The government planned to induce economic growth by pursuing an expansionary budgetary policy on capital account, with particular emphasis on further development of the country's basic industries and on the continued offering of incentives to attract investors. No balance of payment difficulties were encountered, and no fiscal or monetary controls were introduced.

An important milestone in the island's financial his-

MALI
Education. (1965–66) Primary, pupils 161,605, teachers 3,826; secondary, pupils 1,011, teachers 114; vocational, pupils 1,417, teachers 196; teacher training, students 748, teachers 36; higher, students 222, teaching staff 58.
Finance. Monetary unit: Mali franc, with a par value of MFr. 493.71 = U.S. $1 (MFr. 1,184.90 = £1 sterling). Budget (1967–68 est.): revenue MFr. 21.2 billion; expenditure MFr. 24.7 billion. Money supply: (April 1968) MFr. 27,920,000,000; (April 1967) MFr. 23,490,000,000.
Foreign Trade. (1967) Imports MFr. 16,180,000,-000; exports MFr. 6,480,000,000. Import sources: France 30%; China 23%; U.S.S.R. 11%; Ivory Coast 7%; U.K. 6%. Export destinations: Senegal 32%; Ivory Coast 28%; Ghana 15%; France 9%. Main exports: peanuts 31%; cotton 19%; fish 14%.

MALTA
Education. (1966–67) Primary, pupils 45,000, teachers 2,012; secondary, pupils 7,666, teachers 508; vocational, pupils 1,692, teachers 114; teacher training, students 387, teachers 40; higher (including Royal University of Malta), students 970, teaching staff 72.
Finance and Trade. Monetary unit: Maltese pound, at par with the pound sterling (M£1 = U.S. $2.40). Budget (1967–68): revenue M£25,909,654; expenditure M£26,434,554. Foreign trade (1967): imports M£40,509,000 (39% from U.K., 16% from Italy); exports M£9,890,000 (32% to U.K., 9% to Italy, 8% to Libya, 7% to U.S., 15% as ship's stores). Main domestic exports: textile yarns and fabrics 25%; clothing 15%; petroleum products 10%; rubber products 5%; fruit and vegetables 5%. Tourism (1966): visitors 72,-900; gross receipts M£4,750,000.
Transport and Communications. Shipping (1967): merchant vessels 100 gross tons and over 24; gross tonnage 52,483. Ships entered (1966) vessels totaling 1,836,000 net registered tons; cargo loaded (1966) 66,000 metric tons, unloaded 728,000 metric tons. Air traffic (1967): 143,041,000 passenger-km.; freight 1,437,000 net ton-km. Telephones (Jan. 1967) 25,894. Radio receivers (Dec. 1966) 82,000. Television receivers (Dec. 1966) 31,000.

UPI COMPIX

A painting of Pope Paul VI is driven through the streets of Valletta on Oct. 27, 1968, during a procession supporting the pontiff's stand against birth control.

tory was reached by the creation of a central bank and by the setting up of the Malta Development Corp. to administer, on the government's behalf, the grants, loans, and other fiscal benefits operating as aids to industries. In April an agreement was reached between the Maltese and U.K. governments on the financial assistance required from Britain in order that the dockyard might revert to the Maltese government free and unencumbered; funds in addition to the £51 million available under the financial agreement were provided for further development of the yard.

Subsequently, legislation approved by Parliament provided for the transfer of the shares of Bailey (Malta) Ltd. to the government of Malta, the compulsory dissolution of Bailey's, and the establishment of the Malta Drydocks Corp. to take over the main assets of the dockyard.

On September 11 Malta became the 110th member of the International Monetary Fund, with a quota of $10 million. After Malta's appointment of an ambassador to the EEC, exploratory talks were held in Brussels in October on Malta's formal application for a form of relationship with the EEC countries.

In June both Prince Philip, duke of Edinburgh, and Fra Angelo de Mojana, the grand master of the Sovereign Military Order of St. John, paid official visits to Malta.

Steps were taken to reform the laws of the nation by establishing two commissions; one was to revise the criminal code and the other was to make recommendations to the government from time to time on amendments required in Malta's legislation.   (A. G.)

Mathematics

Six new finite simple groups were discovered during 1968. The discussion that follows assumes some general understanding of those sets of elements called mathematical groups. For present purposes let it suffice to say that simple groups are in a sense the building blocks for all groups, and that a classification of all finite simple groups would constitute decisive progress in the subject.

The smallest finite simple group has order 60 (that is, there are 60 elements in the group). The next few orders are 168, 360, 504, 660, and 1,092.

There are some standard finite simple groups that may be called classical; for example, the alternating group on n letters for $n \geqq 5$, and certain groups constructed by appropriately modifying Lie groups. Although substantial technical difficulties were faced in sorting out the classical groups, by the early 1960s these had been thoroughly mastered. A comprehensive survey of the classical groups was presented by R. Carter (*J. Lond. Math. Soc.,* vol. 40, 1965, pp. 193–240).

Thus, the remaining task is to find all the nonclassical finite simple groups. As long ago as 1861, E. Mathieu discovered five such groups. More than 100 years passed before there was an addition to the list. Then Z. Janko found a new one, reported in 1965. By 1967 Janko contributed to the discovery of two more groups, his work being completed by M. Hall and G. Higman.

The table at the end of the column records all the nonclassical finite simple groups that were known to exist as 1968 ended.

The largest of the groups, one credited to J. Conway in the table, arose from a study by J. Leech of close packing of spheres in 24 dimensions. It was remarkable that this group contained copies of most of the others on the list, notably the other two Conway groups and those of Hall-Janko, McLaughlin, and Higman-Sims.

At year's end two more possibilities were reported. D. Held found evidence for the existence of a group of order 4,030,387,200, and J. Thompson discovered a simple group attached to a close packing in 48 dimensions, but it was not known whether this one was new.

It appeared that finite simple groups existed in greater abundance than had been suspected. However, the 14 (possibly 16) examples remained isolated, in that there was as yet no infinite family comparable to the various families that comprise the classical groups. It was noteworthy that some formidable calculations were needed, and were being carried out by a skillful combination of hand work and large, high-speed electronic computers.

Among unsolved problems in mathematics perhaps the best known to the general public is the four-colour problem. If it is required that adjacent countries in a map are to have different colours, how many colours will be needed? An empirical example may be produced with little difficulty to show that four may be needed. It has been proved in mathematical terms that five is enough. There the matter stood as of 1968.

It readily may be seen that the question is exactly the same for maps drawn on a plane or on a sphere. For practical applications it is convenient to switch to a sphere and, once this has been done, it seems reasonable to ask what the answer is for other surfaces, above all for the general orientable surface of genus p. Such a surface can be described as a sphere through which have been punched p holes, where p is

Discoverer	Order of group
E. Mathieu	7,920
E. Mathieu	95,040
E. Mathieu	443,520
E. Mathieu	10,200,960
E. Mathieu	244,823,040
Z. Janko	175,560
M. Hall and Z. Janko	604,800
G. Higman and Z. Janko	50,232,960
J. McLaughlin	898,128,000
D. Higman and C. Sims	44,352,000
M. Suzuki	448,345,497,600
J. Conway	495,766,656,000
J. Conway	42,305,421,312,000
J. Conway	4,157,776,806,543,360,000

an integer. When $p = 1$, for instance, a doughnut-shaped object is produced which mathematicians call a torus. Perversely enough, the problem turned out to be more accessible to treatment for a sphere with holes than for the sphere itself. In 1890, P. J. Heawood found 7 to be exactly the right number of colours for a torus; he conjectured that for any p the answer would be the largest integer not exceeding $\frac{1}{2}(7 + \sqrt{1 + 48p})$. In June 1968 (*Proc. Natn. Acad. Sci. U.S.A.*) G. Ringel and J. Youngs announced a proof that Heawood was right.

March 1968 (*Bull. Am. Math. Soc.*) produced announcements answering two outstanding questions. The first was a basic problem in the theory of games, as presented earlier in *Theory of Games and Economic Behavior* (1944) by J. von Neumann and O. Morgenstern: Does every game have a solution? By a solution, roughly speaking, is meant a stable pattern of behaviour for the players. W. Lucas exhibited a game for ten players not admitting a solution. In the second, J. Stallings answered affirmatively a question that had arisen early in the development of homological algebra, by showing that any finitely generated group of cohomological dimension 1 is free. The proof was of technical interest since it involved a large-scale application of topological techniques to a purely algebraic problem.

In the field of functional analysis there were significant advances in two areas. B. Johnson answered affirmatively two classical problems in the theory of Banach algebras; he proved that any automorphism or derivation of a semisimple Banach algebra is continuous. In the theory of rings of operators it had been known since 1967 that there were infinitely many factors of Type III. For factors of Type II_1 this remained an open question, but W.-M. Ching added a fourth example to three that previously had been found.　　　　　　　　　　　　　　　　(I. KA.)

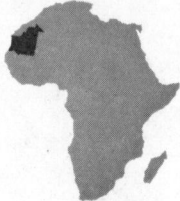

Mauritania

The Islamic Republic of Mauritania is on the Atlantic coast of West Africa, adjoining Spanish Sahara, Algeria, Mali, and Senegal. Area: 397,683 sq.mi. (1,030,000 sq.km.). Pop. (1967 est.): 1.1 million. Cap.: Nouakchott (pop., 1967 est., 15,000). Language: Arabic (national); French (official). Religion: Muslim. President in 1968, Mokhtar Ould Daddah.

Following a congress of the Mauritanian People's Party at which President Ould Daddah announced that the government was to be reshuffled, five out of six high commissions were raised to ministerial level on Jan. 31, 1968. A second government reshuffle was announced on July 4 when the foreign minister, Birane Mamadou Wane, and Fall Papa Daouda, minister of industry, crafts, and mines, were dismissed for alleged embezzlement.

In April diplomatic relations with the U.K., broken off at the time of the 1965 Rhodesian crisis, were restored. Other important events in foreign relations were the strengthening of ties with Communist China, and Ould Daddah's condemnation of the Biafran secession from Nigeria.

Riots in June, paralleling those in Paris in May, took place at Zouérate; eight people were killed. France denied allegations that French troops intervened in this incident.

At the end of the fifth assembly of the Organization of African Unity (OAU) heads of state, held at Algiers

in September, the frontier dispute with Morocco remained unresolved. In this month also Mauritania, which together with Senegal, Guinea, and Mali comprised the Organization of Senegal River States, established a council for coordinating public health projects.　　　　　　　　　　　　　　　　(PH. D.; X.)

Mauritius

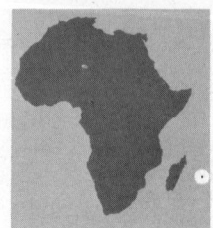

The parliamentary state of Mauritius, a member of the Commonwealth of Nations, lies about 500 mi. E of the Malagasy Republic in the Indian Ocean. Area: 720 sq.mi. (1,865 sq.km.). Pop. (1968 est.): 787,400, including Indian and Pakistani 67%; Creoles (mixed French and African) 29%; Chinese 3.5%; British and French 0.5%. Cap. and largest city: Port Louis (pop., 1968 est., 136,800). Governor-general in 1968, Sir John Rennie; prime minister, Sir Seewoosagur Ramgoolam.

After 150 years of British rule Mauritius became an independent member of the Commonwealth on March 12, 1968. The independence ceremonies were boycotted by the opposition Mauritian Party (PMSD) and followed the worst riots in the island's history, contained, at the request of the government, by the intervention of British troops. A six-year treaty of defense and assistance was established with Britain, which continued to train local security forces and to enjoy existing air and naval facilities. Prompt Communist interest in Mauritius was observed, with both the U.S.S.R. and Communist China applying for the opening of diplomatic relations on March 16.

Independence did not solve urgent political, racial, economic, and population problems. Through the ruling Independence Party the Hindu majority, sup-

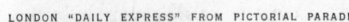

A soldier stands guard in Port Louis on Jan. 29, 1968. The Shropshire Light Infantry was asked to reinforce the island's police force when violence erupted between competing Creole and Muslim youth gangs.

LONDON "DAILY EXPRESS" FROM PICTORIAL PARADE

ported by Chinese and Muslim groups, took over politically, socially, and economically from the Franco-Mauritians, represented by the PMSD, who believed that continued British rule would have best protected minority interests against an ever increasing Indian majority. Racial problems continued to be aggravated by overpopulation (an increase of 80% in the population since 1945 was largely the result of improved medical services, including the eradication of malaria).

With no mineral production and with industry in its infancy, the Mauritian economy remained almost entirely dependent on sugar, which accounted for more than 90% of exports; little further expansion seemed possible as more than 45% of the total land area was already planted with sugar.

During 1966–67 British aid for development and budgetary purposes amounted to £5,876,996. In 1967 Britain contributed an additional £4.3 million to cover the residual deficit for 1967–68. Following independence, financial talks were held in London and another £3 million was approved for development aid for 1968–69. (M. Mr.)

Medicine

The medical scene in 1968 continued to be dominated by heart transplants. To the accompaniment of worldwide public debate provoked by the first operation (performed Dec. 3, 1967; patient died on December 21), the team led by Christiaan Barnard (*see* BIOGRAPHY) at Groote Schuur Hospital in Cape Town, S.Af., carried out a second transplant a month later. The recipient was a 58-year-old dentist, Philip Blaiberg, who had been forced to retire because of disabling heart disease. He received the heart of a young man, Clive Haupt, who had died of a stroke. Following surgery, Blaiberg overcame a critical liver infection and then a lung condition, thought to be the result of rejection reactions, to become the world's longest-surviving heart transplant recipient. By the end of 1968 more than 100 transplants had been carried out in the U.S., India, France, Britain, South America, Canada, Czechoslovakia, and Israel—and more than 40 patients had survived.

Despite early criticisms, the operation clearly was here to stay. It was agreed that the surgical procedure itself was not particularly difficult and that rejection phenomena would in time be overcome. (See *Immunology* and *Surgery,* below.) Moral considerations, however, remained vexing. Fears were expressed that expediency might lead to the use of a heart before the donor's death had occurred, as it is necessary to maintain the integrity of the heart tissue. This provoked attempts to define death. Some suggested that absence of electrical activity in the brain as judged by the electroencephalogram (EEG) would be a satisfactory criterion. Workers in Edinburgh, however, pointed out that a "flat" EEG could be produced by an overdose of sedatives, with subsequent full recovery. As a safeguard, it was suggested that death should be certified by a team of doctors responsible for caring for the dying patient; that is, a team distinct from the doctors waiting to carry out the transplant. The World Medical Association, meeting in Sydney, Austr., found it impossible to give a precise definition of death but agreed to circulate a statement to its members.

A heart transplant was estimated to cost an average of $1,200 a day. The figure accounted only for hospital costs, as surgeons did not charge for the operation. Because the patient must remain in the hospital considerably longer than with other operations, the problem of hospital resources allocation also caused concern. And, because it is possible that demand for suitable hearts will exceed supply for some time, the question was asked: How and by whom are recipients to be chosen?

Comparatively undramatic events in medicine often have broad implications for health, comfort, and longevity. Asthma research in 1968 provided examples. A sharp increase in mortality from asthma among young people was noted in many parts of the world. Between 1959 and 1966 in England and Wales the death rate increased 250% in asthmatics between the ages of 5 and 34 and 800% in the age group 10 to 14. Death was often sudden and unexpected, and two causes were suggested: sudden failure of the adrenal glands due to the use of corticosteroids, and excessive inhalation of sympathomimetic aerosols, particularly those containing isoprenaline. Neither of these could be implicated with certainty, but the latter seemed the more likely and led to an official warning against their abuse. Substances such as adrenaline, ephedrine, and isoprenaline, widely employed in treatment, were found, when used in excessive dosage, to cause abnormal ventricular rhythms with danger of sudden cardiac arrest.

By contrast, new hope for asthma sufferers was provided by the discovery that disodium cromoglycate, a drug that inhibits the release of various mediators of the anaphylactic (allergic) response, was valuable in preventing attacks. Several clinical trials showed that the drug lessened the amount of bronchospasm in patients with asthma precipitated by external allergens. Moreover, its continued use could lead to a reduction in the amount of aerosols and corticosteroids needed to control the disease. The drug was administered in the form of an inhalant, and no toxic effects were reported. The discovery provided a promising new approach to the treatment of allergic diseases.

One of the major allergens causing asthma is house dust. Research in the Netherlands led to the isolation of an acarine mite (*Dermatophagoides*), which was thought to be responsible. The mite grows best on human dander and is found in mattresses.

Public medicine was another area of change. A survey in the 20th year of Britain's Health Service showed that 95% of the citizenry were satisfied with it, despite continued complaints within the service of shortages of money and manpower. Much bitterness was aroused by the reintroduction of prescription charges. Far-reaching administrative changes were

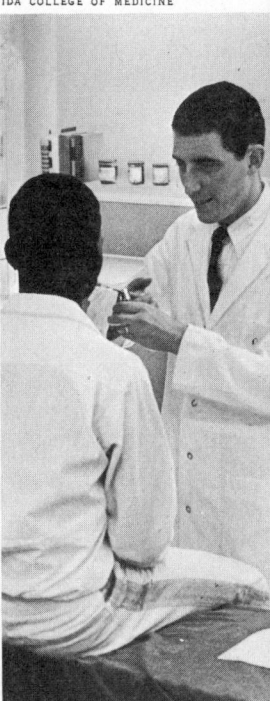

COURTESY, UNIVERSITY OF FLORIDA COLLEGE OF MEDICINE

Volunteer from Florida State Prison receives a flu-vaccine spray as part of a study by microbiologists at the University of Florida under the direction of Robert H. Waldman.

Meat:
see Agriculture; Food

forecast by the government: a single-area health board might replace the existing tripartite system under which hospitals, general practice, and local community health services were controlled by separate bodies. Much closer integration of health and welfare services was also proposed. (AL. PA.)

Three Americans—Robert W. Holley of the Salk Institute, Har Gobind Khorana of the University of Wisconsin, and Marshall Warren Nirenberg of the National Heart Institute—shared the 1968 Nobel Prize for Medicine or Physiology for their contributions to deciphering the genetic code. (*See* BIOGRAPHY.)

Medical science in the United States during the year was exemplified (along with advances mentioned in the specialty sections that follow) by work on such diverse subjects as emphysema, the role of interferon in viral disease, and cancer of the cervix.

Emphysema was said to be second only to heart disease as a cause of adult disability. Reports of deaths from emphysema had doubled every five years since 1945. Cigarette smoking and air pollution are perhaps implicated. The disease is characterized initially by weakness, difficulty in breathing, and a mild cough, and eventually by serious shortness of breath. Pathologists classify people with emphysema into two types: PP (pink and puffing) and BB (blue and bloated). The ninth Emphysema Conference, held at Aspen, Colo., concluded that neither the cause nor a specific method of treatment had yet been demonstrated.

In the search for drugs that can be used for the prevention and treatment of diseases caused by viruses a substance called interferon was found to be effective. It is derived from viruses that have been inactivated with hydroxylamine. These viruses not only reproduce themselves but also produce interferon. Among the inducers of interferon release are live and inactivated viruses, polysaccharides, and microbial toxins. Arthur P. Grollman of the Albert Einstein College of Medicine found that an industrial dye, auriatricarboxylate, can block the entrance of RNA into the cell; its action is like that of interferon in blocking viral action.

Cancer of the cervix (neck of the uterus) is diagnosed in 40,000 women in the U.S. each year. At Baylor University, W. E. Rawls and associates found type 2 herpes virus in the genital organs and on the cervix of women who were studied. (The type 1 herpes virus is the one that causes cold sores around the mouth.) About 80% of women with cancer of the cervix had antibodies to herpes 2, but among 44 cancer-free women used as experimental controls only 9 (20%) had such antibodies. Other controls were women with cancer at places other than the cervix, and 37 randomly selected children and adults; none of them had evidence of the herpes virus. Emory University researchers confirmed the Baylor observations. Establishment of a relationship between the virus and cancer would open the possibility of antiviral treatment with a vaccine. (M. FI.)

ANESTHESIOLOGY

In 1968 an estimated 50,000 doctors throughout the world were specialists in anesthesia (or anesthesiology). In the United Kingdom, for example, anesthesia had become the largest medical specialty in the hospital system. The World Federation of Anesthesiologists (founded 1955) held its quadrennial congress in London in 1968 with 4,132 persons attending. Francis Foldes, of New York City, was elected president. The 1972 congress was scheduled to convene in Tokyo. Regional and continental associations meet between world congress sessions. All these meetings have progressed toward establishing universal standards for anesthetic drugs and apparatus. At the same time there has been considerable interest in ways of improving professional education. The World Health Organization established in Caracas, Venezuela, a training centre like the one started earlier in Copenhagen, and in the U.S. in 1967 the Macy Foundation sponsored a conference on education in anesthesiology.

The general shortage of medical manpower makes it economically impossible to provide fully trained physician anesthetists for all surgical procedures; and they are increasingly in demand outside the operating room—in intensive care units, at the patient's bedside, and in pain clinics. The U.K. and Australia presently restrict the practice of anesthesia to physicians, but nurse or technician anesthetists are used in many European and Asian countries. The American Society of Anesthesiologists' policy of discouraging the use of nurse anesthetists has resulted in a relative increase in the number of physician anesthetists in the United States, with resulting improvement in teaching and practice.

Increased demand for the skills of the anesthetist reflects the changing concept of his place in medicine. An anesthetist used to be simply a person who made the patient insensible to the pain of surgery; today he is more likely to be a doctor especially trained to maintain the viability of the patient while a surgical or medical cure is effected and healing takes place. In this broadened role the anesthetist has become expert in the artificial control of various bodily functions: consciousness, ventilation, temperature, circulation. In a phrase, reanimation and resuscitation have become his responsibility.

Intensive care units have been established in most major hospitals, usually under the control of an anesthetist. Such a unit requires a highly trained staff as well as elaborate and expensive equipment. In addition to serving as resuscitation centres, intensive care units often are equipped to give artificial assistance in cases of cardiac, circulatory, respiratory, or kidney failure. Establishment of these units, together with the anesthetist's interest in the artificial control of bodily functions, has resulted in a demand for sophisticated electrical monitoring apparatus. This in turn has fostered a paramedical industry, sometimes called bioelectronics. (See *Instrumentation*, below.) Clinical measurement has developed as a subspecialty. The use of on-line computers is extending the usefulness of patient-monitoring facilities. Computers are being used in several centres in Europe and the U.S. to analyze electrocardiograms and perform other physician-assistance functions.

Anesthetists are investigating, in fresh detail, the nature of the bodily changes produced with various methods of anesthesia. New hypotheses of the anesthetic state have been proposed. The chemist Linus Pauling has suggested that anesthesia is induced by formation of hydrates within the cell; however, extensive study thus far has failed to establish this as the complete explanation.

New anesthetics under test included methohexitone, a barbiturate; propanidid, a eugonal derivative; and γ-hydroxybutyric acid. Methohexitone had found a place as an alternative to thiopentone in cases where the rapid recovery of full consciousness is desirable; *e.g.*, in dental treatment or outpatient surgery.

Whether propanidid and γ-hydroxybutyric acid offer advantages over thiopentone was as yet uncertain.

Halothane remains the most popular volatile anesthetic: its nonexplosive character makes it the safest, and its great versatility and nonirritant vapour make it one of the easiest to use. However, possible disadvantages have been reported. One is the tendency of halothane to produce postoperative headaches. Another is the suspicion that it causes liver damage. A study of one million administrations of various anesthetics in the U.S. indicated that the incidence of massive liver necrosis following the use of halothane was no higher than with any other agent. There are, however, many well-documented cases of patients developing jaundice after repeated halothane anesthesia. The reaction seems to require a previous exposure that sensitizes the liver to halothane. Animal experiments have failed to produce the condition.

Certain combinations of drugs cause dissociation of mental processes along with analgesia. This state of chemical hypnosis—called neurolept anesthesia—has been found advantageous to the neurosurgeon who wishes to elicit the patient's verbal reaction to surgical interference with a particular area of the brain.

Physical and chemical properties of a drug influence its effectiveness as an anesthetic by altering the rate at which it is taken up by various body tissues. From pharmacokinetics—the study of the uptake, distribution, and elimination of drugs—has come the concept of minimal alveolar concentration (MAC), which is defined as the concentration of an anesthetic that must be present in the lungs before anesthesia can be achieved.

In obstetrics, the hazards to the mother and baby resulting from administration of an analgesic by inhalational techniques are now known to be far greater than the risks accompanying regional block. This is reflected in the increasing resort to continuous epidural (spinal) anesthesia, either by the lumbar or the caudal route, as a means of pain relief in childbirth. The use of combinations of nitrous oxide and oxygen, premixed in cylinders, has been advocated (mainly in the U.K.) as a safe analgesic for self-administration, especially during the first stage of labour. Mixtures containing more than 50% nitrous oxide have been found to be unsafe if stored where the temperature may fall to $-7°$ C ($19.4°$ F). At this point the gases separate, and, if the cylinder is not vigorously shaken, pure nitrous oxide may be released after the oxygen has been used. The need for vigilance in maintaining standards of purity and safety was emphasized by two deaths in the U.K. from the administration of nitrous oxide containing large amounts of the higher oxides of nitrogen. Investigation into this "chance in a million" led to the imposition of more stringent precautions in the production of this agent. (See *Gynecology and Obstetrics,* below.) (S. A. F.)

CANCER

Environmental factors, such as chromates, nickel, iron, asbestos, and a great range of vegetable products, as possible causes of cancer continued to attract wide attention. The outstanding example remained that of lung cancer attributable to cigarette smoking. While the overall mortality from this disease in England and Wales continued to increase at a rate of approximalely 5% a year, this increase had ceased for younger men.

As for the mechanisms of action of chemical carcinogens, a growing number of classes of these seemed to involve interaction with nucleic acids. However, the generality of such mechanisms remained open to doubt. An important event was the publication of James D. Watson's *The Double Helix.* An article by L. D. Hamilton, "DNA: Models and Reality," in *Nature* (218:633–637) was similarly useful. Apart from the disintegrative effects of the alkylating and other carcinogens upon nucleic acid structure, much more attention was devoted in 1968 to the consequent processes of molecular repair. An outstanding conference on "Biological Effects of Alkylating Agents" was held at the New York Academy of Sciences.

Of central significance were numerous studies of the tumour-forming and other mechanisms of many DNA-RNA viruses and so-called mycoplasma in the induction of cancer and the leukemias; but the specific role of these agents in human cancer was still obscure. Research in tumour immunology continued, with special reference to the action of adjuvant and antibody-stimulating systems. The immunological field remained closely linked with fundamental studies of order, disorder, and cellular differentiation.

A rather neglected field was examined in a conference of the New York Academy of Sciences, "Psychophysiological Aspects of Cancer." (AL. HA.)

DERMATOLOGY

Several cutaneous markers of internal disease were attracting interest. For example, a peculiar two-toned ("half-and-half") colour change in fingernails is said to indicate chronic renal insufficiency; but some disagreement prevails as to the specificity of this sign. Both electrocardiographic and structural heart abnormalities are now known to be associated with a hereditary disorder in which affected family members are covered with pigmented frecklelike macules (lentigines). The possibility of phenylketonuria is suspected where a retarded child develops lesions of circumscribed scleroderma; this was previously believed to be an entirely innocuous disorder. Information concerning the early recognition of melanomas ("black cancer") has been collated and systematized, and for the first time the general physician will have an ordered approach to the diagnosis of pigmented moles and melanomas. Narrated clinical films on melanoma recognition have been produced by Massachusetts General Hospital under the sponsorship of the National Cancer Institute.

Awareness of the hazards of antibacterial (*i.e.*, deodorant) additives in commercial toilet soaps was growing: halogenated salicylanilides are now regarded as established causes of abnormal sensitiveness to ultraviolet light. What degree of disability may be sustained by sensitized individuals remained to be clarified.

Other advances have occurred in the classification of such disease constellations as the ichthyoses ("fish skin" diseases) and the primary hyperlipemic states, or xanthomatoses (subcutaneous fatty tumours). In these conditions the abnormal mechanisms are better understood, and more meaningful therapeutic courses can be charted. Common to all the ichthyoses, it seems, is increased production of epidermal cells; in the case of dominantly inherited ichthyosis vulgaris, however, horny cells appear merely to adhere as excess scaly material. Therapeutic agents (*e.g.*, antimetabolites) that inhibit cell growth may prove to be useful in the management of the more disabling proliferative ichthyoses. D. S. Fredrickson's classification of the hyperlipidemias similarly offers a more rational

therapeutic approach in terms of counteracting the specific metabolic defect.

Another metabolic disorder with cutaneous stigmata has recently been elucidated: the fascinating, and fortunately uncommon, inherited disease known as the Lesch-Nyhan syndrome. Affected male children show self-induced maceration of the lips and fingers, chorea-like tics, tortuous movements of the hands and feet, and mental retardation. There is marked accumulation of uric acid in the blood. The metabolic abnormality is due to the absence of an enzyme important in nucleic acid metabolism (J. E. Seegmiller and others). In Refsum's disease, whose expression may include an ichthyosiform dermatosis, deficiency of phytanic acid oxidase has been shown to be the link between the genetic defect and the abnormal accumulation of phytanate. Angiokeratoma corporis diffusum, still another inherited multisystem disease with cutaneous manifestations, has been explained: accumulation of sphingolipid in various tissues is caused by deficiency of ceramide trihexoxidase. This disease may also be attributable in part to abnormal function of lysosomes. These organelles probably will continue to interest investigators both in cutaneous physiology (complexes with transferred melanosomes) and in pathophysiology (cellular inclusions in Chédiak-Higashi syndrome, photosensitive mechanisms in the porphyrias, etc.).

Further research at the subcellular level in patients with fatal granulomatous disease of childhood has revealed an abnormality of aerobic metabolism in certain white blood cells (neutrophils) that may be due to deficiency of nicotine-adenine-dinucleotide oxidase. Affected male children show multiple suppurative, granulomatous skin lesions and invariably succumb to sepsis or pulmonary disease early in life.

A remarkable achievement of the past two years has been the control of sun-induced keratoses by topical application of 5-fluorouracil (5-FU) in cream or lotion form. This treatment, which was developed by C. J. Dillaha of Little Rock, Ark., and E. Klein of Buffalo, N.Y., has become generally accepted. The keratoses—localized, sandpaperlike excrescences on skin much exposed to the sun—become markedly inflamed after three to ten days' treatment with 5-FU; the treatment is then stopped, and the keratoses disappear without a trace. Indeed, 5-FU will destroy keratoses that are subclinical, *i.e.*, not discernible on the skin.

In the management of malignant or "premalignant" cutaneous growths, progress is being made in providing simpler, less toxic, topical modes of therapy as possible alternatives to systemic cancer chemotherapy. Topical nitrogen mustard has been endorsed by H. A. Haynes and E. J. Van Scott as a valid method of treating a relatively common skin lymphoma, mycosis fungoides. Another antitumour drug, methotrexate, a folic acid antagonist, has been used topically with variable success against psoriasis. Heretofore, systemic administration of methotrexate had been widely considered the best means of long-term control of both these diseases. Authorities on congenital malfunctions have long been familiar with the deleterious effects of folic acid deprivation on the developing fetus. A report of multiple anomalies in the live offspring of a woman who took oral methotrexate during the first trimester suggests the need for caution.

Reports from Europe have extolled manipulation of the diet in treatment of various dermatoses allegedly associated with structural abnormalities of the gastrointestinal tract. Gluten restriction, for instance, ostensibly improves both dermatitis herpetiformis and the accompanying villous enteropathy, but the evidence is not wholly convincing.

N. Orentreich and co-workers, after achieving good results with the so-called punch replacement autograft technique in the treatment of male-pattern baldness, recently extended their studies to include patients with baldness due to scarring. Up to now, the outlook for hair regrowth in scarred skin has been dismal.

Betamethasone 17-valerate, a topical steroid derivative introduced to the U.S. from England, appears promising in the management of psoriasis, which has often been refractory to other steroid preparations.

Oral contraceptive agents, once widely heralded as perhaps the definitive treatment for severely disfiguring acne in girls, are being prescribed with greater caution following reports of adverse side effects, such as prolonged post-treatment amenorrhea and fatal thromboembolic phenomena. The evidence for the latter seems incontrovertible.   (J. T. K.; T. B. F.)

EAR, NOSE, AND THROAT DISEASES

The adverse reaction of the human ear to excessive noise is a problem familiar to engineers who design industrial facilities and motor-driven equipment. Sound levels of over 85 decibels require control or the protection of those who are exposed. C. T. Yarington, Jr., reviewed noise-induced hearing loss in military personnel exposed to turbines, aircraft, rocket launchers, missiles, and ordinary weapons. A study of the attenuation performance of standard ear protectors presented a discouraging outlook for the success of hearing conservation programs in the military or in civilian life. Music as a source of acoustic trauma was studied by C. P. Lebo. He found that the sounds of rock 'n' roll and discotheque bands and amplification of psychedelic music frequently reach peaks of 120 decibels at frequencies between 500 and 4,000 cycles per second. This intensity is only 10 decibels less than that of a large pneumatic riveter and is loud enough to produce a temporary shift in the hearing threshold. If such exposure is continued four hours a day, two days a week, for a year or more, permanent hearing loss may result. Thus the hearing deficits formerly associated with aging may now occur in teenagers. Furthermore, the "big sound" may produce adverse psychological and physiological effects in susceptible individuals. Public health authorities warn that the urban environment is at times already excessively noisy and can be expected to get worse in terms of total time exposure. Samuel Rosen, investigating the quiet environs of the Mabaan people of the southeastern Sudan, found a low incidence of hypertension, heart disease, and hearing loss in comparison with these disabilities in the adult population of the U.S.

R. M. Butler and F. H. Moser noted that the "padded dash syndrome" in automobile accidents, while seldom fatal, may produce permanent damage unless adequate treatment is begun early. The type of face or neck injury is related to the position of the passenger at the time of the crash. The driver usually is injured by contact with the steering wheel, but the other occupant of the front seat is in a more vulnerable position and is likely to be thrown upward and forward onto the dashboard or through the windshield. The soft tissues of the face are readily torn, and often there are fractures of the nose, orbits, and upper and lower jaws. A threat of suffocation exists when the victim, especially if unconscious, bleeds excessively into the throat or has sustained an injury to the

larynx. In such cases an air passage must first be provided by tracheotomy. After control of bleeding, treatment of shock, and stabilization of the obvious injuries, an assessment for less apparent traumatic effects should be carried out by X-ray examination of all vulnerable sites about the head and neck. Displaced fractures should be reduced promptly so as to avoid deformity. Hyperextension of the neck as it strikes the edge of the padded dashboard may result in severe laryngotracheal trauma without damaging the soft tissues of the anterior neck. Air in the tissues of the neck is indicative of disruption of the mucous membrane; this calls for cervical and chest X rays, with indirect and direct laryngoscopy. The full extent of injury may not be determined without external surgical exploration, when repositioning of the cartilaginous structures and repair of soft tissues are achieved with the aid of intralaryngeal stents or molds. The authors believe that the padded dash syndrome can be prevented by a shoulder-waist combination seat belt to be worn by all passengers.

Tonsillectomy performed on 40,000 patients on an outpatient basis was reported by T. M. Chiang, A. E. Sukis and D. E. Ross. They stressed the care with which the patients were scheduled. Those with allergies are not operated on during the pollen season, and no one receives surgery within four or five weeks after an acute attack of tonsillitis. This is paramount if postoperative bleeding is to be reduced. The authors reported an incidence of only 0.006%, compared with an estimated 4–8% overall figure for the U.S. Other essentials are a well-equipped surgical suite; the services of surgeons who are board-certified throat specialists and of experienced anesthetists; attentive recovery room care; and instructions to the patient before his dismissal on the afternoon of the operation. The rising cost of care and the shortage of hospital beds strongly favour tonsillectomy on an outpatient basis—but only if all the above guidelines and high standards are followed.

Rhinitis, nasal polyps, and bronchial asthma in more than 1,000 aspirin-sensitive nonatopic patients were reported on by M. Samter and R. Beers, Jr. In many instances nasal and bronchial symptoms preceded the development of intolerance to aspirin by months or years. Salicylates other than acetylsalicylic acid (aspirin) failed to produce symptoms in aspirin-sensitive patients. Other substances, unrelated to aspirin—strong minor analgesics, including pyrazolones and indomethacin—did produce similar symptoms. The authors believe these act on peripheral chemoreceptors and initiate a series of reflexes that might produce either urticaria (angioedema), or rhinitis and bronchial asthma, or all of these. A significant number of the patients did not know they were sensitive to aspirin. Testing for sensitivity is not to be taken lightly. Positive evidence requires anticipation of severe angioedema, bronchial asthma, cyanosis, asphyxia, and possibly coma, any of which may require the presence of a specialized team prepared to maintain an air passage. Obviously it is safer to administer aspirin under controlled hospital conditions to patients with suspected intolerance. Rhinologists have been alerted to the fact that surgical removal of nasal polyps in aspirin-sensitive persons may precipitate the alarming symptoms of status asthmaticus. Intolerance to aspirin has been known for more than 50 years; it is now apparent that an educational campaign is needed to point out the possible complications from this commonplace drug.   (F. L. Lr.)

ENDOCRINOLOGY

Growth hormone was long believed to possess diabetogenic and fat-mobilizing properties; in fact, a rise in titre of plasma-free fatty acids (FFA) was accepted as an index of one of the acute metabolic effects of human growth hormone (HGH). Now, however, O. Trygstad of Oslo has shown that the lipid-mobilizing factor (LMF) is different from HGH. Removal of LMF fraction from crude human pituitary extracts before preparation of HGH eliminated the lipotrophic agent from this hormone. The LMF induced hyperglycemia (increase of sugar in the blood) and fat mobilization, but no growth, whereas highly purified HGH produced growth and no lipid mobilization.

The relation of elevated serum phosphorus and the increased titres of growth hormone seen in acromegaly (pituitary-induced enlargement of the bones and soft parts of the hands, feet, and face) has been brought closer to solution. F. Camanni and his group at the University of Torino, Italy, found that the increased phosphorus concentration was associated with increased reabsorption of phosphorus from the urine in the kidney tubules. HGH secretion in primary hypothyroidism was studied by a Japanese group headed by H. Iwatsubo of Osaka University. The group found a significant decrease in HGH response to insulin-induced lowering of blood sugar in primary hypothyroidism, and a satisfactory recovery in this response after treatment with desiccated thyroid. The findings suggested that HGH secretion in human subjects is dependent on adequate thyroid function.

Treatment of diabetes insipidus with posterior pituitary powder or vasopressin is quite understandable. The paradoxical use of chlorothiazide diuretics has been substantiated. But the treatment of this condition with chlorpropamide, a hypoglycemic agent, was one of the surprise observations of the year. J. Reforzo-Membrives and colleagues in Buenos Aires, Arg., while treating a diabetic who incidentally had diabetes insipidus, found that this agent also had antidiuretic properties. Their investigation revealed that of all the hypoglycemic agents only chlorpropamide had this capacity, and that it behaved much like vasopressin and was far superior to the chlorothiazide diuretic agents.

Treatment of hypoparathyroidism may be greatly facilitated by administration of an alkali, such as

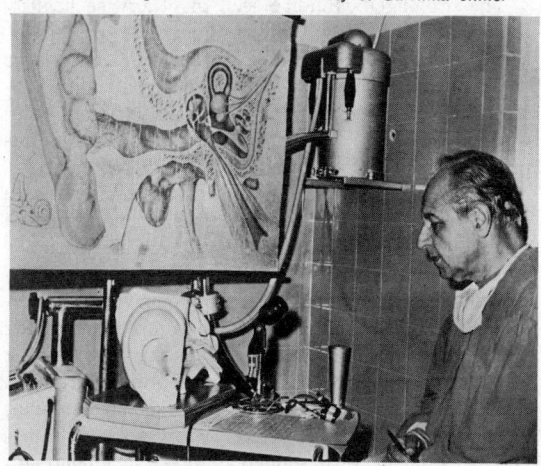

Greek surgeon G. Yannoulis uses diagram to explain the successful eardrum transplant technique that he perfected and used in three operations during 1968 at the University of Salonika clinic.

calcium carbonate. Thomas and colleagues at the University of Florida noted that alkaline salts improved calcium kinetics but that acid salts reversed the effect. The administration of 10 to 18 grams a day of calcium carbonate effectively increased serum calcium levels in 12 patients by 2.5 to 4 mg/100 ml.

Persistent spontaneous milk flow together with suppression of the menses following childbirth may be due to isolation of the pituitary gland from control by the hypothalamus. It is known that a neurohumoral agent in the hypothalamus inhibits the release of prolactin from the pituitary. Management of the condition has proved difficult. The occasional association of this syndrome with hypothyroidism was shown to be a distinct entity, differing from the classical postpartum lactation *cum* amenorrhea known as Chiari-Frommel syndrome in that it is amenable to thyroid medication. (See *Gynecology and Obstetrics*, below.)

Follicle-stimulating hormone (FSH) has always been considered important in the development of the primary ovarian follicle, whereas a surge of luteinizing hormone (LH) at the time of ovulation has been thought responsible for the rupture of the graafian follicle. B. D. Goldman and V. B. Mahesh, of the Medical College of Georgia, experimenting with rats, found that rupture of the graafian follicle resulting in ovulation could be induced by injecting FSH containing less than 5% of the ovulatory dose of LH as contaminant. In the hamster, injection of a mixture of FSH and LH antiserum at the time of ovulation blocked ovulation, whereas anti-LH alone had no effect. These findings may indicate a need to revise classical concepts of the gonadotropic control of ovulation.

The importance of varicocele (swelling of veins of the spermatic cord) as a factor in partial and absolute human male sterility is being increasingly recognized. McLeod of Cornell University has shown that the degree of motility and sperm morphology are more important than numbers. Tying off of the left internal spermatic vein brought some improvement in sperm morphology and variable changes in sperm count. More interesting was a striking increase in sperm motility. Fertile union has followed ligation in men with sperm counts much below 10 million per cm^3, and this has been attributed to the increased motility. The hormonal factor in relation to varicocele remained speculative.

Human skin is capable of transforming dehydroepiandrosterone into testosterone, according to A. J. Gallegos and D. L. Berliner of the University of Utah. The search for a biologically active androgen responsible for hirsutism and virilization was continuing. Wilson and co-workers at Southwestern Medical School, Dallas, Tex., isolated 5α-dihydrotestosterone, a new steroid that is more active biologically than testosterone. Incubation of skin from the pubic region in both males and females with testosterone showed abundant conversion to 5α-dihydrotestosterone. Such conversion is lacking in male pseudohermaphrodites, with the syndrome of feminizing testes, in whom there is complete absence of sexual hair. The skin, it appears, is the largest organ in the human body participating in steroid biotransformation.

(R. B. GT.)

GASTROENTEROLOGY

Persistent hiccups, ordinarily attributed to stimulation of the phrenic nerve supplying the diaphragm, may have several causes, including irritation of the brain, according to J. V. Sonadjian and J. C. Cain. Stimulation of the pharynx with a small rubber tube introduced through the nose relieved uncontrolled hiccups.

Measurement of acid production by the stomach, induced in part by the hormone gastrin, remained an important guideline in the medical and surgical management of peptic ulcer. Synthetic preparations of gastrin were being used as a simple test of acid secretion. In complicated peptic ulcer with non-beta cell islet tumours of the pancreas (Zollinger-Ellison syndrome), gastrin overproduction was found to be important. The increased incidence of duodenal ulcer in patients with hyperparathyroidism further emphasized the hormonal relationships.

The incidence of stomach cancer declined in the United States, but it continued to be a major source of cancer deaths. Earlier diagnosis—for example, in the examination of vulnerable groups, such as persons with pernicious anemia—was facilitated (in addition to X rays) by the new fibregastroscope with camera and by study of the surface cells. (See *Instrumentation*, below.)

The ileum (last portion of the small intestine) is important in the normal metabolism of bile salts. Disease of this area (regional enteritis) or surgical removal of the ileum results in bile salt deficiency, deconjugation of the salts, and fatty diarrhea. Poorly absorbed bile salts also interfere with normal absorption of water and minerals from the colon. G. G. Rowe found that medication with cholestyramine, which absorbs the irritating bile salts, relieved the abdominal cramps and diarrhea.

Medium-chain triglycerides (MCT) are hydrolyzed and absorbed more rapidly from the small bowel than ordinary long-chain triglycerides. They are transported directly to the liver, not by way of the intestinal lymphatic system, and thus are helpful in the management of malabsorptive disorders.

In men over 70 with evidence of arteriosclerosis, abdominal pain, alteration of bowel function, and rectal lesions have been recognized as signs of vascular injury to the bowel. D. A. Morowitz and co-workers found that in inflammatory bowel disease, especially regional enteritis (Crohn's disease), blood platelets rise to very high levels, with the likelihood of bleeding or clotting. Another study indicated that persons who had undergone surgery for ulcerative colitis adapted well to removal of the colon and an ileostomy, provided their condition was accepted by key people (family, employer).

The prolonged jaundice seen in otherwise healthy babies breast-fed by their mothers was explained: a chemical constituent of the mother's milk interferes with normal disposition of the pigment bilirubin. Substitution of cow's milk or breast milk from other women decreased the jaundice. The condition improved as the babies matured.

During the year, drug-induced liver reactions were common, and mimicked hepatitis or obstructive jaundice. Plasma exchange (removal of the patient's plasma followed by return of the patient's packed red blood cells and fresh-frozen donor plasma) relieved otherwise refractory liver coma. Exchanging only the plasma overcame the difficulty of obtaining large amounts of fresh whole blood and reduced the risk of severe transfusion reactions. Clinical studies identified a hepatitis associated with prolonged alcohol ingestion or with sudden increase in alcohol in-

take. Treatment included withdrawal of alcohol, prolonged bed rest, adequate diet, and doses of adrenal corticosteroids. Liver abscesses in returnees from Southeast Asia caused chills, fever, malaise, poor appetite, and pain in the right upper abdomen. Treatment consisted of prompt surgical drainage and the administration of antibiotics.

A. M. Large reported that X rays of the gallbladder and of the bile ducts might be repeatedly normal even though gallstones were actually present. Alterations in the chemistry of the bile, especially saturation with cholesterol, are important in the formation of gallstones, according to W. H. Admirand and D. M. Small. Gallbladder disease was common among Indians in the southwestern United States, with higher operative mortality.

Examination of cells in the fluid removed from the distended pancreatic duct at the time of abdominal operation aided the diagnosis of cancer of the pancreas. Numerous X-ray techniques have been devised for viewing the pancreas. (J. B. KR.)

GENETICS

Unlike heart surgery, organ transplants, and wonder drugs, discoveries in medical genetics seldom make the headlines. In 1968, however, a bit of genetic material—a Y chromosome—became newsworthy. Actually there is nothing unusual about a Y chromosome: every normal man has one in almost every cell (that is actually what makes him a man), but, it was discovered, some men have two—and therein lies a newsworthy tale, the tale of so-called "supermales."

Normally all men and women have 46 chromosomes per cell, grouped into 22 pairs of autosomes (which determine the numberless factors that make up an individual's many and various characteristics) and two sex chromosomes—a pair of X's in the female and an XY combination in the male. Half of each of the 23 pairs of chromosomes come, during fertilization and subsequent cell division, from the mother and half from the father. During the past ten years, as chromosome-study techniques were developed and refined, it was found that chromosome abnormalities occurred as a result of cell division accidents during gametogenesis, in the zygote or even later. Such accidents may produce, in approximately 1 out of 400–600 "male" births, an XXY sex-chromosome constitution that gives rise to Klinefelter syndrome—sparse body hair, long legs, enlarged breasts, and sterility. This anomaly, however, has not been linked with criminality.

The presence of an extra Y chromosome, it was found in 1968, appears to lend extra maleness, over-aggressiveness, and potential criminal tendencies to an individual. The XYY pattern, although found only once in 1,500 males examined for a variety of reasons and not at all in 266 newborn and 209 adult, randomly selected, males, by contrast was discovered among male inmates of maximum security prisons and institutions for the criminally insane with frequencies of 7 in 197, 16 in 100, 1 in 21, and 5 in 129. The XYY individuals averaged 6 ft. 1 in. tall as opposed to an average of 5 ft. 7 in. for the other inmates. According to one geneticist, these men are "unstable and immature . . . committing apparently motiveless crimes." The purported finding in 1968 of the XYY karyotype in an individual on trial for murder focused attention on the legal and social aspects of the observation. A medical editor made the comment, ". . . the doctor, the lawyer, the sociologist, and the criminologist are on the spot—a spot not marked with the conventional

X, but with a fascinating Y, a spot surrounded with a garland of question marks."

Utilizing cells obtained by transabdominal sampling of amniotic fluid (amniocentesis), combinations of cell culture, cytogenetic, and biochemical methods were applied to the prenatal detection of cytogenetic and hereditary metabolic errors. Such application is particularly useful in mothers who have previously borne children with inherited abnormalities and in whom therapeutic abortion might be indicated. Successful diagnosis, beginning after approximately the tenth week of pregnancy, has been obtained for an increasing variety of conditions including the translocation form of Down's syndrome (mongolism), galactosemia, and Hurler's syndrome (gargoylism).

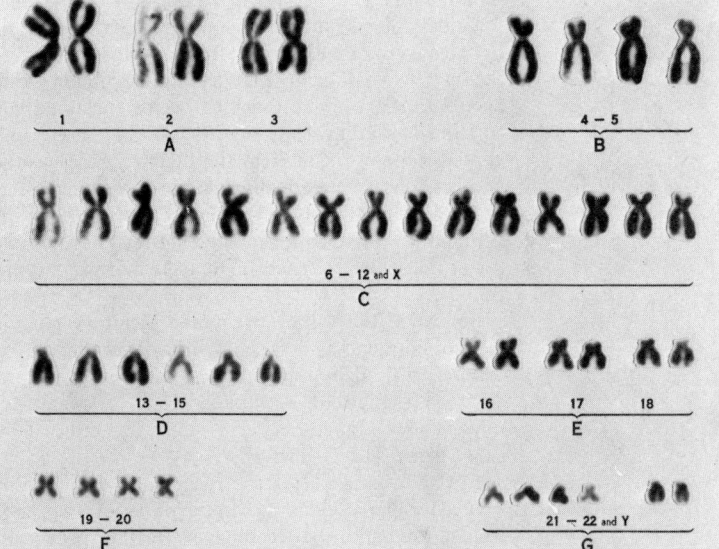

Chromosomes of XYY male institutionalized for antisocial tendencies. To determine chromosome patterns, or karyotypes, tissue cells are taken from the individual to be typed, grown on a culture medium, and then "swollen" by immersion in hypotonic salt solution. The "swelling" separates out the chromosomes, which are then stained, mounted on slides, and photomicrographed. From the enlarged photograph, pairs of chromosomes are cut out, sorted into seven groups, and numbered from 1 to 22, the Denver classification.

Not all inherited metabolic variations are rare. Some are sufficiently common to have considerable social and economic importance. For example, most if not all Africans and Orientals have inherited low-level activity of an intestinal enzyme: lactase. As a result these people are unable to adequately metabolize the milk sugar lactose into its constituent simple sugars, and upon ingestion of a glass or more of milk they develop abdominal cramps and subsequent osmotic and fermentative diarrhea. Thus milk as a basic unmodified food may be largely limited in its usefulness to individuals of European ancestry. (S. H. Bo.)

GYNECOLOGY AND OBSTETRICS

The prenatal use of decompression suits by expectant mothers, in which the atmospheric pressure over the pregnant abdomen is temporarily reduced, continued to be popular in Great Britain in 1968. Impressed by claims that babies born after this treatment were remarkably intelligent, these expectant mothers attended decompression clinics in the last ten weeks of pregnancy. R. Liddicoat conducted a survey of the babies (to age three) of 255 mothers, half of whom had been decompressed and half of whom had been given physiotherapy. No significant difference in intelligence between the two groups of infants was detected; but the number of treatments, whether de-

compression or physiotherapy, did seem to be correlated with the intelligence of the children.

A call for the widespread use of continuous epidural (spinal) anesthesia in childbirth was issued by R. de Vere at the fourth World Congress of Anesthesiology in London. He pointed out that it renders labour and delivery virtually pain-free and is safe for mother and child. However, it requires an expert anesthetist to insert the catheter into the epidural space. An easier way of relieving pain in labour was described by D. H. Gudgeon. He injected the long-acting drug bupivacaine 0.25% with 1 in 400,000 adrenaline on each side of the cervix and obtained good results safely in 87% of cases. Others had noticed an ominous slowing of the fetal heart rate when stronger solutions of local anesthetic or adrenaline were used. (See *Anesthesia*, above.)

Urinary stress incontinence was successfully treated by means of an electronic implant inserted under the vaginal wall near the urethral sphincter. Connected to a battery, the device causes sustained contraction of the levator ani muscles and thereby prevents escape of urine from the bladder. S. Alexander and D. Rowan were equally successful with an electric pessary connected to a miniature battery-operated stimulator carried in a shoulder holster. The stimulator is normally switched off only to permit micturition.

Following the taking of human pituitary gonadotrophic hormone as a fertility drug, Mrs. Sheila Ann Thorns was delivered in Birmingham, Eng., by cesarean section of sextuplets—four girls and two boys. They weighed between 2 lb. 6 oz. and 3 lb. 13 oz. at birth. Three survived.

Breast feeding delays the recurrence of menstruation after parturition. In many parts of the world women prolong breast feeding as a way of preventing conception; *i.e.*, they postpone the onset of ovulation. T. J. Cronin found that the average time for nonlactating women to menstruate was 7 weeks after childbirth but that fertile ovulation preceded menstruation in one woman in five. By continuing to lactate, women could postpone menstruation for up to 6 months; but, in two women out of five, fertile ovulation preceded menstruation. Breast feeding for a few weeks only neither delayed the onset of menstruation nor postponed the time of ovulation. Cronin concluded that women who breast-fed their babies were infertile for at least 12 weeks after delivery, but that women who did not lactate were infertile for only 6 weeks.

Women who do not wish to breast-feed are customarily given estrogen, but D. G. Daniel and co-workers found that such therapy increased the risk of thromboembolism by raising the blood level of factor IX, one of the substances responsible for clotting. G. B. Hill and W. A. Wilson analyzed 160,622 births and reported thromboembolic complications in 809, or 0.5%. The risk was twice as high when the delivery ended in stillbirth. After corrections had been made for age, parity, and type of delivery, suppression of lactation with estrogen seemed to be the main factor responsible for the thromboembolism in these cases.

In two reports to the Committee on Safety of Drugs in Great Britain, W. H. Inman, M. P. Vessey, and R. Doll claimed to have established a strong relationship between the use of oral contraceptives and thromboembolic disease. They compared the contraceptive methods used by 384 married women who

died of pulmonary, cerebral, or coronary thrombosis with a similar number of matched controls. By subtracting the death rate in nonusers of oral contraceptives they estimated the mortality from these three diseases in healthy women taking the pill at 2.2 per 100,000 of those aged 20–34 and 4.5 per 100,000 of those aged 35–44. They also calculated that the likelihood of hospital admission for nonfatal venous thromboembolism was about ten times greater in women who used oral contraceptives (1 in 2,000) than in those who did not. The risk of thromboembolism was not associated with the use of any particular oral contraceptive.

J. Martinez-Manautou and co-workers gave chlormadinone acetate, an antiestrogenic progestogen, in a continuous daily dose of 0.5 mg. to 1,045 women in Mexico for a combined total of 8,652 months. Pregnancy was successfully prevented without inhibiting ovulation. The contraceptive effect probably was achieved by causing cervical mucus to become hostile to spermatozoal activity. Since many of the side effects of oral contraceptives—increase in weight, headache, anxiety and depression, reduced libido, thromboembolism—appear to be caused by the estrogenic component, it was hoped that the incidence of side effects might be reduced by this new approach to conception control. However, irregular menstruation, amenorrhea (absence of menses), or breakthrough bleeding occurred in nearly one-third of the patients. Meanwhile, in Thailand, Chile, and the United States, injections of depot medroxyprogesterone acetate (MPA), 150 to 300 mg., chlormadinone acetate, 100 mg., or norethisterone enanthate, 200 mg., given to women once every three months, successfully inhibited ovulation but caused irregular bleeding or were followed by prolonged amenorrhea. (For related matters see *Endocrinology*, above.)

(T. L. T. L.)

HEART AND CIRCULATORY DISEASES

Human heart transplants—among the most sensational events of the year—are discussed in the introductory section.

In 1968 a wave of enthusiasm was directed toward encouraging regular and rather strenuous physical activity in coronary heart disease (specifically that caused by "hardening" of the coronary arteries) in an attempt to improve collateral blood flow to the heart muscle and possibly help through other mechanisms. Easy running (jogging), bicycling, and like forms of exercise were popular in Europe and the United States to "help your heart." The magnitude of benefits from such measures was unclear, but specialists generally agreed this was probably a movement in the right direction. Clearly, participants in the program felt better.

Active investigation during the year concerned the study of the tissue in the heart responsible for the generation and conduction of electrical impulses that cause the heart to beat. According to a familiar concept, electrical activity normally arises in the right upper chamber of the heart in the area called the sinus, or pacemaker, node; spreads freely through the muscle of the two upper chambers (atria) to an area called the atrioventricular (AV) node; and then passes down specialized conduction tracts in the central wall (septum) of the heart to stimulate the muscle of the two main pumping chambers (ventricles). Recent studies have shown that there are indeed three specialized conduction tracts linking

the sinus and AV nodes. The AV node is a complex structure, probably transmitting the electrical impulses slowly in one part and more rapidly in another part. But in some cases electrical activity of the heartbeat can be present in the sinus and AV nodes and in their interconnecting tracts without any muscle response. The whole subject is under new scrutiny.

Recent evidence suggests that certain cases of congenital heart disease may be attributable to mumps during pregnancy—as with German measles. However, this needs further evaluation, as do the reports that maternal infection with a Coxsackie virus may also result in heart damage in the infant.

A major complication and hazard in the use of artificial heart valves was reported in 1968: the tissues around these foreign objects are highly vulnerable to infection. The organism responsible was often a staphylococcus (the bacterium that causes boils on the skin). The infections were difficult to treat; some cases did respond, however, to large doses of antibiotics. In certain instances replacement of the artificial valve was required because of damage to the sutures from the infection. Another heart condition caused by infection was decreasing in most parts of the world: acute rheumatic fever with acute rheumatic heart disease. Better means of recognition and treatment, and prevention of infection by the causative bacteria, beta-hemolytic streptococci, were major factors in the lessened incidence.

In every community and every large hospital a sizable number of persons have heart disease of unknown origin. Some of these cases seem to be the result of prior undetected infection of the heart by a virus, but proof is usually lacking. Others are thought to result somehow from the heavy use of alcohol, though the idea that this is frequent was challenged in 1968. In still other puzzling cases, local enlargements of the heart muscle occur during contraction, resulting in obstruction of the blood flow out of one of the ventricles. During 1968 certain drugs known as blocking agents were tested as means of modifying the contraction of the heart muscle and thus lessening the difficulty caused by this obstructing process. In severe cases an operation to remove a portion of the offending muscle tissue was tried.

Clarifications of the extent and course of high blood pressure were reported in a book, *Epidemiology*

of Hypertension, edited by J. and R. Stamler and T. Pullman. In almost all parts of the world other than certain Pacific islands the blood pressure rises with age. The rise is chiefly an elevation of the pressure resulting from the heartbeat (systolic pressure); it is much less often a rise in the pressure existing in the blood vessels between beats (diastolic pressure). Elevated blood pressure (hypertension) has been studied in obese persons, diabetics, U.S. Negroes, and persons with a family history of high blood pressure. The consensus among contributors to this book was that a clear dividing line between a normal blood pressure and an elevated one does not exist. However, even modest elevations of blood pressure (*e.g.,* 150/90) have an unfavourable influence on longevity. A U.S. Veterans Administration study confirmed that the treatment of severe high blood pressure with drugs currently available had significantly reduced morbidity and mortality.

Cells of the body wear out, and at least some are known to be freely replaced. J. Post and J. Hoffman, in a review of cell renewal patterns, noted that the muscle cells forming the mass of the heart appear to be capable of significant division (*i.e.,* renewal) only in early life; essentially, the heart muscle of an adult lacks this ability. Damaged cells can be replaced by scar tissue, which is invaluable in binding the remaining cells together; however, scar tissue cannot contract. The authors speculated on the evolutionary implications of this limitation. In prior centuries the average man died young, of malnutrition and infection; renewal of the heart was therefore not important. Today the average life span exceeds 70 years, and failure of cell renewal in the heart has become crucial.　　　　　　　　　　　　　　(O. Pl.)

HEMATOLOGY

New approaches, which should lead to improved management, have been found for sorting out "bleeders." People who bleed excessively after trauma, including minor surgery and tooth extractions, are usually referred to as bleeders. Two groups of bleeders are already well defined: those who have hemophilia and allied conditions caused by inherited deficiencies of essential blood-clotting factors, and those who are deficient in blood platelets, blood elements that are essential for proper hemostasis. But the majority of bleeders do not fit into either of these groups. These patients have prolonged bleeding time. Most of them show normal results with other tests for blood-clotting function, but a few are deficient in antihemophilic globulin. The prolonged bleeding time is partly due to an inherited inability of the capillary vessels to contract properly after damage and partly to a qualitative defect in the blood platelets (which are, however, present in normal numbers). When a blood vessel is damaged, platelets adhere to the damaged area and to each other; the adhering platelets then aggregate to form a mass that eventually plugs the hole in the vessel. If either of these functions is defective, bleeding after trauma will be excessive. In the third group of bleeders, platelet adhesiveness is deficient but platelet aggregation seems to be normal. (The bleeding that is sometimes troublesome in patients with failing kidneys is similarly due to defective platelet function.) A factor has now been found in plasma concentrates prepared for hemophilia that will correct the defective adhesiveness, and special laboratories are engaged in investigations that should reveal much more about this group of sufferers.

WIDE WORLD

Philip Blaiberg, the longest-surviving heart transplant patient, received his new heart on Jan. 2, 1968, in an operation performed by Christiaan Barnard.

Coronary patient receives high-pressure oxygen from a one-bed hyberbaric unit which enables doctors to avoid exposure to the treatments. Tests with the unit at London's Westminster Hospital showed a decreased mortality rate in cardiac patients.

VICKERS LTD. FROM "MEDICAL WORLD NEWS"

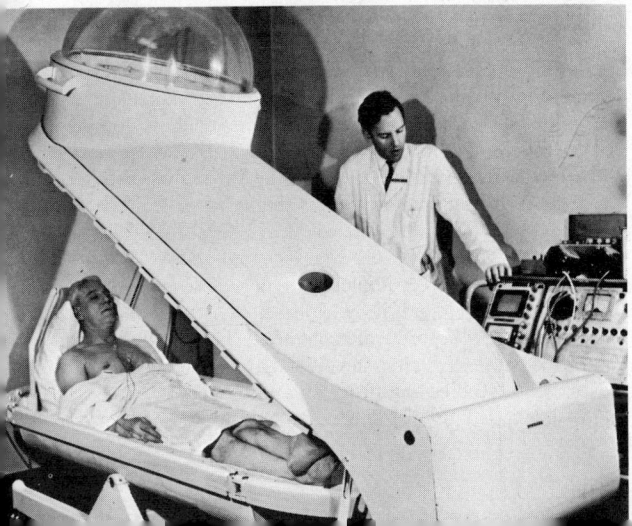

A new technique for the preparation of concentrates of antihemophilic globulin has proved to be of much practical value. Cryoprecipitation, so-called because it is effected at low temperature, enables the antihemophilic factor from a pint of blood to be concentrated in a volume of only 10 ml. So small a volume can be administered intravenously in a few minutes by using an ordinary syringe. The cryoprecipitate is put into plastic bags for deep-freeze storage at various centres where it is most conveniently available for the treatment of hemophilic patients. This is particularly valuable in the control of bleeding into large joints—one of the chief afflictions of hemophilia. If the patient is treated within 48 hours of onset much of the joint damage can be prevented. Prevention of joint damage is a major factor in keeping hemophilic patients mobile and able to follow normal occupations. Until now the physician has had to rely on snap-frozen plasma, which is much bulkier and is stored at only a few centres.

Leukemia therapy continued to be subject to change. Four years ago it seemed there was a good chance of identifying a virus as the cause of human leukemia, since a virus was known to be responsible for leukemia in fowls and mice. Unfortunately, the viruses found in connection with human leukemia proved to be noncausative; indeed, they are probably harmless. The most recent research indicates that if there is a human leukemia virus it is likely to belong to the class of so-called RNA viruses, which have properties different from those of viruses causing common infectious diseases.

In ordinary viruses the amount of virus in infected tissue increases as the disease progresses; thus it is possible to isolate the virus in the later stages of the illness, although tests made at the beginning were negative. The tests depend on the ability of the virus to kill infected cells. With RNA viruses, replication does not cause death of cells; rather, RNA viruses tend to stimulate growth, and experiments have now shown that they can (under admittedly artificial conditions so far) cause malignancies. A further difference is that the amount of RNA virus recoverable from infected tissues depends only on the size of the initiating dose of virus; this may be very small, and the amount does not increase as the disease progresses. Consequently, new techniques have had to be devised to detect the lowest effective dose of these viruses, and more sensitive methods will have to be worked out to permit their identification.

Of the alkaloids isolated some eight years ago from the periwinkle plant (*Vinca*), experience has shown that two, vincristine and vincaleukoblastine, have therapeutic value. Vincristine, combined with steroids, is proving useful in treating acute leukemia of children when the disease has become refractory to cytotoxic drugs like 6-mercaptopurine. Vincaleukoblastine is most useful in the treatment of conditions like Hodgkin's disease. Here, too, fresh remissions have been obtained when the patient has become refractory to radiotherapy and mustard drugs. Another, quite different, material being used in the treatment of leukemia is asparaginase. Certain lymphomas were known to be inhibited by guinea-pig serum, and the source of the inhibition was traced to L-asparaginase by J. D. Broome. Asparaginase can also be recovered from cultures of *Escherichia coli*. Crude active materials prepared from both these sources appear to be helpful against acute lymphatic leukemia, especially in children. (M. C. G. I.)

HOSPITALS

Heart transplant surgery presented a strong challenge to hospital management. Serious objections had been raised to performing these operations on a large scale before the problem of transplant rejection was fully mastered; nevertheless, it was certain that the number of organ transplants would increase. In many countries medical care institutions were planning to remodel their operating rooms and to obtain the specialized equipment necessary to perform transplant surgery.

Increase in costs and shortage of manpower remained two of the most important problems in hospital management. The low salaries formerly earned by hospital personnel discouraged recruitment at a time when sophistication of hospitals was demanding more highly skilled personnel, and the shortage thus created had led to wage increases. The situation was not yet stabilized, despite a heavy drain to developed countries of personnel trained in less developed countries. This drain was a matter of concern to international organizations that were trying to meet the latter countries' dire needs for health personnel.

The replacement of costly hospital facilities by private nursing homes for convalescents had been advocated as a way to keep costs down. This extension of the "progressive patient care" concept runs into difficulties when short-term, longer-term, and convalescent care are given in institutions that are administratively and financially independent of each other.

An advisory committee of the U.S. Public Health Service recommended that every hospital come under the jurisdiction of an area health service planning agency. This scheme, which aimed at ensuring the orderly development of essential health programs while avoiding duplication of facilities, was endorsed by the American Hospital Association. The rapid spread of comprehensive national health insurance was being advocated by an increasing number of responsible bodies in the U.S. This had already been implemented in most Canadian provinces.

The number of patients' visits to clinics and community health centres, as well as hospital admissions, increased significantly in the U.S. in 1967–68. As a consequence, private patients' visits to practitioners fell off from their 1966 level by close to 50 million, according to the National Disease and Therapeutic Index Study. The decline occurred despite a 10% increase in visits by elderly people following the implementation of Medicare.

The Ontario Hospital Services Commission recommended that the metric system be adopted in Canada as soon as feasible, in order to reduce risk of errors and facilitate the future use of computers in hospitals.

Staffing of hospitals with nurses and auxiliary personnel continued to be complicated by the language difficulties of recently immigrated personnel belonging to different ethnic groups.

In Great Britain the ten-year hospital plan was in progress. For England and Wales the value of work in progress as 1967 ended was about £256 million, and £93 million worth of work was scheduled for 1968. Forty hospitals were completed or nearly so in 1968.

Methods developed in various fields were being introduced into hospital management. They included operations research, first developed for military purposes; work studies and program and budgetary planning, originated by private industry; application of

the queuing theory and stochastic models, evolved by mathematicians; and methods of cost-benefit analysis and econometrics, adopted by economists.

(R. F. Br.)

IMMUNOLOGY

The tempo for acceptance of organ transplantation as commonplace was increased by dramatic events in cardiac allografting. The surgical techniques have been perfected and the moral and legal aspects are being explored, but the main problem—immunologic rejection—has not been solved. The current approach includes leukocyte matching to minimize the histocompatibility differences between donor and recipient and then the use of a combination of immunosuppressive drugs such as azothioprine and cortisone and, more recently, intramuscular injections of heterologous antilymphocyte serum. With the international Kidney Transplantation Registry recording more than 4,000 such procedures, the number of heart transplants more than 100 (through 1968), and spleen, liver, and lung transplants constantly on the increase, the efficacy of current means of prolonging organ survival can be adequately assessed. It appears that existing immunosuppressive therapy is adequate when measured against our knowledge of the immune response in general and the immune response in transplantation in particular.

In the early period of transplantation experiments there was considerable debate as to whether the rejection phenomenon was mediated by a circulating antibody or by a sensitized cell of the delayed hypersensitivity type. The consensus in 1968 was that both are operative—the cell-mediated rejection being the more active, if not exclusively so, in the acute rejection phenomenon in the absence of, or with inadequate, immunosuppressive therapy, whereas both are operative in the prolonged, or chronic, rejection. An exception is suggested by recent evidence that antiserum infiltrated around a viable primary skin graft will lead to prompt rejection of the graft within 24 hours of such treatment. Possibly a synergistic or additive effect of both mechanisms may be responsible for this kind of accelerated rejection.

Leukocyte grouping, commonly called tissue typing, is based on the concept that all nucleated cells carry most of the histocompatibility antigens on their surfaces and therefore can be employed in assessing relationships between prospective donors and recipients. The antiserum most often employed is obtained from either multitransfused or multiparous human beings and is subsequently absorbed with leukocytes to make them as monospecific as possible. The human transplantation system, called the HL-A complex, consists of a number of antigenic markers genetically controlled by two recognized subloci with some evidence of additional ones on a pair of autosomal chromosomes. Examination of the data accumulated over the past several years from almost 1,000 renal allografts in which leukocyte matching was used with satisfactory results shows that mismatching in the face of adequate immunosuppressive therapy is not injurious to the outcome of the graft during the first year, but close matching definitely enhances the survival rate thereafter. There is no evidence that Rh incompatibility or any of the other minor blood group antigens are involved, but ABO incompatibility definitely influences the graft adversely.

Approximately 85% of all persons who die under immunosuppressive therapy following transplantation do so from infectious diseases, not from graft failure. Investigators therefore have been searching for alternative methods of achieving suppression. One method currently under trial is the use of antilymphocyte serum. Its precise mode of action is not completely understood, nor is evaluation in vitro satisfactory in determining its efficacy. Moreover, it gives rise to considerable side reactions and may evoke a serum sickness reaction. Recently an additional hazard has become apparent: a number of malignancies (usually lymphomas or other malignancies of the reticuloendothelial system) have appeared in patients undergoing this therapy. Perhaps the homeostatic monitoring mechanism that nature has devised for scavenging mutant cells that arise with this treatment can no longer operate, leaving the malignant cells free to replicate.

In an effort to employ specific immunologic barriers to the rejection phenomenon, more attention has been given to the isolation and chemical characterization of soluble transplantation antigens in the hope of using such materials to induce "tolerance," inhibition, "blindfolding," etc. Although several reports indicate that the goal is being approached, the precise chemical nature of the antigenic determinant grouping remains uncertain. The cautious view at present is that the anatomic locus of the histocompatibility grouping is most likely within or on the membrane architecture; and most of the recent investigations have started with membrane preparations prior to extraction procedures. Chemically, cell membranes are composed of a protein-carbohydrate-lipid mosaic. Since the capacity of pure polysaccharides or lipids to sensitize a host for cellular hypersensitivity remains to be established, by default one must guess that a histocompatibility antigen will either be a polypeptide or a glycopeptide, a lipoprotein, or a lipopolysaccharide. Most materials that have been shown so far to possess transplantation activity have either been polypeptides or glycopeptides.

A source of transplantation antigens has been found in the cell membranes of group A streptococci. In the course of animal experiments such materials have behaved analogously to allogenic transplantation antigens in effecting the viability of skin grafts. Such an observation does not negate the concept of immunologic specificity of the histocompatibility antigens, as it is well known that nature has duplicated carbon-to-carbon linkages or amino acid sequences in laying down structural components. This view is especially acceptable if one thinks in terms of molecular evolution whereby certain chemical structures are retained because of their physiologic function. Hence it may be no accident that the streptococcal cell membrane, which is physiologically related to mammalian cell membranes, contains mammalian cross-reactive histocompatibility groupings.

All this research suggests that routinely successful transplantation will depend on specific immunologic interference. This, in turn, depends on prior knowledge of the chemical nature of the histocompatibility antigen.

(See *Surgery,* below.)   (A. S. M.)

INSTRUMENTATION

Important contributions to medical instrumentation in 1968 from the general field of electronics included the development of transducers and amplifiers of ever smaller dimensions. Miniature telemetric ampli-

Electronic "Boston Arm" developed by Liberty Mutual Insurance Companies with cooperation from Massachusetts General Hospital, Harvard, and MIT. The battery-powered arm (right) is activated with electric signals from the muscles in the amputee's stump.

fiers for the electroencephalograph and the electro-cardiograph were matched by implants of suitable size for the measurement of arterial pressure and arterial flow and by implantable telestimulators for muscle and brain tissue. This kind of telemetric apparatus widens the possibilities of fundamental research on the circulatory and locomotor systems.

Because attachment of pickup elements directly to the organs is seldom feasible during diagnostic examinations, the reflections and projections of phenomena must be sensed, by one means or another, from the surface of the body. This is called noncontact sensing. One such method is based on a law of fluid dynamics: when a fluid is flowing through a tube, a difference of potential arises in the direction of the current, and this constitutes a measure of the flow. The blood flow of portions of the body can be studied by this method. The computer is being used increasingly to correlate signals obtained by noncontact sensing of fundamental organ processes. At the same time, new techniques have been introduced for presenting data in a simpler, more direct manner. Advances of this kind are exemplified by the Stereofluoricon. This X-ray unit has two cathodes, approximately two inches apart. Electrical pulses to the tube cause each cathode to fire sequentially, so that one X-ray beam passes through the patient every $\frac{1}{60}$ second. Because the two beams are slightly separated, each produces an image of the body from a slightly different angle, as in stereoscopic vision. In this way the observer is offered a spatial image— a great help in the localization of foreign bodies, nailing of bones, and catheterization of the heart. The properties of light and sound waves causing interference in the body (holography) make spatial reproduction possible. This faculty is also exploited by means of special microscopes. Visualization of soft tissues in two and three dimensions was achieved by the discovery of ultrasonic holography.

For decompression monitoring to prevent caisson disease ("the bends"), echography has become a useful aid. Skin thickness varies with the degree of the compression. By pinching up a portion of skin and bringing it between an ultrasonic transmitter and receiver, the thickness of the skin is measured. A special echograph has been devised for this purpose.

Patient monitoring was much used in 1968. Alongside the usual continuous recorders of pulse rate and arterial pressure, a venous-pressure monitoring system has been developed; thus the capability of the heart to deal with the return blood can be watched continuously.

External monitoring of implanted pacemakers is a growing possibility. By means of a telemetric signal a pacemaker can be made to indicate externally the heart muscle excitability threshold and the pacemaker electrode impedance. For the power supply of an implanted pacemaker it has been necessary to use the batteries in the apparatus, but pacemakers may now be supplied with accumulators chargeable by induction from a magnetic field created externally. Pacemakers also have been constructed in which charging takes place with the aid of piezoelectric generators driven by the mechanical action of the heart.

The chances of treating hydrocephalus by ventricle drainage have improved. Drainage can now be regulated with the aid of an implanted pump. A system has been designed in which the flow is regulated by means of a magnetic field built up outside the skull.

A portable TV camera, coupled to an acoustic perception system, now enables a blind person to locate obstacles in his path (see *Physiology*, below).

Hydraulic actuation for artificial limbs has been improved by a swing control unit. Combined swing-stance control units have also been devised. The sensory motor control of artificial limbs has been aided by development of suitable muscle transducers and attachment methods. Efforts are being directed toward selection of muscle sites that would provide reliable and isolated outputs. An electronic logic network has been developed for the conversion of coded muscle transducer outputs into control signals to operate a prosthesis. An arm brace has been altered so that a three-dimensional movement can be performed, as with a normal arm.   (G. P. M. H.)

MEDICAL EDUCATION

Overview. The number of students admitted to the medical schools of the world has increased greatly in each of the past ten years. The establishment of new schools continued in 1967 and 1968, though with great difficulty in the less-developed countries. In many countries, notably in Great Britain, existing schools were enlarged. Expansion everywhere was impeded, however, as much by the scarcity of teachers as by the high and still-rising cost of medical education. Despite expansion, the world's serious shortage of doctors continued—few if any countries being satisfied with their doctor-population ratios.

The growing gap between demand for, and supply of, health services continued to enforce an inexorable (but not universally popular) concentration of available resources. Doctors were being drawn together centrally, and paramedical personnel were serving the periphery. This pattern, long visible in the U.S.S.R., began to emerge more clearly in many other countries. In Britain, a traditional home of the independent general practitioner, there was sudden general acceptance in 1968 of the necessity for him to join an interdependent team in a health centre built for team use and properly equipped with the facilities for contemporary medicine. Changes of this kind in the pattern of medical care influenced thought on the objectives of medical education. The quick production of large numbers of young men and women ready for single-handed service in isolated communities, hitherto thought by many to be a major aim, began to be recognized as neither desirable nor possible.

In Britain and Sweden, royal commissions recommended to the parliaments a two-stage preparation for all doctors: basic medical education (comprising a university course and internship) designed to prepare

the individual for a lifetime of change, followed by postgraduate professional training designed to equip him for the current practice of a particular branch of medicine. A license, at the end of the first stage, to practice under supervision would be followed at the end of the second by a license to practice in the particular branch.

These recommendations were in accord with existing trends in many of the developed countries, where they already apply in principle to medical specialists. In such countries little further attempt was being made to provide comprehensive coverage of all aspects of medicine in the university course; instead, the tendency was toward a core curriculum of required content together with much time (up to half the course) for study in subjects thought most suitable for the individual student. Thus, undergraduate medical education was becoming more student-oriented and less class-oriented, with consequent need for a redeployment of teachers into integrated, systematized instruction on the one hand, and into personal or small-group educational guidance and encouragement on the other.

In some countries, particularly those of continental Europe, a strong tradition of independent departments, each completely under the control of one professor, continued to inhibit the interdepartmental collaboration on which the systematized program of studies depends. A long, crowded, compartmentalized program of studies lingered on, allowing the student little opportunity to study subjects of his choosing under more personal supervision. Student unrest was particularly noticeable in such medical schools in 1968.

Another feature of the year was the continuing migration of young medical graduates from countries poorly equipped to provide postgraduate training to countries where they could more easily receive it. The growing realization that medical education everywhere required an undergraduate education leading to postgraduate training emphasized the scope, complexity, and cost of this area of higher education. The consequent importance of developing new techniques of self-instruction was appreciated by some, but no large-scale, coordinated, and well-supported attack on this problem was anywhere under way. (J. R. EL.)

United States. A shortage of manpower in every phase of medical service in the United States led to significant changes in medical education in 1968. New medical schools were in process of development; most held their first classes during the fall of 1968, and some would be ready a year or so later. Among those that opened in 1968 were the University of California at Davis, the University of California at San Diego, the University of Connecticut, Mount Sinai School of Medicine (in New York City), and the University of Texas (in San Antonio). Opening in 1969 would be the Louisiana State University Medical School (in Shreveport) and the Medical College of Ohio (in Toledo). In 1970 first-year medicine would begin at the University of Massachusetts School of Medicine (in Worcester) and in 1971 at the University of South Florida College of Medicine and the State University of New York at Stony Brook. As of 1968 the U.S. had 85 fully accredited medical schools, 4 schools approved in the basic medical sciences, and 5 new schools, which began classes in 1966 and 1967 in connection with the University of Arizona, the University of Hawaii, Michigan State University, Pennsylvania State College, and Brown University.

The year was marked by numerous studies and reports on medical education—especially the need for graduate medical education. A special committee of the American Medical Association (AMA) was concerned with education for family practice. And there were many reports on health manpower. The medical schools, as also the universities, were disturbed by student activism—several organizations of students seeking to speak on organization of the curriculum, examination and promotion procedures, and the quality of teaching. A liaison was established between the AMA and the largely black National Medical Association in an effort to increase the number of black physicians.

The secretary of health, education, and welfare announced the formal establishment of the Lister Hill National Center for Biomedical Communications as a part of the National Library of Medicine. The centre was named for former Sen. Lister Hill of Alabama, a sponsor of key medical legislation.

The Association of American Medical Colleges (AAMC), which had assumed increasing importance in the field of medical education, established an annual assembly, to include all the deans and representatives of academic societies and teaching hospitals. The AAMC would cooperate more closely with the AMA in considering problems of manpower shortage and the distribution of physicians. The AAMC decided to move its headquarters from Evanston, Ill., to Washington, D.C., because of the increasing role of federal agencies in health education and medical manpower procurement. (M. FI.)

MICROBIOLOGY

B. Woodson reviewed recent advances in research on the pox viruses. These relatively large viruses cause a number of diseases, including smallpox in man and vaccinia (cowpox) in cattle. Most of the steps in the reproduction of these viruses now can be traced. A pox virus has an outer coat and an inner core containing the genetic (DNA) unit. After entry into a susceptible tissue cell the coat is lost and the genetic unit takes over the economy of the invaded cell. This results in the production of large numbers of virus particles—not by division of the original virus particle (*i.e.*, not like bacterial reproduction) but by action of the host cell itself under the influence of the viral substance. This take-over of cell function begins within 30 to 60 minutes after infection and is complete in 4 to 5 hours. After 24 hours there may be as many as 10,000 virus particles in the cell—all the result of invasion of the cell by a single virus particle.

Many of the microbial diseases of man that were

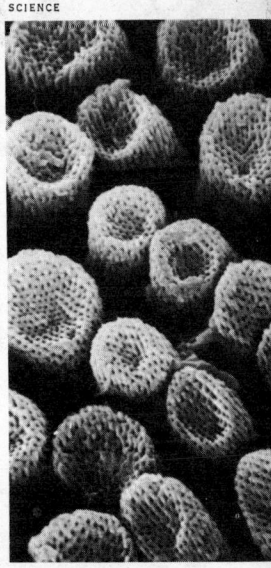

Pictures made with a scanning electron microscope: above, detail of the internal surface of one of the cuplike suckers on the arm of Octopus vulgaris; left, receptor organ of the tenebrio beetle. The scanning electron microscope provided a three-dimensional view of specimens at magnifications ranging from 30 to 50,000 times.

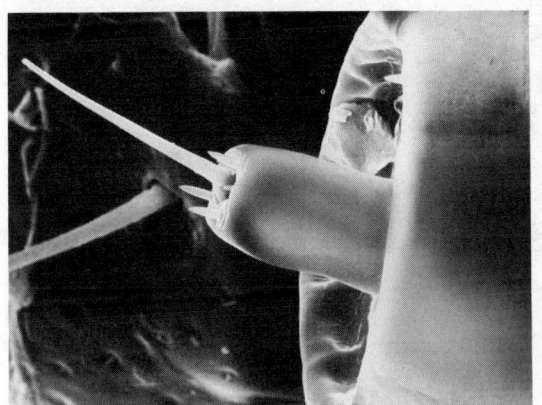

epidemic at one time have been either markedly reduced in importance or literally eliminated in recent times. Some, however, have either remained essentially constant or have increased in occurrence. Among these is salmonellosis, which occurs most frequently as a food-borne infection. There are some 1,200 species in the genus *Salmonella*. Many of them inhabit the digestive tract of animals and are capable of causing acute gastroenteritis in man. Sometimes a human being becomes a carrier, transmitting infection to others. A number of domestic animals, but particularly poultry, contain species of *Salmonella* in their digestive tracts. The meat of these animals may become contaminated during preparation for market. Quick-freezing may preserve the bacteria for a long time, and, if the product is not thoroughly cooked, those who eat it may become infected. In 1967 (latest compilation) 29 outbreaks of salmonellosis, involving 5,761 persons, were reported in the United States. Eighteen of the outbreaks were traced to a specific contaminated food. In addition, an unknown number of individual infections undoubtedly occurred but were not reported as part of the outbreaks. One reason for the persistence of salmonellosis is the ability of these bacteria to acquire resistance to antibiotics through the transfer of certain genetic factors to susceptible strains from those already resistant. The most recent studies show, however, that the considerable increase in resistance of *Salmonella* to antibiotics between 1948 and 1962 has been followed by a period, since 1962, of little change.   (JA. G. S.)

NEUROLOGY

More and more drugs have been found useful in the treatment of epilepsy, but individual successes remained quite often a matter of trial and error, and side effects were still important considerations. To the person who has suffered from epileptic attacks, treatment is only one of the problems weighing on his mind. General ignorance and taboo remain as strong as ever. Many countries refuse admission to an immigrant who is a mild sufferer, and even the well-controlled epileptic is denied a license to drive a motor vehicle. Attempts were being made, however, to change the licensing rules so that some epileptics might drive while still on the medication that affords greater safety.

A common condition that has seen many changes in outlook and emphasis in a relatively short time is cervical spondylosis. This condition of the spine may show itself in one or several ways, including pain, weakness, sensory impairment, or progressive paralysis. The initial problem of establishing the diagnosis is followed by the much more difficult task of treat-

ment. Rest, physiotherapy, traction, osteopathy, the use of a collar, and surgery all have their advantages, with varying degrees of success. The fact that in many instances the process arrests itself makes evaluation of any one form of treatment exceedingly difficult.

Stereotactic surgery in the treatment of parkinsonism, and particularly of the more severe degrees of tremor, is well established. Now the drug treatment of the condition has been advanced by the introduction of DL-DOPA and L-DOPA—the racemic and levo forms, respectively, of α-amino-β-(3,4-dihydroxyphenyl) propionic acid. Relief of tremor and rigidity can be quite remarkable, but possible side effects of blood and liver derangement, and the heavy cost, make general use impractical.

Spinal angiomas (vascular malformations of the spinal cord) are difficult to diagnose. Bleeding is usually inside the cord, and there may be no extravasation of blood into the spinal fluid. The presence of a focal spinal lesion, with variable symptoms and signs, may lead to a false diagnosis of multiple sclerosis. Myelography may suggest the presence of an angioma by the demonstration of serpiginous indentations in the column of contrast material. By means of intercostal arteriography the feeding artery can be selectively injected and the site and extent of the angioma, with all its ramifications, can be demonstrated. A surgical approach is then feasible.

Encephalitis is a dramatic illness with clinical features of disturbance of brain function; epilepsy may be either prominent or absent. In most cases a virus cause has been suspected. A particular form of encephalitis, accompanied by regular motor excitation with sudden muscular jerkings, a typical electroencephalographic record, and an abnormal cerebrospinal fluid, is known as subacute sclerosing leucoencephalitis; and it is probably the same condition as inclusion-body encephalitis. In children and young adults suffering from this form of encephalitis the blood serum and cerebrospinal fluid contain a large quantity of antibodies to measles virus, and virus particles resembling measles virus have been found in the brain. It appeared as if this form of encephalitis is due to an altered immunity reaction of the brain tissue to measles virus. This opened up various possibilities in other, unexplained examples of encephalitis.

Research in multiple sclerosis and muscular dystrophy did not advance notably during the year. A metabolic disorder, porphyria, achieved prominence as a result of historical research suggesting that George III's illness, with periodic episodes of madness, was due to exacerbation of porphyria: the mental disturbance, the attacks of abdominal pain, and the appearance of red urine are all in keeping. Porphyria has also been suggested as the explanation of the illnesses of other royal persons, among them King James I, Mary, queen of Scots, and Frederick the Great of Prussia.   (K. J. Z.)

NUTRITION

Poverty and hunger in the United States received unprecedented nationwide attention in 1968. The concern served to emphasize the lack of information available on the extent and severity of ill health caused by malnutrition. A preliminary investigation by M. L. Myers and co-workers elucidated links between inadequate diet and poor health among more than 300 Negro and Caucasian children, aged 9 to 13, living in a Boston slum. During two or more of the four school days surveyed, of all the children studied 27%

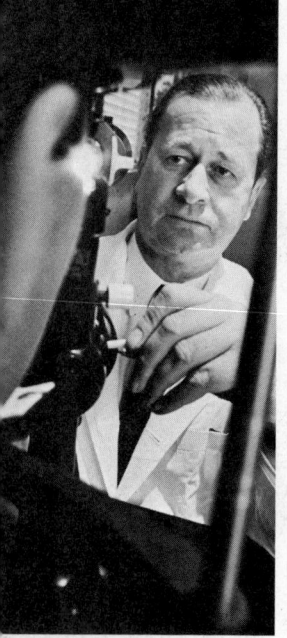

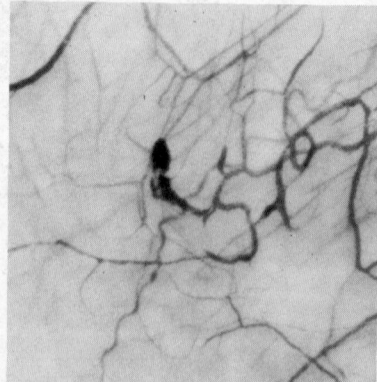
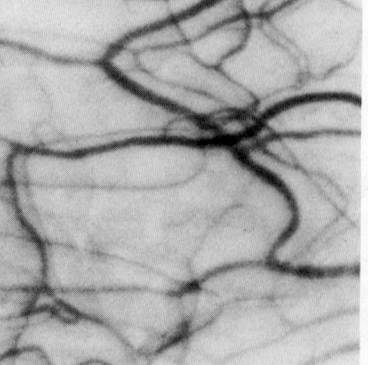

Above, Frank A. Elliott, professor of neurology at the University of Pennsylvania, examines a patient's eye for signs of tortuosity in the conjunctival vessels. Studies indicate that tortuosity of these vessels (below left) may be a means of identifying potential stroke victims. Normal vessels (below right) are quite linear.

had nutritionally inadequate breakfasts; 33%, inadequate lunches; 14%, inadequate dinners; and 9% had both unsatisfactory breakfasts and lunches. These children displayed signs of poor health that could be related to inadequate nutrition.

On the basis of animal studies it is thought that large intakes of sodium early in life may be a factor in the development of high blood pressure in man. L. K. Dahl and co-workers found that high intakes of sodium chloride for only two to six weeks early in life induced permanent, and often fatal, hypertension in rats predisposed to develop this condition. When constant high-salt feeding was delayed until three to six months after weaning, hypertension developed more slowly and was less severe. Relevant, then, is the possible effect of sodium overnutrition in Western infants in their first year of life. Infants can obtain their normal daily requirements of sodium from milk; on the basis of need there seems to be no justification for adding salt to commercial baby foods such as meat and vegetables—30 samples of which were reported five years ago by Dahl and associates to have a sodium content far in excess of that of unprocessed foods.

Changes in the amount or type of dietary fat and cholesterol can reduce the elevated levels of serum cholesterol characteristic of Western adult populations. Whether these changes will reduce the risk of coronary heart disease is a key question. The Committee on Diet and Heart Disease, formed in 1960 with the support of the National Heart Institute, estimated that a study population large enough to confirm reliably a reduction in the incidence of coronary heart disease over four or five years would have to include about 100,000 initially healthy men, aged 45–54. Faced with the many unknowns in a field study of this magnitude, the committee recommended a smaller-scale study, designed, not to determine whether a reduction in serum cholesterol affected coronary disease, but rather to illuminate the practicability of modifying diets to the point of significantly reducing serum cholesterol levels among middle-aged men. In Baltimore, Boston, Chicago, Minneapolis-St. Paul, and Oakland, 1,211 volunteers, all healthy married men aged 45–54, participated for one year in such a "feasibility trial," known as the National Diet-Heart Study. In a second year 745 more men took part. Cooperating were 225 male inmates of a mental institution. All volunteers were randomly assigned to experimental and control groups on the basis of blood pressure, body weight, cigarette smoking habit, and base-line serum cholesterol level. The experimental group was assigned to one of two diets, each restricted in saturated fat and cholesterol and rich in polyunsaturated fat but one richer than the other in polyunsaturates. The control diet was similar to the average American diet: high in saturates and cholesterol, low in polyunsaturates. Neither participants nor study personnel knew to which group the assignments were made, and dietitians gave equivalent detailed dietary advice to all three groups. The difference in fat consumption was achieved by the use of specially manufactured fat-modified foods, each made up in three different varieties of essentially identical appearance and taste yet containing different amounts and types of fats. These foods were purchased by the participants and delivered to their homes from warehouses established in each city. The final report on the National Diet-Heart Study was published in 1968. Before the onset of special diets, mean serum cholesterol of participants in all five cities was 229 mg. per 100 ml. over the base-line period. The overall mean decreases in serum cholesterol for the two experimental groups were 11.7 and 13.1%, respectively, and for the control group, 3.1%. Additional studies carried out during the second year produced no compromise in cholesterol response. In both years of study the smaller responses in serum cholesterol in the five cities, averaging about two-thirds of the responses in the institution, were largely due to nonadherence. In each of the two years, dropout rates were about 10% annually. Before dropping out, these men had a cholesterol response only half as great as the nondropouts—evidence, presumably, of their flagging interest and failure to adhere to the diet. The study demonstrated the feasibility of large-scale manipulative dietary studies—studies demanding a degree of cooperation and persistence probably well worth the effort, in view of the number of deaths from coronary heart disease.   (P. R.; F. J. SE.)

OPHTHALMOLOGY

More attention was being paid to blindness in premature infants. The problem arises chiefly in those that weigh less than three pounds at birth and have breathing difficulties. The respiratory distress may be alleviated by administration of high concentrations of oxygen; however, such concentrations are known to cause disorderly growth of blood vessels within the eye, leading to scar tissue formation and, often, complete blindness. The pediatrician and ophthalmologist thus have a difficult choice: to treat the breathing problem and risk blindness or to leave the respiratory distress untreated and risk death. Fortunately, these infants may require concentrated oxygen for only a brief period—so brief that scarring has no time to develop. By daily inspection of the vessels within the eye it is generally possible to determine whether or not scarring is likely to occur. If the vessels dilate normally when the infant is taken out of the concentrated oxygen atmosphere, this indicates that the child may be safely treated with concentrated oxygen for the next 24 hours. If normal dilation does not occur, the first stage of retinal scarring is developing, and the possibility of blindness is greatly increased by further exposure. All who are responsible for the welfare of the premature infant must make certain that oxygen is administered, in every case, for the shortest period compatible with survival.

Several years ago various kinds of glue to hold living tissues together were developed. Investigators have found that these glues may be useful in treating some conditions of the eye in which there is swelling of the cells of the cornea. The swelling causes an irregularity of vision like that experienced when one swims underwater with his eyes open. The condition is painful and often blinding. A small contact lens glued to the front surface of the eye forms a smooth optical surface permitting better vision and relieving the pain. This technique gives promise of restoring some vision to those having blind, painful eyes. Additionally, the glue may be used to plug openings in the eye and permit normal healing. These techniques, while still in a developmental stage, have been used successfully in a number of instances.

The retina apparently can be damaged by illumination previously considered entirely safe. It is well known that exposure of the eye to high levels of sunlight—for example during a day at the seashore—causes delayed adaptation to darkness; hence night

503

Medicine

UPI COMPIX

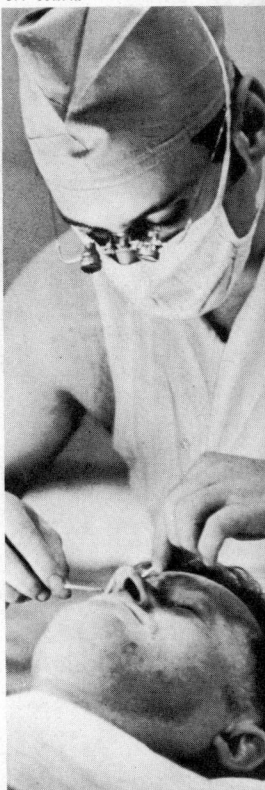

Bernie Zucker performs Canada's first artificial human cornea implant at Scarborough General Hospital in Toronto. Normal vision was restored for Gordon Sheppard, who had been blind for 22 years.

driving is dangerous after exposure to bright sunshine for a prolonged period. However, such exposure had never been considered particularly harmful to the eye itself. Experimentation has now shown that when newborn rats are exposed to bright levels of illumination, permanent damage to the eye ensues. This raises the question whether some of the instruments used in examining the eye may cause permanent injury. Most likely they do not, but an important area of study has been opened.

Several thousand persons in Czechoslovakia have successfully used a plastic contact lens that is soft and molds itself to the contours of the cornea. Furthermore, the material permits oxygen from the air to pass through to the cornea and thus does not interfere with the normal metabolism of the tissues, as occurs with hard contact lenses. The soft lenses are said to cause less discomfort than the hard lenses.

(F. W. N.)

ORTHOPEDICS

The ninth International Leprosy Congress, held in London in 1968, assessed progress in the treatment of one of the world's commonest causes of crippling. Since leprosy can normally be controlled by the sulfone drugs, patients with paralysis of the hands and feet, caused by the neural form of the disease, could be treated in much the same way as those with nerve injuries or poliomyelitis; therapy could be given in ordinary hospitals. In the upper limb the paralysis affects the small muscles of the hand, and nerve damage causes loss of sensibility. The disturbance of grip, which causes undue pressure on the fingertips, damages the skin and underlying bones. The result is ulceration that can lead to progressive mutilation. Muscle balance can be restored by tendon transplantation techniques, devised by P. W. Brand, with great improvement in function despite persistent anesthesia. Similar affliction of the feet can be even more crippling, because weight-bearing quickly causes the skin of the sole to break down, particularly if the foot is deformed. The emphasis here is on use of inexpensive protective footwear, education on care of the feet, correction of deformity by operation on the bones, and tendon transplantation to abolish foot drop, a result of paralysis of the muscles that dorsiflex the ankle. The problem was that where the need was greatest—most of the 15 million leprosy sufferers in the world lived in the tropics—there was a shortage of doctors and hospitals. Much of the work could be done by trained auxiliaries; but the operative treatment, particularly of the paralyzed hand, calls for considerable surgical skill and is time consuming. In Africa attention was, therefore, concentrated on lower-limb paralysis, so that the patient would at least be mobile.

Industry had produced yet another type of injury. Fluid and semifluid substances—oils, paint, cement—are delivered, for various purposes, by machines generating pressures of 70 to 500 kg/cm^2 (about 1,000 to 7,200 lb/in^2). The skin can be penetrated as if it were paper, and the fluid diffuses widely around the deep structures, of which tendons are the most important. A pinhole defect in a high-pressure delivery tube is a sufficient hazard. The point of entry may not be detectable, and there may be little pain. Then the foreign material sets up an inflammatory reaction simulating that caused by infection. If treatment for the latter is applied the result will be disastrous: the digit may be lost. The only remedy is

early recognition of the accident and prompt removal of the foreign material, which can be done only by delicate surgery. Prevention is all-important and, in automobile service stations, for example, was already fairly effective.

Osteoarthritic joints were on occasion being treated by total replacement with a prosthesis, usually wholly metallic. The main damage in these joints is loss of articular cartilage. It would be advantageous if the cartilage could be induced to grow again or if it could be repaired by transplantation. The disconcerting feature of cartilage transplantation is that, depending on the source of the graft, age of donor, and site of implantation, it is more likely to induce the formation of fibrous tissue or of bone (according to M. R. Urist of Los Angeles) than to reproduce itself. Cartilage is mostly a physically homogeneous matrix, composed of collagen and mucopolysaccharide, secreted by the cells (chondrocytes) embedded in it. In 1965 Audrey Smith of Great Britain described a method of isolating chondrocytes by digestion of the matrix. These cells can survive cooling to −70° C (−94° F), which makes storage and transportation possible; they are capable of forming new matrix, *i.e.*, they manufacture cartilage; and, most important of all, cells transplanted from one animal to another of the same species do not provoke the immune reaction that is the most disturbing feature of tissue homotransplants. It had been shown by A. U. Smith and P. J. Chesterman that chondrocytes will lay down cartilage, admittedly imperfectly, when grafted onto an articular surface that has been denuded of its normal cartilaginous covering. Thus there was at least hope that a biological form of repair of damaged joints was within sight.

(HE. SE.)

PEDIATRICS

Newest of the vaccines to become commercially available was the live attenuated mumps virus vaccine, and all studies established its effectiveness. R. E. Weibel and co-workers found no appreciable diminution in protective antibodies in vaccinated children over a two-year period. The level of protection is not so great as that attained after natural infection, but W. C. Sugg and associates, who conducted field trials, estimated the vaccine to be 95.6% effective. There has been considerable debate about which children should receive the vaccine. Some physicians have argued that because the natural disease is mild in young children, inoculation should be restricted to children approaching puberty who have not had the disease. From this point of view, preadolescent boys would be the most logical recipients, since testicular involvement is the most feared complication and this occurs in males after reaching puberty. Other physicians recommend that all children receive the vaccine. The difference of opinion probably reflects the increasing emphasis on the need to limit immunization procedures to the essential minimum. G. Edsall and associates, for example, pointed out that tetanus toxoid boosters are being given too frequently. They deplored the recommendation by some directors of summer camps for children that each camper be given an annual tetanus toxoid booster: too frequent injections are likely to induce sensitivity to the material and produce reactions such as hives and fever. Careful studies indicated that a tetanus booster every ten years sufficed. Additional injections are needed at the time of a penetrating injury; such emergency boosters give adequate protection for at least a year

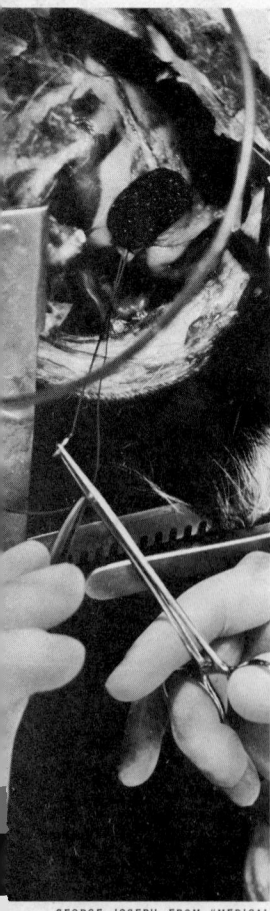

Medical researcher implants iron filings impregnated in plastic in the right ventricle of a dog's heart. A team headed by David Grob at Maimonides Medical Center in New York City was exploring the use of magnetic force to activate nonfunctioning muscles.

and need not be repeated within the year in the event of another accident.

Acute hemorrhagic cystitis, a disease seen in children and adults alike, causes blood to appear in the urine and produces fever and frequent painful urination. Y. Numazaki and co-workers reported for the first time the isolation of a virus as the cause. They succeeded in culturing adenovirus type II from the urine in nine infected children between the ages of 7 and 15 years. No bacteria were cultured from the specimens, and children without the illness did not yield any viral agent. As soon as red blood cells disappeared from the urine and symptoms had disappeared, the virus could no longer be recovered. The isolation of this agent fully explains a disorder that had been most puzzling.

Prolonged bed rest in acute rheumatic fever, a time-honoured practice, was challenged by B. J. Grossman, who studied the effects of early ambulation in 122 children who had suffered a first attack lasting 18 days or less. All were treated with cortisone and initially placed on bed rest; then they were assigned to two groups. In the first the children were kept on bed rest throughout 12 weeks of cortisone treatment and for an additional 3 weeks after the drug was stopped. In the second group bed rest was discontinued when the sedimentation rate returned to normal, and full hospital activity was allowed for the remainder of the period. Grossman found no difference between the groups at the end of 15 weeks and at the end of one year of follow-up study. He concluded that in patients treated with cortisone, prolonged bed rest following the subsidence of the signs of the acute inflammatory reaction of rheumatic fever does not ameliorate the amount of damage.

An important development in the understanding of the methods by which the human body controls infection was reported almost simultaneously by separate teams led by B. Holmes and P. B. Quie. The investigators had been studying a strange, fatal disease of childhood first described in 1957, known as chronic familial granulomatosis. The condition occurs in males; beginning in infancy, it usually causes

Doctors at Children's Hospital Medical Center in Boston use a new X-ray fluoroscope system to position a catheter in the heart of a "blue baby" in an attempt to save its life. Picker Corporation's Custom Medical Engineering Department developed the system.

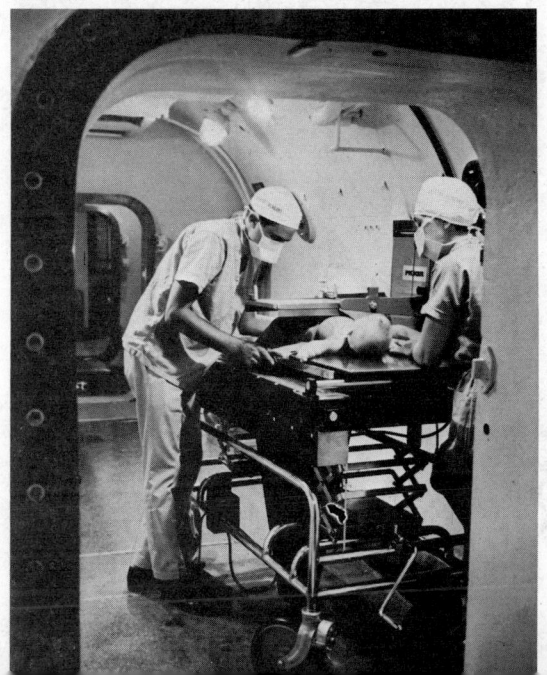

death before the sixth birthday. The children develop enlargement of glands, which may soften and discharge to the surface; major skin infections; repeated pneumonias; and severe anemia. They may also have low gamma globulin levels. The disease progresses in spite of administration of antibiotics and human gamma globulin. The recent studies showed that the defect in infection control lies in the circulating white blood cells. They engulf bacteria normally but do not destroy the organisms. Discovery of this defect not only permits a logical approach to treatment but may prove to be a key to the further understanding of other infectious diseases.   (S. S. G.)

PHARMACOLOGY

General. The existence of pharmacology as a discipline and as a separate subject in the medical curriculum has been questioned. But pharmacology is not only the application of various physicochemical and biochemical techniques to the practice of medicine, it also provides a special way of viewing and interpreting the interactions of drugs with the living organism. One aspect of expanding pharmacodynamic research with direct applications in medicine is perinatal pharmacology, concerned with the effect on the fetus of drugs given to the mother and the effect of drugs on the newborn. Another is called "pharmogenetics," and deals with metabolic defects of hereditary origin that account for eccentric responses to drugs by some individuals. For example, in most persons the muscle-relaxing drug succinylcholine, commonly used in anesthesia, is rapidly destroyed; but some individuals are deficient in the enzyme that decomposes this agent, and they may remain paralyzed for hours. It was thought that research in this field would result in the development of simple tests of ability to handle important medications in the expected manner and in suggestions for alternative medications if a defect is present.

New Drugs. Because of strict requirements of the official agencies and the difficulties of therapeutic research, the number of new drugs introduced during 1968 was relatively low; of several "new" antibiotics and central nervous system drugs, most were chemical modifications of existing agents. Propanolol is an important new drug, already in use in Europe, which affects rate and rhythm of the heart and may be helpful in angina pectoris. Carbamazepine has been found effective in a good proportion of patients suffering from severe neuralgia of the face and head. Thiebendazole was introduced as a treatment of intestinal-tract infestations, which occur in large segments of the population, especially in less developed countries; it may also have value in trichinosis. A group of naturally occurring lipid-soluble acids called prostaglandins, first described about 35 years earlier, attracted new interest. These substances are found in seminal fluid and in several other organs and tissues. Prostaglandins have a variety of actions upon the circulation, sex functions, and metabolism, and they are effective in very small quantities. Synthesis of one of the prostaglandins was recently achieved, so their possible usefulness could be explored more readily.   (R. K. R.)

Narcotics. Production of opium in those countries that report to the United Nations declined to 782 tons in 1966 from 901 tons in 1965 (latest available figures). India, the U.S.S.R., and Turkey accounted for 55.8, 25.8, and 17.7%, respectively, of this output—the U.S.S.R. and Turkey a little more than in the

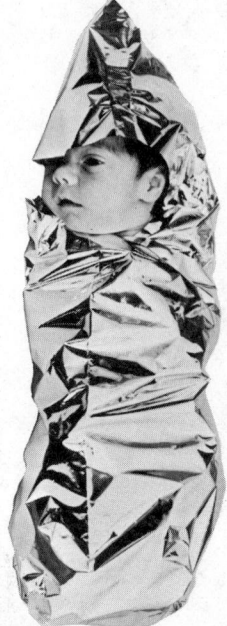

DR. DAVID BAUM, INSTITUTE OF CHILD HEALTH AT HAMMERSMITH HOSPITAL, LONDON

British physicians have used aluminum foil to wrap newborn infants, thereby cutting heat loss by at least half. The technique was considered particularly useful with premature babies.

previous year, India less (thus continuing the fall in production noted in the four preceding years). Some 430 tons of the opium went into the manufacture of morphine. The 149 tons of morphine manufactured from opium (75.5%) and from poppy straw (or its concentrate) compared with 123 tons manufactured the previous year. As usual, most of the morphine was converted into codeine.

Bolivia and Peru continued to be the main producers of coca leaves, with harvests in 1966 of 6,272 tons and 9,091 tons, respectively. Most of the product was used for chewing. The government of Peru was trying to reduce the area under cultivation and was promoting an educational campaign to combat the coca habit.

Manufacture of pethidine, a widely used synthetic drug, continued to increase; 20.6 tons were produced in 1966, compared with 19.5 tons in 1965.

Southeast Asia and the Near and Middle East remained the chief areas of illicit production of opium, morphine, and heroin; South America, of coca leaf and cocaine; and Africa and the Near and Middle East, of cannabis. Total seizure of all these drugs in 1966 amounted to some 416 tons, compared with 196 tons in 1965. The amount of raw opium seized was 52 tons, compared with 37.6 in 1965; of cannabis, 361.7 tons, compared with 157 tons in 1965. Further effort was made to substitute beneficial cash crops for poppy and cannabis cultivation. Lebanon, for example, launched a major program for replacing cannabis with sunflower.

Scientists from Spain, Thailand, Iran, Syria, and Japan completed studies on narcotics in 1967 at the United Nations Laboratory under UN technical assistance or WHO fellowships.   (N. F. C.)

PHYSIOLOGY

Erythropoietin is a hormonelike substance found in the blood and tissues of a number of experimental animals. It stimulates the production of erythrocytes, and it generally increases following hemorrhage or hypoxia. It was once thought to be produced solely in the kidney, but erythropoiesis has been shown to continue at a reduced rate after the kidney is removed.

Current research shows that nephrectomized animals have a slight erythropoietic response to hypoxia and that this response is not abolished by removal of the pituitary; in other words, the pituitary does not play an essential role in this response. In other studies of the role of erythropoietin in the early stages of hematopoiesis, bone marrow was transplanted into mice in which the original had been destroyed by irradiation. Administration of erythropoietin stimulated the growth of the erythroid colony formation from these grafts, showing that erythropoietin is necessary in the establishment of the early stages of erythropoiesis.

A number of disease states have a genetic basis. Rats bred selectively, for example, for a high level of blood pressure become a colony of hypertensive animals. The mesenteric arteries of hypertensive rats are known to have higher-than-normal vasoconstrictor responses to norepinephrine and angiotensin.

Other studies showed that innervated perfused hind-limb blood vessels of hypertensive rats also give a higher-than-normal response to norepinephrine. These data supported the hypothesis that increased vascular responsiveness may play some part in the genesis of hypertension.

During the past two decades a substance has been found in the brain that stimulates smooth muscle and exerts vascular effects. This is a polypeptide (or a family of polypeptides) differing from plasma kinins, posterior pituitary hormones, and angiotensin. Attempts to purify it have led to isolation of a polypeptide that elicits vasodilatation more potently than bradykinin does. Recent studies have detected this principle in perfusates of the somatosensory cortex of anesthetized cats. It has also been found in the spinal cord of the frog. The possible physiological role of this principle in the central nervous system remains to be determined.

Radio receivers were connected to electrodes implanted into the occipital lobe of the right cerebral hemisphere of a 52-year-old blind patient. Appropriate signals caused the subject to experience sensations of light in the left half of the visual field. The most common sensation caused by stimulation through a single electrode was a tiny spot of white light at a constant position in the visual field; less frequently the sensation was two or more spots of light or a small cloud of light. When weak stimuli were used the cortical visual field corresponded roughly to the maps derived from studies of patients with war wounds. When stronger stimuli were used, additional spots of light appeared in a pattern roughly identical to the classical map inverted about the horizontal meridian. On the basis of experience with these methods it might be possible to make prosthetic devices permitting the blind to avoid obstacles in their path or even to read print and handwriting, perhaps at speeds comparable to those achieved by sighted people.   (D. J. I.)

Boston pathologist John Craighead produced diabetes mellitus in laboratory mice by inoculating them with encephalomyocarditis virus. Normal cell structure (top) gives way to disorganization and necrosis (bottom) after injection of the virus.

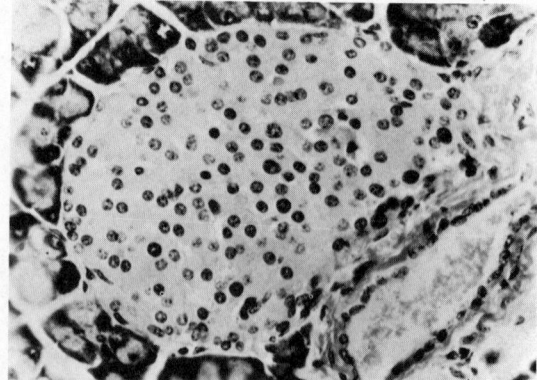

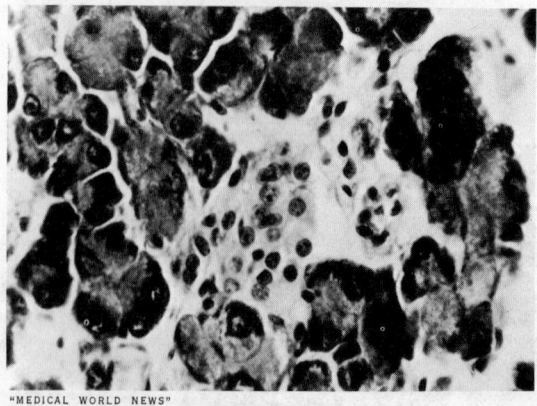

PSYCHIATRY

Major trends in studying schizophrenia in the Soviet Union were reported by M. G. Shchirina and M. E. Vartanyan. A multidisciplinary approach was favoured, and the Institute of Psychiatry of the Moscow Academy of Medical Sciences concentrated its resources on research in the disorder. Three main developmental courses of the illness had been distinguished: continuous (incessant) forms, periodic (recurrent) forms, and intermittent, progressive forms. A long-term clinical study of the course of schizophrenia in 5,000 patients led to the differentiation of nine different syndromes: asthenic, affective, pseudoneurotic, paranoid, hallucinatory, hallucinatory-paranoid, paraphrenic, catatonic, and terminal stationary.

Clinical regularities in the occurrence and development of schizophrenia suggest biological correlates. The Soviets found indications that the blood serum of schizophrenics contains pathological metabolites that disturb the functions of a variety of animals and plants. There was also evidence of change in the permeability of cell membranes in schizophrenia. This was demonstrated for red blood cells (erythrocytes) of the peripheral circulation; the resistance of their membranes to a weak solution of hydrochloric acid was significantly lower among schizophrenics. Similar changes were found for manic-depressive psychotics but not in psychiatric disorders of established organic origin. This finding suggested to the Moscow researchers that endogenous psychoses form a distinct group.

The level of erythrocyte resistance in schizophrenics as a possible consequence of some metabolic disorder was investigated experimentally. Serum from schizophrenic patients was found to affect abnormally the structure of red-cell membranes in vitro. Further, the serum had a destructive effect on chicken erythrocytes. Similar results were not observed with serum from control subjects. "Schizophrenic" serum also produced patchy demyelinization in nerve fibres of chickens, while no such effect was found for control-group serum. Chromatography and electrophoresis indicated that the biologically active factor in schizophrenia involves the protein fraction of the serum. The fraction had the mobility of beta globulin and contained beta lipoproteins. It was assumed that the change in cell-membrane resistance and the action of pathological blood metabolites had released intracellular proteins, leading to autoimmune processes against tissue antigens.

This hypothesis was supported when lymphocytes from schizophrenics showed a reaction typical of those seen in autoimmune processes; lymphocytes from control subjects did not. When "schizophrenic" lymphocytes were introduced into a tissue culture from the brain of a human embryo, both lymphocytes and culture cells were destroyed; no similar reaction was observed for "normal" lymphocytes. Before their destruction the "schizophrenic" lymphocytes formed extensions connecting them with the cells of the tissue. These "bridges" were found to be full of DNA. Observed in samples from schizophrenics five times as often as in control samples, the bridges seemed to be a morphological expression of a transfer of immunological information. Microlymphocytes of schizophrenics were found to contain less DNA than did those of controls; also, more lymphocytes with a characteristic abnormality of the nucleus were found in schizophrenics than in controls. These evidences

of abnormal autoimmune processes were especially marked in more severe forms of schizophrenia.

A number of blood relatives of schizophrenics have exhibited similar reactions, and it is cautiously held that none of these abnormal phenomena are specific to schizophrenia. Some of them also were observed in other endogenous psychoses, and some could be correlated with the course and malignancy of the schizophrenic process. However, the findings as a whole did seem to demonstrate the importance of biological processes in schizophrenia.

The role of experiential factors in schizophrenia was being reappraised. Silvano Arieti of New York City suggested a four-stage sequence of psychodynamic development, in which only the last phase could be considered psychotic. He said that most children pass the first stage (from birth until about age five) without succumbing to disorder. Psychoanalysts have tended to regard this period as the most important etiologically—the primary factor being a "schizophrenogenic" mother. In the light of his researches Arieti dissociated himself from that view, which he seemed to feel overemphasizes interpersonal factors; he recently wrote that intrapsychic factors are at least equally important.

In the second stage psychological defenses against chronic dangers from without and within are held to be built up in anticipation of future events. In the third phase, coinciding with puberty, Arieti observed that those defenses often become less effective, and ideas about the reactions of those close to the person and of the world at large grow important for the person's self-image. Extreme loneliness may be experienced and lead to preschizophrenic panic.

According to Arieti the ultimate defense is manifested in the fourth stage: only then does the psychosis begin. Arieti does not seem to agree that schizophrenia reflects a kind of sickness of society that is responsible for individual disorder.

The clinicobiological approach of the Soviet workers was not necessarily incompatible with the psychodynamic orientation cultivated in the United States. It may be that failure to pass successfully through Arieti's four phases can result from intrapsychic deficiencies that reflect organic dysfunction. (E. ST.)

PUBLIC HEALTH

Engineering. In 1968 responses to the widening scope of public health engineering were exemplified in activities of the World Health Organization (WHO), the International Bank for Reconstruction and Development (the World Bank), and agencies of the U.S. government.

Marking its 20th anniversary in 1968, WHO could report substantial accomplishments in environmental health during the past ten years. (See *World Health Organization*, below.) Seventy-two member states were assisted in establishing or bettering environmental health services at national, provincial, or municipal levels; 16 of these projects are ongoing in Africa. Between 1961 and 1968 nearly a dozen technical conferences on housing and urban development were held in such diverse places as Madrid, Mexico City, Pittsburgh, Pa., and Stockholm. Three of these, including the 1968 conference, were held in Moscow. Housing studies and training aid had reached Colombia, Ethiopia, Iran, Iraq, Sudan, the United Arab Republic, and Venezuela. In 1968, WHO had 169 community water supply projects in 83 countries and 38 intercountry projects. With a budget of only $1

million a year for community water supplies, WHO works by assisting countries in training technicians; in advising on national policy and planning; by developing water-quality standards and stimulating their adoption, as 23 countries have done; and by establishing, in 1968, an international reference centre at Delft, Neth., to coordinate research and act as an information clearinghouse.

Feasibility studies to help countries and cities to prepare loan applications with supporting engineering and management data have been fruitful. Each WHO dollar devoted to this has produced $375 in loan capital. Community water supply loans in the period 1958–67 totaled $675 million from four international lending agencies and from the U.S., West Germany, and the United Kingdom. Because of organizational and technological readiness, 65% of these funds were being expended in Latin America; 50% of the world's total loans for this purpose were from the Inter-American Development Bank. It was estimated that 70% of the world's urban population had a water supply that was unsafe or insufficient and that full improvement would cost $10 billion.

The World Bank and its affiliate, the International Development Association, made major loans in 1968 for water supply projects in Kuala Lumpur, Malaysia, and Bogotá, Colombia, and for a sewerage project in Singapore. The three loans amounted to $23.6 million toward the total cost of $65.4 million. In 1968 World Bank-supported water systems were completed for Jerusalem, Singapore, and Zarqua, Jordan. The total cost of work under way in 1968 was $230 million, of which the World Bank's lending share was $84.4 million.

In the U.S., the Federal Water Pollution Control Administration of the Department of the Interior is responsible for the restoration of clean water in streams, lakes, and estuaries. In addition to specific regulatory actions, the effort was moving forward in three ways. The first was by grants to cities for constructing waste treatment plants. In 1968, 663 grants totaling $173 million generated $669 million of state and local funds for treatment plants. Since 1956 there had been 8,676 such grants totaling $1,160,000,000, with $4,070,000,000 committed by the states and cities; but an estimated $100 billion would be needed to overcome pollution and then keep the waters clean.

The second way was by accelerating research in waste disposal and treatment, along with innovative and comprehensive river-basin planning. For this, funds were provided by grants, contracts, and fellowships. Since 1961, 3,057 proposals had been supported at a cost of $123 million. The third way was by establishing quality standards for surface waters. Under the Water Quality Act of 1965, states were submitting quality standards, for waters under their jurisdiction, to the secretary of the interior for approval. Through 1968, 15 states, 2 territories, and the Delaware River Basin Commission had received full approval of their standards, and 23 states and the District of Columbia had been given partial approval. Should a state fail to act, the secretary was empowered to develop applicable and enforceable standards for it.   (E. T. Ch.)

Epidemics. The intensified global program of smallpox eradication that started in 1967 no doubt also resulted in the improvement of statistical reporting. Throughout the world 119,095 cases were reported in 1967 (latest compilation year). Africa

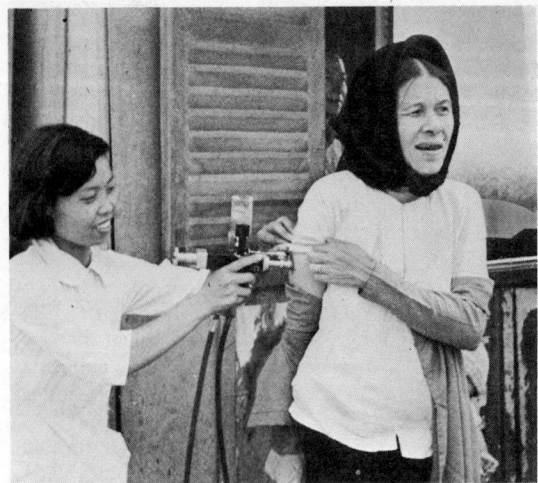

UPI COMPIX

Nurse administers an anti-bubonic plague injection to a Vietnamese woman in Saigon. Nearly 6,000 plague cases were reported in South Vietnam during 1967, up from 353 in 1966, but incidence was said to be down in 1968.

had 15,177 cases in 27 countries. Asia had 99,638 cases in 10 countries, notably India (80,174), Pakistan (11,193), and Indonesia (7,859). South America had 4,275 cases in only 2 countries, Brazil and Argentina. Five cases were imported into 3 European countries (Czechoslovakia 1, West Germany 2, United Kingdom 2).

No further spread of cholera was reported in 1967 (but see *Tropical Medicine*, below). The disease was reported from only nine countries, all in Asia, with 22,912 cases and 3,188 deaths. The main endemic countries were India (11,922 cases of the El Tor variety), South Vietnam (7,664), the Philippines (1,749), and Pakistan (652 cases caused by classical *Vibrio cholerae*).

Yellow fever (jungle type) was reported from Argentina, Brazil, Colombia, and Peru, with a total of 11 cases, all fatal. Liberia had 5 cases and 3 deaths.

Plague was reported from three African countries, four South American countries, the United States (3 cases), and four Asian countries, for a world total of 6,010 cases. Of these, 5,619 cases were reported from South Vietnam, where the disease had been endemic since 1898. Continuous warfare had increased the risk of infection throughout the country, and more than half of the 44 provinces of South Vietnam were now affected. Villages and towns damaged by military action provide ample breeding places for rats, and the human population was forced to live close to infected rat populations. However, the outstanding feature of plague in South Vietnam was the success in patient care. The mortality rate for patients receiving early diagnosis and treatment was only 1 to 5%, in contrast with the 60 to 90% mortality rate in an untreated population.

The 8,372 cases of louse-borne typhus reported in 1967 were chiefly in Ethiopia (4,096) and Burundi (3,669). Louse-borne relapsing fever was reported from three African countries (4,943 cases). Mosquito-borne hemorrhagic fever (2,585 cases) continued to spread in the western Pacific and in Southeast Asia.

Outbreaks of serious disease occurred simultaneously in the West German cities of Frankfurt and Marburg and in Belgrade, Yugos., among laboratory workers who had handled tissues of African green monkeys, or vervets (*Cercopithecus aethiops*), imported from Uganda. Thirty cases, with seven deaths,

occurred. A previously unknown, probably viral, agent was isolated from patients' blood, urine, throat mucus, and liver biopsy material. Antibodies against this newly isolated agent were found in 50% of serum samples from African green and other species of monkeys.

Influenza outbreaks were reported in 1967–68 (see *Respiratory Diseases,* below) from many parts of the world.

Poliomyelitis incidence had risen recently in many countries having warm climates. Serious outbreaks in 1967 were reported in six Latin-American countries: Nicaragua (461 cases), Guatemala (241), Colombia (422), Peru (207), Ecuador (796), and Mexico (636). In Africa outbreaks were reported from the Congo (Kinshasa) (437 cases), the Congo (Brazzaville) (354), Kenya (170), Tanzania (112), Libya (158), and Senegal (114). Most of the victims were children under five years of age. A relatively high incidence of paralytic poliomyelitis was still being reported from Turkey (814 cases) and Spain (341)—an indication that these and perhaps some other countries would have to intensify their immunization programs. The importance of immunization was clearly shown by the low number of cases reported in 1967 by countries with systematic programs. The United States and Canada, for example, with about 222 million inhabitants, had 47 cases, whereas all the other American countries— so far without systematic immunization programs —reported 3,512 cases among 268 million inhabitants.

The ever increasing international trade in foods of animal origin and livestock feeds such as bone meal and fish meal, together with changing habits of diet in the world in the last 30 years, had deeply influenced the spread of salmonellosis in man and animals. The number of *Salmonella* bacteria types circulating in man and animals in European countries multiplied during 1967 and the number of outbreaks of salmonellosis increased considerably. At the suggestion of WHO a surveillance program was instituted. (See *Microbiology,* above.)

Arthropod-borne encephalitis outbreaks were reported from different parts of the world but especially from the Americas. In the U.S., 1,561 cases of primary encephalitis occurred in 1967; and toward the end of the year a serious outbreak of Venezuelan equine encephalitis, with several hundred human and equine cases, was reported from Colombia. (See *Tropical Medicine,* below.) (K. RA.)

RADIOLOGY

Specialization continued in diagnostic radiology. In pediatric radiology, for example, considerable advances were being made. Both Europe and America have societies in this field. Pediatric radiologists are particularly interested in urinary and bladder lesions and in skeletal growth and its abnormalities in infants and children. This kind of specialization suggested a need for new training procedures to include general basic diagnosis followed by specialty training in approved centres.

In radiotherapy, progress continued in the use of hyperbaric oxygen. H. A. S. Van den Brenk, after surveying this field, concluded that hyperbaric oxygen improves the effectiveness of radiotherapy in achieving regression of advanced primary tumours and lymph-node metastases in certain loci, such as the mouth, throat, and bladder.

The use of contrast media had increased in recent years, not only in routine radiological investigations but also in vascular radiology. Radiologists can expect to experience only a few instances among their patients of serious reactions to the injectable contrast media, but the overall number of such reactions is considerable. A symposium held in Chicago considered evidence that the adverse effects do not appear to be antibody-antigen reactions; rather, they seem to be most closely related to hypertonicity and to contrast-protein interactions. These interactions may produce alterations in the diffusibility of certain endogenous substances, alterations in the fluid and electrolyte composition of tissues, and inhibition or activation of enzyme systems. The biochemical effects may be manifested by effects on red blood cells, white blood cells, blood vessel walls, nerves, and clotting. Hemodynamic reactions to angiographic media were also considered, and some ways of minimizing them were laid down.

Electronic subtraction was being used in many radiological centres, particularly in cerebral angiography. This technique greatly enhances the information on the radiographs, for it allows the arterial and venous stages of the arteriogram to be followed. Now colour could be added to subtraction by the use of a colour filter during the process—enabling the arterial phase to be reproduced as red and the venous phase as green; the background mixture of red and green gives yellow. This new technique was described by F. G. J. Haendle. (Jo. W. McL.)

REHABILITATION

The national Citizens' Advisory Committee on Vocational Rehabilitation reported in 1968 that nearly 2% of the population of the United States needed rehabilitation services for physical and mental disability but were not receiving them.

During the year 208,000 handicapped persons were restored to gainful employment through the federal-state program of vocational rehabilitation. This was nearly double the number rehabilitated in 1962. The number of persons newly disabled each year is about 450,000. Each $1,000 spent by federal and state agencies on vocational rehabilitation results in an increase of more than $35,000 in the lifetime earnings of a typical rehabilitated citizen.

Skiing was added to the rehabilitation program for amputees at the U.S. Army's Fitzsimons General Hospital in Denver. Patients benefit both physically and psychologically from the program.

The U.S. Congress in 1968 greatly increased vocational rehabilitation appropriations for the next three years. The Citizens' Advisory Committee recommended that special efforts be made to reach certain large groups, including the culturally disadvantaged, public offenders, the non-English-speaking population, social security disability beneficiaries, the aged, families on welfare, and migratory workers. It also recommended that regional facilities be established for persons with multiple handicaps, the blind, those with neurological disorders such as spinal cord injury, stroke, and epilepsy, those with speech disorders, and those suffering from drug abuse. Illustrative of the need for such services are the 125,000 paraplegics and quadriplegics, whose ranks increase by from 3,000 to 6,000 each year. Some 35,000 in this group were not receiving adequate care.

Lack of personnel remained the major obstacle to expansion of the U.S. rehabilitation effort. The nation had 16,000 physical therapists working full-time or part-time in 1968, and 1,200 new therapists graduate yearly; but 8,000 graduates are needed each year for replacement and new positions. Similar shortages existed in all of the other rehabilitation disciplines: occupational therapy, prosthetics and orthotics, social work, speech pathology and audiology, rehabilitation counseling, and specialized work with the blind, the deaf, and the mentally retarded.   (H. A. Ru.)

RENAL DISORDERS

Recent developments in the treatment of chronic renal failure by dialysis and kidney transplants have overshadowed progress on the preventive side. This is much less dramatic, involving as it does a piecemeal attack on the great variety of disease processes that can lead to a final common state of renal insufficiency. Though no outstanding advances (comparable, say, to successful kidney transplants) were reported in 1968, this may be the time to look at the possibilities.

There are two obvious and compatible approaches to the problem. One is to distinguish those few causes that account for the great mass of patients with chronic renal failure. The other is to make a special search for such causes, even rare ones, as may be ameliorated by appropriate treatment. In terms of frequency, four causes of chronic renal failure stand out above the rest: glomerulonephritis, pyelonephritis, arterial disease affecting the kidney, and obstruction of the urinary tract. Glomerulonephritis (usually called nephritis) may start acutely, as when it follows a streptococcal infection; or it may appear in its later stages with no history of an acute attack. With the second of these modes of onset the chances of prevention are negligible. Acute nephritis seems to be diminishing in frequency—perhaps because of the practice of treating sore throats with penicillin at an early stage. There are objections to this practice, as only a minority of sore throats are due to streptococcal infection. (During an established outbreak of streptococcal sore throat penicillin is, of course, justified.) Because only a few strains of streptococci are nephritogenic, there is no point in following up an attack of acute nephritis with long-term penicillin therapy, as would be done after rheumatic fever: the risks associated with the medication outweigh those of recurrence of the nephritis.

The incidence of pyelonephritis seems to be increasing both in the United States and in Britain. Insofar as the increase is absolute, and not relative to the declining incidence of glomerulonephritis, it is at first sight puzzling, inasmuch as the treatment of urinary infection should have been improved by the increased range of antibiotic agents. Several possible explanations come to mind. Not every attack of acute urinary infection is treated as seriously as it deserves to be, either by the patient or by the doctor, but this situation should be improving as general medical knowledge grows. More suggestive is the change in the age structure of the population: urinary infection is relatively common in the elderly, and with the birthrate falling and life expectancy rising there is an increase in the number of elderly people. Finally, there is a good deal of evidence that renal damage resembling pyelonephritis can be produced by the abuse of analgesic agents, to which our drug-oriented society is prone.

Little can be done at present to prevent the kidney from sharing in the damage caused to all organs by gradual arterial degeneration, but the vigorous treatment of severe hypertension in younger people can save kidneys (as well as eyesight). The prevention of obstructive damage to the kidney depends on early effective surgery of the urinary tract.

The second approach to prevention lies in the curative treatment even of rare causes. Examples include the removal of parathyroid tumour; substitution, where appropriate, of allopurinol for uricosuric agents in gouty nephropathy; protection from nephrotoxic agents; and treatment of tuberculosis, which may cause amyloid degeneration of the kidney. These are concerns of competent general medical care, rather than of nephrology per se, but they perhaps make the point, to the specialist, that a patient is not just an envelope surrounding a pair of kidneys. (D. A. K. B.)

RESPIRATORY DISEASES

In the winter of 1967–68 a major epidemic of influenza A2 (Asian flu) occurred in the United States, especially in the East. The outbreak was marked by excesses in total mortality, in influenza-pneumonia deaths, and in mortality among persons over 65. Much of the influenza around the world in 1967–68 was also of the A2 variety. Large epidemics occurred in South Africa, Japan, the United Kingdom, several European countries, Chile, and Argentina. Influenza B outbreaks occurred in Asia in the fall of 1967, with some cases in western Canada and the western U.S. and scattered outbreaks in Japan in the spring of 1968.

In July 1968 an outbreak of major proportions began in Hong Kong, but the disease was mild. By mid-August the Hong Kong epidemic had subsided but Singapore was experiencing its biggest epidemic since 1957; this was followed by similarly extensive epidemics in the Philippines, Taiwan, and Indonesia. The virus, of A2 type, varied significantly from previous strains, indicating a major antigenic drift. In the U.S. vaccines incorporating the new strain were prepared, but the disease reached epidemic proportions in the late fall and early winter, before adequate supplies had been manufactured and distributed.

Animal reservoirs of influenza have long been suspected, in that outbreaks have been known to occur among swine in the U.S. and among horses in northern Asia. J. A. Kasel, R. J. Byrne, and E. W. Harvey reported the production of experimental human B influenza virus infection in Chincoteague ponies. The finding of a high frequency of influenza antibodies in horses near Toronto confirmed earlier findings by J. Ditchfield and co-workers of influenza B antibodies in horse serum, also in Canada.

Many features of infections with *Mycoplasma*

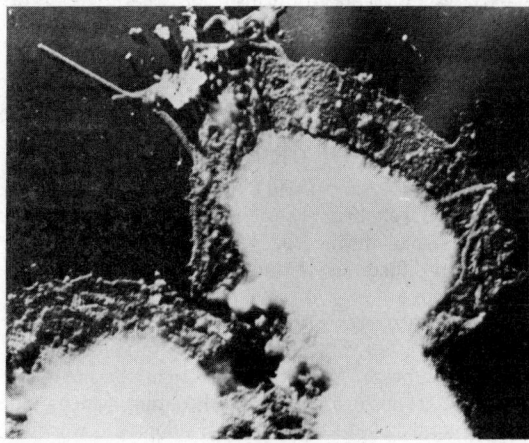

Electron microgram of a "Hong Kong" flu virus coating a red blood cell. Medical authorities feared a worldwide influenza epidemic during the winter of 1968–69.

pneumoniae are being elucidated. S. C. Copp and co-workers described an outbreak of respiratory disease in La Crosse, Wis., in which this agent was implicated in 48% of the cases. Family spread was common, with the initial case usually in a teen-ager. Almost all sufferers had pneumonia, seven also had a rash, and seven had middle-ear involvements. Another study, of eight families followed five months, was made by N. Balassanian and F. C. Robbins in Cleveland, O. More than half of the 48 members of the families were already found to be infected when the initial case in each family was discovered. Clinical pneumonia occurred in one-third of the cases; a somewhat larger proportion had respiratory infection without pneumonia; six persons were infected without symptoms; and only in three did the investigators fail to demonstrate the presence of *M. pneumoniae.* The organism persisted for at least four to six weeks in half of those with infection even after antibodies developed and after specific treatment—although the organisms remained sensitive to the antibiotics that were used. P. C. Fleming of Toronto observed a serious generalized type of skin and mucous membrane lesion (Stevens-Johnson syndrome) associated with pneumonia caused by *M. pneumoniae.* H. P. Lambert of Glasgow ascribed rheumatic manifestations in three patients to infection with this microbe.

Attempts to prevent or treat *M. pneumoniae* infections have given variable results. W. J. Mogabgab tested an inactivated vaccine given by injection to 10,000 U.S. Air Force trainees (against a placebo control). Adverse reactions were inconsequential, and three-fourths of those who got the vaccine developed demonstrable antibodies (which were not appreciably increased by a second dose). The antibody levels were equivalent to those known to protect against natural infection, and there was a significant reduction in pneumonia caused by *M. pneumoniae* among the vaccinated (45% reduction in all pneumonias; less reduction in pharyngitis and bronchitis). J. C. Maisel and co-workers gave prophylactic antibiotics or a placebo, alternately, to naval recruits as they appeared with upper respiratory infection in a dispensary during an unusually severe epidemic. About one-fifth of them were expected to develop pneumonia. The pneumonia cases were not prevented, but those that occurred among men who had received antibiotics resulted in a shorter illness, with fewer relapses and complications, than occurred among those who got the placebo.

(M. Fd.)

SURGERY

Organ transplantation continued in 1968 to be the main field of advance in surgery. (For details of heart transplants, *see* the introductory section.) From the biological point of view it seems that the human heart can be treated rather like a kidney. If the heart fails, however, there is no satisfactory long-term mechanical substitute comparable to dialysis when the kidneys fail. This gives the surgeon far less leeway in managing the recipient before and immediately after grafting and also makes it very difficult to perform a second heart transplant if the first does not succeed.

Although it has received far less publicity than the heart transplant, the more difficult surgical procedure of liver transplantation has been carried out successfully in man with, in one case, postoperative survival of almost a year.

The results of kidney transplantation without anti-lymphocyte serum have improved throughout the world. This applies to both live-donor and cadaver-donor transplants. Approximately 80% of kidneys from live related donors remained functioning after a year, with a small falloff in subsequent years; a survival rate of 60% has been reported in transplantations from unrelated cadaver donors. These improvements closely parallel improved results in the replacement of heart valves. With no obvious new developments in prosthesis construction or in the heart-lung machine, the expectation of success has still increased. These changes probably are due to ever increasing experience in patient care and surgical technique.

The scope of organ replacement surgery in therapeutic medicine has yet to be defined. It is likely that transplantation will prove to be the treatment of choice for chronic renal failure in the near future. The place of heart transplantation is less clear. Most recipients have suffered from myocardial infarction or myopathy. It seems that, provided the heart is the only organ that is severely diseased and that no other treatment is available, heart transplantation may well be indicated. Unfortunately, severe secondary diseases have already developed in many cases; thus transplantation of a perfectly functioning heart may not suffice to restore the patient's health to normal. (The frequency of fatal disease limited to the heart in relatively young people is probably high, but reliable statistics are not available.)

Lack of suitable methods of support for patients

Surgical team at the University of Puerto Rico administers a transfusion to a 6½-month fetus. Doctors throughout the world were developing diagnostic techniques and treatments for the unborn baby.

UNIVERSITY OF PUERTO RICO SCHOOL OF MEDICINE

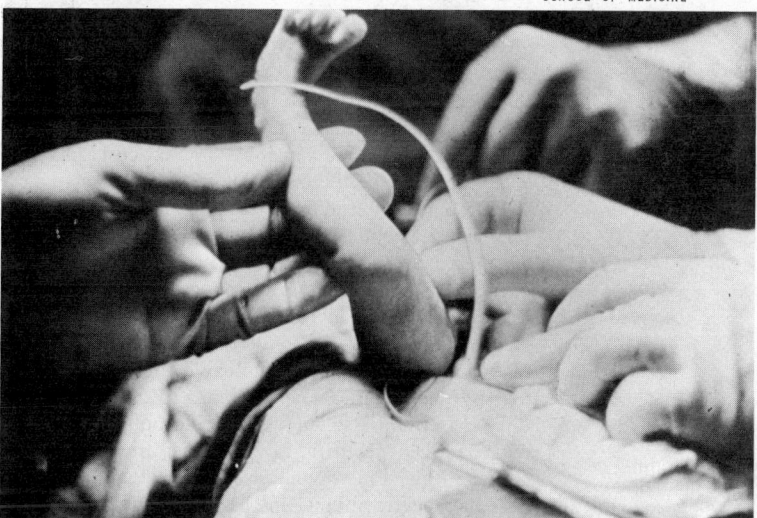

with liver failure has seriously limited the application of liver transplantation. The successes so far have been in patients with primary malignancy of the liver or biliary atresia, where residual function permitted the patient to survive the operation. Developments in support of a patient with liver failure by means of exchange blood transfusion, cross-circulation with another person or an animal, or ex vivo perfusion through a human or animal liver have all been successful in treating patients with acute liver failure in which cell damage was potentially recoverable. These methods, however, are not suitable for chronic liver disease. (R. Y. C.)

TROPICAL MEDICINE

An important recent trend in tropical medicine is the practice of epidemiological surveillance—the intensive collection and detailed analysis of data relating to the spread of disease. The analysis provides a basis for assessing the efficacy of measures taken against an epidemic or endemic situation and for predicting, in new situations, what measures are most likely to succeed. Ineffectual efforts thus can be avoided with considerable savings. Epidemiological surveillance has been applied notably to malaria control and eradication campaigns.

Cholera of the El Tor variety continued to be widely prevalent. Until 1961 this particular infection had been known only in the Celebes. Since then it has spread as far west as Iraq and has tended to replace the classical cholera. The reason for the sudden spread of El Tor cholera is unknown. Subclinical cholera is more frequent than the clinical manifestation and is spoken of as an "iceberg disease," in that the greater part of it remains inscrutable. The existence of this great reservoir of infection renders control a much more difficult problem than had been supposed.

The World Health Organization in 1968 revised its scheme for global malaria eradication, which had begun in many countries in 1955. Eradication is now considered to be unattainable as long as basic medical services necessary for detection and treatment of residual malaria remain insufficiently developed in many countries. Also, malaria refractory to eradication has become apparent in some areas. The latter difficulty may be due in part to the mosquito vectors' having acquired resistance to available insecticides. Resistance has been brought about, in some instances, by exposure to insecticides used in agriculture. Even so, of the 1,692,000,000 people formerly endangered by malaria throughout the world, more than two-thirds now live in regions entirely free from the infection or in places where work toward eradication is being actively pursued. The low cost of eradication in certain areas is remarkable. In Venezuela, for example, malaria has been eradicated from two-thirds of the original endemic area at a lower annual cost than the expenditure for refuse collection in Caracas.

Resistance of the malaria parasite *Plasmodium falciparum* to chloroquine—one of the most valuable antimalarial drugs—was causing problems in Vietnam (acutely so among American troops), in other parts of the Far East, and in Brazil. Acute infections due to chloroquine-resistant *P. falciparum* can be treated effectively with 1 g. sulformetoxine together with 50 mg. pyrimethamine. The antileprotic drug diaminodiphenylsulfone also suppresses chloroquine-resistant malaria when given in weekly doses of 25 mg. together with a similar amount of pyrimethamine.

A therapeutic adjunct in the treatment of cerebral malaria was introduced during 1968: the injection of large doses (10 to 20 mg.) of dexamethasone at the start of treatment. This greatly reduces cerebral edema, which is often responsible for coma and death. (See *Public Health,* above.) (A. W. Wo.)

WORLD HEALTH ORGANIZATION

The 20th anniversary of WHO was celebrated in 1968. *The Second Ten Years of the World Health Organization,* published during the year, traced the achievements and difficulties of the past decade. (See *Public Health,* above.)

As the 21st assembly convened, Southern Yemen was admitted as a full member and Bahrain as an associate member of WHO. This brought the membership to 131 nations, including Lesotho, which had joined in July 1967. The assembly adopted a working budget of $60,747,800 for 1969, an increase over 1968 of a little more than 8%, and it recommended an increase of about 9% for 1970. The assembly approved Director General M. G. Candau's proposal to reexamine the global strategy of malaria eradication. This would involve critical assessment by teams consisting of economists, public health administrators, statisticians, and malariologists. (See *Tropical Medicine,* above.)

About 120,000 cases of smallpox were reported in 1967—the worst year since 1963.

The rising incidence of syphilis attracted attention to the need for control techniques much broader than the use of the highly effective drugs available for individual treatment. The search for an immunizing agent was being pursued in several laboratories. Current trends in the epidemiology of syphilis and gonorrhea reflected the promiscuity associated with more effective contraceptive measures, altered moral codes, travel and population movements, urbanization, and industrialization.

Histological Typing of Lung Tumours, the first volume in the "International Histological Classification of Tumours" series, was well received. Work was continuing on the classification of breast, soft-tissue, and oropharyngeal tumours.

Ischemic (arterial insufficiency) heart disease was singled out as WHO's main object of interest in the field of cardiovascular disorders because of its increasing incidence, particularly among young people. A large-scale cooperative trial aimed at prevention by lowering blood lipid levels in healthy subjects was under way.

Work was begun on the establishment of standards for clinical trials with fertility-regulating agents (intrauterine devices and hormones) and on guidelines for the collection and evaluation of data. Special attention was being given to the training of university teachers and professional staff in the health aspects of population dynamics. (WHO)

See also Dentistry; Insurance; Molecular Biology; Psychology; Social Services; Vital Statistics.

ENCYCLOPÆDIA BRITANNICA FILMS. *Alcoholism* (1952); *Allergies* (1952); *Antibiotics* (1952); *Drug Addiction* (1952); *Mental Health (Keeping Mentally Fit)* (1952); *Cancer* (1953); *The Skeleton* (1953); *Bacteria—Friend or Foe* (1954); *First Aid on the Spot* (1954); *Heart Disease— Its Major Causes* (1955); *The Human Brain* (1955); *Immunization* (1955); *The Spinal Column* (1956); *Tuberculosis* (1956); *Work of the Blood* (1957); *The Housefly* (1958); *Health in Our Community* (1959); *DNA—Molecule of Heredity* (1960); *The Blood* (1961); *Mitosis* (1961); *Bacteria* (1962); *Meiosis: Sex Cell Formation* (1962); *Eyes and Vision* (1963); *Gene Action* (1963); *Laws of Heredity* (1963); *Natural Selection* (1963); *The Digestive System* (1965); *The Hospital* (1966); *Chromosomes of Man* (1967); *The Eyes and Seeing* (1968); *The Work of the Heart* (1968).

Mental Health:
see Medicine;
Psychology

Merchandising

Most of the industrialized world enjoyed unprecedented prosperity during 1968. In the U.S. business activity continued to expand and showed no sign of softening; there was no indication that the federal income tax surcharge had yet begun to cool off the economy. Retail sales in the U.S. rose at an accelerating rate during the first three quarters. During April, May, and June sales were running 6.5, 7.9, and 5.6% higher than in the corresponding months of the preceding year. During July and August, however, the rate of expansion increased dramatically. Retail sales during these months totaled $29.1 billion and $29.2 billion, respectively, representing slightly more than a 10% increase over 1967 levels.

Studies did not give a clear indication of consumers' intentions during the remainder of the year. An index of consumer sentiment, calculated by the Survey Research Center of the University of Michigan, indicated that people were neither notably optimistic nor extremely pessimistic. The centre expected changes in the rate of spending to be minor.

Retail sales in Canada during the first four months of 1968 totaled $8,150,000,000, or 7% above the comparable period of 1967. At midyear consumer spending was up 9% despite higher taxes. This trend was supported by increases in personal income, which during the first quarter was 6% above the first quarter of 1967 and 1.6% higher than in the fourth quarter of the preceding year.

Europe also enjoyed prosperity during 1968. According to the Organization for Economic Cooperation and Development, the prospects for continued expansion were encouraging. The British economy was expected to expand 3% during 1968, up from 1.4% in 1967. The rate of expansion stood at 4% in the first six months, but then decelerated to 2.5%. OECD predicted that business investment would recover, but the restrictive budget of March was depressing overall domestic demand. OECD also predicted a 3.5% rise in GNP for France during 1968, compared with 4.4% in 1967, and West Germany's GNP was expected to grow by 4.5%, compared with the recession year of 1967, when output shrank by 0.3%. However, the rate of expansion slowed from 5% in the first half of the year to around 3.5% during the second half.

Italy continued its three-year expansion, but there were signs that the rate of growth was slowing. Growth in GNP was projected at 5% for the year, down from 5.9% in 1967. Consumer spending, which had expanded significantly during the preceding two years, did not continue at the same rate. New car sales were down 3.3% in the first six months compared with the corresponding period in 1967, and appliance sales also failed to reach expected levels. In August the government announced a number of proposals to stimulate the economy.

In the U.S. the trend toward fewer, larger stores continued during 1968, according to the 15th National Sample Census of Retail Distribution conducted by Audits & Surveys, Inc. There were 1,794,744 retail outlets in operation, 14,170 fewer than in 1967. During the preceding decade, 72,000 stores—mainly small specialty shops—had vanished while multiline discount, department, and automotive stores had increased in number and importance. Furniture and furnishings stores, eating and drinking establishments,

and food outlets suffered the greatest decline during the ten-year period.

Dramatic changes had also occurred in the relative importance of different types of retail institutions. In 1967 supermarkets had a sales volume of $50.3 billion, followed by conventional department stores with $17.7 billion and discount department stores with $16.6 billion. Discounters continued to be the fastest growing type of retail outlet, enjoying an increase in sales of 245% during the 1961–67 period. The second fastest growing type of outlet—men's and boys' clothing stores—increased by only 52% during the same period.

The gain in department store sales of 6 to 7% was exceeded by chain stores. During the first seven months of 1968, the sales of the major variety chains were 16.5% above the corresponding months of 1967, while general merchandise and mail-order chains enjoyed a 12.3% sales increase during both periods. Several factors accounted for this. Nearly half of the increase represented price inflation. Another factor was that new stores, particularly discount outlets, were being opened at a record rate.

The profit picture was not so encouraging. Of the 25 largest retailers in the U.S., only 52% experienced increases in dollar profits from 1966 to 1967, and 60% suffered a decline in their profit margins. With the retroactive corporate income tax increase and predicted rises in wages and other operating expenses, the industry was not optimistic about improving profit margins in 1968.

New supermarkets opened in 1967 differed in several respects from those opened in previous years, according to a study published by the Super Market Institute. New stores were larger, averaging 21,000 sq.ft., compared with 20,800 sq.ft. in 1966. Average sales per square foot amounted to $3.07 a week—3% above the previous year and the highest ever recorded. Two out of three new supermarkets were erected as part of a new shopping centre, the largest proportion to date. The number of customer transactions declined from the preceding year—7,000 a week rather than 7,500—but the average sale per transaction rose from $5.24 to a new high of $5.88.

Supermarkets continued to engage in a number of activities designed to combat adverse public opinion resulting from the 1966 housewives' boycott, as well as charges leveled by civil rights advocates that supermarkets in ghetto areas charged higher prices for inferior merchandise and failed to hire and/or promote minority group employees. In 1967 and 1968, the National Association of Food Chains held a series of 25 consumer conferences in major U.S. cities to determine what the consumers' complaints were and what could be done to resolve them. The conferences showed that consumers thought supermarkets were much more profitable than was actually the case—housewives estimated profits to be 10 to 70% of sales, although the industry average was only 1.19%—and they felt that the elimination of trading stamps and other promotional programs would lower food prices. As a result, the industry was studying a number of pilot programs aimed at restoring public confidence.

Attempts to operate co-op supermarkets in underprivileged areas met with mixed results. A co-op set up by the U.S. Office of Economic Opportunity to give the poor in the San Francisco Hunters Point area a break on prices was losing about $1,000 a week at midyear. Several reasons were given for the failure, among them that residents of the area had not been

educated to use the store, that the co-op did not give trading stamps, and that the appeal of dividing profits among customers on the basis of patronage had little effect since the store had failed to produce a profit in two years of operation. The outlook for a supermarket co-op in Harlem was considerably brighter. The store was financed by co-op memberships at $5 a share, supplemented by grants from several companies. Observers were confident that the venture would prove successful.

Credit continued to become more of a factor in merchandising. In 1967 several small supermarket chains in California had begun to experiment with selling food on credit, despite the fact that similar plans adopted by other supermarkets in recent years had not been successful. In September 1968 the world's largest food chain, A & P, startled the food industry by introducing credit and a credit card in six stores in small communities in Ohio and West Virginia. The card, valid for 30 days, was good for a predetermined amount—normally $400. At the end of the 30-day period, if the consumer's record was satisfactory the card was automatically renewed. Cardholders paid

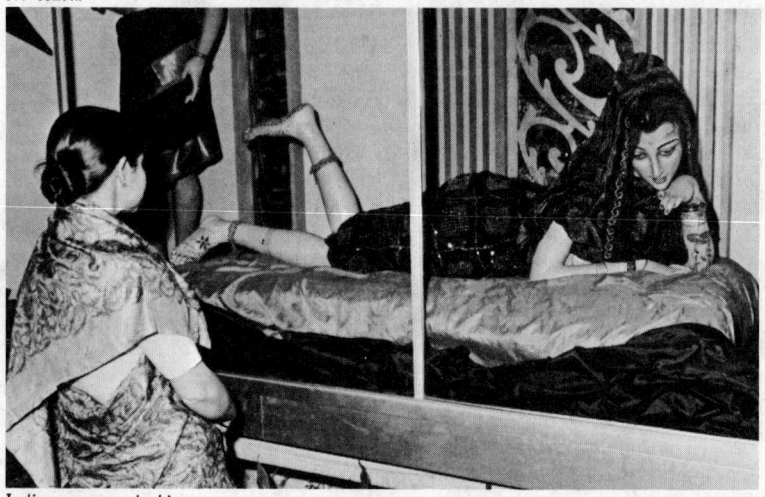

Indian woman looking at a "mini-sari" in a New Delhi store window. This departure from tradition created considerable controversy in India.

no service charge for the first 30 days; thereafter they paid 1¾% of the unpaid balance.

Bank credit cards became a more important source of credit. Although at midyear they accounted for only $1.5 billion, compared with the $81 billion of installment credit in existence in the U.S., they were growing at an impressive rate. During the summer months, outstanding debt under credit cards and similar bank plans was increasing at an annual rate of 26%. Three years earlier, fewer than 70 banks offered a charge card service. At the end of 1967, more than 625 banks offered such services, approximately 10 million consumers held cards, and 400,000 merchants honoured one or more cards.

Throughout the Western world, significant changes occurred in the structure and activities of merchandisers. In Amsterdam, 25 department store chains from 18 nations and three continents formed one of the world's largest wholesale purchasing pools. The 25 chains that made up the International Association of Department Stores represented a retail volume of over $5 billion. Having already pooled their efforts in advertising and display, they decided to use the same approach to obtain large cost savings on quantity purchases.

In Britain, 33% of the retail food market was served by multiple shop organizations in 1968, and

2,400 supermarkets accounted for 11–12% of total national food sales. Of the 250,000 retail food establishments, 21,000 were self-service operations.

In West Germany the number of *Verbrauchermärkte* (VM), or consumer discount stores, had increased from less than a dozen to more than 100 since 1965. There was intensified competition between the VM's and the major department stores, and many of the latter responded by adapting certain discount operation techniques.

Mail-order houses continued to grow in importance in Europe. According to European Free Trade Association analysts, for a decade mail-order selling had been the fastest growing form of retailing in Britain.

Mail-order sales in West Germany totaled $1.4 billion in 1967 (4% of the retail market), but the volume continued to grow, partly because of the country's 6:30 P.M. retail store closing laws. Supermarkets were also increasing at an impressive rate in West Germany, and self-service establishments, combining trading stamps and product lines comparable to department stores, were achieving significant competitive inroads.

July 1, 1968, was a significant date for the EEC. As of that date, tariffs were eliminated on thousands of manufactured products traded among Common Market countries. This amounted to about $25 billion in annual internal EEC trade. Simultaneously, EEC countries began charging a common external tariff on goods imported from outside the six-nation bloc. Originally these tariffs were to be at an average of 12.8% for manufactured goods. However, the EEC decided to make the first two of five scheduled reductions under the Kennedy Round tariff-cutting arrangement, bringing the average external EEC tariff on manufactured goods down to 10.7%. The external tariff changes would affect over $31 billion of EEC imports from other countries, in addition to approximately $32 billion of exports.

Among several important legislative developments that occurred during the second session of the U.S. 90th Congress was the passage of a "Truth-in-Lending" bill requiring lenders and merchants to disclose the cost of credit as an annual rate. Meanwhile, regulatory agencies and industry officials wrestled with problems involved in enforcing the "Truth-in-Packaging" law passed by Congress in 1966. Over 50 industry groups were in the process of examining the need for standards, either on their own or in cooperation with the Department of Commerce. Industry officials were optimistic that this approach would work better than simply waiting for regulations from the Food and Drug Administration or the Federal Trade Commission.

During the year, a new National Commission on Product Safety was appointed. The commission published a list of more than 200 products that it might investigate for safety hazards. The commission would recommend changes to manufacturers and, if it did not get the necessary cooperation, would seek congressional or federal agency action. The commission planned to give priority to power lawnmowers, electric power tools, and toys.

In October the U.S. Federal Trade Commission conducted hearings to explore the possibility of setting up a nationwide system of consumer complaint offices. The offices would be located primarily in low-income areas. The FTC also proposed new guidelines on promotional allowances offered by manufacturers to retailers. The proposed rules would require all com-

panies that grant such allowances to notify every retailer of their availability. Formerly, a manufacturer had been responsible for notifying only those customers with whom it dealt directly.

In its annual report to Congress, the FTC asked for greater powers. Specifically, it asked Congress for the authority to obtain court injunctions that would temporarily block a company from engaging in practices that might violate any of the laws that the FTC enforces. It also proposed that deliberate deception be punished as a misdemeanour; that cigarette advertisements include a health hazard warning and tar and nicotine yield statements; and it called for amendments to the Clayton Act providing for advance notice to the FTC when certain types of mergers are contemplated and also that FTC decisions in Clayton Act cases may be used as prima facie evidence in private damage litigation.

Antitrust enforcement took on a new dimension as a result of the U.S. Supreme Court's decision in the United Shoe Machinery (USM) Corp. case. In 1953 USM had 85% of the shoe machinery market in the U.S. In response to a suit brought by the Justice De-

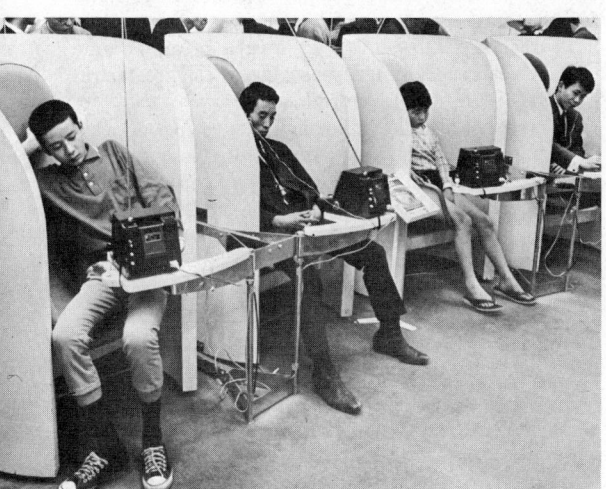

WIDE WORLD

Shoppers relaxing in a Tokyo department store that provides booths in which tired patrons can watch television.

partment the U.S. District Court in Boston ordered USM to take several steps to increase competition in the market, and the company was given until 1965 to make the order work. In 1965 the Justice Department complained to the district court that the order had reduced USM's market share only to 60%. The court refused to reopen the case. In an 8–0 ruling, the Supreme Court ordered the case reopened. The opinion, written by Justice Abe Fortas, stated that the original order had allowed a ten-year time limit, and that if it had not worked in this period, "the time has come to prescribe other, and if necessary more definitive means to achieve the result." This meant that, for the first time, the government could take back to court a previously settled monopoly case in order to force a company to take more drastic steps to end its market domination. Hundreds of these cases existed.

In *U.S.* v. *Arnold Schwinn & Co.* and *U.S.* v. *Sealy, Inc.*, the Supreme Court clarified the conditions that render territorial and customer restrictions by a manufacturer legal, rather than being in violation of sec. 1 of the Sherman Act. In the Sealy case, the government had attacked the territorial restrictions imposed by Sealy on licensed manufacturers of its mattresses

and other bedding products. Sealy contended that the territorial restraints were legal vertical limitations rather than illegal horizontal restraints, since Sealy was substantially owned by the licensees. The Supreme Court disagreed. It found that the common ownership and control of Sealy by the stockholders in their own interest rendered the division of markets by exclusive territorial limitations and the carefully policed common pricing patterns an "aggravation of trade restraints" and a horizontal rather than a vertical arrangement.

In the Schwinn case the court concluded that restrictions on distributors limiting the customer relationship to franchised dealers, and Schwinn's policy of prohibiting retailers from selling to customers other than consumers, was a per se violation of sec. 1 of the Sherman Act. However, the court ruled that if Schwinn did not sell its bicycles—that is, when the role of distributors and retailers was that of agent or consignee—the restrictions imposed violated the Sherman Act only if they were "unreasonably restrictive of competition." The court stated that two other conditions were necessary to legalize the restrictions. First, the restrictions, when evaluated in terms of availability of competitive products, the freedom of dealers to handle other competitive products, the freedom of the restrictions from "intermixture with price fixing," and the competitive justification for the program, must be reasonable. Second, even though "nonpredatory motives and sound business purposes" rather than injury to competitors motivate the manufacturer, the restrictions must not be "substantially adverse to competition in the market place."

In *Burke, et al.* v. *Ford and Kunc, et al.*, the Supreme Court clarified the difference between interstate and intrastate commerce. In this case the complaining parties were liquor retailers and the defendants, Ford and Kunc, were liquor wholesalers in Oklahoma. Ford and Kunc purchased all their liquor from outside the state and stored it in their own warehouses. They had an agreement among themselves that divided the state both by geography and by brand. Burke brought action under sec. 1 of the Sherman Act to enjoin the alleged statewide market division. However, the lower courts dismissed the case on the ground that only intrastate commerce was involved. The Supreme Court, in reversing the decision, reasoned that horizontal territorial divisions typically reduce competition, and when this occurs prices increase as unit sales decrease. The division of the wholesalers' territories almost surely resulted in fewer sales to retailers, and hence fewer purchases from out-of-state distillers than would have occurred had free competition prevailed. Moreover, the market-sharing arrangement reduced the number of wholesale outlets where these brands could be purchased. Thus, interstate commerce was affected.   (D. T. K.)

See also Advertising; Consumer Expenditures; Industrial Review; Prices.

Metallurgy

The major demands made on metallurgy during 1968 were for lower costs and higher reliability—two aspects of the same problem in most cases, since industry was keenly aware of the cost savings resulting from the use of highly uniform, defect-free metals. The concept of "characterization" was attracting much attention, though its practical achievement remained

Merchant Marine:
see Transportation

Metals:
see Industrial Review;
Metallurgy; Mining

nearly as remote as before a name was adopted for the idea. Characterization is the description of a material, not by the usual specifications alone, but by everything that might affect its serviceability, including its response to all the operations involved in the production of the finished part and how it might fail in normal use or as a result of accident. Since a practical routine test seldom reproduces actual conditions in detail, characterization required not only highly sophisticated testing and inspection, but also a deep understanding of the meaning of the test results. The main effect of characterization thus was in testing, especially the development of methods using any phenomena that could be adapted to automatic, 100% inspection or that might give improved correlation with processing or service behaviour. The need for rigorous quality control from the very first steps in metal production was being increasingly stressed.

Two continuous steelmaking processes using oxygen were in advanced stages of development. A pilot plant in Japan was producing low carbon steel by flowing liquid iron from the blast furnace through troughlike furnaces with oxygen blowing over the iron. A spray process being developed in England used a jet of oxygen to atomize a stream of blast furnace iron to which the necessary slag-forming materials had been added. The metal spray, heated far above the melting point by the burning of impurities, falls into a ladle where the oxidized impurities, including even phosphorous, float out in the slag and the superheated steel can melt an appreciable amount of scrap and alloying elements in the ladle.

Canada's program to develop nuclear reactors using natural—rather than enriched—uranium required hafnium-free zirconium for many reactor parts because of its low neutron absorption. A new plant gave Canada a domestic source of zirconium and introduced a new process. First, zirconium and hafnium nitrates are made from zircon ore and are separated by solvent extraction in one of the first applications of that process in the metal industry outside of uranium refining. Pure zirconium tetrachloride is made from the nitrate and is then heated and reduced to the metal. The furnace used for this process was capable of producing either alloy or pure metal ingots, rather than the usual porous zirconium sponge which requires subsequent remelting and alloying.

Poland, which has no natural supplies of bauxite, began production of aluminum oxide from clay and fly ash in a plant with a potential production rate of 100,000 tons per year. Portland cement was obtained as a by-product.

Interest in automation continued in the foundry industry, which was attempting to maintain the cost advantage of casting. The computer-controlled automatic casting line still appeared remote, but many advances were made on the basis of existing technology. Increases in the size and variety of permanent mold and die castings were achieved, largely through the use of new mold materials. Continuous charging and tapping of an electric furnace using carefully selected scrap and prereduced iron pellets was shown to be practical, pointing to a solution to the hot metal supply problem for an automatic steel foundry. Since a lower percentage of scrap is used in the new basic oxygen furnace than was used in open-hearths, scrap was readily available to foundries. The mechanical properties of thin-walled castings were brought nearer to those of wrought parts by a process in which a cold core was dipped into the molten metal, which

quickly solidified around it, and was then withdrawn. The resulting excellent properties were thought to be due to the rapid freezing and cooling. Castings made from a new aluminum alloy containing silver, in addition to other elements, had properties close to those of competing wrought alloys. It was shown that 0.5% silver added to any of several aluminum alloys raised the endurance limit and increased the corrosion resistance.

A solution to the problem of forming refractory metals into shapes too complex for casting or conventional powder metallurgy was achieved by mixing the metal powder with wax and pressing at low pressure. The wax vaporizes during sintering, yielding a sound part.

A uniformity of composition impossible to achieve in cast tool steel ingots was realized by atomizing the steel with a high-velocity jet of inert gas, then pressing and sintering the powder. The life of cutting tools made from the ingots was more than double that of the older types. Producing metal powder, collecting it, and consolidating it into billets in a vacuum was shown to eliminate completely the lack of bonding between particles, making it possible to use the metal for the most critical applications. Melting, casting, heat treating, and welding in a vacuum all became more widespread, primarily because of the greater reliability of the resulting products.

Interest continued to grow in various types of coatings, both superficial and, especially, those diffused into the metal surface. A layer of mixed chromium and chromic oxide electrodeposited one millionth of an inch thick on steel gave excellent protection from corrosion and made a superior base for lacquer. It was being suggested as a substitute for tin in food and beverage containers, adding still another material to this highly competitive market in which nonmetallics were making rapid advances.   (D. F. C.)

See also Industrial Review; Mining; Physics.

ENCYCLOPÆDIA BRITANNICA FILMS. *The Miner* (1967).

Meteorology

The volume of technical and scientific literature published during 1968 in the realm of meteorology, weather, and climate was almost twice that published in 1960, according to the American Meteorological Society (AMS). In applied meteorology, the number of weather bulletins and forecasts published every day by radio, television, and newspapers for use by the public had reached an incredible estimated total of three million or more.

Government monies expended for meteorological purposes exceeded $3 billion for the world as a whole, with the U.S. accounting for approximately half the total. Official backing was given to the advancement of knowledge of the earth's atmosphere, as well as to closer international cooperation in the application of meteorology for the benefit of mankind. This was apparent as various national and intergovernmental bodies enacted special resolutions or adopted programs in support of the World Weather Watch (WWW) and the Global Atmospheric Research Program (GARP).

Basic Research. Investigations during the year again covered the spectrum, from the microscale of condensation nuclei and cloud droplet electrical charges to the planetary waves in the atmosphere which often govern major weather changes. As the re-

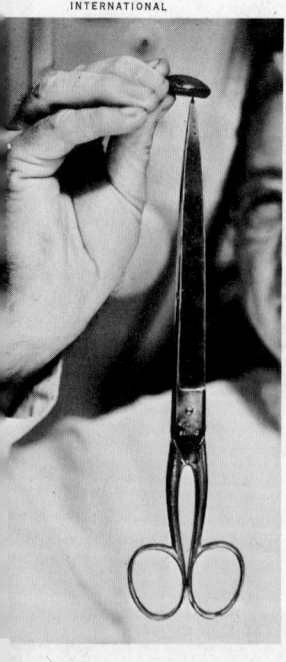

Powerful small magnet developed in 1968 by Bell Telephone Laboratories is cast from rare earth elements, samarium or cerium. The magnet may be produced in extremely small size and in varying shapes, making it more versatile than magnets made from conventional materials.

AUTHENTICATED NEWS INTERNATIONAL

sult of a chain of scientific developments, beginning with the high-altitude rocket photographs of cloud systems many years earlier and the launching of the first Tiros weather satellite in 1960, truly global analysis of the general circulation of the atmosphere, based on data from direct "observations" rather than on speculative interpolations, was at last becoming a possibility.

Perhaps the most spectacular component of this global approach during 1968 was provided by ATS-1 and ATS-3. These applications technology satellites were placed in orbit over the Equator at an altitude of about 22,000 mi. This gave the satellites an angular revolution around the earth equal to the earth's angular rotation, thus keeping the satellites in apparent fixed positions above points on the earth's surface. ATS-1 hovered over the mid-Pacific, ATS-3 above a point near the mouth of the Amazon. From these positions the two satellites, through their Vidicon-telecom systems, provided almost instantaneous photo views of the most active hurricane and typhoon areas of the Atlantic, the Caribbean, the Gulf of Mexico, and the Pacific Ocean. Photographs every 20 minutes gave virtual time-lapse pictures of the easterly wave disturbances that sometimes become tropical cyclones. Research meteorologists who studied the ATS output described it as among the most exciting and promising material ever obtained as regards insight into the general circulation of the atmosphere over the tropics and contiguous areas of the temperate or extratropical zones. New concepts of the mechanisms of the major circulation patterns between latitudes 35° N and 35° S were being considered.

These worldwide efforts in weather research were combined in GARP, the purpose of which was to bring together into a well-coordinated and cooperative effort basic atmospheric-research data and the most capable research scientists from all member countries of the UN. Among the many facets of meteorology to be integrated into this approach were the complex phenomena of solar radiation and the reflection and reradiation of portions of this energy intercepted by the earth, and the absorption characteristics of the atmosphere, especially the variable quantities of ozone and water vapour. Ozone, by its "greenhouse effect," tends to raise the temperature of the air near the surface of the earth, permitting passage of the shortwave radiation from the sun so that it warms the ground and to some extent the oceans and lower layers of the atmosphere. By partially obstructing passage of the longer-wave return radiation from the earth, the ozone in the upper atmosphere raises the temperature at which the incoming and outgoing radiation are in balance, thus determining the heat budget of the earth. GARP also took cognizance of the more specific problems of meteorology, such as the causes and characteristics of severe storms, the nature of condensation processes of water vapour in the air, cloud physics, hail formation, and the role of atmospheric electricity.

Variations in the solar constant—that is, in the intensity and spectral distribution of the total energy emitted by the sun—had long been a subject of study and controversy. Theoretically such variations might account for variations in climate and even—though this was unlikely—for ice epochs. If the sun's energy and the earth's atmospheric circulation are considered as fundamentally a heat engine, with weather and climate as an end product, a variation in the input of energy from the sun would lead to a variation in the weather. High-altitude rockets and space satellites had

COURTESY, U.S. AIR FORCE

Unusual cloud phenomenon which appeared over Vandenberg Air Force Base, California, in February 1968. Weathermen felt that the most probable cause of the formation was penetration of the cirrocumulus layer by aircraft.

Table I. Weather Headlines, 1968

Place	Date	Weather event	Unusual features
Upper Chesapeake Bay and Delaware Canal	Jan. 7–14	Unusually heavy ice jams	Ice paralyzed water traffic; piled ashore, blocked highway
Northern California	Jan. 30–Feb. 2	Prolonged heavy rainfall; 16 deaths	Analysis of storm form and movement aided by space satellite Essa 6, showing jet stream branch
Flagstaff, Ariz.	February	Exceptionally long-lasting and heavy snowfall	Snow piled up to average depth over 6 ft.; during 8 days almost continuous snow over entire area
Vandenberg Air Force Base, Calif.	Feb. 23	Photo "pie-in-the-sky"	Almost perfect circle hole in cloud cover; cirrus tufts; unexplained formation
Oak Ridge, Tenn.	March 12	Hail "jackstones"	Numerous hailstones with cross spikes and other odd shapes
New England states	March 12–18	Prolonged and heavy rainfall	Analysis of storm and predictions aided by Essa 6 photos
Belfast, Ire.	April 3	Hailstorm	Many cone-shaped hailstones and other unusual forms
Guam, Saipan, and western Pacific waters	April 6–15	Tropical cyclone; Typhoon Jean	Early Typhoon Jean, first of 1968 season; tracked by Essa
Iceland	May	Extensive ice fields over ocean east of Iceland	Pack ice wider than anytime in 80 years for that area
Tracy, Minn.	June 13	Tornado caused 9 deaths and injured 100	Rare photos of tenuous and swaying funnel cloud
Midlands and southern England	July 1	Dust cloud, many coloured fine dust particles	Strong winds from Spain and North Africa brought dust at high altitudes
Chile	July and August	Acute drought, worst in a hundred years	The rainfall in August, usually Chile's wettest month, only 10% of normal
Florida	Oct. 16–21	Hurricane Gladys, heavy damage near Tampa, etc.	Erratic movement and standstill made predictions very difficult
Roanoke, Va.	Oct. 18	Rainfall, 6 in. in one day	Stationary rain front, possibly influenced by Hurricane Gladys, rare for that locality
Moscow, U.S.S.R.	Oct. 27	First snowstorm of season	Snow to depth of several inches, not usual that early
Italy north of Turin	Nov. 1–5	Several days heavy rain brought disastrous floods	Worst flooding in 100 years in some valleys, more than 100 deaths

Table II. Selected Meteorological Satellites, 1968*

Satellite	Date launched	Days in operation	Usable photographs	Storms predicted	Other features
Essa 3	Oct. 2, 1966	750 plus	91,000	2,000 plus	One camera still operating
Essa 5	April 20, 1967	550 plus	55,000	800 plus	Both cameras operating
Essa 6	Nov. 10, 1967	350 plus		†	Both cameras operating
Essa 7	Aug. 16, 1968	50 plus	4,000 plus	150 plus	One camera
ATS-1	Dec. 6, 1966	650 plus	‡	Typhoons	Special uses
ATS-3	Nov. 5, 1967	300 plus	‡	Hurricanes	Special uses

*Data in the table are approximate as of November 1968. Essa satellites are in near-circular orbits about 850–900 statute miles from the earth's surface. ATS (applications technology satellites) are about 22,000 mi. from the earth at an altitude that gives them an angular revolution equal to that of earth's rotation and thus makes them appear stationary above points on earth. Nimbus satellites are primarily experimental and have differing orbits. They give only occasional radiation measurements for meteorological uses. Other satellites give occasional data for meteorology, but Essa and ATS are the main operational ones.
†Essa 6 sends pictures on demand to different localities; consequently figures are not available for total pictures, storm advisories, or predictions based thereon.
‡ATS satellites are multipurpose and are used to picture hurricanes and typhoons when occasion demands. Data for column headings are not separated.

yielded some further evidence of variation in the solar constant, but nothing in the scientific literature had as yet furnished conclusive proof of the theory.

Among the many studies of the atmospheric content of ozone were two in the *Journal of Geophysical Research* (Aug. 15, 1968). One reported to have found apparently correlated relationships between the thermal structure of the atmosphere and the vertical distribution of ozone; the second focused on ozone studies in the air over San Francisco Bay and found, among other things, that there were several distinct zones, with height related to ozone production and vertical mixing in the air.

Several research papers reported some degree of refinement in theoretical models of the major wind systems of the atmosphere as a whole. These moderate improvements applied to physical as well as mathematical models, the latter being the basis for the methods of weather prediction by numerical process under development since 1950. GARP procedures were expected to lead eventually to realistic models that would increase the accuracy and time range of weather forecasts. Certain essential parameters were not yet included in models because they could not be measured and expressed in the available equations; *e.g.,* boundary layer and radiation processes. However, the consensus among scientists seemed to be that the 1968 models were sophisticated and remarkably accurate if the complexities of the problem and the wide gaps in data and knowledge of the global circulation were taken into account.

Two new but geographically limited experiments designed to analyze typical segments of the general circulation were the Barbados Oceanographic and Meteorological Experiment (BOMEX) and the trade-winds study based on observations from a linear chain of islands in mid-Pacific known as the Line Islands Experiment. BOMEX was expected to make use of a grid covering more than 300 sq.mi., with data-collecting stations including ocean buoys, buoy tender vessels, oceanographic survey ships, aircraft, space satellites, and land-based stations.

Basic research continued into cyclonic storms and other aspects of the mesoscale or so-called secondary circulation of the atmosphere, including tropical cyclones (hurricanes and typhoons), mid- and high-latitude lows, and tornadoes. Progress was evident, but no major new discoveries or techniques were reported during 1968. Among the more important advances was a refinement in knowledge of the relationships between jet streams in the upper air over the Southwestern U.S. and the sequence of tornado formation.

Microscale events in the atmosphere, such as condensation of water vapour, accretion of raindrops, snowflakes, hail, etc., and the role of electricity in the generation and development of storms, had long received attention from research institutions. Even so, 1968 brought only a modicum of progress in this area, and many basic questions about these common weather processes remained unanswered. More than 150 scientific papers were presented at the international conference on cloud physics, held in Toronto, August 26–30; many made impressive contributions to refinement of details, but little progress was reported on fundamental problems.

An excellent review of the fundamentals for producing precipitation as they occur in nature was published by R. Braham (*AMS Bulletin,* April 1968). His diagrams showed at a glance the complexities and present scope of knowledge of precipitation sequences in the

open atmosphere. Other research studies published during the year treated the many aspects of condensation nuclei, both from natural sources and as a result of chemical particles introduced artificially into the air, either intentionally for purposes of cloud seeding or unintentionally as a result of industrial processes.

Scientific literature on the effects of electricity in the atmosphere was voluminous. During 1968 the National Center for Atmospheric Research (NCAR), Boulder, Colo., speculated that shock waves from discharges of lightning might cause cloud droplets to coalesce into the bigger drops characteristic of thunderstorm rainfall. Some scientists had held that lightning released electrical charges from droplets that had been kept apart by their mutually repelling forces. NCAR reported experiments with shock waves shot into the cloud plume of Old Faithful geyser in Yellowstone Park, but the results were inconclusive.

Applied Meteorology. Once again, interest centred on ideas for modification or control of certain undesired weather conditions, such as hailstorms and hurricanes. Although for the most part these control measures remained conjectural in 1968, they involved techniques and research of more general meteorological significance.

In their efforts to probe storms and to collect the comprehensive data needed for their national weather services and for participation in the WWW and GARP, the 130 member states and territories of the World Meteorological Organization used every conceivable method of sensing and measuring the properties of the air—conventional weather apparatus, pilot balloons, radar, radiosondes, rocket sondes, space satellites, ocean buoys, ocean station vessels, selected merchant vessels, and other devices. Satellite photo mosaics showing nine tropical cyclones at the same time indicated that many more such storms occurred than had been detected heretofore and gave promise of improved forecasts. Additional radar and satellite evidence of the distinguishing features of tornadoes, which would permit detection of these storms while they were still invisible to an observer's eye, was gathered. The identifying cloud systems accompanying jet streams from over Mexico and the adjoining eastern Pacific were found to be precursors to tornado formation when jet streams from the southwest came into a certain orientation with respect to high-level jets from the west or northwest. Although meteorologists had speculated that eddies from jet streams might generate tornado vortices, no evidence to this effect was found.

Clear air turbulence (CAT), a growing hazard as the altitude and speed of aircraft increased, was investigated by radar, reconnaissance aircraft, and space satellite photos. Radar probing gave some hope—as yet uncertain—for a means of "seeing" sharp discontinuities in wind flow—jet stream boundaries, eddies, and other invisible turbulence forms. Laser radar was also reported to have possibilities; it had been successfully used to "see" the boundaries of wind "rivulets" in the lower atmosphere. The importance placed by science and industry on the use of radar in detecting CAT, together with the many other applications of radar in meteorology, was apparent at an international conference in Montreal, August 20–23, devoted exclusively to this subject. Another conference on atmospheric turbulence was convened in Boston under the auspices of the AMS on September 4. Among the approximately 100 research papers presented at these two conferences was one on the possible relationship between microscale surface pressure waves and major

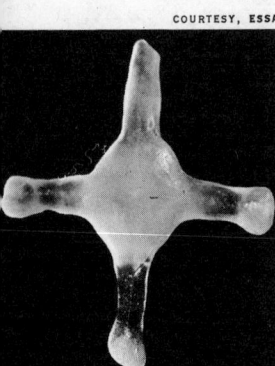

COURTESY, ESSA

Odd-shaped hailstone was found after storm at Oak Ridge, Tenn., on March 12, 1968. A variety of other shapes were also found. The most striking features of the hailstones were the long spikes that were generally coplanar and sometimes remarkably symmetrical.

Methodists:
see Religion

jet streams, as well as CAT. It was hoped that this line of research would lead to ways of identifying severe turbulence by observations with microbarographs on the ground.

Progress in Weather Forecasting. Several mechanical and numerical devices for use in forecasting were said to have been improved during 1968. A cathode-ray tube method for contouring isopleths in experiments on the general circulation was described in the *AMS Bulletin* for September. Automatic meteorological observing stations were improved, but installations of these ocean buoys to eliminate the wide gaps in weather observations at sea still awaited funding. The GHOST (global horizontal sounding technique) balloon project, another device for closing the gaps in synoptic measurements of upper air conditions, was in a very preliminary experimental stage, although trial runs were proving highly successful. One GHOST balloon, which remained floating on the winds at high altitude for more than a year, had circumnavigated the Southern Hemisphere more than 20 times.

In the face of international emphasis on extending the system of synoptic reports for the WWW, it was unfortunate that the U.S., the leader in the movement for a global attack on weather problems, was forced to close many of its weather offices as an economy measure. Another loss was the Washington Daily Weather Maps, which had been published continuously from July 1, 1878, to April 14, 1968.

Longer-range weather forecasting was summarized by J. Namias in an address published in the *AMS Bulletin* of May 1968. The paper tabulated the methods used by pioneers in long-range forecasting throughout the world, summarized progress, and ventured an optimistic outlook for improvement based on further use of numerical techniques and the results of WWW and GARP.

Status of Weather Modification Experiments. The first National (U.S.) Conference on Weather Modification took place in Albany, N.Y., April 28–May 1. In its eight sessions, 64 papers were presented on a broad range of research studies, including hail suppression, fog dispersal, shower-cloud seeding, and planned and unplanned artificial changes in weather and climate. The conference brought together leading experimenters in this specialty from many countries. Very briefly stated, the weather modification techniques of 1968 were shown to be successful in dispelling subfreezing fog and cloud under certain environmental conditions, and in augmenting amounts of precipitation by about 10% in special cases. While reports of success in hail suppression had come from many countries, among them Australia, Canada, Italy, Kenya, Switzerland, the U.S., and the U.S.S.R., the experimental controls used in these operations often were inadequate and doubts remained about the validity of the claims. Similar doubts applied to most other forms of intentional weather modification. The subject was considered to be of great potential importance, but it was still highly controversial.

Public alarm about air pollution continued, and many analyses of local air pollution cases were published in the daily press and in technical journals. The inevitability of dangerous contamination of the atmosphere and of eventual changes in weather and climate if present industrial practices continued had been demonstrated. For example, one published article gave data to prove that winter precipitation around Elkhart and La Porte, Ind., had been modified by the effluents from the factories in Gary.

Operation Stormfury, an experimental program for "controlling" hurricanes by cloud seeding, still awaited the appearance of a storm suitably located for a test. The year brought many studies and hurricane models relating basic research on tropical meteorology to theories on hurricane modification. Not forgotten in the scientific reports was that hurricane rains, however destructive, often end droughts. (F. W. RR.)

See also Astronautics; Conservation; Disasters; Oceanography.

ENCYCLOPÆDIA BRITANNICA FILMS. *The Climates of North America* (1963); *Origins of Weather* (1963); *Weather Forecasting by Satellite* (1964); *Weather Satellites* (1965); *What Makes Clouds?* (1965); *What Makes the Wind Blow?* (1965); *Whatever the Weather* (1967).

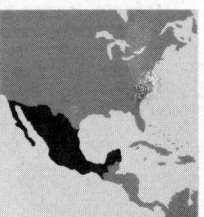

Mexico

A federal republic of Middle America, Mexico is bounded by the U.S., British Honduras, and Guatemala. Area: 761,601 sq.mi. (1,972,547 sq.km.). Pop. (1968 est.): 47,267,000, including about 70% mestizo and 28% Indian. Cap. and largest city: Mexico City (pop., 1968 est., 3,418,471). Language: Spanish. Religion: predominantly Roman Catholic. President in 1968, Gustavo Díaz Ordaz.

When President Díaz Ordaz delivered his state of the nation address on September 1, he could point to another year—his fourth in office—of high accomplishment, with many of the targets established

WIDE WORLD

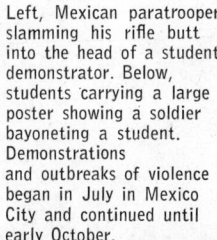

UPI COMPIX

Left, Mexican paratrooper slamming his rifle butt into the head of a student demonstrator. Below, students carrying a large poster showing a soldier bayoneting a student. Demonstrations and outbreaks of violence began in July in Mexico City and continued until early October.

MEXICO

by his administration for 1966–70 already reached or passed. A new coordinated plan for 1971–75 was already under study; it was to be preceded by an aerial survey of the whole country that would allow an assessment of its natural resources and by a population census in 1970–71, on which preliminary work had begun. Construction, manufacturing, petroleum, and electricity were some of the most dynamic sectors of the economy, but increasing attention was being paid to agriculture and livestock with a view to closing the gap between rural and urban incomes. Growing difficulties in finding plots for landless peasants had not prevented the government from distributing 3.8 million ha. to 69,000 farmers in 12 months, bringing the total appropriated since the Díaz Ordaz administration took office to 12.3 million ha. and the number of beneficiaries to 238,000.

Despite economic successes—to which the holding of the Olympic Games in Mexico was an additional stimulus—the country's much-praised political stability began to be seriously questioned both at home and abroad after incidents that took place during the summer. In July Mexico City witnessed the worst outbreaks of violence in decades when students barricaded themselves at the Polytechnic School and other buildings of the National University, following some minor students' squabbles that the police repressed with alleged brutality. Tension increased for many weeks indicating that the causes of the malaise had deeper roots than had at first been assumed. President Díaz Ordaz acknowledged this in his speech of September 1, stressing that Mexico's way of government, originally intended to suit the needs of a less developed economy and society, now called for considerable reforms. Increased efficiency was urgently needed both in government and in private enterprise. Unfortunately, these long-term objectives could not be matched with immediate moderate actions by a government committed to restore order before the opening of the Olympics, which, under the provisions of the International Olympic Committee, could only be held if civil peace prevailed in the host country. In fact, all possible measures to subdue the revolt were taken; the university was occupied by the armed forces, and patrols surrounding the Olympic stadium were very much in sight even after the Games had started on October 12. Violence, however, remained the keynote during the preceding weeks, reaching a climax in early October when probably well over 50 people were killed.

Nevertheless, the state of turmoil that predominated in Mexico City interfered only marginally with the preparation for the Olympics, and by the time they opened, most of the work planned had been completed. Total expenditure in installations was calculated at 1,915,000,000 pesos. The financial disadvantages had no doubt been outweighed by the prestige of being the first Latin-American and Spanish-speaking country to act as a host country. Evidently the wish to appear in the best possible light to the rest of the world was an important factor in eventually restraining both the authorities and the students. An uneasy truce followed, but it was clear that the students and dissident groups within the official Partido Revolucionario Institucional were gathering strength to influence basic changes, including the choice of the next presidential candidate.

The year was one of great economic activity in Mexico. Final statistics for 1967 had shown that the country's progress toward industrialization was well maintained that year: the gross national product increased by 6.4% in real terms to 113.4 million pesos, slightly less than in 1966 but still 2.9% ahead of the population growth; the balance of payments showed an overall surplus of $39.8 million for the year, achieved mainly through net inflows of short- and long-term capital far exceeding those of 1966 and more than making up for larger deficits in visible trade and services. Foreign trade, on the other hand, continued to be one of the weakest spots of the Mexican economy, the import bill rising by almost three times between 1950 and 1967 to $1,749,000,000, while the value of exports merely doubled over the same period to $1,148,000,000.

As 1968 progressed it soon became clear that the year would end with an even greater growth rate, estimated by some at between 7 and 8%. Expectations for an improved foreign trade performance based on promising crops and abundant water in the reservoirs—an indirect benefit of the storms that devastated many areas in 1967—failed to materialize in the period from January to June when the gap of $381.3 million was $97.8 million greater than that for the first half of 1967; imports rose by 12.5% while exports, despite substantial increases in sugar, coffee, and cotton, totaled only 1.5% more than in the previous year because of declines in such commodities as corn and shrimps. The signs, however, were that final statistics for the whole year would show considerable improvement.

Microbiology:
see Medicine

The peso, which retained the stability of recent times, was used during the year by the International Monetary Fund in operations with such countries as Canada, France, and the U.K. At the end of August the Banco Nacional de México was holding $623 million in international reserves ($34 million more than 12 months earlier), and secondary reserves of $500 million were available to support the peso. The policy of leaning toward other capital markets rather than exclusively toward the U.S. for external borrowing, initiated in 1967, was pursued further, and several bond issues were floated on Western European markets, including the West German and the Swiss. France provided substantial loans to modernize Mexico's telecommunications system and to install several petrochemical plants, in addition to helping with the construction of an underground railway in the Federal District. Nevertheless, bond issues continued to be placed in the U.S. and Canada, and substantial funds were received from the World Bank for hydroelectric programs; from the Inter-American Development Bank for irrigation, road building, and the export of railway components to Colombia; and from the Eximbank for railways, buses, and petrochemical installations. At the end of 1967 the government debt amounted to 42,393,000,000 pesos, of which 6,259,-000,000 pesos represented the foreign debt. (M. Pu.)

Encyclopædia Britannica Films. *Arts and Crafts of Mexico:* Part I, *Pottery and Weaving* (1961), Part II, *Basketry, Stone, Wood, and Metals* (1961); *Mexico—The Land and the People* (1961).

Middle East

The political scene in the Middle East, excluding Turkey and Iran, continued to be dominated by the Arab-Israeli problem. The fundamental disagreement between the conservative Arab regimes and the Arab socialist republics remained, but because of Arab preoccupation with Israel it was much less prominent than in previous years. However, the clash continued above the surface in Yemen where the civil war between the royalists, supported by Saudi Arabia, and the republicans receiving some support from the new republican regime in Southern Yemen and from Syria and Algeria, dragged on following the withdrawal of both British and U.A.R. forces from the area during 1967. In the Persian Gulf, Britain's announcement that it would be withdrawing all its forces by 1971 caused the rulers of nine Arab sheikhdoms to agree to form a federation. The Arabs in this area were afraid that Iran might attempt to dominate the Persian Gulf after the British withdrawal, but Saudi Arabia made strong diplomatic efforts to reach an understanding with Iran.

Arab-Israeli Enmity. During 1968 efforts to reach a solution of the Arab-Israeli problem were concentrated on the Swedish diplomat Gunnar Jarring (*see* Biography), whose mission arose out of the Nov. 22, 1967, UN Security Council resolution which called, among other things, for an Israeli withdrawal from territory occupied since June 5, 1967, and the ending of the state of belligerency between Middle East states. Jarring traveled tirelessly throughout the year, between Israel, the Arab states, his own headquarters in Cyprus, and New York. Occasional bouts of international optimism, inspired by a belief that both sides had accepted the November 22 resolution, soon gave way to much longer periods of pessimism

in which leaders of both sides declared that there was no hope of a "political solution" since the other clearly had no real desire for peace. The Arabs made frequent and detailed charges of harsh and repressive treatment by the Israelis of the inhabitants of the occupied territories. They also accused the Israelis of attempting to persuade or force the Arab inhabitants to leave those territories, especially Gaza. The Israelis denied all these charges, saying that the measures being used were the minimum necessary to counter Arab acts of terrorism.

The Suez Canal remained closed throughout 1968. British-led efforts to free 15 merchant ships trapped in the southern end failed in January when the U.A.R. announced that canal clearance would cease because the Canal Authority's ships had been shelled by the Israelis. Meanwhile, the Israelis went ahead with plans to build an oil pipeline from Eilat on the Gulf of Aqaba to Ashdod and to expand Eilat as the staging point for an overland trade route from the Red Sea to the Mediterranean. The U.A.R. also planned to build a pipeline from Suez to a point near Alexandria.

Jordan and the U.A.R., the two Arab states most directly involved in the dispute with Israel, declared unequivocally that they accepted the November 22 resolution (which admittedly was ambiguously worded). Syria and Algeria rejected the resolution, while the other Arab states were prepared to await developments. Israel's attitude was more doubtful. U.A.R. government spokesmen said that Jarring had informed them of Israel's acceptance, but in June the influential Israeli defense minister, Moshe Dayan, was quoted by the Israeli newspaper *Ma'ariv* as saying that it was "in direct conflict with Israeli interests." He was repudiated by Levi Eshkol, the Israeli prime minister, but his view undoubtedly reflected a large body of opinion inside Israel. Eshkol himself told the Israeli Labour Party Central Committee in June that Israel would not be advancing any peace plan of its own since this would enable the Arabs to haggle over its terms before negotiations. However, Dayan had already announced his own plan, which was for Jordan's West Bank (that part of Jordan west of the Jordan River) to become an autonomous Arab region in which there would be Israeli military bases. Another proposal, which became known as the Allon Plan, provided for the return to the Arabs of most of the West Bank with an Israeli corridor north of Jericho and Jerusalem; a row of fortified Israeli settlements on the heights overlooking the river; and Arab access routes to the Mediterranean.

Israeli doubts about the November 22 resolution were at least partly due to the fact that it made no mention of direct negotiations between the two sides, the one thing upon which they insisted most strongly and which the Arabs refused. Meanwhile, U.A.R. and Jordanian diplomacy concentrated on extracting from Israel full acceptance of the resolution. The theme of direct negotiations was played down somewhat in the nine-point peace plan presented to the UN General Assembly in October by the Israeli foreign minister, Abba Eban, but the plan did not include acceptance of the resolution and it was rejected by the U.A.R.

There were two main factors that might influence Israel to relax its attitude on direct negotiations

CAMERA PRESS—PIX FROM PUBLIX

Jordanian Bedouins peering across Israeli frontier on the Jordan River. The area was the scene of heavy artillery duels and Arab commando raids throughout 1968.

Arab diver preparing to submerge to clean the hull of a ship stranded in the Bitter Lakes area of the Suez Canal. Fifteen ships that had been there since June 1967 were waiting to be freed following the removal of a sunken U.A.R. ship.

"But this year's parade was nothing like last year's. . . . .This year we stayed in Israel." —Waite, "The Sun," London.

or spelling out its terms for peace beforehand. One was the attitude of the U.S. government and the other was the continued and growing insecurity on the new frontiers. After the June 1967 war Israel became heavily dependent on U.S. support. Some Israelis, such as former Prime Minister David Ben-Gurion, found this alarming, but most accepted it as a reality. It did mean that Israel had to be deeply concerned with the development of U.S. Middle East policy—a situation that was underlined by the evident Israeli distress when former Pennsylvania Gov. William Scranton, on a fact-finding tour for Pres.-elect Richard Nixon, stated that U.S. policy as between Israel and the Arabs should be more "even-handed." It had long been assumed in Washington that the best hope for a peaceful Middle East settlement lay in some form of U.S.-Soviet agreement which, with the support of all the great powers, could if necessary be imposed. Despite the apparent wide differences between the U.S.S.R. and the U.S. on the Middle East, and their frequent sharp clashes in the UN Security Council, there was some measure of agreement between the two.

The U.S.S.R. declared that it accepted Israel as a reality and used its influence to persuade the Arabs to do likewise. Its action in building up its fleet in the eastern Mediterranean was seen as being intended to strengthen the defensive and bargaining position of its principal Arab friends, the U.A.R. and Syria, rather than as encouraging them to take offensive action against Israel. In September the U.S.S.R. reaffirmed the terms of the November 22 resolution as its peace plan for the Middle East.

However, the U.S. and other NATO powers were seriously concerned with the Soviet naval buildup in the eastern Mediterranean. By the end of the summer 108 Soviet warships had moved from the Black Sea into the Mediterranean and only 62 had returned. The U.S. 6th Fleet was still more powerful, but the gap was closing. However, the U.S. saw this as another good reason for reaching an understanding with the U.S.S.R. on the Middle East. It was noticeable that while the Israeli response to the Soviet "peace plan" was cool and even contemptuous, the U.S. government regarded the initiative as important. U.S. Pres. Lyndon Johnson's moderate and carefully balanced remarks on the Middle East in a speech at the end of September and his long delay before agreeing to begin negotiations on the sale of Phantom fighters to Israel could be seen as attempts to meet the U.S.S.R. halfway. The Soviet intervention in Czechoslovakia did not seem to affect Soviet-U.S. relations in the Middle East.

The year 1968 also showed that the new security many Israelis hoped for behind their broader, though shorter and more defensible, frontiers was an illusion. Throughout the year there were frequent heavy artillery duels in the Jordan Valley, and Israeli settlements in the Beisan area were shelled. The Suez Canal was relatively quiet until September, when a four-hour duel showed that U.A.R. artillery on the west bank of the canal had been strongly reinforced. Throughout the year there were constant terrorist incidents, inside the occupied territories and in Israel itself. The Arab commandos presented no real military threat: Israeli countermeasures were often successful and the commando casualty rate was extremely high. Nevertheless, with the encouragement and help the commandos were receiving from the Arabs there seemed every likelihood that their activities would grow. Above all, they increased bitterness between Israelis and Arabs in the occupied territories, because of both the official Israeli reprisals in blowing up the houses of suspects and the Israeli public's tendency to take the law into its own hands (as in Jerusalem and Tel Aviv where Israeli youths attacked Arabs after bomb incidents). All this reduced Israeli chances of reaching a direct settlement with the Palestinian Arabs, as some Israelis had hoped would be possible. The chances for peace receded even further in December, when Israeli helicopters destroyed 13 civil aircraft at the Beirut airport. The raid, made in reprisal for an earlier attack on an Israeli airliner in Athens by two Beirut-based commandos, emphasized Israel's intention of holding the Arab governments responsible for commando activities on their territory; of Israel's immediate neighbours, Lebanon had held most aloof from the Arab-Israeli struggle.

Several different organizations of Palestinian Arabs existed, of which the most significant were Al Fatah (with its commando wing Al Assifa), the Palestine Liberation Organization (PLO), and the Popular Front for the Liberation of Palestine. At a meeting of

Palestinian organizations in Cairo in June, a 100-member Palestinian National Assembly was formed and a new Central Executive Committee was elected. In the same month Al Fatah and the PLO announced that they had carried out their first joint commando raid. However, the Palestinians remained seriously weakened by internal dissensions, and in August there was a mutiny in the Palestinian Liberation Army at Damascus against the new leadership appointed in Cairo.

Despite their lack of unity the Palestinian commandos emerged as a new element of major importance on the Middle East scene. They raised the morale of all the Arabs after their humiliating defeat. When Israel launched one of its heavy reprisal raids against their bases in the Jordan Valley in March, they fought back and inflicted heavier casualties on the Israelis than had been normal on such occasions. Within Jordan they seemed to be forming a state within a state; in November King Husain came to an agreement with the commandos formalizing their relationship with the government and limiting their activities to military operations, but his control over the movement on his territory appeared tenuous at best. U.A.R. Pres. Gamal Abd-al-Nasser's attitude was equivocal. He expressed support for the commandos and offered to assist them with arms and training, but he made it clear that he believed the burden of recovering lost territory lay with the regular Arab forces.

During 1968 the Arabs recovered a large part of the military strength lost in the 1967 defeat. The U.A.R. was reequipped by the Soviet Union, and Jordan received some military supplies from the U.S. There was little doubt, however, that the Israelis still enjoyed military superiority.

Arab Rivalries. An Arab summit meeting arranged for January 17 in Rabat, Morocco, was postponed indefinitely on the recommendation of the U.A.R. after Syria and Saudi Arabia had both declared their opposition to it. Syria objected to all summits in principle, while King Faisal of Saudi Arabia held the view that no new step should be taken until Jarring had declared the results of his mission. Persistent efforts by King Husain of Jordan and the prime minister of Sudan, Muhammad Ahmed Mahgoub, failed to change his mind on this matter. The latent antagonism between conservative and socialist regimes in the Arab world had remained below the surface since the Arab-Israeli war and especially since the August 1967 summit meeting in Khartoum when a kind of bargain was struck between the two sides. As long as such conservative nations as Saudi Arabia and Kuwait were subsidizing the U.A.R., the dispute was unlikely to come out into the open. However, King Faisal resented the fact that the U.A.R. did not consult him or the other Arab states before deciding to accept the November 22 resolution. Although Saudi Arabia had hardly suffered from the war, certain circumstances were unfavourable to the conservatives. In general the Soviet Union was much more popular than the West in the Arab world, and King Husain, formerly Faisal's most significant royal ally, was obliged to coordinate his policies with Nasser.

The conservative-republican dispute continued in southern Arabia although it was less of a focus of attention than before. Royalist hopes of a comeback after the U.A.R.'s withdrawal from Yemen were dashed when the republicans raised the siege of San'a' in February. But the royalists regrouped and by the end of the year the republicans were expecting a fresh attack. The newly independent People's Republic of Southern Yemen, though torn by internal troubles, was able to lend assistance to the republicans.

The Persian Gulf. Elsewhere in the Arabian Peninsula, the outlook was considerably affected by Britain's announcement in January that all its forces would be withdrawn from the area by 1971. This created alarm (and some anger) among the ruling sheikhs of the region, who felt they had been let down. The ruler of Abu Dhabi was quoted by *The Times* (London) as offering to subsidize a continued military presence, but the British Labour government stood by its decision (Conservative opposition leaders said they would reverse it if they came to power). The ruling sheikhs were alarmed by the prospect of facing Arab nationalist elements in their own states without British protection and by the outside threat of Iran, which had been strengthening its military forces in the area. This particularly affected Bahrain, which was claimed by Iran and had a large minority population of Iranian origin. The sheikhs took steps to link themselves together. On February 19, Abu Dhabi and Dubai, the two principal states in the Trucial Coast, announced that they had formed a federation. Later that month all the rulers of the Trucial States, together with Bahrain and Qatar, met and agreed in principle to form a Federation of Arab Amirates. Difficulties arose as the states divided into two camps, with Qatar, Dubai, and Ras al Khaimah on one side and Bahrain, Abu Dhabi, and other Trucial States, on the other. However, a compromise was reached on July 7, when a council of the nine Arab states was formed; the deputy ruler of Qatar was named chairman to work out a constitution which would have to be approved by the Supreme Council of nine rulers. Iran promptly denounced the federation, which was supported by Iraq, Saudi Arabia, and most other Arab states. However, the efforts of Saudi Arabia and Kuwait to mediate with the shah of Iran bore some fruit and it seemed possible that Iran might accept the results of a referendum on self-determination in Bahrain. (P. Md.)

See also Refugees; also articles on the various political units.

Encyclopædia Britannica Films. *Egypt and the Nile* (1954); *The Middle East* (1955); *Planning Our Foreign Policy (Problems of the Middle East)* (1955); *Iran—Between Two Worlds* (1957); *The Mediterranean World* (1962); *The Nile Valley and Its People* (1962); *The Suez Canal—Gateway to World Trade* (1962); *Turkey—Emergence of a Modern Nation* (1963).

Mining

The wave of expansion and excitement that had characterized mining for several years subsided in 1968. Many production or expansion plans were reduced or eliminated. The increased availability of minerals forced the U.S. government to curtail the disposals from its stockpile surpluses. Mineral requirements in the U.S. for the Vietnam war were met with little disruption of civilian industrial supply. Despite pressure on prices due to currency inflation, the overall price structure for mineral commodities was remarkably stable, and prices of some major minerals weakened or declined. The settlement of a long major labour strike in the base metals industries was an important turning point in the metals industries economy.

Gold became prominent in the news in 1968 as new international monetary policies were adopted to halt a drain of U.S. gold reserves and dampen gold specula-

Military Affairs:
see Defense

Mineralogy:
see Geology

tion. Silver continued newsworthy as speculators kept the market in a ferment, and the U.S. saw its silver coins disappear from use to be replaced by new sandwich-type nickel-copper coins.

The worldwide search for minerals continued at a slower tempo than in recent years. Australia, Canada, and Ireland were focal points for exploration, and the improved outlook for political stability in Indonesia attracted attention there. There were an unusual number of mergers of mining firms, stimulated in part by the high cost of discovery and development of large mining ventures. Major oil companies showed an increasing interest in exploration for minerals and metals.

It appeared probable that U.S. mineral production would reach a new high value in 1968 for the seventh consecutive year. The rise was supported mainly by higher unit values and by a larger output of fuel and energy minerals. The volume was expected to be less than in 1967 for some of the major industrial and construction minerals.

The rate of disposal of mineral commodities from the U.S. national stockpile of strategic and critical materials declined sharply from more than $1 billion in fiscal 1966 to $600 million in fiscal 1967 and only $207 million in fiscal 1968. The 1968 value included sales of silver totaling $62 million from U.S. Treasury Department stocks. Aluminum, mercury, and tin were the other principal metals sold from the stockpile in 1968. Industry sought the release of nickel and platinum, and disposal legislation concerning them was pending in Congress.

Industry Developments. An 8½-month work stoppage idled about 90% of U.S. copper-mine production from July 15, 1967, through March 1968. Despite an estimated loss of about one million tons of refined copper, a major shortage did not develop, because the deficit was made up by large industry stocks, imports, U.S. government stockpile releases, and secondary supplies. Prices rose in a highly fragmented market, with the quoted European price approaching 70 cents per pound and negotiated small lot prices much higher. After the strike the U.S. price was set at 42 cents per pound, compared with 38 cents when the shutdown began. Because of uncertain supply and high prices during the strike, fears were expressed that consumers would no longer want so much copper. However, producers' confidence was reflected in plans to expand

mine capacity of copper in the non-Communist world by at least 1.5 million tons by 1972 from the 5.4 million-ton level in 1967. About one-third of the increase was to be in North America, mostly in the U.S.

Copper-mine developments planned or under way in Chile and Peru could increase capacity in that area from one million to 1.6 million tons a year by 1972. In addition to expansions at several existing mines, three new large mines were being developed in Chile. Several porphyry copper deposits with combined total reserves estimated at 1.5 billion tons of ore were being explored or developed in Peru. At the Exotica mine in Chile waste overburden was being removed at a rate of 130,000 tons daily, and production of 112,000 tons of copper per year was scheduled for 1970. Two large underground mines, the El Salvador and the Rio Blanco, were being developed.

In south-central Africa, the world's third largest copper-producing area, some expansion was under way; in Zambia, however, mining ran into transportation difficulties, and a major effort was required to maintain production. Output was reduced by about 20% from April to August. The Zambian government introduced economic reforms in April that limited the remission of dividends abroad by foreign-controlled companies, including copper-mining firms.

The precious metals—gold, silver, and platinum—drew widespread public attention in 1968. The most notable event was an agreement in March by seven major industrial countries to establish a "two-tier" gold-marketing system. By the terms of the arrangement gold could be sold freely in the open market, while existing official gold reserves of leading nations were to be frozen for purposes of international monetary exchange. The value of monetary gold remained fixed at $35 per ounce, while the free-market gold price fluctuated in a narrow range up to about $42 per ounce but tended to stabilize at about $39 late in the year. There was an adequate supply of gold for industrial and artistic uses as newly mined gold competed with releases from speculators' stocks and secondary gold in the free market.

Gold mining in the U.S. was aided somewhat by the higher price obtained for its output in the free market. Success of the newly opened Carlin open-pit mine in northern Nevada encouraged intensive prospecting and exploratory drilling nearby in a 200-mi.-long geologically favourable area. Another open pit, the Cortez mine, was being developed about 40 mi. to the south. South Africa, the world's leading gold producer, seemed likely to approach its record output of 30.9 million oz., set in 1966.

Because of a favourable outlook for high silver demand, there was vigorous exploration for new mine supplies. Throughout the world lead-zinc deposits containing a high proportion of silver showed the most promise of contributing additional silver, but there was concern that this would lead to surpluses of lead and zinc. Successful exploration in the Coeur d'Alene region of Idaho promised to keep that area the leading U.S. silver producer. For the second year Canada replaced the U.S. as the leading world silver producer, registering an output of 24 million oz. in the first six months, compared with 19 million oz. in the same period of 1967. A production expansion was under way at the Kidd Creek mine in Ontario, already the top silver-producing mine in the world.

A second platinum producer was developing a 100,000-oz.-per-year mine on the Bushveld Complex in South Africa. Combined with an expansion planned

New gold mine in Kloof, S.Af., was officially opened on Jan. 22, 1968. The circular shaft lined with concrete provides the most economical method of construction commensurate with the strength obtained.

COURTESY, CONSOLIDATED GOLD FIELDS LTD.

there by Rustenberg Platinum Mines Ltd., the capacity of the complex was expected to exceed one million ounces a year by 1970. Intensive exploration of the entire platinum-bearing area was under way. The Soviet Union continued as a major source of platinum, but little information was available on mine developments there.

A world surplus of lead, zinc, and tin began to develop in 1968, dampening the recently enthusiastic development of new discoveries. In the U.S. plans to exploit vast lead reserves in southeast Missouri were slowed, but nevertheless a 300,000-ton-per-year increase in output was likely in the period 1967–69. The price of lead dropped twice in 1968, but an increase in October brought it to 13 cents per pound, compared with 16 cents about two years earlier. The quoted zinc price held at $13\frac{1}{2}$ cents a pound, but negotiated prices were lower and the market was weak. The U.S. mine capacity for zinc rose somewhat, but the increasing supply came principally from Canada, where four new projects in 1967–68 added about 600,-000 tons a year to capacity.

The worldwide effort aimed at developing larger nickel supplies continued unabated in 1968, and a doubling of output in five years seemed likely. Early results of a more than $1 million evaluation of large copper-nickel deposits in northern Minnesota were not known by the end of the year. In a new development the Anaconda Co. announced that nickeliferous deposits were being explored in the Stillwater Complex in Montana. Major sulfide-type nickel deposits were being explored or prepared for mining in Australia, Rhodesia, Botswana, and Canada.

A five-year sulfur shortage eased abruptly in 1968, and the long period of reduction of stocks was reversed. The change was due in part to lessened demand for manufactured fertilizer, the principal outlet, and to greater supplies of sulfur and sulfuric acid from by-product sources. Spurred by higher prices, several new Frasch-type mines were opened or being developed in the U.S. and Mexico.

The U.S. retained its position as the leading iron-ore producer in the non-Communist world, but rising world demand was being met by mine expansions elsewhere. Australia was the scene of the most activity, but there were many important projects planned or under way, particularly in Africa and South America. The continued rapid growth in aluminum production was accompanied by major mine and processing-plant installations in Australia and the Caribbean area. In September a $64.5 million loan agreement between the World Bank and Guinea revived plans for exploiting the huge Boké bauxite deposit.

Exploration for uranium was pursued vigorously, despite the uncertainty of the market. The growth rate for nuclear-powered electric utility plants was hotly debated, and the adequacy of uranium supplies for nuclear fuel was contested. Although the renewed search for nuclear fuel was without spectacular success, the U.S. reserves were increased, mainly in New Mexico and Wyoming. The uranium search also was intensified in the Elliot Lake area of Ontario. Gold-mining companies in South Africa began to reap increased benefits from by-product uranium, as the demand increased and prices firmed.

Technological Developments. Engineering improvements in equipment, along with larger sizes and superior automated controls, characterized changes in mining technology in 1968. Advances were particularly rapid in the design and use of rotary drilling and large-

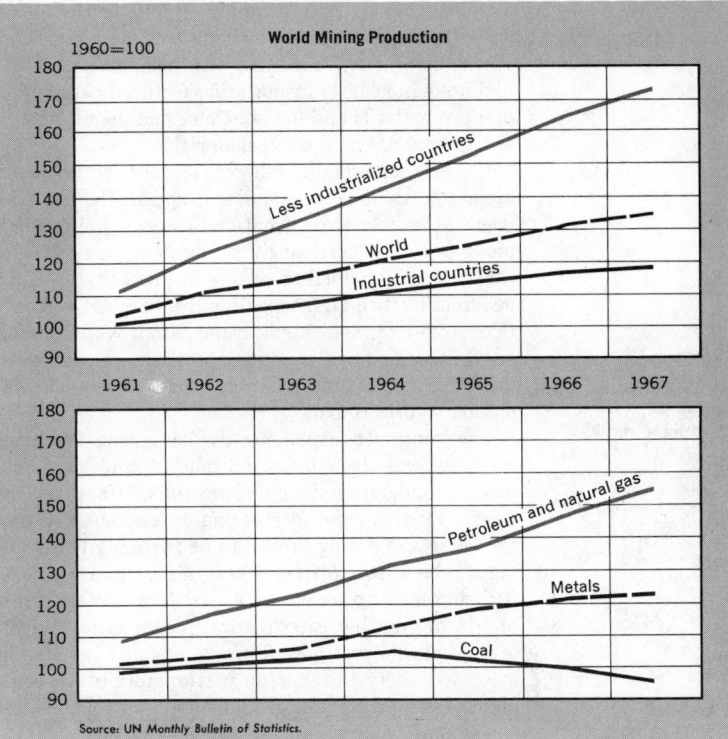

Source: UN Monthly Bulletin of Statistics.

diameter boring machines. As machine performance improved and new types of equipment were introduced, it became apparent that only through thoughtful design of integrated mining systems could the full advantages of highly automated mechanized mining be realized.

Surface mining made the most progress toward mechanization, probably because of its widespread and increasing application and the space restrictions imposed by underground mining. In 1968, however, there was a perceptible intensification of research effort in underground mining. The new enthusiasm may have reflected belated recognition of the rapid growth in underground excavation and mining. The ability to discover deeply buried mineral deposits was improving steadily with better geophysical techniques, fast and efficient exploratory drilling methods, electronic devices for logging drill-hole data, and improved prediction techniques. It also became apparent that resources of such essential metals as lead, silver, gold, platinum, and, to a lesser extent, zinc occurred chiefly in deposits that must be mined underground.

In a report prepared for the U.S. Bureau of Mines, the U.S. National Academies of Science and Engineering recommended a $200 million, ten-year research effort aimed at developing revolutionary techniques that would make underground excavation three times faster than in 1968 at 30% lower cost. According to the report, the new techniques were needed both to enable lower-cost mining of deep mineral deposits and to excavate stable underground rooms and passageways for utilities, transportation, and other purposes.

Drilling rigs and other pit equipment became more highly automated during the year. Tungsten carbide-tipped tricone rotary blasthole drilling was more widely adopted. Improved control mechanisms for power shovels were expected to hasten the next generation of units larger than the 12-to-15-cu.yd. size in current use. As the versatility of rubber-tired front-end loaders won them an expanding role in both underground and surface mining, increasing varieties of them were designed. Special types were designed for

loading, hauling, and dumping. While trucks dominated haulage of run-of-mine rock in open pits, conveyor belts were used for crushed material, and hydraulic pipeline transportation featured handling of dredged material and long-distance hauling of crushed and ground ores and waste materials.

Underground mining followed surface technology in increasing the size of equipment and in the development of rubber-tired front-end-loader type haulage units, powered increasingly by diesel engines. Use of catalytic units helped to cleanse engine exhaust. Low-headroom articulated models were designed for particular underground applications. Improved controls on drilling jumbos permitted console operation of drills, quicker and more flexible setups, and rapid completion of drill rounds.

The continued expanding use of boring machines probably was the most significant technological feature of underground mining in 1968. More designs were available, and performance continuously improved. Raise boring proved to be particularly advantageous because 4–6-ft. diameter raises could be driven for lengths of up to 800 ft. Costs were less and rates of advance much greater than with conventional drilling and blasting methods. Raise boring also resulted in increased safety and superior performance of the completed raise, and fewer ground support problems.

The first experimental nuclear blast to recover minerals was detonated in December 1967. The trial, called Gasbuggy, was designed to accelerate the flow of natural gas by opening fractures and creating heat and pressure in reservoir rocks. This was the forerunner of other experiments with nuclear blasts to shatter copper deposits for in-place leaching or oil shale for in-place fracturing and retorting. (P. F. Y.)

Production. Total world mineral production continued its upward trend and reached a new high in 1967, according to statistics compiled by the U.S. Bureau of Mines. On the basis of data assembled for 65 minerals and mineral products, which normally account for a large proportion of the value of all mineral output, the bureau estimated that production of 34 commodities (20 metals, 12 nonmetals, and 2 fuels) reached new peaks in 1967. Two showed gains over 1966 without establishing new highs; one commodity (peat) remained unchanged from the 1966 level; and the remaining 28 recorded decreases.

Of the precious metals gold output declined 2% in 1967, and silver dropped 2.8%. Platinum-group metals, however, increased by 3.6%. World production of steel ingots and castings in 1967 rose 3.5% over 1966, but the increase in pig-iron output was only 2.5%. Aluminum output was 8.6% higher than the former record set in 1966, while bauxite production rose by 11.7%. Mine production of lead, zinc, and tin rose 2, 10, and 2%, respectively. Conversely, world mine production of copper declined 5%.

Coal continued to decline, with the output for 1967 lower than that of the previous year by 3.8%. Petroleum and marketed natural gas improved their share of total energy, with production increases of 7.3 and 7.5%, respectively.

Total elemental sulfur output increased by 4.3%, and phosphate rock by 3.8%. Hydraulic cement rose by 3.3%, a lower gain than the 6.7% recorded in 1966. Other nonmetals registering increases in 1967 were both gem and industrial diamonds, fluorspar, potash, salt, and talc.

The U.S. was the leading producer of 24 of the 51 minerals for which fairly complete world data were

COURTESY, THE INTERNATIONAL NICKEL COMPANY OF CANADA, LIMITED

Jumbo drill in a nickel mine near Thompson, Man. When fully developed, three new mines in the area would produce 25% of the non-Communist world's nickel.

available. The non-Communist world produced 70.1% of world steel output; the U.S. led with 23.4%. Japan increased its share of world steel production from 10.1% in 1966 to 12.6%. The non-Communist world produced 87% of the gold and 80% or more of the aluminum, bauxite, beryl, bismuth, copper, molybdenum, crude petroleum, silver, and sulfur.

Communist countries ranked first in the production of 16 minerals, 12 of them accounted for by the U.S.S.R. These included cement, chromite, coal, high-temperature coke, smelter copper, iron ore, lead (mine and smelter), magnesite, manganese, peat, and platinum-group metals. North Korea led in the production of graphite, while East Germany ranked first in low-temperature coke and fuel briquettes. Communist China was the leading producer of tungsten and ranked second to South Africa in the output of antimony. It is significant that Communist Chinese output for 1967 was lower than that for 1966 in the case of 27 commodities of the 38 for which estimates were made, chiefly because of civil disorders. Reduced production estimates for Communist China were the principal factor in the decline in the estimated total world output of six commodities (antimony, iron ore, magnesite, coal, manganese ore, and metallurgical coke) and contributed significantly to lower levels for mercury and hydraulic cement.

Aluminum. World production of aluminum reached a new record of 7,451,000 metric tons in 1967, 8.6% higher than in 1966. U.S. output was 10.1% higher at 2,965,823 metric tons. The U.S.S.R. remained the second largest producer with an estimated output of 965,000 tons. The free world provided 81.6% of total primary production, with 51.8% from North America (U.S. 39.8%, Canada 11.7%). Western Europe provided 20.8%, and production in Communist countries accounted for 18.4%.

Antimony. Production of antimony ores fell 5% to 58,000 metric tons during 1967. Output was lower in most countries except Bolivia, Morocco, Spain, and South Africa, which replaced Communist China as the principal producer with an output estimated at 21.3% of the total. Communist China contributed an estimated 20.7%, and the U.S.S.R. an estimated 11%. Free-world output was 64.9% of the total.

Asbestos. Production of asbestos rose by 0.5% during 1967 to a total of 2,992,000 metric tons. Although it continued to be the leading producer, Canada suffered a 2.5% decline in output to 1,309,078 tons, 43.8% of the total. The U.S.S.R. contributed an estimated 25.7%. The series of asbestos production data for 1963–67 was adjusted downward by the exclusion of quantities of material from the U.S.S.R. that had been recorded as asbestos produced but that, because of its low grade, could not or had not been processed to a quality suitable for use in

World Production of Major Metals and Minerals, 1962–66 (average) and 1967, World Totals and Leading Producers

ALUMINUM
In 000 short tons

	1962–66	1967
World	6,493	8,213
U.S.	2,541	3,269
U.S.S.R.*	925	1,065
Canada	795	963
France	356	398
Japan	284	392
Norway	285	399
Germany, West	239	279

COAL
In 000,000 short tons, all grades

	1962–66	1967
World	2,993	3,000
U.S.S.R.	610	656*
U.S.	498	563
China*	320	250
Germany, East	280	278*
Germany, West	268	231
U.K.	213	193
Poland	149	163
Czechoslovakia	111	100*

COPPER
In 000 short tons (metal content of ore)

	1962–66	1967
World	5,359	5,496
U.S.	1,294	955
U.S.S.R.*	740	880
Chile	683	732
Zambia	683	730
Canada	483	603
Congo (Kinshasa)	320	354
Peru	194	200

DIAMONDS, INDUSTRIAL
In 000 carats

	1962–66	1967
World	29,687	33,295
Congo (Kinshasa)	18,195	17,890
S. Africa	2,834	4,900
U.S.S.R.*	3,500	5,600
Ghana	2,467	2,283

GOLD
In 000 troy oz., fine metal

	1962–66	1967
World	44,475	45,614
S. Africa	28,694	30,533
U.S.S.R.*	4,700	5,700
Canada	3,778	2,962

IRON ORE
In 000 short tons

	1962–66	1967
World	632,556	693,680
U.S.S.R.	159,807	185,188
U.S.	91,358	94,281
France	66,078	54,256
China*	40,000	31,000
Canada	36,273	46,652
Sweden	28,765	31,162
India	24,285	28,833
Brazil	17,710	25,904
Venezuela	16,742	18,745
Liberia	12,578	20,088
Australia	7,649	20,739

IRON, PIG and FERROALLOYS
In 000 short tons

	1962–66	1967
World	340,944	391,933
U.S.	82,885	89,479
U.S.S.R.	68,956	82,453
Japan	27,387	45,239
Germany, West	27,942	30,166
China*	20,000	15,000
U.K.	17,635	16,971
France	16,649	17,284

*Estimate.

normal asbestos applications. World production on the new basis increased slightly.

Bauxite. World production of bauxite rose by 11.7% to a new record of 44,608,000 metric tons in 1967. The free world supplied 83.8%, of which 47.9% was produced in the Western Hemisphere. The U.S.S.R. accounted for 11.2% of Eastern Europe's output of 15.4%. At the year's end alumina productive capacity in the free world was an estimated 14,-710,000 metric tons.

Cement. Output of cement totaled 479,909,000 metric tons in 1967, compared with 464,445,000 tons in 1966. This represented an increase of 3.3% and a new record. Western Europe produced 31.5% of the total (West Germany 6.6%, Italy 5.5%, France 5.1%, U.K. 3.7%), Eastern Europe had 25.4% (U.S.S.R. 17.7%), Asia 18.9% (Japan 9%), North and Central America 16.9% (U.S. 13.7%), South America 3.6%, Africa 2.7%, and Oceania 1%.

Chromium. World production of chromium rose slightly in 1967 to 5,094,000 metric tons. Principal producing countries were the U.S.S.R. 30.8% (est.), South Africa 22.6%, Turkey 12.1%, Philippines 8.2%, Rhodesia 7.9% (est.), and Albania 6.2%. Voluntary sanctions were imposed against Rhodesia in 1966 by various countries, and on Dec. 16, 1966, the UN Security Council passed a resolution that imposed mandatory sanctions.

Cobalt. World production of cobalt dropped by 8.2% to 19,100 metric tons during 1967. The decline, of about 2,000 tons, from the 1966 output occurred almost entirely in the Congo (Kinshasa), where the government took over the Union Minière mines for two months. The dispute was settled by a technical agreement whereby Société Générale des Minerais de Belgique was given the right to manage the newly formed Congolese company's (Gecomin) properties and market the metals produced therefrom. Principal producing countries were the Congo (Kinshasa) 50.9%, Morocco 10.1% (est.), Canada 7.8%, Zambia 7.6%, U.S.S.R. 7.3% (est.), and Finland 6.5% (est.).

Copper. World mine production of copper dropped 5% in 1967 to 4,986,000 metric tons. In the U.S. a strike that began on July 15, 1967, and extended until the spring of 1968 gave that country only 17.4% of the world output. Chile and Canada

increased their shares to 13.3 and 11%, respectively, and Peru had 3.6%. The U.S.S.R. produced 16%, Zambia 13.3%, the Congo (Kinshasa) 6.4%, and South Africa 2.6%. World smelter output of copper declined 5.7% in 1967 to 5,394,000 metric tons. The U.S. total dropped to 14.5% of world production, while Chile contributed 11.7%, Canada 8.4%, and Peru 2.9%. The U.S.S.R. produced 14.8%, Zambia 11.4%, Japan 8.7%, West Germany 7.1%, and the Congo (Kinshasa) 5.9%.

Diamonds. World production of diamonds rose by 6% during 1967, totaling 42,388,000 carats; this exceeded all previous records. Industrial diamond production rose 7.2% to 33,295,-000 carats, setting a new high. Gem diamonds continued an upward trend and were 2% higher at 9,093,000 carats. African countries accounted for 82.4% of the total industrial diamonds, followed by the U.S.S.R. with 16.8% (est.); South American countries and India produced a negligible quantity. The Congo (Kinshasa) was the main producer with 53.7% of the total, though a portion of this was attributed to the Congo (Brazzaville). In gem diamonds Africa provided 81.9% (est.) of the total (South Africa 23.1%, South West Africa 18.7%, Angola 11%, Sierra Leone 6.6%, the Congo [Kinshasa] 6.2%, and Tanzania 5.4%).

Gold. For the first time in 14 years, world production of gold declined, falling 2% from 46,567,000 troy ounces in 1966 to 45,614,000 oz. in 1967. This loss of nearly a million ounces was accounted for by reductions in output by several countries. The U.S. produced 12% less in 1967, partly because of labour strikes in the copper mines. South Africa's decrease of almost 350,000 oz. indicated a leveling-off period in that country and probably heralded a decline in years to come. In 1967 Africa produced 70.4% (South Africa 66.9%), U.S.S.R. 12.5% (est.), North and Central America 10.8% (Canada 6.5%, U.S. 3.5%), Asia 2.6% (Philippines 1.1%), Oceania 1.7% (Australia 1.4%), and South America 1.4%.

Iron and Steel. World production of iron ore, at 625,370,-000 metric tons, was 1.5% less in 1967 than in 1966; pig-iron (including ferroalloy) output rose 2.5% to 355,560,000 tons, and output of steel ingots and castings was 3.6% higher at 492,930,000 tons. The principal iron-ore-producing areas, with

continued on page 530

Table I. Mineral and Metal Prices in 1968

New York market January $	September $	Units	Grade	Commodity	Grade	London market Units	January £	s.	d.	September £	s.	d.
0.25	0.26	Pound	99.5% ingot	Aluminum	99.5%	Long ton	228	13⅓	...	238	...	...
5.80	5.80	S.T. unit	60% Sb	Antimony, ore	50–55% Sb	L.T. unit	...	50	...	...	50	...
0.44	0.44	Pound	Domestic, bulk	Antimony	Domestic, 99%	Long ton	360	...	...	360	...	...
87.00	87.00	Short ton	White oxide, car lots	Arsenic	Foreign, 98–100%		45	...	...	45	...	...
4.00	4.00	Pound	Ton lots	Bismuth	Ton lots	Pound	...	33	4	...	33	4
2.65	2.65		Commercial sticks—ton lots	Cadmium	99.95%		...	21	9	...	21	9
35.00	35.00	Short ton	48–50% Cr₂O₃, 3½ Cr : 1 Fe	Chromium, ore	Rhodesian, 1st grade	Long ton	‡	...	...	‡	...	...
0.96	0.96	Pound	98.5%, spot-aluminothermic	Metal	98–99%	Pound	...	7	3	...	7	3
0.197	0.197	"	67–71% Cr*	Ferroalloy	4–6% C, 60% Cr	Long ton	75	...	...	77	...	...
1.85	1.85	"	99% Co-500-lb. lots	Cobalt		Pound	...	15	6	...	15	6
‡	0.41719		Domestic	Copper	Fire ref., high grade	Long ton	540	...	...	465	...	...
0.54923	0.47491		Export		Wire bars	"	576	...	...	464	...	...
35.00	40.27	Ounce†		Gold	Official	Ounce†	...	291	11¼	$40	...	...
2.75	2.50		99.97% In (small lots)	Indium			...	19	2	...	19	2
190.00	190.00		Sponge, powder	Iridium	Sponge and powder		79	...	...	79	...	...
10.55	10.55	Long ton	Mesabi, non-Bessemer	Iron, ore			‡			‡		
‡	‡	Short ton	80%, Joplin, Mo.	Lead, ore	70–80%	Metric ton	$20	...	...	$20	...	...
0.14	0.125	Pound	New York	Metal	Foreign, soft	Long ton	93	5	...	105	15	...
0.3525	0.3525	"	99.8% car lots	Magnesium, ingots		Pound	...	2	5	...	2	5
				sticks	Bars		...	3	1½	...	3	1
‡	‡	L.T. unit	48% Atlantic ports	Manganese, ore	48% Mn	L.T. unit	...	...	78	...	...	70
0.2985	0.3025	Pound	99.9% Mn (f.o.b.-ton lots)	Metal	99.9% Mn-(electro)	Long ton	240	...	...	235	...	...
167.50	164.50	Long ton	74–76%	Ferroalloy	78% Mn (standard)	"	51	5	...	51	5	...
90.00	90.00	Long ton	19–21% Mn	Spiegel	20% Mn	"	34	5	...	34	5	...
528.318	541.85	(76 lb.) Flask		Mercury		(76 lb.) Flask	220	...	...	225	...	...
1.62	1.62	Pound	Mo, Climax, Colo.§	Molybdenum, ore	85% MoS₂	Pound	...	13	6	...	13	6
3.75	3.75	"	99.95% Mo	Metal	Powder		...	40	...	...	40	...
2.17	2.17	"	58–64% Mo* powder	Ferroalloy	65–70% Mo*		...	18	4	...	18	1
0.94	0.94		Cathodes	Nickel	Refined	Long ton	902	...	...	902	...	...
37.00	45.00	Ounce†	23–26% P, car lots	Palladium		Ounce†	16	5	...	19	10	...
120.00	120.00	Gross ton		Phosphorus, ferro-	20–25% P	Long ton	40	...	...	40	...	...
109.00	120.00	Ounce†	Wholesale	Platinum	U.K. and empire, refined	Ounce†	52	...	...	52	...	...
250.00	250.00			Rhodium			104	...	...	104	...	...
6.00	6.00	Pound	High purity	Selenium	99.5%	Pound	...	37	6	...	37	6
‖	‖		98% Si, spot (lump)	Silicon	98% Si	Long ton	137	...	...	137	...	...
0.131	0.139	"	50% Si*	Ferroalloy	45% Si	"	50	17	8	50	...	...
0.151	0.154	"	75% Si*		75% Si	"	71	13	1	70	1	...
1.78955	2.2085	Ounce†	Foreign, New York	Silver	Official, spot	Ounce†	...	...	210½	...	...	226.5
‡	‡	Pound	60% Ta₂O₅-Cb₂O₅*	Tantalum, ore	60% Ta₂O₅	L.T. unit	...	1,910	...	...	1,820	...
60.00	60.00	"	Sheet, high-grade	Metal	Powder	Pound	...	‡		...	‡	
6.00	6.00	"	Powder, 100-lb. lots	Tellurium	99% Lump, powder		...	50	...	...	50	...
1.47966	1.47813	"	Straits	Tin	99%+	Long ton	1,321	...	...	1,304	...	...
1.35	1.35	Short ton	25–40% Ti* Low carbon	Titanium, ferroalloy	20–25% Ti	"	230	...	...	230	...	...
24.00	24.00	Gross ton	54% TiO₂	" , ilmenite	52–54% TiO₂, Malayan	"	9	10	...	9	10	...
121.00	121.00		96% TiO₂	" , rutile	95–97% TiO₂, Australian	"	50	...	...	50	10	...
43.00	43.00	S.T. unit	Wolfram-65% WO₃	Tungsten, ore	65% Wolframite	L.T. unit	422	6	...	415	...	...
43.00	43.00		Scheelite-65% WO₃		65% Scheelite, Korean	"	‡			‡		
2.03	3.71	Pound	70–80% W*	Ferroalloy	80–85% W*	Pound	...	26	9	...	25	6
2.75	2.75	"	98.8% W, 1,000-lb. lots	Powder	98–99% W*		...	31	...	...	30	6
1.30	1.30	"	Domestic¶	Vanadium, ore	98% Fused oxide¶	"	...	8	4	...	7	8
3.45	3.45	"	57% V*	Ferroalloy	50–60% V*	"	...	22	...	...	20	...
84.00	84.00	Short ton	60%, Joplin, Mo.	Zinc, ore	52–55% Zn (sulfide)	Metric ton	$47	...	...	$48	...	...
0.135	0.135	Pound	E. St. Louis	Metal	G.O.B., foreign	Long ton	111	15	...	111	10	...

*Per pound of base metal contained. §Per pound of contained Mo, f.o.b. Climax, plus cost of containers.
†Troy ounces. ‖Contracts negotiated.
‡Not quoted. ¶Per pound of V₂O₅ contained.

Source: *Metals Week incorporating E. & M. J. Metal and Mineral Markets* (New York); *Metal Bulletin* (London).

(B. B. M.)

Table II. World Mineral and Metal Production in 1967

Metric tons unless otherwise specified; Th. indicates thousands, and Mi. millions of units

Country	Aluminum (Th.)	Bauxite (Th.)	Antimony*	Arsenic†	Asbestos (Th.)	Barite (Th.)	Beryl	Bismuth	Cadmium‡	Cement (Th.)	Chromite (Th.)
North America											
Canada	874.0	—	564	272	1,309.1	181.1	—	246.0	816.0	7,160	—
Central America	—	—	30	—	—	—	—	—	‡	835	—
Mexico	21.5	—	3,738	15,423	—	223.3	—	504.0	‡168.0	6,258?	—
United States	2,965.8	1,680.3	809	4,709[9]	111.8	856.5	p	p	3,901.8	65,807	—
West Indies	—	10,734.2	—	—	—	—	—	—	—	1,771	30.0?
South America											
Argentina	—	—	—	p	0.2	18.0[6]	268	p	—	3,552	—
Bolivia	—	—	11,268	—	p	—	—	502.2	—	62	—
Brazil	36.0?	261.0?	—	222	1.7[6]	54.5	1,310	p	—	6,405	6.9
Chile	—	—	—	—	—	4.7	—	—	—	1,203	—
Colombia	—	—	—	—	—	9.0?[6]	—	—	—	2,116	—
Ecuador	—	—	—	—	—	—	—	—	—	430?	—
Guyana	—	3,381.2	—	—	—	—	—	—	—	—	—
Peru	—	—	635	295	—	110.0	—	795.6	150.8	1,042	—
Surinam	31.1	5,300.0?	—	—	—	—	—	—	—	—	—
Venezuela	3.1	—	—	—	—	—	—	—	—	2,248	—
Europe											
Austria	78.7	—	192	p	—	2.5	—	—	19.0	4,548	—
Belgium	—	—	—	p	—	—	—	—	185.8	5,820	—
Bulgaria	—	—	—	—	1.3?	p	—	p	p	3,358	p
Czechoslovakia	65.0?	—	2,000?	p	p	P	—	—	—	6,200?	—
Finland	—	—	—	p	12.0?	—	—	—	—	1,514	30.0?
France	361.2	2,812.6	279[6]	10,200?[6]	10.1[5]	95.0	—	59.0?	450.0?	24,600	—
Germany, East	50.0?	—	—	p	—	P	—	p	12.0?	7,188	—
Germany, West	252.9	3.5?	—	104	—	428.2	—	—	399.0	31,507	—
Greece	72.0	1,692.0	—	—	—	150.0	—	—	—	3,450	50.0?
Hungary	61.8	1,649.0	—	p	—	—	—	—	—	2,656	—
Ireland	—	—	—	—	—	76.0	—	—	—	1,298	—
Italy	127.8	242.0	440?	—	100.7	154.1	—	12.0?	218.0	26,272	—
Luxembourg	—	—	—	—	—	—	—	—	—	183	—
Netherlands	32.0?	—	—	—	—	—	—	—	100.0?	3,349	—
Norway	362.2	—	—	—	—	—	—	—	83.0	2,066	—
Poland	92.3	—	—	—	—	47.0?	—	—	430.0?[6]	11,138	—
Portugal	—	—	23	194[6]	p	0.2	37	—	—	1,836	—
Romania	50.0?	220.0?	—	—	p	55.0?	—	—	—	6,338	p
Spain	69.8	4.2[5]	122	129	—	55.5[5]	—	0.1[5]	60.0?[6]	13,099	—
Sweden	34.3	—	—	20,200	—	—	—	30.0?	—	3,837	—
Switzerland	72.3	—	—	—	—	—	—	—	—	4,176	—
U.S.S.R.	965.0?	5,000.0?	6,400?	7,000?	769.0?	260.0?	1,200?	40.0?	2,200.0?	84,800	1,570.0?
United Kingdom	39.1	—	—	p	—	37.0	—	—	208.7	17,577	—
Yugoslavia	44.6	2,131.0	2,297	p	9.0	90.0?	—	107.5	50.0?	3,313	47.2
Africa											
Algeria (incl. Sahara)	—	—	64	—	—	80.0?	—	—	—	670	—
Angola	—	—	—	—	—	—	—	—	—	279	—
Congo (Kinshasa)	—	—	—	—	—	—	111□	—	404.0	260?	—
Ethiopia	—	—	—	—	—	—	—	—	—	150	—
Gabon	—	—	—	—	—	—	—	—	—	—	—
Ghana	—	351.0	—	—	—	—	—	—	—	—	—
Kenya	—	—	—	—	0.1	0.2	—	—	—	479	—
Liberia	—	—	—	—	—	—	—	—	—	—	—
Malagasy Republic	—	—	—	—	—	—	30	—	—	60	—
Morocco	—	—	1,590	—	—	90.5	—	—	—	869	—
Nigeria	—	—	—	—	—	—	—	—	—	784	—
Rhodesia	—	2.0?	185?[5]	65?[5]	160.0?[6]	2.0?	43?	—	—	250?	500.0?[6]
Sierra Leone	—	341.6	—	—	—	—	—	—	—	—	—
South Africa	—	—	12,335	—	243.6	1.5	104	0.1	—	3,810	1,149.1
South West Africa	—	—	—	40[6]	—	—	22[6]	p	120.0	—	—
Tanzania	—	—	—	—	—	—	—	—	—	149	—
Tunisia	—	—	—	—	—	—	—	—	—	472	—
Uganda	—	—	—	—	—	—	314	0.5	—	139	—
United Arab Republic	—	—	—	—	1.9[6]	6.8[6]	—	—	—	2,736	—
Zambia	—	—	—	—	—	—	—	—	10.0?	244	—
Asia											
Burma	—	—	150	—	—	8.0?[6]	—	—	—	130	—
China	80.0?	350.0?	12,000?	p	150.0?	100.0?	—	250.0?	—	8,000?	—
Cyprus	—	—	—	—	33.5	—	—	—	—	187	21.8
India	96.4	759.0	—	—	6.9[6]	46.6	4,905	—	—	11,700	104.0
Indonesia	—	912.3	—	—	—	—	—	—	—	300	—
Iran	—	—	—	—	—	52.0?	—	—	—	1,394?	180.0?
Israel	—	—	—	—	—	—	—	—	—	805	—
Japan	355.5	—	58	643	24.0	37.6	—	643.0	1,899.0	42,993	45.2
Jordan	—	—	—	—	—	—	—	—	—	300	—
Korea, South	—	—	—	—	2.2	—	—	100.0?[6]	—	2,440	—
Malaysia	—	899.6	—	—	—	—	—	—	—	835?	—
Pakistan	—	—	61[5]	—	—	7.8[6]	—	—	—	2,040	30.0?
Philippines	—	—	—	—	0.5[6]	p	—	—	—	2,112	419.7
Taiwan	15.4	—	—	—	1.5?	—	—	—	—	3,487	—
Thailand	—	—	1,026	—	—	—	—	—	—	1,737	—
Turkey	—	21.5	965	—	2.2	31.6	—	—	—	4,249	615.4
Vietnam, South	—	—	—	—	—	—	—	—	—	176?	—
Oceania											
Australia	92.4	4,236.1	900?	—	12.2[6]	14.5	42	—	523.9	3,817	p
New Caledonia	—	—	—	—	—	—	—	—	—	—	1.8
New Guinea	—	—	—	—	—	—	—	—	—	—	—
New Zealand	—	—	—	—	—	—	—	—	—	814	—
Pacific Islands	—	—	—	—	—	—	—	—	—	47	—
World total (estimate)	7,450.6	44,608.0	58,000	54,700	2,992.0	3,508.0	8,600	3,330.0	12,409.0	479,909	5,094.0

Country	Coal (Mi.)	Coke (high-temp.) (Mi.)	Cobalt	Copper (in ore) (Th.)	Copper (smelter) (Th.)	Diamonds (Th. carats)	Feldspar (Th.)	Fluorspar (Th.)	Fuel Briquettes (Th.)	Gold (Th. oz.)	Graphite (Th.)	Gypsum (Th.)	Ilmenite (Th.)	Iron Ore (Th.)	Pig Iron (Th.)	Steel (Th.)
North America																
Canada	10.34	4.02	1,499	546.7	453.6	—	9.6	80.0?	53?[6]	2,962.0	—	4,465.6	546.5	38,395	6,449	8,795
Central America	—	—	—	9.3	—	—	—	—	—	184.1	—	35.3	—	10	—	—
Mexico	2.16	1.08	—	56.0	54.5	—	—	785.1	—	181.5	40.7	976.4	—	2,696	1,666	3,023
United States	510.98	58.59	1,057[9]	865.5	782.3	—	625.3	268.2	308?[6]	1,584.2	P	8,521.0	848.3	85,530	81,174	115,406
West Indies	—	—	1,045?	8.7	—	—	—	—	—	5.1[6]	—	314.4	—	—	—	—
South America																
Argentina	0.40?	0.40[6]	—	0.4	—	—	19.2	15.0	—	0.1?	0.2	268.0	—	224	610?	1,326
Bolivia	—	—	—	6.1	—	—	—	—	—	55.1	—	p	—	—	—	—
Brazil	4.34	1.31	—	4.2?	3.0	320?	p	p	—	172.0	2.9	80.2[6]	15.0	23,500	3,030?	3,770
Chile	1.50	0.20?[6]	—	663.9	630.7	—	0.9	0.5	—	56.0	—	132.8	—	11,025	498	638
Colombia	3.10?	0.32[6]	—	—	—	—	19.1[6]	—	—	258.2	—	115.0?[6]	—	808	207	252
Ecuador	—	—	—	0.2[6]	—	—	—	—	—	10.9[6]	—	p	—	—	—	—
Guyana	—	—	—	—	—	95	—	—	—	2.4	—	—	—	—	—	—
Peru	0.18	0.04	—	181.1	156.7	—	2.5	—	—	95.6	—	65.0	—	7,659	29	79
Surinam	—	—	—	—	—	—	—	—	—	4.5	—	—	—	—	—	—
Venezuela	0.03	—	—	—	—	70	—	—	—	19.0	—	86.0?[6]	—	17,005	422	703
Europe																
Austria	4.62	1.41	—	1.9	17.4	—	2.5	—	—	—	32.5	738.0	—	3,473	2,144	3,023
Belgium	16.44	6.86	—	—	—	—	—	—	867	—	—	—	—	88	8,992	9,635
Bulgaria	29.27?	0.75?[6]	p	31.0?	27.0?	—	—	p	1,500?[5]	p	—	180.0?	—	2,700?	992	1,239
Czechoslovakia	90.80?	9.47	—	p	—	—	P	—	780?	p	p	356.0?[6]	—	2,000?	6,400?	9,800?
Finland	—	0.04	1,250?	28.8	34.2	—	35.0	—	25?	14.0?	—	—	125.0	643	1,038	394
France	50.56	12.63	—	0.6	—	—	222.2[6]	240.0?	4,839	6.4?	—	5,272.2[6]	—	49,220	15,680	19,675
Germany, East	251.80?	3.25?	p	20.0?	20.0?	—	—	80.0?	60,000?	p	—	262.0?	—	1,750	2,520	4,700?
Germany, West	209.70	35.25	p	1.2	382.4	—	297.9	98.0?	14,641	1.1?	11.9	1,116.0	—	8,553	27,366	36,744
Greece	5.00?	—	—	—	—	—	—	—	100	—	—	150.0	—	17	—	160
Hungary	27.03	0.64	—	p	—	—	—	—	1,068	p	—	—	—	715	1,645	2,739
Ireland	0.18	—	—	3.5	—	—	—	—	309	—	—	218.0?[6]	—	—	—	66?[6]
Italy	2.61	6.25	—	1.8	—	—	147.5	205.2	70?	—	1.9	3,300.0?[6]	—	737	7,464	15,890
Luxembourg	—	—	—	—	—	—	—	—	—	—	—	11.0	—	6,304	3,960	4,481
Netherlands	8.07	3.31	—	—	—	—	—	—	1,118	—	—	—	—	—	2,579?	3,405
Norway	0.81?	0.24?	—	14.2	19.9	—	85.0?	—	—	—	8.0?	—	400.0?	3,232	1,230?	790
Poland	147.80	13.93	p	17.3?	42.2	—	28.0?[6]	—	936[6]	—	—	760.0[6]	—	3,125?	6,581	10,451
Portugal	0.48	—	—	5.2?	—	—	1.6[6]	—	39	27.0?	—	112.9[6]	0.4	196	287?	302
Romania	14.24	1.20	—	—	—	—	p	—	330?	p	—	p	—	2,796	2,200?	4,087
Spain	15.03	2.89	—	8.2	30.3	—	25.6[5]	242.7	480	0.5[6]	—	3,092.0[5]	37.9	5,085	2,730?	4,594
Sweden	0.02?	0.54?	—	14.5?	47.7	—	40.0?	—	40?[6]	78.0[6]	—	—	—	28,270	2,513	4,768
Switzerland	—	—	—	—	—	—	—	—	—	—	—	p	—	4	24	444
U.S.S.R.	595.00?	69.00?	1,400?	800.0?	800.0?	7,000?	240.0?	380.0?	8,900?	5,700.0?	65.0?	4,500.0?	p	168,000	74,800	102,200
United Kingdom	174.93	15.59	—	—	—	—	—	142.0	1,038	—	—	4,593.0	—	12,944	15,396	24,279
Yugoslavia	26.46	1.22	—	61.1	73.0?	—	42.0?	—	24?	86.0?	—	170.0?	—	2,580	1,177	1,832
Africa																
Algeria (incl. Sahara)	0.50?	—	—	1.1	—	—	—	—	—	—	—	175.0	—	2,000?	—	—
Angola	—	—	—	—	—	1,300?	—	—	—	—	—	12.0	—	1,154	—	—
Congo (Kinshasa)	0.13	—	9,718	320.5	320.5	18,453?	—	—	—	153.5	—	—	—	—	p	—
Ethiopia	—	—	—	—	—	—	0.4	—	—	23.6	—	6.1	—	—	—	—
Gabon	—	—	—	—	—	—	—	—	—	34.4[6]	—	—	—	—	—	—
Ghana	—	—	—	—	—	2,537	—	—	—	762.6	—	—	—	—	—	—
Kenya	—	—	—	p	—	—	—	—	—	33.4	—	40.4	—	—	—	—
Liberia	—	—	—	—	—	550	—	—	—	5.1	—	—	—	18,224	—	—
Malagasy Republic	p	—	—	—	—	—	—	—	—	0.8	16.4	—	1.9	—	—	—
Morocco	0.48	—	1,930?	2.5	—	—	—	—	20?[6]	—	—	90.0?	—	884	—	—
Nigeria	0.20?	—	—	—	—	—	—	—	—	p	—	—	—	—	—	—
Rhodesia	2.74	0.21	—	17.4?	17.1?	—	0.2?[5]	0.2?	—	550.0?[6]	—	—	—	700?	260	130?
Sierra Leone	—	—	—	—	—	1,400?	—	—	—	—	—	—	—	2,098	—	—
South Africa	49.30	2.88[6]	—	127.5	127.5	7,000?	25.0	95.3	—	30,532.9	0.7	207.6	—	7,737	3,420	3,652?
South West Africa	—	—	—	33.8	31.7	1,900?	1.2[6]	—	—	—	0.4[6]	—	—	38?	—	—
Tanzania	p	—	—	—	—	988	—	—	—	18.5	—	15.5	—	—	—	—
Tunisia	—	—	—	—	—	—	—	1.7	—	—	—	25.0?	—	918	—	—
Uganda	—	—	p	14.4	14.4	—	—	—	—	—	—	—	—	—	—	—
United Arab Republic	0.02?[6]	0.28?	—	—	—	—	3.5[6]	—	—	—	—	250.0?	2.4[6]	500?	215?	200?
Zambia	0.39	—	1,455	662.2	616.8	—	—	—	—	5.0?	—	—	—	—	—	—
Asia																
Burma	0.02?	—	—	0.1?	—	—	—	p	—	0.2?	—	2.0?	—	—	—	—
China	225.0?	13.00?	—	80.0?	90.0?	—	P	250.0?	—	50.0?	30.0?	500.0?	—	28,000?	14,000?	11,000?
Cyprus	—	—	—	15.2	—	—	—	—	—	—	—	45.0?	—	—	—	—
India	73.40	10.00?	—	8.6	8.6	7	27.5	1.3	—	97.3	p	1,148.0	38.0	26,157	6,954	6,387
Indonesia	0.21	—	—	—	—	3	—	—	p	7.8	—	—	—	—	—	—
Iran	0.30?	0.02?	—	p	—	—	—	—	—	—	—	1,810.0?	—	80?[6]	—	—
Israel	—	—	—	8.5[6]	—	—	—	—	—	—	—	85.0?	—	—	—	—
Japan	47.41	21.29	—	117.7	470.0	—	53.5	11.7	3,839	252.8	1.7	587.0	5.7	2,508	41,040	62,154
Jordan	—	—	—	—	—	—	—	—	—	—	—	—	—	—	—	—
Korea, South	12.44	—	—	1.4	3.7	—	16.8	57.0	6,738[5]	63.3	63.9	—	—	698	31?	329
Malaysia	—	—	—	p	—	—	—	—	—	3.8	—	—	90.8	5,436	—	—
Pakistan	1.40?	—	—	—	—	—	p	—	p	—	—	113.0[6]	—	5?[6]	—	—
Philippines	0.07	—	—	83.8	—	—	8.6[6]	—	—	500.4	—	15.2	—	1,506	—	—
Taiwan	5.08	0.21?	—	2.2	3.0	—	—	—	—	32.4	—	11.5	—	—	86?	300?
Thailand	0.34	—	—	—	—	—	—	133.2	—	p	—	61.7	—	549	—	—
Turkey	9.73?	1.12[6]	—	31.0	25.4	—	—	1.5[6]	30[6]	—	—	220.0?	—	1,485	847	1,056
Vietnam, South	—	—	—	—	—	—	—	—	30?	—	—	—	—	—	—	—
Oceania																
Australia	59.03	3.65	100?	89.1	74.1	—	5.0	—	1,873	627.2	—	787.0	547.7	18,814	4,804[6]	6,201
New Caledonia	—	—	—	—	—	—	—	—	—	—	—	—	—	204	—	—
New Guinea	—	—	—	—	—	—	—	—	—	27.6	—	—	—	—	—	—
New Zealand	2.41	0.01[6]	—	—	—	—	—	—	20	9.0[6]	—	—	—	3[6]	—	—
Pacific Islands	—	—	—	—	—	—	—	—	—	111.3	—	—	—	—	—	—
World total (estimate)	2,721.52	304,978	19,100	4,986.0	5,394.0	42,388	1,987.0	3,192.0	110,000	45,614.0	378.0	46,626.0	2,710.3▲	625,370	355,556	492,929

Additional production of certain minerals was as follows: asbestos, Swaziland 38(?); beryl, Mozambique 169; chromite, Albania 317(?); columbium-tantalum, Mozambique 163.6; graphite, Ceylon 10.4, North Korea 75(?); iron ore, Hong Kong 144, Mauritania 7,500(?), North Korea 6,500(?), Swaziland 1,744; manganese ore, Ivory Coast 149.4; peat, Denmark 10(?); petroleum, Bahrain 25.37, Sarawak and Brunei 38.29, Iraq 445.82, Kuwait 836.72, Kuwait-Neutral Zone 152.86, Libya 636.50, Qatar 118.08, Saudi Arabia 948.11, Trucial States 139.47; phosphate rock, Senegal 1,266, Togo 1,123, North Korea 250(?), North Vietnam 1,050(?)

Country	Lead (in ore) (Th.)	Lead (smelter) (Th.)	Crude Magnesite (Th.)	Magnesium (Th.)	Manganese Ore (Th.)	Mercury (Flasks)	Mica	Molybdenum	Nickel (Th.)	Nitrogen§ (Th.)	Peat (Th.)	Petroleum (Mil. bbl.)	Phosphate Rock (Th.)	Platinum‖ (Th. oz.)	Potash¶ (Th.)	Pyrite (Th.)	Salt (Th.)	Silver (Th. oz.)	Sulfur (elemental) (Th.)	Talc (Th.)	Tantalum¶ (Th.)	Tin (in ore) (Long tons)	Tin (smelter) (Long tons)	Tungsten Conc.δ	Vanadium	Zinc (in ore) (Th.)	Zinc (smelter) (Th.)
North America																											
Canada	308.2	172.6	p	7,879	—	—	—	9,764	224.0	438.0?	251	352.53	54	403.2?	2,207.2	340.5	4,855	36,426	2,106.7	53.9	1,925.0	237	—	1,506⁶	—	1,133.1	359.4
Central America	12.3	0.1	—	—	11.0	23,874	884	132	13.3	7.0?	—	133.04	36,079	—	—	—	3,330	37,939	1,891.2	2.9	1.5	662?	960?	149	—	13.3	75.7
Mexico	171.0?	161.7	478.7³	88,365	11.4	23,784	107,513	39,714	26.6?	171.0?	560	3,215.74	116	16.3?	2,992.8	874.7	35,343	51	8,415.6	818.7	4,934.0	9?	3,048	3,765	4,502	288.4	851.7
United States	287.5	344.6	—	—	75.0?	—	—	—	—	5,535.0	—	65.75	—	—	—	30.0?	1,137?	—	34.1?	—	—	—	—	—	—	498.4	—
West Indies	—	—	—	—	—	—	—	—	—	76.5?	—	—	—	—	—	—	—	—	—	—	—	—	—	—	—	—	23.07
South America																											
Argentina	32.2	22.0	127.1⁶	—	20.2	100	996	—	2	4.0?	2	114.74	p	—	—	—	819	2,207⁶	32.8	25.4	—	802	1,018	105	—	27.2	1.3ᵃ
Bolivia	19.7	0.2	0.2?	—	1,145.0	184	1,018⁶	4,877	1.1	6.4	—	14.53	—	—	14.5?	—	1,040	4,275	50.3	58.0⁶	—	26,890	2,100?	1,585	1,172	16.8	5.3ᵃ
Brazil	23.3?	17.2	—	—	14.9	100?	—	—	—	150.0?	—	53.52	390?	11.14⁶	—	170.0?	418	3,066	6.2	3.2	—	1,600?	—	285	—	1.1	—
Chile	0.4	—	—	—	178.6	—	—	—	—	40.0	—	68.38	16	—	—	352.0⁶	469	110	56.0	1.2?	—	—	—	—	—	0.6?	—
Colombia	0.6ᵃ	—	—	—	1.1	—	—	—	—	—	—	2.20	—	—	—	516.5?	35?	77⁶	21.0	—	—	68	—	256	—	0.2	—
Ecuador	0.1	—	—	—	—	—	—	—	—	—	—	—	—	—	—	—	—	—	0.1⁶	—	—	—	—	—	—	—	—
Guyana	—	—	—	—	—	—	—	—	—	—	—	—	65	—	—	—	—	—	—	—	—	—	—	—	—	—	—
Peru	158.2	81.8	—	—	—	2,980	—	924	—	43.4?ᵃ	—	25.86	—	—	—	—	141	35,870	—	4.5	—	—	—	—	—	317.9	63.0
Surinam	—	—	—	—	—	—	—	—	—	—	—	—	30?	—	—	—	—	—	—	—	—	—	—	—	—	—	—
Venezuela	—	—	—	—	—	—	—	—	—	—	—	1,292.88	—	—	—	—	85?	—	—	—	—	—	—	—	—	—	—
Europe																											
Austria	4.8	7.8	1,535.3	—	—	—	—	—	27	234.5	27	18.73	—	—	—	—	424	93⁶	5.0?	77.7	—	—	—	114	—	8.1	14.2
Belgium	45.1ᵃ	107.8	—	—	43.0?	—	—	p	—	419.5	—	—	—	—	—	170.0?	150?	—	12.0?	—	—	—	6,068	—	—	—	227.3
Bulgaria	1.8	92.0?	—	—	p	900?	—	—	—	297.4?	152?	3.64	22?⁶	—	—	352.0⁶	200?	2,400?	—	—	—	—	—	—	—	67.5	80.0?
Czechoslovakia	14.07	14.5?	2,106.8	—	248.0	—	223⁶	—	3.2?	107.0	61	1.42	—	—	—	516.5?	4,500?	2,003	75.0?	5.0?	53.2	150	—	1,107	—	60.4	185.7
Finland	4.2?	115.9?	—	4,170	112.0?	—	—	—	p	223.5	1,609⁶	—	36⁶	—	1,780.2	P	2,200?	4,800?	1,645.0	225.0	—	452	1,200?	75	—	25.0?	14.07
France	25.0?	25.0?ᵃ	—	200?	8.4	9,00?	13⁶	—	p	1,273.5	—	20.64	—	—	2,200.0?	556.0	2,200?	2,000?	130.0?	42.0	5.0	1,000?	1,622	84⁶	—	12.0?	102.7
Germany, East	59.5	136.3	—	—	—	—	—	—	—	1,301.3	—	57.26	—	—	2,300.0?	180.0	6,468?	238	105.0	5.0	—	—	—	—	—	106.0	—
Germany, West	9.8	5.5	425.0	—	15.0	—	—	—	—	1,081.9	—	12.86	—	—	—	—	95	647	3.5?	—	—	—	—	p	p	10.4	1.57ᵃ
Greece	1.4?ᵃ	0.2?	—	—	215.0?	—	—	7,000?	—	167.2	657?	11.60	—	—	—	—	—	1,219.0?	—	—	—	—	—	—	—	3.3?ᵃ	—
Hungary	58.3	60.5	4.5	6,000?	47.1	48,066	4,500?	—	1.3?	34.0?	4,732	—	90?	—	250.0?	—	2,577	1,382	85.8	118.5	p	—	—	—	—	24.8ᵃ	89.0
Ireland	—	—	—	—	—	—	—	—	—	950.1	p	—	—	—	—	1,411.0	1,926	—	46.0⁶	—	—	—	—	—	—	123.7⁶	—
Italy	38.7	—	—	28,500?	—	15,890	557	2600	—	684.1	400?	15.44	—	—	—	633.7	2,500?	1617	476.5⁶	80.0?	—	617	13,739	—	670?	12.2?	35.7
Luxembourg	—	—	—	—	—	—	—	—	—	355.0	107	3.34	—	—	—	240.0?⁶	143?	357	6.3⁶	—	—	—	—	—	—	196.1	54.7
Netherlands	—	—	—	—	—	—	—	—	—	462.4	60?	—	—	—	468.0	528.0	1,963?	—	0.8?	130.0?	—	—	—	—	—	0.5	196.0
Norway	3.4?	44.3	42.0?	—	9.7	190	—	p	1.37	264.2	—	—	907	—	—	360.0?	1,857?	3,707	42.8	27.8?	203.6?	—	619	1,815	—	59.1	69.7
Poland	40.7	40.0?	—	—	—	50,000?	—	—	—	1,201.5?	150?	98.38	—	—	2,760?	2,391.0	—	—	—	19.0?	—	113	1,534?	—	1,900?	86.2?	—
Portugal	62.6	52.1	100.6⁵	—	112.0?	—	—	—	—	120.3	—	0.56	—	—	—	440.0?	216	—	—	—	5.0	—	—	6,200?	1,400?	—	—
Romania	71.6	42.0	—	—	—	—	—	—	—	737.1?	—	—	—	—	—	—	9,500?	—	—	370.0?	—	25,000?	25,000?	—	—	535.0?	540.0
Spain	106.0	93.9	3,000.0?	40,000?	9.8	45,000?	—	—	95.0?	99.9	195,000?	2,116.00	16,350?	1,900.0?	—	3,500.0?	7,095	35,000?	40.5?	10.0?	p	1,475	23,317	p	—	89.1	104.3
Sweden	—	—	424.8	—	—	—	—	—	—	—	—	—	—	—	—	—	—	—	—	—	—	—	—	—	—	—	53.2
Switzerland	—	—	—	3,800?	—	—	—	—	—	—	—	0.65	—	—	—	—	—	3,075	—	—	—	—	—	p	p	12.0?	—
U.S.S.R.	400.0?	400.0?	—	—	7,200.0?	—	—	—	—	2,930.0?	—	17.66	350?	—	—	425.0?	—	—	—	—	—	—	—	6,000?	—	—	—
United Kingdom	—	—	—	—	—	—	—	—	—	—	—	—	—	—	—	—	—	—	—	—	—	—	—	—	—	—	—
Yugoslavia	106.0	—	—	—	—	—	—	—	—	99.9	—	—	—	—	—	—	—	4202	—	—	—	8,467?	—	343?	—	121.6	61.5
Africa																											
Algeria (incl. Sahara)	4.0?	13.0?	—	—	33.2	—	—	—	—	78	—	282.20?	—	—	—	60.0	1177	1,840	—	—	—	—	—	—	—	—	—
Angola	1.0?	90.0?	—	—	271.6	20,000?	—	1,500?	—	—	—	3.88	—	0.28	—	—	78	—	—	—	—	—	—	907	—	—	—
Congo (Kinshasa)	3.0	2.4	253.0	—	1,124.6	—	—	—	6.0	309.0?	—	—	—	—	—	—	260	—	—	150.0?	—	8,467?	—	8,000?	—	—	—
Ethiopia	—	—	—	—	12.0?	—	21,173	—	—	7	—	—	13	—	—	1,200.0?	49	93	—	135.0	—	259	—	—	—	5.3	4.57
Gabon	0.4	—	40.0?	—	498.4	—	—	—	—	—	—	42.19	10?	—	—	—	307	—	—	—	—	—	—	—	—	—	—
Ghana	—	70.4	80.0	—	41.1	—	536	—	—	25.0?	207?	185.00?	147	—	—	—	309	—	1.2?	—	4.5?	20,000?	13,597	391	—	24.0?	—
Kenya	22.0?	—	5.5⁴	6,400?	340.2	—	111⁶	—	0.4?	24.8	707	952.41?	1,300?	828.40?	380.0?	552.7	57	3,064	5.8?	9.1	0.9?	1,761	659	p	—	22.6	516.2
Liberia	70.2	150.0	2.0	—	1,817.0	—	253	278	—	1,801.2?	100?	0.96	p	6.40	—	—	807?	1,450	—	—	4.57	720?	1,666	2,025	—	262.2	2.5
Malagasy Republic	63.6	3.0	2.0	—	85.1	2,612	2,311	—	5.4	80.9	—	5.54	—	—	—	4.4	973	10,834	316.6	1,369.5	27.7	341	73,851	p	—	13.7	—
Morocco	77.7	21.4	—	—	286.1	—	25⁵	—	—	—	—	—	2,810?	—	—	—	36?	588	—	123.2	—	111	—	38	—	—	—
Nigeria	1.5?	—	—	—	0.2?	—	217	—	0.77	—	—	116.52	—	—	—	82.0?	300?	p	11.7?	—	—	72,121	—	—	—	4.2	—
Rhodesia	3.0	—	—	—	23.0?	4,612	—	—	—	—	—	—	—	—	—	—	27	—	—	0.4?	88.9	24	—	—	—	54.4	—
Sierra Leone	—	—	5.5⁴	—	—	—	—	—	—	—	—	0.74	1	—	—	146.2	—	—	—	41.3	—	—	—	—	—	4.6?	—
South Africa	12.4	13.2	—	—	24.0?ᵃ	250?	—	—	0.17	157.3ᵃ	—	17.07	—	—	—	38.7	627?	750?	—	—	—	—	—	—	—	90.0?	80.0?
South West Africa	—	—	2.0	—	25.0	—	—	41	—	93.4⁶	—	42.00?	—	—	—	125.0	431⁶	917	—	3.3⁶	—	—	20,000?	p	—	5.5	—
Tanzania	0.1	—	—	—	—	—	—	—	—	—	—	—	—	—	—	—	116	600?	—	—	—	—	1,000?	—	—	—	—
Tunisia	3.5	—	85.0	—	78.6	3,500?	—	—	6.0	158.0	—	0.25	1	—	—	—	517	93	p	—	6.5?	1,170	—	—	—	1.5	—
Uganda	2.4	—	0.5	—	23.0?	—	—	—	—	32.7	—	0.057	—	—	—	—	110?	—	25.4	—	46.0	407	26,582	442	—	6.0?	197.6
United Arab Republic	—	—	—	—	—	—	—	—	—	—	—	17.46	6,107	—	—	—	285⁴	p	—	—	—	22,489	—	p	—	—	—
Zambia	—	—	—	—	—	—	—	—	—	—	—	—	—	—	—	—	160?	p	—	—	—	—	—	—	—	—	—
Asia																											
Burma	15.0	13.0?	800.0?	1,000?	700.0?	20,000?	p	—	—	—	—	4.45	—	—	—	1,500.0?	169	1,396	250.0?	150.0?	—	20,000?	—	8,000?	—	4.6?	80.0?
China	90.0?	90.0?	—	—	7	—	p	—	—	30.3?	169	80.30?	1,000?	—	1,200.0?	1,200.0?	13,000?	600?	—	—	—	20,000?	20,000?	p	—	90.0?	—
Cyprus	—	—	—	—	—	—	—	—	—	—	—	—	—	—	—	—	7	—	p	—	—	—	—	—	—	—	4.57
India	—	—	—	—	1,599.0	—	557	—	—	—	—	42.19	1,300?	—	—	—	5,625	93	1.2?	135.0	—	13,597	1,000?	—	—	5.3	—
Indonesia	—	—	—	—	12.0?	—	—	—	—	—	—	185.00?	—	—	—	—	250?	309	25.0?	—	—	13,597	—	—	—	—	—
Iran	—	—	—	—	41.1	—	1⁶	—	—	25.0?	100?	952.41?	600?	—	—	—	57	—	—	—	—	—	—	p	—	—	—
Israel	—	—	—	—	—	—	—	—	—	24.8	—	0.96	973	—	380.0?	—	12	—	—	—	—	—	—	—	—	—	—
Japan	—	—	6,400?	—	340.2	4,612	2,311	253	5.4	1,801.27?	707?	5.54	—	6.40	—	4,527.0	524	10,834	316.6	1,369.5	4.4	1,170	73,851	p	—	262.2	516.2
Jordan	—	—	—	—	—	—	—	—	—	—	—	—	2,810?	—	—	—	524	588	—	123.2	—	—	—	—	—	13.7	2.5
Korea, South	9.7	3.0	—	—	7.2	—	25⁵	278	—	80.9	100?	—	147	—	—	4.4	431⁶	1,396	p	0.3⁶	88.9	72,121	—	p	—	13.7	—
Malaysia	—	0.1	2.0	—	85.1	—	—	—	—	93.4⁶	—	3.77	1	—	—	—	116	116	—	0.4	—	72,121	—	907	—	1.5	—
Pakistan	0.1	—	—	—	86.5	—	—	—	—	—	—	—	—	—	—	146.2	517	—	—	41.3	—	—	—	—	—	—	—
Philippines	—	—	2.0	—	86.5	2,612	—	—	—	—	—	—	—	—	—	38.7	1107	—	p	—	6.5?	—	—	—	—	—	—
Taiwan	3.5	—	—	—	78.6	—	—	—	—	158.0	—	0.057	—	—	—	125.0	285⁴	p	25.4	—	46.0	407	—	442	—	6.0?	—
Thailand	2.4	—	85.0	—	23.0?	3,500?	—	—	6.0	32.7	—	17.46	—	—	—	—	160?	p	—	—	—	22,489	26,582	p	—	—	—
Turkey	—	—	0.5	—	—	—	—	—	—	—	—	—	—	—	—	—	—	—	—	—	—	—	—	—	—	—	—
Vietnam, South	—	—	—	—	—	—	—	—	—	—	—	—	—	—	—	—	—	—	—	—	—	—	—	—	—	—	—
Oceania																											
Australia	378.2	291.1	22.0?	—	550.0?	—	624	—	61.6	39.0?	—	7.59	2,450?	6	—	270.0?	655⁵	19,765	19.0	19.0	23.4	5,379	3,594	956	—	404.4	197.6
New Caledonia	—	—	—	—	—	—	—	—	—	—	—	—	—	—	—	—	17	17	—	—	—	—	—	p	—	—	—
New Guinea	—	—	—	—	—	—	—	—	—	—	—	—	—	—	—	—	—	—	—	—	—	—	—	—	—	—	—
New Zealand	—	—	0.6	—	17.3	—	—	—	—	—	—	p	—	—	—	—	36⁶	61	—	—	—	—	—	—	—	6.0?	—
Pacific Islands	—	—	—	—	—	—	—	—	—	—	—	—	—	—	—	—	—	—	—	—	—	—	—	—	—	—	—
World total (estimate)	2,914.0	2,769.0	10,057.0	183,100	17,073.0	242,000	140,000ᵃ	64,750	439.0?	21,200.0	203,100	12,889.71	78,703	3,180.00	15,400.0	22,410.0	118,262	260,915	17,435.0	4,013.0	9,458.3?	216,100	219,100	28,100	9,644⁶	4,916.0	4,129.0

Notes: A ? indicates an estimate or no data available. The letter "p" indicates a small production, unknown in amount or less than the minimum base of the table: "P" indicates a larger but unknown production. *Metal content of ore. †White arsenic. ‡To avoid duplication of figures, cadmium exported in concentrates, flue dust, etc., is not included in the total. §Nitrogen content of fertilizer compounds not including nitrogen for industrial uses. (Fiscal year ending June 30, 1966.) Source: *United Nations Statistical Yearbook.* ¶Includes combined tantalum and columbium concentrates. δ 'W' basis. ¹,²,³,⁴,⁵ indicate data for 1959, 1963, 1964, 1965, or 1966 where 1967 figures are lacking. ⁶Free world only. ‖Includes all platinum-group metals. ¶1 k₂O equivalent of salts produced (marketable). ᵃIncludes West Irian. ᵇIncludes Rwanda and Burundi. (B.B.M.)

World Production of Major Metals and Minerals, 1962–66 (average) and 1967, World Totals and Leading Producers

LEAD
In 000 short tons
(smelter production)

	1962-66	1967
World	2,797	3,052
U.S.	416	380
U.S.S.R.*	380	440
Australia†	309	321
Mexico	194	178
Canada	166	190
Japan	111	165
Germany, West	130	150
France	98	128*
China*	105	100
Yugoslavia	111	103
Belgium‡	106	119
Bulgaria	80	101*
Peru	91	90
South West Africa	53§	78

†Incl. lead content of base bullion. ‡Includes scrap.
§Average for 1963-66.

MANGANESE ORE
In 000 short tons

	1962-66	1967
World	17,549	18,820
U.S.S.R.	7,658	8,000*
S. Africa	1,621	2,003
India	1,607	1,763
Gabon	960	1,240
Brazil	1,413	1,262
China*	1,100	800

NICKEL
In 000 short tons
(metal content of ore)

	1962–66	1967
World	417	484
Canada	234	247
U.S.S.R.*	86	105

SALT
In 000 short tons

	1962–66	1967
World	111,609	130,361
U.S.†	32,450	38,959
China*	12,500	14,300
U.S.S.R.*	10,400	10,500
U.K.	7,419	7,821
Germany, West	6,073	7,130*
India	4,917	6,200
France	4,608	5,000*
Canada	4,091	5,352
Italy	3,386	4,494
Mexico	1,946	3,671

†Incl. Puerto Rico.

SILVER
In 000 troy oz., smelter output

	1962–66	1967
World	253,852	260,915
U.S.	38,370	32,119
Mexico	41,608	37,939
Canada	31,149	36,426
Peru†	34,416	35,870
U.S.S.R.*	30,000	35,000
Australia	18,356	19,765
Bolivia‡	4,535	4,275
Germany, East*	4,800	4,800
Sweden	3,536	3,707
Yugoslavia	3,876	3,075
Japan	9,099	10,834

†Recoverable.
‡Exports.

TIN
In short tons (ore content)

	1962–66	1967
World	220,349	242,032
Malaysia	69,689	80,776
Bolivia	26,136	30,117
Thailand	19,594	25,188
China*	29,000	22,000
U.S.S.R.*	24,000	28,000
Indonesia	16,537	15,229

ZINC
In 000 short tons
(smelter production)

	1962–66	1967
World	4,086	4,551
U.S.	949	939
U.S.S.R.*	510	595
Japan	365	569
Canada	328	396
Belgium†	248	251
Australia	207	218
France	202	205
Poland	205	216
Germany, West	127	113
U.K.	115	115
China*	100	88

†Incl. production from scrap.
*Estimate.

continued from page 527
their share of the world total, were: Eastern Europe 29.1% (U.S.S.R. 26.9%), North and Central America 20.3% (U.S. 13.7%, Canada 6.2%), Western Europe 19.4% (France 7.9%, Sweden 4.5%, U.K. 2.1%), Asia 11.7% (China 4.5% [est.], India 4.2%), South America 9.5%, and Africa 7%. Steel was produced in nearly 50 countries, but more than 86% of the world total came from the following 12 nations: U.S. 23.4%, U.S.S.R. 20.7%, Japan 12.6%, West Germany 7.5%, U.K. 4.9%, France 4%, Italy 3.2%, Communist China 2.2% (est.), Poland 2.1%, both Belgium and Czechoslovakia 2%, and Canada 1.8%.

Lead. World mine production of lead rose 2% from 2,860,000 metric tons in 1966 to 2,910,000 tons in 1967. The free world produced 73.7%, of which North and Central America supplied 26.8% (Canada 10.6%, U.S. 9.9%, Mexico 5.9%), Western Europe 15.3%, Australia 13%, South America 8% (Peru 5.4%), and Africa 6.5%. The remainder came principally from Eastern Europe with 21% (U.S.S.R. 13.7%, Bulgaria 3.5%) and Communist China with 3.1%. World smelter production of lead rose by 1.8% to 2,769,000 tons, the chief producing areas being North and Central America 24.5% (U.S. 12.5%, Canada 6.2%), Asia 11.4% (Japan 5.4%, Communist China 3.3%), Western Europe 22.5% (West Germany 4.9%, France 4.2%, Belgium 3.9%, Yugoslavia 3.4%), Eastern Europe 22.2% (U.S.S.R. 14.5%, Bulgaria 3.3%), Australia 10.5%, and Africa 4.5% (South West Africa 2.5%).

Manganese. Because world steel production increased by almost 4%, reaching a new peak during 1967, overall manganese consumption must have been correspondingly higher. Total world production of manganese dropped less than 1%, to 17,073,000 metric tons. The U.S.S.R. remained the largest producer with 42.2% of the total.

Mercury. World production of mercury, which dropped slightly in 1966 from 1965, continued to decline to 242,042 flasks (of 76 lb. each) in 1967, lower by 8.7% than the previous year's total. Production in the U.S. rose 8%, principally because of increased output in Nevada. Spain continued to be the largest producer, accounting for 20.7% of the total.

Molybdenum. The situation of a short supply of molybdenum, which had prevailed during the past few years, reversed itself to one of oversupply in 1967. World production totaled 64,750 metric tons, only 0.2% higher than in 1966. The U.S. produced 61.4%, Canada 15.1%, U.S.S.R. 10.8%, Chile 7.5%, and Communist China 2.3%.

Nickel. Consumption of nickel, which had risen by 70% from 1963 to 1966 in the free world, suffered a slight decline there in 1967. This was due in part to a worldwide shortage of the metal. To meet the Western European shortage, nickel was purchased from Communist countries, and the European Economic Community suspended the customs tariff on ferronickel, effective until June 30, 1968. World production rose 10.3% to 439,000 metric tons. North America provided 60.2% (Canada 51.1%, Cuba 6.1% [est.], U.S. 3%), while the U.S.S.R. produced 21.7% and New Caledonia 14%.

Phosphates. The rise in world production of phosphate rock continued, with an increase in 1967 from 1966 of 3.8%, to 78.7 million metric tons. Of this total the free world produced 76.2%. Principal producing countries were the U.S. 45.8%, U.S.S.R. 20.7%, Morocco 13.4%, and Tunisia 3.6%. In the U.S. production increased only 1.9% to 36,079,000 metric tons. This contrasted with the exceptional increase of 33% in domestic marketable production in 1966 over 1965. Although demand was 4% greater than in 1966, it was not enough to absorb the increased output, and the oversupply situation worsened in the U.S. The greatest increase in production took place in the Soviet Union. A large deposit in the Spanish Sahara was being worked, but it was not expected to yield salable phosphate rock for several years.

Platinum-Group Metals. World production of platinum-group metals in 1967, at 3,180,000 troy ounces, was almost 4% larger than in 1966. Apparent world demand continued to exceed production, as the supply-demand imbalance continued to push world markets toward higher price levels for most platinum metals. The U.S.S.R. led in production with 59.7% of the total. The free world produced 40.3% of the total (South Africa 26.1%, Canada 12.7%), with small outputs in the U.S., Colombia, and Japan.

Potash. World production of potash rose by 5.5% during 1967, to 15.4 million metric tons. Of this total 31.2% came from Western Europe (West Germany 15%, France 11.6%), 33.9% from North America (U.S. 19.5%, Canada 14.4%), and 32.3% from Eastern Europe (U.S.S.R. 18%, East Germany 14.3%). Production expansion in many countries again exceeded world demand, resulting in a generally weak price structure. Facing strong competition from other countries, U.S. producers began to curtail output. In Canada, however, potash production in Saskatchewan rose by 22%.

Salt. Production of salt increased by 6.2% to 118,260,000 metric tons in 1967, setting a new record. The free world produced 74.4% of the total. In the U.S., the major producer, output rose 6.8% to 35,340,000 tons, representing 29.9% of the total. Other important producing areas were: Western Europe 23.2% (U.K. 6%, West Germany 5.5%, France 3.8%), Asia 19.8% (Communist China 11%, India 4.8%), and Eastern Europe 13.9% (U.S.S.R. 8%).

Silver. World production of silver dropped 2.8% in 1967 to 261 million troy ounces from 268.6 million oz. in 1966. Output fell in the U.S., Mexico, Bolivia, Yugoslavia, and Sweden. The free world supplied 83.1% of the metal, with Eastern European countries accounting for 16.4%. Mexico became the leading producer with 14.5% of the total, followed by Canada with 14%, Peru 13.7%, U.S.S.R. 13.4% (est.), U.S. 12.3%, Australia 7.6%, and Japan 4.1%. A number of countries, including Australia, Canada, Japan, South Africa, and the U.S., began to replace their silver coinage with easily obtainable and less expensive metals.

Sulfur. Both the production and consumption of sulfur set new records in 1967, with an increase in world production of 4.3% to 17,435,000 metric tons. Of this, 11,150,000 tons were native sulfur and 6,285,000 tons were by-product elemental sulfur, recovered mainly from oil and natural-gas operations. The U.S. (63.9%) and Mexico (16.5%) produced most of the native sulfur, with the balance coming chiefly from Eastern Europe at 13.7% (U.S.S.R. 9.4%, Poland 4.3%). Canada was the leading producer of by-product sulfur, with 33.4% of the total, followed by France 26.2%, U.S. 20.5%, and U.S.S.R. 7.1%. World consumption of sulfur in all forms increased to 27 million tons, a gain of 1 million tons over 1966.

Tin. Both mine and smelter production of tin rose in 1967, mainly because of higher outputs in Malaysia. It was the first time in many years that mine production equaled and slightly exceeded the reported consumption of tin metal. World mine production rose by 2.5% to 216,100 long tons, while smelter production of tin was 7.6% higher at 219,100 long tons. The free world accounted for 78.5% of the tin mined and 79% of the metal smelted. Mine production was divided as follows: Asia 60.2% (Malaysia 33.3%, Thailand 10.4%, Communist China 9.3% [est.], Indonesia 6.3%), Bolivia 12.5%, U.S.S.R. 11.6%, and Africa 9.7% (Nigeria 4.3%). Principal countries smelting tin were Malaysia with 33.7% of the total, Thailand 12.1%, U.S.S.R. 11.4% (est.), U.K. 10.6%, Communist China 9.1% (est.), the Netherlands 6.3%, Nigeria 4.2%, and Belgium 2.8%. Tin prices declined considerably to their lowest point since 1963.

Tungsten. World production of tungsten declined 1.7% in 1967 to 28,100 metric tons of contained tungsten. The industry was marked by higher and relatively stable prices, which encouraged the reopening of several idle mines in the free world. Communist China, the U.S.S.R., and North Korea accounted for 28.4, 22, and 7.6%, respectively, of total world production. Output in the free world was 42% of the total (U.S. 13.4%, South Korea 7.2%, Bolivia 5.6%, Portugal 3.9%, and Australia 3.4%).

Uranium. Production of uranium in the free world dropped 2.3% to 16,900 metric tons in 1967. The U.S. produced 49.1% of the free-world total, with Canada providing 20.2%, South Africa 18.1%, France 6.5%, Gabon 2.7%, and Australia 1.8%. No data were available for the U.S.S.R. Because nuclear energy had become established as a competitive source of power, a steeply rising demand for uranium seemed likely. Exploration for new sources of supply was active in the U.S., Canada, Australia, Gabon, and South Africa.

Zinc. Both mine and smelter production of zinc reached new records in 1967 despite a loss in production due to strikes at mines and refineries in the U.S. that were associated with copper production. A drought caused a shortage of hydroelectric power and thereby curtailed the output of the Electrolytic Zinc Co. of Australasia Ltd. World mine production rose by 9.5% to 4,916,000 metric tons, distributed as follows: North and Central America 39.3% (Canada 23%, U.S. 10.1%, Mexico 5.9%), Eastern Europe 16.6% (U.S.S.R. 10.9%, Poland 4%), Western Europe 12.5%, Asia 10.3% (Japan 5.3%, North Korea 2.3%), Australia 8.2%, Africa 5.4% (Congo [Kinshasa] 2.5%). Smelter production of zinc metal, at 4,129,000 tons, was less than 1% higher. Of this total 76.1% was produced in the free world. World consumption of zinc declined about 2% from 1966. (B. B. M.)

See also Fuel and Power; Geology; Industrial Review; Metallurgy.

Molecular Biology

Biochemistry. Major activity in biochemistry in 1968 centred around inquiries into the origins of life on earth. E. S. Barghoorn and J. W. Schopf of Harvard reported finding amino acids in chert fossils from South Africa, Australia, and Canada that were one to three billion years old and had the same composition as those found in living organisms today. It was generally agreed that no life existed on earth 4.5 billion years ago because the primeval atmosphere contained no free oxygen, consisting instead largely of methane, ammonia, hydrogen, and water. Sidney Fox of the University of Miami maintained that heat from volcanoes or hot streams could provide the energy source needed to create amino acids. He produced 14 amino acids experimentally by passing com-

mon atmospheric elements through simulated volcanic environments. Philip Abelson of the Carnegie Institution of Washington (D.C.), on the other hand, proposed that poisonous hydrogen cyanide was the principal ingredient of a primeval "soup" engulfing the earth and that ferridoxin, a simple enzyme basic to all cells, was an early evolution from such an atmosphere. Organic compounds such as adenine and amino acids evidently occur also in asteroids, indicating that the prerequisite materials for life might exist elsewhere than on earth.

Stanley L. Miller and others assumed that the primeval energy source was ultraviolet rays, but as the earth grew older, a blanket of upper atmosphere ozone began to shut out part of the ultraviolet spectrum of light. Chlorophyll, a "booster" chemical that can convert energy from ordinary sunlight into chemical energy (photosynthesis), developed. A typical photosynthesis product is hydrocarbons. Abelson and Melvin Calvin, of the University of California at Berkeley, were seeking clues to early organic chemistry in hydrocarbons. Phytane and pristane, components of the chlorophyll molecule, had been found in oil-bearing rocks three billion years old. Calvin, a Nobel laureate, vastly expanded knowledge of how photosynthesis helps transform CO_2 through a complex process into carbohydrates, fats, and proteins. One other product of photosynthesis, of course, is free oxygen, prerequisite to animal life.

In 1967 Par Edman of Melbourne, Austr., announced development of a "protein sequenator" that would reveal genetic secrets locked in proteins by splitting off amino acid molecules in a carefully controlled series of chemical reactions and identifying them. It was believed that accurate knowledge of the complex structure of proteins obtained by the device could lead more quickly to their synthesis. It might also identify structural differences between proteins from normal and from cancer cells and throw new light on how cancer develops. Within two or three years the machines were to be available in quantities to perform all these functions, according to Charles G. Sibley of Yale University.

In July 1968, 11 of 16 heart transplant surgeons, meeting in Cape Town, S.Af., agreed that a blood globulin known as ALG (antilymphocyte globulin) should be given all future heart transplant patients. ALG suppresses lymphocytes, white blood cells that infiltrate and destroy foreign tissue. The ALG was produced by injecting human lymphocytes into horses. The horses produced blood globulins (antibodies) that destroy the invading cells. The horse globulin, ALG, removed from equine blood, had also been used successfully in kidney and liver transplants. While it was still too early to determine what immunosuppressive means promised best results, the secret to success in organ transplants seemed to lie more in selective suppression of the body's rejection mechanism than in the surgery itself.

Ajay K. Bose and associates of Stevens Institute of Technology, Hoboken, N.J., outlined two new methods of synthesizing isomers of penicillin V. These processes supplemented the synthetic process of John C. Sheehan and was potentially important because of the resistance of new strains of bacteria to older forms of penicillin. Oxytetracycline, one of the more complex tetracycline compounds, was synthesized after ten years of research by Hans H. Muxfeldt and co-workers of Cornell University.

A Harvard group under E. J. Corey reported the

531

Molecular Biology

Nobel Prize winning geneticists Joshua Lederberg (left) and Arthur Kornberg of Stanford University appearing before the Senate subcommittee on government research on March 8, 1968, to testify in favour of increased federal funds to support research.

synthesis of five prostaglandins, lipid-soluble acids that affect the heart rate, blood pressure, mobilization of fatty acids, smooth muscle contraction, and the firing rate of nerves. Availability of prostaglandins could speed research on their possible roles in hormone or metabolism regulation within the cell.

Further experimental trials of L-DOPA, a drug that promised dramatic relief to sufferers from Parkinson's disease, which is characterized by muscular tremor and rigidity, were projected in 1968 by a national committee under George C. Cotzias of Brookhaven National Laboratory Medical Research Center, Upton, N.Y. (J. S. Sw.)

Biophysics. The large range of radioactive compounds available as tracers in biological systems in conjunction with the electron microscope was revolutionizing thinking about the structure and functioning of the cell. Perhaps one of the greatest achievements in 1967 was made by Mehran Goulian and Arthur Kornberg, who synthesized viral core DNA that was indistinguishable from natural DNA. This could in no way be considered as the creation of "life in a test tube," because two other substances found only in living things were found necessary for its synthesis —DNA-polymerase, the enzyme catalyzing in vivo synthesis, and DNA itself. Nevertheless, it represented a great step forward in increasing understanding of how viruses function within cells.

Since proteins in the cell are only synthesized at specific times in a definite sequence, the idea of repression of gene action was introduced and the popular model of François Jacob and Jacques Monod suggested that the repressive control of protein synthesis occurs at the level of transcription—the point where genetic information is transferred from DNA to messenger ribonucleic acid (mRNA). Some recent experiments appeared to contradict this model since DNA activity is not always synchronized with specific protein synthesis. There would now appear to be good evidence that part of the control of gene action also implicates RNA at the translation level where mRNA gives rise to specific proteins. Moreover, there was a suggestion that instead of sequential gene readout, as had hitherto been supposed, there was some evidence for readout in overlapping sequence or in groups, so that many genes can be transcribed simultaneously. One recent finding of a gene repressor system was made by Robert Ward of the University of California at Berkeley where he demonstrated that certain molecules from the protein coat of a virus, which sheds its coat when it infects a cell, were able to control viral reproduction. This repression was found to be specific for a particular type of nucleic acid.

Missiles: see Defense

The detailed study of mitochondria had become fashionable. The existence of mitochondrial DNA in addition to nuclear DNA now seemed to be well established. There was also good evidence for the presence of ribosomes and transfer RNA within the inner compartment of the mitochondrion, which is capable of synthesizing its own protein and replicating itself.

Without enzymes there is no expression of the genetic code and indeed no DNA or RNA synthesis. Much work had been concentrated on the study of the allosteric enzymes whose functioning depends on their three-dimensional structure. A new tool, the relaxation spectrometer, was announced; the spectrometer enables the basic chemical steps in enzyme reactions to be studied by disturbing a given enzyme substrate system from its equilibrium, or steady state, and observing the relaxation spectrum; *i.e.*, the time taken to return to the stable condition. The principal experimental procedures for perturbing the system were temperature change, electric field pulse, and pressure shock waves. In this way the rates of single reaction steps could be obtained. More information about the intermediates in enzyme reactions was expected.

In much the same way as RNA acts as a messenger for genetic information in the cell, cyclic AMP (adenosine 3′,3′-monophosphate) was reported to act as a transmitter of hormonal messages that control the rates of cellular metabolism. In this new concept the hormones are considered as the first messengers to travel to the target cells where they excite the formation of cyclic AMP. The AMP was thought to act as a regulatory agent to alter the activity of the enzymes and the membrane permeability. Changes effected by cyclic AMP cover a wide range—an increased rate of cell aggregation, an increased kidney permeability, a decrease in the incorporation of amino acids into proteins, and a loss of tone of smooth muscle. A great difference in sensitivity had also been observed in the effect of AMP on different tissues; phosphorylase activity was greatly increased in the liver, but brain phosphorylase activity was not affected.

The increased interest in the appearance and function of cell membranes resulted in three whole volumes being devoted to this subject by *Biochimica et Biophysica Acta* in two years. The first three-dimensional pictures of cancer cells had been made by E. J. Ambrose *et al.*, using a stereoscan electron microscope, at the Chester Beatty Research Institute in London. The pictures confirmed that cell migration across tissue surfaces is made by membrane movement. They also showed that cancer cells adhere more avidly to surfaces of differing textures than do normal cells. This was probably a result of the greater irregularity and undulating nature of the cancer cell membranes they had observed. In addition, they found a decrease in the mutual adhesiveness of cancer cell membranes, suggesting that a chemical change had occurred. The researchers claimed that these properties help explain the ability of cancer cells to invade normal tissues.

The transport of ions through cell membranes also attracted much attention, and perhaps the most revolutionary concept in recent studies was that put forward by G. N. Ling: that the membrane of the cell is not a rate limiting barrier to the passage of water and other solutes between the cell and its external environment. He suggested that cell water exists as polarized multilayers on protein surfaces within the cell and that the physical state of this water is what determines the concentration of different elements within the cell. Ling also contended that the resting cell is not capable of delivering sufficient energy to satisfy the needs of "permeases" and "pumps" as in the classic membrane model. (E. L. Lл.)

Genetics. A central problem of molecular genetics in 1968 remained the determination of how DNA, the genetic material, replicates. All that was certain about DNA replication was that it is semiconservative. A new model, the rolling circle model of DNA replication, stirred interest. It had been proposed in order to explain aspects of bacterial and phage (a bacterial virus) DNA replication. In it the DNA template consists of two complementary strands, each in the form of a closed loop or circle. All bacterial and phage chromosomes studied in detail were known to have this configuration at some time in their existence. One of the strands opens and is peeled away from its complement. As this is done, a new complement or replica is made to take its place and is attached to the free end of the original complement that is last to come off the circular strand. This process is repeated, resulting in replicas attached end to end. These replicas become templates for new complementary strands. There were two important features of this model. First, the replication points for each strand could be at different sites, a condition termed asynchronous replication. Second, and genetically significant, was the use of one of the two parental DNA strands to transmit hereditary information to daughter molecules, aptly described as master-strand replication. Some evidence existed to support this mode of replication. The model explained some observations made on replicating phage chromosomes; *e.g.*, the existence of concatenate structures or a series of phage chromosomes structurally continuous end to end.

Two laboratories reported that newly synthesized DNA appears as short segments. This would be expected if the Kornberg DNA polymerase is the in vivo replicating enzyme, since it only synthesizes continuously in the 5′ to 3′ direction. DNA synthesized in the 3′ to 5′ direction by this enzyme could be made only in a discontinuous fashion producing short segments. Some data had been interpreted to show that all newly made DNA is synthesized in a discontinuous manner. Further work would be necessary to clarify this issue.

Studies on order and control of chromosome replication in bacteria indicated that replication is initiated at one of a few sites on the chromosome. Once initiated, it proceeds in one direction from that site. Replication in animal cells appears to be initiated at many sites in a complex chromosome. Recent evidence showed that chromosome replication initiated in Chinese hamster cells proceeds in two directions from the point of initiation. Further work would determine whether or not this mode of replication was of general significance in animal cells. Replicating DNA in animal cells appears to be attached to the nuclear membrane, a situation analogous to the attachment of replicating bacterial DNA to the cellular membrane.

Reports showed that two recombinational systems exist in lambda phage. A generalized system accounts for the genetic recombination that occurs during vegetative reproduction. A site-specific recombination system directs recombination in the prophage attachment region and brings about the insertion of the phage genome into that of its bacterial host, a relationship called lysogeny. Increasing evidence indicated that bacterial-phage interactions are strikingly similar to

those between animal viruses and the complex animal cells they infect.

That DNA of evolutionarily higher organisms contained repeated sequences was detected in experiments designed to measure the rate of reannealing of separated single-stranded DNA molecules to the double-stranded or native form. The rate of reannealing for a fraction of the DNA was more rapid than expected for genomes containing large amounts of DNA if all sequences of a certain size were unique. It was proposed that during evolution the repeated sequences change slowly and diverge from each other. Occasionally, certain segments of DNA were extensively reduplicated, which replenished the dwindling redundancy. The function of these repeated sequences may be to provide for high rates of synthesis, for ribosomal RNA, for example. An intriguing question remained whether or not the same sequences are repeated in different tissues from the same animal.

In contrast, the genome of the phage T4 does not contain recurring nucleotide sequence chains with more than 12 links. It was thought that any freely recombining haploid genome that has two identical sequences larger than this size has a high probability of losing part of its information content through internal recombination. Evidently a mechanism to prevent such loss in higher organisms must exist.

The most recent achievement involving the in vitro replication system derived from the RNA phage Qβ was the cloning of different RNA molecules. That meant a collection of molecules could be isolated, all having the same single molecule as their parental template. Thus, "mutant" molecules were being studied for their particular properties and eventually the sequence of each would be analyzed. The different molecules had to be treated in a way analogous to that used in working with different strains of bacteria or viruses. This system provided a novel approach to studying the properties of self-replicating macromolecules. An artificial "universe" could be created in the test tube, and the effects of different "natural selections" could be determined as the evolution of these molecules proceeded in a controlled manner.

Finally, work was continuing on the total synthesis of the gene for yeast alanine transfer-RNA. The DNA molecule was being built segment by segment in known sequence. Once the gene was made, it would be attached to the DNA of lambda phage, which would then be used to infect a spheroplast, a cell-wall deficient cell of *Escherichia coli*. In this way the man-made gene would be amplified, and the gene product could be isolated and its functionality determined.

(JA. C. C.)

See also Biological Sciences; Medicine.

Monaco

A sovereign principality on the northern Mediterranean coast, Monaco is bounded on all land sides by the French *département* of Alpes-Maritimes. Area: 0.579 sq.mi. (1.51 sq. km.). Pop. (1967 est.): 23,700. Language: French. Religion: Roman Catholic. Prince, Rainier III; minister of state in 1968, Jean-Émile Reymond.

As the result of a decision of the Supreme Court of Monaco, Prince Rainier regained control of the Société des Bains de Mer (SBM) by purchasing Aris-

MONACO
Education. (1964–65) Primary, pupils 1,476, teachers 87; secondary, pupils 967, teachers 45; vocational, pupils 160, teachers 9.
Finance. Monetary unit: Monégasque franc, at par with the French franc (Fr. 4.94 = U.S. $1; Fr. 11.85 = £1 sterling). Budget (1967): revenue Fr. 131,692,-000; expenditure Fr. 131,270,000. Tourism (1966): visitors 88,000; gross receipts Fr. 30,116,000.

totle Onassis' shares for $8 million; the SBM controls the Monte Carlo casino and most of the hotels. The prince adopted a policy of Americanization designed to increase the company's efficiency and to promote the principality's appeal to American tourists. An agreement was negotiated with Pan American Airways under which that company agreed to take over and manage the principal hotels of the state. In addition, Rainier chose an American, Wilford Groote, to replace Onassis as director of the SBM.

Rainier appointed Martin Dale, another American, to direct the Monaco Economic Development Corporation (MEDC), the organization charged with planning the principality's future. The steps taken by Rainier to raise Monaco from its economic doldrums contributed to a worsening of Franco-Monégasque relations, which had failed to improve after the 1963 tax agreement dictated from Paris. In addition, Princess Grace denounced French state-controlled television for its anti-U.S. attitude. Prince Rainier and Princess Grace visited the U.S. in September.

Tourism, a major source of revenue, showed some signs of improving during 1968. Approximately five congresses or conventions met in the principality each month during the year. In addition, the SS "Constitution" has made Monaco a port of call. An active program of concerts, opera, exhibits, sporting events, and theatre graced the summer season and contributed to the stabilization of the tourist industry. However, the continued controls on American tourists and funds limited expansion.

(R. D. Ho.)

Money and Banking

The somewhat nervous mood that marked the money and capital markets in the months immediately preceding the U.K. devaluation showed little sign of relaxation in the period to June 1968. Indeed, the effect of nearly all major economic and political developments during this period was such as to exacerbate it.

Whereas 1967 had seen a broad similarity in financial developments in the major industrial countries, with a slowing down of general economic expansion, an easing of monetary controls, and a relatively easy supply/demand situation for loanable funds, 1968 saw a much greater variety of experiences. In the U.S., Canada, and Japan there was fairly rapid expansion, a tighter borrowing position, and renewed monetary restriction. Circumstances were slightly different in the U.K., in that the need for monetary stringency was dictated first and foremost by external conditions linked with devaluation rather than by considerations of overrapid internal expansion and domestic inflation. In France, where the situation in the early part of the year was reflationary rather than inflationary, a policy of monetary ease was continued despite the political disturbances of May and June.

These disturbances did, admittedly, produce the need for a substantial increase in the discount rate to stem the loss of reserves, but they also led to a further easing of lending policy to assist in financing the exceptional business expenditures that arose from the eventual settlement of the disputes. It was not until mid-November that monetary policy became unequivocally restrictionary. In West Germany the persistent external surplus and ever strengthening rumours about revaluation of the currency dictated a continuation of the easy money policy initiated in early 1967. In Italy, Belgium, and the Netherlands economic recovery proceeded smoothly and did not produce the need for any great restraint.

Common to both 1967 and 1968 were the internationally high level of interest rates and the tendency of many rates to be strongly influenced by factors other than the prevailing supply/demand situation for funds to which they related. This applied particularly to the U.S., where fluctuations in the prospects for peace in Vietnam and the uncertainty attending the presidential elections gave rise to frequent reassessments of future financial prospects. More specifically, rates tended to move up and down in accordance with assessments of, among other things, the implications of current developments for future Treasury financing requirements. This expectations factor was particularly important in late 1967 and early 1968, since forecasts of a large borrowing requirement could not be qualified by any optimism regarding fiscal intervention. Later developments became more difficult to interpret, as political factors likely to increase the borrowing requirement coincided with factors likely to diminish it.

At the shorter end of the market, the extremely speculative character of international capital movements exerted a significant influence on the upward shift of money market rates in several countries. Pressures on sterling were strong before and, for a while, after devaluation. Both the Canadian dollar and the Swedish krona came under speculative attack during the early part of the year, but in both cases the attacks were short-lived. The dollar was under consistent pressure, and the volume of gold purchases from September until the suspension of gold sales by the Gold Pool countries in mid-March was unprecedented. Later on the franc was brought under what seemed to be irresistible pressure as the disparity between the exchange value of the franc vis-à-vis the Deutsche Mark became increasingly evident. In the countries most affected by these influences, the combination of international pressures and internal restraint led to general increases in short-term lending rates, and these were quickly reflected in higher rates on the international Eurodollar market.

In both Britain and the U.S., a substantial part of the period was characterized by an undesirable imbalance between monetary and fiscal policies, which heightened the influence of expectations on market behaviour. In the U.S. the inability of the administration to persuade Congress to accept the tax increases put forward in August 1967 meant that for several months monetary weapons had to stand alone against the rising tide of inflation. The eventual enactment of the tax measures in midyear produced a welcome relaxation of the market uncertainty that had prevailed for nearly a year. In the U.K. cuts in government expenditure were announced soon after devaluation. Nevertheless, unwillingness to advance the traditional spring budget did leave monetary policy to bear an unreasonably heavy burden in the months between devaluation and the announcement of the budget. In particular, the period saw a boom in consumption expenditure, arising from expectations regarding the stringency of the budget, which made it difficult for some financial institutions to adhere to the lending restrictions that had been laid down for them.

In general, the third quarter of the year was more settled than the first two, though there was no significant easing of monetary restraint in those countries where it was being practised. Speculative influences generally receded, except against the franc and in favour of the Deutsche Mark. The pound looked much stronger after the Basel (Switz.) agreement to diminish the volatility of the sterling balances, and the two-tier gold system turned out to be a more effective stabilizer than had been expected. The balance between monetary and fiscal policy looked healthier after the enactment of the U.S. tax measures and the very stringent British budget. Expectation of cuts in interest rates began to strengthen in Britain, the U.S., and Canada. Canada was the first to give them official support when, at the end of July, the discount rate was cut to 6.5%. The U.S. Federal Reserve Board followed suit with what was, in effect, a purely nominal cut of $\frac{1}{4}$% in the middle of August, and the Bank of England with a $\frac{1}{2}$% cut in the U.K. bank rate in the middle of September. It was not until mid-November, when pressure against the franc greatly intensified, that this healthier tone came to an end.

Eurocurrency and Eurobond Markets. The Eurodollar deposit rate had fallen in the earlier part of 1967 in the face of the easier credit situation in the U.S., the repayment of Eurodollar borrowing by U.S. banks, and large money exports by the West German banks. Later in the year the U.S. banks again became net borrowers and, a month prior to the U.K. devaluation, their demands had pushed the rate to about 1% above the April low of 4.6%. The general interest rate increases associated with devaluation accelerated the upward pressures, as did the extremely heavy gold purchases that followed. The rate reached a peak near the end of September but declined by something over

Selected Interest Rates								
		1966	1967			1968		
Country		June	June	Sept.	Dec.	March	June	Sept.
Belgium	A	5.25	4.50	4.25	4.00	3.75	3.75	3.75
	B[1]	3.50	3.52	2.85	2.54	2.45	2.64	2.80
	C	5.84	5.92	5.77	5.71	5.54	5.50	5.49
France	A	3.50	3.50	3.50	3.50	3.50	3.50	5.00
	B	4.79	4.29	4.34	4.76	5.07	5.76	6.76
	C	5.40	5.95	5.73	5.60	5.84	5.94	5.95
Germany, West	A	5.00	3.00	3.00	3.00	3.00	3.00	3.00
	B[2]	5.00	2.75	2.75	2.75	2.75	2.75	2.75
	C	8.40	6.90	6.70	6.80	6.70	6.40	6.30
Italy	A	3.50	3.50	3.50	3.50	3.50	3.50	3.50
	B	...	...	...	...	...	...	...
	C	5.54	5.62	5.60	5.61	5.59	5.66	5.64
Netherlands	A	5.00	4.50	4.50	4.50	4.50	4.50	4.50
	B[2]	5.09	4.68	4.60	4.51	4.34	4.56	4.39
	C	6.28	5.97	6.03	6.11	6.12	6.24	6.25
Switzerland	A	2.50	3.50	3.00	3.00	3.00	3.00	3.00
	B[1]	3.75	2.82	1.09	2.69	1.25	2.69	2.63
	C	4.04	4.75	4.32	4.55	4.35	4.34	4.34
United Kingdom	A	6.00	5.50	5.50	8.00	7.50	7.50	7.50
	B[2]	5.69	5.27	5.34	7.52	7.25	7.21	6.76
	C	6.98	6.87	6.95	7.13	7.18	7.46	7.43
United States	A	4.50	4.00	4.00	4.50	5.00	5.50	5.25
	B[2]	4.54	3.48	4.45	5.01	5.14	5.54	5.20
	C	4.63	4.86	4.99	5.36	5.39	5.23	5.09
Canada	A	5.25	4.50	5.00	6.00	7.50	7.50	6.00
	B[2]	5.06	4.34	4.50	5.80	6.93	6.75	5.62
	C	5.66	5.87	6.19	6.55	7.01	6.77	6.60
Japan	A	5.48	5.48	5.84	5.84	6.21	6.21	5.84
	B[1]	5.84	6.21	6.94	7.30	8.03	8.03	8.03
	C	6.80	6.80	6.80	—	—	—	—

A = Central bank's discount rate.
B = Money market rate.
  B[1] = Day-to-day money.
  B[2] = 90-day Treasury bills.
C = Long-term government bond yield.

half a point to close the year at 6.4%. Estimates produced by Milton Gilbert of the Bank for International Settlements indicated that the size of the market grew by a further $3.5 billion in 1967, and that the volume of credit channeled in Eurocurrencies was something of the order of $19 billion.

Somewhat surprisingly, the rates in Eurodollar markets fell in the first two months of 1968, despite anticipations that there would be increased demand from the U.S. as a result of the growing tightness of banking funds. West German and Canadian banks were shifting substantial dollar balances out of U.S. banks and into Eurodollars, thereby increasing the supply of funds to the market. At the same time, the impact of the U.S. demand was at first tempered by the preference of many institutions for building up larger credit lines for use later in the year rather than for actual and immediate borrowing.

The development of these cyclical trends was sharply interrupted by the gold crisis of March. It was estimated that between mid-November and mid-March, sales of gold by members of the Gold Pool amounted to a massive total of over $3 billion, and it was clear that a substantial proportion of this had occurred in just a few days in March. Large Euro-dollar borrowings were drawn on to help finance this speculation and, in the face of this unprecedented demand, the Eurodollar deposit rate was forced up more than one and a half points to a mid-March peak of $7\frac{5}{16}\%$. The support given by central banks during this difficult period testified to the importance of this market as part of the international financial system.

Pressure on the rate was compounded by the accelerating demand for funds from U.S. banks. It was estimated that in the first half of the year the volume of funds taken in by the head offices of U.S. banks from their overseas branches totaled about $6 billion, some 50% more than under the extremely stringent credit conditions of 1966.

Subsequently, several developments encouraged a modestly declining trend in rates. The resale of speculative gold purchases following the Washington conference of March 16–17 was the first, but it was not until after the middle of the year, when the demands of the U.S. banks began to slacken in the face of an improving inflow of domestic deposit funds, that the trend really became apparent. By the end of August the rate had declined to a little over 6.1% but it rose sharply again in October and November in response to renewed speculation in international currency markets.

The level of activity in the Eurobond markets was very heavy in 1968, mainly because of restrictions on overseas investment imposed by the U.S. balance of payments program. The amounts raised were $728 million, $956 million, and $1.1 billion in the first, second, and third quarters, respectively, compared with $484 million, $455 million, and $335 million in the corresponding three quarters of 1967. An increasing proportion of these totals was accounted for by subsidiaries of U.S. firms. In the first three quarters, issues by these subsidiaries accounted for $1,677,000,-000 (60% of the total), compared with $525 million (28%) in all of 1967.

Rates on loans rose, at least in the first part of the year, with the general upward movement of rates in the major financial centres. A feature of the market was the increased popularity of convertible bond issues (fixed-interest issues that may, subject to certain conditions, be converted to holdings of preferred

"They ain't just a whistlin' Dixie, Wilbur!"
—Hy Rosen, "Albany Times-Union."

or ordinary shares of the company issuing them). In the six months to June 1968 there were 19 convertible bond issues (for a total of $524 million), compared with only one (for $20 million) in the corresponding period of 1967. In the third quarter of 1968, there were a further 18 such issues.

In the second half of the year, the growing speculation about possible revaluation of the Deutsche Mark provoked heavy activity in Deutsche Mark issues. In the third quarter, Deutsche Mark issues accounted for almost a third of total issues, compared with less than 5% in the third quarter of 1967.

United States. The renewed economic expansion of the second half of 1967 was not accompanied by any immediate tightening of the supply/demand situation for funds nor by any monetary restraint. Under these circumstances, it was apparent that expectational factors were causing rates to trend upward to levels little different from those reached in the extreme credit squeeze 12 months previously. The market uncertainty that produced this situation was itself the outcome of three principal factors: the continuing desire of business to restructure debt on a longer-term basis; forecasts of a need for heavy Treasury financing in 1968; and, above all, concern that the apparent inability of the administration to secure the 10% tax surcharge would inevitably produce the need for greater stringency in monetary policy.

This uncertainty affected the rates on both government and corporate securities. Its effect was felt most strongly at the long end of the market, but it also reflected on the shorter maturities. Thus a new seven-year government bond issue announced in October carried a $5\frac{3}{4}\%$ coupon rate, higher than on any Treasury issue for 46 years. The yield on new corporate securities stood several points higher in December 1967 than had been the case a year earlier, and the six-month Treasury bill rate, at 5.5%, was also up a fraction. The new $4\frac{1}{2}\%$ discount rate that followed the November 18 devaluation of the pound was seen merely as a complement to interest rate trends that were already well established.

The fears that the absence of a fiscal compromise between Congress and the administration would create the need for monetary stringency were justified when, in the last days of 1967, the Federal Reserve announced a $\frac{1}{2}\%$ increase in reserve requirements against bank demand deposits in excess of $5 million. This increase, which was expected to raise member banks' required reserves by $550 million, was the first since September 1966 and the first against demand deposits since 1960. It marked the beginning of a six-

KEYSTONE

London stockbrokers on Throgmorton Street reading morning newspapers on March 15, 1968, when the London Gold Market was closed in cooperation with a request from the U.S.

month period during which monetary instruments were asked to bear almost the full burden of restraining domestic inflation and easing the external deficit. This move, together with the temporarily more settled appearance of international currency markets, dissolved some of the uncertainties of the domestic capital market, and for the first time in several months investors seemed willing to commit funds on a long-term basis and at prevailing yields. This improvement was continued into January and February by the president's announcement of his program for dealing with the balance of payments deficit. By contrast, Treasury bill rates continued to rise through the turn of the year because of aggressive selling following news that a decision on the tax increase could not be made until the new year.

The gold crisis of March dictated a further $\frac{1}{2}\%$ increase in the discount rate, taking it to the highest level in nearly 40 years. This change gave another upward twist to short rates and reversed the modest downward move of rates on longer maturities that had been apparent in January and February. In mid-April the discount rate was increased yet again, by the same amount, in a further attempt to correct the disequilibriums in the economy by monetary means. May saw a peak in most rates, as increasing concern over the fiscal deadlock combined with the effects of the turmoil in France and new worries on the international monetary scene. The tax increases and government expenditure cuts finally became effective in July, and expectations of a moderation of growth and reduced credit requirements quickly established themselves. These expectations were given some hesitant official support when the discount rate was reduced by $\frac{1}{4}\%$ in the middle of August. Short-term rates moved up again, however, as the level of activity seemed temporarily unresponsive to the fiscal pressures and as speculative influences once again became important. The discount rate was raised to $5\frac{1}{2}\%$ on December 17.

The reintroduction of credit restraint at the close of 1967 produced a deterioration of the reserve position of the commercial banks and, consequently, a tightening of the availability of finance. By the end of June, the free reserves of the banks had fallen to an average of minus $350 million, compared with a positive average of $100 million at the turn of the year. This was about the worst position reached, however, and it was far from being as serious as in the second half of 1966.

Demand components varied in the extent to which

they contributed to turning this reduced availability of funds into an actual shortage. Inventory investment, which had been a major factor in reestablishing the boom in the autumn of 1967, was sluggish at first as the growth of consumption expenditures accelerated. Despite the recovery of this component later in the year, business loans for short-term purposes grew at rates marginally below those of the previous year. Real estate loans continued to grow rapidly in the first part of the year, but this growth moderated later as the banks became unwilling to make long-term commitments in light of their reduced deposit inflow. Bank loans for consumption purposes grew much more rapidly than had been the case in the second part of 1967.

The strain on the banks was accentuated as their relative competitiveness in attracting domestic deposits gradually declined. As early as December 1967, rates on certificates of deposit (the more interest-sensitive of bank deposits) were placed near the official ceiling of $5\frac{1}{2}\%$, but even so there were substantial net withdrawals. Most of these losses were made good in the somewhat easier conditions of early 1968, but losses began again when competing rates resumed their upward move in March. In April the Federal Reserve raised the general $5\frac{1}{2}\%$ ceiling to $5\frac{3}{4}\%$ on 60–89-day maturities, to 6% on 90–179-day maturities, and to $6\frac{1}{4}\%$ on longer-dated maturities. This move served to moderate the net outflow of funds from the banks, but could not halt it, and it was only with the decline in short rates in June that any improvement became evident. Later in the year the banks were able to achieve a good inflow of deposit funds even though they were offering rates somewhat below the maximum allowed.

Even in the first part of the year, however, the banks were able to meet the demands on them by making use of the heavy liquidity acquired in the previous year and by mobilizing their reserves of secondary liquidity. As has already been noted, they were heavy borrowers in the Eurodollar market and, in addition, they were heavy sellers of Treasury bills—a major factor contributing to the strong upward trend of rates on these instruments. The business sector was also partially able to insulate itself against the effects of restraint. In particular, businesses were able to draw down assets accumulated in the previous year and to borrow extensively on the international issues market. There can be little doubt that this second factor caused a substantial diversion of demand away from domestic markets.

Paralleling the heavy consumer loans by the banks, loans by finance companies and other purveyors of installment credit grew very rapidly. Dominant in this development were the large increase in automobile sales and the continued reliance of such sales on some form of installment credit. The effect of this increased demand was to produce rather more restrictive lending standards and somewhat higher lending rates, but moves in these directions did not go nearly as far as they had in the tight conditions of 1966. The finance houses continued to move away from bank loans as a means of financing their requirements, and by August their commercial paper debts amounted to more than three times their outstanding bank loans. The inflow of funds to savings and loan associations and mutual savings banks moderated parallel with that to the commercial banks, but since the typical investor in these institutions is less interest sensitive than the bank investor, the trend never went quite as far. Nev-

ertheless, it did contribute to some significant tightening of mortgage funds by midyear. A number of states with low interest ceilings on mortgages took steps to alleviate the tightness by raising them, and savings and loan associations maintained a steady growth of their mortgage lending by borrowing heavily from Federal Home Loan Banks.

United Kingdom. After the introduction of mild reflationary measures in mid-1967, the renewed selling pressures on the pound and the dismal prospects for the external balance prompted the devaluation of sterling's dollar parity to $2.40. Both fiscal and monetary measures were enacted to support this move, but since no moves were taken to advance the traditional spring budget, monetary measures were asked to bear the brunt of restraint between November and March. These measures included an increase in the bank rate to 8%, a tightening of installment credit on cars, and a "request" to the commercial banks to regard their mid-November level of advances as an aggregate ceiling that was not to be exceeded. This new ceiling applied to all lending outside the public sector except that associated with exports.

Despite these moves, the level of economic activity rose substantially in the latter part of 1967 and in 1968. The boom in consumers' expenditure persisted, and only showed signs of being halted by the extremely stringent budget of March 19. Bank advances also rose substantially; given the exemptions to the November ceiling, it was not possible to assess whether the ceiling was being exceeded, but it seems reasonable to assume that it was. In late May the Bank of England imposed a further tightening of credit and ruled that advances should be held at 104% of the November level, the new limit to include loans for exports. The banks had some difficulty in complying with this limit, but by September the Bank of England was able to note with appreciation that advances were within it. As part of the deflationary package of November 22 banks were asked for a further £100 million cut in advances by March 1969.

Rates on installment credit rose sharply in the first part of the year as the finance houses bid for funds to help finance the continuing consumption boom. The rise continued until May, when it was confirmed to the finance houses that the November ceiling would continue to apply to their lending. This announcement moderated the growth of business as well as the increase in borrowing rates. By September the level of outstanding installment credit stood at £1,230 million, as against £1,210 million in November, while the typical borrowing rate had fallen from a peak of something like 8¾% to about 7¾%. These trends were accentuated at the end of October by a somewhat surprising tightening of lending conditions as applied to car purchases and on November 22 by the imposition of further restraints comparable to that applied to the banks.

For the first part of the year, official short-term rates remained near the high levels they had reached at the time of devaluation. After that a belief that rates would fall caused the discount houses to raise their Treasury bill bid regularly through the end of March, by which time the tender rate was down ½% from its December level of 7¾%. The ½% reduction in the bank rate on March 21 caused the houses to raise their bid further; by April the tender rate stood at a fraction over 7%. A similar fall occurred when the bank rate was further reduced in September.

Rates on local authority temporary money rose quite sharply in February as a result of the general shortage of funds, the seasonal slack in the revenue inflow, and unwillingness to borrow on a longer-term basis. At one point in March, the rate on seven-day money exceeded 9½%. Rates fell by the end of March following the cut in the bank rate, but rose again in April. Thereafter the position eased considerably, with funds becoming more plentiful. By August the short-term rate was in a more normal position, about ½% below the long-term borrowing rate.

Prices of gilt-edged securities were steady at first following their sharp fall in November. They suffered setbacks during the gold crisis of March, however, and showed some recovery following the Washington gold conference and the upswing of prices in the U.S. The equity markets remained basically strong and prices rose significantly. The debenture market was kept quiet by the high level of yields and by the moderate nature of the demand for funds.

The consumption boom, coupled with a less rapid growth in personal disposable income, conspired to produce a significant reduction in the personal savings rate. This was especially serious from the point of view of the building societies which, with their relatively inflexible borrowing rates, suffered a reduction in their inflow of share and deposit funds—from £587 million in the second half of 1967 to £342 million in the first half of 1968. By the end of March this had resulted in severe rationing in the granting of new mortgages finance. Corrective steps were taken in April, when the Building Societies Association announced increases in borrowing rates and a new recommended advances rate of 7⅞%. This improved the situation, and in the first three quarters of the year, the growth of mortgages outstanding was significantly greater than in the same period of 1967.

Canada. Following the credit relaxation in the earlier part of 1967, wage costs and prices once again began to move upward in a rather disturbing fashion. The ½% increase in the discount rate in September marked the reintroduction of restraint, and tax increases and government expenditure cuts in November confirmed the reversal of policy. In the same month a new 6% discount rate was announced, both as an aid in dealing with the inflationary domestic situation and as a consequence of the U.K. devaluation. Considerable international speculation against the Canadian dollar built up early in the new year, despite the favourable reserve position and reasonable prospects for the balance of payments. Substantial capital transfers across the border by U.S. subsidiaries contributed to a worsening of the situation, and the Bank of Canada requested banks not to provide finance for such transfers. The bank rate was raised to 7% in January in response to the exchange pressures and a further ½% increase occurred in March in response to the gold crisis.

Short-term interest rates rose sharply in sympathy with this trend, and by the end of June the Treasury bill rate stood at 6.75%, compared with 4.34% a year earlier. With capital expenditures by both business and government running at levels only modestly above those of the previous year, pressures on longer rates were weaker and long and short rates remained very close together.

Indicators of the state of the economy were contradictory in the early part of the year; inflationary pressures seemed to be coexisting with symptoms of recession, such as a high level of unemployment. There was certainly no evidence that the boom was as

strong as in the U.S., and as soon as price pressures showed signs of easing, steps were taken to bring interest rates back to more normal levels. This was made even more necessary by pressures from an inflow of foreign funds. The discount rate was reduced in three steps, the last of which brought it down to 6% by the first week of September.

EEC Countries. The French economic recovery picked up again in the second part of 1967 in response to an easing of installment credit controls and the liquidity positions of the banks, and to expansionist fiscal measures. Further reflationary measures followed the announcement of the U.S. balance of payments program. The easier monetary policy was not sufficient to produce any reduction of interest rates, however. Both long and short rates rose steadily until the end of the year, despite a constant 3.5% discount rate.

The political disturbances of May and June caused a fundamental break in the general trend of the economy. The substantial capital outflow necessitated the reintroduction of exchange controls. The call-money rate rose to $5\frac{3}{4}\%$ by June and in July the discount rate was raised a full $1\frac{1}{2}\%$. While external considerations subsequent to the crisis seemed to dictate a continuation of high interest rates, the economic slack internally, the financing problems of corporations in the face of substantially inflated wage costs, and the political need for reduced unemployment all argued for a somewhat easier policy. In the event, the Banque de France opted for an easy policy with substantial purchases of securities on the open market. At the same time it sought a continuation of high short-term rates.

By September the loss of foreign exchange had slowed but was still serious, prices were rising rapidly, and the import bill had increased significantly. The economic problems arising from the crisis were therefore far from solved, and the prospects for the monetary situation far from certain. In mid-November moves to restrain credit were forced by renewed heavy losses of reserves. The discount rate was raised to 6%, the compulsory deposits of the banks with the Banque de France were raised, liquidity ratios were raised, and quantitative restrictions on lending were imposed. The loss of reserves, however, continued and it was only by recourse to heavy deflation at home that devaluation was avoided.

Recovery from the 1966–67 recession in West Germany began in the autumn of 1967, largely as a result of increased federal spending. Monetary factors did play their part, however, and the reduction of the reserve requirements of the banks throughout 1967 had a considerable effect. The banks continued to make use of part of their increased liquidity to purchase overseas assets, and this resulted in some deterioration in their domestic liquidity position in the early part of 1968. Long-term interest rates continued to fall, despite a somewhat higher level of government investment. Exports became the main component in what was by then a rapid growth of the national product, but consumption remained sluggish.

A major factor in the situation was the persistence of West Germany's massive current account surplus, giving rise to an outflow of long-term capital in the first six months amounting to $1,671,000,000, compared with $335 million in the first half of 1967. With prices remaining constant as the result of enormous productivity increases, monetary policy had no alternative but to remain easy. Even then, with heavy

Sir Leslie O'Brien, governor of the Bank of England, after returning from a meeting with other central bankers in Basel, Switz., July 9, 1968. He announced massive support for the pound from 12 of the world's richest nations and ruled out any further devaluation.

speculative inflows of short-term capital, the prospects for a revaluation of the parity became ever stronger. Germany refused to revalue but on November 21 it announced that its banks would have to surrender to the central bank all new receipts of foreign short-term funds. This move, it was hoped, would halt the massive inflow of speculative capital.

In the Netherlands the economic recovery proceeded more rapidly than had at first been anticipated, with the growth of industrial production in the year to September reaching approximately 6%. Exports were a major factor, and the current account deficit of the previous year was eliminated. The government was able to finance part of its deficit by short-term borrowing, but the difficulties of continuing this in the face of expansion gave rise to moderate interest-rate increases. Public-sector borrowing in the capital market was lower in the first part of the year, compared with the corresponding period of 1967. Private sector borrowing more than compensated for this, and the pressure on long rates persisted.

The cyclical recovery in Belgium continued to be assisted by easy money conditions, and a further $\frac{1}{4}\%$ reduction in the discount rate was made in March. At first the relative sluggishness of the domestic components of demand kept the pressure off interest rates and, as a result, both short and long rates moved in a rather different way from the international trend. By midyear, when the shorter rates did show signs of edging upward in response to increased domestic demand, international pressures on rates had, if anything, diminished. The Italian economy continued to experience stable growth in 1968. Interest rates remained steady, despite growing demands for funds. In the absence of any serious pressure on resources, monetary policy remained rather easy.

Japan. Economic expansion proceeded strongly through the end of 1967 and into 1968, and monetary policy was aimed in the restrictive direction. The September 1967 increase in the discount rate was followed by one of the same size in January 1968, bringing the rate to 6.205%. In addition, banks were requested to limit their increase in lending in the first quarter to 71% of that recorded a year earlier, and to 78% in the second quarter. Economic activity was definitely slowing by midyear and, with a considerable improvement in the current account balance, there were some expectations that policy would ease.   (A. R. R.)

See also Cooperatives; Economics; Economy, World; Government Finance; Housing; Investment, International; Merchandising; Payments and Reserves, International; Stock Exchanges.

Mongolia

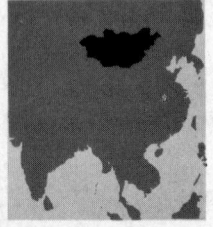

A people's republic of Asia lying between the U.S.S.R. and China, Mongolia occupies the geographical area known as Outer Mongolia. Area: 604,247 sq.mi. (1,565,000 sq. km.). Pop. (1967 est.): 1,156,200. Cap. and largest city: Ulan Bator (pop., 1966 est., 250,000). Language: Mongolian. Religion: Lamaistic Buddhism. First secretary of the Mongolian People's Revolutionary (Communist) Party and chairman of the Council of Ministers (premier) in 1968, Yumzhagiyin Tsedenbal; chairman of the Presidium of the Great People's Khural, Zhamsarangibin Sambuu.

Speaking at Ulan Bator on July 11, at the celebra-

MONGOLIA

Education. (1961–62) Primary, pupils 107,468; secondary, pupils 7,368; teachers (primary and secondary; 1960–61) 3,743; higher (at University of Ulan-Bator; 1963–64), students 7,700.

Finance. Monetary unit: tugrik, with an official parity of 4 tugriks to U.S. $1 (9.60 tugriks = £1 sterling) and a tourist rate of 6 tugriks to U.S. $1 (14.40 tugriks = £1 sterling). Budget (1966 est.): revenue 1,543,000,000 tugriks; expenditure 1,535,000,000 tugriks.

Foreign Trade. (1962) Imports 102.6 million rubles; exports 68.5 million rubles. Import sources (1960): U.S.S.R. 62%; China 23%; Czechoslovakia 5%. Export destinations: (1960) U.S.S.R. 75%; Czechoslovakia 8%; China 5%. Main exports (1960): wool 44%; cattle 34%; butter and meat 8%; hides 6%.

Transport and Communications. Roads (1960) c. 75,000 km. (including c. 7,500 km. motorable). Railways (route length, including cross-border links with U.S.S.R. and China; 1965) 1,427 km. Telephones (Jan. 1967) 14,200. Radio receivers (Dec. 1961) 25,000.

Agriculture. Production (in 000; metric tons; 1966; 1965 in parentheses): wheat c. 325 (c. 300); potatoes c. 27 (c. 27). Livestock (in 000; 1965): cattle 2,093; sheep 13,838; goats 4,786; pigs 20; horses 2,433; camels 685.

Industry. Production (in 000; metric tons; 1965): coal 45; crude oil 16; electricity 199,000 kw-hr.

tion of the 47th Independence Day, Premier Tsedenbal stated that the Soviet-Mongolian alliance, renewed on Jan. 15, 1966, for 20 years, was the surest guarantee of Mongolian sovereignty and freedom. He added that thanks to the economic help from the Soviet Union and other member countries of the Council for Mutual Economic Assistance, Mongolia was being transformed into a modern industrial-agrarian state.

In September two prominent guests from the Communist bloc visited Mongolia: Willi Stoph, chairman of the Council of Ministers of East Germany, and Marshal Marian Spychalski, chairman of the Council of State of Poland. According to the old Mongol tradition, both were greeted at the airport with a drink of curdled mare's milk and shouts of *Nairamdal!* ("Friendship!").

Stoph and Tsedenbal signed on September 12 a new 20-year treaty of friendship and cooperation, mainly economic and technical. During Spychalski's visit on September 24 a trade agreement for 1969 was signed. Spychalski also visited a division of the Mongolian Army and the new industrial town of Darkhan (Blacksmith), built by Soviet, Polish, Czechoslovakian, and Hungarian technicians.

Because of Mongolia's friendship with the Soviet Union, relations with Communist China continued to be tense. In addition to the Soviet motorized infantry division stationed in Mongolia since 1966, the presence of Soviet mobile ground-to-air rocket batteries, as well as medium-range ballistic missiles, was reported in 1968; the weapons were placed near the town of Choybalsan, linked directly to the Soviet Trans-Siberian Railway. (K. SM.)

Morocco

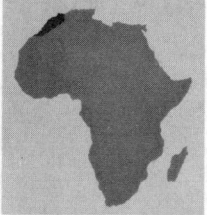

A constitutional monarchy of northwestern Africa, on the Atlantic Ocean and the Mediterranean Sea, Morocco is bordered by Algeria and Spanish Sahara. Area: 174,471 sq.mi. (451,880 sq.km.). Pop. (1966 est.): 13,882,-000. Cap.: Rabat (pop., 1960, 227,445). Largest city:

Casablanca (pop., 1960, 965,277). Language: Arabic; Berber. Religion: Muslim. King, Hassan II; prime minister in 1968, Muhammad Benhima.

The year in Morocco was dominated by economic problems. The 1968–72 development plan was launched at the beginning of the year. Its drafting, its adoption, and the search for the means to finance it occupied a large part of the government's attention both at home and abroad.

The plan envisaged a total investment of about 5 billion dirhams ($1 billion). Its aim was to raise the national income of Morocco by 5%, allowing for an increase in population of 3.2% per annum. One-third of the credits allowed were to be devoted to agriculture, dams, and irrigation projects. Of the total, 1.8 billion dirhams were to be raised from external and 1.5 billion dirhams from internal resources, leaving 1.7 billion dirhams to be found in 1968 to complete the financing of the plan.

With this aim the Moroccan authorities issued a compulsory loan during the course of the year and developed contacts with international organizations and with various countries, in particular France. In the case of France the launching of the five-year plan would provide an opportunity to improve a relationship that had deteriorated as a result of the "freeze" on Franco-Moroccan relations following the kidnapping and presumed killing of Mehdi ben Barka in Paris three years earlier. An agreement was signed

MOROCCO

Education. (1965–66) Primary, pupils 1,124,078, teachers 27,621; secondary, pupils 170,890, teachers 8,100; vocational, pupils (1964–65) 19,052; teacher training, students 1,057, teachers (1964–65) 88; higher (including 3 universities), students 8,535, teaching staff 437.

Finance. Monetary unit: dirham, with a par value of 5.06 dirhams to U.S. $1 (12.15 dirhams = £1 sterling). Gold and foreign exchange, central bank: (June 1968) U.S. $83 million; (June 1967) U.S. $73 million. Budget (1968 est.): revenue 2,365,000,000 dirhams; expenditure 2,486,000,000 dirhams. Money supply: (May 1968) 4,310,000,000 dirhams; (May 1967) 3,859,000,000 dirhams. Cost of living (Casablanca; 1963 = 100): (June 1968) 105; (June 1967) 103.

Foreign Trade. (1967) Imports 2,617,000,000 dirhams; exports 2,146,000,000 dirhams. Import sources (1966): France 40%; U.S. 8%; West Germany 7%. Export destinations (1966): France 46%; West Germany 7%; U.K. 5%. Main exports (1966): phosphates 25%; citrus fruit 15%; tomatoes 7%; fish 6%.

Transport and Communications. Roads (1966) 24,175 (including 14 km. expressways). Motor vehicles in use (1966): passenger 168,602; commercial 61,276. Railways: (1964) 1,756 km. (including 760 km. electrified); traffic (1966) 449 million passenger-km., freight 2,216,000,000 net ton-km. Shipping (1967): merchant vessels 100 gross tons and over 35; gross tonnage 65,343. Air traffic (1966): 238,410,000 passenger-km.; freight 4,451,000 net ton-km. Telephones (Dec. 1966) 143,074. Radio receivers (Dec. 1966) c. 748,000. Television receivers (Dec. 1966) 36,000.

Agriculture. Production (in 000; metric tons; 1967; 1966 in parentheses): wheat 1,090 (814); barley 1,100 (506); corn 255 (154); oranges 614 (596); dry peas 32 (32); dry broad beans 52 (54); chick-peas 67 (41); wine c. 130 (c. 210); olive oil c. 20 (c. 17); figs (1966) 59, (1965) 79; dates (1966) 90, (1965) 85; tomatoes (1966) 303, (1965) 291; linseed c. 7 (8). Livestock (in 000; 1965–66): cattle c. 3,000; sheep c. 14,500; goats c. 7,600; asses c. 1,035; horses and mules c. 705; camels c. 212. Fish catch (in 000; metric tons) (1966) 303, (1965) 215.

Industry. Production (in 000; metric tons; 1966): coal 451; iron ore (55–60% metal content; 1967) 892; phosphate rock 9,438; manganese ore (metal content) 161; lead concentrates (metal content; 1967) 78; zinc concentrates (metal content; 1967) 35; crude oil 103; cement (1967) 873; electricity 1,431,000 kw-hr.

Monophysite Churches: *see* Religion

Montserrat: *see* Dependent States

Mormons: *see* Religion

between the two countries in August, as a result of which France was to provide the necessary credits for the building of a sugar refinery in the Casablanca region, for the purchase of a Caravelle airliner, and for the purchase of railway equipment.

Events in France in May and June had serious repercussions in Morocco in the economic field. First the strikes and then the protectionist measures taken by the French government caused a reduction in Moroccan exports of fruit and early vegetables for the French market.

These unexpected happenings gave further encouragement to the Moroccan authorities to seek wider outlets for their exports. As a result, a far-reaching trade agreement was signed with the U.S.S.R. in June by which the U.S.S.R. would buy 200,000 tons of citrus fruit from Morocco and so become its second largest customer for those products.

The crisis in France had another effect: it led the Moroccan government to make a particular effort in regard to the youth of the country. In July the Ministry of Education was divided into four new departments: for primary education; for secondary and technical education; for higher education; and for culture. The Moroccan leaders were deeply disturbed by the threat that an extremist minority of students could pose to a state such as France, which was considered to be strong and stable. King Hassan II wanted to widen his scope of action as much as possible by dividing up the Ministry of Education and by making the different ministers responsible directly to him.

In the diplomatic field Morocco wished to take the initiative with regard to inter-Arab and inter-Muslim relations. In December 1967 it proposed an Arab summit conference to be held in Rabat in January 1968. However, the meeting was finally postponed indefinitely because of the doubts of the so-called progressive Arab countries. From then on Morocco wished to widen the discussion and to interest Muslim countries generally (and not only the Arab countries) in finding a solution to the Arab-Israeli dispute, thus returning to the idea of an "Islamic alliance."

In April King Hassan II undertook a tour of the Middle East which took him to Turkey, Iran, Saudi Arabia, and Tunisia. In return, the shah of Iran visited Morocco in June for a few days, thus giving the two rulers an opportunity to discuss problems involving the Mediterranean basin.   (D. Da.)

ENCYCLOPÆDIA BRITANNICA FILMS. *Mediterranean Africa* (1952).

Motor Sports

Automobiles. Automobile racing suffered triumphs and tragedies in 1968 but continued to grow in technological virtuosity, in popularity, and in competition facilities. The death in April of Jim Clark of Scotland (*see* OBITUARIES), twice world driving champion and winner of a record 25 Grand Prix races, cast a pall over the year. Clark's Lotus Formula II car hit a tree at Hockenheim, W.Ger., when a tire seemed to flat out, and he was killed instantly. He had just won the Tasman Cup, symbolic of racing supremacy in New Zealand and Australia, and the South African Grand Prix.

The year was generally one of close competition. The Grand Prix title was not decided until the final race in Mexico City, and the U.S. National Association

for Stock Car Auto Racing (NASCAR) and the United States Auto Club (USAC) championships were also undecided until the final races. In Europe BMW won the touring car crown on the final race while Porsche won the hill climb championship. It was also a year in which the race courses at Monte Carlo, Le Mans, France, and Sebring, Fla., were revised and a new Michigan International Speedway was utilized for major events.

Grand Prix racing was continued under the formula stipulating the use of normal gasoline as fuel and an engine size not exceeding 3,000 cc. The drivers' world championship was in doubt up to the final race of the series in Mexico City in November, when Graham Hill of the U.K. clinched the title for the second time in his career, driving for the Lotus-Cosworth team. The engine used in these cars, which achieved the manufacturers' championship, was sponsored by the Ford Motor Company.

Technical innovations in Grand Prix racing included very wide-section tires to enable the full power of the three-litre engines to be transmitted to the road, aerofoils to give greater adhesion during cornering, new rubber mixes and tread patterns for racing tires in the ever-present battle to find the ideal wet/dry-road tire, and a new Honda air-cooled Grand Prix car which was unfortunately raced without sufficient testing and crashed on its first appearance, its inexperienced driver being burned to death.

After Jim Clark had won the South African Grand Prix in his Lotus in January (his 25th Grand Prix win, thereby beating Juan Fangio's previous record of 24), the Grand Prix season warmed up with a world championship contest in Spain, over 90 laps of the Jarama circuit. Hill won at an average speed of 84.358 mph, and the only other competitor to complete 90 laps was Denis Hulme, the 1967 world champion, in a McLaren-Cosworth. The return of France to international motor racing was reflected in the fastest lap being made by J.-P. Beltoise in a Matra-Cosworth, at 86.192 mph. In the Monaco race at Monte Carlo in May there were only five finishers and only two cars ran the full 80 laps of the famous round-the-streets circuit. The winner again was Hill (Lotus-Cosworth), 77.773 mph, with R. Attwood (BRM V-12) in second place. Accidents eliminated Bruce McLaren, Jack Oliver, and Pedro Rodriguez. The Belgian Grand Prix followed in June, over the fast Spa course. In this race there were seven finishers, of whom three went the full distance. McLaren won at 147.138 mph in his McLaren M7A-Cosworth V-8 from Rodriguez (BRM V-12) and Jacky Ickx (Ferrari V-12). The fastest race-lap was established by John Surtees in the Japanese Honda V-12, who set a new record of 149.748 mph.

The Dutch Grand Prix took place as usual over the Zandvoort circuit in the Netherlands and Jackie Stewart of Scotland brought a Matra-Cosworth V-8 home first at 84.608 mph, an Anglo-French victory because the Cosworth engine had been made in England. Beltoise's Matra, with a Matra V-12 engine, was second and Rodriguez' BRM was third. Accidents befell Lucien Bianchi, McLaren, Jack Brabham, and Piers Courage, and out of 19 starters 10 finished. The 1968 French Grand Prix was held at Rouen and was run in heavy rain. It was marred by the aforesaid accident to Jo Schlesser in the new V-8 Honda, who had had little experience either with this car or with Formula I racing. Ickx gained the day for Ferrari, his V-12-engined car averaging 100.5 mph

in winning from Surtees in an older Honda and Stewart in a Matra-Cosworth. J. Servoz-Gavin crashed his Cooper-BRM. It was the turn of Brands Hatch to stage the British Grand Prix, and in good weather Jo Siffert brought a Lotus-Cosworth home first, winning from Chris Amon and Ickx, both driving Ferrari V-12s. Siffert's speed was 104.83 mph, and the Lotus 49B made the fastest lap, at the record speed of 106.290 mph. The German Grand Prix, over the very difficult Nürburgring, was rendered a dangerous and miserable race by rain and mist. Stewart proved himself a master, displaying great skill and courage which gave him a well-deserved victory in an aerofoil-equipped Matra MS-10-Cosworth V-8. In spite of the very poor conditions and one wrist in a plaster cast, Stewart averaged 86.816 mph and set the fastest lap, at 88.617 mph. Surprisingly, 14 of the 20 starters finished. Second place went to Hill's Lotus.

The world championship returned to a fast circuit, at Monza, for the Italian Grand Prix in September. Hulme was the winner, in a McLaren-Cosworth, at 145.328 mph with Servoz-Gavin's Matra-Cosworth second and Ickx's Ferrari V-12 third. This was after Oliver had set a fastest lap of 148.609 mph in a

The Porsche team finished second and third, the drivers being R. Steinemann-D. Spoerry and R. Stommelen-J. Neerpasch, ahead of three Italian Alfa Romeo Tipo 33s. The last remaining open-road race, the strenuous Targa Florio over the Sicilian mountains, resulted in a win for the Porsche 907 eight-cylinder, 2.2-litre car from Germany, driven by Vic Elford and U. Maglioli, but it was challenged strongly by the Alfa Romeo Tipo 33 V-8s. Other important long-distance European sports-car races were the Monza and the Nürburg 1,000-km. The former was taken by a Team Gulf Ford GT-40 of Paul Hawkins from Porsche and Alpine Renault cars, and the latter was won by the Siffert-Elford Porsche 3-litre 908, with a Porsche 907 second and the Hawkins-Ickx Ford GT-40 third.

In international rallying the Monte Carlo Rally was a Porsche benefit, two Porsche 911s leading home a BMC Mini-Cooper. The Royal Automobile Club (RAC) Rally was won by a Swedish Saab (S. Lampinen-J. Davenport) with another Saab placing second. The RAC world rally championship, decided after seven rallies, was won by Porsche from Ford. The rally season concluded with the great London-

Cooper-BRM V-12 and Chris Amon, John Surtees, and the rally driver Vic Elford had crashed. The Grand Prix competition then moved to the American continent for the concluding three championship races. The Canadian Grand Prix at Mont Tremblant, Que., saw Hulme first home in a McLaren-Cosworth at 97.192 mph, McLaren second in a similar car, and Rodriguez third for BRM. Only seven cars finished. At Watkins Glen, N.Y., for the United States Grand Prix, Stewart came in first for Matra, at 124.815 mph, but Hill was second in a Lotus and Surtees managed third place for Honda. Again, many drivers were forced to drop out.

At the final race in Mexico, Hill won after a drive lasting 1 hr. 56 min. 43.95 sec., with McLaren second and Oliver third. The drivers' world championship had been between Hill, Stewart, and Hulme, but in this decisive event Hulme crashed and Stewart's engine developed trouble.

In Europe the Le Mans 24-hour sports-car race was postponed because of the French strikes, but it was held late in the year and its popularity was undiminished. It proved a victory for Ford of the U.S. for the third successive year, the winning car being a GT-40 entered by J. W. Automotive and driven by Rodriguez and Bianchi. They had the 4.9-litre V-8 Ford engine and covered 2,765.238 mi. in the 24 hours.

Start of the British Grand Prix at Brands Hatch, July 20, 1968, won by Jo Siffert driving a Lotus-Cosworth. The airfoils seen over most of the cars are used to increase traction while braking and cornering.

Sydney Marathon sponsored jointly by the London *Daily Express* and the Sydney *Daily Telegraph*. The race was won by the Rootes team (driver A. Cowan) with a Hillman Hunter.

The USAC continued to dilute the importance of the world's oldest and richest race, the Indianapolis 500, by miring itself in technological and legal controversy. After winning a lawsuit brought by turbine engine exponent Andy Granatelli, USAC officials—who were further to restrict turbines and four-wheel drive—watched as the already radically restricted Colin Chapman-designed turbine cars again almost won the 500. During the qualifying trials Joe Leonard in a turbine car had achieved the pole position with an all-time record speed of 171.523 mph. The weather was warmer on race day, which hurt the turbines' fuel-air mixture, but Leonard was leading at the 191-lap mark when a fuel system component sheared, handing the race and $171,523 to Bobby Unser of Albuquerque, N.M., and his turbocharged Eagle-Offenhauser. Britain's Graham Hill had crashed his turbine early, while Art Pollard of the U.S. had to drop out with the same trouble that stopped Leonard. Second in the 500 was American Dan Gurney in a

stock block Ford, while Mel Kenyon finished third and New Zealander Denis Hulme, fourth. Only 11 of the 33 starters finished the race as Unser set a record average speed of 152.822 mph. Other USAC titlists were veteran A. J. Foyt in the stock car division and Larry Dickson in the sprint cars.

NASCAR remained the organization that conducted the most races and the most events in the U.S., drawing crowds of 50,000 or more. But decreased manufacturer support and generally bad weather contributed to a year of less excitement than usual.

In the Daytona 500, a stock car classic, Cale Yarborough of Timmonsville, S.C., qualified for the race at a speed of 189.22 mph, but his winning time was only 143.251 mph, 11 mph slower than the record. Yarborough went on to win three other major events, including a car-length victory over Ford's David Pearson in the Southern 500, at Darlington, S.C., probably the most exciting race of the NASCAR season. He also won the Atlanta 500 and the Daytona Firecracker 400 en route to a NASCAR money-winning record of $136,786.

Ford's David Pearson and Dodge's Bobby Isaac fought all season for the point championship with defender Richard Petty, a late challenger for Plymouth. Petty won the Rockingham (N.S.) 500, the final major race of the season, to tie Pearson in most Grand National victories (16), but Pearson's second-place finish earned him enough points to win the season championship, worth about $50,000. Isaac, who finished second in the point standings, was sidelined late in the Rockingham race with a broken valve.

The fastest growing racing organization during 1968 was the Sports Car Club of America (SCCA) which, late in the year, split into separate professional and amateur divisions. SCCA continued to have great success with its two Group Seven car series, the United States Road Racing Championship and the Canadian-American Challenge Cup, as well as with its Trans-American Sedan Championship. Mark Donohue of Media, Pa., won the Trans-American Sedan series easily for Chevrolet Camaro, finishing first in 10 of 13 events. Ford Mustang won the other three to fight off a surprisingly strong American Motors Javelin challenge. Donohue also won his second straight U.S. Road Racing crown in a Penske Sunoco McLaren-Chevrolet. And he was a major contender in the Can-Am, richest series of all for two-seater racing cars with engines of six and seven litres. In this series he won the Bridgehampton (N.Y.) Grand Prix after

Hulme had won the annual race at Elkhart Lake, Wis. Hulme added a victory in Edmonton, Alta. Donohue's dream of winning the Can-Am and thus three championships in a single year went glimmering in the final race of the season when a last-minute ignition defect prevented him from starting the Stardust Grand Prix in Las Vegas, Nev. That left the Can-Am title to a contest between the New Zealanders, Hulme and defending champion Bruce McLaren, who had won the rich *Los Angeles Times* Grand Prix at Riverside, Calif. Hulme won the Stardust and the title easily, as McLaren was involved in an early accident.

The two U.S. endurance classics in Florida early in the season seemed to indicate that Porsche would easily win the title. The 24-Hours of Daytona in February saw the West German cars finish first, second, and third, led by the team of Vic Elford and Jochen Neerpasch. The Sebring 12-hr. race ended with Hans Hermann-Jo Siffert in a Porsche leading the Daytona winners across the line.

Defending champion Mario Andretti piloted three different cars at the Riverside, Calif., 300 in a vain effort to overtake Bobby Unser in the point standings. Dan Gurney won the race in his Olsonite Eagle, with Unser second. Both Unser and Andretti, with 4,330 and 4,319 points, respectively, shattered a championship point total record that had been set before World War I.   (R. J. Fe.; W. C. Bo.)

Motorcycles. The international road-racing season ended with three men sharing five world titles. Giacomo Agostini of Italy, riding three-cylinder MV Agusta machines, headed the 350-cc. and 500-cc. classes; Englishman Phil Read on Yamaha two-strokes brought off victories in both the 125-cc. and 250-cc. groups (the first time this had occurred since 1960 when Italian Carlo Ubbiali achieved it); and, for the third successive year, Hans Georg Anscheidt of West Germany won the 50 cc. on a Japanese Suzuki two-stroke.

Much of the interest in the racing was diminished by the withdrawal from competition of the Honda factory, following that of Suzuki. This meant that Mike Hailwood, the most consistently successful rider of recent years, was unable to compete in championship events on his four- and six-cylinder Hondas, leaving Agostini with little real opposition in the 350-cc. and 500-cc. classes. In 125-cc. and 250-cc. events the leading exponents, Phil Read and Bill Ivy, were under contract to the same factory, Yamaha; for lack of any worthwhile competition from other riders, they came up with intense duels which, partway through the series, at the Czechoslovakian Grand Prix in July, degenerated into a personal feud. On this occasion Read, after clinching the 125-cc. world title, ignored Yamaha team orders virtually to step aside for Ivy's domination of the 250-cc. class. This latter title was in dispute until the Italian Grand Prix at Monza in September, when Read won the 250-cc. event, allowing him to tie Ivy for the title.

Hailwood, though unable to compete in world championship events, had the use of factory machines on a "private" owner basis in certain international meetings, notably the Race of the Year at Mallory Park (U.K.) and the Hutchinson 100 and Race of the South meetings at Brands Hatch, Eng. In the Race of the Year, riding his 297-cc. Honda in all events open to him, he won as he pleased, proving that he was a match for Agostini even when giving away 200 cc. of engine capacity when the Italian was riding his full-size 500.

Table I. U.S. Motorboat Offshore Champions

Inboard
   Don Aronow
   Miami, Fla.
Outboard
   Bob Magoon
   Miami, Fla.

Three Porsches crossing the finish line nearly simultaneously to sweep the top positions in the 24 Hours of Daytona international race, Feb. 4, 1968.

LONDON "DAILY EXPRESS" FROM PICTORIAL PARADE

Tommy Sopwith and his co-driver Charles de Selincourt driving their 600-hp. "Telstar" to a first-place finish in the English Channel International Daily Express Offshore Powerboat Race, Aug. 31, 1968.

The championship season ended with the news that Yamaha, too, was withdrawing from racing. The only major firms still entering race teams were MV Agusta and Benelli of Italy and MZ of East Germany.

In world championship moto cross the 1968 winners were Paul Friedrichs of East Germany (500 cc.) and Joel Robert of Belgium (250 cc.), both riding Czechoslovakian CZ machines. Two leading British riders in the championships in recent years, Dave Bickers and Jeff Smith, announced their retirement from moto-cross championship competition.

The much-publicized British effort to capture the chief prizes in the International Six Days Trial, held at San Pellegrino in the Italian Alps in October, ended in the worst U.K. performance in many years. West Germany won, breaking East Germany's record of five successive victories in the main Trophy class, while Britain finished last of the seven competing teams.

Motorcycle production in Britain in 1968 continued to soar, but U.K. ownership declined. More than three-quarters of the production of the leading factories of BSA, Triumph, and Norton-Villiers was exported. (C. J. AY.)

Motorboats. Unlimited hydroplane racing suffered its sixth fatality in two years when Warner Gardner died of injuries received in the Gold Cup Race on the Detroit River September 8. Gardner's Eagle Electric became airborne in the final race for the Cup and flipped at more than 125 mph. Gardner, a 52-year-old retired U.S. Air Force colonel from Bay City, Mich., died the following day.

Gardner had shared domination of the unlimited circuit with Seattle's Bill Schumacher, the U.S. national champion. Schumacher, the 26-year-old driver of "Miss Bardahl," virtually took turns with Gardner in winning most of the races during the year. Schumacher won the Gold Cup Race, his second straight victory in that event. He averaged 111.248 mph, compared with his 1967 winning average of 104.691.

Schumacher and Gardner had been heavy favorites in the world unlimited hydroplane championship, which took place August 4 at Seattle, Wash. Both were plagued with mechanical problems, however, and the title went to Bill Muncey, who finished first, second, and third in the three heats.

On the international scene, an Italian industrialist and sportsman became the first European to win the world ocean powerboat racing championship. Vin-

cenzo Balestrieri began with a victory March 2 in the Sam Griffith Memorial Race at Fort Lauderdale, Fla. The diminutive Milanese became the first European ever to defeat the U.S. competitors, who had invented modern offshore powerboat racing in their own waters. The Fort Lauderdale event was the first race in 1968 offering points toward the world driving championship, and it started Balestrieri on his way toward the crown.

With U.S. mechanic Don Pruett, the Italian skipper moved on to the European part of the ocean racing circuit. He placed second in the Wills International race off the coast of England June 29, but followed this with a string of victories: the Naples (Italy) Trophy Race, July 14; the Viareggio-Bastia-Viareggio Race, July 21; France's Dauphin D'Or, August 4; and the Swedish International, August 11. These performances gave Balestrieri five wins in six races, an accomplishment that no offshore racer had ever previously achieved in Union of International Motorboating events.

Bad luck followed when Balestrieri and Pruett sank in the English Cowes-Torquay Race on August 31. And back in the U.S. for the Miami-Nassau Ocean Powerboat Race, a flash fire shortly after the start put Pruett in the hospital with burns. But Balestrieri had gained 51 points on the international circuit and had piled up a lead that guaranteed him the world driving championship no matter who won the few races left on the calendar. None of the previous winners of the Hennessy-Sam Griffith Memorial Trophy, symbolizing the international championship, had ever ended the season so many points ahead as Balestrieri. (JA. E. M.)

Mountaineering

The winter of 1967–68 saw further first winter ascents of difficult routes in the Alps. Among these were the northeast face of Piz Badile, by M. Darbellay, C. Bournissen, D. Troillet, P. Armando, G. Calcagno, and A. Cogna; the north face of the Dent Blanche by C. Bournissen (solo, by a line near the Vaucher route); the west face of the Weisshorn, by R. and F. Theytaz; the north face of the Aiguille Blanche de Peuterey by four Polish climbers; the northeast face of the Lenzspitze by P. Etter and H. Wenin; and the east face of the Watzmann by F. Rasp (solo). The summer of 1968 was one in a recent series of bad seasons, and few climbers were able to carry out ambitious programs; the new routes made were mostly small or on lesser peaks. Noteworthy was the solo ascent of the Walker Spur of the Grandes Jorasses by A. Cogna.

In Norway several difficult new routes were made in the Romsdal area in 1967 by British and French parties. In 1967, also, an expedition from the University of St. Andrews, Scot., climbed 17 peaks on Upernavik Island, Greenland, and in 1968 an Irish expedition made several ascents in the Tasermuit Fjord area near Cape Farewell, N.Z.

Himalayan climbing continued to be restricted by the ban on expeditions imposed by the Nepalese government. This ban was lifted at last in 1968, and ascents of major peaks were expected in 1969. Meanwhile, only minor ascents could be recorded. In the Annapurna Range in 1967, P. Lammerer and H. Scharschinger, with porters, attempted the east face of Lamjung Peak (22,638 ft.) and climbed Charim

Motor Vehicles:
see Disasters;
Industrial Review;
Motor Sports;
Transportation

A British expedition led by Ian Clough climbed the Fortress (above) in the Chilean Andes, for the first time, reaching the summit on Jan. 7, 1968, after five weeks. Blizzards (left) and sheer rock faces (below) make this one of South America's most formidable peaks.

Kokero in the Ganesh Himal (19,849 ft.). A Chinese scientific expedition reached the North Col of Everest early in 1967. In Kulu (India) a British expedition succeeded in climbing Mukar Beh (19,910 ft.) in June 1968 after several other attempts, including one in which a party of three had died in its tent, had failed.

Many parties had been active in the Hindu Kush in the latter part of 1967. Japanese and English expeditions climbed in the central Afghan Hindu Kush. An Austrian group explored the Yarkhun Range and ascended several peaks. A West German party from Munich led by A. Linsbauer climbed Koh-i-Chiantar (21,037 ft.) and 12 other peaks. A Czech party ascended Tirich Mir and made the first ascent of Tirich West I (24,564 ft.).

The summer of 1967–68 was a good one in New Zealand and much climbing was done. The most noteworthy of the new routes were done on the south faces of Hooker and Crosscut; other new face routes were on Haidinger, Tutuko, and Talbot. Tasman, the second highest mountain in New Zealand, was climbed via the couloir from the Fox Glacier, which had been used as a means of descent once previously.

Sir Edmund Hillary's expedition to the Ross Dependency in the Antarctic made the first and second ascents of Mt. Herschel (11,700 ft.) on the Ross Sea coast from Hallett Base. Official New Zealand parties climbed many summits in the far northwest of the dependency while engaged in survey work. The American Antarctic Mountaineering Expedition climbed Mt. Tyree (16,290 ft.), the second highest peak in Antarctica, and five other mountains early in 1967.

In Alaska a U.S. expedition made the first ascents of Mt. Willard Gibbs (12,525 ft.) and Blackcliff Mountain (10,270 ft.) in the Chugach Range. Another U.S. party made a 90-mi. traverse of the Kenai Range and the first ascents of Truuli Peak (6,612 ft.) and Node Nunatak (5,912 ft.). A Japanese party failed in an attempt on King Peak, in the St. Elias Range. Mt. St. Elias itself received its fifth ascent, by the southeast ridge, and Mt. Fairweather its third ascent, by the west ridge. The southeast face of Lotus Flower Tower in the Logan Mountains was climbed by a highly mechanized route, perhaps the most difficult to date in this area. In the Yukon the north face

of Mt. Kennedy was climbed. The ascent required 26 days.

In the Canadian Rockies new routes were made on Mt. Assiniboine in 1967. In 1968 the Appalachian Mountain Club expedition to the northern Selkirks climbed 14 peaks, including Mt. Sir Sandford. The first ascent of the east ridge of this peak was made by another U.S. party. Ascents in the U.S. in 1968 included very hard mechanized climbs in the Yosemite Valley, California, on Longs Peak, Colorado, and on Cathedral Ledges, New Hampshire.

South America was once again the scene of great activity, and still presented as much scope for pioneering as anywhere in the world. While a Japanese expedition to the Sierra Nevada de Santa Marta in Colombia had climbed 15 new peaks in 1967 and a U.S. party had ascended the north ridge of Chimborazo in Ecuador in 1968, most of the activity was occurring in the Peruvian Andes.

Along the western slopes the Cordillera Blanca saw many parties at work where in 1967 a Japanese expedition made several new routes, including one on Santa Cruz Norte (19,125 ft.) by the west face. A Spanish expedition climbed three new peaks, attempted Chopicalqui, and made the third ascent of Alpamayo (19,510 ft.) and the second of Tayapampa (18,615 ft.). The first ascent of Chopicalqui Norte was made by a U.S. party. Another U.S. party climbed Nevado Ango and three unnamed peaks in the Ruri Chinchoy area. Another ascended Atlante (17,930 ft.) and the south peak of Akilpo, Quebrada Honda.

On the eastern side in the Cordillera de Carabaya, a New Zealand expedition climbed 19 peaks in 1967, including 4 virgins and 5 new routes. The Cordillera de Huayhuash saw two Japanese expeditions in 1967, one of them climbing three new peaks. The New Zealand Andean Expedition of 1968 made the first ascent of the northwest spur and north ridge of Yerupaja (21,765 ft.); a U.S. party climbed its northeast face direct. In the Urubamba region a Japanese party made the second ascent of Veronica (18,861 ft.) in 1967. A German party climbing in central Peru in 1967 bagged 14 new peaks in the region between the Yauyos and Cochas groups. Italians in 1967 climbed Condoriri (18,556 ft.) in the Cordillera Real by a new route on the east face. Germans climbed Illampu (20,873 ft.) by the southwest face.

In the Northern Andes of Chile a Chilean expedition made the first ascent of El Ermitado (20,145 ft.) in 1967. Farther south, the Patagonia region of Argentina saw considerable activity in the summer of 1967–68. A British expedition attempted a new route on Cerro Torre, in the Fitzroy Range, by the southeast ridge, but were foiled by the notorious weather of this region. In the Cordillera de Paine (Chile) a British expedition led by I. Clough climbed the Fortress (9,040 ft.), while an Italian expedition ascended the nearby Shield (8,038 ft.). A Chilean expedition in the area at the same time made the first ascent of Principal Cuernos (8,048 ft.).

The annual meeting of the Union Internationale des Associations d'Alpinisme was held in London in October 1968. Among the proposals put to the meeting for its approval was one for an international system for grading the difficulty of climbs, to replace the numerous systems used in climbing guidebooks to the various ranges of the world. The international system was based on a numerical assessment of technical difficulty, separately numbered for free and artificial climbing and for the use of expansion bolts. (Jo. N.)

Museums and Galleries

Museums and galleries continued to enjoy sustained growth during 1968 and in many respects reflected the social and economic changes taking place throughout the world. The second International Campaign for Museums, organized by the International Council of Museums (ICOM), was opened on Oct. 1, 1967, at a ceremony held in the National Museum in Warsaw and ended a year later. Special exhibitions and programs on the role of museums were held in many countries and ICOM launched a series of articles on "The Museum and the Public" as part of the campaign. Of special concern was the fact that statistics on growing museum attendance and the actual growth in numbers of museums reflected, in part, the increase in the number of special exhibitions, which appeared to be attracting the same persons over and over, rather than the overcoming of the passivity and indifference to museums of much of the public.

Two examples of international cooperation were the exhibition of Gothic art organized by the Council of Europe in which many major as well as little known objects were brought together, and the exhibition of Renaissance frescoes sent to the Metropolitan Museum of New York by the city of Florence as a gesture of appreciation. (*See* ART EXHIBITIONS.) Unusual acquisitions included the transfer of the Temple of Dendur to the Metropolitan Museum of New York as a gesture of appreciation by the United Arab Republic for the U.S. role in the international campaign to salvage the sites and monuments along the Nile. The U.A.R. also ceded the Temple of Elleisya to the Museum of Art in Turin, Italy, and decided to give Debod Temple to Spain and Taffe to the Netherlands.

Major exhibitions organized in U.S. museums included "Dada, Surrealism, and Their Heritage," produced by the Museum of Modern Art in New York City and subsequently seen in Chicago and Los Angeles; Los Angeles County Museum's Chaim Soutine show; the Isamu Noguchi and Franz Kline retrospectives at New York City's Whitney Museum; and "Romantic Art in Britain," shared by the Detroit Institute of Arts and the Philadelphia Museum of Art. The Cleveland Museum of Art presented the exotic "Chinese Art Under the Mongols," the first time that this 14th-century art had been so surveyed. The most unusual show of the year was organized by the Philadelphia Museum of Art. A 15th-century German printmaker, known only through the monogram on his very rare surviving prints and, therefore, as the "Master E.S.," was given his first one-man show. Also to be mentioned was the growing number of shows in U.S. museums of the new technologically based art. "The Magic Theatre," eight environmental works utilizing lights, computers, photoelectric cells, and stroboscopic units and sound systems, was commissioned by and shown at the Nelson-Atkins Gallery in Kansas City, Mo. "Options," organized by the Milwaukee Art Centre, featured work that could be manipulated by the viewer. On the West Coast, there were a number of exhibitions reflecting that region's involvement with plastic as an art medium. The Museum of Modern Art in New York City presented an exhibition of the prizewinning works in a world-wide competition sponsored by the Experiments in Art and Technology (EAT) group. The program was an attempt to evaluate the present state of the inter-

KEYSTONE

The National Gallery of West Berlin, designed by Ludwig Mies van der Rohe, was opened Sept. 15, 1968. The sculpture standing at the entrance of the steel and glass structure is "Têtes et Queue" by Calder.

action that EAT was trying to foster between engineers and artists.

Among projects of direct interest to the museum profession carried out by UNESCO was one to encourage the reconstitution of dismembered works of art. To publicize its project, UNESCO negotiated the temporary reconstitution of a large 16th-century carpet half of which was in the collection of Wilanow Castle, Cracow, Pol., and the other in the collection of the Musée des Arts Décoratifs, Paris. The carpet was a Tabriz school design and was one of the spoils brought to the Cathedral of Cracow from the Battle of Parkany (1683) by King John III (Sobieski) of Poland. The reunited carpet was exhibited together with other reassembled works by UNESCO and also at the Musée des Arts Décoratifs and Wilanow Castle.

The problems of conserving cultural property were also in the news. Underwater excavations at Port Royal, Jamaica, for example, yielded many fragile items, including bottles, which had crumbled upon drying when exposed to air. Experimenting with the objects at the National Gallery's laboratory in London, UNESCO devised a method to ensure their conservation. As excavations yield more material, authorities planned to establish a permanent laboratory to ensure that appropriate treatment could be carried out and the objects eventually exhibited.

Museum Buildings. During 1968 three galleries of contrasting designs were completed. Ludwig Mies van der Rohe completed what some critics considered to be his greatest achievement, the new National Gallery of West Berlin, based on ideas he had developed in 1942 for a theoretical design of a museum for a small city. The podium or sunken ground floor housed the museum's permanent collection; the upper gallery, which dominated the structure, was designed for temporary exhibitions. Eight burnished steel columns, tapering slightly, created an illusion of verticality. The centre of the roof was raised to compensate for foreshortening, giving the illusion of a plane surface, and to direct weight toward the supporting columns. As in the case of many recent art museums, the exhibition gallery was bare of features.

The Hayward Art Gallery, London, designed by Sir Hubert Bennett of the Greater London Council, was strikingly different. The mass of cubed and wedged forms in unfinished rough gray concrete was crowned by a series of translucent pyramids set upon the roof. These structures let in daylight which was automatically mixed with artificial lighting to maintain the level of illumination within. The galleries had bold strips of recessed lights, massive staircases, and prominently sculptured walls.

African masks
in the exhibition "Art
of the Congo"
at the Museum of Primitive
Art in New York City.
The traveling exhibition
was organized
by the Walker Art Center,
Minneapolis, Minn.,
from the collection
of the Musée Royal
de l'Afrique Centrale
in Tervuren, Belg.

A more modest goal was achieved in the design of the historical museum on the Hohen Ufer (Hanover, W.Ger.). The architect, Dieter Osterlen, was required to incorporate into the building the tower of the city wall, dating from 1357, and the walls surrounding the arsenal (1643–49). In his design the concrete roof of the museum surmounted but did not touch the old walls and linked them visually with the new building. Because the northern side of the museum faced a row of small, half-timbered, medieval houses, the wall was staggered to duplicate the rhythm of the buildings.

Among the major museum building projects either in plan or in progress in the U.S. were three facilities in California at Pasadena, Berkeley, and Oakland. Completed were the Everson Museum of Art in Syracuse, N.Y., and additions to the Des Moines Art Center, both designed by I. M. Pei. The Kimbell Art Center in Fort Worth, Tex., with Louis Kahn as architect, was scheduled for construction. Plans to add a large three-story building to the Art Museum at the Carnegie Institute, Pittsburgh, Pa., were announced. Reflecting on this activity in the U.S. and elsewhere, the Museum of Modern Art in New York City held an exhibition, "Architecture of Museums," an attempt to study both the phenomenon and its stylistic manifestations.

In Washington, D.C., the long-awaited National Portrait Gallery opened, as did the National Collection of Fine Arts. Both were adjuncts of the Smithsonian Institution, and their exhibition galleries shared the old Patent Office Building. The Mall in the capital city was to be the site of a new structure to house the gift to the nation of the Joseph Hirschhorn Collection of contemporary art. A gift of $20 million from the Mellon family was to be used to enlarge the National Gallery. One of the new wings would house the new Center for Advanced Study in the Visual Arts.

Paralleling the increase in art interest and the growth of private collecting was the tendency of U.S. universities to establish museums of their own. Major facilities at Cornell University, the University of Chicago, and the University of Iowa were being added to the many museums already existing at universities throughout the country. Perhaps even more remarkable was the growth of art centres and museums in urban areas with populations under 100,000. Among these was the Kohler Art Center in Sheboygan, Wis., where new building plans were announced.

The museum explosion was breeding more and more acquisitions. It had been estimated that the holdings of public art collections in New York City alone now totaled several million works. No central file for art, comparable to the Library of Congress catalog for

books, had ever been established. This urgent need was to be met by the Museum Computer Network, a central, computerized archive for visual works. Its first, relatively modest goal was to catalog 15 museums in New York City and the National Gallery of Art in Washington, D.C., providing verbal data, such as titles and bibliographical notations. Eventually, and most importantly, the reference file would include visual images of the works themselves, and would be expanded on a national, or even international basis.

Museum Personnel. The eighth General Conference of ICOM was held from July 29 to August 8 in Cologne and Munich with Arthur van Schendel, director of the Rijksmuseum of Amsterdam, re-elected as president. Under the theme of "Museums and Research," the conference discussed the role of museums in university programs, the use of collections and scientific documentation, and the training of curatorial staff at the university level. The constant growth of museums and their programs was being accompanied by the need for trained personnel, especially in less developed countries where the change of personnel from Europeans to nationals had accelerated markedly. Most of these countries required staffs to ensure the preservation of rapidly disappearing objects of the local culture, the preservation of which served to encourage a sense of national identity and continuity with the past.

UNESCO training projects, carried out with the cooperation of the host governments, included the reopening of the Regional Centre in Jos, Nigeria, to train museum technicians in Africa south of the Sahara. In Mexico City the project to train restorers for Latin-American museums had 16 students enrolled in an intensive ten-month course and 8, primarily Mexicans, in a four-year course. In Honolulu the Academy of Arts and the Bishop Museum began a program to train museographers for Asia and the Pacific area. A seminar was held in Algiers in April, with the cooperation of the Algerian government, on the staff problems of Arabian institutions. Participants discussed ways of developing curatorial personnel in spite of competition from universities and ministries and the need for technical personnel to reinforce rapidly disappearing skills in the arts and crafts.

As part of the overall program to raise personnel standards, ICOM began a worldwide survey of existing training facilities. It found that courses are given in approximately 80 different centres throughout the world. The inquiry took into account the status accorded to those trained in museography (techniques) and university educated specialists as well as the widespread nature of the different types of specialists found in museums.

Museum Costs. In the face of rising costs, museums throughout the world were concerned with financial problems. In the case of government-operated museums, which were common in most of the world, these problems fell within overall government financing. Private museums, too, tended to seek government support, based on the justification that they performed a public service. This was particularly true in the U.S., where, with the exception of the Smithsonian Institution, its associated museums, and a few federally or state-operated museums, most museums were privately owned or endowed.

U.S. Treasury Department regulations, however, now allowed tax benefits to those contributing to museums that qualified as "publicly supported" organizations. Many museums also used their facilities to

cooperate with state or federal government projects, which provided special funds as well as serving to integrate museums more closely with their communities.

Problems Posed by Affluence. Budgets for the new acquisitions proved to be woefully inadequate, and the few major works of art that appeared on the market, especially those of the Impressionists, commanded very high prices. As prices being paid for works of art, historical objects, and archaeological material by newly affluent collectors rose to new heights, the instance of thefts from private and public collections increased. Museums had to make increased outlays for security. Another phenomenon was the increased manufacture and sale of forgeries of paintings and many other items of cultural property. Illegal excavations and the illicit sale and transport of archaeological material were reported in Iran, Mexico, Peru, and Italy. Efforts by UNESCO to develop an international convention on the means of prohibiting the illicit export, import, or transfer of cultural property were being frustrated. One of the principal preventive means being advocated, that of customs control, ran counter to international trends to liberalize border formalities, particularly at airports. Another problem was that few countries had adequate legislation controlling the export or import of cultural property.

With full-scale rioting occurring not only in the major cities but also in several cities of medium size, museum security suddenly grew from a serious consideration into a most immediate concern. Heretofore security concepts had been focused on vandalism and theft occurring during the hours of public attendance and to a lesser extent on the possibility of after-hours break-in. Now security thinking was shifted to the prospect of large-scale vandalism and nihilistic arson. The year's most sensational theft occurred in Milan where several Leonardo da Vinci folio sheets valued at over $1 million were taken from a display case. The culminating experience of violence during 1968 was the fire set by a bomb in the Imperial War Museum in London in October by a "student" protesting the Vietnam war.

Faced with such possibilities as these, major U.S. museums, including the Art Institute of Chicago and the Detroit Institute of Arts, installed full-window protective grating throughout their buildings; and in-

Hayward Art Gallery designed by Sir Hubert Bennett was completed during 1968 in London.

GREATER LONDON COUNCIL

terior electronic and radar devices were either installed or extended, often at great expense, in museum facilities throughout the U.S. While the larger museum could more readily afford these systems, the museums in the middle-sized urban centres were faced with the dilemma of how best to use their available funds. And, for those, maximum security unfortunately became a binding concept. In many places it was becoming necessary to engage guards who were accustomed to and prepared for rough handling instead of elderly, retired men. Shortage of personnel and the dangers of street violence at night in some urban centres were curtailing the practice of opening museums in evening hours. Some museums considered or adopted the policy of placing tempered glass shields before valued works of art, or of using stands with railings to keep the public away from displays, thus preventing the interested and serious visitor from examining a work closely.

New Rules for Museums. Almost antithetical to these concerns was the U.S. museum's search for a definition of its role. The controversy that attended the Metropolitan Museum of Art's display of an 86-ft.-long painting by pop artist James Rosenquist served as the dramatic focus of the problem. The painting was entitled "F-111" after the giant jet bomber that appears throughout the length of the work interspersed among other aspects of current American life. Under its new director, Thomas Hoving, who was very much in favour of museum "involvement with the public," the Metropolitan displayed this painting together with historical paintings—for example, the 17th-century "Rape of the Sabine Women" by Nicolas Poussin and Emanuel Leutze's "Washington Crossing the Delaware." Those antagonistic to this open museum approach felt that the museum should not involve itself with the unproven present and should not move out into other areas such as theatre, music, and "inter-media" happening-like presentations. Buffalo's Albright-Knox Gallery, with its second annual Festival of the Arts Today, was an outstanding example of the latter kind of involvement, and many smaller museums had given avant-garde productions both opportunity and encouragement. That "a museum should be for the eye; a refuge in our hectic times" was opposed by the sentiment that "great works of art change social conditions; our times demand a wider museum commitment to parallel the changing scope and function of art."

Within the framework of the desire to offer more to the socially and culturally disadvantaged, an extension of the thinking surrounding the museum's role in a volatile civilization, the "mobile" museum concept of taking art out to where the people are, was becoming more widespread. The American Museum of Natural History was planning to sponsor neighbourhood natural-science study centres. In Washington, D.C., the Anacostia Museum was opened in a ghetto area and, in New York City's Harlem, the Studio Museum was founded. Aside from providing the usual museum exhibition space, both would serve to bring artists into contact with the people. Artists were to be invited to move into a section of the Studio Museum and then work with whatever members of the community might be interested in talking about and aiding in the creation of large, involved works. An international seminar held in Cracow, Pol., during September discussed the "Museum and the New Public." The growing leisure resulting from rapid social and economic changes was presenting museums and their

"LONDON DAILY EXPRESS" FROM PICTORIAL PARADE

Stones of the Temple of Dendur awaiting shipment to New York City. The temple was a gift from the United Arab Republic to the U.S. in appreciation for aid in salvaging Nubian monuments. The temple would be reconstructed and exhibited as part of the Metropolitan Museum of Art.

staffs with problems of presenting and interpreting cultural works to people from lower socioeconomic classes than those to whom museums were accustomed. The seminar recommended further studies on visitor reactions to exhibitions, to discover whether the goals of the curator were being met.

In a year marked by a leveling off after the Expo 67 frenzy, Canadian museums continued their expansion and vital activity. The Art Gallery of Ontario planned a major building program; the Edmonton Art Gallery stood almost complete; Alberta's Provincial Museum and Archives was in progress. The exhibition of the work of James Rosenquist at the National Gallery in Ottawa marked the first time that the National Gallery had honoured a U.S. artist with a one-man show. New buying policies with respect to the U.S. were expected to offer the Canadian public a more comprehensive view of contemporary trends. The Vancouver Art Gallery proved by its exhibition schedule to be the most open to current avant-garde art, while the James Tissot show organized by the Art Gallery of Ontario demonstrated the newly awakened interest in the art of minor 19th-century artists. Under the National Museums Act, proclaimed in April, museum activity in Canada was to be coordinated and the National Gallery to be administered by a 12-member board of trustees. (H. Du.; J. Ki.)

See also Historic Buildings; Photography.

Music

An extraordinary proliferation of music festivals marked the musical calendar for 1968. Some were sumptuous affairs, put on with the participation of visiting opera companies, European and American orchestras, chamber music ensembles, choral groups, and celebrated soloists. One of the most distinguished was the 22nd annual Edinburgh International Festival, organized in association with the Corporation of the City of Edinburgh, the Scottish Arts Council, and the British Council.

The festival opened on August 18 with a concert by the London Symphony Orchestra, under the direction of Istvan Kertesz, in a program of works by England's most noted living composer, Benjamin Britten; Yehudi Menuhin was soloist in Britten's *Violin Concerto.* The Scottish National Orchestra, conducted by Alexander Gibson, gave a concert of classical music on August 22. Daniel Barenboim, the young Israeli conductor and pianist, demonstrated his versatility by appearing in both capacities with the English Chamber Orchestra (August 23). The State Orchestra of the U.S.S.R. gave two concerts. One, conducted by Evgeny Svetlanov, featured the famous Soviet cellist Mstislav Rostropovich as soloist in Britten's *Cello Symphony* (August 24). The other was conducted by David Oistrakh, who also appeared as solo violinist (August 25). The New Philharmonia Orchestra presented Mahler's monumental Ninth Symphony, under the direction of the octogenarian master conductor Otto Klemperer (August 30). Other conductors of the group included Claudio Abbado (August 28), Carlo Maria Giulini (August 31), and Britten, who conducted his *War Requiem* (September 1).

The Symphony Orchestra of the Bavarian Radio, under the direction of Rafael Kubelik, appeared in three varied programs (September 2, 3, 4). The Soviet pianist Sviatoslav Richter was soloist with the BBC

Scottish Symphony Orchestra in Britten's Piano Concerto, conducted by the composer (September 5). The English Opera Group presented a puppet opera, *Punch and Judy,* by the young British composer Harrison Birtwistle (August 22), and Britten's three parables for church performance, *The Prodigal Son* (August 26), *Curlew River* (August 27), and *The Burning Fiery Furnace* (August 30). Four performances of Britten's opera *Peter Grimes* were given by the Scottish Opera (August 19, 21, 23, 26). The Hamburg State Opera presented a week of German opera (August 29–September 7), including *Elektra* and *Ariadne auf Naxos* by Richard Strauss and Wagner's *Der fliegende Holländer.*

Other festivals with programs of varied content were:

Tenth Festival du Son, presenting concerts and industrial exhibits (Paris, March 7–12); second 20th-Century Festival in Cardiff, Wales, in programs comprising eight new British works (April 21–29); Wiesbaden, Ger., Festival (May 1–June 3); Festival of Flanders, with concerts in Antwerp, Ghent, Brussels, and Bruges, featuring appearances by the Bulgarian Opera, the New York Philharmonic, and other foreign ensembles (May 6–June 8); International Festival of Lausanne, Switz., in programs of opera, ballets, and symphonic works (May 7–June 15); Prague Spring Festival (May 12–June 4); Helsinki, Fin., Festival (May 16–30); Portugal Gulbenkian Festival (May 16–June 7); Bordeaux, France, Festival of Music (May 17–June 2); Vienna Festival Weeks (May 18–June 16); Bergen, Nor., International Grieg Festival (May 22–June 5); Strasbourg, France, International Festival (June 7–23); Holland Festival, presenting opera, orchestra, and chamber music, in Amsterdam, The Hague, and Rotterdam (June 15–July 9); Spoleto, Italy, Festival of Two Worlds (June 21–July 14); English Bach Festival, in Oxford and London (June 22–July 7); Coblenz, Ger., Festival (July 1–September 2); Cheltenham, Eng., Festival, with the participation of the Budapest Symphony Orchestra (July 3–12); Aix-en-Provence, France, Open Air Festival (July 7–28); City of London Festival (July 8–20); Dubrovnik, Yugos., Festival of Music, Drama, and Folklore, which included concerts given on 26 open-air stages (July 10–August 25); Haslemere, Eng., Festival (July 12–20); Athens Festival (July 15–September 15); Munich, Ger., Festival of Opera (July 16–August 10); Bayreuth, Ger., Richard Wagner Festival (July 25–August 28), featuring the centennial production of Wagner's *Die Meistersinger,* staged by Wagner's grandson Wolfgang; Salzburg, Aus., Music Festival (July 26–August 30); International Festival of Music of Lucerne, Switz. (August 14–September 8), with the participation of the Swiss Festival Orchestra conducted by Bernard Haitink and William Steinberg, the New York Philharmonic conducted by Leonard Bernstein, the Berlin Philharmonic conducted by Sir John Barbirolli and Herbert von Karajan, and the New Philharmonia Orchestra conducted by Otto Klemperer and Rafael Kubelik; Montreux, Switz., Festival, "Musique du 21ᵉ siècle" (August 30–October 6), with the participation of the Radio Symphony of Berlin conducted by Lorin Maazel, the Orchestre de la Suisse Romande conducted by Leopold Stokowski, the New York Philharmonic conducted by Leonard Bernstein, and the Hallé Orchestra of Manchester, Eng., conducted by Sir John Barbirolli; Besançon, France, International Music Festival (September 3–15); Stockholm Festival, with the presentation of five concerts of new Scandinavian music (September 19–29); Perugia, Italy, Festival (September 21–October 4); West Berlin Festival (September 22–October 10); East Berlin Festival (September 29–October 13).

For the first time a festival—featuring programs of sacred music—was presented in Lourdes, France, site of the famous Roman Catholic shrine (April 20–September 1). A centennial festival to commemorate the death of Gioacchino Rossini was presented in his birthplace, Pesaro, Italy (June 13–August 31). The Israel Festival of Music was inaugurated in Jerusalem on July 30 with the first performance of an oratorio, *Testimonium,* written collectively by five composers and tracing the history of Jerusalem through the ages; the festival concluded on August 31 with a concert by the New York Philharmonic conducted by Leonard Bernstein. The fourth Inter-American Music Festival

was held in Washington, D.C., under the general direction of Guillermo Espinosa, chief of the Music Division of the Pan American Union (June 20–30); music by 57 composers from the Western Hemisphere and Spain was presented, including 16 world premieres. Avant-garde music was given special emphasis. The Lincoln Center Festival in New York City opened on June 22 with the presentation of Mozart's *Le Nozze di Figaro* by the Rome Opera.

Several important festivals of modern music were presented by college groups. The most opulent and musically significant was the Congregation of the Arts at Dartmouth College, Hanover, N.H., under the direction of Mario di Bonaventura, which featured 12 especially commissioned compositions; among them were the *Concerto for Violoncello and Orchestra* by the Argentine composer Alberto Ginastera (July 7), *Concerto for Flute and String Orchestra* by the American composer Easley Blackwood (July 28), *Instant Remembered* for soprano and orchestra by Ernst Krenek (August 1), *Concerto for Violino Grande* (a specially constructed instrument with five strings) by the Polish modernist Krzysztof Penderecki (August 4), and *Chamber Symphony* by the American composer Andrew Imbrie (August 11). Niels Viggo Bentzon of Denmark, composer in residence at the Congregation of the Arts at Dartmouth, presented five new works of chamber music. Two newly discovered early works by Anton von Webern were performed for the first time (August 1, 2).

The 42nd annual Festival of the International Society for Contemporary Music took place in Warsaw, September 21–29. The programs were as follows:

September 21: *Symphony for Wind Instruments* by Ton de Leeuw (Netherlands); *Capriccio II* by Krzysztof Penderecki (Poland); *Spiegel I* by Friedrich Cerha (Austria); *Requiem* by Gyorgy Ligeti (Hungary).

September 22, noon concert of chamber music: *Amores* by John Cage (U.S.); *Canticle I* by Lou Harrison (U.S.); *Éspace et Rythme* by Tiberiu Olah (Romania); *Solo for Sliding Trombone* by Cage; *Sequenza V* by Luciano Berio (Italy). Evening concert of vocal music: *Canti* by Antonio Tauriello (Argentina); *Stabil-Instabil* by Georg Becker (Germany); *Ayelet*, opera by André Bloch (France).

September 23, afternoon concert: *Symphony* by Boguslav Schäffer (Poland); *Philomel* by Milton Babbitt (U.S.); *Telemusik* for mixed media by Karlheinz Stockhausen (Germany); *Heterozygote* by L. Ferrari (Italy). Evening concert: *Tytania i Osiol*, ballet by Zbigniew Turski (Poland); *Dreadnought Potemkin*, ballet-pantomime by Juliusz Luciuk (Poland).

September 24, afternoon concert of orchestral music: *Crescendo-Diminuendo* by Edison Denisov (U.S.S.R.); *Divertimento d'Improvisation* by Lazar Nikolov (Bulgaria); *Divertimento* by Bela Bartok (Hungary). Evening concert: *Iris* by Per Nørgaard (Denmark); *Tenebrae* by Klaus Huber (Switzerland); *Et exspecto resurrectionem mortuorum* by Olivier Messiaen (France).

September 25, afternoon concert of chamber music: *Training 68* by Wojciech Kilar (Poland); *Pour quatre* by Wlodzimierz Kotonski (Poland); *Plus-minus* by Karlheinz Stockhausen (Germany); *4 Monologi* for oboe solo by Witold Szalonek (Poland). Evening concert: *Tragoedia* by Harrison Birtwistle (England); *Quick Are the Mouths of Earth* by Roger Reynolds (U.S.); *La Passion selon Sade,* mimed oratorio by Sylvano Bussotti (Italy).

September 26: *Piano Concerto* by Kees van Baaren (Netherlands); *Paroles tissées* by Witold Lutoslawski (Poland); Second Symphony by Sergei Prokofiev (U.S.S.R.).

September 27, afternoon concert: *Spheron* by Vladan Radovanovic (Yugoslavia); *Labirintus II* by Berio. Evening concert: *Epiphany* by Berio; *4 × 5* by Constantin Regamey (Switzerland); *Figures, Doubles, Prismes* by Pierre Boulez (France); *Serenada II* for flute and orchestra by Jan van Vlijmen (Netherlands).

September 28, concert of Soviet music: *To the Memory of the Victims of the Siege of Leningrad* for orchestra by Andrei Petrov; *Piano Concerto* by Rodion Shchedrin; Tenth Symphony by Dmitri Shostakovich.

September 29, noon concert of chamber music: *Sonata per archi* by Hans Werner Henze (Germany); *The Dorian*

Horizon by Turo Takemitsu (Japan); *Lineas y puntos* by Cristóbal Halffter (Spain). Evening concert: *Second Concerto* for oboe and orchestra by Bruno Maderna (Italy); *Fifth Symphony* by Boleslaw Szabelski (Poland).

The following works were given for the first time in 1968:

Third Symphony: A Prayer by Nicolas Nabokov (New York, January 4); *Piano Concerto* by Jean Papineau-Couture (Quebec, January 5); *Chimes* for orchestra by Rodion Shchedrin (New York, January 11); *Second Symphony* by Richard Rodney Bennett (New York, January 18); *Eleventh Symphony* by Roy Harris (New York, February 8); *Sixth Symphony* by Howard Hanson (New York, February 29); *Ricercare* for orchestra by Walter Piston (New York, March 7); *Music for New Orleans* for orchestra by Darius Milhaud (New Orleans, March 12); *Second Piano Concerto* by Benjamin Lees (Boston, March 15); *Fra Angelico* for orchestra by Alan Hovhaness (Detroit, March 21); *Fourth Symphony* by Klaus Egge (Detroit, March 28); *Symphony* by Ulysses Kay (Macomb, Ill., March 28); *Estudios Sinfónicos* by Alberto Ginastera (Vancouver, B.C., March 31); *Concerto for Piano and Orchestra* by John Corigliano (San Antonio, Tex., April 7); *Cello Concerto* by Bernd Alois Zimmermann (Strasbourg, France, April 8); *Piano Concerto* by John Ogdon (Cardiff, Eng., April 21); *First Symphony* by Rudolf Kelterborn (Vienna, April 26); *Eighth Symphony* by Roger Sessions (New York, May 2); *Cello Concerto* by Halsey Stevens (Los Angeles, May 12); *The Choir Invisible*, choral symphony by John Joubert (Halifax, Eng., May 18); *Invocation-Concerto* for violin and orchestra by Ralph Shapey (New York, May 24); *Concerto for Double-bass and Orchestra* by Gunther Schuller (New York, June 27); *Violin Concerto* by Don Banks (London, August 14); *Nomos* for orchestra by Harrison Birtwistle (London, August 23); *To Thee Old Cause* for orchestra by William Schuman (New York, October 3); *Sinfonia* by Luciano Berio (New York, October 10); *Fifth Symphony* by Karl Weigl (New York, October 27); *Sixth Symphony* by Hans Werner Henze (Berlin, November 6); *Epitaph for the Victims of Katyn* for orchestra by Andrzej Panufnik (New York, November 17); *Concerto for Two Pianos and Orchestra* by Paul Creston (Montavallo, Ala., November 18); *The Story of Ivan the Fool* by Alexandre Tcherepnin, after a tale by Tolstoy, for narrator, vocalists, chorus, orchestra, and electronic devices (BBC tape recording, London, December 24).

Some curiosity was aroused by the appearance of Oliver Knussen, a 15-year-old English schoolboy, who conducted the London Symphony Orchestra in the first performance of his First Symphony (London, April 7).

The musical avant-garde was extremely active in 1968. Concerts and demonstrations of multimedia were given in schools, colleges, theatres, museums, warehouses, and barns, in a variety of musical, non-musical, unmusical, and antimusical presentations. Some of them used shock techniques—deafening sounds in the 100–150 decibel range—and extraneous attractions (or revulsions), including nudity, eroticism, psychedelic séances, and protracted immobile

George Szell conducting the Cleveland Symphony Orchestra during a 1968 recording session.

Paul Sacher conducting the Collegium Musicum Orchestra of Zürich at the International Music Festival in Lucerne, Switz., August–September 1968.

silences. A typical example was the production of two *Schooltime Compositions* by Cornelius Cardew, given by the Focus Opera Group at the International Students House in London on March 11, with "matrices arranged around vocal sounds, triangles, newspapers, balloons, noise, desire, keyboard, with many people working." Of undoubted musical interest was a *Concerto for Synket and Orchestra* by Jerome Rosen, scored for a portable electronic instrument (University of Washington, Seattle, April 21). (N. Sy.)

Opera. There were a number of important administrative changes during 1968. At La Scala, Milan, the composer Luciana Chailly was appointed artistic director, in succession to Gianandrea Gavazzeni; Heinrich Reif-Gintel succeeded the late Egon Hilbert as director of the Vienna State Opera; and Ulrich Erfurth replaced Harry Buckwitz as administrator of the Frankfurt (W.Ger.) Opera.

United States. In New York City, the Metropolitan Opera production of *Carmen* by Jean-Louis Barrault in December 1967 was considered unsatisfactory, and there was some disappointment at Karajan's *Die Walküre,* brought from Salzburg's Easter Festival the previous month. The revival in February of *Luisa Miller,* with Montserrat Caballé in the title rôle, was well received, as was the new production of *Tosca,* with Birgit Nilsson and Franco Corelli, which opened the 1968–69 season in October. At the New York City Opera, a double bill of Stravinsky's *Oedipus Rex* and Carl Orff's *Carmina Burana* was presented in March; other new productions during the season included a much lauded *Manon* (producer, Tito Capobianco), Alberto Ginastera's notorious *Bomarzo,* and Douglas Moore's *Carry Nation.* The 1968–69 season opened with the premiere of Hugo Weisgall's *Nine Rivers from Jordan* in October. At Philadelphia, the U.S. premiere of Renzo Rossellini's *A View from the Bridge* was given in October 1967, and Bellini's *Il pirata,* with Montserrat Caballé, in March. Also in March, Seattle gave *The Crucible.*

In October 1967 the San Francisco Opera presented Schuller's *The Visitation.* The 1968 season included a triple bill consisting of Arnold Schoenberg's *Erwartung,* Kurt Weill's *Royal Palace,* and Darius Milhaud's *Christopher Columbus.* The revived Chicago Lyric Opera opened in September with *Salome,* Felicia Weathers in the title part. The Santa Fe (N.M.) house, rebuilt after having burned down in 1967, presented the U.S. premieres of Schoenberg's *Die Jakobsleiter* and Henze's *The Bassarids.*

United Kingdom. The Covent Garden Opera Company presented a lavish new production of *Aida* in January, as well as notable revivals of Leos Janacek's *Jenufa,* conducted by Rafael Kubelik, in February, Sir Michael Tippett's *The Midsummer Marriage* in April, and a new production of *Cosi fan tutte* in July. The first new production of the 1968–69 season was *Manon Lescaut* in November. The Sadler's Wells Opera Company moved its home to the London Coliseum, a much larger house than the Sadler's Wells Theatre itself. The company opened there in August with a controversial production of *Don Giovanni.*

The Scottish Opera gave the premiere of Robin Orr's *Full Circle* at Perth in April, and the Welsh National Opera opened its 1968–69 season with a new production of *Boris Godunov* at Cardiff in September. The Scottish company also gave *Peter Grimes* in a new production by Colin Graham at the Edinburgh Festival in August. The Aldeburgh Festival opened with the first performances of Birtwistle's *Punch and*

UPI (UK) LTD.
Leonard Delany as Don Giovanni and Margaret Neville as Zerlina in the Sadler s Wells Opera Company's production of "Don Giovanni," presented at the London Coliseum on Aug. 17, 1968.

Judy and of Britten's third church opera, *The Prodigal Son,* in June. At the Glyndebourne Opera Festival, there was a new production of *Eugene Onegin* by the Bulgarian Michael Hadjimischev. A new group, called the London Opera Society, gave its first concert performance in January—Meyerbeer's *Les Huguenots,* with Joan Sutherland and Martina Arroyo in the cast.

West Germany. The Munich and Stuttgart companies arranged an exchange of productions. At Munich, new productions included *Macbeth* in November 1967; *Oberon* (new edition by Walter Panovsky) in May; *Salome,* Orff's *Prometheus,* and Haydn's *L'infideltà delusa* during the summer festival; and, in October, Rossini's *Il Turco in Italia.* Stuttgart gave the premiere of the Orff work, produced by Gustav Rudolf Sellner, in March; *Der Freischutz,* produced by Walter Felsenstein, in December 1967; and *Turandot,* in both a German and an Italian version, in July. The first performance of Luigi Dallapiccola's *Odysseus* was given in West Berlin at the end of September. Gian-Carlo Menotti's *Help, the Globolinks* premiered in Hamburg in December. Cologne revived Rimsky-Korsakov's *The Legend of the Invisible City of Kitezh* (February). At the Bayreuth Festival, Wolfgang Wagner produced *Die Meistersinger* to celebrate the work's centenary. There was also a memorable performance of *Tristan und Isolde,* with Birgit Nilsson.

Austria. At the Salzburg Easter Festival, Karajan continued his *Ring* cycle with *Das Rheingold,* Dietrich Fischer-Dieskau singing his first Wotan. At the summer festival, Karajan produced and conducted a new *Don Giovanni,* Jean-Pierre Ponnelle produced a witty and memorable *Il barbiere di Siviglia,* and Emilio de' Cavalieri's *La Rappresentazione di anima ed di corpo* (1600) was revived. In Vienna, Hans Hotter produced *Die schweigsamme Frau* by Richard Strauss.

Italy. La Scala gave new productions of *Lucia di Lammermoor* and *Boris Godunov* (both in December 1967), Alfredo Catalani's *Loreley* (February), with Elena Suliotis, and *La Fille du regiment* (February). This last opera was also given in January at the Rome Opera, which added Giordano's *Fedora* and Alban Berg's *Lulu* to its repertory in February. Other outstanding events in Italy were the premiere of Angelo Musco's *Il gattopardo* (*The Leopard*) at Palermo, Boris Christoff in Rimsky-Korsakov's *Ivan the Ter-*

Gwyneth Jones and Grace Bumbry in the Covent Garden Opera Company's new production of "Aida" in January 1968.

DOUGLAS H. JEFFERY

rible at Trieste, and new productions of Donizetti's *Il campanello* and Verdi's *I due Foscari* at Naples. In Florence's Maggio Musicale, Joan Sutherland appeared in *Semiramide,* and Meyerbeer's *Robert le diable,* much cut, was revived. At the Spoleto Festival in July, Gian-Carlo Menotti produced an unorthodox *Tristan und Isolde.*

France. Jacques Dupont produced *Turandot* at the Paris Opera in December 1967, and the Opéra-Comique gave a triple bill of Menotti's *The Medium* and *The Telephone* and Puccini's *Gianni Scicchi.* At Rouen, Guillaume Landré's *La Symphonie pastorale* had its premiere in April; and at Monte Carlo, Renzo Rossellini's seventh opera, *L'avventuriere,* had its first performance in February.

Other Operatic Events. The Ghent, Belg., opera revived Meyerbeer's *L'Africaine.* In Sweden, the Stockholm Royal Opera gave the premiere of the 19th-century romantic opera *Queen of Golconda* by Franz Berwald in April, with Elisabeth Söderström in the title role; at Malmö, Laci Boldemann's *The Hour of Folly* had its first performance in March. In Buenos Aires, where the new director was Enzo Valentino Ferro, *Bomarzo* was banned. There was a double premiere in Prague: Isa Krejic's *Antigone* and Martinu's *Theatre Behind the Gate;* at the Spring Festival, Smetana's *Two Widows* had a new production. There were three interesting revivals in October at the Wexford (Ire.) Festival: Bizet's *La jolie Fille de Perth,* Rossini's *L'equivico stravagante,* and Mozart's *La clemenza di Tito.* (A. G. Bl.)

Jazz. Even more than the previous year, 1968 was notable as a time when the dialogue between generations was becoming difficult to the brink of impossibility. As the older, more traditional instrumentalists pegged away with the approaches that had been in favour all their working lives, the new men continued to formulate theories designed to free them from the daunting proposition that the art of jazz is, after all, finite, and there is a limit to harmonic expansion. By the early 1960s, the music had reached so advanced and sophisticated a stage that the more adventurous soloist, adding passing chords, substituted chords, and similar refinements to the sparse harmonic skeleton of most jazz themes, barely had time to think of the niceties of melodic invention as he followed his own devious patterns. It was noticeable that in the playing of the tenor saxophonist Sonny Rollins, perhaps the most gifted musician of the decade, the old forms were stretched to the breaking point and beyond.

Since the death in 1967 of his great rival, John Coltrane, Rollins was virtually the only master of conventional forms devoting himself to avant-garde effects, although even in his most arcane moments Rollins reflected strongly the traditions established by the late Charlie Parker in the great harmonic revolution of the 1940s. Rollins symbolized to perfection the attitudes of the latter-day musician, in that he almost totally abandoned the conventions of performance that had held good since jazz migrated upriver from New Orleans. Not only did he pay no attention to his audience, but he would often begin playing on the march, as it were, en route from dressing room to bandstand. What was even more striking, Rollins abandoned once and for all the old precept that a jazz musician must finish any piece he started. When he became bored by his own abstractions, Rollins would simply change themes without any discernible break in the music, leaving the analysts utterly bewildered as they tried to distinguish actual switches of theme from mere extra-

neous quotes interpolated into the original theme from other sources.

In the meantime, the younger avant-gardists neither gained ground nor lost it, except that by now each of them was a year older and still no nearer, it seemed, to the definitive recorded masterpieces that had summed up all past eras in jazz. Little new was heard from the fiercely experimental saxophonists such as Ornette Coleman, Charles Lloyd, and Archie Shepp. Although there was copious evidence that these players had inspired many disciples, the avant-garde could regard 1968 as a year of many words and little achievement.

The sole exception was the 25-year-old vibraphonist Gary Burton, who finally established himself in 1968 as an unquestioned virtuoso in the jazz idiom. Burton was something of a musicological test case, since he was the first jazzman of any stature to incorporate into his own playing and that of his quartet some of the broad, almost elemental rhythmic devices of pop music. In the past the traffic had always been the other way, with jazz being plagiarized unmercifully by the sharks of commercialism. Burton's group was perhaps the first in jazz history to reverse this process and borrow from the armoury of popular music. Burton himself was a remarkable technician, who time and again showed his mastery of modern harmony, his perfect control over four beaters being used at once, and his rare dynamism as an improviser.

Jazz suffered its usual depletions through death and

Gary Burton, vibraphonist, was widely hailed in 1968 as one of the top jazz performers in the U.S.

VALERIE WILMER

illness. In particular, Chicago style, that hardy legend of prohibition days, lost two of its great champions in drummer George Wettling and the trombonist Cutty Cutshall. By far the most significant loss of the year, however, was that of guitarist Wes Montgomery (*see* OBITUARIES), easily the most gifted player on his instrument to appear in the last 20 years. Montgomery, whose death at the age of 43 was reported in June, had revolutionized the concept of jazz guitar, and had been known particularly for his astonishing ability to produce extended improvised lines played in octaves. At the time of his death, Montgomery had to some extent been taken up by major recording companies, which were trying to place his music in a semicommercial large-orchestral frame. So complete was Montgomery's style, however, that his playing showed not the slightest signs of ill effect from this operation.

The greatest centre of jazz outside the U.S. continued to be London, and 1968 saw a repeat on a more lavish scale of the successful 1967 jazz festival, "Jazz Expo." To mark this second mass migration of U.S. musicians to Europe, the BBC made 26 television

films of the 100 or so musicians involved, setting them somewhat incongruously at Aldeburgh, until then associated exclusively with the more formal music of Benjamin Britten. It was one more step along the road to respectability that began in the 1930s with the conquest of the ballrooms, developed with the postwar capture of the world's concert halls, and reached its apogee in 1968, at least as far as Great Britain was concerned, with Arts Council grants for young but needy jazz musicians. It had been a long haul indeed from the brothels of Storyville, but the sneaking suspicion would not be denied that in the process something of the red-blooded zest of the music had been drained away. (B. Gr.)

Popular. The pop-music columnists had intended 1968 to be the year of the rock revival. In fact, "Rock Around the Clock" was reissued, and Bill Haley gave a concert at the Albert Hall in London that proved to be the ultimate in nostalgia for former Teddy types. But although the pluggers worked day and night, rock was never truly revived. What actually happened was that the public, sated with the surrealism (Procol Harum, whose "A Whiter Shade of Pale" was the most successful single of 1967), psychedelia (light shows and LSD), and Flower Power of the previous year, turned to simpler music.

The British public, at least, found what it wanted in January, when a brassy number called "Judy in Disguise with Glasses," by the U.S. group John Fred and his Playboy Band, was released in the U.K. It eventually reached the top three, and its success—and classification as "rock 'n' roll"—triggered off a "revival" fever. Even Wink Martindale's old monologue "Deck of Cards" was reissued. But although people wanted rock style, they still demanded new material; so while the reissues smoldered around the bottom of the charts, the Beatles' "Lady Madonna," with its controversial lyric and marked jazz influences, blazed a trail to the top. It was followed later by the Equals, Tommy James and the Shondells, and the Rolling Stones, whose "Jumpin' Jack Flash" provided them with a spectacular comeback after a year's obscurity.

Another popular style in 1968 was that of the beat number with orchestral backing. It was initiated in February by a new group, the Love Affair, whose "Everlasting Love" brought them into conflict with the musicians' union when it was discovered that, in fact, only one member of the group, the singer Steve Ellis, was heard on the record. He was backed by session musicians who received no label credit.

In May came one of the outstanding records of the year—"MacArthur Park," written by Jim Webb and sung by the Irish actor Richard Harris. This beautiful ballad, undoubtedly a masterpiece in the idiom, became a best seller all over the world. It ran for $7\frac{1}{2}$ minutes, and started a craze for records of similar length; one of these was the Beatles' August release "Hey Jude."

It was an important year for the Beatles. Following the death of their mentor, Brian Epstein, in 1967, they took on the entire management of their affairs with considerable success. They ventured into business with their Apple Corps, an organization that included shops, a film company, and, naturally, a recording company. In August came the premiere of "Yellow Submarine," a cartoon film based on the Beatles' songs and personal mythology. It drew high praise from the critics, but surprisingly the public was less enthusiastic. The Beatles were experimenting in many ways, treading ground where few, if any, pop stars had ventured be-

Narcotics:
see Medicine

National Guard:
see Defense

National Incomes:
see Income, National

National Parks:
see Parks

Natural Fibres:
see Agriculture;
    Industrial Review

Naturalization:
see Immigration and
    Emigration

WIDE WORLD

Top left, Janis Joplin, lead singer with Big Brother and the Holding Company, singing at the Newport Folk Festival. Above right, Aretha Franklin enjoyed increasing popularity in 1968. Below, Bob Dylan recorded the album "John Wesley Harding," his first since a near-fatal motorcycle accident.

KEN REGAN—CAMERA 5

fore. Yet they remained first and foremost a recording group, and once more topped the British charts with "Hey Jude," the first issue on their Apple label.

The British pop scene was lively in other ways. Cliff Richard and the Shadows celebrated their tenth year in show business; in March, Cliff gained second place for Britain in the Eurovision Song Contest, with "Congratulations." Several girl singers, including Lulu and Sandy Shaw, were given their own television series. Of the legion of newcomers, the most promising was Don Partridge, whose one-man-band sound earned him two big hits, "Rosie" and "Blue Eyes." In February Esther and Abi Ofarim, international cabaret stars, made their name in Britain with "Cinderella Rockefella," a delightful comedy number that held the number one position for five weeks.

The most important group to appear during 1967–68 was undoubtedly the Bee Gees—Barry, Robin and Maurice Gibb, Vince Melouney, and Colin Petersen. They arrived in Britain from Australia in the fall of 1967, and in November reached number one with "Massachusetts." Their influence was considerable; in particular they gave new musical and dramatic dis-

tinction to the slow ballad style. In March 1968 they gave a concert at the Albert Hall, accompanied by the RAF band, full chorus, and a 75-piece orchestra. Later they took the orchestra on tour with them—one of the first times that a group had done so. The Gibb brothers were much in demand as songwriters; not only did they provide the group's own material, but their compositions were recorded by many other artists. They had a flair for melody, and their lyrics were unconventional and vivid. The Bee Gees were particularly popular in Europe, where their "crying songs" gained preference over hard rock.

In the U.S. pop activity was centred largely along the West Coast, where the music ranged from the happy harmonies of the Beach Boys to the hypnotic involvements of the Doors. Black singers enjoyed increased popularity; the prevailing style was an updated form of gospel music known as soul, exemplified by Aretha Franklin (see BIOGRAPHY) and the late Otis Redding. Bob Dylan returned after a long absence following a motorcycle accident; and such groups as the Ohio Express perpetrated naïve, bouncy "bubblegum music." The overall quality of American pop was vastly improved, and throughout the year it battled with British pop for chart honours. The intense competition meant a rise in standards; the public would no longer accept any old dud—even if it was recorded by last week's top group. The records released in 1968 included some of the best ever made, and it seemed probable that the 1969 crop would be even better.

(H. R. Mo.)

Folk Music. In 1968 there was a marked increase in the collection and study of folk music, particularly in the countries of Africa. Music played a prominent part in the second International Congress of Africanists, held at Dakar, Senegal, and conferences on African music, as well as courses of instruction, were organized by a number of U.S. universities. With the assistance of the Ford Foundation, the African Music Society initiated a project for the production of textbooks with the aim of ensuring that the musical languages of Africa, hitherto perpetuated by oral transmission, should not be discarded by those who had acquired habits of literacy. The recording of folk music continued throughout Africa. Of particular interest were the polyphonic songs recorded in Ethiopia from farmers of the mountain highlands and nomads of the desert.

Intensive recording and filming expeditions were undertaken in many other countries. Some of the most fruitful were those made in Japan, India, Korea, the Cook Islands of New Zealand, and Australia, where the Institute of Aboriginal Studies added considerably to its collection. A considerable number of recordings were made in Europe, both through the agency of official institutions and by private collectors; in Czechoslovakia, the Institute of Musicology of the

Slovak Academy of Sciences was particularly active.

The International Folk Music Council (IFMC), with headquarters in Copenhagen, held no major conferences, but there were meetings of study groups concerned with folk instruments, the systematization of folk music, historical sources of folk music, and folk-dance terminology.

Traditional singers and dancers were encouraged to perpetuate the practice of their art through the holding of national and regional festivals. Among the many festivals, most of them annual events, that held at Keszkemet, Hungary, the birthplace of Zoltan Kodaly, and the numerous festivals in Romania were especially noteworthy. In England many traditional dancers celebrated their own seasonal ceremonies, such as the May Hobby Horse at Padstow, Cornwall, the Whitsun Morris at Bampton, Oxfordshire, and the September Horn Dance at Abbots Bromley, Staffordshire.

The number of international folk music festivals and competitions increased. In the U.K. there were the well-established Eisteddfod at Llangollen and the second Tees-side Eisteddfod at Middlesborough, in which groups from some 16 countries competed. Smaller international festivals included that sponsored by the English Folk Dance and Song Society at Sidmouth and the International Folklore Week at Folkestone.

The practice of folk music—both song and dance—continued to extend far beyond its traditional boundaries and to achieve widespread popularity. Festivals, weekend gatherings, public performances, and, above all, the innumerable folk-song clubs provided increased opportunities for its enjoyment. Though the "folk" label continued to be attached to popular songs of an entirely different genre, there was a growing appreciation of the distinctive character of genuine folk songs.

Radio and television had contributed considerably to the popularity of folk music, with programs ranging in content from unaccompanied folk song by traditional exponents to performances by concert artists with instrumental accompaniment. The question of the presentation of authentic folk music was discussed by representatives of radio and television organizations at a meeting held in Copenhagen under the auspices of the IFMC.

Publications included *Researches into the Medieval History of Folk Music* by L. Vargyas; *Rumanian Folk Music* by Bela Bartok, edited by Benjamin Suchoff (3 vol.); *Folk Song in England* by A. L. Lloyd; *Sowjetische Volkslied– und Volksmusikforschung* by E. Storkmann; *Opere* by Constantin Brailoiu; and *Die Volkmusikinstrumente Ungarns* by Bálint Sarolsi.

(MA. KA.)

See also Cinema; Dance; Television and Radio; Theatre.
ENCYCLOPÆDIA BRITANNICA FILMS. *Listening to Good Music (The String Quartet)* (1955); *Playing Good Music (The String Quartet)* (1955); *The Brass Choir* (1956); *Conducting Good Music* (1956); *The Percussion Group* (1956); *The String Choir* (1956); *The Symphony Orchestra* (1956); *The Woodwind Choir* (1956); *Casals Conducts, 1964* (1965).

Nauru

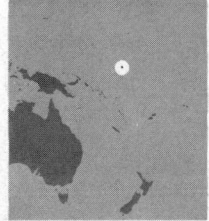

An island republic in the Pacific Ocean, Nauru lies about 12,000 mi. E of New Guinea. Area: 8.2 sq.mi. (21 sq.km.). Pop. (1967 est.): 6,053. President in 1968, Hammer de Roburt.

On Jan. 31, 1968, the trust territory of Nauru be-

came the world's smallest democratic republic. The Nauruans rejected proposals by the administering authority (Australia, Britain, and New Zealand) that Australia should handle their defense and external affairs. Like the Western Samoans they insisted on unqualified independence, though they thought it inappropriate to seek membership in the UN.

In constitution making, too, Nauru followed Samoan precedents. A draft constitution was drawn up by experts and discussed by a constitutional convention composed of 27 elected members and the 9 elected members of the Legislative Council. Pending its completion, executive authority was vested in a five-member Council of State, elected by and from the 18 members of the Legislative Assembly, who were themselves elected by Nauruan citizens of 20 years and over. The Council of State elected Hammer de Roburt, head chief of the Advisory Nauruan Local Government Council, as its chairman. On May 17 de Roburt became Nauru's first president and chief minister in a five-member Cabinet.

Valuable deposits of phosphates made the Nauruans "the richest less developed people in the world." In June 1967 it was agreed that their government would purchase, over the next three years, the assets of the British Phosphate Commission (representing the three partner governments) and then take over the control of the industry. Until 1970 the partner governments would retain exclusive rights of purchase. Increased royalty payments would provide not only sufficient income for existing needs but also funds for Nauru to purchase the industry by installments, restore worked-out land, and build up investments to an estimated $400 million.

At Canberra, in June, de Roburt tried to induce the partner governments to pay a higher price and permit sales to other countries. A Japanese offer of a four-year renewable contract at a substantially higher price gave him a useful lever. A measure of his success was a contract in September with the Japanese-owned company, which agreed to pay $3 a ton more than did Australia. (MY. B. B.)

Nepal

A constitutional monarchy of Asia, Nepal is in the Himalayas between India and Tibet. Area: 54,362 sq.mi. (140,797 sq.km.). Pop. (1968 est.): 13,107,-000. Cap. and largest city: Katmandu (pop., 1968, 157,262). Language: Nepali (official); also Newari and Bhutia. Religion: Hindu 85%; Buddhist 8%; Muslim 2%. King, Mahendra Bir Bikram Shah Deva; chairman of the Council of Ministers (prime minister) in 1968, Surya Bahadur Thapa.

Navies:
see Defense

The confrontation between Communist China and India inevitably continued to dominate the external relations of Nepal and increasingly made the country a battleground where the big powers vied with one another in giving economic and financial assistance. In June 1968, India, which had already spent more than Rs. 100 million on irrigation projects and roads in Nepal, sanctioned an additional Rs. 54 million to be spent before March 31, 1969, on agricultural projects, on two new industrial estates, new buildings for staff quarters, and a water supply system for Tribhubana University. New telecommunications linked Calcutta and Delhi with Katmandu.

In May the deputy prime minister, Kirti Nidhi Bista, was warmly welcomed in Peking where he signed a trade agreement with Ch'en Yi, the Chinese foreign minister. The Sino-Nepalese treaty signed in 1962 provisionally for five years was terminated by China. The Nepalese consulate remained the only foreign mission that functioned in Tibet.

The U.S.S.R. sent its first parliamentary delegation to Nepal in December 1967 and showed great interest in the supply of tractors, technical training, and fertilizers, especially in the Terai. Soviets were helping to conduct a survey for oil and natural gas. Pakistan was setting up jute mills. Under special funds supplied by the UN, ambitious plans were being made to harness the Karnali River for a giant-size irrigation and hydroelectric project. Japanese engineering consultants submitted a seven-volume report for building ten dams at different sites along the stream.

Roads in Nepal continued to constitute a major international interest. In September Britain formally announced its intention to build a 75-mi. sector of the east-west highway at a cost of £4,250,000, with a provisional target date of 1972–73.

The election system promulgated under the 1962 constitution, in which political parties were abolished, had become firmly established. In July Subarna Shamsher, who had led, from Calcutta, the only organized opposition group, returned to Katmandu. He announced the willingness of the Nepali Congress Party to cooperate with King Mahendra under the constitutional system. Accordingly, in October B. P. Koirala, the Nepali Congress leader and former prime minister, was released from detention, and an amnesty was granted to 22 former politicians, who might now be expected to play a part in building up the *panchayat* system. (D. WN.)

Netherlands

A kingdom of northwest Europe on the North Sea, the Netherlands, a Benelux country, is bounded by Belgium on the south and West Germany on the east. Overseas parts of the realm include the Netherlands Antilles and Surinam. Area: 14,139 sq.mi. (36,621 sq.km.). Pop. (1968 est.): 12,661,095. Cap. and largest city: Amsterdam (pop., 1968 est., 857,635). Language: Netherlandic (Dutch). Religion (1960): Roman Catholic 40.4%; Dutch Reformed 28.3%; Reformed Churches 9.3%. Queen, Juliana; prime minister in 1968, Piet J. S. de Jong.

The government, which had come to power in April 1967, was composed of six members of the Catholic People's Party, three members of the People's Party for Freedom and Democracy (Liberals), three members of the Antirevolutionary Party, and two members of the Christian Historical Union. Ten parties were represented in Parliament (elected February 1967). On Feb. 27, 1968, four members of Parliament left the Catholic People's Party, and on April 27 they founded a new party, the Political Party Radicals. On June 25 there was a split in the parliamentary Farmers' Party.

The economic situation continued to be difficult. Unemployment remained a problem, especially in the northern, eastern, and southern parts of the country, although at the end of August it was lower than in August 1967. Mergers took place in many sectors of the economy. Those in the shipbuilding sector attracted the most attention, especially those between Verolme United Shipyards in Rotterdam and the Netherlands Drydock & Shipbuilding Co. of Amsterdam in July, and between the Verenigde Machinefabrieken, the Rijn-Schelde Machinefabrieken, and Wilton-Feyenoord-Bronswerk in September. Other important mergers took place between banks, breweries, and publishing companies, respectively.

A government decision of May 21 to freeze wage increases for six months led to protests from the trade unions. A protest meeting organized by the Christian, Roman Catholic, and Socialist trade unions on May 25

555
Netherlands

Crown Princess Beatrix (left) and her husband, Prince Claus, on Feb. 9, 1968, officiating at the opening ceremonies for the Rotterdam subway system.

ALGEMEEN NEDERLANDSCH PERS-BUREAU

was attended by 15,000 workers. This was the first time that the three trade unions had organized a meeting jointly. After extensive parliamentary debate, the government revised its decision. On September 11 a government bill on the regulation of wages was introduced in Parliament; it would replace part of a royal decree of 1945, which had governed postwar labour relations. A bill to regulate minimum income passed Parliament on September 25.

In his report on the year 1967, published in April, the president of the Netherlands Bank, Jelle Zijlstra, announced a rise in productivity of 6½% and a rise in wages of 8% (a disparity of 1½%). The Dutch competitive position was thus improved, since in countries trading with the Netherlands, the difference between the rise in productivity and the rise in wages was as much as 3½%. The total balance of payments throughout 1967 showed a surplus of 617 million guilders, but this could not be interpreted too optimistically, since the running account of the balance of payments showed a deficit of 355 million guilders. On July 16 the Netherlands Bank forbade any individual to export more than 25 guilders in metal coin from the country, since the silver content of the coins now exceeded the face value.

In May and June there was some unrest among students. The main issue was the Maris Report on the future structure of the universities. Published on

---

NETHERLANDS

Education. (1965–66) Primary, pupils 1,409,-017, teachers 44,996; secondary, pupils 530,919, teachers 27,954; vocational, pupils 554,647; teacher training, students 11,431; higher (including 10 universities), students 148,590.

Finance. Monetary unit: guilder or florin, with a par value of 3.62 guilders to U.S. $1 (8.69 guilders = £1 sterling). Gold and foreign exchange, central bank: (June 1968) U.S. $1,922,-000,000; (June 1967) U.S. $2,094,000,000. Budget (1968 est.): revenue 24,055,000,000 guilders; expenditure 26,826,000,000 guilders. Gross national product: (1967) 82,270,000,000 guilders; (1966) 74,810,000,000 guilders. Money supply: (May 1968) 20,920,000,000 guilders; (May 1967) 19,310,000,000 guilders. Cost of living (1963 = 100): (May 1968) 126; (May 1967) 122.

Foreign Trade. (1967) Imports 30,182,000,-000 guilders; exports 26,381,000,000 guilders. Import sources: EEC 55% (West Germany 25%, Belgium-Luxembourg 18%, France 6%); U.S. 11%; U.K. 6%. Export destinations: EEC 55% (West Germany 26%, Belgium-Luxembourg 15%, France 9%, Italy 5%); U.K. 9%; U.S. 5%.

Main exports: chemicals 12%; electrical machinery 9%; machinery (nonelectric) 7%; textiles 7%; petroleum products 6%; meat products 6%; fruit and vegetables 5%; dairy produce 5%.

Transport and Communications. Roads (1967) c. 71,900 km. (including 690 km. expressways). Motor vehicles in use (1967): passenger 1,803,000; commercial 285,800. Railways: (1966) 3,231 km. (including 1,641 km. electrified); traffic (1967) 7,394,000,000 passenger-km., freight 3,236,000,000 net ton-km. Inland shipping (1966): navigable inland waterways 6,044 km. (including 2,452 km. for ships of 1,000 tons and over); freight traffic 25,240,000,000 ton-km. Oceangoing shipping (1967): merchant vessels 100 gross tons and over 1,739; gross tonnage 5,123,237. Ships entered (1966) vessels totaling 88,891,000 net registered tons; goods loaded (1967) 38,057,000 metric tons, unloaded 130,-632,000 metric tons. Air traffic (1966): 3,901,-546,000 passenger-km.; freight 241,643,000 net ton-km. Telephones (Dec. 1966) 2,515,298. Radio receivers (Dec. 1966) 3,134,000. Television receivers (Dec. 1966) 2,370,000.

Agriculture. Production (in 000; metric tons; 1967; 1966 in parentheses): wheat 739 (597); rye 239 (190); barley 447 (416); oats 365 (357); potatoes 4,840 (4,394); sugar, raw value (1967–68) c. 739, (1966–67) 573; dry peas 48 (35); rapeseed 15 (13); linseed c. 10 (19); flax fibre 13 (20); beef and veal (1966) 257, (1965) 246; pork (1966) 503, (1965) 505; milk (1967) 7,536, (1966) 7,236; butter (1967) 98, (1966) 100; cheese (1967) 269, (1966) 233; hen eggs (1966) 248, (1965) 251. Livestock (in 000; May 1967): sheep 558; pigs 3,918; cattle (May 1967) 4,030; horses used in agriculture 105; chickens 45,285. Fish catch (in 000; metric tons) (1966) 353, (1965) 377.

Industry. Production (in 000; metric tons; 1967): coal 8,065; crude oil 2,260; natural gas (deliveries) 7.2 million cu.m.; manufactured gas 1,647,000 cu.m.; electricity 30,054,000 kw-hr.; pig iron 2,580; crude steel 3,408; zinc 39; tin 14; cement 3,352; cotton yarn 58; wool yarn 17; rayon filament yarn 33; rayon staple fibre 10. Merchant vessels launched (100 gross tons and over; 1967) 333,000 gross tons. Index of industrial production (1963 = 100): (1967) 129; (1966) 123.

March 20, the report suggested a more centralized administration. On June 19 open talks, held between the minister of education and science, G. H. Veringa, and the Netherlands Students Council, were brought to an untimely end by the detonation of a smoke bomb. The Academic Council, a national committee of professors representing the universities, decided on June 22 to reject the Maris Report proposals. Meanwhile, in most universities extensive debates among professors, staff, and students were taking place on the structure of scientific education.

On August 15 the State Advisory Committee on Constitutional Changes and the Electoral System published its first report. The committee suggested the abolition of compulsory voting and proposed some minor revisions of the electoral law.

Queen Juliana opened the new session of Parliament on September 17. In her speech from the throne she said that the government would pay special attention to the problems of air pollution, slum clearance, and improvement of housing. The number of houses to be built in 1969 would be maintained at 125,000. The budget, presented by the finance minister, Hendrik J. Witteveen, forecast a deficit for 1969 of 2,540,000,000 guilders, or 237 million guilders below the estimated deficit for 1968. Expenditure for 1969 was estimated at 26,093,000,000 guilders, of which 26% would go to education and sciences, 13.4% to defense, and 11.5% to social programs. Aid to less developed countries was to be increased by 92 million guilders to 632 million guilders.

Foreign Minister Joseph M. A. H. Luns paid official visits to Hungary in February, to Yugoslavia in March, to Morocco, Portugal, and the U.A.R. from May 26 to June 5, and to Indonesia in July. On July 7 treaties for economic and cultural cooperation between Indonesia and the Netherlands were signed. The Malaysian vice-prime minister and the Austrian foreign minister paid official visits to the Netherlands in May and June, respectively.

On September 25 a second son was born to Crown Princess Beatrix and Prince Claus. He was named Johan Friso Bernhard Christiaan David, and became third in the line of succession to the throne (after his mother and his brother Willem Alexander). Meanwhile, on April 17, a son had been born to Princess Margriet and Pieter van Vollenhoven. He was named Mauritz Willem Pieter Hendrik.

A bill to raise the income of the crown from 2.5 million to 4,750,000 guilders per annum passed the lower house of Parliament in October, by 128 votes to 8. Recently, because of the inadequacy of the grant, the queen had been obliged to supplement it from her private means.

On February 9 Princess Beatrix officially opened the first section of the Rotterdam subway, the first of its kind in the country.   (G. H. v. E.)

ENCYCLOPÆDIA BRITANNICA FILMS. *People of the Netherlands* (1957); *Holland: Hold Back the Sea* (1967).

New Zealand

The Dominion of New Zealand, a parliamentary state and member of the Commonwealth of Nations, is in the South Pacific Ocean, separated from southeastern Australia and Tasmania by the Tasman Sea. The country proper consists of North and South islands and Stewart, Chatham, and other minor islands. Area: 103,736 sq.mi. (268,686 sq.km.). Pop. (1968 est.):

2,755,092. Cap.: Wellington (pop., 1968 est., 133,700). Largest city: Christchurch (pop., 1968 est., 165,000). Largest urban area: Auckland (pop., 1968 est., 577,-300). Language: English; also Maori. Religion (1961): Protestant 70.6%; Roman Catholic 12.9%. Queen, Elizabeth II; governor-general in 1968, Sir Arthur Porritt; prime minister, Keith J. Holyoake.

A single day and a single event dominated 1968. On April 10, in a hurricane that swept down the east coast of New Zealand, a 9,100-ton car ferry, the Union Steamship Company's "Wahine," entering the heads of Wellington Harbour in the early morning on its overnight run from Lyttleton, was battered onto rocks, refloated, and driven by wind to the harbour channel where it foundered. More than 600 people found their way ashore, but 51 died either in the sea or shortly after they were thrown onto rocks. Salvage experts began to remove cars from the wreck more than four months later, and prepared to inject a foam plastic to refloat and remove the ship. An inquiry, which opened on June 25 and lasted for 25 days, ended with a preliminary decision to return their credentials to the ship's master, chief officer, and chief engineer.

Sea disasters were a theme. Seven died as fire swept the former royal yacht "Gothic," now a Shaw Savill freighter, when it was four days outward bound from Invercargill early in August. Nine died when a coaster, the "Maranui," foundered in atrocious weather off Coromandei in June. A shark took a skin diver in Otago Harbour in September. A commercial tragedy was the failure, in September, of a publicly subscribed fishing company, Sea Products Export. Another disaster was an earthquake on May 24 (followed for months by aftershocks) that destroyed the settlement of Inangahua Junction in the Buller Gorge on South Island. Volcanic activity in North Island's Tongariro National Park looked ominous in August, with ash rising to 12,000 ft., but the eruptions eventually died away.

The nation's economy, which had passed through a crisis in the previous year, began to revive in 1968. Unemployment had reached 8,665 at midyear, when the economy began to react favourably to the easing of building and other controls in March and to the provision of special projects. By the end of October unemployment was down to 5,630. The price of wool, the disastrously low price of which had precipitated the crisis, began to recover, so that it became possible to start to dispose of a huge stockpile. On April 5 the Wool Commission made a brave decision to sell the stockpile at market price, and the decision seemed vindicated by an improving world market. Dairy farmers received the lowest guaranteed price in 18 years for butterfat, but an improving market enabled the price cut to be canceled late in the year. Rates for refrigerated freighting to Britain increased by 3.7%, and for wool by 8.5%, renewing public interest in the feasibility of New Zealand operating its own freight line. The Conference Lines revealed plans to introduce containers by 1972, and rivalry over the provision of facilities for containerized ships increased among possible terminal authorities.

The minister of finance, Robert David Muldoon, in his first full year with the portfolio, was generally credited with reviving the economy. In October he said the current account deficit, which a year earlier was running at NZ$136 million on an annual basis, had been transformed into a surplus of NZ$63 million. He attributed the improvement to an increase in ex-

NEW ZEALAND

Education. (1966) Primary, pupils 486,905, teachers 17,495; secondary, pupils 162,138, teachers 7,983; vocational, pupils 87,619, teachers 578; teacher training, students 6,010, teachers 388; higher (at 7 universities), students 24,646, teaching staff 1,452.

Finance. Monetary unit: New Zealand dollar, with a par value of NZ$0.89 to U.S. $1 (NZ$2.14 = £1 sterling). Gold and foreign exchange, central bank: (June 1968) U.S. $169 million; (June 1967) U.S. $123 million. Budget (1967–68 est.): revenue NZ$1,165,362,000; expenditure NZ$1,095,934,000. Gross national product: (1966–67) NZ$3,937,000,000; (1965–66) NZ$3,736,000.000. Money supply: (June 1968) NZ$721.7 million; (June 1967) NZ$709.4 million. Cost of living (1963 = 100): (2nd quarter 1968) 121; (2nd quarter 1967) 117.

Foreign Trade. (1967) Imports NZ$695.6 million; exports NZ$725.4 million. Import sources: U.K. 33%; Australia 21%; U.S. 11%; Japan 7%; Canada 5%. Export destinations: U.K. 45%; U.S. 15%; Japan 9%; Australia 6%. Main exports: wool 19%; lamb and mutton 17%; butter 16%.

Transport and Communications. Roads (1967) 92,926 km. Motor vehicles in use (1967): passenger 801,058; commercial 162,697. Railways (state; 1967): 5,169 km.; traffic 553 million passenger-km., freight 2,394,000,000 net ton-km. Shipping (1967): merchant vessels 100 gross tons and over 137; gross tonnage 216,740. Air traffic (1967): 1,112,556,000 passenger-km.; freight 22,990,000 net ton-km. Telephones (Dec. 1966) 1,085,133. Radio receivers (Dec. 1966) 646,000. Television receivers (Dec. 1966) 515,250.

Agriculture. Production (in 000; metric tons; 1967; 1966 in parentheses): wheat 322 (292); barley 124 (114); oats 35 (44); potatoes 280 (325); dry peas 29 (29); apples 101 (119); mutton and lamb 536 (470); beef and veal 318 (292); milk 6,240 (6,135); butter 259 (258); cheese 105 (107); wool c. 244 (235); timber (1966) 6,600 cu.m., (1965) 6,300 cu.m. Livestock (in 000; Jan. 1967): cattle 7,747; sheep (June 1967) 60,003; horses c. 87; pigs 603; chickens (April 1966) c. 4,600. Fish catch (in 000; metric tons) (1965) 48, (1964) 44.

Industry. Fuel and power (in 000; metric tons; 1967): coal 594; lignite 1,812; manufactured gas 163,000 cu.m.; electricity (excluding most industrial production) 11,488,000 kw-hr. Production (in 000; metric tons; 1967): cement 813; superphosphates (1966) 1,637.

ports and a reduction in "invisible" payments. The government initialed an agreement with Comalco Aluminium Ltd. for development of an aluminum smelter at Bluff in Otago that would use power from the new Manapouri hydroelectric scheme, the tail-race tunnel for which was holed through in October. Approval also was given for hydroelectric development of the Waitaki Valley situated on the Canterbury-Otago border.

A by-product of the economic crisis, which threatened an ugly industrial situation, was a decision of the Court of Arbitration (June 17) to grant no part of an application by the Federation of Labour for a general wage increase. Protest demonstrations, including one before the Parliament House in Wellington on June 26, were fanned by public indignation that while prices had been allowed to advance, wages were being held down for those who could least afford it. A crisis was reached on July 10 when the government declined to alter regulations in order to virtually force a general wage increase. Employers and the federated unions averted anarchy by getting together on an endorsed application to the court for a new wage order. This was granted, at 5%, on August 5.

Members of Parliament had anticipated public reaction to the 7.5% increase in their salaries which an independent tribunal had recommended. When the workers finally received their 5% the way seemed open to accept this raise, but the only non-major party member, Social Credit's Vernon Cracknell, demanded a House discussion of the matter, and the government would not face it. Prime Minister Keith Holyoake visited U.S. Pres. Lyndon B. Johnson in October and returned a visit by Pres. Pak Chung Hi of South Korea, as well as calling in South Vietnam where New Zealand troops were still engaged. The Labour Party retained the Hutt seat made vacant by the death of its most eminent former leader, 86-year-old Sir Walter Nash, but with a reduced majority. Organization began for the formation of a new political party more conservative than the ruling National Party.

Subjects of controversy included a bill proposing a breathalyser test for motorists and a petition seeking amendment of the Crimes Act to allow homosexual acts in private between consenting males. New Zealanders also debated whether the government should consent to the installation of an Omega navigational aid, which opponents claimed would invite attack in nuclear warfare. A demerits system for traffic offenses had its first victims when motorists who had accumulated 100 demerit points were disqualified from driving.

In transport, the first tourist expedition, by chartered ship, to Antarctica, occurred in January, and the domestic airline, NAC, began jet service with the delivery of Boeing 727s in October. The Post Office decided to establish a ground station to receive TV programs broadcast by satellite from other countries. Local elections held in October were spectacular, with mayors defeated in three of the main cities and in many boroughs. Visitors during the year included the prime minister of India, Mrs. Indira Gandhi (in late May); the newly elected prime minister of Australia, John G. Gorton (late March); and Prince Philip, who viewed the tunnel construction at Manapouri and appeared on a television panel during his visit in May.

(Jo. A. K.)

See also **Dependent States.**

Nicaragua

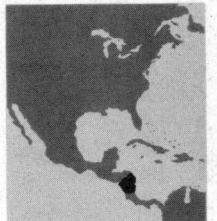

The largest country of Central America, Nicaragua is a republic bounded by Honduras, Costa Rica, the Caribbean Sea, and the Pacific Ocean. Area: 49,173 sq.mi. (127,358 sq.km.). Pop. (1968 est.): 1,809,477, including mestizo 70%; white 17%; Negro 9%; Indian 4%. Cap. and largest city: Managua (pop., 1968 est., 380,966). Language: Spanish. Religion: Roman Catholic. President in 1968, Brig. Gen. Anastasio Somoza Debayle.

Following his election in 1967, Anastasio Somoza Debayle appeared firmly established in the president's chair in 1968. Opposition to the Somoza family still existed, but it was fragmented and unable to put up a forceful united front, while guerrillas operating in the northern mountains and in Managua did not seem to present any immediate threat. Somoza's position was buttressed not only by a well-entrenched political machine of three decades' standing, but also by a progressive program designed to advance the nation's development. Under these circumstances the murder trial of Maj. Oscar Morales, a longtime Somoza associate, was embarrassing but not dangerous.

The nation's gross national product had been growing rapidly for the past few years, though probably not at the rate of 27% annually reported by some sources; 6 to 8% would be a more realistic figure. During 1966 and 1967 the boom had slowed because of abnormally dry weather, but in 1968 the drought ended and the agricultural outlook was promising. In a statement made in January 1968, the president put the greatest emphasis on improving the country's agriculture, the aim being to raise and diversify production in order to make the country's export income less vulnerable to bad weather and the other dangers inherent in a "one-crop economy." In this case it was

a "three-crop economy" with cotton, coffee, and sugar making up 71% of the 1967 export trade. Cotton alone accounted for 41% of the total exports, and it was the crop most seriously damaged by the drought.

Nicaragua hoped to become a major food supplier for Central America within a short period. In line with this aim, the raising of grain, cattle, and bananas (which had been virtually wiped out by disease a few years earlier) was being encouraged. The raising of cattle for export received special emphasis, and beef was already an important foreign exchange earner.

In an attempt to achieve an agricultural-industrial balance, Nicaragua continued its policy of actively promoting industry through a variety of inducements, including total tax exemption for five years, additional partial tax exemptions for certain industries, exemption of customs duties for materials to construct and operate plants and for raw materials and semimanufactured goods, and unrestricted repatriation of profits. Most of the industries in operation as of 1968 were based on the processing of local raw materials. Tourism was also receiving attention, and two luxury hotels were under construction. In May the World Bank extended a loan of $15,250,000 for improvements in Nicaragua's power supply; the project, the total cost of which would amount to $24.7 million, involved an addition to a thermal plant in Managua and construction of a hydroelectric plant on the Viejo River.

With the opening to traffic of the long-delayed Rama Road, coast-to-coast surface transportation in Nicaragua at last became a reality. This road, as well as a number of spurs extending from the Pan-American Highway along much of its length, opened up a large area of potentially good but previously isolated farmland. A new cargo and passenger terminal was opened at the Las Mercedes Airport in the spring.

In October 1968 the Cerro Negro volcano, long dormant, began emitting lava, smoke, and ash. The activity was still negligible at the year's end, but it posed a potential threat. The danger was not so much from lava flow as from the fallout of volcanic ash, since the volcano was located in the cotton-growing area.

(A. W. O.)

Niger

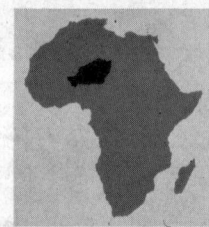

A republic of north central Africa, Niger is bounded by Algeria, Libya, Chad, Nigeria, Dahomey, Upper Volta, and Mali. Area: 458,993 sq.mi. (1,188,794 sq.km.). Pop. (1967 est.): 3,546,036, including (1962) Hausa 49%; Djerma 16%; Peuls 11%; Tuareg 9%. Cap. and largest city: Niamey (pop., 1967 est., 64,692). Language: French and Sudanic dialects. Religion (1960 est.): 1.8 million Muslims; 725,000 animists; 10,000 Christians. President in 1968, Hamani Diori.

At the January conference, held in Niamey, of the African and Malagasy Common Organization (OCAM) the heads of the member states reelected Pres. Hamani Diori of Niger as president. Diori was then empowered to negotiate the renewal of the Yaoundé Convention, which provided for the association of French-speaking African states with the European Economic Community (EEC).

Reports in March emphasized the continuing political stability of the country. With the collapse of the pro-Chinese Sawaba Party, the president had been able to offer an amnesty to all political prisoners arrested before Jan. 1, 1967. In addition, Diori appointed as governmental minister a member of the separatist Tuareg tribe, thus lessening the tension between Niger and Algeria, the home of many Tuaregs.

Although he declared in April that there was no question of his government recognizing the breakaway Biafran regime in Nigeria, President Diori continued his efforts to negotiate a peaceful solution to the war. As a member of the Organization of African Unity's Consultative Committee on Nigeria, he met Maj. Gen. Yakubu Gowon of Nigeria in July and declared himself ready to meet Biafran leader Odumegwu Ojukwu.

In August a $150,000 biennial grant by UNICEF toward increasing the health of mothers and children throughout the country was announced.

NICARAGUA

Education. (1965–66) Primary, pupils 206,349, teachers (including preprimary) 6,066; secondary, pupils 18,754, teachers 1,118; vocational, pupils 3,001, teachers 184; teacher training, students 4,822, teachers 351; higher (including 2 universities), students 3,343, teaching staff 430.

Finance. Monetary unit: córdoba, with a par value of 7 córdobas to U.S. $1 (16.80 córdobas = £1 sterling). Gold and convertible currency, central bank: (March 1968) U.S. $36,730,000; (March 1967) U.S. $59,320,000. Budget (1968 est.) balanced at 661.2 million córdobas. Gross national product: (1967) 4,485,000,000 córdobas; (1966) 4,201,000,000 córdobas. Money supply: (March 1968) 606.8 million córdobas; (March 1967) 635.2 million córdobas. Cost of living (Managua; 1963 = 100): (Dec. 1967) 113; (Dec. 1966) 113.

Foreign Trade. (1967) Imports 1,427,200,000 córdobas; exports 1,025,300,000 córdobas. Import sources (1966): U.S. 46%; West Germany 7%; Costa Rica 6%; El Salvador 5%; Japan 5%. Export destinations (1966): Japan 30%; U.S. 23%; West Germany 15%. Main exports: cotton 38%; coffee 14%; meat 9%.

Transport and Communications. Roads (1966) 6,124 km. (including 368 km. of Pan-American Highway). Motor vehicles in use (1965): passenger 13,000; commercial (including buses) 5,000. Railways (1965): 403 km.; traffic 51 million passenger-km., freight 13 million net ton-km. Air traffic (1966): 45,050,000 passenger-km.; freight 875,000 net ton-km. Telephones (Jan. 1967) 12,713. Radio receivers (Dec. 1966) 105,000. Television receivers (Dec. 1966) c. 19,000.

Agriculture. Production (in 000; metric tons; 1967; 1966 in parentheses): rice c. 38 (c. 35); corn c. 172 (c. 190); cotton, lint c. 119 (c. 115); coffee (1966) c. 29, (1965) c. 28; sugar, raw value (1967–68) c. 104, (1966–67) c. 102; dry beans (1966) c. 38, (1965) c. 37. Livestock (in 000; 1965–66): cattle c. 1,310; pigs c. 450.

Industry. Production (in 000; metric tons; 1966): cement 79; gold (exports) 150 troy oz.; electricity 335,000 kw-hr.

NIGER

Education. (1965–66) Primary, pupils 61,948, teachers 1,484; secondary, pupils 2,562, teachers 161; vocational, pupils 441, teachers 113; teacher training, students 416, teachers 43.

Finance. Monetary unit: CFA franc, with a parity of CFA Fr. 50 to the French franc (CFA Fr. 246.85 = U.S. $1; CFA Fr. 592.45 = £1 sterling). Budget (1967–68 est.) balanced at CFA Fr. 9.6 billion.

Foreign Trade. (1967) Imports CFA Fr. 11,352,000,000; exports CFA Fr. 6,301,000,000. Import sources (1966): France 52%; China 5%. Export destinations (1966): France 52%; Nigeria 21%; Italy 10%. Main exports (1966): peanuts 58%; livestock 13%; peanut oil 9%.

Transport and Communications. Roads (1967) 7,532 km. Motor vehicles in use (1967): passenger 5,842; commercial 1,549. Telephones (Jan. 1967) 2,630. Radio receivers (Dec. 1966) 70,000.

Agriculture. Production (in 000; metric tons; 1966; 1965 in parentheses): peanuts c. 305 (c. 251); rice c. 20 (c. 12); dates c. 5 (c. 5). Livestock (in 000; 1965–66): cattle 4,000; sheep c. 2,150; goats c. 5,600.

Nickel:
see Mining

Throughout the year the president paid several visits to EEC capitals in order to represent the African point of view. Despite differences in political attitude toward the civil strife in Nigeria, relations with France remained good, and Diori was several times received at the Elysée Palace by French Pres. Charles de Gaulle.

Attempts were made during the year to diversify the economy (which in the past had relied almost entirely on agricultural production) by exploiting Niger's mineral resources. In order to exploit the large uranium deposits discovered at Arlit, a new town was envisaged, together with an extended transportation network.

During September 9–20 an international conference on nomads in the southern Sahara, organized by the International Labour Organization, was held in Niamey. Niger, Ethiopia, Mali, Mauritania, Somalia, Sudan, and Chad were represented, together with a number of interested international organizations, such as UNESCO and the World Health Organization.

(PH. D.; X.)

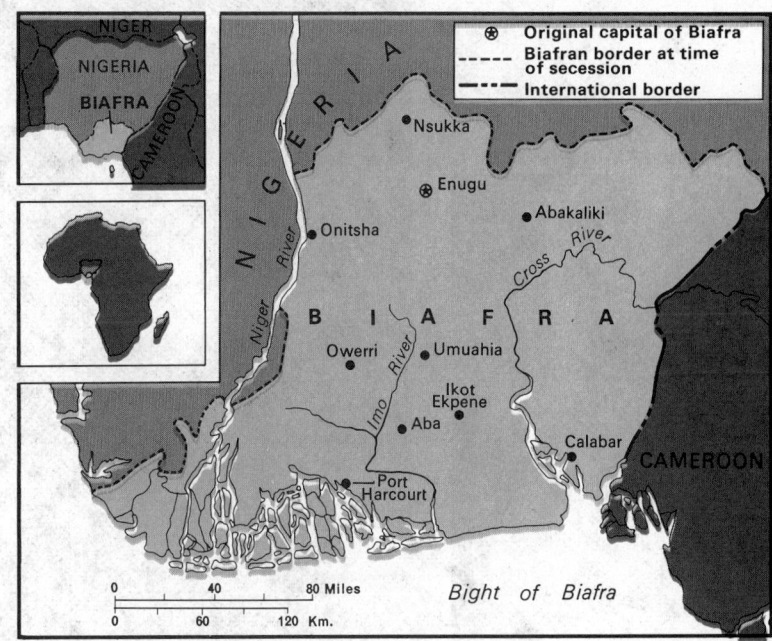

Original capital of Biafra
Biafran border at time of secession
International border

Bight of Biafra

Nigeria

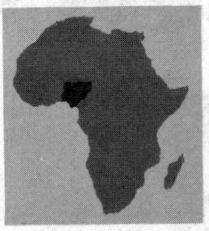

A federal republic and a member of the Commonwealth of Nations, Nigeria is located in Africa on the north coast of the Gulf of Guinea, bounded by Dahomey, Niger, Chad, and Cameroon. Area: 356,669 sq.mi. (923,774 sq.km.). Pop. (1966 est.): 58.6 million, including (1963 est.) Hausa 18%; Ibo 16%; Yoruba 14%; Fulani 10%. Cap.: Lagos (pop., 1963, 665,246). Language: English (official). Religion: Muslim 48%; Christian 23%. Head of provisional military government in 1968, Maj. Gen. Yakubu Gowon.

In Nigeria bitter civil war between the federal government and the breakaway state of Biafra continued throughout 1968. By August, the capture by federal troops of Port Harcourt, Onitsha, and Calabar had driven Biafran forces into a small heartland in southeastern Nigeria from which access by air to the outer world was difficult. The federal government continued to maintain that the war was a domestic suppression of rebellion and that any recognition of Biafra was unwarranted interference in internal affairs and a gross violation of the Organization of African Unity (OAU) Charter: furthermore, Nigeria claimed that it was fighting a war for all independent Africa against neocolonialism and tribalism which could fragment the

continent and return it to its 19th-century condition. In this context, the federal government saw even relief measures to Biafra as an unnecessary prolongation of the war and as hostile aid to rebellion. Fear of domination by the Ibos, the ruling group of Biafra, continued to bolster federal determination.

Biafra attempted to internationalize the civil war, and with the aid of considerable publicity succeeded in obtaining a great deal of world sympathy. Actual recognition by four African states—Tanzania, Zambia, Ivory Coast, and Gabon—was followed by virtual recognition by France. Much private relief organized for Biafra was flowing in under Portuguese auspices via Equatorial Guinea. The Roman Catholic Church was particularly sympathetic (Catholicism was strong in Biafra), and in July 1968 the pope revealed that the International Conference of Catholic Charities (Caritas Internationalis) was flying in charter planes with food and medical supplies. Other recognized agencies, apart from those specially sponsored, were the International Red Cross and the World Council of Churches. British agencies combined in a disaster emergency committee, and the Scandinavian countries were also active. Following the June visit to Nigeria of Lord Shepherd, minister of state for Commonwealth affairs, the British government agreed to allocate £250,000 for civilian relief, and a team headed by Lord Hunt visited Nigeria to assess the best use of the grant.

NIGERIA
Education. (1965–66) Primary, pupils 2,911,-742, teachers 87,074; secondary, pupils 209,026, teachers 10,904; vocational, pupils 12,646, teachers 760; teacher training, students 29,245, teachers 1,925; higher (including 5 universities), students 9,378, teaching staff 1,344.
Finance. Monetary unit: Nigerian pound, with a par value of N£0.36 to U.S. $1 (N£0.86 = £1 sterling). Gold and foreign exchange, official: (June 1968) U.S. $117 million; (June 1967) U.S. $151 million. Federal budget (1967–68 est.) balanced at N£161 million (including N£67.7 million for regional governments). Gross domestic product: (1964–65) N£1,219 million; (1963–64) N£1,208 million. Money supply: (May 1968) N£128.2 million; (May 1967) N£166.7 million. Cost of living (Lagos; 1963 = 100):

(June 1968) 113; (June 1967) 112.
Foreign Trade. (1967) Imports N£223.6 million; exports N£242.8 million. Import sources: U.K. 29%; U.S. 12%; Japan 8%; Italy 5%. Export destinations: U.K. 30%; Netherlands 13%; West Germany 11%; France 9%; U.S. 8%; Italy 6%. Main exports: crude oil 30%; cocoa 22%; peanuts and oil 17%.
Transport and Communications. Roads (1966) c. 80,000 km. (including c. 16,000 km. with improved surface). Motor vehicles in use: passenger (1966) c. 64,300; commercial (including buses; 1964) 25,900. Railways: (1965) 3,010 km.; traffic (1967) 380 million passenger-km., freight 1,593,000,000 net ton-km. Shipping (1967): merchant vessels 100 gross tons and over 35; gross tonnage 63,293. Air traffic (1966):

201,630,000 passenger-km.; freight 6,215,000 net ton-km. Telephones (Jan. 1967) c. 75,000. Radio receivers (Dec. 1964) c. 600,000. Television receivers (Dec. 1966) 40,000.
Agriculture. Production (in 000; metric tons; 1966; 1965 in parentheses): corn c. 1,300 (c. 1,135); sweet potatoes c. 13,600 (c. 13,600); cassava c. 7,000 (c. 7,300); peanuts (1967) c. 1,719, (1966) c. 1,792; palm oil c. 530 (c. 515); cocoa 264 (184); cotton, lint 44 (44); rubber, exports 71 (69). Livestock (in 000; 1965–66): cattle c. 7,518; sheep 5,070; pigs 680; horses, Northern Region only, 356.
Industry. Production (in 000; metric tons; 1967): crude oil 15,745; tin 9.3; electricity 1,087,000 kw-hr.

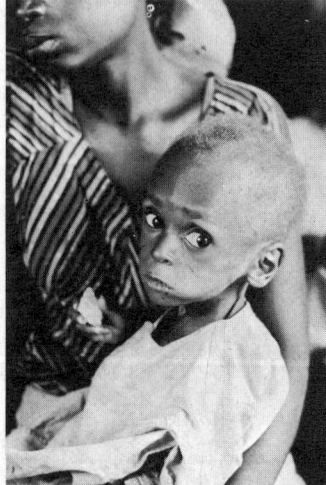

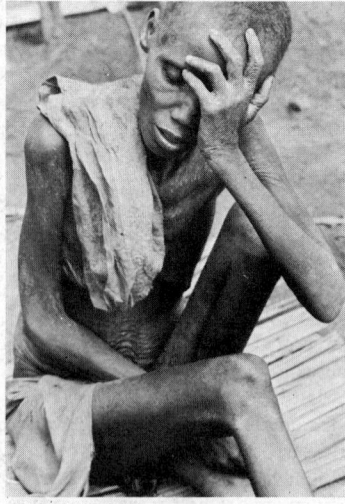

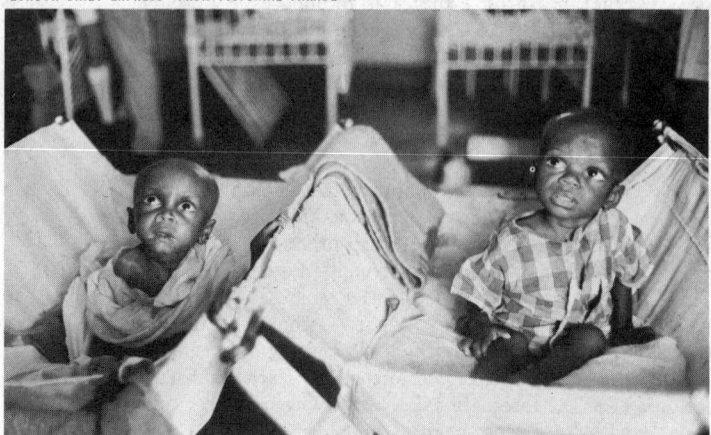

The continuing tight blockade by the Nigerian government against secessionist Biafra brought suffering and starvation to the Ibo people during 1968. Airlifts of supplies from world relief organizations were unable to stem the growing civilian casualty toll.
Above, children as well as adults were victims of the famine.

After several abortive attempts early in the year and preliminary discussions in London in May, a series of unsuccessful peace talks were launched on the basic issues of the war. At the Kampala (Uganda) meeting on May 23, Biafra demanded a cease-fire, an end to the blockade, and withdrawal of federal troops to a prewar position; the federal government insisted on renunciation of secession as a precondition. At Niamey (Niger) in July the OAU Consultative Committee on Nigeria met in the hope of finding some solution, but it became clear that the Biafrans preferred defeat and guerrilla tactics to a settlement that they believed would mean death and enslavement. The suggestion of a plebiscite in the region by Biafran leader Col. Odumegwu Ojukwu was refused. Both sides did, however, consider the possibility of an international police force being stationed in the area following the acceptance of peace terms.

Agreement on a "mercy corridor" for Biafran relief failed, with the Biafrans maintaining that federal control would result in the food being poisoned and the federal government holding that without control sup-

plies would be used to feed troops and the corridor would be misused for arms smuggling. Since much private relief was carried in planes that were also flying in arms for Biafra on the Lisbon run, there were grounds for federal concern.

A further meeting at Addis Ababa, Eth., under the chairmanship of Ethiopian Emperor Haile Selassie, took place in August, with an agenda including relief and peace settlement terms. Although this also failed to achieve peace, the federal government made it clear to the British that it would only consider OAU mediation. An international team of military observers, including two from the OAU, arrived in Nigeria at the end of the month.

Despite the fall of Okigwi and the threat to his last stronghold, Umuahia, Colonel Ojukwu continued to claim that the Ibos would hold out by means of guerrilla warfare and arms from Gabon. His greatest problem was to maintain an airstrip and the health of the civilian population until his cause was officially recognized as of international concern. For a discussion of the military aspects of the war, see DEFENSE.

The British position in relation to the federal government and Biafra was difficult, with blame accruing from both sides. While the U.K. government main-

tained a correct diplomatic position of supporting a fellow Commonwealth member in trying to preserve its territorial integrity, and was supplying arms—as was the Soviet Union—to the federal government, it also strove to promote peace through Commonwealth machinery in the face of public and press sympathy for Biafra. The Soviet Union in November signed a $140 million economic assistance agreement with Nigeria.

The civil war had begun seriously to affect the economy in the second half of 1967. A rapid decline in foreign exchange reserves (N£84.4 million in December 1966; N£27.7 million in February 1968) was little improved by measures to stem the imbalance taken by Chief Obafemi Awolowo, federal finance

Rats being sold as food to starving Biafrans in a village marketplace. This village, near Enugu, Biafra, was under the control of the Nigerian federal government.

WIDE WORLD

commissioner, in a supplementary budget in October 1967. In April 1968 General Gowon, therefore, introduced a stricter budget for 1968–69, which estimated recurrent expenditure at N£150 million with revenue at N£152 million. Foreign private investment was negligible, and loan assistance from both overseas governments and international agencies declined. The economy was bolstered by easing government bank loans, increasing liquidity in reserves, and, mainly, by agricultural exports—peanuts, cocoa, timber, rubber, and tin. The Mid-West Region oil fields, with reserves estimated at 40% of Nigeria's total, went into operation again after the Biafran withdrawal from that area, and the construction of a new N£15 million pipeline and offshore terminal was begun. Industrial development was hard hit by the war.

The remainder of the national development plan was abandoned, and approximately 75% of firms were operating below capacity. Vital works, such as the Kainji Dam and the Lagos Bridge, continued, and some industrial projects in the north were completed. Although some of the 12 new federal states had formidable problems and deficits, the Mid-West continued to operate as a model, with a 1968–69 revenue estimated at N£15 million, five times greater than in the first year of its life, and with federal contributions to it declining 23%.

Once the federal blockade prevented major exports of oil and palm oil products, the Biafran economic situation became totally unviable, with the loss of Port Harcourt and of the major food-producing areas making even subsistence impossible. Though the Nigerian economy deteriorated, it did not break and in the areas physically untouched by war domestic production was stimulated by import restrictions. It was evident that postwar reconstruction and rehabilitation would require much external aid. A report made in 1967 pointed out that training of Africans for managerial posts was being hampered and that more than 2,000 existing staff had resigned and returned to their own tribal areas for reasons of personal safety. Lack of financial confidence and of labour mobility remained the main obstacles to future economic development. (M. Mr.)

ENCYCLOPÆDIA BRITANNICA FILMS. *West Africa (Nigeria)* (1963).

Norway

A constitutional monarchy of northern Europe, Norway is bordered by Sweden, Finland, and the U.S.S.R.; its coastlines are on the North Sea, the Norwegian Sea, and the Arctic Ocean. Area: 125,181 sq.mi. (324,219 sq.km.), excluding the Svalbard Archipelago, 23,957 sq.mi., and Jan Mayen Island, 144 sq.mi. Pop. (1968 est.): 3,802,200. Cap. and largest city: Oslo (pop., 1968 est., 484,300). Language: Norwegian. Religion: Lutheran (96.2%). King, Olav V; prime minister in 1968, Per Borten.

Of vital concern for the Norwegian economy as a whole were the wage negotiations conducted in the spring of 1968. The negotiations were exceptionally difficult, but finally both sides accepted a compromise proposal put forward by the official mediator. It was estimated that the agreement added almost 500 million kroner to Norway's wage bill in 1968 and would add between 700 million and 1 billion kroner in 1969.

Also in the spring, the Storting (parliament) cut the working week from 45 to 42½ hours, to come into effect on July 1. This was the third cut in working hours since 1918, when the 48-hour week was established. In 1958 the length was reduced to 45 hours.

Production continued to increase during the year, although at a lower rate than previously. Investments showed a decline, but industrial activity maintained a high level, largely as a result of brisk export demand. The trade balance improved and the balance of payments improved even more, principally because of high freight earnings by the merchant fleet coupled with reduced imports of ships and increased sales abroad of old tonnage.

The fisheries experienced mounting difficulties, caused by seasonal catch failures and also by market problems abroad. Exports of dried cod (stockfish) were seriously reduced by the civil war in Nigeria, the principal market. Norway sent out only 5 factory ships for the 1967–68 Antarctic whaling season, as against 21 the previous year, and of the quota of 731 units allowed to Norway by the International Whaling Commission, only 292 units were caught. Subsequently A/S Kosmos, Sandefjord, the last Norwegian company engaging in the whaling industry, decided to send no ships at all for the 1968–69 season and saw no prospect of reviving the practice in later

Non-Chalcedonian Eastern Churches: *see* Religion

North Atlantic Treaty Organization: *see* Defense

Northern Ireland: *see* United Kingdom

Northern Rhodesia: *see* Zambia

Crown Prince Harald (right) standing on a palace balcony with his new bride and King Olav V immediately following the wedding ceremony at the Oslo Cathedral on Aug. 29, 1968. The bride, the former Sonja Haraldsen, was the daughter of an Oslo clothing manufacturer.

years. Their withdrawal marked the end of an epoch, Norway having sent whaling factory ships to the Antarctic regularly since 1904.

The chairman of the government's Oil Council, Jens Evensen, said in October that the finds of natural gas and condensate in the Norwegian part of the North Sea by the Phillips Group of prospecting companies might mean that Norway would become a petroleum-producing nation. However, the Phillips Group had not yet decided whether the finds were sufficiently profitable to start production.

Official and industrial circles were greatly disturbed by the British government's decision to support the construction of three aluminum smelters. The establishment of an aluminum industry in Britain was seen as a subsidized venture that would inhibit the sale of Norwegian aluminum, produced competitively on the basis of cheap hydroelectricity. A number of bilateral and EFTA meetings discussed the dispute, but the Norwegians did not succeed in halting the British plans.

Prospects for joining the EEC were still remote.

NORWAY

Education. (1965–66) Primary, pupils 412,157, teachers 19,177; secondary, pupils 190,031, teachers 14,587; vocational, pupils 65,029, teachers 9,313; teacher training, students 7,787, teachers 876; higher (including 3 universities), students 19,528, teaching staff 1,976.

Finance. Monetary unit: Norwegian krone, with a par value of 7.14 kroner to U.S. $1 (17.14 kroner = £1 sterling). Gold and foreign exchange, central bank: (June 1968) U.S. $622.2 million; (June 1967) U.S. $558.8 million. Budget (1968 est.): revenue 13,532,000,000 kroner; expenditure 13,297,000,000 kroner. Gross national product: (1966) 54,177,000,000 kroner; (1965) 50,093,000,000 kroner. Money supply: (May 1968) 11,140,000,000 kroner; (May 1967) 10,-310,000,000 kroner. Cost of living (1963 = 100): (June 1968) 122; (June 1967) 119.

Foreign Trade. (1967) Imports 19,617,000,000 kroner; exports 12,402,000,-000 kroner. Import sources: Sweden 19%; U.K. 14%; West Germany 14%; Japan 8%; U.S. 6%; Denmark 6%. Export destinations: U.K. 19%; Sweden 16%; West Germany 12%; U.S. 8%; Denmark 8%. Main exports: manufactured goods 24%; ships 12%; aluminum 9%; fish 8%; paper 8%.

Transport and Communications. Roads (1967) 68,292 km. Motor vehicles in use (1967): passenger 569,199; commercial 134,200. Railways: (state only; 1966) 4,297 km. (including 2,079 km. electrified); traffic (state only; 1967) 1,710,000,000 passenger-km., freight 2,396,000,000 net ton-km. Shipping (1967): merchant vessels 100 gross tons and over 2,847; gross tonnage 18,381,867. Ships entered (1966) vessels totaling 13,638,000 net registered tons; goods loaded (1967) 29,612,000 metric tons, unloaded 15,079,000 metric tons. Air traffic (including Norwegian apportionment of international operation of Scandinavian Airlines System; 1966): 1,197,066,000 passenger-km.; freight 38,022,000 net ton-km. Telephones (Dec. 1966) 945,573. Radio receivers (Dec. 1966) 1,110,000. Television receivers (Dec. 1966) 574,000.

Agriculture. Production (in 000; metric tons; 1967; 1966 in parentheses): barley 493 (405); oats 123 (91); potatoes 807 (1,090); apples 44 (41); milk c. 1,690 (1,658); butter 20 (21); cheese 49 (48); beef and veal (1966) 57, (1965) 56; pork (1966) 59, (1965) 59; timber (1965–66) 6,800 cu.m., (1964–65) 8,200 cu.m. Livestock (in 000; June 1967): cattle 996; sheep 2,067; horses 53; pigs 590; goats 108; chickens (June 1966) 5,073. Fish catch (in 000; metric tons) (1966) 2,849, (1965) 2,307. Whale oil production (in 000; metric tons) (1966–67) 18, (1965–66) 22.

Industry. Fuel and power (in 000; 1967): coal (Svalbard mines) 408 metric tons; manufactured gas 29,160 cu.m.; electricity 52,814,000 kw-hr. Production (in 000; metric tons; 1967): iron ore (65% metal content) 3,231; pig iron 1,235; crude steel 791; zinc 55; copper 14; aluminum 362; cement 2,064; nitrogenous fertilizers (N content; 1966–67) 355; mechanical wood pulp (1966) 969; chemical wood pulp (1966) 843; newsprint 450; other paper (1966) 713. Merchant vessels launched (100 gross tons and over; 1967) 526,000 gross tons. Dwelling units completed (1967) 31,300.

Norway engaged in important discussions with the other Nordic countries, including a meeting of ministers in Oslo in October, with a view to achieving closer economic cooperation, leading possibly to a Nordic customs union. A comprehensive report was prepared by experts for submission to the governments at the end of the year, preparatory to a further meeting in January 1969. Meanwhile, at home, the government announced certain income tax reductions in October and intimated that proposals would be made for the introduction of a new value-added tax to replace the existing sales tax.

Politically, the domestic scene remained quiet, but interest gradually mounted in advance of the parliamentary elections scheduled for 1969. Public opinion polls indicated no significant decline in support for the parties—Conservative, Centre, Liberal, and Christian Popular—forming the coalition government set up in 1965 after the Labour Party's long reign. Significantly, however, polls taken in the autumn showed that the Communist Party and the Socialist People's Party lost support following the Soviet intervention in Czechoslovakia, while the Labour Party's strength went up correspondingly.

Popular interest centred on the engagement of Crown Prince Harald to a commoner, Sonja Haraldsen, daughter of an Oslo businessman. The marriage took place in Oslo Cathedral on August 29 in the presence of four reigning kings, two presidents, and a large gathering of international notables. While a few voices expressed regret that the crown prince had married a commoner and predicted the eventual demise of the monarchy, the general mood was one of rejoicing over what was generally described as a "fairy story love match." In April King Olav paid a seven-day state visit to the U.S., starting in Washington and proceeding to a number of other cities. In November he spent two days in England, at Newcastle upon Tyne, receiving the freedom of the city and opening a new civic centre.

A notable event in the cultural sphere was the opening on August 23 of Oslo's modern art gallery, at nearby Høvikodden. The gallery, the gift of former ice-skating star Sonja Henie and her shipowner husband, Niels Onstad, was designed to house their large collection of modern paintings.

In March the Storting decided unanimously to establish two more universities, at Tromsø in northern Norway and at Trondheim in western Norway. Trondheim University would be based on the existing Institute of Technology; it was estimated that by 1975 it would have 7,000 students, of whom more than half would be studying engineering. Hitherto, Norway had had universities only in Oslo and Bergen.

In October the Nobel Committee of the Storting announced that the 1968 Peace Prize had been awarded to a French lawyer, René Cassin (see BIOGRAPHY), president of the European Human Rights Tribunal since its creation. Forty-eight candidates, more than usual, had been nominated. No peace prizes had been awarded for 1966 and 1967.

Norwegian sportsmen did well at the Winter Olympic Games in Grenoble, France, winning six gold, six silver, and two bronze medals for a total of 103 points, 11 points more than the next-best nation, the U.S.S.R. At the summer games in Mexico in October, Norway won one gold and one silver medal.

(O. F. K.)

ENCYCLOPÆDIA BRITANNICA FILMS. *Scandinavia—Norway, Sweden, Denmark* (1962).

Nuclear Energy

Beyond question the most important developments in nuclear energy in 1968 centred on the proposed Treaty on the Non-Proliferation of Nuclear Weapons and its progress toward wide international acceptance. In January a year-long impasse was broken when the U.S. and the Soviet Union, acting in concert, presented complete, identical drafts of a nonproliferation treaty to the United Nations-sponsored 18-Nation Disarmament Committee in Geneva. Within three months the text was approved, essentially unchanged, for submission to the UN General Assembly. Debate by the Political Committee—the General Assembly by another name—began late in April. After only six weeks of discussion and a few more relatively insignificant changes, the draft was approved. An overwhelmingly favourable vote by the General Assembly followed immediately, as a matter of course, and on July 1 the treaty was signed by 56 nations and the three depositary countries, the U.K., the U.S.S.R., and the U.S. Forty ratifications plus those of the depositary countries who sign the treaty were required to bring it into effect.

Essentially, the treaty provided that: (1) the nuclear weapons powers which adhered to it would not supply nuclear weapons or weapons technology to nonnuclear weapons nations; (2) the latter would undertake not to acquire nuclear weapons by any means; and (3) the nonnuclear nations would accept the International Atomic Energy Agency's safeguards system —or an equivalent system—as a means of ensuring that their nuclear installations and materials were not being used for military purposes.

The treaty also included general assurances that signatories could continue peaceful nuclear activities with minimal interference and that the nuclear weapons powers who signed it would negotiate to reduce their atomic armaments. It was supplemented by a UN Security Council resolution to the effect that the council or individual members of it could intervene if any nation was attacked or threatened with attack by nuclear weapons.

While the General Assembly vote seemed to imply that the treaty commanded enthusiastic and virtually universal support, the reverse was true. Heavy, sustained pressure by the U.S., the U.S.S.R., and their closest allies was required to achieve its acceptance. A measure of resistance was the fact that, at the year's end, a number of important countries, including West Germany, Japan, Italy, India, Israel, Argentina, and Brazil, had not yet signed. Indeed, as the General Assembly debate brought out, few nations were prepared to give the treaty wholehearted support, and many clearly considered it little better than no treaty at all.

One of the many reasons given for these reservations was that two of the five nuclear weapons powers, France and Communist China, had reaffirmed that they would not adhere to the treaty. An even more important criticism was the often-repeated contention that, while the treaty would require real sacrifices of the nations that had no nuclear weapons, it offered them no guarantees that the nuclear powers would limit their armaments or forgo their use.

Those who took this line did not fail to point out that the U.S. and the Soviet Union were continuing to expand and diversify their nuclear arsenals. That criticism was undercut when the two nations announced that they would begin direct nuclear disarmament negotiations soon. Even after the Soviet occupation of Czechoslovakia had made it politically necessary for the U.S. to postpone these discussions, the pledge remained a potent factor supporting the treaty's acceptance.

Since it was obvious that few ratifications would be filed until the U.S. acted, U.S. Pres. Lyndon Johnson pressed hard for early approval of the treaty by the Senate. In that case, again, the invasion of Czechoslovakia proved to be a formidable obstacle. Richard M. Nixon, the Republican presidential candidate, let it be known that he thought quick ratification might be construed as an acceptance of the Soviet action. Opposition to the treaty then began to firm up and, late in the congressional session, the Senate Democratic leadership decided not to risk a vote. Although Nixon, after he was elected, affirmed that, as president, he would urge the Senate to approve the treaty promptly, this assurance did not console those who felt that any loss of momentum could have serious consequences abroad.

Weapons and Weapons Tests. While the U.S. and the Soviet Union were cooperating on behalf of the nonproliferation treaty, their nuclear weapons programs were not standing still. Reacting to the U.S.S.R.'s creation of the nucleus of an antiballistic missile defense system, the U.S. budgeted for the first installment of funds to construct a "thin" antimissile defense screen, using the nuclear-armed Sentinel missile. With some reluctance Congress approved the appropriation.

Fortunately, there was considerable evidence that neither country was eager to incur the enormous costs that continued rivalry in this field would entail, particularly since it seemed doubtful that any defense could do much to neutralize a massive attack or counterattack. Provisional estimates put the cost of a full-scale antimissile defense complex in the U.S. at roughly $40 billion.

No such restraints affected the two powers' efforts to develop more sophisticated offensive capabilities. The Soviet Union continued a series of tests, dating back to at least 1967, of a high-altitude missile, designed to return to earth after making less than one complete orbit of it. Such "suborbital" missiles are not prohibited by a U.S.-sponsored treaty that precludes the use of nuclear weapons in space. The U.S. tested, with apparent success, two intercontinental multiple-warhead missiles, designed to overwhelm any defense: the Poseidon, to be launched from modified Polaris submarines, and a version of the land-based Minuteman missile.

Inevitably, the adequacy of offensive nuclear armaments vis-à-vis the U.S.S.R. became an issue in the U.S. presidential campaign. Richard M. Nixon, who became the president-elect, called for quick action to ensure that the U.S. would retain a large numerical superiority in all strategic nuclear armaments and argued that this would strengthen the U.S. position in any disarmament negotiations. Vice-Pres. Hubert H. Humphrey, defending the Johnson administration's position that approximate "parity" is not necessarily to be feared, contended that mere numbers are not a meaningful criterion of adequacy.

Whether the two candidates' exchanges reflected a real and significant difference of opinion was hard to determine. The issue receded into the background after the U.S. Department of Defense released data showing that the U.S. had approximately three inter-

Three phases of the first French hydrogen bomb being exploded over Fangataufa atoll in the Pacific on Aug. 24, 1968.

Norwegian Literature: *see* Literature

continental nuclear-armed missiles to the Soviet Union's two (approximately 1,700 to 1,100), and about four times as many "nuclear capable" long-range aircraft.

Beginning in July and continuing into September, France carried out a series of tests which demonstrated that it could produce thermonuclear weapons (hydrogen bombs). The tests, in Polynesia, were conducted above ground: France, unlike the U.S., the U.S.S.R., and the U.K., had never adhered to the limited test-ban treaty of 1963, which banned nuclear explosions in the open air.

After a lapse of a year Communist China resumed its nuclear weapons testing with a presumably thermonuclear explosion in the atmosphere on December 27. The explosion, which had a yield of three megatons, was reported to have occurred in the Lop Nor region of Sinkiang Province. It was China's second successful thermonuclear test.

The U.S. Atomic Energy Commission conducted more than 20 weapons development tests underground —about the same number as in 1967—and reported that the Soviet Union had apparently conducted seven. Britain's nuclear weapons development program, long virtually suspended, showed no signs of activity.

KEYSTONE

The "Otto Hahn," Germany's first nuclear-powered freighter, was launched during 1968.

Nuclear-Powered Ships. At the year's end the U.S. had in commission 41 Polaris missile-firing submarines and 39 attack vessels, 6 more than a year earlier. Under construction or design were three new nuclear-propelled aircraft carriers, two frigates, and four fleet escort ships to supplement the three other nuclear ships already in service with the surface fleet.

The Soviet nuclear fleet was reported to consist of 15 ballistic missile-firing submarines, 25 submarines of the "cruise missile type," and 15 more of the "anti-submarine type." The total of 55 was 10 more than in 1967.

France's nuclear submarine fleet, building or planned for service in 1970–75, consisted of four ballistic missile-firing vessels. Britain had four Polaris and six attack submarines commissioned, under construction, or authorized.

West Germany's first nuclear-powered merchant ship, the "Otto Hahn," underwent its first full-scale sea trials preparatory to beginning regular service as an ore carrier. In Japan the building of that country's first nuclear ship, a small cargo vessel, got under way in earnest. Italy organized a government-industry effort to construct a nuclear naval-support vessel. Discouraged in its efforts to obtain a supply of enriched uranium fuel from the U.S., Italy arranged to borrow

part of its needs from France. The first and only U.S. nuclear merchant ship, the NS "Savannah," was refueled for the first time after having logged 330,000 mi. in more than six years, mostly in commercial service.

Nuclear-Electric Power. Superficially, the year's developments were favourable to the fast-growing U.S. nuclear-electric power industry. Utilities awarded contracts for the construction of 14 nuclear-fueled generating plants with a combined capacity of approximately 13 million kw. While this was, roughly, 50% less than in the record year 1967, it was generally considered satisfactory, since the utilities also ordered fewer fossil-fueled units. At the year's end, U.S. nuclear-generating plants in service, under construction, and on order represented a combined output of about 64 million kw., considerably more than twice the nuclear total for all other nations together, and a capital investment of about $10 billion.

None of the newly ordered U.S. plants was small, and about half were rated at more than a million kilowatts each. The trend toward ever larger projects was exemplified by a single order, placed by a utility system, for a three-unit station designed to generate 2.4 million kw.; such a commitment would have been almost unimaginable a few years ago.

Reacting to the new contracts, the five manufacturers of power reactors in the U.S. and the many companies involved in the complex business of supplying nuclear fuels continued to expand their operations and the range of their interests. Perhaps the most spectacular increase occurred in the uranium production sector. According to U.S. government data, about 80 companies, including many of the nation's largest petroleum and gas producers, actively joined in the new uranium rush in the western U.S. Drilling to discover and develop new ore deposits was carried on at the rate of about 40 million ft. a year, more than twice as much as in the most active earlier year. Concern that low-cost uranium fuel might soon be in short supply faded as favourable results from the drilling were reported.

This apparent prosperity masked, however, a number of increasingly acute problems. At the year's end nuclear generating capacity actually operational in the U.S. was still discouragingly small, and there was little evidence to confirm that the many large units ordered since 1963 could be completed on schedule and brought into regular service without costly interruptions. In some of the most notorious cases construction delays were traceable to equipment manufacturing problems that would, presumably, not arise in later projects. There was less reason to be optimistic about another frequent cause of delay: the increasingly complicated process of obtaining local and federal permits to build and operate nuclear units.

For the utilities that had made the heaviest commitments to nuclear power, these uncertainties were a source of serious concern. Moreover, capital costs of nuclear power plants, which had risen sharply in 1967, continued to mount somewhat faster than the costs of fossil-fuel-burning units. All of these developments, while they did not seem to shake long-term confidence in the economic advantages of nuclear power, did raise doubts about prospects in the next few years.

Outside of the U.S. there was a perceptible quickening of nuclear power activity and some encouraging evidence of growing industrial maturity. The new nuclear generating capacity actually contracted for was not impressively large, about two-thirds the U.S.

total, and many of the individual plants were small by U.S. standards. However, most of the heavily industrialized non-Communist countries strongly confirmed their intention to rely heavily on nuclear power, and a number of relatively less developed countries planned to buy their first units.

Contracts to build multi-unit stations were announced in Britain, Canada, and Sweden, and important new orders were awarded or pending in Belgium, Italy, West Germany, Switzerland, and Japan. West Germany sold its first nuclear unit abroad, to Argentina: it was not only that country's first unit but also the first in South America. Brazil prepared to place its first order, as did South Korea. Both Nationalist China (Taiwan) and Thailand let it be known that they would be customers soon.

Perhaps the clearest evidence of nuclear-industrial vigour was the reaction to a bidding invitation by Dutch utilities for the Netherlands' first commercial-sized nuclear unit. The list of those who responded included 12 companies from 7 nations.

Sharp competition also served, however, to underline the fact that no solution had yet been found for one of the serious, chronic problems besetting the nuclear power industry outside the U.S. This was that, as in many other fields of manufacturing, almost every industrialized nation was committed to maintaining uneconomic, undernourished industrial and research capabilities. The problem was exemplified by the fact that no fewer than eight manufacturing plants, designed solely to produce fuel for one of the basic types of power reactor, were operating or under construction in Europe and Japan, and several more were planned. By contrast five similar but much larger plants served the U.S. market. The same contrast was evident in almost every other sector of the nuclear power industry overseas.

Fortunately, there were indications of increased willingness to cooperate and consolidate for the sake of efficiency and potential growth. Thus, in Britain the government began a drastic reorganization of the entire nuclear power industry, and in the process reduced the number of reactor manufacturers from three to two. In West Germany the two biggest reactor and fuel manufacturing companies pooled their interests by creating a new power plant construction subsidiary, and in both Canada and Sweden state-owned and private reactor design organizations were merged.

Virtually all of the industrialized countries continued to carry on more or less aggressive efforts to develop the reactor generally considered to offer the greatest long-term promise: the sodium-cooled, plutonium-fueled "breeder." National rivalry was the rule in this field, and there was much duplication in the elaborate and costly programs under way in the U.S., Britain, France, Italy, and Japan. An exception was the effective cooperation of West Germany, the Netherlands, and Belgium.

In Communist Eastern Europe, particularly Czechoslovakia, Poland, and Romania, plans for large nuclear-electric projects were announced. However, as in the past, it was difficult to judge when or whether any of these would actually get under way. The Soviet Union itself continued to concentrate on developing the "breeder" reactor, primarily to meet long-range needs. (Jo. H. S.)

The first steps toward building nuclear-powered "energy centres," which would use nuclear-powered desalting plants to provide fresh water and electricity in agroindustrial production complexes in arid regions, were taken by the U.S. Atomic Energy Commission. A study was under way to determine the potential of these centres. A similar plan was proposed for the Indo-Gangetic Plain in India. Consideration was given to developing a nuclear-powered industrial complex, in which heavy industry would be based around a large nuclear power facility that would act as the complex's energy source.

Both in the U.S. and in Britain the policy that restricted nuclear stations to more remote parts of the country was being changed. In Britain the minister of power announced that sites much closer to built-up areas could now be used, while in the U.S. applications were made to build nuclear power stations in the Hudson and East rivers near New York City. (Sy. Ho.)

Other Nonmilitary Uses. One of the most surprising results of the debates that led to the UN General Assembly's approval of the nonproliferation treaty was the emergence of a wide, intense, and, probably, premature interest in the use of nuclear explosives for excavation or recovery of minerals. The U.S. Atomic Energy Commission conducted one major excavation experiment—its first in several years—and evaluated a test sponsored by the government and industry that was carried out late in 1967 to determine whether underground nuclear detonations could free trapped natural gas and create a profitable well. Generally, the results were encouraging, and plans were made for similar experiments in gas, oil, and copper production; the creation of underground reservoirs; and water recovery.

The Soviet Union said nothing about any similar work it might be doing. Experts pointed out, however, that Soviet civil engineers often used large quantities of conventional explosives for excavation and speculated that the nuclear alternative must have been investigated. Britain evinced no interest in nuclear explosives. France, while it had little to say about the explosives, was widely believed to be investigating their use. Communist China's position remained unknown. Many of the nonnuclear weapons countries expressed keen interest.

In the U.S., the absence of a definite, approved program of space exploration for the 1970s seriously threatened one of the most glamorous—and costly—nonmilitary projects: the effort to develop a nuclear rocket engine, primarily for interplanetary missions. Exposed to heavy pressures in Congress, it nevertheless emerged with a budget of more than $90 million.

Another major program, the Atomic Energy Commission-sponsored construction of a 200-Bev (billion electron volt) particle accelerator, was not so fortunate, for Congress postponed appropriating the funds to build it. The huge machine, estimated to cost some $400 million, was scheduled to be built in northern Illinois, near Chicago.

In Western Europe a similar project was more seriously threatened when Britain decided that it could not afford to contribute to the construction of a 300-Bev machine proposed by the multinational European Centre for Nuclear Research. Ultimately, the construction budget was drastically cut to about $300 million, and planning continued on that basis. The choice of a site was narrowed to two possibilities, Italy and the Netherlands. (Jo. H. S.)

See also Defense; Fuel and Power; Physics.

ENCYCLOPÆDIA BRITANNICA FILMS. *Atomic Radiation* (1953); *Carbon Fourteen* (1953); *Atomic Energy—Inside the Atom* (1961); *Electrons at Work* (1961); *Evidence for Molecules and Atoms* (1961).

Obituaries 1968

The following is a selected list of prominent men and women who died during the year 1968.

ADAMS, JOHN JAMES ("JACK"), U.S. hockey player (b. Fort William, Ont., June 14, 1895—d. Detroit, Mich., May 1, 1968), elected to hockey's Hall of Fame in 1959, was general manager of the Detroit Red Wings (1927–62) and a founder (1962) and president of the Central Professional Hockey League.

AGAYANTS, IVAN IVANOVICH, major general, U.S.S.R. secret police (b. Yalisavetpol [now Kirovabad], Azerbaijan, Aug. 28, 1911—d. announced Moscow, U.S.S.R., May 14, 1968), who in 1967 became a deputy chief, one of the six highest ranking officers, in the Soviet State Security Committee (KGB), after having served as chief of the "Department of Disinformation" from 1959.

AILLERET, CHARLES-LOUIS-MARCEL, general, French Army (b. Gassicourt, France, March 26, 1907—d. Réunion Island, March 9, 1968), was chairman of the Joint Chiefs of Staff (from 1962) and director of France's atom-bomb project.

AKIMOV, NIKOLAI, Soviet theatre director and designer (b. St. Petersburg, Russia, 1901—d. Moscow, U.S.S.R., Sept. 6, 1968), was director of the Leningrad Comedy Theatre from 1936.

ALBERT, ÉDOUARD, French architect (b. Paris, France, July 8, 1910—d. Paris, Jan. 18, 1968), was trained at the École des Beaux-Arts and became a professor there in 1958. He gave Paris its first International Style skyscraper, the apartment block at 33, rue Croulebarbe.

ALEXANDER, HATTIE E., U.S. pediatrician (b. Baltimore, Md., April 5, 1901—d. New York, N.Y., June 24, 1968), an authority on the treatment of bacterial meningitis, was emeritus professor of pediatrics at the College of Physicians and Surgeons, Columbia University.

ALLEN, HERBERT WARNER, British journalist (b. Godalming, Surrey, Eng., March 8, 1881—d. Wallingford, Berkshire, Eng., Jan. 12, 1968), who, during World War I, was British press representative in France, Italy, and Germany (writing *The Unbroken Line,* 1916, and *Our Italian Front,* 1920). He was foreign editor of the *Morning Post* (1925–28), London editor of the *Yorkshire Post* (1928–30), and assistant deputy director of the Ministry of Information's foreign division (1940–41). Other books included *A History of Great Vintage Wines from Homer to the Present Day* (1961) and *The Wines of Portugal* (1962); the detective stories *Trent's Own Case* (with E. C. Bentley) and *The Uncounted Hour* (both 1936); and *The Timeless Moment* (1946).

ALVARO DA SILVA, AUGUSTO CARDINAL, Brazilian prelate of the Roman Catholic Church (b. Recife, Braz., April 8, 1876—d. Salvador, Braz., Aug. 14, 1968), archbishop of Bahia and Brazil's first cardinal, was ordained on March 5, 1899, and elevated to cardinal by Pope Pius XII on Jan. 12, 1953.

ARBUZOV, ALEKSANDR Y., Soviet organic chemist (b. Kazan, Russia, 1877—d. Kazan, U.S.S.R., Jan. 22, 1968), discoverer of the catalytic reaction of the rearrangement of neutral phosphites (Arbuzov rearrangement) and recipient of two Orders of Lenin, a Stalin Prize, and the title Hero of Socialist Labour; he was also a member of the Supreme Soviet.

ARCE, JOSÉ, Argentine diplomat (b. Loberia, Arg., Oct. 15, 1881—d. Buenos Aires, Arg., July 28, 1968), was a representative to the United Nations (1947–49), a member of Congress at various times between 1913 and 1938, and Argentina's ambassador to China in 1945–46.

ARMOUR, THOMAS DICKSON ("TOMMY"), U.S. golfer (b. Edinburgh, Scot., Sept. 24, 1895—d. Larchmont, N.Y., Sept. 11, 1968), played as an amateur with British teams before going to the United States in 1921. He became a professional in 1924 and won the Florida East Coast Open in 1925, the U.S. Open in 1927, the PGA in 1930, and the British Open in 1931.

ARNO, PETER, U.S. cartoonist (b. New York, N.Y., Jan. 8, 1904—d. Port Chester, N.Y., Feb. 22, 1968), was with *The New Yorker* magazine from 1925 until the time of his death. His cartoons were collected in several volumes, including *Peter Arno's Cartoon Revue* (1941), *Whoops, Dearie,* and *Man in the Shower.*

ASQUITH, ANTHONY, British film director (b. London, Eng., Nov. 9, 1902—d. London, Feb. 20, 1968), studied film making in Hollywood, Calif., before returning to England to join British Instructional Films. His famous collaboration with playwright Terence Rattigan began with *French Without Tears* (1940) and continued during and after World War II. His best-known films included *Pygmalion* (1938), *The Demi-Paradise* (1943), *The Importance of Being Earnest* (1953), *The Young Lovers* (1954), *Orders to Kill* (1958), and *The Doctor's Dilemma* (1959).

AUSTRAL, FLORENCE (FLORENCE WILSON), Australian soprano (b. Melbourne, Austr., April 26, 1894—d. Newcastle, New South Wales, Austr., May 16, 1968), won a scholarship at the Melbourne Conservatory in 1914, and studied in New York in 1918. She refused a contract by the Metropolitan Opera House, and made her first appearance (1921) at Covent Garden with the British National Opera Company in the role of Brünnhilde.

BABCOCK, HAROLD DELOS, U.S. astronomer (b. Edgerton, Wis., Jan. 24, 1882—d. Pasadena, Calif., April 8, 1968), a staff member of the Mount Wilson and Palomar observatories from 1908 until 1948, who in 1959 reported his discovery that the sun's magnetic field reverses itself periodically.

BAINTER, FAY (MRS. REGINALD S. H. VENABLE), U.S. stage and screen actress (b. Los Angeles, Calif., Dec. 7, 1893—d. Hollywood, Calif., April 16, 1968), won an Academy Award in 1938 for her portrayal of Auntie Belle in *Jezebel.*

BAKER, DOROTHY DODD (MRS. HAROLD BAKER), U.S. novelist (b. Missoula, Mont., April 21, 1907—d. Terra Bella, Calif., June 18, 1968), author of *Young Man with a Horn* (1938), *Trio* (1943), *Our Gifted Son* (1948), and *Cassandra at the Wedding* (1962).

BANKHEAD, TALLULAH, U.S. actress (b. Huntsville, Ala., Jan. 31, 1903—d. New York, N.Y., Dec. 12, 1968), achieved her first success in London in *The Dancers* (1923). After eight years on the London stage she returned to the U.S. and made a number of Broadway appearances during the 1930s. Her most successful roles were Regina in *The Little Foxes* (1939) and Sabrina in *The Skin of Our Teeth* (1942), for each of which she received the year's award for best acting of the season from the New York Drama Critics Circle. Her most popular film was *Lifeboat* (1944). An autobiography, *Tallulah,* was published in 1952.

BARODA, MAHARAJA OF, SIR PRATAPSINHA GAEKWAR, Indian prince (b. June 29, 1908—d. London, Eng., July 19, 1968), was ruler of Baroda, an important Indian princely state, from 1939 to 1951. He was deposed in 1951 by the government for opposing the absorption of Baroda into the then Bombay state. Still the possessor of a great personal fortune, he went to live in England where he was well known as a successful racehorse owner.

BARRY, SIR GERALD REID, British journalist (b. Surbiton, Surrey, Eng., Nov. 20, 1898—d. Belgravia, London, Eng., Nov. 21, 1968), entered journalism after World War I and became editor of the *Saturday Review;* from 1936 until 1947 he was managing editor of the daily *News Chronicle.* From 1948 to 1951 he headed the committee supervising the Festival of Britain. He was also a co-founder of Political and Economic Planning.

BARTH, KARL, Swiss theologian (b. Basel, Switz., May 10, 1886—d. Basel, Dec. 9, 1968), who, as an unknown country pastor, in 1919 presented to the world his book *The Epistle to the Romans,* expressing his idea of the radical transcendence of God, which "landed like a bombshell in the playground of the theologians." Known as the "Red Pastor," Barth joined the Social Democratic Party in 1915, took up the post of professor of Reformed theology at the University of Göttingen in 1921, then in 1925 became professor of dogmatics and New Testament exegesis at the University of Münster in Westphalia. His *Doctrine of the Word of God* appeared in 1927, and in 1932, while professor of systematic theology at Bonn, he published the first part of the massive *Church Dogmatics,* which had grown to 12 volumes by 1962 when he retired.

BARTLETT, EDWARD LEWIS, U.S. senator (from 1959) from Alaska (b. Seattle, Wash., April 20, 1904—d. Cleveland, O., Dec. 11, 1968).

BASDEVANT, JULES, French jurist (b. Anost, France, April 15, 1877—d. Anost, Jan. 6, 1968), member (1939–64), vice-president (1946–49), and president (1949–52) of the International Court of Justice.

BEA, AUGUSTIN CARDINAL, German prelate of the Roman Catholic Church (b. Riedböhringen, Baden, Ger., May 28, 1881—d. Rome, Italy, Nov. 15, 1968), president of the Vatican Secretariat for Christian Unity, was the main architect of the church's ecumenical policy. He entered the Jesuit novitiate in the Netherlands, and was ordained in 1912. He was put in charge of the Jesuits' Institute for Higher Ecclesiastical Studies in Rome in 1924, moving in 1928 to the Pontifical Biblical Institute, of which he became rector in 1930. He was confessor to Pope Pius XII from 1941. Pope John XXIII created him a cardinal in December 1959 and in 1960 made him president of the Secretariat for Christian Unity, which was responsible for introducing the decrees on ecumenism, religious liberty, and relations with non-Christians promulgated by the second Vatican Council.

BEATTY, SIR (ALFRED) CHESTER, British mining engineer and industrialist (b. New York, N.Y., Feb. 7, 1875—d. Monte Carlo, Monaco, Jan. 19, 1968), established the Zambian copper belt as a major mining area.

BELLENGER, FREDERICK JOHN, British politician (b. Abertillery, Monmouthshire, Wales, July 23, 1894—d. London, Eng., May 11, 1968), was secretary of state for war (1946–47). After serving in France throughout World War I, he became an estate agent and a Conservative councillor for Fulham (London). Joining the Labour Party (1928), he defeated Malcolm MacDonald (son of the then prime minister) at Bassetlaw, Nottinghamshire, in 1935, and held the seat until his death.

BENADERET, BEA (MRS. GENE TWOMBLEY), U.S. radio and television actress (b. New York, N.Y., April 4, 1906—d. Hollywood, Calif., Oct. 13, 1968), starred in the TV comedy series "Petticoat Junction" from its introduction in 1963 until the time of her death.

Anthony Asquith   Tallulah Bankhead   Karl Barth   Augustin Cardinal Bea

BEN-GURION, PAULA (Monbaz or Moonmess), wife of David Ben-Gurion, prime minister of Israel from 1948 until 1963 (b. Minsk, Russia, 1892—d. Beersheba, Israel, Jan. 29, 1968).

BENIOFF, HUGO, U.S. seismologist (b. Los Angeles, Calif., Sept. 14, 1899—d. Mendocino, Calif., Feb. 29, 1968), designer of many instruments used to study and record earthquakes, became a full professor (emeritus from 1964) at the California Institute of Technology in 1950. He was a contributor to *Encyclopædia Britannica*.

BENITZ-REIXACH, LUCIENNE ("La Mome Moineau" [kid sparrow]), French popular singer and entertainer (b. 1905—d. Paris, France, Jan. 18, 1968), who at age 15 was selling flowers on the Champs Elysée in Paris; in the early 1920s (under the patronage of Paul Poiret, a fashionable couturier) she became a popular cabaret singer. After a last stage appearance in 1930, she retired and her eccentric exploits in fashionable French society made her a legendary figure.

BERG, PAAL OLAV, Norwegian jurist (b. Hammerfest, Nor., Jan. 18, 1873—d. Oslo, Nor., May 24, 1968), president of the Supreme Court (1929–40, 1945–46), was minister of social affairs (1919–20), minister of justice (1924–26), member of the governing body of the International Labour Organization (1937–45) and its president in 1938–39. He was also a member (1954–62) of the Council of Europe's Commission on Human Rights. He published books on the Norwegian constitution, human rights, and labour legislation.

BIDDLE, FRANCIS, U.S. jurist (b. Paris, France, May 9, 1886—d. Hyannis, Mass., Oct. 4, 1968), who was U.S. attorney general from 1941 until 1945, also served as chairman of the National Labor Relations Board (1934–39), U.S. circuit court judge (1939), U.S. solicitor general (1940), and, following World War II, as a judge at the Nürnberg trials of Nazi war criminals. In later years he was chairman of Americans for Democratic Action (ADA) and an adviser to the American Civil Liberties Union. He wrote several books including *Fear of Freedom* (1951) and his memoirs, *In Brief Authority* (1962).

BLOMDAHL, KARL-BIRGER, Swedish composer (b. Växjö, Swed., Oct. 19, 1916—d. Stockholm, Swed., June 16, 1968), who gained an international reputation with a space opera, *Aniara*, in 1959, also composed the Third Symphony (1948), *In the Hall of Mirrors* (a choral cycle), *Sisyfos* (a choreographic suite), and a second opera which was scheduled to be premiered in the 1969-70 season in Stockholm.

BOGGESS, LYNTON R. ("Dusty"), U.S. baseball umpire (b. Terrell, Tex., 1904—d. Dallas, Tex., July 8, 1968), was with the National League from 1944 until 1962; his memoirs, *Kill the Ump!*, were published in 1966.

BOISSIER, LÉOPOLD, Swiss executive (b. Geneva, Switz., July 16, 1893—d. Geneva, Oct. 22, 1968), president of the International Red Cross Committee during 1955–64. He held diplomatic posts in London and Rome (1917–20), and was president of the International Parliamentary Union, 1933–53.

BONNARD, ABEL, French man of letters (b. Poitiers, France, Dec. 17, 1883—d. Madrid, Spain, May 31, 1968), made his name in the 1920s in the Paris literary salons as a poet and a wit. A series of biographies and travel books won his election to the Académie Française in 1932. He was converted to Nazism by an interview with Hitler and during World War II was appointed minister of education by Pierre Laval in the Vichy government of 1942, despite Marshal Pétain's protest. At the liberation of France in 1944, he escaped to Spain but was sentenced to death, in absentia, by a French court in 1945 and expelled from the Académie Française. He voluntarily returned to France in 1958, was tried again in 1960, and sentenced to ten years' banishment. This sentence was considered as having been served by his exile, and he was permitted to return to Spain.

BOROVSKY, ALEXANDER, U.S. concert pianist (b. Mitau, Latvia, March 18, 1889—d. Waban, Mass., April 27, 1968), was one of the first artists to record the 30 *Inventions* of Bach and all of the Liszt Hungarian rhapsodies; his last recording (in 1956) was Bach's "Forty-eight Preludes and Fugues." Borovsky was soloist with the Boston Symphony Orchestra at more than 30 concerts and was professor of piano at Boston University from 1956.

BOWDEN, FRANK PHILIP, British scientist (b. Tasmania, Austr., May 2, 1903—d. Cambridge, Eng., Sept. 3, 1968), a specialist in problems connected with the surfaces of metals, who became professor of surface physics and director of the subdepartment of surface physics at the Cavendish Laboratory, Cambridge University, in 1965. His best-known work was, with D. Tabor, *The Friction and Lubrication of Solids,* 2 vol. (1950, 1964).

BOYD, JAMES DIXON, British medical anatomist (b. Brooklyn, N.Y., Sept. 29, 1907—d. Cambridge, Eng., Feb. 7, 1968), a leading authority on embryology and placentology, in 1951 became professor of anatomy at Cambridge University, where he remained until his death. He was co-author of a standard textbook on embryology.

BRENNAN, FRANCIS CARDINAL, U.S. prelate of the Roman Catholic Church (b. Shenandoah, Pa., May 7, 1894—d. Philadelphia, Pa., July 2, 1968), head of the Congregation of Sacraments, was with the Roman Curia for almost 30 years. He was the first American to be named to the Sacred Roman Rota (1940), the first American appointed chief judge of the Rota (1959), and the first American chosen to direct a congregation (1968). He was elevated to cardinal in 1967.

BRIDGES, THOMAS ("Tommy"), U.S. baseball player (b. Gordonsville, Tenn., Dec. 28, 1906—d. Nashville, Tenn., April 19, 1968), whose entire 16-year major league career was spent as a pitcher for the Detroit Tigers (1930–46); his record of 194 games won and 138 lost included a 4–1 World Series record.

BRINTON, CRANE, U.S. educator and historian (b. Winsted, Conn., Feb. 2, 1898—d. Cambridge, Mass., Sept. 7, 1968), became McLean professor of ancient and modern history at Harvard University in 1942, having been associated with that institution since 1923. He was the author of 15 books including *The Anatomy of Revolution* (1938).

BROD, MAX, Austrian novelist, critic, and playwright (b. Prague, Aus., May 27, 1884—d. Tel Aviv, Israel, Dec. 20, 1968), friend and biographer of Franz Kafka, for some years editor of the *Prager Tagblatt.* A convinced Zionist, he went to Palestine in 1939 to work with the Haima Theatre. His several historical novels included *Tycho Brahes Weg zu Gott* (1916; trans. as *The Redemption of Tycho Brahe,* 1928). His autobiography, *Streitbares Leben,* appeared in 1960 and a volume of reminiscences, *Der Prager Kreis,* in 1967.

BROOKES, SIR NORMAN, Australian tennis player (b. Melbourne, Austr., 1877—d. Melbourne, Sept. 28, 1968), who played on Davis Cup teams from 1905 until 1920, won the Wimbledon singles championships in 1905, 1907, and 1914. He was president of the Lawn Tennis Association of Australia from 1926 until 1955.

BROWN, ELMER, U.S. union executive (b. Tennessee, 1902—d. Colorado Springs, Colo., Feb. 27, 1968), president of the International Typographical Union from 1958 until the time of his death.

BROWN, JOE B., U.S. jurist (b. Dallas, Tex., June 9, 1908—d. Dallas, Feb. 20, 1968), was the district court judge who presided at the murder trial of Jack Ruby (d. 1967), slayer of Lee Harvey Oswald, the alleged assassin of Pres. John F. Kennedy (d. 1963).

AGIP FROM PICTORIAL PARADE   UPI (UK) LTD.

Abel Bonnard   Sir Alexander Cadogan

BROWNE, BENJAMIN CHAPMAN, British scientist (b. April 29, 1911—d. Balsham, Cambridge, Eng., Aug. 14, 1968), who made an important contribution to the measurement of gravity, was head of the Department of Geodesy and Geophysics at Cambridge University from 1948 to 1960. In assessing the effect of the movements of a ship on the measurement of gravity he showed that a correction of the usual method, since known as the "Browne Correction," was necessary.

BRUCKER, WILBER M(ARION), U.S. politician (b. Saginaw, Mich., June 23, 1894—d. Detroit, Mich., Oct. 28, 1968), governor of Michigan (1930–32), served in the Eisenhower Cabinet as secretary of the army from 1955 until 1961.

BUCHANAN, SCOTT MILROSS, U.S. philosopher, author, and educator (b. Sprague, Wash., March 17, 1895—d. Santa Barbara, Calif., March 25, 1968), during the 1930s pioneered in the "great books" programs that were introduced at the University of Chicago and St. John's College at Annapolis, Md. In 1957 he joined the Fund for the Republic and continued working with its offshoot, the Center for the Study of Democratic Institutions. Buchanan published a number of books, including *Poetry and Mathematics* (1929) and *Essays in Politics* (1953).

BURNEY, SIR CHARLES DENNISTOUN, British naval officer and inventor (b. Upham, Hampshire, Eng., Dec. 28, 1888—d. Hamilton, Bermuda, Nov. 11, 1968), who designed the paravane (a device to protect ships against mines), developed an interest in aeronautics in 1911, doing research for Sir George White's Bristol aviation works. In 1913 he was engaged on antisubmarine defense, and urged the use of shipborne aircraft. In World War I he devised the paravane which saved at least 90 ships during that war. Attracted by the concept of the airship in the 1930s, he joined with Vickers to form the Airship Guarantee Co. which built the R100. He was the author of *The World, the Air and the Future.*

CADOGAN, SIR ALEXANDER GEORGE MONTAGU, British diplomat and civil servant (b. Nov. 25, 1884—d. London, Eng., July 9, 1968), held a position of crucial importance during World War II, and accompanied Winston Churchill to the Yalta and Potsdam Conferences. He entered the diplomatic service in 1908, serving at Constantinople and Vienna; he was counselor at the Foreign Office (1928); minister (1933–35) and then ambassador (1935–36) at Peking; deputy undersecretary of state for foreign affairs from 1936 until 1946; and Britain's permanent representative at the UN (1946–50).

CAM, HELEN MAUD, British medieval historian (b. Abingdon, Eng., Aug. 22, 1885—d. Orpington, Kent, Eng., Feb. 9, 1968), Zemurray Radcliffe professor of history at Harvard University from 1948 to 1954, was the first woman to hold a full professorship on the Harvard faculty of arts and sciences. Her publications included *The Hundred and the Hundred Rolls* (1930) and *Liberties and Communities in Medieval England* (1944).

CARLSON, CHESTER F., U.S. physicist (b. Seattle, Wash., Feb. 8, 1906—d. New York, N.Y., Sept. 19, 1968), invented the reproduction process known as xerography ("dry writing"), which was developed by the Battelle Memorial Institute of Columbus, O., and introduced commercially in 1959 by Haloid-Xerox (later the Xerox Corp.) of Rochester, N.Y.

CARNAHAN, A(LBERT) S(IDNEY) J(OHNSON), U.S. congressman (1945–47, 1949–61) from Missouri (b. Ellsinore, Mo., Jan. 9, 1897—d. Rochester, Minn., March 24, 1968), served as the first U.S. ambassador to Sierra Leone from 1961 until 1963.

CARR, MICHAEL, British composer (b. Leeds, Eng., 1904—d. London, Eng., Sept. 16, 1968), wrote such popular favourites of the 1930s and 1940s as "Did Your Mother Come from Ireland?," "Hang Out the Washing on the Siegfried Line," and "South of the Border."

CARROLL, PAUL VINCENT, Irish dramatist (b. Dundalk, County Louth, Ire., July 10, 1900—d. Bromley, Kent, Eng., Oct. 20, 1968), achieved success with *Shadow and Substance* (Abbey Theatre, Dublin, 1937; New York, 1938), which won the Casement Award of the Irish Academy of Letters and the New York Drama Critics Circle's Foreign Award. *The Watched Pot* (1931; his first play), *The Things That Are Caesar's* (1932; Abbey Theatre Award), and *The Wise Have Not Spoken* (1933) were produced at the Abbey. With the Abbey's rejection, as anticlerical, of *The White Steed* (1939; also a Drama Critics award winner), Carroll moved to the U.S., but returned to Britain in 1941. Later plays included *The Strings, My Lord, Are False* (Dublin, 1942), *The Old Foolishness* (1945), *The Devil Came from Dublin* (1952), and *The Wayward Saint* (1955). Of filmscripts, notable was that for Sir Alexander Korda's *Saints and Sinners* (1948). In Glasgow he founded the Curtain Theatre (1933) and the Glasgow Citizens' Theatre (1943), of which he remained a director until his death.

CASTELNUOVO-TEDESCO, MARIO, U.S. composer (b. Florence, Italy, April 3, 1895—d. Hollywood, Calif., March 15, 1968), whose last opera, *The Merchant of Venice,* was awarded the $8,000 Campari Prize in Italy in 1961.

CASTRO, JUAN JOSÉ, Argentine composer and conductor (b. Buenos Aires, Arg., March 7, 1895 —d. Buenos Aires, Sept. 3, 1968), for many years director of the Teatro Colòn of Buenos Aires, was dismissed in 1944 for his outspoken disapproval of the Axis powers. He then conducted his own symphony orchestra in 1946–47, but because of public disagreement with Pres. Juan D. Perón was compelled to leave Argentina. In 1951 Castro won the La Scala contest for his composition "Prosperina," and in 1954, at the first Inter-American Music Festival in Caracas, Venez., he won first prize for his "Corales Criollos No. 3." He returned to Brazil in 1956 and conducted at the Teatro Colòn for about a year, then joined the faculty of the new National Conservatory at San Juan, P.R. Other works included "Sinfonia Argentina," "Sinfonia Biblica," and "Suite Breve."

CHAPPELL, MATTHEW N., U.S. psychologist (b. Wakefield, R.I., July 26, 1900—d. Amityville, N.Y., Feb. 10, 1968), professor (emeritus from 1961) and chairman of the department of psychology at Hofstra University, Hempstead, N.Y.; wrote *In the Name of Common Sense* (1938; reissued 1949).

CHATEAUBRIAND BANDEIRA DE MELLO, FRANCISCO DE ASSIS ("CHATÔ"), Brazilian publisher (b. Umbuzeiro, Paraíba, Braz., April 10, 1891—d. São Paulo, Braz., April 4, 1968), was the owner of a Latin-American communications empire that included 32 newspapers, 18 TV stations, 24 radio stations, 4 magazines, and 1 news agency.

CHRYSOSTOMOS, ARCHBISHOP (THEMISTOCLES S. HADJISTAVROU), prelate of the Greek Orthodox Church (b. Aydin, Asia Minor, 1880— d. Athens, Greece, June 9, 1968), took office as primate of Greece and archbishop of Athens in 1962 and was deposed in May 1967 by the military regime that took over his country. After ordination he served in Eastern Macedonia but

fled to escape a prison sentence for having organized Greek guerrilla fighters. He was consecrated a suffragan bishop in 1910 and given his first see, in Turkey, three years later. In the mid-1920s he was appointed to the new diocese of Kavalla in Greek East Macedonia, where he served for 38 years. He presided at the 1961 Pan-Orthodox Conference, held on the island of Rhodes, of the 12 main Orthodox churches of the world, the largest such conference in 12 centuries.

CHURCHILL, RANDOLPH (FREDERICK EDWARD SPENCER), British author, journalist, and politician (b. London, Eng., May 28, 1911— d. East Bergholt, Suffolk, Eng., June 6, 1968), only son of Sir Winston Churchill, was a popular journalist in the 1930s. He thrice failed to enter Parliament before becoming Conservative member for Preston (1940–45). During World War II he served as an intelligence officer in the Middle East and Yugoslavia. He was unsuccessful in parliamentary elections in 1945, 1950, and 1951. His books on controversial topics included *What I Said About the Press* (1957), *The Rise and Fall of Sir Anthony Eden* (1959), and *The Fight for the Tory Leadership* (1964). He wrote a historical study, *Lord Derby: King of Lancashire* (1960), and by his death had published two volumes of a definitive biography of his father.

CLARK, JAMES ("JIM"), Scottish auto racing champion (b. Berwickshire, Scot., 1936—d. Hockenheim, W.Ger., April 7, 1968), was killed when his Lotus-Ford went out of control during the German Formula II championship race. The "Flying Scot" was the youngest driver to win a Formula I world championship, attained in 1963. In 1965 he again won the Formula I championship, and then added the Indianapolis 500 to his record. At the time of his death Clark had won a record 25 Grand Prix races.

COBB, STANLEY, U.S. neurologist (b. Brookline, Mass., Dec. 10, 1887—d. Cambridge, Mass., Feb. 25, 1968), Bullard professor emeritus of neuropathology at Harvard University, joined the Harvard faculty of medicine in 1919 and retired in 1954. Cobb wrote a number of books, including *Borderlands of Psychiatry* and *Emotions and Clinical Medicine*. In 1956 he received one of the first Albert Einstein Awards.

COGNY, RENÉ, general (ret.), French Army (b. 1904—d. in the Mediterranean, Sept. 11, 1968), killed in the crash of a French airliner, was field commander of the French forces in North Vietnam that lost the battle of Dien Bien Phu in 1954, leading to France's withdrawal from Indochina. Cogny was commander in chief of French forces in Morocco in 1956, and for French Central Africa in 1959.

COHEN, SIR ANDREW BENJAMIN, British civil servant (b. Berkhamsted, Eng., Oct. 7, 1909—d. London, Eng., June 17, 1968), did much to make possible the grant of independence to the British colonies and protectorates in Africa. Except for a period of three years in Malta during World War II, Cohen served continuously in the Colonial Office from 1933 to 1951. As head of the African division of that department from 1947 he used his influence and his great talents in preparing his African charges for independence. Later, as governor of Uganda (1951–57), he introduced many political and economic reforms. British representative on the Trusteeship Council of the UN (1957–61), Cohen was at the time of his death permanent secretary to the Ministry of Overseas Development.

COMINSKY, JACOB ROBERT, U.S. publisher (b. Rochester, N.Y., April 11, 1899—d. Asbury Park, N.J., Aug. 2, 1968), was vice-president of the McCall Corp. and publisher of the *Saturday Review*.

CONCEPCIÓN DE GRACIA, GILBERTO, Puerto Rican lawyer (b. 1909—d. San Juan, P.R., March 15, 1968), leader of Puerto Rico's Independence Party from its founding in 1946.

CONSTANT, HAYNE, British aeronautical engineer (b. Gravesend, Kent, Eng., Sept. 26, 1904— d. Jan. 12, 1968), who helped develop the jet aircraft engine by his work on axial flow compressors, began working on gas turbines in 1936, joined the National Gas Turbine Establishment, becoming director in 1948, and was made chief scientist (RAF) at the Ministry of Defense in 1964. He was awarded the Royal Aeronautical

Society's gold medal in 1963 and was a fellow of the Royal Society.

COREY, WENDELL, U.S. actor (b. Dracut, Mass., March 20, 1914—d. Woodland Hills, Calif., Nov. 8, 1968), star of the television series "Eleventh Hour," first won motion picture stardom in *The Accused* (1948), and continued playing major roles through the 1950s and 1960s. Among his better known films were *Rear Window* (1954), *The Rack* (1956), and *The Rainmaker* (1957).

CROSS, SIR RONALD HIBBERT, British administrator (b. May 9, 1896—d. London, Eng., June 3, 1968), was high commissioner in Australia during a critical period of World War II. Educated at Eton, he served in World War I and thereafter became a merchant banker. He entered Parliament as a Conservative in 1931 and became minister of economic warfare in 1939. In 1940 he was minister of shipping but went to Australia as high commissioner in 1941. During 1941–45, when Australia was in danger of Japanese attack, Cross had the responsible task of explaining British policy to the Australian public. He was later governor of Tasmania (1951–58).

CUMMINS, CLESSIE L., U.S. transportation executive (b. 1889—d. Sausalito, Calif., Aug. 18, 1968), who, during the 1930s, developed the diesel engine for use in highway transportation.

DALE, SIR HENRY HALLETT, British physiologist (b. London, Eng., June 9, 1875—d. Cambridge, Eng., July 23, 1968), won the 1936 Nobel Prize (with Otto Loewi) for Physiology or Medicine for his work on the chemical transmission of nerve impulses. Educated at Cambridge University and St. Bartholomew's Hospital, London, he began his research career in 1904 at the Wellcome Physiological Research Laboratories, of which he was director from 1906 to 1914. During this period he investigated the chemical composition and effects of ergot of rye, and developed his important researches into the pharmacologically active substances histamine and acetylcholine. In 1914 Dale joined the staff of what later became the Medical Research Council and from 1928 to 1942 was director of the National Institute for Medical Research. Among other offices he held were the presidency of the Royal Society (1940–45) and of the British Association for the Advancement of Science (1947). He was knighted in 1932 and awarded the Order of Merit in 1944.

DAVIES, WILLIAM, British scientist (b. London, Eng., April 20, 1899—d. Reading, Eng., July 28, 1968), won an international reputation for his work on grassland productivity. Trained at Aberystwyth under the famous grassland expert George Stapledon, he worked for a time in New Zealand and Australia, and during 1933–40 completed the first grassland survey of England and Wales. From 1949 to 1964 he was director of the Grassland Research Institute at Hurley.

DAWSON, WARREN ROYAL, British egyptologist (b. London, Eng., Oct. 13, 1888—d. Bletchley, Buckinghamshire, Eng., May 5, 1968), was an expert on the methods employed in mummification; he was a contributor to *Encyclopædia Britannica*.

DE BLANK, JOOST, British Anglican clergyman (b. Rotterdam, Neth., Nov. 14, 1908—d. London, Eng., Jan. 1, 1968), who as archbishop of Cape Town from 1957 to 1963 ceaselessly proclaimed the incompatibility of apartheid with Christianity, was ordained in 1931. He served as an army chaplain during World War II, and

Juan José Castro   Archbishop Chrysostomos

Randolph Churchill   James Clark

filled a pastorate at Harrow from 1948 until 1952 (described in his book *The Parish in Action*); he became a canon of Westminster Abbey in 1964.

DEHN, ADOLF ARTHUR, U.S. painter and printmaker (b. Waterville, Minn., Nov. 22, 1895—d. New York, N.Y., May 19, 1968), who was a successful lithographer, turned to watercolours in 1936 and became a leading artist in that medium. Dehn wrote several books and a number of magazine articles; he was also a contributor to *Encyclopædia Britannica.*

DEL PIERRE, FRANCINE (JEANNINE BON SAINT-ANDRÉ), French potter (b. Paris, France, Dec. 2, 1912—d. Paris, Jan. 1968), whose mature work was influenced by Bernard Leach (whom she met in 1952) and by Hamada. She was associated with the Sèvres factory. Her awards included the Grand Prix and gold medal of the Milan Triennale (1957).

DE MAISTRE, ROY, Australian painter (b. Bowral, New South Wales, Austr., March 27, 1894—d. London, Eng., March 1, 1968), was known for his modern religious paintings, portraits, and still lifes. After early years in Australia and Paris, he emigrated to London. His "Stations of the Cross" at Westminster Cathedral was installed in 1956. In 1960 a retrospective exhibition of his work was held at the Whitechapel Art Gallery, London.

DERTINGER, GEORG, East German government official (b. Berlin, Ger., Dec. 25, 1902—d. Leipzig, E.Ger., Jan. 21, 1968), was the first foreign minister for East Germany (1949–53).

D'HARNONCOURT, RENÉ, U.S. museum director (b. Vienna, Aus., May 17, 1901—d. New Suffolk, N.Y., Aug. 13, 1968), was the director of the Museum of Modern Art, New York City, from 1949 until his retirement in 1968.

DILLON, GEORGE HILL, U.S. poet and editor (b. Jacksonville, Fla., Nov. 12, 1906—d. Charleston, S.C., May 9, 1968), who published his first book of poems, *Boy in the Wind,* in 1927, won the 1932 Pulitzer Prize in poetry for his second, *Flowering Stone.* In the 1920s he became associated with *Poetry* magazine and served as its editor from 1937 until 1949.

DIMITROFF, GEORGE Z., U.S. astronomer (b. Svistove, Bulg., Aug. 24, 1901—d. Hartland, Vt., Jan. 1, 1968), in 1946 became professor of astronomy (emeritus from 1966) at Dartmouth College, Hanover, N.H.; he was superintendent (1937–42) of the Oak Ridge, Mass., station of the Harvard Observatory.

DIRKS, RUDOLPH, U.S. cartoonist (b. Heide, Ger., Feb. 26, 1877—d. New York, N.Y., April 20, 1968), created the "Katzenjammer Kids" in 1897 and continued to produce the comic strip for the rest of his life. The long-running "bad boys of the funnies" strip, retitled several times ("Hans and Fritz," "The Captain and the Kids"), was scheduled to keep on appearing under the guidance of Dirks's son John.

DOBI, ISTVÁN, Hungarian statesman (b. Szöny, Hung., Dec. 31, 1898—d. Budapest, Hung., Nov. 24, 1968), joined the Smallholders' Party in the 1930s and soon became one of its officials; in World War II he served in the Hungarian Army. Elected to the National Assembly in 1945, he was minister of state from November 1945 to February 1946, then minister of agriculture until November. In January 1947 he was appointed to the five-member committee to purge his party of anti-Communist elements. So, when his old leaders had been deposed, he became chairman of his party in May 1947. After being minister of agriculture again from April 1948, he became premier on Dec. 9, 1948. He retained this post until Aug. 14, 1952, when he became head of state. He joined the Hungarian Socialist Workers' (Communist) Party in 1959 and was elected to its Central Committee. He was superseded as head of state in April 1967.

DOBSON, SIR ROY HARDY, British aircraft designer and manufacturer (b. Horsforth, Yorkshire, Eng., Sept. 27, 1891—d. Midhurst, Sussex, Eng., July 7, 1968), joined A. V. Roe, aircraft company, as a fitter in 1914. He was chairman of the Hawker Siddeley Group from 1963 until 1967. During World War II he was largely responsible for the development and production of the four-engined Lancaster bomber. He was knighted in 1945.

DONDERO, GEORGE A., U.S. congressman (1933–57) from Michigan (b. Greenfield Township, Mich., Dec. 16, 1883—d. Royal Oak, Mich., Jan. 29, 1968), author of the St. Lawrence Seaway bill.

DÖNGES, (THEOPHILUS) EBEN(HAEZER), president-elect of South Africa (b. Klerksdorp, Transvaal, S.Af., March 8, 1898—d. Cape Town, S.Af., Jan. 10, 1968), who was stricken with illness three weeks before his inaugural ceremony on May 31, 1967, had served as minister of the interior (1948–58) and finance minister (1958–66); he was elected president in January 1967.

DORLING, HENRY TAPRELL, British naval officer and writer (b. Duns, Berwickshire, Scot., Sept. 8, 1883—d. London, Eng., July 1, 1968), was widely known under the pseudonym "Taffrail" for his books on ships and the sea and on life in the Royal Navy in war and peace. He was press liaison officer to the commander in chief, Mediterranean (1942–45), and after World War II became well known as a broadcaster.

DREYER, CARL, Danish motion-picture director (b. Feb. 3, 1889—d. Copenhagen, Denmark, March 20, 1968), a pioneer in silent films, introduced many effective techniques in lighting, close-ups, and composing of scenes. Among his 14 feature films were *The Passion of Joan of Arc* (1928), *Day of Wrath* (1948), and *Ordet* (1955).

DUCHAMP, MARCEL, French–U.S. painter (b. Blainville, France, July 28, 1887—d. Neuilly, France, Oct. 1, 1968), whose painting "Nude Descending a Staircase" caused a sensation at the 1913 Armory Exhibit in New York City, was an exponent of Cubism and a founder of Dada. Another work, on transparent glass, "The Bride Stripped Bare by Her Bachelors, Even," was never finished, since Duchamp gave up painting at the age of 36. However, his short painting career influenced the moderns and paved the way for the pop and op art of the 1960s. The Pasadena (Calif.) Art Museum presented the first Duchamp retrospective in 1963, and in 1966 the Tate Gallery in London mounted a survey of his work.

DUNOYER DE SEGONZAC, PIERRE, general (ret.), French Army (b. Toulon, France, March 10, 1906—d. Paris, France, March 13, 1968), obtained leave from the Army after the Franco-German armistice of June 1940 for the purpose of founding the École Nationale des Cadres (in Uriage) as a training centre for future officers. The school was suppressed by the government in 1942 and went underground, while Dunoyer de Segonzac organized the armed maquis of the anti-German resistance. During the liberation of France, he led his "Bayard" volunteers and took part in the invasion of Germany (1945). He was promoted general of brigade in 1959 and retired in 1963.

DURYEA, DAN, U.S. actor (b. White Plains, N.Y., Jan. 23, 1907—d. Hollywood, Calif., June 7, 1968), whose first screen appearance was in *The Little Foxes* (1941), made a total of more than 60 motion pictures, of which *Flight of the Phoenix* (1965) was one of the most memorable. Duryea also was credited with about 75 television parts, including the lead in "The Adventures of China Smith" series (1952) and a continuing role in the "Peyton Place" series.

EDWARDS, NESS, British trade unionist and Labour politician (b. Abertillery, Monmouth-

shire, Wales, April 5, 1897—d. Caerphilly, Glamorgan, Wales, May 3, 1968), was postmaster general from 1950 to 1951. A miner from the age of 13, he held various union appointments (1927–38) in South Wales before becoming (1939) member of Parliament for Caerphilly. As parliamentary secretary to the Ministry of Labour and National Service (1945–50) he did much to maintain smooth labour relations after World War II. In protest against its defense policy, he resigned (1960) from Hugh Gaitskell's shadow cabinet, becoming chairman (1964) of the Labour Parliamentary Trade Union Group.

EISLER, GERHART, German Communist (b. Leipzig, Ger., Feb. 20, 1897—d. Armenian Soviet Socialist Republic, March 21, 1968), during the 1940s spent a number of years in the United States directing the Communist movement. In 1947 he refused to testify before the House Committee on Un-American Activities and was sentenced to a year in jail. While his case was pending appeal Eisler jumped bail and fled to East Germany, where he became a leading Communist propagandist as chairman of the Central Committee's radio and television committee.

EKELÖF, GUNNAR, Swedish poet (b. Stockholm, Swed., Sept. 15, 1907—d. Sigtuna, Swed., March 16, 1968), was the author of 15 volumes of poetry, including an English translation, *Selected Poems,* published in 1967. He also wrote several books of essays and some works on art. In 1964 he was awarded the Grand Prize for Poetry by the Danish Academy, and he received the prize of the Scandinavian Council in 1966 for his poem "Diwan."

ELMAN, ZIGGY (HARRY FINKELMAN), U.S. jazz trumpeter (b. Philadelphia, Pa., May 26, 1914—d. Los Angeles, Calif., June 26, 1968), was featured with the big bands of Benny Goodman and Tommy Dorsey during the 1930s and 1940s, and later formed his own group. His best-known recordings included "And the Angels Sing," "Zaggin' with Zig," and "Forgive My Heart."

ELZE, JUPP, German boxer (b. Cologne, Ger., Dec. 14, 1939—d. Cologne, W.Ger., June 20, 1968), who was middleweight champion of West Germany from May 1964, died of injuries received June 12 during a 15-round TKO bout with European middleweight champion Carlos Duran of Italy. Elze's record (from 1961) stood at 35 professional bouts won, 6 lost, 1 draw, and 1 no decision.

ENRIGHT, ELIZABETH (MRS. ROBERT GILLHAM), U.S. writer (b. Oak Park, Ill., 1909—d. Wainscott, N.Y., June 8, 1968), was the author of about 50 short stories for children and adults. Her *Thimble Summer* won the 1938 Newbery Medal; later works included the "Gone-Away Lake" series (1955–57).

ERIXON, SIGURD EMANUEL, Swedish ethnographer (b. Söderköping, Swed., March 26, 1888—d. Stockholm, Swed., Feb. 18, 1968), was for many years professor and curator at the Nordiska Museet in Stockholm. A leading authority on Scandinavian folklore, he published many works including *Skultuna bruks historia* (1921–35), *Svensk byggnadskultur* (1947), and contributions to the first volume of the *International Dictionary of Regional European Ethnology and Folklore.*

EWING, THE REV. J. FRANKLIN, U.S. anthropologist and Roman Catholic clergyman (b. New York, N.Y., Oct. 14, 1905—d. Peekskill, N.Y., May 20, 1968), director of research services at Fordham University, Bronx, N.Y., from 1953, who was co-director of the archaeological diggings at Ksar 'Akil (Lebanon) in 1948 when the 20,000-year-old cranium of an early Aurignacian boy was uncovered.

FABRY, JEAN, French parliamentarian (b. Villefranche-de-Rouergue, France, June 6, 1876—d. June 1, 1968), was an officer during World War I, serving as *chef de cabinet* to Marshal Joffre. A member of the Chamber of Deputies from 1919 to 1936, he was minister for the colonies during 1924 and minister of war in Édouard Daladier's second Cabinet, which took office in January 1934 during the outcry over a govern-

Gerhart Eisler   Ziggy Elman

ment scandal. Fabry, protesting the handling of the situation, resigned. However, the following year he was minister of war again. From 1936 until 1945 he was senator for Doubs *département*.

FALKENHORST, NIKOLAUS VON, German Army officer (b. Breslau, Prussian Silesia, Jan. 17, 1885—d. West Germany, June 18, 1968), served in Finland during World War I and in Poland at the start of World War II before being German commander in chief in Norway from 1940 to 1944. Though he was recalled from Norway because he disagreed with Nazi policy there, he was subsequently tried by a British military court in 1946 and sentenced to death for having delivered captured British commando troops from the custody of the Army to that of the *Sicherheitsdienst,* which killed them. The sentence was commuted to one of 20 years' imprisonment, from which Falkenhorst was released in 1953.

FEARNSIDES, WILLIAM GEORGE, British geologist (b. Horbury, Yorkshire, Eng., Nov. 10, 1879—d. Sheffield, Eng., May 15, 1968), who did pioneer work on the structure of metallic alloys, published his first paper on the Arenig Mountains of North Wales in the early 1900s. He combined the duties of Sorby professor of geology at Sheffield from 1913 to 1945 with advising on substitute raw materials in World Wars I and II.

FERBER, EDNA, U.S. novelist (b. Kalamazoo, Mich., Aug. 15, 1885—d. New York, N.Y., April 16, 1968), author of more than a dozen best sellers, including *So Big,* a Pulitzer Prize winner of 1924, and *Show Boat* (1926), which was made into a hit musical by Oscar Hammerstein II and Jerome Kern and later appeared in three different film versions. Some of her other popular novels were *Cimarron* (1929), *American Beauty* (1931), *Saratoga Trunk* (1941), *Giant* (1952), and *Ice Palace* (1958), most of which were adapted for motion pictures. *A Peculiar Treasure* (1939) and *A Kind of Magic* (1963) were autobiographical. With George S. Kaufman, Miss Ferber wrote several plays: *Dinner at Eight, The Royal Family,* and *Stage Door.*

FERNANDES, RAÚL, Brazilian diplomat (b. Valença, Braz., Oct. 24, 1877—d. Rio de Janeiro, Braz., Jan. 6, 1968), last surviving signer of the Treaty of Versailles (1919), also represented his country at the Paris peace conference in 1946.

FLECK, ALEXANDER FLECK, 1ST BARON, British industrialist (b. Glasgow, Scot., Nov. 11, 1889—d. London, Eng., Aug. 6, 1968), chairman of Imperial Chemical Industries (ICI) from 1953 to 1960, who, during World War I, became chief chemist to the Castner Kellner Co., which in 1926 merged with other companies to form ICI, one of the world's largest industrial combines. He joined the board in 1944 and became deputy chairman in 1946. He served as chairman of the Coal Board Organization Committee (1953–55) and of the Nuclear Safety Advisory Committee (1960–65). He was knighted in 1955 and created a baron in 1961.

FLOREY, HOWARD WALTER FLOREY, BARON, British scientist (b. Adelaide, Austr., Sept. 24, 1898—d. Oxford, Eng., Feb. 21, 1968), developed during the early 1940s the clinical use of the

antibiotic penicillin. For this work he received the Nobel Prize for Physiology or Medicine in 1945, together with Sir Alexander Fleming, who had first discovered penicillin, and Ernst B. Chain. He was president of the Royal Society (1960–65) and provost of Queen's College, Oxford, from 1962 until his death. Born in Australia, Florey received his early education there, then went to Magdalen College, Oxford, as a Rhodes scholar in 1921. After an early career in medicine, he was professor of pathology at Oxford University from 1935 to 1962.

FOLEY, RED (CLYDE JULIAN FOLEY), U.S. country and Western singer (b. Blue Lick, Ky., 1918—d. Fort Wayne, Ind., Sept. 19, 1968), well known for his recording of "Chattanooga Shoe Shine Boy," was a regular member of the "Grand Ole Opry" radio show from 1946 until 1954 and again from 1963. In the intervening years he had been host of the TV series "Ozark Jubilee" and a star in the "Mr. Smith Goes to Washington" series.

FONTANA, LUCIO, Italian abstract painter and sculptor (b. Rosario, Arg., Feb. 19, 1899—d. Varese, Italy, Sept. 7, 1968), exhibited in the 1930s with the Abstraction-Création group in Paris and from 1939 to 1946 taught in Argentina, where in 1946 he published his "White Manifesto," proposing the concept of "Spatialism."

FORGIONE, FRANCESCO (PADRE PIO DA PIETRALCINA), Italian Capuchin friar (b. Pietralcina, Benevento, Italy, May 25, 1887—d. San Giovanni, Italy, Sept. 23, 1968), reputedly received the stigmata on Sept. 20, 1918. He entered the convent at Morcone, Benevento, in 1902, was ordained priest in 1910, and in 1916 went to San Giovanni Rotondo to which, in due course, rumours of his supernatural powers attracted numerous pilgrims. With the gifts he received he founded a hospital. In 1960 Pope John XXIII sent an apostolic visitor to investigate conditions at San Giovanni Rotondo. As a result, the Vatican took over the hospital, and Padre Pio was forbidden to say Mass or solemnize marriages.

FOUJITA, (TSUGUJI), Japanese-French painter (b. Tokyo, Jap., Nov. 27, 1886—d. Zürich, Switz., Jan. 29, 1968), noted for his prints and paintings of cats, is represented by several works in the National Museum of Modern Art in Paris.

FRANCESCHETTI, ADOLPHE, Swiss surgeon (b. Zürich, Switz., Oct. 11, 1896—d. Geneva, Switz., March 7, 1968), was a specialist in eye surgery. He was professor of ophthalmology at the University of Geneva from 1933 until his retirement. He served as president of the Swiss Academy of Medical Sciences and was the author of more than 450 scientific papers.

FRANCIS, KAY (KATHERINE GIBBS), U.S. stage and screen actress (b. Oklahoma City, Okla., Jan. 13, 1905—d. New York, N.Y., Aug. 26, 1968), made her Broadway debut in 1925 and her first film, *Gentlemen of the Press,* in 1930. She later starred in more than 50 pictures, including *Give Me Your Heart* (1936) and *Four Jills in a Jeep* (1944). In 1946 she returned to Broadway in *State of the Union.*

FRASER, BLAIR, Canadian journalist (b. Nova Scotia, 1915—d. Algonquin National Park, Ontario, May 12, 1968), from 1943 was associated with *Maclean's* magazine as a correspondent and commentator.

FRY, THE REV. FRANKLIN CLARK, U.S. clergyman (b. Bethlehem, Pa., Aug. 30, 1900—d. New Rochelle, N.Y., June 6, 1968), was president

of the Lutheran Church in America from 1962 until May 31, 1968; from 1944 until 1962 he had served as president of the United Lutheran Church, one of the four Lutheran bodies that merged to form the Lutheran Church in America. He also was head of the central committee of the World Council of Churches.

FULLER, THE REV. CHARLES E., U.S. clergyman and radio evangelist (b. Los Angeles, Calif., April 25, 1887—d. Los Angeles, March 19, 1968), conducted "The Old Fashioned Revival Hour," which was heard by ten million persons each week during the 1940s.

FULLERTON, ELMER GARFIELD, Canadian aviation pioneer (b. Pictou, Nova Scotia, 1894—d. Calgary, Alta., March 6, 1968), first person to fly north of the Arctic Circle (1921), served briefly in the Royal Air Force during World War I, then returned to Canada and joined the Royal Canadian Air Force. In 1938 he was awarded the McKee Trophy for his outstanding contribution to Canadian aviation, and in 1945 he received the Air Force Cross. Fullerton retired from the service the following year.

GAGARIN, YURI ALEKSEYEVICH, Soviet cosmonaut (b. near Gzhatsk, U.S.S.R., March 9, 1934—d. near Kirzhach, U.S.S.R., March 27, 1968), who was the first man to orbit the earth, was killed in the crash of a special plane he was testing. Gagarin made his one-orbit space flight around the earth on April 12, 1961, in a Vostok space capsule launched from a pad in Kazakhstan. He never made a second space flight but was active in the U.S.S.R. space program as commander of cosmonauts and chief of training experiments. Gagarin's many honours included Hero of the Soviet Union and the Order of Lenin. (Killed with Gagarin was Col. Vladimir S. Seryogin, a test pilot.)

GAMOW, GEORGE, U.S. physicist and author (b. Odessa, Russia, March 4, 1904—d. Boulder, Colo., Aug. 19, 1968), received the 1956 UNESCO Kalinga Prize for his nontechnical writing on scientific subjects for the layman. His later books included *A Planet Called Earth* (1963), *A Star Called the Sun* (1964), and *Thirty Years That Shook Physics: The Story of Quantum Theory* (1966); he also contributed to *Encyclopædia Britannica.*

GARROD, DOROTHY ANNIE ELIZABETH, British archaeologist (b. London, Eng., May 5, 1892—d. Cambridge, Eng., Dec. 18, 1968), a leading authority on the Paleolithic Age, was a research fellow at Newnham College, Cambridge, and the holder of a Leverhulme research fellowship. She carried out the excavation of Paleolithic cave dwellings in Mt. Carmel, Palestine (1932–34), on which she wrote the monograph *The Stone Age of Mount Carmel* (1937).

GERRITY, THOMAS P., general, U.S. Air Force (b. Harlowton, Mont., Dec. 8, 1913—d. Wright-Patterson Air Force Base, Ohio, Feb. 24, 1968), head of the U.S. Air Force Logistics Command from Aug. 1, 1967, until the time of his death, had served in the Pacific theatre during World War II.

GERSTENFELD, RABBI NORMAN, U.S. leader of Reform Judaism (b. Croydon, Eng., Sept. 1, 1904—d. Washington, D.C., Jan. 27, 1968), rabbi of the Washington Hebrew Congregation from 1939, was a member of the advisory committee of the Central Conference of American Rabbis and of the national board of governors of the American Jewish Committee. His series of radio sermons, "The Message of Israel" and "The Church of the Air," were broadcast during the 1950s.

GIEDION, SIGFRIED, Swiss architecture historian (b. Aargau Canton, Switz., April 14, 1893—d. Zürich, Switz., April 10, 1968), author of *Space, Time and Architecture: The Growth of a New Tradition* (1941).

GISH, DOROTHY, U.S. actress (b. Massillon, O., March 11, 1898—d. Rapallo, Italy, June 4, 1968), who, with her sister Lillian, started in silent films in 1912 with D. W. Griffith and his Biograph Company. Dorothy Gish's screen appearances were mostly in silent films and included *Orphans of the Storm, Hearts of the World,* and a dozen others. She made few sound films—the last in which she had a role was *The Cardinal* (1963). Her stage career continued through 1956 when she starred on Broadway as Vinnie in *Life with Father.*

Edna Ferber   Howard Florey   The Rev. Franklin Fry   Yuri A. Gagarin

GLASSCO, J. GRANT, Canadian executive (b. Los Angeles, Calif., Jan. 20, 1905—d. Toronto, Ont., Sept. 20, 1968), president and chairman (1968) of the Brazilian Light and Power Co., Ltd., was chairman of the Canadian Royal Commission on Government Organization from 1960 until 1963.

GOLDBLOOM, ALTON, Canadian pediatrician (b. Montreal, Que., Sept. 23, 1890—d. Montreal, Feb. 3, 1968), chairman of the department of pediatrics (1948–54) and emeritus professor at McGill University, was physician in chief of Children's Memorial Hospital, Montreal, from 1947 until 1954. He was the author of *Care of the Child* (1928).

GOOCH, GEORGE PEABODY, British historian (b. London, Eng., 1873—d. Chalfont St. Peter, Buckinghamshire, Eng., Aug. 31, 1968), editor of *The Contemporary Review* from 1911 to 1960, was primarily a specialist in diplomatic history. He was Liberal member of Parliament for Bath (1906–10), but after failing in two subsequent elections (1910 and 1913), abandoned politics. His books included *Germany and the French Revolution* (1920), *A History of Modern Europe* (1923), and contributions to the *Cambridge Modern History*. Gooch was joint editor of *The Cambridge History of British Foreign Policy*: *British Documents on the Origins of the War, 1898–1914*. He received the order of merit in 1963.

GRANT, ULYSSES SIMPSON, III, major general (ret.), U.S. Army (b. July 4, 1881—d. Clinton, N.Y., Aug. 29, 1968), the namesake and grandson of the U.S. Civil War general and 18th president of the United States, served in World Wars I and II and, after retiring in 1945, was chosen as vice-president of George Washington University (1946–51). In 1961 he was named chairman to the Civil War Centennial Commission.

GRAY, HAROLD, U.S. cartoonist (b. Kankakee, Ill., Jan. 20, 1894—d. La Jolla, Calif., May 9, 1968), who drew the "Little Orphan Annie" comic strip, which first appeared in the *New York Daily News* of Aug. 5, 1924, and by the mid-1960s was a feature in more than 400 papers.

GRIGORIEV, SERGE, Soviet ballet dancer and regisseur (b. Tikhvin, near St. Petersburg, Russia, 1883—d. Kensington, London, Eng., Aug. 28, 1968), was responsible for the preservation of some of the most famous works created for the Diaghilev Russian ballet. He studied at the Imperial School of Drama and Ballet in St. Petersburg, and during 1909–29 was with Diaghilev's ballet company, first as dancer, then as regisseur. In the 1930s he was regisseur for Colonel de Basil's various ballet companies, reviving many works from the Diaghilev repertory. During the 1950s he worked for the Royal Ballet, Covent Garden, the Festival Ballet, and La Scala, Milan, producing in particular four ballets by Fokine. His book *The Diaghilev Ballet, 1909–1929* was published in 1953.

GROHMANN, WILL, German educator, art historian, and critic (b. Bautzen, Saxony, Ger., Dec. 4, 1887—d. West Berlin, May 6, 1968), was associated with the Bauhaus at Weimar. His writings included works on Ernst Ludwig Kirschner (1925), Paul Klee, Karl Schmidt-Rottluff, and Oskar Schlemmer.

GUARDINI, ROMANO, Italian-born German Catholic theologian, philosopher, and liturgist (b. Verona, Italy, Feb. 17, 1885—d. Munich, W.Ger., Oct. 1, 1968), was a professor of Christian philosophy at Munich University and a member of the liturgical commission set up by Pope John XXIII before the second Vatican Council. Taken to Germany as a child, he was ordained priest in 1910, and in 1923 was appointed professor of philosophy and religion at Berlin University. He wrote extensively on such varied figures as St. Augustine and Kierkegaard, Freud and Rainer Maria Rilke.

GUARESCHI, GIOVANNI, Italian journalist and novelist (b. Fontenelle di Parma, Italy, May 1, 1908—d. Cervia, Italy, July 22, 1968), creator of Don Camillo, the simple-seeming, quick-witted parish priest, whose first Don Camillo collection, *The Little World of Don Camillo* (1951), became a best seller in Italy after success in the U.S. as a Book-of-the-Month Club choice. It was later filmed by Julien Duvivier with Fer-

nandel in the name part. Guareschi in 1945 founded *Candido*, the promonarchist periodical that made headline news in 1954 with Guareschi's sensational trial for publishing two political documents libeling the former Italian premier Alcide de Gasperi, claimed by De Gasperi to be forgeries dating from the Mussolini period. Already under suspended sentence for libel against President Einaudi, Guareschi was sent to prison for a year, and while there wrote the script for his third Don Camillo film. Other books included *Don Camillo and His Flock* (1952), *The House That Nino Built* (1953), and *Don Camillo and the Devil* (1957).

HACKENSCHMIDT, GEORGE ("THE RUSSIAN LION"), British wrestler (b. Dorpat, Estonia, 1877—d. London, Eng., Feb. 19, 1968), who was billed as "the strongest man in the world," won the world Greco-Roman championship in 1898 and from 1900, when he turned professional, until 1911 when he retired, was undefeated. He set several weightlifting records, including a one-hand lift of 269¼ lb. In later years he wrote a number of philosophical books, including *Man and Cosmic Antagonism to Mind and Spirit* (1935).

HAHN, OTTO, German nuclear chemist (b. Frankfurt am Main, Ger., March 8, 1879—d. Göttingen, W.Ger., July 28, 1968), won the 1944 Nobel Prize for Chemistry for his 1938 discovery that nuclear fission was possible. At the Kaiser Wilhelm Institute for Chemistry in Berlin-Dahlem, Hahn and his associate Fritz Strassmann had worked for several years on the problem of the identity of radioactive elements produced by neutron bombardment of uranium. When their experiments finally showed the products to be barium, lanthanum, and cerium, the team was reluctant to accept the implication that the uranium atom actually had been split. They published their findings in the German scientific journal *Die Naturwissenschaften* of Jan. 6, 1939, with the statement that the report covered only experimental observations, and stopped short of analyzing the results. In 1966 Hahn shared the $50,000 Enrico Fermi Award with the nuclear physicist Lise Meitner, a long-time associate, and Strassmann. Hahn's autobiography appeared in 1962 (Eng. trans., *Otto Hahn: A Scientific Autobiography*, 1966).

HALL, DONALD A., U.S. aircraft designer (b. Brooklyn, N.Y., Dec. 7, 1898—d. San Diego, Calif., May 2, 1968), who designed and constructed the "Spirit of St. Louis," the plane that Charles A. Lindbergh flew across the Atlantic and landed in Paris on May 21, 1927.

HAMMOND, BRAY, U.S. banker and historian (b. Springfield, Mo., Nov. 20, 1886—d. Middlebury, Vt., July 20, 1968), was the author of *Banks and Politics in America: From the Revolution to the Civil War* (1957), awarded the 1958 Pulitzer Prize in history.

HANCOCK, ANTHONY JOHN ("TONY"), British comedian (b. Birmingham, Eng., May 12, 1924—d. Sydney, Austr., June 25, 1968), proceeded from the stage of the London Windmill Theatre in the late 1940s to appearances on radio and TV. There, with Sid James, he created a new kind of comedy, with strong elements of social satire.

HANI, NASSER AL-, Iraqi diplomat (b. Ana, Iraq, 1920—d. Baghdad, Iraq, Nov. 11, 1968), taught literature as an assistant professor in Baghdad University before he turned to diplomacy and became ambassador first to Lebanon and then to Washington. He was foreign minister for a short time in 1968 before Pres. Ahmed al-Bakr dismissed the Nayef Cabinet.

HARRIS, JOHN EDWARD, British zoologist (b. Lincoln, Eng., Sept. 15, 1910—d. Bristol, Eng., June 24, 1968), vice-chancellor and professor of animal biology at Bristol University, graduated from Cambridge and began a distinguished career in zoological research at Cambridge, and in the U.S. at Columbia University and the Guggenheim School of Aeronautics, New York University. He was elected fellow of the Royal Society in 1956.

HARRISON, GEORGE MacGREGOR, U.S. labour leader (b. Lois, Maries Co., Mo., July 19, 1895—d. Cincinnati, O., Nov. 30, 1968), president (1928–63, emeritus from 1965) of the National Brotherhood of Railway Clerks.

HARRISON-GRAY, MAURICE, British bridge expert (b. Ingatestone, Essex, Eng., Nov. 13, 1899—d. London, Eng., Nov. 24, 1968), was one of the world's leading players and a well-known writer on bridge problems. He represented Great Britain many times in European bridge championships, including those of 1948–50 when he was player captain, and in the world championships of 1950 and 1965, and won many personal trophies. Among the publications for which he wrote bridge articles were the *Evening Standard* and *Country Life*.

HARROUN, RAY, U.S. inventor and auto racer (b. Spartansburg, Pa., Jan. 12, 1879—d. Anderson, Ind., Jan. 19, 1968), won the first Indianapolis 500 in 1911 and was one of the ten original members of the American Auto Racing Hall of Fame.

HARTMAN, CARL G., U.S. zoologist (b. Reinbeck, Ia., June 3, 1879—d. Plainfield, N.J., March 1, 1968), was director of the Ortho Research Foundation, specializing in research in family planning, from 1947 until 1957. Hartman's work in embryology and gynecology advanced the basic principles of birth control. His studies established the part played by the endocrine system in the reproductive process (the rhythm method) and are summed up in *Science and the Safe Period*, published in 1962.

HARVEY, LILIAN (LILIAN MURIEL HELEN PAPE), British film actress (b. London, Eng., Jan. 19, 1907—d. Antibes, France, July 27, 1968), who became famous in musical pictures in the early 1930s, began her career in Berlin as a dancer, her talents first being recognized by the film director Richard Eichberg. Lilian Harvey's best known film was *Congress Dances*, directed by Erik Charell (1932), in which she played the part of a glove seller who captivated the czar of Russia at the Congress of Vienna. Other films included *Suzanne the Chaste*, *Miquette and Her Mother*, *Serenade*, and *Blonde Dream*.

HASELDEN, THE REV. KYLE EMERSON, U.S. clergyman and editor (b. Latta, S.C., Feb. 12, 1913—d. Evanston, Ill., Oct. 2, 1968), from 1964 editor of the *Christian Century* magazine, was the author of *The Racial Problem in Christian Perspective* (1959), which was awarded the 1960 Brotherhood Award of the National Conference of Christians and Jews.

HAY, GEORGE D., U.S. radio director (b. 1886—d. Virginia Beach, Va., May 9, 1968), originated the "Grand Ole Opry" program, which he introduced by that name over radio station WSM (Nashville, Tenn.) in 1927 and directed until retiring in 1956.

HEARTFIELD, JOHN (HELMUT HERTZFELDE), German pioneer of photomontage (b. Berlin, Ger., 1891—d. East Berlin, April 26, 1968), who used his technique for dramatic political effect, lived in Britain from 1938 to 1946, when he returned to Germany and became a professor and a member of the East German Academy of Arts. He also did theatre designs for the Deutsche Theater and for Brecht's plays. Exhibitions of his photomontages were shown in 1967 in Stockholm and other European capitals.

HERRERA ORIA, ANGEL CARDINAL, Spanish prelate of the Roman Catholic Church (b. Santander, Spain, Dec. 19, 1886—d. Madrid, Spain,

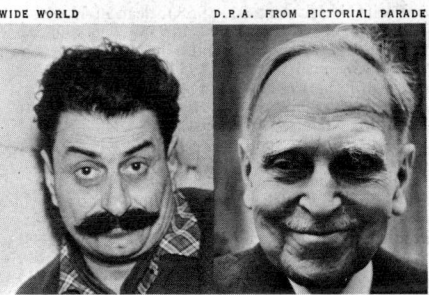

Giovanni Guareschi   Otto Hahn

July 28, 1968), who did not enter the priesthood until he was 50 years of age, was ordained in 1940 and appointed as a curate in Santander. In 1947 he was named bishop of Málaga, and in 1965 elevated to cardinal. He resigned his bishopric in 1966, following a ruling by the pope that high churchmen should retire by age 75.

HEYMANS, CORNEILLE (JEAN FRANCOIS), Belgian physiologist (b. Ghent, Belg., March 28, 1892—d. Knokke, Belg., July 18, 1968), was awarded the 1938 Nobel Prize for Physiology or Medicine for his work on the respiratory and circulatory systems, which demonstrated the existence of the carotid sinus reflex. Heymans became professor of pharmacology and director of the Institute of Pharmacodynamics and Therapeutics at the University of Ghent in 1930, and was a member of more than 40 medical societies in Europe and the United States.

HEYSEN, SIR HANS, Australian painter (b. Hamburg, Ger., Oct. 8, 1877—d. Adelaide, Austr., July 2, 1968), became eminent as a traditional landscapist of the Australian school in the first decades of the 20th century. He studied in Paris and held his first successful exhibition in Melbourne in 1908. His later work was mostly in watercolour. He was knighted in 1959.

HILBERT, EGON, Austrian musical director (b. Vienna, Aus., May 19, 1899—d. Vienna, Jan. 18, 1968), was in Dachau concentration camp for most of World War II; released by the British in 1945, he went to Salzburg, then to Vienna where, as chief of the Austrian Bundestheaterverwaltung, he aided in reestablishing the Vienna State Opera. In the mid-1950s he was in Rome as head of the Austrian Institute, but was recalled in 1960 to reorganize the Vienna Festival, which under his direction became one of the principal cultural events in Europe. In 1963 he was appointed director of the Vienna State Opera.

HOLMES, JULIUS CECIL, U.S. diplomat (b. Pleasanton, Kan., April 24, 1899—d. Washington, D.C., July 14, 1968), was a political adviser to Gen. Dwight D. Eisenhower during World War II and served as ambassador to Iran from 1961 to 1965.

HORD, J. RAYMOND, Canadian clergyman (b. Ilderton, Ont., 1919—d. Toronto, Ont., March 1, 1968), was ordained in 1942 in the United Church of Canada, and served as executive secretary of the church's Board of Evangelism and Social Services from 1962 until the time of his death.

HORNER, ARTHUR, British trade unionist and Communist (b. Merthyr Tydfil, Wales, April 5, 1894—d. London, Eng., Sept. 4, 1968), served as general secretary of the National Union of Mineworkers from August 1946 until his retirement in 1959. He was converted to Marxism in the Rhondda collieries, where his activities led to his dismissal and blacklisting. He refused to fight in World War I, fled to Ireland, and was imprisoned on his return. During 1936–46 he served as president of the South Wales Miners Federation, playing an important role in the nationalization of the coal industry. His autobiography, *Incorrigible Rebel*, was published in 1960.

HORTON, THE REV. DOUGLAS, U.S. ecumenical leader (b. Brooklyn, N.Y., July 27, 1891—d. Berlin, N.H., Aug. 21, 1968), dean of Harvard University Divinity School (1955–59), was head of the Congregational Christian Churches from 1938 until 1955. In 1957 he negotiated the merger of the Congregational Christian Churches and the Evangelical and Reformed Church into the United Church of Christ. The last of the 14 books that he wrote, *Toward an Undivided Church*, was published in 1967.

HOWARD, ANDRÉE, British choreographer (b. Oct. 3, 1910—d. London, Eng., April 18, 1968), studied dancing with Marie Rambert and later with expatriate Russian ballerinas in Paris. She danced with the Rambert company and in 1933 joined the Ballet Russe de Monte Carlo, but had to retire because of ill health. She made a repu-

tation as a choreographer and was appointed the first resident choreographer of the newly formed Sadler's Wells Theatre Ballet in 1945. Her ballets included *Our Lady's Juggler* (1933) and *Mermaid* (1934), both in collaboration with Susan Salaman, *La Fête étrange* (1940), and *The Sailor's Return* (1947).

HURST, FANNIE (MRS. JACQUES S. DANIELSON), U.S. author (b. Hamilton, O., Oct. 18, 1889—d. New York, N.Y., Feb. 24, 1968), wrote hundreds of short stories and about 30 novels. Among her best known works are *Lummox* (1923), *Back Street* (1930), *Imitation of Life* (1933; adapted for the screen in 1934 and remade in 1959), and *Fool, Be Still* (1964). Her autobiography, *Anatomy of Me*, was published in 1958.

HUTCHINGS, JOHN FENWICK, British naval officer (b. Dundee, Scot., May 17, 1885—d. Bishopsteignton, Devon, Eng., Sept. 20, 1968), commanded Naval Force Pluto during 1943–45. He won a DSO in 1919, having served in the Submarine Service in World War I; later he headed the experimental department at the Fort Blockhouse submarine depot. In World War II he was in command of Operation Pluto, responsible for laying a pipeline under the English Channel to supply fuel to the Allied forces in Europe after the Normandy invasion in 1944. He was created CBE in 1944.

HUYSMANS, CAMILLE, Belgian Socialist leader (b. Bilsen, Belg., May 26, 1871—d. Antwerp, Belg., Feb. 25, 1968), prime minister of Belgium (1946–47).

ICHIMURA, KIYOSHI, Japanese industrialist (b. 1900—d. Tokyo, Jap., Dec. 16, 1968), president of the Ricoh Company, Japan's largest producer of photocopying equipment, whose manufacturing empire included a dozen other companies as well.

INFELD, LEOPOLD, Polish physicist (b. Cracow, Pol., Aug. 20, 1898—d. Warsaw, Pol., Jan. 16, 1968), who specialized in the areas of field theory and the theory of relativity, was director of the Theoretical Physics Institute of Warsaw University from the early 1950s. He was co-author with Albert Einstein of *The Evolution of Physics: The Growth of Ideas from Early Concepts to Relativity and Quanta* (1938).

ISSERLIS, JULIUS, British-Russian pianist (b. Kishinev, Russia, Nov. 7, 1889—d. London, Eng., July 23, 1968), at the age of 16 won the gold medal of the conservatory in Moscow, where he was later appointed (1911) professor of piano. As a virtuoso he toured Europe and the U.S., settling in Britain in 1938. Although his repertory was wide-ranging, he was especially regarded for his performances of Chopin.

JACKSON, CHARLES, U.S. author (b. Summit, N.J., April 6, 1903—d. New York, N.Y., Sept. 21, 1968), whose novel *The Lost Weekend* (1944) was adapted for the screen and won the Academy Award for the best picture of 1945. Other works included *The Fall of Valor* (1945), *The Outer Eagles* (1948), and *A Second-Hand Life* (1967).

JARA, HERIBERTO CORONA, major general (ret.), Mexican Army (b. Orizaba, Mex., July 10, 1879—d. Mexico City, Mex., April 17, 1968), was a leader in the revolution (1910–11) that overthrew the dictator Porfirio Díaz. In 1914 Jara became secretary-general of the revolutionary government of Veracruz, and in 1916

was named interim governor and military commander of the state of Tabasco. Elected to the constituent congress, he aided in drawing up a new constitution (1917) for Mexico. Jara also served as ambassador to Cuba (1919–20), governor of Veracruz, and as minister of the navy (1941–46). He was awarded the U.S. Legion of Merit (1943) and the Lenin International Peace Prize (1951).

JARVIS, SIR JOHN LAYTON, British racehorse trainer (b. Exning, Newmarket, Suffolk, Eng., Dec. 28, 1887—d. Newmarket, Eng., Dec. 19, 1968), who won nearly 2,000 races and more than £1.5 million in prize money, was long associated as a trainer with the earls of Rosebery. Jarvis was knighted in 1967, the first trainer to be thus honoured.

JEFFERSON, HILTON W., U.S. jazz saxophonist (b. Danbury, Conn., 1903—d. New York, N.Y., Nov. 14, 1968), played alto sax in the big bands of the 1930s–1950s, including those of Cab Calloway and Duke Ellington.

JOHNS, WILLIAM EARL, British author (b. Hertford, Eng., Feb. 5, 1893—d. London, Eng., June 21, 1968), won fame as the creator of a British-type character for juvenile fiction called "Biggles," whose exploits were published in over 80 books, translated into several languages. "Biggles," who first appeared in short stories in 1932, was based on the type of airman Johns had known in the Royal Flying Corps during World War I. Johns also wrote popular books on aviation and was founder and editor of the magazine *Popular Flying*.

JOHNSON, DANIEL, Canadian political figure (b. Danville, Que., April 9, 1915—d. Manicouagan, Que., Sept. 26, 1968), became premier of Quebec Province in 1966 when his French-oriented Union Nationale won the election over the Liberal Party.

JONES, BOB (ROBERT REYNOLDS JONES), U.S. evangelist (b. Dale County, Ala., Oct. 30, 1883—d. Greenville, S.C., Jan. 16, 1968), was a fundamentalist preacher who conducted revival meetings all over the United States from the 1920s through the 1940s. In 1927, in order to train young persons for evangelism, Jones founded Bob Jones College at Lynn Haven, Fla.; in 1933 the school was moved to Cleveland, Tenn., and in 1947 it was relocated in Greenville, S.C., and became a university.

KAHANAMOKU, DUKE PAOA, U.S.-Hawaiian swimming champion (b. near Waikiki, Hawaii, Aug. 26, 1890—d. Waikiki, Jan. 22, 1968), won the 100-m. freestyle race in the 1912 and 1920 Olympic Games; he also competed in the 1924 and 1928 Games, and for those 16 years held every international swimming record up to the half mile. He was sheriff of the city and county of Honolulu from 1932 until 1961 when he became Hawaii's official greeter.

KANE, FRANK, U.S. author (b. Brooklyn, N.Y., July 19, 1912—d. Manhasset, N.Y., Nov. 29, 1968), who wrote the adventure-mystery stories of Johnny Liddell, private eye, which sold more than 30 million paperback copies in 17 languages, also wrote the scripts for "The Shadow," a 1945–50 radio series.

KEILBERTH, JOSEPH, German conductor and opera director (b. Karlsruhe, Ger., April 19, 1908—d. Munich, W.Ger., July 20, 1968), born into a family of musicians and at age 17 became a coach at the Karlsruhe State Opera, where, within ten years, he was appointed principal conductor. He later was appointed conductor of the Hamburg Philharmonic Orchestra, working also with the Hamburg State Opera, the Berlin State Opera, and the radio orchestra in Cologne.

KELLER, HELEN ADAMS, U.S. leader in education of the handicapped (b. Tuscumbia, Ala., June 27, 1880—d. Westport, Conn., June 1, 1968), who through illness became blind, deaf, and mute at the age of 19 months, but learned to read, write, and speak under the guidance of her teacher, Anne Mansfield Sullivan. Miss Keller graduated cum laude from Radcliffe College, Cambridge, Mass., in 1904, and began her work on behalf of other handicapped persons, by writing and by lecturing. She established the Helen Keller Endowment Fund for the American Foundation for the Blind, and served many years as counselor on national and international relations for the foundation. Miss Keller's books

WIDE WORLD   WIDE WORLD

Leopold Infeld   Duke Kahanamoku

included *The Story of My Life* (1902), *Optimism* (1903), *The World I Live In* (1908), *Out of the Dark* (1913), *My Religion* (1927), *Helen Keller's Journal* (1938), *Let Us Have Faith* (1940), and *The Open Door* (1957).

KELLY, THE VERY REV. JOHN M., U.S. clergyman and editor (b. Nov. 9, 1918—d. Chicago, Ill., Sept. 18, 1968), served as assistant editor (1950–56) and editor (from 1956) of the *New World,* Roman Catholic weekly for the Chicago archdiocese.

KELTON, PERT, U.S. actress (b. Great Falls, Mont., 1907—d. Ridgewood, N.J., Oct. 30, 1968), the original Alice Kramden of Jackie Gleason's "Honeymooners" television series, played on Broadway during the 1920s and appeared in many films, including *The Music Man* (1957).

KEMSLEY, JAMES GOMER BERRY, 1ST VISCOUNT, British publisher (b. Merthyr Tydfil, Wales, May 7, 1883—d. Monte Carlo, Monaco, Feb. 6, 1968), was owner and editor in chief of the *Sunday Times* from 1937 to 1959. With his elder brother, William (afterward Viscount Camrose), and Sir Edward (later Baron) Iliffe, he built up a press empire that included the *Sunday Times,* the *Financial Times,* and the *Daily Telegraph.* When the three men divided their property (1937), Berry retained a group that included the *Sunday Times,* which he sold to Roy (afterward Baron) Thomson in 1959.

KENNEDY, ROBERT FRANCIS, U.S. senator (from 1965) from New York (b. Brookline, Mass., Nov. 20, 1925—d. Los Angeles, Calif., June 6, 1968), was assassinated in a Los Angeles hotel just after he had claimed victory in the California Democratic presidential primary. Kennedy had interrupted his studies at Harvard to serve in the U.S. Navy during World War II, but returned to the university and graduated in 1948. After receiving his law degree from the University of Virginia Law School in 1951, he began his political career in Massachusetts the next year with the management of his brother John's successful campaign for the U.S. Senate. Robert Kennedy first came into national prominence in 1953, when he was an assistant counsel to the Senate Permanent Subcommittee on Investigations, headed by Joseph R. McCarthy (he resigned in mid-1953, returning in 1954 as counsel to the Democratic minority). In 1957 he was chief counsel to the Senate select committee conducting investigations into labour racketeering, which led to his long-standing feud with James R. Hoffa of the teamsters' union. Kennedy resigned from the committee staff in 1960 to conduct his brother's campaign for the U.S. presidency, and was subsequently appointed (1961) attorney general in the Cabinet of Pres. John F. Kennedy. After the assassination of his brother in 1963, Robert resigned (1964) his Cabinet post to run on the Democratic ticket for U.S. senator from New York. As senator, he was active in promoting civil rights legislation and frequently opposed the Johnson administration's conduct of the war in Vietnam. He declared his candidacy for the Democratic presidential nomination in the spring of 1968. Kennedy wrote several books: *The Enemy Within* (1960), *Just Friends and Brave Enemies* (1962), and *Pursuit of Justice* (1964).

KHALDI, ISMAIL RAGIB, Saudi Arabian political expert (b. 1916—d. Beirut, Leb., Sept. 2, 1968), was associated with the United Nations for 19 years, principally as a political affairs officer.

KIANG, CHIPING H. C., Chinese diplomat (b. Shanghai, China, 1899—d. New Rochelle, N.Y., Sept. 9, 1968), joined the Chinese mission to the United Nations in 1948 and served as a permanent delegate from the Republic of China (Taiwan) until his retirement in 1967.

KIMMEL, HUSBAND EDWARD, rear admiral (ret.), U.S. Navy (b. Henderson, Ky., Feb. 26, 1882—d. Groton, Conn., May 14, 1968), was commander of the U.S. Pacific Fleet when Japan attacked Pearl Harbor, Hawaii, Dec. 7, 1941. Criticized for supposed dereliction of duty, he resigned from the Navy in 1942, but four years later a joint congressional committee, completing an investigation, charged him with "errors in judgment" only.

KING, THE REV. MARTIN LUTHER, JR., U.S. clergyman and civil rights leader (b. Atlanta, Ga., Jan. 15, 1929—d. Memphis, Tenn., April 4, 1968), recipient of the 1964 Nobel Peace Prize, was assassinated outside a Memphis motel where he was staying prior to heading a march by striking city sanitation workers. King graduated from Morehouse College in Atlanta in 1948, continued his education at Crozer Theological Seminary in Chester, Pa., and at Boston University, where he received his Ph.D. in 1955. He had been ordained a minister in 1947 at his father's church, Ebenezer Baptist in Atlanta; in 1954 he accepted the pastorate of the Dexter Avenue Baptist Church in Montgomery, Ala., and in 1959 returned to Atlanta to become co-pastor at his father's church. King's leadership in the civil rights movement began in 1956 when he was placed in charge of a city-wide boycott of Montgomery public transportation by Negro riders protesting against Jim Crow practices. The boycott was successful, and King became the most prominent leader in the nonviolent civil rights movement that led to passage of the civil rights acts of 1964 and 1965. In 1966 King, who to that time had been active chiefly in the South, chose Chicago for his first Northern drive. The effort was less than completely successful, and King's leadership was increasingly rejected by younger, more militant black leaders. Most polls, however, showed that he still had a vast following within the black community. His last efforts were directed toward the Poor People's Campaign, slated for the summer of 1968. He was president of the Southern Christian Leadership Conference, founded in 1960, and had been instrumental in forming the Student Nonviolent Coordinating Committee (SNCC). His writings included *Stride Toward Freedom* (1958), *Strength to Love* (1963), and *Why We Can't Wait* (1964).

KIR, FÉLIX-ADRIEN, French ecclesiastic (b. Alise-Sainte-Reine, Côte-d'Or, France, Jan. 22, 1876—d. Dijon, France, April 25, 1968), who from 1940 until 1968 was prominent in Burgundian and national politics, worked as a simple priest until in his 50s, when he was appointed to a canonry at Dijon, where he edited a weekly paper, *Le Bien du Peuple.* When the Germans occupied Dijon in June 1940, Canon Kir was nominated by local French authorities to sit on the "delegation" that took the place of the municipal council. He helped more than 4,000 prisoners of war escape, and took an anti-German line in his weekly paper. Arrested in October 1940, he was sentenced to death, but on December 7 was released. In January 1944 the pro-German French militia tried to assassinate him, but he went into hiding until the liberation. Elected mayor of Dijon in 1945, he remained in that office until his death. He was also elected to the Constituent Assembly in 1945 as one of the deputies of the Côte-d'Or and was constantly reelected as an independent to the successive National Assemblies until 1967.

KONSTAM, KENNETH, British bridge player (b. 1906—d. Juan-les-Pins, France, May 21, 1968), played for Great Britain in 12 European championships (from 1937) and was a member of the winning team in 6 of them (1948, 1949, 1950, 1954, 1961, and 1963). In world events he played in 1950, 1955, 1962, 1964 (the Olympiad), and 1965, his greatest triumph being that of 1955, when the British won the Bermuda Bowl. Besides serving on the directing committees of bridge in London, he was active as a journalist.

KOSSAK, ZOFIA, Polish historical novelist (b. Kosmin, Volhynia Russia, Aug. 8, 1890—d.

Bielsko-Biala, Pol., April 9, 1968), best known for her story of St. Francis of Assisi, *Blessed Are the Meek* (Eng. trans. 1944); she wrote an account of her World War II internment in the concentration camp at Auschwitz in *Back from the Abyss.*

KOSTOPOULOS, STAVROS, Greek parliamentarian and statesman (b. Kalamata, Greece, Sept. 14, 1900—d. Athens, Greece, June 23, 1968), was elected to Parliament as Liberal deputy for Kalamata in 1928 and for Messenia almost continuously from 1932 through 1958. During this period he was minister of national economy (1932, 1947); of supply (1948); of coordination and of merchant shipping successively (1950); and of economic affairs (1950–51). After 1958, he was parliamentary spokesman of the transient National Regeneration Movement (1960–61), then led his followers into the Centre Union and was reelected deputy for Messenia in 1961, 1963, and 1964. He was minister of the interior in the Papandreou government of 1963 and foreign minister in that of 1964–65. After Papandreou's resignation (July 1965), he was minister of defense until finally excluded from political life by the military coup of April 1967.

KURNITZ, HARRY, U.S. playwright (b. New York, N.Y., Jan. 5, 1908—d. Los Angeles, Calif., March 18, 1968), turned out more than 40 filmscripts including *Witness for the Prosecution, See Here, Private Hargrove,* and *A Shot in the Dark;* for the stage he wrote *Reclining Figure* (1954) and *Once More with Feeling.* Among his several mystery stories were *Fast Company* (1937) and *The Shadowy Third.*

LAMBERT, WALTER D., U.S. mathematician and geodesist (b. West New Brighton, N.Y., 1879—d. Washington, D.C., Oct. 27, 1968), was chief of the gravity and astronomy section of the U.S. Coast and Geodetic Survey from 1941 to 1947. He wrote for the Coast and Geodetic Survey publications and was a contributor to *Encyclopædia Britannica.*

LANDAU, LEV DAVIDOVICH, Soviet theoretical physicist (b. Baku, Russia, Jan. 22, 1908—d. Moscow, U.S.S.R., April 1, 1968), recipient of the 1962 Nobel Prize for Physics, received his doctorate from the University of Leningrad in 1927, the same year he advanced a concept for energy called the density matrix, which came to be commonly used in quantum mechanics. Later he studied low-temperature physics and formulated a series of mathematical equations explaining certain phenomena within that field. In the 1930s, at the Ukrainian Physical and Technical Institute at Kharkov, Landau made significant contributions in the study of the scattering of light by light and on the absorption of sound by solids. In 1962 he was almost totally incapacitated as the result of an auto accident and, although able to retrain his mind and body to some extent, never regained his full powers. In addition to the Nobel Prize, he also held a Stalin Prize, a Lenin Prize, the Order of Lenin, and the Max Planck Medal.

LANE, ROSE WILDER, U.S. novelist (b. De Smot, S.D., Dec. 5, 1887—d. Danbury, Conn., Oct. 30, 1968), was the author of *Let the Hurricane Roar* (1933), *Free Land* (1938), and *The Discovery of Freedom* (1943).

WIDE WORLD   UPI COMPIX   WIDE WORLD   CAMERA PRESS

Helen Adams Keller   Robert Francis Kennedy   The Rev. Martin Luther King, Jr.   Lev Davidovich Landau

LATOURETTE, KENNETH SCOTT, U.S. church and Oriental historian (b. Oregon City, Ore., Aug. 9, 1884—d. Oregon City, Dec. 26, 1968), became associated with Yale University in 1921, serving as chairman of the department of religion (1938–46), director of graduate studies at the Divinity School (1946–53), and Sterling professor of missions and Oriental history (1950–53, emeritus from 1953). Among his more than 80 works were *The Chinese: Their History and Culture* (2 vol., 1934; 3rd ed. 1946), *The History of the Expansion of Christianity* (7 vol., 1937–45), *A History of Japan* (1947), and *Christianity in a Revolutionary Age* (5 vol., 1958–62). He was also a contributor to *Encyclopædia Britannica.*

LAURENDEAU, ANDRÉ, Canadian journalist (b. Montreal, Que., 1912—d. Ottawa, Ont., June 1, 1968), editor in chief of the Montreal French-language newspaper *Le Devoir* (from 1957), was co-chairman of the Royal Commission on Bilingualism and Biculturalism from the time of its establishment in 1963.

LAWRENCE, ROBERT DANIEL, British physician (b. Aberdeen, Scot., Nov. 18, 1892—d. London, Eng., Aug. 27, 1968), a leading authority on diabetes and among the first to be treated (in 1923) with the newly discovered insulin. He became head of the diabetic department at King's College Hospital, London, in 1939. He was founder (1935) of the Diabetic Society and his book *The Diabetic Life* (17th ed., 1965) was translated into several languages.

LAYCOCK, SIR ROBERT EDWARD, major general (ret.), British Army (b. London, Eng., April 18, 1907—d. Doncaster, Yorkshire, Eng., March 10, 1968), was a commando leader in World War II and governor and commander in chief of Malta from 1954 to 1959. Commissioned in the Royal Horse Guards in 1927, he volunteered during World War II for special service with the commando units that became known as "Layforce." After participating in the raid on Gen. Erwin Rommel's headquarters in Libya and the Salerno landing, he became chief of combined operations in 1943.

LAZURICK, ROBERT, French journalist (b. Pantin, France, April 3, 1895—d. Paris, France, April 18, 1968), who, after a period as a Communist (1920–23), joined the Socialist Party (SFIO) in 1925 and was chosen by Pierre Laval, then minister of public works, to manage his personal office. Subsequently returning to journalism, he ran a daily paper, *Le Soir,* for seven years. Elected mayor of Saint-Amand-Montrond in 1935, he also represented Cher *département* in the Chamber of Deputies (1936–40). He founded two more newspapers, *La Justice* and *Le Cher,* in 1939, and during the Vichy regime (with the former premier Joseph Paul-Boncour) launched *L'Aurore* as a clandestine newspaper. After the liberation *L'Aurore* became an important Paris daily, and Lazurick, who resigned from the Socialist Party in 1945, came to be regarded as a spokesman of the moderate right.

LEDUC, RENÉ-HENRI, French jet aviation pioneer (b. Saint-Germain-les-Corbeil, France, April 24, 1898—d. near Paris, France, March 10, 1968), patented his stato-reactor engine in 1933. From 1949 to 1957 the Leduc engine was incorporated into French test aircraft, one of which reached twice the speed of sound.

LEEPER, SIR REGINALD WILDIG ALLEN ("REX"), British diplomat (b. Sydney, Austr., March 25, 1888—d. London, Eng., Feb. 2, 1968), was concerned in opposing Nazi propaganda during World War II, and was a pioneer in the use of embassies to promote cultural relations. He was permanently appointed to the diplomatic service in 1920; served at Warsaw (1923–24; 1927–29); and was ambassador to the Greek government (1943–46) and to Argentina (1946–48).

LEITH-ROSS, SIR FREDERICK, British banker and civil servant (b. 1887—d. Isle of Man, Aug. 22, 1968), chief economic adviser to the government, 1932–46, joined the Treasury in 1909 and became deputy controller of finance (1925–32), being for many years chief British delegate at international financial conferences. From 1951 until his retirement in 1966, he was deputy chairman of the National Provincial Bank, and his autobiography, *Money Talks,* was published shortly before his death.

LEONARD, ROBERT Z., U.S. film director (b. Chicago, Ill., Oct. 7, 1889—d. Beverly Hills, Calif., Aug. 27, 1968), who, during a 40-year career, directed such pictures as *Strange Interlude, Susan Lenox: Her Fall and Rise* (1931), *The Great Ziegfeld* (1936), and *Maytime* (1937).

LEWANIKA, SIR MWANAWINA, III, Zambian tribal leader (b. Feb. 7, 1888—d. Lusaka, Zambia, Nov. 13, 1968), was the *litunga* (paramount chief) of the Lozi people living in Barotseland, having assumed the throne in 1948.

LEWIS, GEORGE, U.S. jazz clarinetist (b. New Orleans, La., July 13, 1900—d. New Orleans, Dec. 31, 1968), a traditionalist who played with many of the great bands of the 1920s and 1930s, was rediscovered in the 1950s when he led his New Orleans jazz band to acclaim in the U.S. and Europe.

LICHTENBERGER, THE RIGHT REV. ARTHUR, U.S. churchman (b. Oshkosh, Wis., Jan. 8, 1900—d. Bethel, Vt., Sept. 3, 1968), was presiding bishop of the Episcopal Church of the United States from 1958 until 1964.

LIE, TRYGVE HALVDAN, Norwegian diplomat (b. Oslo, Nor., July 16, 1896—d. Geilo, Nor., Dec. 30, 1968), first secretary-general of the United Nations, was elected on Feb. 1, 1946, and served until April 10, 1953. Under his leadership the UN dealt with such controversial problems as the seating of Communist China, the Berlin blockade (1948), and the start of the Korean War (1950). However, his more positive contributions were attested to by the Israeli-Arab armistice of 1948, and by the establishment of an independent Indonesia in 1950. Included in his writings were several volumes of memoirs: *In the Cause of Peace* (1954), *Leve eller dø* (1955; "To Live or to Die"), *Med England i ildinjen* (1956; "With England in the Front Line"), and *Hjemover* (1958; "Homeward Bound").

LINDEGREN, (J.) ERIK, Swedish poet (b. Luleå, Swed., Aug. 5, 1910—d. Stockholm, Swed., May [?] 1968), was, with Gunnar Ekelöf (*q.v.*), one of the foremost exponents of the lyric modernism that flourished in Sweden, particularly during the 1940s, and of which his *Mannen utan väg* ("The Man Without a Way"; 1942) is typical. Lindegren wrote the libretto of Karl-Birger Blomdahl's space opera *Aniara,* and other librettos, and translated into Swedish the works of T. S. Eliot, R. M. Rilke, Graham Greene, Dylan Thomas, William Faulkner, Paul Claudel, and others. He was elected to the Swedish Academy in 1962.

LINDSAY, HOWARD, U.S. playwright, actor, director, and producer (b. Waterford, N.Y., March 29, 1889—d. New York, N.Y., Feb. 11, 1968), collaborated with Russel Crouse in writing *Life with Father* (1939), based on sketches by Clarence Day. Lindsay played the role of Father Day in the Broadway production that ran for more than seven years. Other plays and musicals by Lindsay and Crouse included *State of the Union* (1946 Pulitzer Prize), *Arsenic and Old Lace* (1941), *Call Me Madam* (1950), the libretto for *The Sound of Music* (1959), and *Mr. President* (1962).

LITTLE, W. LAWSON, U.S. golf champion (b. Newport, R.I., June 23, 1910—d. Pebble Beach, Calif., Feb. 1, 1968), won the U.S. and British amateur championships in 1934 and 1935; after turning professional in 1936 he won the Canadian Open and in 1940 the National Open and the Los Angeles Open.

LLOYD, EDWARD MAYOW HASTINGS, British civil servant (b. Nov. 30, 1889—d. London, Eng., Jan. 27, 1968), aided in the planning of food rationing in World Wars I and II.

LLOYD, SIR THOMAS INGRAM KYNASTON, British civil servant (b. June 19, 1896—d. Radlett, Hertfordshire, Eng., Dec. 10, 1968), was undersecretary of state for the colonies during 1947–56 when some of the largest colonies such as Ceylon, Malaya, and Ghana were achieving independence.

LODOVICI, CESARE VICO, Italian playwright, editor, and translator (b. Carrara, Italy, Dec. 18, 1885—d. Rome, Italy, March 25, 1968), who was best known for his translation of Shakespeare's plays, also wrote many comedies, including *La Ruota,* performed by Luigi Pirandello's company in 1932.

LOHR, LENOX RILEY, U.S. engineer and museum executive (b. Washington, D.C., Aug. 15, 1891—d. Chicago, Ill., May 28, 1968), was president of Chicago's Museum of Science and Industry from 1940.

LOMBARDO TOLEDANO, VICENTE, Mexican labour leader (b. Teziutlán, Mex., July 16, 1894—d. Mexico City, Mex., Nov. 16, 1968), was the founder (1936) and first president of the Confederation of Mexican Workers (CTM); he was also the head of the Popular Socialist Party during the early 1950s.

LORNE, MARION, U.S. actress (b. Philadelphia, Pa., Aug. 12, 1888—d. New York, N.Y., May 9, 1968), played comedy roles in television's "Mr. Peepers" series, the "Garry Moore Show," and later in the "Bewitched" series.

LOUW, ERIC HENDRIK, South African politician (b. Jacobsdal, Orange Free State, Nov. 21, 1890—d. Cape Town, S.Af., June 24, 1968), entered politics as Nationalist member for Beaufort West in 1924. In 1925 he was appointed trade commissioner of South Africa in Canada and the U.S., and four years later became minister plenipotentiary in Washington. In 1937 he joined the Malanite Nationalist Party, and became minister of economic affairs when it came to power in 1948. Under J. G. Strijdom he later became minister of finance and during 1956–63 minister for external affairs (foreign minister).

LUCAS, SCOTT WIKE, U.S. senator (1939–50) from Illinois (b. Chandlerville, Ill., Feb. 19, 1892—d. Rocky Mount, N.C., Feb. 22, 1968), also served as a member of the U.S. House of Representatives (1935–39) and was the Senate majority leader in 1949–50.

McALEAVY, HENRY, British scholar (b. Manchester, Eng., Jan. 11, 1912—d. London, Eng., Oct. 25, 1968), an expert on Chinese history, taught English for five years in Chinese middle schools (1935–40), and at the time of his death was reader in Oriental laws at the School of Oriental and African Studies, London University. His publications included *A Dream of Tartary* (1963), *The Modern History of China* (1967), and *Black Flags in Vietnam* (1968).

McCABE, STANLEY JOSEPH, Australian cricketer (b. Grenfell, New South Wales, July 16, 1910—d. Sydney, Austr., Aug. 25, 1968), one of Australia's most famous batsmen, who during 1930–38 played in 39 test matches, scoring 2,748 runs for an average of 48. His finest innings was probably against D. R. Jardine's English team at Sydney, during the 1932–33 test series, when he scored 187.

McGOVERN, JOHN, British politician (b. Glasgow, Scot., Dec. 13, 1887—d. Glasgow, Feb. 14, 1968), was Independent Labour Party member of Parliament for the Shettleston division of Glasgow (1930–47) and Labour Party member for the same constituency (1947–59). He was an outspoken champion of the underprivileged, and his forcible expression of his views led to several suspensions from the House of Commons (1931, 1933, 1936, 1937).

MACKAY, ROLAND PARKS, U.S. neurologist (b. Atlanta, Ga., Oct. 25, 1900—d. Hinsdale, Ill., Feb. 20, 1968), professor of neurology at Northwestern University, Evanston, Ill., from

WIDE WORLD   CAMERA PRESS

Trygve Halvdan Lie   Eric Hendrik Louw

1961, was president of the American Neurological Association (1954) and author of about 60 scientific papers.

McLEAN, ALICE THROCKMORTON, U.S. social service executive (b. 1886—d. Baltimore, Md., Oct. 25, 1968), founded the American Women's Voluntary Services (AWVS) in 1940.

McLEAN, JOHN MILTON, U.S. ophthalmologist (b. New York, N.Y., Oct. 24, 1909—d. New York, May 2, 1968), professor of surgery at Cornell University Medical College who devised a technique for wound closure in cataract surgery, was credited with establishing the first corneal eye bank. He was the author of two textbooks, *The Atlas of Cataract Surgery* and *The Atlas of Glaucoma Surgery.*

McNAIR, JOHN BABBITT, Canadian politician (b. Andover, N.B., Nov. 20, 1889—d. Fredericton, N.B., June 14, 1968), was New Brunswick's premier (1940–52), chief justice of the New Brunswick Supreme Court (1955–64), and lieutenant governor of New Brunswick from 1965 until Jan. 31, 1968.

MacNIDER, HANFORD, lieutenant general (ret.), U.S. Army (b. Mason City, Ia., Oct. 2, 1889—d. Sarasota, Fla., Feb. 17, 1968), served in World War I, winning more medals than any other soldier except Gen. John J. Pershing, and in World War II, during which he received numerous other U.S. medals and decorations. During the 1920s and 1930s General MacNider served as assistant secretary of war and as minister to Canada.

MACRAE, ELLIOTT BEACH, U.S. book publisher (b. Staten Island, N.Y., June 13, 1900—d. New Canaan, Conn., Feb. 13, 1968), president of E. P. Dutton & Co., Inc., from 1944 until the time of his death.

MADGE, JOHN, British social scientist (b. June 19, 1914—d. London, Eng., Aug. 27, 1968), who made a major contribution to urban sociology and social science research methods, was a prolific writer, his most notable work being *The Tools of Social Science* (1953). He was sociologist to the Building Research Station (1952–60), and afterward deputy director of Political and Economic Planning. From 1965 he was director of the Sociological Research Unit, University College, London, and chief consultant to Political and Economic Planning.

MAGNUSON, PAUL BUDD, U.S. orthopedic surgeon (b. St. Paul, Minn., June 14, 1884—d. Washington, D.C., Nov. 5, 1968), chief medical director of the U.S. Veterans Administration for three years during the late 1940s, was the founder of the Rehabilitation Institute of Chicago. His autobiography, *Ring the Night Bell,* was published in 1960.

MARIA-FRANCISCA, princess of Orléans-Braganza (b. Sept. 8, 1914—d. Lisbon, Port., Jan. 15, 1968), wife of Dom Duarte Nuno, duke of Braganza and pretender to the throne of Portugal.

MARINA, PRINCESS, Greek-born princess, widow of George, duke of Kent, a son of the English king George V (b. Athens, Greece, Dec. 13, 1906—d. London, Eng., Aug. 27, 1968), was one of the most popular members of the British royal family, greatly admired for her beauty, elegance, and charm. A daughter of Prince Nicolas of Greece and the grand duchess Helen of Russia, she lived in Greece until her family was forced into exile in 1917. She was married to her cousin, Prince George, on Nov. 29, 1934, and her children, the present duke of Kent, Princess Alex-

andra, and Prince Michael, were born in 1935, 1936, and 1942. A month after Prince Michael's birth her husband was killed (August 25) in a plane accident in Scotland. The duchess, who took a full share in the public duties of the royal family, was perhaps most frequently seen at the Wimbledon championships, which, as president of the All England Lawn Tennis and Croquet Club, she attended regularly. On her elder son's marriage (1961) she became known again as Princess Marina.

MARSH, MAE (MRS. LOUIS LEE ARMS), U.S. silent-screen star (b. Madrid, N.M., Nov. 9, 1895—d. Hermosa Beach, Calif., Feb. 13, 1968), played the role of Flora in the D. W. Griffith classic *The Birth of a Nation* (1915). With Griffith and then as the original "Goldwyn Girl," she made more than 60 silent pictures before retiring in the late 1920s. She resumed her career in the 1930s in character parts and appeared in films and television until the early 1960s.

MARTIN, (WARREN) HOMER, U.S. labour leader (b. near Marion, Ill., 1901—d. Los Angeles, Calif., Jan. 22, 1968), was the first president of the United Automobile Workers (1936–39).

MARTIN, JOSEPH W., JR., U.S. congressman (1924–66) from Massachusetts (b. North Attleboro, Mass., Nov. 3, 1884—d. Hollywood, Fla., March 6, 1968), was twice speaker of the House of Representatives (1946–48, 1952–54) and was chairman of five Republican national conventions, 1940 through 1956.

MASKELL, VIRGINIA, British actress (b. 1937 [?]—d. Stoke Mandeville, Buckinghamshire, Eng., Jan. 25, 1968), made her screen debut in *Virgin Island* (1959); among her other films were *Jet Storm* (1960), *Doctor in Love* (1961), *Only Two Can Play* (1962), and her last, *Interlude,* with Oskar Werner.

MASTERTON, WILLIAM, U.S. hockey player (b. 1938—d. Edina, Minn., Jan. 15, 1968), who was centre with the Minnesota North Stars of the National Hockey League, died of head injuries received in a game against the Oakland Seals on January 13.

MATTHEWS, ZACHARIAH KEODIRELANG, Botswanian diplomat (b. Kimberley, S.Af., 1901—d. Washington, D.C., May 11, 1968), ambassador to the United States from 1966, also served as permanent representative of Botswana at the United Nations.

MAYO, CHARLES WILLIAM, U.S. surgeon (b. Rochester, Minn., July 28, 1898—d. Rochester, July 28, 1968), the son of Charles C. Mayo and the nephew of William J. Mayo, co-founders (1889) of the Mayo Clinic in Rochester, Minn., was the last family member to practice at the clinic, having served as senior surgeon and board member until retiring in 1963. Mayo was an alternate delegate to the United Nations General Assembly (1953) and president of the American Association for the UN (1954). His autobiography was published in 1968.

MEIN, JOHN GORDON, U.S. diplomat (b. Cadiz, Ky., Sept. 10, 1913—d. Guatemala City, Guat., Aug. 28, 1968), U.S. ambassador to Guatemala from 1965, was slain by machine-gun fire as his car was being driven along the city streets.

MEITNER, LISE, Austrian physicist (b. Vienna, Aus., Nov. 7, 1878—d. Cambridge, Eng., Oct. 27, 1968), a pioneer in the field of radioactivity, was joint discoverer of nuclear fission. After acquiring a doctorate (1906) at the University of Vienna (one of the first women to do so), she studied under Max Planck in Berlin and joined the chemist Otto Hahn in research on radioactivity, a partnership that lasted for over 30 years. Among their discoveries was that of the element protactinium. Subsequently she did valuable work in clarifying the relation between the beta and gamma rays of radioactive substances. In 1938 she escaped from Nazi-occupied Austria to Sweden, where she worked on nuclear physics until her retirement to England in 1960. In 1966 she shared the Enrico Fermi Award with Hahn and Fritz Strassmann for their joint researches that led to the discovery of uranium fission in the late 1930s.

MENÉNDEZ PIDAL, RAMÓN, Spanish academic scholar (b. La Coruña, Spain, March 13, 1869—d. Madrid, Spain, Nov. 14, 1968), specialized in the poetry and chronicles of the Middle Ages. His first major work was a comprehensive study of

the legend of the Infantes of Lara in 1896. He became professor of Romance philology at Madrid in 1899, a member of the Royal Spanish Academy in 1902, and founder-editor of *Revista de filología española* in 1914. His *Manual de gramática histórica española* (1904; 8th ed. 1949) was followed by an edition of the *Primera crónica general* (1906) and by his commentary on the Poem of the Cid (*Cantar de mio Cid;* 1908–11; new ed. 1944–46). His numerous works included *L'Épopée castillane à travers la littérature espagnole* (1910; Sp. ed. 1945); *La Primitiva Poesía lírica española* (1919); *Poesía juglaresca y juglares* (1924); *Orígenes del español* (1926; 3rd ed. 1950); and *La España del Cid* (1929; Eng. trans. 1934; 4th Sp. ed. 1947). The monumental *Historia de España,* which he had begun to edit in the 1930s and for which he wrote an important prologue—*Los españoles en la historia* (1947; Eng. trans. 1950)—was incomplete at the time of his death; but he published a final *Romancero hispánico* in 1953, a work on the *Chanson de Roland* in 1959, and a controversial book on Bartolomé de las Casas in 1963.

MENNEN, WILLIAM G., U.S. executive (b. Newark, N.J., Dec. 20, 1884—d. Montclair, N.J., Feb. 17, 1968), took over leadership of the Mennen Company, manufacturer of babies' and men's toiletries, in 1912, and in 1916 became president; in 1965 he was named chairman of the board.

MENZIES, SIR STEWART GRAHAM, major general (ret.), British Army (b. Jan. 30, 1890—d. London, Eng., May 30, 1968), head of Britain's Secret Intelligence Service (MI6) from 1939 to 1951, served in the Life Guards from 1910 until he became head of MI6.

MERTON, THOMAS (FATHER M. LOUIS), U.S. Trappist monk (b. Prades, France, Jan. 31, 1915—d. Bangkok, Thailand, Dec. 10, 1968), entered the Trappist monastery of Gethsemani at Bardstown, Ky., in 1941 and began writing of the spiritual life and of religious devotion. His works included *Thirty Poems* (1944), *Seven Storey Mountain* (1948), *The Waters of Siloe* (1949), *Seeds of Contemplation* (1949), *The Sign of Jonas* (1952), *No Man Is an Island* (1955), and the later *Conjectures of a Guilty Bystander* (1966) and *Mystics and Zen Masters* (1967).

MILLER, ARTHUR AUSTIN, British geographer (b. Wrangle, Lincolnshire, Eng., July 6, 1900—d. Reading, Berkshire, Eng., March 31, 1968), emeritus professor of geography, Reading University, where he was appointed in 1926 and served continuously for 40 years, first as a lecturer and later as a professor. His major work was *Climatology* (1931).

MILLER, EDWARD T., U.S. congressman (1947–59) from Maryland (b. Woodside, Md., Feb. 1, 1895—d. Easton, Md., Jan. 20, 1968).

MILLIN, SARAH GERTRUDE, South African writer (b. Lithuania, 1889—d. Johannesburg, S.Af., July 6, 1968), was best known for her novels, especially *God's Step-Children* (1924; new ed. 1952), in which she treated with impartiality and imaginative insight the problems of race and colour. Brought up in the slums of Barkly West, she used her early experience in this and other novels—*The Dark River* (1920), *Adam's Rest* (1922), and *The Sons of Mrs. Aab* (1931). Other books about her adopted country included the novels *The Jordans* (1923), *The Coming of the Lord* (1928), and *The Herr Witch Doctor* (1941); the historical *King of the Bastards* (1950) and *The Burning Man* (1952); biographies of Cecil Rhodes (1933; rev. ed. 1952) and Gen. J. C. Smuts (1936); the political and historical study *The South Africans* (1926; revised as *The People of South Africa,* 1950); and her war diaries *World Blackout* (1944) and *The Reeling Earth* (1945).

MILLIS, WALTER, U.S. author, editor, and historian (b. Atlanta, Ga., March 16, 1899—d. New York, N.Y., March 17, 1968), was associated with the *New York Herald Tribune* from 1924 until 1954, when he joined the staff of the Center for the Study of Democratic Institutions. Millis was the editor of the James V. Forrestal diaries,

CAMERA PRESS   WIDE WORLD

Princess Marina   Lise Meitner

author of eight books, and wrote many articles on the war in Vietnam.

MILLS, PERCY HERBERT MILLS, 1st Viscount, British industrialist (b. Thornaby-on-Tees, Yorkshire, Eng., Jan. 4, 1890—d. London, Eng., Sept. 10, 1968), controller general of machine tools during World War II, joined the Conservative government as an adviser to the minister of housing, Harold Macmillan, in 1951. He served as minister of power (1957–59), then became paymaster general. During 1961–62 he was minister without portfolio, and he was deputy leader of the House of Lords during 1960–62 (having been raised to the peerage in 1957). He retired from politics in 1962, was made a viscount, and became director of Electric and Musical Industries, Ltd.

MIRGHANI, SAYYID ALI AL-, Sudanese religious leader (b. Dongola Province, Sudan, 1879—d. Khartoum, Sudan, Feb. 21, 1968), was for many years prominent in Sudanese political life. Head of the Khatmia religious sect, he was the principal opponent of the influence of the Mahdi's family in the early 20th century. He supported the policy of union with Egypt after World War II.

MITCHELL, ARTHUR W., U.S. congressman (1935–43) from Illinois (b. Chambers Co., Ala., Dec. 22, 1883—d. Petersburg, Va., May 9, 1968), the first Negro Democrat to serve in the U.S. House of Representatives, was elected by the 1st district in Chicago.

MONTGOMERY, WES, U.S. jazz musician (b. Indianapolis, Ind., March 6, 1925—d. Indianapolis, June 15, 1968), top-selling jazz recording artist of 1967, was named best jazz guitarist of 1968 by the *Down Beat* magazine poll. His first successful album, "Movin' Wes," was followed by "Bumpin'" (both in 1965), "Goin' Out of My Head," a Grammy Award winner (1966), and "A Day in the Life" (1967).

MORANE, ROBERT CHARLES, French aeronautical engineer (b. Paris, France, March 10, 1886—d. Paris, Aug. 28, 1968), founded the Morane-Saulnier Aircraft Co. in 1911. In World War I he supplied the Allied armies with aircraft and in World War II equipped the French Air Force with the NS-406. He also founded the first French airline, the forerunner of Air France.

MORANO, FRANCESCO CARDINAL, Italian prelate of the Roman Catholic Church (b. Caivano, Italy, June 8, 1872—d. Vatican City, July 12, 1968), at the time of his death the oldest cardinal in the church, was ordained in 1897. He was appointed as an assistant in the Vatican Observatory in 1900 and began his 59-year service in the Vatican, attaining the post of secretary to the supreme tribunal of the Signatura Apostolica (ecclesiastical court); he held that position until 1959, the year in which Pope John XXIII elevated him to cardinal.

MO TEH-HUI, Nationalist Chinese government official (b. 1881—d. T'ai-pei, Taiwan, April 17, 1968), served in the first Parliament of the Republic of China, which was established in 1912; he was the governor of Feng-t'ien Province; and during the 1920s was president of the Chinese Eastern Railway, being dismissed in 1932 when the Japanese took over the railroad. Mo was senior adviser to Chiang Kai-shek from 1948 until 1954.

MOUTET, MARIUS, French parliamentarian (b. Nîmes, France, April 19, 1876—d. Paris, France, Oct. 29, 1968), joined the Socialist Party in 1895, and was first elected to the Chamber of Deputies by the Rhône *département* in 1914; he was minister for the colonies during 1936–38. During World War II he was interned after voting against the delegation of power to Marshal Pétain (1940). After the war he was minister for the colonies overseas (1946–47), then elected to the Senate as representative of French Sudan in 1947 and of the Drôme *département* from 1948.

MULLINS, CLAUD, British magistrate (b. Sept. 6, 1887—d. Chichester, Sussex, Eng., Oct. 23, 1968), writer on law reform, became chairman of Courts of Referees (Unemployment Insurance) in 1930, and a metropolitan magistrate in 1931. He was vice-president of the London Marriage Guidance Council and of the Family Planning Association. His works included *In Quest of Justice* (1931), *Crime and Psychology* (1943), and his autobiography, *One Man's Furrow* (1963).

MUNCH, CHARLES, French conductor (b. Strasbourg, Ger., Sept. 26, 1891—d. Richmond, Va., Nov. 6, 1968), founder (1935) of the Paris Philharmonic Orchestra and its director until 1938, when he became head of the Société des Concerts du Conservatoire in Paris. From 1949 until 1962 he was conductor of the Boston Symphony Orchestra. At the time of his death he was in the U.S. for the first tour of the Orchestre de Paris, which he organized in 1967.

NASH, SIR WALTER, New Zealand statesman (b. Kidderminster, Eng., Feb. 12, 1882—d. Wellington, N.Z., June 4, 1968), pioneer of the welfare state, was prime minister from 1957 until 1960. He emigrated at the age of 27 and soon had a leading part in the New Zealand labour movement. He entered Parliament in 1929, was minister of finance and customs (1935–49), and was responsible for piloting New Zealand's prototype social security legislation through Parliament in 1938 while simultaneously holding the Social Security portfolio.

NEWMAN, BERNARD, British writer and lecturer (b. Ibstock, Leicestershire, Eng., May 8, 1897—d. London, Eng., Feb. 19, 1968), author of more than 125 books about spies and travel, entered the civil service in 1920 and from 1924 was a lecturer on espionage, travel, and European affairs.

NEY, ELLY, German pianist (b. Düsseldorf, Ger., Sept. 27, 1882—d. Tutzing, W.Ger., March 31, 1968), a leading interpreter of Beethoven, who made her U.S. debut in October 1921, gave her last concert only three weeks before her death.

NICOLSON, SIR HAROLD GEORGE, British man of letters (b. Teheran, Persia [Iran], Nov. 21, 1886—d. Sissinghurst Castle, Kent, Eng., May 1, 1968), whose officially commissioned *King George the Fifth: His Life and Reign* (1952) gained him the K.C.V.O. (knight commander of the Royal Victorian Order) in 1953. As a biographer of his own times he wrote *Lord Carnock* (1930), both a life of his own father and a study in pre-World War I diplomacy, followed by *Peacemaking* (1933) and *Curzon: The Last Phase* (1934). Among his other works were: *Marginal Comment* (1939) and *Friday Mornings* (1944), both collected from the *Spectator*, for which he wrote occasional columns; *Benjamin Constant* (1949); *Sainte-Beuve* (1957); *Monarchy* (1962); and his *Diaries and Letters* (3 vol., 1966–68).

NOONAN, TOMMY (Thomas Patrick), U.S. comic actor, director, and producer (b. Bellingham, Wash., April 29, 1922—d. Hollywood, Calif., April 24, 1968), after acting in, or directing, more than 200 stage plays made his film debut in *Scandals of 1945;* he also appeared in *Gentlemen Prefer Blondes* (1953), *A Star Is Born* (1955), and *Bundle of Joy* (1956).

NORDHOFF, HEINRICH, German engineer and industrialist (b. Hildesheim, Prussia, Jan. 6, 1899—d. Wolfsburg, W.Ger., April 12, 1968), who built the Volkswagen concern into one of the largest car plants in the world, worked with the Bayerische Motorenwerke (BMW) in Munich (1926–30) before joining the Adam Opel Automobile Company; he became manager of its truck plant at Brandenburg in 1942. In 1948 he was appointed president of the then derelict Volkswagen plant at Wolfsburg and the VW, whose beetle shape he refused to change over the years, soon became one of Germany's most successful exports.

NORTH, JOHN DUDLEY, British aircraft designer and executive (b. Jan. 2, 1893—d. Bridgenorth, Shropshire, Eng., Jan. 10, 1968), was head of Boulton Paul Aircraft Ltd., for which he designed (in the 1920s and 1930s) Royal Air Force twin-engined aircraft such as the Sidestrand, Overstrand, and Defiant.

NOTH, MARTIN, German Old Testament scholar, historian, philologist, and archaeologist (b. Dresden, Ger., Aug. 3, 1902—d. Negev, Israel, May 30, 1968), was director of the Evangelical Institut für Altertumswissenschaft des Heiligen Landes, and represented German-speaking members of the editorial board of the periodical *Vetus Testamentum*. After teaching at Greifswald (1927–28) and Leipzig (1928–30), he became professor of theology at Königsberg (1930–45) and at Bonn (1945–65). His main work concerned the early history of Israel. His books included *Die Welt des Alten Testaments* (1962; Eng. trans. 1966), *Geschichte Israels* (1962), and commentaries on various books of the Old Testament. Those on Exodus and Leviticus were translated into English.

NOVARRO, RAMON (José Ramón Gil Samaniegos), U.S. motion-picture actor (b. Durango, Mex., Feb. 6, 1899—d. Hollywood Hills, Calif., Oct. 31, 1968), starred in the silent pictures *The Prisoner of Zenda, Ben Hur, Scaramouche, The Student Prince,* and *The Midshipman* (all in the 1920s), and in *Mata Hari* with Greta Garbo in 1932. In the 1960s he appeared frequently in television shows, including an episode of "High Chaparral" in 1967.

O'CONNOR, EDWIN GREENE, U.S. novelist (b. Providence, R.I., July 29, 1918—d. Boston, Mass., March 23, 1968), who won the 1962 Pulitzer Prize for fiction with his novel *The Edge of Sadness,* also wrote *The Last Hurrah* (1956) and several other novels and plays.

O'KEEFE, DENNIS (Edward Vanes Flanagan, Jr.), U.S. actor (b. Fort Madison, Ia., 1908—d. Hollywood, Calif., Aug. 31, 1968), was a popular leading man of the 1930s and 1940s, who appeared in the films *Brewster's Millions, The Story of Dr. Wassell,* and *Walk a Crooked Mile.* In 1958 he ventured into television with "The Dennis O'Keefe Show," and in 1964 starred in the Broadway hit *Never Live Over a Pretzel Factory.*

ORE, OYSTEIN, Norwegian-U.S. mathematician and educator (b. Oslo, Nor., Oct. 7, 1899—d. Oslo, Aug. 13, 1968), Sterling professor emeritus of mathematics at Yale University, where he had become a full professor in 1929. His writings included *Cardano: The Gambling Scholar* (1953), *Niels Henrik Abel: Mathematician Extraordinary* (1957), and *Invitation to Number Theory* (1968); he also contributed to *Encyclopædia Britannica.*

ØVERLAND, ARNULF, Norwegian poet (b. Kristiansund, Nor., April 27, 1889—d. Oslo, Nor., March 25, 1968), whose series of poems written and clandestinely distributed in Norway after the German invasion of 1940, and which led to his imprisonment in Sachsenhausen, were collected in *Vi overlever alt* (1945). Later collections were *Sverdet bak døren* (1956) and *Livets minutter* (1965). After his return from Germany Øverland was honoured as Norway's poet laureate.

PANOFSKY, ERWIN, U.S. art historian (b. Hanover, Ger., March 30, 1892—d. Princeton, N.J., March 14, 1968), was emeritus professor of art history at the Institute for Advanced

WIDE WORLD · WIDE WORLD · CAMERA PRESS · MARIO DE BIASI, COURTESY MONDADORIPRESS

Sir Walter Nash · Georgios Papandreou · Konstantin G. Paustovsky · Salvatore Quasimodo

Study in Princeton, N.J., where he became a member of the faculty in 1935. He wrote three major works on the history of art: *Studies in Iconology* (1939), *Albrecht Dürer* (1943), and *Early Netherlandish Painting* (1953).

PAPANDREOU, GEORGIOS, Greek statesman (b. Kalentzi, Greece, Feb. 13, 1888—d. near Athens, Greece, Nov. 1, 1968), who was three times prime minister of his country, entered national politics in 1923 and in 1935 founded the Democratic Socialist Party. During World War II he set up a government in exile (October 1944); but on Dec. 31, 1944, he resigned. He served as minister without portfolio (1946), minister of the interior (1947), and vice-premier (1950–51), until the electoral landslide to the right in 1952 forced him into a decade of opposition. During that time he merged his Democratic Socialists with the Liberal Party, and then in 1961 organized a new bloc, the Centre Union. In 1963 the CU won a bare majority and Papandreou became prime minister on November 7, but resigned the next month, since he wanted a greater majority. Winning an absolute majority in the next election, Papandreou formed a new government on Feb. 19, 1964. A crisis developed in mid-1965 because of Papandreou's insistence on giving ministerial posts to his son Andreas, who was suspected of links with Aspida (a left-wing group subversively infiltrating the Army), and on July 15, King Constantine dismissed the prime minister. Papandreou was arrested following the military coup of April 21, 1967, but was later released.

PARRAN, THOMAS, U.S. physician and public official (b. St. Leonard, Md., Sept. 28, 1892—d. Pittsburgh, Pa., Feb. 15, 1968), was surgeon general, U.S. Public Health Service, from 1936 to 1948, and a founder of the World Health Organization (WHO).

PARSONS, EDWIN CHARLES, rear admiral (ret.), U.S. Navy (b. Holyoke, Mass., Sept. 24, 1892—d. Sarasota, Fla., May 2, 1968), a fighter pilot in World Wars I and II, was the last surviving ace of the Lafayette Escadrille of World War I fame.

PAULHAN, JEAN, French writer (b. Nîmes, France, Dec. 2, 1884—d. near Melun, France, Oct. 9, 1968), became professor of Malagasy at the École Nationale des Langues Orientales (1912) and produced his anthology of Malagasy poems in his own translation, *Les Hain-Teny merinas* (1913). He joined the staff of the *Nouvelle Revue française* and, in 1925, became its editor in chief. During World War II he founded a clandestine weekly, *Les Lettres françaises* (1941), but after the war resumed his editorial work (Gallimard's "Pléiade" series and *La Nouvelle N.R.F.*). His most important work, perhaps, was *Les Fleurs de Tarbes* (1941; new ed. 1945, 1963); he wrote a controversial vindication of the marquis de Sade (1951) and a preface, "Le Bonheur dans l'esclavage," to Pauline Réage's *Histoire d'O* (1954; Eng. trans. 1959). Elected to the Académie Française in 1963, he published a collected edition of his works in 1966.

PAUSTOVSKY, KONSTANTIN G., Soviet author (b. Moscow, Russia, May 31, 1892—d. Moscow, U.S.S.R., July 14, 1968), became known to the Western world in 1964 with the translation and publication of his autobiographical work, *The Story of a Life*. Paustovsky, who began publishing adventure stories in 1911, later turned to biographies and historical novels. An advocate of younger liberal writers, he often defended them before the board of the Soviet Writers Union; this, along with his own outspoken opinions, occasioned public censure by N. S. Khrushchev in 1962–63. However, in 1967 Paustovsky was awarded the Order of Lenin.

PEAKE, MERVYN, British artist and writer (b. Kuling, central China, July 9, 1911—d. Oxfordshire, Eng., Nov. 17, 1968), was best known for his fantasy novels, *Titus Groan* (1946), *Gormenghast* (1950), and *Titus Alone* (1959).

PETTER, WILLIAM EDWARD WILLOUGHBY, British aircraft designer (b. Aug. 8, 1908—d. France, May 1968), was technical director for the Westland Aircraft Co. from 1935 until 1944. During this period he designed the Lysander reconnaissance plane and the Whirlwind two-engined fighter. Later he produced for English Electric Ltd. the Canberra bomber and for Folland Aircraft the Gnat supersonic fighter.

PHOLIEN, JOSEPH, Belgian political leader (b. Liège, Belg., Dec. 28, 1884—d. Brussels, Belg., Jan. 4, 1968), was prime minister of Belgium from 1950 to 1952.

PISSARRO, OROVIDA CAMILLE, British painter (b. Epping, Essex, Eng., Oct. 8, 1893—d. London, Eng., Aug. 8, 1968), was a painter of animals, especially horses and tigers, in the Oriental manner. Her work is represented in many public collections, including the British Museum and the New York Public Library.

PIZZETTI, ILDEBRANDO, Italian composer (b. Parma, Italy, Sept. 20, 1880—d. Rome, Italy, Feb. 13, 1968), whose works included the operas *Fra Gherardo* and *Assassinio nella cattedrale* (1955; from T. S. Eliot's play *Murder in the Cathedral*); the symphonic *Concerto dell' estate, Canti dalla stagione alta,* and the Violin Concerto; and the choral works *Messa di Requiem* (1922) and *Cantico di gloria* (1948).

PLATT, JOSEPH BRERETON, U.S. industrial and interior designer (b. Plainfield, N.J., 1895—d. Wayne, Pa., Feb. 6, 1968), who in 1938 designed the interior sets for the film *Gone with the Wind.*

PLA Y DENIEL, ENRIQUE CARDINAL, Spanish prelate of the Roman Catholic Church (b. Barcelona, Spain, Dec. 19, 1876—d. Toledo, Spain, July 5, 1968), a strong supporter of Gen. Francisco Franco during the Spanish Civil War of 1936–39, was ordained in 1900 and appointed to the faculty at the Seminario de Barcelona. He became a canon at the Cathedral of Barcelona in 1912, and in 1919 was consecrated bishop of Avila. In 1935, as the new bishop of Salamanca, he began restoring the diocese's church property, which had been destroyed in the war, and by 1940 had completed the rebuilding of the Pontifical Ecclesiastic University. He was named archbishop of Toledo in 1941 and succeeded in establishing cordial relations between the church and the Franco government. At a consistory on Feb. 18, 1946, he was proclaimed cardinal by Pope Pius XII.

POIRIER, LÉON, French film director (b. Paris, France, Aug. 25, 1884—d. Urval, France, June 1968), produced his first films for Gaumont, which he joined in 1913. He directed many adaptations, including Balzac's *La Peau de chagrin* (1921), and films based on historical events. In the mid-1920s he became interested in documentary films, producing *La Croisière noire* to publicize the Citroën trans-Sahara trek (1925–26). His biggest success was *Verdun* (1928; sound version 1931), with Albert Préjean. *L'Appel du silence,* his first talking film, won the French cinema's Grand Prix in 1936.

POLING, DANIEL ALFRED, U.S. Protestant clergyman (b. Portland, Ore., Nov. 30, 1884—d. Philadelphia, Pa., Feb. 7, 1968), who conducted a nationwide weekly radio program over the NBC network during the 1920s, was the editor of the *Christian Herald* magazine from 1925 to 1965.

POOL, JOE RICHARD, U.S. congressman (from 1963) from Texas (b. Tarrant Co., Tex., Feb. 18, 1911—d. Houston, Tex., July 14, 1968).

POWER, CHARLES GAVAN, Canadian member of Parliament (b. Sillery, Que., Jan. 18, 1888—d. Quebec, Que., May 30, 1968), whose record of parliamentary service, beginning in 1917, spanned more than 50 years.

PRICE, MARGARET (MRS. HICKMAN PRICE, JR.), U.S. political party official (b. New York, N.Y., Oct. 15, 1912—d. New York, July 23, 1968), served as national vice-chairman of the Democratic Party and as chairman of the Democratic Women's Division from 1960.

PRITCHARD, JOHN LAURENCE, British writer (b. Shrewsbury, Eng., Feb. 25, 1885—d. Dorking, Surrey, Eng., April 23, 1968), secretary of the Royal Aeronautical Society (1925–51) and editor of the society's journal (1920–45), was an authority on aircraft structures. In addition to his aeronautical books, among which was *Sir George Cayley: The Inventor of the Aeroplane* (1961), he wrote over 20 novels.

PUCCI-NEGRI, ANNA MARIA, wife of an Italian entertainer (b. Carpena, near Forli, Italy, 1929—d. Rome, Italy, April 25, 1968), was the youngest and favourite child of Benito Mussolini.

PURDIE, EDNA, British scholar (b. Nov. 27, 1894—d. London, Eng., June 17, 1968), was distinguished for her contribution to Germanic studies and her administrative abilities. She was the first British woman professor of German (University of London, Bedford College, 1933–62; emeritus, 1962–68). Her first notable work, *Friedrich Hebbel: A Study of His Life and Work* (1932), remained a classic in Germany and in England; others included editions of Hebbel's *Herodes und Mariamne* (1943) and *Poems* (1953); and *Studies in German Literature of the 18th Century* (1965). She was chairman of the management committee of the Warburg Institute from its incorporation into the university in 1945 to 1966; helped to found and administer the Institute of Germanic Languages and Literatures (after 1950, of Germanic Studies); and represented the university on the governing body of the Royal College of Music.

PYRYEV, IVAN A., Soviet film director (b. 1901—d. Moscow, U.S.S.R., Feb. 7, 1968), made his first motion picture, *The Alien Woman,* in 1929. This was followed by *The Party Membership Card* in 1936, and three comedies filmed in the latter 1930s, for which he received a Stalin Prize in 1941. He received five more Stalin awards for films made in the 1940s.

QUASIMODO, SALVATORE, Italian poet (b. Modica, Sicily, Italy, Aug. 20, 1901—d. near Naples, Italy, June 14, 1968), recipient of the 1959 Nobel Prize for Literature, was professor of Italian literature at the Guiseppe Verdi Conservatory of Music in Milan from 1935. His first volume of poetry, *Acque e terre* ("Waters and Land"), appeared in 1930, and was followed by others in fairly rapid succession. Three works, *La vita non e' un sogno* ("Life Is No Dream") and *Il falso e vero verde* ("The False and True Green"), both published in 1949, and *La terra impareggiabile* ("The Incomparable Earth"), published in 1958, were cited in the Nobel Prize announcement.

RAISZ, ERWIN, U.S. cartographer (b. Hungary, 1893—d. Bangkok, Thailand, Dec. 1, 1968), who in 1945 founded the cartography section of the Association of American Geographers, was the author of several works including *Principles of Cartography* (1962) and *Atlas of Florida* (1964).

RAKOTOMALALA, LOUIS, Madagascan diplomat (b. Tananarive, Madagascar, Sept. 11, 1901—d. Spring Valley, N.Y., July 1, 1968), from 1960 was ambassador from the Malagasy Republic to the United States and permanent representative from his country to the United Nations.

RAND, CHRISTOPHER TAMPLE EMMET, U.S. foreign correspondent (b. New York, N.Y., 1912—d. Mexico City, Mex., Sept. 26, 1968), who covered World War II and the Korean War, was a member of *The New Yorker* magazine staff from 1951. He was the author of a number of books, including *Los Angeles: The Ultimate City* (1967).

REDFEARN, ERIC REGINALD, British biochemist (b. 1924—d. Great Glen, Leicestershire, Eng., March 6, 1968), whose main work concerned the biosynthesis of vitamin A and the biological role of ubiquinones in animal cells. After studying at the University of Liverpool (1948–54), he lectured in biochemistry at Queen's University, Belfast (1954–57), and at Liverpool (1957–62); he was a senior lecturer at Leicester (1962–64) before being appointed to a professorship there. Redfearn was an editor of the *Biochemical Journal* and of *Biochimica et Biophysica Acta.*

REID, THOMAS, Canadian legislator (b. Scotland, 1886—d. Surrey, B.C., Oct. 11, 1968), Liberal member of Parliament for New Westminster from 1930 until 1949, when he was appointed senator; he served in that position until the time of his death.

RIBAR, IVAN, Yugoslav politician (b. Vukmanic, near Karlovac, Croatia, Jan. 21, 1881—d. Zagreb, Yugos., Feb. 2, 1968), was president of the National Assembly (Skupstina) of the Kingdom of Serbs, Croats, and Slovenes from 1920 to 1922. He supported the United Opposition to the government during the regency for King Peter (1934–41). During World War II he rallied to Tito and joined the Communist Party (1942). He was

president successively of the executive committee of the Antifascist Council of National Liberation of Yugoslavia, the Presidium of the Provisional Assembly, the Presidium of the Constituent Assembly, and the Presidium of the National Assembly of Federal Yugoslavia (1945).

RICH, ARNOLD RICE, U.S. pathologist (b. Birmingham, Ala., March 28, 1893—d. Baltimore, Md., April 17, 1968), Baxley professor (emeritus from 1958) of pathology at Johns Hopkins University Medical School, and author of a standard textbook, *The Pathogenesis of Tuberculosis* (1944; rev. ed. 1951).

RICH, ROBERT FLEMING, U.S. congressman (1930–43, 1944–51) from Pennsylvania (b. Woolrich, Pa., June 23, 1883—d. Jersey Shore, Pa., April 28, 1968).

RICHARDS, JOHNNY (JOHN CASCALES), U.S. jazz composer and arranger (b. Mexico, Nov. 2, 1911—d. New York, N.Y., Oct. 7, 1968), who was an associate of Stan Kenton during the Kenton progressive jazz period, composed "Cuban Fire," "The Rites of Diablo," "Annotations of the Muses," and the popular "Young at Heart."

RICHAUD, PAUL CARDINAL, French prelate of the Roman Catholic Church (b. Versailles, France, April 16, 1887—d. Bordeaux, France, Feb. 5, 1968), who was trained as a lawyer, entered a seminary in 1909 and was ordained priest in 1913. After further studies in Rome, he returned to Versailles, where he was active in charitable and welfare work. In 1933 he was consecrated auxiliary bishop of Versailles; in 1938 he became bishop of Laval; and in 1950 he was named archbishop of Bordeaux. He was created cardinal in November 1958.

RICHTER, CONRAD MICHAEL, U.S. novelist (b. Pine Grove, Pa., Oct. 13, 1890—d. Pottsville, Pa., Oct. 30, 1968), was the author of *The Town,* awarded a 1950 Pulitzer Prize, and *The Waters of Kronos,* winner of the 1960 National Book Award. Other works included *The Lady* (1957), *Over the Blue Mountain* (1967), and *The Aristocrat* (1968).

RIVKIND, ISAAC, U.S. Zionist scholar (b. Lodz, Pol., 1895—d. New York, N.Y., Feb. 17, 1968), emeritus chief of Hebraica of the library at the Jewish Theological Seminary of America, was the author of *Bar Mitzvah: A Study in Jewish Cultural History* and *A Study of Five Centuries of Jewish Poetry and Cultural History.*

ROATTA, MARIO, general (ret.), Italian Army (b. Modena, Italy, Jan. 2, 1887—d. Rome, Italy, Jan. 6, 1968), was chief of staff of the Italian Army (1941); commander of the 2nd Army in Croatia and later of the 6th Army in Sicily; then again became chief of staff in June 1943. After Italy's surrender to the Allies, he was dismissed from the Army. Arrested a year later on charges of having abetted Fascism, he escaped to Spain; the Italian government sentenced him in absentia to life imprisonment but subsequently he was acquitted in 1948.

ROBB, SIR JAMES, air chief marshal, Royal Air Force (b. Hexham, Northumberland, Eng., Jan. 25, 1895—d. Bognor Regis, Sussex, Eng., Dec. 18, 1968), commander in chief of Air Forces, Western Europe, 1948–51, served as chief of staff (air) to Gen. Dwight Eisenhower 1944–45, and

as vice-chief of air staff, 1947–48. In 1951 he was made inspector general of the RAF.

ROBERTSON, CHARLES, British educationalist and administrator (b. Scotland, Feb. 23, 1874—d. London, Eng., Jan. 6, 1968), a member of the London County Council (1931–52) and its chairman (1945–46), was a pioneer of comprehensive schools. He worked for the Egyptian education services from 1902 to 1925. As chairman (1937–45) of the LCC's education committee, he did much to ensure the education of London schoolchildren evacuated during World War II.

ROBERTSON, NORMAN ALEXANDER, Canadian diplomat (b. Vancouver, B.C., March 4, 1904—d. Ottawa, Ont., July 16, 1968), was ambassador from Canada to the United States, 1957–58, and twice high commissioner for Canada to the United Kingdom, 1946–49 and 1952. After retiring from the Foreign Service Office in 1965, Robertson became director of the Graduate School of International Affairs of Carlton University, Ottawa.

ROKOSSOVSKY, KONSTANTIN K., marshal (ret.), Soviet Army (b. Warsaw, Pol., Dec. 21, 1896—d. Moscow, U.S.S.R., Aug. 3, 1968), a leading general in World War II, was commander of the forces defending Stalingrad and Moscow, and later commander of the six Soviet armies of the Don front. Following the war he was sent to Poland and served as that country's minister of defense from 1949 until 1956. He returned to the U.S.S.R. in the latter year and was deputy defense minister in Moscow until 1958. Rokossovsky held the Gold Star of a Hero of the Soviet Union and in 1966 was awarded the Order of Lenin.

ROSE, ARNOLD M., U.S. sociologist (b. Chicago, Ill., July 2, 1918—d. Minneapolis, Minn., Jan. 2, 1968), professor of sociology at the University of Minnesota, was the author of *The Negro in America* (1948; paperback ed. 1965) and *The Negro's Morale: Group Identification and Protest* (1949). He also contributed to *Encyclopædia Britannica.*

ROWLEY, ARTHUR HENDERSON, BARON, British socialist politician (b. Newcastle upon Tyne, Eng., Aug. 27, 1893—d. London, Eng., Aug. 28, 1968), was a Labour member of Parliament for 24 years and after holding several junior ministerial appointments served as secretary of state for air from 1947 to 1951. He was created a life peer in 1966.

SABARTÉS, JAIME, Spanish poet (b. 1881—d. Paris, France, Feb. 16, 1968), a long-time secretary to Pablo Picasso and author of a biography of the artist: *Picasso: Toreros* (1961).

ST. DENIS, RUTH (RUTH DENNIS), U.S. interpretive dancer (b. Newark, N.J., Jan. 20, 1877/80[?]—d. Los Angeles, Calif., July 21, 1968), was a pioneer in the development of modern choreography, especially Eastern-inspired dances. Her original numbers, *Incense, Radha, The Cobra, Yogi,* and *Nautch,* featured her as soloist (1909–10). In 1914 Miss St. Denis was married to her partner, Ted Shawn, and the team established the Denishawn Company and School. For 17 years they toured the U.S. and many countries abroad, but in 1931, with the separation of the two principals, the company was disbanded. Around 1950 the couple reunited to produce a series of demonstrated lectures and, until 1955, Miss St. Denis appeared regularly at Shawn's Jacob's Pillow Dance Festival (Lee, Mass.). In 1963 she appeared in a revival of *Incense* at New York Central Park's Delacorte Theater, and in 1964, in celebration of their golden wedding anniversary, she and Shawn danced before an invited audience at the Jacob's Pillow Festival. Her autobiography, *Unfinished Life,* was published in 1939.

ST. JOHN, EARL, U.S. film producer (b. Baton Rouge, La., June 14, 1892—d. Torremolinos, Spain, Feb. 26, 1968), who made his reputation in England, was executive producer for Pinewood Studios where he was responsible for such films as *Genevieve* and *Doctor in the House.* From 1951 he was executive producer for J. Arthur Rank Productions, Ltd. His other films included *Above Us the Waves, A Tale of Two Cities,* and *A Night to Remember.*

SALMOND, SIR JOHN MAITLAND, marshal, Royal Air Force (b. July 17, 1881—d. Eastbourne, Eng., April 15, 1968), was a pioneer leader of the Royal Flying Corps and the RAF. After early service as an army officer he took up

flying and was seconded to the RFC in 1912. He commanded an air squadron in France in 1914 and, after rapid promotion, took command of the newly formed RAF in France in 1918. An air marshal in 1923, he organized the air defense of Great Britain and in 1930 became chief of the air staff. After retirement he served (1939–41) in the Ministry of Aircraft Production.

SANDE, EARL, U.S. jockey (b. Groton, S.D., Nov. 13, 1898—d. Jacksonville, Ore., Aug. 20, 1968), a member of the Racing Hall of Fame, brought in 967 winners during his riding career which began in 1917. His victories included three Kentucky Derby firsts—Zev in 1923, Flying Ebony in 1925, and Gallant Fox in 1930—and earned almost $3 million in purses.

SCARFIOTTI, LODOVICO, Italian racing driver (b. Turin, Italy, Oct. 18, 1933—d. near Berchtesgaden, Ger., June 8, 1968), was killed when his Porsche 910 crashed in the German Alps during trials for the mountain driving championship. Scarfiotti had won the European mountain driving title twice, in 1962 and 1965; other victories included the Italian and the Syracuse Grand Prix races of 1967, the year he was ranked tenth in Formula I world championship ratings.

SCHINDLER, RUDOLF, U.S. gastroenterologist (b. Berlin, Ger., May 10, 1888—d. Munich, W.Ger., Sept. 9, 1968), who in 1932 invented the flexible gastroscope for viewing the interior of the stomach.

SCHLUMBERGER, JEAN, French literary figure (b. Guebwiller, Alsace-Lorraine, Ger., May 26, 1877—d. Paris, France, Oct. 25, 1968), collaborated with André Gide in founding *La Nouvelle Revue Française* in 1908–09 and with Jacques Copeau in founding the Théâtre du Vieux-Colombier in 1913. His fiction included *Heureux qui comme Ulysse* (1906; reworked as *L'Inquiète Paternité,* 1913); *Un Homme heureux* (1921); *Le Camarade infidèle* (1922); *Le Lion devenu vieux* (1924); *Les Yeux de dix-huit ans* (1928); *Saint-Saturnin* (1931); *Histoire des quatre potiers* (1935); and *Stéphane le glorieux* (1940).

SCHNEIRLA, T(HEODORE) C(HRISTIAN), U.S. animal psychologist (b. Bay City, Mich., July 23, 1902—d. New York, N.Y., Aug. 20, 1968), curator of the department of animal behaviour, American Museum of Natural History (New York City), from 1947; wrote *Principles of Animal Psychology* (with N. R. F. Maier, 1935) and contributed to *Encyclopædia Britannica.*

SCOTT, WINFIELD TOWNLEY, U.S. poet (b. Haverhill, Mass., April 30, 1910—d. Santa Fe, N.M., April 28, 1968), author of *Wind the Clock* (1941), *The Sword on the Table* (1942), *To Marry Strangers* (1945), *Mr. Whittier and Other Poems* (1948), *The Dark Sister* (1958), *Scrimshaw* (1959), and *Collected Poems 1937–1962* (1962).

SEARS, ELEONORA ("ELEO"), U.S. socialite and sportswoman (b. Boston, Mass., Sept. 28, 1881—d. Palm Beach, Fla., March 26, 1968), pioneered the way for the entrance of women into major sports. The first woman squash champion (1928), she held more than 240 trophies for competition in tennis, squash, horsemanship, and a variety of other sports.

SEGAL, MOSHEH ZEVI HIRSCH, Jewish rabbi and biblical scholar (b. Maishad, Lithuania, October 1876—d. Kfar Sava, Israel, Jan. 11, 1968), emeritus professor of Bible at the Hebrew University of Jerusalem, was a tutor in Old Testament and Semitic languages at Oxford University (1906–09), then served as a rabbi in various parts of England. He went to Israel in 1925 and became head of the Bible department at the Hebrew University in 1926. He pioneered the study of Hebrew phonetics, wrote a grammar of Mishnaic Hebrew, and published an edition of Ecclesiasticus.

SERAFIN, TULLIO, Italian opera conductor (b. near Venice, Italy, Dec. 8, 1878—d. Rome, Italy, Feb. 2, 1968), was conductor for La Scala in Milan (1909–13), then spent some time in London, Paris, and Buenos Aires before becoming principal conductor for the Metropolitan Opera Company in New York City. During his time at the Met (1924–34), he conducted the world premieres of Deems Taylor's *Peter Ibbetson* and of Louis Greunberg's *The Emperor Jones.*

SEROV, VLADIMIR ALEKSANDROVICH, Soviet artist (b. Emmaus [now in Kalinin Oblast],

Norman Alexander
Robertson

Ruth St. Denis

Russia, July 21, 1910—d. Moscow, U.S.S.R., Jan. 19, 1968), president of the Soviet Academy of Arts from 1962, received Stalin prizes in 1948 and 1951 for his paintings "Lenin Proclaiming the Soviet Regime" (1947) and "Peasant Petitioners to Lenin" (1950).

SHAPIRO, JOSEPH M., U.S. designer and manufacturer (b. Borisov, Russia, Sept. 25, 1888—d. La Jolla, Calif., July 29, 1968), founder and president (1927–49) and chairman of the board (1949–67) of the Simplicity Pattern Company.

SHEPPARD, LAWRENCE BAKER, U.S. executive and horse breeder (b. Baltimore, Md., Dec. 13, 1897—d. Hanover, Pa., Feb. 26, 1968), was founder, president, and general manager of Hanover Shoe Farm, largest U.S. Standardbred breeding farm. Among his famous trotters and pacers were Dean Hanover, onetime world record holder, and Adios, sire of Bret Hanover, 1964 harness horse of the year (owned by R. Downing).

SILVERMAN, (SAMUEL) SYDNEY, British politician (b. Liverpool, Eng., Oct. 8, 1895—d. London, Eng., Feb. 9, 1968), Labour member of Parliament for Nelson and Colne (1935–68), helped end capital punishment in Britain by piloting through Parliament his private member's Murder (Abolition of Death Penalty) Bill, 1965.

SIMAGIN, VLADIMIR PAVLOVITCH, Soviet chess grand master (b. 1920—d. Kislovodsk, U.S.S.R., Sept. 26, 1968), although he was not in the front rank of Soviet grand masters, his theoretical innovations to the openings such as those in the queen's gambit and the Ruy Lopez will be long remembered.

SIMPSON, SIR JOSEPH, British police official (b. Dawley, Shropshire, Eng., June 26, 1909—d. London, Eng., March 20, 1968), rose from the rank of constable to become commissioner of metropolitan police at Scotland Yard in 1958. The policy of letting the public "have a go" at apprehending smash-and-grab raiders, bank robbers, and so on was introduced during his commissionership.

SINCLAIR, UPTON (BEALL), U.S. author and Socialist (b. Baltimore, Md., Sept. 20, 1878—d. Bound Brook, N.J., Nov. 25, 1968), whose concern with trade unions, child labour, birth control, Prohibition, utopian Socialism, educational reform, civil liberties, and a multitude of other causes was expressed in the more than 90 books he wrote. An early work, *The Jungle* (1906), led to the passage of the first U.S. Food and Drug Act; other protest works included *King Coal* (1917), *The Profits of Religion* (1918), *The Goose-Step* (1923), *Oil!* (1927), and *The Flivver King: A Story of Ford-America* (1937). His later work was in historical fiction, including 11 volumes of the Lanny Budd series (1939–49), one of which, *Dragon's Teeth*, was awarded a 1943 Pulitzer Prize. His autobiography appeared in 1962.

SIPLE, PAUL ALLMAN, U.S. polar explorer (b. Montpelier, O., Dec. 18, 1908—d. Arlington, Va., Nov. 25, 1968), who at 19 was chosen from 600,000 Boy Scouts to accompany Adm. Richard E. Byrd on his first voyage to Antarctica (1928). Siple made six subsequent trips to the South Pole, including one (1956–57) in connection with the International Geophysical Year. From 1967 he was special science adviser to the U.S. Army. Siple was the author of several books including *90° South* (1959). His many honours included the Hubbard Medal of the National Geographic Society (1958).

SMATHERS, EUGENE, U.S. clergyman (b. Bath Co., Ky., Dec. 4, 1907—d. Big Lick, Tenn., Aug. 16, 1968), head of the United Presbyterian Church in the U.S.A., was elected moderator by the general assembly of the church in May 1967.

SMITH, JAMES LEONARD BRIERLEY, South African ichthyologist (b. Graaff-Reinet, S.Af., 1897—d. Grahamstown, S.Af., Jan. 7, 1968), was professor of ichthyology at Rhodes University from 1949 until the time of his death. Early in 1939 he identified the (supposedly extinct) coelacanth that had been caught in the Indian Ocean on Dec. 22, 1938. He wrote of the discovery in *The Search Beneath the Sea: The Story of the Coelacanth* (1956); he was also a contributor to *Encyclopædia Britannica.*

SMITH, RONALD GREGOR, Scottish theologian (b. Edinburgh, Scot., April 17, 1913—d. Hull,

Eng., Sept. 26, 1968), from 1956 primarius professor of divinity at Glasgow University, was educated at the universities of Edinburgh, Munich, Marburg, and Copenhagen. He was a minister at Selkirk (1939–44), chaplain to the forces (1944–46), and a member of the Control Commission in Germany (1946–47). Associate editor (1947–50) and editor (1950–56) of the Student Christian Movement Press, he wrote *The New Man* (1956), but he was best known as the translator of Martin Buber's *Ich und Du (I and Thou,* 1937).

SOKOLOVSKY, VASILY DANILOVICH, marshal (ret.), Soviet Army (b. Kozliki, then Russian Poland, 1897—d. Moscow, U.S.S.R., May 10, 1968), who during World War II served as chief of staff (1941–43) of the Western front and led his troops in the recapturing of Smolensk, was commander of the Soviet forces in East Germany (1946–49) when the four-power Allied Control Council struggle ended in the Berlin blockade. In 1949 he returned to Moscow and became first deputy defense minister; in 1952 he was named chief of staff of the Soviet armed forces (until 1960) and became a member of the Central Committee. Sokolovsky was made a Hero of the Soviet Union and was a seven-time recipient of the Order of Lenin.

SOLH, ABD-AL RAHIM SAMI ES-, Lebanese political leader (b. Acre [then in Palestine], 1890—d. Beirut, Lebanon, Nov. 6, 1968), five times prime minister of Lebanon (1942–43, 1945, 1952, 1954–55, and 1956–58), entered politics and the Lebanese Legislative Council in 1924, during the period of the French mandate. His career covered a stormy period in Lebanese political life and this accounted for his many short-lived premierships. After failing to win a seat in the 1960 general election he retired into private life.

SOROKIN, PITIRIM, U.S. sociologist (b. Touria, Russia, 1889—d. Winchester, Mass., Feb. 10, 1968), first chairman of the sociology department at Harvard University, who retired in 1955, wrote more than 30 books, including a four-volume study, *Social and Cultural Dynamics* (1937–40). Among other works were *Social Philosophies of an Age of Crisis* (1950), *Forms and Techniques of Altruistic and Spiritual Growth* (1954), and *Sociological Theories of Today* (1966). His autobiography, *A Long Journey,* was published in 1963.

SOWERBY, LEO, U.S. composer and organist (b. Grand Rapids, Mich., May 1, 1895—d. Port Clinton, O., July 7, 1968), won the 1946 Pulitzer Prize for musical composition with his secular work *Canticle of the Sun.*

SPECTOR, MAURICE, Canadian Communist (b. Russia, 1898—d. New York, N.Y., Aug. 1, 1968), was a founder of the Communist Party in Canada (1921) and of the Trotskiist Party in Canada and the United States (in the 1930s).

STAFFORD, HANLEY (ALFRED JOHN AUSTIN), U.S. radio actor (b. Hanley, Staffordshire, Eng., 1899—d. Hollywood, Calif., Sept. 11, 1968), played the Daddy role opposite Fanny Brice in the "Baby Snooks" radio series from 1938 until the mid-1940s; he also played Mr. Dithers in the "Blondie" series during approximately the same period.

STALLINGS, LAURENCE TUCKER, JR., U.S. playwright and screenwriter (b. Macon, Ga., Nov. 25, 1894—d. Pacific Palisades, Calif., Feb. 28, 1968), in 1924 collaborated with Maxwell Anderson in writing the World War I play *What Price Glory?*

STEGMEYER, WILLIAM JOHN, U.S. composer and clarinetist (b. Detroit, Mich., Oct. 8, 1916—d. Syosset, N.Y., Aug. 19, 1968), played with the bands of Glenn Miller and Bob Crosby in the late 1930s; he was an arranger for Billy Butterfield (1946–47) and for the television show "Your Hit Parade" (1950–58). He wrote "The Jazzman Blues" and "Blue Manhattan."

STEINBECK, JOHN ERNST, U.S. author (b. Salinas, Calif., Feb. 27, 1902—d. New York, N.Y., Dec. 20, 1968), winner of a Nobel Prize for Literature, had little success with his first novel, *Cup of Gold* (1929, which sold about 1,500 copies), or with the next two. *Tortilla Flat*, published in 1935, became a best seller. It was followed by *In Dubious Battle* (1936) and

Of Mice and Men (1937); the latter as a stage play was chosen for a New York Drama Critics Circle award and later made into a motion picture. In 1939 Steinbeck published *The Grapes of Wrath*, winner of a 1940 Pulitzer Prize. This was followed by *The Moon Is Down* (1942) and by a filmscript for *Lifeboat* (1944), starring Tallulah Bankhead (q.v.). Next came *Cannery Row* (1945), *The Wayward Bus* (1947), and *A Russian Journal* (1948). *East of Eden* (1952; the film version starred James Dean) was his major contribution during the 1950s. *The Winter of Our Discontent* was published in 1961, and in 1962 Steinbeck was awarded the Nobel Prize for Literature, being cited for his "sympathetic humor and social perception." His *Travels with Charley*, a whimsical account of a jaunt across the U.S. in company with his dog, was a 1962 best seller.

STERN, LINA SOLOMONOVNA, Soviet physiologist (b. Libava [now Liepaja], Latvia, 1878—d. Moscow, U.S.S.R., March 7, 1968), the Soviet Union's most illustrious woman scientist, pioneered study of the chemical basis of physiological processes, especially in the central nervous system. Brought up in Switzerland, she became professor of physiological chemistry at the University of Geneva (1917–25). Moving to Moscow, she became professor of physiology at the Second Moscow Medical Institute, but was dismissed in 1949 for allegedly sharing scientific secrets with foreigners. Rehabilitated after Stalin's death, she was from 1954 head of the physiology laboratory of the U.S.S.R. Academy of Sciences.

STRACHEY, PHILIPPA, British pioneer for women's rights (b. 1872—d. Aug. 23, 1968), became secretary to the London Society for Women's Suffrage in 1907 when she organized the first open-air rally which became the prototype for such demonstrations. She was honorary secretary to the Fawcett Society after her retirement in 1951.

STROMBERG, HUNT, U.S. film producer (b. Louisville, Ky., July 12, 1894—d. Santa Monica, Calif., Aug. 23, 1968), who was voted "Champion of Champion Producers of All Time" in 1947, produced such films as *Red Dust* (1925), *Blonde Bombshell* (1933), *The Thin Man* and two sequels (1934–39), *Naughty Marietta* (1935), *The Great Ziegfeld* (Academy Award, 1936), *Rose Marie* (1936), *Maytime* (1937), and *Dishonored Lady* (1947). He retired in 1951.

SULZBERGER, ARTHUR HAYS, U.S. newspaper publisher (b. New York, N.Y., Sept. 12, 1891—d. New York, Dec. 11, 1968), published the *New York Times* from 1935 until 1961, becoming chairman of the board in 1957.

SWALLOW, JOHN, British polymer chemist (b. March 4, 1903—d. July 20, 1968), helped discover polythene in 1933, and thereafter continued to research the processes of its manufacture and its uses. He was research director from 1942 and chairman (1952–63) of the plastics division of Imperial Chemical Industries.

SWING, RAYMOND GRAM, U.S. radio commentator (b. Cortland, N.Y., March 25, 1887—d. Washington, D.C., Dec. 22, 1968), whose Monday-through-Thursday broadcasts attracted 37 million listeners in the U.S. and abroad during the 1930s and 1940s, was later a political commentator for the "Voice of America." His auto-

CAMERA PRESS   WIDE WORLD

Vasily D. Sokolovsky   John Steinbeck

biography, *Good Evening! A Professional Memoir*, was published in 1964.

SYDNEY, BASIL, British actor (b. St. Osyth, Essex, Eng., April 23, 1894—d. London, Eng., Jan. 10, 1968), who was as successful in interpreting Shakespeare, Shaw, or Sartre as in creating leading roles in light comedies such as *Love from a Stranger* and *The Man About the House,* made his first stage appearance in 1909. In 1914 he first visited the U.S., where he spent much of the 1920s and 1930s. His chance came in 1917, when he took over the dual role in *Romance,* and for 30 years he played leading parts in plays as varied as they were popular. Notable successes included Romeo in his own London production (1919); and in the U.S., *The Devil's Disciple, She Stoops to Conquer, Children of Darkness* (retitled *Knave and Queen* when he took it to London in 1930), *Dinner at Eight, Pygmalion, The Dark Tower* (with which he finally returned to London in 1937), *Hamlet* (1944, and later in Sir Laurence Olivier's film version), also *Crime Passionel* and *Altona.* His last stage appearance was in 1966, at the New Arts Theatre, London.

SYPHERS, GRANT E., U.S. government official (b. Arcadia, Calif., Jan. 15, 1911—d. San Diego, Calif., Feb. 5, 1968), was sworn in as U.S. interstate commerce commissioner on July 31, 1967, for a seven-year term.

TALMAN, WILLIAM WHITNEY, U.S. actor (b. Detroit, Mich., Feb. 4, 1917—d. Encino, Calif., Aug. 30, 1968), played the part of Hamilton Burger, district attorney, in the "Perry Mason" television series from 1957 until 1966. He also appeared in a number of motion pictures including *The Hitch-Hiker* (1953) and *The Ballad of Josie,* released in 1968.

TECCHI, BONAVENTURA, Italian novelist (b. Bagnoregio, Viterbo, Italy, Feb. 11, 1896—d. Rome, Italy, March 31, 1968), professor of letters and philosophy at Rome University and director of the Italian Institute for Germanic Studies, was best known for his long short stories, including the collections *Il vento tra le case* (1928), *Tre storie d'amore* (1931), and *La presenza del male* (1947).

TEMPLETON, KATHRYN KELLET, U.S. author and scouting adviser (b. Butte, Mont., 1910—d. Mount Kisco, N.Y., June 1, 1968), a member of the Girl Scouts national staff, was the author of the *Brownie Girl Scout Handbook.*

TENGBOM, IVAR JUSTUS, Swedish architect (b. Vireda, Swed., April 7, 1878—d. Drottningholm, Swed., Aug. 6, 1968), known for his buildings in Stockholm such as the Högalids Church (1916–23) and the neoclassic Concert Hall (1920–26), which had much influence in England in the 1930s. Tengbom was professor of architecture at Stockholm College of Art (1916–20) and director general of the Swedish Office of Works (1924–36). In 1938 he was awarded the gold medal of the Royal Institute of British Architects.

TEVIOT, CHARLES IAIN KERR, 1ST BARON, British politician (b. May 3, 1874—d. London, Eng., Jan. 7, 1968), was chairman of the Liberal National Party from 1940 to 1956. He was Liberal National member of Parliament for Montrose Burghs from 1932 to 1940 (chief whip, 1937–39), and in 1937 became a lord commissioner of the treasury from 1939 to 1940. He was comptroller of his majesty's household from 1939 to 1940.

THIL, MARCEL, French boxer (b. St.-Dizier, France, May 4, 1904—d. Cannes, France, Aug. 14, 1968), was world middleweight champion, 1932–37.

THOMAS, GEORGE A., U.S. Indian leader (b. 1910—d. Syracuse, N.Y., Oct. 22, 1968), was chief of the 16,000-member Iroquois Indian Confederacy of the United States and Canada from 1957 until the time of his death.

THOMAS, NORMAN MATTOON, U.S. Socialist (b. Marion, O., Nov. 20, 1884—d. Huntington, N.Y., Dec. 19, 1968), who was his party's nominee for the U.S. presidency six times (1928 through 1948), received a divinity degree in 1911 from Union Theological Seminary and continued in pastoral work until 1931. He joined the Socialist Party in 1918, and later edited *The World Tomorrow* for the Fellowship of Reconciliation. As well as campaigning in his many attempts to win public office, Thomas lectured at least two or three times a week and wrote innumerable articles on world peace, anti-Communism, civil liberties, and related subjects. His 20 books included *A Socialist's Faith* (1951), *The Great Dissenter* (1961), and *Socialism Re-examined* (1963).

THOMPSON, (LAFAYETTE) FRESCO, U.S. baseball executive (b. Centreville, Ala., June 6, 1903—d. Fullerton, Calif., Nov. 20, 1968), vice-president (from 1950) and general manager (from June 1968) of the Dodgers baseball team (in Brooklyn and Los Angeles). As a player he achieved a batting average of .298 for nine seasons (1925–34).

THOMPSON, SYLVIA ELIZABETH, British novelist (b. Sept. 4, 1902—d. Reigate, Surrey, Eng., April 27, 1968), began her second, most successful novel, *The Hounds of Spring* (1925), while an undergraduate. Her output of competent, readable works continued with *Chariot Wheels* (1929), *Winter Comedy* (1931; U.S. title, *Portrait of Caroline*), *Summer's Night* (1932), *Helena* (1933; U.S. title, *Unfinished Symphony*), *Golden Arrow* (a play, with V. Cunard, 1935), *Third Act in Venice* (1936), *Recapture the Moon* (1937), *The Gulls Fly Inland* (1941), *The People Opposite* (1949), and *The Candle's Glory* (1953).

TONE, FRANCHOT, U.S. stage and screen actor (b. Niagara Falls, N.Y., Feb. 27, 1905—d. New York, N.Y., Sept. 18, 1968), starred in more than 100 motion pictures including *Lives of a Bengal Lancer* (1935), *Mutiny on the Bounty* (1935), *Three Comrades* (1938), *Five Graves to Cairo* (1943), and *Advise and Consent* (1962). He also appeared in a number of Broadway plays.

TOSCANO, MARIO, Italian historian (b. Turin, Italy, June 3, 1908—d. Rome, Italy, Sept. 17, 1968), was a specialist in the study of diplomacy whose works included *Il Patto di London* (1934) and *Le origini del Patto d'acciaio* (1948–56; Eng. trans., *The Origins of the Pact of Steel,* 1968).

TRACY, (WILLIAM) LEE, U.S. actor (b. Atlanta, Ga., April 14, 1898—d. Santa Monica, Calif., Oct. 18, 1968), played chiefly newspaper reporter roles starting with *The Front Page* on Broadway in 1928 and continuing through more than 50 motion pictures. His stage appearances in later years included *The Best Man* (1960) and *Minor Miracle* (1966).

TRUSSELL, C(HARLES) P(RESCOTT), U.S. news correspondent (b. Chicago, Ill., Aug. 3, 1892—d. Washington, D.C., Oct. 2, 1968), who was with the Washington bureau of the *New York Times* from 1941 until 1965, won a Pulitzer Prize in 1949 for his reporting of national affairs.

TSIRIMOKOS, ELIAS, Greek statesman (b. Lamia, Greece, Aug. 2, 1907—d. Athens, Greece, July 13, 1968), a leftist, was elected to Parliament as a Liberal in 1936. During World War II he became a leader of the resistance to the German occupation of Greece. When the Communist-dominated National Liberation Front set up its "Political Committee" as a sort of government in March 1944, Tsirimokos became secretary for justice, but in September he joined the Athens government as minister for the national economy. On a decision to disarm all former resistance groups, Tsirimokos and his friends resigned from the government (December 1944), and civil war ensued until February 1945. Secretary-general of a "unified" Socialist Party, he was elected to the short-lived Parliament of 1950, then again elected to Parliament in 1958 as an independent. He then founded a new Democratic Union Party, which in 1961 merged into Georgios Papandreou's Centre Union. When the latter came to power Tsirimokos was chosen as president of the Parliament in 1963 but not in 1964; however, he became minister of the interior in January 1965. In the long crisis following King Constantine's dismissal of Papandreou, Tsirimokos was actually prime minister from Aug. 20 to Aug. 29, 1965. Subsequently he was deputy prime minister and minister of foreign affairs from Sept. 17, 1965, to April 11, 1966, when he resigned in a disagreement over Cyprus.

UPSON, RALPH HAZLETT, U.S. aeronautical engineer (b. New York, N.Y., June 21, 1888—d. Burien, Wash., Aug. 13, 1968), a balloon-racing champion whose victories included the 1913 International Balloon Race from Paris to England and the American National Balloon Race in 1913, 1919, and 1921. He later designed dirigibles and planes, and participated in the U.S. space program. He retired in 1964.

VAN DONGEN, KEES (CORNÉLIUS THÉODORUS MARIE VAN DONGEN), Dutch-French painter (b. Delfshaven, Neth., Jan. 26, 1877—d. Monte Carlo, Monaco, May 28, 1968), a member of the group of artists known as Les Fauves ("the Wild Beasts") because of their violent use of colour, exhibited at the third Salon d'Automne at Paris in 1905, when the group was first called by that name. His later work moved into a range of cold though still intense colour, and included portraits of many noted persons—the Aga Khan, Anatole France, King Leopold of Belgium, Maurice Chevalier, and Brigitte Bardot.

VAN PAASSEN, PIERRE ANTHONIE LAURUSSE, U.S. clergyman and writer (b. Gorcum, Neth., Feb. 7, 1895—d. New York, N.Y., Jan. 8, 1968), was an ordained minister of the Unitarian Fellowship and the author of more than a dozen works on Jewish culture and political history, including *Days of Our Years,* a 1939 best seller.

VAN VOORHIS, WESTBROOK, U.S. radio and television announcer (b. New Milford, Conn., Sept. 21, 1903—d. New Milford, July 13, 1968), was best known as the narrator for *The March of Time* radio and film documentaries of the 1930s and 1940s.

VESTINE, ERNEST HARRY, U.S. geophysicist (b. Minneapolis, Minn., May 19, 1906—d. Santa Monica, Calif., July 18, 1968), an authority on geomagnetism and auroral sciences, received the John Fleming Award from the American Geophysical Union in 1967. He was a contributor to *Encyclopædia Britannica.*

VEUILLOT, PIERRE CARDINAL, French prelate of the Roman Catholic Church (b. Paris, France, Jan. 5, 1913—d. Paris, Feb. 14, 1968), was ordained in 1939 and received an appointment as curate in a Paris suburb. In 1949 he was chosen by Pope Pius XII as aide for French affairs under Giovanni Battista Montini (later Pope Paul VI), who was then acting secretary of state for Pius. Veuillot was appointed bishop of Angers by Pope John XXIII in 1959; in 1961 he became archbishop coadjutor of the Paris archdiocese and in 1966, archbishop. He was elevated to cardinal in the 1967 consistory.

VIAN, SIR PHILIP LOUIS, British admiral of the fleet (b. June 15, 1894—d. Ashford Hill, Berkshire, Eng., May 27, 1968), World War II commander of the destroyer "Cossack" which rescued 299 British merchant seamen held prisoner in the German supply ship "Altmark" in a Norwegian fjord. He commanded the 4th destroyer flotilla in the Norwegian campaign (1940) and in action against the "Bismarck." In 1941–42 he commanded the 15th cruiser squadron in the Mediterranean, took part in the invasion of Sicily, in the Salerno landing, and in the invasion of Normandy in 1944. In 1944–45 he commanded the British carrier force in the Pacific which joined in the final air attack on the Japanese home islands. He was fifth sea lord (1946–48) and commander in chief of the home fleet (1950–52).

VOGT, WILLIAM, U.S. naturalist and writer (b. Mineola, N.Y., May 15, 1902—d. New York, N.Y., July 11, 1968), who served as national director of the Planned Parenthood Federation of America from 1951 until 1961, was the author of *Road to Survival* (1948) and *People! Challenge to Survival* (1960).

Kees van Dongen   Pierre Cardinal Veuillot

VORONOV, NIKOLAI NIKOLAEVICH, chief marshal (ret.), Soviet Army (b. St. Petersburg, Russia, 1899—d. Moscow, U.S.S.R., Feb. 28, 1968), began his career during the Russian Revolution, as a volunteer for the Red Army from 1918 and as a Communist Party member from 1919. He completed his education at the Frunze Military Academy, Moscow, in 1930, was made commander of the Soviet Army's main artillery administration in 1937, and chief marshal of artillery in 1944. In World War II he served on the Leningrad, Southwestern, Voronezh, Bryansk, and Stalingrad fronts. He left his command in 1950 and became president of the Academy of Artillery Sciences and, in 1953, head of the Artillery Academy.

WALLACE, LURLEEN BURNS, U.S. public official (b. Tuscaloosa, Ala., Sept. 19, 1926—d. Montgomery, Ala., May 7, 1968), 47th governor of Alabama who in January 1967 succeeded her husband, George C. Wallace. Under her leadership the state legislature voted to provide more funds for mental hospitals.

WALTER, JOHN, British newspaperman (b. London, Eng., Aug. 8, 1873—d. Hove, Sussex, Eng., Aug. 12, 1968), proprietor and director of *The Times* from 1922 to 1966, was a great-great-grandson of the newspaper's founder, John Walter (d. 1812). After working as a foreign correspondent for *The Times*, he became chairman of The Times Publishing Co. Ltd. on the death of his father in 1910. This was at a time when Alfred Harmsworth (afterward Lord Northcliffe) had secured control of the company. In 1922 Walter, in association with Maj. John Astor (the future Lord Astor of Hever), acquired Northcliffe's shares, and thus became co-chief proprietor of the newspaper.

WANGER, WALTER (WALTER FEUCHTWANGER), U.S. film producer (b. San Francisco, Calif., July 11, 1894—d. New York, N.Y., Nov. 18, 1968), who, during his 44-year career, produced such motion pictures as *Queen Christina,* starring Greta Garbo (1933); *52nd Street* (1937); *Stage Coach* (1939); *Foreign Correspondent* (1940); *Joan of Arc,* starring Ingrid Bergman (1951); *I Want to Live,* for which Susan Hayward received an Academy Award (1959); and his last, *Cleopatra,* with Elizabeth Taylor and Richard Burton, released in 1963. He was president of the Academy of Motion Picture Arts and Sciences from 1939 until 1945.

WARE, KEITH L., major general, U.S. Army (b. Denver, Colo., Nov. 23, 1915—d. Bin Long Province, S.Viet., Sept. 13, 1968), commander of the U.S. 1st Infantry Division in Vietnam, was killed in a helicopter crash. In 1944 he was awarded the Medal of Honor while serving in the European theatre during World War II.

WEDGWOOD, JOSIAH, British industrialist (b. Elswick, Newcastle upon Tyne, Eng., Oct. 20, 1899—d. London, Eng., May 5, 1968), was chairman (1947–67) and managing director (1930–60) of the pottery firm of Josiah Wedgwood and Sons, Ltd., of Barlaston. He served as vice-chairman of the British Pottery Manufacturers' Federation (1942–45), was a director of the Bank of England (1942–46), chairman of the advisory council of the Royal College of Art, and one of the original members of the Council of Industrial Design. In 1929 he published *The Economics of Inheritance.*

WEEGEE (ARTHUR H. FELLIG), U.S. photographer (b. Zloczew, Pol., June 12, 1899—d. New York, N.Y., Dec. 26, 1968), excelled in capturing the candid shot or, as he himself called it, "life in the Naked City."

Josiah Wedgwood   Sir Donald Wolfit

WEIGELT, KURT, German airline magnate (b. Berlin, Ger., June 4, 1884—d. Bad Homburg, W.Ger., Aug. 4, 1968), who revived the Lufthansa airline after World War II, began his career in 1913 with the Deutsche Bank. In 1918 he was appointed to the executive board of Deutsche Petroleum AG, besides serving as a deputy director of the Deutsche Bank; later he was concerned in setting up the Deruluft airline, and, in particular, the original Lufthansa.

WETTLING, GEORGE, U.S. jazz drummer (b. Topeka, Kan., 1906—d. New York, N.Y., June 6, 1968), who played Chicago-style jazz, was with Artie Shaw in 1936; during 1938–40 he was with Paul Whiteman, and from 1940 through 1943 he played for Muggsy Spanier.

WHEELER, BERT (ALBERT JEROME), U.S. comedian (b. Paterson, N.J., April 17, 1895—d. New York, N.Y., Jan. 18, 1968), whose 50-year career included the *Ziegfeld Follies,* motion pictures, and television. During the 1930s he teamed with Robert Woolsey and the two made more than 30 films together, including *Rio Rita* (1930), *Girl Crazy* (1932), *Kentucky Kernels* (1934), and *Mummy's Boys* (1936).

WHITE, GEORGE (GEORGE WEITZ), U.S. theatrical producer (b. New York, N.Y., 1890—d. Hollywood, Calif., Oct. 10, 1968), who staged 13 productions of his *Scandals* from 1921 through 1939, also acted in the *Ziegfeld Follies* (1915) and produced *Manhattan Mary* (1927) and *Flying High* (1930) on Broadway.

WILLAN, HEALEY, Canadian composer (b. Balham, Surrey, Eng., Oct. 12, 1880—d. Toronto, Ont., Feb. 16, 1968), was professor of music at the University of Toronto from 1937 until 1950. He composed more than 300 works, including symphonies, motets, and choral, orchestral, chamber, liturgical, and organ pieces.

WILLARD, JESS, U.S. boxer (b. Pottawatomie Indian land, Kan., Dec. 29, 1881—d. Los Angeles, Calif., Dec. 15, 1968), gained the heavyweight championship on April 5, 1915, in Havana, when he knocked out Jack Johnson in the 26th round of a scheduled 45-round fight, a battle that ran 1 hr. 45 min. in 100° heat. At Toledo, O., on July 4, 1919, Willard was ousted from the championship by Jack Dempsey when he was unable to answer the bell for the fourth round. In Willard's 36 fights he scored 20 KO's, 4 decisions won and 3 lost, 1 lost on an unintentional foul, 4 no-decisions, and 1 draw; he was knocked out twice, once by Dempsey and once by Luis Firpo.

WILLEN, PEARL LARNER (MRS. JOSEPH WILLEN), U.S. social worker (b. Chicago, Ill., Jan. 2, 1904—d. Kenya, March 17, 1968), was president of the International Council of Jewish Women (1954–57) and of the National Council of Jewish Women (1963–67).

WILLIAMS, ALWYN TERRELL PETRE, British educator and Anglican clergyman (b. Barrow-in-Furness, Lancashire, Eng., July 20, 1888—d. Bridport, Dorset, Eng., Feb. 18, 1968), bishop of Durham (1939–52) and Winchester (1952–61), was from 1950 chairman of the committee preparing the *New English Bible: New Testament* (1961). Ordained in 1913, he was headmaster of Winchester College (1924–34) and dean of Christ Church, Oxford (1934–39).

WILLIAMS, R(ICHARD) NORRIS, II, U.S. tennis champion (b. Geneva, Switz., 1891—d. Philadelphia, Pa., June 2, 1968), on seven U.S. Davis Cup teams and winner of more than ten national championships, was elected to the National Tennis Hall of Fame in 1957.

WINTERS, (ARTHUR) YVOR, U.S. educator, poet, and critic (b. Chicago, Ill., Oct. 17, 1900—d. Palo Alto, Calif., Jan. 25, 1968), professor of English (1949–60) and Albert Guerard professor of literature (1961–66) at Stanford University, was the author of *Collected Poems* (1952; rev. ed. 1960). His critical works included *In Defense of Reason* (1947; reissued 1950) and *The Functions of Criticism* (1957). In 1960 he received Yale University's Bollingen Prize and a Creative Arts gold medal from Brandeis University; in 1961 he was awarded the Harriet Monroe Poetry Prize.

WOLFIT, SIR DONALD, British actor and stage manager (b. Newark-on-Trent, Nottinghamshire, Eng., April 20, 1902—d. London, Eng., Feb. 17, 1968), first appeared on the London stage in 1924. He formed his own company in 1937 and

during World War II made special tours to garrison theatres in France and Belgium and immediately after the war visited the U.S. He was most famous for Shakespearean roles, particularly King Lear and Shylock. He was appointed Commander Order of the British Empire in 1950 and knighted in 1957. His autobiography, *First Interval,* appeared in 1955.

WOOD, JOHN S., U.S. congressman (1932–36, 1944–52) from Georgia (b. Cherokee Co., Ga., Feb. 8, 1885—d. Atlanta, Ga., Sept. 12, 1968), was chairman of the U.S. House Committee on Un-American Activities (1945–47, 1949–52).

WOOLRICH, CORNELL, U.S. writer (b. New York, N.Y., 1904—d. New York, Sept. 25, 1968), was the author of about 20 mystery stories, many of which were adapted for the screen, including *No Man of Her Own* (released in 1950), *Rear Window* (1954), and *The Bride Wore Black* (1967). Under the pen name George Hopley, he wrote *The Night Has a Thousand Eyes* (1945) and *Fright* (1950). He also wrote under the name William Irish.

WORLEY, ROBERT F., major general, U.S. Air Force (b. Riverside, Calif., Oct. 12, 1919—d. near Da Nang, S.Viet., July 23, 1968), deputy commander of the U.S. 7th Air Force in Vietnam, was killed when his RF-4C was hit by enemy fire.

XENIA, ARCHDUCHESS OF HABSBURG, descendant of the nobility of old Russia (b. 1933—d. near Soigny, France, Sept. 6, 1968), wife of Archduke Rudolf, youngest son of Charles I, last emperor of Austria-Hungary.

YASHIN, ALEKSANDR, Soviet writer (b. 1915—d. July 12, 1968), was the author of *Levers* (1956), censured by the Soviet Writers Union, and *Vologda Wedding* (1962), a story denounced by *Pravda* as giving a false picture of rural life in the U.S.S.R. His *Political Control of Literature in the U.S.S.R., 1946–56* was published in the U.S. in 1962.

YEATMAN, ROBERT JULIAN, British writer (b. 1898—d. London, Eng., July 13, 1968), was, with Walter Carruthers Sellar (d. 1951), author of the best-selling humorous account of English history, *1066 and All That* (1930; 35th ed. 1963; stage versions, 1932, 1935, 1937, 1947). His literary partnership with Sellar also produced *Horse Nonsense* (1933), *And Now All This* (1934), and *Garden Rubbish* (1936).

YEATS, GEORGINA HYDE-LEES, Irish writer (b. 1893—d. Dublin, Ire., Aug. 24, 1968), was the biographer of her husband, the Irish poet William Butler Yeats, whom she married on Oct. 21, 1917, and who died on Jan. 28, 1939.

YUDIN, PAVEL F., Soviet scholar and diplomat (b. Sept. 7, 1899—d. [announced] Moscow, U.S.S.R., April 11, 1968), Soviet ambassador to China (1953–59), was a noted Marxist theoretician and the author of about 150 works on science, philosophy, and history. He held the Order of Lenin (1959) and won the Stalin Prize (1943) for his history of philosophy.

ZBYSZKO, WLADEK, U.S.-Polish wrestler (b. Cracow, Pol., 1893—d. Savannah, Mo., June 10, 1968), who wrestled professionally in Europe and the Americas during the 1920s and 1930s, claimed the world championship for a short time in the 1920s.

ZWEIG, ARNOLD, German-Jewish writer (b. Gross-Glogau, Ger., Nov. 10, 1887—d. East Berlin, E.Ger., Nov. 26, 1968), best known for *Der Streit um den Sergeanten Grischa* (1927; *The Case of Sergeant Grischa,* 1934), one of the outstanding novels inspired by World War I; he later wrote *De Vriendt kehrt heim* (1932; *De Vriendt Goes Home,* 1933), on the Zionist aspiration, and *Das Beil von Wandsbek* (1947; *The Axe of Wandsbek,* 1947), a massive treatment of Nazi Germany. A drama, his Jewish tragedy *Ritualmord in Ungarn* (1914), was produced as *Die Sendung Samaels* in 1920. Expelled from Germany in 1933, he lived in Haifa, Palestine, until 1948, when he returned to East Germany. He received the Lenin Peace Prize in 1958.

Oceanography

The most significant oceanographic event of 1968 was the successful initial voyage of the "Glomar Challenger," marking the first field operations of the Deep Sea Drilling Project of the U.S. National Science Foundation. This project was the outgrowth of planning by the Joint Oceanographic Institutions Deep Earth Sampling Program group, consisting of the Woods Hole (Mass.) Oceanographic Institution, the Lamont Geological Laboratory of Columbia University, Palisades, N.J., the Institute of Marine Science at Miami, Fla., and the Scripps Institution of Oceanography at La Jolla, Calif. Stated most simply, the purpose of the operation was to drill and obtain cores of the sediments of the deep ocean basins down to the underlying basement. These sediments, which range up to 6,000 ft. in thickness, contain the relatively un-

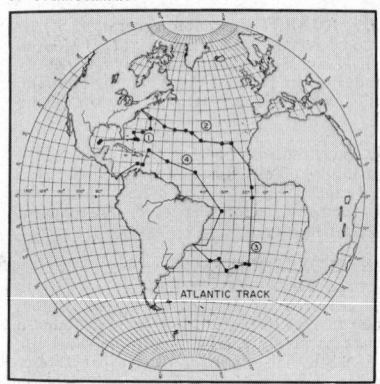 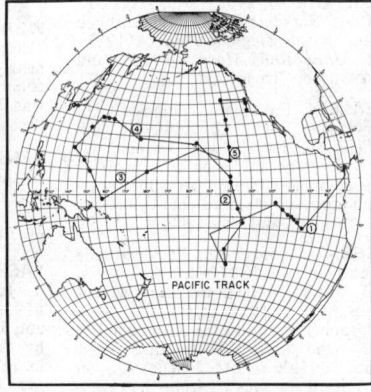

Planned route of the research ship "Glomar Challenger" while carrying out the Deep Sea Drilling Project of the National Science Foundation. The Atlantic portion of the voyage was to be completed by March 1969 and the Pacific portion by December 1969. The black dots indicate drilling sites.

disturbed record of the last 100 million years of oceanic processes.

All previous information on the basins had been based largely on indirect evidence—bathymetric, acoustic penetration, magnetic, and thermal. The only direct information was based on relatively shallow cores and dredged samples. It had long been recognized that real progress could not be made unless tangible samples were returned from all levels of the sediments and from geographically well distributed areas in the Atlantic and Pacific oceans. Scientific interest in the project was heightened by the sea-floor spreading hypothesis introduced by H. H. Hess and F. J. Vine of Princeton University, which assumes a continuous lateral spreading of the sea floor away from the mid-oceanic ridges. The possibilities of mineral wealth in the ocean floor were not ignored, of course; at one of the first holes drilled (at the Sigsbee Knolls in the Gulf of Mexico) traces of oil were found at a depth greater than 11,000 ft.

The 400-ft.-long "Glomar Challenger," built by the Levingston Shipbuilding Co. in Orange, Tex., was a fully equipped drilling vessel with a 142-ft. derrick and conventional offshore drilling gear. It had drilled and cored in depths as great as 18,000 ft. and into almost 2,800 ft. of sediment to the basement. The first leg of its expedition started in the Gulf of Mexico and ended at New York; the chief scientists were Maurice Ewing and J. Lamar Worzel. The second leg was to go from New York to Dakar, Senegal, and the chief scientists were Melvin Peterson and Terence Edgar.

The Global Marine Corp. was the owner and operator of the vessel, under subcontract to the Scripps Institution of Oceanography.

A series of major efforts to study the important mechanism of the air-sea interaction was under way. These fundamental studies were related to such phenomena as long-range climatic variations in time and space, the physical and chemical state of the upper ocean layers (the thermocline), oceanic productivity, and military problems such as antisubmarine warfare. The Office of Naval Research, the U.S. Coast Guard, the Scripps Institution of Oceanography, and the Convair Corp. joined in a massive effort of buoy implantation 1,000 mi. N of Hawaii. The field consisted of a large number of relatively small buoys anchored in the deep ocean, with a so-called monster buoy in the centre of the field. The smaller buoys recorded the physical parameters of the upper oceanic layers and the properties of the atmosphere close to the sea surface. These records were read out periodically by a visiting ship. The monster buoy made the same measurements but it transmitted the record by radio to California on command.

A similar and very important operation called BOMEX (Barbados Oceanographic and Meteorological Experiment) was being planned to study the waters off Barbados, with the object of gaining a better understanding of the mechanics of hurricane formation. Ships from almost every major U.S. laboratory would be involved in taking the measurements.

The Eastropac expedition concluded with an extended series of operations on both sides of the Equator in the eastern Pacific. The expedition, sponsored by the U.S. Bureau of Commercial Fisheries with the cooperation of a number of oceanographic institutions and the Office of Naval Research, had as its primary purpose a thorough exploration of the fisheries possibilities of this part of the ocean, along with the related oceanographic and atmospheric variables. It would be several years before the vast amount of data could be assimilated, reduced, and published.

Scientists on board the "Eltanin" demonstrated the existence of a western boundary current in the South Pacific. This is a major current system of great importance to the climate of Australia. Studies of another western boundary current in the South Pacific produced a startling find: the northward current of the deeper waters in the South Pacific is concentrated into a relatively narrow region east of the oceanic ridge extending northward to the Tonga Islands. To the north there is an east-west oceanic ridge with a gap near Samoa, and the flow is further constricted, yielding the anomalously high velocity of about one-third of a knot. Further investigation of this phenomenon was called for.

A different kind of current study was being made of the Gulf Stream. A neutrally buoyant, manned research submarine would spend several weeks drifting with the stream to study its properties in situ and in depth. Unrelated but equally important was a series of buoy experiments designed to study the properties of the stream. The year 1968 marked the end of the eight-nation study of the Kuroshio Current off Japan.

The U.S. Navy continued its study of the problems of man in the sea with the installation of Sealab III near San Clemente Island, off the coast of southern California. The project would last two months and would involve approximately 50 aquanauts, working in teams at a depth of 600 ft., or approximately three times the depth of Sealab II. The program would con-

sist of a variety of exercises on the part of the divers, who would periodically emerge from the Sealab habitat to go to greater depths. These exercises would involve a variety of biological, engineering, and physiological experiments to test and develop man's ability to operate at ever increasing depths.

Offshore engineering was developing at a very rapid rate, chiefly because of the stimulation provided by the offshore petroleum industry. As an indication of that industry's importance, 15% of the gasoline used in California automobiles in 1968 came from offshore wells, and at least one successful well had come in at a depth of more than 600 ft. A significant accomplishment demonstrating the state of the art in ocean engineering was the location of the sunken nuclear submarine USS "Scorpion" by the oceanographic research vessel USS "Mizar." This vessel, equipped with the best automated survey equipment, obtained photographs of the submarine in deep waters 400 mi. SW of the Azores. Such an operation would have been impossible only a few years earlier.

In October the experimental miniature submarine "Alvin" became detached from its mother ship during a launch operation off Cape Cod, Massachusetts, and sank in 4,500 ft. of water. No one was aboard at the time. Since the submarine had been built to withstand depths greater than 4,500 ft., there was some hope that it might be salvaged. The "Alvin," which was operated by the Woods Hole Oceanographic Institution, had been used to retrieve an atom bomb

WIDE WORLD

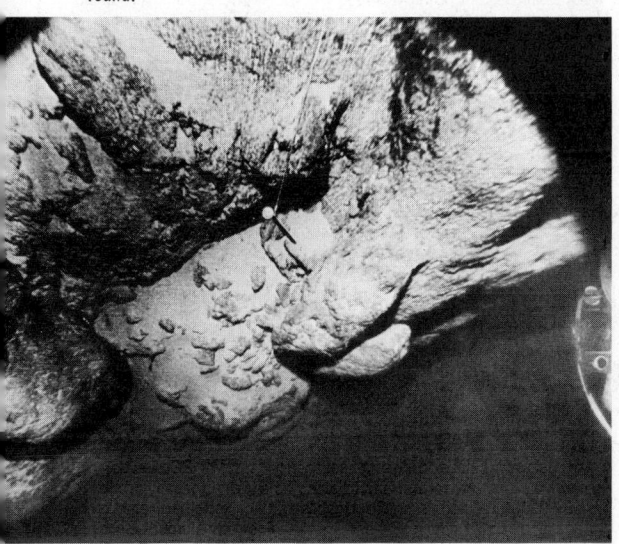

Above, USS "Mizar," the oceanographic research vessel that obtained photographs of parts of the hull of the sunken nuclear submarine "Scorpion" at a depth of more than 10,000 ft. Below, ocean floor in the region where the "Scorpion" wreckage was found.

COURTESY, U.S. NAVY

that fell into deep water off the coast of Spain when a U.S. Air Force bomber and a tanker plane collided in 1966.

The year 1968 saw an acceleration of interest in the political and diplomatic aspects of oceanography and activities in the field were carried on at all levels of government. Marine science councils had been formed in many of the major countries. In the U.S. both the Commission on Marine Sciences and Technology and the Marine Sciences Council had been in operation for a year, and would shortly issue a report on a national program for developing the ocean potential. On the international scene, official conferences were being held under the sponsorship of the UN and its specialized agencies.

The most intense debate seemed to be focused on the future status of the sea bed. The international convention governing the continental shelves and operations on these shelves had been in operation for about ten years, and questions had arisen with regard to both changes in definition of the shelf and the freedoms that are to be accorded to research vessels operating there. More difficult was the resolution of proposals to internationalize and/or demilitarize the ocean beds. These were important questions for the future involving both the military and the economic security of the world. The success of the "Glomar Challenger" and the "Mizar" only intensified these concerns. (W. A. Ni.)

See also Antarctica; Biological Sciences; Geography; Geology; Law; Seismology.

Encyclopædia Britannica Films. *Ocean Tides (The Bay of Fundy)* (1956); *The Marine Biologist* (1963); *Plankton —Pastures of the Ocean* (1965); *Waves on Water* (1965).

Pakistan

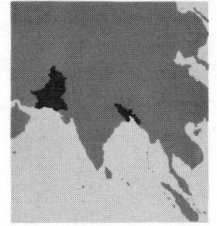

A federal republic and member of the Commonwealth of Nations, Pakistan is divided into two parts, separated by India. West Pakistan, the main part of the country, is bordered on the south by the Arabian Sea and on the west by Afghanistan and Iran; East Pakistan lies on the Bay of Bengal. Total area: 365,529 sq.mi. (946,721 sq.km.), excluding the Pakistani-controlled section of Kashmir. Pop. (1968 est.): 109,-519,831. Cap.: Islamabad (pop., 1967 est., 226,000); legislative cap.: Ayubnagar (pop., 1968 est., 459,861). Largest city: Karachi (pop., 1968 est., 2,186,236). Language: officially Urdu, Bengali, English. Religion (1961): Muslim 88.1%; Hindu 10.7%; Christian and Buddhist minorities. President in 1968, Field Marshal Muhammad Ayub Khan.

The severe illness of President Ayub Khan, who contracted virus pneumonia in January and was ill until April, caused widespread concern. When the president recovered, Sharifuddin Pirzada, the foreign minister, reverted at his own request to his former post of attorney general; he was replaced by Arshad Husain, a career diplomat. The tenth anniversary of the coup that had brought President Ayub Khan to power was celebrated in October. Shortly afterward, however, student disorders erupted, necessitating the calling out of the Army, and an attempt was made on the life of the president. Former Foreign Minister Zulfikar Ali Bhutto and several other opposition leaders were arrested.

A new opposition leader emerged, however, in the person of the chief of the Air Force, Air Marshal Muhammad Asghar Khan, who in a series of speeches called for an end to graft and privilege. On December

22 Marshal Asghar Khan was ordered to appear in court in January 1969 on charges of having violated the government prohibition against the assembly of more than five persons in a public place. On December 28, Bhutto, who was challenging his arrest in the courts, declared that he would be a candidate in the presidential elections of January 1970.

Throughout the year, the country continued to make encouragingly rapid economic progress. There was a real breakthrough in agriculture; wheat production increased by more than 40% to a record 6 million tons; rice, with a 15% rise, attained more than 12 million tons. It was confidently hoped that the country would be self-sufficient in food by 1970. These advances were not wholly attributable to a fairly favourable season or to improved strains of seed. U.S. observers noted that among the consequences of land reform and the achievement of greater political power by the masses had been a steady and continuous pressure from below upon the planning authorities for even more rapid improvements in agricultural techniques, extensions of irrigation, development of communications, and improved marketing facilities.

During the first three years of the third five-year plan, the average annual growth in crop output exceeded 4%. In industrial growth the record was equally striking. Taking production in 1959–60 as 100, the figure rose to 201 in 1964–65 and to 213 in 1966–67, while all the indications were that the index for 1968, as the World Bank mission that visited Pakistan early in 1968 foresaw, would show a rise of 7% over 1967 in the gross national product. This, indeed, might be an underestimate, for figures published after the mission's visit appeared to confirm a rise of 8.3%.

The strength of Pakistan's financial position was shown when the budget for 1968–69 was introduced into the National Assembly in June. Capital receipts were estimated at PakRs. 5,396,000,000 and disbursements at PakRs. 5,456,000,000. Taxation adjustments without new imposts were estimated to yield a small surplus of PakRs. 3 million. Deficit financing was again eliminated. This prudent financial management, along with the exceptional growth rate in the economy, was of great service to Pakistan's quest for foreign aid. The World Bank, along with the consortium of countries pledged to aid the development program, expressed satisfaction at the progress achieved in 1967–68, and agreed to provide external finance to the amount of $498 million toward the estimated cost—$827 million—of the immense new Tarbela Dam to be built on the Indus River 40 mi. NW of Rawalpindi.

President Ayub Khan's policy of shaping Pakistan's foreign relations to secure friendship with all well-disposed nations without damage either to its own interests or to the interests of others again gained substantial help from countries belonging to the Communist bloc as well as from the West. In April Soviet Premier Aleksei N. Kosygin visited Pakistan, and a fresh agreement for financial and technical aid was concluded. Soviet assistance was promised for a metallurgical plant at Kalabagh, for an electrical complex near Chittagong, for oil exploration, for the provision of high-power medium- and short-wave transmitters, and for an inquiry into the feasibility of setting up a nuclear plant in East Pakistan. A five-year trade agreement, to be operative from 1971, was to provide machinery and equipment valued at 60 million rubles. As a token of its determination to "play fair with everyone," Pakistan gave notice to the U.S. that after 1969 it would not renew the lease of the U.S. communications base near Peshawar (from which the U-2 surveillance plane that was downed in the U.S.S.R. in 1960 had taken off).

Pakistan's closest international connections were still those with its partners, Iran and Turkey, in the Regional Cooperation for Development (RCD) organization, which celebrated its fourth anniversary during the year. The evaluation of the organization that took place at that time showed that out of 33 projects approved for joint activities by the three countries, 17 were on the point of completion and several others were already operating. Tourism and communications were stepped up, and it was expected that the new RCD highway would be opened at the end of the year.

It was only with India that Pakistan's relations remained bad. The release by the Indian authorities of Sheikh Abdullah, former prime minister of Kashmir, in January was followed by renewed agitation in Indian-held Kashmir for a plebiscite and by anti-Muslim disturbances in India. Feeling in Pakistan was bitter. On the Indian side there was violent resentment at the finding of the international tribunal constituted to settle the dispute (1965) over the Rann of Cutch. The verdict, given in February, allocated to Pakistan about 300 sq.mi. of territory on the border of Sind. The remaining 3,200 sq.mi. were allocated to India. Pakistan accepted the finding without protest, but there were angry protests in India.

(L. F. R. W.)

ENCYCLOPÆDIA BRITANNICA FILMS. *India (Pakistan and the Union of India)* (1952); *Pakistan* (1955).

PAKISTAN

Education. (1965–66) Primary, pupils 6,920,-632, teachers 181,625; secondary, pupils 2,585,-258, teachers 90,607; vocational, pupils 22,196; teacher training, students 15,488, teachers (1964–65) 1,119; higher, students 274,857, teaching staff 11,062.

Finance. Monetary unit: Pakistan rupee, with a par value of PakRs. 4.76 to U.S. $1 (PakRs. 11.43 = £1 sterling). Gold and foreign exchange, official: (June 1968) U.S. $183 million; (June 1967) U.S. $176 million. Budget (1967–68 est.): revenue PakRs. 6,383,800,000; expenditure PakRs. 5,159,300,000. Gross national product: (1965–66) PakRs. 52,630,000,000; (1964–65) PakRs. 48,260,000,000. Money supply: (June 1968) PakRs. 10,119,000,000; (June 1967) PakRs. 9,952,000,000. Cost of living: (Karachi; 1963 = 100): (June 1968) 128; (June 1967) 127.

Foreign Trade. (1967) Imports PakRs. 5,243,-000,000; exports PakRs. 3,164,000,000. Import sources: U.S. 33%; U.K. 13%; Japan 9%; West Germany 9%; Australia 5%. Export destinations: U.S. 13%; U.K. 13%; China 6%; Japan 6%; Hong Kong 5%. Main exports: textiles 30%; jute 22%; cotton 11%.

Transport and Communications. Roads (1967) c. 110,000 km. (including 41,505 main roads). Motor vehicles in use (1967): passenger 125,221; commercial 41,047. Railways: (1963–64) 11,328 km.; traffic (1965–66) 12,540,000,-000 passenger-km., freight 9,155,000,000 net ton-km. Shipping (1967): merchant vessels 100 gross tons and over 155; gross tonnage 473,363. Air traffic (1967): 1,350,356,000 passenger-km.; freight 56,956,000 net ton-km. Telephones (Dec. 1966) 145,680. Radio receivers (Dec. 1964) 549,-000. Television receivers (Dec. 1966) c. 16,000.

Agriculture. Production (in 000; metric tons; 1967; 1966 in parentheses): rice c. 18,000 (16,-410); wheat 4,393 (3,933); barley 104 (96); corn 795 (590); millet (1966) 371, (1965) 370; sorghum (1966) 277, (1965) 274; dry beans (1966) 107, (1965) 94; chick-peas 578 (583); sugar, raw value (1967–68) c. 460, (1966–67) 461; gur (indigenous raw sugar; 1967–68) 1,881, (1966–67) 1,911; tobacco (1966) 137, (1965) 110; tea (1966) 29, (1965) 27; lentils 81 (67); rapeseed and mustard seed 307 (278); sesame (1966) 34, (1965) 31; jute (1966) 1,161, (1965) 1,154; cotton, lint 510 (457). Livestock (in 000; 1965–66): cattle c. 35,550; sheep c. 10,950; goats c. 11,380; buffaloes c. 8,690; horses 497; asses 925; camels 601; chickens (1962–63) 11,345. Fish catch (in 000; metric tons) (1966) 412, (1965) 379.

Industry. Production (in 000; metric tons; 1967): cement 2,038; crude oil (1966) 508; coal and lignite (1966) c. 1,200; electricity (1966) 3,903,000 kw-hr.; natural gas (1965) c. 1,620,-000 cu.m.; chrome ore (oxide content; 1966) 13; jute manufactures (1966) 415; cotton yarn 247; woven cotton fabrics 708,000 m.

Panama

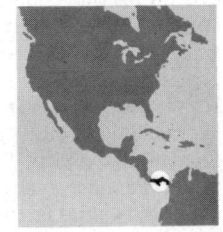

A republic of Central America, bisected by the Panama Canal Zone, Panama is bounded by the Caribbean Sea, Colombia, the Pacific Ocean, and Costa Rica. Area: 29,783 sq.mi. (77,138 sq.km.). Pop. (1968 est.): 1,-372,200. Cap. and largest city: Panama (pop., 1968 est., 373,200). Language: Spanish. Religion: Roman Catholic 93%. Presidents in 1968, Marco Aurelio Robles to October 1, Arnulfo Arias to October 12, and, from October 12, provisional president of civilian-military government, Col. José M. Pinilla.

For many months prior to the presidential elections on May 12, 1968, Panamanians engaged in a spirited political contest. It centred on a split in the usually united wealthy oligarchy controlling governmental power, for the two principal antagonists were Arnulfo Arias and Marco A. Robles, both members of the ruling families. The latter was the incumbent president, chosen and maintained in office until November 1967 by virtue of the support of a coalition of the ten political parties. The former, twice elected president and twice deposed during 1940–51 and an unsuccessful candidate in 1964, had the fervid backing of the poor and the strong support of a six-party coalition.

Basic differences on issues between the two political camps were lacking. Instead, Arias and his followers burned with resentment over his defeat in 1964 by allegedly fraudulent means and over the suspicion that his opposition would again resort to fraud in 1968. Robles, by constitutional prohibition unable to suc-

Below, troops supporting impeached Pres. Marco Robles barring Max Delvalle from the National Assembly Building on March 26, 1968. Above, rioting in Panama following the presidential election in May 1968.

WIDE WORLD

PANAMA
Education. (1964–65) Primary, pupils 196,412, teachers 6,480; secondary, pupils 32,786, teachers 1,733; vocational, pupils 16,887, teachers 735; teacher training, students 1,351; teachers 56; higher (including 2 universities; 1966), students 7,964, teaching staff 343.
Finance. Monetary unit: balboa, at par with the U.S. dollar (2.40 balboas = £1 sterling). Total reported dollar assets: (June 1968) U.S. $150.1 million; (June 1967) U.S. $144.6 million. Budget (1968 est.) balanced at 129.9 million balboas. Gross national product: (1966) 697.8 million balboas; (1965) 630.4 million balboas. Money supply (deposits only): (March 1968) 69.8 million balboas; (March 1967) 66.8 million balboas. Cost of living (Panama City; 1963 = 100): (2nd quarter 1968) 106; (2nd quarter 1967) 104.
Foreign Trade. (1967) Imports 229,370,000 balboas; exports 91,340,000 balboas. Net service receipts from Canal Zone (1966) 84.9 million balboas. Main import sources: U.S. 40%; Venezuela 20%. Main export destinations: U.S. 78%; Panama Canal Zone 8%; Canada 5%. Main exports: bananas 53%; refined petroleum 25%; shrimps 10%.
Transport and Communications. Roads (1966) 6,633 km. Motor vehicles in use (1966): passenger 32,500; commercial (including buses) 10,700. Railways (1966) 684 km. (including 169 km. state controlled). Shipping (1967): merchant vessels 100 gross tons and over 757 (mostly owned by U.S. and other foreign interests); gross tonnage 4,756,154. Telephones (Dec. 1966) 47,967. Radio receivers (Dec. 1965) c. 500,000. Television receivers (Dec. 1966) c. 77,000.
Agriculture. Production (in 000; metric tons; 1966; 1965 in parentheses): rice 140 (151); sugar, raw value (1967–68) c. 65, (1966–67) c. 64; bananas c. 600 (c. 583); oranges c. 35 (41); coffee 5.1 (4.4); cocoa 0.7 (1). Livestock (in 000; 1965–66): cattle 1,011; pigs 167; horses c. 160.
Industry. Production (in 000; 1967): electricity (Panama and Colón) 422,000 kw-hr.; manufactured gas 20,400 cu.m.; cement (1966) 149 metric tons.

ceed himself, backed his former finance minister and candidate of the National Liberal Party, David Samudio. This support gave the opposition forces a rallying cry, for the Panamanian constitution prohibited the authority in power from giving aid to a candidate and provided for removal from office for such an offense. Robles was charged with violating this prohibition, and the National Assembly named an investigating committee, which recommended impeachment. On March 14 the National Assembly accepted the recommendation and ordered Robles to stand trial on March 24. The Assembly deputies, meeting as a court of justice but with the pro-Robles members absenting themselves, convicted the president. Robles denied that he had violated the constitution and was supported by a restraining order from a magistrate's court.

The Arias forces, in control of the National Assembly, rejected the validity of the court injunction and proceeded to support a new executive. The first vice-president, Max Delvalle, was sworn in as president. In ruling on the restraining order of the lower court, the Supreme Court, in effect, was to decide whether the Robles administration or this newly constituted authority held the legal power of government. Its decision (April 5) favoured Robles by 8–1.

From the time the impeachment of Robles was submitted to the decision of the Supreme Court, Panama experienced a tumultuous period, marked by demonstrations and riots in which several people were killed and much property was damaged. In these circumstances of disorder, Brig. Gen. Bolívar Vallarino and the National Guard attempted to keep peace with tear gas and rubber hoses. Vallarino announced that the Guard would uphold the existing regime pending the decision of the Supreme Court on the validity of the actions of the National Assembly. When the court favoured the Robles government, the Guard gave its support, and Arias had no means to counteract it. He could only await the election on May 12.

On that day approximately 320,000 Panamanians voted in an atmosphere of violence. Amid charges of fraud and intimidation, Arias was declared the victor and was supported by the National Guard. However, 11 days after his inauguration on October 1,

Palestine: see Israel; Jordan

Arias was overthrown by a military coup of the Guard. Most constitutional guarantees were suspended, and the National Assembly was dissolved. After a two-day interval in which a two-man junta ruled, Col. José M. Pinilla was sworn in as provisional president and a new Cabinet was appointed. Arias took sanctuary in the Canal Zone and called for a general strike and forceful resistance, but the Panamanian people did not respond.

The political agitation throughout the year did not help Panama's lethargic economy—although shipping through the Panama Canal reached new heights of volume. The three proposed treaties between the U.S. and Panama concerning the sovereignty and operation of the canal, its defense, and the construction of a new canal were victims of the political turmoil.

(A. R. W.)

ENCYCLOPÆDIA BRITANNICA FILMS. *The Panama Canal* (1961).

Paraguay

A landlocked republic of South America, Paraguay is bounded by Brazil, Argentina, and Bolivia. Area: 157,047 sq.mi. (406,752 sq.km.). Pop. (1967 est.): 2,161,000. Cap. and largest city: Asunción (pop., 1964 est., 321,187). Language: Spanish (official), though Guaraní is the language of the majority of the people. Religion: Roman Catholic. President in 1968, Gen. Alfredo Stroessner.

Presidential and congressional elections were held on Feb. 11, 1968. In the presidential election Gen. Alfredo Stroessner was reelected by more than a two-thirds majority over the combined number of votes cast for his three opponents. The Colorado Party won 40 out of the 60 seats in the Chamber of Deputies and 20 of the 30 seats in the Senate. President Stroessner began his new term of office on August 15. It was expected that in his forthcoming five years he would vigorously attack the problems hindering economic growth in Paraguay.

The Paraguayan economy was faced with considerable difficulties in 1968. At the end of July there was a trade deficit of $9.9 million; exports were adversely affected by a considerable decline in the production of livestock and agricultural goods. It was hoped that the abundant natural resources of the country would eventually make up for this deficiency once efficient export industries were established and the effects of the significant influx of foreign capital into Paraguay began to be felt.

A group from the Inter-American Committee for the Alliance for Progress visiting Asunción in September made recommendations for a reform of the tax system and export sector. It was stressed that unless these reforms were carried out, Paraguay would suffer critical balance of payments difficulties for the next three years. Greater participation was expected from Paraguay in the integration of the countries of the Río de la Plata Basin, an area of 1.6 million sq.mi. comprising all or part of Argentina, Bolivia, Brazil, Paraguay, and Uruguay.

A favourable development during the year was the expanding tourist market. In 1967 about 43,000 tourists visited Paraguay, bringing about $5 million into the country. Flights to Asunción increased, in part because there was more passenger service on the Paraná and Paraguay rivers and because the development of the area around the magnificent Brazilian Iguaçu Falls had caused an extension of roads from Asunción to the Brazilian border.

In August the government forced the closing of the Roman Catholic newspaper *Comunidad*. The only privately owned paper in the country, it had been hostile to President Stroessner.

(D. J. Ro.)

PARAGUAY
Education. (1965) Primary, pupils 356,728, teachers 11,796; secondary, pupils 30,404, teachers (1964) 2,674; vocational (1964), pupils 3,054, teachers 529; teacher training, students 3,285; higher (at National University and Catholic University), students 6,030, teaching staff 960.
Finance. Monetary unit: guaraní, with free rates (October 1968) of 126 guaranies to U.S. $1 and 302 guaranies to £1 sterling. Gold and foreign exchange, central bank: (June 1968) U.S. $8,530,000; (June 1967) U.S. $10,910,000. Budget (1968 est.): revenue 8,973,000,000 guaranies; expenditure 9,889,000,000 guaranies. Gross national product: (1966) 58,120,000,000 guaranies; (1965) 55,120,000,000 guaranies. Money supply: (June 1968) 5,301,000,000 guaranies; (June 1967) 4,890,000,000 guaranies. Cost of living (Asunción; 1963 = 100): (June 1968) 111; (June 1967) 111.
Foreign Trade. (1967) Imports 7,603,800,000 guaranies; exports 5,964,700,000 guaranies. Import sources: Argentina 21%; U.S. 19%; West Germany 16%; Italy 9%; U.K. 5%. Export destinations: U.S. 25%; Argentina 24%; U.K. 16%; Netherlands 6%; Uruguay 6%. Main exports: meat 36%; timber 16%; oilseeds 9%; tobacco 7%; cotton 5%.
Transport and Communications. Roads (1965) c. 12,500 km. (including 4,370 km. highways). Motor vehicles in use (1965): passenger 5,442; commercial (including buses) c. 5,900. Railways (1964): 1,147 km.; traffic 39 million passenger-km., freight 20 million net ton-km. Navigable inland waterways (including Paraguay-Paraná River system; 1965) c. 3,000 km. Telephones (Dec. 1966) 14,033. Radio receivers (Dec. 1962) c. 160,000.
Agriculture. Production (in 000; metric tons; 1967; 1966 in parentheses): corn 225 (166); peanuts 21 (20); cassava (1966) 1,437, (1965) 1,512; sweet potatoes (1966) 90, (1965) 100; sugar, raw value (1967–68) c. 39, (1966–67) 36; tobacco (1966) 8.8, (1965) 17; oranges 204 (198); tannin (1962) **37**, (1961) 37; cotton, lint 9 (9). Livestock (in 000; 1965–66): cattle 5,461; sheep 442; horses 624; pigs 861; chickens 6,610.
Industry. Production (1966): cement 26,000 metric tons; electricity 205 million kw-hr.

Parks

Europe. In the United Kingdom, the Countryside Act of 1968, which went into force on August 3, renamed the National Parks Commission as the Countryside Commission and gave it new functions and responsibilities. Where previously financial aid from the central government had been confined mainly to activities in national parks and "areas of outstanding natural beauty," it was now extended to allow provision for outdoor recreation as well as conservation on a countrywide scale. The commission was charged with reviewing all matters relating to the conservation and enhancement of the natural beauty of the countryside, the provision and improvement of such facilities as country parks and picnic and camping sites, and the provision of public access to the countryside. The commission would make recommendations regarding the allocation of central government grants to local authorities, and could make grants or loans to non-public bodies furthering the purposes of the act.

The designation of four "areas of outstanding natural beauty"—South Hampshire (30 sq.mi.), Anglesey (83 sq.mi.), Norfolk Coast (194 sq.mi.), and Kent Downs (326 sq.mi.)—was confirmed in 1968. In April the Welsh government purchased some 13,000 ac. in

Panama Canal Zone:
see Dependent States; Panama

Paper Industry:
see Industrial Review; Timber

Papua-New Guinea:
see Dependent States

Parachuting:
see Sporting Record

the Caernarvonshire section of Snowdonia National Park, including the summit and northern slopes of Mt. Snowdon, the southwestern slopes of the Glyder range, the greater part of the Llanberis Pass, and part of the Nantlle Ridge west of Rhyd-ddu. A detailed study was being made, covering particularly the ecological and conservation aspects of the area, attitudes of residents and visitors, the incidence of visitor use, and an economic analysis of agricultural and recreational development in the area.

In Brecon Beacons National Park, the British Waterways Board and the Breconshire and Monmouthshire county councils reached agreement on the restoration of 32 mi. of the Monmouthshire and Brecon Canal as a recreational and scenic attraction. The Youth Hostel and National Park Information Centre was completed at Once Brewed in the Northumberland National Park, close to the point where the Pennine Way and Roman Wall cross. In the Yorkshire Dales National Park, agreement was reached with respect to public access to 13,821 ac. of Barden Moor and Barden Fell. Warden service in the parks increased and the new post of youth liaison warden was introduced in the Peak District National Park. In Northern Ireland, negotiations for the designation of part of County Fermanagh as a national park reached an advanced stage, and the Ulster Countryside Committee recommended to the Ministry of Development that an area in County Armagh be designated a national park. Consultations with supporting local authorities and other interested bodies were beginning.

In France development work was carried out in the Parc National de Port-Cros to facilitate connections with the continent at Port-Cros Bay and for scientific research at Fort du Moulin. Other developments included water points and restoration of the network of roads and pathways. Visitors to the park had numbered approximately 40,000. Adjoining the Parc National des Pyrénées-Occidentales, the nature reserve of Néouvielle (9 sq.mi.) was created. In Italy, on May 4, 1968, Calabria Park (58 sq.mi.) in the provinces of Reggio di Calabria, Catanzaro, and Cosenza was officially proclaimed. It consisted of three distinct zones: integral natural reserve, bush and pasture land for educational and recreational purposes, and a tourist area. Forests of larch pines in Calabria formed part of the wide variety of woodlands of the region, and its fauna included wild pig, marten, badger, and wild boar. Part of Stelvio National Park was being reserved specifically for nature protection. In Gran Paradiso National Park the problem of compensation to owners of pasture land on the mountains was being studied. Following intensified study of natural environment conducted in collaboration with Italian universities, the capture of game by narcotic guns was permitted.

Two new parks were created in West Germany: Rheingau-Untertaunus (about 232 sq.mi.) and Cham-Waldmünchen (251 sq.mi.), both with predominantly mountainous landscape. In all of the West German parks progress was made in improving pathway networks and in providing parking places and protective huts. The Ormtjernkampen Park (under $\frac{1}{2}$ sq.mi.) was established in the southeast highlands of Norway. It consisted of virgin mountain forest, mainly spruce. In Sweden, the recorded number of park visitors was approximately 80,000. A new national park centre was established at Zernez, Switz., to provide space for information and exhibits. The centre, which included a conference room, was open during the summer, when visitors to the park averaged 160,000.

Hikers looking toward Challenger Glacier in the newly established 1.2 million-ac. North Cascades National Park in Washington State.

North America. On Oct. 2, 1968, U.S. Pres. Lyndon B. Johnson signed bills establishing the 34th and 35th national parks. Redwood National Park (58,000 ac.), in northern California, was the outgrowth of a long, bitter fight between lumber and conservation interests. The park would cost $92 million, more than all other U.S. national parks combined, and would necessitate the purchase of 10,000 ac. of privately owned stands of old growth virgin redwoods towering as high as 367 ft. North Cascades National Park was established on 1.2 million ac. in the part of the Pacific Northwest often called the "American Alps."

Other federal legislation provided for a national system of urban and rural trails to start with the Appalachian Trail, extending 2,000 mi. from Maine to Georgia, and the Pacific Coast National Scenic Trail, running from Mexico to British Columbia. Studies were to be made of 14 other trails that might be included in the system. The National Wild and Scenic Rivers System was established to preserve the unspoiled sections of 8 rivers and to study 27 other rivers that might be added. Federal areas established in 1968 were the San Rafael Wilderness Area (143,000 ac.) in Los Padres National Forest in southern California and Flaming Gorge National Recreation Area on the Utah-Wyoming border. Visitors to areas under the administration of the National Park Service numbered 139,675,600 in 1967; a record 150 million visitors was estimated for 1968.

A seven-man team was preparing a new master plan for Yosemite National Park and meetings were being held to obtain public comments. Suggestions covered new and different means of transportation and routes within the park, the removal or relocation of facilities intruding upon park resources, air pollution abatement, future use of the park for winter sports, and long-range plans for the management of wildlife.

The National Park Service launched a new interpretative program to increase the usefulness of national park areas to schools. Work was under way on a model plan of environmental instruction, the National Environmental Educational Development Program, that would provide schoolchildren with a series of environmental experiences to heighten their enjoyment of future national park visits and to create in them an understanding of the importance of careful usage and protection of the parks. Dovetailed with the pro-

gram was the establishment of 27 environmental study areas on National Park Service properties along the populous East Coast and in Tennessee, West Virginia, the District of Columbia, and Puerto Rico.

In Canada in April, a 7,000-sq.mi. area in Ontario, fronting on James Bay and Hudson Bay, was declared Polar Bear Provincial Park. The nation's second largest provincial park, it had the most southerly population of polar bears, as well as bearded seals, walrus, Arctic fox, and a seasonal herd of woodland caribou. The area was also the breeding ground for snow and blue geese.

Africa. In March 1968 the Kenya government announced the establishment of two marine national parks, Malindi (about $2\frac{1}{4}$ sq.mi.) and Watamu (about $4\frac{1}{2}$ sq.mi.). Both parks also had natural reserves adjacent to them. The areas were designed to protect spectacular specimens of fish, aquatic plants, and animals visible at close range. The Kenyan side of Mt. Elgon constituted the first national park (about 65 sq.mi.) in western Kenya in which the forest stand of podo was accorded complete protection. Mt. Elgon includes a substantial part of the main watershed of Lake Victoria. The highest peak of the mountain is recorded as approximately 14,000 ft. Special attention was given to the construction and maintenance of roads in all Kenyan parks. Lodges of high international standards were erected at Tsavo West and Tsavo East. The standard of existing game blinds was raised.

Two new parks were established in Tanzania. Gombe (60 sq.mi.), on the shores of Lake Tanganyika and north of Kigoma, was designed mainly to ensure the protection of the 200 wild chimpanzees inhabiting the hilly and wooded area. Tarangire (1,000 sq.mi.) is an area of savannah country 90 mi. S of Arusha that is provided with water year round from the Tarangire River. It is the dry-season retreat of much of the wildlife from southern Masailand. Work was begun on the construction of wildlife viewing tracks.

In Serengeti National Park in Tanzania an all-season north-south road was completed, and the area was extended 300 sq.mi. to include game migration. Hotels were being erected at Lobo, 40 mi. NE of Seronera, and in Mikumi National Park. The Ngurdoto and Meru craters were united to form the Arusha National Park, an area of only 50 sq.mi. but with a range in altitude of over 10,000 ft., from Lake Momela to the summit of Mt. Meru. The road in Arusha National Park, to provide access to the Meru crater and ash cone, was nearing completion. Visitors to all parks in Tanzania totaled 70,468.

In the Republic of South Africa, Groenkloof Park (about 17 ac.), situated on Muckleneuk Hill in the heart of Pretoria, was established on March 26, 1968. The new headquarters of the National Park Board of Trustees was to be built there shortly. Six visitor accommodation huts were built in Addo Elephant National Park; a youth hostel for groups of visiting schoolchildren was erected in Mountain Zebra National Park; and the Brandwag camp was established in Golden Gate Highlands National Park. Visitors to the nine parks numbered approximately 400,000, including some 250,000 to Kruger National Park. The total number of visitors to the Kafue National Park in Zambia exceeded 3,000. Dindir National Park in the Sudan was scheduled for development as a major tourist attraction and funds were being negotiated for this purpose. Visitors to the park numbered approximately 1,500.

Oceania. A new National Parks and Wildlife Act went into force in New South Wales, Austr., on Oct. 1, 1967. Its chief aims were to prevent alienation of lands in national and state parks and historic sites, to present an effective obstacle to mining and logging in those areas, and to provide a management plan for each area. Under the act, full management of the Royal, Kuring-gai Chase, Kosciuske, Dharug, and Kinchega parks passed to the National Parks and Wildlife Service. A new state park, Mt. Warning (about 8 sq.mi.), approximately 10 mi. from Murwillumbah, was established. Mt. Warning, a volcanic spire rising 3,800 ft. from a surrounding dense rain forest, was the central feature. Visitors to all parks in New South Wales totaled nearly 4 million.

Four new parks were established in Queensland. Timber Reserve 165 (about 5 sq.mi.) is comprised mainly of broken granite hills rising sharply from relatively flat surroundings and supporting a flora and fauna peculiar to these drier granite areas. The crown land in the Black Trevethan Range (3 sq.mi.) contains the unique geologic feature of Black Mountain, which is composed of huge granite boulders towering above the surrounding forest. Timber Reserve 1244 ($4\frac{1}{2}$ sq.mi.) is mainly a flat and gently sloping series of tablelands rising in places to rugged ranges. Its complex structure and relatively open forest floor rendered the area a valuable habitat for a diversity of arboreal and ground mammals. The valley of Barratt Creek ($5\frac{1}{2}$ sq.mi.), a tributary of the Daintree River, contains a heavily timbered area with tropical rain forest in the gullies and wet eucalyptus forest on the upper slopes. Park 133, which already embraced the greater part of the watershed of the Mossman River, was enlarged to include the Rex Creek Catchment Area (about 10 sq.mi.). Two miles of track were constructed, bringing the total length of track system to over 268 mi. The walking track system within the parks was maintained and expanded, and visitor facilities were improved in a number of parks. Visitors to Queensland parks totaled approximately one million persons; south Queensland parks received a record 870,000 visitors.

Government attention focused on acquisition in South Australia. The ten newly established parks included Yumbarra (410 sq.mi.); Simpson Desert (2,670 sq.mi.), which adjoined Simpson Desert Park, Queensland; Mount Boothby ($15\frac{1}{2}$ sq.mi.); Elliot

Citizens of Tokyo strolling through the new Imperial Palace East Garden, formerly the site of Edo Castle, which was opened as a public park in 1968.

Price Wilderness (250 sq.mi.), which included a dry salt lake (Lake Eyre); and Mambray Creek (13 sq.mi.). These areas were mostly arid or semiarid and contained several varieties of kangaroo, dingo, emu, and wallaby, various desert, mallee, and pink gum vegetation, and, in one case, aboriginal relics. New parks under 1 sq.mi. were: Buck's Lake, a swampy lakebed; Morialta, in the Adelaide Hills (Mt. Lofty Ranges) and adjoining the Morialta National Pleasure Resort; Mt. Magnificent; Jip Jip; and the coastal dunes of Guichen Bay. This brought the total area controlled by the National Parks Commission to 4,234 sq.mi.

In Tasmania, the creation of a scenic reserve of approximately $\frac{1}{2}$ sq.mi. at St. Patrick's Head on the east coast brought the total area of reserved land to 952 sq.mi., or approximately 3.6% of the state's total area. This was the highest percentage of land reserved specifically for national parks and scenic reserves in any Australian state. Two new family accommodation units were erected at Lake St. Clair and two overnight accommodation huts established in the central portion of the Cradle Mountain-Lake St. Clair National Park.

In Victoria new staff quarters and guest flats were built in the Wilson's Promontory National Park and the cafe was improved and extended. In Wyperfeld National Park an ironclad catchment was completed. New tourist facilities were constructed in Mt. Buffalo National Park, and in Fraser National Park the nature trail was extended.

Two new parks were proclaimed in Western Australia: Yalgorup (12 sq.mi.), an undulating, lightly timbered landscape that is rich in flora, with small limestone hills and outcrops, and Namburry (62 sq.mi.), which included Pinnacles Reserve. This interesting country of limestone caves and natural formations, including pinnacles 12–14 ft. high, was also noted for its attractive wildflowers found in the hinterland. A very substantial firebreak construction program was undertaken principally in Kalbarri, Stirling Range, Kalamunda, Neerabup, Walyunga, and Greenmount parks. A major access road and track construction program in the Walpole-Nornalup Park and Park Lands Reserve was a scenic asset as well as a means of dividing up this heavily timbered area into small compartments for fire control.

Hauraki Gulf in New Zealand, of prime popularity for maritime activities, was created a maritime park in November 1967 and was proving a tremendous success. The park contained $19\frac{1}{2}$ sq.mi. and embraced the islands of Motutapu, Motuora, Poor Knights, Little Barrier, and part of Kawau, and land at the north head of Whangaruru Harbour. Arrangements were made for Rangitoto and Motuihe island domains and Brown Island to be included on transfer from local authority control. Pending establishment of a park board, an interim committee carried out programs for controlling noxious animals and planting 1,430 trees on Motutapu Island. On Kawau Island a lease was negotiated to ensure the continued operation of Mansion House, former home of Sir George Grey, as a high-standard tourist centre. Arrangements were made for $12\frac{1}{2}$ sq.mi. of state forest land and almost 1 sq.mi. of scenic reserve to be added to Westland National Park. This would increase the park area to 342 sq.mi. and link it with Mount Cook National Park by bringing within its boundaries the entire length of the western portion of the Copland Track. The National Parks Authority adopted a system defining four classes of park use—scientific, wilderness, natural environment,

and development—as a basis for maintaining an orderly balance between use by the public and conservation. Poor winter conditions reduced the visits to Tongariro and Egmont national parks.

Other Countries. On March 2, 1968, the government of Peru set aside a large region (about 4,750 sq.mi.) to form Manú National Park. The area covered the entire basin of the Manú River and included a succession of tropical, subtropical, and temperate forests. It contained undistributed populations of almost all the fauna of the southwest Amazon region.

A master plan was prepared for the establishment of the Goreme Park, an area of approximately 36 sq.mi. within the Hasan Dag-Erciyas Degi volcanic region of central Anatolia, Turk. The park and its immediate environs are part of a large erosion basin of a former plateau. Rock-carved churches excavated in tuffs by early Christians added historical and archaeological value to the geologic formations and rural landscape of the park. Its main features were the great volcanic cones of Mt. Erciyas and Mt. Hasan, the Tuz Golu (Salt Lake) depression, and Ak Dag, a great erosional remnant of layered volcanic tuffs. In Uludag National Park two new hotels and two tele-ski lines were constructed, a meteorological station was established, and a nature conservancy building erected, all in accordance with the master plan. The plan was amended to provide for a new ski and lodging site for international skiing events. A main highway for Samsundag National Park was begun. During studies in the Manyas Kus Cenneti Park pelicans were seen to nest and hatch on willow trees, a very rare and interesting event. (M. F. B. B.)

See also Conservation; Tourism.

Payments and Reserves, International

Against the background of the international monetary crises of confidence discussed elsewhere in these pages, this article reviews the balance of payments trends, developments, and policies of some of the large industrial countries. The Federal Republic of Germany achieved—through restoration of monetary stability in its free-market economy and intensive export promotion—a very large merchandise trade surplus. It also experienced substantial inflows of funds, partly in anticipation of future commitments for payments in Deutsche Marks. To hold down additions of dollars to official reserves, the authorities encouraged and facilitated capital exports. Nevertheless, Germany added substantial amounts of dollars to its already large official reserves.

Following recurrent rumours that the mark might be upvalued—as it had been, in 1961, by 5%—expectations erupted in mid-November that the exchange rate for the mark was bound before long to be changed upward. Upvaluation would, among other things, raise the price of goods that Germany exported and would lower the price of the goods it imported. In the German view, however, a further upswing in the economy was sufficient—along with the elimination of excess demand in the United States, the United Kingdom, and France—to reduce the surplus on current account to amounts that could be accommodated by capital exports. As spokesmen for the Deutsche Bundesbank repeatedly noted, an upvaluation of the mark could be regarded only as a

means of last resort if other measures failed to curb inflationary trends. While declining to adjust the exchange rate, however, Germany decided to lower export rebates on manufactures and border taxes on imports from an average 11 to 7%—a move tantamount to a selective upvaluation of the mark by around 3%. It also decided to sterilize foreign funds and enact incentives to encourage German industry to make direct investments abroad.

France met the political and social unrest of extraordinary magnitude and complexity in May and June 1968 by sudden and large increases in wages, and endeavoured to find its way out of the difficulties by spurring economic expansion. It trod a delicate path. A forced economic expansion—evidenced, among other things, by a very rapid rise in domestic credit and money supplies and by a sharp increase in prices—inevitably encountered many pitfalls, including anticipatory buying of foreign exchange to finance imports, delayed selling of export proceeds for francs, and plain capital flight. The rise in the Bank of France discount rate from 5 to 6% on November 12 and emergency measures to curb domestic credit expansion, together with the prospects of a large increase in income and inheritance taxation, were yet other

contributory factors in the crisis of confidence. The upsetting factor in the flight of capital was the expectation that the German mark might, before long, be upvalued.

Contrary to widespread expectations that the franc would be devalued, the French government decided to "complete our recovery from the aftermath of the disturbances of last May and June without having recourse to devaluation." To win "the war of the franc," the budget deficit for 1969 would be reduced from the equivalent of $2.3 billion to $1.3 billion; prices and wages would be maintained at current levels; and exports would be stimulated by tax relief. France also reestablished exchange controls. It accepted an offer of a $2 billion credit package from other governments.

In the United Kingdom, the switch of resources from domestic consumption to production for export and to import saving was slower than had been hoped to take advantage of sterling devaluation. During the first nine months of 1968, exports expanded by 16% in sterling value over a year earlier; in foreign currency terms—and this is what really mattered—British exports rose but moderately above the predevaluation level in line with the growth of world trade. The booming domestic demand sucked in disappointingly large imports. The attainment of the government's target of a balance of payments surplus was repeatedly postponed, and was finally put off until 1969. Some relief for sterling came from a new international credit facility to reduce the switches by overseas sterling countries of their reserves from sterling into gold and dollars. Confidence remained fragile.

To make devaluation work, fiscal and monetary restraints were successively strengthened; but a ceiling on wages, regarded as essential by the government, was strongly resisted. When in November poor foreign trade figures were reported once again and further pressures on sterling developed in the wake of expectations that the German mark might be upvalued, Britain imposed additional taxes on consumer goods and further restraints on bank lending. To curb imports of manufactured products, importers were required to deposit 50% of the value of such goods with British customs for six months.

By and large, therefore, the three governments sought a way out not through open adjustments in exchange rates but through back-door changes in export and import taxation, and, in the case of Britain, through a device that, while absorbing domestic liquidity, also made imports more expensive. Furthermore, France and Germany had recourse to direct controls over the movements of capital.

The U.S. balance of payments was marked by a substantial deterioration on trade account and a substantial improvement on capital account. After allowing for exports financed by U.S. government aid, there was a sizable trade deficit—a deficit attributable primarily to a large increase in imports, the obvious accompaniment of booming domestic demand.

In contrast, the United States imported more private capital from abroad than it exported, for the first time since World War II. Some of the factors behind this dramatic shift were undoubtedly transitory, but others appeared more solid. In particular, purchases by foreigners of U.S. stocks reached record levels—reflecting a recognition abroad of the prospects for capital growth in the dynamic U.S. economy, the breadth of U.S. markets, and the belief that, in

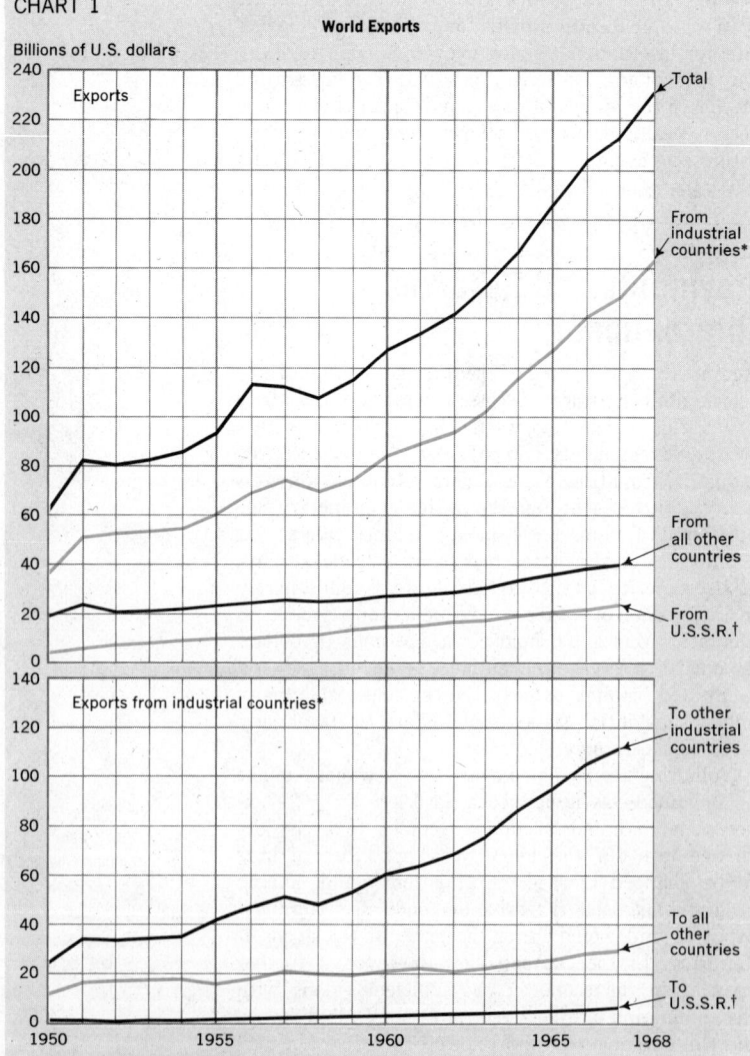

CHART 1

World Exports

Billions of U.S. dollars

Exports

Total

From industrial countries*

From all other countries

From U.S.S.R.†

Exports from industrial countries*

To other industrial countries

To all other countries

To U.S.S.R.†

1950 1955 1960 1965 1968

*United States, Canada, Western Europe, Australia, New Zealand, South Africa, and Japan.

†U.S.S.R. and other Eastern Europe, Communist China, Mongolia, North Korea, and North Vietnam.

continued on page 595

continued from the article Economy, World
on page 307

root cause is the lack of confidence in the ability and willingness of governments to maintain reasonable monetary stability.

From the vantage point of the U.S. national interest, it is argued that a higher gold price would not help the U.S. balance of payments. For, in practical reality, the United States could not devalue the dollar against other currencies unless the other countries would allow the United States to do so. A rise in the price of gold would, therefore, set off a worldwide wave of currency adjustments in terms of gold that would, in all likelihood, leave the exchange relationships between the dollar and other currencies substantially unchanged.

Views like these are in turn countered by pointing out that a gold price rise would relieve the United States from some of the pressures it was experiencing in 1968. Above all, the United States would witness a substantial improvement in its net gold position, because of the increase in the value of its gold stock relative to its liabilities to foreign governments (see Chart III). Furthermore, an immediate increase in, and a large long-run supply of, international liquidity as a result of a higher gold price would undoubtedly provide an incentive to U.S. exports and to world trade all around. Further relief might come from purchases of U.S. securities with some of the funds obtained through massive private gold sales abroad.

It is sometimes said that an increase in the dollar price of gold would ruin the dollar as an international currency. Obviously, there would be disappointment on the part of governments holding primarily dollars in monetary reserves. On second thought, however, it would be realized that interest income on reserves held, over the years, in the form of dollars would have made good —or might have even exceeded—the profit that would have accrued from gold revaluation had the reserves been held in gold. Most decisively, a currency is not judged on the basis of its past history but by its current and prospective monetary and fiscal conditions and policies. The increase in the dollar price of gold in 1934 did not prevent the dollar from becoming subsequently the foremost international reserve currency. In brief, the dollar would not die from a rise in the gold price—provided that the rise, after 35 years of stability despite a great world war, would be generally recognized as necessary and would be made to stick.

3. Kindling the Fires of Inflation. A gold price rise would add fuel to the worldwide fires of inflation. The revaluation of present gold reserves would give rise to book profits that, in practice, would be very difficult to sterilize in the face of the propensity of governments and legislatures to expand spending. It would bring about further weakening of the already weakened attitude toward fiscal discipline. The psychological effect of a gold price rise would be decidedly bullish. In countries where gold may be held privately, a massive dishoarding would increase money supplies. One cannot stop people from dancing around the golden calf.

In trying to envisage the shape of things to come, it must be recognized that a gold appreciation might accentuate the already seemingly intractable inflationary pressures. The difficulties of countering inflation in the aftermath of a gold price rise must not be underestimated. But more determined and more skillful efforts to hold inflation in check would have to be made whether or not the price of gold was raised, for inflation would undermine not only the world's monetary system but the dollar as well and, with it, the American economy. While an increase in the gold price would give time to work toward financial prudence, the elbowroom it would provide would be all the more limited because people would be very alert for the possibility of yet another increase. This greater alertness would, of course, itself be a stabilizing factor.

The difficulties of holding inflation in check after a gold price rise are often exaggerated. Inflation would follow only if governments were to tap revaluation profits to finance all kinds of public expenditures. But the revaluation profit could be offset against government debts to central banks which are large prac-

tically everywhere (Switzerland is the main exception). In the United States, which would undoubtedly receive gold following the price rise, the accretions to the Treasury stock could be offset, if needed, through sales from the very substantial Federal Reserve holdings of government bonds. These thoughts rest, of course, on the assumption that governments and central banks—above all, those of the large industrial nations—would follow prudent fiscal and monetary policies.

The money value of private gold holdings would also increase in the wake of a gold price rise. In countries where private holdings were large—France, in particular—dishoarding would bring about increases in money in circulation. The size of dishoarding would depend on the circumstances of the moment, above all, the degree of credibility of the new price; but even if private gold sales were massive, central banks would not be defenseless. No such problem would, obviously, arise in the United States where private ownership of gold—except for collectors' items— is prohibited.

How does an individual protect himself against a rise in the price of gold? In countries where private gold ownership is legal, holders of paper money can buy gold. Frenchmen can also buy two French government long-term bonds, issued in the 1950s, featuring, in addition to generous tax exemptions, a gold clause designed to restore the confidence of people in government paper and to help break the vicious circle of inflation. Elsewhere in the world, gold clauses—the pledge that a debtor will repay in money having the same value in terms of gold as he received—are dead. In the United States, they were abrogated in 1933 in circumstances recalled in the insert:

Abrogation of Gold Clauses— Unhappy Memories of 1933 Recalled in 1969.

Until a generation ago, gold clauses—the pledge that a debtor will repay money having the same value in terms of gold as he received—were widely used in the United States. In fact, for more than a hundred years prior to 1933, they were a matter of routine in mortgage deeds and bonds, including most of the securities issued by the federal government. The popularity of gold clauses reflected a concept that gold was the only true money, the foundation of the credit system, and the final denominator of all values.

The use of gold clauses was abruptly ended in June 1933. Following the suspension of the gold standard in April 1933, Congress passed a joint resolution declaring gold clauses to be "against public policy." At the same time, it provided that "public and private debts" could be discharged, "dollar for dollar," in any coin or currency that "at the time of payment" was legal tender, which gold ceased to be.

Creditors, understandably, resisted. In several famous cases, the Supreme Court in 1935 recognized the constitutionality of the joint resolution. By a vote of 5 to 4, it held that the enforcement of gold clauses in private contracts was inconsistent with the power of Congress to regulate money. As to the federal government's own bonds, the court declared that Congress could not "disregard the obligations of the Government at its discretion," but it dismissed the bondholders' claims on the ground that they suffered no injury as a result of the payoff in paper money. In 1935, it should be recalled, domestic price levels were virtually the same as in 1933. The theory that a loss of purchasing power would give bondholders a right to compensation would have subsequently led to extreme embarrassment had not Congress, in 1935, passed a resolution cutting off litigation against the government on the ground of abrogated gold clauses.

The debate was dramatic and momentous. In the light of the subsequent shrinkage in the value of the dollar and the pervasive impact of inflation on people's minds, attitudes, and actions, the opinion of the Supreme Court minority, written by Justice James C. McReynolds, is worth remem-

bering: "Loss of reputation for honorable dealing will bring us unending humiliation; the impending legal and moral chaos is appalling."

For Americans concerned about protection of their savings, what matters is what the dollar buys in day-to-day life. As already noted, the 1968 dollar was worth only 39 cents of the 1934 dollar. In the event that the official gold price were readjusted, the prices of goods and services would not rise *pari passu* and immediately. Even prices of imported goods would not rise automatically since a gold revaluation would be carried out by other countries as well—though not necessarily to the same degree—with the result that the existing exchange rate structure would not be greatly disturbed. Whether or not in the longer run prices would rise at a faster pace after a gold price readjustment than during recent years would depend on government policies. Protection against a gold price rise is, therefore, protection against domestic inflation. Fundamentally, of course, the only way people can protect themselves against an unacceptable degree of depreciation of money is through responsible government at all levels.

4. The "Dialogue of the Deaf" Concluded The arguments and counterarguments about the price of gold in the world today, just summed up, are a veritable "dialogue of the deaf." The issues are intellectually provocative and monetarily and politically explosive, but the protagonists are seldom converted.

In matters governing gold, there is nothing of the inexorableness of the Greek drama. A rise in the dollar price of gold is not inevitable. Responsible fiscal and monetary policies in the United States and a reasonable measure of wage self-discipline—coupled with good luck in the process of disengagement from Vietnam and in the handling of the problems of the disturbed cities—would undoubtedly salvage the present price of gold. International monetary cooperation would thus be offered a chance to establish "paper gold," on the basis of the present price of gold, as a form of international reserves continuously acceptable to governments in large amounts.

Amid all the uncertainties, however, this most favourable course of events and developments may not materialize. If so,

two other courses of the shape of things to come must be envisaged. A rise in the price of gold might come about as a result of a concerted decision by governments, preferably at the U.S. initiative—a decision motivated by considerations commanding logical acceptance and intellectual respect, and implemented in an orderly manner. And, alternatively, a gold price rise might come either as a consequence of a breakdown of international monetary cooperation or as a move forced upon governments as an expedient of last resort. Of the two courses, the one that would bring the change in an orderly and efficient way would obviously be preferable to disorder and waste.

Getting Rid of the "Constraints of Gold." Some students of international liquidity want to cut loose from gold and thus liberate the United States from the "constraints of gold." Such an action—so we hear from the ivory towers—would enable the United States to make full use of the intrinsic strength of its rich, productive, and efficient economy, thereby greatly increasing the freedom of domestic policy making. Other large industrial nations, which are vitally dependent on exports to maintain their output, incomes, and employment at home, would—so concludes this school of thought—have little choice but to continue accepting dollars even if these were not convertible into gold; otherwise, they would have to allow their own currencies to appreciate in terms of the dollar and thus inflict upon themselves a competitive disadvantage, relative to the United States, in export markets as well as in their own domestic markets.

Thoughts like these—discarding as they purport to do the ancient fetish of gold and invoking the modern concept that the value of the dollar does not depend on the hoards of gold in Fort Knox but on the productive power of the U.S. economy—appeal to many of those who have become impatient or irritated over the difficulties the United States has encountered in financing its balance of payments deficit. This school of thought regards the convertibility of dollars into gold as a fiction maintained to reassure continental Europe and to comply with certain technicalities of the IMF charter.

Cutting loose from gold has been variously described as re-

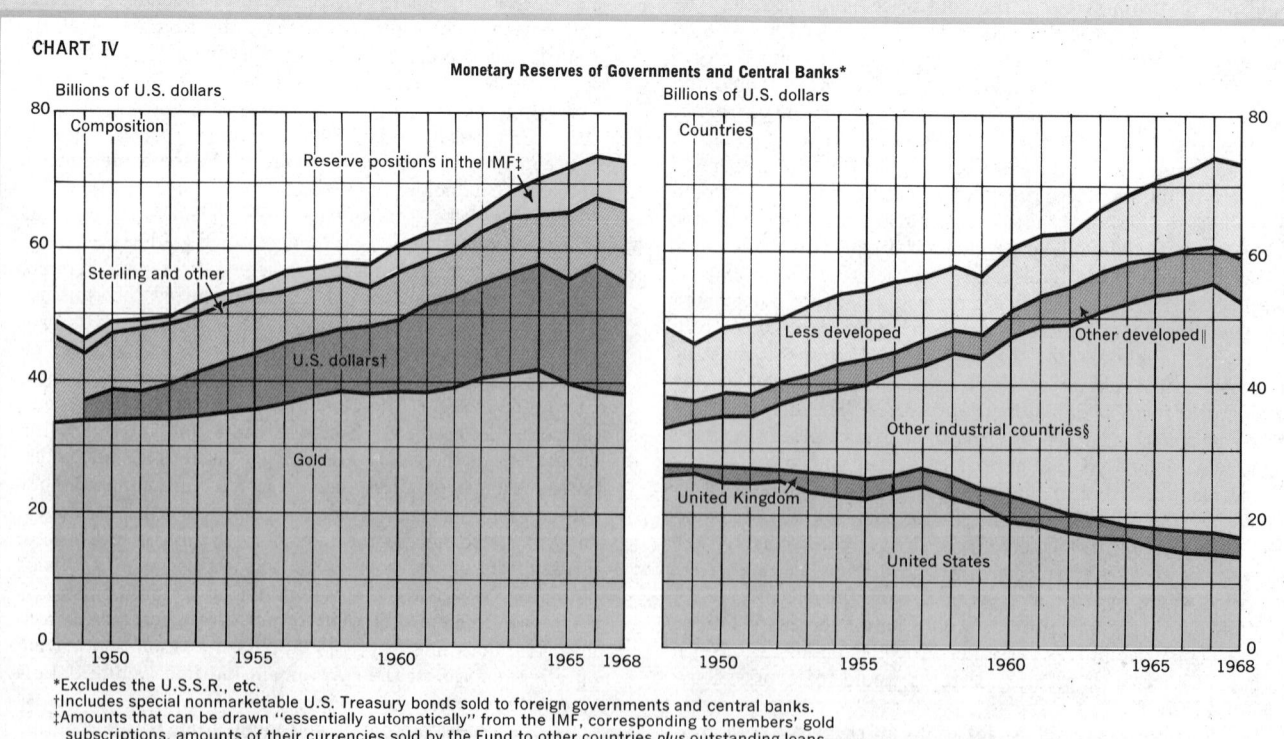

CHART IV

Monetary Reserves of Governments and Central Banks*

*Excludes the U.S.S.R., etc.
†Includes special nonmarketable U.S. Treasury bonds sold to foreign governments and central banks.
‡Amounts that can be drawn "essentially automatically" from the IMF, corresponding to members' gold
   subscriptions, amounts of their currencies sold by the Fund to other countries *plus* outstanding loans
   to the Fund.
§Belgium, Canada, France, West Germany, Italy, Japan, the Netherlands, Norway, Sweden, Switzerland.
‖Other European countries, Australia, New Zealand, South Africa.

fusal to sell gold, suspension of the convertibility of dollars into gold, or a gold embargo. The U.S. Treasury has, of course, no commitment to sell (or to buy) gold; the policy could be changed without notice. In practical reality, however, cutting the dollar loose from gold would throw the whole system of international trade and payments into confusion.

Thought is also being given to permitting greater flexibility in exchange rates than exists today. Under the IMF system, fluctuations in exchange rates are limited within narrow margins, and adjustments are allowed only in the case of "fundamental disequilibrium." Adjustment is, however, a hard problem to deal with—as evidenced by the November 1968 currency crisis reviewed elsewhere.

The best argument for greater exchange flexibility is that it would obviate the need for back-door changes in currency values such as those made in Germany, France, and the United Kingdom in November 1968 and described in PAYMENTS AND RESERVES, INTERNATIONAL. The rub is that governments could not be expected to disinterest themselves in matters as vital as exchange rates. They would intervene. Judging from past behaviour, they would, at times, support the exchange rate to calm apprehensions of their own people alarmed over a shrinking rate for the national currency. At times, they might let the rate go down in order to make imports more expensive and exports cheaper, and thus to secure a competitive advantage in the world market.

Furthermore, no one can be certain how greater flexibility might work in practice when applied to the U.S. dollar. Because of the size of its economy and because of the use made internationally of the dollar, the United States cannot expect to bring about, at its own initiative, any effective change in its exchange rates vis-à-vis other currencies. Any attempt to initiate a change in the dollar rate against other currencies—either through "devaluation" under the fixed exchange rate system or through forced depreciation under a flexible rate system—might be resisted. Other governments might take offsetting actions in order to defend what they would regard as their national interest.

Thus, other currencies can fluctuate against the dollar. But acceptance by other industrial nations of a fluctuating exchange rate for the dollar would presuppose a degree of willingness to help increase the competitiveness of U.S. exports—and help decrease the competitiveness of their own exports into the United States—that these nations give no evidence of possessing.

Should the dollar nevertheless be allowed to fluctuate in terms of other currencies, its use as the standard in exchange markets would, of course, come to an end. With it, the dollar would cease to be the intervention and reserve currency. All this would require far-reaching changes in the working rules in exchange markets and would give rise to difficult problems for governments that would decline to place their currencies on a full dollar standard. It would also weaken the position of the United States as the international financial centre—a weakening that would, in turn, affect the position of the United States in world affairs.

Finally, with flexible or floating exchange rates, balance of payments deficits and gold losses would no longer be an impediment to domestic inflation. Flexible or floating exchange rates would thus remove yet another of the few remaining barriers to persistent depreciation of the domestic buying power of money.

The merit of the present system, which emerged from the disastrous experience with the "managed" exchange flexibility of the 1930s, is to assure order in the international exchange structure—order that is, by no means, rigid. The International Monetary Fund—while standing for stability in exchange rates—also makes possible orderly changes in these rates. The Fund thus aims to provide a pattern of exchange rates sufficiently rigid to enable traders and investors to count on reasonable exchange stability, and yet supple enough to permit such orderly adjustments of rates as might be required to deal with a fundamental disequilibrium in the balance of payments.

Letting the dollar float in foreign exchange markets would be a much greater evil than raising the official price of gold. Either step would mean political embarrassment and damage to the U.S. position in the world. But the first evil would be compounded by confusion and disorder in exchange markets—disorder that would lend itself to competitive depreciation, protectionism, restrictionism, and, sooner or later, economic warfare.

It is illusory to expect that a system of exchange rate permissiveness would somehow lead to a worldwide demonetization of gold. Amid uncertainties about currency values, international monetary cooperation would be severely damaged, and nations would insist on settlements in gold; even the United States would have to pay out gold if it sought any semblance of order in the exchange markets. Paradoxically, the consequence of foreign exchange permissiveness might well be to raise gold to unchallenged primacy in international settlements—to the detriment of the dollar and, needless to say, the SDR's.

The evolutionary process that has reduced the monetary functions of gold within countries was, so far ahead as could be seen, quite unlikely to encompass the demonetizing of gold in international monetary relationships. For, given all the circumstances of the real world, there is deep-seated rationality in gold. The rationality has, of course, nothing to do with the mystical properties of gold. For reasons set forth earlier in this essay, it rests on the qualities of gold as "outside money" —money independent of any government or group of governments and, therefore, more suitable as international money than a national reserve currency like the dollar or money controlled by an international board. In a politically, institutionally, and culturally diverse world, which is monetarily unsettled, insecure, and suspicious, the international gold standard—as modernized through the elements of international credit that had been built into it, subject to limits, rules, and safeguards—gives nations a degree of monetary autonomy and independence that they could not otherwise secure.

The Early 1930s and Today—Does History Repeat Itself?

Concern was sometimes expressed lest another gold crisis toll the bell for world prosperity. Those who put forward ideas like these saw a parallel between the monetary conditions of the late 1920s and the early 1930s and those of 1968.

From 1918 to 1931, despite World War I inflation and its aftermath, the monetary structure among most of the leading currencies was defended on the basis of the pre-1914 gold price —at the cost of unemployment and loss of output, particularly in the United Kingdom. In the end, the pound sterling was devalued in 1931, the dollar in 1933, and the French and Swiss francs and the Dutch guilder in 1936. As the gold standard was suspended in one country after another, the world passed through a series of monetary crises and floating exchange rates, which led to sharp currency depreciations in terms of gold. At the end of the devaluation cycle, however, the exchange rates among the dollar, sterling, and other leading currencies (except the French franc, which suffered several amputations) were not too different from what they had been at the beginning; only the world gold price was higher. The hardships suffered to sustain the price of gold proved unnecessary. The realignments of major currencies, partly in relation to each other but fundamentally in relation to gold, helped the world's economic recovery.

Equating the uncertainties surrounding the $35 gold price with the threat of world deflation overlooks the fact that mankind is in the midst of its biggest technological and inventive revolution. World industrial output, which had experienced dramatic setbacks in the early 1930s, has over the past 20 years been rising steadily. Unemployment, which then exceeded 20% of the labour force in the United Kingdom and 25% in the United States, is, in comparison, very small. World trade, which had

been more than halved between mid-1920 and the early 1930s, has more than doubled since 1958.

In the United States of 1968, the differences with the early 1930s were striking:

During the early 1930s, in an environment of a severe depression, the Federal Reserve allowed money supplies and credit to decline by 30%; in 1968, given the mood of the country, it seemed to want to apply enough restraint to slow down the boom but stop well short of the severity that would spell recession of employment, output, incomes, and profits. It would not kill off economic growth by restricting credit and money supplies.

During the 1930s, President Roosevelt was elected on a platform of a balanced federal budget; and when he unbalanced the budget, he did it in amounts that, in today's circumstances, appear quite moderate. The bias in 1968 was for deficit spending.

In the 1930s, agricultural prices and incomes fell disastrously; in 1968, they were supported by the federal government. Besides, agriculture represented a very much smaller portion of the U.S. gross national product than it did in the 1930s.

Then, wages and salaries were deliberately cut down; today, given all the pressures, they can only rise. Then, unemployment insurance and other social services were nonexistent; in 1968, they were built into the economy.

On the eve of the 1970s, the course of the U.S. economy remained the single dominant influence in the world. The crucial issue was whether the United States could control its inflation and its balance of payments deficits through processes of adjustment orderly enough not to hurt world business. Nations abroad were anxiously watching whether the United States could bring about a sustainable balance in its domestic economy and in its international payments without precipitating a deflation. For a

deflation in the United States would damage world trade and, hence, employment, output, and incomes of people everywhere. An assured expansion of world trade was particularly vital for Britain's postdevaluation comeback.

As long as the U.S. balance of payments was out of joint, much also depended on the views, attitudes, and policies of the surplus nations of continental Europe. All of them would like to see the United States exercise more discretion in the use of economic stimulants than had been the case during recent years. But if the U.S. economy were depressed and the administration and the Federal Reserve were to respond with expansionary monetary and fiscal policies, nations abroad would undoubtedly cooperate with the United States in countering international monetary stresses and strains. For they themselves have a large stake in the maintenance of high and rising levels of business in the country that provides the largest import market in the world.

Hopefully, and this is a comforting thought, nations would, sooner or later, want to resist the forces pushing the world into economic and monetary disorder and disintegration. They would want to resist at all cost even if this were to bring about changes in the established gold arrangements and practices, for these exist not for their own sake but only to promote and safeguard a workable, open, and integrated international monetary system and world prosperity. The most essential single task is to face the matters governing gold squarely in an emotion-free atmosphere so as to avoid misunderstanding, mistrust, and mishandling.

Among the greatest values to be preserved is a stable, reliable, and respected dollar, domestically as well as internationally. This is an economic and social imperative, for prolonged inflation wreaks havoc on economic growth and social justice. It is also a political imperative, for "good money is coined freedom."

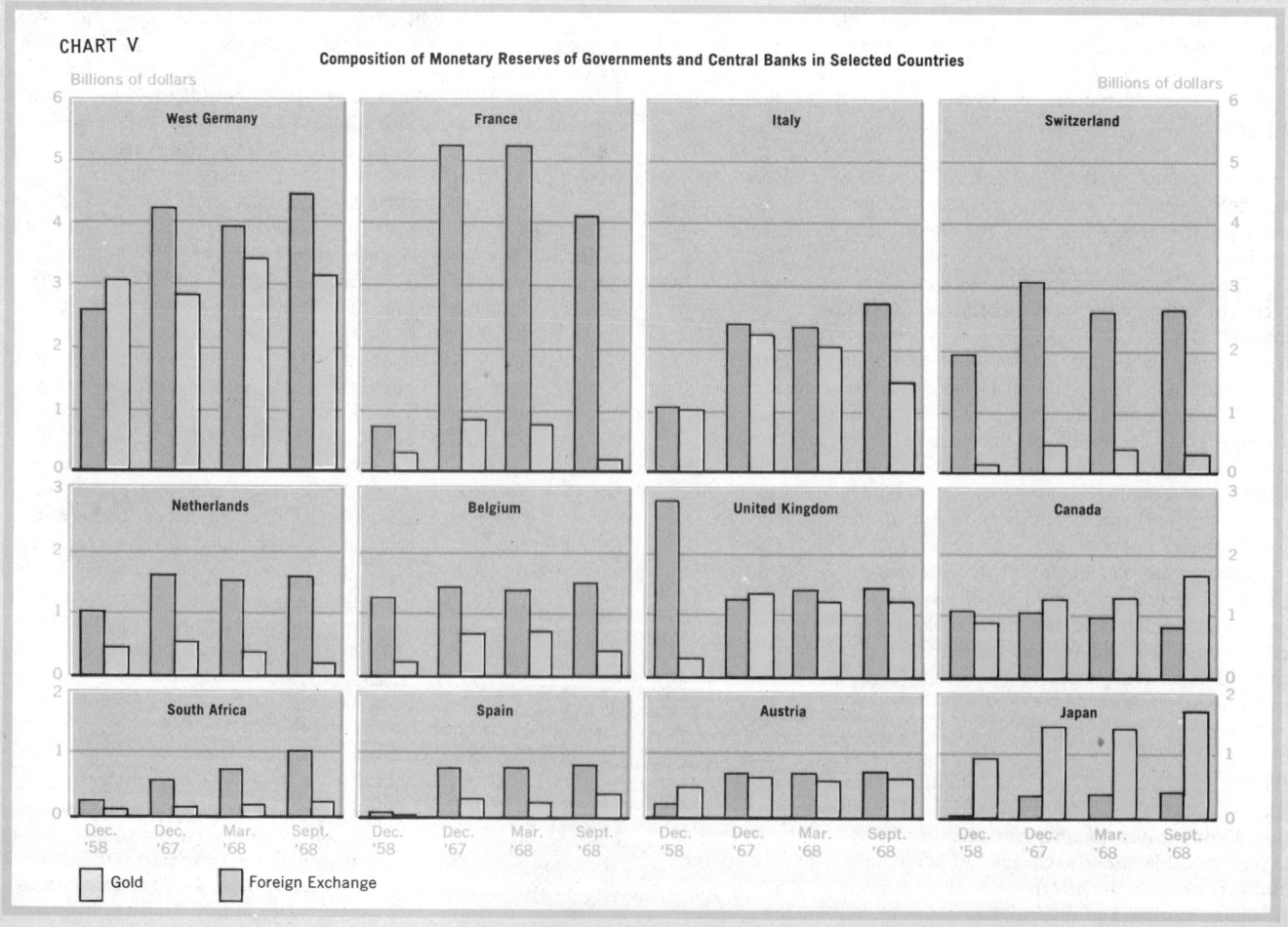

CHART V

Composition of Monetary Reserves of Governments and Central Banks in Selected Countries

Gold   Foreign Exchange

continued from page 590

an unsettled world, the United States was a safe depository for invested funds.

Flows of new U.S. funds for direct investment abroad declined markedly. This was, in part, the result of business compliance with government balance of payments controls and, in part, a natural slowdown from unusually large outflows because of lower rates of return in Europe and other factors. At the same time, the remarkable growth of international markets for Eurodollars and Eurobonds enabled American businesses and banks to secure a large volume of foreign financing. U.S. interest rates were more in line with those in markets abroad than in earlier years; this narrowing of interest rate differentials also helped the U.S. balance of payments.

In assessing the U.S. balance of payments performance, account must also be taken of the draining of dollars caused by defense and other U.S. commitments abroad, notably the war in Vietnam. These drains increased still further in 1968—to over $3 billion, of which about one-half was statistically attributable to Vietnam. In an unsettled and insecure world, the United States had to provide for its defense; at the same time, however, it could not remain strong politically and monetarily unless it had a strong and respected currency.

Good sense demanded that U.S. balance of payments deficits be reduced—but not necessarily eliminated. Ironically enough, nations that had payments surpluses in counterpart of the U.S. deficit wanted to eat their cake and still have it; they resented unwanted dollars but were apprehensive of the consequences of a sharp and sudden swing of the U.S. payments into a surplus.

As 1969 was shaping up, therefore, the United States would be expected to correct the inflationary pressures in its economy and improve substantially its balance of payments. What mattered, however, was that the process of disinflation and balance of payments adjustment be orderly so that it would not cloud the business horizons, damage world trade and, hence, employment, output and incomes of people everywhere.

Processes of balance of payments adjustment—forces bearing on aggregate demand through prices, costs, and interest rates—worked rather disappointingly. During the past two years the U.S. wage costs per unit of output rose; German costs declined. Discrepancies also appeared in export prices (Chart 1).

In the United States and the United Kingdom, much emphasis was placed on the "duties of creditors" to expand domestic demand and imports and thereby help to bring about reduced balance of payments surpluses. Germany, Italy, and other countries repeatedly replied, however, that they were set on an expansionary course in their domestic economies, but that they were determined not to inflate.

By year's end, an uneasy but tense calm returned to the world's foreign exchange markets. Looking forward into 1969, it was evident that, in a world of convertibility and with large amounts of funds moving through foreign exchange markets, a sustainable international monetary order was conditioned on orderliness in the domestic financial and economic affairs of each of the major nations.

The strains and stresses in the world's exchange rate structure had no adverse effect on international trade, which rose at a near-record rate (Chart 2). This strong expansion was not, however, well balanced.

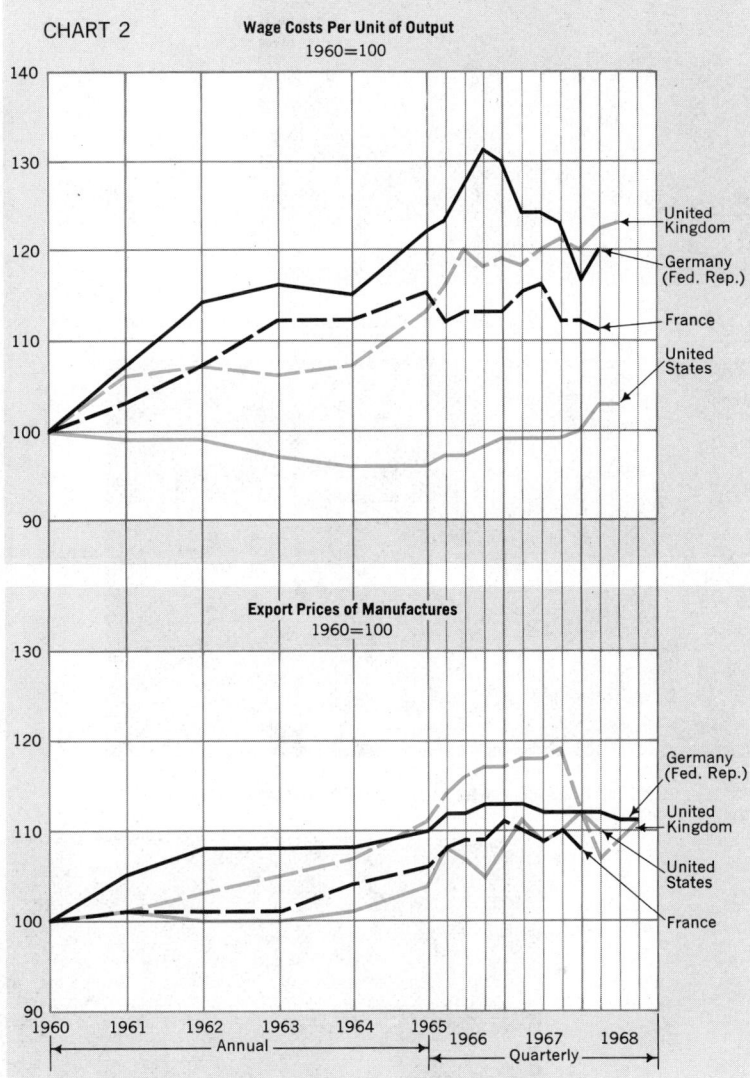

Much of it stemmed from the surge of imports into the United States and the United Kingdom. Moreover, as in earlier years, primary-producing countries benefited from the rise in demand for raw materials in the industrial world but experienced a slowdown in the growth of their own imports as they received less private long-term capital and foreign aid—yet another consequence of the world's balance of payments problems. (M. A. K.)

See also Commercial Policies; Commodities, Primary; Economics; Economy, World; Investment, International; Money and Banking; Prices; Trade, International.

Peace Movements

Experimentation with dramatic new forms of organization and protest marked 1968 for world peace movements. While the major preoccupation continued to be the conflict in Vietnam, peace activists also focused on such areas as electoral politics, the escalating arms race, the simmering Middle East crisis, the nuclear nonproliferation treaty, and the Soviet-led military intervention in Czechoslovakia. In the U.S. 1968 witnessed the growth of movements of draft resistance and university reform.

In Europe, antiwar and university reform groups broadened their challenges to prevailing systems, most

UPI COMPIX
U.S. citizens of Eastern European descent picketing the UN.

THE "NEW YORK TIMES" FROM WIDE WORLD
West 16th Street for Peace Committee members dedicating their "Peace Mural" in New York City.

WIDE WORLD
Japanese students in Sasebo burning U.S. flag to protest visit of nuclear-powered carrier USS "Enterprise."

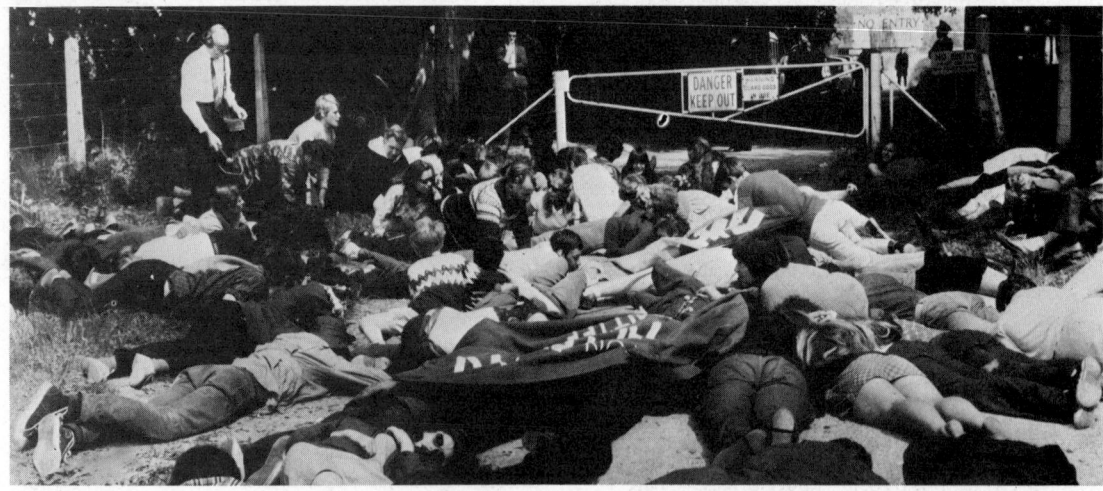

UPI COMPIX
Demonstrators conducting a protest on the grounds outside the Microbiological Research Establishment at Porton Down, Wiltshire, Eng.

"Peace in Vietnam" rally in New York City's Central Park.

A.F.P. FROM PICTORIAL PARADE

Paris youths staging a march in support of the people of South Vietnam.

"PARIS MATCH" FROM PICTORIAL PARADE

LONDON "DAILY EXPRESS" FROM PICTORIAL PARADE

U.S. and North Vietnamese negotiating teams meeting in the Hotel Majestic in Paris to discuss terms for holding peace talks aimed at ending the war in Vietnam.

conspicuously in France and West Germany, indicating the continued growth of a viable world student movement. In Czechoslovakia the predominantly non-violent resistance of the populace to Soviet-led invasion forces provided notable examples of creative defenses of freedom. In the U.S.S.R. itself, poet Yevgeny Yevtushenko and physicist Pavel Litvinov risked jail and exile to protest the Soviet action.

Some peace spokesmen offered a more pessimistic reading of events, however. The assassinations of the Rev. Martin Luther King, Jr., and Sen. Robert F. Kennedy removed two American leaders sympathetic to peace movement concerns. Further, as the war in Vietnam continued and American domestic tensions heightened, the divergence between the "antiwar" and "peace" movements widened. The antiwar elements, harsh in their denunciation of the U.S. and not necessarily pacifistic, tended to view a militarist and imperialist foreign policy as the primary root of the war system. Some leaders of Students for a Democratic Society (SDS), for example, criticized the "social fascism" of American corporate liberals as the adversary rather than the resurgent right wing. Such unorthodox manifestations of protest as the iconoclastic Youth International Party (Yippies) satirized conventional institutions.

The more traditional peace effort, including such organizations as SANE, the United World Federalists, the World Without War Council, and the Fellowship of Reconciliation, tended to view international conflict as a function of interaction between nation-states rather than simply as the result of "aggression" by any single state. While severely critical of U.S. military intervention in Vietnam, these groups, together with liberal left organizations such as Americans for Democratic Action (ADA), urged action within traditional peace education and electoral processes.

A temporary convergence of the antiwar and peace movements occurred in Chicago at the Democratic national convention. The SDS, the National Mobilization to End the War in Vietnam, supporters of Eugene McCarthy's presidential candidacy, Yippies, and pacifists sponsored demonstrations in the streets and parks. While peace leaders regretted the actions of some protesters, they vehemently criticized what they characterized as the repressive violence of police countertactics.

Opposition to the draft continued to grow. The noted pediatrician Benjamin Spock, Yale chaplain William Sloane Coffin, Jr., writer Mitchell Goodman, and Harvard graduate student Michael Ferber were found guilty of conspiring to urge resistance to the Selective Service System. Sentenced to two years in jail and fines up to $5,000, the defendants promptly appealed. Nine Roman Catholics who had seized and burned Selective Service records in Catonsville, Md.,

were found guilty of destroying government property.

Moderate critics of U.S. policy, such as the Council for a Livable World and the National Committee for a Political Settlement in Vietnam, led by educator Clark Kerr, continued their efforts. ADA chairman John Kenneth Galbraith and Mrs. Martin Luther King, Jr., among others, reinforced the attempts of UN Secretary-General U Thant to obtain an unconditional halt to the U.S. bombing of North Vietnam. The International Liaison Committee of the Stockholm Conference on Vietnam, meeting in Rome in June, announced that over 600 organizations in 41 countries signed a similar statement. South Vietnam's 17 Roman Catholic bishops issued a surprising call for an end to the bombing as a first step toward peace. Peace spokesmen felt their efforts were at least partially responsible for Pres. Lyndon Johnson's order to halt bombing of the North as of November 1.

In the academic world, a student movement initiated by SDS successfully disrupted Columbia University, merging attacks on the war system with demands for far-reaching structural changes within the university. Elsewhere, faculty and student groups moved to abolish university complicity with biochemical warfare and counterinsurgency research. Others entertained radical proposals to utilize the universities as "sanctuaries" and to create model "counterinstitutions," noting such suggestive examples as worker councils in Yugoslavia, the Soka Gakkai in Japan, and the Extra-Parliamentary Opposition (APO) in West Germany.

The growing APO encompassed diverse organizations and individuals, none formally represented in the Bundestag. Some elements sought formal representation there, while the radical wing, including most of the Socialist Students' League urged decentralized, decision-making at the grass roots. Leaders such as Rudi Dutschke (*see* BIOGRAPHY) and Karl Dietrich Wolff moved from protest to revolutionary resistance. Their credo was notably similar to that of the French student movement that revolted against the Gaullist establishment in late spring. While in both Germany and France success was problematic, the students offered powerful challenges to the establishment. (*See* FRANCE; GERMANY.)

Japanese peace leaders witnessed a tentative coalescence of the fragmented antiwar movement around opposition to the Japanese-U.S. security treaty, renewable in 1970. Markedly ideological in temper, Japanese antiwar groups opposed U.S. bases in Japan, protested the visit to Sasebo of the nuclear-powered aircraft carrier "Enterprise," and continued their opposition to the war in Vietnam.   (R. Hy.)

Peru

A republic on the west coast of South America, Peru is bounded by Ecuador, Colombia, Brazil, Bolivia, Chile, and the Pacific Ocean. Area: 496,222 sq.mi. (1,285,216 sq.km.). Pop. (1967 est.): 12,012,000, including approximately 52% whites and mestizos and 46% Indians. Cap. and largest city: Lima (pop., 1966 est., 1,883,700). Language: Spanish; Indians speak Quechuan or Aymaran. Religion: Roman Catholic. Presidents in 1968, Fernando Belaúnde Terry and, from October 3, president of the military government, Maj. Gen. Juan Velasco Alvarado.

An event of great significance for Peru was the military coup of October 3, which ousted President Belaúnde. The coup was engineered by Gen. Juan Velasco Alvarado, who became president and installed a military Cabinet with civilian technical advisers.

The coup took place soon after a dispute arose involving the International Petroleum Co., Ltd. (IPC, a subsidiary of Standard Oil of New Jersey), the Empresa Petrolera Fiscal (EPF, the state petroleum agency), and the government. The issue related to the amount of freedom foreign companies should have in the exploitation of Peru's national resources and originated as early as 1924, when IPC obtained rights to exploit the La Brea y Pariñas oil field in the north of Peru. Various sectors of opinion at that time believed that the terms granted to IPC were too generous, and a prolonged debate ensued; it lasted until 1959, when President Belaúnde declared he would soon solve the problem. However, the problem was still not solved on Aug. 13, 1968, when IPC handed over its rights to La Brea y Pariñas to the nation but maintained rights to refine and market the oil.

The EPF disagreed with the government over the terms of the contract, which had been drawn up by the latter in what appeared to have been a hasty manner. What was at first a disagreement over technical matters was soon turned into a political "scandal" fed by currents of nationalistic opinion, particularly when the entire board of EPF resigned. As a result of popular clamour, the government was forced to retract the contract with IPC, and the Cabinet resigned. Belaúnde formed a new Cabinet, but it lasted less than a day before it was replaced by the military junta which expropriated all of IPC's interests. At year's end the U.S., which recognized the military regime on October 25, was attempting to encourage negotiations between Peru and the IPC regarding compensation.

The less obvious cause for military intervention was the split in Belaúnde's Acción Popular (AP) Party and the resulting lack of political stability. The split was largely the work of Edgardo Seoane Corrales, vice-president, party leader, and official AP candidate in the presidential elections due to be held in 1969. He had little support from Belaúnde, who evidently regarded the powerful finance minister, Manuel Ulloa, with considerably more sympathy.

The junta began effectively to undertake the administration of Peru and enjoyed some support. High priority was given to completing refinancing arrangements, begun by Manuel Ulloa, to guarantee the existing exchange system and to restore economic stability. In October, Gen. Ernesto Montagne Sánchez, the new premier and war minister, announced that the junta proposed to hold a referendum on whether a new constitution should be drawn up. No date was suggested.

Fernando Belaúnde Terry, former president of Peru, was ousted in a military coup Oct. 3, 1968, after a dispute over the rights to be given a foreign oil company.

FLASH PRESS—PIX FROM PUBLIX

The coup followed a year of uncertain economic progress. The short-term outlook for Peru following the devaluation of the sol on Sept. 1, 1967, appeared gloomy. To remedy what was an increasingly precarious economic position, the Belaúnde government took drastic measures to strengthen the economy under emergency powers lasting from June 21 to August 16. Taxation, both direct and indirect, was increased; an import surcharge of 15%, later reduced to 10%, was imposed on all items except essentials; borrowing abroad by the government and its agencies was severely limited; installment sales were discouraged; and banking operations were placed under greater surveillance and control by a series of new decrees.

Devaluation and the measures outlined above had the greatest effect upon exports in an economy whose health was poor in contrast to former years. A trade surplus was recorded for every month from October 1967 to August 1968, when the amount of the surplus was $28 million. But the deficit on capital and nontrade services for August amounted to $24 million, leaving a relatively small net surplus figure of $4 million. An external public debt service of $140 million for 1968 explained why the balance of payments on capital account still registered a deficit, and therefore why the positive effects of a trade surplus were diminished. The net decline in reserves between January and

PERU

Education. (1966) Primary, pupils 2,157,246, teachers (1964) 52,390; secondary, pupils 362,551, teachers (1964) 16,069; vocational, pupils 72,718, teachers (1964) 6,645; teacher training, students 16,464; higher (1963), students 46,334.

Finance. Monetary unit: sol, with a free exchange rate (Oct. 1968) of 43.75 soles to U.S. $1 (104.50 soles = £1 sterling). Gold and foreign exchange, central bank; (June 1968) U.S. $90.9 million; (June 1967) U.S. $102.7 million. Budget (1967–68 est.) balanced at 32,936,000,000 soles. Gross domestic product: (1967) 176.2 billion soles; (1966) 152.1 billion soles. Money supply: (Jan. 1968) 15,580,000,000 soles; (Jan. 1967) 13,860,000,000 soles. Cost of living (1963 = 100): (June 1968) 187; (June 1967) 151.

Foreign Trade. (1967) Imports 24,478,000,000 soles; exports 23,261,000,000 soles. Import sources: U.S. 37%; West Germany 12%; Japan 8%; Argentina 6%. Export destinations: U.S. 42%; Japan 14%; West Germany 11%; Belgium-Luxembourg 6%; Netherlands 6%. Main exports: copper 27%; fish meal 23%; iron ore 8%; cotton 7%; sugar 7%; zinc 5%.

Transport and Communications. Roads (1965) 42,817 km. (including 22,428 km. with improved surface). Motor vehicles in use (1966): passenger 178,-200; commercial (including buses) 107,800. Railways (1965): 3,345 km.; traffic 236 million passenger-km., freight 646 million net ton-km. Shipping (1967): merchant vessels 100 gross tons and over 231; gross tonnage 250,779. Air traffic (1966): 541,926,000 passenger-km.; freight 12,644,000 net ton-km. Telephones (Jan. 1967) 142,589. Radio receivers (Dec. 1964) c. 2.1 million. Television receivers (Dec. 1966) c. 275,-000.

Agriculture. Production (in 000; metric tons; 1967; 1966 in parentheses): wheat c. 140 (c. 140); sugar, raw value 732 (c. 814); rice 458 (360); barley c. 180 (c. 175); corn (1966) c. 550, (1965) 591; potatoes (1966) c. 1,512, (1965) c. 1,643; cassava (1966) c. 540, (1965) 449; dry beans (1966) c. 42, (1965) 52; citrus fruit (1966) c. 200, (1965) 213; cotton, lint 92 (121). Livestock (in 000; 1965–66): cattle 3,644; sheep 15,218; horses 1,108; pigs 1,843; goats 3,959; poultry c. 20,000. Fish catch (in 000; metric tons) (1966) 8,798, (1965) 7,462.

Industry. Fuel and power (in 000; metric tons; 1966): coal 68; crude oil 3,075; electricity 4,080,000 kw-hr. Production (in 000; metric tons; 1967): lead 82; zinc 61; copper 36; iron ore (metal content; 1966) 4,672; pig iron (1966) 12; steel (1966) 80; tungsten concentrates (oxide content; 1966) 0.4; silver (1966) 1.02; gold (1966) 110 troy oz.; fish meal (1966) 1,470.

September 1968 was $232 million, compared with a decline of $92 million over the corresponding period of 1967, which indicated that business confidence was still low. Inflationary pressures still existed: the cost of living went up by 7.6% in the first half of 1968, and the cost of imports rose.

Despite recent amendments to the U.S. Foreign Aid Act, which threatened penalties to Latin-American countries increasing their armaments, Peru in 1968 bought 14 Mirage supersonic jet fighters and 78 Amex-13 light tanks from France, while the U.K. was to deliver 6 Canberra bombers in 1969.   (D. J. Ro.)

Encyclopædia Britannica Films. *Peru: People of the Andes* (1959).

Philately and Numismatics

Philately. The major international exhibition of the year was held in Prague, Czech., in June and July. The Grand Prix International was won by H. Knapp of West Germany and the Grand Prix National (for Czech stamps) by Z. Kvasnicka of Czechoslovakia. The annual International Philatelic Exhibition, EFIMEX '68, was held in Mexico City, November 1–9. Eleven Latin-American nations, the United States, and Canada formally created a functioning Philatelic Federation of the Americas.

Two auction sale records were broken. One of philately's greatest prizes, an envelope with two copies of the 1847 Post Office one-penny orange of Mauritius, was sold late in the year for $380,000, the highest price ever paid for a single stamped envelope. The cover was part of the collection assembled by the late Alfred F. Liechtenstein and by his late daughter, Louise Boyd Dale. Portions of this collection were to be sold in ten auctions. The previous record for a single stamped envelope had been set earlier in the year when a Finnish stamped envelope of 1850 sold for $9,600. The Josiah K. Lilly Collection of World Wide Stamps broke the single-sale record when it sold at auction for more than $3 million.

Thefts of stamps from both dealers and collectors increased at an alarming rate during 1968. Philatelic publications offered advice and warning to philatelists, who until recently had appeared to be safe from robberies that had plagued coin dealers and collectors.

Prices for Vatican City stamps, after the inflated boom of the two previous years, fell to their lowest level in several years, particularly for issues of the last five years. The stamps of the U.K. rose sharply during 1968, and the trend toward higher prices for U.S. stamps continued steadily, particularly for older U.S. stamps. A June auction of such stamps, expected to realize about $100,000, brought $129,947.

By early 1968 Anguilla, in the West Indies, had established itself as an independent administration following its nonacceptance of "associated statehood with Great Britain" when the parent colony of St. Kitts-Nevis acquired that status. Anguilla's first issue of 16 stamps, consisting of St. Kitts issues with a local overprint, made history with a starting price of £1,000 for the basic normal set, largely because only 100 of the 60-cent St. Kitts stamp were available for overprinting.

During the year, Thomas DeLaRue Co. of Colombia perfected its "Delacryl" (basically lithographic) process, which was used for an increasing quantity of British Commonwealth stamps. After a 100-year absence the name of Perkins, Bacon and Co. came back

SOVFOTO
XIX Olympiad stamp issued by the U.S.S.R. in 1968.

Law and order commemorative stamp issued by the U.S. on May 17, 1968.

CANADIAN PRESS
Stamp commemorating the 50th anniversary of the 1918 Armistice issued by Canada on Oct. 15, 1968.

U.S. airmail 50th anniversary stamp issued May 15, 1968.

to the stamp catalogs as a stamp printer, also using a lithographic process. (The company's fame a century ago was founded on recess printing.)

In April, Stanley Gibbons Ltd., of London, became the first philatelic firm to go to the public for capital, offering 950,000 5s. shares. Apart from the 65,000 shares allocated to the company's staff at 12s. 6d., the allotments were finally made at 20s. per share. With the directors' holdings, this placed a value of £1.6 million on the company. Trading in the shares began on April 16. The peak quotation during the year was 31s. 9d. The same month J. and H. Stolow of New York announced the discovery of the first printing error on UN stamps, the 1960 World Bank issue being found imperforate. A market value of $1,000 a pair was placed on the stamps.

The 1968 elections by the Philatelic Congress of Great Britain to the Roll of Distinguished Philatelists were: Herbert J. Bloch, a U.S. professional expert; Francis J. Field of the U.K., a pioneer aerophilatelist; Michel Liphschutz of France, a leading authority on Russian philately; and Achille Rivolta of Italy, a specialist in the postal history of Lombardy-Venetia. The 1968 Philatelic Congress Medal was awarded to Kenneth K. Chapman, editor of *Stamp Collecting*.

U.S. Representative Thaddeus J. Dulski (Dem., N.Y.), chairman of the House Post Office and Civil Service Committee, had introduced a bill in 1967 to permit the illustration of both U.S. and foreign stamps in colour. On June 12, 1968, this bill passed Congress and was signed by Pres. Lyndon B. Johnson. Thus, for the first time, newspapers and magazines were permitted to picture canceled stamps in colour in any size. Uncanceled stamps, both U.S. and foreign, must be reproduced in colour at a size less than $\frac{3}{4}$ or more than $1\frac{1}{2}$ times the original.   (K. F. C.; R. F. Mi.)

Numismatics. Although the U.S. struck no commemorative coins in 1968, a number of other countries did: Finland, 10 markkaa, silver, 50th anniversary of independence; Israel, 10 pounds, gold, and 100 pounds,

Petroleum Industry:
see Fuel and Power; Industrial Review

Pharmacology:
see Medicine

Top and third,
the first two decimal
coins placed
in circulation
in the United Kingdom
on April 23, 1968,
with their nondecimal
counterparts.
These coins initiated
the change
to the decimal currency
system, which was
to become effective
Feb. 15, 1971.

gold, victory issues; U.S.S.R., 10, 15, 20, 50 kopecks, and one ruble, nickel silver, 50th anniversary of the October revolution; Hungary, 25, 50, 100, silver, 500 and 1,000 forints, gold, 85th birthday of Zoltan Kodaly; West Germany, 5 Deutsche Marks, silver, von Humboldt anniversary; Czechoslovakia, 25 koruny, silver, 150th anniversary of the National Museum in Prague; Mexico, 25 pesos, silver, Olympic Games. U.S. citizens were denied the right to purchase or to possess current gold coins without a special permit from the Department of the Treasury. Several countries issuing gold coins were the Bahamas, United Kingdom, South Africa, Canada, and Thailand.

Some record-breaking prices for U.S. coins realized at auction were: 1841 $2.50 gold piece for $18,000 to a dealer; $20 gold for $3,125; 1933 $10 gold piece, $4,600; 1879-CC $10 gold piece for $1,375. Aubrey Bebee turned down an offer of $60,000 for the James V. McDermott specimen of the 1913 Liberty Head nickel. He paid $46,000 for it in August 1967.

The sale of 1,400 numismatic books held in the offices of Hans Schulman in New York City was attended by a select group of buyers representing some of the largest numismatic libraries; E. T. Newell's *Coinage of Eastern Seleucid Mints* and *Numismatic Studies Number 4* each brought $325; R. B. Whitehead, *Catalogue of Coins in the Punjab Museum,* $200; L. Forrer, *Biographical Dictionary of Medallists,* $1,300; H. A. Grueber, *Coins of the Roman Republic in the British Museum,* $260; G. E. Rizzo, *Monete Greche della Sicilia,* $450; J. T. Medina, *Hispano Americanas,* $575.

Yugoslavian aluminum coins minted in 1953–63 (5, 2, 1, and ½ dinar) were taken out of circulation. Old 100-dinar bank notes with the dates of May 1, 1955, and 1963 were withdrawn from circulation. The reddish coloured bank notes ceased to be legal tender as of Feb. 1, 1968. In Brazil the Banco Central began the distribution of a second type of 10-cruzeiro bank note. The dominating colour of the new notes was purple. Brazilian cruzeiro bank notes in denominations of 1,000 old cruzeiros and less were being withdrawn.

The secessionist province of Biafra issued its own currency. This currency was not approved by the Nigerian central government, and official circles in Lagos warned the public, especially foreign businessmen, against accepting Biafran currency.

The shift to decimal currency in the U.K. was begun on April 23, when Britain issued the new five-pence and ten-pence coins, equal, respectively, to the old one-shilling and two-shilling pieces. Complete changeover to decimal currency (100 pence = £1 sterling) was set for Feb. 15, 1971.   (EL. G. B.)

See also Postal Services.

Commemorative medals
minted in Tübingen,
W.Ger., and issued
during August 1968.

Philippines

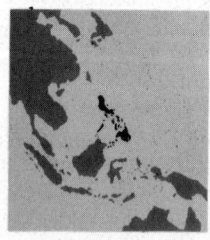

Situated in the western Pacific Ocean off the southeast coast of Asia, the Republic of the Philippines consists of an archipelago of about 7,100 islands. Area: 115,830 sq.mi. (300,000 sq.km.). Pop. (1968 est.): 35,883,000. Administrative capital and largest city: Manila (pop., 1968 est., 1,499,000). Legal capital: Quezon (pop., 1965 est., 545,500). Language: Tagalog or Filipino (official), English, Spanish, and many dialects. Religion: Roman Catholic 84%; Aglipayan 5%; Muslim 5%; Protestant 3%. President in 1968, Ferdinand Marcos.

The economic outlook for the Philippines in 1968 was generally brighter than it had been previously. The presidential economic staff announced at the beginning of the year that the total of goods and services produced in 1967 had increased 5.6%, or 0.4% higher than the target originally set. Agricultural output had risen by 7.2%, mining and manufacturing by 7.3%, construction by 12.7%, transportation and communication by 6.6%, commerce by 7.7%, and services by 5.2%. President Marcos' economic development program had manifested itself in the appearance of six-lane highways between many cities and towns, greatly aiding transportation and communication for isolated areas. New roads built in 1967 added up to 1,480 mi. The demand for more classrooms had been partly met by erecting 5,000 prefabricated schools.

At the end of 1967, the Rice and Corn Administration announced self-sufficiency in rice. After half a century of importing this principal item in the Filipino diet, the country expected a surplus of over 400,000 tons of rice and was prepared to reexport half of the 377,000 tons of rice previously imported. The International Rice Research Institute in Los Baños had developed several varieties of "miracle" rice that mature faster, yield up to four times as large a crop as the regular variety, and are more responsive to fertilizers and more resistant to disease. This had initiated a massive information and distribution campaign by the government among the farmers in a concerted effort to increase both the food supply of the country and the personal income of its farmers. Furthermore, 30,000 tons of the newly developed seeds were to be distributed abroad. By late 1968 at least 60 other countries had imported the new strains. This attainment of self-sufficiency in rice was expected to save the nation $50 million in foreign exchange.

However, rising living costs tended to cancel out the effect upon the average worker's budget of the general increase in the gross national product. The consumer price index rose 6% on account of increased interest rates and higher prices for materials and services. Although the average per capita income increased from the equivalent of $140 per year in 1967 to $163 in 1968, it obviously fell far short of what was considered adequate by Western standards.

A land reform program, designed to relieve farmers of the burden of tenancy by allowing them to own their own land, was just barely getting under way in 1968. One of the chief objectives of the program was to check social unrest, which existed most threateningly in the form of the Hukbalahap, or People's Liberation Army, movement. The Huks, as members

of the organization were known, although described as Communist, were not considered to be so ideologically oriented. They were believed to consist of "old-time idealist reformers, Communists, farmers who are so poor they have decided to join the movement to assure themselves of three meals a day, persons with pending criminal cases, . . . and plain gangsters who have found it extremely profitable to operate their protection rackets 'in the name of the Huk organization.'" In addition, the organization had approximately 30,000 supporters who were not active members of the movement but whose votes could make the Huks a potential political force in, at least, Pampanga Province of central Luzon Island. The Huks were generally believed to wield significant influence over some local government officials.

While the Huk movement was commonly considered confined to Luzon Island in the north, the presence of insurgency in the south was implied by the Philippine government. A training camp on Corregidor Island in Manila Bay, described as a site for survival training for members of a Philippine special force devoted to counterguerrilla tactics aimed at insurgents in the southern islands of the Philippines, was the site of a mutiny in March. Trainees at the camp protested rigorous training methods.

Malaysia, upon whose state of Sabah the Philippines had laid claim, received assurances from Philippine Foreign Secretary Narciso Ramos that the Philippines had no aggressive intentions toward Sabah and that no infiltrators had been sent there. Sabah,

UPI COMPIX

Taal volcano, 40 mi. S of Manila, during an eruption in July 1968. Many families were evacuated from their homes when the volcano became active.

once ruled by the sultan of Sulu in the Philippines, is a 29,388 sq.mi. region located on the northern tip of Borneo. The Philippines claimed it on the ground that it was Philippine territory until the sultan of Sulu ceded part of North Borneo to a British syndicate in 1878. The territory, which has valuable oil, timber and fishery resources, became part of Malaysia in 1963.

On July 15 Malaysia formally rejected the Philippines' claim to Sabah, and by July 21 President Marcos had recalled the Philippine ambassador and most of his staff from Malaysia, virtually cutting off diplomatic relations. In mid-September Marcos signed into law a bill declaring Sabah to be part of the Philippines and promised to use "peaceful means" to pursue the claim. In December, however, the foreign ministers of the two countries agreed to restore diplomatic relations and to observe a year-long "cooling-off period" on the Sabah issue.

Early on the morning of August 2 an earthquake smashed five buildings and cracked a large number of others in Manila, filling hospitals with casualties. A five-story apartment house, erected just a year earlier, collapsed, completely burying people under 14-in.-thick slabs of broken concrete and killing more than 300 residents. More than 350 aftershocks were recorded during the following weekend.

Another major natural disaster occurred earlier in the year when 7,943-ft. Mt. Mayon volcano, located 200 mi. SE of Manila, erupted in late April after 21 years of dormancy. At least seven villages in the area were evacuated when the volcano started to erupt on April 22. More than 20,000 refugees were reported to have arrived at nearby Legaspi.   (RA. PA.)

ENCYCLOPÆDIA BRITANNICA FILMS. *The Philippines: Land and People* (1960).

PHILIPPINES
Education. (1964–65) Primary, pupils 5,577,901, teachers 168,237; secondary and vocational, pupils 1,037,256, teachers 30,694; higher (including 29 universities), students 450,833, teaching staff 22,855.
Finance. Monetary unit: peso, with a par value of 3.90 pesos to U.S. $1 (9.36 pesos = £1 sterling). Gold and foreign exchange, central bank: (June 1968) U.S. $177 million; (June 1967) U.S. $142 million. Budget (1967–68 est.): revenue 2,754,000,000 pesos; expenditure 2,688,000,000 pesos. Gross national product: (1967) 24,540,000,000 pesos; (1966) 22,340,-000,000 pesos. Money supply: (May 1968) 3,230,-000,000 pesos; (May 1967) 2,864,000,000 pesos. Cost of living (Manila; 1963 = 100): (June 1968) 124; (June 1967) 121.
Foreign Trade. (1967) Imports 4,601,000,000 pesos; exports 3,164,000,000 pesos. Import sources: U.S. 34%; Japan 28%; West Germany 5%. Export destinations: U.S. 43%; Japan 34%; Netherlands 5%. Main exports: coconut products 26%; timber 26%; sugar 17%.
Transport and Communications. Roads (1967) 56,180 km. Motor vehicles in use (1966): passenger 174,400; commercial (including buses) 134,700. Railways: (1965) 1,026 km.; traffic (1967) 1,015,000,-000 passenger-km., freight 146 million net ton-km. Shipping (1967): merchant vessels 100 gross tons and over 248; gross tonnage 720,286. Air traffic (1966): 973,530,000 passenger-km.; freight 16,770,000 net ton-km. Telephones (Jan. 1967) 188,144. Radio receivers (Dec. 1964) 1,225,000. Television receivers (Dec. 1966) c. 160,000.
Agriculture. Production (in 000; metric tons; 1967; 1966 in parentheses): rice 4,341 (4,165); corn 1,483 (1,435); sweet potatoes and yams 681 (657); cassava 590 (580); copra (1966) 1,610, (1965) 1,446; sugar, raw value (1967–68) c. 1,705, (1966–67) 1,560; abaca (1966) 95, (1965) 108; bananas (1966) c. 650, (1965) 623; tobacco (1966) 58, (1965) 46; timber (1965–66) c. 8,700 cu.m., (1964–65) c. 8,800 cu.m. Livestock (in 000; March 1966): pigs 6,914; cattle (March 1967) 1,600; buffaloes 3,633; goats 616; horses 257; chickens 68,122.
Industry. Production (in 000; metric tons; 1967): cement 1,670; coal 56; chrome ore (oxide content; 1966) 195; manganese ore (metal content; 1966) 12; copper ore (metal content) 86; iron ore (55–60% metal content) 1,240; silver (1966) 0.04; gold (1966) 454 troy oz.; electricity 4,800,000 kw-hr.

Philosophy

Increasing opposition to established authority in 1968 led to a growing interest in issues relating to civil disobedience, revolution, and punishment. Such problems as ghetto education, mass communications, and overpopulation increased the literature on the concepts of equality, community, and social value and brought the principles of ethics and aesthetics into close conjunction with the behavioural sciences.

Moral and Social Philosophy. Edward H. Madden, in *Civil Disobedience and Moral Law*, traced the basic issues of protest and social reform through the religious and moral thought of 19th-century Amer-

ica. He described the academic versions of Christian orthodoxy, transcendentalism, and evolutionary theory as the dominant factors affecting the moral philosophy of the period. *The Concept of Order*, edited by Paul G. Kuntz, was a study of ideas on the meaning of order. It considered the relation of order to chaos, and of freedom to predictability, as well as a possible dialectic in the processes of order.

J. Roger Saydah described *The Ethical Theory of Clarence Irving Lewis* as based on four rational imperatives: cognitive, technical, prudential, and moral. In *Life or Death: Ethics and Options*, papers presented at a Reed College symposium probed the issue of the worth and quality of life in the light of the modern pressures that threaten historic concepts. The legal, political, medical, and moral facets of the problem were examined. The problem of technology and human values was treated by philosophers, social scientists, and economists in *Values and the Future*, edited by Kurt Baier and Nicholas Rescher.

Essays in the Theory of Society by Ralf Dahrendorf of the University of Constance attempted a coherent theory of the social process. Bertram Morris, in *Institutions of Intelligence*, held that the productive activities of science cannot be divorced from moral principles and that the arts should be regarded as the basic units of society. In *The Improvement of Mankind*, John M. Robson identified the ethical system underlying the logical and political work of John Stuart Mill. In *The Political Philosophy of Rousseau*, Roger D. Masters attempted to guide the "serious" reader in what Rousseau called a "more reflective reading" of his work.

Metaphysics, Method, and the Theory of Knowledge. The uniqueness of human action, its relation to reason and its common ground with inanimate action, was the subject of *Action* by D. G. Brown of the University of British Columbia. In *Metaphysical Analysis*, John W. Yolton of New York University argued in favour of a plurality of languages that convey a plurality of meanings. Richard Rorty's volume *The Linguistic Turn* was a useful presentation of the recent movement of philosophy toward logical and linguistic analysis. *Intellect and Hope*, edited by T. A. Langford and W. H. Poteat, examined various disciplines in terms of Michael Polanyi's thesis on "personal knowledge," which, according to some of the writers, can overcome the alienation of science from human affairs.

The official papers of the fourth East-West Philosophers' Conference at the University of Hawaii, edited by the late Charles A. Moore, discussed *The Status of the Individual in the East and West*. Moore also edited three volumes of papers on the foundations of Indian, Chinese, and Japanese cultures. *Four Modern Philosophers*, by the Norwegian Arne Naess (translated by Alastair Hannay) described the logical empiricism and existentialism of Rudolf Carnap, Ludwig Wittgenstein, Martin Heidegger, and Jean-Paul Sartre. Frederick Sontag's *The Existentialist Prolegomena* argued that existential writings have provided the empirical basis for metaphysics demanded by Kant.

Logic, Language, and the Philosophy of Science. In *Languages of Art* Nelson Goodman moved toward a general theory of symbols by examining the nonlinguistic symbols and systems of the arts. Whitehead's changing theories of perception were examined by Paul F. Schmidt in *Perception and Cosmology in Whitehead's Philosophy*. Victor Preller's *Divine Science and the Science of God* employed the-

ological treatises of Thomas Aquinas as models for his argument that the term "God" can be given referential status in religious language.

Philosophy of Religion. Lionel Rubinoff edited *Faith and Reason,* essays by R. G. Collingwood that "sought to remove religion from the charge of irrationalism." Charles Hartshorne's *A Natural Theology for Our Time* defended the rational argument that God exists necessarily. John A. T. Robinson, bishop of Woolwich, continued the discussion of the life or death of God and the relevance of religion to modern man in *Exploration into God*. Eugene Thomas Long published *Jaspers and Bultmann: A Dialogue Between Philosophy and Theology in the Existentialist Tradition*. Vernard Eller's *Kierkegaard and Radical Discipleship* was intended to exhibit Kierkegaard as essentially a religious thinker and to describe him as in the stream of "classic Protestant sectarianism." James C. S. Wernham compared the personalities and ideas of Nicholas Berdyaev and Lev Shestov in *Two Russian Thinkers* by relating them especially to Dostoevski. Shestov's *Kierkegaard and the Existential Philosophy* was translated by Elinor Hewitt.

Scholarly and Historical Studies. A major contribution to philosophical scholarship was *The Philosophy of Martin Buber* edited by Paul Arthur Schilpp and Maurice Friedman, the 12th volume in the "Library of Living Philosophers." The volume contained Buber's intellectual autobiography, 30 critical essays on his philosophy, his reply to his critics, and a bibliography. Writers on his philosophy included Gabriel Marcel, Charles Hartshorne, Nathan Rotenstreich, Emil Brunner, Herbert W. Schneider, and Walter Kaufmann. Buber's commitment to the I-Thou relationship as the bearer of spiritual and moral meaning and value was evident throughout the dialogue with his critics.

In *The Concept of the Categorical Imperative*, T. C. Williams attempted to construct an unambiguous definition of the categorical imperative and to determine Kant's theory of the relation of the formal imperative to concrete morality. In *Probability and Opinion*, Edmund F. Byrne found the background of modern probability theory in the knowledge theory of Aquinas. *Unamuno: Creator and Creation* was edited by José Rubia Barcia and M. A. Zeitlin from papers read at the centennial celebration of the Spanish philosopher's birth at the University of California, Los Angeles. Daniel S. Robinson, who had already influenced the course of idealism in America, edited a volume of essays by Josiah Royce and William Ernest Hocking— *Royce and Hocking: American Idealists*. Nathan Rotenstreich of the Hebrew University, Jerusalem, presented a systematic account of *Jewish Philosophy in Modern Times: From Mendelssohn to Rosenzweig*. Nicholas Rescher issued *Studies in Arabic Philosophy*.

New Journals and Conferences. *Man and World*, a multilingual international philosophical review, began publication at State College, Pa. The first issue of *Transactions of the Charles S. Peirce Society*, to be published triannually, appeared in January 1968. *Philosophy and Rhetoric*, a quarterly, issued its first number in January 1968. The 14th International Congress of Philosophy was held in Vienna, September 2–9. The Association for Symbolic Logic met in Warsaw, August 30–31.   (S. M. Mc.)

ENCYCLOPÆDIA BRITANNICA FILMS. *Aristotle's Ethics: The Theory of Happiness* (1963); *Athens—The Golden Age* (1963); *Plato's Apology: The Life and Teachings of Socrates* (1963); *Emperor and Slave: The Philosophy of Roman Stoicism* (1965); *The Spirit of Rome* (1965).

Photography

The long-term growth trend of the photographic industry in the United States continued through 1968 at an annual rate approximately three times the annual increase in the U.S. gross national product. A major explanation for this rapid growth was the increase in sales to other countries and the expansion of the industry's productive capability. By the end of the year the U.S. photographic industry produced approximately 70% of the world's output of photographic equipment and materials. An additional impetus to sales was given by the 1968 Photokina exposition in Cologne, W.Ger. Exhibits of photographic materials, equipment, and related services at this show covered about one million square feet, and approximately 183,000 persons attended. In order to provide international coverage of new developments in photography, the Photokina exposition was scheduled to be held in future even years, and the National Association of Photographic Manufacturers planned Photo Expo to be held in June of off-Photokina years. International sales were also stimulated by continuing rounds of tariff reductions on various categories of photographic products.

Dry Photographic Processes. Interest began developing in dry photographic processes that used silver in one form or another; aside from convenience, these processes used considerably less silver than conventional ones, which was an advantage in terms of economy. One U.S. corporation, the 3M Co., utilized such a dry process in one of its office copiers; in this particular process a sheet coated with a substituted alpha-naphthol is exposed to light in contact with an original. The light exposure destroys the ability of the coating to couple with the silver compound, and the process, thus, is direct positive. After exposure the sheet is placed in contact with another sheet coated with silver behenate, and the two are heated; a black silver image then appears on the transfer sheet, and the originally exposed sheet is discarded.

The Eastman Kodak Co. also was working on a dry photo process utilizing silver; like the 3M process described above, it was also sensitive only to ultraviolet, though Kodak stated that it was possible to sensitize the material to other colours. In this process a single sheet is used; after an image-forming exposure, it is briefly heated and then exposed to an intense fogging light that brings out the image.

In their paper on photosoluble silver halide systems, E. F. Haugh and J. F. Strange showed that both conventional and solubilization images can exist in the same emulsion. In this paper they discussed the behaviour of the two types of latent image, suggested uses for each, and suggested a possible use for both images in combination.

In photopolymer systems that polymerize by the free-radical addition of monomer units, the free radicals frequently react with oxygen faster than with the monomer. This reaction with oxygen inhibits or postpones polymerization until the absorbed oxygen is exhausted. Where diffusion replenishes the oxygen, the photopolymer may never polymerize. Oxygen inhibition can cause a serious image-quality problem in materials that have a coating thickness greater than 0.01 in., such as E. I. du Pont de Nemours & Co.'s Dycril Photopolymer printing plates. The problem is usually avoided by holding the plates in carbon di-

"Photo Graphics" by Hein Gravenhorst was included in one of the first exhibits at the newly opened Galerie Clarissa in Hanover, W.Ger.

PICTORIAL PARADE

oxide until the oxygen is desorbed. G. A. Thommes, however, showed that the same reactions by which oxygen inhibits polymerization can be used to remove the oxygen from the plates in only a few minutes. D. K. Smith, of du Pont, published a paper that presented in mathematical terms the mechanism of photometric oxygen removal by preexposure of the plate to green light.

Polaroid Corp. continued its work on several new materials. In one, a highly concentrated fixing bath is used in the pod, in addition to the usual developer. This traps the unexposed silver grains in the original negative sheet, preventing the migration that usually forms a positive image in the receptor sheet. The reaction is of considerable violence, and the exposed grains are expelled to the receptor sheet, wherein they form a second negative image. The silver layer thus produced is very thin but of high covering power; this, it was claimed, would make it possible to attain

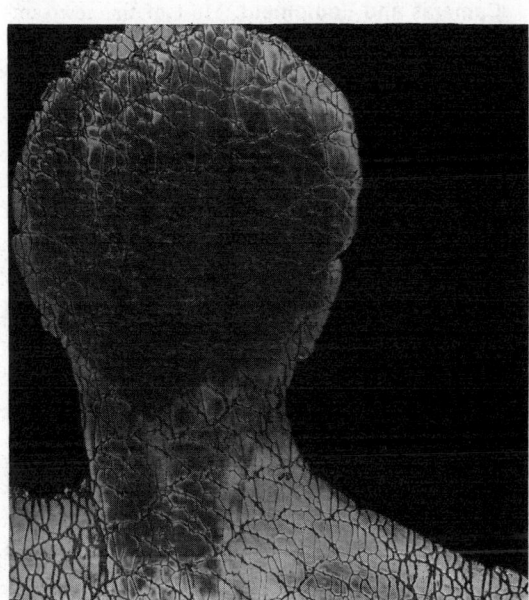

"Enmeshed Man," a photoengraved silver-plated copper plate with painted additions by Naomi Savage from the show "Photography as Printmaking" at the Museum of Modern Art, March 19–May 26, 1968.

COLLECTION, PETER C. BUNNELL, NEW YORK, COURTESY MUSEUM OF MODERN ART

emulsion speeds for the system ranging from ASA 6,000 to as high as ASA 25,000. This system was expected to find its major use in radiography, where the negative image is normal for its intended use.

Another new Polaroid material was a large-format packet for cameras measuring 8 × 10 in. and larger. When this material is used, the processed image is dry when removed from the camera and does not require coating.

Two new Polaroid colour materials were also shown during the year. Both of these were designed to produce transparencies rather than paper prints. No marketing date for the two was given; it was emphasized that the materials were still under development and that some colour deficiencies that were noted would be rectified before the material was made available. Polaroid also showed a new office copier using silver-coated paper. It was stated that the coating used only a very small quantity of silver and that the

Detail of the Avebury Stone Circle, Avebury, Eng., from Paul Caponigro's one-man show of recent photographs at the Museum of Modern Art, Oct. 8–Dec. 8, 1968.

difference in cost between this coated paper and plain white paper was very small.

Cameras and Equipment. Most of the new cameras marketed during 1968 were fairly conventional. Some did, however, add through-the-lens metering or microprism focusing to conventional single-lens reflex systems. A representative sample of this type of improvement was the new Leicaflex SL by Ernst Leitz, Wetzlar. In this camera the external photocell of the original Leicaflex was replaced by an internal one that reads the light transmitted by the lens.

Polaroid began marketing a new hand-held aerial camera, Model M-10, for instant reconnaissance pictures. It used the regular 3¼ × 4¼ in. Polaroid film packs, and the images develop outside the camera so that there is no delay in taking additional pictures.

Projection of slides and 8-mm. motion pictures was said to be greatly enhanced by the use of a new screen material developed by Kodak. During certain tests of narrow-angle materials, it was found that so-called "pack-rolled" aluminum foil, in which two sheets of aluminum are rolled into foil in contact with a lubricant between them, had a surface that acted as a

screen material in a highly desirable manner. The surface is composed of microscopic crystals randomly but regularly oriented, and the light reflectance of this material is highly uniform over an angle of from 15° to 25°, dropping off to very nearly zero at angles beyond that. A screen made of this material shows a very bright image over a viewing angle area of about 15°, with a light gain of as much as 11 times over a pure diffuser. The viewing angle can be increased to about 25° by curving the surface of the screen, to a radius of about 4.5 times the screen width. Because the screen has almost no diffusing power, any light striking it from outside the projection angle and viewing area is merely reflected to the opposite side, and the viewer does not receive it at all. The result is that a full, bright image can be produced on this material in a brightly lighted room, provided only that the ambient light comes from a direction differing from that of the projected image by at least 25°. Because of this critical angular reflectance, the material is quite sensitive to wrinkling, and the curved surface is essential if a reasonably large seating area for an audience is to be attained; these two factors rule out the possibility of making the new screen in a roll-up form. It seemed possible, however, that flat screens could be developed if the surface is formed into Fresnel-type elements.

Holography. L. H. Lin and K. S. Pennington of Bell Laboratories and G. W. Stroke and A. B. Lebeyrie of the University of Michigan devised a system for making multicolour holograms. They achieved this by combining two or more laser beams of different colours to form a single beam. Laser light for viewing is usually required where the original hologram is made with an angle of 30° to 90° between the main and reference beams. By increasing the angle between the two beams to 160°, however, it was found that "packing" of interference fringes in the emulsion of the negative is increased to the point where ordinary white light rather than laser light can be used for reconstruction; the resulting image is three dimensional and multicoloured.

Another type of hologram developed at Bell Laboratories allowed the viewer to see a three-dimensional image rotate through a full circle of 360° merely by moving his head sideways in front of the hologram. This hologram is made by exposing narrow strips of a photographic plate sequentially; after each exposure the exposing mask is shifted by an amount equal to its own width, while the object being photographed is rotated a fraction of a revolution. Adjustments are then made so that the exposure of the entire plate width is completed at the same time that the object has been rotated 360°. Such "flat" holograms can be viewed with a monochromatic filter and a strong white light source; laser viewing devices are not needed.

Photographic Exhibitions. The year was noted for a diversity of subject matter and methods of presenting photographic images included at exhibitions. The undercurrent of interest in collecting photographic prints and forming private collections was also more evident than during previous years.

"Photography as Printmaking," which was exhibited in several U.S. museums, was one of the most controversial shows of 1968, representing the century-old tradition of the fine and the unique (one of a kind) photographic print traced from 1842 to the present. The core concept of the show, as stated by show director Peter Bunnell, was ". . . photography as print-

making seeks to make the medium visible, whereas the so-called 'straight' approach seeks to make it invisible." This exhibition demonstrated the immense variety of photographic media currently available to photographers and all types of artists as a vehicle of expression. Techniques included letterpress, lithography, serialography, engraving, electrostatic image formation, and other hand and photomechanical techniques used singly and in multiple combinations.

"The Destruction of Lower Manhattan" by Danny Lyon at South Street Seaport Museum, New York City, was a show with a historic purpose: the preservation of Americana that would be lost without the photographic record. This show could set a trend in pictorial preservation of other historic areas that are being demolished throughout the United States for urban renewal and normal replacement.

Henri Cartier-Bresson's photographs of the preceding ten years and earlier were shown at the Museum of Modern Art in New York City. As usual, his work surmounted the technical limitations that prevent many photographers from achieving pictorial excellence. John Szarkowski, director of the museum's department of photography, mentioned that ". . . Cartier-Bresson discovered a new formal order that had been hidden within the flux of movement and change . . . and concerns himself first of all with the quality of ordinary life." Cartier-Bresson was one of the original users of 35-mm. photography and pioneered hand-held spontaneous exposures. He stated that photography "is at one and the same time the recognition of a fact in a fraction of a second and the rigorous arrangement in the forms visually perceived which give to that fact expression and significance."

The multiprojection presentation of contemporary social issues, "Conscience: The Ultimate Weapon," was based on photographs by Benedict J. Fernandez and opened at the George Eastman House in Rochester, N.Y. Nathan Lyons, the exhibition director, helped design the show to point out the photographer's personal observations as they related to the use and abuse of photographs to persuade and elicit response. Eleven projection units with 880 slides and 4 synchronized sound units were employed to create a thematic environmental experience.

"Eyewitness: Czechoslovakia, 1938—August, 1968" was a show to set a new precedent of "instant museumology," according to Oriol Farb, director of the Riverside Museum, New York City, joint sponsor of the show with the Fund for Concerned Photography. Jan Lukas, Sonja Bullaty, Angelo Lomeo, and Hilmar Pabel had, with their cameras, covered historic occurrences of the period and also the August 1968 Soviet occupation of Prague. The show was planned and presented within ten days after the event to serve as an eyewitness report.

The "Brassaï: Photographs" exhibition at the Museum of Modern Art contained 75 prints taken from 1932 to 1958. They included scenes of the city of Paris at night, showing its café life, its people, its scribbled walls, and its famous artists and poets. The photographer believes "The photograph has a double destiny. . . . It is the daughter of the world of externals, of the living second, and as such will always keep something of the historic or scientific document about it; but it is also the daughter of the rectangle, a child of the beaux arts, which requires one to fill up the space agreeably or harmoniously with black-and-white spots or colors."

The largest assemblage of photographs displayed during the year at one location was the more than 1,600 prints organized into various exhibits at the Photokina 1968 World Fair of Photography in Cologne. The exhibitions included "The Measure of All Things," which followed the idea of Heinz Haber, who through photography invaded the realms of very small and very large objects. Using man as a reference, the subjects ranged from atom traces 10^{-10} the size of a man to the Milky Way galaxy, 10^{10} the size of man. Karl Pawek's second world exhibition was built around the theme "Woman" and contained 525 prints that ". . . reveal feminine fascination as well as the drama of man in woman's existence." The "World Show of Youth Photography" displayed examples chosen from the work of approximately 10,000 photographers aged 25 or younger from 50 countries; its 275 photographs attempted to depict youth's picture of mankind's life together. "Youth Behind the Cine Camera" offered a theatre where young moviemakers demonstrated their ability. The display "Colour Avantgarde: Gene Laurents—Max Maxwell" produced some striking dynamic and static colour photographs that took everyday subjects and gave them emotional impact by means of dynamic composition and effective colour balance. The effect of the photographs was heightened by mounting them

COURTESY, THE MUSEUM OF MODERN ART

"Greek Island, c. 1963" from the show "Cartier-Bresson: Recent Photographs" at the Museum of Modern Art, June 25–Sept. 2, 1968.

on free-standing panels in a hallway, so that viewers had to thread their way among them.

An outstanding one-man show was by the young photographer Paul Caponigro, at the Museum of Modern Art. His photographs were described as possessing ". . . the depth of the artist's inspiration, the dignity of his seeing, and the lucidity of his craftsmanship," according to the show director. Caponigro's work is in the tradition of the so-called straightforward photographers: Minor White, Edward Weston, Paul Strand, and Alfred Stieglitz.

"Light 7," as directed by Minor White at the Hayden Gallery of the Massachusetts Institute of Technology, demonstrated different levels of light consciousness. Prints showing the recording of images and the manipulation of the medium or effects of light on a photosensitive material were represented. Attempts were made by White to establish standards of permanency for archival processing and handling of prints as an aid to museum and private collectors of fine photographic prints.

606

" 'Kiki' singing
in a Montparnasse cabaret,
1933" from the
retrospective exhibition
"Brassai: Photographs"
at the Museum of Modern
Art, Oct. 29, 1968–
Jan. 5, 1969.

COURTESY, THE MUSEUM OF MODERN ART

"The Circular Image" was a selection of 40 circular photographs displayed at George Eastman House and taken with the Kodak cameras No. 1 and No. 2 during 1888 to 1896. This format no doubt held a fascination for photographers of that era similar to the effect on today's photographers of fish-eye and extreme-wide-angle types of lenses.

Imogen Cunningham, in a one-man show at the Smithsonian Institution, Washington, D.C., was first in a series of exhibitions planned by Eugene Ostroff featuring women photographers. Miss Cunningham, now in her 80s, began exhibiting her work in 1912.

The husband-and-wife photography of Ruth-Marion Baruch and Pirkle Jones produced "The Black Panthers, a Photographic Essay" at the M. H. de Young Memorial Museum in Golden Gate Park, San Francisco. This group of 125 prints, 11 × 14 in. and 16 × 20 in., showed events and activities of this organization of U.S. Negro militants from July to October. The photographers moved freely, with the sanction of the organization's leaders, through Black Panther rallies and other events not normally photographed. (D. O. M.)

See also Astronautics; Cinema.

Physics

Particle Physics. Recent evidence seems to confirm that leptons are conserved. Results from C. S. Wu et al. (*Phys. Rev. Lett.*, vol. 26B, p. 112, 1967) in studies of double beta decays suggest that in all cases the two electrons emitted are accompanied by two neutrinos (as conservation theory requires).

New determinations of $g-2$, the anomalous magnetic moment for the muon and electron, show small departures from theoretically predicted values. The electron value reported by A. Rich (*Phys. Rev. Lett.*, vol. 20, p. 967, 1968) was lower; the muon value, reported by F. Farley at the 1968 Washington, D.C., American Physical Society (APS) meeting, is higher than theoretical. The latter discrepancy supports the idea that the muon may emit another photon-like particle, of spin I and large mass, that would affect the muon magnetic moment as observed.

Experiments by D. Dorfan et al. and by S. Bennett et al. (*Phys. Rev. Lett.*, vol. 19, 1967) seemed to imply that the phenomenological description of CP violation in K-meson decay was at last complete. However, two papers read at the Chicago APS meeting (*Physics Today*, April 1968) suggest that the ratio of the two-neutral-pion decay rate of K_2^0 to that of a similar decay in K_1^0 is still unknown.

Solid-State Physics. Until recently neutron diffraction was the only way of studying the spin systems of magnetic crystals. When the magnetic and chemical unit cells differ, additional lines in the diffraction pattern arise from scattering of the neutron spins by the unpaired electron spins. Similarly, there should be additional scattering of incident electrons by the unpaired electrons in a magnetic material; except for very low-velocity electrons, however, these reflections should be extremely weak. P. W. Palmberg et al. detected such "coherent exchange scattering" (*Phys. Rev. Lett.*, vol. 21, p. 682, 1968) from the surface of a nickel oxide crystal using a fluorescent screen to display the electron diffraction pattern. It was claimed that this experimental arrangement provides the most direct means for studying the role of spin exchange in electron scattering.

Yu. A. Osip'yan and I. B. Savchenko discovered that illumination increases the mechanical strength of Cds (*JETP Lett.*, vol. 7, p. 100, 1968). The effect is held to result from absorption of light energy; this may ionize atoms in the crystal to affect the ease of movement of lattice dislocations.

The Gunn effect (a source of electrical oscillations in the microwave region) previously has been produced by applying intense electric fields to GaAs, n-type Ge, or some polar semiconductors. Recent work at the IBM Watson Research Center by J. F. Smith, Jr., indicates that these oscillations can also be produced by applying pressures of the order of 10,000–20,000 atm. along the (III) axis in n-type Ge. The uniaxial stress is held to alter the conduction band, allowing electron transfer to higher energy levels.

Liquid Helium. H. A. Notarys has shown that a strong electric field applied to liquid helium can suppress the lambda point (*Phys. Rev. Lett.*, vol. 20, p. 258, 1968). The only previously known way to suppress it was to apply pressure. Perhaps the effect is attributable to electrostriction, in which the density of the liquid is greater in a region of high electric field; the lambda point thus should be lowered by the pressure increase.

C. M. Surko and F. Reif (*Phys. Rev. Lett.*, vol. 20, p. 582, 1968) have produced a previously unreported kind of neutral excitation in superfluid helium that travels centimetres without scattering. The excitation is believed to be a long-lived metastable state of the helium atom that finally is converted to electrons and He_2^+ ions.

Laser Physics. A first step in developing an X-ray counterpart of the laser is the construction of a

tunable X-ray resonator (proposed by R. M. J. Cotterill, *Appl. Phys. Lett.*, vol. 12, p. 403, 1968). The resonator consists of sets of single crystals placed so that the X rays can be reflected from crystal planes around closed paths by undergoing successive Bragg reflections. An even number of parallel pairs of crystal reflectors are used so that all the reflections are at the same Bragg angle and the whole resonator is in one plane. This system can be used over a range of wavelengths because the symmetry of the set is independent of the exact Bragg angle used. The resonator can be tuned by altering the temperature of the crystals to change the lattice spacing.

Self-induced transparency found with a ruby laser by E. L. Hahn and S. L. McCall (*Phys. Rev. Lett.*, vol. 18, p. 908, 1967) was verified by K. Patel and R. Slusher (*Phys. Rev. Lett.*, vol. 19, p. 1019, 1967). A short, intense pulse from a Q-switched CO_2 laser was applied to gaseous sulfur hexafluoride, making the gas transparent to 10.6 micron radiation. This technique would be useful for studying relaxation times of individual transitions in gases and gas mixtures.

General. V. Szebehely and C. F. Peters formulated a complete solution of the Pythagorean three-body problem (*Astron. J.* [U.S.], vol. 72, p. 876 and p. 1187, 1967). In the final configuration two of the bodies form a close binary system and the third moves away to infinity. More recently (*Bull. Astron.* [France], vol. 3, no. 1, 1968) these authors offer a generalization of their method to an *n*-body problem. This will have astronomical uses in the study of globular cluster development.

Papers by R. Davis *et al.* and by J. Bahcall *et al.* (*Phys. Rev. Lett.*, vol. 20, 1968) seriously question current ideas of how nuclear fusion produces solar luminosity. Bahcall estimates the neutrino flux on the earth at $5 \pm (3 \times 10^6)$ particles cm^2/sec. Davis found no neutrinos in excess of the background count of his apparatus, leading to an estimate of less than 2×10^6 particles cm^2/sec. These results lead one to infer that less than 9% of the solar energy is produced by the carbon-nitrogen cycle.　　(S. B. P.)

See also Astronautics; Astronomy; Chemistry; Electronics; Nuclear Energy.

ENCYCLOPÆDIA BRITANNICA FILMS. *Laws of Motion* (1952); *Archimedes' Principle* (1953); *Atomic Radiation* (1953); *Magnetism* (1953); *Atmospheric Pressure* (1955); *The Speed of Light* (1955); *Fuels—Their Nature and Use* (1958); *Electrons at Work* (1961); *Evidence for Molecules and Atoms* (1961); *Energy and Work* (1961); *Forces* (1961); *How to Bend Light* (1961); *How to Measure Time* (1961); *How to Produce Electric Current with Magnets* (1961); *Light and Color* (1961); *Magnetic, Electric and Gravitational Fields* (1961); *Vibrations* (1961); *Waves and Energy* (1961); *What Is Electric Current?* (1961); *What Is Space?* (1961); *What Is Uniform Motion?* (1961); *Molecular Theory of Matter* (1965).

Poland

A people's republic of Eastern Europe, Poland is bordered by the Baltic Sea, the U.S.S.R., Czechoslovakia, and East Germany. Area: 120,664 sq.mi. (312,500 sq.km.). Pop. (1968 est.): 32,065,000, including (1963 est.) Poles 30.7 million; Ukrainians 180,000; Belorussians 165,000; Jews 31,000; Slovaks 21,000; Russians 19,000; Lithuanians 10,000; Germans 3,000; Czechs 2,000; others 22,000. Cap. and largest city: Warsaw (pop., 1967 est., 1,272,200). Language: Polish. Religion: predomi-

Polish military troops crossing the Czechoslovakian border into Poland on Oct. 24, 1968, after assisting other Warsaw Pact nations in the occupation of Czechoslovakia.
WIDE WORLD

nantly Roman Catholic; Orthodox and Lutheran minorities. First secretary of the Polish United Workers' (Communist) Party in 1968, Wladyslaw Gomulka; chairman of the Council of State, Edward Ochab and, after April 11, Marshal Marian Spychalski; chairman of the Council of Ministers (premier), Jozef Cyrankiewicz.

The year began with the so-called "March incidents," which resulted in a violent campaign against the "revisionists" and "Zionists" within the ruling party ranks; following that there was Polish participation in the military occupation of Czechoslovakia by five member states of the Warsaw Treaty Organization; and the year ended with the fifth congress of the Polish United Workers' (Communist) Party (PZPR) coupled with celebrations of the 50th anniversary of the restoration of the Polish state.

In January the Warsaw National Theatre presented a new and successful production of *Forefathers' Eve*, a 19th-century patriotic drama by Adam Mickiewicz, Poland's national poet. Mickiewicz' anticzarist lines in the play became the occasion for expressions of anti-Soviet feelings. The government eventually decided to suspend performances of the play, and on January 30 approximately 100 students marched in protest from the theatre to the Mickiewicz monument. Claiming that the protest march had been organized by "revisionist" elements within the PZPR, the government expelled from Warsaw University two alleged ringleaders, the sons of prominent party members of Jewish origin. A month later the Warsaw branch of the Polish Writers' Union adopted a resolution condemning the "excesses of censorship," appealing for a genuine democratization of public life, and urging the government to authorize the revival of *Forefathers' Eve*. On March 8 about 4,000 students held a meeting at the Warsaw University campus, demanding the reinstatement of their two colleagues. Party activists and militia units tried to disperse them, and the demonstration became violent. In the following days students throughout the country joined their Warsaw colleagues, protesting against what they claimed were the biased press reports of the Warsaw incidents and demanding the freedom of speech and respect for civil rights guaranteed by the 1952 constitution. More than 1,800 students were subsequently arrested. Many were drafted into the Army or sentenced to short terms of imprisonment, and the rest—except for the alleged ringleaders—were released and allowed to continue their studies.

Speaking on March 12 to the important Warsaw party organization, Jozef Kepa, its first secretary, described the student demonstrations as a political movement engineered by the "revisionists." He mentioned some names, many of which belonged to the sons and daughters of party officials of Jewish extraction. A campaign identifying "revisionists" with "Zionists" started, supported by the Partisans led by Mieczyslaw Moczar, minister of the interior. Wladyslaw Gomulka, first secretary of the PZPR, tried to

Physiology:
see Medicine

Pipelines:
see Fuel and Power; Transportation

Planning, Economic:
see Economic Planning

Plastics Industry:
see Industrial Review

Poetry:
see Literature

POLAND

Education. (1965–66) Primary, pupils 5,176,-588, teachers 182,760; secondary, pupils 426,846, teachers 19,210; vocational, pupils 1,283,404, teachers 108,592; teacher training, pupils 78,378, teachers 5,994; higher (including 17 universities), students 251,864, teaching staff 22,960.

Finance. Monetary unit: zloty, with a foreign trade exchange of 4 zlotys to U.S. $1 (9.60 zlotys = £1 sterling) and a tourist rate of 24 zlotys to U.S. $1 (57.60 zlotys = £1). Budget (1967 est.): revenue 321 billion zlotys; expenditure 316 billion zlotys. National income (net material product): (1966) 567.2 billion zlotys; (1965) 531.3 billion zlotys. Cost of living (1963 = 100): (Dec. 1966) 104; (Dec. 1965) 104.

Foreign Trade. (1967) Imports 10,582,000,-000 zlotys; exports 10,108,000,000 zlotys. Import sources: U.S.S.R. 35%; East Germany 11%; Czechoslovakia 9%; U.K. 7%. Export destinations: U.S.S.R. 36%; Czechoslovakia 8%; East Germany 7%; U.K. 6%. Main exports: machinery, industrial and transport equipment 36%; raw materials 33%; agricultural products and foodstuffs 16%; consumer goods 15%.

Transport and Communications. Roads (1967) 272,725 km. (including 139 km. expressways). Motor vehicles in use (1967): passenger 331,893; commercial 212,669. Railways (1966) 26,739 km. (including 2,568 km. electrified); traffic (1967) 35,447,000,000 passenger-km., freight 88,543,000,000 net ton-km. Shipping (1967): merchant vessels 100 gross tons and over 421; gross tonnage 1,209,574. Air traffic (1966): 309,048,000 passenger-km.; freight 4,445,000 net ton-km. Telephones (Dec. 1966) 1,411,481. Radio receivers (Dec. 1966) 5,593,000. Television receivers (Dec. 1966) 2,540,000.

Agriculture. Production (in 000; metric tons; 1967; 1966 in parentheses): wheat 3,934 (3,-646); rye 7,691 (7,700); barley 1,420 (1,418); oats 2,802 (2,625); potatoes 48,574 (46,144); sugar, raw value (1967–68) c. 1,913, (1966–67) 1,684; rapeseed 650 (448); linseed (1966) 74, (1965) 77; dry peas (1966) 38, (1965) 61; apples (1966) 794, (1965) 200; onions (1966) 320, (1965) 325; tobacco (1966) 48, (1965) 52; flax fibre (1966) 56, (1965) 57; hemp fibre (1966) 20, (1965) 19; butter (1966) 193,

(1965) 178; beef and veal (1966) 426, (1965) 434; pork (1966) 1,312, (1965) 1,306. Livestock (in 000; June 1966): horses 2,590; cattle (June 1967) 10,768; pigs 14,251; sheep 3,164; chickens 132,500. Fish catch (in 000; metric tons) (1966) 335, (1965) 297.

Industry. Production (in 000; metric tons; 1967): coal 123,881; brown coal 23,922; coke (1966) 14,700; crude oil 450; natural gas 1,568,-000 cu.m.; electricity 51,227,000 kw-hr.; manufactured gas (1966) 6,308,000 cu.m.; iron ore (30% metal content) 3,077; pig iron 6,581; crude steel 10,450; zinc 196; copper 42; lead 45; cement 11,140; sulfuric acid 1,213; nitrogenous fertilizers (pure N; 1966) 462; superphosphates (1966) 1,485; passenger cars 28 units; commercial vehicles 36 units; cotton fabrics 824,000 m.; woolen fabrics 90,000 m.; rayon and synthetic fabrics 114,000 m. Merchant vessels launched (100 gross tons and over; 1967) 391,000 gross tons. New dwellings completed (1966) 175,800. Index of industrial production (1963 = 100): (1967) 140; (1966) 128.

stem the tide, and on March 19, in a nationally televised speech, attacked the "revisionists," while minimizing the "Zionist" influence among them. His appeal for moderation was ignored by the Warsaw and other provincial party organizations, and during the following three months a few hundred Polish and Jewish "revisionists," including government officials, party leaders, university professors, and journalists, were dismissed.

On July 9 in a speech at the plenary meeting of the party Central Committee Gomulka said that the anti-Zionist campaign had got out of hand. "There were many abuses," he went on, "which must be condemned. We should unmask revisionism, but not dress it in the name of Zionism." In current Communist terminology, revisionists were generally former Stalinists, who had become antisocialist or, at least, anti-government after Stalin's death.

On August 20–21, Polish divisions took part in the occupation of Czechoslovakia by the armed forces of five Warsaw Treaty Organization countries. The Polish units were directed to East Slovakia region. Their hostile reception by the population was not concealed by the Polish press. Speaking in Warsaw on August 31, Jozef Cyrankiewicz, the premier, explained why Poland agreed to send its divisions to Czechoslovakia. He said that in the haste of enacting their just reforms the Czechoslovak comrades had

Granite statue of Pope John XXIII, designed by Lodovica Nitsch, during the unveiling ceremony in Wroclaw. Although many priests attended the ceremony, the undertaking was generally opposed by the Polish Catholic hierarchy.

PATELLANI—PIX FROM PUBLIX

not foreseen the consequences; that is, that antisocialist forces, at home and abroad, had started a "peaceful, semisecret counterrevolution with the aim of wresting Czechoslovakia from the socialist camp." Thus, by the terms of this argument, Czechoslovakia's allies could not observe such antisocialist activities with indifference, especially as Czechoslovakia's geographic position was crucial from the point of view of common security. In general, the Poles approved this principle, but not all approved of the method of persuasion used and some protested publicly.

The fifth congress of the PZPR was held in Warsaw, November 11–16. There were 1,764 delegates representing more than two million members. About 40 Communist and Workers' parties from other nations were represented by their leaders, including Leonid Brezhnev, general secretary of the Communist Party of the Soviet Union. The Chinese, Yugoslav, Albanian, and Swedish parties were not invited. In his opening speech Gomulka insisted that the first condition of a purposeful leadership of a Communist party was to adhere staunchly to the Marxist-Leninist principles of democratic centralism at home and of proletarian internationalism in foreign policy.

The congress elected a new Central Committee of 91 members, including 36 newcomers and 91 deputy members. As the majority of the delegates represented the party's mainstream, faithful to Gomulka, it was not surprising that the elections of the new Politburo confirmed the first secretary in his office. Of the other 11 members of this policy-making body, Edward Ochab resigned in March and was replaced in July by Boleslaw Jaszczuk, a candidate member. Three other members disappeared from the Politburo after the November 16 election; Adam Rapacki, Eugeniusz Szyr, and Franciszek Waniolka. The newly elected members were: Stanislaw Kociolek, 35, secretary of Gdansk Province; Wladyslaw Kruczek, 57, secretary of Rzeszow Province; and Jozef Tejchma, 41, a secretary of the Central Committee.

On April 8 Ochab resigned from the chairmanship of the Council of State and three days later Marshal Marian Spychalski, minister of defense and a close friend of Gomulka, was elected as Ochab's successor. Lieut. Gen. Wojciech Jaruzelski, 45, former chief of staff, was appointed minister of defense. In December, in one of several governmental changes, Rapacki was replaced as foreign minister by Stefan Jedrychowski. (K. Sm.)

Police

Membership of the International Criminal Police Organization (Interpol) was 103 countries in 1968. At the General Assembly held in Teheran, Iran, during October 1–8, Paul Dickopf (W.Ger.) was elected president for a five-year term, succeeding F. Franssen (Belg.). J. Népote (France) remained secretary-general. The international increase in armed crime led to demands that regulations on the ownership and sale of firearms should be enforced and that national registries of those owning firearms should be established.

The second inter-American regional conference was held in Lima, Peru, Sept. 10–15, 1968. Symposia conducted by Interpol covered fingerprinting problems, international frauds, international police liaison by phototelegraphy, and road traffic offenses.

The work of most Interpol bureaus increased in 1967; 1,877 arrests resulted from cooperation between the bureaus. Between October 1967 and September 1968, the General Secretariat handled 5,711 cases leading to 231 arrests and supplied bureaus with 5,471 items of information; 453 persons were the subject of international notices. As in previous years, Interpol took a close interest in the work of the UN Commission on Narcotic Drugs and participated in two UN regional conferences on drugs, in New Delhi and Beirut. The organization also followed with great interest the treatment of offenders, took part in the Council of Europe's work on crime problems, met with experts in West Germany on the question of extradition, and was represented at the meeting of the International Air Transport Association (IATA) fraud-prevention group in Geneva.

Uprisings by students and youthful protesters presented problems for police throughout the world in 1968. In March, London police confronted thousands of anti-Vietnam demonstrators who hurled stones and steel pellets at the U.S. embassy. On October 27, however, when an estimated 50,000 marchers swarmed through London, fears of a major clash with police proved groundless. In Mexico City student agitation extended over many weeks. One of the bloodiest battles, on the night of September 24, resulted in several deaths and injury to dozens of policemen and students. Clashes in an area in the northwest part of the city raged for 12 hours before army reinforcements

aided police and restored order. It had been feared that students would attempt to disrupt the Olympic Games, but most of the agitation had ceased by October 12.

In Argentina in June police used tear gas to remove 400 students from La Plata National University. On September 25, in Lima, Peru, tear-gas barrages and water cannon were used to disperse angry bands of youthful demonstrators as a large police force maintained guard on the city's thoroughfares. In June, during three days of student disorders, the U.S. embassy in Rio de Janeiro was stoned and rioters fought police. In Tokyo, on September 4, policemen broke through barricades of desks and chairs to end a three-month sit-in by 100 students at Nihon University. On August 16, 1968, the Manila police fired in the air to disperse 300 students who stormed a police cordon around the U.S. embassy. Feelings ran high following the killing of a Filipino who had strayed into a U.S. military base.

Following a police-student clash in Warsaw on March 8, students held sympathy meetings in eight Polish cities. In Paris violence broke out in May as rebellious students and other youths clashed with the police. On May 24, thousands of police fought with tens of thousands of students supported by some workers. In Belgrade, Yugos., more than 1,000 students battled policemen in the streets in June. Students were occupying the administration building of the University of Belgrade and threatened to hold it until their demands for educational and economic reforms were met. The University of Madrid was closed on March 28 following student disturbances and was reopened on May 6. New disturbances broke out later and on May 16, 800 students shouting slogans against the government stoned police.

In Rome policemen and students clashed in March, as a result of nationwide agitation for university reform. In June the police had to break up a battle between opposing factions of Rome University students. In West Germany students headed massive demonstrations for several days in April. Chancellor Kurt Georg Kiesinger warned of tougher police measures as left-wing protesters continued to demonstrate in many cities. About 200 leftist students armed themselves with clubs as they occupied the Free University of Brussels in May. Policemen and students clashed in Istanbul in July following a visit to Turkey by a unit of the U.S. 6th Fleet.

North America. *United States.* Civil disorders continued to present major problems to police through-

Left, police battling antiwar protesters near the Conrad Hilton Hotel in Chicago, Aug. 28, 1968, during the week of the Democratic national convention. Below, Chicago policeman displaying weapons allegedly taken from demonstrators.

WIDE WORLD

Special antiriot equipment was being acquired by police departments in many cities: left, Los Angeles County sheriff's M8 armoured car; above, new helmets issued to New York City police protect face and neck; right, face mask and plastic shield used by Montreal's police department; far right, Victoria, Austr., policeman wearing armour that can stop a .32 calibre bullet fired from 10 ft.

out the U.S. in 1968. A national survey revealed that 41% of the municipalities with populations over 100,-000 had racial disturbances in 1967. To meet anticipated crises in 1968, conferences on civil disorders for chiefs of police and their city managers or mayors were conducted in Washington by the International Association of Chiefs of Police at the behest of U.S. Attorney General Ramsey Clark, and were followed by regional sessions for police captains and watch commanders. Many police departments purchased added equipment; one manufacturer reported that over 3,000 agencies purchased the Mace spray gun.

Following the assassination of civil-rights leader the Rev. Martin Luther King, Jr., in Memphis, Tenn., on April 4, violence erupted in many cities and the police were overwhelmed. Particularly hard hit were Washington, Baltimore, and Chicago. In Chicago, 5,000 federal troops and 6,700 Illinois National Guardsmen were dispatched to aid police. Mayor Richard J. Daley was publicly critical of the Chicago Police Department for having failed to take more aggressive action when the rioting started. His announcement on April 15 that, in the future, the Chicago police were instructed to "shoot to kill" arsonists and "shoot to maim" looters received nationwide publicity, was vigorously denounced by civil-rights leaders, and subsequently was modified. The 46 deaths that occurred nationally during April made it the worst month of rioting in recent years with the exception of July 1967, when 81 persons were killed.

By the middle of July serious racial disturbances had occurred in 211 cities. During the summer months of June, July, and August, however, there was a significant decline in the number and severity of riots: 19 deaths were recorded, as compared with 87 during the same period in 1967; National Guard assistance was required 6 times (18 the previous summer).

A study by the National Students Association revealed that from Jan. 1 to June 15, 1968, there were 221 major demonstrations at 101 colleges and universities. Involved were 38,911 persons, or 2.6% of the students enrolled in the institutions studied. In 59 instances a college or university building was taken over. The study did not include Columbia University, scene of one of the most serious uprisings.

The biggest confrontation between police and demonstrators occurred during the Democratic national

convention in Chicago, August 26–29. Thousands of dissidents flocked to Chicago to protest against the war in Vietnam, the Democratic administration, and the "establishment." Leaders of some of the groups announced that plans were made to disrupt the convention and paralyze the city. Before the convention, television newscasts showed groups practicing tactics they intended to use if violence erupted. Prominent leaders of these groups were Jerry Rubin of the Youth International Party (Yippies), Tom Hayden of the Students for a Democratic Society, and David Dellinger of the National Mobilization Committee to End the War in Vietnam. Dellinger organized a Chicago project committee with Rennie Davis as one leader. Literature distributed before the convention referred to the police as "pigs" and announced that the police would be shown up "as the brutes they are."

In anticipation of trouble, a barricade was placed around the Amphitheatre, in which the convention was to be held. The National Guard was called in and federal troops were flown to Chicago and kept in a state of readiness. Chicago's police force was placed on a 12-hour shift. Confrontations between police and protest demonstrators were numerous, the most serious occurring near the Conrad Hilton Hotel.

During the disorders, 198 Chicago police officers were injured, including victims of tear gas. Persons arrested totaled 641. Television cameras recorded many instances of clubbings by police but the police claimed that acts of provocation were not shown. Mayor Daley backed the action of the police department and, on September 6, issued a supporting white paper entitled "The Strategy of Confrontation." Investigations of the disorders were initiated by the FBI, a federal grand jury, the President's Commission on the Causes and Prevention of Violence, and the House Committee on Un-American Activities. Late in the year the President's Commission published a report on the convention disorders compiled for it by a study group headed by Chicago attorney Daniel Walker. The report detailed instances of provocation on the part of the demonstrators and of excessive reaction on the part of the police. The greatest controversy was created by a statement in the summary, written by Walker, that characterized the violence as a "police riot."

In most of the major confrontations between police

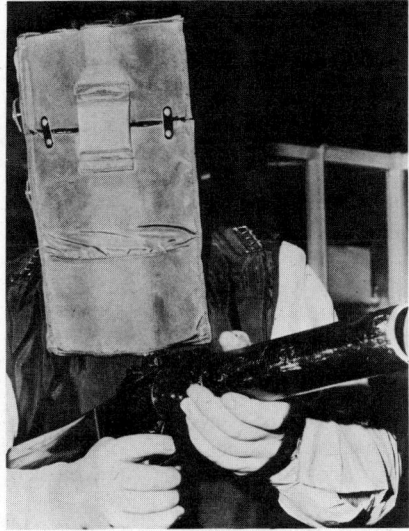

CENTRAL PRESS FROM PICTORIAL PARADE

and protest groups, there were charges of police brutality. There were also numerous charges of police underreaction—failures to make arrests or take action. Receiving considerably less attention, however, was the growing violence against law officers. The FBI *Uniform Crime Reports* revealed that 76 law-enforcement officers were killed by criminal action in 1967, as compared with the annual average of 48 for 1960–66. Assaults on police officers increased 11% in 1967 to 26,755.

Assaults on police in 1968 included the attack on August 2 on two men answering an emergency call in the Crown Heights section of Brooklyn. Assailants hidden in bushes opened fire with shotguns. Two days later, a bomb exploded inside a police call box in Jackson Heights. In Orlando, Fla., on February 11, a man remarked to a bystander, "Watch this." He then shot a policeman between the eyes, killing him. In attempting to flee, the assailant, who later described his occupation as "thief," wrecked two automobiles. In Washington on July 2, two officers were shot when attempting to arrest a Negro for disorderly conduct. A militant organization, the Black United Front, adopted a resolution stating that the slaying of the "honky cop" was "justifiable homicide." In Cleveland, on the night of July 23, five men described as black nationalists opened fire on a police task force car and riddled it with bullets. In the sniper battle that followed on Cleveland's East Side, three officers were killed. In Pittsburgh a patrolman was attacked, his wife beaten, and his home damaged by a mob on June 16. The Fraternal Order of Police filed a petition with the city Human Relations Commission charging a Negro group with brutality against a policeman.

Notwithstanding the growing demands for police services, the personnel strength of U.S. police departments remained almost static. In 1967, 3,596 cities having a population of 112,760,000 had a total of 227,008 police employees, or two employees per 1,000 inhabitants. Excluding civilian employees, the number of police per 1,000 inhabitants was 1.8. On the average, during 1967, 11.8% of all city police employees were civilians, up from 11% in 1966.

Recruitment was a major problem in many cities. In June Attorney General Clark, calling on U.S. mayors to raise police standards and salaries, asserted that "the average rookie policeman makes less than what the government says is necessary to support a family of four." Fact-finding panels and patrolmen's associations called for pay raises in many cities. Policemen employed picket lines, strike threats, and wild-cat strikes to dramatize their demands.

Many departments recognized the need for greater representation from minority groups. In Detroit a 20-man recruiting team, including 16 Negroes, was formed and, in a general revision of recruitment standards, arrest or conviction for a felony was removed as a disqualification for appointment, providing criminal records were expunged by a court.

The New Jersey State Department of Community Affairs allocated $35,000 to finance a plan to recruit at least 90 Negroes and Puerto Ricans for the Newark Police Department and provide them with jobs while preparing them for entrance tests. A similar program, begun in New York City in 1966, was reduced to one-fifth its original size in 1968 because of the large number of dropouts in the program and a reduction of federal funds backing it.

Also in effect was a U.S. Army program allowing police authorities to visit military bases to interview and sign up applicants. Attorney General Clark reported in April that during the preceding 30 months, the Law Enforcement Assistance Act (LEA) had provided about $19 million to 330 projects throughout the U.S. and its possessions. The American Telephone and Telegraph Co. announced an intention of gradually establishing 911 as an emergency telephone number throughout the country. On July 1, New York became the first major city to employ the three-digit emergency number.

Canada. The Montreal Police Department formed an antiriot squad following serious disorders on St. Jean Baptiste Day, June 24, 1968. Plastic shields, long batons, and face masks were acquired and 450 men were to be trained in riot-control methods. Two members of the Penticton detachment of the Royal Canadian Mounted Police were removed from the force following a series of thefts from a number of businesses in Alberta. (V. W. P.)

Europe. *United Kingdom.* Police strength in England and Wales at the end of 1968 had increased to 92,000, the highest total ever. There were 1,207,354 offenses during 1967, an increase of 0.6% over 1966 but a marked improvement on the 5.8% increase for 1966 over 1965. The introduction of pocket radio sets and the wider use of vehicles provided an effective interchange of information and improved efficiency. Police amalgamation plans continued. It was expected that by April 1969 the number of police forces in England and Wales would have been reduced from 105 to 47.

A national crime-prevention campaign was launched by the Home Office in February on the lines of a similar 1966–67 campaign, and steps were taken to encourage forces to set up local crime prevention organizations. With the cooperation of the Society of Motor Manufacturers and Traders, the principal motor manufacturers and importers undertook to fit an anti-theft locking device to all new models of cars and pickup trucks by Jan. 1, 1970. With art theft remaining a major concern, the Art Theft Squad, attached to the Interpol section of New Scotland Yard, was revitalized early in 1968. Information on stolen art works was to be published in the *Arts Review,* a periodical bought by most dealers.

In 1968 recruitment to Scottish forces remained good, and on August 31 the strength of Scottish

forces was 9,902 men and 386 women, an increase of 141 men and a decrease of 7 women over 1967. Greater use was made of civilians to release police officers for more important duties. After successful pilot experiments the "unit beat policing" system was extended by some forces to all suitable parts of their areas. The Scottish Crime Squad, a new investigation and intelligence agency, was established on August 5. Amalgamations reduced the number of Scottish forces from 25 to 22. Procedures to amalgamate the forces of Caithness, Orkney, and Zetland were under way.

France. Reforms proposed in the law of July 9, 1966, began on January 1 with the amalgamation of the National Criminal Investigation Department and the Prefecture of Police. Police training facilities were expanded and the structure of the Central Public Security Services changed to place both the urban police and the CRS (*Compagnies républicaines de sécurité—*riot police) under the same authority. The reorganization of General Intelligence and the Judicial Police was due by the end of 1968. In the regional services, the Prefecture of Police was amalgamated with the National Police, to become an external state service with particular emphasis on the maintenance of order in Paris. Other reforms created a homogeneous police structure for the whole Paris region.

The events of May and June 1968 led the government to propose increasing police strength in the 1969 budget. Priority would go to mobile forces, such as the CRS and the "intervention units" of the Prefecture of Police.

West Germany. Traffic violations, previously considered punishable acts in West Germany, were transformed into cases of "disorderly conduct." Policemen were empowered to impose and collect "warning fees" not exceeding DM. 20. The number of crimes and offenses, excluding crimes against state security and traffic offenses, increased 8.2% over 1967. Among the causes of the spring student protests was an amendment to the Basic Law that enabled the federal government under certain conditions of extreme disorder to use border police, and even the Army, for police functions.

Italy. To synchronize police activities in each field and throughout Italy, in 1967 the police administration set up Criminalpol (the National Centre for the Coordination of Criminal Police Operations). The Technical Evidence and Documentation Section used specially equipped squads to carry out collection of evidence and registration of every sort. A central bureau for stolen cars began operation.

Scandinavia. In 1967, Norway's 5,000 police dealt with 51,400 criminal cases, a 6% increase over the previous year. Offenses against public order, malicious damage, and larcenies showed the largest rises. The Investigation Unit of the Criminal Police headquarters in Oslo completed its first full year of operation. The abuse of narcotic drugs further increased and appeared to spread to smaller towns; branches of an international distribution system were uncovered. The largest case of illicit traffic in alcohol since World War II was revealed. Most of the alcohol originated in East Germany and Poland and was carried by fast-moving fishing craft to ports in Norway.

In Sweden clashes with demonstrators against the Vietnam war and against South Africa and Rhodesia (particularly at Båstad in May, during the Davis Cup tennis matches) brought accusations of police brutality. Nevertheless, an opinion poll revealed that 92% of those asked thought that the police were "usually

very friendly." Of those in urban areas, 73% thought that more police should be recruited—reflecting possibly a noticeable increase in armed robbery and street violence.

The Danish police force would face an acute manpower problem in the near future, as 50% of the entire force was recruited in the 1939–45 period. A committee was appointed during 1968 to consider this problem. Despite an overall increase in crime, sexual crimes decreased by more than 20%. This might prove to be related to the legitimization of pornography in 1967.

U.S.S.R. Complaints multiplied in 1968 about the People's Brigade, the large volunteer police force (numbering six million in 1968) recruited from workers, peasants, and students mainly to deal with drunkenness and delinquency. A denunciation of their overzealous activities appeared in *Komsomolskaya Pravda* in February. It was claimed, however, that crime in general had decreased spectacularly. Militia bodies were increasingly using new techniques, and the scientific organization of work had been started.

Oceania. During 1968, the increase in crime noted in Australia in recent years continued unabated. There was particular concern about the rise in armed robberies and in offenses committed by juveniles. A special parliamentary committee was established to investigate pack rape by juveniles. Australian police forces renewed their search for new methods of crime detection and prevention, including the use of computers.

Like other countries, Australia witnessed many public protests and demonstrations resulting in violent clashes between the police and demonstrators. Following a special university study that revealed that only 65% of the population had great respect for the police, attempts to improve police public relations in traffic-law enforcement were made.   (X.)

See also Crime; Law; Prisons and Penology; Race Relations; United States.

Encyclopædia Britannica Films. *The Policeman* (3rd ed., 1966).

Army helicopter dropping chemical riot control agents during a special demonstration at Ft. Belvoir, Va., for military and civilian police officials.

Political Parties

The following table is intended to provide a general world guide to political parties. All countries that were independent on Dec. 1, 1968, are included, but there are a number for which no analysis of political activities is given. Some of these cases are explained in the notes at the foot of the table.

Parties are included in most instances only if represented in parliaments (in the lower house in bicameral legislatures), but the figures in the last column of the table do not necessarily add up to the total number of seats in parliament because independents and certain small political groupings are sometimes omitted. The date of the most recent general election follows the name of the country.

The code letters in the affiliation column show the relative political position of the parties within each country; there is, therefore, no entry in this column for single-party states. There are obvious difficulties involved in labeling parties within the political spectrum of a given country. The key chosen is as follows: F—fascist; ER—extreme right; R—right; CR—centre right; C—centre; L—non-Marxist left; SD—social-democratic; S—socialist; EL—extreme left; and K—communist.

The percentages in the column "Voting strength" indicate proportions of the valid votes cast for the respective parties, or the number of registered voters who went to the polls in single-party states.

COUNTRY AND NAME OF PARTY	Affiliation	Voting strength	Parliamentary representation
Afghanistan (1965)			
Royal government with an elected House of the People (Wolesi Jirga)	—	—	216
Albania (1966)			
Albanian Labour (Communist)	—	99.99%	214
Algeria			
Military government since June 19, 1965	—	—	—
Andorra			
No parties*	—	—	24
Argentina			
Military government since June 28, 1966	—	—	—
Australia (1966)			
Country (Conservative)	R	...	21
Liberal	CR	...	61
Democratic Labor (DLP)	C	...	—
Australian Labor (ALP)	L	...	41
Austria (1966)			
Freiheitliche Partei Österreichs	R	5.4%	6
Österreichische Volkspartei	C	48.4%	85
Sozialistische Partei Österreichs†	SD	42.6%	74
Barbados (1966)			
Barbados National Party	R	...	2
Democratic Labour Party	C	...	14
Barbados Labour Party	L	...	8
Belgium (1968)			
Volksunie (Flemish)	R	9.8%	20
Parti pour la Liberté et le Progrès	CR	20.9%	47
Parti Social-Chrétien	C	31.7%	69
Parti Socialiste Belge	SD	28.0%	59
Parti Communiste Belge	K	3.3%	5
Bhutan			
No parties‡	—	—	130
Bolivia (1966)			
Frente de la Revolución Boliviana	R	79.7%	82
Comunidad Demócrata Cristiana	C	16.2%	19
Movimiento Revolucionario Paz-Estenssorista	L	...	1
Botswana (1965)			
Botswana Democratic Party	C	...	28
Botswana People's Party	L	...	3
Brazil (1966)			
Aliança Renovadora Nacional§	—	...	409
Bulgaria (1966)			
Bulgarian Communist / Agrarian Union / Nonparty } Fatherland Front	—	99.8%	416
Burma			
Military government since March 2, 1962	—	—	—

COUNTRY AND NAME OF PARTY	Affiliation	Voting strength	Parliamentary representation
Burundi			
Military government since Nov. 28, 1966	—	—	—
Cambodia			
Royal government with a single party	—	...	77
Cameroon (1965)			
Union Nationale Camérounaise	—	...	50
Canada (1968)			
Social Credit	R	0.7%	—
Progressive Conservative	CR	31.4%	72
Liberal	C	45.5%	155
Rassemblement des Créditistes	C	4.8%	14
New Democratic	L	16.7%	22
Central African Republic			
Military government since Jan. 1, 1966	—	—	—
Ceylon (1965)			
United National	R	41.1%	66
Sri Lanka Freedom	CR	31.4%	41
Federal (Tamil)	C	5.6%	14
Lanka Sama Samaja (Trotskiist)	SD	8.2%	10
Mahajana Eksath Peramuna	S	3.0%	2
Communist	K	2.8%	4
Chad (1963)			
Union pour le Progrès du Tchad	—	99%	75
Chile (1965)			
Partido Conservador	R	5.6%	3
Partido Liberal	CR	7.7%	6
Partido Radical	C	14.1%	20
Partido Demócrata-Cristiano	C	45.0%	82
Partido Democrático-Nacional	L	3.6%	3
Partido Socialista Chileno	S	10.9%	15
Partido Comunista del Chile	K	13.0%	18
China, People's Republic of			
Communist (Kungchan-tang)	—	—	—
China (Taiwan), Republic of			
Nationalist (Kuomintang)	—	—	773
Colombia (1968)			
Alianza Nacional Popular	R	...	38
Partido Conservador	R }	...	} 141
Partido Liberal	C }	...	
Congo (Kinshasa), Dem. Rep. of			
Military government since Nov. 25, 1965	—	—	—
Congo (Brazzaville), Rep. of			
Military government since September 1968	—	—	—
Costa Rica (1966)			
Partido de Liberación Nacional	R	...	28
Partido de Unificación Nacional	C	...	27
Unión Cívica Revolucionaria	L	...	2
Cuba			
Partido Comunista de Cuba	—	—	—
Cyprus			
Civil war since December 1963	—	—	—
Czechoslovakia (1964)			
Communist / Socialist / People's } National Front	—	99.9%	300
Dahomey			
On July 28, 1968, a popular referendum approved the appointment by the Revolutionary Military Committee of a civilian president of the republic	—	—	—
Denmark (1968)			
Conservative	R	20.4%	37
De Uafhaengige (Independents)	R	0.5%	—
Venstre (Agrarian)	C	18.6%	34
Centre (Liberal)	C	1.3%	—
Radical-Liberal	C	15.0%	27
Social Democratic	SD	34.0%	62
Socialist People's	S	6.1%	11
Communist	K	1.0%	—
Left Socialists	—	2.0%	4
Dominican Republic (1966)			
Partido Reformista	R	...	48
Partido Revolucionario Dominicano	C	...	26
Ecuador (1968)			
Alianza Popular	R	...	...
Izquierda Democrática	L	...	...
El Salvador (1966)			
Partido de Conciliacion Nacional	R	60.0%	31
Partido Demócrata Cristiano	C	28.8%	15
Partido Acción Renovadora	C	7.7%	4
Partido Popular Salvadoreño	L	1.8%	1
Equatorial Guinea (1968)			
Movimiento por Unión Nacional de Guiné Ecuadorial (MUNGE) }			
Idea Popular de Guiné Ecuadorial (IPGE) }	—	...	35
Movimiento Nacional por Liberación de Guiné Ecuadorial (MONALIGE) }			
Ethiopia (1965)			
Imperial government with an elected Yeheg Memria (lower chamber)	—	—	250
Finland (1966)			
Kansallinen Kokoomus Poulue (Cons.)	R	13.8%	26
Svenskapartiet	R	6.0%	12
Keskusliitto (Centre)	C	21.1%	49
Kansan Poulue (Liberal)	C	6.5%	9
Sosialidemokraatinen Poulue	SD	27.7%	55
Communist-controlled SKDL‖	K	21.1%	41

COUNTRY AND NAME OF PARTY	Affili-ation	Voting strength	Parlia-mentary represen-tation
France (1968)			
Extreme right	ER	0.2%	—
Gaullists¶	CR	38.1%	292
Independent Republicans	CR	5.1%	61
Centre Démocrate⁹	C	10.8%	33
Fédération de la Gauche Démocrate et Socialiste	L	18.0%	57
Parti Socialiste Unifié	EL	4.1%	10
Parti Communiste Français	K	22.1%	34
Gabon (1964)			
Bloc Démocratique Gabonais	—	—	31
Opposition (2 parties)	—	—	16
Gambia, The (1966)			
People's Progressive Party	C	...	24
United Party	L	...	8
German Democratic Republic (1967)			
Sozialistische Einheitspartei Christlich-Demokratische Union National-Demokratische Partei Liberal-Demokratische Partei Demokratische Bauernpartei	National Front	98.82%	434
Germany, Federal Republic of (1965)			
Christlich-Demokratische Unionð	R	47.6%	245
Freie Demokratische Partei	C	9.5%	49
Sozialdemokratische Partei Deutschlands	SD	39.3%	202
Ghana			
Military government since Feb. 24, 1966	—	—	—
Greece			
Military government since April 21, 1967	—	—	—
Guatemala (1966)			
Movimiento de Liberación Nacional	R	...	...
Partido Revolucionario	C	54%	30
Partido Institucional Democrático	C	...	...
Guinea (1968)			
Parti Démocratique de Guinée	—	—	75
Guyana (1968)			
People's National Congress	C	...	30
United Force	L	...	4
People's Progressive Party	EL	...	19
Haiti			
Presidential dictatorship since 1957	—	—	—
Honduras (1965)			
Partido Nacional	R	...	35
Partido Liberal	C	...	29
Hungary (1967)			
Hungarian Socialist Workers' National Peasant Party Smallholders' Party	Patriotic People's Front	99.7%	349
Iceland (1967)			
Independence (Conservative)	R	37.5%	23
Progressive	C	28.1%	18
Social-Democratic	SD	15.7%	9
United People's Socialist	K	17.6%	10
India (1967)			
Jan Sangh (Hindu Nationalist)	ER	...	35
Swatantra (Freedom)	R	...	42
Dravida Munnetra Kazhagam□	R	...	25
Indian National Congress	C	...	281
Praja Socialist	SD	...	13
Samyukta Socialist	S	...	23
Communist (pro-Soviet)	K	...	23
Communist (pro-Chinese)	K	...	19
Indonesia			
Military government since Oct. 1, 1965	—	—	—
Iran (1967)			
Iran Novin (New Iran)	R	...	180
Mardom (People's) Party	C	...	20
Pan-Iranian Party	C	...	5
Iraq			
Military governments since 1958	—	—	—
Ireland (1965)			
Fianna Fail (Sons of Destiny)	C	...	72
Fine Gael (United Ireland)	C	...	47
Labour	L	...	22
Israel (1965)			
Gahal (Herut and Liberal)	R	...	26
National Religious	R	...	11
Agudat Israel	C	...	4
Poalei Agudat Israel	C	...	2
Independent Liberal	C	...	5
Mapai (Israeli Labour)	L	...	45
Rafi (Ben-Gurion's splinter group)	L	...	10
Mapam (United Workers')	S	...	8
Communist (pro-Israel)	K	...	1
Communist (pro-Soviet)	K	...	3
Italy (1968)			
Movimento Sociale Italiano	F	4.5%	24
Partito Democratico Italiano di Unitá Monarchica	R	1.3%	6
Partito Liberale Italiano	CR	5.8%	31
Partito Democrazia Cristiana	C	39.1%	266
Partito Socialista Italiano	SD	14.5%	91
Partito Socialista Italiano di Unitá Proletaria◇	EL	4.5%	23
Partito Comunista Italiano	K	26.9%	177
Südtiroler Volkspartei		...	3
Ivory Coast (1960)			
Parti Démocratique de la Côte d'Ivoire	—	...	85
Jamaica (1967)			
Jamaica Labour Party	L	...	33
People's National Party	L	...	20

COUNTRY AND NAME OF PARTY	Affili-ation	Voting strength	Parlia-mentary represen-tation
Japan (1967)			
Komeito▲	ER	5.38%	25
Liberal-Democratic	CR	48.80%	277
Democratic Socialist	SD	7.40%	30
Socialist	S	27.89%	140
Communist	K	4.76%	5
Jordan			
Royal government, no parties	—	—	60
Kenya (1963)			
Kenya African National Union	—	—	171
Korea, Republic of (1967)			
Democratic Republican Party	R	...	130
New Korea Party	C	...	44
Taejung Dang (Party of the Masses)	EL	...	1
Korea, People's Democratic Republic of (1967)			
Korean Workers' (Communist) Party	...	100%	300
Kuwait			
Princely government	—	—	30
Laos (1965)⁺			
Independents	R	...	27
Neutralist Party	C	...	13
Social Democrats	L	...	11
Rally of the Lao Party	EL	...	8
Lebanon (1964)			
Chamber of Deputies elected by universal suffrage according to the proportional division between Christians and Muslims	—	—	99
Lesotho (1965)			
Lesotho National Party	CR	41.6%	31
Lesotho Congress Party	C	39.6%	25
Marematlou Freedom Party	L	16.4%	4
Liberia (1968)			
True Whig Party	—	...	41
Libya (1968)			
Royal government, no political parties but members of the Chamber of Deputies are elected	—	...	91
Liechtenstein (1966)			
Vaterländische Union	CR	42.6%	7
Fortschrittliche Bürgerpartei	C	48.5%	8
Christlich-Soziale Partei	C	8.9%	—
Luxembourg (1968)			
Parti Chrétien-Social	CR	35.3%	21
Parti Libéral	C	16.6%	11
Parti Ouvrier Socialiste	SD	32.3%	18
Parti Communiste	K	15.5%	6
Malagasy Republic (1965)			
Parti Social-Démocrate	C	...	104
Malagasy Independence Party	L	...	3
Malawi (1964)			
Malawi Congress Party	CR	...	50
Malawi Constitutional Party	L	...	3
Malaysia			
Republican constitution adopted following plebiscite in March 1968			
Maldive Islands (1965)			
Government by the Didi family	—	...	54
Mali			
Military government since Nov. 19, 1968	—	—	—
Malta (1966)			
Nationalist Party	R	...	28
Malta Labour Party	SD	...	22
Mauritania (1965)			
Parti du Peuple Mauritanien	—	92%	40
Mauritius (1967)			
Independence Party (Indian-dominated)	C	...	39
Parti Mauricien Social-Démocrate	L	...	23
Mexico (1967)			
Partido Acción Nacional	CR	...	12
Partido Revolucionario Institucional	L	90%	189
Partido Auténtico de la Révolución Mexicana	L	...	3
Partido Popular Socialista	S	...	6
Monaco (1968)			
Union Nationale et Démocratique	—	...	18
Mongolia (1967)			
Mongolian People's Revolutionary Party	—	99%	295
Morocco			
Royal government since June 8, 1965	—	—	—
Nauru (1968)			
No political parties	—	...	18
Nepal			
Royal government since December 1960	—	—	—
Netherlands (1967)			
Staatkundig Gereformeerde Partij	R	2.01%	3
Boerenpartij (Farmers' Party)	R	4.77%	7
Anti-Revolutionaire Partij	CR	9.90%	15
Christelijk Historische Unie	CR	8.15%	12
Katholieke Volkspartij	C	26.51%	42
"Democraten '66"	C	4.46%	7
Volkspartij voor Vrijheid en Democratie	C	10.74%	17
Partij van de Arbeid	SD	23.55%	37
Pacifistisch Socialistische Partij	S	2.68%	4
Communistische Partij	K	3.61%	5
New Zealand (1966)			
National (Conservative)	CR	43.4%	44
Social Credit Party	C	14.7%	1
Labour Party	L	41.5%	35
Nicaragua (1967)			
Partido Liberal Nacionalista (Somoza)	R	...	36
Partido Conservador Tradicionalista	R	...	15
Partido Demócrata Cristiano	C	...	2
Partido Liberal Independenta	C	...	1
Niger (1965)			
Parti Progressiste Nigérien	—	...	50

COUNTRY AND NAME OF PARTY	Affili-ation	Voting strength	Parlia-mentary represen-tation
Nigeria			
Military governments since Jan. 15, 1966; civil war since May 30, 1967	—	—	—
Norway (1965)			
Høyre (Conservative)	R	20.1%	31
Kristelig Folkeparti	CR	7.8%	13
Senterpartiet (Agrarian)	CR	9.4%	18
Venstre (Liberal)	C	10.1%	18
Arbeiderpartiet (Labour)	SD	43.3%	68
Sosialistisk Folkeparti	S	6.0%	2
Norges Kommunistiske Parti	K	1.4%	—
Pakistan (1965)			
Conventionist Muslim League	—	...	118
Combined opposition	—	...	32
Panama			
Presidential elections in May 1968 were followed by a military coup			
Paraguay (1967)			
Partido Colorado (Stroessner)	R	69.4%	80
Partido Liberal Radical	C	21.5%	29
Partido Liberal	C	6.2%	8
Partido Revolucionario (Febrerista)	SD	2.8%	3
Peru (1963)			
Unión Nacional Odriista	R	...	23
Partido Acción Popular	C	...	48
Partido Demócrata-Cristiano	C		
Partido del Pueblo[e]	L	...	57
Philippines (1965)			
Partido Nacionalista	R	...	65
Partido Liberal	CR	...	39
Poland (1965)			
Polska Zjednoczona Partia Robotnicza			255
Zjednoczone Stronnictwo Ludowe	—	96.5%	117
Stronnictwo Demokratyczne			39
Nonparty			49**
Portugal (1965)			
União Nacional	—	...	130
Romania (1965)			
Partidul Comunist Romîn	—	99.8%	465
Nonparty			
Rwanda (1965)			
Parmehutu Party	—	...	47
San Marino (1964)			
Partito Democratico-Cristiano	C	...	29
Partito Social-Democratico	SD	...	10
Partito Socialista	S	...	6
Partito Comunista	K	...	14
Saudi Arabia			
Royal government	—	—	—
Senegal (1968)			
Union Progressiste Sénégalaise	—	...	80
Sierra Leone			
Military government since March 26, 1967	—	—	—
Singapore (1968)			
People's Action Party	C	...	58
United People's Party	EL	...	—
Somali Republic (1964)			
Youth League	R	...	95
National Congress	CR	...	13
Democratic Union	L	...	6
South Africa (1966)			
Nationalist Party	R	...	126
United Party	C	...	39
Progressive Party	L	...	1
Southern Yemen, Rep. of			
National Liberation Front			
Spain (1967)			
Movimiento Nacional (nonparty and Falange†† Party members, the latter in minority)	—	...	564
Sudan (1968)			
Umma Party (Sadiq el-Mahdi)	R	...	36
Umma Party (Hadi el-Mahdi)	R	...	30
Democratic Unionist Party	C	...	101
Sudan African National Union	L	...	15
Southern Front	L	...	10
Communist Party	K	...	1
Swaziland (1968)			
Imbokodvo Party	...	...	...
Sweden (1968)			
Högerpartiet (Conservative)	R	13.7%	32
Centerpartiet (Agrarian)	CR	16.1%	39
Folkpartiet (Liberal)	C	15.0%	34
Socialdemokratiska Arbetarepartiet	SD	50.9%	125
Vänsterpartiet-Kommunisterna	K	3.0%	3
Switzerland (1967)			
Conservative Christian-Social	R	...	45
Evangelical People's	CR	...	3
Liberal Democratic	CR	...	6
Farmers, Artisans, and Middle Class	C	...	21
Radical Democratic	C	...	49
Independents	C	...	16
Social Democratic	SD	...	51
Communist (Partei der Arbeit)	K	...	5
Syria			
Baath and military government	—	—	—
Tanzania (1965)			
Tanganyika African National Union	C	...	107
Zanzibar Afro-Shirazi Party	L	...	52
Thailand			
Royal and military government	—	—	—
Togo			
Military government since Jan. 13, 1967	—	—	—

COUNTRY AND NAME OF PARTY	Affili-ation	Voting strength	Parlia-mentary represen-tation
Trinidad and Tobago (1966)			
People's National Movement	C	...	24
Democratic Labour Party	L	...	12
Tunisia (1964)			
Destourian Socialist Party	—	—	90
Turkey (1965)			
Turkish Justice	R	...	240
Republican Nation's	R	...	31
Republican People's	C	...	134
New Turkey	C	...	19
Republican Peasants'	L	...	11
Turkish Workers'	EL	...	15
Uganda			
Uganda People's Congress	—	...	...
Union of Soviet Socialist Republics (1966)			
Communist Party of the Soviet Union	—	99.7%	767
United Arab Republic (1968)			
Arab Socialist Union	—	—	350
United Kingdom (1966)			
Conservative and Unionist	R	41.9%	253
Liberal‡‡	C	8.5%	12
Labour	L	48.1%	364
Communist§§	K	0.2%	—
United States (1968)			
American Independent	R	13.5%	—
Republican	CR	43.5%	192
Democratic	C	43.0%	243
Upper Volta			
Military government since Jan. 3, 1966	—	—	—
Uruguay (1967)			
Partido Nacional (Blanco)	R	39.6%	41
Partido Colorado	C	49.8%	50
Partido Demócrata Cristiano	C	3.0%	3
Frente Izquierdista de Liberación	K	5.7%	5
Venezuela (1968)			
Cruzada Cívica Nacional‖‖	ER	11.4%	21
Unión Republicana Democrática	R	9.6%	17
Frente Nacional Democrático	R	2.6%	5
Fuerza Democrática Popular	C	5.5%	10
Social Christians (COPEI)¶¶	C	25.4%	57
Acción Democrática	C	28.0%	68
Movimiento Electoral del Pueblo	L	14.5%	27
Unión para Avanzar (Communist)99	K	2.8%	5
Vietnam, North (1964)			
Lao Dong (Communist Party)	—	...	366
Vietnam, South (1967)			
National coalition	—	...	137
Western Samoa (1967)			
No political parties	—	...	45
Yemen			
Civil war since Sept. 27, 1962	—	—	—
Yugoslavia (1967)			
League of Communists of Yugoslavia / Socialist Alliance of the Working People	—	...	670
Zambia (1968)			
United National Independence Party	—	...	81
African National Congress	—	...	23
Independents	—	...	1

*Council General elected by heads of families of the six parishes.

†The Kommunistische Partei Österreichs presented in 1966 only one (unsuccessful) candidate in Vienna; in all other constituencies it supported Socialist candidates.

‡The National Assembly (Tsongdu) meets once a year.

§In October 1965 all political parties were banned, but two months later an official party, the Alianca Renovadora Nacional, was created, and an official opposition, the Movimento Democratico Brasileiro, was authorized. The latter declared that it would not participate in any indirect elections.

‖Suomen Kansan Demokraatinen Liitto or Finland's People's Democratic League.

¶After the 1968 election the Gaullists took the name of Union des Démocrates pour la République.

9After the 1968 election the Centre Démocrate took the name of Progrès et Démocratie Moderne.

δIncluding 50 members of the Bavarian Christlich-Soziale Union.

□A right-wing opposition party based mainly in the Tamil speaking Madras State.

°A breakaway group from the Socialist Party formed in December 1963; it opposes the centre-left coalition government.

▲Komeito, a "Clean Government Party," was formed in November 1964; it is a political arm of the Soka Gakkai Buddhist movement.

+Theoretically Laos has a coalition government; in fact, it is a divided country with a pro-Communist Neo Lao Hak Sat party controlling territory bordering North Vietnam.

ᵉFormerly Alianza Popular Revolucionaria Americana founded in 1924 by Víctor Raúl Haya de la Torre.

**Including 13 Catholic deputies, namely 5 from "Pax," 5 from "Znak," and 3 from the Christian-Social Association.

††The full name of this only allowed political party was: Falange Española Tradicionalista y de las Juntas de Ofensiva Nacional-Sindicalistas.

‡‡Out of 630 constituencies, the Liberals contested only 311, forfeiting their deposits in 104.

§§The Communist Party of Great Britain presented its candidates in 57 constituencies only, forfeiting their deposits in all of them. A candidate forfeits his deposit of £150 if he fails to poll more than one-eighth of the total votes cast.

‖‖New party formed by former dictator Marcos Pérez Jiménez.

¶¶Comitado Organización Política Electoral Independiente.

99Partido Comunista Venezuelano was declared illegal in 1963.

(K. Sm.)

Political Science

Books and scholarly articles published in many countries in 1968 showed a renewal of interest in the state of the discipline and in its methodological problems. The new lines of theory and research developed in previous years—for example, systems analysis (David Easton), structural-functional analysis (Gabriel Almond and James Coleman), and the use of automatic retrieval of information as well as computer analysis of data—found their way increasingly into works that were no longer considered pioneering, even though subject to severe criticism. The gap seemed to be widening, however, between political science in the advanced English-speaking countries and Scandinavia and in the rest of the world, where political scientists were barely becoming aware of the newer developments. In countries with authoritarian regimes, whether of the left or of the right—the U.S.S.R. and Eastern Europe, Greece, Spain, much of Latin America, and most of the developing countries—the possibilities of expansion and innovation in political science research and instruction remained very slight.

In France the need for evaluation was recognized by the French Political Science Association, which met at the end of the year after the vote on the new law on higher education. The lines along which research and teaching in political science ought to be organized were vigorously debated while the rigid university structure in force for generations was replaced (as a result of the student and labour disorders in May and June) by a system emphasizing flexibility and self-government. It was still not clear whether political scientists would be able to put the new opportunities to good use and shake the hold of the legalistic approach, imposed on many of them by their membership in the law schools.

In the United States the political science profession continued to be agitated throughout 1968 by the war in Vietnam, and many political scientists participated in the primary campaigns of Sen. Eugene McCarthy, Gov. Nelson Rockefeller, and Richard M. Nixon; then in the campaigns of the Republican and Democratic candidates, Nixon and Vice-Pres. Hubert H. Humphrey. Such support was not readily available to third-party candidate George Wallace, whose effect on public opinion came as a surprise to most specialists.

The Committee on Professional Standards and Responsibilities of the American Political Science Association (APSA), appointed in April 1967 and presided over by C. Herman Pritchett, published its report and recommendations in June 1968. Focusing on the ethical problems of academic political scientists (to the exclusion of political scientists serving as government employees), the report (a truly remarkable document) reviewed the setting and complexity of these problems, then discussed them under four headings: teacher-student relations; conduct of officers and employees of APSA; political activity of academic political scientists; and freedom and integrity of research. Twenty-one rules of conduct were recommended, plus guidelines for research contract relations between government and university and for the conduct of foreign area research under government contract.

According to a study by the National Academy of Sciences, the typical 1966 recipient of a doctorate

in political science granted by a U.S. university was male, married, and 31½ years old. In 1966 approximately 2.25% of all doctorates awarded were in political science. Seventy-seven institutions reported granting Ph.D.'s; the five institutions producing the greatest number during 1964–66 were, in descending order, New York University, Columbia University, American University, Harvard University, and the University of California (Berkeley). The proportion of Ph.D.'s in political science who began their careers as teachers increased from 67% in 1961–63 to 74% in 1964–66. Of those receiving Ph.D.'s in political science, almost half (49%) had their bachelor's degrees in other fields. The median time spent in academic training from the bachelor's degree to the doctorate was 8.6 years, with 5.2 years in graduate school; for all fields, the corresponding figures were 7.9 and 5.7 years.

APSA, which in 1968 numbered over 16,000 members, held its 64th annual meeting September 3–7 in Washington, D.C. The president for 1968–69 was David Easton (University of Chicago) and the new president-elect was Karl W. Deutsch (Harvard). The fifth edition of the APSA *Biographical Directory* was published in May 1968.

Political science was included for the first time in 1968 in the National Register of Scientific and Technical Personnel. APSA, under a grant from the National Science Foundation, would compile the political science section of the register. After the initial survey, the association would analyze the data collected and prepare a report on the discipline.

In March 1968, under the terms of a special Ford Foundation grant, APSA sponsored, jointly with the Louisiana State Legislative Council, orientation sessions for newly elected members of the Louisiana legislature. Similar programs were co-sponsored by the association in 1966 and 1967 in Illinois, Iowa, and Wisconsin, and it was intended that the association should establish state legislative service projects in about 25 states in the next five years.

The vitality of political science was proved in many countries by the creation of new university chairs and departments and by an increase in the number of dissertations and books. New journals in countries already well equipped included the *Indian Political Science Review* and the *Indian Journal of Politics* and (in the U.S.) *Comparative Political Studies* and *Comparative Politics*. The problems raised by the number and structure of the some 23 journals in the U.S. that publish scholarly articles of interest to political scientists were examined by a special APSA Committee on Journals; the need for a similar study was felt increasingly at the international level.

Under its new president, Carl J. Friedrich of Harvard, and its new secretary-general, André Philippart (Brussels), the International Political Science Association held its annual round table meeting at Salzburg, Aus., Sept. 16–20, 1968. The two topics discussed were "Political Problems of Planning" (general rapporteur: Hans J. Arndt, University of Heidelberg) and "Modernization of Politics" (general rapporteur: Ghita Ionescu, Manchester University and London School of Economics and Political Science). Plans were made for future meetings in Turin, Italy; Moscow; and Santiago, Chile, and for the eighth World Congress of Political Science, to be held in London in September 1970.   (SE. H.)

ENCYCLOPÆDIA BRITANNICA FILMS. *Political Parties* (1952); *Presidential Elections* (1952).

Political Security:
see Intelligence Operations

Polo:
see Sporting Record

Populations and Areas

World population reached 3.5 billion by the end of 1968, an increase of 70 million in one year: 118 million babies were born and 49 million persons died. This meant that the daily tally was approximately 324,000 live births and 133,000 deaths. With growth in population continuing at the rapid rate of 2% a year, the earth appeared headed for a doubling of its 1968 population by the year 2006, according to compilations based on United Nations statistics. Increases, however, were uneven. Fastest gains were scored in the less developed nations of Africa, Asia, and Latin America, which already claimed 70% of the world's population. There, growth by 2 and 3% a year was severely straining economies of nations ill equipped to feed, house, and educate their present inhabitants. Though crisis conditions in many of these countries had stirred interest in family planning and birth control programs, there were few signs that any of these programs had, as yet, produced any drop in birthrates.

It was only in the economically developed nations of Europe, North America, and Oceania that low birthrates suggested any use of birth control. But most of these low rates of growth were traceable to the decisions of individuals rather than to government policies. In most cases, there was a direct correlation between low birthrates and economic status.

Europe, excluding the U.S.S.R., contained approximately 455 million people. Per capita income was $1,069. Each year the continent was experiencing a modest 0.7% growth rate, which, if it continued, would double the population in 100 years. The world's slowest growths, due to low birthrates, were reported in Hungary (0.2%) and East Germany (0.3%). At these rates Hungary would double its population in 233 years, East Germany in 350.

The Soviet Union, with 239 million people and a per capita income of $928, was growing annually by 1.1%, as was the United States, where income was $2,893 per capita. Both countries would now take 63 years to double their populations. Although the U.S. had passed a milestone by going over the 200 million mark in population in 1967, it achieved another distinction in the area of population early in 1968: the birthrate dropped to a historic low of 17.9 per 1,000. It was this trend toward fewer children on the average that was decelerating population growth in the U.S.

In fast-growing Asia, only industrially developed Japan, with an annual per capita income of $696, showed the signs of birth control. The 1.1% rate of growth matched that of both the U.S. and the U.S.S.R. Through most of the Asian continent, high birthrates (averaging 39 per 1,000) worked with death rates (averaging 17 per 1,000) to produce a 2.2% gain each year. This meant that Asia would have to provide for another two billion people in 32 years in nations where incomes were currently running about $128 for each person. In addition, this vast continent had five of the seven nations of the world with populations exceeding 100 million: China, a demographic mystery with estimates setting the population at from 728 million to over 900 million; India, with 523 million; Pakistan, 126 million; Indonesia, 113 million; and Japan, 101 million.

One country, however, contradicted the rule that high birthrates typified "have not" nations and low birthrates marked "have" nations. Oil-rich Kuwait in the Middle East boasted the highest per capita income in the world, $3,184. It also had the distinction of being the fastest-growing nation; a typical Middle Eastern birthrate of 47–49 combined with an unusually low death rate of 6–7 to yield a growth rate of 5.1% annually. At this pace, Kuwait would double its 500,000 population in 14 years. But, unlike its neighbours, Kuwait could afford the pressures created by new waves of people.

With accelerations in population growth closely following that of Kuwait but with one-tenth the per capita income, the less fortunate nations of Central America were rushing toward doubling their populations in 20 years. El Salvador, with a $236 per capita income, was moving fastest. Its 3.7% annual growth rate suggested a doubling in 19 years. What was true of the smaller nations of Central America was also true of the rest of Latin America, particularly the more northern, less economically developed nations, where birthrates were in the 40–45 range. It appeared that Latin America would add an equal number of people to its present population of 268 million within 24 years.

Much the same could be said of the less developed nations of Africa were it not for high death rates, averaging 22 per 1,000, which slowed down annual increases. Because of a lack of medical facilities and proper diet, a typical country, Gabon, had a birthrate of 35–42, only slightly in excess of its death rate of 27–32. This meant a growth rate as low as 0.3% a year, comparable to that of Hungary. In Guinea, where a birthrate of 50 was practically at the physiological upper limits, the inordinately high death rate of 38 kept growth to 1.1%. Improved medical care would doubtless lower the death rates in African

continued on page 620

Display booth in New York City sponsored by the Association for Voluntary Sterilization, Inc., which was seeking to inform the general public about one method of birth control.

WIDE WORLD

Table I. The Ten Largest Nations by Area and by Population*

Rank		Area in sq.mi.	Rank		Population
1	U.S.S.R.	8,649,489	1	China	850,000,000
2	Canada	3,851,809	2	India	524,080,000
3	China	3,691,502	3	U.S.S.R.	234,396,000†
4	United States	3,615,211‡	4	United States	201,750,000
5	Brazil	3,286,470	5	Indonesia	110,000,000†
6	Australia	2,967,877	6	Pakistan	109,519,831
7	India	1,232,560	7	Japan	100,510,000
8	Argentina	1,072,156	8	Brazil	89,376,000
9	Sudan	967,491	9	Germany, West	60,165,000
10	Algeria	919,590	10	Nigeria	61,450,000†

*Based on independent countries, Dec. 31, 1968. Areas are latest official data available; populations are 1968 estimates.
†1967 estimate.
‡Excludes Great Lakes waters and territorial sea, 94,485 sq.mi.

Table II. World Census Data

POLITICAL UNIT	Year of census	ENUMERATED POPULATION			AGE DISTRIBUTION			ECONOMICALLY ACTIVE		
		Total	Male	Percent urban*	0 to 15	16 to 45	46 and over	Total	Agriculture	Mining and manufacturing
Albania	1960	1,626,315	834,384	30.9	...	...	...	730,800	...	...
Algeria	1966	11,833,126	6,079,900	...	5,947,800	4,387,700	1,744,800	2,335,200	1,300,000	183,500
American Samoa	1960	20,051	10,164	24.5	9,946	7,731	2,374	5,889	2,840	...
Angola	1960	4,830,449†	2,459,015	10.6	2,011,378‡	2,177,631‡	641,440‡	1,421,966	944,716	26,508
Antigua	1960	54,060§	25,230	60.1	23,154	20,964	9,942	16,873	12,564	4,084
Argentina	1960	20,008,945	10,034,544	...	5,772,043§	10,486,674§	3,663,094§	7,599,071	1,460,541	1,959,041
Australia	1966	11,550,462	5,816,359	83.2	3,392,488	4,873,899	3,284,073	4,856,455	...	1,368,468
Austria	1961	7,073,807	3,296,400	50.1	1,660,615	2,729,599	2,683,593	3,369,815	767,604	1,093,046
Bahama Islands	1963	130,220||	63,485	24.0||	57,452¶	51,924¶	20,844¶	51,948	5,882	...
Bahrain	1965	182,203†	99,384	20.1	83,667	80,589	17,947	50,935	4,348	7,185
Barbados	1960	232,327	105,519	40.3	88,882‡	88,636‡	54,809‡	85,040	22,440	13,468
Belgium	1961	9,189,741	4,496,860	66.4	2,333,846	3,543,729	3,312,166	3,512,463	253,922	1,326,732
Bermuda	1960	42,640	21,233	9.6	14,199	18,179	9,470	19,498	309	322
Botswana	1964	543,105	264,535	...	242,424	204,797	80,198	250,678	227,009	1,800||
Brazil	1960	70,119,071†	35,010,717	46.3	29,931,481¶	32,976,869¶	7,210,721¶	22,651,263	11,697,798	3,364,232
British Honduras	1960	90,505	44,659	53.7	40,369	34,615	15,521	26,029	8,833	3,329
British Solomon Islands	1959	124,076	65,550	2.3	64,940	43,960	16,140	8,000	3,061	2,508
British Virgin Islands	1960	7,338	3,930	12.1	3,793	2,737	808	2,128	629	107
Brunei	1960	83,877	43,676	43.6	39,109‡	33,059‡	11,709‡	24,830	8,317	5,171
Bulgaria	1965	8,227,866	4,114,167	46.4	2,112,364	3,789,130	2,326,372	4,267,793	1,891,398	1,124,885
Cambodia	1962	5,740,115	2,880,780	16.0	2,513,300‡	2,381,215‡	845,600‡	...	...	...
Canada	1966	20,014,880	10,054,344	73.6	6,591,757‡	8,325,686‡	5,097,437‡	6,458,156	648,910	1,101,553
Canal Zone	1960	42,122†	23,278	31.9	15,204¶	19,888¶	7,030¶	17,085	336	...
Cape Verde Islands	1960	199,661	94,027	23.2	99,023◊	69,816◊	29,358◊	105,570	42,387	1,294
Cayman Islands	1960	8,511†	3,974	41.4	3,020	3,515	1,976	3,132	...	...
Ceylon	1963	10,624,507	5,503,000	18.8	4,616,920	4,408,550	1,564,590	2,542,920	1,272,800δ	258,170
Channel Islands										
Guernsey	1961	47,099	22,718	33.3	11,262‡	17,410‡	18,427‡	...	...	...
Jersey	1961	63,550	30,715	...	12,534	25,643	25,373	30,696	3,259	2,028
Chile	1960	7,374,115	3,612,807	68.2	3,075,036	3,062,143	1,236,936	2,388,667	662,379	519,974
Christmas Island (Australian)	1966	3,381	2,151	...	...	...	...	...	...	...
Colombia	1964	17,484,508	8,614,652	52.8	8,155,529□	7,022,627□	2,306,508□	5,134,059	2,427,059	81,279
Costa Rica	1963	1,336,274†	668,957	34.5	636,665‡	516,395‡	183,214‡	395,273	194,309	46,459
Cyprus	1960	573,566†	281,983	35.9	221,656‡	226,612‡	125,298‡	241,823	93,287	37,718
Czechoslovakia	1961	13,745,577†	6,704,674	47.6	3,960,752	5,370,682	4,414,143	...	...	...
Denmark	1965	4,767,597	2,362,000||	77.1	1,215,000||	1,957,000||	1,596,000||	2,251,000||	608,000||	1,282,000||
Dominica	1960	59,916	28,167	25.6	26,802‡	21,599‡	11,515‡	22,477	11,693	2,553
Dominican Republic	1960	3,047,070	1,535,820	30.1	1,440,900‡	1,218,440‡	387,730‡	820,710	504,820	58,890
Ecuador	1962	4,476,007	2,236,476	36.0	2,014,505	1,838,160	623,342	1,442,591	800,390	215,617
El Salvador	1961	2,510,984	1,236,728	38.5	1,176,744	1,011,819	322,421	807,092	486,213	104,227
Equatorial Guinea	1960	245,989	132,293	...	...	...	...	...	...	...
Faeroe Islands	1965	37,122	...	...	...	...	...	...	...	...
Falkland Islands	1962	2,172	1,195	49.4	568◊	1,134◊	470◊	930	359	...
Fiji	1966	476,727	242,747	33.4	232,826	190,543	53,112	125,809	656,921	10,451
Finland	1960	4,446,222†	2,142,263	38.4	1,338,991	1,831,849	1,275,382	2,033,268	720,817	444,516
France	1962	46,520,271†	22,595,000	63.0	14,967,160▲	25,654,380▲	5,834,720▲	18,956,380	3,849,700	5,666,460
French Guiana	1961	33,295†	16,288	75.1	12,127¶	14,296¶	6,872¶	11,981	3,273	...
French Polynesia	1962	84,550	43,106	...	45,232	34,591	3,643	25,593	9,484	5,715
French Somaliland	1964	82,100	...	57.4	...	...	...	...	...	...
Gabon	1960-61	444,264†	204,698	16.7	135,574	210,611	98,079	311,959	153, 414	21,512
Gambia, The	1963	315,486	160,849	8.8	118,586‡	155,834‡	41,066‡	160,000||	135,000||	2,500||
Germany, East	1964	17,011,931†	7,751,862	72.9	4,262,941	6,338,075	6,410,915	7,657,786	1,267,257	3,140,721
Germany, West	1961	56,174,826†	26,413,362	77.8	12,184,784	22,935,570	21,054,478	26,527,328	3,587,000	12,908,000
Ghana	1960	6,726,815	3,400,270	23.1	2,996,506‡	2,894,238‡	836,071‡	2,723,026	1,581,331	282,168
Gibraltar	1961	21,785†	10,436	100.0	5,456	9,336	6,993	9,292	...	783
Gilbert and Ellice Islands	1963	48,780	23,927	5.4	22,521	18,192	8,067	11,884	8,272	902
Greece	1961	8,388,553	4,091,894	43.3	2,392,514	3,710,437	2,285,602	3,638,601	1,960,446	510,087
Greenland	1965	39,600	20,354	...	19,091	15,752	4,757	13,248	3,651	300
Grenada	1960	88,677	40,660	8.2	42,268‡	30,472‡	15,937‡	15,219	10,895	2,657
Guadeloupe	1961	283,222†	138,435	38.8	119,950‡	110,508‡	52,764‡	97,494	46,959	12,311
Guam	1960	67,044	39,211	...	28,014	31,709	7,321	26,304	411	535
Guatemala	1964	4,287,328	2,174,077	33.5	2,032,540	1,680,180	574,608	1,362,944	861,140	151,180
Guyana	1960	560,330	279,128	15.5	259,228‡	215,228‡	85,874‡	174,730	59,790	32,371
Honduras	1961	1,884,765	939,029	23.2	940,827	730,153	213,785	567,988	379,125	45,779
Hong Kong	1966	3,716,400	1,880,870	86.9	1,571,440	1,493,630	643,850	1,454,730	27,970	557,300
Hungary	1961	9,961,044	4,804,043	39.7	2,691,036	4,096,392	3,173,616	5,312,831	1,872,730	1,378,987
Iceland	1966	196,933	...	...	...	...	...	...	...	...
India	1961	439,234,771†	226,293,201	18.0	188,500,020	192,142,333	58,294,565	188,675,500	131,142,816	18,561,671
Indonesia	1961	96,318,829	47,493,854	14.8	40,544,678	42,458,049	13,316,102	34,578,234	23,516,197	1,943,546
Iran	1966	25,078,923	12,981,665	38.1	11,639,200+	9,861,700+	3,642,800+	7,584,085	3,168,515	1,293,912
Iraq	1965	8,261,527	4,205,201	44.1	...	...	...	...	...	...
Ireland	1966	2,884,002	1,449,032	49.2	...	...	...	1,106,000	330,000δ	277,000
Isle of Man	1966	50,423	23,226	56.0	10,385	16,450	23,588	13,837	1,829	...
Israel	1961	2,179,491†	1,106,069	77.9	786,196‡	869,045‡	524,250‡	751,230	96,420	168,895
Italy	1961	50,623,569†	24,791,683	47.7	11,549,626□	22,903,305□	16,170,638□	20,096,693	5,657,446	7,886,181⊕
Jamaica	1960	1,609,814†	773,439	32.0	662,508‡	646,281‡	301,025‡	677,003	229,718	94,172
Japan	1965	98,274,961†	48,244,445	68.9	27,390,062	48,894,840	21,990,059	48,268,767	10,866,693	12,018,479
Jordan	1961	1,706,226	867,597	47.4	815,910**	638,732**	251,584**	389,978	137,757	41,932
Kenya	1962	8,636,263	4,276,963	7.8	3,975,500‡	3,530,300‡	1,130,400‡	...	...	...
Korea, South	1966	29,207,856	14,700,966	33.5	12,851,456‡	11,975,220‡	4,381,178‡	9,325,000	4,826,000	940,000
Kuwait	1965	467,339	286,312	71.0	184,967	247,905	34,467	179,284	1,983	31,925
Lesotho	1966	969,634	465,784	...	370,390‡	306,208‡	172,756‡	...	...	...
Liberia	1962	1,016,443	503,588	19.7	394,509	471,553	150,381	411,794	298,404	22,913
Libya	1964	1,564,369†	813,386	...	683,431‡	630,379‡	249,160‡	405,258	146,709δ	43,636
Liechtenstein	1960	16,628	8,130	...	4,792	6,267	5,569	7,575	962	3,273
Luxembourg	1966	334,790	164,575	...	75,450‡	138,781‡	120,559‡	164,575	14,554	45,864
Macao	1960	169,299†	83,897	95.2	68,556	60,472	40,271	37,905	1,717	22,000††
Malaysia										
West Malaysia	1957	6,278,758	3,237,579	26.5	2,752,208‡	2,576,252‡	950,298‡	2,164,861	468,317	58,499
East Malaysia	1960	1,198,950	612,462	15.0||	197,826‡	199,091‡	57,504‡	470,911	381,941	7,451
Maldive Islands	1965	97,743	51,964	...	49,124▲	48,619▲		...	...	...
Malta	1967	318,806	150,467	...	100,671	134,601	82,833	94,303	...	...

Table II. World Census Data (Continued)

POLITICAL UNIT	Year of census	ENUMERATED POPULATION Total	Male	Percent urban*	AGE DISTRIBUTION 0 to 15	16 to 45	46 and over	ECONOMICALLY ACTIVE Total	Agriculture	Mining and manufacturing
Martinique	1961	290,679†	140,011	29.1	122,340‡	112,124‡	56,215‡	100,000‖	33,000‖	...
Mauritius	1962	681,619	342,306	34.2	323,007	258,285	100,327	187,401	70,866	27,560
Mexico	1960	34,923,129	17,415,320	50.7	16,205,849	13,999,075	4,718,205	11,332,016	6,144,930	2,147,963
Monaco	1961	22,297	9,933	...	2,742‡‡	14,962‡‡	4,570‡‡	10,580	9	1,700
Mongolia	1963	1,018,800†	508,800	39.5	411,300	378,100	227,700	483,400	279,200	41,900
Montserrat	1960	12,167†	5,407	16.0	5,198	3,946	3,023	4,282	1,881	...
Morocco	1960	11,626,232†	5,809,172	29.3	5,307,824	4,738,350	1,580,058	3,290,950	1,721,000‖	...
Mozambique	1960	6,578,604†	3,149,270	...	...	...	...	...	...	...
Nauru	1966	6,048	3,696	...	...	...	...	...	...	...
Nepal	1961	9,387,661	4,619,973	2.8	3,684,000‖	4,258,000‖	1,445,000‖	...	...	...
Netherlands	1960	11,461,964†	5,706,874	55.4	3,516,623‡‡	6,952,166‡‡	993,175‡‡	4,168,626	446,695	1,306,480
Netherlands Antilles	1960	192,538†	94,811	...	79,683‡	77,069‡	35,786‡	59,806	1,029	16,059
New Caledonia	1963	86,519	45,640	43.1	41,657▲	39,878▲	4,984▲	30,471	11,213	4,906
New Guinea, Territory of	1966	1,578,650	821,899	47.3	694,633	700,669	183,348	889,287	818,739	9,023
New Zealand	1966	2,676,919	1,343,858	62.4	...	...	...	...	...	...
Nicaragua	1963	1,535,588	757,922	40.9	740,729	603,072	191,787	474,960	283,106	59,644
Nigeria	1963	55,670,046	28,112,118	16.1	25,514,354	25,980,055	4,175,637	18,267,669	10,209,122	2,205,476
Norway	1960	3,591,234†	1,789,406	32.1	989,927	1,396,484	1,204,823	1,406,358	188,431	367,296
Pakistan⁺	1961	93,831,982†	49,308,645	13.1	40,178,518	36,322,838	13,781,318	30,205,981	22,441,788	...
Panama	1960	1,075,541	545,774	41.5	491,102	435,207	149,232	336,969	155,690	25,964
Papua	1966	606,336	318,460	87.7	274,873	270,698	60,765	312,748	269,076	4,375
Paraguay	1962	1,816,890	895,551	36.1	866,052	684,563	266,275	596,555	312,647	91,077
Peru	1961	10,420,351§§	4,925,518	47.4	4,290,084¶	4,143,473¶	1,468,200¶	3,124,579	1,555,560	477,393
Philippines	1960	27,087,685†	13,662,869	29.9	12,377,240◻	11,310,181◻	3,400,264◻	10,692,000‖	5,768,000‖	1,120,000‖
Poland⁺	1960	29,775,508	14,404,218	47.7	9,935,779‡	11,871,906‡	7,598,044‡	13,907,442	6,636,632ⵠ	3,237,814
Portugal	1960	8,889,392†	4,254,373	22.6	2,757,895	3,792,171	2,339,326	3,316,472	1,393,624	717,117
Portuguese Guinea	1960	521,336	260,650	...	...	...	...	...	...	...
Portuguese Timor	1960	517,079	267,783	...	...	...	...	...	...	...
Puerto Rico	1960	2,349,544	1,386,968	44.2	1,058,750	863,849	426,945	551,688	135,100	95,504
Réunion	1961	349,282	170,046	...	155,803‡	137,625‡	52,832‡	88,340	38,195	50,145
Rhodesia	1961–62	3,857,470	1,984,050	21.6	1,866,850	1,990,620		713,640	247,030	147,710
Romania	1966	19,105,056	9,356,715	38.2	...	...	...	...	...	...
Rwanda	1965	3,744,723†	1,493,963	...	1,397,928◻	1,235,648◻	487,147◻	1,136,378	...	...
Ryukyu Islands	1960	883,122†	422,843	...	367,553‡	355,641‡	159,799‡	356,249	152,041	20,474
St. Helena	1966	4,649	2,233	...	1,944¶	1,501¶	1,204¶	1,562	...	...
St. Kitts-Nevis and Anguilla	1960	56,693†	26,149	32.9	25,920	19,378	11,395	32,023	8,565	2,078
St. Lucia	1960	86,108	40,693	24.9	38,109	33,122	14,877	28,544	15,144	3,485
St. Vincent	1960	79,948	37,561	...	39,305‡	28,267‡	12,376‡	23,310	9,954	2,868
São Tomé and Príncipe	1960	63,485†	35,259	...	...	...	...	...	...	...
Seychelles	1960	41,425	20,289	25.4	15,934	16,491	9,000	17,665	5,910	2,151
Sierra Leone	1963	2,180,355	1,081,123	...	800,404‡	1,016,240‡	363,711‡	...	682,588	88,846
Sikkim	1961	162,189	85,285	4.2	68,019	73,748	20,422	2,728	249	64
South Africa	1960	16,002,797	8,043,493	46.7	6,418,492‡	6,945,380‡	2,638,925‡	5,696,060	1,700,958	1,285,113
South West Africa	1960	526,004	265,312	21.9	217,541	227,238	81,225	203,271	118,996	18,647
Spain	1960	30,430,698	14,763,388	42.5	8,365,000	13,506,800	8,652,900	11,634,214	4,803,316	2,749,419
Spanish Sahara	1960	23,793	13,070	...	...	...	...	...	...	...
Surinam⁺	1964	324,211	161,855	40.1	147,927‡⁺	122,897‡⁺	46,668‡⁺	80,199§§	19,922§§	12,713§§
Swaziland	1966	374,571	178,795	12.5	174,455	145,618	54,498	121,063	85,103	23,480
Sweden	1960	7,495,316†	3,738,881	72.8	1,648,906‡	3,035,606‡	2,810,804‡	3,244,084	446,952	1,167,877
Switzerland	1960	5,429,061†	2,663,432	42.0	1,361,210	2,302,312	1,765,539	2,512,411	280,191	1,006,038
Syria	1960	4,565,121	2,344,224	41.9	2,014,509	1,656,452	680,094	1,016,347	518,933	128,954
Taiwan	1966	13,512,143	7,159,850	...	...	...	...	...	...	...
Tanzania	1967	12,231,342	5,969,107	53.8	...	...	...	...	...	...
Thailand	1960	26,257,916	13,154,149	12.5	11,823,535	10,949,932	3,484,393	13,836,984	11,334,382	500,595
Togo	1958–60	1,439,772	689,556	9.6	695,411	558,839	185,550	566,868	452,889	...
Tonga	1966	77,429	39,157	...	...	...	...	...	...	...
Trinidad and Tobago	1960	827,957	411,580	17.0	351,050‡	336,730‡	140,177‡	262,570	52,528	53,617
Trust Territory of the Pacific	1960	75,836†	38,721	...	33,332	27,139	15,092	...	...	...
Tunisia	1966	4,533,351	2,314,419	40.1	2,191,088	1,678,465	663,798	1,093,735	448,296	103,582
Turkey	1965	31,391,207	15,945,768	...	13,844,128	12,775,996	4,771,083	13,591,822	9,764,652	1,025,022
Turks and Caicos Islands	1960	5,668†	2,667	...	2,557	1,975	1,136	2,034	393	...
Uganda	1959	6,536,616	3,283,230	4.8	2,846,000	2,796,000	895,000	...	...	...
Union of Soviet Socialist Republics	1959	208,826,650	94,050,303	47.9	63,495,768**	94,205,904**	51,116,616**	99,130,212	38,425,967	36,575,187
United Arab Republic	1966	30,053,861	15,168,000	40.5	...	...	...	...	...	...
United Kingdom	1961	52,708,934	25,480,791	79.0	12,335,703‡	20,784,033‡	19,589,198‡	23,616,620	865,129	6,975,166
United States	1960	179,323,175	88,331,494	69.9	55,786,173‡	70,919,666‡	52,617,336‡	64,639,252	4,256,734	18,167,092
Uruguay	1963	2,592,563	1,289,454	...	721,500‡	1,143,600‡	727,500‡	1,015,500	181,800	213,600
Venezuela	1961	7,523,999§§	3,823,569	62.5	3,538,949	3,022,725	962,325	2,406,725	773,650	1,633,075
Vietnam, North	1960	15,916,955	7,687,814	9.5	7,055,544‖‖	7,556,129‖‖	1,305,282‖‖	8,119,286	6,377,024	537,761
Virgin Islands of the United States	1960	32,099	15,930	57.9	12,768‡	12,510‡	6,821‡	10,845	610	894
Western Samoa	1966	131,379	67,809	19.2	...	...	...	...	...	...
Yugoslavia	1961	18,549,291†	9,043,424	28.8	5,770,817‡	8,168,259‡	4,610,215‡	8,340,400	4,674,856	1,137,848
Zambia	1961–63	3,493,590	1,734,860	21.3	1,492,150	3,092,400	401,190	693,000	220,000	72,000
DEMOGRAPHIC AND/OR SAMPLE SURVEYS										
Burundi	1962	2,319,540	1,104,266	...	...	...	...	...	...	...
Central African Republic	1959–60	1,177,000	577,000	6.8	429,000‡	661,000‡	81,000‡	610,000	461,000	52,000
Chad	1964	3,254,000	1,567,000	7.8	...	...	...	950,000	600,000	60,000
Congo (Brazzaville)	1960–61	794,400†	...	...	...	...	...	...	...	...
Cuba	1965	7,630,700	2,895,155	53.0	2,808,190¶¶	4,009,110¶¶	813,400¶¶	2,546,000	838,000	390,000
Dahomey	1961	2,106,000	...	...	...	...	...	...	...	...
Malagasy	1966	6,200,000	3,049,000	...	2,882,000‡	2,326,000‡	992,000‡	2,733,000	2,396,000	337,000
Malawi	1963	3,753,000†	...	...	...	...	...	...	...	...
Mali	1960–61	4,100,000	...	...	1,763,000	2,127,900	209,100	...	...	...
Niger	1959–60	2,556,211	...	...	...	...	...	1,506,490	703,610	4,510
Senegal	1960–61	3,109,840†	1,531,760	23.7	1,320,680	1,641,420	147,720	1,317,580	1,087,020	73,800
Upper Volta	1960–61	4,400,000	2,208,800	4.6	1,830,400	1,892,000	677,600	2,627,000	1,300,000	...

Note: Data reflect results of enumerations conducted 1957 to 1967, as available.
*That population defined as urban by the political unit.
†De jure population.

‡0–14, 15–44, 45 and over.
§0–13, 14–49, 50 and over.
‖Estimate.
¶0–14, 15–49, 50 and over.
⌀0–19, 20–49, 50 and over.
δIncludes forestry, hunting, and fishing.
◻0–14, 15–45, 46 and over.

◇0–15, 16–49, 50 and over.
▲0–19, 20–64, 65 and over.
⁺Age distribution excludes unknown.
Iran 474,322; Pakistan 3,437,939;
Poland 369,779; Surinam 6,719.
◻Includes public utilities and construction.

**0–15, 16–44, 45 and over.
††Includes transportation.
‡‡0–14, 15–64, 65 and over.
§§Excludes Amerindian.
‖‖0–15, 16–55, 56 and over.
¶¶0–14, 15–54, 55 and over.

continued from page 617

countries or, more particularly, the infant mortality rates, which claimed close to one-quarter of the live births in Gabon, Guinea, and Niger. This rate was ten times the infant mortality rate in the U.S. and about 30 times those recorded in Iceland and the Netherlands.

One of the most persistent population trends continued to be urbanization. Fully 19% of the world's population, or close to 700 million people, lived in 1,700 cities with populations in excess of 100,000; 100 cities passed the mark into this group during 1968. There were at least 80 cities with more than one million inhabitants; 39 were in Asia, 18 in Europe, 7 in the U.S.S.R., 7 in South America, and 9 in North America. Tokyo, with 8.9 million people in the city proper, ranked first. When the full urban agglomeration was considered, however, the 16 million persons in New York City's consolidated area represented the largest concentration of people in the world.

Because runaway population growth had come to be associated with deprivation and starvation, malnutrition, and low productivity, heavy emphasis was being placed on birth control programs. The Indian government, seeing the addition of approximately 12 million people annually as a heavy burden on an al-

ready overtaxed economy, set a goal of cutting its growth rate to 1% by 1985. With varying degrees of enthusiasm, Tunisia, Turkey, and Pakistan had established official lines toward a population policy. In the Roman Catholic countries of Latin America, a variety of programs had been created to deal with the problems caused by population growth. Because of the Vatican's stand against birth control, the policy in a number of places was to give population programs semiofficial recognition or to officially ignore their existence.

The hope, in many places, was that Pope Paul VI, after studying the plight of the world's teeming millions in less developed nations, would sanction the use of contraceptive devices such as the pill. On July 29, 1968, however, in his encyclical *Humanae Vitae* ("Of Human Life"), the pope completely rejected artificial contraception. He reaffirmed the proclamation made 38 years before by Pope Pius XI that "each and every marriage act must remain open to the transmission of life."

In discussing the population explosion, the pontiff asserted that its threat depended "on a lack of wisdom in government, on an insufficient sense of social justice," and "on blameworthy indolence in confronting the efforts necessary to insure the raising of living standards of a people." Quoting his predecessor, John XXIII, the pope reiterated that the only morally acceptable solutions to the demographic problem were

"Well, boys, this means it'll be a race to the finish with them."—Wetzel.

BEN ROTH AGENCY

—Abu, the "Guardian," London.

—Mahood, "The Times," London.

". . . Go on and multiply."—Behrendt, "Algemeen Handelsblad," Amsterdam.

Table III. Populations and Areas of the Countries of the World

Continent and state	Area in sq.mi.	Population in 000	Persons per sq.mi.
World total	58,327,230	3,580,940	67.8*
AFRICA	12,095,413	330,522	27.3
Algeria	919,590	12,943	14.1
Botswana	222,000	611	27.5
British island dependencies	330	54	—
Burundi	10,707	3,340	311.9
Cameroon	183,591	5,493	29.9
Central African Republic	240,540	1,488	6.2
Chad	495,750	3,410	6.9
Congo (Brazzaville)	134,749	860	6.4
Congo (Kinshasa)	905,063	15,918	17.6
Dahomey	43,243	2,577	59.6
Equatorial Guinea	10,830	277	25.6
Ethiopia	471,776	23,644	50.1
French dependencies	10,727	807	—
Gabon	103,089	474	4.6
Gambia, The	4,361	343	78.7
Ghana	92,100	8,376	90.9
Guinea	94,925	3,750	29.5
Ivory Coast	123,503	4,010	32.5
Kenya	224,960	10,209	45.4
Lesotho	11,716	1,018	86.9
Liberia	43,000	1,110	25.8
Libya	679,536	1,743	2.6
Malagasy Republic	226,657	6,562	29.0
Malawi	45,725	4,130	90.3
Mali	479,000	4,741	9.9
Mauritania	397,683	1,100	2.8
Mauritius	720	787	109.3
Morocco	174,471	14,140	81.0
Niger	458,993	3,546	7.7
Nigeria	356,669	61,450	172.3
Portuguese dependencies	1,282,032	13,149	—
Rhodesia	150,820	4,580	30.6
Rwanda	10,169	3,321	326.6
Senegal	76,124	3,670	48.2
Sierra Leone	27,699	2,475	89.3
Somali Republic	246,000	3,000	12.2
South Africa	471,445	18,733	39.7
South West Africa	317,827	610	1.9
Spanish dependencies	103,282	102	—
Sudan	967,491	14,355	14.8
Swaziland	6,704	398	59.4
Tanzania	361,800	12,231	33.8
Togo	21,853	1,746	79.9
Tunisia	63,378	4,560	71.9
Uganda	91,076	7,934	87.1
United Arab Republic	385,237	31,693	82.3
Upper Volta	105,886	5,040	47.6
Zambia	290,586	4,014	13.8
ANTARCTICA	5,500,000†		0.2
Australian dependencies	2,472,113	—	—
British Antarctic Territory‡	650,000		0.1
French Southern and Antarctic Lands	157,874		0.1
Norwegian dependencies	119§		—
Prince Edward and Marion Islands (South African)	110	—	—
Ross Dependency (New Zealand)	160,000	—	—
ASIA (exclusive of U.S.S.R.)	10,642,975	2,052,494	193.0
Afghanistan	251,000	16,113	64.2
Australian dependencies	58	4	—
Bahrain‖	256	200	781.2
Bhutan (Indian protected state)	18,000	770	42.8
British dependencies	428	3,927	917.5
Brunei‖	2,226	107	48.1
Burma	261,789	25,811	98.6
Cambodia	69,898	6,557	93.8
Ceylon	25,332	11,701	46.8
China, Communist	3,691,502	850,000	230
Cyprus	3,572	618	173.0
India (incl. Kashmir)	1,232,560	524,080	425.2
Indonesia	735,268	112,311	152.7
Iran	636,292	26,315	41.4
Iraq¶	169,284	8,547	50.5
Israel	8,000	2,750	343.7
Japan	142,799	100,510	703.8
Jordan	37,737	2,145	56.8
Korea, North	46,540	12,800	275.0
Korea, South	38,022	30,469	801.4
Kuwait	7,450	532	713.5
Laos	91,428	2,770	30.3
Lebanon	4,015	2,520	62.8
Malaysia	127,672	10,021	78.5
Maldive Islands	115	104	904.3
Mongolia	604,247	1,170	1.9
Muscat and Oman‖	82,000	750	9.1
Nepal	54,362	13,107	241.1
Pakistan	365,529	109,520	299.6
Philippines	115,830	35,883	309.8
Portuguese dependencies	5,769	840	—
Qatar‖	4,000	80	20.0
Ryukyu Islands (United States)	848	969	1,114.3
Saudi Arabia¶	873,972	6,990	8.0
Sikkim (Indian protected state)	2,774	187	67.4
Singapore	224	1,974	8,812.5
Southern Yemen	111,000	1,170	10.5
Syria	71,498	5,652	79.1
Taiwan	13,885	13,941	100.4
Thailand	198,445	33,693	169.8
Trucial States‖	32,278	180	5.6
Turkey	301,380	33,539	111.3
Vietnam, North	61,293	20,100	328.0

Continent and state	Area in sq.mi.	Population in 000	Persons per sq.mi.
Vietnam, South	67,108	16,067	239.4
Yemen	75,290	5,000	66.4
AUSTRALIA and OCEANIA	3,286,919	18,633	5.6
Australia	2,967,877	11,991	4.0
Australian dependencies	179,113	2,186	—
British dependencies	18,952	699	—
British-French condominium	5,700	78	13.7
French dependencies	8,971	206	—
Nauru	8.2	6	727.3
New Zealand	103,736	2,755	26.6
New Zealand dependencies	192	27	—
Tonga‖	261	79	302.7
United States dependencies	991	178	—
United States-British condominium	27	370	13.7
Western Samoa	1,091	137	125.6
EUROPE (exclusive of U.S.S.R.)	1,906,228	453,935	238.1
Albania	11,100	2,000	180.2
Andorra	175	14	80.0
Austria	32,374	7,323	226.2
Belgium	11,781	9,606	815.4
British dependencies	304	187	—
Bulgaria	42,823	8,257	192.8
Czechoslovakia	49,370	14,362	291.0
Denmark (incl. Faeroe Islands)	17,169	4,892	—
Finland	130,128	4,676	35.9
France	212,950	50,100	235.3
Germany, East	41,766	17,090	409.2
Germany, West (incl. W. Berlin)	95,964	60,165	627.0
Greece	50,944	8,716	170.9
Hungary	35,919	10,240	285.1
Iceland	39,702	200	5.0
Ireland	27,136	2,910	107.2
Italy	116,316	53,656	461.3
Liechtenstein	62	20	322.6
Luxembourg	999	335	335.3
Malta	122	319	2,614.8
Monaco	0.6	24	40,000.0
Netherlands	14,139	12,661	895.5
Norway (incl. Svalbard and Jan Mayen Land)	149,282	3,805	—
Poland	120,664	32,065	265.7
Portugal	35,553	9,415	264.5
Romania	91,699	19,248	209.9
San Marino	24	18	750.0
Spain	194,884	32,411	166.3
Sweden	173,649	7,893	49.7
Switzerland	15,941	6,071	393.8
United Kingdom of Great Britain and Northern Ireland	94,222	55,069	591.7
Vatican City	0.2	0.9	5,029.4
Yugoslavia	98,766	20,186	227.4
NORTH AMERICA	9,360,527	309,414	33.1
Barbados	166	248	1,493.9
British dependencies	14,774	816	—
Canada	3,851,809	20,744	5.4
Costa Rica	19,652	1,567	79.7
Cuba	44,218	7,937	179.5
Dominican Republic	18,708	4,029	215.4
El Salvador	8,056	3,210	398.5
French dependencies	1,199	649	—
Greenland (incl. icecap; Danish)	840,000	40	0.05
Guatemala	42,042	4,864	115.7
Haiti	10,714	4,674	439.6
Honduras	43,277	2,532	58.5
Jamaica	4,244	1,893	446.0
Mexico	761,601	47,267	62.2
Netherlands Antilles	394	211	535.5
Nicaragua	49,173	1,809	39.6
Panama (excl. Canal Zone)	29,208	1,329	45.5
Trinidad and Tobago	1,980	995	502.5
United States	3,615,210	201,750	56.8
United States dependencies	4,112	2,850	—
SOUTH AMERICA	6,885,679	180,399	26.2
Argentina	1,072,156	23,707	22.1
Bolivia	424,162	3,852	9.1
Brazil	3,286,470	89,376	27.4
Chile	292,256	9,351	32.0
Colombia	439,735	19,829	45.1
Ecuador	109,483	5,695	52.0
Falkland Islands (British)	6,270	2	0.3
French Guiana	35,135	40	1.1
Guyana	83,000	677	8.2
Paraguay	157,047	2,231	14.2
Peru	496,222	12,772	25.7
Surinam (Netherlands)	63,064	363	5.8
Uruguay	68,536	2,818	41.1
Venezuela	352,143	9,686	27.5
U.S.S.R.	8,649,489	235,543	27.2

Note: A dash (—) indicates none or negligible.
*In computing the world density the area of Antarctica is omitted.
†Estimated area, including some unclaimed territory.
‡Includes some territory claimed by Argentina and Chile.
§Insular dependencies only. Norwegian claims to continental Antarctica are undefined.
‖British protected state.
¶Excluding Iraq-Saudi Arabia neutral zone of 7,000 sq.mi.

those that did not do "violence to man's essential dignity" and that were not based on "an utterly materialistic conception of man himself and of his life." Solutions would have to come in the form of "social and economic progress" of a kind that "respects and promotes true human values."

In making his stand the pope had accepted the general principle asserted by the second Vatican Council that the uniting quality of conjugal love and procreation shared equally as the ends of marriage. He rejected, however, the majority interpretation of a Vatican study commission that the morality of sexuality rested on the total approach of the married couple to its obligations and not on the significance or motive of any given act.

Reaction was swift, both within and without the Roman Catholic world. By the end of November the bishops of Belgium, West Germany, England and Wales, the Netherlands, Canada, France, and the U.S. had issued statements that reflected their dilemmas between loyalty to the pope and responsibility to their national laity. In general, they pointed out that the statements in the encyclical must be taken seriously but were not infallible. Most noted that the pope had not said that use of the pill was a mortal sin. Curiously, in Latin America, one of the areas where birth control programs might have their profoundest effects, the major concern of 161 bishops meeting at Medellín, Colombia, in September was the morality of armed revolution against bad governments. Their conference endorsed the pope's ban on artificial contraception.

In the U.S., 671 Catholic theologians and priests signed a statement taking broad exception to the pope's conclusions. They insisted his ban was not binding on Catholics. A Gallup poll revealed that 54% of American Catholics opposed the pope's stand, while 28% favoured it; the remainder had no opinion. The American bishops endorsed the encyclical in full, saying it must be obeyed to the letter. In Washington, D.C., 44 priests who publicly refuted the encyclical were subjected to disciplinary action. At their national conference in November, however, the U.S. bishops issued a pastoral letter that tempered endorsement of the encyclical and allowed that "circumstances may reduce moral guilt."

Despite the potential political hazards of directing a population policy, the 90th U.S. Congress overcame its tendency to cut budgets by actually boosting funds for the population program of the Agency for International Development (AID) from $35 million to $50 million for 1969. There was fear that political pressure might be applied to prevent federal government involvement in programs of population study and birth control. But, in fact, references to the explosion of population in the less developed countries were now a part of American political jargon. In their 1968 platforms both major U.S. political parties called for "priority attention" to population control. World Bank president Robert McNamara proposed bank action to spark interest in the study of population and the use of financial aid to improve family planning methods and administration. (W. EI.)

The accompanying table of World Census Data reflects the principal results of population censuses held between 1959 and 1967. In the case of political units holding more than one enumeration during that period, the latest available data have been included.

See also Food; Heads of State; Immigration and Emigration; Vital Statistics; articles on individual political units.

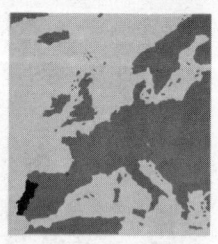

Portugal

A unitary corporative republic of southwestern Europe, Portugal shares the Iberian Peninsula with Spain. Area: 35,553 sq.mi. (92,082 sq.km.), including the Azores (893 sq.mi.) and Madeira (308 sq.mi.). Pop. (1967 est.): 9,415,-000. Cap. and largest city: Lisbon (pop., 1967 est., 824,800). Language: Portuguese. Religion: Roman Catholic. Portugal has seven overseas provinces (*see* DEPENDENT STATES). President in 1968, Rear Adm. Américo Deus Rodrigues Tomás; premiers, António de Oliveira Salazar and, from September 27, Marcello José das Neves Alves Caetano.

The most important event to take place in Portugal for many years occurred in September 1968. After 36

PORTUGAL

Education. (1965–66) Primary, pupils 892,603, teachers 27,966; secondary, pupils 159,246, teachers 8,073; vocational, pupils 164,037, teachers 8,135; teacher training, students 3,710, teachers 418; higher (including 4 universities), students 31,414, teaching staff 1,997.

Finance. Monetary unit: escudo, with a par value of 28.75 escudos to U.S. $1 (69 escudos = £1 sterling). Gold and foreign exchange, official: (March 1968) U.S. $1.2 billion; (March 1967) U.S. $1,039,000,000. Budget (including extraordinary; 1968 est.): revenue 22,337,000,000 escudos; expenditure 22,335,000,000 escudos. Gross national product: (1966) 117,028,000,-000 escudos; (1965) 107,866,000,000 escudos. Money supply: (March 1968) 75,160,000,000 escudos; (March 1967) 72,410,000,000 escudos. Cost of living (Lisbon; 1963 = 100): (June 1968) 124; (June 1967) 115.

Foreign Trade. (1967) Imports 29,135,000,000 escudos; exports 19,685,000,000 escudos. Import sources: West Germany 15%; U.K. 14%; Angola 8%; U.S. 7%; France 7%; Italy 6%; Mozambique 5%; Spain 5%. Export destinations: U.K. 20%; Angola 14%; U.S. 10%; Mozambique 9%; West Germany 5%; France 5%. Main exports: textile yarns and fabrics 20%; cork 8%; wine 8%; fish 7%; clothing 6%; fruit and vegetables 6%; precious stones 6%.

Transport and Communications. Roads: continent (1966) 29,244 km.; islands (1961) 2,058 km. Motor vehicles in use (1967): passenger 316,000; commercial (including buses) 92,500. Railways (continent; 1966) 3,591 km.; traffic (1967) 3,271,000,-000 passenger-km., freight 727 million net ton-km. Shipping (1967): merchant vessels 100 gross tons and over 335; gross tonnage 755,000. Air traffic (1966): 932,343,000 passenger-km.; freight 13,679,000 net ton-km. Telephones (Dec. 1966) 581,780. Radio receivers (Dec. 1966) 1,235,000. Television receivers (Dec. 1966) 211,000.

Agriculture. Production (in 000; metric tons; 1967; 1966 in parentheses): wheat 560 (312); barley 87 (49); oats 124 (63); rye 204 (145); corn 426 (565); rice 147 (159); potatoes 1,251 (923); dry broad beans 35 (24); other dry beans 50 (58); chickpeas 35 (23); wine 770 (893); figs (1966) c. 365, (1965) c. 365; oranges (1966) 143, (1965) c. 158; olive oil 72 (38); apples (1966) 86, (1965) c. 90; pears (1966) 43, (1965) c. 55; meat (1966) 177, (1965) 173; timber (1966) 6,100 cu.m., (1965) 6,100 cu.m. Livestock (in 000; 1965–66): cattle c. 1,092; sheep c. 5,818; pigs c. 1,675; horses c. 75; mules c. 138; asses c. 255; goats c. 607; chickens c. 8,100. Fish catch (in 000; metric tons) (1966) 502, (1965) 554.

Industry. Fuel and power (in 000; metric tons; 1967) coal 443; lignite 38; electricity 6,006,000 kw-hr.; manufactured gas (Lisbon only) 103,000 cu.m. Production (in 000; metric tons; 1967): iron ore (50% metal content) 197; sulfur (1966) 257; cement 1,836; tin concentrates (metal content) 0.6; manganese ore (metal content; 1966) 3.3; tungsten concentrates (oxide content; 1966) 1.2; gold (1966) 18 troy oz.; cotton yarn 70; woven cotton fabrics 43; preserved sardines (1966) 52; cork products (1966) 334.

years as premier, Salazar suffered a brain hemorrhage on September 16, following an operation to remove a blood clot from his brain, and on September 25 Marcello José das Neves Alves Caetano, a 62-year-old lawyer and former minister of colonies, was appointed to succeed him. Caetano had been a close collaborator of Salazar and architect of the corporate state, but he did not always share Salazar's strict views and had retired from the government some years earlier.

A few weeks before his illness, Salazar had announced surprising changes in his Cabinet, involving the ministries of Finance, Communications, Education, Health, the Army, Navy, and the Ministry of the Interior, where a newcomer to politics, António Manuel Gonçalves Rapazote, replaced one of the most powerful political figures in the country, Alfredo dos Santos. Salazar also appointed as chief of the general staff of the Portuguese armed forces the former governor-general of Angola, Gen. Venâncio Deslandes, who had lost prestige with the government a few years before. A few ministerial changes were made by Caetano when he assumed office; these involved the ministers of state, defense, health, and public works. A Secretariat for Information and Tourism was created early in October. It appeared that the new government would follow the general lines of policy of the Salazar regime, but that a gradual liberalization was being introduced. Press censorship was relaxed, and it was decided that the elected leaders of trade unions and other professional bodies would no longer require governmental approval before taking up their posts.

In March a prominent lawyer and leading member of the opposition, Mario Soares, was arrested and banished to the island of São Tomé in the Gulf of Guinea; he was released after Caetano came to power. News of a clandestine Paris- or Brussels-based organization composed of former members of the armed forces, the League of Union and Revolutionary Action (LUAR), appeared in the foreign press at the end of 1967; some of its members were captured in Spain and Portugal during the year. A so-called Committee of Free Portugal was also set up in Paris in the middle of the year by Portuguese exiles; its purposes were to carry out propaganda against the Portuguese government and to help other Portuguese established in France.

There was a movement in June for a wage increase by the Lisbon streetcar and bus workers. Strikes and public gatherings being illegal in Portugal, the workers occupied the central depot for 15 minutes after their working hours for two weeks and refused on one day to collect passenger fares. They succeeded in obtaining a 20 escudo-a-day increase.

The situation in the overseas provinces remained unchanged. About 40 million escudos of the 1968 budget were allocated to military expenditure to maintain security in Angola, Mozambique, and Portuguese Guinea. A decree extended compulsory military service from one to three or four years and admitted women volunteers to noncombatant positions in the armed forces. In February Pres. Américo Tomás visited Portuguese Guinea and Cape Verde, apparently to disprove rumours that part of Portuguese Guinea was controlled by rebels.

Economic development in Portugal showed a slight improvement in 1967 and 1968, following the depression of 1966. The gross national product registered an increase of 5.5% in 1967, against 3% in 1966, and it was expected to increase annually by 7% under the third development plan (1968–73). Investments un-

der the plan in 1968 were forecast at 18.5 billion escudos (out of a total of 167.5 billion escudos for the entire plan), the main allocations being directed to industry, transport and communications, power generation, and agriculture.

Early in the year the minister of finance, Ulisses Côrtes, introduced new financial measures, including the establishment of a new investment bank, new regulations for medium- and long-term operations by banks, and the modification of certain taxes. The government floated several loan issues, and the fishing and tourist industries and the merchant navy were authorized to issue bonds for the improvement and reequipment of their respective sectors. The telephone and airline companies and some electrical companies were also allowed to raise external loans. The government granted loans totaling 150 million escudos for the purchase of agricultural machinery and equipment; this was in addition to subsidies of up to 20% of the cost of such machinery introduced in 1967.

Agricultural production proved to be favourable and industrial output registered an increase, especially in manufactured products in the first nine months of 1968. Both exports and imports rose during the first half of the year. Following a sharp increase in the cost of living in 1967, prices in the first nine months of 1968 were remarkably stable.

The economy of Angola and Mozambique continued to develop, particularly in the mining and manufacturing sectors. Several foreign, local, and Portuguese firms were engaged in the exploration and development of iron ore and petroleum deposits. Work on the huge Cahorabassa hydroelectric project in the Zambezi Valley in Mozambique was begun.   (I. A. B.)

Marcello Caetano, top, was appointed premier after António Salazar, bottom, suffered a brain hemorrhage on Sept. 16, 1968.

Postal Services

The number of member countries of the Universal Postal Union (UPU) rose to 137 in 1968. The executive council, at its annual meeting in Bern, Switz., examined various questions connected with international cooperation and technical aid among postal authorities. These would be discussed at the Universal Postal Congress, scheduled to take place in Tokyo in 1969. The UPU continued to increase its technical aid activities and took an increasing part in the UN Development Program (UNDP). In 1967–68 the allocation to the UPU for this program of aid within the UNDP amounted to $1,085,478.

Progressive automation, the utilization of satellite communications, and the introduction of new postal services were features of 1967–68 for the Australian Post Office. The extension of subscriber trunk dialing facilities continued with the completion of more automatic trunk switching centres and the spread of the broadband trunk systems—the country's main telecommunications network. International telephone traffic to and from Australia had risen 516% in the six years to June 30, 1968. Australia had international service to 205 countries and during 1967–68 more than 835,000 international calls were made or received.

Australia's first commercial earth station, at Moree, New South Wales, opened in March, and bids had been requested for the second, at Ceduna, South Australia. Both would work with Intelsat III satellites over the Pacific and Indian oceans. During the year the country's 4,054 Telex subscribers made 5.4 million calls, all but about 4% automatically. Automatic Telex call facilities between Australia and England

Portuguese Overseas Provinces:
see Dependent States

"THE VANCOUVER SUN" FROM CANADIAN PRESS

Postal workers in Vancouver, B.C., left this strike message spelled out in unsorted mail as they joined a nationwide walkout, July 18, 1968.

were introduced. About 2,700,000,000 articles of mail were handled during 1967–68. Electronic equipment in the Sydney Mail Exchange operated throughout the year, processing about 1.5 million letters a day. By June 1968 more than 70% of mail carried the new four-figure postal address code, introduced in 1967.

The New Zealand Post Office had a difficult year. Traffic volume and business figures, which had shown a steady upward trend since World War II, fell off. Postings declined by 1.4%, telegrams handled by 15%, and telephone toll calls by 2%. Outward overseas telecommunications increased, however. The financial year 1966–67 had ended in a loss of NZ$2 million. Rates were increased from April 1, 1967, and there was a profit of NZ$5.8 million for the year ended March 31, 1968. The Post Office recommendation that an earth station be built in New Zealand was approved by the government.

In France the postal services carried and delivered some 33 million items of correspondence on every working day in 1968. The aim, successful in 85% of cases, of ensuring delivery of letters and comparable items on the day following posting (except Sundays and holidays) required constant improvement in the means of transport. With this in view, the French Post Office further developed its internal air postal network, hitherto chiefly centred on Paris. Night air routes were established linking Bordeaux with Clermont-Ferrand and Rennes with Clermont-Ferrand. During the year, 1,700 new motorized delivery routes served by light vans were set up: 350 in towns and 1,350 in the country, where they replaced bicycle routes. A new type of delivery was introduced. Known as CEDEX (Courrier d'Entreprise à Distribution Exceptionnelle, or Extraordinary Business Mail Delivery), it consisted of a postbox offered free of charge in a sorting office to clients who received a very large volume of mail and who could thus collect their mail on its arrival. Mechanization of large sorting and delivery offices made progress: 11 were equipped during the year and the automatic sorting office at Paris-Gare d'Austerlitz became fully operational. After June 1968, French post offices were closed on Saturday afternoons.

The West German Post Office dealt with about 9,400,000,000 letter mail items and 291.6 million parcels in 1967; 5,200,000,000 local telephone calls and 2,300,000,000 trunk calls were made, and 18.5 million telegrams were handled. At the end of 1967, the number of television broadcast receiving licenses amounted to 13.8 million and sound broadcast receiving licenses totaled 18.5 million. The Post Office's efforts to run its business on a profit basis (a profit of DM. 441.2 million was recorded for 1967) required an increasing degree of rationalization. The West German Post Office was the largest commercial user of electronic

data-processing systems in Europe (35 systems in more than 80 different fields of activity). In telephony the subscriber trunk dialing service accounted for 99% of inland traffic and 87% of traffic with foreign countries (563,875 new main stations were installed in 1967). For many years, the entire inland Telex traffic and 93% of the international traffic had been fully automatic. In 1967 systematic rationalization efforts based on profitability calculations, work studies, and analytical accounting resulted in the elimination of 3,265 jobs.

In Pakistan the expansion of postal services, especially in rural areas, continued according to the national development plan. In 1968, 507 new post offices (465 in rural areas) were added, bringing the total to 13,036. The scheme for establishing closer postal relations with other countries was extended to include the U.A.R. and Jordan. Inland postage rates were applied for surface mails intended for Ceylon, India, Indonesia, Iran, Iraq, Lebanon, Jordan, Nepal, Saudi Arabia, Turkey, and the U.A.R., and all these countries except one applied similar reduced rates in return. From July 1968, postcards were transported by air as normal practice wherever this would expedite delivery. Good progress was made in mechanization, and a program to provide more government buildings for the main post offices was under way.

A five-digit postal code system was introduced in Sweden in March, designed to expedite not only the sorting of letters sent from one locality to another but also local delivery sorting in a number of towns. The postal codes were adapted to an entirely new postal sorting and transport system introduced on May 12. Previously the sorting had been done mainly in traveling post offices, and the mail had been delivered to its destination more or less directly from the trains. After May 1968 Sweden was divided into 41 sorting areas. The post to each area was sent to its sorting centre by mail, and after sorting was distributed to all places within the region, mainly by road. All this was done during the night and early morning. To make it easier and less expensive for firms with big mailing registers to adopt the codes, the Post Office provided address plates and other means of mechanical addressing. Dur-

Berlin postman spraying a dog with an aerosol container of cayenne pepper and mineral oil which was issued to the city's 600 mail carriers in 1968.

D.P.A. FROM PICTORIAL PARADE

ing 1967 the postal staff was reduced (by 3.4%) for the first time in over 40 years.

Efforts to improve the U.K. postal services were continued during 1968. Among the studies carried out were analyses of the operations in large sorting offices, which resulted in a number of improvements.

One of the major developments in British postal history took place on September 16 with the introduction of an entirely new form of inland letter service to replace the established letter, printed-paper, sample, and postcard services. Customers paid according to the speed of service required—first class (5d.) or second class (4d.)—instead of according to the type of missive or to the content of the envelope, which under the new system could be sealed in all cases. An important aim of the new service was to maintain the high quality of the overnight letter service by removing the less urgent mail from the growing pressure of evening and night peak periods. In its early stages the system was received with some hostility and many complaints were published in the press. By mid-October, however, the postmaster general claimed that 94% of first-class mail was being delivered on the day after posting (92% under the old system) and 93% of second-class mail was arriving within 48 hours of posting. Britain's national Giro service, providing a current account banking and payment transfer facility operated by the Post Office, was opened on October 18.

The profit on the postal service for 1967–68 was £4 million. Income increased by £19.3 million to £359.9 million, largely as a result of the full-year effect of rate changes made in 1966–67. Expenditure amounted to £355.9 million, £21.9 million greater than in the previous year; £14.8 million of this was due to pay awards. The number of letters, postcards, printed papers, and newspapers posted rose by 100 million to a new record of 11,500,000,000. The total number of parcels handled in 1967–68 was 216.6 million, nearly 6 million fewer than in the previous year.

In the U.S.S.R. the Post Office delivered over 6,-000,000,000 letters in 1967, as well as 600 million money orders and pensions. Post offices were also charged with the delivery of pensions to collective farmers and grants to mothers with large families and unmarried mothers. In addition, 148 million parcels and 254 million telegrams were handled. The volume of deliveries of publications was increasing every year. An estimated 30,000,000,000 newspapers and magazines were delivered in 1968, compared with 27,300,-000,000 in 1967. The number of new post offices opened in 1967 and in the first six months of 1968 totaled 2,290; this brought the total network of communication centres to nearly 78,000, of which more than 57,000 were in rural localities. Postal air traffic rose by 19.7% in 1967. (X.)

In the U.S. a special commission appointed by Pres. Lyndon B. Johnson recommended that the Post Office Department be converted from a Cabinet-level agency to a public, nonprofit corporation chartered by Congress. The commission, headed by Frederick R. Kappel, retired chairman of the American Telephone and Telegraph Co., presented its report in July after more than a year of work.

The commission recommended turning the Post Office into a self-supporting organization that could set its own rates after public hearings and issue revenue bonds to finance badly needed capital improvements instead of going to Congress for annual appropriations to cover the gap between costs and revenue. It was estimated that within a few years this would save the nation about $1 billion a year, nearly the amount of the deficit for fiscal 1968.

A nine-man board would head the revamped agency, of whom six would be chosen by the president with Senate confirmation; they in turn would choose the other three, who would be the actual operating executives. Postal employees would be appointed and promoted on a nonpolitical basis. The recommendations were generally applauded by large mail users. However, the postal workers' union, which over the years had acquired considerable influence with Congress, remained skeptical.

The recommendations of the Kappel commission were presented as the Post Office recorded another year of unprecedented volume: 81,500,000,000 pieces for fiscal 1968, an increase of 4% over the preceding year. Predictions were that mail volume for fiscal 1969 would reach 84,000,000,000 pieces. Net postal revenue for the fiscal year ended June 30 was $5.6 billion. Total costs came to $6.8 billion, all but $1.4 billion of which went to payroll costs. Revenues came to slightly more than $5.6 billion, and congressional appropriations were required to make up the resulting deficit. More than $600 million of this deficit, however, was written off as public service costs.

Direct mail companies expressed concern over a new law, effective April 14, 1968, empowering recipients of mail they considered offensive to demand that officials prohibit the sending of such mail to them in the future. The law was aimed at cutting down the flow of pornographic material, but representatives of the direct mail industry feared it would be used to limit the flow of advertising.

In midsummer, a halt in Saturday residential deliveries and post office window services was narrowly averted when Congress exempted the Post Office from cutbacks ordered throughout the federal government. The increased volume of heavy commercial mail, especially publications such as catalogs and magazines not easily transported by air, led officials to seek new ways of moving them. One method that came under discussion was creation of special "all mail" trains.

Marvin Watson became the 62nd postmaster general on April 26, replacing Lawrence O'Brien.

(Jy. L.)

See also Philately and Numismatics; Telecommunications.
ENCYCLOPÆDIA BRITANNICA FILMS. *Our Post Office* (1965).

Prices

Taking both industrial and less developed countries as a group, there was no great change in the rates at which prices increased in 1968, compared with the rises recorded a year earlier. In developed market economies the cost of living went up, on the average, by 4.3% in 1968 and 4.1% in 1967. The situation was somewhat better, again on the average, in the less developed countries, where the respective increases were 3.9 and 3.6%. (Brazil, Chile, and Argentina, which continued to experience exceptionally heavy rates of inflation, were excluded from the calculation.) As for wholesale prices, the evidence indicated deterioration in a number of industrial economies and improvement in many less developed countries. In the former, the average increase was 1.7% in 1968, as against 0.8% in 1967. The comparable figures for less developed countries (excluding Brazil, Chile, and Argentina) were 2.1% in 1968 and 3.4% in 1967.

Consumer Prices. In the period 1967–68, increases in the cost of living among developed market economies ranged from the very small changes in West Germany (0.9%), Belgium (1.7%), and Sweden (1.7%) to the unusually rapid rises experienced by Denmark (11.6%), Finland (8.8%), and Japan (6.7%). (*See* Table I.) In the case of Belgium and Sweden, the relative stability was achieved mainly at the expense of growth. In the former, economic recovery in the first half of 1968 was rather modest—and this was especially true of consumer expenditure. Moreover, the stability of food prices helped to keep domestic prices in check generally. In Sweden, where unemployment went up during the period, the rise in consumer prices might have been even smaller except for the higher prices of certain services and imported fuels and an increase in taxes on alcohol. On the other hand, the stability achieved by West Germany was quite remarkable because it was maintained over a period when the economy showed all the signs of a recovery more rapid than originally expected. (The country had virtually full employment in the middle of 1968.) The change to a value-added tax pushed the cost of living up early in the year, but the index remained stable afterward.

At the other extreme, devaluations of the markka and the krone in the last quarter of 1967 were undoubtedly responsible for a large proportion of the price increases in Finland and Denmark. Moreover, the system of linking changes in incomes to changes in the cost of living tended to aggravate the problem in Finland and was abandoned in March 1968. The devaluation of the pound sterling in November 1967 had a similar though more moderate effect on the U.K.'s price level. (Actually the overall increase in the cost of living, most of which took place early in 1968, was smaller than anticipated.) However, it should be borne in mind that since the middle of 1966 the British economy had been subjected to the longest and most severe squeeze since World War II. New Zealand was one of the countries that followed the U.K. and devalued in November 1967; again, there was little doubt that a very tight squeeze, maintained since 1967, helped to keep the increase in the cost of living to a relatively moderate rate. Furthermore, in the summer of 1968 the government imposed a two-month freeze on prices of most consumer goods. In certain cases, however, manufacturers and wholesalers were allowed to apply for exemptions.

In Norway, where the cost of living went up by 4.3%, the government increased subsidies in order to keep prices of certain foodstuffs down. A similar rise in consumer prices was experienced by France where, following the upheavals of May and June, there were substantial increases in both incomes and taxes. Faced with the possibility of very serious inflation, the authorities reinforced their surveillance of prices but refused to resort to a price freeze. However, new price controls, including some freezes, were instituted late in the year as part of the program to relieve pressure on the franc. In Italy the increase in the cost of living was much more in line with that in other EEC countries, excluding France. This was also a period of relatively modest economic progress—by Italian standards—and the government introduced a series of measures designed to stimulate economic expansion and, in particular, to increase the level of fixed investment. The measures included, among other things, a reduction in the tax on electricity consumption for domestic use, intended to encourage the sale of household appliances. The U.S. lost its position as the industrial country with the most stable price level. The unprecedented growth performance of the U.S. economy since 1960 continued through most of 1968, even after the introduction of the tax surcharge, and consumer prices increased more rapidly than in any other year in the 1960s. The tax surcharge, however, was expected to lead to more balanced growth toward the end of the year and in 1969.

In the centrally planned economies of Yugoslavia and Hungary, consumer prices rose by less than in the year before. In Yugoslavia the change in the cost of living was influenced considerably by an administrative increase in rents. In Hungary the index actually declined by 0.9%. In judging the country's performance, however, it is important to bear in mind that, even after the new reforms went into effect in January 1968, 50% of all retail prices were still firmly controlled by the authorities. Of the remainder, 25% were subject to a ceiling, leaving only 25% that could

Table I. Cost of Living—Selected Countries

Country	Index (1963 = 100)			Annual percentage changes over preceding year			
	1966	1967	1968*	1960–65 Average	1966	1967	1968†
Developed market economies							
Finland	120	127	136	5.2	3.4	5.8	8.8
Denmark‡	116	126	135	5.1	6.4	8.6	11.6
Japan	117	122	128	6.2	4.5	4.3	6.7
Netherlands	117	121	124	3.4	5.4	3.4	3.3
Sweden	115	121	122	3.7	5.5	5.2	1.7
Norway	114	119	122	4.1	3.6	4.4	4.3
New Zealand	110	117	120	2.6	2.8	6.4	4.3
U.K.	112	115	120	3.5	3.7	2.7	5.3
Italy	113	118	119	5.0	1.8	4.4	2.6
Switzerland	112	117	118	3.3	4.7	4.5	2.6
Belgium‡	113	115	118	2.4	4.6	1.8	1.7
Austria	111	116	118	3.9	1.8	4.5	2.6
Australia	110	114	116	1.8	3.8	3.6	3.6
France	109	112	116	2.9	2.8	2.8	4.5
Canada	108	112	116	1.6	3.8	3.7	5.4
Germany, West	110	111	112	2.9	3.8	0.9	0.9
U.S.	106	109	112	1.2	2.9	2.8	3.7
Centrally planned economies							
Yugoslavia	184	199	211	13.4	22.7	8.2	5.0
Hungary	106	107	105	0.4	3.9	0.9	−0.9
Less developed countries							
Brazil	443	575	676	62.1	46.7	29.8	24.3
Chile	231	273	326	27.0	22.9	18.2	25.4
Argentina	207	268	306	23.3	31.8	29.5	23.4
Korea, South	164	181	198	15.2	12.3	10.4	12.5
Peru	141	155	180	9.2	9.3	9.9	21.6
Colombia	146	158	166	11.4	19.7	8.2	6.4
India	137	156	160	6.2	10.5	13.9	6.0
Ghana	148	139	147	11.4	5.0	−6.1	3.5
Spain	129	137	143	7.1	6.6	6.2	5.9
Zambia‡	128	129	141	2.3	15.3	0.8	11.9
Turkey	115	131	136	3.8	9.5	13.9	6.2
Bolivia	121	130	136	5.1	7.1	7.4	6.2
Israel	122	124	127	7.2	8.0	1.6	1.6
Pakistan	119	127	126	2.2	10.2	6.7	0.0
Philippines	118	125	124	4.8	6.3	5.9	1.6
Ireland	115	119	124	4.3	2.7	3.5	5.1
Portugal	112	119	124	2.8	3.7	6.2	6.9
Tunisia	115	119	121	2.1	3.6	3.5	3.4
Ecuador	113	117	121	4.0	5.6	3.5	4.3
Uganda‡	122	128	120	5.3	−3.9	4.9	−6.2
Mexico§	110	114	116	1.8	3.8	3.6	3.6
South Africa‖	110	114	115	2.0	3.8	3.6	1.8
Thailand	107	111	113	1.4	3.9	3.7	2.7
Nigeria	115	111	112	3.1	8.5	−3.5	−1.8
Jamaica	107	110	112	2.9	1.9	2.8	3.7
Greece	109	111	110	1.6	4.8	1.8	−1.8
Kenya‡	107	110	110	2.0	2.9	2.8	0.9
Iran	106	107	110	2.0	0.0	0.9	0.0
Ceylon	103	106	110	1.6	0.0	2.9	5.8
Taiwan	102	105	110	2.4	2.0	2.9	5.8
Cambodia	105	105	109	4.3	−0.9	0.0	3.8
Dominican Republic	108	108	108	2.6	8.0	0.0	0.0
Malta	104	105	108	2.0	0.0	1.0	2.8
Morocco	106	106	107	4.2	−1.9	0.0	0.9
Costa Rica	103	104	107	2.3	0.0	1.0	3.9
El Salvador	101	102	106	0.2	−1.0	1.0	5.0
Cyprus	100	101	104	0.4	0.0	1.0	2.0
Iraq	99	101	104	0.8	1.0	2.0	2.0
Guatemala	100	100	102	0.2	1.0	0.0	2.0

*January–June (average).
†First half 1968 over first half 1967.
‡Excluding rent.
§Excluding rent and miscellaneous.
‖White population only.
Sources: International Monetary Fund, *International Financial Statistics; United Nations, Monthly Bulletin of Statistics.*

be set freely. At the same time, the intention of the reforms was that the full introduction of free prices would be implemented over a period of several years. The existing fixed prices would gradually be decontrolled proportionately with increases in the supply of the goods concerned.

Among less developed countries, those of South America were still suffering from extremely high rates of inflation. The increases in consumer prices experienced by Chile (25.4%), Brazil (24.3%), Argentina (23.4%), and Peru (21.6%) were not equaled nor even approached by any other country for which data were available. Brazil again depreciated the exchange rate of the new cruzeiro in August 1968—the first step in a new series of more frequent adjustments, to be made on the basis of movements in the internal prices, the state of reserves, and the rate of price increase in the country's most important trading partners. Colombia, on the other hand, achieved further success in stabilizing the cost of living.

Elsewhere, consumer prices showed considerable stability. In Africa by far the biggest increase took place in Zambia (11.9%) while, at the other extreme, prices declined by 6.2% in Uganda. In Ghana, where the cost of living had stabilized markedly in recent years, the authorities decided in 1968 to establish a Prices and Incomes Commission to control prices and all increases in incomes.

Consumer prices were also rather stable in Asia, where the biggest rises were recorded in South Korea

"It's all right, Barbara . . . . You're quite safe here!"— Garland, "Sunday Telegraph," London.

(12.5%) and India (6%). Turkey experienced a similar increase, but this was in fact a substantial improvement over 1967. Higher levels of capacity utilization made it possible for the producers of certain products to reduce their prices—after negotiations with the government—by as much as 10%. The government also decided to continue its support of agricultural prices.

So far only changes in the aggregate cost of living have been compared. Table II shows something slightly different: the extent to which food prices were increasing at a higher (or lower) rate than those of consumer goods and services in general. This is of great importance in the less developed countries where, because of the low level of income, a high proportion of consumer expenditure goes to foodstuffs.

Table II. Indices of Food Prices in Relation to Cost of Living Index

1963 = 100

Country	1965	1966	1967	1968*
Developed market economies				
Finland	103	103	102	104†
Japan	102	101	102	104‡
Australia	103	102	103	103
Belgium	101	102	102	101†
New Zealand	102	101	102	101
Norway	102	101	101	101
Sweden	102	102	101	100
U.S.	100	102	101	100
Canada	100	102	100	100‡
Denmark	101	99	100	100‡
Austria	102	101	101	99†
France	100	100	99	98
U.K.	98	98	98	98
Italy	100	100	98	97
Germany, West	100	99	98	96
Less developed countries				
Thailand	102	105	108	107
Philippines	104	106	109	106
India	102	103	105	106‡
Uganda	108	106	108	105
Ceylon	101	103	104	105
Pakistan	105	104	105	104
Hungary	102	105	105	104
South Africa§	104	104	104	104
Kenya	102	104	104	104
Iran	103	102	103	104‡
El Salvador	100	99	102	103‡
Tunisia	102	102	102	102
Costa Rica	101	102	102	102
Malta	101	101	100	102
Dominican Republic	102	100	99	102
Zambia	101	103	104	101
Greece	102	102	101	101
Mexico	102	101	101	101
Cyprus	100	101	101	101
Guatemala	100	100	99	101
Portugal	103	105	101	100
Morocco	102	100	100	100
Chile	104	103	100	99†
Colombia	101	103	100	99
Ireland	101	98	97	99‡
Argentina	103	98	98	98
Spain	100	99	96	96‡
Israel	97	94	95	96
Nigeria	97	106	98	94
Brazil	97	98	94	91
Cambodia	91	91	89	90

*January–June (average) except where stated otherwise.
†January–July (average).
‡January–May (average).
§White population only.
Source: United Nations, *Monthly Bulletin of Statistics.*

Table III. Wholesale Prices for Selected Countries

Country	Index (1963 = 100) 1966	1967	1968*	Annual percentage changes over preceding year 1960–65 Average	1966	1967	1968†
Developed market economies							
Finland	116	119	130	3.9	1.8	2.6	10.2
U.K.‡	111	113	117	2.8	2.8	1.8	4.5
Australia§	112	115	116	0.4	4.7	2.7	1.8
Netherlands	115	115	114	2.3	4.5	0.0	-1.7
Austria	110	113	114	2.8	1.8	2.7	1.8
Denmark	109	110	114	2.9	2.8	0.9	3.6
Sweden	112	112	113	3.2	2.8	0.0	0.9
New Zealand	107	107	113	1.8	0.9	0.0	5.5
Norway	110	112	112	2.2	1.8	1.8	0.9
Canada	106	108	110	1.7	3.9	1.9	3.8
U.S.	106	106	108	0.4	1.8	0.0	1.9
Italy	107	106	107	2.7	1.9	-0.9	0.9
Belgium	108	107	106	1.8	1.9	-0.9	-1.9
Japan	103	105	106	0.4	2.0	1.9	1.0
France	105	105	105	2.3	1.9	0.0	0.0
Switzerland	104	104	104	2.1	2.0	0.0	0.0
Germany, West	105	104	99	1.2	1.9	-1.0	-4.8
Less developed countries							
Brazil‖	389	496	579	59.4	39.9	27.5	22.2
Chile	230	274	346	25.5	23.0	19.1	30.6
Argentina	188	236	254	23.1	20.5	25.5	14.9
Korea, South	162	172	184	17.3	8.7	6.2	8.9
Colombia	149	159	168	12.0	17.3	6.7	7.0
India	138	160	156	5.6	13.1	15.9	0.6
Yugoslavia¶	134	137	137	2.4	11.7	2.2	0.0
Spain	116	117	122	2.4	2.6	0.9	3.4
Turkey	113	119	122	2.3	4.6	5.3	1.7
Philippines	112	117	122	2.5	4.7	4.5	7.0
Ireland	112	115	121	3.2	1.8	2.7	5.2
Thailand	111	119	114	0.4	16.8	7.2	-3.4
South Africa	110	112	113	2.0	3.8	1.8	0.9
Mexico	108	111	112	1.8	1.9	2.8	1.8
Morocco	113	116	111	2.4	1.8	2.6	-4.3
Greece	112	112	111	3.0	2.8	0.0	-2.6
Dominican Republic	107	104	111	3.7	-1.8	-2.8	9.9
Ecuador	108	110	110	2.9	2.8	1.8	0.0
Iran	106	106	108	1.8	-0.9	0.0	0.0
El Salvador	105	106	105	0.6	0.0	1.0	-0.9
Taiwan	99	102	104	2.2	1.0	3.0	2.0
Costa Rica	99	101	102	0.6	2.1	2.0	2.0

*January–June (average).
†First half 1968 over first half 1967.
‡Prices of finished goods only.
§Domestic goods.
‖Excluding coffee.
¶Producers' prices of industrial products.
Sources: International Monetary Fund, *International Financial Statistics;* United Nations, *Monthly Bulletin of Statistics.*

The figures in Table II were obtained, in each case, by dividing the index of food prices by the aggregate index of consumer prices. Consequently, the figures over 100 indicate that prices of foodstuffs were rising faster than those of consumer goods and services as a whole, and vice versa. The table shows clearly that a relatively faster growth of food prices occurred in only 6 out of 15 developed market economies, but in no fewer than 20 out of 31 less developed countries. (Hungary was included in this group because of the lack of data for other centrally planned economies. In both 1967 and 1968, food prices in Hungary were adversely affected by exceptionally bad weather: an unusually long period of drought, followed, early in 1968, by rather severe spring frosts that caused considerable damage to crops.) The tendency of food prices to increase at a relatively more rapid rate was particularly evident in the heavily populated countries of the Far East. Both India and Pakistan featured rather prominently in this group, although the situation in those two countries improved in 1968.

Wholesale Prices. It was pointed out above that wholesale prices deteriorated slightly, on average, between 1967 and 1968 in developed market economies. From Table III it can be seen that this was due mainly to the rate at which they increased in Canada and in the four countries that devalued their currencies in the last quarter of 1967: Finland, New Zealand, the U.K., and Denmark. The changes in the wholesale price index experienced by other industrial countries were rather normal, except in three cases where they declined sharply: West Germany (4.8%), Belgium (1.9%), and the Netherlands (1.7%). Wholesale prices in West Germany were apparently influenced to a considerable extent by the downward trend in industrial producers' prices and building prices. The rise in the U.S. (1.9%), on the other hand, although similar to the one recorded in 1966, was well above the annual rate (0.4%) in the first half of the 1960s.

As usual, wholesale prices were also rather stable in the less developed countries. (Because of the lack of comparable data for other centrally planned economies, Yugoslavia was included in this group in Table III.) Indeed, there were strong signs of improvement in most of the countries, including Brazil and Argentina, where (as in Chile) the annual increases in prices were still exceptionally high. Excluding the three South American countries, only the Dominican Republic (9.9%), South Korea (8.9%), Colombia (7%), and the Philippines (7%) experienced wholesale price rises significantly higher than in the advanced countries. (M. Pan.)

See also Commodities, Primary; Economy, World; Employment, Wages, and Hours; Income, National; Industrial Review; Investment, International; Merchandising; Money and Banking; Payments and Reserves, International; Stock Exchanges; Trade, International.

Prisons and Penology

From the standpoint of penology 1968 was neither an outstandingly good or bad year in the United States. It was another 12-month period of occasional prison riots, sporadic criticism of penal conditions and practices, and isolated instances of progressive reform. There were 11 major prison riots, including one that resulted in $2 million damage to the Oregon State Penitentiary in Salem. Five persons died in a North Carolina disturbance, and a conflict at the Ohio State Penitentiary at Columbus left five prisoners dead after

National Guard troops stormed the prison to free hostages. When asked if there was a common cause of the disturbances, a federal Bureau of Prisons spokesman produced a newspaper article written in 1952 and said that its thesis was as true in 1968 as the day it was written. According to that article the underlying causes are that prison plants are obsolete and overcrowded, rehabilitation programs are uninspired or ineffective, and personnel are inadequate in both training and number.

In Philadelphia the U.S. district attorney's office investigated reports of sexual assaults on prisoners by other inmates and announced that an estimated 2,000 such attacks had taken place recently. Earlier in the year at an Arkansas prison farm three unidentified skeletons were found buried in what some former inmates charged was a clandestine cemetery for prisoners murdered by guards.

These incidents and more came to light during the year and the public, apparently, forgot about them as soon as possible. In an attempt to explain the public's apparent indifference, Karl Menninger wrote *The Crime of Punishment,* which was published during the year. In the book he suggested a reason that penologists publicly ignored and privately scoffed at: "The inescapable conclusion is that society secretly wants crime, needs crime and gains definite satisfaction from the present mishandling of it. . . ."

Some manifestations of a more "enlightened" approach to penology were to be seen during the year. In December the Robert F. Kennedy Youth Center was dedicated in Morgantown, W.Va. This $10 million federal facility was designed as a model rehabilitation centre for juvenile delinquents. Elsewhere, at San Quentin Prison in California, a pilot program was initiated in which one "serious offender" was enabled to take a regular job in San Francisco and commute to work daily without an escort. The California Correctional Institute at Tehachapi initiated conjugal visits —the first U.S. prison to do so outside Mississippi. In Canada a progressive move was made when a five-year national moratorium was placed on capital pun-

Columbus policeman standing guard in front of the Ohio State Penitentiary during a riot on June 24, 1968, in which prisoners set fire to a number of prison buildings.

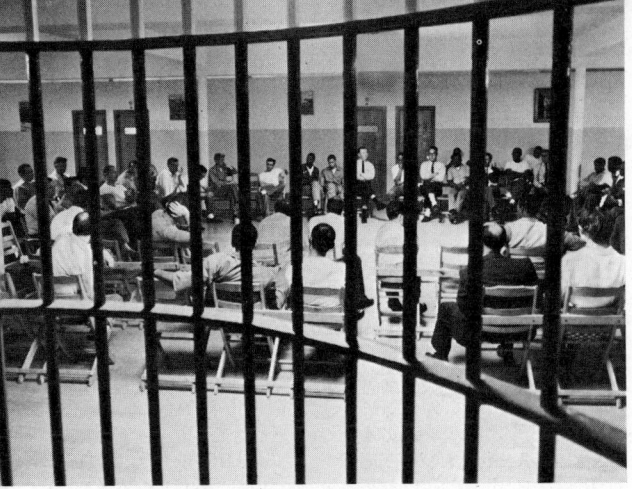

"THE NEW YORK TIMES" FROM WIDE WORLD

Inmates of Clinton State Prison in Dannemora, N.Y., attending a meeting where they attempt to work out mutual problems among themselves. The meetings were part of an experimental program set up to determine if the recidivism rate of persistent felons could be significantly lowered.

ishment to test whether the threat of execution was a deterrent to criminals.

There were 20,247 inmates in U.S. federal institutions at the end of fiscal 1968, 700 more than a year earlier, which had marked the lowest year-end prison population since 1954. The increase was partly due to the 14% rise in men convicted of Selective Service violations and to the fact that the more stringent sentences given narcotics violators starting a decade ago resulted in fewer of them being eligible for parole. The total U.S. prison population at the beginning of 1968 was reported as 196,000, 2% less than 12 months earlier. (PH. K.)

See also **Crime.**

Propaganda

There was no slackening in the intensity of propaganda on the international scene in 1968. The Soviet Union's invasion of Czechoslovakia preceded and overshadowed what at the time was its space "first"—the sending of Zond 5 around the moon and its recovery in the Indian Ocean. An even more spectacular space feat was carried off by the U.S. at Christmastime when it successfully sent three of its astronauts on a lunar "tour"—ten close orbits around the moon with live television coverage beamed back to many countries on earth—and then safely brought them back home. An uneasy peace was kept in the Middle East, despite a major arms race and an increase in Arab terrorism and Israeli reprisals. This was accompanied by intensified Soviet propaganda stressing the complicity of the U.S. with Israel in a conspiracy to keep the Arab nations subjugated to the West. Protests and violent confrontations in the U.S., combined with the assassinations of the Rev. Martin Luther King, Jr., and Sen. Robert Kennedy and magnified by the increasing partisanship of the U.S. election campaign, provided ample material for Communist exploitation.

Opposition to U.S. policy in Vietnam continued to provoke a massive volume of anti-American propaganda, and some American public opinion experts found a steadily declining respect for U.S. leadership and policies abroad.

Radio broadcasts most quickly and clearly reflected changes in propaganda lines, in target emphasis, and even in official policies for all countries—Communist and non-Communist, developed and less developed.

Analysis of such broadcasts revealed a pattern of events and issues around which major propaganda campaigns were constructed. Soviet external radio output continued to be the largest in the world.

The Czechoslovak Crisis. No single event of recent years so split the Communist world as the invasion of Czechoslovakia. The liberalization moves made in Czechoslovakia beginning in January quickly aroused anxieties in the Soviet Union and other Eastern European nations. In the early stages of the polemic, which was in full swing by March, the Soviets took the approach that efforts by slanderous Western propagandists to read into the situation signs that the fraternal solidarity among the Warsaw Pact states was loosening were ludicrous and treacherous.

However, as the Czechoslovaks stubbornly continued to insist on upholding free—and often candid and critical—press and radio, the Soviets took a harsher stance and began to denounce by name several highly placed Czechoslovak liberals. Throughout these polemics the Czechoslovaks pleaded repeatedly for tolerance. "For God's sake," a Czechoslovak radio broadcaster was saying as early as May 9, "let us not have . . . a repetition of the tragic history of Yugoslavia or perhaps even that of Budapest in 1956."

The invasion of Czechoslovakia on August 20–21 by Soviet and other Warsaw Pact troops was described by the U.S.S.R. as a mission of brotherly assistance aimed at putting down "the threat emanating from the counterrevolutionary forces which have entered into a collusion with foreign forces hostile to socialism." The Soviet radio said: "The [Czechoslovak] population is calm. Many Czech citizens express their gratitude to soldiers of the allied armed forces for their timely arrival." Czechoslovak broadcasts, while exhorting the citizenry to act with calm and dignity in order to avoid provocation and bloodshed, emphasized that the invasion took place without the knowledge of Czechoslovak leaders.

The Chinese did not even mention the Soviet-Czechoslovak quarrel until August 10, and then they labeled it as "a dogfight between Soviet and Czech revisionist renegades." The invasion, they said, was "the deathbed struggle of the Soviet revisionist renegade clique in an attempt to avert the crisis of disintegration and imminent destruction of the entire modern revisionist bloc."

The BBC and Voice of America (VOA) had both been on top of developments in Czechoslovakia from an early stage, and both had emphasized the danger that Czechoslovakia's Communist partners would not be able to tolerate the infectious example of Czechoslovak liberal reform. Both intensified their coverage of the Czechoslovak story after the invasion, and both were subjected to rigorous Soviet jamming for the first time since 1963.

The French government of Pres. Charles de Gaulle found in the Czechoslovak invasion a convenient platform from which to launch its most vehement anti-Anglo-American campaign in years. The basic cause of the invasion was seen as the "odious" Yalta agreements of 1945, in which the French had not been invited to participate. In this view, the Yalta agreements had divided the world into spheres of influence controlled by the Soviet bloc and the so-called free-world group, and Czechoslovakia clearly demonstrated the correctness of the de Gaulle prescription that the only safe and honourable place is outside both of the two big hegemonies.

UPI COMPIX

Photograph of a little girl holding a toy machine gun and a wooden workman's hammer was released by the Albanian government official news agency to mark International Children's Day, June 1, 1968.

Hanoi residents watching a game introduced at about the time of the Tet offensive in which President Johnson and Gen. William Westmoreland, then commander of U.S. forces in Vietnam, serve as targets for arrows.

Student Protests. A growing worldwide rebellion against the role of authority was evident in student protests and violent confrontations. Chinese propagandists used student expressions of unrest and dissent as one of the most fertile fields for sowing the seeds of their ideology. Student dissent in a host of countries—including the U.S., France, Yugoslavia, Japan, Mexico, Ecuador, Venezuela, Brazil, Colombia, Chile, and Argentina—was highlighted by the Chinese, and the same interpretation was invariably given: the class contradictions in the students' countries were sharpening, and the students, gaining enlightenment and courage from the wisdom of Chairman Mao Tse-tung, were entering into the revolutionary struggle in ever increasing numbers.

The Soviets did not stress this subject as heavily as the Chinese, and for the most part they confined their attentions to students of "capitalist" countries. They allotted a higher ratio of reportage to editorializing and their tone was less vituperative, but the same theme of leftist correction of rightist injustice was present.

VOA, in keeping with its role as an interpreter of U.S. life and happenings for foreign audiences, devoted the greatest share of its coverage of student dissidence to what was taking place in the U.S. In addition to reporting the actual events, VOA broadcast feature programs dealing with the problem of the limits of dissent. BBC broadcasts to Western and uncommitted countries stressed the difficulties of controlling the student movements, but also highlighted the adverse effects of meeting force with force in the absence of constructive solutions. Its main theme in broadcasts to Communist countries was that the suppression of the useful aspects of student protest, as in Poland, or its reckless encouragement, as in the earlier stages of China's Cultural Revolution, were features of societies without flexible institutions.

The upheavals that rocked France in May and June, although ultimately involving millions of workers, originated with dissident students. During the height of the turmoil, propagandists in all quarters daily concentrated great attention on it, but after the de Gaulle government's victory in the June parliamentary elections, the interest of propagandists rapidly waned. Internally, the French government broadcasting organization, ORTF (Office de Radiodiffusion-Télévision Française), which during the disorders had abandoned its long-established role as a mouthpiece for de Gaulle and taken a much more objective stance, was subjected to a swift, thoroughgoing crackdown. Over a hundred of the rebellious ORTF workers found themselves out of work, a number of others were transferred to the provinces, and the minister of information, the director general, and the chairman of the board of directors of ORTF were replaced.

Vietnam. The war in Vietnam continued to divide Americans and to offer abundant material for anti-American propaganda. The Chinese called for a military victory, and in their overall coverage tended to stress the military aspects of the struggle. When the North Vietnamese and the U.S. agreed to begin talks in Paris, Radio Peking delayed several weeks before making comment, then cited Pres. Lyndon B. Johnson's letter to Congress of May 21, requesting additional appropriations for the Vietnam conflict, as proof that the talks were a "hoax." The Chinese also roundly condemned the Soviets as collaborators with the United States.

In keeping with its policy of favouring a diplomatic settlement of the Vietnam conflict (while publicly applauding the military successes of the Vietnamese Communists), the Soviet Union devoted considerable attention to the Paris peace talks, emphasizing the importance of world public opinion and even assigning it a causal influence. The halt in the bombing of North Vietnam shortly before the U.S. elections was viewed, for example, as a result of the pressure of U.S. and world public opinion.

The Soviets attributed the peace talks completely to the initiative of the North Vietnamese; the Chinese said they came about as a result of the "historic inevitability" that guarantees success to national liberation movements. Both the Chinese and the Soviets insisted that the U.S. was being defeated in the military theatre, but the Chinese went on to conclude that the purpose of the talks was to enable the U.S. to acquire diplomatically what it could not acquire in a military way. The Soviets, on the contrary, maintained that the U.S. was doing everything possible to undermine the talks and, simultaneously, was activating its forces in hopes of a military victory.

The North Vietnamese attitude vis-à-vis the Soviet and Chinese positions was equivocal. On the one hand, Hanoi spoke of the need for a negotiated settlement and often stressed the importance of world public opinion—two typically Soviet lines. At the same time, they echoed the Chinese by asserting that the sweeping military victories of the Tet offensive, as well as other less dramatic successes, were proofs of the "invincibility of a people's war."

VOA, in its coverage of the war, gave a great deal of attention to rural development in South Vietnam and attempts to develop democratic institutions. Reports were broadcast from VOA's two regular correspondents in South Vietnam and two special correspondents covering the Paris peace talks, and in its broadcasts to North Vietnam VOA gave all official U.S. statements in full.

U.S. Election Campaign. There was a striking contrast between the coverage given to the campaign by the Soviets and by the Chinese. Soviet international broadcasts gave the various candidates wide coverage, while the Chinese dismissed the campaign as "an election farce." At first the Soviets were not certain whether to interpret President Johnson's announced decision not to seek reelection as an admission that

U.S. policy in Vietnam had failed or simply as a pre-election maneuver aimed at improving his political image. Very soon, however, they acknowledged the possibility of his sincerity and interpreted his decision as an admission of failure in Vietnam.

The assassination of Senator Kennedy (following closely after that of King) elicited an outburst of anti-American propaganda from a variety of sources. The Soviets attributed the murder to a climate of violence in the U.S. and speculated on "the sinister role played by the FBI and the CIA," implying that Kennedy was killed for his criticism of U.S. policy in Vietnam. Radio Cairo, although acknowledging the Arab origins of Sirhan Sirhan, Kennedy's alleged assassin, portrayed him as someone who had spent his formative years in America and therefore was "a natural product of the atmosphere of crime in the United States." At the same time, his act was seen as the result of frustration caused by "American discrimination against the Arabs."

The VOA, which from the primaries on had correspondents with all the major candidates, reported the assassination in detail, without speculating on Sirhan's motives. It gave heavy emphasis to American and world reactions of shock.

The conventions of the two major parties were given considerable attention by the Soviets, who also discussed favourably the decision of the U.S. Communist Party to run its first presidential slate since 1940. Two Soviet correspondents covered the Republican convention in Miami, Fla., where they commented on the relative scarcity of Negroes among delegates and the strong proportion of businessmen. Richard Nixon was portrayed as an opportunist.

In Chicago the Soviets covered not only the Democratic convention itself but the demonstrations outside as well. They reported that the nomination of Hubert Humphrey surprised few since "a majority of the delegates had been handpicked by party bosses." The Chinese ignored the convention, giving all their attention to the demonstrations. VOA covered both conventions live, including the Chicago demonstrations, while avoiding any station-originated comment.

The outcome of the election was virtually ignored by the Chinese, while the Soviets emphasized the closeness of the race, the high cost of electioneering, and the dangers and "undemocratic" nature of the electoral college system. The election of Nixon was viewed more as a repudiation of the Democrats than as a victory for the Republicans.   (H. H. Sa.)

Psychology

Rioting occurred in more than 100 so-called black or Negro ghettos in the U.S. following the assassination of Martin Luther King, Jr. (April 1968); for the previous year 164 instances of such violence (including major rioting in Detroit, Mich., and Newark, N.J.) were recorded by the National Advisory Commission on Civil Disorders. Interviews with residents of the Detroit and Newark ghettos (*Scientific American*, p. 15, August 1968) yielded no support for the popular hypothesis that black rioters are poorer, less educated, or more disturbed than Negro nonrioters. About half of those who identified themselves as rioters wanted to be called "black" (rather than "Negro" or "coloured"), while only about a third of the nonrioters favoured that label. It was concluded "that the continued exclusion of Negroes from Ameri-

can economic and social life is the fundamental cause of riots . . . and is most galling to young Negroes who perceive it as arbitrary and unjust."

However, social factors do not seem to be the only correlates of violent behaviour. Most male criminals show the normal number of 46 chromosomes, one of which (the so-called Y-chromosome) is not found in normal females. Yet, a recent study of 129 men in institutions for criminals (*Science*, vol. 159, p. 1249, 1968) reveals 11 "supermales" (men with two Y-chromosomes to give a total of 47). This is a significantly greater incidence of chromosomal abnormality than is found in the general population. On the basis of such data it has been suggested that the surplus "Y-chromosome represents a double dose of those potencies that may under certain conditions facilitate the development of aggressive behavior." (*Psychology Today*, p. 46, October 1968.) Similar findings had been reported earlier in England.

The order in which children are born into their families also seems to be related to their behavioural tendencies (*American Psychological Association, Annual Proceedings*, p. 165, 1968). According to one hypothesis, firstborns should find the prospect of painful stimulation more frightening than do children of later birth order. If this is so, firstborns should be unusually prone to avoid high-risk physical activities (*e.g.*, contact sports). A questionnaire survey of the New York Giants football team, the New York Mets baseball team, and two large samples of students from Ivy League universities produced convincing evidence in support of the prediction (*Journal of Personality and Social Psychology*, vol. 8, p. 351, 1968).

According to one theory, the effects of learning are stored chemically in ribonucleic acid (RNA), a compound found throughout the body, including brain cells. Earlier studies indicated that these effects could be transferred by injecting untrained animals with chemical extracts taken from the brains of those previously trained. But these results have not been verified consistently, perhaps because the extracts can vary widely in composition (*Psychological Bulletin*, vol. 68, p. 160, 1967). Experimental data reported during recent months (*Nature*, vol. 217, p. 1259, 1968) indicated positive transfer of learning to untrained mice that had been injected with materials taken from the brains of rats trained to prefer lighted environments over darkened places. Significantly, evidence was offered that the substance involved in the transfer is not RNA, but another type of material that chemists call a peptide.

More than three decades ago, a distinction was drawn between classical and instrumental conditioning. Classical conditioning involves the pairing of an unconditioned stimulus (*e.g.*, food) with a neutral stimulus (*e.g.*, a buzzer) that then comes to elicit the previously unconditioned response (*e.g.*, salivation). In instrumental conditioning a behavioural response is more likely to recur when followed by a reward; a punishing stimulus correspondingly decreases the likelihood of that response recurring. Traditionally it has been held that only classical conditioning can modify such automatic responses as the pupillary reflex, galvanic skin responses, heart rate, and vasoconstriction; *i.e.*, those mediated by the autonomic nervous system. A recent series of experiments offers strong evidence that such responses can be instrumentally conditioned. Deeply curarized rats, maintained on artificial respiration, were trained to increase or decrease heart rate, to vary intestinal contractions, and to increase or de-

Protected States:
see Dependent States
Protestant Episcopal Church:
see Religion
Psychiatry:
see Medicine

Supervisory personnel wearing masks while playing the role of hard-core unemployed job candidates. Masks are part of a "sensitivity kit" used by Human Development Institute, Inc., in an attempt to increase understanding on the part of supervisory personnel of problems faced by the untrained and unskilled.

crease urinary output by using electrical brain stimulation as a reward (*American Psychological Association, Annual Proceedings*, p. 259, 1968). Curarized rats likewise can learn to increase or decrease heart rate to escape or avoid mild electric shock. Also reported was evidence that the voltage of brain waves has been altered by instrumental conditioning; such learning transfers from the curarized to the non-curarized state. Assuming that human heart rate can be instrumentally conditioned to increase or decrease according to the direction rewarded, the implications for psychosomatic medicine are most hopeful. For example, such dangerous or distressful symptoms as excessively rapid or irregular heartbeat or high blood pressure could be altered in the direction of safety and comfort with appropriate reconditioning.

Psychological research is being conducted at an unprecedented pace, and it has become evident that researchers need to take into account those social and psychological factors that influence the behaviour of experimental subjects in a systematic but uncontrolled way. It has been suggested that rigorous research strategies (*i.e.*, clear definitions of the problems and relevant variables, control of subjects, and so on) themselves may lead to situations that contaminate rather than clarify results (*Psychological Bulletin*, vol. 70, p. 185, 1968). Drawing on information from organization theory, the journal article just cited postulates that the relationships involved in this kind of research strikingly parallel the situation of management and labour, researchers being cast in the role of management and subjects playing the role of labour. The researcher expects (as does management) that the subject-employee will behave in a passive, compliant style with noncritical acceptance of the researcher's definition of the task. According to the journal article, the unintended consequences predictable from organization theory might well include such behaviour as the following: A subject may withdraw as a participant; or he may express covert hostility toward the researcher, second-guess the research design, and find a way around it as well as engaging in other ploys that may influence and shape the nature of his involvement. The influence of these factors depends on the subject's sophistication, his appraisal of the meaningfulness of research, of the trustworthiness of the researcher, and the extent to which being manipulated and controlled is acceptable to him.

(J. T. G.; C. CE.)

Public Health:
see Medicine

Public Utilities:
see Cooperatives;
    Fuel and Power;
    Industrial Review;
    Transportation

See also Medicine; Sociology.

Publishing

Magazines. Continued, unspectacular change marked the year 1968. Publishers placed more emphasis on specialized audiences, personalized journalism, innovative formats, and higher prices for both advertisers and subscribers. In the U.S. the moves seemed effectively to counter a 1967 revenue setback and the boost in postal rates. During the first six months of 1968 the number of advertising pages dropped 4%, yet thanks to business streamlining, the industry reported a 1% increase in overall revenue. The most striking news, however, was the slimming operation forced on two big companies, the Curtis Publishing Co. in the U.S. and the West German publishing empire of Axel Springer (*see* BIOGRAPHY; *Newspapers*, below).

Springer's reductions followed a government report critical of the extent of his control of the West German press. In June he sold the weekly *Das Neue Blatt* (circulation 1.2 million) and offered four other weeklies to the Hamburg group of Gruner und Jahr, publishers of the weekly *Stern*. This offer was refused, but two days later a Berlin group, Weitpert, bought four of Springer's magazines: *Jasmin* (circulation 1.5 million), described as "erotic and gay"; *Eltern* (1.2 million) for parents of young children; *Bravo* (728,000) for teen-agers; and *Twen* (165,000) for clothes-conscious young men.

Unable to meet its bank loan payments and losing advertising, Curtis, under its new president, Martin Ackerman: (1) sold the *Ladies' Home Journal* and *American Home* for a reported $5.4 million in Downe Communications, Inc., stock; (2) planned to revise the editorial policy of *Holiday;* (3) purchased Igor Cassini's *Status,* possibly to challenge Hearst's *Town and Country;* and (4) trimmed three million subscribers from the *Saturday Evening Post* to cut circulation costs and change the *Post* from a mass medium magazine to a special interest book for families in the upper educational-income brackets. A $5 million loan from Time Inc. made it possible to switch lower income subscribers to *Life.* Due to faulty computers, Arkansas Gov. Winthrop Rockefeller and Ackerman himself received cancellation notices; the *Wall Street Journal* had a holiday depicting the reactions of imaginary subscribers on being told they were unwanted as future *Post* readers.

A shake-up in British magazines began early in the year when International Publishing Corporation (IPC) merged its competing general and women's magazines into a general magazines division, and its trade and technical journals into a business publications division. In a move toward unified control of trade publications within the Thomson Organization, Northwood Industrial, Ltd., was to take over Associated Trade Publications, Ltd. In December the British versions of *Good Housekeeping* and *House Beautiful*, published by the National Magazine Co., Ltd., were merged.

Scholarly and scientific magazines multiplied at the usual alarming rate. *Ulrich's International Periodicals Directory*, in its 12th edition, boasted 8,700 new listings in the arts, humanities, business, and social sciences. The total, including science and technology publications, was over 30,000. And while no one was certain how many magazines were issued in the U.S., the growth rate seemed to run from 150 to 200 new magazines per year. That specialized publishing was

very profitable was apparent in the high price ($37.2 million) paid by Capital Cities Broadcasting Corp. for Fairchild Publications, Inc., publishers of *Women's Wear Daily* and seven other trade newspapers.

Another facet of the mass medium syndrome took shape in 1968. One group suggested the elimination of paid subscriptions for magazines of over one million circulation. Profit would come from controlled circulation that guaranteed advertisers a well-defined market. Potential customers would be flooded with free copies of the magazine. On this premise the Consumer Communications Corp. launched *Homemaker's Digest* and sent it without charge to ten million families in key target areas. Out of Cleveland, O., *Dare* continued its free circulation to 95,000 college students and reported that it was doing well.

Using somewhat the same approach, house organ circulations rose as companies used them to seek goodwill. IBM's *Think* and the *Ford Times* continued to enjoy a lead. The Bank of America was to sponsor a monthly magazine for the nearly two million families who used its credit card system. United Air Lines' *Mainliner* became as familiar in libraries as on airplanes. The 700 or so corporation magazines grossed over $110 million in nontaxable advertising—serious competition for private enterprise.

In order to survive, consumer magazines felt obliged to offer advertisers more selective audiences. *Look* developed an edition aimed at subscribers in zip-code zones with a predominantly upper income class. *Fortune* offered advertisers an edition especially tailored for top echelon manufacturers. Improved printing and distribution methods suggested numerous other combinations.

The U.S. public, clamouring for personalized journalism, found its hero in Norman Mailer. Reporting on the Washington peace march and the Republican and Democratic conventions for *Harper's*, he told it like it was, Mailer-wise. *Atlantic*'s Dan Wakefield used a similar approach on the national mood over Vietnam, and *Esquire* published admittedly biased reports on Mayor Richard Daley's Chicago by Jean Genet, Wil-

Japanese newsboy delivering "Asahi Shimbun," the newspaper with the world's largest circulation, to a worker in a rice paddy. About 98% of the paper's circulation of 9 million was home delivered.

MCGRAW-HILL WORLD NEWS

liam Burroughs, and Allen Ginsberg. The highest figure ever paid for an article went to the estate of the late Robert Kennedy for his story of the 1962 Cuban missile crisis; *McCall's* paid $1 million for the 25,000 words. Even cartoonists, a minor drawing card for most magazines, assumed new personal importance. David Levine found himself featured on the cover of *Time* and *Newsweek* in the same week; Edward Sorel, in *Ramparts, Esquire,* and *Atlantic,* did much to blast the figures of the Johnson administration; and Jules Feiffer gained new popularity.

The more successful new publications in the U.S. followed the dictum of a specialized audience. For a whopping $50, Marshall McLuhan promised immediate reports on technological and electronic breakthroughs in his monthly printed newsletter, *Dew-Line*. *Psychology Today* and *Careers Today* proved that a newcomer (a University of Chicago group) can break into the field.

Of the new British ventures, most interesting was that of Helen Vlachos, whose right-wing papers in Greece had been suspended. In London in May she began the monthly *Hellenic Review* of Greek current affairs but closed it in November when her husband was placed under surveillance in Greece. An IPC-supported monthly, *Help,* was launched in May to "attack bureaucratic humbug"; despite an impressive list of contributors and subscribers, however, it did not appeal to any audience. In March the Nottingham-based Illustrated Country Magazine Group relaunched the *Tatler and Bystander,* with a social section supervised by the editor of *Burke's Peerage.* Of the new magazines aimed at an affluent male readership, Seerey-Lester's *Man About* tried but failed to acquire wide circulation without photographs of nudes or political articles.

International ventures in 1968 included the launching of an Austrian family monthly, *Sie,* by Hurst Barnard, independent British printers, using editorial material from the National Magazine Co.'s *She.* Two daily newspapers, the Paris evening *Le Monde* and the Vatican's *L'Osservatore Romano,* started English-language weeklies.

No major new children's magazines appeared on the scene, and educators and librarians alike bemoaned the lack of innovative periodicals in this area. A different complaint came from Canada where a Western Ontario University study revealed that Canadian college freshmen chose U.S. magazines over Canadian ones and scored 1.1% higher on knowledge of U.S. current

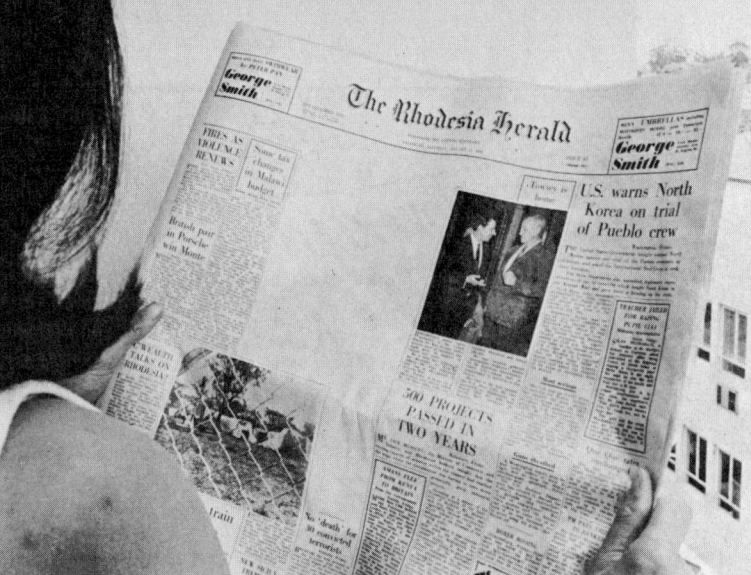

WIDE WORLD

Editors of the "Rhodesia Herald" (Salisbury), frequent critics of the Ian Smith regime, leave blank spaces in the paper to call attention to news stories that have been censored by the government.

"Just so you won't talk about us after we've gone." —King, "Daily Telegraph," Australia.

events than on Canadian events. Canadian publishers, forced to specialize, continued to do well enough with literary magazines. *Tamarack Review* celebrated its 12th anniversary and *The Malahat Review, Prism,* and *Canadian Literature* reported they were doing well.

In the U.S., the hippie newspapers, often closer to magazines in approach and content, proved a financial and cultural hit. Although filling a different type of gap for young people than most educators and librarians envisioned, the underground claimed a readership of 4.6 million, 50 to 280 different papers, and at least two news services.

Regardless of purpose or content, publishers were promising new approaches to format—*e.g.,* records, instructional courses—and McLuhan even offered "sensory training units." Thanks to a psychedelic layout, *Eye* boosted circulation to over 300,000 by year's end. Depending more on the public's familiarity with names than on format *Mayday* started in New York. Modeled in part after the successful *I. F. Stone's Weekly,* it boasted an editorial staff of two former *Time* correspondents, Andrew Kopkind and Robert Sherrill, and James Ridgeway of the *New Republic.* But it took more than personality to save a magazine. After 19 years Max Ascoli's *The Reporter,* founded as a liberal publication, went under, primarily because it supported the Johnson administration. The subscrip-

Police and students battling outside the Springer Press Building in West Berlin after an attempted assassination of student leader Rudi Dutschke. Springer publications were under attack because of criticism of student opinions and activities.

tion list and many of the writers went to *Harper's.* In contrast, one controversial current affairs monthly, *Ramparts,* became a biweekly. The British Broadcasting Corporation's *Listener* ran into legal difficulties in late October when the Periodical Publishers Association claimed that since August 1967 it had contained "much more" than the 10% of nonbroadcast material allowed under the BBC charter.

Across the industry the cost of advertising and subscriptions jumped in 1968. Announcements of future boosts in advertising rates accounted for 18 pages in *Consumer Magazine and Farm Publication Rates and Data* for Oct. 27, 1968, and more were to follow. At the same time, the annual subscription price index, as reported in the *Library Journal,* "continued to move upward at a sobering pace." In the U.K., prices for many "quality" women's and general magazines and reviews were raised.

More involved with the message than the medium (or the reader or the advertiser), the ubiquitous little magazines increased in numbers. Some 1,200 publications carried new poetry, opinion, and prose to readers who rarely numbered over 500. Unexpected help continued to come from the Coordinating Council of Literary Magazines, which had received a $50,000 grant from the National Endowment for the Arts. After repeated crises, the *Adam International Review* was to be saved; though still edited in London, it would be published by the University of Rochester, N.Y.

Recognition that old magazines could be valuable became evident at auctions. Movie magazines, comics, and social commentary journals brought prices as high as $100 per copy. Reprints of little and radical magazines cost from $5 to $40 per volume. By year's end Kraus Reprint had published in book form nearly every issue of 104 U.S. and British little magazines.

On April 22 the U.S. Supreme Court upheld a New York law banning sales to children of "suggestive" publications. By year's end dozens of states and municipalities had passed or studied laws patterned on the New York statute, and the Magazine Publishers Association urged the government to keep its hands off the industry. On May 28, however, the court, in an unsigned opinion, declared vague and unconstitutional the section specifically prohibiting the sale of "any magazine which would appeal to the lust of persons under the age of 18 years."

In a time of increased freedom of sexual expression, such magazines as *Playboy* and its feminine counterpart, *Cosmopolitan,* built followings. Another advocate of the same freedom, Ralph Ginzburg, won an appeal of a five-year jail sentence for publication of *Eros,* among other works. Advertisements for his *Avant Garde* cashed in on the case's continued publicity. *Evergreen Review* literally received a censorship blast in July. The Grove Press offices where the magazine was edited were bombed. Apparently Cuban exiles retaliated for the issue publishing excerpts of "Che" Guevara's diary. In the U.K. *New Worlds,* saved in 1967 by an Arts Council grant, stopped publication after W. H. Smith and Sons Ltd. refused to handle the March issue because it used "four-letter" words.

(A. N. F.; W. A. KA.)

Newspapers. Strikes in the U.S., France, and Britain were among 1968's common denominators in Western newspaper publishing. Worst in the U.S., in France they formed part of the general May–June wave of industrial unrest (*see* FRANCE), and in Britain they affected mainly the national dailies. Even more serious, however, were the threats to press freedom that came

from political dictatorships, the judiciary, government action on disclosure of "secret" information, efforts to protect personal privacy, and mergers and take-overs leading to monopoly controls.

Journalists played important roles in major world news stories of 1968. Of special significance in the crisis in Czechoslovakia was the fact that the Czechoslovak government had abolished press censorship in January and that "lacky" journalists turned into real heroes in the liberalization movement. During the first few days following the August invasion, clandestine radio stations and newspapers had great influence in bringing about a passive but united show of solidarity. As might have been expected, the Soviets forced the Czechoslovakian National Assembly to reestablish direct censorship of the mass media.

In the U.S., reporters for the print and electronic media actually made part of the news at the Democratic national convention rather than just covering it. The August convention in Chicago was held under tight security arrangements because of the thousands of protesters who had gathered. When trouble broke out between police and demonstrators, several dozen reporters and photographers were injured by police. Chicago Mayor Richard Daley was severely castigated by some sections of the press, particularly the television networks. The news media, however, did not seem to be entirely in agreement as to what happened and why it happened.

In the announcement of the 1968 Pulitzer Prizes for journalism, the most interesting element was the awarding of three prizes to one newspaper organization. John S. Knight, editorial chairman of the Knight Newspapers, won the editorial writing prize. The staff of the *Detroit Free Press,* a Knight newspaper, grabbed honours for general local reporting and became the first newspaper to receive the award while not publishing. Eugene Gray Payne of the *Charlotte (N.C.) Observer,* another Knight newspaper, was honoured for his editorial cartooning.

Of the high-level disagreements during 1968, the most dramatic was that between Cecil Harmsworth King and his fellow directors of the IPC, the world's largest publishing empire. King's much-publicized political pronouncements reached their high point when, in mid-May in a front page article in the *Daily Mirror,* a pro-Labour publication, he demanded "a new start under a new leader." On May 30, King was dismissed from the IPC board.

A widely publicized example of objections to invasion of privacy was the criticism of the *Daily Express*'s publication of family snapshots of the queen taken soon after Prince Andrew's birth. *Paris-Match,* which also used the pictures, had been praised for "the best royal pictures yet."

Several clashes between government and the press in the U.S. during 1968 revolved around charges of antitrust violations. Early in the year Federal District Judge James A. Walsh officially ruled that the joint operation of the *Tucson Daily Citizen* and the *Arizona Star* by William A. Small, Jr., was a violation per se of the Sherman Anti-Trust Act. Prior to 1965 the *Citizen* and the *Star* had been under separate ownership but had operated jointly in selling advertising, providing circulation service, and printing the newspapers. When the *Citizen* purchased the *Star* in 1965, the U.S. Justice Department challenged not only the purchase but the whole concept of a joint operation of business functions. Both Judge Walsh and the Justice Department had indicated approval of a joint

printing arrangement only, but considered the addition of joint circulation and advertising sales an activity that restrained trade and eliminated any possibility of additional competition. There were 21 other U.S. cities in which two independent newspapers had entered into some type of agreement that joined all or part of the printing, circulation, and advertising operations. These papers would be subject to federal prosecution if the lower court ruling was upheld by the Supreme Court.

Legislation that would exempt newspapers engaged in agency arrangements from antitrust action had been introduced in 1967 by Sen. Carl Hayden of Arizona. The Senate Judiciary Subcommittee on Antitrust and Monopoly and the House Judiciary Committee held hearings in 1968 on the bill, entitled the Newspaper Preservation Act. Most smaller publishers, especially those in suburban areas, expressed opposition to the bill. Publishers from cities where the joint operations were in existence were favourable, as was the American Newspaper Publishers Association. The financial problems of starting a new daily paper were pointed out by the continued failure in New York to replace the *World Journal Tribune* and so provide a rival to the *Post,* the surviving afternoon paper.

Elsewhere on the antitrust scene, the *Los Angeles Times* was denied a hearing by the U.S. Supreme Court on a decision rendered in 1967. The Times Mirror Corp. had been ordered to divest itself of the newspapers in San Bernardino, Calif., that had been purchased in 1964. E. W. Scripps Co., threatened with an antitrust action by the Justice Department over its ownership of a majority holding in the *Cincinnati* (O.) *Enquirer,* agreed to sell its 58% stock interest within 18 months. Scripps had purchased more than 50% of the *Enquirer* stock in 1956, and two years later had bought the *Times-Star,* which was then merged with the Scripps newspaper, the *Post.*

Justice Department activities against newspapers even reached into the circulation area with a Supreme Court decision early in the year that the *St. Louis* (Mo.) *Globe-Democrat* had been guilty of violating the Sherman Anti-Trust Act when it tried to fix the resale price of its newspaper through an independent dealer. A bad year was made worse when the Federal Communications Commission began discussing limitations on newspaper ownership of broadcast facilities.

Attacks on alleged monopolistic practices were not confined to the U.S. Axel Springer, the West German press magnate, took his lumps from a government-appointed commission. In a June report, the commission suggested that when one newspaper owner had 20% of the circulation in the country, press freedom was endangered and that when that circulation rose to 40%, press freedom was "directly prejudiced." Newspapers owned by Springer accounted for over 39% of the West German newspaper circulation, and his magazines had 17% of the circulation. In addition to the government suggestion that he cut down his circulation, student demonstrations in the spring attempted to halt distribution of some of his magazines. Apparently in response to all of this, Springer sold five of his magazines in June.

One of the year's major acquisition attempts began in October, when Robert Maxwell of Pergamon Press offered £26 million for the *News of the World,* the largest-selling English-language Sunday paper, which was heavily in debt with profits down from 32% of capital in 1961 to 12% in 1967. This was refused by Sir William Carr, chairman of the News of the World

"We can't advance. We don't have any troops. These are all news correspondents." —Pearson, "Knickerbocker News," Albany, N.Y.

Organisation. Maxwell, who was more interested in the underemployed plant than in the paper, then raised his price to more than £34 million. Carr, however, made a deal with an associated Australian group, News Ltd., that gave him 51% control. Possible action by various antitrust groups, and Maxwell's independent bid for Australian interests, held up the final disposition and confused the issues involved.

The longest strike in the history of U.S. newspapers was ended during 1968. The *Detroit News* was struck by the teamsters when the contract expired at midnight Nov. 15, 1967, and resumed publication on Aug. 9, 1968—some 267 days later. The *Detroit Free Press* closed down on November 18 in accordance with a publishers' agreement. Both newspapers ended up having to settle strikes with 13 other unions after reaching an agreement with the teamsters. Detroit had a long history of newspaper blackouts, and there were indications that the management of both newspapers would resist future strikes by operating without union help if necessary. The establishment of a single expiration date for all contracts was expected to produce better interunion cooperation.

In Los Angeles, the Hearst owned *Herald-Examiner* continued to publish without union employees, as it had since Dec. 15, 1967. The situation became particularly emotional, with acts of violence becoming part of the conflict. The Los Angeles dispute gave rise, in part, to a strike of the *San Francisco Examiner* and *Chronicle* from January 5 to February 25, when pickets from the Los Angeles strike appeared at the San Francisco papers. There was even a three-day strike of newspapers in Washington, D.C., in July.

In Britain, the most serious strike, by the Society of Lithographic Artists and Designers (SLADE), began on August 5 with a demand for higher pay without any form of productivity agreement, and ended on September 6. Beginning with a strike in October by Manchester *Daily Mirror* employees (ended by local settlement), demands for higher pay rates to preserve London-provincial differentials spread to London and Glasgow papers.

In France almost all Paris and provincial papers ceased publication during early summer, exceptions being the Communist Party daily *L'Humanité* and the Paris evening *Le Monde*, which printed some 300,000 more copies than usual. In autumn the Paris daily *Le Figaro*, proud of its 112-year record of rarely (ex-

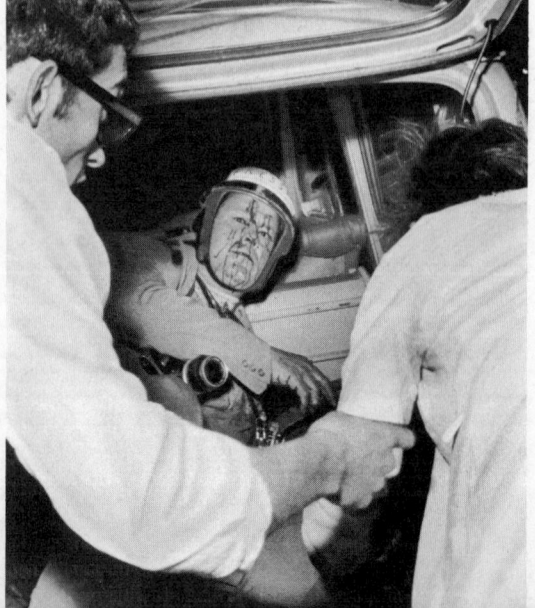

Londoner looking at the front-page photograph of the royal family taken shortly after the birth of Prince Edward. The picture appeared in the Oct. 2, 1968, issue of the "Daily Express." The "Express" was criticized for publishing this and similar photographs without permission from the queen.

cept in wartime) missing an edition, was threatened with a serious strike. A token strike in October showed workers' determination to resist industrialist-owner Jean Prouvost's intention to assert the editorial control that had been denied him in 1949, when he bought the paper, because he had served in the Vichy government.

The battle between the press and the legal profession over appropriate coverage of criminals and criminal trials took a definite turn against the news media in the U.S. The Reardon Report, which recommended considerable restriction on the amount and type of information that should be released to the press by law enforcement agencies, was adopted by the House of Delegates of the American Bar Association in February. While it was unlikely that all or even most of the state bar associations would adopt the report, as a practical matter the mere existence of its recommendations had encouraged many judges to place limitations on trial coverage. Extremely tight rules were placed on coverage related to the trials of James Earl Ray, accused of murdering the Rev. Martin Luther King, Jr., in Memphis, and Sirhan Sirhan, charged with the murder of Sen. Robert F. Kennedy in Los Angeles.

In Britain, disquiet resulted from clashes between papers and legal authorities on what constituted "contempt of court" in political reporting. Growing liberalism on the part of the High Court was shown in the decision by Lord Chief Justice Lord Parker of Waddington to absolve the *Sunday Times* editor of blame for publishing a photograph caption describing "Michael X" (Michael Abdul Malik) as "brothel keeper, procurer, and property racketeer" while he was awaiting retrial under the Race Relations Act, 1965. Lord Devlin, the Press Council chairman, in a foreword to the March 1968 annual report, stressed that part of the council's duty was to repel "unjustifiable attacks on the press"—a welcome change from its former policy of almost always finding against the newspaper.

Newspapers were more severely hit by devaluation than other sectors of British publishing. Price increases reflected the high rise in the cost of imported newsprint, the restriction of advertising by deflation-

ary policy, and expensive strike settlements. The increase of 1d. for the *Daily Mirror* led to court action when the National Federation of Retail Newsagents, Booksellers, and Stationers boycotted the newspaper because the increase had been accompanied by a 1% reduction in wholesale and retail terms. The court settled in favour of the *Mirror*. Cost of newspaper development was highlighted in Britain by *The Times*'s achievement by October 1968 of a two-thirds increase over its May 1966 circulation—at a cost to Lord Thomson of considerably more than £1 million a year for extensive advertising, editorial, and format changes.

Elsewhere in the world there were both pluses and minuses pertaining to freedom of the press. Prior censorship of the press in Rhodesia was ended on April 6. It had been instituted in November 1965, at the time Rhodesia separated itself from Britain. The press in Greece was still operating under a military dictatorship, but censorship of newspapers and magazines was ended about the middle of the year. It was suggested by the government that the key to continued "freedom" was satisfactory "self-control." In Spain, in July, 168 journalists in a letter to the government protested the series of restrictions and penalties that had been imposed on the press since May. Most serious was the suspension of the afternoon *Madrid* for failure to pay "due respect" to government bodies. In articles criticizing French Pres. Charles de Gaulle as "an old man clinging obstinately to office," *Madrid* had drawn comparisons to the Spanish political situation.

There was even a flicker of liberty in the U.S.S.R. where four Western newspapers were given permission to be sold over the counter in Moscow. The London *Times, Neue Zürcher Zeitung* (Switzerland), *Le Monde,* and the international edition of the *New York Herald Tribune* began making sales in large hotels over the summer months. In the autumn a Central Committee decree, attributing lack of interest in press reports to poor presentation, suggested use of "actual examples" in explaining policy, selectivity and simplification in reporting decrees and speeches, and greater attention to "letters to the editor." One assessment, made in 1968 for 1967, suggested, however, that there had been an overall reduction in the amount of press freedom throughout the world. The study was conducted by the Freedom of Information Center at the University of Missouri.

A year of problems also extended to the wire services. In the U.S. the *Chicago Tribune* abandoned its wire news service; in Britain, Exchange Telegraph confined itself to financial news. The end of the 50-year noncompetitive agreement between Reuters and the Associated Press's Dow Jones service led to rivalry for the U.S. financial news: Reuters flashed the news of possible Vietnam peace talks just as Wall Street opened, scooping Dow Jones by eight minutes.

(A. N. F.; M. D. Bu.; X.)

Books. Further technological advances in printing (*see* INDUSTRIAL REVIEW: *Printing*) and the application of scientific methods to market research, cost, production, and distribution could be noted throughout the book publishing industry in 1968. Publishers' trade missions and sales of translation and publication rights opened up new markets; shared production, information, sales, and distribution services helped to develop them. Execution overseas of large printing orders used underemployed facilities in smaller countries, and kept prices competitive. Paperbacks

World Daily Newspapers and Circulations, 1967–68*

Country	Daily newspapers	Circulation per 1,000 of population	Country	Daily newspapers	Circulation per 1,000 of population
AFRICA			China, Communist	392	19
			Cyprus	12	136
Algeria	3	15	Hong Kong	16	349
Angola	4	9	India	459	13
Cameroon	1	4	Indonesia	72	7
Central African Republic	1	†	Iran	14	15
Ceuta	1	58	Iraq	4	12
Chad	1	†	Israel	20	143
Congo (Brazzaville)	3	1.3	Japan	116	465
Congo (Kinshasa)	6	2	Jordan	3	8
Dahomey	2	1	Korea, North	7	‡
Ethiopia	6	2	Korea, South	29	51
Gabon	1	1	Kuwait	4	28
Ghana	4	37	Laos	4	5
Guinea	1	†	Lebanon	33	97
Ivory Coast	1	3	Macao	1	171
Kenya	3	9	Malaysia	35	57
Liberia	1	4	Mongolia	2	88
Libya	5	5	Nepal	13	3
Malagasy Republic	6	9	Pakistan	90	18
Mali	2	†	Philippines	16	27
Mauritius	13	122	Ryukyu Islands	9	366
Melilla	1	60	Saudi Arabia	5	8
Morocco	7	17	Singapore	7	268
Mozambique	5	6	Syria	3	11
Niger	1	†	Taiwan	31	64
Nigeria	18	7	Thailand	18	22
Portuguese Guinea	1	2	Turkey	372	45
Réunion	1	61	Vietnam, North	3	10
Rhodesia	2	15	Vietnam, South	34	51
Senegal	1	6	Yemen	5	18
Seychelles	2	47	Total	1,874	
Sierra Leone	2	10			
Somali Republic	1	2	**EUROPE**		
South Africa	21	57			
South West Africa	2	12	Albania	2	45
Sudan	10	5	Austria	27	249
Tanzania	8	3	Belgium	47	285
Togo	2	6	Bulgaria	12	187
Tunisia	5	27	Czechoslovakia	23	288
Uganda	6	8	Denmark	91	347
United Arab Republic	10	15	Finland	59	358
Upper Volta	2	†	France	101	245
Zambia	1	8	Germany, East	40	421
Total	174		Germany, West	473	332
			Gibraltar	1	120
NORTH AMERICA			Greece	98	125
			Hungary	24	187
Bahama Islands	2	114	Iceland	5	435
Barbados	2	112	Ireland	7	243
Bermuda	2	334	Italy	85	113
British Honduras	2	55	Luxembourg	6	477
Canada	114	218	Malta	7	‡
Costa Rica	4	77	Netherlands	80	292
Cuba	9	88	Norway	88	381
Dominican Republic	5	27	Poland	41	179
El Salvador	8	47	Portugal	27	68
Guadeloupe	1	9	Romania	9	161
Guatemala	9	31	Spain	73	153
Haiti	4	5	Sweden	101	501
Honduras	7	19	Switzerland	107	344
Jamaica	2	69	U.S.S.R.	457	274
Leeward Islands	2	33	United Kingdom	119	488
Martinique	1	9	Vatican City (Holy See)	1	§
Mexico	132	116	Yugoslavia	21	80
Netherlands Antilles	6	138	Total	2,232	
Nicaragua	7	49			
Panama (incl. Canal Zone)	11	78	**OCEANIA**		
Puerto Rico	4	96			
Trinidad and Tobago	2	102	American Samoa	1	37
United States	1,749	312	Australia	63	370
Virgin Islands (U.S.)	4	170	Cook Islands	1	29
Windward Islands	1	8	Fiji Islands	1	20
Total	2,090		French Polynesia	1	73
			Guam	1	272
SOUTH AMERICA			New Caledonia	1	65
			New Zealand	40	380
Argentina	86	148	Niue	1	60
Bolivia	12	26	Tonga	12	16
Brazil	68	33	Total	122	
Chile	34	118	Grand total	6,886	
Colombia	38	52			
Ecuador	16	45			
French Guiana	1	42			
Guyana	4	73	*Only newspapers issued four or more times weekly are included. Areas not listed had no known daily newspapers. †Total circulation less than 1 per 1,000 population. ‡Not available. §Circulation largely outside territory.		
Paraguay	4	37			
Peru	72	47			
Surinam	5	49			
Uruguay	28	314			
Venezuela	26	70			
Total	394				
			Sources: For numerical count: *Newspaper Press Directory 1968, Benn's Guide to Newspapers and Periodicals of the World;* for U.S. and Canada, *Editor & Publisher International Yearbook* (1968); other secondary sources. For circulation estimates: *UN Statistical Yearbook 1967* (1968).		
ASIA					
Afghanistan	15	6			
Burma	10	9			
Cambodia	11	11	(W. A. Ha.)		
Ceylon	9	43			

tightened their hold on "quality" markets in the U.S. and the U.K., and elsewhere began to take an important share in sales. Injections of foreign capital— from the U.S. in Britain and elsewhere; from Britain in Africa, Australia, and New Zealand—provided competition, new ideas and techniques, and new potential markets. International ventures begun in 1968 reflected the interest in diversification on the part of large companies. The take-over of Corgi Books, Britain's third largest paperback series (after Penguin and Pan), by a U.S. theatrical, film, and television company in May 1968 carried with it chances for film and television tie-ins. The acquisition by McGraw-Hill Book Co. Inc., of a 10% interest in Penguin Books (announced in June) opened new markets for Penguins. Encyclopædia Britannica's purchase of a minority interest in the Weidenfeld Group reflected its increasing interest in general book publishing. In addition, it was reported in the fall of 1968 that the Italian publishers Arnoldo Mondadori, which already produced 25 million books in 20 languages for 40 countries, were considering entry into the British market.

The first co-publishing agreement between a capitalist and a Communist book company was announced at the Frankfurt (W.Ger.) Book Fair in September. Yugoslavia's state publishing house, Mladinska Knijga, was to print and distribute, first in Yugoslavia and eventually throughout Eastern Europe, scientific and technical books published by McGraw-Hill Book Co. Inc., of the U.S. The books would be printed in English and produced at much lower costs than were possible in the U.S. In a test project in 1967, six U.S. classics had been printed by the Yugoslav house and had sold out quickly at the equivalent of $1 each. Two other U.S. publishers, Doubleday & Co. and Time-Life, also completed plans to have their books printed by the Yugoslav company.

While some mergers were opening new opportunities, there was growing concern about the changes caused by the transition of book publishing into a technological industry. Although publishing houses generally claimed that their mergers with big corporations, primarily in the electronics field, did not affect either their quality or their independence, there were exceptions and a shift in top editorial personnel was noted in several U.S. publishing houses.

While some of the changes were outgrowths of shifts in the emphasis of a house's business after a merger, *i.e.*, from trade books to textbooks, others reflected influences on the business as a whole. The federal government diverted to the Vietnam war about $150 million that had been spent in previous years to purchase books for schools and libraries. In addition, some U.S. paperback publishers had overextended, producing too many books for the market.

In 1967, 28,762 titles were published in the U.S., according to *Publishers' Weekly*. The decrease of 1,288 titles from the 1966 total reflected revisions in *Publishers' Weekly* counting procedures to make the figures more representative of U.S. book output and to bring them more in line with UNESCO's standards on book statistics and the proposed U.S. standards. The two main changes in policy were the counting of each volume in a set separately only if it had a separate title and formed a separate whole, and the counting of imports only if no more than a year had lapsed between the time a book was published and the time it was available in the U.S.

In the major acquisitions and mergers in 1967–68, Harcourt, Brace and World, Inc., acquired Guidance Associates, a producer of educational films; Columbia Broadcasting System merged with Holt, Rinehart and Winston; Cowles Communications, Inc., acquired Cambridge Book Co., Inc.; Litton Industries, Inc., acquired American Book Co.; Encyclopædia Britannica acquired Technomics, Inc., of California; and Scott, Foresman and Co. acquired William Morrow Co. and agreed to a merger with South-Western Publishing Co. In addition, Field Enterprises Educational Corp. bought the Harr Wagner Publishing Co.; Doubleday added Communications Films, Inc., of Monterey Park, Calif.; New Jersey Lithographers acquired Rocappi, Inc., a pioneer firm in the use of computer-operated typesetting; Charles E. Merrill Publishing Co. became a subsidiary of Bell & Howell Co.; and Xerox Corp. purchased the R. R. Bowker Co.

Critics of publishing centralization found support for their fears in June when Hobart Lewis, president of Reader's Digest Association, Inc., ordered Funk & Wagnalls to halt distribution of S. S. Baker's *The Permissible Lie,* a critical study of advertising. Lewis noted that the publisher "is our subsidiary," and Baker's book ran counter to Digest philosophy. Since he asked for no refund of advances and gave the printing plates to Baker, Lewis denied censorship.

The bitterest copyright dispute of the year also had an international character. The British publishing house, Bodley Head, claimed it had obtained the world translation rights for *The Cancer Ward,* a two-volume novel by Soviet author Aleksandr I. Solzhenitsyn, and had sold the U.S. rights to Farrar, Straus & Giraux. Bodley Head issued a translation of the first volume with the second promised at the end of the year. On October 15, however, Dial Press of New York put out a translation of both sections, listing La Société Y.M.C.A.-Press of Paris as the copyright source. Bodley Head obtained a summons from London's High Court charging that the Dial edition was unauthorized and constituted unfair competition.

Perhaps the most practical international advance in 1968 was virtual adoption at the first International Standard Book Number Conference (September, London) of an International Standard Book Number (ISBN) system, based on the English-language system, introduced in the U.K. in May 1967.

Developments in particular countries highlighted general tendencies. In Australia, publishers' activity showed expansion potential. Angus and Robertson, Ltd., oldest and largest Australian publishers, set up in Singapore a cooperative distribution centre for Southeast Asia to be used by all Australian-based publishers; Paul Hamlyn Pty., Ltd. (established 1967), began a big expansion program; Longmans, Green, and Co., Ltd., acquired a 20% interest in Rigby Ltd., last wholly Australian-owned public company. Concern over printing abroad (especially in Hong Kong) of Australian books led publishers and printers to negotiate with the government to bridge the gap between home and overseas printing costs.

In France the value of books exported outside the European Economic Community was some Fr. 26 million higher than that of those imported. Big imports of art books from Italy and religious books from Belgium reversed the proportions within EEC trade. The big problem remained the size of the nonbook-reading public, though inquiries showed that 15–19-years-olds bought 37% of all books sold; and that television owners bought more books than those without TV.

In West Germany book production reached a record of 30,863 new titles in 1967. Turnover, after the 1966 recession, showed an increase of some 5%. Record book and periodical exports were valued at DM. 434 million; imports also rose by some DM. 10 million to DM. 143.5 million. At the Frankfurt Book Fair the peace prize went to Léopold Sédar Senghor, first president of the republic of Senegal—an outstanding African poet and founder of the Franco-African *négritude* movement.

New markets for British books (*e.g.*, in Europe, Borneo, the Philippines) replaced those in Africa and the Middle East disturbed by political crises. The rise in value of books exported from the U.K. was maintained, with £55 million of 1967's total turnover (some £126 million) earned overseas. Though new titles decreased by 405, total titles published in 1967 (29,619) increased by more than 750. Controversy arose over introduction of U.S.-type "simultaneous book clubs." From Sept. 1, 1967, cheaper book club editions could be published on the day of a book's publication. Formerly, book club publication had been possible only a year later.

Two legal decisions in 1968 affected book publishing: the ruling (March 1) that publishers might maintain resale prices of books, and the reversal in July of the November 1967 conviction under the Obscene Publications Act, 1959, of Calder and Boyars, Ltd., British publishers of U.S. author Hubert Selby, Jr.'s *Last Exit to Brooklyn*.

In the Netherlands several publishers' mergers in late 1967–early 1968 concentrated staffs and standardized methods, in an effort to achieve larger printings at lower costs. The relatively small size of the Dutch-speaking population and the lack of overseas markets meant that, to use facilities thus made available, publishers had to undertake big foreign orders.

Quality paperback production was rising in Norway, but expansion was limited by population size. Of 1,230 new titles in 1967, 126 were new paperback titles; 58 of these were "literary" fiction. Equally high sales for technical and general nonfiction paperbacks, however, suggested a specific "paperback market." Of the 4,895 titles put out in Denmark, 1,026 were paperbacks (764 fiction).

In the U.S.S.R., 1967 saw a 1.5% increase over the 1966 total of books and pamphlets; 90% of the 74,081 books were new titles. A rise in political and socioeconomic works to 17% of books printed resulted in part from large printings of the works of Marx, Engels, and L. I. Brezhnev's *Fifty Years of Socialist Achievement* to mark the 50th anniversary of the Revolution.

In Swiss book publishing in 1967, the value of books exported (19% higher than in 1966) considerably exceeded that of chocolate, and for first time exceeded imports value. Notable was the expansion in exports to Britain, from SFr. 3.3 million in 1966 to SFr. 7.7 million. Imports rose most steeply from Italy. In Italy, after a long dispute, an agreement reached in 1967 allowed kiosks to sell low-priced books and some bookshops in each province to sell newspapers —a notable difference from other countries where the need was to broaden markets.

Best sellers in the U.S. in 1967 were:

Hardcover fiction: *The Arrangement* by Elia Kazan; *The Confessions of Nat Turner* by William Styron and *The Chosen* by Chaim Potok (tied for second place); *Topaz* by Leon Uris; and *Christy* by Catherine Marshall. Hardcover nonfiction: *Death of a President* by William Manchester; *Misery Is a Blind Date* by Johnny Carson;

Games People Play by Eric Berne, M.D.; *Stanyan Street* by Rod McKuen; and *A Modern Priest Looks at His Outdated Church* by Father James Kavanaugh. Mass market paperbacks: *Valley of the Dolls* by Jacqueline Susann; *The Hobbit, The Lord of the Rings* trilogy, and *The Tolkien Reader* by J. R. R. Tolkien; *Games People Play* by Eric Berne, M.D.; *The Adventurers* by Harold Robbins; and *The Source* by James A. Michener. Trade paperbacks: *In Wildness Is the Preservation of the World* by Eliot Porter; *Psycho-Cybernetics* by Maxwell Maltz; "Peanuts" books by Charles M. Schulz; *Summerhill: A Radical Approach to Child Rearing* by A. S. Neil; and *The Stranger* by Albert Camus.   (P. B. St.; X.)
See also **Law.**

Race Relations

In race relations, as in other fields, 1968—or International Human Rights Year, as it was proclaimed by the UN in celebration of the 20th anniversary of its Declaration on Human Rights—was, as the British shadow chancellor of the Exchequer, Iain Macleod, commented, "the year of the hothead and the demagogue and the peddler of panaceas." In Britain this was mainly confined to verbalization, but in some other parts of the world confrontations flared into violence, civil disorder, and even war.

The need for, or inevitability of, a "race war" between the white "have" nations and the nonwhite "have-nots" was propagated assiduously and major skirmishes continued between black African nationalist guerrillas and the South African, Portuguese, and Rhodesian forces along the frontiers of black-ruled and white-ruled Africa. (*See* AFRICA: *Special Report*.) Less attention was paid to ethnic divisions and disputes characteristic of many newly independent African states once the unifying hand of the colonial power was withdrawn. In recent years ethnic tensions had exploded tragically in the Congo, Rwanda, Burundi, and the Sudan. Throughout 1968 the most serious flare-up was in Nigeria. The deep and ancient enmity between the largely Muslim northerners and the southerners, particularly the Ibos, had led to the tragic and destructive war between Nigeria and the breakaway state of Biafra.

An even more specific legacy of the colonial era was the Asian minorities in East Africa. These self-segregating communities, occupying niche positions in the economy and administration, were at risk once they lost the protection of the colonial powers. The predicament was particularly noticeable among the Asians, mainly Indians, in Kenya. A settlement was reached between Britain and India whereby the latter agreed to receive those Asians who wished to settle there.

In Southeast Asia the various overseas Indian and Chinese communities continued to be the objects of greater or lesser hostility, envy, or apprehension from the Malays, Thais, Fijians, and others among whom they lived. There had been an upsurge of pan-Malay feeling during riots in Penang in November 1967. In India itself the militant Hinduism of the Jan Sangh Party was reported to be gaining strength in 1968.

In the birthplace of ethnic nationalism, Europe, the retreat from world domination or influence seemed to have stimulated old regional or ethnic feelings and demands for decentralization. Catalans and Basques in Spain, Bretons in France, Scots, Welsh, and Northern Irish Catholics in the British Isles—all were demanding greater cultural and political self-determination. This trend was also discernible in the Eastern European states and even in such integrated Soviet republics as the Ukraine. With it went a certain re-

"... and if we don't stop them coming, we'll end up with a multi-racial society ... Celts, Romans, Saxons, Goths. ..." —Jon, "London Daily Mail."

vival of anti-Semitism, dressed up politically as anti-Zionism, a term that made it possible to accuse Jewish Israelis with "fascist aggression" and the West Germans with "revanchism." Some resurgence of anti-Semitism was noticeable, not only in the European extreme right-wing circles where it was traditional, but also in the thinking of the extreme left, the "third world" anti-imperialists, and the Black Power spokesmen.

South Africa. Several measures taken in 1968 by the South African Parliament set the seal on political apartheid. Chief among them was the Prohibition of Political Interference Act, promulgated in March, which made it a punishable offense to belong to or assist a multiracial political party. As an immediate consequence, the Progressive Party, which for ten years had been the only multiracial party to be represented in Parliament, decided "under protest and under compulsion" to confine its membership to whites. Faced with the alternative of disbanding and leaving the field open to the Nationalists and the United Party, the Progressives chose rather to "fight on as an uniracial party until one day we can become multiracial again."

On the other hand, in April the 3,000-member Liberal Party, which was the only existing political party with white members that advocated ultimate universal suffrage for all races, decided to disband. Commenting on the implication of the Liberal Party's dissolution, the *Johannesburg Star* noted: "It is not large. But its disappearance will, quite disproportionately to its numbers, reduce the area of political dialogue and dissent. . . . That is of course what the Nationalists have always wanted."

Meanwhile, as the 11-man UN Council for South West Africa failed to establish even token UN authority over the territory, the government tabled a White Paper authorizing the take-over of the "White Area" of the territory. A bill for the development of self-government for the native nations of South West Africa also came before Parliament in Cape Town. This made provision for the establishment of at least six Bantustans, self-governing authorities for indigenous groups: Ovamboland (for 270,900 Ovambos), Damaraland (50,200), Hereroland (40,000), Okavangoland (31,500), Eastern Caprivi (17,900), and Kaokoland (10,500).

The *Rand Daily Mail* saw the proposals as nothing more than a reductio ad absurdum of the self-determination ideal: "These insignificant ethnic offshoots are solemnly being adorned with the trappings of self-determination and promised independence in the end if they want it. And to accomplish this extraordinary aim, more than 134,000 people, a quarter of the territory's indigenous population, will have to be moved from where they are now living in order to fit in with the new pattern of emerging mini-states."

Another move toward "large apartheid" was the announcement of a plan to make Zululand into yet another Bantustan. The long-term difficulties of implementing the separate development policy, however, were highlighted by the fact that the year's budget allocated R 39.7 million for Bantustan development, as compared with R 252.7 million for defense. Moreover, the allocation for the purchase of land for the geographic consolidation of the African homelands was cut from R 10 million in 1965 to R 8 million in 1967 and R 5 million in 1968. A recent visitor to the Bantustans commented that, with the exception of the Transkei, they still did not exist but were "a host of tiny spots, some no bigger than a few square miles of

mission land, scattered like a rash across the face of Africa."

Meanwhile, over 200,000 Africans from the urban areas had been resettled in the homelands and more progress had been made in clearing the 469 "black spots" (African enclaves in white areas); by 1967 these had been reduced to 267 and at least 73,000 Africans had been moved "voluntarily," according to M. C. Botha, minister of Bantu administration. The situation with regard to the border industrial areas appeared somewhat less bleak—nearly R 387 million was spent between 1960 and 1967 (about R 243 million by private white industrialists) to provide jobs for some 50,000 Africans. This, however, fell far short of the 20,000 new jobs annually recommended by the Tomlinson report in 1954, and also of the 9,000 new jobs needed annually for African males to keep pace with the increase in the reserves alone, not to mention any resettlement of Africans from outside.

While the government determinedly pressed on with its economic apartheid policy, proclaiming 37 industrial areas as "controlled areas" where no new industrial development involving African labour might be undertaken without permission, demographic and economic factors combined to work against it. Population estimates released in October 1967 showed that the gap between the white and African populations had widened by nearly a million in the past five years. By the year 2000, Africans would number 28 million and the whites would constitute only 15% of the total population, as compared with 19% currently. A survey by the Trade Union Council of South Africa (TUCSA) also showed that the proportion of white workers in South Africa's manufacturing industry had dropped by a steady average of 1% each year, from 30% in 1961. Accepting the logic of this, TUCSA in 1968 reaffirmed its decision to admit Africans, despite governmental pressure and the fact that African unions could not be registered officially.

Notable instances of "petty apartheid" were the massive forced removals under the Group Areas Act and influx control (latest available figures for the latter, about 220,000 between 1959 and 1965).

Outside its borders South Africa continued to pursue the policy of establishing relations with black African countries. This was working well with Malawi and moderate neighbours such as Lesotho, Botswana, and the newly independent Swaziland. The intransigence of the white Rhodesian regime and the possibility of changes in the status of the Portuguese African territories following the replacement of the Portuguese premier, António de Oliveira Salazar, posed problems for the future. A more immediate setback was the International Olympic Committee's decision to withdraw its invitation to South Africa to send a team to the 1968 Olympics in Mexico. This was followed by the commotion over the delayed decision of Britain's Marylebone Cricket Club to include the Cape Coloured cricketer Basil D'Oliveira in the team to be sent to South Africa, the South African government's refusal to allow such a team to play, and the MCC's withdrawal from the tour. This badly handled affair seemed likely to cut off South African sportsmen still further from international events.

Finally, mention should be made of the South African medical achievement of a successful transplantation of a "coloured" heart into a "white body"—which seemed to some to undermine all the biological and social myths supporting racial separateness, and

to others to reflect an almost "veterinary" approach to human life and death in a country where colour determined the way in which people were allowed to live their lives.

United Kingdom. The issue of coloured Commonwealth immigration remained precariously neutralized between the two major British political parties up to the early part of 1968, although there was intensified activity from the late summer of 1967 onward by the Conservative anti-immigrationists—notably Sir Cyril Osborne, Duncan Sandys, and—a relative newcomer to the field—Enoch Powell (*see* BIOGRAPHY).

The campaign concentrated on two major themes. The first was that there was a danger of an intractable U.S.-type situation emerging in Britain, with ghettos, black militants, and race riots (the implication being that white and nonwhite cannot live together peacefully in a single society). This danger was unceasingly underlined by the detailed television and press coverage of the violence and disorder that exploded in U.S. cities after the assassination of the Rev. Martin Luther King, Jr., in April. The second theme posited a threat to the British way of life and the swamping of the British nation itself.

The measures proposed for dealing with the immigration problem were invariably negative and preoccupied with numbers: even more drastic restrictions and controls, more effective prevention of "evasions," and assisted repatriation. In the absence of positive government directives and massive assistance to "twilight areas" in the west Midlands and elsewhere, where shortages of housing, schools, and welfare services were being exacerbated by an inflow of dependents, this negative and hostile line was widely approved.

The actual number of permanent immigrants from the nonwhite Commonwealth in 1967 was made up of 4,721 holders of work vouchers (5,141 in 1966) and 50,080 dependents (40,130 in 1966). In the first eight months of 1968, 30,724 more dependents from the nonwhite Commonwealth entered Britain (about the same number as in 1967). The most immediate effects of this flow of dependents were felt by the schools. In some areas where no dispersal policies were applied, a few schools had between 50 and 90% immigrant

"It's not just you—I'm against all races."
—Waite, "The Sun," London.

BEN ROTH AGENCY

pupils in the fall of 1968. The latest available figures for England and Wales (January 1967) showed that 2.2% of all pupils in maintained schools were immigrants (*i.e.,* 165,725 out of a total of 7,328,110), as compared with 1.8% a year earlier.

There was also increasing preoccupation with a "loophole" in the Commonwealth Immigrants Act, 1962, whereby something over one million Commonwealth citizens who held or could legally claim a U.K. passport could enter Britain freely. Those most likely to make use of this loophole were the Kenya Asians, variously estimated at between 100,000 and 170,000, who had failed to apply for Kenya citizenship before the deadline and whose jobs were being steadily "kenyanized." The numbers entering Britain were rising monthly and the matter was raised in the press and Parliament. But apparently no contingency plan was worked out before the renewed anti-immigration campaign in February, led by Powell and Sandys, in conjunction with the intransigence of the Kenya government, set off a hectic beat-the-ban exodus of Asians to Britain.

This led to the panic passing in a single week of the Commonwealth Immigrants Act, 1968. This measure (criticized by the International Commission of Jurists as creating a "sort of second-class citizen" and violating the rule of law) brought under control the entry of U.K. passport holders with no substantial connection with the United Kingdom, giving them a special allocation of 1,500 employment vouchers in addition to the existing statutory ceiling of 8,500. The act also contained provisions further restricting the entry of dependents and dealing with the problem of evasion and clandestine entry. In the single week before curbs came into force on March 1, an estimated 5,000 Kenya Asians entered, compared with a total of about 25,000 in the preceding eight months.

The Kenya Asians affair intensified the generally unfavourable climate of opinion in Britain, and further tension built up in March and April, as the government returned to its preparations for extending anti-discrimination legislation to cover employment, housing, and the provision of goods, facilities, and services to the public. On April 20 came a second event which caused the climate of British opinion to become even more explosive—a speech by Powell, in which for the first time a major politician and public figure talked of coloured immigration in the exaggerated, personalized, and highly flavoured terminology of the public house and workingman's club. This led to Powell's dismissal from the Conservative shadow cabinet and triggered off a massive explosion of anti-immigration, antiliberal, and antimetropolitan feeling, and of public support for Powell himself, expressed in a flood of letters and protest strikes or marches by London dockers, meat porters, and other workers up and down the country.

It was in this febrile and antagonistic atmosphere that the Race Relations Bill, 1968, began its slow but ultimately successful progress through Parliament. Meanwhile, the Race Relations Board, the body responsible for operating the more limited 1965 act, published an analysis of the complaints received from the start of its operations up to April 1, 1968. Of the total of almost 1,200 complaints, 959 had been outside the scope of sec. 1 of the act, 412 were related to employment, 112 to housing, and 98 to the police (whose treatment of coloured immigrants and other minorities was increasingly called in question during the year). Of the 234 complaints that fell within the

KEYSTONE
London police using a hacksaw to free Cameron Wottell, a West Indian student, after he had chained himself to the main door of a government building, Atlantic House in Holborn, as a protest against racial discrimination in employment practices in the U.K.

act, 153 related to public houses and 45 to cafés or clubs; 63 cases were settled by conciliation, 87 were not sustained, 5 were referred to the attorney general, and 69 were still under investigation.

There were some resignations from the National Committee for Commonwealth Immigrants after the passing of the Commonwealth Immigrants Act, 1968, but the committee contrived to expand its work of integration, particularly with local voluntary liaison committees. Part III of the Race Relations Act, 1968, made provision for the ultimate replacement of the committee by a new Community Relations Commission, which would have approximately the same functions and staff.

The militancy and protest noted in 1966 among a minority of coloured immigrants and their radical white supporters were increased. The hitherto highly effective multiracial Campaign Against Racial Discrimination (CARD) was split, and a number of Black Power, Maoist, and other splinter groups preached black revolution and war against the whites at Speakers' Corner in Hyde Park and via the mass media, which were often extremely generous with their coverage. There were indications of an increasing linkup between black militancy, student militancy, and the anti-Vietnam war issue, with the police as the major scapegoat.

A different kind of protest was found among such immigrant communities as the Sikhs, many of whom organized demonstrations against the continuing refusal of a few local authorities such as Wolverhampton to employ them as busmen unless they discarded the beards and turbans which have a religious significance. The strong internal organization and desire for self-segregation of these and similar immigrant groups reinforced the host society pressures toward ghettoization. The increasing consolidation of coloured quarters in turn made educational and later job dispersal more difficult for the next generation.

In May the government announced a new urban program aimed at helping the 57 areas of highest immigration, but there were many criticisms of its inadequacy. The new Conservative-dominated Birmingham City Council called for a ban on future immigration to the area but later published a report suggesting a readiness to tackle the rehousing of the majority of its 80,000 coloured Commonwealth immigrants.

In September 1968, after a long wet summer, Powell returned to the attack on current immigration policy, calling it "a potential threat to our very nationhood." He also spoke in the immigration debate at the Conservative Party conference in Blackpool, where about a third of the delegates seemed to share his views, which included large-scale repatriation (whether voluntary or compulsory was not clear). The party leader, Edward Heath, who had previously outlined a policy for stricter limitation and controls involving the introduction of legislation affecting aliens and Commonwealth immigrants, rejected the idea that repatriation would solve the problem or that British citizens should be forcibly deported because of their colour. He won a record ovation of nearly eight minutes, and for the time being, at least, moderate views and policies seemed likely to prevail over Powellism.   (SH. P.)

United States. Competition and conflict were the catchwords in 1968 as black Americans strove for increased power and the American Indian was ignored. Congress, in a thrifty mood, cut millions from urban programs for training and employment of hard-core

poor and largely ignored the more than 3,000 poor who went to the nation's capital. A great black statesman and a white politician who championed civil rights were murdered, and the cries were for law and order and elimination of crime in the streets. Civil rights were subjugated to civil order; militant blacks came into open conflict with authorities.

Militants and moderates were talking past each other as the National Association for the Advancement of Colored People (NAACP) and the Urban League repudiated violence while the Black Panthers advocated it. Black Panthers, angry young blacks organized into armed groups whose stated purpose was to protect black communities from police, had chapters in many major cities. They urged full employment, decent housing, black history courses, and an end to consumer exploitation, police brutality, and the murder of blacks.

Relations between the police and black militants were critical. Huey Newton (see BIOGRAPHY) and Eldrige Cleaver, both leaders of the Oakland, Calif., chapter of the Black Panthers, were arrested. Newton was convicted of voluntary manslaughter and sentenced to 2–15 years. Cleaver skipped bail and disappeared. In Brooklyn, N.Y., off-duty white policemen entered a court building and assaulted some Panthers charged with holding a rally without a permit. In Cleveland, O., a miniature guerrilla war broke out as three police and seven blacks were killed. The National Guard was called in to restore order.

In the black ghettos of metropolitan areas, the police had become symbols of rigidity and of the city governments' failure to act. For instance, in Wilmington, Del., a city of 86,000 (40% black), the National Guard took up posts in April and were still there in November. Wilmington was a city patrolled night and day by troops. Gov. Charles L. Terry, Jr., refused to withdraw the troops "because decent white and Negro citizens want the Guard there." In force was an antiriot law that applied to three or more people engaging in disorderly conduct, a 10 P.M. curfew for all juveniles, and a catchall law for "night prowlers."

In early March, the National Advisory Commission on Civil Disorders issued its 1,485-page report. The commission, headed by Gov. Otto Kerner of Illinois and Mayor John Lindsay of New York City, said that "our nation is moving toward two societies, one black, one white—separate and unequal," and that such a polarization would destroy basic democratic values. The commission stated that white institutionalized racism, barring blacks from decent employment, education, and housing and from equal protection under the law, was responsible for the riots of the summer of 1967.

The report called for creation of two million jobs over the next three years, half of which would be in the private sector; elimination of de facto segregation in schools; on-the-job training by employers of the hard-core unemployed with reimbursement to the employer; passage of a federal open-housing law to cover sale or rental of all housing; and provision to low- and moderate-income families of six million units of decent housing in the next five years. The typical rioter, according to the commission, was a black teenager or young adult—a high school dropout extremely hostile to both whites and middle-class Negroes. Most conservatives and Southerners concluded with F. Edward Hébert, Louisiana Democrat, that the report was "propaganda ad nauseam."

Less than a month after the report was issued a

strike of the Memphis, Tenn., sanitation employees over union recognition had profound implications for its contents. Mayor Henry Loeb, a conservative with solid white support, refused to recognize the union, which was 90% black. Until this time, the city had had what whites would call good race relations—meaning a nonassertive, servile Negro population—but, because of the city's intransigence, the union turned for support to the black community (40% of the population of Memphis). The sanitation men became symbols of the fight for better economic conditions and equal rights, and the labour dispute was transformed into a major civil rights confrontation ending months later only after disturbances and the death of the Rev. Martin Luther King, Jr.

On March 28, 1968, King came to Memphis to lead a march in support of the striking sanitation workers. Police prevented students from joining the march, and violence erupted as the students hurled rocks at the officers. A few marchers became unruly and some

AMERICA'S FORGOTTEN RACE PROBLEM

The Navaho, poorest of the poor, have been largely ignored and abused by white society. In 1868 the Navaho nation (12,000), after having been held captive for three years at Ft. Sumner, N.M., was herded onto a scrub-grass, desert reservation and given 35,000 sheep. Even after Negroes were emancipated, many Navaho women and children were sold into slavery. Despite a century of programs, poverty was still a way of life, with an average family income of less than $500 per year. Navahos still lived in hogans—mud structures without windows and with a smoke hole in the top—as they had 100 years before. Robert F. Kennedy was appalled when he visited Indian schools in January and found the emphasis on silvercraft, typing, and home economics instead of on preparation for the industrial world. Late in December 1967 the Navaho were snowed in and many of their sheep and cattle perished in the 56-in. drifts. Because they lacked adequate housing and food, many became ill and nine died. At the end of a week the government air-dropped food, medical supplies, and hay.

windows were smashed. Police responded with billy clubs and tear gas and attacked all the marchers; 4,000 National Guardsmen were called in to restore order. On April 3, 1968, addressing a rally, King said:

Like anybody, I would like to live a long life. Longevity has its place. But I'm not concerned about that now. I just want to do God's will. . . . I've looked over, and I've seen the promised land. I may not get there with you, but I want you to know tonight that we as a people will get to the promised land.

Less than 24 hours later, he was dead. King was leaving for a Thursday evening dinner at a friend's home when he stepped onto the balcony at the Lorraine Motel. A bullet from a high-powered rifle struck him in the neck, and he died within the hour. Stokely Carmichael, a militant black leader, said, "white America has declared war on black America," and, in 125 cities across the nation, young blacks took to the streets in a widespread convulsion of disorder. The disturbances lasted two to three days in many cities.

Washington, a city 66% black, was hardest hit. After two days and nights of looting and burning, Pres. Lyndon B. Johnson ordered 6,000 Guardsmen into the city. In Chicago, angry blacks burned down blocks and, in the end, 12,500 troops were needed to bring the city under control. In New York, a cool mayor kept violence to a minimum by walking the streets of Harlem three nights in a row, but many wondered if nonviolence was dead. At the final count, 46 persons had died and over 55,000 troops were used; the National Guard accounted for 34,000 and the regular Army for 21,000. In addition, another 22,000 regular Army troops had been put on standby.

King was buried the following week in Atlanta, Ga. Most of the nation's leaders attended, including Robert F. Kennedy, who was to be felled by an assassin's bullet barely two months later. Over 100,000 blacks and whites marched in the three-and-a-half mile processional. The Rev. Ralph Abernathy (*see* BIOGRAPHY) was named King's successor as leader of the Southern Christian Leadership Conference, and he pledged to carry out King's Poor People's Campaign, a drive by the poor for decent jobs, housing, and education.

In early May, the Poor People's Campaign got under way with a mule train and Southern violence. In Marks, Miss., a poverty-ridden village, one of the march's advance men, Willie Bolden, was jailed for coaxing students to demonstrate. When 200 youths went to the courthouse either to free Bolden or to be arrested with him, state troopers charged the group, clubbing them with billy clubs and gun butts. Abernathy arrived and restored a semblance of order.

As the first marchers reached Washington for their stay at Resurrection City (plywood structures stretching along the Lincoln Memorial's reflecting pool), Abernathy was experiencing financial and managerial difficulties. The march needed $3 million, the housing units were slow in going up, and the local citizens were edgy about rioting. As the project developed, it was plagued by ghetto gangs who abused newsmen, by drinking, by petty thievery, and by nature, which turned the city into a muddy swamp. Furthermore, the blacks, whites, and Indians were not cooperating, and each group set off in its own direction. The largest number of poor, mostly blacks, in Resurrection City at any time was about 2,600 and eventually the rains drove all but 500 away. The campaign ended with a march for which 50,000 turned out.

The 1968 Civil Rights Act, passed in April, contained an open-housing clause which, by Jan. 1, 1970, would cover 34.9 million housing units; only owner-sold single dwellings and apartments with less than four units, one of which is occupied by the owner, were excepted. The Supreme Court went further in June when it upheld an 1866 statute declaring that all citizens are entitled to sell, lease, and hold property equally, thus immediately banning discrimination in sale or rental by anyone. In November, the high court agreed to rule on Adam Clayton Powell's suit against the House of Representatives for illegally removing him from office. The decision could have profound implications regarding the court's power to rule on the constitutionality of the House's rules.

The power struggle in education intensified in both South and North. The Justice Department ordered nine Southern school districts to replace their freedom-of-choice pupil-assignment plans with more effective desegregation measures. The Supreme Court ruled in May that freedom-of-choice plans were inadequate

Above right, the Rev. Martin Luther King, Jr. (centre), standing on the balcony of a Memphis motel with the Rev. Jesse Jackson (left) and the Rev. Ralph Abernathy, April 3, 1968. The next day King was killed by an assassin's bullet while standing in approximately the same place. Below left, federal troops on guard at the U.S. Capitol in Washington, D.C., following King's assassination. Outbreaks of arson and looting occurred in many U.S. cities including Pittsburgh, above left, and Washington, D.C., below, in the days after King's death.

if they did not desegregate as fast as other methods. A Northern community, South Holland, Ill., was ordered to end de facto segregation, a result of the "neighbourhood school" policy. Under this policy, followed widely throughout the nation, pupils attended schools in their neighbourhoods, so that the schools reflected housing patterns.

In New York City, a fight for local control of the schools brought about a power struggle with marked racial overtones between the United Federation of Teachers and the community. Blacks (and many others) maintained that inner-city school systems across the nation had failed to meet the needs of the black pupils, and of the Puerto Rican and Mexican-American pupils as well. The children were retarded in reading and, in general, neglected. In Brooklyn, decentralized, locally controlled, demonstration schools were set up in an attempt to solve these problems. One of the schools was in the predominantly black Ocean Hill-Brownsville district with over 9,000 black pupils. In May, the local board requested transfer of 13 teachers and 6 administrators, charging that they were sabotaging the experiment. Superintendent of Schools Bernard E. Donovan ordered the 19 back to their assignments, but the local board refused to take them. When the schools reopened in September, the members of the teachers' union, feeling their job security threatened, staged a boycott that kept over one million pupils out of school and that was not settled until November. Of the 60,000 teachers, only

6,000 to 6,500 were black.

In universities across the nation, black students and their allies confronted administrators. At Columbia, demonstrators seized university buildings in protest against, among other things, a gym being built in a park adjoining Harlem and the university's ownership of ghetto property. The demonstrators were forcibly evicted by the police. In May, black students staged a sit-in at Northwestern University with specific demands for housing, admission of more black students, and scholarships. Northwestern's administration negotiated with the students and found most of their demands acceptable. In November and December, black students at San Francisco State College demanding the creation of a Department of Black Studies were supported by members of the Mexican-American, Oriental, and New Left contingents on campus.

In the political arena, by and large, blacks did not fare well. In Mississippi, Charles Evers, brother of slain civil rights leader Medgar Evers, ran in a congressional primary but faced a runoff in a predominantly white district. After losing the contest, Evers said, "Win, lose, or draw, we've already won. They're scared to death. They're going to pay attention to us from now on."

In June, Sen. Robert F. Kennedy, perhaps the only white politician with an enthusiastic black following, was murdered.

In August, the Republicans nominated Richard

Nixon and Spiro Agnew as their presidential and vice-presidential candidates. To many blacks the "law and order" plank in the Republican platform meant perpetuation of institutional racism. Nixon spoke of "black capitalism," a system of tax incentives and credits to enable black Americans to own and manage their own businesses. He said that he would alter the welfare system that leads many blacks into a cycle of dependency. Yet he also declared that, because of high present expenditures and international problems, he would not commit billions to the cities. He supported the 1954 school desegregation ruling but was against withholding federal funds from noncomplying districts.

In Chicago, under siegelike security, the Democrats nominated Hubert Humphrey and Edmund Muskie. Humphrey, long a civil rights advocate, was hampered by ties to the unpopular Johnson administration. George Wallace, former governor of Alabama, ran as an independent candidate and embodied the radical segregationist trend in America. In the end, although about 90% of the blacks voted for Humphrey, he lost narrowly to Nixon. (*See* UNITED STATES: *Special Report.*)

Adam Clayton Powell was overwhelmingly reelected to the House by voters in Harlem. For many black Americans, Powell symbolized hope for equal status in a white-dominated society. It appeared likely that he would be readmitted to the House in 1969.

In the South, ever since the advent of Jim Crow legislation, whites had controlled the courts, but blacks were making inroads. In November, three members of the Ku Klux Klan went on trial in a federal district court in Mississippi for violation of the civil rights of Ben Chester White, a Negro murdered in 1966. Two of the three had been tried and acquitted of murder by the state court. After the evidence was in, Judge William H. Cox instructed the four white and eight black jurors to find the defendants guilty. The jury did so, and assessed them $21,500 in actual damages and $1 million in punitive damages.

During the year, some private companies such as IBM indicated interest in helping the poor get and hold jobs. Their concern was, in part, promoted by a government subsidy of $3,500 per job to train and employ the hard-core poor. Meanwhile, Congress cut poverty and Job Corps funds; for example, in Newark, where riots had occurred in 1967, federal aid was cut 25%. Cuts in "war on poverty" funds forced the closing of 16 Job Corps centres. At the same time, Congress passed a $400 million law-and-order measure.

The protest and the violence so evident in 1968 involved a large, discriminated-against lower class defined on the basis of race. Its members were poor, poorly housed, poorly educated, and underprivileged in their access to political power, to economic opportunity, and to human dignity. But the protest and the violence were relatively new, whereas black Americans had been underprivileged and discriminated against for over three centuries. It could be concluded, therefore, that neither peaceful protests nor large-scale riots resulted simply from the existence of an oppressed class.

This was not to say that oppression was not a causative factor. The various studies on the current civil unrest pointed out that throughout most of its history, oppression in the U.S. had not resulted in militant protest or in widespread violence. They also tried to determine what had been added to the pattern of oppression in the past two decades that led to

the need for a National Advisory Commission on Civil Disorders.

Four factors were generally conceded to differentiate black Americans in 1968 from their parents, grandparents, and enslaved ancestors: (1) marked upward mobility in education, leading to (2) markedly higher expectations for equality of opportunity, for human dignity, for access to political power, and for economic payoff in the society's reward structure, leading to (3) social organization to protest the discrimination that blocked access to these goals, with all three of these occurring at the same time that black Americans were suffering (4) the dislocation of mass migration, which had removed them from their traditional rural Southern homes to Northern urban ghettos.

(R. W. MA.; L. J. RE.)

See also Crime; Law; Police; Sociology; South Africa; United States.

Below, "Resurrection City" in Washington, D.C., May 20, 1968, housed thousands who joined in the Poor People's Campaign conceived by the Rev. Martin Luther King, Jr., to dramatize demands for better living conditions, education, and employment opportunities. Right, the Rev. Ralph Abernathy, leader of the campaign, confronting Secretary of the Interior Stewart Udall on the problems of poverty.

UPI COMPIX

Refugees

Although refugee influxes continued in various parts of the world during 1968, two events—the civil war in Nigeria and the invasion of Warsaw Pact troops into Czechoslovakia—carried with them the seeds of new refugee problems.

By September 10, when the government of Czechoslovakia issued a proclamation assuring personal freedom and urging people to return home, it had been reported that 750 Czechoslovaks had applied for political asylum in Austria, and that there were 10,000 Czechoslovaks in Austria, 8,500 in West Germany, and 1,200 in Italy. Although Austrian agencies had begun to organize aid programs, the Czechoslovaks were considered tourists and it 'was impossible to determine how many would actually become refugees. By the end of October, various governments were accepting refugees under special immigration provisions. Canada had been accepting 800 Czechoslovaks a month since the invasion; Australia, interested in attracting intellectuals and artists, was actively soliciting immigrants; and the U.S. government planned to fly 160–170 Czechoslovak refugees to the U.S. every week until March 1969.

The Intergovernmental Committee for European Migration reported on October 22 that it expected to transport 46,000 refugees in 1968, the largest number since 1956, the year of the Hungarian uprising. The committee had transported 1,200 refugees, mainly Jewish, from Poland, a 25% increase over the year before; 1,100 Hungarians, a 15% increase; and 862 Albanians who had been moved to Italy, an increase of 110%.

Throughout the last half of 1968 international concern focused on the food crisis in the secessionist republic of Biafra. In the Nigerian civil war, which had begun on May 30, 1967, an estimated four million persons had been displaced by the advancing federal forces. Although many international organizations had provided large quantities of food, very little was reaching the refugees. The Nigerian federal government persisted in refusing to allow mercy flights over the battle areas during the day, and Biafran leaders rejected any plan that allowed the food to pass through Nigerian hands for fear that the food would be poisoned. Only limited supplies were being brought into Biafra by plane. As various attempts at negotiation were frustrated, the estimated number of deaths from starvation rose from 6,000 a day in July to a projected estimate for December of 25,000 a day. The minimum food supply needed per month was 40,000 tons. The key to a Middle East peace settlement within the United Nations appeared to rest largely with an acceptable solution to the Arab refugee problem. For 20 years the UN Relief and Works Agency (UNRWA) had been attempting to relieve the plight of 1.5 million Arab refugees, mainly through the distribution of food and clothing. Following the June 1967 war over 120,000 refugees fled into Jordan. Although some attempts at repatriation were made, fewer than 12,000 returned at the close of hostilities. Nearly 100,000 refugees fled into Syria. The cost of resettling the refugees was estimated at $2,500 per head. In 1968 UNRWA continued to operate its health and education facilities in the area, cooperating extensively with UNESCO.

Statistics on South Vietnamese refugees during 1968 were not reliable. The Ministry of Health, Social Welfare, and Relief worked through a network of 44 provincial representatives with aid from some 30 private voluntary agencies, and figures covered both those who had been resettled and those still in temporary camps. Based on cumulative statistics from Jan. 1, 1964, it was estimated that by Dec. 31, 1967, 2,114,197 persons had become refugees, of whom 1,320,253 had been resettled.

By Aug. 31, 1968, an additional 1,456,855 persons had become refugees or had been made homeless as a result of a general increase in the level of military activity throughout the country, particularly two major attacks by the Viet Cong on urban population centres. Of this number, 1,070,308 were classed as "war victims," since their jobs or means of livelihood generally had not been destroyed by the Viet Cong attacks and their refugee status would be only temporary. The South Vietnamese government, under Operation Recovery, aided in rebuilding homes and, by the end of August, all but 31,808 persons had been resettled. The remaining 386,547 were primarily nonurban refugees and were likely to remain in refugee status for an extended period of time.

Throughout 1968, about 900 persons continued to be airlifted each week from Cuba to Miami, Fla., in accordance with the memorandum of understanding initiated on Dec. 1, 1965, by the U.S. and Cuban governments. The number of Cubans reaching Miami on these flights passed the 131,000 mark by December. As of August 2, over 295,000 Cubans had registered for services at the Cuban Refugee Center in Miami and the majority had been resettled throughout the U.S. The refugees were assisted by the Cuban Refugee Program of the U.S. Department of Health, Education, and Welfare, and by several national voluntary agencies. The lack of an agreement allowing for the return of refugees to Cuba had resulted in a large number of hijackings in 1968 in which pilots of U.S. airliners were forced to fly to Havana.

In February 1968, the Indian government reported a marked increase in the number of Tibetan refugees in India. By mid-November 1967, 867 Tibetans had crossed into India, as compared with 240 for all of 1966. Of the 51,000 Tibetans who had arrived in India since March 1959, nearly all had been resettled.

Homeless South Vietnamese children reaching for pills being given out by a medic at the Cho Ray Hospital in the Cholon section of Saigon.   UPI COMPIX

During 1968 various projects of the Office of the UN High Commissioner for Refugees reached the stage where they could be included in wider programs for social and economic development. On November 1, the U.S. became the 26th party to accede to the protocol relating to the status of refugees.

(J. F. Th.; X.)

See also Immigration and Emigration.

Religion

According to a Gallup poll taken during 1968, U.S. citizens were pessimistic about the state of religion and morality; 78% said morals were declining and 50% said life was "worse" in terms of religion. Percentage opinions in other Western nations indicated that equally grim opinions were held: in the Netherlands 77% said life on the religious level was worse; in Switzerland, 65%; Great Britain, 61%; Sweden, 60%; Canada, 58%; and Finland, 54%.

Other Gallup poll findings indicated that religion was losing its influence on American life. In a series of five polls conducted over 11 years, there had been a decided increase in the number of persons who believed that religion's influence was waning. In 1957, 69% thought that religion was increasing its influence on American life, but in 1968 this was practically reversed with 67% believing that religious influence was diminishing.

There were also indications that not as many young men were enrolling in seminaries as in past years. Pope Paul VI declared that a significant decline in the ratio of priests to parishioners had taken place since 1960 in Europe, the U.S., and Africa. Protestant theological educators expressed similar concerns.

Unity. The Bible became a symbol of Christian unity, as Protestant and Roman Catholic biblical scholars met to set up ecumenical guidelines as a basis for all common Bible translation. The United Bible Societies, a federation of 35 Protestant groups, and the Vatican Secretariat for Promoting Christian Unity designated specific editions of Greek and Hebrew manuscripts to be used by scholars. The scholars agreed that the Apocrypha—which most Protestants do not recognize as canonical—should be published between the Old and New Testaments. Roman Catholic translators agreed that footnotes to passages relating to doctrine should be descriptive rather than doctrinal. Heretofore canon law had required such notes to passages relating to Catholic doctrine, while Protestants had generally published the Scriptures without comment.

Several steps toward church unity were taken during the year. The United Methodist Church was formed, linking together the 10.3 million-member Methodist Church and the 728,000-member Evangelical United Brethren Church. Conversations on this union extended as far back as 1803. In 1871 the Evangelical Association, a forerunner of the EUB body, approved a union by one vote, but merger never came about. The Presbyterian Church in the U.S. (Southern Presbyterians) voted overwhelmingly to approve a plan of union with the Reformed Church in America, although the Reformed Church's vote for union was less enthusiastic. The proposed denomination would link more than 960,000 Presbyterians in 16 Southern and Southwestern states with nearly 400,000 Reformed Church members who are concentrated in the Northeast and Midwest. The basic theology and form of government of both communions are similar. In Canada, the Anglican and United churches set 1974 as the target date for union. Meanwhile, the two communions began joint action in many areas and heard recommendations that the churches immediately combine programs in a number of fields, including finance,

Estimated Membership of the Principal Religions of the World

Religions	North America*	South America	Europe†	Asia	Africa	Oceania‡	World
Total Christian	214,258,000	150,426,000	442,006,000	61,473,000	42,056,000	14,055,000	924,274,000
Roman Catholic	126,468,000	147,219,000	226,303,000	47,622,000	28,751,000	4,107,000	580,470,000
Eastern Orthodox	3,675,000	47,000	114,103,000	2,819,000	4,956,000	84,000	125,684,000
Protestant§	84,115,000	3,160,000	101,600,000	11,032,000	8,349,000	9,864,000	218,120,000
Jewish‖	6,035,000	705,000	4,025,000	2,460,000	238,000	74,000	13,537,000
Muslim¶	166,000	416,000	13,848,000	374,167,000	104,297,000	118,000	493,012,000
Zoroastrian⚲	—	—	12,000	126,000	—	—	138,000
Shintoठ	31,000	116,000	2,000	69,513,000	—	—	69,662,000
Taoist▢	16,000	19,000	12,000	54,277,000	—	—	54,324,000
Confucian▢	96,000	109,000	55,000	371,261,000	9,000	57,000	371,587,000
Buddhist◇	187,000	157,000	8,000	176,568,000	—	—	176,920,000
Hindu▲	55,000	660,000	160,000	434,447,000	1,205,000	218,000	436,745,000
Totals	220,844,000	152,608,000	460,128,000	1,544,292,000	147,805,000	14,522,000	2,540,199,000
Population⁺	304,439,000	174,246,000	636,993,000	1,907,481,000	328,134,000	18,127,000	3,369,420,000

*Includes Central America and the West Indies.

†Includes communicants claimed by established churches; includes also the U.S.S.R., in which the effect of a half-century of official Marxist ideology upon religious adherence is much disputed among specialists.

‡Includes New Zealand and Australia as well as islands of the South Pacific.

§Protestant statistics usually include "full members" rather than all baptized persons and are not comparable to those of ethnic religions or churches counting all adherents. The World Council of Churches in 1968 constituted a working committee to seek uniform nomenclature and reporting procedures.

‖Based on 1968 estimates of Jewish Statistical Bureau.

¶The chief base of Islam is still ethnic, and the statistics are largely derived from demographic studies. Evangelistic work is now carried on by Muslim renewal movements, and major gains have been made in Europe and the U.S. (viz. Black Muslims).

⚲A declining number of Zoroastrians are found in Iran, Pakistan, and India.

ठA Japanese ethnic religion, Shinto's strength has declined since the emperor gave up claim to divinity (1947). Japanese religious statistics are highly problematical because adherents frequently are related to several different religions simultaneously. In 1968 the Japanese government instituted a statistical survey to clarify the status of different religions, cults, and movements, several of which claim millions of new adherents since World War II.

▢Figures on China are highly speculative, including the number of remaining Muslims. The effect of Mao's Cultural Revolution upon Taoism and Confucianism is not yet to be measured. Moreover, there is a long-standing dispute among scholars as to whether Confucianism should be counted as a "religion" at all.

◇Buddhism has several modern renewal movements which have won adherents in Europe and the U.S. The shift from ethnic to missionary base is evident in some areas not formerly ethnic-Buddhist.

▲Hinduism's strength in India has been enhanced by nationalism, and modern Hinduism has also developed renewal movements which have reached into Europe and the U.S. for converts.

⁺Source: 1968 United Nations survey.

(F. H. Li.)

Participants in one of the experimental worship services held in Uppsala, Swed., in July 1968. This part of the service was intended to increase physical contact and communication between worshipers.

evangelism, and Christian education. The Church of England and the Methodist Church in England had begun studying blueprints for reunion which, if accepted by their church governments, could give England a united church by 1980. (See *Protestant Churches*, below.)

One of the largest made-in-America denominations, the Christian Church, known also as the Disciples of Christ, was formally constituted as an organized church of nearly 6,000 congregations, mostly in the Midwest and Southwest, with a total of 1.4 million members. The Christian Church, which started on the American frontier in the early 19th century as a protest against rigid creeds, had always been in the forefront of Christian unity movements.

The Consultation on Church Union continued its discussions toward the goal of merging ten major Protestant denominations in America by 1970.

The Church in Action. The concern of the churches over social matters was apparent at the fourth assembly of the World Council of Churches, held in Uppsala, Swed., in July (*see* Special Report), as well as in individual countries and within the individual church bodies.

American churches played a significant part in the setting up of Resurrection City on the Mall, between the Washington Monument and the Lincoln Memorial, in Washington, D.C. The "city," consisting of hundreds of canvas and plywood shanties, was a dramatic aspect of the Poor People's Campaign, proposed by the Rev. Martin Luther King, Jr., to make poverty visible.

The high point of the campaign was reached on June 19, when more than 75,000 persons gathered in Washington for a poor people's march. The population of Resurrection City, which had been plagued by disorders, rain, and disagreements among the leaders, shrank in the following week from 3,000 to about 50, and it was closed by the authorities. However, it had made church people increasingly aware of the presence of poverty in the U.S., and many denominations allocated large sums to alleviate suffering, especially in the inner city.

On the other hand, many militant black clergy had been negatively inclined toward the Poor People's Campaign and felt that white churches were unrealistic in their support. The Rev. Albert B. Cleage, Jr., of Detroit stated that whites gave money only out of a "feeling of sentimental memory" for King. Cleage, who preached that Jesus was a "black Messiah" and called his church (affiliated with the United Church of Christ) the Shrine of the Black Madonna, said that he was attempting to restore Christianity as a black man's religion.

In the area of civil rights generally, the churches found that some of their efforts to obtain equality for Negroes were not completely appreciated. Negro clergymen from a dozen major denominations held a closed-door caucus at the University of Chicago at which they agreed that black churches should serve as rallying points for gaining black control over all church programs affecting urban areas. Black clergymen of various denominations also met during the year to demand greater representation in their church councils.

The war in Vietnam continued to exacerbate churchmen's consciences. Two Roman Catholic priests, the brothers Daniel and Philip Berrigan, forcibly entered the headquarters of the Catonsville, Md., draft board and burned draft records; they were sentenced to federal prison for their actions. In Milwaukee, Wis., a group of Roman Catholic priests burned draft records. The Rev. William Sloane Coffin, Yale University chaplain, was sentenced to a prison term for allegedly counseling draft resistance. Some churches were also granting sanctuary to draft resisters, but FBI agents or military police simply entered the churches to arrest them.

A long-term set of social action programs, to be administered at the diocesan level, was adopted by more than 200 Roman Catholic bishops in the U.S. The attack on the racial crisis would be waged in the areas of education, job opportunity, housing, and welfare assistance. Church investments would be used to assist the urban poor. Some black priests, however, expressed dissatisfaction and insisted that the Roman Catholic Church in the U.S. was "primarily a white racist structure."

The publication of the papal encyclical *Humanae Vitae*, upholding the traditional Roman Catholic stand on birth control, aroused a storm of controversy, both inside and outside the church. Compliance with the encyclical was not consistent among countries or even among dioceses in the U.S. Protestant leaders generally tended to feel that the encyclical might hinder ecumenical developments.

Citizens for Educational Freedom, an organization with a membership of 150,000 in 36 U.S. states, continued to lobby for state aid to private schools. Legislatures of Michigan, Rhode Island, Pennsylvania, and Louisiana had bills under consideration that would provide tax money for parochial schools. The U.S. Supreme Court, in *Board of Education* v. *Allen*, opened the courts to taxpayers' suits challenging federal assistance to parochial schools. In upholding the constitutionality of a New York free textbook law, the court found that the religious training given in a parochial school does not prevent the state from extending aid to children enrolled in such schools.

Experiments. Churches continued to experiment with new forms of worship designed to make churchgoing more meaningful and relevant. Liturgical dancing by a Roman Catholic nun was part of a joint Roman Catholic-Protestant service at Stanford (Calif.) University. Dialogue sermons involving wor-

shipers and the preacher in discussion were frequent, especially among college congregations.

New, imaginative means of bringing scriptural teachings to the public included religious television programs that examined moral problems in a realistic and uninhibited manner. *The Cotton Patch Version of Paul's Epistles* by Clarence Jordan was a freewheeling paraphrase of the Pauline letters in colloquial, Georgian dialect. At an Episcopalian church in California there was a hippie ordination to the accompaniment of rock settings of hymn tunes.

At the annual meeting of the United Presbyterian Church a radical litany, composed for the occasion, was recited by the delegates. The litany focused on modern issues in contemporary language. Tactile liturgies in which worshipers embraced, shook hands, touched, or kissed one another were also being practiced in various churches. The basis for this was the idea of God's touch infusing strength, as demonstrated in Scripture.

The "underground church" movement, at first a liturgical experiment, was the subject of several conferences in both Protestantism and Roman Catholicism. While the movement was vaguely structured, the fact was that an increasing number of Christians were searching for a new form of basic Christian community to replace the socially inadequate parish. *The Underground Church*, edited by Malcolm Boyd (*see* BIOGRAPHY), described the clandestine and semi-clandestine underground cells for worship and fellowship.   (A. P. KL.)

PROTESTANT CHURCHES

Anglican Communion. Dominating the life and thought of the Anglican Communion in 1968 was the Lambeth Conference, held in London from July 25 to August 25, under the presidency of Arthur Michael Ramsey, archbishop of Canterbury, and attended by 462 Anglican bishops from all over the world.

This latest in the series of episcopal conferences, held normally at ten-year intervals since 1867, differed in several respects from its predecessors. The number of bishops attending was much larger than ever before, necessitating the transfer of the conference meetings from Lambeth Palace, the archbishop of Canterbury's London residence, to Church House, Westminster, the administrative centre of the Church of England. For the first time also, 26 theological consultants accepted invitations to attend the conference and give expert guidance to the bishops. An additional innovation was the presence of 76 official observers from other churches, including the Roman Catholic Church. Partly because of pressure from the American bishops, all the main sessions of the conference were open to the press. This had the paradoxical result of making the bishops more than usually cautious in their debates.

The theme chosen for the conference was the renewal of the church in faith, in ministry, and in unity, and the work of the conference was accordingly divided into three main sections. The subject of faith presented the bishops with their greatest difficulties, in view of recent much publicized radical criticisms (emanating from the U.S. but spreading throughout the communion) of traditional orthodox belief. The conference eventually decided to avoid any clear reassertion of orthodox Christian faith, preferring instead to imply general approval of the radical ferment while at the same time calling on Anglicans to deepen their spiritual life in prayer, sacrament, and worship.

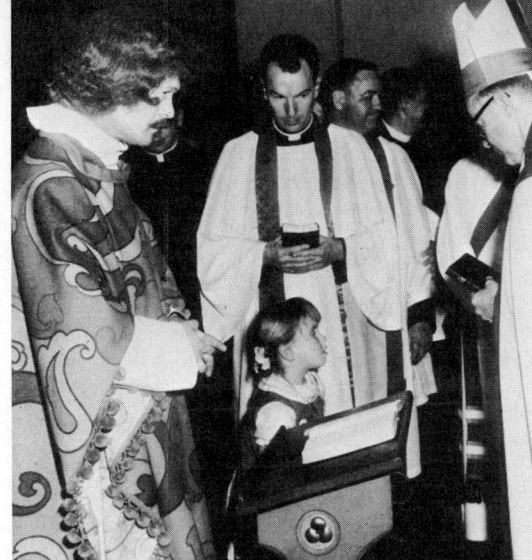

Episcopal Bishop G. Richard Millard (right) ordaining the Rev. Richard York (left) at St. Mark's Church in Berkeley, Calif., March 10, 1968, in a service that included Indian sitar music and a hippie litany. The Rev. York served Berkeley's Telegraph Avenue hippie community.

WIDE WORLD

In their anxiety to emphasize the relevance of the church to the modern world, the bishops devoted much of the section on faith to the expression of their views on current social, economic, and technological problems.

On the subject of ministry, the conference gave powerful support to the modern trend that stressed the ministry of all members of the church. Despite an enthusiastic advocacy of the ordination of women to the priesthood from Donald Coggan, archbishop of York, the conference declared that the question was still an open one. The bishops recommended, however, that women should be ordained as full members of the diaconate, with power to perform all clerical functions except to absolve, to conduct marriages, and to celebrate Holy Communion.

On unity, the conference gave its enthusiastic blessing to the various negotiations for church reunion in which Anglicans were engaged in different parts of the world, including the scheme (published dur-

John Cardinal Heenan, archbishop of Westminster, embracing the Most Rev. A. Michael Ramsey, the archbishop of Canterbury, on the altar steps of London's Westminster Cathedral, Jan. 23, 1968, when Ramsey became the first Protestant bishop to preach in the cathedral.

"THE TIMES," LONDON FROM PICTORIAL PARADE

ing the year) for Anglican-Methodist reunion in England and Wales and the plans for united churches in North India and Ceylon, and the more preliminary discussions taking place in the United States, Canada, and elsewhere.

Among other recommendations were the suggestion that bishops should forgo some of their external signs of dignity, and an important proposal—which owed much to the initiative of the bishop of Huron (Canada)—for the establishment of a permanent Anglican Consultative Council, composed of bishops, clergy, and laity representative of all Anglican churches. It was widely believed that such a council might make future Lambeth Conferences unnecessary.

On August 6, by a unanimous vote, the conference dissented from the teaching promulgated in Pope Paul VI's encyclical *Humanae Vitae,* and reaffirmed the endorsement of contraceptive practices made by the Lambeth Conference of 1958.

Throughout the year opposition to the proposed Anglican-Methodist merger increased among Anglicans of various theological positions. It was decided that all beneficed and licensed clergy in England and Wales should be secretly polled on the subject.

In the U.S. Bishop James Pike, long a controversial figure in the Episcopal Church, again made headlines by publishing a book in which he claimed to have contacted his dead son through a medium.

(R. L. R.)

Baptists. The Baptist World Alliance (BWA) reported the number of Baptists in the world in 1968 at 29,817,707, compared with 27,183,622 in 1967.

The seventh Baptist World Youth Conference, held from July 22 to July 28 at Bern, Switz., drew about 6,000 young people from 65 countries. About 3,800 came from the U.S. and 1,000 from Europe. Among the speakers were the American evangelist Billy Graham and Paul Tournier, Swiss physician and author.

World Baptist leaders meeting in Monrovia, Liberia (July 30–August 1), were particularly concerned with problems of world peace and the relief of want. They urged greater financial support and more direct aid through the donation of surplus food supplies to impoverished nations. This was the first worldwide Baptist meeting ever held in Africa. The BWA Executive Committee created a Study Commission on Cooperative Christianity, charged with the "study of Baptist relations with other Christians." The BWA already had four study commissions, dealing with, respectively, doctrine, Christian teaching and training, missions and evangelism, and religious liberty and human rights.

Ernest A. Payne, former general secretary of the Baptist Union of Great Britain and Ireland, was elected one of the six presidents of the World Council of Churches at Uppsala. He had taken part in the work of the WCC since 1948.

For the first time since 1944, Baptists in Romania were able to receive an official visit of representatives of the BWA. The visitors were greatly impressed by the crowded houses of worship and the lively services. In the Soviet Union, Baptists won permission to teach Bible correspondence courses to 100 persons.

In the U.S., the annual session of the 11 million-member Southern Baptist Convention, held at Houston, Tex., heard a disturbing report on the large number of young persons leaving the denomination. A woman college student attributed this to three "hang-ups": "1. The Baptist tendency to [emphasize] interest in spiritual things to the neglect of the physical. 2. Emphasis on faith to the detriment of works. 3. . . . over-emphasis on negative things, smoking, drinking, to the detriment of poverty, war, inhumanity." Controversy developed as to the guilt of Southern whites for the condition of blacks, and over failure to denounce war and to seek abolition of poverty and social injustice. Open membership was approved. W. A. Criswell of Dallas, Tex., was elected president.

The American Baptist Convention met in Boston. The General Council responded sympathetically to a list of demands presented by black churchmen. A report on conversations between ABC officials and the Church of the Brethren regarding union was favourably received. A resolution that "the termination of pregnancy prior to the end of the 12th week at the request of the individuals concerned" be permitted was adopted, and emphasis was laid on the necessity of active interest in poverty, civil rights, and the crisis of the cities.

The National Baptist Convention, U.S.A., Inc. (black), meeting in Atlanta, Ga., September 4–8, approved a $9 million housing project for low- and moderate-income families; implemented its self-help program by extending $100,000 to Natchez (Miss.) College; took under advisement the development of a cooperative loan plan to help weak churches secure first mortgages; and recommended that institutes on "Citizenship Under the Law" be carried on in individual churches.

In Britain a Joint Baptist Publications Committee was established to survey the field of denominational publishing, encourage authors to submit manuscripts to fill obvious gaps, and obtain a wider field for the sale of certain publications. The Baptist Women's League celebrated its diamond jubilee.

(R. E. E. H.; R. W. T.)

Christian Science. Expanding activities marked the year for Christian Science. Denominational nursing-care facilities for those relying on spiritual means of healing were enlarged and extended, and recruitment and training of Christian Science nurses received increased attention. Some 4,400 Christian Science lectures were given in 56 countries during the year.

The First Church of Christ, Scientist, in Boston published and distributed over 75 million pieces of literature (including the *Christian Science Monitor*) in English and other languages. Advertising and sales of the Bible and the denominational textbook, *Science and Health with Key to the Scriptures* by Mary Baker Eddy, rose. Books published included the first volume of *The Continuity of the Bible,* a compilation of a series appearing in the monthly *Christian Science Journal.*

L. Ivimy Gwalter retired from the Christian Science Board of Directors after 20 years of service. Mrs. Lenore D. Hanks was selected as the new director. At the annual meeting in June, which was attended by more than 8,000 persons, Gordon V. Comer was elected president of the Mother Church for 1968. Comer retired as clerk of the denomination and was succeeded in that office by Charles Henry Gabriel. David E. Sleeper was appointed to the newly created post of executive administrator, and J. Buroughs Stokes became manager of committees on publication.

Full-scale construction on the 16-ac. site of the new Church Center, world headquarters for the denomination, was begun in Boston in August. Completion of

continued on page 652

UPPSALA: 1968

By J. Robert Nelson

Behold, I make all things new," the promise of God in Revelation, was the general theme of Bible studies and addresses at the fourth assembly of the World Council of Churches, held July 4–19, 1968, at Uppsala, Swed. In troubled times, it bade men take heart, in faith that God is ever renewing his creation.

The assembly is the highest governing body of the council, meeting at intervals of approximately six years. Uppsala was thus in succession to Amsterdam (1948), Evanston, Ill. (1954), and New Delhi (1961). The council's 237 member churches, including Orthodox, Anglican, Old Catholic, Lutheran, Reformed (Presbyterian), Methodist, Baptist, United, and several smaller denominations, sent 720 official delegates to the assembly. Observers, guests, youth participants, staff, and the press brought the total to more than 2,000 persons.

Much of the council's business is transacted annually by the 120-member Central Committee and by specialized committees. The assembly's decisions, therefore, were few but important. Strong demands from Negro delegates led to the election of an increased number of nonwhites to the Central Committee. Recognition of the important place of laymen resulted in the choosing of 31 lay members. An Indian layman, M. M. Thomas, was elected chairman.

Of several resolutions voted, the most notable was a clear invitation to the Roman Catholic Church to become a member church of the council. Further, for the first time in its history the council included individual Catholics in its elected commissions: nine theologians were chosen members of the Commission on Faith and Order.

Other important decisions included those to launch a coordinated study on the meaning of man = *humanum* in the light of Christian faith and contemporary knowledge; to establish a secretariat on questions of education and another on medical questions; and to authorize a committee to examine the existing structure of the council in order to promote efficiency and economy.

All participants in the assembly were divided among six study sections, dealing with The Holy Spirit and the Catholicity of the Church; Renewal in Mission; World Economic and Social Development; Toward Justice and Peace in International Affairs; The Worship of God in a Secular Age; and Toward New Styles of Living. As is the practice, the reports of the sections were not adopted but were received by the assembly and commended to the churches and the public.

Among the many speeches given in plenary sessions, appeals for economic and technical aid to the "third world" nations were made by Barbara Ward (Lady Jackson) of England and Pres. Kenneth Kaunda of Zambia. The American novelist James Baldwin and Lord Caradon of England spoke on racism, and the technological revolution was discussed by André Dumas of France. Roberto Tucci, S.J., the first Roman Catholic ever to address a full assembly of the council, spoke on the need for still closer collaboration with his church.

At every ecumenical conference the experience of worship is both ambiguous and memorable; as Christians the participants sense a profound oneness, even while the diversities of practice and intention remind them of traditional divisions. At Uppsala there was a formal opening service in the cathedral, attended by the Swedish king. The closing service was informal and remarkably intimate, marked especially by a spontaneous "sermon" in the quotations on placards carried by youth.

Leaders of the world's churches and King Gustav VI of Sweden (centre right) meeting at one of the sessions of the fourth assembly of the World Council of Churches held in Uppsala, Swed., July 4–19, 1968.

"LONDON DAILY EXPRESS" FROM PICTORIAL PARADE

continued from page 650

the first portion of the $26 million centre, which was to expand and replace badly outdated facilities, was expected in 1971. (J. B. St.)

Churches of Christ. The greatest growth in mission effort in 1968 was in the Latin-American countries, rather than in the traditional fields of Europe and Africa. More families moved to Belo Horizonte, Braz., as part of Operation 1968, a team evangelism effort; they joined some 200 families who had settled there in 1967.

Missionaries were evacuated from Eastern Nigeria (Biafra) and, for a time, from Israel and the Arab lands. As a result of the civil war, about 60,000 Nigerian Christians were left with indigenous leadership and no outside financial aid. Mass evangelism, combined with door-to-door calling by volunteer workers, strengthened the church in Germany and France. There was more emphasis on vocational missionaries and on the training of preachers in their native land.

A new church building was opened in New York City, and in Madison, Tenn., the largest Church of Christ occupied a new building seating 3,000. Among the Churches of Christ generally, however, emphasis on buildings was giving way to emphasis on helping to meet community needs. Efforts to minister to the inner city were strengthened. Houses of the Carpenter in Detroit, Boston, and Camden, N.J., and the Lighthouse in Los Angeles provided after-school recreation, day care, and tutoring for children. In Philadelphia a coffeehouse and a Christian service centre ministered to teen-age groups, and in several sections of New York City subsistence-salaried workers from Camp Shiloh ministered to ghetto children.

Apartment, hospital, and prison ministries were increased, and several nursing homes and homes for the elderly were constructed. Since Churches of Christ have no central organization, each of these works was under the direction of one congregation or under a separate board of trustees.

The magazine *20th Century Christian* celebrated its 30th anniversary. A 19-volume series of commentaries on the New Testament, the *Living Word Commentary,* was edited. "World Radio" entered its eighth year of multilingual broadcasting to countries behind the iron curtain. (M. N. Y.)

Church of Jesus Christ of Latter-day Saints. Church membership in 1968 totaled approximately 2.6 million. Approximately 12,500 full-time and 5,000 part-time missionaries were serving in the missions and stakes of the church. Among new stakes organized outside the U.S. were those in Nukualofa, Tonga; Auckland, N.Z.; and Perth, Austr. The church completed the building of 389 chapels. A new church school complex of 27 buildings was dedicated in Mexico City.

Through the church's Welfare Program, relief assistance was furnished to victims in several disaster-stricken areas. The Deseret Industries, an arm of the Welfare Program providing work opportunities for handicapped persons unemployable by private industry, increased the number of its units and enlarged its facilities. The women's Relief Society of the Church, with a membership of 300,000 women in 58 countries, carried forward a twofold program of education and welfare, including specialized services requiring licensed status for adoption and foster-home care of children.

Church recreational programs for the young included all-church golf, softball, and basketball tourna-

ments and various other sports and summer activities. Youth seminars, which were held throughout the church, brought large numbers of young people together to participate in spiritual, social, and recreational activities. In the U.S. 83% of the boys in the church were enrolled in the Boy Scouts of America.

A collection of Egyptian papyri, once owned by Joseph Smith, founder of the church, was given to the church by the Metropolitan Museum of Art in New York City. Part of the material related to the *Pearl of Great Price,* one of the standard doctrinal works of the church. (Jo. A.)

Congregational Churches. The International Congregational Council (ICC) and the World Alliance of Reformed Churches (WARC) agreed in July that they had received a mandate from their member churches to unite in 1970. Only a few of the member churches had voted against the proposal. Subsequently, the secretariat of the ICC moved from London to Geneva. Frederik Kaan had earlier been appointed secretary to the ICC in succession to Norman Goodall and had also accepted office within WARC. (See *Presbyterian and Reformed,* below.)

In August the United Church of Christ in Madagascar (Congregational) joined with the Evangelical Church of Madagascar (Paris Mission) and the Friends Church to form the Church of Jesus Christ in Madagascar. The event coincided with the 150th anniversary of the arrival of the first Protestant missionaries on the island.

A decision as to the constitution of the new church to be formed by the union of the Congregational Church in England and Wales and the Presbyterian Church of England was delayed for a further year. One of the questions under discussion was the adoption by the new church of a lifelong ordained eldership. The proposed name of the new church was changed from the Reformed Church in England and Wales to the United Church.

Paton Congregational College, Nottingham, closed to unite with Northern Congregational College, Manchester. Negotiations were initiated toward the union of Western College, Bristol, with Northern Congregational College. This would reduce the number of Congregational theological colleges to three from the eight that had existed just over ten years earlier. The intake of students during the year was reported to be smaller than at any time for a century. There was also a decline in the appointment of Congregational overseas missionaries, but this was partly offset by those offering their services overseas on a lay professional basis.

At the annual assembly of the Congregational Church in England and Wales, increasing pressure was exerted toward the grouping of churches under one minister, partly for economic reasons, but also because of the shortage of ministers.

World membership of Congregational churches was estimated in 1968 at about 3.2 million. (See *United Church of Canada; United Church of Christ,* below.) (R. F. G. C.)

Disciples of Christ (Christian Church). The 119th annual assembly of the International Convention of Christian Churches (Disciples of Christ), held in Kansas City, Mo., Sept. 27–Oct. 2, 1968, adopted a design for reorganization that brought about the reconstitution of the convention and its related bodies as "Christian Church (Disciples of Christ)."

Involved in the restructuring were the central organization of the International Convention, 21 member

agencies that reported to the annual assembly, 39 state and area organizations, and 34 member institutions of higher education. The reconstituted Christian Church would include approximately 6,000 local congregations with 1.4 million members.

The design for restructure recognized the manifestation of the church at three levels—local, regional, and general. Each manifestation, while recognizing the "integrity, self-government, authority, rights and responsibilities" of the others, was bound by covenantal relationships.

The general church structure provided for a biennial assembly of delegates chosen from local congregations and regional bodies of the church. There would be a General Board of 280 persons, half elected by the General Assembly and half by the regional manifestations of the church. The chief executive of the Christian Church would be the general minister and president, elected to serve for a term of six years.

There were 10,492 registered members of the Kansas City assembly, of whom 4,739 were voting representatives. Less than 100 voted against adoption of the new structure.

The 1968 assembly also went on record as favouring new U.S. legislation to provide for selective conscientious objection (objection to specific wars) and called on the U.S. and Canada to ratify all of the conventions on human rights. It called upon member congregations to study the Christian response to world revolution.
(A. D. Fl.)

Jehovah's Witnesses. This society of Christian ministers was active in 200 countries during 1968. Over 25,000 congregations operated under the direction of 94 branch offices. During the year more than 82,000 new ministers (members) were baptized, increasing the total membership to more than 1.2 million.

Series of "Good News for All Nations" assemblies were held in over 125 cities in some 30 countries, the majority of them in the Northern Hemisphere, and additional assemblies of the same series were held in Central and South America and other areas later in the year. More than 925,000 persons heard the main talk, "Man's Rule About to Give Way to God's Rule." A Bible study book, *The Truth that Leads to Eternal Life,* was released for use in a new six-month Bible study program.

The Brooklyn headquarters printing plant produced over 12 million bound books and Bibles and over 169 million magazines during the year. Circulation of *The Watchtower,* the official journal of Jehovah's Witnesses, rose to 5,450,000 in 72 languages, and its companion, *Awake!,* attained a circulation of 5.2 million in 26 languages. Work began on the construction of a new office and residence building in Brooklyn to meet the needs of the growing headquarters staff. An average of 20 new meeting halls were constructed each month during 1968 in the U.S.

Opposition to the work of Jehovah's Witnesses continued in Eastern Europe, Spain, Portugal, and several Arab and African countries. (N. H. K.)

Lutherans. An increase of nearly 600,000 baptized members of Lutheran churches in 1968 brought the worldwide total above the 75 million mark, according to statistics compiled by the Lutheran World Federation (LWF). Applications from churches in West Germany, Malaysia, and South Africa for membership in the LWF were accepted by the Federation Committee. With the three new churches, the LWF would include 78 full members and 14 recognized congregations.

Senior officials of 18 Lutheran bodies in seven East Asian countries met at Hong Kong for discussion of church structures, mission relationships, economic life, and ecumenical involvement. Ecumenical activity among Lutherans included doctrinal discussions with Eastern Orthodox representatives at a two-day meeting in New York City. The theological consultation was devoted chiefly to "Scripture and Tradition," preceded by a review of the faith and life of the respective churches today. The first study commission of Roman Catholic and Lutheran theologians representing the Roman Catholic Church and the LWF, respectively, met in Zürich, Switz. The group was to meet again from time to time during the next few years to study "The Gospel and the Church."

The death of Franklin Clark Fry (*see* OBITUARIES) overshadowed all other developments for U.S. Lutheranism during 1968. Fry had headed the Lutheran Church in America since it was formed by a four-way merger in 1962 and had been president for 18 years of one of its predecessor bodies, the United Lutheran Church in America. Robert J. Marshall of Chicago was elected to fill Fry's unexpired two-year term as head of the nation's largest Lutheran body (3.3 million members). The Lutheran Church in America became one of the first Protestant communions to endorse selective conscientious objection. Other Lutheran groups had rejected such a stand.

The 2.6 million-member American Lutheran Church, at its fourth biennial convention, declared pulpit and altar fellowship with the Lutheran Church in America, the 2.8 million-member Lutheran Church-Missouri Synod, and the 21,400-member Synod of Evangelical Lutheran Churches (SELC). All four bodies cooperated in the Lutheran Council in the U.S.A., a common agency for theological study and Christian service. The action was subject to ratification by the American Lutheran Church's districts and acceptance by the Missouri Synod and SELC conventions in 1969. The Lutheran Church in America had already offered officially to enter into fellowship with other Lutherans. (Altars of churches in fellowship are open to communicants of their sister communions and their pulpits are open to the pastors of those churches.)

A joint effort to arrive at uniform wordings for major worship and liturgical materials was initiated in 1968 by the Inter-Lutheran Commission on Worship, the Commission on Worship of the Consultation on Church Union, and the International Committee on English in the Liturgy of the Roman Catholic Church. After two meetings, the three groups issued common texts for the Lord's Prayer, the Apostles' Creed, the Nicene Creed, the Sanctus, and the Gloria; the texts would be recommended to the parent organizations for approval.

For the first time in history, the more than 350 Lutheran deaconesses in the U.S. were united as members of the Lutheran Deaconess Conference in America. A Coordinating Committee of Black Lutheran Clergymen was organized during the year and charged with the task of developing a program to overcome racism in the church.

At its first general convention the Evangelical Lutheran Church of Canada, organized in 1967, called for a four-church merger to create a single Lutheran Church in Canada. A committee was instructed to initiate union negotiations with the three Canadian jurisdictional units of the Missouri Synod, the Lutheran Church in America, and the SELC. Such a merger would encompass some 304,000 members in 1,085

congregations. It would be the fourth largest Protestant body in Canada. (E. W. M.; W. Vö.)

Methodists. The birth of a new church in the U.S. was the high point of 1968 within the Methodist family, as the Methodist Church, largest of the Wesleyan denominations, and the Evangelical United Brethren (EUB) joined to form the United Methodist Church. The merger, which officially took place on April 23 in Dallas, Tex., brought into being a denomination with more than 11 million members in the U.S. and approximately 1 million more in 50 other nations. First the bishops and then some 1,300 delegates to the Uniting Conference clasped hands to declare: "Lord of the Church, we are united in Thee, in Thy Church, and now in The United Methodist Church."

The Methodist-EUB union brought together what only 29 years earlier had been five denominations. The Methodists had a three-way merger in 1939 and the Evangelical and United Brethren groups joined in 1946. EUB organization and doctrines were closely related to those of the larger denomination. Long separated by language differences (EUB work was traditionally among the German-speaking), the churches had worked cooperatively through most of their two-century existence.

The union was only the largest of many ecumenical developments within Methodism during the year. Others included: the granting of permission to Methodists in 14 nations (India, Belgium, Hong Kong, Pakistan, Sierra Leone, Malaysia-Singapore, Costa Rica, Panama, Peru, Chile, Bolivia, Uruguay, and Argentina) to become autonomous units or to join union churches; formalizing of cross-representation between the United Methodist Church and the British Methodist Conference; and merger of the Wesleyan Methodist and Pilgrim Holiness churches (U.S.) into the 122,000-member Wesleyan Church. The three Negro Methodist denominations in the U.S. reiterated

their intention to work toward union among themselves. In Britain the final report of the Anglican-Methodist Unity Commission was published on April 4. The British Methodist Conference accepted in principle proposals for the joint training of theological students in an ecumenical college at Edgbaston, Birmingham.

The formation of the United Methodist Church signaled the end of an era in which most black members of the Methodist Church were separated into the Central Jurisdiction, with guarantees of black leadership. By midyear there remained only ten all-black annual (regional) conferences of the 17 extant in 1964; a black had been elected bishop by a nonsegregated jurisdiction for the first time; and all six black bishops were supervising predominantly white areas. As in many other denominations in the U.S., a new all-black group, the Black Methodists for Church Renewal, was formed.

In the executive committee of the World Methodist Council (WMC), which met in Helsinki, Fin., September 9–12, a resolution was passed calling upon Methodist churches throughout the world to observe Aldersgate Sunday (the Sunday nearest to May 24—the date of John Wesley's conversion) over the next five years as a day of fasting, in remembrance of the needs of the world's poor and hungry. The British Methodist Conference, which met in London in June, pledged to give one day's income on Good Friday 1969 for world poverty projects through Christian Aid. Mervyn M. Temple, a Methodist minister and missionary in Zambia for 25 years, sat in Westminster Abbey near the tomb of David Livingstone and fasted for two weeks from May 20 to call attention to what he regarded as the church's misuse of its resources in the face of the world's poor.

On Dec. 2, 1967, 150 Methodists had met 150 Roman Catholics in Westminster Cathedral Great Hall for two hours of informal dialogue. The second meeting of the group, appointed by the WMC and the Roman Catholic Secretariat for Promoting Christian Unity, took place in London, Aug. 31–Sept. 4, 1968. The subjects discussed were the Eucharist and authority in the church.

Daniel T. Niles, president of the Methodist Church, Ceylon, was elected as one of the presidents of the World Council of Churches at the fourth assembly, and Miss Pauline M. Webb was the first woman to become a vice-chairman of the council's Central Committee. Bishop Odd Hagen was elected president of the Swedish Free Church Council, which celebrated its 50th anniversary during the year.

Membership showed a slight decline in both the American and British churches. In early 1968, the Methodist Church showed a drop of some 21,000 to 10,289,214 in the U.S. British figures fell some 12,000 to 666,713. The EUB total of 737,762 as 1968 opened was diminished by some 10,000 in the Canadian Conference, which was permitted to withdraw and join the United Church of Canada. (M. W. Wo.; W. H. Ta.)

Presbyterian and Reformed. The 1968 meeting of the executive committee of the World Alliance of Reformed Churches (WARC; World Presbyterian Alliance) was held at Cluj, Rom., June 25–29, at the invitation of the Reformed Church of Romania.

In 1968 the total membership of WARC reached 110 churches, of which 66 were so-called younger churches. Those admitted into membership during the year were the Christian Church of Sumba (Indonesia), the Presbyterian Church of Guyana, the Evangelical

Bishop Lloyd C. Wicke of the Methodist Church and Bishop Reuben H. Mueller of the Evangelical United Brethren clasping hands during ceremonies in Dallas, Tex., April 23, 1968, when the two groups merged to form the United Methodist Church.

BOB W. SMITH

Church of Morocco, and the Evangelical Church of Madagascar.

Apart from observers from the Lutheran World Federation (LWF) and the Orthodox Church of Romania, three fraternal delegates from the International Congregational Council (ICC) attended the Cluj meeting. Central to the discussions on interchurch relationships was the planning for the intended merger in 1970 of WARC and the ICC. Increased cooperation between these two world confessional organizations has already found expression in the appointment of the new minister-secretary of the ICC (Frederik Kaan) as a staff member (secretary for information) of WARC. Moreover, the quarterly magazine *Reformed and Presbyterian World* became a joint publication of the two organizations.

A joint WARC-ICC executive committee meeting was held at Uppsala on July 13, at which a report was received on replies sent in by member churches of the two organizations regarding the proposed merger. Of the (then) 109 member churches of WARC, 76 had so far replied; 73 were in favour of the union and 3 were against it. Of the 19 member churches of the ICC, 15 were in favour of the union; 2 indicated that they would not oppose the union, though full membership would be impossible for them; and 2 churches had not replied. The members of the two executives unanimously voted "that we have received a mandate from our member churches to proceed with the union."

Further evidence of the increasing cooperation between the Reformed and Congregational church families was an important theological consultation held in Stockholm (July 22–23). A statement on "the significance of the Reformed position in an Ecumenical age" was drafted, and work was begun on the content and preliminary study of the theme for the 1970 uniting General Council: "God reconciles and makes free."

The General Synod of the Reformed Church in America voted 183–103 to approve and recommend to its 45 classes (lower judicatories) full organic merger with the Presbyterian Church in the U.S. The General Assembly of the Presbyterian Church in the U.S., by a vote of 406–36, also voted to approve the Plan of Union and sent it to the presbyteries for their consideration. This was the first of three necessary steps. Approval by the presbyteries and classes would bring the issue to the 1969 General Assembly and General Synod for a final vote, with the united assemblies scheduled for 1970.

Continuation of the dialogue between the Lutheran World Federation and WARC was assured as a proposal for the setting up of a Lutheran-Reformed joint committee was approved at the Cluj meeting. The joint committee was to consist of "four on each side representing both theological and administrative leadership in the churches, including one executive committee member from both bodies." The executive committee at Cluj also resolved to appoint a committee to explore, with representatives of the World Council of Churches and the Roman Catholic Church, "the elements in the new situation that might make the initiation of Reformed Roman Catholic dialogue wise at this time." The North American area of WARC engaged in conversations with the Ecumenical Commission of the Standing Committee of Orthodox Bishops in America.

A major action of the General Synod of the Associate Reformed Presbyterian Church (U.S.) was the approval of a new constitution that would permit women to serve as ministers, elders, and deacons. The first woman minister in the Presbyterian Church in Canada, Miss Shirley Jeffery, was ordained in May.

(F. H. KA.; W. B. MI.)

Religious Society of Friends. In June 1968 Bronson P. Clark was appointed executive secretary of the American Friends Service Committee, which continued to operate worldwide programs on a budget of some $7 million. Among new undertakings were a relief mission to Nigeria/Biafra, the sending of Quaker representatives to the Middle East and Southeast Asia, and support for the Southern Christian Leadership Conference's campaign for jobs and income. Draft counseling and programs of medical assistance to both North and South Vietnam increased during the year.

At the end of the sessions of the Friends General Conference, at Cape May, N.J., in June, some 300 Quakers went to Washington, D.C., to demonstrate their support of the Poor People's Campaign. At the climax of this witness, 34 Friends were arrested, along with more than 40 persons from the SCLC, for holding an illegal religious service on a terrace of the Capitol.

The Friends World Committee for Consultation named William E. Barton to a new position as associate secretary to head up special efforts toward international cooperation in mission and service. For the past 12 years he had been general secretary of the Friends Service Council (London).

A Quaker body shared in forming a new united national church for the first time when the 8,000 members of the Malagasy Yearly Meeting, known officially as the Friends Church of Madagascar, joined two other Protestant bodies in August to form the Church of Jesus Christ in Madagascar.

British Friends, anxious to see the government increase aid to less developed countries, decided in 1968 to tax themselves voluntarily to help relieve world poverty. Individual Friends would give 1% of their net income each year, in addition to any other charitable commitments, to finance projects to assist poorer nations and communities.

A group of Friends and a group of Unitarians met in London in "a quest for understanding," but discussions were not continued. (CD. H.; E. B. BR.)

Salvation Army. In the U.K. the "For God's sake care" public appeal ended with a total of £2.5 million, received in cash or realizable promises, for the 28 new social centre enterprises launched in the centenary year, 1965. The largest, Booth House, was declared open by Queen Elizabeth II in March.

The Joystrings, a British rhythm group organized by the Salvation Army, performing in Paris. The group disbanded in July 1968 after participating in the Army's "Youth Year" celebration.

The Army's international leader, Gen. Frederick Coutts, campaigned in India and Pakistan, his engagements ranging from an audience with the president of India to tent meetings lit by hurricane lamps for villagers. In Japan the emperor received General Coutts, and Princess Chichibu opened a new wing of a Salvationist hospital for TB patients. The general also traveled extensively in Europe.

In the U.S., World Youth Year was observed in all four territories, and special events and programs attracted young Salvationist participants from every part of the nation.

The formation of the Salvation Army Refugee and Rehabilitation Program on behalf of Vietnamese refugees was announced by the national commander, Commissioner Samuel Hepburn, in early March. The program, inaugurated at the request of the Vietnamese consulate in Hong Kong, was designed to provide food, housing, clothing, and medical attention for refugees.

Chosen from scores of worldwide submissions, a British ITV film on the Salvation Army, entitled *The Warmongers,* was acclaimed at the World Assembly of the World Association for Christian Broadcasting in Oslo.

Denmark issued a 60 øre postal stamp to mark the 80th year of Army work there. A 10 øre surcharge would help finance Salvationist projects.

(J. Gr.; W. P.)

Seventh-day Adventists. Church activities were carried on in nearly 200 countries during 1968, in some 1,068 languages and dialects. Several new medical institutions were opened. Literature produced and sold by Adventist publishing houses totaled nearly $24 million, up 5% from 1967. Church membership reached a new high of 1,780,000 (including 406,000 in the U.S.), and tithes and offerings totaled $166.9 million. During the year more than 800 workers were sent overseas from home bases. One-third were educators, another third were health workers, and one-third were ministerial and administrative personnel.

For the first time in history the annual Autumn Council of the General Conference was held outside the U.S. Meeting in Toronto, Ont., October 8–16, the council voted a world budget that included appropriations of $46,985,537, a new high. Early in the year the church voted an appropriation of $100,000 to provide educational, welfare, and medical facilities in ghetto areas.

The church-operated Home Study Institute, a worldwide correspondence school with headquarters in Washington, D.C., enrolled its 100,000th student. The Southern Union Bible correspondence school, Atlanta, Ga., merged with the Faith for Today television correspondence school of New York. Nearly 400,000 students were enrolled in free Bible correspondence schools.

In the first eight months of the year, assistance valued at nearly $1.5 million was provided to victims of natural disasters by SAWS (Seventh-day Adventist Welfare Service). Included were 2,000 CARE packages for earthquake victims in Turkey. (K. H. W.)

Unitarians and Universalists. March 17, 1968, marked the 400th anniversary of the establishment of the oldest Unitarian Church still holding services. Although institutional Unitarianism had begun some years earlier in Poland, this church in Cluj, Rom., constituted the movement's Transylvanian beginnings. The International Association for Religious Freedom (IARF) was represented at the celebrations in Transylvania by its president, Peter Dalbert of Switzerland.

Unitarian Universalist churches throughout the U.S. reflected in their dominant emphases during the year the racial unrest and independence from authority manifest in the nation itself. The search for ways of coping with these crises most effectively created such deep religious concern that a record 1,350 delegates were drawn to the seventh annual General Assembly of the Unitarian Universalist Association in Cleveland, O., May 23–28.

The conference theme was "Determining Our Priorities." Most of the controversy centred around a proposed Black Affairs Council (BAC), independent of the association itself, which sought to handle the main thrust of the Unitarian Universalist race program nationally. Objecting to this proposal was Black and White Action, a group that favoured a primarily integrated attack on racial problems, with responsibility to the entire movement.

After hours of emotional debate, the delegates voted 836–327 to entrust the chief action on race to BAC. The group comprised six black and three white members, selected by and responsible to a black activist minority. The assembly provided $250,000 annually for four years to underwrite this pioneering approach to ghetto problems. Only history could disclose whether this experiment would eventually draw blacks and whites closer together or whether it would strengthen sentiment and pressure for black nationalism and/or increased racial separatism.

The delegates endeavoured to reduce centralization of power in the Unitarian Universalist Association by adopting a bylaw that required the General Assembly to elect a 27-member Board of Trustees, consisting of three officers elected by the General Assembly (the moderator, the president, and the special financial adviser), plus four trustees elected at large and one trustee elected directly by each geographical district. Another radical innovation in a movement usually noted for its insistence on individual freedom was a decision to make substantial financial contributions for support of the association mandatory for churches and fellowships after 1969. Otherwise a church or fellowship could not legally share in association meetings, elections, or department and district services. The provision would go into effect if approved in final reading at the next General Assembly.

Mirroring the times, the assembly recommended that all churches study, in the coming year, the (Kerner) Report of the National Advisory Commission on Civil Disorders. General resolutions passed by a greater than two-thirds vote dealt with Vietnam, self-determination for black and other ethnic groups, equal opportunity in housing, the right of dissent, abortion, the Poor People's Campaign, and the National Advisory Commission on Civil Disorders.

The British General Assembly of Unitarian and Free Christian Churches held its annual meetings in London, April 8–11. The important features were a full discussion of the report of a team that had visited the Unitarian Universalist churches in the U.S. in the previous year and a discussion of a report prepared by the Foy Society on the state of the churches.

The council of the assembly set up a Review Commission, which reported in October on the headquarters administration. A report on the organization of the assembly was also in preparation. In November a subcommittee reported to the council on national Unitarian membership, and another subcommittee reported on the Unitarian press. The council also set up a Theological Panel, charged with the study of theo-

logical questions and theological articles in non-Unitarian publications.

The Religious Education Department produced a study of religious education in British Unitarian churches (*Growing Vision*), and this led to a considerable movement in the Sunday schools to adopt a more modern approach. More use was to be made of material prepared by the Beacon Press of the Unitarian Universalist Religious Education Department. A school for Sunday school teachers was held in August in Oxford, with Muriel Davies, director of religious education in the Washington, D.C., area, as one of the main speakers.

An exploratory conference of Unitarians and Quakers was held under the auspices of the Interfaiths Subcommittee. (J. N. B.; JN. KY.)

United Church of Canada. For the first time in the history of the United Church of Canada, a layman, Robert B. McClure, was elected moderator. McClure, who had spent most of his life outside Canada, had devoted 45 years to medical work in China, on the Burma Road, among Arab refugees in the Gaza Strip, and finally as head of the Ratlam Christian Hospital in India. Confessedly he was neither an administrator nor a theologian, but it was expected that he would attract the interest of the young in the church's mission, show the laity that they also have a ministry, and make a strong plea for support of the less developed nations.

Perhaps the chief feature of the General Council in 1968 was the attention given to world poverty. The council undertook to increase by $1,250,000 the amount devoted to direct relief overseas, while continuing practical assistance in many fields. In the Congo (Kinshasa), the Community Development Program operated in the areas of agriculture, trades, and public health. In Brazil it provided technical guidance and supervision in a new settlement at Gurupi. In India, the Malwa Economic Development Society stressed food and water relief and training in mechanical skills.

In all such projects the trend was toward the employment of more laity and a stress on technical skills for the relief of poverty. Perhaps most important of all, because of its ultimate consequences, was the increasingly ecumenical pattern in missionary programs, involving not only various Protestant bodies but the Roman Catholic Church as well.

At the General Council the report of the Commission on the Ministry resulted in the formation of a new Division of Ministry and Personnel Services, which would attempt to cope with the problems of ministry and with issues arising from new forms of ministry for both ordained ministers and laymen. The report on the church in the field of social welfare emphasized the need for church people to participate in community programs and for the church, as a body, to act where state and community organizations were not at work. In addition, it proposed the training of professional and volunteer workers through cooperation between the church and its colleges and schools of social work.

The Commission on Union between the Anglican Church of Canada and the United Church was fully organized, with subcommissions and a director from each church in one office. It was hoped that union would be achieved by 1974. The two churches had already agreed on amalgamation of the official church papers as soon as possible and were working together on a new hymnbook.

The General Council approved a new service book to replace the former Book of Common Order, but it shelved an "experimental" creed. (A. G. R.)

United Church of Christ. Like other mainstream Protestant denominations, the United Church of Christ, which came into existence in 1957 through a union of the Congregational Christian Churches and the Evangelical and Reformed Church, counted as its main task the finding of new ways to confront the world with the old truth of the Gospel. Two words could well describe the thrust of the church during these 12 years.

The first word was "ecumenical." On many occasions the church had made it plain that it would not do anything alone that could be done as well or better in company with other churches. This was true in local communities, where the United Church of Christ and its predecessor bodies had always been in the forefront in establishing and supporting local councils of churches. On the national scene, the United Church of Christ was one of the staunch supporters of the National Council of Churches, and on the world scene it was a member church of the World Council of Churches. It was also engaged in negotiations looking toward the establishment of a united church.

The second word was "experimental." Wedded to no old or traditional ways of setting forth the claims of the Gospel on men, the church was seeking new modes that would speak to this day and generation in inescapable terms. The chief emphasis in this effort was being placed on strengthening the local church. On the world scene, the Board for World Ministries was cooperating with other denominations, namely the Disciples of Christ and the United Presbyterian Church in the U.S.A., in establishing joint staff arrangements. Almost all the work in the world mission field was done ecumenically. The church was also committed to meeting the needs of the urban crisis in the U.S. and to the establishment of peace through a Peace Priority Program.

Officers of the church in 1968 were Ben M. Herbster, president; Joseph H. Evans, secretary; and Charles H. Lockyear, treasurer. (B. M. H.)

ROMAN CATHOLIC CHURCH

The most dramatic event in the Roman Catholic Church was the publication of the long-delayed encyclical on birth control, *Humanae Vitae* ("Of Human Life"), on July 29. Though compassionate in tone, it reiterated the 1930 ban on the use of artificial contraceptives and stated that "every marriage act must remain open to the transmission of life." The encyclical aroused varied reactions, ranging from enthusiastic support (especially in some less developed countries where contraception was often regarded as a form of "neocolonialism") to fierce rejection (especially in the Anglo-Saxon world). The pastoral consequences of the encyclical were spelled out in a series of collective pastoral letters from national hierarchies, but they too varied greatly in the stress they placed on the rights of conscience. The debate continued. (*See* POPULATIONS AND AREAS.)

However, in spite of the encyclical and in spite of the note of caution that had crept into papal pronouncements generally, the trend in 1968 was outward looking, with an emphasis on ecumenism and on social and political problems.

In the work for church unity, 1968 was a year of conferences. Notable among these was the fourth assembly of the World Council of Churches at Uppsala,

at which Roman Catholic observers were present and warmly welcomed. For the first time, Roman Catholics participated as full members of the Commission on Faith and Order. Shortly afterward (July 25–August 25), Roman Catholic observers attended a Lambeth Conference of Anglican bishops for the first time. Though *Humanae Vitae* distressed many Anglicans, the observers spoke at the conference and contributed to the work of drafting documents. There was great cordiality among Roman Catholics and Anglicans. The third and final meeting of the Joint Preparatory Commission, set up to investigate the difficulties of reunion, took place in Malta in January. The archbishop of Canterbury was invited to preach in Westminster Cathedral, London, and was received with applause; later in the year, John Cardinal Heenan preached at Westminster Abbey.

In April representatives of the Roman Catholic Church and the World Council of Churches met economic experts of the UN to discuss world poverty and the problems of the less developed countries. The meeting was held at Beit Meri near Beirut, Lebanon, and a strong joint statement was issued.

The personal concern for peace of Pope Paul VI (*see* BIOGRAPHY) was much in evidence throughout the year. Late in 1967 he had received U.S. Pres. Lyndon B. Johnson and pleaded for an end to the bombing of North Vietnam. New Year's Day was declared a day of prayer for peace, especially in Vietnam and Nigeria. Throughout the year these pleas were repeated. In July, Pope Paul admitted that Caritas Internationalis, the Vatican relief organization, had been flying supplies to the secessionist state of Biafra, where thousands were reported to be starving.

In August Pope Paul went to Bogotá, Colombia, on the occasion of a Eucharistic Congress. It was the first visit of a pope to South America. He was cheered by the poor. Though insistent on the need for radical social reform, he offered no encouragement to those who advocate revolution, which could only "delay in-

A.F.P. FROM PICTORIAL PARADE

stead of advancing that social progress to which you lawfully aspire." This teaching was repeated by the Latin-American bishops, who met after the Eucharistic Congress at Medellín, Colombia, but they urged even more strongly the "pressing need for the reform of political structures and agricultural policies."

The year saw the long-awaited reform of the Roman Curia begin to take effect. The new rules, intended to internationalize the Curia and make it more pastoral in spirit, came into force on March 1. Throughout the early part of the year, many curial cardinals resigned, mostly on grounds of age or ill health. The most important resignation was that of Alfredo Cardinal Ottaviani, head of the Congregation for the Doctrine of the Faith and the church's best known conservative. He was replaced by Franjo Cardinal Seper, a Yugoslav and a moderate progressive.

In the U.S. the growth of the "underground church," a revolutionary Christian movement bypassing official church structures, led to much discussion on the nature of the church and on the relations between bishops and laity, the charismatic and the institutional. In an attempt to provide a doctrinal basis for these discussions, the bishops of the U.S. joined together to write a pastoral letter, based on the documents of the second Vatican Council. Later in the year, they produced another joint statement on the racial crisis calling for "collaborative peaceful solutions," and the pastoral letter issued by the National Conference of Catholic Bishops in November included an endorsement of selective conscientious objection and urged an end to the war in Vietnam. Other talking points of the year were clerical celibacy and the changing nature of the priestly ministry, and the ethical problems surrounding heart transplants. But from July the birth-control question and the nature of papal authority were at the centre of discussion. In December the pope announced the convening of an extraordinary session of the Synod of Bishops for October 1969 to discuss "better cooperation and more fruitful contacts" between the Holy See and the national hierarchies.

The note of caution in papal pronouncements, mentioned earlier, was found not only in the encyclical but also in the pope's *Credo* issued in late June. The

Below, members of the Parents Aid Society picketing St. Patrick's Cathedral in New York City on July 30, 1968, to protest Pope Paul VI's edict against birth control. Above right, Archbishop Terence J. Cooke, the seventh Roman Catholic archbishop of New York, during his installation ceremonies on April 4, 1968.

WIDE WORLD

pope strongly emphasized traditional positions on clerical celibacy, papal infallibility, and the Marian dogmas. The timing of the *Credo*—just before the World Council of Churches assembly—was thought by many to be unfortunate, but there could be no doubt that it brought reassurance and comfort to many traditional Catholics. (P. A. H.)

EASTERN CHURCHES

The Orthodox Church. The year 1968 was marked by several events of Pan-Orthodox significance. On the initiative of the Ecumenical Patriarchate, representatives of all autocephalous churches—with the exception of Czechoslovakia, Georgia, and Albania—met in Chambéry, near Geneva, June 8–15, to discuss the agenda of a future Great Council of the Orthodox Church. The churches agreed that an "Inter Orthodox Commission for the preparation of the Great and Holy Council of the Orthodox Church" would prepare materials on six subjects: the sources of revelation; more active lay participation in worship and the life of the church in general; *oikonomia* and "strictness" in the church; readaptation of fasting rules; obstacles to marriage; and problems related to the liturgical calendar. The commission would have the services of a general secretariat.

Although the delegations were, as usual, divided along political lines—which explained the lack of any statement on social or political issues—the conference offered new proof of spiritual unity in theological problems and concerns. It contributed to the preparations for Orthodox participation in the fourth assembly of the World Council of Churches in Uppsala.

In Moscow, from May 26 to June 2, the Russian Patriarchate celebrated the 50th anniversary of its reestablishment in November 1917. Delegations from abroad included the Greek patriarch of Jerusalem and the patriarchs of Serbia, Romania, and Bulgaria, as well as official representatives of Roman Catholicism and Protestantism. The previously announced visit to Moscow of the ecumenical patriarch, Athenagoras I, again failed to materialize.

As these official celebrations were taking place, the internal ferment, noted in previous years, continued inside Russian Orthodoxy. In a letter addressed to Patriarch Alexis of Moscow and dated February 20, the former archbishop of Kaluga, Yermogen, protested violently against state interventions in the appointment of clerics and criticized the Patriarchate of Moscow for its docility to government orders.

On May 19 a new Orthodox patriarch of Alexandria (U.A.R.), Nicholas, was enthroned in Cairo Cathedral. He thus became the spiritual leader of the small Orthodox minority in the U.A.R. and of larger communities scattered around Africa, including missions in Uganda, Kenya, and Tanzania.

The Orthodox represented the largest confessional group at the fourth assembly of the World Council of Churches. Three Orthodox speakers—Ignatius Hazim, metropolitan of Latakia (Syria), Metropolitan Nicholas Corneanu of Banat (Romania), and John Meyendorff of the U.S.—were among those who addressed the assembly plenum. The patriarch of Serbia, German, was elected as one of the council's presidents. In general the Orthodox, without denying the social responsibility of Christians, failed to sympathize with the tendency of the assembly to identify the Christian commitment with social "causes."

On May 15 the Standing Conference of Orthodox Bishops in America approved an appeal to the Pan-

UPI COMPIX

Pope Paul VI (right) receiving newly elected Patriarch Ignace Antoine II Hayek of Antioch in the Vatican on June 20, 1968.

Orthodox meeting in Chambéry calling for action toward the establishment of an administratively united Orthodox Church of America. The Orthodox of America were organized according to the nationality of the immigrants whose descendants constituted the major part of church membership—Greeks, Russians, Serbians, and others. The refusal of the Ecumenical Patriarchate to put the issue on the agenda, which had been previously fixed, provoked much criticism in America. The Clergy-Laity Congress of the Greek Archdiocese of America, the largest single American administrative body, met in Athens and adopted a resolution calling for the creation of a united American Synod under the jurisdiction of the Ecumenical Patriarchate. This and several other developments, including an appeal for Orthodox unity in the "Diaspora" published by Syndesmos, the world association of Orthodox youth movements, seemed to indicate that Orthodox unity in the New World was becoming a major issue.

As the Orthodox communities in America matured, their isolation from each other and their dependence on centres in the Old World seemed more and more unnatural. This maturity was symbolized in 1968 by the celebration in October of the centennial of the Orthodox parish of San Francisco and by the 30th anniversary of St. Vladimir's Orthodox Theological Seminary in Crestwood, N.Y. The latter celebration was marked by the granting of honorary degrees to Orthodox scholars and leaders from Greece, Yugoslavia, the U.S.S.R., Lebanon, and the U.S.

Eastern Non-Chalcedonian Churches. June 1968 was marked by a significant event in the history of the Coptic Church of Egypt: the dedication of a new and imposing patriarchal cathedral in Cairo. The U.A.R. government had contributed a large sum for its erection, thus affirming its sympathy toward the Coptic Christian minority. In the past, relations between the Muslim authorities of Egypt and the Copts were often strained, and the government had tended to deemphasize their numbers and influence on Egyptian society.

In May the Armenian Catholicos Vasghen of Echmiadzin (Soviet Armenia) paid a long visit to the U.S., where he dedicated a new cathedral in New York. The visit strengthened the spiritual and material ties between the prosperous Armenian communities of America and the mother see of Echmiadzin. (J. Me.)

JUDAISM

The year 1968 (5728–29, according to the Jewish calendar) was a disturbing one for the Jewish people. The elation engendered by Israel's victory over the Arabs in June 1967 gave way to a more sober assessment of the political implications and to concern over the fate of many Jewish communities in the Diaspora, especially in the Arab countries and in Eastern Europe.

Remnants of the ancient and once great Jewish communities in the Arab countries continued to bear the brunt of the aftermath of the six-day war. Many Jews in the U.A.R., Syria, and Iraq remained in prisons and concentration camps; their economic life was slowly strangled, and they were objects of hostile propaganda and incitement, denied the opportunity of emigration. In spite of repeated requests to the UN secretary-general to intervene on their behalf, it was impossible for representatives of humanitarian organizations to obtain access to the imprisoned' Jews or to inquire into the living conditions and well-being of those not incarcerated. About 14,000 Jews left Libya, Tunisia, and even Morocco, where the authorities made valiant efforts to protect Jewish citizens.

In Eastern Europe circumstances and events took a sharp turn for the worse. In Poland the bitter intra-party struggle for power resulted in an onslaught on the small Jewish community (estimated at about 30,-000). Many hundreds of Jews were dismissed from their posts and expelled from the Communist Party. About 3,000 emigrated (mainly to Israel), and hundreds more applied for exit visas. The famous Yiddish theatre directed by Ida Kaminska was disbanded, and the activities of many Jewish educational and cultural institutions were curtailed.

"Zionists" and "Zionism" also emerged as the main targets for Eastern European attacks on Czechoslovakian "liberalization." Jewish political and cultural leaders, such as Eduard Goldstuecker and Frantisek Kriegel, had to flee the country. In the wake of the Soviet invasion about 1,500 left Czechoslovakia, but—at least for the time being—Jewish communal and religious institutions were allowed to function undisturbed.

The climate of hostility toward Israel and the intensified propaganda against "Zionism" caused renewed concern for the future of the three million Soviet Jews. Although the Soviet leaders and propagandists were meticulous in distinguishing between "Jews" and "Zionists," the borderline became blurred. Trofim Kychko, whose anti-Semitic tract *Judaism Unmasked* was officially condemned by the Central Committee of the Soviet Communist Party in 1964, produced a further attack in *Judaism and Zionism*. The 100,000-strong Jewish community in Romania under the courageous leadership of the chief rabbi, David Moses Rosen, and that of Yugoslavia (7,500) remained the last islands of hope for Jewry in Eastern Europe.

In Britain some stir was caused by the report of the Statistical and Demographic Unit of the Board of Deputies of British Jews, which showed that the Jewish population in Britain was 410,000, about 40,000 below the previous estimate. The chief rabbi, Immanuel Jakowovitz, carried through a plan, first formulated in 1967, to decentralize authority by establishing a so-called cabinet of rabbis to work with him.

Efforts to achieve some degree of cooperation between the Orthodox and Reform wings of Judaism in Britain and in Israel were not very successful. The conservative World Council of Synagogues held its meeting in London in July but failed to make any impact on the religious establishment. The World Union of Progressive Judaism met in Jerusalem but made no noticeable impression. A proposal to hold a prayer service at the Western Wall where men and women would worship together provoked a violent reaction and led to fears of disorders at the Jewish holy places.   (P. GL.)

A significant event in American Jewish life was the formal opening of the Reconstructionist Rabbinical College in Philadelphia on October 13, under the auspices of the Jewish Reconstructionist Foundation. The new rabbinical college took its place beside the Hebrew Union College-Jewish Institute of Religion, of Cincinnati, O., and the Jewish Theological Seminary of America, of New York City, as an institution of higher learning serving the non-Orthodox segment of the Jewish community.

The Jewish Reconstructionist Foundation was established by Mordecai M. Kaplan in order to promote his concept of Judaism as a religious civilization. The Reconstructionist philosophy takes as its starting point the historical-spiritual unity of the Jewish people. The

WIDE WORLD

Yehuda Leib Levin, chief rabbi of Moscow, during his visit to New York City in June 1968. This was the first visit to the United States by a leader of Russian Judaism in more than 50 years, and his visit caused a controversy among Jews in the U.S.

unifying bond is not simply secular nationalism, nor the Thirteen Principles of Faith, nor the blind impetus of history, but the feelings of fellowship and kinship, sublimated by a long tradition into the shared quest of the good life. In brief, it is the ideal of "peoplehood," in which national loyalty is balanced by dedication to the universal society and religion is articulated in a pattern of living and an interpretation of the destiny of the people. In the past three decades, Reconstructionism influenced all trends in Judaism by the vigour and range of its criticism. It challenged all ideologists to take account of the secularizing trends in society, of the emergence of Israel, and of the new developments in contemporary thought.

In respect of the Jewish-Christian dialogue, the year began with the realization that the theological implications of the rebirth of Israel were not clarified, in either Jewish or Christian circles. Is the state viewed by Jews as the fulfillment of the *eschaton*, the promised End? Or is it to be seen within the mundane context of political-military struggles? Does its very existence run counter to basic Christian axioms? Within Judaism and at interfaith convocations, these questions would loom large in the coming years.

The chief rabbi of Moscow, Yehuda Leib Levin, visited the U.S. Though many Jewish leaders resented the fact that the visit was sponsored by the American Council for Judaism and the Friends of Jerusalem, both anti-Zionist, it served as a reminder that, despite half a century of atheistic propaganda, many hundreds of thousands of Soviet Jews remained loyal to their religious and cultural heritage.   (J. B. A.)

Though Jewish education in the U.S. was estimated to be a $100 million-a-year business, and though 10 new Hebrew day schools were founded in 1968, bringing the total to 387, Jewish leaders were concerned that fewer than 90,000 students were enrolled in such schools. In a major educational development, Yeshiva Torah Vodaath and Mesivta, the world's largest Orthodox seminary with an enrollment of more than 2,000 students, dedicated its new $4 million campus in Brooklyn, N.Y.

Disturbing instances of anti-Semitism continued to appear among some militant segments of the black community in the U.S. This was especially apparent during the strike of public-school teachers in New York in the fall. The strike originated in a dispute between the teachers' union, in which Jewish members were prominent, and a predominantly nonwhite school district in Brooklyn, where a group of community leaders was attempting to exert local control. In one incident a group of about 15 persons hung a swastika in P.S. 148 in the Bronx and demanded the transfer of the Jewish principal. A related dispute arose when John F. Hatchett, author of "The Phenomenon of the Anti-Black Jews and the Anglo-Saxons: A Study in Educational Perfidy," an article in *Forum,* the organ of the African-American Teachers, was appointed by New York University as director of the new Martin Luther King, Jr., Afro-American student centre.

(C. U. L.)

BUDDHISM

The year 1968 (2511 according to the Buddhist calendar) brought many important events in the world of Buddhism. The most ecumenical and inclusive Buddhist organization, the World Fellowship of Buddhists (WFB, with its permanent secretariat in Bangkok), held its tenth biennial conference at Dacca, Pak., in November. The cause of Buddhist unity, especially as regarding the Theravada (Southern) and Mahayana (Northern) traditions, had received enthusiastic approval at the last meeting of the 22-nation World Sangha Council.

The Indian Buddhist Society, which boasted a membership of 20 million, mostly converts from the scheduled caste (untouchables), demanded that the Indian Buddhists be provided with representation in the legislature. The Dalai Lama, who was in exile in India, reported that Red Guards had repeatedly rampaged in many parts of Tibet, destroying monasteries and killing monks. He planned to establish a miniature Tibet in India for the preservation of Tibetan Buddhism and culture. A bill was introduced in the House of Representatives in Ceylon providing for the establishment of a university for the education of monks (*bhikkus*).

In Burma a group of monks were visiting isolated villages and conducting social service activities. The Thai government planned to forbid begging by Buddhist nuns on the ground that most of them were not registered with the authorities. In Vietnam the Buddhists were still sharply split between the militant wing led by Thich Tri Quang and the moderate wing led by Thich Tam Chau. The militant wing, alarmed by the success of the Roman Catholics in the 1967 elections, continued to demonstrate against the Saigon regime. In Indonesia, where Buddhists claimed ten million adherents, Ida Bagus Giri, a nephew of former President Sukarno, was ordained as a Theravada monk.

Buddhist establishments in many parts of Communist China were reported to have been devastated by the Red Guards. In Taiwan, where Buddhists were building numerous temples and schools, a new institute for the training of priests was established in T'ai-pei in honour of the celebrated philosopher T'ai-'hsü (d. 1947). Both the established Buddhist schools and the Buddhist-related "new religions" continued to carry on multidimensional activities in Japan. The Japanese Buddhist Association laid the cornerstone for the new Japanese Temple at Buddha Gaya, India.

Ever growing Buddhist activities in the West included formation of the German Buddhist Union and the new Dutch Buddhist Society and the establishment of the first Theravada Buddhist vihara in Rio de Janeiro. The government of Czechoslovakia did not allow the formation of a Buddhist organization, however. A higher ordination ceremony (*Upasampada*) was conducted for the first time in England in 1967. It was reported that the Indian Buddhists' Society in the U.K. had 100,000 members.

Archaeology had contributed greatly to Buddhist studies during the last two years. Two inscriptions, one in Greek and the other in Aramaic, of King Asoka (3rd century B.C.) were discovered in Afghanistan. In India, Buddhist relics, containing 2,000-year-old copperplate inscriptions, were found in the districts of Broach and Mehsana, and the remains of a 1st- or 2nd-century stupa (Buddhist mound) were unearthed in the Osmanabad district. Most spectacular was a series of discoveries by Soviet scholars—a Buddhist monastery in Karatepe, Turk.; an ancient commentary to the *Pratimoksha* (monastic rules), written on 250 palm leaves, near the town of Merv in Central Asia; and a gigantic statue of a reclining Buddha in Adzinatepe near Dushanbe. An ancient gilded bronze image of the Buddha was unearthed in the outskirts of Seoul, Korea.

(J. M. KA.)

ISLAM

For Muslims, especially in the Middle East, the year 1968 was one of continued concentrated attention on the Israeli-Arab territorial situation, which remained from the six-day war in 1967. Many Muslims continued to express concern for the status of Jerusalem and its holy places; a conference called in February by the Institute of Islamic Research in Rawalpindi, Pak., and attended by some 70 scholars representing most Muslim lands, called for a concerted Muslim effort to recover Jerusalem. In spite of the general tension and occasional military encounters, however, it was possible for organized groups from Israeli-occupied territory to go on the pilgrimage to Mecca. Again in 1968 the total number of pilgrims appeared to have been a record; estimates put the figure in excess of 300,000.

Communal relations between Hindus and Muslims in India continued to be marked by violence. A number of outbreaks through the year took the lives of more than 200 persons, with many more injured. The Kashmir issue remained the major point of dispute between India and Pakistan. Sheikh Abdullah was released from imprisonment at the beginning of the year by the Indian government. He returned to Srinagar in March after a three-year absence and took up his leadership in the agitation against Indian control.

Some other areas of past tension seemed to be quieter. There was little violence between the Turkish and Greek Cypriot communities, even during the presidential election, and relations between Greece and Turkey seemed to have improved compared with the previous year. In Iraq the Kurdish problem also

An ancient handwritten copy of the Holy Koran housed in the mosque where the head of Husain, Muhammad's grandson, is buried. The special chamber containing eight of Muhammad's personal possessions was opened to the public for the first time during the Muslim pilgrimage to Mecca in 1968.

tended to remain out of the news, in spite of sporadic violence and the government coups of July and August. Pakistani students in Lahore damaged some U.S. business property in February in a riot protesting the publication of a "portrait" representing Muhammad that was printed in the American magazine *Scientific Digest.*

Other developments were of less immediate note, but some were of long-range importance. Anti-Muslim pressures were reported in Communist China in January and February, especially in the provinces of Ningsia and Sinkiang. In February President Suharto approved the formation of a new Indonesian Muslim political party, headed by the moderate H. Djarnawi. Jordan reaffirmed its cooperation with Syria and Saudi Arabia in March for speeding rebuilding of the Hejaz railway. Air-conditioned cars would be provided. The project would also help relieve some of the acute unemployment problems caused by the 1967 war with Israel. In April the U.A.R. released some 200 Muslim Brethren from prison; the organization, important in previous years, had been identified as anti-Nasser.

The new nation of Southern Yemen spent much of its first year facing internal disturbances, including an attempted coup. By September, however, there was a report that the last traces of Negro slavery in South Arabia had gone with the downfall of former sheikhs. The People's Republic of Southern Yemen had come into existence Nov. 30, 1967, upon the formal withdrawal of Great Britain from the area. It embraced the former lands of Aden and the South Arabian Federation.   (R. W. Sм.)

RELIGIONS OF ASIA

Religious development in Asia during the year was marked by a number of contradictory trends, complicated by the fact that it was becoming increasingly difficult to isolate "religion" from other aspects of life. In the main, despite serious efforts on the part of leaders to consolidate their respective religious communities, the chasm between the intellectuals who attempt to find a meaningful faith in the modern world and the aspirations of the masses who are motivated by simple piety had not been bridged. Many religions in Asia tended to be concerned with the spiritual and mundane welfare of the people within the framework of ethnic, regional, and/or national communities. Inevitably, many of the domestic and interstate problems in Asia seemed to have semireligious overtones.

An important step had been taken to cement Hindu-Buddhist friendship in April 1967 when S. Radhakrishnan, on behalf of the government of India, presented the first Jawaharlal Nehru Award to U Thant, the UN secretary-general and a devout Buddhist, for his contribution to international understanding. Also in 1967 Maharishi Mahesh Yogi, a Hindu guru and the founder of the Spiritual Regeneration Movement, which claimed 100,000 members, made headlines when the Beatles and some Hollywood celebrities announced plans to join his ashram in India.

Meanwhile, the government of India, which adhered to the principle of a secular state, was plagued by rebellious "communalist" movements espoused by various religious, ethnic, and linguistic groups, and by the growing assertiveness of conservative Hindus. In 1967 India's Home Ministry had charged that some foreign missionaries had encouraged the Mizo rebels in Assam, and ordered all missionaries to leave the Mizo Hills. While the ruling Congress Party had received 59 million votes in the 1967 parliamentary elections, the conservative, pro-Hindu Jan Sangh had rolled up 14 million. The Jan Sangh bitterly criticized the 1968 settlement that turned over to Pakistan a small portion of the desolate Rann of Cutch, and even demanded that the Indian government send troops to the insignificant island of Kachchativu to safeguard it against a recent claim by the government of Ceylon. Occasional anti-Muslim incidents continued to occur inside India's borders.

In Ceylon, tension between the Sinhalese Buddhist majority and the sizable Tamil Hindu minority was further complicated by the presence of one million "Indian Tamils," so called to distinguish them from the "Ceylon Tamils," who were old-time settlers. The government, which included members of minority groups, had been criticized by the Sinhalese for compromising the cause of Buddhism. In the meantime, a series of intercaste incidents had arisen in the north, and it was reported that 300,000 depressed Tamils were willing to embrace Buddhism if the government would protect them from caste discrimination.

All the nations of Southeast Asia continued to be deeply concerned with the war in Vietnam. In most cases the dominant religious and cultural groups in the Southeast Asian nations had not developed realistic measures for dealing with religious or ethnic minority groups, with the result that many of the governments were relatively unstable. Insurgents controlled nearly a tenth of the population and two-fifths of the territory of Burma, and insurgency in Thailand had been intensified, especially in the northeast. The government of South Vietnam, which continued to suffer from tensions between Roman Catholics and Buddhists, was attempting to secure the support of the animistic mountain tribesmen called *montagnards,* thousands of whom had moved to Cambodia following an abortive rebellion in 1963.

In his *Asian Drama,* published in 1968, the Swedish sociologist Gunnar Myrdal (*see* BIOGRAPHY) criticized the influence of Asian religions which, he felt, encouraged social inertia. On the other hand, Pres. Zakir Husain of India, speaking at an international inter-religious symposium on peace held in January 1968 at New Delhi, stressed the fact that, in spite of all the advances in science and technology, it would be unwise for anyone to ignore religious influence in finding "solutions" to world problems.   (J. M. KA.)

ENCYCLOPÆDIA BRITANNICA FILMS. *Major Religions of the World (Development and Rituals)* (1954).

Rhodesia

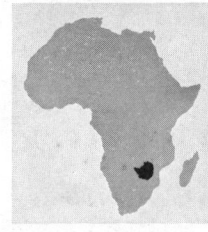

Though Southern Rhodesia declared its independence and assumed the name Rhodesia on Nov. 11, 1965, it remained a British colony in the eyes of other independent nations. It is bounded by Zambia, Mozambique, South Africa, and Botswana. Area: 150,820 sq.mi. (389,622 sq.km.). Pop. (1968 est.): 4,580,000, of whom 94% are African and 5% white. Cap. and largest city: Salisbury (pop., 1968 est., 186,000). Language: English (official) and Bantu. Religion: predominantly traditional tribal beliefs; Christian minority. Queen, Elizabeth II; British governor in 1968, Sir Humphrey Gibbs; prime minister (not recognized by British government), Ian D. Smith.

After the failure of the talks between George Thomson, British Commonwealth secretary, and Ian Smith in November 1967, Sir Alec Douglas-Home visited Rhodesia early in 1968 in the hope that a leading British Conservative might be able to achieve a greater measure of understanding. On his return to Britain Sir Alec was guardedly optimistic, but his report was almost immediately pushed into the background by the events of March 6 when three Africans, sentenced to death before Rhodesia declared itself independent, were executed on the order of Smith's government. The executions had been preceded by judicial hearings in the Appellate Division of the Rhodesian High Court, which had refused a stay of execution and rejected a right of appeal to the judicial committee of the Privy Council; this judgment had

Above, relatives of condemned prisoners waiting outside Salisbury Prison, Rhodesia, for the posting of execution notices. Left, the death sentences of James Dhlamini (left) and Victor Mlambo were commuted to life imprisonment by Queen Elizabeth II. On March 11, 1968, they were hanged in defiance of the royal reprieve.

the effect of recognizing the Smith regime as the de facto government. Furthermore, the execution was carried out despite the exercise by the queen of her royal prerogative of mercy and in defiance of the Privy Council, which had already started proceedings to review the case.

The judges of the Rhodesian High Court were divided in their opinion of the action taken. Because the 1961 constitution appeared to have been set aside, Justice John Fieldsend went so far as to ask the governor to relieve him of his duties as a judge. The British government's immediate response to these events was to announce that the Rhodesian chief justice, Sir Hugh Beadle, would no longer be recognized as deputy to the governor in the event of the latter's being unable to fulfill his duties, and the British prime minister emphasized that contact with Rhodesia could no longer be maintained. On March 11, however, two more Africans were executed, while later about 60 of more than 100 prisoners were reprieved.

Britain's next step was to propose a resolution, approved by the UN Security Council on May 29, which imposed comprehensive mandatory sanctions on trade with Rhodesia. An order in council to give effect to the resolution met with resistance in the British House of Lords, some of whose members disliked the imposition of sanctions by the UN rather than by Britain, but having made their protest the critics allowed the order to go forward on a second hearing.

Already the proposals contained in the report of the Rhodesian constitutional commission under the chairmanship of a Salisbury lawyer, W. R. Whaley, had suggested that the Smith regime saw virtually no possibility of an agreement either with the British Labour Party government or with some future Conservative Party successor. There was no direct suggestion for a republic, and the ultimate goal was said to be racial parity. But the achievement of the latter seemed to have been safely postponed by the recommendation

Demonstrators at Rhodesia House in London on March 11, 1968, opposing the execution policy of Ian Smith's government in Rhodesia. Judith Todd (right), daughter of the former premier of Rhodesia, was one of the demonstrators.

RHODESIA

Education. African (1965): primary, pupils 638,370; secondary, pupils 11,495; vocational, pupils 832; teacher training, students 2,819; teachers (all African schools) 18,544. Non-African (1967): primary, pupils 32,762; secondary, pupils 19,879; primary and secondary, teachers 2,344. African and non-African higher (University College of Rhodesia), students 717, teaching staff 129.

Finance. Monetary unit: Rhodesian pound, with an exchange rate of R£0.36 to U.S. $1 (R£0.86 = £1 sterling). Budget (1967–68) est.: revenue R£76,138,000; expenditure R£81,378,000. Gross national product: (1966) R£358.2 million; (1965) R£358.9 million.

Foreign Trade. (1967) Imports R£93.5 million; exports R£100.6 million. Import sources (1965): U.K. 30%; South Africa 23%; U.S. 7%; Japan 6%. Export destinations (1965): Zambia 29%; U.K. 20%; South Africa 11%; West Germany 8%; Malawi 6%; Japan 5%. Main exports (1965): tobacco 29%; asbestos 7%.

Transport and Communications. Roads (1966) 73,278 km. (including 5,798 km. with improved surface). Motor vehicles in use (1966): passenger 109,408; commercial (including buses) 32,515. Railways: (1966) 3,330 km.; freight traffic (Rhodesia and Zambia; 1965–66) 8,671,000,000 net ton-km. (railway traffic for Rhodesia and Zambia operated separately from 1967). Air traffic (apportionment of traffic of Central African Airways; 1966): 72,112,000 passenger-km.; freight 891,000 net ton-km. Telephones (Dec. 1966) 105,594. Radio receivers (June 1966) 85,271. Television receivers (June 1966) 31,796.

Agriculture. Production (in 000; metric tons; 1966; 1965 in parentheses): tobacco 113 (126); corn 602 (472); tea 2.3 (1.6); sugar, raw value (1967–68) c. 157, (1966–67) c. 260; peanuts c. 112 (c. 112). Livestock (in 000; 1965–66): cattle 3,527; sheep 427; goats c. 622; pigs c. 126.

Industry. Production (in 000; metric tons; 1966): coal c. 3,040; chrome ore (oxide content; 1965) 281; asbestos 160; iron ore (metal content; 1965) 824; gold 550 troy oz.; electricity 4,217,000 kw-hr.

that the Legislative Assembly should consist of 80 members, of whom 40 should be elected by European voters, 20 by the common roll, which would be dominated by European voters for some time to come, and 20 by African electors.

The confiscation by Britain of the passport of Sir Frederick Crawford, resident director in Rhodesia of the Anglo-American Corporation of South Africa, because he had cooperated unduly with the Smith regime, was important mainly because it demonstrated the British government's determination to prosecute its campaign against Smith as vigorously as possible. More significant was the report on the effect of selective sanctions on Rhodesia's trade, which was presented to the UN Security Council by the UN secretary-general on June 13. Data made available by reporting nations showed that imports from Rhodesia had fallen from $330 million in 1965 to $40 million in 1967, while exports to Rhodesia had fallen from $187 million in 1965 to $54 million in 1967.

In July signs that a right-wing section of the Rhodesian Front Party was dissatisfied with the Whaley constitutional proposals led to the resignation, at Smith's request, of the minister of internal affairs, W. J. Harper. Two months later Lord Graham, minister of external affairs and defense, resigned from the government, and several prominent members of the Rhodesian Front left the party. The supporters of this right-wing movement were opposed to African membership in the Legislative Assembly, at least for the time being. Smith, however, still appeared to command the support of the great majority of Europeans in Rhodesia, and many thought that his position might have been strengthened by the defection of some of his more extreme colleagues.

In October the British government again proposed talks, and the British prime minister, Harold Wilson, met Smith on board HMS "Fearless" off Gibraltar. Wilson again made it clear that Britain would not give way on the principle of unimpeded progress toward equal political rights for black Rhodesians, but he was prepared to make some concessions that might make acceptance of his proposals more feasible in Rhodesia. Smith, however, was firm in his refusal to accept the ultimate authority of the Privy Council, and the proposals made by Wilson were received with reserve by the whites in Rhodesia, who feared he was asking too much, and also by the black Rhodesians, who were afraid that he had given too much away. Early in November Thomson, the British minister responsible for Rhodesia, flew to Salisbury for talks with Smith, declaring that relations between the two countries, though improving, were still marked by important differences.   (K. I.)

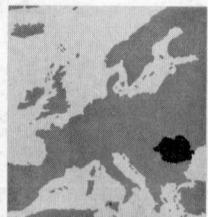

Romania

A socialist republic on the Balkan Peninsula in southeastern Europe, Romania is bordered by the U.S.S.R., the Black Sea, Bulgaria, Yugoslavia, and Hungary. Area: 91,699 sq.mi. (237,500 sq.km.). Pop. (1968 est.): 19,720,984, including (1968) Romanian 87.8%; Hungarian 8.4%. Cap. and largest city: Bucharest (pop., 1968 est., 1,431,993). Religion: Romanian Orthodox 70%; Greek Orthodox 10%. General secretary of the Romanian Communist Party and chairman of the State Council in 1968, Nicolae Ceausescu; chairman of the Council of Ministers (premier), Ion Gheorghe Maurer.

BEN ROTH AGENCY

"Only a little harmless maneuver, Ceausescu! How else shall we find our way around your country when the imperialistic West threatens you?"—Backes, Nürnberg, W.Ger.

Romania continued to expound its own independent concept of Communism in 1968, despite increased tensions with the Soviet Union and the other Warsaw Pact countries that invaded Czechoslovakia in August. These policies gained Ceausescu's regime increased international prestige but left unclear Romania's future role in the Warsaw Pact and in the Council for Mutual Economic Assistance, the economic organ of the countries allied with the Soviet Union. In essence,

ROMANIA

Education. (1965–66) Primary, pupils 2,987,240, teachers 128,253; secondary, pupils 359,836, teachers 13,117; vocational, pupils 271,180, teachers 17,220; teacher training, students 12,703, teachers 475; higher (including 5 universities), students 130,614, teaching staff 13,038.

Finance. Monetary unit: leu, with an official exchange rate of 6 lei to U.S. $1 (14.40 lei = £1 sterling) and a tourist rate of 18 lei to U.S. $1 (43.20 lei = £1). Budget (1967 est.): revenue 124.1 billion lei; expenditure 123.1 billion lei.

Foreign Trade. (1966) Imports 7,279,300,000 lei; exports 7,116,900,000 lei. Import sources: U.S.S.R. 32%; West Germany 12%; East Germany 7%; Czechoslovakia 6%; France 5%. Export destinations: U.S.S.R. 35%; Czechoslovakia 8%; Italy 6%; West Germany 6%; East Germany 6%. Main exports: machinery 17%; raw materials (cereals, timber, etc.) 14%; petroleum products 10%; chemicals 6%.

Transport and Communications. Roads (1966) 76,598 km. (including 9,376 km. with improved surface). Motor vehicles in use: passenger (1965) c. 250,000; commercial (1966) 34,000. Railways: (1966) 11,007 km.; traffic (1967) 15,775,000,000 passenger-km., freight 37,296,000,000 net ton-km. Inland waterways (1964) 1,673 km. Shipping (1967): merchant vessels 100 gross tons and over 52; gross tonnage 244,687. Air traffic (1967): 236,032,000 passenger-km.; freight 6,225,000 net ton-km. Telephones (Dec. 1966) 510,257. Radio receivers (Dec. 1966) 2,925,000. Television receivers (Dec. 1966) 712,000.

Agriculture. Production (in 000; metric tons; 1967; 1966 in parentheses): wheat 5,820 (5,065); rye 71 (100); barley 531 (483); oats (1966) 170, (1965) 124; corn 6,858 (8,022); potatoes (1966) 3,323, (1965) 2,169; sugar, raw value (1967–68) c. 450, (1966–67) 508; tobacco (1966) 40, (1965) 34; sunflower seed (1966) 671, (1965) 563; dry peas (1966) 163, (1965) 123; plums (1966) 837, (1965) 695; apples 234 (234); grapes 910 (954); cheese (1966) 54, (1965) 53. Livestock (in 000; Jan. 1967): cattle 5,198; pigs 5,400; sheep 14,109; horses 705; poultry 43,966.

Industry. Production (in 000; metric tons; 1967): coal 5,112; lignite 7,791; coke (1966) 1,103; crude oil 13,200; natural gas 20,503 cu.m.; electricity 24,765,000 kw-hr.; iron ore (30–35% metal content) 2,797; pig iron 2,456; crude steel 4,088; cement 6,338; sulfuric acid 679; superphosphates (1966) 155; nitrogenous fertilizers (1966) 264; cotton fabrics 358,000 sq.m.; woolen fabrics 50,000 sq.m.; newsprint 51; other paper (1965) 192; commercial motor vehicles 23 units. New dwellings completed (1966) 114,233. Index of production (1963 = 100): (1967) 163; (1966) 143.

Romania's foreign policy was based on the view that every Communist country was entitled to follow its own course, free from interference or pressure from other powers.

In keeping with this policy, Romania continued to improve relations with many countries at odds with the U.S.S.R., including Israel, Communist China, and West Germany. Together with Yugoslavia, Romania expressed strong support for Czechoslovakia, both before and after the August 20–21 invasion. Nevertheless, Romania and the Soviet Union ostensibly remained on friendly terms. Ceausescu seemed able to avoid the pitfalls that had caused so much trouble for Czechoslovakia.

As part of its independent foreign policy, Romania dispatched Alexandru Birladeanu to the U.S. as head of an important scientific delegation in June. He met with high U.S. officials and became the first Communist leader to visit Cape Kennedy, Fla. A two-year cultural exchange agreement was signed by the U.S. and Romania in November.

Because of its refusal to follow the Soviet line blindly, Romania walked out of a meeting of Communist parties held in Budapest, Hung., in February and was not invited to a succession of Warsaw Pact meetings that apparently plotted the Czechoslovak invasion.

In domestic affairs, Romania continued to ease restrictions on its population and to institute certain changes in the structure of the society. The administration of the country was altered from the Soviet-style regional system to the prewar county system. This involved the dismissal of many party leaders and their replacement by men loyal to Ceausescu.

The party also took the unusual step of rehabilitating certain key figures of the past who were unjustly convicted and executed under the regime of Gheorghe Gheorghiu-Dej. Gheorghiu-Dej, who was revered as a national hero after his death a few years earlier, was held directly responsible for the trials and executions of Lucretiu Patrascanu, a former minister of justice, and Stefan Foris, a wartime general secretary of the party. The downgrading of Gheorghiu-Dej was accompanied by the purging from party leadership of former Minister of the Interior Alexandru Draghici, who at one time was thought to be Ceausescu's possible successor. Draghici lost both his party and government positions. Western analysts believed the attacks on Gheorghiu-Dej and Draghici were not only linked to the decision to liberalize life in Romania but were also designed to underline Ceausescu's primacy.

Romania's educational system was changed, with the emphasis placed on giving universities more autonomy. This change resembled that in the economic sphere, where a new program of economic "improvement" was launched to give more independence to individual enterprises. The economic program was far from the profit-motivated reforms instituted in Czechoslovakia and other Eastern European countries, however.

Romania again reported outstanding economic growth. For calendar 1967, Romania's industrial growth rate was 13.5% above 1966; national income was up 7.5%; production costs decreased by 2.8%; and labour productivity rose by 9.4%. Agricultural production did not rise as high as expected, however; grain production fell to 13.5 million tons, as against 13.9 million in 1966. Foreign trade increased 22.4%, with the non-Communist countries accounting for almost 50%. (B. M. G.)

Rowing

The rowing highlight of 1968 was the Olympic competition in Mexico in October, which attracted 102 entries from 30 countries. East Germany, West Germany, the Soviet Union, and the United States were the only countries to contest all seven events. East Germany with two gold medals and the Netherlands, West Germany, the U.S.S.R., Italy, and New Zealand took the major honours. The U.S. was the only country to reach every final, but it finished with only two minor medals.

West Germany beat Australia in the eights, and the

CENTRAL PRESS FROM PICTORIAL PARADE

Cambridge crew (right) holds lead over Oxford in annual race on the Thames, March 30, 1968. Cambridge, loser in previous three races, went on to beat Oxford.

U.S.S.R. triumphed over the Netherlands in the double sculls by 0.98 sec., but the closest verdict was the East German triumph by only 0.15 sec. over the United States in coxless pairs. All the other finals were decided by two seconds or more. In the coxed fours New Zealand scored its first Olympic rowing victory; Henri Wienese recorded the Netherlands' first win in single sculls; Italy took the coxed pairs; and East Germany won its second gold medal in the coxless fours.

No European championships were held in 1968, but there was a special pre-Olympic regatta in late July in Amsterdam. In the finals, lasting two days, East German crews won the eights, coxed fours, and coxless fours. Potomac Boat Club (U.S.) did likewise in coxless pairs, and so did Laga for the Netherlands in coxed pairs.

The Netherlands and K. Dwan of Great Britain won the double and single sculls on the first day. However, on the second day Dwan caught an outsize "crab" at the start, and Wienese triumphed for the Netherlands. In the double sculls East Germany scored its fourth victory of the day. The East German eight and both their fours were quite decisively the fastest crews in their events; so was the United States coxless pair. In coxed pairs the Netherlands, East Germany, and another Potomac crew finished within three seconds of one another.

East German domination of the European rowing scene continued in the women's European championships, held in East Berlin. The East Germans won in eights, double sculls, and single sculls; they also placed second and third in the quadruple sculls and coxed fours, respectively. The U.S.S.R. was pushed out of second place by Romania, with the Netherlands finishing fourth among the 12 competing nations. The Soviet oarswomen won first place in coxed fours and Romania won in the quadruple sculls.

Sixteen nations competed in Amsterdam at the second Fédération Internationale Sociétés d'Aviron (FISA) Junior Regatta in August. The only notable absentee was the U.S.S.R., which had earlier been defeated by East Germany in all seven events in the Communist countries' Junior Regatta in Bled, Yugos. The East German youngsters won the eights, coxed fours, coxless fours, and coxless pairs.

In England, the Henley Royal Regatta in mid-July was bedeviled by exceptional midsummer floodwater and suffered from an almost complete absence of European entries because the date—a week later than usual—clashed with a regatta at Lucerne, Switz. United States entries were also fewer than usual, and the only overseas winner was J. E. B. Stuart High School (U.S.), which became the third U.S. winner of the Princess Elizabeth Cup for schoolboy eights.

Britain's oldest rowing club, Leander, celebrated its 150th anniversary with a victory over Cornell University (U.S.), the defending champions in the Thames Cup. In the 114th boat race between Oxford and Cambridge universities, held in March, the Cambridge eight won by three and a half comfortable lengths. (K. L. O.)

Rubber

World production of natural rubber in 1967 was estimated at 2,452,500 long tons, an increase of 52,000 long tons over 1966. Production for the first six months of 1968 was estimated at 1,187,000 long tons, up 10,000 long tons compared with the corresponding period of 1967.

The management committee of the International Rubber Study Group (IRSG), meeting in London at the end of May 1968, estimated world production and consumption of new rubber in 1968 as follows: natural rubber supply (including deliveries from government stockpiles), 2,670,000 long tons; synthetic rubber supply in member countries, 3,845,000 long tons; natural rubber consumption (*i.e.*, turned into manufactured goods), 2,670,000 long tons; synthetic rubber consumption in member countries, 3,690,000 long tons. The U.S.S.R., Communist China, and some countries in Eastern Europe were not members of the IRSG.

The New York spot price for no. 1 ribbed smoked sheet continued the downward trend that had started in June 1967—partly as a result of the prolonged strike in the U.S. rubber industry—until March 1968, when it bottomed out at $16\frac{1}{2}$ cents per pound. Thereafter, the price recovered rather sharply to 21 cents per pound at the end of September.

Exports of natural rubber latex from producing countries totaled an estimated 209,000 long tons (dry basis) in 1967. In the U.S., natural and synthetic latex consumption in 1967 totaled an estimated 192,000 long tons (dry basis), of which 25.6% was natural rubber latex. Reported world consumption of natural and synthetic rubber latex in 1967 reached a total of 387,900 long tons (dry basis), of which 46.3% was natural rubber latex.

About 86% of Malaysian estate acreage was under high-yielding rubber in 1967, compared with 80% in 1966. The total acreage there of smallholdings (plantings of less than 100 ac.) under high-yielding rubber remained at 57%. On March 23, 1968, the Malaysian Industrial Arbitration Court handed down a decision

that tappers must be paid a basic daily wage of M$3.10 (U.S. $1.02), to be in effect for three years. Details of incentive pay and vacations also were included in the decision.

World production of all types of synthetic rubber for 1967 (excluding the Soviet Union and other countries not reporting) was 3,415,000 long tons (including latices), of which the U.S. produced 1,243,968 long tons (including oil content). World production of all types in the first six months of 1968 was estimated at 1,967,000 long tons, compared with 1,640,000 long tons for the corresponding period of 1967. Reported stocks (worldwide) of synthetic rubber at the end of May 1968 totaled 544,000 long tons.

World production of reclaimed rubber for 1967 was 344,585 long tons (France not reporting). For the first six months of 1968 world production was estimated at 198,000 long tons, compared with 162,581 long tons for the corresponding period of 1967. World consumption of reclaimed rubber in 1967 (France not reporting but included at 30,000 long tons) was estimated at 372,171 long tons, which was equivalent to 6.4% of total world consumption of new (natural and synthetic) rubber.

Bridgestone Tire Co. of Japan announced a new nickel catalyst for making cis-polybutadiene and Goodyear Tire and Rubber Co. announced the use of cerium halides for the same polymerization. There were now at least four known co-catalysts for the cis-polybutadiene polymerization: cerium halides, cobalt compounds, nickel halide, and titanium iodide. Each of these co-catalysts is used in conjunction with an alkyl aluminum halide.

Copolymer Rubber and Chemical Corp. announced it had solved the slow curing rate problem of ethylene-propylene-diene monomer rubber by incorporating larger amounts of diene monomer (in this case, ethylidene norbornene), using an undisclosed polymerization catalyst. Such rubbers will co-vulcanize with good physical properties in blends with highly unsaturated rubbers such as styrene-butadiene rubber.

Table I. Natural Rubber Production

In 000 long tons

Country	1963	1964	1965	1966	1967
Malaysia	851	890	934	983	985
Indonesia	573	638	706	704	750*
Thailand	187	218	213	204	211
Ceylon	103	110	116	129	141
Vietnam	71	73	60	48	40
Cambodia	40	45	48	51	53
India	37	44	49	52	62
Brazil	20	28	29	24	21
Others	185*	189*	187*	202*	189*
Total	2,067*	2,235*	2,342*	2,397*	2,452*

*Estimate.

Table II. Synthetic Rubber Production

In 000 long tons

Country	1963	1964	1965	1966	1967
United States	1,608	1,765	1,814	1,970	1,912
Canada	179	197	203	200	197
United Kingdom	125	153	172	191	200
West Germany	106	136	161	182	180
France	97	128	146	161	186
Japan	90	120	159	228	276
Italy	94*	110*	118*	121*	116*
Netherlands	85*	90*	100*	111*	125*
Brazil	29	32	35	53	51
Czechoslovakia	—	20*	30*	30*	33*
Australia	17	18	21	20	26
Belgium	—	15*	21*	20*	20*
India	7	12	16	15	22
South Africa	—	6	16	18	24
Argentina	—	—	3	10	17
Spain	—	—	—	—	10*
Mexico	—	—	—	—	20*
Total	2,437*	2,802*	3,015*	3,330*	3,415*

*Estimate.

Source: International Rubber Study Group.

World consumption of new rubber in 1966 was again at a record high—5,822,500 long tons, of which 42.4% was natural and 57.6% was synthetic. World consumption of new rubber in the first six months of 1968 was estimated at 3,260,000 long tons, of which 41.6% was natural.

In the U.S., sales of the bias-belted tire to both motorists and auto manufacturers began to rise rapidly in 1968. Armstrong Rubber Co. had offered such a tire in 1966, built with a nylon cord carcass and fibre glass overhead belts. Early in 1968 Goodyear Tire and Rubber Co. introduced its Polyglas bias-belted tire, with polyester cord in the carcass and fibre glass belts, and by year's end most tire manufacturers were offering their own versions. Some regarded this as an interim development on the way to large-scale adoption of the radial tire. There was a shift in European markets toward radial tires: 75% of the tires manufactured in France, 30–35% in the U.K. and Benelux countries, 25% in West Germany, and 40% in Italy were radials.

The world's largest automated curing press was introduced by the McNeil Corp., based in Akron, O. The 90-ton press, standing two stories high, could handle tires up to seven feet in diameter, three feet wide, and weighing up to 2,200 lb.

Some 16 million winter (mud and snow) tires were sold in the U.S. in 1967–68, about four million of which were fitted with metal studs. All but five states, located in the South, permitted the use of studded tires on their highways. (E. B. Nn.)

Rwanda

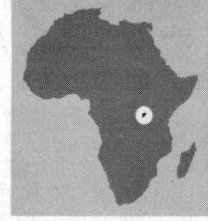

A republic in eastern Africa, Rwanda is bordered by the Congo (Kinshasa), Uganda, Tanzania, and Burundi. Area: 10,169 sq.mi. (26,338 sq.km.). Pop. (1967 est.): 3,239,350, composed of Tutsi (Watutsi), Hutu (Bahutu), and Twa (Batwa) tribes. Cap. and largest city: Kigali (pop., 1967 est., 20,000). Language: French (official); tribal dialects. Religion: traditional or tribal beliefs 50%; Roman Catholic. President in 1968, Grégoire Kayibanda.

In December 1967 the Katangese soldiers from the Congo (Kinshasa) who had taken refuge in Rwanda

RWANDA
Education. (1963–64) Primary, pupils 359,542, teachers 4,892; secondary, pupils 2,268; vocational, pupils 3,370, teachers 84; teacher training (state only), students 2,016, teachers 103.
Finance and Trade. Monetary unit: Rwanda franc, with a par value of RwFr. 100 to U.S. $1 (RwFr. 240 = £1 sterling) and a free market rate (October 1968) of RwFr. 133.33 to U.S. $1 (RwFr. 320 = £1). Foreign exchange, central bank: (June 1968): U.S. $4,-610,000; (June 1967) U.S. $2.1 million. Budget (1967 est.): revenue RwFr. 1,360,000,000; expenditure RwFr. 1.5 billion.
Foreign Trade. (1966) Imports RwFr. 1,776,800,-000 (30% from Belgium-Luxembourg, 16% from Japan, 14% from Uganda, 8% from West Germany); exports RwFr. 1,083,000,000 (57% to U.S., 33% to Belgium-Luxembourg). Main exports: coffee 60%; tin 29%.
Agriculture. Production (in 000; metric tons; 1966; 1965 in parentheses): dry beans c. 90 (87); coffee 8.8 (10.2); potatoes c. 45 (43); sweet potatoes c. 260 (203); cassava c. 180 (178). Livestock (in 000; July 1966): cattle c. 600; sheep c. 145.

along with more than 100 white mercenaries earlier in the year were repatriated. However, in spite of the statement by Congo Pres. Joseph Mobutu in the last week of December that Rwanda intended to extradite the white mercenaries to the Congo also, President Kayibanda insisted that Rwanda would abide by the decision of the Organization of African Unity that the mercenaries should be repatriated to their own countries. As a result, the Congo broke off diplomatic relations with Rwanda on Jan. 11, 1968. In April, however, President Mobutu agreed that the mercenaries should return to their homes, and in the latter part of the month they were flown to Europe on the understanding that their own countries would never permit them to return to Africa. With this obstacle removed, a reconciliation was arranged with the mediation of Pres. Ismail al-Azhari of the Sudan.

Rwanda's basic coffee export quota was raised to 9,000 tons under the new International Coffee Agreement which came into force in November, with an adjustment clause allowing an increase to 15,600 tons.

(K. I.)

Sailing

Single-handed ocean sailing, whether or not racing was involved, had during recent years caught the imagination of yachtsmen in all categories—power, sail, racing, and cruising—and extended far beyond to a large and enthusiastic public. Sponsoring and other forms of financial backing, high-pressure public relations, and the machinery of modern communications all played their parts in promoting an activity that had proved to give vicarious satisfaction to millions. Thus, 1968 was a year in which more people than ever before became aware of how oceans are crossed in small craft and also a year in which the world had its greatest share yet in experiences, at second hand, of single-handed ocean sailing. During the year one event in this category ran its full course, another came to completion, and a third was begun; respectively, these were the third single-handed transatlantic race; the arrival home of Alec (later Sir Alec) Rose from his voyage around the world; and the start at intervals of competitors round the world in pursuit of the "Golden Globe."

The outstanding features of the third transatlantic race were the large size of the boats involved and the number of multihulled craft that were entered. It was now appreciated that, if designed especially for the purpose, the fastest yacht for a single-handed seaman might be larger than anything believed to be suitable in 1960 when the first race was organized. The current interest in multihulled craft was revealed by the fact that of the 43 original entries from 10 nations, 15 were of the catamaran, trimaran, or prau types.

On June 1 the fleet sailed from Plymouth, Eng., on the 3,700-mi. course to Newport, R.I. The winner was one of the largest yachts in the race, "Sir Thomas Lipton" (sailed by Geoffrey Williams, U.K.), a 57-ft. ketch especially designed and built for the contest. Though the race had been widely regarded as inimical to enthusiasm for multihulled craft, a number of which broke up or gave up, the fact that three out of the seven leading craft were of this type made their record far from undistinguished. But their greater liability to trouble on ocean passages meant that in 1968 they were still inferior, despite their speed potential,

"THE TIMES," LONDON FROM PICTORIAL PARADE

Alec Rose, who sailed around the world alone in a 36-ft. sailboat, greeting crowds outside the Guildhall in Portsmouth, Eng., where a reception was given in his honour July 5, 1968. Queen Elizabeth II knighted him in recognition of his successful voyage.

to conventional craft. A special study of safety in multihulled boats was being conducted in 1968 by the Amateur Yacht Research Society (U.K.).

The rapt public attention given to Alec Rose's circumnavigation was somewhat surprising, since it followed that of Sir Francis Chichester in 1966–67 so closely. The voyage was not commercially sponsored; radio communication was minimal; and the yacht, although of good design and construction, was 20 years old and not built for the voyage. Serious rigging failures occurred on the voyage from Portsmouth, Eng., to Melbourne, Austr.; this leg of the trip took 154 days, during which Rose, then aged 59, proved his outstanding qualities as a seaman. Additional rigging trouble made it necessary to put into Bluff, southern New Zealand, for a few days. The voyage was continued round Cape Horn, and after a total of 320 days spent at sea after leaving Portsmouth, "Lively Lady" returned up the same harbour channel into Portsmouth from which she had sailed, escorted by a dense fleet of craft. On his return Rose was knighted at Buckingham Palace.

At intervals during June–October yachts began leaving on the single-handed "Golden Globe" race round the world sponsored by the London *Sunday Times.* Conditions prescribed for the event were that competitors had to sail from the British Isles before October 31; to round Capes Leeuin, Good Hope, and Horn; and not to enter a port or to receive outside assistance without disqualification. Apart from the Golden Globe itself, to be awarded to the first seaman completing the nonstop circumnavigation, £5,000 would be received by the competitor making the fastest time. Whether the race was a seamanlike concept might be argued; certainly it was a harsher test of man and boat than the transatlantic or even the voyages of Chichester and Rose. By the deadline date seven yachtsmen, four British, two French, and one Italian, were well on their way; but shortly afterward one of the most promising competitors, "Galway Blazer II" (W. L. King, U.K.), was forced to retire with one mast lost and the other damaged.

Immediately after Christmas 1967 the most important offshore race of the Southern Hemisphere was sailed in Australian waters, from Sydney to Hobart, with a record entry of 67 yachts. The fleet made a ludicrous start, having to search for a missing mark buoy that had broken adrift. At a late stage it appeared that "Pen Duick III," the French entry skippered by Eric Tabarly, winner of the second transatlantic single-handed race, would be the first yacht home and the winner on corrected time. But toward the end the yacht ran into baffling calms, giving the victory to "Rainbow II," owned and skippered by a professional sailmaker from New Zealand.

In other events "Indigo," skippered by 76-year-old Samuel Wellman of the U.S., won the 3,524-mi. Bermuda-to-Travemünde (W.Ger.) transatlantic race. James Hunt of Massachusetts won the Mallory Cup, symbolic of the North American sailing championship. "Robin," a Class C yacht owned by Ted Hood of the U.S., won the Newport-to-Bermuda competition, while the 42-ft. "Comanche" won the storm-plagued Chicago-to-Mackinac race.

In Australia preparations for the America's Cup challenge, scheduled for 1970, were continuous, which suggested the dedication now required for competing in this event. The challenge, issued by the Royal Sydney Yacht Squadron on behalf of the newspaper proprietor Sir Frank Packer and his syndicate, was to be

made by a 12-metre yacht being designed by Alan Payne, architect of the 1962 Australian challenger, "Gretel." There was also speculation that France planned to challenge for the cup. While racing for the America's Cup had for a long time had much in it prejudicial to the purer spirit of sailing, the event retained its peculiar significance as carrying on the old tradition of yacht racing in first-class craft of large size.

The Olympic Games brought to racing under sail a category of sport analogous to America's Cup racing, but in smaller boats. In the 1968 Olympics the medals were shared among the nations as follows: Flying Dutchman—gold, U.K., silver, West Germany, bronze, Brazil; Dragon—gold, U.S., silver, Denmark, bronze, East Germany; Star—gold, U.S., silver, Norway, bronze, Italy; 5.5-metre—gold, Sweden, silver, Switzerland, bronze, U.K. (*See* also SPORTING RECORD: *Special Report.*)

The International Catamaran Challenge, known generally as the Little America's Cup, was again successfully defended by the British craft "Lady Helmsman" against "Yankee Flyer" (U.S.), making the eighth U.K. victory in the series and the third in succession by the same defender.

Races for the fourth One Ton Cup contest were held off Heligoland Island, W.Ger., during July 15–23. The 1967 winner had been the West German boat "Optimist," and in 1968 the same boat and helmsman won an even more convincing victory. The four nominally "inshore" races were in effect almost ocean races, with lumpy seas and the next mark never within sight until part of the leg was sailed. There were 22 boats entered from 11 nations, apart from the French and Australian entries which various unfortunate circumstances prevented from reaching Heligoland. Aside from the widely international character of the event, another outstanding feature, typifying modern yachting, was the number of sailmakers taking part, including entries from the United States, the United Kingdom, New Zealand, and West Germany. While the great majority of the sails in the fleet were made in the U.S., the spars, of light alloy, came mainly from the U.K.

"Optimist" won three of the inshore races and gained second place to the Italian "Kerkyra II" in

". . . or is it Alec Chichester in Gypsy Lady IV and Francis Rose in Lively Moth?"—Spencer, "London Daily Mail."

Paul Lyons and David Haddleton winning the 505 Class championship at the Vancouver Sea Festival in Vancouver, B.C., on July 20, 1968.

another; she also won the 210-mi. distance race. The final results were: (1) "Optimist" (G. Kohler, West Germany); (2) "Rainbow II" (G. B. Bouzaid, New Zealand); (3) "Kerkyra II" (M. Spaccarelli, Italy).

During the International Boat Show in London in January, Charles Gardner won the award of Yachtsman of the Year for 1967. His immediate distinction was in powerboat racing (*see* MOTOR SPORTS), but his yachting achievements had been many.

During the last 20 years of yachting, two outstanding trends seem worth recording: first, the steady replacement of the traditional wood by plastics for the hull construction of all kinds of craft, a revolution that by 1968 had made new construction in timber the exception rather than the rule; second, the widespread use of multihulled craft, raising this type of vessel from the position of a marine curiosity to one of assured recognition.   (D. H. C. P.-B.)

San Marino

A small republic, San Marino is an enclave in northeastern Italy, 14 mi. SW of Rimini. Area: 24 sq.mi. (61 sq.km.). Pop. (1968 est.): 18,150. Cap. and largest city: San Marino (pop., 1968 est., 4,150). Language: Italian. Religion: Roman Catholic. San Marino is united with Italy by a customs union. The country is governed by two *capitani reggenti,* or coregents, appointed every six months by a Grand and General Council.

Capitani reggenti in 1968 were Romano Michelotti and Domenico Forcellini to March 31; Marino Benedetto Belluzi and Dante Rossi from April 1 to September 30; and, from October 1, Aldo Zavoli and Pietro Giancecchi.

Economic indicators for San Marino remained very stable during 1968. The sale of postage stamps was unchanged from 1967 highs while the number of tourists visiting the republic increased by about 1%. Revenues gained from these two sources accounted for over 80% of San Marino's gross national product.

With general elections scheduled for 1969, political activities were on the increase. Because of the abolition of absentee balloting by mail, the main parties of the government coalition—the Christian Democrats and the Social Democrats—were expected to decline slightly in strength.

The successful negotiation of a large loan from Italy virtually assured the construction of a large, modern hospital in the republic. San Marino and Italy also renegotiated the convention governing their mutual relations. Italy was to double its annual payments to the state, and the two countries would raise their mutual representation to the diplomatic level.

San Marino signed the nuclear nonproliferation treaty in December.   (R. D. Ho.)

SAN MARINO
Education. (1965–66) Primary, pupils 1,337, teachers 72; secondary, pupils 740, teachers 41.
  Finance. Monetary unit: Italian lira (625 lire = U.S. $1; 1,500 lire = £1 sterling). Budget (1967–68 est.) balanced at 5,026,832,365 lire. Tourism (1966) 2,247,866 visitors.
  Transport and Communications. Roads (1965) *c.* 100 km. Electric funicular railway 32 km. Telephones (Dec. 1966) 1,712. Radio receivers (Dec. 1966) 3,000. Television receivers (Dec. 1966) 1,800.

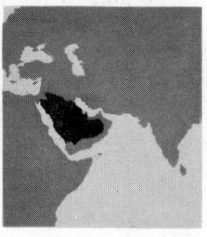

Saudi Arabia

A kingdom occupying four-fifths of the Arabian Peninsula, Saudi Arabia has an area of 873,972 sq.mi. (2,263,587 sq.km.). Pop. (1966 est.): 6,870,000. Cap. and largest city: Riyadh (pop., 1963, 170,000). Language: Arabic. Religion: Muslim. King and prime minister, Faisal ibn 'Abd al-'Aziz ibn 'Abd al-Rahman Al Sa'ud.

In the political sphere 1968 was a relatively inactive year for Saudi Arabia. King Faisal, who in 1966–67 had visited many Muslim countries, remained at home except for a brief visit to Kuwait. In January he received a state visit from Pres. Cevdet Sunay of Turkey. The king did not attempt to take any strong lead in the Arab world. He refused to agree to the holding of a new Arab summit meeting on the ground that this should await the outcome of the mission of Gunnar Jarring (*see* BIOGRAPHY), the UN special envoy. His view was that, since some Arab countries (such as Jordan and the United Arab Republic) had accepted the terms of the Nov. 22, 1967, UN Security Council resolution on the Middle East while others (such as Syria) had rejected it, there was no use meeting until it was seen whether the resolution had any success as a basis for a settlement. In press interviews the king continued to warn against the grave dangers of external Communist influence in Arab and Muslim countries. He denied being opposed to the purchase of Soviet arms but said that the Arabs, having rid themselves of Ottoman and Western control, should not replace it with Soviet influence.

King Faisal did pursue his efforts to achieve a rapprochement between Iran and the Arab states and to avert the real danger of a Saudi-Iranian clash of interests in the Persian Gulf area. The matter was of the greatest urgency in view of Britain's decision to withdraw all its forces from the Persian Gulf region by

SAUDI ARABIA
Education. (1965–66) Primary, pupils 244,010, teachers (1963–64) 9,628; secondary, pupils 28,027, teachers (1964–65) 1,002; vocational, pupils 2,789; teacher training, students 6,339, teachers (1963–64) 465; higher (1964–65), students 1,568, teaching staff 175.
  Finance. Monetary unit: riyal, with a par value of 4.50 riyals to U.S. $1 (10.80 riyals = £1 sterling). Gold and foreign exchange, official: (June 1968) U.S. $870 million; (June 1967) U.S. $839 million. Budget (1967–68 est.) balanced at 4,937,000,000 riyals (including, in 1965–66, revenue from oil companies of 3,145,000,000 riyals). Money supply: (March 1968) 2,111,000,000 riyals; (March 1967) 1,922,000,000 riyals.
  Foreign Trade. (1966–67) Imports 2,194,300,000 riyals; exports 7,605,700,000 riyals. Import sources: U.S. 23%; U.K. 8%; Lebanon 8%; Italy 8%; West Germany 6%; Netherlands 5%. Export destinations: Italy 13%; U.K. 8%; Spain 5%; Bahrain 5%; Netherlands 5%; West Germany 5%. Main exports: (1965–66) crude oil 76%; petroleum products 13%.
  Transport and Communications. Roads (1967) *c.* 22,000 km. (including 5,802 km. main roads). Motor vehicles in use (1966): passenger 27,092; commercial 19,703. Railways (1967): Ad Damman–Riyadh 584 km.; Hejaz line 567 km. Telephones (Jan. 1967) *c.* 28,500. Radio receivers (Dec. 1964) *c.* 77,000. Television receivers (Dec. 1964) 30,000.
  Agriculture. Production (in 000; metric tons; 1966; 1965 in parentheses): wheat 149 (148); barley 34 (32); millet *c.* 15 (*c.* 15); sorghum *c.* 50 (*c.* 50); dates 375 (354). Livestock (in 000; 1965–66): cattle 105; sheep 3,500; goats 2,500; camels 350.
  Industry. Production (in 000): crude oil (1967) 128,923 metric tons; electricity (excluding most industrial production; 1965) 268,000 kw-hr.

1971. The shah of Iran abruptly canceled a state visit to Saudi Arabia, but the matter was later smoothed over, and the two leaders agreed in November to try to maintain peace in the Gulf area.

The Saudi government refused to recognize the new People's Republic of Southern Yemen and continued to support the royalists against the republicans in Yemen. Saudi Arabian hopes for an outright royalist victory after the withdrawal of U.A.R. troops at the end of 1967 were at least temporarily disappointed.

At midyear it was announced that oil revenues for 1967 had amounted to $909 million, an increase of 15% from 1966. This was partly due to an 8% increase in output and partly to improved terms from one of the major oil producers, the Arabian American Oil Co. Saudi Arabia paid £50 million in 1968 to aid Jordan and the U.A.R., but increased revenues enabled it to do this and maintain a balanced budget.   (P. Mₚ.)

Encyclopædia Britannica Films. *The Middle East* (1955).

Savings and Investment

There was a marked difference in the behaviour of savings and investment in most countries in 1968 as compared with 1967 and 1966 as financial markets—which act as one of the important links between countries—and, above all, international capital and money markets showed a further considerable development and played a steadily increasing role.

The availability of domestic savings, together with such external resources as can be obtained, limits the volume of investment that any economy can undertake. Investment—which includes spending on plant and machinery, buildings and houses, as well as additions to inventories and work in progress—can be financed by the three main types of economic units (households, enterprises, and various units in the public sector) either through use of the unit's own surplus of income over expenditure, or by supplementing it by borrowing through the intermediary of financial institutions or the capital market.

Each sector, of course, is made up of a multitude of units, each spending and receiving income but also borrowing from or lending to the other sectors through the financial markets. To distinguish such financial transactions, the term savings is now used to denote the contribution each individual sector makes toward the creation of tangible assets. The total of the acquisitions of real assets, as well as financial assets net of changes in indebtedness, is described as financial surplus (or deficit).

While the development of savings and investment is of crucial significance from the point of view of the economy as a whole, for the financial markets it is the behaviour of the financial surpluses or deficits that each sector generates—denoting its capacity to lend to other sectors—that is of immediate importance.

Periods of rapid increases in investment, which generate additional income and savings, tend to be periods of rapid expansion or upswings, and tend also to raise the share of these two components in total output or gross national product (GNP). If domestic savings are insufficient in relation to total investment, both domestic and external, balance of payments deficits as well as pressure on prices frequently develop, forcing the authorities to adopt measures that will bring savings and investment into closer balance; this is generally accomplished by slowing down the expansion of investment. Such restrictive measures are also often taken to reduce the rate of increase in prices even if external accounts remain in a healthy state, but the effects on investment and savings are similar. Once initiated, the process of slowing down investment and savings may gather momentum, moving the economy into stagnation or recession as the volume of investment and savings falls below what the economy can produce. Once this happens measures are adopted to raise investment and savings.

Developments in 1967 covered both these phases. During the first half of the year investment was slowing down in most of the industrial countries of the West, but the turning point was reached in the second half. The recovery that began then continued during the first three quarters of 1968, with the pace of the upswing gradually gaining strength.

Although this cyclical pattern was common to almost all the advanced countries, the timing and intensity differed. In the U.S. and Canada a sharp slowdown in fixed investment and inventory building in the first half of 1967 was followed by a rapid recovery in the third and fourth quarters, the intensity of which increased so much that the authorities were compelled to impose restraints in the first half of 1968. The behaviour of the Canadian economy corresponded very closely to that of the U.S., except that investment in plant and machinery actually declined and Canada's recovery lagged behind that of its neighbour.

In Western Europe, West Germany experienced a very pronounced fall in all types of fixed investment. The decline, amounting to some 15% as compared with 1966, contributed to the fall in GNP. This decline, which started in 1966, continued until the first quarter of 1968. There was a recovery in the second quarter of 1968, however, which continued to gain strength thereafter.

Among the other members of the European Economic Community, only Belgium experienced a decline in fixed investment in 1967, and it passed the turning point in the first half of 1968. In France and Italy there was an increase in fixed investment—accompanied, however, by a decline in the foreign balance as well as a reduction in inventory building.

In the U.K. there was a gradual slowing down of

Table I. Changes in Gross National Product, Fixed Domestic Investment, and Its Components in Selected Countries					
Country	Year	Percent increase in GNP	Change in total fixed domestic investment	Changes in fixed investment	
				Housing	Plant and equipment
U.S.	1966	5.8	4.4	−12.7	9.2
	1967	2.6	−0.6	−4.8	0.3
Canada	1966	6.5	13.0	−3.9	16.1
	1967	2.8	−1.7	0.5	−2.0
France	1966	4.9	5.8	0.1	8.6
	1967	4.2	6.9	...	...
West Germany	1966	2.3	0.2	2.5	−0.1
	1967	−0.1	−7.7	−10.0	−7.2
Italy	1966	5.7	3.4	−1.3	5.9
	1967	5.9	10.1	4.1	13.1
Netherlands	1966	2.5	6.8	7.3	6.6
	1967	4.8	6.8	12.8	5.3
Belgium	1966	2.7	5.6	−7.8	10.4
	1967	2.7	1.2	...	...
U.K.	1966	1.6	1.5	−3.2	2.6
	1967	1.0	5.4	8.9	4.5
Sweden	1966	2.9	5.9	−2.0	8.5
	1967	3.6	6.7	15.6	4.1
Norway	1966	3.9	5.9	4.5	6.1
	1967	4.3	8.6	9.9	8.4
Denmark	1966	1.9	3.0	1.8	3.3
	1967	3.4	7.1	13.0	5.9
Japan	1966	10.7	9.5	7.2	7.2
	1967	13.7	21.7	17.3	17.3

Source: Bank for International Settlements, *38th Annual Report.*

fixed investment in 1967, accompanied by a growing external deficit and a considerable reduction in inventory building. This trend changed partially in 1968, as foreign balance and inventory building began to change direction. Fixed domestic investment showed some tendency to accelerate in the second half of 1968.

In Japan fixed domestic investment and inventory building rose sharply in 1967, while the foreign balance deteriorated very markedly. Distinctive signs of a slowdown in domestic outlays occurred in the first half of 1968, and there was a dramatic improvement in foreign trade position.

The records of the more developed primary producing countries were mixed. In Australia the pace of advance of fixed domestic investment declined in 1967, but that of inventory building rose. New Zealand experienced some slowing down, while restrictive government policy in South Africa had an adverse effect on domestic investment.

In Eastern Europe and the Soviet Union, economic expansion gained momentum in 1967, but the behaviour of fixed investment outlays differed. They expanded faster than in 1966 in Hungary, Poland, and East Germany, but grew at reduced rates in Bulgaria and Czechoslovakia. All the Eastern European countries appeared to have succeeded in improving their foreign trade balances to a greater or lesser extent.

To help understand how the investment demand of the various sectors and of the economy as a whole is met and the effects that the process of bringing investment and savings into balance has on the rate of growth, some of the advanced, industrial countries compile financial accounts; *i.e.*, flow-of-funds accounts, showing investment in tangible and financial assets—the latter being the result of the borrowing and lending transactions that each sector undertakes. Such accounts giving details of changes in the various types of financial assets and liabilities that give rise to them have a direct bearing on ability and willingness to spend in excess of current income; *i.e.*, to undertake investment. They are affected by—and, in turn, affect—the terms and conditions of borrowing and lending, as well as the volume of resources available.

The factors determining the financial surpluses and deficits of each of the sectors and of the economy as a whole are many and complex. They include income earned and real investment undertaken on the one hand, and government financial and monetary policy, as well as access to and activities in foreign markets, on the other. The size of these surpluses and deficits does not by itself provide any indication of the financial problems involved nor of their repercussions. It does, however, throw light on some general aspects of the situation, such as the location of finance between different sectors and the relative importance of internal savings and external finance. Both of these are of the utmost significance to the authorities in the context of the cyclical policies they pursue and of the long-term objectives of generating sufficient volume of financial resources and ensuring their smooth and rapid transfer in the optimum manner.

Because of differences in methods and coverage, the existing flow-of-funds accounts do not permit a comparison of the structure of financing and savings from country to country. Simplified capital accounts for the nonfinancial sectors of three of the main industrial countries, the U.S., the U.K., and West Germany, for 1967 are given in Table II. They show that investment by business in the U.S. declined by over $2 billion as compared with 1966, but that the foreign sector provided some $2.4 billion of resources. While the financial surplus (including transfers) of the households sector increased, the deficit of business units declined, reflecting a fall in investment and the difficulty of raising external finance—which was predominantly going to meet the requirements of the public sector. This process of transferring the financial resources to public authorities was assisted by monetary policy, and was accompanied by pressures on financial markets and interest rates.

A similar trend developed in the U.K. A sharp rise in public investment, which resulted in a large increase in the government's financial deficit, had to be financed by transfers not only from the households and business sectors but also from abroad. To reduce the balance of payments deficit, while still making it possible for government plans to be fulfilled, monetary policy had to be tightened.

In West Germany the 15% fall in investment outlays and the policy of expansion adopted by the au-

Table II. Savings and Investment in U.S., U.K., and West Germany

Item	Households		Enterprises		Public sector		Foreign sector		Total	
	1966	1967	1966	1967	1966	1967	1966	1967	1966	1967
U.S. (in $000,000,000)										
Gross saving	112.2	122.0	77.0	78.4	−3.3	−19.7	−4.0	−2.9	181.9	177.8
Gross investment	92.0	93.0	98.3	93.1	—	—	—	—	190.3	186.1
Financial surplus (+) or deficit (−)	+20.2	+29.0	−21.3	−14.7	−3.3	−19.7	−4.0	−2.9	−8.4	−8.3
Net transfers and adjustment	+12.1	+12.5	+2.3	+3.4	−1.0	−2.6	−0.4	−0.5	+13.0	+12.8
U.K. (in £000,000)										
Gross saving	2,033	1,924	2,796	2,759	2,239	2,116	+31	+514	7,099	7,313
Gross investment	1,011	1,019	2,811	2,505	3,178	3,712	—	—	6,900	7,236
Financial surplus (+) or deficit (−)	+552	+273	+303	+526	−849	−1,486	+31	+514	+199	+77
Net transfers and adjustment	−166	−156	+25	+204	+141	−48	—	—	—	—
West Germany (in DM. 000,000,000)										
Gross saving	34.9	30.5	59.8	66.8	30.3	22.0	−1.2	−10.5	123.9	105.9
Gross investment	—	—	103.1	85.8	20.8	20.1	—	—	123.9	105.9
Financial surplus (+) or deficit (−)	+34.9	+30.5	−43.3	−19.0	+9.5	+2.1	−1.2	−10.5	—	—
Net transfers and adjustment	−3.4	−4.1	+12.8	+14.1	−10.2	−10.6	+0.8	+0.6	—	—

Note: For the U.S.: Households investment includes consumer average; enterprises include noncorporate business; all public expenditure regarded as current expenditure. For the U.K.: Households expenditure includes noncorporate business; public enterprises included in public sector; "unidentified" item included in financial surplus or deficit. For West Germany: Households are assumed not to invest. Their housing expenditure regarded as transfer to enterprise sector; enterprises investment includes noncorporate business and public enterprises.
Sources: *Federal Reserve Bulletin* (August 1968); Bank of England *Quarterly Review* (June 1967); *Monthly Report* of the Deutsche Bundesbank (April 1968).

thorities caused the public sector surplus to be turned into a deficit. The domestic slowdown, however, was accompanied by large foreign investment, which increased to DM. 10.5 billion. This represented part of the savings the economy generated.

The behaviour of savings and investment in these three countries had profound effects on developments in the Western world and in its capital and money markets. Restrictive monetary policies in the U.S. and U.K., together with other associated measures, led corporate and other borrowers to raise funds abroad—especially in the international capital markets. This contributed to pressure on interest rates which had not been decisively reversed in late 1968.

(T. M. R.)

See also Money and Banking; Stock Exchanges.

Seismology

For several years, seismologists and geologists had been intrigued by a series of earthquakes in the Denver, Colo., area. In 1961 the U.S. Army Corps of Engineers began disposing of waste fluids at the Rocky Mountain Arsenal, near Denver, by injecting them into a 3,638-m. well drilled into sedimentary rocks. Because of a suggested relationship with earthquakes in the area, the injection was stopped in February 1966. Subsequently, numerous earthquakes were recorded, with the strongest in August and November 1967. The fluid injection was believed to have triggered the earthquakes by reducing frictional resistance to faulting. The implication that the rocks were stressed to near their breaking strength before the injection was in accord with available data. On Sept. 1, 1968, the Army began removing fluid from the well at a very slow rate, in the hope that earthquake occurrences would be reduced. However, a number of small earthquakes were recorded after September.

The possibility of earthquake activity was significantly affecting the selection of nuclear reactor sites in the U.S. If a reactor is to be located in a historically active earthquake state, rather stringent factors are imposed on the design and, in some cases, there is a question as to whether safety can be assured. As a consequence, proposed sites were being rejected, even though construction of a reactor was deemed essential to the growth and industrial development of the areas in question.

In studying earthquake mechanisms with a view toward the eventual prediction of earthquakes, seismologists have considered many geophysical parameters including fault displacement, creep, anomalous gravity, and heat flow. California Institute of Technology scientists measured heat flow along the San Andreas fault near Hollister, Calif., and found that 50% more heat is flowing east of the fault (temperature about 600° F) than west of it (about 430° F). This was deduced from measurements made by drilling eight holes about 1,000 ft. deep and 8 mi. apart spanning the fault. The increase in heat loss being detected in a broad area east of the fault indicates that the heat did not originate from creep but from other geologic conditions. The high rate of creep in the area might actually be the result of heat flow, rather than the cause of it. The heat may cause the rock to become more plastic and to creep more readily.

The Lunar Passive Seismic Experiment, conducted by the Space Physics Division at the Earth Sciences Laboratory in Pasadena, Calif., in collaboration with the Lamont Geological Observatory in New York, was expected to provide the most sophisticated instrument ever produced for earth-based operation. The instrument would measure both long- and short-period seismic activity (moon tides and moon quakes) for one year. Information from the experiment would add to knowledge of the moon and might yield specific data about lunar morphology.

The Pan-American Conference on the Upper Mantle Project, jointly organized by the Institute of Geophysics of the National Autonomous University of Mexico and the Pan-American Institute of Geography

Left, road destroyed by severe earthquake that ravaged northern Japan on May 16, 1968, killing 47 persons. Below, a surviving youngster watching as rescue teams search the ruins for victims of resulting landslides that caused major property damage.

ORION PRESS—PIX FROM PUBLIX

and History, was held in Mexico City, March 18–21, 1968. Nearly 90 participants from seven countries were in attendance. The program included technical papers on the mechanism of Late Cenozoic tectonics of the southwestern U.S.; comparison of major fault systems in parts of North and South America; and the use of earthquake surface waves to determine geophysical structure beneath the Gulf of California and adjacent regions.

About 100 Soviet scientists and 75 geodesists and geologists from outside the U.S.S.R. participated in the third Symposium on Recent Crustal Movements, held in Leningrad, May 23–29. Papers were presented on crustal movements, crustal movements and seismicity, and continental drift. Special studies of crustal movements were under way in the U.S., but they had been limited, in general, to seismic activity in areas of abnormal subsidence caused by the withdrawal of water or oil.

The Intergovernmental Oceanographic Commission convened the first meeting of the International Coordinating Group for the Pacific Tsunami Warning System in Honolulu, March 25–28. Delegates were present from the U.S., the U.S.S.R., Canada, Japan, and Chile. The establishment of the International Tsunami Information Center at Honolulu was reported, and its functions were defined as: (1) ensuring dissemination of tsunami (seismic sea wave) warnings to all countries participating in the warning system; (2) collecting tsunami data on a real-time basis; (3) encouraging tsunami research; and (4) promoting exchange of scientific and technical personnel and data among participating nations. (L. M. M.)

See also Disasters.

Senegal

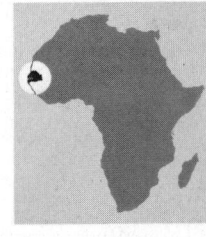

A republic of northwestern Africa, Senegal is bounded by Mauritania, Mali, Guinea, and Portuguese Guinea, and by the Atlantic Ocean. The independent nation of The Gambia forms an enclave within the country. Area: 76,124 sq.mi. (197,161 sq.km.). Pop. (1966 est.): 3,580,000. Cap. and largest city: Dakar (pop., 1965 est., 576,-093). Language: French (official); Wolof; Peular (Fulani); other tribal dialects. Religion: Muslim; pagan, Christian minority. President in 1968, Léopold Sédar Senghor.

Reelected president on February 25 by 93% of the electorate, Léopold Senghor excluded from the government Doudou Thiam, minister of state for foreign affairs, who had long been considered the second most important man in the nation. In May Thiam was censured by the government's political bureau (of which, however, he remained assistant secretary-general), and shortly afterward he was deposed from the chairmanship of the Economic and Social Council.

In May also the government was faced with serious disturbances at the University of Dakar, in direct consequence of the student disturbances during May in Paris. Despite government warnings members of the Democratic Union of Senegalese Students went on strike to demand longer and increased university grants. In the wave of labour strikes that followed, with union members expressing their solidarity with student views, order was restored by official intervention: approximately 30 arrests were made, and 36 people were tried and summarily sentenced.

In a government reshuffle in June President Senghor named himself minister of defense in order to strengthen his ability to control any future disturbances. Also in June a decision was taken to raise the rate of basic wages. Senghor in July announced the partial closing of the University of Dakar. This decision, however, was to be reconsidered before the start of the 1968–69 session.

President Senghor was received by French Pres. Charles de Gaulle several times during the year—notably in April, when discussions took place concerning the problems imposed by the diminution of French aid to African states, and in July, when the theme was the necessity of revising the University of Dakar's constitution.

At the invitation of West Germany, Senghor visited Frankfurt in September to receive a peace prize.

There, he was the subject of student demonstrations organized in protest against his attitude to Senegalese students. (As a result of these demonstrations Daniel Cohn-Bendit [see BIOGRAPHY], who had played an important part in the incidents in Paris earlier in the year, was arrested and received a suspended sentence of eight months' imprisonment.)

In June the death was announced at Dakar of Lamine Gueye, president of the National Assembly and a leading Senegalese political figure. His post in the National Assembly was taken by Amadou Cissé Dia. (PH. D.)

Sierra Leone

A parliamentary state within the Commonwealth of Nations, Sierra Leone is a West African nation located between Guinea and Liberia. Area: 27,699 sq.mi. (71,-740 sq.km.). Pop. (1968 est.): 2,475,000, including (1962 est.) Mende and Temne tribes 60%; other tribes 38.5%; Creole 1.2%. Cap. and largest city: Freetown (pop., 1968 est., 163,000). Language: English (official); tribal dialects; Hausa. Religion: Christian; pagan; Muslim minority. Queen, Elizabeth II; acting governor-general from April 22, 1968, Banja Tejan-Sie; chairman of the National Reformation Council until April 18, Col. Andrew Juxon-Smith; head of the National Interim Council from April 18, Patrick Conteh; prime minister from April 26, Siaka Stevens.

Army warrant officers overthrew the National Reformation Council (NRC) in April 1968 and restored constitutional government. Previously, after its own coup in March 1967, the NRC had appointed commissions under High Court judges to clarify the political situation. The Dove-Edwin Report, which had found that the 1967 election (held before the NRC coup) had been "rigged and corrupt" throughout, was published in December 1967. At that time, a 74-member Civilian Rule Committee, made up of representatives of various political bodies and other organizations, was appointed. Meeting on Feb. 21, 1968, the committee quickly recommended a return to civilian rule.

The Beoku-Betts (after his death, Percy Davies) Commission, appointed to investigate the activities of certain ministries, resulted in some firms and individuals being ordered to repay considerable sums to the government, including 302,000 leones each from former Prime Minister Sir Albert Margai and a French firm. The Forster Report (March 1968) on the assets of ex-ministers and ex-deputy ministers resulted in

SENEGAL
Education. (1965–66) Primary, pupils 218,795, teachers 5,133; secondary, pupils 25,574, teachers 885; vocational, pupils 4,330, teachers (1964–65) 364; teacher training, students 826, teachers 80; higher (at University of Dakar), students 2,139, teaching staff 187.
Finance. Monetary unit: CFA franc, with a parity of CFA Fr. 50 to the French franc (CFA Fr. 246.85 = U.S. $1; CFA Fr. 592.45 = £1 sterling). Budget (1966–67 est.): revenue CFA Fr. 44,927,000,000; expenditure CFA Fr. 33,975,000,000.
Foreign Trade. (1967) Imports CFA Fr. 39,170,-000,000; exports CFA Fr. 33,890,000,000. Import sources (1966): France 53%; West Germany 6%; U.S. 5%; China 5%. Export destination (1966) France 74%. Main exports (1966): peanuts 42%; peanut oil 36%; phosphates 6%.

SIERRA LEONE
Education. (1966–67) Primary, pupils 123,287, teachers 3,729; secondary, pupils 20,247, teachers 879; vocational, pupils 814, teachers 58; teacher training, students 802, teachers 87; higher, students 930, teaching staff 158.
Finance and Trade. Monetary unit: leone, with a parity of 0.83 leones to U.S. $1 (2 leones = £1 sterling). Budget (1967–68 est.): revenue 42.2 million leones; expenditure 40.7 million leones. Foreign trade (1967): imports 65,270,000 leones; exports 50,460,000 leones. Import sources: U.K. 28%; Japan 11%; U.S. 11%; France 7%; Netherlands 6%; West Germany 5%. Export destinations: U.K. 71%; Netherlands 12%; West Germany 5%. Main exports: diamonds 59%; iron ore 18%.
Agriculture and Industry. Production (in 000; metric tons): palm kernels (1966) 55, (1965) 50; coffee (1966) c. 7.2, (1965) 6; iron ore (metal content; exports; 1966) 1,331; diamonds (1966) 1,252 metric carats.

Margai being charged an additional 771,037 leones, while 20 other individuals had to pay sums varying from 61 leones to 52,957 leones. An introduction to the report said that the period between the death of Prime Minister Sir Milton Margai in 1964 and the general elections of March 1967 was one of which no self-respecting Sierra Leonean could be proud. It further stated that stealing from the government had become as comon as petty larceny of private property.

The counterrevolutionaries of the April coup arrested Col. Andrew Juxon-Smith and about 40 senior army and police officers. Calling themselves the Anti-corruption Revolutionary Movement, they said power would be handed over to civilian rule as soon as possible. A National Interim Council (NIC) was formed and freedom of the press was restored, but political parties remained banned. Constitutional provisions concerning the office of governor-general were revived. On April 22 Banja Tejan-Sie, the chief justice, was sworn in as acting governor-general.

Meetings on April 26 led to the choice of Siaka Stevens (*see* BIOGRAPHY) as prime minister.

A second meeting of elected national legislators then agreed on a national government and invited Stevens to lead it. He was sworn in by the officiating governor-general and announced to the people that they now had an elected national government.

Stevens' Cabinet consisted of eight All People's Congress (ALP) members, four Sierra Leone People's Party (SLPP) members, three tribal chiefs, and two independent members. After warnings to subversive elements, he took impartial steps against them. More than 20 prominent persons were arrested, including several NIC leaders. Later, ten of the former NRC leaders, including Juxon-Smith, were charged with treason for unlawfully overthrowing the government.

Parliament met to elect a speaker and swear in members on June 5. It then adjourned till the formal opening on June 20. Later in the year violence was reported in provincial areas, and on November 20 a state of emergency was proclaimed.

The World Bank granted a loan of $3.9 million to Sierra Leone for expanding electric power facilities.
(W. H. Is.)

UPI COMPIX

Prime Minister Siaka Stevens waving to the crowd from his motorcade in Freetown, following the swearing-in ceremony on April 26, 1968.

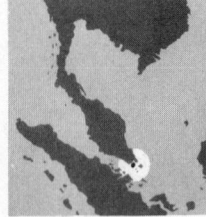

Singapore

The republic of Singapore occupies a group of islands, the largest of which is Singapore, at the southern extremity of the Malay Peninsula. Area: 224.5 sq.mi. (581.5 sq.km.). Pop. (1968 est.): 1,974,600, including approximately 80% Chinese, 12% Malays, and 7% Indians and Pakistanis. Cap. and largest city: Singapore (pop., 1965 est., 1,150,000). Language: official languages are Malay, Chinese, Tamil, and English. Religion: Malays are Muslim; Chinese, mainly Buddhist; Indians, mainly Hindu. President in 1968, Inche Yusof bin Ishak; prime minister, Lee Kuan Yew.

In the general election held in April the ruling People's Action Party, which had been in power since 1959, won all the 58 seats; there was no opposition for 51 seats.

The year saw continued progress and success, both at home and abroad. Industrial output was up by 21%; bank deposits by 31%, reflecting the confidence of investors abroad; external trade by 9%; and private construction by 27%. An annual rate of a little more than 9% was maintained for economic growth,

SINGAPORE
Education. (1965–66) Primary, pupils 362,672, teachers 12,202; secondary, pupils 107,219, teachers 4,255; vocational, pupils 10,419, teachers 723; higher (including 3 universities; 1964–65), students 16,228, teaching staff 926.
Finance and Trade. Monetary unit: Singapore dollar, with a par value of Sing$3.06 to U.S. $1 (Sing$7.35 = £1 sterling). Budget (1968 est.): revenue Sing$646,-730,000; expenditure Sing$616,450,000. Foreign trade (1966): imports Sing$4,065,670,268; exports Sing$3,-373,602,436. Import sources: Malaysia 29%; Japan 11%; U.K. 10%; China 7%; U.S. 5%; Australia 5%. Export destinations: Malaysia 35%; South Vietnam 8%; U.K. 6%; U.S. 5%. Main exports: rubber 23%; petroleum and products 18%; ship and aircraft stores 6%.
Transport and Communications. Roads (1966) 1,830 km. (including 1,067 km. government maintained). Motor vehicles in use (1967): passenger 114,-739; commercial 24,503. Railways (1967) 45 km. Shipping traffic (1967): goods loaded 12,136,000 metric tons, unloaded 18,691,000 metric tons. Telephones (Dec. 1966) 94,089. Radio receivers (Dec. 1964) 389,000. Television receivers (Dec. 1966) 74,-000.

and since the population increase had been held at 2.1%, this meant a steady improvement in living standards. The good performance of Singapore's economy, according to the finance minister, Goh Keng Swee, was due to the growth of trade with Indonesia, continued expansion of exports to South Vietnam, and a substantial increase in the inflow of Hong Kong industry into Singapore.

Despite the healthy condition of the economy, however, the future gave no cause for complacency. Singapore was faced with a severe challenge to its economic prosperity posed by the British decision to withdraw its forces by the end of 1971, which would mean not only an increase in the number of unemployed but also an eventual end to the local expenditure that the British base facilities generated. In 1967 British expenditure in Singapore accounted for 16% of the national income. Considerable energy was being expended to meet the economic and defense gaps resulting from the withdrawal.

On the international front, the republic's nonalignment policy and its willingness to seek trade and friendship with all who were prepared to reciprocate yielded dividends. During the year North Korea, North Vietnam, Romania, and Israel set up permanent trade missions in Singapore. Diplomatic relations were established at the ambassadorial level with the U.S.S.R., Yugoslavia, and Bulgaria. Trade missions from Romania, the U.S.S.R., Pakistan, Italy, Australia, Yugoslavia, Argentina, Indonesia, Israel, Burma, and the United Arab Republic visited Singapore, and trade agreements were signed with several of them. Singapore also sent missions abroad. One of them was a 28-member mission to Eastern European countries and to Denmark, West Germany, Austria, and Greece. Several heads of state made official visits to Singapore during the year, including, for the first time, the vice-president of North Korea, Kang Ryang Wook, the highest ranking Asian Communist yet to have come to the republic.
(M. S. R.)

Skiing

The establishment of additional mountain resorts and the opening of many more mechanical ascents reflected a continued worldwide growth of interest and participation in skiing during 1968. At Sallent, Spain,

4,500 ft. high in the Pyrenees, a complete new ski resort opened an uphill transport network extending 3,000 ft. above the town, where ideal snowfields promised to put Spain more certainly on the skier's map.

The most spectacular structural developments in Switzerland were four new cableway systems, providing access to a wide selection of good skiing terrain at altitudes above 5,000 ft. In Canada two modern trends were signified by 50 lighted night-skiing trails augmented by artificially manufactured snow when required. Some of Australia's 12 ski centres were boosted by visits from leading U.S. and European performers who took advantage of, for them, good out-of-season training facilities. In Britain more than 40 plastic ski training slopes and nearly 200 pre-ski schools helped to satisfy the demand for training facilities. The number of officially qualified instructors rose in the United States to 2,424. France and Japan each had approximately 2,000; Austria 1,424; Switzerland 1,226; and Italy 469.

From intensive equipment research evolved new all-plastic boots which, though not yet ideal, appeared to be a promising advance. Skis made of fibre-glass–epoxy plastics gained more favour over metal and wooden ones. New instruments to test and ensure more reliable settings for safety bindings were a breakthrough toward the future prevention of unnecessary accidents.

The 13 February days of winter sports including world and Olympic Games ski championships at Grenoble, France, drew 623,680 spectators. Approximately 102,000 saw the Alpine events at Chamrousse; 58,000 the jumping at Saint-Nizier; and 41,000 the Nordic competitions at Autrans. Thirty-seven countries entered 684 competitors. Incidentally, these figures included an Indian slalom racer whose performance counted in the Olympic Games but not in the world championship records because India then had no national association affiliated with the International Ski Federation.

Alpine Racing. The world championships, contested by 248 competitors and decided concurrently with the Grenoble Olympic contests (*see* SPORTING RECORD: *Special Report*), included Alpine combination titles separate from the Olympic honours. Jean-Claude Killy of France, winner of the downhill, slalom, and giant slalom, was indisputable men's champion. Matched only by that of the Austrian Toni Sailer in 1956, Killy's achievement could not be marred by a dispute over the result of his final event, the slalom. Austria's Karl Schranz asked for an inquiry after his disqualification for allegedly missing a gate when covering the course in a faster time than Killy, but the jury's decision was upheld. Dumeng Giovanoli (Switz.) was runner-up in the Alpine combined scoring and Heinrich Messner (Aus.) third.

Victor in the giant slalom and runner-up in the slalom, Canadian Nancy Greene won the women's combined title. Marielle Goitschel and Annie Famose, both of France, were second and third, respectively. Visibility was sometimes poor on the Chamrousse courses, but the runs were otherwise good, technically difficult, and a fair challenge to the world's best performers.

A controversy about allowing manufacturers' trademarks on skis, so often prominent in photographs of the stars, was an aspect of the crypto-professionalism impossible to eradicate, magnifying the impracticability of enforcing with fairness any definition of amateur status. Suggestions that future championships become officially open to professional skiers appeared realistic but not yet in line with official Olympic wishes.

For a second season, World Alpine Skiing Cup awards were based on each skier's highest score in any 3 of approximately 15 selected top international events during the year. Presented after the final race, at Heavenly Valley, Calif., on April 7, the cups were retained by their previous holders and Olympic champions, Killy and Miss Greene. The men's runner-up was Giovanoli, with Herbert Huber (Aus.) third. Second and third women's prizes went to French girls, Isabelle Mir and Florence Steurer, respectively.

Nordic Events. As with the Alpine events, the Nordic world championships were decided concurrently with the Grenoble Olympic contests, 435 competitors taking part in the cross-country and jumping. That the medal winners in these included, for the first time, competitors from Austria, Czechoslovakia, Italy, and Switzerland emphasized the increase of Nordic skiing skill among Alpine nations. Toini Gustafsson, a Swede who won the 5-km. and 10-km. events, became the first individual since 1952 to break a Soviet run of victories in women's cross-country racing. Franco Nones (Italy), who won the 30 km., and Josef Haas (Switz.), who was third in the 50 km., both broke into the traditional Scandinavian monopoly in men's cross-country events. Jiri Raska made a corresponding and equally unexpected breakthrough by winning the 70-m. jump for Czechoslovakia.

At the 70th Holmenkollen Games, in Oslo on March 15–17, John Bower became the first U.S. skier to win the Nordic combined title and King's Cup, defeating the Olympic champion, Franz Keller of West Germany.

The most progressive development in Nordic skiing during 1968 was a successful organization of the first European championships for juniors, held at Morez-les-Rousses, France, on February 2–4. Age limits were 20 for men and 17 for women, and the entry of 177 competitors from 16 nations was a gratifying start. Finnish entrants proved collectively the most successful, with Norwegians next best.   (H. B.)

Some 8,000 amateurs testing the Grand Feria run on one of the opening days of the annual cross-country race of Vasa in central Sweden during March 1968.

France's Jean-Claude Killy on his way to winning the men's slalom at the American International Team Meet in Sun Valley on March 23, 1968.

Social Services

With many countries already having adopted social security schemes, new legislation in 1968 dealt mainly with improvements in existing programs. In this connection, there was an increased awareness of the value of international discussion and the exchange of information between different countries. For example, in September members of the United Nations and its related agencies participated in an international con-

Skating:
see Hockey; Ice Skating; Sporting Record

Snooker:
see Sporting Record

Soccer:
see Football

ference of ministers responsible for social welfare. The conference had been called by the Economic and Social Council to examine the role of welfare programs in national development and to make recommendations for further UN action in this field.

The International Social Security Association continued to assist in promoting satisfactory social security schemes in various countries. A report was issued of the 16th general assembly of the association, held in Leningrad in May 1967, with 140 member organizations from 62 countries taking part. The working sessions were opened by the discussion of a report on "Developments and Trends in Social Security, 1964–66." Attention was drawn to the difficulties of discovering distinct trends and common denominators in the evolution of the social security schemes in different countries, since each scheme reflects the demographic, socioeconomic, and cultural conditions of the nation concerned. Nevertheless, certain common trends became apparent when social security evolution was observed with reference to each branch of insurance. The general trend toward extension of social security coverage to all classes of the population was manifest.

In discussing the relationship between cash benefits and services in kind in the less developed countries, it was noted that the cash benefit solution may be preferable in protecting urban wage earners, but it may be unworkable when the problem is to offer some minimum degree of social protection to the masses of people who live on the products of traditional agriculture and do not have a steady income. Industrialized countries that give cash benefits rely on the utilization of already existing social services by the beneficiaries. In the less developed countries, on the other hand, the creation of such social services appeared to be among the first tasks of governments and social security institutions.

A report was issued of a research study on the conditions of the elderly in the U.S., the U.K., and Denmark. Comparable data were obtained from interviews of some 2,500 elderly people in each country. Among the matters on which information was obtained was the economic condition of the elderly. Absolute incomes were found to be higher in the U.S., but the elderly were more prosperous in relation to the rest of the community in Denmark, as a result of more adequate old-age pensions and supplements for those over 80 years of age.

Another comparative study concerned the member countries of the EEC. Comparative tables, prepared jointly by the EEC Commission and the High Authority of the European Coal and Steel Community (ECSC), covered contributions; sickness, maternity, and unemployment benefits; retirement or old-age pensions; survivors' benefits; and family allowances. In the EEC countries (with the exception of the Netherlands), retirement pensions were related to earnings over some prescribed period, and the formula for calculating pensions varied. The schemes were at different stages of maturity, so that many people might be getting pensions at a lower rate than the formula would eventually provide. Unlike the U.K., where sickness benefit was a purely cash benefit and all medical care was provided under the National Health Service and financed mainly from taxation, in the EEC countries medical care was part of the contributory sickness insurance scheme, the cost being reimbursed in whole or in part to the individual. The cash value of family allowances varied widely in the EEC countries;

it was highest in France and lowest in West Germany. These allowances were provided at the expense of the employer, except in West Germany where, as in the U.K., they were financed out of general taxation. Total social expenditure in the EEC countries represented at least 20% of the national income and sometimes more. The greater part of the expenditure was on social security. Proportional individual and employers' contributions to social insurance in the EEC countries are shown in Table I.

Table I. Social Security Contributions in EEC Countries
Percent of employed person's earnings

Country	By employee (%)	By employer (%)
France	6.57	32.48
Germany, West	13.15	14.65
Belgium	10.55	27.20
Italy	7.05	50.06
Netherlands	17.85	18.85
Luxembourg	10.00	16.00

The part that voluntary organizations should take in cooperating with statutory bodies in the social services received special consideration in several countries. In Canada and the U.K. it was becoming increasingly apparent that voluntary organizations could no longer rely on private income but needed financial help from governmental and local authority sources. In both countries some voluntary bodies, which could not function properly on their private income, were reluctant to seek aid from public funds for fear of interference. In other cases the public authority was not willing to give grant aid because the organization in question was not thought to be efficient. The annual report of the Canadian Welfare Council showed that coordination and cooperation between public and private bodies on the neighbourhood level was intellectually accepted, though there was not always agreement that services should be financed jointly from voluntary and public sources.

On the other hand, concern was sometimes felt over the extent to which monies raised for voluntary activities were spent on the cost of fund raising and over the business efficiency of some such organizations. In Canada more than Can$45 million was raised in the year for more than 2,000 voluntary agencies whose annual expenditure totaled three times that amount. Their accounting and reporting systems were sometimes inadequate, however. Accordingly, standards were suggested for all voluntary organizations by the national biennial conference of Community Funds and Councils of Canada, and the Canadian Welfare Council offered to help smaller organizations reorganize their accounting systems. Help to voluntary agencies in the improvement of financial procedures was also provided by the National Agency Review Committee. In the U.K. criticisms had also been raised concerning the fund-raising activities of charitable bodies. The National Council of Social Service thought it would be useful to examine the possibility of drawing up a code of conduct for fund raising, to which voluntary organizations could subscribe. At the request of the Charity Commission, a working party was set up with this end in view.

United Kingdom. Family allowances were increased from 8s. to 15s. a week for the second child in the family and from 10s. to 17s. a week for each subsequent child. Benefits for certain children under the national insurance scheme were also altered, so that, for widow's benefit, child's special allowance, and guardian's allowance, benefit and (where payable)

family allowances together normally provided a total of £2 5s. 6d. a week (increased from £2 2s. 6d.) for each child. For other benefits the total was £1 8s. for each child.

Considerable public concern was expressed about the effect of the wage stop on low-income families. The statutory provision in question limited the amount of any supplementary benefit paid to an unemployed man, who was required to register for work, so that his income did not exceed what it would be if he were at work full time in his normal occupation. After conducting field inquiries into the living conditions of affected families, the Supplementary Benefits Commission, the body responsible to the minister of social security for administering the wage stop, decided to make a number of changes so as to ensure that the wage stop would be administered in as fair and sympathetic a way as possible. By mid-March the adoption of standard local authority wage rates, together with more favourable rules about expenses, had been brought into use as a measure of net earning capacity, rather than the regionally prescribed figures that had been used previously. The commission decided that consideration should be given to withdrawing the requirement of registering for work, and with it the wage stop, from blind persons who had been unemployed for two years or more. It also decided to review all wage-stopped cases with an element of disability.

Under the Supplementary Benefits scheme, a retirement pensioner is entitled to a supplementary pension if his resources, as calculated under the Ministry of Social Security Act, are below a guaranteed level. This level was raised to £5 1s. for a single householder and £7 19s. for a married couple, plus—in each case—an allowance for rent and rates. For a non-householder the level was fixed at £4 15s., which included an allowance toward the rent. These levels could be increased when the pensioner had exceptional expenses. In calculating whether the resources of a person without a retirement pension were below these levels, the first £1 of private income (including charitable payments) was to be disregarded.

Over 22 million claims for benefits and allowances were made in 1967. Those made under the three main categories (retirement, sickness, and unemployment) are shown in Table II.

Table II. United Kingdom: Claims for Social Security Benefits and Allowances

Item	1967	1966
Retirement pensions	643,000	598,000
Sickness benefit	10,048,000	10,925,000
Unemployment benefit	3,275,000	2,633,000

The annual costs of benefits at the rates applying at the end of 1967 was about £2,900 million a year. (*See* Table III.)

Table III. United Kingdom: Cost of Social Security Benefits
In £000,000

Item	1967	1966
From Exchequer money:		
War pensions	128	117
Family allowances	168	150
Supplementary benefits	385	353
Supplementary pensions	183	192
Supplementary allowances	202	161
Total	681	620
From the National Insurance and Industrial Injuries Funds:		
Retirement pensions	1,480	1,270
Other benefits	755	670
Total	2,335	1,940

The proportions of the main groups receiving supplementary benefit from the Supplementary Benefits Commission at the end of 1967 were: persons of pension age 70%; sick 12%; unemployed 9%; others 9%.

The National Old People's Welfare Council reported increased activities throughout the country in promoting the welfare of the elderly. This had been stimulated in some areas by local authority grants for the employment of paid organizers, though the main work was undertaken by voluntary helpers. Citizens' advice bureaus continued to expand. It was accepted that there should be a bureau in every town with a population of 30,000 or more, and in selected smaller towns acting as centres for surrounding areas. Following the British model, an Old People's Welfare Council was established in Ireland, and local councils of social service were set up in some areas.

As a result of discussions on the ways in which service to the community by youth might be encouraged, the government promoted the establishment of an independent foundation to provide an advisory and consultative service. The foundation set up a unit with a full-time staff of young people. On invitation, the unit would send small teams into an area to help in setting up machinery for stimulating and sustaining the interest of young people in community service.

The report of a government-appointed committee on local authority and allied personal social services was published. Far-reaching alterations in the existing system were recommended, including the establishment of a new social service department by each health and welfare authority—the councils of counties, county boroughs, and the London boroughs—so that the provision of personal social services by the various authorities could be unified. The new departments would be responsible for the welfare services provided under the National Assistance Act, 1948, as well as a variety of welfare services provided under other statutes. Importance was attached to the participation of volunteers and voluntary organizations in the social services. It was suggested that, within the framework of the service, volunteers could assume many of the duties that do not need to be carried out by a professionally qualified worker.

Other European Countries. In Belgium the pension schemes for wage earners, salaried employees, mine workers, and seamen were amalgamated. Contributions were brought into line so as to provide a uniform rate of 12.5% of earnings. The contribution limit on earnings for salaried employees was raised to BFr. 13,200 a month, to be increased to BFr. 15,000 in 1969. Later it would be adjusted annually in the light of increases in real earnings. Provision was also made for a comprehensive state subsidy of BFr. 6 billion, which would increase annually by 4% and would be adjustable according to fluctuations in retail prices.

The French social security scheme was reformed to make it self-supporting. Contribution rates for sickness, maternity, invalidity, and death insurance were fixed at 15% on an income up to Fr. 200 a month (11.5% by the employer and 3.5% by the employee). On any part of the wage exceeding the limit, there was a contribution of 3% (2% by the employer and 1% by the employee). For old-age insurance, up to the above minimum limit, there was a contribution of 8.5% (5.5% by the employer and 3% by the employee).

The pension insurance scheme in West Germany was extended to all salaried employees, irrespective of the amount of their earnings. The earnings limit for

calculating contributions was raised from DM. 1,400 to DM. 1,600 a month. In Spain new rates of contributions were fixed to take fluctuations into account; they varied according to whether workers were paid by the day or by the month. In Switzerland there were improvements in the invalidity insurance scheme. Contributions were based on a percentage of earnings rather than being treated as a supplement to the contributions to the old-age and survivors' insurance scheme. The age for entitlement to invalidity benefit was reduced from 20 to 18 years and the allowance for cost of assistance to totally disabled persons was no longer conditional on proof of indigence. Help to the disabled was put on a new footing, based on a concept of social protection in which vocational rehabilitation took precedence over the payment of cash benefit.

Sickness insurance rates in the U.S.S.R. were raised to the following percentages of the relevant wage: for up to three years of uninterrupted employment, 50%; from three to five years, 60%; from five to eight years, 80%. Additional categories of wage earners undertaking exacting types of work were included among those entitled to receive the old-age pension at special rates before normal retirement age.

North America. *Canada.* The rate of the old-age security pension was adjusted according to the pension index; for 1968 it was Can$6.50. Other pensions were similarly increased, and there was an increase of 2% in payments under the guaranteed income supplement. These were the first increases to take place under the system whereby pension payments were linked to the pension index. The ceiling for maximum pensionable earnings was raised from $5,000 to $5,100, and maximum contributions in respect of employed persons from $79.20 to $81 a year.

Information obtained by the Economic Council of Canada showed that at least one in every five Canadians suffered from poverty (assessed on the basis of spending more than 70% of income on food, clothing, and shelter). This would mean an income of less than $1,500 a year for an unmarried man and $4,000 for a married man with a large family. About four million people, or 27% of the nonagricultural population, fell within this category in 1961, and the council saw no reason why this proportion should have changed. One-third to one-fifth of the poor lived in the western parts of Quebec, commonly thought of as prosperous.

The Medical Care Act of 1966 came into operation.

Table IV. Social Security Programs, by Country, 1967 and 1958

Type of program available

Country	Old age, invalidity, survivors 1967	1958	Health, sickness 1967	1958	Work injury 1967	1958	Unemployment 1967	1958	Family allowances 1967	1958
Afghanistan					X	X				
Albania	X	X	X	X	X	X			X	
Algeria*	X		X		X				X	
Argentina	X	X	X		X	X			X	X
Australia	X	X	X	X	X	X	X	X	X	X
Austria	X	X	X	X	X	X	X	X	X	X
Barbados*	X				X					
Belgium	X	X	X	X	X	X	X	X	X	X
Bolivia	X	X	X	X	X	X			X	X
Botswana*					X					
Brazil	X	X	X	X	X	X			X	X
Bulgaria	X	X	X	X	X	X	X	X	X	X
Burma			X	X	X	X				
Burundi*	X				X					
Cambodia*					X				X	
Cameroon			X		X				X	
Canada	X	X	X	X	X	X	X	X	X	X
Central African Rep.*	X				X				X	
Ceylon	X	X	X		X	X				
Chad*					X				X	
Chile	X	X	X	X	X		X	X	X	X
China, Communist	X	X	X	X	X					
Colombia	X		X	X	X	X			X	
Congo (Brazzaville)*	X				X				X	
Congo (Kinshasa)*	X				X				X	
Costa Rica	X	X	X	X	X	X				
Cuba	X	X	X		X	X				
Cyprus*	X		X		X		X			
Czechoslovakia	X	X	X	X	X	X			X	X
Dahomey*					X				X	
Denmark	X	X	X	X	X	X	X	X	X	X
Dominican Rep.	X	X	X	X	X	X				
Ecuador	X	X	X	X	X	X	X	X		
El Salvador			X	X	X					
Ethiopia*			X		X					
Finland	X	X	X	X	X				X	X
France	X	X	X	X	X	X	X	X	X	X
Gabon*	X				X				X	
Gambia, The*					X					
Germany, East	X	X	X	X	X	X	X	X	X	X
Germany, West	X	X	X	X	X	X	X	X	X	X
Ghana	X		X		X					
Greece	X	X	X	X	X	X	X		X	
Guatemala			X	X	X	X				
Guinea*	X				X				X	
Guyana*	X				X					
Haiti	X		X		X	X				
Honduras			X		X	X				
Hungary	X	X	X	X	X	X	X		X	X
Iceland	X	X	X	X	X	X	X	X	X	X
India	X	X	X	X	X	X				
Indonesia			X		X					
Iran	X	X	X	X	X	X			X	X
Iraq	X	X	X	X	X	X				
Ireland	X	X	X	X	X	X	X	X	X	
Israel	X	X	X	X	X	X			X	
Italy	X	X	X	X	X	X	X	X	X	X
Ivory Coast*	X				X				X	
Jamaica*	X				X					
Japan	X	X	X	X	X	X	X	X		
Jordan					X	X				
Kenya*	X				X					
Korea, South					X					
Lebanon	X		X		X	X			X	
Liberia*	X				X					
Libya	X	X	X	X	X	X				
Luxembourg	X	X	X	X	X	X	X	X	X	X
Malagasy Rep.*			X		X				X	
Malawi*					X					
Malaysia	X	X	X		X		X			
Mali*	X		X		X				X	
Malta*	X		X		X		X			
Mauritania*	X		X		X				X	
Mexico	X	X	X	X	X	X				
Morocco	X	X	X		X	X			X	X
Netherlands	X	X	X	X	X	X	X	X	X	X
New Zealand	X	X	X	X	X	X	X	X	X	X
Nicaragua	X	X	X	X	X					
Niger*	X		X		X				X	
Nigeria*	X		X		X					
Norway	X	X	X		X	X	X	X	X	X
Pakistan			X		X					
Panama	X	X	X	X	X	X				
Paraguay	X	X	X	X	X	X				
Peru	X	X	X	X	X	X				
Philippines	X	X	X	X	X	X				
Poland	X	X	X	X	X	X			X	X
Portugal	X	X	X	X	X	X			X	X
Romania	X	X	X	X	X	X			X	X
Rwanda*	X				X					
Saudi Arabia*	X				X					
Senegal*			X		X				X	
Sierra Leone*					X					
Singapore*	X	X	X		X					
Somali Rep.*					X					
South Africa*	X	X	X		X	X	X	X	X	X
Spain	X	X	X	X	X	X	X	X	X	X
Sudan*					X					
Sweden	X	X	X	X	X	X	X	X	X	X
Switzerland	X	X	X	X	X	X	X	X	X	X
Syria*	X		X		X					
Taiwan*	X	X	X	X	X	X				
Tanzania*	X		X		X					
Thailand					X					
Togo*			X		X				X	
Trinidad and Tobago*	X				X					
Tunisia			X		X	X			X	X
Turkey	X	X	X	X	X	X				
Uganda*					X					
U.S.S.R.	X	X	X	X	X	X			X	X
U.A.R.	X	X	X	X	X	X	X			
United Kingdom	X	X	X	X	X	X	X	X	X	X
United States	X	X	X	X	X	X	X	X		
Upper Volta*	X		X		X				X	
Uruguay	X	X	X		X	X	X	X	X	X
Venezuela	X		X		X	X				
Vietnam, North	X				X				X	X
Vietnam, South			X		X				X	X
Yugoslavia	X	X	X	X	X	X	X	X	X	X
Zambia*					X					

*Country not reported prior to 1964.

Source: U.S. Department of Health, Education, and Welfare, Social Security Administration, Office of Research and Statistics, *Social Security Programs Throughout the World.*

Federal contributions became available to the provinces for provincially administered medical care programs on the basis of half the per capita cost of all insured services under the provincial plan, multiplied by the average number of insured persons in the particular province.

In the year ending March 1968, $2.5 million was allocated under the National Welfare Grants program, established in 1962 to help develop and strengthen welfare services, research, and professional training throughout Canada. The proportion of government expenditure on health and social welfare generally continued to grow. In 1966–67 family allowances totaled $556 million; old-age security, $1,033,000,000, plus $40 million for three months under the Guaranteed Income Supplement Program which began to operate in January 1967; and unemployment insurance benefits, $307 million. The federal-provincial income maintenance program required $42 million for old-age assistance and $260 million for unemployment assistance.

United States. In January 1968 monthly benefit awards under the Old Age, Survivors, Disability, and Health Insurance program (OASDHI) totaled about 266,000—the lowest number in more than a year and about 12% fewer than in December 1967. The most substantial decline (17%) was in survivors' benefit awards. At the end of January benefits were payable to about 23.8 million persons at a monthly rate of $1.8 billion. Approximately $1.2 billion went to about 15.2 million retired workers and their dependents; $149 million to 2.2 million disabled workers and their dependents; $392 million to 5.7 million survivor beneficiaries; and $25 million to 724,000 special "aged 72" beneficiaries. The number in the last category was lower by 55,000 than in January 1967.

At the end of January 1968, approximately 19.6 million persons aged 65 and over were covered by the hospital insurance program under health insurance for the aged (Medicare), and 18.1 million had voluntarily enrolled in the medical insurance program. During January more than 555,000 hospital admission notices for aged individuals covered by the scheme were received by the Social Security Administration from 6,862 hospitals. Since the beginning of the fiscal year 1967–68, more than 3.2 million hospital admission notices had been received. More than one-half of those receiving old-age assistance (OAA) under state and federal programs received cash benefits under OASDHI.

The annual report of the Department of Health, Education, and Welfare showed that almost 87 million workers contributed to the social security program in 1967. In June 1967 the average retirement benefit being paid to a retired worker who had no dependents receiving benefit was $81 a month; when the worker and his wife were both receiving benefits, the average for the family was $144. For families composed of a disabled worker and a wife under 65 with one or more children, the average was $213; and for families consisting of a widowed mother and two children, the average was $222. The average monthly benefit for an aged widow was $75.

By 1968 about 100 million people had worked in covered employment long enough to be eligible for benefits. Some 63 million were permanently insured. About 95% of young children and their mothers would be eligible for benefit if the father died. Of the population under 65, an estimated 88 million were insured at the beginning of 1968; 17.5 million—90% of the 19.5 million persons aged 65 or over—were eligible for benefits under the program, including noninsured persons aged 72 and over. Some 82% were actually receiving benefits, and an additional 7% would have received them if they or their spouses had not been receiving substantial income from working.

The Social Security Amendments law of 1967 made changes in the cash benefits of the social security program, including an increase of 13% in insurance benefits, with a minimum monthly benefit of $55 for a person retiring at or over 65; an increase from $35 to $40 in the special age-72 payments; an increase from $1,500 to $1,680 in the amount a person might earn in a year and still receive full benefit; cash benefits for disabled widows at age 50 at reduced rates; and an increase in the contribution and benefit base from $6,600 to $7,800. Among other changes, the law included new provisions for aiding families with dependent children, under which the federal government would match state payments to families with absent parents.

Although about 8.4 million persons were receiving public assistance payments in 1967, less than one-half of the people who were needy and eligible under federal provisions were actually being aided. Not all states participated in the program, and many states placed restrictions on their public assistance program for fiscal and other reasons. The average public assistance money payment under federally aided categories was little more than one-half of the minimum amount required for subsistence according to the generally accepted poverty level, and in some states the average was less than one-quarter. The average varied considerably between states—from $9 a month for a dependent child in Mississippi to $56 in New Jersey. For old-age assistance, the rates varied from a low of $38 in Mississippi to a high of $105 in California.

A research study published in March 1968 showed that in 1966 a total of 29.7 million persons—one out of every seven Americans not in institutions—were in households with a money income for the year that fell below the poverty level. They were distributed in 11 million households which contained about one-sixth of the nation's children under 18. The total of those in poverty, however, showed a drop of 9.2 million as compared with 1959. Two out of five households consisting of one aged person or an elderly couple fell below the poverty line. Among the poor, women outnumbered men by eight to five.

Other Countries. In Argentina an old-age pension on the grounds of advanced age was introduced to replace the reduced retirement pension. Insured persons became entitled to the ordinary retirement pension after 30 years' employment on reaching the age of 60 for men and 55 for women. The old-age pension was payable on the ground of advanced age at 65 if the beneficiary had been employed for at least 15 years, including at least 5 years during the 8 years preceding retirement. The advanced age pension was to be calculated at 3.33% of the ordinary pension for each year of service taken into account.

The social security scheme in Brazil was generally improved, and the income ceiling on which contributions were based was raised to ten times the amount of the highest minimum wage.

Distress caused by flooding continued to be a major problem in some parts of Ceylon. It was the responsibility of the Social Service Department to help victims in various ways, including temporary re-housing, cash payments, and replacement of lost implements of

trade. Voluntary agencies extended their help to the department in providing homes for the aged. Maintenance grants were made by the state for persons in homes, together with grants toward buildings and equipment. A proposal to declare begging a cognizable offense was awaiting government action.

In Pakistan the National Council of Social Welfare sanctioned grants amounting to PakRs. 1,360,000 and PakRs. 1,311,430 for 825 voluntary agencies in East Pakistan and 248 in West Pakistan for the year 1967–68.

In India the constitution enjoins the government to endeavour to bring about prohibition of the consumption of intoxicating liquor and drugs. A central prohibition committee reviewed the progress of the program, coordinated activities in the different states, and kept in touch with their practical difficulties. Progress had varied considerably among the states, and several state governments decided either to scrap the program or to amend the relevant legislation. Progress continued in the campaign to eradicate untouchability. A committee set up in 1965 was still reviewing the situation.

The legislative, economic, social, and political rights of the tribal people were being given special attention in India. Welfare activities consisted mostly of introducing some innovations in the tribal culture, but they were not always readily accepted. Research showed that the planning of welfare programs for the tribes must be based on thorough knowledge of the culture, including an anthropological study of tribal life to identify the aspects where improvement was needed. It was accepted that efforts must be made to secure the services of this tribe's own men and women as social workers, and that the few tribal men having any degree of literacy must be encouraged to help.

(JN. M.)

See also Education; Housing; Insurance; Labour Unions; Medicine; Race Relations; Refugees.

Sociology

Although race relations continued to be a major concern of many U.S. sociologists, the wave of riots that followed the assassination of Negro civil rights leader the Rev. Martin Luther King, Jr., appeared to mark the crest of the Negro revolt in 1968. While subsequent incidents, such as the attack on a detachment of Cleveland, O., police, were highly dramatic in character, they were, for the most part, the work of small bands of dedicated revolutionaries who lacked the support of the larger Negro community. Rumours that Negroes would storm the national convention of the Democratic Party in Chicago were found to be baseless. Most Negroes were aware that many leading white Democrats were becoming increasingly responsive to their demands. In Cleveland and in Gary, Ind., the support of national Democratic politicians had helped to elect Negro mayors. After having appointed the first Negroes to the Cabinet and to the Supreme Court of the United States, U.S. Pres. Lyndon B. Johnson also appointed the first Negro mayor of Washington, D.C. Furthermore, as the Johnson administration drew to a close it was evident that educational and occupational opportunities for Negroes had increased substantially. While Negroes in the ghettos of U.S. cities still faced great problems, many black nationalist leaders had come to the opinion that such problems could be solved peaceably. It was true

that many whites continued to hold strong prejudices against Negroes, but such prejudices could not nullify the economic, political, and social gains made by Negroes in recent years.

In 1968, more than in any previous year, U.S. sociologists pondered the question of whether or not to use their professional organizations for political purposes. To many it seemed that a stand against the Vietnam war policy of the Johnson administration was desirable; therefore, the American Sociological Association (ASA) polled its members on two questions. In one question, each member was asked if he favoured or opposed a certain prepared statement criticizing the Vietnam war policy. The second question asked members whether the ASA should take an official position regarding U.S. policy in Vietnam. Of the 4,429 voting members, 2,881 returned their ballots before the deadline. Of the 2,881, 1,472 favoured the critical statement, 1,247 opposed that statement, and 162 were undecided. On the second question, 989 held that the ASA should take an official position on Vietnam, but 1,874 opposed such action and 18 were undecided. In view of these results, the American Sociological Association refrained from taking an official position on the matter.

On another political matter, at Omaha, Neb., in April 1968, supporters of U.S. Sen. Eugene McCarthy for the Democratic nomination for president of the United States sought to obtain an official endorsement for their candidate from the convention of the Midwest Sociological Society (MSS). They were unable to obtain it, although, as individuals, many members of the MSS favoured McCarthy. In late August, however, the American Sociological Association did, in effect, take a political stand by canceling its 1969 convention in Chicago as a protest against the severe treatment of McCarthy supporters and other demonstrators by the Chicago police during the 1968 Democratic convention.

In Latin America the publication of the first *Annario de Sociologia de los Pueblos Ibericos* consolidated gains made by sociologists in the Spanish- and Portuguese-speaking areas of the world since World War II. This work was an accomplishment of the Asociación de Sociólogos de Lengua Española y Portuguesa (ASLEP) under the presidency of Hernan Godoy of the Universidad Católica de Chile in Santiago. ASLEP included members in Spain, Portugal, and the Philippines, as well as in all Latin-American countries.

With problems of urbanism reaching the acute stage on all continents, sociologists frequently found it challenging and rewarding to join other specialists in carrying on research and planning aimed at control of the stresses and strains related to urban industrial expansion. Vigorous interdisciplinary enterprises were in operation at the office of El Comite Interdisciplinario de Desarrollo Urbano (CIDU), affiliated with the Universidad Católica de Chile; at the Centro de Estudios Urbanos y Regionales (CEUR), associated with the Instituto Di Tella in Buenos Aires, Arg.; and at the Athens Centre of Ekistics. The director of the latter centre, Constantinos Doxiadis, defined "ekistics" as "the science of human settlements."

In the United States, also, a number of universities had founded centres for urban studies, while interest in rural sociology continued to decline. In India and Pakistan, however, the sociological associations were stressing the use of empirical research methods in the study of rural sociology and demography. Since both

of these countries were still heavily rural, urban sociology had low priority despite the recent growth of cities. In the Soviet Union, sociological studies had challenged several revered Marxist positions, including the classless society. Surveys had indicated that opportunities for education above the secondary level were significantly lacking for children of workers in agricultural, service, and manual occupations, but were significantly available to sons and daughters of persons in skilled, white collar, and professional vocations. Such studies had been encouraged by Communist Party General Secretary Leonid I. Brezhnev, who declared them to be as important as the achievements of the natural sciences, and Premier Aleksei N. Kosygin, who stated that sociological research was playing an increasing role in the solution of practical problems.

(J. E. McK.)

See also Anthropology; Psychology; Social Services.

ENCYCLOPÆDIA BRITANNICA FILMS. *The Living City* (1953); *Man and His Culture* (1954); *Megalopolis—Cradle of the Future* (1962); *Population Ecology* (1964); *Operation Bootstrap* (1968).

Somali Republic

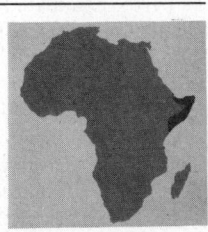

A republic of northeast Africa, the Somali Republic, or Somalia, is bounded by the Gulf of Aden, the Indian Ocean, Kenya, Ethiopia, and the French Territory of Afars and Issas. Area: 246,155 sq.mi. (637,541 sq.km.). Pop. (1968 est.): 3 million, predominantly Hamitic, with Arabic and other admixtures. Cap. and largest city: Mogadishu (pop., 1968 est., 172,120). Language: Cushitic Somali with some Arabic influence. Religion: orthodox Muslim. President in 1968, Abd-i-Rashid Ali Shermarke; prime minister, Muhammad Haji Ibrahim Egal.

Following the negotiations with Kenya and Ethiopia at the end of 1967 in regard to the disputed Somali areas of those countries, diplomatic relations were resumed with Britain in January 1968 after a five-

year interval. In March the Somali prime minister visited Britain, Italy, West Germany, and the U.S. As a result of his tour, Prime Minister Egal reported that he had gained support from the U.S. and the European Economic Community countries for his proposal to establish a £40 million development project in the Juba River basin that would produce sufficient foodstuffs to make the republic self-supporting. Egal also announced that the UN geological survey had discovered deposits of more than a quarter of a million tons of high-grade uranium ore about 250 mi. from Mogadishu.

The prime minister was appointed ex officio leader of the Somali Youth League Party (SYL) at its annual conference in February. In May a new electoral law was approved by the National Assembly requiring civil servants to resign their posts six months before they could stand as parliamentary candidates (without the possibility of automatic reappointment if they were unsuccessful). The system of allocating seats in Parliament was also changed in such a way as to discourage the growth of small parties, which had already proliferated in anticipation of the 1969 general election. In May, for the first time, a Somali judge, Abdulrahman Sheikh, was appointed president of the Supreme Court—an office previously filled by Italian lawyers. In August the new National Advisory Council, consisting of 600 delegates from all walks of life, met for the first time and discussed with the government a series of proposals for the improvement of social and other services. One resolution proposed that ministers, civil servants, and members of Parliament should be prohibited from engaging in trade while in office.

(I. M. L.)

South Africa

A republic occupying the southern tip of Africa, South Africa is bounded by South West Africa, Botswana, Rhodesia, Mozambique, and Swaziland. Lesotho forms an enclave within South African territory. Area: 471,445 sq.mi. (1,221,037 sq.km.), excluding Walvis Bay, 372 sq.mi. Pop. (1967 est.): 18,733,000, including Bantu 68.1%; white 19%; Coloured 9.9%; Asian 3%. Administrative cap.: Pretoria (metro. pop., 1967 est., 523,000); judicial cap.: Bloemfontein (pop., 1967 est., 197,000); legislative cap.: Cape Town (metro. pop., 1967 est., 758,000). Largest city: Johannesburg (metro. pop., 1967 est., 1,309,000). Language: Afrikaans and English. Religion: mainly Christian. State presidents in 1968, Theophilus E. Dönges to January 3, Jozua F. Naudé (acting president) to April 10, and Jacobus J. Fouché; prime minister, Balthazar J. Vorster.

Domestic Affairs. Theophilus E. Dönges, who had been elected state president in January 1967 to succeed Charles R. Swart but could not assume office because of serious illness, died in January (*see* OBITUARIES). Jozua F. Naudé acted as president until April 10, when Jacobus J. Fouché (*see* BIOGRAPHY) took office. Cabinet changes involving a number of portfolios were made in February and August. As a result, there was a reshuffle of departments and four ministers were replaced. Four new deputy ministers were appointed.

In May legislation was adopted establishing an armaments corporation (Armscor), functioning under the Munitions Board, with a minimum capital of R 100 million, to make South Africa more self-supporting in

Pongolapoort arch dam
on the Orange River
was still under construction
in 1968. When completed
in 1970 the dam would be
293 ft. in height and have
a storage capacity
of two million ac.-ft.
JOLYON RHIND

arms production. South Africa's first missile base, for experimental tests and launchings, was planned for the east coast in Zululand. Changes were made in the supreme command to promote efficiency and arms production.

The first steps were taken toward establishing an aluminum smelting complex, estimated to cost R 48 million, at the proposed new harbour at Richards Bay in Natal. From there the construction of an oil pipeline through Durban to the Witwatersrand was begun. At Durban three major international oil companies were authorized to build a tanker terminal to accommodate vessels of up to 200,000 tons, at an estimated cost of R 5 million. Large-scale explorations for oil, in the interior as well as offshore, continued.

In February South Africa and Lesotho agreed on the joint construction of the Oxbow (Orange River) water and power project to serve both countries. Work began in November on the R 245 million hydroelectric and irrigation scheme at Cahorabassa on the Zambezi River in Mozambique to supply water and power to South Africa, Mozambique, South West Africa, and Malawi. Negotiations were continued with Portugal for a similar project on the Kunene River to serve South West Africa and Angola.

A government commission was appointed to devise a new national flag to be introduced on the tenth anniversary of the republic (May 31, 1971). Preliminary preparations were begun for the institution of a new population register and a comprehensive identification system ("book of life"). Following the world's first heart transplant (December 1967) performed at Groote Schuur Hospital, Cape Town, by a team under Christiaan Barnard (*see* BIOGRAPHY), a heart research foundation and an international heart transplant register were established at Cape Town.

Race Relations. Three measures were passed by Parliament to deal with the political status and future of the Coloured (racially mixed) people. Under the Separate Representation of Voters Amendment Act their representation in Parliament, based on a separate voters' roll limited to Cape Province, was to be entirely abolished when the life of the current Parliament expired in 1971. Their representation in the Cape Provincial Council would, under the same act, end in 1970 when a new council was elected. The Coloured Persons' Representative Council Amendment Act provided for the enlargement of the existing Coloured Representative Council. The members would be partly nominated and partly elected for the whole country on a basis of universal franchise for the Coloureds, and would have limited legislative and administrative powers affecting Coloured affairs. By a third measure, the Prohibition of Political Interference Act, members of one racial group could not belong to a political party whose members were predominantly of another racial group.

In the Transkei, the first of the partially self-governing Bantu regions, the ruling National Independence Party was returned to power. The second general election for the Legislative Assembly was held in October. In its final session the first Legislative Assembly adopted resolutions asking for the incorporation of certain "white" areas into the Transkei, and for the furtherance of industrial development in the territory to provide employment for the local population and check the outflow to other areas. The Transkei also sought an extension of its legislative control over matters hitherto reserved for the central government, and for the employment of more Bantu in the higher administrative posts in the territory. Two Bantu magistrates were appointed to replace white officials. In November the tribal territorial authority of the Ciskei was reconstituted as a Legislative Assembly; similar arrangements were planned for Tswanaland, Zululand, and other Bantu homelands. The system was also extended to South West Africa (*see* below).

SOUTH AFRICA

Education. (1966) Primary, secondary, and technical, pupils 3,292,035 (including 732,283 European), teachers 84,237; teacher training (1962), students 15,742 (including 9,032 European), teachers 1,086; higher (including 11 universities), students 64,388 (including 57,211 European), teaching staff 4,493.

Finance. Monetary unit: rand, with a par value of R 0.71 to U.S. $1 (R 1.71 = £1 sterling). Gold and foreign exchange, official: (June 1968) U.S. $1,121,000,000; (June 1967) U.S. $618 million. Budget (1967–68 est.): revenue R 1,438,100,000; expenditure R 1,387,300,000. Gross national product: (1967) R 9,363,000,000; (1966) R 8,545,000,000. Money supply: (June 1968) R 1,782,000,000; (June 1967) R 1,626,000,000. Cost of living (1963 = 100): (June 1968) 115; (June 1967) 114.

Foreign Trade. (1967) Imports R 1,916,000,000; exports (excluding gold) R 1,352,700,000 (outflow of gold R 773 million). Import sources: U.K. 26%; U.S. 17%; West Germany 12%; Japan 6%. Export destinations (excluding gold): U.K. 30%; Japan 13%; U.S. 8%; West Germany 6%. Main exports: diamonds 12%; wool

7%; nonferrous metals 10%; fruit and vegetables 8%.

Transport and Communications. Roads (1967) *c.* 350,000 km. (including 10,030 km. main roads). Motor vehicles in use (1967): passenger 1,316,000; commercial 342,000. Railways (1967): 19,762 km. (excluding South West Africa, 2,340 km.); freight traffic (including South West Africa) 45,671,000,000 net ton-km. Shipping (1967): merchant vessels 100 gross tons and over 230; gross tonnage 470,187. Air traffic (1967): 1,654,308,000 passenger-km.; freight 45,259,000 net ton-km. Telephones (Dec. 1966) 1,260,692. Radio receivers (Dec. 1965) 2.6 million.

Agriculture. Production (in 000; metric tons; 1967; 1966 in parentheses): corn 9,299 (4,907); wheat, farms and estates only 1,023 (567); sorghum (1966) 336, (1965) 438; oats 204 (98); raisins (1966) *c.* 9.9, (1965) *c.* 8.8; tobacco (1966) 29, (1965) 22; peanuts 422 (200); potatoes (1966) *c.* 430, (1965) *c.* 425; sugar, raw value (1967–68) *c.* 1,805, (1966–67) 1,628; oranges (1966) *c.* 510, (1965) *c.* 495; wine 420 (425); wool

(1966) *c.* 66, (1965) *c.* 72; meat (1966) 586, (1965) 574; milk (1966) *c.* 2,600, (1965) *c.* 2,540; butter (1966) 42, (1965) 42. Livestock (in 000; 1965–66): sheep *c.* 42,102; cattle *c.* 12,500; horses *c.* 460; pigs *c.* 1,500; goats *c.* 5,394; poultry, farms and estates *c.* 11,375. Fish catch (in 000; metric tons) (1966) 532, (1965) 664. Whaling: catch (1965–66) 4,148, (1964–65) 5,398; whale and sperm oil (1965–66) 16,000 metric tons, (1964–65) 18,000 metric tons.

Industry. Fuel and power (in 000; 1967): coal 49,367 metric tons; electricity 37,867,000 kw-hr. Production (in 000; metric tons; 1967): iron ore (60–65% metal content) 7,736; pig iron 3,600; crude steel 3,648; copper ore (metal content) 128; cement 4,011; asbestos (1966) 251; chrome ore (oxide content; 1966) 473; antimony concentrate (metal content; 1966) 11; manganese ore (metal content; 1966) 790; gold (1966) 30,530 troy oz.; diamonds (1966) 6,037 metric carats. New dwellings completed (private construction only in 18 principal urban areas; 1967) 12,000. Index of manufacturing production (1963 = 100): (1967) 138; (1966) 130.

Legislation enacted by the central Parliament in 1968 made provision for white entrepreneurs to start industries in the homelands as agents of Bantu development corporations appointed by the government for the different territories, under conditions which would prevent industrialists from acquiring a permanent footing there. Additional economic concessions were granted to industries located on the borders of the Bantu homelands where the Bantu employees could work in a "white" area while living in an adjoining homeland area. New regulations were enforced for the employment of migratory Bantu labour.

The Trade Union Council of South Africa, one of the major coordinating labour organizations, decided to allow Bantu unions, which could not be legally registered, to be affiliated members; and it advocated the official recognition of such unions and the granting to them of legal bargaining power on the basis of "the rate for the job." The government opposed the decisions, and several "white" unions resigned from the council.

A ban by the government on the appointment of a Bantu lecturer to the staff of the University of Cape Town, because of his race, was followed by a series of student protest demonstrations at several universities.

Foreign Affairs. Resolutions passed by large majorities condemning South Africa's race policies and administration of South West Africa continued to figure in the proceedings of the General Assembly of the UN at the end of 1967 and in 1968. A resolution adopted in December 1967 called, among other measures, for an international campaign against apartheid (South Africa's official policy of racial separation) and for Security Council action to force a change in that policy. In a report presented at the 1968 session, the UN Apartheid Committee declared that South Africa's policies and actions constituted a threat to international peace.

In regard to South West Africa, the General Assembly demanded the withdrawal of South Africa from the territory in compliance with the earlier UN decisions terminating South Africa's mandate. The South African government issued a White Paper in June declaring that, although the mandate had lapsed, the territory would continue to be administered in the spirit of its provisions. A series of constitutional and financial changes for the territory were proposed, and legislation for the development of self-government for the Bantu peoples was enacted. A legislative council for Ovamboland was opened in October, under a federal system representing the seven tribes in that area.

In accordance with the South African government's "outward policy" toward black African nations, diplomatic missions were exchanged with Malawi. Technical and other forms of assistance were given to Botswana and Lesotho. Extradition treaties, excluding political refugees, were signed with these states and with Swaziland, which became independent in September.

Because of Britain's embargo on the sale of arms to South Africa under a UN resolution, the minister of defense, P. W. Botha, stated in February that British defense forces would be denied the free use of dockyard and air facilities at the naval base of Simonstown except when it was considered to be in South African interests.

A decision by the International Olympic Committee to permit South Africa to compete in the 1968 Olympic Games in Mexico City, subject to satisfactory arrangements for the selection of racially mixed teams, was later revoked as a result of international agitation.

The Economy. The minister of finance, N. J. Diederichs, introducing the 1968 budget on March 27, said that its principal aim was to continue the struggle against inflation and that it embodied no dramatic change in fiscal policy or taxation. Relief was given to public servants, pensioners, farmers, and the family man. Assistance was given to marginal gold mines, and there were increased tax allowances to exporters under the policy of encouraging exports. An uncertain factor of significance, said the minister, was the future of the price of gold. Recent events, such as the devaluation of the British pound, the wave of speculation in gold, and the establishment of the two-tier gold price added to the uncertainties, but South Africa could face them with confidence. Concerning the future marketing of newly mined gold, South Africa would await events. Accordingly, gold was sold at intervals in limited quantities on the free market, at a premium which was distributed among gold producers. The bulk of the gold output was retained. Gold and foreign assets held by the Reserve Bank rose to R 902 million in October, compared with R 430 million in October 1967. Serious flooding in October at the West Dreifontein gold mine, South Africa's biggest, caused widespread repercussions in gold share markets.

Internally there was a large influx of foreign capital, and this added to the problems of excess liquidity. Exchange and import controls were relaxed; further credit restrictions were imposed on commercial banks; and tax-free investments were offered by the state and by building societies to stimulate savings. In August the Reserve Bank rate was reduced from 6 to 5.5%.

(L. H.)

See also Race Relations.
ENCYCLOPÆDIA BRITANNICA FILMS. *The Republic of South Africa* (1963).

Southeast Asia

As a region of nations that are small or underdeveloped or both, Southeast Asia is highly sensitive to outside influence. In 1968 North Vietnam was Communist, approximately but by no means entirely in the Chinese manner; Burma and Cambodia had tried since independence to steer a path between the demands of the contending great powers, Burma by remaining neutral so far as possible on every issue and Cambodia by playing Communist China and the U.S. off against each other. In the other countries the rulers' innate anti-Communism was reinforced by economic and military aid from the United States and other Western countries.

Southeast Asia Treaty Organization (SEATO). The cornerstone of Western military power in the region in 1954, when it was founded after the French defeat in Indochina, SEATO had by 1968 become a shadow of itself. The organization was based on the belief that Communist China might take overt military action against its neighbours, a belief supported by the Chinese intervention in Korea in 1950. But Communist expansionism had since taken other forms—subversion, insurgency, and infiltration, in which the hand of Peking was not always evident—and SEATO had proved unsuited to handle this problem.

The organization's 13th annual meeting, which opened at Wellington, N.Z., on April 2, closed with a declaration that Communist aggression in Southeast Asia "must not be allowed to succeed." However, if such aggression did occur, SEATO did not seem to

UPI COMPIX

Prince Norodom Sihanouk of Cambodia greeting an elderly citizen on Nov. 5, 1968, in Battambang where he was entertaining members of the diplomatic corps.

South Arabia: *see* Southern Yemen

be an organization capable of stopping it. Cracks in the alliance had appeared in 1962, during the civil war in Laos. U.S., British, Australian, and New Zealand troops were rushed to Thailand in that year, but France and Pakistan held back. This failure to achieve the unanimity required by the alliance caused the obligations of its members to be redefined as "individual as well as collective." Under this formula five SEATO members went to the assistance of South Vietnam, which was covered by the SEATO protocol, but not France (neutralist), Pakistan (an ally of China), or Britain (which felt militarily overextended already).

U.S. Pres. Lyndon B. Johnson's announcement of the cessation of the bombing over most of North Vietnam and his call for peace negotiations on March 31 again called in question the usefulness of SEATO as a framework for joint cooperative action. Not only did Johnson fail to consult the United States' SEATO allies, but his move also cast doubt on U.S. determination to stand firm in Vietnam and Southeast Asia. Dean Rusk, the U.S. secretary of state, who represented the U.S. at the SEATO meeting, only partly succeeded in convincing the allies that the U.S. had no intention of abandoning its commitments in the area. All the delegates were fully aware of the political and economic pressures on Washington to find a way out of the war.

SEATO's future was put further in doubt by Britain's decision to accelerate its military withdrawal from Asia (except for Hong Kong). This led to Britain's announcement that its commitment to SEATO would have to change. The defense White Paper published in July 1967 had envisaged completion of the pullout from Asia by the mid-1970s, but British Prime Minister Harold Wilson announced on Jan. 16, 1968, that the date was to be advanced to the end of 1971. This news caused dismay in Singapore, Malaysia, Australia, and New Zealand; during 1967 they had urgently reminded London of the fragility of peace in Southeast Asia and the contribution to its tranquility made by a British presence there.

Britain, it seemed, was ending an era for the sake of financial stability and in order to concentrate its political and military interests in Europe. That Britain should be prepared to do this despite its political ties and enormous economic stake in the East seemed especially ominous to the Asian SEATO countries.

At Wellington the SEATO nations, in an effort to conciliate U.S. opinion, "endorsed unreservedly" President Johnson's "bold and generous decision" for a degree of unilateral de-escalation of the fighting. In private, the Thais and South Vietnamese—the latter being present with the South Koreans to participate in a conference of nations fighting in Vietnam that succeeded the SEATO meeting—freely expressed their anxieties. Thanat Khoman, foreign minister of Thailand, was especially outspoken: Thailand might, he said, be wiser not to "put all its eggs in one basket"; *i.e.,* to rely on support from the U.S.

Association of Southeast Asian Nations. Proposals from Thailand for a SEATO joint security force and from the Philippines for an armed Association of Southeast Asian Nations (ASEAN) outside SEATO were coldly received. Nevertheless, Asian fears had to be allayed, and, if possible, Asians had to be taught to help themselves. Hence, the communiqués issued at Wellington expressed strong support for ASEAN. Thanat Khoman and Paul Hasluck, the Australian minister for external affairs, particularly

stressed the role ASEAN could play, Hasluck seeming to envisage cooperation for security purposes between ASEAN and SEATO.

All projects for regional cooperation in the underdeveloped world probably derive much of their impetus from a desire for nonalignment vis-à-vis the great powers, to which the Indonesians in particular gave expression. But most of the hopes placed in ASEAN were economic: for the liberalization of trade among members, harmonization of regional development, and provision of scope for projects likely to interest such international organizations as the Asian Development Bank and some UN agencies. Obviously, the disparity in the stages of economic growth reached by the various countries would cause difficulties. Nevertheless, such promising ideas as a payments union among member countries came up for discussion almost immediately, and the erection of an administrative framework of standing and other committees and a national secretariat in each country went quickly ahead.

The second ASEAN meeting of foreign ministers, held at Jakarta, Indon., in early August, drew up a list of inexpensive projects for immediate action, such as the exchange of information, experts, and training facilities. The ministers agreed to set up a number of permanent bodies to carry out projects in such fields as communications, shipping, food production, and aviation, and to study the possibility of establishing a central fund on which members could draw to finance development projects.

A suggestion from Tunku Abdul Rahman, prime minister of Malaysia, that ASEAN should merge with the Asian and Pacific Council (ASPAC) had no result. ASPAC, which was formed by Australia, Japan, South Korea, Malaysia, New Zealand, the Philippines, Taiwan, Thailand, and South Vietnam at Seoul in 1966, was primarily a forum for discussion of measures to be taken against Communist aggression. Its third ministerial meeting, held at Canberra, Austr., in late July, issued a communiqué emphasizing the Communist threat to Korea and the region generally.

The Philippines-Malaysia dispute over Sabah threw its shadow over ASEAN in 1968. Pres. Ferdinand Marcos of the Philippines signed a bill "annexing" Sabah, and immediately Malaysia abrogated an agreement by which it had helped to prevent the smuggling of cigarettes and other goods from Sabah into the Philippines. An ASEAN meeting to discuss cooperation in commerce and industry, due to open at Manila on September 23, was delayed for a week by Malaysia-Philippines dissension. ASEAN then agreed to form a group of experts to examine the possibility of a Southeast Asian common market, but Malaysia proved unresponsive, pleading its ties with the Commonwealth. At year's end the question of Sabah remained unsolved, although an agreement between the Philippine and Malaysian foreign ministers for a "cooling-off" period gave some hope of eventual settlement.

ASEAN indeed appeared to be falling victim to Southeast Asia's competitive nationalisms. These formed a problem with which powers outside the region also had to contend. Thus, when Britain, Australia, New Zealand, Malaysia, and Singapore met in June to discuss ways of filling the gap after the departure of the 30,000 British troops in the region, the conference was clouded by the bad feeling between Malaysia and Singapore. Tunku Abdul Rahman emphasized on this occasion the necessity of a "defense

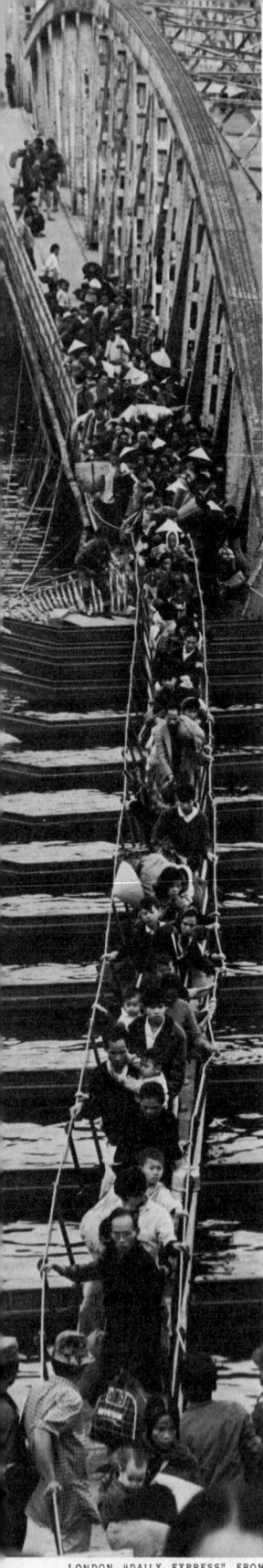

Vietnamese refugees fleeing across the Perfume River in Hue on a makeshift pontoon footbridge in February 1968 during the Viet Cong Tet offensive.

umbrella" for the region, but it remained doubtful how far Malaysia and Singapore would help themselves by cooperating to run the installations Britain would leave behind; they could hardly cooperate to run Malaysia-Singapore Airlines. Similarly, U.S. problems in Southeast Asia had been enormously increased by the impossibility of being friends with Thailand, Cambodia, and South Vietnam simultaneously.

A UN World Economic Survey published in mid-July indicated that all the ASEAN countries produced roughly the same commodities—tin, rubber, rice, and timber. Less than 21% of their trade was with one another, and their economies were competitive rather than complementary. These factors, together with Singapore's free port tradition, jeopardized the chances of a customs union. In short, the prospects for cooperation in the economic field seemed little better than in the political sphere. However, there was hope that multilateral groupings might serve to cushion national animosities.

Development Projects. The outstanding example of the above-mentioned groupings was the Mekong Development Scheme. Cambodia was at loggerheads with its three partners—Laos, Thailand, and South Vietnam—on the committee to develop this project, and did not even have diplomatic relations with the latter two; it was also determined to pursue "complete independence" before surrendering any sovereignty at all. In February 1966, and again in April 1967, Cambodia boycotted meetings of the committee. Nonetheless, work was completed on two projects in Thailand, the Nam Pung and Nam Pong dams, and was started on the Nam Ngum project, 43 mi. N of Vientiane in Laos. In 1968 the committee was trying to finance construction of a dam at Prek Thnot in Cambodia. A year earlier Prince Norodom Sihanouk of Cambodia had declared that he did not want the dam, to which U Thant, secretary-general of the UN, replied that unless the prince reconsidered his policy, Cambodia could no longer expect to benefit from the outside financial aid supplied to the committee. In August, Sihanouk informed U Thant that the Prek Thnot project was too advantageous to Cambodia to be abandoned. An agreement on financing of the dam was signed by 11 nations in November.

By early 1968 the Mekong Committee was receiving aid from 23 countries, a dozen UN agencies, four foundations, and a number of private business organizations; more than $135 million had been collected or promised, nearly a third of it by the Mekong countries themselves, for the financing of approximately 70 projects. During the year the main projects under study were a dam at Pa Mong, to span the river between Laos and Thailand just above Vientiane, and two dams in Cambodia, at Sambor, 140 mi. above Phnom Penh, and on the Tonle Sap. An alternative was a project for a large mainstream dam at Stung Treng in Cambodia, from which both Cambodia and South Vietnam might be expected to benefit enormously in terms of flood control and irrigation.

Cambodia's attitude to these projects remained uncertain but was probably less intransigent than was Burma's toward the Asian Highway. By the end of 1967 about 35,000 mi. of this had been completed, chiefly by the improvement of existing roads, but a long gap remained in the middle owing to Burma's refusal to allow any sort of transport through its territory.

The Colombo Plan for Cooperative Economic Development in South and East Asia, inaugurated in Colombo, Ceylon, in 1950, continued its attempts to combine multilateral and bilateral approaches. While it studied the problems of Southeast Asia as a whole and kept them in view when working out regional requirements, negotiations for assistance were made directly between donor and receiving countries. The multilateral approach was embodied mainly in the annual meetings of the plan's Consultative Committee, of which the 18th was held at Rangoon from Nov. 21 to Dec. 8, 1967. The meeting was primarily devoted to the topic of increasing food supplies in the region. The plan provided a major channel through which its "donor" members—Australia, Britain, Canada, Japan, New Zealand, and the United States—could give aid to the countries of the region.

The UN Economic Commission for Asia and the Far East (ECAFE, founded at Shanghai in 1947 and located at Bangkok, Thailand, since 1949) held its 24th conference at Canberra in April, with 29 nations attending. The economic survey that served as a working paper for the meeting remarked that the region's problems had been alleviated to a large degree by the $1 billion a year currently being injected into

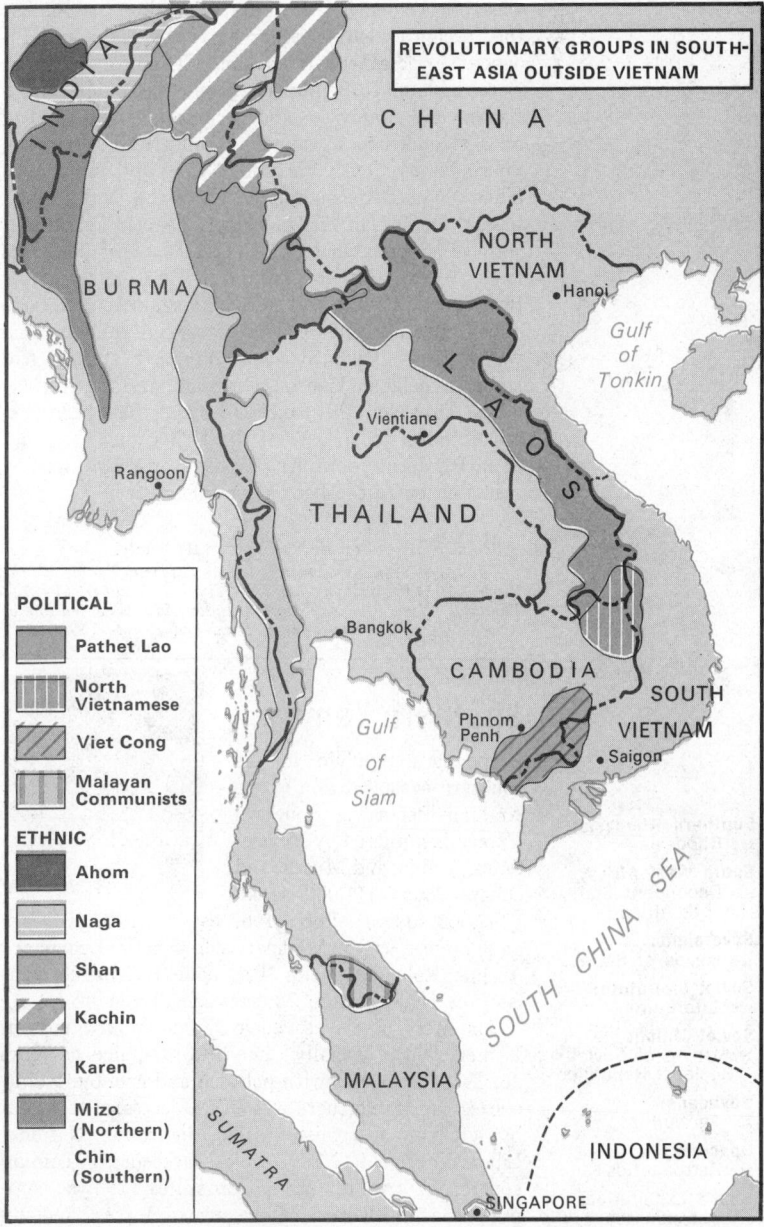

REVOLUTIONARY GROUPS IN SOUTHEAST ASIA OUTSIDE VIETNAM

POLITICAL
- Pathet Lao
- North Vietnamese
- Viet Cong
- Malayan Communists

ETHNIC
- Ahom
- Naga
- Shan
- Kachin
- Karen
- Mizo (Northern) Chin (Southern)

its trading economy by the requirements of the Vietnam war. An end to the war would almost certainly present serious difficulties for the economies of Taiwan, South Korea, Singapore, and Thailand in particular. As it was, the great desire to import goods by the region's developing countries, basically a consequence of their desire for a "modern" economic and cultural life, had caused a serious expansion of trading deficits. Despite the call of U Nyun, ECAFE's executive secretary, for an "action-oriented" approach, few concrete proposals were approved. One was for establishment of a regional trade promotion centre in Bangkok; another was that the UN be requested to increase its allotment of funds for economic development in the region.

Perhaps ECAFE's most useful achievement was the launching on Aug. 22, 1966, of the Asian Development Bank, whose membership was limited to members or associate members of ECAFE or to governments belonging to the UN or its specialized agencies; Communist China, North Vietnam, and North Korea were thus excluded. The bank opened for business on Dec. 19, 1966, with its headquarters at Manila. The first loan from the bank's ordinary capital resources was approved on Jan. 25, 1968: $5 million to augment the foreign exchange resources of the Industrial Finance Corporation of Thailand. Three more loans were made up to September 1968—to Ceylon, South Korea, and Malaysia; and technical assistance had been extended to a number of countries—Indonesia, South Korea, South Vietnam, Nepal, and the Philippines. Some criticism was heard of the bank's slowness in lending, but its president, Takeshi Watanabe, stated in September that he expected the value of its loans to reach $50–$60 million in 1968, to be double that figure in 1969, and to double again in 1970. He added that concrete pledges of special funds, which would be available for loans on "soft" terms, had come from Japan, Canada, Denmark, and the Netherlands. However, the bank's members had been disappointed at the failure of the U.S. Congress to act upon President Johnson's proposal for a $200 million contribution to the bank's special funds.

(P. H. M. J.)

See also articles on the various political units.

ENCYCLOPÆDIA BRITANNICA FILMS. *Burma, People of the River* (1957); *Malaya, Land of Tin and Rubber* (1957); *Thailand, Land of Rice* (1957); *Indonesia—New Nation of Asia* (1959); *The Philippines: Land and People* (1960).

Southern Yemen

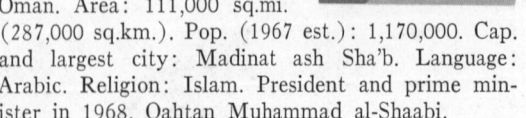

A people's republic in the southern coastal region of the Arabian Peninsula, Southern Yemen is bordered by Yemen, Saudi Arabia, and Muscat and Oman. Area: 111,000 sq.mi. (287,000 sq.km.). Pop. (1967 est.): 1,170,000. Cap. and largest city: Madinat ash Sha'b. Language: Arabic. Religion: Islam. President and prime minister in 1968, Qahtan Muhammad al-Shaabi.

The first year of the People's Republic of Southern Yemen, which officially came into existence on Nov. 30, 1967, was beset with political and economic difficulties. In March there was an unsuccessful rebellion by left-wing extremists within the ruling National Liberation Front (NLF), which succeeded in gaining control of two eastern governorates. It was suppressed with the aid of the armed forces, and six

weeks later President al-Shaabi (*see* BIOGRAPHY) felt strong enough to declare a general amnesty. But in May there was another left-wing revolt, led by the minister of justice, Abd-al-Mahfoudh Khalifa, which temporarily gained control of three towns east of Aden. In September a violent dispute within the Army led to the exiling to Algeria of 22 officers.

In the summer matters looked serious for the NLF regime as there were signs of joint action between its former rival, the Front for the Liberation of Occupied South Yemen, the conservative South Arabian League, and the republican government of Yemen, which was reported to be alarmed by the activities of left-wing extremists in Southern Yemen. However, President al-Shaabi's government held talks with the Yemeni government in August, and its forces joined hands with the republicans against Yemeni royalists who had occupied the town of Harib on the border between the two republics.

Relations with Britain were unsatisfactory. In February the government expelled all British military experts who had remained with the Southern Yemeni forces, and in May talks with Britain in Aden on a financial settlement ended in failure. Southern Yemen was asking for £60 million over three years as compensation for Britain's alleged exploitation and distortion of the South Arabian economy, but Britain was offering £1 million. With the removal of the British military base and the closing of the Suez Canal, the republic's economy was in a perilous condition. In May the government announced sharp tax increases to help the budgetary position. (P. MD.)

Spain

A nominal monarchy of southwest Europe, Spain is bounded by Portugal, with which it shares the Iberian Peninsula, and by France. Area: 194,884 sq.mi. (504,-750 sq.km.), including the Balearic and Canary islands. Pop. (1968 est.): 32,411,407, including the Balearics and Canaries. Cap. and largest city: Madrid (pop., 1967 est., 2,680,769). Language: Spanish. Religion: Roman Catholic. Chief of state and premier in 1968, Gen. Francisco Franco Bahamonde.

Contrary to expectations, no political announcements were made during 1968, and Prince Juan Carlos' 30th birthday in January was not followed by his installation as king, a decision that General Franco had

hinted at years earlier. Considerable monarchist feeling, however, was expressed when the dowager queen, Victoria Eugénie, visited Spain in February after 37 years in exile, and the expulsion in December of Prince Xavier de Bourbon-Parma and his son Prince Carlos Hugo seemed to foreshadow the imminent nomination of Prince Juan Carlos as Franco's successor. In the Basque provinces, nationalism created considerable turmoil. In April San Sebastián in the Basque region was cordoned off by a massive display of police force to prevent a nationalist demonstration, and in August the whole primarily Basque province of Guipúzcoa was put under a "state of emergency."

The year was one of marked student unrest in Spain. A series of incidents in the early months culminated in May Day demonstrations shared by many workers but repressed by the police. The academic year was all but lost for many in the higher education centres, but the students scored two victories: the replacement of the minister of education and science in April, and, in September, the right to set up their own unions (*i.e.,* free of state control) and to participate in the ruling bodies of universities and technical schools. By the end of the year, however, there had been no rush for new unions to be formed and the students were still in a militant mood. A portrait of Franco was burned by University of Madrid students on October 31, and they sacked the office of the dean of the law faculty. As a result, the authorities closed the university for a few days. The workers, encouraged by the illegal though increasingly strong *comisiones obreras* (workers' committees), kept pressing for reforms, and at the plenary session of the state-controlled *sindicatos* (unions), proposals were made that union officials should in the future be elected rather than appointed. The press also ran into difficulties, and several measures taken during the year pointed to a hardening of the official attitude in the interpretation of the so-called "freedom of the press" in operation since 1966. In May the afternoon daily *Madrid* was suspended for several months and its editor heavily fined, allegedly for other charges, but in fact for the publication of an article criticizing French Pres. Charles de Gaulle as an old man "clinging obstinately" to power which left the readers in no doubt as to the intended parallel with Franco.

Throughout 1968 the economy moved under the effects of the change in the parity of the peseta adopted on Nov. 19, 1967, the day after the British devaluation. The change (from 60 to 70 pesetas to the U.S. dollar) was immediately supplemented by a series of austerity measures. These included a severe restraint on government spending; a freeze until the end of 1968 at predevaluation levels of wages and salaries, rents, dividends, and prices; a rise in taxation affecting company profits; an increase in the Banco de España discount rate; and duty reductions combined with official subsidies on imports of certain foods, raw materials, and other products. These measures kept prices stable in December 1967, but even so the cost of living showed an increase of 6.5% for the whole of the year.

When 1968 began it was expected that measures would be taken to restore economic growth to the fast pace achieved in the early 1960s. Outstanding among those should have been the launching of the 1968–71 *Plan de Desarrollo* as the successor to the first four-year plan that had just ended. Devaluation, however, by upsetting the statistics on which many of the projections were based, forced the authorities first to postpone the launching of the plan for three months and later to leave it in abeyance until the end of the year, when it was published in a revised form. The economy, left to its own devices virtually all year, was slow to show improvement. Lack of confidence in the immediate future restrained investment, and except for shipbuilding, electricity, construction, and chemicals, industry showed little recovery. For agriculture, the 1967–68 season was a good one, despite setbacks in citrus fruit and olives, but the prospects of good crops were felt only over the second half of the year when agricultural produce began to be marketed. Where the benefit of the austerity measures showed more clearly was in the cost of living, which rose by only 1.3% in the first eight months. Price increases were, nevertheless, expected in the last quarter, partly because certain wage readjustments were allowed in October despite the general wage freeze. Foreign trade, spurred by devaluation, was showing substantial improvement, with exports rising by 14.5% and imports falling by 3.5% in the first nine months, while tourist income and long-term capital

GAMMA—PIX FROM PUBLIX

Policemen patrolling the streets of Madrid as workers participated in silent demonstrations against Franco's regime to celebrate May Day in 1968.

SPAIN

Education. (1965–66) Primary, pupils 3,357,-813, teachers (1964–65) 107,627; secondary, pupils 800,380, teachers (1964–65) 25,725; vocational, pupils 292,071, teachers 13,941; teacher training, students 64,316, teachers 1,022; higher (including 15 universities), students 125,879, teaching staff (1964–65) 6,096.

Finance. Monetary unit: peseta, with a par value of 70 pesetas to U.S. $1 (168 pesetas = £1 sterling). Gold and foreign exchange, official: (June 1968) U.S. $959 million; (June 1967) U.S. $990 million. Budget (1968–69) balanced at 224 billion pesetas. Gross national product: (1966) 1,474,000,000,000 pesetas; (1965) 1,-287,000,000,000 pesetas. Money supply: (May 1968) 546.6 billion pesetas; (May 1967) 486.6 billion pesetas. Cost of living (1963 = 100): (May 1968) 144; (May 1967) 137.

Foreign Trade. (1967) Imports 241,920,000,-000 pesetas; exports 96,880,000,000 pesetas. Import sources: EEC 37% (West Germany 14%, France 11%, Italy 7%); U.S. 17%; U.K. 9%. Export destinations: EEC 32% (West Germany 10%, France 10%, Netherlands 5%, Italy 5%); U.S. 15%; U.K. 10%. Main exports: citrus fruit 10%; vegetables 8%; machinery 7%; chemicals 6%; petroleum products 5%. Tourism (1966):

visitors 15,835,300; receipts 74,742,000,000 pesetas.

Transport and Communications. Roads (1966) 131,808 km. (including 60 km. expressways). Motor vehicles in use (1966): passenger 1,052,506; commercial 444,035. Railways: (1966) 17,336 km. (including 3,788 km. electrified); traffic (state system only; 1967) 12,-440,000,000 passenger-km., freight 8,727,000,000 net ton-km. Shipping (1967): merchant vessels 100 gross tons and over 1,969; gross tonnage 2,570,890. Air traffic (1967): 3,071,295,000 passenger-km.; freight 54,582,000 net ton-km. Telephones (Dec. 1966) 3,053,879. Radio receivers (Dec. 1966) 6,010,000. Television receivers (Dec. 1966) *c.* 2,325,000.

Agriculture. Production (in 000; metric tons; 1967; 1966 in parentheses): wheat 5,602 (4,-812); barley 2,632 (2,006); oats 492 (419); rye 336 (353); corn 1,178 (1,154); potatoes 4,197 (4,423); rice 367 (375); chick-peas 149 (127); lentils (1966) 38, (1965) 23; dry beans (1966) 124, (1965) 118; dry broad beans 130 (126); tomatoes (1966) 1,296, (1965) 1,330; apples 320 (362); oranges 2,079 (2,329); lemons 72 (89); sugar, raw value (1967–68) 582,

(1966–67) *c.* 617; olive oil 300 (464); wine 2,358 (3,240); onions 774 (768); bananas (1966) 350, (1965) 372; dates (1966) 21, (1965) 18; figs (1966) 158, (1965) 147; tobacco (1966) 26, (1965) 34; cotton, lint 66 (89); meat (1966) 595, (1965) 577. Livestock (in 000; 1965–66): horses 305; mules 694; asses 442; cattle (1966–67) 3,844; sheep 18,-785; goats 2,309; chickens 39,186. Fish catch (in 000; metric tons) (1966) 1,357, (1965) 1,341.

Industry. Fuel and power (in 000; metric tons; 1967): coal 11,753; lignite 2,435; electricity 40,013,000 kw-hr.; manufactured gas 542,000 cu.m. Production (in 000; metric tons; 1967): iron ore (50% metal content) 5,085; pig iron 2,764; crude steel 4,521; manganese ore (metal content; 1966) 6.2; zinc 70; copper 72; lead 52; cement 12,970; potash (oxide content; 1965) 431; sulfur (1966) 1,129; cotton yarn 121; cotton fabrics 109; wool yarn 33; rayon filament yarn 18; rayon staple fibre 27. Merchant vessels launched (100 gross tons and over; 1967) 401,000 gross tons. Index of industrial production (1963 = 100): (1967) 144; (1966) 140.

investment were also well above the 1967 levels. All these factors taken into account, it was estimated that the balance of payments would be in equilibrium by the end of 1968, a considerable feat when contrasted with the deficit of $125 million in 1967.

In international relations the most important event was the decision taken by the Spanish government not to renew the last of the military agreements with the U.S. in operation since 1953, which lapsed September 26. Conversations held in Washington, D.C., failed to yield positive results, but both sides left the door open for further negotiations. If no agreement was reached by March 26, 1969, the U.S. would have one year to dismantle its military installations in Spain. Another important decision was the granting of independence to Equatorial Guinea on October 12. (*See* EQUATORIAL GUINEA.)   (M. Pu.)

ENCYCLOPÆDIA BRITANNICA FILMS. *People of Spain* (1955); *Spanish Children* (1964).

Speleology

As a result of further survey in 1968, the Flint Ridge Cave System in Kentucky became the longest known cave in the world at 63.18 mi. The Hölloch (Switzerland), previously the longest, was explored further but its total length was still only 61.1 mi.

There was still some doubt as to which was the deepest cave. The 1967 expedition to the Gouffre Berger (France) measured a depth of 3,786 ft., but in 1968 this was revised to 3,755 ft. by the Spéléo-Club de la Seine. More accurate surveys on the surface showed that the bottom of the cave could be more than 3,700 ft. lower than the entrance. The Gouffre de la Pierre Saint-Martin in the French Pyrenees, at 3,779 ft., would thus appear to hold the record. However, French explorers discovered a cave in the Sornin Plateau (Isère), the Gouffre d'Engins, which might be deeper.

A group of British speleologists was reported to have reached a depth of 3,000 ft. in the Grotta di Eolo in Tuscany, which thus became the deepest known cave in Italy and the third deepest in the world. Cavers from Texas explored a new deep cave in Mexico; they were stopped by a wet pitch at a depth of about 2,000 ft., but the water from the cave did not come to the surface until 4,000 ft. below this, so further attempts were expected.

A British Army expedition from the 16th Parachute Brigade reached the bottom of the Proventina pothole in Greece, at 1,350 ft. The entrance shaft, a sheer drop of 1,298 ft., was the deepest known single pitch in the world. The Association for Mexican Cave Studies, from the U.S., explored the Sotano de las Golondrinas and claimed that its entrance pitch of 1,070 ft. was the second deepest. It was not clear if this was so, however; the Gouffre de la Pierre Saint-Martin was a contender and, although its entrance pitch was commonly said to be 1,017 ft. deep, the explorers who descended it by winch measured it as 1,091 ft. This entrance shaft of the Pierre Saint-Martin cave was descended by a U.S. party using a single rope and no winch. They descended by rappelling and climbed by a technique using Prusik knots, which take the weight of the climber but can be slid freely up the main rope.

A large new cave was discovered in Banff National Park, Canada. An expedition from McMaster University, Hamilton, Ont., spent six days in it and estimated its total length to be 12 mi. or more, by far the

longest cave in Canada. The Nakimu Cave (Canada) was explored further during a four-day underground camp in 1967, in midwinter when many of the formations in the cave were of ice. The party was flown to the cave by helicopter and the bottom was reached at a depth of 850 ft. A British expedition to Norway explored a connection between the Okshola and Kristihola caves; their combined length of 11,000 ft. made this the longest known cave in Norway. Caves formed in gypsum are not common and a new discovery in 1968, Parks' Ranch Cave, 8,700 ft. long, was now the biggest gypsum cave known in the U.S. In Australia the deepest known cave, Mini Martin, was now 720 ft. It contains a 360-ft. pitch.

An important new discovery was made at Gaping Gill (Yorkshire, Eng.); 9,000 ft. of passage was entered, leading to within 100 yd. of Ingleborough Cave where the Gaping Gill stream reappears. The cave was now known to be about 6½ mi. long. An underground camp in Dan-yr-Ogof (South Wales) at Easter aided the discovery of several thousand feet of passage. New passages found in Ogof Ffynnon Ddu (South Wales) increased the total vertical extent of the cave to 870 ft., making it the deepest in Britain. A new extension of Gingling Hole on Fountains Fell made this cave 580 ft. deep and the deepest in Yorkshire.

The record for the longest stay underground stood at 181 days, completed by Jean-Pierre Mairetet on Nov. 29, 1966.

Caves of scientific importance continued to be threatened by quarrying and by contamination that might destroy the animal life in them. The Batu Caves Protection Association was formed in Malaysia to preserve this cave area as an attractive feature close to Kuala Lumpur. Shelta Cave in Alabama was bought by the National Speleological Society to protect it.

The Petralona Cave near Salonika, Greece, is an extensive stalactite cave containing Pleistocene animal remains. Among these a skull of Neanderthal man was found, the first to be discovered in Greece. Prehistoric Olmec paintings (800–400 B.C.) were discovered in the Juxtlahuaca Cave in Mexico.

Pollen analysis research enabled the permanent ice in the Dachstein-Rieseneishöhle (Austria) to be dated. The oldest ice there was formed in the 13th or 14th century A.D. In France, Michel Cabidoche was awarded a doctorate for his researches on cave fauna in the Pyrenees.

The newly found manuscript diaries (1839–74) of William Metcalf describe historic early visits, previously unknown, to the caves of Yorkshire. Thus Gaping Gill was first explored in 1846, 49 years before Edouard A. Martel's famous descent. The hundredth anniversary of William Beard's death fell in 1968; he was well known for over 40 years as the discoverer and proprietor of the Banwell Bone Cave (England). His collection of fossil bones was in the Taunton Museum. The year also marked the 150th anniversary of the publication of William Westall's classic book of engravings, *Views of the Caves near Ingleton.* . . .

The most important book on speleology to appear in 1968 was *Höhlen-Kunde* by H. Trimmel, an authoritative work on many aspects of the subject. A valuable study of the caves of the Nullarbor Plain, Australia, was published by the Speleological Research Council of the University of Sydney. The University of Bristol Spelaéological Society published a book on the karst geomorphology of *The Caves of North-West Clare, Ireland*—the result of 20 years' work in which 35 mi. of caves were surveyed.   (T. R. Sh.)

Yves Peter is rescued from a ledge in Berger Cave (France) where he fell while exploring the chasm with 19 other cave explorers in August 1968.

Sporting Record

ARCHERY

Event	Winner	Country
EUROPEAN CHAMPIONS		
Men's individual	K. Laasonen	Finland
Women's individual	M. Maczynska	Poland
Men's team		U.K.
Women's team		Poland
U.S. CHAMPIONS		
Men	H. Ward	
Women	V. Cook	

AVIATION CONTESTS

Event	Winner	Country
AEROBATICS		
WORLD CHAMPIONSHIPS		
Men	P. Kahle	East Germany
Women	M. Delacroix	France
Team		East Germany
Men's figures*	I. Yegorov	U.S.S.R.
Men's overall*	P. Kahle	East Germany
Women's figures*	M. Fleck	East Germany
Women's overall*	M. Fleck	East Germany

*Results unofficial, events being abandoned on account of unfavourable weather.

Event	Winner	Country
GLIDING		
WORLD CHAMPIONS		
Open class	H. Woedl	Austria
Standard class	A. Smith	U.S.

BADMINTON

Event	Winner	Country
FRENCH OPEN CHAMPIONS		
Men's singles	S. Jonsson	Sweden
Men's doubles	H. Losch, G. Kucki	West Germany
Women's singles	E. Twedberg	Sweden
Women's doubles	E. Twedberg, K. Dittberner	Sweden, West Germany
Mixed doubles	H. Liedelmeyer, J. Termetz	Netherlands
EUROPEAN CHAMPIONS		
Men's singles	S. Jonsson	Sweden
Men's doubles	D. Eddy, R. Powell	U.K.
Women's singles	I. Latz	West Germany
Women's doubles	M. Boxall, S. Pound	U.K.
Mixed doubles	A. Jordan, S. Pound	U.K.
ALL-ENGLAND CHAMPIONS		
Men's singles	R. Hartono	Indonesia
Men's doubles	H. Borch, E. Kops	Denmark
Women's singles	E. Twedberg	Sweden
Women's doubles	R. Minarni, R. Koestijah	Indonesia
Mixed doubles	A. Jordan, S. Pound	U.K.
ENGLISH NATIONAL CHAMPIONS		
Men's singles	R. Sharp	
Men's doubles	C. Beacom, A. Jordan	
Women's singles	A. Bairstow	
Women's doubles	M. Boxall, S. Pound	
Mixed doubles	R. Mills, G. Perrin	
NORDIC CHAMPIONS		
Men's singles	E. Kops	Denmark
Men's doubles	P. Walsoe, S. Andersen	Denmark
Women's singles	J. Foege	Denmark
Women's doubles	P. Moelgaard Hansen, A. Flindt	Denmark
Mixed doubles	P. Nielsen, P. Moelgaard Hansen	Denmark
U.S. CHAMPIONS		
Men's singles	C. Ratana Saeng Suang	Thailand
Men's doubles	J. Poole, D. Paup	U.S.
Women's singles	T. Barinaga	U.S.
Women's doubles	H. Tibbetts, T. Barinaga	U.S.
Mixed doubles	L. Saben, C. Starkey	U.S.

BILLIARDS AND SNOOKER

Event	Winner	Country
BILLIARDS		
European 71/2 championship	R. Ceulemans	Belgium
World professional championship	R. Williams	U.K.
World cushion championship	R. Ceulemans	Belgium
European 47/2 championship	H. Scholte	Netherlands
World pocket championship	I. Crane	U.S.
U.S. open championship	J. Baisis	U.S.
SNOOKER		
World professional championship	J. Pulman	U.K.
World amateur championship	D. Taylor	U.K.
U.K. amateur championship	D. Taylor	U.K.

BOBSLEDDING

Event	Winner	Country
European two-man championship	W. Zimmerer, P. Utzenschneider	West Germany
European four-man championship	J. Wicki, H. Candrian, W. Hofmann, W. Graf	Switzerland
North American two-man championship	C. McDonald, J. Handley	U.S.
North American four-man championship	L. Fenner, A. Hatchigan, J. Dezalia, A. Lowe	U.S.

CHECKERS

Event	Winner	Country
World champion	A. Andreiko	U.S.S.R.

CROSS-COUNTRY

Event	Winner	Country
INTERNATIONAL CHAMPIONS		
Senior, individual	M. Gammoudi	Tunisia
Senior, team		England
Junior, individual	J. Bednarski	England
Junior, team		England
Women, individual	D. Brown	U.S.
Women, team		U.S.
NATIONAL CHAMPIONS		
Belgium	G. Roelants	
England	R. Hill	
France	J. Wadoux	
Morocco	B. El Ghazi	
Northern Ireland	D. Graham	
Scotland	J. L. Stewart	
Spain	M. Haro	
U.S.	K. Moore	
Wales	A. Joslyn	

CURLING

Event	City or country
WORLD CHAMPIONS	
Men	Canada
U.S. CHAMPIONS	
Men	Superior (Wisconsin)
Women	St. Paul (Minnesota)

CYCLING

Event	Winner	Country
WORLD CHAMPIONS—TRACK		
Professional sprint	G. Beghetto	Italy
Professional individual pursuit	H. Porter	U.K.
Professional motor-paced	L. Proost	Belgium
Amateur motor-paced	G. Grassi	Italy
Amateur sprint	L. Borghetti	Italy
Amateur 4,000-m. pursuit	M. Frey	Denmark
WORLD CHAMPIONS—ROAD		
Professional, men	V. Adorni	Italy
Amateur, men	V. Marcelli	Italy
MAJOR RACE WINNERS		
Baracchi Trophy	F. Bracke, E. Merckx	Belgium
Tour of Mexico	A. Pachon	Colombia
Tour of Sardinia	E. Merckx	Belgium
Paris–Nice	R. Wolfshohl	West Germany
Milan–San Remo	R. Altig	West Germany
French national criterium	R. Poulidor	France
Paris–Roubaix	E. Merckx	Belgium
Flèche Wallonne	R. Van Looy	Belgium
Ghent–Wevelghem	W. Godefroot	Belgium
Liège–Bastogne–Liège	V. Van Sweefelt	Belgium
Berlin–Prague–Warsaw	A. Peschel	East Germany
Tour of Britain	G. Pettersen	Sweden
Tour of Italy	E. Merckx	Belgium
Manx international road race	J. Bettinson	U.K.
Manx professional road race	A. Metcalfe	U.K.
Tour de France	J. Janssen	Netherlands
Tour of Switzerland	L. Pffeninger	Switzerland
Tour of Spain	F. Gimondi	Italy
NATIONAL ROAD CHAMPIONS		
Belgium	J. Stevens	
France	L. Aimar	
Great Britain	C. Lewis	
Luxembourg	E. Schutz	
Netherlands	L. Dolman	
Spain	L. Ocana	
Switzerland	K. Brand	
West Germany	R. Wolfshohl	
Italy	F. Gimondi	
CYCLO-CROSS WORLD CHAMPIONS		
Professional, individual	E. de Vlaeminck	Belgium
Professional, team		Belgium
Amateur, individual	R. de Vlaeminck	Belgium
Amateur, team		Belgium

Event	Competitor, country	Performance
WORLD RECORDS SET IN 1968		
PROFESSIONAL		
5,000-m. individual pursuit	O. Ritter, Denmark	5 min. 57.4 sec.
5 km.	O. Ritter, Denmark	5 min. 51.6 sec.
10 km.	O. Ritter, Denmark	11 min. 58.4 sec.
20 km.	O. Ritter, Denmark	24 min. 17.4 sec.
1 hr.	O. Ritter, Denmark	48.66 km.
AMATEUR		
1,000-m. time trial	P. Trentin, France	1 min. 03.91 sec.
100-km. team time trial	G., T., E., and S.	
	Pettersen, Sweden	1 hr. 57 min. 8.2 sec.
3,000-m. individual pursuit, women	M. Tartagni, Italy	4 min. 10.8 sec.
4,000-m. individual pursuit	M. Frey, Denmark	4 min. 37.54 sec.
4,000-m. team pursuit	West Germany	4 min. 15.76 sec.
4,000-m. indoor pursuit	R. Kratzer,	
	West Germany	4 min. 57.59 sec.

EQUESTRIAN SPORTS

Event	Winner	Country
MAJOR EVENT WINNERS		
European junior show jumping		
championship	Ann Moore	U.K.
Burghley three-day event	Sheila Willcox	U.K.
European men's show jumping		
championship	P. d'Inzeo	Italy
European women's show jumping		
championship	Anneli Drummond-Hay	U.K.
Badminton three-day event	Jane Bullen	U.K.

FENCING

Event	Winner	Country
WORLD JUNIOR CHAMPIONS		
Men's foil	J. Kaczmarek	Poland
Men's épée	I. Samochkin	U.S.S.R.
Men's sabre	V. Krovupuskov	U.S.S.R.
Women's foil	N. Kozlenko	U.S.S.R.
EUROPEAN CHAMPIONS' CUP WINNERS		
Men's team épée	Dynamo Moscow	U.S.S.R.
U.S. NATIONAL CHAMPIONS		
Men's foil	H. Okawa	Japan
Men's épée	P. Pesthy	U.S.
Men's sabre	J. Keane	U.S.
Women's épée	J. Romary	U.S.
AMATEUR FENCING ASSOCIATION		
NATIONAL CHAMPIONS (U.K.)		
Men's foil	G. Paul	
Men's épée	R. Johnson	
Men's sabre	A. Leckie	
Women's foil	S. Green	

FISHING

Event	Winner	Country
World champion, individual	G. Grebenstern	West Germany
World champion, team		France
U.K. champion, individual	D. Groom	
U.K. champion, team	Leighton Buzzard	
U.S. champion, all-round	Z. Willson, Jr.	

FOOTBALL

Event	Winner	Country
ASSOCIATION FOOTBALL		
MAJOR TOURNAMENT WINNERS		
Inter-Continental Club Championship		
Cup (1967)	Racing, Buenos Aires	Argentina
European Championship	Italy	
European Champions' Cup	Manchester United	England
European Cup-winners' Cup	AC Milan	Italy
Inter-Cities Fairs' Cup	Leeds United	England
South American Club Championship		
Cup	Estudiantes de La Plata	Argentina
African Champions' Cup	Cape Coast Dwarfs	Ghana
Football League Cup	Leeds United	England
African Nations' Cup	Congo (Kinshasa)	
UEFA Youth Tournament	Czechoslovakia	
Asian Nations' Cup	Iran	
British Isles Championship	England	
NATIONAL CUP WINNERS		
Albania	FC Partizan	
Austria	Rapid Vienna	
Belgium	FC Bruges	
Brazil	Palmeiras	
Bulgaria	Spartak Sofia	
Czechoslovakia	Slovan Bratislava	
Denmark	Randers Freja	
East Germany	Union Berlin	
England	West Bromwich Albion	
France	St. Étienne	
Greece	Olympiakos Piraeus	
Hungary	Vasa Gyor	
Iceland	KR Reykjavik	
Ireland	Shamrock Rovers	
Italy	Torino	
Luxembourg	Ruemilingen	
Netherlands	ADO	
Northern Ireland	Crusaders	

Event	Winner
Norway	Lyn Oslo
Poland	Gornik Zabrze
Portugal	Porto
Romania	Dynamo Bucharest
Scotland	Dunfermline
Spain	Barcelona
Sweden	Malmö FF
Switzerland	FC Lugano
Turkey	Altay Izmir
U.S.S.R.	Dynamo Moscow
Wales	Cardiff City
Yugoslavia	Red Star, Belgrade
NATIONAL LEAGUE CHAMPIONS	
Argentina	San Lorenzo
Austria	Rapid Vienna
Belgium	RSC Anderlecht
Bolivia	Wilstermann Cochabamba
Brazil (Rio Grande League)	Gremio de Porto Alegre
Brazil (Pernambuco League)	Nautico de Recife
Brazil (Metropolitan Carioca	
League)	Botafogo
Brazil (São Paulo League)	Santos
Brazil (Minas Gerais League)	Cruzeiro de Belo Horizonte
Bulgaria	Levski Sofia
Chile	Universidad de Chile
Colombia	Magdalena
Costa Rica	Deportivo Saprissa
Czechoslovakia	Spartak Trnava
Denmark	Academisk Boldklub
East Germany	Carl Zeiss, Jena
Ecuador	Nacional Quito
England	Manchester City
France	St. Étienne
Greece	AEK Athens
Iceland	FC Valur
Ireland	Waterford
Italy	AC Milan
Luxembourg	Jeunesse d'Esch
Mexico	Toluca
Netherlands	Ajax Amsterdam
Northern Ireland	Glentoran
Norway	Rosenborg Trondheim
Paraguay	Guarani
Peru	Universitario do Deportos
Poland	Ruch Chorzow
Portugal	Benfica
Romania	Steau Bucharest
Scotland	Glasgow Celtic
Spain	Real Madrid
Switzerland	FC Zürich
Turkey	Fenerbache
Uruguay	Penarol Montevideo
U.S.S.R.	Dynamo Kiev
U.S. (North American	
Soccer League)	Atlanta Chiefs
Venezuela	Deportivo Portugeses
West Germany	FC Nürnberg
Yugoslavia	Red Star, Belgrade

Event	Winner	Country
RUGBY UNION		
International Championship		France
RUGBY LEAGUE		
World Cup		Australia
Rugby League Cup	Leeds	U.K.

GYMNASTICS

Event	Winner	Country
ARTISTIC GYMNASTICS		
World champion (women)	E. Karpukhina	U.S.S.R.
U.S.S.R. CHAMPIONS		
Men	M. Voronin	
Women	N. Kuchinskaya	
U.S. (AAU) CHAMPIONS		
Men	M. Sakamoto	
Women	L. Metheny	
BRITISH CHAMPIONS		
Men	M. Booth	
Women	M. Bell	

HANDBALL

Event	Winner	Country
European Champion Clubs' Cup		
(indoors)	Steau Bucharest	Romania
European Champion Clubs' Cup, women		
(indoors)	Zhalgiris Kaunas	U.S.S.R.
U.S. 4-wall singles	W. Yambrick	
U.S. 4-wall doubles	R. and O. Obert	
U.S. Masters doubles	R. Brady and	
	R. McGuire	

HORSESHOE PITCHING

Event	Winner	Country
WORLD CHAMPIONS		
Men	E. Hohl	Canada
Women	L. Thomas	U.S.

continued on page 696

THE 1968 OLYMPICS: GRENOBLE AND MEXICO CITY

By Howard Bass, Norris McWhirter, and Ross McWhirter

Winter Olympics. The X Winter Olympic Games at Grenoble, France, from Feb. 6 to 18, 1968, were accompanied by abnormally mild weather, which was very agreeable for the skating sports but caused inconvenient rescheduling for some of the bobsled, toboggan, and Alpine ski events. Probably these Games will be remembered most for the three gold medals won in Alpine skiing by Jean-Claude Killy of France and for allegations of professionalism, which seemed neither to be proved nor disproved to general satisfaction.

Even Killy's achievements and Guy Perillat's second place in the downhill could not obscure the fact that France did not dominate the men's Alpine events to the extent that it had in the world championships in 1966. On the technically demanding Olympic courses, the Swiss were more successful than in 1966 with Willi Favre, Daniel Daetwyler, and Dumeng Giovanoli particularly prominent. Heinrich Messner and Karl Schranz kept Austria well in the picture, too.

Victor in the giant slalom and runner-up in the slalom, Canadian Nancy Greene was the most successful competitor in the women's Alpine events, her success the more creditable because she had been hampered by an ankle injury during the preceding weeks. Marielle Goitschel, France's world champion in 1966, only matched her previous best form when winning the slalom but was the next best all-rounder. The petite Annie Famose of France proved that physical size was not essential in order to win giant slalom silver and slalom bronze medals. Isabelle Mir finished close behind her two compatriots, and only Florence Steurer among the French girls failed to win a medal—by one one-hundredth of a second in the giant slalom.

If Killy was the man of the Winter Olympics, the title of outstanding woman surely belonged to a Swedish cross-country skier, Toini Gustafsson. She gained two gold medals, for the 5 km. and 10 km., and a silver as one of the Swedish relay team in the 15-km. event won by Norway.

An Italian disturbed the normal pattern in the men's cross-country skiing at Autrans, when Franco Nones led home the Scandinavians in the 30 km. Two Norwegians, Harald Groenningen and Ole Ellefsæter, took the 15 and 50 km., respectively, and both were also members of the winning Norwegian 40-km. relay team. Another Norwegian, Magnar Solberg, won the individual biathlon, but his team lost to the U.S.S.R. in the biathlon relay. Franz Keller of West Germany won the Nordic combination, comprising a 15-km. race and jumping.

Perhaps the biggest upset came in the special jumping, which used to be won consistently by Scandinavians. A Czech, Jiri Raska, led two Austrians in the 70-m. jump at Autrans, with Norway's world champion, Bjørn Wirkola, humbled in fourth place. The spectacular final event was the lofty 90-m. jump at Saint-Nizier. Vladimir Beloussov's victory for the U.S.S.R., thanks to a gigantic leap of 101.5 m., was less startling than the name of the competitor who tied for second best jump (though not the runner-up), Takashi Fujisawa—heralding a significantly rising level of performance by Japanese athletes.

The bobsled events were a sentimental triumph for the veteran

---

WINTER GAMES, GRENOBLE

Event	Winner and country	Performance
	Skiing	
NORDIC EVENTS	Men	
15-km. cross-country	H. Groenningen (Norway)	47 min. 54.2 sec.
30-km. cross-country	F. Nones (Italy)	1 hr. 35 min. 39.2 sec.
50-km. cross-country	O. Ellefsaeter (Norway)	2 hr. 28 min. 45.8 sec.
Relay (40 km.)	Norway	2 hr. 8 min. 33.5 sec.
Jumping (70-m. slope)	J. Raska (Czechoslovakia)	216.5 pt.
Jumping (90-m. slope)	V. Beloussov (U.S.S.R.)	231.3 pt.
Combined (15 km. and jumping)	F. Keller (West Germany)	449.04 pt.
Biathlon	M. Solberg (Norway)	1 hr. 13 min. 45.9 sec.
Biathlon relay	U.S.S.R.	2 hr. 13 min. 2.4 sec.
	Women	
5-km. cross-country	T. Gustafsson (Sweden)	16 min. 45.2 sec.
10-km. cross-country	T. Gustafsson (Sweden)	36 min. 46.5 sec.
Relay (15 km.)	Norway	57 min. 30.0 sec.
ALPINE EVENTS	Men	
Downhill	J. Killy (France)	1 min. 59.85 sec.
Slalom	J. Killy (France)	1 min. 39.73 sec.
Giant slalom	J. Killy (France)	3 min. 29.28 sec.
	Women	
Downhill	O. Pall (Austria)	1 min. 40.87 sec.
Slalom	M. Goitschel (France)	1 min. 25.86 sec.
Giant slalom	N. Greene (Canada)	1 min. 51.97 sec.
	Skating	
FIGURE SKATING		
Men	W. Schwarz (Austria)	1,904.1 pt.
Women	P. Fleming (U.S.)	1,970.5 pt.
Pairs	Oleg and Ludmila Protopopov (U.S.S.R.)	315.2 pt.
SPEED SKATING	Men	
500 m.	E. Keller (West Germany)	40.3 sec.
1,500 m.	K. Verkerk (Netherlands)	2 min. 3.4 sec.*

Event	Winner and country	Performance
5,000 m.	A. Maier (Norway)	7 min. 22.4 sec.*†
10,000 m.	J. Höglin (Sweden)	15 min. 23.6 sec.*
	Women	
500 m.	L. Titova (U.S.S.R.)	46.1 sec.
1,000 m.	C. Geijssen (Netherlands)	1 min. 32.6 sec.*
1,500 m.	K. Mustonen (Finland)	2 min. 22.4 sec.*
3,000 m.	J. Schut (Netherlands)	4 min. 56.2 sec.*
	Ice Hockey	
Winner	U.S.S.R.	
	Tobogganing (Luge)	
	Men	
Single	M. Schmid (Austria)	2 min. 52.48 sec.
Two-man	K. Bonsack and T. Köhler (East Germany)	1 min. 35.85 sec.
	Women	
Single	E. Lechner (Italy)	2 min. 28.66 sec.
	Bobsledding	
Two-man	E. Monti and L. De Paolis (Italy)	4 min. 41.54 sec.
Four-man	Italy (E. Monti, L. De Paolis, R. Zandonella, M. Armano)	2 min. 17.39 sec.

*Olympic record.
†World record.

Distribution of Medals

	Gold	Silver	Bronze	Total
Norway	6	6	2	14
U.S.S.R.	5	5	3	13
France	4	3	2	9
Italy	4	0	0	4
Austria	3	4	4	11
Netherlands	3	3	3	9
Sweden	3	2	3	8
West Germany	2	2	3	7
United States	1	5	1	7
East Germany	1	2	2	5
Finland	1	2	2	5
Czechoslovakia	1	2	1	4
Canada	1	1	1	3
Switzerland	0	2	4	6
Romania	0	0	1	1

Commemorative
medal of the
1968 Winter
Olympic Games.

A.F.P. FROM PICTO-
RIAL PARADE

UPI (UK) LTD.
Jean-Claude Killy

UPI (UK) LTD.

Marielle Goitschel   KEYSTONE

Erhard Keller   AUTHENTICATED
NEWS INTERNATIONAL

Peggy Fleming

COURTESY, ABC

Franco Nones

UPI COMPIX

Italy's winning four-man bobsled team

Italian driver Eugenio Monti, who at the age of 40 took gold medals in both the two-man and four-man contests. These were the first Olympic victories for the winner of nine world titles. Although Horst Floth piloted his West German two-man sled so that it had an aggregate time equal to Monti's, he was ruled second by the little-known regulation that, in such circumstances, the fastest single run is the deciding factor.

An unfortunate incident of the Winter Games occurred during the tobogganing (luge) when three East German women were disqualified for illegally heating their metal runners. The toboggan run, along with the bobsled course, suffered several postponements because of melting ice. As usual, the Austrians, Poles, and East and West Germans filled most of the top places in this sport, a notable exception being the victory of the Italian Erica Lechner in the women's single toboggan. In the men's event, Manfred Schmid of Austria edged the East German Thomas Köhler, but Köhler had the consolation of winning the two-seater event with Klaus Bonsack.

In seven of the eight speed skating events, one new world record time was established and no fewer than 52 racers beat the previous Olympic record for their respective distances. These performances confounded those who had claimed beforehand that the rink would not be as fast as those at higher altitudes. Perhaps the answer lay in the ice itself, which was manufactured from chemically purified water and thus minimized friction.

Anton Maier of Norway and Kees Verkerk of the Netherlands were the leading male skaters. Maier clipped 3.8 sec. off his own world best time to win the 5,000 m. in 7 min. 22.4 sec. Verkerk and his Dutch team colleague Petrus Nottet also broke Maier's previous record. The major surprise was the victory of Sweden's Johnny Höglin over Maier in the 10,000 m. The performance of Erhard Keller of West Germany in the 500 m. suggested that he was the world's best sprinter on skates.

Three silver medals in one event by competitors from the same country was an Olympic occurrence without precedent. It hap-

pened when a U.S. trio, Jenny Fish, Dianne Holum, and Mary Meyers, tied for second in the women's 500 m.

In the ice hockey finals the U.S.S.R. steadily deflated the zealous Canadians to gain a 5–0 triumph that emphasized the solid Soviet defensive covering whenever their sharpshooting forwards lost command. The U.S.S.R.'s earlier 5–4 defeat by the Czechs was the best and most memorable match of the series. Had Czechoslovakia not been held by Sweden to a 2–2 draw, the Czechs would have won the tournament. Anatolii Firsov (U.S.S.R.) led the final scoring list with 12 goals in 7 games.

Peggy Fleming gained the women's figure skating title with that easy, imperturbable style which, in recent years, had so clearly distinguished her from all her contemporaries. The zenith of her always graceful performance came when a superb double axel was sandwiched between two smoothly controlled spread-eagles. A surprising lapse of form in the compulsory figures robbed the men's favourite, Emmerich Danzer, of success, the winner being his fellow Austrian Wolfgang Schwarz. The classical Soviet masters of synchronized skating, Oleg Protopopov and his wife, Ludmila Belousova (see BIOGRAPHY), climaxed a great career by retaining their pairs title at the ages of 35 and 32, respectively.

The youngest of all the competitors was a Romanian figure skater, Beatrice Hustiu, 11 years old. The most experienced was Evgenii Grichine, the Soviet speed skater, appearing in his fourth Winter Olympics.   (H. B.)

Summer Olympics. More than 6,000 competitors from 112 nations converged on Mexico City to compete for the 172 championships of the XIX Olympic Games in 15 days of intense competition on Oct. 13–27, 1968—72 years after King George I of Greece had been able to invite all the competitors to breakfast at the first modern-era Games in Athens in 1896.

The "oxygen debt" effects of the host city's altitude—more than $1\frac{1}{4}$ mi. above sea level (7,347 ft.)—were as had been predicted. The reduced atmospheric pressure benefited the sprinters

and jumpers, but it meant that each inhalation of breath by a middle-distance or long-distance runner achieved only about 90% of the oxygen intake he could get at sea level. The crossover point at which the benefit of reduced pressure was outweighed by the thinness of the air occurred after 2 to 2½ min. of continuous exertion; that is, after 1,000 m. of running or 150 m. of swimming.

The track and field program of 24 men's and 12 women's events provided some of the most outstanding moments of the Games, with world records being broken or equaled more than 30 times in 16 events. Judged by the amount of improvement, the two greatest feats were the 8.90-m. (29-ft. 2⅜-in.) long jump of Bob Beamon (U.S.) and the 400-m. hurdles, won by 7 yd. by David Hemery (U.K.). Beamon must have cleared a height above his own stature (6 ft. 3 in.) on the way to his extraordinary record—over 21½ in. beyond any previous validly measured long jump.

The 400-m. hurdles provided the greatest track event, insofar as all preexisting standards were destroyed. The favourites, Ron Whitney (U.S.) and Geoffrey Vanderstock (U.S.), finished sixth and fourth, respectively. The winner, Hemery, drawn in lane 6, reached the halfway mark in an unprecedented 23 sec. and switched his stride pattern from 13 to 15 after the sixth hurdle. He flashed over the tenth hurdle and won by a yawning margin in 48.1 sec.—a full second faster than the pre-1968 world record.

The 100 m. was brilliantly won by Jim Hines (U.S.) in 9.89 sec. (returned as 9.9 sec.) to equal the pending world record. In the 200 m. the ground-eating stride of Tommie Smith (U.S.) carried him, arms raised, through the tape in a world record 19.8 sec. The victory ceremony for this race was used by the gold and the bronze medal (John Carlos) winners as an opportunity for a "Black Power" demonstration. Their black-gloved salutes caused particular offense to many since they were made during the playing of the U.S. national anthem. The U.S. Olympic Committee ordered the two athletes to return home.

The 400 m. was won by Lee Evans (U.S.) in a world record

43.8 sec.—the first time that anyone had come close to running this race in under "even time," i.e., averaging better than 10 sec. per 100 yd. Evans and his two compatriots Larry James and Ron Freeman also engaged in a milder Black Power demonstration on the rostrum.

The favourite for the 800-m. title, Wilson Kiprugut (Kenya), was unexpectedly beaten by an Australian, Ralph Doubell, in the world record-equaling time of 1 min. 44.3 sec. The 1,500-m. race was affected by the altitude but produced probably the greatest middle-distance running feat yet seen when Kipchoge Keino (Kenya) ran away from the field over the last two laps to win by more than 15 yd.—in the Olympic record time of 3 min. 34.9 sec.—from the world record holder, Jim Ryun (U.S.). The normally unbeatable Ryun appeared to be at a considerable disadvantage in competing against a man born at 6,500 ft.

The oxygen problem became highly apparent in the 5,000 and 10,000 m., in which two Kenyans, a Tunisian, and an Ethiopian won all the medals. Keino, Naftali Temu of Kenya, and Mamo Wolde of Ethiopia were all born at high altitude, while Mohamed Gammoudi of Tunisia had spent over a year at Font Remeau in the Pyrenees. The reigning world record holder, Ron Clarke (Australia), had to be resuscitated after his brave but unavailing effort in the 10,000 m., and there were those who doubted the medical wisdom of permitting him to run in the 5,000 m. Wolde won the marathon in impressive style; though his time was about 8 min. slower than the winning time at sea level in Tokyo, it was clear that the flow rate of oxygen consumption was a less severe problem at marathon tempo than in the 5,000 and 10,000 m.

Both relays produced victories and very decisive world records for the U.S. quartets. An expected Olympic record came in the 110-m. hurdles, won by Willie Davenport (U.S.). The unknown Amos Biwott (Kenya) won the 3,000-m. steeplechase from his compatriot Benjamin Kogo; Biwott's name did not appear on even the most complete Kenyan ranking lists in 1967.

WIDE WORLD
Daniel Morelon

KEYSTONE
Tommie Smith

Bill Steinkraus   WIDE WORLD

Al Oerter
WIDE WORLD

Dick Fosbury
UPI COMPIX

Debbie Meyer   KEYSTONE

Gold medal for the 1968 summer Olympic Games maintains the design used since 1928.
UPI COMPIX

WIDE WORLD

WIDE WORLD

Spencer Haywood

Klaus Dibiasi leaving platform, left, and entering water, below.

SUMMER GAMES, MEXICO CITY

Complete List of Winners

Basketball

Winning team U.S. (beat Yugoslavia 65–50 in final)

Boxing

Light flyweight	F. Rodriguez (Venezuela)
Flyweight	R. Delgado (Mexico)
Bantamweight	V. Sokolov (U.S.S.R.)
Featherweight	A. Roldan (Mexico)
Lightweight	R. Harris (U.S.)
Light welterweight	J. Kulej (Poland)
Welterweight	M. Wolke (East Germany)
Light middleweight	B. Lagutin (U.S.S.R.)
Middleweight	C. Finnegan (U.K.)
Light heavyweight	D. Pozdniak (U.S.S.R.)
Heavyweight	G. Foreman (U.S.)

Canoeing

Men

1,000-m. Canadian singles	T. Tatai (Hungary)	4 min. 36.14 sec.
1,000-m. Canadian pairs	Romania	4 min. 07.18 sec.
1,000-m. kayak singles	M. Hesz (Hungary)	4 min. 02.63 sec.
1,000-m. kayak pairs	U.S.S.R.	3 min. 37.54 sec.
1,000-m. kayak fours	Norway	3 min. 14.38 sec.

Women

500-m. kayak singles	L. Pinaeva (U.S.S.R.)	2 min. 11.09 sec.
500-m. kayak pairs	West Germany	1 min. 56.44 sec.

Cycling

1,000-m. sprint	D. Morelon (France)	10.68 sec. (Best 200 m.)
1,000-m. time trial	P. Trentin (France)	1 min. 03.91 sec.*†
2,000-m. tandem	France	9.83 sec. (Best 200 m.)
4,000-m. individual pursuit	D. Rebillard (France)	4 min. 41.71 sec.*†
4,000-m. team pursuit	Denmark	4 min. 22.44 sec.*
100-km. team time trial	Netherlands	2 hr. 07 min. 49.06 sec.
Road race (196.2008 km.)	P. Vianelli (Italy)	4 hr. 41 min. 25.24 sec.

Equestrian Sports

Dressage—individual	I. Kizimov (U.S.S.R.) on Igor
Dressage—team	West Germany
3-day event—individual	J. Guyon (France) on Pitou
3-day event—team	United Kingdom
Show jumping—individual	W. Steinkraus (U.S.) on Snowbound
Show jumping—team	Canada

Fencing

	Individual	*Team*
Foil	I. Drimba (Romania)	France
Épée	G. Kulcsar (Hungary)	Hungary
Sabre	J. Pawlowski (Poland)	U.S.S.R.
Women's foil	E. Novikova (U.S.S.R.)	U.S.S.R.

Football (Soccer)

Winning team Hungary (beat Bulgaria 4–1 in final)

Gymnastics

Men

Combined exercises individual	S. Kato (Japan)
Combined exercises team	Japan
Parallel bars	A. Nakayama (Japan)
Horizontal bar	A. Nakayama (Japan); M. Voronin (U.S.S.R.)
Rings	A. Nakayama (Japan)
Pommeled horse	M. Cerar (Yugoslavia)
Long horse	M. Voronin (U.S.S.R.)
Floor exercises	S. Kato (Japan)

Women

Combined exercises individual	V. Caslavska (Czechoslovakia)
Combined exercises team	U.S.S.R.
Long horse	V. Caslavska (Czechoslovakia)
Uneven parallel bars	V. Caslavska (Czechoslovakia)
Balance beam	N. Kuchinskaya (U.S.S.R.)
Floor exercises	V. Caslavska (Czechoslovakia); L. Petrik (U.S.S.R.)

Hockey (Field)

Winning team Pakistan (beat Australia 2–1 in final)

Modern Pentathlon

Individual	B. Ferm (Sweden)	4,964 pt.
Team	Hungary	14,325 pt.

Rowing

Single sculls	J. Wienese (Netherlands)	7 min. 47.80 sec.
Double sculls	U.S.S.R.	6 min. 51.82 sec.
Coxed pairs	Italy	8 min. 04.81 sec.
Coxless pairs	East Germany	7 min. 26.56 sec.
Coxed fours	New Zealand	6 min. 45.62 sec.
Coxless fours	East Germany	6 min. 39.18 sec.
Eights	West Germany	6 min. 07.00 sec.

Shooting

Free pistol (50 m.)	G. Kosykh (U.S.S.R.)	562 pt.*
Free rifle (300 m.)	G. Anderson (U.S.)	1,157 pt.*†
Small-bore rifle (50 m., prone)	J. Kurka (Czechoslovakia)	598 pt.*§
Small-bore rifle (3-position)	B. Klinger (West Germany)	1,157 pt.
Rapid-fire pistol	J. Zapedzki (Poland)	593 pt.*
Trapshooting	J. Braithwaite (U.K.)	198 targets‡§
Skeet shooting	E. Petrov (U.S.S.R.)	198 targets†‖

Swimming and Diving

Men

100-m. freestyle	M. Wenden (Australia)	52.2 sec.*†
200-m. freestyle	M. Wenden (Australia)	1 min. 55.2 sec.*
400-m. freestyle	M. Burton (U.S.)	4 min. 09.0 sec.*
1,500-m. freestyle	M. Burton (U.S.)	16 min. 38.9 sec.*
100-m. breaststroke	D. McKenzie (U.S.)	1 min. 07.7 sec.‖
200-m. breaststroke	F. Muñoz (Mexico)	2 min. 28.7 sec.
100-m. butterfly	D. Russell (U.S.)	55.9 sec.‖
200-m. butterfly	C. Robie (U.S.)	2 min. 08.7 sec.
100-m. backstroke	R. Matthes (East Germany)	58.7 sec.*
200-m. backstroke	R. Matthes (East Germany)	2 min. 09.6 sec.*
200-m. individual medley	C. Hickcox (U.S.)	2 min. 12.0 sec.‖
400-m. individual medley	C. Hickcox (U.S.)	4 min. 48.4 sec.
400-m. free-style relay	United States	3 min. 31.7 sec.*†
800-m. free-style relay	United States	7 min. 52.3 sec.
400-m. medley relay	United States	3 min. 54.9 sec.*†
Platform diving	K. Dibiasi (Italy)	164.18 pt.
Springboard diving	B. Wrightson (U.S.)	170.15 pt.

Women

100-m. freestyle	J. Henne (U.S.)	1 min. 00.0 sec.
200-m. freestyle	D. Meyer (U.S.)	2 min. 10.5 sec.‖
400-m. freestyle	D. Meyer (U.S.)	4 min. 31.8 sec.*
800-m. freestyle	D. Meyer (U.S.)	9 min. 24.0 sec.‖
100-m. backstroke	K. Hall (U.S.)	1 min. 06.2 sec.*†
200-m. backstroke	L. Watson (U.S.)	2 min. 24.8 sec.‖
100-m. breaststroke	D. Bjedov (Yugoslavia)	1 min. 15.8 sec.‖
200-m. breaststroke	S. Wichman (U.S.)	2 min. 44.4 sec.*
100-m. butterfly	L. McClements (Australia)	1 min. 05.5 sec.
200-m. butterfly	A. Kok (Netherlands)	2 min. 24.7 sec.‖
200-m. individual medley	C. Kolb (U.S.)	2 min. 24.7 sec.‖
400-m. individual medley	C. Kolb (U.S.)	5 min. 08.5 sec.*
400-m. free-style relay	United States	4 min. 02.5 sec.*
400-m. medley relay	United States	4 min. 28.3 sec.*†
Platform diving	M. Duchkova (Czechoslovakia)	109.59 pt.
Springboard	S. Gossick (U.S.)	150.77 pt.

Track and Field

Men

100 m.	J. Hines (U.S.)	9.9 sec.*†
200 m.	T. Smith (U.S.)	19.8 sec.*†
400 m.	L. Evans (U.S.)	43.8 sec.*†
800 m.	R. Doubell (Australia)	1 min. 44.3 sec.*§
1,500 m.	K. Keino (Kenya)	3 min. 34.9 sec.*
5,000 m.	M. Gammoudi (Tunisia)	14 min. 05.0 sec.
10,000 m.	N. Temu (Kenya)	29 min. 27,4 sec.
Marathon	M. Wolde (Ethiopia)	2 hr. 20 min. 26.4 sec.
110-m. hurdles	W. Davenport (U.S.)	13.3 sec.*
400-m. hurdles	D. Hemery (U.K.)	48.1 sec.*†
3,000-m. steeple-chase	A. Biwott (Kenya)	8 min. 51.0 sec.
400-m. relay	United States	38.2 sec.*†
1,600-m. relay	United States	2 min. 56.1 sec.*†
20-km. walk	V. Golubnichy (U.S.S.R.)	1 hr. 33 min. 58.4 sec.
50-km. walk	C. Hohne (East Germany)	4 hr. 20 min. 13.6 sec.
High jump	R. Fosbury (U.S.)	2.24 m. (7 ft. 4 3/16 in.)*
Long jump	R. Beamon (U.S.)	8.90 m. (29 ft. 2⅜ in.)*†
Pole vault	R. Seagren (U.S.)	5.40 m. (17 ft. 8⅝ in.)*†
Triple jump	V. Saneev (U.S.S.R.)	17.39 m. (57 ft. 0⅝ in.)*†
Shot put	R. Matson (U.S.)	20.54 m. (67 ft. 4 11/16 in.)*
Discus	A. Oerter (U.S.)	64.78 m. (212 ft. 6⅜ in.)*
Hammer throw	G. Zsivotzky (Hungary)	73.36 m. (240 ft. 8 3/16 in.)*
Javelin	Y. Lusis (U.S.S.R.)	90.10 m. (295 ft. 7¼ in.)*
Decathlon	W. Toomey (U.S.)	8,193 pt.*

Women

100 m.	W. Tyus (U.S.)	11.0 sec.*†
200 m.	I. Kirszenstein-Szewinska (Poland)	22.5 sec.*†
400 m.	C. Besson (France)	52.0 sec.‡
800 m.	M. Manning (U.S.)	2 min. 00.9 sec.*†
80-m. hurdles	M. Caird (Australia)	10.3 sec.*§
400-m. relay	United States	42.8 sec.*†
High jump	M. Rezkova (Czechoslovakia)	1.82 m. (5 ft. 11⅝ in.)
Long jump	V. Viscopoleanu (Romania)	6.82 m. (22 ft. 4½ in.)*†
Shot put	M. Gummel (East Germany)	19.61 m. (64 ft. 4 1/16 in.)*†
Discus	L. Manoliu (Romania)	58.28 m. (191 ft. 2½ in.)*
Javelin	A. Nemeth (Hungary)	60.36 m. (198 ft. 0⅜ in.)
Pentathlon	I. Becker (West Germany)	5,098 pt.

Volleyball

Winning men's team U.S.S.R. Winning women's team U.S.S.R.

Water Polo

Winning team Yugoslavia (beat U.S.S.R. 13–11 in final)

Weight Lifting

Bantamweight	M. Nassiri (Iran)	367.5 kg. (810¼ lb.)*§
Featherweight	Yoshinobu Miyake (Japan)	392.5 kg. (865¼ lb.)
Lightweight	W. Baszanowski (Poland)	437.5 kg. (964½ lb.)*
Middleweight	V. Kurentsov (U.S.S.R.)	475.0 kg. (1,047¼ lb.)*
Light heavyweight	B. Selitsky (U.S.S.R.)	485.0 kg. (1,069¼ lb.)*§
Middle heavyweight	K. Kangasniemi (Finland)	517.5 kg. (1,141 lb.)*
Heavyweight	L. Zhabotinsky (U.S.S.R.)	572.5 kg. (1,262¼ lb.)‡

	Freestyle	Greco-Roman
Flyweight	S. Nakata (Japan)	P. Kirov (Bulgaria)
Bantamweight	Y. Uetake (Japan)	J. Varga (Hungary)
Featherweight	M. Kaneko (Japan)	R. Rurua (U.S.S.R.)
Lightweight	A. Movahed (Iran)	M. Mumemura (Japan)
Welterweight	M. Atalay (Turkey)	R. Vesper (East Germany)
Middleweight	B. Gurevitch (U.S.S.R.)	L. Metz (East Germany)
Light heavyweight	A. Ayuk (Turkey)	B. Radev (Bulgaria)
Heavyweight	A. Medved (U.S.S.R.)	I. Kozma (Hungary)

Yachting

5.5-m. class	Sweden ("Wasa IV")	8 penalty pt.
Dragon Class	United States ("Williwaw")	6 penalty pt.
Flying Dutchman class	United Kingdom ("Superdocious")	3 penalty pt.
Star class	United States ("North Star")	14.4 penalty pt.
Finn Monotype class	V. Mankin (U.S.S.R.)	11.7 penalty pt.

*Betters Olympic record.
†Betters recognized world record.
‡Equals Olympic record.
§Equals recognized world record.
‖Olympic record (new event).

The winning high jump "back flip" style of Dick Fosbury (U.S.), at a height of 2.24 m. (7 ft. $4\frac{3}{16}$ in.), caused vast interest and amusement. This reverse dive probably heralded an eventual improvement in the world record of 2.28 m. (7 ft. $5\frac{3}{4}$ in.). The pole vault competition, the greatest in the history of the event, captivated the stadium. A three-way tie at 5.40 m. (17 ft. $8\frac{5}{8}$ in.) was resolved in favour of Bob Seagren (U.S.) because he had fewer misses. In the triple jump Viktor Saneev (U.S.S.R.) set a new world record of 17.39 m. (57 ft. $\frac{5}{8}$ in.) in the final.

The four throwing events, in which the advantage of reduced air pressure was less significant, produced no world record performances. The outstanding achievement was that of Al Oerter (U.S.), who, almost incredibly, retained the discus championship which he first won at Melbourne (1956), and retained at Rome (1960) and Tokyo (1964). Oerter won easily with an Olympic record of 64.78 m. (212 ft. $6\frac{3}{8}$ in.). Olympic records were also set by Randy Matson (U.S.), in the qualifying competition of the shot put; by Gyula Zsivotzky (Hungary), in the hammer throw; and by Yanis Lusis (U.S.S.R.), in the javelin event with his last and winning throw of 90.10 m. (295 ft. $7\frac{1}{4}$ in.).

The decathlon was won by Bill Toomey (U.S.), with an Olympic record 8,193 pt. This event struck a balance between the advantages of low air pressure in the sprints and the disadvantage of high altitude in the tenth and cruelest trial over 1,500 m.

New women's world records were set in the 100 and 200 m., the 400-m. sprint relay and long jump, with a bonus in the shot put when Margitta Gummel (East Germany) put the shot a prodigious 19.61 m. (64 ft. $4\frac{1}{16}$ in.). Wyomia Tyus (U.S.) became the first woman sprinter ever to retain an Olympic title when she won the 100 m. in a world record 11 sec.; and the U.S. sprinters lowered the recognized world sprint relay record by an extraordinary 1.1 sec. to 42.8 sec. In the 200 m. Irina Kirszenstein-Szewinska (Poland) improved her own world record by $\frac{1}{5}$ sec. Colette Besson (France) floated past the more favoured Lillian Board (U.K.) to take the 400 m. in the Olympic record-equaling time of 52 sec.

The sheer burden of national expectations appeared too much for the pending world 800-m. record holder, Vera Nikolic (Yugoslavia), who failed to complete the competition. Madeline Manning (U.S.) won the event by 10 yd. in an Olympic and world record 2 min. 0.9 sec. Australia placed first and second in the 80-m. hurdles with Maureen Caird winning over the former world record holder, Pamela Kilborn. The high jump was won by Miloslava Rezkova of Czechoslovakia.

The long jump was a triumph for Viorica Viscopoleanu (Romania) with 6.82 m. (22 ft. $4\frac{1}{2}$ in.). Lia Manoliu, at the age of 36 and in her fifth Olympics, won the discus also for Romania with a record 58.28 m. (191 ft. $2\frac{1}{2}$ in.).

In basketball, the U.S. team won its seventh consecutive set of gold medals, preserving its unbroken monopoly since the sport was admitted at Berlin in 1936. The second-place Yugoslavs played well to defeat the Soviet team, which finished third in a play-off against Brazil. Vladimir Andreev of the U.S.S.R. team

measured 7 ft. 2 in. in height and was thus the tallest competitor in any sport in all Olympic history.

The outstanding boxer to emerge from the Games was George Foreman, the heavyweight champion from the U.S. On the night of the finals the home crowd cheered Mexican victories in the flyweight over a Pole and in the featherweight by disqualification. Jerzy Kulej of Poland and Boris Lagutin of the U.S.S.R. retained their light-welterweight and light-middleweight titles won in the 1964 Games at Tokyo. The victory of Chris Finnegan (U.K.) in the middleweight division puzzled a crowd that did not appreciate that in amateur boxing defense scores as heavily as attack. The tournament was remarkable for the number of boxers from countries with no long-established tradition in the sport who survived to the quarterfinals. A South Korean, Yong-Ju Jee (light-flyweight), a Ugandan, Eridadi Mukwanga (bantamweight), and a Cameroon welterweight, Joseph Bessala, all won silver medals.

The five cycling track events were dominated by France with four gold medals. Pierre Trentin (France) lowered the world record for the 1,000-m. (standing start) time trial with an average speed of 56.330 kph (35.002 mph.). The winner of the 196.2008-km. (121.9133-mi.) road race was Pierfranco Vianelli (Italy) at an average speed of 41.831 kph (25.99 mph.), while the Netherlands took the 100-km. (62.137-mi.) time trial, at an average of 47.881 kph (29.752 mph.), from Sweden and Italy.

During the cross-country obstacle course on the second day of the three-day equestrian event staged at Avandaro, a flash flood occurred, drowning two horses. The team event was won by Great Britain. The Grand Prix Dressage at Campo Marte was won by the Soviet horse Igor, ridden and trained by Ivan Kizimov (U.S.S.R.), while the team event was taken by a West German trio. The individual Grand Prix jumping was a triumph for the U.S. team captain Bill Steinkraus. The silver medal was taken by Marion Coakes (U.K.), the first woman ever to take an individual medal in Olympic equestrian competition. In the team Grand Prix des Nations show jumping Canada won over France.

Transcending all other gymnasts, male or female, was the blonde Czechoslovak Vera Caslavska. In Mexico, having won the individual combined exercises gold medal, she swept the horse and asymmetrical bars and was deemed unlucky only to tie first in the floor exercises for a fourth gold medal.

The greatly expanded swimming program involved the addition of 11 new events. Though the facilities of the superb new Olympic swimming pool were ideal, the altitude factor kept the number of new world records to five events. Outstanding among the male swimmers was Australia's Mike Wenden who lowered the world 100-m. freestyle record to 52.2 sec. and took a second gold medal in the 200-m. freestyle. The aquatic heroine was Debbie Meyer, the 16-year-old multiple world record holder from Sacramento, Calif., who won the 200-, 400-, and 800-m. freestyle events. Other men's world records were set in the 400-m. freestyle relay, which the U.S. quartet swam in 3 min. 31.7 sec., and in the 400-m. medley relay, in which the U.S. team recorded 3 min. 54.9 sec. In the women's events, Kaye Hall (U.S.) lowered the 100-m. backstroke record to 1 min. 06.2 sec., and the U.S. 400-m. medley relay team recorded 4 min. 28.3 sec. The long U.S. monopoly of men's high diving was broken in the platform event by an Italian, Klaus Dibiasi.

Only seven countries were involved in the distribution of the 16 wrestling titles. Japan won four titles; the U.S.S.R. three; Bulgaria, East Germany, Hungary, and Turkey took two each; and Iran won the remaining one.

The yachting events were staged at Acapulco on the Pacific coast. Only the United States scored more than one success when they took the Star Class with Lowell North (helm) and Peter Barrett (crew) and the Dragon Class with George Friedrichs (helm) and Barton Jahncke and Gerald Schreck (crew). The British Flying Dutchman "Superdocious," with Rodney Pattisson (helm) and Iain Macdonald-Smith (crew), set an overall Olympic regatta record in crossing the line first in its first six races and finishing second in the seventh. (N. McW.; R. McW.)

continued from page 690

JUDO

Event	Winner	Country
EUROPEAN CHAMPIONS		
Lightweight	A. Martkoplishvili	U.S.S.R.
Light middleweight	G. Magaltadze	U.S.S.R.
Middleweight	W. Hoffmann	West Germany
Light heavyweight	P. Hermann	West Germany
Heavyweight	K. Glahn	West Germany
Unlimited weight	G. Saunin	U.S.S.R.
Teams		France
U.S. (AAU) CHAMPIONS		
139-lb.	Y. Koga	
154-lb.	T. Hiraoka	
176-lb.	M. Yamashita	
205-lb.	M. Watanabe	
Over 205-lb.	A. Coage	
Open	T. Itoh	
Overall	M. Watanabe	

KARTING

Event	Winner	Country
World championship, individual	T. Nilsson	Sweden

LACROSSE

Event	Winner
U.S. Club champions	Long Island AC
U.S. National champions	Johns Hopkins University

MODERN PENTATHLON

Event	Winner	Country
NATIONAL CHAMPIONS		
U.S.S.R.	P. Lednyev	U.S.S.R.
Sweden	P. Lednyev	U.S.S.R.
U.K.	J. Fox	U.K.
U.S.	J. Moore	U.S.
MAJOR INTERNATIONAL EVENTS		
Fontainebleau (France), individual	J. Fox	U.K.
Fontainebleau team		Hungary
Arborfield (U.K.), individual	F. Torok	Hungary
Arborfield team		Hungary
Halle (East Germany), individual	A. Balczo	Hungary
Halle team		U.S.S.R.
Moscow (U.S.S.R.)	A. Balczo	Hungary

MOTOR (AUTOMOBILE) RACING

Event	Winner (with machine)	Country
WORLD CHAMPIONSHIP FORMULA 1 EVENTS		
South African Grand Prix	J. Clark (Lotus-Ford)	U.K.
Spanish Grand Prix	G. Hill (Lotus-Ford)	U.K.
Monaco Grand Prix	G. Hill (Lotus-Ford)	U.K.
Belgian Grand Prix	B. McLaren (McLaren-Ford)	New Zealand
Dutch Grand Prix	J. Stewart (Matra-Ford)	U.K.
French Grand Prix	J. Ickx (Ferrari)	Belgium
British Grand Prix	J. Siffert (Lotus-Ford)	Switzerland
German Grand Prix	J. Stewart (Matra-Ford)	U.K.
Italian Grand Prix	D. Hulme (McLaren-Ford)	New Zealand
Canadian Grand Prix	D. Hulme (McLaren-Ford)	New Zealand
U.S. Grand Prix	J. Stewart (Matra-Ford)	U.K.
Mexican Grand Prix	G. Hill (Lotus-Ford)	U.K.
World champion driver	G. Hill	U.K.
OTHER MAJOR RACE WINNERS		
Indianapolis 500	R. Unser (Eagle-Offenhauser)	U.S.
Daytona 24 hr.	V. Elford, J. Neerpasch (Porsche 907)	U.K., West Germany
Sebring 12 hr.	J. Siffert, H. Hermann (Porsche 907)	Switzerland, West Germany
Brands Hatch 500 mi.	J. Ickx, B. Redman (Ford GT 40)	Belgium, U.K.
Monza 1,000 km.	D. Hobbs, P. Hawkins (Ford GT 40)	U.K., Australia
Targa Florio	V. Elford, U. Maglioli (Porsche 907)	U.K., Italy
Nürburgring 1,000 km.	V. Elford, J. Siffert (Porsche 908)	U.K., Switzerland
Spa 1,000 km.	J. Ickx, B. Redman (Ford GT 40)	Belgium, U.K.
Watkins Glen 6 hr.	J. Ickx, L. Bianchi (Ford GT 40)	Belgium
Austrian Grand Prix	J. Siffert (Porsche 907)	Switzerland
Le Mans 24 hr.	P. Rodriquez, L. Bianchi (Ford GT 40)	Mexico, Belgium
RALLY-DRIVING		
Monte Carlo Rally	V. Elford, D. Stone (Porsche 911T)	U.K.
Acropolis Rally	R. Clark, J. Porter (Ford Escort)	U.K.
London–Sydney	A. Cowan (Hillman Hunter)	U.K.

MOTO-CROSS

Event	Winner	Country
WORLD 250-cc. CHAMPIONSHIP		
Spanish Grand Prix	T. Hallman	Sweden
Czechoslovak Grand Prix	O. Andersson	Sweden
Dutch Grand Prix	J. Robert	Belgium
West German Grand Prix	J. Robert	Belgium
Luxembourg Grand Prix	T. Hallman	Sweden
U.S.S.R. Grand Prix	T. Hallman	Sweden
Yugoslav Grand Prix	T. Hallman	Sweden
Finnish Grand Prix	K. Vehkonen	Finland
Swedish Grand Prix	T. Hallman	Sweden
U.K. Grand Prix	J. Robert	Belgium
Belgian Grand Prix	J. Robert	Belgium
Austrian Grand Prix	J. Robert	Belgium
Overall champion	J. Robert	Belgium
WORLD 500-cc. CHAMPIONSHIP		
Austrian Grand Prix	B. Aberg	Sweden
Finnish Grand Prix	P. Friedrichs	East Germany
East German Grand Prix	P. Friedrichs	East Germany
Czechoslovak Grand Prix	P. Friedrichs	East Germany
British Grand Prix	V. Eastwood	U.K.
French Grand Prix	J. Banks	U.K.
Belgian Grand Prix	B. Aberg	Sweden
Dutch Grand Prix	J. Banks	U.K.
Luxembourg Grand Prix	V. Eastwood	U.K.
Belgian Grand Prix	B. Aberg	Sweden
Swiss Grand Prix	P. Friedrichs	East Germany
Overall champion	P. Friedrichs	East Germany

MOTORCYCLING

Event	Winner (with machine)	Country
WEST GERMAN GRAND PRIX		
50 cc.	H. Anscheidt (Suzuki)	West Germany
125 cc.	P. Read (Yamaha)	U.K.
250 cc.	W. Ivy (Yamaha)	U.K.
350 cc.	G. Agostini (MV Agusta)	Italy
500 cc.	G. Agostini (MV Agusta)	Italy
SPANISH GRAND PRIX		
50 cc.	H. Anscheidt (Suzuki)	West Germany
125 cc.	S. Canellas (Bultaco)	Spain
250 cc.	P. Read (Yamaha)	U.K.
500 cc.	G. Agostini (MV Agusta)	Italy
ISLE OF MAN T.T.		
50 cc.	R. Smith (Derbi)	New Zealand
125 cc.	P. Read (Yamaha)	U.K.
250 cc.	W. Ivy (Yamaha)	U.K.
350 cc.	G. Agostini (MV Agusta)	Italy
500 cc.	G. Agostini (MV Agusta)	Italy
Sidecar	S. Schauzu (BMW)	West Germany
DUTCH GRAND PRIX		
50 cc.	P. Lodewijk (Jamathi)	Netherlands
125 cc.	P. Read (Yamaha)	U.K.
250 cc.	W. Ivy (Yamaha)	U.K.
350 cc.	G. Agostini (MV Agusta)	Italy
500 cc.	G. Agostini (MV Agusta)	Italy
Sidecar	J. Attenberger (BMW)	West Germany
BELGIAN GRAND PRIX		
50 cc.	H. Anscheidt (Suzuki)	West Germany
250 cc.	P. Read (Yamaha)	U.K.
500 cc.	G. Agostini (MV Agusta)	Italy
Sidecar	G. Auerbacher (BMW)	West Germany
EAST GERMAN GRAND PRIX		
125 cc.	P. Read (Yamaha)	U.K.
250 cc.	W. Ivy (Yamaha)	U.K.
350 cc.	G. Agostini (MV Agusta)	Italy
500 cc.	G. Agostini (MV Agusta)	Italy
CZECHOSLOVAK GRAND PRIX		
125 cc.	P. Read (Yamaha)	U.K.
250 cc.	P. Read (Yamaha)	U.K.
350 cc.	G. Agostini (MV Agusta)	Italy
500 cc.	G. Agostini (MV Agusta)	Italy
FINNISH GRAND PRIX		
125 cc.	P. Read (Yamaha)	U.K.
250 cc.	P. Read (Yamaha)	U.K.
500 cc.	G. Agostini (MV Agusta)	Italy
ITALIAN GRAND PRIX		
125 cc.	W. Ivy (Yamaha)	U.K.
250 cc.	P. Read (Yamaha)	U.K.
350 cc.	G. Agostini (MV Agusta)	Italy
500 cc.	G. Agostini (MV Agusta)	Italy
WORLD CHAMPION		
50 cc.	H. Anscheidt	West Germany
125 cc.	P. Read	U.K.
250 cc.	W. Ivy and P. Read	U.K.
350 cc.	G. Agostini	Italy
500 cc.	G. Agostini	Italy

ORIENTEERING

Event	Winner	Country
WORLD CHAMPIONS		
Men's individual	K. Johansson	Sweden
Men's relay	S. Björk, K. Johansson, S. Carlström	Sweden
Women's individual	U. Lindkvist	Sweden
Women's relay	A. Roedmyr, A. Hansen, I. Hadler	Norway

PARACHUTING

Event	Winner	Country
WORLD CHAMPIONS		
Men's precision	J. Kalous	Czechoslovakia
Men's figures	T. Gurniy	U.S.S.R.
Men's combined	T. Tkachenko	U.S.S.R.
Men's team precision	East Germany	
Men's team combined	U.S.	
Women's precision	H. Tomsikova	Czechoslovakia
Women's figures	T. Voinova	U.S.S.R.
Women's combined	T. Voinova	U.S.S.R.
Women's team precision	Czechoslovakia	
Women's team combined	U.S.S.R.	

POLO

Event	Winner
U.S. Open championship	Midland, Tex.
U.S. 20-Goal championship	Oak Brook, Ill.
U.S. 16-Goal championship	Milwaukee, Wis.
U.S. 12-Goal championship	Midland, Tex.

RACKETS

Event	Winner	Country
World champion	G. Atkins	U.K.

REAL (COURT) TENNIS

Event	Winner	Country
World open champion	N. Knox	U.S.
U.K. open champion	F. Willis	
U.K. amateur champion	H. Angus	
U.S. amateur doubles champions	N. Knox, W. Talbert	
U.S. amateur singles champion	G. Bostwick	

ROLLER HOCKEY

Event	Winner
World Championship	Portugal

ROLLER SKATING

Event	Winner	Country
WORLD FIGURE SKATING CHAMPIONS		
Men	J. Courtney	U.S.
Women	A. Bader	West Germany
Pairs	J. Courtney, S. Truman	U.S.
Dance	D. Rudalewicz, R. Smith	U.S.

SHOOTING

Event	Winner	Country
World running-boar championship	M. Nordfors	Sweden
World clay-pigeon championship, women	E. von Soden	West Germany
European clay-pigeon championship	M. Carrega	France
European clay-pigeon championship, women	E. von Soden	West Germany
European skeet championship	K. Wirnhier	West Germany
European skeet championship, women	L. Gurevich	U.S.S.R.
U.S. skeet championship	J. Bellows	
U.S. skeet championship, women	J. Armour	

SPEEDWAY

Event	Winner	Country
World championship, individual	I. Mauger	New Zealand
World championship, team		U.K.

SQUASH RACKETS

Event	Winner	Country
MAJOR TOURNAMENT WINNERS		
British amateur championship (men)	J. Barrington	U.K.
British open championship (men)	J. Barrington	U.K.
British open championship (women)	H. McKay	Australia
Australian championship (men)	J. Barrington	U.K.
U.S. amateur championship (men)	C. Adair	Canada
U.S. amateur championship (women)	N. Meade	U.S.
U.S. open championship (men)	M. Khan	U.S.

SURFING

Event	Winner	Country
WORLD CHAMPIONS		
Men	F. Hemmings, Jr.	U.S.
Women	M. Godfrey	U.S.

TABLE TENNIS

Event	Winner	Country
EUROPEAN CHAMPIONS		
Men's singles	D. Surbek	Yugoslavia
Men's doubles	J. Stipancic, D. Vecko	Czechoslovakia
Women's singles	I. Vostova	Czechoslovakia
Women's doubles	M. Luzova, J. Karlikova	Czechoslovakia
Mixed doubles	S. Gomoskov, Z. Rudnova	U.S.S.R.
Men's team	Sweden	
Women's team	West Germany	
SOUTHEAST ASIA/PACIFIC AREA CHAMPIONS		
Men's singles	N. Hasegawa	Japan
Men's doubles	N. Hasegawa, S. Ito	Japan
Women's singles	Choi Jung Sook	South Korea
Women's doubles	Yoon Ki Sook, Kim In Ok	South Korea
Mixed doubles	S. Ito, M. Fukuno	Japan
Men's team	Japan	
Women's team	Japan	
ENGLISH OPEN CHAMPIONS		
Men's singles	S. Gomoskov	U.S.S.R.
Men's doubles	I. Korpa, D. Surbek	Yugoslavia
Men's team	Yugoslavia	
Women's singles	E. Mihalca	Romania
Women's doubles	S. Grinberg, Z. Rudnova	U.S.S.R.
Women's team	Czechoslovakia	
Mixed doubles	S. Gomoskov, Z. Rudnova	U.S.S.R.
U.S. OPEN CHAMPIONS		
Men's singles	Dal Joon Lee	South Korea
Men's doubles	B. Bukiet, D. Sweeris	U.S.
Women's singles	V. Nesukaitis	Canada
Women's doubles	B. Kaminsky, V. Nesukaitis	U.S., Canada
Mixed doubles	D. and C. Sweeris	U.S.

TRACK AND FIELD

Event	Winner and country	Performance
EUROPEAN MEN'S INDOOR CHAMPIONS		
50 m.	J. Hirscht (West Germany)	5.7 sec.
400 m.	A. Badenski (Poland)	47.0 sec.
800 m.	N. Carroll (Ireland)	1 min. 56.6 sec.
1,500 m.	J. Whetton (U.K.)	3 min. 50.9 sec.
3,000 m.	V. Kudinsky (U.S.S.R.)	8 min. 10.2 sec.
50-m. hurdles	E. Ottoz (Italy)	6.5 sec.
High jump	V. Skvortsov (U.S.S.R.)	7 ft. 1½ in.
Pole vault	W. Nordwig (East Germany)	17 ft. 0¾ in.
Long jump	I. Ter-Ovanesyan (U.S.S.R.)	26 ft. 9¼ in.
Triple jump	N. Dudkin (U.S.S.R.)	54 ft. 10 in.
Shot put	H. Birlenbach (West Germany)	61 ft. 2¼ in.
3x364 m. relay	Poland	2 min. 48.9 sec.
3x1,000 m. relay	U.S.S.R.	7 min. 13.6 sec.
Medley relay	U.S.S.R.	3 min. 52.2 sec.
EUROPEAN WOMEN'S INDOOR CHAMPIONS		
50 m.	S. Telliez (France)	6.2 sec.
400 m.	N. Pechenkina (U.S.S.R.)	55.2 sec.
800 m.	K. Burneleit (East Germany)	2 min. 7.6 sec.
50-m. hurdles	K. Balzer (East Germany)	7.0 sec.
High jump	R. Schmidt (East Germany)	6 ft. 0½ in.
Long jump	B. Berthelsen (Norway)	21 ft. 1¼ in.
Shot put	N. Chizhova (U.S.S.R.)	59 ft. 7¾ in.
4x182 m. relay	West Germany	1 min. 28.8 sec.
Medley relay	U.S.S.R.	4 min. 28.3 sec.

Event	Winner and Affiliation	Performance
U.S. NATIONAL COLLEGIATE ATHLETIC ASSOCIATION CHAMPIONS (OUTDOORS)		
100 m.	L. Miller, Southern California	10.1 sec.*
200 m.	E. Taylor, Ohio University	20.8 sec.
400 m.	L. Evans, San Jose State	45.0 sec.†
800 m.	B. Dyce, New York University	1 min. 47.3 sec.
1,500 m.	D. Patrick, Villanova	3 min. 39.9 sec.†
5,000 m.	G. Lindgren, Washington State	13min.57.2sec.†
10,000 m.	G. Lindgren, Washington State	29 min. 41.0 sec.
3,000-m. steeplechase	K. Pearce, Univ. of Texas, El Paso	8 min. 50.8 sec.
110-m. high hurdles	E. McCullouch, Southern California	13.4 sec.*
400-m. hurdles	D. Hemery (U.K.), Boston University	49.8 sec.
440-yd. relay	Southern California	39.5 sec.
1-mi. relay	Villanova	3 min. 8.6 sec.
High jump	R. Fosbury, Oregon State	7 ft. 2¼ in.†
Pole vault	J. Vaughn, UCLA	17 ft. 0¼ in.
Long (broad) jump	P. Pousi, Brigham Young	26 ft. 3½ in.
Triple jump	L. Burgher, Nebraska	53 ft. 1¼ in.†
Shot put	S. Marcus, UCLA	61 ft. 7¾ in.
Discus	J. Van Reenen, Washington State	194 ft. 10 in.
Hammer throw	R. Narcessian, Rhode Island	202 ft. 1 in.
Javelin	C. O'Donnell, Washington State	258 ft. 11 in.
Team	Southern California	58 pt.
	Washington State	57 pt.

*Ties meet record.
†Meet record.

U.S. NATIONAL COLLEGIATE ATHLETIC ASSOCIATION CHAMPIONS (INDOORS)		
60 yd.	J. Green, Kentucky	6.0 sec.*
440 yd.	L. James, Villanova	47.0 sec.†
600 yd.	T. Albright, Colgate	1 min. 10.6 sec.
880 yd.	D. Patrick, Villanova	1 min. 52.0 sec.
1,000 yd.	R. Arrington, Wisconsin	2 min. 9.3 sec.
1 mi.	J. Ryun, Kansas	4 min. 6.8 sec.
2 mi.	J. Ryun, Kansas	8 min. 38.9 sec.
60-yd. high hurdles	R. Flowers, Tennessee	7.0 sec.*
1-mi. relay	Villanova	3 min. 14.4 sec.†
2-mi. relay	Harvard	7 min. 26.8 sec.†
Distance medley relay	Villanova	9 min. 49.6 sec.
High jump	R. Fosbury, Oregon State	7 ft. 0 in.*
Pole vault	P. Wilson, Southern California	16 ft. 8 in.
Long jump	R. Beamon, Univ. of Texas at El Paso	27 ft. 2¾ in.‡
Triple jump	R. Beamon, Univ. of Texas at El Paso	52 ft. 3½ in.

Event	Winner and Affiliation	Performance
Shot put	J. Van Reenen, Washington State	62 ft. 1 in.
35-lb. weight	R. Narcessian, Rhode Island	65 ft. 5¾ in.†
Team	Villanova	35⅓ pt.

*Ties meet record.
†Meet record.
‡World indoor best.

U.S. NATIONAL AAU MEN'S CHAMPIONS (OUTDOORS)

Event	Winner and Affiliation	Performance
100 m.	C. Greene, Husker AA	10.0 sec.
200 m.	Tommie Smith, Santa Clara Valley Youth Village	20.3 sec.*
400 m.	L. Evans, Santa Clara Valley Youth Village	45.0 sec.*
800 m.	W. Bell, Oregon Track Club	1 min. 45.5 sec.*
1,500 m.	J. Mason, Fort Hays State	3 min. 43.1 sec.
5,000 m.	R. Day, U.S. Army	13 min. 50.4 sec.*
10,000 m.	Tracy Smith, U.S. Army	28 min. 47.0 sec.*
3,000-m. steeplechase	G. Young, unatt., Casa Grande, Ariz.	8 min. 30.6 sec.†
100-m. high hurdles	E. McCullouch, Southern California Striders	13.5 sec.
400-m. hurdles	R. Whitney, Southern California Striders	49.6 sec.*
3,000-m. walk	D. DeNoon, unatt., Long Beach, Calif.	12 min. 38.0 sec.*
High jump	E. Hanks, Brigham Young Univ.	6 ft. 11 in.
Pole vault	R. Railsback, Southern California Striders	17 ft. 0¼ in.
Long jump	R. Beamon, Houston Striders	27 ft. 4 in.*
Triple jump	A. Walker, Southern California Striders	53 ft. 9¼ in.*
Shot put	R. Matson, Houston Striders	67 ft. 5 in.*
Discus	J. Silvester, unatt., Logan, Utah	203 ft. 9 in.
Hammer throw	E. Burke, Southern California Striders	217 ft. 0 in.
Javelin	F. Covelli, Pacific Coast Club	269 ft. 6 in.
Team	Southern California Striders	127 pt.

*Meet record.
†U.S. record.

TRAMPOLINE

Event	Winner	Country
WORLD CHAMPIONS		
Men's individual	D. Jacobs	U.S.
Men's pairs	M. Budenberg, C. Foerster	West Germany
Women's individual	J. Wills	U.S.
Women's pairs	U. Czech, C. Mohrlang	West Germany

VOLLEYBALL

Event	Winner
U.S. CHAMPIONS	
Men	Westside Jewish Community Center
Women	Long Beach Shamrocks
EUROPEAN CHAMPIONS	
Men	U.S.S.R.
Women	U.S.S.R.
Western European Cup (men)	Netherlands
Western European Tournament (women)	Netherlands

WATER POLO

Event	Winner	Country
European Champion Clubs' Cup	Mladost Zagreb	Yugoslavia

WATER SKIING

Event	Winner	Country
EUROPEAN CHAMPIONS		
Men's overall	R. Zucchi	Italy
Men's slalom	R. Zucchi	Italy
Men's jumps	P. Clerc	Switzerland
Men's tricks	J. Tillement	France
Women's overall	S. Hulsemann	Luxembourg
Women's slalom	S. Hulsemann	Luxembourg
Women's jumps	J. Stewart-Wood	U.K.
Women's tricks	S. Hulsemann	Luxembourg
Team overall		France
U.S. CHAMPIONS		
Men's overall	M. Suyderhoud	
Men's slalom	M. Suyderhoud	
Men's jumps	M. Suyderhoud	
Men's tricks	A. Kempton	
Women's overall	L. Allan	
Women's slalom	L. Allan	
Women's jumps	L. Allan	
Women's tricks	L. Allan	

WEIGHT LIFTING

Event	Competitor, country, date	Performance
WORLD RECORDS SET IN 1968		
Bantamweight		
Press	I. Foldi (Hungary); April 21	273¼ lb.
Jerk	M. Nassiri (Iran); June 19	321¾ lb.
	M. Nassiri (Iran); June 23	324 lb.
Total	G. Chetin (U.S.S.R.); Aug. 24	809¾ lb.
Middleweight		
Press	V. Kurentsov (U.S.S.R.); April 6	352½ lb.
	V. Kurentsov (U.S.S.R.); June 22	354¾ lb.
Jerk	V. Kurentsov (U.S.S.R.); Aug. 31	408 lb.
Total	V. Kurentsov (U.S.S.R.); April 6	1,041¼ lb.
	V. Kurentsov (U.S.S.R.); Aug. 31	1,064 lb.

Event	Competitor, country, date	Performance
Light heavyweight		
Snatch	V. Belyaev (U.S.S.R.); Feb. 24	331¾ lb.
Middle heavyweight		
Press	E. Sharipov (U.S.S.R.); Feb. 21	376¾ lb.
	V. Golovanov (U.S.S.R.); Feb. 21	378 lb.
	V. Golovanov (U.S.S.R.); Feb. 25	378¼ lb.
	B. Johansson (Sweden); June 3	380¼ lb.
	K. Pumpurin (U.S.S.R.); June 25	385¾ lb.
	K. Kangasniemi (Finland); July 27	386¾ lb.
Snatch	J. Talts (U.S.S.R.); Feb. 24	336 lb.
	J. Talts (U.S.S.R.); April 6	337 lb.
	J. Talts (U.S.S.R.); May 18	338¼ lb.
	K. Kangasniemi (Finland); July 7	342¾ lb.
	K. Kangasniemi (Finland); Aug. 24	347 lb.
Jerk	J. Talts (U.S.S.R.); Feb. 24	429¾ lb.
	J. Talts (U.S.S.R.); April 6	430¾ lb.
	J. Talts (U.S.S.R.); Aug. 31	432 lb.
Total	J. Talts (U.S.S.R.); April 6	1,124¼ lb.
	J. Talts (U.S.S.R.); June 24	1,129½ lb.
	K. Kangasniemi (Finland); July 7	1,135 lb.
	K. Kangasniemi (Finland); Aug. 24	1,140½ lb.
	K. Kangasniemi (Finland); Aug. 24	1,151½ lb.
Heavyweight		
Press	G. Pickett (U.S.); Feb. 25	445 lb.
	J. Dube (U.S.); March 23	449 lb.
	R. Bednarski (U.S.); June 9	455¼ lb.
	J. Dube (U.S.); Aug. 31	462½ lb.
Snatch	L. Zhabotinsky (U.S.S.R.); June 25	388 lb.
Jerk	L. Zhabotinsky (U.S.S.R.); May 19	485 lb.
	R. Bednarski (U.S.); June 9	486 lb.

Event	Winner	Performance
U.S.S.R. CHAMPIONS		
Bantamweight	G. Chetin	766 lb.
Featherweight	E. Karimov	815½ lb.
Lightweight	N. Nogaitsev	920¼ lb.
Middleweight	V. Kurentsov	1,019½ lb.
Light heavyweight	G. Koshiyev	1,036 lb.
Middle heavyweight	J. Talts	1,102 lb.
Heavyweight	Y. Yablonovsky	1,090¾ lb.
Super heavyweight	L. Zhabotinsky	1,289½ lb.
U.S. CHAMPIONS		
Bantamweight	F. Baez (Puerto Rico)	740 lb.
Featherweight	W. Imahara	795 lb.
Lightweight	S. Mansour	820 lb.
Middleweight	R. Knipp	955 lb.
Light heavyweight	J. Puleo	1,025 lb.
Middle heavyweight	P. Grippaldi	1,055 lb.
Heavyweight	J. Murray	1,035 lb.
Super heavyweight	R. Bednarski	1,280 lb.
EUROPEAN CHAMPIONS		
Bantamweight	I. Foldi (Hungary)	771¼ lb.
Featherweight	M. Nowak (Poland)	837½ lb.
Lightweight	W. Baszanowski (Poland)	936½ lb.
Middleweight	V. Kurentsov (U.S.S.R.)	1,019¼ lb.
Light heavyweight	B. Selitsky (U.S.S.R.)	1,041¼ lb.
Middle heavyweight	J. Talts (U.S.S.R.)	1,129½ lb.
Heavyweight	L. Zhabotinsky (U.S.S.R.)	1,256¼ lb.

WRESTLING

Event	Winner	Country
WORLD FREESTYLE CHAMPIONS		
Flyweight	S. Nakata	Japan
Bantamweight	A. Aliev	U.S.S.R.
Featherweight	A. Kaneko	Japan
Lightweight	A. Mohaved	Iran
Welterweight	D. Robin	France
Middleweight	B. Gurevich	U.S.S.R.
Light heavyweight	A. Ayik	Turkey
Heavyweight	A. Medved	U.S.S.R.
Team	U.S.S.R.	
EUROPEAN FREESTYLE CHAMPIONS		
Flyweight	B. Baev	Bulgaria
Bantamweight	A. Aliev	U.S.S.R.
Featherweight	Z. Dinev	Bulgaria
Lightweight	E. Vulchev	Bulgaria
Welterweight	D. Robin	France
Middleweight	V. Shovrebov	U.S.S.R.
Light heavyweight	P. Golotkin	U.S.S.R.
Heavyweight	A. Medved	U.S.S.R.
Team	Bulgaria	
EUROPEAN GRECO-ROMAN CHAMPIONS		
Flyweight	I. Kotyergin	U.S.S.R.
Bantamweight	K. Traykov	Bulgaria
Featherweight	Y. Grigoryev	U.S.S.R.
Lightweight	V. Novochatko	U.S.S.R.
Welterweight	S. Acar	Turkey
Middleweight	O. Bliadze	U.S.S.R.
Light heavyweight	F. Kiss	Hungary
Heavyweight	P. Kment	Czechoslovakia

	U.S. CHAMPIONS	
	Freestyle	Greco-Roman
Flyweight	A. Chavez	A. Chavez
Bantamweight	R. Sofman	I. Yamamoto (Japan)
Featherweight	M. Ichiguchi	J. Hazewinkel
Lightweight	R. Douglas	F. Lett
Welterweight	M. Gallego	L. Lyden
Middleweight	R. Camilleri	W. Baughman
Light heavyweight	H. Schenk	J. Lewis
Heavyweight	L. Kristoff	R. Johnson

(D. K. R. P.)

Squash Rackets:
see Sporting Record

Stamp Collecting:
see Philately and Numismatics

Steel Industry:
see Industrial Review

See also Baseball; Basketball; Bowling and Lawn Bowls; Boxing; Chess; Contract Bridge; Cricket; Football; Golf; Hockey; Horse Racing; Ice Skating; Motor Sports; Rowing; Skiing; Swimming; Tennis; Track and Field Sports.

Stock Exchanges

Stock prices throughout the world generally increased in 1968. The trend of business activity, fears of actual or potential inflation, balance of payments policies, a flight from important currencies, as well as monetary policy decisions of central banks themselves were all important influences on stock price movements during the year. Eleven of the 12 major world stock price indexes posted higher prices on the average in 1968. (*See* Table I.) In addition, countries with relatively minor exchanges generally experienced rising stock markets.

Fears of inflation in many of the world's major countries were often related to efforts by leading financial nations to create monetary stability. The threatened collapse of the postwar exchange system of the Western countries led to a series of international monetary conferences between March and November. Stock markets in the three leading Western European countries—Great Britain, France, and West Germany—were greatly influenced by those events.

In early March an unprecedented demand for gold by investors and speculators caused the United States and six Western European nations to meet in Washington. A dual-market, or two-tier, system for trading gold was established. The U.S. agreed to uphold the $35-per-ounce gold price for dealings among central bankers, while permitting gold prices in private transactions to fluctuate freely on the open market.

At the end of March nine nations met in Stockholm and agreed to begin creating special drawing rights from the International Monetary Fund (IMF) to supplement reserves being used in international transactions. Under this plan the IMF would establish special credits that could be drawn in place of gold or dollars by a member nation with a balance of payments problem.

On September 9 in Basel, Switz., central bankers of 12 Western nations developed a $2 billion credit plan aimed at supporting the British pound. And on November 20, in response to the threatened devaluation of the French franc and revaluation of the West German mark, financial leaders of ten major industrial nations met in Bonn, W.Ger., to cope with the problem. France was granted a $2 billion credit line from other central banks to use in defending the franc. West Germany, on the other hand, agreed to take steps to restore a better trade balance with its neighbours, and to impose some controls aimed at keeping so-called "hot money" out of the country. In the end, the values of the French franc and the West German mark were intact, but instability in the world's monetary system remained. For the year as a whole, the London Stock Exchange, the West German stock markets, and the Paris Bourse showed higher prices.

The Scandinavian countries also had generally higher stock prices. Stock markets in Sweden, Finland, and Denmark revealed strong bullish patterns, while stock prices in Norway declined. Central banks in Sweden and Denmark pursued an easy-money policy, which helped to sustain the rise in stock prices. Improved balance of payments prospects in Finland increased the confidence of investors there.

In other European stock markets, higher prices prevailed in Switzerland, the Netherlands, Belgium, Spain, and Italy. Generally higher industrial produc-

tion and inflationary expectations caused a brisk demand for equities in those countries, except in Spain and Italy where prices mainly rose on the rebound from an oversold market. Austria was the only Western country for which a full year's data were available that experienced a bear market in 1968. Apparently, the lack of demand for equities reflected investor concern about the long-term growth prospects of the Austrian economy.

Other countries where stock price information was available revealed strong performances, especially in Japan, Australia, and New Zealand, and for South African gold stocks. Stock markets in the Philippines, India, and South America were also higher.

United Kingdom, West Germany, and France. The British stock exchanges experienced a bull market in 1968. The *Financial Times* index of 30 British industrial stocks rose steadily throughout the year, reaching a peak in September before declining slightly during the final weeks of 1968. From the end of 1967 to the end of 1968, the index was up 30%. This increase in stock prices continued the rise that began after the pound was devalued in November 1967.

After a relatively modest increase during the first three months of the year, British stock prices picked up steam and ended the first half with a 21% gain. This remarkable performance occurred despite a mon-

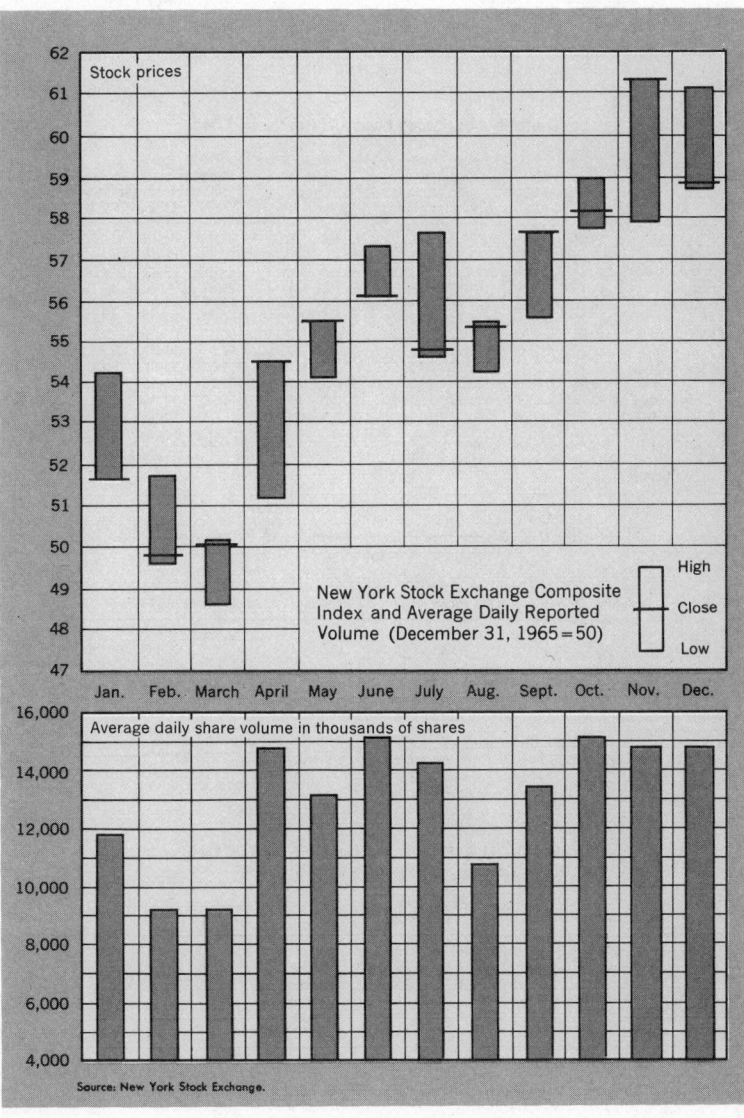

New York Stock Exchange prices and average daily volume, 1968.

etary crisis in March, practically no improvement in corporate profits, relatively high unemployment, and an increase in corporate tax rates in March from 40 to 42.5%. The Bank of England lowered its lending rate from 8 to 7.5%. Hourly wage rates in June were about 1% higher than in January. During this period retail prices rose by more than 3%. Clearly, inflationary fears were the motivating force behind the rise in stock prices.

The second half of the year saw stock prices on the London Stock Exchange increase 7%. During the November monetary crisis stock values declined 17% from the September high. In response to this crisis, the British government announced further domestic restrictions in the form of a sales tax increase and a reduction in credit for the private sector of the economy. The discount rate, however, was reduced another

0.5% to 7%. The demand for equities as protection against real or potential inflation was relatively strong as 1968 came to a close.

The West German stock market reflected the economy's expanding industrial production and the nation's strong position in international trade. For 1968 as a whole the average rise in stock prices was 13%. From January to June prices rose 16%. This increase continued during the September quarter, but a sharp downtrend in stock prices set in as a result of the November monetary crisis.

During the year the West German economy recovered strongly from the recession of 1966–67. Industrial productivity increased faster than wages. The cost of living was practically stable. The discount rate remained at 3% throughout the year. In fact, the strength of the West German mark in foreign exchange markets precipitated the monetary crisis in November. The restrictive measures imposed by the government, however, depressed the hopes of investors for continued gains in business activity.

The influence of economic and monetary crises was especially apparent in the French stock market. Average share prices on the Paris Bourse increased 10% from the end of 1967 to the end of 1968. Between the end of 1967 and the first week of May, however, stock prices showed a gain of 18%. Then, striking French workers, inspired by student disorders, virtually paralyzed the nation's economy. The Paris Bourse was closed during much of the rioting.

Despite the subsequent restoration of order in France, stock prices continued to decline and in early July reached a point about 2% lower than the 1967 close and almost 20% below the high for the year. Stock prices then rallied throughout the early fall, regaining most of the summer's losses; by mid-October the average was up 6% for the year as a whole. Then, however, the threat of devaluation of the French franc in November nearly wiped out these gains. After central bankers agreed to defend the franc, the market rallied and ended the year 9% above the low recorded in November. As the year came to a close, France's economic situation was still under the influence of the loss of about $3 billion in reserves—nearly $1.1 billion in gold—between May and November.

Scandinavian Countries. In Sweden the increase in equity prices in 1968 (40%) was the largest among the major world stock market indexes. Prices rose virtually without pause throughout the year, with final 1968 levels at an all-time high. The increase in total production of goods and services in 1968 was expected to be 4%, or twice as much as in 1967.

Finland also reflected a bull market through the end of October. Average share prices in October were 42% higher than in the fourth quarter of 1967, when Finland devalued its currency in response to devaluation of the British pound. Finnish exports exceeded imports in mid-1968 for the first time in a decade. As a result, balance of payments prospects greatly improved.

In November 1967, Denmark also followed the U.K. and devalued its currency. From the third quarter of 1967 to the third quarter of 1968, the average rise in industrial stock prices in Denmark was about 9%. Most of this increase occurred during the second and third quarters of 1968. The most serious problem in the country continued to be inflation and a relatively high balance of payments deficit.

In Norway, stock prices on the average declined

Table I. Selected Major World Stock Market Price Indexes*

	1968 range High	1968 range Low	Year-end indexes 1967	Year-end indexes 1968	Percent change
Australia	621	444	446	600	+35%
Austria	1,901	1,743	1,881	1,789	− 5
Belgium	92	83	85	91	+ 7
France	120	97	100	110	+10
West Germany	124	106	104	117	+13
Italy	64	57	62	63	+ 2
Japan	1,851	1,266	1,283	1,715	+34
Netherlands	470	359	374	460	+23
South Africa (gold stocks)	88	62	68	79	+16
Sweden	309	220	220	309	+40
Switzerland	337	238	246	337	+37
United Kingdom	522	385	389	506	+30

*Limited to countries for which full year's data were available.
Source: Barron's, The Economist, New York Times.

Table II. U.S. Stock Market Prices and Yields

Month	Railroads (20 stocks) 1968	Railroads (20 stocks) 1967	Industrials (425 stocks) 1968	Industrials (425 stocks) 1967	Public utilities (55 stocks) 1968	Public utilities (55 stocks) 1967	Composite (500 stocks) 1968	Composite (500 stocks) 1967	Yield (200 stocks; %) 1968	Yield (200 stocks; %) 1967
January	43.38	44.48	103.11	89.88	68.02	70.63	95.04	84.45	3.40	3.55
February	42.35	46.13	98.33	93.35	65.61	70.45	90.75	87.36	3.49	3.56
March	41.68	46.78	96.77	95.86	62.62	70.03	89.09	89.42	3.47	3.44
April	44.79	45.80	104.42	97.54	63.66	71.70	95.67	90.96	3.22	3.31
May	48.00	47.00	107.02	99.59	62.92	70.70	97.87	92.59	3.22	3.44
June	51.72	48.19	109.73	98.61	65.21	67.39	100.53	91.43	3.16	3.39
July	51.01	49.91	109.16	100.38	67.55	67.77	100.30	93.01	3.21	3.25
August	48.80	50.43	106.77	102.11	66.60	68.03	98.11	94.49	3.20	3.30
September	51.11	49.27	110.53	103.84	66.77	67.45	101.34	95.81	3.18	3.19
October	54.26	46.28	113.29	104.16	66.93	64.93	103.76	95.66	3.17	3.27
November	53.74	42.95	114.77	100.90	70.59	63.48	105.40	92.66		3.31
December		43.46		103.91		64.61		95.30		3.24

Source: U.S. Department of Commerce, Survey of Current Business. Prices are Standard and Poor's monthly averages of daily closing prices with 1941-43=10. Yield figures are Moody's index of 200 stocks.

Table III. U.S. Government Long-Term Bond Prices and Yields
Average price in dollars per $100 bond

Month	Average 1968	Average 1967	Yield (%) 1968	Yield (%) 1967	Month	Average 1968	Average 1967	Yield (%) 1968	Yield (%) 1967
January	73.09	81.54	5.18	4.40	July	73.99	76.39	5.09	4.86
February	73.30	80.73	5.16	4.47	August	74.48	75.38	5.04	4.95
March	70.98	80.96	5.39	4.45	September	73.95	75.04	5.09	4.99
April	72.06	80.24	5.28	4.51	October	72.44	73.01	5.24	5.18
May	70.89	77.48	5.40	4.76	November	71.27	70.53	5.36	5.44
June	72.58	76.37	5.23	4.86	December		71.22		5.36

Source: U.S. Department of Commerce, Survey of Current Business. Average prices are derived from average yields on the basis of an assumed 3% 20-year taxable U.S. Treasury bond. Yields are for U.S. Treasury bonds that are taxable and due or callable in ten years or more.

Table IV. U.S. Corporate Bond Prices and Yields
Average price in dollars per $100 bond

Month	Average 1968	Average 1967	Yield (%) 1968	Yield (%) 1967	Month	Average 1968	Average 1967	Yield (%) 1968	Yield (%) 1967
January	77.2	85.9	6.17	5.20	July	76.1	81.1	6.24	5.58
February	77.5	86.4	6.10	5.03	August	78.1	80.3	6.02	5.62
March	76.9	85.6	6.11	5.13	September	78.4	80.0	5.97	5.65
April	76.2	85.4	6.21	5.11	October	77.0	78.5	6.09	5.82
May	75.3	83.4	6.27	5.24	November	75.7	76.8		6.07
June	76.6	81.7	6.28	5.44	December		75.9		6.19

Source: U.S. Department of Commerce, Survey of Current Business. Average prices are based on Standard and Poor's composite index of A1+ issues. Yields are based on Moody's Aaa domestic corporate bond index.

7% from the fourth quarter of 1967 through November. This reflected a decline in capital expenditures and a slowing down in the growth of internal demand.

Other European Stock Exchanges. The performance of the Swiss stock market was one of the best in the world. Average share prices on the Zürich Stock Exchange rose 37% from the end of 1967 to the end of 1968. This was particularly impressive after the strong market in 1967, when stock prices increased 44%. The precipitous rise during the second and fourth quarters of 1968 was probably triggered by the expectation of possible devaluations of the dollar and the French franc during the respective monetary crises of March and November.

The Netherlands' stock market was also a star performer in 1968. Its equity price index increased 23%. The demand for stocks was influenced largely by a relatively sharp increase in industrial production, accompanied by surging domestic consumption. Prices and wages also showed a marked rise.

Prices on the Brussels Stock Exchange rose 7% in 1968. All but 1% of the increase came during the period from July through September. The market remained relatively firm throughout the closing months of 1968 with year-end prices only 1% below the September high. During 1968 industrial production continued the uptrend that began in the fourth quarter of 1967.

In Spain, stock prices gave some evidence of reversing a long decline that began in 1963. Average share prices through October were 7% higher than during the fourth quarter of 1967 but still were roughly 20% below the 1963 peak. Price controls, without a similar freeze on wages, squeezed profit margins. Consequently, corporate profits were severely depressed.

After experiencing a general decline in share prices in 1967 and throughout most of 1968, the Italian stock price index rallied in December, finishing the year about 2% higher than in 1967. Throughout most of 1968 industrial production on a month-to-month basis rose substantially above levels for the same months in 1967. The relatively depressed condition of share prices on the Milan Stock Exchange could be attributed to investor concern about the stability of the government and dissatisfaction over taxes imposed on dividends.

Austria experienced lower stock prices in 1968. The decline in prices on the Vienna Stock Exchange, which began in April 1966, continued throughout most of 1968 with the average ending the year approximately 5% lower than the 1967 close. Prices fell sharply in the second quarter and at a lesser rate during the summer. A recovery began in early September, but the year closed with prices only 2% above the lows recorded in August. This poor performance occurred in the face of rising industrial production and an average rise of 3% in the cost of living through August. Apparently, investment psychology was influenced by uncertainty over the outcome of proposed government legislation to improve the growth, structure, and competitiveness of the Austrian economy.   (R. H. TR.)

United States. The year 1968 was encouraging to investors in the U.S. stock market, as prices in all major segments rose irregularly to record levels. The volume of trading was so overwhelmingly large that emergency procedures were invoked to avert a breakdown in the processing of purchase orders. Blue-chip

stocks were relatively unpopular as inflationary pressures in 1968 fostered a contagious speculative mood with certain aggressive mutual funds leading even formerly staid institutional investors into small new issues offering a chance for quick profits. On the New York Stock Exchange the Dow Jones industrial average was up only 4.3% for the year. The New York Stock Exchange index, embracing all stocks on the exchange, rose 9.4%. Meanwhile, on the American Stock Exchange the average price of shares was up 33% for the year. Between 1966 and 1968 the price-earnings ratio on American Stock Exchange stocks rose from 10 times to more than 26, while, in contrast, the prices of stocks in the Dow Jones industrial average dipped from 17.2 times earnings in 1967 to 16.7 during 1968.

The year was marked more by wide swings in public sentiment regarding the outlook for the economy than by changes in the direction of the economy itself.

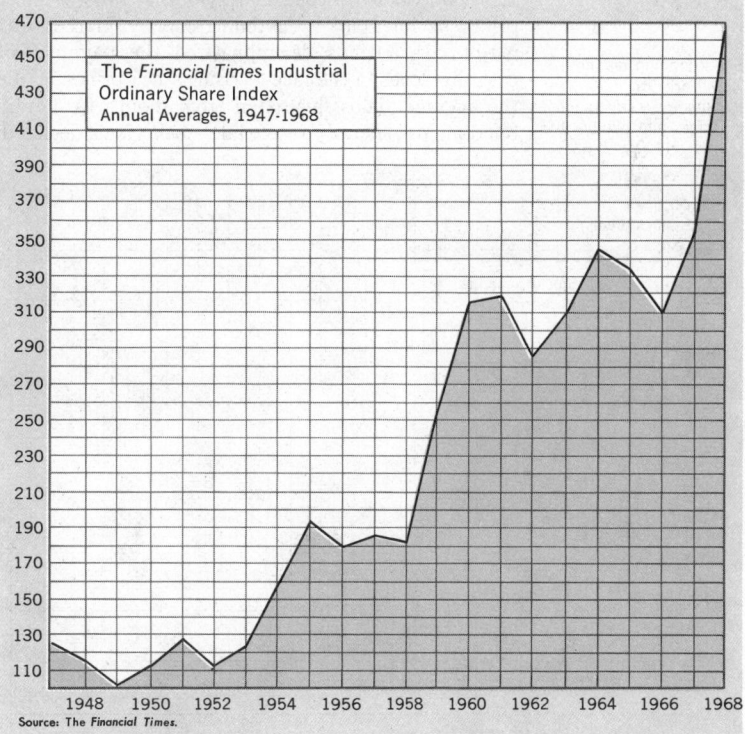

Index of industrial ordinary share prices on the London Stock Exchange, 1947–68.

Real economic growth was well above the 4% figure that the U.S. Department of Commerce considered consistent with the long-term increase in the labour force and productivity. By the end of 1968 forecasters were predicting a recession in the first half of 1969 accompanied by tight money. In the face of this prediction, however, the economy continued to finish its eighth consecutive year of expansion, and in the stock markets working hours were being shortened to accommodate the enormous flood of paper work as 25 million investors followed the financial news with increasing interest. Special television channels were used to accommodate the public interest in the movement of stock prices, allowing an investor to watch the stock price quotation boards on his TV set.

Railroad prices, as shown in Table II, began 1968 on a declining trend during the first quarter and then made a recovery which carried the averages to a level about 20% above the previous year's close. Favourable action on several major railroad mergers, with the promise of substantial economies of operation and

the prospects of better earnings from diversification, made railroads more attractive to investors. The industrials dipped in the first months of 1968, in line with other prices, and then, beginning in April, broke out of the doldrums and rose to a peak level in November that was about 14% higher than in the corresponding month of 1967. Public utility stocks traded within a narrower range than most other groups and tended to be lower priced than in 1967 until the last quarter of 1968, when they rose modestly above the previous year's levels. Standard and Poor's composite index of 500 stocks declined from a level of 95.04 in January to a low of 89.09 in March and then rose to a June level of 100.53 before dipping again to an August average of 98.11. During the last quarter of 1968 this index rose to an all-time high monthly average level of 105.40.

Stock yields continued their long-term decline and dipped irregularly month by month to a level of 3.17% in October. The reverse spread between stock and bond yields widened sharply during 1968, as bond prices declined in a tightening money market and major corporations de-emphasized the payment of cash dividends in the face of rising stock prices. While the average yields fluctuated from month to month, bond yields generally rose while stock yields declined.

U.S. government long-term bond prices, as seen in Table III, rose and fell irregularly throughout 1968, although the general trend was one of gradual decline. This decline was not nearly as steep as in 1967, but its impact in increasing yields helped force interest rates in the money markets up to record levels. The Federal Reserve Board's monetary policy, which was moderately restrictive during the first quarter of 1968 as contrasted with the unusually expansive policy followed in much of 1967, became expansive again between May and November. In December, however, there was a return to restrictiveness. The easy-money policy, coupled with a record-high (since World War II) $25 billion budget deficit, aggravated inflationary pressures, which the government sought to curb by increasing the cost of money. On Dec. 18, 1968, major banks raised their prime interest rates on business loans to 6.75%, a record high. At the Dec. 20, 1968, auction of 91-day bills the average yield was 6.278%, while on 182-day bills it was 6.401%; these rates represented record high costs of money for the government. The Federal Reserve Board in December raised the discount rate from 5.25 to 5.5%, but kept the ceiling on rates for certificates of deposit. This resulted in a drain of about $3 billion from the banking system and led to tighter credit by the end of the year.

U.S. corporate bond prices were relatively steady throughout 1968, as shown by Table IV, although average prices were well below 1967 levels throughout the year. The price downtrend, which had become apparent in early 1967, continued at a less rapid rate through much of 1968. In part, the weakness of the corporate bond market was attributable to a record amount of new financing by corporations. There was also much concern, however, about the international outlook and the need for unorthodox financing to overcome the restraints imposed by the government via the interest equalization tax, which penalized investors in foreign securities to the extent of about 18.75%.

One of the factors that made for bullishness in the 1968 stock market was a rapid expansion in the mutual fund business, the total assets of which rose to about $55 billion. Merger activity was up sharply, one authority reporting that there were 4,462 such transactions in 1968, an increase of 50% over the previous high of 2,975 recorded in 1967. Mergers were almost certainly an important stimulant to the stock market in 1968. Odd-lot selling (selling fewer than 100 shares of stock to a customer at a time), generally regarded as a bullish sign, was the highest in history during September and October. The confidence of the public was manifested in many other ways, including a record high rate of automobile sales at a level of 9.6 million, a high rate of housing starts, and a high level of overall retail sales. Consumer saving, as a percentage of disposable personal income, declined to the lowest rate in three years during the third quarter of 1968, and the amount of installment credit outstanding rose rapidly all through the year.

The principal sources of anxiety in the market seemed to arise from a feeling that the economy had expanded too rapidly and that a recession was overdue. The slow pace of peace talks in Paris relating to the Vietnam conflict, continuing urban unrest in the U.S., a persistent balance of payments deficit, and fears about spiraling inflation also posed problems.

Probably the leading development affecting all of the stock exchanges in 1968 was the "backroom crisis."

Stock trading on the New York Stock Exchange: yearly range of prices and number of shares sold, 1947–68.

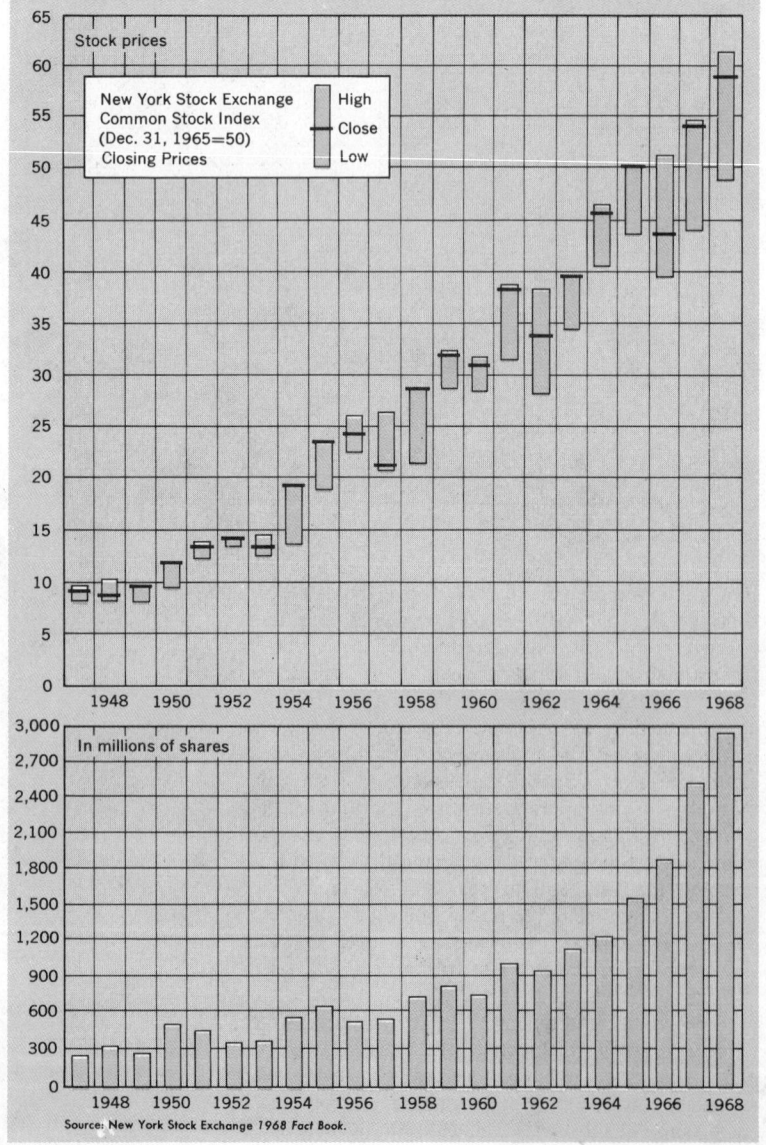

New York Stock Exchange Common Stock Index (Dec. 31, 1965=50) Closing Prices

High
Close
Low

Stock prices

In millions of shares

Source: New York Stock Exchange *1968 Fact Book.*

The volume of trading, which averaged more than 20 million shares a day on all exchanges combined, overwhelmed the capacity of stock-brokerage firms to meet their obligations for five-day delivery of securities. Oct. 29, 1929, had formerly been the busiest day on the New York Stock Exchange, with 16.4 million shares traded. On April 1, 1968, there were 17.7 million shares traded, and the 1929 record was surpassed on 20 different days during 1968. To meet this problem, daily trading hours on the exchanges were shortened by 90 minutes from January 22 until early March. Beginning June 12 the exchanges closed one day a week for the rest of the year. A result was 226 trading days in 1968, as compared with 251 in 1967. Some brokers cut back on activity by closing offices and firing many of their customers' men; some would accept no orders for less than $1,000 on listed stocks or $5,000 for over-the-counter stocks. Correspondent relationships among brokerage firms were cut back, and restrictions on accounts a salesman might maintain were common.

On the New York Stock Exchange there were 2,931,365,000 transactions in 1968, up from 2,529,-785,834 in 1967. As recently as 1964 the volume had been only 1,238,885,223. During the year 1,784 issues were traded on the exchange, as contrasted with 1,713 in 1967. The prospects for increasing volume were enhanced with the abolition on December 5 of a brokerage fee-splitting arrangement known as "customer-directed give-ups," whereby mutual funds placed orders on regional exchanges as a means of directing commissions to nonmember firms. The end of give-ups served to divert business back to the major exchanges.

The American Stock Exchange volume of activity was up to a level of 1,435,597,381 in 1968 from the volume of 1,145,090,300 experienced in 1967, a gain of 25.3%. In 1964 the volume on this exchange had only been 374,500,114 shares traded. In 1968, 1,088 issues were traded, compared with 1,067 in 1967.

The Pacific Coast Stock Exchange, continuing its rapid expansion, had total transactions of 143.3 million shares in 1968, compared with 114 million shares in 1967. The volume on the Pacific Coast Stock Exchange was 25% above 1967, and dollar volume was up 15.5%. In 1964 volume on this exchange was only 56,216,672 shares. Of the 721 Pacific Coast Stock Exchange stocks listed, 535 were also traded on the New York Stock Exchange and another 149 on the American Stock Exchange. This system of secondary market trading on regional exchanges was common. On the Boston Stock Exchange, for example, volume rose from 5.5 million shares in 1963 to 40 million in 1968, largely on the basis of secondary market trading of nationally listed securities.

Canada. Canadian stock prices were generally lower for the first few months of 1968, with the bottoms for the year reached in March. A strong bullish trend began after that date, in tandem with the U.S. markets, and it continued to gain strength with senior industrial, utility, bank, paper, base metal, and western oil indexes achieving their highs for the year during November. Gold and real estate issues did almost as well. Stock prices showed a net increase of nearly 18% for the year, after being down 10% in mid-March.

The Canadian bond market paralleled that of the U.S. The rise in interest rates during the first four months of the year was largely a result of an international monetary situation that placed several cur-

rencies, including the Canadian and U.S. dollars, under pressure. The March 31 appeal to the U.S. Congress by the president of the U.S. for passage of the tax surcharge bill signaled the beginning of a decline in most interest rates, and when the bill passed in June, the bond markets in both the U.S. and Canada were enjoying a rally. At mid-December yields ranged from 6 to 6.5% for short-term Canada bonds, 6.75 to 7.25% for mid- and long-term Canada bonds, 7.5 to 8% for provincial bonds, and 7.5 to 9% for municipal and corporate issues. (I. Pr.)

Other Countries. Among the other nations for which stock price index information was available, all showed higher stock prices for 1968 as a whole. Japan experienced one of the strongest stock markets in the world (+34%). During the first quarter, prices on the Tokyo Stock Exchange showed a modest increase over the depressed levels of November 1967 after the British pound was devalued. Then, however, prices climbed sharply for six consecutive months, reaching an all-time high on October 2 of 44% above the 1967 close. A decline followed with stock prices at the end of December 7% below the historic peak. Surging export sales, higher family incomes, strong consumer demand, and improving profits were the driving force behind the market.

The Australian stock market was not only one of the better performing markets in the Western world but also one of the most volatile. Its rise of 35% was bettered only by Sweden and Switzerland. Between May and mid-August the Australian stock price index rose 14%. By late September the index, however, had plunged 19% below the mid-August peak as a result of a sharp decline in prices of mining shares. A rebound then took place so that at the end of December stock prices were 14% above the September close. Several newer discoveries of oil, nickel, and uranium, together with discoveries over the past 20 years of iron ore and copper, attracted large amounts of foreign capital.

Strong performances were also turned in by the New Zealand stock market and South African gold stocks. Through September the average rise of industrial shares in New Zealand was 33% over the fourth quarter of 1967. The market appeared to be responding to a near-record surplus in the country's trade balance. South African gold stocks (traded in London) were up 16%. Prices reached a peak during a period of frantic gold buying in Europe during early March. The passage of the special drawing rights agreement by the IMF and the credit lines extended to support the British pound and French franc then dampened speculation. Prices rose, however, after the Bonn conference in November.

Higher stock markets also prevailed in the Philippines, India, Chile, Peru, and Venezuela. In the Philippines the Manila Stock Exchange experienced a bull market in the prices of both mining and sugar shares. Late in 1968 prices of mining shares were up about 31% from the second quarter of 1967. Sugar stocks showed an even larger increase (46%) during the same period. In India share prices rose about 6% through November. The Chilean stock market experienced an average rise of 45% from the fourth quarter of 1967 through September, while the comparable gain for Peru was 6%. Industrial share prices in Venezuela through August were also higher (5%) than in the final quarter of 1967. (R. H. Tr.)

See also Economy, World; Investment, International; Money and Banking; Savings and Investment.

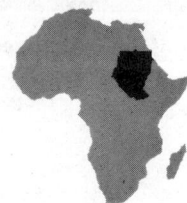

Sudan

A republic of northeast Africa, the Sudan is bounded by the U.A.R., the Red Sea, Ethiopia, Kenya, Uganda, the Congo (Kinshasa), the Central African Republic, Chad, and Libya. Area: 967,491 sq.mi. (2,505,805 sq.km.). Pop. (1967 est.): 14,148,000, including Arabs in the north and Negroes in the south. Cap.: Khartoum (pop., 1967 est., 188,000). Largest city: Omdurman (pop., 1967 est., 203,000). Language: Arabic; various tribal languages in the south. Religion: Muslim in the north; predominantly pagan in the south. Acting head of state in 1968, the Supreme Council, with Ismail al-Azhari as president; prime minister, Muhammad Ahmed Mahgoub.

The 1½-year-old split in the Umma Party, the country's leading political party, continued to mark Sudanese politics in 1968. Prime Minister Muhammad Ahmed Mahgoub, heading the conservative wing of

Sudanese farmer watching an airplane spraying a cotton crop in the Gezira region.

Small band of the Anya'nya rebel organization in action in southern Sudan. The revolt of the Africa-dominated south against the Arab-dominated north has lasted six years with the loss of 500,000 lives.

the Umma and well surrounded by a broad alliance of Muslim sects, moderates, and less progressive elements, decided to take action against the Constituent Assembly (parliament), ostensibly for failure in its prime task of drawing up a permanent constitution. He was reinforced by the successes of 1967: the holding of the fourth Arab summit conference in the Sudan and the settlement of frontier problems with Chad, Uganda, the Congo (Kinshasa), and the Central African Republic. In February the Constituent Assembly was dissolved and general elections were called for April. Sadik al-Mahdi, heading the progressive wing of the Umma, challenged the decision and took the matter to court as a breach of the constitution. This brought the political rivalry between the two Umma wings to its highest pitch. Prior to this, President al-Azhari, leader of the National Unionist Party, Sudan's second major political grouping, in December 1967 had merged his party with the People's Democratic Party. The new organization, the Democratic Unionist Party (DUP), was led by al-Azhari.

In spite of protests, general elections took place in April. They resulted in a new distribution of parliamentary seats, as follows: 101 DUP, 36 Umma of Sadik al-Mahdi's wing, 33 Umma of Mahgoub's wing, and a lesser number of seats for other parties. A coalition government comprising the DUP, the Umma (Mahgoub's wing), and the Southern Front (ten parliamentary seats) was constituted under Mahgoub as prime minister. In May the Constituent Assembly re-elected al-Azhari to the presidency of the Supreme Council.

Early in 1968, southern insurgents violently re-

newed their activities in the three southern provinces. The Army and police dampened the revolt, but incidents continued to take place occasionally. While on a tour of the south, William Deng, leader of a minor party, was killed. A peace conference for the south was held and was attended by Army leaders in that region and ambassadors of countries bordering on the Sudan. The conferees decided to halt the anti-Sudanese activities of southern Sudan refugees. The government followed this by drawing up a development plan for the south, and a ministerial committee was formed to put this plan into effect.

The government was very active during the year in African affairs. President al-Azhari worked to bring about the resumption of relations between the Congo (Kinshasa) and Rwanda and also helped achieve the airlift of mercenary soldiers from the Congo.

(M. B. A.)

ENCYCLOPÆDIA BRITANNICA FILMS. *The Nile Valley and Its People* (1964).

SUDAN

Education. (1965–66) Primary, pupils 492,085, teachers 10,895; secondary, pupils 92,407, teachers 4,453; vocational, pupils 6,391, teachers 479; teacher training, students 1,680, teachers 174; higher (including 3 universities), students 7,701, teaching staff 737.

Finance. Monetary unit: Sudanese pound, with a par value of Sud£0.35 to U.S. $1 (Sud£0.84 = £1 sterling). Foreign exchange, official: (June 1968) U.S. $50.1 million; (June 1967) U.S. $53 million. Budget (1967–68 est.): revenue Sud£91,866,077; expenditure Sud£85,659,317. Gross national product: (1965–66) Sud£473.6 million; (1964–65) Sud£483 million. Money supply: (June 1968) Sud£74,610,000; (June 1967) Sud£71,190,000. Cost of living (1963 = 100): (May 1968) 102; (May 1967) 116.

Foreign Trade. (1967) Imports Sud£69,520,000; exports Sud£74,520,000. Import sources (1966): U.K. 21%; India 10%; Japan 8%; U.S. 8%; West Germany 7%; China 6%. Export destinations (1966): Italy 13%; India 11%; West Germany 8%; Netherlands 7%; U.K. 6%; Japan 6%; China 6%; France 5%. Main exports: cotton 42%; gum arabic 11%; peanuts 8%.

Transport and Communications. Roads (1965) *c.* 50,000 km. (mainly tracks, including *c.* 2,500 km. with improved surface). Motor vehicles in use: passenger (1966) *c.* 26,000; commercial (including buses; 1965) 16,900. Railways: (1965) 5,403 km.; freight (1966) 2,253,000,000 net ton-km. Navigable waterways (1965) 4,068 km. Air traffic (1966): 108,545,000 passenger-km.; freight 2,065,000 net ton-km. Telephones (Jan. 1967) 38,469. Radio receivers (Dec. 1964) *c.* 225,000. Television receivers (Dec. 1966) *c.* 11,000.

Agriculture. Production (in 000; metric tons; 1966; 1965 in parentheses): millet 253 (253); sorghum 875 (1,094); cotton, lint 159 (152); durra (1965) 1,274, (1964) 1,035; sesame 134 (160); dates *c.* 45 (*c.* 45); bananas *c.* 10 (*c.* 10); peanuts 324 (305). Livestock (in 000; 1965–66): cattle 7,500; sheep 8,660; goats 6,850; camels *c.* 2,040; horses *c.* 22; asses *c.* 590.

Industry. Production (in 000; 1966): salt 43 metric tons; electricity (public supply only) 262,000 kw-hr.

Swaziland

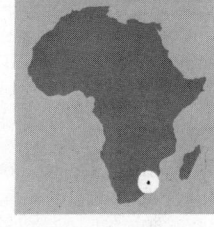

A landlocked constitutional monarchy of southern Africa, Swaziland is bounded by South Africa and Mozambique. Area: 6,704 sq.mi. (17,296 sq.km.). Pop. (1968 est.): 398,400. Cap. and largest city, Mbabane (pop., 1966 est., 13,803). Language: Swazi. Religion: Christian 60%. King in 1968, Sobhuza II; prime minister, Prince Makhosini Dlamini.

The kingdom of Swaziland, last of the three British High Commission Territories in Africa (the other two, Botswana and Lesotho, gained independence in 1966), became independent on Sept. 6, 1968. More fortunate than many new countries in being racially homogeneous, Swaziland also enjoyed rich supplies of minerals, good soil, and ample water supplies. The independence constitution, which was closely modeled on the self-government constitution adopted in 1966, combined traditional administration with a modern elective legislature. The *ngwenyama* ("lion"), King Sobhuza II, was recognized as constitutional king and head of state, and the royalist Imbokodvo Party won all the elective seats in the 1967 elections. Its leader, Prince Makhosini Dlamini, became the country's first prime minister.

King Sobhuza on September 6 officially received the instruments of his nation's independence at a formal ceremony in the new national stadium at Mbabane. More than 50,000 Swazis attended the event, which marked the climax of a week-long series of independence celebrations. After the formal ceremony the king and the prime minister, both wearing traditional tribal dress, joined in mass dancing.

Striking economic development had taken place in the last few years, exports alone increasing by 220% during 1960–67. The majority of the people were farmers, and, with irrigation, the land was rapidly developed for sugar, rice, and citrus fruit. Sugar exports doubled in value to $14.4 million between 1962 and 1967. The export of forest products, under the aegis of the Usutu Pulp Co., rose from $1 million in 1962 to $10,270,000 in 1966.

The exports from the Havelock mine, one of the five main producers of asbestos in the world, were valued at nearly $6 million in 1966, while iron ore exports (to Japan) for the same year were worth approximately $9,360,000. The railway, completed in 1964 and linking the ore mine at Ngwenya with Lourenço Marques (Mozambique), also enabled large coal resources to be developed. A comprehensive survey of the Usutu Basin was under way and was expected to lead to hydroelectric development as well as to the exploitation of mineral potential.

Swaziland relied on British aid to balance its budget. The Commonwealth Development Corp. had committed more than £21 million to investment projects in Swaziland, covering sugar, timber, iron ore, and forestry. Other British aid over the last five years totaled £11 million. Landlocked between Mozambique and South Africa, Swaziland remained largely dependent on the latter, with which it shared a common currency and customs union (more than 80% of imports were estimated to come from South Africa) and which supplied a market for Swazi labour and goods. More important, South African technical aid, private investment, entrepreneurs, and farmers played a crucial role in Swaziland's economic development. Prime Minister Dlamini in September summed up Swazi policy by saying that the country's very existence depended on its trade relations with African and overseas nations.

(M. Mr.)

Sweden

A constitutional monarchy of northern Europe lying on the eastern side of the Scandinavian Peninsula, Sweden has common borders with Finland and Norway. Area: 173,649 sq.mi. (449,750 sq.km.). Pop. (1968 est.): 7,892,774. Cap. and largest city: Stockholm (pop., 1968 est., 767,606). Language: Swedish, with some Finnish and Lappish in the north. Religion: predominantly Lutheran. King, Gustaf VI Adolf; prime minister in 1968, Tage Fritiof Erlander.

The most remarkable event of 1968 in Sweden was the totally unexpected return of the Social Democrats to power at the general election on September 15. The Conservative, Liberal, and Centre parties had had high hopes that they would at last be able to form a coalition government, based largely on a feeling that, after 36 years in office, the Social Democratic Party had burned itself out. The public was suspicious of the evident swing to the left that had been taking place over the past three years, as shown above all in a changed attitude toward nationalization and an increasingly "selective" neutrality that was critical of the U.S. and tolerant of the U.S.S.R. There was discontent with the chronic housing shortage, as the admittedly high building rate of 11.6 new homes a year per 1,000 Swedes was almost canceled out by the high demolition rate. Finally, there was a prevailing condition described by the finance minister as "tax fatigue." Sweden's rate of taxation—41% of the gross national product in 1968—was the world's highest.

The 1968 election was the last under the old two-chamber system (to be replaced in 1971 by a single-chamber system). The campaign was unusually hard fought and the poll, at 88.7%, was the highest ever recorded. In the event the Social Democrats were not only returned again, but they obtained their first absolute majority since 1940, with 50.9% of the votes and 12 new seats, while the Communists, losing 5 out of their 8 seats, suffered their biggest setback since they first emerged as a political party. This complete reversal of expectations was generally attributed to the invasion of Czechoslovakia, which rearoused Sweden's traditional fears of Russian aggression and put the government's conciliatory policy toward the U.S.S.R. in a more favourable light.

Above, Nguyen Tho Chanh, North Vietnamese ambassador to Moscow, and Olof Palme, Swedish minister of education, leading a torchlight parade in Stockholm supporting North Vietnam. Below, Bill Jones of the U.S. telling a Stockholm group of the establishment of an "International Deserters" organization with chapters in Stockholm, Paris, and Tokyo.

wines and spirits, which actually met with general approval. It was further proposed to shift from the present retail turnover tax, standing currently at 10%, to a value-added tax on Jan. 1, 1969. Since this measure would involve a loss of about 240 million kronor in 1968–69, it was decided to introduce a special payroll tax of 1% to offset it. Machinery and other capital equipment were to be exempted from the turnover tax immediately (hitherto 60% of the purchase price had been subject to tax).

Lower industrial profits in 1967 had affected investment, resulting in the merging or closing down of several hundred of the less viable industries. With unemployment increasing, wages were expected to rise by only 7% per man-hour, as against an average annual rise of 9% during the 1960s. The reasonable success of the government's measures seemed confirmed by the revised national budget submitted to the Riksdag on May 3, in which it was stated that the gross national product was now expected to rise by just over 4% during the year, as against an original estimate of 3.5%, and exports to rise by 6.5%, as against 5.5% in 1967. Production in the second quarter rose at a faster rate than in the first quarter, and this improvement was expected to continue.

If the foreign policy of neutrality remained unchanged, it was expressed in 1968 with a new vigour. This was linked, perhaps, with the greater public awareness of and involvement in foreign affairs that had been a growing phenomenon of the past decade. Student demonstrations were rife. In January a highly placed U.S. official was pelted with eggs and snowballs as he entered the Stockholm Chancellery. The government apologized, but the anti-Vietnam demonstrators were supported by the UN movement in Sweden. (At the end of October an information office was opened in Stockholm by the National Liberation Front, the political arm of the Viet Cong, which received some government aid.) In May, demonstrations prevented the holding of the Sweden-Rhodesia Davis Cup match, which had to be transferred to France.

More serious repercussions followed an incident in February when the North Vietnamese ambassador to Moscow, Nguyen Tho Chanh, who had come to present his government's views on Vietnam, headed a 6,000-strong torchlight procession in Stockholm, accompanied by Olof Palme, minister of education, who made a fighting speech championing North Vietnam and criticizing the U.S. The U.S. ambassador to Stock-

The government at once set about exploiting its victory by introducing a greatly increased degree of nationalization. Only 5% of Swedish industry was state-owned, and 4% had already been nationalized when the Social Democrats first came to power in 1932. In September Krister Wickman, the economics minister, stated that it would not be unreasonable for the state to own or acquire a controlling interest in 25% of industry. Only in this way could unemployment, which had reached 2.3%, be cured, and the concentration of power in a few private families be checked (it had been found that 15 families controlled one-fifth of industry). The instruments of this changeover were to be a new Industrial Department of the Economics Ministry and the state-owned Investment Bank, created the previous year to provide low-interest, long-term loans to industry in return for the right to acquire shares and hold directorships in the companies it aided. New undertakings were to be set up in the depressed areas of Norrbotten, the northern mining province, and Borås and Norrköping, where the textile industry was declining.

In the budget presented in January, still under the constant shadow of inflation, it was estimated that expenditure would rise by only 6% in the year beginning July 1 and income slightly more; thus the deficit was expected to drop from about 2.8 billion kronor in the current year to 2.1 billion kronor in 1968–69. The only immediate rise in taxation was another 10% on

---

SWEDEN

Education. (1965–66) Primary, pupils 636,884, teachers 30,000; secondary, pupils 367,102, teachers 34,906; vocational, pupils 234,701; teacher training, students 7,623; higher (including 8 universities), students 71,413, teaching staff (1964–65) 2,296.

Finance. Monetary unit: krona, with a par value of 5.17 kronor to U.S. $1 (12.42 kronor = £1 sterling). Gold and foreign exchange, central bank: (June 1968) U.S. $763 million; (June 1967) U.S. $859 million. Budget (1968–69 est.): revenue 36,386,000,000 kronor; expenditure 38,535,000,000 kronor. Gross national product: (1966) 110,335,000,000 kronor; (1965) 102,025,000,000 kronor. Money supply: (April 1968) 20,980,000,000 kronor; (April 1967) 18,470,000,000 kronor. Cost of living (1963 = 100): (June 1968) 123; (June 1967) 120.

Foreign Trade. (1967) Imports 24,329,000,000 kronor; exports 23,425,000,000 kronor. Import sources: West Germany 19%; U.K. 15%; U.S. 9%; Denmark 7%; Norway 6%; France 5%; Netherlands 5%. Export destinations: U.K.

13%; Norway 12%; West Germany 11%; Denmark 9%; U.S. 7%; Finland 5%; France 5%. Main exports: machinery 24%; wood pulp 10%; paper 9%; motor vehicles 7%; timber 6%; ships and boats 6%.

Transport and Communications. Roads (1967) 169,770 km. (including 283 km. expressways). Motor vehicles in use (1967): passenger 1,966,600; commercial 137,795. Railways: (1966) 13,070 km. (including 7,568 km. electrified); traffic (state system only; 1967) 4,840,000,000 passenger-km., freight 12,572,000,000 net ton-km. Shipping (1967): merchant vessels 100 gross tons and over 1,092; gross tonnage 4,634,648. Air traffic (including Swedish apportionment of international routes of Scandinavian Airlines System; 1967): 1,825,015,000 passenger-km.; freight 67,809,000 net ton-km. Telephones (Dec. 1966) 3,572,630. Radio receivers (Dec. 1966) 2,946,000. Television receivers (Dec. 1966) 2,160,000.

Agriculture. Production (in 000; metric tons; 1967; 1966 in parentheses): wheat 1,095 (576);

barley 1,677 (1,408).; oats 1,425 (1,077); rye 193 (85); potatoes 1,269 (1,355); sugar, raw value (1967–68) c. 262, (1966–67) 229; rapeseed 244 (95); butter 65 (74); timber (1965–66) 48,400 cu.m., (1964–65) 50,700 cu.m. Livestock (in 000; June 1966): horses 95; sheep 238; cattle (June 1967) 2,111; pigs 1,898; chickens 8,386.

Industry. Production (in 000; metric tons; 1967): iron ore (60% metal content) 28,753; coal (1966) 40; electricity (90% hydroelectric in 1966) 53,840,000 kw-hr.; pig iron 2,350; crude steel 4,750; cement 3,836; copper 48; lead (1966) 44; silver (1966) 0.11; gold (1966) 78 troy oz.; mechanical wood pulp (1966) 1,300; chemical wood pulp (1966) 5,253; newsprint 704; other paper (1966) 2,493; cotton yarn 15; wool yarn 9. Merchant vessels launched (100 gross tons and over; 1967) 1,308,000 gross tons. New dwellings completed (1967) 100,200. Index of industrial production (1963 = 100): (1967) 126; (1966) 123.

holm was recalled to Washington shortly afterward for consultation and, though he returned two months later, it appeared for a time that diplomatic relations might be severed. In a heated Riksdag debate on March 21, all parties supported the official attitude on the war in Vietnam, and a new principle was enunciated: that Sweden's neutrality was no neutrality of opinion. It was Sweden's duty as a neutral power to give expression to its opinions. This same principle had already been applied when the Swedish ambassador to Greece was recalled indefinitely in December 1967 in protest against the military government in Athens. The Soviet premier, Aleksei N. Kosygin, was cordially received on a visit in July, when it was learned that the U.S.S.R. was highly critical of Sweden's attempts to enter the EEC.

The establishment from 1969 of a new international award, to be known as the Prize in Economic Sciences in Memory of Alfred Nobel, was announced on May 15 by the Riksbank in connection with its tercentenary celebrations. It would be equal in value to the Nobel Prizes and would be awarded with them.

Modernization measures included the introduction of a five-digit postal code for all kinds of mail, which came into full effect on May 12. Though it was one of the most advanced systems in the world, it caused bad delays at first, but the authorities promised that they would soon be eliminated. The year also saw the passing of the time-honoured "student examen" with all its romantic associations; the 104th and last was held in May. Henceforth anyone would be entitled to wear the student's white cap. In an extension of reforms to the penal code, an experiment was begun in which 100 prisoners at Tillberga Prison were to receive standard wages, pay for their own board and lodging, support their families, and pay taxes. In September, on the first anniversary of the changeover to right-hand traffic, the measure was said to have saved 250 lives and attracted 11% more tourists. (J. C. B. B.)

Encyclopædia Britannica Films. *Scandinavia—Norway, Sweden, Denmark* (1962).

Swimming

The assault on world records in swimming, a feature of each year during the 1960s, reached a peak in 1968 when 26 of the 31 were broken, 19 by U.S. swimmers. Actually, more world records were broken in previous years, but there were twice as many records to be broken then. In October 1968, the Federation Internationale de Natation Amateur (FINA), the world governing body of swimming, decided not to recognize records at linear (yardage) distances. Henceforth records would be at metric distances only.

The change made little difference to the swimmers. The men broke 14 of their 16 world records (8 by Americans), the women 12 of 15 (11 by Americans). The most prominent record-breakers were 16-year-old Debbie Meyer and 21-year-old Mike Burton, both distance freestylers. Miss Meyer came from Sacramento, Calif., and Burton from neighbouring Carmichael, Calif., and both swam for the Arden Hills Swim Club of Carmichael.

The 5-ft. 7-in. Miss Meyer broke four world records during the year. Three came in the U.S. Olympic trials: 2 min. 6.7 sec. for the 200-m. freestyle; 4 min. 24.5 sec. for the 400-m. freestyle; and 9 min. 10.4 sec. for the 800-m. freestyle. She then won all three races in the Olympic Games, October 12–27 at Mex-

ico City. Five weeks before the trials, in the Los Angeles invitation meet, Miss Meyer set perhaps the most significant record of the year, 17 min. 31.2 sec. for the 1,500-m. freestyle. That time would have won the 1956 Olympic and 1962 European championships—for men.

Burton, a compact, 5-ft. 9-in. senior at UCLA, continued to break records by wide margins. His finest performance came in the Olympic trials when he set a world record of 16 min. 8.5 sec. for the 1,500-m. freestyle and established a record en route of 8 min. 34.3 sec. for 800 m. "It was the best race of my life," he said. Seven weeks later, he won the Olympic 1,500-m. freestyle title in another outstanding performance and also won the Olympic 400-m. freestyle title.

Miss Meyer and Burton were consistent winners. In her four most important meets—the Amateur Athletic Union (AAU) national short-course (indoor) championships April 17–20 at Pittsburgh, Pa.; the AAU men's and women's national long-course (outdoor) championships July 31–August 4 at Lincoln, Neb.; the Olympic trials; and the Olympic Games—Miss Meyer won 11 of the 12 longest freestyle races. Burton won the 1,500-m., or 1,650-yd., race for men in those four meets plus the National Collegiate Athletic Association (NCAA) championships March 28–30 at Hanover, N.H. He bettered world, U.S., Olympic, and/or meet records in each of the five meets.

It was also a year of great triumphs for Charles Hickcox of Phoenix, Ariz., and Claudia Kolb of Santa Clara, Calif., the world's best in the individual medley events, and Kaye Hall, a backstroker from Tacoma, Wash. It was a year of triumph mixed with disappointment for Mark Spitz of Santa Clara and Don Schollander and Catie Ball of Jacksonville, Fla.

In the U.S. Olympic trials the 21-year-old Hickcox set world records in the individual medley of 2 min. 10.6 sec. for 200 m. and 4 min. 39 sec. for 400 m. He then won both races in the Olympics. He also won six AAU and NCAA titles, two in the individual medley and four in the backstroke.

Miss Kolb, a 1964 Olympic silver medalist at the age of 14, continued her dominance of the women's individual medley. In the U.S. Olympic trials she set world records of 2 min. 23.5 sec. for 200 m. and 5 min. 4.7 sec. for 400 m., and then captured both races in the Olympics. She also took three of the four AAU races in her specialty, once finishing second to Sue Pedersen of Sacramento, Calif.

The 17-year-old Miss Hall became America's best backstroker in four years. In the two AAU meets, Olympic trials, and Olympics, she won five of eight races and only once finished worse than third.

By ordinary standards Spitz had a most successful year. The 18-year-old schoolboy won five AAU butterfly and freestyle titles and qualified for the Olympic team in six events, including three relays. He hoped to finish first in all six events, but he swam in only five and won only two gold medals, both in relays.

Schollander had become the hero of the 1964 Olympic Games at Tokyo when he won four gold medals, unprecedented for a swimmer. In 1968 Schollander was a 22-year-old senior at Yale University and was not able to devote as much time to swimming as he had earlier. He did, however, set a world record of 1 min. 54.3 sec. for the 200-m. freestyle in the Olympic trials though he placed second in that event in the Olympics.

WIDE WORLD

Above, Debbie Meyer winning a gold medal in the 800-m. freestyle in an Olympic record time of 9:24.0 at Mexico City, Oct. 24, 1968. Below, Catie Ball setting a new world record of 2:38.5 for the 200-m. breaststroke in the Olympic trials at Los Angeles, Aug. 27, 1968.

WIDE WORLD

© UPI COMPIX

Mike Burton, who set a world record of 16:08.5 in the 1,500-m. freestyle at Long Beach, Calif., on Sept. 3, 1968.

Swedish Literature: *see* Literature

WIDE WORLD

Above, Michael Wenden of Australia winning an Olympic gold medal in the 200-m. freestyle, Oct. 24, 1968. Below, Roland Matthes of East Germany, who held the world record of 2:07.5 in the 200-m. backstroke, winning the third heat at the Olympic Games. He went on to win the gold medal in this event.

WIDE WORLD

did produce several distinguished performances. The best non-U.S. swimmers were Roland Matthes of East Germany and Michael Wenden of Australia, each the winner of two Olympic gold medals. Matthes, an 18-year-old backstroker, also set world records of 58 sec. for 100 m. and 2 min. 7.5 sec. for 200 m. Wenden, an 18-year-old freestyler, won in the Olympics at 100 m. (52.2 sec., a world record) and 200 m.

The stars of the British Amateur Swimming Association championships, August 5–10 at Blackpool, Eng., were 18-year-old Martyn Woodroffe of Cardiff, Wales, and 19-year-old Alan Kimber of Southampton. Woodroffe won five gold medals. Kimber, who won four in 1967, took three but was not chosen for the British Olympic team.

In the Australian championships and Olympic trials, February 23–25 at Melbourne, Karl Byrom won three individual gold medals among the men, while Lyn Watson gained four and 14-year-old Karen Moras three among the women. Wenden took the 100-m. and 200-m. freestyle races.

In the Canadian championships and Olympic trials, August 13–17 at Winnipeg, Man., Elaine Tanner finished with six gold medals, while Angela Coughlan had four and Ralph Hutton three. Miss Tanner, primarily a backstroker, also gained six gold medals in the South African championships, February 26–March 1 at Bloemfontein.

For Olympic Games results, *see* SPORTING RECORD: *Special Report.* (F. L.)

Switzerland

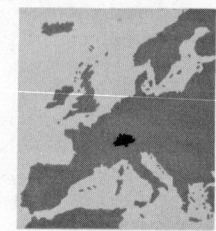

A federal republic in west central Europe consisting of a confederation of 22 cantons, Switzerland is bounded by Germany, Austria, Liechtenstein, Italy, and France. Area: 15,941 sq.mi. (41,288 sq.km.). Pop. (1967 est.): 6,071,000. Cap.: Bern (pop., 1967 est., 168,800). Largest city: Zürich (pop., 1967 est., 436,200). Language (1960): German 69.3%; French 18.9%; Italian 9.5%; Romansh 0.9%. Religion (1960): Protestant 52.6%; Roman Catholic 45.6%. President in 1968, Willy Spühler.

The agitation of the French-speaking Jura separatists, and the measures taken to cope with it, continued to be an outstanding issue in 1968. In July the federal government discussed the Jura problem officially for the first time and offered its services to the separatists and the cantonal Bernese authorities to mediate in the conflict. The Bernese government appointed a committee to study the matter and propose solutions. In August the report of a previously appointed committee was published, containing contributions of some 60 political, economic, and cultural groups from all over Switzerland.

At the same time it was revealed that troops stationed in the Jura region for regular training purposes had been assigned by the federal government to "protect federal property endangered by separatist excesses." Even those who considered the government's action justified objected to the delay in informing the public, and in November the order alerting the troops was rescinded. Meanwhile, most of the groups directly involved, as well as the Swiss people at large, appeared to favour the holding of a plebiscite in the area to determine whether or not the French-speaking

When the 17-year-old Miss Ball contracted mononucleosis and missed the AAU indoor meet, there were doubts as to whether she could regain world supremacy in the breaststroke. She did, winning both breaststroke titles in the AAU outdoor meet and then setting world records in the U.S. Olympic trials of 1 min. 14.2 sec. for 100 m. and 2 min. 38.5 sec. for 200 m. But, suffering from influenza during the Olympics, she finished fifth in the 100-m. final and was not able to compete in the 200-m.

The Santa Clara Swim Club retained the team titles in the AAU men's outdoor and women's indoor and outdoor championships. Santa Clara was dethroned in the AAU men's indoor meet by Indiana University. The Santa Clara teams were coached by George Haines, who also coached the U.S. men's Olympic team. Indiana, coached by James Counsilman, won the NCAA title for the first time, largely because of its diving strength. Jim Henry of Dallas, Tex., and Edwin ("Win") Young of Phoenix were the leading Indiana divers.

With United States swimmers winning 21 of the 29 Olympic gold medals (plus 2 of 4 in diving) and 52 of the 77 medals available to them (plus 6 of 12 in diving), little was left for other countries. But they

World Records Set in 1968			
Event	Name	Country	Time
MEN			
100-m. freestyle	Michael Wenden	Australia	52.2 sec.
200-m. freestyle	Don Schollander	U.S.	1 min. 54.3 sec.
400-m. freestyle	Ralph Hutton	Canada	4 min. 6.5 sec.
800-m. freestyle	Mike Burton	U.S.	8 min. 34.3 sec.
1,500-m. freestyle	Mike Burton	U.S.	16 min. 8.5 sec.
100-m. breaststroke	Nikolai Pankin	U.S.S.R.	1 min. 6.2 sec.
200-m. breaststroke	Vladimir Kosinsky	U.S.S.R.	2 min. 27.4 sec.
100-m. butterfly	Mark Spitz	U.S.	55.6 sec.
100-m. backstroke	Roland Matthes	East Germany	58.0 sec.
200-m. backstroke	Roland Matthes	East Germany	2 min. 7.5 sec.
200-m. individual medley	Charles Hickcox	U.S.	2 min. 10.6 sec.
400-m. individual medley	Charles Hickcox	U.S.	4 min. 39.0 sec.
400-m. freestyle relay	U.S. (Z. Zorn, S. Rerych, M. Spitz, K. Walsh)		3 min. 31.7 sec.
400-m. medley relay	U.S. (C. Hickcox, D. McKenzie, D. Russell, K. Walsh)		3 min. 54.9 sec.
WOMEN			
200-m. freestyle	Debbie Meyer	U.S.	2 min. 6.7 sec.
400-m. freestyle	Debbie Meyer	U.S.	4 min. 24.5 sec.
800-m. freestyle	Debbie Meyer	U.S.	9 min. 10.4 sec.
1,500-m. freestyle	Debbie Meyer	U.S.	17 min. 31.2 sec.
100-m. breaststroke	Catie Ball	U.S.	1 min. 14.2 sec.
200-m. breaststroke	Catie Ball	U.S.	2 min. 38.5 sec.
100-m. backstroke	Kaye Hall	U.S.	1 min. 6.2 sec.
200-m. backstroke	Karen Muir	South Africa	2 min. 23.8 sec.
200-m. individual medley	Claudia Kolb	U.S.	2 min. 23.5 sec.
400-m. individual medley	Claudia Kolb	U.S.	5 min. 4.7 sec.
400-m. freestyle relay	Santa Clara S.C., U.S. (L. Gustavson, P. Watson, P. Carpinelli, J. Henne)		4 min. 1.0 sec.
400-m. medley relay	U.S. (K. Hall, C. Ball, E. Daniel, S. Pedersen)		4 min. 28.3 sec.

Catholic Jura region wanted and would be allowed to form a separate canton. At the end of the year such a plebiscite seemed the most likely future development.

The question of government control over television and other mass media was widely debated, but remained undecided at the end of the year. The organization and functioning of the universities was another urgent topic of discussion, partly because of the considerable increase in the number of students and partly in response to student unrest at home and abroad. The federal authorities concerned themselves with a program that included expansion of facilities, more autonomy for the universities, and more participation by students in curricula and administration.

The right of women to vote made some halting progress on the cantonal and communal levels, although it was rejected in two cantons and was still lacking on the federal level. Optimists nevertheless believed that an evolution "from the bottom up" would eventually lead to unrestricted suffrage for women. A woman became mayor of the city of Geneva. Mean-

UPI (UK) LTD.

Part of the group of 24 new Mirage III jet fighters that were assigned to Flying Corps 16 and 17 of the Swiss Air Force in March 1968.

while, the continued lack of women's suffrage was one of the reasons Switzerland had not as yet signed the European Convention on Human Rights, a fact that was widely noted in view of the 20th anniversary of the UN Declaration of Human Rights.

The issue of *Überfremdung* ("overalienation"; i.e., the high percentage of foreign workers in Switzerland) continued to make news. A popular initiative to restrict the number of aliens to 10% was published in the summer but was withdrawn in the face of widespread opposition. For economic reasons Switzerland continued to need large numbers of foreign workers, but for political and cultural reasons it feared to accept them.

The economic situation continued more or less at the boom level achieved in recent years, with foreign trade and payments moving around the established limits and the position of the Swiss franc strong. The labour market remained very tight, while wages and prices tended to rise. In March the federal government halted speculative foreign trading in Swiss silver coins by prohibiting their exportation, smelting, and hoarding; the traditional silver coins used for minor change were replaced by coins made of an inferior alloy.

A new law, effective in March, allowed conscientious objectors to serve their sentences in hospitals, road-building projects, or agriculture rather than in prison.

The government increased its collaboration in international economic and social, cultural, and humanitarian activities, especially those carried on by the specialized agencies of the UN. While its neutrality prevented the government from participating in the sanctions imposed on Rhodesia, it reaffirmed that it would continue to refrain from any action that would help to circumvent those sanctions. The occupation of Czechoslovakia by Soviet troops aroused a great deal of articulate sympathy for the Czechoslovak reformers, and the government gave the widest possible interpretation to its traditional policy of granting asylum to political refugees. Through the International Committee of the Red Cross in Geneva, aid was extended under difficult circumstances to the people of Biafra and Nigeria.

A development of particular interest was the submission by the Swiss government to the conference of nonnuclear states in Geneva of two draft resolutions concerning the nonproliferation of nuclear weapons. The first called for restricting the control of the International Atomic Energy Agency in Vienna to plutonium and highly enriched uranium; the second

SWITZERLAND

Education. (1964–65) Primary, pupils 468,664, teachers (excluding craft teachers; 1961–62) 23,761; secondary, pupils 242,249, teachers (full time; 1961–62) 6,583; vocational, pupils 19,500 (excluding 131,-897 in apprenticeship training schools); teacher training, students 10,410; higher (including 8 universities; 1965–66), students 32,921, teaching staff 2,342.

Finance. Monetary unit: Swiss franc, with a par value of SFr. 4.37 to U.S. $1 (SFr. 10.50 = £1 sterling). Gold and foreign exchange, central bank: (June 1968) U.S. $3.4 billion; (June 1967) U.S. $3,329,-000,000. Budget (1968 est.): revenue SFr. 6,493,-380,700; expenditure SFr. 6,318,502,300. Gross national product: (1967) SFr. 68.2 billion; (1966) SFr. 64.5 billion. Money supply: (June 1968) SFr. 33,940,000,000; (June 1967) SFr. 30,280,000,000. Cost of living (1963 = 100): (June 1968) 119; (June 1967) 117.

Foreign Trade. (1967) Imports SFr. 17,744,000,-000; exports SFr. 15,032,000,000. Import sources: EEC 60% (West Germany 29%, France 14%, Italy 10%); U.S. 8%; U.K. 8%. Export destinations: EEC 37% (West Germany 13%, France 9%, Italy 9%); U.S. 10%; U.K. 7%; Austria 5%. Main exports: machinery 30%; chemicals 20%; clocks and watches 14%; textile yarns and fabrics 7%. Tourism (1966): visitors 5,936,800; gross receipts SFr. 2,421,000,000.

Transport and Communications. Roads (1967) 57,923 km. Motor vehicles in use (1967): passenger 1,081,386; commercial 111,812. Railways: federal (1966) 2,934 km. (including 2,906 km. electrified); private (1965) 2,121 (including 1,912 km. electrified); traffic on federal railways (1967) 7,383,000,000 passenger-km., freight 5,665,000,000 net ton-km.; traffic on private railways (1965) 1,138,000,000 passenger-km., freight 373 million net ton-km. Shipping (1967): merchant vessels 100 gross tons and over 33; gross tonnage 198,850. Air traffic (1967): 2,994,481,000 passenger-km.; freight 82,047,000 net ton-km. Telephones (Dec. 1966) 2,395,123. Radio receivers (Dec. 1966) 1,685,000. Television receivers (Dec. 1966) 752,000.

Agriculture. Production (in 000; metric tons; 1967; 1966 in parentheses): wheat (including spelt) c. 330 (358); barley (1966) 107, (1965) 95; oats 30 (33); rye (1966) 47, (1965) 51; potatoes (1966) 1,049, (1965) 1,005; apples (1966) 360, (1965) 255; pears (1966) 153, (1965) 100; sugar, raw value (1967–68) c. 64, (1966–67) 58; wine (1966) 77, (1965) 90; milk (1966) 3,153, (1965) 3,117; butter 41 (34); cheese 83 (77); meat (1966) 273, (1965) 267. Livestock (in 000; April 1966): horses 67; sheep 266; cattle (April 1967) 835; pigs 1,513; goats 74; chickens 6,191.

Industry. Production (in 000; metric tons; 1967): cement 4,176; iron ore (1966) 66; aluminum (1966) 69; rayon yarn 11; rayon staple fibre (1966) 9; cigarettes (1966) 15,606,000 pieces; watches (1966) 38,015 units; electricity 30,795,000 kw-hr.; manufactured gas (1966) 383,000 cu.m. Index of industrial production (1963 = 100): (1967) 116; (1966) 113.

proposed that the nonnuclear powers be given access to advanced technology, especially with regard to the enrichment of uranium and the use of fissionable materials for peaceful purposes. The Swiss government had previously expressed its reservations about the nonproliferation treaty worked out at Geneva by the United States and the Soviet Union.   (M. F. S.)

ENCYCLOPÆDIA BRITANNICA FILMS. *Switzerland: Life in a Mountain Village* (1963).

Syria

A republic in southwestern Asia on the Mediterranean Sea, Syria is bordered by Turkey, Iraq, Jordan, Israel, and Lebanon. Area: 71,498 sq.mi. (185,180 sq.km.). Pop. (1967 est.): 5,652,000. Cap. and largest city: Damascus (pop., 1966 est., 594,426). Language: Arabic (official); also Kurdish, Armenian, Turkish, and Circassian. Religion: predominantly Muslim. Chairman of the Presidency Council in 1968, Nureddin al-Attassi; premiers, Yussef Zayen and, from October 28, Nureddin al-Attassi.

In 1968 the Syrian neo-Baathist regime maintained a hard line of total rejection of any political solution to the Arab-Israeli problem. However, there were few military incidents in the Golan Heights, the Syrian territory occupied by the Israelis, and Syria was accused by other Arab states of failing to back up its tough words with any action. At home, the government continued to deal severely with Palestinian refugees who were a potential challenge to its authority. In Damascus the situation remained tense and uncertain, although the widely expected coup did not occur. The regime was alarmed by the activities of Syrian exiles in Beirut, Lebanon, and its anxieties were increased by the July coup in Baghdad which brought to power in Iraq the orthodox Baathists of the kind ousted in Syria in 1966. In Syria a division appeared in the ruling group between Maj. Gen. Salah Jadid, assistant secretary-general of the Baath Party in Syria, who wished to pursue Syria's independent radical line, and

the defense minister, Maj. Gen. Hafez al-Assad, who favoured a rapprochement with the Iraqi Baathists and disliked Syria's constantly increasing dependence on the U.S.S.R. Jadid had been the real power in Syria for the previous two years, and in February he succeeded in ousting the army chief of staff, Maj. Gen. Ahmed Sweidani, and replacing him with Maj. Gen. Mustafa Tlas. In October, when Baath Party elections were held and Nureddin al-Attassi was reelected as head of the party in Syria, it seemed that Jadid and his supporters had strengthened their position. However, when al-Attassi took the premiership later in the month from the former premier, Yussef Zayen, and Foreign Minister Ibrahim Makhos also lost his post, it was interpreted as a victory for al-Assad.

In March the Soviet defense minister, Marshal Andrei A. Grechko, paid a five-day visit to Syria. In May all the Syrian leaders went to Cairo, where they urged that the United Arab Republic associate itself more closely with Syria. U.A.R. Pres. Gamal Abd-al-Nasser's reply was that for the strengthening of the Arab front the first essential was a rapprochement between Syria, Iraq, and Jordan.

In March work was inaugurated on the giant Euphrates Dam, which was to be built at Tabaqah with Soviet aid. It was estimated that the dam would cost S£2,400 million and increase Syria's national income by about S£700 million. It was expected to add 640,000 ha. (1,580,000 ac.) to the nation's irrigated area. On May 1 the premier inaugurated a 405-mi. pipeline built by an Italian firm from the oil fields of northeastern Syria to the port of Tartus, and in late July the first Syrian oil was exported.

In August a major dispute arose with Lebanon when Syria imposed heavy taxes on all goods in transit through Syrian territory from Lebanon. The Syrian action was partly intended as a warning to Lebanon against the activities of Syrian exiles in Beirut, but there was also an economic motive, as was shown by the special facilities Syria offered Jordan so that Jordan would export phosphates through Tartus rather than Beirut. The dispute was settled in October.

While the government continued to concentrate on large-scale public works and nationalized industries, the private sector remained stagnant. The government did make intensive efforts to improve cotton output over the poor level of the previous year. Prices for farmers were raised and acreage was increased.

(P. MD.)

ENCYCLOPÆDIA BRITANNICA FILMS. *The Middle East* (1955); *The Mediterranean World* (1961).

SYRIA

Education. (1965–66) Primary, pupils 688,165, teachers 19,040; secondary, pupils 177,174, teachers 7,326; vocational, pupils 8,030, teachers 945; teacher training, students 7,038, teachers 572; higher (including 2 universities), students 31,993, teaching staff 839.

Finance. Monetary unit: Syrian pound, with a par value of S£2.19 to U.S. $1 (S£5.26 = £1 sterling), an effective controlled rate of S£3.82 to U.S. $1 (S£9.17 = £1), and a free rate (Oct. 1968) of S£4.20 to U.S. $1 (S£10 = £1). Gold and foreign exchange, central bank: (June 1967) U.S. $46 million; (June 1966) U.S. $53 million. Budget (1966 est.) balanced at S£783 million. Money supply: (March 1968) S£1,512 million; (March 1967) S£1,228 million. Cost of living (Damascus; 1963 = 100): (March 1968) 117; (March 1967) 123.

Foreign Trade. (1967) Imports S£1,009,091,000; exports S£591,271,000. Import sources: Italy 11%; U.S.S.R. 10%; West Germany 8%; France 8%; Iraq 6%; U.K. 6%; China 5%; Romania 5%. Export destinations: Lebanon 20%; U.S.S.R. 12%; France 7%; Japan 7%; China 5%. Main exports: cotton 43%; wool 4%.

Transport and Communications. Roads (1966) *c.* 15,000 km. (including 8,490 km. with improved surface). Motor vehicles in use (1966): passenger 26,497; commercial 13,308. Railways (1966): 844 km.; traffic 68 million passenger-km., freight 85 million net ton-km. Ships entered (1966) vessels totaling 12,920,000 net registered tons; goods loaded (1966) 25,773,000 metric tons, unloaded 1,507,000 metric tons. Air traffic (1966): 198,105,000 passenger-km.; freight 350,000 net ton-km. Telephones (Dec. 1966) 85,911. Radio receivers (Dec. 1965) 1,745,000. Television receivers (Dec. 1966) *c.* 100,000.

Agriculture. Production (in 000; metric tons; 1967; 1966 in parentheses): wheat 1,060 (559); barley 599 (203); millet and sorghum (1966) 15, (1965) 44; grapes (1966) 206, (1965) 206; raisins (1966) 8.1, (1965) 7.6; figs (1966) 54, (1965) 54; olive oil *c.* 21 (24); tobacco (1966) 10, (1965) 12; chick-peas (1966) 16, (1965) 46; lentils (1966) 22, (1965) 66; cotton, lint 122 (135); wool (1966) 5.6, (1965) 6.6. Livestock (in 000; 1965–66): cattle 524; sheep 5,422; horses 67; mules 66; asses 198; goats 832; chickens 4,600.

Industry. Production (in 000; metric tons; 1966): petroleum products 1,052; cement (1967) 688; cotton yarn 18; electricity 658,000 kw-hr.

Taiwan

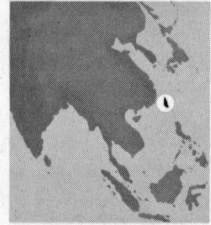

Taiwan, which consists of the islands of Formosa and Quemoy and other surrounding islands, is the seat of the Republic of China (Nationalist China). It is situated north of the Philippines, southwest of Japan and Okinawa, and east of Hong Kong. The island of Formosa has an area of 13,807 sq.mi. (35,760 sq.km.); including its 77 outlying islands (14 in the Taiwan group and 63 in the Pescadores group), the area of Taiwan totals 13,885 sq.mi. Pop. (1968 est.): 13,941,006, excluding armed forces and aliens. Cap. and largest city: T'ai-pei (pop., 1967 est., 1,199,934). President in 1968, Chiang Kai-shek; vice-president

and premier (president of the Executive Yuan), C. K. Yen.

When the Republic of China celebrated its 57th anniversary on October 10, its government had been in refuge on Taiwan for nearly two decades. However, the turmoil created by the Cultural Revolution in Communist China and its diplomatic setbacks in Indonesia and several African countries strengthened Nationalist China's international position. As of October, 66 countries, including 20 African states, maintained diplomatic relations with Nationalist China, while 45 maintained relations with Communist China. A number of countries recognized neither regime. In the United Nations General Assembly, 58 of 126 members voted against the resolution on seating Communist China in November 1968, compared with 47 of 114 members in 1965, while the number of countries voting for Communist China's admission declined from 47 to 44 during the same period.

The two-China solution to the problem of Chinese representation in the UN continued to be opposed vehemently by both Communist and Nationalist China. On June 8, speaking to a group of Japanese journalists, Chiang Kai-shek reaffirmed his government's firm opposition to the two-China policy and warned that Nationalist China would sever relations with any country recognizing the Communist regime in Peking. Referring to reports that Japan intended to increase official contacts with Communist China, Chiang stated that if the Japanese government should decide to recognize Peking, Japan would have to break off diplomatic ties with Nationalist China.

TAIWAN

Education. (1965–66) Primary, pupils 2,257,720, teachers 54,610; secondary, pupils 543,019, teachers 19,882; vocational, pupils 117,575, teachers 6,194; teacher training, students 3,159, teachers 225; higher (including 10 universities), students 85,346, teaching staff 9,411.

Finance. Monetary unit: New Taiwan dollar (NT$40.10 = U.S. $1; NT$96.24 = £1 sterling). Gold and foreign exchange, official: (June 1968) U.S. $416 million; (June 1967) U.S. $392 million. Budget (1965–66 actual): revenue NT$25,320,000,000; expenditure NT$23,888,000,000. Gross national product: (1967) NT$141,570,000,000; (1966) NT$125.5 billion. Money supply: (June 1968) NT$23,960,000,000; (June 1967) NT$18,760,000,000. Cost of living (1963 = 100): (May 1968) 112; (May 1967) 103.

Foreign Trade. (1967) Imports U.S. $805.8 million (including U.S. $42.3 million of U.S. aid); exports U.S. $640.7 million. Import sources: Japan 41%; U.S. 31%. Export destinations: U.S. 26%; Japan 18%; South Vietnam 12%; Hong Kong 8%; West Germany 6%. Main exports (1966): sugar 10%; rice 6%.

Transport and Communications. Roads (1966) 16,581 km. Motor vehicles in use (1966): passenger 19,200; commercial (including buses) 21,300. Railways (1966): 4,600 km.; traffic 4,642,000,000 passenger-km., freight 2,435,000,000 net ton-km. Shipping (1967): merchant vessels 100 gross tons and over 174; gross tonnage 775,397. Air traffic (1967): 287,279,000 passenger-km.; freight 3,932,000 net ton-km. Telephones (Jan. 1967) 191,532. Radio receivers (Dec. 1966) 1,362,000. Television receivers (Dec. 1966) 108,000.

Agriculture. Production (in 000; metric tons; 1967; 1966 in parentheses): rice c. 3,400 (2,960); sweet potatoes 3,719 (3,460); cassava (1966) 264, (1965) 265; peanuts 133 (115); tea (1966) 21, (1965) 21; sugar, raw value (1967–68) c. 873, (1966–67) c. 780; bananas (1966) 528, (1965) 452; jute 15 (11). Livestock (in 000; Dec. 1966): cattle 367; pigs 3,110; goats 158; chickens (Dec. 1965) 9,868.

Industry. Fuel and power (in 000; 1967): coal 5,077 metric tons; natural gas 527,000 cu.m.; electricity 8,411,000 kw-hr. Production (in 000; metric tons; 1967): cement 3,487; pig iron 85; petroleum products (1966) 2,187; cotton yarn 70; paper (1966) 214.

Nationalist China's friendly relations with several countries in the Asia-Pacific region were strengthened in 1968 by the conclusion of trade and economic cooperation pacts. After an exchange of state visits and the holding of a Sino-Thai Economic Cooperation Conference in T'ai-pei in June, an agreement on economic and technical cooperation was signed whereby Nationalist China would send an agricultural technical mission to help Thailand boost its agricultural production while Thailand would dispatch urban development and highway experts to render technical services to Nationalist China. The fourth Sino-Korean Ministerial Economic Cooperation Conference took place in T'ai-pei in July, and the two countries agreed to increase trade and to work together in deep-sea fishing, agriculture, science, and technology. China also agreed to send agricultural demonstration teams to Iran and the Philippines to help them increase their rice production.

Prior to the convocation of the General Assembly of the UN, special envoys on a goodwill mission from Nationalist China toured 11 Latin-American nations and practically all the African countries with which it maintained diplomatic relations. In May the Central African Republic resumed diplomatic relations with T'ai-pei. In September, four days after it achieved independence, Swaziland exchanged ambassadors with Nationalist China. This brought to 20 the number of African countries having formal diplomatic relations with T'ai-pei.

Reporting to the Legislative Yuan on the state of the nation in February, Premier Yen warned that the Chinese Communists might stir up trouble in the Taiwan Straits as a diversionary move in support of the Viet Cong offensive in South Vietnam. In the meantime, it was reported that the U.S. was considering a request to Chiang to withdraw his forces from the islands of Quemoy and Matsu, from which the Nationalists had recently intensified their psychological warfare directed at Communist China. The exchange of artillery shells containing mainly propaganda messages between Nationalist and Communist troops continued, but more Communist defectors were reported to have reached Quemoy and Matsu in recent months. Chiang remained firm in keeping a garrison on the offshore islands. In March it was reported that the U.S. had given Nationalist China assurances that it would not press Chiang to remove his troops from Quemoy and Matsu, but that it expected T'ai-pei to pay a larger share of its military expenditures; U.S. military aid had been averaging about $100 million a year. Nationalist military expenditure was known to be about 10% of its gross national product and constituted the biggest portion of the government's budget outlays. It remained to be seen whether Nationalist China could maintain its present large military forces without external aid or without seriously affecting its rate of economic growth.

Two important measures were introduced for national modernization. To promote science education as well as to curb the loss of leading scientists to other countries, the Science Development Guidance Committee of the National Security Council worked out a ten-year program for the development of science and technology. In September a nine-year program of free education was inaugurated, and graduates of primary school, which was compulsory and free, were allowed to continue their education at tuition-free, publicly operated schools without taking entrance examinations, as formerly required.

Table Tennis:
see Sporting Record

At the fourth local elections for the provincial assembly on April 21, 3.7 million of 5,260,000 eligible voters cast their votes. Candidates of the Kuomintang, the party headed by Chiang Kai-shek, captured 61 of the 71 seats.   (H. T. Ch.)

See also China.

Tanzania

This republic, an East African member of the Commonwealth of Nations, consists of two parts: Tanganyika, on the Indian Ocean, bordered by Kenya, Uganda, Rwanda, Burundi, the Congo (Kinshasa), Zambia, Malawi, and Mozambique; and Zanzibar, just off the coast, including Zanzibar Island, Pemba Island, and small islets. Total area of the united republic: 361,800 sq.mi. (937,058 sq.km.). Total pop. (1967 est.): 12,231,342 (approximately 98% Africans and 1% Arabs). Cap. and largest city: Dar es Salaam (pop., 1967, 272,515), in Tanganyika. Language: primarily Bantu, of which Swahili serves as the lingua franca. Religion: predominantly pagan; many Muslims in coastal areas and in up-country settlements; Christian minority. President in 1968, Julius Nyerere.

After the Tanganyika African National Union (TANU) national conference, held in Mwanza in October 1967, President Nyerere appeared to be in a stronger position than ever before. His policy of self-reliance won wholehearted approval, while the all-important role of the central government was emphasized by party reorganization involving the abolition of the offices of secretary-general, formerly held by Oscar Kambona, and national treasurer and the disbanding of the TANU Cabinet on the ground that it no longer served any useful function.

Yet Kambona was not without sympathizers, as indicated by letters to the press, criticizing the president. In January 1968 Kambona himself broke silence after the arrest and detention of two of his brothers, along with Abdullah Kassim Hanga, former vice-president of Zanzibar and once a minister in the Tanzania government. From London Kambona challenged Nyerere to appoint a commission to inquire into the allegations that he had opened illegal banking accounts and purchased five houses in contravention of government regulations. Nyerere, however, rejected the challenge and was soon threatening with dismissal any members of Parliament or leading civil servants who were drawing more than one salary, receiving income from directorships, or employing workmen in any trade or profession. That his policy did not lack support was soon demonstrated when the National Assembly rejected a proposal that ministers and senior officials on restricted salaries should be paid bonuses.

Four years after the revolution that had brought about the overthrow of the sultan and had led to union with Tanganyika, Zanzibar continued to manage most of its own affairs, although the Tanzanian National Assembly was becoming increasingly dissatisfied with the Zanzibar regime. After new measures for the treatment of offenders in Zanzibar had been announced in July by Sheikh Abeid Karume, Tanzania's first vice-president, members of the Assembly went so far as to demand democratic elections on the island; others strongly urged the amalgamation of TANU and the Afro-Shirazi Party in order to make the union more effective. Despite lavish aid from no less than six Communist countries there were still no signs of buoyancy in the island's economy.

KEYSTONE

Students and youths demonstrating in front of the Soviet embassy in Dar es Salaam to protest the Soviet invasion of Czechoslovakia.

To mark the fourth anniversary of the union, Nyerere addressed a public rally on April 26 in Dar es Salaam. In the course of his speech he declared that African nations were not compelled to respect boundaries drawn up in the colonial era. The immediate implication of this for Tanzania was not clear unless it related to claims against Malawi, but the long-term effect as far as the policy of the Organization of African Unity (OAU) was concerned was considerable. So, too, was Tanzania's recognition of Nigeria's secessionist state of Biafra, which was also announced in April. This was the first time that any African country had recognized the right of secession from an independent African state, and Nyerere defended Tanzania's action on the ground that unity can only exist with the general consent of the people involved.

Relations with Britain became strained in June when Tanzania declared its intention of ceasing payment of pensions to expatriate civil servants who had left the country before independence. By arrangement between the U.K. and Tanganyika governments prior to independence, the former had offered to make a loan that would enable the new government to pay the pensions for some years until it was able to bear the burden itself.

This loan was now virtually exhausted, and the time for repayment was approaching. Tanzania's decision, however, meant that 70% of the loan would not be repaid and that Britain would have to assume responsibility for the pensions itself. Britain responded to the news by bringing to an end its program of aid

TANZANIA

Education. (1965) Primary, pupils 710,200, teachers 13,576; secondary, pupils 21,915, teachers 1,064; vocational, pupils 2,842, teachers 147; teacher training, students 2,270, teachers 299; higher (at the Dar es Salaam University College), students 440.

Finance. Monetary unit: Tanzanian shilling, with a par value of TShs. 7.14 to U.S. $1 (TShs. 17.14 = £1 sterling). Budget (1967–68 est.): revenue TShs. 939 million; expenditure TShs. 1,566,400,000. National income (mainland only): (1966) TShs. 5,038,000,000; (1965) TShs. 4,551,000,000. Cost of living (Dar es Salaam; 1963 = 100): (June 1968) 119; (June 1967) 118.

Foreign Trade. *Mainland.* (Excluding trade with Kenya and Uganda; 1967) Imports TShs. 1.3 billion; exports TShs. 1,582,000,000. Import sources: U.K. 29%; Italy 11%; U.S. 8%; West Germany 6%; Iran 6%; Japan 5%; China 5%. Export destinations: U.K. 30%; Hong Kong 7%; India 7%; West Germany 5%; U.S. 5%. Main exports: cotton 16%; coffee 15%; diamonds 14%; sisal 13%. *Zanzibar.* (1966) Imports TShs. 91 million; exports TShs. 104 million. Main exports (1965): cloves 57%; copra 19%.

Transport and Communications. Roads (1966) *c.* 50,000 km. (including *c.* 13,000 km. all-weather and *c.* 990 km. in Zanzibar and Pemba). Motor vehicles in use (1966): passenger *c.* 38,000; commercial (including buses) *c.* 12,500. Railways (1966) 2,977 km. (for traffic *see* KENYA). Shipping traffic (mainland only; 1967): goods loaded 1,254,000 metric tons; unloaded 1,633,000 metric tons. Telephones (Dec. 1966) 24,869. Radio receivers (Dec. 1966) *c.* 120,000.

Agriculture. Production (in 000; metric tons; 1967; 1966 in parentheses): cotton, lint (mainland) 68 (80); sisal (mainland) 233 (227); corn (mainland; 1966) 1,150, (1965) 512; peanuts, commercial (mainland) 8 (12); millet and sorghum (1966) *c.* 1,100, (1965) 1,100; sugar, raw value (mainland) 83 (76); rice (1966) *c.* 143, (1965) 84; cassava (1966) *c.* 1,130, (1965) *c.* 1,130; timber (1966) *c.* 11,600 cu.m., (1965) *c.* 11,500 cu.m. Livestock (in 000; 1965–66): cattle *c.* 10,514; sheep (mainland) 2,974; goats *c.* 4,470; asses 161; pigs (mainland) 16. Fish catch (in 000; metric tons) (1966) 92, (1965) 103.

Industry. Production (in 000; metric tons; 1966): salt 37; tin concentrates (metal content) 0.4; gold 55 troy oz.; diamonds 906 metric carats; electricity (mainland; public supply) 252,000 kw.-hr.

for Tanzania and by ceasing to recruit technical assistance staff to help Tanzania's development program. On July 4, however, diplomatic relations between the two countries, broken off in 1965 by Tanzania in protest against Britain's Rhodesia policy, were restored, but no immediate steps were taken to resume financial and technical aid.

A new press ordinance giving the president power to ban any newspaper if he considered it in the public interest to do so aroused adverse comment outside Tanzania in May. More reassuring was the first report of Chief Erasto Mang-Enya, Tanzania's ombudsman, also published in May, which dealt with the 1,627 complaints he had heard against Tanzanian officials and in which he stated that the public was gaining confidence in his office as the realization grew that complaints did not result in reprisals against those who made them.   (K. I.)

ENCYCLOPÆDIA BRITANNICA FILMS. *East Africa (Kenya, Tanganyika, Uganda)* (1962).

Telecommunications

Telecommunications authorities throughout the world in 1968 made and heard proposals for bringing order to the disarray wrought by rapidly advancing technology. Committees chartered by international organizations and national governments released the results of studies and reported plans for untangling the communications problems generated by modern technology.

The Soviet Union and its allies proposed a rival to the U.S.-led International Telecommunications Satellite Consortium (Intelsat). The competitive organization, called Intersputnik, was designed to be governed by each member nation on an equal-vote basis. This was intended to counteract Intelsat's use of a weighted membership, basing ownership on the amount of international communications used by the country. There was also a suggestion in 1968 that Latin-American countries set up a coordinated network of high-capacity communications links.

A new trend was noted in the United States. The Federal Communications Commission (FCC) began edging toward a new regulatory philosophy by pro-

Technicians installing a new antenna at Bouchette, Que., which would eventually relay voice and television signals into northern Canada in conjunction with a satellite communications system.

CANADIAN PRESS

moting competition among communications companies in the hopes that competition itself would become a regulatory device.

The importance of international news reporting, beamed via communications satellites, increased during 1968. The first commercial telecast using satellites between the U.S. and Australia carried a speech by U.S. Pres. Lyndon B. Johnson on March 31.

During 1968, criticism of the FCC intensified, and a number of different groups began laying the groundwork for completely overhauling the organization. The U.S. House of Representatives Commerce Committee in a series of legislative hearings criticized the FCC for "sloppy administrative procedures" in the licensing of broadcasters. In May, one of the FCC's commissioners, Robert T. Bartley, suggested replacing the FCC with two independent agencies and a third authority for handling frequency allocations. He said that the multi-agency arrangement for communications would result in "more effective management" of telecommunications resources.

Satellites. An attempt to dramatize the effectiveness of satellite communications failed to materialize. Intelsat had hoped to provide "live" coverage in Europe of the Olympic Games from Mexico City. But the spacecraft, first in a new series of high-capacity satellites, was dumped into the Atlantic Ocean in September when its booster rocket failed. Consequently, the U.S. space agency supplied the television service for the Olympics.

Even with this setback, 1968 was a good year for Intelsat. Its membership grew to 63, and the number of earth stations equipped to receive and send satellite signals was increased to 22. A second satellite was launched successfully from Cape Kennedy, Fla., in mid-December.

Even after the loss of the first Intelsat 3 satellite, consortium officials confidently predicted that the long-term goal of global coverage would be a reality in 1969 or 1970. Intelsat contracted for six satellites in buying the Intelsat 3s. The first three were planned for positioning at various points over the Equator, and a fourth was to be located over the Indian Ocean to complete a global system. All were to be orbited at an altitude of 22,300 mi. where they would be "stabilized" relative to the movement of the earth. Each satellite was designed to be capable of 1,200 two-way telephone circuits, about five times the capacity of the Intelsat 2s.

The Intelsat 3s featured a number of technical improvements in addition to the extra capacity. They were designed to last longer—five years, compared with three for the Intelsat 2s. Also, a new antenna directed the satellite's energy toward the earth at all times, preventing a waste of power.

Late in 1968 Intelsat decided to begin construction of satellites more technically advanced than the Intelsat 3s. Hughes Aircraft Co. was awarded a $72 million contract to build the 5,000-circuit Intelsat 4 series.

An international agreement to organize Intelsat permanently was to be negotiated in 1969. The interim agreement in effect until then divided ownership in relation to the use a country made of international communications. On that basis the U.S., through its Communications Satellite Corp. (Comsat), held 53% of Intelsat. U.S. officials hinted, however, at a willingness to reduce ownership. The negotiations were scheduled to begin in February 1969, at a conference in Washington, D.C.

UPI COMPIX

New Jersey Bell Telephone Co. supervisors repairing a cable cut on April 17 near Newark Airport. Forty cables were cut in the first four days of a strike against the company.

Tariffs:
see Commercial Policies; Trade, International

Taxation:
see Government Finance

Tea:
see Agriculture

COURTESY, STC

U.S. negotiators planned to urge, at the conference, that Intelsat governing countries recognize regional satellite systems within the framework of Intelsat. A number of countries, notably the U.S., Canada, and the Soviet Union, were considering domestic or regional systems. An Intelsat provision for regional satellites would also aid planners of the proposed Latin-American coordinated network. The $300 million complex of microwave systems, submarine cables, and satellites had been suggested to the members of the Inter-American Telecommunications Commission (CITEL) by the World Bank.

Comsat gained financial stability as its Intelsat responsibilities grew in 1968. Earnings for the first six months of 1968 amounted to 33 cents per share, compared with 21 cents per share during the same period of 1967. During the year Comsat hired its 800th employee and moved its business offices into L'Enfant Plaza, near U.S. government buildings in Washington, D.C.

In addition to making a spirited drive for domestic satellite business, Comsat continued its legal fight to increase its ownership of ground terminals used in the U.S. for international service. By the terms of an interim policy established by the FCC, Comsat owned 50% of the U.S. stations, while the remainder were owned by other communications companies: AT & T, 28.5%; RCA Global Communications, 10.5%; ITT World Communications, 7%; and Western Union International, 4%. Comsat planned to request FCC authority to own more than 50% of the terminals. FCC Chairman Rosel Hyde told Comsat that permanent ownership arrangements would be worked out early in 1969.

Development of space communications, at present independent of Intelsat, was being carried out by France and West Germany with a 4% Belgian participation. This program, announced at the UN space conference in Vienna in August, envisaged the launching by a Europa II vehicle of three Symphonie satellites from the French base in French Guiana during late 1971 and early 1972. Coverage would include South America, Africa, Europe, and the east coast of the United States and Canada; the satellites would be used principally for experimental television transmissions and also for radio, telephony, telegraphy, and data transmissions.

Telephone Service. At the beginning of 1967 there were 208.5 million telephones throughout the world. About 106 million were in North America and 67 million in Europe. The highest urban telephone density was in Washington, D.C., with 94.7 telephones per 100 inhabitants. In Europe, Stockholm headed the list with 77.5 telephones per 100 inhabitants, followed by Zürich with 65.9. The use of telephones increased throughout the world in 1968. During the year the Dominican Republic, Israel, and Venezuela joined 23 other countries that could be dialed directly by U.S. overseas operators. AT & T's Bell System, with about 85% of the phones in the U.S., reported that 16.1 million overseas phone calls were made in 1968. The total in 1967 was 12.6 million.

Profits of U.S. telephone companies increased in 1967, and the 57 companies reporting to the FCC handled more than 141.9 million calls. AT & T spent $4.7 billion in 1968 to build new facilities. The company announced plans for a $170 million underground cable between St. Louis and Los Angeles. The cable, called L-5, would be able to carry about 90,000 telephone conversations simultaneously. Previously, no cable system had been able to carry more than 36,000 circuits.

The new high-capacity cable reopened the debate over the economic wisdom of using satellites instead of cables for long-distance communications within the U.S. Officials of the Bell companies estimated that cables were more economical than satellites for telephone service between points less than 1,300 mi. apart. The average long-distance call in the U.S. was for 400 mi.

The most hotly contested regulatory issue during 1968 involved how much a customer could modify the equipment supplied to him by the telephone company —either to save money or to obtain a wider range of services. The issue was brought to a head by Carter Electronics Co. of Dallas, Tex., a small firm which built a device to connect mobile radio system signals to the regular telephone company network. The phone companies, led by the Bell System, first contested Carter's right to market the systems. But the FCC ruled that Bell's prohibition was not legal, and the giant company weakened its regulations.

At the urging of the FCC, AT & T agreed to convert its pay station phones in such a way as to make it possible to dial an emergency number without paying for the call. A nationwide emergency number—911— was established. The conversion was estimated to have cost the company about $50 million.

Europe's first electronic switching telephone exchange (EAX—Electronic Automatic Exchange) with stored program control was opened in Belgium in December 1967. Calls were metered on a magnetic drum.

A new telegraph relay centre to speed up the handling of overseas telegrams was opened in November 1967 in London. Initially, it handled 35,000 to 40,000 telegrams a day, most of them automatically. When fully equipped, it would be the largest automatic centre in the world network.

Pulse code modulation (PCM), the British invention that provides 24 speech circuits on two pairs of

Engineer making test measurements on a pulse code modulation (PCM) encoder card. This equipment, which provides 24 speech channels on two pairs of wires, was supplied for the London-Sudbury PCM link.

Countries Having More Than 100,000 Telephones
Telephones in service, 1967

Country	Number of telephones	Percentage increase over 1957	Telephones per 100 population	Country	Number of telephones	Percentage increase over 1957	Telephones per 100 population
Algeria*	140,000	...	1.15	Korea, South	324,049	544.8	1.11
Argentina	1,526,767	32.2	6.68	Lebanon	120,323	212.6	4.84
Australia	2,978,336	74.8	25.81	Malaysia	137,726	...	1.40
Austria	1,087,007	101.1	14.88	Mexico	930,940	142.9	2.07
Belgium	1,665,508	78.8	17.43	Morocco	143,074	14.6	1.06
Brazil	1,431,653	68.9	1.67	Netherlands	2,512,826	104.4	20.05
Bulgaria	306,361	...	3.70	New Zealand	1,087,133	91.3	39.87
Canada	7,880,471	75.1	38.91	Norway	945,573	49.7	25.09
Chile	281,532	84.4	3.19	Pakistan	145,689	192.0	0.14
China, Communist†	244,028	...	0.05	Peru	142,589	110.2	1.17
Colombia	479,134	142.3	2.53	Philippines	188,144	196.8	0.55
Cuba*	234,000	22.8	2.95	Poland	1,411,481	151.6	4.44
Czechoslovakia	1,582,852	125.1	11.09	Portugal	581,780	108.1	6.31
Denmark	1,411,040	52.9	29.09	Puerto Rico	218,658	235.4	8.14
Finland	892,300	83.5	19.19	Rhodesia	105,599	93.5	2.36
France	6,554,441	97.8	13.19	Romania*	510,000	...	2.66
Germany, East	1,723,814	61.6	10.09	South Africa	1,260,692	64.7	6.86
Germany, West	9,532,417	120.5	15.89	Spain	3,072,214	156.2	9.60
Greece	579,076	323.2	6.69	Sweden	3,757,495	62.5	47.90
Hong Kong	301,673	373.1	7.97	Switzerland	2,395,123	85.1	39.25
Hungary	597,376	63.5	5.86	Taiwan	191,532	306.6	1.47
India	961,063	205.2	0.19	Turkey	385,560	121.9	1.17
Indonesia	164,373	107.5	0.15	U.S.S.R.*	8,400,000	149.6	3.58
Iran	213,420	233.9	0.83	United Arab Republic*	335,000	86.1	1.10
Ireland	225,000	82.0	7.80	United Kingdom	11,376,000	57.6	20.70
Israel	301,008	315.5	11.33	United States	98,789,000	64.1	49.87
Italy	6,467,597	147.9	12.44	Uruguay*	190,000	55.0	6.87
Japan	16,011,745	329.6	16.08	Venezuela	308,898	177.0	3.36
				Yugoslavia	452,248	157.9	2.27

*Estimate. †1948.
Source: American Telephone and Telegraph Co., The World's Telephones, 1957 and 1967.

wires in existing telephone cables, went into full commercial operation in Britain. The first PCM link was inaugurated in November 1967, and it was expected that more than 1,000 would be in operation by the end of 1969.   (W. D. Hi.; T. C. J. C.)

International Telecommunication Union. The 23rd session of the Administrative Council of the International Telecommunication Union (ITU) took place in May at ITU headquarters in Geneva. The council emphasized the importance of the ITU in space radiocommunications by adopting three resolutions. They dealt with ITU activities in the field of space telecommunications, the role of the ITU in this field, and the convening of a world conference during the latter part of 1970 or early 1971 for a duration of five weeks. The proposed objectives of this conference included, in particular, the following items: (1) to revise existing administrative and technical regulations and to adopt such new provisions as would be necessary for both the space radio services and the radio-astronomy service to ensure the efficient use of the radio frequency spectrum; (2) to consider, and revise as necessary, the provisions of the Radio Regulations pertaining to the Aeronautical Mobile and the Maritime Mobile services and to navigation insofar as the use of space techniques was concerned; (3) to consider and provide, as far as possible, additional radio frequency allocations for the space radio services; and (4) to revise and supplement, as appropriate, the existing technical criteria for frequency sharing between space and terrestrial systems and to establish criteria for sharing between satellite systems.

The International Consultative Committees' (CCI) Study Groups held numerous meetings during the year. The two CCI's were ITU organs devoted to studying technical and operating questions relating to radiocommunications (CCIR) and to telegraphy and telephony (CCITT). Sound and television broadcasting, broadcasting in the tropics, radio propagation, space systems and radio astronomy, radio relay systems, transmission of sound and television signals over long distances, and data transmission were some of the questions under study. In particular, the CCIR was requested by UNESCO and the Economic Commission for Africa to draw up specifications for one or more types of low-cost television receivers. The receivers had to be suitable for mass production and suited to the needs of countries where, for economic, geographical, or technical reasons, the number of television receivers available was inadequate.

The CCITT held its fourth Plenary Assembly from September 23 until October 25 in Mar del Plata, Arg. The first part of this conference dealt with the drawing up of recommendations devoted, for example, to the introduction of worldwide automatic telephony and to transmissions between computers.

The World Telecommunication Plan 1967–1970–1975 was issued following the meeting of the ITU's World Plan Committee in Mexico at the end of 1967. This plan made a broad statistical survey of intercontinental communications as they currently existed. It also allowed provision for the future in the light of foreseeable short-term (1970) and longer-term (1975) developments in international telecommunications, with particular reference to the use of communications satellites.   (ITU)

See also Industrial Review; Television and Radio.

Encyclopædia Britannica Films. *Development of Communications (From Telegraph to TV)* (1955).

Television and Radio

The rapid growth rates of television and radio began to slow down in 1968 as opportunities for further expansion became more and more limited. With television in operation in more than 100 countries and radio in more than 200, it appeared likely that the costs of setting up new systems would keep future growth rates at more moderate levels than in the past. The latest official report, compiled by the United States Information Agency in 1964, estimated that 162 million television sets and more than 500 million radio sets were in use throughout the world. Private broadcasting industry sources estimated that the totals had reached 213 million television sets and 595 million radio sets by late 1968.

More than one-third, or about 78 million, of the TV sets were in the U.S. The U.S.S.R. had approximately 25 million, Japan 20.5 million, the United Kingdom 19 million, West Germany 13.5 million, France 10 million, Italy 8.2 million, Canada 6.2 million, Poland 2.5 million, and Australia 2.4 million, according to estimates compiled by *Broadcasting* magazine and *Broadcasting Yearbook* in late 1968.

Television stations operating or under construction throughout the world numbered approximately 5,520 in 1968. Western Europe had about 2,000, the Far East 1,300, the U.S. 1,030, Eastern Europe 900, South America 165, and Africa 30. About 12,550 radio stations were in operation or under construction. Most of these were amplitude modulation (AM) radio stations, but the total also included frequency modulation (FM) stations and the relay or booster operations used in many countries to carry radio programming into remote areas. More than half of the 12,550 radio stations, or 6,828, were in the U.S., and more than one-third, or 2,499, of the U.S. total were FM, according to records compiled by *Broadcasting* in November. Approximately half of the world's 595 million radio sets, or about 300 million, also were in the U.S., with the rest distributed among the world's countries in proportions ranging from less than 1 set per 100 population to more than 1 set for every 2 persons.

Organization. Though cutbacks in expenditure in the U.S. and Europe affected expansion, technological progress continued. The Olympic Games, held in Mexico in October, were successfully transmitted by satellite, and despite failure to launch Intelsat 3 from Cape Kennedy, Fla., full coverage was provided. The picture was routed via the U.S. National Aeronautics and Space Administration's (NASA) ATS-3 satellite, in orbit over the Atlantic, and the sound via Intelsat 1 (Early Bird), with Intelsat 2 transmission to Asia. Links with the U.S.S.R.'s Molniya 1 satellite system covered the Soviet Union. An estimated potential audience of approximately 600 million was served jointly by the European Broadcasting Union (EBU), American Broadcasting Company (ABC), and Japan's Nippon Hoso Kyokai (NHK), with about 40 hours of transmission daily by the Telesistema Mexicano (TSM) network. The Winter Olympics at Grenoble, France, had been equally successfully covered by the French Office de Radiodiffusion-Télévision Française (ORTF), with its first large-scale, widely transmitted outdoor colour broadcasts, and by separate colour facilities for ABC on the U.S. 525-line National Television System Committee's (NTSC) system.

Plans continued to extend and improve the interna-

tional satellite system. Intelsat 3 would lead a four-satellite global system, with two satellites over the Atlantic, one over the Pacific, and one over the Indian Ocean, each with about quadruple Intelsat 2's capacity and carrying at least 12 colour-TV channels, as well as relaying telephone communications. (*See* TELE-COMMUNICATIONS.) By 1968 the International Tele-communications Satellite Consortium (Intelsat) had 62 member nations; stations in Australia, Canada, Chile, France, West Germany, India, Indonesia, Italy, Japan, Mexico, Panama, the Philippines, Spain, Thailand, the U.S., and the U.K.; and stations under construction in more than 40 other countries. Intelsat's

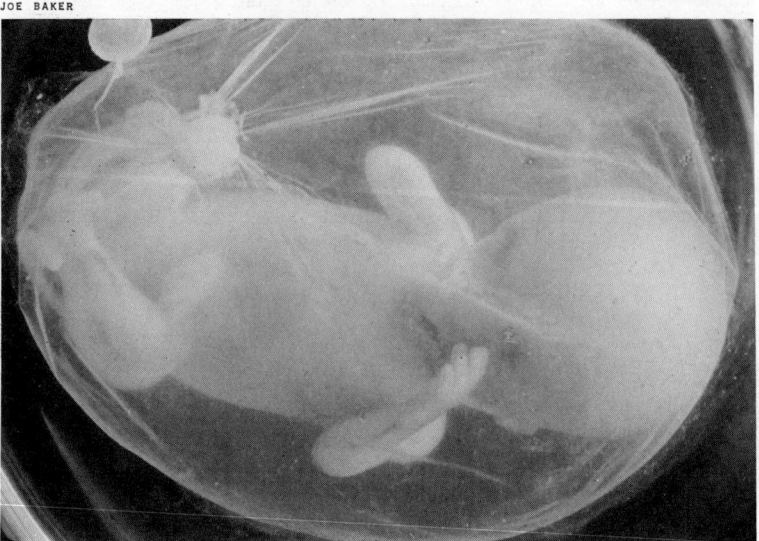

Rare view of a human fetus from the ABC News special "How Life Begins," which documented prenatal development and included actual scenes of a birth.

aim—to establish a single shared global system—seemed likely to be thwarted by development of other systems, however. The Soviet Union (not an Intelsat member) at a UN conference in August announced plans for Intersputnik, an international system with Bulgaria, Cuba, Czechoslovakia, Hungary, Mongolia, Poland, and Romania among founder-members. It would be financed by members in proportion to their use of the communications channels provided, and membership by countries belonging to other systems would be allowed. It would probably use the Molniya 1 network, successfully tested for international use.

Another development forecast was replacement, wholly or partially, of terrestrial distribution networks by distribution satellites. Research continued, particularly in the U.S., Canada, and Japan. Use of satellites for mass education was being considered in less developed areas, notably India, Indonesia, and Brazil.

United States. Colour became more and more dominant in 1968. Black-and-white programming on the three television networks was rare: a survey by *Broadcasting* in January showed that the National Broadcasting Company (NBC) had converted 100% of its regular programming to colour, the Columbia Broadcasting System (CBS) 91%, and ABC 87%, and the ratios for CBS and ABC increased as the year progressed. Most stations, even in small communities, were capable of presenting at least some colour programming. By October an estimated 17,450,000 homes, more than 30% of all those with television, had colour sets, an increase of 41% in 12 months. The public's rush to colour brought manufacturers' set sales to the point where, for the first time, colour was outselling black and white on a year-to-date basis; the crossover occurred in mid-October, when the Electronics Indus-

tries Association reported that 1968 sales to that time totaled 4,351,681 colour and 4,343,243 black-and-white sets. Colour sales were running 10% ahead of their 1967 pace, while black-and-white sales were up 1.9%.

The president's task force on telecommunications policy, appointed by U.S. Pres. Lyndon B. Johnson in 1967 and assigned to find the answers to many fundamental telecommunications problems, was completing its work in the closing months of 1968 but did not appear likely to propose basic changes in the broadcasting field. The final draft of the task force staff's recommendations for television, reported in *Broadcasting* in September, anticipated that community antenna television (CATV)—which many broadcasters had feared as a threat to, if not an eventual replacement of, broadcast television—would supplement broadcast TV rather than supplant it.

Commercial broadcasters heard little but bad news from the government in 1968. In midyear the Federal Communications Commission (FCC) imposed a freeze on applications for new AM radio stations and for major improvements in existing stations, announcing it would make no more grants in those categories until it had completed a review of its AM allocations policies. This review included, for the first time, the question as to whether AM and FM should be considered a single aural radio service. Earlier in the year the FCC called for a hearing on a proposal to prevent any company or person from acquiring more than one station—AM, FM, or TV—in a single community. The proposal did not contemplate immediate divestiture of stations by owners already having AM, FM, or TV combinations in the same market, but the U.S. Department of Justice thought that it should and urged that divestiture be required.

But the biggest trouble seemed to lie in Congress. Democrats, incensed by the reporting of riots and other disorders during the Democratic national convention in Chicago in August, planned congressional hearing that seemed likely to keep network officials testifying for months to come. The question of "violence" in television programming, and its potential effects on society, was also explored at length by a presidential commission set up following the assassination of Sen. Robert F. Kennedy in June.

CATV was in the news in 1968. With more than 2,000 widely distributed systems serving nearly 3.5 million subscribers, many offering up to 12 channels and also carrying FM radio broadcasts, it raised general problems for broadcasting. A legal dispute was resolved in June by a U.S. Supreme Court ruling that under copyright law as then in force CATV systems were not liable for copyright payments for programs distributed. Thus, CATV owners avoided big back payments for programs already broadcast. The Supreme Court also upheld FCC jurisdiction over CATV.

Though the Vietnam war, the international monetary situation, and the disturbed domestic economy called for reduced expenditure on broadcasting, the Corporation for Public Broadcasting (CPB) was formally constituted in March, with a $9 million allocation for 1969. Later financing was to be either by a levy on commercial broadcasters or by a tax on receivers. However, the Public Broadcast Laboratory (PBL), established in November 1967 as a unit of National Educational Television (NET) with a $10 million Ford Foundation grant, was forced to reduce its worldwide foreign correspondents' network. The experimen-

tal Midwest Program on Airborne Television Instruction (MPATI), transmitted from a DC-6 plane flying at 23,000 ft. over a 210-mi. radius, ended for lack of support from schools.

Canada. Under legislation enacted earlier in the year, the Canadian Radio-Television Commission (CRTC) came into being on April 1, replacing the Board of Broadcast Governors (BBG) as the regulatory authority for television and radio. The new body represented an almost complete change in top regulatory personnel: the CRTC chairman, Pierre Juneau, who had been vice-chairman of the BBG, was one of only two members of the old body named to serve on the new one. The five full-time members of the CRTC, all named to seven-year terms and authorized to serve as the CRTC's executive committee, were given far-reaching powers, including licensing authority. The general function of the ten part-time members was to provide regional representation; the executive committee was required to consult with them but was not bound by their views.

The management of the government-owned Canadian Broadcasting Corporation (CBC) also was reorganized early in 1968, with two men named to share the responsibilities formerly carried by J. Alphonse Ouimet, who retired in December 1967 after 15 years as president. George F. Davidson, who had been secretary of the Treasury Board, was named president of CBC and given responsibility for policy matters; Laurent A. Picard, a member of the committee for higher education of the Superior Council of Education in Quebec, was named vice-president and given charge of CBC's day-to-day operations.

Europe. For many Western European countries the year's main problem was how to cut budgets while at the same time increasing television transmission and introducing colour or raising colour programs to an economic level. (In many countries the high prices of colour sets, combined with the small amount of program time in colour, caused sales to lag.) The introduction or extension of commercial broadcasting was also one of 1968's preoccupations. A related problem was the elimination or reduction of nonpayment of radio license fees by TV-set owners.

The year saw the end of the so-called "colour war" between the French Système en Couleurs à Mémoire (SECAM) and German Phase Alternation Line (PAL) systems with the realization that for major international relays, transcoding was the answer. Its use for transmission from SECAM to PAL of the Winter Olympic Games led to an exchange of patent agreements between the patent holders of SECAM and PAL. PAL colour transmission, begun in 1967 in Britain, West Germany, the Netherlands, and Sweden, was introduced in 1968 in Switzerland and Austria and was to be adopted by Italy in 1971. SECAM, used by France and the Soviet Union since 1967, would be introduced in Poland (1969), and Bulgaria, Czechoslovakia, East Germany, Hungary, Luxembourg, and Yugoslavia (1970–71). Belgium, Denmark, Norway, and Finland all chose PAL.

In countries with colour television in operation, its extension was a top-priority policy objective. In West Germany both First and Second Programs increased colour transmission during 1968 from a minimum of four hours to between eight and ten hours weekly: 20–25% of all their offerings. Cost held back expansion: despite a steady rise in sales from a January estimate of 100,000, by October only 0.7% of West Germany's viewers had colour sets. Investment in col-

our was expected to reach approximately $25 million by late 1970. To meet costs an extra license fee for colour might be introduced.

Norway, though including colour installations in a new TV centre completed late in 1968, was uncertain whether to give priority to introduction of a Second Radio Program, more necessary in a country where radio remained the main communications channel to the offshore islands. TV coverage (almost nationwide on the mainland by 1968) was to be extended to the nearer islands in 1969, with programs videotaped and locally transmitted from Longyearbyen, Vestspitsbergen. On the mainland colour programs were available from Eurovision and Sweden in many regions.

In Austria a ten-year plan was launched to provide 95% coverage by three radio and two television channels, with more than 1,000 new transmitters and relays. The TV centre at Küniglberg, near Vienna, was to be rebuilt at an estimated cost higher than $160 million. Italy increased television coverage in 1968 on both channels, achieving 98% on the first and 87% on the second, among the highest in Europe.

In the U.K. economic problems hindered development: the government asked both the British Broadcasting Corporation (BBC) and the Independent Television Authority (ITA) to reduce expenditure for 1968–70 by some £4 million. Though retailers cut makers' list prices by up to 10%, colour-set sales remained below the year's 150,000 target. Deflationary policy, high cost, and less than full coverage made the public unwilling to invest in colour, still only available on BBC-2 but to become nearly nationwide in November 1969 with extension to BBC-1 and ITV.

Commercial broadcasting, accepted for television, was opposed for radio. The Greater London Council's (GLC) plan to set up commercial radio stations in London, supervised by a Greater London Radio Authority, was rejected by the government, which also opposed extension of low-power broadcasts by Manx Radio (only official British commercial radio station).

Experimental coin-in-the-slot TV, begun by Pay-TV, Ltd., in London in 1966 and extended to Sheffield with a total of 26,000 viewers, was ended suddenly in October by government unwillingness to spend the more than £100 million needed to make it a nationwide alternative to BBC-TV and ITV.

Elsewhere, commercial television increased. In France, despite strong opposition, advertising began on October 1, with a daily two minutes of "spots," to

WIDE WORLD

Left, members of a Chicago youth gang, the Blackstone Rangers, rehearsing with Tommy Smothers for a guest appearance, Jan. 21, 1968, on the "Smothers Brothers Comedy Hour." Above, Pat Paulsen, comic on the Smothers Brothers show, campaigned for president on the Straight Talking American Government (STAG) Party ticket.

WIDE WORLD

be doubled beginning January 1969. It was estimated that this advertising would bring in about $30 million a year, to be administered (as in Italy and Switzerland) by a specially formed company and used to extend TV coverage, improve quality, and do research on colour television. The Netherlands, which began commercial television on March 1, reported high public acceptance, with an estimated annual $2 million revenue. In Norway in October three members of a government-appointed commission voted for limited TV advertising, with three against; interested organizations were to be consulted before a bill was drafted.

Middle East. By 1968 experimental television transmission in Turkey had reached two to three hours daily, five days a week, in the Ankara region. In several Arab countries French money and ORTF experts were helping to develop broadcasting services. In Iran, where a national radio service had been set up in 1940 but where television was privately owned until 1966, ORTF had agreed in 1963 to help establish a national television network and build a radio and television centre in Teheran; in October 1967 a provisional national transmitter, installed by ORTF, began operation.

The situation in Lebanon was complex; two commercial television stations, the French-controlled Compagnie Libanaise de Télévision (CLT; established 1959) and Télé-Orient (1962), in which Lord Thomson owned majority shares, competed for audiences, advertising, and foreign capital. The government, though rejecting a single nationalized system in 1965, proposed one station with 20% government participation but could only revoke the 15-year licenses of the two existing stations for a fully nationalized system. French interest in extending its SECAM colour system and Télé-Orient's higher ratings encouraged both stations to try for monopoly. Government authorization was needed for colour installation, however, and the choice of which colour system to use (Télé-Orient being likely to prefer PAL) would probably affect that of the whole Arab world. A 1967 proposal for a merger of the two stations, with a government share in financing, policy, and programming, was defeated because of political opposition to increased state control and because of rumours that the French company had interests in Israeli TV. If Lebanon became able to establish a strong national system, it would probably become a producer of programs for transmission and sale to all Arab countries. The issue, therefore, was of more than local importance.

Africa. In Ghana, where a commercial radio service began in 1967, the Ghana Broadcasting Corporation (GBC) reorganized in 1968 to provide three channels: one in English, one in the main national languages (with emphasis on audience participation and national music), and one commercial. The Accra-based GBC television service (begun in 1966, and one of the best equipped in Africa) concentrated, like those in other African countries, on educational programs, especially for adult illiterates.

Another notable educational TV experiment in Africa was in operation in Niger, where a program for elementary education for children and adults was taken over by television, thus releasing fully trained teachers for secondary schools. In Uganda, educational programs were available to 60% of the population, while Algeria was experimenting with teacher training via TV. The Broadcasting Corporation in Malawi planned to improve medium-wave radio coverage in 1968 by installing extra transmitters in the Northern, Central, and Southern regions.

Far East. In India the Chanda Committee report (1967) recommended a crash program to extend television to 113 cities and some 250,000 villages, transmitted from a network of 16 earth stations and several satellites. Japan, with 92.6% of the population owning television sets by 1968, made further progress, with full changeover during the year to ultrahigh frequency (UHF) channels, increased colour programs, and routine use of satellites for quick news transmission.

(S. Tf.; R. W. Cr.; Ja. Ma.)

Programming. News remained a fundamental concern of television and radio broadcasters throughout the world in 1968 and was one of the most popular forms of programming with viewers and listeners. Use of communications satellites to relay U.S. programs to European countries and Japan was almost commonplace: they were used extensively to carry coverage surrounding such events as the assassinations of the Rev. Martin Luther King, Jr., in April and of Sen. Robert F. Kennedy in June; the Republican and Democratic conventions in August; and the election to the presidency of Richard Nixon over Hubert Humphrey in November. To a considerable but somewhat lesser extent satellites were also used to carry coverage of events in Europe and Latin America to the U.S. and other countries, as at the start of the Paris peace talks in May, aimed at ending the Vietnam war; the student riots in Paris later the same month; the Soviet-bloc invasion of Czechoslovakia in August; and the Olympic Games in Mexico City in October.

Westerns, mysteries, and comedies produced and shown in the U.S. remained among the most popular fare in most of the major television countries, but increasingly these nations were developing their own locally produced programs. In Japan, for instance, there were fewer U.S. programs among the top-rated shows, and, according to a study by the A. C. Nielsen Co. of Chicago, program preferences not only followed nationalistic lines but also differed between the country's leading cities, with Tokyo viewers preferring "rather sophisticated fare, with a heavy emphasis on news [and] serious drama," while Osaka audiences were inclined more toward "entertainment, comedy and participation programs." In some areas the increase in local production was less a matter of preference than of necessity; Latin-American broadcasters in particular said they were turning more to local production because U.S. television's emphasis on theatrical motion pictures and special programming had reduced the supply of the type of entertainment that Latin Americans preferred. (S. Tf.; R. W. Cr.)

Australia and New Zealand. As usual there was a notable contrast between Australian and New Zealand broadcasting in 1967–68. In Australia, locally produced programs topped the polls, while New Zealand remained dependent on imports for entertainment, drama, variety shows, and serials. In both countries, radio tended to be more experimental; in New Zealand music, radio drama, and serious imported drama rated higher than in Australia, and in both, locally produced current affairs programs were successful.

Australia achieved greatest success with Channel 9's new serial, "Skippy, the Bush Kangaroo," and the same channel's "Sound of Music" (begun autumn 1967), both regularly in the top ten in most polls in 1968; the latter was voted 1967's most popular program in the national *TV Week*'s end-of-the-year readers' survey and won a Logie Award. The big success on Channel 7 was "The Battlers," a serial showing an Aboriginal boxer struggling to adapt himself to the white man's

world, with Vincent Gill as the boxer and Mark McManus as his trainer.

New Zealand's most popular imports were the serialized dramatization of John Galsworthy's *The Forsyte Saga;* Jeremy Sandford's moving documentary drama of homeless families in Britain's welfare state, "Cathy Come Home" (1963); and the dramatization of Evelyn Waugh's trilogy *Sword of Honour.* Successful locally produced TV programs were mainly current affairs series and light musicals. Radio current affairs programs remained popular, notably the late night news review "Checkpoint" and the weekly survey "Aspect."

Japan. Celebration in 1968 of the centenary of the so-called Meiji Restoration that led to Japan's emergence as a modern industrialized nation was responsible for outstanding educational and cultural programs, which took the opportunity to trace Japanese history in the last 100 years and evaluate Japan's place in the modern world. Among them were the television series "A Century of Industrial Development," and "Meiji Album," a pictorial evocation of an era; and on radio, "A Hundred Years in the Life of the People," a monthly program in the "Wisdom of Life" series, and "Fountainhead of History." Also connected with the celebrations was the popular Sunday evening serial "Ryoma-ga Yuko," begun in January, a lavish, full-colour costume production.

A new television series enjoying wide audiences and prestige was "Diagnosing Japan," which combined experimental and established techniques to treat subjects of topical interest. After public opinion polls and research surveys had determined a subject, computers assessed a particular region or group's awareness of and general attitude to it, with live informal interviews to highlight and personalize particular aspects and responses.

Western Europe. In many countries, though colour television coverage was not complete, 1967–68 was notable for an increase in programs, more experimental use of colour, and "prestige programs." Sports continued popular, and viewing was dominated by the winter and summer Olympic Games, while the staple fare remained much as usual. In general, discussion programs gained in popularity with greater audience participation; news presentation became snappier; and "serious" works won high ratings if well presented.

In France, colour, introduced on Oct. 1, 1967, on the Second Program and later extended to cover 75% of the country, with a weekly average of 22 hours, gained international prestige with transmission of the winter Olympic Games from Grenoble. Other journalistic triumphs in colour included a live broadcast of parachute jumping ("Arc en ciel à Biscarosse") and coverage of the whole of the 24-hour Le Mans sports car race. In the studio, colour was dazzlingly used for productions by Jean-Christophe Averty, notably in "C'est la vie" (Maurice Chevalier and Diahann Carroll), "Montand chante Prévert" (composer Jacques Prévert, singer Yves Montand), and the variety series "Au risque de vous plaire." A successful experiment in colour television was André S. Labarthe's program "Bleu comme une orange," a review of colour in the contemporary arts.

In West Germany colour began officially on Oct. 25, 1967, and, as elsewhere, gained publicity with the winter Olympic Games and increased the popularity of such programs as films about wildlife and the undersea world ("Expedition ins Tierreich," "Der Eroberung des Meeres") and travel films. Well-received new pro-

Tiny Tim with Dick Martin on "Laugh-In." During 1968, after years of performing only at private parties and Greenwich Village coffeehouses, Tiny Tim made several network TV appearances and issued a best-selling record album.

grams included the cultural review "Titel, Thesen, Temperamente" and two current affairs reviews: "Pro und Contra," treating controversial topics of wide general interest, and "Kontraste," concerned with East-West relations. Crime series continued popular, with increased ratings for the Second Program's "Aktenzeichen XY . . . ungelöst," showing the police at work on real-life cases.

In 1967–68, programs achieving high ratings in Portugal included the live broadcast of the midnight Mass (Christmas Eve, 1967) from the sanctuary of Fátima, a filmed survey of Pres. Américo Tomás' visit (February 1968) to Portuguese Guinea and the Cape Verde Islands, and the swearing-in of new Premier Marcello Caetano, with part of his first speech to the nation.

In the Netherlands, with colour and commercial television introduced in 1967, 1968 was a year of assessment. Reactions to colour, officially tested by schoolchildren in March when a football match between two top teams was broadcast in colour, were extremely favourable. The first play in colour was Ivan Turgenev's *The Provincial Lady,* given its Netherlands premiere in a production by Max Douwes. Dutch television continued to treat controversial subjects boldly. In a series on health, a discussion between experts on the sex life of the elderly evoked a surprisingly enthusiastic response, as did "Present and Future," in which a Christian, a Jew, and a Muslim were asked rapid-fire questions on their faith.

Italian television Channel 2's new 1968 midday (12:30 P.M.–2 P.M.) program proved popular: it included news and comment, variety, cartoons, cultural reviews, and documentary series. Other successful documentaries discussed the tourist industry and holidays, costume and fashion, and the development of modern theatre and cinema. Dramatizations won high ratings, most notably Ugo Gregoretti's Channel 1 Sunday-night serial adaptation of Charles Dickens' *Pickwick Papers.*

Vatican Radio caused a sensation by introducing beat music and "pop" singers in a regular program on its Italian service, and also by transmitting to foreign stations; it was an experimental attempt to bridge the gap between youth and the church. Difficulty was found in discovering enough suitable music: a first series, "Spiritual Values in Songs of Today," ceased for lack of songs that were both sufficiently "spiritual" and popular.

In Britain both BBC and ITV were under fire in 1968. Attacks were leveled at their treatment of politics and politicians, at a preference for sensation rather than information in news programs, at interviewers' excessive powers and lack of taste and tact,

CBS Television's seven-part series "Of Black America" included Bill Cosby with Mrs. Lovely Billups and her fourth-grade class, above, in "Black History: Lost, Stolen, or Strayed," and World War I American Negro soldiers returning home wearing the Croix de Guerre of France, below, in "The Black Soldier."

and at an increasing tendency to pander to public opinion rather than to lead or educate it. Inevitably, attack concentrated on the BBC, uneasily poised between an "official" educational tradition and the struggle with ITV for high audience ratings, and with a tendency to avoid controversy. Suspicions that caution controlled BBC program policy were seen as confirmed by last-minute cancellations of commissioned programs on controversial topics—race relations, censorship in the arts, and relations between the police and the public. In contrast, there were complaints (mainly from physicians) about "alarmist" programs on drug taking and the side effects of birth-control pills. Listeners and viewers mourned the loss of old favourites (ITV's "Double Your Money," "Take Your Pick," and "Armchair Theatre" were casualties of the July contract reshuffle; and in the autumn the BBC's dropping of Radio 2's theatre organ program raised a surprising storm of indignant distress). Critics, on the other hand, complained of programs overdue for honourable retirement: though ITV's nine-year-old "Coronation Street" was still enjoyed, with "The Avengers" a close runner-up, BBC-1's "Dixon of Dock Green" and ITV's "Z-Cars" were felt to be expendable.

There was much to praise, however. Large audiences watched BBC-2's presentation of Henry James's *The Portrait of a Lady* (though critics felt that the dramatization turned a great novel into a merely good story). The new sobriety of BBC-1's "Man Alive" was preferred to its overdramatic treatment of social problems, and BBC-1 and 2 presented excellent series of musical biographies. Both BBC and ITV covered the Czechoslovak crisis and the Olympic Games with dignified restraint and untiring effervescence, respectively. ITV's "World in Action" gave interesting programs on a variety of subjects, including detective agency methods in dealing with industrial espionage, the problems of 15-year-olds who sign on for 12 years at sea and outgrow their enthusiasm, and an unusually balanced view of Castro's Cuba. Also highly praised were John Betjeman's nostalgic "Contrasts" journey from Marble Arch to Edgware (BBC-1), and "Alf Garnett" (Warren Mitchell, voted Radio Club of Great Britain's TV Personality of the Year for his acting in BBC-1's comedy serial "Till Death Do Us

Part"). Acclaim for Kenneth Horne's Radio Personality Award was less wholehearted, and, as usual, David Frost (*see* BIOGRAPHY), continuing to bite and sparkle, received both praise and criticism. Malcolm Muggeridge remained, perhaps, the most influential and unpredictable of interviewers.

Opinion continued sharply divided between critics and public about Radio 1, which celebrated its first birthday in September with the announcement that listeners had risen from a daily average of 2 million to 27 million. The largest increase was for the 10 A.M.–12 noon "Jimmy Young Show."

Competition for ratings between BBC and ITV, with all its problems, continued to act as a stimulant: ITV challenged BBC's control of sports contracts by scooping the November indoor tennis Dewar Cup tournament. The BBC responded to increased ratings for ITV's sports reviews by replacing midweek "Sportsview" with a trendier "Sportsnight with Coleman." BBC-television kept top ratings at Christmas 1967, with 11 A.M.–11 P.M. programs watched by an average of 15 million (ITV: 4.7 million).

Eastern Europe. The year's most dramatic and moving programs were unplanned and unscripted: the last broadcasts, as Soviet troops moved in, from hidden Free Czechoslovak radio stations. They would not soon be forgotten by those who heard (direct, or transmitted by the Voice of America and the BBC) the repeated announcements that "with this broadcast, Free Czech radio says goodbye. . . ." only to return minutes, hours, and days later from a new hideout. When jamming made voices inaudible, the stations continued to broadcast music and, finally, occasional signals. They symbolized the spirit that had made Czechoslovak radio and television influential instruments of the liberalization movement.

Official Eastern European broadcasting followed familiar lines: increased internationalism, close cooperation within the Soviet bloc, and emphasis on educational and cultural programs with audience participation. In the Soviet Union developments were mainly educational. On Channel 3, the "Radio University of Culture" courses, begun in 1965, had by 1968 made progress toward production of courses for transmission from all local TV stations. Channel 4, opened in November 1967 to popularize science and general culture, raised its output to three hours daily, with series on such topics as "Man and His World" (modern society), "Time Machine" (social history), "The Inquisitive Camera" and "Window into the World" (natural sciences), "Literary Review," "Theatre," and "Palette" (on painting techniques). Channel 5 (colour), beginning on Oct. 1, 1967, as part of the 50th anniversary of the Revolution celebrations, had only achieved an average 30 minutes of colour transmission per day in 1968, but completion of the new Ostankino (Moscow) TV centre was expected to extend colour considerably. The establishment (November 1967) of the Orbita satellite system allowed programs from Moscow to be made available in 23 cities of the U.S.S.R., as well as abroad.

During 1967–68 the Soviet Union began national television festivals: at the Moscow festival (December 1967) 104 films (14 in colour) were submitted by 62 regional studios, winners being the documentary series "Chronicle of Half a Century" and the feature film *Major Vikhr.* The Soviet Union won a special prize at the seventh Monte Carlo International TV Film Festival for "Not Every Bear Hibernates in Winter," and Czechoslovak TV won the *grand prix* for Stanislaw

Barabas' production of Dostoevski's *The Tender Girl.* Czechoslovak TV also won second prize at the 1968 International TV Film Festival (first to be held in Australia, at Adelaide).

Winners of the 1968 Czechoslovak TV's International Television Film Festival included British Granada (ITV), with "A Group of Partisans" (best documentary photography); scriptwriter Derek Hart, for the U.S. (CBS), "Don't Count the Candles"; West Germany's "Murder in Frankfurt" (cameraman's prize and viewer's prize); and Algerian Television (progress prize). Czechoslovak TV won the Praha Grand Prix and critics' and viewers' prizes for the best documentary with "The Advertisement."

A popular new Bulgarian evening "Radio Diary" included eyewitness reports by foreign commentators (from Western as well as Eastern Europe) of the day's events, and discussions on topical subjects. Sofia Radio celebrated the 25th anniversary of the Bulgarian socialist revolution with "Passport to Victory," jointly organized by Bulgarian Radio and the Central Trade Council.

Hungarian Television's quiz-competition "Show What You Know!" was enthusiastically received; winners took part in a World Youth Week at Sofia. The joint Hungarian-Soviet radio "Youth Meets Youth" was also popular: youth clubs in Moscow and Budapest discussed problems and exchanged music and poetry readings.

A popular East German program was the new "Frankly and Openly" series, based on listeners' answers to questions such as "What does the Communist Manifesto offer today?" Of programs for children most notable was East Germany's 14-day winter holiday competition; plays were presented, comments invited, and essays, stories, poems, paintings, etc., on the play's themes and characters were awarded prizes. Perhaps most popular was Czechoslovak TV's "Merry Go Round," an operatic series by Vaclav Trojan in which a group of children enjoyed wish-fulfillment dream adventures. (X.)

U.S. U.S. programs remained best sellers in other nations around the world, but the foreign market for such programming was, in the opinion of some producers, shrinking. As the television systems of other nations grew and became more nationalistic, they used fewer imported shows. In addition, some countries, such as Canada, Japan, and the United Kingdom, had firm quotas on program imports. Even so, aided considerably by an easing of tensions between U.S. distributors and Australian broadcasters over program prices, foreign sales of U.S. programs in 1968 were expected by *Broadcasting* to reach $80 million to $85 million, a new record. Among the best-selling U.S. programs in foreign markets, according to *Broadcasting,* were "Bonanza," a Western; "Bewitched," a fantasy-comedy; "Perry Mason," a detective series; and "20th Century," a public-affairs program. All four were being seen in 60 to 80 foreign countries. Other U.S. programs popular in overseas markets included "Wide World of Sports," "Voyage to the Bottom of the Sea," "Lost in Space," "Peyton Place," "Man From U.N.C.L.E.," "Daktari," "Flipper," and a series of specials presented in the U.S. by the National Geographic Society.

For U.S. audiences, the three TV networks were spending close to $260 million for the production of regularly scheduled nighttime programs for the 1968–69 season. This estimate, by *Broadcasting,* represented an increase of $20 million over 1967–68 production costs. The total did not include network commitments for the production of approximately 235 "specials" on subjects as diverse as "Man and the Universe," "How Life Begins," "Pogo," *A Midsummer Night's Dream, Heidi,* and the Olympic Games. Nor did the total include about 200 specials being planned by independent producers and group station owners, many of them as ambitious and as costly as some of the network specials.

News—often unexpected news—was 1968's big contribution to broadcasting, however. From the spring and summer primary campaigns through the Republican and Democratic national conventions, the elections in November, and the flight of Apollo 8 around the moon in December, TV and radio news crews were kept busy. They also had to cover news breaks that could not be anticipated: the seizure of the USS "Pueblo" by North Korea in January; the assassination of the Rev. Martin Luther King, Jr., in April and the riots that followed; the assassination of Sen. Robert F. Kennedy in June; and the invasion of Czechoslovakia in August. In all, *Broadcasting* estimated that the news costs of the three TV networks alone would exceed $150 million for 1968, not counting the losses—which might be even higher—of revenues from normal programs preempted by the news coverage.

Coverage of the Democratic convention in Chicago in August was especially costly, not only in dollars but also in prestige. Many Democrats were offended by the showing and reporting of the disorders and demonstrations that occurred while the convention was being held. TV-radio newsmen, along with other newsmen, were no less angered by the sometimes rough treatment they received at the hands of the police, but the end result was that they were called on, by both the FCC and congressional committees, to defend their coverage. In addition, Chicago Mayor Richard J. Daley demanded that the networks give him an hour in which to present "Chicago's side" of what happened during convention week. The networks refused, but more than 100 TV and "several hundred" radio stations carried the Daley program, according to an estimate by *Broadcasting.*

The national concern over "violence," which developed after the assassinations of King and Senator Kennedy, had a considerable effect on programming. Network and independent producers spent a hectic summer revising scripts and, in many instances, re-shooting scenes and rescheduling entire programs already on film in an effort to reduce the number of killings, fights, and other forms of violence depicted in the shows that started in September. The effect on the next year's programming appeared likely to be even greater. A survey by *Broadcasting* in October found that of the approximately 65 new programs under development for the 1969–70 season, virtually none relied on plot lines requiring the use of force to resolve conflicts. The growing public concern with racial and social problems also was reflected on television and radio as more and more programs were directed to the problems of black people, the ghettos, schools, and the urban crisis generally.

Sports and movies remained the most popular entertainment fare, although audience measurements in the opening weeks of the 1968–69 season indicated that movies might be losing some of their popularity. Sports, especially professional football, continued to command huge audiences.

In noncommercial broadcasting, the Public Broadcast Laboratory (PBL) received mixed reviews for

most of its first year's offerings, and its plans for 1968–69 suggested it was seeking a better popular response. PBL, created by a two-year, $10 million grant by the Ford Foundation to show what educational TV could do if it were given a chance, had got off to a bad start. The first of its weekly programs, in November 1967, was a controversial study with a racial theme that provoked widespread political as well as artistic criticism. There were frequent differences between PBL's management and its editorial board, which was finally dissolved, and the public response to its programs was less enthusiastic than many had expected. Presentations planned for the new season were to deal with such subjects as how television affects children, the European money market, and the problems of U.S. universities. (S. Tf.; R. W. Cr.)

Amateur Radio. During 1968 the worldwide amateur radio movement continued steady growth. By the end of the year there were more than 450,000 individuals who operated their own amateur radio stations; over 275,000 of those were in the U.S. With the admission of Monaco, Mauritius, and Surinam, the International Amateur Radio Union (IARU), a global federation of national noncommercial amateur radio societies, grew to a membership of 80. During May IARU held a congress of Asian and Oceanic societies in Australia to strengthen the union's organizational structure.

Public service remained a predominant theme for radio amateurs in the United States. Countless times during the year, amateurs provided emergency communications in situations ranging from searching for a lost boy to recovering from a devastating natural disaster. Many amateurs also volunteered their services to handle messages to and from U.S. servicemen in Vietnam and aboard hospital ships. President Johnson lauded the amateurs for providing a significant boost to morale. More than 12,000 U.S. and Canadian amateurs participated in the annual Field Day event sponsored by the American Radio Relay League, a binational association of amateurs in those two countries. Field Day is a contest activity designed to give amateurs practice in operating during situations similar to times of emergency.

Seeking to upgrade their operating privileges, many amateurs gained and demonstrated increased technical knowledge and Morse code ability before the FCC, the licensing authority for U.S. amateur operators. The FCC had readopted a system of amateur licensing whereby certain operating privileges were available only to holders of upper grades of licenses; as an amateur upgrades his license, he is rewarded by increased privileges. In other actions, the FCC expanded amateur privileges in the 160-m. band and provided for slow-scan picture transmission in the high-frequency amateur bands. A rule was proposed to make the novice amateur license (currently available only on a one-time basis) available to former amateurs.

Technologically, amateurs continued to make greater use of solid-state devices and digital circuitry in their stations. Experimental communications continued at very-high and ultrahigh frequencies, using the moon as a passive reflector, and development was under way on several amateur communications satellites. (Wi. D.)

See also Advertising; Astronautics; Cinema; Education; Music; Photography; Telecommunications.

Encyclopædia Britannica Films. *Development of Communications (From Telegraph to TV)* (1955); *Getting the News* (1967).

Tennis

Momentous changes took place in tennis in 1968. In December 1967 the British Lawn Tennis Association amended its rules to abolish all distinction between amateurs and professionals, effective April 22, 1968. This amendment violated the rules of the International Lawn Tennis Federation (ILTF), whose management committee announced that from that date Great Britain would be suspended. At a special general meeting of the ILTF in Paris at the end of March a compromise was reached. Member nations unanimously agreed on a change of rules permitting each nation self-determination so far as amateurism and professionalism were concerned. At the same time, the British delegates agreed to restrict full open tournaments, that is, those open to professionals under contract to promoters and not under the control of national associations, to a limited number specifically sanctioned by the management committee of the ILTF.

About this time many leading amateurs signed professional contracts with promoters. They included the Australians Roy Emerson, Tony Roche, and John Newcombe; Roger Taylor of the U.K.; the South African Cliff Drysdale; Nikola Pilic of Yugoslavia; and, unusually, four women, Billie Jean King and Rosemary Casals of the United States, Françoise Durr of France, and Ann Jones of the U.K.

The new legislation of the ILTF, confirmed at the annual general meeting in July, allowed for a new category, the "registered" player. Such a competitor was permitted to receive expenses without limitation and to compete for prize money, but would be under the disciplinary control of his or her national association. In due course the regulations of the Davis Cup were amended to permit participation by registered players, but professionals under contract to promoters continued to be excluded.

Accordingly 1968 brought professionals and those who used to be called amateurs together in tournaments for the first time. The first tournament open to all classes was the British Hard Court Championships at Bournemouth, and it was notably successful. The French championships in Paris were open, as were the U.K.'s Wimbledon tournament and the German championships in Hamburg. The United States retained its old Amateur Championships, staging all events at the Longwood Cricket Club in Brookline, Mass., and then inaugurated the first U.S. Open Championships at Forest Hills, N.Y. For the latter event $100,000 was given in prize money, the largest amount by far.

Davis Cup. West Germany and Spain were winners of the two sections of the European Zone. The German victory was mainly brought about by the excellent form of Wilhelm Bungert, who was unbeaten against Switzerland, Bulgaria, Czechoslovakia, and South Africa. Spain, led by Manuel Santana, was extended to 3–2 in the first round by the Netherlands, but subsequently won more easily over Sweden, Great Britain, and Italy. The entry of South Africa and Rhodesia brought some repercussions, particularly in Sweden where the courts at Båstad were wrecked by demonstrators against Rhodesian participation. Rhodesia's match with Sweden had to be played in Bandol, France, because the demonstrations made it impossible to stage it in Sweden. Romania refused to play South Africa and conceded to it to express anti-

apartheid policy. (A motion by the U.S.S.R. to expel South Africa at the meeting of the ILTF failed.)

The United States had no difficulty in winning the American Zone. They played Spain in Cleveland, O., and won 4–1, the only Spanish victory being that of Santana against Clark Graebner.

The U.S. took the Davis Cup away from Australia for the first time since 1963 by winning 4–1 at Adelaide in December. Arthur Ashe defeated Ray Ruffels, Clark Graebner triumphed over Ruffels and Bill Bowrey, and the U.S. doubles team of Bob Lutz and Stan Smith beat Ruffels and John Alexander. Australia's only victory was that of Bowrey over Ashe.

Men's Competition. *Singles.* At the first major meeting, the Australian championships in January, Bill Bowrey of Australia won the title by defeating the Spaniard Juan Gisbert in the final. In the South African championship Tom Okker of the Netherlands showed the strong form that he had maintained throughout the season by winning the title from Marty Riessen of the U.S. 12–10, 6–1, 6–4.

Okker also won the Italian championship in Rome, defeating the South African Bob Hewitt 10–8, 6–8, 6–1, 3–6, 6–0. The Italian authorities chose to keep the meeting amateur, even though sanction of the event as open would have been automatic. The first open championship of the world, the British Hard Court meeting at Bournemouth, was won by Ken Rosewall when, a little surprisingly, he beat his professional colleague Rod Laver 3–6, 6–2, 6–0, 6–3.

In the next open championship, the French meeting in Paris, Rosewall once more was successful. He again defeated Laver in the final, this time 6–3, 6–1, 2–6, 6–2. The French event was notable for the good play of the 40-year-old Richard ("Pancho") Gonzales of the U.S., who lost to Laver in the semifinals.

The Wimbledon championship, with a prize of £2,000 for the singles winner, saw Laver prove himself the world's outstanding performer. Pacing his effort with expert discretion, he won his quarterfinal against the U.S. professional Dennis Ralston 4–6, 6–3, 6–1, 4–6, 6–2; a semifinal against U.S. amateur Arthur Ashe 7–5, 6–2, 6–4; and the final against the Australian professional Tony Roche 6–3, 6–4, 6–2.

In the German championship at Hamburg John Newcombe of Australia was the winner. He beat Riessen, who had turned professional not long before, 3–6, 4–6, 6–4, 6–0, 6–1 in the quarterfinal; Pilic 3–6, 6–4, 6–4, 6–3 in the semifinal; and Drysdale 6–3, 6–2, 6–4 in the final.

The U.S. Amateur Championship in Brookline was convincingly won by Ashe, the first Negro to take it (*see* BIOGRAPHY). He went on to achieve more striking success in the U.S. Open meeting in Forest Hills, a tournament that provided many surprises. Drysdale upset Laver in the fourth round, while Gonzales beat Roche at the same stage. In the quarterfinals Graebner beat Newcombe, and Ashe defeated Drysdale. Okker beat Gonzales while Rosewall won over Ralston to be the only professional survivor. In the semifinals Ashe beat Graebner 4–6, 8–6, 7–5, 6–2, and Okker defeated Rosewall 8–6, 6–4, 6–8, 6–1. Ashe then went on to win the final against Okker 14–12, 5–7, 6–3, 3–6, 6–3.

Laver's Wimbledon victory confirmed his stature as the accepted master player of the world. Ashe, a semifinalist at Wimbledon and winner of both the U.S. Amateur and Open championships, made a spectacular advance to fame. So did Okker as winner of the South African and Italian championships and as finalist in the U.S. Open.

Doubles. Okker and Riessen took the South African, Italian, and German titles. Rosewall and Fred Stolle of Australia won the French title but yielded to Newcombe and Roche in the final at Wimbledon.

Women's Competition. *Singles.* Billie Jean King of the U.S., then still an amateur, won the Australian title when she beat Margaret Court 6–1, 6–2. Mrs. Court, formerly Margaret Smith, had returned to the game after more than a year's absence. She took the South African championship, beating Virginia Wade of the U.K. 6–4, 6–4.

The Australian Lesley Bowrey, formerly Lesley Turner, defeated Mrs. Court 2–6, 6–2, 6–3 to win the Italian title. The French championship went to the U.S. amateur Nancy Richey when she beat Mrs. King 2–6, 6–3, 6–4 in the semifinal, and won the final against the U.K.'s Ann Jones 5–7, 6–4, 6–1.

At the semifinal stage at Wimbledon Mrs. King narrowly beat Mrs. Jones 4–6, 7–5, 6–2, while Judy Tegart of Australia played the greatest tennis of her career in defeating Miss Richey 6–3, 6–1. In the final Mrs. King won over Miss Tegart 9–7, 7–5.

The U.S. Amateur title went to Mrs. Court with a final win against Maria Bueno of Brazil 6–2, 6–2. The U.S. Open title went surprisingly to Miss Wade, who achieved a fine sequence of victories. She beat the U.S. professional Rosemary Casals 6–4, 7–5; Miss Tegart 6–3, 6–2; her professional compatriot Mrs. Jones 7–5, 6–1; and Mrs. King in the final 6–4, 6–2.

Doubles. Mrs. Annette du Plooy (formerly Annette van Zyl) and Pat Walkden, both of South Africa, won the South African and German titles. Mrs. Court and Miss Wade won the Italian. The French championship had professional winners, Françoise Durr of France and Mrs. Jones. So did Wimbledon, with Mrs. King and Miss Casals taking the title. Miss Bueno and Mrs. Court won both the U.S. Amateur and Open titles, the latter by defeating Mrs. King and Miss Casals.

Wightman Cup. Great Britain, playing at Wimbledon, won the trophy for the first time since 1960, with Miss Wade as the main instrument of success. Mrs. Gerald Janes, formerly Christine Truman, was her principal supporter in a 4–3 victory over the United States, led by Miss Richey and Mary Ann Eisel.

Federation Cup. Played in Paris, the women's team championship of the world was won by Australia for the third time since the competition began in 1963. The former titleholder, the U.S., was upset 2–1 in the semifinal by the Netherlands, against whom Australia, represented by Mrs. Court and Kerry Melville, won 3–0 in the final. (L. O. T.)

Arthur Ashe, returning the ball to his Soviet opponent, V. Korotkov, in the London Open Championship on June 17, 1968. Ashe received noteworthy acclaim in 1968 as the first Negro winner of the U.S. Amateur Championship.

Thailand

A constitutional monarchy of Southeast Asia, Thailand is bordered by Burma, Laos, Cambodia, and Malaysia. Area: 198,455 sq.mi. (514,000 sq.km.). Pop. (1968 est.): 33,693,000. Cap. and largest city: Bangkok (pop., 1967 est., 2,136,432). Language: Thai. Religion (1964): Buddhist 93.7%; Muslim 3.9%. King, Bhumibol Adulyadej; prime minister in 1968, Field Marshal Thanom Kittikachorn.

The launching of Thailand's new constitution by means of a royal proclamation on June 21 brought certain political groups into the open for the first time in almost ten years. The 183-article constitution made Thailand a constitutional monarchy with the king as head of state and provided for a bicameral legislature comprising an elected lower house of 210 members (one member for 150,000 persons) and a Senate appointed by the king consisting of about 150 members. The Council of Ministers was not to include members of Parliament. A majority vote of all members of both houses would be required for a motion of censure against the government or for amending the constitution.

THAILAND

Education. (1965) Primary, pupils 4,165,352, teachers 126,813; secondary, pupils 316,736, teachers 17,490; vocational, pupils 35,011, teachers 3,460; teacher training, students 14,173, teachers 436; higher (including 6 universities), students 50,722, teaching staff 4,956.

Finance. Monetary unit: baht, with a par value of 20.80 baht to U.S. $1 (49.92 baht = £1 sterling). Gold and foreign exchange, official: (June 1968) U.S. $1,027,000,000; (June 1967) U.S. $995 million. Budget (1966–67 est.): revenue 13,321,000,000 baht; expenditure 18,484,000,000 baht. Gross national product: (1967) 105,290,000,000 baht; (1966) 96,207,000,000 baht. Money supply: (March 1968) 18.5 billion baht; (March 1967) 17.8 billion baht. Cost of living (Bangkok; 1963 = 100): (June 1968) 115; (June 1967) 110.

Foreign Trade. (1967) Imports 20,663,000,000 baht; exports 14,252,000,000 baht. Import sources (1966): U.S. 37%; Japan 26%; U.K. 6%; West Germany 6%. Export destinations (1966): Japan 21%; India 10%; Malaysia 8%; U.S. 7%; Singapore 7%; Hong Kong 7%; Bermuda 6%. Main exports: rice 33%; tin 13%; rubber 11%; corn 10%; kenaf 6%; tapioca 5%.

Transport and Communications. Roads (1965): c. 15,000 km. (including c. 4,500 km. with improved surface). Motor vehicles in use (1966): passenger 68,900; commercial (including buses) c. 79,600. Railways (1966): 3,765 km.; traffic 3,305,000,000 passenger-km., freight 1,655,000,000 net ton-km. Shipping traffic (Bangkok only; 1966): goods loaded 4,863,000 metric tons, unloaded 6,106,000 metric tons. Air traffic (1967): 378,410,000 passenger-km.; freight 4,402,000 net ton-km. Telephones (Dec. 1966) 86,008. Radio receivers (Dec. 1966) 2,765,000. Television receivers (Dec. 1966) c. 210,000.

Agriculture. Production (in 000; metric tons; 1967; 1966 in parentheses): rice c. 11,200 (c. 13,500); peanuts c. 134 (c. 130); sweet potatoes (1966) 196, (1965) 180; corn c. 1,000 (c. 1,277); rubber (1966) 207, (1965) 217; soybeans c. 20 (19); cassava (1966) c. 1,500, (1965) 1,475; sesame (1966) c. 18, (1965) 18; sugar, raw value (1967–68) c. 378, (1966–67) c. 410; tobacco (1966) c. 80, (1965) 76; cotton, lint (1966) c. 22, (1965) 20; kenaf, hard fibre (1966) c. 550, (1965) 529; timber (1966) 3,900 cu.m., (1965) 4,600 cu.m. Livestock (in 000; 1965–66): cattle 5,300; buffaloes c. 6,900; pigs c. 4,700; horses c. 108; chickens c. 34,000. Fish catch (in 000; metric tons) (1966) 708, (1965) 615.

Industry. Production (in 000; metric tons; 1967): tin concentrates (metal content) 23; cement 1,696; tungsten concentrates (oxide content; 1966) 0.3; lead concentrates (metal content) 6.7; electricity (Bangkok and Thonburi only) 1,908,000 kw-hr.

On June 20 the king selected a 120-member provisional Senate, composed of 81 officers of the Army, Navy, Air Force, and police, and 39 civilians. More were to be appointed after the general election which, it was stipulated, should take place within 240 days of the promulgation of the constitution.

In September the government published a Political Parties Bill which expressly ruled out the formation of Communist or pro-Communist parties in Thailand. On September 1 the first municipal elections in more than a decade were held in Bangkok. The Democratic Party, a liberal opposition party led by a former prime minister, M. R. Seni Pramoj, won a landslide victory, taking 22 out of the 24 seats contested. Fears that the government might refuse municipal power to the opposition Democrats proved groundless as the Democratic nominee, Rear Adm. Chalit Kulkamthorn, was officially installed as lord mayor on October 21. Also in October, the government lifted martial law in all areas except the Communist terrorist-infested districts of the north and northeast provinces.

Communist terrorism, which had first raised its head in 1965, was officially described as being less than in 1967. The number of terrorists was reduced from 2,500 at its peak in 1967 to 1,500. The government, however, noted that the terrorists, led by men trained in Communist China and North Vietnam, had plans to reorganize and coordinate their activities to launch more daring attacks. On July 26 the first organized Communist commando raid on a U.S. air base occurred in Udon Thani, 400 mi. N of Bangkok. One Thai security guard was killed, four Americans were wounded, and two U.S. aircraft were damaged. The first use of artillery by the guerrillas was reported in December, when an armoured personnel carrier was blown up near the Laotian border. In the southern border regions remnants of the Malayan Communist movement killed 15 members of a Malaysian police patrol. The Thai-Malaysian Joint Border Defense Committee decided to intensify measures to eliminate the approximately 500 terrorists believed to be operating in the area.

Thailand stepped up its Vietnam commitment on the side of the allies by sending a fully trained combat regiment of 5,000 men, called the "Black Panthers," to South Vietnam in September. The strength of the Black Panthers was to be increased to 10,000 by the end of the year. The number of U.S. soldiers and airmen in Thailand reached 50,000 by mid-1968.

Aided by the "Vietnam boom," the Thai economy continued to prosper, but significant declines in agricultural output and export earnings occurred in the first half of 1968 compared with the same period in 1967. The economic growth rate was expected to be only about 6%, compared with 7.2% the previous year. Earnings from U.S. military expenditure, tourism, and foreign investments, however, were keeping Thailand's foreign exchange position strong. The government budgeted for a record total expenditure of 23,690,000,000 baht for the fiscal year beginning October 1968; this was an excess of 5.4 billion baht over revenue.

(G. U.)

Theatre

Great Britain and Ireland. The most important single event of 1968 for British theatre (though not for Ireland, where no official state censorship of stage performances operates) was the abolition of the lord chamberlain's power to censor plays to be performed

Textiles:
see Industrial Review

on the public stage. Fears that the Theatres Act (which became law in September 1968) would result in a spate of lewd productions were not realized: nudity, though banned (except in revues), had been tacitly allowed before the act came into force, as, for example, in Clifford Williams' production (Stratford-upon-Avon, June) of Christopher Marlowe's *Dr. Faustus,* in which the Helen of Troy conjured up for Faustus' delight by Mephistophilis appeared naked. Indeed, disrobing provided much—even most—of the fun in several of the year's plays, from *The True History of Squire Jonathan and His Unfortunate Treasure,* John Arden's erotic duologue at the Ambiance, one of London's restaurant cellar club theatres (which took on new importance with the ending of censorship), to the riotous U.S. musical *Hair,* at the Shaftesbury.

Censorship had also been instrumental in keeping off the London stage for 18 months West German drama-tist Rolf Hochhuth's *Soldiers* (*Soldaten*), a dramatic presentation of Sir Winston Churchill as wartime leader, first performed in West Berlin in October 1967. A proposal by Sir Laurence Olivier and Kenneth Tynan (April 1967) to give it its English-language and, indeed, world premiere in an Old Vic Company production at London's National Theatre had been re-jected by Lord Chandos, chairman of the National Theatre Board and one of Churchill's World War II colleagues. This was done, apparently, partly out of respect for the family (some members of which did object when it was performed in 1968). With official censorship gone, however, Tynan persuaded two com-mercial impresarios to join him, and with John Colicos, who had played the lead in the Toronto English-lan-guage premiere, repeating his remarkable impersona-tion of Churchill, the play reached the New Theatre, London, in November. In this drastically cut version, Churchill's reputation emerged unscathed, and many wondered what all the fuss had been about.

The National Theatre had a successful year, cele-brating the Old Vic Company's 150th anniversary; touring Canada and Europe; and getting an official go-ahead from the government and the Greater London Council for its new home on the south bank of the Thames. Olivier, returning after severe illness, was greeted enthusiastically, as was Frank Dunlop, a new director. Among highlights of 1968 were Sir Tyrone Guthrie's production of Ben Jonson's *Volpone,* in which actors squawked and flapped like feathered monsters; Peter Brook's unorthodox version of Sen-eca's tragedy *Oedipus,* in which Sir John Gielgud as the king and Irene Worth as Jocasta, his wife-mother, were joined by an imposing, well-drilled chorus, wear-ing practice costumes, in an imaginative ritual ending; and Joan Plowright's moving rendering of the nitwit heroine of Natalia Ginzburg's *The Advertisement* (winner of the 1968 Italian Marzotta theatre prize), ably translated by Henry Reed.

There were changes at the Royal Shakespeare Com-pany early in the year. Paul Scofield, a director and leading actor, resigned in February just after Peter Hall(who had built up the company) had given up as managing director. Dispute was denied, though sur-prise was felt that Scofield should abandon the thea-tre's stage as well as its directorate, for "something new in the West End." A new directorial hierarchy of five included 28-year-old Trevor Nunn, who had joined the company in 1965, as artistic director; Derek Hornby, who had joined in 1967, as administrative director (thus dividing Peter Hall's directorate, with Hall remaining a director with special responsibility

for films and for the new Barbican Theatre); and Dame Peggy Ashcroft, on contract with the company since 1960, as a new director.

Peter Daubeny's fifth World Theatre Season at the Aldwych broke all attendance records and became a leading international event. It featured companies from France (Jean-Louis Barrault's Théâtre de France, presenting a new version and production of Paul Claudel's *Partage de midi,* with Édwige Feuil-lère); Czechoslovakia (a return visit by Prague's The-atre on the Balustrade); Italy (the Rome Stabile's first foreign tour); Ireland (the Dublin Abbey Theatre with a revival of Dion Boucicault's Victorian melo-drama *The Shaughraun*); Sweden (the Stockholm Royal Dramatic Theatre company's first London visit); and Japan (the Bunraku National Puppet The-atre, on its first European tour). Most outstanding of these in retrospect were the offerings of the Théâtre de France, Ingmar Bergman's production of *Hedda Gabler,* and the exotic charm of the Japanese puppet plays.

At Stratford Trevor Nunn's *King Lear* (with Eric Porter as Lear) and *Much Ado About Nothing* won critical acclaim. The press made more of *Dr. Faustus,* but rather for Maggie Wright's nude Helen of Troy than for Porter's admirable Faustus. There was en-thusiasm for John Barton's *Troilus and Cressida,* which stressed the erotic aspect of Shakespeare's bitter comedy. *The Merry Wives of Windsor* and *Julius Caesar* transferred to the Aldwych and almost equaled in popularity the previous year's transfers: *Macbeth* and *All's Well That Ends Well.* Original productions by U.S. directors (to mark, as Nunn said, "presidential election year") were variously critical of "the Amer-ican way of life." The world premiere of Arthur Kopit's *Indians,* directed by Jack Gelber, was a sad tale of genocide and 19th-century opportunism; Paddy Chayefsky's *The Latent Heterosexual* and Jules Feif-fer's *God Bless* had already been seen in the U.S.

London's third major subsidized theatre, the Royal Court, also had a year to be proud of. It put D. H. Lawrence back on the theatrical map, winning first prize at the Belgrade Theatre Festival with Peter Gill's pleasantly realistic production of *The Daughter-in-Law,* starring Judy Parfitt, as well as staging two new plays by John Osborne (*see* BIOGRAPHY) and reviv-ing his *Look Back in Anger,* still topical after 12 years. *Time Present* (starring Osborne's fourth wife, Jill

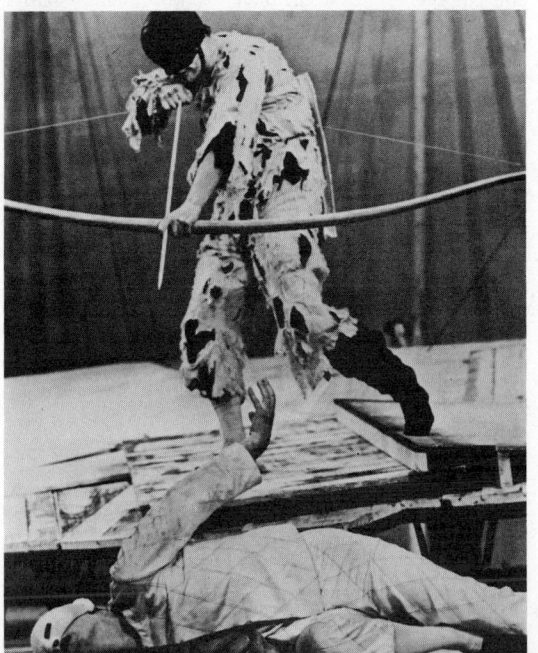

Helmut Griem (standing) and Martin Benrath portray Philoctetes and Odysseus in "Philoctetes" by East German playwright Volker Braun. The play, a modern interpretation of a Greek saga, was premiered in Munich on July 13, 1968, in the Staatstheater.

Bennett) and *Hotel in Amsterdam* (starring Paul Scofield) had typical Osborne protagonists: an actress who is a failure and an insecure writer, respectively.

One of the lord chamberlain's last actions was to ban Edward Bond's satire on Queen Victoria and 19th-century politics, *Early Morning,* which was threatened with police prosecution after only two club performances at the Royal Court (though it later became a success at Stockholm). However, William Gaskill, the manager, announced a Bond season for early 1969, with three plays in repertory: the earlier *Saved, Early Morning,* and the new *Narrow Road to the Deep North.* This most recent effort was also a drama about violence and war, set in a mythical Orient. It was commissioned for and produced at Coventry Cathedral's 1968 Conference on Cities and People.

At London's other repertory theatres talking points were the Mermaid's *Hadrian VII* and the Hampstead Theatre Club's *Spitting Image,* the former with a homosexual hero, the latter with two. In *Hadrian VII,* adapted from the 1904 autobiographical fantasy of

GUNTER ENGLERT

A scene from "Vietnam Diskurs" by Peter Weiss during its world premiere on March 20, 1968, in the Frankfurt Stadttheater. The stage designs were by Gunilla Palmstierna-Weiss, the author's wife.

Frederick Rolfe (Baron Corvo), Alec McCowen acted superbly as the malcontent priest who dreamed that he became the second English pope; in *Spitting Image* by Colin Spencer, two homosexuals scandalized society and the medical establishment by producing a baby. Hampstead also staged John Bowen's *Little Boxes,* a neatly written double bill about misfits in an enclosed world, and a dramatization of *The Ha-Ha,* Jennifer Dawson's novel about a mental breakdown, starring Angela Pleasence.

Transfers to the West End, as usual, helped resolve financial problems, especially for smaller managements using experimental theatres for tryouts. With the censor gone, however, not every experimental theatre had its eye on an eventual transfer. At the Open Space, a cellar theatre that opened in the summer with Canadian John Herbert's *Fortune and Men's Eyes,* which dealt with the dangers of sexual perversion in prison and achieved notoriety by showing actors undressing in full view of the audience, several plays put on by New York-born owner-manager Charles Marowitz were not specifically intended for transfer. The Ambiance (also run by an American, Ed Berman) showed British and foreign "far-out" playlets (*e.g.,* U.S. Negro Ed Bullins' *The Electronic Nigger and Others*) that had little apparent potential for a West End run.

Emergence into prominence of theatres of this kind was a feature of the London season, the Arts Laboratory (run by American Jim Haines) being an extreme, and early, example. All of them produced plays not likely to pass the censor, as did the Royal Court at its "members only" Sunday or late night performances.

Transfer was no guarantee of success, however. Threats to pull down or convert theatres in London and the provinces were growing, the famous Birmingham "Rep" being a particularly regretted possible target for destruction. The London Coliseum was saved by reverting to its original function as opera house for the Sadler's Wells Company, which had been deprived by government economies of its home on the south bank next to the National Theatre. Even some musicals, seemingly set for long runs, closed suddenly; *e.g., Cabaret, Man of La Mancha,* and *Golden Boy.* However, in *Canterbury Tales,* a ribald British musical produced with vigour and swing, Neville Coghill and Martin Starkie exploited the "bawdy Chaucer" to general, and lasting, satisfaction; and John Hanson's revival of *The Student Prince* also found audiences responsive. Newcomers were not discouraged. John Gale scored a box-office success at the Savoy with William Douglas Home's *The Secretary Bird,* a shallow, but wittily performed, marital comedy.

Among best performances were those by the National Youth Theatre company in Peter Terson's play about the football-mania menace, *Zigger-Zagger;* Ian McKellen, with Dorothy Reynolds, in *The White Liars,* Peter Shaffer's one-act curtain-raiser to a revived *Black Comedy;* and Bryan Pringle, John Woodvine, Colin Douglas, and a group of children led by John White in *Close the Coalhouse Door,* Alan Plater's documentary, based on short stories by Sid Chaplin with songs by Alex Glasgow, about coal miners and the labour movement.

Outside London the year was notable for the Oxford Experimental Theatre Club's British premiere of Günter Grass's *The Plebeians Rehearse the Uprising,* a brave attempt at a play neglected by both commercial and state-aided theatres; a stylish production of Alfred de Musset's *Un Caprice* (written 1837) at Guildford's Yvonne Arnaud Theatre; and Enid Bagnold's new play, *Call Me Jacky,* at the Oxford Playhouse, with Dame Sybil Thorndike dominating play, cast, and stage. A depressingly leaden-footed piece was *Confession at Night* by the Soviet playwright Aleksei Arbusov (Nottingham Playhouse).

At the Dublin Theatre Festival, the Olympia welcomed Prague's Black Theatre, a puppet mime theatrical company run by Jiri Srnec, with assistants and sets in black. Also at the Dublin Festival, the Gaiety revived Boucicault's *The Colleen Bawn;* Thomas Kilroy's *The Death and Resurrection of Mr. Roche* was given at the Olympia; Thomas Murphy's *The Orphans* was presented at the Gate; and the Abbey put on a satisfying version of *The Cherry Orchard,* transplanting Russian poignancy to Irish turf in the playing of Cyril Cusack and Siobhan McKenna.

France. The turbulent political troubles of spring and early summer—culminating in closed playhouses; the despoliation of the Odéon, Paris' second national theatre; premature closing of the Théâtre des Nations festival and the dismissal of its director, Jean-Louis Barrault—made 1968 a sad year for French theatre. Barrault's world-famous Théâtre de France was split up, and the experimental program devised by Peter Brook for it under Barrault's direction at the Théâtre des Nations moved to London's Roundhouse,

the new theatre at the Institute of Contemporary Arts. The effects of the student riots spread to Avignon, where Jean Vilar's festival collapsed, with the withdrawal after three performances of the U.S. Living Theater company, which had been featuring its iconoclastic *Paradise Now.* Barrault returned to the theatre (though not to the Odéon) in December, staging a dramatization from Rabelais; and his wife, Madeleine Renaud, made her Théâtre National Populaire (TNP) debut in *L'Amante anglaise,* a talkative "antiplay" by Marguerite Duras about a woman who murders without motive. Soon after Georges Wilson's grandiose revival of Jean-Paul Sartre's *Le Diable et le Bon Dieu* (not performed since 1951), the TNP made headlines when Sartre read from the stage a virulent—and widely supported—attack on the government for yielding to pressure from abroad by banning Armand Gatti's poetical documentary about Spanish emigration, despite earlier formal approval.

The year had begun well, with the first production of Henry de Montherlant's 17-year-old tragedy of unspeakable goings-on at a Jesuit college, *La Ville dont le prince est un enfant,* carried over from 1967 and sensitively handled by Jean Meyer, who took over the Lyons Théâtre Celestins during the year. It ended with Anouilh's black comedy, his first play in six years, *Le Boulanger, la boulangère, et le petit Mitron.* The title of this surprisingly fanciful box-office success echoed the tragic fate of France's last royal family (that of the "bourgeois king," Louis Philippe) and symbolized Anouilh's hatred for bourgeois family morality. As a counterpart to the Parisian suburban Théâtre de l'Est Parisien, where Guy Retoré's stirring version of Sean O'Casey's *The Silver Tassie* appeared as *La Coupe d'argent,* the Théâtre de l'Ouest Parisien opened in Boulogne. The city of Paris appointed Jean Mercure to manage its first full-time civic theatre, the Théâtre de la Ville (formerly the Sarah-Bernhardt). Retaining its classical facade, it was refitted with a new stage and single-tier auditorium. Mercure's model inaugural production of Pirandello's *Six Personnages en quête d'un auteur* was followed by Shakespeare's *Much Ado About Nothing,* ostentatiously updated by director Jorge Lavelli and designer Michel Raffaelli.

At the Comédie Française (which made history by traveling 4,000 mi. to take part in the first International Arts Festival in Teheran, Iran), Jean-Paul Roussillon showed promise as director of a Molière double bill and Robert Hirsch designed and played the lead in a new production of Molière's *Tartuffe.* Ariane Mnouchkine, taking her cue from the revolutionary Polish Shakespearean producer Jan Kott, staged *A Midsummer Night's Dream* as a macabre nightmare in a circus.

Switzerland, Germany, Austria, Belgium. The Swiss playwright Max Frisch returned to the theatre with *Biographie,* a metaphysical play in which the hero, a scientist, is offered a chance by a supernatural stage director to live his life piecemeal over again. Friedrich Dürrenmatt deserted Zürich for Basel, as co-manager and author of a macabre, politically oriented version of Shakespeare's *King John.* Politics continued to occupy German-language writers. At Stuttgart, Peter Palitzsch and Jörg Welhmeier completed their *Henry VI* cycle with a penetrating, modern *Der Dritte Richard (Richard III),* starring Hans Christian Blech as a coldly calculating Hitlerian villain; this was followed by *Toller,* Tancred Dorst's dramatic analysis of the abortive Bavarian Soviet secessionist regime. Peter Weiss's crude, cautionary his-

torical reassessment of the Vietnam war, its original 42-word title reduced to *Vietnam Diskurs,* was brilliantly staged at Frankfurt by Harry Buckwitz shortly before he retired from management of the Stadttheater. The later version, by the Berliner Ensemble, directed by Ruth Berghaus, achieved an even higher degree of stylization. In another Berliner Ensemble production, Bertolt Brecht's *Saint Joan of the Stockyards,* Weiss's daughter Hanne Hiob, in the title role, helped to keep Manfred Wekwerth and Joachim Tenschert's directorial genius afloat.

There was trouble in East Berlin, with the resignation of Benno Besson from the Deutsches Theater after his beautiful, faithfully Molièresque production of *Don Juan;* and with an ideologically motivated attack on Wolfgang Heinz for his Brechtian treatment of *Faust I,* in which the hero was portrayed (by Fred Düren) as a doubting agnostic and Mefisto (by Dieter Franck) as something of a clown. Trouble, too, dogged Hamburg, where Egon Monk was fired after only two months at the Schauspielhaus, during which he had made a disastrous beginning as manager and principal director. In West Berlin, the Schiller Theater staged two acceptable productions (of *Macbeth* and *The Seagull*) by the controversial Romanian guest director, Liviu Ciulei. In Munich highlights of the season in-

Barrie Ingham as Buffalo Bill in the Royal Shakespeare Company's production of "Indians," a satirical examination of the myth of the U.S. Western hero by Arthur Kopit.

ANTHONY CRICKMAY

cluded Hans Lietzau's ascetic production of East German playwright Volker Braun's new version of *Philoctetes,* at the Staatstheater; and, at the Stadttheater, Brecht's *Die Dreigroschenoper (The Threepenny Opera)* was given a new look by Prague producer Jan Grossman. In Düsseldorf Karl Heinz Stroux staged the world premiere of two short plays by the Polish playwright Stawomir Mrozek, banned in Poland because they criticized political tyranny. In Vienna, where producers are usually reluctant to stage controversial plays, the Burgtheater presented Fritz Hochwälder's *The Command* (which raked up the mud of a Nazi criminal's past), and the Josefstadt staged *The Grand Inquisitor,* exiled Hungarian dramatist Julius Hay's antidictatorship thriller. Flemish Paul Willems, a favourite with Viennese audiences, had *La Ville à voile,* a fey parable about seafaring folk, staged not in Austria (as had been expected) but in French at Brussels, at the Belgian National Theatre. Similarly, the Austrian Peter Handke's fourth play, *Kaspar,* a verbal pyrotechnic display on the theme of identity, premiered in West Germany.

Italy. During the year Giorgio Strehler resigned from the Milan Piccolo, which he had helped found in 1968, ostensibly to devote himself to more experimental work but also undoubtedly in protest against the

authorities' refusal to fulfill their promise to give him either the money or the equipment essential for his work. The Rome Stabile won new laurels, notably during their first visit abroad, to the London World Theatre Season, in Giuseppe Patroni Griffi's version of two early comedies by Raffaele Viviani. Giorgio de Lullo's third Pirandello production, of the little-known *The Wives' Girl-Friend,* starring Romolo Valli and Rossella Falk, proved as challenging a dramatic tidbit as its predecessors.

Eastern Europe. In the U.S.S.R. the Moscow Art Theatre celebrated its 70th anniversary, and several younger theatres incurred official disapproval for alleged failure to cater to popular taste. Thus, Anatoli Efros' *The Three Sisters,* hailed in 1967 at the Malaya Bronnaya (to which he had been banished from the Lenin Komsomol Theatre), was struck out of the repertoire, and even the highly acclaimed Yuri Liubimov at the Taganka fell foul of officialdom in the continuing ideological struggle. The virus spread to Czechoslovakia in the summer, after the armies of its Warsaw Pact allies had stopped its liberalization policy; though stage censorship did not follow immediately, the National Theatre in Bratislava shelved its production of *The Red Cavalry,* adapted from Isaac Babel's stories. Several leading Czechoslovak directors and theatre artists fled after the invasion, and Prague's progressive Theatre on the Balustrade suffered eclipse. In Warsaw the National Theatre's head, Kazimierz Dejmek, was dismissed. In Bucharest, however, the theatre forged ahead, with outstanding productions at Radu Beligan's Comedy Theatre of Eugène Ionesco's *Tueur sans gages;* at Horia Lovinescu's theatre of several modern works; at Ciulei's City Theatre of his own modern-dress *Macbeth* and Andrei Serban's timeless production of *Julius Caesar;* and at Radu Penciulescu's Little Theatre of Mikhail Sadoveanu's *The Hatchet,* dramatized for the first time. In Budapest the revival at the National Theatre of Imre Madach's neglected 19th-century classic, *Moses,* revealed it as a surprisingly modern play, Endre Marton as a brilliant director, and Imre Sinkovits as a great actor.

Scandinavia. The Swedish National Theatre in Helsinki was the only Swedish-speaking theatre to tackle Hochhuth's *Soldiers.* The Finnish-born director, Ralf Långbacka, after a time at Göteborg, made his debut in Stockholm's Royal Dramatic Theatre with an eye-catching production of Carlo Goldoni's *Village Trilogy.* Alf Sjöberg surpassed himself with Brecht's *The Tutor* and later capped it with *Alcestis* and *The*

Father, all starring George Rydeberg. A new movement toward collectively staged performances was reflected in the Royal's documentary, *Gipsies,* and in the Göteborg Civic Theatre's plays about contemporary problems of various kinds, *The Old People's Home* and *The Sandbox.* The artistic and popular smash hit of the season proved to be Bond's *Early Morning* at the Royal Dramatic, whose third revival of Bergman's laconic production of Ibsen's *Hedda Gabler* was another highlight of the year.   (O. Tr.)

U.S. and Canada. Suddenly a time of innovation and quickening seemed to have begun for the American theatre; perhaps it would quickly pass and leave little behind, but even in that case the interim was exciting. During the 1967–68 season the avant-garde appeared to have passed decisively under the influence of the French actor, director, playwright, and poet Antonin Artaud (1896–1948), the theoretician of the "Theatre of Cruelty." Artaud was frustrated to the point of fury by the conventional theatre of his time and demanded something far more urgent and intense: a theatre of shock, of "extreme action," "a theatre which events do not exceed." Like the Absurdists (the avant-garde of the late 1950s and early 1960s), Artaud rejected the theatre of realism, but his rejection went much further: he rejected the whole idea of the theatre as an institution devoted first of all to the interpretation of texts. He demanded "a theatre which eliminates the author in favour of . . . the director, but a director who has become a kind of manager of magic, a master of sacred ceremonies."

Words themselves are deemphasized in the Theatre of Cruelty, which experiments instead with chanting, humming, gymnastics, etc. Plot and character are deemphasized in favour of ritual. The boundaries between actor and audience are broken down; the spectator "is engulfed and physically affected" by the action.

Artaud's American disciples modified his teachings in various ways. They not only "engulfed" the spectator but also invited him to participate in the action. And they added one significant point that Artaud himself did not particularly emphasize: sexual exhibitionism. By the end of the 1967–68 season there was no word in the language that could not be said on the public stage in New York, and no part of the body that could not be shown. Audience confrontation and sexual explicitness, thus, were the most striking and widespread innovations of the "new theatre."

In the fall of 1968, the Living Theater, under the leadership of Julian Beck and his wife Judith Malina, returned to the U.S. for a national tour after four years of self-imposed European exile. This pioneer avant-garde group had begun experimenting with Artaudian techniques even before their exile; while in Europe, they had carried their experiments much further. Their newest work, *Paradise Now,* was a scriptless affair that varied greatly from night to night, depending on the contributions of the audience, who were screamed at, caressed, and engaged in political arguments. The company performed in loincloths and bikinis; often, members of the public stripped to their shorts in emulation. The Living Theater greatly excited many young people, but it disappointed many critics, including some who tended to be sympathetic to the avant-garde.

By the time the Living Theater returned, a number of other American theatre groups were working along more or less similar lines. Richard Schechner, for instance, editor of *The Drama Review* and a professor at New York University, produced and directed a very free version of Euripides' *The Bacchae,* entitled *Dio-*

Charles Lewson (left) and Terence Knapp in a scene from the dramatic madrigal "Naboth's Vineyard" by Alexander Goehr, which had its premiere at the London Festival in July 1968.

DOUGLAS H. JEFFERY

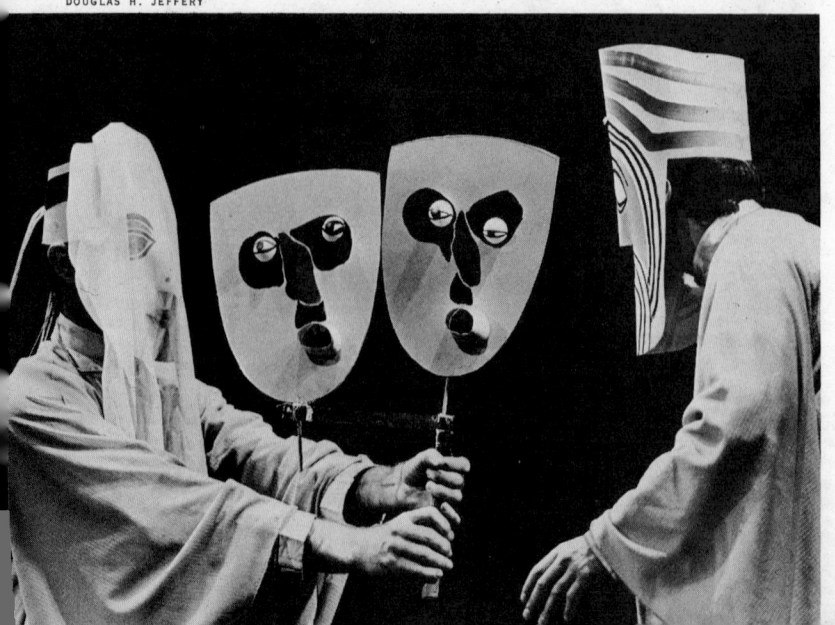

nysus in '69; it opened in June in a former garage in downtown Manhattan. *Dionysus* went to great lengths in its attempt to involve the audience physically in the action; it also made extensive use of improvisation, gymnastics, and ritual. What made the production particularly significant was that these techniques were used to develop a strong and coherent plot, suggesting that the "new theatre" and the conventional theatre of plot and character need not be mutually exclusive.

Another exponent of neo-Artaudian theatre was Tom O'Horgan (*see* BIOGRAPHY), who had been working for several years off-off-Broadway with the La

Mama Troupe. O'Horgan's productions of *Tom Paine* by Paul Foster and *Futz!* by Rochelle Owens, both originally staged at the Café La Mama, were subsequently moved to off-Broadway. O'Horgan's most important production, however, was the tremendously successful rock musical *Hair* (book and lyrics by Gerome Ragni and James Rado, music by Galt MacDermot). *Hair* originally opened off-Broadway in October 1967, under Gerald Freedman's direction, as the first production of the New York Shakespeare Festival's Public Theater. In this first incarnation it was a good-natured hippie pastoral, a bit of picturesque East Village local colour. O'Horgan's version, rewritten, recast, and restaged, opened on Broadway in April 1968. It was nastier, more militant, more basic than the old *Hair;* it had become a lurid, galvanic, plotless, free-form phantasmagoria, a ritual of alienation. Onstage and in the aisles, the performers did their best to insult, offend, and unnerve the audience, and the audience (attracted, perhaps, by the coed nude scene, a Broadway first) responded by making *Hair* the season's biggest musical hit.

Hair aside, the Broadway season of 1967–68 was dominated by British imports. *Rosencrantz and Guildenstern Are Dead,* by a young Englishman, Tom Stoppard, used the fate of Hamlet's two schoolfellows as the occasion for a dramatic meditation on the human condition that reminded many people of *Waiting for Godot. The Prime of Miss Jean Brodie* was adapted by Jay Allen from Muriel Spark's novel about a gallant, romantic, slightly mad Scottish schoolteacher; it was notable above all for Zoe Caldwell's virtuoso performance. *Everything in the Garden* by Giles Cooper, an ironic comedy about a suburban cou-

Left, Jenny Egan (top), Lucille Patton, and Conrad Yama performing in "Box-Mao-Box," a play combining two interlocking playlets by Edward Albee, during the March 1968 premiere at the Studio Arena Theater in Buffalo, N.Y. Above, a scene from the antiestablishment rock musical production "Hair," which opened on Broadway in April 1968 under the direction of Tom O'Horgan.

ple corrupted by the love of money, was adapted for U.S. audiences by Edward Albee; the irony was cleverly underlined by casting Barbara Bel Geddes and Barry Nelson, the clean-cut protagonists of so many happy comedies, in the leading roles. And *The Birthday Party,* Harold Pinter's first full-length play, finally received a New York production.

The 1967–68 Broadway season was a sad one as far as most U.S. playwrights were concerned. *The Price,* Arthur Miller's new play, was a box-office success; *The Seven Descents of Myrtle,* Tennessee Williams' new play, was not, in spite of an extraordinary performance by Estelle Parsons. Both plays inspired many viewers with a strong sense of déjà vu. There was also a new play by Robert Anderson, entitled *I Never Sang for My Father.* Ingrid Bergman returned to Broadway in *More Stately Mansions,* a posthumous work by Eugene O'Neill; the play was almost universally condemned.

The most popular of a bad lot of Broadway comedies was *Plaza Suite* by Neil Simon, a bill of three short plays about the funny sorrows of middle age, all set in the same suite at the Plaza Hotel in New York City. Except, once again, for *Hair,* there were no noteworthy new Broadway musicals.

For off-Broadway, which had appeared to be dying just a few years ago, 1967–68 was commercially the best season in history; it was a good season artistically as well. There were two successful revivals, *Iphigenia in Aulis* by Euripides and *A Moon for the Misbegotten* by O'Neill. *Your Own Thing,* an extremely slick and up-to-date rock musical based on the transvestite theme of Shakespeare's *Twelfth Night,* was enormously popular. But the season was chiefly notable for introducing a number of new playwrights. The novelist and short-story writer Bruce Jay Friedman made his playwriting debut with *Scuba Duba,* a wryly fantastic farce-comedy about a neurotic young man whose wife has just left him, or so he believes, for a Negro scuba diver; *The Boys in the Band,* a comedy-drama by Mart Crowley, was an explicit, naturalistic account of life in the homosexual subculture. Other young playwrights were Paul Foster (*Tom Paine*), Rochelle Owens (*Futz!*), Michael McClure

James Earl Jones playing the leading role in "The Great White Hope" by Howard Sackler, a Broadway production based on the life of prizefighter Jack Johnson, the first Negro heavyweight champion.

INGE MORATH FROM MAGNUM

Kate Reid, Pat Hingle, and Arthur Kennedy in Arthur Miller's psychological problem drama "The Price," in which two brothers meet for the first time in 16 years to dispose of their dead parents' belongings.

(*The Beard*), Israel Horovitz (*The Indian Wants the Bronx*), Sam Shepard (*Red Cross*), and John Guare (*Muzeeka*). The American Place Theatre's offerings included *The Electronic Nigger and Others* by Ed Bullins, which transferred to a commercial off-Broadway house for a brief run, and *Endecott and the Red Cross* by Robert Lowell.

Two new resident professional theatres opened their doors in New York late in 1967, and both had successful first seasons. The Anspacher Theater, the new winter headquarters of Joseph Papp's New York Shakespeare Festival, followed its production of *Hair* with *Hamlet*, staged as a parody of itself by Papp; *Ergo* by the Austrian novelist and playwright Jakov Lind; and *The Memorandum* by the Czechoslovakian dramatist Vaclav Havel. The Negro Ensemble Company offered *Song of the Lusitanian Bogey* by Peter Weiss (author of *Marat/Sade*), *Summer of the Seventeenth Doll* by Ray Lawler, *Kongi's Harvest* by the Nigerian playwright Wole Soyinka (*see* BIOGRAPHY), and *Daddy Goodness* by Louis Sapin, adapted by Richard Wright.

Outside New York, the regional theatres seemed in general to be making some progress toward stability. The Tyrone Guthrie Theatre of Minneapolis, Minn., presented a winter season in neighbouring St. Paul, opening in December 1967; its successful Minneapolis season the following summer featured a brilliant production of *The Resistible Rise of Arturo Ui,* Brecht's play about Hitler. In July 1968, Cincinnati's Playhouse in the Park inaugurated a spectacularly austere new 672-seat, thrust-stage auditorium.

In Canada the Stratford (Ont.) Shakespearean Festival took on a new name, the Stratford National Theatre of Canada, and prepared to become a year-round operation, with winter headquarters in Ottawa. A new company, Theatre Toronto, began its career in January 1968; in addition to two new Canadian plays, it offered the English-language premiere of Hochhuth's *Soldiers;* this production was subsequently transferred to Broadway.

The regional theatre continued to sustain itself mainly with revivals, but it also began to offer some new U.S. plays of genuine interest. In fact, the beginning of the new 1968–69 Broadway season was dominated—for the first time in history—by U.S. plays that had received their first productions at the hands of theatre companies outside the New York City area during the previous season. *Box* and *Quotations from Chairman Mao Tse-tung* (usually shortened to *Box-Mao-Box*), a double bill of elegantly minimal Absurdist playlets by Edward Albee, was produced at the Studio Arena Theatre in Buffalo, N.Y., in March 1968 and opened in New York City six months later. *We Bombed in New Haven* by Joseph Heller, a first play by the author of *Catch-22,* was given its world premiere by the Repertory Theatre of the Yale School of

Theology:
see Religion

Tibet:
see China

Drama in December 1967; it came to Broadway (in a new production) the following October. *The Great White Hope* by Howard Sackler, a huge, sprawling, powerful chronicle-play based on the life of the Negro prizefighter Jack Johnson, was first produced in December 1967 by the Arena Stage in Washington, D.C. It was directed by Edwin Sherin, associate producing director of the Arena Stage; James Earl Jones played the leading role. This production, with Jones still in the lead, opened on Broadway in October 1968. It received enthusiastic notices and was obviously going to be one of the successes of the new season. (J. No.)

See also Dance; Literature; Music.

ENCYCLOPÆDIA BRITANNICA FILMS. *The Age of Sophocles* (1959); *The Character of Oedipus* (1959); *Hamlet: The Age of Elizabeth* (1959); *Hamlet: The Poisoned Kingdom* (1959); *Hamlet: The Readiness Is All* (1959); *Oedipus Rex: Man and God* (1959); *Our Town and Ourselves* (1959); *The Recovery of Oedipus* (1959); *The Theatre: One of the Humanities* (1959); *Thornton Wilder: Our Town and Our Universe* (1959); *What Happens in Hamlet?* (1959); *Macbeth: The Politics of Power* (1964); *Macbeth: The Secret'st Man* (1964); *Macbeth: The Themes of Macbeth* (1964); *The Cherry Orchard I—Chekhov: Innovator of Modern Drama* (1967); *The Cherry Orchard II—Comedy or Tragedy?* (1967); *A Doll's House I—The Destruction of Illusion* (1967); *A Doll's House II—Ibsen's Themes* (1967).

Timber

The world's output of forest products, which had showed substantial increases in both volume and value during the 1950s and early 1960s, continued to rise in 1966, the last year for which figures were available. Estimates by the Forestry and Forest Products Division of the UN Food and Agriculture Organization (FAO), based on reports from 180 countries, placed total removals of roundwood from the forests of the world in 1966 at 2,049,100,000 cu.m. (1 cu.m. = 35.31 cu.ft.). The comparable figure ten years earlier (1957) was 1,829,300,000 cu.m. In terms of U.S. dollars based on constant 1960 prices, world production in 1966 was valued at $41.9 billion, compared with $34 billion in 1960 and $28.9 billion in 1955. Production of the more highly processed products, such as panel and pulp products, showed the greatest gain.

Of the $41.9 billion value of the world's output of forest products in 1966, $15.2 billion represented the value of sawn wood (lumber, railway sleepers, and boxboards). The value of wood pulp products (paper and paperboard) was $17.3 billion; of panel products (veneers, plywood, particle board, fibreboard), $4.6 billion; and of all other wood products, $4.8 billion.

Of the 2,049,100,000 cu.m. of roundwood cut from the world's forests in 1966, 1,137,400,000 cu.m. was removed for industrial uses, the remainder being cut for fuel wood and other domestic or nonindustrial purposes. Estimated removals of industrial wood rose about 20% in the decade 1957–66. For all uses, removals of coniferous (softwood) roundwood and of broad-leaved (hardwood) roundwood in 1966 were about equal in volume. For industrial uses, however, coniferous roundwood accounted for nearly 80% of the total.

Sawn wood or lumber accounted for about one-third of total removals. Although world production of sawn wood in 1966 was about 20% above the figure of ten years earlier, it failed to equal the record high achieved in 1965. The 1966 total was 370,328,000 cu.m. (1 cu.m. lumber measure = 424 bd.-ft.). FAO's revised estimate for 1965 was 373,707,000 cu.m. For both years, about 80% of the total was coniferous sawn wood. The temperate regions of the Northern Hemi-

sphere accounted for about 90% of coniferous sawn wood production.

The U.S.S.R. ranked first in production of sawn wood in 1966, with a reported total of 106.8 million cu.m. This almost equaled the combined total of 109,-552,000 cu.m. for the U.S. and Canada. Europe, excluding the U.S.S.R., produced 72,172,000 cu.m.; Asia, 60,355,000 cu.m.; South America, 10,122,000 cu.m.; the Pacific area, 5,108,000 cu.m.; Central America, 3,129,000 cu.m.; and Africa, 3,091,000 cu.m.

Among individual nations, the U.S. ranked second to the U.S.S.R. in 1966 sawn wood production, with 85,982,000 cu.m. Japan was third, with 35.3 million cu.m.; and Canada fourth, with 23,570,000 cu.m. Communist China's 1966 sawn wood production was not reported; its production for 1965 was estimated by the FAO at 11.5 million cu.m. Sweden had a 1966 output of 10,068,000 cu.m.; West Germany, 9,010,-000 cu.m.; Poland, 6,923,000 cu.m.; Finland, 6,055,-000 cu.m.; Romania, 5,399,000 cu.m.; Austria, 4,-944,000 cu.m.; Czechoslovakia, 3,648,000 cu.m.; and Yugoslavia, 2,887,000 cu.m. France produced 7,782,000 cu.m. in 1965; 1966 production was not reported. Brazil's production of sawn wood in 1966 was reported at 6,072,000 cu.m. Other countries producing more than one million cubic metres in 1966 were East Germany, Italy, Norway, Spain, Bulgaria, Portugal, Switzerland, Mexico, Turkey, Malaysia, Thailand, Australia, and New Zealand.

Preliminary estimates of U.S. lumber production, based on information compiled by the National Forest Products Association, were available for 1967. The total 1967 output was 34,595,000,000 bd.-ft., including 27,410,000,000 of softwood lumber and 7,185,-000,000 of hardwood lumber. The combined output of softwood and hardwood lumber showed a decided drop from the 36,433,000,000 bd.-ft. (revised estimate) produced in 1966. The postwar high of 38.9 billion bd.-ft. was reached in 1950. U.S. exports totaled 1,134,-000,000 bd.-ft. in 1967. Imports were 5,145,700,000 bd.-ft. The wholesale price index of lumber at the end of 1967 was 111.8, up 7% from December 1966 (1957–59 = 100).

Total Canadian production of lumber in 1966 was reported at 9,993,680,000 bd.-ft., a substantial drop from the 10,829,384,000 bd.-ft. (revised figure) produced in the preceding year. About 95% of the total was softwood lumber. Canada exported about two-thirds of its annual lumber production.

World production of pulp continued the rapid increase of recent years, rising to 83.4 million metric tons in 1966, compared with 78.5 million in 1965. Expansion of output in North America and the Soviet Union accounted for a major portion of the rise. Chemical (including semichemical) pulp represented more than 70% of 1967 world output, the remainder being mechanical wood pulp (about 24%) and pulp from materials other than wood (about 6%). In 1966 pulp and paper accounted for 41% of the total value of the world output of forest products, compared with 37% in 1960 and 36% in 1950.

North America accounted for about 55% of the world total of pulp production. The U.S. produced 32.3 million metric tons and Canada, 14.5 million. Among European producers, Sweden led with 6.5 million tons, followed by Finland (5.7 million), Norway (1.8 million), France (1.5 million), and West Germany (1.4 million). The U.S.S.R. reported 1966 production of 4.3 million tons. Japan's production was 5.7 million tons. Brazil, Mexico, Chile, Communist China, New Zealand, Australia, and South Africa were important producers, although none produced as much as one million tons.

World production of newsprint in 1966 reached 18 million metric tons, compared with 16.9 million in 1965. More than half of the total was produced in North America; Canada produced 7.6 million tons and the U.S., 2 million. Finland (1.3 million), Japan (1.2 million), the U.S.S.R. (882,000), the U.K. (780,-000 in 1965), Sweden (689,000), France (461,000), Italy (407,000), Norway (345,000), and Communist China (350,000 estimated in 1965) were other leading producers.

World production of plywood, according to FAO reports, rose from 24,309,000 cu.m. in 1965 to 25,315,-000 cu.m. in 1966. The U.S., with an output of 12.8 million cu.m., accounted for more than half of the world total. Japan produced 3,101,000 cu.m.; Canada, 1,803,000 cu.m.; the U.S.S.R., 1,772,000 cu.m.; West Germany, 631,700 cu.m.; Finland, 550,000 cu.m.; and France, 494,400 cu.m. Plywood production in a number of Asian and African countries rose at significant rates. Taiwan's output increased from 250,000 cu.m. in 1965 to 312,000 cu.m. in 1966; the Philippines increased production from 269,800 cu.m. to 328,-200 cu.m.; Malaysia, from 26,800 cu.m. (including veneers) to 53,800 cu.m.; and Singapore, from 31,800 cu.m. to 45,300 cu.m. South Korea achieved high rank among Asian countries as production there rose from 313,600 cu.m. to 515,200 cu.m. In Africa, Gabon was a leading producer in 1965 with 88,600 cu.m. (1966 output not reported). Brazil ranked first among Latin-American countries with a 1966 output of 220,-000 cu.m. Australia's plywood production dropped from 96,000 cu.m. in 1965 to 89,000 cu.m. in 1966.

Particle board production continued its rapid growth, although the rate of expansion slowed down somewhat compared with previous years. The world output in 1966 was 5,899,000 metric tons, more than 13% above the 1965 figure (1965 had shown increases of 25% over 1964 and 200% over 1960). Europe continued to account for nearly two-thirds of the total; West Germany, with a 1966 output of 1,198,600 metric tons, was the leading producer. The U.S. ranked second with 900,000 tons, and the U.S.S.R. was third with 672,900 tons. Other leading producers were France (404,000), Italy (270,000), East Germany (226,000), the U.K. (164,900), Japan (153,000), Austria (144,700), Spain (144,000), Romania (130,-000), Sweden (129,000), Finland (127,400), Switzerland (107,000), Czechoslovakia (102,000), and Yugoslavia (101,100). Canada, where the industry had been expanding rapidly, increased its production from 99,000 tons in 1965 to 116,000 tons in 1966. Particle board production in the U.S. rose sixfold from 1958 to 1966. Measured in square feet, $\frac{3}{4}$-in. basis, the 1966 output was 783.5 million. Production in 1967 was expected to exceed 900 million sq.ft.

In the U.S., lack of agreement among producers continued to prevent the adoption of a new standard for softwood lumber, although the older standard was considered inadequate and misleading and was expected to be withdrawn by the Department of Commerce. Under existing authority, the secretary of commerce was not authorized to promulgate a mandatory new standard, but could assist the industry to develop a voluntary standard.

The largest sale of national forest timber ever made by the U.S. Forest Service was completed in September 1968, when U.S. Plywood-Champion Papers, Inc.,

signed a 50-year contract for the purchase of 8,750,-000,000 bd.-ft. of timber in the Juneau unit of the Tongass National Forest in Alaska. The agreement required the purchaser to install a mill or mills in the area for the manufacture of pulp and other wood products. Approximately 200 million bd.-ft. of hemlock and spruce timber, mostly overmature, would be used annually for the manufacture of lumber and chemical grade paper pulp. The contract contained strict requirements designed to prevent water pollution and damage to salmon streams and waterfowl nesting areas. (C. E. R.)

See also Industrial Review.

ENCYCLOPÆDIA BRITANNICA FILMS. *The Temperate Deciduous Forest* (1962); *The Lumberman* (1965); *Trees and Their Importance* (1966); *Science Conserves Forests* (1967).

Tobacco

With hopes for a constitutional settlement between the U.K. and Rhodesia declining, interest in the future of Rhodesia's leaf crops waned. On the basis of figures gleaned from Rhodesia, it seemed likely that some £20 million worth of tobacco from the 1966 and 1967 crops must have been sold to manufacturers between the time sanctions began and June 1968, although Rhodesia's small domestic industry could have used little of this. In any case, the decisive switch in Britain's leaf imports continued. The latest import figures showed the U.S. supplying 44% of Britain's imported unmanufactured leaf, as against 33% in 1967, while Canada (22%) and India (20%) showed substantial comparative declines. Stocks in the U.K. at the end of July 1968 were 419 million lb., slightly higher than a year before.

An interesting feature of the U.K. import market was an increase of nearly one-third in manufactured cigars and cheroots during the first seven months of 1968, as compared with a year earlier. This occurred despite a lively home-produced cigar market stimulated by a plethora of new brand introductions. Displaced some years ago from its traditional role of leading cigarette exporter, the U.K. went some way toward recovering that position. Exports of cigarettes rose by a further one-tenth, with Kuwait the biggest single market.

Britain's 1968 budget impost of 4s. 4d. brought the total tobacco duty to 91s. 8½d. per pound. This was followed shortly by the expected manufacturers' price increase without, however, any increase in margins for the distributive trade, which the manufacturers were barred from incorporating into the price by the Prices and Incomes Board. Retailers and wholesalers, however, still considered that their margins needed urgent improvement, and set about preparing their own case for the board.

In Zambia and Malawi mixed results were reported. During the first 14 weeks of the Lusaka auctions, sales of flue-cured totaled approximately 13 million lb., or about seven-eighths of the crop, and the average price was 44.0d. per pound. By the corresponding date in 1967, sales had amounted to just over 9.5 million lb., averaging 53.4d. Sales at the Limbe auctions totaled 31.5 million lb. by August 29, about 1 million lb. below the estimate for the total crop. Average prices for flue-cured were markedly below those for 1967, but prices for other types were considerably higher.

Indian exports of unmanufactured tobacco in the first five months of 1968 amounted to 62 million lb.,

29% more than a year earlier and 86% more than in January–May 1966. Of the total exports in the first five months, 53% went to the U.K.

Canadian tobacco production in 1967 amounted to 213 million lb., 9% below the record crop harvested in 1966. Because of unfavourable weather, the average yield per acre fell by 285 lb. to 1,514 lb.—the lowest figure since 1959. The latest estimate for the total U.S. crop stood at 1,972,147,000 lb., with flue-cured leaf of better quality than in the previous year. The proportion of the crop under government support increased. Exports of unmanufactured tobaccos rose further in June, but shipments for the first half of the year, at 244 million lb., were nearly 3% less than in January–June 1967. The chief destination was the U.K., which took 46.4 million lb., 8.6 million lb. more than in the first five months of 1967. Shipments to West Germany, however, were reduced by almost one-half to 27.3 million lb. Shipments to Japan rose spectacularly, to 12.9 million lb. in January–May from 4 million lb. a year earlier. The 6.9 million lb. shipped to Taiwan had no 1967 counterpart. Total stocks of unmanufactured tobacco held in the U.S. on April 1 amounted to 5,309,000,000 lb., or 30 million lb. more than a year earlier.

Exports of unmanufactured tobacco from Turkey in the first half of 1968, at 79 million lb., were 25 million lb. below the corresponding period of 1967, mainly because of reduced shipments to the U.S. Shipments to EEC countries showed an even more marked decline, but exports to Eastern Europe remained level. Duty-paid imports of unmanufactured tobacco into the Netherlands in the first half of the year, at 48 million lb., were 5 million lb. below the corresponding period of 1967, with imports from the U.S. representing just over one-third of the total.

Easily the largest tobacco producer in Latin America, Brazil provided varying estimates of the 1967 crop. Conservative sources placed it at about 280 million lb., of which about 180 million was dark air-cured (including cigar) and 90 million lb. was flue-cured. Spain remained the chief target for Brazil's tobacco exports.

The U.S. was still the main source of unmanufactured tobacco for Australia, but its share was declining; still small but increasing amounts were received from countries in Eastern Asia. Fifth among tobacco growing countries in the world, Japan produced an estimated 462.7 million lb. in 1967 from an enlarged acreage. Despite heavy domestic production, 1967 imports, at 65 million lb., were nearly twice those of 1963. The South African tobacco crop was estimated at the end of January 1968 at 74.1 million lb., of which 41 million lb. was flue-cured, 18.9 million lb. dark air-cured, and 9.8 million lb. light air-cured. Although the Soviet Union's domestic production had reached recent peaks of over 500 million lb., it continued to rank among the world's main importers of tobacco; Bulgaria was the principal source.

Lower domestic growth in the U.S. seemed one likely reason for the flurry of foreign acquisitions and licensing deals by U.S. companies. Industry sales and production fell in the second quarter of 1968, probably because taxes went up, but the setback was expected to be only temporary. Menthol brands continued to show the best growth, while the 100-mm. (super king) size seemed to have reached a peak at 12% of the market. The possibility remained that TV advertising of cigarettes might be banned by government action or dropped by the companies, although

European experience suggested that this sort of action had little effect on industry growth.

In Britain, U.S. take-overs and the abandonment by the manufacturers of resale price maintenance created a puzzling situation. By securing 66% of the common stock of Britain's second largest manufacturer, Gallaher (27% of the cigarette market), American Tobacco Co. obtained an important overseas potential. The Philip Morris take-over of Godfrey Phillips took the former into India, Pakistan, and Ceylon, where there were almost no existing U.S. interests. A spate of price cutting followed abandonment of the resale price maintenance case. Multipacks of 60, 80, 100, and 200 were offered in supermarkets at prices clearly below apparent economic levels; Imperial and Gallaher claimed there were no "hidden" discounts, but Carreras did not deny suggestions of special promotion and marketing allowances to supermarkets. The most intriguing development was the bulk purchase by South Wales wholesalers and retailers from cooperative outlets of a king-size brand selling at a price less than that normally paid by traders direct to this manufacturer. The general impression of the conventional distributive trade was that deep price cutting would be a nine-day wonder, though most faced the fact that the supermarkets would increase their share of the market.   (PE. M.)

Togo

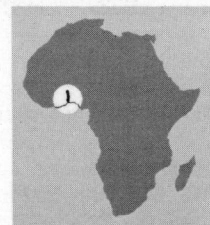

A West African republic, Togo is bordered by Ghana, Upper Volta, and Dahomey. Area: 21,853 sq.mi. (56,600 sq.km.). Pop. (1968 est.): 1,746,400. Cap. and largest city: Lomé (pop., 1968 est., 90,600). Language: French (official). Religion: pagan; Muslim and Christian minorities. President in 1968, Gen. Étienne Eyadema.

On January 12 President Eyadema emphasized the trend toward a resumption of civilian rule with the announcement that when the constitution, then in preparation, was ready, democratic elections would take place. Disturbed by developments in Nigeria's civil war, he announced (while visiting Paris in May) his willingness to act as mediator in that conflict. Divergent statements on that and other issues by members of the Organization of African Unity (OAU) and by the African and Malagasy Common Organization (OCAM), he said, were liable to divide these associations, and Eyadema urged OCAM members—unsuccessfully—to meet and discuss the problem.

TOGO
Education. (1965–66) Primary, pupils 155,803, teachers 3,097; secondary, pupils 11,330, teachers 492; vocational, pupils 1,796, teachers 70; teacher training, students 66, teachers 13; higher, students 73, teaching staff 7.
Finance. Monetary unit: CFA franc, with a parity of CFA Fr. 50 to the French franc (CFA Fr. 246.85 = U.S. $1; CFA Fr. 592.45 = £1 sterling). Budget (1967 rev. est.): revenue CFA Fr. 5,274,000,000; expenditure CFA Fr. 5,875,000,000.
Foreign Trade. (1967) Imports CFA Fr. 11,133,-000,000; exports CFA Fr. 7,894,000,000. Import sources: France 29%; Japan 13%; West Germany 10%; U.K. 8%; China 5%; Ghana 5%. Export destinations: France 38%; Netherlands 18%; West Germany 11%; Belgium-Luxembourg 7%; Italy 5%; Australia 5%. Main exports: phosphates 38%; cocoa 30%; coffee 11%; palm nuts 5%.

Togo became closely involved with Dahomean politics because three Dahomey ex-presidents had taken residence there in July (having previously lived in exile in Paris after being expelled from their own country). The Togo government decided to close the Togo-Dahomey border in order to prevent any accusation of interference in Dahomey's internal affairs.

In March Togo joined Air Afrique, the multinational airline created in 1961 by 11 French-speaking African states. On April 27 President Eyadema inaugurated new deepwater port facilities at Lomé, built with West German finance totaling $16.8 million. The port was designed to accommodate vessels of up to 12,000 tons and to handle 500,000 tons of cargo annually. Following an agreement with West Germany to postpone repayments until December 1970, it was decided to abolish a 2% reduction of wages and salaries in public employment intended to help finance Togo's five-year development plan.   (PH. D.; X.)

Tourism

An important step toward the recognition of tourism as one of the world's major economic and social activities had been the designation of 1967 as International Tourist Year by the General Assembly of the United Nations. Because of its close relationship with income levels and leisure time, tourism was largely an activity of the developed areas of the world, but by its very nature, it tended to spread its benefits in an ever widening area.

In 1967 and 1968 the overall growth of world tourism slowed considerably as compared with the mid-1960s; the political and economic situations in two regions, Europe and the Middle East, were mainly responsible for this. In other regions of the world, growth continued more or less unabated. It was anticipated that the early 1970s would see a tremendous increase in tourism embracing all levels of the populations of the economically developed countries and increasingly benefiting the less developed countries, due to rising levels of prosperity and cheaper air transportation.

The trends toward lower-spending tourists, traveling independently by road, or in organized groups by air, continued. The accommodations industry tended to find itself with either not enough capacity or too much of the wrong sort. Both vertical integration (airlines building hotels) and horizontal integration (growth of hotel chains) took place to the benefit of the whole tourist industry.

The Volume and Value of Tourism. *Domestic Tourism.* While the volume and value of international tourism was comparatively easy to measure, the size of domestic tourism was much harder to gauge. This was due to the fact that there were no frontier crossings or foreign exchange transactions involved. Several countries in Europe and North America, however, could measure domestic tourism through accommodation records and by sample surveys. It was estimated that domestic tourism probably represented some 75% of the total world expenditure on tourism, international tourism representing the other 25%. During 1967–68, the growth of domestic tourism in Europe slowed compared with previous years, but the experience of several countries, notably the U.K. and West Germany, showed that domestic tourism demand resisted periods of poor overall economic growth better than demand for international tourism.

International Tourism. In the decade before 1967, world international tourist arrivals and receipts had grown steadily at an annual average rate of 10–12%. In 1967, however, world international tourist arrivals and receipts grew by only 6 and 7%, respectively. International tourist receipts totaled $14 billion in 1967, excluding transport payments. This distinctly lower rate of growth was mainly due to the preponderant influence of Europe, which recorded 72% of the world's arrivals and 60% of the receipts, and where receipts and arrivals grew by only 3 and 4%, respectively. (*See* Tables I and II.) The main cause of the lower rate was the stagnant economic situation in the main tourist generating markets—West Germany, France, the U.K., the Netherlands, and the Scandinavian countries.

A further cause of the poor growth of world tourism in 1967 was the war in the Middle East in June. Not only did tourist arrivals and receipts in that region drop by 20 and 30%, respectively, but tourism to the eastern Mediterranean, including Turkey, Greece, and Cyprus, and to the countries of North Africa (Libya, Tunisia, Algeria, and Morocco) was also affected. While in central and southern Africa tourism grew strongly, in North Africa tourism's growth slowed and even showed a decline in Morocco and Algeria. In other regions the growth of international tourism tended to be above average.

In Central and North America, international tourism surged ahead, mainly influenced by the overwhelming success of Expo 67, held during the summer in Montreal. Canada's tourist receipts rose by 55%, to $1,209,000,000, principally due to the increased expenditures of U.S. visitors. The Caribbean and South American countries also registered record numbers of tourist arrivals, which grew at average, or above average, rates.

In eastern Asia, tourism continued its rapid rise despite a poor performance by Hong Kong, the major tourist attraction in the area. Other countries such as Singapore (arrivals up 59%), Nationalist China (up

38%), and Cambodia (up 16%) experienced record years. Oceania too had a very good year for international tourism in 1967; tourist arrivals and receipts rose 18%. Similarly, Southeast Asia—mainly India, Iran, and Pakistan—had an above average year and tourist arrivals grew by 16%.

An inauspicious start was given to 1968 when U.S. Pres. Lyndon B. Johnson appealed to Americans to restrict travel outside the Western Hemisphere to the bare minimum. This appeal was brought on by the greatly increased deficit on travel account that the U.S. had suffered during 1967. This deficit, however, was due almost entirely to the increased spending by U.S. tourists attracted by Expo 67. In any case, restricting travel to the Western Hemisphere did not tackle the major reason for the dollar outflow. Although the taxes on travel proposed by the administration were not accepted by Congress, the president's message began to take effect. The travel trade in Europe reported consistently lower U.S. bookings and the eastward flood of U.S. tourists was greatly cut back.

In Europe, meanwhile, the continuing difficulties of the U.K. economy and the stagnation of that of West Germany boded ill for tourism during 1968. These countries were, with France, the major generators of tourists. The French crisis of May helped to deter even more Americans from traveling to Europe and drastically affected France's tourist performance for the year. The occupation of Czechoslovakia in August was yet another blow to European tourism and effectively stopped, for a time at least, the hitherto growing flow of West-East traffic. However, some countries, drawing benefit from their devalued currencies (Spain and the U.K.), experienced distinctly better years in 1968, while others, such as Switzerland and Austria, had marginally better years.

In the Middle East, the main tourist receptors, Lebanon, Israel, Jordan, and the U.A.R., recovered a little of their lost ground; this was particularly true of Lebanon and Israel. Growing tensions at the end of the summer of 1968, however, set back the restoration of confidence, and tourist arrivals and receipts in the region as a whole were still well below those of 1966.

Other regions of the world experienced quite good tourism growth in 1968. The North African countries, especially Tunisia, experienced a considerable increase in tourist arrivals, and central and southern Africa continued to benefit from growing flows of tourists from Europe and North America. In the Americas, tourism's growth benefited from President Johnson's appeal for U.S. tourists to restrict their travel to the Western Hemisphere. The Caribbean and Latin-American countries experienced strong U.S. demands, at the same time that the Olympic Games in Mexico were attracting overseas visitors to the continent. The East Asian countries, such as Singapore, Cambodia, Thailand, and Nationalist China, seeing increasingly the potential benefits of tourism and making strenuous efforts, achieved larger shares of the market.

Trends in Tourism. With the extension of paid vacations and rising income levels, more and more people had the means to travel abroad during 1967–68. At the same time, the increased availability of promotional air fares and, in particular, of package vacations, lowered the price of travel. The trend was toward travel by the lower-spending tourists who stayed for shorter periods. This affected the airlines, which experienced increased traffic without commensurate rises in revenue, and the tourist industries of the various

Table I. International Tourist Arrivals, 1966–67

Region	Arrivals		Change	
	1967	1966	Absolute	Percent
Africa	1,926,000	1,833,000	+ 93,000	+ 5
Americas				
South America	1,017,000	869,000	+ 148,000	+17
Central and North America	27,379,000	23,753,000	+3,626,000	+15
Caribbean	2,462,000	2,218,000	+ 244,000	+11
Total	30,858,000	26,840,000	+4,018,000	+15
Europe	100,322,000	95,975,000	+4,347,000	+ 4
Middle East	2,510,000	3,138,000	− 628,000	−20
Pacific areas				
Eastern Asia	2,114,000	1,810,000	+ 304,000	+17
Oceania	421,000	356,000	+ 65,000	+18
Total	2,535,000	2,166,000	+ 369,000	+17
Southeast Asia	549,000	474,000	+ 75,000	+16
Total	138,700,000	130,426,000	+8,274,000	+ 6

Source: International Union of Official Travel Organizations, Geneva.

Table II. International Tourist Receipts, 1966–67
In $000,000

Region	Receipts		Change	
	1967	1966	Absolute	Percent
Africa	210	191	+ 19	+10
Americas				
South America	369	321	+ 48	+15
Central and North America	3,870	3,252	+618	+20
Caribbean	326	290	+ 36	+13
Total	4,565	3,863	+702	+18
Europe	8,378	8,194	+184	+ 3
Middle East	245	359	−114	−32
Pacific areas				
Eastern Asia	385	333	+ 52	+16
Oceania	139	118	+ 21	+18
Total	524	451	+ 73	+16
Southeast Asia	117	102	+ 15	+15
Total	14,039	13,160	+879	+ 7

Source: International Union of Official Travel Organizations, Geneva.

countries, which found they were providing increased services to international tourists but were not receiving proportional increases in tourist receipts.

The case of U.S. tourists was illustrative of this trend; between 1963 and 1967 U.S. tourist numbers rose by 72%, but, due to a fall of 20% in the average expenditure from $563 to $448, total expenditures of U.S. tourists had risen only 37%. These tendencies were accelerated by the fact that the numbers of business travelers, habitually higher spenders (and covered by the international definitions of "tourist"), did not grow at the same rate as pleasure travelers. This trend naturally affected the nature of the services demanded and, in particular, the type of accommodation required. The steady growth of camping and trailer-park sites in Europe, and of medium-price accommodations elsewhere, bore witness to this effect.

As to the kind of transport used, the trend differed according to the type of tourism involved. For intracontinental traffic, that is, within Europe or North America, the ascendancy of the automobile tended to be reinforced while the decline of the railroads continued. Air transport, while representing a comparatively small part of such traffic, grew in importance.

For intercontinental tourism, the trend toward air traffic and away from sea transport continued. On North Atlantic routes the number of air passengers rose by 17% to 5.5 million in 1967 while the number of sea passengers fell by 17% to 506,000. The shipping companies offered 12% less capacity in 1967 but, due to the greater fall in passengers, load factors fell by 4% to 62%. The selling of the "Queen Mary" and "Queen Elizabeth" by Cunard was a sad symptom, although it made economic common sense. On world international air routes as a whole, scheduled passenger traffic rose by 14% in 1967. Nonscheduled passenger traffic, that is, charter and package tour flights, was estimated to have increased by 55% in 1967, bringing its total volume to nearly 15% of world air passenger traffic. This was symptomatic of the whole trend toward organized travel. Similarly, the growth of travel clubs in 1967 and 1968, in both Europe and North America, reinforced the trend toward group tours.

The problem of seasonality was one that conditioned much of the tourist-serving sector and created many of the difficulties, such as low profitability, high prices, and shortage of skilled staff. Despite several years of trying, the countries of Europe had not found a solution to the situation.

Equipment and Services. *The Accommodations Industry.* During 1967 and 1968 various serious problems manifested themselves in the accommodations industries. A lack of suitably priced accommodations was felt in many countries. This lack was directly related to the scarcity and high cost of investment funds and to high operating costs. In several countries with fairly low levels of international tourist flows and considerable unexploited tourist potential, the main obstacle to tourism's growth was acknowledged to be not a demand, but a supply constraint, that is, a lack of suitable accommodations and other facilities.

One of the main features of the accommodations industry in these two years was the realization by the airline companies of the threat that the lack of accommodations posed to their future traffic. This was particularly alarming at a time when the airlines were embarking on massive reequipment programs involving purchases of stretched jets, jumbo jets, and airbuses. The airlines felt forced to enter the hotel industry, generally in association with established hotel chains. Examples were an expansion of activities by Pan American's subsidiary Intercontinental Hotels, the take-over by TWA of Hilton International, and the activities of BOAC in association with Fortes, Trust Houses, and Intercontinental. These activities were centred both in Europe and in such developing tourist areas as East Africa, the Pacific, and Asia.

The more forward-looking hotel and motel chains also began to realize what the shortage of accommodations could mean to them. The use of strict quantity and quality control, of computerized booking and accounting procedures, and of mass production of standardized equipment gave the chains the chance to enter the international market and provide high quality lodgings at reasonable price levels.

In Europe, there was no apparent shortage of hotel capacity; occupancy rates fell in many countries. It was in the gateway cities (London, Paris, Amsterdam, Zürich, Copenhagen) that the shortage of accommodations existed and it was in these cities that the airline companies entered the hotel industry. In North America, the decline of the hotel and the rise of the motel continued. Between 1963 and 1967 hotel capacity fell by 1% in the U.S. while the number of rooms available in motels rose by 12%.

Outside of North America and Europe, some governments themselves invested in hotels, while others provided favourable tax and credit facilities to encourage foreign and domestic investments in hotels. In all these countries one of the major problems was the maintenance of local charm (and, therefore, attractiveness) while achieving the internationally accepted standards of comfort at reasonable prices.

Transport Facilities. While the means of transport increased in number and size, the facilities for them did not; the roads in Europe became steadily more crowded during the peak summer months, and airports around the world became jammed with people and aircraft. The situation in midsummer 1968 at Kennedy International Airport in New York, where planes circled for hours waiting to land, was indicative of what was in store for the rest of the world's airports unless massive steps were taken quickly. The airlines estimated that not one airport outside of North America would be prepared or equipped for the jumbo jets by their expected date of introduction (late 1969).

Organization and Promotion of Tourism. The authority and power of national and international tourist organizations grew considerably during 1967–68. In many countries national tourist offices were reorganized and their powers reinforced (Australia, Ceylon). This was due to the growing recognition that the or-

"PARIS MATCH" FROM PICTORIAL PARADE

The French Paquet Line inaugurated the first musical cruise of the Mediterranean during 1968. Above, Tessa Beaumont dancing on the deck of the SS "Renaissance" accompanied by pianist George Solchany, flutist Jean-Pierre Rampal, and the Vegh Quartet.

ganization of tourism—promotion, development and planning, professional training—required strong central control. The total budgets of the national tourist offices increased considerably and in 1968 some $82 million (60% of the total tourism budget) was spent on promotional activities. These activities were supplemented by the vast promotional efforts of the airline companies, travel agents, and tour operators. The airlines were estimated to have spent close to $200 million on promotion in 1968.   (JE. S. B.)

See also Parks; Transportation.

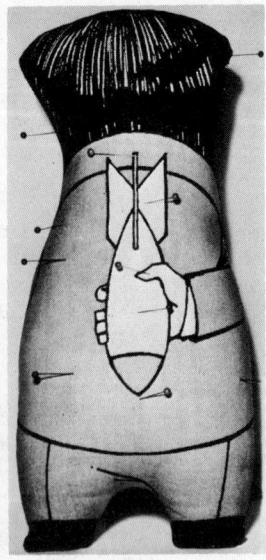

Voodoo doll of Mao Tse-tung depicting his dual character. A shipment of these Irish-made dolls caused considerable controversy when the International Longshoremen's Association, convinced that the crates contained Communist propaganda, refused to unload the cargo in New York City.

Toys and Games

The international aspect of toy and game production on all continents—the feeling that the whole globe should be treated as one vast market—seemed to gain fresh impetus for manufacturers during 1968. Various national economic upsets in no way checked the continuing success of the major toy fairs; rather, they contributed to that success in large part.

The trade exhibitions at Nürnberg, W.Ger., Brighton and Harrogate, Eng., Paris, France, Milan, Italy, and Tokyo, Japan, were truly international in fact as well as in name. Europe, indeed, added yet another show to its yearly calendar with "Bimbo Sud" in Naples, Italy, in June. One of the aims of the new exhibition was to attract buyers from the Middle East, although it was also intended as an opportunity for a midyear recapitulation of the lines introduced during the previous winter.

The Australian fair, too, continued successfully, while future U.S. toy fairs, held in New York City, could be expected to make an even greater international impact than in the past. Already a major source of ideas, as well as actual products, the U.S. Toy Fair would greatly increase its attraction for buyers by opening its doors in 1970 for the first time to foreign exhibitors. The decision to admit foreign exhibitors was the result of a poll taken by the show's sponsors, the Toy Manufacturers of America, Inc., among current exhibitors. Announcing the change in policy, the president, William R. McLain, said that "the growing interest in foreign trade has made this a matter for study. . . . This move to reciprocate the courtesies of the foreign manufacturers should further the cause of international trade in the toy field."

Toy promotion in Europe received a massive boost with the introduction of a toy week, already hugely successful in some countries on the continent—in the Netherlands it was backed by a consumer competition. West Germany and Austria planned to support theirs by heavy television and press advertising. Future Dutch plans discussed at a meeting of the European Association of Toy Retailers included a mobile exhibition on a whistle-stop railway tour, while the Belgians planned to repeat their "Keep Smiling" campaign to support the week.

Space-age toys continued to dominate the world market in both volume and variety. Many of these were the product of modern merchandising at its most high powered; in Britain the latest of the puppet films designed for television by Gerry Anderson had as great an impact as its predecessors "Captain Scarlet" and "Thunderbirds." Also from Century 21, the Project S.W.O.R.D. range of toys received a boost from a merchandising tie-in with the film *2001: A Space Odyssey*.

In a similar vein, a Canadian best seller, Billy Blast-

Talking Christie doll, the black counterpart of the white Barbie doll by Mattel. During 1968 many companies produced Negro dolls to meet the growing demand of the Negro market.

Town Planning: *see* Cities and Urban Affairs

off, exploited the interest in all things extraterrestrial, while the most recent launch of all, Major Matt Mason (and his men and equipment), seemed likely to corner much of the Christmas market in the U.S. and Britain at least. Created by the U.S. firm Rosebud Mattel, the off-world Major Matt Mason was highly "realistic," with both men and equipment produced in great detail, from space station to remote control "Reconjet pak" and an eight-legged space crawler.

Hong Kong ingenuity added a further refinement to toy spaceship design in a model that included a sound control device. This battery-operated spaceship made by Kota "responds solely to the human voice and whistling."

The year 1968 also saw the launch of what could be a successor to the record-setting Hula Hoop craze. This was the Ride-a-Roo Kangaroo Jockey Ball, a large bouncy globe on which children or adults could sit and bounce high in the air; it enjoyed immediate international success. Another toy that gained great popularity during the year appeared to hark back to the Hula Hoop for its inspiration. Called Footsee, it consisted of a plastic ankle ring to which was attached a 30-in. string with a bell-shaped weight at the end. The object was to keep the bell and string twirling around one foot while hopping over it with the other.

At the other end of the size-scale was a U.S. puzzle game called Instant Insanity. This comprised four cubes, each with six differently coloured sides. The trick was to align them so that four different colours were visible on each side of the group. It was calculated that there were 80,000 possible alignments, only one of which was right.

A device illustrating Newton's Third Law of Motion —for every action there is an equal and opposite reaction—enjoyed considerable success during the year. Produced and sold under such varying names as Swinging Wonder and Motion Teaser, it consisted of five large ball bearings suspended by string from a wooden or plastic frame. When the balls were drawn apart and allowed to collide, they rebounded in a variety of patterns that illustrated Newton's principle.   (J. M. TH.)

Track and Field Sports

Blazing speed in the running events, including the relays and 400-m. hurdles, with special emphasis on the sprints; prodigious performances in the jumps and throwing events; and, at the Olympic Games, complete domination of all distance races, from the 1,500 m. through the marathon, by a handful of astonishing athletes from Africa provided the highlights of the 1968 track and field season.

The most monumental single effort of the season, and possibly in the entire history of track and field,

UPI COMPIX

was the amazing long jump of Bob Beamon of the U.S. in the Olympics. Beamon shattered all previous marks in this event by nearly two feet. He completely scorned the 28-ft. bracket as he leaped right over it to extend the world record from 27 ft. 4¾ in. (Ralph Boston, U.S., 1965, and Igor Ter-Ovanesyan, Soviet Union, 1967) to 29 ft. 2⅜ in.

Male athletes shattered all world outdoor records from 100 m. through 600 m. and tied the listed world record at 800 m. in altitudes corresponding to the oxygen-starved air of Mexico City's 7,347-ft. height. During the year they set new world standards at 2, 10, and 20 mi.; in the 3,000-m. steeplechase; both the 20- and 50-km. walks; the 400-m. hurdles; the pole vault, long (broad), and triple jumps; the discus, javelin, and hammer throws; the 400-m. and 1,600-m. relays, the distance medley relay, and the 480-yd. shuttle hurdles relay; and the pentathlon.

Women athletes, meanwhile, were setting new world records in the 100-m. and 200-m. dashes; in the 800-m., 3,000-m., one-hour, and 10-mi. runs; in the 400-m. and 800-m. relays, the medley relay, and 3 × 800 m. relay; in the 80-m. and 100-m. hurdles; and in the shot put, discus throw, and long jump.

All told, world outdoor records were broken or tied 85 times in 44 events by the combined performances of men and women athletes. Indoor world marks were set or tied by men and women 39 times in 24 events.

Sprints and Hurdles. The evening of June 20 witnessed one of the most sensational one-day displays of sprinting in the annals of track and field. The occasion was the 100-m. dash in the U.S. national Amateur Athletic Union (AAU) championships at Sacramento, Calif. Before the event was concluded with Charlie Greene of the Husker AA, Nebraska, defeating Jim Hines of the Houston Striders and Lennox Miller of Jamaica, AAU hand timers had officially clocked Hines, Greene, and Ronnie Ray Smith (Southern California Striders) in world-record times of 9.9 sec. Smith was so timed while running second to Hines in a semifinal heat. There were 13 non-wind-aided recordings tying the old world record of 10 sec., and a total of 32 clockings of 10.1 sec. or faster.

Out of this mass assault on the world record there emerged five men who reached the eight-man final of the Olympic Games 100 m. at Mexico City. These were Hines, first in the Olympics in an official 9.9; Miller, second in 10; Greene, third in 10; Roger Bambuck of France, fifth in 10.1; and Mel Pender of the U.S. Army, sixth in 10.1.

Paul Nash of South Africa, ineligible for the Olympic Games because his country had been banned for its racial policies, had two official and several wind-aided clockings at 10 sec., and Oliver Ford of the United States had one.

Tommie Smith of the U.S. ran faster than his previous world 200-m. record in winning the Olympic gold medal in 19.8 sec., but in a final team trial at South Lake Tahoe, Calif., John Carlos, also U.S., had lowered the world record to 19.7 sec. Carlos' record, however, was set while wearing illegal "brushspike" shoes. Smith and Carlos were split at the Olympics by the silver medalist from Australia, Peter Norman.

During the year U.S. stars Lee Evans, Larry James, and Vincent Matthews at various times took several tenths off Tommie Smith's world record of 44.5 sec. for 400 m. Evans then won the Olympic 400 m. in a record 43.8 sec., with James finishing second at 43.9.

The women's 100-m. record of 11.1 sec. was tied five times prior to the Olympic Games, where defend-

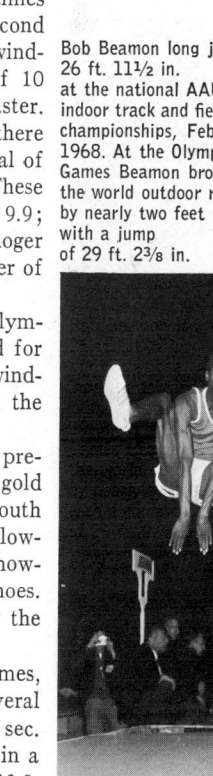

Bob Seagren clearing 17 ft. 4¼ in., a new world's best indoor performance, in the Millrose Games at Madison Square Garden, Jan. 25, 1968.

Bob Beamon long jumping 26 ft. 11½ in. at the national AAU indoor track and field championships, Feb. 24, 1968. At the Olympic Games Beamon broke the world outdoor record by nearly two feet with a jump of 29 ft. 2⅜ in.

WIDE WORLD

Event	Competitor, country, date	Performance
Records broken		
100 m.	Jim Hines, U.S., June 20 (heat)	9.9 sec.
	Ronnie Ray Smith, U.S., June 20 (heat)	9.9 sec.
	Charlie Greene, U.S., June 20 (heat)	9.9 sec.
	Jim Hines, U.S., October 14	9.9 sec.
200 m.	John Carlos, U.S., September 12	19.7 sec.*
	Tommie Smith, U.S., September 12	19.9 sec.*
	Tommie Smith, U.S., October 16	19.8 sec.
400 m.	Vince Matthews, U.S., August 31	44.4 sec.
	Lee Evans, U.S., September 14	44.0 sec.*
	Larry James, U.S., September 14	44.1 sec.
	Lee Evans, U.S., October 18	43.8 sec.
	Larry James, U.S., October 18	43.9 sec.
	Ron Freeman, U.S., October 18	44.4 sec.
600 m.	Tom Farrell, U.S., July 27	1 min. 16.5 sec.
	Lee Evans, U.S., August 31	1 min. 14.3 sec.
2 mi.	Ron Clarke, Australia, Aug. 24	8 min. 19.6 sec.
10 mi.	Ron Hill, U.K., November 9	46 min. 44 sec.
20 mi.	Ron Hill, U.K., n.a.	1 hr. 36 min. 38 sec.
20-km. walk	Gennadiy Agapov, U.S.S.R., n.a.	1 hr. 25 min. 21.4 sec.
50-km. walk	Bernhard Nemerich, West Germany, n.a.	4 hr. 4 min. 8.2 sec.
	Christoph Hohne, East Germany, June 2	4 hr. 6 min. 23.4 sec.
3,000-m. steeplechase	Jouka Kuha, Finland, July 17	8 min. 24.2 sec.
400-m. hurdles	Geoff Vanderstock, U.S., September 11	48.8 sec.
	Boyd Gittins, U.S., September 11	49.1 sec.
	David Hemery, U.K., October 15	48.1 sec.
400-m. relay	U.S. national team (Charlie Greene, Mel Pender, Ronnie Ray Smith, Jim Hines), October 20	38.2 sec.
1,600-m. relay	U.S. national team (Vince Matthews, Ron Freeman, Larry James, Lee Evans), October 20	2 min. 56.1 sec.
2-mi. relay	West Germany (Bodo Tummler, Walter Adams, Harald Norpoth, Franz-Josef Kemper), June 13	7 min. 14.6 sec.
Distance medley relay	U.S. Army, Ft. MacArthur (Robert Tobler, Darnell Mitchell, Tom Von Ruden, Preston Davis), April 27	9 min. 33.4 sec.
480-yd. shuttle hurdles relay	Southern California Striders (Ralph Boston, Ron Copeland, Leon Coleman, Tom White), April 20	55.4 sec.
4-mi. relay	University of Oregon (Roscoe Divine, Wade Bell, Arne Kvalheim, David Wilborn), May 30	16 min. 5.0 sec.
56-lb. weight (for height)	Jim Hannefield, U.S., March 2	17 ft. 6½ in.
Discus throw	Jay Silvester, U.S., May 25	218 ft. 4 in.
	Jay Silvester, U.S., September 18	224 ft. 5 in.
Javelin throw	Yanis Lusis, U.S.S.R., June 23	301 ft. 9½ in.
Hammer throw	Gyula Zsivotzky, Hungary, September 14	242 ft. 0 in.
Pole vault	Robert Seagren, U.S., September 12	17 ft. 9 in.
Long jump	Robert Beamon, U.S., October 18	29 ft. 2⅜ in.
Triple jump	Giuseppe Gentile, Italy, October 17	56 ft. 6 in.
	Viktor Saneev, U.S.S.R., October 17	57 ft. ⅝ in.
Pentathlon	Rein Aun, Soviet Union, July 18	4,079 pt.

*May not be officially ratified; illegally spiked "brush" shoes used.

KEYSTONE

Kipchoge Keino of Kenya winning the finals of the 1,500-m. run at the Olympic Games in Mexico City, Oct. 23, 1968. His time of 3 min. 34.9 sec. set a new Olympic record.

WIDE WORLD

Barbara Ferrell running the last leg of the medley relay for the Los Angeles Mercurettes at the national AAU indoor championships, Feb. 24, 1968. The team established a new indoor record of 1 min. 45.1 sec.

ing champion Wyomia Tyus of Tennessee State reduced it to 11 sec. Also at the Olympics Irina Kirszenstein-Szewinska of Poland lowered her own 200-m. world record to 22.5 sec. Maureen Caird, a 17-year-old Australian, upset favoured Pam Kilborn, also of Australia, in the women's 80-m. hurdles at the Olympics to tie the world record. Vyera Korsakova of the Soviet Union claimed a record 10.2 sec. in that event on June 16, but a dispute over the time might result in rejection of the claim.

On March 9 Pam Kilborn lowered the world record for the 100-m. hurdles to 13.4 sec. after a previous record performance of 13.6. This was of importance because in future Olympic Games the women's hurdle race would be 100 m. rather than 80 m.

The old world record of 49.1 sec. for the 400-m. hurdles, held by Rex Cawley of the U.S., was lowered to 48.8 sec. by Geoff Vanderstock and tied by Boyd Gittins, both of the U.S. At the Olympics, however, David Hemery of the U.K. turned in what was perhaps the most spectacular mark made by any athlete in a running race during the entire Olympics, setting a new world record of 48.1 sec.

Distance Events. While it was the Africans who dominated the distance events in the Olympics, the high altitude at Mexico City made it impossible for them to come within many seconds of the world records in events beyond 1,500 m. At that distance Kipchoge Keino of Kenya won a gold medal by upsetting the world record holder at the mile, Jim Ryun of the U.S., by 20 yd. Keino's time, 3 min. 34.9 sec., was a new Olympic record and second only to Ryun's 1967 world record of 3:33.1, made at sea level.

Other outstanding performances in distance running were 1:44.3 by Ralph Doubell of Australia in the 800 m., tying Peter Snell's world record and setting a new Olympic standard; Australian Ron Clarke's new world two-mile record of 8:19.6 at London on August 24; and a world record 800-m. race by Vera Nikolic of Yugoslavia in 2:00.5 on July 20 at London.

In addition to the magnificent performances of the Kenyans in the Olympics, Africa also produced Mamo Wolde of Ethiopia, who won first place in the marathon and second in the 10,000 m.; and Muhammad Gammoudi of Tunisia, first in the 5,000 m. and third at 10,000 m. Kenya's medals went to Keino (1,500 m.), Naftali Temu (10,000 m.), and Amos Biwott (steeplechase), gold; to Wilson Kiprugut (800 m.), Benjamin Kogo (steeplechase), Keino (5,000 m.), and the 1,600-m. relay team, silver; and to Temu (5,000 m.), bronze.

Relays. National teams, either before or during the Olympics, set many new world records. U.S. foursomes at Mexico City broke the records at 400 m., for both men and women, and at 1,600 m. for men. Charles Greene, Mel Pender, Ronnie Ray Smith, and Jim Hines were clocked in 38.2 sec., 0.4 sec. under Southern California's all-time best in the 400-m. relay; Vincent Matthews, Ronald Freeman, Larry James, and Lee Evans cut the 1,600-m. record to 2:56.1 (old record 2:59.6) as Kenya tied the former record. Cuba, France, and Jamaica also bettered the old 400-m. record of 38.6, and East Germany tied it. Poland's old 400-m. record for women of 43.6 sec. was lowered to 42.8 sec. by Barbara Ferrell, Margaret Bailes, Mildrette Netter, and Wyomia Tyus of the U.S.

On June 13 a West German team of Bodo Tummler, Walter Adams, Harald Norpoth, and Franz-Josef Kemper set a world record of 7:14.6 in the two-mile relay. A British team made up of Maureen Tranter,

Table II. World Outdoor Records—Women

Event	Competitor, country, date	Performance
Records broken		
100 m.	Wyomia Tyus, U.S., October 15	11.0 sec.
200 m.	Irina Kirszenstein-Szewinska, Poland, October 18	22.5 sec.
800 m.	Vera Nikolic, Yugoslavia, July 20	2 min. 0.5 sec.
3,000 m.	Ann O'Brien, Ireland, September 10	10 min. 5.4 sec.
1 hr.	Ann O'Brien, Ireland, September 12	9 mi. 1,133 yd.
10 mi.	Ann O'Brien, Ireland, September 12	1 hr. 2 min. 7 sec.
80-m. hurdles	Vyera Korsakova, U.S.S.R., June 16	10.2 sec.*
100-m. hurdles	Pam Kilborn, Australia, March 6 (heat)	13.6 sec.
	Pam Kilborn, Australia, March 9	13.4 sec.
400-m. relay	U.S. Olympic team (Barbara Ferrell, Margaret Bailes, Mildrette Netter, Wyomia Tyus), October 20	42.8 sec.
800-m. relay	U.K. Olympic team (Maureen Tranter, Della James, Janet Simpson, Valerie Peat), August 24	1 min. 33.8 sec.
Medley relay (220 yd., 110 yd., 110 yd., 440 yd.)	Los Angeles Mercurettes (Barbara Ferrell, Pernetta Glenn, Dee DeBusk, Jarvis Scott), April 13	1 min. 41.9 sec.
2,400-m. relay (3 x 800)	Netherlands national team (Ilja Keizer, Tilly van der Made, Maria Gommers), August 20	6 min. 15.5 sec.
Shot put	Nadyezhda Chizhova, Soviet Union, April 28	61 ft. 3 in.
	Margitta Gummel, East Germany, September 22	61 ft. 11 in.
	Margitta Gummel, East Germany, October 20	64 ft. 4¹⁄₁₆ in.
Discus throw	Christina Spielberg, East Germany, May 26	202 ft. 2½ in.
	Liesel Westermann, West Germany, July 25	205 ft. 2 in.
Long jump	Viorica Viscopoleanu, Romania, October 14	22 ft. 4½ in.
Records tied		
60 m.	Diana Burge, Australia, March 13	7.2 sec.
100 m.	Wyomia Tyus, U.S., April 21	11.1 sec.
	Margaret Bailes, U.S., August 18 (heat)	11.1 sec.
	Margaret Bailes, U.S., August 18	11.1 sec.
	Lyudmila Samotyesova, U.S.S.R., August 15 (heat)	11.1 sec.
	Irina Kirszenstein-Szewinska, Poland, October 14 (heat)	11.1 sec.
80-m. hurdles	Maureen Caird, Australia, October 18	10.3 sec.
400-m. relay	Soviet Union Olympic team (Ludmilla Zharkova, Vyera Popkova, Lyudmila Samotyesova, Galina Bukharina), September 27	43.6 sec.
	Cuba Olympic team (Marien Elejarde, Fulgencia Romay, Violetta Quezada, Miguelina Cobian), October 4 (heat)	43.6 sec.

*Questionable timing.

Table III. World's Indoor Best Performances—Men*

Event	Competitor, country, date	Performance
Records broken		
50 m.	W. Gaines, U.S., February 17	5.4 sec.
200 m.	B. Jacob, West Germany, March 2	21.6 sec.
	D. Hubner, West Germany, March 2	21.6 sec.
220 yd.	J. Green, U.S., January 13	21.7 sec.
300 yd.	W. Hurd, U.S., March 23	29.8 sec.
440 yd. (11-lap track)	L. James, U.S., March 15	47.0 sec.
2 mi.	K. Pearce, Australia, February 3	8 min. 27.2 sec.
3 mi.	T. Smith, U.S., March 1	13 min. 15.2 sec.
60-yd. low hurdles	G. Byers, U.S., March 1	6.5 sec.
Pole vault	R. Seagren, U.S., January 25	17 ft. 4¼ in.
Long jump	R. Beamon, U.S., January 20	27 ft. 1 in.
	R. Beamon, U.S., March 15	27 ft. 2¾ in.
Triple jump	M. Sauer, West Germany, March 2	55 ft. ¼ in.
880-yd. relay	Western Michigan, March 23	1 min. 28.1 sec.
2-mi. relay	Villanova (I. Hamilton, C. Messenger, F. Murphy, D. Patrick), February 17	7 min. 23.8 sec.
Records tied		
50-yd.	W. Turner, U.S., January 6	5.1 sec.
	H. Washington, U.S., March 9	5.1 sec.
	H. Washington, U.S., March 23	5.1 sec.
45-yd. high hurdles	E. McCullouch, U.S., January 13	5.4 sec.
50-yd. high hurdles	W. Davenport, U.S., March 1	5.9 sec.
	M. Butler, U.S., March 9 (heat)	5.9 sec.
	M. Butler, U.S., March 9	5.9 sec.
60-yd. low hurdles	G. Byers, U.S., February 22 (heat)	6.6 sec.
	G. Byers, U.S., February 22	6.6 sec.
	G. Byers, U.S., March 1 (heat)	6.6 sec.
60-yd. high hurdles	E. McCullouch, U.S. (semifinal), February 24	6.8 sec.
300 yd.	G. Crosby, U.S., February 25	29.9 sec.

*The International Amateur Athletic Federation does not officially recognize world indoor records but refers to them as "world best."

Della James, Janet Simpson, and Valerie Peat set a world 800-m. relay record of 1:33.8 in London on August 24. There were other new records of less importance in medley and shuttle hurdles relays, but worthy of note was the 3 × 800 m. women's record of 6:15.5 set by a Netherlands team made up of Ilja Keizer, Tilly van der Made, and Maria Gommers at Frankfurt an der Oder in August.

Field Events. It is probable that no single performance in the history of field events cooled off other competitors in the field as completely as did Bob Beamon's world record 8.90 m. (29 ft. 2⅜ in.) in the long jump at the Olympic Games. Defending champion Lynn Davies of the U.K. was prepared to battle it out in the 27- or 28-ft. bracket with Beamon, Ralph Boston and Igor Ter-Ovanesyan.

Twice during the Olympic competition the world triple jump record was broken, first by Giuseppe Gentile of Italy and, in the finals, by Viktor Saneev from the Soviet Union with a mark of 17.39 m. (57 ft. ⅝ in.). During the year Robert Seagren of the U.S. broke both the indoor pole vault record (17 ft. 4¼ in.) and the outdoor standard (17 ft. 9 in.). The latter might officially be reduced to 17 ft. 8¾ in.

All records in the throwing events except the shot put were broken during the year. Prior to the Olympics, Yanis Lusis of the Soviet Union advanced the javelin throw mark to 301 ft. 9½ in., and Gyula Zsivotzky of Hungary threw the hammer 242 ft. Both won gold medals at the Olympics, but Jay Silvester of the U.S. never threatened in the Olympic discus after having set new records during the year of 218 ft. 4 in. and 224 ft. 5 in. Silvester was fifth, while Al Oerter of the U.S. won his fourth successive gold medal with an Olympic record of 64.78 m. (212 ft. 6⅜ in.). Oerter thus became the only athlete ever to win four straight Olympic gold medals in the same event.

Three times during the season the women's world record for the shot put was broken: first, by Nadyezhda Chizhova of the Soviet Union, at 61 ft. 3 in.; then by Margitta Gummel of East Germany, 61 ft. 11 in. in September, and finally again by Margitta Gummel at 19.61 m. (64 ft. 4 1/16 in.) in winning the gold medal in the Olympics. Christina Spielberg of East Germany set a discus record of 202 ft. 2½ in. in May, but this was broken in July by Liesel Westermann of West Germany with a throw of 205 ft. 2 in. In the Olympics final, Viorica Viscopoleanu of Romania set a world long-jump record for women of 6.82 m. (22 ft. 4½ in.).

Best all-around athletes for 1968 were Bill Toomey, who won the decathlon for the U.S. with an Olympic record of 8,193 points, and West Germany's Ingrid Becker, champion in the women's pentathlon with 5,098 points.

Championship Meets. The Southern California Striders won the national AAU outdoor championships with 127 points. The indoor AAU team title, however, went to the Pacific Coast Club of Long Beach, Calif., with 30 points. The outdoor AAU meet for women was won by the Crown Cities Club of Pasadena, Calif., with 45. The national indoor meet for women was won by Tennessee State with 24 points.

The University of Southern California edged Washington State, 58 points to 57, to win the National Collegiate Athletic Association (NCAA) outdoor championship. Villanova won the NCAA indoor meet with 35⅓ points.   (MA. S.)

See also Sporting Record.

Trade, International

The value of world trade was expanding quite rapidly in 1968 after a period of rather slow growth during 1967. In the first three quarters of 1968 the value of world trade was about 9.5% higher than in the same period of 1967, and preliminary figures suggested that for the year as a whole the growth would be in the region of 10–11%. The slowing down in growth and its subsequent acceleration in 1968 can be seen from the following figures: in the first half of 1966 the increase in the value of trade compared with one year earlier was 11%; in the second half of 1966, 9%; in the first half of 1967, 6%; and in the second half of 1967, 3%. For 1968, however, the growth rate was 7% in the first six months and 13% in the second six months. These statistics largely reflected the pattern of growth in industrial production in the major economies.

The slowing down in the growth of world trade in 1967 was not quite so marked in terms of the volume of goods as it was in terms of value. For the first time since 1962, the average price of goods in world trade fell. This was the result of a 3% fall in the price of primary products and stability in the price of manufactured goods. In 1968 this position was reversed; primary product prices recovered while those of manufactures fell by 1–2%.

The growth pattern of world trade in recent years is shown in Table I. The deceleration in 1967 was more marked in primary producing countries than in industrial countries, although both groups recovered in 1968. One of the most rapidly increasing trade flows continued to be trade between industrial countries, but the expansion of 7% in 1967 did not compare favourably with the annual average of 11% in the previous five years. Trade between the Sino-Soviet countries and the rest of the world expanded more

			Exports to			
			Primary producing countries			
Exports from		Industrial countries	More developed*	Less developed†	Sino-Soviet countries	World
Industrial countries‡	1964	14	17	9	30	14
	1965	11	15	7	2	10
	1966	11	4	9	22	11
	1967§	7	5	2	29	6
Primary producing countries More developed*	1964	12	20	13	15	13
	1965	−1	8	10	23	4
	1966	12	10	19	−3	11
	1967§	5	−3	10	15	6
Less developed†	1964	9	6	18	28	11
	1965	6	9	−1	19	5
	1966	8	3	4	−1	6
	1967§	3	4	1	−4	2
Sino-Soviet countries	1964	13	33	22	7	8
	1965	15	4	13	4	7
	1966	15	15	6	2	6
	1967§	7	0	3	9	7
World	1964	13	17	11	27	12
	1965	9	13	6	9	9
	1966	11	5	8	4	9
	1967§	6	4	2	7	5

Table I. Growth in Value of World Trade
Percentage change from previous year

*Australia, New Zealand, South Africa, and primary producing countries in Europe.
†All other primary producers.
‡Excludes U.S. military exports.
§Figures for 1967 are preliminary estimates.
Source: International Monetary Fund, *Annual Report*.

"We'll join the European market as soon as you've solved your problems!"—Behrendt, "Algemeet Handelsblad," Amsterdam.

rapidly in 1967 than it had in 1966 and more rapidly than world trade in general.

In 1968 exports of industrial countries were expanding somewhat faster than those of the less developed economies. An important factor here was the 20% expansion in Japanese exports in the first half of 1968 compared with one year earlier and 9% increases recorded by the European Economic Community (EEC) and North America.

Primary Producing Countries. The exports of primary producing countries increased little in 1967, and their value was stable in late 1967 and early 1968. After growth rates of 5 and 8% in 1965 and 1966, the increase in 1967 was no more than 3%. This slackening was largely the result of the poor performance of exports from the less developed economies; exports from the more advanced primary producers fared better, increasing to about 7%. Imports into these countries continued to rise in the first half of 1967, as in 1966, and reached a level some 9% above

that of a year earlier. Many countries' imports, however, were sharply cut back in response to falling or stagnant export receipts and in the second half of 1967 were some 3% lower than in the first half.

These divergent trade flows resulted in a sharp deterioration in the combined balance of trade of these countries from mid-1966 to mid-1967. With the cutback in imports the deficit was reduced. About two-thirds of the $4.7 billion deficit shown in Table II actually occurred before mid-1967. In 1968 imports began to increase and, with no export growth, the trade balance deteriorated sharply in the first quarter. In the second quarter exports expanded to a level some 10% above that of mid-1967, and the trade deficit was reduced. In the first half of 1968 the deficit was at about the same annual rate as in 1967. The average price of primary producers' exports, after rising a little in recent years, fell by about 1% in 1967 as import prices rose by a similar amount. There was, thus, a deterioration in their terms of trade, which dropped to a level similar to 1963. With export prices recovering in the early part of 1968, there was some improvement in the terms of trade.

These overall figures concealed the divergent trends in the prices of particular commodities that were important to many countries. Particularly sharp declines were recorded in the 1967 prices of wool, rubber, sisal, and lead. Prices of foodstuffs, in general, rose during 1967 but went into a steady decline in 1968. Agricultural raw material prices, which had fallen by almost 10% in 1967, began a steady recovery early in 1968, led by rubber and cotton prices. Even so, the level of these prices in mid-1968 was little above that of a year earlier. Metal prices, after a 20% rise in 1966, fell by 7% in 1967 and, apart from a short-lived increase in copper prices at the end of 1967, continued to drift downward in 1968.

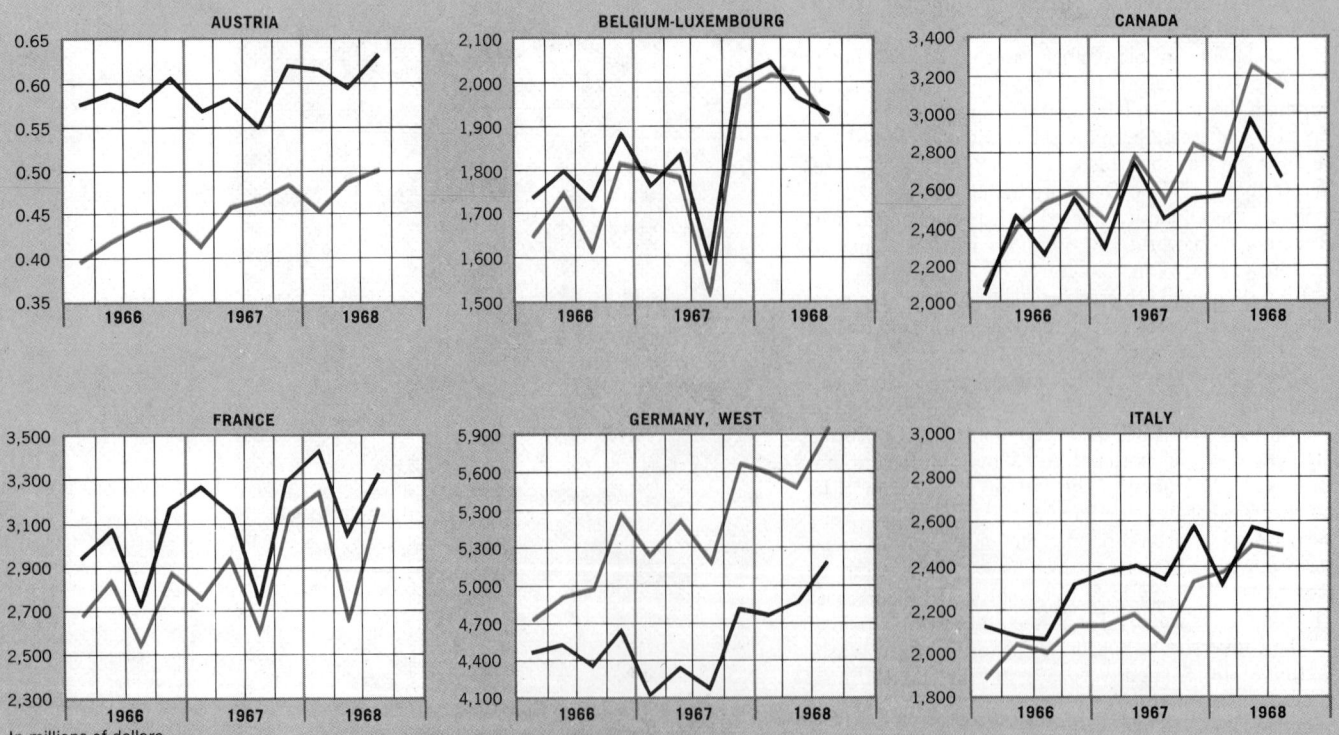

In millions of dollars

The worsening of the trade balance in 1967 was due entirely to the poor performances of the less developed primary producers; the more advanced countries recorded the same deficits as in 1966. As Table II shows, there were important regional variations. Most of the major countries in Latin America recorded poorer trade balances in 1967. Argentina and Uruguay were affected by lower wool prices and toward the end of the year by the U.K.'s ban on meat imports from countries where foot-and-mouth disease was endemic. In addition, Argentine wheat exports fell. Brazil, along with Colombia, was hit by falling coffee prices, and its cotton exports, like those of Mexico, declined sharply in value. By making very sharp cuts in imports, Colombia managed to show a marked improvement in its balance of trade. Both Peru and Chile benefited from the high level of mineral prices, although their trade balances were not so favourable as in 1966. By mid-1968 the trade surplus in Latin America had increased to an annual rate of $1.3 million.

In Asia, an important factor in the overall deficit increase in 1967 was the decline in rubber, tin, and fibre prices. In Indonesia and the Philippines trade surpluses in 1966 were converted into deficits in 1967. There was a marked decline in Pakistan's exports to the EEC, due to the economic slowdown in Europe, and manufactured exports to Africa were not maintained; imports increased by 25%. In Thailand lower prices for major exports and drought, which reduced the rice crop, lowered exports receipts; with imports of capital equipment and consumer goods rising, the trade deficit worsened.

Middle Eastern economies were affected by the Israeli-Arab hostilities in June 1967 and by the closing of the Suez Canal. The overall trade of the region increased by $350 million as imports fell slightly and exports rose 6%. With the exception of Iran, the exports of oil-producing countries rose much less rapidly than in recent years, and in some cases actually declined, largely because of an Arab embargo on oil shipments to certain industrial countries. Oil exports from Iran increased sharply in the second half of 1967 and were up 25% for the year. Exports from Iraq fell by 17% in 1967, the effect of the embargo being accentuated by a pipeline closure early in the year. Exports from Israel, many of which were manufactured and processed goods not affected by primary commodity prices, increased in value by 12%; imports fell and the trade balance improved by $120 million.

Trade of African countries in 1967 was affected by a number of adverse factors—the Nigerian civil war, Rhodesian independence, the closing of the Suez Canal, and poor harvests in many countries in the north. Overall, there was a slight improvement in the trade balance, in some cases at the expense of economic growth. Ghanaian exports recovered from their abnormally low 1966 level and, with a reduction in imports, the balance of trade improved by $75 million. In Libya petroleum exports continued to rise, though not as fast as they had in 1966. In Zambia the rate of economic growth accelerated after the dislocation caused by the Rhodesian declaration of independence. In Nigeria exports, which had expanded considerably in the first half of 1967, were cut back by the civil war; for the year as a whole, both imports and exports were down some $120 million. East African economies suffered from the lower coffee prices.

Industrial Countries. Exports by industrial countries increased by 6% in 1967—their smallest annual increase since 1962 but still larger than that recorded by the less developed economies. This growth was concentrated in the first quarter of the year; exports in the last quarter were less than 1% above the first quarter level. World industrial production, which

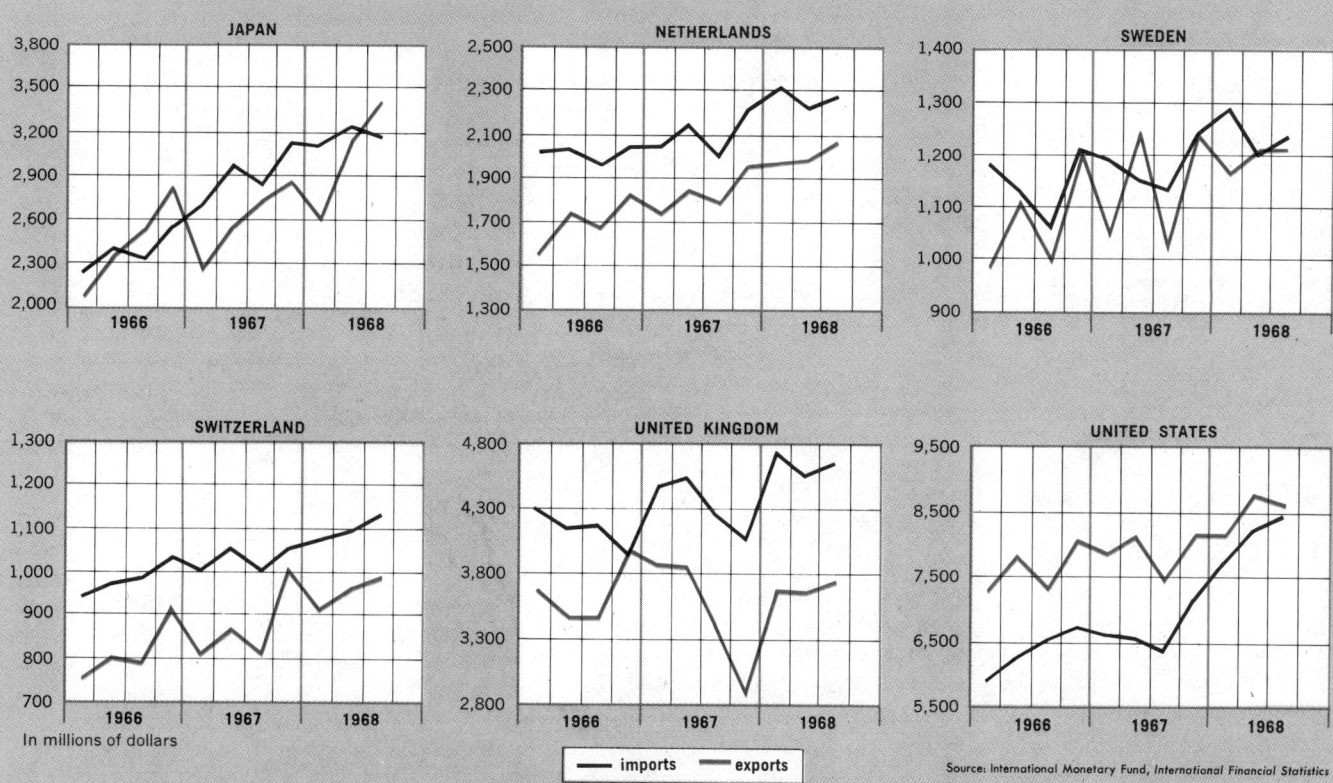

In millions of dollars

— imports — exports

Source: International Monetary Fund, International Financial Statistics

Table II. Primary Producing Countries' Foreign Trade

In $000,000

Area	1966			1967		
	Exports	Imports*	Balance of trade	Exports	Imports*	Balance of trade
More developed countries	13,374	16,918	−3,544	14,110	17,636	−3,526
Less developed countries						
Latin America	11,427	10,005	1,422	11,320	10,439	881
Asia	7,981	10,645	−2,664	8,231	12,104	−3,873
Middle East	5,180	4,363	817	5,468	4,299	1,169
Africa	4,552	3,927	625	4,655	3,973	682
	29,140	28,940	200	29,674	30,815	−1,141
All primary producers	42,514	45,858	−3,344	43,784	48,451	−4,667

*Imports in most cases exclude freight and insurance charges.
Source: IMF, Annual Report.

Table III. World Exports of Manufactured Goods

	Total value in $000,000,000*	United States	United Kingdom	Percent of total value West Germany	France	Italy	Japan	Other†
1955	34.0	24.5	19.8	15.5	9.3	3.4	5.1	22.4
1960	52.4	21.6	16.3	19.3	9.7	5.1	6.9	21.0
1964	73.2	20.4	14.2	19.7	8.9	6.4	8.3	22.2
1965	82.8	20.5	13.5	19.2	8.8	6.8	9.4	21.8
1966	92.4	20.2	12.9	19.5	8.6	6.9	9.8	22.1
1967	99.2	20.5	11.9	19.7	8.5	7.0	9.8	22.6
1968‡	107.8	20.3	11.4	19.1	8.2	7.1	10.6	23.3

*Excluding arms.
†Belgium, Luxembourg, Canada, Netherlands, Sweden, and Switzerland.
‡First half of year (seasonally adjusted) at annual rates.
Source: National Institute of Economic and Social Research, Economic Review.

failed to rise noticeably until late in 1967, continued to increase in 1968. The import demands generated by this growth pushed industrial countries' exports up sharply in 1968, particularly in the third quarter. The level of their exports in the first nine months of 1968 was some 10% above the corresponding period in 1967, accompanied by a 2% reduction in world export prices of manufactured goods. Imports also rose in the first half of 1968, and the combined trade balance worsened a little. The rapid upsurge in exports in the third quarter reduced the deficit somewhat.

Table III shows the share of each of the major industrial countries in total manufactured exports. The major feature here was the steady decline in

recent years in the U.K. share. The U.S. share, which had been declining until the early 1960s, had stabilized. Similarly, the previous steady rise in the West German share had leveled off, and the Japanese share maintained its very steady growth.

The combined trade balance of industrial countries showed no marked change from 1966 to mid-1968. There were, however, important movements within this broad figure. In 1967 the trade balance of European Free Trade Association (EFTA) countries deteriorated by $1.1 billion, due almost entirely to the increased U.K. deficit. The small Japanese surplus of 1966 became a sizable deficit in 1967. The U.S. and Canadian balances remained approximately the same, while the balance of EEC countries improved by $2.5 billion because of the West German improvement. In the first half of 1968 the overall deficit of industrial countries was similar to that in 1967, but in the third quarter there were definite signs of an improvement even though the EFTA figures were again adversely affected by the larger U.K. deficit.

In the second quarter of 1968 the U.S. recorded its smallest surplus on merchandise trade for many years. At an annual rate of $1,360,000,000 by midyear, the surplus was one quarter of the average rate in the previous decade. The 1967 surplus had been very similar to that of 1966, and exports had remained at the same level. Imports, although falling somewhat in the middle of the year as industrial stocks were run down, had accelerated in the fourth quarter and continued to grow rapidly in 1968. Certain special factors, such as the copper strike and an expected steel strike, influenced this, but so did growth in industrial production and a rebuilding of stocks. At the same time, exports were feeling the effects of reduced demand from Europe. By mid-1968 exports were less than 5% higher than a year before, but imports were 22% higher. As trade with Europe increased in the third quarter of 1968, exports moved up and the import rise declined, with a consequent improvement in the trade balance.

Table V. World Exports by Provenance and Destination, 1967

F.o.b. value in U.S. $000,000

Exports from	World*	Economic class I†	Economic class II‡	Economic class III§	United States	Canada	Latin America	Total‖	EEC¶	Western Europe Total	EFTA United Kingdom	Other Northern♀	Southern♂
World*	214,140	147,330	41,680	23,530	26,000	9,670	10,560	95,390	52,780	32,850	15,510	2,620	7,150
Economic class I†	149,350	112,230	30,290	6,270	18,440	8,790	8,170	74,060	40,750	25,890	10,810	2,110	5,310
Economic class II‡	39,960	29,190	8,100	2,240	7,370	780	1,500	16,470	9,900	5,360	3,930	150	1,070
Economic class III§	24,820	5,900	3,300	15,020	180	100	890	4,860	2,140	1,600	770	360	770
United States	31,250	21,210	9,850	195	.	7,070	4,080	10,060	5,610	3,260	1,970	160	1,030
Canada**	10,560	9,550	750	250	6,800	.	315	1,960	640	1,250	1,090	20	53
Latin America	11,700	8,710	2,190	780	3,830	290	1,160	3,980	2,420	1,140	720	60	360
Western Europe‖	90,850	71,460	13,910	5,010	7,890	1,350	3,210	58,050	33,090	19,090	5,990	1,850	4,020
EEC¶	56,130	45,050	8,230	2,530	4,420	550	1,970	38,390	24,510	10,420	2,850	620	2,840
EFTA	28,670	22,120	5,040	1,430	2,850	770	990	16,120	6,950	6,950	2,010	1,190	1,050
United Kingdom	13,860	9,990	3,330	570	1,690	590	460	5,790	2,650	1,890	.	730	520
Other: Northern♀	2,390	1,910	115	350	175	12	52	1,670	440	1,170	890	20	39
Southern♂	3,650	2,390	520	710	440	23	190	1,860	1,190	550	245	22	92
Eastern Europe¶□	22,820	5,230	2,460	14,550	180	79	820	4,510	1,940	1,470	700	350	760
U.S.S.R.	9,650	2,240	1,450	5,530	39	23	580	1,820	720	495	305	255	355
South Africa**	1,910	1,490	345	4	150	31	5	1,050	340	650	600	42	23
Developing Africa††	8,520	6,900	890	560	590	84	29	5,790	3,990	1,490	1,050	31	275
Northern○	3,260	2,640	190	405	69	22	14	2,510	1,990	355	210	11	160
Japan**	10,440	5,340	4,570	530	3,050	275	500	1,440	550	730	295	38	125
Developing Asia													
Western▲	7,530	5,710	1,460	155	285	100	115	3,790	2,240	1,230	960	31	295
Other	10,180	6,170	3,260	740	1,900	160	120	2,250	1,040	1,070	890	22	115
Communist China, etc.+	2,000	670	840	.	4	21	70	350	200	125	72	9	13
Australia,** New Zealand	4,350	3,170	860	285	550	69	61	1,500	520	910	870	8	56
Rest of world⊗	2,030	1,700	295	2	780	150	81	660	210	420	315	6	26

Note: The data cover world trade with the exception of the trade with one another of: Communist China, Mongolia, North Korea, and North Vietnam. For most countries they represent the official export figures, converted to U.S. dollars. Where official figures are not available, estimates, based on imports reported by partner countries and on other subsidiary data, are used. A dash (—) means none or less than $500,000; (.) means not applicable.
*The figures for total exports include certain exports which, because their regions of destination could not be determined, are not included elsewhere in the table.
†United States, Canada, Western Europe, Australia-New Zealand, South Africa, and Japan.
‡Sum of regions other than economic classes I and III.
§U.S.S.R. and other Eastern Europe, Communist China, Mongolia, North Korea, and North Vietnam.
‖Includes Turkey and Yugoslavia.
¶The transactions between West Germany and East Germany have been omitted. Based on data reported by the sender, they were $371 million from West Germany to East Germany and $295 million from East Germany to West Germany.
♀Finland, Iceland, Ireland.

Canadian exports grew faster than imports in 1967–68, and the trade balance improved steadily from the very low levels of 1966. Export growth slackened after the first quarter of 1967 but resumed later with the upswing in the U.S. economy. Lower sales to the U.S.S.R. and China decreased wheat exports, but mineral exports, especially copper and petroleum, rose. The biggest single factor, the sale of motor vehicles to the U.S., accounted for over 60% of the total rise in exports. Exports in 1967 were 11% higher and imports 6% higher than in 1966, and in the first three quarters of 1968, exports were up 18% with imports up 10%.

EEC trade in 1967–68 reflected the level of industrial production in member countries—relatively little growth until the fourth quarter of 1967 and then a forward burst into 1968 disturbed by the French strikes in May. Exports increased by 7% in 1967, while imports rose by only 2.5%. Intra-EEC trade, which had increased by 11.5% in 1966, rose by only 5.5% in 1967, due largely to the West German recession; but the combined trade balance moved into surplus for the first time since 1961, mainly because the German surplus was up $2,150,000,000. A big improvement in the Italian balance helped the trade surplus increase further in 1968.

Exports by EFTA countries increased by only 2.5% in 1967, the lowest increase since 1958. This deceleration from a 7% growth in 1966 reflected the 2% fall in the dollar value of U.K. exports caused by devaluation. Imports increased by over 5%, and the trade balance worsened by over $1 billion to $6.6 billion. The $1.3 billion deterioration in the U.K. deficit offset improvements in other EFTA countries. The Austrian trade balance showed major improvement; imports fell slightly while exports increased by 7%. Half of the exports increase was in sales to other EFTA countries; sales to the EEC fell. Switzerland reduced its trade deficit in 1967 for the third successive year and, although exports to the U.K. rose by 23%, the growth rates of imports and exports both slack-ened. In the first quarter of 1968 the deficit widened. Sweden also recorded an improved trade balance; as in many countries, a slowdown of imports was achieved by damping the domestic economy.

Imports into EFTA countries in 1968 continued to grow faster than exports, and there was a further deterioration in the trade balance. This was due to a large extent to the failure of U.K. trade, especially imports, to respond quickly and significantly to the devaluation of the pound in November 1967. In the first three quarters of 1968 the combined deficit of the EFTA countries was at an annual rate of $6.8 billion, about $200 million worse than in 1967.

Imports into the U.K. in 1967 rose by 8%, more than double the average rate of increase in the previous decade. Exports were 0.5% lower than in 1966 and, in the second half of the year—partly because of dock strikes—were some 10% below the first half. Exports to the U.S. fell by 2%. About 75% of the increase in imports was in manufactured goods, which rose by 20%.

Devaluation increased the average price of imports but seemed to have relatively little effect on their

Table IV. Trade of Industrial Countries

Country	1967 Exports	1967 Imports†	1967 Balance of trade	1968* Exports	1968* Imports†	1968* Balance of trade
United States	31.16	26.72	4.44	32.60	32.14	1.36
Canada	10.56	10.08	0.48	12.48	11.22	1.26
EEC	56.16	54.96	1.20	60.16	57.82	2.34
EFTA	29.12	35.72	−6.60	30.36	36.98	−6.62
Germany, West	21.72	17.36	4.36	22.94	18.98	3.96
France	11.40	12.40	−1.00	11.60	12.48	−0.88
Italy	8.72	9.68	−0.96	9.82	9.54	0.28
Netherlands	7.28	8.32	−1.04	8.00	8.90	−0.90
United Kingdom	12.06	15.35	−3.29	14.46	18.87	−4.41
Japan	10.44	11.68	−1.24	12.26	12.38	−0.12
Total	137.44	139.16	−1.72	147.86	149.64	−7.78

*First half of year (seasonally adjusted) at annual rate.
†Imports are valued c.i.f. except for U.S. and Canada; insurance and freight costs on U.S. and Canadian imports are approximately 7% of value of the goods.
Source: National Institute of Economic and Social Research, *Economic Review.*

Eastern Europe□ Total¶	U.S.S.R.	South Africa	Developing Africa Total	Northern°	Japan	Developing Asia Western▲	Other	Communist China+	Australia, New Zealand	Rest of world®	Exports from
21,140	8,300	2,490	8,330	2,820	9,680	5,050	14,600	2,390	4,100	3,160	World*
5,040	1,870	2,170	6,290	1,930	5,280	3,690	10,170	1,230	3,480	1,970	Economic class I†
1,880	1,020	315	1,200	270	3,680	950	3,270	360	570	1,180	Economic class II‡
14,220	5,410	—	840	620	720	410	1,160	810	46	2	Economic class III§
195	60	425	730	290	2,670	880	3,530	—	980	630	United States
170	120	74	35	8	530	24	260	85	185	115	Canada**
670	385	22	50	23	590	57	92	110	11	830	Latin America
4,370	1,500	1,470	4,500	1,580	1,060	2,360	2,940	640	1,650	900	Western Europe‖
2,100	590	610	2,970	1,250	580	1,340	1,510	425	495	445	EEC¶
1,230	350	840	1,360	205	410	900	1,350	200	1,120	435	EFTA
460	175	720	880	125	225	630	1,000	105	970	335	United Kingdom
335	280	11	22	11	13	20	18	12	21	5	Other: Northern¶
700	290	8	145	115	52	100	64	3	11	15	Southernδ
13,740	5,110	—	720	560	445	370	550	810	19	1	Eastern Europe¶
5,040	.	—	395	340	355	170	300	495	2	—	U.S.S.R.
4	—	.	310	—	240	3	27	—	19	2	South Africa**
490	225	135	520	77	285	135	170	72	29	32	Developing Africa††
360	170	7	81	36	26	33	42	41	1	20	Northern°
230	160	155	680	43		335	2,930	295	425	130	Japan**
											Developing Asia
130	51	104	270	84	1,230	510	500	27	195	67	Western▲
590	365	54	330	80	1,520	245	2,470	155	290	100	Other
.	.	—	120	60	270	42	610	.	27	1	Communist China, etc.+
75	26	49	42	9	780	87	475	210	225	200	Australia,** New Zealand
2	1	5	25	8	60	5	36	—	50	150	Rest of world®

δGreece, Spain, Turkey, Yugoslavia.
□Albania, Bulgaria, Czechoslovakia, East Germany, Hungary, Poland, Romania, and the U.S.S.R.
°Algeria, Libya, Morocco, Tunisia, U.A.R.
▲Middle East countries in Asia including Cyprus and Iran.
+Estimates based partly on import data of trading partners. Where exports to Taiwan could not be distinguished from exports to Communist China they are shown as exports to Communist China. Exports of and to Mongolia, North Korea, and North Vietnam are included under this heading. The intertrade of these countries and their trade with Communist China are excluded.
®Mainly the islands of the Caribbean and Pacific areas.
**General trade.
††Including trade between countries of former British East Africa: Kenya, Tanzania, and Uganda; and between member states of former Federation of Rhodesia and Nyasaland; Malawi, Rhodesia, and Zambia.
Source: United Nations, *Monthly Bulletin of Statistics.*

(B.N.D.)

volume, which was 9% higher in the first three quarters of 1968 than in the same period of 1967. The value of imports increased by 24%. Imports of industrial materials rose by 20%, and imports of manufactured goods, the area most responsible for the deficit troubles, increased by 33%. Devaluation improved the competitive position of British goods and, coupled with an expansion in world trade, helped to increase exports by 17% in the first three quarters of 1968. Sales to the U.S. increased by 40% and to the EEC by 22%. There were signs that the deficit would be reduced to manageable proportions in 1969.

Sino-Soviet Area. The 7% growth in exports by Sino-Soviet countries to the rest of the world in 1967, a rate very similar to that of the preceding few years, was due entirely to exports from Eastern Europe and the U.S.S.R. to EEC countries (up 10%) and to Japan (up over 50%). Chinese exports fell by 10% and, because of this sharp reduction, exports from the Sino-Soviet countries to primary producing countries showed only a small increase.

Sino-Soviet imports increased by 7% in 1967, a faster growth than in 1966. The major expansion occurred in purchases from the more developed primary producers. Imports from industrial countries expanded by only 7%, in line with the world total but much less than the 1966 increase. As in the case of exports, the major part of this growth was accounted for by the Soviet countries in Europe; Chinese imports increased by little more than 5%. (A. G. A.)

See also Commercial Policies; Commodities, Primary; Payments and Reserves, International.

ENCYCLOPÆDIA BRITANNICA FILMS. *World Trade for Better Living* (1951); *Round Trip: The U.S.A. in World Trade* (1952); *Food and People* (1956); *Britain: World Trader* (1964).

Transportation

Although no revolutionary breakthroughs were recorded in 1968, steady advances in both the technological and the operational fields heralded considerable changes in the transport scene by the 1970s. The Soviet Tu-144 supersonic transport (SST) made a successful trial flight at the end of the year. Progress, though slower than planned, was made on the prototypes of the Concorde, for which trial flights were scheduled for early 1969—as they were also for the jumbo jets. The first commercial service using the large SR-N4 Hovercraft began operating across the English Channel and, despite some technical difficulties, additional services were planned for 1969.

The most significant operational progress continued to be in the rapid and successful expansion of containerization. Ports the world over were constructing facilities to cope with the new methods of mechanical handling required for movement by container and in bulk. At the same time the trend toward larger vessels continued, and the world's first tanker of more than 300,000 tons deadweight was unloaded in Bantry Bay, Ire., in October 1968.

These operational changes, involving the use of several transport modes, were leading governments and operators to formulate policies for the greater integration and more effective coordination of transport. Thus in the U.K. the Transport Bill enacted in 1968 provided for centralization of the freightliner container services of British Railways and of the nationalized road haulage and roll-on/roll-off services

under a single authority. On the international level action was taken to facilitate movement across national frontiers, and the UN held a world conference in Vienna in the fall to update the road traffic conventions first signed in Geneva in 1949.

The railways too were modernizing their facilities and adjusting their services in order to meet these new demands and to compete more effectively with air and road transport. Many new, fast, scheduled container trains were introduced by railway authorities in the U.S. and Europe. Roll-on/roll-off services were greatly extended on the short-sea routes between the U.K. and the continent, raising doubts as to the necessity for a Channel tunnel. The construction of such a tunnel, although accepted in principle by the British and French governments, was again put back in October pending final financial arrangements. Otherwise, the railways' main efforts were directed toward raising speeds through the maximum exploitation of electronics and automation. Running speeds exceeding 100 mph were common, and research on new forms of traction to operate at far higher speeds was intensified. Introduction of gas-turbine trains in the U.S. was again delayed, but a gas-turbine train began regularly scheduled runs between Toronto and Montreal. British Railways, with government support, was researching even more advanced trains, both gas-turbine driven and employing the Hovercraft principle.

Despite these technological improvements, road transport continued to increase its proportion of total carryings of both passengers and freight, and the growth in the number of motor vehicles in use continued unabated. Nor did road transport neglect development of improved vehicle power units. Considerable attention was given to development of small electric cars for city use, and even the steam car was again being investigated. (E. A. J. D.)

AVIATION

The year 1968 might well go down as one in which the transport aircraft design technicians found that they had taken on more than they could immediately handle. The very advanced U.S. variable-geometry (swing-wing) supersonic transport to be built by Boeing ran into serious design difficulties, and even the more conventional fixed-delta-wing Anglo-French Concorde (British Aircraft Corp. and Sud-Aviation) was much more than six months late in its forecast first-flight date.

Plans to build the Boeing SST prototype were deferred because, with the immense structural-weight penalty involved in the use of variable geometry and in the associated mounting of the engines in the tail plane (which was to be an integral part of the lifting surface when the main planes were swept back to form a delta wing), it was not a usefully economic proposition from which a production design could be developed. The entire program was delayed by 12–15 months so that Boeing and the Federal Aviation Administration (FAA) could reconsider the project.

Late in 1968 it seemed probable that a more conventional fixed-wing Boeing SST would be designed and built. One of the disappointments for the design team stemmed from the fact that, because the pivots for the wing had to be outside the fuselage (to allow for undercarriage mounting and retraction, and for other reasons), the high-lift advantages at low speeds were considerably reduced. At the year's end it seemed likely that the U.S. SST would go ahead—but on a more conventional fixed-wing basis and with a smaller

Concorde supersonic transport, developed jointly by British Aircraft Corp. and Sud-Aviation of France, undergoing brake tests in August 1968 in Toulouse, France.

(250-seat) passenger capacity than had been envisaged earlier. The swing-wing design remained as a possible prospect for a second-generation SST development.

More than a year had passed since the British-French-West German "memorandum of understanding" had been signed in Bonn in September 1967, but a firm start on the A-300 European Airbus program continued to be delayed. The two U.S. medium-haul tri-jet airbus projects, the Douglas DC-10 and the Lockheed L-1011, were given a go-ahead early in 1968. A decision to buy 25 DC-10s (with an option on another 25) was announced by American Airlines in February, although the power-plant type, whether Rolls-Royce RB.211 or General Electric CF6/36, had not yet been selected. Less than two months later, on March 29, Lockheed announced a go-ahead for the 1011 and, more important—at least for the British aircraft industry's future—the selection of the Rolls-Royce advanced technology engines. The initial orders from Eastern Airlines (for 50 aircraft), Trans World Airlines (44), and Air Holdings Ltd. of London (30 plus an option on 20) represented a sales value for Rolls-Royce of about £150 million, with the possibility of eventual sales of up to £2,000 million. A week later two more U.S. carriers, Delta Air Lines and Northeast Airlines, placed orders for 24 and 4 aircraft, respectively. It seemed to be a landslide to Lockheed, but within a month United Air Lines ordered 30 DC-10s to add to the 25 for American Airlines, and the decision to use General Electric engines was announced. The result was a satisfactorily competitive situation, with two aircraft manufacturers and two engine manufacturers—one British and one U.S.—involved.

A portent of a longer-term nature was the first flight in June of the military Lockheed C-5A Galaxy. As the L-500 civil freighter, it could knock the bottom out of cargo rates in the mid-1970s.

The situation regarding the A-300 European Airbus project was discussed on August 2 by ministers of the three countries involved, and the manufacturers were given four months in which to improve the economics of the proposed aircraft, reduce estimated costs, and complete preliminary designs. A revised version, with 250 seats instead of 300, was announced in December. A decision to go ahead still depended, officially, on a minimum initial order for 75 aircraft from the three national airlines, Air France, British European Airways (BEA), and Lufthansa, but the last two showed little inclination to place more than token orders.

BEA, whose request for permission to order the British Aircraft Corp.'s projected 185-seat Two-Eleven was rejected on the ground of cost at the end of 1967, continued to insist that an intermediate-sized aircraft would be needed before an aircraft of the capacity of the Airbus could be put into service. Meanwhile, with a form of compensation for lost lead time

since their original request in 1966 for permission to buy Boeing 727s and 737s, the airline had ordered Hawker Siddeley Trident 3s in July.

During the first part of the year there were signs of a general slowdown in airline traffic growth, at least in some areas. Because of the British economic situation and the reduction in the personal travel allowance, a slowdown in Europe, and particularly on services to and from the U.K., could be expected. In May, for instance, BEA, the biggest intra-European airline, recorded an increase in passenger-miles on international services of only about 1% over May 1967. European airlines as a whole, represented by the members of the European Airlines Research Bureau, showed no increase in passenger-miles in that month in comparison with a year earlier, and a growth of only 6% in the 12 months through June 1968 compared with the corresponding period of 1966-67. Cargo continued to show a healthy growth, however, with a 20% increase in May in comparison with May 1967.

More significant, perhaps, was the slowdown on the North Atlantic route, generally considered to be a barometer of airline traffic health. During the first six months of the year passengers increased only about 4% over the first half of 1967, and load factors were down badly. Cargo rose 23% overall.

Preliminary financial figures for the world's airlines in 1967 also showed a decline in the growth of operating profits, which increased on an average, worldwide, by only 3% (15% for 1966). In the U.S. traffic reached record highs and revenues were up nearly 20%, but expenditures rose by 16%. The reason for the profit lag was the inability of the airlines to reduce operating costs per unit of traffic. The outlook for fare reductions was not bright, and even the introduction of the really big jets—the Boeing 747s—at the end of 1969 was not likely to change the situation in the short term. Only after several years of operation would the introductory costs have been reduced and traffic have been built up to the point where the prospectively low seat-mile costs could be reflected in lower fares.

By comparison with 1967, statistically the "safest" year ever for the world's scheduled airlines, 1968 did not have a particularly good safety record. In the first eight months more than 600 passengers were killed on scheduled flights. Assuming, with normal traffic growth, that a total of about 125,000,000,000 passenger-miles had been flown by all the airlines (excluding the U.S.S.R. and China) during that period, the fatality rate was 0.5 per 100 million passenger-miles for the eight months. The 1967 figure was 0.4, representing 674 fatalities in about 171,000,000,000 passenger-miles.

There were 29 fatal accidents in 1967 but, unlike

World Transportation

Country	Railways Route length in 000 km.	Railways Traffic Passenger in 000,000 pass.-km.	Railways Traffic Freight in 000,000 net ton-km.	Motor transport Road length in 000 km.	Motor transport Vehicles in use Passenger in 000	Motor transport Vehicles in use Commercial in 000	Merchant shipping Ships of 100 tons and over Number of vessels	Merchant shipping Gross reg. tons in 000	Air traffic Total km. flown in 000	Air traffic Passenger in 000 pass.-km.	Air traffic Freight in 000 net ton-km.
EUROPE											
Austria	5.9*	6,319*	8,326*	93.0	966.6	103.6			8,235	301,426	3,539
Belgium	4.4*	7,783*	6,287*	91.7	1,667.1	262.1	218	940	32,255	1,953,857	98,308
Bulgaria	4.1	5,119	11,449	28.9†	9.3†	20.4†	97	471	...	273,141†	3,724†
Czechoslovakia	13.3	19,653	57,652	133.0†	156.0†	151.5	8	78	19,195	751,949	15,283
Denmark	3.8	3,163*	1,426*	61.3†	878.8	250.2	1,072	3,014	18,812‡	1,058,105‡	40,845‡
Finland	6.0*	2,131*	5,611*	70.1	551.4	97.1	415	1,064	14,502	455,086	7,480
France	37.7	38,400	64,000	784.0	10,565.0	1,756.0	1,538	5,576	141,432	8,986,688	273,146
Germany, East (excluding Berlin)	15.7	17,386	45,743	160.0	721.0	172.6	347	756	...	...	...
Germany, West (excluding Berlin)	34.7	35,536	55,787	412.0	11,292.9§	991.3§	2,679	5,990	84,712	4,619,750	216,474
Greece	2.6†	1,151	552	34.0	122.5	72.4	1,600	7,433	16,277	864,727	17,099
Hungary	8.8	13,743	17,618	113.8	144.6	42.0†	...	...	...	2,355†	1,311†
Ireland	2.3†	547	391	53.0	314.4	45.6	79	143	18,216	1,072,965	30,497
Italy	20.9	29,874	16,022	282.0	7,311.4	693.1	1,445	6,219	86,316	4,679,831	141,883
Netherlands	3.2	7,603	3,272	71.9	1,803.0	285.8	1,739	5,123	68,533	3,901,546	241,643
Norway	4.3*	1,748*	2,123*	68.3	569.2	134.2	2,847	18,382	27,376‡	1,197,066‡	38,022‡
Poland	26.7	34,877	85,014	272.7	331.9	212.7	421	1,211	9,860	309,048	4,445
Portugal	3.6	3,124	677	31.3	316.0	92.5	335	755	20,519	932,343	13,679
Romania	11.0	14,652	34,541	76.6	250.0†	34.0	52	245	6,865	193,319	5,171
Spain	17.3	12,523*	7,882*	131.8	1,052.5	444.0	1,969	2,571	51,783	2,698,519	44,241
Sweden	13.1	5,133*	14,081*	169.8	1,966.6	137.8	1,092	4,635	34,541‡	156,099‡	60,042‡
Switzerland	2.9*	7,718*	5,354*	57.9	1,081.4	111.8	33	199	49,340	2,688,109	83,727
U.S.S.R.	132.5	219,400	2,016,031	1,363.5†	1,100.0†	4,500.0†	2,238	10,617	...	...	...
United Kingdom	22.1‖	29,697‖	23,858‖	345.7	9,447.0	1,434.0	4,156	21,716	250,526	13,938,958	457,296
Yugoslavia	11.6	12,196	16,554	78.9	253.3	77.5	351	1,196	10,064	299,330	3,093
ASIA											
Burma	4.3	2,496	894	25.0†	25.2†	24.8†	30†	39†	3,320	63,445	1,183
Cambodia	0.4	108	39	8.3	18.9	10.1	...	...	1,406	45,672	1,021
Ceylon	1.5	2,473	321	37.3	83.7	28.5	...	...	2,562	100,405	2,032
China, Communist	32.0	45,670†	265,260†	550.0	40.0†	250.0†	247	772	...	63,882†	1,967†
India	57.6	96,756	98,891	928.2	477.2	264.8	369	1,887	49,782	2,162,172	77,077
Indonesia	6.8	6,262†	951†	81.0†	162.0	110.0	458	624	12,170	509,556	10,760
Iran	3.5	1,142	2,232	34.5†	142.0	49.4	29	73	7,293	306,934	2,847
Iraq	1.6†	431†	818†	17.5	74.7	44.6	...	...	2,993	72,140	1,012
Israel	0.7	368	318	8.3	97.4	47.9	109	688	17,147	1,452,812	37,181
Japan	27.9†	258,381	55,112	996.8	3,836.4	6,531.8	6,409	16,883	100,230	5,371,006	157,628
Korea, South	3.1	8,665	5,518	34.7	17.5	31.6	196	306	2,400	56,850	185
Malaysia	1.8	610¶	983¶	19.8	192.8	54.0	110	64	5,846◊	190,479◊	2,024◊
Pakistan	11.3†	12,540	9,155	110.0	125.2	41.0	155	473	18,471	1,093,803	41,408
Philippines	1.0	983	143	56.2	174.4	134.7	248	720	31,610	973,530	16,770
Syria	0.8	68	85	15.0	26.5	13.3	...	...	5,800	198,105	350
Thailand	3.8	3,305	1,655	15.0	68.9	79.6	...	...	9,028	314,536	3,528
Turkey	8.0	4,189	5,485	69.1	106.5	90.9	285	611	9,475	271,855	2,603
Vietnam, South	1.5†	4	14	20.3	42.3	44.9	...	...	6,781	242,816	2,723
AFRICA											
Algeria	3.8†	681†	2,130†	35.5†	210.0†	95.5†	...	...	5,980	247,550	2,720
Central African Republic	—	—	—	19.0	6.3	2.6	...	...	1,169δ	53,033δ	3,001δ
Chad	...	...	...	11.8†	3.3†	4.8†	...	...	1,345δ	56,253δ	3,122δ
Congo (Brazzaville)	0.8	117	351	10.8†	9.0†	6.8†	...	...	2,059δ	66,578δ	3,181δ
Dahomey	0.6	70	56	6.5	7.8	5.1	...	...	1,169δ	53,033δ	3,001δ
Gabon	0.6	...	...	5.1†	3.2†	5.8†	...	...	2,509δ	70,138δ	3,161δ
Ghana	1.0	417	310	33.0	30.3	18.6	58	132	3,866	137,434	5,070
Ivory Coast	0.6	517	311	36.2	38.6	24.4	...	...	1,502δ	56,034δ	3,078δ
Kenya	2.1	4,004†□	3,936†□	41.9†	75.0	14.1	...	...	4,733◊	133,170◊	3,629◊
Malawi	0.5	49†	135	10.6	8.4	5.9	...	...	628▲	16,024▲	199▲
Mali	0.6	56†	125†	12.0	5.4	5.5	...	...	2,429	50,651	2,768
Morocco	1.8†	449	2,216	24.2	168.6	61.3	35	65	5,270	238,410	4,451
Nigeria	3.0†	380	1,593	80.0	64.3	25.9	35	63	6,180	201,630	6,215
Rhodesia	3.3	...	8,671*	73.3	109.4	32.5	...	...	2,834▲	72,112▲	891▲
Senegal	1.2	268	206	13.0†	29.8	18.8	...	...	1,359δ	58,543δ	3,011δ
South Africa	22.1⊖	...	43,479⊖	350.0	1,316.0	342.0	230	470	27,273	1,654,308	45,259
Tanzania	3.0	4,004†□	3,936†□	50.0	38.0	12.5	...	...	4,733◊	133,170◊	3,629◊
Uganda	0.9	4,004†□	3,936†□	24.0	25.3	11.2	...	...	4,733◊	133,172◊	3,631◊
United Arab Republic	4.2*†	6,170*	3,387*	47.7†	105.3	27.5	121	236	17,011	658,336	7,419
Zambia	1.0	...	8,671*	34.1†	42.1	14.9	...	...	2,834▲	72,112▲	891▲
NORTH AND CENTRAL AMERICA											
Canada	69.2	4,164	138,840	557.9	5,499.5	1,427.8	1,236	2,306	151,081	8,976,251	197,563
Costa Rica	0.7	67	28	10.0	27.2	14.3	44†	92†	2,879	95,128	7,417
El Salvador	0.7	...	...	8.4	27.6	12.9	...	...	...	...	...
Guatemala	1.2	...	133	11.2†	33.3	18.3	...	...	4,000	73,300	3,570
Honduras	1.2†	...	...	3.3†	11.8	8.7	45	75	3,858	79,187	6,877
Mexico	23.7†	4,062	18,407	180.0	850.0	460.0	99	330	43,000	1,961,040	36,800
Nicaragua	0.4†	51†	13†	6.1	13.0†	5.0†	...	...	1,560	45,050	875
Panama	0.7	...	...	6.6	32.5	10.7	757	4,756	...	...	...
United States	340.4	27,620	1,090,162	5,951.2	80,458.3	16,193.6	3,303	20,333	2,385,766	158,912,939	5,072,925
SOUTH AMERICA											
Argentina	41.8	14,089	13,459	135.2†	925.3†	542.1†	315	1,240	33,964	1,140,790	15,804
Bolivia	3.6	236†	300†	28.0	17.2	6.2	...	...	3,619	59,795	1,343
Brazil	32.0	13,724	19,253	803.1†	1,337.0	1,059.9	394	1,305	95,235	3,124,170	97,765
Chile	8.4†	2,096	2,758	60.0	108.2	96.9	134	279	15,699	529,285	26,479
Colombia	3.4†	419	1,114	41.4†	135.3	115.8	42	196	44,061	1,491,232	53,576
Ecuador	1.3†	53	72	16.7†	19.4	21.9	...	...	7,309	160,685	2,822
Paraguay	1.1†	39†	20†	12.5†	5.4†	5.9†	...	...	...	...	...
Peru	3.3	236	646	42.8†	178.2	107.8	231	251	15,552	541,926	12,644
Uruguay	3.1	...	...	41.6†	114.0†	82.0†	40	126	3,120	93,990	625
Venezuela	0.5*†	45	26	31.1†	384.9†	165.9†	88	350	25,777	740,175	35,049
OCEANIA											
Australia	40.3*	3,504*,**	18,850*	896.9	3,193.5	893.3	307	803	139,678	5,613,597	181,642
New Zealand	5.2*	553*	2,394*	92.9	801.1	162.7	137	217	30,005	1,105,020	22,935

Note: Data are for 1966 or 1967 unless otherwise indicated.

...Indicates not known.

*State system only.

†Data given are the most recent available.

‡Including apportionment of traffic of Scandinavian Airlines System.

§Including West Berlin.

‖Excluding Northern Ireland.

¶Including Singapore.

◊Apportionment of traffic of Malaysia-Singapore Airlines.

δIncludes apportionment of traffic of Air Afrique.

□Total for Kenya, Tanzania, and Uganda (East African Railways Corporation).

◊Includes apportionment of traffic of East African Airways Corp. and Caspair Ltd.

▲Apportionment of traffic of Central African Airways.

+Total for Rhodesia and Zambia.

⊖Including South West Africa.

**Excluding New South Wales and Queensland.

Sources: UN, *Statistical Yearbook 1967*; *Monthly Bulletin of Statistics*; *Annual Bulletin of Transport Statistics for Europe* (1966); Lloyd's Register, *Statistical Tables* (1967); International Road Federation, *World Road Statistics 1967*.

(M. C. MacD.)

the previous year, none in which more than 100 passengers were killed. With 250-passenger aircraft due to enter service on the world's long-haul air routes by the end of 1969, the safety situation, in terms of fatalities per accident, did not look promising. Undoubtedly the statistical fatality rate would continue to improve, but unless there were big improvements in the levels of operating safety, accidents involving disturbingly heavy death tolls seemed inevitable. Since 1959 the total loss rate (not necessarily involving passenger fatalities) for the jets had been averaging about 1% per annum; in other words, with 2,500 jets in airline service, an average of 25 could be written off every year in passenger-carrying, training, or other accidents. It was unlikely that this average would be improved upon by the new big jets— at least during the first year or two of service.

In relation to the enormous productivity of its air transport, the U.S. safety record continued to be well above the world average. In 1967 the supplemental (nonscheduled) carriers recorded no accidents on passenger-carrying services, despite a 162% increase in passenger-miles flown. The scheduled airlines, domestic and international, suffered eight fatal accidents involving 226 passenger fatalities. With 103,-381,000 passenger-miles flown, this represented about 0.22 fatalities per 100 million passenger-miles.

The big jets offered one hopeful feature. With their spacious cabins, many doors, and generally improved "crashworthiness," the prospects of survival for passengers in noncatastrophic accidents should be much higher than in the earlier generations of transport aircraft. The new safety rules introduced by the FAA in 1967 should also improve the situation. These rules included the demonstration of passenger evacuation in 90 seconds with only half the exits in use; larger and differently located exits; self-extinguishing fabrics; and many other important features designed primarily to improve the chances of survival in crash fires and to reduce the rate of fire propagation.

The long-forecast effects of the saturation of U.S. airspace and airport capacity and the overloading of the air traffic control system were seen early in July. Landing delays of up to 2½ hours, with multiple diversions, were experienced in the congested New York area, and there were lesser delays at Chicago and Washington, D.C. A fourth major airport for New York had been under consideration for a number of years, though no suitable site had been agreed upon, but the real problem there and elsewhere was the inevitable peaking of traffic at periods when passengers wished to travel and competitive scheduling by different airlines operating over similar routes.

In its search for a cure, the U.S. Civil Aeronautics Board (CAB) was prepared at one stage to permit consultation between the airlines for the revision of schedules in order to ease congestion, a procedure that would cut across the competitive system and would probably be contrary to the antitrust laws. Another solution would be the imposition of flow control —in other words, the regulation of departures according to the available capacity of the air traffic control system.

In an effort to avoid the congestion troubles being experienced in the U.S., efforts had been made in Britain to hasten development of a third airport for London. After many years of delay and contention, the choice of Stansted, an already existing airport some 34 mi. N of London, seemed to be firm at the end of 1967. In February 1968, however, the British

government, in the face of strong anti-Stansted pressures, reversed its decision and decided on a new, wide-ranging inquiry. A commission to examine the whole situation in detail was set up in May.

Meanwhile, the Edwards Committee, set up in 1967 to examine British air transport—and, in particular, airline licensing—policy, continued through 1968 to look at both foreign and British methods of organizing the industry. It seemed unlikely that its recommendations would become available before the spring of 1969. The knowledge that big changes might be proposed and agreed to by the government inevitably led the authorities concerned to defer important policy decisions and the private airlines to avoid making expensive long-term plans. The closing down of British Eagle in November, precipitated by the withdrawal of financial support by backers who had lost confidence in the face of continuing setbacks and losses, could be considered as symptomatic of the uneasy environment in which the British private airlines had been operating during an economically difficult year.

In the U.S. the charter airlines, or "supplementals," also suffered a period of uncertainty when the U.S. Supreme Court ruled that the CAB had no power to approve international inclusive-tour charters—the all-in-one-price package flights. It was feared at the time that, if the U.S. supplementals were denied these tours, the CAB or the U.S. government might, in self-defense, be forced to ban similar flights by foreign carriers. However, the U.S. Congress approved a bill, amending the Federal Aviation Act of 1958, that gave the necessary authority to the CAB. The board was also empowered to approve such flights by the scheduled airlines, though they and the supplementals were specifically precluded from selling tours directly to the public. (*See* INDUSTRIAL REVIEW: *Aerospace.*)

(H. A. TA.)

COMMERCIAL MOTOR TRANSPORTATION

Progress was made toward the coordination of road traffic rules on an international basis, as the world conference called by the UN met in Vienna in October 1968 to complete and approve the revised Draft Conventions on Road Traffic and Road Signs and Signals. The new conventions, which would replace those signed at Geneva in 1949, covered the whole field of road traffic rules, the regulation of traffic, standardization of traffic signs and markings, and the regulation and conditions of operation of international road traffic.

Considerable progress was also made toward establishing a common transport policy for the EEC, as provided for in the Treaty of Rome. Following a meeting of the Council of Transport Ministers of the

A British-made Aston Martin valued at $14,400 smashing into concrete block during test of new U.S. automobile safety regulations. Results of the test were successful; the passenger compartment remained intact and the steering column moved less than an inch.

LONDON "DAILY EXPRESS" FROM PICTORIAL PARADE

six countries in December 1967, further steps were taken to formulate a system of competition for transport, for introduction in 1968, that would be appropriate to the special structure of transport markets while at the same time forming part of the Community's general competition policy. Accordingly, in July 1968 the Council of Ministers adopted European Commission proposals that (1) laid down conditions of competition for road, rail, and inland waterways; (2) introduced Community quotas for licenses for intra-Community road-freight traffic; (3) determined allowances for duty-free fuel in vehicle tanks; (4) harmonized working conditions for truck and bus drivers; and (5) fixed rate brackets for intra-Community road transport.

Under the quota system, until Dec. 31, 1971, 1,200 Community licenses would be issued, permitting the holders to operate freight traffic between all the member countries. Of the 1,200 licenses, 161 would go to Belgium; 286 to France; 286 to West Germany; 194 to Italy; 33 to Luxembourg; and 240 to the Netherlands. The range allowed between minimum and maximum rates was 23%, and rates had to be published. Decisions were postponed on the harmonization of member states' subsidies to rail, road, and inland waterways and on the double taxation of vehicles engaged in intra-Community trade. Also pending were decisions regarding the termination of discrimination and the harmonization of taxation. The European Conference of Ministers of Transport (ECMT) continued its task of drawing up a European Highway Code, to become obligatory in all member countries.

Meanwhile, further steps for the liberalization of international road transport were taken at the national level. In several countries policies were introduced to facilitate coordination, integration, and regulation of the different forms of transport. West Germany proposed to introduce a transport policy program for 1968–72, directed at the regulation of road, rail, and inland waterways. It included interim measures to limit heavy long-distance road hauls, simultaneously with the development of combined road/rail transport, so as to divert long-distance road traffic to the railways. It also involved heavy taxation of road haulage and an embargo on long-distance transport by road. The scheme was abandoned in the face of

strong opposition, including that of the European Commission which considered it incompatible with the transport policies of the EEC member states and with the Rome Treaty.

In the U.K. the Transport Bill, which became law in October 1968, introduced far-reaching changes in the licensing system for freight vehicles; the existing system had been in effect since the early 1930s. Certain provisions of the act—introduction of quantitative licensing, abolition of the differential between public haulage and carrying on own account, and establishment of quantitative control for all vehicles of more than 16 tons laden weight operating on long distance—were not to operate until the new railway freightliner services were deemed sufficiently comprehensive to offer satisfactory alternative services, probably during 1970. This form of licensing would apply to about 100,000 freight vehicles making journeys of more than 100 mi. (for bulk carriers the limit would be 25 mi.). Meanwhile, 900,000 vehicles of up to 30 cwt. unladen weight were to be excluded from the licensing system. Qualitative licensing, which would apply to all the 600,000 vehicles over this weight and would require proof of the operators' financial status and ability to maintain working standards, was expected to come into operation in the fall of 1969. The act also amended road haulage drivers' working conditions and reduced the maximum working and driving hours. The publicly owned road haulage vehicles were to be transferred to the National Freight Corp. on Jan. 1, 1969.

In Austria mandatory rates for road hauls exceeding 130 km. came into effect in 1968. In Belgium the supervision of rates and terms of carriage was introduced for the first time, and mandatory professional qualifications were required to obtain an international carrier's license. In Portugal measures for the coordination of land-borne transport were adopted. Taxes on road vehicles in Sweden were raised 50%, and in Yugoslavia steps were taken to stimulate coordination between road and rail.

To the extent that data were available, it was evident that the number of registered freight vehicles increased during the year in most countries, Italy and West Germany being notable exceptions. Tonnage carried also tended to rise, particularly on international journeys; the Netherlands recorded the largest increase—about 13%—and West Germany nearly 7%, but road freight traffic crossing the frontiers of the Belgium-Luxembourg economic union rose by less than 2% on average. Unusually large increases were recorded in international traffic across the Spanish borders: import traffic was up by 38.5%, export traffic by 45.2%, and transit traffic by 12.5%. Road traffic between the U.K., the continent, and Ireland increased sharply with the development of roll-on/roll-off services in 1967–68. Over one million unit and container loads passed through Southampton, Hull, Immingham, and King's Lynn, compared with 642,000 loads in 1966—an increase of 68%. To assist in this traffic, a number of inland customs and excise and clearance depots were established in industrial centres.

The U.K. recorded an increase of 500 million freight vehicle-km. during the year, and France registered an increase of 900 million. In the U.S.S.R. a freight turnover of 28 billion ton-km. was achieved during the first six months of 1968, representing an increase of 18% over the corresponding period of 1967. In the

continued on page 752

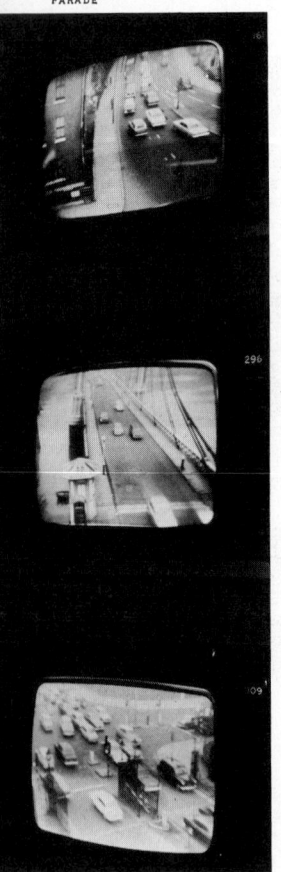

Below, closed-circuit TV camera monitoring traffic on the Texas Gulf Freeway in Houston. Above, TV screens showing three intersections in London. Both systems incorporated electronic devices that improve traffic flow by controlling traffic lights.

URBAN TRANSPORTATION SYSTEMS

By Ernest Davies

The major problem of the 20th century facing planners and engineers, city managers and local politicians, is how our towns and cities can cope with the automobile explosion. It is not only a question of providing facilities for vehicle movement and storage, but of deciding what kind of city, environment, and urban way of life should be planned now for the 21st century. The urban problem is one that has to be solved not for this generation but for the next and the one after that. Many new concepts are being put forward by those concerned: from the fantasies of the dreamers to the imaginative concepts of the inventors, and from the detached theories of the scientists to the mechanical and physical constructions of the engineers, architects, and designers —curbed perhaps by the restraining influences of the economists and the human realities of the community as a whole.

Taming the Automobile. Up to the 1950s, it was all too readily accepted that enough roads and parking places could be provided to cope with the growing automobile population. The effect on the city structure and the urban way of life gave concern to few. Hence the new freeways radiating from suburbia to the city centre, the parking lots and other eyesores, and the decline of the central business districts which died when the commuter sped homeward at the end of his working day. There followed inevitably a decline in mass transportation, a deterioration in services, loss of patronage and sometimes financial bankruptcy for the transit companies. This was the result of the never ending growth of car usage in America. By the '60s European cities were experiencing these phenomena to an increasing degree, but since they lagged behind the United States, they were able to learn from it and seriously to consider calling a halt to the merry-go-round in which facilities chased cars with no prospect of the construction of the one ever overtaking the growth of the other.

By the early 1960s the realization had dawned that entirely new approaches were needed. The urban problem was no longer seen as one of building facilities fast enough to provide for the increase in automobiles, but as both an urban and a human problem, one that required study in depth and a comprehensive solution, embracing the whole urban scene. It was recognized that the use to which land was put—the activities taking place on it— was the source of movement, the generator of travel. The two were indivisible, and the intelligent planning of the one could influence the demand for the other. Planning was not the answer but a means for finding it. Just as there are many uses for land, so there are many means of movement; all had to be considered, fitted into a pattern, and an overall plan evolved. In sum, there had to be a systems approach, one that covered a whole town or city in relation to the region of which it was a part and that provided for the movement of its citizens, services, goods, and commodities by all available transport modes. In the U.S. this concept was converted into legislation, and land use-transportation studies were required before government funds were granted for urban redevelopment, transportation systems, or new road and traffic networks. Europe followed suit.

From such studies, bold and imaginative plans emerged. Some

attempted to resuscitate the downtown areas by the provision of integrated transit systems and the stimulation of centralized activities in the city centre, as in Philadelphia; others by the creation of environmental areas, linked together and with the city centre by appropriate forms of transport, as in Stockholm; but each aimed at establishing balanced public and private transportation systems. Elsewhere new towns were planned, providing for the full use of the motorcar by building a hierarchy of roads and segregating vehicles and pedestrians, as at Cumbernauld, Scot. A great variety of new ideas appeared, but most of them were based on the fundamental principle that the city is a natural centre of activity that should be preserved and the motorcar would destroy it if allowed to run riot. A balance had to be struck between the demands of ever increasing mobility and accessibility, made possible by personal ownership of the automobile, and the retention of the existing environment. The urban way of life had to be adapted to the motorcar or it would be destroyed. A compromise between the two had to be sought.

With the drawing of plans in this context, man's imagination expanded. He began to look beyond present physical structures and transport forms to cities of the future with different modes of movement—transport forms exploiting new technologies, automation, and electronics. The old transport systems had failed to attract sufficient patronage to prevent the drift to the private car and could not be adapted to prevent it in the future. New forms had to be evolved that could meet the need for movement at least as well as—and preferably better than—the automobile, and that at the same time would permit a style of living within an urban environment acceptable to and desired by the community.

Great technological advances are already taking place in transport—supersonic planes are being built; new forms of traction are seeking railway speeds of 200 and 300 mph; a container revolution is taking place in shipping—but urban mass transportation has made no comparable advance. For the most part it is still based on the bus, streetcar, or rapid rail transit, and though there have been a few innovations, in the main public transport offers little more than it did before World War II—often, because of traffic congestion and the competition of the private car, it offers far less. The bus has changed little in the last 30 years and the subway operates much as it did in the 19th century. Further, more often than not the different transport modes operate independently, and there is little or no coordination.

Monorail and Duorail. New forms are being conceived, however, and their integration into a balanced transport system, providing for all movement within a given area, is envisaged. These new forms range from the monorail, which is no new invention but has never been in general use, to automatic taxi trains, now undergoing development in Britain; from the Transit Expressway, in experimental operation near Pittsburgh, Pa., to Travolators or moving platforms; from minibuses to electric cars.

The only true monorail systems are those suspended from a single rail without any lateral restraint and with the gyroscopically stabilized system running with double flanged wheels on a single rail. There are, however, pseudo-monorail systems that go under this name, for example, the Alweg bottom-supported monorail vehicles with rubber tires for support and guidance, running on a concrete beam. This system has been used in amusement parks, such as Disneyland, but the speeds of such systems are low and no efficient switching system has been devised. The Safege is another suspended monorail system; its vehicles, with rubber running and guidance tires, operate on a concrete beamway with wooden running surfaces. It has been tried experimentally but as of 1968 it was not in operation. None of these systems is truly revolutionary in concept; all are propelled by conventional electric traction motors and have the passenger compartments supported on or hung from wheeled axles. Studies have shown that the capital cost of such systems is no less than that of conventional rapid transit. A commercial monorail runs from the centre of Tokyo to the airport, but it has not proved successful.

The Westinghouse Transit Expressway comprises lightweight, rubber-tired vehicles with horizontal guide wheels that run on concrete surfaces and are guided along a steel beam. An experimental system in South Park near Pittsburgh included 9,340 ft. of roadway, mainly elevated; three vehicles resembling buses; an elevated platform; and one at-grade station. The vehicles were computer-controlled singly or in trains, required no guards or drivers, and ran continuously 24 hours a day. It is claimed that such a system is economically feasible for urban areas with traffic densities of 8,000 to 20,000 passengers an hour. The system has two shortcomings, however: cost and size. It is as costly as existing rapid transit and too large to run through a central area on an elevated surface. If these problems could be overcome, it would be of great interest, since—like a building elevator—it requires no operators and has a high degree of safety.

A study of possible monorail systems for London by the Greater London Council led to the conclusion that the monorail had no significant advantage over the more conventional rail—for comparison now known as the duorail. In fact, the latter was considered superior because of the vast fund of experience gained during its development and operation and because of its cost advantages. Further, a monorail overhead system posed major environmental problems. A comparative study of several rapid transit systems and concepts, including monorail and Transit Expressway, prepared for the city of Manchester, Eng., reached a similar conclusion: on grounds of cost, comfort, and convenience, the duorail was the most practical of all systems studied.

Because the duorail is presently favoured, the new rapid transit systems being built in the metropolitan areas of the Americas and Europe are underground railways powered by electric traction. In Canada subway systems came into operation in Toronto in 1954 and Montreal in the 1960s, and in the San Francisco-Oakland area of California the 75-mi. Bay Area Rapid Transit (BART) System was under construction; similar systems were planned for Washington, D.C., Los Angeles, and Atlanta, Ga. Systems were being built in several European cities, including Munich and Frankfurt in West Germany, Stockholm, Swed., and Milan, Italy. The pace in technological development was probably being set by BART; designed to operate at 80 mph and controlled by electronic computer, it would be entirely automatic, as is the Victoria Line extension to London's underground system opened in 1968.

In continental Europe, where streetcar systems have long been favoured, a compromise was being effected in many cities; the streetcar systems continued to run on their reserved rights of way, partly in a tunnel or cut, but so built that they could be converted easily into full-scale underground railways should the need arise.

Automated Taxi and Moving Sidewalk. Developments were also taking place in bus transport, as regards both type of service and control. In Washington, D.C., a 20-seater minibus system underwent successful trials, carrying two million passengers in the first year; speeds were slow, however, averaging only four miles per hour in heavy traffic. Studies by the British Road Research Laboratory showed that small buses of this kind have great advantages compared with the traditional large buses, particularly the double decker so familiar to Londoners. They reduce waiting and provide faster traveling time because of their great maneuverability. Proposals have been made in the U.S. for using minibuses directed by computer-radio control in low-density residential areas, where public transport is difficult to operate economically; the buses would pick up people en route like a taxi, but at less cost. Because manpower accounts for as much as 60% of operating costs and congestion makes for poor service, the final answer to improved bus travel must lie in the development of automated systems segregated above or below other traffic. This was recognized by the planners of the New Town of Runcorn in Cheshire, Eng., where public transport was confined to bus services operating on reserved tracks.

The most revolutionary development in surface transport systems is the automatic, self-routing, public taxi service for towns and cities. The system is intended to transport cars containing up to four passengers between preselected destinations, the routing being controlled by computer. Small four-seater vehicles would be available at stations and operated only as required. The occupant would press a button designating his destination, and the vehicle would then automatically feed into the totally segregated network, join other vehicles, and be separated from the network when it reached the selected point. The unique features of the auto-taxi are, therefore: passengers travel independently in a small vehicle, either alone or in a group of up to four adults (as in a private car); all stations are off the main line, so the average speed is high because there is no stopping at intermediate stations; the vehicles are driverless and route themselves automatically. Empty vehicles are routed by computer to where they are required; computers also control the issuing of tickets, line and station loading, safety, and maintenance and cleaning procedures. This system was under active development by the British government's National Research and Development Corporation.

A somewhat similar system, known as Teletrans, was being tried out in the U.S. Teletrans has small two-seater cars in an enclosed tube; on paying, passengers take a card for the desired station, which they fit into the control; they are then automatically driven to their destination. One disadvantage of such systems is that they require a reserved right of way that would almost certainly have to be elevated and would impinge upon the environment.

While such developments in public transport systems would speed the journey to the city centre, the passenger still has to reach his final destination, such as his place of work. With vehicle-free areas, pedestrian precincts, and shopping malls planned in many cities, and with the increasing reluctance to use one's feet to move around, provision has to be made for completing the journey. This is an area where development is lacking. Moving pavements appear to be the obvious method of moving pedestrians horizontally, as escalators do vertically, but few have been introduced. Such systems could be routed to serve the needs of pedestrian movement within the city, however. They would not need to be much faster than walking pace, but they would have to be continuous, with no waiting at boarding points, and with a system of graduated speeds to permit boarding.

Two systems of moving pavement were in production in 1968. One was the Travolator, which consists of a series of aluminum platforms driven by chains and running on wheels on a track similar to that used in an escalator. A Travolator is in use at the Bank Underground Station, London; it rises at a gradient of 1 in 7,300 ft. and has a theoretical capacity of 16,200 passengers an hour. The other system is the pedestrian conveyor. These conveyors use a grooved rubber belt, can run level or ramp up to 1 in 10, and vary in width from 24 to 60 in., depending on the required capacity. A wide belt may have side access at intermediate points or a parallel belt can be used. The longest pedestrian conveyor in operation, at Sydney, Austr., was 700 ft. long and was used to connect a garage with the central business district.

The New Automobile. Computer-controlled automated and segregated systems—both conventional, such as subways, and new types like the auto-taxi—appear to be the most likely developments in public transport. In private transport, changes may well be more revolutionary, as regards both the vehicle and its usage. The automobile as we know it today might be superceded in the city by much smaller cars with different power systems, and the use of larger cars might well be restricted. New types of vehicles, tailored to the narrow streets of existing towns, would be small, compact, maneuverable, of uniform size, capable of steady rather than high speeds, and easy to get into and out of quickly. Electric cars seem to fit these specifications most closely; they do not emit fumes, need little attention, have low fuel costs, require minimal maintenance, have a long life, and are simple to operate.

"Tomorrow's travellers will be piped from city to city says transport expert."—Waite, "The Sun," London.

Carpeted rolling sidewalks which move at a speed of two miles per hour link four subway lines at the Montparnasse station in Paris.

Model of an automatic, self-routing public taxi system being developed in Britain by Auto Taxi Development Ltd. and the National Research and Development Corporation.

Many types of electric cars were being developed in the 1960s. The prototypes in operation were battery driven, but research was being conducted on cars driven by fuel cells, and these are a likely development in the not too distant future. In Britain the nationalized electricity industry and several private companies had demonstrated a number of electrically propelled cars, but none had been perfected. Maximum speed of lead acid battery electric cars is about 40 mph and the maximum range is 50 to 60 mi. Recharging is a slow process, and the batteries take up most of the space normally occupied by the rear seats.

In the U.S. an electric car with a top speed of 25 mph and a range of 50 mi. was in production. Others were being built in Italy and elsewhere. Ford of Britain launched a prototype of its electric city or shopping car, the Comuta, in 1967. It was only 6 ft. 8 in. long, had a turning circle of 18 ft., and was equipped with automatic shift. The rear wheels were driven directly by two electric motors. It had a range of 40 mi. at a steady speed of 25 mph and was powered by conventional batteries. The Ford Motor Co. in both Great Britain and the U.S. was engaged in a program designed to develop a low-cost electric city car with a new form of electric storage, the sodium-sulfur battery, said to be able to store 15 times the electrical energy of the lead acid storage battery. Another new development, the zinc air battery, was capable of storing five to seven times the energy of the lead acid type. Research was also being undertaken into steam-powered cars, stimulated by the need to curb air pollution caused by the internal combustion engine.

The Working Group set up by the British minister of transport to consider future trends in the design of cars for use in cities envisaged a personal transport system based on small vehicles with a 40-mph speed limit in towns, operating on reserved road space. Some of the segregated road space would be provided by building a new lightweight overhead network and the rest by setting aside existing space. The "citycars" would be garaged at home and driven on the ordinary road system, moving onto the segregated space where available. Near its destination, the city-car would be parked or would move off the reserved right of way and reenter the ordinary street system to complete its journey. It was estimated that such a system would enable twice as many people to travel by car as at present. Little attention was paid to this report, and it was pigeonholed.

Movement of Goods. All this has referred only to the movement of persons, although the movement of goods is also important in the urban transport picture. New ideas are being formulated for the distribution of merchandise and commodities within urban areas, most schemes being directed at reducing surface transport and eliminating the congestion arising from loading and unloading. Thus urban redevelopment schemes frequently incorporate special off-the-highway servicing facilities; some go so far as to provide special access into stores and warehouses, as in

Rotterdam, where ramps for freight vehicles run up several floors into the main shopping area.

A variety of automated systems have also been suggested. One of the most interesting on paper is that for an as yet hypothetical new town of Etarea, designed as an urban unit for some 130,000 inhabitants, ten miles from Prague, Czech. The town centre and ten district centres would be linked with the centre of Prague by monorail, below which conveyor belts would be installed to transport goods to the centre of the new town. For distribution of goods within the city, the plan proposes an underground system of automatically controlled electric battery trolleys, running in tubes and linking the main distribution centres. For distribution from shops to homes, another unique system is suggested: magnetically guided containers would be propelled by compressed air through a system of 220-mm.-diameter tubes from distribution centres, located under the district centres, directly into the individual homes. This would enable direct delivery within a few minutes of the receipt of an order. It may be a pipe-dream today, but—given the pace at which automation is developing—it could be a reality tomorrow.

Whatever the form of developments in transport systems and their hardware, and however much control is exercised over movement in cities, the trend will be toward planning and control of the system rather than of the mode. Urban transport systems of the future will still comprise a modal mix, but the types that make it up will be integrated into a balanced transport system, with easy interchanges between one form and another.

Ultimately, movement of both persons and goods in cities may become fully automated, but that is not for this century. Today's planners have enough difficulty finding solutions for the present transport dilemma of too many vehicles and too few facilities to concern themselves overmuch with science fiction, even though that "fiction" may well become fact in the 21st century.

Transportation

continued from page 748

U.S. new truck registrations in 1967 exceeded 1.5 million, bringing the total to more than 16 million. Ton-miles operated in 1967 were estimated at 400,-000,000,000, representing about 31% of the ton-mileage carried by all forms of transport and 52% of all intercity tonnage of manufactured products excluding petroleum and coal. Truck operating revenues for fiscal 1967 rose about 3% to a new all-time high.

Road passenger traffic followed the trends of recent years: travel by private car continued to rise with the uninterrupted growth in private automobiles, and journeys by public transport remained static or declined further. Action was being initiated in a number of countries, however, to resuscitate mass transportation by such measures as government financing of infrastructure, subsidizing of uneconomic services, and the provision of preferential treatment for public transport in urban areas. In the U.K. preliminary steps were taken to set up the public transport authorities provided for by the Transport Act, 1968. Under the act the minister of transport was authorized to designate any area outside London as a Passenger Transport Area, but initially only four were to be set up—in the conurbations of Greater Manchester, Merseyside, West Midlands, and Tyneside.

A passenger transport authority and a passenger transport executive were to be established in each area, and their task would be to integrate and develop the public transport services. The authority, with the majority of its members appointed by the local authorities, would be responsible for broad policy, and the executive, appointed by the authority, would run the public transport system. They would have powers to carry passengers themselves or through subsidiaries, and to make contracts with other operators. They would take over all the municipal passenger transport undertakings in their areas and would make agreements with the new National Bus Co. and with the Railways Board for services required from these bodies.

The National Bus Co., scheduled to begin operations on Jan. 1, 1969, would take over the bus companies operated by the nationalized Transport Holding Co. except for the Scottish Bus Group. During the year the Holding Co. had purchased the British Electric Traction Group of companies, giving it control of virtually all the U.K.'s major bus and coach concerns outside of those operated by the Scottish Bus Group, the municipalities, and London Transport. The new company would own more than 20,000 buses and would be responsible for the basic network of services outside the main municipalities. A Scottish Transport Group was to be established to take over the 5,000 buses of the Scottish Bus Group. Legislation was to be introduced during 1969 to transfer the London Transport Board, with its monopoly of bus and underground railways in the Greater London area, to the Greater London Council.

Bus operating revenues in the U.S. achieved new highs during the year; revenues for fiscal 1967 were up nearly 6%. Most of the increase was accounted for by intercity services, which recorded nearly one-quarter of all passenger-miles of common carriers. Local and suburban commuter services generally showed a decline. (*See* Special Report.)

PIPELINES

The most interesting pipeline development under way in 1968 was the project of the great European chemi-

cal companies to construct an international pipeline grid to link the ethylene producers and balance distribution of the product. The Dutch State Mines and five West German companies agreed to construct a 25-cm., 200-km. line with an annual capacity of 250,000 tons to link the former's plant with the Ruhr and Cologne. A line from Cologne to Frankfurt and Raunheim was already under construction, and there was a network of lines serving the complex of refineries and chemical plants around Rotterdam and Antwerp.

A further feature of pipeline development was the widening range of natural gas transport in Europe. Over 25,000 km. of natural-gas lines had been completed by the end of the year. Developments were largely designed to extend the pipelines from the prolific Slochteren field in the Netherlands to neighbouring countries; the connection with Paris was completed, export lines to West Germany were being extended to the Rhine-Ruhr industrial area, and a separate line was built from the Netherlands-West German frontier via Hamburg to the Baltic coast. In Great Britain gas from the North Sea fields flowed into the national pipeline transmission system, parts of which were still under construction. The U.S.S.R.–Czechoslovakia line from the Ukraine was extended to Austria, and supplies began to flow through this branch in September.

The U.S.S.R. claimed that by 1970 its gas-pipeline network would total 70,800 km., compared with the existing network of 56,300 km. Pipes of much larger diameter were being developed, and construction of the first (120-cm.) pipeline began in 1968. It would run northward from the Turkmen Soviet Socialist Republic (Central Asia) to Saratov, which it was expected to reach by 1970. Plans were also being made to lay a line linking Western Siberia with European Russia, using pipes of 2.5-m. diameter.

The first pilot schemes to use pipelines for the transport of milk in East Germany were considered sufficiently successful to justify further lines, and 480 km. were expected to be in service by 1970. In the U.S. a pipeline transportation system was being developed for moving 500 to 3,000 tons of wood chips a day between the forest source and the processing centre.

The Great Lakes pipeline project comprising a 1,000-mi. network to carry natural gas from western to eastern Canada through the U.S. was completed in 1968. It extended from the Manitoba border through Minnesota, Wisconsin, and Michigan to Ontario. The total cost was estimated at $212 million. A natural-gas pipeline 260 mi. long was being built in Australia from Roma to Brisbane and another, 110 mi. long, from Dutson near Sale to Dandenong near Melbourne. In New Zealand a 450-mi. line was being constructed to carry gas from the fields near Kapuni to Auckland and Wellington. The Titas gas field in East Pakistan was being linked with Dacca by a 50-mi. pipeline.

With the development of the European pipeline networks, transport of both crude oil and oil products continued to grow; 57.5 million tons were transported during 1967, and ton-kilometres totaled 14,557,-410,725, 8.8% above 1966. France recorded the highest flow in Western Europe with 67.1 million tons. West Germany, with 9,165,000,000 ton-km., came next, and the flow through the Rotterdam–Rhine line increased by 25%. Exceptionally, the Rhine–Danube pipeline experienced a sharp decrease because of competition from the Central European (Genoa–Inglo-

stadt) line. The new continuous crude-oil line alongside the Rhine from Rotterdam to Ludwigshafen in southern Germany came into operation, as did the Burghausen pipeline (Munich–St. Christoph–Burghausen), and work began on the Venlo (Neth.)–Dinslaken (W.Ger.) products pipeline. In Austria work started on the construction of a 418-km., 46-cm. spur from the Trans-Alpine pipeline to Schwechat near Vienna, to be completed by 1970. In Belgium oil started to flow through the Zeebrugge–Ghent pipeline, and in July the government approved in principle the construction of a $20 million crude-oil pipeline linking Rotterdam-Europoort and Antwerp.

In the U.K. authority was sought to build a 180-mi. line from Milford Haven to the Midlands. The Stanlow–Haysham crude-oil pipeline and the Stanlow–Runcorn products lines were in service. In the U.S.S.R. plans were completed to build a second "Friendship" oil pipeline; it would run parallel to the main existing section and its southern branch across the Carpathian Mountains, and would connect the oil fields on the Volga and in the Ukraine with Czechoslovakia and Hungary.

Agreement was reached between the U.S. and Canadian governments for the construction of a 412-mi. line from Superior, Wis., to Sarnia, Ont., via Chicago. Construction of a 1,200-mi., large-diameter common carrier pipeline from the Texas-Louisiana Gulf Coast refineries to the Midwest, terminating in Chicago, was authorized, and the line was expected to be in operation by the mid-1970s. The 640-mi. Capline, the largest crude-oil pipeline in the U.S., bringing oil from southern Louisiana to Illinois, came into operation in July.

During 1967 the first pipeline in the Caribbean islands had been opened in Puerto Rico, running for 80 mi. from Penuelas on the southern coast to San Juan in the north, with a spur to the airport at Isla Verde. In Argentina construction began on a $21 million, 1,365-km., 36-cm. products pipeline from the Lujan de Cuyo refinery in the province of Mendoza to the cities of Córdoba and Buenos Aires. The first stage, a 1,000-km.-long line to Córdoba, was in operation by the end of the year. The whole project was due for completion early in 1970.

Israel began construction of the link from Eilat on the Gulf of Aqaba to Ascalon, south of Tel Aviv, and the U.A.R. was considering building a large-diameter pipeline from Suez to the Mediterranean, terminating at Alexandria. The latter would be of greater importance since it would also serve the Persian Gulf.

Algeria was to build a fourth major crude-oil pipeline that would increase the flow of Saharan crude oil to Mediterranean ports by 60%. Scheduled for completion in early 1970, the new 90-cm. line would link the region of Mesdar (approximately 100 km. SE of Hassi Messaoud) to the port of Skikda, a distance of 700 km. The line would be Algeria's largest, with an ultimate capacity of 30 million tons a year. A system of gathering lines to bring crude from new fields in the east and southeast to the Mesdar terminal would be built at the same time. The most important of these would be a 40-cm. line running 250 km. to the El Borma field on the Tunisian border. Until the new line was completed, El Borma crude would be carried to Arzew via the Trapes and Sonatrach pipelines.

Libya was considering construction of a new pipeline system from Zaggut in the Defa field to Es Sider. The 141-mi.-long Nafovra–Amal–Ras Lanof line was completed in August. The 1,060-mi. products pipeline linking the Dar es Salaam refinery in Tanzania with Ndola in northern Zambia went into operation in July. In South Africa work was due to start on the 420-mi., 18-in. crude-oil pipeline from the new tanker terminal being built at Richard's Bay, north of Durban, to the refinery under construction at Sasolburg.

RAILWAYS

Consolidation of railway systems, progress with modernization, and adaptation of services to changing needs—including the introduction of high-speed passenger and containerized services—were the main features of 1967–68. The closing of unremunerative lines continued at a much reduced rate, and only in Spain and the U.S. was this done on any substantial scale. There was a growing tendency for governments to subsidize uneconomic lines that needed to be kept open for social reasons. This policy was endorsed by the report on the financial situation of the railways made by the ECMT, which recommended that governments should define public service obligations and that, where services could no longer be justified on economic grounds but met essential needs, compensation should be paid. Other recommendations were that railway services should be adapted to suit the changing pattern of demand and that the optimum size of railway networks should be determined.

Advances toward the normalization of railway accounts were being made by both the ECMT and the Economic Commission for Europe. The purpose of this was to ensure that the financial cost of obligations and constraints imposed on railways, but not on other means of transport, by public policy should be isolated in order that appropriate financial adjustments might be made in the railways' favour. In July the Council of Ministers of the EEC adopted measures in connection with the institution of a common transport policy, which laid down conditions of competition between different transport modes, including rail. In the U.K. the Transport Act, 1968, wrote off a substantial part of British Railways' capital debt and provided for subsidization of socially desirable services and for the reorganization of the railways as a viable system. British Railways' rapidly developing freightliner container services, together with its parcels and sundries services, were to be transferred to the new publicly owned National Freight Corp. (which would also be in charge of the nationalized road freight services) in January 1969. The purpose of the new corporation would be to provide integrated road and rail freight services in Great Britain.

In West Germany the transport program presented at the end of 1967 provided for the reorganization, concentration, and rationalization of the Bundesbahn, with better operating services and improvements on the technical and commercial side. In the U.S. consolidation through the merging of systems continued. The Interstate Commerce Commission reaffirmed the merger of the Chicago and North Western Railway with the Chicago Great Western Railway after an appeal by the Soo Line. The merger, which became effective in July 1968, brought 12,000 mi. in 11 Midwestern states under unified control. Control of the Chicago and Eastern Illinois railroad by the Missouri Pacific was authorized.

In the less developed countries progress was made on the construction of new lines, often with aid from the World Bank. In India the Dharmapuri–Bangalore

UPI (UK) LTD.

4,000-hp. Hawker Siddeley Kestrel, the world's most powerful single-engined diesel electric locomotive, capable of maintaining speeds up to 110 mph. It was intended for use in areas where electrification was impractical.

section of the Salem–Bangalore metre-gauge line was opened for freight traffic in June. The 65 mi. metre-gauge Jaisalmer–Pokaran line was opened early in 1968, linking Jaisalmer by rail with the rest of India for the first time. On the South Eastern Railway, the Kottavalasa–Kirandul line came into full operation. In East Pakistan a railway from Faridpur to Barisal was under construction. Iran received aid from the U.S.S.R. for a number of railway projects, including the Isfahan–Kerman section of the link with the Pakistan system at Zahedan. Studies were completed and plans submitted by the Soviet Union for a Damascus to Homs line in Syria, to replace the existing single-track, narrow-gauge line. In Iraq conversion of the Baghdad–Basra railway to standard gauge was completed. The Economic Commission for Asia and the Far East (ECAFE) furthered the project for a trans-Asian railway from Istanbul to Singapore, and surveys were begun. The line would ultimately connect up existing lines and would include new links in Iran, Afghanistan, India, Pakistan, Burma, Thailand, and Malaysia, the whole system totaling some 14,000 km. in length. In Africa construction began early in 1968 on the trans-Cameroon railway between Belabo and Ngaoundéré, and a 65-mi. line was to be built in Malawi to provide an alternative rail outlet to the sea at Nacala, Mozambique. A further step toward construction of the Tanzania–Zambia railway by the Chinese was taken with the appointment of a joint railway authority.

The Canadian National Railways undertook a feasibility study of a rail link to the Yukon. Also in Canada, the Pacific Great Eastern Railway proposed to build an 80-mi. extension from Fort St. James to Takla Lake and a 300-mi. extension from Fort St. John to Fort Nelson. In Bolivia the first section of

the Santa Cruz de la Sierre–Sucre line, from Santa Cruz to Monteres, was scheduled to open early in 1969. Colombia obtained a loan of $18.3 million from the World Bank to assist the five-year program of the National Railways. In Australia the standard-gauge link between Port Pirie in South Australia and Perth in Western Australia was completed, closing the last gap in the trans-Australian standard-gauge system. In Japan work advanced on the 162-km. extension to Okayama of the high-speed Tokaido line from Tokyo to Osaka; the extension had a design speed of 155 mph. Spain was the only European country to undertake considerable new construction; the line between Madrid and Burgos was opened in July and the second transportation plan provided for several new rail links. Some new links were under construction in Switzerland and Greece.

Accelerated modernization characterized railway development during the year. Computers, automation, and mechanization were being applied in all feasible areas of operation, while research and development gave promise of even more sophisticated apparatus and installations. To permit safe operation at higher speeds, track replacements, the laying of long welded rails, and the building of new stations were being undertaken. Considerable progress was made in the development of better signaling facilities and automatic block systems, and in the installation of automatic control points, centralized control operations, and better telecommunications. Elimination of steam traction proceeded, but the pace of electrification slackened further. Nonetheless, the number of electric locomotives continued to rise steadily; 9,655 units were operating in Western Europe at the end of 1967, while the number of steam locomotives declined by 4,000 during the year to 11,000.

In August 1968 the last steam locomotives in the U.K. were withdrawn from service, diesel and electric traction having replaced the 19,000 steam locomotives that were operating in 1955. The next stage

Network of main-line railway track in the U.S. Major new companies resulting from mergers during the years 1962–68 are listed with the names of the railways that were involved in each merger. The Burlington-Northern Pacific merger was being examined by the Justice Department in 1968.

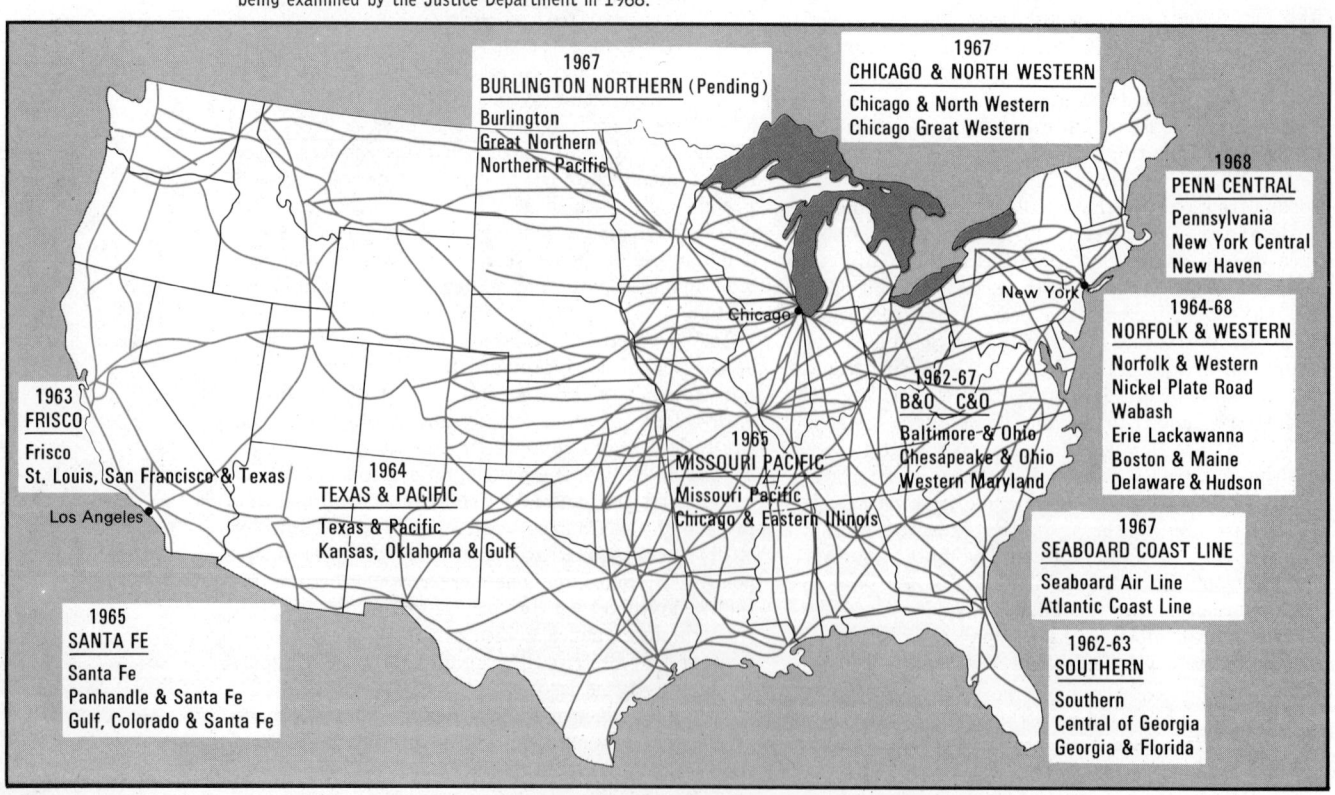

of development would be the removal of bottlenecks and the carrying out of engineering works to enable speeds of 125 mph to be attained. The most rapid electrification continued to be in the U.S.S.R. (2,000 km. a year), where it was planned to have 35,000 km. electrified by 1970. In Western Europe more than 1,600 more kilometres of line were electrified, bringing the total to more than 77,000 km. With conversion of the Osnabrück–Bremen–Hamburg and Hamm–Minden–Wunsdorf lines completed in September 1968, electrification of the (West) German Federal Railways main lines was virtually finished and about a quarter of the whole system was electrified. In France, with the Paris–Le Havre line completely electrified, the chief work in progress was on the Dijon–Bourg and Dôle–Mulhouse lines and on the Marseilles–Ventimiglia line, where the section from Les Arcs to Saint Raphaël was completed during the year. In Italy electrification was completed on the S. Mauro La Bruca–Sapri and Verbicaro–Belvedere sections of the Battipaglia–Reggio and Calabria lines and on the S. Benedetto del Tronto–Ros to degli Abbruzzi section of the Ancona–Pescara line. Electrification of the Coutumil–São Romão line in Portugal was finished, and in Hungary electrification began on the 70-km. Budapest–Cegled section. Conversion to electric and diesel traction progressed in India and Pakistan. India planned to convert by 1970–71 all sections of Indian railways having a traffic density of 20,000 net ton-km. per route-kilometre per day during 1966. Electrification of the 178-mi. Lahore–Khanewal section of the Pakistan Western Railway neared completion.

Railway traffic generally made a poor showing during the year. In Western Europe passenger traffic declined in terms of both numbers carried and passenger-kilometres, with the latter registering a sharper rate of decline than during the previous year. The only countries recording an increase in passengers were Italy, Portugal, and Luxembourg. Freight traffic also showed a declining tendency, but less so than passenger traffic. Tons carried rose by 8.1% in Italy and 11.1% in Norway. Other countries recording increases included Belgium, Denmark, Portugal, Spain, Ireland, and Switzerland. The largest decreases were in Greece (down 12%) and in the U.K. (down nearly 6%). The pattern for ton-kilometres was similar.

To counteract the decline, attempts were made to adjust services to public requirements by raising the scheduled speeds of passenger services and by introducing new types of freight services—particularly those involving containerization—and coordinating these with other transport modes. In the U.K. the freightliner service of standardized container trains was further extended; by mid-1968, 17 terminals were open and 31 services carried 7,000 containers a week, equivalent to about 3.5 million tons a year. Investment of a further £12.3 million in five new terminals and the expansion of three others was approved. Coordination of these services with the short-sea routes progressed substantially. The German Federal Railways was to have 450 container terminals, of which 25 were operating by the end of 1968. In the U.S. nearly half of freight revenue came from container traffic and piggyback (trailer on flatcar) services. U.S. railway companies were becoming increasingly interested in capitalizing on containerization through the concept of the "land bridge," in which high-speed, coast-to-coast trains would be used to bypass the slower sea route through the Panama Canal. It was estimated that, even with existing routes and equip-

ment, the time required for shipment between the Far East and Europe could be up to 20 days less than via the Cape and 10 days less than via the Panama Canal.

During fiscal 1967 net income of the U.S. Class I railroads was at its highest level since 1955, but the increase was due to higher freight earnings; passenger carryings—except for commuter traffic—continued to decline though at a decreasing rate. In the U.S.S.R. record carryings were achieved during 1967 and the trend continued into 1968, with traffic reaching 1,343,000,000,000 tons and 1,137,000,000,000 ton-km. during the first six months of the year.

Technical development on new forms of high-speed traction continued. The French tracked Hovercraft aerotrain, powered by both an aircraft propeller and a rocket, attained speeds of 300 mph during its 1968 trials; the next stage would be construction of an experimental Hovertrain line between Paris and the University of Orléans. In Great Britain preliminary work continued in preparation for the setting up of a trial track and construction of a test vehicle for the Hovertrain experiment, with a target speed of 300 mph.

At Lyons, France, a new "flying bus," suspended by air suction from a raised aluminum rail and powered by a linear electric motor, was demonstrated. Known as the URBA, it had lightweight coaches designed to carry large numbers of passengers at commercial speeds or small numbers at speeds up to 250 mph.

The advanced gas-turbine passenger train being developed by British Railways at its Derby works was to obtain government support on a 50–50 basis. With a top speed of 150 mph, the train was to be powered by a development of the Rolls Royce Dart gas-turbine engine. A second project was to develop, from existing rolling stock, a high-speed train using the 400-hp gas-turbine traction unit developed by British Leyland.

In the U.S.S.R. an experimental jet-driven train was being developed at the Kalinin works; two aviation jet engines, installed on the roof, would drive the unit at speeds approaching 200 mph.   (E. A. J. D.)

WATER TRANSPORTATION

Shipping. The shipping industry was going through a period of rapid technical advance in 1968. Suddenly an activity that for centuries had been regarded as unique was seen to be susceptible to the new techniques and management systems applied ashore. Shipping was being viewed simply as one part of the in-

UPI (UK) LTD.

The new Cunard liner "Queen Elizabeth II" edges into Port Glasgow for fitting out before her maiden voyage. Cunard subsequently refused delivery until engine defects had been corrected.

756

Transportation

creasingly sophisticated and integrated worldwide through-transport systems.

Possibly the most striking example during 1968 was the tanker "Universe Ireland," 312,000 tons deadweight, delivered in Japan in the summer. This was not just because of her huge size—she exceeded the largest standard supertankers under construction at the time by nearly 100,000 tons—but because her size prevented her from delivering her cargo to its final destination, the European refineries of the Gulf Oil Co. With her five sister ships, she was specifically designed for transshipment to smaller ships in deep water at Bantry Bay in Ireland, for onward delivery to the refineries.

The economies of scale obtained from the "Universe Ireland" during the main part of the voyage from the Persian Gulf would be more than enough to pay the cost of transshipment. The next step in bulk shipment (which might still be some years off, however) would clearly be transshipment at sea from much larger ships—500,000–1 million-tonners—incapable of entering even deepwater harbours. Another of the big oil companies, Shell, was already developing this technique with smaller ships.

Similar trends were observable in general cargo, with the container as their focal point. During the year several new container ships entered service on the trunk routes out of North America across both the Atlantic and the Pacific, speeding up delivery of manufactured goods and playing havoc with existing shipping and port practices. The advent of the container ship, in which cargo is prestowed in boxes and slotted into the cellular holds of the ship, seemed certain to lead within a decade to the greatest transformation on the main trade routes since the coming of steam, probably accompanied by sporadic freight wars.

This was already happening in the short-sea trades, particularly around Britain and Europe, where the introduction of container and roll-on/roll-off ships was more advanced than in the deep-sea trades. Freight rates across the North Sea between England and northern Europe were cut by up to 50% in the course of the year, threatening the survival of those lines, however well established, that were ill-equipped to meet the new competition.

The Suez Canal remained closed after the Arab-Israeli conflict of 1967, but the effect of this on world shipping and trade had become negligible. With almost 200 very large tankers delivered or on order, the oil industry was rapidly making itself independent of the canal, and cargo liner services had been adjusted to take account of longer voyages round the Cape. It seemed unlikely that the canal would ever recapture its role as a vital trade artery. Possibly the greatest effect (apart from that on the economies of countries adjacent to the canal) was on passenger shipping, which was diverted not only over longer distances but in many cases away from attractive routes. This would no doubt accelerate the decline of the passenger ship as a trunk-route carrier and help to concentrate those liners remaining in service on pleasure cruising.

The world merchant fleet continued to grow steadily, exceeding 200 million tons by the year's end, and—despite various political upheavals—operated in relatively stable commercial conditions. The United Kingdom Chamber of Shipping tramp freight index fluctuated around 120–130 points (1960 = 100) for the greater part of the year. (M. By.)

Hovercraft. For the first time since its conception some ten years earlier, the Hovercraft came into its

COURTESY, BRITISH HOVERCRAFT CORPORATION LTD.

The 165-ton SR-N4, the world's largest Hovercraft, crossing the English Channel on a regularly scheduled trip from Dover to Boulogne. Service was inaugurated in August 1968.

own in 1968 with the introduction of a car-carrying craft on a 25-mi. international route from Dover, Eng., to Boulogne, France. The craft was the 165-ton SR-N4 "Mountbatten," made by the British Hovercraft Corp. (BHC), and the inaugural run was made on August 1—a target date set two years previously when the craft was still on the drawing board. However, technical faults and weather problems reduced the craft's availability to below 80% during the ten weeks it was in service before a layoff for modifications. A second SR-N4 was to enter service in 1969.

The "Mountbatten" carried 250 passengers and 30 cars and was by far the largest Hovercraft in existence—the Boeing 747 of an industry less than a decade old. It was this time scale that to a great extent explained the craft's teething troubles, for there was no great wealth of experience available upon which the now booming Hovercraft industry could draw.

Other BHC designs, the Winchester and Warden classes, were used by civil and military operators throughout the year in places as far apart as the Falkland Islands, Canada, and Malaysia. In Great Britain, Hovertravel Ltd., a completely independent commercial operator, logged its millionth passenger on a nine-minute run from Southsea to Ryde on the Isle of Wight, using a Winchester craft. Other commercial operations with the Winchester, of which more than 30 had been built, included a run between Naples, Capri, and Ischia, off southern Italy, and a route in Japan operated by a craft built there under license from BHC.

Another British manufacturer, Hovermarine, was producing the HM2, a nonamphibious Hovercraft propelled by water screws and having rigid sidewalls instead of an all-round flexible skirt. The HM2 was operated off the south coast of England by two companies during the summer and was scheduled to be used in the Bahamas before the end of the year. The first French-built craft, the Sedam N.300, began trials off the Côte d'Azur, and a completely Japanese design, the Mitsui MV-PP5, was launched near Tokyo. The only U.S. craft, the Bell SK-5, a derivative of the BHC Warden class, saw its first service as a military assault craft in Vietnam. (J. B. Be.)

Docks and Harbours. The trend toward unit loads, containerization, larger and more specialized ships, and the further development of mechanized methods for cargo handling continued unabated during 1968. Ports the world over were engaged in adapting their facilities to the radical changes. Several new container berths with apron hinterlands came into operation, and work began or was in progress on many others.

In the U.K. £50 million was spent on such moderni-

zation during the year ending March 1968, £5 million more than a year earlier, and further expenditure on at least this scale was expected for several years to come. The British Transport Docks Board (owner of 19 ports) alone had plans for spending £71 million during the five years ending 1972. The Port of London Authority decided to concentrate its facilities at its modern developments, particularly at Tilbury, and announced the closing of the London and St. Katharine docks by the end of 1968. The new facilities at Tilbury for handling container traffic neared completion, and three of the six new berths were in operation. The £1 million Liverpool Gladstone container terminal, which this project would adjoin, became operational in May.

A £2.5 million container terminal was completed on the River Clyde at Greenock. At Southampton a new container berth, also costing £2.5 million, was under construction, and work started on the first phase of the scheme to extend the Western Docks. Meanwhile, two new roll-on/roll-off terminals were finished. Two more such terminals came into use at Hull and a new marine terminal for 100,000-ton tankers was well under way at Immingham. Work continued on the £17 million tidal harbour at Port Talbot in South Wales; it would be operational for 100,000-ton ore carriers in 1969 and would eventually accommodate ships of 150,000 tons.

Ambitious schemes were begun at several of Europe's major ports, particularly Rotterdam-Europoort, Amsterdam, Antwerp, Hamburg, Le Havre, and Marseilles. At Europoort work continued on the massive development plan, and the authorities were looking ahead to extension of the harbour and industrial sites adjacent to the New Waterway and the Westerschelde. The first 200,000-ton tanker arrived in the port in December 1967. At Amsterdam the widening and deepening of the North Sea canal and construction of adjoining harbours to take 85,000-ton ships was proceeding.

Access channels and docks at Le Havre were being deepened to about 49 ft. to accommodate ships between 300,000 and 350,000 tons by 1970, and imaginative possibilities were being explored for construction of an artificial island 17 mi. off the harbour mouth to take tankers up to one million tons. At Marseilles a $240 million project, to be completed in 1978, would enable the port to handle total annual cargo of 170 million tons. The channel at Hamburg was being deepened to take 80,000–90,000-ton tankers; the fifth of 14 planned container berths came into use in 1968, and two more were under construction. In Scandinavia container roll-on/roll-off facilities were also being developed at major ports. In Cyprus plans were prepared for a $2.4 million port at Limasol, with work expected to start in 1969.

On balance, traffic through Europe's major ports improved. Rotterdam maintained its position as the world's busiest port, handling international seaborne traffic of 141.4 million tons in 1967, against 130.4 million tons in 1966. The Port of London handled 60.1 million tons (59 million in 1966). Among French ports, Le Havre experienced a 22% rise in 1967, whereas traffic through Marseilles declined slightly. Most West German ports also suffered a fall in traffic, Hamburg's decline being 5.5%. Traffic at Antwerp rose about 4%, and there was a further increase in the first six months of 1968.

Developments in Asia during the year included improvements in India's major ports to meet growing traffic, which reached a new peak of 55.8 million tons. The 1968 modernization program required an investment of Rs. 429.7 million. What was said to be the world's largest shipping berth, built at a cost of $12 million in the middle of Tokyo Bay, began operation in August. The East Lagoon area at Singapore was being developed at a cost of $21.6 million to take container ships.

During 1967 the Port of New York Authority spent $20.4 million on the development and construction of marine facilities, and the 1968 program totaled $27 million for further projects. Construction of the Sea-Land container terminal at Elizabeth, N.J., continued, with five new berths brought into use and five being built. On completion in 1975, this facility would have 25 deep-sea vessel berths. At Newark, N.J., work continued on construction of six new container berths. Total cargo tonnage handled by the authority rose to 8.9 million tons in 1967 (1966: 8.7 million). At Baltimore the Port Authority started work on four additional container berths, making a total of six in all. At Galveston, Tex., a $9 million terminal complex to handle container services was planned.

Canada's first container berth went into operation in the Port of Montreal, and two new berths were under construction at Halifax. Work began on the $65 million Roberts Bank Super Port Development near Vancouver, B.C., scheduled for completion in 1970. The Callao (Peru) port expansion progressed, with some new facilities coming into operation. In Argentina the government sponsored an investigation to determine a site for a new port near Buenos Aires capable of handling the world's largest tankers.

In Australia work began on the modernization of facilities at Darling Harbour, Sydney. Two inner berths of the four-berth overseas passenger terminal at Melbourne were being modernized, and the draft within the port was being increased from 31 to 44 ft. Construction of the land-backed berth at Port Hedland was completed. In New Zealand the Napier Harbour Board approved an $8,160,000 development plan.

With the Suez Canal still closed, South African ports continued to boom; Durban handled 41 million tons during the year. Several projects for port development were under consideration, including extensive facilities at Cape Town and construction of tanker ports at Richards Bay near the Portuguese border on the Natal coast and at Saldanha Bay, a magnificent natural harbour 70 mi. N of Cape Town.

Inland Waterways. Helped by good weather conditions, traffic on European inland waterways rose during 1967. On the Netherlands waterways, for example the total exceeded that for West Germany for the first time in recent years. Tonnage totaled 223 million and ton-kilometres, 28 million, representing increases of 24 million and 3 million, respectively, over the preceding year. At Rotterdam international transport of goods by inland shipping rose by 3%, from 49.9 million to 51.4 million tons, of which 45.5 million tons was related to Rhine shipping. In West Germany traffic handled totaled 214.4 million tons, but ton-kilometres were up by only 900,000. Traffic rose by 5.8 million tons in Belgium. In France tonnage increased by 4.5%; activity at the port of Strasbourg remained steady at 11.3 million tons in 1967, only slightly below that in 1966. Italy's tonnage increased 16.7%.

Freight movements across the West German-Netherlands frontier on the Rhine—a customary criterion for measuring traffic—increased 12.8% from January to October 1967, to 82.9 million tons. In Luxembourg

Inclined lift for canal traffic at Ronquières, Belg., was completed in 1968. Ships up to 1,000 tons are raised 190 ft. in 15 min.

tonnage handled through the Grevenmacher Lock on the Moselle rose to 4.8 million tons in 1967 from the 1966 total of 4.6 million tons, an increase of 4.3%. Contrary to the general trend, tonnage carried on the Swiss waterways fell by 5.9%, with traffic handled at the port of Basel declining from the 1966 total of 8.4 million tons to 7.9 million tons. Traffic on the Danube also declined, with the Austrian figures well below those for the previous year. In Yugoslavia competition from both road and rail led to a decline of more than one-third in passengers, but freight traffic rose by 4.1% and ton-kilometres by 3.5%. The relatively small amount of traffic carried on U.K. inland waterways declined even further, by 6.8% for tons carried and 18.9% for ton-kilometres. The U.S.S.R. registered an increase from 279 million tons in 1966 to 306.6 million tons in 1967.

Work on the improvement of European inland waterways progressed so satisfactorily that the ECMT decided to draw up a new map showing the latest changes. The EEC continued its efforts to formulate a common policy with regard to access to the market in inland-waterway freight transport. Proposed regulations had been submitted to the Council of Ministers by the European Commission in November 1967, and recommendations were made in September 1968 regarding measures to be taken by national governments for rationalizing capacity on inland waterways.

In West Germany development work on the Rhine between Neuburgweier–Lauterburg and St. Goar was accelerated; the first stage on the Oberwesel–St. Goar section was completed and work began on the Rüdesheim–Bingen section. The first 32-km. stretch on the Bamberg–Nürnberg section of the canal that would link the Rhine to the Danube via the Main River was opened to shipping in March 1968. Completion of this canal would make a new water connection between northwest and southeast Europe, usable by ships of up to 1,500 tons and stretching more than 3,218 km. from Rotterdam to the Black Sea.

In Belgium, because of flood damage during the winter of 1966–67, the Charleroi–Brussels (Charleroi–Clabeq section) and Basse–Sambre canals were not opened until April 1968. The gigantic inclined lift at Ronquières eliminated 28 locks, cut journey time from Antwerp to Brussels and Charleroi from 35 to 14 hours, and provided navigation for boats of 1,000 tons with a draft of 2.30 m. A new lock at Zenst was scheduled for completion in 1971. Improvements on the Ghent circular canal and its branches, to be completed in 1969, would permit navigation for boats of 2,000 tons. Work began on the New Scheldt–Rhine canal with construction of the Kreekrak Lock in the Netherlands.

After five years of radical reconstruction, the 56-km. Saimaa Canal linking Lake Saimaa in Finland with the Baltic Sea came into operation as a joint Finnish-Soviet enterprise. The canal would constitute a major artery for the transport of oil and coal for Finland's eastern regions.

In the 1967 season, the ninth of its operation, the St. Lawrence Seaway experienced a 10% decrease in tonnage from the record set in 1966; the decline, which occurred on both sections of the seaway, was caused largely by a decrease in wheat sales and a five-week shipping strike. A total of 9,603 ship transits moved 60.9 million tons of cargo through the system, of which 47.4 million tons were domestic traffic (*i.e.*, of Canadian or U.S. origin) and 13.5 million tons were foreign. Oceangoing ships carried 22.2% of the ton-

nage and lakers 77.8%, compared with 21.2 and 78.8%, respectively, for 1966. Cargoes on the Montreal–Lake Ontario section decreased 11.6% from the 1966 record, and traffic through the Welland Canal section was down 6.4 million tons. The total income of the Seaway Authority was $17.3 million, the same as in 1966. Negotiations between the U.S. and Canada on the level and sharing of tolls were concluded during the year, with Canada's share increasing from 71 to 73%. The combined net operating profit of the seaway before interest was $3.7 million, an increase of $400,-000 over 1966, while the combined net loss rose from $13,280,000 to $50 million.

Work on federally aided inland waterway projects in the U.S. during fiscal 1968 included channel and lock improvements on the Alabama, Arkansas, Ohio, and Columbia rivers. Progress was made on the Chesapeake-Delaware Canal, the cross-Florida barge canal, the Illinois Waterway, and the Mississippi Gulf outlet.

(E. A. J. D.)

See also Cities and Urban Affairs; Engineering Projects; Industrial Review; Labour Unions.

ENCYCLOPÆDIA BRITANNICA FILMS. *The Living City* (1953); *Inland Waterways* (1956); *Development of Transportation* (1958); *The Gasoline Age* (1958); *The Steam Age* (1958); *The St. Lawrence Seaway* (1959); *The Panama Canal* (1961); *The Suez Canal* (1962); *Our Shrinking World—Jet Pilot* (1964).

Trinidad and Tobago

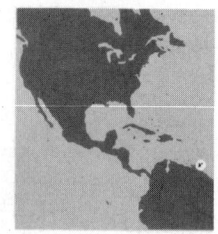

A parliamentary state and a member of the Commonwealth of Nations, Trinidad and Tobago consists of two islands off the coast of Venezuela, north of the Orinoco River delta. Area: 1,980 sq.mi. (5,128 sq.km.). Pop. (1967 est.): 1,016,000, including (1960) Negro 43.3%; East Indian 36.5%; mixed 16.3%. Cap. and largest city: Port-of-Spain (pop., 1965 est., 85,100). Language: English (official); Hindi, French, Spanish. Religion

---

TRINIDAD AND TOBAGO

Education. (1965–66) Primary, pupils 216,063, teachers 6,301; secondary (1963–64), pupils 33,641, teachers 1,017; vocational (1963–64), pupils 1,051, teachers 57; higher, students 910, teaching staff 120.

Finance and Trade. Monetary unit: Trinidad and Tobago dollar, with an exchange rate of TT$2 to U.S. $1 (TT$4.80 = £1 sterling). Budget (1967 est.): revenue TT$232.3 million; expenditure TT$225 million. Foreign trade (1967): imports TT$714.7 million; exports TT$768.2 million. Import sources: Venezuela 40%; U.S. 15%; U.K. 15%; Canada 5%. Export destinations: U.S. 43%; U.K. 13%; Sweden 6%. Main exports: petroleum and products 78%; sugar 5%.

Transport and Communications. Roads (1966) 4,067 km. Motor vehicles in use (1966): passenger 59,-200; commercial (including buses) 16,800. Shipping traffic (1966): goods loaded 18,093,000 metric tons, unloaded 13,638,000 metric tons. Air traffic (1967): 381,308,000 passenger-km.; freight 4,155,000 net ton-km. Telephones (Jan. 1967) 42,487. Radio receivers (Dec. 1966) 200,000. Television receivers (Dec. 1964) 44,000.

Agriculture. Production (in 000; metric tons; 1966; 1965 in parentheses): rice *c.* 10 (*c.* 10); sweet potatoes *c.* 15 (*c.* 15); oranges *c.* 15 (16); grapefruit *c.* 24 (29); sugar, raw value (1967–68) 248, (1966–67) 203; copra *c.* 13 (13). Livestock (in 000; 1965–66): cattle *c.* 56; pigs *c.* 43; sheep *c.* 5; poultry *c.* 950.

Industry. Production (in 000; metric tons; 1967): crude oil 9,196; petroleum products (1966) 19,550; asphalt 142.

(1960): Christian 66%; Hindu 23%; Muslim 6%. Queen, Elizabeth II; governor-general in 1968, Sir Solomon Hochoy; prime minister, Eric Williams.

During 1968 there was a rise in revenues accruing from U.S. sources, while a prices commission successfully sought to curb price increases on imports. In January Prime Minister Williams, who was also the finance minister, presented a budget providing for TT$330 million in expenditure, with decreases in income and withheld taxes but with increases in corporation and purchase taxes. Attention was drawn to the country's overdependence on oil and the relatively low level of investment and taxation.

At the end of the year, the prime minister announced plans to establish a national oil corporation and to purchase television and radio interests and the local branch of Cable and Wireless. A national lottery was established, formation of a national insurance scheme was in its concluding stages, and the Central Bank was broadening its range of activities. The Agricultural Development Bank and the Industrial Development Corporation were reorganized with assistance from the Inter-American Development Bank. The unemployment rate rose from 14 to 15%, despite a significant downturn in population growth.

A by-election in February and local government elections in June were marked by record low participation, but the opposition Democratic Labour Party brought to an end its policy of silence in the House of Representatives, begun as a protest against the use of voting machines. A shake-up was promised in the ruling People's National Movement, though its hierarchy remained unchanged at the annual party elections.

(RA. R.)

ENCYCLOPÆDIA BRITANNICA FILMS. *The West Indies* (1965).

Tunisia

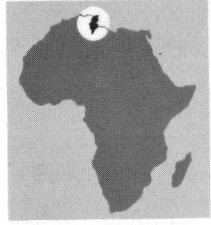

A republic of North Africa, lying on the Mediterranean Sea, Tunisia is bounded by Algeria and Libya. Area: 63,378 sq.-mi. (164,150 sq.km.). Pop. (1967): 4,560,000. Cap. and largest city: Tunis (pop., 1966, 462,979). Language: Arabic (official). Religion: Muslim; Jewish and Christian minorities. President in 1968, Habib Bourguiba.

In January the resignation of Muhammad Mestiri from his post as secretary of state for the presidency and his replacement by Bahi Ladgham was interpreted as a protest by Mestiri against President Bourguiba's decision to designate his own successor. In fact, it seemed to indicate deep disagreement between Mestiri and the president.

Student demonstrations in March led to the exclusion of five students from Tunis University, and in September the newly created State Security Court, in a trial of 134 students and teachers, passed severe sentences, giving terms of imprisonment ranging from 10 to 14 years to several of those convicted. A Neo-Destour Socialist Party report alleged that the accused had tried to overthrow the government. Throughout the year this affair continued to grow in importance because of the movement of solidarity with the students started by a number of French teachers working in Tunisia and because of the sympathy of the French left for the Tunisian students.

However, despite the expulsion of several French teachers in September, it was expected that in October France would send 3,300 teachers to Tunisia for the beginning of the new academic year. The student unrest had the result of bringing about the appointment of Ahmed ben Salah to the post of secretary of state in the Ministry of Education and the creation of the State Security Court in July.

In April a Franco-Tunisian financial agreement was signed in Paris, where Habib Bourguiba, Jr., secretary of state for foreign affairs, had stayed during the preceding month. In July two protocols to this agreement were signed. Bahi Ladgham visited Paris in October to strengthen Franco-Tunisian cooperation.

In April an agreement was signed with Algeria concerning the demarcation of their border. However, the fact that the Tunisian government had given refuge to Algerian Col. Tahar Zbiri in June, when he had been implicated in an attempt to overthrow Algerian Pres. Houari Boumédienne, annoyed the Algerian leaders, although Zbiri did not stay more than three weeks in Tunisia.

Relations with other Arab states remained poor, particularly as a result of Bourguiba's unorthodox stand in the Arab-Israeli dispute. In May Tunisia broke off diplomatic relations with Syria. In September Bourguiba decided once again to boycott the Arab League. The Tunisian president paid official visits to Canada and the United States in May. On this occasion he presented a plan for a Middle East settlement to the UN General Assembly. In July Bourguiba was the official guest of Romania, thus reaffirming his government's intention of following a policy of political nonalignment. (PH. D.)

ENCYCLOPÆDIA BRITANNICA FILMS. *Mediterranean Africa* (1952).

TUNISIA

Education. (1965–66) Primary, pupils 734,216, teachers 12,878; secondary, pupils 103,339; vocational, pupils 6,394; secondary and vocational (state only), teachers 1,293; teacher training, students 4,745; higher (including University of Tunis), students 6,230.

Finance. Monetary unit: dinar, with a parity of 0.52 dinars = U.S. $1 (1.26 dinars = £1 sterling). Gold and foreign exchange, central bank: (June 1968) U.S. $31.5 million; (June 1967) U.S. $28.7 million. Budget (1968 est.) balanced at 124 million dinars. Gross national product: (1966) 488.6 million dinars; (1965) 483.7 million dinars. Money supply: (March 1968) 152,770,000 dinars; (March 1967) 144,980,-000 dinars. Cost of living (1963 = 100): (June 1968) 120; (June 1967) 119.

Foreign Trade. (1967) Imports 137,090,000 dinars (32% from France, 25% from U.S., 8% from West Germany, 6% from Italy); exports 78,360,000 dinars (28% to France, 12% to Italy, 8% to West Germany, 5% to Libya). Main exports: phosphates 30%; crude oil 13%; olive oil 10%; wine 7%.

Transport and Communications. Roads (1967) 17,110 km. Motor vehicles in use (1967): passenger 56,602; commercial 30,864. Railways: (1966) 2,021 km.; traffic (1967) 408 million passenger-km., freight 1,188,000,000 net ton-km. Air traffic (1967): 134,-926,000 passenger-km.; freight 2,014,000 net ton-km. Telephones (Dec. 1966) 53,322. Radio receivers (Dec. 1966) c. 370,000. Television receivers (Dec. 1966) 5,500.

Agriculture. Production (in 000; metric tons; 1967; 1966 in parentheses): wheat c. 370 (459); barley c. 80 (110); wine c. 85 (126); dates (1966) 20, (1965) 54; figs (1966) 24, (1965) 20; olive oil c. 55 (22); oranges c. 80 (c. 85); lemons (1966) 14, (1965) 16. Livestock (in 000; 1965–66): sheep 3,767; cattle 592; horses c. 86; asses c. 163; mules c. 54; goats 527; camels 150; poultry c. 5,500.

Industry. Production (in 000; metric tons; 1967): iron ore (55% metal content) 918; phosphate rock (1966) 3,190; lead 13; cement 470; electricity (public supply) 488,000 kw-hr.

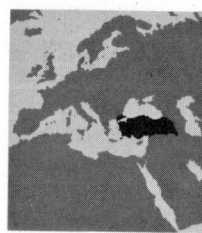

Turkey

A republic of southeastern Europe and Asia Minor, Turkey is bounded by the Aegean Sea, the Black Sea, the U.S.S.R., Iran, Iraq, Syria, the Mediterranean Sea, Greece, and Bulgaria. Area: 301,380 sq.mi. (780,576 sq.km.), including 9,158 sq.mi. in Europe. Pop. (1968): 33,539,000. Cap.: Ankara (pop., 1968, 1,082,350). Largest city: Istanbul (pop., 1965, 1,750,642). Language: Turkish 90.7%; Kurdish 6.7%; Arabic 1.3%. Religion: predominantly Muslim. President in 1968, Gen. Cevdet Sunay; prime minister, Suleyman Demirel.

Increased student militancy and decreased U.S. aid in 1968 posed some awkward problems for the Justice Party administration of Prime Minister Suleyman Demirel, but midterm Senate elections and local government elections held simultaneously on June 2 showed that the party had preserved a broad base of popular support. In the elections to fill one-third of the Senate seats, the Justice Party (JP) won 50% of the votes, as against 27% for the Republican People's Party (RPP) and 9% for the new Reliance Party, which had earlier broken away from the RPP. In the previous Senate elections, held two years earlier in a different set of constituencies, the JP's share had been 57%. In terms of seats won (JP, 38; RPP, 13), the JP benefited from an amendment to the electoral law, passed in March, which did away with the national pooling and redistribution of wasted votes ("the national residue"), changing the system to one of proportional representation in multimember constituencies. In the local government elections, the JP won 61% of the seats in provincial councils and obtained control of 56% of all the municipalities.

A few days after the elections the vast majority of university students started a boycott of classes and, in many cases, occupied academic premises. The authorities made no attempt either to eject or to penalize the students, thus avoiding any incidents, and the movement ended at the beginning of July with a number of agreements, embodying concessions to student demands and allowing approximately 80,000 students to take their end-of-year examinations a little later than usual. Nonetheless, boycotts, although on a much smaller scale, recurred when classes were resumed in October. Militant left-wing students succeeded in staging violent incidents when the U.S. 6th Fleet

Students from Istanbul University burning the North Atlantic star during the Anti-NATO Campaign Week declared in May 1968.

visited Istanbul in July, and one student was killed when the riot police occupied a university hostel. Other incidents followed: also in July, an attempt by left-wing militants to stage a rally in the conservative city of Konya, in central Turkey, led to a riot in which right-wing activists destroyed book shops, restaurants serving alcoholic drinks (forbidden to Muslims), and other examples of alien cultural influences. In August a visit by the 6th Fleet to Izmir was marked by fights between left-wing and right-wing students. While government and opposition accused each other of encouraging or condoning extremism, the National Security Council—representing the two pillars of political power in Turkey, the government and the Army—endorsed the government's policy of controlling violence without recourse to extraordinary measures.

Statements by the prime minister and the foreign minister deploring the occupation of Czechoslovakia, without, however, once naming the U.S.S.R., reflected the Turkish government's concern to avoid giving any offense to the Soviet leaders, while remaining in the NATO and CENTO alliances and working for their continued effectiveness. This policy, which was clearly

TURKEY

Education (1966–67) Primary, pupils 4,273,977, teachers 93,398; secondary, pupils 655,251, teachers 23,458; vocational, pupils 194,323, teachers 11,507; teacher training, students 54,637, teachers 1,737; higher (including 7 universities), students 60,654, teaching staff 4,217.

Finance. Monetary unit: Turkish pound or lira, with a par value of 9 lire to U.S. $1 (21.60 lire = £1 sterling). Gold and foreign exchange, central bank: (June 1968) U.S. $123 million; (June 1967) U.S. $116 million. Budget (1968–69 est.): revenue 21,112,211,000 lire; expenditure 21,612,211,000 lire. Gross national product: (1966) 92,480,000,000 lire; (1965) 79,690,000,000 lire. Money supply: (May 1968) 11,070,000,000 lire; (May 1967) 9,540,000,000 lire. Cost of living (Istanbul; 1963 = 100): (June 1968) 138; (June 1967) 133.

Foreign Trade. (1967) Imports 6,216,000,000 lire; exports 4,703,000,000 lire. Import sources: West Germany 20%; U.S. 18%; U.K. 13%; Italy 7%. Export destinations: U.S. 18%; West Germany 16%; Italy 7%; U.K. 7%; France

6%; U.S.S.R. 5%; Switzerland 5%; Japan 5%. Main exports: cotton 25%; tobacco 23%; hazelnuts 16%.

Transport and Communications. Roads (1967) 69,069 km. (including 42,000 km. allweather). Motor vehicles in use (1967): passenger 106,500; commercial 90,900. Railways (1966): 8,008 km.; traffic 4,189,000,000 passenger-km., freight 5,485,000,000 net ton-km. Shipping (1967): merchant vessels 100 gross tons and over 285; gross tonnage 611,078. Air traffic (1966): 271,855,000 passenger-km.; freight 2,603,000 net ton-km. Telephones (Dec. 1966) 385,560. Radio receivers (Dec. 1966) 2,637,000. Television receivers (Dec. 1966) c. 2,500.

Agriculture. Production (in 000; metric tons; 1967; 1966 in parentheses): wheat (including spelt) 10,940 (9,715); barley 4,500 (3,800); oats 510 (510); corn 1,000 (1,000); rye 980 (850); onions (1966) 450, (1965) 450; potatoes (1966) 1,750, (1965) 1,680; sunflower seed (1966) 200, (1965) 160; chick-peas (1966) 89, (1965) 89; dry beans (1966) 138, (1965) 142;

lentils (1966) 100, (1965) 90; oranges 375 (360); lemons 90 (85); apples 500 (440); pears 182 (135); grapes 2,900 (3,100); raisins (1966) 250, (1965) 389; figs (1966) 215, (1965) 210; sugar, raw value (1967–68) c. 793, (1966–67) 701; olive oil c. 70 (155); tobacco (1966) 168, (1965) 132; cotton, lint c. 385 (382); linseed c. 13 (11); meat (1966) 188, (1965) 197. Livestock (in 000; Dec. 1966): cattle 13,232; sheep 34,663; horses (Dec. 1965) 1,199; mules (Dec. 1965) 225; asses (Dec. 1965) 1,971; buffaloes 1,253; goats 20,932; camels 43; chickens (Dec. 1965) 28,687.

Industry. Fuel and power (in 000; metric tons; 1967): crude oil 2,320; coal 5,030; lignite 3,420; electricity 6,300,000 kw-hr. Production (in 000; metric tons; 1967): iron ore (55–60% metal content) 1,527; pig iron 847; crude steel 996; copper 8; sulfur (1966) 58; sulfuric acid 28; cement 4,237; superphosphates (1966) 222; manganese ore (metal content; 1966) 8.2; chrome ore (oxide content; 1966) 277; cotton yarn 127; woven cotton fabrics 710,000 m.; wool yarn 24.

stated in the communiqué on the visit to Turkey of West German Chancellor Kurt Georg Kiesinger in September, was endorsed by the main opposition Republican People's Party. Nor was Turkey's support for a unified NATO command structure weakened by the state visit paid by French Pres. Charles de Gaulle at the end of October. But while the opposition leader, Ismet Inonu, advocated official Turkish neutrality in the Arab-Israeli dispute, the state visits paid by the Turkish president, Cevdet Sunay, to Saudi Arabia, Libya, Iraq, and Afghanistan were marked by a reiteration of Turkish support for "legitimate" Arab rights, as defined in UN resolutions.

Tension over Cyprus decreased following the decision taken in March by the government of President Makarios of Cyprus to lift all restrictions on the Turkish Cypriot community. On April 13, Rauf Denktash, chairman of the Turkish-Cypriot Communal Chamber, was allowed to return to the island, and, after a meeting between the Turkish and the Cypriot foreign ministers in May, the way was opened to direct talks between the two communities. Thereafter, the Turkish government gave the talks every encouragement, while reserving its rights under the 1959–60 settlement and announcing that for its part it would initiate a plan of economic aid for Turkish Cypriots. There was a parallel improvement in relations with Greece. On January 20 Turkey became the first NATO country to recognize the military regime in Athens after the failure of King Constantine's countercoup. On August 15 an agreement on minorities came into force, allowing Greeks in Turkey and Turks in Greece to be taught in their own languages.

The U.S. decision, announced in January, to reduce aid to Turkey from $135 million to $60 million endangered imports necessary to implement the second five-year plan. However, as aid from other sources, including the U.S.S.R., was maintained, and as there was a residue of unspent credit, progress in 1968 was not seriously impaired. The survey published in July by the Organization for Economic Cooperation and Development stated that 1967 had been another year of rapid growth, with real GNP rising by over 6.5%; the organization forecast further growth in 1968. The report called for greater efforts to develop Turkish exports, and in September the authorities announced measures to supply exporters with cheaper credits and to decrease their tax liability. (A. J. A. M.)

See also Cyprus; Greece.

ENCYCLOPÆDIA BRITANNICA FILMS. *The Middle East* (1955); *Turkey: Emergence of a Modern Nation* (1963).

Uganda

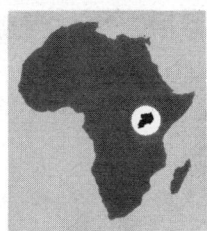

A federal parliamentary state and a member of the Commonwealth of Nations, Uganda is bounded by the Sudan, the Congo (Kinshasa), Rwanda, Tanzania, and Kenya. Area: 91,076 sq.mi. (235,886 sq.km.), including 16,364 sq.mi. of inland water. Pop. (1967 est.): 7,934,000, about 99% of whom are African. Cap. and largest city: Kampala (pop., 1965 est., 76,597). Language: Bantu, Nilotic, Nilo-Hamitic, and Sudanic. Religion: pagan, with Hindu, Muslim, and Christian minorities. President and prime minister in 1968, Apollo Milton Obote.

Disturbances along the Sudan border continued to worry the government, and in May the defense minister, Felix Onama, protested to the Organization of African Unity (OAU) about alleged raids into Uganda from the Sudan. It was claimed that Sudanese troops had pursued rebels from that country into Uganda territory and had even become involved in fighting against Uganda forces.

In Uganda itself, rumours of an army plot to overthrow the government were vigorously disclaimed by President Obote, as well as by the army commander, Maj. Gen. Idi Amin. Observers, however, were unable to agree as to whether the political situation was becoming more relaxed. The release from detention in October of Prince Simbwa, brother of the former kabaka of Buganda (a part of Uganda) who had been held since the time of the kabaka's overthrow, and three Buganda chiefs aroused some hopes of a relaxation of tension. These, however, were sharply reversed later in the month with the arrest and detention of Rajat Neogy, editor of the magazine *Transition*, and of Abubaker Mayanja, a former minister of education in the kabaka's government.

Peace talks between representatives of the federal government of Nigeria and of the breakaway state of Biafra were held in Kampala in May. President Obote took an active part in the proceedings, which failed, however, to reach a satisfactory conclusion. Three weeks earlier a disagreement between leaders of Uganda's labour movement grew so serious that it became necessary for the minister of internal affairs, Basil Bataringaya, to close the offices of the Uganda Labour Congress in Kampala.

It was announced in August that the U.S.S.R. had presented the Uganda government with a number of jet fighter aircraft to swell the Uganda Air Force,

MARION KAPLAN

A Tutsi instructor teaching math to Rwandan refugee children in an open-air school at Kyangwali, Uganda, where refugees were received during 1968.

UGANDA
Education. (1965) Primary, pupils 526,833, teachers 16,319; secondary, pupils 68,946, teachers 930; vocational, pupils 3,219, teachers 333; teacher training, students 3,883, teachers 269; higher (at the Makerere University College of the University of East Africa), students 1,240.

Finance. Monetary unit: Uganda shilling, with a par value of UShs. 7.14 to U.S. $1 (UShs. 17.14 = £1 sterling). Budget (1967–68 est.): revenue UShs. 880 million; expenditure UShs. 722 million. Gross domestic product: (1966) UShs. 4,852,000,000; (1965) UShs. 4,460,000,000. Cost of living (Kampala; 1963 = 100): (June 1968) 123; (June 1967) 132.

Foreign Trade. (Excluding trade with Kenya and Tanganyika; 1967) Imports UShs. 826 million; exports UShs. 1,311,000,000. Import sources: U.K. 34%; West Germany 13%; U.S. 7%; Japan 6%; Italy 5%. Export destinations: U.K. 23%; U.S. 21%; Japan 9%. Main exports: coffee 53%; cotton 23%; copper 8%.

Transport and Communications. Roads (1966) 24,000 (including c. 12,000 km. all-weather). Motor vehicles in use (1966): passenger 25,265; commercial 11,152. Railways (1966) 850 km. (for traffic *see* KENYA). Telephones (Dec. 1966) 21,089. Radio receivers (Dec. 1965) 200,000. Television receivers (Dec. 1965) 5,800.

Agriculture. Production (in 000; metric tons; 1966; 1965 in parentheses): sweet potatoes c. 1,500 (c. 1,600); cassava c. 1,500 (c. 1,480); dry beans c. 140 (c. 160); cotton, lint (1967) c. 78, (1966) 81; coffee c. 185 (220); tea 11.2 (8.4); peanuts c. 163 (c. 163); sugar, raw value (1967) 149, (1966) 139; sesame c. 30 (c. 30); timber (1965–66) c. 10,800 cu.m., (1964–65) c. 10,800 cu.m. Livestock (in 000; Jan. 1966): cattle 3,627; sheep 791; goats 1,998; pigs c. 20; chickens c. 9,500. Fish catch (in 000; metric tons) (1966) 83, (1965) 76.

Industry. Production (in 000; metric tons; 1967): cement 140; copper, smelter 14; tin concentrates (metal content) 0.1; beryl (exports) 0.31; salt (1966) 6; phosphate rock (1966) 16; electricity 704,000 kw-hr.

Turks and Caicos Islands: *see* Dependent States

which had recently been brought into being with the assistance of Israel, Czechoslovakia, and the U.S.S.R.

Figures for Uganda's economic performance in 1967 showed an improved trading position compared with 1966 and an increased export balance of £21 million. The main area of growth was in the manufacturing sector, while in agriculture improvement in the output of tea, tobacco, and sugar only served to offset the disappointing coffee and cotton crops. At a summit meeting of leaders of East and Central Africa held in Kampala in December 1967, it was agreed that the 12 nations represented would, whenever possible, buy manufactured goods from other African countries in preference to making purchases outside Africa. In the same month the Treaty for East African Cooperation became effective. The treaty established the East African Community, comprising Kenya, Uganda, and Tanzania. The treaty also provided for a common market among the three nations. An East African Development Bank was set up under the treaty and was opened in July 1968 in Kampala with an initial capital of £20 million. (K. I.)

ENCYCLOPÆDIA BRITANNICA FILMS. *East Africa (Kenya, Tanganyika, Uganda)* (1962).

Union of Soviet Socialist Republics

The Union of Soviet Socialist Republics is a federal state covering parts of eastern Europe and northern and central Asia. Area: 8,649,489 sq.mi. (22,402,200 sq.km.). Pop. (1968 est.): 235,543,000, including Russians 55%; Ukrainians 18%; Belorussians 4%; Uzbeks 3%; Tatars 2%. Cap. and largest city: Moscow (pop., 1967 est., 6,507,000). Language: officially Russian, but many others are spoken. Religion: some 40 religions are represented in the U.S.S.R., the major ones being Christian denominations. General secretary of the Communist Party of the Soviet Union in 1968, Leonid I. Brezhnev; chairman of the Presidium of the Supreme Soviet (president), Nikolai V. Podgorny; chairman of the Council of Ministers (premier), Aleksei N. Kosygin.

The year 1968 in the Soviet Union was one of ideological toughness, a reinforcement of orthodox Communist doctrine that was marked above all in external affairs by the military intervention in Czechoslovakia in August. This invasion took place in accordance with a new Soviet doctrine about the "international duty" of socialist countries to intervene in situations to protect the gains of socialism, wherever they may be threatened.

The year thus demonstrated a halt in the U.S.S.R. to the processes of democratization and liberalization, which had already been noticeably slowed down during preceding years. This hard line was in evidence as early as January with the harsh sentences pronounced by a Moscow court against the writers Aleksandr Ginzburg, Yuri Galanskov, and their friends. It was not only the severity of these sentences (five and seven years' imprisonment) that was disturbing to the Soviet liberals, but, above all, the fact that the trial was not open to the general public; foreign observers were excluded, and numerous irregularities in the conduct of the proceedings were reported. The prosecution attacked the accused for collusion with the Narodno-Trudovoi Soyuz (NTS), an anti-Soviet emigrants' organization dealing in espionage and ideological subversion. In this way the authorities were trying to indict the NTS, to isolate the accused from their fellow writers, and carefully to avoid any discussion of the basic problems, especially those concerning freedom of artistic expression. The accused denied the charges against them, and the prosecution was unable to offer formal and public proof of any guilty association with the NTS. Nevertheless, the "confession" of Aleksei Dobrovolsky, one of the accused, and the suspect "evidence" of a student awaiting trial for his cooperation with the NTS (he eventually benefited from a reprieve) persuaded the court to bring in a verdict of guilty.

The sentences created a considerable stir in intel-

PICTORIAL PARADE

Soviet TU-16 medium-range bomber photographed in low flight near the USS "Essex" just before it crashed and burned May 25, 1968, off the coast of Norway. Plane allegedly buzzed U.S. ships during training exercises.

lectual and scientific circles. Petitions flowed in, first demanding that the proceedings of the trial be made public and then appealing for reprieves. This wave of demands worried the authorities. Among the most outspoken authors of the petitions were Pavel Litvinov, grandson of a former minister of foreign affairs, and Larisa Bogoraz-Daniel, wife of an imprisoned writer. Both were eventually arrested and sentenced in October to five and four years in exile, respectively, for having helped organize a small and short demonstration in Red Square against the Soviet intervention in Czechoslovakia. In the trials of Litvinov and Mrs. Bogoraz-Daniel the authorities once again avoided any discussion of basic political problems, and the charges against the two related solely to disorder on the public highway and libel against the Soviet Union. This time, however, some publicity for the trial was ensured, first by means of an official who reported the proceedings in the court to foreign journalists and second because of information "leaks" to which the authorities apparently turned a blind eye. The defense and statements by the accused were consequently given wide coverage abroad. By their gesture Litvinov and Mrs. Bogoraz-Daniel expressed publicly a feeling of condemnation of the action against Czechoslovakia shared by the vast majority of Soviet intellectuals.

Reinforcement of Orthodox Ideology. The events that shook Eastern Europe from the beginning of the year constituted the major concern of the Soviet leaders. They believed that the trend toward liberalization, especially in Czechoslovakia, would prove contagious and possibly become a threat in their own country. As a result, the plenum of the Central Committee, meeting in April, once more adjourned the debate on agriculture and concentrated its work on ideological questions. Without even waiting for the meeting of this group, Brezhnev, in a speech on March 29, had initiated a campaign of "ideological rectification," and he denounced the leading heresies of nationalism and "revisionism." This denunciation was directed not only at the Romanians and the Czechoslovaks but also at those in the Soviet Union who, in official terms, "lack political maturity." Those who hoped for the building of socialism under conditions of political liberty were accused of, consciously or otherwise, playing into the hands of the "class enemy." In short, the official directive was: no peaceful coexistence in the ideological field. Brezhnev emphasized the need for a strengthening of discipline, an "iron" discipline, which, he declared, was needed as much today as in the historic moments of the revolutionary struggle in the 1920s.

Thus, Moscow replied by a hardening of its line to the liberal developments that had taken place in Eastern Europe. Immediately after the April meeting a purge began inside the Communist Party, affecting many writers and artists. But unlike previous purges this was mild, though it affected not only persons who had signed petitions and manifestos, but also those who strayed from the orthodox line. The authorities asked only for retractions from signatories to petitions and for an agreement from the others to conform. Basically, what the government wanted was to set off a reflex of self-criticism. Among those excluded from the party were such men as Nikolai Karinakin and the writer Grigori Sverski, both of whom had violently attacked censorship, and also the critic Lev Kopelev, who had denounced tendencies toward a rehabilitation of Stalin. Mathematicians were also purged, particularly those at Moscow University, where numerous petitions had circulated, notably one on behalf of the

KEYSTONE

Pres. Ludvik Svoboda of Czechoslovakia (left) raising bouquet with Soviet Communist Party leader Leonid I. Brezhnev in gesture of friendship during summit meeting in Bratislava, Czech., Aug. 7, 1968. Aleksei N. Kosygin (behind Svoboda) and Alexander Dubcek (right) attended with other officials of both countries.

poet-mathematician Aleksandr Yesenin-Volpin, who had been imprisoned. There were, in fact, hardly any retractions, but the atmosphere of surveillance discouraged artistic creation.

The Aleksandr Solzhenitsyn affair illustrated the difficulties of the writer's condition in the U.S.S.R. Solzhenitsyn (*see* BIOGRAPHY), a leading author, had protested in April against the foreign publishers who had issued certain of his works without his permission. Despite this protest, in June *Literaturnaya Gazeta*, official organ of the Soviet Writers' Union, published a violent attack, accusing him of ignoring the warnings given by the union, of not protesting against the anti-Soviet use made of his writings, and of not dissociating himself publicly from the ideological enemies of the Soviet Union. In short, they accused Solzhenitsyn of having, consciously or unconsciously, played into the hands of bourgeois propaganda. The union did not expel Solzhenitsyn, but it prevented the publication of his work in the U.S.S.R.

The official attitude to cultural problems was fairly clearly defined by Brezhnev in April. At the School Teachers' Congress he admitted the need for variety in styles, forms, and techniques, and he emphasized that the Communist Party opposed "any attempt to efface the individual qualities of each artist." But at the same time he set limits to this creative freedom: "The party and the people," he said, "only demand that a work of art should represent the great historical achievements of the Soviet people and educate mankind in the spirit of the great Communist ideology." And he denounced "one-sided description of the negative aspects of the building of socialism, which our opponents would like to place at the summit of free artistic creation. . . ." More than ever the official directive was one of vigilance toward bourgeois ideologists, who attempted to export "openly or secretly, anti-communism, nationalism, and individualism."

There was great concern during the year about the attitude of young people and, more especially, about.

continued on page 766

CRISIS IN THE COMMUNIST WORLD

By François Fejto

Agence France-Presse

Certainly since the Sino-Soviet split of 1963, no event produced such serious upheavals within the international Communist movement as the challenge offered to Moscow by democratization in Czechoslovakia and the firm way in which the U.S.S.R. and its four closest allies—Poland, East Germany, Hungary, and Bulgaria—replied to it on August 20–21. The use of force against socialist Czechoslovakia produced a new demarcation line that would henceforth set a wide gap between the Warsaw Pact group and the Communist parties of the capitalist West.

On the eve of the Czechoslovak crisis the Soviet Union was involved in two far-reaching parallel operations. The first aimed to reestablish the unity and the cohesion of those Communist parties that had remained within the Soviet orbit following the breakaway of China, and the second to reinforce the discipline of the Warsaw Pact, which had been disrupted by the semi-dissidence of Romania. And it quite soon appeared that there were considerable difficulties in harmonizing the means used to achieve these two aims. As far as the international movement was concerned, the failure of Khrushchev's efforts at a collective condemnation of the Chinese heresy taught his successors that unity was no longer possible except in diversity. After many years of opposition to the "polycentrist" theses of the Italians and the Yugoslavs, the Kremlin leaders at last realized that their only hope of regaining preeminence lay in renouncing their former supremacy, at least at the beginning and in the formal sense.

It was in this open-minded and undogmatic mood that the Soviet Union in 1967 developed its campaign to organize a new international conference to set the seal on the rediscovered unity of the movement. Without overcoming the reluctance of all those concerned—especially of the Yugoslavs, Romanians, and Japanese—the increased flexibility of their approach brought results. The representatives of 18 Communist parties, gathering in Moscow for the celebration of the 50th anniversary of the October Revolution (November 1967), revived the proposal for an international conference. A preparatory consultative meeting was called in Budapest at the end of February 1968, and of the 81 parties invited 67 sent representatives. Admittedly the absence of 6 of the 14 parties in power, and of almost all the Asian parties, diminished the significance of the meeting; and the spectacular walkout of the Romanians, in reply to the criticism directed against their "chauvinist and isolationist attitude" by the Syrians, spotlighted the difficulties of the undertaking. It was continued nonetheless, and a further meeting at the end of April —this time without the Romanians—fixed the date of the conference for November 25 in Moscow.

At the same time, however, in contradiction to its assertions of belief in pluralism, the Kremlin was showing an "interventionist" attitude toward Czechoslovakia, which had set out in search of a new road after the fall of Antonin Novotny. The Dresden conference in March 1968, to which the new Czechoslovak leaders had been called to give an account of themselves, was the start of a whole series of discussions terminating, after the failure of various types of pressure, in the occupation of Czechoslovakia by the troops of the "Five" and revealing the very relative nature of the way in which the U.S.S.R. observed the principles of sovereignty and noninterference.

Separate Development. The Sino-Soviet split had highlighted the fundamental socioeconomic, historical, and cultural disunity between the U.S.S.R. and China. From the Chinese point of view (shared by Latin-American Castroites and many "third world" revolutionaries) the Soviet leadership appeared to be presiding over a revisionist country, in process of becoming bourgeois. But the Czechoslovak threat was directed against another aspect, the backward and backward-looking characteristics of the Soviet Union. It expressed the rejection by the Eastern European countries, with their distinctive traditions and structures, of the transplant of the ponderous bureaucratic system of the U.S.S.R.

No doubt the Kremlin apologists were not entirely wrong in pointing to nationalism as the common characteristic of the Chinese and Czechoslovak, as well as Romanian and Yugoslav, deviations. This did not alter the fact that the two challenges combined to bring about a sort of return to Stalinism in the Soviet Union. China's ceaseless condemnation of revisionism obliged Soviet leaders to emphasize the Marxist-Leninist purity of their doctrine and the primacy that they were giving to the anti-imperialist struggle. In fact, Czechoslovak de-Stalinization gathered strength at the very moment when Soviet policy, particularly regarding party relations with the intelligentsia, was in process of returning to the habits and forms of the Stalinist era. The fear aroused by developments in Czechoslovakia accentuated this tendency. It was this growing divergence in the political and social climates in Czechoslovakia and the U.S.S.R. that explained the "misunderstandings" mentioned by Alexander Dubcek and his companions, and that they tried in vain to dispel during their many meetings with the Soviet leaders and their allies between January and August 1968.

The Meaning of the Czechoslovak Challenge. The Soviet, East German, and Polish leaders betrayed a pessimism on the subject of the new road adopted by Czechoslovakia from the very start, and this pessimism was derived much more from a priori considerations than from the situation and the real balance of forces prevailing in Czechoslovakia. The Czechoslovak leaders, although aware of the risks they were taking by relaxing restrictions, were convinced right to the very end that they would be able to "exercise political leadership otherwise than by bureaucratic and police methods," through a "just policy, supported by the population as a whole."

Unfortunately for Dubcek, the Soviet leaders could see only the dangers involved in the experiment. They were convinced that democratization, and in particular freedom of speech, could lead only to counterrevolution. They were further irritated by Czechoslovakia's claim that it had discovered a perfected, civilized, and attractive model of socialism. It was all very well for the Czechoslovaks to insist that they were not pretending that their actions were universally valid and that they were merely exercising the right, recognized by the U.S.S.R., of adapting the socialist system to the conditions of their country: conservative leaders in all the Communist countries could detect a repudiation of their policies in the harsh criticism contained in the Czechoslovak action program. The chief factor that caused the downfall of the Dubcek team was the power of seduction and encouragement in their program of "humanist socialism" for all who aspired to progress in the other countries of the bloc.

It would be wrong also to underestimate the importance of the strategic and economic interest represented for the Kremlin in the control, through intermediaries, of Czechoslovakia. Until recent years Czechoslovakia had been the U.S.S.R.'s most faithful ally—and an unconditional ally. So, although the aims of Dubcek and his team in the field of foreign policy and trade were moderate in comparison with those of Romania, they foreshadowed a change of direction. As democratization proceeded, the traditional sympathies of the Czechs and Slovaks for the West were exposed. Demonstrations of solidarity with the Yugoslavs and the Romanians revealed the outlines of a rebirth of the *petite entente* of former times. Admittedly, only someone showing a very crude understanding of politics could have seen in this an

immediate danger for the U.S.S.R., or one that could not have been warded off by political means. But the Soviet leaders, especially the military leaders, were known to be already exasperated by the many insubordinate acts of the Romanians, and Walter Ulbricht and Wladyslaw Gomulka incited them to intransigence. Ideological passion was all that was needed to bring the Kremlin around to the use of force to put a strong brake on the disintegration of their territorial and doctrinal legacy.

New Doctrine, New Disagreements. The operation was carried out on August 20–21 in the form of a lightning invasion, the technical virtuosity of which excited the admiration and envy of strategists throughout the world (*see* DEFENSE). Its success was all the more complete since the Czechoslovaks, demonstrating considerable realism and discipline, offered no armed resistance. At very little cost (about 150 dead on the Czechoslovak side) the U.S.S.R. demonstrated that it was no less able in 1968 than in 1956 to maintain the Soviet order in central Europe, and to do so without endangering its "peaceful coexistence" with the Western powers.

The problem was to dress up in the unsullied garments of Marxism-Leninism, for the benefit of sister parties, this "restoration of certain elements of Stalinist bloc policy" and this new act of hegemony. A new doctrine of "limited sovereignty" and of "double responsibility" had been worked out progressively from the spring and expressed in the letter of the "Five" to the Czechoslovak Central Committee on July 15:

Our parties must answer for their actions not only to their own working-class, but also to the international working-class and to the international Communist movement. . . . We must join together for the defense of the achievements of socialism, of our security, and of our international position.

This implied the right of intervention in cases where "the essential common interests of other socialist countries" were threatened by developments in one of their number and was what Soviet ideologists were subsequently to certify as "a truly Marxist-Leninist interpretation of sovereignty." But all their dialectic acrobatics were not enough to divert attention from the fact that the new doctrine was utterly incompatible with the "Leninist" principles of sovereignty and noninterference, which were reaffirmed in other respects.

To dilute the arbitrary character of their theoretical construction, the Soviets attempted to justify the intervention by an "appeal for aid" that had allegedly been made to them. But as they were unable to produce any authors of this appeal, the argument —the emptiness of which even Fidel Castro denounced—rebounded against them. In addition, Communists of other countries were unable to admit that a "counterrevolutionary" situation had existed in Czechoslovakia on the eve of the intervention. Finally, the unanimous and prolonged resistance of the official media, of Communist militants, and of the Czech and Slovak people, transformed the military success into a political fiasco that seriously damaged Soviet prestige and aggravated divisions in the international Communist movement.

Two socialist countries—Romania and Yugoslavia—protested officially and rejected the "new doctrine." The least one might say was that the Soviet action increased their mistrust of their powerful ally. The fear spread to the Albanian leaders, who hastened to strengthen their links with China. Thus the Balkans —with the Bulgarians fully underwriting the Soviet line—had once more become a region of dangerous tensions and rivalries. The overriding factor in Eastern Europe, as at the time of the Middle East war, was the solidarity of small nations, which had been assaulted and humiliated, against the "superpower," which had just led their governments into an unnatural participation in the repression. Moreover, the most Russophile of central European peoples, the Czechoslovaks, henceforth would be violently anti-Soviet.

Paradoxically, while China attacked the Soviet action as "social-imperialist," and saw in it a further outcome of Soviet-U.S. collusion for the division of the world, Moscow obtained the approval of three Communist governments that attach great importance to their independence: those of North Vietnam, North Korea, and Cuba. Nevertheless, in these countries the opinion prevailed that the intervention would result in the U.S.S.R.'s taking on a stronger engagement toward the resolutely anti-imperialist Communist countries, and in a reinforcement inside the Soviet bloc of barriers against revisionism. The Vietnamese, Koreans, and Cubans tended to see Czechoslovak revisionism as an extension of Khrushchevism, which symbolized to them the drift of Soviet society toward a bourgeois way of life.

It was precisely the anti-Khrushchevite and antiprogressive nature of the Soviet action that so deeply disturbed relationships between Moscow and the Communist parties of the West. These parties, especially in France and Italy, had long sought to reconcile their traditional regard for the primacy of Moscow with the desire to develop strategy and tactics adapted to conditions in their own countries. In their protests one could detect nuances and vacillations explicable by the weight of tradition and by the fact that a considerable number of rank-and-file militants were loath to break with the comforting myth of Kremlin infallibility.

Neither the Italian nor the French Communist parties denounced the dictatorial terms of the Soviet-Czechoslovak agreements of August 26 and October 16. Nor did the Western parties take full advantage of the means of bringing pressure to bear on the U.S.S.R. represented by the Soviet desire to organize the international conference. Instead of making their participation in the conference depend on the withdrawal from Czechoslovakia of the Warsaw Pact troops, they were satisfied, when a further meeting of the preparatory commission was held in November, by an adjournment of the conference until May 1969. But the fixing of even this represented a success for the Soviets.

This success, however, was more apparent than real. A few days before the meeting of the Budapest commission, at the congress of the Polish party, Gomulka brutally insisted on the "special role of the parties of the socialist countries," which constitute "the main strength of socialism and the main support for working-class and national liberation movements." Thus, in place of the concept of the "leading party," which they had rejected, Western Communist parties were offered that of the primacy of the socialist camp—a concept all the less acceptable since it concerned a remarkably diminished camp, with only 5 of the 14 socialist countries effectively belonging to it.

Furthermore, an increasing number of Western Communists had realized that what had just been condemned in Czechoslovakia was basically the line that they themselves were defending. In June 1948 all the Communist parties joined in the condemnation of the Yugoslav heresy. In November 1956 the crushing of the Hungarian uprising produced some upheavals, but no Western party protested publicly. In August 1968 all (with the exception of the West German Communists) expressed objections. During this time all these parties, following in the footsteps of the most imaginative of them, the Italian party, had become more closely integrated into the reality of the situations in their countries and had undertaken revisions of doctrine, both for tactical reasons and from conviction. Aiming for "unity of the left," they repeatedly declared, for the benefit of the public and of their potential allies, their desire of ensuring "the transition to socialism with plurality of parties and in democracy." Czechoslovak democratization, compensating for unhappy memories of the "Prague coup" of 1948, added to the credibility of their statements.

Whether they liked it or not, the Communist parties of Western Europe were now forced to admit that the myth of the identification of their interests, and of the working-class interests they hoped to represent, with those of the Soviet Union had had its day. Unless they were to recant, they could not accept the doctrine of "limited sovereignty" and of the "primacy of the 'Five.'" These parties would be increasingly vulnerable to the tendency to nationalize Communism, which first had appeared in Communist countries in direct contact with Soviet hegemony— Yugoslavia, China, Albania, and eventually Czechoslovakia.

continued from page 763

Union of Soviet Socialist Republics

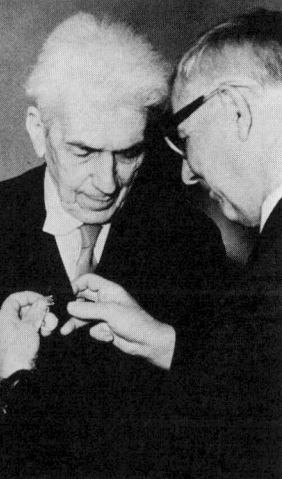

CAMERA PRESS—PIX FROM PUBLIX

Soviet Academician
P. N. Fedoseyev (right)
awarding Endre Sik,
chairman of the Hungarian
National Peace Council,
the 1968 International
Lenin Peace Prize.

the gaps in the ideological education of the young. The estrangement, indifference, and lack of concern about politics of many young people were attacked again and again in the newspapers. In June there was a major reshuffle of the leadership of the Komsomol (All-Union Leninist Communist League of Youth). Sergei Pavlov lost the post of first secretary of the organization, which he had held for nine years, and his closest collaborators were also dismissed.

This reorganization in no way pointed to a move toward liberalization but on the contrary represented a tougher policy and a reassertion of government control over the Komsomol. Evidently, the serious defects that had been revealed in the political education of the young were thought to demand new men, able to understand the aspirations of a younger generation with concerns seemingly different from those of their counterparts 20 years ago. In fact, the younger age groups were still excluded from leading state bodies: while more than 50% of party members were between 35 and 45, in high organizations only the secretary of the Central Committee belonged to that age group. The party remained under the leadership of "old men."

Despite the military intervention in Czechoslovakia there was no change in the U.S.S.R.'s top government positions, in spite of rumours that one or more of the leaders were to be made scapegoats for the insufficiently prepared Czechoslovak operation. Until the October plenum the government maintained complete silence on the subject of the military action of August 20–21, and at the year's end it was still not known by whom the decision to invade was taken. The intervention, together with the whole of Soviet foreign policy, was finally officially approved by the plenum of the Central Committee in October. But experienced observers were convinced that there had been a bitter struggle within the Politburo between those who favoured and opposed the military action. It was reported that the Army finally tipped the scales in favour of intervention. (*See* Special Report.)

Industry and Agriculture. In internal affairs there was no change in the major economic policies. After considerable delay a consultative conference, bringing together representatives of ministries and administrative bodies, economists, and heads of firms, met in Moscow in the spring to assess the current industrial

reforms and to outline future developments. The discussion, though academic, was instructive about the reforms, which continued to spread. The number of firms and enterprises working under the new system of planning and economic incentives reached more than 25,000 by late 1968, and they represented about half the total industrial output of the country. Nonetheless, it appeared that the reform had run into difficulties: certain directors of concerns were unable to change their routines and take on their new responsibilities. There was also opposition at the top between the "orthodox" economists, who were worried by the undermining of centralized planning, and the "modernists," who wanted to see further reductions in the powers of the central administration so that business enterprises could be run under a system by which they would pay their own way completely. Yevsei Liberman, chief instigator of the reform, was attacked by his opponents in February. They denounced the idea of profit and emphasized the importance of central planning and of price control. But Liberman held to all his positions in the belief that ideas of profit and competition should not be rejected and that they in no way implied a return to capitalism, because they were conceived in a different context. (*See* Economic Planning: *Special Report.*)

However, despite the efforts of the government, serious economic failings remained, particularly in the areas of consumer goods and production of articles for ordinary consumption. Soviet workers, whose average wages in cash had risen by 18% since 1963, according to official statistics, were not able to utilize fully their increased buying power despite the fact that the government had devoted more than 1 billion rubles to the production of clothing, washing machines, and refrigerators. Moreover, in a speech in Minsk in February Premier Kosygin admitted that the Soviet Union was still behind the United States both in amount of industrial output and in productivity. According to him there was still insufficient organization and efficiency in Soviet industrial production, and the quality of many products left much to be desired.

Brezhnev showed comparable frankness on the subject of agriculture when speaking to the Central Committee in October. He admitted notorious insufficiencies in cattle raising, construction of agricultural machinery, and the returns from *sovkhozes* (state pilot

---

U.S.S.R.

Education. (1965–66) Primary, pupils 38,-343,000, teachers 1,449,000; secondary, pupils 4.8 million, teachers 251,000; vocational (including teacher training), pupils 3,659,300, teachers 134,000; higher (including 45 universities), students 3,860,500, teaching staff 201,000.

Finance. Monetary unit: ruble, with an exchange rate of 0.90 rubles to U.S. $1 (2.16 rubles = £1 sterling). Budget (1968 est.): revenue 123,-912,000,000 rubles; expenditure 123,604,000,000 rubles.

Foreign Trade. (1966) Imports 7,122,000,000 rubles; exports 7,957,000,000 rubles. Import sources: Sino-Soviet area 64% (East Germany 16%, Czechoslovakia 12%, Poland 9%, Bulgaria 8%, Hungary 6%, Romania 5%). Export destinations: Sino-Soviet area 64% (East Germany 16%, Czechoslovakia 10%, Poland 9%, Bulgaria 8%, Hungary 6%, Cuba 5%). Main exports: machinery 21%; iron and steel 8%; crude oil 7%; timber 7%.

Transport and Communications. Roads (1965) 1,363,500 km. (including 379,000 km. surfaced). Motor vehicles in use (1965): passenger *c.* 1.1 million; commercial *c.* 4.5 million. Railways (1966): 132,500 km. (including 27,000 km.

electrified); traffic 219,400,000,000 passenger-km., freight 2,016,031,000,000 net ton-km. Navigable inland waterways: (1965) 142,700 km.; freight (1966) 137,582,000,000 ton-km. Shipping (1967): merchant vessels 100 gross tons and over 2,238; gross tonnage 10,617,418. Telephones (Dec. 1966) *c.* 7.9 million. Radio receivers (Dec. 1966) *c.* 76.8 million. Television receivers (Dec. 1966) 19 million.

Agriculture. Production (in 000; metric tons; 1967; 1966 in parentheses): wheat 77,300 (100,-499); barley 24,600 (27,879); oats 11,500 (9,-199); rye 13,000 (13,146); corn 9,100 (8,416); rice 890 (712); millet 3,200 (3,101); potatoes 94,995 (87,853); sugar, raw value (1967–68) 10,174, (1966–67) *c.* 8,966; cotton, lint (1966) 2,045, (1965) 1,937; flax fibre (1966) 461, (1965) 480; tobacco (1966) *c.* 235, (1965) *c.* 194; sunflower seed 6,587 (6,150); dry peas (1966) *c.* 4,738, (1965) *c.* 4,625; soybeans *c.* 610 (586); tea (1966) 55, (1965) 45; wine 1,780 (1,586); wool (1966) 223, (1965) 214; eggs (1966) 1,742, (1965) 1,596; meat (1966) 7,866, (1965) 7,246; milk (1966) 76,000, (1965) 72,563; butter (1966) 1,157, (1965) 1,184; timber (1966) *c.* 373,400 cu.m., (1965)

c. 378,100 cu.m. Livestock (in 000; Jan. 1966): cattle 93,028; pigs 59,576; sheep 129,764; goats 5,552; horses 7,977; poultry 490,508. Fish catch (in 000; metric tons) (1966) 5,349, (1965) 5,100.

Industry. Fuel and power (in 000; metric tons; 1967): coal and lignite 594,900; crude oil 288,-000; natural gas 158,400,000 cu.m.; electricity 589,000,000 kw-hr. Production (in 000; metric tons; 1967): iron ore (60% metal content) 168,-000; pig iron 74,900; steel 102,200; aluminum (1966) *c.* 1,300; copper (1966) *c.* 900; zinc (1966) *c.* 470; lead (1966) *c.* 370; gold (1965) *c.* 6,100 troy oz.; silver (1966) *c.* 27,000 troy oz.; manganese ore (metal content; 1966) *c.* 3,500; tungsten concentrates (oxide content; 1966) *c.* 6.9; magnesite (1966) *c.* 2,900; superphosphates (1966) 13,916; nitrogenous fertilizers (1966) 2,920; sulfuric acid 9,740; cement 84,-800; newsprint (1966) 888; other paper (1966) 4,324; passenger cars (1966) 230 units; commercial vehicles (1966) 655 units; cotton fabrics 6,015,000 sq.m.; woolen fabrics 547,000 sq.m.; rayon and synthetic fabrics 938,000 sq.m. Index of industrial production (1963 = 100): (1967) 139; (1966) 127.

farms), but he maintained that the general picture was encouraging. Agricultural production, per head of population, increased by 11% between 1965 and 1967. The grain harvest for 1968 was more than 165 million tons (as against 133 million tons in 1962–64 and 145 million tons between 1965 and 1967). Targets in the milk and meat industry were only 80% achieved, however, and if grain production was to achieve the desired level of 190 to 200 million tons, it was essential, according to Brezhnev, that returns from cereal crops should increase even more quickly.

Foreign Policy. Soviet foreign policy did not deviate during 1968 from the cautious line that it had taken in recent years. Aid to liberation movements and peaceful coexistence with states having different political and social structures continued to form the mainstays of this policy. Thus, aid to North Vietnam was not seen as contradicting the search for an agreement with the U.S. Despite noisy propaganda the Soviet Union's main concern still seemed to be to avoid a direct confrontation with the U.S. and to look for an area in which understanding between the two powers could be reached. In any case the military success of the Viet Cong at the beginning of the year justified, in Soviet eyes, a policy that rejected the Chinese theories on the inevitability of world conflict. These Viet Cong triumphs, obtained mainly because of Soviet military aid and without threatening world peace, led the Soviet Union to the conclusion that war was not a necessary precondition for the success of such insurgent movements. The halt to the U.S. bombing of North Vietnam was, of course, hailed as a step in the right direction and as a realistic, though doubtless belated, gesture, calculated to bring about a negotiated settlement of the conflict. But the Soviet Foreign Office was careful, at least publicly, not to intervene or to bring pressure to bear on North Vietnam.

As far as Soviet-U.S. relations were concerned, they did not appear to have been unduly affected by the Vietnam war. Admittedly the current negotiations were not making progress, but the signing of the treaty on nonproliferation of nuclear weapons created a favourable climate. In June the Soviet government confirmed its intention to study with the U.S. the question of limiting rocket systems, both offensive and defensive. The invasion of Czechoslovakia interrupted those negotiations, which had been prepared and gotten underway by the U.S. ambassador in Moscow, Llewellyn Thompson. But by means of talks with various U.S. officials late in the year, Kosygin clearly confirmed the Soviet government's desire to resume and extend its dialogue with the United States.

On the subject of the Middle East, despite many ostentatious demonstrations of solidarity with the Arab countries, the Soviet government did not deviate from the prudent policy that it had followed previously. Soviet diplomacy continued to support a negotiated settlement and tactfully attempted to dissuade the Arabs from any ill-considered military action. But this prudent diplomacy was counterbalanced by the presence in the Mediterranean of large Soviet naval forces. At the year's end, the Soviet Union had at its disposal in the Mediterranean a large force for intervention, which, according to Moscow, was only there to act as a counterweight to the U.S. 6th Fleet.

(HI. P.)

See also Astronautics; Communist Movement; Propaganda.

Encyclopædia Britannica Films. *The Soviet Challenge* (*The Industrial Revolution in Russia*) (1962).

United Arab Republic

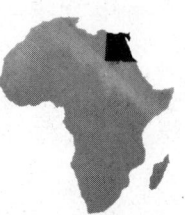

A republic of northeast Africa, the United Arab Republic (U.A.R.) is bounded by Israel, Sudan, Libya, the Mediterranean Sea, and the Red Sea. Area: 385,-237 sq.mi. (997,765 sq.km.). Pop. (1968): 31,693,000. Cap. and largest city: Cairo (pop., 1968 est., 4,585,-000). Language: Arabic 97%. Religion: Muslim 91%; Christian 8%. President and prime minister in 1968, Gamal Abd-al-Nasser.

In 1968 the U.A.R. went some way toward physical recovery from the previous year's defeat by Israel although it was unable to recover any of the territory it lost in that war. By the end of the year President Nasser was still fairly securely in control although he had been obliged to contend with and respond to various demands for changes in his regime.

On February 20 the military court that had been trying senior air force officers accused of criminal negligence in the Arab-Israeli war passed sentences of 15 years' imprisonment on Gen. Muhammad Sidky

GAMMA—PIX FROM PUBLIX

A soldier of the U.A.R. poses as an Israeli fighter and is captured by troops during training exercises reportedly aided by Soviet military technicians during 1968.

Mahmud, the former air force commander, 10 years' imprisonment on another officer, and acquitted two more. During the following days there was serious rioting by workers at Hulwan and by students in Cairo and Alexandria in which scores were injured. Initially, the rioters were protesting against the leniency of the sentences, but some of the demonstrators began to call for freedom of the press and the dissolution of the Arab Socialist Union (ASU). The riots reflected widespread dissatisfaction with the regime for failing to make any fundamental changes since the war. Nasser responded by forming a new government on March 20, still under his own premiership but with several new civilian ministers drawn from universities and the professions. At this time Deputy Prime Minister Zakaria Mohieddin, a former prime minister and a leading member of the regime, resigned all his offices, mainly because he disagreed with the government's economic policies and its failure to apply austerity measures to industrial workers.

Ten days later Nasser announced what came to be known as the "March 30 program to revitalize the revolution." Its basis was the holding of democratic elections to complete the pyramidal structure of the ASU, from the basic units throughout the country to

Unions:
see Labour Unions

Unitarians:
see Religion

UNITED ARAB REPUBLIC

Education. (1965–66) Primary, pupils 3,450,-338, teachers 87,390; secondary, pupils 819,373, teachers 34,819; vocational, pupils 127,734, teachers 9,975; teacher training, students 49,448, teachers 4,531; higher (including 5 universities), students 177,123, teaching staff (1964–65) 10,-406.

Finance. Monetary unit: Egyptian pound, with a nominal par value of E£0.35 to U.S. $1 (E£0.84 = £1 sterling) and an effective exchange rate of E£0.43 to U.S. $1 (E£1.04 = £1 sterling). Gold and foreign exchange, central bank: (June 1968) U.S. $198 million; (June 1967) U.S. $231 million. Budget (1967–68 est.): revenue E£1,-176 million; expenditure E£1,217 million. Money supply: (June 1968) E£649.2 million; (June 1967) E£668.7 million. Cost of living (Cairo: 1963 = 100): (Feb. 1968) 130; (Feb. 1967) 131.

Foreign Trade. (1967) Imports E£344,360,-000; exports E£246,137,000; receipts from Suez Canal dues (1966) E£95.3 million. Import sources: U.S.S.R. 21%; U.S. 9%; West Ger-many 7%; Romania 5%; India 5%; France 5%. Export destinations: U.S.S.R. 25%; Czechoslovakia 7%; East Germany 5%. Main exports: cotton 49%; cotton yarn 12%; rice 12%; cotton textiles 5%.

Transport and Communications. Roads (1964) c. 47,700 km. (including 17,058 km. with improved surface). Motor vehicles in use (1966): passenger 105,300; commercial (including buses) 27,500. Railways: (state only; 1964) 4,231 km.; traffic (state only; 1965–66) 6,170,000,000 passenger-km., freight 3,387,000,000 net ton-km. Shipping (1967): merchant vessels 100 gross tons and over 121; gross tonnage 235,995. Air traffic (1966): 658,336,000 passenger-km.; freight 7,-419,000 net ton-km. Telephones (Jan. 1967) 335,-000. Radio receivers (Dec. 1965) 1,613,000. Television receivers (Dec. 1966) 375,000.

Agriculture. Production (in 000; metric tons; 1967; 1966 in parentheses): corn c. 2,200 (2,-358); wheat c. 1,500 (c. 1,620); barley c. 110 (102); sorghum (1966) 862, (1965) 806; potatoes (1966) 324, (1965) 441; sweet potatoes and yams (1966) 83, (1965) 86; rice 2,300 (c. 2,000); sugar, raw value (1967–68) c. 383, (1966–67) c. 380; tomatoes (1966) 1,366, (1965) 1,242; dry broad beans 188 (381); lentils (1966) 44, (1965) 61; cotton, lint 440 (462); flax fibre 7.6 (7.1); linseed c. 8 (9); dates (1966) 390, (1965) 386; oranges (1966) 409, (1965) 399; lemons (1966) 85, (1965) 83; bananas (1966) 68, (1965) 64; grapes (1966) 90, (1965) 90; onions (1966) 724, (1965) 691. Livestock (in 000; 1965–66): horses 57; mules 11; asses 1,162; sheep 1,947; cattle 1,630; buffaloes 1,646; camels 176; goats c. 790; chickens 23,319. Fish catch (in 000; metric tons) (1965) 94, (1964) 115.

Industry. Production (in 000; metric tons; 1967): crude oil 5,716; iron ore (metal content; 1966) 220; cement 2,742; phosphate rock (1966) 661; manganese ore (metal content; 1966) 47; salt (1966) 627; asbestos (1966) 1.9; cotton yarn 158; cotton fabrics 697,000 m.; electricity (1966) 5,895,000 kw-hr.

CAMERA PRESS—PIX FROM PUBLIX

Col. Kamal Habib Ayub was stripped of his rank and sentenced to penal servitude for criminal negligence in the war against Israel after trials that ended in February 1968.

United Church of Canada: see Religion

United Church of Christ: see Religion

the National Congress at the apex. In April the president held a meeting with university student and faculty representatives to discuss their grievances and agreed that students should be allowed to form their own union and be free from political supervision. On May 2 the March 30 program was approved by a national plebiscite in which 99.99% of the votes were in the affirmative. On June 25 the first round of the ASU elections was held, with 180,000 candidates contesting 75,000 seats in 7,584 basic units. The National Congress met on July 23 and, on Nasser's advice, elected a General Committee to draft an agenda for it to follow. The 1,701 members of the Congress met again two months later and elected a 150-member Central Committee with a core of 25 nominated by the president. On October 10 the Central Committee empowered Nasser to nominate 20 of its members for the Supreme Executive Committee, of whom 10 would be selected by the committee.

On November 14 the president dissolved the 350-member National Assembly, which had been elected in 1964, and it was announced that new elections would be held on Jan. 8, 1969. On November 24 the president ordered the closing of all U.A.R. universities and higher education institutes after further student riots and demonstrations in favour of more democratic government.

Throughout the year the U.A.R.'s policy on the Arab-Israeli question was to maintain that it stood by the Nov. 22, 1967, resolution of the UN Security Council, which, in its view, required Israel to withdraw from all territory occupied since June 5, 1967. U.A.R. government spokesmen expressed pessimism about the prospects of the Middle East peace mission led by Gunnar Jarring (*see* BIOGRAPHY) but showed no desire for it to be brought to an end. Nasser repeated that he was ready for a settlement but not for surrender. Although he said on several occasions that another war with Israel was inevitable, he restrained those elements in the U.A.R. forces that favoured immediate offensive action against the Israelis. With Soviet help the U.A.R. built up its defenses on the Suez Canal until it had about ten times as many troops in the area as the Israelis and more powerful artillery. There were fierce duels on July 8, September 8, and October 26. Suez town was severely damaged, but most civilians were evacuated. The Israelis hit the Suez refinery on October 26, but the Egyptians inflicted heavy punishment on the Israeli positions. Is-rael retaliated on October 31 by a commando raid against the Nej Hammedi power station and the Qina Bridge over the Nile River in Upper Egypt. The U.A.R. claimed that new defense measures would ensure that Israel would not repeat the exploit, but it considered the incident as a potential threat to the Aswan High Dam. The U.S.S.R. issued a warning that it would protect the high dam. Soviet warships, which were entering the eastern Mediterranean in increasing numbers, made frequent use of Alexandria and Port Said as refueling stations.

In early July Nasser paid a visit to Moscow, where he agreed with the Soviet leaders on the need for a political settlement in the Middle East. Shortly after his return to Cairo, he caused widespread alarm in the U.A.R. by announcing that he would be going back to the U.S.S.R. for medical treatment. This gave rise to rumours about the state of his health, especially as he appeared to be in some pain. However, the official version that he was suffering from defective circulation in his leg as a side effect of diabetes was generally accepted and he returned from the U.S.S.R. in improved health.

Economically, the U.A.R.'s position was less alarming than it might have been after the loss of its Suez Canal revenues. This was partly because of the £95 million annual payments that it continued to receive from Saudi Arabia, Kuwait, and Libya under the Khartoum agreement of August–September 1967. But the U.A.R. was also able to increase its agricultural exports, notably rice, which rose to one million tons in 1968. The agricultural terms of trade had turned in the U.A.R.'s favour, and it was able to import wheat and flour for substantially less than it had budgeted for. Also, the full benefits of the high dam, of which the main body had been completed by the end of the year, were beginning to affect the economy. The installation of the dam's first hydroelectric power units resulted in a supply of cheap power to industry. In August the Phillips Petroleum Co. began to produce oil from the Alamein field in the Western Desert, and in September the Pan-American Company discovered a new offshore field in the Red Sea near Murgan. By the end of the year the U.A.R. had become a net oil producer.

(P. MD.)

See also Middle East; Yemen.

ENCYCLOPÆDIA BRITANNICA FILMS. *Mediterranean Africa* (1952); *Egypt and the Nile* (1954); *The Middle East* (1955); *The Suez Canal* (1962); *The Nile Valley and Its People* (1964).

United Kingdom

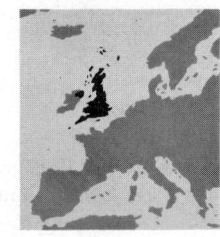

A constitutional monarchy in northwestern Europe, the United Kingdom comprises the island of Great Britain (England, Scotland, and Wales) and Northern Ireland, together with many small islands. Area: 94,222 sq.mi. (244,034 sq.km.), excluding 1,160 sq.mi. of inland water, the crown possession of the Isle of Man, and the crown dependencies of the Channel Islands. Pop. (1967 est.): 55,068,600. Cap. and largest city: London (pop. [Greater London], 1967 est., 7,880,760). Language: English is spoken almost universally, but some Welsh and Gaelic are also used. Religion: mainly Protestant. Queen, Elizabeth II; prime minister in 1968, Harold Wilson.

Domestic Politics. Once again in 1968 the most important issue in United Kingdom politics was economic policy, made more pressing by the devaluation of the pound in November 1967. To switch resources into exports, wage advances had to be held back at a time when prices were rising, government spending had to be cut, and government projects had to be curbed. It was a disenchanting year for a Labour government that had encountered almost continuous economic difficulties since taking office in October 1964. The first major political pronouncement of the year came from Prime Minister Harold Wilson (*see* BIOGRAPHY) in the House of Commons on January 16, when an extensive program of economies totaling £325 million for the year 1968–69 was announced. Many of the economies touched acutely on Labour policy. The raising of the school-leaving age from 15 to 16 was deferred for two years; *i.e.*, until 1973. Free milk for pupils in secondary schools was to be ended in September. Various university and higher education projects were postponed. National Health Service prescriptions were no longer free of charge. The housing program and the roads program were cut.

Two months later there followed the most severe peacetime budget on record. Introduced by the chancellor of the exchequer, Roy Jenkins (*see* BIOGRAPHY), on March 19, it increased taxes by £775 million; these increases were widely spread over income from investment (a surtax), corporation tax, purchase tax, the selective employment tax, and taxes on wines and liquor, tobacco, gasoline, and betting. These restrictions, accompanied by tight credit policies for bank lending and for installment buying, were tightened in May and again in October, for consumer expenditure still obstinately increased and by autumn was 2% over the budget forecast. There was satisfactory progress in increasing exports, but the level of imports remained alarmingly high, and so the balance of payments continued to give concern. Though in October and early November Jenkins was forecasting progress toward a substantial surplus, a monetary crisis involving the Deutsche Mark and the French franc caused him (November 22) to announce a 10% increase in the main indirect taxes, and a new requirement on importers of most manufactured and semimanufactured goods to deposit with the government for six months a prior payment of up to half the value of the goods imported.

In such circumstances it was hardly surprising that the Labour Party had a calamitous year in parliamen-

tary by-elections, losing some of its supposedly safest seats in the industrial Midlands and Lancashire. In March Labour lost Dudley, near Birmingham, with a swing of 21.2% to the Conservatives. In London the Labour candidate in the Conservative area of South Kensington polled so few votes that he lost his deposit, and in the working-class area of Acton the Labour vote was almost halved. This constituted the worst by-election record for a party in power in more than 30 years. Labour did not do quite so badly in another round of by-elections in June, though the party lost two Lancashire seats at Oldham West and at Nelson and Colne which it had held for many years. In July in a mining area of Wales, at Caerphilly, the Labour candidate was almost pushed out by a Welsh Nationalist. In the autumn, before the November economic crisis, Labour was doing a little better in by-elections. The opinion polls, which had recorded an astonishing 25-point lead by Conservatives over Labour in the spring and early summer, showed the Conservative lead cut to 10 points in the autumn, but

Workmen removing loose chalk and flints from the "white cliffs" above the harbour at Dover. The work was part of a project to lessen the danger of falling debris caused by erosion and water seepage.

by December the gap had widened again to more than 20 points. Meanwhile, in local elections in May, fewer than 500 Labour councillors were returned in 2,800 seats contested in the boroughs of England and Wales. Labour was left controlling only 4 boroughs in the area of Greater London, and outside London only 3 of the 32 largest boroughs with populations of more than 150,000. Labour lost Sheffield for the first time in 41 years. There was no electoral defeat of comparable proportions in recent British political history—to find comparisons commentators had to go as far back as the collapse of the Labour government in 1931. Yet one factor made comparisons of any kind uncertain, that being the extraordinary volatility of political opinion.

Popular discontent with the Labour government was echoed by disaffection among Labour members of Parliament (M.P.'s). Substantial numbers of them abstained in House of Commons votes on health service charges and, in particular, at different stages in the passage of the Prices and Incomes Act—in May, 48 Labour M.P.'s signed a motion to reject the bill at its second reading, and 23 defied the strictest party injunction in voting against one section of the bill. During the spring and summer there was some talk of "Wilson must go," but this came to nothing, and Wilson was able to reestablish his hold on the leadership

770

United Kingdom

Prince Charles, below, was confronted by a hostile group of Welsh nationalists, above, during a visit to Cardiff on June 28, 1968.

CENTRAL PRESS FROM PICTORIAL PARADE

at the party's autumn conference. Later there were back-bench rumblings of dissent over proposals for a Rhodesia settlement, and on October 22, 49 Labour rebels voted against the government on the Rhodesia issue.

It was also an uneasy year in the Cabinet. George Brown, foreign secretary since August 1966, resigned on March 15, complaining that he had not been consulted on policy concerning the gold and dollar crisis and giving as his reason for going, "the way this government is run." This statement referred to his view that Wilson relied too heavily on inner groups of ministers within the Cabinet. Brown was succeeded by Michael Stewart, who had been Brown's predecessor at the Foreign Office.

In an extensive Cabinet reconstruction on April 5 Barbara Castle (*see* BIOGRAPHY) took over at the Ministry of Labour, which was reconstituted as the Department of Employment and Productivity; she was given special responsibility for the prices and incomes policy. At the Department of Education and Science, Patrick Gordon Walker was replaced by Edward Short. In other principal changes Frederick Peart moved from Agriculture to be leader of the House of Commons and lord privy seal; Ray Gunter moved from Labour to Power; Richard Marsh from Power to Transport; and Cledwyn Hughes to Agriculture. Lord Shackleton had become leader of the House of Lords

in January. At the same time Wilson announced the formation of a Parliamentary Committee of the Cabinet, which was taken to reflect his preference for working through smaller groups rather than through the whole Cabinet. The members were Wilson, Stewart, Jenkins, Lord Gardiner, Richard Crossman, Barbara Castle, James Callaghan, Denis Healey, and Peart. The resignation on June 30 of Ray Gunter, like George Brown a long-time trade union member of the party, reflected some continuing discontent in the higher ranks of the government with Wilson's methods. Some further changes announced in October marked another rearrangement of responsibilities, with Richard Crossman taking charge of the new Department of Health and Social Security. The Commonwealth Office was merged with the Foreign Office without new appointments being made. Judith Hart entered the Cabinet as paymaster general, and at 44 she became the second woman Cabinet minister—the first time there had been two women members of the Cabinet.

The Conservative leader Edward Heath made a number of changes in the Conservatives' shadow cabinet during the year. He dismissed Enoch Powell (*see* BIOGRAPHY) in April after Powell gave a speech on race relations that Heath said was inflammatory. In a reshuffle of responsibilities on November 14 Reginald Maudling became chairman of the party's Policy Advisory Committee—a key position in the hierarchy. Other principal Conservative parliamentary spokesmen were: defense, Geoffrey Rippon; housing, land, and local government, Peter Walker; transport, Margaret Thatcher; foreign and Commonwealth affairs, Sir Alec Douglas-Home; economic affairs, Iain Macleod; home affairs, Quintin Hogg; education, Sir Edward Boyle; trade, Sir Keith Joseph; party chairman, Anthony Barber.

Legislation. Acts of Parliament passed during the 1967–68 session included the Prices and Incomes Act, which gave the government statutory powers to bar unjustified increases in prices and increases in wages and salaries that either exceeded the prevailing rate of economic growth or were unjustified by improvements in productivity. The Town and Country Planning Act was designed to modernize the system of development planning and would require planning authorities to arrange for public participation in the preparation of development plans. The act also provided for the appointment of commissions of inquiry

UNITED KINGDOM

Education. (1965–66) Primary, pupils 5,416,-926; secondary, pupils 3,541,438; vocational, pupils 1,580,053; teachers, primary, secondary, and vocational 434,553; higher (1964–65), students 386,252.

Finance. Monetary unit: pound sterling, with a par value of £0.42 to U.S. $1 (£1 = $2.40). Gold and convertible currency, official: (June 1968) U.S. $2,683,000,000; (June 1967) U.S. $2,834,000,000. Budget: (1968–69 est.): revenue £12,875 million; expenditure £11,489 million. Gross national product: (1967) £39,200 million; (1966) £37,650 million. Money supply: (March 1968) £14,375 million; (March 1967) £12,912 million. Cost of living (1963 = 100): (June 1968) 121; (June 1967) 116.

Foreign Trade. (1967) Imports £6,442 million; exports £5,210 million. Import sources: EEC 20% (West Germany 5%, Netherlands 5%); U.S. 13%; Canada 7%. Export destinations: EEC 20% (West Germany 5%); U.S. 12%; South Africa 5%; Australia 5%. Main exports: machinery 27%; motor vehicles 10%; chemicals 10%; textile yarns and fabrics 5%; iron and steel 5%.

Transport and Communications. Roads (1966) 354,725 km. (including 668 km. expressways). Motor vehicles in use (1967): passenger 9,447,000; commercial 1,434,000. Railways (excluding Northern Ireland; 1966): 22,082 km.; traffic 29,697,000,000 passenger-km., freight (1967) 22,054,000,000 net ton-km. Shipping (1967): merchant vessels 100 gross tons and over 4,156; gross tonnage 21,716,148. Ships entered (1967) vessels totaling 118,726,000 net registered tons; goods loaded (1966) 35,680,000 metric tons, unloaded 160,330,000 metric tons. Air traffic (1967): 14,068,707,000 passenger-km.; freight 464,615,000 net ton-km. Telephones (Dec. 1967) 11,289,000. Radio licenses (including combined sound-television; Dec. 1967) 17,493,000. Television licenses (Dec. 1967) 14,910,000.

Agriculture. Production (in 000; metric tons; 1967; 1966 in parentheses): wheat 3,898 (3,475); barley 9,391 (8,724); oats 1,362 (1,120); potatoes 7,201 (6,575); sugar, raw value (1967–68) c. 964, (1966–67) 935; apples (1966) 479, (1965) 615; pears (1966) 47, (1965) 77; dry peas (1966) 44, (1965) 47; dry broad beans (1966) c. 80, (1965) c. 80; toma-

toes (1966) 82, (1965) 81; onions (1966) 87, (1965) 84; hen eggs (1966) 827, (1965) 835; beef and veal 920 (882); mutton and lamb 288 (272); pork 802 (879); wool (1967) 39, (1966) 39; milk (1967) 13,200, (1966) 12,750; butter 42 (34); cheese 120 (108). Livestock (in 000; June 1967): cattle 12,369; sheep 28,885; pigs 7,107; chickens 120,147. Fish catch (in 000; metric tons): (1967) 849, (1966) 904.

Industry. Fuel and power (in 000; 1967): coal 174,920 metric tons; manufactured gas 25,514,-000 cu.m.; electricity 207,820,000 kw-hr. Production (in 000; metric tons; 1967): iron ore (25–30% metal content) 12,940; pig iron 15,400; crude steel 24,280; superphosphates (1966) 479; nitrogenous fertilizers (1966) 732; cement 17,-580; passenger cars 1,552 units; commercial vehicles 385 units; agricultural tractors 187 units; aircraft 0.31 units; aeroengines 1.04 units; cotton fabrics 684,000 m.; woolen fabrics 246,000 sq.m.; rayon and other synthetic fabrics 485,000 m. Merchant vessels launched (1967) 1,303,000 gross tons. Permanent houses and flats completed (1967) 415,455. Index of industrial production (1963 = 100): (1967) 112; (1966) 112.

to consider development proposals of nationwide concern; the first of these was set up to examine proposals for a third London airport. The Countryside Act established a Countryside Commission, replacing the National Parks Commission, and provided powers for the development of the countryside for leisure use as well as for its preservation (*see* PARKS). The Gaming Act imposed restrictions on gambling intended to end profiteering and racketeering in gambling clubs. The Trade Descriptions Act introduced new powers to deal with inaccurate descriptions of goods and services and false statements about price and to regulate the labeling of goods and the inclusion of information in advertisements. The Transport Act, one of the longest measures ever to come before Parliament, provided for the integration of road, rail, and freight services; for a new financial structure for the railways, including state support for uneconomic commuter services in urban areas; and for the closer regulation of safety rules and working conditions in road haulage. (*See* TRANSPORTATION.)

Plans for reform of the House of Lords has been discussed in interparty talks begun in November 1967. But rejection by the upper chamber in June of a government order for increased sanctions against Rhodesia caused the prime minister to end the discussions, and on November 1 a White Paper was issued, outlining the basis on which legislation for reform of the House of Lords would be introduced during the parliamentary session of 1968–69. The government aimed at the establishment of a second chamber of about 230 members, which would have the power to delay for a period of six months ordinary public bills sent up from the House of Commons. Membership would be on a two-tier structure, comprising voting and nonvoting peers. All in the former class would be "created"; *i.e.*, holders of first-creation or life peerages. Some existing hereditary peers might, by the grant of such fresh titles, be made into voting peers. Otherwise, existing members of the House of Lords would continue as nonvoting peers, with the right to speak and serve on committees. On their deaths, however, their successors would receive no writ of summons. Thus, the nonvoting section of the House would gradually decline. Voting peers, who would be paid, would be expected to attend regularly and would probably retire at the age of 72.

Government Inquiries. The Royal Commission on Trade Unions and Employers' Associations under Lord Donovan reported on June 13. It criticized the prevailing conflict between national and local agreements and negotiations, arguing that company and factory agreements should be the basis of industrial relations. It rejected the case for legislation to outlaw unofficial strikes or to make collective agreements enforceable at law, holding that the law should be kept out of industrial relations as far as possible. The report suggested the setting up of an industrial relations commission to investigate disputes, of labour tribunals to hear individual complaints about contractual rights, and of an industrial relations body to which unions could bring complaints of unfair treatment or electoral malpractice.

Lord Fulton's committee on the civil service reported in June. Criticizing as obsolete the philosophy of the gifted amateur and generalist moving from job to job as the ideal of the civil servant, the report called for more professionalism and specialization in the civil service, with more training for management. The government adopted the Fulton committee's recommendation that a new civil service department directly responsible to the prime minister be set up with the task of supervising the civil service as a whole.

Foreign Policy. British foreign policy continued to be beset by frustrations of long standing—the application for membership in the European Economic Community (EEC); the pursuit, as an intermediary, of peace in Vietnam; the search for a Rhodesia settlement; and the dispute with Spain over Gibraltar. Added to this list of problems in 1968 was the civil war in Nigeria.

The British approach to the EEC was again blocked by France. A plan for closer links between the six EEC nations and the countries applying for membership was vetoed by the French in April, and they rejected another mutual tariff-cutting plan in September. In spite of these setbacks the foreign secretary insisted that Britain would persevere with its application for membership.

On Gibraltar, the U.K. maintained Gibraltar's right

CAMERA PRESS—PIX FROM PUBLIX

Above, members of the Scottish National Party marching to a rally at Bannockburn. Below, a caricature of the secretary of state for Scotland. The party claimed that the government in London was not doing enough about problems of housing and unemployment in Scotland.

CAMERA PRESS—PIX FROM PUBLIX

to self-determination, as expressed in the referendum of September 1967 which produced a vast majority in favour of retaining the link with Britain. In July Britain gave Gibraltarians greater responsibility in domestic affairs. Meanwhile, Spain tightened up restrictions on movements from Gibraltar across the Spanish border.

Wilson's visits to the U.S.S.R. in January and to the U.S. and Canada in February were primarily concerned with Vietnam. The Moscow visit was unfruitful. In Washington, Wilson counseled the U.S. to "show restraint in the face of exasperation." He expressly refused to dissociate the British government from U.S. action in Vietnam, although he was under political pressure to do so from the left wing of his party at home.

Wilson reiterated the policy of strengthening sanctions against Rhodesia, ruled out resort to force, and continued to pursue a negotiated settlement. This culminated in new talks between Wilson and the Rhodesian prime minister, Ian Smith, on the Royal Navy assault ship "Fearless" at Gibraltar in October.

BEN ROTH AGENCY

"With the lapse of a generation or so we shall at last have succeeded—to the benefit of nobody—in reproducing 'in England's green and pleasant land' the haunting tragedy of the United States. (Enoch Powell)" —Garland, "Daily Telegraph," London.

In Nigeria a succession of British initiatives in Lagos failed to end the war with the secessionist state of Biafra. The Wilson government was criticized for apparently condoning Nigeria's plans to finish the war by a final attack at a time when reports of starvation in Biafra were being widely publicized.

Defense. In announcing cuts in government expenditure on January 16, Wilson declared that Britain's military contribution must be commensurate with its economic strength. He announced that the withdrawal of British military troops east of Suez would be completed by the end of 1971 instead of by the mid-1970s as at first intended. The entire order for 50 U.S. F-111 military aircraft was canceled, and there was to be a reduction in military manpower of 75,000. In the annual defense White Paper on February 22 it was emphasized that the first priority was the fullest possible support for the North Atlantic alliance, with a stronger contribution to NATO as one aspect of withdrawal from the Far East and from the Middle East. A supplementary defense White Paper on July 11 listed the impending disappearance of a number of Army units, including a famous Scottish regiment, the Argyll and Sutherland Highlanders—a decision that provoked widespread popular protest in Scotland. The defense minister, Denis Healey, explained that when withdrawals and economies were complete the British defense budget would fall to about 5% of the gross national product. Conservatives were critical of the withdrawal from east of Suez.   (W. H. Ts.)

The Economy. The course of the economy in 1968 was dominated by the working out of the decision, Nov. 18, 1967, to devalue the currency. Economic policy was designed to back up the devaluation decision by securing, against undue erosion, the cost and price advantage it conferred and by ensuring that excessive home demand would not frustrate the effort to increase exports. To this end, the government announced cuts (January 16) in its own spending program and a little later (March 19) introduced an austerity budget. Estimates at the time gave the deflationary effects of the budget on the volume of consumers' expenditure as equivalent to a cut of $1\frac{3}{4}$-2%. These measures complemented earlier actions that had been taken at the time of devaluation and had as their purpose the creation of low domestic demand, which would permit the expected increase in exports while holding imports down and moderating the rate of wage and price inflation. Prices and incomes policy was given renewed life in a further effort to hold back the erosion of the cost and price advantages obtained through devaluation.

Despite these supporting policies, the firstfruits of the devaluation were disappointing. The deficit on the balance of payments in 1968 was larger than it had been in 1967, and although there was improvement later in the year, a sustained surplus position had not yet been reached by its end. The response of exports to devaluation was reasonably encouraging; in the second and third quarters of the year goods exported were 25% higher than in the corresponding period of 1967 (in sterling terms) and three-fifths of this rise was in volume. It was on the import side that the trouble seemed to lie. Although the prices of imports (in sterling terms) rose as expected in consequence of the devaluation, there seemed no sign that this was causing the hoped-for displacement of imported goods by home-produced goods. Indeed, in certain categories there were dramatic increases; imports of finished manufactured goods, for example, rose by nearly 29%

in value between the second and third quarters of 1967 and the corresponding period in 1968, and the greater part of this was due to increased volume.

An additional disappointment was the failure of private investment to recover more substantially before the end of the year. After two years of a low rate of investment in manufacturing it had been expected that substantial new capacity would be developed during 1968. In fact, there was little change from the 1967 level; however, nonmanufacturing private investment did show improvement.

The earlier measures to keep down the level of home demand proved not wholly successful. Although consumer spending slumped heavily in the three months after the budget, this turned out to be merely a short-lived reaction to the boom that had preceded it (it had been well known that the budget would be harsh and spending had risen in anticipation). In the third quarter of the year consumers' expenditure again rose sharply, provoking further deflationary measures, the need for which was reinforced by the European monetary crisis in November. Hire purchase (installment buying) restrictions were tightened early in the month, bank credit and tax rates later.

Output rose erratically, largely reflecting the swings in consumers' expenditure. Thus, it rose sharply in the first quarter, fell back slightly in the second, again moved up strongly in the third quarter, and showed a modest rise in the fourth. For the year as a whole, output was up by more than $3\frac{1}{2}$% from 1967.

The growth in output was accompanied by large gains in productivity. Unemployment reached a peak in August (after seasonal adjustment and including those leaving school) but thereafter fell back, standing in the autumn at levels of about 2.3% of the labour force. This was approximately the same percentage as it had been a year before.   (M. J. A.)

Home Affairs. Race relations became increasingly a matter of controversy. During the winter of 1967–68 there was a sharp increase in the number of Kenyan Asians coming to Britain as immigrants holding British passports. After a request for the tightening up of immigration controls by Conservative leaders, the government hurried a Commonwealth Immigrants Bill through Parliament in the last few days of February. This imposed immigration control on citizens of the United Kingdom and its colonies who held passports issued by the British government but who had "no substantial connection" with Britain. The measure was strongly criticized for introducing a principle of racial classification. Controversy later centred on a speech in April by Enoch Powell proposing the cessation of immigration and a scheme for voluntary repatriation. Meanwhile, a Race Relations Bill was passed through Parliament. It made racial discrimination unlawful in employment, housing, insurance, and credit, and in the provision of goods, facilities, and services. (See RACE RELATIONS.)

A gas explosion in May in Ronan Point, a 23-story block of flats in east London, led to the progressive collapse of 18 adjoining floors, with the loss of five lives. An inquiry found that the system of jointing of large prefabricated panels was liable to such a collapse if one panel was displaced. Gas supplies were disconnected as a safety precaution from tall buildings constructed in a similar manner, and it was believed that more than 200 buildings would have to be strengthened. As many as 400 were to be inspected.

An exceptionally wet summer in southern England brought widespread flooding in the southwest when

more than three inches of rain fell in 12 hours in some places on July 11, and there was also widespread flooding in the London area and the southeast when more than five inches of rain fell in certain areas, September 14–16.

As the winter of 1968–69 drew on, the switch to year-round "British Standard Time," which meant that morning darkness lasted one hour longer than usual, aroused some protest, especially in Scotland and the North.

Northern Ireland. The old feud between Protestants and Roman Catholics in Ulster broke out with the launching of a civil rights campaign during the summer. This followed a period during which the Northern Ireland prime minister, Terence O'Neill, had sought to liberalize the relations between Protestants and Catholics and between the governments of Northern Ireland and the Republic of Ireland. Complaints of discrimination against Roman Catholics in voting arrangements, in allocation of housing, and in appointment to official posts were taken to the European Court of Human Rights in Strasbourg, France, in July. On October 5 a civil rights demonstration in Londonderry, where a large Roman Catholic population complained of disfranchisement by the property qualification required for voting, was broken up by the police, and nearly 100 persons were injured. A few days later there was another clash with the police in Belfast when the ultra-Protestant followers of the self-styled moderator of the Free Presbyterian Church, Ian Paisley, challenged a Catholic civil rights demonstration.

The dispute between the Protestants and the Roman Catholics centred on the claim of "one-man, one-vote." In local elections in Northern Ireland the vote was restricted to taxpayers and their wives, and to the occupiers of business property who exercised a plural vote related to the amount of tax they paid. It was further claimed that ward boundaries were so arranged as to favour the Protestants and that local authority housing (which carried with it a vote) was allocated with discrimination in favour of Protestants. In Londonderry, where about a quarter of the electorate lacked the vote, the government set up a Londonderry commission to take over all municipal activities and to initiate reforms. The business property plural vote was to be ended, and local authorities were told to introduce a points system for the fair allocation of houses. The government agreed to appoint an ombudsman to hear complaints. One effect of these promises was to inflame the hostility of the extreme Protestant factions.   (W. H. Ts.)

ENCYCLOPÆDIA BRITANNICA FILMS. *The British Isles—The Land and the People* (1963); *Britain—Searching for a New Role* (1964).

United Nations

From the vantage point of UN Secretary-General U Thant the international situation deteriorated through most of 1968. The Middle East was filled with frustration and tension; the Soviet invasion of Czechoslovakia, in U Thant's words, "cast a long shadow and created a feeling of uneasiness and insecurity which will take determination and sustained effort to overcome"; a halt to the U.S. bombing of North Vietnam, which the secretary-general had long regarded as the key to successful negotiations, was not ordered until October 31; the UN Conference on Trade and Development (UNCTAD) fell short of the hopes of the less developed states; and the old problems of decolonization, apartheid (racial separation in South Africa), and the UN budget persisted and may even have worsened. Some progress did, however, take place in disarmament when, on June 12, the General Assembly approved a Treaty on the Nonproliferation of Nuclear Weapons.

Middle East. Tension and frustration in the Middle East arose from the inability of interested parties, including the secretary-general's special representative, Ambassador Gunnar Jarring (*see* BIOGRAPHY), to bridge the gap between Israel and the Arab states

U.S. Ambassador Arthur Goldberg addressing the Security Council on Jan. 26, 1968. He presented his nation's position that the USS "Pueblo" was in international waters when captured by North Korea.

UPI COMPIX

that remained after the June 1967 war. Israel at first insisted upon negotiating directly with the Arabs. It later agreed to talk with the Arabs through Jarring but still required a broad, negotiated political settlement before it would withdraw from the territory it had occupied in 1967. The Arabs, before they would agree to move toward a political accommodation, wanted Israel to withdraw from the occupied territory. As the secretary-general reported to the UN Security Council on July 31, the differences between the two sides even prevented him from establishing the humanitarian mission, which in 1967 the General Assembly and Security Council had wanted him to send to the Middle East as a first step toward improving the lot of the civilian population. The council on September 27 deplored the delay in implementing its resolutions "because of the conditions still being set by Israel." (Israel wanted Ambassador Jarring's mandate widened to permit him to consider the treatment of Jewish minorities in the Arab countries along with the Arab refugee question.) The Security Council requested Israel to receive the special representative, cooperate with him, and facilitate his work. Despite this resolution U Thant had to report on October 15 that he could not dispatch the representative because Israel would not receive him unless Ambassador Jarring's instructions were changed. On December 19 the General Assembly established a three-man committee to investigate Israel's acts in the occupied territory, a step opposed by Israel.

In the meantime, humanitarian work went forward in the Middle East, although shortages of funds, food, supplies, and equipment handicapped the work of the UN Relief and Works Agency for Palestine Refugees in the Near East (UNRWA). A UNRWA appeal on March 2 for funds and tents, and a joint appeal, with the director general of the Food and Agriculture Organization, on April 30, brought meagre responses. The agency expected that it would need $42.5 million

in 1969 to carry on its current programs but received only $35.7 million in pledges from 38 governments at a pledging conference held December 6. On December 19 the General Assembly issued its own appeal to UN members to support UNRWA and extended the agency's life three years until 1972.

Ambassador Jarring, charged with establishing and maintaining contacts to promote agreement and to assist efforts to settle Middle Eastern problems peacefully, moved among the parties from his two head-

Table I. Member States of the United Nations
Dec. 31, 1968

Afghanistan	Dominican Rep.*	Lebanon*	Saudi Arabia*
Albania	Ecuador*	Lesotho	Senegal
Algeria*	El Salvador*	Liberia*	Sierra Leone
Argentina*	Equatorial Guinea†	Libya	Singapore
Australia*	Ethiopia*	Luxembourg*	Somalia
Austria	Finland	Malagasy Rep.	South Africa*
Barbados	France*	Malawi	Southern Yemen
Belgium*	Gabon	Malaysia	Spain
Belorussia*	Gambia, The	Maldive Islands	Sudan
Bolivia*	Ghana	Mali	Swaziland§
Botswana	Greece*	Malta	Sweden
Brazil*	Guatemala*	Mauritania	Syria*
Bulgaria	Guinea	Mauritius‡	Tanzania
Burma	Guyana	Mexico*	Thailand
Burundi	Haiti*	Mongolia	Togo
Cambodia	Honduras*	Morocco	Trinidad and
Cameroon	Hungary	Nepal	Tobago
Canada*	Iceland	Netherlands*	Tunisia
Central African	India*	New Zealand*	Turkey*
Rep.	Indonesia	Nicaragua*	Uganda
Ceylon	Iran*	Niger	Ukraine*
Chad	Iraq*	Nigeria	U.S.S.R.*
Chile*	Ireland	Norway*	United Arab Re-
China*	Israel	Pakistan	public
Colombia*	Italy	Panama*	United Kingdom*
Congo (Kinshasa)	Ivory Coast	Paraguay*	United States*
Congo (Brazz.)	Jamaica	Peru*	Upper Volta
Costa Rica*	Japan	Philippines*	Uruguay*
Cuba*	Jordan	Poland*	Venezuela*
Cyprus	Kenya	Portugal	Yemen
Czechoslovakia*	Kuwait	Romania	Yugoslavia*
Dahomey	Laos	Rwanda	Zambia
Denmark*			

*Signatories to original charter.
†Admitted Nov. 12, 1968.
‡Admitted April 24, 1968.
§Admitted Sept. 24, 1968.

Table II. Council Membership
Years indicate date membership expires

Country	Security Council	Economic and Social Council	Trusteeship Council
China	Permanent		Permanent
France	Permanent	1969	Permanent
U.S.S.R.*	Permanent	1971†	Permanent
United Kingdom*	Permanent	1971†	Permanent‡
United States*	Permanent	1970	Permanent‡
Algeria	1969		
Argentina		1970	
Australia*			‡
Belgium		1969	
Bulgaria*		1970	
Chad		1970	
Colombia	1970		
Congo (Brazz.)		1970	
Finland*	1970		
Guatemala		1969	
Hungary	1969		
India*		1970	
Indonesia		1971	
Ireland		1970	
Jamaica		1971	
Japan		1970	
Kuwait		1969	
Libya		1969	
Mexico		1969	
Nepal	1970		
Norway		1971	
Pakistan	1969	1971	
Paraguay	1969		
Senegal	1969		
Sierra Leone*		1969	
Spain	1970		
Sudan		1971	
Tanzania*		1969	
Turkey		1969	
Upper Volta		1970	
Uruguay		1971	
Yugoslavia*		1971	
Zambia	1970		

*Members of the Committee of 24 on colonization in addition to: Afghanistan, Chile, Ethiopia, Honduras, Iran, Iraq, Italy, Ivory Coast, Malagasy Republic, Mali, Poland, Syria, Tunisia, and Venezuela.
†Reelected.
‡Administering authorities.

quarters on Cyprus and in New York City, but he was unable to fulfill his mandate. He did help Israel and the United Arab Republic (U.A.R.) exchange prisoners according to plans announced on January 11. And he seemed to have made some progress in arranging to remove 15 ships stranded in the Suez Canal until U.A.R. survey operations moved beyond a line Israel had specified; the Israelis then opened fire on the survey vessels, and the operations were suspended.

The dangers of failing to settle the Middle East crisis became apparent as incidents erupted throughout the year along unstable military lines. On March 21 Israel and Jordan asked the council to consider the Israeli raid on the Karameh refugee camp in eastern Jordan, allegedly undertaken in retaliation for commando activities supposed to have originated there. On March 24 the council unanimously condemned Israel's reprisal and deplored all cease-fire violations. While Jordan was dissatisfied with the council because it had not applied sanctions against Israel under Ch. VII of the UN Charter, Israel proclaimed its "right and duty" to take all necessary steps needed for the security of its territory and people. The council met again to consider fighting that broke out March 29 between Israel and Jordan and held other meetings (August 5 and 16) to consider cease-fire violations in the area.

At the August 16 meeting the council again condemned Israel's attacks against alleged commando bases in Jordan. On September 4 and 5 the council discussed an Israeli charge of a U.A.R. ambush carried out across the Suez Canal against an Israeli jeep, in which two Israeli soldiers were killed and a third kidnapped. An exchange of fire along the canal broke out on September 8 and was discussed by the council on that day and also on September 10 and 11, during which the council president, George Ignatieff (Canada), expressed the council's deep regrets over the loss of life and stated that the council "requires the parties strictly to observe the cease-fire" called for in earlier resolutions. The council met again later in the year: on September 18, it "insisted," by a vote of 14–0–1, "that its cease-fire orders be rigorously respected"; on November 1 and 4 it discussed U.A.R. charges that Israel had violated its airspace and Israeli charges of U.A.R. cease-fire violations.

The year ended with a flurry of border incidents, including several air strikes by Israeli planes against targets in Jordan, and then with a major air strike by Israel on December 28 against the Beirut International Airport in Lebanon. Israel claimed that the attack, which destroyed several Lebanese civil aircraft, was in retaliation for terrorist activities against Israel by commandos based in Lebanon and especially was a response to the severe damage and one death caused by an attack by two Arab terrorists on an Israeli airliner in Athens on December 26. The Security Council met on December 29, 30, and 31 and unanimously condemned Israel's "premeditated military action." The council issued a "solemn warning to Israel" to the effect that "if such acts were . . . repeated, the Council would have to consider further steps to give effect to its decisions."

Intervention in Czechoslovakia. The U.S.S.R. on August 23 cast a veto to defeat an eight-power (Brazil, Canada, Denmark, France, Paraguay, Senegal, the U.K., and the U.S.) resolution condemning the August 20–21 armed intervention by the U.S.S.R. and other

continued on page 776

HUMAN RIGHTS

By Sir Dingle Foot

All we have of freedom, all we use or know
This our fathers bought for us, long and long ago.

Ancient Right unnoticed as the breath we draw
Leave to live by no man's leave underneath the Law.

Kipling's "ancient right" and the Englishman's acceptance of what are now called human rights are rooted in Magna Carta and in the English common law, with its emphasis on individual rights and remedies. Earlier generations of Englishmen, however, were concerned more with their own rights than with the rights of man. The idea of human rights as being of universal application originated in the 18th century with the U.S. Constitution, Thomas Paine, and the French Revolution.

It was the French Revolution's National Constituent Assembly which in 1789 proclaimed the Declaration of the Rights of Man and of the Citizen, and the principles that it formulated had a profound effect on the whole of the Western world. In France, someone could always be found to champion the individual or the minority against the pretensions of the state. Perhaps the most remarkable chapter in the internal history of France before World War I was the Dreyfus case. The whole country was riven into warring sections, divided by the utmost bitterness, because one man, without friends or influence, had been the victim of injustice. It could at least be argued that the real originators of the United Nations' Universal Declaration of Human Rights were the Dreyfusards.

Interest in the Dreyfus case was not confined to France. Indeed, manifestations of sympathy in cases of real or suspected injustice have never been confined within national frontiers. When, in 1914, labour union leaders were expelled from South Africa, indignant British workers staged a memorable demonstration in Hyde Park. And when, in the '20s, Sacco and Vanzetti were sent to the electric chair in Massachusetts for robbery and murder that many believed they had not committed, there were furious mass meetings of protest throughout the capitals of Europe. Nevertheless, as a matter of law the preservation of human rights remained a strictly national concern. Public international law dealt only with relations between governments. There was no supranational tribunal to which the individual could have recourse. It did not occur to anyone at Versailles that the League of Nations should concern itself with injustice to individual citizens of its member states. It was set up only as a peace-keeping instrument.

A New Departure. The change came when the United Nations Organization was created at San Francisco in 1945. The preamble to the UN Charter reaffirms "faith in fundamental human rights, in the dignity and worth of the human person, in the equal rights of men and women and of nations large and small." Later articles imposed obligations to promote or encourage respect for human rights and fundamental freedoms. They offered no guarantee and provided no means of enforcement; nevertheless, they symbolized a new approach. They were the result of five years of war against Nazi Germany, and the realization that the same government that had denied all human rights had waged aggressive war on a scale unparalleled in modern history. So one finds a wholly novel conception running through the Charter. The fate of individuals had become a matter of international concern.

On Dec. 10, 1948, the General Assembly of the United Nations adopted the Universal Declaration of Human Rights. This was proclaimed as "a common standard of achievement for all peoples and all nations." It provided a model that has since been followed on many occasions in the constitutions of new countries. Everyone was to be entitled to all the rights and freedoms set forth in the Declaration without distinction of any kind—colour, sex, language, religion, political or other opinions, national or social origin, property, birth, or other status. All were to be equal before the law. No one was to be subjected to arbitrary arrest, detention, or exile; everyone was to have the right to freedom of movement and residence within the borders of each state and the right to leave any country, including his own, and to return to his country. Freedom of thought, conscience, and religion, of opinion and expression, and of peaceful assembly and association were to be guaranteed. Everyone was to have the right to take part in the government of his country, directly or through freely chosen representatives.

So far, the Declaration was concerned with what are generally described as civil liberties. But in its later articles it went further. It provided for social security, the right to work, free choice of employment—and protection against unemployment—the right to rest and leisure, to an adequate standard of living, to education, and to participation in the cultural life of the nation. The European Convention on Human Rights, signed in 1950, was less ambitious in its scope. It did not seek to ensure social benefits, but confined itself to civil liberties. Its importance lay in the provisions for enforcement. It set up the European Commission of Human Rights and the European Court of Human Rights. The function of the Commission is to investigate alleged breaches of the Convention and to secure, if possible, a friendly settlement. If this proves unobtainable, the matter may be referred to the Committee of Ministers at Strasbourg or to the Court of Human Rights. Most important of all is the provision for the right of individual petition. This is not mandatory for all the signatories to the Convention. It is exercisable only where a national government has declared that it recognizes the competence of the Commission to receive petitions from individuals. Such recognition has now been accorded by 11 nations. Here is a new departure of the highest significance. For the first time in history, individual citizens who allege that their rights have been infringed can appeal over the heads of their governments to an international tribunal. The governments are bound by the Convention to abide by the decisions of the court.

It was not until 1966 that the government of the United Kingdom acceded to the right of individual petition. Two such petitions, both lodged in June 1967 by Commonwealth immigrants to the U.K., may be cited as examples of the many complaints laid before the European Commission—a comparatively small number of which have been referred to the court. In one case an Indian living in the United Kingdom complained that his father in India had not been allowed to come and join him. In the other, a Pakistani made a similar complaint in respect of his son. Both alleged a violation of article 8 of the European Convention, which lays down that "everyone has the right to respect for his private and family life, his home and his correspondence." The Commission dismissed the Indian's petition as not disclosing a prima facie case. It allowed the Pakistani petition, however, and the matter went forward. It was later settled.

Widening Circles. The Universal Declaration and the European Convention have served as models for other instruments. For example, various constitutions drawn up when former British colonial territories became independent included provisions for fundamental rights couched in similar terms. And there have been various occasions when jurists drawn from different parts of the world, at the invitation of the International Commission of Jurists, have reasserted, in different forms, fundamental human rights and liberties. Such assertions were made at Athens, Greece, in 1955; Delhi, India, in 1959; Lagos, Nigeria, in 1961; Rio de Janeiro, Braz., in 1962; and Bangkok, Thailand, in 1965. In 1966, at Colombo, Ceylon, a colloquium was held on the rule of law, consisting of the representatives of seven countries in Southeast Asia and also of the United Kingdom and Israel. They pressed for an enforceable covenant of human rights, for the setting up

of a United Nations high commissioner for human rights, for regional conventions on human rights, and, on the national level, for more effective constitutional entrenchment of human rights.

These were merely recommendations, but later in the same year the General Assembly adopted the United Nations Covenant on Civil and Political Rights, which was to come into force when it had been ratified by 35 countries. Under article 2, each state undertakes to respect and ensure to individuals within its territory and subject to its jurisdiction the rights recognized in the Covenant, without any distinction. These rights cover much the same ground as the Universal Declaration of 1948, but, unlike the Universal Declaration, the Covenant provides for supervision and enforcement. A Human Rights Committee was established. The states that are parties to the Covenant undertake to submit reports on the measures they have adopted which give effect to the rights recognized therein and on the progress made in the enjoyment of those rights. Under article 41 a state that is party to the Covenant may at any time declare that it recognizes the competence of the committee to receive complaints by one state against another, if the latter is not fulfilling its obligations under the Covenant. Thereafter, there is elaborate provision for communication between the complainant and defendant states and for conciliation under the auspices of the committee. These provisions do not go as far as the European model. In the last resort, the committee cannot pass an enforceable judgment. Nevertheless, they contemplate that a state that is alleged to have violated human rights shall be answerable to an international organization.

Over the years a series of conventions on particular human rights has been drawn up under the auspices of the United Nations. These conventions include a covenant on the abolition of slavery and forced labour, a convention concerning discrimination in respect of employment and occupation, a convention concerning equal remuneration for men and women workers for work of equal value, and a convention concerning freedom of association and protection of the right to organize. In London in June 1968 the representatives of 28 nations considered freedom of association.

Hope for the Future. No one concerned with human rights in 1968 can fail to be struck by two contrasts. The first is between the countries of Western Europe and, for the most part, the Afro-Asian countries on the one hand and, on the other, the Communist states and the white supremacist countries of southern Africa. On the one side there is the general acceptance (at least in theory) of civil liberties and the rule of law. There is no such acceptance on the other. In particular, the Communist states repudiate any suggestion involving the submission of disputes between individuals and governments to an international tribunal.

The second contrast is between principle and performance. It not infrequently happens that guarantees of human rights, although embodied in national constitutions, prove of little real value. There is nearly always a provision that such rights may be abrogated during an emergency. Since the government itself is the sole judge of the existence of an emergency, it can lock up its opponents without trial and prohibit all freedom of expression regardless of the constitutional guarantees.

Nevertheless, anyone who studies the history of the 23 years that have passed since the UN Charter was promulgated must be struck by the emphasis on the supreme importance of human rights. Of course it has frequently happened—and certainly not least in 1968—that these rights have been invaded or ignored and constitutional guarantees have been made to appear as so much waste paper. Perhaps some comfort may be drawn from English history. The provisions of Magna Carta were frequently violated. On many occasions political recusants were proceeded against without due process of law. But a standard had been established that was never forgotten and came to be maintained.

The Charter, the Universal Declaration, and the Covenant of 1966 represent the Magna Carta of the world.

776

continued from page 774

Warsaw Pact members in Czechoslovakia and calling on those nations to withdraw their forces forthwith. Algeria, India, and Pakistan abstained, and Hungary joined the U.S.S.R. in opposing the resolution; the final vote was 10–2–3. The council had discussed the problem at meetings held daily August 21–24. The council majority also attempted to request the secretary-general to send a special representative to Prague to seek the release and to guarantee the personal safety of Czechoslovak leaders then being detained. On August 27 the Czechoslovak representative to the UN requested that the council remove the item concerning his country from the agenda "in view of the agreement . . . reached on the substance of the problem during Soviet-Czechoslovak talks held in Moscow from 23 August to 26 August." In a statement on August 21 U Thant's spokesman indicated that he regarded developments in Czechoslovakia "as yet another serious blow to the concepts of international order and morality which form the basis of the Charter."

Vietnam. During the year the secretary-general called repeatedly on the powers involved to reduce their military efforts in Vietnam. He met various North Vietnamese officials in New Delhi, India, and Paris in February and was assured that productive talks would follow an end to the U.S. bombing. In a speech at the University of Alberta on May 13 U Thant reiterated his belief that it was crucial for the U.S. to stop the bombing of North Vietnam, and he maintained the same view in introducing his annual report to the UN in September. Agreement to stop the bombing finally came on October 31, after preliminary peace talks had started in Paris in May. U Thant on November 1 characterized the move as "a first and essential step toward peace."

Peace-keeping. During 1968 tensions between Greek and Turkish Cypriots seemed to relax somewhat, and shooting and other incidents were fewer than in 1967. The government of Cyprus, meanwhile, was reducing restrictions it had placed upon Turkish Cypriots. In May the secretary-general's special representative, Bibiano F. Osorio-Tafall (Mexico), arranged for direct talks between the Greek and Turkish communities on Cyprus, the first serious contacts between them in more than four years. U Thant stated in September that some "real promise of progress" was being made toward a settlement. In the meantime, the UN Peace-Keeping Force in Cyprus (UNFICYP) continued to carry out its obligations on the island, despite a deficit of more than $16 million. Voluntary financing was clearly proving inadequate to meet UNFICYP expenses, but the Security Council decided three times to extend the life of the force, on March 18 for three months, and on June 18 and December 5 for six. The council members optimistically expected that the end of each period would see enough progress toward a final solution so that UNFICYP could withdraw or be substantially reduced.

The Special Committee on Peace-Keeping Operations (Committee of 33), established in 1965 to undertake "a comprehensive review of the whole question of peace-keeping operations in all their aspects," was asked to report by July 1 on progress made regarding "a study on matters related to facilities, services, and personnel which member states might provide in accordance with the Charter for United Nations peace-keeping operations." The committee met under these instructions on March 4. Adopting an attitude, sug-

gested by Italy, that it concentrate on what united it rather than what divided it, the committee on April 8 established a working group; by the end of May the group had agreed to make, as a first model, a study of UN military observers established or authorized by the Security Council. If the committee could, indeed, move on from its first model to others, the UN might find itself in a position to discuss establishing military forces under art. 43 and 47 of the UN Charter and even to liquidate the organization's mounting deficit. By June 30 this deficit exceeded $260 million, largely because of refusals by France and the U.S.S.R. to pay their shares of the cost of several UN forces.

Disarmament. The Treaty on the Non-proliferation of Nuclear Weapons marked the successful outcome of ten years of effort by the conference of the 18-Nation Disarmament Committee (ENDC). The treaty, approved by the resumed 22nd session of the assembly (April 24–June 12), was open for signatures on July 1. By the end of the year more than 80 states had signed it, and the U.K., Ireland, and Nigeria had ratified it. It would go into effect when ratified by the U.S.S.R., the U.S., and 38 other nations. The treaty aimed at preventing nuclear weapons from spreading to countries which did not already possess them and established a safeguards system for verifying the obligations that states assumed under its provisions. The ENDC met four times in January and eight times in March to deal with the treaty. It met again July 16–August 28 to consider its agenda: further effective measures aimed at ending the nuclear arms race and promoting nuclear disarmament; nonnuclear disarmament measures; and general and complete disarmament under strict and effective international control. It also asked the General Assembly to have the secretary-general appoint experts to study the effects of the possible use of chemical and bacteriological weapons in war. (*See* DEFENSE: *Special Report.*)

A UN Conference of Non-Nuclear-Weapon States met from August 29 to September 28 in Geneva. The conference approved (71–0–1) a declaration urging nations to do all they could to increase international security, particularly the security of nonnuclear states, until such time as general and complete disarmament became possible. It called for steps to prevent proliferation of nuclear weapons and encouraged states to undertake disarmament measures relating to nuclear weapons and to develop cooperative programs for using nuclear energy peacefully. Invitations to attend the conference went to all nuclear *powers*, not states, in order to allow the People's Republic of China (not a UN member) to attend. The Communist regime refused to accept the invitation, but France, the U.S.S.R., the U.K., and the U.S. all attended.

Many nonnuclear states, led by Argentina, Italy, Brazil, Pakistan, and Yugoslavia, attempted to reactivate the UN Disarmament Commission, composed of all UN members, as a permanent sounding board on nuclear issues. The U.S. and U.S.S.R. convinced them that they could not muster enough votes, and the sponsors settled for a resolution (adopted December 20) asking the 24th assembly in 1969 to consider reconvening the commission.

Human Environment. Increasing concern over pollution in all environments led the General Assembly on December 3 to adopt unanimously a resolution calling for an international conference in 1972 to explore the possibilities of cooperating to "eliminate the impairment of human environment." Swedish Ambassador Sverker C. Astrom, sponsoring the resolution,

spoke of the price of polluting the seas, the atmosphere, and the earth: "Even if we avoid the risk of blowing up the planet," he said, "we may, by changing its face, unwittingly be parties to a process with the same fateful outcome."

At its summer meetings the 18-Nation Disarmament Committee had warned against an arms race on the bed of the sea. The sea was also the principal concern of an ad hoc committee of the General Assembly "to study the peaceful uses of the seabed and the ocean floor beyond the limits of national jurisdic-

"Of course we failed in Kashmir, South West Africa, the Middle East, Hungary and Czechoslovakia, but we darn well put the Rhodesian sportsmen in their place." —King, "Daily Telegraph," Australia.

tion." The committee, established in 1967, met March 18–27, June 17–July 9, and August 19–30, 1968. The 35 members generally agreed that states should use the seabed exclusively for peaceful purposes and should prevent all military uses, although some believed that a state might use the seabed for military purposes so long as the use conformed with provisions of the UN Charter. A U.S. proposal for an International Decade of Ocean Exploration received general support as did an Icelandic proposal to prevent sea pollution.

Outer Space. A UN Conference on the Exploration and Peaceful Uses of Outer Space met in Vienna August 14–27 to hear more than 180 papers on space themes prepared by governments and organizations. Besides scientists and nonscientists from 79 countries, the 600 delegates included representatives of nine UN agencies and four specialized organizations. Proposals presented to the conference included an Eastern European plan to establish an international synchronous communications satellite system, Intersputnik. The conference discussed its possible relation to the existing International Telecommunication Satellite Consortium and the possibilities and problems involved in establishing a UN space agency at some time in the future. A paper, prepared by the late Soviet cosmonaut Yuri Gagarin, described the selection and training of cosmonauts. Still other papers dealt with direct broadcast television from synchronous satellites; UN use of communications satellites; the relevance of space programs to less developed countries; and aspects of outer space relating to biology, medicine, oceanography, and water resources. One report indicated the feasibility by 1970 of using satellites to transmit educational programs to all schools within areas as large as India or Brazil. Another spelled out the use of navigation satellites in guiding aircraft and ships, in warning against hazards to shipping, and in helping rescue operations.

The Legal Sub-Committee of the UN Committee on the Peaceful Uses of Outer Space worked June 4–28 on an agreement on liability for damage caused by launching objects into space. The subcommittee draft included articles relating to exoneration from liability, joint and several liability, presentation of claims by states on behalf of their nationals, and pursuit of available remedies. The assembly also charged the committee with defining "outer space," but by the end of the year the committee had been unable to identify scientific or technical criteria that would permit a precise and lasting definition.

Human Rights. The year 1968 was the 20th anniversary of the Universal Declaration of Human Rights and was proclaimed by the General Assembly as the International Year for Human Rights. The major anniversary celebration took the form of an International Conference on Human Rights in Teheran, Iran (April 22–May 13), attended by representatives from 84 countries. (*See* Special Report.)

UNCTAD. The second session of the UN Conference on Trade and Development (UNCTAD; February 1–March 29) in New Delhi failed to improve the access of less developed countries to export markets for commodities and manufactured goods, nor did it ease the terms of aid to help alleviate the burdens such countries encountered in servicing their debts. The developed countries maintained that they could do no more to help because of British and U.S. balance of payments problems, the world monetary crisis, and the Vietnam war. Agreeing that military expenses in developed nations were staggering, U Thant observed nonetheless that the developed countries seemed to have forgotten that they could make a "truly constructive contribution to their own security and to the reduction of the basic causes of unrest and insecurity by working towards the elimination of poverty and want in the world."

In spite of general disappointment about the results of the New Delhi conference, UNCTAD made several important decisions. The conferees rejected the view that expanding East-West trade would harm trade between the industrial and less developed countries and decided to work with the regional economic commissions on trade problems; the less developed countries announced that they were determined to negotiate arrangements among themselves to expand their own trade and promote integrated economic undertakings; the developed states announced their willingness to negotiate concrete schemes for financial and technical assistance with less developed countries.

UNDP. The United Nations Development Programme (UNDP) held its 1968 pledging conference in New York City on October 17 and received pledges from 97 governments amounting to nearly $115 million for operations in 1969. Some governments, including the U.S., planned to announce their pledges later. These would probably bring the 1969 pledges close to $200 million, the target for the year. For 1969, 50 governments increased their contributions. UNDP, a partnership of virtually all UN organizations, remained dedicated to increasing the development power of low-income countries and in 1967–68 spent about $176 million pursuing its objectives. The recipient governments themselves contributed substantially to the program—almost $200 million in 1968. UNDP was also administering a $30 million fund for the development of West Irian; a $6 million fund for the Congo (Kinshasa); a $500,000 fund from Sweden to train administrative personnel for Lesotho;

Demonstrators outside United Nations headquarters in New York City protesting the Nigerian government's blockade of Biafra.

and, jointly with the UN Industrial Development Organization (UNIDO), a $7 million Special Industrial Services Fund.

Food and Population. The race between available supplies of food and the size of the world's population continued to concern various UN bodies. The International Conference on Human Rights declared it a "basic right" of couples "to decide freely and responsibly on the number and spacing of their children," and the Economic and Social Council (ECOSOC) in its 45th session (July 8–August 2) debated "population and its relation to economic and social development." On July 30 ECOSOC adopted a resolution endorsing or recommending many activities and research studies relating to population problems and trends.

Organizational Matters. Emilio Arenales Catalan, minister of foreign affairs of Guatemala, was elected president of the General Assembly at its 23d session (September 24–December 21). Three new members of the United Nations made their appearance in 1968: Mauritius, recommended by the Security Council on April 18 and admitted by the General Assembly on April 24; Swaziland (September 11 and September 24); and Equatorial Guinea, formerly Spanish Guinea (November 6 and November 12). The organization's membership thus rose to 126.

On November 19 the People's Republic of (Communist) China failed by a vote of 44–58–23 (one member absent) to replace the Republic of (Nationalist) China on the Security Council and General Assembly. The vote in 1967 was 45–58–17.

At the Security Council meeting of December 30, members rose for a moment of silent tribute to Trygve Lie, first UN secretary-general (1946–53), who died that day in Oslo. (*See* OBITUARIES.)   (R. N. S.)

UNESCO. In 1968—the International Year for Human Rights—UNESCO laid increasing stress on the economic and social advancement of the people of the less developed nations, particularly in Africa, Asia, and Latin America. While carrying out its programs aimed at promoting international cooperation in the fields of education, science, culture, and communications, UNESCO also worked for more widespread action in favour of human rights and international understanding.

UNESCO and the Organization of African Unity jointly convened a conference in Nairobi in July on "Education and Scientific and Technical Training in Relation to Development in Africa." The 165 delegates from 36 African countries agreed on the need for reform in primary education, the training of more African teachers, and the introduction of more scientific and technical education.

More than 300 delegates attended a conference in August at UNESCO headquarters in Paris on educational planning. The conference report stressed the importance of education as a preliminary investment and the need to integrate education in overall economic and social planning.

A meeting at UNESCO in September—the Conference on the Scientific Basis for Rational Use and Conservation of the Resources of the Biosphere—called on the UN General Assembly to consider the advisability of a Universal Declaration on the Protection and Betterment of the Human Environment.

On October 19 Director General René Maheu was unanimously renominated to a second term of office. This was the first time UNESCO had renominated a director general.   (R. C. LeB.)

United States

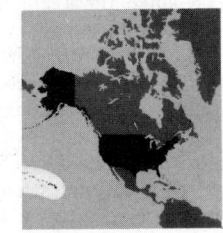

The United States of America is a federal republic composed of 50 states, 49 of which are in North America and one of which consists of the Hawaiian Islands. Area: 3,615,210 sq.mi. (9,363,405 sq.km.), including 66,237 sq.mi. of inland water but excluding the 60,306 sq.mi. of the Great Lakes that lie within U.S. boundaries. Pop. (1968 est.): 201,750,000, including (1960) white 88.6%; Negro 10.5%. Language: English. Religion (1963 est.): Protestant 64,435,000; Roman Catholic 42,-877,000; Jewish 5,365,000; Orthodox 2.8 million. Cap.: Washington, D.C. (pop., 1968 est., 854,000). Largest city: New York (pop., 1968 est., 8,125,000). President in 1968, Lyndon Baines Johnson.

A year of tragedy and turmoil in both domestic and foreign affairs ended in a surprisingly close presidential election won by the Republican nominee, Richard M. Nixon. Nixon's triumph came eight years after he had lost an even closer presidential election to John F. Kennedy. He thus became the first man since William Henry Harrison in 1840 to win the presidency for the first time after a previous unsuccessful attempt. Complete, official returns gave Nixon 31,770,237 popular votes (43.4%) and 301 electoral votes, as against 31,270,533 popular votes (42.7%) and 191 electoral votes for Democratic nominee Hubert H. Humphrey and 9,906,141 popular votes (13.5%) and 46 electoral votes for American Independent Party nominee George C. Wallace. A scattering of minor-party candidates received a total of 239,908 popular votes (0.4%).

The closeness of the presidential race was reflected in the results of the congressional elections. The Republicans scored a net gain of five seats in the Senate, making the new composition 58 Democrats and 42 Republicans. In the House of Representatives, the Republicans failed in their well-organized and heavily financed campaign to become the majority party. They gained only four seats for a total of 192 as compared with 243 for the Democrats. As a result, Nixon became the first president-elect since Zachary Taylor in 1848 not to bring in at least one house of the new Congress of his own political party in his initial election. On the other hand, the Republican Party won 13 of the 21 state gubernatorial elections, giving it a total of 31 governorships.

Prominent among the new members of the Senate was Barry M. Goldwater (Ariz.), the 1964 Republican presidential nominee, who previously had been a U.S. senator from 1953 to 1965. Goldwater won the seat of retiring Democratic Sen. Carl Hayden, who had served continuously in the House and Senate since 1912. Republican newcomers to the Senate included Robert W. Packwood (Ore.), William B. Saxbe (O.), and Charles M. Mathias, Jr. (Md.). Among Democrats winning election to the Senate for the first time were Harold E. Hughes (Ia.), Alan Cranston (Calif.), and Thomas F. Eagleton (Mo.). Of the 435 members of the House elected on November 5, no fewer than 396 were incumbents (223 Democrats and 173 Republicans) and only 39 (20 Democrats and 19 Republicans) were newcomers. Adam Clayton Powell, a New York Democrat, who was not allowed to take his seat in the 90th Congress, was reelected by his Harlem constituents. Allard K. Lowenstein, a leader of the movement to deny renomination to President Johnson, was a surprise winner in a suburban Long Island, N.Y., district.

President-elect Nixon introduced the 12 men designated for Cabinet positions in his administration in a nationwide television program on December 11. Assuming that all would be confirmed by the Senate, Nixon's Cabinet would consist of the following men: William P. Rogers, secretary of state; Melvin R. Laird, secretary of defense; David M. Kennedy, secretary of the treasury; John N. Mitchell, attorney general; Winton M. Blount, postmaster general; Walter J. Hickel, secretary of the interior; Clifford M. Hardin, secretary of agriculture; Maurice H. Stans, secretary of commerce; George P. Shultz, secretary of labour; Robert H. Finch, secretary of health, education, and welfare; George W. Romney, secretary of housing and urban development; and John A. Volpe, secretary of transportation.

Foreign Affairs. The Vietnam war headed toward a possible negotiated settlement in 1968. In the same March 31 speech in which he announced that he would not seek reelection, President Johnson said that he had ordered—"unilaterally"—a halt to the U.S. air and naval bombardment of North Vietnam "except in the area north of the Demilitarized Zone where the continuing enemy buildup directly threatens Allied forward positions and where the movements of troops and supplies [is] clearly related to that threat." The president added: "We are prepared to move immediately toward peace through negotiations. So tonight, in the hope that this action will lead to early talks, I am taking the first step to de-escalate the conflict."

Responding to Johnson's address, the North Vietnamese government on April 3 "declared its readiness" to arrange for a meeting with a U.S. representative "with a view to determining . . . the unconditional cessation of the U.S. bombing raids and all other acts of war against the Democratic Republic of Vietnam so that talks may start." A month of wrangling over a mutually acceptable site for negotiations followed. Finally, on May 3, the U.S. and North Vietnam agreed

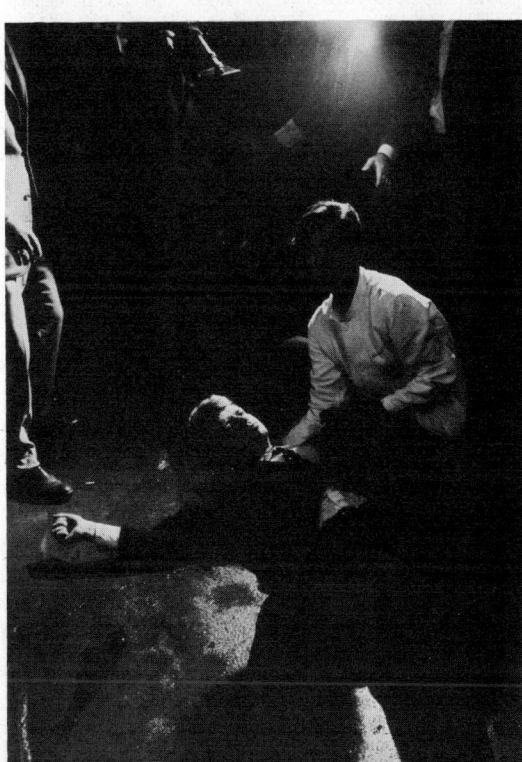

BILL EPPRIDGE, "LIFE" MAGAZINE © TIME INC.

Sen. Robert F. Kennedy lying mortally wounded in a corridor of the Ambassador Hotel in Los Angeles after being shot by an assassin on June 5, 1968.

UPI COMPIX

Mrs. Martin Luther King, Jr., comforting her daughter Bernice during funeral services for her slain husband in the Ebenezer Baptist Church, Atlanta, Ga., April 9, 1968.

to hold preliminary peace talks in Paris. Exactly one week later, talks opened there between a U.S. delegation headed by Ambassador-at-large W. Averell Harriman and a North Vietnamese delegation headed by Minister of State Xuan Thuy (*see* BIOGRAPHY).

Months of negotiation brought no appreciable progress. The deadlock was finally broken by President Johnson's announcement on October 31 that all air, naval, and artillery bombardment of North Vietnam would cease the following day. Because of the bombing halt, Johnson said, the U.S. could "now expect . . . prompt, productive, serious and intensive negotiations in an atmosphere that is conducive to progress." The president added that North Vietnam had agreed, in

exchange for a bombing halt, to permit the South Vietnamese government to take part in the Paris talks. The United States in turn agreed to permit the National Liberation Front (NLF), political arm of the Viet Cong, to participate. The expanded talks were to have begun on November 6, but South Vietnamese Pres. Nguyen Van Thieu announced that his government would not attend unless North Vietnam agreed to negotiate without the NLF participating as a separate delegation. Although Thieu finally relented and sent a delegation headed by Vice-Pres. Nguyen Cao Ky to Paris, a dispute over conference-table seating arrangements further delayed the opening of the expanded talks, which had still not begun by the end of 1968.

Seizure of the U.S. Navy intelligence ship "Pueblo" and its 83 crew members off the coast of North Korea on January 23 proved a major embarrassment to the Johnson administration. The ship and its crew were captured by four North Korean patrol boats and taken to the port of Wonsan. The U.S., insisting that the "Pueblo" had been in international waters about 25 mi. off the coast, demanded the release of the ship and its men. But a North Korean broadcast claimed that the "Pueblo" was captured legally because it had been inside the 12-mi. limit of North Korean territorial waters. U.S.-North Korean talks on the release of the "Pueblo" were held periodically at Panmunjom, and finally resulted in the freeing of the crew and their return to the U.S. in late December. North Korea, however, kept possession of the ship. In the meantime, North Korea had exploited the situation for its propaganda value.

U.S. reaction to the foremost international crisis of the year, the Soviet-led invasion of Czechoslovakia by

continued on page 784

UNITED STATES

Education. (1965–66) Primary (including preprimary), pupils 31,961,500, teachers 1,134,000; secondary and vocational, pupils 17,127,500, teachers 830,000; higher (including junior colleges and teacher-training colleges), students 5,526,325, teaching staff 429,000.

Finance. Monetary unit: U.S. dollar ($2.40 = £1 sterling; $35 = 1 troy oz. of gold). Gold and foreign exchange, official: (June 1968) $13,160,000,000; (June 1967) $13,910,000,000. Federal administrative budget (1968 rev. est.): revenue $126,937,000,000; expenditure $135,033,000,000. Gross national product: (1967) $789.7 billion; (1966) $747.6 billion. Money supply: (June 1968) $183.3 billion; (June 1967) $173.2 billion. Cost of living (1963 = 100): (June 1968) 113; (June 1967) 109.

Foreign Trade. (1967) Imports $26,893,000,000; exports (excluding military aid to the value of $592 million) $31,035,000,000. Import sources: Canada 26%; Japan 11%; West Germany 7%; U.K. 6%. Export destinations: Canada 23%; Japan 9%; U.K. 6%; West Germany 5%. Main exports: machinery 26%; chemicals 9%; motor vehicles 9%; cereals 9%.

Transport and Communications. Roads (1966) 3,697,960 mi. (including 13,816 mi. state primary system expressways). Motor vehicles in use (1967): passenger 80,458,317; commercial 16,193,618. Railways: (1966) 211,514,000 mi.; traffic (1967) 15,199,952,-940 passenger-mi., freight 718,749,411,120 net ton-mi. Inland waterways freight traffic (1965) 255,999,874,-832 ton-mi. (including [1964] 105,892,342,400 ton-mi. on Great Lakes system and 89,350,944,800 ton-mi. on Mississippi River system). Oceangoing shipping (1967): merchant vessels 100 gross tons and over 3,017; gross tonnage 18,440,199. Great Lakes shipping (1967): merchant vessels 100 gross tons and over 286; gross tonnage 1,892,427. Shipping traffic (including Great Lakes international traffic; 1967) goods loaded 189,038,449 short tons, unloaded 272,276,-082 short tons. Air traffic (1967): 78,743,732,906 passenger-mi. (including 84,265,342,772 passenger-mi. on internal services); freight 3,474,669,541 ton-mi. (in-

cluding 2,373,259,040 net ton-mi. on internal services. Telephones (Dec. 1966) 98,789,000. Radio receivers (Dec. 1966) 262.7 million. Television receivers (Dec. 1966) *c.* 74.1 million.

Agriculture. Production (in 000; short tons; 1967; 1966 in parentheses): corn 132,219 (115,285); wheat 45,730 (39,351); oats 12,510 (12,820); barley 8,885 (9,435); rye 674 (778); rice 4,481 (4,250); linseed 557 (654); sorghum 21,436 (20,020); dry beans 780 (1,001); soybeans 29,181 (27,853); dry peas 187 (186); peanuts 1,254 (1,204); potatoes 15,295 (15,-345); sweet potatoes (1966) 684, (1965) 776; tobacco 986 (944); sugar, raw value (1967–68) *c.* 4,763, (1966–67) *c.* 4,767; apples 2,896 (3,032); oranges 5,683 (8,473); grapefruit 1,726 (2,293); lemons 740 (779); grapes 3,007 (3,733); cotton, lint 1,828 (2,298); wool 49 (51); beef and veal 10,075 (10,-308); pork 6,188 (5,862); milk 59,645 (60,114); butter 628 (567); cheese 946 (928); hen eggs (1966) 4,322, (1965) 4,271; hardwood timber (1966) 3,301,-901,000 cu.ft., (1965) 3,270,118,200 cu.ft. Livestock (in 000; Jan. 1967): cattle 108,645; sheep *c.* 23,900; horses *c.* 2,800; pigs (Jan. 1966) 47,414; chickens (Jan. 1966) 393,019. Fish catch (in 000; short tons) (1966) 2,772, (1965) 3,002.

Industry. Fuel and power (in 000; short tons; 1967): coal 558,593; crude oil 479,141; natural gas 668,483,384 cu.yd.; electricity 1,314,298,000 kw-hr. Production (in 000; short tons; 1967): iron ore (50–55% metal content) 94,298; pig iron (1966) 94,002; crude steel 126,919; newsprint 2,321; sulfuric acid 28,212; caustic soda 7,892; superphosphates (1966) 2,804; nitrogenous fertilizers (N content; 1966–67) 6,101; plastics and resins 6,312; synthetic rubber 2,141; passenger cars 7,437 units; commercial vehicles 1,540 units. Merchant vessels launched (100 gross tons and over; 1967) 250,000 gross tons. New dwellings started (1967) 1,322,000. Index of industrial production (1963 = 100; 1967; 1966 in parentheses): total 127 (126); mining 114 (112); manufacturing 128 (127); electricity and gas 132 (124); construction 102 (106). Unemployment: (1967) 3.8%; (1966) 3.8%.

AN INCREDIBLE YEAR IN U.S. HISTORY

By Bruce L. Felknor

Richard Nixon, Hubert Humphrey, and George Wallace as interpreted by Gerald Scarfe, political cartoonist for "The Sunday Times" of London. The life-size papier-mâché sculptures of the three presidential candidates were among caricatures done by Scarfe for the U.S. election campaign.

COURTESY, WADDELL GALLERY, NEW YORK

Murders and riots, along with an unpopular war and unexpected peace moves, shaped the incredible U.S. election year of 1968. An incumbent president was challenged and withdrew and was finally succeeded by a man many had come to regard as an "easy to beat" loser. A popular liberal became the stereotype of reaction to many fellow Democrats—yet he reunited a sundered party and lost the presidency only narrowly. A third-party candidate waxed and waned, and a nation called divided watched a president and his successor launch one of the smoothest transitions of administration in history. It took two days of counting to determine that Richard Nixon had won a plurality of half a million popular votes and a majority of the electoral votes, and that his Republican Party had gained four seats in the House of Representatives, five seats in the Senate, and five governorships.

The story that ended in that long count had begun a year earlier, when Minnesota's Democratic senator, Eugene J. McCarthy, challenged Pres. Lyndon B. Johnson on his Vietnam war policies. The roots, however, went back even further. Lyndon Johnson, who had succeeded to the presidency after the assassination of John F. Kennedy and who had been overwhelmingly reelected in 1964, completed the unfinished agenda of Franklin Roosevelt's New Deal, and early in his term his popularity was immense. But then U.S. involvement in Vietnam, which had escalated invisibly under Presidents Dwight D. Eisenhower and Kennedy, became highly visible with rapidly increasing U.S. death tolls. The war's unpopularity mounted, and with it that of Lyndon Johnson. The 1966 elections reinstated the Republicans as a large minority in Congress, and social legislation, competing with the Vietnam war for the available money, slowed. Many U.S. Negroes found their race's gains were too little, too late, and too slow, and they responded with the call for "Black Power" to achieve their goals. A general crime increase and sporadic violence in the cities raised apprehension in white communities. A call for "law and order" was the response, and it became not only an issue, but, many believed, a code word for Negro repression.

Early in the year Michigan's Republican Gov. George Romney announced that he was a candidate for the presidency. New York's Gov. Nelson Rockefeller, also a Republican, was thought to be available. George Wallace, former governor of Alabama, began hinting of his interest in the office. Peace factions and black militants talked of nominating their own candidates, and a rerun of the four-way race of 1948 seemed possible.

The Primaries. In this setting, McCarthy, whose criticism of the administration on its Vietnam policies had become increasingly caustic, announced his candidacy for president and entered the nation's first primary, in New Hampshire. Rockefeller denied that he was a candidate, but said that he would accept a draft; 30 Republican leaders endorsed him. At this time, Richard Nixon declared that new leadership could end the war; he entered the New Hampshire primary and announced his serious candidacy.

McCarthy was the only major Democrat on the New Hampshire ballot, but shortly before the March 12 voting, Democratic

regulars, alarmed by the effectiveness of his legion of young amateur campaign workers, mounted a desperate write-in campaign for the president. Johnson won 48% of the vote, but McCarthy, with 42%, won 20 of the 24 delegates. Nixon won the Republican primary; Romney, with the polls indicating a disaster for him, withdrew from the primary and the presidential race. A few days later, Robert Kennedy announced that he would enter the race on the Democratic side.

Then President Johnson stunned the nation by announcing an end to the bombing of most of North Vietnam—and his decision not to seek reelection. Two days later, McCarthy won a somewhat diluted triumph over the president in the Wisconsin primary. The following Thursday, April 4, Negro leader Martin Luther King, Jr. (*see* OBITUARIES), was assassinated in Memphis, Tenn. Negro grief, shock, and anger found expression in rioting and violence in 125 cities, and some white citizens took a second look at George Wallace, who was stressing "law and order" and promising to be on the ballot in 50 states.

After the King funeral, McCarthy, unopposed, won a preferential primary but no delegates in Pennsylvania and took all the delegates in the Massachusetts primary. The upset Republican winner in Massachusetts was Rockefeller, for whom a hasty write-in campaign had been contrived by amateurs. He beat Gov. John Volpe, who was on the ballot, and Richard Nixon, who was not, and reversed his decision not to run.

Vice-Pres. Hubert Humphrey took four weeks to assess his chances after Johnson's withdrawal. He then declared his candidacy and hurriedly assembled an organization to hunt delegates.

In the Indiana primary Robert Kennedy defeated both McCarthy and Gov. Roger Branigan. He won in the District of Columbia and trounced McCarthy in Nebraska. In Oregon, McCarthy won his only primary victory over an active opponent who was on the ballot, handing Kennedy his first election defeat and winning 45% of the vote to Kennedy's 39%. The next week, on June 4, Kennedy scored a solid victory over McCarthy in California. But on the night of the election, as the votes were still being counted, he was assassinated (shortly after midnight) in Los Angeles (*see* OBITUARIES).

Nixon, meanwhile, had won every Republican primary he entered; the Massachusetts write-in effort for Rockefeller had

been his only reverse. Rockefeller had intensified his campaign and in mid-July finished a 44-state tour as his $3 million advertising campaign reached a peak.

Humphrey entered no primaries, but he was able to gain enough delegates in those states without primaries to give him apparent control over the convention. But dissenters were taking an increasingly hard line against him and the administration. To ardent liberals, Humphrey—until recently denounced by rightists as a dangerous radical—was becoming the very image of the establishment.

The Conventions. The national conventions of the two parties could hardly have been more dissimilar. The Republicans convened amid the orderly opulence of Miami Beach, Fla., where the only hot question was whether Rockefeller, California Gov. Ronald Reagan, and assorted favourite sons could stop Nixon. The answer was no, partly because one of the favourite sons, Maryland's Gov. Spiro Agnew, released his delegation and declared for Nixon as the convention opened.

Just after the Soviet Union moved its Warsaw Pact troops into Czechoslovakia, the Democrats met—mired in disorder inside and outside the hall—in a tense Chicago. The city resembled one under siege, and the main question seemed to be whether the convention could go on at all, given disabling telephone, taxi, and bus strikes.

Security had been no problem for the Republican convention, with the only disorder occurring miles away on the Florida mainland. But the Democrats were beset by organized plans to disrupt the convention proceedings within the hall and throughout the city. The Coalition for an Open Convention had brought about 1,200 dissenting Democrats to Chicago two months in advance to plan challenges of delegate credentials and also a platform repudiating the Democratic administration.

Throughout 1968 various peace groups, notably an amalgam of new leftists, the National Mobilization Committee to End the War in Vietnam ("the Mobe" to its adherents), and the lesser and more whimsical Youth International Party, or "Yippies," planned massive demonstrations. Before the convention opened, the leaders had trained "parade marshals" in the harassment and penetration of police lines and were preparing themselves to lead the expected scores of thousands of youthful demonstrators into confrontation with the police. They succeeeded completely. The threat of huge crowds of dissenters had put Chicago's 11,900-man police force on 12-hour duty and brought some 13,000 National Guard and federal troops to the city. The harassment tactics—throwing rocks and bottles and using obscene language—precipitated recurring battles between demonstrators and police. During these conflicts it was charged that some police removed their badges, while others ignored orders from superiors to stop beating demonstrators. Many, as one Chicago reporter put it, "went animal," clubbing demonstrators repeatedly, even those already on the ground, making newsmen a secondary target, and charging bystanders when they ran out of kids and cameramen. The majority of the police acted responsibly and with minimum force, but they simply formed a backdrop for the excesses of the rabid ones. The most notorious scene took place on Wednesday night, August 28, when the organizers assembled their followers where the television cameras were, outside the convention headquarters hotel, the Conrad Hilton. Television filmed most of the 18-minute donnybrook touched off by brickbats, bottles, and bags hurled at police by agitators. The television film was played to the nation the rest of the week.

In peaceful Miami Beach, the Republicans lacked even the excitement of delegate credentials fights. Two Negro protests over lily-white Southern delegations were filed too late for action. But in Chicago the Democrats faced challenges involving a record of 17 state delegations. In response, they threw out the entire Mississippi regular delegation in favour of an integrated challenge slate, seated an integrated Georgia challenge delegation alongside Gov. Lester Maddox's regulars and split the vote between them, and made Alabama delegates sign a

"negative loyalty oath" that they would not support the nominee of another party.

The Republicans made one mildly worded and uncontroversial rule change prohibiting discrimination in selecting future delegates. (There were 26 Negroes among the 1,333 GOP delegates; 212 of 3,099 Democratic delegates were black.) The Democrats, after rancorous debate, outlawed the unit rule (that an entire delegation must vote the will of its majority) at the 1968 convention and prohibited it at every level down to the precinct in selecting delegates for 1972. In addition, the Democrats required delegates to the 1972 convention to be chosen in that calendar year rather than long in advance.

In Miami Beach any controversy over the platform was smoothed out in committee; a hard-line plank on Vietnam was watered down. But in Chicago the long-brewing fight over the Vietnam war policy went to the convention floor in a historic two-hour debate that was finally resolved for the majority (relatively hard-line) plank in a 60–40% roll-call vote.

The only significant surprise at the Republican convention was Nixon's choice of Agnew, relatively inexperienced and ambiguous on civil rights. The move angered many liberals, who tried to draft an alternative. Newscasts reported a flurry for New York City Mayor John Lindsay, who had rejected the idea months before. Even as the Lindsay "boom" was being reported, he was on his way to second Agnew's nomination. The Democratic vice-presidential nominee, Edmund Muskie, was a respected and seasoned U.S. senator, twice governor of Maine, while Agnew had been a governor for only a year and a half and had limited local government experience before that.

Humphrey's nomination as the Democratic candidate for president was no surprise, although the news media had made much of a last-minute draft attempt for Sen. Edward Kennedy. After a couple of days, the Massachusetts senator asked that his name not be placed in nomination. In spite of entering no primaries, Humphrey had gained the necessary delegate votes weeks earlier. After the increasing bitterness of the preconvention campaign between McCarthy and Humphrey, it was not surprising that McCarthy told supporters he could not endorse the nominee. A relative surprise, perhaps, was the dignity, grace, and sportsmanship of Sen. George McGovern (S.D.), who became a candidate on the eve of the convention to rally Robert Kennedy's supporters but said he would support the party's nominee. He quickly came to Humphrey's side after his acceptance speech.

But the big winner at Chicago's bloodbath was "the Mobe." Among the losers were about 1,000 demonstrators treated for tear gas and injuries, 101 of them hospitalized; 192 injured police, 49 hospitalized; 63 newsmen attacked by police, 13 with their camera or recording equipment deliberately damaged; the city of Chicago; and—gravest casualties of all—the Democratic Party and its candidate.

Campaigns and Election. Hubert Humphrey opened his campaign on Labor Day in New York City. He urged Senate ratification of the nuclear nonproliferation treaty, chiding Nixon for advocating delay. The confident Nixon, who launched his crisply organized campaign in Chicago a few days later, wanted to reassess the "posture and intentions of the Soviet Union," in light of that nation's invasion of Czechoslovakia, before endorsing the treaty.

For the first month of the campaign Nixon seemed to be the only American listening to his rival. Wherever Humphrey went, he was literally drowned out by hecklers, who accused him of following President Johnson's policies and whose thunderous chants made it impossible for audiences to hear the candidate.

In dealing with the important "law and order" issue, Nixon called Humphrey "tragically naïve" about the "crime crisis." Humphrey, who as mayor of Minneapolis had rehabilitated an outmoded and corrupt police force, dealt with the problem by advocating federal aid to obtain improved salaries, training, and equipment for police. He spoke of "order and justice" instead of "law and order."

Events at the Democratic convention in Chicago: above, Chicago's Mayor Richard J. Daley and members of the Illinois delegation shouting at Sen. Abraham Ribicoff (Conn.); right, Georgia delegate Julian Bond declining vice-presidential nomination; far right, cheering delegates.

Spiro Agnew, talking "law and order," rebuffed Republican colleagues who urged him to substitute "order with justice." The Maryland governor's rhetoric got him into trouble repeatedly. He called Humphrey "squishy soft on Communism," and used the terms "Polack" and "fat Jap." Aghast Republicans demanded apologies. For the Democrats, Edmund Muskie concentrated his campaign largely on crime, the Wallace candidacy, and Vietnam. He was becoming better known and appeared to be adding strength to the Democratic ticket.

That strength was needed. During the early part of the campaign Humphrey trailed Nixon badly in the polls. The Nixon campaign appeared to run effortlessly, on a five-day week that left the candidate free to relax on weekends at Key Biscayne, Fla. Not so Humphrey, who was angered and frustrated at his inability to penetrate the sound barrier raised by his ever-present hecklers, and also depressed by the polls. But at last his campaign organization began to hum instead of creak under the practiced hand of former Kennedy aide Lawrence O'Brien. Humphrey pledged, if elected, to stop bombing North Vietnam as "an acceptable risk for peace." Muskie invited a heckler to the platform to air his views. Young people began to listen, and hecklers were shouted down by growing Humphrey crowds.

George Wallace was nominated as the presidential candidate of the newly formed American Independent Party. He had no running mate until October, when he selected retired Air Force Gen. Curtis LeMay. But Wallace hardly seemed to need a running mate. He had one speech, which the faithful received with joyous shouts and rebel yells wherever he went. He found "rednecks and peckerwoods" in Boston and New York and other

unlikely places outside the piney woods. They liked everything they heard from the diminutive Southern firebrand. He was against "pointy-head intellectuals" and anarchists, and for "law and order." Until the very end of the campaign the polls indicated that he had the support of about 20% of the electorate.

The Wallace candidacy did one interesting and useful favour for the political system otherwise so sorely beset in 1968: it offered political action and an emotional outlet to haters and other Americans frightened about prospective Negro encroachments on their jobs, neighbourhoods, and schools. These frightened Americans supported Wallace who never in public uttered the word "nigger," and who gave the good white folk up North and down South all the trappings of respectable conservatism, but with the emotional lift of a wild excursion into bigotry. As a result, gutter literature attacking Negroes and "race-mixers," of the sort so often directed at both Humphrey and Nixon in the past, was all but nonexistent.

By mid-October the Humphrey campaign began to catch fire. The candidate's ebullience, submerged by the jeers and inattention of September, resurfaced, and he began campaigning in the old, zesty, give-'em-hell style, bringing his crowds along with him. He was bringing the opinion polls along with him, too.

As the GOP campaign sailed on its serenely even keel of dignified confidence—but not overconfidence, it was announced weekly—Nixon's standing in the polls hardly wavered. Neither had Humphrey's; he remained near the midpoint between Nixon and Wallace until late October. Then Humphrey began to climb, cutting into both Wallace and undecided votes.

Now Nixon, who had not been on a major television inter-

Below, CBS newsman Mike Wallace being removed from the floor. Charges of "Gestapo tactics" were leveled at Mayor Daley for use of National Guard troops (right) and for security measures including barbed wire around the convention hall (left).

view program in two years, consented to appear on CBS' "Face the Nation" two Sundays before the election and on NBC's "Meet the Press" a week later. On the CBS show he maintained his composure and sidestepped difficult questions with ease. On the usually acerb and hard-hitting "Meet the Press," he handled comfortably a series of uncommonly benign queries which enabled him to state his position on key issues with calm and statesmanlike dignity.

A week before election day, Eugene McCarthy diffidently suggested that Humphrey's position had come close enough to his own to make it possible for him to vote for Humphrey, and he hoped his supporters would, too.

On Thursday, October 31, five days before the election, President Johnson lobbed the last bombshell into election year 1968: the following morning U.S. bombing would stop everywhere over North Vietnam. After weeks of negotiation, North Vietnam had agreed to substantive peace talks in Paris. Rumours of such progress had been current for months. In September Nixon had said he knew the president to be driving hard for a break in the negotiations, and not just to aid Humphrey's campaign. Nixon handled the new situation with discrimination and dignity, although some of his supporters saw the move as politically motivated.

Humphrey's last-minute surge, although considerable, came too late to save his campaign. The precise measure of Nixon's victory was unclear for a week after the polls closed, but its general dimensions were apparent within a day or two. The Republicans carried 32 states with 302 electoral votes (one elector pledged to Nixon voted for Wallace, however); 270 were needed to win. Humphrey won 13 states and the District of Columbia with 191 electoral votes, 79 short. Wallace took 5 states with 45 electoral votes.

Nixon won 31,770,237 popular votes (43.4%) to Humphrey's 31,270,533 (42.7%), to Wallace's 9,906,141 (13.5%). Thus Nixon's margin over Humphrey—499,704—nearly quadrupled that by which John Kennedy beat Nixon in 1960, but was still the second-smallest margin in 76 years.

While Wallace polled nearly nine times Strom Thurmond's 1948 vote as a third-party candidate, he carried only one more state and six more electoral votes than had the South Carolinian. Wallace demonstrated scant electoral potential outside the South, but he did play the most effective spoiler role since 1912, when Theodore Roosevelt siphoned away from William Howard Taft the votes that could have beaten Woodrow Wilson. In 18 of Nixon's 32 states Wallace's vote exceeded Nixon's margin over Humphrey, although the Wallace vote probably came about evenly from Democrats and Republicans.

The Republican gain of four seats in the House of Representatives was a modest 1%, but in the Senate the party picked up five seats, reducing the Democrats' numerical superiority from 63–37 to 58–42. Thus Nixon became the first president since Zachary Taylor in 1848 who would not have his party in the majority in either house of Congress at the beginning of his first term.

One impact of the election was that elimination or revision of the Electoral College seemed more likely now than ever. The 1968 election was a classic close call: a shift of 1% of the 5.5 million votes cast in Ohio and Missouri would have denied Nixon an electoral majority, and the House of Representatives would most probably have had to elect the president.

In the final analysis, the very narrowness of Nixon's victory, as well as the freedom from stridency of his campaign, should help him unite the nation. Great electoral margins between the candidates, such as that between Johnson and Goldwater in 1964, generally reflect ideological gulfs—fundamental differences between a large group and a small one that speak more of implacable hostility than of potential harmony. Electoral "horse races," such as the one just ended—and like the Kennedy-Nixon election of 1960—indicate that the nation is undecided because the goals of the two men are so similar.

784

continued from page 780

five Warsaw Pact nations, was relatively restrained. In a brief television address on August 21 President Johnson said: "The Soviet Union and its allies have invaded a defenseless country to stamp out a resurgence of ordinary human freedom. It is a sad commentary on the Communist mind that a sign of liberty is deemed a fundamental threat to the security of the Soviet system." Following a Cabinet meeting on the invasion, U.S. Secretary of State Dean Rusk said that the United States was not planning any "retaliatory actions or sanctions" against the Soviet Union, and he appealed to Moscow and its Warsaw Pact allies "to bring about a prompt withdrawal of their forces." It was reported in Washington that the U.S. and the Soviet Union had reached agreement, just prior to the invasion of Czechoslovakia, on the details of the opening of bilateral talks on missile disarmament. The agreement was shelved, at least for the time being.

Domestic Affairs. Despite such stinging defeats as those inflicted on the foreign aid program and on his nomination of Associate Justice Abe Fortas to be chief justice of the United States, President Johnson compiled a generally successful record with Congress in his final year as president. Election-year pressures, rising discontent with U.S. involvement in Vietnam, and cutbacks in appropriations did not prevent the passage of several landmark administration proposals, including the Housing and Urban Development Act of 1968, the Civil Rights Act of 1968, and the Omnibus Crime Control and Safe Streets Act. Johnson won less visible but equally significant victories in health, education, and general welfare as he saw his formerly controversial programs for aid to education, to the cities, and to the poor extended and funded with relatively little debate. The antipoverty appropriation of $1.9 billion, although somewhat less than the president's request, was the largest in that program's history. The price of victory, however, often was some modification of the original request. Appropriations for many programs did not match the budget amount, due to the general spending cut imposed by Congress, yet were still substantially increased from fiscal 1968 amounts. The 10% tax surcharge sought by President Johnson passed only when linked to the spending cut. The crime bill contained wiretapping provisions strongly opposed by the president, while the gun-control bill did not contain the licensing and registration requirements sought by Johnson.

Congress expanded the president's requested $2.3 billion housing bill by passing the Housing and Urban Development Act, which authorized a $5.3 billion, three-year housing program. This bill included a wide variety of new programs designed to encourage and facilitate homeownership among low-income families, to stimulate the development of new communities and increased area planning, and to attract private capital into the area of housing and urban renewal. Giant steps in conservation were taken by Congress with the establishment of the long-sought Central Arizona Project, the Redwood National Park, and systems of scenic rivers and scenic trails. Congress also authorized the creation of a National Water Commission and additional revenues for the Land and Water Conservation Fund.

The omnibus crime bill, authorizing new programs of crime prevention, control, and correction, along with the Juvenile Delinquency Prevention Act and

measures concerning alcoholic rehabilitation and drugs, reflected a growing concern with issues of "law and order," which figured prominently in the presidential campaign. The Civil Rights Act, with its controversial open-housing provisions, passed Congress in spite of substantial opposition. Only minimum funds were later granted, however, for the enforcement of those provisions. A truth-in-lending bill headed a long list of consumer-protection bills approved by Congress. Head Start, the Teacher Corps, vocational education, family planning assistance, food stamps, rent supplements, and model cities programs were all extended and financed with only minimal debate.

Among the serious legislative defeats for President Johnson were the severe cutting of his foreign aid request and the failure of the Senate to ratify the international Treaty on the Non-proliferation of Nuclear Weapons. An already record-low budget request for foreign aid was sliced by $1.2 billion to the smallest amount appropriated for such assistance since the advent of the Marshall Plan two decades earlier. Other administration defeats were the minimal funding of the highway beautification program, the failure of the Oil Pollution Control Act, the mere one-year extension of the farm program, and the failure of the proposed Occupational Safety and Health Act.

King Assassination. The assassination on April 4 of the Rev. Martin Luther King, Jr., Negro civil rights leader and Nobel Peace Prize laureate, had far-reaching consequences. King was shot as he leaned over the second-floor railing outside his room at the Lorraine Motel in Memphis, Tenn. He was pronounced dead at a hospital one hour later (*see* OBITUARIES). It was presumed that the assassin had fired the single shot from a rooming house only 50–100 yd. away and then had fled. James Earl Ray, who was charged with slaying King, was arrested in London on June 8.

The King assassination precipitated rioting in predominantly Negro sections of Washington, D.C., Chicago, and other cities. More than 20,000 regular federal troops and 34,000 National Guardsmen were sent to the troubled cities during the week after King's death as local authorities called for help to end the disorders. By the end of the week more than 30 persons had been killed and thousands injured and arrested.

Before his death King had planned a Poor People's Campaign in Washington, D.C., with the aim of persuading Congress to enact legislation that would reduce poverty in the United States. His successor as head of the Southern Christian Leadership Conference, the Rev. Ralph Abernathy, carried out those plans. The first nine caravans of poor people, most of them black, arrived in the capital on May 11 to begin construction of Resurrection City, a temporary town consisting mainly of plywood shacks near the Lincoln Memorial.

Resurrection City was plagued from the outset by quarrels among its leaders and by disciplinary problems among its residents. Unusually rainy weather during the month of May turned the formerly grassy site into a sea of mud. Administration officials and members of Congress sympathetic to the Poor People's Campaign complained that Abernathy and other leaders failed to put forward specific legislative proposals. The climax of the campaign was the June 19 Solidarity Day demonstration at the Lincoln Memorial. Reminiscent in some ways of the ebullient 1963 March on Washington for Jobs and Freedom, Solidarity Day nevertheless was a sombre occasion. Speakers expressed sorrow and anger over the assassinations of King and Kennedy, condemned the Vietnam war as racist and immoral, and warned that Solidarity Day might be the last peaceful demonstration of its kind.

Student Unrest. College campuses became the stage in 1968 for unruly demonstrations, sometimes involving clashes between students and local police. In April normal operations at Columbia University in New York City were virtually suspended for the remainder of the academic year after a group of leftist white students and a group of Negro students and nonstudents seized and occupied five campus buildings on April 23 and 24. The seizures were designed as a protest against Columbia's construction of a gymnasium in city-owned Morningside Heights Park and against the university's ties with the Institute for Defense Analysis, which was involved in military research. The demonstrators held the buildings until April 30, when, after efforts to negotiate an end to the take-over had failed, the university administration summoned city police. About 700 persons were arrested and 148 injured as police ended the occupation.

Use of police on campus provoked a general student-faculty strike. The focus of the new protest extended to questions of the structure of the university and of the role of faculty and students in determining university policy. Similar issues were raised in demonstrations on other college campuses. Organizers of a student sit-in at Howard University in Washington, D.C., demanded "faculty control over academic affairs and student control over student affairs" as well as establishment of a "black-oriented curriculum." Harvard and Yale agreed to demands by black student organizations that courses in Afro-American studies be introduced. At San Francisco State College one of the numerous demands by striking students was the unlimited admission of Negroes.

Wallace Campaign. Student disorders, street crime, and rioting in big cities gave rise to widespread fear in 1968 that lawlessness in the U.S. was out of control. Former Alabama Gov. George C. Wallace skillfully exploited this fear in his presidential election campaign. In an interview published in the *New York Times* on September 26, Wallace advocated stronger police action to "stop this group of militants and anarchists from threatening the mass of people in the country."

Wallace campaign rallies often turned into vivid demonstrations of "anarchy and violence." Screaming demonstrators would try to drown out Wallace, sometimes successfully. Fistfights occasionally broke out. Wallace returned the demonstrators' contempt. The most popular line from his basic campaign speech was, "If you elect me president and an anarchist lies down in front of my automobile, it's going to be the last automobile he'll want to lie down in front of."

Wallace's high standing in national public opinion polls early in the campaign seriously worried Democratic and Republican officials. The high-water mark of Wallace strength, as reflected in the polls, was reached at the end of September, when both the Gallup Poll and the Harris Survey reported that 21% of adult Americans would vote for him if the election were held then. But Wallace began to lose support after he chose Gen. Curtis E. LeMay, former Air Force chief of staff, as his vice-presidential running mate on October 3. Appearing with Wallace at a nationally televised news conference that day, LeMay said he "would use anything that we could dream up, including nuclear weapons, if it was necessary" to win the Vietnam war.

WIDE WORLD

The former Jacqueline Kennedy and her new husband, Aristotle Onassis, emerging from the chapel following their wedding on Skorpios Island, Greece, Oct. 20, 1968.

Public Service Strikes. An important development on the labour front in 1968 was the growing militancy of such public employees as teachers, firemen, policemen, and sanitation workers. New York City was subjected to a city-wide health emergency when sanitation workers went on a nine-day strike in February. Sanitation workers went on strike also in Atlanta, Memphis, and St. Petersburg, Fla. Newark, N.J., was left unprotected briefly at the end of the year by a walkout of city firemen and policemen.

Strikes by teachers occurred in cities throughout the country, including East St. Louis, Ill.; Salt Lake City, Utah; East Chicago, Ind.; Cumberland, R.I.; East Haven, Conn.; and approximately 20 school districts in Michigan. The longest teachers' strike occurred in New York City. Actually, it involved three separate strikes, which paralyzed the city's school system from the beginning of the autumn term on September 9 until a presumably final settlement was reached on November 18.

The dispute centred on the Ocean Hill-Brownsville Demonstration District in Brooklyn, an experimental unit involving eight schools with more than 8,000 pupils, most of them Negro and Puerto Rican, and about 500 teachers, the majority of them white. The Ocean Hill-Brownsville district was one of three special units set up in July 1967 by the New York City Board of Education as an experiment in decentralization and community control of neighbourhood schools. But the experiment soon developed into a racially tinged power struggle between the predominantly Jewish United Federation of Teachers and the predominantly Negro Ocean Hill-Brownsville governing board. The strike settlement approved on November 18 reinstated the teachers transferred out of the district by the local governing board and vested authority over Ocean Hill-Brownsville in a state trustee. But the hostility stirred up by the long strike lingered.   (RI. W.)

ENCYCLOPÆDIA BRITANNICA FILMS. *People Along the Mississippi* (1952); *Southwestern States* (1954); *Far Western States* (1955); *Northwestern States* (1956); *Southeastern States* (1956); *The Wheat Farmer* (1956); *Hawaii—The 50th State* (1959); *Alaska—The 49th State* (1960); *Corn Farmer* (1960); *Chicago—Midland Metropolis* (1963); *Our Changing Way of Life—The Cotton Farmer* (1963); *Our Changing Way of Life—Cattleman (A Rancher's Story)* (1964); *Our Changing Way of Life—The Dairy Farmer* (1965); *Our Changing Way of Life—The Lumberman* (1965); *Washington D.C.—Capital City U.S.A.* (1965); *The Great Plains—Land of Risk* (1966); *The Interior West—The Land Nobody Wanted* (1966); *Making the Desert Green* (1966); *New England Fisherman* (1967); *The Northeast: Gateway for a Nation* (1967); *The Northeast: Headquarters for a Nation* (1967); *The Northeast: Port of New York* (1967); *The Orange Grower* (1967); *The Sheep Rancher* (1967); *Midwest—Heartland of the Nation* (1968); *Problems of Conservation—Air* (1968); *Produce—From Farm to Market* (1968).

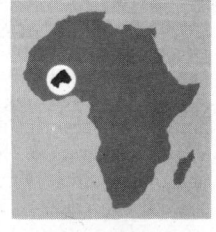

Upper Volta

A republic of West Africa, Upper Volta is bordered by Mali, Niger, Dahomey, Togo, Ghana, and Ivory Coast. Area: 105,869 sq.mi. (274,200 sq.km.). Pop. (1967 est.): 5,054,000. Cap. and largest city: Ouagadougou (pop., 1965 est., 72,337). Language: French (official); various tribal languages and dialects. Religion: pagan; Muslim and Christian minorities. President in 1968, Gen. Sangoule Lamizana.

UPPER VOLTA

Education. (1965–66) Primary, pupils 107,588, teachers (including preprimary) 1,714; secondary, pupils 5,468; vocational, pupils 1,010; teacher training, students 1,164; higher, students 28; secondary, vocational, teacher training, and higher, teachers 226.

Finance. Monetary unit: CFA franc, with a parity of CFA Fr. 50 to the French franc (CFA Fr. 246.85 = U.S. $1; CFA Fr. 592.45 = £1 sterling). Budget (1968 est.) balanced at CFA Fr. 8,564,000.

Foreign Trade. (1967) Imports CFA Fr. 8,970,-000,000; exports CFA Fr. 4,430,000,000. Import sources: France 46%; Ivory Coast 21%; Mali 6%. Export destinations: Ivory Coast 50%; Ghana 13%; France 13%. Main exports (1966): livestock 38%; meat products 13%; cotton 8%; peanuts 5%.

The Union of Chiefs, meeting from April 28 to 30 under the leadership of the emperor of the Mossis, Moro-Naba Kougri, issued a communiqué asking the government to end the measures that had compromised its powers since the revolution in January 1966.

Late in May, 35 people charged with plotting against the government in September 1967 were brought before the Special Tribunal of Upper Volta in Ouagadougou. Among those accused were the wife and son of ex-Pres. Maurice Yaméogo and the son of the former president of the National Assembly, Begnon Kone. Sentences of imprisonment, suspended in the case of Félicité Yaméogo, were passed on June 5.

The political situation, however, remained relatively calm. The military regime primarily concerned itself with restoring the national economy. Having managed to balance the 1968 budget by dint of a rigorous reorganization of public finances, the regime continued its already established policy of attempting to encourage greater French investment in the country. With that goal in mind, President Lamizana visited Paris in July. A minimum of CFA Fr. 5 billion was required for the exploitation of manganese deposits at Tambao.

In July, at the first meeting of the Permanent Parity Commission of Mali and Upper Volta held at Bobo-Dioulasso, agreements concerned with establishing a common frontier and with projects for transport and commercial cooperation were reached.   (PH. D.; X.)

Uruguay

A republic of South America, Uruguay is on the Atlantic Ocean and is bounded by Brazil and Argentina. Area: 68,-536 sq.mi. (177,508 sq.km.). Pop. (1968 est.): 2,818,000, including white 89%; mestizo 10%. Cap. and largest city: Montevideo (pop., 1967,

1,280,000). Language: Spanish. Religion: mainly Roman Catholic. President in 1968, Jorge Pacheco Areco.

Long considered one of the most stable, prosperous, and democratic countries in Latin America, Uruguay experienced acute economic and political disorder in 1968. This grew in part from 15 years of ineffective government under a nine-man National Council, the death of Pres. Oscar Diego Gestido in December 1967 after less than one year in office, and the continued expansion of social benefits despite deteriorating financial conditions.

Pres. Jorge Pacheco Areco (*see* BIOGRAPHY), who had served as vice-president under Gestido, inaugurated his administration with vigorous efforts to combat inflation and to reduce the influence of leftist forces in Uruguay. Restrictions on wage and salary increases in both public and private employment aroused strong opposition from the Communist-dominated National Workers Convention (CNT), which controlled about half of the nation's 900,000-man labour force. A series of general strikes called by the CNT kept the country in periodic paralysis throughout most of the year; they were countered by stern government measures.

Public crises were frequent in early 1968 and increased in severity during the year. During February farmers withheld milk from urban markets in protest against low prices, and workers from interior areas marched on the capital in search of employment and higher wages. In late April the Uruguayan peso was devalued, for the fifth time in a 15-month period; the entire Cabinet resigned over congressional criticism, in which a fishing agreement with Argentina and Brazil played an important part. A general strike and demonstration on May 1 left 30 paraders wounded,

while in June about 5,000 employees of the Central Bank were mobilized into the Army to prevent their participation in antigovernment activities.

The worst riot in Uruguayan history occurred in August after the kidnapping of Ulises Pereira Reverbel, a close friend and adviser of President Pacheco, by members of the pro-Chinese Communist group known as the Tupamaru National Liberation Front. In search of Pereira, police raided the University of Uruguay and confiscated quantities of firebombs, ammunition, and other terrorist materials. Pereira was, meanwhile, released unharmed, but clashes between students and police resulted in the deaths of one student in August and two in September. Some decrease in tension was evident by November, and the universities and secondary schools of Montevideo were reopened after being closed for one month. The seventh strike called by the CNT in less than six months brought only limited response from its membership and the battle-weary public.

The Uruguayan economy continued the long-term decline that had reduced the average annual per capita income by 10% during the preceding decade. The cost-of-living index in Montevideo rose by a record 136% in 1967 and continued to rise until mid-1968, when a price freeze proved effective. Exports remained at a sharply reduced level, and prices on the world market for wool and beef, which provided 88% of the nation's foreign exchange, also fell. Loans from the United States, Western Europe, the Soviet bloc, and neighbouring Latin-American countries offset some of the deficit, while the possibility of additional resources was enhanced when Uruguay joined the International Finance Corporation in August.

International relations centred on efforts to achieve economic integration with other member nations of the Latin American Free Trade Association. President Pacheco visited Argentina and Chile, where trade agreements were concluded. Plans were laid for integration of the railroad systems of Argentina, Uruguay, and Paraguay.   (C. W. MI.)

URUGUAY

Education. (1965–66) Primary, pupils 335,089, teachers (including preprimary) 9,152; secondary, pupils 91,371; vocational, pupils 26,298; teacher training, students 4,947; higher, students 17,087, teaching staff (1962–63) 2,031.

Finance. Monetary unit: peso, with an official rate (following devaluation of April 29, 1968) of 250 pesos to U.S. $1 (600 pesos = £1 sterling). Gold and foreign exchange, central bank: (May 1968) U.S. $179 million; (May 1967) U.S. $189 million. Budget (1968 est.): revenue 46.1 billion pesos; expenditure 56.4 billion pesos. Money supply: (Dec. 1967) 27,490,000,-000 pesos; (Dec. 1966) 13,458,000,000 pesos. Cost of living (Montevideo; 1963 = 100): (March 1968) 1,440; (March 1967) 582.

Foreign Trade. (1967) Imports U.S. $170.2 million; exports U.S. $158.7 million. Import sources: U.S. 14%; Brazil 12%; West Germany 10%; U.K. 8%; Argentina 7%; Kuwait 6%. Export destinations: U.K. 22%; Spain 9%; U.S. 7%; Italy 7%; Netherlands 7%; West Germany 6%. Main exports: wool 50%; meat 25%; hides and skins 9%.

Transport and Communications. Roads (1965) 41,620 km. (including *c.* 9,000 km. main roads). Motor vehicles in use (1965): passenger *c.* 114,000; commercial *c.* 82,000. Railways (1966) 3,102 km. Shipping (1967): merchant vessels 100 gross tons and over 40; gross tonnage 126,257. Air traffic (1966): 93,-990,000 passenger-km.; freight 625,000 net ton-km. Telephones (Jan. 1967) *c.* 190,000. Radio receivers (Dec. 1966) 1 million. Television receivers (Dec. 1965) 200,000.

Agriculture. Production (in 000; metric tons; 1966; 1965 in parentheses): wheat 329 (547); barley 31 (28); oats 72 (97); sweet potatoes *c.* 80 (*c.* 80); corn (1967) *c.* 117, (1966) 180; linseed (1967) 40, (1966) 38; sunflower seed (1967) 76, (1966) 99; rice 116 (90); sugar, raw value (1967–68) *c.* 74, (1966–67) *c.* 57; wine *c.* 85 (*c.* 85); wool *c.* 52 (*c.* 50); beef and veal *c.* 237 (*c.* 341); mutton and lamb *c.* 58 (*c.* 71). Livestock (in 000; May 1966): cattle *c.* 8,400; sheep *c.* 21,800; horses *c.* 450.

Industry. Production (in 000; 1966): cement 465 metric tons; electricity 1,841,000 kw-hr.

Vatican City State

This independent sovereignty, surrounded by but not part of Rome, came into being with the signing of the Lateran Treaty between the Holy See and the Italian government on Feb. 11, 1929. As a state with territorial limits, it is properly distinguished from the Holy See, which, being the pope together with the nine congregations of the Roman Curia, constitutes the worldwide administrative and legislative body for the Roman Catholic Church. The area of Vatican City is 108.7 ac. (44 ha.). Pop. (1967): 1,000. As sovereign pontiff, Paul VI is the head of state. Vatican City is administered by a pontifical commission of five cardinals, of which the secretary of state, A. G. Cardinal Cicognani, is president.

Following the reforms of the papal Curia announced in August 1967, decrees introducing important changes in the administration of the papal court were issued on March 29, 1968. The first decree divided the pope's household into two sections, one comprising those concerned with religious ceremonies and the other, those occupied in the government of the church. The decree, which reserved to the pope the nomination of officials, consolidated his power over his entourage. Henceforward offices would be held for a five-year period, whereas in the past ap-

pointments were often made for life or held on a hereditary basis. A second decree set up a consultative body of 24 lay experts to advise the five cardinal members of the pontifical commission that administers the Vatican City State.

Diplomatic occasions during the year included the visit to the Vatican on January 10 of Mika Spiljak, president of the Yugoslav Federal Executive Council. This was the first visit to the Vatican of a Yugoslav statesman since the country became Communist. During August the pope visited Bogotá, Colombia, for the International Eucharistic Congress.

On April 2 the first English-language edition of *L'Osservatore Romano* was published. Weekly editions of the paper, which appeared daily in Italian, were thus available in French, Spanish, and English.
(Mx. B.; X.)

See also Religion.

Venezuela

A republic of northern South America, Venezuela is bounded by Colombia, Brazil, Guyana, and the Caribbean Sea. Area: 352,143 sq.mi. (912,050 sq.km.). Pop. (1967 est.): 9,352,000, including mestizo 69%; white 20%; Negro 9%; Indian 2%. Cap. and largest city: Caracas (metropolitan area pop., 1966 est., 1,764,274). Language: Spanish. Religion: predominantly Roman Catholic. President in 1968, Raúl Leoni.

The year was dominated by the presidential and congressional elections, which were held in December. The four million eligible voters had a choice of six presidential candidates: Gonzalo Barrios (Acción Democrática), Rafael Caldera (Comitado Organización Politica Electoral Independiente), Luis Beltrán Prieto Figueroa (Movimiento Electoral del Pueblo, Partido Revolucionario de Izquierda Nacionalista, and Cruzada Cívica Nacional), Miguel Angel Burelli Rivas (Unión Republicana Democrática Popular), Alejandro Hernández (Partido Socialista Democrático), and Germán Borregales (Movimiento de Acción Nacional).

The election took place on December 1, and the presidential winner was Rafael Caldera. The Acción Democrática candidate, Gonzalo Barrios, placed second, and that party's ten years in the presidency was thus ended. Caldera's party did not gain a majority in Congress, and the new president, therefore, faced the necessity of coalition government. Former dictator Marcos Pérez Jiménez added interest to the election results by winning a Senate seat.

Despite most attention being directed to the elections the political scene was not otherwise uneventful. At the beginning of the year the governing party, Acción Democrática (AD), failed to get its nominees elected as leaders of the Senate and the Chamber of Deputies. President Leoni declared the election invalid, but the Supreme Court ruled otherwise. The coalition party, Unión Republicana Democrática (URD), withdrew from the government in April. New Cabinet ministers were appointed, including the first woman, Aura Celina Casanova, as minister of development. In July, Pérez Jiménez was tried and found guilty of embezzling $13 million of state funds. The court sentenced him to 4 years, 1 month, and 15 days in prison, but as he had already spent over five years there, he was released and departed for Spain. Throughout the year there were sporadic guerrilla outbreaks but none of any consequence.

The strengthening of the economy continued. Venezuela was the largest holder of gold and foreign exchange reserves in Latin America, and on January 16 its reserves reached $839 million, of which $400.7 million were in gold. The Banco Central paid in advance the two remaining installments of a loan granted by the Export-Import Bank of Washington in 1961, thus saving $2.5 million in interest charges. In June the Banco Central announced the renewal of a $50 million agreement with the Bank for International Settlements which, together with the renewal of a similar agreement with the U.S. Treasury, provided Venezuela with secondary reserves of $100 million. The bolívar, accepted by the International Monetary Fund as a hard currency, continued to be stable and freely convertible; it was used by several countries in credit transactions arranged by the Fund. In March the government for the first time made an issue of 45-day treasury bills, to absorb some of the excess liquidity in the economy and to level out the government cash flow (subject to wide fluctuation on account of quarterly tax payments from the oil companies).

The government placed emphasis on developing the country's relations abroad. A trade mission visited Eastern Europe, after which the U.S.S.R., Hungary, Romania, and Bulgaria agreed to exchange permanent trade missions with Venezuela; diplomatic relations with Czechoslovakia were to be renewed, and a tech-

WIDE WORLD

Carlos Betancourt, commander of the Armed Forces of National Liberation (FALN), a guerrilla organization operating in Venezuela.

VENEZUELA

Education. (1965–66) Primary, pupils 1,453,310, teachers 42,623; secondary, pupils 189,583, teachers 9,045; vocational, pupils 93,120, teachers 4,738; teacher training, students 12,831, teachers 1,470; higher (including 7 universities), students 46,825, teaching staff 4,762.

Finance. Monetary unit: bolívar, with an official selling rate of 4.50 bolivares to U.S. $1 (10.80 bolivares = £1 sterling), a rate of 4.40 bolivares to U.S. $1 (10.56 bolivares = £1) for petroleum and iron ore exports, and a rate of 4.48 bolivares to U.S. $1 (10.75 bolivares = £1) for other exports. Gold and foreign exchange, central bank: (June 1968) U.S. $758 million; (June 1967) U.S. $687 million. Budget (1968 est.) balanced at 8,965,000,000 bolivares. Gross national product: (1966) 35,730,000,000 bolivares; (1965) 34,220,000,000 bolivares. Money supply: (April 1968) 4,880,000,000 bolivares; (April 1967) 5,044,000,000 bolivares. Cost of living (Caracas; 1963 = 100): (March 1968) 103; (March 1967) 102.

Foreign Trade. Imports (f.o.b.; 1967) 5,617,000,-000 bolivares; exports (1966) 11,941,000,000 bolivares. Import sources (1966): U.S. 50%; West Germany 10%; U.K. 5%; Canada 5%; Japan 5%; Italy 5%. Export destinations (1966): U.S. 37%; Netherlands Antilles 21%; Canada 8%; U.K. 7%. Main exports: crude oil and refined petroleum products 92%; iron ore 5%.

Transport and Communications. Roads (1965) 31,180 km. (including c. 14,000 km. with improved surface). Motor vehicles in use (1965): passenger 384,900; commercial (including buses) 165,900. Railways: (state only; 1965) 468 km.; traffic (1966) 45 million passenger-km., freight 26 million net ton-km. Shipping (1967): merchant vessels 100 gross tons and over 88; gross tonnage 350,442. Air traffic (1966): 740,175,000 passenger-km.; freight 35,049,000 net ton-km. Telephones (Jan. 1967) 308,898. Radio receivers (Dec. 1966) 1,675,000. Television receivers (Dec. 1965) 650,000.

Agriculture. Production (in 000; metric tons; 1966; 1965 in parentheses): corn 557 (521); sesame 60 (54); sweet potatoes 107 (103); cassava 320 (301); dry beans 47 (42); coffee 61 (54); tobacco 9.8 (9); cocoa 22 (22); sugar, raw value (1967–68) c. 400, (1966–67) 394; cotton, lint 16 (16); meat 199 (196). Livestock (in 000; 1965–66): horses 406; asses 471; cattle 6,702; pigs 1,932; sheep 77.

Industry. Production (in 000; metric tons; 1967): cement 2,264; crude oil 185,406; natural gas 7,511,-000 cu.m.; petroleum products (1966) 60,092; iron ore (62% metal content) 17,005; gold (1966) 17 troy oz.; diamonds (1966) 85 metric carats; electricity (1966) 8,735,000 kw-hr.

nical and scientific agreement with Poland was proposed. In August Venezuela signed an agreement with Tunisia for increased economic, cultural, and technical cooperation.

In the same month, in an attempt to promote commercial, cultural, and tourist relations within the Caribbean Sea region, Venezuela and the Netherlands Antilles formed a joint commission to study a reciprocal treaty. Decisions relating to the Andean Development Corp., formed to control investment, to encourage integration, and to provide financial assistance among the Andean countries, were delayed by the considerable opposition of private business.

A marked expansion in the petroleum sector was evident. Because of the uncertainty of some traditional sources of oil, there was increased demand for Venezuelan oil. During the first seven months of 1968 petroleum production was up 3.8% over the 1967 figure. As most of the existing concessions to oil companies were due to expire in 1983, the government introduced a plan to replace the concession scheme with service contracts involving a form of partnership between the private operating companies and the state oil company, Corporación Venezolana del Petróleo. The first area submitted for bidding was southern Lake Maracaibo; on the July 3 closing date, 11 bids had been submitted by 17 oil companies. The next area to be discussed was to be the Gulf of Venezuela; a seismographic survey of the area, completed in 1968, revealed that it contained one of the largest deposits of petroleum in the world. Another recently published survey revealed that reserves equivalent to 700,000,000,000 bbl. of heavy crude oil and tars are located in the Orinoco bituminous belt, which extends from the delta of the Orinoco River to Calabozo in the state of Guárico.

Venezuela continued its efforts to increase investment in other sectors of the economy. In the field of petrochemicals, work began on at least 11 projects, of which one was expected to start production in 1968 and one in 1969–70. The most important complex was under construction at El Tablazo, on Lake Maracaibo, where a production capacity of 900,000 tons, mainly of ammonia and other nitrogen-based products, was envisaged and where annual sales were expected to amount to about $150 million. Development of the iron and steel industry was also being actively extended through the exploration of deposits of iron ore in the Guayana region; a plant to produce briquettes with an 86.5% iron content was to be built there. A centrifugal tube plant to produce pipes mainly for water supplies was under construction at Puerto Ordaz. Satisfactory progress was maintained on the construction of a hydroelectric project at Guri, which would eventually supply large quantities of power for heavy industrial projects. Three of the electric generators were to begin operation in November.

Various projects to improve communications were under discussion throughout the year. A call for bids from contractors for the Caracas underground railway was to be made at the end of the year. The first stretch of 12½ mi. was expected to be completed in 1973 and the remainder by 1975. A project to enlarge the nation's railway network was under consideration, and a complete overhaul of the postal system was to be made. Finally, it was hoped that the broadcasting of colour television programs would begin before the end of 1968.   (J. C. Bd.)

Encyclopædia Britannica Films. *Colombia and Venezuela* (1961).

Veterinary Medicine

For many years foot-and-mouth disease had been a major problem in many parts of the world, and in 1968 it was recognized by the UN Food and Agriculture Organization (FAO) as the most important single disease of livestock. Throughout much of central Europe and in most of the less developed nations it regularly caused substantial losses, resulting from reduced animal productivity and the cost of vaccination. In countries where eradication measures were employed, there was also the direct cost of those measures. Its greatest economic impact, however, resulted from restriction of trade, and in this regard it was probably more important than all other animal diseases combined.

The outbreak of foot-and-mouth disease that began in England during October 1967 and continued until the last infected or in-contact animal was destroyed in March 1968 forcefully demonstrated the havoc such a disease can cause in a country that has been free of the infection. This outbreak, which apparently originated in a shipment of meat from South America, involved some 2,300 farms and resulted in the death or destruction of more than 400,000 animals. Animal movement was severely restricted and embargoes were placed on meat imports from all infected countries. The direct cost of eradication included more than £26 million in government indemnities paid to farmers for livestock destroyed, and total losses, including disruption of breeding operations, were estimated to exceed £150 million.

This British outbreak also made apparent the problems faced by countries (including the U.S. and Canada) that had been largely successful in keeping out such diseases, and where rigorous eradication measures were employed as the primary means of combating the disease once it gained a foothold. There were numerous protests by well-meaning persons over the presumed brutality and economic waste involved, and television coverage of slaughter operations caused veterinarians to be depicted as "cow butchers." The question of whether it would be possible to maintain a disease-free status under modern conditions of rapid transport was raised, and the supposed merits of vaccination were argued. The forces favouring total eradication, which included the organized veterinary profession, were successful in promoting stringent recommendations to permit earlier and more efficient handling of any subsequent epidemic.

Isolated outbreaks of rinderpest in cattle and buffaloes were effectively controlled by mass vaccination in various parts of Asia, and considerable progress was made in controlling the disease in Africa. The third phase of a campaign against rinderpest, conducted by several African nations jointly with the FAO, had satisfactory results in West Africa, and a fourth phase covering East Africa was implemented.

The Veterinary College (Tierärtzliche Hochschule) of Vienna celebrated the 200th year of its founding; it had been one of the earliest veterinary schools in Europe and the first established in a German-speaking country. Establishment of a school in Louisiana, the 19th in the U.S., was implemented by the appointment of a dean and the nucleus of a faculty.

In the U.S. the national hog cholera (swine fever) eradication program made further progress, with the addition of several states to the list of those already

Vegetables:
see Agriculture; Food;
Gardening

declared cholera-free. The use of live-virus vaccines had been outlawed, and when certain attenuated vaccines were found to have a cholera-spreading potential they were also withdrawn.

An outbreak of screwworm infestation in the southwest U.S. reached emergency proportions. Stepped-up efforts at eradication were made by releasing sterile (irradiated) male flies above and below the Mexican border. Once the female fly has mated with a sterile male, it cannot produce eggs. Normally the eggs are deposited in skin wounds on cattle, and the larval "screwworms" emerge from them.

A matter of broad concern to the U.S. veterinary profession was the proposed strict regulation, by the Food and Drug Administration, of antibiotics for use in animal health products. Antibiotics were widely used for treatment of disease in all species, and most meat-producing animals were fed antibiotic-medicated feeds to promote growth and prevent disease.

The U.S. marked its first year in recorded history without a human death from rabies, although there were two cases involving persons who contracted the disease outside the country. As in the U.S., rabies in wildlife (sylvatic rabies) became an increasingly serious problem in Europe, where member nations of the World Health Organization were advised to undertake wholesale destruction of the fox population in affected areas. With a sharp decline in value of pelts, the number of wild fox had been rising steadily, and it was feared that a dangerous rabies reservoir would develop. West Germany was the centre of this virus pool during 1968.

African swine fever reappeared in Italy in 1968, only six months after the disease first appeared and was believed to have been eradicated. In Australia, further progress was made in eradicating contagious bovine pleuropneumonia, a disease that in the past had decimated herds in Europe and Britain. Contagious caprine pleuropneumonia was recorded for the first time in the U.S. and Mexico.

So-called green monkey disease, hitherto entirely unknown, appeared in West Germany in late 1967 and infected some two dozen persons before it was recognized as a new disease entity. The mortality rate among affected monkey handlers was about 25%. Importation of green monkeys from Uganda was halted. (J. F. Ss.)

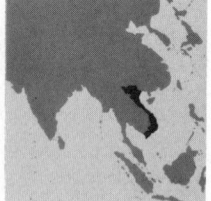

Vietnam

A country comprising the easternmost part of the Indochinese Peninsula, Vietnam, from July 21, 1954, was divided de facto into two republics.

Republic of Vietnam (South Vietnam). This is bordered by North Vietnam (along the 17th parallel), the South China Sea, Cambodia, and Laos. Area: 67,108 sq.mi. (173,809 sq.km.). Pop. (1967 est.): 16,067,000, including (1967 est.) Vietnamese 87%; Chinese 8%; Cambodian and Laotian 2%; others 3%. Cap. and largest city: Saigon (pop., 1967 est., 1,623,000). Language: Vietnamese. Religion: Buddhist; pagan; Confucian; Christian. President in 1968, Nguyen Van Thieu; premiers, Nguyen Van Loc and, after May 25, Tran Van Huong.

The War in Vietnam. Presidents Nguyen Van Thieu and Lyndon Johnson met in Canberra, Austr., in December 1967, in one of their periodic U.S.-South Vietnamese reviews of the war. A joint statement at the conclusion of the conference referred to "good

UPI COMPIX

Support units moving supplies to U.S. Marines following a six-day battle for Hill 689 near Khe Sanh, South Vietnam.

progress" in the military situation. It was noted that "there was no sign that North Vietnam was prepared to take any of the many avenues to peace that had been opened. They agreed that in these circumstances there was no alternative to continuing appropriate military actions."

There were indications at that time in Saigon, however, that the Viet Cong and North Vietnamese were preparing to strike a major military blow. It came in a series of carefully coordinated attacks on January 30, directed against all 40 of South Vietnam's major urban centres in what became known as the Communist Tet (lunar new year) offensive. It was more savage and massive than allied intelligence had anticipated.

U.S. military commander Gen. William C. Westmoreland and other U.S. officials insisted that they had been aware of the impending attacks on the cities. U.S. troops were alerted, but many of the South Vietnamese military and national police were given leaves for the lunar new year holiday. Few defense positions in the country were adequately manned when the Communists attacked.

The Tet offensive was preceded by broadcasts from the clandestine "Liberation Radio," in which the National Leadership Committee of the Alliance of National and Peace Forces exhorted the South Vietnamese people to rise in open revolt against the Saigon government. Citizens were called on "to side with the ranks of the people and to give their arms and ammunition to the revolutionary armed forces."

Fighting was particularly intense in Saigon and Hue. In the capital, guerrillas penetrated the presidential palace and the compound of the U.S. embassy. En-

U.S. soldier and South Vietnamese interpreter interrogating a Vietnamese youngster in a village 35 mi. S of Da Nang.

WIDE WORLD

trenched units in Cholon, the Chinese district of Saigon, were blasted out in fierce fighting that demolished large numbers of dwellings. Viet Cong and North Vietnamese units occupied the walled fortress of Hue, the ancient capital, until they were finally driven out by U.S. and South Vietnamese forces on February 24. It was estimated that only 7,000 of Hue's 17,000 homes were left standing after the battle for the city. Throughout the country 75,000 homes were destroyed or damaged. Property replacement costs were estimated at $173 million. Official government figures showed that 7,721 civilians were killed during the Tet offensive, while another 18,516 were wounded. More than 670,000 persons were declared refugees, raising the total number in South Vietnam to about 1.5 million.

The Communists paid dearly for their attacks. According to U.S. Information Service estimates, 60,000 Viet Cong and North Vietnamese were killed. More than 24,000 weapons were captured. Never before had the Communists absorbed such losses in the war. U.S. and South Vietnamese casualties during the Tet offensive were 12,727, including more than 2,600 killed.

U.S. and South Vietnamese officials declared that the Communists had suffered a resounding military defeat. It was, nonetheless, a psychological victory for the Viet Cong and the North Vietnamese. Although unable to spark a popular uprising, they proved that they were still able to launch major offensives against the cities despite large-scale search-and-destroy operations by the allied forces and the concentrated firepower they had been subjected to since the massive U.S. military involvement began in 1965. Even after the Tet offensive, the Communists regrouped sufficiently to launch a second attack on Saigon. For two weeks, beginning on May 5, the guerrilla and main force units fought in the streets of the capital city, holding wide sections before being dislodged in heavy fighting.

There were repeated warnings of a third major offensive, but the Communists did not, or perhaps could not, mount another major thrust against Saigon and other population centres. U.S. and South Vietnamese officials said that the Communists were set back in their plans by the deployment of highly mobile forces in areas where the Communists were trying to build strength, and by intense artillery and aerial bombardment.

During the summer the Communists subjected Saigon to 40 days of rocket and mortar attacks. Thousands of rounds were fired indiscriminately into the city. There were widespread civilian casualties and extensive property damage. Acts of terrorism and harassment took place in many other cities during the year without abatement.

Harsh fighting took place in other parts of the country, most notably in the area immediately below the Demilitarized Zone, which was, in fact, heavily militarized. A U.S. Marine Corps combat base at Khe Sanh, located astride strategic land routes from Laos and North Vietnam into South Vietnam, was under siege for two months. Because of the preliminary peace talks which had begun in Paris and which followed President Johnson's decision to declare a partial bombing halt over North Vietnam, it was assumed that the Communists sought an impressive battlefield victory to enhance their bargaining position. Khe Sanh was finally relieved in April when allied forces reached the besieged base. The U.S. relief columns encountered little opposition as the North Vietnamese

withdrew, apparently electing to fight elsewhere and with better odds.

Early in July Gen. William Westmoreland was succeeded by Gen. Creighton W. Abrams as the senior U.S. military commander in Vietnam. General Abrams undertook to modify operations, preferring a strategic concept of searching out the enemy with smaller numbers of troops and following through with greater artillery and air strikes. General Westmoreland's methods of employing massive search-and-destroy missions to draw the enemy into battles of attrition were no longer emphasized. General Abrams began using B-52 bombers of the U.S. Strategic Air Force in a more flexible, tactical manner.

General Abrams also moved more vigorously to "de-Americanize" the war, although U.S. forces continued to play a role as prominent as that of the South Vietnamese government forces. In April, U.S. Secretary of Defense Clark Clifford said "that the increasing effectiveness of the South Vietnamese government and its fighting forces will now permit us to level off our effort and in due time to begin the gradual process of reduction." To this end, the U.S. Military Command in Vietnam established urgent priorities on equipping the South Vietnamese Army with more modern weapons, including the M-16 automatic rifle. The M-16s permitted the South Vietnamese an equality of firepower to match the Communist Chinese-manufactured AK-47, the standard weapon of the Viet Cong and North Vietnamese. Modernization of the South Vietnamese armed forces was one of the major items covered by Presidents Thieu and Johnson when they met in Honolulu on July 19 and 20.

In addition to modernization of the South Vietnamese military, steps were taken by the Thieu government to increase the size of the armed forces. Under the new General Mobilization Law compulsory military service was extended to 18- and 19-year-olds for the first time, while veterans and reserve officers were recalled to active duty. The effect was to bring 135,000 more men into uniform.

The total number of men under arms in Vietnam reached new highs on both sides during the year. As of late November there were an estimated 791,000 South Vietnamese regular troops, 178,000 South Vietnamese paramilitary forces, 599,000 allied troops of which more than 530,000 were U.S., 95,000 North Vietnamese regulars, 35,000 Viet Cong, and about 100,000 Communist guerrillas and support forces.

Efforts to pacify the countryside were dealt a crippling blow by the Tet offensive. South Vietnamese military units were forced to pull back from the rural

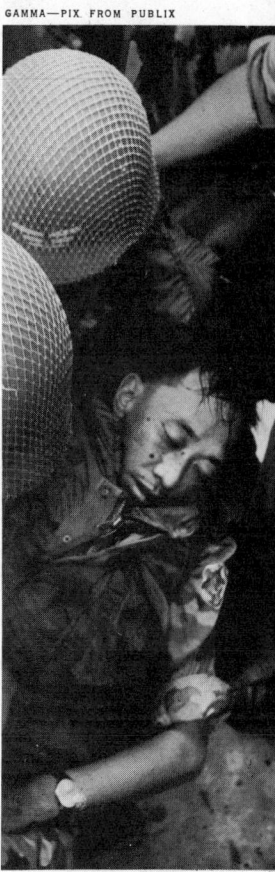

Top, South Vietnamese national police chief Brig. Gen. Nguyen Ngoc Loan executing a Viet Cong officer in Saigon, Feb. 1, 1968. Bottom, soldiers aiding General Loan after he was wounded by Viet Cong attack on Saigon, May 5, 1968.

areas, where they had provided security screens, to help defend the besieged cities. Until then, the revamped U.S.-directed pacification program had been making commendable headway. After Tet, however, the military demands were such that civilian protection efforts were sharply reduced. In March, U.S. officials reported that only 4,093 of the nation's 12,-736 hamlets and villages were securely under government control. Of the remaining rural centres, 4,084 were considered as "contested" and the remainder under Viet Cong control. South Vietnamese military forces began returning to pacification duties in the spring. By the end of October they were able to re-secure many hamlets and villages, and it was estimated that slightly more than 50% of the population in the countryside lived in pacified areas. The remainder of the villagers resided, in almost equal proportions, in "contested" or Viet Cong-controlled areas.

Domestic Politics. President Thieu solidified his political base in 1968, bringing to South Vietnam greater stability than the country had known since the early years of the administration of the late Ngo Dinh Diem. In May, Thieu reshuffled the Cabinet, naming Tran Van Huong as premier. Huong had campaigned in opposition to Thieu for the presidency in 1967, coming in fourth. As a native South Vietnamese, Huong enjoyed widespread public support. Many South Vietnamese resented the leadership imposed upon the country by North Vietnamese-born politicians and military officers, such as Thieu.

The new Cabinet also reflected a de-emphasis of the officer class in the ruling establishment. Only 2

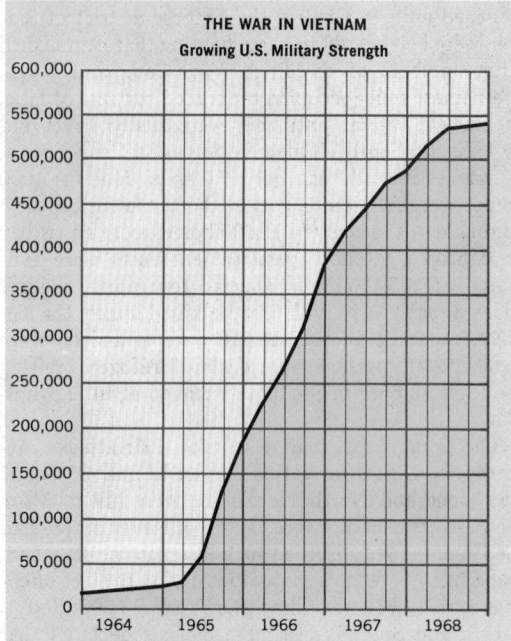

THE WAR IN VIETNAM
Growing U.S. Military Strength

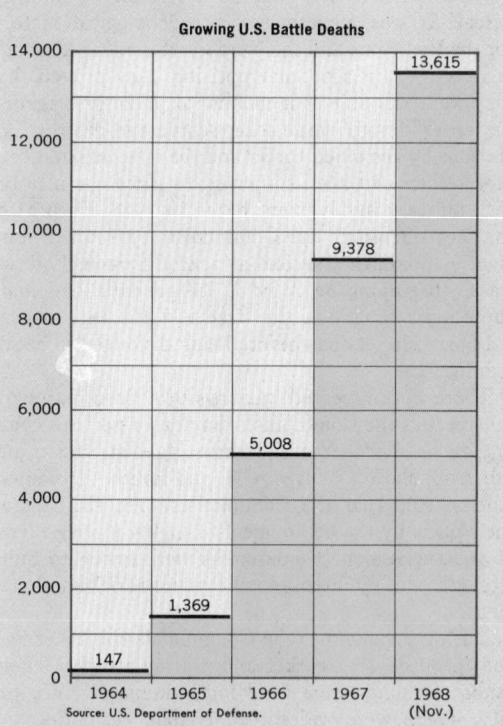

Growing U.S. Battle Deaths

Source: U.S. Department of Defense.

U.S. troop strength and battle deaths in Vietnam for the years 1964 to 1968. Estimated number of U.S. troops in Vietnam as of Dec. 31, 1968, was 542,100. Battle deaths for the five-year period totaled 29,517.

VIETNAM: Republic

Education. (1965) Primary, pupils 1,660,968, teachers 28,803; secondary, pupils 370,668, teachers 9,903; vocational, pupils 7,565, teachers (full time) 355; teacher training, students 2,497, teachers 54; higher, students 27,105, teaching staff 904.

Finance. Monetary unit: piastre, with an official exchange rate of 80 piastres to U.S. $1 (192 piastres = £1 sterling) and a principal effective rate of 118 piastres to U.S. $1 (283.20 piastres = £1). Gold and foreign exchange, central bank: (June 1968) U.S. $352 million; (June 1967) U.S. $373 million. Budget (1967 est.): revenue 58 billion piastres; expenditure 75 billion piastres. Money supply: (April 1968) 106,110,000,000 piastres; (April 1967) 71,190,000,000 piastres. Cost of living (Saigon; 1963 = 100): (June 1968) 347; (June 1967) 274.

Foreign Trade. (1967) Imports 12,507,000,000 piastres; exports 1,250,000,000 piastres. Import sources (1966): U.S. 40%; Japan 15%; Taiwan 14%. Export destinations (1966): France 39%; U.K. 16%; Japan 14%; West Germany 10%; Italy 6%. Main export rubber 81%.

Transport and Communications. Roads (1966) 20,255 km. (including 371 km. main roads). Motor vehicles in use (1967): passenger 42,272; commercial (including buses) 44,941. Railways: (1965) *c.* 1,500 km.; traffic (1966) 3.6 million passenger-km., freight 14 million net ton-km. Air traffic (1967): 377,252,-000 passenger-km.; freight 3,302,000 net ton-km. Telephones (Jan. 1967) 24,837. Radio receivers (Dec. 1966) 1.3 million.

Agriculture. Production (in 000; metric tons; 1966; 1965 in parentheses): sweet potatoes 246 (278); cassava 280 (236); rice (1967) 4,688, (1966) 4,336; rubber 57 (65); tea 5.2 (5.9). Livestock (in 000; 1965–66): cattle 1,101; buffaloes 733; pigs 3,474; horses 8. Fish catch (in 000; metric tons) (1966) 701, (1965) 640.

Industry. Production (in 000; metric tons; 1966): salt 88; cotton yarn 8.7; woven cotton fabrics (1965) 121,000 m.; electricity (public supply) 602,000 kw-hr.

VIETNAM: Democratic Republic

Education. (1965–66) Primary, pupils 2,270,000, teachers 34,730; vocational, pupils 49,600; higher (including University of Hanoi), students 15,900; vocational and higher, teaching staff 920.

Finance and Trade. Monetary unit: dong, with an official exchange rate of 3.50 dong to U.S. $1 (8.40 dong = £1 sterling). Budget (1963) balanced at 1,779,288,000 dong. Foreign trade: total turnover (1965) 780 million dong (85% with China, U.S.S.R., and other Eastern European countries).

Transport. Roads (1965) *c.* 9,000 km. Railways (1965) 938 km.

Agriculture. Production (in 000; metric tons; 1966; 1965 in parentheses): rice *c.* 4,500 (*c.* 4,600); corn *c.* 250 (*c.* 265); tobacco *c.* 5 (5); sweet potatoes *c.* 800 (*c.* 800); tea *c.* 3 (*c.* 3.6); timber (1961) 760 cu.m. Livestock (in 000; 1965–66): buffaloes *c.* 1,550; cattle *c.* 820; pigs 5,800. Fish catch (in 000; metric tons) (1962) 289, (1961) 223.

Industry. Production (in 000; metric tons; 1966): coal *c.* 3,500; apatite ore *c.* 1,000; salt *c.* 150; cement *c.* 750; cotton textiles (1962) 56,100 m.; silk textiles (1961) 2,200 m.; electricity (1964) 548,000 kw-hr.

of the 19 Cabinet members were military men. Buddhists were also given a greater voice in policy making.

Equally important in the reshuffling was the erosion of Vice-Pres. Nguyen Cao Ky's political power. Thieu and Ky had long been at odds. Those officials loyal to Ky were shunted out of office. The rivalry reached a stage in June that compelled Ky to appear on national television to deny that the rift had reached crisis proportions. By then, however, Ky had no alternative. His power was reduced to its lowest level since he began his political ascendancy in 1965. Late in the year, however, Thieu appointed Ky as head

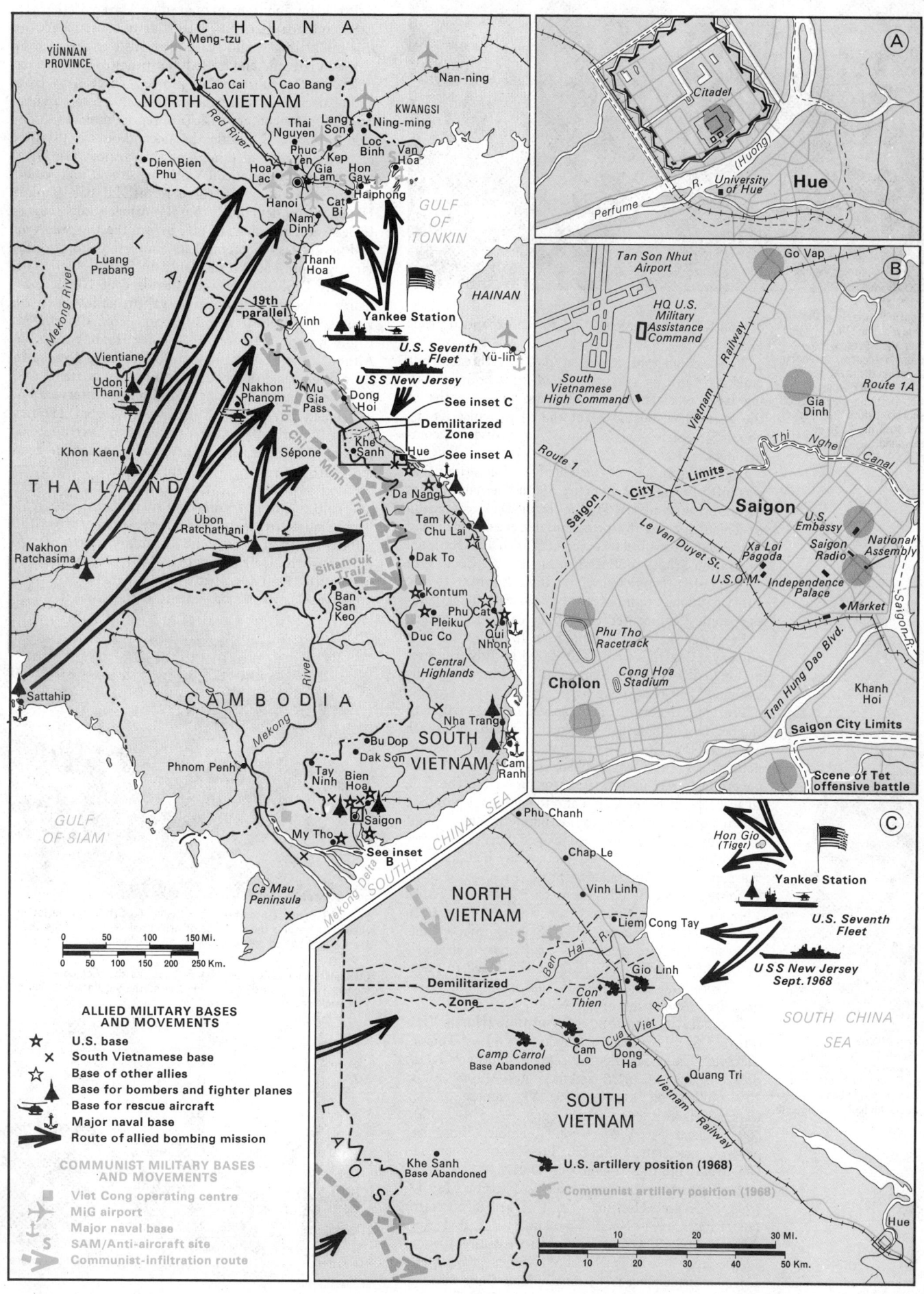

South Vietnamese Pres. Nguyen Van Thieu (right) and Vice-Pres. Nguyen Cao Ky (centre) attending a national prayer service with Premier Nguyen Van Loc (left) on May 1, 1968, shortly before Premier Loc and his Cabinet resigned.

of South Vietnam's delegation to the expanded peace talks.

Thieu eliminated Ky as a political threat while cracking down on corruption and graft and dismissing inept officials. During the first nine months of the year Thieu ousted 21 of the 44 province chiefs, about 50 district chiefs, and 3 Army division commanders.

One of the actions of the Thieu administration that was bitterly resented by many South Vietnamese was the imprisonment of Truong Dinh Dzu, runner-up to Thieu in the 1967 presidential election. Dzu had campaigned for direct peace talks with the National Liberation Front, political arm of the Viet Cong. Dzu was arrested, convicted of "actions harmful to the anti-Communist fighting spirit of the South Vietnamese people," and sentenced to five years' hard labour.

Press censorship was reimposed following the Tet offensive. Controls were again lifted in July, the first major policy decision announced by Huong when he assumed the premiership.

President Thieu did not conceal his opposition to the partial bombing halt of North Vietnam on March 31, or to the complete bombing halt which was announced by President Johnson on October 31. His government was under great pressure from the U.S. to agree to the latter action and to endorse it publicly. Thieu, however, referred to the complete bombing halt as a "unilateral" action and balked until December at sending an official South Vietnamese delegation to the expanded peace talks in Paris. In November he suggested two-way talks between North and South Vietnam with the U.S. and the National Liberation Front in secondary roles; the U.S. later rejected this proposal. All four delegations had arrived in Paris by the year's end, although Thieu continued to resist any procedural arrangements that might be interpreted as recognition of the NLF.   (Ro. Go.)

Gen. Duong Van Minh, known as "Big Minh," was allowed to return to Saigon in 1968 from Bangkok, Thailand, where he had been in exile.

Democratic Republic of Vietnam (North Vietnam).
This is bordered by China, the Gulf of Tonkin, the South China Sea, South Vietnam, and Laos. Area: 61,293 sq.mi. (158,750 sq.km.). Pop. (1967 est.): 20.1 million, including (1960) Vietnamese 85.1%. Cap. and largest city: Hanoi (pop., 1965 est., 500,-000). Language: Vietnamese. Religion: Buddhist; pagan; Confucian; Christian. President in 1968, Ho Chi Minh; premier, Pham Van Dong.

According to a statement made in Paris on May 18, 1968, by Averell Harriman, the U.S. peace negotiator (*see* BIOGRAPHY), North Vietnam had at that time approximately 85,000 men in South Vietnam, of whom 72,000 were in wholly North Vietnamese units while 13,000 were serving in nominally Viet Cong units.

President Johnson announced on March 31 that the U.S. bombing that had begun as a consequence of this infiltration would cease over 90% of the area of North Vietnam, and called for prompt and serious talks "on the substance of peace." Three days later Hanoi declared "its readiness to send its representatives to make contact with U.S. representatives to decide with the U.S. side the unconditional cessation of bombing and all other war acts against the DRV [Democratic Republic of Vietnam] so that talks could begin." Acceptance in these terms did not commit Hanoi to any deviation from its former stand: nevertheless, an agreement to talk before the war was won and before U.S. bombing had completely stopped obviously represented a new shift in policy.

Many U.S. officials were surprised at North Vietnam's response to this initiative, or, at least, at the rapidity of it. Fear of obstruction from Communist China was probably one reason for Hanoi's reaction. Although the Cultural Revolution in China seemed to have diminished that country's influence in Hanoi and to have reduced the danger of Chinese intervention, it seemed likely that China would resent Hanoi's action. In early 1968 China was said to have approximately 40,000 men in North Vietnam engaged in road and rail repair, and to be supplying aid in the form of food and other consumer goods, trucks, shipping and ship-repairing equipment, small arms, and artillery. China was estimated to have sent perhaps $150 million worth of arms and $100 million worth of economic aid to North Vietnam in 1967, a total increase of about $75 million over 1966.

Chinese news media failed to mention the U.S.

South Vietnamese fishermen near Quang Tri City continue folding their nets despite the presence of armoured vehicles of the U.S. 1st Cavalry, which was conducting a sweep through the area.

Civilians fleeing Saigon on May 5, 1968, as the Viet Cong launched their second major offensive of the year against South Vietnam's capital.

Photograph released by North Vietnam through a Japanese news agency reportedly shows two captured U.S. pilots meeting with a North Vietnamese official in Hanoi.

offer until April 5, but before then reiterated a saying of Chairman Mao Tse-tung that "by persevering in protracted war the Vietnamese people will surely drive the U.S. aggressors out of their country." They then described President Johnson as "using the swindle of stopping bombing to lead to peace talks." On April 26, Chen Yi, the Chinese foreign minister, accused the United States of "trying to gain at the negotiating table what it could not get on the battlefield," and Chinese comment continued in this strain of veiled condemnation of Hanoi's tactics until, on September 2, at a National Day reception at North Vietnam's embassy in Peking, Chou En-lai declared "the scheme of peace talks in Vietnam" to be "jointly devised by U.S. imperialism and Soviet revisionism."

Some observers considered that the Soviet Union viewed the war as a dangerous threat to world peace with a risk of victory for Chinese policies; others thought that Moscow saw in it mainly such advantages as a closer alliance with the Eastern European Communist countries and a serious loss of U.S. influence and prestige throughout the world. Possibly the only fixed principles of Soviet policy were fear of giving an advantage to China in the competition for leadership of the Communist world, and determination to win the greatest possible influence in Hanoi. Hence in late 1967, when Hanoi was belligerent, Moscow did nothing to push it toward the conference table. During 1968 the U.S.S.R. greatly increased its economic and military aid to North Vietnam, supplying surface-to-air missiles, antiaircraft guns, radar equipment, MiG fighter planes and ammunition, and a few bombers and tanks.

The value of Soviet military aid to North Vietnam was estimated at about $500 million in 1967, as against $350 million in 1966, though Moscow was said to have only about 2,000 military personnel in the country, in noncombat advisory, technical, and training roles. Soviet economic aid to North Vietnam in 1967 was estimated at $200 million, as against $150 million in 1966, and was reported to include petroleum, trucks, tractors, rail equipment, bridge components, barges, machinery, food, and fertilizers. North Vietnam's response to the U.S. offer of peace talks apparently took Moscow by surprise, but on April 5 it announced its full support for Hanoi's decision. The U.S.S.R. announced in November that its 1969 aid to North Vietnam would emphasize civilian goods rather than military equipment.

After a long exchange of notes, both parties agreed on Paris as a site for the talks; the two delegations arrived on May 9. Xuan Thuy (*see* BIOGRAPHY), the leader of the North Vietnamese delegation, empha-

sized on arrival that the first topic for the talks was "unconditional cessation of the bombing and all other American acts of war" against his country; this would initiate a process leading to the end of U.S. "aggression" in Vietnam. That U.S. "restraint," as President Johnson put it on March 31, should be "matched by restraint in Hanoi" seemed out of the question for North Vietnam.

The talks opened on May 13 with Averell Harriman renewing previous offers to withdraw the U.S. forces from Vietnam if and when the North pulled its forces out of South Vietnam and the "level of violence" subsided. Xuan Thuy replied that the U.S. had been defeated but was continuing its "aggression."

By late October little progress had been made, and, in particular, no answer had been given to the repeated U.S. question "what step toward peace will you make if we stop the bombing altogether?" Nonetheless, on October 31 President Johnson ordered an end to all U.S. aerial and naval bombardment of North Vietnam. Hanoi's first encouraging response was to agree to South Vietnam's participation in expanded Paris peace talks.

On April 22 the Hanoi newspaper *Nhan Dan* declared on the 98th anniversary of the birth of Soviet leader Lenin that each Communist country faced distinctive problems and should meet them in its own way. Despite this "declaration of independence," Hanoi appeared to be working in close coordination with Moscow during the period of the Paris talks, so much so that it immediately approved the Warsaw powers' invasion of Czechoslovakia. The U.S.S.R. clearly found this support valuable, though Hanoi subsequently showed a disposition to back-pedal on this issue. Moreover, the intervention in Czechoslovakia, besides supplying an unwelcome precedent for similar Chinese action in Vietnam, strengthened the hand of the U.S. "hawks" and discredited Moscow's attacks on U.S. imperialism in Vietnam.

No change seemed to have occurred in the composition of North Vietnam's leadership from late 1967 to late 1968. The veteran revolutionary Pres. Ho Chi Minh, aged 78, was reported in poor health, but it was quite uncertain who would inherit his power. According to one report, in November 1967 he had designated as his successor the premier, Pham Van Dong, a cautious man and probably less belligerent than most of his colleagues. However, the most powerful man in the country after Ho appeared in 1968 to be Le Duan, who had succeeded Ho as first secretary of the ruling Lao Dong (Workers') Party in 1961. He was said to take a hard line on the war with no thought except total victory.

For six or seven years commentators had usually distinguished a pro-Soviet faction in North Vietnam comprising Pham Van Dong; Vo Nguyen Giap (the victor of Dien Bien Phu and later minister of defense); the deputy premier, Pham Hung; the minister of the interior, Ung Van Khiem; and the economist Le Thanh Nghi. The pro-Chinese faction was believed to consist of Truong Chinh, chairman of the Standing Committee of the National Assembly; Le Nuc Tho; and the foreign minister, Nguyen Duy Trinh. On April 28 Truong Chinh made a speech in a factory on the "need to go on fighting" and criticized "right deviationist and conservative ideas and fear of difficulties." This statement echoed Chinese utterances on the Paris talks and seemed to constitute a warning from the local hardliners. (P. H. M. J.)

See also Defense; Propaganda; Southeast Asia.

British ship lying at anchor in the North Vietnamese port of Haiphong. Despite U.S. appeals several Western nations continued trade with North Vietnam during 1968.

Vital Statistics

New editions of the standard certificates of birth and death became effective in the U.S. in 1968, leading to revision by the states of the basic certificates. The standard report forms had been the principal means of attaining uniformity of information for compilation of national vital statistics in the U.S., as the control of registration of vital events was vested in the individual states. Since 1900 the degree of uniformity necessary for national data on births and deaths had been obtained by periodic issuance of recommended standards from the responsible national agency (since 1946, the U.S. Public Health Service) and their cooperative adoption by the separate states. Representatives of the state systems advised and assisted in the development of the standard forms. This was the first thorough revision since 1949.

Two other developments of 1968 were significant for vital statistics. One was adoption of the Eighth Revision of the International Classification of Diseases (ICDA) for classifying diseases and causes of death. Despite expectations in 1965, when the International Conference for the Eighth Revision was convened by the World Health Organization to agree on the ICDA, the new revision was put to use for 1968 data in few of the member countries. Exceptions were the U.S. and the U.K., where the latest of the internationally accepted systems for coding causes of death was applied to national statistics beginning in January 1968.

Also noteworthy was the biennial meeting of the Public Health Conference on Records and Statistics (PHCRS) held in June 1968 in Washington, D.C. This was the 12th national meeting for the PHCRS, a consultative and collaborative study program that functions under the aegis of the National Center for Health Statistics to provide a forum for representatives of the U.S. vital statistics system and various federal agencies. It stimulates the delineation and discussion of problems in vital records and public health statistics and provides a focus and continuity for unifying the national system. At the 1968 meeting the participants, numbering over 400, concentrated on the hard facts for comprehensive health planning, a broad topic of major concern to all health professionals since the Comprehensive Health Planning and Public Health Services Amendments of 1966 required a broadening of health services to assure "the highest level of health attainable for every person."

Birth Statistics. Not quite 3.5 million births were registered in the U.S. in the 12 months ending with August 1968, or 3% fewer than in the comparable period ending with August 1967, for which the provisional total was 3.6 million live births. The birthrate of 17.4 per 1,000 population for the more recent period was about 4% below the rate for the earlier period. Thus, the decline continued into 1968 from the peak reached in 1957. The birthrate of 17.9 for 1967 was below the previous low of 18.4 seen in 1933, in 1936, and again in 1956. The fertility rate for 1967, however, was well above the low level recorded right after the depression. It was 87.8 births per 1,000 women 15–44 years of age (the childbearing period used to calculate the fertility rate), as compared with 75.8 for 1936. These differences between 1936 and 1967 in the levels of the birth and fertility rates resulted from changes in the proportion of women of childbearing ages in the total U.S. population. In 1936 women of reproductive age made up 24% of the total population; in 1967 they comprised only 20%. Due to this decrease in the proportion of women in the childbearing bracket, the higher fertility rate of women in 1967 was only large enough to keep the crude birthrate close to the low level of the mid-1930s.

The decline in the birthrate was not expected to continue much past 1968. The number of women of reproductive age was increasing rapidly because of the spurt in the birthrate at the end of World War II and the large numbers of births between 1948 and 1957. The babies born in those years were reaching young adulthood and had been contributing to the upturn in the marriage rate in the U.S.

The U.S. birthrate was not unlike the rates for other developed countries, though these were considerably below the rates appearing in Table I for less developed nations. The rate in Japan, after dropping to an exceptional low of 13.7 in 1966, a year that according to folklore boded ill for baby girls, swung back in 1967 to about 19. The rates for most Latin-American countries remained high.

Death Statistics. The death rate for the U.S. in the 12 months ending with August 1968 was 9.6 per 1,000 population, or 3% higher than the provisional rate of 9.3 for the comparable period of 1966–67. Somewhat higher rates were recorded in the first eight months of 1968, except during the spring. In most of 1967 there was a relatively low incidence of pneumonia and influenza, but in January and February 1968 extremely high death rates were observed for influenza.

Since 1955, when the long downward trend of the mortality rate came to an end, the general death rate for the entire U.S. had fluctuated over a narrow range, depending largely on the presence or absence of major influenza outbreaks. The estimated rate for 1967

Table I. Birthrates and Death Rates per 1,000 Population and Infant Mortality per 1,000 Live Births in Selected Countries, 1967*

Country	Birth-rate	Death rate	Infant mortality	Country	Birth-rate	Death rate	Infant mortality
Africa				Poland	16.3	7.7	38.0
Mauritius	30.4	8.5	64.2	Portugal	21.1	10.0	59.3
South Africa (white)	22.8†	8.6†	25.9‡	Romania	27.1	9.3	46.8
United Arab Republic	39.3	14.3	83.2	Spain	21.1	8.7	33.2
Asia				Sweden	15.5	10.1	12.6
Ceylon	31.5	8.2	55.8	United Kingdom	17.5	11.2	18.8
Cyprus	25.6	6.5	26.7	England & Wales	17.2	11.2	19.0
Hong Kong	23.0	5.1	25.6	N. Ireland	22.4	9.8	23.4
Israel	24.8	6.6	25.3†	Scotland	18.6	11.5	21.0
Japan†	19.3	6.7	13.3	Yugoslavia	19.5	8.7	61.3
Jordan†	46.2	5.0	36.3				
Malaysia, West††	37.3	7.6	50.0	**North America**			
Singapore	27.1	5.4	25.8†	Canada	18.0	7.3	23.1
Syria	32.1	4.5	28.1	Costa Rica	39.2	6.9	69.9†
Taiwan	28.5	5.5	20.2†	El Salvador	44.2	9.2	62.0†
Europe				Guatemala†	44.2	16.6	91.5
Albania	34.0†	8.6†	86.8§	Jamaica	35.4	7.0	35.4†
Austria	17.4	13.0	26.4	Mexico	42.7	8.9	62.9†
Belgium	15.2	12.2	23.7	Panama	40.2	6.9	45.0†
Bulgaria†	15.0	9.0	32.9	Puerto Rico	26.2†	5.5†	36.7§
Czechoslovakia†	15.6	10.0	23.7	Trinidad & Tobago	30.2	7.1	35.3
Denmark†	18.4	10.3	16.9	United States	17.9	9.4	22.1
Finland	16.5	9.4	15.0	Virgin Islands (U.S.)	40.5	6.6	30.2
France	16.8	10.8	17.1				
Germany, East	14.8	13.2	21.2	**Oceania**			
Germany, West‖	17.3	11.2	23.5	American Samoa†	36.5	5.5	36.1
Gibraltar†	23.8	8.2	11.8	Australia	19.5	8.8	18.2
Greece	18.5	8.3	34.7	Guam†	33.4	4.1	20.4
Hungary	14.5	10.7	38.4	New Zealand	22.4	8.4	17.7
Iceland†	23.9	7.1	13.7				
Ireland	21.1	10.7	24.4	**South America**			
Italy	18.1	9.7	34.3	Argentina	22.5	8.8	58.3
Luxembourg	14.8	12.3	20.4	Chile†	30.6	10.4	127.5
Malta	16.5	9.4	27.5	Ecuador†	41.5	11.2	90.4
Netherlands	18.9	7.9	14.7	Uruguay†	21.4	9.0	43.3
Norway	18.0	9.2	16.8				
				U.S.S.R.	17.4	7.6	26.0

*Registered births and deaths only.
†1966.
‡1965.
§1964.
‖Not including West Berlin.

Sources: United Nations, *Monthly Bulletin of Statistics* (October 1968), *Population and Vital Statistics Report* (July 1, 1968), *Demographic Yearbook* (1967).

was 9.4 per 1,000 population, as compared with 9.5 for 1966. This was lower than the rates given in Table I for many of the Western European countries, but higher than rates reported by other countries in North America. The age and ethnic composition of the national populations, as well as their stage of economic development, influenced the general death rate.

No marked changes occurred in the rank of the ten leading causes of death in the U.S. between 1966 and 1967. A small decrease (1.3%) was reported for the leading cause, diseases of the heart, the estimated rate for 1967 being 366.2 per 100,000 population. Deaths from this cause accounted for 39% of all deaths. Next in rank were malignant neoplasms (159 per 100,000), followed by vascular lesions affecting the central nervous system, or "stroke" (102.6 per 100,000), and then accidents, with a death rate of 55.1, in fourth place. The first three of the leading causes resulted in 67% of all deaths; accidents caused 6% of the total; the remaining six causes in the list of ten were responsible for 13% of the total 1,852,000 deaths.

Although accident mortality in the U.S. was close to that for Canada, it compared unfavourably with the 1966 experience of certain other English-speaking countries. The rate was 58 for the U.S. versus 57.3 for Canada, 54 for Australia, 53.1 for New Zealand, and 39.7 for England and Wales. While the difference between the U.S. and the U.K. was due largely to a higher motor-vehicle accident death rate, 27.1 per 100,000 population in contrast to 15.5, the death rate for accidents exclusive of motor-vehicle accidents in the U.S. (30.9) was also higher than the rates of about 25 for the U.K. and Australia. The latter country's motor-vehicle accident death rate was 28.3, or slightly above the U.S. rate.

With travel by plane, automobile, and train commonplace, it was revealing to see the National Safety Council's estimates of the relative risk of death in these modes of transportation. The accident death rates for passengers per 100 million mi. in the U.S. are shown below.

	1967	1965–67 (average rate)
Passenger automobiles and taxis	2.40	2.40
Passenger automobiles on turnpikes	1.10	1.20
Buses	0.20	0.19
Railroad passenger trains	0.09	0.10
Scheduled air transport planes (domestic)	0.29	0.25

There was a striking difference of over tenfold between the death rate for occupants of buses vis-à-vis passenger cars and taxis, when allowance was made for the number of occupants and mileage traveled on streets and highways by the different classes of vehicles. A similar, though smaller, relative difference was seen between scheduled air transport planes and autos, including taxis. Travel by railroad passenger trains showed an even greater advantage.

Infant and Maternal Mortality. In contrast to the general death rate, infant mortality in the U.S. declined in the first eight months of 1968. For the 12 months ended with August 1968, the rate was 21.9 infant deaths per 1,000 live births, whereas for the year ended in August 1967 it was 22.4. In calendar 1967 there were 78,200 deaths to infants under one year of age, resulting in an infant mortality rate of 22.1 per 1,000 live births. This was 6% lower than the rate of 23.4 for 1966. Both the neonatal (infants under 28 days old) and postneonatal (infants 28 days through 11 months of age) rates declined in 1967.

About one-fourth of the total decline in 1967 was attributed to lower mortality from influenza and pneumonia, except pneumonia of the newborn.

Despite the steady decline since 1962 in the U.S. infant mortality rate, it had not reached the low level attained by some other countries, notably in Europe—Denmark, England and Wales, the Netherlands, Norway, and Sweden—and Australia and New Zealand. It was thought that the difference was due in part to the greater availability and utilization of prenatal and postnatal care under the social insurance systems of those countries.

In 1967 maternal mortality in the U.S. remained close to the level reached in 1966. The rates for the two years were, respectively, 28.9 and 29.1 deaths from conditions associated with childbirth per 100,000 live births. Since 1960, when the rate was 37.1, there had been a significant decline.

Expectation of Life. In 1967 the estimated expectation of life at birth was 70.5 years for the total population of the U.S., the highest yet attained. The comparable figure for 1966 was 70.1 years. The latest available data by sex for various countries are shown

Table II. Life Expectancy at Birth, in Years, for Selected Countries

Country	Period	Male	Female
Africa			
Gabon	1960–61	25.0	45.0
Mauritius	1961–63	58.7	61.9
United Arab Republic	1960	51.6	53.8
Upper Volta	1960–61	32.1	31.1
Asia			
Cambodia	1958–59	44.2	43.3
Hong Kong	1961	63.6	70.5
India	1951–60	41.9	40.6
Israel (Jewish population)	1966	70.9	73.7
Japan	1966	68.3	73.6
Korea, South	1955–60	51.1	53.7
Taiwan	1959–60	61.3	65.6
Western Malaysia	1956–58	55.8	58.2
Europe			
Albania	1960–61	63.7	66.0
Austria	1966	66.8	73.5
Belgium	1959–63	67.7	73.5
Bulgaria	1960–62	67.8	71.4
Czechoslovakia	1964	67.8	73.6
Denmark	1964–65	70.2	74.7
Finland	1956–60	64.9	71.6
France	1965	67.8	75.0
Germany, East	1963–64	68.3	73.3
Germany, West	1964–65	67.6	73.5
Greece	1960–62	67.5	70.7
Hungary	1964	67.0	71.8
Iceland	1961–65	70.8	76.2
Ireland	1960–62	68.1	71.9
Italy	1960–62	67.2	72.3
Malta	1964–66	67.5	71.1
Netherlands	1961–65	71.1	75.9
Norway	1961–65	71.0	76.0
Poland	1960–61	64.8	70.5
Portugal	1959–62	60.7	66.4
Romania	1963	65.4	70.3
Spain	1960	67.3	71.9
Sweden	1961–65	71.6	75.7
Switzerland	1958–63	68.7	74.1
United Kingdom			
England and Wales	1963–65	68.3	74.4
Northern Ireland	1964–66	67.8	73.0
Scotland	1964–66	66.6	72.6
Yugoslavia	1961–62	62.4	65.6
North America			
Canada	1960–62	68.4	74.2
El Salvador	1960–61	56.6	60.4
Guatemala	1963–65	48.3	49.7
Jamaica	1959–61	62.7	66.6
Mexico	1956	55.1	57.9
Puerto Rico	1959–61	67.1	71.9
Trinidad and Tobago	1959–61	62.2	66.3
United States	1966	66.7	73.8
Oceania			
Australia	1960–62	67.9	74.2
New Zealand	1960–62	68.4	73.8
South America			
Argentina	1960–65	63.7	69.5
Venezuela	1960	61.2	65.6
U.S.S.R.	1965–66	66.0	74.0

Source: United Nations, *Demographic Yearbook* (1967).

Virgin Islands: *see* Dependent States

in Table II. Over the past decade life expectation at birth for males in the U.S. showed little change, but it increased almost one year for females. Values as high or higher were reported by Western European countries, Israel, and Japan. However, the differences in the periods to which the data relate and the validity of the population estimates, together with variations among the countries in the completeness of death registration, limit meaningful comparisons between all of the areas listed.   (E. H. HA.)

Marriage and Divorce. Generally, the marriage rates for the 44 areas for which there were reported statistics in the UN *Monthly Bulletin of Statistics* remained fairly constant for 1967 as compared with 1966. The marriage rate during this period increased in about the same number of countries as it decreased. No rates were reported for India, Communist China, and the U.S.S.R., among others.

During 1967 the countries with the highest marriage rates per 1,000 population were Puerto Rico (9.7), the U.S. (9.7), Japan (9.5), Hungary (9.4), and the Netherlands (9.1); the countries with the lowest marriage rates were El Salvador (3.3), Panama (3.8), Jamaica (4.1), Mauritius (5.1), Trinidad and Tobago (5.4), and Costa Rica (5.6). Data referred to marriages performed, marriage licenses issued, or marriages registered. In countries where the number of consensual marriages was large, rates based on recorded marriages were correspondingly low.

The marriage rates for all other countries that reported data ranged between 6.2 and 8.9. Reporting areas with rates between 8 and 8.9 were Australia, Canada, Finland, West Germany, Greece, New Zealand, Portugal, Romania, Ryukyu Islands, the U.K., and Yugoslavia; with rates between 7 and 7.9 were Austria, Belgium, Chile, Israel, Italy, Norway, Poland, Spain, Sweden, Switzerland, and Taiwan; with rates between 6 and 6.9 were France, East Germany, Luxembourg, Malta, Mexico, and Tunisia.

From 1962 to 1967 the marriage rate of five countries with populations of five million or more increased 10% or more (Australia, Canada, Hungary, Netherlands, and the U.S.), while this rate decreased 10% or more for Austria, East Germany, Italy, and Romania. The change in the marriage rate for other reporting countries of this size was less than 10%. The marriage rate of 9.7 for the U.S. in 1967 marked the fifth successive increase in the annual rate. These increases followed a five-year period when the marriage rate (8.4 in 1958 and 8.5 in 1959–62) was lower than for any year in the 38 years between 1920 and 1957 except for 1932.

Statistics on divorce were published by a number of countries, but frequently this information was not available until two or more years after the year in which the divorces occurred. A few countries reported the divorce rate per 1,000 population. For those countries not giving this figure, it could be approximated from the estimated population. Estimates of the divorce rates of several countries for 1966 (or 1965) were: Australia, 0.8; Belgium, 0.6 (1965); Czechoslovakia, 1.4; Denmark, 1.4; France, 0.6; West Germany, 1; East Germany, 1.6; Iceland, 1; Mexico, 0.6 (1965); the Netherlands, 0.5; New Zealand, 0.8; Poland, 0.8; Portugal, 0.1; Romania, 1.4; Sweden, 1.3; Switzerland, 0.8 (1965); and the U.K., 0.8. The divorce rate of 2.7 for the U.S. in 1967 was the highest rate since 1949; that for Canada in 1967 remained unchanged at 0.5 per 1,000.   (W. W. E.)

See also Populations and Areas.

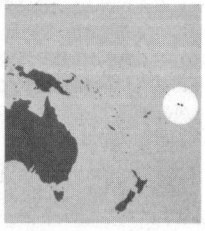

Western Samoa

An independent parliamentary state, Western Samoa is an island group in the South Pacific Ocean, about 1,600 mi. E of New Zealand and 2,200 mi. S of Hawaii. Area: 1,097 sq.mi. (2,842 sq.km.), with two major islands, Savai'i (622 sq.mi.) and Upolu (435 sq.mi.), and seven smaller islands. Pop. (1968 est.): 137,300. Cap. and largest city: Apia (pop., 1968 est., 26,600). Language: Samoan and English. Religion: about 80% Protestant, 20% Roman Catholic. Head of state (*O le Ao o le Malo*) in 1968, Malietoa Tanumafili II; prime minister, Fiame Mata'afa Faumuina Mulinu'u II.

Just as it was recovering from the 1966 hurricane, Western Samoa suffered more storm damage, on Feb. 10, 1968. This aggravated the need for capital to implement the 1966–70 economic development program. Australia made a grant of A$20,000 as emergency relief, while New Zealand postponed for one year the beginning of payments on the NZ$150,000 hurricane restoration loan. The Samoan government signed an agreement with the World Food Program for food to labourers rehabilitating the banana industry.

New Zealand offered a new NZ$1.2 million three-year aid program, little more in scale but rather different in form from that for 1965–68. Of the total, NZ$250,000 would be granted annually for educational and administrative assistance, while NZ$150,000 would be in loan form, although Samoa's "strictly limited" capacity to service loans was recognized.

Prospects of advances to planters were improved by legislation to increase the share capital of the Bank of Western Samoa from NZ$126,000 to NZ$225,000. To enable the Samoan government to maintain its 45% proportion, the Bank of New Zealand agreed to lend it NZ$99,000, payable over ten years at 5%. A reconnaissance visit by Asian Development Bank officials encouraged hopes of further aid.

After almost four years of secret negotiations and sometimes widespread and bitter debate, legislation was passed authorizing Potlatch Forests Inc. to develop a timber industry on Savai'i, and the government signed an agreement giving the company a 40-year concession.

Afioga Tupua Tamasese Leolofi IV was appointed to the Council of Deputies, which henceforth would have two members.   (My. B. B.)

WESTERN SAMOA
Education. (1965) Primary, pupils 26,827, teachers 888; secondary and vocational, pupils 7,459, teachers 310; teacher training, students 187, teachers 9.
    Finance. Monetary unit: Western Samoa thaler (dollar), with a par value of WS$0.72 to U.S. $1 (WS$1.72 = £1 sterling). Budget (1966 rev. est.): revenue WS$4,670,000; expenditure WS$4,824,000.
    Foreign Trade. (1966) Imports WS$5,728,000; exports WS$3,160,000. Import sources: New Zealand 30%; Australia 24%; U.K. 10%; Japan 7%; U.S. 5%. Export destinations: Netherlands 26%; New Zealand 25%; West Germany 19%; U.K. 12%; U.S. 6%; Denmark 5%. Main exports: copra 52%; cocoa 38%; bananas 5%.
    Transport and Communications. Roads (1965) 768 km. (including 160 km. surfaced). Motor vehicles (1965): passenger 683; commercial 673; buses 115. Telephones (Jan. 1965) 1,405. Radio receivers (Dec. 1966) 15,000.

Words and Meanings, New

The words, phrases, and some other forms listed below achieved some currency in the information media during 1968. Additional words and terms will be found and defined in the *Book of the Year* in articles in which they are pertinent. This list has been prepared by the permanent editorial staff of G. & C. Merriam Company, Springfield, Mass., publishers of *Webster's Third New International Dictionary* and a subsidiary of Encyclopædia Britannica, Inc.

A

acid rock *n* : rock 'n' roll songs whose titles or lyrics make cryptic references to drugs

air battery *n* : a rechargeable battery in which current is generated as a result of oxidation of a metal (as zinc) that takes place in pressurized air and releases free electrons at the anode with the fine particles of oxide so formed precipitating into a circulating electrolyte and then being filtered and stored

airbus *n* : a short-range or medium-range subsonic jet passenger airplane

algeny *n* : controlled alteration (as by modification of DNA or transfer of factors from one cell line to another) of genetic material

allogeneic *also* **allogenic** *adj* : genetically dissimilar <*allogeneic* skin grafts> <*allogenic* mice>

alphametic *n* : a mathematical puzzle that consists of letters substituted for the numerical figures of a problem with the solution to be obtained by mathematical reasoning whereby the original figures may be inferred

atmospherium *n* 1 : an optical device for projecting images of meteorological phenomena (as clouds, thunderstorms, rainbows, or auroras) on the inside of a dome 2 : a building or room housing an atmospherium

automanipulation *n* : physical stimulation of the genital organs by oneself—**automanipulative** *adj*

autonumerologist *n, Brit* : a person who interests himself in distinctive automobile registration numbers and their owners

auto-train *n* : a passenger train that includes one or more cars onto which travelers drive their own automobiles for transportation while they themselves remain in the automobiles or go into another of the train's cars

avalement *n* : a folding of the legs by a skier as he leans back and shoots his feet forward so as to keep the skis in contact with the snow in skiing and turning at high speed on bumpy terrain

B

be-in *n* : an informal public gathering (as in a park) for expressing love and happiness

bioclean *adj* : free or almost free of harmful or potentially harmful organisms (as bacteria) <*bioclean* room for assembly of spacecraft>

bioproduct *n* : a biologically active material (as a chemical or a vaccine) used for a specific purpose <a *bioproduct* to protect a plant against mildew>

birdyback *or* **birdieback** *n* : the movement of loaded truck trailers by airplane

block home *n* : a dwelling or commercial establishment designated in each block of a community as a refuge for children in distress

button *n, specif* : a low-ranking member or employee of a crime syndicate (as the Mafia)—called also *soldier*

BZ *n* : a gas that when breathed produces incapacitating physical and mental effects (as disorientation)

C

cabbish *n* : RADAGE

calcitonin *n* : THYROCALCITONIN

caporegime *n* : a lieutenant in a crime syndicate (as the Mafia)

carbecue *n* : a large oven for melting away unsalvageable material from a junked car rotated on a spit

cassette *n, specif* : a plastic case containing two small reels for insertion into a tape recorder with the tape on one reel passing to the other without having to be threaded

chameleon *vb* : to change suddenly and markedly in personality or personal appearance

chemical mace *n* : MACE

chicerino *n* : one who is chic

childrenese *n* : an oral language designed to enable parents to communicate with their children tactfully and authoritatively

chipmunk *n, specif* : a sportswriter who concentrates on human-interest stories rather than on facts and statistics

closet queen *n* : a homosexual who for fear of discovery lives an ostensibly heterosexual life

contour suit *n* : a man's suit tailored primarily for comfort usually without inner construction or waistbands

cottontail *n, specif* : one who is not a nudist—used by nudists

cowbell *n* : a mixed drink made from Scotch whisky and milk

crash pad *n, specif* : an apartment where hippies may obtain free lodging

D

dating bar *n* : a bar that caters especially to young unmarried men and women

deadee *n* : a portrait painted (as from a photograph) after the death of the subject

Denver boot *n* : a metal clamp that locks onto an automobile wheel and must be unlocked before a motorist can drive off (as after payment of a fine)

dime bag *n* : an amount of marijuana having a market value of ten dollars

disintermediation *n* : diversion of savings from institutions (as savings banks) with governmentally imposed interest ceilings to direct investment in higher-yielding securities (as bonds)

disposable *n* : something (as a paper blanket) that is disposable

downies *n pl* : BARBITURATES

dox *n pl* : documentary films

dual fund *n* : a closed-end investment company whose capitalization consists half of income shares entitled to the entire income of the company and half of capital shares entitled to all capital gains and appreciation—called also *dual-purpose fund*

dustoff *n* : a helicopter used to evacuate the dead and wounded from a combat area

dybosphere *n* : a realm of artificially created things that behave in a lifelike manner

E

econymical *adj* : of, relating to, or engaged in the study of the names of houses from a sociological, psychological, and linguistic point of view

ego plate *n* : an automobile license plate bearing distinctive letters, numbers, or a combination of these and usually available at extra cost : VANITY PLATE

electrodelic *adj* : imitating the effects of psychedelic drugs especially through the use of lighting <an *electrodelic* environment>

electromagnetic interaction *n* : a fundamental interaction experienced by most elementary particles that is responsible for the emission and absorption of photons and for electric and magnetic forces

episome *n* : a genetic determinant or group of determinants (as of a bacterium) capable of alternating between an autonomous existence and attachment to a chromosome—**episomal** *adj*—**episomic** *adj*

erectarine *n* : a rhythm instrument consisting of a mopstick with bottle caps attached

Eurobond *n* : a bond of a United States corporation that is sold outside the United States but that is denominated and paid for in dollars and yields interest in dollars

executive park *n* : an area that is at a distance from the center of a city and that is designed chiefly for a community of business offices (as of corporations)

expanded cinema *n* : MEDIA MIX

F

fiberfill *n* : man-made fibers (as of polyester) used as a filling material (as for cushions, comforters, or apparel)

fireflood *n* : the process of injecting compressed air into a petroleum reservoir and igniting the oil so that the small amount of oil that burns produces heat and combustion products that drive the remainder of the oil into producing wells—called also *fireflooding*

fireman *n, specif* : a dishonest tableman in a gambling casino—called also *mechanic*

fire painting *n* : an artistic work (as a panel) produced by the action of fire on its surface

fly-tipping *n, Brit* : the dumping of unwanted household goods onto the street

found *adj, specif* : presented as or incorporated into an artistic work essentially as found by an artist <a sculpture of fabric, wood, and other *found* materials>

found poem *n* : a poem consisting of words found in a nonpoetic context (as a telephone directory) and usually rearranged by the poet into poetic form—**found poetry** *n*

fractional orbital bombardment system *n* : a system for delivering a nuclear warhead from orbit by slowing it down by a retrorocket before completion of an orbit

frost high *n* : a high induced by sniffing a coolant used to frost highball glasses

funk art *n* : sculptural art characterized especially by the use of unconventional materials, sexual and scatological imagery, an irreverent spirit, and intentional ungainliness

G

ghosting *n* : the sharing by several individuals of a room (as in a hotel) for which only two have registered

girlcott *n* : a boycott carried out by housewives (as against a supermarket) to protest rising food prices—**girlcott** *vb*

gravitational collapse *n* : the tendency of particles to move toward a common center of gravity that results in the formation of stars, star clusters, and galaxies from the dilute gas of interstellar space and that causes some stars to collapse to the extent that there is conversion of appreciable mass into explosive energy

gravitational interaction *n* : an interaction that along with the electromagnetic interaction, the strong interaction, and the weak interaction is one of the fundamental interactions in nature but is the weakest of these interactions and that is hypothesized to act between elementary particles but has been observed only on a larger scale

gray collar *n* : a worker employed in one of the service industries especially in a small business and often on a part-time basis

gregarian *n* : one who is gregarious

grok *vb* : to enjoy what is happening especially among fellow hippies—**grokker** *n*

grubs *n pl* : blue jeans with legs cut short and often ragged

guava *n* : a bomb within a cluster bomb unit that explodes antipersonnel pellets

gunship *n* : a helicopter armed with rockets and machine guns and used especially for protecting from ground fire helicopters transporting troops into combat areas

H

helilift *vb* : to transport military personnel by helicopter

high energy physics *n* : a branch of physics dealing with the constitution, properties, and interactions of elementary particles especially as revealed by experiments involving particle accelerators

hominology *n* : a generalized study of man without regard to traditional academic disciplines (as philosophy and religion)

honkie *or* **honky** *also* **honkey** *n* : a white man—usually used disparagingly

I

idiot light *n* : a colored light on an automobile instrument panel designed to give a warning (as of an overheated engine or a low fuel tank)

ilth *n* : production that tends to increase prices and that does not contribute to long-term economic growth

intellectocracy *n* : a controlling or influential class of intellectuals

IPI *n* : instruction (as in mathematics or reading) through individually prescribed assignments geared to the student's ability: individually prescribed instruction

ironmonger *n, specif* : a dealer in illicit weapons

J

jocko *n, pl* **jockos** : a professional athlete

juvenocracy *n* : a state whose ruling or influential class is youth

K

kiss of life *Brit* : artificial respiration by the mouth-to-mouth method

L

lame *n, specif* : a person who is not in the know : SQUARE—**lame** *adj*

leotites *n pl* : tights for wear especially with a miniskirt

light show *n* : a kaleidoscopic display of colored lights, slides, and film loops designed to imitate the effects of psychedelic drugs

lunarnaut *n* : one that travels to the moon

M

mace *n, specif* : a temporarily disabling liquid for squirting in the faces of rioters and causing tears, dizziness, confusion, immobilization, and sometimes nausea—called also *chemical mace*

maxi *n* : a long skirt that extends often to the ankle—called also *maxi-skirt*

mechanic *n, specif* : FIREMAN

media mix *n* : a presentation (as in a theater) in which several media (as films, tapes, and slides) are employed simultaneously—called also *expanded cinema*

medionym *n* : a term that is medial in meaning between antonyms—called also *meronym*

mellotron *n* : an electronic musical instrument programmed to imitate the sounds of orchestral instruments

meronym *n* : MEDIONYM

middlescent *n* : a middle-aged individual; *esp* : one who has just turned 40—**middlescence** *n*

midi *n* : a calf-length dress or skirt—called also respectively *midi dress* or *midi skirt*

mind-expanding *adj* : causing an exposure of normally repressed psychic elements : PSYCHEDELIC

minibus *n, specif* : a small bus for comparatively short trips (as in a shuttle service)

minimal sculpture *n* : sculpture in the idiom of minimal art

mobilography *n* : the study of the typical routes by which an executive reaches the top of a large organization (as a corporation)

moontel *n* : a hostelry on the moon

morning-after pill *n* : an oral drug that blocks implantation of a fertilized egg in the human uterus and thereby interferes with pregnancy

multilemma *n* : a problem involving a choice from many alternatives no one of which is clearly satisfactory

N

Naderism *n* : a protest against defective consumer goods in the manner of the American lawyer Ralph Nader

notchback *n* **1** : a back on a closed passenger automobile having a distinct deck as distinguished from a fastback **2** : an automobile having a notchback

O

olfactronics *n* : a science dealing with the detection and measurement of odors by analytical instruments

open enrollment *n* : the voluntary enrollment of a student in a public school other than the one he is assigned to on the basis of his residence

ornithogolfing *n* : bird-watching with emphasis on the number of bird species seen

P

pantihose *or* **panty hose** *n pl* : a one-piece garment for women combining the function of panties and hose for wear especially with a miniskirt

parkicide *n* : disfigurement of the natural features of a park by building recreational facilities inside it

partocracy *n* : absolute rule by one political party through a government subject to its dictates—**partocratic** *adj*

patterning *n, specif* : a physiotherapeutic technique designed to improve damaged neural controls by means of feedback from patterns of muscular activity either passively imposed or obliquely induced

pepperette *n* : a co-ed who performs a dance routine during a suspension of play at an athletic contest

psychedelia *n* : the world of people or items associated with psychedelic drugs

psychotogen *n* : a chemical agent (as a drug) that induces a psychotic state—**psychotogenic** *adj*

pulsar *n* : a celestial source of pulsating radio waves characterized by a short interval (as 1.33 or 0.25 seconds) between pulses and uniformity of the repetition rate of the pulses

Q

quote-drop *vb* : to use familiar quotations for rhetorical effect in public speaking—**quote-dropper** *n*

R

radage *n* : a hybrid between a radish and a cabbage—called also *cabbish*

radial-ply tire *n* : a pneumatic tire in which the ply cords that extend to the beads are laid at approximately 90 degrees to the center line of the tread—called also *radial tire*

radiosterilized *adj* : sterilized by irradiation (as with X rays or gamma rays) <*radiosterilized* mosquitoes> <*radiosterilized* syringes>—**radiosterilization** *n*

replicase *n* : an enzyme that promotes the synthesis of a particular RNA in the presence of a suitable template

Rita *n* : a member of the armed forces who resists his country's war effort

rolamite *n* : a nearly frictionless elementary mechanism consisting of two or more rollers inserted in the loops of a flexible metal or plastic band and suitably housed with the band acting to turn the rollers whose movement can be directed to perform various functions (as operating a control or registering a change in speed)

roll bar *n* : an overhead metal bar in an automobile designed to protect riders in case of a turnover

S

sanitize *vb, specif* : to make more acceptable by removing unpleasant or undesired features

schnorrologist *n* : one who is adept at raising funds especially for an educational institution

sculpfest *n* : an exhibition of sculpture

shadow *adj, specif* : of, produced by, or being a publisher of books whose proprietary rights are often uncertain and which appear in editions that resemble those of other publishers

skinoes *n pl* : footwear resembling miniature canoes and enabling the wearer to walk on water

skylounge *n* : a passenger vehicle carried by helicopter from a downtown terminal to an airport

skystreet *n* : a street on an upper level (as of an apartment building)

soldier *n, specif* : BUTTON

speed *n, specif* : a synthetic drug used especially as a stimulant for the central nervous system : METHAMPHETAMINE

spoiler *n, specif* : a metallic device (as a turned-up or snowplow-shaped piece) used on the front or on the rear deck of an automobile and especially a racer to divert airflow and thus reduce the tendency to lift off the road at high speeds

sprint car *n* : a rugged racing automobile that is midway in size between midget racers and ordinary racers, has about the same horsepower as the larger racers, and is usually raced on a dirt track

STP *n* : a psychedelic drug chemically related to mescaline and amphetamine

suicidology *n* : the study of suicide and suicide prevention

surfari *n* : a group of surfboarders who travel together in search of good surfing areas

surfari *vb* : to travel with a group of surfboarders

syntactic foam *n* : a plastic in which preformed cells (as tiny hollow glass spheres) have been incorporated, which can withstand great pressures (as at ocean depths), and which floats

T

taxback *n* : an unconditional transfer of federal tax revenue to the state government

telelecture *n* 1 : a loudspeaker connected to a telephone line for amplifying voice communication 2 : a lecture delivered to an audience by telelecture

Texas toast *n* : a thick slice of bread warmed and covered with butter

thermal pollution *n* : the discharge of liquid (as waste water from a factory) into a natural body of water at such a high temperature that harm to the plant and animal life may result

thyrocalcitonin *n* : a polypeptide hormone from the thyroid gland that tends to lower the level of calcium in the blood plasma

topic book *n, Brit* : a book published as one of a series (as on educational topics)

tunnel rat *n* : a soldier who crawls through a tunnel in search of weapons, documents, or enemies

twofer *n, specif* : a blazer with matching trousers

U

ufologist *n* : one who is interested in unidentified flying objects

urban-grant university *n* : a university receiving governmental funds and involving itself deeply in urban affairs

V

virion *n* : a complete virus particle with membrane intact : the extracellular infective form of a virus

vodkatini *n* : a cocktail made after a martini recipe with vodka instead of gin

W

wayoutitude *n* : the quality or state of being unconventional : EXTREMENESS

white-out *n* : a protest in which an artist covers his work on display in a gallery with a sheet

wok *n* : a bowl-shaped cooking utensil used especially in the preparation of Chinese food

Z

zinc-air battery *n* : an air battery having a zinc electrode

Yemen

A country situated in the southwestern coastal region of the Arabian Peninsula, Yemen is bounded by Southern Yemen, Saudi Arabia, and the Red Sea. Although Yemen was largely republican controlled, the imam continued to rule in the remoter parts of the north, and his royalist government was recognized by some countries. Area: 75,290 sq.mi. (195,000 sq.km.). Pop. (1967 est.): 5 million. Cap. and largest city: San'a' (pop., 1960 est., 60,000). Language: Arabic. Religion: Muslim. Republican Yemen: president in 1968, Qadi Abdul Rahman al-Iryani; premier, Maj. Gen. Hassan al-Amri. Royalist Yemen: imam, Muhammad al-Badr; premier in 1968, Sayf al-Islam al-Hassan.

The Saudi-United Arab Republic (U.A.R.) agreement on Yemen of August 1967 failed to bring peace

Female textile factory workers in San'a' participating in a marching drill as part of their training to help defend the republican regime.
UPI COMPIX

to the country in 1968, and the three-nation conciliation committee comprising Iraqi, Moroccan, and Sudanese members, which arose out of the agreement, had to admit failure in its efforts to help establish a compromise regime. The republicans continued to accuse Saudi Arabia of helping the royalists with money, arms, and training facilities for mercenaries. This was vigorously denied by the Saudis. All the U.A.R. troops had been withdrawn from the country by the end of 1967, but the royalists accused the republicans of using Communist help and claimed to have shot down a republican plane with a Soviet pilot.

In January the royalists, who had succeeded in occupying most of the hills surrounding San'a', came close to taking the capital but the republicans rallied their forces with emergency assistance from Syria, Algeria, and the U.S.S.R. and succeeded in lifting the siege. The main San'a'-Ta'izz road, however, remained periodically cut by the royalists. In May a serious rift

YEMEN
Education. (1965–66) Primary, pupils 69,139, teachers 1,726; secondary, pupils 1,949, teachers 126; vocational, pupils 45, teachers (1963–64) 2; teacher training, students 125, teaching staff 5.
Finance and Trade. Monetary unit: Maria Theresa dollar, called the riyal, with a value of 1 riyal to U.S. $0.39 (2.57 riyals = £1 sterling). Budget (1967–68) balanced at 50,948,500 riyals. Trade with the U.K. (1967): imports £15,000 (but most British goods enter via Southern Yemen); exports £133,000.
Agriculture. Production (in 000; metric tons; 1966; 1965 in parentheses): wheat *c.* 27 (*c.* 26); dates *c.* 60 (*c.* 60); coffee *c.* 3.6 (*c.* 4.5). Livestock (in 000; 1965–66): cattle *c.* 1,230; sheep *c.* 11,700; camels *c.* 56; horses *c.* 3.

Yemen, People's Republic of Southern:
see Southern Yemen

Yiddish Literature:
see Literature

in the royalist ranks appeared. Opposition to the imam, Muhammad al-Badr, was led by his cousin Prince Muhammad ibn Husain, and a new Imamate Council and royalist Cabinet were announced in which al-Badr's name was not included. In September al-Badr reappeared, and the royalists claimed to have closed ranks behind him, but at year's end signs of disagreement were still apparent.

The republicans also had their divisions: between conservatives and young radicals and between Zaydis and Shafi'ite Sunnis, the two Yemeni Islamic sects. In August the premier, Maj. Gen. Hassan al-Amri, resigned as commander in chief in protest against dissidence within the republican forces, but he later withdrew his resignation. Later in the month there was serious fighting with heavy casualties between republican factions, but al-Amri succeeded in ending the strife and on September 15 formed his sixth government with seven Shafi'ite Sunnis and nine Zaydis. In October al-Amri visited Moscow, where he was promised continued Soviet aid. As winter approached republicans warned that the royalists were massing for new attacks. (P. Md.)

ДВАДЕСЕТ ТОДИНА

"Joseph, Joseph, when will you finally understand that you are really dead." "Politika," a major Yugoslavian daily newspaper published this cartoon following the Soviet invasion of Czechoslovakia.

Yugoslavia

A federal socialist republic, Yugoslavia is bordered by Italy, Austria, Hungary, Romania, Bulgaria, Greece, and Albania. Area: 98,766 sq.mi. (255,804 sq.km.). Pop. (1968 est.): 20,186,000. Cap. and largest city: Belgrade (pop., 1967 est., 697,000). Language: Serbo-Croatian, Slovenian, and Macedonian. Religion (1953): Orthodox 41.4%; Roman Catholic 31.8%; Muslim 12.3%. President of the republic and secretary-general of the League of Communists in 1968, Marshal Tito (Josip Broz); president of the Federal Executive Council (premier), Mika Spiljak.

During 1968 there were major shifts of emphasis in Yugoslavia's foreign policy, and also the fear of external attack, which contributed to greater cohesion at home. In a New Year speech President Tito lamented the estrangement of intellectuals and young people from the League of Communists, but by the end of the year the number of young party members was rapidly increasing.

Domestic Affairs. Sweeping reforms were envisaged following an eight-day sit-in strike by students at Belgrade University in early June which brought sympathetic action from intellectuals and workers throughout the country. In the name of socialism the students called for more thoroughgoing economic self-management, greater emphasis on social ownership, and more jobs for university graduates, many of whom had found it necessary to emigrate to the West for employment. They demanded further democratization of the League of Communists, guaranteed freedom of public assembly, and equal student representation on university administrative bodies. On June 10 President Tito promised redress of some of their grievances and an investigation into the behaviour of the police during the two days of bloody clashes that sparked off the protest. Opening the sixth Congress of Yugoslav Trade Unions in Belgrade at the end of June, the Yugoslav president repeated his pledge to speed reform. Elections to the 107-member Trade Union Central Council were by secret ballot and without a fixed list of candidates. In July the former vice-president, Milovan Djilas, had his confiscated manuscripts returned and was given a passport for foreign travel.

The Economy. In economic life decentralization continued. The Yugoslav Federal Economic Chamber sanctioned in January the creation of special local, regional, republican, and federal economic councils composed of private craftsmen. In May workers

pooled their savings to set up their own textile mill in Orahovica. In June the Crvena Zastava automobile factory in Kragujevac, together with the Yugoslav Investment Bank of Belgrade, issued 6% bonds to finance modernization of the plant. During the first seven months of 1968 industrial production rose 4.6% over the 1967 output for the same period, surpassing plan targets. This led Yugoslav economists to conclude that the period of economic stagnation was over, but they were less hopeful about reducing the 1967 balance of payments deficit of 5,684,000,000 dinars ($455 million). During the first half of 1968 Yugoslavia drew heavily on its $135 million worth of frozen capital tied up in the Council for Mutual Economic Assistance (Comecon). The problem of increasing exports to hard currency countries, with which Yugoslavia did more than 60% of its trade, was slightly eased after diplomatic relations were established with West Germany in January. West Germany promised to double its imports of Yugoslav textiles, enlarge its purchases of Yugoslav wines, and plead the case for giving Yugoslavia's agricultural produce preferential treatment in the European Economic Community.

Foreign Affairs. In January Yugoslavia pledged full support to Alexander Dubcek's reform program in Czechoslovakia, and kept aloof from the flurry of Soviet-sponsored Communist conferences in the following months. Tito late in April reportedly warned the Soviets against a military intervention in Czechoslovakia, and the Yugoslav press chided the U.S.S.R. and its allies for their misrepresentations of Eastern European events. In August the Yugoslav president demonstrated his solidarity with the Czechoslovak government in a three-day visit to Prague. After the five-power Communist invasion of Czechoslovakia later that month, the Yugoslav Communist Politburo and Secretariat registered the country's "deep indignation and bitterness," and President Tito called the occupation "a grievous blow to the world's socialist and progressive forces." Approximately 200,000 Czechoslovak sympathizers staged one of the biggest political demonstrations ever seen in Belgrade, while the country made emergency plans to accommodate thousands of Czechoslovak tourists, including five members of the government, who were temporarily stranded in Yugoslavia.

At the United Nations Security Council the Yugoslav representative, Anton Vratusa, warned that the intervention "constituted a serious danger to peace and stability" and repeated Tito's message that the Yugoslav people were "prepared to defend their independence at all costs." On August 24 Tito conferred in secret with the Romanian leader Nicolae Ceausescu, and reports indicated that they discussed the possibility of joint action should either country be invaded. In response to bitter attacks in the Soviet and allied press, Yugoslavia was put in a state of military readiness. All leaves were canceled, reserve officers with technical expertise were called up, and there was some redeployment of troops along the borders with Bulgaria, Hungary, and Romania. In October the Yugoslav Parliament voted an 8.2% increase in defense spending for 1969, to more than $561 million. Throughout the year there were heated exchanges with Bulgaria over disputed territory in the Macedonian region of Yugoslavia, and after August there were repeated suggestions in the Yugoslav press that the U.S.S.R. was urging Bulgaria to resurrect claims to Macedonia as a possible pretext for invasion.

Throughout 1968 President Tito and his ministers worked tirelessly for a conference of nonaligned nations, and a provisional arrangement was made to stage it in the Ethiopian capital some time in 1969. But there was disappointment when at the fourth conference of Mediterranean Communist and "progressive" parties in Rome in April, Yugoslavia failed to get endorsement for a resolution calling for the removal of Soviet as well as U.S. warships from the Mediterranean area. Later there was concern at the failure of the United Arab Republic, India, and other leading nonaligned countries to condemn outright the invasion of Czechoslovakia. Meanwhile, relations with the United States showed signs of improvement, and correspondents regarded as significant the discussions in October between Tito and the U.S. undersecretary of state, Nicholas Katzenbach. Relations with the Vatican improved dramatically, and Eugene Cardinal Tisserant, dean of the College of Cardinals, was given a warm welcome during his 12-day visit to Yugoslavia in June. (G. H. St.)

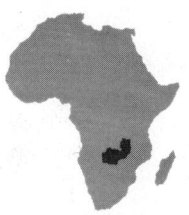

Zambia

A republic and a member of the Commonwealth of Nations, Zambia is bounded by Tanzania, Malawi, Mozambique, Rhodesia, South West Africa, Angola, and the Congo (Kinshasa). Area: 290,587 sq.mi. (752,621 sq.km.). Pop. (1968 est.): 4,014,000, of whom 99% are Africans. Cap.: Lusaka (pop., 1968 est., 154,000). Language: English and Bantu. Religion: predominantly pagan beliefs; Europeans are Christian. President in 1968, Kenneth Kaunda.

In a statement of economic policy on April 19 President Kaunda (see BIOGRAPHY) reaffirmed that nothing would be done to encourage Zambian capitalism, although there was nothing wrong in the ownership of property by individuals. What mattered was how they had acquired it. In an attempt to reduce the domination of economic activity by Europeans and Asians and to encourage Zambian participation, measures were to be taken to require banks and building so-

Demonstrators in Lusaka listening to speeches on UN Human Rights Day. Placards denounced white-rule regimes and Great Britain.

THE "NEW YORK TIMES" FROM WIDE WORLD

cieties to restrict loans for business purposes to companies having Zambian membership or shareholders and to partnerships or individuals who were Zambian. In agriculture, Kaunda said, it was important to utilize the country's manpower and not to concentrate upon big projects. He was disappointed by the lack of development in the mining industry since independence, a situation that he attributed largely to the distribution of more than 80% of profits as dividends. In the future, he declared, no more than 50% of profits might be sent abroad as dividends and the remainder must be reinvested in the industry. Foreign investors would nevertheless be welcome, and the government planned to enact legislation to safeguard approved foreign investments.

On January 16 Zambia changed to the decimal currency system with a new unit of currency, the kwacha ($1.40). No appreciation or depreciation of Zambian currency was involved.

The 1,058-mi. oil pipeline from Dar es Salaam to Ndola, constructed by an associate of the Italian state oil company, ENI, and financed by a loan from a consortium of Italian banks, went into operation on July 22. The opening brought to an end the severe fuel crisis that had existed since Rhodesia's declaration of independence from the U.K. in November 1965. Following the destruction of two spans of the important 1,000-ft. Luangwa Bridge by saboteurs in June a plastic pipeline was constructed across the Luangwa River to maintain supplies of oil to Zambia from Salima in Malawi. In August, too, President Kaunda announced that Zambia intended to go ahead with the construction of a power station on the north bank of the Kariba River.

Much of Zambia's economic policy was closely related to external problems, in particular to the situation in Rhodesia. Throughout the year Kaunda continued to urge upon Britain a firmer attitude toward

Workmen constructing a section of the 1,058-mi. pipeline from Dar es Salaam to Ndola, which went into operation on July 22, 1968.

Zanzibar:
see Tanzania

Zinc:
see Mining

Zoology:
see Biological Sciences

ZAMBIA
Education. (1965) Primary, pupils 410,150, teachers 8,036; secondary, pupils 17,187, teachers 921; vocational, pupils 1,931, teachers 66; teacher training, students 1,571, teachers 127.
    Finance. Monetary unit: kwacha (decimal currency introduced on Jan. 16, 1968), with a par value of 0.71 kwachas to U.S. $1 (1.71 kwachas = £1 sterling). Gold and foreign exchange, central bank: (June 1968) U.S. $95.9 million; (June 1967) U.S. $82.5 million. Budget (1968 est.): revenue 250.1 million kwachas; expenditure 195.8 million kwachas. Gross national product: (1966) 722.8 million kwachas; (1965) 601.4 million kwachas. Cost of living (1963 = 100): (May 1968) 143; (May 1967) 127.
    Foreign Trade. (1967): Imports 306,350,000 kwachas; exports 470,009,000 kwachas. Import sources: South Africa 24%; U.K. 21%; U.S. 11%; Rhodesia 11%; Japan 6%. Export destinations: U.K. 27%; Japan 20%; West Germany 9%; Italy 9%; France 8%; South Africa 5%; U.S. 5%. Main export copper 89%.
    Transport and Communications. Roads (1965) 34,130 km. (including 7,110 km. with improved surface). Motor vehicles in use (1966): passenger 42,100; commercial (including buses) 14,900. Railways (1965) 1,046 km. (for traffic *see* RHODESIA). Air traffic (apportionment of traffic of Central African Airways; 1966): 72,112,000 passenger-km.; freight 891,000 net ton-km. Telephones (Dec. 1966) 38,368. Radio receivers (1967) *c.* 80,000. Television receivers (1967) *c.* 10,000.
    Agriculture. Production (in 000; metric tons; 1966; 1965 in parentheses): corn *c.* 305 (*c.* 297); peanuts *c.* 36 (*c.* 36); tobacco 7.6 (9.3). Livestock (in 000; 1965–66): cattle *c.* 1,275; sheep *c.* 37; goats *c.* 150; pigs *c.* 61.
    Industry. Production (in 000; metric tons; 1967): copper 534; zinc 45; lead 19; manganese ore (metal content; 1966) 14; electricity 608,000 kw-hr.

the regime of Ian Smith in Rhodesia. In the course of a visit to London in July he tried unsuccessfully to convince the British government that force was the only answer to the Rhodesian problem, but he was more successful in his request for arms to enable Zambia to defend itself against external aggression. He also stated that he had been offered financial assistance to offset the cost to his government of sanctions against Rhodesia.

There was trouble in internal politics early in the year. In February, in the course of a conference of the ruling United National Independence Party (UNIP), Kaunda briefly resigned the presidency in protest against tribal wrangles within the party and was induced to retain office only when the party members agreed to dedicate themselves again to a national policy. Then, in by-elections held in the southern province in March, the opposition African National Congress (ANC) retained all the four seats that had been vacated when four members of Parliament had resigned from the ANC to join UNIP. As a result, Parliament was not dissolved until October. In the meantime, the opposition United Party was proscribed in August, and three of its leaders, including Nalumino Mundia, were arrested following disturbances near the Congo border. With the disappearance of the United Party, Harry Nkumbula's ANC became the only opposition party. In the elections in December, Kaunda was elected to a second term; UNIP obtained 81 seats in the 105-seat legislature, the ANC won 23, and 1 went to an independent. However, tribal divisions were emphasized by lack of support for Kaunda in Barotse Province.

(K. I.)

Zoos and Botanical Gardens

Zoos. The Federation of Zoological Gardens of Great Britain and Ireland formed in 1968 a Conservation and Breeding Committee, which planned to maintain a register of all rare animals and their births at member zoos and also act as an animal "mating bureau" by keeping a register of unmated animals. As part of this scheme, Chester Zoo received two pygmy hippos from Whipsnade, to be mated with its male. At the London Zoo an attempt was again made to mate its female giant panda, Chi-Chi, with the male An-An from Moscow, but, as in 1966 in Moscow, the effort was unsuccessful.

The ages reached by animals in captivity came under review. A Philadelphia, Pa., zoo owned a gorilla aged 37 years and a pair of 50-year-old orangutans. Elephants' longevity was found often to be overstated; one that died at Sydney, Austr., in 1939 was thought to have been 69, but so far as was known no others had lived for more than 60 years in captivity. A Siberian crane died at Washington, D.C., having reached an age of 61 years.

Zoos continued to breed many species threatened by extinction in the wild state. An orangutan born in West Berlin was the sixth to be born there since 1963. Others were born at Chester, Eng., Rotterdam, Neth., St. Louis, Mo., and Tarpon Springs, Fla.; twin orangutans were born at Seattle, Wash. Prolific zoo breeders were a pair of tigers at Crandon Park, Fla., which had produced 18 offspring since 1964. At Tokyo a spotless reticulated giraffe was born; the coloration was light brown all over. Both parents were typically marked reticulated giraffes.

All species of rhinoceros were becoming scarce in

LONDON "DAILY EXPRESS" FROM PICTORIAL PARADE

Mother dolphin at New Zealand's Napier Marineland with her 16-lb. baby, the first dolphin born alive in captivity in Australia or New Zealand.

the wild state but fortunately were being bred at zoos. Black rhino births were recorded in the U.S. at Washington, D.C., Kansas City, and Oklahoma City, and at Chester and Bristol, Eng. A white rhino was born at Pretoria, S.Af., and a great Indian rhino at Basel, Switz. The Hanover (W.Ger.) Zoo recorded the birth of two Asiatic elephants within one month, a unique breeding record, as was also the birth of a hairy saki at Frankfurt am Main.

Gorillas have always been difficult to breed in captivity, and most young ones have required rearing by their keepers. Frankfurt maintained a studbook of all the gorillas in captivity, and twin lowland gorillas were born at its zoo. A lowland gorilla birth was also recorded in the U.S., at Columbus, O., and the mother was taking care of the youngster.

Zoos were responsible for breeding a number of rare birds. The Chester Zoo successfully bred and reared a superb bird of paradise, believed to have been the first breeding in captivity of this species. Other outstanding successes, possibly firsts, were a thick-billed parrot bred at Tucson, Ariz., four green-billed toucans at Walsrode, W.Ger., a king vulture at Naples, Italy, and a ribbon-tailed bird of paradise at the London Zoo. A Colombian red-eyed cowbird died at Washington, D.C., after 11 years, and so far as was known it was the only one of its species to be found since 1866 when they were declared extinct.

Many zoological buildings were opened in which animals were housed in near natural conditions. Milwaukee, Wis., opened a new aquarium-reptile building with a 52,000-gal. dolphin pool, an Amazon River exhibit, and a 65,000-gal. Wisconsin lakes exhibit. Cities building barless enclosures for their hoofed animals included Winnipeg, Man., Duisburg, W.Ger., and West Berlin. Philadelphia was constructing the largest hummingbird exhibit of its type in the world. At Antwerp, Belgium's Jubilee project was designed to include accommodations for large carnivores, bears, dolphins, nocturnal animals, and birds of prey.

(G. S. Mo.)

Botanical Gardens. In 1968 the Royal Botanic Gardens, Kew, London, established a modern card index recording system to account for every newly acquired plant, as well as, ultimately, the whole collection. In the U.S. the Arnold Arboretum, in Jamaica Plain, Mass., continued to serve as the national registration centre for cultivars and woody genera not otherwise handled by specialist societies. Richard A. Howard, director of the Arnold Arboretum, was appointed chairman of the Plant Records Centre Committee of the American Horticultural Society. The centre was formed to place the records of botanical gardens into a computer system permitting electronic data processing and recovery. A standard information

form was developed for all botanical gardens wishing to record information on their accessions and holdings to facilitate electronic data processing.

Research on the propagation of native Australian plants was undertaken at King's Park Botanic Garden, Perth, and the information was then passed on to growers elsewhere. After its official opening in 1965 the garden had by 1968 amassed 1,200 indigenous species in 61 ac., including nearly all the trees native to the southern half of the state. Several acres were also devoted to Californian, South African, and Mediterranean plants. Gardens in other parts of the world reported collections of their native flora or of that of certain regions, thereby reflecting scientific interest in conservation of vegetation and its constituent species. A special collection of plants endemic to Chatham Island was established at Christchurch, N.Z. The National Botanic Gardens of South Africa continued to concentrate almost entirely on the rich indigenous flora, and each garden was devoted to particular aspects of it according to climatic conditions and available habitats. Linked with these projects was the fight against invasive alien plants and the preservation of native species in their own habitats.

Modernization was undertaken in most botanic gardens. At the University Botanic Garden, Cambridge, Eng., an oil-fired, pressurized, high-speed hot-water system replaced the 80-year-old solid-fuel appliance. Singapore Botanic Gardens reported the installation of path lighting and the completion of an extension for the herbarium and library. A precedent was created at the Royal Botanic Garden, Edinburgh, Scot., by the provision for visitors of a 35-minute sound-guide tour of the greenhouses. Another trend at Kew was the landscaping of the interior of several greenhouses to accommodate the plants in more natural surroundings. A large rural extension of Kew, at Wakehurst Place in Sussex, was opened to the public in October.

The 150th anniversary of the Geneva Botanic Garden was marked by an international symposium on "the many functions of a botanic garden," which was attended by numerous guests from many countries. Also celebrating its 150th anniversary during 1968 was the University Botanic Garden in Warsaw.

In Britain a national garden centre of more than 55 ac. was established at Syon House, Brentford, at a cost of £500,000. Facing the Royal Botanic Gardens across the Thames River, and close to London's Heathrow Airport, the site was expected to be ideal for holding international conferences.   (F. N. HE.)

UPI COMPIX

Colo, the first gorilla born in captivity, holding her baby born Feb. 1, 1968, at the Columbus (O.) Zoo. The baby was the first second-generation gorilla born in captivity.

"There, the trouble's not genetic, it's geopolitical."—King, "The Telegraph," Australia.

RUSSIANS GO HOME!

BEN ROTH AGENCY

Index

The black type entries are article headings in the *Book of the Year*. These black type article entries do not show page notations because they are to be found in their alphabetical position in the body of the book. They show the dates of the issues of the *Book of the Year* in which the articles appear. For example "Agriculture 69, 68, 67, 66" indicates that the article "Agriculture" is to be found in the 1969, 1968, 1967 and 1966 *Book of the Year*.

The light type headings that are indented under black type article headings refer to material elsewhere in the text related to the subject under which they are listed. The light type headings that are not indented refer to information in the text not given a special article. Biographies for 1969 are listed in the index alphabetically with page numbers. Those previous to 1969 are listed as cross references to the article "*Biography*" for the year in which they appeared. All obituaries are listed as cross references to the article "*Obituaries*" for the year in which they appear. References to illustrations are preceded by the abbreviation "il."

All headings, whether consisting of a single word or more, are treated for the purpose of alphabetization as single complete headings. Names beginning with "Mc" and "Mac" are alphabetized as "Mac"; "St." is treated as "Saint." All references below show the exact quarter of the page by means of the letters *a, b, c,* and *d,* signifying, respectively, the upper and lower halves of the first column and the upper and lower halves of the second column. Exceptions to this rule are tables, illustrations, and biographies.

A

Aaltonen, Waeinoe Waldemar: *see* **Obituaries 67**
Aaron, Hank (baseball player) 134b
Abdullah, Sheikh 402c; 661d
Abdullah as-Salim as-Sabah: *see* **Obituaries 66**
Abelson, Philip (biochemist) 531a
Abernathy, Ralph David (biog.) 140; il. 141
  Poor People's Campaign 643c; ils. 644, 645; 785b
Abortion 650c; 161
Abrams, Creighton Williams, Jr. (biog.) 140; il. 141
  defense 265a; 791c
Absorption (atmosphere) 517b
Academic freedom 317b
Accidents and safety 286a
  advertising 66c
  air transportation 745a
  cities and urban affairs 206c
  defense 262c
  engineering projects 327a
  industrial design 408c
  industrial review 412
  insurance 422d
  medicine 492d; 504b
  merchandising 514d
  mining 526a
  U.S. (Special Report) 782d
  vital statistics 797a
Ackerley, J. R. 470c
Ackley, (Hugh) Gardner: *see* **Biography 68**
Acromegaly 493d
Acute hemorrhagic cystitis 505a
ADA (Americans for Democratic Action) 597b
Adam, Karl: *see* **Obituaries 67**
Adams, John James ("Jack"): *see* **Obituaries 69**
Adams, Michael: *see* **Obituaries 68**
Aden: *see* Southern Yemen
Adenauer, Konrad: *see* **Obituaries 68**
Adenine 169b
Adler, Rabbi Morris: *see* **Obituaries 67**
Advertising 69, 68, 67, 66
  food 345b
  publishing 632c
  religion 650d
  tobacco 732d
AEC: *see* Atomic Energy Commission, U.S.
Aerospace 411; 744d
  accident risk 797b
  Australia 129d
  Busby, Sir Matthew 145
  cities and urban affairs 206a
  defense 257a
  disasters 286a
  electronics 319b
  fire fighting 227a
  geography 366c
  gold crisis 303b
  industrial design 407d
  insurance 423d
  nuclear energy 564a
  tourism 734d
  United Nations 777d
  see also Astronautics
Afars and Issas, French Territory of 273c
Affinity groups 315a
Afghanistan 69, 68, 67, 66
  Buddhism 661c

defense 267 (table)
education 311 (table)
electric power 359 (table)
fairs and shows 336c
France 356b
internat. organizations 431 (table)
political parties 613 (table)
publishing 637 (table)
social services 678 (table)
AFL-CIO 454b
Africa 69, 68, 67, 66
  "Agenda For the Future" (Johnson) 19b
  agriculture 84b
  China 198c
  commodities, primary 215d
  Commonwealth of Nations 219a
  cooperatives 234b
  defense 269a
  dependent states 273c
  development, economic 282b
  domestic arts and sciences 289b
  education 309b
  engineering projects 329b
  European Unity 334b
  food 342d
  football 350b
  France 356c
  fuel and power 360
  housing 392d
  industrial review 418 (table)
  inter-American affairs 428a
  Israel 440b
  mining 528 (table)
  Mondlane, Eduardo 158
  museums and galleries 546c
  populations and areas 617a
  publishing 638a
  race relations 639c
  religion 647a
  television and radio 718b
  trade, international 741a
  transportation 746 (table)
  veterinary medicine 789d
  vital statistics 797 (table)
  see also under various countries
"Africa: A Divided Continent" (Special Report) 71a
African and Malagasy Common Organization (OCAM) 71b; 74c
  commercial policies 214c
  Ivory Coast 443b
  Niger 558c
Afro-Americans: *see* Negroes, American
AFT (American Federation of Teachers) 313b
Agayants, Ivan Ivanovich: *see* **Obituaries 69**
Agency for International Development 344c; 622b
"Agenda For the Future: A Presidential Perspective" (Lyndon B. Johnson) 17
Agnew, Spiro Theodore (biog.) 140; il. 141; 782a
  race relations 645a
Agnon, Samuel Joseph: *see* **Biography 67**
Agrarian reform 80c
  Honduras 389a
  inter-American affairs 428a
  Mexico 520a
  Philippines 600d
Agricultural Development Law (Peru, 1968) 80d
Agricultural Producers Marketing Act (U.S., 1968) 78c
Agriculture 69, 68, 67, 66
  "Agenda For the Future" (Johnson) 25c

Chavez, César Estrada 145
  commercial policies 213b
  commodities, primary 215c
  conservation 225d
  cooperatives 234c
  defense 266c
  development, economic 284d
  employment, wages, and hours 321d
  European Unity 333c
  fairs and shows 337b
  Faure, Edgar 150
  food 342c
  gardening 365c
  gold crisis 594a
  income, national 401a
  inter-American affairs 427d
  tobacco 732a
  trade, international 740c
  unemployment 298d
  veterinary medicine 789c
  see also under various countries
Agriculture, U.S. Department of 80a
Aguiyi-Ironsi, Johnson Thomas Umunanke: *see* **Obituaries 67**
Ahidjo, Ahmadou (pres. Camer.) 183d
AID: *see* Agency for International Development
Ailleret, Charles-Louis-Marcel: *see* **Obituaries 69**
Air battery (elec.) 799
Airbus (aero.) 799; 745a
  electronics 319b
  industrial review 411
Air Force, U.S. 271c
Air pollution: *see* Pollution
Air Quality Act (U.S., 1968) 205c
Aiyar, Sir Chetpat Pattabhirama Ramaswami: *see* **Obituaries 67**
Akebia quinata (bot.) 170a
Akeley, Mary Jobe: *see* **Obituaries 67**
Akhmatova, Anna Andreyevna: *see* **Obituaries 67**
Akimov, Nikolai: *see* **Obituaries 69**
Akintola, Samuel Ladoke: *see* **Obituaries 67**
ALA (American Library Association) 464d
Alabama (state, U.S.) 688c
  Wallace, George C. 168
Alaska (state, U.S.) 100d
  archaeology (Special Report) 101a
  furs 363b
  mountaineering 544b
  timber 732a
Albania 69, 68, 67, 66
  China 196b
  Communist movement 221b
  Czechoslovak crisis 765b
  defense 267 (table)
  fuel and power 360
  income, national 401 (table)
  internat. organizations 431 (table)
  political parties 613 (table)
  propaganda il. 629
  publishing 637 (table)
  refugees 646a
  religion 659a
  social services 678 (table)
Albareda (Gioacchino), Anselmo Maria Cardinal: *see* **Obituaries 67**
Albatross 172c
Albert, Edouard: *see* **Obituaries 69**
Alberta (prov., Can.) 185d; 361
Albizu Campos, Pedro: *see* **Obituaries 66**
Albright-Knox Gallery (Buffalo, N.Y.) 114a
Alcindor, Ferdinand Lewis, Jr. (biog.) 140
  basketball 136c; il. 138
Alcoholic Beverages 69, 68, 67, 66
  Castle, Barbara 145
  industrial review 419
  religion 650c
Aldabra, coral atoll, Ind.O. 172c
Alegría, Ciro: *see* **Obituaries 68**
Alexander, Hattie: *see* **Obituaries 69**
Alexander of Hillsborough, Albert Victor Alexander, 1st earl: *see* **Obituaries 66**
Al Fatah 441a; 268b
Alfieri, Odoardo D.: *see* **Obituaries 67**
ALG: *see* Antilymphocyte globulin
Algae 169c
Algeny (genetics) 799
Algeria 69, 68, 67, 66
  Africa (Special Report) 71b
  "Agenda For the Future" (Johnson) 20d
  agriculture 84b
  border incidents 460a
  defense 262a
  disasters 286d
  education 311 (table)
  engineering projects 330b
  fuel and power 361
  internat. organizations 431 (table)
  Middle East 521b
  mining 528 (table)
  museums and galleries 546d
  Niger 558d
  political parties 613 (table)
  publishing 637 (table)
  social services 678 (table)
  telecommunications 714 (table)
  tourism 734a
  transportation 746 (table)
  Tunisia 759c
  United Nations 776c
  Yemen 801d
All-Blacks (football team) 349c

Allen, Sir Carleton Kemp: *see* **Obituaries 67**
Allen, Florence E.: *see* **Obituaries 67**
Allen, Henry: *see* **Obituaries 68**
Allen, Herbert Warner: *see* **Obituaries 69**
Allen, Ralph: *see* **Obituaries 67**
Alliance for Progress 425d; 79c
Alliluyeva, Svetlana: *see* **Biography 68**
Allingham, Margery (Louise): *see* **Obituaries 67**
Allison, Samuel K.: *see* **Obituaries 66**
Allogeneic (genetics) 799
Allon Plan 521d
Allport, Gordon Willard: *see* **Obituaries 68**
All-Union Economic Conference (Moscow, 1968) 297c; 296d
Almonds 82d
Alphametic (math.) 799
Alps, mts., Europe 543d
Altizer, Thomas Jonathan Jackson: *see* **Biography 67**
Altrock, Nick: *see* **Obituaries 66**
Aluminum 216a; 528 (table)
  Ghana 373b
  medical use il. 505
  metallurgy 516c
  Norway 562a
  photography 604b
  South Africa 682a
Alvarez, Luis W. (biog.) 140; il. 141
Alvaro da Silva, Augusto Cardinal: *see* **Obituaries 69**
Amateur radio 722a
Amazon River, S.Am. 368a
Ambrose, E. J. (biophysicist) 532b
Amer, Abdel Hakim: *see* **Obituaries 68**
American Antarctic Mountaineering Expedition 544b
American Ballet Theatre 248b
American Bar Association 636d
American Broadcasting Company 715d
American Federation of Teachers (AFT) 313b
American Friends Service Committee 655c
American Heart Association 142
American Independent Party 779a
American Institute of Architects 105b
"American Kinship: A Cultural Account" (Schneider) 99a
American League (baseball) 133c; 158
American Library Association (ALA) 464d
American literature 466a
American Meteorological Society (AMS) 516d
American Paleo-Arctic tradition 100d
American Samoa, Pac.O. 275 (table)
  publishing 637 (table)
Americans for Democratic Action (ADA) 597b
American Telephone and Telegraph Co. (AT & T) 714d
America's Cup (sailing) 668b
Amico, Gianni 200d
Amino acids 169a; 530d
Amis, Kingsley 471d
Amri, Hassan al- 801c
Anastasi, P. (athlete) 348c
Anastassy (Gribanovsky), Metropolitan: *see* **Obituaries 66**
Andean Common Market 426b
Andean Development Corporation 81a
  Venezuela 789a
Anders, William (astronaut) 121d
Anderson, Douglas D. 100d
Andorra 69, 68, 67, 66
  political parties 613 (table)
Andrews, Laverne: *see* **Obituaries 68**
Anesthesiology 490b
Angell, Sir Norman: *see* **Obituaries 68**
Angiokeratoma corporis diffusum 492a
Anglican Communion 649a
  Boyd, Malcolm 143
Angola 74c
  coffee 89 (table)
  defense 270c
  dependent states 273d
  mining 528 (table)
  Portugal 623b
Anguilla, W.I. 273d
  philately 599b
Animal behaviour 170c
Ankrah, Joseph A. 372b
Anniversaries
  Declaration of the Rights of Man 145
  "Encyclopædia Britannica" 143
  Israel celebration ils. 439, 440
  New York City Ballet 251b
  race relations 639c
  Russian Revolution (1917) 480a
  Taiwan 711a
  Tanganyika and Zanzibar 712c
  theatre 725c
  Veterinary College of Vienna 789d
  Vietnam 795c
Antarctica 69, 68, 67, 66
  biological sciences 170b
  dependent states 274 (table)
  mountaineering 544b
  New Zealand 557c
Antarctic Treaty 97a
Anthropology 69, 68, 67, 66
  skull il. 103
Antibiotics
  chemical and biological warfare 254d
  gardening 366a
  veterinary medicine 790a
Antigens 499b

INDEX 821
Mansfield / Mosbacher

Mansfield, Jayne: *see* **Obituaries 68**
Mansfield, Mike 258c
Manship, Paul H.: *see* **Obituaries 67**
Manson-Bahr, Sir Philip (Henry): *see* **Obituaries 67**
Mansur, Hassan Ali: *see* **Obituaries 66**
Manufacturing 409c; 215c
  chemical and biological warfare 253d
  employment, wages, and hours 322a
  European Unity 333c
  food 347a
  inter-American affairs 430a
  investment, international 433c
  merchandising 514d
  nuclear energy 564d
  race relations 640c
  trade, international 739c
  see also various countries
Manuscripts 118c
Manville, Thomas Franklyn ("Tommy"): *see* **Obituaries 68**
Mao Tse-tung: *see* **Biography 68**
  China 195c; 266b
  Communist movement 221b
  education 316c
  propaganda 630b
  Vietnam 795a
Maple sugar 76c
Mara, John V.: *see* **Obituaries 66**
Marathon (sports) 738b
Marcos, Ferdinand (pres., Phil.) 600c
Marcus, James L. (crime) 239b
Marcuse, Herbert (biog.) 158
Margesson, Henry David Reginald Margesson, 1st Viscount: *see* **Obituaries 66**
Margrethe, (crown princess, Den.) 272b
Maria-Francisca, Princess of Orleans and Bragança: *see* **Obituaries 69**
Marie Byrd Land Survey (Antarctica) 97d
"Mariée à double face, La" (Chagall) 115d
Marijuana 239d
Marina, Princess: *see* **Obituaries 69**
Marine biology 173a; 97b
Marine Midland Building (New York, N.Y.) 105c; il. 109
Maris Report (Neth.) 555d
Maritime law 461b
Marketing: *see* Merchandising
Marmstedt, (Sigfrid) Lorens: *see* **Obituaries 67**
Marriage: *see* Vital statistics
Mars 169b
Marsh, Mae: *see* **Obituaries 69**
Marshall, Herbert: *see* **Obituaries 67**
Marshall, Thurgood: *see* **Biography 68**
Marshall, Caroline, and Mariana Islands, Pac.O. 275 (table)
Martin, Edward: *see* **Obituaries 68**
Martin, (Warren) Homer: *see* **Obituaries 69**
Martin, John Leonard: *see* **Obituaries 66**
Martin, Joseph W.: *see* **Obituaries 69**
Martin, Kingsley (author) 471a
Martin, William McChesney, Jr.: *see* **Biography 66**
Martinique, W. I. 275 (table)
Martino, Gaetano: *see* **Obituaries 68**
Masaryk, Alice G.: *see* **Obituaries 67**
Masefield, John: *see* **Obituaries 68**
Maskell, Virginia: *see* **Obituaries 69**
Masner, P. (biol.) 171d
Massamba-Debat, Alphonse (pres., Congo, Rep. of) 225a; 70d
Mass extinction 170c
Massey, Vincent: *see* **Obituaries 68**
Masson, André (art.) 113a
Masson, Roger: *see* **Obituaries 68**
Ma Ssu-tsung (Ma Sitson): *see* **Biography 68**
Master-strand replication (biol.) 532c
Masterton, William: *see* **Obituaries 69**
  hockey 388b
Mathematics 69, 68, 67, 66
Matthes, Roland (swimmer) 708c
Matthews, Zachariah Keodirelang: *see* **Obituaries 69**
Maugham, William Somerset: *see* **Obituaries 66**
Maurer, Ion Gheorghe (Rom.) 664b
Mauritania 69, 68, 67, 66
  Africa 75b
  agriculture 85d
  dependent states 273c
  internat. organizations 432 (table)
  political parties 614 (table)
  social services 678 (table)
Mauritius 69
  Africa 69c
  conservation 227a
  education 311 (table)
  employment 322 (table)
  internat. organizations 432 (table)
  political parties 614 (table)
  publishing 637 (table)
  sugar 89 (table)
  United Nations 778c
  vital statistics 798a
Maurois, André: *see* **Obituaries 68**
Mayo, Charles W.: *see* **Obituaries 69**
Mays, Willie (baseball player) 135c
M'ba, Léon: *see* **Obituaries 68**
  Bongo, Albert Bernard 143
Meat 344a; 216a; 741a
Mechanic (Fireman) (gambling) 800
Media mix (Expanded cinema) 800
Medicaid 40d
Medical education 500c
Medicare 679b; 40a
  Canada 375d
  insurance 423a
Medicine 69, 68, 67, 66
  astronautics 120a
  Barnard, Christiaan 142
  chemical and biological warfare 253c
  dentistry 272b
  Ghana 372c
  law 458b
  Maldive Islands 486a
  refugees 646b
Medionym (Meronym) (lang.) 800
Megalopolis 108c
Meier, Norman C.: *see* **Obituaries 68**
Mein, John Gordon: *see* **Obituaries 69**
  assassination 239d
Meinertzhagen, Richard: *see* **Obituaries 68**
Meitner, Lise: *see* **Obituaries 69**
Mekong delta 228d
Mekong Development Scheme 685a
Melachrino, George: *see* **Obituaries 66**
Melanoma 491d
Mellotron (mus.) 800
Memphis, Tenn.
  King, Martin L., Jr. 785a
  race relations 643a
Mendès-France, Pierre: *see* **Biography 68**
Méndez Montenegro, Julio César 379c
Menéndez Pidal, Ramón: *see* **Obituaries 69**
Menken, Helen: *see* **Obituaries 67**
Mennen, William G.: *see* **Obituaries 69**
Menninger, William Claire: *see* **Obituaries 67**
Menon, Vapal Pangunni: *see* **Obituaries 67**
Menzies, Sir Robert Gordon: *see* **Biography 66**
Menzies, Sir Stewart Graham: *see* **Obituaries 69**
Mercenaries
  Congo (Kinshasa) 223d; il. 224
Mercer, David: *see* **Biography 67**
Merchandising 69, 68, 67, 66
  alcoholic beverages 93a
  economic policy 299b
  philately 599a
  prices 625d
  trade, international 742c
Merckx, Eddy (athlete) 243c
Mercury 529 (table)
Mercy, Prerogative of 457d
Meredith, James Howard: *see* **Biography 67**
Mergers
  Netherlands 555a
  publishing 632d
  stock exchanges 701d
Mérode, Cléo de: *see* **Obituaries 67**
Meronym (Medionym) (lang.) 800
Merton, Thomas (Father M. Louis): *see* **Obituaries 69**
Meson 606c
Messenger ribonucleic acid 531d
Metallurgy 69, 68, 67, 66
  food 346c
  fuel and power 357c
Meteorology 69, 68, 67, 66
  Arctic regions 110d
  astronautics 125a
  geology 367b
Methodists 654a
Methohexitone (drug) 490d
Methotrexate (drug) 492b
Metropolitan Museum of Art (New York City) 114b; 545a
Mexico 69, 68, 67, 66
  agriculture 79c
  alcoholic beverages 94 (table)
  architecture 109a
  crime 239d
  defense 267 (table)
  disasters 287c
  economy, world 302 (table)
  education 311 (table)
  employment 325 (table)
  engineering projects 329a
  fisheries 342a
  food 345a
  fuel and power 361
  Fuentes, Carlos 151
  housing 393d
  immigration and emigration 398d
  income, national 399 (table)
  industrial review 410 (table)
  inter-American affairs 430a
  internat. organizations 432 (table)
  literature 478d
  mining 528 (table)
  motor sports 541b
  museums and galleries 546c
  Norway 562d
  political parties 614 (table)
  prices 626 (table); 627 (table)
  propaganda 630a
  publishing 637 (table)
  rubber 666 (table)
  social services 678 (table)
  speleology 688b
  sports 135c; 175d
  tourism 734d
  trade, international 741a
  transportation 746 (table)
  veterinary medicine 790b
  vital statistics 798b
Mexico City, Mex.
  architecture 109a
  Brundage, Avery 144
  cycling (Olympic Games) 243a
  football 347b
  philately 599a
  riots 609b
  Summer Olympics 692d
  track and field sports 737a
Meyer, Albert Gregory Cardinal: *see* **Obituaries 66**
Meyer, Debbie (swimmer) 707b
Miami, Fla. 782a; 646c
Mica 529 (table)
Micara, Clemente Cardinal: *see* **Obituaries 66**
Michener, (Daniel) Roland: *see* **Biography 68**
Micombero, Michel 182c
Microbiology 501c
  biological warfare 254d; il. 255
  chemical and biological warfare 254a
  defense 258a
  dentistry 272c
  food 346c
Microblade (archae.) 102a
Middle East 69, 68, 67, 66
  "Agenda For the Future" (Johnson) 20c
  commodities, primary 215d
  defense 266b
  dependent states 276b
  development, economic 282b
  European Unity 335a
  food 342c
  France 356b
  fuel and power 362
  gold crisis 303b
  industrial review 411
  Jarring, Gunnar V. 153
  populations and areas 617c
  propaganda 629b
  refugees 646b
  television and radio 718a
  tourism 734a
  trade, international 741a
  United Nations 773c
  U.S.S.R. 767b
  see also Middle Eastern countries
Middlescent (sociol.) 800
Midway Islands 275 (table)
Mies van der Rohe, Ludwig 109d; 545d
Migration: *see* Immigration and emigration
Mikita, Stan (hockey player) 387d
Military, Air, and Naval Affairs: *see* **Defense 69, 68, 67.** *See* **Military, Air, and Naval Affairs 66**
Military Counterespionage Service (MAD) 424c
Milk: *see* Dairy and dairy products
Miller, Arthur Austin: *see* **Obituaries 69**
Miller, Arthur Lewis: *see* **Obituaries 68**
Miller, Edward T.: *see* **Obituaries 69**
Miller, Lennox (athlete) 737d
Miller, Max: *see* **Obituaries 68**
Miller, Stanley L. (biochemist) 531a
Millet 85c
Millin, Sarah G.: *see* **Obituaries 69**
Millis, Walter: *see* **Obituaries 69**
Mills, Frederick Percival: *see* **Obituaries 66**
Mills, Percy Herbert Mills, 1st viscount: *see* **Obituaries 69**
Minibus (transportation) 750b; 800
Minimal sculpture (art) 800
Mining 69, 68, 67, 66
  Australia 131a
  conservation il. 226
  dependent states 279a
  disasters 287a
  fuel and power 358
  geology 368a
  gold crisis 307b
  investment, international 433c
  Italy 443c
  Lesotho 462b
  oceanography 582b
  South Africa 683c
  stock exchanges 703c
  trade, international 741a
Mink 363a
Minnesota (state, U.S.)
  baseball 133c
  hockey 388b
Minton, Sherman: *see* **Obituaries 66**
Miquelon: *see* St. Pierre and Miquelon
Mirghani, Sayyid Ali al-: *see* **Obituaries 69**
Miró, Joan (art.) 112d
Mirsky, Samuel K.: *see* **Obituaries 68**
MIRV (Multiple independently targeted reentry vehicle) 257d
Missiles: *see* Rockets and missiles
Mitchell, Arthur W.: *see* **Obituaries 69**
Mitochondria (biol.) 532a
Mitterrand, François Maurice: *see* **Biography 67**
"Mizar" (submarine) 583a
Mobilography (sociol.) 800
Mobutu, Joseph 223d
  Burundi 182c
  Ivory Coast 443d
  Rwanda 667c
Modern art 116a
Model Cities Program 36b
Mohammad Reza Pahlavi (shah, Iran) 435d
Mohammad Zahir Shah (k. Afg.) 68d
Molecular Biology 69
  Nirenberg, Marshall W. 160
Mollusk 169c
Molniya (communications satellite) 715d; 122 (table)
Molybdenum 529 (table)
Momsen, Charles B.: *see* **Obituaries 68**
Monaco 69, 68, 67, 66
  chess 193d
  education 311 (table)
  internat. organizations 432 (table)
  political parties 614 (table)
Monckton of Brenchley, Walter Turner Monckton, 1st Viscount: *see* **Obituaries 66**
Mondlane, Eduardo Chivambo (biog.) 158; 273b
Money and Banking 69, 68, 67, 66
  cities and urban affairs 203c
  cooperatives 234c
  crimes against banks 239a
  development, economic 282b
  economics 298b; 294d; 699a
  employment, wages, and hours 323c
  European Unity 334a
  gold crisis 302d
  housing 394b
  inter-American affairs 430a; 429a
  investment, international 434c
  mining 524c
  payments and reserves 590a
  Southeast Asia 684c
  stock exchanges 699a
  see also various countries
Mongolia 69, 68, 67, 66
  China 198b
  Communist movement 221b
  internat. organizations 432 (table)
  political parties 614 (table)
  publishing 637 (table)
Monod, Jacques: *see* **Biography 66**
  molecular biology 531d
Monopoly
  merchandising 515a
Monorail 749d
Monte Carlo, Monaco 533c; 540c
Montet, Pierre: *see* **Obituaries 67**
Montgomery, Wes: *see* **Obituaries 69**
  music 551d
Montherlant, H. (novelist) 474d
Montreal, Que., Can.
  architecture 105d
  baseball 134b
  hockey 387d
  police 611c
Montserrat 275 (table)
  Barbados 133a
Monuments 385a
Moon
  astronautics 121d; ils. 123
  seismology 672b
Moontel (housing) 800
Moore, Brian 472a; il. 471
Moore, Henry (biog.) 159; il. 158
  art exhibitions 112d
Moore, Lillian: *see* **Obituaries 68**
Moore, O'Neal: *see* **Obituaries 66**
Moran, Charles McMoran Wilson, Baron: *see* **Biography 67**
Morane, Robert Charles: *see* **Obituaries 69**
Morano, Francesco Cardinal: *see* **Obituaries 69**
Moreau, Jeanne: *see* **Biography 66**
Morehead, Albert Hodges: *see* **Obituaries 67**
Morgan, Edwin (poet) 473a
Morgan, Sir Frederick (Edgworth): *see* **Obituaries 68**
Morgenthau, Henry H., Jr.: *see* **Obituaries 68**
Morison, Stanley: *see* **Obituaries 68**
Morning-after pill (med.) 800
Moro, Aldo (Italy) 441b
Morocco 69, 68, 67, 66
  Africa (Special Report) 71b
  agriculture 84d
  defense 267 (table)
  dependent states 273c
  education 311 (table)
  electric power 359 (table)
  employment, wages, and hours 322 (table)
  fisheries 342 (table)
  food 344b
  income, national 399 (table)
  internat. organizations 432 (table)
  mining 528 (table)
  political parties 614 (table)
  prices 626 (table)
  publishing 637 (table)
  religion 655a
  social services 678 (table)
  telecommunications 714 (table)
  tourism 734a
  transportation 746 (table)
Morphine 506a
Morrison, Charles Clayton: *see* **Obituaries 67**
Morrison, Norman R.: *see* **Obituaries 66**
Morrison of Lambeth, Herbert Stanley Morrison, Baron: *see* **Obituaries 66**
Morse, Sir Arthur: *see* **Obituaries 68**
Mortgage 394b
Mosbacher, Emil, Jr.: *see* **Biography 68**

S

States Statistical Supplement

ENCYCLOPÆDIA BRITANNICA, INC.

17 68

Developments in the states in 1968

It is more than likely that in terms of government action 1968 was one of the states' most active years. This occurred despite the fact that 1968 was what used to be considered an off year, when legislatures were not supposed to be in session. Continuing a recently established trend, the states responded more strongly than ever to the demands for social and political reform that have dominated the 1960s. Also, the role of the states in this area continued to grow as the federal government became less active. A striking aspect of this new strength and responsibility was the increased activity of the smaller and traditionally less-active states, which were busy in 1968 modernizing their structures and initiating new programs. Prominent among these were Delaware, Vermont, Maryland, and South Dakota. Indeed, in a year of trials for the nation as a whole, when bad news so often dominated the headlines, the states' quiet and unsung progress toward dealing with domestic problems offered a measure of optimism for the future.

The states' new energy was manifested on two fronts: within their boundaries, through widespread structural reforms, extensive legislative innovation, and intensive expansion of programs; and in Washington, D.C., through concentrated efforts to increase their role or improve their position in intergovernmental affairs. By and large, they met with substantial success on both fronts. One notable feature of this effort was congressional enactment of the Intergovernmental Cooperation Act of 1968, which ratified many of the new trends in state-federal relations and gave them legislative roots from which to be further developed. Other features included the addition of three more "block grants" programs to give the states greater flexibility in using federal funds.

Among the most important structural changes was the continued increase in the number of states holding annual legislative sessions. Seven states—Florida, Idaho, Iowa, Mississippi, Ohio, Utah, and Wisconsin—approved the holding of annual sessions in 1968, bringing the total number of annual sessions in 1968, bringing the total

to almost three-fifths of all the states. Changes in gubernatorial tenure, another vital issue in current state reform efforts, were also noticeable in 1968, as an increasing number of the minority of states still restricting gubernatorial terms of office eliminated their restrictions.

Constitutional ratification of legislative reapportionment took place in at least 7 states, bringing the total number that had done this to 17. All but three states had completed reapportionment of their legislatures and had valid new plans in effect.

The expansion of both municipal and county home rule was another major aspect of constitutional reform in 1968, with comprehensive changes being achieved in Florida and Iowa and smaller changes in many other states. On the other hand, 50 constitutional amendment proposals were on the ballot in Louisiana, the state with the longest and most detailed constitution, and most of them involved local issues.

The states became increasingly active in the federal "model cities" program in 1968. According to federal reports, New Jersey and Pennsylvania financed more model cities with their own money than the federal government had designated. New York, Connecticut, Ohio, Vermont, California, Texas, Kentucky, Illinois, and Tennessee, among others, provided assistance by assigning personnel representing relevant state agencies to help in the planning of model cities programs in their communities. The states were also involved more heavily in most other efforts undertaken to meet urban problems.

Perhaps the biggest "new" issue of the year was that of "law and order." Both the states and the federal government responded to the loud public outcries on this subject by acting on a number of fronts. Gun control was a primary topic of concern, particularly in the aftermath of the assassinations of the Rev. Martin Luther King, Jr., and Sen. Robert F. Kennedy.

Reflecting the revived concern with cultural pluralism in the United States, Louisiana reversed a long-standing policy and began to encourage the French-Acadian culture of the southern parts of

that state. The Louisiana legislature went so far as to create a council to develop French and made study of the language mandatory in the state's elementary and secondary schools.

State Government. New York established a seven-member Council of Economic Advisers with broad economic research, advisory, and planning powers. Massachusetts initiated a study as to how its state government could best obtain and utilize advice on scientific and technological matters. Maine established a State Planning Office, while Arizona initiated a statewide economic development program to be headed by its governor. North Carolina's Planning Task Force inaugurated a major planning effort involving many state agencies and supported by federal funds.

Oregonians authorized their legislature to extend the state's ocean boundaries. Wyoming established procedures for initiative and referendum proposals. Oklahoma's legislature enacted a general code of ethics for all public officials and employees, to be enforced by separate commissions for legislative and nonlegislative officials.

Constitutional Revision. The year 1968 was an unusually active year for constitutional reformers, with more than half the states engaged in efforts to change their basic documents. Thirty-four states considered 216 constitutional amendments in the November elections, and more than 100 of them were adopted. Two states, Florida and Hawaii, adopted entirely new documents, while others achieved significant constitutional changes by amending their existing ones.

Highlights of the new Florida constitution included revisions of the sections on suffrage and elections, and the local government article. Governors were allowed to succeed themselves for a second four-year term, and the legislature was to meet annually and be automatically reapportioned every ten years. Counties were given home rule, and property tax and state bonding interest rate ceilings were raised.

The new Hawaii constitution provided for reapportionment after 1970 and regularly every eight years thereafter. The length of the second-year legislative session was extended, and a carry-over of bills from the first year was provided. Legislators' salaries were increased substantially, and future raises by law were authorized. State budgeting was put on a two-year basis, and both the state and county debt limits were raised.

Oklahoma voters approved ten constitutional amendments during 1968 in a major effort to update the state's constitution. Nebraska voters approved 13 of 17 proposed amendments in a major effort to broaden the powers of their state's legislature and increase Nebraska's fiscal

flexibility. A majority of New Hampshire voters approved a ten-amendment "package" to that state's constitution, but only eight of the measures received the two-thirds vote needed for passage.

Pennsylvania, in another major effort at constitutional change, unified the administration of the state's courts under the State Supreme Court, abolished the existing state debt limit and established a flexible ceiling based on total state income over the previous five years, required regular reapportionment of local government boards after each census, abolished the constitutional limit on local government debt and granted the legislature power to establish debt limits for local government units based on their incomes, and, finally, granted local governments power to adopt home rule charters.

One new trend to emerge in recent years was the creation of special commissions to set legislators' salaries, thus overcoming the problem of either allowing the legislators to set their own compensation or rigidly fixing salaries within the state constitution. The most recent additions to the list of states using the commission method, alone or in combination with legislative action, included Oklahoma and Idaho. Michigan created a seven-man commission to set salaries of all state government officials, including legislators.

Alabama and Florida provided that their governors and other major executive officers could succeed themselves for a second four-year term. Arizona voted to give its governor and his Cabinet four-year terms. Colorado provided for the election of governor and lieutenant governor as a team. Iowa's governor was given an item veto over appropriations measures. Provisions for runoff elections and gubernatorial succession were altered in Georgia in reaction to Lester Maddox's 1966 victory with only a plurality of the vote. Massachusetts governors were given up to ten days to act on measures passed by the legislature.

Judicial reform amendments of varying extent were adopted in Louisiana, Alaska, Oklahoma, Idaho, Oregon, Utah, and Washington. Most were concerned with the retirement or removal of judges, though Washington's provided for the establishment of a state court of appeals.

Voters in Arkansas, Illinois, and New Mexico approved the calling of unlimited constitutional conventions; those in Tennessee approved a limited constitutional convention and, via the initiative method, the Massachusetts electorate required that a constitutional convention proposal be placed on the ballot in 1970. Virginia appointed a Commission on Constitutional Revision, whose recommendations were to be considered by the 1969 session of the legislature. South Carolina

voters adopted a "gateway" amendment to facilitate a major constitutional revision, article by article, in 1970 and 1972. The Tennessee convention was to be confined to property-tax matters, as the voters of that state rejected all other proposed topics.

Legislatures and Legislative Procedures. Legislators' pay was raised in Ohio. Expense allowances for 34 chairmen and senior minority members of legislative committees were instituted in New York. The Illinois legislature gave its 14 major standing committees between-sessions research functions and provided them with appropriate staffs and financing. The Florida legislature took steps in the same direction, including the abolition of the Legislative Council as its inter-session research agency at the end of 1968 and the transferring of the council's powers and functions to the standing legislative committees. Florida also created a Fiscal Account Division, with a six-member Joint Legislative Management Committee to supervise it and assume the general functions of the Legislative Council. The Kentucky legislature established a Joint Legislative Committee on Un-American Activities and assumed sole control over its own finances and personnel. The Rhode Island legislature overrode a gubernatorial veto to assume similar powers. The Maryland legislature instituted the prefiling of bills and joint resolutions, and established a Department of Fiscal Services to handle its legislative postaudit. The Kentucky legislature adopted a far-reaching reorganization of its committee system, greatly reducing the number of standing committees. Vermont imposed a registration fee on lobbyists.

The National Legislative Conference Committee on Legislative Rules presented a model act that established a code of fair procedures for investigations by state legislatures. Maryland instituted such a code of procedures for its legislative committees. The Pennsylvania legislature adopted a code of ethics. A committee to draft such a code was appointed by the Delaware legislature, which also enacted legislation forbidding legislators to hold other state offices.

Administration. A major topic of concern in 1968 was the right of public employees to bargain collectively with the state and its subdivisions and to strike. By and large, steps were taken to permit and even encourage collective bargaining while strikes continued to be prohibited. The California legislature required all public employers to bargain collectively with their employees' recognized labor organizations. The new Hawaii constitution permitted such collective bargaining. A Pennsylvania study commission recommended that most state and local employees be granted a limited right to strike. Gov. Spiro Agnew of Maryland

appointed a commission to look into the matter, and Delaware permitted its merit system employees to join unions and establish procedures for collective bargaining with them. Meanwhile, New York sponsored an all-state National Conference on Public Employment in October to study the new problems in the field.

In another major reorganization, the New Mexico legislature abolished eight obsolete state agencies, created two new departments in the fields of health and social services, and established a Property Control Division to centralize management of state property. Vermont instituted a veterans' preference system for state jobs. A uniform merit system for all state employees was established by Arizona, which also raised the pay of state and county officials. The Colorado legislature implemented a 1966 constitutional amendment that consolidated 148 state agencies within 17 departments and gave the governor more direct lines of control over the executive branch.

Judiciary and Law Enforcement. By far the major "new" issue of the year, law enforcement produced an unprecedented amount of state action. The states acted to strengthen law enforcement institutions and to expand state and local law enforcement powers, in regard to both individual criminals and mass disturbances. At the same time, they took many important steps toward implementing new protections for the rights of those accused of crimes, particularly juveniles, and toward the improvement of their correctional systems.

The states that had not already done so inaugurated crime commissions or law enforcement councils, while those that already had such commissions expanded their scope, principally to take advantage of the federal funds that were to become available under the 1968 Crime Control Act. Many of the conferences of state officials devoted their sessions to the problems of crime control.

Delaware created a Department of Justice, while Arizona established a public safety division under the governor, a state crime laboratory, and a statewide police-training program. The Oregon Criminal Law Revision Commission began revising that state's criminal law. Vermont ratified the New England Police Compact. Kentucky's new Law Enforcement Council was authorized to establish training schools and programs for policemen and regulations for police training and certification. Maryland set up a new division within its Department of State Police to make agreements with local governments concerning the provision of police services. New Jersey established a bipartisan State Commission on Investigation, similar to New York's, to investigate organized crime and governmental corruption. Alaska instituted a central-

ized criminal information exchange and a Governor's Planning Council on the Administration of Criminal Justice. Alabama's State Law Institute was activated; it was to advise the legislature in matters involving the codification and simplification of Alabama law, including continuous code revision, improving the administration of justice, and conducting legal research.

The Maine legislature enacted a measure allowing the state to grant immunity to implicated witnesses if they testified against others. The state was also given the right to appeal dismissals of cases based on technical legal errors. A similar provision was enacted in Rhode Island. An Ohio act allowed the examination of a judge's charge to the jury before closing arguments. Vermont broadened its "right to counsel" law, provided for more representative juries in its courts, and reformed its procedures for handling cases of juvenile delinquency. Oklahoma enacted a new juvenile code that strengthened the state's ability to deal with dependent, neglected, or delinquent children. Colorado tightened the arrest provisions for juvenile misdemeanors in its children's code and permitted felony prosecutions of minors of 14 and above who commit major crimes.

Responding to the epidemic of crime in the state, the New York legislature permitted the issuance of court orders permitting wiretapping and electronic eavesdropping when justified. It also broadened the rights of policemen and private citizens to shoot to kill suspected criminals and intruders.

Illinois enacted a "stop and frisk" act, increased penalties for aggravated assault, and applied them to any assault committed in a public place. The legislature also authorized cities and villages to hire part-time police and granted railroad and public transit police the power to make arrests beyond the normal limits of their jurisdictions when in pursuit of suspects.

Texas set a five-year penalty for carrying weapons on premises where alcoholic beverages are sold, served, or consumed.

New drug-control-and-abuse laws were enacted in South Dakota, Vermont, and Colorado. California judges were given discretionary powers to decide whether a first conviction on drug possession would be considered a felony or a misdemeanor. Connecticut initiated a handgun sale information exchange with the rest of the New England states, New York, and New Jersey. Gun-control legislation was strengthened in Delaware.

Riot control came in for its share of attention in 1968. The Ohio legislature expanded the state's authority to control riots. New York gave its mayors the power to deal with riots or potential riots

by allowing them to impose curfews, close public places, and control sales of arms and ammunition. The governor of Maryland was given the power to declare a state of emergency and designate special emergency areas. Similar legislation was enacted in Oklahoma. Michigan passed new legislation that defined riots and provided heavy penalties for rioting, incitement, interference with firemen and other public employees in the line of duty, and willful blocking of streets or traffic. A state police reserve force was authorized, to be used in extreme emergencies.

The state courts were also busy, mostly ratifying the new legislation dealing with law enforcement. The New Jersey Supreme Court ruled that it had the authority to reduce the death penalty through its "inherent" power to modify sentences of judges and juries, thus assuming powers previously confined to juries and governors in that state.

In regard to corrections, Nebraska established a Board of Parole. In the aftermath of an unresolved prison scandal, a special session of the Arkansas legislature created a Department of Correction under the supervision of a Board of Correction. The Michigan General Assembly set new guidelines for gubernatorial pardons of former convicts. Those pardons that could be granted had to meet with the unanimous approval of the state parole board. California instituted a program providing for two-day visits to prisoners nearing their release time, by their wives, children, and parents, with three-bedroom apartments provided.

Finance and Taxation. The 1968 report in this field continued to be a familiar one: taxes of one kind or another were raised in more than half of the 24 states submitting budgets in an even-numbered year, thereby setting a record; more states entered the $1 billion budget category; and the need for funds outran the available revenues. Collections by the states in fiscal 1968 rose 14% to $36.4 billion. Two other developments were prominent in 1968: the attempt to improve the efficiency of existing taxes and the increasing action of the states to improve local revenue-raising abilities.

By constitutional amendment, Oklahoma voters abolished the state's intangibles tax. Oklahoma and Missouri voters authorized the legislature to fix the state income tax as a percentage of its federal counterpart. California voters approved their legislature's plan for homestead exemptions that would reduce their real property taxes. Idahoans voted to amend their constitution to allow state endowment funds to be invested in the private sector as well as in government bonds. Louisiana extended its veterans' homestead tax exemption provisions, and Nebraska authorized its legislature to provide general homestead exemptions. **3**

Twenty-five bond issues involving more than $2 billion were passed in 12 states, while 8 other issues involving $1.3 billion failed. California voters defeated a $250 million education bond issue.

Massachusetts and Michigan voters overwhelmingly rejected a graduated income tax. Montana voters initiated a reclassification of property for tax purposes that would set a 1% tax limit on many kinds of property. Nebraskans turned down another effort to eliminate their state income tax.

The New Mexico Supreme Court ordered the state to set a statewide uniform rate for assessment of state property taxes by 1969, ending a tradition that allowed each county to set its own ratio. The Illinois Supreme Court created a financial crisis in that state by holding a 1967 legislative plan for broadening the sales tax unconstitutional.

Interstate Cooperation. There were a number of practical steps in interstate cooperation in 1968. The New England Board of Higher Education adopted a program permitting New England residents, if they met the proper criteria, to attend any of 30 junior colleges in the region for the same tuition they would pay in their own states. The Coastal Plains Regional Commission, uniting North Carolina, South Carolina, and Georgia, established an advisory panel of scientists and businessmen to plan the development of marine resources in the region's tidewater areas.

The Appalachian Regional Commission (ARC) work advanced during 1968 on both an interstate and an intrastate basis. Falling into both categories was West Virginia's legislation authorizing its border counties and municipalities to create interstate regional planning commissions in cooperation with the political subdivisions of neighboring states. As a result of the commission's work, a number of states initiated comprehensive statewide planning in various fields. Pennsylvania, for example, developed a water-resources plan, which the state planning department, using its ARC mandate, was able to prepare for the state as a whole.

In a unique step, Florida and New York entered into a bistate agreement to assist families migrating from the first to the second by preparing them for urban life through job training and social adjustment programs. The first such project involved people from Sanford, Fla., who were planning to migrate to Rochester, N.Y. (an established pattern of movement). Vocational-education programs for those people were to be established in both cities and paid for by their respective states.

In *Elkind* v. *Byck,* a case important for its interstate implications, the California Supreme Court ruled that a father who had moved from Georgia to California

could be compelled by California welfare authorities to furnish greater support to his child, then living in New York, despite a Georgia court decree barring revision of support payments. Because both states adopted the Uniform Reciprocal Enforcement of Support Act, "the federal system now espouses the principle that no state may freeze the obligations flowing from the continuing relationship of parent and child."

Politics and Elections. Mississippi cut its state residency requirement to one year, while Alaska voted to introduce voter registration. Louisiana amended its constitution to allow new residents to vote for president and vice-president of the U.S. if such residents were qualified voters in their previous states. A new South Dakota election law made it a misdemeanor not to report campaign expenses.

The spread of the two-party system in the Southern states was not only visible in the presidential elections but in other ways as well. At the beginning of 1968 Georgia's eight Republican state senators organized a weekly caucus. In an unusual occurrence a Democratic senator in Delaware shifted his party allegiance in midsession, causing a reorganization of the Delaware Senate under the Republicans.

State-Federal Relations. The year saw increased efforts by both the federal and state governments to work out ways to bring together the various strands of federal aid within each state. Approximately one-third of the states had opened offices in Washington, D.C., by the fall of 1968, and nearly every governor had appointed a coordinator of state-federal relations.

A pilot program to consolidate grant financing and reporting procedures was developed by Nebraska and the U.S. Department of Health, Education, and Welfare (HEW). It was to go into effect on July 1, 1969. Under the program HEW would issue a single letter of credit to Nebraska covering all of its grants, which previously had required 11 separate letters to a number of different agencies.

On the federal side, the major development of the year was the passage of the Intergovernmental Cooperation Act of 1968 after more than four years of congressional consideration. The new act required: provision of full information to state officials on federal grants to the states; improved scheduling of transfers of federal funds under the various grant programs; federal technical or specialized services to state and local governments on a reimbursible basis; congressional review of grant-in-aid programs; and uniform application in the formulation, evaluation, and review of federal programs with an impact on community development.

The states were also given increased flexibility in two new grant programs enacted by Congress, the Omnibus Crime Control and Safe Streets Act and the Juvenile Delinquency Prevention and Control Act. The weapons-control acts passed by Congress in 1968 rejected the demands for preemptive federal action and instead adopted proposals that "backstopped" state efforts at gun regulation rather than replacing them. States were given the right to permit their residents to purchase arms in adjacent states despite the general federal ban on interstate arms sales.

In the 1967 fiscal year public assistance replaced highway construction as the leading recipient of federal grant funds with a total of $4.2 billion (a rise of 17% in one year) as against $4 billion. Agricultural aid was third with $3.5 billion, followed by education with $3 billion. Public health completed the top five with $1.4 billion. The total amount of federal grants-in-aid to the states and localities reached $15 billion, or 15% of the total federal tax collections for the fiscal year, up 2% from fiscal 1966.

The major state-federal conflict during the year revolved around the lifting of federal tax exemptions for state and municipal industrial development bonds. Despite great pressure from the states and localities and the municipal bond market, Congress subjected to federal taxes most industrial development bond issues of more than $1 million used to finance facilities for private, taxable tenants. Exempted were convention and trade-show facilities, stadiums, airports, and piers and terminals for mass community facilities. Failure to exempt other public-purpose facilities, such as hospitals and educational institutions, led to the immediate introduction of bills to correct that situation, none of which had been passed by year's end.

U.S. Legislation. Congressional action in the consumer protection field was considerable in 1968. New legislation affecting the states included the Consumer Credit Protection Act (popularly known as the "truth-in-lending" act); the Poultry Products Inspection Act, which applied federal standards to poultry sold intrastate and required the states to enforce those standards within two to three years or risk federal preemption; and the Natural Gas Pipeline Safety Act. The Consumer Credit Protection Act provided that finance charges must be clearly disclosed in writing before completion of a business transaction, restricted state garnishment of wages, permitted federal enforcement of state usury laws when a violation involved interstate traffic in loans, placed restrictions on second mortgage practices, and required interest-rate disclosure in credit advertising. The Poultry Inspection Act authorized matching

grants to aid states in upgrading their poultry inspection programs. The Pipeline Safety Act allowed the states to certify their compliance with federal standards.

Passage of the Civil Rights Act of 1968 extended external federal protection to the housing field. Like the other civil rights acts, it provided a major role for the states, using federal authority only as a "backstop."

Congress extended and expanded the Elementary and Secondary Education Act. Several new programs were established, including aid for bilingual education for certain children and demonstration projects to prevent students from dropping out of school.

The Federal Courts and the States. The U.S. Supreme Court in 1968 bound the states to provide trial by jury, holding that this was a fundamental right of U.S. citizens whenever imprisonment was a possible punishment. In *Witherspoon* v. *Illinois* the court ruled that a person may not be condemned to death by a jury from which all persons opposed to capital punishment are automatically excluded. States could, however, still exclude people who said that they would not even consider returning a verdict that required the death penalty.

In a major but not entirely unprecedented decision the court ruled that the Civil Rights Act of 1866 banned all racial discrimination, public or private, in the sale or rental of real property. The court emphasized that their ruling in no way diminishes the Civil Rights Act of 1968, which was viewed as a means to enforce the constitutional mandate.

On April 1 in *Avery* v. *Midland City, Texas,* the U.S. Supreme Court extended the "one-man, one-vote" principle to units of local government by requiring the apportionment of legislative bodies of general local governments strictly according to population.

In *Maryland* v. *Wirtz* the court also upheld the controversial 1966 Fair Labor Standards Amendments, which applied federal minimum-wage and overtime provisions to state and local employees serving hospitals, schools, certain transit authorities, and other public institutions. The statute had been challenged by 28 states and a school board on the ground that it infringed upon the sovereign powers of the states.

In *King* v. *Smith* the court upheld a lower federal court decision that held unconstitutionally discriminatory Alabama's denial of aid-to-dependent-children benefits to families where the woman of the household had a man other than the father living with her. The ruling affected 19 states with similar regulations.

The possibilities for extending state aid to parochial schools were increased through one major Supreme Court deci-

sion. In *Board of Education* v. *Allen,* the court upheld New York's Textbook Loan Act, which required school districts to lend textbooks to grades 7 through 12 of private and parochial schools within their districts. At the same time, in *Flast* v. *Cohen,* the court opened the door for taxpayers' suits challenging the constitutionality of federal aid to state educational programs that assisted parochial schools. One larger constitutional consequence of this last decision was a modification of the doctrine established in *Frothingham* v. *Mellon* (1923), which held that the individual taxpayer has too little financial stake in federal expenditures to bring suit as to their constitutionality.

Attacking a basic tradition of U.S. political life, the U.S. District Court for Nebraska ruled that candidates for the U.S. House of Representatives did not have to live in the district they sought to represent. This decision was reached on the ground that the states could not add to the qualifications for the office set by the U.S. Constitution, which only demanded residence in the state at the time of election.

A U.S. District Court in Missouri ruled that tax-supported colleges and universities had a right to establish their own rules of student discipline within broad limits, even if they were more strict than those applied to the general public. This could be done because attendance was not compulsory, and students, in effect, consented to those rules by applying for admission.

In an opinion that raised historical echoes by directly challenging John Marshall's landmark decision of 1819, *McCulloch* v. *Maryland,* the New York Court of Appeals held that a national bank in the state was not exempt from state and county taxes. In so ruling the court followed a Massachusetts Supreme Court decision of July 1967.

Reapportionment. As of July 1, 1968, reapportionment of all 50 state legislatures was virtually completed. Forty-seven states had valid plans in effect; the Georgia and Kansas plans were under court review; and, after a gubernatorial veto, Massachusetts still had to redraw its senatorial district lines and have its house districts approved by the courts. Attention was redirected to the reapportionment of congressional districts. In a summary decision, the U.S. Supreme Court prohibited the use of any congressional districts in Indiana other than those that had been created by the federal district court. By year's end, 37 states had redrawn their congressional districts, and all the rest, except possibly Indiana, Missouri, and New York, met court standards.

State Programs and Nationwide Concerns. The daylight savings time issue involved the states in 1968 after Con-

gress established nationwide daylight savings time but allowed the individual states to opt out. After the Michigan and South Dakota legislatures refused to opt out, initiative petitions placed the issue on the ballot in both states, and in both the voters upheld the legislatures.

Fire and police officers and first-aid rescue squads in South Dakota were exempted from liability for civil charges for rendering emergency aid. Vermont passed a "Duty to Aid the Endangered Act," which provided that a person must render assistance if he could do so without peril to himself.

Antipoverty Programs. State assistance was making itself felt on the antipoverty front. The Pennsylvania Department of Public Welfare inaugurated two programs to train public assistance recipients and other needy jobless people for careers in state health and welfare institutions. Both programs were financed by federal antipoverty funds. The Wisconsin Department of Local Affairs and Development organized and implemented eight antipoverty projects in Milwaukee, which were at least partially managed by the ghetto residents involved.

Job-training efforts to move people off welfare roles continued in 1968, with some states making useful innovations. California transferred all programs related to job and vocational training from the welfare system to the State Department of Employment. At the same time, the California legislature authorized supplemental welfare payments for employed heads of families whose wages fell below the outright welfare grant to which they were entitled when unemployed.

Business Regulation and Consumer Protection. The states, like the federal government, continued to be active in the expanding field of consumer protection. Oklahoma voters approved constitutional amendments authorizing the legislature to prescribe maximum interest rates, license and regulate money lenders, and enact a truth-in-lending code that would meet the new federal standards. Truth-in-lending laws were also passed by Vermont, Rhode Island, Kentucky, and New York. Illinois voters approved an amendment to the state banking law authorizing state-chartered banks to open branches in foreign countries without changing the ban on branch banking in the state. Nebraskans authorized business promotion lotteries and raffles for charity.

Federal meat-inspection standards were adopted by South Dakota, Kentucky, Oklahoma, New York, Pennsylvania, and West Virginia. Nevada, on the other hand, repealed its 1967 meat inspection law on the ground that the federal standards set up intolerable procedures for Nevada slaughterers.

Virginia established the first state insurance pool program to provide coverage

for potential riot areas. Administered by the newly created Virginia Rating Bureau, it went into effect on June 28. The state-created pool provided coverage for any property otherwise insurable except for its location.

Church and State. The Massachusetts Supreme Judicial Court held that state aid for the construction and financing of facilities for sectarian institutions would not violate the commonwealth's constitution, unlike more direct aid for the training of religious personnel. By the end of 1968, Pennsylvania, Michigan, New York, and Rhode Island were providing limited financial aid to parochial schools and had initiated a study of the financial needs of private and parochial schools for long-range planning purposes. Pennsylvania enacted what was, in effect, a revenue-sharing measure with parochial schools to assist them with any expenditures in the fields of mathematics, modern foreign languages, physical science, and physical education. Delaware authorized public school districts to provide transportation for nonpublic school pupils. New York permitted direct aid to nonpublic colleges and universities.

Civil Rights. With the legal as well as other battles for Negro rights increasingly concentrated on the state and local levels, several important developments took place in 1968. In May the Illinois Supreme Court upheld the constitutionality of a 1963 state law requiring school boards to draw district lines so as to counteract de facto segregation; this reversed the court's 1967 decision regarding the constitutionality of the same law. South Dakota created a State Human Relations Commission to hear complaints of discrimination on the grounds of race or religion. Oklahoma adopted a civil rights act embodying the principles of the federal Civil Rights Act of 1964 and strengthening the State Human Rights Commission.

Many states took action against discrimination in housing. Vermont added a fair housing amendment to its Anti-Discrimination Act. Washington voters added discrimination in the sale of housing as a ground for suspension of real estate licenses. Kentucky passed an open housing law prohibiting discrimination in the sale or rental of property, with the exception of private transactions and small rental units. Rhode Island eliminated most exemptions in its open housing law and established procedures for court injunctions to ensure that the law was enforced. Michigan passed a comprehensive fair housing law. Maryland voters rejected their state's newly enacted open housing law on an initiative vote, thus bringing the state under the more stringent federal law.

Economic Development. Mississippi amended its constitution to pave the way for the construction of offshore oil wells. Kentucky reorganized its Department of Commerce into three divisions: industrial development to create jobs; research and planning to work with the federal government and other state agencies; and community services to manage the states' out-of-state economic promotion offices.

Pennsylvania enacted legislation to make bank credit directly available to small businesses during periods of tight money at a rate of $5 per $100. South Dakota initiated a program to induce new plants to locate in that state. Among other things, the state would train workers for new industries.

Education. South Dakota voters approved the creation of a State Commission on Elementary and Secondary Education to reorganize the state's school districts. The state legislature also created a South Dakota Education Policies and Goals Commission to prepare an evaluation of state and local financial responsibility for elementary and secondary education. Florida created the Florida Public School Board and redefined the state's uniform system of free public schools so that all would provide 13 years of instruction beginning with kindergarten and would also provide facilities for exceptional children. Delaware authorized state support for kindergartens and provided for the consolidation of school districts. In order to give local school boards greater flexibility in curriculum construction, California reduced the number of state-required subjects but added a requirement that the role of racial minorities in the development of California and the nation be taught in all schools.

State expenditures for education continued to rise rapidly, along with proposals that the states assume full responsibility for financing local schools. The Rhode Island General Assembly's Special Commission on Education recommended the abolition of local education agencies and the creation of a state board of regents to govern all public schools. Vermont provided that the state would pay 75% of the cost of constructing special education classrooms and facilities. New York changed its per pupil allotment formula to increase the amount of state aid to public schools and also provided special aid to urban school districts with poverty problems. Michigan revised its aid formula to give poorer districts a larger share of state aid.

The big new issue in the field of education in 1968 was the question of teachers' strikes. Though there were many local strikes in 1968 that involved state governments, the only statewide strike took place in Florida, with mixed results. One result was state legislature authorization of local school boards to hire people without certificates to teach in times of emergency.

School decentralization emerged as a major issue in the urban states in 1968. New York led the way by enacting legislation that provided for the gradual decentralization of New York City's school system.

Environmental Pollution Control. Michigan voters approved a $335 million bond issue and Washington a $25 million issue for water pollution control. Part of a bond issue approved by Ohio voters was also to be used for water pollution control. The California State Water Resources Control Board adopted a statewide water quality policy applicable to all water in the state. Oklahoma created a Department of Pollution Control to ensure the quality of the state's waters.

Vermont required industries to install air pollution control equipment. California enacted a measure that would establish in 1970 the strictest automobile exhaust control standards in the nation.

On the other hand, Illinois failed to muster sufficient voters to meet the constitutional requirement for the approval of a $1 billion bond issue to finance a comprehensive air and water pollution control program, even though the proposal was approved by a majority of those voting on it.

Health and Welfare. Californians amended their constitution to authorize the legislature to make loans for hospital construction and equipment. Virginia passed a $13,770,000 bond issue for the support of mental hospitals and appointed a commission to study the state's mental hospital and clinic program. Rhode Island took an important step toward controlling patient costs in hospitals by requiring hospitals to obtain Health Department approval for any new construction, substantial alterations, or purchases of new equipment. Pennsylvania also implemented a program designed to use available health care facilities more efficiently in its state medical assistance program.

Maryland passed one of the most comprehensive alcoholism control acts in the nation, modeled after the code proposed by the American Medical Association. The act created a Division of Alcoholism Control within the Department of Mental Hygiene and a new crime of disorderly intoxication, which applied to any person who becomes intoxicated in a public place and causes a public disturbance. North Carolina's new law on chronic alcoholics permitted the courts to retain jurisdiction over persons acquitted of public drunkenness by reason of chronic alcoholism for purposes of supervising their treatment.

Abortion reform continued to be a solely state issue that attracted much public attention. Beginning in 1967 five states enacted legislation to permit therapeutic abortions.

The issue of human organ transplanta-

tion took on new importance for the public and the states in 1968 as a result of the introduction of heart transplant surgery. As in the case of abortions, the laws regulating such operations were solely the province of the states. Maryland legally authorized the donation of all or part of a human body for transplants. New York, moving more cautiously, created a temporary state commission to study transplantation of vital organs of human beings. California enacted legislation that established legal procedures for the transplanting of vital human organs.

California and the National Institute of Mental Health initiated the first exchange of mental health personnel under a 1966 federal act authorizing such exchanges. Two high-level staff members traded positions for a two-year period. The program was designed to open both governments to new ideas and a better understanding of their counterparts.

Highways. West Virginia voters authorized the issuance of up to $350 million in bonds for highway construction. The Maryland legislature limited the veto power of counties in highway planning. Oklahoma enacted an omnibus highway code, harmonizing and modernizing its highway laws and ensuring their conformity with federal requirements.

Vermont enacted a comprehensive billboard control law that prohibited visible commercial off-premise signs near any road or highway in the state and limited the size of on-premise signs. Delaware became the 15th state to sign an agreement with the Federal Highway Administration to regulate outdoor advertising under the provisions of the Highway Beautification Act of 1965. Maryland and Oklahoma also enacted legislation to meet the federal standards.

In the four years through June 30, 1968, the states and the federal government invested nearly $1.2 billion in 17,580 spot improvement projects designed to make existing highways more safe. State funds alone paid for 13,380 projects, while the other 4,200 were financed jointly and about equally.

Housing. New Jersey voters approved a $12.5 million bond issue for construction and improvement of low- and moderate-income housing via low-interest loans designed to rehabilitate or construct approximately 5,000 units through private initiative. The state also initiated a cooperative housing inspection program whereby local housing inspectors would carry out state enforcement of safety, construction, and maintenance regulations for hotels, motels, and apartment buildings, at state expense.

Rhode Island initiated a comprehensive program to improve rental housing and protect tenants in that state. Its legislature enacted a measure that allowed rent money paid by tenants of sub-standard housing to be held in escrow and used to pay maintenance costs and remove safety violations in those housing units. Vermont established the Vermont Home Mortgage Credit Agency to help finance homes of up to $20,000 in value for persons of moderate income, and a State Housing Authority with the power to lease buildings and rent apartments to low-income families and the elderly. California introduced a system of tax incentives to encourage private agencies to provide real-estate loans to families in slum neighborhoods for the purchase of moderate- or low-cost housing.

Labor. Arkansas voters approved an initiative measure improving the state's workmen's compensation law. New York raised workers' disability and unemployment benefits.

Alaska's local labor autonomy law, enacted in 1967 and requiring all unions with 100 or more members in the state to maintain a state-chartered local union, was held unconstitutional by a federal court; this decision prevented the state from protecting its residents against a Seattle-based construction union that dominated the Alaska contracting market and discriminated against local construction workers.

Major occupational safety and health legislation was enacted by a number of states in 1968. Vermont adopted a strong and comprehensive law to be administered by the state labor commissioner. In a special session that found the legislature working an extra 11 payless days, Arizona structured its Industrial Commission, creating a commission to handle compensation of injured workers and a board to administer the insurance fund. Laws regulating the use of nuclear energy and the provision of radiation protection were enacted in Delaware, Tennessee, and Virginia.

Local Government and Urban Affairs. The states' role as initiator and experimentor in the urban field expanded during 1968. The states also showed a greater willingness to give their local subdivisions the power to adapt their governmental structures and revenue systems to changing needs.

Michigan authorized local urban development agencies to function under the supervision of local governments in clearing, replanning, rehabilitating, and reconstructing major areas in central cities. Vermont established local and regional planning and development commissions whose task would be to prepare and administer comprehensive planning programs. New York created an Urban Development Corporation with powers to finance, undertake, and promote development of city core areas. Florida granted its counties home rule. Iowa granted home rule to municipal corporations, excluding only issues of taxation, which continued to require state legislative authorization.

Three national groups were formed during 1968 to deal with urban problems. One, the States Urban Action Center, was the creation of several leading governors. It was designed by the states particularly to assist the governors in dealing with urban problems and received a $350,000 Ford Foundation grant to develop its program.

National and Civil Defense. Maryland ratified the National Guard Mutual Assistance Compact, while Delaware provided for state employees called to active duty with the Guard to be paid the difference between their military pay and state salaries.

As usual in wartime, the states began to make provision for aiding returning veterans. Oregon liberalized its veterans' farm- and home-loan laws. Pennsylvania and Vermont extended their veterans' bonus programs to Vietnam returnees. Several states granted additional property-tax relief to veterans.

Parks and Recreation. Michigan voters approved a $100 million bond issue and Washington voters a $40 million issue for recreational land acquisition and development. New Mexico authorized a $1 million severance-tax bond issue for the same purpose. Georgia announced plans for a state park designed especially for the handicapped.

Regulation of Public Morals. Michigan liberalized its liquor laws to permit the issuance of special liquor licenses for commercial airports and allow Sunday liquor sales in restaurants and hotels, subject to local option in both cases. The Rhode Island legislature passed a bill to create a film classification board to determine which movies should be banned for persons under 18 years of age. The law provided that if a theater was showing a movie so classified, it must prominently display that classification.

Transportation. New Jersey voters approved a $640 million bond issue to improve mass transportation and highway facilities. Delaware created a Department of Transportation, while West Virginia authorized creation of mass transportation authorities by counties, municipalities, or any combinations thereof.

Vermont issued $600,000 in bonds for the operation of a regional airport system. Maryland created an Airport Authority with the power to acquire certain existing airport facilities and construct and maintain new ones.

DANIEL J. ELAZAR
Director,
Center for the Study of Federalism
Temple University, Philadelphia

Area and Population

Area and population of the states

State	AREA in sq.mi. Total	AREA in sq.mi. Inland water*	RESIDENT POPULATION April 1, 1960, census	RESIDENT POPULATION July 1, 1968, estimate†	RESIDENT POPULATION Percent increase 1960–68
Alabama	51,609	549	3,266,740	3,566,000	9.2
Alaska	586,400	15,335	226,167	277,000	22.4
Arizona	113,909	334	1,302,161	1,670,000	28.3
Arkansas	53,104	605	1,786,272	2,012,000	12.6
California	158,693	2,120	15,717,204	19,221,000	22.3
Colorado	104,247	363	1,753,947	2,048,000	16.8
Connecticut	5,009	110	2,535,234	2,959,000	16.7
Delaware	2,057	79	446,292	534,000	19.7
District of Columbia	69	8	763,956	809,000	5.9
Florida	58,560	4,308	4,951,560	6,160,000	24.4
Georgia	58,876	602	3,943,116	4,588,000	16.3
Hawaii	6,424	9	632,772	778,000	23.0
Idaho	83,557	849	667,191	705,000	5.7
Illinois	56,400	470	10,081,158	10,974,000	8.9
Indiana	36,291	106	4,662,498	5,067,000	8.7
Iowa	56,290	258	2,757,537	2,748,000	−0.4
Kansas	82,264	216	2,178,611	2,303,000	5.7
Kentucky	40,395	532	3,038,156	3,229,000	6.3
Louisiana	48,523	3,417	3,257,022	3,732,000	14.6
Maine	33,215	2,203	969,265	979,000	1.0
Maryland	10,577	703	3,100,689	3,757,000	21.2
Massachusetts	8,257	390	5,148,578	5,437,000	5.6
Michigan	58,216	1,197	7,823,194	8,740,000	11.7
Minnesota	84,068	4,059	3,413,864	3,646,000	6.8
Mississippi	47,716	493	2,178,141	2,342,000	7.5
Missouri	69,686	548	4,319,813	4,627,000	7.1
Montana	147,138	1,402	674,767	693,000	2.6
Nebraska	77,227	615	1,411,330	1,437,000	1.8
Nevada	110,540	752	285,278	453,000	58.9
New Hampshire	9,304	290	606,921	702,000	15.6
New Jersey	7,836	315	6,066,782	7,078,000	16.7
New Mexico	121,666	156	951,023	1,015,000	6.7
New York	49,576	1,637	16,782,304	18,113,000	7.9
North Carolina	52,712	3,645	4,556,155	5,135,000	12.7
North Dakota	70,665	1,208	632,446	625,000	−1.2
Ohio	41,222	250	9,706,397	10,591,000	9.1
Oklahoma	69,919	1,032	2,328,284	2,518,000	8.1
Oregon	96,981	733	1,768,687	2,008,000	13.5
Pennsylvania	45,333	326	11,319,366	11,712,000	3.5
Rhode Island	1,214	156	859,488	913,000	6.2
South Carolina	31,055	783	2,382,594	2,692,000	13.0
South Dakota	77,047	669	680,514	657,000	−3.5
Tennessee	42,244	482	3,567,089	3,976,000	11.5
Texas	267,338	4,499	9,579,677	10,972,000	14.5
Utah	84,916	2,577	890,627	1,034,000	16.1
Vermont	9,609	333	389,881	422,000	8.2
Virginia	40,815	977	3,966,949	4,597,000	15.9
Washington	68,192	1,483	2,853,214	3,276,000	14.8
West Virginia	24,181	102	1,860,421	1,805,000	−3.0
Wisconsin	56,154	1,449	3,951,777	4,213,000	6.6
Wyoming	97,914	503	330,066	315,000	−4.5
Total U.S.	3,615,210	66,237	179,323,175	199,861,000	11.5

*Does not include the Great Lakes and coastal waters. †Preliminary.
Source: U.S. Department of Commerce, Bureau of the Census.

Largest cities by area

July 1, 1968

Rank	City	Area in sq.mi.	Rank	City	Area in sq.mi.
1	Oklahoma City, Okla.	648	11	New Orleans, La.	200
2	Los Angeles, Calif.	463	12	San Antonio, Tex.	183
3	Houston, Tex.	453	13	Memphis, Tenn.	180
4	New York, N.Y.	320	14	Detroit, Mich.	139
5	Kansas City, Mo.	316	15	Atlanta, Ga.	131
6	San Diego, Calif.	310	16	Philadelphia, Pa.	129
7	Dallas, Tex.	295	17	Columbus, Ohio	116
8	Phoenix, Ariz.	248	18	Seattle, Wash.	99
9	Chicago, Ill.	224	19	Denver, Colo.	98
10	Fort Worth, Tex.	200	20	Milwaukee, Wis.	97

On October 1, 1968, Jacksonville, Fla., city proper became coextensive with Duval County (827 sq. mi.).
Source: City Planning Departments.

Largest metropolitan areas by population

Area	Population July 1, 1968, estimate	Area	Population July 1, 1968, estimate
Standard Consolidated Areas		Houston	1,850,000
New York–Northeastern New Jersey	15,953,141*	Newark	1,800,000
Chicago–Northwestern Indiana	7,440,000	Minneapolis–St. Paul	1,751,490†
Standard Metropolitan Statistical Areas		Cincinnati	1,525,000
New York	11,679,858	Milwaukee	1,460,000
Los Angeles–Long Beach	7,120,000	Dallas	1,453,000
Chicago	6,810,000	Paterson–Clifton–Passaic	1,359,610†
Philadelphia	4,800,000	Buffalo	1,350,000
Detroit	4,214,000†	Kansas City	1,347,000
San Francisco–Oakland	3,130,500	Anaheim–Santa Ana–Garden Grove	1,330,701
Washington, D.C.	2,663,000*	San Diego	1,320,500
Boston	2,600,000	Seattle	1,317,947‡
Pittsburgh	2,500,000	Atlanta	1,280,000
St. Louis	2,345,000	Miami	1,215,000
Cleveland	2,175,000‡	Denver	1,157,000
Baltimore	1,992,210	San Bernardino–Riverside–Ontario	1,131,354
		Indianapolis	1,100,000
		New Orleans	1,095,500

*July 1, 1966. †July 1, 1967. ‡April 1, 1968.
Source: City and state governments.

Largest cities by population

Rank in 1968	City	POPULATION April 1, 1960, census	POPULATION July 1, 1968, estimate	Mayor in 1968
1	New York, N.Y.	7,781,984	8,125,000	John V. Lindsay
2	Chicago, Ill.	3,550,404	3,500,000	Richard J. Daley
3	Los Angeles, Calif.	2,481,595	2,935,000	Samuel W. Yorty
4	Philadelphia, Pa.	2,002,512	2,060,000	James H. J. Tate
5	Detroit, Mich.	1,670,144	1,620,000*	Jerome P. Cavanagh
6	Houston, Tex.	938,219	1,230,000	Louie Welch
7	Baltimore, Md.	939,024	909,000	Thomas J. D'Alesandro III
8	Dallas, Tex.	679,684	867,300†	J. Erik Jonsson
9	Washington, D.C.	763,956	854,000	Walter E. Washington
10	Cleveland, Ohio	876,050	789,000‡	Carl B. Stokes
11	Milwaukee, Wis.	741,324	776,000	Henry W. Maier
12	San Francisco, Calif.	740,316	748,700	Joseph L. Alioto
13	San Antonio, Tex.	587,718	735,624	Walter W. McAllister, Sr.
14	St. Louis, Mo.	750,026	699,000	Alfonso J. Cervantes
15	New Orleans, La.	627,525	691,575	Victor H. Schiro
16	San Diego, Calif.	573,224	684,400	Frank E. Curran
17	Boston, Mass.	698,080	616,326	Kevin H. White
18	Pittsburgh, Pa.	604,000	600,000	Joseph M. Barr
19	Kansas City, Mo.	475,539	599,100	Ilus W. Davis
20	Seattle, Wash.	557,087	587,000‡	J. D. Braman
21	Columbus, Ohio	471,316	581,883	M. E. Sensenbrenner
22	Memphis, Tenn.	497,524	540,000	Henry Loeb
23	Phoenix, Ariz.	439,170	527,774	Milton H. Graham
24	Denver, Colo.	439,887	527,500	Thomas G. Currigan
25	Indianapolis, Ind.	476,258	520,000	Richard G. Lugar
26	Atlanta, Ga.	487,455	506,700	Ivan Allen, Jr.
27	Cincinnati, Ohio	502,550	500,000	Eugene P. Ruehlmann

*July 1, 1967. †December 1, 1967. ‡April 1, 1968.
Source: City and state government departments.

Population change

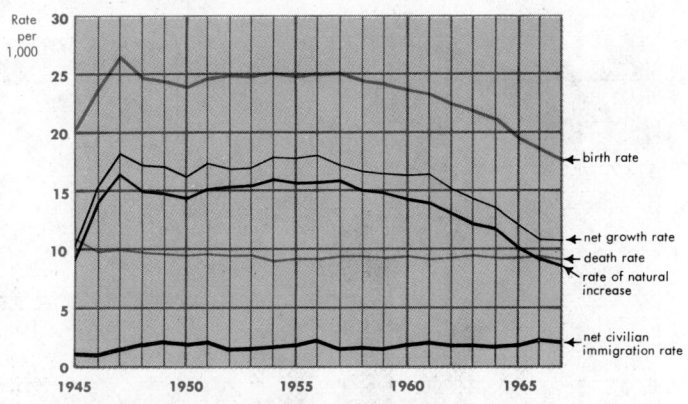

Source: U.S. Department of Commerce, Bureau of the Census.

← birth rate
← net growth rate
← death rate
← rate of natural increase
← net civilian immigration rate

Characteristics of families
March 1967

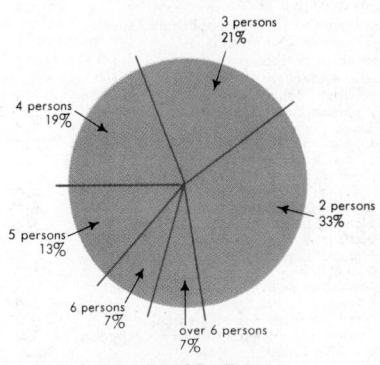

3 persons 21%
4 persons 19%
2 persons 33%
5 persons 13%
6 persons 7%
over 6 persons 7%

size of family

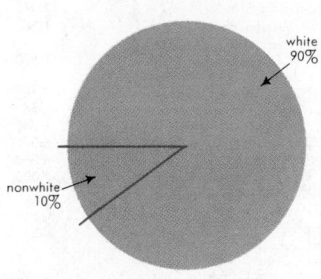

white 90%
nonwhite 10%

color

Expectation of life at birth

in years

Year	TOTAL POPULATION			WHITE			NONWHITE		
	Total	Male	Female	Total	Male	Female	Total	Male	Female
1920	54.1	53.6	54.6	54.9	54.4	55.6	45.3	45.5	45.2
1930	59.7	58.1	61.6	61.4	59.7	63.5	48.1	47.3	49.2
1940	62.9	60.8	65.2	64.2	62.1	66.6	53.1	51.5	54.9
1950	68.2	65.6	71.1	69.1	66.5	72.2	60.8	59.1	62.9
1955	69.6	66.7	72.8	70.5	67.4	73.7	63.7	61.4	66.1
1960	69.7	66.6	73.1	70.6	67.4	74.1	63.6	61.1	66.3
1961	70.2	67.0	73.6	71.0	67.8	74.5	64.4	61.9	67.0
1962*	70.0	66.8	73.4	70.9	67.6	74.4	64.1	61.5	66.8
1963*	69.9	66.6	73.4	70.8	67.5	74.4	63.6	60.9	66.5
1964	70.2	66.9	73.7	71.0	67.7	74.6	64.1	61.1	67.2
1965	70.2	66.8	73.7	71.0	67.6	74.7	64.1	61.1	67.4
1966	70.1	66.7	73.8	71.0	67.6	74.7	64.0	60.7	67.4
1967	70.5	67.0	74.2	71.3	67.9	75.0	64.8	61.2	68.5

Prior to 1960, data excludes Alaska and Hawaii. *Figures by color exclude data for New Jersey.
Source: U.S. Department of Health, Education, and Welfare, Public Health Service,
Vital Statistics of the United States.

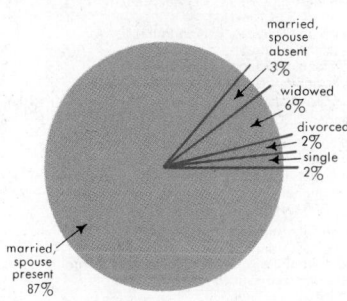

married, spouse absent 3%
widowed 6%
divorced 2%
single 2%
married spouse present 87%

marital status of head

Immigration and naturalization

year ending June 30, 1968

Country or region	Total immigrants admitted	Quota immigrants	NONQUOTA IMMIGRANTS			Aliens naturalized
			Total	Families of U.S. citizens	From Western Hemisphere*	
Europe†	139,360	105,361	33,999	25,694	2,166	58,267
Austria	1,249	931	318	268	16	825
France	3,403	2,454	949	847	52	1,424
Germany	15,919	9,207	6,712	6,409	169	12,692
Greece	13,047	10,479	2,568	2,457	34	3,256
Hungary	2,062	1,429	633	402	41	2,139
Ireland	3,004	2,649	355	257	17	2,959
Italy	23,575	17,248	6,327	5,933	132	9,379
Netherlands	2,243	1,793	450	361	49	2,555
Poland	5,986	4,702	1,284	874	52	3,893
Portugal	12,210	10,928	1,282	1,154	93	1,694
Spain	5,136	1,739	3,397	955	448	713
United Kingdom	28,585	24,392	4,193	3,025	876	8,466
Yugoslavia	6,783	5,333	1,450	631	33	2,067
Other Europe†	16,158	12,077	4,081	2,121	154	6,205
North America	231,028	5,494	225,534	767	129,826	23,167
Canada	27,662	2	27,660	11	27,018	6,984
Mexico	43,560	—	43,560	8	41,290	6,134
Cuba	102,299	—	102,299	7	10,748	6,784
Dominican Republic	9,244	—	9,244	—	9,096	363
Jamaica	17,469	—	17,469	3	17,413	429
Other North America	30,794	5,492	25,302	738	24,261	2,473
South America	21,973	77	21,896	19	21,593	3,081
Argentina	3,425	—	3,425	3	3,357	800
Brazil	2,524	—	2,524	4	2,489	328
Colombia	6,903	—	6,903	3	6,840	587
Ecuador	3,662	—	3,662	—	3,621	362
Other South America	5,459	77	5,382	9	5,286	1,004
Asia	57,211	39,544	17,667	15,799	242	14,980
China‡	12,724	9,241	3,483	2,601	32	3,186
Hong Kong	3,696	3,145	551	510	16	—
India	4,683	4,221	462	398	22	303
Israel	1,989	1,526	463	398	34	2,271
Japan	3,609	1,101	2,508	2,406	14	2,476
Korea	3,814	1,553	2,261	2,188	9	1,776
Philippines	16,698	12,300	4,398	4,083	13	2,807
Other Asia	9,998	6,457	3,541	3,215	102	2,161
Africa	5,077	3,978	1,099	705	59	905
Australia and Oceania	2,588	1,759	829	692	39	461
Other countries	3	1	2	—	1	1,865
Total	457,240	156,214	301,026	43,676	153,926	102,726

Data are preliminary. Immigrants listed by country of birth; aliens naturalized, by country of former
allegiance. *Natives and/or spouses and children. †Includes Turkey and the U.S.S.R. ‡Includes Taiwan.
Source: U.S. Department of Justice, Immigration and Naturalization Service.

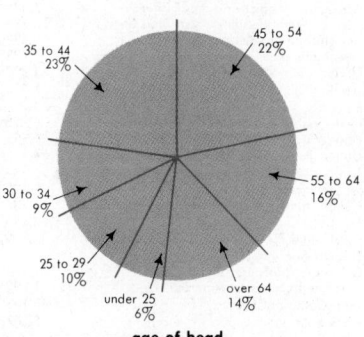

45 to 54 22%
35 to 44 23%
55 to 64 16%
30 to 34 9%
25 to 29 10%
under 25 6%
over 64 14%

age of head

total number of families: 48,921,000

Source: U.S. Department of Commerce, Bureau of the Census,
Current Population Reports.

Church membership

Religious body	Total clergy	Inclusive membership
Adventists, Seventh-day	3,266	384,878
Apostolic Overcoming Holy Church of God	300	75,000
Armenian Apostolic Church of America	34	125,000
Armenian Church, Diocese of North America, Diocese of California	51	136,000
Assemblies of God	11,197	595,231
Baptist Bodies		
American Baptist Association	3,195	745,620
American Baptist Convention	7,352	1,454,965
Baptist General Conference	850	92,806
Conservative Baptist Association of America	2,500	300,000
Free Will Baptists	3,000	250,000
General Association of Regular Baptist Churches	1,556	170,299
General Baptists	910	65,000
National Baptist Convention of America	28,574	2,668,799
National Baptist Convention, U.S.A., Inc.	27,500	5,500,000
National Baptist Evangelical Life and Soul Saving Assembly of U.S.A.	137	57,674
National Primitive Baptist Convention of the U.S.A.	580	1,235,000
North American Baptist Association	3,000	275,000
North American Baptist General Conference	422	54,358
Primitive Baptists	...	72,000
Progressive National Baptist Convention, Inc.	863	521,692
Southern Baptist Convention	...	11,140,486
United Baptists	1,100	63,641
United Free Will Baptist Church	784	100,000
Brethren (German Baptists)		
Church of the Brethren	2,070	189,558
Christian and Missionary Alliance	1,263	68,679
Christian Churches (Disciples of Christ), International Convention	7,590	1,875,400
Churches of God		
Church of God (Anderson, Ind.)	2,753	144,243
Church of God (Cleveland, Tenn.)	3,468	244,129
The Church of God	1,859	74,101
Church of God in Christ	6,000	425,500
Church of the Nazarene	6,364	358,346
Churches of Christ	7,000	2,350,000
Congregational Christian Churches, National Association of	...	110,000
Eastern Churches		
American Carpatho-Russian Orthodox Greek Catholic Church	61	104,500
Bulgarian Eastern Orthodox Church	13	86,000
Greek Orthodox Archdiocese of North and South America	567	1,770,000
Romanian Orthodox Episcopate of America	42	50,000
Russian Orthodox Catholic Church in America, Patriarchal Exarchate	98	152,973
The Russian Orthodox Church Outside Russia	168	55,000
The Russian Orthodox Greek Catholic Church of America	375	56,549
Serbian Orthodox Church in the U.S.A. and Canada	64	65,000
Syrian Antiochian Orthodox Church	81	120,000
Ukrainian Orthodox Church of U.S.A.	131	87,475
Episcopal Church	10,639	3,420,297
Evangelical Covenant Church of America	660	65,496
Friends		
United Meeting of Friends	378	69,353
Independent Fundamental Churches of America	1,251	119,970
International Church of the Foursquare Gospel	2,690	89,215
Jehovah's Witnesses	...	311,378
Jewish Congregations	5,920	5,725,000
Latter-Day Saints		
Church of Jesus Christ of Latter-day Saints	...	1,891,965
Reorganized Church of Jesus Christ of Latter Day Saints	12,878	169,248
Lutherans		
American Lutheran Church, The	5,869	2,575,506
Lutheran Church in America	7,107	3,157,543
Lutheran Church—Missouri Synod	6,572	2,759,308
Wisconsin Evangelical Lutheran Synod	789	358,466
Mennonite Church	1,853	83,627
Methodist Bodies		
African Methodist Episcopal Church	7,089	1,166,301
African Methodist Episcopal Zion Church	2,983	1,100,000
Christian Methodist Episcopal Church	2,598	466,718
Free Methodist Church of North America	1,738	62,090
United Methodist Church*	32,890	11,026,976
Moravian Church in America (Unitas Fratrum)	217	60,574
Pentecostal Assemblies		
Pentecostal Church of God in America, Inc.	1,325	115,000
Pentecostal Holiness Church, Inc.	1,953	67,027
United Pentecostal Church, Inc.	4,160	225,000
Polish National Catholic Church of America	144	282,411
Presbyterian Bodies		
Cumberland Presbyterian Church	736	88,540
Presbyterian Church in the U.S.	4,290	960,776
The United Presbyterian Church in the U.S.A.	12,932	3,268,761
Reformed Bodies		
Christian Reformed Church	870	278,869
Reformed Church in America	1,292	384,751
Roman Catholic Church	60,123	47,468,333
Salvation Army	5,207	324,911
Spiritualists		
International General Assembly of Spiritualists	190	164,072
Unitarian Universalist Association	892	283,000
United Church of Christ	9,047	2,052,857

Table includes churches reporting a membership of 50,000 or more and represents the latest information available.

*Formed in 1968 by a merger of The Methodist Church and the Evangelical United Brethren Church.

Source: National Council of Churches, *Yearbook of American Churches, 1969.*

(C. H. J.)

Birth rates by age of mother

live births per 1,000 women in 1966 in specified age and color

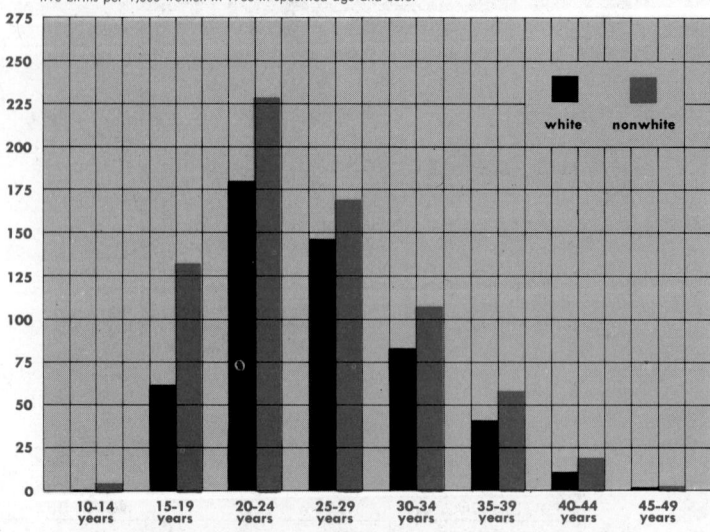

Source: U.S. Department of Health, Education, and Welfare, Public Health Service, *Monthly Vital Statistics Report.*

Marriage and divorce rates

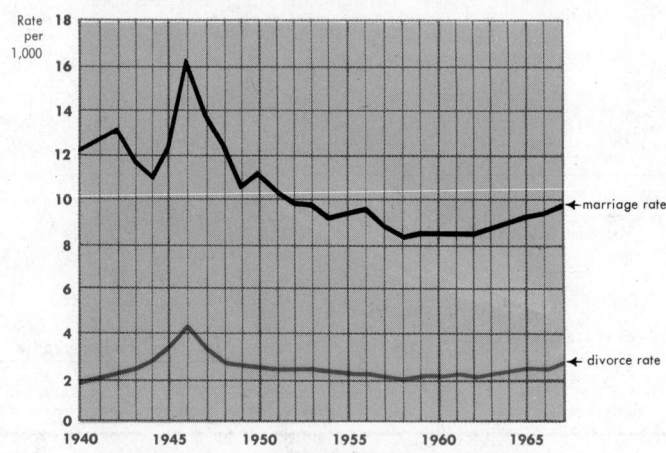

All rates are based on population excluding Armed Forces abroad, except 1941-46 divorce rates which include Armed Forces abroad.
Source: U.S. Department of Health, Education, and Welfare, Public Health Service, *Monthly Vital Statistics Report.*

Causes of deaths

Death rates per 100,000 population

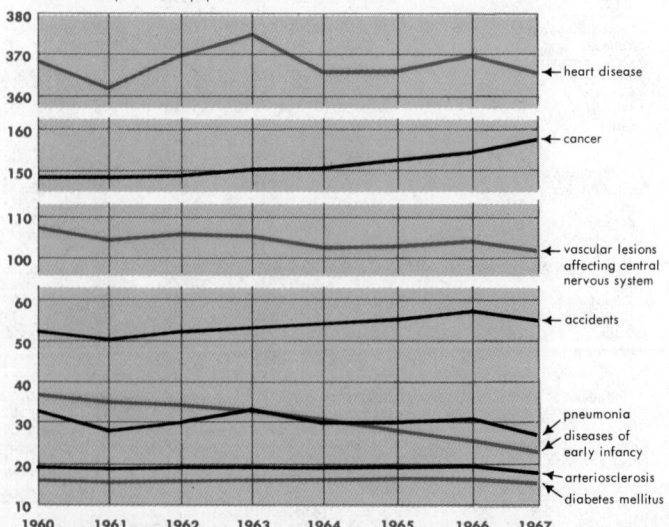

Source: U.S. Department of Health, Education, and Welfare, Public Health Service, *Monthly Vital Statistics Report.*

National Government

The national executive

December 31, 1968

Department, bureau, or office	Executive officer and official title
DEPARTMENT OF STATE	Dean Rusk, secretary
	Nicholas Katzenbach, undersecretary
Political Affairs	Eugene Rostow, undersecretary
	Charles E. Bohlen, deputy undersecy.
Administration	Idar Rimestad, deputy undersecy.
Foreign Service	John M. Steeves, director general
Public Affairs	Dixon Donnelley, asst. secretary
Educational and Cultural Affairs	Edward D. Re, assistant secretary
Economic Affairs	Anthony M. Solomon, asst. secretary
African Affairs	Joseph Palmer II, asst. secretary
Inter-American Affairs	Covey T. Oliver, assistant secretary
European Affairs	John M. Leddy, assistant secretary
East Asian and Pacific Affairs	William P. Bundy, assistant secretary
Near Eastern, South Asian Affairs	Lucius D. Battle, asst. secretary
International Organization Affairs	Joseph J. Sisco, assistant secretary
Agency for International Development	William S. Gaud, administrator
Peace Corps	Jack H. Vaughn, director
U.S. Mission to the UN	James Russell Wiggins, representative
DEPARTMENT OF THE TREASURY	Henry H. Fowler, secretary
	Joseph W. Barr, undersecretary
Monetary Affairs	Frederick L. Deming, undersecretary
Bureau of Customs	Lester D. Johnson, commissioner
Bureau of Engraving and Printing	James A. Conlon, director
Bureau of the Mint	Eva Adams, director
Internal Revenue Service	Sheldon S. Cohen, commissioner
Office of Comptroller of Currency	William B. Camp, comptroller
U.S. Savings Bonds Division	Glen R. Johnson, national director
U.S. Secret Service	James J. Rowley, director
DEPARTMENT OF DEFENSE	Clark M. Clifford, secretary
	Paul H. Nitze, deputy secretary
Joint Chiefs of Staff	Gen. Earle G. Wheeler, chairman
Chief of Staff, U.S. Army	Gen. Harold K. Johnson
Chief of Naval Operations	Adm. Thomas H. Moorer
Chief of Staff, U.S. Air Force	Gen. John P. McConnell
Commandant, Marine Corps	Gen. Leonard F. Chapman, Jr.
Department of the Army	Stanley R. Resor, secretary
	David E. McGiffert, undersecretary
Department of the Navy	Paul R. Ignatius, secretary
	Charles F. Baird, undersecretary
Marine Corps	Gen. L. F. Chapman, Jr., commandant
Department of the Air Force	Harold Brown, secretary
	Townsend W. Hoopes, undersecretary
DEPARTMENT OF JUSTICE	Ramsey Clark, attorney general
	Warren M. Christopher, deputy atty. gen.
Solicitor General	Erwin N. Griswold
Federal Bureau of Investigation	J. Edgar Hoover, director
Bureau of Prisons	Myrl E. Alexander, director
Immigration and Naturalization	Raymond F. Farrell, commissioner
POST OFFICE DEPARTMENT	W. Marvin Watson, postmaster general
	F. C. Belen, deputy postmaster general
Bureau of Operations	W. M. McMillan, asst. postmaster gen.
Bureau of Personnel	R. J. Murphy, asst. postmaster gen.
Chief Postal Inspector	H. B. Montague
DEPARTMENT OF THE INTERIOR	Stewart L. Udall, secretary
	David S. Black, undersecretary
Fish and Wildlife, and Parks	Stanley A. Cain, assistant secretary
	Clarence F. Pautzke, commissioner
National Park Service	George B. Hartzog, Jr., director
Mineral Resources	J. Cordell Moore, assistant secretary
Bureau of Mines	Earl T. Hayes, acting director
Geological Survey	William T. Pecora, director
Public Land Management	Harry R. Anderson, asst. secretary
Indian Affairs	Robert L. Bennett, commissioner
Bureau of Outdoor Recreation	Edward C. Crafts, director
Office of Territories	Ruth Van Cleve, director
Water and Power Development	Kenneth Holum, assistant secretary
Reclamation	Floyd E. Dominy, commissioner
Water Pollution Control	Max N. Edwards, asst. secretary
DEPARTMENT OF AGRICULTURE	Orville L. Freeman, secretary
	John A. Schnittker, undersecretary
Commodity Credit Corporation	John A. Schnittker, president
Rural Development and Conservation	John A. Baker, assistant secretary
Farmers Home Administration	Howard Bertsch, administrator
Forest Service	Edward P. Cliff, chief
Rural Electrification	Norman M. Clapp, administrator
Soil Conservation Service	Donald A. Williams, administrator
International Affairs	Dorothy H. Jacobson, asst. secretary
Marketing and Consumer Services	G. L. Mehren, asst. secretary
DEPARTMENT OF COMMERCE	C. R. Smith, secretary
	Howard J. Samuels, undersecretary
U.S. Travel Service	John W. Black, director
Economic Affairs	W. H. Chartener, asst. secretary
Bureau of the Census	A. Ross Eckler, director
Economic Development	Ross D. Davis, asst. secretary
Science and Technology	John F. Kincaid, asst. secretary
Patent Office	Edward J. Brenner, commissioner
National Bureau of Standards	Allen V. Astin, director
Environmental Science Services	Robert M. White, administrator
Domestic and International Business	Lawrence C. McQuade, asst. secy.

Department, bureau, or office	Executive officer and official title
DEPARTMENT OF LABOR	W. Willard Wirtz, secretary
	James J. Reynolds, undersecretary
Manpower	Stanley Ruttenberg, asst. secretary
Labor-Management Relations	Thomas R. Donahue, asst. secretary
International Affairs	George L-P Weaver, asst. secretary
Wage and Labor Standards	Esther Peterson, asst. secretary
Women's Bureau	Mary Dublin Keyserling, director
Employees' Compensation	Thomas A. Tinsley, director
DEPARTMENT OF HEALTH, EDUCATION, AND WELFARE	Wilbur J. Cohen, secretary
Health and Scientific Affairs	Philip R. Lee, assistant secretary
Public Health Service	William H. Stewart, surgeon general
Food and Drug Administration	James L. Goddard, commissioner
Education	Paul A. Miller, assistant secretary
Office of Education	Harold Howell, commissioner
Social Security Administration	Robert M. Ball, commissioner
Social and Rehabilitation Service	Mary E. Switzer, administrator
DEPARTMENT OF HOUSING AND URBAN DEVELOPMENT	Robert C. Weaver, secretary
	Robert C. Wood, undersecretary
Mortgage Credit and Federal Housing	Philip N. Brownstein, asst. secretary
Renewal and Housing Assistance	Don Hummel, assistant secretary
Metropolitan Development	Charles M. Haar, assistant secretary
Model Cities and Governmental Relations	H. Ralph Taylor, assistant secretary
DEPARTMENT OF TRANSPORTATION	Alan S. Boyd, secretary
	John E. Robson, undersecretary
National Transportation Safety Board	J. J. O'Connell, Jr., chairman
United States Coast Guard	Adm. Willard J. Smith, commandant
Federal Aviation Administration	Gen. William F. McKee, administrator
Federal Highway Administration	Lowell K. Bridwell, administrator
Federal Railroad Administration	A. Scheffer Lang, administrator
St. Lawrence Seaway Development Corporation	Joseph H. McCann, administrator
INDEPENDENT OFFICES AND ESTABLISHMENTS	
Atomic Energy Commission	Glenn T. Seaborg, chairman
Civil Aeronautics Board	John H. Crooker, Jr., chairman
Commission of Fine Arts	William Walton, chairman
District of Columbia	Walter E. Washington, commissioner
Export-Import Bank of the U.S.	Harold F. Linder, pres. and chairman
Federal Communications Commission	Rosel H. Hyde, chairman
Federal Deposit Insurance Corp.	K. A. Randall, chairman
Federal Maritime Commission	John Harllee, chairman
Federal Mediation and Conciliation Service	William E. Simkin, director
Federal Power Commission	Lee C. White, chairman
Federal Reserve System	William McC. Martin, Jr., chairman
Federal Trade Commission	Paul Rand Dixon, chairman
General Services Administration	Lawson B. Knott, Jr., administrator
Indian Claims Commission	John T. Vance, chairman
Interstate Commerce Commission	Paul J. Tierney, chairman
National Aeronautics and Space Administration	James E. Webb, administrator
National Labor Relations Board	F. W. McCulloch, chairman
National Mediation Board	Howard G. Gamser, chairman
National Science Foundation	Leland J. Haworth, director
Railroad Retirement Board	H. W. Habermeyer, chairman
Securities and Exchange Commission	Manuel F. Cohen, chairman
Selective Service System	Lieut. Gen. Lewis B. Hershey, director
Small Business Administration	Robert C. Moot, administrator
Smithsonian Institution	S. Dillon Ripley, secretary
Tennessee Valley Authority	Aubrey J. Wagner, chairman
U.S. Arms Control and Disarmament Agency	William C. Foster, director
U.S. Civil Service Commission	John W. Macy, Jr., chairman
U.S. Information Agency	Leonard H. Marks, director
U.S. Tariff Commission	Stanley D. Metzger, chairman
Veterans Administration	W. J. Driver, administrator
EXECUTIVE OFFICE OF THE PRESIDENT	
The White House Office	Joseph A. Califano, Jr., spec. asst.
Bureau of the Budget	Charles J. Zwick, director
Council of Economic Advisers	Arthur M. Okun, chairman
National Security Council	Walt W. Rostow, spec. asst.
Central Intelligence Agency	Richard M. Helms, director
Office of Economic Opportunity	Bertrand Harding, acting director
Office of Emergency Planning	Price Daniel, director
Office of Science and Technology	Donald F. Hornig, director
QUASI-OFFICIAL AGENCIES	
American National Red Cross	E. Roland Harriman, president
National Academy of Sciences	Frederick Seitz, president
National Academy of Engineering	Eric A. Walker, president

House of Representatives

membership in 1968, and winners in Nov. 5 election

State, district, name, and party	Residence
Ala.—1. *Edwards, W. J. (R)	Mobile
2. *Dickinson, W. L. (R)	Opelika
3. *Andrews, George W. (D)	Union Springs
4. *Nichols, William (D)	Union Springs
5. Selden, Armistead I., Jr. (D)	Greensboro
†Flowers, W. W. (D)	
6. *Buchanan, John (R)	Birmingham
7. *Bevill, Tom (D)	Jasper
8. *Jones, Robert E., Jr. (D)	Scottsboro
Alaska—*Pollock, H. W. (R)	Anchorage
Ariz.—1. *Rhodes, John J. (R)	Mesa
2. *Udall, Morris K. (D)	Tucson
3. *Steiger, Sam (R)	Prescott
Ark.—1. Gathings, E. C. (D)	West Memphis
†Alexander, Bill (D)	
2. *Mills, Wilbur D. (D)	Kensett
3. *Hammerschmidt, J. P. (R)	Harrison
4. *Pryor, David (D)	Camden
Calif.—1. *Clausen, Don H. (R)	Crescent City
2. *Johnson, Harold T. (D)	Roseville
3. *Moss, John E. (D)	Sacramento
4. *Leggett, Robert L. (D)	Vallejo
5. *Burton, Phillip (D)	San Francisco
6. *Mailliard, William S. (R)	San Francisco
7. *Cohelan, Jeffery (D)	Berkeley
8. *Miller, George P. (D)	Alameda
9. *Edwards, W. Donlon (D)	San Jose
10. *Gubser, Charles S. (R)	Gilroy
11. *McCloskey, Paul N. (R)	Portola Valley
12. *Talcott, Burt L. (R)	Salinas
13. *Teague, Charles M. (R)	Ojai
14. *Waldie, Jerome R. (D)	Antioch
15. *McFall, John J. (D)	Manteca
16. *Sisk, B. F. (D)	Fresno
17. King, Cecil R. (D)	Los Angeles
†Anderson, Glenn M. (D)	Los Angeles
18. *Mathias, Robert B. (R)	Visalia
19. *Holifield, Chet (D)	Montebello
20. *Smith, H. Allen (R)	Glendale
21. *Hawkins, Augustus F. (D)	Los Angeles
22. *Corman, James C. (D)	Van Nuys
23. *Clawson, Del M. (R)	Compton
24. *Lipscomb, Glenard P. (R)	Los Angeles
25. *Wiggins, Charles (R)	El Monte
26. *Rees, Thomas (D)	Beverly Hills
27. *Reinecke, Ed (R)	Tujunga
28. *Bell, Alphonzo (R)	Beverly Hills
29. *Brown, George E., Jr. (D)	Monterey Park
30. *Roybal, Edward R. (D)	Los Angeles
31. *Wilson, Charles H. (D)	Los Angeles
32. *Hosmer, Craig (R)	Long Beach
33. *Pettis, Jerry (R)	Loma Linda
34. *Hanna, Richard T. (D)	Fullerton
35. *Utt, James B. (R)	Santa Ana
36. *Wilson, Bob (R)	San Diego
37. *Van Deerlin, Lionel (D)	San Diego
38. *Tunney, John V. (D)	Riverside
Colo.—1. *Rogers, Byron G. (D)	Denver
2. *Brotzman, D. G. (R)	Boulder
3. *Evans, Frank (D)	Pueblo
4. *Aspinall, Wayne N. (D)	Palisade
Conn.—1. *Daddario, Emilio Q. (D)	Hartford
2. *St. Onge, William L. (D)	Putnam
3. *Giaimo, Robert N. (D)	North Haven
4. Irwin, Donald J. (D)	Rowayton
†Weicker, Lowell P., Jr. (R)	Greenwich
5. *Monagan, John S. (D)	Waterbury
6. *Meskill, Thomas J. (R)	New Britain
Del.—*Roth, William V., Jr. (R)	Wilmington
Fla.—1. *Sikes, Robert L. F. (D)	Crestview
2. *Fuqua, Don (D)	Altha
3. *Bennett, Charles E. (D)	Jacksonville
4. Herlong, A. Sidney, Jr. (D)	Leesburg
†Chappell, William (D)	
5. Gurney, Edward J. (R)	Winter Park
†Frey, Louis (R)	Winter Park
6. *Gibbons, Sam (D)	Tampa
7. *Haley, James A. (D)	Sarasota
8. *Cramer, William C. (R)	St. Petersburg
9. *Rogers, Paul G. (D)	West Palm Beach
10. *Burke, J. Herbert (R)	Hollywood
11. *Pepper, Claude (D)	Coral Gables
12. *Fascell, Dante B. (D)	Miami
Ga.—1. *Hagan, G. Elliott (D)	Sylvania
2. *O'Neal, M. (D)	Bainbridge
3. *Brinkley, Jack (D)	Columbus
4. *Blackburn, B. B. (R)	Atlanta
5. *Thompson, S. F. (R)	East Point
6. *Flynt, J. J., Jr. (D)	Griffin
7. *Davis, John W. (D)	Summerville
8. *Stuckey, W. S., Jr. (D)	Eastman
9. *Landrum, Phil M. (D)	Jasper
10. *Stephens, Robert G., Jr. (D)	Athens
Hawaii—*Mink, Patsy (D)	Waipahu
*Matsunaga, Spark M. (D)	Honolulu
Ida.—1. *McClure, James A. (R)	Payette
2. Hansen, G. V. (R)	Pocatello
†Hansen, Orval (R)	Idaho Falls
Ill.—1. *Dawson, William L. (D)	Chicago
2. O'Hara, Barratt (D)	Chicago
†Mikva, Abner (D)	Chicago
3. *Murphy, William T. (D)	Chicago
4. *Derwinski, Edward J. (R)	Chicago
5. *Kluczynski, John C. (D)	Chicago
6. *Ronan, Daniel J. (D)	Chicago
7. *Annunzio, Frank (D)	Chicago
8. *Rostenkowski, Dan (D)	Chicago
9. *Yates, Sidney R. (D)	Chicago
10. *Collier, Harold R. (R)	Berwyn

State, district, name, and party	Residence
11. *Pucinski, Roman C. (D)	Chicago
12. *McClory, Robert (R)	Lake Bluff
13. *Rumsfeld, Donald (R)	Glenview
14. *Erlenborn, J. N. (R)	Elmhurst
15. *Reid, Charlotte T. (R)	Aurora
16. *Anderson, John B. (R)	Rockford
17. *Arends, Leslie C. (R)	Melvin
18. *Michel, Robert H. (R)	Peoria
19. *Railsback, Thomas F. (R)	Moline
20. *Findley, Paul (R)	Pittsfield
21. *Gray, Kenneth J. (D)	West Frankfort
22. *Springer, William L. (R)	Champaign
23. *Shipley, George E. (D)	Olney
24. *Price, Melvin (D)	East St. Louis
Ind.—1. *Madden, Ray J. (D)	Gary
2. Halleck, Charles A. (R)	Rensselaer
†Landgrebe, Earl F. (R)	Valparaiso
3. *Brademas, John (D)	South Bend
4. *Adair, E. Ross (R)	Fort Wayne
5. Roush, J. Edward (D)	Huntington
†Roudebush, Richard L. (R)	Noblesville
6. *Bray, William G. (R)	Martinsville
7. *Myers, John (R)	Covington
8. *Zion, Roger (R)	Evansville
9. *Hamilton, L. H. (D)	Columbus
10. Roudebush, Richard L. (R)	Noblesville
†Dennis, David (R)	Richmond
11. *Jacobs, A., Jr. (D)	Indianapolis
Iowa—1. *Schwengel, Fred (R)	Davenport
2. *Culver, J. C. (D)	Marion
3. *Gross, H. R. (R)	Waterloo
4. *Kyl, John H. (R)	Bloomfield
5. *Smith, Neal (D)	Altoona
6. *Mayne, Wiley (R)	Sioux City
7. *Scherle, W. J. (R)	Henderson
Kan.—1. Dole, Robert (R)	Russell
†Sebelius, Keith G. (R)	Norton
2. *Mize, C. L. (R)	Atchison
3. *Winn, Larry, Jr. (R)	Leawood
4. *Shriver, Garner E. (R)	Wichita
5. *Skubitz, Joseph (R)	Pittsburg
Ky.—1. *Stubblefield, Frank A. (D)	Murray
2. *Natcher, William H. (D)	Bowling Green
3. *Cowger, William O. (R)	Louisville
4. *Snyder, Gene (R)	Jeffersontown
5. *Carter, Tim L. (R)	Tompkinsville
6. *Watts, John C. (D)	Nicholasville
7. *Perkins, Carl D. (D)	Hindman
La.—1. *Hébert, F. Edward (D)	New Orleans
2. *Boggs, Hale (D)	New Orleans
3. Willis, Edwin E. (D)	St. Martinville
†Caffery, Patrick (D)	New Iberia
4. *Waggonner, Joe D., Jr. (D)	Plain Dealing
5. *Passman, Otto E. (D)	Monroe
6. *Rarick, John R. (D)	St. Francisville
7. *Edwards, Edwin W. (D)	Baton Rouge
8. *Long, Speedy O. (D)	Jena
Me.—1. *Kyros, Peter (D)	Portland
2. *Hathaway, W. D. (D)	Auburn
Md.—1. *Morton, Rogers C. B. (R)	Easton
2. *Long, Clarence D. (D)	Ruxton
3. *Garmatz, Edward A. (D)	Baltimore
4. *Fallon, George H. (D)	Baltimore
5. Machen, H. (D)	Hyattsville
†Hogan, Lawrence J. (R)	Hyattsville
6. Mathias, Charles McC., Jr. (R)	Frederick
†Beall, J. Glenn, Jr. (R)	Frostburg
7. *Friedel, Samuel N. (D)	Baltimore
8. *Gude, Gilbert (R)	Bethesda
Mass.—1. *Conte, Silvio O. (R)	Pittsfield
2. *Boland, Edward P. (D)	Springfield
3. *Philbin, Philip J. (D)	Clinton
4. *Donohue, Harold D. (D)	Worcester
5. *Morse, F. Bradford (R)	Lowell
6. *Bates, William H. (R)	Salem
7. *Macdonald, Torbert H. (D)	Malden
8. *O'Neill, Thomas P., Jr. (D)	Cambridge
9. *McCormack, John W. (D)	Dorchester
10. *Heckler, Margaret (R)	Wellesley Hills
11. *Burke, James A. (D)	Milton
12. *Keith, Hastings (R)	West Bridgewater
Mich.—1. *Conyers, J. J. (D)	Detroit
2. *Esch, Marvin (R)	Ann Arbor
3. *Brown, Gary E. (R)	Schoolcraft
4. *Hutchinson, Edward (R)	Fennville
5. *Ford, Gerald R., Jr. (R)	Grand Rapids
6. *Chamberlain, Charles E. (R)	East Lansing
7. *Riegle, D. W., Jr. (R)	Flint
8. *Harvey, James (R)	Saginaw
9. *Vander Jagt, Guy (R)	Cadillac
10. *Cederberg, Elford A. (R)	Bay City
11. *Ruppe, Philip (R)	Houghton
12. *O'Hara, James G. (D)	Utica
13. *Diggs, Charles C., Jr. (D)	Detroit
14. *Nedzi, Lucien N. (D)	Detroit
15. *Ford, W. D. (D)	Detroit
16. *Dingell, John D. (D)	Detroit
17. *Griffiths, Martha W. (D)	Detroit
18. *Broomfield, William S. (R)	Royal Oak
19. *McDonald, J. H. (R)	Detroit
Minn.—1. *Quie, Albert H. (R)	Dennison
2. *Nelsen, Ancher (R)	Hutchinson
3. *MacGregor, Clark (R)	Plymouth Village
4. *Karth, Joseph E. (D)	St. Paul
5. *Fraser, Donald M. (D)	Minneapolis
6. *Zwach, John M. (R)	Walnut Grove
7. *Langen, Odin (R)	Kennedy
8. *Blatnik, John A. (D)	Chisholm

State, district, name, and party	Residence
Miss.—1. *Abernethy, Thomas G. (D)	Okolona
2. *Whitten, Jamie L. (D)	Charleston
3. *Griffin, Charles (D)	Utica
4. *Montgomery, G. V. (D)	Meridian
5. *Colmer, William M. (D)	Pascagoula
Mo.—1. Karsten, Frank M. (D)	St. Louis
†Clay, William (D)	St. Louis
2. Curtis, Thomas B. (R)	Webster Groves
†Symington, James W. (D)	Clayton
3. *Sullivan, Leonor K. (D)	St. Louis
4. *Randall, William J. (D)	Independence
5. *Bolling, Richard (D)	Kansas City
6. *Hull, W. R., Jr. (D)	Weston
7. *Hall, Durward G. (R)	Springfield
8. *Ichord, Richard H. (D)	Houston
9. *Hungate, W. L. (D)	Troy
10. Jones, Paul C. (D)	Kennett
†Burlison, Bill D. (D)	Cape Girardeau
Mont.—1. *Olsen, Arnold (D)	Helena
2. *Battin, James F. (R)	Billings
Neb.—1. *Denney, Robert V. (R)	Fairbury
2. *Cunningham, Glenn (R)	Omaha
3. *Martin, David (R)	Kearney
Nev.—*Baring, Walter S. (D)	Reno
N.H.—1. *Wyman, Louis C. (R)	Manchester
2. *Cleveland, James C. (R)	New London
N.J.—1. *Hunt, John E. (R)	Pitman
2. *Sandman, Charles W. (R)	Cape May
3. *Howard, J. J. (D)	Wall Township
4. *Thompson, Frank, Jr. (D)	Trenton
5. *Frelinghuysen, Peter, Jr. (R)	Morristown
6. *Cahill, William T. (R)	Collingswood
7. *Widnall, William B. (R)	Saddle River
8. *Joelson, Charles S. (D)	Paterson
9. *Helstoski, Henry (D)	E. Rutherford
10. *Rodino, Peter W., Jr. (D)	Newark
11. *Minish, Joseph G. (D)	West Orange
12. *Dwyer, Florence P. (R)	Elizabeth
13. *Gallagher, Cornelius E. (D)	Bayonne
14. *Daniels, Dominick V. (D)	Jersey City
15. *Patten, Edward J. (D)	Perth Amboy
N.M.—1. Walker, E. S. (D)	Santa Fe
†Lujan, Manuel, Jr. (R)	Albuquerque
2. Morris, Thomas G. (D)	Tucumcari
†Foreman, Ed (R)	Las Cruces
N.Y.—1. *Pike, Otis G. (D)	Riverhead
2. *Grover, James R., Jr. (R)	Babylon
3. *Wolff, L. L. (D)	Great Neck
4. *Wydler, John W. (R)	Garden City
5. Tenzer, H. (D)	Lawrence
†Lowenstein, A. K. (D)	Nassau
6. *Halpern, Seymour (R)	Forest Hills
7. *Addabbo, Joseph P. (D)	Ozone Park
8. *Rosenthal, Benjamin S. (D)	Elmhurst
9. *Delaney, James J. (D)	Long Island City
10. *Celler, Emanuel (D)	Brooklyn
11. *Brasco, Frank J. (D)	Brooklyn
12. Kelly, Edna F. (D)	Brooklyn
†Chisholm, Shirley (D	Brooklyn
13. *Podell, B. L. (D)	Brooklyn
14. *Rooney, John J. (D)	Brooklyn
15. *Carey, Hugh L. (D)	Brooklyn
16. *Murphy, John M. (D)	Staten Island
17. Kupferman, Theodore (R)	New York
†Koch, Edwin I. (D)	New York
18. *Powell, Adam C. (D)	New York
19. *Farbstein, Leonard (D)	New York
20. *Ryan, William Fitts (D)	New York
21. *Scheuer, James (D)	Bronx
22. *Gilbert, Jacob H. (D)	New York
23. *Bingham, J. B. (D)	Bronx
24. Fino, Paul A. (R)	New York
†Biaggi, Mario (D)	Bronx
25. *Ottinger, R. (D)	Pleasantville
26. *Reid, Ogden R. (R)	Purchase
27. Dow, John G. (D)	Grand View
†McKneally, M. B. (R)	Newburgh
28. Resnick, J. Y. (D)	Ellenville
†Fish, Hamilton, Jr. (R)	Millbrook
29 *Button, Daniel E., Jr. (R)	Albany
30. *King, Carleton J. (R)	Saratoga Springs
31. *McEwen, Robert (R)	Ogdensburg
32. *Pirnie, Alexander (R)	New Hartford
33. *Robison, Howard W. (R)	Owego
34. *Hanley, James M. (D)	Syracuse
35. *Stratton, Samuel S. (D)	Amsterdam
36. *Horton, Frank J. (R)	Rochester
37. *Conable, B., Jr. (R)	Alexander
38. Goodell, Charles E. (R)	Jamestown
†Hastings, James F. (R)	Allegany
39. *McCarthy, R. D. (D)	Buffalo
40. *Smith, H. P., III (R)	N. Tonawanda
41. *Dulski, Thaddeus J. (D)	Buffalo
N.C.—1. *Jones, Walter B. (D)	Farmville
2. *Fountain, L. H. (D)	Tarboro
3. *Henderson, David N. (D)	Wallace
4. *Galifianakis, Nick (D)	Durham
5. Kornegay, Horace R. (D)	Greensboro
†Mizell, Wilmer (R)	Winston-Salem
6. Preyer, L. R. (D)	Greensboro
7. *Lennon, Alton (D)	Wilmington
8. Ruth, Earl B. (R)	Salisbury
9. *Jonas, Charles Raper (R)	Lincolnton
10. *Broyhill, James T. (R)	Lenoir
11. *Taylor, Roy A. (D)	Black Mountain
N.D.—1. *Andrews, Mark (R)	Mapleton
2. *Kleppe, Thomas S. (R)	Bismarck

State, district, name, and party	Residence
Ohio—1. *Taft, Robert A., Jr. (R)	Cincinnati
2. *Clancy, Donald D. (R)	Cincinnati
3. *Whalen, Charles W., Jr. (R)	Dayton
4. *McCulloch, William M. (R)	Piqua
5. *Latta, Delbert L. (R)	Bowling Green
6. *Harsha, William H., Jr. (R)	Portsmouth
7. *Brown, Clarence J., Jr. (R)	Urbana
8. *Betts, Jackson E. (R)	Findlay
9. *Ashley, Thomas L. (D)	Waterville
10. *Miller, Clarence E. (R)	Lancaster
11. *Stanton, J. W. (R)	Painesville
12. *Devine, Samuel L. (R)	Columbus
13. *Mosher, Charles A. (R)	Oberlin
14. *Ayres, William H. (R)	Akron
15. *Wylie, Chalmers P. (R)	Worthington
16. *Bow, Frank T. (R)	Canton
17. *Ashbrook, John M. (R)	Johnstown
18. *Hays, Wayne L. (D)	Flushing
19. *Kirwan, Michael J. (D)	Youngstown
20. *Feighan, Michael A. (D)	Cleveland
21. Vanik, Charles A. (D)	Cleveland
†Stokes, Louis (D)	Cleveland
22. Bolton, Frances P. (R)	Lyndhurst
†Vanik, Charles A. (D)	Cleveland
23. *Minshall, William E. (R)	Cleveland
24. *Lukens, Donald E. (R)	Middletown
Okla.—1. *Belcher, Page (R)	Enid
2. *Edmondson, Ed (D)	Muskogee
3. *Albert, Carl (D)	McAlester
4. *Steed, Tom (D)	Shawnee
5. *Jarman, John (D)	Oklahoma City
6. Smith, James V. (R)	Chickasha
†Camp, J. N. H. (R)	Waukomis
Ore.—1. *Wyatt, Wendell (R)	Stayton
2. *Ullman, Al (D)	Baker
3. *Green, Edith (D)	Portland
4. *Dellenback, John R. (R)	Medford
Penn.—1. *Barrett, William A. (D)	Philadelphia
2. *Nix, Robert N. C. (D)	Philadelphia
3. *Byrne, James A. (D)	Philadelphia
4. *Eilberg, Joshua (D)	Philadelphia
5. *Green, William J., III (D)	Philadelphia
6. Rhodes, George M. (D)	Reading
†Yatron, Gus (D)	Reading
7. *Williams, L. G. (R)	Springfield
8. *Biester, E. G., Jr. (R)	Furlong
9. *Watkins, G. R. (R)	West Chester
10. *McDade, Joseph M. (R)	Scranton
11. *Flood, Daniel J. (D)	Wilkes-Barre
12. *Whalley, J. Irving (R)	Windber
13. Schweiker, Richard S. (R)	Lansdale
†Coughlin, R. L. (R)	Villanova
14. *Moorhead, William S. (D)	Pittsburgh
15. *Rooney, Fred B. (D)	Bethlehem
16. *Eshleman, Edwin D. (R)	Lancaster
17. *Schneebeli, Herman T. (R)	Williamsport
18. *Corbett, Robert J. (R)	Pittsburgh
19. *Goodling, George A. (R)	Loganville
20. Holland, Elmer J. (D)	Pittsburgh
†Gaydos, Joseph (D)	McKeesport
21. *Dent, John H. (D)	Jeannette
22. *Saylor, John P. (R)	Johnstown
23. *Johnson, Albert W. (R)	Smethport
24. *Vigorito, J. P. (D)	Erie
25. *Clark, Frank M. (D)	Bessemer
26. *Morgan, Thomas E. (D)	Fredericktown
27. *Fulton, James G. (R)	Pittsburgh
R.I.—1. *St. Germain, Fernand J. (D)	Woonsocket
2. *Tiernan, Robert O. (D)	Providence
S.C.—1. *Rivers, L. Mendel (D)	Charleston
2. *Watson, Albert W. (R)	Columbia
3. *Dorn, W. J. Bryan (D)	Greenwood
4. Ashmore, Robert T. (D)	Greenville
†Mann, James R. (D)	
5. *Gettys, Thomas S. (D)	Rock Hill
6. *McMillan, John L. (D)	Florence
S.D.—1. *Reifel, Ben (R)	Aberdeen
2. *Berry, E. Y. (R)	McLaughlin
Tenn.—1. *Quillen, James H. (R)	Kingsport
2. *Duncan, John J. (R)	Knoxville
3. *Brock, W. E., III (R)	Chattanooga
4. *Evins, Joseph L. (D)	Smithville
5. *Fulton, Richard (D)	Nashville
6. *Anderson, W. R. (D)	Waverly
7. *Blanton, Ray (D)	Adamsville
8. *Everett, Robert A. (D)	Union City
9. *Kuykendall, Dan (R)	Memphis
Tex.— 1. *Patman, Wright (D)	Texarkana
2. *Dowdy, John (D)	Athens
3. *‡Collins, James M. (R)	Dallas
4. *Roberts, Ray (D)	McKinney
5. *Cabell, Earle (D)	Dallas
6. *Teague, Olin E. (D)	College Station
7. *Bush, George (R)	Houston
8. *Eckhardt, Robert C. (D)	Houston
9. *Brooks, Jack (D)	Beaumont
10. *Pickle, J. J. (D)	Austin
11. *Poage, W. R. (D)	Waco
12. *Wright, James C., Jr. (D)	Fort Worth
13. *Purcell, Graham (D)	Wichita Falls
14. *Young, John (D)	Corpus Christi
15. *de la Garza, E. (D)	Mission
16. *White, Richard C. (D)	El Paso
17. *Burleson, Omar (D)	Anson
18. *Price, Robert (R)	Pampa
19. *Mahon, George (D)	Lubbock
20. *Gonzalez, Henry B. (D)	San Antonio
21. *Fisher, O. C. (D)	San Angelo
22. *Casey, Robert R. (D)	Houston
23. *Kazen, Abraham (D)	Laredo
Utah—1. *Burton, Laurence J. (R)	Ogden
2. *Lloyd, Sherman P. (R)	Salt Lake City
Vt.—*Stafford, Robert T. (R)	Rutland City
Va.—1. *Downing, Thomas N. (D)	Newport News
2. Hardy, Porter, Jr. (D)	Churchland
†Whitehurst, G. W. (R)	Norfolk
3. *Satterfield, D. E., III (D)	Richmond
4. *Abbitt, Watkins M. (D)	Appomattox
5. Tuck, William M. (D)	South Boston
†Daniel, W. C. (D)	Danville
6. *Poff, Richard H. (R)	Radford
7. *Marsh, John O., Jr. (D)	Strasburg
8. *Scott, William L. (R)	Fairfax
9. *Wampler, William C. (R)	Bristol
10. *Broyhill, Joel T. (R)	Arlington
Wash.—1. *Pelly, Thomas M. (R)	Seattle
2. *Meeds, Lloyd (D)	Everett
3. *Hansen, Julia Butler (D)	Cathlamet
4. *May, Catherine (R)	Yakima
5. *Foley, Thomas S. (D)	Spokane
6. *Hicks, Floyd V. (D)	Tacoma
7. *Adams, B. (D)	Seattle
W.Va.—1. Moore, Arch A., Jr. (R)	Glen Dale
†Mollohan, R. H. (D)	
2. *Staggers, Harley O. (D)	Keyser
3. *Slack, John M., Jr. (D)	Charleston
4. *Hechler, Ken (D)	Huntington
5. *Kee, James (D)	Bluefield
Wis.—1. *Schadeberg, H. C. (R)	Burlington
2. *Kastenmeier, Robert W. (D)	Watertown
3. *Thomson, Vernon W. (R)	Richland Center
4. *Zablocki, Clement J. (D)	Milwaukee
5. *Reuss, Henry S. (D)	Milwaukee
6. *Steiger, William A. (R)	Oshkosh
7. *Laird, Melvin R. (R)	Marshfield
8. *Byrnes, John W. (R)	Green Bay
9. *Davis, Glenn R. (R)	Whitefish Bay
10. *O'Konski, Alvin E. (R)	Mercer
Wyo.—Harrison, William H. (R)	Sheridan
†Wold, John (R)	Casper

*Incumbent, reelected.
†Winner, replacing member listed immediately above.
‡Elected Aug. 24, 1968, to fill a vacancy created by the death of Joe R. Pool, July 14, 1968.

Supreme Court

Chief Justice of the United States: Earl Warren
Associate Justices:

Hugo L. Black	Potter Stewart
William O. Douglas	Byron R. White
John M. Harlan	Abe Fortas
William J. Brennan, Jr.	Thurgood Marshall

Senate

membership in 1968, and winners in Nov. 5 election

State, name, and party	Residence	Term expires
Ala.—Hill, Lister (D)	Montgomery	1969
*Allen, James B. (D)	Gadsden	1975
Sparkman, John (D)	Huntsville	1973
Alaska—Gruening, Ernest (D)	Juneau	1969
*Gravel, Mike (D)	Anchorage	1975
§Theodore F. Stevens (R)	Anchorage	1971
Ariz.—Hayden, Carl (D)	Phoenix	1969
*Goldwater, Barry (R)	Phoenix	1975
Fannin, Paul J. (R)	Phoenix	1971
Ark.—†Fulbright, J. W. (D)	Fayetteville	1975
McClellan, John (D)	Camden	1973
Calif.—Kuchel, T. H. (R)	Anaheim	1969
*Cranston, Alan (D)	Los Angeles	1975
Murphy, George (R)	Beverly Hills	1971
Colo.—†Dominick, Peter (R)	Englewood	1975
Allott, Gordon (R)	Lamar	1973
Conn.—†Ribicoff, Abraham (D)	Hartford	1975
Dodd, Thomas J. (D)	West Hartford	1971
Del.—Williams, John J. (R)	Millsboro	1971
Boggs, J. Caleb (R)	Wilmington	1973
Fla.—Smathers, George (D)	Miami	1969
*Gurney, Edward (R)	Winter Park	1975
Holland, Spessard L. (D)	Bartow	1971
Ga.—†Talmadge, Herman (D)	Lovejoy	1975
Russell, Richard B. (D)	Winder	1973
Hawaii—†Inouye, Daniel K. (D)	Honolulu	1975
Fong, Hiram L. (R)	Honolulu	1971
Ida.—†Church, Frank (D)	Boise	1975
Jordan, Len B. (R)	Boise	1973
Ill.—†Dirksen, Everett (R)	Pekin	1975
Percy, Charles H. (R)	Kenilworth	1973
Ind.—†Bayh, Birch E., Jr. (D)	Terre Haute	1975
Hartke, Vance (D)	Evansville	1971
Ia.—Hickenlooper, Bourke (R)	Cedar Rapids	1969
*Hughes, Harold (D)	Des Moines	1975
Miller, Jack R. (R)	Sioux City	1973
Kan.—Carlson, Frank (R)	Concordia	1969
*Dole, Robert (R)	Russell	1975
Pearson, James B. (R)	Prairie Village	1973
Ky.—Morton, Thruston (R)	Glenview	1969
*Cook, Marlow W. (R)	Louisville	1975
Cooper, John S. (R)	Somerset	1973
La.—†Long, Russell (D)	Baton Rouge	1975
Ellender, Allen J. (D)	Houma	1973
Me.—Muskie, Edmund S. (D)	Waterville	1971
Smith, Margaret Chase (R)	Skowhegan	1973
Md.—Brewster, Daniel (D)	Towson	1969
*Mathias, C. M. Jr. (R)	Frederick	1975
Tydings, Joseph D. (D)	Havre de Grace	1971
Mass.—Kennedy, Edward M. (D)	Boston	1971
Brooke, Edward W. (R)	Boston	1973
Mich.—Hart, Philip A. (D)	Lansing	1971
Griffin, Robert P. (R)	Traverse City	1973
Minn.—McCarthy, Eugene (D)	St. Paul	1971
Mondale, Walter F. (D)	Minneapolis	1973
Miss.—Stennis, John (D)	DeKalb	1971
Eastland, James (D)	Doddsville	1973
Mo.—Long, Edward V. (D)	Bowling Green	1969
*Eagleton, T. F. (D)	St. Louis	1975
Symington, Stuart (D)	Creve Coeur	1971
Mont.—Mansfield, Mike (D)	Missoula	1971
Metcalf, Lee (D)	Helena	1973
Neb.—Hruska, Roman L. (R)	Omaha	1971
Curtis, Carl T. (R)	Minden	1973
Nev.—†Bible, Alan (D)	Reno	1975
Cannon, Howard W. (D)	Las Vegas	1971
N.H.—†Cotton, Norris (R)	Lebanon	1975
McIntyre, Thomas J. (D)	Laconia	1973
N.J.—Williams, Harrison, Jr. (D)	Westfield	1971
Case, Clifford P. (R)	Rahway	1973
N.M.—Anderson, Clinton (D)	Albuquerque	1973
Montoya, Joseph M. (D)	Santa Fe	1971
N.Y.—†Javits, Jacob K. (R)	New York	1975
‡Goodell, Charles E. (R)	Jamestown	1971
N.C.—†Ervin, Sam J., Jr. (D)	Morganton	1975
Jordan, B. Everett (D)	Saxapahaw	1973
N.D.—†Young, Milton R. (R)	La Moure	1975
Burdick, Quentin N. (D)	Fargo	1971
Ohio—Lausche, Frank (D)	Cleveland	1969
*Saxbe, William (R)	Mechanicsburg	1975
Young, Stephen M. (D)	Shaker Heights	1971
Okla.—Monroney, Mike (D)	Oklahoma City	1969
*Bellmon, Henry (R)	Red Rock	1975
Harris, Fred R. (D)	Lawton	1973
Ore.—Morse, Wayne (D)	Eugene	1969
*Packwood, Robert (R)	Portland	1975
Hatfield, Mark O. (R)	Salem	1973
Penn.—Clark, Joseph S. (D)	Philadelphia	1969
*Schweiker, R. S. (R)	Plymouth Meeting	1975
Scott, Hugh (R)	Philadelphia	1971
R. I.—Pastore, John O. (D)	Providence	1971
Pell, Claiborne (D)	Newport	1973
S.C.—†Hollings, Ernest F. (D)	Charleston	1975
Thurmond, Strom (R)	Aiken	1973
S.D.—†McGovern, George (D)	Mitchell	1975
Mundt, Karl E. (R)	Madison	1973
Tenn.—Gore, Albert (D)	Carthage	1971
Baker, Howard, Jr. (R)	Knoxville	1973
Tex.—Yarborough, Ralph (D)	Austin	1971
Tower, John G. (R)	Wichita Falls	1973
Utah—†Bennett, Wallace (R)	Salt Lake City	1975
Moss, Frank E. (D)	Salt Lake City	1971
Vt.—†Aiken, George D. (R)	Putney	1975
Prouty, Winston L. (R)	Newport	1971
Va.—Byrd, Harry F., Jr. (D)	Winchester	1971
Spong, William, Jr. (D)	Portsmouth	1973
Wash.—†Magnuson, Warren (D)	Seattle	1975
Jackson, Henry M. (D)	Everett	1971
W.Va.—Byrd, Robert C. (D)	Sophia	1971
Randolph, Jennings (D)	Elkins	1973
Wis.—†Nelson, Gaylord (D)	Madison	1975
Proxmire, William (D)	Madison	1971
Wyo.—McGee, Gale W. (D)	Laramie	1971
Hansen, Clifford P. (R)	Cathlamet	1973

*Winner, replacing member listed immediately above.
†Incumbent, reelected. ‡Appointed Sept. 10, 1968, to fill vacancy due to death of Robert F. Kennedy.
§Appointed Dec. 23, 1968, to fill vacancy due to death of E. L. Bartlett.

Act	House vote	Senate vote	Date of enactment
Senate Code of Ethics (restricted outside employment for Senate employees, limited use of political funds to campaign expenses and certain office costs, restricted political fund-raising by Senate employees and required confidential disclosure of personal finances by Senators and employees earning more than $15,000 a year)	Not needed	67–1 Yeas: D. 40, R. 27 Nays: D. 0, R. 1 (March 22)	March 22
House Code of Ethics (established a Code of Official Conduct for congressmen and House employees requiring public reports on sources of major income and confidential reports on the amount of such income)	405–1 Yeas: D. 225, R. 180 Nays: D. 0, R. 1 (April 3)	Not needed	April 3
Antiriot—Open Housing (prohibited interference with a person exercising federally-protected rights, prohibited discrimination in the sale and rental of housing, guaranteed constitutional rights of American Indians, and banned travel in interstate commerce with intent to incite or take part in a riot)	326–93 Yeas: D. 165, R. 161 Nays: D. 68, R. 25 (Aug. 16, '67)	71–20 Yeas: D. 42, R. 29 Nays: D. 17, R. 3 (March 11)	Signed April 11
"Truth in Lending" (required all lenders and retail creditors to disclose the annual percentage cost of credit, restricted wage garnishment to 10 percent of a worker's income above $30, established a National Commission on Consumer Finance, and made "loan sharking" a federal crime)	382–4 Yeas: D. 217, R. 165 Nays: D. 3, R. 1 (Feb. 1)	92–0 Yeas: D. 56, R. 36 Nays: D. 0, R. 0 (July 11, '67)	Signed May 29
Safe Streets and Crime Control Act of 1968 (authorized $400.1 million for law-enforcement planning and assistance grants with 85 percent of funds alloted through block grants to the states, provided that confessions were admissible even despite delay in arraignment if federal trial judge found them 'voluntary' and that eyewitness testimony was admissible even if the accused had no counsel during a police lineup, permitted wiretaps and 'bugs' by police in a wide variety of cases, prohibited the mail-order sale of handguns and over-the-counter sale to persons who did not live in the dealer's state)	337–23 Yeas: D. 204, R. 173 Nays: D. 22, R. 1 (Aug. 8,'67)	72–4 Yeas: D. 42, R. 30 Nays: D. 2, R. 2 (May 23)	Signed June 19
Revenues and Expenditures Control Act of 1968 (imposed a 10-percent surcharge on individual and corporate income taxes and required a $6-billion reduction in federal spending for fiscal '69, a $10-billion reduction in projected '69 appropriations and a decrease in the federal work force to the level of June, 1966)	Passed by voice vote (Feb. 29)	57–31 Yeas: D. 27, R. 30 Nays: D. 28, R. 3 (April 2)	Signed June 28
Conservation Fund (augmented revenues for the Land and Water Conservation Fund by using income from oil and gas leases on the outer continental shelf to bring annual intake to at least $200 million during fiscal 1967–73)	Passed by voice vote (May 23)	Passed by voice vote (April 30)	Signed July 15
Housing and Urban Development Act of 1968 (provided federal aid for home ownership for low-income families and low-rental housing and federal reinsurance for insurance industry riot losses and set up flood insurance program and extended and expanded other housing programs)	227–135 Yeas: D. 155, R. 72 Nays: D. 43, R. 92 (July 26)	67–4 Yeas: D. 40, R. 27 Nays: D. 3, R. 1 (May 28)	Signed July 31
Juvenile Delinquency Prevention and Control Act of 1968 (authorized a three-year $150-million program of grants to states, localities and public and private nonprofit agencies to prevent juvenile crime and rehabilitate youth offenders)	Passed by voice vote (Sept. 26, '67)	Passed by voice vote (July 8)	Signed July 31
Natural Gas Pipeline Safety Act of 1968 (authorized Secretary of Transportation to set safety standards for gas pipelines)	351–14 Yeas: D. 191, R. 160 Nays: D. 12, R. 2 (July 2)	78–0 Yeas: D. 49, R. 29 Nays: D. 0, R. 0 (Nov. 9, '67)	Signed Aug. 12
Wholesome Poultry Products Act of 1968 (aided states in developing poultry inspection programs for poultry distributed intrastate which were same as federal inspection programs for poultry sold in interstate commerce)	352–17 Yeas: D. 192, R. 160 Nays: D. 8, R. 9 (June 13)	73–0 Yeas: D. 48, R. 25 Nays: D. 0, R. 0 (July 29)	Signed Aug. 18
Central Arizona Project (authorized construction of the Central Arizona Project and five other water projects in the Colorado River Basin)	Passed by voice vote (May 16)	Passed by voice vote (Aug. 7, '67)	Signed Sept. 30
Redwoods Park (established a 58,000-acre Redwoods National Park in Northern California)	388–15 Yeas: D. 209, R. 179 Nays: D. 13, R. 2 (July 15)	77–6 Yeas: D. 46, R. 31 Nays: D. 6, R. 0 (Nov. 1, '67)	Signed Oct. 2
Vocational Education (amended the Vocational Education Act of 1963 and appropriated $1.2 billion for programs through fiscal 1970)	390–0 Yeas: D. 215, R. 175 Nays: D. 0, R. 0 (July 15)	88–0 Yeas: D. 54, R. 34 Nays: D. 0, R. 0 (July 17)	Signed Oct. 16
College Assistance (extended four higher-education laws through fiscal 1972 with proviso that funds be denied to students who participate in serious campus disorders)	Passed by voice vote (July 25)	83–0 Yeas: D. 51, R. 32 Nays: D. 0, R. 0 (July 15)	Signed Oct. 16
Radiation Control Act of 1968 (authorized Secretary of Health, Education and Welfare to develop standards to control radiation from television sets, microwave ovens, lasers and radar and to ban the sale of those devices that fail to meet federal standards)	381–0 Yeas: D. 207, R. 174 Nays: D. 0, R. 0 (March 20)	Passed by voice vote (Oct. 3)	Signed Oct. 18
Gun Control Act of 1968 (banned interstate shipment of rifles and shotguns and handgun ammunition and restricted out-of-state purchases of rifles and shotguns)	305–118 Yeas: D. 158, R. 147 Nays: D. 79, R. 39 (July 24)	70–17 Yeas: D. 39, R. 31 Nays: D. 13, R. 4 (Sept. 18)	Signed Oct. 22
Drug Abuse Control Act of 1968 (provided criminal penalties for possession of illegally obtained stimulants, depressants or hallucinogenic drugs and increased existing penalties for illegal sale of such drugs)	320–2 Yeas: D. 178, R. 142 Nays: D. 2, R. 0 (July 12)	Passed by voice vote (Oct. 4)	Signed Oct. 24

Key To Electoral Votes Cast

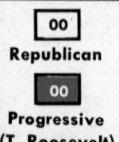
Republican

Progressive (T. Roosevelt)

Democratic

Progressive (LaFollette)

Populist

States' Rights Democratic

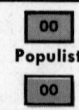
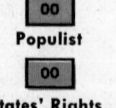
Noncandidates

American Independent

Split vote

One hundred years of presidential elections

State	1868	1872	1876	1880	1884	1888	1892	1896	1900	1904	1908	1912	1916	1920	1924	1928	1932	1936	1940	1944	1948	1952	1956	1960	1964	1968
Alabama	8	10	10	10	10	10	11	11	11	11	11	12	12	12	12	12	11	11	11	11	11	11	10/1	6/5	10	10
Alaska																						Admitted 1959		3	3	3
Arizona												Admitted 1912	3	3	3	3	3	3	3	4	4	4	4	4	5	5
Arkansas	5	**	6	6	7	7	8	8	8	9	9	9	9	9	9	9	9	9	9	9	9	8	8	8	6	6
California	5	6	6	1/5	8	8	8/1	8/1	9	10	10	2/11	13	13	13	13	22	22	22	25	25	32	32	32	40	40
Colorado	Ad. 1876		3	3	3	3	4	4	4	5	5	6	6	6	6	6	6	6	6	6	6	6	6	6	6	6
Connecticut	6	6	6	6	6	6		6	6	7	7	7	7	7	7	7	8	8	8	8	8	8	8	8	8	8
Delaware	3	3	3	3	3	3	3	3	3	3	3	3	3	3	3	3	3	3	3	3	3	3	3	3	3	3
Dist. of Columbia													Constitutional amendment (1961) permitted residents to vote												3	3
Florida	3	4	4	4	4	4	4	4	4	5	5	6	6	6	6	7	7	7	7	8	8	10	10	10	14	14
Georgia	9	8	11	11	12	12	13	13	13	13	13	14	14	14	14	14	12	12	12	12	12	12	12	12	12	12
Hawaii																						Admitted 1959		3	4	4
Idaho				Admitted 1890			3	3	3	3	3	4	4	4	4	4	4	4	4	4	4	4	4	4	4	4
Illinois	16	21	21	21	22	22	24	24	24	27	27	29	29	29	29	29	29	29	29	28	28	27	27	27	26	26
Indiana	13	15	15	15	15	15	15	15	15	15	15	15	15	15	15	15	14	14	14	13	13	13	13	13	13	13
Iowa	8	11	11	11	13	13	13	13	13	13	13	13	13	13	13	13	11	11	11	10	10	10	10	10	9	9
Kansas	3	5	5	5	9	9	10	10	10	10	10	10	10	10	10	9	9	9	8	8	8	8	8	8	7	7
Kentucky	11	12	12	12	13	13	13	12/1	13	13	13	13	13	13	13	13	11	11	11	11	11	10	10	10	9	9
Louisiana	7	**	8	8	8	8	8	8	8	9	9	10	10	10	10	10	10	10	10	10	10	10	10	10	10	10
Maine	7	7	7	7	6	6	6	6	6	6	6	6	6	6	6	6	5	5	5	5	5	5	5	5	4	4
Maryland	7	8	8	8	8	8	8	8	1/7	2/6	8	8	8	8	8	8	8	8	8	8	8	9	9	9	10	10
Massachusetts	12	13	13	13	14	14	15	15	15	15	16	18	18	18	18	18	17	17	17	16	16	16	16	16	14	14
Michigan	8	11	11	11	13	13	9/5	14	14	14	14	15	15	15	15	15	19	19	19	19	19	20	20	20	21	21
Minnesota	4	5	5	5	7	7	9	9	9	11	11	12	12	12	12	12	11	11	11	11	11	11	11	11	10	10
Mississippi	*	8	8	8	9	9	9	9	9	10	10	10	10	10	10	10	9	9	9	9	9	8	8	8	7	7
Missouri	11	15	15	15	16	16	17	17	17	18	18	18	18	18	18	18	15	15	15	15	13	13	13	13	12	12
Montana				Admitted 1889			3	3	3	3	3	4	4	4	4	4	4	4	4	4	4	4	4	4	4	4
Nebraska	3	3	3	3	5	5	8	8	8	8	8	8	8	8	8	8	7	7	7	6	6	6	6	6	5	5
Nevada	3	3	3	3	3	3	3	3	3	3	3	3	3	3	3	3	3	3	3	3	3	3	3	3	3	3
New Hampshire	5	5	5	5	4	4	4	4	4	4	4	4	4	4	4	4	4	4	4	4	4	4	4	4	4	4
New Jersey	7	9	9	9	9	9	10	10	10	12	12	14	14	14	14	14	16	16	16	16	16	16	16	16	17	17
New Mexico												Admitted 1912	3	3	3	3	3	3	3	4	4	4	4	4	4	4
New York	33	35	35	35	36	36	36	36	36	39	39	45	45	45	45	45	47	47	47	47	47	45	45	45	43	43
North Carolina	9	10	10	10	11	11	11	11	11	12	12	12	12	12	12	12	13	13	13	14	14	14	14	14	13	12/1
North Dakota				Admitted 1889			1/1	3	3	4	4	4	5	5	5	4	4	4	4	4	4	4	4	4	4	4
Ohio	21	22	22	22	23	23	1/22	23	23	23	23	24	24	24	24	24	26	26	26	25	25	25	25	25	26	26
Oklahoma											Admitted 1907	7	10	10	10	10	11	11	11	10	10	8	7/1	8	8	8
Oregon	3	3	3	3	3	3	3/1	4	4	4	4	5	5	5	5	5	5	5	5	6	6	6	6	6	6	6
Pennsylvania	26	29	29	29	30	30	32	32	32	34	34	38	38	38	38	38	36	36	36	35	35	32	32	32	29	29
Rhode Island	4	4	4	4	4	4	4	4	4	4	4	5	5	5	5	5	4	4	4	4	4	4	4	4	4	4
South Carolina	6	7	7	7	9	9	9	9	9	9	9	9	9	9	9	9	8	8	8	8	8	8	8	8	8	8
South Dakota				Admitted 1889			4	4	4	4	4	5	5	5	5	4	4	4	4	4	4	4	4	4	4	4
Tennessee	10	12	12	12	12	12	12	12	12	12	12	12	12	12	12	12	11	11	11	12	11/1	11	11	11	11	11
Texas	*	8	8	8	13	13	15	15	15	18	18	20	20	20	20	20	23	23	23	23	23	24	24	24	25	25
Utah				Admitted 1896				3	3	3	3	4	4	4	4	4	4	4	4	4	4	4	4	4	4	4
Vermont	5	5	5	5	4	4	4	4	4	4	4	4	4	4	4	4	3	3	3	3	3	3	3	3	3	3
Virginia	*	11	11	11	12	12	12	12	12	12	12	12	12	12	12	12	11	11	11	11	11	12	12	12	12	12
Washington				Admitted 1889			4	4	4	5	5	7	7	7	7	7	8	8	8	8	8	9	9	9	9	9
West Virginia	5	5	5	5	6	6	6	6	6	7	7	8	7/1	8	8	8	8	8	8	8	8	8	8	8	7	7
Wisconsin	8	10	10	10	11	11	12	12	12	13	13	13	13	13	13	13	12	12	12	12	12	12	12	12	12	12
Wyoming				Admitted 1890			3	3	3	3	3	3	3	3	3	3	3	3	3	3	3	3	3	3	3	3

Total Electoral Votes Cast

	1868	1872	1876	1880	1884	1888	1892	1896	1900	1904	1908	1912	1916	1920	1924	1928	1932	1936	1940	1944	1948	1952	1956	1960	1964	1968
Winner	Grant	Grant	Hayes	Garfield	Cleveland	Harrison	Cleveland	McKinley	McKinley	Roosevelt	Taft	Wilson	Wilson	Harding	Coolidge	Hoover	Roosevelt	Roosevelt	Roosevelt	Roosevelt	Truman	Eisenhower	Eisenhower	Kennedy	Johnson	Nixon
Votes	214	286	185	214	219	233	277	271	292	336	321	435	277	404	382	444	472	523	449	432	303	442	457	303	486	301
Opponent	Seymour	Various cand.	Tilden	Hancock	Blaine	Cleveland	Harrison	Bryan	Bryan	Parker	Bryan	Roosevelt	Hughes	Cox	Davis	Smith	Hoover	Landon	Willkie	Dewey	Dewey	Stevenson	Stevenson	Nixon	Goldwater	Humphrey
Votes	80	63	184	155	182	168	145	176	155	140	162	88	254	127	136	87	59	8	82	99	189	89	73	219	52	191
Third party							Weaver 22					Taft 8			LaFollette 13						Thurmond 39			Jones 1 / Byrd 15		Wallace 46

* No vote for this year.
** Rejected.

Ambassadors and envoys

Country	From the U.S.	To the U.S.	Country	From the U.S.	To the U.S.
Afghanistan	Robert G. Neumann	Abdullah Malikyar	Luxembourg	George J. Feldman	Maurice Steinmetz
Algeria	(Embassy closed June 6, 1967)		Malagasy Republic	David S. King	*René Gilbert Ralison
Argentina	Carter L. Burgess	Alejandro Roca	Malawi	Marshall P. Jones	Nyemba Wales Mbekeani
Australia	William H. Crook	Sir Keith Waller	Malaysia	James D. Bell	Tan Sri Ong Yoke Lin
Austria	Douglas MacArthur II	Ernst Lemberger	Maldive Islands	Andrew V. Corry	Abdul Sattar
Barbados	Fredric R. Mann	Hilton A. Vaughan	Mali	G. Edward Clark	Moussa Léo Keita
Belgium	Ridgway B. Knight	Baron Louis Scheyven	Malta	Hugh H. Smythe	Arvid Pardo
Bolivia	Raul H. Castro	Julio Sanjines-Goytia	Mauritania	(Embassy closed June 8, 1967)	
Botswana	†Charles H. Pletcher	*Phineas P. Makepe	Mauritius	David S. King	Pierre G. G. Balancy
Brazil	John W. Tuthill	*Jorge de Sá Almeida	Mexico	Fulton Freeman	Hugo B. Margáin
Bulgaria	John M. McSweeney	Luben Nikolov Guerassimov	Morocco	Henry J. Tasca	Ahmed Osman
Burma	Arthur W. Hummel	U Hla Maung	Nepal	Carol C. Laise	Padma Bahadur Khatri
Burundi	George W. Renchard	Terence Nsanze	Netherlands	William R. Tyler	Carl W. A. Schurmann
Cambodia	(Embassy closed May 3, 1965)		New Zealand	John F. Henning	Frank Corner
Cameroon	Robert L. Payton	Joseph Owono	Nicaragua	Kennedy Crockett	Guillermo Sevilla-Sacasa
Canada	Harold Francis Linder	A. Edgar Ritchie	Niger	Samuel C. Adams, Jr.	Adamou Mayaki
Central African Republic	Geoffrey W. Lewis	Michel Gallin-Douathe	Nigeria	Elbert G. Mathews	Joe Iyalla
Ceylon	Andrew V. Corry	Oliver Weerasinghe	Norway	Margaret J. Tibbetts	Arne Gunneng
Chad	Sheldon B. Vance	Lazare Massibe	Pakistan	Benjamin H. Oehlert, Jr.	Agha Hilaly
Chile	Edward M. Korry	Domingo Santa Maria	Panama	Charles W. Adair, Jr.	*Arturo Morgan
China (Formosa)	Walter P. McConaughy	Chow Shu-kai	Paraguay	Benigno C. Hernandez	Roque J. Avila
Colombia	Reynold E. Carlson	*José Camacho	Peru	J. Wesley Jones	*Carlos Alzamora
Congo (Brazzaville)	(Embassy closed Aug. 13, 1965)		Philippines	G. Mennen Williams	Salvador P. Lopez
Congo (Kinshasa)	Robert H. McBride	Cyrille Adoula	Poland	Walter J. Stoessel, Jr.	Jerzy Michalowski
Costa Rica	Clarence A. Boonstra	Luis Demetrio Tinoco	Portugal	W. Tapley Bennett	Vasco Vieira Garin
Cyprus	Taylor G. Belcher	Zenon Rossides	Romania	Richard H. Davis	Corneliu Bogdan
Czechoslovakia	Jacob D. Beam	Karel Duda	Rwanda	Leo G. Cyr	Celestin Kabanda
Dahomey	Clinton E. Knox	Maxime-Leopold Zollner	Saudi Arabia	Hermann F. Eilts	Ibrahim al-Sowayel
Denmark	Angier Biddle Duke	Torben Ronne	Senegal	L. Dean Brown	Cheikh Ibrahima Fall
Dominican Republic	John H. Crimmins	Hector Garcia-Godoy	Sierra Leone	Robert G. Miner	Adesanya K. Hyde
Ecuador	Edson O. Sessions	Carlos Mantilla-Ortega	Singapore	Francis J. Galbraith	Wong Lin Ken
El Salvador	William G. Bowdler	Julio A. Rivera	Somali Republic	‡Harold G. Josif	Yusuf O. Azhari
Equatorial Africa	Albert W. Sherer Jr.		South Africa	William M. Rountree	Harold L. T. Taswell
Estonia	(Legation at Tallinn closed)	†Ernst Jaakson	Southern Yemen	*William Eagleton	
Ethiopia	William O. Hall	Minasse Haile	Spain	Robert F. Wagner	Marquis de Merry Del Val
Finland	Tyler Thompson	Olavi Munkki	Sudan	(Embassy closed June 6, 1967)	
France	R. Sargent Shriver	Charles E. Lucet	Swaziland	—	Msindazwe Sukati
Gabon	David Bane	Leonard Antoine Badinga	Sweden	William W. Heath	Hubert de Besche
Gambia	L. Dean Brown		Switzerland	John S. Hayes	Felix Schnyder
Germany, West	Henry Cabot Lodge	Heinrich Knappstein	Syria	(Embassy closed June 6, 1967)	
Ghana	Thomas W. McElhiney	Ebenezer Moses Debrah	Tanzania	John H. Burns	Michael Lukumbuzya
Greece	Phillips Talbot	C. Xanthopoulos Palamas	Thailand	Leonard Unger	Bunchana Atthakor
Guatemala	Nathaniel Davis	Francisco Linares Aranda	Togo	Albert W. Sherer, Jr.	Alexandre Ohin
Guinea	Robinson McIlvaine	Karim Bangoura	Trinidad and Tobago	William A. Costello	Sir Ellis E. I. Clarke
Guyana	Delmar R. Carlson	Sir John Carter	Tunisia	Francis H. Russell	Rachid Driss
Haiti	Claude G. Ross	Arthur Bonhomme	Turkey	Robert W. Komer	Melih Esenbel
Honduras	Joseph J. Jova	Ricardo Midence Soto	Uganda	Henry E. Stebbins	E. Otema Allimadi
Hungary	Martin J. Hillenbrand	János Nagy	U.S.S.R.	Llewellyn E. Thompson	Anatoly F. Dobrynin
Iceland	Karl F. Rolvaag	Petur Thorsteinsson	United Arab Republic	(Diplomatic relations severed June 6, 1967)	
India	Chester Bowles	Nawab Ali Yavar Jung	United Kingdom	David K. E. Bruce	Sir Patrick Dean
Indonesia	Marshall Green	R. M. Soedjatmoko	Upper Volta	Elliott P. Skinner	Paul Rouamba
Iran	Armin H. Meyer	Hushang Ansary	Uruguay	Robert M. Sayre	Juan Felipe Yriart
Iraq	(Embassy closed June 7, 1967)		Venezuela	Maurice M. Bernbaum	*Carlos Perez de la Cova
Ireland	Leo J. Sheridan	William P. Fay	Vietnam, South	Ellsworth Bunker	Bui Diem
Israel	Walworth Barbour	Yitzhak Rabin	Yemen	(Embassy closed June 7, 1967)	
Italy	H. Gardner Ackley	Egidio Ortona	Yugoslavia	C. Burke Elbrick	Bogdan Crnobrnja
Ivory Coast	George Allen Morgan	Timothée N'Guetta Ahoua	Zambia	Robert C. Good	Rupiah B. Banda
Jamaica	Walter N. Tobriner	Sir Egerton R. Richardson			
Japan	U. Alexis Johnson	Takeso Shimoda			
Jordan	Harrison M. Symmes	Abdul Hamid Sharaf			
Kenya	Glenn W. Ferguson	Burudi Nabwera			
Korea, South	William J. Porter	Dong Jo Kim			
Kuwait	Howard R. Cottam	Talat al-Ghousein			
Laos	William H. Sullivan	Khamking Souvanlasy			
Latvia	(Legation at Riga closed)	*Arnolds Spekke			
Lebanon	Dwight J. Porter	Najati Kabbani			
Lesotho	‡Richard St. F. Post	Albert Steerforth Mohale			
Liberia	Ben H. Brown, Jr.	S. Edward Peal			
Libya	David D. Newsom	Fathi Abidia			
Lithuania	(Legation at Kaunas closed)	*Joseph Kajeckas			

U.S. AMBASSADORS TO INTERNATIONAL ORGANIZATIONS

Ambassadors at Large — W. Averell Harriman, George C. McGhee

International Atomic Energy Agency — Henry D. Smyth
North Atlantic Treaty Organization — Harlan Cleveland
Organization of American States — Sol. M. Linowitz
European Office of the UN and other
   International Organizations—Geneva — Roger W. Tubby
European Communities — J. Robert Schaetzel
United Nations — James Russell Wiggins
United Nations Educational, Scientific, and
   Cultural Organization — William Benton

*Charge d'affaires.   †Consul general.   ‡Deputy chief of mission.

Source: U.S. Department of State, *The Department of State Bulletin* and *Diplomatic List* (November 1968).

The federal government dollar

estimates for year ending June 30, 1969

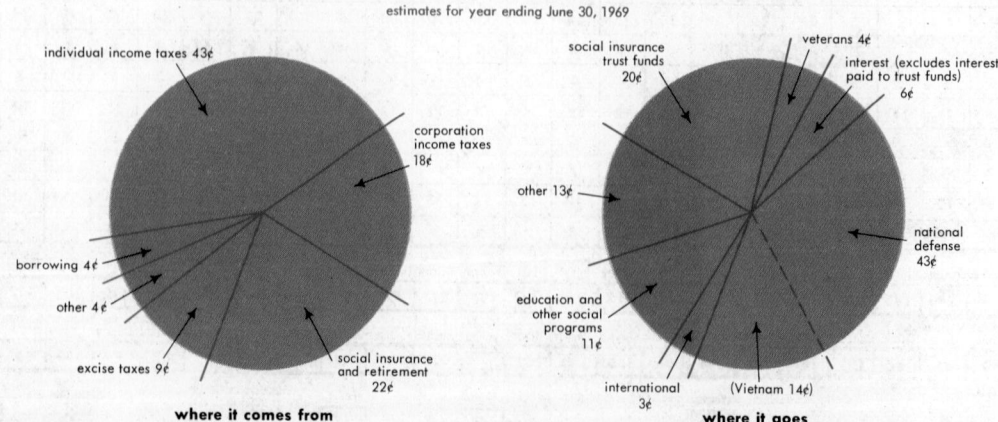

where it comes from
- individual income taxes 43¢
- corporation income taxes 18¢
- social insurance and retirement 22¢
- excise taxes 9¢
- borrowing 4¢
- other 4¢

where it goes
- social insurance trust funds 20¢
- veterans 4¢
- interest (excludes interest paid to trust funds) 6¢
- national defense 43¢
- (Vietnam 14¢)
- international 3¢
- education and other social programs 11¢
- other 13¢

Data are based on federal administrative budget and trust fund receipts and expenditures.

Source: Executive Office of the President, Bureau of the Budget, *The Budget in Brief*.

The federal administrative budget

in millions of dollars

Source and function	1967	1968 estimate	1969 estimate
Budget receipts	149,591	155,830	178,108
Individual income taxes	61,526	67,700	80,900
Corporation income taxes	33,971	31,300	34,300
Excise taxes	13,719	13,848	14,671
Alcohol taxes	4,076	4,242	4,404
Tobacco taxes	2,080	2,172	2,207
Manufacturers' excise taxes	6,129	6,105	6,628
Other excise taxes	1,434	1,329	1,432
Employment taxes	27,823	29,730	34,154
Unemployment insurance	3,652	3,660	3,594
Premiums for other insurance and retirement	1,853	2,049	2,275
Estate and gift taxes	2,978	3,100	3,400
Customs	1,901	2,000	2,070
Miscellaneous receipts	2,168	2,443	2,744
Budget expenditures*	158,414	175,635	186,062
National defense*	70,095	76,491	79,792
Department of Defense military functions	67,608	73,860	76,806
Military assistance	1,943	1,675	1,853
Atomic energy	2,264	2,334	2,546
Defense-related activities	−14	115	242
International affairs and finance*	4,110	4,330	4,478
Conduct of foreign affairs	366	559	438
Economic and financial assistance	2,517	2,417	2,564
Foreign information and exchange activities	245	256	255
Food for Freedom	1,452	1,315	1,444
Space research and technology	5,423	4,803	4,573
Agriculture and agricultural resources*	3,156	4,412	4,474
Farm income stabilization	2,267	3,428	3,459
Financing farming and rural housing	−10	26	32
Financing rural electrification and rural telephones	12	13	13
Agricultural land and water resources	353	362	350
Research and other agricultural services	570	623	662
Natural resources*	2,113	2,416	2,483
Land and water resources	2,335	2,465	2,536
Forest resources	482	518	493
Mineral resources	122	133	131
Fish and wildlife resources	136	153	158
Recreation resources	194	245	309
General resource surveys and administration	275	250	239
Commerce and transportation*	7,308	7,695	7,996
Air transportation	945	950	1,282
Water transportation	792	855	1,000
Ground transportation	4,050	4,385	4,420
Postal service	1,141	1,087	767

Source and function	1967	1968 estimate	1969 estimate
Advancement of business	189	160	153
Area and regional development	137	312	425
Regulation of business	101	100	107
Housing and community development*	577	697	1,429
Aids to private housing	−225	−539	−457
Public housing programs	251	297	350
Urban renewal and community facilities	504	865	1,432
National Capital region	66	90	104
Health, labor, and welfare*	39,512	46,396	51,945
Health services and research	7,722	10,734	12,041
Labor and manpower	1,069	1,326	1,492
Public assistance, excl. medical care for the aged	3,041	3,484	3,605
Retirement and social insurance	27,117	29,946	33,932
Economic opportunity programs	1,485	1,853	1,997
Other welfare services	905	1,102	1,302
Education*			
Assistance for elementary or secondary education	3,602	4,157	4,364
Assistance for higher education	1,859	1,930	1,931
Assistance to science education and basic research	711	1,057	1,065
Other aids to education	415	456	480
	628	730	905
Veterans benefits and services*	6,366	6,798	7,131
Service-connected compensation	2,310	2,435	2,461
Non-service-connected pensions	1,893	2,063	2,101
Readjustment benefits	282	480	611
Hospitals and medical care	1,391	1,458	1,546
Other veterans benefits and services	997	865	924
Interest*	12,548	13,535	14,400
Interest on the public debt	13,391	14,350	15,200
Interest on refunds of receipts	120	134	137
Interest on uninvested funds	13	13	12
General government*	2,452	2,618	2,827
Legislative functions	167	185	198
Judicial functions	87	95	102
Executive direction and management	25	31	35
Central fiscal operations	968	1,007	1,104
General property and records management	620	629	648
Central personnel management	191	212	218
Law enforcement and justice	426	462	529
Other general government	213	203	205
Allowances for pay increase and contingencies	—	100	1,950
Undistributed intragovernment payments	−4,022	−4,591	−5,049
Total deficit (−)	−8,823	−19,805	−7,954

Data are for years ending June 30.
*Totals reflect interfund and intragovernmental transactions and applicable receipts not shown separately.

Source: U.S. Department of Commerce, Bureau of the Census, *Statistical Abstract of the United States.* Data compiled by the Executive Office of the President, Bureau of the Budget.

Federal trust fund receipts and expenditures

in millions of dollars

Description	1960	1965	1966	1967	1968 estimate	1969 estimate
Trust fund receipts	20,342	31,047	34,853	44,725	47,814	53,839
Federal OASI trust fund	10,360	16,417	18,461	23,371	24,005	27,188
Federal disability insurance trust fund	1,062	1,241	1,616	2,332	2,838	3,655
Federal hospital insurance trust fund	—	—	916	3,089	4,278	5,018
Federal supplementary medical insurance trust fund	—	—	—	1,285	1,473	1,809
Unemployment trust fund	2,703	4,132	4,126	4,072	4,119	4,095
Railroad retirement accounts*	1,403	1,342	1,411	1,611	1,629	1,791
Federal employees funds	1,766	2,674	2,834	3,105	3,452	3,638
Highway trust funds†	2,541	3,670	3,925	4,455	4,379	4,805
Veterans life insurance funds	703	711	740	736	752	744
Other trust funds	711	1,500	1,593	1,355	1,530	1,816
Interfund transactions	−908	−638	−770	−686	−641	−720
Trust fund expenditures	21,212	29,637	34,864	38,589	43,946	46,469
Federal OASI trust fund	11,073	15,962	18,769	19,842	21,650	24,567
Federal disability insurance trust fund	561	1,498	1,937	2,071	2,268	2,617
Federal hospital insurance trust fund	—	—	64	2,612	3,452	3,947
Federal supplementary medical insurance trust fund	—	—	—	799	1,612	1,823
Unemployment trust fund	2,736	3,130	2,687	2,868	3,163	3,088
Railroad retirement accounts*	1,136	1,185	1,246	1,429	1,415	1,376
Federal employees funds	852	1,410	1,680	2,091	2,133	2,262
Highway trust funds†	2,945	4,026	3,966	3,973	4,219	4,203
Veterans life insurance funds	665	616	554	970	638	559
Federal National Mortgage Association trust fund	988	91	1,478	807	1,949	590
Other trust funds	755	1,189	1,589	1,813	2,088	2,157
Deposit funds	−78	−210	−520	—	—	—
Interfund transactions	−908	−638	−770	−686	−641	−720
Government-sponsored enterprises	484	1,379	2,184	—	—	—
Trust fund surplus (+) or deficit (−)	−870	+1,410	−12	+6,136	+3,868	+7,370

Years ending June 30.
*Beginning 1966, includes supplemental account.
†Beginning 1966, includes beautification and safety trust funds.
Source: Executive Office of the President, Bureau of the Budget, *Budget of the United States Government.*

Budget expenditures of government agencies

in millions of dollars

Agency	1967	1968 estimate	1969 estimate
Legislative branch	240	274	285
The Judiciary	88	95	102
Executive Office of the President	28	32	33
Funds appropriated to the president	4,872	5,076	5,424
Department of Agriculture	5,828	6,705	7,167
Department of Commerce	738	782	853
Department of Defense			
Military	67,466	73,695	76,657
Civil	1,310	1,378	1,343
Department of Health, Education, and Welfare	35,153	40,859	45,769
Department of Housing and Urban Development	2,793	4,551	3,216
Department of the Interior	529	779	923
Department of Justice	409	444	555
Department of Labor	3,361	3,876	3,800
Post Office Department	1,141	1,087	767
Department of State	419	428	439
Department of Transportation	5,428	5,753	6,282
Department of the Treasury			
Interest on public debt	13,231	14,212	15,065
Other	—133	249	360
Atomic Energy Commission	2,264	2,333	2,546
General Services Administration	131	389	493
National Aeronautics and Space Administration	5,423	4,803	4,573
Veterans Administration	6,846	7,139	7,382
Other independent agencies	4,870	5,185	5,127
Allowance for contingencies		100	1,950
Undistributed intragovernmental payments	—4,022	—4,591	—5,049
Total	158,414	175,635	186,062

Years ending June 30.
Source: Executive Office of the President, Bureau of the Budget, *Budget of the United States Government*.

Internal revenue collections

in millions of dollars

Type of tax	1967	1968
Corporation income tax	34,918	29,896
Individual income and employment taxes	96,329	106,338
Withheld	74,307	82,377
Not withheld	20,626	22,495
Railroad retirement	793	858
Unemployment insurance	603	607
Estate tax	2,729	2,710
Gift tax	286	372
Alcohol taxes	4,076	4,287
Distilled spirits	3,007	3,197
Wines	122	127
Beer	946	963
Tobacco taxes	2,080	2,122
Cigarettes	2,023	2,066
Cigars	56	55
Stamp taxes on documents, other instruments, and playing cards*	68	49
Manufacturers' excise taxes	5,478	5,714
Gasoline	2,933	3,031
Lubricating oils	93	92
Tires and tubes	504	489
Passenger cars, chassis, bodies, etc.	1,414	1,531
Trucks and buses, chassis, bodies, etc.	469	448
Parts and accessories for cars, trucks, etc.†	35	76
Radio and television sets, phonographs, etc.‡	—1	§
Firearms (except pistols and revolvers), shells, cartridges	28	31
Pistols and revolvers	4	5
Retailers' excise taxes‡	4	§
Toilet preparations	1	§
Jewelry	2	§
Miscellaneous excise taxes	1,732	1,859
Admissions taxes‖	3	1
Club dues and initiation fees‖	2	1
Telephone, wire, etc., and equipment services¶	1,102	1,105
Air transportation of persons	170	199
Sugar	104	102
Diesel and special motor fuels	182	202
Use tax on highway motor vehicles weighing over 26,000 lb.	108	109
Unclassified excise taxes	676	288
Total	148,375	153,637

Years ending June 30.
*Tax on playing cards and issues and transfers of stock repealed effective June 22, 1965, and January 1, 1966, respectively. Tax on foreign insurance payable by return on and after January 1, 1966. †Tax on auto parts and accessories repealed effective January 1, 1966. ‡Repealed effective June 22, 1965.
§Less than $1,000,000. ‖Repealed effective noon December 31, 1965.
¶Tax on local and toll telephone and typewriter service reduced to 3% and tax on private communications services, telegraph service, and wire equipment service repealed effective January 1, 1966. Tax on general and toll telephone service and typewriter exchange service is increased from 3% to 10% on bills paid after March 31 for services rendered after January 31.
Source: U.S. Department of the Treasury, Internal Revenue Service.

Ownership of federal securities

June 30, par value, in billions of dollars

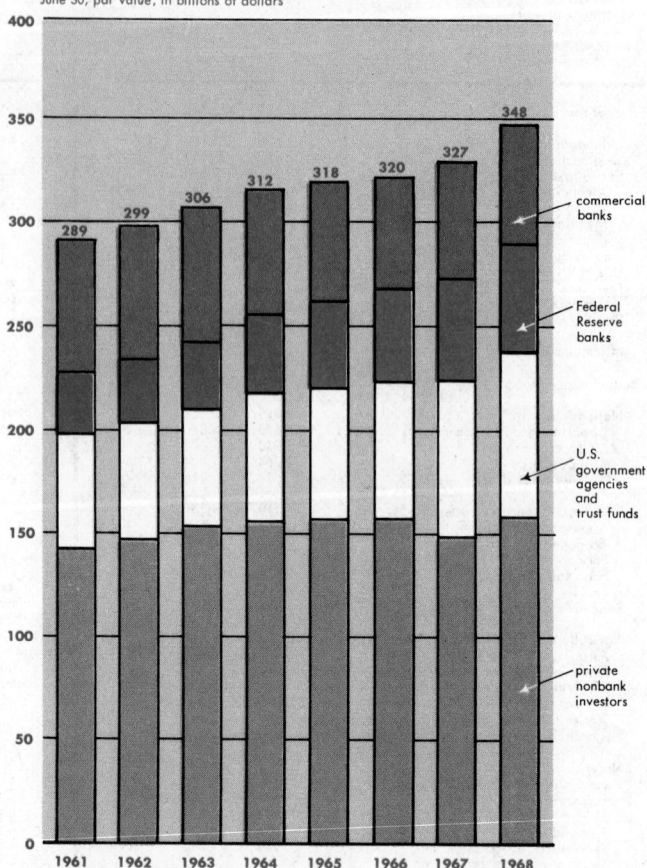

Data refer to securities issued or guaranteed by the U.S. government, excluding guaranteed securities held by the Treasury.
Source: Board of Governors of the Federal Reserve System, *Federal Reserve Bulletin*.

Debt of the federal government

	DEBT OUTSTANDING* on June 30			INTEREST PAID on public debt for fiscal year	
Year	Total in $000,000†	Per capita	Gross public debt in $000,000	Total in $000,000	Percent of federal expenditures
1900	1,263.4	$ 16.60	1,263.4	40	7.7
1905	1,132.4	13.51	1,132.4	25	4.3
1910	1,146.9	12.41	1,146.9	21	3.1
1915	1,191.3	11.85	1,191.3	23	3.0
1920	24,299.3	228.23	24,299.3	1,020	15.9
1925	20,516.2	177.12	20,516.2	882	28.8
1930	16,185.3	131.51	16,185.3	659	19.2
1935	32,823.6	257.95	28,700.9	821	12.6
1940	48,496.6	367.08	42,967.5	1,041	11.5
1945	259,115.3	1,851.70	258,682.2	3,617	3.7
1950	257,376.9	1,696.80	257,357.4	5,750	14.5
1951	255,251.2	1,654.39	255,222.0	5,613	12.7
1952	259,150.7	1,651.13	259,105.2	5,859	9.0
1953	266,123.1	1,667.80	266,071.1	6,504	8.8
1954	271,341.0	1,670.91	271,259.6	6,382	9.4
1955	274,418.4	1,660.37	274,374.2	6,370	9.9
1956	272,824.7	1,621.82	272,750.8	6,787	10.2
1957	270,634.3	1,580.12	270,527.2	7,244	10.4
1958	276,444.4	1,587.47	276,343.2	7,607	10.6
1959	284,816.9	1,606.74	284,705.9	7,593	9.4
1960	286,470.6	1,585.48	286,330.8	9,180	11.9
1961	289,211.2	1,573.89	288,970.9	8,957	10.9
1962	298,645.0	1,599.98	298,200.8	9,120	10.3
1963	306,466.2	1,617.94	305,859.6	9,895	10.6
1964	312,525.9	1,626.72	311,712.9	10,666	10.9
1965	317,864.2	1,633.63	317,273.9	11,346	11.8
1966	320,368.6	1,627.54	319,907.1	12,014	11.2
1967	326,733.1	1,640.90	326,220.9	13,391	10.7
‡1968	348,147.0	1,730.65	347,578.4	14,585§	...

*Includes certain securities not subject to statutory limitation. †Gross public debt plus guaranteed debt of U.S. government agencies held outside the Treasury. ‡1968 data were compiled on a new basis and are not strictly comparable with those before that date. §Preliminary.
Source: U.S. Department of the Treasury, *Annual Report of the Secretary of the Treasury*.

State Government

State finance

Major sources of revenue

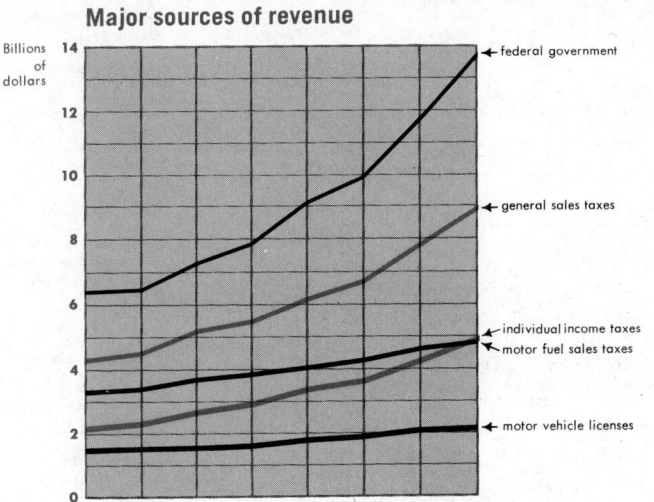

Billions of dollars

federal government
general sales taxes
individual income taxes
motor fuel sales taxes
motor vehicle licenses

1960 1961 1962 1963 1964 1965 1966 1967

Major expenditures

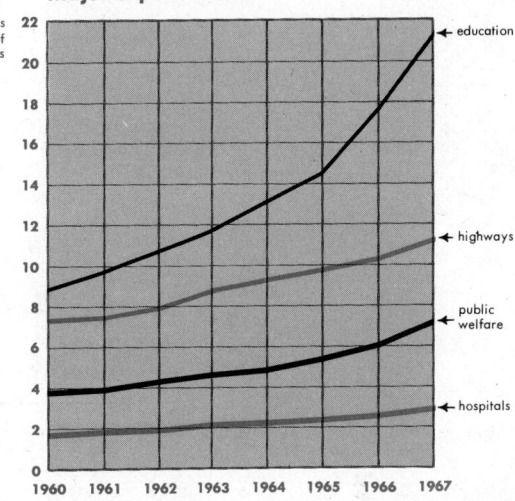

Billions of dollars

education
highways
public welfare
hospitals

1960 1961 1962 1963 1964 1965 1966 1967

Source: U.S. Department of Commerce, Bureau of the Census, *State Government Finances.*

State legislatures

State	Name of house	Composition before November 1968 election			Composition after election†		
		Total Seats*	Demo-crats	Repub-licans	Total seats*	Demo-crats	Repub-licans
Alabama‡	Senate	35	34	1	—	—	—
	House of Representatives	106	106	0	—	—	—
Alaska	Senate	20	6	14	20	9	11
	House of Representatives	40	15	25	40	22	18
Arizona	Senate	30	14	16	30	13	17
	House of Representatives	60	27	33	60	26	34
Arkansas	Senate	35	35	0	35	34	1
	House of Representatives	100	97	3	100	96	4
California	Senate	40	20	20	40	20	20
	Assembly	80	42	38	80	39	41
Colorado	Senate	35	15	20	35	11	24
	House of Representatives	65	27	38	65	27	38
Connecticut	Senate	36	25	11	177	117	60
	House of Representatives	36	24	12	177	110	67
Delaware	Senate	18	9	9	...	...	...
	House of Representatives	35	12	23	...	...	...
Florida	Senate	48	26	22	48	32	16
	House of Representatives	115	76	39	119	77	42
Georgia	Senate	54	46	8	56	49	7
	House of Representatives	205	184	21	195	168	26
Hawaii	Senate	25	15	10	25	16	9
	House of Representatives	51	39	12	51	39	12
Idaho	Senate	35	13	22	35	15	20
	House of Representatives	70	31	39	70	31	39
Illinois	Senate	58	19	37	58	20	38
	House of Representatives	177	78	99	177	83	94
Indiana	Senate	50	29	21	50	15	35
	House of Representatives	100	34	66	100	27	73
Iowa	Senate	61	32	29	61	16	44
	House of Representatives	124	34	90	124	38	86
Kansas	Senate	40	13	27	40	8	32
	House of Representatives	125	48	77	125	38	87
Kentucky	Senate	38	25	12	38	24	14
	House of Representatives	100	63	36	100	56	42
Louisiana‡	Senate	39	39	0	—	—	—
	House of Representatives	105	105	0	—	—	—
Maine	Senate	34	10	24	32	14	18
	House of Representatives	151	55	96	151	66	85
Maryland‡	Senate	43	35	8	—	—	—
	House of Delegates	142	117	25	—	—	—
Massachusetts	Senate	40	26	14	40	27	13
	House of Representatives	240	165	69	240	172	68
Michigan	Senate	38	18	19	‡	—	—
	House of Representatives	110	54	56	110	57	53
Minnesota§	Senate	67	—	—	‡	—	—
	House of Representatives	135	—	—	135	—	—
Mississippi‡	Senate	52	52	0	—	—	—
	House of Representatives	122	122	0	—	—	—
Missouri	Senate	34	23	11	34	23	11
	House of Representatives	163	109	54	163	109	54
Montana	Senate	55	30	25	55	30	25
	House of Representatives	104	40	64	104	46	58
Nebraska§	Unicameral	49	—	—	49	—	—
Nevada	Senate	20	11	9	20	11	9
	Assembly	40	21	19	40	18	22
New Hampshire	Senate	24	10	14	24	9	15
	House of Representatives	400	154	244	400	144	255
New Jersey‡	Senate	40	9	31	—	—	—
	General Assembly	80	22	58	—	—	—
New Mexico	Senate	42	25	17	‡	—	—
	House of Representatives	70	45	25	70	44	26
New York	Senate	57	26	31	57	24	33
	Assembly	150	78	70	150	72	78
North Carolina	Senate	50	43	7	50	38	12
	House of Representatives	120	94	26	120	91	29
North Dakota	Senate	49	5	43	49	7	42
	House of Representatives	98	15	83	98	18	79
Ohio	Senate	33	10	23	33	12	21
	House of Representatives	99	37	62	99	35	64
Oklahoma	Senate	48	39	9	48	38	10
	House of Representatives	99	74	25	99	76	23
Oregon	Senate	30	19	11	30	16	14
	House of Representatives	60	22	38	60	22	38
Pennsylvania	Senate	50	22	28	50	22	27
	House of Representatives	203	96	104	203	107	95
Rhode Island	Senate	50	35	15	50	36	9
	House of Representatives	100	66	33	100	74	21
South Carolina	Senate	50	43	7	46	43	3
	House of Representatives	124	107	17	124	119	5
South Dakota	Senate	35	6	29	35	8	27
	House of Representatives	75	11	64	75	15	59
Tennessee	Senate	33	25	8	33	20	13
	House of Representatives	99	58	41	99	49	49
Texas	Senate	31	29	2	31	29	2
	House of Representatives	150	142	8	150	142	8
Utah	Senate	28	5	23	28	8	20
	House of Representatives	69	10	59	69	21	48
Vermont	Senate	30	8	22	30	8	22
	House of Representatives	150	54	96	150	49	101
Virginia‡	Senate	40	34	6	—	—	—
	House of Delegates	100	85	14	—	—	—
Washington	Senate	49	29	20	49	27	22
	House of Representatives	99	44	45	99	43	56
West Virginia	Senate	34	25	9	34	28	6
	House of Delegates	100	65	35	100	63	37
Wisconsin	Senate	33	12	21	33	10	23
	Assembly	100	46	54	100	48	52
Wyoming	Senate	30	13	17	30	11	19
	House of Representatives	61	27	34	61	16	45

*The total number of seats is not always equal to the number of Democrats plus Republicans because of vacancies and seats held by independents.   †Preliminary.
‡No election held.   §Nonpartisan election.
Sources: State governments.

Executive officials

incumbents, and winners in 1968 elections

State	Governor	Lieutenant Governor	Secretary of State	Treasurer
Alabama	Albert P. Brewer(D)	(vacancy) —	Mabel Amos(D)	Agnes Baggett(D)
Alaska	Walter J. Hickel(R)	—	Keith H. Miller(R)	
Arizona	†Jack Williams(R)	—	†Wesley Bolin(D)	Charles H. Garland(R)
				*Morris Herring(R)
Arkansas	†Winthrop Rockefeller(R)	†Maurice Britt(R)	†Kelly Bryant(D)	†Nancy Hall(D)
California	Ronald Reagan(R)	Robert H. Finch(R)	Frank M. Jordan(R)	Ivy Baker Priest(R)
Colorado	John A. Love(R)	Mark A. Hogan(D)	Byron A. Anderson(R)	Virginia N. Blue(R)
Connecticut	John N. Dempsey(D)	Attilio R. Frassinelli(D)	Ella T. Grasso(D)	Gerald A. Lamb(D)
Delaware	Charles L. Terry, Jr.(D)	Sherman W. Tribbitt(D)	Elisha C. Dukes(D)	Daniel J. Ross(R)
	*Russell W. Peterson(R)	*Eugene D. Bookhammer(R)		
Florida	Claude R. Kirk, Jr.(R)	—	Tom Adams(D)	Broward Williams(D)
Georgia	Lester G. Maddox(D)	George T. Smith(D)	Ben W. Fortson, Jr.(D)	Jack B. Ray(D)
Hawaii	John A. Burns(D)	Thomas P. Gill(D)		
Idaho	Don Samuelson(R)	Jack M. Murphy(R)	Pete T. Cenarrusa(R)	Marjorie Moon(D)
Illinois	Samuel H. Shapiro(D)	(vacancy)	†Paul Powell(D)	Adlai E. Stevenson III(D)
	*Richard B. Ogilvie(R)	*Paul Simon(D)		
Indiana	Roger D. Branigin(D)	Robert L. Rock(D)	Edgar D. Whitcomb(R)	†John K. Snyder(R)
	*Edgar D. Whitcomb(R)	*Richard E. Folz(R)	*William N. Salin(R)	
Iowa	Harold E. Hughes(D)	Robert D. Fulton(D)	†Melvin D. Synhorst(R)	Paul Franzenburg(D)
	*Robert D. Ray(R)	*Roger W. Jepsen(R)		*Maurice E. Baringer(R)
Kansas	†Robert B. Docking(D)	John W. Crutcher(R)	†Mrs. Elwill M. Shanahan (R)	†Walter H. Peery(R)
		*James DeCoursey(R)		
Kentucky	Louie B. Nunn(R)	Wendell H. Ford(D)	Elmer Begley(D)	Thelma Stovall(D)
Louisiana	John J. McKeithen(D)	C. C. Aycock(D)	Wade O. Martin, Jr.(D)	Mary E. Parker(D)
Maine	Kenneth M. Curtis(D)	—	Joseph T. Edgar(R)	Michael A. Napolitano(R)
Maryland	Spiro T. Agnew(R)	—	C. Stanley Blair(R)	John A. Leutkemeyer(D)
Massachusetts	John A. Volpe(R)	Francis W. Sargent(R)	John F. X. Davoren(D)	Robert Q. Crane(D)
Michigan	George Romney(R)	William G. Milliken(R)	James M. Hare(D)	Allison Green(R)
Minnesota	Harold LeVander(R)	James B. Goetz(R)	Joseph L. Donovan(DFL)	Val Bjornson(R)
Mississippi	John B. Williams(D)	Charles L. Sullivan(D)	Heber Ladner(D)	Evelyn Gandy(D)
Missouri	†Warren E. Hearnes(D)	Thomas F. Eagleton(D)	†James Kirkpatrick(D)	M. E. Morris(D)
		*W. S. Morris(D)		*William E. Robinson(D)
Montana	Tim Babcock(R)	Ted James(R)	†Frank Murray(D)	Henry H. Anderson(D)
	*Forrest H. Anderson(D)	*Thomas L. Judge(D)		*Alex B. Stephenson(R)
Nebraska	Norbert T. Tiemann(R)	John E. Everroad(R)	Frank I. Marsh(R)	Wayne R. Swanson(R)

Party affiliations are indicated by (D) for Democrat, (R) for Republican, and (DFL) for Democratic Farmer Labor Party.
*Winner, replacing official listed immediately above.   †Incumbent re-elected.
Source: State governments; The Council of State Governments.

State government revenue, expenditure, and debt

in thousands of dollars

	FISCAL YEAR TOTALS				GENERAL REVENUE, FISCAL 1967				Liquor store revenue fiscal 1967
	Revenue		Expenditure			State	Intergov-	Charges	
State	1960	1967	1960	1967	Total	taxes	ernmental	and other	
Alabama	543,686	969,840	565,342	1,007,067	855,660	483,064	286,137	86,459	55,269
Alaska	74,646	259,481	56,109	272,309	243,250	58,169	147,326	37,755	—
Arizona	296,060	612,116	261,986	591,133	534,505	298,535	166,474	69,496	—
Arkansas	278,621	532,172	261,687	508,791	499,633	283,896	179,272	36,465	—
California	3,752,919	7,710,448	3,583,197	7,791,845	6,177,721	3,485,125	2,179,082	513,514	—
Colorado	358,008	679,206	332,201	642,508	611,743	335,715	182,229	93,799	—
Connecticut	420,958	812,969	446,898	753,687	708,142	468,154	150,374	89,614	—
Delaware	113,116	219,702	120,107	247,442	213,211	140,125	36,789	36,297	—
Florida	812,496	1,440,581	764,831	1,363,312	1,325,143	876,821	332,025	116,297	—
Georgia	613,748	1,185,757	564,300	1,140,064	1,092,022	667,847	334,617	89,558	—
Hawaii	204,980	413,548	192,088	407,140	370,982	220,111	108,469	42,402	—
Idaho	140,271	246,346	131,137	225,740	212,224	128,534	59,098	24,592	17,042
Illinois	1,452,061	2,397,620	1,362,598	2,456,060	2,175,071	1,450,326	527,322	197,423	—
Indiana	683,221	1,308,545	668,466	1,228,424	1,210,529	771,300	246,262	192,967	—
Iowa	526,688	873,969	483,789	808,517	765,733	452,762	220,331	92,640	57,694
Kansas	353,168	617,701	335,321	566,229	580,397	355,165	150,691	74,541	—
Kentucky	431,776	927,690	439,419	949,502	862,307	465,707	299,468	97,132	—
Louisiana	815,037	1,334,541	829,944	1,359,707	1,236,482	690,439	337,303	208,740	—
Maine	187,742	294,689	181,352	288,444	235,693	132,524	69,114	34,055	33,258
Maryland	524,786	1,026,993	491,234	976,205	923,754	641,433	183,910	98,411	—
Massachusetts	852,001	1,645,684	914,283	1,546,015	1,455,483	953,669	376,933	124,881	—
Michigan	1,652,216	2,924,216	1,641,812	2,891,954	2,403,820	1,530,806	568,398	304,616	232,291
Minnesota	628,990	1,229,362	631,621	1,090,132	1,128,230	660,112	316,329	151,789	—
Mississippi	339,277	638,681	350,718	602,271	577,917	307,909	207,459	62,549	28,370
Missouri	587,514	1,104,526	561,443	1,012,284	1,012,259	615,082	310,196	86,981	—
Montana	165,614	257,829	159,118	248,618	210,876	92,823	86,958	31,095	20,458
Nebraska	182,125	314,995	176,582	317,916	301,755	136,459	120,517	44,779	—
Nevada	87,239	200,561	80,186	193,881	166,654	87,236	64,800	14,618	—
New Hampshire	128,109	199,962	122,774	194,229	133,114	66,181	43,529	23,404	49,160
New Jersey	811,011	1,702,788	698,699	1,414,073	1,347,767	833,964	329,632	184,171	—
New Mexico	240,940	465,725	221,381	435,354	434,764	205,765	149,866	79,133	—
New York	3,303,310	6,895,360	3,317,205	6,455,569	5,747,420	4,056,275	1,086,495	604,650	—
North Carolina	734,712	1,366,527	643,510	1,278,989	1,244,692	840,712	287,248	116,732	—
North Dakota	154,290	240,134	155,833	242,904	227,483	86,628	67,166	73,689	—
Ohio	1,841,221	2,822,046	1,686,780	2,512,061	1,922,264	1,157,817	517,616	246,831	273,361
Oklahoma	471,373	827,688	457,316	837,249	793,819	401,030	268,006	124,783	—
Oregon	485,498	767,347	443,697	770,485	601,630	322,742	181,654	97,234	66,620
Pennsylvania	2,065,941	3,441,561	2,131,883	3,193,668	2,596,964	1,769,332	606,959	220,673	312,763
Rhode Island	158,249	287,320	153,308	323,565	237,030	143,447	66,158	27,425	—
South Carolina	381,898	673,451	329,748	618,348	611,911	395,793	148,930	67,188	—
South Dakota	121,683	196,067	117,284	193,121	190,878	83,640	71,106	36,132	—
Tennessee	517,311	962,743	494,351	956,603	889,447	514,442	314,943	60,082	—
Texas	1,419,751	2,497,414	1,304,665	2,336,966	2,308,155	1,335,847	660,764	311,544	—
Utah	209,399	398,230	191,534	397,975	347,486	175,438	123,290	48,758	20,773
Vermont	92,315	179,747	94,239	190,258	148,360	78,675	51,949	17,736	16,276
Virginia	622,126	1,227,169	576,246	1,202,064	1,031,893	634,946	263,642	133,305	129,228
Washington	829,161	1,474,522	767,069	1,354,959	1,162,892	775,641	271,316	115,935	108,105
West Virginia	364,187	610,082	345,956	614,459	507,375	281,657	176,302	49,416	40,109
Wisconsin	686,891	1,496,090	645,248	1,428,878	1,343,505	921,051	283,745	138,709	—
Wyoming	119,391	170,046	109,260	170,950	150,914	55,284	70,877	24,753	8,808
All states	32,837,660	61,081,787	31,595,755	58,610,225	52,070,959	31,926,135	14,289,076	5,855,748	1,469,585

Source: U.S. Department of Commerce, Bureau of the Census, *State Government Finances*.

State	Governor	Lieutenant Governor	Secretary of State	Treasurer
Nevada	Paul Laxalt(R)	Ed Fike(R)	John Koontz(D)	Michael Mirabelli(D)
New Hampshire	John W. King(D) / *Walter R. Peterson, Jr.(R)	—	Robert L. Stark(R)	Robert W. Flanders(R)
New Jersey	Richard J. Hughes(D)		Robert J. Burkhardt(D)	John A. Kervick(D)
New Mexico	†David F. Cargo(R)	†E. Lee Francis(R)	†Ernestine D. Evans(D)	Merrill B. Johns, Jr.(R) / *Jesse D. Kornegay(D)
New York	Nelson A. Rockefeller(R)	Malcolm Wilson(R)	John P. Lomenzo(R)	
North Carolina	Dan K. Moore(D) / *Robert W. Scott(D)	Robert W. Scott(D) / *Hoyt P. Taylor(D)	†Thad Eure(D)	†Edwin Gill(D)
North Dakota	†William L. Guy(D)	Charles Tighe(D) / *Richard F. Larsen(R)	†Ben Meier(R)	†Curtis Olson(R)
Ohio	James A. Rhodes(R)	John W. Brown(R)	Ted W. Brown(R)	John D. Herbert(R)
Oklahoma	Dewey F. Bartlett(R)	George Nigh(D)	John Rogers(D)	Leo Winters(D)
Oregon	Tom McCall(R)	—	†Clay Myers(R)	†Robert W. Straub(D)
Pennsylvania	Raymond P. Shafer(R)	Raymond J. Broderick(R)	Joseph J. Kelley, Jr.(R)	Thomas Z. Minehart(D) / *Grace M. Sloan(D)
Rhode Island	John H. Chafee(R) / *Frank Licht(D)	Joseph H. O'Donnell, Jr.(R) / *J. Joseph Garrahy(D)	†August P. LaFrance(D)	†Raymond H. Hawksley(D)
South Carolina	Robert E. McNair(D)	John C. West(D)	O. Frank Thornton(D)	Grady L. Patterson, Jr.(D)
South Dakota	Nils A. Boe(R) / *Frank L. Farrar(R)	Lem Overpeck(R) / *James Abdnor(R)	†Alma Larson(R)	Al Hamre(R) / *Neal Strand(R)
Tennessee	Buford Ellington(D)	Frank Gorrell(D)	Joe C. Carr(D)	Charles E. Worley(D)
Texas	John B. Connally(D) / *Preston Smith(D)	Preston Smith(D) / *Ben Barnes(D)	Roy Barrera(D)	†Jesse James(D)
Utah	†Calvin L. Rampton(D)	—	†Clyde L. Miller(D)	Linn C. Baker(D) / *Golden L. Allen(R)
Vermont	Philip H. Hoff(D) / *Deane C. Davis(R)	John J. Daley(D) / *Thomas W. Hayes(R)	Harry H. Cooley(D) / *Richard C. Thomas(R)	Madelyn W. Davidson(R) / *Frank H. Davis(R)
Virginia	Mills E. Godwin, Jr.(D)	Fred G. Pollard(D)	Martha B. Conway(D)	Lewis H. Vaden(D)
Washington	†Daniel J. Evans(R)	†John A. Cherberg(D)	†A. Ludlow Kramer(R)	†Robert S. O'Brien(D)
West Virginia	Hulett C. Smith(D) / *Arch A. Moore(R)	—	Robert D. Bailey(D) / *John D. Rockefeller IV(D)	†John H. Kelly(D)
Wisconsin	†Warren P. Knowles(R)	†Jack B. Olson(R)	†Robert C. Zimmerman(R)	†Harold W. Clemens(R)
Wyoming	Stanley K. Hathaway(R)	—	Thyra Thomson(R)	Minnie A. Mitchell(R)

GENERAL EXPENDITURES, FISCAL 1967					Liquor store expenditure fiscal 1967	INSURANCE TRUST FUND, FISCAL 1967				DEBT, FISCAL 1967		
							Expenditures			Gross debt outstanding at end of year	Long-term debt issued	Long-term debt retired
Total	Education	Highways	Public welfare	Hospitals		Revenue	Total	Unemployment compensation	Employee retirement			
922,139	445,889	195,831	127,605	35,223	50,367	58,911	34,561	20,206	14,350	562,246	84,853	21,843
264,353	59,358	116,071	9,547	4,573	—	16,231	7,956	6,710	1,185	153,764	43,795	2,218
551,929	233,965	153,134	37,328	9,661	—	77,611	39,204	11,547	6,766	71,361	26,525	861
487,565	192,458	126,948	82,473	21,168	—	32,539	21,226	11,397	9,824	114,239	16,193	7,881
6,769,554	2,145,461	1,105,610	1,450,728	245,961	—	1,532,727	1,022,291	462,349	265,684	4,719,061	657,090	147,580
608,512	265,069	120,333	97,779	40,695	—	67,463	33,996	9,897	12,557	125,796	10,235	6,878
701,547	217,539	155,202	102,379	57,885	—	104,827	52,140	28,467	23,634	1,295,352	116,635	36,692
239,534	112,250	40,556	16,172	10,664	—	6,491	7,908	7,414	487	368,140	53,749	20,062
1,305,833	561,971	286,858	128,755	61,237	—	115,438	57,479	18,440	38,504	893,113	119,680	21,572
1,101,082	528,434	228,982	133,821	54,374	—	93,735	38,982	17,915	21,067	728,137	168,195	31,640
386,249	176,323	41,181	23,813	17,722	—	42,566	21,192	10,280	10,912	274,890	23,355	54,860
201,057	71,157	54,868	20,751	7,164	12,559	17,080	12,124	7,436	2,923	16,275	1,300	650
2,290,586	900,105	476,331	392,336	193,663	—	222,549	165,474	78,464	86,907	1,227,320	128,258	30,612
1,169,963	609,504	278,506	56,013	73,768	—	98,016	58,461	26,574	31,835	541,273	27,070	13,380
739,668	268,439	233,525	74,589	39,907	45,511	50,542	23,338	9,113	14,224	80,827	13,985	3,570
546,787	240,990	122,317	58,394	38,747	—	37,304	19,442	9,758	9,637	256,062	6,137	2,135
915,068	351,901	256,332	122,497	34,271	—	65,383	34,434	17,387	14,635	963,808	142,295	19,023
1,308,298	497,977	276,381	214,024	79,423	—	98,059	51,409	22,246	29,163	721,487	105,064	35,335
244,768	82,916	66,150	32,130	13,005	23,812	25,738	19,864	7,728	12,136	168,009	17,860	10,848
930,173	316,563	180,166	115,406	64,590	—	103,239	46,032	24,646	18,815	891,713	140,625	64,054
1,392,911	325,927	179,973	270,916	129,033	—	190,201	153,104	90,686	62,356	1,816,435	128,895	82,111
2,531,268	1,253,506	450,437	271,102	152,082	187,923	288,105	172,763	111,368	51,102	983,278	63,371	60,098
1,043,960	466,857	253,821	114,415	62,568	—	101,132	46,172	22,263	23,785	309,914	13,016	18,732
558,792	226,456	138,646	84,034	21,621	29,516	32,394	13,963	6,811	7,138	288,519	47,555	14,793
966,086	382,341	230,456	169,477	60,086	—	92,267	46,198	31,419	14,655	141,912	17,577	6,766
214,018	76,788	77,738	15,616	7,169	17,017	26,495	17,583	5,598	8,183	77,702	7,876	6,697
309,643	92,228	109,175	36,899	23,275	—	13,240	8,273	5,934	2,331	56,117	—	9,539
167,876	59,663	53,891	11,066	2,574	—	33,907	26,005	12,526	5,933	17,909	2,955	988
149,773	47,140	45,539	13,309	9,651	38,173	17,688	6,283	2,469	3,814	141,717	29,325	8,885
1,181,768	428,414	259,543	129,277	93,287	—	355,021	232,305	111,538	90,922	1,193,393	224,100	53,990
420,202	221,688	88,132	39,753	9,053	—	30,961	15,152	6,198	8,954	142,208	26,000	9,143
5,887,562	2,473,015	737,023	864,706	438,304	—	1,147,940	568,002	308,574	180,521	4,796,050	326,500	162,449
1,223,802	630,731	251,555	99,881	66,212	—	121,835	45,187	24,649	20,526	457,015	145,266	22,601
232,241	75,408	60,293	21,496	7,716	—	12,651	10,663	4,739	1,915	31,465	6,485	1,308
1,961,583	685,798	618,458	256,290	99,956	215,889	626,421	334,589	61,603	167,350	1,149,676	109,800	83,278
813,035	302,830	162,493	206,414	31,366	—	33,869	24,214	10,196	11,129	647,142	262,667	31,420
666,613	266,490	161,142	61,377	26,854	41,078	99,097	62,794	27,588	9,589	482,491	51,300	21,367
2,674,332	1,046,115	634,805	323,531	190,387	263,506	531,834	255,830	95,834	119,572	2,119,334	290,120	101,290
288,750	80,661	65,810	47,333	21,046	—	50,290	34,815	12,504	9,437	261,842	20,211	8,791
593,019	282,645	117,954	37,445	29,499	—	61,540	25,329	13,350	11,227	308,323	100,495	30,843
191,198	65,210	66,033	19,695	6,518	—	5,189	1,923	1,581	342	21,349	2,450	297
921,461	399,532	242,299	99,216	45,623	—	73,296	35,142	23,853	11,218	283,187	77,675	13,173
2,244,626	1,075,796	578,018	278,497	103,426	—	189,259	92,340	27,542	64,785	722,692	134,361	25,170
364,309	195,854	80,855	31,407	12,210	14,980	29,971	18,686	9,872	5,500	107,576	1,769	1,047
168,293	53,479	60,616	16,128	5,597	15,834	15,111	6,131	3,610	2,521	98,994	27,860	6,912
1,064,169	425,605	320,660	48,592	77,808	112,974	66,048	24,921	8,906	16,051	266,047	3,965	15,067
1,164,991	521,501	272,633	141,218	40,622	79,177	203,525	110,791	34,085	29,564	584,239	87,973	49,907
542,018	201,529	176,644	63,436	20,603	30,316	62,598	42,125	10,376	14,495	385,976	42,014	34,905
1,364,951	532,154	209,319	113,046	68,866	—	152,585	63,927	38,234	24,677	351,853	52,614	4,800
157,178	55,818	64,805	6,071	5,873	8,218	10,324	5,554	2,272	1,341	54,780	31,089	1,166
53,155,093	21,229,308	11,284,051	7,188,163	2,972,586	1,186,850	7,541,243	4,268,282	1,934,152	1,606,142	32,472,008	4,243,569	1,419,227

Taxation

Tax collections

State	STATE TAX COLLECTIONS fiscal 1968 Total in $000,000	Per capita	FEDERAL TAX COLLECTIONS fiscal 1968 Total in $000,000	Individual income and employment tax in $000,000	Per capita*	LOCAL TAX COLLECTIONS fiscal 1967 Total in $000,000	Per capita
Alabama	532	$149.09	1,122	913	$ 453	197	$ 55.59
Alaska	60	218.06	119	108	737	27	98.16
Arizona	316	189.17	613	540	587	222	135.80
Arkansas	290	143.96	542	441	422	107	54.52
California	4,663	242.62	15,456	12,281	850	4,455	232.59
Colorado	361	176.39	1,936	1,619	674	349	176.81
Connecticut	500	168.92	3,057	2,248	1,013	503	172.10
Delaware	145	271.14	1,115	612	1,150	38	72.08
District of Columbia	—	—	†	†	1,009	275	339.80
Florida	973	157.98	2,986	2,381	645	769	128.34
Georgia	737	160.68	2,488	1,822	533	346	76.69
Hawaii	243	311.90	440	368	697	80	108.93
Idaho	137	194.03	337	291	532	77	110.16
Illinois	1,731	157.70	13,254	9,484	899	1,798	165.11
Indiana	819	161.66	3,861	2,895	710	769	153.82
Iowa	502	182.84	1,305	1,034	666	450	163.57
Kansas	357	155.03	1,067	862	642	361	158.64
Kentucky	509	157.73	2,491	933	493	214	67.07
Louisiana	740	198.40	1,524	1,213	516	265	72.34
Maine	146	149.28	411	340	588	125	128.37
Maryland	771	205.31	4,092	3,285	836	555	150.68
Massachusetts	1,033	190.06	4,755	3,571	824	1,044	192.64
Michigan	1,886	215.75	12,649	7,330	809	1,239	144.02
Minnesota	815	223.57	2,915	2,162	663	619	172.72
Mississippi	323	137.71	531	447	359	154	65.59
Missouri	657	141.99	4,315	3,175	690	583	126.66
Montana	105	$151.48	244	208	$592	117	$167.19
Nebraska	194	134.99	944	739	668	254	176.79
Nevada	104	228.54	308	248	870	82	184.68
New Hampshire	75	107.21	386	328	688	110	160.64
New Jersey	954	134.78	5,856	4,165	877	1,372	195.99
New Mexico	217	213.93	340	298	542	70	70.29
New York	4,447	245.52	30,192	20,052	919	4,339	236.63
North Carolina	900	175.30	3,567	1,743	504	285	56.63
North Dakota	101	162.33	188	166	515	84	130.99
Ohio	1,370	129.38	10,129	7,098	764	1,447	138.33
Oklahoma	428	169.78	1,564	966	568	243	97.59
Oregon	325	161.75	1,151	965	680	305	152.53
Pennsylvania	2,004	171.07	10,504	7,790	747	1,487	127.89
Rhode Island	167	182.53	775	607	764	123	137.00
South Carolina	412	153.19	830	676	446	116	447.48
South Dakota	88	133.75	200	168	488	110	163.50
Tennessee	577	145.20	1,641	1,312	515	310	79.60
Texas	1,438	131.06	6,708	4,721	607	1,152	106.03
Utah	184	177.48	405	330	559	119	116.11
Vermont	88	208.94	190	155	583	49	118.70
Virginia	732	159.16	2,513	1,669	615	449	99.10
Washington	879	268.21	2,303	1,902	751	323	104.60
West Virginia	321	177.60	560	463	509	120	66.96
Wisconsin	991	235.12	3,080	2,205	697	564	134.57
Wyoming	69	218.00	122	102	681	60	190.79
Total U.S.	36,414‡	182.94	153,637§	106,388§	723	29,315‡	148.15

*Federal tax burden as estimated by Tax Foundation, Inc. Federal tax collections data do not accurately reflect the tax burden by state.
†District of Columbia included with Maryland. ‡Data not equal to total due to rounding. §Includes some collections not allocated by state.
Sources: Tax Foundation, Inc. U.S. Department of Commerce, Bureau of the Census, *Governmental Finances* and *State Tax Collections.*
U.S. Department of the Treasury, Internal Revenue Service.

State taxes
fiscal year 1968

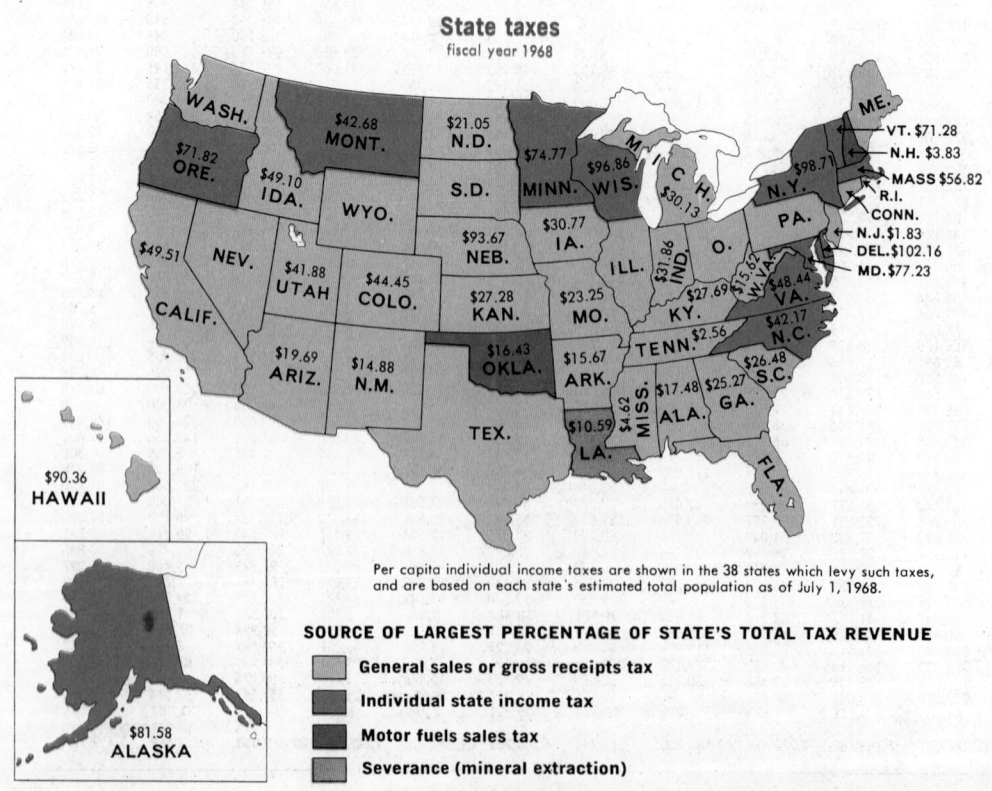

Per capita individual income taxes are shown in the 38 states which levy such taxes, and are based on each state's estimated total population as of July 1, 1968.

SOURCE OF LARGEST PERCENTAGE OF STATE'S TOTAL TAX REVENUE

- General sales or gross receipts tax
- Individual state income tax
- Motor fuels sales tax
- Severance (mineral extraction)

Source: U.S. Department of Commerce, Bureau of the Census, *State Tax Collections in 1968.*

Living Conditions

Income and Expenditures

Personal consumption expenditures

in billions of dollars

Type of expenditure	1960	1965	1967
Food, beverages, tobacco	87.5	107.2	118.6
Clothing, accessories, personal care	38.3	50.9	59.2
Housing	46.3	63.5	70.9
Household operation	46.9	61.8	69.9
Medical care expenses	19.1	28.1	34.0
Personal business	15.0	21.9	26.7
Transportation	43.1	58.2	63.6
Recreation	18.3	26.3	30.6
Private education and research	3.7	5.9	7.8
Religious and welfare activities	4.7	6.0	6.9
Foreign travel and other, net	2.2	3.1	4.0
Total	325.2	432.8	492.2

Source: U.S. Department of Commerce, Office of Business Economics, *Survey of Current Business.*

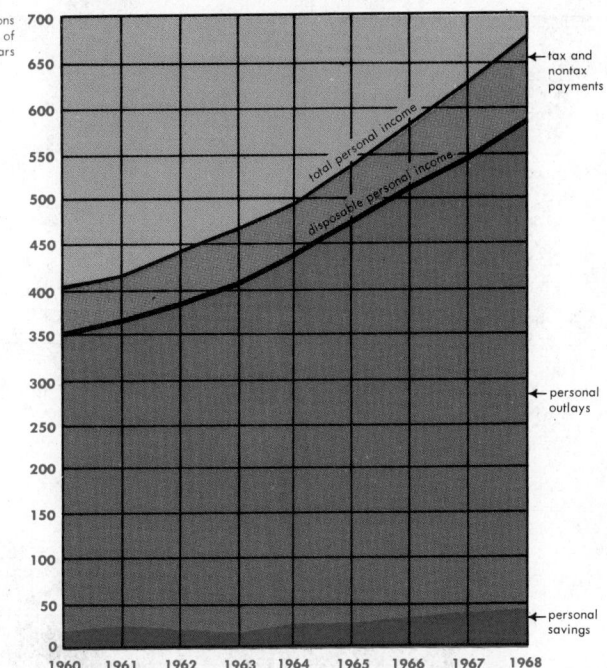

Disposition of personal income

1968 data are for the second quarter, seasonally adjusted at annual rates.
Source: U.S. Department of Commerce, Office of Business Economics, *Survey of Current Business.*

Major sources of personal income, 1967

in millions of dollars

State	Personal income total	WAGE AND SALARY DISBURSEMENTS Total	Farms	Mining	Contract construction	Manufacturing	Wholesale and retail trade	Finance, insurance, and real estate	Transportation	Communications and public utilities	Services	Government	Other labor income	Proprietors' income	Property income	Transfer payments	Less: personal contributions for social insurance
Alabama	7,656	5,259	35	52	288	1,654	753	201	200	142	599	1,321	286	750	868	744	250
Alaska	1,017	854	1	27	82	41	90	18	41	31	66	451	29	64	59	42	32
Arizona	4,444	2,987	60	113	201	562	504	136	106	104	391	802	148	433	604	408	136
Arkansas	4,130	2,433	65	30	178	712	395	97	124	78	265	478	141	642	548	496	129
California	70,204	47,753	616	284	2,523	12,873	7,938	2,209	2,091	1,415	6,431	11,255	2,474	6,154	9,987	6,352	2,515
Colorado	6,191	4,163	72	107	274	726	742	196	214	139	516	1,170	188	670	835	530	195
Connecticut	11,609	7,996	23	7	444	3,672	1,154	449	200	202	916	912	496	846	1,905	728	361
Delaware	1,905	1,246	5	1	82	542	162	44	41	26	127	216	76	135	376	118	46
Dist. of Columbia	3,336	2,203	—	*	66	76	225	81	48	62	447	1,178	67	130	582	463	110
Florida	17,101	10,677	174	56	777	1,810	2,141	603	569	319	1,694	2,489	494	1,554	3,036	1,844	505
Georgia	11,458	8,113	47	37	420	2,343	1,414	373	433	229	817	1,968	413	1,186	1,264	866	384
Hawaii	2,415	1,787	67	*	140	140	261	85	83	49	226	731	70	180	317	141	80
Idaho	1,800	1,054	35	25	73	210	198	39	52	39	136	243	55	352	238	160	59
Illinois	40,850	27,827	67	208	1,686	10,222	5,045	1,391	1,503	747	3,198	3,725	1,619	3,770	6,200	2,766	1,332
Indiana	15,980	11,088	29	59	674	5,138	1,627	402	461	278	858	1,552	695	1,658	1,930	1,117	509
Iowa	8,558	4,646	66	23	308	1,507	867	214	201	142	473	830	255	1,787	1,422	708	260
Kansas	6,961	4,178	34	75	232	1,161	741	173	281	132	430	909	226	1,048	1,149	579	218
Kentucky	7,737	4,996	48	170	332	1,497	756	172	253	135	477	1,149	266	1,065	777	777	242
Louisiana	8,995	5,878	38	409	600	1,135	1,001	238	399	183	650	1,209	310	945	1,342	793	272
Maine	2,585	1,667	21	1	91	606	258	58	57	45	158	365	92	256	382	274	86
Maryland	12,595	9,261	20	13	571	1,994	1,460	404	384	261	1,205	2,934	418	944	1,556	856	439
Massachusetts	19,197	13,141	23	9	689	4,569	2,219	735	442	371	1,964	2,082	760	1,282	2,936	1,708	631
Michigan	29,151	20,424	51	98	1,096	9,570	2,953	650	607	532	1,955	2,888	1,334	2,403	3,841	2,041	893
Minnesota	11,162	7,242	35	111	511	2,111	1,410	355	408	196	909	1,182	399	1,372	1,544	964	360
Mississippi	4,453	2,670	46	39	173	796	390	97	88	82	304	644	150	780	519	457	125
Missouri	13,775	8,845	58	53	501	2,786	1,629	425	563	268	995	1,555	492	1,584	2,061	1,235	443
Montana	1,939	1,125	40	42	87	143	200	39	90	41	117	323	55	360	286	179	66
Nebraska	4,422	2,343	37	10	154	479	459	140	165	76	284	531	114	942	797	355	130
Nevada	1,591	1,181	10	28	76	50	168	40	52	41	467	247	45	111	209	99	54
New Hampshire	2,094	1,438	7	2	90	577	208	58	33	41	165	253	85	157	306	178	70
New Jersey	25,686	18,224	40	31	1,064	7,053	2,984	839	958	507	2,211	2,505	1,094	1,855	3,594	1,807	888
New Mexico	2,484	1,683	20	120	104	109	241	60	68	67	299	593	69	293	304	211	76
New York	68,916	45,332	66	83	2,081	13,101	7,920	3,632	2,468	1,422	6,930	7,550	2,502	5,466	11,840	5,870	2,094
North Carolina	12,267	8,439	83	21	454	3,151	1,283	318	344	183	783	1,805	456	1,469	1,384	916	397
North Dakota	1,589	810	21	12	54	44	176	32	44	33	104	287	33	386	261	148	50
Ohio	33,605	23,462	42	156	1,343	10,504	3,606	827	1,007	574	2,237	3,135	1,533	2,736	4,496	2,545	1,167
Oklahoma	6,594	4,059	30	312	199	733	669	172	210	130	410	1,187	202	800	1,029	704	201
Oregon	6,122	3,974	50	13	254	1,132	759	172	246	126	416	797	229	765	793	557	197
Pennsylvania	37,065	25,038	52	295	1,367	10,366	3,658	1,012	1,154	739	2,753	3,614	1,517	3,140	5,357	3,272	1,259
Rhode Island	2,995	2,076	4	2	120	758	316	93	53	53	220	454	115	198	435	283	112
South Carolina	5,752	4,091	25	9	243	1,563	504	133	108	86	383	1,030	223	600	591	438	191
South Dakota	1,745	818	17	15	45	90	175	37	31	31	112	262	35	494	284	164	49
Tennessee	9,316	6,255	35	37	346	2,249	1,039	253	287	111	681	1,207	356	1,067	1,111	835	307
Texas	29,822	19,639	199	842	1,319	4,373	3,590	907	998	592	2,267	4,520	990	3,311	4,575	2,228	921
Utah	2,667	1,861	12	79	96	327	316	69	120	54	185	601	89	255	352	211	101
Vermont	1,178	755	8	6	57	261	108	28	25	21	118	121	44	132	171	110	35
Virginia	12,719	9,348	42	82	529	1,931	1,290	349	434	217	979	3,481	395	943	1,544	919	430
Washington	10,871	7,330	61	15	500	2,182	1,234	317	384	158	745	1,715	392	1,201	1,374	889	316
West Virginia	4,197	2,803	7	324	175	878	369	72	149	120	233	459	178	323	518	510	136
Wisconsin	13,220	8,562	46	21	526	3,604	1,342	311	314	216	827	1,342	519	1,571	1,941	1,060	433
Wyoming	946	569	20	68	44	45	84	18	46	22	52	170	25	150	153	77	29
Total U.S.	625,068	419,599	2,712	4,648	24,339	134,157	69,031	19,769	19,636	11,868	50,185	82,429	23,250	60,715	90,085	51,737	20,318

Data not equal to total due to rounding.   *Less than $500,000.   Source: U.S. Department of Commerce, Office of Business Economics, *Survey of Current Business.*

Family income levels

by region

1967 INCOME LEVEL	North-east	North central	South	West	Total U.S.
	(Percent distribution)				
Under $1,000	1.4	1.5	3.1	1.7	2.0
$1,000 to $1,999	3.1	3.9	6.8	2.7	4.4
$2,000 to $2,999	4.6	5.4	8.1	4.8	5.9
$3,000 to $3,999	5.5	5.6	8.1	5.4	6.3
$4,000 to $4,999	5.5	5.9	8.2	5.9	6.5
$5,000 to $5,999	7.3	7.1	9.1	7.1	7.7
$6,000 to $6,999	8.7	8.5	8.3	7.6	8.3
$7,000 to $7,999	9.5	9.5	8.1	8.2	8.8
$8,000 to $8,999	8.6	8.9	7.5	8.3	8.3
$9,000 to $9,999	7.6	8.0	5.7	7.1	7.1
$10,000 to $11,999	12.6	12.8	9.9	12.8	11.9
$12,000 to $14,999	11.7	11.1	7.9	12.9	10.6
$15,000 to $24,999	11.1	9.6	7.1	12.3	9.7
$25,000 and over	2.9	2.1	2.1	3.0	2.5
MEDIAN INCOME	$8,530	$8,296	$6,823	$8,808	$8,017

Data do not total 100 percent, due to rounding.
Source: U.S. Department of Commerce, Bureau of the Census, *Current Population Reports.*

Average employee earnings

June figures

Industry	AVERAGE WEEKLY EARNINGS 1967	1968	AVERAGE HOURLY EARNINGS 1967	1968
MANUFACTURING	$114.49	$123.30	$2.82	$3.00
Durable goods	122.89	132.92	2.99	3.18
Ordnance and accessories	128.74	134.37	3.14	3.23
Lumber and wood products	96.63	106.30	2.38	2.58
Furniture and fixtures	93.09	101.52	2.31	2.47
Stone, clay, and glass products	117.46	127.62	2.81	3.01
Primary metal industries	136.12	150.10	3.32	3.54
Fabricated metal products	122.36	132.62	2.97	3.15
Nonelectrical machinery	134.51	141.37	3.18	3.35
Electrical equipment and supplies	111.48	118.15	2.78	2.91
Transportation equipment	141.17	155.55	3.41	3.66
Instruments and related products	117.42	120.88	2.85	2.97
Nondurable goods	101.63	109.47	2.56	2.73
Food and kindred products	108.50	115.36	2.64	2.80
Tobacco manufactures	94.80	102.31	2.40	2.63
Textile mill products	82.82	90.69	2.03	2.18
Apparel and related products	72.52	80.30	2.02	2.20
Paper and allied products	122.41	130.59	2.86	3.03
Printing and publishing	124.86	132.94	3.26	3.48
Chemicals and allied products	128.65	136.27	3.10	3.26
Petroleum and coal products	152.72	158.90	3.56	3.73
Rubber and plastics products	109.03	121.64	2.64	2.91
Leather and leather products	79.28	87.36	2.07	2.24
NONMANUFACTURING				
Metal mining	137.80	151.64	3.25	3.40
Coal mining	154.01	156.11	3.72	3.78
Oil and gas extraction	125.88	135.79	2.99	3.18
Contract construction	153.95	164.74	4.03	4.29
Local and suburban transportation	117.32	124.36	2.78	2.94
Telephone communication	113.87	121.70	2.89	3.05
Electric, gas, and sanitary services	141.66	149.09	3.43	3.61
Wholesale trade	115.66	122.92	2.87	3.05
Retail trade	71.56	75.82	2.01	2.16
Hotels, tourist courts, and motels	56.36	59.37	1.54	1.64

Source: U.S. Department of Commerce, Office of Business Economics, *Survey of Current Business.*

Median family income

by year of school completed by head of family, 1966

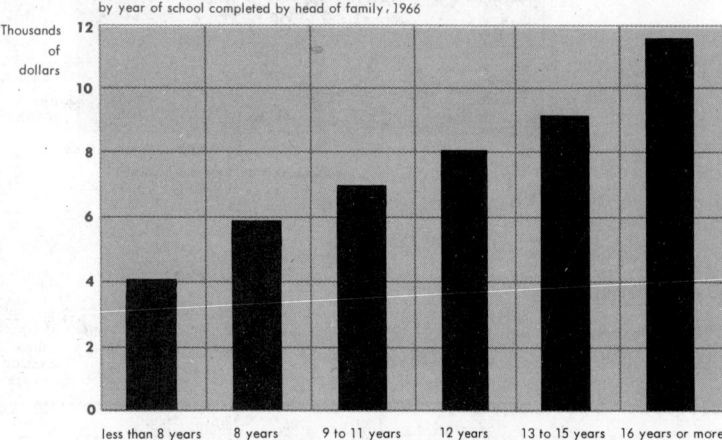

Thousands of dollars

less than 8 years — 8 years — 9 to 11 years — 12 years — 13 to 15 years — 16 years or more

Number of families = 48,922,000

Source: U.S. Department of Commerce, Bureau of the Census, *Current Population Reports.*

Employment

Trends in the labor force

persons 16 years of age and over

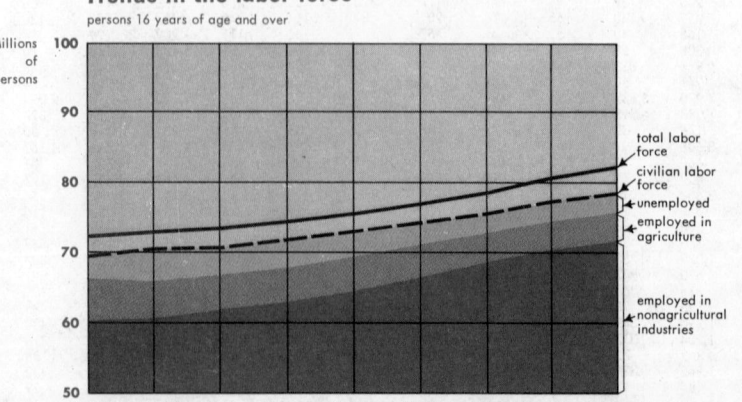

Millions of persons

total labor force
civilian labor force
unemployed
employed in agriculture
employed in nonagricultural industries

1960 1961 1962 1963 1964 1965 1966 1967 1968*

*Average of first three quarters only.
Source: U.S. Department of Labor, Bureau of Labor Statistics, *Employment and Earnings.*

Labor force by age and sex

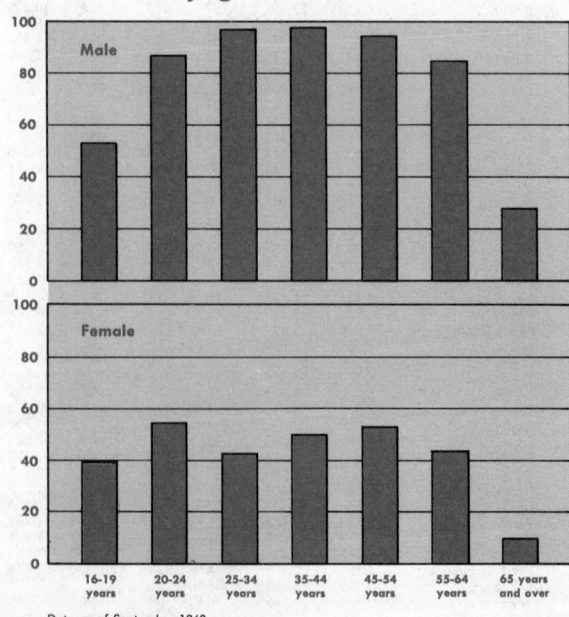

Percent

Male

Female

16-19 years — 20-24 years — 25-34 years — 35-44 years — 45-54 years — 55-64 years — 65 years and over

Data as of September 1968.
Source: U.S. Department of Labor, Bureau of Labor Statistics, *Employment and Earnings.*

Nonagricultural employment

in thousands, July 1968

State	Total	Mining	Contract construction	Manufacturing	Transportation and public utilities	Wholesale and retail trade	Finance, insurance, and real estate	Services	Government
Alabama	961	8	53	302	55	182	41	126	190
Alaska	90	3	9	12	8	12	2	10	33
Arizona	465	18	26	85	27	104	24	76	106
Arkansas	519	5	36	160	30	102	21	71	94
California	6,614	33	301	1,622	454	1,415	338	1,149	1,301
Colorado	680	13	37	107	49	160	35	118	160
Connecticut	1,157	*	57	474	49	209	67	162	137
Delaware	203	†	15	73	11	39	9	27	28
District of Columbia‡	692	†	19	21	31	83	33	125	379
Florida	1,851	9	139	290	134	482	112	334	351
Georgia	1,432	7	83	446	99	296	68	162	270
Hawaii	264	†	20	32	20	58	15	47	70
Idaho	194	4	11	35	14	46	7	30	46
Illinois	4,282	25	201	1,382	285	927	223	653	585
Indiana	1,805	8	101	712	97	348	71	197	271
Iowa	867	4	48	221	52	208	40	134	161
Kansas	671	11	41	145	53	149	28	97	147
Kentucky	850	28	53	232	61	174	34	115	152
Louisiana	1,040	53	93	180	95	228	45	145	201
Maine	332	†	18	119	17	64	12	43	59
Maryland‡	1,240	2	89	282	82	276	64	219	225
Massachusetts	2,212	†	100	683	104	465	122	443	295
Michigan	2,821	14	68	1,096	145	548	105	379	467
Minnesota	1,256	16	75	319	86	296	60	192	212
Mississippi	546	6	33	172	28	101	19	64	122
Missouri	1,624	9	76	464	125	352	87	248	263
Montana	201	6	13	25	19	47	7	30	53
Nebraska	454	2	25	83	37	111	27	74	94
Nevada	181	4	10	7	12	33	6	74	34
New Hampshire	260	§	13	98	9	47	10	52	30
New Jersey	2,471	3	124	861	167	501	110	366	339
New Mexico	279	16	20	18	20	58	11	53	83
New York	7,036	10	280	1,865	491	1,405	559	1,292	1,135
North Carolina	1,607	4	98	668	85	287	63	185	217
North Dakota	154	2	10	9	12	43	7	28	43
Ohio	3,717	20	165	1,430	219	729	146	508	500
Oklahoma	728	43	38	123	53	161	35	102	174
Oregon	679	2	35	174	50	155	33	103	126
Pennsylvania	4,245	41	204	1,566	266	770	180	649	567
Rhode Island	340	†	17	124	14	66	15	52	52
South Carolina	764	2	49	324	33	127	26	76	126
South Dakota	172	2	11	16	10	46	7	30	50
Tennessee	1,237	7	71	440	62	232	51	157	216
Texas	3,448	109	215	713	252	802	176	545	636
Utah	342	12	15	55	24	74	13	51	98
Vermont	146	1	10	44	7	26	5	30	23
Virginia‡	1,388	16	96	357	96	281	62	197	282
Washington	1,095	2	60	287	73	237	55	158	222
West Virginia	512	48	26	132	42	90	15	63	95
Wisconsin	1,476	3	71	511	76	310	58	212	235
Wyoming	110	10	8	7	10	24	4	17	29
Total U.S.‖	68,327	652	3,498	19,729	4,394	14,112	3,407	10,687	11,848

*Combined with construction. †Combined with services.
‡Federal employment in Maryland and Virginia sectors of the Washington Standard
 Metropolitan Statistical Area is included in data for District of Columbia.
§Less than 1,000.
‖Totals differ from the sum of the state figures because methods of computation vary.
 Source: U.S. Department of Labor, Bureau of Labor Statistics, *Employment and Earnings.*

Unemployment trends

quarterly averages, seasonally adjusted

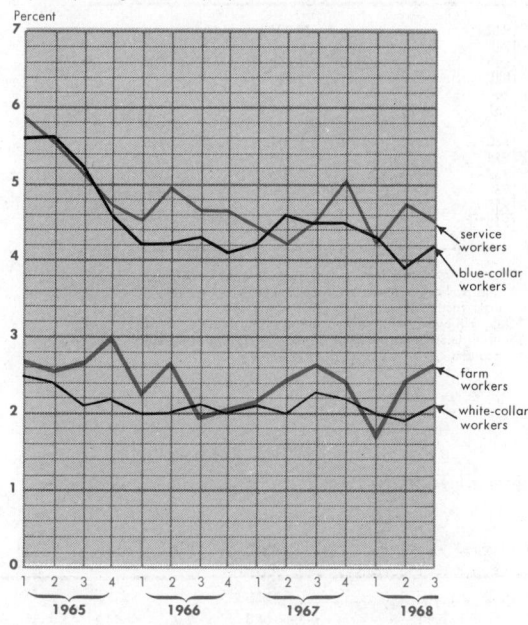

Source: U.S. Department of Labor, Bureau of Labor Statistics,
Monthly Labor Review.

Public employment, 1967

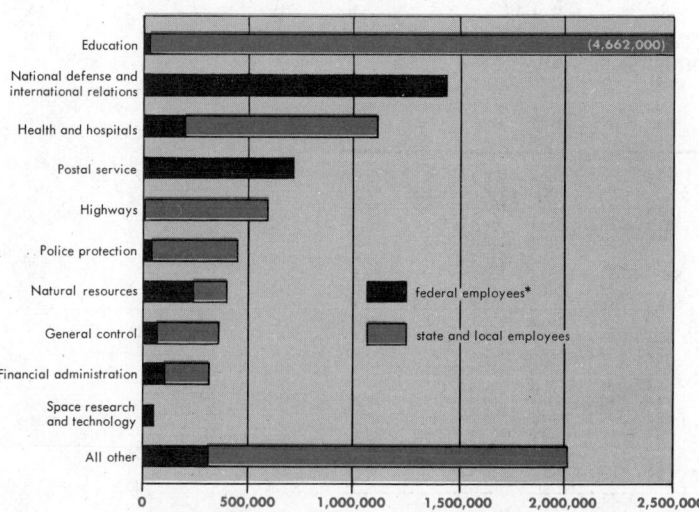

*Civilian employees only, including those outside the United States.
Source: U.S. Department of Commerce, Bureau of the Census, *Public Employment.*

Labor union membership

membership in the United States, by year

Year	Total union membership in 000	TOTAL LABOR FORCE Total in 000	TOTAL LABOR FORCE Percent union members	NON-AGRICULTURAL EMPLOYEES Total in 000	NON-AGRICULTURAL EMPLOYEES Percent union members
1930	3,401	50,080	6.8	29,424	11.6
1940	8,717	56,180	15.5	32,376	26.9
1950	14,267	64,749	22.0	45,222	31.5
1955	16,802	68,896	24.4	50,675	33.2
1960	17,049	72,142	23.6	54,234	31.4
1961	16,303	73,031	22.3	54,042	30.2
1962	16,586	73,442	22.6	55,596	29.8
1963	16,524	74,571	22.2	56,702	29.2
1964	16,841	75,830	22.2	58,332	28.9
1965	17,299	77,178	22.4	60,770	28.5
1966	17,940	78,893	22.7	63,864	28.1

membership by largest unions

Union	1962	1964	1966
Teamsters (Independent)	1,457,000	1,507,000	1,651,000
Automobile workers	1,074,000	1,168,000	1,403,000
Steelworkers	879,000	965,000	1,068,000
Electrical (IBEW)	793,000	806,000	875,000
Machinists	868,000	808,000	836,000
Carpenters	739,000	760,000	800,000
Retail clerks	364,000	428,000	500,000
Laborers	429,000	432,000	475,000
Ladies' garment workers	441,000	442,000	455,000
Hotel and restaurant workers	445,000	445,000	450,000

Unions not identified as Independent are affiliated with the AFL-CIO.
Source: U.S. Department of Labor, Bureau of Labor Statistics.

Prices

Purchasing power of the dollar
1957-59 = $1.00

Year	Wholesale prices	Consumer prices
1940	$2.326	$2.048
1945	1.727	1.595
1950	1.152	1.194
1955	1.073	1.071
1960	.993	.971
1961	.997	.960
1962	.994	.949
1963	.997	.937
1964	.995	.925
1965	.976	.910
1966	.945	.884
1967	.943	.860
1968*	.924	.835

Prior to 1961, wholesale prices exclude data for Alaska
and Hawaii; prior to 1964, consumer prices exclude
data for those states.
*Data are average of first six months only.
Source: U.S. Department of Commerce, Office of Business
Economics, *Survey of Current Business.*

Medical care prices
1957-59 = 100

Year	PROFESSIONAL SERVICES					Drugs and prescrip-tions	Hospital daily service charges	Total medical care
	Physi-cians' fees	Obstet-rical case	Tonsil-lectomy and adenoid-ectomy	Dentists' fees	Optometric examina-tion and eye-glasses			
1940	54.5	43.6	55.8	53.5	70.8	69.3	25.4	50.3
1945	63.3	54.3	65.5	63.3	77.8	73.2	32.5	57.5
1950	76.0	67.7	81.5	81.5	89.5	86.6	57.8	73.4
1955	90.0	90.8	92.7	93.1	93.8	92.7	83.0	88.6
1960	106.0	105.0	107.9	104.7	103.7	102.3	112.7	108.1
1961	108.7	107.3	110.0	105.2	107.0	101.1	121.3	111.3
1962	111.9	110.7	112.5	108.0	108.6	99.6	129.8	114.2
1963	114.4	112.5	115.3	111.1	109.3	98.7	138.0	117.0
1964	117.3	115.2	118.7	114.0	110.7	98.4	144.9	119.4
1965	121.5	117.8	122.2	117.6	113.0	98.1	153.3	122.3
1966	128.5	123.0	127.5	121.4	116.1	98.4	168.0	127.7
1967	137.6	132.3	134.3	127.5	121.8	97.9	200.1	136.7

Prior to 1964, data exclude Alaska and Hawaii.
Source: U.S. Department of Commerce, Bureau of the Census, *Statistical Abstract of the United States.*
Data compiled by the U.S. Department of Labor, Bureau of Labor Statistics, *Price Indexes for
Selected Items and Groups, Annual Averages.*

Retail food prices
in cents per pound, except as indicated

Commodity and unit	1940	1950	1960	1965	1968
Cereals and bakery products					
Flour, wheat	4.3	9.8	11.1	11.6	11.8
Corn flakes (12 oz.)	10.7	18.5	25.8	28.9	31.3
Bread, white	8.0	14.3	20.3	20.9	22.0
Meats, poultry, and fish					
Steak, round	36.4	93.6	105.5	108.4	113.5
Hamburger	...	56.6	52.4	50.8	55.1
Pork chops, center cut	27.9	75.4	85.8	97.3	103.2
Bacon, sliced	27.3	63.7	65.5	81.3	81.0
Frying chickens	...	59.5	42.7	39.0	41.5
Ocean perch, fillet, frozen	...	...	47.4	52.7	53.7
Dairy products					
Milk, fresh (grocery)	11.5	19.3	24.7	23.6	26.3
Butter	36.0	72.9	74.9	75.4	83.4
Cheese, Am. process	25.9	51.8	68.6	75.4	87.8
Fruits and vegetables					
Apples	5.2	12.0	16.2*	17.8	22.2
Oranges, size 200 (doz.)	29.1	49.3	74.8	77.8	93.5
Potatoes	2.4	4.6	7.2	9.4	6.8
Tomatoes	...	24.3	31.6	34.3	43.6
Peas, green, can	13.6	...	20.7	23.7	24.6
Other					
Eggs, Grade A, large (doz.)	33.1	60.4	57.3	52.7	47.8
Margarine	15.9	30.8	26.9	27.9	28.2
Sugar	5.2	9.7	11.6	11.8	12.1
Coffee†	21.2	79.4	75.3	83.3	75.9

Prior to 1965, data exclude Alaska and Hawaii.
*11-month average.   †Beginning 1960, vacuum-pack can only.
Source: U.S. Department of Commerce, Bureau of the Census, *Statistical Abstract of
the United States.* Data compiled by the U.S. Department of Labor, Bureau of Labor
Statistics, *Retail Food Prices by Cities* and *Estimated Retail Food Prices by Cities.*

Consumer prices in selected cities, 1967
1957-59 = 100, except as noted

Standard Metropolitan Statistical Area	Food	Hous-ing	Apparel and upkeep	Medical care	Transpor-tation	All items
Average*	115.2	114.3	114.0	136.7	115.9	116.3
Atlanta	114.2	114.7	117.2	132.2	112.9	115.0
Baltimore	116.3	113.8	116.5	149.6	115.6	116.1
Boston	119.4	120.7	114.0	137.3	119.1	119.8
Chicago†	115.4	111.1	109.9	144.7	112.6	113.6
Cincinnati	112.5	108.7	114.9	141.2	114.8	113.5
Cleveland	111.4	108.6	111.8	143.7	116.1	112.9
Detroit	114.1	109.4	113.5	144.7	114.4	114.9
Honolulu‡	108.3	111.2	105.8	114.4	100.7	107.8
Houston	115.8	110.9	110.5	126.9	113.4	114.4
Kansas City	117.9	112.9	117.0	143.8	119.1	118.7
Los Angeles–Long Beach	114.1	119.7	113.6	134.1	121.0	117.6
Milwaukee	114.5	109.5	111.6	130.9	113.3	112.9
Minneapolis–St. Paul	113.0	113.5	112.5	146.0	117.2	115.9
New York†	115.7	118.1	118.3	138.5	117.1	119.0
Philadelphia	114.5	114.5	120.3	140.6	121.9	116.8
Pittsburgh	111.2	113.5	115.0	144.0	117.0	115.0
St. Louis	119.0	111.6	114.7	132.9	117.9	116.8
San Diego§	107.6	104.6	102.0	113.8	104.2	105.1
San Francisco–Oakland	114.7	122.9	118.0	139.0	115.8	119.0
Seattle	114.6	117.6	115.7	131.3	118.6	117.5
Washington, D.C.	115.9	113.6	117.6	150.7	115.2	116.5

Indexes measure time-to-time changes in prices. They do not indicate whether it costs
more to live in one area than in another.
*1967; 56 cities.
†Standard Consolidated Area.
‡December 1963 = 100.   §February 1965 = 100.
Source: U.S. Department of Commerce, Bureau of the Census, *Statistical Abstract
of the United States.* Data compiled by U.S. Department of Labor, Bureau of
Labor Statistics, *Monthly Labor Review.*

Consumer prices by commodity groups
1957-59 = 100

Commodity	1950	1955	1960	1965	1967	1968*
Food	85.8	94.0	101.4	108.8	115.2	118.0
Food away from home	...	91.8	105.5	117.8	129.6	134.1
Food at home	85.8	94.4	100.6	107.2	112.3	114.8
Housing	83.2	94.1	103.1	108.5	114.3	117.4
Rent	79.1	94.8	103.1	108.9	112.4	114.2
Home ownership	...	92.6	103.7	111.4	120.2	124.1
Fuel and utilities	...	92.8	104.5	107.2	109.0	109.9
Household furnishings and operation	...	97.3	101.5	103.1	108.2	111.8
Apparel and upkeep	90.1	95.9	102.2	106.8	114.0	117.9
Transportation	79.0	89.7	103.8	111.1	115.9	119.0
Private	82.6	89.9	103.2	109.7	113.9	116.7
Public	64.6	89.0	107.0	121.4	132.1	136.9
Health and recreation	...	91.4	105.4	115.6	123.8	128.4
Medical care	73.4	88.6	108.1	122.3	136.7	142.9
Personal care	78.9	90.0	104.1	109.9	115.5	118.7
Reading and recreation	89.3	92.1	104.9	115.2	120.1	124.2
Other goods and services	82.6	94.3	103.8	111.4	118.2	122.5
All items	83.8	93.3	103.1	109.9	116.3	119.7

Prior to 1960, data exclude Alaska and Hawaii.   *6-month average.
Sources: U.S. Dept. of Commerce, Bureau of the Census, *Statistical Abstract of the
United States*; U.S. Dept. of Labor, Bureau of Labor Statistics, *Monthly Labor Review.*

Housing

Homes with selected electrical appliances
number of homes in millions

	1953		1960		1965		1967		1968	
Product	Number	Percent	Number	Percent	Number	Percent	Number	Percent	Number	Percent
Total number of wired homes	42.3	100.0	50.6	100.0	56.4	100.0	58.8	100.0	60.1	100.0
Air conditioners, room	0.6	1.3	6.5	12.8	11.4	20.2	17.6	29.9	22.0	36.7
Bed coverings	3.6	8.6	10.8	21.3	18.3	32.4	22.8	38.7	25.4	42.3
Blenders	1.5	3.5	3.8	7.5	6.2	11.0	9.4	16.0	12.0	20.0
Can openers	...	...	...	...	11.1	19.7	17.5	29.8	20.7	34.5
Coffee makers	21.6	51.0	27.0	53.4	38.6	68.5	44.7	76.0	47.8	79.6
Dishwashers	1.3	3.0	3.2	6.3	6.7	11.8	9.2	15.7	10.9	18.1
Dryers, clothes*	1.5	3.6	9.0	17.8	13.7	24.2	17.9	30.5	20.8	34.6
Food disposers	1.4	3.3	4.8	9.5	7.0	12.5	9.4	15.9	10.8	18.0
Freezers	4.9	11.5	11.2	22.1	13.1	23.2	15.1	25.7	16.3	27.2
Fry pans	...	...	20.6	40.7	26.2	46.4	29.6	50.3	31.1	51.8
Irons	37.9	89.6	44.9	88.6	55.4	98.3	58.4	99.3	59.6	99.3
Mixers	12.6	29.7	27.0	53.4	39.7	70.4	44.7	76.0	47.1	78.5
Radios	43.7	96.2	50.0	96.1	55.2	97.9	58.6	99.5	59.8	99.5
Ranges										
Free-standing	}10.2	}24.1	{14.5	28.7	17.0	30.1	19.1	32.4	20.5	34.1
Built-in			2.7	5.3	5.9	10.5	7.2	12.2	7.7	12.9
Refrigerators	37.8	89.2	49.6	98.0	55.5	98.3	58.6	99.6	59.9	99.7
Television										
Black and white	19.8	46.7	45.5	89.9	53.1	94.1	57.6	97.8	58.9	98.1
Color	—	—	...	...	2.9	5.1	8.8	15.0	15.7	26.2
Toasters	30.0	70.9	40.2	79.4	45.8	81.1	50.8	86.3	52.6	87.6
Vacuum cleaners	25.1	59.4	36.7	72.5	45.8	81.2	53.3	90.6	55.3	92.0
Washers, clothes	32.2	76.2	47.1	93.1	45.0	79.7	51.9	88.2	56.6	94.3

Data as of January 1. *Includes gas dryers.
Source: U.S. Department of Commerce, Bureau of the Census, *Statistical Abstract of the United States.*
Data from *Merchandising Week.*

New private one-family homes sold, or for sale
in thousands of units

	HOMES SOLD DURING MONTH*			HOMES FOR SALE AT END OF MONTH*		
Year and month	Total in 000	Median sale price	Median number of months start to sale	Total in 000	Median intended sale price	Median number of months from start of construction
1967						
January	29	$22,000	4.1	188	$22,800	6.0
February	32	22,400	4.5	185	22,400	6.1
March	41	22,500	3.4	185	22,400	5.9
April	44	22,300	3.1	184	22,500	5.4
May	49	24,000	3.1	182	22,600	4.8
June	47	23,700	3.3	184	22,600	3.9
July	46	23,400	3.3	183	22,400	3.8
August	47	21,600	2.6	177	22,900	3.8
September	43	22,700	2.6	179	22,800	3.8
October	45	22,300	2.5	186	23,200	3.4
November	34	23,100	2.9	188	23,000	3.4
December	31	22,200	3.3	189	23,600	3.8
1968						
January	34	23,400	3.7	188	23,500	4.1
February	42	23,500	3.4	186	23,600	4.5
March	45	24,600	3.4	192	23,600	4.5
April	47	24,500	2.5	202	24,000	3.7
May	44	25,300	2.9	204	24,100	3.6
June	42	25,500	2.5	202	24,100	3.7

*Homes sold include all homes; homes for sale include only completed homes, homes under construction, and homes not yet started for which a building permit has been issued.
Source: U.S. Department of Commerce, Bureau of the Census, and U.S. Department of Housing and Urban Development; *Construction Reports.*

Mortgage loan interest rates
conventional mortgages on single-family homes

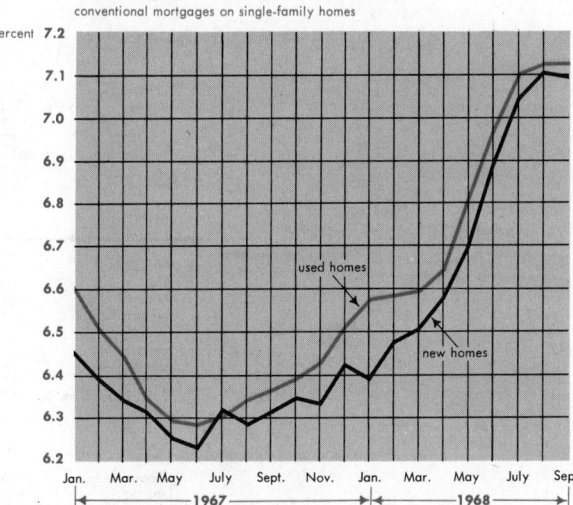

Source: Federal Home Loan Bank Board.

Housing starts
in thousands of units

Year and month	Total	TYPE OF STRUCTURE			OWNERSHIP		LOCATION		GEOGRAPHIC REGION			
		One-family	Two-family	Multi-family	Private	Public	Metro-politan	Nonmetro-politan	North-east	North central	South	West
1967												
January	61.7	40.6	2.5	18.7	59.1	2.6	43.0	18.7	8.8	11.2	30.8	11.0
February	63.2	40.4	2.6	20.1	61.4	1.8	43.9	19.2	9.1	10.3	30.5	13.2
March	92.9	66.6	2.7	23.6	91.5	1.5	62.7	30.3	9.4	21.5	45.3	16.7
April	115.9	79.9	4.5	31.5	113.7	2.2	77.4	38.4	20.2	31.3	47.3	17.1
May	134.2	87.4	5.2	41.5	132.0	2.1	91.7	42.4	23.1	40.0	48.7	22.4
June	131.6	87.7	4.1	39.8	125.4	6.2	88.1	43.5	21.7	37.9	50.9	21.1
July	126.1	82.4	4.6	39.1	125.3	0.9	87.7	38.5	27.8	32.5	45.2	20.7
August	130.2	83.8	4.6	41.9	127.4	2.9	90.0	40.2	18.1	37.7	50.0	24.4
September	125.8	78.2	4.5	43.1	121.9	3.9	88.4	37.4	27.2	29.5	48.1	21.0
October	137.0	81.8	5.4	49.7	135.4	1.6	99.0	38.0	25.0	39.0	51.2	21.7
November	120.2	69.1	3.6	47.6	118.4	1.8	84.9	35.4	21.0	32.3	49.2	17.6
December	83.1	47.1	3.5	32.5	80.1	3.0	63.6	19.5	12.1	20.7	34.1	16.2
1968												
January	82.7	45.3	3.4	34.0	80.5	2.1	63.5	19.2	8.8	15.1	35.6	23.2
February	87.2	55.4	3.8	27.9	84.6	2.5	61.5	25.7	7.5	14.8	43.9	21.0
March	128.6	79.4	4.6	44.6	126.6	2.1	92.1	36.5	12.7	30.1	60.3	25.6
April	165.2	98.0	4.6	62.6	162.0	3.2	118.5	46.7	27.5	45.4	60.7	31.7
May	145.1	87.0	4.7	53.4	140.9	4.3	101.3	43.9	24.5	36.2	55.8	28.6
June	141.3	81.2	6.2	53.9	136.2	5.1	102.3	39.0	21.0	39.4	54.3	26.6

Mobile homes and travel trailers
manufacturers' shipments

	NUMBER OF UNITS		Mobile homes as a percent of total shipments
Year	Mobile homes	Travel trailers	
1960	103,700	40,300	72.0
1961	90,200	40,500	69.0
1962	118,000	57,000	67.4
1963	150,840	72,170	67.6
1964	191,320	90,370	67.9
1965	216,470	107,580	66.8
1966	217,300	122,700	63.9
1967	240,360	130,420	64.8
1968*	144,780	88,900	61.9

*First six months only.
Source: U.S. Department of Commerce, Business and Defense Services Administration, *Construction Review.*

Source: U.S. Department of Commerce, Business and Defense Services Administration, *Construction Review.*

Health and Welfare

Social welfare spending under public programs

years ending June 30

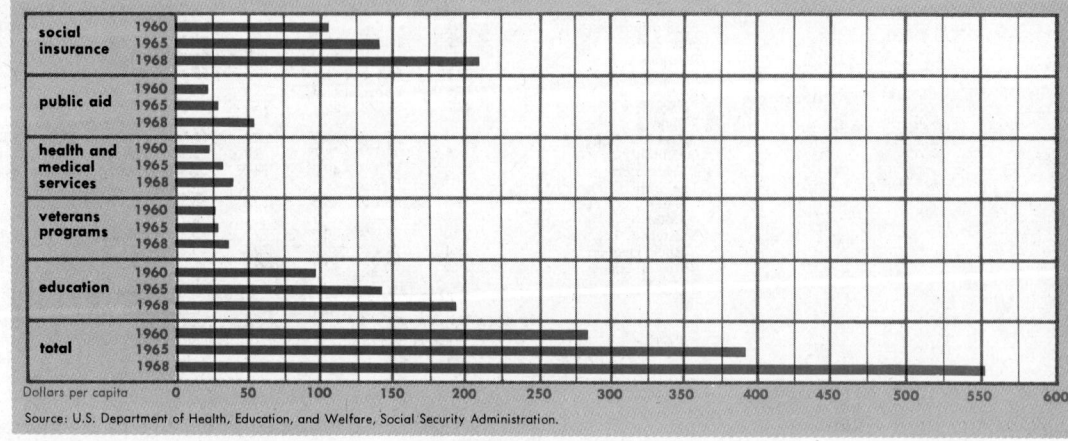

Dollars per capita

Source: U.S. Department of Health, Education, and Welfare, Social Security Administration.

Social insurance beneficiaries and benefits

State	OLD-AGE AND SURVIVORS INSURANCE		DISABILITY INSURANCE			UNEMPLOYMENT INSURANCE State programs	
	Beneficiaries Jan. 1, 1968	Benefits for year ending Jan. 1, 1968 in $000	Beneficiaries Jan. 1, 1968	Benefits for year ending Jan. 1, 1968 in $000	Medicare enrollment Jan. 1, 1968	Beneficiaries* June 30, 1968	Benefits for year ending June 30, 1968 in $000
Alabama	354,238	265,743	56,136	44,313	305,039	12,205	22,653
Alaska	8,851	7,334	830	765	5,805	2,842	8,375
Arizona	155,917	144,282	21,495	19,764	130,149	5,171	12,224
Arkansas	246,864	178,104	35,912	27,709	224,268	6,284	13,471
California	1,798,699	1,716,050	166,574	176,772	1,660,550	144,482	419,286
Colorado	190,556	169,883	16,531	15,332	179,465	1,845	7,535
Connecticut	299,825	307,943	20,554	21,394	276,293	17,348	47,016
Delaware	48,219	45,564	4,745	4,484	42,452	1,503	6,580
District of Columbia	68,519	57,237	6,573	5,961	67,734	3,384	7,988
Florida	847,279	797,172	81,926	74,388	773,184	13,213	21,937
Georgia	388,562	293,525	70,686	53,476	341,700	9,120	18,957
Hawaii	50,905	44,013	4,811	4,355	39,051	2,716	8,713
Idaho	76,619	67,528	6,432	5,982	65,195	2,670	7,347
Illinois	1,163,169	1,122,372	90,999	90,494	1,074,939	35,835	94,131
Indiana	553,516	522,282	45,778	43,419	481,384	14,550	34,364
Iowa	378,527	333,316	21,737	20,145	349,133	4,628	13,798
Kansas	276,305	240,404	18,498	16,735	260,609	3,657	10,551
Kentucky	377,948	291,966	63,693	47,105	327,634	9,226	21,426
Louisiana	308,403	239,111	54,915	41,840	285,839	13,591	30,742
Maine	130,226	112,898	10,675	9,013	116,791	4,418	8,582
Maryland	301,645	276,163	25,175	24,831	268,759	10,963	27,214
Massachusetts	647,113	630,240	45,655	44,538	625,016	32,263	93,072
Michigan	878,036	872,130	77,172	78,033	735,520	39,041	118,529
Minnesota	437,534	385,274	25,604	23,666	399,797	8,082	26,361
Mississippi	247,733	162,679	37,302	26,674	213,313	4,325	8,432
Missouri	574,015	500,328	51,599	45,914	544,605	13,656	35,906
Montana	78,537	70,934	6,584	6,140	67,955	2,128	5,295
Nebraska	189,817	164,103	10,800	9,754	179,360	2,210	6,146
Nevada	29,474	28,430	2,720	2,950	25,812	3,547	9,839
New Hampshire	85,361	79,950	5,714	5,514	78,083	635	2,423
New Jersey	734,418	739,538	55,725	58,673	660,608	49,671	128,934
New Mexico	79,995	62,601	12,244	9,170	64,545	3,251	7,529
New York	2,083,145	2,069,964	168,399	173,040	1,925,138	115,695	285,754
North Carolina.	487,355	366,977	71,915	55,786	382,505	16,526	26,799
North Dakota	76,241	62,835	4,798	3,841	65,321	774	3,953
Ohio	1,078,538	1,028,933	102,544	97,494	973,894	18,866	63,931
Oklahoma	290,362	240,747	36,189	30,842	281,217	7,611	12,353
Oregon	242,044	228,653	20,364	20,394	211,395	10,629	27,946
Pennsylvania	1,383,689	1,326,514	127,179	128,463	1,239,723	47,096	112,296
Rhode Island	110,526	105,877	9,281	9,082	100,983	5,734	14,971
South Carolina	229,091	169,088	42,449	32,534	178,495	6,898	15,601
South Dakota	90,062	74,060	5,405	4,570	79,135	623	2,915
Tennessee	416,371	309,724	55,595	43,930	361,956	12,654	30,753
Texas	1,005,774	812,699	107,312	89,946	908,576	13,313	26,938
Utah	82,462	76,646	6,602	6,263	70,615	3,339	10,661
Vermont	52,546	45,818	5,000	4,205	47,986	1,452	4,635
Virginia	400,328	321,720	59,315	47,733	338,202	3,959	9,027
Washington	343,423	327,360	26,618	26,544	307,380	14,721	39,524
West Virginia	236,106	196,016	55,816	45,222	192,542	7,435	14,330
Wisconsin	520,156	483,516	35,784	34,502	457,342	11,637	42,684
Wyoming	33,294	29,705	2,513	2,381	29,715	436	1,783
Total U.S.	21,566,294†	19,467,599†	2,141,159†	1,938,856†	19,328,912†	777,858	2,032,210

*Weekly average. †Includes data for American Samoa, Guam, Puerto Rico, Virgin Islands, and for beneficiaries or enrollees living abroad.
Source: U.S. Department of Health, Education, and Welfare, Social Security Administration.

Public assistance

June 1968

States	NUMBER OF RECIPIENTS					AVERAGE MONEY PAYMENTS				
	Old-age assistance	Aid to dependent children*	Aid to the permanently and totally disabled	Aid to the blind	General assistance	Old-age assistance	Aid to dependent children, per recipient	Aid to the permanently and totally disabled	Aid to the blind	General assistance
Alabama	113,000	90,400	15,700	1,900	77	$59.35	$15.15	$ 49.65	$ 70.15	$14.40
Alaska	1,500	5,800	460	94	440	80.25	38.10	101.80	108.65	21.15
Arizona	12,900	43,500	6,100	650	5,600	50.50	28.85	65.70	70.20	18.60
Arkansas	62,000	39,000	11,400	1,800	670	54.75	19.25	61.60	69.40	3.95
California	292,000	818,000	125,000	12,500	47,900	99.85	45.55	117.55	138.25	45.70
Colorado	39,000	54,500	7,200	200	3,200	77.50	39.75	67.15	72.05	12.45
Connecticut	6,900	65,700	4,900	240	15,900†	72.25	52.00	92.70	82.25	31.10
Delaware	1,800	17,200	1,100	340	4,100	62.85	32.25	91.50	91.35	28.20
District of Columbia	2,200	26,500	4,200	180	1,000	74.95	38.90	89.60	89.60	73.00
Florida	70,800	149,000	20,300	2,400	...	46.95	15.15	59.45	62.55	—
Georgia	88,500	115,000	29,400	3,200	5,500	51.90	24.90	61.35	62.90	15.40
Hawaii	1,900	19,700	1,600	72	2,400	81.95	44.40	108.65	99.20	57.30
Idaho	3,500	12,200	2,700	100	—	63.85	46.75	74.70	76.75	—
Illinois	37,900	295,000	33,300	1,800	52,100	60.20	43.95	82.15	80.25	44.10
Indiana	17,700	53,200	3,100	1,400	—	46.70	32.65	50.65	65.05	—
Iowa	23,600	52,100	2,400	1,000	6,600	101.45	49.25	128.00	106.20	—
Kansas	16,200	41,000	5,600	390	5,700	87.50	44.00	116.95	89.20	41.70
Kentucky	60,800	109,000	15,300	2,600	—	53.50	28.50	70.70	70.50	—
Louisiana	122,000	141,000	22,300	2,500	7,000	69.85	23.65	53.50	77.05	47.05
Maine	10,100	22,300	2,700	210	7,100	53.75	29.70	76.10	75.15	12.45
Maryland	7,700	111,000	13,200	350	7,700	59.95	39.00	78.20	82.05	71.25
Massachusetts	48,000	149,000	14,900	2,500	20,800	80.45	55.85	94.95	123.90	44.40
Michigan	38,000	197,000	19,500	1,400	69,200	67.05	45.15	87.05	87.90	31.15
Minnesota	24,100	61,600	8,400	800	17,400	62.70	54.00	79.65	80.20	30.75
Mississippi	71,400	103,000	21,800	2,300	1,500	36.05	8.50	44.50	45.25	16.35
Missouri	91,800	116,000	17,200	3,900	12,500	67.85	24.65	73.45	86.85	52.40
Montana	3,700	9,900	1,600	160	3,000	64.00	36.95	77.35	79.50	17.55
Nebraska	8,300	24,500	3,400	350	—	56.80	36.85	70.15	84.60	—
Nevada	2,600	8,600	—	150	—	74.70	30.90	—	100.50	—
New Hampshire	4,100	6,200	700	240	2,100	107.70	43.35	99.50	108.60	20.25
New Jersey	14,000	159,000	9,900	880	35,100	72.65	58.25	89.50	87.80	43.00
New Mexico	9,600	41,400	5,900	370	630	54.20	30.85	69.10	75.20	13.60
New York	76,100	853,000	42,400	3,200	197,000	92.50	71.75	105.65	120.20	67.15
North Carolina	37,400	107,000	23,300	4,600	3,900	65.70	25.85	70.65	78.85	12.05
North Dakota	4,100	9,900	1,900	82	880	74.85	47.90	85.85	81.85	13.55
Ohio	61,500	231,000	24,500	2,800	60,600	60.85	37.50	72.15	72.70	35.35
Oklahoma	77,500	88,700	19,500	1,500	...	71.65	34.40	94.65	104.30	—
Oregon	8,800	39,600	5,200	500	...	57.70	40.25	78.40	89.50	—
Pennsylvania	42,800	306,000	25,900	9,300	43,500	70.60	38.55	72.95	107.45	58.40
Rhode Island	4,100	31,000	3,500	110	11,700	59.10	47.80	82.10	71.40	25.85
South Carolina	20,100	30,900	9,200	1,900	900	46.35	18.45	52.80	59.05	32.90
South Dakota	4,900	13,800	1,300	110	740	61.65	44.45	67.15	85.75	11.45
Tennessee	50,100	100,000	18,600	1,800	3,300	49.30	26.45	65.45	67.35	13.50
Texas	229,000	141,000	15,600	4,200	...	60.25	20.45	56.30	72.70	—
Utah	4,100	27,000	3,800	140	1,500	54.15	38.25	61.15	60.20	68.40
Vermont	4,300	9,200	1,500	100	...	67.95	46.75	82.20	85.90	—
Virginia	10,800	60,600	7,100	1,100	7,800	55.85	30.90	66.90	73.90	27.15
Washington	24,300	65,400	10,300	480	12,600	62.40	47.65	79.40	87.30	52.85
West Virginia	11,300	88,100	6,200	600	2,600	61.60	25.60	54.95	56.55	30.40
Wisconsin	16,300	69,600	5,600	570	10,500	62.25	50.30	62.20	78.75	31.65
Wyoming	2,100	4,600	840	43	520	78.00	38.05	71.00	...	24.30
Total U.S.§	2,019,000	5,609,000	670,000	81,200	737,000‡	67.70	41.85	81.10	91.05	44.65

*Includes children and parents or caretaker relatives in families in which these adults were included in determining amount of assistance. †Estimated.
‡Partly estimated. Excludes Idaho, Indiana, Kentucky, Nebraska, Nevada, Puerto Rico. §Includes Guam, Puerto Rico, and the Virgin Islands.
Source: U.S. Department of Health, Education, and Welfare, Social Security Administration, *Social Security Bulletin.*

Low income counties

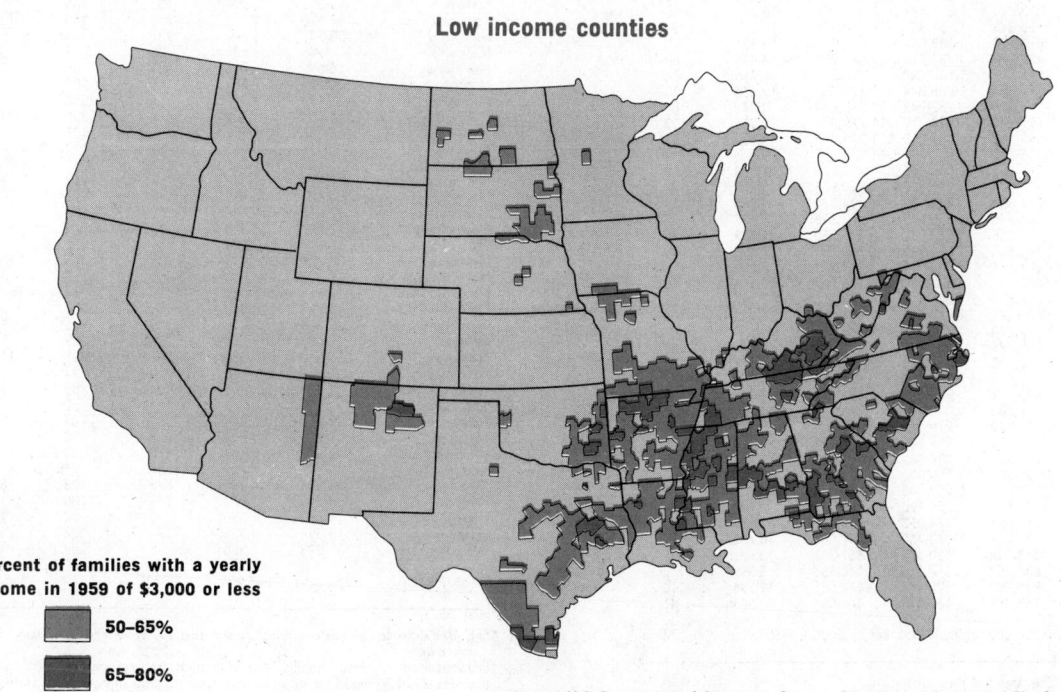

Percent of families with a yearly income in 1959 of $3,000 or less

- 50–65%
- 65–80%

Source: U.S. Department of Commerce, Bureau of the Census, *County and City Data Book.*

Vocational rehabilitation
year ending June 30, 1968

State	DISABLED PERSONS Number rehabilitated	Number in process of rehabilitation June 30	Total federal and state funds
Alabama	5,414	10,064	$12,790,231
Alaska	154	455	483,429
Arizona	1,146	2,490	3,833,546
Arkansas	4,979	8,233	8,767,400
California	10,389	27,313	29,344,085
Colorado	2,527	4,050	5,027,345
Connecticut	2,060	4,360	3,610,422
Delaware	812	1,341	868,553
District of Columbia	2,137	3,100	1,242,980
Florida	9,261	18,805	14,079,524
Georgia	9,001	14,872	16,778,055
Hawaii	565	1,867	1,491,056
Idaho	598	1,264	934,178
Illinois	11,563	14,123	16,666,663
Indiana	2,411	6,907	3,551,814
Iowa	3,139	8,010	5,730,383
Kansas	1,363	2,264	2,093,662
Kentucky	6,184	7,109	5,815,312
Louisiana	3,221	10,774	8,132,451
Maine	537	1,239	1,074,560
Maryland	5,984	8,947	7,670,456
Massachusetts	3,425	6,890	7,284,380
Michigan	6,381	12,956	11,961,487
Minnesota	3,185	8,053	8,568,422
Mississippi	2,982	5,782	6,005,193
Missouri	5,364	8,465	8,952,035
Montana	699	2,103	$ 1,276,150
Nebraska	1,408	3,690	2,649,910
Nevada	316	608	678,210
New Hampshire	324	839	692,446
New Jersey	6,765	9,733	9,510,226
New Mexico	617	1,070	1,234,468
New York	9,341	24,980	26,400,856
North Carolina	8,626	10,808	13,361,105
North Dakota	400	1,726	1,240,000
Ohio	5,943	10,068	11,756,810
Oklahoma	3,815	12,973	7,219,004
Oregon	1,413	3,909	3,997,455
Pennsylvania	14,956	30,867	27,899,219
Rhode Island	1,966	4,298	2,185,793
South Carolina	6,672	11,180	10,744,723
South Dakota	556	1,640	1,373,058
Tennessee	4,726	9,163	7,222,874
Texas	9,558	20,853	19,586,269
Utah	1,204	3,587	2,959,999
Vermont	313	820	1,294,084
Virginia	6,788	9,658	9,492,251
Washington	1,762	4,916	6,143,218
West Virginia	4,791	8,916	7,271,962
Wisconsin	7,289	13,888	11,084,657
Wyoming	371	802	921,111
Total U.S.*	207,918	411,450	$385,592,934

*Includes Guam, Puerto Rico, and the Virgin Islands.
Source: U.S. Department of Health, Education, and Welfare, Rehabilitation Services Administration.

Maternity and child welfare services

State	FEDERAL GRANTS year ending June 30, 1968 Maternal and child health services	Services for crippled children	Child welfare services	CHILDREN RECEIVING SERVICES March 31, 1967 Total	Rate per 10,000 children
Alabama	$ 971,578	$1,104,872	$1,090,905	11,340	74
Alaska	167,549	163,887	124,893	1,138	88
Arizona	343,510	364,647	489,502	4,681	64
Arkansas	608,931	671,443	626,926	1,787	22
California	2,143,084	2,100,373	3,176,047	43,628	57
Colorado	372,555	377,872	497,796	6,823	82
Connecticut	423,537	423,770	503,342	11,606	102
Delaware	189,075	186,825	157,625	2,731	124
District of Columbia	230,114	208,982	169,614	8,143	266
Florida	1,354,581	1,174,470	1,399,659	9,850	42
Georgia	1,297,313	1,321,128	1,281,221	14,202	73
Hawaii	219,655	213,152	222,593	1,197	37
Idaho	202,682	218,104	249,495	1,280	42
Illinois	1,323,810	1,317,389	1,850,707	15,237	35
Indiana	990,348	1,057,831	1,104,843	17,123	83
Iowa	618,690	688,061	669,325	5,531	50
Kansas	422,640	487,210	547,289	4,496	50
Kentucky	978,224	1,038,643	926,235	9,785	74
Louisiana	1,091,664	1,046,344	1,120,461	12,465	76
Maine	294,048	282,043	312,989	4,371	109
Maryland	819,679	624,479	779,094	20,255	132
Massachusetts	690,778	681,057	1,009,715	10,939	52
Michigan	1,433,691	1,484,021	1,772,367	5,666	16
Minnesota	786,652	836,875	882,868	27,583	80
Mississippi	931,443	959,674	836,503	9,019	84
Missouri	874,839	899,479	1,006,046	11,030	63
Montana	207,948	209,503	241,818	1,719	57
Nebraska	325,028	361,922	393,270	1,759	30
Nevada	181,817	179,527	143,587	1,195	62
New Hampshire	201,144	200,901	218,279	3,020	110
New Jersey	811,768	822,589	1,176,709	16,188	60
New Mexico	306,570	297,861	372,386	3,127	63
New York	2,084,182	1,912,694	2,856,303	74,244	108
North Carolina	1,539,200	1,718,718	1,435,955	15,555	73
North Dakota	204,696	231,075	242,679	4,542	160
Ohio	1,812,050	1,882,132	2,205,002	36,409	85
Oklahoma	510,518	576,262	647,609	5,821	61
Oregon	380,211	415,614	463,919	10,323	133
Pennsylvania	2,068,584	2,080,430	2,343,734	34,711	78
Rhode Island	223,062	219,148	240,252	3,578	105
South Carolina	932,634	978,502	866,254	6,916	60
South Dakota	213,321	237,586	255,969	2,118	72
Tennessee	1,032,581	1,150,696	1,103,743	8,971	56
Texas	2,103,339	2,259,445	2,778,915	16,787	36
Utah	289,820	255,120	346,216	3,138	65
Vermont	174,797	174,053	170,483	2,225	132
Virginia	991,759	1,072,750	1,149,084	16,738	90
Washington	573,149	560,372	651,337	12,681	105
West Virginia	636,962	617,516	540,951	8,569	118
Wisconsin	905,187	925,297	984,555	19,246	110
Wyoming	167,353	167,015	145,526	576	41
Total U.S.*	$50,000,000	$50,000,000	$46,000,000	607,900	74

*Includes Guam, Puerto Rico, and the Virgin Islands.
Source: U.S. Department of Health, Education, and Welfare, Welfare Administration.

Physicians and hospital facilities

State	PRACTICING PHYSICIANS* Jan. 1, 1968 Total	Engaged in patient care	In other professional activity†	HOSPITALS 1967 Number	Beds
Alabama	2,766	2,619	147	142	28,210
Alaska	168	162	6	27	1,982
Arizona	1,841	1,790	51	80	9,341
Arkansas	1,585	1,505	80	91	11,758
California	31,928	30,204	1,724	639	137,377
Colorado	3,258	3,013	245	92	15,788
Connecticut	5,141	4,735	406	65	25,347
Delaware	656	635	24	14	5,224
District of Columbia	2,890	2,509	381	21	15,127
Florida	7,360	7,006	354	185	41,123
Georgia	4,314	4,034	280	154	33,900
Hawaii	935	898	37	33	6,346
Idaho	610	598	12	52	3,896
Illinois	14,160	13,313	842	320	105,656
Indiana	4,778	4,516	262	139	38,934
Iowa	2,763	2,566	197	142	20,601
Kansas	2,383	2,228	155	165	19,242
Kentucky	3,010	2,795	215	140	23,340
Louisiana	3,941	3,704	237	149	26,989
Maine	955	935	20	59	9,559
Maryland	6,093	5,466	627	85	33,450
Massachusetts	10,504	9,584	920	202	64,051
Michigan	10,180	9,590	590	256	73,377
Minnesota	5,136	4,802	334	202	34,969
Mississippi	1,687	1,603	84	107	16,367
Missouri	5,461	5,030	431	148	41,091
Montana	656	645	11	63	4,356
Nebraska	1,596	1,479	117	118	12,810
Nevada	423	415	8	22	2,664
New Hampshire	849	797	52	36	6,606
New Jersey	9,061	8,688	373	140	54,145
New Mexico	863	788	75	58	5,973
New York	38,829	36,044	2,785	435	206,694
North Carolina	4,937	4,484	453	163	35,220
North Dakota	554	535	19	64	6,278
Ohio	13,234	12,539	695	251	81,835
Oklahoma	2,365	2,240	125	146	15,818
Oregon	2,605	2,422	183	89	16,239
Pennsylvania	16,560	15,380	1,180	321	117,254
Rhode Island	1,289	1,255	34	24	8,670
South Carolina	2,000	1,906	94	83	18,523
South Dakota	507	503	4	62	6,152
Tennessee	4,278	3,946	332	162	32,357
Texas	11,279	10,644	635	570	73,641
Utah	1,298	1,188	110	40	4,610
Vermont	677	590	87	29	4,829
Virginia	4,887	4,538	349	128	37,785
Washington	4,271	3,973	298	130	18,909
West Virginia	1,683	1,590	93	92	16,099
Wisconsin	4,833	4,539	294	203	36,731
Wyoming	293	288	5	34	3,882
Total U.S.	264,330‡	247,256	17,072	7,172	1,671,125

*Excludes data for physicians temporarily abroad, or whose addresses are unknown.
†Includes medical school faculty, administration, and research.
‡Includes 24,015 physicians in government service not allocated by state.
Sources: American Hospital Association, American Medical Association.

Water pollution

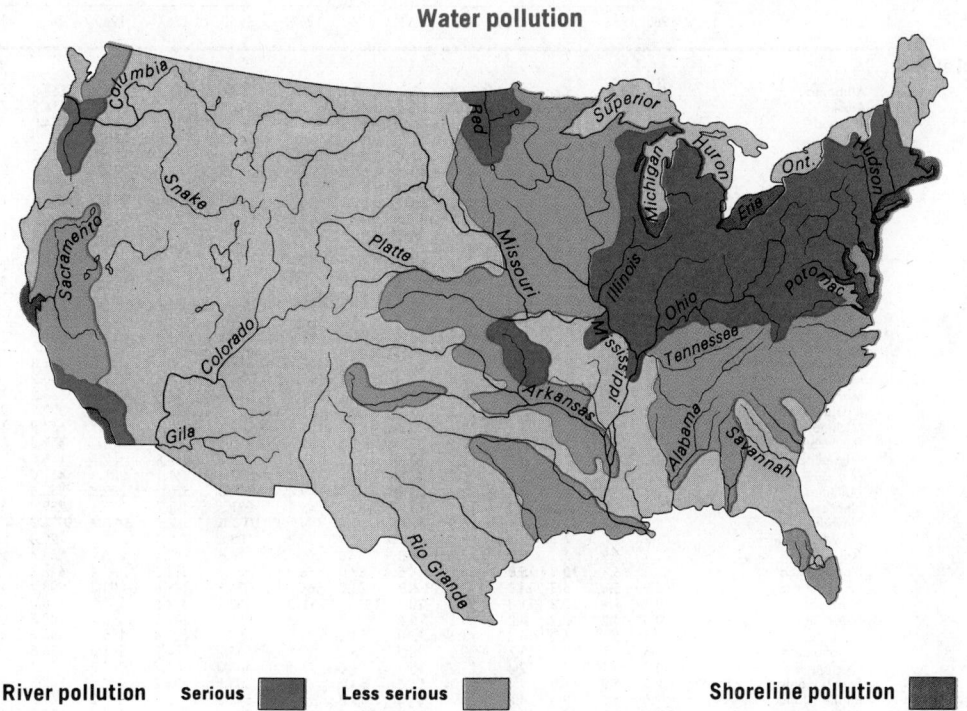

River pollution Serious ▮ Less serious ▯ **Shoreline pollution** ▮

Law Enforcement

Rearrests

within 4 years of 1963 release

Age, and type of release	Percent
Age	
Under 20	70
20–24	67
25–29	65
30–39	61
40–49	51
50 and over	38
All ages	60
Type of release	
Fine and probation	33
Suspended sentence and/or probation	52
Parole	59
Fine	71
Mandatory release	72
Acquitted or dismissed	91

Source: U.S. Department of Justice, Federal Bureau of Investigation, *Uniform Crime Reports.*

Arrests, 1967

Offense charged	UNDER 18 Persons arrested	UNDER 18 Percent change from 1966	18 AND OVER Persons arrested	18 AND OVER Percent change from 1966	ALL AGES Persons arrested	ALL AGES Percent change from 1966
Murder and nonnegligent manslaughter	752	+ 2.9	7,465	+ 9.1	8,217	+ 8.5
Manslaughter by negligence	206	+ 8.4	2,169	− 9.0	2,375	− 7.7
Forcible rape	2,314	+ 6.8	9,085	+ 1.5	11,399	+ 2.6
Robbery	17,858	+20.3	38,223	+18.0	56,081	+18.7
Aggravated assault	17,067	+ 5.8	79,970	+ 1.3	97,037	+ 2.1
Other assaults	34,383	+12.6	168,048	+ 5.0	202,431	+ 6.2
Burglary—breaking or entering	115,915	+11.2	100,371	+13.3	216,286	+12.2
Larceny—theft	226,661	+ 5.2	182,429	+ 9.1	409,090	+ 6.9
Auto theft	66,601	+ 3.8	41,249	+ 8.1	107,850	+ 5.4
Arson	4,592	+ 1.4	2,486	+23.1	7,078	+ 8.1
Forgery and counterfeiting	3,510	+23.5	26,489	+ 6.8	29,999	+ 8.6
Fraud	2,233	+24.6	47,878	+ 1.5	50,111	+ 2.3
Embezzlement	235	+18.1	5,424	− 0.9	5,659	− 0.2
Stolen property; buying, receiving, possessing	9,114	+24.6	16,867	+31.4	25,981	+29.0
Vandalism	73,736	+ 6.0	22,025	+ 8.0	95,761	+ 6.5
Weapons; carrying, possessing, etc.	11,877	+ 7.6	53,101	+19.9	64,978	+17.5
Prostitution and commercialized vice	810	+28.8	37,920	+13.4	38,730	+13.7
Sex offenses (except forcible rape and prostitution)	11,787	− 9.6	37,120	− 7.4	48,907	− 7.9
Narcotic drug laws	19,885	+134.4	75,585	+47.7	95,470	+60.0
Gambling	2,023	−10.7	79,305	−15.9	81,328	−15.8
Offenses against family and children	749	+ 8.4	48,274	− 8.2	49,023	− 8.0
Driving while intoxicated	2,405	+16.8	246,207	+ 6.6	248,612	+ 6.7
Liquor law violations	54,971	+ 6.3	128,223	+ 1.1	183,194	+ 2.6
Drunkenness	30,991	+11.8	1,365,289	− 2.4	1,396,280	− 2.2
Disorderly conduct	100,134	+11.4	395,650	− 4.1	495,784	− 1.3
Vagrancy	9,041	+10.2	90,801	− 0.6	99,842	+ 0.3
All other offenses, except traffic	173,211	+11.6	413,478	+13.4	586,689	+12.9
Suspicion	19,520	+ 8.8	69,969	+10.8	89,489	+10.4
Curfew and loitering law violations	87,030	+ 8.4	—	—	87,030	+ 8.4
Runaways	117,480	+20.1	—	—	117,480	+20.1
Total arrests*	1,197,571	+10.5	3,721,131	+ 2.3	4,918,702	+ 4.2

Data are from 3,678 agencies reporting on estimated population of 129,384,000.
*Excludes arrests for suspicion.
Source: U.S. Department of Justice, Federal Bureau of Investigation, *Uniform Crime Reports.*

Crime rates per 100,000 population

Unit	MURDER* 1960	1967	FORCIBLE RAPE 1960	1967	ROBBERY 1960	1967	AGGRAVATED ASSAULT 1960	1967	BURGLARY 1960	1967	LARCENY† 1960	1967	AUTO THEFT 1960	1967
STATE														
Alabama	12.9	**11.7**	8.3	10.5	26.9	33.0	123.2	183.5	368.6	561.6	183.2	367.6	95.6	146.0
Alaska	10.2	9.6	**20.8**	17.6	28.3	35.3	45.1	98.2	332.1	688.6	352.4	716.9	242.3	404.4
Arizona	6.1	5.6	16.1	16.7	54.6	74.9	120.1	141.0	687.1	1,137.3	415.0	874.9	339.6	407.2
Arkansas	8.6	8.8	8.7	14.2	25.0	35.2	56.7	161.3	273.9	400.4	160.2	310.2	46.5	78.5
California	3.9	5.4	18.3	**25.0**	98.0	149.0	120.2	172.7	913.3	**1,446.0**	494.5	901.2	328.1	508.1
Colorado	4.2	4.1	13.3	20.9	80.0	67.9	41.0	98.9	579.7	789.4	317.3	625.4	217.5	308.4
Connecticut	1.7	2.4	4.2	5.6	9.5	32.2	21.9	55.7	330.7	751.7	179.0	413.0	131.1	321.1
Delaware	6.5	7.8	8.3	10.3	34.5	63.4	21.1	63.5	557.0	771.2	179.3	423.3	162.7	368.7
Florida	10.5	10.5	8.4	15.2	81.1	130.9	114.7	233.6	829.6	1,220.8	366.1	688.2	198.6	285.7
Georgia	12.0	11.1	7.6	12.4	26.6	37.3	98.9	128.5	408.1	591.4	179.4	385.3	153.7	199.9
Hawaii	2.4	2.4	3.3	5.0	10.9	19.8	5.2	52.8	525.9	1,152.4	284.9	581.6	269.9	404.2
Idaho	2.4	4.3	7.0	8.7	13.9	10.9	14.7	44.5	301.3	405.9	265.0	398.3	100.0	112.9
Illinois	5.1	7.3	12.4	17.9	**159.7**	200.9	94.2	168.3	521.4	608.5	340.1	428.6	307.5	421.7
Indiana	4.4	3.7	4.7	11.4	34.4	76.7	37.4	64.9	429.7	651.6	182.8	426.5	162.2	322.7
Iowa	0.6	1.5	3.7	5.6	11.2	21.0	8.7	30.3	233.5	431.6	181.9	361.9	77.1	155.2
Kansas	3.2	4.0	5.3	10.7	20.8	42.2	29.0	86.0	355.4	598.2	168.6	405.8	91.0	184.9
Kentucky	6.8	7.2	5.5	9.1	33.7	47.1	51.8	77.2	376.8	482.9	211.5	396.7	125.7	281.8
Louisiana	8.7	9.3	9.5	16.5	52.8	82.1	78.0	167.2	411.2	656.2	242.8	471.8	225.3	281.3
Maine	1.7	0.4	5.0	6.0	7.9	9.7	10.7	43.3	246.0	403.0	150.7	230.2	117.9	106.4
Maryland	5.5	8.0	7.3	19.6	37.9	212.1	90.1	234.5	366.8	1,014.8	239.7	683.2	184.3	489.1
Massachusetts	1.5	2.8	5.0	7.6	21.2	52.0	20.1	65.2	309.9	675.5	185.1	392.3	215.6	**667.4**
Michigan	4.3	6.2	12.4	22.5	73.7	189.6	96.0	158.5	592.1	1,103.5	273.9	664.9	178.5	384.8
Minnesota	1.3	1.6	2.5	8.6	29.4	67.1	10.8	54.7	360.1	704.4	218.0	459.3	141.8	292.4
Mississippi	10.0	8.7	5.1	5.5	15.0	10.6	66.0	89.0	205.3	257.8	89.8	146.6	48.4	56.7
Missouri	4.6	7.3	11.0	17.1	76.2	130.5	71.6	122.1	523.4	861.1	231.9	411.0	177.0	355.0
Montana	3.9	2.4	7.3	10.3	28.0	21.4	24.5	49.8	401.3	522.3	269.3	482.6	248.1	215.7
Nebraska	2.3	2.7	4.2	8.2	18.0	38.7	16.5	63.6	231.8	491.7	125.6	289.0	125.8	188.2
Nevada	8.8	10.8	12.6	14.4	74.0	117.8	50.5	104.7	913.5	1,066.2	**541.9**	**972.3**	**391.9**	476.8
New Hampshire	1.3	2.0	4.1	3.4	3.0	6.1	4.9	20.3	182.6	342.6	88.5	220.6	57.7	111.8
New Jersey	2.9	3.9	7.9	9.7	46.0	82.5	59.8	92.4	438.6	861.4	236.9	504.4	201.9	425.3
New Mexico	7.3	6.4	12.0	15.0	38.7	44.5	89.0	156.9	434.9	812.3	378.4	647.7	371.1	248.5
New York	2.9	5.4	6.3	14.3	44.1	**217.9**	73.8	165.8	336.3	1,149.6	403.3	903.9	178.2	451.1
North Carolina	10.1	9.4	7.3	11.0	17.0	30.2	**182.1**	261.5	258.2	477.8	140.2	328.0	78.2	131.1
North Dakota	0.5	0.2	2.2	4.7	6.3	5.8	5.2	18.3	199.2	241.2	93.4	243.7	68.5	82.3
Ohio	3.3	5.2	6.0	10.3	41.6	95.0	34.2	74.5	350.4	607.6	195.4	387.7	138.1	325.6
Oklahoma	7.5	6.7	12.8	13.7	40.2	38.5	36.0	85.9	536.7	594.9	261.0	436.5	199.4	188.0
Oregon	2.4	3.1	9.3	12.4	31.9	65.9	26.0	76.1	406.3	857.4	317.3	692.7	130.9	273.4
Pennsylvania	2.8	3.8	9.0	9.4	36.1	56.5	53.7	63.6	308.8	483.2	149.6	242.8	128.2	232.8
Rhode Island	1.0	2.2	2.3	4.8	14.5	31.4	19.8	90.0	517.3	896.9	419.2	479.9	317.3	608.9
South Carolina	**13.3**	11.2	9.4	13.9	20.4	34.9	102.2	170.7	371.4	567.7	205.4	337.6	104.7	155.6
South Dakota	2.1	3.7	5.4	8.3	9.1	12.9	16.0	62.0	247.9	341.5	198.8	300.4	86.6	84.1
Tennessee	8.5	8.9	5.2	12.5	27.8	56.5	50.4	130.5	469.4	711.8	153.5	368.0	132.2	243.1
Texas	8.7	9.8	9.3	13.3	32.8	68.4	111.8	152.3	613.8	816.4	233.1	467.4	168.1	257.3
Utah	1.6	2.7	9.5	7.2	28.1	38.5	34.5	68.2	517.7	685.5	320.1	594.3	207.3	225.3
Vermont	0.3	3.1	2.3	4.3	2.3	1.9	4.6	11.3	242.1	517.0	201.9	171.9	87.7	124.9
Virginia	10.0	7.3	7.3	11.9	25.3	50.9	102.1	122.0	346.3	635.2	212.0	367.8	120.0	228.5
Washington	2.1	3.1	5.9	12.5	31.5	54.6	15.5	83.7	488.7	837.7	331.5	672.5	158.0	281.5
West Virginia	4.4	4.6	4.4	4.7	13.5	19.3	35.5	68.4	239.0	298.4	198.4	175.9	71.5	87.4
Wisconsin	1.3	1.9	2.8	4.6	8.5	28.0	16.9	35.9	199.6	450.3	378.1	385.8	106.4	214.6
Wyoming	4.8	4.8	7.0	7.3	53.6	13.7	51.5	67.9	300.2	506.0	331.8	494.3	114.8	174.9
METROPOLITAN AREA														
Baltimore	7.2	11.3	8.5	27.6	56.5	**353.0**	132.1	**378.3**	424.7	1,269.3	319.2	909.7	245.6	618.5
Boston	1.8	3.2	5.2	7.7	29.4	66.8	28.4	68.7	313.5	621.2	203.0	389.5	262.8	**805.6**
Chicago	6.7	9.5	17.0	24.2	**237.5**	294.5	134.9	229.6	640.8	681.1	451.4	477.1	442.3	581.4
Cleveland	5.3	8.4	5.3	8.6	81.7	188.8	33.0	87.0	265.0	577.3	125.6	377.1	196.3	666.5
Detroit	5.1	8.9	14.6	28.7	130.6	341.3	159.6	197.8	746.3	1,451.4	303.8	823.4	256.1	592.0
Houston	**10.9**	**16.9**	16.1	17.1	53.7	194.8	149.9	189.5	877.8	1,180.4	312.3	580.1	261.7	498.3
Los Angeles—Long Beach	4.4	7.0	**29.0**	35.4	143.9	234.3	**199.1**	269.6	**1,200.9**	**1,774.2**	657.3	1,109.8	**444.3**	687.1
Minneapolis—St. Paul	1.8	2.1	3.9	15.0	62.5	137.6	19.0	101.9	585.7	1,107.8	345.2	682.6	258.2	519.2
Newark	3.8	6.1	12.7	13.9	95.4	152.6	121.0	157.8	663.5	1,229.0	411.9	639.0	332.7	540.0
New York	4.0	7.0	8.4	17.6	64.2	317.5	106.9	224.1	414.2	1,462.0	**565.0**	**1,223.7**	228.4	582.0
Philadelphia	4.8	6.3	16.5	14.6	62.3	81.6	119.4	104.5	430.3	578.7	184.7	290.2	135.9	287.6
Pittsburgh	2.4	3.0	10.6	10.2	47.9	98.4	34.0	67.4	354.9	550.4	212.6	380.3	261.4	451.6
St. Louis	5.7	10.6	17.4	19.9	152.8	169.7	133.0	150.2	785.9	1,025.1	350.7	437.1	279.7	491.6
San Francisco—Oakland	3.5	6.0	11.9	22.2	102.8	226.8	92.9	158.5	739.9	1,706.0	335.7	775.5	320.8	704.5
Washington, D.C.	6.9	8.6	10.2	15.8	67.3	263.0	183.6	187.5	455.1	1,145.2	270.8	631.4	192.6	588.2

Boldface type indicates highest rate for that crime among the states or the listed metropolitan areas.
*Includes nonnegligent manslaughter.   †$50 and over.
Source: U.S. Department of Justice, Federal Bureau of Investigation, *Uniform Crime Reports*.

Deaths by firearms

1962 to 1967

State	Total number of murders	Percent by use of firearm	State	Total number of murders	Percent by use of firearm
Alabama	2,166	63.5	Montana	97	70.3
Alaska	130	62.1	Nebraska	187	67.0
Arizona	531	66.3	Nevada	221	67.6
Arkansas	855	69.1	New Hampshire	86	63.1
California	4,857	52.3	New Jersey	1,310	41.2
Colorado	501	60.3	New Mexico	360	65.2
Connecticut	303	46.5	New York	4,835	34.9
Delaware	170	57.4	North Carolina	2,385	70.2
District of Columbia	788	47.2	North Dakota	46	29.0
Florida	3,132	67.8	Ohio	2,350	63.6
Georgia	2,811	68.7	Oklahoma	776	62.8
Hawaii	109	48.6	Oregon	322	59.4
Idaho	132	68.2	Pennsylvania	2,173	43.9
Illinois	3,721	57.0	Rhode Island	82	34.1
Indiana	991	64.5	South Carolina	1,539	74.1
Iowa	222	64.7	South Dakota	88	61.5
Kansas	423	66.1	Tennessee	1,642	67.1
Kentucky	1,158	77.3	Texas	5,104	70.7
Louisiana	1,728	63.5	Utah	124	74.1
Maine	95	47.0	Vermont	26	83.3
Maryland	1,402	51.3	Virginia	1,763	63.1
Massachusetts	712	39.9	Washington	460	55.4
Michigan	2,073	52.4	West Virginia	459	64.0
Minnesota	312	58.6	Wisconsin	391	59.3
Mississippi	1,197	69.1	Wyoming	84	55.4
Missouri	1,586	67.1	TOTAL U.S.	59,015	58.2

Source: U.S. Department of Justice, Federal Bureau of Investigation, *Uniform Crime Reports*.

Education

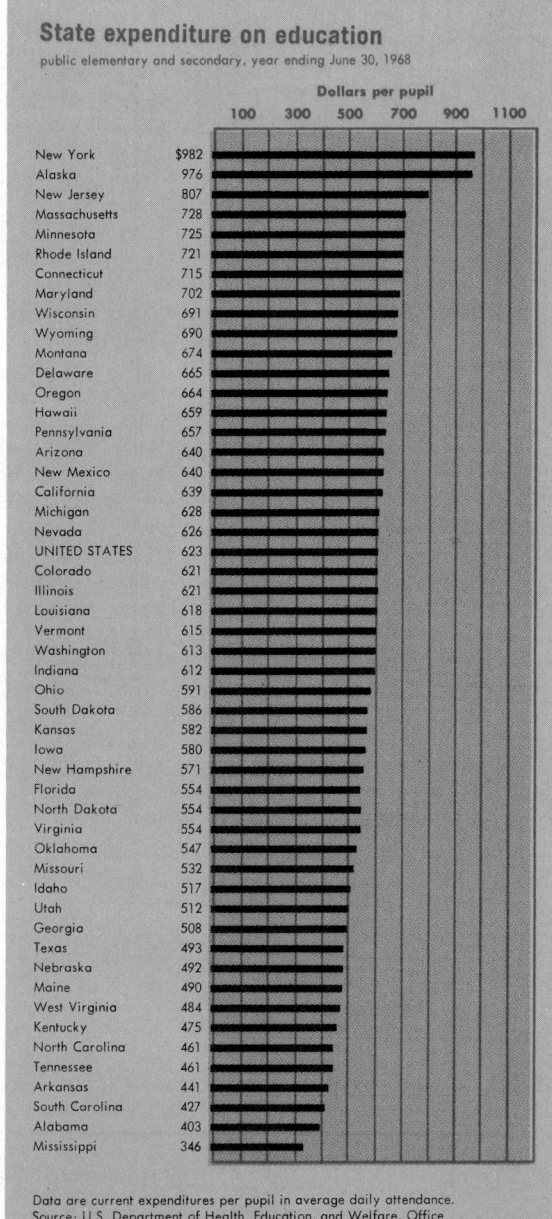

State expenditure on education
public elementary and secondary, year ending June 30, 1968

Dollars per pupil

New York	$982
Alaska	976
New Jersey	807
Massachusetts	728
Minnesota	725
Rhode Island	721
Connecticut	715
Maryland	702
Wisconsin	691
Wyoming	690
Montana	674
Delaware	665
Oregon	664
Hawaii	659
Pennsylvania	657
Arizona	640
New Mexico	640
California	639
Michigan	628
Nevada	626
UNITED STATES	623
Colorado	621
Illinois	621
Louisiana	618
Vermont	615
Washington	613
Indiana	612
Ohio	591
South Dakota	586
Kansas	582
Iowa	580
New Hampshire	571
Florida	554
North Dakota	554
Virginia	554
Oklahoma	547
Missouri	532
Idaho	517
Utah	512
Georgia	508
Texas	493
Nebraska	492
Maine	490
West Virginia	484
Kentucky	475
North Carolina	461
Tennessee	461
Arkansas	441
South Carolina	427
Alabama	403
Mississippi	346

Data are current expenditures per pupil in average daily attendance.
Source: U.S. Department of Health, Education, and Welfare, Office of Education.

Vocational education

	NUMBER OF STUDENTS		
Type of program	1959–60	1964–65	1966–67
Agriculture	796,237	887,529	934,463
Distributive occupations	303,784	333,342	480,380
Home economics	1,588,109	2,098,520	2,185,671
Trades and industry	938,490	1,087,807	1,441,976
Health occupations	40,250	66,772	115,512
Technical education	101,279	225,737	267,338
Office occupations	—	730,904	1,568,900
Total	3,768,149	5,430,611	6,994,240

Data refer to vocational programs receiving federal aid.
Source: U.S. Department of Health, Education, and Welfare, Office of Education, *Digest of Educational Statistics*.

Federal funds supporting education
in thousands of dollars

Funds	Year ending June 30, 1960	Year ending June 30, 1968*	Year ending June 30, 1969*
Supporting education in educational institutions			
Grants, total	$1,512,329	$8,146,756	$8,381,309
Elementary-secondary education	507,170	3,252,046	3,389,180
Higher education†	734,718	3,792,730	3,590,790
Adult, vocational technical, and continuing education (not classifiable by level)	270,441	1,101,980	1,401,339
Loans, total	222,305	641,644	780,722
Elementary-secondary education	394	1,000	1,000
Higher education	221,911	634,596	779,722
Vocational-technical and adult education	...	6,048	...
Other funds for education and related activities			
Research and development‡	545,585	1,144,377	1,144,300
School services	307,926	477,868	499,608
Training of federal personnel	67,738	1,679,767	1,722,337
Library services	18,980	141,790	144,844
International education	53,359	321,305	368,352
Other	62,633	406,596	502,791

*Estimated data.   †Includes funds for basic research.
‡Includes funds for applied research.
Source: U.S. Department of Health, Education, and Welfare, Office of Education, *Digest of Educational Statistics*.

School years completed by persons 25 years old and over
March 1967

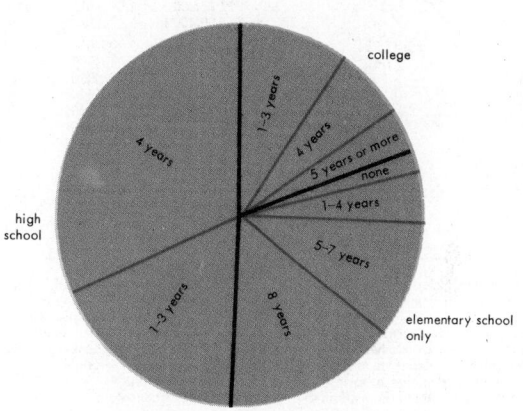

Persons 25 years old and over: 104,864,000

Source: U.S. Department of Commerce, Bureau of the Census, *Current Population Reports*.

Enrollment in special education
programs for exceptional children

Type	1958	1963	1966 estimate
Visually handicapped	12,000	21,531	23,300
Deaf and hard of hearing	20,000	45,594	51,400
Speech impaired	490,000	802,197	989,500
Crippled and special health problems	52,000	64,842	69,400
Emotionally and socially maladjusted	29,000	79,587	87,900
Mentally retarded	223,000	431,890	540,100
Other handicapped conditions	12,000	22,039	32,500
Gifted	52,000	214,671	312,100
Total	890,000	1,682,351	2,106,200

Data are for February of years reported.
Beginning 1963, includes public and private residential schools; 1958, includes public day schools only.
Source: U.S. Department of Health, Education, and Welfare, Office of Education.

Public elementary and secondary schools

1968–69 estimates

State	Operating school districts	Instruction rooms in use*	ENROLLMENT Elementary	ENROLLMENT Secondary	High school graduates	INSTRUCTIONAL STAFF Total	Principals and supervisors	Teachers, elementary Total	Teachers, elementary Men	Teachers, secondary Total	Teachers, secondary Men	TEACHERS' AVERAGE ANNUAL SALARIES Elementary	TEACHERS' AVERAGE ANNUAL SALARIES Secondary
Alabama	118	31,000	482,000	382,000	44,000	33,570	1,420	16,500	845	15,650	6,175	$5,750	$ 6,025
Alaska	28	2,747	54,600	28,000	2,900	3,623	179	1,995	432	1,274	699	...	...
Arizona	296	16,400	324,002	122,245	20,636	19,150	775	12,375	3,125	5,175	3,275	8,025	8,750
Arkansas	388	17,984	250,550	205,576	24,631	20,461	677	9,958	667	9,303	4,227	6,077	6,312
California	1,093	163,900	3,135,000	1,805,000	265,800	195,000	12,400	106,000	21,500	69,000	48,500	9,100‡	10,000‡
Colorado	181	20,121	320,500	230,000	28,800	26,000	1,400	12,350	2,075	11,200	6,275	6,985	7,300
Connecticut	174	24,975	426,000	228,000	32,550	34,221	2,567	17,405	3,481	12,095	6,652	8,325	8,700
Delaware	48	5,075	70,600	54,400	6,550	5,750	270	2,600	442	2,620	1,450	8,000	8,400
District of Columbia	1	4,798	99,057	57,310	4,950	8,500	570	3,875	375	3,375	1,275	...	...
Florida	67	45,427	832,728	659,629	68,967	64,100	2,776	29,838	3,342	26,871	12,817	...	...
Georgia	193	41,094	744,003	393,779	54,908	48,135	2,680	27,556	2,342	17,899	7,159	6,967	7,047
Hawaii	1	6,758	101,000	76,000	9,750	8,455	364	4,276	276	2,958	1,325	8,080	8,140
Idaho	115	7,366	97,000	88,500	11,650	8,478	715	3,687	479	4,076	2,295	5,970	6,490
Illinois	1,275	85,336	1,485,000	804,000	132,000	106,963	3,185	60,603	12,121	41,400	22,675	8,800	9,500
Indiana	342	44,620	701,000	549,000	65,100	55,200	3,500	25,600	4,100	23,100	13,500	7,800	8,210
Iowa	455	29,109	481,000	202,000	43,800	37,000	1,600	20,891	2,716	12,731	7,381	7,364	8,292
Kansas	330	25,495	398,995	157,312	32,600	25,380§	1,348§	12,120§	1,387§	10,681§	6,042§	6,867	7,256
Kentucky	195	25,927	460,000	249,000	37,000	32,075	2,035	17,600	2,400	11,100	5,175	6,325	6,725
Louisiana	66	33,875	545,000	341,000	43,500	40,600	2,200	21,300	2,400	17,100	7,450	6,810	7,192
Maine	250	9,314	171,000	62,000	12,200	11,475	500	6,500	1,350	4,200	2,500	6,425	6,900
Maryland	24	28,903	532,100	371,850	43,600	41,923	2,549	19,420	2,428	17,926	9,142	8,593	9,055
Massachusetts	390	38,647	640,000	480,000	64,000	54,200	3,100	26,050	3,650	22,450	13,000	8,000	8,200
Michigan	644	...	1,218,500	947,500	113,000	96,900	3,900	39,933	5,151	47,067	27,016	9,087	9,499
Minnesota	995	36,144	502,000	410,500	60,000	43,500	2,100	19,700	2,575	19,800	13,075	7,750	8,225
Mississippi	148	21,841	354,000	244,095	28,300	24,366	1,340	12,076	906	9,980	4,250	5,650	5,920
Missouri	665	36,396	782,556	276,929	53,409	47,129	2,849	29,148	5,580	13,045	7,305	7,051	7,232
Montana	733	8,195	115,800	64,600	10,700	8,980	370	5,425	920	2,890	1,870	6,400	7,300
Nebraska	1,589	16,344	200,000	138,000	20,900	17,650	750	8,900	455	7,500	3,990	6,124	7,112
Nevada	17	4,634	3,135,000	1,805,000	265,800	5,555	339	2,568	506	2,342	1,342	8,186	8,528
New Hampshire	160	6,151	92,130	58,490	8,200	7,171	412	3,390	411	3,038	1,721	6,919	7,215
New Jersey	572	53,470	976,000	485,000	83,000	77,500	6,500	38,250	7,650	26,250	15,000	8,227	8,690
New Mexico	89	11,341	160,021	128,883	15,113	12,810	830	6,160	1,050	5,250	3,000	7,160	7,130
New York	750	133,000	1,978,800	1,500,420	194,000	198,000	15,500	87,400	11,000	82,600	41,500	8,700	9,300
North Carolina	157	49,302	867,334	353,198	66,148	53,696	2,470	33,190	4,309	15,686	6,463	6,747	6,953
North Dakota	416	7,312	107,450	46,950	10,000	7,475	310	4,475	675	2,490	1,700	5,600	6,855
Ohio	648	88,387	1,741,120	695,950	138,600	105,555	5,030	54,880	8,280	40,970	22,720	7,450	8,050
Oklahoma	704	26,927	348,260	267,983	35,028	29,454	1,500	14,136	2,332	13,498	7,512	6,548	6,750
Oregon	359	20,137	336,572	153,502	30,323	24,741	1,383	11,707	2,628	9,265	5,516	7,789	8,191
Pennsylvania	610	83,578	1,294,300	1,071,300	148,500	103,960	4,470	46,120	7,420	48,240	27,550	7,731	7,985
Rhode Island	40	6,309	100,400	76,600	9,600	8,970	492	4,012	509	3,880	2,219	8,167	7,973
South Carolina	93	24,123	399,340	267,011	35,955	29,600	1,250	14,350	850	12,150	4,200	5,700	6,100
South Dakota	1,110	8,189	120,100	51,000	11,400	9,204	464	5,887	705	2,853	1,854	5,050	6,300
Tennessee	150	32,624	583,000	332,000	48,100	36,700	1,725	20,325	2,225	13,000	5,400	6,115	6,600
Texas	1,234	107,956	1,941,576	725,424	135,000	125,320	6,579	60,461	7,199	53,204	26,105	6,600	6,638
Utah	40	10,686	174,500	135,300	17,250	12,940	740	5,950	1,135	5,275	3,350	7,025	7,150
Vermont	274	...	62,876	37,518	5,150	4,877	325	2,437	315	1,765	988	6,500	7,000
Virginia	134	...	712,900	374,100	54,700	51,500	3,200	26,300	2,300	22,000	8,350	7,025	7,625
Washington	328	31,277	455,300	364,800	47,500	37,375	2,465	17,500	3,600	14,610	5,600	7,950	8,600
West Virginia	55	16,588	236,800	184,800	26,000	18,475	1,700	8,550	650	7,250	3,000	6,270	6,550
Wisconsin	464	35,662	601,650	401,100	60,373	47,546§	3,502§	23,286§	3,609§	20,758§	12,538§	7,700	8,300
Wyoming	161	4,501	49,039	39,961	5,100	4,825	210	2,250	343	2,140	1,420	7,167	7,345
Total U.S.	19,369	1,709,000⁹	28,952,459	17,432,515	2,526,191	2,132,033δ	119,515	1,067,265	157,221	850,980	455,543	$7,676	$ 8,160

Kindergartens are included in the elementary schools; junior high schools, in the secondary schools.
Enrollment data show cumulative count of pupils registered at any time during the school year in each state.
*At the beginning of the 1967–68 school year.   †Money received from loans, sales of bonds, sales of property purchased from capital funds, and insurance adjustments.
‡Includes extra pay for coaching, supervising intern teachers, etc.   §Excludes vocational and technical-vocational schools.
||Excludes state's share of teacher retirement and social security.   ¶Excludes kindergarten.   ⁹Includes an estimate for nonreporting states.
δIncludes librarians; guidance and psychological personnel; related instructional workers.
Sources: National Education Association, Research Division, *Estimates of School Statistics*, 1968–69 (copyright 1968. All rights reserved. Used by permission).
U.S. Department of Health, Education, and Welfare, Office of Education, *Digest of Educational Statistics*, 1968.

Private elementary and secondary day schools

fall 1968 estimates

State	ENROLLMENT Elementary	ENROLLMENT Secondary	CLASSROOM TEACHERS Elementary	CLASSROOM TEACHERS Secondary	State	ENROLLMENT Elementary	ENROLLMENT Secondary	CLASSROOM TEACHERS Elementary	CLASSROOM TEACHERS Secondary
Alabama	21,300	7,600	870	580	Montana	13,900	4,300	500	270
Alaska	1,400	900	70	100	Nebraska	42,200	14,200	1,520	910
Arizona	25,700	7,200	930	520	Nevada	3,500	1,000	140	60
Arkansas	9,400	3,300	370	230	New Hampshire	23,300	10,800	830	840
California	330,600	98,800	11,810	6,230	New Jersey	248,100	63,500	7,500	4,030
Colorado	32,700	10,400	1,450	880	New Mexico	18,200	5,200	700	420
Connecticut	81,200	37,900	3,010	3,000	New York	666,900	193,300	22,820	11,060
Delaware	14,200	5,400	490	360	North Carolina	16,600	4,900	780	500
District of Columbia	14,300	7,900	620	650	North Dakota	13,500	5,000	560	350
Florida	72,300	17,200	2,870	1,300	Ohio	278,200	85,000	8,450	4,540
Georgia	18,500	9,400	800	770	Oklahoma	13,900	3,700	600	290
Hawaii	18,600	10,200	750	670	Oregon	25,900	7,700	960	560
Idaho	7,400	1,400	240	100	Pennsylvania	434,900	137,800	12,530	7,440
Illinois	414,300	111,300	12,710	5,890	Rhode Island	37,500	10,900	1,270	730
Indiana	107,800	26,700	3,480	1,510	South Carolina	11,600	4,100	570	330
Iowa	70,000	25,400	2,620	1,510	South Dakota	13,100	4,600	550	360
Kansas	37,100	11,700	1,270	740	Tennessee	21,100	12,700	1,000	960
Kentucky	66,600	22,400	2,170	1,430	Texas	124,100	28,600	5,240	2,080
Louisiana	105,200	30,600	3,760	1,820	Utah	4,000	2,000	140	170
Maine	18,200	11,900	600	910	Vermont	9,100	7,200	330	570
Maryland	100,800	31,000	3,410	2,260	Virginia	41,400	18,800	1,790	1,580
Massachusetts	172,300	73,200	5,790	4,780	Washington	42,900	13,600	1,460	890
Michigan	258,000	78,600	7,630	4,060	West Virginia	10,400	3,600	370	280
Minnesota	125,000	29,900	4,430	1,960	Wisconsin	214,800	43,100	7,100	2,530
Mississippi	15,000	5,600	670	400	Wyoming	3,000	800	120	70
Missouri	129,900	37,700	4,350	2,520	Total U.S.	4,600,000	1,400,000	155,000	87,000

Data exclude subcollegiate departments of institutions of higher education and residential schools for exceptional children.
Source: U.S. Department of Health, Education, and Welfare, Office of Education, *Digest of Educational Statistics*.

Total in $000	Federal	State	Local	Nonrevenue receipts† in $000	For day schools	For other programs	Capital outlay in $000
365,000	15.9	60.0	24.1	18,000	300,376	1,600	38,000
73,310	25.7	44.7	29.6	25,423	68,570	480	22,000
274,907	8.0	55.2	36.8	45,000	262,179	...	18,583
225,210	16.9	46.7	36.4	25,000	201,746	2,425	40,109
3,675,000	5.9	34.3	59.9	380,000	2,950,000	385,000	523,000
366,000	7.1	24.0	68.9	35,000	310,000	10,500	46,000
568,000	4.4	31.3	64.3	50,000	470,000	4,000	40,000
108,000	7.4	72.7	19.9	20,000	86,800	200	25,000
178,443	34.9	—	65.1	...	123,300	5,200	36,768
996,990	10.2	56.5	33.3	43,000	837,362	884	181,772
588,665	11.0	63.2	25.7	45,000	537,496	9,000	40,000
153,300	10.0	84.8	5.2	...	110,000	6,000	16,000
102,575	9.3	40.9	49.7	7,000	93,000	600	12,000
1,822,828	5.2	26.7	68.1	143,255	1,498,753	73,048	243,016
908,000	4.8	34.0	61.1	62,100	718,600	14,000	100,000
479,000	4.2	32.6	63.2	40,000	440,000	10,000	60,000
406,981	7.8	29.2	63.0	35,000	308,093	9,874	60,276
411,000	15.8	51.3	32.8	40,000	345,000	3,700	22,000
594,275	10.3	62.8	26.9	80,000	505,000	1,000	85,000
137,931	7.2	34.7	58.0	10,000	120,726	4,290	13,750
781,559	6.7	37.3	56.0	108,172	624,245	27,293	171,232
871,000	6.9	22.4	70.7	80,000	700,000	11,000	74,000
1,697,377	3.9	44.3	51.7	240,000	1,300,000	43,000	240,000
679,000	6.6	43.3	50.1	100,000	580,000	8,000	100,000
295,554	20.0	53.1	26.9	22,000	251,305	18,000	30,000
648,182	6.3	34.3	59.4	55,000	555,638	30,000	97,500
127,000	7.1	27.6	65.4	12,000	113,000	1,800	12,000
187,257	7.6	17.6	74.8	30,000	159,383	9,700	30,600
90,900	7.2	38.8	54.0	15,000	74,000	1,250	10,000
96,892‖	4.9	9.1‖	86.0	18,460	83,597‖	596	19,069
1,305,000	4.6	27.5	67.9	160,000	1,200,000	15,000	175,000
192,847	15.1	61.8	23.1	16,240	160,515	2,863	31,794
4,166,000	4.2	47.8	47.9	475,000	3,527,000	174,000	400,000
645,000	12.9	67.3	19.8	60,000	565,000	27,000	72,000
97,800	7.9	26.1	66.0	9,000	83,000	1,400	16,000
1,589,400	5.3	34.9	59.8	145,000	1,425,000	25,000	200,000
352,000	11.9	32.7	55.4	30,000	280,000	2,500	38,000
432,200	6.7	17.7	75.6	36,000	346,914	20,803	59,836
1,892,683	5.5	45.2	49.3	68,400	1,605,568	57,637	167,888
121,671	6.7	33.6	59.7	20,000	121,671	750	19,000
338,000	12.1	63.6	24.3	15,000	289,300	10,000	35,000
96,400	14.9	11.4	73.7	10,000	86,700	250	17,000
461,800	11.9	48.7	39.4	50,000	405,800	11,000	52,800
1,508,528¶	11.6	47.1	41.3	210,000¶	1,149,540¶	9,000	250,000
182,112	6.1	52.0	41.9	16,250	150,385	4,940	37,448
84,298	4.2	29.7	66.2	9,539	61,000	100	10,750
700,000	9.3	40.7	50.0	80,000	589,200	20,000	110,000
600,000	6.7	60.8	32.5	80,000	510,000	40,000	82,000
225,100	12.2	50.2	37.6	10,000	200,000	3,000	27,000
728,478	4.6	26.0	69.4	110,000	676,336	12,654	111,800
63,000	20.6	25.4	54.0	10,000	58,500	...	8,200
33,692,453	7.3	40.9	51.9	3,404,839	28,219,598	1,130,337	4,329,191

Characteristics of teachers, 1967

public elementary and secondary schools

	Elementary school	Secondary school	Men	Women
	(Percent distribution)			
Experience				
1 year	6.2	9.4	8.9	7.1
2 to 3 years	14.7	18.7	18.2	15.9
4 to 6 years	15.5	18.5	19.5	15.6
7 to 9 years	11.7	13.3	16.3	10.5
10 to 14 years	17.6	13.7	14.8	16.2
15 to 19 years	10.3	10.8	11.7	9.9
20 to 29 years	14.3	8.9	5.7	14.7
30 years or more	9.7	6.7	4.9	10.1
Median years	10.0	7.0	7.0	10.0
Age				
24 years or less	14.0	16.0	13.1	15.9
25 to 29 years	16.1	22.3	25.4	15.8
30 to 34 years	9.7	11.9	15.7	8.2
35 to 39 years	10.7	9.7	13.1	8.8
40 to 49 years	20.8	19.9	20.9	20.2
50 to 59 years	20.2	15.5	9.3	22.3
60 years or more	8.5	4.7	2.5	8.8
Median years	39.0	34.0	33.0	40.0
Highest degree held				
No degree	2.4	0.8	0.8	2.1
2-year degree	7.9	0.7	1.1	6.2
Bachelor's degree	72.9	63.0	58.3	73.1
Master's degree	15.7	34.1	38.1	17.6
Professional degree, 6 years	1.1	1.3	1.5	1.0
Doctor's degree	0.0	0.1	0.2	0.0

Data as of spring of year. Based on sample survey.
Source: U.S. Department of Commerce, Bureau of the Census, *Statistical Abstract of the United States.* Data compiled by the National Education Association.

Universities and colleges

state statistics

State	Total	Public	Total	First-time students	Bachelor's and first professional	Master's, except first professional	Doctor's
	NUMBER OF INSTITUTIONS fall, 1967		ENROLLMENT fall, 1967		EARNED DEGREES CONFERRED 1966–1967		
Alabama	44	24	88,575	22,694	8,371	1,560	127
Alaska	3	1	5,836	766	204	81	2
Arizona	12	9	78,549	21,381	5,675	2,235	233
Arkansas	21	10	48,505	13,421	5,072	848	76
California	189	100	974,426	244,181	50,608	14,501	2,333
Colorado	24	15	93,309	21,216	8,011	2,842	389
Connecticut	42	12	95,796	20,398	7,690	2,965	413
Delaware	4	2	15,173	3,430	1,059	322	48
District of Columbia	22	1	65,104	8,641	6,366	3,567	326
Florida	54	32	179,847	47,554	12,302	2,932	447
Georgia	53	23	98,476	22,259	9,660	1,781	231
Hawaii	4	1	27,847	8,186	1,626	555	28
Idaho	11	6	26,372	8,196	2,013	314	13
Illinois	124	33	343,292	83,864	28,133	9,426	1,397
Indiana	41	5	163,393	36,826	16,757	7,268	863
Iowa	51	17	99,072	27,269	11,058	2,019	530
Kansas	49	24	89,069	23,320	9,142	2,402	249
Kentucky	38	8	90,211	22,496	8,605	1,470	115
Louisiana	21	10	104,171	22,288	9,958	2,315	291
Maine	22	7	25,519	6,012	2,916	363	8
Maryland	46	20	115,510	22,922	8,847	1,759	354
Massachusetts	106	28	252,638	57,975	23,380	8,889	1,280
Michigan	87	36	317,466	75,492	26,201	9,643	1,043
Minnesota	57	23	138,239	31,283	13,606	2,131	408
Mississippi	41	25	64,716	19,381	6,349	1,073	94
Missouri	65	18	153,281	39,484	14,189	3,575	424
Montana	12	9	23,175	6,396	2,749	376	49
Nebraska	24	12	54,955	13,314	6,730	967	171
Nevada	1	1	8,575	2,074	629	127	6
New Hampshire	20	6	25,793	6,342	2,925	424	31
New Jersey	45	14	152,548	29,261	14,080	3,878	463
New Mexico	11	8	33,767	7,104	2,576	941	82
New York	199	62	677,251	123,784	55,832	20,249	2,472
North Carolina	78	34	134,979	36,858	13,696	2,593	438
North Dakota	13	10	26,501	7,345	2,804	461	41
Ohio	80	16	313,956	77,056	30,363	6,418	755
Oklahoma	34	23	100,352	23,842	9,291	2,190	365
Oregon	41	20	90,305	24,179	7,611	2,086	270
Pennsylvania	148	29	347,894	76,450	35,796	8,322	974
Rhode Island	14	3	36,909	8,509	3,489	848	108
South Carolina	33	9	51,812	15,208	5,581	618	53
South Dakota	17	7	27,483	7,195	3,272	577	28
Tennessee	50	11	112,583	26,651	11,763	2,284	237
Texas	110	60	348,481	83,951	29,877	6,192	783
Utah	9	5	75,773	13,499	6,989	1,368	230
Vermont	17	5	16,407	4,968	2,128	501	8
Virginia	57	23	117,531	34,326	9,936	1,714	207
Washington	38	20	144,496	43,442	11,018	2,191	359
West Virginia	21	11	52,688	13,753	5,067	1,305	49
Wisconsin	58	27	156,553	38,187	14,791	3,427	664
Wyoming	6	6	12,010	2,948	1,016	290	45
Total U.S.	2,367	927	6,897,169	1,637,577	587,807	157,183	20,610

All totals exclude data for service academies.
Source: U.S. Department of Health, Education, and Welfare, Office of Education.

Earned degrees conferred, 1966–67

Field of study	Bachelor's or first professional degrees*	Master's or second level degrees	Doctorates
Agriculture	6,258	1,463	564
Architecture	2,867	443	8
Biological sciences	28,993	5,003	2,256
Business and commerce	69,687	14,894	437
Computer science and systems analysis	222	449	38
Education	120,879	55,861	3,529
Engineering	36,188	13,885	2,614
English and journalism	45,949	7,984	871
Fine and applied arts	21,569	5,812	504
Foreign languages and literature	17,025	4,255	578
Forestry	1,631	298	73
Geography	2,163	463	79
Health professions	29,371	3,417	250
Home economics	6,335	850	66
Law	15,339	818	27
Library sciences	701	4,489	16
Mathematical subjects	21,308	5,284	832
Merchant Marine (deck officer)	215	—	—
Military, naval, or air force science	1,716	—	—
Philosophy	5,420	604	249
Physical sciences	17,794	5,412	3,462
Psychology	19,496	3,138	1,231
Religion	8,168	2,272	312
Social sciences	104,771	18,710	2,507
Trade and industrial training	2,741	107	5
Miscellaneous	8,056	1,981	113
All fields	594,862	157,892	20,621

*Includes first-professional degrees requiring at least 6 years.
Source: U.S. Department of Health, Education, and Welfare, Office of Education.

Universities and colleges

Selected list of accredited schools, 1968

Institution and location	Year founded	Total students	Faculty	Bound library volumes	Endowment fund
A					
Abilene Christian Col., Abilene, Tex.	1906	2,936	172	134,000	$ 4,877,000
Abraham Baldwin Ag. Col. (Jr.), Tifton, Ga.	1933	1,257	70	30,000	—
Adams St. Col., Alamosa, Colo.	1921	3,000	135	130,000	—
Adelphi U., Garden City, N.Y.	1896	8,357	304	190,000	1,750,000
Adrian Col., Adrian, Mich.	1859	1,442	107	62,000	2,227,000
‡Agnes Scott Col., Decatur, Ga.	1889	750	85	100,000	11,900,000
Ag., Mech. & Normal Col., Pine Bluff, Ark.	1873	2,997	152	4,000	—
†Air Force Inst. of Tech., Wright-Patterson AFB, O.	1919	621	111	80,000	—
Akron, U. of, Akron, O.	1870	12,878	702	250,000	2,000,000
Alabama, U. of, University	1831	18,370	1,500	1,122,000	13,055,000
Alabama A. & M. Col., Norman	1875	1,288	121	...	—
Alabama Col., Montevallo	1896	2,400	110	105,000	—
Alaska, U. of, College	1917	1,828	229	220,000	2,449,000
Anchorage Comm. Col. (Jr.)	1954	2,379	85	20,000	—
Ketchikan Comm. Col. (Jr.)	1954	309	13	7,000	—
Juneau-Douglas Comm. Col. (Jr.), Juneau	1956	458	25	7,000	—
Matanuska-Susitna Comm. Col. (Jr.), Palmer	1958	183	11	1,000	—
Alaska Methodist U., Anchorage	1957	496	50	35,000	613,000
Albany St. Col., Albany, Ga.	1903	1,516	96	34,000	—
‡Albertus Magnus Col., New Haven, Conn.	1925	675	61	56,000	243,000
Albion Col., Albion, Mich.	1835	1,654	129	140,000	8,476,000
Albright Col., Reading, Pa.	1856	1,505	103	105,000	2,705,000
Albuquerque, U. of, Albuquerque, N.M.	1940	1,407	87	44,000	—
Alcorn A. & M. Col., Lorman, Miss.	1871	2,235	115	45,000	210,000
Alderson-Broaddus Col., Philippi, W.Va.	1871	793	62	41,000	150,000
Alfred U., Alfred, N.Y.	1857	1,598	151	120,000	4,938,000
Alice Lloyd Col. (Jr.), Pippa Passes, Ky.	1923	267	21	17,000	—
Allan Hancock Col. (Jr.), Santa Maria, Calif.	1920	3,324	120	23,000	—
Allegany Comm. Col. (Jr.), Cumberland, Md.	1961	516	35	23,000	—
Allegheny Col., Meadville, Pa.	1815	1,505	116	179,000	8,235,000
Alliance Col., Cambridge Springs, Pa.	1912	608	48	47,000	—
Alma Col., Alma, Mich.	1886	1,182	78	75,000	1,773,000
Alpena Comm. Col. (Jr.), Alpena, Mich.	1952	806	50	12,000	—
‡Alverno Col., Milwaukee, Wis.	1936	1,391	106	70,000	241,000
Alvin Jr. Col., Alvin, Tex.	1949	1,613	94	11,000	—
Amarillo Col. (Jr.), Amarillo, Tex.	1929	2,408	106	28,000	—
American International Col., Springfield, Mass.	1885	1,724	114	70,000	720,000
American River Col. (Jr.), Sacramento, Calif.	1955	10,042	232	34,000	—
American U., Washington, D.C.	1893	13,211	432	176,000	3,968,000
†Amherst Col., Amherst, Mass.	1821	1,206	137	388,000	55,500,000
Anderson Col., Anderson, Ind.	1917	1,449	85	116,000	510,000
Anderson Col., Anderson, S.C.	1911	827	44	12,000	280,000
Andrew Col. (Jr.), Cuthbert, Ga.	1854	420	23	16,000	283,000
Andrews U., Berrien Springs, Mich.	1874	1,515	124	190,000	285,000
Angelo St. Col., San Angelo, Tex.	1928	2,395	110	30,000	25,000
‡Anna Maria Col. for Women, Paxton, Mass.	1946	672	59	28,000	—
‡Annhurst Col., Woodstock, Conn.	1941	420	52	28,000	—
Antelope Valley Col., Lancaster, Calif.	1929	2,465	119	24,000	—
Antioch Col., Yellow Springs, O.	1852	1,845	145	156,000	5,706,000
Antioch-Putney Grad. Sch. of Ed., Putney, Vt.	1964	116	13	...	—
Appalachian St. U., Boone, N.C.	1903	5,487	255	160,000	522,000
Aquinas Col., Grand Rapids, Mich.	1923	1,510	100	68,000	—
Aquinas Inst. Sch. of Philos., River Forest, Ill.; Sch. of Theol., Dubuque, Ia.	1939	283	34	60,000	—
Arizona, U. of, Tucson	1885	21,284	1,841	1,162,000	1,633,000
Arizona St. U., Tempe	1885	21,037	1,013	522,000	597,000
Arkansas, U. of, Fayetteville	1871	10,500	773	550,000	—
Arkansas A. & M. Col., College Heights	1909	1,663	84	40,000	—
Arkansas Col., Batesville	1872	317	28	43,000	1,000,000
Arkansas Polytech. Col., Russellville	1909	2,293	102	50,000	—
Arkansas St. U., State University	1909	5,551	239	182,000	25,000
Arkansas, St. Col. of, Conway	1907	3,546	162	106,000	—
Armstrong Schools of Business, Berkeley, Calif.	1918	383	30	11,000	—
Armstrong St. Col., Savannah, Ga.	1935	1,508	84	48,000	—
Art Center Col. of Design, Los Angeles, Calif.	1930	1,032	93	6,000	526,000
Art Inst. of Chicago (Ill.), The School of The	1866	1,346	82	82,000	1,870,000
Asbury Col., Wilmore, Ky.	1890	1,021	66	73,000	4,400,000
Asheville-Biltmore Col., Asheville, N.C.	1927	664	58	49,000	—
Ashland Col., Ashland, O.	1878	2,403	138	90,000	1,210,000
†Assumption Col., Worcester, Mass.	1904	1,232	64	93,000	613,000
†Athenaeum of Ohio, Norwood, Cincinnati	1829	568	46	76,000	3,734,000
Athens Col., Athens, Ala.	1822	1,105	69	40,000	1,500,000
Atlantic Christian Col., Wilson, N.C.	1902	1,431	94	72,000	957,000
Atlantic Union Col., South Lancaster, Mass.	1882	889	73	65,000	—
Auburn Comm. Col. (Jr.), Auburn, N.Y.	1953	2,713	140	33,000	—
Auburn U., Auburn, Ala.	1856	12,093	770	550,000	3,400,000
Augsburg Col., Minneapolis, Minn.	1869	1,674	113	75,000	494,000
Augusta Col., Augusta, Ga.	1925	2,285	128	67,000	—
Augustana Col., Rock Island, Ill.	1860	1,833	125	134,000	3,774,000
Augustana Col., Sioux Falls, S.D.	1860	1,901	123	95,000	800,000
Aurora Col., Aurora, Ill.	1893	1,200	85	63,000	240,000
Austin Col., Sherman, Tex.	1849	840	95	90,000	2,771,000
Austin Peay St. Col., Clarksville, Tenn.	1927	2,779	131	85,000	—
‡Averett Col. (Jr.), Danville, Va.	1859	586	40	15,000	98,000
‡Avila Col., Kansas City, Mo.	1916	396	41	46,000	—
Azusa Pacific Col., Azusa, Calif.	1899	790	52	43,000	306,000
B					
Babson Inst., Babson Park, Mass.	1919	1,150	52	45,000	4,352,000
Bacone Col. (Jr.), Bacone, Okla.	1880	604	31	20,000	854,000
Baker U., Baldwin City, Kan.	1858	923	64	55,000	3,028,000
Bakersfield Col. (Jr.), Bakersfield, Calif.	1913	8,243	218	37,000	—
Baldwin-Wallace Col., Berea, O.	1845	2,668	174	122,000	4,741,000
Ball St. U., Muncie, Ind.	1918	13,282	511	305,000	—
Baltimore, Comm. Col. of (Jr.), Baltimore, Md.	1947	3,575	217	40,000	—
Bank Street Col. of Ed., New York, N.Y.	1916	802	48	25,000	588,000
‡Barat Col. of the Sacred Heart, Lake Forest, Ill.	1863	676	59	54,000	—
Barber-Scotia Col., Concord, N.C.	1867	315	30	23,000	713,000
Bard Col., Annandale-on-Hudson, N.Y.	1860	557	59	85,000	267,000
‡Barnard Col., New York, N.Y.	1889	1,900	167	110,000	14,250,000
Barrington Col., Barrington, R.I.	1900	631	65	40,000	305,000
‡Barry Col., Miami, Fla.	1940	1,122	93	62,000	257,000
Barstow Col. (Jr.), Barstow, Calif.	1960	1,189	25	14,000	—
Bates Col., Lewiston, Me.	1864	963	70	130,000	7,867,000
Baylor U., Waco, Tex.	1845	8,164	750	500,000	24,801,000
‡Bay Path Jr. Col., Longmeadow, Mass.	1897	500	30	18,000	$ 750,000
‡Beaver Col., Glenside, Pa.	1853	806	81	62,000	232,000
Belhaven Col., Jackson, Miss.	1883	552	51	35,000	1,100,000
Bellarmine-Ursuline Col., Louisville, Ky.	1968	2,164	128	105,000	—
†Belmont Abbey Col., Belmont, N.C.	1878	755	56	65,000	638,000
Belmont Col., Nashville, Tenn.	1951	1,025	55	41,000	600,000
Beloit Col., Beloit, Wis.	1846	1,563	125	200,000	6,816,000
Bemidji St. Col., Bemidji, Minn.	1913	4,484	230	75,000	—
Benedict Col., Columbia, S.C.	1870	975	56	32,000	517,000
‡Bennett Col., Greensboro, N.C.	1873	686	67	56,000	1,900,000
‡Bennett Col. (Jr.), Millbrook, N.Y.	1891	348	38	26,000	1,588,000
‡Bennington Col., Bennington, Vt.	1932	429	67	56,000	1,110,000
Berea Col., Berea, Ky.	1855	1,364	121	165,000	40,000,000
Berkshire Comm. Col. (Jr.), Pittsfield, Mass.	1960	701	63	15,000	—
Berry Col., Mount Berry, Ga.	1926	1,082	73	60,000	10,812,000
Bethany Bible Col., Santa Cruz, Calif.	1919	458	27	...	—
Bethany Col., Bethany, W.Va.	1840	1,091	71	98,000	8,930,000
Bethany Col., Lindsborg, Kan.	1881	517	41	40,000	1,000,000
Bethany Nazarene Col., Bethany, Okla.	1899	1,687	78	64,000	—
Bethel Col., McKenzie, Tenn.	1842	804	52	46,000	945,000
Bethel Col., North Newton, Kan.	1887	531	61	59,000	922,000
Bethel Col., St. Paul, Minn.	1871	977	88	54,000	145,000
Bethune-Cookman Col., Daytona Beach, Fla.	1872	1,160	57	53,000	1,385,000
Biola Col., La Mirada, Calif.	1908	1,284	84	87,000	—
Birmingham-Southern Col., Birmingham, Ala.	1856	1,000	63	75,000	5,847,000
Bishop Col., Dallas, Tex.	1881	1,523	113	61,000	611,000
Bismarck Jr. Col., Bismarck, N.D.	1939	888	47	16,800	—
Blackburn Col., Carlinville, Ill.	1837	498	37	51,000	3,957,000
Black Hawk Col., Moline, Ill.	1946	2,424	155	19,000	—
Black Hills St. Col., Spearfish, S.D.	1883	2,230	100	47,000	—
Blinn Col. (Jr.), Brenham, Tex.	1883	1,391	65	15,000	—
Bloomfield Col., Bloomfield, N.J.	1868	1,376	75	40,000	1,080,000
Bloomsburg St. Col., Bloomsburg, Pa.	1839	3,531	210	103,000	—
Bluefield Col. (Jr.), Bluefield, Va.	1922	410	29	20,000	118,000
Bluefield St. Col., Bluefield, W.Va.	1895	1,343	61	41,000	—
‡Blue Mountain Col., Blue Mountain, Miss.	1873	349	32	29,000	887,000
Bluffton Col., Bluffton, O.	1900	700	61	50,000	1,144,000
Boise St. Col., Boise, Ida.	1932	3,357	252	50,000	—
Borromeo Sem. of Ohio, Wickliffe	1954	202	21	30,000	—
Boston, Col., Chestnut Hill, Mass.	1863	9,729	959	688,000	8,685,000
Boston U., Boston, Mass.	1869	22,602	2,428	750,000	22,100,000
†Bowdoin Col., Brunswick, Me.	1794	911	114	400,000	27,170,000
Bowie St. Col., Bowie, Md.	1867	1,091	56	40,000	—
Bowling Green St. U., Bowling Green, O.	1910	11,426	907	489,000	—
‡Bradford Jr. Col., Bradford, Mass.	1803	431	53	35,000	657,000
Bradley U., Peoria, Ill.	1897	6,333	314	167,000	4,299,000
Brandeis U., Waltham, Mass.	1947	2,649	373	371,000	25,100,000
‡Brenau Col., Gainesville, Ga.	1878	532	58	29,000	1,337,000
Brescia Col., Owensboro, Ky.	1925	1,115	90	43,000	300,000
Brevard Col. (Jr.), Brevard, N.C.	1853	682	44	25,000	840,000
Brevard Jr. Col., Cocoa, Fla.	1960	5,978	150	28,000	—
Brewton Parker Col., Mt. Vernon, Ga.	1904	720	28	16,000	434,000
‡Briarcliff Col., Briarcliff Manor, N.Y.	1903	633	62	40,000	—
Briar Cliff Col., Sioux City, Ia.	1930	1,071	69	55,000	110,500
Bridgeport, U. of, Bridgeport, Conn.	1927	8,617	485	147,000	3,350,000
Bridgewater Col., Bridgewater, Va.	1880	863	64	68,000	886,000
Brigham Young U., Provo, Utah	1875	20,041	1,246	700,000	8,975,000
Brooklyn (N.Y.), Polytech. Inst. of	1854	5,016	387	145,000	4,734,000
Brooks Inst. of Photography, Santa Barbara, Calif.	1945	381	16	1,000	—
Broome Tech. Comm. Col. (Jr.), Binghamton, N.Y.	1946	3,279	228	26,000	59,000
Broward County, Jr. Col. of, Fort Lauderdale, Fla.	1960	4,271	192	33,000	—
†Brown U. (incl. ‡Pembroke Col.), Providence, R.I.	1764	4,953	1,114	1,192,000	63,656,000
‡Bryn Mawr Col., Bryn Mawr, Pa.	1885	1,252	192	350,000	30,000
Bucknell U., Lewisburg, Pa.	1846	2,692	211	258,000	23,000,000
Buena Vista Col., Storm Lake, Iowa	1891	938	59	51,000	566,000
Butler U., Indianapolis, Ind.	1855	4,260	250	185,000	10,000,000
C					
Cabrillo Col. (Jr.), Aptos, Calif.	1959	3,323	85	25,000	—
‡Cabrini Col., Radnor, Pa.	1957	430	40	34,000	—
‡Caldwell Col. for Women, Caldwell, N.J.	1939	904	63	53,000	—
California, U. of (campuses at Berkeley, Davis, Irvine, Los Angeles, Riverside, San Diego, San Francisco, Santa Barbara, Santa Cruz)	1868	142,335	11,076	7,651,000	194,659,000
California Col. of Medicine, Los Angeles	1896	315	584	52,000	—
California Baptist Col., Riverside	1950	779	44	71,000	47,000
California Col. of Arts and Crafts, Oakland	1907	1,021	76	16,000	43,000
California Inst. of the Arts, Los Angeles	1962	806	70	...	—
†California Inst. of Tech., Pasadena	1891	1,520	600	181,000	110,200,000
California Lutheran Col., Thousand Oaks	1959	930	77	50,000	144,000
California St. Col., California, Pa.	1852	4,911	300	95,000	—
California St. Col., Dominguez Hills, Gardena	1962	548	45	55,000	—
California St. Col., Long Beach	1949	23,324	1,344	352,000	—
California St. Col. at Fullerton	1959	9,177	542	141,000	—
California St. Col. at Hayward	1959	3,830	250	123,000	—
California St. Col. at Los Angeles	1947	21,100	1,200	450,000	—
California St. Col. at San Bernardino	1967	918	67	84,000	—
California St. Polytech. Col., Kellogg-Voorhis, Pomona	1966	5,752	363	130,000	—
California St. Polytech. Col., San Luis Obispo	1901	8,081	470	200,000	—
California Western U., San Diego	1924	1,970	130	145,000	1,125,000
Calvin Col., Grand Rapids, Mich.	1876	3,209	172	170,000	360,000
Cameron State Ag. Col., Lawton, Okla.	1909	2,950	112	30,000	—
Campbell Col., Buie's Creek, N.C.	1887	2,299	126	60,000	845,000
Campbellsville Col., Campbellsville, Ky.	1906	957	52	44,000	160,000
Canal Zone Col., Balboa Heights, C.Z.	1933	1,500	53	20,000	—
Canisius Col., Buffalo, N.Y.	1870	3,418	219	123,000	618,000
Capital U., Columbus, O.	1850	1,866	128	69,000	2,059,000
†Cardinal Glennon Col., St. Louis, Mo.	1900	196	29	47,000	—
‡Cardinal Stritch Col., Milwaukee, Wis.	1937	651	54	40,000	150,000
Carleton Col., Northfield, Minn.	1866	1,362	136	232,000	16,500,000
Carnegie-Mellon U., Pittsburgh, Pa.	1967	5,278	434	297,000	93,882,000
Carroll Col., Helena, Mont.	1909	993	65	43,000	3,000,000

†Men's schools, ‡women's schools; the others are coeducational.

Institution and location	Year found-ed	Total stu-dents	Faculty	Bound library volumes	Endowment fund
Carroll Col., Waukesha, Wis.	1846	1,018	84	82,000	$ 2,034,000
Carson-Newman Col., Jefferson City, Tenn.	1851	1,712	104	90,000	1,544,000
Carthage Col., Kenosha, Wis.	1847	1,925	94	75,000	2,920,000
Cascade Col., Portland, Ore.	1918	252	35	29,000	42,000
Case Western Reserve U., Cleveland, O.	1826	10,130	4,146	1,029,000	135,000,000
Casper Col., Casper, Wyo.	1945	2,428	129	24,000	84,000
Castleton St. Col., Castleton, Vt.	1867	964	80	25,000	—
Catawba Col., Salisbury, N.C.	1851	1,046	81	73,000	3,502,000
‡Catherine Spalding Col., Louisville, Ky.	1920	1,766	116	85,000	—
Catholic U. of America, Washington, D.C.	1887	6,591	825	730,000	7,207,000
Catholic U. of Puerto Rico, Ponce	1948	6,363	388	117,000	416,000
‡Cazenovia Col., Cazenovia, N.Y.	1824	553	47	22,000	285,000
‡Cedar Crest Col., Allentown, Pa.	1867	636	50	60,000	2,008,000
Centenary Col., Shreveport, La.	1825	1,465	105	84,000	6,391,000
‡Centenary Col. for Women, Hackettstown, N.J.	1867	665	70	31,000	306,000
Central Col., Pella, Ia.	1853	1,093	73	67,000	1,285,000
Central Connecticut St. Col., New Britain	1849	10,485	564	135,000	—
Central Florida Jr. Col., Ocala	1958	1,090	60	21,000	250,000
Central Methodist Col., Fayette, Mo.	1854	937	65	81,000	3,800,000
Centralia Col. (Jr.), Centralia, Wash.	1925	1,400	75	15,000	—
Central Michigan U., Mt. Pleasant	1892	10,128	530	301,000	108,000
Central Missouri St. Col., Warrensburg	1871	11,080	522	240,000	—
Central St. Col., Edmond, Okla.	1890	8,809	281	118,000	—
Central St. U., Wilberforce, O.	1887	2,684	160	75,000	—
Central Washington St. Col., Ellensburg	1891	5,701	356	164,000	—
Central Wesleyan Col., Central, S.C.	1906	229	20	20,000	215,000
Centre Col. of Kentucky, Danville	1819	697	62	80,000	4,569,000
Cerritos Col., Norwalk, Calif.	1955	10,555	285	38,000	—
Chabot Col. (Jr.), Hayward, Calif.	1961	4,922	187	...	—
Chadron St. Col., Chadron, Neb.	1911	1,852	93	88,000	—
Chaffey Col. (Jr.), Alta Loma, Calif.	1883	6,545	227	43,000	—
Chaminade Col. of Honolulu, Hawaii	1955	725	53	36,000	—
Chapman Col., Orange, Calif.	1861	3,035	252	68,000	1,075,000
Charleston, Col. of, Charleston, S.C.	1770	442	34	34,000	1,000,000
‡Chatham Col., Pittsburgh, Pa.	1869	669	77	76,000	11,000,000
Chattanooga, U. of, Chattanooga, Tenn.	1886	2,638	160	281,000	5,345,000
‡Chestnut Hill Col., Philadelphia, Pa.	1871	1,073	72	77,000	551,000
Cheyney St. Col., Cheyney, Pa.	1837	1,773	128	65,000	—
Chicago, The U. of, Chicago, Ill.	1892	10,531	1,086	2,504,000	181,921,000
Chicago (Ill.) City Jr. Col. (incl. Amundsen-Mayfair, Bogan, Crane, Fenger, Loop, Southeast, Wilson, Wright)	1911	36,000	940	126,000	—
Chico St. Col., Chico, Calif.	1887	7,528	479	180,000	—
Chipola Jr. Col., Marianna, Fla.	1947	1,038	75	21,000	—
Chowan Col. (Jr.), Murfreesboro, N.C.	1848	1,163	72	26,000	220,000
†Christian Brothers Col., Memphis, Tenn.	1871	1,130	78	47,000	300,000
‡Christian Col. (Jr.), Columbia, Mo.	1851	565	39	22,000	117,000
Church Col. of Hawaii, Laie	1955	1,028	75	55,000	—
Cincinnati, U. of, Cincinnati, O.	1819	27,259	2,400	900,000	36,494,000
Cisco Jr. Col., Cisco, Tex.	1940	813	50	11,000	75,000
Citrus Jr. Col., Azusa, Calif.	1915	5,483	230	40,000	—
Claflin Col., Orangeburg, S.C.	1869	779	51	31,000	550,000
Claremont (Calif.) Grad. Sch.	1925	968	285	440,000	17,800,000
†Claremont (Calif.) Men's Col.	1946	737	80	440,000	12,000,000
Clarion St. Col., Clarion, Pa.	1866	3,319	212	150,000	—
Clark Col., Atlanta, Ga.	1869	1,040	89	32,000	1,771,000
Clark Col. (Jr.), Vancouver, Wash.	1933	2,799	115	21,000	—
‡Clarke Col., Dubuque, Ia.	1843	1,106	114	72,000	641,000
Clarke Memorial Col. (Jr.), Newton, Miss.	1908	298	20	13,000	485,000
Clarkson Col. of Tech., Potsdam, N.Y.	1895	2,575	165	75,000	3,791,000
Clark U., Worcester, Mass.	1887	2,733	227	270,000	10,229,000
Clatsop Comm. Col., Astoria, Ore.	1958	1,098	50	11,000	—
Clemson U., Clemson, S.C.	1889	6,057	343	382,000	605,000
Cleveland St. U., The, Cleveland, O.	1964	8,164	469	116,000	—
Coalinga Col. (Jr.), Coalinga, Calif.	1932	607	44	19,000	—
Coe Col., Cedar Rapids, Ia.	1851	1,004	80	126,000	5,754,000
‡Coker Col., Hartsville, S.C.	1908	322	32	45,000	3,500,000
Colby Col., Waterville, Me.	1813	1,479	129	255,000	17,225,000
‡Colby Jr. Col. for Women, New London, N.H.	1837	582	61	39,000	1,315,000
†Colgate U., Hamilton, N.Y.	1819	1,923	168	252,000	22,286,000
‡College Misericordia, Dallas, Pa.	1924	1,134	95	53,000	240,000
Colorado, U. of, Boulder and Denver	1876	26,252	2,324	1,101,000	7,039,000
Colorado Col., Colorado Springs	1874	1,584	150	232,000	10,831,000
Colorado School of Mines, Golden	1874	1,652	135	130,000	400,000
Colorado St. Col., Greeley	1890	7,913	314	280,000	—
Colorado St. U., Fort Collins	1870	14,565	927	425,000	1,000,000
Columbia Basin Col., Pasco, Wash.	1955	2,113	105	17,000	—
‡Columbia, Col., Columbia, S.C.	1854	851	64	58,000	1,300,000
Columbia Union Col., Takoma Park, Md.	1904	1,107	110	73,000	—
Columbia U., New York, N.Y.	1754	17,545	4,183	3,782,000	151,000,000
Columbus Col., Columbus, Ga.	1958	1,167	54	26,000	35,000
Compton District Jr. Col., Compton, Calif.	1927	5,300	155	30,000	—
Concord Col., Athens, W.Va.	1872	1,622	101	70,000	—
Concordia Col., Moorhead, Minn.	1891	2,217	141	109,000	971,000
Concordia Col., St. Paul, Minn.	1905	674	55	52,000	—
Concordia Col. (Jr.), Milwaukee, Wis.	1881	296	21	35,000	—
Concordia Col. (Jr.), Portland, Ore.	1950	147	15	21,000	352,000
Concordia Collegiate Inst., Bronxville, N.Y.	1881	415	45	27,000	—
†Concordia Senior Col., Fort Wayne, Ind.	1957	514	41	43,000	104,000
Concordia Tch. Col., River Forest, Ill.	1864	1,470	131	81,000	396,000
Concordia Tch. Col., Seward, Neb.	1894	1,386	99	50,000	116,000
Connecticut, U. of, Storrs	1881	18,249	1,022	687,000	1,454,000
‡Connecticut Col., New London	1911	1,533	170	235,000	6,449,000
Connors St. Col. (Jr.), Warner, Okla.	1908	600	30	25,000	—
Contra Costa Col. (Jr.), San Pablo, Calif.	1948	5,278	193	38,000	—
‡Converse Col., Spartanburg, S.C.	1889	768	91	74,000	1,738,000
Cooke County Jr. Col., Gainesville, Tex.	1924	1,220	67	16,000	190,000
Cooper Union, New York, N.Y.	1859	1,272	164	100,000	24,131,000
Copiah-Lincoln Jr. Col., Wesson, Miss.	1928	762	51	17,000	—
Coppin St. Col., Baltimore, Md.	1900	647	57	55,000	—
Cornell Col., Mount Vernon, Ia.	1853	983	98	145,000	7,123,000
Cornell U., Ithaca, N.Y.	1865	14,259	3,809	3,200,000	181,566,000
Corning Comm. Col. (Jr.), Corning, N.Y.	1956	2,600	84	34,000	—
‡Cottey Jr. Col., Nevada, Mo.	1884	369	40	35,000	—
Cranbrook Acad. of Art, Bloomfield Hills, Mich.	1927	123	14	15,000	1,100,000
Creighton U., Omaha, Neb.	1878	4,116	605	248,000	5,380,000
Culver-Stockton Col., Canton, Mo.	1853	857	52	81,000	947,000
Cumberland Col., Williamsburg, Ky.	1889	1,117	63	23,000	915,000
Cumberland Col. of Tennessee (Jr.), Lebanon	1842	383	23	17,000	—

Institution and location	Year found-ed	Total stu-dents	Faculty	Bound library volumes	Endowment fund
D					
Dakota Wesleyan U., Mitchell, S.D.	1885	787	51	43,000	$ 1,149,000
Dallas, U. of, University of Dallas Sta., Tex.	1956	1,122	88	57,000	8,000,000
Dallas Baptist Col., Dallas, Tex.	1898	1,088	59	30,000	320,000
Dana Col., Blair, Neb.	1884	1,394	54	57,000	240,000
Daniel Payne Col., Birmingham, Ala.	1889	356	21	9,000	—
†Dartmouth Col., Hanover, N.H.	1769	3,609	510	960,000	110,664,000
David Lipscomb Col., Nashville, Tenn.	1891	2,068	100	68,000	2,261,000
†Davidson Col., Davidson, N.C.	1837	1,004	83	134,000	13,500,000
Davis and Elkins Col., Elkins, W.Va.	1904	729	59	50,000	542,000
Dayton, U. of, Dayton, O.	1850	10,220	528	230,000	2,641,000
Daytona Beach Jr. Col., Daytona Beach, Fla.	1958	2,323	82	33,000	—
Dean Jr. Col., Franklin, Mass.	1865	916	71	24,000	1,000,000
De Anza Col., Cupertino, Calif.	1967	5,891	134	20,000	—
†Deep Springs, Col. (Jr.), Deep Springs, Calif.	1917	18	5	11,000	—
Defiance Col., The, Defiance, O.	1850	1,105	74	52,000	605,000
Delaware, U. of, Newark	1833	11,045	595	670,000	52,000,000
Delaware St. Col., Dover	1891	937	72	53,000	75,000
†Delaware Valley Col. of Sc. & Ag., Doylestown, Pa.	1896	1,055	69	38,000	2,181,000
Del Mar Col. (Jr.), Corpus Christi, Tex.	1935	3,658	176	54,000	—
Delta St. Col., Cleveland, Miss.	1924	2,221	109	70,000	—
Denison U., Granville, O.	1831	1,880	136	160,000	12,821,000
Denver, U. of, Denver, Colo.	1864	8,595	558	545,000	12,655,000
De Paul U., Chicago, Ill.	1898	7,187	490	244,000	1,964,000
De Pauw U., Greencastle, Ind.	1837	2,340	200	272,000	12,423,000
Desert, Col. of the (Jr.), Palm Desert, Calif.	1958	1,293	79	23,000	—
Detroit, U. of, Detroit, Mich.	1877	8,803	525	315,000	3,053,000
Detroit Inst. of Tech., Detroit, Mich.	1891	1,527	92	38,000	77,000
Diablo Valley Col. (Jr.), Pleasant Hill, Calif.	1948	9,383	310	45,000	—
Dickinson Col., Carlisle, Pa.	1773	1,521	121	160,000	8,884,000
Dickinson St. Col., Dickinson, N.D.	1916	1,525	77	50,000	—
Dillard U., New Orleans, La.	1869	1,031	82	61,000	6,503,000
District of Columbia Tch. Col., Washington	1851	2,251	72	91,000	—
District No. 522, Jr. Col., Belleville, Ill.	1946	2,934	190	14,000	—
Dixie Jr. Col., St. George, Utah	1911	1,069	45	25,000	—
Doane Col., Crete, Neb.	1872	717	48	54,000	3,890,000
Dodge City Comm. Jr. Col., Dodge City, Kan.	1935	825	43	13,000	—
Dominican Col., Racine, Wis.	1935	598	49	35,000	—
‡Dominican Col. of San Rafael, Calif.	1890	774	80	57,000	—
Donnelly Col. (Jr.), Kansas City, Kan.	1949	958	42	16,000	—
Drake U., Des Moines, Ia.	1881	7,576	385	260,000	4,100,000
Drew U., Madison, N.J.	1866	1,510	153	286,000	13,966,000
Drexel Inst. of Tech., Philadelphia, Pa.	1891	10,670	688	250,000	13,200,000
Dropsie Col. for Hebrew & Cognate Learning, Philadelphia, Pa.	1907	158	22	95,000	1,611,000
Drury Col., Springfield, Mo.	1873	2,580	148	97,000	2,829,000
Dubuque, U. of, Dubuque, Ia.	1852	907	54	49,000	2,040,000
Duke U., Durham, N.C.	1838	7,581	1,084	1,863,000	60,302,000
‡Dunbarton Col. of Holy Cross, Washington, D.C.	1935	543	59	51,000	41,000
Duquesne U., Pittsburgh, Pa.	1878	6,647	409	257,000	1,839,000
‡D'Youville Col., Buffalo, N.Y.	1908	1,291	110	71,000	129,000
E					
Earlham Col., Richmond, Ind.	1847	1,095	117	147,000	8,447,000
Eastern Indiana Ctr.	0000	698	44	...	—
East Carolina U., Greenville, N.C.	1907	8,671	550	321,000	70,000
East Central Jr. Col., Decatur, Miss.	1928	759	44	10,000	—
East Central St. Col., Ada, Okla.	1909	2,719	101	82,000	—
Eastern Arizona Col. (Jr.), Thatcher	1888	968	50	17,000	—
Eastern Baptist Col., St. Davids, Pa.	1932	470	47	38,000	1,000,000
Eastern Baptist Theol. Sem., Philadelphia, Pa.	1925	195	20	69,000	5,140,000
Eastern Connecticut St. Col., Willimantic	1889	1,818	96	59,006	—
Eastern Illinois U., Charleston	1895	6,165	372	131,000	—
Eastern Kentucky U., Richmond	1906	7,960	411	195,000	—
Eastern Mennonite Col., Harrisonburg, Va.	1917	844	68	46,000	379,000
Eastern Michigan U., Ypsilanti	1849	14,650	920	180,000	70,000
Eastern Montana Col., Billings	1927	3,145	146	92,000	—
Eastern Nazarene Col., Wollaston, Mass.	1918	855	60	50,000	353,000
Eastern New Mexico U., Portales	1934	3,597	200	139,000	—
Eastern Oklahoma St. Col. (Jr.), Wilburton	1909	1,037	41	...	—
Eastern Oregon Col., La Grande	1929	1,366	105	70,000	—
Eastern Utah, Col. of, Price	1938	600	36	16,000	—
Eastern Washington St. Col., Cheney	1890	4,507	273	172,000	—
East Mississippi Jr. Col., Scooba	1928	318	29	11,000	—
East Stroudsburg St. Col., E. Stroudsburg, Pa.	1893	2,528	146	110,000	—
East Tennessee St. U., Johnson City	1911	8,903	542	191,000	—
East Texas Baptist Col., Marshall	1912	629	39	57,000	1,734,000
East Texas St. U., Commerce	1889	7,971	505	365,000	—
‡Edgewood Col., Madison, Wis.	1927	847	65	46,000	—
Edinboro St. Col., Edinboro, Pa.	1857	4,856	246	179,000	—
Eisenhower Col., Seneca Falls, N.Y.	1968	300	24	14,000	50,000
El Camino Col. (Jr.), El Camino College, Calif.	1946	14,263	341	40,000	—
Elizabeth City St. Col., Elizabeth City, N.C.	1891	948	59	28,000	—
‡Elizabeth Seton Col. (Jr.), Yonkers, N.Y.	1960	410	42	21,000	—
Elizabethtown Col., Elizabethtown, Pa.	1899	1,737	100	65,000	1,262,000
Ellsworth Jr. Col., Iowa Falls, Ia.	1895	1,036	56	13,000	40,000
Elmhurst Col., Elmhurst, Ill.	1871	1,390	108	76,000	980,000
Elmira Col., Elmira, N.Y.	1855	1,195	69	106,000	3,350,000
Elon Col., Elon College, N.C.	1889	1,407	84	63,000	1,339,000
Emerson Col., Boston, Mass.	1880	1,173	113	38,000	277,000
‡Emmanuel Col., Boston, Mass.	1919	1,463	132	71,000	—
Emory and Henry Col., Emory, Va.	1836	837	74	90,000	2,980,000
Emory U., Atlanta, Ga.	1836	5,137	1,418	898,000	67,510,000
Oxford Col. of Emory U., Oxford, Ga.	1836	368	34	16,000	—
Emporia, Col. of, Emporia, Kan.	1882	908	54	50,000	625,000
‡Endicott Jr. Col., Beverly, Mass.	1939	850	62	28,000	—
†Epiphany Apostolic Col. (Jr.), Newburgh, N.Y.	1889	32	13	19,000	—
Erskine Col., Due West, S.C.	1839	734	60	45,000	1,384,000
Eureka Col., Eureka, Ill.	1855	518	38	60,000	1,150,000
Evangel Col., Springfield, Mo.	1955	773	60	46,000	—
Evansville, U. of, Evansville, Ind.	1854	4,214	180	80,000	2,025,000
Everett Comm. Col. (Jr.), Everett, Wash.	1941	4,913	150	28,000	—

F

Institution and location	Year founded	Total students	Faculty	Bound library volumes	Endowment fund
†Fairfield U., Fairfield, Conn.	1942	2,738	164	88,000	—
Fairleigh Dickinson U., Rutherford, N.J.	1941	19,042	1,100	369,000	$11,000,000
Fairmont St. Col., Fairmont, W.Va.	1867	2,755	140	72,000	—
Fashion Inst. of Tech. (Jr.), New York, N.Y.	1944	5,220	160	26,000	—
Fayetteville St. Col., Fayetteville, N.C.	1877	1,268	76	55,000	—
Ferris St. Col., Big Rapids, Mich.	1884	6,882	347	130,000	—
Ferrum Jr. Col., Ferrum, Va.	1913	993	54	25,000	336,000
‡Finch Col., New York, N.Y.	1900	393	45	54,000	—
Findlay Col., Findlay, O.	1882	1,339	91	52,000	548,000
Fisk U., Nashville, Tenn.	1867	1,070	105	159,000	9,109,000
Flint Comm. Jr. Col., Flint, Mich.	1923	6,212	224	101,000	—
Florence St. Col., Florence, Ala.	1873	2,688	122	87,000	—
Florida, U. of, Gainesville	1853	16,600	1,400	1,250,000	3,000,000
Florida A. & M. U., Tallahassee	1887	3,783	207	181,000	—
Florida Col. (Jr.), Temple Terrace	1946	362	27	15,000	30,000
Florida Inst. of Tech., Melbourne	1958	2,153	142	25,000	—
Florida Memorial Col., St. Augustine	1892	483	31	35,000	437,000
Florida Southern Col., Lakeland	1885	1,650	100	95,000	1,688,000
Florida St. U., Tallahassee	1857	13,657	985	827,000	69,000
‡Fontbonne Col., St. Louis, Mo.	1917	931	94	62,000	—
Foothill Col. (Jr.), Los Altos Hills, Calif.	1958	8,446	307	50,000	—
Fordham U., Bronx, N.Y.	1841	10,450	539	768,000	10,610,000
Fort Hays Kansas St. Col., Hays	1902	5,115	258	250,000	440,000
Fort Lewis Col., Durango, Colo.	1911	1,450	77	57,000	200,000
Fort Valley St. Col., Fort Valley, Ga.	1895	1,654	85	60,000	82,000
‡Fort Wright Col. of the Holy Names, Spokane, Wash.	1907	411	49	41,000	125,000
Francis T. Nicholls St. Col., Thibodaux, La.	1948	3,836	166	78,000	—
Franklin Col. of Indiana, Franklin	1834	723	62	70,000	3,810,000
†Franklin and Marshall Col., Lancaster, Pa.	1787	1,696	133	194,000	10,025,000
Frank Phillips Col. (Jr.), Borger, Tex.	1946	704	44	18,000	—
Freed-Hardeman Col. (Jr.), Henderson, Tenn.	1908	702	47	28,000	366,000
Fresno City Col. (Jr.), Fresno, Calif.	1910	8,868	188	28,000	—
Fresno St. Col., Fresno, Calif.	1911	10,188	610	235,000	—
Friends U., Wichita, Kan.	1898	995	54	42,000	950,000
Frostburg St. Col., Frostburg, Md.	1898	2,342	109	70,000	—
Fullerton Jr. Col., Fullerton, Calif.	1913	12,133	364	56,000	—
Furman U., Greenville, S.C.	1826	1,639	115	152,000	8,113,000

G

Institution and location	Year founded	Total students	Faculty	Bound library volumes	Endowment fund
Gallaudet Col., Washington, D.C.	1864	640	97	102,000	—
†Gannon Col., Erie, Pa.	1944	2,846	153	81,000	435,000
Gardner-Webb Jr. Col., Boiling Springs, N.C.	1905	1,134	68	32,000	918,000
‡Garland Jr. Col., Boston, Mass.	1872	392	42	11,000	—
Gavilan Col., Gilroy, Calif.	1919	905	35	12,000	—
General Beadle St. Col., Madison, S.D.	1881	1,299	50	35,000	—
General Motors Inst., Flint, Mich.	1919	2,624	235	36,000	—
Geneva Col., Beaver Falls, Pa.	1848	1,741	116	70,000	3,535,000
George Fox Col., Newberg, Ore.	1891	365	45	35,000	945,000
George Peabody Col. for Teachers, Nashville, Tenn.	1875	1,810	170	1,000,000	13,000,000
Georgetown Col., Georgetown, Ky.	1829	1,409	90	87,000	1,411,000
George Washington U., The, Washington, D.C.	1821	12,492	1,670	438,000	13,000,000
George Williams Col., Downers Grove, Ill.	1890	865	52	43,000	743,000
Georgia, U. of, Athens	1785	20,370	1,700	900,000	3,500,000
Georgia Col. at Milledgeville	1889	1,361	84	100,000	425,000
Georgia Inst. of Tech., Atlanta	1885	6,836	455	463,000	1,900,000
†Georgia Mil. Col. (Jr.), Milledgeville	1879	213	20	13,000	—
‡Georgian Court Col., Lakewood, N.J.	1908	605	49	46,000	181,000
Georgia Southern Col., Statesboro	1908	3,993	258	115,000	—
Georgia Southwestern Col., Americus	1926	1,922	87	38,000	—
Georgia St. Col., Atlanta	1913	9,037	435	230,000	18,000
Gettysburg Col., Gettysburg, Pa.	1832	1,840	171	160,000	2,033,000
Glassboro St. Col., Glassboro, N.J.	1923	8,386	313	101,000	—
Glendale Col. (Jr.), Glendale, Calif.	1927	6,623	179	28,000	—
Glenville St. Col., Glenville, W.Va.	1872	1,602	77	42,000	—
Goddard Col., Plainfield, Vt.	1938	744	63	32,000	—
Gogebic Comm. Col. (Jr.), Ironwood, Mich.	1932	530	24	13,000	—
Golden Gate Col., San Francisco, Calif.	1901	2,579	140	50,000	225,000
Gonzaga U., Spokane, Wash.	1887	2,696	203	231,000	655,000
‡Good Counsel Col., White Plains, N.Y.	1923	501	52	52,000	—
Gordon Col., Wenham, Mass.	1889	631	35	50,000	666,000
Gordon Military Col. (Jr.), Barnesville, Ga.	1852	540	27	13,000	—
Goshen Col., Goshen, Ind.	1894	1,230	134	97,000	397,000
‡Goucher Col., Baltimore, Md.	1885	1,052	118	130,000	9,140,000
Graceland Col., Lamoni, Ia.	1895	1,111	76	53,000	450,000
Grambling Col., Grambling, La.	1901	4,154	248	76,000	—
Grand Rapids Jr. Col., Grand Rapids, Mich.	1914	5,031	154	25,000	—
Grand View Col. (Jr.), Des Moines, Ia.	1896	1,421	74	23,000	225,000
Grays Harbor Col. (Jr.), Aberdeen, Wash.	1930	1,737	99	30,000	—
Great Falls, Col. of, Great Falls, Mont.	1932	1,128	56	37,000	291,000
‡Green Mountain Col. (Jr.), Poultney, Vt.	1834	647	46	28,000	344,000
Greensboro Col., Greensboro, N.C.	1838	677	51	53,000	1,549,000
Greenville Col., Greenville, Ill.	1892	748	52	60,000	350,000
Grinnell Col., Grinnell, Ia.	1846	1,155	119	179,000	11,064,000
Grossmont Col. (Jr.), El Cajon, Calif.	1961	5,279	150	25,000	—
Grove City Col., Grove City, Pa.	1876	2,006	108	105,000	2,319,000
Guam, Col. of, Agana, Guam	1952	1,200	75	55,000	7,000
Guilford Col., Greensboro, N.C.	1837	1,499	126	100,000	4,030,000
Gulf Coast Jr. Col., Panama City, Fla.	1957	1,359	70	...	—
‡Gulf Park Col. (Jr.), Long Beach, Miss.	1919	289	30	12,000	—
Gustavus Adolphus Col., St. Peter, Minn.	1862	1,701	131	115,000	1,469,000
‡Gwynedd-Mercy Col., Gwynedd Valley, Pa.	1948	1,051	130	29,000	—

H

Institution and location	Year founded	Total students	Faculty	Bound library volumes	Endowment fund
†Hamilton Col., Clinton, N.Y.	1793	823	82	277,000	18,227,000
Hamline U., St. Paul, Minn.	1854	1,165	96	109,000	8,879,000
†Hampden-Sydney Col., Hampden-Sydney, Va.	1776	559	45	73,000	3,691,000
Hampton Inst., Hampton, Va.	1868	2,398	168	130,000	32,000,000
Hannibal-LaGrange Col. (Jr.), Hannibal and St. Louis, Mo.	1858	643	34	17,000	18,000
Hanover Col., Hanover, Ind.	1827	1,020	71	110,000	6,256,000
Harding Col., Searcy, Ark.	1924	1,762	88	85,000	13,000,000
Hardin-Simmons U., Abilene, Tex.	1891	1,664	112	106,000	$ 4,244,000
Harris Tch. Col., St. Louis, Mo.	1857	1,292	56	40,000	—
Hartford, U. of, West Hartford, Conn.	1957	7,450	487	137,000	3,269,000
‡Hartford (Conn.) Col. for Women (Jr.), Hartford	1933	180	30	...	—
Hartnell Col. (Jr.), Salinas, Calif.	1920	3,050	125	35,000	33,000
Hartwick Col., Oneonta, N.Y.	1928	1,465	97	71,000	4,263,000
†Harvard U., Cambridge, Mass.	1636	16,645	7,450	7,787,000	621,795,000
‡Radcliffe Col.	1879	1,215	...	140,000	19,258,000
Harvey Mudd Col., Claremont, Calif.	1955	292	46	465,000	1,724,000
Hastings Col., Hastings, Neb.	1882	805	63	65,000	2,650,000
†Haverford Col., Haverford, Pa.	1833	570	71	265,000	28,500,000
Hawaii, U. of, Honolulu	1907	20,415	1,089	709,000	6,050,000
Hebrew Tch. Col., Brookline, Mass.	1921	139	15	52,000	300,000
†Hebrew Union Col.-Jewish Inst. of Religion, Cincinnati, O.	1875	224	33	220,000	6,510,000
Heidelberg Col., Tiffin, O.	1850	1,217	85	88,000	3,625,000
Henderson County Jr. Col., Athens, Tex.	1946	1,177	65	15,000	—
Henderson St. Col., Arkadelphia, Ark.	1929	3,256	125	80,000	—
Hendrix Col., Conway, Ark.	1884	833	48	70,000	6,500,000
Henry Ford Comm. Col. (Jr.), Dearborn, Mich.	1938	11,021	521	50,000	—
Hesston Col. (Jr.), Hesston, Kan.	1909	425	35	19,000	31,000
Hibbing St. Jr. Col., Hibbing, Minn.	1916	748	38	11,000	—
Highland Park Col., Highland Park, Mich.	1918	3,600	135	25,000	—
Highline Col., Midway, Wash.	1961	4,003	244	26,000	—
High Point Col., High Point, N.C.	1924	1,284	70	69,000	2,104,000
Hillsdale Col., Hillsdale, Mich.	1844	1,124	65	42,000	4,039,000
Hinds Jr. Col., Raymond, Miss.	1917	2,412	121	25,000	—
Hiram Col., Hiram, O.	1850	1,076	90	95,000	6,672,000
Hiwassee Col. (Jr.), Madisonville, Tenn.	1849	604	32	23,000	347,000
†Hobart and ‡Wm. Smith Colleges, Geneva, N.Y.	1822	1,469	114	125,000	2,904,000
Hofstra U., Hempstead, N.Y.	1935	11,870	703	230,000	6,109,000
‡Hollins Col., Hollins College, Va.	1842	950	97	97,000	4,584,000
Holmes Jr. Col., Goodman, Miss.	1925	1,212	61	19,000	—
†Holy Cross, Col. of the, Worcester, Mass.	1843	2,246	178	229,000	4,843,000
‡Holy Family Col., Manitowoc, Wis.	1935	562	44	35,000	—
‡Holy Family Col., Philadelphia, Pa.	1954	772	51	44,000	500,000
‡Holy Names, Col. of, Oakland, Calif.	1880	1,048	103	84,000	170,000
‡Hood Col., Frederick, Md.	1893	783	76	82,000	2,639,000
Hope Col., Holland, Mich.	1866	1,839	120	106,000	2,294,000
Houghton Col., Houghton, N.Y.	1883	1,162	80	70,000	400,000
Houston, U. of, Houston, Tex.	1934	21,170	1,093	421,000	5,730,000
Howard County Jr. Col., Big Springs, Tex.	1945	1,016	60	15,000	—
Howard Payne Col., Brownwood, Tex.	1889	1,136	75	87,000	2,750,000
Howard U., Washington, D.C.	1867	8,813	1,014	534,000	6,379,000
Humboldt St. Col., Arcata, Calif.	1913	3,850	325	100,000	—
Huntingdon Col., Montgomery, Ala.	1854	876	68	70,000	2,505,000
Huntington Col., Huntington, Ind.	1897	473	40	37,000	520,000
Huron, Col., Huron, S.D.	1883	534	41	42,000	1,580,000
Huston-Tillotson Col., Austin, Tex.	1876	771	59	39,000	212,000
Hutchinson Comm. Jr. Col., Hutchinson, Kan.	1928	1,452	84	19,000	112,000

I

Institution and location	Year founded	Total students	Faculty	Bound library volumes	Endowment fund
Idaho, Col. of, Caldwell	1891	896	89	70,000	1,520,000
Idaho, U. of, Moscow	1889	5,914	433	604,000	14,717,000
Idaho St. U., Pocatello	1901	4,906	344	158,000	17,000
Illinois, U. of, (3 campuses: Urbana-Champaign, Chicago Circle, Medical Center in Chicago), Urbana	1868	42,223	8,513	4,313,000	13,647,000
Illinois Col., Jacksonville	1829	800	49	58,000	3,093,000
Illinois Inst. of Tech., Chicago	1892	7,885	683	1,000,000	7,243,000
Illinois St. U. at Normal	1857	9,508	730	300,000	—
Illinois Valley Comm. Col. (Jr.), La Salle	1924	1,663	81	30,000	—
Illinois Wesleyan U., Bloomington	1850	1,524	145	100,000	5,281,000
‡Immaculata Col., Immaculata, Pa.	1920	1,602	116	73,000	234,000
‡Immaculata Col. of Washington, D.C.	1904	270	36	27,000	—
†Immaculate Conception Sem., Conception, Mo.	1873	325	37	54,000	—
‡Immaculate Heart Col., Los Angeles, Calif.	1916	1,109	94	130,000	208,000
Imperial Valley Col. (Jr.), Imperial, Calif.	1922	1,700	62	15,000	—
‡Incarnate Word Col., San Antonio, Tex.	1881	1,326	101	70,000	1,062,000
Independence (Kan.) Comm. Jr. Col.	1925	483	37	19,000	—
Indiana Central Col., Indianapolis	1902	2,292	113	50,000	635,000
Indiana Inst. of Tech., Fort Wayne	1930	1,036	70	45,000	—
Indiana St. U., Terre Haute	1870	11,716	700	400,000	225,000
Indiana U., Bloomington	1820	45,381	6,945	2,417,000	10,000,000
Indiana U. of Pennsylvania, Indiana	1875	8,300	450	320,000	—
Indian River Jr. Col., Fort Pierce, Fla.	1960	955	56	24,000	—
Inter American U. of Puerto Rico, San German	1912	6,777	271	105,000	830,000
†Iona Col., New Rochelle, N.Y.	1940	3,080	180	92,000	515,000
Iowa, U. of, Iowa City	1847	17,707	3,016	1,354,000	4,144,000
Iowa St. U. of Sc. & Tech., Ames	1858	16,841	910	611,000	2,467,000
Iowa Wesleyan Col., Mt. Pleasant	1842	1,090	65	54,000	1,160,000
Itawamba Jr. Col., Fulton, Miss.	1948	822	43	18,000	—
Ithaca Col., Ithaca, N.Y.	1892	3,211	220	94,000	335,000

J

Institution and location	Year founded	Total students	Faculty	Bound library volumes	Endowment fund
Jackson Comm. Col. (Jr.), Jackson, Mich.	1928	2,949	141	17,000	—
Jackson St. Col., Jackson, Miss.	1877	2,990	126	53,000	—
Jacksonville St. U., Jacksonville, Ala.	1883	4,476	180	120,000	—
Jacksonville U., Jacksonville, Fla.	1934	2,517	150	112,000	2,200,000
Jamestown Col., Jamestown, N.D.	1884	393	44	29,000	1,943,000
Jamestown (N.Y.) Comm. Col. (Jr.)	1950	1,192	94	28,000	—
Jersey City (N.J.) St. Col.	1927	6,450	300	88,000	—
Jewish Theol. Sem. of America, New York, N.Y.	1887	567	98	150,000	17,261,000
John Brown U., Siloam Springs, Ark.	1919	738	48	40,000	12,000,000
John Carroll U., Cleveland, O.	1886	4,459	307	205,000	2,258,000
†Johns Hopkins U., Baltimore, Md.	1876	11,017	2,073	1,618,000	150,200,000
Johnson C. Smith U., Charlotte, N.C.	1867	1,354	85	74,000	2,659,000
Johnson St. Col., Johnson, Vt.	1867	548	39	22,000	—
Joliet Jr. Col., Joliet, Ill.	1901	2,826	130	30,000	—
Jones County Jr. Col., Ellisville, Miss.	1927	2,612	81	22,000	—
Judson Col., Elgin, Ill.	1913	276	31	23,000	600,000
‡Judson Col., Marion, Ala.	1838	450	41	35,000	1,047,000
Juilliard Sch. of Music, New York, N.Y.	1905	1,018	146	35,000	—
Juniata Col., Huntingdon, Pa.	1876	1,107	82	100,000	2,081,000

Institution and location	Year found-ed	Total stu-dents	Faculty	Bound library volumes	Endowment fund

K

Institution and location	Year found-ed	Total stu-dents	Faculty	Bound library volumes	Endowment fund
Kalamazoo Col., Kalamazoo, Mich.	1833	1,223	95	140,000	$11,469,000
Kansas, U. of, Lawrence	1866	17,025	975	1,250,000	24,000,000
Kansas City Kan. Comm. Jr. Col.	1923	1,368	53	13,000	—
Kansas City (Mo.) Art Inst.	1885	503	40	26,000	—
Kansas St. Col. of Pittsburg	1903	5,393	423	282,000	370,000
Kansas St. Tch. Col., Emporia	1863	6,658	376	312,000	975,000
Kansas St. U. of Ag. & Applied Sc., Manhattan	1863	11,073	1,304	472,000	4,356,000
Kansas Wesleyan U., Salina	1886	716	50	55,000	1,309,000
Kaskaskia Col. (Jr.), Centralia, Ill.	1966	1,136	56	...	—
Kearney St. Col., Kearney, Neb.	1905	4,660	216	86,000	148,000
Kellogg Comm. Col. (Jr.), Battle Creek, Mich.	1956	2,942	88	22,000	—
†Kemper Military Sch. & Col. (Jr.), Boonville, Mo.	1844	550	29	18,000	—
Kendall Col. (Jr.), Evanston, Ill.	1934	608	59	19,000	374,000
Kent St. U., Kent, O.	1910	22,946	822	468,000	—
Kentucky, U. of Lexington	1865	13,762	1,150	1,223,000	478,000
Kentucky St. Col., Frankfort	1886	1,535	90	36,000	—
Kentucky Wesleyan Col., Owensboro	1858	1,104	65	44,000	705,000
†Kenyon Col., Gambier, O.	1824	820	68	170,000	6,250,000
‡Keuka Col., Keuka Park, N.Y.	1892	791	70	55,000	1,271,000
Keystone Jr. Col., La Plume, Pa.	1868	682	42	16,000	525,000
Kilgore Col. (Jr.), Kilgore, Tex.	1935	2,184	101	35,000	—
King Col., Bristol, Tenn.	1867	326	30	49,000	1,277,000
†King's Col., Wilkes-Barre, Pa.	1946	1,841	121	85,000	500,000
Knox Col., Galesburg, Ill.	1837	1,309	97	135,000	10,104,000
Knoxville Col., Knoxville, Tenn.	1875	924	75	38,000	1,038,000
Kutztown St. Col., Kutztown, Pa.	1866	3,863	215	108,000	—

L

Institution and location	Year found-ed	Total stu-dents	Faculty	Bound library volumes	Endowment fund
‡Ladycliff Col., Highland Falls, N.Y.	1933	602	48	46,000	—
†Lafayette Col., Easton, Pa.	1826	1,941	166	220,000	24,630,000
LaGrange Col., LaGrange, Ga.	1831	574	43	40,000	4,030,000
‡Lake Erie Col., Painesville, O.	1856	612	58	58,000	1,843,000
Lake Forest Col., Lake Forest, Ill.	1857	1,214	99	100,000	6,831,000
Lakeland Col., Sheboygan, Wis.	1862	545	40	40,000	190,000
Lake Michigan Col., Benton Harbor, Mich.	1946	2,076	84	25,000	—
Lamar St. Col. of Tech., Beaumont, Tex.	1923	9,214	407	138,000	250,000
Lambuth Col., Jackson, Tenn.	1843	863	62	48,000	1,906,000
Lander Col., Greenwood, S.C.	1872	583	41	50,000	—
Lane Col., Jackson, Tenn.	1882	1,034	41	41,000	400,000
Langston U., Langston, Okla.	1897	1,310	83	110,000	—
Lansing Comm. Col. (Jr.), Lansing, Mich.	1957	4,394	171	32,000	—
Laredo Jr. Col., Laredo, Tex.	1947	1,226	37	25,000	—
†La Salle Col., Philadelphia, Pa.	1863	6,292	335	124,000	2,700,000
‡Lasell Jr. Col., Auburndale, Mass.	1851	906	75	21,000	75,000
Lassen Col. (Jr.), Susanville, Calif.	1925	846	38	8,000	—
La Verne Col., La Verne, Calif.	1891	662	46	36,000	1,105,000
Lawrence U., Appleton, Wis.	1847	1,295	112	159,000	20,946,000
Lebanon Valley Col., Annville, Pa.	1866	1,257	78	92,000	2,353,000
Lee Col. (Jr.), Baytown, Tex.	1934	2,209	94	41,000	—
Lee Col., Cleveland, Tenn.	1918	1,113	60	30,000	—
Lees Jr. Col., Jackson, Ky.	1883	319	19	12,000	550,000
Lees-McRae Col. (Jr.), Banner Elk, N.C.	1900	624	38	31,000	750,000
†Lehigh U., Bethlehem, Pa.	1865	4,995	484	472,000	41,074,000
Leicester Jr. Col., Leicester, Mass.	1784	258	23	12,000	410,000
LeMoyne Col., Memphis, Tenn.	1870	641	47	43,000	310,000
Le Moyne Col., Syracuse, N.Y.	1946	1,536	104	73,000	966,000
Lenoir Rhyne Col., Hickory, N.C.	1891	1,264	90	60,000	1,950,000
‡Lesley Col., Cambridge, Mass.	1909	681	53	40,000	275,000
Lewis and Clark Col., Portland, Ore.	1867	1,687	130	75,000	2,533,000
Lewis-Clark Normal School, Lewiston, Ida.	1955	920	53	38,000	89,000
†Lewis Col., Lockport, Ill.	1930	1,663	72	40,000	159,000
‡Limestone Col., Gaffney, S.C.	1845	651	52	37,000	1,042,000
Lincoln Col. (Jr.), Lincoln, Ill.	1865	678	53	13,000	1,051,000
Lincoln Memorial U., Harrogate, Tenn.	1897	688	42	57,000	2,591,000
Lincoln U., Jefferson City, Mo.	1866	2,014	123	86,000	—
†Lincoln U., Lincoln University, Pa.	1854	911	115	100,000	1,707,000
‡Lindenwood Col., St. Charles, Mo.	1827	675	59	59,000	8,339,000
Lindsey Wilson Col. (Jr.), Columbia, Ky.	1904	547	28	16,000	150,000
Linfield Col., McMinnville, Ore.	1849	1,214	78	63,000	3,000,000
Little Rock U., Little Rock, Ark.	1927	3,099	130	64,000	6,000,000
Livingstone Col., Salisbury, N.C.	1879	868	66	62,000	511,000
Livingston St. Col., Livingston, Ala.	1835	1,300	70	40,000	—
Lock Haven St. Col., Lock Haven, Pa.	1870	1,980	140	165,000	—
Loma Linda U., Loma Linda, Calif.	1905	1,277	1,085	135,000	2,266,000
La Sierra Campus, Riverside, Calif.	1922	1,675	125	85,000	124,000
Long Beach (Calif.) City Col. (Jr.)	1927	22,496	803	83,000	—
Long Island U. (incl. Brooklyn Center, C.W. Post Campus, Southampton Campus, and Brooklyn Col. of Pharmacy), Greenvale, N.Y.	1926	20,133	1,054	345,000	3,585,000
‡Longwood Col., Farmville, Va.	1884	1,739	123	97,000	—
Lon Morris Col. (Jr.), Jacksonville, Tex.	1873	373	24	18,000	905,000
†Loras Col., Dubuque, Ia.	1839	1,655	131	165,000	—
‡Loretto Heights Col., Denver, Colo.	1918	941	87	79,000	166,000
Los Angeles (Calif.) City Jr. Col. District:					
East Los Angeles Col.	1945	12,359	175	59,000	—
Los Angeles City Col.	1929	18,816	610	110,000	—
Los Angeles Harbor Col., Wilmington	1949	6,712	260	45,000	—
Los Angeles Pierce Col., Woodland Hills	1947	13,732	250	57,000	—
Los Angeles Trade-Tech. Col.	1949	14,534	778	50,000	—
Los Angeles Valley Col., Van Nuys	1949	16,258	452	74,000	—
Los Angeles (Calif.) Col. of Optometry	1904	169	29	5,000	250,000
Louisburg Col. (Jr.), Louisburg, N.C.	1787	701	49	31,000	670,000
Louisiana Col., Pineville	1906	1,079	61	59,000	2,590,000
Louisiana Polytech. Inst., Ruston	1894	6,490	393	133,000	—
Louisiana St. U. & A. & M. Col., Baton Rouge	1860	16,000	950	1,080,000	553,000
St. U. at Alexandria	1960	610	45	55,000	—
St. U. in New Orleans	1958	6,187	293	300,000	—
St. U. Medical Center, New Orleans	1931	662	216	69,000	—
Louisville, U. of, Louisville, Ky.	1798	7,604	500	500,000	8,111,000
‡Lourdes Jr. Col., Sylvania, O.	1958	115	20	43,000	125,000
Lowell Tech. Inst., Lowell, Mass.	1895	5,816	232	106,000	7,000
Lower Columbia Col. (Jr.), Longview, Wash.	1934	2,190	60	30,000	—
Loyola Col., Baltimore, Md.	1852	2,896	191	75,000	1,867,000
†Loyola U., Los Angeles, Calif.	1911	2,415	161	212,000	2,139,000
Loyola U., Chicago, Ill.	1870	12,651	1,165	470,000	$14,974,000
†Bellarmine Sch. of Theol., North Aurora, Ill.	1934	152	32	120,000	—
Loyola U., New Orleans, La.	1912	4,334	354	235,000	—
Lubbock Christian Col. (Jr.), Lubbock, Tex.	1957	643	42	23,000	250,000
Luther Col., Decorah, Ia.	1861	1,925	124	150,000	1,267,000
Lycoming Col., Williamsport, Pa.	1812	1,444	105	73,000	1,300,000
Lynchburg Col., Lynchburg, Va.	1903	1,763	103	63,000	1,412,000
Lyndon St. Col., Lyndonville, Vt.	1911	531	43	23,000	—

M

Institution and location	Year found-ed	Total stu-dents	Faculty	Bound library volumes	Endowment fund
Macalester Col., St. Paul, Minn.	1885	1,769	148	161,000	26,750,000
MacMurray Col., Jacksonville, Ill.	1846	1,064	73	92,000	4,679,000
Madison Col., Harrisonburg, Va.	1908	3,246	198	132,000	—
‡Madonna Col., Livonia, Mich.	1947	725	44	53,000	—
Maine, U. of (incl. campuses at Portland and Augusta), Orono	1865	7,889	551	472,000	5,101,000
Farmington St. Col., Farmington	1864	870	57	35,000	250,000
Gorham St. Col., Gorham	1879	855	70	35,000	—
Malone Col., Canton, O.	1892	1,129	66	44,000	580,000
Manatee Jr. Col., Bradenton, Fla.	1958	3,000	120	27,000	—
Manchester Col., North Manchester, Ind.	1889	1,418	82	84,000	1,418,000
†Manhattan Col., Bronx, N.Y.	1853	4,598	335	125,000	1,565,000
Manhattan School of Music, New York, N.Y.	1917	693	137	9,000	2,500,000
Manhattanville Col., Purchase, N.Y.	1841	1,402	135	170,000	2,260,000
Mankato St. Col., Mankato, Minn.	1867	10,308	500	220,000	—
Mansfield St. Col., Mansfield, Pa.	1857	2,537	192	82,000	—
Marian Col., Indianapolis, Ind.	1937	1,061	87	55,000	109,000
‡Marian Col. of Fond du Lac, Wis.	1936	472	48	38,000	—
Phoenix Col. (Jr.), Phoenix, Ariz.	1920	11,155	372	61,000	—
Marietta Col., Marietta, O.	1835	1,705	110	156,000	4,478,000
‡Marillac Col., St. Louis, Mo.	1955	407	64	55,000	114,000
Marin, Col. of (Jr.), Kentfield, Calif.	1926	4,674	123	32,000	—
Marion Col., Marion, Ind.	1920	740	44	...	—
†Marion Inst. (Jr.), Marion, Ala.	1842	371	34	14,000	—
Marlboro Col., Marlboro, Vt.	1946	175	31	26,000	12,000
Marquette U., Milwaukee, Wis.	1864	11,611	730	402,000	6,415,000
Marshalltown (Ia.) Comm. Col. (Jr.)	1927	1,201	57	14,000	—
Marshall U., Huntington, W.Va.	1837	7,585	330	163,000	—
Mars Hill Col., Mars Hill, N.C.	1856	1,405	90	61,000	530,000
Martin Col. (Jr.), Pulaski, Tenn.	1870	454	30	11,000	946,000
‡Mary Baldwin Col., Staunton, Va.	1842	708	51	75,000	2,250,000
‡Marycrest Col., Davenport, Ia.	1939	1,089	76	61,000	336,000
‡Marygrove Col. (incl. Monroe campus), Detroit, Mich.	1910	1,366	122	164,000	—
‡Mary Hardin-Baylor Col., Belton, Tex.	1845	993	61	61,000	3,800,000
†Mary Immaculate Sem., Northampton, Pa.	1939	80	13	38,000	—
†Maryknoll Col., Glen Ellyn, Ill.	1949	300	33	42,000	—
Maryland, U. of, College Park	1807	27,995	2,830	800,000	11,241,000
Maryland St. Col. at Princess Anne	1886	765	50	43,000	—
‡Marylhurst Col., Marylhurst, Ore.	1893	780	70	69,000	93,000
‡Mary Manse Col., Toledo, O.	1922	1,284	126	60,000	—
‡Marymount Col., Palos Verde Est., Calif.	1932	351	21	50,000	300,000
Marymount Col., Salina, Kan.	1922	466	63	46,000	—
‡Marymount Col., Tarrytown, N.Y.	1918	1,044	94	64,000	—
‡Marymount Col. of Virginia (Jr.), Arlington	1950	721	50	26,000	—
‡Marymount Manhattan Col., New York, N.Y.	1936	525	72	35,000	245,000
‡Mary Rogers Col., Maryknoll, N.Y.	1931	152	25	48,000	—
Maryville Col., Maryville, Tenn.	1819	829	69	83,000	4,000,000
‡Maryville Col. of the Sacred Heart, St. Louis, Mo.	1872	563	54	57,000	—
‡Marywood Col., Scranton, Pa.	1915	1,900	120	84,000	269,000
Massachusetts, U. of, Amherst and Boston	1863	17,266	1,200	532,000	870,000
Massachusetts Col. of Art, Boston	1873	500	43	18,000	—
Massachusetts Inst. of Tech., Cambridge	1861	7,730	1,646	1,065,000	135,184,000
Massachusetts State Colleges:					
St. Col. at Boston	1852	6,687	321	58,000	—
St. Col. at Bridgewater	1840	5,250	250	50,000	20,000
St. Col. at Fitchburg	1894	3,232	150	50,000	—
St. Col. at Framingham	1839	2,750	140	47,000	—
St. Col. at Lowell	1894	1,930	105	50,000	—
St. Col. at North Adams	1894	1,348	70	40,000	—
St. Col. at Salem	1854	5,666	203	70,000	—
St. Col. at Westfield	1839	4,944	329	46,000	—
St. Col. at Worcester	1871	3,526	106	57,000	—
Mauna Olu Col., Paia, Hawaii	1861	147	18	14,000	21,000
Mayville St. Col., Mayville, N.D.	1889	801	46	56,000	—
McMurry Col., Abilene, Tex.	1922	1,507	87	83,000	2,916,000
McNeese St. Col., Lake Charles, La.	1939	4,366	204	89,000	—
McPherson Col., McPherson, Kan.	1887	753	49	38,000	1,026,000
‡Medaille Col., Buffalo, N.Y.	1937	450	35	53,000	—
Memphis Acad. of Arts, Memphis, Tenn.	1936	510	30	7,000	—
Memphis St. U., Memphis, Tenn.	1909	14,216	586	250,000	—
†Menlo Col., Menlo Park, Calif.	1915	525	52	30,000	—
Mercer County Comm. Col. (Jr.), Trenton, N.J.	1966	2,612	135	26,000	—
Mercer U., Macon, Ga.	1833	1,941	118	140,000	9,000,000
Mercy Col. of Detroit, Mich.	1941	1,226	92	58,000	—
‡Mercyhurst Col., Erie, Pa.	1926	701	62	45,000	—
Meridian Jr. Col., Meridian, Miss.	1937	1,290	65	14,000	—
‡Meredith Col., Raleigh, N.C.	1891	856	67	50,000	1,150,000
Merrimack Col., North Andover, Mass.	1947	2,353	174	50,000	373,000
Merritt Col., Oakland, Calif.	1953	8,465	425	38,000	—
Mesa Jr. Col., Grand Junction, Colo.	1925	2,391	99	30,000	—
Mesabi St. Jr. Col., Virginia, Minn.	1966	629	29	25,000	—
Messiah Col., Grantham, Pa.	1909	447	39	42,000	464,000
Miami, U. of, Coral Gables, Fla.	1925	14,237	585	813,000	18,000,000
Metropolitan Jr. Col., Kansas City, Mo.	1915	5,686	165	40,000	—
Miami-Dade Jr. Col., Miami, Fla.	1960	21,661	730	75,000	—
Miami U., Oxford, O.	1809	10,531	789	469,000	1,667,000
Michigan, U. of, Ann Arbor	1817	37,283	2,277	3,715,000	49,884,000
Michigan St. U., East Lansing	1855	45,949	3,051	1,287,000	4,355,000
Oakland U., Rochester	1957	2,699	150	...	
Michigan Tech. U. (incl. Lake Superior St. Col. at Sault Ste. Marie), Houghton	1885	5,015	358	133,000	1,093,000
Middlebury Col., Middlebury, Vt.	1800	1,357	115	170,000	16,750,000
Middle Georgia Col. (Jr.), Cochran	1928	1,676	82	32,000	—
Middle Tennessee St. U., Murfreesboro	1911	6,041	349	146,000	—
Midland Lutheran Col., Fremont, Neb.	1883	810	52	60,000	656,000

Universities and colleges (continued)

Institution and location	Year founded	Total students	Faculty	Bound library volumes	Endowment fund
‡Midway Jr. Col., Midway, Ky.	1847	180	15	14,000	$ 334,000
Midwestern U., Wichita Falls, Tex.	1922	3,391	150	95,000	—
Millersville St. Col., Millersville, Pa.	1855	3,643	272	130,000	—
Milligan Col., Milligan College, Tenn.	1882	864	60	47,000	—
Millikin U., Decatur, Ill.	1901	1,225	117	98,000	3,655,000
‡Mills Col., Oakland, Calif.	1852	755	85	145,000	10,955,000
‡Mills Col. of Education, New York, N.Y.	1909	520	42	36,000	214,000
Millsaps Col., Jackson, Miss.	1892	935	79	73,000	4,723,000
Milwaukee Tech. Col. (Jr.), Milwaukee, Wis.	1951	8,020	451	27,000	—
Minneapolis (Minn.) School of Art	1886	341	40	28,000	—
Minnesota, U. of, Minneapolis, St. Paul, Duluth, Morris, Crookston	1851	64,558	3,507	2,500,000	78,320,000
Minot St. Col., Minot, N.D.	1913	2,752	130	80,000	—
MiraCosta Col. (Jr.), Oceanside, Calif.	1934	1,688	74	15,000	—
Mississippi, U. of, University	1848	8,641	882	400,000	639,000
Mississippi Col., Clinton	1826	2,102	92	106,000	1,943,000
Mississippi Delta Jr. Col., Moorhead	1911	897	48	16,000	—
Mississippi Gulf Coast Jr. Col. District: Perkinston Col., Perkinston	1911	516	42	16,000	—
‡Mississippi St. Col. for Women, Columbus	1884	2,419	209	144,000	195,000
Mississippi St. U., State College	1878	7,914	694	285,000	410,000
Missouri, U. of, Columbia	1839	19,008	2,353	1,350,000	4,409,000
Missouri, U. of, at Kansas City	1933	8,025	879	312,000	944,000
Missouri, U. of, at Rolla	1870	4,907	502	131,000	627,000
Missouri, U. of, at St. Louis	1963	6,110	225	65,000	—
Missouri Southern Col. (Jr.), Joplin	1937	1,497	67	20,000	—
Missouri Valley Col., Marshall	1888	877	48	58,000	1,628,000
Missouri Western Col. (Jr.), St. Joseph	1915	1,259	63	20,000	—
Mitchell Col. (Jr.), Statesville, N.C.	1852	492	32	15,000	487,000
Modesto (Calif.) Jr. Col.	1921	4,079	230	60,000	8,008,000
Mohawk Valley Comm. Col., Utica, N.Y.	1946	3,292	253	33,000	—
Monmouth Col., Monmouth, Ill.	1853	1,392	98	114,000	2,115,000
Monmouth Col., West Long Branch, N.J.	1933	4,742	264	85,000	1,168,000
Monroe Comm. Col. (Jr.), Rochester, N.Y.	1962	4,337	178	28,000	—
Montana, U. of, Missoula	1893	6,465	358	450,000	1,218,000
Montana Col. of Min. Sc. & Tech., Butte	1893	597	41	36,000	1,600,000
Montana St. U., Bozeman	1893	6,277	660	450,000	3,108,000
Montclair St. Col., Upper Montclair, N.J.	1908	7,884	321	113,000	150,000
Monterey (Calif.) Inst. of Foreign Studies	1955	195	42	21,000	—
Monterey Peninsula Col., Monterey, Calif.	1947	2,349	92	34,000	—
Montgomery Jr. Col., Takoma Park and Rockville, Md.	1946	4,685	305	38,000	—
‡Monticello Col. (Jr.), Godfrey, Ill.	1835	360	41	28,000	623,000
Montreat-Anderson Col. (Jr.), Montreat, N.C.	1916	424	35	28,000	370,000
‡Moore Col. of Art, Philadelphia, Pa.	1844	513	71	20,000	5,000,000
Moorhead St. Col., Moorhead, Minn.	1887	3,884	265	90,000	12,000
Moravian Col., Bethlehem, Pa.	1807	1,126	80	89,000	4,545,000
Morehead St. U., Morehead, Ky.	1922	5,783	277	123,000	—
†Morehouse Col., Atlanta, Ga.	1867	989	81	210,000	4,270,000
Morgan St. Col., Baltimore, Md.	1867	3,864	284	102,000	—
Morningside Col., Sioux City, Ia.	1894	1,314	105	87,000	2,447,000
Morris Brown Col., Atlanta, Ga.	1881	1,142	96	22,000	1,004,000
Morris Harvey Col., Charleston, W.Va.	1888	2,830	129	52,000	1,120,000
Morristown Col., Morristown, Tenn.	1881	280	15	12,000	136,000
Morton Jr. Col., Cicero, Ill.	1924	2,429	146	18,000	—
‡Mt. Aloysius Jr. Col., Cresson, Pa.	1939	431	49	25,000	—
Mt. Angel Col., Mt. Angel, Ore.	1887	378	53	41,000	30,000
†Mt. Angel Sem., St. Benedict, Ore.	1887/89	130	37	50,000	—
‡Mt. Holyoke Col., South Hadley, Mass.	1837	1,806	185	300,000	27,700,000
‡Mt. Marty Col., Yankton, S.D.	1936	472	56	35,000	—
‡Mt. Mary Col., Milwaukee, Wis.	1872	1,100	95	71,000	450,000
‡Mt. Mercy Col., Cedar Rapids, Ia.	1928	651	54	28,000	—
‡Mt. Mercy Col., Pittsburgh, Pa.	1929	1,425	110	75,000	300,000
Mt. Olive Jr. Col., Mt. Olive, N.C.	1951	360	27	13,000	290,000
‡Mt. St. Agnes Col., Baltimore, Md.	1867	482	55	41,000	171,000
‡Mt. St. Clare Col. (Jr.), Clinton, Ia.	1918	280	38	24,000	—
‡Mt. St. Joseph on-the-Ohio, Col. of, Mt. St. Joseph, O.	1854	988	97	76,000	572,000
‡Mt. St. Mary Col., Hooksett, N.H.	1934	303	40	28,000	—
†Mt. St. Mary's Col., Emmitsburg, Md.	1808	862	74	85,000	548,000
‡Mt. St. Mary's Col., Los Angeles, Calif.	1925	1,299	117	88,000	510,000
‡Mt. St. Scholastica Col., Atchison, Kan.	1863	823	60	56,000	—
‡Mt. St. Vincent, Col. of, Bronx, N.Y.	1910	987	80	47,000	470,000
Mt. San Antonio Col. (Jr.), Walnut, Calif.	1946	11,172	444	65,000	—
Mt. Union Col., Alliance, O.	1846	1,305	87	120,000	3,750,000
‡Mt. Vernon Jr. Col., Washington, D.C.	1875	275	32	17,000	350,000
Muhlenberg Col., Allentown, Pa.	1848	1,425	103	132,000	3,795,000
Multnomah Col. (Jr.), Portland, Ore.	1897	860	80	12,000	54,000
‡Mundelein Col., Chicago, Ill.	1930	1,470	101	68,000	241,000
Murray St. Col. of Ag. and Ap. Sc., Tishomingo, Okla.	1908	656	34	14,000	—
Murray St. U., Murray, Ky.	1922	7,017	375	130,000	—
Museum Art School, Portland, Ore.	1909	115	26	3,000	217,000
Muskegon Co. Comm. Col. (Jr.), Muskegon, Mich.	1926	3,475	119	300,000	—
Muskingum Col., New Concord, O.	1837	1,427	114	100,000	6,679,000

N

Institution and location	Year founded	Total students	Faculty	Bound library volumes	Endowment fund
Napa Col. (Jr.), Napa, Calif.	1942	1,534	106	23,000	—
Nasson Col., Springvale, Me.	1912	877	64	45,000	915,000
National Col. of Ed., Evanston, Ill.	1886	1,736	102	54,000	539,000
Navarro Jr. Col., Corsicana, Tex.	1946	1,203	59	19,000	—
‡Nazareth Col., Kalamazoo, Mich.	1924	475	67	47,000	86,000
Nazareth Col. of Kentucky, Nazareth	1814	441	60	42,000	—
‡Nazareth Col. of Rochester, N.Y.	1924	1,362	88	85,000	—
Nebraska, U. of, Lincoln	1869	17,596	937	865,000	2,616,000
Nebraska, U. of, at Omaha	1908	8,288	376	248,000	280,000
Nebraska Wesleyan U., Lincoln	1887	1,369	103	105,000	2,893,000
Nevada, U. of (incl. Nevada Southern U., Las Vegas), Reno, Nev.	1874	10,677	448	360,000	3,550,000
Newark Col. of Engineering, Newark, N.J.	1881	6,170	380	51,000	158,000
Newark St. Col., Union, N.J.	1855	10,458	238	85,000	—
New Church, Acad. of the, Bryn Athyn, Pa.	1876	121	34	70,000	15,063,000
New England Cons. of Music, Boston, Mass.	1867	2,294	175	25,000	—
Newberry Col., Newberry, S.C.	1856	747	55	44,000	857,000
New Hampshire, U. of, Durham	1866	6,756	607	435,000	4,182,000
Keene St. Col., Keene	1909	1,652	98	60,000	—
Plymouth St. Col., Plymouth	1870	1,826	97	45,000	—
New Haven Col., West Haven, Conn.	1920	3,294	265	45,000	$ 60,000
New Mexico, The U. of, Albuquerque	1889	13,024	724	536,000	9,369,000
New Mexico Highlands U., Las Vegas	1893	1,764	87	99,000	—
New Mexico Inst. of Mining & Tech., Socorro	1889	593	65	56,000	1,161,000
†New Mexico Military Inst. (Jr.), Roswell	1891	944	55	50,000	—
New Mexico St. U., University Park Branch, Las Cruces	1889	6,305	307	218,000	1,871,000
New Orleans (La.) Baptist Theol. Sem.	1917	831	45	110,000	800,000
‡New Rochelle, Col. of, New Rochelle, N.Y.	1904	942	106	94,000	1,035,000
New School for Social Research, The New York, N.Y.	1919	11,175	383	53,000	—
‡Newton (Mass.) Col. of the Sacred Heart	1946	838	95	71,000	—
Newton Jr. Col., Newtonville, Mass.	1946	430	49	19,000	—
New York, City U. of, New York, N.Y.	1847	150,847	9,866	1,965,000	12,530,000
Brooklyn Col., Brooklyn	1930	27,054	1,573	443,000	177,000
City Col., New York	1847	28,900	1,900	830,000	2,270,000
Hunter Col., New York	1870	18,000	1,000	433,000	—
Queens Col., Flushing	1937	24,397	1,467	281,000	138,000
Borough of Manhattan Comm. Col. (Jr.), New York	1963	4,828	263	18,000	—
Bronx Comm. Col. (Jr.), Bronx	1957	7,337	414	23,000	—
Kingsborough Comm. Col. (Jr.), Brooklyn	1963	2,876	193	42,000	—
New York City Comm. Col. of Applied Arts & Science (Jr.)	1946	9,344	466	28,000	—
Queensborough Comm. Col. (Jr.), Bayside	1959	6,636	549	30,000	4,000
Staten Island Comm. Col. (Jr.), Staten Island	1955	3,450	183	30,000	3,000
New York, St. U. of, Albany	1948	108,827	7,217	4,445,000	—
St. U. at Albany	1844	9,089	560	313,000	—
St. U. at Binghamton	1946	4,028	268	261,000	—
St. U. at Buffalo	1846	19,113	1,170	891,000	—
St. U. at Stony Brook	1957	5,199	400	214,000	—
Col. at Brockport	1867	4,574	243	134,000	—
Col. at Buffalo	1867	7,561	468	153,000	—
Col. at Cortland	1868	4,127	242	158,000	—
Col. at Fredonia	1867	3,112	196	126,000	—
Col. at Geneseo	1871	3,562	223	135,000	—
Col. at New Paltz	1885	4,519	335	151,000	—
Col. at Oneonta	1887	4,251	287	154,000	—
Col. at Oswego	1861	5,029	346	200,000	—
Col. at Plattsburgh	1889	3,496	215	140,000	—
Col. at Potsdam	1867	3,009	214	112,000	—
Buffalo Health Science Ctr., Buffalo	1846	1,682	(included with St. U. of Buffalo)		
Downstate Health Science Ctr., Brooklyn	1858	884	584	300,000	—
Upstate Health Science Ctr., Syracuse	1834	575	176	83,000	—
Col. of Forestry at Syracuse U.	1911	1,349	107	60,000	—
†Maritime Col., Ft. Schuyler	1874	716	50	85,000	—
Col. of Ag. at Cornell U.	1904	2,989	134	354,000	—
Col. of Ceramics at Alfred U.	1900	541	56	37,000	—
Col. of Home Ec., Cornell U.	1925	993	65	354,000	—
Sch. of Ind. & Labor Relations, Cornell U.	1944	484	32	86,000	—
Veterinary Col. at Cornell U.	1894	306	46	45,000	—
Ag. & Tech. Col. at Alfred	1908	2,751	173	48,000	—
Ag. & Tech. Col. at Canton	1906	1,264	87	27,000	—
Ag. & Tech. Col. at Cobleskill	1911	1,619	92	27,000	—
Ag. & Tech. Col. at Delhi	1913	1,398	89	30,000	—
Ag. & Tech. Col. at Farmingdale	1912	9,041	256	78,000	—
Ag. & Tech. Col. at Morrisville	1908	1,566	103	43,000	—
New York U., New York, N.Y.	1831	40,711	5,503	1,815,000	71,542,000
Niagara U., Niagara University, N.Y.	1856	2,663	169	88,000	218,000
†Nichols Col. of Bus. Adm., Dudley, Mass.	1815	670	39	23,000	437,000
Norman Col. (Jr.), Norman Park, Ga.	1900	264	18	13,000	647,000
North Carolina, U. of, at Chapel Hill	1789	15,110	1,400	1,715,000	15,788,000
North Carolina, U. of, at Charlotte	1946	2,030	123	87,000	1,454,000
North Carolina, U. of, at Greensboro	1891	5,163	334	280,000	—
North Carolina A. & T. St. U., Greensboro	1891	3,930	275	168,000	—
North Carolina Col. at Durham	1910	3,021	230	191,000	—
North Carolina St. U. at Raleigh	1887	10,392	1,541	425,000	1,421,000
North Central Col., Naperville, Ill.	1861	805	73	96,000	2,871,000
North Dakota, U. of, Grand Forks	1883	6,949	425	330,000	1,096,000
North Dakota St. U., Fargo	1890	5,863	432	189,000	2,728,000
Northeastern Illinois St. Col., Chicago	1869	5,779	304	95,000	—
Northeastern Oklahoma A. & M. Col. (Jr.), Miami	1919	1,806	72	22,000	—
Northeastern Jr. Col., Sterling, Colo.	1941	1,404	81	24,000	—
Northeastern St. Col., Tahlequah, Okla.	1846	5,746	185	130,000	—
Northeastern U., Boston, Mass.	1898	31,432	1,526	180,000	22,682,000
Northeast Louisiana St. Col., Monroe	1931	6,328	312	115,000	—
Northeast Mississippi Jr. Col., Booneville	1948	885	60	14,000	—
Northeast Missouri St. Col., Kirksville	1867	5,335	248	157,000	—
Northern Arizona U., Flagstaff	1899	7,493	350	210,000	—
Northern Baptist Theol. Sem., Oakbrook, Ill.	1913	60	11	65,000	418,000
Northern Illinois U., DeKalb	1895	18,718	825	421,000	—
Northern Iowa, U. of, Cedar Falls	1876	6,930	415	246,000	—
Northern Michigan U., Marquette	1899	6,294	286	84,000	—
Northern Montana Col., Havre	1929	1,194	86	42,000	—
Northern Oklahoma Col., Tonkawa	1901	1,074	51	17,000	—
Northern St. Col., Aberdeen, S.D.	1901	2,903	140	100,000	—
North Florida Jr. Col., Madison	1958	961	73	22,000	—
North Georgia Col., Dahlonega	1873	1,113	54	70,000	—
North Greenville Jr. Col., Tigerville, S.C.	1934	474	31	16,000	122,000
North Idaho Jr. Col., Coeur d'Alene	1939	855	57	15,000	—
North Iowa Area Comm. Col. (Jr.), Mason City	1918	1,802	115	22,000	—
Northland Col., Ashland, Wis.	1892	683	63	40,000	1,176,000
North Park Col. and Theol. Sem., Chicago, Ill.	1891	1,606	90	87,000	1,034,000
Northrop Inst. of Tech., Inglewood, Calif.	1942	1,839	100	19,000	—
North Texas St. U., Denton	1890	1,356	803	630,000	—
Northwest Christian Col., Eugene, Ore.	1895	394	23	35,000	135,000
Northwest Comm. Col. (Jr.), Powell, Wyo.	1946	483	32	16,000	15,000
Northwestern Col., Orange City, Ia.	1928	727	59	37,000	415,000
Northwestern Michigan Col. (Jr.), Traverse City	1951	1,210	51	25,000	—
Northwestern St. Col., Alva, Okla.	1897	2,431	92	71,000	—
Northwestern St. Col. of Louisiana, Natchitoches	1884	5,027	273	158,000	—
Northwestern U., Evanston, Ill.	1851	17,356	2,420	1,847,000	239,250,000
Northwest Mississippi Jr. Col., Senatobia	1927	1,341	90	9,000	—
Northwest Missouri St. Col., Maryville	1905	3,936	205	150,000	—
Northwest Nazarene Col., Nampa, Ida.	1913	1,203	65	50,000	159,000
†Norwich U., Northfield, Vt.	1819	1,269	103	90,000	6,800,000
‡Notre Dame, Col. of Belmont, Calif.	1851	1,823	83	62,000	—

Institution and location	Year founded	Total students	Faculty	Bound library volumes	Endowment fund
†Notre Dame, U. of, Notre Dame, Ind.	1842	7,500	669	840,000	$60,000,000
‡Notre Dame Col., Cleveland, O.	1922	513	52	46,000	—
‡Notre Dame Col., St. Louis, Mo.	1954	338	35	65,000	—
‡Notre Dame Col. of Staten Island, N.Y.	1931	500	40	31,000	84,000
†Notre Dame Sem., New Orleans, La.	1923	133	20	45,000	—
Nyack Missionary Col., Nyack, N.Y.	1882	652	48	40,000	—

O

Institution and location	Year founded	Total students	Faculty	Bound library volumes	Endowment fund
Oakwood Col., Huntsville, Ala.	1896	538	14	38,000	300,000
Oberlin Col., Oberlin, O.	1833	2,505	243	640,000	66,667,000
Occidental Col., Los Angeles, Calif.	1887	1,714	122	215,000	15,226,000
Odessa Col. (Jr.), Odessa, Tex.	1946	2,525	176	30,000	—
Oglethorpe Col., Atlanta, Ga.	1835	1,218	39	37,000	500,000
Ohio Dominican Col., Columbus	1911	997	77	44,917	210,000
Ohio Northern U., Ada	1871	2,748	174	68,000	2,600,000
Ohio St. U., Columbus	1870	38,201	3,971	2,000,000	22,365,000
Ohio U., Athens	1804	16,250	780	450,000	1,000,000
Ohio Wesleyan U., Delaware	1842	2,378	160	317,000	8,199,000
Oklahoma, U. of, Norman	1890	17,737	1,331	1,120,000	13,477,000
Oklahoma Baptist U., Shawnee	1911	1,481	100	75,000	2,900,000
Oklahoma Christian Col., Oklahoma City	1950	905	35	36,000	—
Oklahoma City (Okla.) U.	1904	2,485	174	124,000	2,139,000
Oklahoma Col. of Liberal Arts, Chickasha	1908	1,033	61	60,000	—
†Oklahoma Mil. Acad. (Jr.), Claremore	1919	608	42	14,000	—
Oklahoma St. U. of Ag. & Ap. Sc., Stillwater	1890	16,010	1,255	832,000	9,881,000
Old Dominion Col., Norfolk, Va.	1930	9,111	361	130,000	1,239,000
Olivet Col., Olivet, Mich.	1844	730	50	50,000	230,000
Olivet Nazarene Col., Kankakee, Ill.	1907	1,850	102	59,000	—
Olympic Col. (Jr.), Bremerton, Wash.	1946	3,470	200	24,000	—
Orange Coast Col. (Jr.), Costa Mesa, Calif.	1947	14,772	435	34,000	—
Orange County Comm. Col. (Jr.), Middletown, N.Y.	1950	3,064	218	41,000	—
Oregon, U. of, Eugene	1872	12,800	1,350	1,118,000	3,155,000
Oregon Col. of Ed., Monmouth	1856	2,806	180	80,000	—
Oregon St. U., Corvallis	1868	13,358	1,176	515,000	1,275,000
Oregon Tech. Inst., Klamath Falls	1947	962	100	25,000	—
Orlando Jr. Col., Orlando, Fla.	1941	1,871	83	38,000	400,000
Otis Art. Inst. of Los Angeles County, Los Angeles, Calif.	1918	303	31	7,000	—
Ottawa U., Ottawa, Kan.	1865	974	61	60,000	1,218,000
Otterbein Col., Westerville, O.	1847	1,417	101	78,000	2,164,000
‡Ottumwa Heights Col. (Jr.), Ottumwa, Ia.	1925	435	34	23,000	—
Ouachita Baptist U., Arkadelphia and Little Rock, Ark.	1886	2,001	118	86,000	2,553,000
‡Our Lady of Cincinnati Col., Cincinnati, O.	1935	1,062	74	54,000	—
†Our Lady of Hope Sem., Newburgh, N.Y.		37	9	15,000	—
Our Lady of the Elms, Col. of, Chicopee, Mass.	1928	660	59	35,000	—
‡Our Lady of the Lake Col., San Antonio, Tex.	1911	1,421	110	78,000	881,000
‡Owen Col. (Jr.), Memphis, Tenn.	1954	450	32	15,000	—
Ozarks, The Col. of the, Clarksville, Ark.	1834	486	31	55,000	563,000
Ozarks, School of the, Point Lookout, Mo.	1906	773	45	62,000	23,000,000

P

Institution and location	Year founded	Total students	Faculty	Bound library volumes	Endowment fund
Pace Col. (incl. Westchester branch, Pleasantville), New York, N.Y.	1906	8,700	500	150,000	—
Pacific, U. of the, Stockton, Calif.	1851	3,624	604	142,000	4,580,000
Pacific Col., Fresno, Calif.	1944	354	32	50,000	48,000
Pacific Lutheran U., Tacoma, Wash.	1894	2,739	158	96,000	544,000
Pacific Oaks Col., Pasadena, Calif.	1945	217	13	14,000	141,000
Pacific Union Col., Angwin, Calif.	1882	1,750	113	73,000	—
Pacific U., Forest Grove, Ore.	1849	1,035	87	72,000	4,950,000
‡Packer Collegiate Inst. (Jr.), Brooklyn, N.Y.	1845	114	24	17,000	846,000
Paducah Jr. Col., Paducah, Ky.	1932	1,102	64	14,000	—
Paine Col., Augusta, Ga.	1883	668	50	40,000	386,000
Palm Beach Jr. Col., Lake Worth, Fla.	1933	4,611	192	52,000	—
Palomar Jr. Col., San Marcos, Calif.	1946	5,123	154	50,000	—
Palo Verde Col. (Jr.), Blythe, Calif.	1947	405	38	9,000	—
Pan American Col., Edinburg, Tex.	1927	3,821	138	67,000	—
Panhandle A. & M. Col., Goodwell, Okla.	1909	1,255	63	38,000	—
Panola Col. (Jr.), Carthage, Tex.	1948	529	32	12,000	—
Paris Jr. Col., Paris, Tex.	1924	525	34	12,000	—
Park Col., Parkville, Mo.	1875	568	56	76,000	3,167,000
Parsons Col., Fairfield, Ia.	1875	2,110	97	115,000	754,000
Pasadena (Calif.) City Col. (Jr.)	1924	11,443	360	86,000	—
Pasadena (Calif.) Col.	1902	1,208	61	102,000	—
Pasadena (Calif.) Col. of Theatre Arts	1928	195	26	19,000	—
Paterson St. Col., Wayne, N.J.	1855	6,086	269	101,000	—
Peabody Inst., Baltimore, Md.	1857	466	77	275,000	—
‡Peace Col. (Jr.), Raleigh, N.C.	1857	436	26	18,000	1,000,000
Pearl River Jr. Col., Poplarville, Miss.	1912	916	60	17,000	—
Pembroke St. Col., Pembroke, N.C.	1887	1,495	96	46,000	—
Pennsylvania, U. of, Philadelphia	1740	18,273	4,438	2,150,000	150,000,000
Pennsylvania Col. of Optometry, Philadelphia	1919	337	47	9,000	464,000
Pennsylvania St. U., University Park	1855	36,099	2,749	1,030,000	517,000
Pensacola Jr. Col., Pensacola, Fla.	1948	3,912	165	43,000	—
Pepperdine Col., Los Angeles, Calif.	1937	1,521	133	85,000	1,500,000
Peru St. Col., Peru, Neb.	1867	1,076	55	78,000	—
Pfeiffer Col., Misenheimer, N.C.	1885	936	70	53,000	1,800,000
Philadelphia (Pa.) Col. of Art	1876	776	104	14,000	1,005,000
Philadelphia (Pa.) Col. of Pharm. & Sc.	1821	872	92	47,000	6,285,000
Philadelphia (Pa.) Col. of Textiles & Science	1884	1,511	74	30,000	2,184,000
Philander Smith Col., Little Rock, Ark.	1877	609	49	497,000	582,000
Phillips U., Enid, Okla.	1907	1,432	100	145,000	3,500,000
Piedmont Col., Demorest, Ga.	1897	628	37	52,000	1,800,000
Pikeville Col., Pikeville, Ky.	1889	1,185	40	50,000	930,000
‡Pine Manor Jr. Col., Chestnut Hill, Mass.	1911	396	37	17,000	—
Pittsburgh, U. of, Pittsburgh, Pa.	1787	23,261	1,401	1,072,000	76,135,000
‡Pitzer Col., Claremont, Calif.	1963	535	48	625,000	1,500,000
†PMC Colleges, The, Chester, Pa.	1821	2,733	176	57,000	10,991,000
Polytechnic Inst. of Brooklyn, N.Y.	1854	5,283	475	105,000	6,032,000
Pomona Col., Claremont, Calif.	1887	1,274	118	750,000	17,577,000
Porterville (Calif.) Col. (Jr.)	1927	650	47	15,000	—
Portland, U. of, Portland, Ore.	1901	1,741	135	114,000	—
Portland St. Col., Portland, Ore.	1955	8,406	564	217,000	—
Prairie St. Col. (Jr.), Chicago Heights, Ill.	1958	1,720	75	14,000	—
Pratt Inst., Brooklyn, N.Y.	1887	4,445	464	225,000	—
Presbyterian Col., Clinton, S.C.	1880	648	50	65,000	$ 2,145,000
Presbyterian Sch. of Christian Ed., Richmond, Va.	1914	174	11	121,000	1,672,000
†Princeton U., Princeton, N.J.	1746	4,663	854	2,202,000	226,423,000
Principia Col., Elsah, Ill.	1910	698	66	92,000	8,609,000
†Providence Col., Providence, R.I.	1917	2,522	202	90,000	1,250,000
Puerto Rico Jr. Col., Rio Piedras, P. R.	1949	2,700	103	17,000	51,000
Puget Sound, U. of, Tacoma, Wash.	1888	3,613	169	117,000	5,366,000
Purdue U., Lafayette, Ind.	1869	32,036	2,746	900,000	16,248,000

Q

Institution and location	Year founded	Total students	Faculty	Bound library volumes	Endowment fund
‡Queens Col., Charlotte, N.C.	1857	779	73	66,000	3,171,000
Quincy Col., Quincy, Ill.	1860	1,568	96	139,000	808,000
Quinnipiac Col., Hamden, Conn.	1929	2,116	172	39,000	—

R

Institution and location	Year founded	Total students	Faculty	Bound library volumes	Endowment fund
‡Radford Col., Radford, Va.	1910	3,119	185	98,000	—
†Randolph-Macon Col., Ashland, Va.	1830	740	70	67,000	2,977,000
‡Randolph-Macon Woman's Col., Lynchburg, Va.	1891	893	84	113,000	3,687,000
Redlands (Calif.), U. of	1907	1,716	131	154,000	11,600,000
Reed Col., Portland, Ore.	1909	1,083	113	184,000	5,266,000
Reedley (Calif.) Col. (Jr.)	1926	1,695	78	15,000	—
†Regis Col., Denver, Colo.	1888	993	75	70,000	1,300,000
‡Regis Col., Weston, Mass.	1927	1,223	110	99,000	—
Reinhardt Col. (Jr.), Waleska, Ga.	1883	316	21	12,000	653,000
Rensselaer Polytech. Inst., Troy, N.Y.	1824	5,496	617	146,000	54,197,000
Rhode Island, U. of, Kingston	1892	5,809	500	300,000	74,000
Rhode Island Col., Providence	1854	4,806	210	98,000	—
Rhode Island School of Design, Providence	1877	986	108	37,000	13,301,000
Rice U., Houston, Tex.	1912	2,830	350	605,000	84,539,000
Richmond, U. of, Richmond, Va.	1830	4,531	290	185,000	10,494,000
Ricks Col. (Jr.), Rexburg, Ida.	1888	3,498	160	51,000	—
Rider Col., Trenton, N.J.	1865	5,184	269	145,000	2,899,000
Ripon Col., Ripon, Wis.	1850	930	88	86,000	2,412,000
Riverside (Calif.) City Col. (Jr.)	1916	3,514	150	43,000	—
‡Rivier Col., Nashua, N.H.	1933	830	55	55,000	—
Roanoke Col., Salem, Va.	1842	971	65	71,000	1,756,000
Roberts Wesleyan Col., North Chili, N.Y.	1866	674	58	44,000	—
Rochester, U. of, Rochester, N.Y.	1850	8,423	1,678	1,063,000	85,000,000
Rochester (N.Y.) Inst. of Tech.	1829	9,600	712	80,000	21,649,000
Rochester St. Jr. Col., Rochester, Minn.	1915	1,656	77	16,000	—
Rockford Col., Rockford, Ill.	1847	1,152	93	60,000	2,800,000
†Rockhurst Col., Kansas City, Mo.	1910	2,117	137	69,000	—
Rocky Mountain Col., Billings, Mont.	1883	529	55	45,000	840,000
Rollins Col., Winter Park, Fla.	1885	2,715	139	142,000	7,200,000
Roosevelt U., Chicago, Ill.	1945	6,759	226	175,000	1,005,000
‡Rosary Col., River Forest, Ill.	1848	1,308	102	110,000	700,000
‡Rosary Hill Col., Buffalo, N.Y.	1948	1,345	112	53,000	15,000
‡Rosemont Col., Rosemont, Pa.	1921	688	82	92,000	—
†Rose Polytech. Inst., Terre Haute, Ind.	1874	991	65	34,000	4,300,000
‡Russell Sage Col., Troy, N.Y.	1916	1,445	100	90,000	4,164,000
Rutgers, The St. U., New Brunswick, N.J.	1766	25,852	2,963	1,367,000	25,766,000

S

Institution and location	Year founded	Total students	Faculty	Bound library volumes	Endowment fund
Sacramento (Calif.) City Col. (Jr.)	1916	6,640	265	64,000	—
Sacramento (Calif.) St. Col.	1947	12,457	650	245,000	—
‡Sacred Heart, Col. of the, Santurce, P.R.	1935	571	52	40,000	50,000
‡Sacred Heart Col., Belmont, N.C.	1892	410	35	15,000	—
‡Sacred Heart Col. (Jr.), Cullman, Ala.	1940	181	35	12,000	—
‡Sacred Heart Dominican Col., Houston, Tex.	1945	338	83	49,000	38,000
†Sacred Heart Sem., Detroit, Mich.	1919	222	26	35,000	—
†St. Ambrose Col., Davenport, Ia.	1882	1,378	86	60,000	—
St. Andrews Presbyterian Col., Laurinburg, N.C.	1858	888	75	50,000	1,500,000
†St. Anselm's Col., Manchester, N.H.	1889	1,395	119	72,000	—
St. Augustine's Col., Raleigh, N.C.	1867	740	51	25,000	479,000
‡St. Benedict, Col. of, St. Joseph, Minn.	1913	539	58	64,000	193,000
†St. Benedict's Col., Atchison, Kan.	1858	1,135	74	170,000	—
St. Bernard Col., St. Bernard, Ala.	1892	786	54	56,000	153,000
St. Bonaventure U., St. Bonaventure, N.Y.	1859	2,446	192	140,000	292,000
St. Catharine Col. (Jr.), Springfield, Ky.	1931	213	17	15,000	—
‡St. Catherine, Col. of, St. Paul, Minn.	1905	1,316	128	160,000	2,698,000
St. Clair Co. Comm. Col. (Jr.), Port Huron, Mich.	1923	2,456	85	14,000	—
St. Cloud St. Col., St. Cloud, Minn.	1869	7,681	435	166,000	12,000
St. Edward's U. and Maryhill Col., Austin, Tex.	1885	916	69	55,000	4,927,000
‡St. Elizabeth, Col. of, Convent Station, N.J.	1899	979	101	78,000	—
‡St. Francis, Col. of, Joliet, Ill.	1874	904	70	65,000	250,000
St. Francis Col., Fort Wayne, Ind.	1890	1,808	99	60,000	—
†St. Francis Col., Brooklyn, N.Y.	1884	2,221	104	50,000	111,000
St. Francis Col., Loretto, Pa.	1847	1,675	106	84,000	—
†St. Francis Sem., Milwaukee, Wis.	1856	280	19	50,000	—
‡St. John Col. of Cleveland, O.	1928	1,354	96	44,000	—
†St. John Fisher Col., Inc., Rochester, N.Y.	1948	1,180	80	53,000	395,000
St. John's Col., Annapolis, Md. and Santa Fe, N.M.	1696	470	72	62,000	8,239,000
†St. John's Col., Camarillo, Calif.	1939	384	28	60,000	—
St. John's Col. (Jr.), Winfield, Kan.	1893	288	34	31,000	150,000
†St. John's U., Collegeville, Minn.	1857	1,481	132	166,000	5,179,000
St. John's U., Jamaica, N.Y.	1870	11,419	611	405,000	1,070,000
‡St. Joseph Col., Emmitsburg, Md.	1809	645	80	52,000	413,000
‡St. Joseph Col., West Hartford, Conn.	1932	901	88	57,000	293,000
‡St. Joseph's Col., North Windham, Me.	1915	216	30	24,000	—
†St. Joseph's Col., Philadelphia, Pa.	1851	6,592	262	88,000	736,000
†St. Joseph's Col., Rensselaer, Ind.	1889	1,423	87	125,000	460,000
‡St. Joseph's Col. for Women, Brooklyn, N.Y.	1916	610	70	62,000	66,000
†St. Joseph Sem., St. Benedict, La.	1891	119	18	42,000	—
†St. Joseph's Sem. & Col., Yonkers, N.Y.	1833	180	48	70,000	—
†St. Joseph's Seminary of Washington, D.C.	1888	47	10	23,000	—
St. Lawrence U., Canton, N.Y.	1856	1,946	135	193,000	10,368,000
St. Louis-St. Louis County, The Jr. Col. District of St. Louis, Mo.	1962	9,735	520	75,000	—
Florissant Valley Comm. Col.		2,807	177	25,000	—
Forest Park Comm. Col.		3,992	168	25,000	—
Meramec Comm. Col.		2,936	175	25,000	—

Universities and colleges (continued)

Institution and location	Year found-ed	Total stu-dents	Faculty	Bound library volumes	Endowment fund
St. Louis U., St. Louis, Mo.	1818	11,146	1,649	725,000	$21,000,000
†St. Martin's Col., Olympia, Wash.	1895	670	69	61,000	1,055,000
‡St. Mary, Col. of, Omaha, Neb.	1923	657	64	31,000	—
‡St. Mary Col., Xavier, Kan.	1860	604	64	93,000	—
St. Mary of the Plains Col., Dodge City, Kan.	1952	750	52	33,000	—
‡St. Mary-of-the-Woods Col., St. Mary-of-the-Woods, Ind.	1840	619	74	155,000	937,000
‡St. Mary's Col., Notre Dame, Ind.	1844	1,414	133	101,000	853,000
†St. Mary's Col., Winona, Minn.	1912	1,100	85	76,000	250,000
†St. Mary's Col. of California, St. Mary's College	1863	861	86	76,000	1,900,000
‡St. Mary's Dominican Col., New Orleans, La.	1910	557	63	61,000	671,000
St. Mary's Col. of O'Fallon, Mo.	1921	293	32	25,000	—
‡St. Mary's Jr. Col., Raleigh, N.C.	1842	473	37	17,000	530,000
St. Mary's Col. of Maryland, St. Mary's City	1839	417	34	19,000	21,000
†St. Mary's Sem. & U., Baltimore, Md.	1791	725	56	180,000	—
†St. Charles Col. (Jr.), Catonsville, Md.	1831	189	17	40,000	—
St. Mary's U. of San Antonio, Tex.	1852	3,742	320	145,000	557,000
†St. Meinrad Col., St. Meinrad, Ind.	1861	274	43	70,000	—
†St. Meinrad School of Theology, Meinrad, Ind.	1861	153	20	70,000	—
†St. Michael's Col., Winooski, Vt.	1903	1,525	100	57,000	536,000
St. Norbert Col., West De Pere, Wis.	1898	1,553	128	65,000	1,150,000
St. Olaf Col., Northfield, Minn.	1874	2,568	195	210,000	2,513,000
†St. Patrick's Col., Menlo Park, Calif.	1898	173	31	40,000	—
St. Paul's Col., Lawrenceville, Va.	1888	520	43	37,000	589,000
†St. Paul's Col., Washington, D.C.	1889	87	20	36,000	—
†St. Paul Sem., St. Paul, Minn.	1894	206	25	60,000	—
St. Petersburg Jr. Col. (incl. campus at Clearwater), St. Petersburg, Fla.	1927	8,527	314	73,000	—
†St. Peter's Col., Jersey City, N.J.	1872	3,942	284	92,000	1,010,000
†St. Procopius Col., Lisle, Ill.	1887	751	89	70,000	—
‡St. Rose, Col. of, Albany, N.Y.	1920	1,343	100	62,000	364,000
‡St. Scholastica, Col. of, Duluth, Minn.	1912	583	75	60,000	—
†St. Stephen's Col., Dover, Mass.	1955	56	16	17,000	—
‡St. Teresa, Col. of, Winona, Minn.	1907	1,341	132	92,000	800,000
†St. Thomas, Col. of, St. Paul, Minn.	1885	2,230	135	150,000	4,802,000
St. Thomas, U. of, Houston, Tex.	1947	896	83	36,000	1,149,000
†St. Thomas Sem. (Jr.), Bloomfield, Conn.	1891	145	18	33,000	750,000
†St. Thomas Sem., Denver, Col.	1906	231	17	30,000	—
†St. Vincent Col., Latrobe, Pa.	1846	1,031	75	192,000	943,000
‡St. Xavier Col., Chicago, Ill.	1847	1,039	115	90,000	—
Salem Col., Salem, W. Va.	1888	1,557	90	50,000	1,154,000
‡Salem Col., Winston-Salem, N.C.	1772	574	67	70,000	3,090,000
Salisbury St. Col., Salisbury, Md.	1925	851	52	66,000	—
‡Salve Regina Col., Newport, R.I.	1934	847	78	43,000	60,000
Samford U., Birmingham, Ala.	1842	2,757	162	200,000	2,344,000
Sam Houston St. Tch. Col., Huntsville, Tex.	1879	7,108	335	254,000	—
San Antonio Col. (Jr.), San Antonio, Tex.	1925	11,400	450	76,000	—
St. Philip's Col., San Antonio, Tex.	1898	732	46	11,000	—
San Bernardino Valley Col. (Jr.), San Bernardino, Calif.	1926	10,134	403	52,000	—
San Diego (Calif.), U. of, Col. for Men	1949	575	74	70,000	—
San Diego (Calif.), U. of, Col. for Women	1949	580	56	60,000	—
San Diego (Calif.) Jr. Colleges (incl. City Col., Evening Col., Mesa Col.)	1914	17,840	884	65,000	—
San Diego (Calif.) St. Col.	1897	20,046	1,422	475,000	—
San Fernando Valley St. Col., Northridge, Calif.	1958	15,995	825	230,000	—
San Francisco (Calif.), City Col. of (Jr.)	1935	12,061	395	50,000	—
†San Francisco (Calif.), U. of	1855	4,310	230	109,000	1,155,000
San Francisco (Calif.) Art Institute Col.	1871	740	58	14,000	—
‡San Francisco (Calif.) Col. for Women	1921	676	67	139,000	364,000
San Francisco (Calif.) Conservatory of Music	1917	104	60	32,000	550,000
San Francisco (Calif.) St. Col.	1899	17,860	1,277	305,000	—
San Jacinto Col. (Jr.), Pasadena, Tex.	1960	4,797	174	29,000	—
San Joaquin Delta Col., Stockton, Calif.	1935	3,707	187	36,000	—
San Jose (Calif.) City Col. (Jr.)	1921	10,722	397	47,000	—
San Jose (Calif.) St. Col.	1857	22,350	1,348	478,000	191,000
†San Luis Rey (Calif.) Col.	1929	133	10	30,000	—
San Mateo (Calif.), Col. of (Jr.)	1922	19,195	750	70,000	—
Santa Ana (Calif.) Col. (Jr.)	1915	6,468	184	35,000	—
Santa Barbara (Calif.) City Col. (Jr.)	1946	3,932	94	32,000	—
Santa Clara (Calif.), U. of	1851	5,434	296	163,000	12,175,000
Santa Fe, Col. of, Santa Fe, N.M.	1947	1,225	70	60,000	—
Santa Monica (Calif.) City Col. (Jr.)	1929	13,253	470	55,000	—
Santa Rosa (Calif.) Jr. Col.	1918	2,870	120	48,000	4,000,000
‡Sarah Lawrence Col., Bronxville, N.Y.	1926	617	96	100,000	2,300,000
Savannah St. Col., Savannah, Ga.	1890	1,615	83	65,000	—
Scarritt Col. for Christian Workers, Nashville, Tenn.	1892	196	21	25,000	2,254,000
Schreiner Inst. (Jr.), Kerrville, Tex.	1923	402	35	13,000	2,809,000
†Scranton, U. of, Scranton, Pa.	1888	3,081	143	109,000	2,102,000
‡Scripps Col., Claremont, Calif.	1926	470	61	71,000	8,621,000
Seattle Pacific Col., Seattle, Wash.	1891	1,832	137	73,000	509,000
Seattle U., Seattle, Wash.	1891	3,851	228	106,000	—
Sequoias, Col. of the (Jr.), Visalia, Calif.	1925	2,331	108	40,000	—
Seton Hall U., South Orange, N.J.	1856	8,828	661	275,000	3,863,000
‡Seton Hill Col., Greensburg, Pa.	1883	934	79	62,000	—
Shasta Col. (Jr.), Redding, Calif.	1950	2,180	98	28,000	—
Shaw U., Raleigh, N.C.	1865	846	70	37,000	494,000
Shenandoah Col. (Jr.) and Shenandoah Conservatory of Music, Winchester, Va.	1875	531	56	16,000	125,000
Shepherd Col., Shepherdstown, W.Va.	1871	1,560	88	52,000	180,000
Shimer Col., Mt. Carroll, Ill.	1853	391	41	28,000	328,000
Shippensburg St. Col., Shippensburg, Pa.	1871	3,192	220	170,000	—
Shorter Col., Rome, Ga.	1873	695	55	46,000	1,108,000
†Siena Col., Loudonville, N.Y.	1937	1,970	121	120,000	761,000
‡Siena Col., Memphis, Tenn.	1922	309	30	24,000	12,000
‡Siena Heights Col., Adrian, Mich.	1919	677	65	63,000	—
Sierra Col. (Jr.), Rocklin, Calif.	1936	2,615	68	30,000	—
‡Simmons Col., Boston, Mass.	1899	2,147	285	125,000	8,757,000
Simpson Col., Indianola, Ia.	1860	941	73	71,000	3,370,000
Sioux Falls Col., Sioux Falls, S.D.	1883	1,006	52	47,000	388,000
Siskiyous, Col. of the (Jr.), Weed, Calif.	1957	1,800	35	9,000	—
Skagit Valley Col., Mt. Vernon, Wash.	1926	2,332	75	25,000	—
‡Skidmore Col., Saratoga Springs, N.Y.	1911	1,558	141	120,000	2,207,000
Slippery Rock St. Col., Slippery Rock, Pa.	1889	4,160	270	133,000	—
‡Smith Col., Northampton, Mass.	1871	2,471	250	520,000	48,000,000
Snead St. Jr. Col., Boaz, Ala.	1935	413	26	15,000	193,000
Solano Col. (Jr.), Vallejo, Calif.	1945	4,480	161	14,000	—

Institution and location	Year found-ed	Total stu-dents	Faculty	Bound library volumes	Endowment fund
Sonoma St. Col., Rohnert Park, Calif.	1960	2,087	142	83,000	—
†South, U. of the, Sewanee, Tenn.	1858	801	68	174,000	$16,908,000
South Carolina, U. of, Columbia	1801	13,625	750	655,000	2,350,000
South Carolina St. Col., Orangeburg	1896	2,175	104	81,000	—
South Dakota, U. of, Vermillion	1882	4,600	350	215,000	—
South Dakota Sch. of Mines & Tech., Rapid City	1885	1,380	108	46,000	250,000
South Dakota St. U., Brookings	1883	5,213	473	190,000	3,174,000
Southeastern Christian Col. (Jr.), Winchester, Ky.	1949	159	14	11,000	—
Southeastern Iowa Area Comm. Col. (Jr.), Burlington	1920	724	35	8,000	—
Southeastern Massachusetts Tech. Inst., North Dartmouth	1895	2,600	197	77,000	115,000
Southeastern St. Col., Durant, Okla	1909	1,990	100	90,000	—
Southeast Missouri St. Col., Cape Girardeau	1873	5,800	288	120,000	—
Southern Baptist Col. (Jr.), Walnut Ridge, Ark.	1941	686	32	25,000	118,000
Southern California, U. of, Los Angeles	1879	18,692	3,643	1,236,000	25,487,000
Southern California Col., Costa Mesa	1920	478	34	27,000	100,000
Southern Colorado St. Col., Pueblo	1933	5,800	300	62,000	—
Southern Connecticut St. Col., New Haven	1893	9,011	491	165,000	—
Southern Illinois U., Carbondale	1869	26,976	2,829	1,000,000	—
Southern Louisiana Col., Hammond	1925	4,922	327	100,000	—
Southern Methodist U., Dallas, Tex.	1911	8,510	600	875,000	19,000,000
Southern Missionary Col., Collegedale, Tenn.	1892	1,202	118	49,000	—
Southern Mississippi, U. of, Hattiesburg	1910	7,935	396	218,000	—
Southern Oregon Col., Ashland	1926	3,475	220	90,000	—
‡Southern Sem. Jr. Col., Buena Vista, Va.	1867	325	33	13,000	500,000
Southern St. Col., Magnolia, Ark.	1909	2,721	110	46,000	—
Southern St. Col., Springfield, S.D.	1881	1,557	76	35,000	425,000
Southern U. & A. & M. Col., Baton Rouge, La.	1880	6,776	399	201,000	—
Southern Utah, Col. of, Cedar City	1897	1,530	90	50,000	—
South Florida, U. of, Tampa	1960	10,848	480	178,000	168,000
South Georgia Col, (Jr.), Douglas	1906	1,001	48	34,000	—
South Plains Col. (Jr.), Levelland, Tex.	1957	1,505	73	22,000	—
South Texas Jr. Col., Houston	1948	4,602	126	60,000	210,000
Southwest Baptist Col., Bolivar, Mo.	1878	1,167	65	47,000	108,000
Southwestern at Memphis, Tenn.	1848	955	91	100,000	5,487,000
Southwestern Col., Chula Vista, Calif.	1961	4,950	110	26,000	—
Southwestern Col., Winfield, Kan.	1885	645	56	58,000	3,195,000
Southwestern Louisiana, U. of, Lafayette	1898	8,409	490	278,000	—
Southwestern St. Col., Weatherford, Okla.	1901	4,549	179	76,000	—
Southwestern Union Col., Keene, Tex.	1916	298	34	28,000	—
Southwestern U., Georgetown, Tex.	1840	781	68	83,000	7,712,000
Southwest Mississippi Jr. Col., Summit	1929	534	30	20,000	—
Southwest Missouri St. Col., Springfield	1906	6,750	325	170,000	—
Southwest Texas Jr. Col., Uvalde	1946	905	37	15,000	—
Southwest Texas St. Col., San Marcos	1899	6,105	271	178,000	—
Spartanburg Jr. Col., Spartanburg, S.C.	1911	633	34	14,000	26,000
‡Spelman Col., Atlanta, Ga.	1881	780	71	18,000	5,008,000
Spring Arbor Col., Spring Arbor, Mich.	1873	565	44	30,000	32,000
Springfield Col., Springfield, Mass.	1885	2,323	101	88,000	3,338,000
Springfield Jr. Col., Springfield, Ill.	1929	1,002	52	16,000	—
Spring Hill Col., Mobile, Ala.	1830	1,115	97	150,000	1,250,000
Stanford U., Stanford, Calif.	1885	10,924	1,227	3,000,000	217,449,000
Stanislaus St. Col., Turlock, Calif.	1960	1,224	77	66,000	—
Stephen F. Austin St. Col., Nacogdoches, Tex.	1923	7,459	328	152,000	52,000
‡Stephens Col., Columbia, Mo.	1833	1,924	180	81,000	1,417,000
Sterling Col., Sterling, Kan.	1887	592	39	57,000	1,541,000
Stetson U., DeLand, Fla.	1883	2,170	155	172,000	4,824,000
Steubenville, Col. of, Steubenville, O.	1946	1,169	64	55,000	—
†Stevens Inst. of Tech., Hoboken, N.J.	1870	2,600	194	60,000	39,000,000
Stillman Col., Tuscaloosa, Ala.	1876	749	65	35,000	1,100,000
Stonehill Col., North Easton, Mass.	1948	1,243	73	62,000	25,000
Stout St. U., Menomonie, Wis.	1893	3,753	265	77,000	110,000
‡Stratford Col., Danville, Va.	1852	528	44	25,000	350,000
Sue Bennett Col. (Jr.), London, Ky.	1896	386	21	24,000	—
Suffolk U., Boston, Mass.	1906	3,665	139	78,000	1,387,000
‡Sullins Col. (Jr.), Bristol, Va.	1870	351	37	30,000	1,300,000
†Sulpician Sem. of the Northwest, Kenmore, Wash.	1931	184	23	...	—
Sul Ross St. Col., Alpine, Tex.	1920	1,798	106	111,000	—
Susquehanna U., Selinsgrove, Pa.	1858	1,142	100	70,000	1,230,000
Swarthmore Col., Swarthmore, Pa.	1864	998	138	315,000	27,455,000
‡Sweet Briar Col., Sweet Briar, Va.	1901	718	76	128,000	5,089,000
Syracuse U. (incl. Utica Col.), Syracuse, N.Y.	1870	22,866	1,298	1,391,000	38,879,000
T					
Tabor Col., Hillsboro, Kan.	1908	350	44	35,000	236,000
Taft Col. (Jr.), Taft, Calif.	1922	1,229	55	15,000	—
Talladega Col., Talladega, Ala.	1867	397	33	47,000	1,730,000
Tampa, U. of, Tampa, Fla.	1931	2,149	98	85,000	750,000
Tarkio Col., Tarkio, Mo.	1883	756	41	51,000	420,000
Taylor U., Upland, Ind.	1846	1,217	85	70,000	583,000
‡Temple Buell Col., Denver, Colo.	1888	1,091	92	67,000	25,000,000
Temple Jr. Col., Temple, Tex.	1926	999	57	16,000	—
Temple U., Philadelphia, Pa.	1884	28,285	2,071	6,620,000	750,000
Tennessee, U. of (main branches at Martin, Memphis, Nashville), Knoxville	1794	28,393	2,689	1,045,000	4,386,000
Tennessee A. & I. St. U., Nashville	1909	5,614	293	150,000	—
Tennessee Tech. U., Cookeville	1915	5,327	315	250,000	—
Tennessee Wesleyan Col., Athens	1857	832	56	43,000	750,000
Texarkana Col. (Jr.), Texarkana, Tex.	1927	1,618	76	19,000	—
Texas, U. of (incl. branches at Arlington, Dallas, El Paso, Galveston, Houston, San Antonio), at Austin	1881	52,681	3,639	2,654,000	534,400,000
Texas A&M University System:					
Prairie View A. & M. Col., Prairie View	1876	3,686	197	106,000	—
Tarleton St. Col., Stephenville	1899	2,079	103	88,000	—
†Texas A&M U., College Station	1876	10,918	875	500,000	2,813,000
Texas A&I U., Kingsville	1925	5,332	265	185,000	—
Texas Christian U., Fort Worth	1873	6,078	513	600,000	27,500,000
Texas Lutheran Col., Seguin	1891	809	57	60,000	598,000
Texas Southern U., Houston	1947	4,076	232	151,000	—
Texas Southmost Col. (Jr.), Brownsville	1926	1,299	56	61,000	—
Texas Tech. Col., Lubbock	1923	18,646	1,157	950,000	—
Texas Wesleyan Col., Fort Worth	1891	2,056	90	65,000	3,489,000

Institution and location	Year founded	Total students	Faculty	Bound library volumes	Endowment fund
‡Texas Woman's U., Denton	1901	5,051	310	301,000	—
†The Citadel, Charleston, S.C.	1842	2,200	152	102,000	—
Thiel Col., Greenville, Pa.	1866	1,260	86	68,000	$ 1,388,000
Thomas More Col., Ft. Mitchell, Ky	1921	1,874	131	54,000	—
Thornton Jr. Col., Harvey, Ill.	1927	1,860	124	18,000	—
‡Tift Col., Forsyth, Ga.	1847	618	33	36,000	1,589,000
Toledo, The U. of, Toledo, O.	1872	12,051	880	570,000	588,000
Tougaloo Col., Tougaloo, Miss.	1869	682	51	42,000	522,000
Towson St. Col., Baltimore, Md.	1866	7,100	319	109,000	—
Transylvania Col., Lexington, Ky.	1790	802	66	65,000	1,112,000
Trenton St. Col., Trenton, N.J.	1855	8,773	264	147,000	—
Trinidad St. Jr. Col., Trinidad, Colo.	1925	1,372	57	23,000	—
‡Trinity Col., Burlington, Vt.	1925	470	43	35,000	—
†Trinity Col., Hartford, Conn.	1823	1,766	138	475,000	25,000,000
‡Trinity Col., Washington, D.C.	1897	760	83	81,000	729,000
Trinity U., San Antonio, Tex.	1869	2,468	159	251,000	39,500,000
Tri-State Col., Angola, Ind.	1884	1,752	96	39,000	250,000
Troy St. Col., Troy, Ala.	1887	2,557	133	78,000	—
Tufts U. (incl. ‡Jackson Col.), Medford, Mass.	1852	5,022	688	380,000	21,285,000
Tulane U. (incl. ‡Newcomb Col.) of Louisiana, New Orleans	1834	8,094	1,148	1,025,000	39,939,000
Tulsa, U. of, Tulsa, Okla.	1894	6,567	318	350,000	9,000,000
Tusculum Col., Greeneville, Tenn.	1794	548	43	45,000	2,200,000
Tuskegee Inst., Tuskegee Institute, Ala.	1881	2,980	342	159,000	17,745,000
Tyler Jr. Col., Tyler, Tex.	1926	3,271	157	28,000	—

U

Institution and location	Year founded	Total students	Faculty	Bound library volumes	Endowment fund
Union Col., Barbourville, Ky.	1879	872	63	47,000	1,823,000
Union Col., Lincoln, Neb.	1891	1,202	93	79,000	—
Union Col., Cranford, N.J.	1933	1,450	84	30,000	12,000
†Union Col. and U., Schenectady, N.Y.	1795	2,436	159	230,000	31,747,000
Union U., Jackson, Tenn.	1825	780	62	42,000	810,000
†U.S. Air Force Acad., Colorado Springs, Colo.	1954	3,065	572	250,000	—
†U.S. Coast Guard Acad., New London, Conn.	1876	850	97	70,000	—
†U.S. Merchant Marine Acad., Kings Point, N.Y.	1938	922	88	55,000	—
†U.S. Military Acad., West Point, N.Y.	1802	3,210	489	270,000	—
†U.S. Naval Acad., Annapolis, Md.	1845	4,000	639	210,000	—
U.S. Naval Postgrad. School, Monterey, Calif.	1909	1,250	254	316,000	—
Upper Iowa U., Fayette	1857	1,400	66	70,000	934,000
Upsala Col., East Orange, N.J.	1893	2,217	167	106,000	1,171,000
Ursinus Col., Collegeville, Pa.	1869	2,034	124	75,000	5,523,000
‡Ursuline Col. for Women, Cleveland, O.	1871	487	46	43,000	—
Utah, U. of, Salt Lake City	1850	18,488	1,550	975,000	1,700,000
Utah St. U. of Ag. & App. Sc., Logan	1888	7,712	472	541,000	956,000

V

Institution and location	Year founded	Total students	Faculty	Bound library volumes	Endowment fund
Valdosta St. Col., Valdosta, Ga.	1906	2,236	138	72,000	—
Valley City St. Col., Valley City, N.D.	1889	1,256	70	50,000	825,000
†Valley Forge Mil. Jr. Col., Wayne, Pa.	1928	209	35	30,000	1,500,000
Valparaiso U., Valparaiso, Ind.	1859	3,611	269	195,000	1,509,000
Vanderbilt U., Nashville, Tenn.	1872	5,364	1,070	1,048,000	76,406,000
‡Vassar Col., Poughkeepsie, N.Y.	1861	1,650	205	385,000	48,573,000
Ventura Col. (Jr.), Ventura, Calif.	1929	6,703	279	39,000	—
Vermilion St. Jr. Col., Ely, Minn.	1922	239	21	7,000	—
Vermont, U. of, Burlington	1791	5,355	647	426,000	11,681,000
‡Vermont Col. (Jr.), Montpelier	1834	517	43	20,000	192,000
Victoria Col. (Jr.), The, Victoria, Tex.	1925	1,499	58	20,000	—
Victor Valley Col. (Jr.), Victorville, Calif.	1961	1,340	47	20,000	—
‡Villa Julie Col. (Jr.), Stevenson, Md.	1947	210	38	12,000	—
‡Villa Maria Col., Erie, Pa.	1925	764	58	33,000	93,000
Villanova U., Villanova, Pa.	1842	7,440	462	185,000	5,376,000
Vincennes U. (Jr.), Vincennes, Ind.	1806	959	45	15,000	29,000
Virginia, Medical Col. of, Richmond	1838	1,600	850	95,000	12,000,000
Virginia, The U. of, (incl. branch colleges: Clinch Valley, George Mason, Patrick Henry, Eastern Shore) at Charlottesville	1819	10,245	1,001	1,438,000	48,220,000
‡Mary Washington Col., Fredericksburg	1908	2,091	168	180,000	12,000
Virginia Commonwealth U., Richmond	1917	10,063	369	87,000	—
Virginia Intermont Col. (Jr.), Bristol	1884	560	38	23,000	617,000
†Virginia Military Inst., Lexington	1839	1,205	133	150,000	4,228,000
Virginia Polytech. Inst., Blacksburg	1872	8,395	625	431,000	864,000
Virginia St. Col., Petersburg	1882	2,313	232	111,000	183,000
Virginia Union U., Richmond	1865	1,352	95	79,000	1,935,000
‡Viterbo Col., La Crosse, Wis.	1931	581	55	48,000	—
Voorhees Col. (Jr.), Denmark, S.C.	1897	704	53	31,000	118,000

W

Institution and location	Year founded	Total students	Faculty	Bound library volumes	Endowment fund
†Wabash Col., Crawfordsville, Ind.	1832	891	78	178,000	17,500,000
Wagner Col., Staten Island, N.Y.	1883	2,612	179	75,000	1,158,000
Wake Forest U., Winston-Salem, N.C.	1834	3,070	447	388,000	17,500,000
Waldorf Col. (Jr.), Forest City, Ia.	1903	627	40	20,000	69,000
Walker Col. (Jr.), Jasper, Ala.	1938	750	44	16,000	425,000
Walla Walla Col., College Place, Wash.	1892	1,410	110	83,000	—
Warner Pacific Col., Portland, Ore.	1937	344	34	33,000	—
Warren Wilson Col., Swannanoa, N.C.	1894	306	34	28,000	—
Wartburg Col., Waverly, Ia.	1852	1,251	88	89,000	482,000
Washburn U. of Topeka, Kan.	1865	4,025	207	97,000	8,500,000
Washington, U. of, Seattle	1861	27,591	4,907	1,611,000	53,762,000
†Washington and Jefferson Col., Washington, Pa.	1781	853	82	140,000	10,100,000
†Washington and Lee U., Lexington, Va.	1749	1,472	133	210,000	12,943,000
Washington Col., Chesterton, Md.	1782	625	59	82,000	1,983,000
Washington St. U., Pullman	1890	10,739	745	900,000	39,914,000
Washington U., St. Louis, Mo.	1853	11,908	2,944	1,009,000	68,965,000
Wayland Baptist Col., Plainview, Tex.	1908	658	51	50,000	2,803,000
Waynesburg Col., Waynesburg, Pa.	1849	1,045	74	69,000	1,610,000
Wayne St. Col., Wayne, Neb.	1891	2,578	128	86,000	—
Wayne St. U., Detroit, Mich.	1868	32,370	2,069	1,169,000	2,712,000
Weatherford Col. (Jr.), Weatherford, Tex.	1921	951	47	20,000	115,000
†Webb Inst. of Naval Arch., Glen Cove, N.Y.	1889	68	14	16,000	—
Weber St. Col., Ogden, Utah	1889	6,647	311	98,000	70,000
Webster Col., St. Louis, Mo.	1915	845	100	32,000	—
‡Wellesley Col., Wellesley, Mass.	1870	1,742	194	405,000	72,651,000
‡Wells Col., Aurora, N.Y.	1868	615	67	148,000	5,662,000
Wenatchee Valley Comm. Col. (Jr.), Wenatchee, Wash.	1939	1,473	100	14,000	—
†Wentworth Mil. Acad. and Jr. Col., Lexington, Mo.	1880	310	32	17,000	—
Wesley Col. (Jr.), Dover, Del.	1873	884	42	17,000	$ 268,000
‡Wesleyan Col., Macon, Ga.	1836	698	61	70,000	4,018,000
†Wesleyan U., Middletown, Conn.	1831	1,500	253	600,000	105,000,000
‡Westbrook Jr. Col., Portland, Me.	1831	439	45	16,000	184,000
West Chester St. Col., West Chester, Pa.	1812	4,902	314	160,000	—
West Coast U., Los Angeles, Calif.	1909	1,525	64	8,000	—
Western Carolina Col., Cullowhee, N.C.	1889	3,399	184	97,000	191,000
‡Western Col. for Women, Oxford, O.	1853	531	66	60,000	1,886,000
Western Connecticut St. Col., Danbury	1903	2,782	154	78,000	—
Western Illinois U., Macomb	1899	8,368	575	191,000	—
Western Kentucky U., Bowling Green	1906	9,339	427	300,000	138,000
Western Maryland Col., Westminster	1867	1,607	88	80,000	3,102,000
Western Michigan U., Kalamazoo	1903	17,325	753	435,000	41,000
Western Montana Col., Dillon	1893	913	42	42,000	—
Western New England Col., Springfield, Mass.	1919	3,077	132	30,000	643,000
Western New Mexico U., Silver City	1893	1,156	76	73,000	—
Western St. Col. of Colorado, Gunnison	1901	3,282	140	105,000	—
Western Washington St. Col., Bellingham	1899	6,243	432	189,000	51,000
West Georgia Col., Carrollton	1933	3,208	175	62,000	—
West Liberty St. Col., West Liberty, W.Va.	1837	3,400	172	65,000	—
Westmar Col., Le Mars, Ia.	1890	1,040	66	64,000	605,000
†Westminster Col., Fulton, Mo.	1851	779	68	66,000	2,400,000
Westminster Col., New Wilmington, Pa.	1852	2,016	107	95,000	4,200,000
Westminster Col., Salt Lake City, Utah	1875	782	39	26,000	243,000
†Westminster Theol. Sem., Philadelphia, Pa.	1929	141	17	47,000	296,000
Westmont Col., Santa Barbara, Calif.	1940	643	53	62,000	234,000
West Texas St. U., Canyon	1910	6,583	299	140,000	—
West Valley Col. (Jr.), Campbell, Calif.	1966	6,699	...	...	—
West Virginia Inst. of Tech., Montgomery	1895	2,064	142	55,000	—
West Virginia St. Col., Institute	1891	2,811	160	86,000	—
West Virginia U., Morgantown	1867	12,094	1,156	833,000	1,875,000
Potomac St. Col., Keyser	1901	834	48	23,000	—
West Virginia Wesleyan Col., Buckhannon	1890	1,678	115	81,000	1,600,000
Wharton County Jr. Col., Wharton, Tex.	1946	1,868	86	26,000	11,000
‡Wheaton Col., Norton, Mass.	1834	1,098	97	125,000	5,000,000
Wheaton Col., Wheaton, Ill.	1860	1,959	168	148,000	9,575,000
Wheeling Col., Wheeling, W.Va.	1954	795	61	59,000	25,000
‡Wheelock Col., Boston, Mass.	1889	624	54	37,000	228,000
Whitman Col., Walla Walla, Wash.	1859	1,010	89	144,000	13,104,000
Whittier Col., Whittier, Calif.	1901	1,963	125	75,000	4,100,000
Whitworth Col., Spokane, Wash.	1890	1,765	97	57,000	1,738,000
Wichita St. U., Wichita, Kan.	1895	10,535	372	289,000	1,989,000
Wilberforce U., Wilberforce, O.	1856	858	41	34,000	95,000
Wiley Col., Marshall, Tex.	1873	703	54	49,000	1,000,000
Wilkes Col., Wilkes-Barre, Pa.	1933	2,752	172	85,000	3,749,000
Willamette U., Salem, Ore.	1842	1,523	123	111,000	8,800,000
William and Mary, Col. of, Williamsburg, Va.	1693	3,709	361	371,000	3,960,000
William Carey Col., Hattiesburg, Miss.	1906	746	54	43,000	469,000
William Jewell Col., Liberty, Mo.	1849	997	76	92,000	5,430,000
William Penn Col., Oskaloosa, Ia.	1873	1,026	57	57,000	532,000
‡William Woods Col., Fulton, Mo.	1890	898	47	31,000	705,000
†Williams Col., Williamstown, Mass.	1793	1,278	162	290,000	43,567,000
Wilmington Col., Wilmington, N.C.	1947	1,080	85	45,000	—
Wilmington Col., Wilmington, O.	1870	856	67	67,000	1,580,000
‡Wilson Col., Chambersburg, Pa.	1869	714	71	95,000	5,629,000
Wingate Col. (Jr.), Wingate, N.C.	1896	1,572	88	38,000	970,000
Winona St. Col., Winona, Minn.	1858	3,290	180	72,000	—
Winston-Salem St. Col., Winston-Salem, N.C.	1892	1,461	108	66,000	100,000
‡Winthrop Col., Rock Hill, S.C.	1886	3,304	180	218,000	—
Wisconsin, The U. of (all campuses)	1848	56,932	...	2,768,000	20,463,000
Wisconsin-Madison, U. of, Madison	1848	33,000	...	2,233,000	
Wisconsin-Milwaukee, U. of, Milwaukee	1956	15,419	...	374,000	
Freshman-Sophomore Centers at Baraboo, Janesville, Marshfield, Sheboygan, Waukesha, Wausau, West Bend		2,719	...	76,000	
Wisconsin-Green Bay, U. of (campuses at Green Bay, Menasha, Manitowoc, Marinette)	1968	2,454	...	45,000	
Wisconsin-Parkside, U. of (campuses at Racine, Kenosha)	1968	1,405	...	23,000	
Wisconsin St. U.—Eau Claire	1916	5,862	333	152,000	—
Wisconsin St. U.—La Crosse	1909	5,800	350	150,000	—
Wisconsin St. U.—Oshkosh	1871	9,444	550	200,000	—
Wisconsin St. U.—Platteville	1866	4,601	310	130,000	—
Wisconsin St. U.—River Falls	1874	3,691	248	130,000	—
Wisconsin St. U.—Stevens Point	1894	5,907	394	151,000	—
Wisconsin St. U.—Superior	1896	2,953	204	125,000	210,000
Wisconsin St. U.—Whitewater	1868	8,561	523	138,000	—
Wittenberg U., Springfield, O.	1845	3,932	182	175,000	11,599,000
†Wofford Col., Spartanburg, S.C.	1854	968	72	88,000	2,381,000
Woodbury Col., Los Angeles, Calif.	1884	1,815	73	15,000	—
Wood Jr. Col., Mathiston, Miss.	1886	168	13	13,000	260,000
†Woodstock Col., Woodstock, Md.	1869	206	27	140,000	3,000,000
Wooster, Col. of, Wooster, O.	1866	1,657	129	181,000	11,502,000
Worcester Jr. Col., Worcester, Mass.	1938	2,096	113	16,000	600,000
Worcester Polytech. Inst., Worcester, Mass.	1865	1,757	239	67,000	21,628,000
Wyoming, U. of, Laramie	1886	6,883	474	390,000	12,846,000

X

Institution and location	Year founded	Total students	Faculty	Bound library volumes	Endowment fund
†Xaverian Col. (Jr.), Silver Spring, Md.	1931	222	18	31,000	—
†Xavier U., Cincinnati, O.	1831	5,995	251	152,000	—
Xavier U. of Louisiana, New Orleans, La.	1925	1,207	87	98,000	—

Y

Institution and location	Year founded	Total students	Faculty	Bound library volumes	Endowment fund
Yakima Valley Col., Yakima, Wash.	1928	3,071	125	25,000	—
†Yale U., New Haven, Conn.	1701	8,666	2,730	5,184,000	457,952,000
Yankton Col., Yankton, S.D.	1881	576	55	45,000	1,430,000
Yeshiva U., New York, N.Y.	1886	5,539	1,850	450,000	3,600,000
York Col. of Pennsylvania, York	1941	1,813	76	47,000	882,000
Young Harris Col. (Jr.), Young Harris, Ga.	1886	416	33	29,000	2,025,000
Youngstown St. U., Youngstown, O.	1908	13,228	695	165,000	—
Yuba Col. (Jr.), Marysville, Calif.	1927	4,802	156	28,000	—

Army personnel

Military status	1960	1965	1968
Personnel on active duty	873,078	968,313	1,570,408†
Officers	101,236	111,541	166,173
Enlisted	771,842	856,772	1,401,777
Reserve personnel not on			
active duty*	703,000	641,000	700,717
National Guard	402,000	379,000	389,182
Officers	37,000	34,000	31,938
Enlisted	365,000	345,000	357,244
Army Reserve	301,000	262,000	311,535
Officers	50,000	40,000	44,657
Enlisted	251,000	221,000	266,878

Data are for June 30 of years reported.
*Paid status only; excludes personnel in inactive reserve.
†Includes cadets and officer candidates.
Source: U.S. Department of Defense.

Navy and Marine Corps personnel

Military status	1960	1965	1968
Personnel on active duty	788,605	861,196	1,071,791†
Navy	617,984	671,009	764,572
Officers	69,559	77,720	84,540
Enlisted	548,425	593,289	673,610
Marine Corps	170,621	190,187	307,219
Officers	16,203	17,234	24,559
Enlisted	154,418	172,953	282,660
Reserve personnel not on			
active duty*	165,000	169,000	179,370
Naval Reserve	120,000	123,000	131,242
Officers	26,000	23,000	28,102
Enlisted	94,000	100,000	103,140
Marine Corps Reserve	45,000	46,000	48,128
Officers	4,000	3,000	3,364
Enlisted	41,000	43,000	44,764

Data are for June 30 of years reported.
*Paid status only; excludes personnel in inactive reserve.
†Includes cadets and officer candidates.
Source: U.S. Department of Defense.

Air Force personnel

Military status	1960	1965	1968
Personnel on active duty	814,752	823,633	904,850†
Officers	129,689	131,141	139,691
Enlisted	685,063	692,492	761,507
Reserve personnel not on			
active duty*	129,000	123,000	120,999
Air National Guard	71,000	76,000	75,261
Officers	9,000	10,000	9,292
Enlisted	62,000	66,000	65,969
Air Force Reserve	58,000	46,000	45,738
Officers	22,000	11,000	11,978
Enlisted	37,000	36,000	33,760

Data are for June 30 of years reported.
*Paid status only; excludes personnel in inactive reserve.
†Includes cadets and officer candidates.
Source: U.S. Department of Defense.

Coast Guard personnel

Military status	1960	1965	1968
Personnel on active duty	31,406†	31,792†	37,482†
Officers	4,011	4,492	5,372
Enlisted	26,991	26,860	31,311
Reserve personnel not on			
active duty*	14,144	16,578	17,142
Officers	1,712	1,943	1,882
Enlisted	12,432	14,635	15,260

Data are for June 30 of years reported.
*Paid status only; excludes personnel in inactive reserve.
†Includes cadets.
Source: U.S. Department of Transportation,
U.S. Coast Guard.

The Selective Service, 1968

State	Registrants subject to draft as of June 30	Registrants forwarded to Armed Forces year ending June 30*	Inductions year ending June 30	ENLISTMENTS† year ending June 30 Regular	ENLISTMENTS† year ending June 30 Reserves or National Guard
Alabama	450,876	20,535	6,884	10,149	1,528
Alaska	16,522	829	216	475	130
Arizona	154,895	12,275	2,844	3,925	425
Arkansas	246,776	15,513	3,544	6,196	871
California	1,658,034	127,223	35,869	38,999	4,319
Colorado	187,291	10,054	2,944	5,253	463
Connecticut	264,651	17,226	3,518	6,328	1,128
Delaware	46,224	3,109	887	1,194	301
District of Columbia	77,896	5,799	1,290	1,815	121
Florida	513,430	28,214	8,075	16,466	1,791
Georgia	502,401	23,460	8,807	12,022	1,296
Hawaii	73,671	3,603	929	2,660	390
Idaho	82,796	3,725	929	2,223	299
Illinois	1,012,888	54,676	18,768	22,108	2,305
Indiana	496,035	29,726	8,492	12,456	1,660
Iowa	295,617	17,136	5,703	8,053	973
Kansas	232,084	10,999	3,239	6,285	1,061
Kentucky	384,769	23,223	7,340	7,903	911
Louisiana	415,260	24,573	5,210	8,135	1,148
Maine	109,035	4,764	1,486	3,900	319
Maryland	337,773	18,283	5,864	8,245	1,245
Massachusetts	538,712	29,266	4,986	14,295	2,749
Michigan	851,844	53,507	19,745	18,089	1,709
Minnesota	368,876	24,064	6,811	9,097	1,357
Mississippi	306,490	17,793	3,766	5,623	945
Missouri	453,892	15,098	8,274	11,565	1,373
Montana	62,878	4,065	1,252	2,148	416
Nebraska	148,296	8,932	2,283	3,980	699
Nevada	32,705	2,033	708	879	130
New Hampshire	67,857	2,904	687	2,355	252
New Jersey	631,968	31,578	7,247	13,828	2,353
New Mexico	106,471	6,525	1,730	3,003	312
New York	1,725,139	111,609	28,749	33,771	5,121
North Carolina	600,435	41,763	11,851	14,923	1,136
North Dakota	74,751	4,086	1,529	1,754	309
Ohio	1,030,396	60,030	19,904	25,214	2,798
Oklahoma	275,928	17,515	5,230	8,595	1,230
Oregon	195,184	13,204	3,866	6,443	780
Pennsylvania	1,160,681	49,194	16,330	30,285	4,078
Rhode Island	82,273	9,189	1,560	2,282	463
South Carolina	316,037	17,384	5,954	7,829	1,035
South Dakota	82,049	3,662	1,182	2,005	375
Tennessee	461,742	22,404	6,970	10,862	1,179
Texas	1,144,717	66,702	16,291	27,996	2,448
Utah	109,788	6,556	1,812	2,123	758
Vermont	46,149	1,941	420	1,434	230
Virginia	462,805	27,258	7,405	11,902	1,348
Washington	316,137	19,072	4,426	10,103	1,203
West Virginia	236,937	14,070	4,082	7,289	510
Wisconsin	422,087	23,570	7,401	9,851	1,268
Wyoming	36,514	2,071	624	1,097	142
Total U.S.‡	20,326,445	1,186,473	341,404	487,622	61,850

*For preinduction examinations.   †Estimated.
‡Includes Canal Zone, Guam, Puerto Rico, and Virgin Islands.
Source: Selective Service System.

Vietnam

U.S. armed forces and casualties

	1961	1962	1963	1964	1965	1966	1967	Sept. 1, 1968
Military forces	3,200	11,300	16,300	23,300	184,300	385,300	486,600	537,000
Army	2,100	7,900	10,100	14,700	116,800	239,400	320,500	353,500
Navy*	100	500	800	1,100	8,400	23,300	31,700	38,000
Marine Corps	—	500	800	900	38,200	69,200	78,000	84,000
Air Force	1,000	2,400	4,600	6,600	20,600	52,900	55,900	61,000
Coast Guard	—	—	—	—	300	500	500	500
Casualties†								
Battle deaths	11	31	78	147	1,369	5,008	9,378	12,540
Killed	1	19	53	112	1,130	4,179	7,482	10,823
Died of wounds	—	1	5	6	87	517	981	1,363
Died while missing	10	11	20	28	151	309	911	353
Died while captured	—	—	—	1	1	3	4	1
Wounded, nonfatal								
Hospital care required	2	41	218	522	3,308	16,526	32,371	40,953
Hospital care not required	1	37	193	517	2,806	13,567	29,654	37,895

Data are for December 31 of years reported, except as indicated.
*Excludes personnel on ships off Vietnam's shores.
†Represents casualties from enemy action. Deaths exclude servicemen who died in accidents or from disease.
Source: U.S. Department of Defense.

Production

National Product and Income

Gross national product and national income

in billions of dollars

Item	1960	1965	1967	1968*
Gross national product	503.8	683.9	789.7	852.9
By type of expenditure				
Personal consumption expenditures	325.2	433.1	492.2	527.9
Durable goods	45.3	66.0	72.6	81.0
Nondurable goods	151.3	191.2	215.8	228.2
Services	128.7	175.9	203.8	218.7
Gross private domestic investment	74.8	107.4	118.0	105.1
Fixed investment	71.3	98.0	108.2	116.5
Changes in business inventories	3.6	9.4	6.1	10.8
Net exports of goods and services	4.1	6.9	4.8	2.0
Exports	27.2	39.1	45.8	49.9
Imports	23.2	32.2	41.0	47.9
Government purchases of goods and services	99.6	136.4	178.4	195.7
Federal	53.5	66.8	90.6	100.0
State and local	46.1	69.6	87.8	95.6
By major type of product				
Goods output	259.6	346.6	379.6	392.1
Durable goods	99.5	139.5	159.3	175.3
Nondurable goods	160.1	207.1	237.6	253.1
Services	187.3	262.9	314.8	339.2
Structures	56.8	74.4	77.9	85.4

Item	1960	1965	1967	1968*
National income	414.5	562.4	652.9	705.4
By type of income				
Compensation of employees	294.2	393.9	468.2	507.1
Proprietors' income	46.2	56.7	60.7	62.6
Rental income of persons	15.8	19.0	20.3	20.9
Corporate profits and inventory valuation adjustment	49.9	74.9	80.4	89.2
Net interest	8.4	17.9	23.3	25.8
By industry division				
Agriculture, forestry, and fisheries	16.9	21.0	21.4	22.2
Mining and construction	26.5	35.3	39.7	42.6
Manufacturing	125.8	171.8	196.6	214.4
Nondurable goods	52.2	66.3	75.8	82.1
Durable goods	73.6	105.5	120.8	132.3
Transportation	18.2	23.1	26.1	27.9
Communications and public utilities	17.1	22.6	26.0	27.3
Wholesale and retail trade	64.4	84.2	96.8	104.5
Finance, insurance, and real estate	45.9	61.3	70.9	76.2
Services	44.4	63.7	77.0	82.6
Government and government enterprises	52.9	75.2	93.6	102.8
Other	2.4	4.2	4.6	4.9

*Second quarter, seasonally adjusted at annual rates.   Source: U.S. Department of Commerce, Office of Business Economics, *Survey of Current Business.*

Agriculture

Farming trends

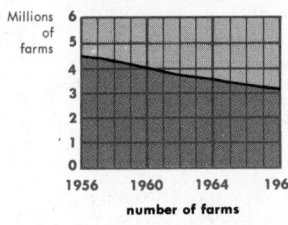

number of farms

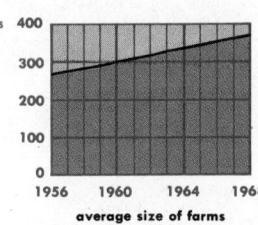

average size of farms

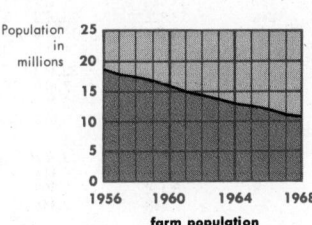

farm population

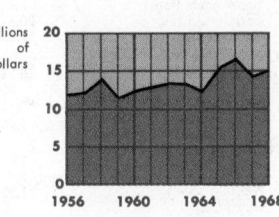

net farm income

Sources: U.S. Department of Agriculture, Statistical Reporting Service, *Number of Farms and Land in Farms;*
U.S. Department of Commerce, Bureau of the Census, Economic Research Service.

Farms and farm income

State	Number of farms 1968*	Land in farms 1968* in 000 acres	CASH INCOME, 1967, IN $000 Farm marketings Crops	Livestock and products	Government payments	Realized net income per farm 1967
Alabama	94,000	15,200	169,078	424,776	89,180	$ 2,294
Alaska	310	1,900†	1,101	3,159	70	497
Arizona	6,100	43,500	288,116	239,403	46,785	25,850
Arkansas	77,000	17,900	426,683	424,577	103,289	3,726
California	64,000	37,200	2,331,754	1,547,457	110,289	13,172
Colorado	31,000	39,500	200,299	684,984	57,606	4,379
Connecticut	5,300	660	66,400	93,444	887	8,280
Delaware	3,900	720	44,574	87,379	1,567	8,147
Florida	35,000	16,200	732,780	329,432	17,643	10,366
Georgia	80,000	18,200	456,904	576,209	77,825	4,760
Hawaii	4,700	2,350	161,611	37,349	8,554	17,311
Idaho	29,400	15,400	292,817	227,081	37,070	5,223
Illinois	131,000	29,900	1,308,084	1,224,145	97,674	5,272
Indiana	101,000	17,800	639,499	752,091	77,317	4,638
Iowa	147,000	34,500	890,541	2,546,951	142,839	6,749
Kansas	91,000	50,100	528,338	951,919	212,379	5,285
Kentucky	136,000	17,000	440,049	380,812	41,527	2,979
Louisiana	56,000	12,000	378,030	216,044	55,463	4,995
Maine	11,000	2,500	79,356	133,041	2,145	4,161
Maryland	19,500	3,300	108,564	219,523	5,317	4,144
Massachusetts	7,000	800	68,595	87,453	656	5,132
Michigan	89,000	13,500	399,689	455,642	56,039	3,230
Minnesota	131,000	32,400	594,016	1,236,728	95,251	4,215
Mississippi	99,000	17,700	396,630	384,246	146,914	4,052
Missouri	150,000	33,500	447,082	895,350	115,838	3,169
Montana	27,100	67,100	220,813	267,156	69,098	6,367

State	Number of farms 1968*	Land in farms 1968* in 000 acres	CASH INCOME, 1967, IN $000 Farm marketings Crops	Livestock and products	Government payments	Realized net income per farm 1967
Nebraska	76,000	48,200	572,990	1,162,431	134,514	$ 6,690
Nevada	2,100	8,800	11,613	45,770	1,687	3,617
New Hampshire	3,900	780	11,905	44,185	675	1,611
New Jersey	9,100	1,050	150,169	101,807	4,201	7,323
New Mexico	14,200	48,600	96,378	221,041	33,315	8,182
New York	61,000	12,100	295,586	698,517	20,215	5,189
North Carolina	165,000	16,100	816,593	463,141	61,696	3,491
North Dakota	45,000	42,000	435,615	281,773	130,850	5,807
Ohio	114,000	17,600	538,031	696,266	70,355	3,437
Oklahoma	92,000	37,200	263,031	543,691	112,097	2,872
Oregon	41,500	20,900	294,566	229,077	22,627	3,583
Pennsylvania	77,000	10,800	230,844	657,441	21,191	3,232
Rhode Island	1,000	97	9,176	10,361	76	1,568
South Carolina	55,000	8,600	281,037	143,799	57,437	3,530
South Dakota	48,500	45,500	218,265	705,795	65,944	6,606
Tennessee	132,000	15,600	242,612	358,696	73,783	1,913
Texas	195,000	145,000	1,153,007	1,368,976	462,163	4,701
Utah	15,000	13,300	45,220	145,371	8,954	2,855
Vermont	8,100	2,410	14,023	122,908	1,715	4,682
Virginia	75,000	11,800	239,562	272,924	17,582	2,190
Washington	46,000	18,100	528,248	253,431	52,321	6,983
West Virginia	31,000	5,400	20,701	72,978	3,884	428
Wisconsin	116,000	20,800	207,931	1,212,178	41,227	4,514
Wyoming	8,900	37,000	34,550	166,267	11,098	4,569
Total U.S.	3,058,610	1,128,567	18,383,056	24,405,175	3,078,829	4,526

*Preliminary.   †Includes about 1,830,000 acres of grazing land leased from the U.S. government.
Source: U.S. Department of Agriculture, Economic Research Service, *Farm Income Situation;* Statistical Reporting Service, *Number of Farms and Land in Farms.*

Principal crops
of the United States and each state

Crops (unit of production)	Amount produced in 000 1968	Acreage harvested in 000 acres 1968	VALUE OF PRODUCTION in $000 1967	1968
UNITED STATES				
Corn, grain (bu.)	4,374,840	55,707	4,939,670	4,601,290
Hay (tons)	125,438	62,570	2,896,858	2,806,035
Soybeans for beans (bu.)	1,079,662	40,659	2,432,564	2,617,069
Wheat (bu.)	1,570,433	55,309	2,110,197	1,920,202
Cotton lint (bales)	10,822	10,175	953,820	1,366,876
Tobacco (lb.)	1,715,573	884	1,315,694	1,195,014
Sorghum grain (bu.)	738,507	13,971	744,666	686,964
Potatoes (cwt.)	293,438	1,377	563,776	609,091
Oats (bu.)	929,524	17,361	525,257	556,458
Rice (cwt.)	105,322	2,353	443,995	526,790
Alabama				
Cotton lint (bales)	405	525	25,793	53,662
Soybeans for beans (bu.)	12,254	557	32,670	30,022
Peanuts harvested for nuts (lb.)	245,700	182	26,414	28,747
Corn, grain (bu.)	22,016	688	43,894	25,539
Hay (tons)	701	485	19,762	18,927
Alaska				
Potatoes (cwt.)	115	1	642	631
Hay (tons)	11	9	770	588
Silage (tons)	23	4	363	351
Arizona				
Cotton lint (bales)	710	296	67,476	96,647
Hay (tons)	1,174	239	34,221	28,763
Sorghum grain (bu.)	18,249	231	23,313	20,621
Cottonseed (tons)	294	...	10,282	15,435
Barley (bu.)	12,848	176	14,040	14,004
Arkansas				
Soybeans for beans (bu.)	85,764	3,989	228,450	210,122
Cotton lint (bales)	1,030	980	71,960	139,050
Rice (cwt.)	24,882	572	111,124	124,410
Hay (tons)	1,358	755	30,532	31,234
Wheat (bu.)	14,200	568	26,562	16,472
California				
Cotton lint (bales)	1,535	687	166,435	214,931
Hay (tons)	7,740	1,864	212,212	193,500
Grapes (tons)	3,270	...	169,483	193,490
Rice (cwt.)	23,328	432	85,378	113,141
Peaches (bu.)	46,045	...	82,777	97,261
Potatoes (cwt.)	22,629	92	75,899	82,529
Barley (bu.)	70,300	1,406	85,202	75,221
Colorado				
Hay (tons)	2,858	1,491	76,896	77,166
Wheat (bu.)	38,745	1,933	47,169	41,841
Sugar beets (tons)	2,621	169	29,680	...
Corn, grain (bu.)	20,418	246	23,828	23,072
Potatoes (cwt.)	11,005	49	20,885	17,870
Connecticut				
Tobacco (lb.)	10,362	7	26,482	30,463
Hay (tons)	220	116	8,724	7,810
Apples (bu.)	1,140	...	3,008	3,722
Potatoes (cwt.)	1,254	6	2,505	3,010
Delaware				
Corn, grain (bu.)	8,673	177	16,943	9,367
Soybeans for beans (bu.)	2,964	156	9,262	7,114
Potatoes (cwt.)	1,539	8	3,468	3,309
Hay (tons)	69	36	2,588	2,346
Florida				
Oranges (tons)	4,523	...	219,444	282,405
Grapefruit (tons)	1,399	...	57,194	78,942
Sugarcane for sugar (tons)	5,846	183	65,551	58,460
Tobacco (lb.)	27,154	15	32,652	29,409
Corn, grain (bu.)	15,666	373	24,695	18,329
Georgia				
Peanuts harvested for nuts (lb.)	934,360	497	112,139	109,320
Tobacco (lb.)	107,731	57	101,007	76,856
Corn, grain (bu.)	58,200	1,455	98,630	66,348
Cotton lint (bales)	265	395	29,386	35,112
Soybeans for beans (bu.)	7,080	472	32,000	17,346
Hawaii				
Macadamia nuts (lb.)	10,166	...	1,964	2,316
Papayas (lb.)	22,960	...	1,691	2,198
Coffee (lb.)	6,180	...	1,545	1,545
Taro (lb.)	8,740	...	579	640
Bananas (lb.)	6,735	...	567	514
Idaho				
Potatoes (cwt.)	59,505	294	102,819	110,710
Hay (tons)	3,397	1,292	70,566	64,543
Wheat (bu.)	56,364	1,236	75,953	61,806
Sugar beets (tons)	3,323	185	38,730	...
Barley (bu.)	24,384	508	23,847	21,458
Illinois				
Corn, grain (bu.)	901,570	10,130	1,100,376	955,664
Soybeans for beans (bu.)	204,435	6,490	471,286	500,866
Hay (tons)	3,559	1,305	83,776	78,298
Wheat (bu.)	53,136	1,476	100,017	63,232
Oats (bu.)	49,896	756	29,378	29,938
Indiana				
Corn, grain (bu.)	416,330	4,898	436,911	424,657
Soybeans for beans (bu.)	95,854	3,043	176,082	225,257
Hay (tons)	2,204	969	48,125	53,998
Wheat (bu.)	35,490	1,014	59,042	39,394
Oats (bu.)	21,735	345	9,469	13,693

Crops (unit of production)	Amount produced in 000 1968	Acreage harvested in 000 acres 1968	VALUE OF PRODUCTION in $000 1967	1968
Iowa				
Corn, grain (bu.)	901,728	9,696	996,195	928,780
Soybeans for beans (bu.)	177,952	5,561	360,662	435,982
Hay (tons)	7,435	2,674	142,058	141,265
Oats (bu.)	110,460	1,841	68,932	68,485
Sorghum grain (bu.)	3,510	45	2,872	3,089
Kansas				
Wheat (bu.)	243,775	9,571	299,187	292,530
Sorghum grain (bu.)	163,325	3,475	140,444	143,726
Hay (tons)	4,741	2,419	108,281	97,190
Corn, grain (bu.)	85,050	1,134	76,405	88,452
Soybeans for beans (bu.)	23,925	957	44,920	55,028
Kentucky				
Tobacco (lb.)	411,620	172	280,406	296,056
Hay (tons)	2,943	1,613	70,096	79,461
Corn, grain (bu.)	69,366	1,051	104,653	77,690
Soybeans for beans (bu.)	12,349	466	26,617	29,638
Wheat (bu.)	6,240	208	10,839	7,613
Louisiana				
Rice (cwt.)	26,481	679	108,192	129,757
Soybeans for beans (bu.)	37,336	1,436	75,095	91,473
Cotton lint (bales)	540	410	61,130	71,550
Sugarcane for sugar (tons)	7,641	283	71,863	67,623
Sweet potatoes (cwt.)	4,240	53	14,488	16,112
Maine				
Potatoes (cwt.)	36,890	155	51,141	62,713
Hay (tons)	436	306	11,525	10,900
Apples (bu.)	1,650	...	3,634	3,881
Oats (bu.)	1,664	32	1,102	1,265
Maryland				
Corn, grain (bu.)	31,944	484	46,151	33,861
Hay (tons)	674	319	23,785	21,568
Tobacco (lb.)	33,000	30	20,440	20,790
Soybeans for beans (bu.)	5,225	209	13,005	12,540
Wheat (bu.)	4,224	132	7,339	4,520
Massachusetts				
Tobacco (lb.)	3,768	3	9,375	11,391
Cranberries (bbl.)	655	...	9,111	10,414
Hay (tons)	263	143	9,588	8,942
Apples (bu.)	2,300	...	5,968	6,215
Potatoes (cwt.)	1,036	6	2,614	2,486
Michigan				
Corn, grain (bu.)	96,216	1,266	88,711	94,292
Hay (tons)	3,379	1,591	72,600	76,028
Beans, dry edible (cwt.)	6,614	624	44,789	51,589
Cherries (tons)	119	...	21,038	36,175
Wheat (bu.)	31,860	885	50,803	34,090
Soybeans for beans (bu.)	12,038	463	25,145	28,891
Apples (bu.)	12,000	...	28,083	28,416
Minnesota				
Corn, grain (bu.)	360,369	4,449	348,778	371,180
Soybeans for beans (bu.)	70,312	3,196	174,360	172,264
Hay (tons)	7,710	3,341	155,452	150,345
Oats (bu.)	183,480	3,058	95,912	100,914
Wheat (bu.)	33,532	1,018	51,411	45,091
Mississippi				
Cotton lint (bales)	1,520	1,105	149,565	209,000
Soybeans for beans (bu.)	55,120	2,120	125,546	135,044
Cottonseed (tons)	629	...	26,818	32,708
Hay (tons)	1,162	625	27,400	27,888
Corn, grain (bu.)	14,430	370	22,403	17,605
Missouri				
Corn, grain (bu.)	245,514	2,958	222,311	257,790
Soybeans for beans (bu.)	100,632	3,594	186,006	241,517
Hay (tons)	5,706	2,869	115,661	119,826
Wheat (bu.)	42,174	1,278	75,892	50,187
Cotton lint (bales)	195	190	8,676	26,812
Montana				
Wheat (bu.)	125,869	4,550	154,040	145,329
Hay (tons)	3,585	2,193	86,940	77,078
Barley (bu.)	42,735	1,155	31,839	32,051
Sugar beets (tons)	1,051	15	14,400	...
Potatoes (cwt.)	1,458	8	3,916	4,957
Nebraska				
Corn, grain (bu.)	302,877	4,149	350,427	333,165
Hay (tons)	6,067	4,292	126,692	127,407
Wheat (bu.)	101,088	3,159	116,308	115,240
Sorghum grain (bu.)	103,008	1,776	110,275	89,617
Soybeans for beans (bu.)	19,067	829	42,932	45,761
Nevada				
Hay (tons)	662	356	20,225	15,557
Barley (bu.)	900	15	1,163	990
Wheat (bu.)	700	13	1,585	904
New Hampshire				
Hay (tons)	206	134	6,903	5,562
Apples (bu.)	1,180	...	3,385	3,234
Potatoes (cwt.)	230	1	592	598
New Jersey				
Hay (tons)	332	145	13,022	10,458
Peaches (bu.)	2,300	...	6,100	8,798
Potatoes (cwt.)	3,570	14	6,448	7,783
Apples (bu.)	2,400	...	6,355	6,577
Corn, grain (bu.)	3,551	53	7,603	4,226

1968 figures are preliminary estimates; 1967 figures are revised estimates.
Boldface type indicates the states which lead in the value of production for the eleven leading crops of the U.S.
Source: U.S. Department of Agriculture, Statistical Reporting Service, Crop Reporting Board, Crop Production and Crop Values.

Crops (unit of production)	Amount produced in 000 1968	Acreage harvested in 000 acres 1968	VALUE OF PRODUCTION in $000 1967	1968
New Mexico				
Hay (tons)	1,049	273	29,372	27,798
Cotton lint (bales)	180	152	24,935	26,372
Sorghum grain (bu.)	15,624	279	18,962	15,468
Wheat (bu.)	7,625	305	5,409	9,226
Cottonseed (tons)	75	...	4,053	3,975
New York				
Hay (tons)	5,504	2,632	137,358	129,344
Apples (bu.)	20,000	...	45,610	47,310
Potatoes (cwt.)	17,158	70	33,966	41,045
Corn, grain (bu.)	16,920	235	24,227	19,627
Oats (bu.)	24,780	420	17,623	16,850
Grapes (tons)	125	...	18,328	14,500
North Carolina				
Tobacco (lb.)	668,785	363	534,846	445,419
Corn, grain (bu.)	80,880	1,348	117,551	86,542
Peanuts harvested for nuts (lb.)	346,525	167	40,294	43,316
Soybeans for beans (bu.)	16,038	972	67,594	39,293
Hay (tons)	609	439	19,313	18,879
North Dakota				
Wheat (bu.)	213,867	7,903	272,982	294,956
Barley (bu.)	107,666	2,626	78,794	81,826
Hay (tons)	3,779	3,314	66,320	58,574
Oats (bu.)	103,390	2,110	34,636	50,661
Flaxseed (bu.)	13,860	1,155	27,205	38,808
Ohio				
Corn, grain (bu.)	242,256	2,884	251,975	244,679
Soybeans for beans (bu.)	68,280	2,276	126,499	163,872
Hay (tons)	3,400	1,646	77,804	85,000
Wheat (bu.)	45,362	1,226	67,434	51,259
Oats (bu.)	45,078	683	17,812	26,145
Oklahoma				
Wheat (bu.)	122,383	5,321	130,373	152,979
Peanuts harvested for nuts (lb.)	229,400	124	22,374	26,840
Cotton lint (bales)	240	385	19,633	26,400
Sorghum grain (bu.)	26,158	638	25,802	24,850
Hay (tons)	3,001	1,598	14,812	13,961
Oregon				
Hay (tons)	2,013	1,017	55,800	49,318
Wheat (bu.)	30,162	982	46,978	38,593
Potatoes (cwt.)	12,290	47	23,155	23,284
Pears (tons)	97	...	22,736	22,892
Cherries (tons)	16	...	15,444	6,924
Pennsylvania				
Hay (tons)	4,085	1,970	119,032	110,295
Corn, grain (bu.)	56,700	810	94,826	64,071
Potatoes (cwt.)	7,585	37	20,338	19,721
Oats (bu.)	26,712	477	16,200	18,966
Wheat (bu.)	12,608	394	22,637	13,995
Rhode Island				
Potatoes (cwt.)	1,260	6	2,690	3,024
Hay (tons)	26	13	999	923
Apples (bu.)	115	...	295	373
South Carolina				
Tobacco (lb.)	122,383	63	106,891	81,140
Cotton lint (bales)	255	340	26,640	38,338
Soybeans for beans (bu.)	11,638	931	59,073	29,095
Peaches (bu.)	8,000	...	16,074	19,552
Corn, grain (bu.)	17,415	387	25,853	18,982
Hay (tons)	366	234	12,285	11,163

Crops (unit of production)	Amount produced in 000 1968	Acreage harvested in 000 acres 1968	VALUE OF PRODUCTION in $000 1967	1968
South Dakota				
Corn, grain (bu.)	110,354	2,399	96,745	115,872
Hay (tons)	5,127	4,425	90,890	94,850
Wheat (bu.)	65,729	2,418	103,655	82,985
Oats (bu.)	106,065	2,357	64,477	57,275
Flaxseed (bu.)	7,882	1,155	19,707	22,070
Tennessee				
Tobacco (lb.)	116,184	59	74,686	80,047
Soybeans for beans (bu.)	25,053	1,193	67,736	60,127
Hay (tons)	1,799	1,256	52,677	50,372
Cotton lint (bales)	330	365	20,614	43,725
Corn, grain (bu.)	30,926	658	51,326	35,565
Texas				
Cotton lint (bales)	3,475	4,125	273,546	367,410
Sorghum grain (bu.)	340,780	6,196	346,920	320,333
Rice (cwt.)	27,462	597	125,476	142,802
Wheat (bu.)	84,150	3,825	77,695	106,029
Hay (tons)	4,587	2,376	94,350	105,501
Cottonseed (tons)	1,452	...	66,402	74,052
Peanuts harvested for nuts (lb.)	420,320	296	37,346	48,757
Utah				
Hay (tons)	1,472	581	39,128	31,648
Wheat (bu.)	7,490	261	12,114	9,091
Barley (bu.)	6,966	129	7,725	6,896
Sugar beets (tons)	504	30	6,046	...
Potatoes (cwt.)	1,072	7	3,014	3,109
Vermont				
Hay (tons)	960	545	25,512	23,040
Apples (bu.)	930	...	2,939	2,548
Maple syrup (gal.)	285	...	1,612	1,568
Potatoes (cwt.)	285	2	720	712
Virginia				
Tobacco (lb.)	115,315	67	83,278	75,541
Hay (tons)	1,861	1,052	52,088	61,413
Corn, grain (bu.)	30,956	436	41,692	33,123
Peanuts harvested for nuts (lb.)	234,600	102	30,150	28,621
Apples (bu.)	9,000	...	15,843	21,507
Soybeans for beans (bu.)	7,068	372	20,091	17,317
Washington				
Wheat (bu.)	108,975	2,766	168,219	142,730
Apples (bu.)	21,400	...	96,348	96,042
Hay (tons)	2,168	882	55,108	53,116
Potatoes (cwt.)	24,173	64	34,130	40,215
Pears (tons)	140	...	25,620	23,963
Sugar beets (tons)	1,362	55	14,412	...
West Virginia				
Hay (tons)	912	602	30,552	27,360
Apples (bu.)	4,800	...	11,922	13,292
Corn, grain (bu.)	2,376	44	4,444	2,946
Tobacco (lb.)	3,802	2	2,482	2,775
Wheat (bu.)	456	16	983	561
Wisconsin				
Hay (tons)	10,783	4,049	200,226	199,486
Corn, grain (bu.)	163,122	1,754	144,414	166,384
Oats (bu.)	106,079	1,739	75,024	68,951
Potatoes (cwt.)	11,895	54	27,028	28,571
Soybeans for beans (bu.)	3,542	161	8,158	8,324
Wyoming				
Hay (tons)	1,680	1,178	37,947	32,760
Sugar beets (tons)	1,000	62	12,395	...
Wheat (bu.)	8,466	290	10,483	8,572
Barley (bu.)	4,794	102	4,422	4,363
Beans, dry edible (cwt.)	660	40	5,079	4,092

(H. R. Sh.)

Farm wage workers, 1967

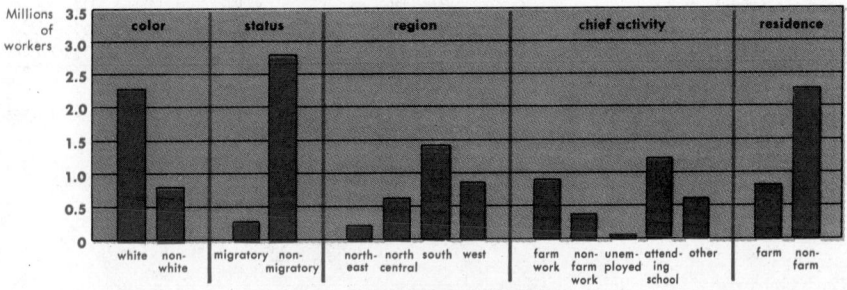

total workers: 3,078,000

Source: U.S. Department of Agriculture, Economic Research Service.

Increased efficiency per man-hour in agriculture

selected activities; 1957-59 = 100

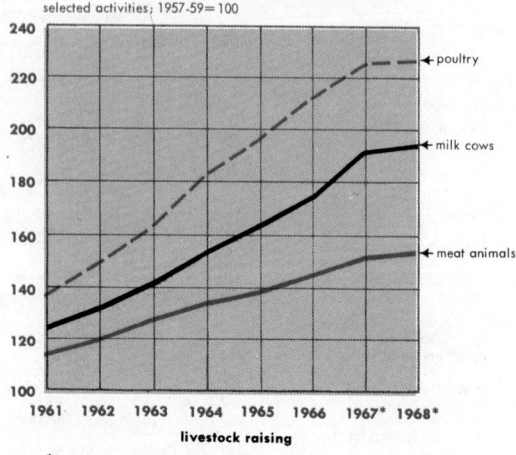

livestock raising

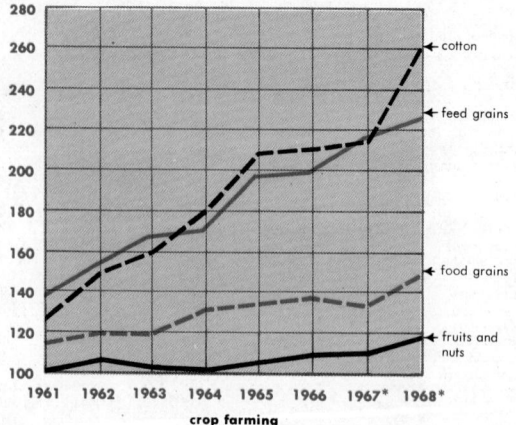

crop farming

*Preliminary estimates.
Source: U.S. Department of Agriculture, Economic Research Service.

Livestock on farms

State	AGGREGATE VALUE OF 5 SPECIES, IN $000		NUMBER, IN 000 HEAD, 1968					VALUE, IN $000, 1968				
	1960	1968	All cattle	Hogs and pigs	Sheep and lambs	Chickens	Turkeys	All cattle	Hogs and pigs	Sheep and lambs	Chickens	Turkeys
Alabama	188,198	257,839	1,915	902	8	18,031	46	218,310	22,821	91	16,408	209
Alaska	...	2,713	9	1	27	37	...	1,828	57	745	83	...
Arizona	138,231	176,616	1,160	47	487	1,540	18	164,720	1,137	8,890	1,771	98
Arkansas	158,292	232,916	1,719	247	10	21,833	138	207,999	5,335	130	18,776	676
California	733,873	964,836	4,927	182	1,535	51,063	1,582	857,298	6,133	37,880	56,169	7,356
Colorado	338,813	472,320	3,021	210	1,384	1,843	56	432,003	5,712	32,465	1,843	297
Connecticut	41,548	40,521	126	10	5	4,960	11	31,374	309	84	8,680	74
Delaware	11,199	8,598	34	35	2	860	7	6,426	1,022	38	1,075	37
Florida	184,463	267,465	1,788	299	6	14,430	13	243,168	8,282	82	15,873	60
Georgia	180,505	285,918	1,833	1,506	6	34,215	115	210,795	38,554	91	35,926	552
Hawaii	...	41,478	241	66	...	1,277	...	35,668	3,320	...	2,490	...
Idaho	212,296	264,161	1,588	116	834	1,151	8*	239,788	2,970	20,189	1,209	44*
Illinois	704,261	730,703	3,413	6,772	402	11,107	58	511,950	200,451	6,934	11,107	261
Indiana	397,221	427,886	1,918	4,111	293	17,432	69	280,028	124,152	5,071	18,304	331
Iowa	1,200,620	1,529,612	7,183	13,740	947	17,352	218	1,048,718	446,550	16,087	17,178	1,079
Kansas	586,828	809,333	5,564	1,541	454	5,173	47	756,704	40,836	7,325	4,242	226
Kentucky	305,185	435,579	2,721	1,403	135	4,193	9	389,103	40,126	2,619	3,690	41
Louisiana	201,423	212,787	1,739	209	30	5,100	5	201,724	5,100	327	5,610	26
Maine	39,353	41,318	151	9	17	6,897	1	29,747	282	248	11,035	6
Maryland	92,172	87,096	422	168	19	2,009	22	78,914	5,090	361	2,612	119
Massachusetts	44,421	39,326	125	92	10	2,964	23	31,000	2,972	157	5,039	158
Michigan	312,427	295,761	1,454	554	255	9,129	109	261,720	16,786	4,831	11,868	556
Minnesota	670,758	764,206	4,080	2,867	568	12,766	907	648,720	88,304	9,651	13,404	4,127
Mississippi	226,717	307,893	2,464	506	21	15,888	12	278,432	12,440	279	16,682	52
Missouri	603,332	798,073	4,748	4,174	349	8,133	438	674,216	110,194	5,282	6,344	2,037
Montana	354,403	493,532	2,984	149	1,275	1,219	8*	459,536	4,351	28,290	1,341	44*
Nebraska	732,337	1,062,688	6,475	2,738	451	6,560	58	964,775	84,330	8,670	4,658	255
Nevada	821,192	93,095	568	9	247	42	...	86,904	225	5,918	48	...
New Hampshire	21,937	21,342	78	13	5	2,176	14	17,160	415	84	3,590	93
New Jersey	75,553	50,653	141	118	8	6,330	17	37,506	4,047	150	8,862	88
New Mexico	181,582	201,225	1,346	40	873	934	8*	183,056	964	16,258	934	44*
New York	486,348	492,077	1,887	86	107	14,110	31	464,202	2,571	1,828	23,282	194
North Carolina	147,463	189,585	1,000	1,426	22	19,396	652	128,000	40,071	350	18,426	2,738
North Dakota	272,321	346,460	2,132	268	394	1,581	25	330,460	8,040	6,466	1,375	119
Ohio	416,831	430,300	2,073	2,340	775	13,093	206	331,680	67,626	14,077	15,712	1,205
Oklahoma	415,872	575,519	4,351	406	139	3,037	48	561,279	9,297	2,053	2,460	230
Oregon	207,397	247,201	1,577	117	550	3,142	248	227,088	3,124	12,148	3,613	1,228
Pennsylvania	436,839	436,285	1,781	460	172	17,748	188	390,039	15,502	3,079	26,622	1,043
Rhode Island	6,453	4,961	15	9	2	450	1	3,870	288	31	765	7
South Carolina	72,952	92,941	617	451	2	6,869	186	72,806	11,681	33	7,556	865
South Dakota	517,669	750,966	4,323	1,615	1,382	7,048	53	665,742	52,488	27,092	5,427	217
Tennessee	252,512	337,882	2,308	986	57	7,377	18	304,656	25,932	952	6,270	72
Texas	1,249,699	1,493,772	10,972	926	4,206	18,582	785	1,393,444	21,761	56,492	18,582	3,493
Utah	125,650	144,217	762	50	1,074	1,670	103	114,300	1,215	26,277	1,920	505
Vermont	81,388	85,263	351	7	7	653	1	83,889	179	112	1,077	6
Virginia	213,161	226,171	1,390	529	205	6,648	244	198,770	14,865	4,223	7,313	1,000
Washington	183,221	221,804	1,354	88	157	6,949	46	207,162	2,649	3,454	8,339	200
West Virginia	77,171	69,522	448	62	173	1,805	94	62,272	1,538	3,218	2,076	418
Wisconsin	812,721	896,805	4,117	1,581	189	7,533	359	835,751	47,746	2,922	8,663	1,723
Wyoming	209,784	261,033	1,420	23	1,847	215	8*	218,680	662	41,410	269	44*
Total U.S.	15,944,672	18,720,053	108,813	54,263	22,122	424,550	7,289	16,183,380	1,610,510	425,444	466,598	34,121

Data are for January 1 of years reported. Total may not equal the sum of the parts due to rounding.
*Data combined for Idaho, Montana, New Mexico, and Wyoming.
Source: U.S. Department of Agriculture, Statistical Reporting Service, *Livestock and Poultry Inventory.*

Mining

Principal minerals produced

in the United States and each state

Mineral (unit of production)	1960 Quantity	1960 Value in $000	1967 Quantity	1967 Value in $000
UNITED STATES		18,032,000		23,736,000
Mineral fuels		12,142,000		16,198,000
Petroleum, crude (000 bbl.)	2,574,933	7,420,181	3,216,715	9,377,516
Natural gas (000,000 cu.ft.)	12,771,038	1,789,970	18,171,325	2,898,741
Coal (000 short tons)				
Bituminous and lignite*	415,512	1,950,425	552,626	2,555,377
Pennsylvania anthracite	18,817	147,116	12,256	96,160
Natural-gas liquids (000 gal.)				
Natural gasoline and cycle products	5,842,507	416,819	7,919,831	549,429
Liquefied petroleum gases	8,444,074	391,566	13,717,861	632,994
Nonmetallic minerals, except fuels		3,868,000		5,205,000
Cement				
Portland (000 376-lb. bbl.)	321,646	1,089,134	{365,570	1,148,208
Masonry (000 280-lb. bbl.)			21,700	62,168
Natural and slag (000 376-lb. bbl.)			94	360
Stone (000 short tons)	616,784	952,555	785,592	1,240,244
Sand and gravel (000 short tons)	709,792	720,432	905,162	980,356
Lime (000 short tons)	12,935	172,731	17,974	241,137
Salt (000 short tons)	25,479	161,140	38,946	251,210
Clays (000 short tons)	49,069	162,411	54,664	223,987
Phosphate rock (000 short tons)	19,620	117,041	39,770	265,947
Sulfur, Frasch-process mines (000 long tons)	5,003	115,494	7,682	251,670
Potassium salts, K_2O equivalent (000 short tons)	2,638	89,676	3,299	105,313
Bromine (000 lb.)	175,010	44,637	349,757	85,391
Boron minerals (000 short tons)	641	47,550	955	74,130
Metals		2,022,000		2,333,000
Copper, recoverable (000 short tons)	1,080	693,468	954	729,401
Iron ore, usable (000 long tons)	82,963	724,131	82,415	817,511
Zinc, recoverable (000 short tons)	435	112,365	549	151,562
Uranium ore (U_3O_8) (000 lb.)	7,970△	152,188△	20,655	165,239
Molybdenum, content of concentrate (000 lb.)	69,941	87,406	81,596	133,604
Lead, recoverable (000 short tons)	247	57,722	317	88,741
Gold (troy oz.)	1,666,772	58,336	1,584,187	55,447
Silver, recoverable (000 troy oz.)	30,766	27,846	32,119	49,784
Alabama		221,802		251,391
Coal, bituminous (000 short tons)	13,011	92,439	15,486	110,696
Cement				
Portland (000 376-lb. bbl.)	12,931	42,706	{15,364	46,510
Masonry (000 280-lb. bbl.)			2,377	6,938
Stone (000 short tons)	13,503	19,970	18,371	33,346
Petroleum (000 bbl.)	7,329	‡	7,348	19,500
Iron ore, usable (000 long tons)	4,068	23,511	1,472	8,286
Alaska		21,860		134,066
Petroleum (000 bbl.)	559	1,230	29,126	91,164
Sand and gravel (000 short tons)	6,013	5,483	22,370	26,248
Arizona		417,225		463,863
Copper, recoverable (000 short tons)	346	345,784	502	383,591
Sand and gravel (000 short tons)	14,490	14,235	16,580	17,017
Molybdenum (000 lb.)	4,359	5,211	9,261	15,385
Silver, recoverable (000 troy oz.)	4,775	4,322	4,588	7,112
Zinc, recoverable (000 short tons)	36	9,239	14	3,967
Arkansas		159,519		179,453
Petroleum (000 bbl.)	30,117	83,424	21,075	56,902
Stone (000 short tons)	10,939	13,555	17,454	23,236
Bauxite (000 long tons)	1,932	20,469	1,571	18,269
Sand and gravel (000 short tons)	8,192	10,262	14,239	15,531
Natural gas (000,000 cu.ft.)	55,451	6,599	116,522	17,828
California		1,422,087		1,696,233
Petroleum (000 bbl.)	305,352	751,166	359,219	829,133
Natural gas (000,000 cu.ft.)	517,535	138,182	681,080	202,290
Cement (000 376-lb. bbl.)	39,712§	128,826§	42,034	137,961
Sand and gravel (000 short tons)	87,679	107,503	116,125	139,212
Natural-gas liquids (000 gal.)	1,203,035	83,978	1,010,627	68,187
Stone (000 short tons)	33,075	49,842	37,186	55,263
Boron minerals (000 short tons)	641	47,550	955	74,130
Lime (000 short tons)	345	5,628	539	8,696
Colorado		345,418		346,235
Petroleum (000 bbl.)	47,469	137,660	33,905	99,003
Molybdenum (000 lb.)	51,615	65,448	52,040	84,728
Coal, bituminous (000 short tons)	3,607	21,090	5,439	25,920
Sand and gravel (000 short tons)	19,053	16,882	21,810	22,904
Zinc, recoverable (000 short tons)	31	8,070	52	14,519
Natural gas (000,000 cu.ft.)	107,404	12,781	116,857	15,542
Uranium ore (U_3O_8) (000 lb.)	1,150△	23,462△	2,537	20,299
Connecticut		15,353		20,619
Stone (000 short tons)	5,057	8,313	5,097	10,141
Sand and gravel (000 short tons)	6,575	5,960	8,320	8,710
Delaware		989		2,383
Sand and gravel (000 short tons)	1,084	907	1,966	1,846
Florida		180,286		309,797
Phosphate rock (000 long tons)	12,321	82,530	‡	‡
Stone (000 short tons)	27,629†	37,419†	33,971	38,723
Clays (000 short tons)	252‖	6,357‖	756	11,574
Titanium concentrate	286	7,489	‡	‡
Georgia		92,305		153,458
Clays (000 short tons)	3,519	40,160	4,953	77,314
Stone (000 short tons)	14,297	37,033	23,418	49,953
Sand and gravel (000 short tons)	3,338	3,047	3,787	4,206
Hawaii		9,367		16,936
Cement (000 376-lb. bbl.)	113	571	1,395	7,360
Stone (000 short tons)	3,535	6,443	4,100	7,207
Idaho		57,606		109,408
Silver, recoverable (000 troy oz.)	13,647	12,351	17,033	26,402
Lead, recoverable (000 short tons)	43	10,040	61	17,188
Zinc, recoverable (000 short tons)	37	9,495	57	15,650
Phosphate rock (000 long tons)	2,177	11,044	‡	‡
Sand and gravel (000 short tons)	7,088	6,594	11,246	11,490
Illinois		589,874		636,801
Coal, bituminous (000 short tons)	45,977	184,087	65,133	252,975
Petroleum (000 bbl.)	77,341	228,929	60,115	181,581
Stone (000 short tons)	41,721	55,593	48,458	66,757
Sand and gravel (000 short tons)	33,138	36,255	38,801	44,175
Cement				
Portland (000 376-lb. bbl.)	9,139	30,732	{9,069	30,186
Masonry (000 280-lb. bbl.)			591	1,851
Natural-gas liquids (000 gal.)	374,862	21,254	‡	‡
Indiana		210,932		244,921
Coal, bituminous (000 short tons)	15,538	61,570	18,772	73,419
Cement (000 bbl.)	14,052	48,310	15,924§	53,123§
Stone (000 short tons)	18,956	34,920	26,977	46,725
Petroleum (000 bbl.)	12,054	35,439	10,081	30,041
Sand and gravel (000 short tons)	20,752	18,377	26,265	25,588
Iowa		99,319		113,222
Cement				
Portland (000 376-lb. bbl.)	12,517	44,204	{13,712	45,394
Masonry (000 280-lb. bbl.)			612	1,853
Stone (000 short tons)	23,185	30,321	26,133	37,912
Sand and gravel (000 short tons)	14,692	13,516	17,734	16,564
Gypsum (000 short tons)	1,283	5,428	1,219	5,186
Kansas		486,534		574,068
Petroleum (000 bbl.)	113,453	329,014	99,200	297,600
Natural gas (000,000 cu.ft.)	634,410	74,226	871,971	116,844
Cement				
Portland (000 376-lb. bbl.)	8,162	26,373	{8,833	25,545
Masonry (000 280-lb. bbl.)			350	1,000
Stone (000 short tons)	11,814†	15,031†	13,551	17,806
Petroleum gases, liquefied (000 gal.)	127,270	6,343	859,230	42,626
Salt (000 short tons)	1,213	14,109	1,069¶	14,686
Kentucky		414,553		535,705
Coal, bituminous (000 short tons)	66,846	282,395	100,294	396,883
Petroleum (000 bbl.)	21,147	60,268	15,535	45,052
Stone (000 short tons)	15,810	21,493	24,812	35,481
Natural gas (000,000 cu.ft.)	75,329	18,380	89,168	21,400
Sand and gravel (000 short tons)	5,113	5,763	7,981	7,859
Louisiana		1,990,895		3,961,750
Petroleum (000 bbl.)	400,832	1,258,138	774,527	2,419,823
Natural gas (000,000 cu.ft.)	2,988,414	511,019	5,716,857	1,057,619
Natural-gas liquids				
Natural gasoline (000 gal.)	875,567	66,214	1,754,603	130,212
Petroleum gases, liquefied (000 gal.)	606,023	28,147	1,844,689	92,234
Sulfur, Frasch-process mines (000 long tons)	2,256	52,639	4,233	139,739
Salt (000 short tons)	4,792	21,959	9,585	48,483
Sand and gravel (000 short tons)	14,319	19,106	20,312	27,442
Maine		14,108		14,882
Sand and gravel (000 short tons)	9,833	3,892	11,627	5,368
Stone (000 short tons)	1,012	3,851	1,159	2,999
Maryland		57,697		72,819
Stone (000 short tons)	7,944	16,962	14,479	28,581
Sand and gravel (000 short tons)	10,076	13,221	12,868	17,724
Coal, bituminous (000 short tons)	748	2,799	1,305	4,548
Massachusetts		28,245		40,612
Sand and gravel (000 short tons)	14,789	13,013	17,881	19,504
Stone (000 short tons)	5,247	12,782	6,203	17,724
Michigan		437,598		610,204
Iron ore, usable (000 long tons)	10,792	95,791	14,130	162,610
Cement				
Portland (000 376-lb. bbl.)	22,361	77,694	{29,645	94,515
Masonry (000 280-lb. bbl.)			1,995	5,296
Copper, recoverable (000 short tons)	56	36,199	58	44,692
Sand and gravel (000 short tons)	46,910	39,304	52,310	49,616
Petroleum (000 bbl.)	15,899	46,266	13,664	39,455
Stone (000 short tons)	31,256	32,274	36,432	39,910
Salt (000 short tons)	4,088	33,759	4,789	42,389
Magnesium compounds, MgO equivalent (000 short tons)	‡	‡	309	26,388
Lime (000 short tons)	1,177	15,730	1,787	21,582
Minnesota		515,521		523,326
Iron ore, usable (000 short tons)	54,723	470,874	49,457	468,623
Sand and gravel (000 short tons)	30,302	24,611	41,212	33,132
Stone (000 short tons)	4,234	10,034	4,160	11,442
Manganiferous ore (000 short tons)	441	‡	237	‡
Mississippi		199,210		217,010
Petroleum (000 bbl.)	51,673	146,235	57,147	155,726
Natural gas (000,000 cu.ft.)	172,478	32,426	139,497	24,133
Sand and gravel (000 short tons)	6,181	5,568	14,039	15,485
Missouri		162,244		236,659
Stone (000 short tons)	27,180	37,878	36,585	53,953
Cement				
Portland (000 376-lb. bbl.)	12,183	42,330	{15,044	52,119
Masonry (000 280-lb. bbl.)			372	51,172
Lead, recoverable (000 short tons)	112	26,196	153	42,742
Iron ore, usable (000 long tons)	365	3,760	1,871	26,673
Lime (000 short tons)	1,254	14,701	1,434	16,371
Sand and gravel (000 short tons)	10,207	11,601	9,716	12,556
Coal, bituminous (000 short tons)	2,890	12,450	3,696	15,573

Principal minerals produced (continued)

Mineral (unit of production)	1960 Quantity	1960 Value in $000	1967 Quantity	1967 Value in $000
Montana		179,406		186,524
Petroleum (000 bbl.)	30,240	72,878	34,959	87,543
Copper, recoverable (000 short tons)	92	59,046	65	50,063
Sand and gravel (000 short tons)	12,589	11,657	12,339	10,655
Stone (000 short tons)	1,183	1,576	4,782	6,037
Zinc, recoverable (000 short tons)	2	3,238	3	925
Silver, recoverable (000 troy oz.)	3,607	3,265	2,066	3,203
Nebraska		103,942		70,868
Petroleum (000 bbl.)	23,825	68,378	13,373	36,775
Sand and gravel (000 short tons)	10,876	8,746	11,739	10,878
Stone (000 short tons)	3,336	5,651	4,846	7,483
Natural-gas liquids (000 gal.)	‡	‡	28,543	1,801
Natural gas 000,000 cu.ft.)	15,258	2,670	8,453	1,454
Nevada		80,892		90,883
Copper, recoverable (000 short tons)	77	49,745	51	38,815
Sand and gravel (000 short tons)	4,085	5,224	10,166	8,644
Iron ore, usable (000 long tons)	740	3,683	641	2,858
Gold (troy oz.)	58,187	2,037	434,993	15,225
Gypsum (000 short tons)	802	2,721	409	1,412
New Hampshire		5,439		8,117
Sand and gravel (000 short tons)	6,621	3,687	8,449	5,137
Stone (000 short tons)	104	594	473	2,887
New Jersey		56,469		72,747
Stone (000 short tons)	10,202	22,814	12,611	28,253
Sand and gravel (000 short tons)	11,594	19,511	18,626	29,975
Zinc, recoverable (000 short tons)	—	—	26	7,031
Clays (000 short tons)	664	1,597	437	1,189
New Mexico		653,766		874,106
Petroleum (000 bbl.)	107,380	305,895	126,144	368,340
Potash, K_2O equivalent (000 short tons)	2,440	82,645	2,883	91,098
Natural gas (000,000 cu.ft.)	798,928	85,485	1,067,510	138,776
Copper, recoverable (000 short tons)	67	43,199	75	57,345
Natural-gas liquids (000 gal.)	966,783	49,200	1,247,282	60,733
Uranium (U_3O_8) (000 lb.)	3,793△	61,827△	11,202	89,615
Sand and gravel (000 short tons)	7,419	7,459	14,672	14,336
New York		260,922		299,318
Stone (000 short tons)	29,802	46,955	33,389	56,615
Sand and gravel (000 short tons)	30,687	35,152	43,500	44,499
Salt (000 short tons)	4,008	30,763	5,320	41,568
Iron ore, usable (000 long tons)	2,484	32,977	‡	‡
Zinc, recoverable (000 short tons)	66	17,122	71	19,534
North Carolina		45,096		77,094
Stone (000 short tons)	14,721	23,296	24,507	41,488
Sand and gravel 000 short tons)	8,801	7,453	10,014	9,962
Feldspar (000 long tons)	271	2,781	266	3,113
Clays‖ (000 short tons)	2,476	1,548	2,977	2,012
Mica, scrap (000 short tons)	47	1,100	69	1,751
North Dakota		78,378		97,538
Petroleum (000 bbl.)	21,992	59,598	25,315	65,818
Sand and gravel (000 short tons)	8,648	6,904	8,822	9,118
Natural gas (000,000 cu.ft.)	19,483	2,221	40,462	6,636
Coal, lignite (000 short tons)	2,525	5,790	4,156	7,967
Natural-gas liquids (000 gal.)	‡	‡	111,949	5,344
Ohio		406,142		498,888
Coal, bituminous (000 short tons)	33,957	130,877	46,014	176,921
Stone (000 short tons)	35,856	59,479	45,458	72,534
Cement				
Portland (000 376-lb. bbl.)	17,480	61,478	14,726	46,860
Masonry (000 280-lb. bbl.)			946	2,730
Lime (000 short tons)	3,117	44,403	3,636	48,817
Petroleum (000 bbl.)	5,405	16,053	9,924	31,427
Sand and gravel (000 short tons)	37,943	44,979	43,196	52,888
Salt (000 short tons)	3,108	24,149	5,407	39,549
Clays (000 short tons)	5,165	14,325	4,670	15,185
Oklahoma		782,579		1,032,126
Petroleum (000 bbl.)	192,913	563,306	230,749	676,095
Natural gas (000,000 cu.ft.)	824,266	98,088	1,412,952	202,052
Natural-gas liquids				
Natural gasoline (000 gal.)	531,995	33,074	568,905	35,846
Petroleum gases, liquefied (000 gal.)	762,258	32,409	1,005,633	49,276
Stone (000 short tons)	14,054†	16,098†	16,355	18,932
Helium (000 cu.ft.)	289,068	4,691	309,100♀	9,835♀
Sand and gravel (000 short tons)	6,424	7,468	4,540	5,280
Oregon		55,772		66,560
Sand and gravel (000 short tons)	17,673	16,170	19,630	25,250
Stone (000 short tons)	16,913	19,721	13,201	20,256
Nickel, content of ore (000 short tons)	13	5,246	15	‡
Lime (000 short tons)		‡	99	2,059
Pennsylvania		838,146		898,398
Coal				
Bituminous (000 short tons)	65,425	345,971	79,412	419,345
Anthracite (000 short tons)	18,817	147,116	12,256	96,160
Cement				
Portland (000 376-lb. bbl.)	38,320	131,763	40,197	114,592
Masonry (000 280-lb. bbl.)			2,929	7,948
Stone (000 short tons)	42,136	74,168	60,155	103,157
Sand and gravel (000 short tons)	13,011	21,204	17,479	29,614
Pennsylvania (continued)				
Natural gas (000,000 cu.ft.)	113,928	36,229	89,966	25,280
Petroleum (000 bbl.)	6,009	27,341	4,387	19,701
Lime (000 short tons)	1,120	16,277	1,719	24,715
Clays‖ (000 short tons)	3,557	16,536	2,994	16,703
Rhode Island		5,727		4,035
Sand and gravel (000 short tons)	1,535	1,355	2,334	2,416
Stone (000 short tons)	1,810	4,372	481	1,618
South Carolina		30,987		48,274
Stone (000 short tons)	7,327	10,593	8,310†	12,366†
Clays (000 short tons)	1,297	6,201	1,733	8,048
Sand and gravel (000 short tons)	3,029	3,048	5,248	7,178
South Dakota		47,675		52,618
Gold (troy oz.)	554,771	19,417	601,785	21,062
Sand and gravel (000 short tons)	13,548	9,359	13,463	13,737
Cement				
Portland (000 376-lb. bbl.)	‡	‡	1,406	4,815
Masonry (000 280-lb. bbl.)	‡	‡	54	178
Stone (000 short tons)	3,149	7,909	1,866	9,694
Tennessee		145,538		189,572
Stone (000 short tons)	20,074	29,942	31,463†	41,958†
Zinc, recoverable (000 short tons)	91	23,579	113,065	31,303
Cement				
Portland (000 376-lb. bbl.)	8,246	27,384	8,062	25,548
Masonry (000 280-lb. bbl.)			1,092	2,992
Coal, bituminous (000 short tons)	5,930	21,154	6,832	26,974
Phosphate rock (000 short tons)	2,172	15,424	2,992	22,571
Sand and gravel (000 short tons)	6,293	7,655	7,975	10,679
Texas		4,126,419		5,406,371
Petroleum (000 bbl.)	927,479	2,748,735	1,119,962	3,375,565
Natural gas (000,000 cu.ft.)	5,892,704	665,876	7,188,900	948,935
Natural-gas liquids				
Natural gasoline (000 gal.)	2,880,906	207,583	4,031,589	277,105
Petroleum gases, liquefied (000 gal.)	4,476,142	200,478	7,449,439	320,326
Cement				
Portland (000 376-lb. bbl.)	23,365	76,577	31,944	99,329
Masonry (000 280-lb. bbl.)			888	2,847
Sulfur, Frasch-process mines (000 long tons)	2,747	62,855	3,448	111,931
Stone (000 short tons)	39,029	45,088	49,424	61,577
Sand and gravel (000 short tons)	29,844	30,754	31,398	39,170
Salt (000 short tons)	4,756	18,222	8,344	36,435
Lime (000 short tons)	821	9,087	1,564	20,713
Helium (000 cu.ft.)	120,921	2,044	1,313,500ð	20,146ð
Utah		432,712		354,477
Copper, recoverable (000 short tons)	218	139,987	169	128,905
Petroleum (000 bbl.)	37,594	103,008	24,048	63,221
Coal, bituminous (000 short tons)	4,955	31,458	4,175	24,281
Uranium (U_3O_8) (000 lb.)	1,090△	27,843△	1,287	10,300
Iron ore, usable (000 long tons)	3,334	23,862	1,708	11,916
Natural gas (000,000 cu.ft.)	51,040	9,187	48,965	6,463
Lead, recoverable (000 short tons)	39	9,219	54	15,068
Sand and gravel (000 short tons)	6,848	6,182	9,412	8,631
Gold (troy oz.)	368,255	12,889	288,350	10,092
Zinc, recoverable (000 short tons)	35	9,153	34	9,483
Vermont		22,903		27,268
Stone (000 short tons)	2,114	17,444	2,761	20,520
Sand and gravel (000 short tons)	1,809	1,218	3,718	2,178
Virginia		208,880		283,685
Coal, bituminous (000 short tons)	27,838	122,723	36,721	171,183
Stone (000 short tons)	19,358	33,019	31,324	52,470
Sand and gravel (000 short tons)	7,666	11,432	9,863	12,494
Lime (000 short tons)	711	8,028	829	10,345
Zinc, recoverable (000 short tons)	20	5,142	19	5,088
Washington		72,404		82,067
Sand and gravel (000 short tons)	25,594	19,459	28,164	27,520
Stone (000 short tons)	13,897	15,796	14,454	19,099
Zinc, recoverable (000 short tons)	21	5,500	22	5,964
Uranium ore (000 short tons)	171	3,223	...	...
Lead, recoverable (000 short tons)	8	1,808	3	773
West Virginia		722,628		937,858
Coal (000 short tons)	118,944	597,222	153,749	800,683
Natural gas (000,000 cu.ft.)	208,757	54,694	211,460	50,962
Natural-gas liquids (000 gal.)	353,085	18,040	‡	‡
Stone (000 short tons)	8,001	14,001	9,445†	16,447†
Petroleum (000 bbl.)	2,300	9,361	3,561	14,244
Sand and gravel (000 short tons)	4,506	9,802	5,827	12,167
Wisconsin		78,760		79,612
Sand and gravel (000 short tons)	35,681	25,648	42,542	32,955
Stone (000 short tons)	16,486	22,302	17,122	24,863
Iron ore, usable (000 long tons)	1,502	‡	...	...
Zinc, recoverable (000 short tons)	18	4,750	29	8,016
Wyoming		439,256		530,696
Petroleum (000 bbl.)	133,910	336,114	136,312	351,685
Natural gas (000,000 cu.ft.)	181,610	21,793	240,074	35,051
Uranium (U_3O_8) (000 lb.)	1,357△	27,387△	4,655	37,243
Iron ore, usable (000 long tons)	‡	‡	1,854	19,186
Clays (000 short tons)	788	9,571	1,495	14,313
Coal, bituminous (000 short tons)	2,024	6,992	3,588	11,876

Boldface type indicates the state which leads in value of production for that mineral.
Production is measured by mine shipments, sales, or marketable production (including consumption by producers).

*Includes small quantity of anthracite mined in states other than Pennsylvania. †Excludes certain stone.
‡Figure withheld to avoid disclosing confidential data of individual company. △Short tons of uranium ore.
§Excludes certain cement. ‖Excludes certain clays. ¶Excludes salt in brine. ♀Grade A. ðIncludes crude.
Source: U.S. Department of the Interior, Bureau of Mines.
(B. B. M.)

Forestry and Fisheries

Forest land

State	Total forest land in 000 acres*	COMMERCIAL FOREST LAND* in 000 acres Total	Federally owned or managed	State, county, municipal	Private	Number of national forests June 30, 1967
Alabama	21,770	21,742	799	202	20,741	4
Alaska	118,487	5,761	5,585	146	30	2
Arizona	19,902	3,870	3,701	34	135	7
Arkansas	21,591	21,530	2,641	205	18,684	3
California	42,541	17,391	9,153	194	8,044	22
Colorado	22,583	12,275	8,907	235	3,133	12
Connecticut	1,990	1,973	1	154	1,818	—
Delaware	392	391	1	8	382	—
Florida	19,904	18,474	1,640	580	16,254	3
Georgia	26,365	26,298	1,674	135	24,489	2
Hawaii	1,982	1,089	9	487	593	—
Idaho	21,815	15,823	11,817	940	3,066	15
Illinois	3,871	3,761	229	11	3,521	1
Indiana	4,018	3,960	177	117	3,666	1
Iowa	2,620	2,595	13	24	2,558	—
Kansas	1,668	1,664	1	—	1,663	—
Kentucky	10,891	10,840	575	77	10,188	2
Louisiana	16,576	16,512	704	181	15,627	1
Maine	17,425	17,169	66	139	16,964	1
Maryland	2,920	2,897	54	160	2,683	—
Massachusetts	3,288	3,259	29	370	2,860	—
Michigan	19,699	19,121	2,540	3,780	12,801	4
Minnesota	19,047	17,056	2,813	6,720	7,523	2
Mississippi	18,008	17,976	1,267	452	16,257	6
Missouri	15,296	14,977	1,361	224	13,392	2
Montana	22,048	17,300	11,801	639	4,860	11
Nebraska	1,140	1,140	66	12	1,062	1
Nevada	12,036	109	32	—	77	4
New Hampshire	5,019	4,907	579	118	4,210	1
New Jersey	2,229	2,120	17	237	1,866	—
New Mexico	18,807	6,083	4,118	161	1,804	7
New York	14,450	12,002	98	797	11,107	—
North Carolina	20,862	20,216	1,247	290	18,679	5
North Dakota	439	424	118	10	296	—
Ohio	5,171	5,121	88	272	4,761	1
Oklahoma	9,235	5,299	423	60	4,816	1
Oregon	30,739	26,613	15,379	923	10,311	15
Pennsylvania	15,186	15,089	485	2,815	11,789	1
Rhode Island	434	430	—	26	404	—
South Carolina	11,640	11,559	837	176	10,546	2
South Dakota	1,837	1,706	1,139	84	483	2
Tennessee	13,907	13,643	834	365	12,444	1
Texas	23,954	11,991	719	34	11,238	4
Utah	14,955	3,999	3,096	240	663	9
Vermont	3,730	3,713	231	98	3,384	1
Virginia	16,492	15,829	1,277	140	14,412	2
Washington	23,050	19,510	8,159	2,200	9,151	9
West Virginia	11,469	11,389	883	153	10,353	3
Wisconsin	15,588	15,396	1,910	3,156	10,330	2
Wyoming	9,777	4,853	3,883	111	859	9
Total U.S.	758,865	508,845	113,176	28,692	366,977	153†

*Data are for January 1, 1963. However, since change in forest land is slow, the data are generally indicative of the current situation.
†Total is less than the sum of the state figures because forests extending into two or more states are shown for each state.
Source: U.S. Department of Agriculture, Forest Service.

Lumber production
in millions of board feet

Kind of wood	1960	1965	1966*
Softwoods	26,672	29,295	28,754
Cedar	...	633	610
Douglas fir	8,832	8,783	8,529
Hemlock	2,032	2,576	2,442
Ponderosa pine	3,169	3,776	3,809
Redwood	1,000	1,087	1,039
Southern yellow pine	5,660	6,628	6,609
Spruce	471	641	644
Sugar pine	408	464	507
White fir	2,224	2,422	2,321
White pine	...	1,151	1,111
Other softwoods	675	1,134	1,133
Hardwoods†	6,254	7,467	7,738
Ash	125	141	153
Basswood	92	87	90
Beech	195	182	175
Birch	126	109	104
Cottonwood and aspen	206	198	211
Elm	195	206	208
Maple	602	786	658
Oak	2,789	3,356	3,678
Sweet (red and sap) gum	331	387	435
Tupelo and black gum	292	385	352
Yellow poplar	592	681	692
Other hardwoods†	709	788	779
Total	32,926	36,762	36,492

*Preliminary.
†Includes estimate for western hardwoods, not reported by species.
Source: U.S. Department of Commerce, Bureau of the Census, Current Industrial Reports; and U.S. Department of Agriculture, Forest Service.

Forest fires
in thousands of acres

Place and cause	1950	1960	1965	1967
Total fires	208,588	103,387	113,684	125,025
On protected areas	105,182	89,627	100,568	113,762
Percent of total	50.4	86.7	88.5	91.0
Lightning	6,518	11,068	8,730	10,335
Campfires	3,802	3,614	3,404	3,405
Smoking	18,287	16,030	16,517	16,844
Debris burning	18,768	21,870	22,882	28,253
Arson	40,127	21,162	26,860	33,116
Machine use	...	...	6,734	8,763
Miscellaneous	17,680	15,883	15,441	13,046

Source: U.S. Department of Commerce, Bureau of the Census, Statistical Abstract of the United States. Data compiled by the U.S. Department of Agriculture, Forest Service.

Commercial fishing
1967 catch, by states

State	Quantity in 000 lb.	Value in $000	State	Quantity in 000 lb.	Value in $000
Alabama	32,049	8,843	Missouri	626	93
Alaska	369,000	47,000	Montana	521	62
Arizona	21	4	Nebraska	349	43
Arkansas	6,000	400	New Hampshire	1,166	683
California	506,988	51,384	New Jersey	123,688	10,716
Colorado	...	...	New Mexico	41	9
Connecticut	4,768	1,768			
Delaware	865	259	New York	38,047	12,711
Florida	205,900	33,400	North Carolina	225,000	8,400
Georgia	16,400	3,700	North Dakota	585	44
Hawaii	11,860	3,076	Ohio	9,909	1,061
			Oklahoma	1,013	126
Idaho	3,071	106	Oregon	91,400	16,000
Illinois	7,271	777	Pennsylvania	478	64
Indiana	3,384	391	Rhode Island	76,347	5,764
Iowa	3,299	307	South Carolina	18,900	3,200
Kansas	50	9	South Dakota	4,267	318
Kentucky	3,319	583			
Louisiana	643,300	37,300	Tennessee	8,879	951
Maine	197,400	23,000	Texas	139,200	49,800
Maryland	73,400	16,900	Utah	728	72
			Virginia	349,400	18,000
Massachusetts	345,700	39,065	Washington	167,000	24,300
Michigan	29,221	2,846	Wisconsin	51,307	2,323
Minnesota	12,357	931			
Mississippi	264,600	9,451	Total U.S.	4,049,074	436,240

Data are preliminary.
Source: U.S. Department of the Interior, Fish and Wildlife Service.

Commercial fishing
principal species caught

Species	QUANTITY in 000 lb. 1960	1965	1967*
Total	4,942,229	4,776,766	4,049,074
Menhaden	2,018,263	1,726,089	1,165,800
Crabs	221,681	335,407	322,700
Salmon	235,447	326,871	206,400
Tuna	298,203	318,895	328,991
Shrimps	249,452	243,645	312,200
Flounder	127,048	180,121	157,800
Haddock	118,697	133,892	98,500
Ocean perch	150,275	111,960	71,500
Herring, sea	239,018	110,293	85,100
Whitings	111,602	82,574	69,600
Clams	49,572	70,849	68,400
Jack mackerel	75,137	66,856	38,300
Oysters	60,000	54,688	57,700
Cod	45,753	46,201	53,000
Mullet	40,839	41,392	34,100
Halibut	51,202	40,825	39,900
Scup	49,229	35,870	19,800
Lobsters, Northern	31,168	30,246	26,800

*Preliminary.
Source: U.S. Department of the Interior, Fish and Wildlife Service.

Power

Mineral fuels and electricity production

in trillions of British thermal units

Year	Total production	MINERAL FUELS				ELECTRICITY*	
		Bituminous coal and lignite	Anthra-cite	Crude petroleum	Natural gas, wet (unprocessed)	Hydro-power	Nuclear power
1960	41,704	10,886	478	14,935	13,822	1,578	5
1961	42,499	10,558	443	15,185	14,691	1,605	17
1962	44,146	11,060	429	15,495	15,365	1,774	23
1963	46,274	12,024	464	15,741	16,271	1,741	33
1964	47,836	12,759	436	15,690	17,056	1,861	34
1965	49,467	13,417	378	15,930	17,652	2,051	39
1966	52,256	13,988	329	16,925	18,894	2,062	58
1967†	55,276	14,436	311	17,994	20,121	2,338	76

The fuel equivalent of hydropower and nuclear power is calculated from the kilowatt-hours of power produced, converted to coal input equivalent, at the prevailing average pounds of coal per kilowatt-hour each year at central electric plants, using 12,000 BTU per pound.
*Includes installations owned by manufacturing plants and mines, as well as government and privately owned public utilities.   †Preliminary.
Source: U.S. Department of the Interior, Bureau of Mines.   (B. B. M.)

Manufacturing

Business activity in manufacturing

Item	1960	1965	1966*
Number of businesses (in 000)			
Sole proprietorships	193	186	180
Active partnerships	47	37	37
Active corporations	166	186	189
Business receipts (in $000,000)			
Sole proprietorships	6,935	7,267	7,145
Active partnerships	7,372	5,596	6,077
Active corporations	364,612	502,982	565,116
Net profit (less loss) (in $000,000)			
Sole proprietorships	645	774	872
Active partnerships	602	589	617
Active corporations	22,145	39,852	44,526

Data cover accounting periods which ended between July 1 of the year shown and June 30 of the following year. *Preliminary.
Source: U.S. Department of the Treasury, Internal Revenue Service, Statistics of Income, U.S. Business Tax Returns, and Corporation Income Tax Returns.

Electric utilities

State	Number of utilities	Number of plants*	Total capacity in kw.	SALES OF ELECTRIC ENERGY in 000 kw-hrs.	
				June 1967†	June 1968†
Alabama	5	28	8,956,198	2,208,713	2,152,902
Alaska	27	47	254,022	58,379	64,206
Arizona	10	35	3,946,190	885,764	965,038
Arkansas	14	31	2,168,680	887,864	955,537
California	22	202	23,932,445	7,815,187	8,665,425
Colorado	31	76	2,350,450	665,383	728,375
Connecticut	9	39	2,522,054	1,008,823	1,080,426
Delaware	4	13	814,940	271,279	304,740
District of Columbia	2	3	536,670	‡	‡
Florida	28	71	10,042,310	3,025,988	3,380,366
Georgia	6	39	4,507,625	1,878,003	2,092,790
Hawaii	5	14	785,667	242,528	278,418
Idaho	10	42	1,260,570	729,543	850,480
Illinois	44	88	13,836,412	4,511,494	4,924,500
Indiana	23	52	8,565,193	2,383,818	2,614,562
Iowa	94	181	3,045,690	976,054	1,064,664
Kansas	80	123	3,358,670	906,732	954,175
Kentucky	10	25	6,586,623	2,196,701	2,348,275
Louisiana	30	62	5,307,581	1,859,418	2,167,314
Maine	15	66	886,223	325,630	356,179
Maryland	11	24	4,100,633	1,655,525‡	1,817,995‡
Massachusetts	22	61	4,518,753	1,568,606	1,653,430
Michigan	50	155	9,278,010	3,799,567	4,020,023
Minnesota	74	160	3,159,087	1,237,708	1,418,340
Mississippi	12	22	1,770,963	934,999	1,050,169
Missouri	61	95	4,831,101	1,806,575	1,990,690
Montana	8	28	1,659,130	589,966	603,653
Nebraska	66	98	1,652,465	498,350	568,149
Nevada	7	23	1,289,759	373,240	401,420
New Hampshire	7	27	753,612	213,839	227,784
New Jersey	8	31	6,740,752	2,443,759	2,601,076
New Mexico	16	30	1,924,468	351,632	368,927
New York	31	186	18,044,321	5,983,743	5,947,417
North Carolina	25	73	7,188,190	2,408,593	2,668,809
North Dakota	13	38	944,948	170,853	183,305
Ohio	38	86	13,731,844	5,928,957	6,311,114
Oklahoma	30	60	3,443,698	1,008,902	1,098,908
Oregon	11	67	3,653,147	1,568,910	1,725,158
Pennsylvania	18	85	12,582,023	4,878,733	5,247,452
Rhode Island	6	11	399,625	240,589	269,117
South Carolina	9	47	3,092,669	1,400,353	1,490,049
South Dakota	30	56	1,708,669	181,118	191,154
Tennessee	5	34	9,337,448	3,790,760	3,856,142
Texas	61	171	19,638,630	6,235,727	6,996,112
Utah	24	76	792,654	329,779	349,207
Vermont	11	60	303,025	139,571	146,337
Virginia	19	49	5,349,124	1,769,054	1,938,487
Washington	20	62	10,671,865	3,120,494	3,204,924
West Virginia	10	20	5,146,884	1,050,591	1,135,102
Wisconsin	46	165	4,835,915	1,571,146	1,718,605
Wyoming	15	41	867,707	291,392	298,556
Total U.S.	1,233§	3,378	267,074,687	90,380,322	97,445,983

Number of utilities and plants and total capacity as of Jan. 1, 1968 (preliminary data).
*Each prime mover at combination plants is counted as a plant. †Total sales for year ending June 30, 1967: 1,070,439,894,000 kw-hrs.; preliminary total for year ending June 30, 1968: 1,144,262,062,000 kw-hrs. ‡District of Columbia included with Maryland.
§Adjusted to exclude duplications because of utilities with generating plants in more than one state.
Source: Federal Power Commission.

Manufacturing activity in major industry groups, 1966

Industry group	ALL EMPLOYEES		PRODUCTION WORKERS			New capital expenditures in $000	Value added by manufacture in $000	Cost of materials* in $000	Value of shipments* in $000
	Number	Payroll in $000	Number	Man-hours in 000	Wages in $000				
Food and kindred products	1,642,145	9,542,116	1,076,357	2,239,475	5,675,932	1,692,045	24,895,940	55,071,497	79,750,949
Tobacco products	72,363	356,171	64,092	122,284	289,448	58,248	1,871,980	2,908,763	4,772,734
Textile mill products	927,339	4,243,454	827,992	1,728,234	3,448,904	887,346	8,028,374	11,723,662	19,599,852
Apparel and related products	1,359,833	4,539,214	1,202,187	2,213,143	4,037,772	202,465	9,220,536	10,943,117	19,971,042
Lumber and wood products	569,837	2,688,677	504,183	1,012,959	2,210,641	485,185	4,788,595	5,992,461	10,715,018
Furniture and fixtures	428,125	2,185,959	360,298	734,026	1,619,659	185,495	3,978,170	3,605,193	7,522,210
Paper and allied products	633,939	4,235,900	503,173	1,075,645	3,070,801	1,421,868	9,417,167	11,112,828	20,413,731
Printing and publishing	1,017,581	6,751,066	619,129	1,208,749	3,831,543	708,514	13,264,493	7,114,912	20,201,718
Chemicals and allied products	822,491	6,130,407	528,551	1,077,548	3,400,854	2,899,023	22,812,263	18,529,285	40,796,724
Petroleum and coal products	140,765	1,128,036	99,900	198,001	741,676	668,667	4,736,880	15,652,518	20,402,817
Rubber and plastics products†	491,823	3,072,031	390,587	802,939	2,174,282	599,919	6,277,082	5,825,468	11,975,964
Leather and leather products	341,078	1,426,049	303,116	574,402	1,125,309	61,475	2,480,757	2,590,313	5,032,590
Stone, clay, and glass products	618,550	3,837,514	491,924	998,856	2,811,708	939,464	8,494,586	6,262,450	14,629,434
Primary metal industries	1,296,541	9,913,533	1,065,737	2,191,793	7,650,316	2,767,655	20,907,888	29,133,125	49,540,612
Fabricated metal products	1,252,294	8,244,878	984,127	2,077,026	5,762,428	933,413	15,791,896	15,306,173	30,904,649
Nonelectrical machinery	1,804,255	13,473,873	1,310,328	2,796,547	8,846,358	1,658,304	27,040,990	20,775,105	46,633,641
Electrical machinery	1,814,302	11,985,113	1,307,527	2,668,286	7,249,270	1,379,901	23,543,922	18,376,939	40,817,084
Transportation equipment	1,890,397	15,454,072	1,406,012	3,032,838	10,314,801	2,019,731	29,250,179	43,009,790	71,511,772
Instruments and related products	362,504	2,521,401	249,278	491,863	1,437,594	307,099	5,844,992	3,214,743	8,847,528
Miscellaneous manufacturing	418,563	2,152,714	342,769	665,693	1,463,329	181,308	4,394,390	3,778,315	7,993,311
Ordnance and accessories‡	300,528	2,395,173	161,162	329,979	1,123,761	173,876	3,972,787	2,574,239	6,460,850
Total	19,121,528§	125,560,849§	13,798,429	28,240,286	78,286,386	20,231,001	251,013,867	293,500,896	538,494,230

Data are preliminary.
*Includes extensive duplication arising from shipments between establishments in the same industry classification.
†Excludes certain products included under other industry groups.
‡Excludes government-owned and operated establishments.
§Includes data for administrative offices and auxiliary units not allocated by industry group.
Source: U.S. Department of Commerce, Bureau of the Census, Annual Survey of Manufactures.

Principal manufacturing industries

In the United States and each state

Industry	Employees 1963	Employees 1965	Value added by manufacture* in $000 1963	Value added by manufacture* in $000 1965
United States	16,960,983	18,047,608	192,103,102	226,974,525
Transportation equipment	1,601,158	1,744,937	22,765,674	27,547,920
Motor vehicles and equipment	693,821	828,914	12,780,577	16,449,974
Aircraft and parts	679,385	643,326	7,867,349	8,347,511
Food and kindred products	1,643,111	1,642,072	21,825,516	23,554,013
Beverages	204,621	210,848	3,724,834	4,150,532
Dairy products	256,828	246,675	3,184,867	3,301,657
Bakery products	280,144	278,132	3,030,822	3,186,390
Canned and frozen foods	244,824	251,147	2,778,810	3,159,518
Meat products	299,576	301,468	2,882,580	3,132,915
Nonelectrical machinery	1,459,377	1,652,836	17,310,599	22,761,953
Metalworking machinery	259,002	299,971	3,037,659	4,036,994
General industrial machinery	233,143	264,805	2,812,672	3,657,255
Construction equipment	210,959	246,776	2,732,269	3,556,033
Chemicals and allied products	737,414	780,265	17,586,138	20,955,645
Basic chemicals	236,652	241,247	6,171,182	7,297,045
Fibres, plastics, rubbers	144,713	163,339	2,865,399	3,602,582
Drugs	99,001	104,963	2,807,331	3,364,230
Cleaning and toilet goods	85,572	90,814	2,866,446	3,306,312
Electrical machinery	1,511,819	1,606,980	17,010,665	20,256,363
Communication equipment	476,849	455,167	5,341,463	5,710,609
Electronic components	288,527	320,556	2,508,117	3,308,439
Household appliances	145,855	157,896	2,097,915	2,417,018
Primary metal industries	1,126,536	1,250,299	15,261,089	18,924,411
Steel rolling and finishing	568,849	640,930	8,617,266	10,594,387
Nonferrous rolling and drawing	167,005	176,892	2,127,688	2,609,637
Fabricated metal products	1,082,102	1,172,781	11,791,081	14,163,970
Structural metal products	325,470	351,453	3,219,813	3,938,866
Printing and publishing	913,243	982,352	10,476,433	12,098,776
Newspapers	306,439	327,731	3,201,872	3,731,677
Commercial printing	300,309	326,058	2,961,069	3,374,217
Apparel and related products	1,279,534	1,335,820	7,861,011	8,687,713
Women's and misses' outerwear	405,466	416,394	2,459,739	2,733,497
Paper and allied products	588,014	609,612	7,395,677	8,430,245
Paper and paperboard products	166,725	176,123	1,962,370	2,322,915
Stone, clay, and glass products	573,859	605,725	7,043,987	7,995,919
Concrete and plaster products	165,848	179,606	2,122,283	2,336,389
Textile mill products	863,246	893,565	6,122,982	7,489,378
Rubber and plastics products†	414,959	465,205	4,653,953	5,681,387
Instruments and related products	305,452	328,722	3,992,131	5,002,202
Lumber and wood products	563,135	570,651	4,020,600	4,470,558
Petroleum and coal products	153,486	143,356	3,713,231	4,168,299
Petroleum refining	119,297	109,653	3,137,603	3,530,272
Furniture and fixtures	376,548	407,079	3,068,287	3,612,408
Household furniture	270,293	293,958	2,047,494	2,413,734
Leather and leather products	327,489	335,701	2,078,572	2,322,019
Tobacco products	77,330	74,555	1,680,594	1,765,725
Alabama	243,800	271,725	2,518,314	3,138,701
Primary metal industries	40,078	43,715	693,292	807,808
Steel rolling and finishing	21,774	23,071	494,292	556,234
Textile mill products	35,474	37,296	219,338	295,508
Chemicals and allied products	8,490	9,756	216,531	281,934
Food and kindred products	22,420	23,046	203,421	224,483
Paper and allied products	11,675	12,944	165,574	222,667
Alaska	5,809	5,912	84,954	106,490
Food and kindred products	2,860	2,695	39,819	50,544
Arizona	57,039	62,223	627,141	719,882
Electrical machinery	9,131	14,415	86,431	151,171
Electronic components	5,776	8,906	48,687	89,671
Nonelectrical machinery	5,771	10,922	51,324	134,366
Arkansas	113,658	129,224	960,886	1,216,370
Food and kindred products	17,878	19,984	155,929	202,201
Lumber and lumber products	21,198	22,045	119,830	140,293
Sawmills and planing mills	14,101	13,820	81,067	78,354
Paper and allied products	7,224	6,889	118,853	122,814
California	1,398,611	1,406,211	17,162,564	18,876,132
Transportation equipment	202,090	211,115	2,665,830	3,000,342
Motor vehicles and equipment	27,000	32,067	583,424	786,813
Food and kindred products	155,731	154,173	2,412,559	2,649,985
Electrical machinery	187,965	173,382	2,192,114	2,178,960
Communication equipment	96,738	82,400	1,166,416	1,068,284
Ordnance and accessories	136,447	116,855	1,743,355	1,790,302
Nonelectrical machinery	93,308	101,647	1,086,421	1,330,076
Fabricated metal products	88,535	91,756	1,036,525	1,189,023
Chemicals and allied products	35,703	39,295	809,488	974,817
Printing and publishing	74,407	79,730	846,820	924,920
Colorado	93,722	96,636	1,193,828	1,225,941
Food and kindred products	18,597	18,323	252,251	277,762
Nonelectrical machinery	5,172	6,729	65,722	107,531
Primary metal industries	7,642	8,180	91,813	94,820
Printing and publishing	7,618	7,858	75,559	79,441
Connecticut	419,412	441,624	4,495,878	5,296,356
Transportation equipment	84,784	88,074	898,047	1,088,379
Aircraft and parts	65,193	65,837	706,556	859,850
Nonelectrical machinery	58,587	62,477	684,061	797,791
Fabricated metal products	40,334	43,174	422,235	504,732
Electrical machinery	43,302	45,254	483,694	497,598
Primary metal industries	25,865	27,117	321,769	441,647
Chemicals and allied products	11,087	12,703	265,890	355,505
Delaware	58,395	68,712	658,189	889,614
Food and kindred products	6,124	7,992	54,634	130,617
Primary metal industries	2,282	2,360	19,371	22,273
Leather and leather products	1,718	1,982	13,503	15,639
District of Columbia	22,147	27,702	256,813	287,047
Printing and publishing	13,153	14,928	162,058	191,736
Periodicals	3,257	3,693	57,186	71,868

Industry	Employees 1963	Employees 1965	Value added by manufacture* in $000 1963	Value added by manufacture* in $000 1965
Florida	215,447	231,714	2,351,973	2,670,785
Food and kindred products	39,593	40,334	499,694	511,217
Chemicals and allied products	18,143	18,829	346,897	386,640
Paper and allied products	13,594	14,175	204,604	274,767
Printing and publishing	16,331	17,563	154,644	174,053
Electrical machinery	15,125	17,160	153,347	169,866
Transportation equipment	16,667	18,647	132,541	168,199
Georgia	354,023	393,328	3,254,007	4,060,703
Textile mill products	93,482	99,532	618,226	850,803
Transportation equipment	30,357	38,713	514,266	700,417
Food and kindred products	41,949	43,340	441,953	493,310
Paper and allied products	20,484	21,589	339,327	414,933
Apparel and related products	57,145	64,175	323,163	350,541
Hawaii	25,144	25,109	261,147	288,928
Food and kindred products	15,231	14,789	166,986	108,122
Canned and frozen foods	7,502	7,285	63,012	73,942
Idaho	30,487	32,724	366,411	436,362
Food and kindred products	9,881	10,876	111,086	129,441
Lumber and wood products	10,288	9,900	88,581	101,698
Illinois	1,210,802	1,315,273	14,640,121	17,587,028
Nonelectrical machinery	178,573	202,909	2,264,672	2,845,799
Construction and like equipment	52,590	60,072	735,987	941,678
Food and kindred products	116,063	117,922	2,059,037	2,286,573
Electrical machinery	167,834	187,698	1,806,838	2,185,646
Fabricated metal products	121,879	128,803	1,366,458	1,638,101
Primary metal industries	97,851	109,944	1,176,747	1,568,649
Chemicals and allied products	47,468	49,631	1,218,465	1,384,657
Printing and publishing	95,476	102,138	1,197,739	1,379,718
Indiana	609,840	664,396	7,726,942	9,248,741
Primary metal industries	93,613	108,175	1,456,412	1,689,100
Steel rolling and finishing	59,295	68,586	1,056,396	1,160,497
Electrical machinery	91,105	106,066	1,125,703	1,468,496
Transportation equipment	91,203	93,988	1,119,585	1,348,776
Motor vehicles and equipment	60,226	60,988	775,522	927,213
Nonelectrical machinery	54,501	62,678	678,261	858,954
Food and kindred products	45,401	46,515	642,850	713,592
Iowa	178,199	191,630	2,287,001	2,632,611
Food and kindred products	50,356	47,974	653,155	676,127
Meat products	25,659	24,261	281,560	287,720
Nonelectrical machinery	35,496	41,428	476,926	586,186
Farm machinery and equipment	21,605	24,664	287,319	362,750
Electrical machinery	19,635	22,128	252,644	291,181
Kansas	114,288	121,293	1,460,374	1,707,000
Transportation equipment	34,610	35,179	446,673	489,050
Food and kindred products	21,225	21,200	239,227	269,225
Chemicals and allied products	6,224	6,499	179,704	222,844
Nonelectrical machinery	8,486	11,970	97,032	141,982
Petroleum and coal products	3,954	3,749	115,621	132,924
Kentucky	180,460	203,284	2,548,531	3,135,372
Food and kindred products	23,849	23,844	444,202	484,688
Beverages	10,003	10,846	288,516	329,881
Electrical machinery	21,319	25,772	350,172	441,544
Chemicals and allied products	11,189	12,304	273,669	344,274
Nonelectrical machinery	16,156	19,047	231,352	340,095
Louisiana	139,511	148,949	1,915,625	2,255,262
Chemicals and allied products	15,629	19,037	435,387	618,505
Basic chemicals	10,865	14,004	308,005	473,496
Food and kindred products	29,588	29,512	367,891	350,944
Transportation equipment	11,327	18,301	112,083	255,800
Paper and allied products	15,574	14,079	202,566	227,456
Maine	99,926	104,885	785,730	889,178
Paper and allied products	16,537	17,313	232,399	248,401
Paper mills, except building	13,526	14,248	190,688	199,445
Leather and leather products	24,699	26,923	135,204	158,856
Maryland	263,672	271,137	3,001,468	3,342,878
Primary metal industries	36,035	38,086	509,289	542,679
Food and kindred products	35,881	35,575	419,836	475,676
Chemicals and allied products	14,227	16,080	298,182	356,522
Transportation equipment	31,671	21,373	403,388	327,747
Electrical machinery	26,871	24,634	312,625	290,861
Massachusetts	674,023	675,669	6,403,789	7,327,404
Electrical machinery	96,183	93,775	985,805	1,087,516
Nonelectrical machinery	67,673	70,126	714,596	832,873
Fabricated metal products	39,608	41,695	450,999	529,388
Food and kindred products	41,037	38,872	506,119	520,680
Printing and publishing	40,578	43,825	439,640	515,576
Michigan	961,090	1,091,991	13,090,328	16,719,481
Transportation equipment	281,870	347,657	5,090,843	6,942,132
Motor vehicles and equipment	263,442	327,659	4,906,456	6,739,676
Nonelectrical machinery	134,256	152,404	1,794,126	2,268,122
Metalworking machinery	49,673	57,824	661,570	910,041
Primary metal industries	81,807	90,390	1,155,577	1,489,326
Fabricated metal products	86,619	101,498	1,025,281	1,318,117
Chemicals and allied products	33,595	34,525	761,996	889,076
Food and kindred products	52,472	51,656	729,211	791,821
Minnesota	245,931	258,711	2,806,116	3,360,285
Nonelectrical machinery	37,532	43,404	482,493	670,004
Food and kindred products	48,619	47,081	587,507	637,082
Electrical machinery	18,953	20,335	225,256	269,008
Printing and publishing	21,879	23,455	206,341	232,195
Paper and allied products	13,505	14,193	177,998	217,809
Chemicals and allied products	5,646	6,148	166,551	208,661
Stone, clay, and glass products	10,961	11,585	158,740	197,200

Principal manufacturing industries
(continued)

Industry	EMPLOYEES 1963	EMPLOYEES 1965	VALUE ADDED BY MANUFACTURE* in $000 1963	VALUE ADDED BY MANUFACTURE* in $000 1965
Mississippi	128,506	146,505	1,016,962	1,199,091
Lumber and wood products	20,914	23,946	130,696	159,302
Food and kindred products	14,641	15,333	130,946	157,588
Apparel and related products	31,435	31,402	131,465	123,795
Missouri	391,254	429,914	4,296,036	5,122,161
Transportation equipment	58,206	72,932	998,328	1,234,690
Motor vehicles and equipment	23,467	32,951	632,520	787,735
Food and kindred products	48,188	48,829	629,933	681,955
Chemicals and allied products	19,558	20,579	395,319	459,445
Nonelectrical machinery	26,449	29,537	275,562	368,141
Printing and publishing	27,643	29,357	286,952	341,059
Montana	20,247	21,176	236,230	284,809
Lumber and wood products	8,297	8,841	70,670	75,376
Primary metal industries	3,261	3,528	47,795	72,443
Nebraska	64,882	66,059	746,597	870,155
Food and kindred products	26,698	25,368	316,634	338,303
Meat products	12,613	11,718	115,537	128,298
Electrical machinery	5,348	6,151	64,379	73,821
Nevada	6,768	7,039	106,278	106,897
Chemicals and allied products	849	703	22,273	21,672
New Hampshire	84,107	88,593	636,088	770,940
Electrical machinery	11,508	11,765	100,912	132,535
Nonelectrical machinery	8,002	9,904	78,269	113,458
Leather and leather products	20,137	20,110	104,325	110,319
New Jersey	829,201	343,517	9,957,333	11,231,732
Chemicals and allied products	84,490	88,808	2,103,260	2,546,097
Basic chemicals	30,209	30,523	654,206	753,483
Drugs	16,775	17,785	539,611	722,591
Electrical machinery	127,564	121,930	1,315,329	1,478,323
Food and kindred products	61,098	59,842	1,034,623	1,058,716
Nonelectrical machinery	57,384	62,832	703,081	837,822
Fabricated metal products	57,451	59,050	687,255	755,028
Transportation equipment	39,471	37,968	620,314	710,236
New Mexico	15,324	16,127	149,641	141,627
Food and kindred products	3,595	3,877	34,537	38,744
Stone, clay, and glass products	1,353	1,436	19,264	19,966
New York	1,853,050	1,924,702	19,559,120	22,730,453
Printing and publishing	171,593	182,913	2,576,592	2,878,830
Apparel and related products	316,522	322,193	2,472,531	2,602,435
Women's and misses' outerwear	136,918	136,818	1,077,315	1,086,891
Electrical machinery	185,978	196,498	1,964,932	2,420,093
Nonelectrical machinery	134,680	145,477	1,541,141	2,337,595
Food and kindred products	128,774	120,741	1,846,827	1,809,743
Transportation equipment	99,811	94,958	1,342,730	1,693,287
Instruments and related products	75,499	77,300	1,259,704	1,634,524
Photographic equipment	39,401	41,469	882,624	1,227,787
Chemicals and allied products	61,352	63,853	1,373,598	1,513,426
Primary metal industries	68,539	73,797	916,516	1,049,600
North Carolina	530,646	573,534	4,566,547	5,509,481
Textile mill products	220,929	233,927	1,425,377	1,783,410
Knitting mills	68,203	72,901	385,621	468,076
Yarn and thread mills	47,992	52,275	312,216	420,892
Tobacco manufactures	29,187	26,341	849,989	858,754
Cigarettes	19,507	18,817	792,928	805,559
Furniture and fixtures	47,994	53,394	337,299	416,149
Household furniture	44,371	49,302	311,142	380,746
Electrical machinery	23,195	26,291	279,179	373,386
North Dakota	6,507	6,424	72,445	94,138
Food and kindred products	3,063	2,774	36,747	35,173
Ohio	1,239,515	1,333,956	15,506,118	18,352,110
Transportation equipment	164,408	176,998	2,459,304	2,874,045
Motor vehicles and equipment	112,368	124,558	1,895,276	2,234,645
Primary metal industries	155,447	173,206	2,197,734	2,705,210
Steel rolling and finishing	92,152	103,891	1,441,640	1,784,162
Nonelectrical machinery	167,277	190,503	2,036,679	2,640,357
Electrical machinery	117,182	120,454	1,547,622	1,743,724
Fabricated metal products	115,296	126,299	1,345,844	1,647,926
Food and kindred products	76,265	77,976	1,051,910	1,159,364
Rubber and plastics products†	80,471	85,306	968,715	1,147,155
Oklahoma	97,691	103,629	978,774	1,096,262
Food and kindred products	14,212	13,318	148,173	156,998
Nonelectrical machinery	11,032	11,683	120,244	139,155
Transportation equipment	7,801	12,300	67,542	113,833
Oregon	145,164	153,904	1,574,816	1,833,324
Lumber and wood products	69,975	71,676	700,535	761,015
Millwork and related products	27,982	29,056	284,488	303,525
Sawmills and planing mills	27,199	27,972	252,005	266,637
Food and kindred products	19,938	19,926	234,720	263,524

Industry	EMPLOYEES 1963	EMPLOYEES 1965	VALUE ADDED BY MANUFACTURE* in $000 1963	VALUE ADDED BY MANUFACTURE* in $000 1965
Pennsylvania	1,392,922	1,488,061	14,043,602	17,003,315
Primary metal industries	210,388	236,239	2,663,777	3,524,999
Steel rolling and finishing	161,235	183,151	2,155,134	2,881,539
Nonelectrical machinery	112,607	124,580	1,257,664	1,582,480
Electrical machinery	107,010	117,227	1,190,613	1,562,410
Food and kindred products	107,508	109,323	1,355,664	1,446,840
Fabricated metal products	104,800	107,974	1,085,860	1,260,665
Chemicals and allied products	45,805	47,342	987,162	1,183,230
Apparel and related products	173,130	178,331	876,008	971,136
Transportation equipment	66,339	77,374	733,011	939,788
Rhode Island	113,940	118,973	958,575	1,193,646
Miscellaneous manufacturing	21,239	24,878	152,303	207,456
Jewelry and silverware	8,467	11,121	71,953	103,331
Textile mill products	22,863	21,094	155,023	167,913
Nonelectrical machinery	9,106	10,122	88,643	134,681
Primary metal industries	9,096	9,029	94,983	129,735
Nonferrous rolling and drawing	6,425	6,961	60,568	97,210
South Carolina	261,655	282,701	2,111,117	2,737,735
Textile mill products	130,375	138,271	941,238	1,234,160
Weaving mills, cotton	67,371	66,270	426,634	546,383
Weaving mills, synthetics	23,087	26,054	170,690	238,814
Chemicals and allied products	16,181	17,328	342,833	452,273
Fibres, plastics, rubbers	5,625	7,997	141,351	240,934
South Dakota	13,234	14,158	140,042	157,449
Food and kindred products	7,905	7,952	94,923	93,746
Meat products	4,922	4,758	59,676	59,131
Tennessee	339,108	376,559	3,302,688	4,096,238
Chemicals and allied products	39,820	43,410	826,807	985,247
Basic chemicals	16,299	15,705	403,979	471,849
Fibres, plastics, rubbers	16,582	20,553	300,809	368,421
Food and kindred products	31,928	32,466	349,348	407,119
Apparel and related products	52,140	62,813	251,859	336,057
Electrical machinery	17,530	20,483	230,442	313,495
Texas	513,802	566,848	7,086,283	8,611,722
Chemicals and allied products	43,538	45,577	1,644,714	1,989,212
Basic chemicals	27,130	28,605	1,215,258	1,496,406
Petroleum and coal products	35,963	35,139	1,016,211	1,147,878
Petroleum refining	33,700	32,356	986,911	1,117,437
Food and kindred products	75,351	76,662	929,542	1,029,724
Transportation equipment	50,099	60,329	615,617	874,997
Nonelectrical machinery	41,949	49,515	510,362	655,481
Utah	53,504	47,760	710,627	683,163
Food and kindred products	8,463	8,205	99,108	95,984
Nonelectrical machinery	3,150	4,367	33,689	40,900
Petroleum and coal products	1,000	971	25,238	39,085
Vermont	33,740	39,280	309,253	444,456
Electrical machinery	1,871	3,211	19,939	109,225
Nonelectrical machinery	6,398	7,216	68,140	82,101
Virginia	302,084	320,186	3,046,268	3,576,061
Chemicals and allied products	35,106	37,268	609,341	736,966
Fibres, plastics, rubbers	21,888	25,010	395,447	500,189
Food and kindred products	32,048	32,450	326,468	350,354
Textile mill products	35,961	38,473	260,606	327,431
Tobacco manufactures	13,740	13,453	308,014	316,765
Transportation equipment	25,432	26,923	263,314	299,845
Washington	224,375	223,399	3,028,577	3,179,104
Transportation equipment	72,402	67,230	1,058,202	995,379
Lumber and wood products	42,440	43,980	360,706	423,153
Food and kindred products	26,704	25,111	360,950	383,542
Paper and allied products	17,985	19,171	330,262	356,998
Primary metal industries	9,768	11,710	202,202	244,147
Chemicals and allied products	10,908	8,183	238,150	208,572
West Virginia	117,026	123,371	1,887,148	2,033,122
Chemicals and allied products	22,573	22,044	783,235	865,025
Basic chemicals	14,915	14,298	606,027	668,315
Primary metal industries	21,652	24,096	389,749	431,489
Steel rolling and finishing	14,771	16,214	272,193	304,059
Wisconsin	461,807	493,684	5,363,153	6,157,761
Nonelectrical machinery	85,113	96,247	1,004,641	1,270,069
Food and kindred products	58,714	59,538	754,500	821,990
Electrical machinery	49,762	51,074	596,348	679,439
Transportation equipment	42,975	41,124	734,560	632,888
Motor vehicles and equipment	37,721	35,510	692,595	580,546
Paper and allied products	36,339	37,577	501,795	560,134
Wyoming	6,797	6,326	81,678	93,882
Petroleum and coal products	2,127	1,819	37,222	44,253

*Adjusted. Represents value of products shipped less cost of materials, supplies, fuel, electric energy, and contract work plus the net change in finished products and work-in-process inventories.
†Excludes certain products.
Boldface type indicates the state which leads in the value added by manufacture for that industry.
Source: U.S. Department of Commerce, Bureau of the Census, *1963 Census of Manufactures* and *1965 Annual Survey of Manufactures*.

Distribution and Services

Services

Kind of service	NUMBER OF SERVICES* First quarter		EMPLOYEES Mid-March pay period	
	1966	1967	1966	1967
Hotels and other lodging places	53,912	53,232	659,955	700,093
Hotels, tourist courts, and motels	37,505	36,855	560,625	589,414
Rooming and boarding houses	6,829	6,777	63,829	72,104
Personal services	186,072	184,800	1,001,230	1,025,260
Laundries, cleaning, dyeing plants	50,350	49,714	540,106	644,828
Photographic studios	6,977	7,048	32,651	34,524
Beauty shops	64,730	66,423	233,787	250,086
Barber shops	32,550	30,745	69,465	65,902
Funeral services, crematories	13,804	13,620	62,410	63,188
Miscellaneous business services	77,806	80,014	1,157,468	1,271,868
Advertising	7,613	7,617	106,319	110,397
Credit reporting and collection	5,887	5,565	65,399	58,809
Duplicating, mailing, stenographic	4,963	4,964	63,529	67,768
Building services	12,976	13,413	196,584	218,921
Private employment agencies	3,646	3,949	30,615	39,586
Research and testing laboratories	2,793	2,893	110,348	123,314
Business consulting services	12,960	13,971	140,541	161,457
Detective agency and protective services	2,418	2,558	85,057	96,614
Auto repair, services, and garages	68,558	67,218	330,299	339,549
Auto rentals, without drivers	4,409	4,443	41,530	45,506
Auto parking	4,431	4,287	36,232	37,256
Auto repair shops	54,020	52,599	186,551	188,678
Miscellaneous repair services	38,650	37,838	179,803	188,293
Electrical repair shops	13,037	12,751	49,047	51,617
Motion pictures	11,160	10,967	166,837	168,544
Picture production, distribution	2,389	2,434	44,908	47,560
Motion picture theaters	8,346	8,083	112,214	111,001
Other amusement, recreation services	40,475	39,970	370,886	390,302
Producers, orchestras, entertainers	6,792	6,660	52,513	56,937
Bowling alleys, billiard parlors	11,430	11,037	98,902	97,693
Golf clubs, country clubs	4,032	4,131	69,366	73,891
Race tracks, stables	1,445	1,417	24,290	25,813
Medical and other health services	201,503	203,581	2,136,888	2,362,174
Physicians' and surgeons' offices	102,667	102,985	303,362	319,160
Dentists', dental surgeons' offices	59,703	60,766	122,537	130,471
Hospitals	5,220	5,223	1,342,897	1,479,698
Medical, dental laboratories	6,299	6,392	37,275	40,401
Legal services	66,995	67,191	196,720	202,994
Educational services	27,391	28,332	695,656	761,702
Elementary and secondary schools	19,293	20,043	229,886	245,798
Colleges and universities	1,687	1,726	386,840	426,538
Correspondence and vocational schools	2,928	3,011	38,632	43,463
Museums, botanical gardens, zoos	688	705	14,353	15,015
Nonprofit membership organizations	115,927	116,969	887,820	967,796
Business associations	11,657	11,645	64,686	67,236
Labor organizations	19,905	20,041	121,134	126,138
Civic, social, fraternal organizations	28,348	28,083	219,440	226,107
Religious organizations	39,690	40,137	237,284	249,752
Charitable organizations	6,863	6,840	125,164	133,163
Miscellaneous services	56,058	56,412	482,735	503,771
Engineering, architectural services	21,207	21,260	243,370	250,465
Nonprofit research agencies	3,301	3,341	82,920	88,689
Accounting, auditing, bookkeeping	27,310	27,500	132,623	141,654
Total†	947,232	949,163	8,320,158	8,938,459

*Each business is counted as only one service in each county for each kind of service it performs, regardless of the number of establishments it operates.
†Includes administrative and auxiliary businesses, not shown separately.
Source: U.S. Department of Commerce, Bureau of the Census, *County Business Patterns.*

Sales of merchant wholesalers
in millions of dollars

Kind of business	1960 total	1965 total	1967 total	1968 1st half
Durable goods	56,803	76,232	90,447	48,052
Motor vehicles, automotive equipment	7,883	10,945	14,195	8,102
Electrical goods	8,660	11,248	14,141	6,980
Furniture, home furnishings	2,910	3,392	4,440	2,239
Hardware, plumbing, heating equipment, supplies	6,422	7,947	8,876	4,649
Lumber, construction materials	6,680	7,747	8,614	4,699
Machinery, equipment, supplies	14,287	20,279	23,836	12,498
Metals, metalwork (except scrap)	5,708	8,796	9,692	5,488
Scrap, waste materials	3,296	4,590	4,474	2,398
Jewelry	960	1,294	...	...
Nondurable goods	80,477	101,354	114,740	58,026
Groceries and related products	27,661	36,478	41,287	21,536
Beer, wine, distilled alcoholic beverages	7,424	9,496	10,427	5,044
Drugs, chemicals, allied products	5,370	6,859	8,074	4,250
Tobacco, tobacco products	4,164	4,856	5,357	2,709
Dry goods, apparel	6,675	8,614	9,772	4,977
Paper, paper products (excluding wallpaper)	4,153	5,234	6,236	3,228
Farm products (raw materials)	11,683	12,808	14,244	6,412
Other nondurable goods	13,346	17,008	18,876	9,869
Total	137,281	177,587	205,187	106,080

Source: U.S. Department of Commerce, Bureau of the Census, *Monthly Wholesale Trade Report.*

Retail sales
in millions of dollars

Kind of business	1960 total	1965 total	1967 total	1968 1st half
Durable goods stores	70,733	93,718	99,669	52,896
Automotive group	39,509	56,266	57,556	32,273
Passenger car, other automotive dealers*	36,981	53,217	53,695	30,355
Tire, battery, accessory dealers	2,528	3,049	3,861	1,918
Furniture and appliance group	10,598	13,737	15,700	7,751
Furniture, home furnishings stores	6,770	8,538	9,384	4,744
Household-appliance, TV, radio stores	3,828	4,223	5,245	2,507
Lumber, building, hardware, farm-equipment group	14,819	16,274	17,259	8,498
Lumberyards, building-materials dealers†	8,618	9,302	9,350	4,844
Hardware stores	2,693	2,813	3,061	1,474
Nondurable goods stores	148,796	190,232	213,834	107,966
Apparel group	13,708	15,752	18,105	8,541
Men's, boys' wear stores‡	2,619	3,258	3,822	1,777
Women's apparel, accessory stores§	5,329	6,243	6,994	3,299
Family clothing stores	2,728	2,981	3,586	1,596
Shoe stores	2,450	2,571	2,947	1,528
Drug and proprietary stores	7,530	9,335	10,894	5,578
Eating and drinking places	16,096	21,423	24,887	12,867
Food group	53,837	66,920	72,137	37,285
Grocery stores	48,339	61,068	66,146	34,246
Meat markets	1,560	1,552	1,586	823
Bakeries	1,034	1,142	1,177	581
Gasoline service stations	17,594	21,765	24,011	12,510
General merchandise group	24,007	35,840	42,174	19,849
Department stores and dry goods, general merchandise stores	16,994	27,939	33,329	15,739
Variety stores	3,899	5,320	6,078	2,847
Mail-order houses (department store merchandise)	1,857	2,581	2,767	1,263
Liquor stores	4,880	6,305	7,120	3,538
Total	219,529	283,950	313,503	160,862

*Includes both franchised and nonfranchised car dealers. †Includes lumberyards, building materials dealers; paint, plumbing, and electric stores. ‡Includes men's, boys' clothing, furnishings stores, and custom tailors. §Includes women's ready-to-wear; other apparel, accessory, specialty shops; and furriers.
Source: U.S. Department of Commerce, Bureau of the Census, *Monthly Retail Trade Report.*

Business activity in wholesaling, retailing, and services

Item	WHOLESALING			RETAILING			SERVICES		
	1960	1965	1966*	1960	1965	1966*	1960	1965	1966*
Number of businesses (in 000)									
Sole proprietorships	306	265	281	1,548	1,554	1,513	1,966	2,208	2,271
Active partnerships	41	32	29	238	202	200	159	169	172
Active corporations	117	147	152	217	288	299	121	188	202
Business receipts (in $000,000)									
Sole proprietorships	17,061	17,934	19,808	65,439	77,760	78,610	23,256	29,789	31,991
Active partnerships	12,712	10,879	11,142	24,787	23,244	23,987	9,281	12,442	13,660
Active corporations	130,637	171,414	188,425	125,787	183,925	201,936	22,106	36,547	41,790
Net profit (less loss) (in $000,000)									
Sole proprietorships	1,305	1,483	1,651	3,869	5,019	5,177	8,060	11,008	11,990
Active partnerships	587	548	506	1,612	1,654	1,715	3,056	4,402	4,924
Active corporations	2,130	3,288	3,946	2,225	4,052	4,454	849	1,505	1,886

Data cover accounting periods which ended between July 1 of the year shown and June 30 of the following year.
*Preliminary figures.
Source: U.S. Department of the Treasury, Internal Revenue Service, *Statistics of Income, U.S. Business Tax Returns* and *Corporation Income Tax Returns.*

Foreign Aid and Commerce

International investment position

in millions of dollars

Type of investment	January 1, 1967	January 1, 1968*
U.S. assets and investments abroad	111,840	122,292
Private investments	86,321	93,287
Long-term	75,715	81,442
Direct	54,711	59,267
Foreign dollar bonds	9,513	9,666
Other foreign bonds	1,030	1,113
Foreign corporate stocks	4,324	5,238
Banking claims	3,980	3,711
Short-term assets and claims	10,606	11,845
U.S. government credits and claims	25,519	29,005
Long-term credits†	21,054	23,545
Foreign currencies and short-term claims	2,818	2,695
IMF gold tranche position and monetary authorities' holdings of convertible currencies	1,647	2,765
Foreign assets and investments in the U.S.	60,410	69,613
Long-term	27,006	31,962
Direct	9,054	9,923
Corporate stocks	12,643	15,511
Corporate, state, and municipal bonds	2,042	2,159
Short-term assets and U.S. government obligations	33,404	37,651
Private obligations	20,799	22,901
U.S. government obligations	12,605	14,750
Bills and certificates	8,064	9,325
Marketable bonds and notes	1,969	2,381

*Preliminary. †Excludes World War I debts not currently being serviced.
Source: U.S. Department of Commerce, Office of Business Economics, *Survey of Current Business.*

Major recipients of foreign assistance

in millions of dollars

Program, region, and country	1958	1959	1960	1961	1962	1963	1964	1965	1966	1967	1968*
Total	5,312	5,557	5,050	5,604	6,282	6,588	5,917	5,799	6,692	6,818	6,425
By program											
Economic assistance programs	2,908	3,396	3,206	4,138	4,755	4,643	4,377	4,486	5,249	5,290	5,051
Agency for International Development†	1,620	1,916	1,866	2,012	2,508	2,297	2,136	2,026	2,545	2,249‡	2,170‡
Loans	417	626	564	707	1,329	1,343	1,328	1,122	1,219	1,087	1,079
Grants	1,203	1,291	1,302	1,305	1,180	954	808	904	1,326	1,162	1,091
Social Progress Trust Fund§	—	—	—	—	226	127	42	101	24	2	...
Food for Freedom	784	858	997	1,170	1,443	1,561	1,591	1,484	1,754	1,040	1,439
Export-Import Bank long-term loans	480	603	246	867	344	294	354	405	418	1,457	850
Other economic programs‖	23	19	97	88	234	363	254	470	509	541	485
Military assistance programs	2,404	2,160	1,845	1,466	1,527	1,945	1,540	1,313	1,442	1,528	1,374
By region and country											
Africa	110	192	221	471	512	499	388	347	406	420	407
Congo (Kinshasa)	—	¶	1	75	83	73	43	27	40	47	36
Ethiopia	14	15	15	47	26	25	19	28	64	28	9
Ghana	—	2	1	22	130	3	3	3	9	35	38
Ivory Coast	—	—	—	2	3	7	9	4	6	2	37
Morocco	34	48	81	96	50	72	46	37	68	55	79
Nigeria	¶	2	2	14	25	29	51	35	30	18	26
Tunisia	27	34	59	110	48	65	49	54	20	56	49
Asia	3,205	3,259	3,190	3,031	3,456	3,653	3,114	3,408	3,475	3,114	3,084
Ceylon	20	17	9	9	6	4	3	4	14	11	28
Greece	204	121	184	85	81	134	109	133	80	46	48
India	308	366	687	570	745	687♀	666♀	721♀	917♀	606	690♀
Indonesia	27	66	72	36	69	104	36	—1	16	65	99
Iran	125	138	127	156	100	107	53	92	115	182	125
Israel	85	53	56	78	80	76	40	74	39	14	79
Japan	195	172	108	115	136	151	76	94	52	127	102
Korea, South	621	463	405	449	327	355	342	355	420	335	354
Laos	37	33	55	64	64	379	42♀	48♀	55♀	55♀	64♀
Pakistan¶	158	229	292	168	422	355	380	348	142	233	362♀
Philippines	50	132	43	111	44	115	28	48	40	66	39
Ryukyu Islands	4	2	6	5	25	11	11	17	16	39	39
Saudi Arabia	69	13	—1	5	6	6	4	8	3	68	29
Taiwan	262	338	261	205	157	154	171	143	145	92	94
Thailand	46	77	51	48	87	90	68	78	101	84	53
Turkey	357	394	219	307	341	337	281	321	258	270	223
Vietnam, South	242	249	251	209	287	376	403	543	900	542δ	540δ
Canada	—	—	—	9	—	—	—	—	—	—	30
Europe	1,387	1,153	1,119	869	695	680	565	431	564	981	640
Germany, West	182	59	138	17	2	1	¶	¶	2	14	9
Italy	176	139	128	165	105	123	91	88	46	151	87
Norway	64	40	34	13	25	23	41	35	43	34	18
Poland	25	9	3	5	7	8	15	4	7	5	11
Spain	216	187	187	149	66	54	76	104	158	178	17
Sweden	—	—	—	—	—	—	—	—	—	48	32
United Kingdom	23	136	116	14	27	12	¶	¶	86	407	396
Yugoslavia	139	175	76	147	114	111	73	87	140	12	12
Latin America	402	630	395	963	1,148	1,063	1,268	1,231	1,352	1,475	1,483
Argentina	¶	141	1	49	60	134	13	16	34	13	55
Bolivia	22	25	14	30	38	65	79	14	39	31	23
Brazil	45	154	47	304	249	152	362	287	402	286	362
Chile	49	48	46	142	182	109	137	139	116	290	118
Colombia	99	9	15	112	83	134	131	39	107	151	121
Dominican Republic	1	1	¶	¶	35	53	16	77	110	62	72
Guatemala	17	22	9	32	11	16	15	14	5	22	19
Mexico	64	108	49	31	50	46	107	106	37	102	88
Nicaragua	4	4	12	12	15	9	8	25	21	13	32
Panama	5	2	2	16	25	10	25	24	14	36	22
Peru	26	43	21	72	90	25	87	44	53	39	27
Uruguay	6	19	17	5	10	24	9	2	9	5	41
Venezuela	¶	13	25	68	64	54	55	47	18	47	79
Oceania	6	30	11	8	7	26	33	36	176	311	271
Australia	—	25	6	2	1	12	18	19	151	263	181
Trust Territory of the Pacific Islands	6	5	5	6	6	9	15	17	18	23	28
Nonregional	201	293	115	252	463	667	548	345	717	516	510

Years ending June 30. Economic assistance data on net obligation and loan authorization basis, rather than expenditure basis. Military assistance data represent value of goods delivered. *Preliminary. †A.I.D. predecessor agencies prior to Nov. 3, 1961. ‡Excludes $43.1 million reimbursements in 1967 and $34.6 million reimbursements in 1968 by Department of Defense for grants to Vietnam. §Administered by Inter-American Development Bank as part of Alliance for Progress. ‖Principal programs include capital subscriptions to Inter-American Development Bank and International Development Association, Peace Corps, Philippine War Damage Claims, United Nations bond issue. ¶Less than $500,000. ♀Economic assistance only. δEconomic assistance only. Military assistance transferred to Department of Defense funding. Military assistance data classified.
Source: U.S. Department of State, Agency for International Development.

Trade by commodity groups

in millions of dollars

Commodity group	EXPORTS								IMPORTS							
	1960	1961	1962	1963	1964	1965	1966	1967	1960	1961	1962	1963	1964	1965	1966	1967
Food and live animals	2,684	2,960	3,245	3,657	4,083	4,003	4,562	4,064	2,996	3,018	3,243	3,401	3,487	3,460	3,948	4,003
Beverages and tobacco	483	506	498	531	554	517	624	649	396	437	431	462	535	553	642	698
Crude materials, inedible, except fuels	2,805	2,794	2,226	2,493	2,969	2,855	3,070	3,280	2,711	2,487	2,670	2,678	2,826	3,047	3,266	2,965
Mineral fuels and related materials	842	797	828	978	953	947	976	1,104	1,574	1,738	1,887	1,924	2,030	2,221	2,262	2,250
Animal and vegetable oils and fats	295	272	301	303	414	472	357	338	95	93	98	105	119	116	146	122
Chemicals	1,776	1,789	1,876	2,009	2,364	2,402	2,675	2,803	821	726	760	701	702	769	955	963
Machinery and transport equipment	6,992	7,313	8,026	8,243	9,369	10,147	11,155	12,573	1,467	1,363	1,674	1,823	2,216	2,948	4,823	5,791
Other manufactured goods	3,791	3,646	3,753	4,007	4,655	4,839	5,278	5,376	4,559	4,420	5,178	5,526	6,178	7,521	8,635	8,963
Other transactions	718	675	676	841	794	954	1,187	960	401	435	450	518	590	730	866	1,060
Total	20,383	20,754	21,431	23,062	26,156	27,135	29,884	31,147	15,019	14,716	16,392	17,140	18,684	21,366	25,542	26,816

Export data exclude reexports.
Import data show commodities released for domestic consumption during each year.
Source: U.S. Department of Commerce, Bureau of the Census, *Statistical Abstract of the United States.*
Data compiled by U.S. Department of Commerce, Bureau of International Commerce.

Principal trading partners

by exports and imports, in millions of dollars

Country	EXPORTS				Country	IMPORTS			
	1960	1963	1965	1967		1960	1963	1965	1967
North America	5,394	5,864	7,680	9,507	North America	4,429	5,358	6,579	9,073
Bahamas	49	78	107	153	Canada	2,901	3,829	4,832	7,099
Canada	3,715	4,120	5,585	7,146	Costa Rica	35	42	57	70
Dominican Republic	41	91	76	96	Dominican Republic	110	140	111	134
Guatemala	63	74	95	90	Honduras	34	32	72	70
Honduras	34	44	54	70	Jamaica	54	103	125	144
Jamaica	48	62	87	125	Mexico	443	594	638	749
Mexico	822	861	1,105	1,222	Netherlands Antilles	265	264	319	311
Netherlands Antilles	65	78	75	78	Panama	24	32	60	76
Nicaragua	30	45	69	70	Trinidad and Tobago	55	111	142	184
Panama	89	109	125	139	South America	2,435	2,492	2,624	2,663
South America	2,103	1,840	2,142	2,319	Argentina	98	165	122	140
Argentina	351	189	266	227	Brazil	570	562	512	559
Brazil	433	382	329	531	Chile	193	188	209	175
Chile	196	162	235	245	Colombia	299	249	277	240
Colombia	247	240	196	214	Ecuador	65	76	106	101
Ecuador	55	57	78	98	Peru	183	215	241	310
Peru	143	194	281	255	Venezuela	948	936	1,018	982
Venezuela	552	509	624	585	Europe	4,268	4,811	6,292	8,232
Europe	6,561	7,116	8,852	9,752	Austria	49	52	66	72
Belgium and Luxembourg	439	524	643	700	Belgium and Luxembourg	364	379	494	584
Denmark	111	147	185	202	Denmark	98	125	147	183
France	583	681	902	1,013	Finland	52	62	84	93
Germany, West	1,077	1,120	1,502	1,563	France	396	431	615	690
Greece	64	97	121	100	Germany, West	897	1,003	1,341	1,955
Ireland	40	46	69	77	Greece	33	53	44	68
Italy	653	884	864	951	Ireland	28	43	58	130
Netherlands	734	781	1,055	1,225	Italy	393	493	620	856
Norway	90	96	130	138	Netherlands	213	211	251	372
Portugal	39	50	74	75	Norway	66	105	124	135
Spain	190	278	447	516	Poland	39	43	66	91
Sweden	301	255	330	383	Portugal	35	47	56	69
Switzerland	254	312	352	428	Spain	88	97	133	217
Turkey	126	218	164	134	Sweden	170	181	243	330
United Kingdom	1,412	1,162	1,565	1,815	Switzerland	198	239	306	383
Yugoslavia	86	165	149	96	Turkey	60	65	83	103
Asia	3,652	4,812	5,495	6,768	United Kingdom	993	1,079	1,405	1,710
Hong Kong	123	146	191	254	Yugoslavia	41	47	61	87
India	642	817	928	955	Asia	2,721	3,192	4,528	5,352
Indonesia	86	109	42	68	Hong Kong	139	193	343	498
Iran	117	90	162	192	India	228	295	348	298
Israel	126	167	201	186	Indonesia	216	113	165	182
Japan	1,343	1,714	2,058	2,666	Iran	51	65	88	83
Korea, South	153	238	202	329	Israel	27	47	62	87
Kuwait	41	60	66	108	Japan	1,149	1,498	2,414	2,999
Pakistan	170	388	336	347	Korea, South	5	23	54	117
Philippines	298	323	336	422	Malaysia	175*	188*	212	196
Saudi Arabia	43	69	129	129	Philippines	307	357	369	381
Taiwan	111	137	172	266	Taiwan	20	55	93	166
Thailand	65	96	107	164	Thailand	56	39	41	96
Vietnam, South	53	115	191	297	Australia and Oceania	266	502	453	581
Australia and Oceania	477	531	848	911	Australia	142	317	311	406
Australia	389	446	696	786	New Zealand and Western Samoa	119†	173	130	156
New Zealand and Western Samoa	75†	72	126	89	Africa	534	777	878	905
Africa	767	992	1,224	1,167	Angola	26	38	48	63
Libya	42	44	64	85	Ghana	52	51	59	57
South Africa	278	278	438	426	South Africa	108	259	226	227
United Arab Republic	151	210	158	66	Unidentified	19	6	12	8
Unidentified‡	1,625	2,192	1,238	1,109	Total	14,654	17,138	21,366	26,816
Total	20,578	23,347	27,478	31,534					

*Federation of Malaya. †New Zealand only. ‡Special Category commodities (exports not identified by country of destination for security reasons).
Source: U.S. Department of Commerce, Bureau of the Census, *Statistical Abstract of the United States.*

Major commodities traded, 1967

in millions of dollars

Item	Total	Canada	American republics	Western Europe*	Far East†	Other areas
EXPORTS						
Total‡	31,534	7,173	4,126	10,099	6,252	3,884
Agricultural commodities						
Grains and preparations§	2,681	102	235	781	1,242	321
Fruits, nuts, and vegetables§	492	196	41	178	48	29
Tobacco, unmanufactured	498	4	8	371	77	38
Soybeans, not canned	772	63	4	458	217	30
Cotton, including linters, waste	464	33	1	113	296	21
Nonagricultural commodities‖						
Ores and scrap, metal	520	78	31	116	291	4
Coal, coke, and briquettes	501	144	34	189	132	2
Petroleum products	447	61	69	129	111	77
Chemicals	2,803	421	527	928	580	347
Machinery‖	8,251	2,211	1,309	2,486	1,097	1,148
Industrial machinery‖	5,311	1,338	872	1,629	714	758
Agricultural machines and tractors, and parts	844	352	141	138	82	131
Electrical apparatus	2,097	520	296	719	302	260
Road motor vehicles‖	2,448	1,504	402	164	114	264
Automobile parts, nonmilitary	1,110	794	148	70	34	64
Aircraft, civilian, and parts for all aircraft	1,213	170	119	600	144	180
Pulp, paper, and manufactures	726	98	129	281	126	92
Metals and manufactures	1,734	526	265	456	301	186
Iron and steel-mill products¶	539	181	92	84	114	68
Textile yarn, fabrics, and made-up articles	531	134	75	150	56	116
Other agricultural and nonagricultural exports, including re-exports and "Special Category" items	7,453	1,428	877	2,699	1,420	1,029
IMPORTS						
Total	26,816	7,099	3,853	8,055	5,059	2,750
Agricultural commodities						
Meat and preparations	645	39	117	177	3	309
Fruits, nuts, and vegetables	556	27	292	107	105	25
Coffee	964	—	670	♀	41	253
Sugar	588	♀	334	1	178	75
Nonagricultural commodities						
Alcoholic beverages	528	138	3	382	2	3
Pulp, paper, and manufactures	1,381	1,256	2	100	13	10
Ores and scrap, metal	974	409	231	19	38	277
Petroleum, crude and partly refined	1,167	380	523	3	43	218
Petroleum products	921	11	444	39	♀	427
Chemicals	963	270	84	416	80	113
Machinery	3,103	782	20	1,471	811	19
Transport equipment	2,688	1,476	♀	1,033	175	4
Automobiles, new	1,695	818	♀	804	73	—
Iron and steel-mill products¶	1,289	102	30	606	532	19
Nonferrous base metals	1,477	534	299	352	199	93
Textile yarn, fabrics, and made-up articles	812	17	38	248	481	28
Fish, including shellfish	522	136	118	55	111	102
Other agricultural and non-agricultural imports	8,238	1,522	648	3,046	2,247	775

*Includes Greece and Turkey.   †Asia, excluding the Near East.
‡Includes commodities classified as "Special Category" for security reasons.
§Includes shipments for relief by individuals and private agencies.
‖Excludes "Special Category" commodities.
¶Excludes pig iron.   ♀Less than $500,000.
Source: U.S. Department of Commerce, Bureau of the Census, *Statistical Abstract of the United States*. Data compiled by the U.S. Department of Commerce, Bureau of International Commerce.

Components of surplus or deficit in the balance of payments

in billions of dollars

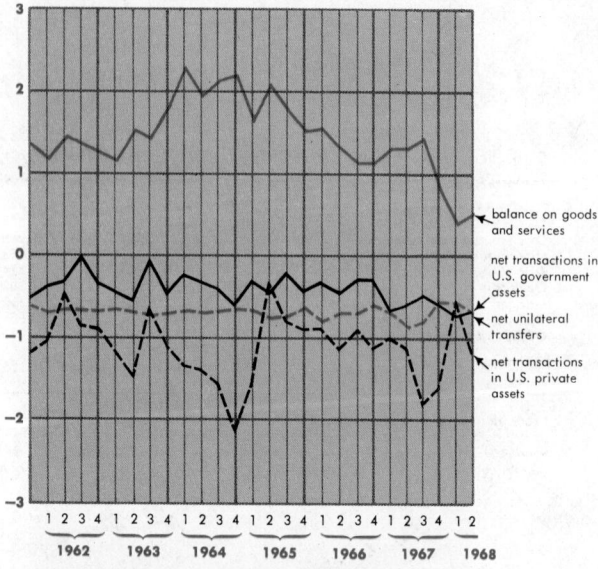

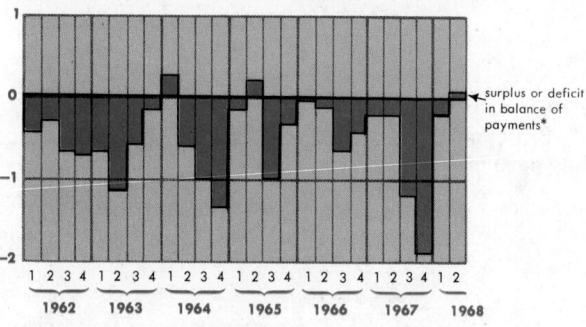

Data in top grid are seasonally adjusted and exclude military grant aid. Negative amounts are net increases in assets abroad and net unilateral transfers to foreigners.
*Measured by increase in U.S. official reserve assets and decrease in liquid liabilities to all foreigners.
Source: U.S. Department of Commerce, Office of Business Economics, *Survey of Current Business*.

Transactions in the balance of payments

in millions of dollars

Type of transaction	1961	1962	1963	1964	1965	1966	1967	1968 1st quarter	1968 2nd quarter
Exports of goods and services	30,040	31,817	33,821	38,288	40,621	44.036	46,661	11,904	...
Merchandise	19,954	20,604	22,071	25,297	26,276	29,168	30,468	7,892	8,504
Military transfers	1,867	2,195	2,139	2,077	2,472	1,844	2,145	535	...
Transportation	1,805	1,964	2,115	2,324	2,415	2,589	2,701	659	709
Foreign travel in U.S.	885	878	934	1,095	1,212	1,573	1,646	374	467
Miscellaneous services	1,588	1,751	1,908	2,103	2,345	2,617	2,843	726	756
Income on investments abroad	3,941	4,425	4,654	5,392	5,901	6,245	6,858	1,719	1,919
Imports of goods and services	−22,954	−25,148	−26,442	−28,468	−32,036	−37,937	−40,989	−11,036	−12,038
Merchandise	−14,510	−16,187	−16,992	−18,621	−21,488	−25,510	−26,991	−7,749	−8,279
Military expenditures	−2,981	−3,083	−2,936	−2,834	−2,881	−3,694	−4,340	−1,110	−1,143
Transportation	−1,943	−2,128	−2,316	−2,462	−2,691	−2,914	−2,982	−718	−862
U.S. travel abroad	−1,735	−1,885	−2,090	−2,201	−2,400	−2,657	−3,195	−511	−795
Miscellaneous services	−851	−809	−837	−946	−930	−1,088	−1,189	−300	−284
Income on foreign investments in U.S.	−934	−1,056	−1,271	−1,404	−1,646	−2,074	−1,293	−648	−676
Net unilateral transfers (to foreigners [−])	−4,051	−4,215	−4,266	−4,095	−4,422	−3,922	−3,981	−887	...
Private remittances	−497	−512	−605	−600	−628	−647	−835	−164	−194
U.S. government transfers	−3,554	−3,703	−3,661	−3,495	−3,794	−3,275	−3,146	−713	...
Net transactions in U.S. private assets (increase [−])	−4,180	−3,425	−4,456	−6,523	−3,690	−4,213	−5,504	−817	−1,111
Net transactions in U.S. government assets (increase [−])*	−926	−1,094	−1,664	−1,674	−1,575	−1,531	−2,411	−734	−751
Net transactions in U.S. official reserve assets (increase [−])	606	1,533	378	171	1,222	568	52	904	−137
Net transactions in foreign assets in the U.S. (increase [+])	2,471	1,691	2,981	3,312	309	3,301	6,704	725	2,127
Net errors and omissions	−1,006	−1,159	−352	−1,011	−429	−302	−532	−60	−108

*Excluding transactions in official reserve assets.
Source: U.S. Department of Commerce, Office of Business Economics, *Survey of Current Business*.

Finance

Money stock and money in circulation

In millions of dollars, except per capita

		MONEY HELD IN TREASURY			MONEY OUTSIDE OF TREASURY		
Year	Stock of money in U.S.*	In trust against gold and silver certificates	Treasury cash	For federal reserve banks and agents	Held by federal reserve banks and agents	In circulation† Amount	In circulation† Per capita
1960	53,071	(21,455)	395	16,213	4,398	32,065	177.46
1961	51,947	(19,662)	379	14,440	4,724	32,405	176.35
1962	52,195	(18,435)	379	13,342	4,705	33,770	180.92
1963	53,335	(17,585)	369	12,641	4,855	35,470	187.30
1964	55,451	(16,997)	391	12,369	4,957	37,734	196.46
1965	56,690	(14,559)	747	13,669	2,554	39,720	204.33
1966	60,362	(13,595)	1,049	12,992	3,768	42,554	213.99
1967	61,408	(13,006)	1,472	12,607	2,616	44,712	225.97
1968	61,506	(10,026)	838	10,024	3,003	47,640	238.37

Data are for June 30 of each year.
*Does not include duplications, which are shown in parentheses.
†Includes any paper currency held outside the U.S.
Source: Board of Governors of the Federal Reserve System, *Federal Reserve Bulletin.*

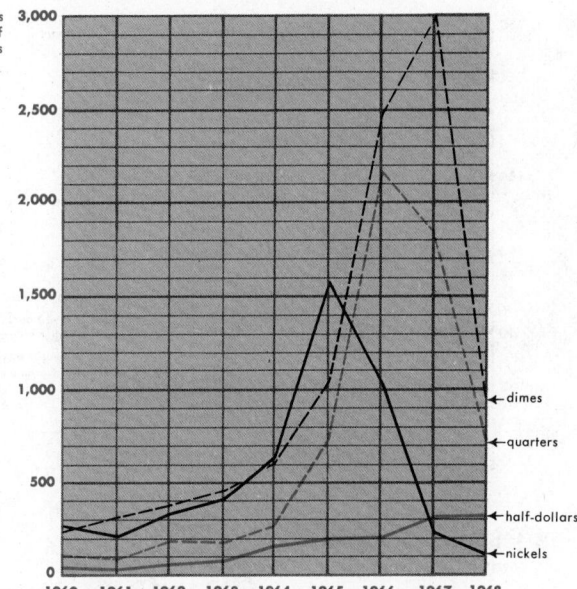

Coin production
years ending June 30

Millions of pieces

← dimes
← quarters
← half-dollars
← nickels

After July 1965, because of the silver shortage, dimes and quarters were minted of copper and cupronickel, and the silver in half dollars was reduced to 40%.
Source: U.S. Department of the Treasury, Bureau of the Mint.

Banks

June 29, 1968

State	Number of banks	Total assets or liabilities in $000,000	SELECTED ASSETS in $000,000 Loans*	SELECTED ASSETS Invest-ments	SELECTED ASSETS Cash and balances with other banks	SELECTED LIABILITIES in $000,000 Deposits Total	Deposits Inter-bank	Deposits Other Demand	Deposits Other Time	Capital accounts
Alabama	268	4,347	2,106	1,484	664	3,882	146	1,937	1,798	370
Alaska	14	463	246	140	59	426	3	190	233	30
Arizona	14	2,878	1,868	602	294	2,592	18	1,058	1,516	199
Arkansas	248	2,580	1,305	795	420	2,305	104	1,222	979	224
California	174	47,416	27,681	10,910	6,886	41,327	1,058	15,989	24,280	3,196
Colorado	257	3,853	2,216	936	592	3,411	134	1,588	1,690	309
Connecticut	137	9,737	6,533	2,188	822	8,711	83	2,408	6,220	793
Delaware	21	1,573	861	448	236	1,391	20	687	685	142
District of Columbia	14	2,910	1,435	899	517	2,602	80	1,486	1,036	218
Florida	457	11,097	4,985	4,126	1,656	9,982	488	4,785	4,709	824
Georgia	429	6,603	3,628	1,694	1,030	5,765	293	2,930	2,542	579
Hawaii	11	1,452	795	385	206	1,284	26	596	662	140
Idaho	26	1,151	688	296	135	1,036	3	482	551	83
Illinois	1,072	34,141	17,552	10,834	4,739	28,985	1,438	12,918	14,629	2,675
Indiana	420	9,854	4,890	3,253	1,529	8,780	235	4,175	4,370	697
Iowa	674	5,853	2,965	2,021	778	5,280	212	2,374	2,693	489
Kansas	601	4,475	2,130	1,685	588	4,016	137	2,032	1,847	408
Kentucky	346	4,531	2,245	1,457	751	4,080	230	2,092	1,758	384
Louisiana	229	5,761	2,722	1,927	1,000	5,145	339	2,652	2,153	487
Maine	76	1,991	1,225	586	139	1,750	17	455	1,278	177
Maryland	129	5,872	3,340	1,596	775	5,202	147	2,411	2,645	486
Massachusetts	335	21,813	13,861	5,419	2,079	18,692	745	5,377	12,570	1,826
Michigan	339	19,526	11,222	5,629	2,232	17,656	363	5,874	11,418	1,228
Minnesota	724	8,905	4,753	2,824	1,152	7,844	419	2,895	4,531	643
Mississippi	187	2,760	1,396	864	433	2,451	115	1,386	950	223
Missouri	666	10,935	5,439	3,603	1,683	9,623	765	4,495	4,363	945
Montana	135	1,400	755	447	164	1,253	26	558	668	102
Nebraska	440	3,062	1,599	930	473	2,725	182	1,396	1,146	270
Nevada	9	962	524	286	115	868	7	403	459	71
New Hampshire	109	1,987	1,398	441	116	1,754	18	358	1,378	176
New Jersey	250	16,217	9,240	5,011	1,623	14,570	141	5,472	8,957	1,202
New Mexico	64	1,228	637	373	181	1,103	18	593	491	95
New York	450	137,199	83,875	24,449	23,984	114,721	9,104	40,529	65,088	10,442
North Carolina	124	6,367	3,499	1,770	915	5,463	239	2,584	2,640	497
North Dakota	169	1,374	667	554	128	1,239	16	509	714	115
Ohio	529	20,777	10,994	6,592	2,791	18,476	423	7,826	10,227	1,681
Oklahoma	423	4,902	2,385	1,589	828	4,356	246	2,226	1,884	439
Oregon	51	3,862	2,226	969	506	3,446	40	1,350	2,056	257
Pennsylvania	523	31,325	18,072	8,807	3,715	27,199	952	10,018	16,228	2,677
Rhode Island	21	2,744	1,858	657	174	2,443	19	623	1,801	224
South Carolina	124	1,993	1,044	592	309	1,753	36	1,175	542	176
South Dakota	165	1,332	689	466	151	1,207	17	535	655	105
Tennessee	300	6,578	3,554	1,824	1,034	5,728	420	2,550	2,758	538
Texas	1,149	23,203	12,052	6,216	4,230	20,479	1,636	10,124	8,718	1,898
Utah	56	1,735	975	461	248	1,533	40	612	881	132
Vermont	52	1,018	708	226	67	922	2	228	691	76
Virginia	243	6,986	3,990	1,960	872	6,234	134	2,584	3,516	537
Washington	101	6,439	4,000	1,435	789	5,741	107	2,210	3,424	460
West Virginia	195	2,514	1,186	957	313	2,208	49	1,079	1,080	240
Wisconsin	605	8,658	4,489	2,902	1,071	7,809	226	3,029	4,554	632
Wyoming	69	689	376	202	93	612	12	268	332	60
Total U.S.†	14,225	527,091	298,911	136,739	76,292	458,109	21,732	183,348	253,029	40,884

*Includes Federal Funds sold and securities purchased under agreement to resell.   †Includes a member bank in the Virgin Islands.
Source: Board of Governors of the Federal Reserve System, *Federal Reserve Statistical Release.*

Assets of commercial banks

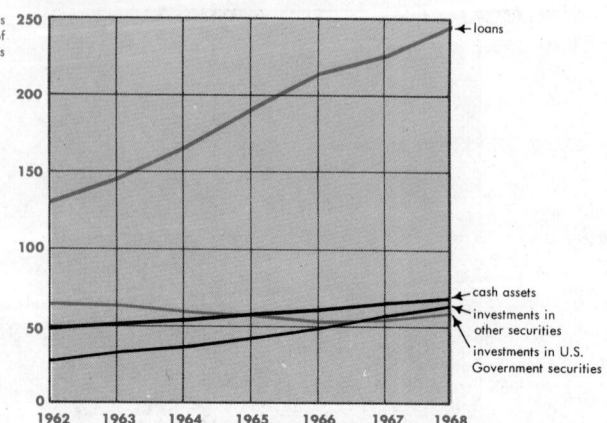

Billions of dollars

- loans
- cash assets
- investments in other securities
- investments in U.S. Government securities

1962 1963 1964 1965 1966 1967 1968

Data are for June 30 of years reported.
Source: Board of Governors of the Federal Reserve System, *Federal Reserve Bulletin*.

Credit unions

dollar figures in millions

Year	Number of active credit unions	Number of members	Savings*	Loans outstanding to members†	Reserves	Assets
1955	16,201	8,153,641	$ 2,447	$ 1,934	$110	$ 2,743
1956	17,256	9,061,339	2,914	2,326	137	3,271
1957	18,203	9,819,452	3,382	2,778	165	3,813
1958	18,838	10,431,606	3,870	3,078	198	4,346
1959	19,452	11,262,581	4,436	3,708	232	5,024
1960	20,047	12,037,533	4,975	4,377	272	5,653
1961	20,615	12,882,793	5,636	4,818	326	6,383
1962	20,951	13,762,047	6,331	5,477	381	7,186
1963	21,369	14,586,988	7,166	6,171	441	8,131
1964	21,807	15,619,210	8,242	7,046	510	9,361
1965	22,119	16,753,106	9,249	8,095	590	10,552
1966	22,692	17,897,351	10,106	9,003	678	11,609
1967‡	23,207	19,070,105	11,143	9,910	769	12,749

*Shares and deposits.
†Includes some loans to other credit unions before 1960.
‡Preliminary.
Source: CUNA International, Inc.

Savings and loan associations

dollar figures in millions

State	NUMBER OF ASSOCIATIONS Total	State	ASSETS Total	State	Mortgage loans outstanding	Savings capital
Alabama	56	8	$ 1,019	$ 142	$ 863	$ 922
Alaska	3	0	58	0	47	50
Arizona	14	12	816	475	675	685
Arkansas	63	23	772	147	645	694
California	264	192	27,967	18,884	23,583	23,500
Colorado	56	36	1,759	898	1,491	1,487
Connecticut	38	20	1,227	328	1,052	1,082
Delaware	31	28	97	51	83	42
District of Columbia	23	15	2,251	1,665	1,996	1,929
Florida	136	6	6,639	119	5,613	5,949
Georgia	106	7	2,277	32	1,958	1,983
Hawaii	14	12	540	436	454	450
Idaho	13	5	272	32	237	212
Illinois	575	436	12,370	5,875	10,524	10,666
Indiana	209	107	3,276	778	2,753	2,944
Iowa	92	47	1,588	604	1,327	1,415
Kansas	100	71	1,712	735	1,502	1,480
Kentucky	134	46	1,623	281	1,387	1,452
Louisiana	105	69	1,900	1,444	1,635	1,680
Maine	30	22	194	127	164	173
Maryland	306	240	2,641	775	2,239	2,244
Massachusetts	195	160	3,534	1,913	3,015	3,103
Michigan	71	33	3,719	1,173	3,174	3,287
Minnesota	75	25	2,691	126	2,310	2,346
Mississippi	80	49	655	184	548	585
Missouri	144	99	3,344	1,800	2,883	2,915
Montana	16	8	$ 230	$ 79	$ 194	$ 206
Nebraska	47	26	1,021	591	857	911
Nevada	6	5	634	550	432	451
New Hampshire	25	18	290	81	252	253
New Jersey	376	350	5,377	4,623	4,640	4,760
New Mexico	37	27	439	218	352	386
New York	212	127	8,869	2,821	7,691	7,780
North Carolina	184	147	2,626	1,695	2,293	2,306
North Dakota	15	7	389	195	319	340
Ohio	540	403	11,275	6,607	9,151	9,855
Oklahoma	58	28	1,301	358	1,134	1,175
Oregon	32	14	1,159	387	993	991
Pennsylvania	707	574	6,681	2,740	5,798	5,823
Rhode Island	8	6	406	356	363	338
South Carolina	78	31	1,388	374	1,192	1,219
South Dakota	20	12	193	35	163	172
Tennessee	68	0	1,538	0	1,301	1,362
Texas	275	190	6,195	4,129	5,233	5,428
Utah	20	14	684	377	573	574
Vermont	8	6	78	14	69	66
Virginia	78	46	1,435	450	1,237	1,262
Washington	68	33	2,450	609	2,086	2,112
West Virginia	38	15	386	50	322	343
Wisconsin	146	102	3,310	2,019	2,829	2,867
Wyoming	12	3	151	23	128	135
TOTAL U.S.	6,007	3,960	143,446	68,405	121,760	124,390

Data are for January 1, 1968, for all federally chartered and state chartered savings and loan associations and cooperative banks.
Source: United States Savings and Loan League.

Consumer credit outstanding

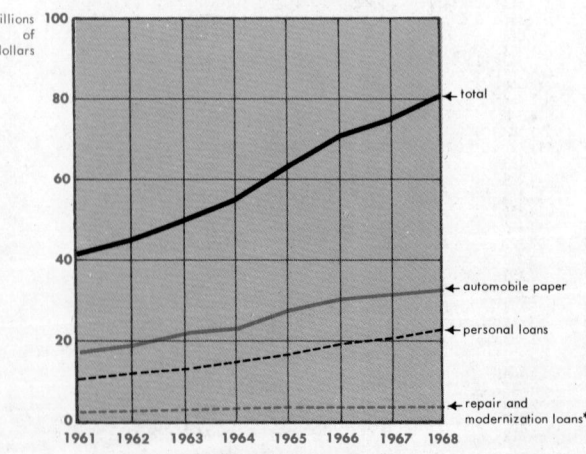

Billions of dollars

- total
- automobile paper
- personal loans
- repair and modernization loans*

1961 1962 1963 1964 1965 1966 1967 1968

installment credit

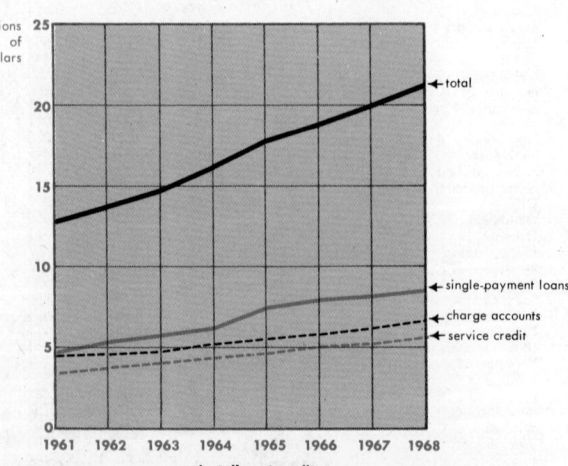

Billions of dollars

- total
- single-payment loans
- charge accounts
- service credit

1961 1962 1963 1964 1965 1966 1967 1968

noninstallment credit

Graphs cover loans outstanding as of June 30, to individuals for households, family, and other personal expenditures, except real estate mortgage loans.
*Holdings of financial institutions only.
Source: Board of Governors of the Federal Reserve System, *Federal Reserve Bulletin*.

Health insurance

Item	1960	1965	1967
Premiums received (in $000,000)	7,485	12,130	...
Insurance companies	4,671	7,352	...
Other*	2,814	4,778	...
Benefit payments (in $000,000)	5,688	9,617	...
By type of insurer			
Insurance companies	3,069	5,160	5,987
Other*	2,619	4,457	5,050
By type of benefit			
Hospital expense†	3,207	5,695	6,262
Surgical and medical expense†	1,642	2,876	3,565
Loss of income	839	1,046	1,210
Number of persons covered, Dec. 31 (in 000)			
Insurance companies‡			
Hospital expense	78,885	97,042	100,298
Surgical expense	75,305	93,717	93,618
Regular medical expense	41,312	58,398	64,604
Blue Cross, Blue Shield, and Medical Society			
Hospital expense	58,050	64,495	68,432
Surgical expense	50,281	55,420	59,840
Regular medical expense	45,017	52,042	56,247
Independent plans§			
Hospital expense	5,542	7,376	7,450
Surgical expense	6,573	8,974	8,880
Regular medical expense	6,773	8,718	8,680

*Blue Cross, Blue Shield, and other insuring organizations.
†Includes benefits from major medical expense policies.
‡Persons covered by more than one insurance company are counted
 only once.
§Industrial plans, community plans, private group clinics, college health
 plans, and consumer-sponsored plans.
Source: Health Insurance Institute.

Life insurance
dollar figures in millions

Item	1960	1965	1967	1968
Number of companies	1,442	1,610	1,726	1,758
Amount in force	$560,000	$849,000	$1,030,000	$1,140,000
Value of purchases*	72,989	108,989	127,357	148,628
Ordinary	52,382	78,122	90,952	99,566
Group	13,706	23,506	29,339	42,229
Industrial	6,901	7,361	7,066	6,833
Benefit payments				
Death payments	3,253	4,643	5,446	5,976
Matured endowments	652	933	998	994
Policy dividends	1,541	2,416	2,796	2,995

Years ending June 30.
*Exclusive of revivals, increases, dividend additions, and reinsurance
 acquired.
Source: Institute of Life Insurance.

Sales of stocks and bonds
in millions

Year and month	Market value of all sales	STOCKS*		BONDS†	
		Market value	Number of shares	Market value	Principal amount
1967					
November	$15,068	$14,477	381	$567	$536
December	15,477	14,919	412	532	519
1968					
January	18,246	17,662	517	552	504
February	12,432	12,008	321	403	392
March	13,095	12,632	336	435	433
April	18,139	17,571	453	523	499
May	20,622	20,012	567	550	521
June	19,072	18,582	509	446	429
July	16,975	16,529	444	389	375
August	14,442	14,038	376	364	343
September	14,166	13,733	388	398	398

*Includes voting trust certificates, certificates of deposit for stocks, American
 depository receipts for stocks; excludes rights and warrants.
†Excludes U.S. government bonds.
Source: U.S. Securities and Exchange Commission, *Statistical Bulletin*.

Stock dividends
July data, at annual rates per share

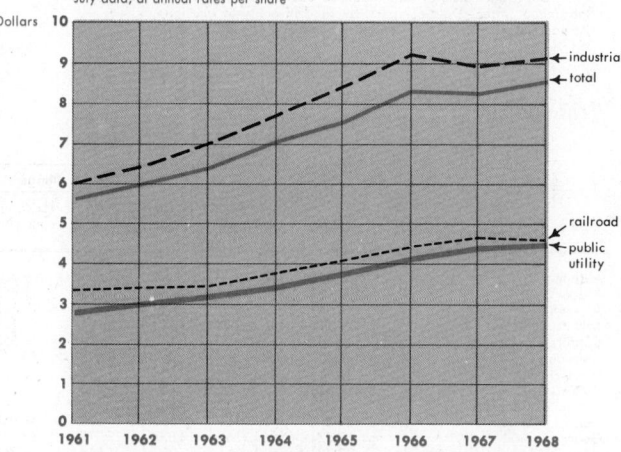

Source: U.S. Department of Commerce, Office of Business Economics, *Survey of
Current Business*. Data compiled by Moody's Investors Service, Inc.

Stock market prices
1941-43 = 10

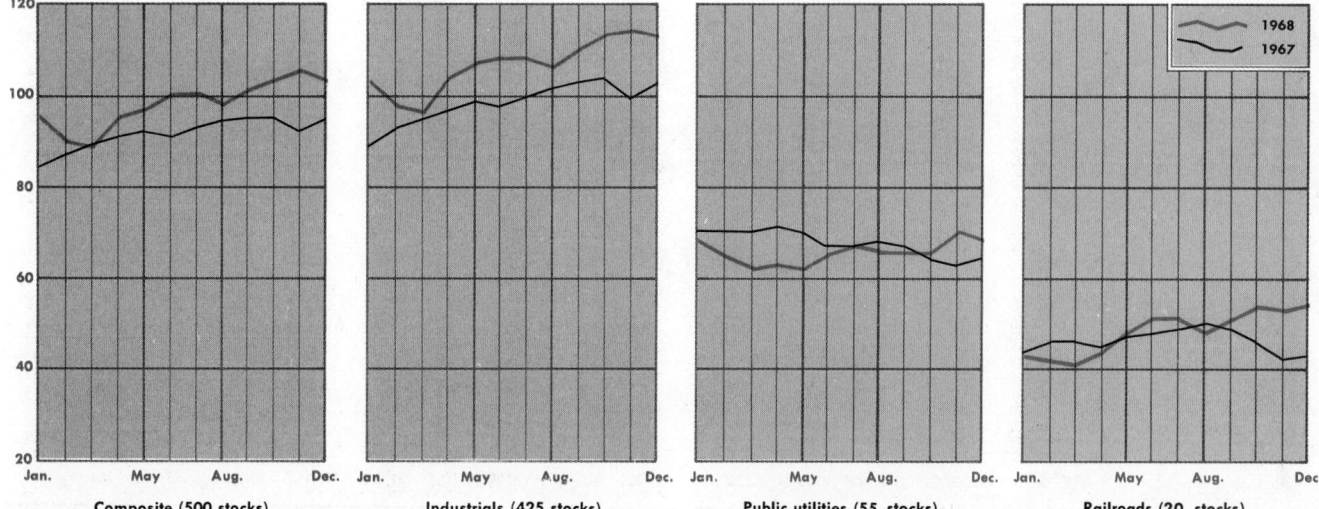

Composite (500 stocks)   Industrials (425 stocks)   Public utilities (55 stocks)   Railroads (20 stocks)

Monthly averages except December 1968 which is the closing price.
Source: U.S. Department of Commerce, Office of Business Economics, *Survey of Current Business*. Data compiled by Standard & Poor's Corporation.

Transport and Communications

Automobile ownership

Unit	1950	1955	1960	1965	1967
Total number of families in the U.S. (000,000)	45.2	49.1	53.4	58.4	60.2
Percent of families owning automobiles	59	70	77	79	78
Owning 1 automobile	52	60	62	55	53
Owning 2 or more automobiles	7	10	15	24	25
Age of automobiles owned, by percent					
Less than 2 years old	17	12	14	16	17
2 and 3 years old	19	22	20	21	22
4 to 7 years old	6	43	41	33	33
8 years old and over	58	23	25	30	28
Total automobiles purchased (000,000)	...	13.6	14.1	18.3	19.1
New cars (000,000)	...	4.4	5.2	7.2	7.6
Average price paid	...	$2,730	$3,140	$3,140	$3,250
Used cars (000,000)	...	9.2	9.1	11.1	11.5
Average price paid, gross	...	$ 780	$ 980	$ 920	$ 880
Method of financing purchases, by percent					
Full cash (including trade-in allowance)	47	38	38	48	48
Installment credit and other borrowing	52	60	62	52	52

Source: U.S. Department of Commerce, Bureau of the Census, *Statistical Abstract of the United States*. Data compiled by The University of Michigan, Survey Research Center, *Survey of Consumer Finances*.

Traffic accidents

	PERSONS KILLED				PERSONS INJURED			
Type of action	1950	1960	1965	1967	1950	1960	1965	1967
Driver action:								
Number	26,700	30,400	41,600	52,200	1,210,000	2,600,000	3,682,000	4,200,000
Percent distribution								
Speeding	49.8	36.1	41.1	39.0	39.3	38.5	42.2	20.9
Wrong side of road	17.8	17.0	16.4	13.1	8.7	6.7	6.8	5.2
No right-of-way	10.4	12.8	13.0	14.3	26.6	22.5	18.9	20.1
Drove off road	5.2	16.6	10.5	13.2	2.9	8.3	6.9	8.9
Reckless driving	8.5	12.5	14.9	15.4	9.0	13.5	19.2	38.9
Other*	8.3	5.0	4.1	5.0	13.5	10.5	6.0	6.0
Pedestrian action:								
Number	9,400	7,600	9,000	9,500	299,500	255,500	274,700	256,000
Percent distribution								
Crossing at intersection								
With signal	4.6	6.2	4.8	5.5	10.1	11.9	8.6	10.9
Against signal	6.3	7.1	8.6	8.5	9.4	8.5	9.5	11.5
No signal	13.5	15.9	7.4	9.6	13.6	12.3	8.1	8.3
Crossing between intersections	39.8	37.1	40.8	41.6	26.1	32.2	31.6	23.8
Children playing in street	5.8	5.3	3.3	2.9	16.6	6.6	6.3	6.0
At work in road	3.1	2.9	2.8	2.4	2.7	2.2	1.8	1.8
Coming from behind parked car	6.7	6.2	6.9	3.4	9.1	15.7	16.8	13.2
Walking on rural highway	13.0	10.0	15.6	14.1	2.3	2.4	7.6	7.7
Not on roadway	3.5	4.2	4.7	4.2	6.5	4.5	3.6	4.8
Other†	3.7	5.1	5.1	7.8	3.6	3.7	6.1	12.0

*Cutting in; improper passing; improper or no signalling; movement of driverless car; miscellaneous. †Standing on safety isle; getting on or off other vehicle; riding or hitching on vehicle; miscellaneous.

Source: U.S. Department of Commerce, Bureau of the Census, *Statistical Abstract of the United States*. Data compiled by The Travelers Insurance Companies, Hartford, Conn., annual report, *The Travelers Book of Street and Highway Accident Data*.

Transportation

	ROAD AND STREET MILEAGE Jan. 1, 1968					AUTOMOBILES, TRUCKS, AND BUSES registrations, in 000, 1967				RAILROAD MILEAGE OWNED Jan. 1, 1968		AIRPORTS‡ Jan. 1, 1968		CIVIL AIRCRAFT Jan. 1, 1968	
				Rural mileage			Private and commercial									
State	Total*	Total surfaced	Municipal mileage	State controlled	Locally controlled	Total	Auto-mobiles	Trucks and buses	Publicly owned†	Total	Class 1	Total	Private	Total	Eligible
Alabama	77,850	70,181	11,435	19,861§	46,554	1,735	1,393	317	25	4,579	3,900	123	47	2,100	1,494
Alaska	6,582	2,746	540	4,291	1,655	110	74	32	4	20	—	626	168	3,076	1,807
Arizona	40,843	19,603	5,592	5,132	17,389	890	680	191	19	2,052	1,879	191	98	2,794	1,775
Arkansas	79,211	55,234	8,247	12,885	56,192	983	682	289	11	3,611	3,320	127	64	2,233	1,530
California	162,809	115,721	41,131	13,482	70,563	10,849	9,035	1,663	151	7,485	6,663	684	443	22,736	15,603
Colorado	81,228	47,426	6,323	8,192	66,662	1,242	940	279	22	3,746	3,629	177	64	2,700	1,955
Connecticut	17,980	17,822	12,696	1,509	3,775	1,545	1,369	159	17	734	679	75	12	1,418	963
Delaware	4,826	4,807	1,380	3,446§	—	268	225	39	4	292	—	21	17	601	464
District of Columbia	1,083	1,071	1,083	—	—	247	219	19	9	31	12	3	—	927	708
Florida	82,898	57,271	19,526	16,304	47,068	3,393	2,946	398	48	4,469	3,957	281	172	7,081	4,549
Georgia	97,524	64,776	14,077	15,247	68,140	2,164	1,739	396	29	5,474	3,730	169	73	3,184	2,338
Hawaii	3,401	3,231	923	1,018	1,369	336	295	35	6	—	—	46	30	351	196
Idaho	53,484	29,885	2,793	4,682	26,809	455	310	132	12	2,668	2,478	164	53	1,430	1,030
Illinois	128,479	119,368	26,022	13,081	89,376	4,818	4,187	578	54	10,928	9,144	433	364	7,481	5,349
Indiana	90,878	85,868	12,613	10,112	68,153	2,632	2,119	487	26	6,488	3,428	153	105	4,104	3,036
Iowa	112,409	104,222	12,701	9,165	90,543	1,651	1,293	329	29	8,291	7,874	228	138	2,915	2,294
Kansas	133,232	94,770	9,905	9,944	113,383	1,441	1,036	382	23	7,871	7,847	266	157	3,656	2,636
Kentucky	70,225	55,825	4,954	23,712	41,295	1,632	1,293	319	20	3,529	3,091	63	19	1,117	831
Louisiana	51,759	46,604	10,513	14,208§	27,038	1,634	1,300	312	22	3,807	3,496	224	160	2,786	1,878
Maine	21,267	19,450	2,320	10,964‖	7,819	452	361	85	6	1,679	1,523	136	93	782	497
Maryland	25,585	25,512	3,978	4,887	16,600	1,612	1,401	194	17	1,128	564	83	70	1,894	1,308
Massachusetts	27,544	25,963	20,093	1,088	6,334	2,223	1,993	201	30	1,520	1,316	113	86	2,257	1,522
Michigan	113,895	95,019	18,998	7,968	86,929	4,133	3,570	505	58	6,372	4,212	251	132	6,412	4,647
Minnesota	126,879	113,801	16,170	11,509	97,386	1,997	1,608	362	26	7,990	7,867	260	138	4,211	3,136
Mississippi	65,525	62,567	6,246	9,788	49,252	1,012	748	248	16	3,653	3,170	159	90	1,953	1,310
Missouri	114,285	102,621	14,665	29,993	68,982	2,211	1,748	439	23	6,414	5,785	265	185	4,209	3,050
Montana	75,747	39,547	2,180	11,606	51,310	451	298	143	10	4,937	4,900	188	74	1,877	1,382
Nebraska	103,374	70,214	6,213	9,390	87,307	888	647	226	14	5,498	5,498	260	179	2,154	1,578
Nevada	46,798	14,723	1,743	6,232§	38,822	287	214	63	10	1,635	1,474	79	36	1,287	896
New Hampshire	14,613	11,919	4,672	3,037	6,827	349	290	50	8	815	679	44	29	492	332
New Jersey	33,183	30,418	16,116	1,776	15,291	3,200	2,850	307	43	1,789	941	138	122	3,574	2,476
New Mexico	66,350	19,333	3,957	11,546	45,642	571	418	141	13	2,225	2,151	124	62	1,636	1,149
New York	102,292	92,124	16,896	13,975	71,411	6,060	5,378	586	96	5,689	4,763	338	283	7,717	5,342
North Carolina	84,219	75,142	12,955	69,811§	—	2,423	1,907	450	66	4,222	2,960	181	132	2,835	2,044
North Dakota	107,163	66,551	3,016	6,402	97,194	405	260	137	7	5,165	5,097	180	110	1,300	942
Ohio	108,049	106,248	22,952	16,596	68,501	5,305	4,715	538	52	8,031	4,690	397	330	7,032	4,950
Oklahoma	106,955	75,737	12,921	11,454	82,580	1,542	1,107	413	22	5,506	5,200	206	107	3,520	2,363
Oregon	88,329	55,119	5,843	8,829	34,776	1,190	964	202	24	3,091	2,780	177	92	3,354	2,448
Pennsylvania	113,166	92,873	23,053	43,768	46,128	5,335	4,647	632	57	8,477	5,555	443	377	5,149	3,666
Rhode Island	4,883	4,623	3,896	499	488	434	384	45	5	155	112	11	6	224	174
South Carolina	58,766	37,524	6,181	29,904	22,681	1,180	960	199	21	3,140	2,123	100	51	1,214	913
South Dakota	83,941	57,504	2,890	8,594	70,797	407	282	116	10	3,818	3,818	108	44	1,231	873
Tennessee	77,182	75,153	9,015	8,266	58,882	1,870	1,517	325	27	3,285	2,603	101	42	2,124	1,604
Texas	237,769	170,045	40,775	59,397	137,597	5,894	4,577	1,231	86	14,051	13,396	900	676	12,811	9,030
Utah	38,684	21,701	4,279	5,197	20,350	562	432	119	11	1,771	1,707	71	21	967	686
Vermont	14,109	12,135	932	2,325	10,764	194	159	32	3	770	326	37	25	333	242
Virginia	59,781	58,569	7,953	49,257§	766	1,932	1,617	281	34	4,025	3,314	138	99	2,085	1,444
Washington	72,424	59,906	9,578	10,908	39,568	1,852	1,444	371	37	4,943	4,827	198	104	4,121	2,727
West Virginia	35,700	26,225	3,552	31,256§	—	765	611	143	12	3,569	3,136	48	33	702	470
Wisconsin	101,295	95,482	13,491	10,647	77,095	1,954	1,624	299	31	6,006	5,695	225	130	3,043	2,189
Wyoming	78,461	17,124	1,220	5,564	66,710	226	146	74	6	1,848	1,841	86	45	794	582
Total U.S.	3,704,914	2,827,303	521,203	698,704	2,320,753	96,945¶	80,014¶	15,518¶	1,413¶	209,292	179,150	10,099	6,287	165,984	116,408

*Includes federally controlled rural roads. †Excludes vehicles owned by military services. ‡Includes seaplane bases, heliports, and military fields having joint civil-military use. §Includes mileage of state-controlled county roads. ‖Includes the state-aid system. ¶Data not equal to total due to rounding.

Sources: Interstate Commerce Commission; U.S. Department of Transportation, Federal Aviation Administration; Federal Highway Administration, Bureau of Public Roads.

Passengers carried by public urban transportation

In billions

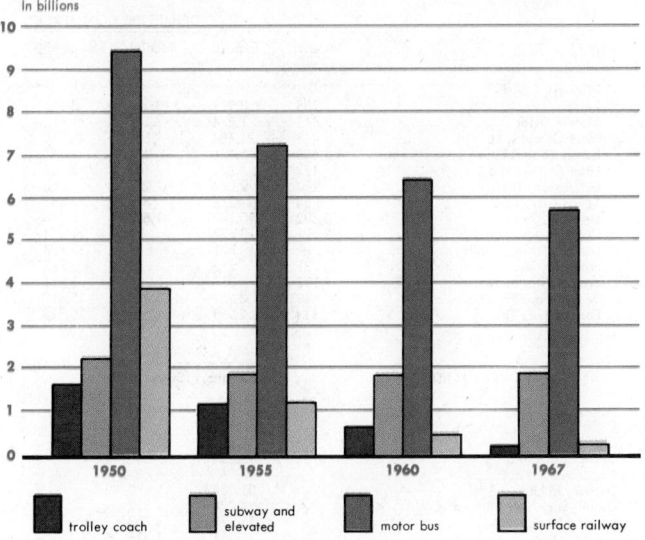

Source: American Transit Association, *Transit Fact Book*.

Legend:
- trolley coach
- subway and elevated
- motor bus
- surface railway

Aviation

Item		1960	1967
CIVIL FLYING			
Total aircraft		111,580	166,598
Hours flown*	(000)	13,121	22,154
Miles flown*	(000,000)	1,769	3,336†
Aircraft accidents*		4,793	5,425†
Aircraft accident fatalities*		787	1,069†
Pilot licenses		348,062	611,465
SCHEDULED AIR CARRIERS			
Aircraft operating‡		1,822	2,129
Fixed wing		1,797	2,129
Four-engine		1,141	997
Twin-engine		651	711
Express and freight flown§	(000 ton-miles)	578,518	2,111,373
Mail flown	(000 ton-miles)	239,258	966,699
Domestic operations‖			
Number of operators§		39	40†
Route miles in operation¶		101,414	104,703†
Revenue passengers carried	(000)	56,352	128,479
Revenue passenger-miles flown	(000,000)	30,557	75,487
International operations‖			
Number of operators§		10	9†
Route miles in operation		148,303	145,898†
Revenue passengers carried	(000)	5,904	14,020
Revenue passenger-miles flown	(000,000)	8,306	23,259

*Excludes civil flying performed by public carriers. †1965.
‡Excludes aircraft used for crew training and general utility purposes, those held for disposal, and those operated by the scheduled all-cargo carriers.
§Excludes all-cargo operators. ‖Operations between conterminous U.S. and Hawaii and Alaska included with international. ¶Excludes intra-Alaska.
Source: U.S. Department of Transportation, Federal Aviation Administration, *FAA Statistical Handbook of Aviation*.

Railroads

years ending December 31

Item		1960	1965	1966
Number of operating companies*		407	372	375
Miles of road owned, first track†		217,552	211,384	210,573
Total miles operated		381,745	370,636	370,104
Number of locomotives in service		31,178	30,061	30,124
Number of passenger-train cars in service‡		25,746	20,022	18,974
Operating revenues	($000,000)	9,642	10,425	10,880
Operating expenses	($000,000)	7,657	8,003	8,277
Net income§	($000,000)	473	866	957
Passenger revenue	($000,000)	641	556	547
Passengers carried	(000,000)	327	306	308
Passenger-miles	(000,000)	21,284	17,454	17,162
Revenue per passenger-mile	(cents)	3.014	3.185	3.188
Average journey per passenger	(miles)	65.05	57.07	55.72
Freight revenue	($000,000)	8,152	9,037	9,487
Freight revenue-tons originated	(000,000)	1,301	1,479	1,544
Tons carried one mile	(000,000)	575,360	705,705	746,699
Revenue ton-miles per mile of road	(000)	2,497	3,121	3,312
Revenue per ton-mile	(cents)	1.417	1,281	1,271
Haul per ton				
U.S. as a system	(miles)	442.14	477.15	483.70
Individual railroad	(miles)	238.83	257.40	261.93
Revenue per ton				
U.S. as a system	(dollars)	6.26	6.11	6.15
Individual railroad	(dollars)	3.38	3.30	3.33
Average number of employees	(000)	793	655	645
Compensation of employees	($000,000)	4,957	4,887	4,975

All data are for Classes I and II.
*Includes unofficial companies.
†Includes lessors, proprietary and unofficial companies.
‡Includes switching and terminal companies.
§Includes lessors.
Source: Interstate Commerce Commission.

U.S. postal service

Year ending June 30	Number of post offices	FINANCES in $000,000		Postage stamps issued, in 000	MONEY ORDERS ISSUED in $000,000		Pieces of mail handled, in 000,000
		Net revenue	Expend- iture		Domestic	Inter- national	
1960	35,238	3,276.8	3,874.0	23,773,570	5,030.6	39.9	63,674.6
1961	34,955	3,423.1	4,249.4	23,001,808	4,957.6	35.3	64,932.9
1962	34,797	3,557.0	4,331.6	25,405,929	4,787.4	33.7	66,493.2
1963	34,498	3,879.1	4,698.5	31,669,175	4,709.1	33.4	67,852.7
1964	34,040	4,276.1	4,927.8	24,692,326	4,719.4	32.3	67,676.5
1965	33,624	4,420.8	5,274.8	22,652,248	4,519.7	31.8	71,628.0
1966	33,121	4,682.5	5,629.6	23,503,959	4,606.0	28.9	75,800.0
1967	32,626	4,962.7	6,133.4	26,320,662	4,697.3	26.2	79,165.0
1968	32,261	5,505.3	6,635.8	34,500,000*	...	...	81,500.0

*Approximate.
Source: U.S. Post Office Department.

Sources of major air pollutants

in millions of tons per year

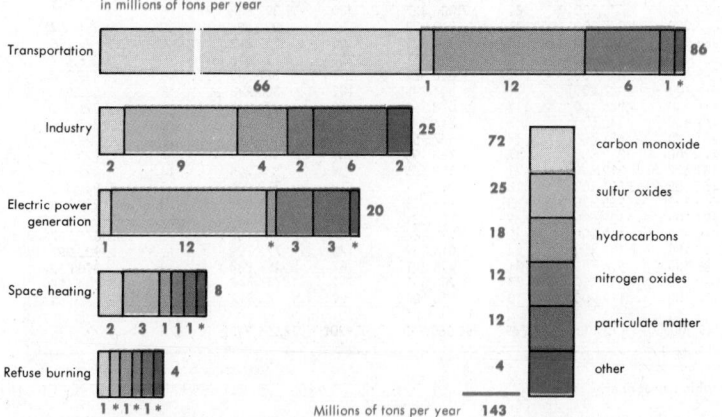

Transportation — 86
66 1 12 6 1*

Industry — 25
2 9 4 2 6 2

Electric power generation — 20
1 12 * 3 3 *

Space heating — 8
2 3 1 1 1*

Refuse burning — 4
1* 1* 1*

72	carbon monoxide
25	sulfur oxides
18	hydrocarbons
12	nitrogen oxides
12	particulate matter
4	other

Millions of tons per year 143

*Less than one million tons.
Source: U.S. Public Health Service.

Intercity freight traffic

in percent by year

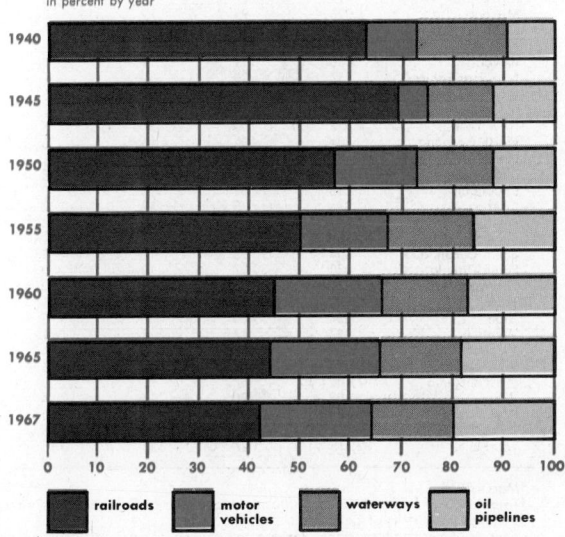

Years: 1940, 1945, 1950, 1955, 1960, 1965, 1967

Legend:
- railroads
- motor vehicles
- waterways
- oil pipelines

Air freight is not shown, since it is less than one percent.
Source: Interstate Commerce Commission.

Commerce of selected ports

1967, in thousands of short tons (cargo)

Port	Imports	Exports	DOMESTIC COMMERCE* Receipts	Shipments	Port	Imports	Exports	DOMESTIC COMMERCE* Receipts	Shipments
COASTAL PORTS					Gulf coast				
Atlantic coast					Tampa, Fla.	1,735	8,912	10,379	3,525
Portland, Me.	18,790	69	3,227	584	Mobile, Ala.	8,873	1,874	237	1,877
Salem, Mass.	510	—	1,045	15	New Orleans, La.	5,469	21,794	1,892	28,718
Boston, Mass.	7,645	710	11,093	799	Baton Rouge, La.	6,658	5,156	464	9,157
Providence, R.I.	1,381	173	6,565	599	Lake Charles, La.‡	153	1,231	159	3,356
New Haven, Conn.	2,638	254	6,807	1,654	Galveston, Tex.	200	2,064	216	56
Bridgeport, Conn.	388	64	2,138	389	Texas City, Tex.	54	276	396	4,155
Norwalk, Conn.	—	—	1,186	—	Houston, Tex.	3,632	10,149	1,856	18,084
New York, N.Y. and N.J.	49,284	6,979	29,464	19,635	Corpus Christi, Tex.	3,021	2,634	76	11,674
Hempstead, N.Y.	—	—	2,083	1,979	Harbor Island, Tex.	—	721	—	4,600
Port Jefferson, N.Y.	717	—	1,301	17	Freeport, Tex.	91	993	30	977
Albany, N.Y.	1,531	305	1,890	42	Brazos Island, Tex.	1,902	860	2	1,681
Delaware River ports†	46,126	3,133	32,858	8,441	Beaumont, Tex.	48	3,257	1,168	15,612
Baltimore, Md.	17,793	4,546	3,780	1,173	Port Arthur, Tex.	114	2,291	4,568	10,528
Norfolk, Va.	3,710	27,152	1,931	2,675					
Newport News, Va.	683	8,886	—	1,563					
Wilmington, N.C	1,110	219	2,128	130				ALL COMMERCE	
Charleston, S.C.	1,709	920	2,623	75	**GREAT LAKES PORTS**			Receipts	Shipments
Savannah, Ga.	1,864	884	1,729	86					
Jacksonville, Fla.	3,065	993	3,889	610	Ashtabula, Ohio			5,691	1,389
Port Everglades, Fla.	1,930	254	5,149	267	Buffalo, N.Y.			13,682	484
Pacific coast					Chicago, Ill.			13,501	12,497
Long Beach, Calif.	3,285	4,837	2,069	1,943	Cleveland, Ohio			19,950	538
Los Angeles, Calif.	5,279	5,049	6,749	6,057	Conneaut, Ohio			7,565	6,436
San Francisco Bay area, Calif.	5,944	5,616	12,788	8,257	Detroit, Mich.			31,088	1,260
Stockton, Calif.	218	1,045	167	69	Duluth-Superior, Minn. and Wis.			4,494	32,832
Portland, Ore.	1,031	4,387	4,043	385	Indiana Harbor, Ind.			13,778	4,704
Longview, Wash.	128	2,236	472	47	Lorain, Ohio			3,647	1,419
Tacoma, Wash.	1,617	1,987	177	101	Milwaukee, Wis.			4,527	1,777
Seattle, Wash.	1,733	1,495	3,095	981	Sandusky, Ohio			101	5,690
Honolulu, Hawaii	1,229	161	3,004	2,202	Toledo, Ohio			6,166	32,382

Data exclude purely local port traffic and commerce with ports on internal rivers and canals.
*Domestic commerce figures for coastal ports exclude commerce with Great Lakes ports.
†Includes tributaries. ‡Includes Calcasieu River and Pass.
Source: U.S. Department of the Army, Corps of Engineers, *Waterborne Commerce of the United States.*

Communication facilities

State	Post offices Sept. 15, 1968	AM radio stations Jan. 1, 1967	TELEVISION STATIONS Jan. 1, 1968 Commercial	Educational	TELEPHONES Jan. 1, 1968 Total	Residence	NEWSPAPERS Daily Number Feb. 1, 1968	Circulation Oct. 1, 1967	Weekly Mar. 1968 Number	Circulation	Sunday Number Feb. 1, 1968	Circulation Oct. 1, 1967
Alabama	680	126	15	7	1,338,100	987,900	21	721,626	100	387,503	14	624,250
Alaska	203	15	7	0	74,000	41,400	6	60,426	6	6,205	2	15,575
Arizona	219	53	11	2	742,800	501,400	13	390,521	53	112,356	5	319,376
Arkansas	713	80	6	1	707,500	520,900	34	433,653	131	273,179	11	341,092
California	1,179	226	42	8	11,734,800	8,276,300	134	5,810,060	457	2,432,606	35	4,769,021
Colorado	433	64	11	1	1,140,300	793,300	26	680,046	131	262,385	9	710,640
Connecticut	256	37	5	3	1,815,700	1,334,400	25	905,636	52	227,290	5	483,412
Delaware	57	9	0	1	316,100	229,300	3	151,061	13	36,809	—	—
Dist. of Columbia	1	6	6	1	818,300	424,000	3	1,002,624	…	…	2	959,095
Florida	473	183	20	9	3,259,700	2,255,500	49	1,899,657	136	371,353	29	1,696,166
Georgia	663	163	12	10	1,922,300	1,383,600	32	981,177	186	472,436	13	905,987
Hawaii	80	25	10	2	364,700	245,000	5	215,491	2	13,248*	3	171,325
Idaho	278	42	6	1	300,100	214,600	14	165,453	70	105,923	5	132,893
Illinois	1,307	119	21	4	6,374,800	4,593,600	85	3,907,390	602	2,227,669	20	2,911,921
Indiana	773	79	18	2	2,493,200	1,830,200	86	1,707,648	211	428,586	18	1,130,375
Iowa	978	69	12	1	1,439,600	1,107,300	44	999,556	362	670,295	9	871,891
Kansas	740	59	12	1	1,140,300	855,700	51	659,954	259	380,380*	14	431,305
Kentucky	1,384	98	7	1	1,219,300	909,100	28	759,073	135	351,069	13	558,941
Louisiana	554	88	15	1	1,530,300	1,140,700	22	759,864	96	258,467	12	677,243
Maine	524	33	7	4	423,400	315,500	9	265,850	37	82,967	1	109,282
Maryland	446	50	5	0	2,070,800	1,515,400	12	764,883	68	381,326	4	722,866
Massachusetts	462	60	10	2	3,131,700	2,220,300	46	2,383,276	144	615,684	8	1,626,591
Michigan	890	121	19	4	4,507,900	3,368,000	54	2,492,252	291	959,396	11	2,166,680
Minnesota	896	81	13	4	1,906,200	1,427,700	29	1,128,092	361	724,837	8	1,072,166
Mississippi	497	87	8	0	724,900	544,400	19	300,712	104	135,347	7	177,056
Missouri	1,026	95	19	2	2,405,600	1,765,000	53	1,853,858	293	616,046	14	1,569,927
Montana	396	40	8	0	318,900	231,000	15	189,374	73	107,344	9	178,997
Nebraska	571	45	14	7	762,000	573,100	19	483,660	204	380,913	5	360,408
Nevada	100	19	7	0	255,300	153,500	7	135,380	18	38,445	4	116,055
New Hampshire	257	25	2	1	344,900	257,900	9	147,348	31	63,037	1	48,544
New Jersey	528	31	1	0	4,144,700	3,083,100	31	1,758,166	226	1,144,554	7	1,100,590
New Mexico	349	53	7	1	426,500	280,300	19	201,204	25	31,719	12	171,643
New York	1,658	150	27	6	11,239,700	7,773,300	82	7,483,827	430	1,398,608	16	6,940,591
North Carolina	801	182	16	6	1,877,200	1,397,700	47	1,219,228	137	236,026	18	881,654
North Dakota	487	23	11	1	283,900	209,100	10	151,925	105	159,412	2	92,125
Ohio	1,096	111	25	8	5,481,400	4,098,000	97	3,490,331	258	1,127,600	18	2,216,117
Oklahoma	668	61	10	3	1,249,600	895,200	52	866,877	211	377,548	43	809,256
Oregon	374	78	12	2	1,015,100	727,800	21	641,845	102	303,598	5	523,561
Pennsylvania	1,882	164	23	8	6,585,400	4,965,100	112	4,078,311	252	774,033	10	2,895,378
Rhode Island	59	15	3	1	471,800	345,500	7	316,143	12	59,135	2	216,922
South Carolina	404	93	11	5	927,000	681,700	17	547,759	77	136,569	7	428,004
South Dakota	440	27	10	2	295,200	222,800	12	166,136	149	185,389	4	120,478
Tennessee	611	134	14	3	1,631,600	1,212,800	31	1,119,565	124	354,225	14	892,603
Texas	1,592	275	50	5	5,168,100	3,581,100	110	3,081,877	519	762,981	80	2,943,412
Utah	234	30	3	5	510,800	365,300	5	258,413	50	108,021	4	253,145
Vermont	297	17	1	1	194,100	139,500	9	105,831	15	27,382	—	—
Virginia	999	117	13	4	2,040,900	1,462,000	32	992,136	103	302,186	12	675,707
Washington	511	93	13	6	1,698,100	1,221,400	24	1,014,049	145	778,799	11	922,997
West Virginia	1,102	57	9	0	683,700	516,700	31	498,321	83	196,984	9	390,712
Wisconsin	803	90	15	4	2,070,300	1,508,100	37	1,200,061	252	616,465	7	864,188
Wyoming	184	29	3	0	170,700	119,900	10	70,187	29	54,513	2	25,962
Total U.S.	32,115	4,027	625	151	103,749,800	74,822,400	1,749	61,560,952†	7,930‡	22,258,848‡	573	49,224,125

*March 1967.
†Total has been adjusted to account for double listings of Covington, Ky., edition of Ohio newspaper.
‡Excludes the District of Columbia.
Sources: American Newspaper Representatives, Inc. American Telephone and Telegraph Co. Federal Communications Commission.
Television Digest, Inc., *Television Factbook* (Copyright 1968. All rights reserved. Used by permission). The Editor & Publisher Co., Inc.
International Year Book (Copyright 1968. All rights reserved. Used by permission). U.S. Post Office Department.

Printed in U.S.A. by R. R. Donnelley & Sons Company